"*Information U.S.A., billed as 'The Ultimate Source of Information on Earth,' more than lives up to the boast. [It] not only gives the browser a fascinating idea of government's scope but of its services. There is something here to interest everyone.*" —**King Features Syndicate**

"*If you have the questions, Matthew Lesko's* Information U.S.A. *has the answers. . . . None to ask? Leafing through the 900-page book is fun, anyway. If you enjoy browsing, this is the way to go.*"
—**Chicago Sunday Sun-Times**

"*Information U.S.A. is intended to help the uninitiated locate government information sources and specialists. Author Lesko, the founder of Washington Researchers, comes to this task with impressive experience in locating and obtaining government information.*" —**Booklist**

"*A vast and detailed compendium of advice on how to get information from the U.S. Government on, seemingly, every subject under the sun.*"
—**The Washington Post**

"*[Information U.S.A. is] of value to anyone tackling the bureaucracy for the first, or last, time.*" —*John McKelway,* **Washington Times**

"*Matthew Lesko [the author of* Information U.S.A.*] operates Washington Researchers, a consulting firm that helps such giants as 20th Century-Fox and Chase Manhattan Bank mine the informational treasures of Washington. . . . Information U.S.A. . . . provides names, addresses, and phone numbers—many toll-free—of sources on almost any subject.*"
—**Washingtonian**

"*One could well say that this compilation is more than one would ever want to know about the federal government, but the table of contents and a very extensive index make this tome manageable. Must be seen to be believed.*" —**American Council on Consumer Affairs**

"*Four years ago, Matthew Lesko decided to make a list of all the . . . information you can get, free or almost free, from the U.S. government, everything from census data to how to remove crayon stains from carpeting. A thousand pages and 10,000 listings later,* Information U.S.A. *has appeared, a 2¼-pound handbook that gives you new respect for the phrase 'your tax dollars at work.'*" —**Philadelphia News**

Penguin Handbooks

INFORMATION U.S.A.

Matthew Lesko is president of Information U.S.A., Inc., a firm he founded to help private and business clients draw on the informational resources of the federal government. His activities have included a monthly column for *Good Housekeeping*, a regular broadcast on National Public Radio, appearances on over five hundred radio and television talk/interview shows, including *The Phil Donahue Show, The David Letterman Show, The Larry King Show, Good Morning America,* and the *Today* show. He is a contributing editor to *Success Magazine* and has written feature articles for publications ranging from *The Washington Post* to *Consumer Digest*. He frequently speaks to consumer and professional groups about the art of obtaining information. Mr. Lesko's other books include *Getting Yours: The Complete Guide to Government Money* (available from Penguin), *The Maternity Sourcebook* (coauthored by Wendy Lesko), *The Computer Data and Database Source Book,* and *Lesko's New Tech Sourcebook*.

INFORMATION U.S.A.

REVISED EDITION

Matthew Lesko

Research Director, First Edition: Eudice Daly

Research Director, Second Edition: Sharon Zarozny

Viking

Penguin Books

PENGUIN BOOKS
Published by the Penguin Group
Penguin Books USA Inc.,
375 Hudson Street, New York, New York 10014, U.S.A.
Penguin Books Ltd, 27 Wrights Lane, London W8 5TZ, England
Penguin Books Australia Ltd, Ringwood, Victoria, Australia
Penguin Books Canada Ltd, 10 Alcorn Avenue,
Toronto, Ontario, Canada M4V 3B2
Penguin Books (N.Z.) Ltd, 182–190 Wairau Road,
Auckland 10, New Zealand

Penguin Books Ltd, Registered Offices:
Harmondsworth, Middlesex, England

First published in 1983 in simultaneous hardcover and
paperback editions by Viking Penguin Inc.
This revised edition first published in 1986 in simultaneous
hardcover and paperback editions by Viking Penguin Inc.
Published simultaneously in Canada

10 9 8 7 6

LIBRARY OF CONGRESS CATALOGING IN PUBLICATION DATA
Information U.S.A.
Includes index.
1. Information services—United States—Directories.
2. Federal government—United States—Information
services—Directories. 3. Government information—
United States—Directories. I. Lesko, Matthew.
II. Zarozny, Sharon. III. Title: Information USA.
Z674.U5I53 1986 020′.25′73 85-40628
ISBN 0-670-80972-1
ISBN 0 14 046.745 9 (pbk.)

Printed in the United States of America

Set in Times Roman

This book is dedicated to all federal bureaucrats,
the true possessors of institutional knowledge
in our federal government.

Acknowledgments

I'd like to thank the thousands of federal workers who shared their time to insure the accuracy and completeness of the manuscript. Thanks as well to Eudice Daly, whose research and writing skills, along with her special dedication and friendship, made the project a joy. And my special gratitude to my agent, Rafe Sagalyn, whose patience, support, and clear vision of the future are truly responsible for making Information U.S.A. *happen.*

Again I would like to thank federal government workers for their help with updating this book for the second edition. Many offices were extremely kind in sending corrections even before they were contacted by our researchers.

Sharon Zarozny's dedication to quality was probably the most important aspect of this edition. Toni Murray deserves praise for her enthusiasm and for seeing the project through from fact-checking to editing. I would also like to thank Ingrid Reeves, Max Murray, and Amy Summers for their efforts in ferreting out new material for the book; Marye Cotton for her enthusiastic contribution to the "Sampler Section" and word processing; and Natalie Hartman for being so pleasant despite many manuscript revisions.

I look forward to thanking more people in the third edition.

Contents

Sampler Section
PAGE 1

Departments
PAGE 343

Agencies, Boards, Commissions, Committees, and Government Corporations
PAGE 789

Executive Branch
PAGE 1091

Judicial Branch
PAGE 1097

Legislative Branch
PAGE 1103

Quasi-Official Agencies
PAGE 1169

Index
PAGE 1193

Introduction to Revised Edition

IF YOU ARE a reader who also purchased the first edition of *Information U.S.A.*, I thank you, thank you, thank you. I cannot tell you how thrilled I am over the success of the first edition. I had no idea that people would so readily see the value of the vast resources that lie untapped in our nation's capital. I thought that it would take years of work before any recognition would come. But the book buyers who showed such enthusiasm for the first edition made this book a national bestseller (it marked the first time a $20 paperback made *The New York Times* bestseller list) and helped the American Library Association choose it as one of the "Outstanding Reference books of the Year."

Besides the sales success, what was even more gratifying was hearing success stories from readers. One reader from New York City called me while I was on the Larry King radio show and told me how buying *Information U.S.A.* helped turn him from a poor immigrant into a successful businessman, with two companies with over $1 million in sales each. He told the audience how this book directed him to willing free experts and enough cheap money to help him start a bicycle business and a cheese business. This was a great thrill to hear (especially with millions of people listening in).

A friend in Washington, D.C., told me how he used the book to solve a problem his father was having. His dad, living in a Florida retirement community, encountered a medical problem that cut off the circulation to his foot. Because he was a golfer, this caused him great concern. His doctors in central Florida were not much help but did mention a new operation in which a device could be used to clear out the blood vessels in the leg. No physician in central Florida performed such a procedure or knew its specifics. Learning of his father's problem, my friend used my book to contact the National Institutes of Health and was immediately connected with a doctor who had spent the last few years studying this new procedure. The NIH expert sent my friend very current literature (*not* full of incomprehensible medical jargon) describing the procedure along with details of all the associated risks and benefits. He was also given the names and telephone numbers of the best experts in the country who can perform this procedure and was then told that if his father wanted to have it done *for free,* he could probably qualify to have it done at the National Institutes of Health, because they are heavily involved in studying this procedure.

A New York shipping broker called me to say that no businessman should be without this book. A lobbyist for a Fortune 500 company remarked that the four pages on export help are the best he has seen anywhere. A teenager from Boston told me that he used my book to get a $2,500 loan from the U.S. Department of Agriculture's Youth Loan Program to start a lawnmowing business that now provides the money for his college tuition.

As the book became more popular I heard many other such stories. The successes that are most meaningful to me are those in which *Information U.S.A.* may have enhanced the quality of someone's life. I have to admit that selling books is a primary motivation, but to hear that my work may have changed someone's life for the better is something that is more valuable than what I can take to the bank.

All was not a bed of roses with the first edition—there were problems. The index was limited, the Sampler Section was short, and some of the listings were out of date. There constantly lurked the possibility that the current Administration would cut out most of the programs that comprise the book. In this new edition we have improved the index, reorganized and beefed up the Sampler Section, and worked on keeping the information as current as possible. However, the quest for accuracy is a never-ending battle that is somehow never won. Particularly to first-time buyers, but also to veteran users of *Information U.S.A.*, may I strongly encourage you to look over the main introduction to the book. It will show you how best to use this book and deal with government bureaucrats.

As far as the Reagan Administration's effect on this book is concerned, we were pleasantly surprised to find that the federal government is spending more money than ever before and has more bureaucrats on its payroll. As a result, *Information U.S.A.* has grown. Although there are some programs that have been cut back and others that have been eliminated, most of the government is simply operating at a *slower rate of growth* than in the past, and some priorities have shifted. For example, the large number of energy experts at the Department of Energy in the Carter Administration have been reduced, but we now have a large number of high-tech experts at the Department of Defense. And remember, they still are accessible if you know where to find them.

I believe that more important problems besides the growth or lack of growth of the government have emerged during President Reagan's tenure. Even if the Administration cut the government by 50 percent it would not affect the size of *Information U.S.A.* To tell you the truth, this book could be five times as large. My biggest job is selecting what *should* be included. This book represents only a small fraction of available government resources, and most readers only use a small fraction of them. There is just too much that continues to go unused because no one knows it exists. The headlines about budget cuts have increased this problem because they have led taxpayers into believing that the government is no longer available to them. This is certainly not true. As a matter of fact, there are greater opportunities for those who use the government because now

fewer people are using it when there is so much available. Also, in the atmosphere of budget cutting, many departments and agencies cut back in areas that help taxpayers learn about available information and programs, but the government did little cutting in the actual amount of available information and assistance. For example:

1. Free publications that explained the results of studies were eliminated, but the money supporting the research continued.
2. Support services, like one at the Bureau of the Census that helped show people how to get and use the data, were cut back, when we still spent over $1 billion on the 1980 census.
3. Toll-free hotlines, like the one assisting students in finding financial assistance, were taken out, when the government actually gave out *more* student aid than ever before.

It seems to me that cutting out free publications that may cost thousands of dollars is a disservice to the taxpayer unless we also cut out the billions spent each year to collect the information that was put into free publications. The best way that taxpayers have of getting their money's worth is by knowing about and using the information generated.

The present situation has the government creating more information and telling less. I hope *Information U.S.A.* continues to help solve this ever-ending problem for many thousands of its readers.

Introduction

IT IS NOT AN exaggeration to say that information is the life-blood of modern American society. In business we rely on data to plan our agendas. Every day in our personal lives we make decisions—in buying and selling, entertainment, travel, education, and so many other areas—based largely on information that is available to us. What we do is shaped by what we learn from information sources—television, books, films, radio, newspapers, newsletters, magazines, and so on. Access to information, then, is a necessary tool for living.

By far the most comprehensive, yet the most unexplored, source of information in the United States is our federal government. Washington, DC, it can unequivocally be said, is the information capital of the world. We call the 2,880,000 employees of the government "bureaucrats." But "bureaucrats" is really a misnomer. Some 710,000 of these government workers are really information specialists. As taxpayers we pay their salaries and fund their research. As information consumers, we are entitled to a return on our investment.

These specialists work in every cubbyhole of the government bureaucracy, from cabinet-level agencies to independent government commissions, and from the Department of Agriculture to the Library of Congress to the Small Business Administration. This book pinpoints the information sources and specialists in our government: who they are, what they do, how they can help *you*.

I was certainly not the first person to recognize the phenomenal information resources that are available in Washington. I simply discovered a way to run a business that exploits their expertise. In 1975 I founded Washington Researchers, a company designed to bridge the gap between the information source and the information user. In four years, Washington Researchers grew from an undercapitalized company with a staff of one—me—to a million-dollar enterprise with a staff of 35 workers.

As so often happens in a fledgling enterprise, my first client was a friend. His problem was this: could I, within 24 hours, describe the basic supply and demand for Maine potatoes? How I supplied the information he wanted illustrates perfectly how you can put government specialists to work for you.

My client represented a syndicate of commodity investors who invested millions of dollars in Maine potatoes. When he called me, these potatoes were selling at double their normal price; he wanted to know why. I knew absolutely nothing about potatoes, but I thought I knew where to find this out. We decided that I would be paid for my service only if I found the information within a day.

I immediately called the general office at the Department of Agriculture and asked to speak to an expert on potatoes. The operator referred me to a Mr. Charlie Porter. I wondered: Was he the department functionary for handling crank calls or could he really help me? The operator assured me Porter was an agriculture economist specializing in potatoes. I called the number given and, to my surprise, he answered his telephone. I began by saying I was a struggling entrepreneur who knew nothing about potatoes and needed his help to answer a client's request. Charlie graciously gave me much of the information I needed, adding that he would be happy to talk at greater length either on the phone or in person at his office. I decided to go see him.

For two and one half hours the next morning, Charlie explained in intimate detail the supply and demand for Maine potatoes. He showed me computer printouts that explained why their price had doubled in recent weeks. For any subject that came up during our conversation, Charlie had immediate access to a reference source. He had rows of books covering all aspects of the potato market. A strip of ticker tape that showed the daily price of potatoes from all over the country lay across his desk. Here in this office, I thought, was everything you would ever want to know about potatoes. My problem, it turned out, was not in getting *enough* information, but *too much!* Once Charlie started talking, it was hard to stop him. I sensed that Charlie Porter had spent his lifetime studying the supply and demand for the potato and *finally* someone with a genuine need sought his expertise.

Charlie then pointed me across the hall in the

direction of a potato statistician whose sole responsibility was to produce a monthly report showing potato production and consumption in the United States. In the statistician's office, I learned all the various categories of potatoes that were tallied. I was surprised to learn that even the number of potato chips produced each month was counted.

My client couldn't have been more satisfied. And I realized that I was on to something big—and profitable.

The Art of Obtaining Information from Bureaucrats

ONCE YOU find your Charlie Porter you must make your information request carefully. Remember that the expert you find is probably a mid-level bureaucrat who has spent most of his career studying a narrow subject area. Moreover, his work goes largely unnoticed by top management. Bureaucrats are under no obligation to share their expertise with you: They receive the same paycheck no matter how useful they are to you. The success you have in rallying them to your cause will determine how fully your problem is solved.

Following are ten techniques developed by Washington Researchers to help insure a rewarding relationship with federal bureaucracy:

1. *Introduce yourself cheerfully.* The way you open the conversation will set the tone for the entire interview. Your greeting and initial comments should be cordial and cheery. They should give the feeling that yours is not going to be just another anonymous telephone call, but a pleasant interlude in your source's day.

2. *Be open.* You should be as candid as possible with your source since you are asking the same of him. If you are evasive or deceitful in explaining your needs or motives, your source will be reluctant to provide you with information. If there are certain facts you cannot reveal because of client confidentiality, for example, explain why. Most people will understand.

3. *Be optimistic.* Throughout your entire conversation, you should exude a sense of confidence. If you call a source and say, for example, "You don't have any information that can help me, do you?" it makes it easy for your source to say, "You're right. I can't help you." A positive attitude will encourage your sources to stretch their minds to see the various ways they can be of assistance.

4. *Be humble and courteous.* You can be optimistic and still be humble. Remember the old adage that you can catch more flies with honey than you can with vinegar. People in general, and experts in particular, love to tell others what they know, as long as their positions of authority are not questioned or threatened.

5. *Be concise.* State your problem in the simplest possible manner. If you bore your source with a long-winded request, your chances for a thorough response are diminished.

6. *Don't be a "gimme."* A "gimme" is someone who says "give me this" or "give me that," and has no consideration for the other person's feelings.

7. *Be complimentary.* This goes hand in hand with being humble. A well-placed compliment about your source's expertise or insight into a particular topic will serve you well. In searching for information in the government, you are apt to talk to people who are colleagues of your source. It would be reassuring to your source to know he is respected by his peers.

8. *Talk about other things.* Do not spend the entire time talking about the information you need. If you can, discuss briefly a few irrelevant topics, such as the weather, the Washington Redskins, or this year's pennant race. The more social you are, the more likely it is that your source will respond favorably.

9. *Return the favor.* You might share with your source some bits of information, or even gossip, you have learned from other sources. However, be certain not to betray anyone's trust. If you do not have any information to share at the moment, it would be a good idea to call back when you are further along in your research and obtain something of interest to your source.

10. *Send thank-you notes.* A short note, typed or handwritten, will help insure that your source will be just as cooperative in the future.

How to Use *Information U.S.A.*

BEFORE you use the directory portion of this book, review the "Sampler" section. This section will give you a feeling for both the breadth and depth of information presented in the directory portion.

There are essentially two ways to use the directory section. If you know exactly what you're looking for, the first—and quickest—way is to choose key words (e.g., earthworms, franchising, heart disease) that characterize your area of interest and turn to the subject index at the back of the book. This will refer you directly to those agencies where your information can be found. Alternatively, you can turn to a department or an agency whose name makes it sound as if it might be of value to you. For example, to research solar energy, look under U.S. Department of Energy; for business loans, look under the Small Business Administration. The description of each agency's "mission" will give you a good idea how useful that agency will be. Be sure to glance at the subject headings of the information sources listed. Although these might not be topics that directly meet your needs, there may be a related subject area listed.

As you begin to use government resources regularly, you'll be constantly surprised by the amount of information available. As I discovered in my meeting with Charlie Porter at the Department of Agriculture, my happy dilemma was not in finding enough information, but finding almost too much!

Some of the services you request will be available for free; some, such as booklets, directories, newsletters, etc., at a minimal cost. Keep the following in mind when you ask for such items:

If you do not know what to ask for specifically, describe your problem and ask how you can be helped, or request a listing of products or services that are available. Then request that your source send you the items you can use that are available.

Be sure to state that you authorize any costs that may be incurred on your behalf, up to a maximum amount.

For any items above your maximum amount, ask for descriptions and prices.

Include your name, address, and telephone number in all correspondence.

When requesting a publication, be sure to include the complete title and order number (if applicable).

Unless otherwise indicated, the government prefers to receive requests on a postcard.

The Objectives and Limitations of *Information U.S.A.*

THE FEDERAL GOVERNMENT spends more than $700 billion a year. Much of that money goes toward accumulating expertise and information; *Information U.S.A.* is an attempt to catalog these resources. However, because of the herculean dimensions of this objective and because of the changing nature of the information, it is virtually impossible for this book to be thoroughly complete and up-to-date. What it *will* do is:

Expand your mind to see that somewhere in the federal government there is a free source of information on almost any topic you can think of.

Save you time in locating where in the federal government your needed source is located.

Help you realize that, large as this book is, it is still only the tip of the iceberg. If you cannot find the exact source you need in this book, with a little effort and ingenuity you can probably find the expert you need.

The reader should be warned that, like any directory, this book is out of date as soon as it is printed. Some of the addresses and telephone numbers may have changed by the time you use them. Do not be discouraged. Just knowing that an office or expert exists is the most important part of getting the information you need, for then it is not overly difficult to track down the correct address or phone number. If you get stuck in your search here are some tips:

Call the government operator at 202-655-4000 for the correct address or phone number.

Contact your local Federal Information Center, listed in the Sampler Section under "Resources Close-To-Home" or in your telephone book under "U.S. Government."

Contact the local office of your Congressman or Senator.

Each of these sources can help you locate what you need from the federal government.

SAMPLER SECTION

Introduction

While the news from Washington has been of budget cuts, staff reductions, and drastic cutbacks in free publications and services, the fact is there still are thousands of free—and nearly free—resources in this vast treasure trove. And they are all yours for the asking—as long as you know how to uncover them!

INFORMATION USA is written to help you do just that. This new, reorganized Sampler Section will help you quickly identify the most frequently sought after information. Before delving into the Sampler though, we suggest you scan the Table of Contents to get an idea of the variety of categories covered here. There are sections for kids through senior citizens. You can use the Sampler to shop for gifts, locate surplus property, find the answers to information needed by you and your family, help your plants, get assistance in conducting business, learn how to find an expert, plan your trips, and more. We also suggest you read "The Art of Obtaining Information from Bureaucrats" in the Introduction so that you will become more adept at using the leads provided here.

Designed to introduce you to the incredible wealth of resources available from Uncle Sam, the Sampler is meant to be used as a starting-point in your search for assistance, especially since the book's chapters on specific departments and agencies offer many more resources than we could possibly list in this section. We hope the Sampler will help you become resourceful and creative in your use of the remainder of the book.

INFORMATION USA describes hotlines, publications, gifts and unique services—many, especially those mentioned in the "The Best of The Freebies," which are only available from your rich and resourceful Uncle Sam. We hope you take advantage of what's offered. After all, it is estimated that you work at least 1 hour and 43 minutes out of an 8 hour work day—just to pay for it all via your federal taxes. So use what's here—you've earned it!

3

The Best of the Freebies

Uncle Sam offers hundreds of free items and services of interest to the general public. In this section we have pulled together some of what we consider to be the "best" freebies. These range from free airplane rides for kids to information about wine and cheese-making at home. Occasionally you'll notice there is a small fee charged for something we've included here. In such a case, we felt the item to be so unique or worthwhile that it deserved to be highlighted in this "Best of" section.

Accommodations, Airplane Rides and More for Youth Groups

The U.S. Air Force provides a variety of free, unique experiences for our nation's youth, especially national scouting groups. The Air Force opens its facilities to these groups for special events, such as olympics, jamborees, conferences, and meetings. Overnight accommodations ranging from camping sites to beds in barracks are also available. Youth can participate in training exercises, obtain orientation plane rides, and take tours of the Air Force facilities. Aerospace education, career programs, and sometimes surplus properties are also available. Films, on topics as diverse as expert motorcycle riding, space communications, the history of the Air Force, and missile development in space can be borrowed. For information, assistance or support in any of the above areas, scout and youth groups should contact the Youth Organization Project Officer at the Air Force Installation where they wish to conduct an activity. Address correspondence to: Base Commander, (List Appropriate Name) Air Force Base, State, Zip Code, Attention: Youth Organization Project Officer. For national and regional events, youth groups should write the appropriate regional liaison officer or the director. A list of these officers appears below.

Director, Air Force Office of Youth Relations, Kelly Air Force Base, Texas 78241-5000/ 512-925-5384.

Northeast Region, Air Force Office of Youth Relations, McGuire Air Force Base, New Jersey 08641-5000/609-724-2905/3728.

Southeast Region, Air Force Office of Youth Relations, Dobbins Air Force Base, Georgia 30069-5000/404-424-4990.

East Central Region, Air Force Office of Youth Relations, O'Hare ARF Facility, Illinois 60666-5000/312-694-6088.

South Central Region, Air Force Office of Youth Relations, Carswell Air Force Base, Texas 76127-5000/817-735-7134.

North Central Region, Air Force Office of Youth Relations, Whiteman Air Force Base, Missouri 65305-5000.

Western Region, Air Force Office of Youth Relations, Travis Air Force Base, California 94535-5260/707-438-5100.

Adopt-A-Horse

In order to control the population of wild horses and burros grazing on public land, the U.S. Department of the Interior offers these animals for adoption to qualified applicants. For further information and adoption applications contact: Adopt-A-Horse, Bureau of Land Management, U.S. Department of the Interior, Washington, DC 20240.

Anger—Helping Children Cope

A free pamphlet entitled *Plain Talk About Dealing with the Angry Child* (502N) suggests ways of helping a child cope with feelings of anger and aggression. Available from: Consumer Information Center, P.O. Box 100, Pueblo, CO 81002.

Anorexia Nervosa

A 7-page booklet entitled *Facts About Anorexia Nervosa* (411N, 50 cents) describes symptoms, causes, and treatments of this potentially fatal eating disorder. It also gives sources for more information and assistance. Available from: Consumer Information Center, P.O. Box 100, Pueblo, CO 81002.

Anti–Jet Lag Diet
This freebie provides information about how you can reduce the adverse side effects of air travel by altering your diet. To obtain a copy, send a stamped, self-addressed envelope to: Anti–Jet Lag Diet, Office of Public Affairs, Argonne National Laboratory, 9700 South Cass Avenue, Argonne, IL 60439.

Art Museum Exhibits for Rent
The Smithsonian Museum provides specially designed exhibits to organizations and institutions across the country, and abroad, at the lowest possible rental fees. More than 120 exhibitions of paintings, sculptures, prints, drawings, decorative arts, history, children's art, natural history, photography, science and technology are circulated every year. Lists of available exhibitions and information about future bookings are available. Contact: Smithsonian Institution Traveling Exhibition Service, Smithsonian Institution, 900 Jefferson Drive SW, Washington, DC 20560/ 202-357-3168.

Art on Loan
Educational materials, including color slide programs, films and videocassettes based on works in the National Gallery of Art's collection and special exhibitions can be borrowed without charge. A free catalogue is available. Write: Extension Programs, National Gallery of Art, Washington, DC 20565.

Arts America
The International Communication Agency assists qualified artists and performers in arranging private tours overseas. Its aim is to present a balanced portrayal of the American scene. ICA has sponsored: a major exhibition of American crafts shown in China; a modern dance company's visit to the USSR, Spain, and Portugal; and a jazz ensemble's tour of Nigeria, Senegal and Kenya. Contact: Arts Liaison Advisor, Office of the Associate Director for Programs, International Communication Agency, United States Intelligence Agency, 301 4th Street SW, Room 568, Washington, DC 20547/202-485-2779.

Art Slides from the National Gallery
Slides of the Gallery's collection are available on a loan basis to organizations, schools, and colleges without charge. Contact: Slide Library, National Gallery of Art, Washington, DC 20565/202-737-4215.

Baldness Treatments (553N)
This freebie discusses products which are supposed to restore hair or prevent hair loss. Write: Consumer Information Center, P.O. Box 100, Pueblo, CO 81002.

Best and Worst Food Buys for Coming Months
A free subscription to the *National Consumer Buying Alert* will keep you informed about which foods will be cheaper or more expensive in coming months. The monthly publication also provides general consumer tips, such as how to deal with a wet basement, how to insulate your home or how to reduce gas consumption. For a free copy write: Consumer Information Center, Pueblo, CO 81009.

Bibliographies
Free listings of Government publications on more than 240 subjects ranging from accounting to veteran's affairs can be easily obtained. For a brochure on the subjects covered write to: Superintendent of Documents, U.S. Government Printing Office, Washington, DC 20402/202-783-3238.

Biking and Hiking Maps
Brochures with maps of trails throughout the National Park Service are available free of charge. When placing your order, specify the geographical area you are interested in. Contact: U.S. Department of Interior, 18th and C Streets NW, Room 1013, Washington, DC 20240/202-343-4747. (Note: If you call, you will at first hear a recording. Stay on the line if you wish to speak with someone.)

Birthday and Anniversary Greetings from the President
The President will send birthday greetings to individuals 80 or over and anniversary greetings to couples married 50 years or longer. You must notify the President of the event, in writing, at least 2 weeks (preferably 1 month or more) before the celebrated occasion. Include in your letter: the name(s) and address, including zip code of the person(s) to be honored, and information about the event including the date, number of years being celebrated and whether it is a birthday or anniversary. Write: White House, Greetings Office, Washington, DC 20500.

Boating Lessons
A variety of free courses, ranging from 1 to 13 classes, on safe boating are offered by the U.S.

Coast Guard. For further information contact your local U.S. Coast Guard Office, or Commandant (G-BAU-1), U.S. Coast Guard, Washington, DC 20592/202-426-1077.

Breast Cancer

A pamphlet is available summarizing information about breast cancer, biopsy, mammography, reconstruction and rehabilitation. For a free copy write: Public Inquiries Office, National Cancer Institute, National Institutes of Health, Bethesda, MD 20205.

Brides Information Package

Available to new homemakers, this packet contains an assortment of home and garden bulletins relating to budgeting, consumer tips, cooking, etc. Contact: Your Congressman, U.S. Congress, Washington, DC 20515/202-224-3121.

Business Loans for Children and Teenagers

The U.S. Department of Agriculture lends up to $10,000 to youths from ten to 21 years of age. The loans can be used to support both farm and non-farm ventures, such as small crop farming, livestock farming, roadside stands and custom work. They are normally made in conjunction with youth groups and require parental consent. Contact: Production Loan Division, Farmers Home Administration, Department of Agriculture, Washington, DC 20250/202-447-4572.

Calendars

Each congressional office has a large stock of hanging wall calendars, containing beautiful photographs of Washington Scenes. For a free calendar contact: Your Congressman, U.S. Congress, Washington, DC 20515/202-224-3121.

Child Support Handbook

The *Handbook on Child Support Enforcement* is a "how-to" guide for getting the child support payments which are owed to you and your children. Information is provided about applying for child support enforcement services, obtaining help in finding the absent parent, establishing paternity, collecting child support, and collecting payments in another state. The free publication is available by writing: Consumer Information Center, P.O. Box 100, Pueblo, CO 81002.

Christmas Trees

Free Christmas trees are available to nonprofit organizations. Commercial organizations and individuals can obtain trees at fair market value, and for $1.00 you can cut your own tree. The trees are located on federal land in ten western states. Contact: Your local office of the Bureau of Land Management, the Forest Service, or: Division of Forestry, Bureau of Land Management, Department of the Interior, Room 5620, Washington, DC 20240/202-343-3229.

Chronic Pain

A free booklet describing causes and possible cures for pain, including headaches, lower back pain, cancer pain and arthritis pain is available from: Chronic Pain, National Institute of Neurological and Communicative Disorders and Stroke, Room 8A-06, Building 31, Bethesda, MD 20205.

Coaches—Drug and Alcohol Prevention Program

A nationwide program, developed in conjunction with the National High School Athletic Coaches Association, is designed to help coaches prevent drug and alcohol abuse. Free information packets, publications, a slide show and video tape are all available to coaches. Clinics and workshops for coaches will be held throughout the United States at which Drug Enforcement Agency Special Agents, professional athletes, and amateur sports figures will address a variety of topics pertaining to drug and alcohol prevention. Contact: Preventive Programs, Drug Enforcement Administration, Department of Justice, 1405 I Street NW, Washington, DC 20537/202-633-1437.

Computerized Databases and Searches Available

The Federal Government maintains hundreds of in-house, computerized databases on subjects ranging from acid rain to women in development. Often staff will search their database for you and send you a print-out either free of charge or on a cost-recovery basis. Approximately 200 of these databases are described in *Information USA*. For more information, look up "Computerized Databases" entry under the *Major Information Sources* sections of this book.

Computerized Databases—Free Public Access

For the price of a phone call, computer users, with telephone link-up equipment, can dial directly into several data bases operated by the federal government:

ALTERNATIVE FUEL DATA BANK (AFDB)—AFDB, designed for direct public access, can be searched by most home computer users having a telephone linkup. The data bank contains information about the utilization of alternative fuels. It has three types of data: bibliographies of publications, synopses of ongoing research activities and discussions of topics of current interest. AFDB focuses on the use of non-petroleum sources and non-conventional fuels from petroleum sources in transportation. Examples of fuels covered include syncrudes from shale, coal, alcohols, hydrogen, ethers and broadcut. Information is collected from periodicals, abstract news service publications, technical society papers, conference proceedings, and project progress and final reports. Data retrieval programs are interactive and designed for easy use by the general public.

Searches and direct-access privileges are available free of charge. Contact the Center to obtain a free user's manual and I.D. number. If you don't have the equipment to search AFDB yourself, the Center will query the system for you and send you a printout. Contact: Alternative Fuel Data Bank, Bartlesville Energy Technology Center, P.O. Box 2128, Bartlesville, OK 74005/918-337-4267.

CLIMATE ASSESSMENT DATA BASE—this database designed for easy public access provides users with information about short-term climate conditions in the United States and throughout the world. Anyone with a compatible terminal (most home computers are) and telephone linkup can obtain a password and dial directly into the system. Users can then select from a menu of 12 databases summarizing meteorological data on a weekly, monthly and seasonal basis. Examples of data include: temperature, precipitation, weather indexes, heating and cooling days, energy conditions, and assessment of climate on crops. The system contains global surface data collected from 8,000 stations worldwide. Currently, most data is in tabular form, but plans are under way to include graphical presentations. To obtain a password for this system contact: NOAA, National Meteorological Center, W353, WWB, Room 201, Washington, DC 20233/301-763-8071.

COMPUTER STANDARDS AND TECHNOLOGY BULLETIN BOARDS—the Institute for Computer Science and Technology sponsors two free electronic bulletin boards which provide information about conferences, articles, and other literature dealing with new standards and technology in computers and software. One bulletin board deals with computer performance evaluation and the other microprocessors. Contact: Institute for Computer Science and Technology, National Bureau of Standards (NBS), Washington, DC 20234/301-921-2731.

CRUDE OIL ANALYSIS DATA BANK (COA)—this data bank contains analyses of nearly all crude oils discovered in the United States and representative crude oils from foreign countries. COA is the world's largest collection of data about crude oil physical properties, distillation and refining. Examples of retrievable properties include: gravity, sulphur content, nitrogen content, viscosity, color and pour point. Other retrievable information includes the oil's geochemistry, its source and financial value. The database can be searched by any parameter in the analyses (i.e., type of oil, location, specific property, etc.). The system is designed for easy use by the general public.

COA was started in the 1920's and it currently contains more than 10,000 analyses. Searches and direct access privileges are available free of charge. If you don't have the equipment to search COA yourself, the Center will query the system for you and send you a printout. To obtain a free User's Guide or more information, contact: Crude Oil Analysis Data Bank, Bartlesville Energy Technology Center, U.S. Department of Energy, P.O. Box 1398, Bartlesville, OK 74003/918-336-2400 (ext. 256).

TIME DATABASE (USNO-ADS)—the U.S. Naval Observatory—Automated Data Service (USNO-ADS) collects the latest available time data, and most owners of home computers with a telephone hook-up can dial directly into the system's numerous files. By inputting appropriate information, users can obtain data such as: the time of sunrise, sunset, twilight and moonrise on a given day at any location on Earth; the times when transit satellites will pass over their area during the upcoming 25 hours; the direction and distance (in nautical and statute miles) between any two points on Earth; the Universal Time; and much more. The Naval Observatory has designed most of the programs on ADS, but they will help individuals and organizations (such as universities) run their own programs on the system. Staff will also search their database for you at no cost. Contact: Time Service Division, U.S. Naval Observatory, Washington, DC 20390/202-254-4548.

Computerized Decisionmaking for Consumers, Families, Businessmen, and Farmers

The Computerized Management Network (CMN) is a software system of more than 60 interactive programs developed to help the decisionmaking process for farmers, consumers, families, and businessmen. Designed to be used by non-computer-oriented individuals, the system covers areas such as: finance and accounting; taxes and estate planning; human nutrition and health; home, farm, and crop management; information retrieval; and much more.

You can obtain access to CMN through most Cooperative Extension Service (CES) offices nationwide. Subscribing CES offices will either search the system for you or possibly let you conduct a search yourself. Individuals and organizations can also obtain direct-access privileges for a minimum usage fee of $25.00 per month. The cost of running CMN programs varies from 50 cents for a very simple analysis to $15.00 for complex linear models. Contact your local Extension Service Office (listed under Department of Agriculture in your telephone book) or Computerized Management Network, Plaza 1, Building D, Extension Division, Virginia Polytechnic Institute, Blacksburg, VA 24061/703-961-5184.

Congressional Pages and Interns
Approximately 100 pages work for Members of Congress during the school year. More positions for pages as well as interns are available during the summer months. Contact your U.S. Senator and Representative for more information.

Consumer Publications—Best Freebies List
The Consumer Information Center is the main distributor of free and low-cost consumer oriented publications issued by the federal government. Below is a representative listing of some of the Center's most popular publications.

For copies of these publications, or to order a free publications catalogue, contact: Consumer Information Center, Pueblo, CO 81009.

Cancer Prevention: Good News, Better News, Best News (571N)—provides advice on what you can do to help protect yourself against cancer, including latest nutrition information.
Child Support (501N)—describes help available from the government to enforce child support obligations, locate missing parents, and establish paternity.
Consumer Credit Handbook (591N)—explains how to apply for credit, what to do if you are denied, and how consumer credit laws can help you.
Student Guide—Five Federal Financial Aid Programs (513N)—gives important information about five grant and loan programs for college, vocational, and technical school students.
Back Pain (569N)—describes common causes and treatments of this all too common ailment.
Your Social Security (515N)—explains all about Social Security and Medicare benefits, including who gets them and how to apply.

Checklist for Going into Business (516N)—discusses important considerations before starting a small business.
A Consumer's Guide to Life Insurance (592N)—this is a comprehensive guide to different types of policies, costs, and coverage; includes a glossary of commonly used terms.
How to Choose and Use a Lawyer (601N)—provides questions and answers about fees, advertising, referrals, and other legal resources. It also covers what to do when you have a problem with a lawyer.
Some Things You Should Know About Prescription Drugs (560N)—even prescription drugs can be dangerous; here are tips for safe use.
How to Buy a Telephone (600N)—gives facts about costs, selection, installation, and repair.
Consumer's Guide to Telephone Services (618N)—describes the best area services available.

Consumer's Resource Handbook (613N)
A comprehensive guide to how to complain and get results, this lists corporate consumer representatives, private consumer organizations, and federal, state, and local government agencies with consumer responsibilities. The 111-page guide is available free of charge from: Consumer Information Center, P.O. Box 100, Pueblo, CO 81002.

Contraception: Comparing the Options (554N)
This free fold-out chart lists the nine common methods of birth control and the pros and cons of each. For a copy write: Consumer Information Center, P.O. Box 100, Pueblo, CO 81002.

Cosmetics
A free pamphlet entitled *Questions Concerning Cosmetics* (548N) provides answers to seven commonly asked questions regarding ingredients in various cosmetics. Write: Consumer Information Center, P.O. Box 100, Pueblo, CO 81002.

Crime Resistance: A Way to Protect Your Family Against Crime
This 16-page booklet provides tips for how you and your family can make yourself safe from crime in your home as well as when you go about your daily routines—commuting to and from work, traveling in the family car, walking to school and shopping. For a free copy write: FBI, Office of Congressional and Public Affairs, Room 6236, 10th Street at Pennsylvania Avenue SW, Washington, DC 20535.

Depression and Manic-Depressive Illness
This publication describes the wide range of

depression states, the biological factors related to depression and the treatments available. To obtain a free copy write: Information Office, National Institutes of Health, Clinical Center, Room 5C305, Bethesda, MD 20205.

Diet and Weight-Loss Gimmicks

Below are 2 freebies available from: Consumer Information Center, P.O. Box 100, Pueblo, CO 81002.

About Body Wraps, Pills, and Other Magic Wands (564N)—this discusses weight-loss gimmicks, untested diet aids, and their potential dangers.
Diet Books Sell Well But . . . . . . (566N)—presents the fallacies and hazards of some popular diets, as well as advice about selecting a healthy diet to lose weight.

Disaster Handbook

In Time of Emergency . . . A Citizen's Handbook, provides information and guidance about what families can do to enhance survival in the event of natural or man-made disasters, such as fires, floods, hurricanes, tornadoes, winter storms, earthquakes, tidal waves, nuclear power plant accidents or nuclear attacks. Free from: Federal Emergency Management Agency, P.O. Box 8181, Washington, DC 20024.

Duck Stamp Contest

Artists are invited to participate in the Duck Stamp Contest, one of our nations' oldest and most successful wildlife conservation efforts. Generally, beginning in July of each year, artists can submit a rendition of any living species of North American migratory duck, goose or swan for the contest. A winner is selected, and he or she receives a sheet of stamps (worth $225) and owns the copyright of the painting which can be of great value. The stamps, which must be purchased yearly by waterfowl hunters, are sold by the U.S. Post Office for $7.50 each. The proceeds are then used to buy wetlands for the National Wildlife Refuge System. A free pamphlet entitled *The Duck Stamp Story* presents the background of the Duck Stamp Program. To order, or obtain further information, contact: Public Affairs, Fish and Wildlife Service, Washington, DC 20240/202-343-5634.

Employment Roadmaps

The Congressional Caucus for Science and Technology, established to serve members of Congress, can tell you about the impact of science and technology on training and retraining. The Caucus

plans to develop *Employment Roadmaps* which will highlight employment opportunities, as well as training and educational requirements, for current and prospective jobs. Staff can answer questions about high tech related legislation and they will refer science and technology oriented inquiries to the Caucus' research arm, the Research Institute for Space, Science and Technology. Contact: Congressional Caucus for Science and Technology, House Annex Building #2, H2-226, 2nd and D Streets SW, Washington, DC 20515/202-226-7788.

Exercise and Your Heart

This free booklet explains the relationship between exercise and a healthy heart and it offers practical information about what you can do to improve your heart. Available from: National Heart, Lung, and Blood Institute, Information Office, Building 31, Room 4A21, Bethesda, MD 20205.

Films You Can Borrow—or Buy

The U.S. Government has produced more than 13,500 films on subjects as varied as foreign relations, drug abuse, preparing your taxes, business management, space exploration and sexual assault. The Government's National Audio Visual Center catalogues, loans, rents and sells these films. Upon your request the clearinghouse will send you a listing of its holdings on any subject you choose. A free catalogue listing 3,000 titles on subjects of interest to the general public is available free of charge. Often there is a small fee for films borrowed from the Center. Contact: National Audio Visual Center, Information Services DW, Washington, DC 20409/202-763-1896.

Several government agencies distribute films they have produced directly to the public. Listed below, by broad subject area, are agencies from which you can borrow films free of charge. Films offered by these offices range from expert motorcycle riding, courtesy of the Air Force, to recreational films from the U.S. Corps of Engineers. Most of these offices will send you a free catalogue listing films you can borrow or purchase.

AGRICULTURE—motion pictures on a variety of agricultural subjects are available for loan through various State Extension Services film libraries. Contact: National Audio-Visual Center, Attention: Information Services, Washington, DC 20409/301-763-1896.
AIR AND SPACE—films are available on topics such as the Apollo missions, the planets, earth-sun relationships, the atmosphere, weather, and

National Aeronautics and Space Administration research projects. For information and a free film catalogue contact: NASA, Motion Pictures, Office of Public Affairs, Washington, DC 20546/202-755-3500.

AIR FORCE MOTION PICTURES—for information on motion picture films created or acquired by the Air Force and cleared for public distribution, contact: DAVA-N-LD, Norton Air Force Base, CA 92409/714-382-2394. A film catalog, "Air Force Regulations 95-2, Vol. 2," is available for $10.00 from: Superintendent of Documents, U.S. Government Printing Office, Washington, DC 20402/202-783-3238.

AIR FORCE STOCK FOOTAGE—stock footage of Air Force films is available from: DAVA-DAV-COM Divisions, Building 248, Motion Media Depository, Norton Air Force Base, CA 92409/714-382-2307.

ARMY FILMS—for Army films available to the public, contact: Commander, U.S. Army Audio Visual Center, 1010 MOAV-MO, Room 5A470, Pentagon, Washington, DC 20310/202-694-4548.

CAPTIONED FILMS—a free catalog listing free educational and entertainment films for the deaf is available from: Modern Talking Picture Service, Inc., 5000 Park Street N, St Petersburg, FL 33709/813-541-7571.

CITIZENSHIP EDUCATION—citizen education films are available at no charge to civic, patriotic, educational and religious groups. There are also about 15 textbooks on citizenship available, consisting of teachers' manuals and student textbooks at various reading levels. These books are distributed free to public schools for applicants for citizenship. Contact: Naturalization, Immigration and Naturalization Service, Department of Justice, 425 Eye Street NW, Room 7228, Washington, DC 20536/202-633-3320.

DEFENSE LOGISTICS AGENCY FILMS—for information on films available for public showing to present and potential contractors, contact: Headquarters, Defense Logistics Agency, Department of Defense, Cameron Station, Room 3C547, Alexandria, VA 22314/202-274-6075.

DOCUMENTARY FILMS AND NEWSREEL FOOTAGE—approximately 91 million feet of documentary and newsreel footage and other government-produced films constitute this collection. Materials can be screened and footage may be purchased. For more information, contact: Motion Picture and Video and Sound Branch, National Archives and Records Administration, 8th and Pennsylvania Avenue NW, Room G-13, Washington, DC 20408/202-786-0041.

DRUG EDUCATION—drug education films are available free of charge to civic, educational, private and religious groups. Contact: Preventive Programs, Office of Public Affairs, Drug Enforcement Administration, Department of Justice, 1405 Eye Street NW, Room 1209, Washington, DC 20537/202-633-1249.

EDUCATIONAL FILMS—ERIC Clearinghouse described in the "Information on Anything and Everything" section of this Sampler, frequently loans audiovisual materials. For further details contact the ERIC Clearinghouse covering the subject in which you are interested.

ENVIRONMENTAL AND RECREATION—the Army Corps of Engineers offers public informational films on subjects including navigation, flood control, hydroelectric power, recreation, emergency operations management, environmental enhancement and boating safety. Various exhibits and audiovisual presentations produced by the Corps are available for touring. For short, descriptive lists and information, contact: Public Affairs, Army Corps of Engineers, Department of the Army, Department of Defense, 20 Massachusetts Avenue NW, Room 8122C, HQDA (DAEN-PAV), Washington, DC 20314/202-272-0017. Requests for loan of these films should be sent to: Modern Talking Picture Service, Inc., 5000 Park Street N, St. Petersburg, FL 33709/813-541-7571.

GEOLOGY AND MAPPING—films about geology, topographic mapping, water resources, astrogeology, aerial photography, and other subjects are available. For information and a free film catalogue contact: Visual Information Services, U.S. Geological Survey, 790-National Center, Reston, VA 22092/703-860-6171.

LAW ENFORCEMENT FILMS—films and videotape recordings can be borrowed for education and information purposes. Contact: National Criminal Justice Research Service, 1600 Research Boulevard, Rockville, MD 20850/301-251-5500.

NATURAL RESOURCES—films are available describing many of the country's natural resources. For information and a free catalogue contact: Bureau of Mines, Motion Pictures, 4800 Forbes Avenue, Pittsburgh, PA 15213/412-621-4500.

NAVAL STOCK FOOTAGE—collections of official film photography covering the activities of the U.S. Navy since 1958 (anything prior to that year is kept in the National Archives) are maintained. For information on the collection and ordering, contact: DAVA-N-DDEP, Norton Air Force Base, CA 92409-6518/714-382-2307.

SAFETY RELATED FILMS—films are available on safety-related topics such areas as outdoor power equipment, playground equipment, poison prevention packaging, and toys. A free catalogue is available. Contact: Consumer Product Safety Commission, Washington DC 20207/Hotline: 800-638-2772.

SEXUAL ASSAULT—films explaining how to protect yourself against sexual assault, as well as how to help a victim of an attack, are available from: The National Center for the Prevention and Control of Rape, 5600 Fishers Lane, Room 6C-12, Rockville, MD 20852/301-443-1910.

TAXES—the Internal Revenue Service loans a variety of films on subjects such as the history of taxes, how a tax return is processed, taxpayer rights, and how to organize a business for tax purposes. For a free film listing and information, contact your local IRS office or: Public Affairs Division, Internal Revenue Service, Department of the Treasury, 1111 Constitution Avenue NW, Washington, DC 20224/202-566-6860.

U.S. FOREIGN RELATIONS—HISTORY—a four-part color film series, 30 minutes each, with accompanying discussion guides, may be bought or borrowed without charge. The series starts with the militia diplomacy of the Revolution and ends with the development of U.S. foreign policy through 1975. Contact: Films Officer, Office of Public Communication, Public Affairs, Department of State, 2201 C Street NW, Room 4827A, Washington, DC 20250/202-632-8203.

YOUTH ORIENTED FILMS—a free booklet listing films, both informative and educational, for youth organizations is available from the Air Force. The films, on topics from expert motorcycle riding to space communications, as well as Air Force history, may be borrowed. For a copy of the booklet, "Air Force Films for National Youth Groups," contact: Aerospace Audio-Visual Service, United States Air Force Central Audio-Visual Library, Norton Air Force Base, CA 92409-6518/714-382-2307.

Firewood

Firewood, for personal use, is available for a minimal fee from 155 National Forests in the U.S. A local forest ranger will identify the fallen and dead wood which can be cut and/or carried away. Contact your local Forest Service Office for a free fact sheet. For a map showing Forest Service land write: Forest Service, Department of Agriculture, P.O. Box 2417, Washington, DC 20013/202-447-3957.

Food Buying

You will find the 2 publications described below

helpful. Order from: Consumer Information Center, P.O. Box 100, Pueblo, CO 81002.

Making Food Dollars Count (409N, 50 cents)—a two-week plan, including recipes, to help the shopper on a limited budget meet nutritional needs.

How to Buy Economically: A Food Buyer's Guide (436N, 50 cents)—this provides advice about how to cut costs on meat, poultry, eggs, milk, fruits and vegetables. It identifies months during which you can get the best buys on a variety of fruits and vegetables.

Funeral Information

A booklet entitled *Consumer Guide to the FTC Funeral Rule* (425N, 50 cents) explains your legal right to information concerning prices and options of funeral services. Available from: Consumer Information Center, P.O. Box 100, Pueblo, CO 81002.

Future Trends

What's Next is a free bimonthly newsletter reporting about social, technical and political trends that could be important in the future. It is written to help Congressional Representatives think about the future as they prepare legislation. You too can subscribe by contacting: Your U.S. Congressional Representative's office and asking his/her staff to place you on the newsletter's mailing list.

Gender Gap at the Dinner Table (524N)

This publication describes how men and women differ in nutritional needs, provides weight and energy expenditure charts, and discusses nutritional disorders. Available free of charge from: Consumer Information Center, P.O. Box 100, Pueblo, CO 81002.

Government Surplus Property

Throughout the year the Federal Government gives away surplus property to select groups and offers hundreds of millions of dollars worth of property and goods to the public at bargain prices. For information about what's available and how you can take advantage of these bargains consult the "Surplus Property" Section of the Sampler.

Great Outdoors

The free catalogue *Recreation and Outdoor Activities* (SB-017) is a listing of Federal government publications on biking, water sports, national recreation areas, winter activities and more. Available from: Superintendent of Documents, U.S. Government Printing Office, Washington, DC 20402/202-783-3238.

Handicrafts

A pamphlet containing information and a bibliography about crafts, both as an art and as a business, is available free of charge from: U.S. Small Business Administration, 1441 L Street NW, Washington, DC 20416, or your local SBA office.

Hotline to the President

Call 456-7198 in DC area or 800-424-9090 elsewhere to hear the President announce the latest news from the White House.

How to Strike It Rich in the Government Oil and Gas Lottery

Individuals can participate in public lotteries which offer the rights to extract oil and gas from federally owned land. For an application and further information contact: Bureau of Land Management, Department of Interior, 18th and C Street NW, Room 3560, Washington, DC 20240/202-343-5717.

Infant Care

A free publication from the U.S. Department of Health and Human Services describes how to develop the skills necessary to care for a baby so that he or she can grow into a healthy, able child and adult. Copies are available from: LSDS, Department 76, Washington, DC 20401.

Infertility and How It's Treated (578N)

This 2-page pamphlet discusses the causes of infertility and methods of treatment. Available free of charge from: Consumer Information Center, P.O. Box 100, Pueblo, CO 81002.

Information Guides

The Library of Congress has published more than 100 *Tracer Bullets,* which are reference guides designed to help a reader begin to locate information on a subject about which he or she has only a general knowledge. Examples of these bullets are listed below. Each cites books, reports, periodicals, abstracting services and organizations for a particular topic. A complete listing of these guides appears under *Tracer Bullets* in the "Library of Congress" section of this directory. To order a bullet or obtain further information contact: Science and Technology Division, Reference Section, Library of Congress, Washington, DC 20540/202-287-5580.

> *Biotechnology*
> *Japanese Science and Technology*
> *Alcoholism*
> *Extraterrestrial Life*
> *Women in the Sciences*

> *Manned Space Flight*
> *Personal Computing/Home Computers*
> *Aging*
> *Stress: Physiological and Psychological Aspects*
> *Human Diet and Nutrition*
> *Chemical and Biological Warfare*

Insomnia (579N)

This freebie covers the common causes of sleeplessness and ways to cope without medication. For a copy, write: Consumer Information Center, P.O. Box 100, Pueblo, CO 81002.

International Youth Exchange Programs

Your Guide to International Youth Exchange (512N) lists guidelines for selecting the right exchange program as a student, host family, or community volunteer. The guide also contains a directory of selected programs and services. The 64-page publication is available free of charge from: Consumer Information Center, P.O. Box 100, Pueblo, CO 81002.

Kids—Toys and Other Freebies!

Uncle Sam has many free things for kids including toys, comic books, coloring books and services. To learn what he has for you, look up "Especially For . . . . Kids and Teens" in the Sampler Section entitled "Free Help and Information for You and Your Family."

Lista de Publicaciones Federales en Espanol para el Consumidor (602N)

This 8-page freebie lists all free federal consumer publications in Spanish. Write: Consumer Information Center, P.O. Box 100, Pueblo, CO 81002.

Mailing Help

All you ever wanted to know about certified mail, forwarding mail, express mail, return receipts, postage meters, COD, and much more is described in a free 21-page booklet called *A Consumer's Directory of Postal Services and Products.* Copies can be obtained from your local post office or by writing to: Consumer Information Center, Department 532, Pueblo, CO 81009.

Medical Care—Free or Low-Cost at 5,000 Places Nationwide

Call 800-638-0742 in Maryland or 800-492-0359 elsewhere for information about free and low-cost care in hospitals and other health facilities nationwide. Staff will send you a list of facilities in your area participating in the federal Hill-Burton Free Care Program. They will also send you a brochure describing eligibility guidelines and advise you about filing any complaints you may have about the program or care you may have received. Information can also be obtained by writing: BHMORD-JRSA, 5600 Fishers Lane, Rockville, MD 20857. (Note: Residents of Alaska and Hawaii must write for information, as the toll-free numbers do not service either state.)

Menstrual Discomforts
A freebie entitled *Doing Something About Menstrual Discomforts* (574N)—discusses common problems related to menstruation and treatments, including a list of non-prescription drugs that relieve specific symptoms. Write: Consumer Information Center, P.O. Box 100, Pueblo, CO 81002.

Mental Health Services
A Consumer's Guide to Mental Health Services (544N)—provides information on services ranging from financial aid to different kinds of therapy. The 21-page guide is available by writing: Consumer Information Center. P.O. Box 100, Pueblo, CO 81002.

Microwave Oven Radiation (539N)
Information on microwave radiation and safe oven operation is provided in this 7-page publication available from: Consumer Information Center, P.O. Box 100, Pueblo, CO 81002.

Military Service Records
You can obtain the service record of anyone who retired from the U.S. Military 75 or more years ago. Under certain circumstances you can also obtain information about individuals who retired earlier. A free booklet describing the process for obtaining these records is available from: Public Affairs Office, Department of Defense, Pentagon, Washington, DC 20301/202-697-5737.

Mining, Prospecting and Drilling on Public Lands
Prospecting is still possible! You can look for and mine "hard rock" minerals on public lands administered by the federal government. You can also lease certain public lands to obtain oil, gas, coal, geothermal resources, and other mineral products. For information and free publications about this opportunity, contact the local offices of your U.S. Forest Service (USDA), or Bureau of Land Management (Department of Interior). You can also contact: United States Department of Agriculture, U.S. Forest Service, 12th and Independence Avenue SW, P.O. Box 2417, Washington, DC 20013/703-235-8010.

Missing and Exploited Children Resources Guide
A free publication entitled *Directory of Support Services and Resources for Missing and Exploited Children* describes nonprofit or public support groups throughout the country dedicated to assisting missing and exploited children and their parents. For a copy contact: National Center for Missing and Exploited Children, 1835 K Street NW, Suite 700, Washington, DC 20006/202-634-9821.

Missing Persons Locator
Both the Social Security Administration and the U.S. military offer locator services.

FIND A LOST LOVED ONE—The Social Security Administration will help you locate a missing parent, lost child or other close relative—as long as your reasons are humane. To activate the search, write a letter to your missing person and send it with as much personal information as possible, e.g. date of birth and place of residence, to the Social Security Administration. If the Administration can locate the person in its files, it will forward your letter to him or her. The Administration will not, however, give you the missing person's current address. For further information contact your local Social Security Information Office or send your missing person letter, along with pertinent information to: Social Security Administration, Public Inquiries, Department of Health and Human Services, 6401 Security Boulevard, Baltimore, MD 21235/301-594-5970.

PAST AND PRESENT MILITARY PERSONNEL—trying to locate someone who is, or has been, in the military? Each branch of the Armed Services has a worldwide locator number you can call for information. The operator needs the full name, and if available the birth date and Social Security number, of the military person you are trying to locate. This service is free for military personnel or members of the immediate family. All other users must pay a fee of $2.85 and submit their request by mail.

Air Force   512-652-5774
                 Mailing Address:
                 AF MPC/MPC D003
                 9504 IH 35 N
                 San Antonio, TX 78233-6636
                 (Make checks payable to Air
                 Force, Randolph Air Force Base)

Army 317-542-3647
Mailing Address:
USAEREC
ATTN: Locator Branch
Ft Harrison, IN 46249-5301
(Make checks payable to the U.S. Treasury)

Marine Corps 202-694-1861
Mailing Address:
CMC MMRB-10
HQs U.S. Marine Corps
Washington, DC 20380
(Make checks payable to the U.S. Treasury)

Navy 202-694-3155
Mailing Address:
To find non-family members:
Naval Military Personnel
Command N 0216
Washington, DC 20370-5021

To find a family member:
Naval Military Personnel
Command N 036CC
Washington, DC 20370-5036
(Make checks payable to the U.S. Treasury)

Money-Saving Directory of Drugs
A directory entitled *Approved Prescription Drug List With Therapeutic Equivalent Evaluation* shows how to substitute one drug for another, often at a substantial savings. Available from: Division of Drug Information Resources, FDA, Department of Health and Human Services, 5600 Fishers Lane, Room 8B37, Rockville, MD 20857/301-443-3204.

Motorcycle Safety
The booklet answers questions like: Is motorcycling safe? How does it compare to driving a car? What are the causes of motorcycle accidents and how can they be reduced? Free from: U.S. Department of Transportation, NHTSA, NTS/31, 400 7th Street SW, Washington, DC 20590.

Office Automation and Working Women: Issues for the Decade Ahead
This publication discusses the most important issues women workers face in the electronic office. Single copies can be obtained free of charge. There is a nominal fee for multiple copies. Contact: Women's Bureau, U.S. Department of Labor, 200 Constitution Avenue NW, Washington, DC 20210/202-523-6611.

Organic Farming and Gardening
A free bibliography on this subject, containing over two hundred citations, is available from: National Agricultural Library, 10301 Baltimore Boulevard, Beltsville, MD 20705/301-344-3704.

Overseas Travel Programs for Americans
The United States Information Agency (USIA) will pay American experts, who can contribute to foreign societies' understanding of the United States, to travel abroad and participate in seminars, colloquia or symposia. Subjects covered by American participants have included economics, international relations, U.S. social and political processes, arts and humanities, and science and technology. A free booklet *American Participants,* which describes the program, is available. Contact: American Participants, Office of Program Coordination and Development, U.S.I.A., 1750 Pennsylvania Avenue NW, Room 200, Washington, DC 20547/202-724-1900.

Pamphlets Unlimited
The free leaflet *Vacations Unlimited!* catalogs many low-cost ($2.25–$7.00) travel publications available from the Federal Government. Available from: *Vacations Unlimited!,* Superintendent of Documents, U.S. Government Printing Office, Washington, DC 20402/202-783-3238.

Parental Kidnapping Handbook
Written to assist the parent of a child who has been taken by a non-custodial spouse, this free publication is available from: National Center for Missing and Exploited Children, 1835 K Street NW, Suite 700, Washington, DC 20006/202-634-9821.

Park Rangers' Outdoors Classes
Most National Parks offer free educational programs for visitors. Taught by Park Rangers, the programs generally introduce visitors of all ages to the natural, cultural, and historical significance of a park. Classes range from bodysurfing lessons to nature walks, to slide shows of an area's history. For further information check with the Park's Information Office or contact: Activities and Protection Division, National Park Service, Department of the Interior, Room 3324, Washington, DC 20240/202-343-4874.

Pension Plans—Your Rights
A freebie entitled *Know Your Pension Plan* (511N) provides checklists to help you understand your rights and benefits under your retirement plan. Available free of charge from: Consumer Information Center, P.O. Box 100, Pueblo, CO 81002.

Pick Your Own Fruits and Vegetables
Many farmers allow consumers to pick products directly from their fields at substantial savings. For a directory of farms which offer these direct marketing programs contact your state department of agriculture or a state extension service. For help in locating your local office contact: Administrative Office, Department of Agriculture, Extension Service, Room 340-A, Washington, DC 20250/202-447-3377.

Physical Fitness and Sports
The President's Council on Physical Fitness and Sports will supply information and expertise for those who wish to establish physical fitness programs. Available free publications include:

Aqua Dynamics, Physical Conditioning Through Water Exercise
Exercise and Weight Control
An Introduction to Physical Fitness
Physical Education—A Performance Checklist
The Physically Underdeveloped Child

Contact: President's Council on Physical Fitness and Sports, Department of Health and Human Services, 450 5th Street, Suite 7103, Washington, DC 20001/202-272-3430.

Police Radar—Is It Reliable?
A free issue paper entitled *Police Traffic Radar* examines the use of police radar; the effects of interference from CB radios and cars' ignition, etc; and makes recommendations about improving the effectiveness of radar trafficking. For a copy write: National Bureau of Standards, Public Information Division, Department of Commerce, Washington, DC 20234/301-921-3161.

Posters
A variety of colorful, professionally illustrated posters are available from Uncle Sam. Examples of these freebies are described below.

ARBORETUM—a beautiful poster of azaleas and other flowers is available from: U.S. National Arboretum, Department GH, 3501 New York Avenue NE, Washington, DC 20002/202-475-4857.

AGING—each year a new poster celebrating Older American Month is available from: National Clearinghouse on Aging, Development Services, Department of Health and Human Services, 330 Independence Avenue SW, Room 4247, Washington, DC 20201/202-245-0827.

ENERGY—several energy-related posters are available: a poster illustrating 6 energy tips in cartoon format; a poster presenting a photograph of the sun overlooking a country landscape and promoting solar and renewable energy; and 2 energy conservation posters showing children enjoying their natural environment. Information Center, Department of Energy, P.O. Box 62, Oak Ridge, TN 37831/615-576-1301.

ENVIRONMENT—a simple drawing of a bird in soft colors with a message encouraging environmental protection is available from: Environmental Protection Agency, Public Inquiry Center, 401 M Street SW, Room 211B, Washington, DC 20460/202-382-7550.

FOOD—a fold-out poster entitled *Snack Facts (505N)* is designed to show how snacking can harm your teeth. It provides an attractive chart of snack foods that are least likely to cause decay. Available from: Consumer Information Center, P.O. Box 100, Pueblo, CO 81002.

HOUSING—a black and white poster stating *Fair Housing: More Than A Right—A Responsibility For All* is available from: Fair Housing and Equal Opportunity, U.S. Department of Housing & Urban Development, Room 5110, Washington, DC 20410.

TRAFFIC—a colorful poster called *Let the Gipper Win One for You . . . Fasten Your Seatbelt* is available from: National Highway Traffic Safety Administration, Publications Department, 400 7th Street SW, Washington, DC 20230/202-287-3220.

Productivity Center
This Clearinghouse can provide you with information about how to improve your organization's productivity, competitiveness, and quality. It also has information about other nations, including Japanese productivity and management techniques. Staff can provide you with literature, reference/referral services and reading lists—all free of charge. Contact: Commerce Productivity Center, U.S. Department of Commerce, 14th and Constitution Avenue NW, Room 7413, Washington, DC 20230.

Reading is Fundamental
Reading is Fundamental develops community projects to motivate young people to read by letting them choose and keep books. It supports these programs with publications, training aids and publicity such as film and public service announcements. For additional information contact: Reading is Fundamental, Smithsonian Institution, 600 Maryland Avenue SW, Suite 500, Washington, DC 20560/202-287-3220.

Recycling Paper

A free pamphlet, *What You Can Do To Recycle More Paper*, explains what you can do around your home or at work to help the nation cope with the problem of solid waste disposal. Write: Public Inquiries Center (PM211B), U.S. Environmental Protection Agency, Washington, DC 20460.

Resort Guides

Free resort guides are available for various areas of the United States. They contain a seasonal breakdown of weather and recreational opportunities. They stress elements of interest for each season, along with a table of activities best suited for each season. Contact: Resort Guides, National Oceanographic Data Center, NOAA/NESDIS, Department of Commerce, Washington, DC 20235/ 202-634-7500.

Sexual Assault—Protect Yourself

A free 25-page booklet entitled *How to Protect Yourself Against Sexual Assault* and films on the subject, loaned free of charge are available from: The National Center for the Prevention and Control of Rape, 5600 Fishers Lane, Room 6C-12, Rockville, MD 20852/301-443-1910.

Sexually Transmitted Diseases

A free booklet providing information about the symptoms, diagnosis, treatment and complications of diseases spread through sexual contact is available from: The National Institute of Allergy and Infectious Diseases, Building 31, Room 7A32, Bethesda, MD 20205.

Smoking—Kicking the Habit

A publication entitled *Clearing the Air: A Guide to Quitting Smoking* (543N) offers no-nonsense tips on kicking the habit and staying "clean." Available free of charge by writing: Consumer Information Center, P.O. Box 100, Pueblo, CO 81002.

Space and Aerospace Freebies

NASA has prepared many beautifully illustrated publications about space and aerospace activities. Many are geared toward students and the general public. The publications listed below are all available free of charge, while the supply lasts, from NASA Educational Publications, NASA Headquarters, Code LEP, Washington, DC 20546. Once NASA's supply is exhausted the publications can be purchased, for a minimal fee, from the Superintendent of Documents, U.S. Government Printing Office, Washington, DC 20402/202-783-3238.

Aboard the Space Shuttle—this describes what it would be like to live in space—how you would get there, what the trip would be like, what you would eat, how you would exercise and sleep and finally, how you would return home.

Aerospace Bibliography—the bibliography provides a listing of fiction and nonfiction books and pamphlets available from both commercial and government sources. Reading level, which ranges from Grade 1 through Adult, is indicated.

Elementary School Aerospace Activities—a resource guide for teachers, this manual provides activities, research project ideas, bibliographic information and more to help instructors teach students about the story of man and flight, with emphasis on flight into space.

Mars: The Viking Discoveries—the booklet includes photographs and information about Mars.

NASA 1958–1983—A beautifully illustrated history of NASA, covering events such as the Apollo mission and man's landing on the moon. The publication includes photographs taken in space.

Spacelab—This publication explains what Spacelab is, introduces you to the crew, describes Spacelab experiments, and takes you through a day aboard the aircraft.

Spacelab Poster—A 3½ × 4 foot color illustration of Spacelab.

Spacestation: The Next Logical Step—With pictures and narrative, this booklet shows you what the spacestation will look like, how it will work, the ways industry will set up shop in space, and what the spacestation means to nations and individuals.

Sun, Earth and Man: the Need to Know and the Quest for Knowledge of Sun-Earth Relations— This discusses the relationship of the sun, earth and man covering the time before Sputnik, the Age of Space, the Eighties, and the future.

The Space Shuttle at Work—The booklet describes the space transportation system: how it came to be, why it is designed the way it is, what we expect of it, and how it may grow.

The Voyager Flights to Jupiter and Saturn—This describes, with pictures and narrative, the Voyager Flights to Jupiter and Saturn.

The World of Tomorrow: Aerospace Activities for 8 to 10-Year-Olds—A guide for leaders of children's groups and teachers of the lower grades, this presents projects kids can work on.

Viking: The Exploration of Mars—This includes information about Viking's mission and findings. The booklet also displays pictures taken in space.

What's New on the Moon?—This answers questions such as: Is there life on the moon? What is the moon made of? How old is the moon?—and more.

Space Shuttle Trips
While NASA is not yet taking reservations for the space shuttle, it does have an office coordinating opportunities for private citizens to fly on space shuttle missions. As opportunities develop, such as the first teacher in space, they will be announced in newspapers and on television. For a free fact sheet *Space Flight Participant Program* contact: Manager, Space Flight Participant Program, Mail Code ME, NASA Headquarters, Washington, DC 20546/ 202-453-2556.

Stamp Collecting Guide
Anyone interested in philately, the collecting and study of stamps, can receive a free booklet called *Introduction to Stamp Collecting* from: Stamp Division, Postal Service, 475 L'Enfant Plaza West SW, Washington, DC 20260/202-245-5778.

Star Wars Defense Program
The office of Assistant Secretary of Defense for Public Affairs can supply you with information about the overall Star Wars defense program, the Defense Advanced Research Projects Agency's (DARPA) efforts in this area, and the DOD Laser and Space Program. Fact sheets, press releases, congressional testimony, and reports about strategic defense initiative programs and studies are available. Contact: Public Correspondence Branch, Office of Assistant Secretary of Defense for Public Affairs, Department of Defense (DOD), Pentagon, Room 2E777, Washington, DC 20301-1400/202-697-5737 (Public Inquiries), 202-659-0192 (Press Inquiries).

Stress
Learn what stress is and how to deal with it from the free pamphlet *Plain Talk About Stress* (580N). Write: Consumer Information Center, P.O. Box 100, Pueblo, CO 81002.

Suicide
The free publications and films (available on a loan basis) listed below all deal with depression and suicide, particularly among teenagers. They are available from: National Institute of Mental Health, 5600 Fishers Lane, Rockville, MD 20857/301-443-4573.

Publications: *Dealing With the Crisis of Suicide Adolescence and Depression* (ADM 841337) *Information Packet*

Films: *Last Cry for Help*
Teenage Suicide: Is Anyone Listening?
Help Me—The Story of a Teenage Suicide
Teenage Suicide—Don't Try It!

Sun Tan (582N)
This free pamphlet reports on the hazards of over-exposure to the sun and safe sunscreen ingredients. It also explains the rating system of sunscreens. For a copy write: Consumer Information Center, P.O. Box 100, Pueblo, CO 81002.

Teacher Tours of the Navy
High school and college educators may apply to the Navy for a free orientation visit to a Naval facility. These visits are arranged to provide educators with first-hand knowledge of Navy programs and specialties, such as oceanography, math and high technology, medicine, submarines and more. Chosen teachers receive free travel and accommodations. For further information contact the Educational Specialist at the nearest Navy Recruiting District Office or Public Information Division, Department of the Navy, Department of Defense, The Pentagon, 2E337, Washington, DC 20350/202-695-0965.

Tell the President What You Think
White House operators at 202-456-7639 will take messages for the President. You can also write to the President and tell him what you think about current issues. His address is: White House, 1600 Pennsylvania Avenue NW, Washington, DC 20500.

Ulcer Treatments (583N)
Described in this booklet are ulcer symptoms, who is likely to be affected, diagnostic tests, and common forms of treatment. Available free of charge from: Consumer Information Center, P.O. Box 100, Pueblo, CO 81002.

Ultrasound
A free pamphlet *The Unknowns of Ultrasound* (562N) explains how this technique is used to monitor fetal growth and development, the latest research on its safety, and other medical uses. Available free of charge from: Consumer Information Center, P.O. Box 100, Pueblo, CO 81002.

Weather Hazards: Protect Yourself
The following publications will help you better identify and cope with potential weather hazards. Free copies are available from: Office of Public

Affairs, National Oceanic and Atmospheric Administration, U.S. Department of Commerce, Room 6013, Washington, DC 20230.

The Amateur Weather Forecaster—gives you the basics for observing, recording and forecasting the present, past and future weather conditions.

Spotter's Guide For Identifying and Reporting Severe Local Storms—descriptions and photographs illustrate important cloud features which commonly precede tornado and severe weather events.

Winter Storms and *Rules for Riding Out Winter Storms Wallet Card*—describes the causes and effects of winter storms, defines terms like "storm watch" and "storm warning," and tells you how to deal with such storms on the road or in your home.

Lightning the Underrated Killer—describes the causes and effects of lightning and the ways in which it is the chief killer in stormy weather.

Lightning Safety Wallet Card—describes the best ways to protect yourself in lightning storms and how to administer first aid to lightning victims.

Tornado Safety—this booklet is designed to increase your understanding and awareness of the tornado hazard, explain the National Weather Services Watch and Warning Program, and provide lifesaving safety precautions.

Floods, Flash Floods and Warnings—describes the safety rules and warning signs for this hazard which annually drives an average of 75,000 Americans from their homes. It kills about 90 people and destroys or damages more than $250 million worth of property annually.

Wife Abuse

A factsheet entitled *Plain Talk About Wife Abuse* (581N) explores the causes, the emotional and physical consequences, and where an abused wife can get assistance. Available free of charge from: Consumer Information Center, P.O. Box 100, Pueblo, CO 81002.

Wine and Cheese Making at Home

The U.S. Department of Agriculture has accumu-lated documentation and expertise to assist you in making wine and cheese at home. For a review on these topics, contact: USDA, National Agriculture Library, Beltsville, MD 20705/301-344-3755. For expertise in cheese contact: Dairy Laboratory, Department of Agriculture, AR-NER, Eastern Regional Research Center, 600 East Mermaid Lane, Philadelphia, PA 19118/215-233-6462.

White House Fellows Program

This program provides gifted and highly motivated young Americans with first hand experience in the process of governing the nation, and a sense of personal involvement in the leadership of society. The Fellows Program seeks to draw exceptional, promising young people from all sectors of our national life—professions, business, government, the arts, and the academic world. The term of the Fellowship is one year. A free brochure which explains the program and its purpose is available. For further information contact: White House Fellows Program, 712 Jackson Place NW, Washington, DC 20503/202-395-4522.

You and Your Medicines

This free 12-page report explains why there is such a high level of drug-induced illness in people over 65, and suggests ways to avoid it. For a copy write: Special Committee on Aging, U.S. Senate, G33 Dirksen Office Building, Washington, DC 20240.

Youth Programs from the Navy

Guided tours of Naval facilities, as well as films and speakers on a wide variety of subjects, are available from the U.S. Navy. A free brochure, *Navy and Youth,* outlines the activities available in the Navy Youth Program. A Youth Program Petty Officer is assigned to each Navy Recruiting Office to aid youth organizations or educational groups. For further information contact the Youth Program Petty Officer at the nearest Navy Recruiting Office or Public Information Division, Department of the Navy, Department of Defense, The Pentagon, 2E337, Washington, DC 20350/202-695-0965.

Gifts from Uncle Sam

Whether you're thinking of spending $0 or $10,000, your Uncle Sam has hundreds of items from which to choose. Many can't be found elsewhere—so you may be able to find a unique gift for that special someone who has everything.

The shopping list below highlights some favorites and it will give you an idea of what is available. A listing of gift catalogues is provided at the end of this section in case you would like to find out about more of Uncle Sam's offerings. Many catalogues contain color illustrations, and most are available free of charge.

After browsing through this list, you might also check the rest of the Sampler, and other sections of the book, as they too contain items that just might be a good gift for someone you know—or yourself!

Free!!!

The "Best of the Freebies" section of the Sampler identifies many items which would make great gifts. Some favorites are:

Adopt-a-Horse
Biking and Hiking Maps
Birthday and Anniversary Greetings from the White House
Boating Lessons
Bride's Information Package
Calendar of Washington, DC
Christmas Trees
Mining and Prospecting Rights
Gas or Oil Lottery Ticket
I Spy at the FBI—a fun minipage for kids
Posters
A picture of the President or First Lady (see Presidential Pictures)
Space and Aerospace posters and booklets
Stamp Collecting Guide
Winter Storm Survival Wallet Card (see Weather)

Other sections of the Sampler (and the remainder of the book) also give leads to interesting gifts. For example:

"Especially for . . . Kids" describes coloring books, comic books, litter bags, and more that kids would enjoy.

"Tracing Your Roots" tells you how to get a free booklet which will help an amateur genealogist determine family history.

"Traveling Abroad" mentions several free publications that would make a nice gift for someone going overseas.

"Help from Your Congressional Representative" identifies a free 200-page pictorial history book about Congress and the U.S. Capitol.

"Especially for . . . Parents and Parents-to-Be" describes a variety of publications which would be appreciated by new fathers and mothers.

The possibilities are endless . . . have fun shopping!

For $5.00 and Under. . . . .

Aboard the Space Shuttle—a fascinating color booklet that shows what it would be like to be aboard the space shuttle. Describes the clothes you would wear, how the launch would feel, what you would eat, etc. Order for $2.75 from: Superintendent of Documents, U.S. Government Printing Office, Washington, DC 20402/202-783-3238.

American Dolls—full-color poster of cloth sesquicentennial dolls. The 34″ × 22½″ poster is available for $2.00 from: Smithsonian Institution, P.O. Box 1949, Washington, DC 20013/202-357-3168. Please add $2.50 for shipping and handling.

Aviation Sea Survival Techniques—set of "flash cards" for the study of survival in an aviation sea environment. Order for $2.50 from: Superintendent of Documents, U.S. Government Printing Office, Washington, DC 20402/202-783-3238.

Black People and Their Culture—this book examines the cultural links between black Americans and the peoples of Africa, Latin America, and the Caribbean in areas such as music, dance, material culture, and the spoken word. Available for $6.45 from: Smithsonian Institution Press, P.O. Box 1579, Washington, DC 20013/202-357-1743.

Bookmark and Greeting Card—this custom designed leather bookmark with the Library of Congress seal and a silhouette of the Jefferson Building comes in a greeting card with envelope. Choice of blue, black, red, green, or brown, for $5.00 from: Library of Congress, Information Office, Box A, Washington, DC 20540/202-287-5112.

Children's Books—list compiled by the Library of Congress includes bibliographic information, prices, and annotations for publications that are suitable for preschool to junior-high school age children. Order for $1.00 from: Superintendent of Documents, U.S. Government Printing Office, Washington, DC 20402/202-783-3238.

Egg Art and Paper Cutting—10-page booklet describing egg-decorating and paper-cutting techniques. Booklet comes with its own envelope and has space for an inscription of a creative friend. 4½ × 4½ inches, Order for $4.00 from: Library of Congress, Information Office, Box A, Washington, DC 20540/202-287-5112.

Graphics—11 × 14 inch reproductions from the National Gallery of Art. Paradise with Christ in the Lap of Abraham by Anonymous (Lower Saxony), The Crucifixion Master of Jesus in Bethany, Battle of the Nudes by Antonio Pollaiuolo, Portrait of a Young Man by Gian Lorenzo Bernini, Young Woman in Netherlandish Dress by Albrecht Durer, The Beautiful Virgin of Regensburg by Albrecht Altdorfer, Self-Portrait by Rembrandt van Ryn, Lion by Peter Paul Rubens, Converture de l'estampe originale by Henri de Toulouse-Lautrec, Dancers at the Old Opera House by Edgar Degas, Cardinal Grosbeak by John James Audubon, and Unemployment by Kathe Kollwitz. Each graphic is .50, with a $2.00 minimum order. From: Publications Service, National Gallery of Art, Washington, DC 20565/202-737-4215. Include $2.00 handling charge with order.

Homesteading—rather than let run-down homes stand empty, the government turns these houses over to local communities, which in turn sell them to lower-income families for just a small amount of money (usually one dollar). To find out if your community is involved in this program, and if you qualify, contact your local officials at the Department of Housing and Urban Development: or Urban Homesteading Division, Office of Urban Rehabilitation, Community Planning and Development, Department of Housing and Urban Development, 451 7th Street SW, Room 7168, Washington, DC 20410/202-755-8702.

Immigrant & Passenger Arrivals: A Select Catalog of National Archives Microfilm Publications. Order for $2.00 from: National Archives BOOKS, NEPS, Room 505, Washington, DC 20408/202-523-3236.

National Archives and Records Service—contains ship passenger records from 1820, military records from the Revolutionary War, and census forms from 1790 to 1910. Anyone in the USA can rent microfilm on the census 1790–1910 or the Revolutionary War from the local public, college or genealogical library. The cost is $3.25 per reel for a one-month rental. Three catalogues are available listing films on census (1) 1790–1890, (2) 1900, and (3) 1910 at $5.00 each. The Revolutionary War catalogue is a 3-volume issue at $1.50 total. Contact: DDD Company, P.O. Box 2940, Hyattsville, MD 20784.

Old Maps and Patent Drawings—copies of elaborate patent and trademark drawings from the 19th Century can be purchased from the National Archives. Reproductions of original maps and architectural drawings are available, with a patent or trademark number, from: Cartographic and Architectural Branch, National Archives and Records Administration, 8th and Pennsylvania Ave. NW, Washington, DC 20408/202-523-3236.

Our Nation's Capitol Coloring Book—$2.50 from: United States Capitol Historical Society, 200 Maryland Avenue, N.E., Washington, DC 20515/202-543-8919.

Pocket Guide—summary information on the customs, currency, sights, people, and language of the subject country. Useful information for tourists. Available from: Superintendent of Documents, U.S. Government Printing Office, Washington, DC 20402/202-783-3238. Cost varies according to country—be sure and list country of your choice. Puerto Rico, for $3.50, Germany for $4.25, Japan for $4.50, Low Countries: Belgium, Luxembourg, The Netherlands for $4.25, Portugal for $4.50, United Kingdom for $4.75, Israel for $4.25, Korea for $4.50, and Philippines for $4.50.

Ships, Aircraft, and Weapons of the US Navy—a series of illustrated fact sheets on significant Navy weapons systems in five general categories: ships, fixed wing aircraft, helicopters, missiles, and weapons. Available for $3.00 from: Superintendent of Documents, U.S. Government Printing Office, Washington, DC 20402/ 202-783-3238.

Smithsonian Coloring Books—handsome coloring books based on some of the Smithsonian's most popular collections. Each book features 29 illustrations accompanied by informative captions. Four books available: *Aircraft, Balloons, Dinosaurs, and First Ladies' Gowns.* $2.50 each from: Smithsonian Institution Press, P.O. Box 1579, Washington, DC 20013/202-357-1743. Please include $1.50 for the first book and .50 for each additional book ordered.

Space Shuttle Wallsheet—presents a cutaway view of the space shuttle to show its inner workings. 30 × 42 inches. Order for $3.50 from: Superintendent of Documents, U.S. Government Printing Office, Washington, DC 20402/202-783-3238.

Subways—by Peter Blake. Includes 20 articles on the design, history, technology, and future of subways worldwide. 32 page tabloid for $3.50 from: Mail Order Dept., Cooper-Hewitt Museum, 2 East 91st Street, New York, NY 10128/212-860-6868.

The Comet Halley Handbook, An Observer's Guide—contains updated orbit that includes recovery observations of the comet. Order for $4.75 from: Superintendent of Documents, U.S. Government Printing Office, Washington, DC 20402/202-783-3238.

The First Ladies—includes biographies and portraits of the First Ladies. Paperbound $3.25, clothbound $4.50 from: White House Historical Association, 740 Jackson Place, N.W., Washington, DC 20506/202-737-8292.

The Living White House—tells about the families who have lived, worked, and entertained in the White House. Paperbound $3.75, clothbound $5.50 from: White House Historical Association, 740 Jackson Place N.W., Washington, DC 20506/202-737-8292.

The Presidents of the United States of America—the biographies and official portraits. Paperbound $3.25, clothbound $4.50 from: White House Historical Association, 740 Jackson Place, N.W., Washington, DC 20506/202-737-8292.

The White House: An Historic Guide—illustrated guidebook—visit the rooms and learn about the historical furnishings. Paperbound $3.75, clothbound $5.50 from: White House Historical Association, 740 Jackson Place, N.W., Washington, DC 20506/202-737-8292.

United States General Reference Atlas Maps—showing populated places, transportation routes and highest elevation in each State, with insets of Alaska and the principal islands of Hawaii. Available for $3.10 from: Branch of Distribution, Eastern Region, U.S. Geological Survey, 1200 South Eads Street, Arlington, VA 22202. West of the Mississippi River: Branch of Distribution, Central Region, U.S. Geological Survey, Box 25286, Federal Center, Denver, CO 80225.

Washington: Man and Monument—a biography of the first President with panoramic views of the city named for him. Available in paperbound for $2.75, and in clothbound for $4.25 from: White House Historical Association, 740 Jackson Place, N.W., Washington, DC 20506/202-737-8292.

Washington Past & Present—historical book available for $4.50 from: United States Capitol Historical Society, 200 Maryland Avenue, N.E., Washington, DC 20515/202-543-8919.

We, the People—paperback historical book available for $4.00 from: United States Capitol Historical Society, 200 Maryland Avenue, N.E., Washington, DC 20515/202-543-8919.

We, the People Calendar—a history lesson each day with full color pictures of the Capitol. Available for $4.00 from United States Capitol Historical Society, 200 Maryland Avenue N.E., Washington, DC 20515/202-543-8919.

Workers and Allies: Female Participation in the American Trade Union Movement, 1824–1976— reference book includes introduction by Bella Abzug, chronology of labor events, and biographies of over 100 women. Available for $4.50 from: Smithsonian Institution, P.O. Box 1949, Washington, DC 20013/202-357-3168.

Your Trip Abroad—a brochure that can help you prepare for a trouble-free, rewarding experience. Basic information about passports, visas, vaccinations, customs, money, help from American consuls, legal aid and more. Available for $1.00 from Superintendent of Documents, U.S. Government Printing Office, Washington, DC 20402/202-783-3238.

For $6.00 to $15.00. . . . .

A Guide to the Study and Use of Military History—a series of essays by military experts which explore the nature and value of military history. Available for $9.00 from: Superintendent of Documents, U.S. Government Printing Office, Washington, DC 20402/202-783-3238.

And Now a Message—A Century of American Advertising, 1830–1930—full color reproduction of the Nabisco boy in his yellow slicker. Available for $7.50 from: Smithsonian Institution, P.O. Box 1949, Washington, DC 20013/202-357-3168.

Animal Sound Boxes—cylindrical boxes depict a cow, cat, goat, lamb, and bird. When turned upside down, delight small children. Approx. 2″ high, available for $15.00 from: Smithsonian Institution, P.O. Box 2456, Washington, DC 20013/703-455-1700.

Appointment Book—elegant 6 × 7 inch book contains 160 pages with 77 beautiful color illustrations of Near and Far Eastern art from the Freer Collection. Available for $15.00 from: The Freer Gallery of Art, Smithsonian Institution, Washington, DC 20560/202-357-1432.

Baroque-Style Recorder—simple for either adults or children to master. A joy to play alone or in groups. Soprano available for $12.00 from: Smithsonian Institution, P.O. Box 2456, Washington, DC 20013/703-455-1700. The Recorder Guide provides excellent instruction for beginning and advanced players. Also available for $9.95, from above address.

Bright Ideas—a game based on Thomas Edison's inventions and his lifetime that spanned 84 years. Game board is printed in full color and measures 20″ × 20″, with 4 markers, 60 "Idea" cards and 12 "Patent" cards, plus instructions. It is available for $6.00 from: Smithsonian Institution, P.O. Box 1949, Washington, DC 20013/202-357-3168.

Bureau of the Census Catalog: 1984—includes abstracts for all products from the 1977 Economic Censuses, and updates the 1982–83 Census Catalog. Available for $7.00 from: Superintendent of Documents, U.S. Government Printing Office, Washington, DC 20402/202-783-3238.

Butterflies Colorwise—6 identical posters, that when colored and cut out, the six butterflies form a mobile. (Age 7 plus). Available for $7.50 from: Smithsonian Institution, P.O. Box 1949, Washington, DC 20013/202-357-3168.

Carpenter's Lace—a boxed set of 12 activity cards on Victorian architecture. Written for children, the activities include quizzes and guessing games. The box folds up to form the walls of a Victorian house. (Age 10 plus) Order for $6.00 from: Smithsonian Institution, P.O. Box 1949, Washington, DC 20013/202-357-3168.

Collection of White House Books—*The White House: An Historic Guide, The Living White House, The Presidents of the United States of America,* and *The First Ladies* in a set with slipcase. Available in paperbound for $14.00, and in clothbound for $20.00 from: White House Historical Association, 740 Jackson Place, N.W., Washington, DC 20506/202-737-8292.

Computer Chip Tie Tack—actual computer chip surrounded by a design modeled after a chip carrier. Gold-plated brass with black enamel, for ties or lapels. ⅝ inch diameter. Available for $12.00 from: Smithsonian Institution, P.O. Box 2456, Washington, DC 20013/703-455-1700.

Double Matted Reproductions—from The National Gallery of Art. Mat Size is 14 × 18 inches. Still Life; Le Jour by Georges Braque, The Lovers by Pablo Picasso, Oarsen at Chatou by Auguste Renoir, The Boating Party by Mary Cassatt, The Sacrament of the Last Supper by Salvador Dali, Banks of the Seine, Vetheuil by Claude Monet, and A Young Girl Reading by Jean-Honore Fragonard. Each $4.00 from: Publications Service, National Gallery of Art, Washington, DC 20565/202-737-4215. Include $2.00 for handling with order.

Faberge: Jeweler to Royalty—by A. Kenneth Snowman. Relates the history of the jewelry and objets d'art of the virtuoso goldsmith Peter Carl Faberge. 112 page paperbound available for $11.95 from: Mail Order Dept., Cooper-Hewitt Museum, 2 East 91st Street, New York, NY 10128/212-860-6868.

Famous Personalities of Flight Cookbook—tells what famous flyers like the Wright Brothers, Charles Lindbergh, and Amelia Earhart had for dinner when they came down from the clouds. Their recipes and those of other air and space personalities are included along with anecdotes, photographs, etc. Paperbound $6.45 from: Smithsonian Institution Press, P.O. Box 1579, Washington, DC 20013/202-357-1743.

From Sundials to Atomic Clocks: Understanding Time and Frequency—explores the riddle of time, tells how we find and keep time and outlines the uses of time. Order for $7.00 from: Superintendent of Documents, U.S. Government Printing Office, Washington, DC 20402/ 202-783-3238.

George Washington Proof Coin—commemorative half dollar to recognize the 250th anniversary of the birth of our nation's first President. Coin has frosted relief design and high luster background. Available for $12.00 from: Bureau of the Mint, 55 Mint Street, San Francisco, CA 94175.

George Washington Uncirculated Coin—with a brilliant coin finish. Produced by the same high standard coining techniques used for circulating coins. Available for $10.00 from: Bureau of the Mint, 55 Mint Street, San Francisco, CA 94175.

Golden Eagle Passports—for persons under 62. This is an annual entrance permit to parks, monuments, historic sites and recreation areas in the National Park System that charge entrance fees. The passport costs $10.00, not refundable nor transferable, and is good for one calendar year. Available by mail from: The National Park Service, Room 1013, U.S. Department of the Interior, 18th and C Streets NW, Washington, DC 20240.

Greeting Cards—vaudeville set designed in the 1930's for the Federal Theatre Project by James Stewart Morcan with no greeting. A set of 12 available for $7.75 from: Library of Congress, Information Office, Box A, Washington, DC 20540/202-287-5112.

Hair—by Brooks Adams and David Revere McFadden. Entertaining and informative history of styles and symbols in hair design from ancient times to the present. 32 page paperbound book available for $6.95 from: Mail Order Dept., Cooper-Hewitt Museum, 2 East 91st Street, New York, NY 10128/212-860-6868.

Human Rights in Latin America, 1964–1980—a 257 page, selected annotated bibliography. Available for $13.00 from: Superintendent of Documents, Dept. 39-LC, U.S. Government Printing Office, Washington, DC 20402/202-783-3238.

Ideas and Weapons: The U.S. Air Force Special Studies—a history of the evolution of weapons in the period of the World Wars. The book explores the background of the contemporary air weapon, along with the history and development of the early weapons up to the present time. Available for $9.50 from: Superintendent of Documents, U.S. Government Printing Office, Washington, DC 20402/202-783-3238.

If You Want to Fight, Join the Marines—20 × 28″ poster. Order for $7.50 from National Archives, NEPS, Room 505, Washington, DC 20408/ 202-523-3236.

I Want You for the U.S. Army—20 × 28″ poster. Order for $7.50 from National Archives, NEPS, Room 505, Washington, DC 20408/202-523-3236.

I Wish I Were a Man—I'd Join the Navy—20 × 28″ poster. Order for $7.50 from National Archives, NEPS, Room 505, Washington, DC 20408/ 202-523-3236.

Jack-in-the-Box—snap open the wooden box and up pops a jolly clown with painted face and sparkling costume. 3½″ square. Available for $8.75 from: Smithsonian Institution, P.O. Box 2456, Washington, DC 20013/703-455-1700.

Jigsaw Puzzles—measure 18 × 24 inches when completed and contains 551 pieces. Two designs, Cat and Butterfly or Puppies in the Snow. Each available for $10.50 from: The Freer Gallery of Art, Smithsonian Institution, Washington, DC 20560/202-357-1432.

Library of Congress Engagement Calendar—each calendar page covers one week and gives ample space for appointments and reminders. Over 70 color and black-and-white images drawn from collections of the Library of Congress. Available for $12.00 from: Library of Congress, Information Office, Box A, Washington, DC 20540/ 202-287-5112.

Nostalgic Tin Eggs—feature charming lithograph designs similar to advertisements in the Smithsonian Collection of Business Americana. Eggs open to hold treasures or treats. Set of 5 eggs, $8.00 from: Smithsonian Institution, P.O. Box 2456, Washington, DC 20013/703-455-1700.

Note Cards—pen and ink sketches of the White House, includes north and south exteriors, the

Rose Garden, and the Blue Room. 16 note cards and envelopes available for $6.00 from: White House Historical Association, 740 Jackson Place, N.W., Washington, DC 20506/ 202-737-8292.

Occupational Outlook Handbook—a comprehensive book on the most current information available on the characteristics of work today and on hiring trends of tomorrow. 396 page-paperback available for $8.50, from: Superintendent of Documents, U.S. Government Printing Office, Washington, DC 20402/202-783-3238.

On the Rocks: The Story of Prehistoric Art—the book introduces cave paintings and rock art to children ages 10 and over through interesting stories. Order for $6.00 from: Smithsonian Institution, P.O. Box 1949, Washington, DC 20013/202-357-3168.

Patterns and Sources of Navajo Weaving—fully-illustrated catalog of the rugs from Harmsen's Western Americana Collection. Essays on weavings by the Navajo and other Southwest weavers. Available for $8.50 from: Smithsonian Institution, P.O. Box 1949, Washington, DC 20013/202-357-3168.

Plaques—reproductions from the National Gallery of Art. Pot of Geraniums by Henri Matisse, Breezing Up by Winslow Homer, The Lackawanna Valley by George Inness, Children Playing on the Beach by Mary Cassatt, The Lovers by Pablo Picasso, A Girl with a Watering Can by Auguste Renoir, Fatata te Miti by Paul Gauguin and Ville d'Avray by Jean-Baptiste-Camille Corot. Available for $3.50 each from: Publications Service, National Gallery of Art, Washington, DC 20565/202-737-4215. Include $2.00 for handling charge.

Pottery: A Notebook for New Potters—innovative book with instructions for digging your own clay, processing it, making pots without a wheel, and firing them without a kiln. Available for $8.45 from: Smithsonian Institution, P.O. Box 1949, Washington, DC 20013/202-357-3168.

Puzzle Postcards—five different views of the Library of Congress in puzzle form. A clever way to say hello and a great stocking stuffer. A set of five available for $7.95 from: Library of Congress, Information Office, Box A, Washington, DC 20540/202-287-5112. Include $2.00 for shipping and handling.

Railroad Maps of the United States—brief history of American railroad mapping, with entries that include maps covering the entire United States and maps of individual railroads in a 112 page, paperbound book. Available for $5.50 from: Superintendent of Documents, Dept. 39-LC,

U.S. Government Printing Office, Washington, DC 20402/202-783-3238.

Records—an anthology of 15 records highlighting themes in American music, as love, marriage, jazz, country, blues, and ethnic music. Available for $7.00 per record or the 15-record set for $100.00. Please specify. Religious Music, Congregational and Ceremonial; Songs of Love, Courtship, and Marriage; Dance Music, Breakdowns and Waltzes; Dance Music, Reels, Polkas, and More; Dance Music, Ragtime, Jazz, and More; Songs of Migration and Immigration; Songs of Complaint and Protest; Songs of Labor and Livelihood; Songs of Death and Tragedy; Songs of War and History; Songs of Humor and Hilarity; Songs of Local History and Events; Songs of Childhood; Solo and Display Music; Religious Music: Solo and Performance. From: Library of Congress, Information Office, Box A, Washington, DC 20540/202-287-5112. Include $2.00 for shipping and handling.

Ride On—two color poster of Thomas Stevens, the first American to circle the globe on a bicycle. Available for $6.00 from: Smithsonian Institution, P.O. Box 1949, Washington, DC 20013/202-357-3168. Please add $2.50 for shipping and handling.

Robert Frost—reads fourteen of his most-loved poems on record available for $9.00 from: Library of Congress, Information Office, Box A, Washington, DC 20540/202-287-5112. Include $2.00 for shipping and handling.

Sandstone Paperweights from the East Front Extension of the U.S. Capitol. Available for $6.00 from: United States Capitol Historical Society, 200 Maryland Avenue N.E., Washington, DC 20515/202-543-8919.

Set of four color posters by Norman Rockwell—includes *Freedom from Fear, Freedom from Want, Freedom of Speech, and Freedom of Worship.* Available for $12.50, product code 6600, from: National Archives, NEPS, Room 505, Washington, DC 20408/202-523-3236.

Smithsonian Illustrated Library of Antiques—a comprehensive series of the history and design of antiques. The series provides a background on each subject. Included are: Boxes, Clocks, Enamels, Furniture I: Prehistoric through Rococo; Furniture II: Neoclassic to The Present, Glass, Jewelry, Miniatures, Needlework, Oriental Rugs, Porcelain, Pottery, Prints, Silver, and Toys and Games. Clothbound books are available for $9.95 each from: Mail Order Dept., Cooper-Hewitt Museum, 2 East 91st Street, New York, NY 10128/212-860-6868. Include $2.50 UPS charge for first book and $1.00 for each additional book. Please specify the volume wanted.

Spacelab—describes Spacelab and its scientific mission. Contains full-color photos and illustrations and details a typical day onboard. Available for $7.00 from: Superintendent of Documents, U.S. Government Printing Office, Washington, DC 20402/202-783-3238.

Space Shuttle Pen—silver-colored pen writes forward, backward—even upside down, with a gold-toned model of the shuttle "Columbia." Available for $12.50 from: Smithsonian Institution, P.O. Box 2456, Washington, DC 20013/703-455-1700.

The World Factbook, 1984—gives a brief resume of each country of the world with vital information on land, nationality, religion, language, literacy, political parties, and much more. Available for $11.00 from: Superintendent of Documents, U.S. Government Printing Office, Washington, DC 20402/202-783-3238.

The Written Word Endures: Milestone Documents of American History—the preservation of our historical past is available for $15.00 from: National Archives and Records Administration, NEPS, Room 505, Washington, DC 20408/202-523-3236.

Uncirculated Coin Proof Sets—contains a proof half dollar, quarter, dime, nickel, and one cent coin produced and sealed into plastic cases, with Mint-mark "S." Available for $11.00 per set from: United States Mint, 55 Mint Street, San Francisco, CA 94175.

Unicorn Dragon Kite—framed by a crescent moon, trailing a majestic tail made of mylar that sparkles in the sun. Easy to fly, approx 50 feet long available for $8.50 from: Smithsonian Institution, P.O. Box 2456, Washington, DC 20013/703-455-1700.

Vertical Flight (The Age of the Helicopter)—a history told by those pioneers who endured the hardships, blind alleys, and failures of the early days and emerged triumphant. Available for $12.45 from: Smithsonian Institution Press, P.O. Box 1579, Washington, DC 20013/202-357-1743.

Volcanic Eruptions of 1980 at Mount St. Helens: The First 100 Days—a nontechnical description of the volcanic events surrounding the 1980 eruptions. Fully illustrated with a glossary of volcanic terms. Available for $8.50 from: Superintendent of Documents, U.S. Government Printing Office, Washington, DC 20402/202-783-3238.

Wives Who Earn More Than Their Husbands—discusses characteristics of those couples in which the wife is the primary wage earner. Available for $1.50 from: Superintendent of Documents, U.S. Government Printing Office, Washington, DC 20402/202-783-3238.

For $16.00 to $50.00. . . . .

American Military History—this book surveys American military history from colonial times to the Vietnam era. Available for $19.00 from: Superintendent of Documents, U.S. Government Printing Office, Washington, DC 20402/202-783-3238.

American Popular Song—six decades of songwriters and singers. 110 of America's greatest popular songs by 62 of America's most appealing artists. #1500, 7-LP boxed set with 148-page booklet or #1501, 4 90-minute Dolby cassettes in a boxed set with 148-page booklet for $47.96 from: Smithsonian Collection of Recordings, Smithsonian Institution Press, Smithsonian Customer Service, P.O. Box 10229, Des Moines, Iowa 50336/800-247-5072. In Iowa: 800-532-1526.

Archival Videodiscs—The National Air and Space Museum is reproducing its entire photo archives on videodiscs. Videodisc 1 has one hundred thousand color and black and white photographs of U.S. and foreign aircraft from the Museum's archives, and Videodisc 2 contains one hundred thousand photographs including balloons, airships, commercial airlines, etc., not covered in Videodisc 1. $35.00 per disc from: Smithsonian Institution Press, P.O. Box 1579, Washington, DC 20013/202-357-1743. Include $1.50 for the first book and .50 for each additional book or disc ordered.

A Smithsonian Book of Comic-Book Comics—a carefully produced study of the seminal comic books and their creators—great for any devotee of comic and satiric art. Clothbound are available for $26.50 from: Smithsonian Institution Press, P.O. Box 1579, Washington, DC 20013/202-357-1743.

Celebrate A Special Day By Flying Your Flag Over the Capitol—for the cost of a flag ($7.00 to $16.00) your congressman can have the Architect for the Capitol fly your personal stars and stripes over the Capitol Building on the day you specify. Be sure to state the day to be flown and the name of the recipient. Contact: local office of your Congressman or write Capitol, Washington, DC 20515.

Classic Flower Brick—made of glazed crackle stoneware, this useful vase has an insert plate to hold stems that is removable to allow for larger arrangements. Available for $22.50 from: Smithsonian Institution, P.O. Box 2456, Washington, DC 20013/703-455-1700.

Desk Accessories—Mother-of-Pearl, Peonies and Willows, or Pheasant on a Camellia Branch on a 14 × 20½ Desk Pad available for $20.00. Accordion File in Mother-of-Pearl or Peonies and Willows at $33.50 with a 22 pocket capacity. Other items for the desk, as well as playing cards, tallies and score pads from: The Freer Gallery of Art, Smithsonian Institution, Washington, DC 20560/202-357-1432. Include $2.50 for postage for items up to $16.00, $3.50 for items up to $24.00 and $5.00 for an order up to $50.00.

Framed Prints—from The National Gallery of Art. Child in a Straw Hat by Mary Cassatt, Miss Willoughby by George Romney, Girl with a Hoop by August Renoir, Woman Seated under the Willows by Claude Monet, Madonna and Child on a Curved Throne by Byzantine School, XIII Century. Available for $15.00 each from: Publications Service, National Gallery of Art, Washington, DC 20565/202-737-4215. Include $2.00 handling charge.

Friendly Song Sparrow—sculpted in warmly hued stoneware by Maine craftsmen. $18.00 from: Smithsonian Institution, P.O. Box 2456, Washington, DC 20013/703-455-1700.

Good Show—A Practical Guide for Temporary Exhibitions—provides information on every aspect of temporary exhibitions. Security and evaluation are addressed, as well as a special chapter on planning installations for handicapped access. An invaluable reference book. Available for $20.00 from: Smithsonian Institution, P.O. Box 1949, Washington, DC 20013/202-357-3168. Please add $2.50 for shipping and handling.

Guide to Genealogical Research in the National Archives—a wealth of information about individuals, including census records, military service, pension files, ship passenger arrival lists, and more, 304 pages, 40 illustrations. Clothbound copies available for $25.00, Paperbound copies available for $19.00 from National Archives BOOKS, NEPS, Room 505, Washington, DC 20408/202-523-3236.

Heart Thimble—reproduced from the original in

the Mary Gallatin Hoppin Collection at the Smithsonian. Approx. ⅞″ high, $32.00 from: Smithsonian Institution, P.O. Box 2456, Washington, DC 20013/703-455-1700.

Historic America: Buildings, Structures, and Sites—a collection of photographs, drawings and data sheets produced by the Historic American Buildings Survey to document our nation's significant historic architecture. Clothbound book available for for $29.00 from: Superintendent of Documents, Dept. 39-LC, U.S. Government Printing Office, Washington, DC 20402/202-783-3238.

Lockheed P-38L Lightning Model Kit—you can create one of the most famous fighter planes of World War II—a twin-engine balsa wood model with plastic parts, features movable controls, retractable landing gear, droppable bombs, and decals. Instructions included, wingspan 40″, scale ¾″. Available for $35.00 from: Smithsonian Institution, P.O. Box 2456, Washington, DC 20013/703-455-1700.

Louis Armstrong and Earl Hines, 1928—two enduring jazzmen, in an epoch-making collaboration. A 2-LP record set available for $16.98 from: Smithsonian Customer Service, P.O. Box 10229, Des Moines, Iowa 50336/800-247-5072. In Iowa: 800-532-1526.

Major Legislation of the Congress—provides summaries of topical congressional issues and major legislation introduced. Approx. 10 issues per Congress (2-year period). A subscription of $39.00 to domestic addresses and $48.75 to a foreign address. Order (MLC) from: Superintendent of Documents, U.S. Government Printing Office, Washington, DC 20402/202-783-3238.

Map—map of Manhattan drawn on site in 1639 for the West India Company of Holland. The panel identifies each property owner by name and locates his farm or plantation. Available for $17.00 from: Library of Congress, Information Office, Box A, Washington, DC 20540/202-287-5112.

Map—vellum chart of the Mediterranean made in 1559 by a Majorcan cartographer. Available for $22.00 from: Library of Congress, Information Office, Box A, Washington, DC 20540/ 202-287-5112.

McGuffey's Eclectic Readers—7 volume set of the classics that have taught generations of Americans to read. First published in 1881, the series is laced with moral lessons, while teaching the alphabet, penmanship, vocabulary, and spelling. Hardback copies available for $39.95 from: Smithsonian Institution, P.O. Box 2456, Washington, DC 20013/703-455-1700.

Medal of the Presidents of the United States—most designed especially for the President at the time he was in office. 3-inch bronze medal of your favorite President or Presidents in a display box with an easel and a biography enclosed with each medal available for $16.00 each from: United States Mint (Medals), P.O. Box 500, Philadelphia, PA 19105. Please list President or Presidents desired.

Needlepoint—was created for the Library of Congress, includes needle, color design displayed on cotton canvas, easy-to-follow instructions, and durable 3-ply yarn. Can be framed to use as a pillow top. Cat design from 1894 lithograph by Theophile Alexandre Steinlen, $22.95 or Seasons adapted from drawings by Kate Greenway for the 1897 Almanack and Diary, 12 × 14 inches, $24.95 from: Library of Congress, Information Office, Box A, Washington, DC 20540/202-287-5112. Include $2.00 for shipping and handling.

Now I Lay Me Down to Eat: Notes and Footnotes on the Lost Art of Living—by Bernard Rudofsky. Spirited commentary of mankind's everyday habits of eating, sleeping, sitting, bathing, and cleansing from ancient times to today. 189 pages, and illustrated, for $22.90 from: Mail Order Dept., Cooper-Hewitt Museum, 2 East 91st Street, New York, NY 10128/212-860-6868.

Our Musical Past—two-record album with a selection of band, vocal, and piano music popular in America in the 1850's and 1860's. Available for $16.00 from: Library of Congress, Information Office, Box A, Washington, DC 20540/202-287-5112.

Phoenix Kite—magnificent Chinese bird kite is a favorite flyer. Available in silk for $19.00, paper for $6.50 from: Smithsonian Institution, P.O. Box 2456, Washington, DC 20013/703-455-1700.

Plush Teddy Bear—with a special place in American folklore. This honey-colored bear is soft and cuddly with movable arms and legs, 16″ high. Available for $20.00 from: Smithsonian Institution, P.O. Box 2456, Washington, DC 20013/703-455-1700.

Porcelain Bead Necklace—in the water lily motif associated with rebirth and new life. Made in China, each bead is painted by hand. Approx. 24″ long. Available for $48.00 from: Smithsonian Institution, P.O. Box 2456, Washington, DC 20013/703-455-1700.

Railroad Maps of North America—includes 92 maps (some in color) showing the development of cartographic style and technique. Informative text for the historian, railroad buff, or collector. Available for $28.00 from: Superintendent of Documents, U.S. Government Printing Office, Washington, DC 20402/202-783-3238.

Red Phoenix (The Rise of Soviet Air Power, 1941–1945)—An historical survey of the Soviet Air Force during World War II. Available for $24.00 from: Smithsonian Institution Press, P.O. Box 1579, Washington, DC 20013/202-357-1743.

Remember the Hindenburg?—a newly released book gives an expert's opinion on what caused the Hindenburg to burn that fateful day—May 6, 1937—and how the airship's chances for development as a major commercial vehicle were thereby destroyed. *The Golden Age of the Great Passenger Airships, Graf Zeppelin and Hindenburg* is a 200 page, illustrated clothbound book for $26.45 from: Smithsonian Institution Press, P.O. Box 1579, Washington, DC 20013/202-357-1743. Please include $1.50 for the first book and .50 for each additional book ordered.

Robot—Mr. Technoman Kit—clap your hands and watch him go. A friendly little robot as represented in the National Museum of American History, like the robot of Star Wars fame. Kit comes with a sound sensor control unit ready made and includes screwdriver, batteries, and assembly instructions. Ages 12 and up. 5″ tall. Available for $25.00 from: Smithsonian Institution, P.O. Box 2456, Washington, DC 20013/703-455-1700.

Sandstone Bookends from the East Front Extension of the Capitol, each piece with a small plaque noting its origin. $23.50 from United States Capitol Historical Society, 200 Maryland Avenue N.E., Washington, DC 20515/202-543-8919.

Silk Aviator Scarf—reminiscent of the early days of flight when long silk scarves did more than add pizzazz to the panache of the pilot, but had several practical uses in the cockpit. Fringed, tubular, approx. 72″ × 8½″ in white for $24.00 from: Smithsonian Institution, P.O. Box 2456, Washington, DC 20013/703-455-1700.

Slides of the White House—a 40-slide set with cassette tape containing a narration with background music by the U.S. Marine Band. Available for $16.50 from White House Historical Association, 740 Jackson Place, N.W., Washington, DC 20506/202-737-8292.

Statistical Abstract of the United States—1984—summary of statistics on the social, political, and economic status of government and business in the US. Available for $23.00 from: Superintendent of Documents, U.S. Government Printing Office, Washington, DC 20402/202-783-3238.

The Birds of China—use as a field guide and as a

descriptive catalog, this book is the first systematic guide in English on Chinese birds, with a history of ornithology in China. 602 pages with black and white and color plates. Clothbound is available for $45.00, and paperbound for $29.95 from: Smithsonian Institution Press, P.O. Box 1579, Washington, DC 20013/202-357-1743. Include $1.50 for the first book and .50 for each additional book ordered.

The Original White House Cookbook—first published in 1887, included in the Political History Collection of the National Museum of American History. Recipes from biscuits to details of Presidential State Dinners are included. 619 pages for $24.95 from: Smithsonian Institution, P.O. Box 2456, Washington, DC 20013/703-455-1700.

The Phenomenon of Change—an illustrated anthology of various aspects of change in the twentieth century. 192 page paperbound book for $15.95 from: Mail Order Dept., Cooper-Hewitt Museum, 2 East 91st Street, New York, NY 10128/212-860-6868.

The United States and Russia: The Beginning of Relations 1765–1815—the history of our relationship with the Soviet Union. Available for $17.50 from: National Archives and Records Administration, NEPS, Room 505, Washington, DC 20408/202-523-3236.

The Velveteen Rabbit—classic tale of a toy rabbit and a child whose love made the toy real. Book and 9¾″ toy bunny for $21.45 from: Smithsonian Institution, P.O. Box 2456, Washington, DC 20013/703-455-1700.

Thread of Life: The Smithsonian Looks at Evolution—a lively, comprehensive, up-to-the-minute account of the evolution of life. Available for $22.95 from: Smithsonian Customer Service, P.O. Box 10229, Des Moines, Iowa 50336/800-247-5072. In Iowa: 800-532-1526.

Wild Rose Needlepoint Kit—kit includes imported Zweigart canvas with hand silk-screened full-color design, 3-ply Persian wool, needles and instructions. Finishes to 12″ square. Available for $32.00 from: Smithsonian Institution, P.O. Box 2456, Washington, DC 20013/703-455-1700.

Wright Flyer Kite—learn about aircraft structure and the history of early flight while constructing this spruce wood and paper kite based on the Wright Flyer in the National Air and Space Museum. Available for $14.00 from: Smithsonian Institution, P.O. Box 2456, Washington, DC 20013/703-455-1700.

For $51.00 to $100.00. . . . .

African Giraffes—graceful giraffe tenderly mothering her young portrays a sublime moment of spring's new life. Carved of olivewood in Kenya and signed by the craftsman. Approx. 11″ high × 7″ wide. Available for $55.00 from: Smithsonian Institution, P.O. Box 2456, Washington, DC 20013/703-455-1700.

DeWitt Clinton Electric Train Set—one of America's early steam-operated trains made its maiden run on August 9, 1831. HO scale commemorates this historic train—includes locomotive, tender, 3 coaches, plug-in terminal rerailer track, 45″ × 36″ of oval track, power pack, and instructions. Plastic cars available for $65.00 from: Smithsonian Institution, P.O. Box 2456, Washington, DC 20013/703-455-1700.

Needlework Kits from a Japanese Screen—Edo period, 18th century. Kits contain handpainted 14 inch canvas, 3 ply Persian yarns, needle and instructions. Finished size 12½ × 13 inches, suitable for wall hangings or pillow. Two styles, Shrikes on a Loquat Branch or Hoopoe Birds. Available for $56.50 each from: The Freer Gallery of Art, Smithsonian Institution, Washington, DC 20560/202-357-1432.

Red Telescope—lets you zoom in 150 times closer. Interchangeable 4mm and 12.5 mm eye lenses, rack and pinion focusing, diagonal prism. Metal rubber-tipped tripod. Available for $59.95 from: Smithsonian Institution, P.O. Box 2456, Washington, DC 20013/703-455-1700.

The Papers of the Continental Congress 1774–1789—5 Volumes. This comprehensive index covers all the papers of the Continental Congress except the Journals and two manuscript indexes. 6,615 pages. Clothbound $85.00 from National Archives BOOKS, NEPS, Room 505, Washington, DC 20408/202-523-3236.

The Stars Above—find your way among the stars and plot celestial movements, including Halley's Comet with a planisphere. The opaque horizon dome turns inside the blue bowl of stars to reveal the visible night sky at any hour. Instructions included 14½ inches diameter. Available for $65.00 from: Smithsonian Institution, P.O. Box 2456, Washington, DC 20013/703-455-1700.

For $101.00 to $500.00. . . . .

Bronze Exeter Sundial—similar to those in the Mathematics Division at the Smithsonian. Cast in solid bronze, the authentic instrument is accurate at any latitude and built to withstand years of weathering. 9″ diameter sphere, 18″ arrow $125.00 from: Smithsonian Institution, P.O. Box 2456, Washington, DC 20013/703-455-1700.

Butterfly Collection—delightful display of butterflies in a limited edition of 250, each plexiglass box includes a diagram with the name and locale of each non-endangered butterfly. Available for $120.00 from: Smithsonian Institution, P.O. Box 2456, Washington, DC 20013/703-455-1700.

Cloisonne Necklace—dramatically accented with 6mm black onyx and rose quartz beads. Available for $165.00 from: Smithsonian Institution, P.O. Box 2456, Washington, DC 20013/703-455-1700.

Gemstone Champleve Necklace—twist choker of mother-of-pearl, amethyst, rose quartz, and aventurine strands, highlights gemstones from the National Museum of Natural History. Enamel on brass clasp is signed by the artist. Available for $280.00 from: Smithsonian Institution, P.O. Box 2456, Washington, DC 20013/703-455-1700.

Lapis Turtle—carved by hand from a single piece of lapis, this is a replica of the world famous collection of Minerals and Gems housed in the National Museum of Natural History. Rests on a footed wooden display stand. Available for $150.00 from: Smithsonian Institution, P.O. Box 2456, Washington, DC 20013/703-455-1700.

Smithsonian Elephant—cold-cast bronze miniature of the African Bush Elephant as it stands in the National Museum of Natural History. 7″ × 3½″ with a walnut base. Available for $130.00 from: Smithsonian Institution, P.O. Box 2456, Washington, DC 20013/703-455-1700.

Sterling Silver Dresser Set—by Gorham, reproduced from a 19th-century silver dresser set, is representative of those on display in the Arts and Industries Building. In Dresden Rose Pattern, the three-piece set includes comb and brush with natural boar bristles, 10″ mirror, rosewood base. Available for $475.00 from: Smithsonian Institution, P.O. Box 2456, Washington, DC 20013/703-455-1700.

Victorian Engagement Ring—reproduced from the original circa 1870. A faceted garnet set off by 18 seed pearls in a 14K gold setting. Sizes 5, 6, 7, and 8. Available for $380.00 from: Smithsonian Institution, P.O. Box 2456, Washington, DC 20013/703-455-1700.

For $501 and over. . . . .

Opportunities to donate money or memorials to assist in the beautification of our National Park Service are many. Examples of needed gifts include:

Creek Crossing—Give a concrete ford with pedestrian bridges across creeks, to replace dirt crossings that wash out during rains are $2,500.

Chumash Demonstration Village—Donations to provide a place where visitors will be invited to participate in traditional activities as preparing food, basketmaking, beadworking, stonework-ing, plank canoe making and other crafts are needed in total of $10,000. A single Chumash Indian house is $2,000.

Cultural Center—You can provide for the renovation of an existing structure to provide a center for interpreting local Native American Indian culture. Cost: $10,000. To furnish the cultural center is $7,000, and interpretive displays of the cultural center are $300 each.

Ranch Animals—You can adopt a ranch animal and provide for its care and feeding for $50 a week, $200 a month or $2,400 per year.

Barns and Stables—Improvements are needed for buildings on the Rancho Sierra Vista ranch at $5,000 per building.

Horse Care and Tack for the Mounted Patrol—are needed; tack is $1,000 per horse, and care and feeding for one horse is $1,700 per year.

The above items, plus many more donations of time and money, are available through the U.S. Department of the Interior, Information Office, National Park Service, 18th and C Streets NW, Washington, DC 20240.

Bibliography of Gift Catalogs

American Indians: A Select Catalog of National Archives Microfilm Publications. Available for $2.00 from: National Archives BOOKS, NEPS, Room 505, Washington, DC 20408.

Black Studies: A Select Catalog of National Archives Microfilm Publications. Available for $2.00 from: National Archives BOOKS, NEPS, Room 505, Washington, DC 20408.

Bureau of the Mint, 55 Mint Street, San Francisco, CA 94175. (published as new coins are minted).

Congressional Information Service, Inc., 4520 East-West Highway, Suite 800, Bethesda, MD 20814/800-638-8380 (toll free). 301-654-1550. (published once a year).

Cooper-Hewitt Museum, The Smithsonian Institution, National Museum of Design, 2 East 91st Street, New York, NY 10128/212-860-6868. (published once a year).

Library of Congress, Card and Gift Catalog, Information Office, Box A, Washington, DC 20540/202-287-5112. (published once a year).

Library of Congress, Selected Publications, Publishing Office, Washington, DC 20540/202-287-5112. (published once a year).

National Archives Trust Fund Board, Publications Sales Department, Washington, DC 20408/202-523-3164. (published periodically).

National Gallery of Art, Publications Service, Washington, DC 20565/202-842-6466. (published once a year; must enclose $1.00 when requesting the catalogue or make check out to: Publications Fund).

SITES, Smithsonian Institution Traveling Exhibition Service, Smithsonian Institution, P.O. Box 1949, Washington, DC 20013/202-357-3168. (published once a year).

Smithsonian Books, Public Inquiry Mail Service, Smithsonian Institution, Washington, DC 20560/202-357-2700. (published once a year).

Smithsonian Institution Press, Public Inquiry Mail Service, Smithsonian Institution, Washington, DC 20560/202-357-2700. (published once a year, with periodic 'New Book' supplements).

Superintendent of Documents, U.S. Government Printing Office, Washington, DC 20402/202-783-3238. (published once a year).

The Freer Gallery of Art, Sales Catalogue, Smithsonian Institution, Washington, DC 20560/202-357-1432. (published once a year).

The Smithsonian Collection of Recordings, Public Inquiry Mail Service, Smithsonian Institution, Washington, DC 20560/202-357-2700. (published once a year).

The Smithsonian Gift Catalogue, Public Inquiry Mail Service, Smithsonian Institution, Washington, DC 20560/202-357-2700. (published 3 or 4 times a year).

United States Capitol Historical Society, 200 Maryland Avenue NE, Washington, DC 20515/202-543-8919. (published once a year).

United States Department of the Interior, Geological Survey, National Cartographic Information Center, Reston VA 22092/703-860-7444.

White House Historical Association, 740 Jackson Place NW, Washington, DC 20506/202-737-8292. (published once a year).

Surplus Property: Red Tag Specials from Uncle Sam

Throughout the year, the Federal government offers hundreds of millions of dollars worth of property and goods at never-heard-of-before bargain prices. Very few people or organizations know about these unique bargains because the Federal government spends little or no money advertising the availability of its surplus goods and services. Described below are 34 of Uncle Sam's Red Tag Specials. Contact the appropriate offices and discover how you can get some of your taxes back by participating in these programs.

Auctions—Customs Service
Federally seized items are auctioned approximately once a year through the U.S. Customs Service in your geographic region. Jewelry, cameras, shoes, rugs, cases of wine, leather goods, perfumes, and even a double-decker bus have been available for purchase. Items not included are firearms, liquor, art objects and artifacts. Contact: Your local U.S. Customs Service Office; or U.S. Customs Service, P.O. Box 7118, Washington, DC 20044.

Auctions—Internal Revenue Service
The Collection Division of the Internal Revenue Service holds regular auctions to dispose of items seized from businesses and individuals who have failed to pay their taxes. Real estate, household goods, cars, furniture and boats are sold. To be notified of upcoming auctions in your area, call your local Internal Revenue Service, Collections Division Office, and ask to be placed on the IRS auctions mailing list.

Auctions—Postal Service
The regional Dead Parcel Branches of the U.S. Postal Service auction unclaimed merchandise. Many of these branches also include their own surplus office equipment among the auctioned items. Recent bargains have included a $500 limited edition plate for $85 and a camel saddle for $100. Books are the most plentiful items offered. For information about upcoming auctions contact: Your local Post Office and ask for the closest Dead Parcel Office; or the U.S. Postal Service, 475 L'Enfant Plaza, West Building, Washington, DC 20260/202-523-2253.

Auctions—Small Business Administration
You can own a liquor store, an ice cream parlor or art gallery. The Small Business Administration obtains entire businesses and business supplies through its foreclosure of business loans. Most newspapers run ads about auctions in the Classified Section under Bids and Proposals, usually on weekends. Businesses valued over $5,000 are auctioned on the premises. Goods, machinery and some real estate may be sold by negotiation or sealed bids. Contact: the Liquidation Officer at your local Small Business Administration office; or the U.S. Small Business Administration, General Agency Information, 1441 L Street NW, Washington, DC 20416.

Auctions and Donations—Department of Defense
The Defense Properties Donations Services disposes of excess or surplus properties throughout its

offices around the world. Almost anything you can imagine is auctioned or donated to nonprofit organizations. Items have included: tents, cots, jeeps, firearms, armored combat vehicles, aircraft, ships, explosives, machinery and office supplies. To be notified of future auctions in your area or to investigate donation possibilities contact: U.S. Department of Defense, Surplus Sales, P.O. Box 1370, Battle Creek, MI 49016; or Director Sales Division, Office of Property Management, Office of Federal Supply and Services, General Services Administration, Washington, DC 20405/703-557-0814.

Books—Library of Congress
The Library of Congress will give schools, public libraries or nonprofit organizations its surplus and duplicate books. Profit making groups can submit bids to purchase the books. Your Congressman's district office can help you with your selection or you can contact: Gift and Exchange Division, Library of Congress, Washington, DC 20540/202-287-6171.

Cannons, Combat Materials and More—Department of Defense
Cannons, obsolete combat material and books, drawings, plans, models, etc. are available on loan or as a donation to veterans' organizations, soldiers' monument associations, state museums, incorporated museums and incorporated municipalities. The cost of packing and handling must be paid by the recipient. Applications for donations or loans are handled by the Secretary of the Military Department which has control of the desired items. Contact: Your nearest military installation for general information; or Headquarters: (Appropriate Military Department), Pentagon, Washington, DC 20301.

Cars, Boats, Airplanes, etc.—General Services Administration
Federal surplus items are available to State and local public agencies for carrying out or promoting public purposes, and for use in areas such as parks, education, public health, public safety, etc. Items such as office machines, furniture, boats, airplanes, special purpose motor vehicles are donated to eligible recipients within the State on a fair and equitable basis. Items not donated are made available for sale to the general public. For information contact: Director: Donation Division, Office of Property Management, General Services Administration, Washington, DC 20406/202-557-1234.

Christmas Trees—Bureau of Land Management
Free Christmas trees are available to nonprofit organizations. Commercial organizations and individuals can obtain trees at fair market value. And for $1.00 you can cut your own evergreen! The trees are located on federal land in ten Western states. Contact: your local office of the Bureau of Land Management, the Forest Service, or Division of Forestry, Bureau of Land Management, U.S. Department of the Interior, Room 15620, 18th and C Streets, NW, Washington, DC 20240/202-343-3229.

Decorations and Gifts—General Services Administration
A list of all decorations and gifts given to federal departments and agencies by foreign governments is published annually in the *Federal Register*. The gifts are described and their value is estimated. Gifts not used by the government are donated to public institutions or sold to the public by the General Services Administration. For information, contact: Office of Protocol, Department of State, 2201 C Street NW, Room 1238, Washington, DC 20520/202-632-0907.

Donations and Auctions—General Services Administration
Regularly scheduled sales of surplus Federal property are held at government buildings throughout the country. Most items are sold at 80% to 90% of their original value. Examples include automobiles, furniture, typewriters, office equipment, oven cookers, stainless kitchen items, star scanners, sawdust vacuum machines and magnetic tape readers. These same items are also donated to nonprofit organizations. Contact your nearest Regional Surplus Sales office to identify donations and sales in your area. The three regional offices are: 1) General Services Administration, Surplus Sales Branch, 7th & D Streets SW, Washington, DC 20407; 2) General Services Administration, Surplus Sales Branch, 75 Spring Street, Atlanta, GA 30303; and 3) General Services Administration, Surplus Sales Branch, 525 Market Street, San Francisco, CA 94105.

Energy Equipment—Department of Energy
Used energy equipment is granted to nonprofit education institutions of higher learning for use in energy-oriented educational programs in the life, physical and environmental sciences and engineering. In 1983 alone, 32 pieces of equipment were donated to nine universities. For information contact: Larry Barker, University and Industry Programs Division, Office of Field Operations

Management, DOE, Washington, DC 20585/202-252-6833.

Firewood—Forest Service

Within the 187 million acres of national forest throughout the United States, you may gather firewood free of charge. You must have a "free use" permit and a copy of the rules. Only dead or felled timber is available and there is a limit of 13 pick-up loads. You must cut, split, stack and haul your own load, and the wood must be gathered for your own use. Contact: your local U.S. Forest Service Office or Forest Service, U.S. Department of Agriculture, P.O. Box 2417, Washington, DC 20013/202-447-3957.

Food—Food and Nutrition Service

Charitable and rehabilitative institutions are usually eligible to receive surplus commodities stored by the U.S. Department of Agriculture. The commodities available include dairy products, oil, grain and peanuts. Contact: Food Distribution Program, Food and Nutrition Service, 500 12th Street SW, Washington, DC 20250.

Fruits and Vegetables—Department of Agriculture

Many farmers allow consumers to harvest their fields at substantial savings. For a directory of farms which offer these direct Marketing Programs, contact your state department of agriculture or a state county extension service office. For help locating your local office contact: Administrator's Office, U.S. Department of Agriculture, Extension Service, Room 340A, Washington, DC 20250/202-447-3377.

Homes and Land—Department of Housing and Urban Development

Hundreds of reasonably priced homes in 96 cities throughout the United States are available through the U.S. Department of Housing and Urban Development. These properties have been acquired by HUD Properties Disposition Department through FHA and VA federally insured loan default. Properties are advertised in local newspapers and are sold by commercial real estate brokers. For information about properties in your area contact: The local office of the Department of Housing and Urban Development; or Program Information Center, U.S. Department of Housing and Urban Development, 451 7th Street SW, Washington, DC 20410/202-755-5324.

Homes and Land—Farmers Home Administration

The Farmers Home Administration (FHA) Rural Housing Office maintains a listing of reasonably priced rural single-family properties identified for sale by local FHA offices. The current listing includes 8,800 properties acquired through loan default. Eligible areas are rural, open counties with populations of not more than 10,000 and in areas where credit is scarce. Land properties are also available. Purchasers must show intent to become a resident. For further information contact: FHA Rural Housing Properties, U.S. Department of Agriculture, 14th and Independence Avenue SW, Washington, DC 20250/202-447-7967.

Horses—Department of the Interior

In order to control the population of wild horses and burros grazing on public land, the U.S. Department of the Interior offers these animals for adoption to qualified applicants. Individuals are granted titles to ownership after a one-year period of humane treatment as certification by a veterinarian. Since the program began 33,000 healthy animals have been relocated nationwide. Applications for adoption are available by writing Consumer Information Center, Adopt-a-Horse Program, Box 4007, Pueblo, Colorado 81003.

Houses for $1.00—Department of Housing and Urban Development

Under the Urban Homesteading program, the U.S. Department of Housing and Urban Development gives cities and towns abandoned single-family homes that the government had insured. For one reason or another, the owner let the house run down and then abandoned it without paying back the loan. Rather than let these homes stand empty, the government turns the dwellings over to local communities which, in turn sell them to low-income families for practically nothing, usually for $1.00. To find out whether your community is participating in the program and whether you qualify, contact: Your local U.S. Department of Housing and Urban Development; or Urban Homesteading Division, Office of Urban Rehabilitation, Community Planning and Development, U.S. Department of Housing and Urban Development, 451 7th Street SW, Washington DC 20410/202-755-8702.

Icebreaker Travel—U.S. Coast Guard

Scientists and researchers can travel on U.S. Coast Guard Icebreaker expeditions into the Arctic. Passage is granted on a space-available basis, and applicants are selected according to the value of the project they are working on. Occasionally representatives of government agencies, academic institutions, and nonprofit organizations can travel free of charge; for the most part, though, travel is on a reimbursement basis. For details contact: Ice \ Operations Division, U.S. Coast Guard Headquarters, Washington, DC 20593/202-426-1881.

Jeeps, Trucks, and more—Postal Service
Local Post Offices continually sell used jeeps, trucks, tractors and wreckers to the public. Jeeps less than 10 years old with only 20,000 miles of use will sell for as little as $1,300. Contact: Motor Vehicle Service Department of your local Post Office.

Land and Buildings—Department of Health and Human Services
Eligible organizations and institutions can obtain surplus real properties to carry out health programs including research. Property is awarded to the applicants whose programs or use are determined to be in the highest public interest. To find out what is available and how to apply for it contact: Chief, Division of Realty, Office of Real Property, Office of Facilities Engineering, Department of Health and Human Services, Washington, DC 20201/202-245-1926.

Land for Builders—Department of Housing and Urban Development
The U.S. Department of Housing and Urban Development sells and donates surplus federal land and property to those who use it for low or moderate-income housing and related commercial and industrial use. Contact: Office of Surplus Land and Housing, New Communities Development Corporation, U.S. Department of Housing and Urban Development, 451 7th Street SW, Washington, DC 20410/202-426-3500.

Oil and Gas Lotteries—Bureau of Land Management
Individuals can participate in public lotteries that offer the rights to extract oil and gas from federally owned land. Most winners sell these rights to energy companies for large sums of money. For further information about how to participate in these lotteries contact: Bureau of Land Management, U.S. Department of the Interior, 18th and C Streets NW, Room K5623, Washington, DC 20240/202-343-7753.

Plants and Shrubs—Soil Conservation Service
Individuals, nonprofit organizations, and state and local governments are all eligible for seeds, plants, shrubs, etc., to be used for soil erosion, windbreak or water conservation. Contact: Your county government for the local office of the Soil Conser-

vation Service; or Soil Conservation Service, U.S. Department of Agriculture, P.O. Box 2890, Washington, DC 20013/202-447-4630.

Property Sales and Donations—General Services Administration
Surplus property is offered for sale or use as public parks, recreation areas, public health centers or educational centers. The property is generally offered for sale to the public on a competitive bid basis. State and local government agencies and tax exempt agencies and schools are eligible to apply for this property. For information contact: Assistant Commissioner, Office of Real Property, Federal Property Resource Service, General Services Administration, Washington, DC 20405/202-535-7084.

Rent a Museum—Smithsonian Institution
Many organizations can take advantage of Smithsonian exhibits through the SITES program sponsored by the federal government. A broad range of exhibitions are available on a traveling basis to museums of all sizes and character, art galleries, and educational organizations. To be eligible an applicant must satisfy the requirements of appropriate space, lighting, environmental controls, police and fire protection, and handling of exhibitions. Exhibitions are offered for a four or six week period. For information contact: Assistant Director for Program Analysis, Smithsonian Institution Traveling Exhibition Service, Office of Museum Programs, Smithsonian Institution, Washington, DC 20560/202-357-3168.

Ship Sales—Department of Transportation
Merchant ships no longer used by the government are sold on a competitive bid basis to the public. Those who need a ship for non-transportation or dismantling purposes may purchase ships under prescribed conditions. For further information contact: Chief, Division of Ship Disposals and Foreign Transfers, Office of Ship Operations, Maritime Administration, Department of Transportation, Washington, DC 20590/202-426-5821.

Schools—Department of Education
The Department of Education will sell or lease surplus Federal Real Property at fair market value. Property must be used for educational purposes including higher education, elementary and secondary education, libraries, central administrative facilities, educational TV and radio and vocational education and research. For information contact: Federal Real Property Assistance Program, Office of the Under Secretary, Department of Education,

400 Maryland Avenue SW, Washington, DC 20202/202-755-2083.

Stock Your Pond—Department of the Interior
As a result of some old oil conservation policies, ponds can be stocked free of charge with bass and bluegills. Depending on which state is involved, the U.S. Department of the Interior or the state government will provide the fish. To find out if you qualify, contact: Your local game warden or the local county agent from the U.S. Department of Agriculture; or Fish and Wildlife Service, Department of the Interior, Washington, DC 20240/ 202-653-8746.

Swimming and Boating—Department of Agriculture
The U.S. Department of Agriculture gives money to small landowners to help them turn their property into recreation areas for the public. Most of these areas are in attractive, out-of-the-way places for those who wish to avoid crowds. For information about the program, or help in locating an area near you or where you intend to vacation, contact: Recreation Staff, Forest Service, U.S. Department of Agriculture, P.O. Box 2471, Washington, DC 20013/703-235-1071.

Tools for Schools—Department of Defense
Surplus tools that can be used by nonprofit public schools and vocational training centers are available for the cost of packing and shipping. The U.S. Department of Defense Logistics Agency's program, "Tools for Schools" will give these organizations tools it no longer uses. This program was initiated in an attempt to develop skilled manpower for industrial preparedness. Contact: Commander, Defense Industrial Plant Equipment Center, Defense Depot, Memphis, TN 38114.

Use of Minerals—Bureau of Land Management
Free-use-permits are granted to governmental units to allow them use of mineral material on lands under the jurisdiction of the Bureau of Land Management. Permits are granted to nonprofit organizations for mineral material not to exceed 5000 cubic yards during any consecutive twelve month period. Contact: Chief, Division of Mining Law and Saleable Minerals, Bureau of Land Management, Department of the Interior, Washington, DC 20240/202-343-8537.

Wild Animals—National Park Service
The Department of the Interior will restock wildlife ranges, zoo display animals and research animals, and scientific specimens. For further information applicants, including American Indians, can contact: The appropriate National Park Service regional office; or Chief, Biological Resources Division, National Park Service, Department of the Interior, 18th and C Streets, NW, Washington, DC 20240/202-343-8125.

Hotlines and Recorded Messages

Uncle Sam provides nearly 200 Hotlines and Recorded Messages you can call to obtain information, file a complaint, or keep up-to-date about newsworthy government statistics and activities. Below you will find a listing of Hotline numbers followed by a listing of Recorded Message telephone numbers. Many of these calls are free of charge!

Hotlines

The following toll-free numbers handle complaints or provide information to the public.

Agency for International Development
Fraud, waste and abuse hotline for whistle blowers: (call collect) 703-235-3528.

Agriculture, Department of
Fraud, waste and abuse hotline for whistle blowers: 800-424-9121, DC: 202-472-1388.
Economic Statistics Hotline: 800-424-7964. DC: 202-488-8358.

Commerce, Department of
Roadmap Program—Information and Referrals on subjects of interest to callers (not toll free): 202-377-3176.
Fraud, waste and abuse hotline: 800-424-5197, DC: 202-724-3519.
Export Financing Hotline: 800-424-5201, DC: 202-566-8860.

Commodity Futures Trading Commission
Information on commodity brokers: 800-424-9838, DC: 202-254-8630.

Consumer Product Safety Commission
Product recall information, complaints, and fact sheets: 800-638-2772, MD: 301-492-6626.
Commission for Hearing Impaired: 800-638-8270, MD: 800-492-8104.

News—Media Inquiries: 202-634-7780.
News—Public Inquiries: 301-492-5713.
Information on Recalls, Complaints, Free Pamphlets and Fact Sheets: 800-638-8326, MD: 800-492-8363. AK, HI, Puerto Rico & Virgin Islands: 800-638-8333

Defense, Department of
To collect information from those who participated in nuclear weapons tests in Nevada or Marshall Islands from 1945 to 1962, and from anyone who went into Japan three months after the nuclear bombs were dropped: 800-336-3068. DC: 202-274-9161.

Fraud Hotline: 800-424-9098. DC: 202-693-5080.
Air Force Retiree Counsel: 800-531-7502. TX: 800-292-5222.
Army Recruiting: 800-USA-ARMY.
Retired Army Pay: 800-428-2290. IN: 317-542-3911 (call collect).
Marine Corps Recruiting: 800-423-2600. CA: 800-252-0241.
National Guard—Recruiting Support Service: 800-638-0936 (ex NJ). 800-638-1802 (ex MD). 800-638-7600 (ex MI).
National Guard Bureau—Army: 800-446-4010.

Navy Finance Center: 800-321-1080. OH: 216-522-5955.

Navy Recruiting: 800-327-6289. GA: 800-342-5855.

Navy Deserters Information Point: 800-336-4974. VA: 800-572-0266.

Navy Employment Information: 800-327-6289. FL: 800-432-1884.

Navy Prisoner of War and Missing in Action (not toll free): 202-694-3197.

Education, Department of

Student Financial Assistance: 800-241-4710. GA: 800-282-1050. Atlanta: 221-2018.

National Clearinghouse for Bilingual Education: 800-336-4560. VA: 703-522-0710 (call collect).

Public Affairs Office: DC: 202-472-3850.

Recorded Message: DC: 202-472-2729.

Loan Monitoring—Financial Aid: 800-621-3115. IL: 800-972-3189. Chicago: 353-7910.

Federal/Student Aid: 800-638-6700. MD: 800-492-6602.

Clearinghouse on the Handicapped Ecucational Services: 800-424-8567. DC: 202-287-5100.

Emergency Management Agency, Federal

Crime Insurance Information: 800-638-8780. DC & MD: 202-652-2637.

Flood Insurance Information: 800-638-6620. DC: 202-731-5300.

Energy, Department of

Conservation and Renewable Energy: 800-523-2929. PA: 800-462-4983. AK & HI: 800-233-3071.

National Appropriate Technology Assistance Service: 800-428-2525. MT: 800-428-1718.

Efficiency Labeling for Consumer Products: 800-523-2919. MD: 800-462-4983.

News Features: 800-424-9128. DC: 202-252-9500.

Environmental Protection Agency

Fraud, waste and abuse hotline for whistle blowers: 800-424-4000. DC: 202-382-4977.

Information on Dangerous Chemicals: 800-424-9065. DC: 202-554-1404.

Information on Pesticides: 800-531-7790. TX: 800-292-7664.

National Pesticide Information Clearinghouse: 800-858-7378.

Information on Hazardous Waste Material: 800-424-9346. DC: 202-382-3000.

Small Business Hotline: 800-368-5888.

Export—Import Bank

Small Business Advisory Hotline: 800-424-5201 or 5202. DC: 202-566-8860.

Federal Deposit Insurance Corporation

Information and Complaints Concerning FDIC Banks: 800-424-5488. DC: 202-389-4353.

Federal Election Commission

Information on Political Fund Raising Laws: 800-424-9530. DC: 202-523-4068. Alaska and Hawaii call DC number collect.

Federal Home Loan Bank Board

Information: 800-424-5405. DC: 202-377-6988.

Federal Trade Commission

Consumer Education Resources Network: 800-336-0223. VA: 703-522-4616.

General Accounting Office

Fraud Prevention Task Force: 800-424-5454. DC: 202-633-6987.

General Services Administration

Fraud, waste and abuse hotline for whistle-blowers: 800-424-5210. DC: 202-566-1780.

Sexual harassment of GSA Employees: 800-424-5210. DC: 202-566-1780.

Health and Human Services, Department of

(See also "Health Information Hotlines and Helps" in Health Matters section of sampler)

Second Opinion on Non-Emergency Surgery: 800-638-6833. MD: 800-492-6603.

Cancer Information: 800-638-6694. MD: 800-492-1444.

Health Service Corps Medical Scholarships: 800-638-0824. DC and MD: 301-443-1650.

Venereal Disease Hotline: 800-227-8922. CA: 800-982-5883.

To Report Denial of Treatment at a Health Care Facility because you are a Medicaid/Medicare Recipient: 800-638-0742. MD: 800-492-0359.

Parents Anonymous (child abuse): 800-421-0353. CA: 800-352-0386.

National Health Information Clearinghouse: 800-336-4797. VA: 703-522-2590.

National Runaway Switchboard (for parents and runaways to leave messages): 800-621-4000. IL: 800-972-6004.

Civil Rights discrimination in Health and Human Services programs: 800-368-1019. DC: 202-863-0100.

Fraud, waste and abuse hotline for whistle blowers: 800-368-5779. MD: 301-597-0724.

Acquired Immune Deficiency Syndrome (AIDS) Information Hotline: 800-221-AIDS. Alaska and Hawaii only: 202-245-6867 (call collect).

Children's Defense Fund (for information on current legislation in Congress as it affects children): 800-424-9602. DC: 202-628-8789.

Better Hearing Institute: 800-424-8576. DC: 202-638-7577.

Library of Congress National Library Service for the Blind and Physically Handicapped: 800-424-8567. DC: 202-287-5100.

Medicare/Medicaid—To report complaints regarding fraud, waste and abuse: 800-368-5779. MD: 301-597-0724.

National Abortion Federation: 800-772-9100. DC: 202-546-9060.

National Center for Stuttering: 800-221-2483. NY: 212-532-1460.

National Federation of Parents for Drug Free Youth: 800-554-KIDS. MD: 301-649-7100.

National Hotline for Missing and Exploited Children: 800-843-5678. DC: 202-634-9821.

National Institute on Drug Abuse Prevention Branch: 800-638-2045. MD: 301-443-2450.

National Parkinson's Disease Foundation: 800-327-4545. FL: 800-433-7022. Miami: 305-547-6666.

Hill-Burton Hospital Free Care: 800-638-0742. MD: 800-492-0359.

National Retinitis Pigmentosa Foundation: 800-638-2300. MD: 301-655-1011.

Women's Sports Foundation: 800-227-3988. CA, AK & HI: 415-563-6266.

National Health Information Hotline: 800-424-2481.

Housing and Urban Development, Department of
Housing Discrimination Complaints: 800-424-8590. DC: 202-426-3500.

News: 800-424-8530. DC: 202-755-7395.

Solar Information Hotline: 800-523-2929. PA: 800-462-4983. AK & HI: 800-523-4700.

Interior, Department of
Fraud, Waste and Abuse Hotline: 800-424-5081.

Abandoned Mine Reclamation Information (not toll free) 202-343-7937.

Internal Revenue Service
Federal Internal Revenue Service for TDD users: 800-428-4732. IN: 800-382-4058.

Federal tax information: 800-242-1040. DC: 202-488-3100. AK & HI: 800-428-4732.

Interstate Commerce Commission
Complaints about Moving Household Goods (not toll free) 202-275-0860.

Rates, Service and Claims Handling via Inland Waterways, Rail, Truck, and Service Freight Forwarders: 800-424-9312. DC: 202-275-0860.

Justice, Department of
Crime Insurance information: 800-638-8780. AK, HI & MD (call collect if necessary): 301-652-2637.

Juvenile Justice Clearinghouse—information on juvenile justice matters: 800-638-8736. MD: 301-251-5500.

National Center for Missing and Exploited Children: 800-843-5678. DC: 202-634-9821.

Labor, Department of
Information on Fraud Reporting Hotline: 800-424-5409. DC: 202-376-6995.

Library of Congress
Information on programs and books for the blind and physically handicapped: 800-221-4792. DC: 202-727-2142.

Talking Books Program: 800-424-9100. DC: 202-287-5100.

National Referral Center—free referrals to information sources (not toll free): 202-287-5670.

Recordings for the Blind: 800-221-4792. DC: 202-727-2142.

Merit System Protection Board
Fraud, waste and abuse hotline for whistle blowers: 800-872-9855. DC: 202-653-7188.

National Aeronautics and Space Administration
Fraud, waste and abuse hotline for whistle blowers: 800-424-9182. DC: 202-755-3402.

National Consumer Co-Op Bank
Information on Loans and Notes: 800-424-2481, DC: 202-673-4300.

Overseas Private Investment Corporation
Information Hotline: 800-424-6742. DC: 202-653-2800. AK & HI: 800-424-9704.

Peace Corps
Volunteer Program Information: 800-424-8580. DC: 202-254-6886.

Small Business Administration
Business Desk—Loan Management: 800-368-5855. DC: 202-653-7561.

Publications Information: 800-433-7212. TX: 800-792-8901. DC: 202-653-6365.

Teachers Service Organization
Credit and Banking Information and Services: 800-523-1888. PA. 800-492-2500.

Transportation, Department of
Fraud, waste and abuse hotline for whistle blowers: 800-424-9071. DC: 202-755-1855.
News (not toll free): 202-426-4321.
Complaints and Information on Auto Safety: 800-424-9393. DC: 202-426-0123.
Coast Guard Recruiting: 800-424-8883. DC: 202-426-7914.
Coast Guard Military Pay Center (retired): 800-638-0250.
To Report Oil Spills: 800-424-8802. DC: 202-426-2675.
United States Coast Guard (boating safety): 800-368-5647.
Information & Referral on Research, Development & Technical Assistance: 800-225-1612.
News features: 800-484-8807. DC: 202-426-1921.

Treasury, Department of
To Report Thefts, Losses or Discoveries of Explosive Materials: 800-424-9555. DC: 202-566-7777.

Veterans Administration
Fraud, waste and abuse hotline for whistle blowers: 800-368-5899. DC 202-389-5394.
Veterans Supply Depot: 800-323-0238. IL: 312-681-6877.

White House
News: 800-424-9090.
President's Daily Schedule: 202-456-2343.
First Lady's Daily Schedule: 202-456-6269.

Women's Economic Development Corps
Information Hotline: 800-222-2933.

Recorded Messages

The following recorded messages will give you information today that you are likely to read in the newspaper tomorrow.

Agriculture, Department of
Consumers' spot news: 202-488-1110
National grain market summary: 202-447-8233
Features and highlights: 202-488-8358 or 202-488-8359.

Botanic Garden, U.S.
Upcoming activities: 202-225-7099.

Commerce, Department of
Economic News: 202-393-4100
News highlights: 202-393-1847
Weekend preview: 202-393-4102.

Education, Department of
News: 202-472-2729.

Federal Communications Commission
News: 202-632-0002.

Federal Energy Regulatory Commission
Actions: 202-357-8555.

Federal Trade Commission
FTC Meetings: 202-528-3806
News: 202-523-3540
Public Affairs: 202-523-3830
Public Reference Desk: 202-523-3598.

Government Jobs
Federal Job Information Center: 202-737-9616
Agriculture, Department of: 202-447-2108
Energy, Department of: 202-252-4333
Environmental Protection Agency: 202-755-5055
General Accounting Office: 202-275-6361
Interior, Department of: 202-343-2154
Justice, Department of: 202-633-3121
National Institutes of Health: 301-496-1209
National Oceanic and Atmospheric Administration: 301-443-8274
Smithsonian Institution: 202-357-1452
State, Department of: 202-632-0580.

House of Representatives, U.S.
Floor activity, Democrat: 202-225-7400
Floor activity, Republican: 202-225-7430
Democratic legislative program: 202-225-1600
Republican legislative program: 202-225-2020.

Housing and Urban Development, Department of
News: 800-424-8530
202-755-7395.

Interior, Department of
News: 202-343-3020.

Labor, Department of
Press release information: 202-523-6899.

National Capital Parks
Washington, DC Area Activities: 202-426-6975.

President's Daily Schedule
News: 202-456-2343.

Senate
Floor activity, Democrat: 202-224-8541
Floor activity, Republican: 202-224-8601.

Smithsonian Institution
Dial-A-Museum: 202-357-2020
Dial-A-Phenomenon: 202-357-2000.

Transportation, Department of
News: 800-484-8807
202-426-1921.

Treasury, Department of
Bureau of the Public Debt: A lesson in government securities: 202-287-4091
Auction results and auction dates for government securities: 202-287-4100
Treasury Bills 202-287-4091
Bonds and Notes 202-287-4088 Information Center 202-287-4113

Time Within Milli-seconds
Naval Observatory Master Clock: 202-653-1800

White House
News outside Washington, DC: 800-424-9090.
President's Daily Schedule: 202-456-2343.
President's Voice Announcing News Items: 202-456-7198 in DC area, 800-424-9090 elsewhere.

Free Help and Information For You and Your Family

The Government offers lots of resources, from hotlines to comic books, on all sorts of topics of interest to you and your family. This section is designed to introduce you to what's available and how you can make use of it—whether you are a kid, parent, traveler or consumer.

Immigration, Naturalization, and Citizenship

The government offers films, publications and services designed to help you help yourself—or others—immigrate and prepare for U.S. citizenship. Many of these materials are also helpful resources for learning more about our U.S. heritage.

Bibliography
A variety of citizen education materials are available from the government, including publications designed to help you help yourself—or others—prepare for the U.S. Citizenship test. For a free copy of Subject Bibliography SB-069 contact: Superintendent of Documents, U.S. Government Printing Office, Washington, DC 20402/202-783-3238.

Citizenship Education
Citizen education films are available at no charge to civic, patriotic, educational and religious groups. There are also about 15 textbooks on citizenship available, consisting of teachers' manuals and student textbooks at various reading levels. These books are distributed free to public schools to help

applicants for citizenship. Contact: Naturalization, Immigration and Naturalization Service, Department of Justice, 425 Eye Street NW, Room 7228, Washington, DC 20536/202-633-3320.

Visa Information for Aliens Waiting to Enter the United States
This office provides general or specific information and visas for aliens wishing to enter the United States. Inquiries about the status of specific cases should be directed to the U.S. consul in the country where the application is made. A list is available of American diplomatic and consular offices that issue visas. Contact: Visa Services, Bureau of Consular Affairs, Department of State, SA 13th Floor, Washington, DC 20520/202-632-1972.

Tracing Your Roots

The following assistance is available to those trying to find information about their family background. Most of this help is provided free of charge.

Family Folklore

The pamphlet, *Family Folklore* (188N) $1.75, describes how to record family stories and traditions to add to genealogical research. To obtain a copy write: Consumer Information Center, Pueblo, CO 81002.

Genealogy Research

The staff at the National Archives is eager to help individuals researching their family heritage. A 20-page booklet, "Genealogy Records in the National Archives," is available free of charge. Contact: Reference Service Branch, National Archives and Records Administration, 8th and Pennsylvania Avenue, Room 205, Washington, DC 20408/202-523-3218.

Library of Congress

Local History and Genealogy Section, General Reading Room, Washington, DC 20540/202-287-5537. This section contains a number of "finding aids" and indexes arranged by family names and geographic location. Reading Room contains card catalogue of published genealogy by surname—now being put on computer terminal.

National Archives and Records Service

Central Reference Division, Washington, DC 20408/202-523-3218. This division has ship passenger records from 1820, military records from the Revolutionary War, and census forms from 1790 to 1910. Anyone in the USA can rent microfilm on the census 1790–1910 or the Revolutionary War from the local public, college or genealogical library. To do this contact: DDD Company, P.O. Box 2940, Hyattsville, MD 20784/301-731-4595 or your local library. The cost is $3.25 per reel for a one-month rental. Three catalogues are available listing films on census (1) 1790–1890, (2) 1900, and (3) 1910 at $5.00 each. The Revolutionary War catalogue is a 3-volume issue at $1.50 total. All of the above are also available for rental in Canada.

Especially For . . . . . .

Uncle Sam has something for everyone—from kids to senior citizens. This section is designed to help you understand what's available for you. It includes sections for: 1) Parents and Parents-To-Be; 2) Kids and Teens; 3) Women; and 4) Senior Citizens.

Parents and Parents-to-Be

The Federal government spends billions of dollars trying to determine the healthiest way to have a baby and raise a child. As taxpayers we can tap into this resource and thereby have access to the latest research developments and techniques. Described below are free services and publications designed to help you in your role as a parent. The Sampler sections entitled "Health Matters" and "Social Injustices and Crime" also contain resources of interest to parents.

SERVICES

All services described below are available free of charge. In addition to these entries, also feel free to contact the centers which put out the publications described later in this section.

RAISING A CHILD: HOW MUCH WILL IT COST?

The table below presents the average annual cost of raising an urban child in the northeastern United States at a moderate standard of living. The prices are in 1984 dollars. Estimates are also available for different regions, standards of living, and cost factors. Contact: Department of Agriculture, Science and Education Administration, Family Economics Research Group, Federal Building, Room 338, Hyattsville, MD 20782.

Age of Child (years)	Total	Food at Home	Clothing	Housing	Medical Care	Education
Under 1	$3,134	$487	$120	$1,301	$219	$ 0
1	3,236	509	120	1,301	219	0
2–3	2,198	583	172	1,108	188	0
4–5	3,031	640	172	1,108	188	0
6	3,025	640	240	960*	188	65
7–9	3,128	743	240	869	188	65
10–11	3,256	871	248	969	188	65
12	3,482	871	326	987	188	65
13–15	3,584	975	326	897	188	65
16–17	3,847	1,141	377	1,025	188	65
TOTAL	$55,077	$14,085	$7,426	$18,886	$3,446	$780

*By the time a child is 6 years old he or she probably has siblings; therefore per capita expenses in the household will drop.

Local Family Experts Offer Free Advice

Over 3,000 county Cooperative Extension Service offices throughout the country offer the services of home economists and family-life specialists, free for the asking. These experts provide information and assistance for almost any area of family living. To identify your local family life specialist, call information and ask for the Cooperative Extension Service for your county. If you cannot locate your local office, contact: Executive Officer, Department of Agriculture, SEA/Extension, Room 332A, Administration Building, Washington, DC 20250/202-447-3304.

Hotline to Health Questions

The Health Information Clearinghouse maintains a staff of information specialists who can locate a source of information for any health related problem that may be encountered while bringing up children. The staff's services are free. Contact: National Information Clearinghouse, P.O. Box 1133, Washington, DC 20013/toll-free 800-336-4797/in Virginia call collect 703-522-2590.

Hotline for Advice About Buying Toys and Children's Furniture

Before you purchase a toy or furniture for your child, you can call the Consumer Product Safety Commission's toll-free number and find out if there have been any complaints about the product you wish to buy, or if it has been recalled by the manufacturer. The publications described below are free of charge.

Contact: Office of Communication, Consumer Product Safety Commission, Washington, DC 20207/toll-free 800-638-2772.

Crib Safety—Keep Them on the Safe Side
Toys—A Fact Sheet
Playground Equipment Guide
A Toy and Sports Equipment Safety Guide

Child Entrepreneurs

The U.S. Department of Agriculture lends up to $10,000 to youths between 10 and 21 years of age. The loans can be used to support both farm and non-farm ventures such as small crop growing, livestock farming, roadside stands or custom work. The loans are normally made in conjunction with youth groups and require parental consent. Contact: Production Loan Division, Farmers Home Administration, Department of Agriculture, Washington, DC 20250/202-447-2288.

PUBLICATIONS AND EXPERTISE

The listing below represents only a small fraction of the materials and expertise available to make pregnancy and child raising a healthier and happier experience. The centers distributing many of the publications often have staff available to answer your questions or refer you elsewhere.

Help Before Having A Baby

The following publications and services provide assistance during pregnancy:

Prenatal Care (OHDS 73-30017)—this bestseller gives the expectant mother advice on caring for herself during pregnancy. It also describes the needs of a newborn baby. Free from Department of Health and Human Services, Office of Human Development Services, LSDS, Department 76, Washington, DC 20401.

Alcohol and Pregnancy—the following publications discuss the effects of alcohol on pregnancies: *Should I Drink?, Think First of Your Unborn Child* (also available in Spanish), *Preventing Fetal Alcohol Effects.* They are free from National Clearinghouse for Alcohol Information, P. O. Box 2345, Rockville, MD 20852/301-468-2600.

Drugs and Pregnancy—these publications contain practical information and research results on the effects of drugs on pregnancies: *Drug Dependence in Pregnancy, Research Issues #5, Drugs and Pregnancy.* They are free from National Clearinghouse for Drug Abuse Information, P. O. Box 416, Kensington, MD 20795/301-443-6500.

Smoking and Pregnancy—free publications, including *Pregnancy and Infant Health,* and information assistance are available from: Office of Smoking and Health, Department of Health and Human Services, 5600 Fishers Lane, Park Building Room 1–58, Rockville, MD 20857/301-443-1575. Ask for literature on smoking and pregnancy.

Caffeine and Pregnancy—results of a recent FDA study linking caffeine to birth defects in animals are available. Basic facts about caffeine, its known effects on health, and a list of foods and drugs containing caffeine can also be obtained. Free from Consumer Information Center, Pueblo, CO 81009.

X-Rays and Pregnancy—shows what special precautions to take if you must have an x-ray during pregnancy. Free from Consumer Information Center, Pueblo, CO 81009.

Down's Syndrome and Pregnancy After 35—*Facts About Down's Syndrome for Women Over 35* explains the increased chances of bearing a child with mongolism for women over 35 years of age. Free from Office of Research Reporting, National Institute of Child Health and Human Development, Building 31, Room 2A-32, National Institutes of Health and Human Development, 9000 Rockville Pike, Bethesda, MD 20205/301-496-5133.

Premature Birth—*Little Babies: Born Too Soon—Born Too Small* shows expectant mothers how to take precautions against premature birth and low birth weight in full-term infants. Free from Office of Research Reporting, National Institute of Child Health and Human Development, Building 31, Room 2A-32, National Institutes of Health, 9000 Rockville Pike, Bethesda, Md 20205/301-496-5133.

Child Care: Infant through 12 years

The publications below are available from: Superintendent of Documents, U.S. Government Printing Office, Washington, DC 20402/202-783-3238. Please include title of book and stock number with a check made out to Superintendent of Documents. They will also take VISA and Master Card when ordering by phone.

Infant Care (017-091-00228-2)—this popular booklet covers the basics of caring for an infant (e.g., feeding, clothing, bathing, health care). It is written for parents who want to make sure their baby has a good start in life. $4.75.

Your Child from 1 to 6 (017-091-00219-2)—describes the growth of children from 1 to 6 years of age. Emphasizes the child's emotional needs and his or her relationship to other members of the family. $5.00.

Your Child from 6 to 12 (017-091-00070-1)—brings together the opinions of many specialists on how parents can help their children mature into healthy, well-adjusted, and socially responsible people. $5.00.

Childhood Diseases and Other Health Problems

A Parent's Guide to Childhood Immunization—describes measles, polio, rubella (German measles), mumps, diphtheria, pertussis (whooping cough), and tetanus. Shows how vaccinations should be given and includes record-keeping forms. Free from Consumer Information Center, Pueblo, CO 81009.

A Tale of Shots and Drops For Parents of Young Children (017-092-00058-8) $3.25—provides information regarding the need for immunization against childhood diseases. Available from: Superintendent of Documents, U.S. Government Printing Office, Washington, DC 20402/202-783-3238. Please include book title, stock number and a check made out to Superintendent of Documents. They will also take VISA and Master Card when ordering by phone.

Young Children and Accidents in the Home (017-091-00191-0) $4.25—describes the major causes of children's accidents in the home. Includes a checklist by age group of accident causing situations and how to avoid them, and a tear-out sheet with first aid information. Available from: Superintendent of Documents, U.S. Government Printing Office, Washington, DC 20402/202-783-3238. Please include book title, stock number and a check made out to Superintendent of Documents. They will also take VISA and Master Card when ordering by phone.

A Word of Caution About Treating Flu or Chicken Pox. (506N) Important facts about Reye Syndrome, a life-threatening condition that may affect children with flu or chicken pox. Free from Consumer Information Center, Pueblo, CO 81009.

Lead Poisoning in Children (HSA 78-5142)—discusses problems of lead paint poisoning and emphasizes essential steps in preventing death or permanent harm. Free (single copies only) Contact: National Center for Education in Maternal and Child Health, 3520 Prospect Street NW, Washington, DC 20057/202-625-8400.

Facts About Sudden Infant Death Syndrome (Crib Death) (HSA 81-5259)—provides basic facts, answers most-frequently-asked questions, discusses problems of grief, and refers to sources of help and information. Free (single copies only) Contact: National Center for Education in Maternal and Child Health, 3520 Prospect Street NW, Washington, DC 20057/202-625-8400.

Obesity in Childhood—free from Office of Research Reporting, National Institute of Child Health and Human Development, Building 31, Room 2A-32, National Institutes of Health, 9000 Rockville Pike, Bethesda, MD 20205/301-496-5133.

Child Abuse—free (single copies only) publications and information assistance are available from the Clearinghouse on Child Abuse and Neglect Information, P. O. Box 1182, Washington, DC 20013/202-245-2840

Child Mental Health—the following publications are free from National Clearinghouse for Mental Health Information, Room 11A-21, 5600 Fishers Lane, Rockville, MD 20857/301-443-4513.

Caring about Kids: Dyslexia (ADM 80-616)

Caring about Kids: Stimulating Baby's Senses (ADM 77-481)

Plain Talk About Children with Learning Disabilities (ADM 79-825)

Plain Talk About Dealing with the Angry Child (ADM 79-781)

Plain Talk About Feelings of Guilt (ADM 78-580)

Plain Talk About Raising Children (ADM 79-875)

Plain Talk About When Your Child Starts School (ADM 80-1021)

Day Care and Babysitters

A Parents Guide to Day Care (017-091-00231-2) $4.75—this guide provides parents with information on how to select proper in-home care, family day care, or a center-based care facility. Available from: Superintendent of Documents, U.S. Government Printing Office, Washington, DC 20402/202-783-3238. Please include book title, stock number and a check made out to: Superintendent of Documents. They will also take VISA and Master Card when ordering by phone.

A Pocket Guide to Babysitting (017-091-00236-3) $4.50—this handy guide describes the responsibilities of babysitting and also includes practical information needed by babysitters. It is a useful document for both the parent and the babysitter. Available from: Superintendent of Documents, U.S. Government Printing Office, Washington, DC 20402/202-783-3238. Please include book title, stock number and a check made out to: Superintendent of Documents. They will also take VISA and Master Card when ordering by phone.

The Super Sitter—this booklet outlines responsibilities of the babysitter. Free from Office of Communication, Consumer Product Safety Commission, Washington, DC 20207/toll-free 800-638-2772.

Child Physical Fitness

Children and Youth in Action: Physical Fitness in Sports (017-092-00079-1) $4.50—discusses the importance of physical activity from birth to 18 years of age. Available from: Superintendent of Documents, U.S. Government Printing Office, Washington, DC 20402/202-783-3238. Please include book title, stock number and a check made out to: Superintendent of Documents. They will also take VISA and Master Card when ordering by phone.

Youth Physical Fitness (017-001-00432-4) $4.75—describes physical fitness programs for children from 4 to 18 years of age. Available from: Superintendent of Documents, U.S. Government Printing Office, Washington, DC 20402/202-783-3238. Please include book title, stock number and a check made out to: Superintendent of Documents. They will also take VISA and Master Card when ordering by phone.

Parenting

The following publications are all available from

the Consumer Information Center, Pueblo, CO 81009.

An Adolescent in Your Home. (107N)—$3.50. Ways to cope with the physical and emotional stresses of adolescents.

Child Development in the Home. (108N)—$3.00. How to build self-confidence and self-discipline in the preschool child.

Child Safety Program Handbook. (402N)—50¢. A guide for parents who want to educate themselves and their community to the problems of missing children and what can be done.

Child Support. (501N)—Free. Help available from the government to enforce child support obligations, locate missing parents, and establish paternity.

Cognitive Development. (110N)—$2.75. How children learn and how parents can help.

Footsteps: A Parenting Guide. (190N)—$2.50. Practical advice for parents of young children on sibling rivalry, teaching values, independence, creativity, and more. Viewer guide for TV show "Footsteps," but can stand alone as reference.

The importance of Play in Child Development. (112N)—$2.00. Play is a child's way of learning social skills, creativity, and responsibility; how parents can enhance this learning.

The New Teen Titans. (403N)—50¢. This comic book depicts youngsters and their families dealing with alcohol and drug abuse with the help of the superheroes, the Teen Titans. Written for late elementary school children.

Plain Talk About Dealing with the Angry Child. (502N)—Free. Helping a child cope with feelings of anger and aggression.

Food and Nutrition

Breast Feeding (HSA 80-5109)—provides information to help mothers make decisions about breast feeding. It also includes "how-to" techniques. Single copies are available free of charge from: National Center for Education in Maternal and Child Health, 3520 Prospect Street NW, Washington, DC 20057/202-625-8400.

Recommendations for Feeding Normal Infants (HSA 79-5108)—contains information about breast feeding, infant formula, other foods, and flouride before and after six months of age. Single copies are available free of charge from: National Center for Education in Maternal and Child Health, 3520 Prospect Street NW, Washington, DC 20057/202-625-8400.

Nutrition—Copies of the following publications are available from: Superintendent of Documents, U.S. Government Printing Office, Washington, DC 20402/202-783-3238. Please include book title, stock number and a check made out to: Superintendent of Documents. They will also take VISA and Master Card when ordering by phone.

Family Fare: A Guide to Good Nutrition (001-000-03777-3) $5.50.

Keeping Food Safe to Eat: A Guide for Home-makers (001-000-03832-0) $2.25.

Your Money's Worth in Foods (001-000-04431-1) $2.25.

Nutrition and Your Health: Dietary Guidelines for Americans (001-000-04248-3) $2.25.

Copies of the following publications are available free of charge from: Consumer Information Center, Pueblo, CO 81009.

The Confusing World of Health Foods (543H)

Consumer's Guide to Food Labels (588H)

Nutrition and Your Health (656H)

Some Facts and Myths About Vitamins (550H)

Microwave Oven Radiation (553H)

Snack Facts (505N)

The Thing the Professor Forgot (437N, 50 cents)—a coloring book to teach children about good nutrition. Available from: Consumer Information Center, Pueblo, CO 81009.

(See also Coloringbooks, Comic Books and Toys in Sampler section.)

For Kids and Teens

Adults aren't the only ones who benefit from Uncle Sam's research, services and publications. Many things are put out just for kids, teens and young adults. And both the President and your Congressional Representative will write back to you if you write and tell them what you think about our country, kids, and international issues. Described below are things for kids through young adults.

Abused and Neglected?

A national center can provide help, send you things to read, and tell you who to contact in your home area for help. Contact: National Center on Child Abuse and Neglect, P.O. Box 1182, Washington, DC 20013/301-251-5157.

Abused or Kidnapped—Where to Get Help

There's a place that can help you if you think you are being sexually abused or if you have been taken from your home and need help. Staff at this center will put you in touch with people near you who can be of help. The Center can also send you things to read that could be of help. Contact: National Center for Missing and Exploited Children, 1835 K Street NW, Suite 700, Washington, DC 20006/202-9821.

Adventures

These publications are available from the Consumer Information Center, Pueblo, CO 81002.

Aboard the Space Shuttle (115N)—$2.75. An illustrated guidebook to a flight aboard the Space Shuttle—from take-off through daily routine to landing.

Comparing the Planets (116N)—$3.50. Full-color wall-chart featuring close-up pictures and important data on our neighbors in the solar system. Folded poster (56" x 31").

Environmental Coloring Book (117N)—$1.75. Charlie Chipmunk teaches preschoolers about the wonders of the forest.

Finding Your Way with Map and Compass (423N)—50¢. A layman's guide to using a compass and topographic map. 2 pp. 1982.

Space Shuttle (119N)—$3.50. Colorful illustration of the orbiter, with details of the interior design and equipment. Also includes a brief history. Folded poster (42" x 30").

Stars in Your Eyes: A Guide to the Northern Skies (195N)—$1.50. How to locate the best known constellations. Relates the legends of how they were named.

The Story of Checks and Electronic Payments (405N)—50¢. Comic book for teenagers on how banks started and how they work today.

Visiting People on a Dairy Farm (438N)—50¢. For early elementary school children, an illustrated tour of a dairy farm: What daily life on a farm is like, the hard work, and the rewards.

Airplane Rides, Overnight Stays and More—Free From the Air Force

At the request of your scout troop or youth group, the Air Force will provide a wide variety of free activities—all at no cost. The Air Force will let you use its facilities for special activities such as olympics, jamborees, and meetings. Your group can arrange to stay overnight on bases—either at camping sites or in the barracks. You can take part in training exercises, have plane rides around the base, tour airforce compounds, and learn about a variety of careers. Your group can also borrow films, on topics as varied as expert motorcycle riding, space communications, and careers in the airforce. For further information, contact the Youth Organization Project Officer at the Air Force base you want to visit or use for an activity.

Address your letter to: Base Commander, (use person's name), Air Force Base, State, Zip Code, Attention: Youth Organization Project Officer. If you are planning a national or regional event, you should write to the region's liaison officer or director. Listed below are the addresses and phone numbers of the U.S. Air Force Regional Liaison Offices.

Director, Air Force Office of Youth Relations, Kelly Air Force Base, Texas 78241-5000/ 512-925-5384.

Northeast Region Air Force Office of Youth Relations, McGuire Air Force Base, New Jersey 08641-5000/609-724-2905/3728.

Southeast Region Air Force Office of Youth Relations, Dobbins Air Force Base, Georgia 30069-5000/404-424-4990.

East Central Region, Air Force Office of Youth Relations, O'Hare ARF Facility, Illinois 60666-5000/312-694-6088.

South Central Region, Air Force Office of Youth Relations, Carswell Air Force Base, Texas 76127-5000/817-735-7134.

North Central Region, Air Force Office of Youth Relations, Whiteman Air Force Base, Missouri 65305-5000.

Western Region, Air Force Office of Youth Relations, Travis Air Force Base, California 94535-5260/707-438-5100.

Alcohol Abuse

Information and publications about alcohol abuse are available free of charge from: National Clearinghouse for Alcohol Information (NCALI), P.O. Box 2345, Rockville, MD 20852/301-468-2600.

Alcohol and Drug Abuse Prevention Network

The National Partnership to Fight Drug and Alcohol Abuse is a national network of individuals, professional and lay, concerned with preventing substance abuse, especially among young people. Staff can supply you with information about literature and programs, on a national to local level, which deal with these problems. Anyone interested in obtaining information, or in joining the partnership, should contact: National Partnership, Office of Juvenile Justice and Delinquency Prevention, Department of Justice, Washington, DC 20530/ 202-724-5911.

Amnesty and Military Deserter Policies

For information on amnesty programs, contact: Office of the Assistant Secretary of Defense, (MRA and L-MPFM, Legal Policy), The Pentagon, Washington, DC 20301/202-697-3387. For information on deserter programs, contact: Director of Legislation and Legal Policy, OSD (M) (MP and FM) (LLP), Department of Defense, The Pentagon, Room 3D823, Washington, DC 20301/202-697-3387.

Anorexia Nervosa
A booklet called *Facts about Anorexia Nervosa* (411N) will tell you about this eating problem and places you can contact for help. It costs 50¢ and can be ordered from: Consumer Information Center, P.O. Box 100, Pueblo, CO 81002.

Careers
Many agencies such as the Federal Bureau of Investigation (FBI), Central Intelligence Agency, NASA, Department of Defense and Peace Corps put out publications describing careers. The Department of Labor publishes lots of surveys and some directories describing overall career opportunities. Check these chapters for further information, or call the Public Affairs or Recruiting Office for the agencies you would be interested in working for. If you want to work with the federal government, check with the Civil Service Commission for information about opportunities. See also "Careers and Education" in this section of the Sampler.

COLORING BOOKS
You can get free coloring books from many places in the government. Examples are:

Water'n Kids—is a simple coloring and activity book reminding children that safe boating is fun boating. Contact: Commandant (G/BAU), U.S. Coast Guard, Washington, DC 20593/202-426-1079.

Charlie Brown Cleans the Air—The coloring book is available from: Environmental Protection Agency, Public Information Center, 820 Quincy Street NW, Washington, DC 20011/202-829-3535.

Safety—Two coloring books *Play Happy, Play Safety* and *Think Toy Safety*, are available from Office of Communication, Consumer Product Safety Commission, Washington, DC 20207/ toll-free 800-638-2772.

Stay-Well Card (508N)—this coloring book on the importance of immunization with a check list for parents on vaccinations young children need is available from: Consumer Information Center, Pueblo, CO 81009.

Winter Survival Coloring Book—this 8-page coloring book shows children how to deal with some of the hazards of winter. Free from: Federal Emergency Management Agency, Washington, DC 20472.

COMIC BOOKS
The following comic books are available from: Federal Reserve Bank of New York, Publications Section, 33 Liberty Street, New York, New York 10045.

The Story of Banks—shows how banks serve as financial supermarkets in our society as well as acting as go-betweens linking savers with borrowers.

The Story of Checks and Electronic Payments—describes in simple terms how checks are used in our society and how they are processed in our banking system.

The Story of Consumer Credit—describes the impact that consumer credit has on all of our lives.

The Story of Inflation—shows how inflation is one of the most damaging of all economic ills and the most difficult to end because its roots are so deeply entwined in our economic and political system.

The Story of Money—describes how coin, paper, and checkbook money have evolved over the ages.

Computer Users
You can use your computer and modem to get into several government sponsored databases which give information on time, climate, fuel, and computer standards and technology. For information about these databases, see "Computerized Databases—Free Public Access" in the Freebies section.

Congressional Pages and Interns
Each year about 100 pages work for Members of Congress during the school year. Many more youth get jobs working as interns or pages during the summer months. To learn about these opportunities, contact your Senator and Congressional Respresentative for more information.

Contraception: Comparing the Options (554N)
This free fold-out chart lists the nine common methods of birth control and the pros and cons of each. For a copy write: Consumer Information Center, P.O. Box 100, Pueblo, CO 81002.

Cosmetics

A free pamphlet entitled *Questions Concerning Cosmetics* (548N) provides answers to seven commonly asked questions regarding ingredients in various cosmetics. Write: Consumer Information Center, P.O. Box 100, Pueblo, CO 81002.

Depression and Manic Depressive Illness

This freebie describes the wide range of depressive states, the biological factors related to depression and the treatments available. To obtain a copy write: Information Office, National Institutes of Health, Clinical Center, Room 5C305, Bethesda, MD 20205.

Diet and Weight-Loss Gimmicks

Below are 2 freebies available from: Consumer Information Center, P.O. Box 100, Pueblo, CO 81002.

About Body Wraps, Pills, and Other Magic Wands (564N)—this discusses weight-loss gimmicks, untested diet aids, and their potential dangers.

Diet Books Sell Well But . . . . . (566N)—presents the fallacies and hazards of some popular diets, as well as advice about selecting a healthy diet to lose weight.

Drug Abuse

Informational materials about drugs, drug abuse, and its prevention are available free of charge. Examples include:

Controlled Substance Chart: Use, Abuse and Effects—a 4-page chart free to the general public in limited quantities (up to 25).

Drugs of Abuse—a 40-page booklet, written especially for law enforcement officers, educators, health and other professionals, containing full color illustrations of drugs controlled under the Controlled Substances Act 1970 (CSA)-1970, administered by the Drug Enforcement Administration (DEA), it also gives concise, factual, accurate scientific descriptions of the drugs, their effects and the consequences of abuse. It contains a chart summarizing scientific data about controlled licit and illicit drugs and a glossary of slang terms. The Controlled Substances Act-1970 is summarized.

Soozie and Katy—a 26-page activities and coloring book for children ages 5 to 9, which teaches them the consequences of drug abuse and emphasizes the theme, "Only sick people need drugs."

These, film rentals, and more are available from: National Clearinghouse on Drug Abuse, 5600 Fishers Lane, Rockville, MD 20857/301-443-6500. Publications are also available from: Drug Enforcement Agency Publications, 1405 Eye Street NW, Washington, DC 20537/202-633-1127.

Drunk Driving

A free pamphlet tells "How You Can Help Fight Drunk Drivers." Contact: National Highway Transportation Safety Administration, Public Affairs, DOT, 400 7th Street SW, Washington, DC 20590/202-426-9550.

FBI Freebies

The FBI has many free publications of interest to kids. Described below are some you might enjoy reading. To order a copy, write: FBI, Office of Congressional and Public Affairs, Room 6236, 10th Street at Pennsylvania Avenue, NW, Washington, DC 20531.

I Spy at the FBI—this freebie has puzzles, interesting facts, fingerprinting information and more to help you learn about the FBI.

Fingerprint Identification—provides a history of how fingerprints came to be.

99 Facts about the FBI—this 29-page booklet, with sketches, covers all aspects of the FBI including its history, jurisdiction, and operation. Done in a question and answer format, it is geared toward the general public.

The FBI: The First 75 Years—prepared in 1983, this 29-page booklet traces the history of the FBI providing information about topics such as the gangster era, spying, World War II activities, and the training of FBI agents.

Films You Can Borrow

The Freebies section of the Sampler describes films, on all different topics, that can be borrowed at no cost from the government. You will probably have to arrange a loan through your school or youth group. To learn more about these films, look-up Films in the Freebies section.

International Youth Exchange Program

Your Guide to International Youth Exchange (512N)—lists guidelines for selecting the right exchange program as a student, host family, or community volunteer. The Guide also contains a directory of selected programs and services. The 64-page publication is available free of charge from: Consumer Information Center, P.O. Box 100, Pueblo, CO 81002.

Loans for Kids 10 to 21 Years Old

The U.S. Department of Agriculture makes loans of up to $10,000 to kids aged 10 to 21. Often these loans are made to youth groups, and your parents must agree to your receiving the loan. These loans are made for both farm and non-farm business ventures. Money has been loaned for setting up road-side sales stands, growing crops, and doing specialized work. For information, contact: Production Loan Division, Farmers Home Administration, Department of Agriculture, Washington, DC 20250/202-447-2288.

KIDS' PUBLICATIONS

Uncle Sam has put together the following just for you!

I Spy at the FBI—is a mini-page publication to help parents and teachers introduce children to the FBI, both its services and its building. The 4-page publication contains puzzles, interesting facts, fingerprinting information and more. Write: FBI, Office of Congressional and Public Affairs, Room 6236, 10th Street at Pennsylvania Avenue NW, Washington, DC 20535

Dennis Takes a Poke at Poison (507N)—in this freebie Dennis the Menace learns about poisons in the home and how to tell if something is safe to eat. Available from: Consumer Information Center, Pueblo, CO 81009.

Fish, Storms and Lightning—the following pamphlets are available free from: Office of Public Affairs, National Oceanic and Atmospheric Administration, U.S. Department of Commerce, Washington, DC 20230.

Fish: The Most-Asked Questions—this pamphlet answers dozens of interesting questions about fish like: How long do fish live? What is the world's largest fish? The smallest?

Owlie Skywarn's Lightning Book—this pamphlet describes how lightning occurs and how children can protect themselves from its killing effects.

Watch Out . . . Storms Ahead—Owlie Skywatch Weather Book—this 28-page book provides basic information in a cute format about hurricanes, tornadoes, lightning, flash floods, and winter storms.

Motorcycle Safety

This booklet answers questions like: Is motorcycling safe? How does it compare to driving a car? What are the causes of motorcycle accidents and how can they be reduced? Free from: U.S. Department of Transportation, NHTSA, NTS/31, 400 7th Street SW, Washington, DC 20590.

Pets

The government has written several things to help you in taking care of your pets. For more information, see the "Pets and Plants" section of the Sampler.

Runaways

If you call the National Runaway Switchboard at 800-972-6004 in Illinois or 800-621-4000 elsewhere, you can leave a message for your parents or anyone else you would like to reach. These calls are free and the person answering the phone will not make you tell where you are staying.

SPACE AND AEROSPACE

NASA has put together many publications with beautiful pictures of space, the planets, the moon, and spacecrafts. You can get the publications described below for free, as long as NASA has copies. Contact: NASA Educational Publications, NASA Headquarters, Code LEP, Washington, DC 20546. When NASA runs out of these publications, you will have to buy copies, for a small fee, from: The Superintendent of Documents, U.S. Government Printing Office, Washington, DC 20402/202-783-3238.

Aboard the Space Shuttle—this describes what it would be like to live in space—how you would get there, what the trip would be like, what you would eat, how you would exercise and sleep and finally, how you would return home.

Aerospace Bibliography—this bibliography provides a listing of fiction and nonfiction books and pamphlets available from both commercial and government sources. Reading level, which ranges from Grade 1 through Adult, is indicated.

Mars: The Viking Discoveries—the booklet includes photographs and information about Mars.

Spacelab—this publication explains what Spacelab is, introduces you to the crew, describes Spacelab experiments, and takes you through a day aboard the aircraft.

Spacelab Poster—a 3½ x 4 foot color illustration of Spacelab.

Spacestation: The Next Logical Step—with pictures and narrative, this booklet shows you what the spacestation will look like, how it will work, the ways industry will set up shop in space, and what the spacestation means to nations and individuals.

Sun, Earth, and Man: the Need to Know and the Quest for Knowledge of Sun-Earth Relations—this discusses the relationship of the sun, earth and man covering the time before Sputnik, the Age of Space, the Eighties, and the future.

The Space Shuttle at Work—this booklet describes the space transportation system: how it came to be, why it is designed the way it is, what we expect of it, and how it may grow.

The Voyager Flights to Jupiter and Saturn—this describes with pictures and narrative the Voyager Flights to Jupiter and Saturn.

The World of Tomorrow: Aerospace Activities for 8- to 10-Year-Olds—a guide for leaders of children's groups and teachers of the lower grades, this presents projects kids can work on.

Viking: The Exploration of Mars—this includes information about Viking's mission and findings. The booklet also displays pictures taken in space.

What's New on the Moon?—this answers questions such as: Is there life on the moon? What is the moon made of? How old is the moon?—and more.

Stamp Collecting Guide
A free booklet called *Introduction to Stamp Collecting* tells you lots of things about stamps and how to collect them. Order from: Stamp Division, Postal Service, 475 L'Enfant Plaza West SW, Washington, DC 20260/ 202-245-5778.

Student Guide—Federal Financial Aid Programs
Published annually, this informative booklet by the department of Education, contains descriptive listings of the major types of financial assistance available to students of higher education. Coverage includes Pell Grants, Work Study Programs, National Direct Student Loans, Guaranteed Student Loans, and other Supplemental Educational Grants. It also covers general information topics such as eligibility, applications, deadlines, and contacts for student aid. The publication is free and available from: Federal Student Aid Programs, Department DEA-85, Pueblo, CO 81109, or contact: Federal Student Aid Programs, U.S. Department of Education, Washington, DC 20202/301-984-4070.

Suicide and Depression
To help you or your friends who might be depressed or suicidal, the government has put together the free publications and films (which can be borrowed) listed below. Contact: National Institute of Mental Health, 5600 Fishers Lane, Rockville, MD 20857/301-443-4573.

Publications: *Dealing With the Crisis of Suicide Adolescence and Depression*

(ADM 841337) Information Packet

Films: *Last Cry for Help*
Teenage Suicide: Is Anyone Listening?
Help Me—The Story of a Teenage Suicide
Teenage Suicide—Don't Try It!

Tell the President What You Think
You can write to the President and let him know what you think about things in the United States, plus you can give him ideas about making problems better. And, when the President gets your letter he'll write back to you! His address is: White House, 1600 Pennsylvania Avenue NW, Washington, DC 20500.

TERM PAPER HELP—FREE FOR THE ASKING
Using the resources mentioned in *Information USA*, you can put together an original paper that will also be fun to research. Once you've selected your topic, call the appropriate offices mentioned in this book and interview the experts for information and literature recommendations. As long as you have narrowed your subject matter and know exactly what you are looking for, you'll find government offices to be a wonderful resource. Described below are examples of places to start. Also check the Sampler section "Information About Anything and Everything" for additional leads.

Your Congressional Representative's office can send you reports put out by Congressional Committees or the highly regarded Congressional Research Service. Often these reports cover the historical, present and future aspects of a particular subject.

The National Referral Center, part of the Library of Congress, can recommend experts, associations, and literature helpful on nearly every subject imaginable. Contact: National Referral Center, Library of Congress, Washington, DC 20540/202-287-5670.

Tracer Bullets, described under "Information Guides" in the Freebies section, will help you identify literature, experts and organizations you can consult for information about a particular topic. These are excellent bibliographic resources.

Data Experts, listed in many of this book's chapters, can supply you with statistics, perspective, and reports relating to their field of expertise.

The Public Affairs Office of all government agencies will send you free literature on the subject areas their agency is responsible for. Public Affairs staff can also direct you to someone in their agency who covers the subject you are researching.

Department of State Country Desk Officers, listed in the Department of State chapter, can supply you with all types of information about the country they cover.

Federal Depository Libraries, described in the "Resources-Close-to-Home" section of the Sampler, house government publications. One of these libraries probably exists near your home.

Tours, Films and Speakers from the Navy—All Free!

You and your youth group can get tours of navy bases. You can also get films and speakers for your group on all different kinds of subjects. At each Navy Recruiting Office there is a naval officer to help you and your group in obtaining these services or planning activities. A free brochure, *Navy and Youth,* will tell you about things available. To get the brochure and further information contact the Youth Program Petty Officer at your nearest Navy Recruiting Office or Public Information Division, Department of the Navy, Department of Defense, The Pentagon, 2E337, Washington, DC 20350/ 202-695-0965.

Toys: Fun in the Making (017-090-00052-6)—This publication offers ideas for making toys and games from throw-away materials you have at home. Simple and fun to make, the toys and games will help you learn about colors, shapes, sizes of things, counting and words. It is available for $3.75 from Superintendent of Documents, U.S. Government Printing Office, Washington, DC 20402/202-783-3238.

TOYS

Uncle Sam has several toys you might enjoy.

Ecology—
Buttons, decals, posters and children's educational materials, all related to ecology, are available from: Environmental Protection Agency, Public Information Center, 820 Quincy Street NW, Washington, DC 20011/202-829-3535.

Energy Activities—A wide range of educational materials are available for teachers and children at all levels. Most of the materials are aimed at illustrating certain principles and problems related to various forms of energy and to their development, use and conservation. A free catalogue of available materials can be obtained from: Technical Information Center, Department of Energy, P.O. Box 62, Oak Ridge, TN 37830/615-576-1301.

Smokey Bear—Children who write INDIVIDU-ALLY can receive Smokey Bear's *Junior Forest Ranger Kit.* Write to: Smokey Bear, Washington, DC 20252. Smokey Bear is the only person in the U.S. with his very own zip code!

Spunky Squirrel—The Spunky Squirrel program is concerned with environment in urban and community forestry. Two brochures available: *Spunky's Tree Care Checklist* or *Spunky's Gypsy Moth Fact Sheet.* Please specify which you desire. Contact: Trees, P.O. Box 2000, Department GH, Washington, DC 20013.

Woodsy Owl—Litter bags, coloring books, song sheets, photographs, posters, bike stickers, and wallet cards are available from: Woodsy Owl, Forest Service, Department of Agriculture, Room 3124, South Building, P.O. Box 2417, Washington, DC 20013/202-447-7013.

Women

The publications and services described below are designed especially for women. Many other sections in the Sampler also contain resources for women, especially "Social Injustices and Crime," "Parents and Parents-to-Be," and "Household Tips and Information."

Continuing Education for Women
Information is available on programs which allow women to study part-time in school or at home in order to get formal educational qualifications. A free publication, *How to Get Credit for What You Know: Alternative Routes to Educational Credit,* lists organizations which offer information about adult education programs and opportunities. Contact: Women's Bureau, Department of Labor, 200 Constitution Ave. N.W., Room S3005, Washington, DC 20210/202-523-6668.

Female/Male Differentials in Countries Worldwide
Women in Development is a computerized database with demographic, social and economic data concerning female/male differentials in 120 countries throughout the world. Variables include: breakdowns by age, sex, urban/rural residence; marital status and fertility; birth and death rates; income and labor statistics; literacy and education levels; religion; ethnicity; and household data. Tables are included. The database was started in 1980 and contains 62,000 records. Searches and printouts are available free of charge. Tapes can be purchased for $140.00 from the U.S. Census Bureau. Contact: Ellen Jamison, International Demographic Data Center, Scuderi Building, Room 302, U.S. Census Bureau, Washington, DC 20233, 301-763-4221.

Help Yourself to a Midlife Career Change (122N)—
$2.25. This publication describes the basic steps involved in a career change: assessing your skills, personality, interests, and values; and transferring your abilities to new work situations. It also lists the "Ten Hottest Transferrable Skills." The booklet is available by writing Consumer Information Center, Pueblo, CO 81002.

Nutrition
The 2 publications described below are available free of charge by writing: Consumer Information Center, P.O. Box 100, Pueblo, CO 81002.

The Gender Gap at the Dinner Table (524N)— How men and women differ in nutritional needs; weight and energy expenditure charts; and discussion of nutritional disorders.
Please Pass That Woman Some More Calcium and Iron (607N)—Why a diet rich in calcium and iron is important to a woman's health.

Office Automation and Working Women: Issues for the Decade Ahead
This publication discusses the most important issues women workers face in the electronic office.

Single copies can be obtained free of charge. There is a nominal fee for multiple copies. Contact: Women's Bureau, U.S. Department of Labor, 200 Constitution Avenue NW, Washington, DC 20210/202-523-6611.

A Woman's Guide to Social Security
Describes what women in any situation should know about Social Security, e.g. working women, wives, widows, widows with children, career interruptions, etc. Available free from your local Social Security Administration office listed in your telephone book, or by writing: Consumer Information Center, P.O. Box 100, Pueblo, CO 81002.

Women in Defense
The Department of Defense publishes an illustrated booklet, *Going Strong,* which recognizes how vital women are to the national security of our country. It outlines policies and programs which ensure the continued recognition, opportunities and contributions of women. *Going Strong* is available free from: Office of the Assistant Secretary of Defense for Manpower, Installation and Logistics, Department of Defense, Washington, DC 20301-4000/202-783-3238.

Working Women Information Source
The Women's Bureau of the U.S. Department of Labor follows the impact women have on the U.S. workforce as well as the conditions and special problems encountered by working women. The Bureau is currently studying the impact of high technology on labor and its findings will be released in early 1985. The office has studied a variety of issues affecting women, including equal opportunity, women in non-traditional careers, employment goals, and women in management. Staff tracks legislative proposals affecting women such as sex discrimination laws, job training partnerships, and state labor laws. A free listing of publications and bibliographies produced by the Bureau, as well as program models, are available upon request. Contact: Women's Bureau, U.S. Department of Labor, 200 Constitution Avenue, NW, Washington, DC 20210, 202-523-6611.

Women's Bureau Publications
A variety of free publications are available from the Women's Bureau of the U.S. Department of Labor. Listed below are examples of materials that can be obtained by writing: Division of Information and Publications, Women's Bureau, U.S. Department of Labor, #53306, Washington, DC 20210.

Economic Recovery Tax Act: Selected Provisions of Interest to Women—Describes how the new tax laws affect women's income and assets. Covers child care credit, retirement and saving, charity, and estate and gift taxes. (Enclose a self-addressed stamped envelope if this is the only publication ordered.)

Brief Highlights of Major Federal Laws on Sex Discrimination in Employment—Shows how women in the work force are protected under the Fair Labor Standards Act, the Civil Rights Act, and other laws. Also shows who to contact if you feel discriminated against because of sex. (Enclose a self-addressed, stamped envelope if this is the only publication ordered.)

A Women's Guide to Apprenticeship—Describes the various apprenticeship programs available to women and provides information about how to apply.

Employers and Child Care: Establishing Services Through The Workplace—This 83-page book shows the need for establishing such programs and provides the reader with necessary information about setting up such a program.

Working Woman's Guide to Her Job Rights (128N) Employment services, minimum wage, overtime pay, and maternity leave are among the rights—for women and men—discussed in this helpful guide. It is available for $2.25 from: Consumer Information Center, Pueblo, CO 81002.

Senior Citizens
The government offers a variety of services and publications geared toward senior citizens. Below are examples of what is available.

Special Committee on Aging
This Committee of the U.S. Senate is an advocate for older Americans and their special needs. Staff have prepared several free publications designed to be helpful guides for the elderly. A sampling of these publications is listed below. To obtain a publication or information write: Special Committee on Aging, U.S. Senate, G33 Dirksen Office Building, Washington, DC 20240.

Heat Stress and Older Americans—a free booklet which describes how heat affects the body and what measures can be taken to avoid serious complications.

Frauds Against the Elderly—a free 132 page book, which is a reprint of a U.S. Senate Committee Hearing on the subject, shows you how not to be taken in by phony arthritis cures, work-at-home

schemes, distribution swindles, or medical frauds. It also contains reprints of three helpful consumer pamphlets on the subject.

Protecting Older Americans Against Overpayment of Taxes—a free booklet that can serve as a checklist for itemizing deductions. The checklist is designed to protect older Americans from overpaying their federal income tax.

You and Your Medicines—Guidelines for Older Americans—this 12-page booklet explains why there is such a high level of drug-induced illness in people over 65, and it tells how to avoid this pitfall.

Administration on Aging
This office, and its regional offices throughout the country, can provide information about aging. For more details, contact your local Agency on Aging or the Administration of Aging, 330 Independence Avenue SW, Washington, DC 20201/202-245-0641.

Office of Human Development Service
The office has several free publications of interest to the elderly, including *A Winter Hazard for the Old* and *Accidental Hypothermia*. Contact: Office of Human Development Service, Department of Health and Human Services, 330 Independence Avenue SW, Room 4146, Washington, DC 20201/202-245-2158.

Pension Plans—Your Rights
A free publication entitled *Know Your Pension Plan* (511N) provides useful checklists to help you understand your rights and benefits under your retirement plan. Available free of charge from: Consumer Information Center, P.O. Box 100, Pueblo, CO 81002.

Age Pages (147N)
This publication has practical advice for older people on a variety of topics including sexuality, exercise, foot care, incontinence, and more. Available for $2.00 from: Consumer Information Center, P.O. Box 100, Pueblo, CO 81002.

Travel Tips for Senior Citizens
A variety of information is available including: health advice, emergency help, general information, customs hints for returning U.S. residents, visa requirements of foreign governments, foreign country information, passports and visas and clothing. Contact: Bureau of Consular Affairs, Office of Public Affairs, Department of State, 2201 C Street NW, Room 6811, Washington, DC 20520/202-632-1489.

Social Injustices and Crime

Described in this section are services, publications and films designed to help victims of abuse or crime. Resources to help you protect yourself and your family against these injustices are also included.

Abuse, Fraud and Waste Hotlines
The Federal Government sponsors several toll-free numbers you can call to report fraud, abuse, and/or waste in the federal government. A list of these numbers is given in the "Hotline and Recorded Messages" section of the Sampler.

Alcohol Abuse Information
Information and publications about alcohol related subjects are available from: National Clearinghouse for Alcohol Information (NCALI), P.O. Box 2345, Rockville, MD 20852/301-468-2600.

Alcohol and Drug Abuse Prevention Network
The National Partnership to Fight Drug and Alcohol Abuse is a national network of individuals, professional and lay, concerned with preventing substance abuse, especially among young people. Staff can supply you with information about literature and programs, on a national to local level, which deal with these problems. Anyone interested in obtaining information, or in joining the partnership, should contact: National Partnership, Office of Juvenile Justice and Delinquency Prevention, Department of Justice, Washington, DC 20530/202-724-5911.

Amnesty and Military Deserter Policies
For information on amnesty programs, contact: Office of the Assistant Secretary of Defense, (MRA and L-MPFM, Legal Policy), The Pentagon, Washington, DC 20301/202-697-3387. For information on deserter programs, contact: Director of Legislation and Legal Policy, OSD (M) (MP and FM) (LLP), Department of Defense, The Pentagon, Room 3D823, Washington, DC 20301/202-697-3387.

Antisocial and Violent Behavior
The National Institute of Mental Health supports research focusing on violent behavior of individuals and related legal and mental health interactions. Its studies contain information about the biological, behavioral, psychosocial and empirical legal aspects of such behavior. It also has information about the victims of crime. Information, including the following free publications are available from the Center for Antisocial and Violent Behavior, 5600 Fishers Lane, Room 6C-15, Rockville, MD 20857/ 301-443-3728.

The Future of Crime
Observing the Law
The Functions of the Police in Modern Society
Research on Victims of Crime

Battered Women and Domestic Violence
Free fact sheets and information about women and domestic violence are available from: Center for Women Policy Studies, 2000 P Street NW, Suite 508, Washington, DC 20036/202-872-1770.

Child Abuse and Neglect
Information and a variety of publications, many free, are available from the Clearinghouse on Child Abuse and Neglect information. A free publications catalogue is also available. Examples of free publications are listed below. Contact: National Clearinghouse on Child Abuse and Neglect Information, P.O. Box 1182, Washington, DC 20015/301-251-5157.

Everything You Always Wanted to Know About Child Abuse and Neglect
Child Sexual Abuse: Tips to Parents
Clearinghouse on Child Abuse and Neglect Information
Educators Role in the Prevention and Treatment of Child Abuse and Neglect
The Role of Law Enforcement in the Prevention and Treatment of Child Abuse and Neglect
Adolescent Maltreatment: Issues and Program Models
National Study of the Incidence and Severity of Child Abuse and Neglect: Executive Summary

Children—Missing and Exploited
The National Center maintains a toll-free number for the use of individuals who believe they have information that could lead to the location and recovery of a missing child. Because these calls literally can be a matter of life or death, the Center asks that the Hotline number be used by those individuals who have this critical information. If you know the location of a missing child, please call 1-800-843-5678.

As a Clearinghouse, the Center can provide information, assistance and publications regarding child abduction and exploitation, including pornography and prostitution. Listed below are examples of publications available free of charge to the public. Anyone seeking information or wishing to contribute information about the problem should contact: National Center for Missing and Exploited Children, 1835 K Street, NW, Suite 700, Washington, DC 20006/202-634-9821.

Directory of Support Services and Resources for Missing and Exploited Children—a descriptive listing of nonprofit or public support groups throughout the country, dedicated to assisting missing and exploited children and their parents.

Education and Prevention Guidelines—safety and precaution tips for preventing child abductions and exploitation.

Parental Kidnapping Handbook—a handbook to assist the parent of a child who has been taken by a noncustodial spouse.

Summary of Selected State Legislation—a guide to the most effective state child-protection laws in the country.

Child Support (501N)

This free booklet describes help available from the government to enforce child support obligations, locate missing parents, and establish paternity. For a copy write: Consumer Information Center, P.O. Box 100, Pueblo, CO 81002.

Child Support Handbook

The *Handbook on Child Support Enforcement* is a "how-to" guide for getting the child support payments which are owed to you and your children. Information is provided about applying for child support enforcement services, obtaining help in finding the absent parent, establishing paternity, collecting child support, and collecting payments in another state. The free publication is available by writing: Consumer Information Center, P.O. Box 100, Pueblo, CO 81002.

Computer Crime and Security

The Bureau of Justice Statistics, which acts as a clearinghouse on computer crime and security, and has issued five one-time publications dealing with these topics. The Bureau is an excellent source of legal and technical information regarding computer crime and security. The five volumes are:

Computer Crime: Expert Witness Manual—deals with issues relevant to the selection of witnesses to use in computer crime trials.

Computer Crime: Legislative Resource Manual—(Pub. #027-000-01135-7) deals with issues relevant to the selection of witnesses to use in computer crime trials.

Computer Crime: Criminal Justice Resource Manual (Pub #027-000-00870-4) describes different types of computer crime strategies—available for $10.00.

Computer Crime: Computer Security Techniques—(Pub #027-000-01160-1) describes different security techniques used to control computer crime—available for $7.50.

Computer Crime: Electronic Fund Transfer Systems and Crime—(Pub #027-000-01170-5) describes electronic fund transfer crimes and discusses available sources of data—available for $7.00.

These reports are available from: Superintendent of Documents, U.S. Government Printing Office, Washington, DC 20402/202-783-3238. Contact Bureau of Justice Statistics, U.S. Department of Justice, 633 Indiana Avenue NW, Washington, DC 20531.

Corrections Information Center

The Center provides information on all aspects of corrections as well as in specialty areas such as volunteers in corrections, staff development and training and legal matters. Contact: National Institute of Prisons, Department of Justice, 1790 30th Street, Suite 130, Boulder, CO 80301/ 303-444-1101.

Crime Bibliographies

Listed below are 4 *Subject Bibliographies* covering different aspects of crime. The free catalogues cite all publications you can purchase from the Government Printing Office. To order contact: Superintendent of Documents, U.S. Government Printing Office, Washington, DC 20402/202-783-3238.

Child Abuse and Neglect
Crime and Criminal Justice
Juvenile Delinquency
Law Enforcement

Crime in the United States

An annual report called *Uniform Crime Reports* contains information on the types of crimes committed (murder, rape, robbery, motor vehicle theft, etc), victim/offender relationships, types of weapons, motives, persons arrested, crime trends, and geographical areas in which crimes were committed. Other published reports include: *Bomb Summary,* and *Law Enforcement Officers Killed.* Contact: Uniform Crime Reporting Section, Federal Bureau of Investigation, Department of Justice, 9th Street and Pennsylvania Avenue NW, Room 7437, Washington, DC 20535/ 202-324-2820.

Crime Prevention Booklets
Got a Minute? You Can Stop Crime is the first in a series of crime booklets available free of charge from the Distribution Service, National Criminal Justice Reference Service, National Institute of Justice, Department of Justice, P.O. Box 6000, Rockville, MD 20850/ 301-251-5500.

Criminal Justice Bibliographies
The National Crime Justice Reference Service maintains the following bibliographies. When requesting a bibliography, ask for the latest available update.

Affirmative Action-Equal Employment Opportunities in the Criminal Justice System (NCJ 61834)
Alternatives to Institutionalization (NCJ 58518)
Arson (NCJ 58366)
Basic Sources in Criminal Justice (NCJ 49417)
Bibliographies in Criminal Justice (NCJ 62014)
Community Crime Prevention (NCJ 43628)
Crime and Disruption in Schools (NCJ 56588)
Crimes Against the Elderly in 26 Cities (NCJ 76709)
Criminal Justice and the Elderly (NCJ 55197)
Criminal Justice Periodicals (NCJ 57168)
Etiology of Criminology: Nonbehavioral Science (NCJ 60117)
Female Offender (NCJ 55637)
Firearm Use in Violent Crime (NCJ 52677)
Halfway Houses (NCJ 46851)
International Policing (NCJ 46190)
Jail-Based Inmate Programs (NCJ 60331)
Jury Reform (NCJ 48232)
Paralegals (NCJ 57986)
Plea Negotiation (NCJ 66559)
Police Consolidation (NCJ 67142)
Police Crisis Intervention (NCJ 48005)
Police Discretion (NCJ 46183)
Police Stress (NCJ 59352)
Prison Industries (NCJ 49701)
Private Security (NCJ 47367)
Publications of the National Institute of Law Enforcement and Criminal Justice (NCJ 49700)
Publications of the National Institute of Law Enforcement and Criminal Justice (NCJ 57987)
Restitution (NCJ 62011)
Speedy Trial (NCJ 48110)

Spouse Abuse (NCJ 54427)
Standards of Care in Adult and Juvenile Correctional Institutions (NCJ 61443)
Strategies for Reintegrating the Ex-Offender (NCJ 61571)
Team Policing (NCJ 35887)
Techniques for Project Evaluation (NCJ 43556)
Terrorism Supplement (NCJ 45005)
Variations on Juvenile Probation (NCJ 62010)
Victimless Crime (NCJ 43630)
Victim/Witness Assistance (NCJ 49698)
White Collar Crime (NCJ 69331)

Contact: NCJRS Distribution Service, Department of Justice, P.O. Box 6000, Rockville, MD 20850/301-251-5500.

Criminal Justice Reference Service
This office acts as an international clearinghouse, serving both the criminal justice profession and the general public, in subjects such as courts, police, corrections, juvenile justice, human resources, and fraud and abuse of government programs. It also provides an evaluation and statistics service for victims of crime, and has information about civil and criminal dispute resolution. The service publishes a monthly announcement of significant publications, audiovisual material and events that relate to specific areas of interest. It maintains a reading room and a reference library which is open to the public. The library contains holdings from NIJ, NIJJ and Delinquency Proceedings, Bureau of Justice Statistics, Office for Victims of Crime, and Federal Justice Research Programs. A bimonthly journal, *NIJ Reports,* gives news of criminal justice research, abstracts of important publications and announcements of new products and services available from OJARS. Contact: National Criminal Justice Reference Service, National Institute of Justice, Department of Justice, P.O. Box 6000, Rockville, MD 20850/ 301-251-5500.

Domestic Violence
Project Share can supply you with information about books, journals, and unpublished reports pertaining to battered spouses, family violence and child abuse. Free public information packets and resource kits are available. Staff will also answer your questions about the subject. Contact: Project Share, P.O. Box 2309, Rockville, MD 20852/301-231-9539 or 301-231-9540.

Drug and Alcohol Prevention Program—Coaches
This nationwide program, developed in conjunction with the National High School Athletic

Coaches Association, is designed to help coaches prevent drug and alcohol abuse among high school athletes and students. Free information packets, publications, a slide show and video tape are all available to coaches. Clinics and workshops for coaches will be held throughout the United States at which DEA Special Agents, professional athletes, and amateur sports figures will address a variety of topics pertaining to drug and alcohol prevention. Contact: Preventive Programs, Drug Enforcement Administration, Department of Justice, 1405 I Street NW, Washington, DC 20537/202-633-1437.

Drug Abuse Warning Network (DAWN)
The network identifies and evaluates the scope and magnitude of drug abuse in the United States. More than 900 hospital emergency rooms and medical examiner facilities supply data to the program. DAWN identifies drugs currently being abused; determines existing patterns of abuse/abuser in Standard Metropolitan Statistical Areas; monitors systemwide abuse trends; detects new abuse entities and polydrug combinations; provides data for the assessment of health hazards and abuse potential of drug substances; and provides data needed for rational control and scheduling of drugs of abuse. Contact: Information Systems Unit, Office of Drug Enforcement, Division Control Administration, Department of Justice, 1405 Eye Street NW, Room 419, Washington, DC 20537/202-633-1316.

Drug Education and Information
Staff at the National Clearinghouse for Drug Abuse Information will answer your questions, loan you films, and send you free informational materials about drugs, drug abuse and prevention. Examples of available freebies are described below. Contact: National Clearinghouse for Drug Abuse Information, P.O. Box 416, Kensington, MD 20795/301-443-6500.

Controlled Substance Chart: Use, Abuse and Effects—a 4-page chart free to the general public in limited quantities (up to 25).
Drugs of Abuse—a 40-page booklet, written especially for law enforcement officers, educators, health and other professionals, this contains full color illustrations of drugs controlled under the Controlled Substances Act 1970 (CSA)-1970, administered by the Drug Enforcement Administration (DEA). It also gives concise, factual, accurate scientific descriptions of the drugs, their effects and the consequences of abuse. The booklet contains a chart summarizing scientific

data about controlled licit and illicit drugs and a glossary of slang terms. The Controlled Substances Act-1970 is also summarized.
Soozie and Katy—a 26-page activities and coloring book for children ages 5 to 9, which teaches them the consequences of drug abuse and emphasizes the theme, "Only sick people need drugs."

Drunk Driving
A free pamphlet explains "How You Can Help Fight Drunk Drivers." Contact: National Highway Transportation Safety Administration, Public Affairs, DOT, 400 7th Street SW, Washington, DC 20590/202-426-9550.

Emergency Programs Center
This office coordinates Department of Justice activities in three main areas—civil disorder, terrorism, and nuclear incidents (criminal aspects only—extortion, theft, etc.) It also responds to special crises and special security events such as coordinating responsibilities for the Winter Olympics and the Cuban refugees. Contact: Emergency Programs Center, Department of Justice, 10th Street and Constitution Avenue NW, Room 6101, Washington, DC 20530/202-633-4545.

Federal Bureau of Investigation
A variety of publications, reports and article reprints are available free of charge from the FBI. Topics cover all aspects of criminal justice, from crime prevention to the history of the FBI. Listed below are examples of current materials. Contact: FBI, Office of Congressional and Public Affairs, Room 6236, 10th Street at Pennsylvania Avenue NW, Washington, DC 20535.

Crime Resistance: A Way to Protect Your Family Against Crime—this 16-page booklet provides tips on how you and your family can make yourself safe from crime in your home as well as when you go about your daily routines—such as commuting to and from work, traveling in the family car, walking to school, and shopping.
Fingerprint Identification—provides a history of how fingerprints came to be.
How You Can Help the FBI Combat White Collar Crime—in a question and answer format, this brochure describes what white collar crime is, gives examples, and provides a listing of FBI offices you can contact to report such crime.
I Spy at the FBI—is a "Mini-Page" publication to help parents and teachers introduce children to the FBI, both its services and building. The

4-page publication contains puzzles, interesting facts, fingerprinting information and more.

99 Facts about the FBI—this 29-page booklet, with sketches, covers all aspects of the FBI including its history, jurisdiction, and operation. Done in a question and answer format, it is geared toward the general public.

The FBI: The First 75 Years—prepared in 1983, this 29-page booklet traces the history of the FBI providing information about topics such as the gangster era, spying, World War II activities, and the training of FBI agents.

The NCIC and You—a booklet describing the National Crime Information Center and the computerized information system the FBI maintains on behalf of law enforcement agencies across the U.S. The NCIC computerized data base contains information about missing children and adults, as well as stolen property such as cars, boats, planes and guns.

You, Yours and Crime Resistance—a self-help booklet with tips for making your home, car and habits safer to avoid being victimized by crime.

Fingerprint Records to Private Citizens

An individual may obtain a copy of his/her arrest record by submitting a written request directly to the FBI Identification Division, together with a set of rolled, inked fingerprint impressions taken on a fingerprint card which indicates the individual's name and birth data. There is an $11.00 fee for this service. This office also complies with court-ordered expungements and purge requests received from criminal justice agencies. Contact: Identification Division, Federal Bureau of Investigation, Department of Justice, 9th Street and Pennsylvania Avenue NW, Room 11255, Washington, DC 20535/202-324-5454.

Foreign Agent Information

The public can look through the records of foreign agents for their initial statements upon registration and their six-month follow-ups. These statements provide details on the country, payments, contracts, missions and everything else that involves the agent's relationship with the foreign country. A list of Public Agents is available for $11.00. Contact: Public Office, Internal Security Section, Criminal Division, Department of Justice, 315 9th Street NW, Room 100, Washington, DC 20530/202-724-6926.

Frauds and White Collar Crimes

This section directs and coordinates the federal effort against white-collar crime. It focuses on frauds involving government programs and procurement, transnational and multi-district trade, the security and commodity exchanges, banking practices, and consumer victimization. Contact: Fraud Section, Criminal Division, Department of Justice, 315 9th Street NW, Room 832, Washington, DC 20530/202-724-7038.

Frauds—How to Protect Yourself

This free 132-page booklet entitled *Frauds Against the Elderly* is a reprint of a U.S. Senate Committee Hearing, which will show you how not to be taken in by phone arthritis cures, work-at-home schemes, distribution swindles, or medical frauds. The book also contains reprints of three helpful consumer pamphlets on the subject. Write for a copy from: Special Committee on Aging, U.S. Senate, G33 Dirksen Office Building, Washington, DC 20240.

Paternity and Adoption

For general information about paternity claims and adoption proceedings involving members and former members of the Armed Forces, contact: Manpower, Reserve Affairs and Logistics, Department of Defense, The Pentagon, Room 3D823, Washington, DC 20301/202-697-5947.

Runaway Hotline

The National Runaway Youth Hotline provides advice to both parents and runaways. The service is confidential and operates 24 hours a day. Call toll-free 800-621-4000; 800-972-6004 in Illinois.

Runaway Youths

For information and expertise on Runaway Youth Programs or for a directory of available programs, contact: Division of Runaway Youth Programs, Adminstration for Children, Youth and Families, Department of Health and Human Services, P.O. Box 1182, Washington, DC 20013/202-755-0593.

Sexual Assault

The National Center for the Prevention and Control of Rape can provide you with information, free publications, and films about protecting yourself against sexual assault and how you can help a rape victim. Contact: The National Center for the Prevention and Control of Rape, 5600 Fishers Lane, Room 6C-12, Rockville, MD 20852/301-443-1910.

Victims Resource Center

A clearinghouse of national scope, this Center will refer victims of all types to places that can be of help. The Center will also provide reading lists, bibliographic references, audio visuals, and startup kits to individuals or organizations interested in starting victims assistance programs. Information about state efforts to compensate victims and provide assistance is also available from the Center. Contact: National Victims Resource Center, Office of Victims of Crime, Department of Justice, Room 1352, 633 Indiana Avenue NW, Washington, DC 20531/202-724-5947.

Wife Abuse
A fact sheet entitled *Plain Talk About Wife Abuse* explores the causes, the emotional and physical consequences, and where an abused wife can get assistance. Available free of charge from: Consumer Information Center, P.O. Box 100, Pueblo, CO 81002.

Health Matters

The federal government spends billions of dollars studying the latest techniques and developments for every conceivable illness and ailment. Information about the results of this research as well as technical assistance for your specific health problem are available for the asking. This section includes information centers, publications and hotline numbers you can consult for help on health matters ranging from arthritis to second opinions for surgery. (Note: see also Department of Health and Human Services chapter for additional resources.)

Health Information Clearinghouses
The following centers can provide you with information and assistance regarding health matters within their area of interest. Often publications, audiovisuals, and referrals to experts and support groups are available from these centers. If you do not see a subject area in this listing which meets your needs, contact the following clearinghouse for an appropriate referral: National Health Information Clearinghouse, P.O. Box 1133, Washington, DC 20018/toll-free 800-336-4797 (Virginia residents call collect 703-522-2590.)

Aging
Adminstration on Aging, 330 Independence Avenue, S.W., Washington, DC 20201/ 202-245-0641. Provides some information on aging. To learn what's available contact your local Area Agency on Aging, listed under "Aging" in the government section of your telephone book.

AIDS—Acquired Immune Deficiency Syndrome
Center for Disease Control, Office of Public Affairs, 1600 Clifton Road, NE, Building 1, Room 2167, Atlanta, GA 30333. This Center administers AIDS research which is being conducted at four agencies within the Department of Health and Human Services. Information about AIDS is available free of charge in the form of a question and answer fact sheet and reprints of articles summarizing studies currently being conducted.

Alcohol
National Clearinghouse for Alcohol Information (NCALI), P.O. Box 2345, Rockville, MD 20852/301-468-2600. Gathers and disseminates current knowledge on alcohol-related subjects.

Arthritis
Arthritis Information Clearinghouse, P.O.Box 9782, Arlington, VA 22209/703-558-8250. Identifies materials concerned with arthritis and related musculo-skeletal diseases and serves as an information exchange for individuals and organizations involved in public, professional, and patient education. Refers personal requests from patients to the Arthritis Foundation.

Breast Cancer
Public Inquiries Office, National Cancer Institute, National Institutes of Health, Bethesda, MD 20205. A pamphlet is available summarizing information about breast cancer, biopsy, mammography, reconstruction and rehabilitation. Free from the above address.

Cancer
Cancer Information Clearinghouse, National Cancer Institute, 805 15th Street N.W., Room 500, Washington, DC 20005/202-496-4070. Collects and disseminates public, patient, and professional cancer education materials to organizations and health care professionals.

Office of Cancer Communications (OCC), Public Inquiries Section, 9000 Rockville Pike, Building 31, Room 10A18, Bethesda, MD 20205/301-496-5583. Answers requests for cancer information from patients and the general public.

Child Abuse
National Center on Child Abuse and Neglect, P.O. Box 1182, Washington, DC 20013/ 301-251-5157. Collects, processes, and disseminates information on child abuse and neglect.

Consumer Information
Consumer Information Center, Pueblo, CO 81009/303-544-5277, ext. 370. Distributes consumer publications on topics such as children, food and nutrition, health, exercise and weight control. The *Consumer Information Catalog* is available free from the Center and must be used to identify publications being requested.

Dental Research
National Institute of Dental Research, National Institutes of Health, Bethesda, MD 20205. Conducts research in dental areas. A free pamphlet entitled *Good Teeth for You and Your Baby* shows how to watch your diet and practice good dental habits during pregnancy to protect your teeth. It is available by writing the above address.

Diabetes
National Diabetes Information Clearinghouse, Box NDIC, Bethesda, MD 20205/301-468-2162. Collects and disseminates patient information materials and coordinates the development of materials and programs for diabetes education. A Diabetes Dictionary is available for 50¢ (covers postage).

Digestive Diseases
National Digestive Diseases Education and Information Clearinghouse, 1555 Wilson Blvd., Suite 600, Rosslyn, VA 22209/703-496-9707. Provides information on digestive diseases to health professionals and consumers.

Drug Abuse
National Clearinghouse on Drug Abuse Information, P.O. Box 416, Kensington, MD 20795/ 301-443-6500. Collects and disseminates information on drug abuse. Produces informational materials on drugs, and drug abuse and prevention.

Family Planning
National Clearinghouse for Family Planning Information, PO Box 12921, Arlington, VA 22209/

703-558-7923. Collects family planning materials, makes referrals to other information centers, and distributes and produces materials. Primary audience is federally funded family planning clinics. Professionals in the field and the general public can request information.

Food and Drugs
Food and Drug Administration (FDA), National Agricultural Library Building, Room 304, Beltsville, MD 20705/301-344-3719. Serves the information needs of persons interested in human nutrition, food service management, and food technology. Acquires and lends books, journal articles, and audiovisual materials dealing with these areas of concern.

The Handicapped
Clearinghouse on the Handicapped, 330 C Street S.W., Washington, DC 20202/202-732-1245. Responds to inquiries from handicapped individuals and serves as a resource to organizations that supply information to, and about, handicapped individuals.

Health Education
Bureau of Health Information (BHE), 1300 Clifton Road, Building 14, Atlanta, GA 30333/ 404-329-3235. Provides leadership and program direction for the use of health education in prevention of disease, disability, premature death, and unnecessary health problems. Inquiries on health education can be directed to BHE.

Health Indexes
Clearinghouse on Health Indexes, National Center for Health Statistics, Office of Analysis and Epidemiology Programs, 3700 East-West Highway, Hyattsville, MD 20782/301-436-7035. Provides informational assistance in the development of health measures to health researchers, administrators, and planners.

Health Information
National Health Information Clearinghouse, P.O. Box 1133, Washington, DC 20013/ toll-free 800-336-4797/703-522-2590 in Virginia. Helps the public locate health information. Health questions are referred to appropriate health resources that, in turn, respond directly to inquirers. NHIC does not diagnose, gives no medical advice or recommend treatment.

Health Planning
National Health Planning Information Center, 5600 Fishers Lane, Room 9A33, Rockville, MD

20857/301-443-2183. Provides information which can be used to analyze issues and problems related to health planning and resource development. Information services are only provided for health systems agencies and state health planning and development agencies.

Health Standards

National Health Standards and Quality Information Clearinghouse, 11301 Rockville Pike, Kensington, MD 20895/301-881-9400. Collects materials concerning standards for health care and health facilities, qualifications of health professionals, and evaluation and certification of health care providers serving federal beneficiaries. While free to federal agency personnel, searches are done on a cost-recovery basis for others.

High Blood Pressure

High Blood Pressure Information Center, 1501 120/30 National Institutes of Health, Bethesda, MD 20205/301-496-1809. Provides consumers and health professionals with information on the detection, diagnosis, and management of high blood pressure.

Injuries

National Injury Information Clearinghouse, 5401 Westbard Ave., Room 625, Washington, DC 20207/301-492-6424. Collects and disseminates injury data and information relating to the causes and prevention of death, injury, and illness associated with consumer products. Requests of a general nature are referred to the Consumer Product Safety Commission's Communications Office.

Maternal and Child Health

National Center for Education in Maternal and Child Health, 3520 Prospect Street NW, Washington, DC 20057/202-625-8400. The Center is a major link between sources of information/services, the health professional and the general public in areas of maternal and child health, including medical genetics.

Medical Care—Free or Low Cost at 5,000 Places Nationwide

Call 800-638-0742 in Maryland or 800-492-0359 elsewhere for information about free and low-cost care in hospitals and other health facilities nationwide. Staff will send you a list of facilities in your area participating in the federal Hill-Burton Free Care Program. They will also send you a brochure describing eligibility guidelines and advise you about filing any complaints you may have about the program or care you may have received. Information can also be obtained by writing: BHMORD-JRSA, 5600 Fishers Lane, Rockville, MD 20857. (Note: Residents of Alaska and Hawaii must write for information, as the toll-free numbers do not service either state.)

Mental Health

National Institute of Mental Health, 5600 Fishers Lane, Rockville, MD 20857/301-443-4513. Acquires and abstracts the world's mental health literature, answers inquiries from the public, and has some free publications available. Will send single copies only.

Occupational Safety

Library and Inquiry Response Section, Technical Information Branch, National Institute for Occupational Safety, 4676 Columbia Parkway, Cincinnati, OH 45226/513-684-8328. Provides technical information for National Institute for Occupational Safety and Health research programs and supplies information to others on request.

Patient Admittance to NIH Studies

Physicians can recommend patients to participate in clinical research programs conducted by the National Institutes of Health. Patients are admitted to a program if their case fits into an ongoing research project. The patient then receives free medical care. To recommend a patient, physicians can call the Warren Grant Magnuson Clinical Center's Patient Referral Services Unit at 301-496-4891. Physicians can also obtain further information about these programs by writing to the Director of the Clinical Center, Building 10, Room 1N212, National Institutes of Health, Bethesda, MD 20205.

Physical Fitness

President's Council on Physical Fitness and Sports, 450 5th Street, NW, Suite 7103, Washington, DC 20001/202-272-3421. Conducts a public service advertising program and cooperates with governmental and private groups in promoting the development of physical fitness leadership, facilities, and programs. Produces informational materials on exercise, school physical education programs, sports, and physical fitness for youth, adults, and the elderly.

Poison Surveillance Branch

Adverse Reaction and Poison Surveillance Branch, Division of Drug and Biological Product Experience, Office of Epidemiology and Biostatistics, FDA, Room 15B-23, HSN 730, 5600 Fishers

Lane, Rockville, MD 20857/ 301-443-6260. Works with the national network of 600 Poison Control Centers to reduce the incidence and severity of acute poisoning. Directs toxic emergency calls to a local poison control center.

Product Safety

Consumer Product Safety Commission, Washington, DC 20207/toll-free 800-638-8326/ except: 800-492-8363 in Maryland; 800-638-8333 in Alaska, Hawaii, Virgin Islands and Puerto Rico. Evaluates the safety of products sold to the public. Provides printed materials on different aspects of consumer product safety on request. Does not answer questions from consumers on drugs, prescriptions, warranties, advertising, repairs, or maintenance. Also, toll-free 800-638-2772.

Rape Information

National Center for the Prevention and Control of Rape, 5600 Fishers Lane, Room 6C-12, Rockville, MD 20857/301-443-1910. Maintains a listing of rape prevention and treatment resources to help people locate services available in their community and to facilitate networking among those working in the field of sexual assault.

Rehabilitation Information

National Rehabilitation Information Center, Catholic University of America, 4407 8th St. N.E., Washington, DC 20017/202-635-5822. Supplies publications and audiovisual materials on rehabilitation, and assists in locating answers to questions such as dates, places, names, addresses, or statistics. Its collections include materials relevant to the rehabilitation of all disability groups.

Sexually Transmitted Diseases

The National Institute of Allergy and Infectious Diseases, Bldg. 31, Room 7A32, Bethesda, MD 20205. Collects and provides information on symptoms, diagnosis, treatment and complications for diseases spread through sexual conduct. A free booklet about sexually transmitted diseases is available from the Institute.

Smoking

Office on Smoking and Health, Park Building, Room 110, 5600 Fishers Lane, Rockville, MD 20857/301-443-1575. Offers bibliographic and reference services to researchers and others, also publishes and distributes a number of titles in the field of smoking, such as *Why People Smoke Cigarettes.*

Sudden Infant Death Syndrome (SIDS)

Sudden Infant Death Syndrome Clearinghouse, 1555 Wilson Blvd., Suite 600, Rosslyn, VA 22209/703-528-8480. Provides information on SIDS to health professionals and consumers. A publication, *What Parents Should Know About SIDS,* is available free of charge from the Clearinghouse.

Surgical Opinion

National Second Surgical Opinion Program, Health Care Financing, Administrative Office of Public Affairs, 330 Independence Ave. S.W., Washington, DC 20201/202-245-6183/ toll-free 800-639-6833/800-492-6603 in Maryland. Provides information for people who are faced with the possibility of non-emergency surgery. Sponsors the toll-free number to assist the public in locating a surgeon or other specialist. The publication, *Thinking of Having Surgery,* is also available from the above address.

Hotlines and Helps

Listed below are toll-free telephone numbers you can call for help regarding health matters. Many of these hotlines are federally funded endeavors, others are privately supported. We have included both in the hope that you will be able to find whatever health information you need.

Abortion Advice and Referral: 800-438-8039. NC: 800-532-6713.

Abortion Information Service: 800-321-0575. OH: 800-362-1205.

Acquired Immune Deficiency Syndrome Hotline (AIDS): 800-342-2437. DC: 202-646-8182.

Advice for Children and Parents of Runaways: 800-621-4000. IL: 800-972-6004.

Alzheimers Disease and Related Disorder Association: 800-621-0379. IL: 800-572-6037.

AMC Cancer Information: 800-525-3777.

American Association of Mental Deficiency: 800-424-3088. DC: 202-387-1968.

American Council of Blind: 800-424-8666. DC: 202-833-1251.

American Kidney Fund: 800-638-8299. MD: 800-492-8361.

Asthma-Allergy Hotline: 800-558-1035. WI: 414-272-1004 (call collect).

American Medical Radio News: 800-621-8094.

Better Hearing Institute: 800-424-8576. DC: 202-638-7577.

Cancer Information: 800-422-6237. 800-638-6694. AK: 800-638-6070. MD: 800-492-6600.

Children's Defense Fund (current legislation affecting children): 800-424-9602. DC: 202-628-8789.

Childfind: 800-431-5005. NY: 914-255-1848.

Child Help USA (counseling on Child Abuse): 800-422-4453.

Cardio-Care Testing: 800-822-4826. NY: 718-520-2700 (call collect).

Epilepsy Information Line: 800-426-0660. WA: 206-323-8174.

Second Opinion on Non-Emergency Surgery: 800-638-6833. MD: 800-492-6603.

⚹If denied treatment at a health care facility because you are on Medicare/Medicaid or low-income assistance call Hill-Burton Hospitals: 800-638-0742. MD: 800-492-0359.

International Association of Pacemaker Patients: 800-241-6993. GA: 800-282-3119.

Library of Congress National Library Service for the Blind and Physically Handicapped: 800-424-8567. DC: 202-287-5100.

Medical Scholarships from Health Services Corps: 800-638-1824. MD: 301-436-6453.

Miss You, Runaway (in San Diego area): 800-647-7968. CA: 800-448-4663.

National Abortion Federation: 800-772-9100. DC: 202-546-9060.

National Association for Hearing and Speech Action Line: 800-638-8255. MD: 301-897-8682 (HI, AK, & MD call collect).

National Asthma Center: 800-222-5864. CO: 303-398-1477.

National Center for Stuttering: 800-221-2483. NY: 212-532-1460.

National Hearing Aid Helpline: 800-521-5247. MI: 313-478-2610.

National Cocaine Hotline: 800-COC-AINE.

National Down Syndrome Society Hotline: 800-221-4602. NY: 212-764-3070.

New York Cancer Research: 800-223-7874. NY State: 800-522-5022. NY City: 212-688-7515.

National Federation of Parents for Drug Free Youth: 800-554-KIDS. MD: 301-649-7100.

National Gay Task Force Crisisline: 800-221-7044. NY, AK & HI: 212-807-6016.

National Health Information Clearinghouse: 800-336-4797. DC, VA, AK, & HI: 703-522-2590.

National Hotline for Missing Children: 800-843-5679.

National Institute on Drug Abuse Prevention Branch: 800-638-2045. MD: 301-443-2450.

National Parkinson's Disease Foundation: 800-327-4545. FL: 800-433-7022. Miami: 305-547-6666.

National Pregnancy Hotline: 800-344-7211. 800-831-5881.

National Retinitis Pigmentosa Foundation: 800-638-2300. MD: 301-655-1011.

National Runaway Switchboard: 800-621-4000. IL: 800-972-6004.

Organ Donor Hotline: 800-24-DONOR.

Parents Anonymous Hotline (child abuse): 800-421-0353. CA: 800-352-0386.

Personal Health Profile (General Health Risk Assessment): 800-424-2775. DC: 202-965-4881.

Practitioner Reporting System (report problems with drugs or medical devices): 800-638-6725. MD: 301-881-0256 (call collect).

Pregnancy Crisis Center: 800-368-3336. VA: 800-847-6828.

Runaway Hotline—Information, Referral, will pass messages from parent to child: 800-231-6946. TX: 800-392-3352.

Shriners Hospital Referral Line (free care for children under 18 needing orthopedic & burn treatment): 800-237-5055. FL: 800-282-9161.

Spina Bifida Information and Referral: 800-621-3141. IL: 312-663-1562.

The Living Bank (organ transplants): 800-528-2971. TX: 713-528-2971.

Venereal Disease Hotline: 800-227-8922. CA: 800-982-5883.

Women's Sports Foundation: 800-227-3988. CA, AK, & HI: 415-563-6266.

Publications To Write For

Health-related publications are available from a wide variety of sources. Many of the Clearinghouses described earlier in this section have pamphlets, brochures, and reports which staff will send you free of charge. Listed below are examples of materials available at no cost.

MISCELLANEOUS GOVERNMENT CENTERS

Depression and Manic-Depressive Illness—identifies and describes the wide range of depression states, the biological factors related to depression and treatments available. Available from: Information Office, National Institutes of Health, Clinical Center, Room 5C305, Bethesda, MD 20205.

Exercise and Your Heart—this booklet explains the relationship between exercise and a healthy heart. It offers practical information to enhance the prospects of a healthy heart. Available from: National Heart, Lung and Blood Institute, Information Office, Building 31, Room 4A21, Bethesda, MD 20205.

Good Teeth for You and Your Baby—this pamphlet shows how to watch your diet and practice good dental habits during pregnancy to protect your teeth. Available from: National Institute of Dental Research, National Institutes of Health, Bethesda, MD 20205.

How Children Grow—this booklet gives a detailed explanation of how babies and children grow and how genetic and environmental factors can influence their development. Available from: Office of Science and Health Reports, National Institutes of Health, Division of Research Resources, Building 31, Room 5B10, Bethesda, MD 20205.

Is Your Drinking Water Safe?—a free booklet which describes the laws put into effect to solve the problem of the illness linked to drinking water every year in the United States. Available from: Public Information Center, PM 211A, U.S. Environmental Protection Agency, Washington, DC 20460.

Approved Prescription Drug List With Therapeutic Equivalent Evaluation—shows how to substitute one drug for another, often at substantial savings. Available from: Division of Drug Information Resources, FDA, Department of Health and Human Services, 5600 Fishers Lane, Room 8B37, Rockville, MD 20857/301-443-3204.

CONSUMER INFORMATION CENTER

This Center distributes publications, produced by government agencies, to the general public. Many materials are available free of charge, others can be obtained for a minimal fee. Described below, clustered by Freebies and then For Sale, are the health-related publications you can order from: Consumer Information Center, P.O. Box 100, Pueblo, CO 81002.

Freebies

About Body Wraps, Pills, and Other Magic Wands (564N)—Weight-loss gimmicks, untested diet aids, and their potential dangers.

Acne (567N)—Causes and methods of treatment, including recently approved drugs.

Antidepressant Drugs (550N)—Discusses different types of depression and the effects of specific drug treatments.

Antihistamines (551N)—How these drugs work to treat allergies, motion sickness, ulcers, and much more; lists generic and brand names.

Arthritis (568N)—Snake venom, vibrating chairs, special diets, and other frauds perpetrated as cures for arthritis, rheumatism, and gout; major forms of the disease and medically sound treatments; information on DMSO.

Aspirin (552N)—Proper use and possible risks; what to do in case of an overdose.

Back Pain (569N)—Common causes and treatments of this all too common ailment.

Baldness Treatments (553N)—Discusses products supposed to restore hair or prevent hair loss.

Breast Exams: What You Should Know (570N)—Eighty percent of breast lumps are not cancer: how to check for lumps, how doctors examine them, what types of treatment are available.

Cancer Prevention: Good News, Better News, Best News (571N)—Advice on what you can do to help protect yourself against cancer, including latest nutrition information. 20 pp. 1984.

Cellulite (565N)—All about those "lumps and bulges you couldn't lose before" and the many gimmicks supposed to help women get rid of fat on hips and thighs.

Clearing the Air: A Guide to Quitting Smoking (543N)—No-nonsense tips on kicking the habit and staying "clean."

The Colon (572N)—While this part of the body is not generally discussed, it performs important functions and is the site of many problems such as colitis, diverticulitis, and cancer.

The Common Cold (573N)—Effectiveness of various cough, cold, allergy, and asthma remedies; labeling information.

A Consumer's Guide to Mental Health Services (544N)—Information on services ranging from financial aid to different kinds of therapy.

Contraception: Comparing the Options (554N)—Fold-out chart listing nine common methods of birth control and the pros and cons of each. 1982.

The Dental Plaque Battle is Endless, But Worth It. (608N)—Early signs of gum disease; how to avoid it by taking good care of your gums and teeth.

Diet Books Sell Well But . . . (566N)—Fallacies and hazards of some popular diets; selecting a healthy diet to lose weight.

Does Your Medicine Chest Need First Aid? (555N)—Medical supplies to have in the home and tips for safe storage.

Doing Something About Menstrual Discomforts (574N)—Common problems related to menstruation; and treatments including a list of non-prescription drugs that relieve specific symptoms.

Everything Doesn't Cause Cancer (575N)—Facts about the causes and prevention of cancer, with toll-free cancer information numbers.

Facing Surgery? Why Not Get a Second Opinion? (545N)—Answers this and other questions of the prospective patient. A toll-free number for locating specialists around the country is included.

Flu/Cold (576N)—Describes differences in symptoms between the flu and common cold; different strains of flu; recommended precautions and treatments.

Food and Drug Interactions (556N)—How commonly used drugs affect nutritional needs; how some foods affect drug actions; and how to avoid ill effects.

For Treating Arthritis, Start With Aspirin (557N)—Describes the major forms of arthritis and drugs commonly used for treatment.

Generic Drugs: How Good Are They? (558N)—What they are, how they can save you money, and the generic names of 14 commonly prescribed drugs.

Glaucoma (577N)—Facts about this often painless cause of blindness, including causes, symptoms, and methods of treatment.

Guide to Health Insurance for People with Medicare (546N)— What Medicare pays and doesn't pay, and what to look for in private insurance.

Herbs—Magic or Toxic? (559N)—Describes which commonly used herbs are toxic and their dangers.

Infertility and How It's Treated (578N)—Causes of infertility and methods of treatment.

Insomnia (579N)—Common causes of sleeplessness and ways to cope without medication.

Plain Talk About Biofeedback (604N)—Biofeedback is a system that teaches you to control involuntary body functions, such as blood pressure. This fact sheet reviews common medical uses.

Plain Talk About Feelings of Guilt (605N)—How excessive guilt can cause serious emotional problems; suggestions on ways to handle guilt.

Plain Talk About Mutual Help Groups (547N)—Gaining strength through sharing with others who have similar problems; an overview of the many support groups available.

Plain Talk About Physical Fitness and Mental Health (609N)—Suggests appropriate forms of exercise for children, adults, the elderly, and the physically and mentally handicapped. Discusses the importance of exercise to the physical and mental well-being of all people.

Plain Talk About Stress (580N)—What stress is and how to deal with it.

Plain Talk About Wife Abuse (581N)—This fact sheet explores the causes, the emotional and physical consequences, and where an abused wife can get assistance.

Questions Concerning Cosmetics (548N)—Provides answers to seven commonly asked questions regarding ingredients in various cosmetics.

Some Things You Should Know About Prescription Drugs (560N)—Even prescription drugs can be dangerous; here are tips for safe use.

Sun Tan (582N)—Hazards of over-exposure to the sun and safe sunscreen ingredients; explains rating system of sunscreens.

The Surgeon's Newest Scalpel is a Laser (561N)—How lasers work and why they have become a valuable tool for medical treatment.

Ulcer Treatments (583N)—Describes symptoms, who is likely to be affected, diagnostic tests, and common forms of treatment.

The Unknowns of Ultrasound (562N)—How this technique is used to monitor fetal growth and development; latest research on its safety; other medical uses.

A Winter Hazard for the Old: Accidental Hypothermia (584N)—Dangers of exposure to even mild cold; causes, including medication for other problems; symptoms; and prevention.

For Sale

Adult Physical Fitness (151N)—$4.50. Graduated physical fitness program for adults who have not exercised regularly, including illustrations and instructions.

Age Pages (147N)—$2.00. Practical health advice for older people on a variety of topics including sexuality, exercise, foot care, incontinence, and more.

Calories and Weight (153N)—$2.25. Handy pocket guide with calorie tables for hundreds of popular foods and beverages.

Chronic Pain (155N)—$3.75. Illnesses such as migraine headaches, back problems, arthritis, and cancer may involve chronic pain. Discusses research findings on pain, different kinds of treatment, and where they are available.

Facts About Anorexia Nervosa (411N)—50¢. Describes symptoms, causes, and treatments of this potentially fatal eating disorder; gives sources for more information and assistance.

Facts About Caesarian Childbirth (412N)—50¢. Describes the procedure, why its use has increased, benefits, and risks.

Facts About Oral Contraceptives (410N)—50¢. Recent research findings on the risks, side effects, and benefits.

FDA Consumer (148N)—$17.00. Recent developments in the regulation of foods, drugs, and cosmetics by the Food and Drug Administration. Annual subscription—10 issues.

First Aid (149N)—$2.50. Pocket guide for treating burns, poisoning, bleeding, shock, heart attacks, etc.; instructions for moving the injured.

Headaches (156N)—$2.75. Types of headaches; causes, and relief.

How to Cope with Arthritis (157N)—$2.50. Types,

symptoms, and treatment of arthritis and related diseases.

An Introduction to Physical Fitness (154N)—$2.75. Guide to fitness tests, warm-up and conditioning exercises, and a graduated jogging program.

Poison Ivy Allergy (158N)—$2.00. What causes the allergic reaction to poison ivy, oak, and sumac; treatment; how to spot and destroy these plants.

Protect Your Lifeline—Fight High Blood Pressure (159N)—$2.00. What high blood pressure is, how it affects your body, and what to do about it.

Shingles (160N)—$3.00. Symptoms of this painful viral infection and its relation to chicken pox.

Stroke (161N)—$1.75. Latest research reverses some old ideas about stroke: victims can recover and it can be prevented. An overview of causes, diagnosis, treatment, and prevention.

Treating Alcoholism (162N)—$3.00. If you're concerned about your own drinking or someone else's, here are facts you should know: warning signs, nature of alcoholism, types of treatment for the alcoholic and family, where to go for help.

Varicose Veins (163N)—$2.25. What causes veins to enlarge and methods of treatment.

Walking for Exercise and Pleasure (192N)—$1.00. You can walk to get fit. Here's how to warm up and suggestions on how far, how fast, and how often to walk for best results.

You Are Not Alone (164N)—$2.25. Recognizing and dealing with depression, mood changes, and related stress in yourself and others; and where to look for help.

Exercise and Diet

The resources described below will help you in your quest for physical fitness. In addition to this section, also check the "Health," and "Travel USA" sections of the Sampler.

Physical Fitness and Sports

The President's Council on Physical Fitness and Sports will supply information and expertise for those who wish to establish physical fitness programs. Available free publications include:

Aqua Dynamics: Physical Conditioning Through Water Exercise
Exercise and Weight Control
An Introduction to Physical Fitness
Physical Education—A Performance Checklist
The Physically Underdeveloped Child

Contact: President's Council on Physical Fitness and Sports, Department of Health and Human Services, 450 5th Street, Suite 7103, Washington, DC 20001/202-272-3430.

Exercise and Your Heart

This free booklet explains the relationship between exercise and a healthy heart, and it offers practical information about what you can do to improve your heart. Available from: National Heart, Lung, and Blood Institute, Information Office, Building 31, Room 4A21, Bethesda, MD 20205.

Exercise and Weight Control

Below are several publications, many free, available from: Consumer Information Center, P.O. Box 100, Pueblo, CO 81002.

About Body Wraps, Pills, and Other Magic Wands (564N)—Free. Weight-loss gimmicks, untested diet aids, and their potential dangers.

Adult Physical Fitness (151N)—$4.50. Graduated fitness program for adults who have not exercised regularly, including illustrations and instructions.

Calories and Weight (153N)—$2.25. Handy pocket guide with calorie tables for hundreds of popular foods and beverages.

Cellulite (565N)—Free. All about those "lumps and bulges you couldn't lose before" and the many gimmicks supposed to help women get rid of fat on hips and thighs.

Diet Books Sell Well But . . . (566N)—Free. Fallacies and hazards of some popular diets; selecting a healthy diet to lose weight.

An Introduction to Physical Fitness (154N)—$2.75. Guide to fitness tests, warm-up and conditioning exercises, and a graduated jogging program.

Walking for Exercise and Pleasure (192N)—$1.00.

You can walk to get fit. Here's how to warm up and suggestions on how far, how fast, and how often to walk for best results.

Mental Health and Exercise
A free booklet entitled *Plain Talk About Physical Fitness and Mental Health* (609N) suggests appropriate forms of exercise for children, adults, the elderly, and the physically and mentally handicapped. It also discusses the importance of exercise to the physical and mental well-being of all people. For a copy, write: Consumer Information Center, P.O. Box 100, Pueblo, CO 81002.

Nutrition
All but the last publication described below are available free of charge from: Consumer Information Center, Pueblo, CO 81002.

Freebies
Cholesterol, Fat, and Your Health (519N)—What cholesterol is, how it affects your heart, and what to do about it.

A Compendium on Fats (520N)—All about fats— saturated, unsaturated, and polyunsaturated— and what they do to your blood.

The Confusing World of Health Foods (521N)— Common sense about health food claims.

Consumer's Guide to Food Labels (522N)—Explains dating, symbols, grades, and nutrition information on food labels.

Food Additives. (523N)—Why chemicals are added to foods and how additive use is regulated.

The Gender Gap at the Dinner Table (524N)— How men and women differ in nutritional needs; weight and energy expenditure charts; and discussion of nutritional disorders.

The Latest Caffeine Scorecard (526N)—Caffeine content of coffee, tea, chocolate, and soft drinks.

Please Pass That Woman Some More Calcium and Iron (607N)—Why a diet rich in calcium and iron is important to a woman's health.

A Primer on Dietary Minerals (527N)— Describes necessary minerals and best food sources.

RDA's: Key to Nutriton (528N)—Federal requirements for nutrition labeling of packaged foods and RDA's—Recommended Daily Allowances.

Roughage (529N)—Claims and facts about high fiber diets and health; good food sources.

Saccharin, Cyclamate, and Aspartame (530N)— Safety and risks of these artificial sweeteners.

Sodium (531N)—What sodium does for the body and how to reduce sodium intake. Fold-out poster.

Some Facts and Myths About Vitamins (532N)— What vitamins are and are not, and which foods are the best sources.

Sugar (533N)—Different types of sugar, how they work, and their caloric and carbohydrate values.

That Lite Stuff (534N)—FDA requirements for low-calorie, sugar-free, or diet foods.

Vegetarian Diets (535N)—Benefits, possible risks, and important nutrition considerations.

What About Nutrients in Fast Foods? (536N)— What's good and bad about them and the nutritional effect of a regular fast food diet.

For Sale
Nutritive Value of Foods (136N)—$4.50. Tables on nutritive value of 730 foods, volume and weight equivalents. Recommended Daily Dietary Allowances, and more.

Careers and Education

Described below are services and publications you'll find helpful as you plan your education and explore career and employment options.

Careers and Employment
Many agencies such as the Federal Bureau of Investigation (FBI), Central Intelligence Agency, NASA, Department of Defense and Peace Corps put out publications describing careers. The Department of Labor publishes lots of surveys and some directories describing overall career opportunities. Check these chapters for further informa-

tion, or call the Public Affairs or Recruiting Office of the agencies you would be interested in working for. If you want to work for the federal government, check with the Civil Service Commission for information about opportunities.

Changing Careers
Help Yourself To A Midlife Career Change (122N)

describes the basic steps involved in a career change: assessing your skills, personality, interests, and values; transferring your abilities to new work situations; and more. It also lists the "Ten Hottest Transferrable Skills." The booklet is available for $2.25 from: Consumer Information Center, P.O. Box 100, Pueblo, CO 81002.

Career Information Systems Program
This program was launched to improve the quality and dissemination of occupational and educational information. This includes descriptions of occupations such as duties, tasks, special tools and equipment needed, working conditions, career advancement, types of employer and occupation requirements. It also distributes also information about the economy, current employment outlook, earnings and fringe benefits, data on training, education and other ways to prepare for an occupation. Contact: Career Information Services Division, Office of Policy, Evaluation and Research, Employment and Training Administration, Department of Labor, 601 D St. N.W., Room 9122, Washington, DC 20213/202-376-7264.

CETA Programs
The Comprehensive Employment Training Administration (CETA) program provides economically disadvantaged persons, who are unemployed or underemployed, training, upgrading, retraining, education, and other services to help them qualify for jobs. Contact: Comprehensive Employment and Training Program, Comprehensive Employment Development, Employment and Training Administration, Department of Labor, 601 D St. N.W., Room 5014, Washington, DC 20213/202-376-6254.

Child Labor Laws
Certain provisions of the Fair Labor Standards Act apply to minors employed in nonagricultural occupations. Violators of the child labor laws are subject to civil penalties of up to $1,000 for each violation. Contact: Child Labor Branch, Wage and Hour Division, Employment Standards Administration, Department of Labor, 200 Constitution Ave. N.W., Room S3030, Washington, DC 20210/202-523-7640.

Collective Bargaining Agreements
The public has access to copies of some 5,000 agreements in private industry and government, including all those covering 1,000 employees or more, exclusive of railroads and airlines. Contact: Public File of Collective Bargaining Agreements, Union Contracts Section, Industrial Relations Section, Office of Wages and Industrial Relations, Bureau of Labor Statistics, Department of Labor, 441 G St. N.W., Room 1288, Washington, D.C. 20212/202-523-1143.

Compensation Trends and Current Wage Developments
Data are available showing amount and nature of changes in wages and related benefits for collective bargaining agreements. Data are identified by individual company and union, with number of workers affected listed by industry group and location. Contact: Division of Occupational Pay and Employee Benefit Levels, Office of Wages and Industrial Relations, Bureau of Labor Statistics, Department of Labor, 441 G St. N.W., Room 1284, Washington, DC 20212/202-523-1246. For description of the division, call Charles O'Connor, 202-523-1246.

Current Employment Analysis
Detailed analyses are conducted on data from the Current Population Survey conducted by the Bureau of the Census showing employment, unemployment and the number of persons not in the labor force. Studies include: characteristics of special groups in the labor force; changing patterns in work time and leisure; absence from work; employment status of noninstitutional population 16 years and over; hours of work, annual average employment levels for detailed occupational and industry groups; and employed persons by major occupational and industry groups. Contact: Current Employment Analysis, Office of Current Employment Analysis, Division of Employment and Unemployment, Bureau of Labor Statistics, Department of Labor, 441 G St. N.W., Room 2486, Washington, DC 20212/202-523-1944.

Current Wage Development
This monthly publication reports on collective bargaining settlements, wage and benefit data, and compensation and wage trends. Available for $12.00/year from: Superintendent of Documents, Government Printing Office, Washington, DC 20402/202-783-3238. For detailed information on content, contact: Office of Wages and Industrial Relations, Bureau of Labor Statistics, Department of Labor, 441 G St. N.W., Room 1916, Washington, DC 20212/202-523-1319.

Employment Projections
Long-term economic projections which include projections of aggregate labor force, potential demand, and industrial output and employment by industry and occupation are available from:

Office of Economic Growth, Bureau of Labor Statistics, Department of Labor, 441 G St. N.W., Room 4860, Washington, DC 20212/202-523-1450.

Employment Research and Development
Federally funded research and development programs cover various aspects of labor-related subjects including: education, public employment programs, supported employment, training and apprenticeship, upgrading and job restructuring, welfare recipient programs, worker assessment and orientation, supportive services for workers and trainers, worker attitudes, employer practices, labor force, labor demand and economic and social policies. The annual publication, *Research and Development Projects,* summarizes funded projects. Contact: Office of Research and Development, Office of Policy, Development and Research, Employment and Training Administration, Department of Labor, 601 D St. N.W., Room 9100, Washington, DC 20213/202-376-7244.

Employment Roadmaps for Science and Technology
The Congressional Caucus for Science and Technology, established to serve members of Congress, can share its information about the impact of science and technology on training and retraining. The Caucus plans to develop *Employment Roadmaps* which will highlight employment opportunities, as well as training and educational requirements, for current and prospective jobs. Staff can answer questions about high tech related legislation and they will refer science and technology oriented inquiries to the Caucus' research arm, the Research Institute for Space, Science and Technology. Contact: Congressional Caucus for Science and Technology, House Annex Building #2, H2-226, 2nd and D Streets SW, Washington, DC 20515/202-226-7788.

Employment Service
The Employment Service and affiliated State Employment Service Agencies operate nearly 2500 local offices to serve both those seeking employment and those providing it. Local offices in most states are now identified as the Job Service. Services include outreach, interviewing, testing, counseling, and referral. Contact: Employment Service, Employment and Training Administration, Department of Labor, 601 D St. N.W., Room 8000, Washington, DC 20213/202-376-6289.

Employment Standards and Reporting Unfair Practices
The Employment Standards Administration has the authority to correct a wide range of unfair employment practices. It enforces laws and regulations, sets employment standards providing workers' compensation to those injured on their jobs, and requires federal contractors and subcontractors to provide equal employment opportunity. Contact: Office of Information and Consumer Affairs, Employment Standards Administration, Department of Labor, 200 Constitution Ave. N.W., Room C4331, Washington, DC 20210/202-523-8743.

Employment Structures and Trends
Detailed data are available on employment, wages, hours, earnings, and turnover; monthly estimates of states and local area unemployment; occupational employment for most industries; and employment in major nonagricultural industries. Contact: Office of Employment Structure and Trends, Bureau of Labor Statistics, Department of Labor, 441 G St. N.W., Room 2919, Washington, DC 20212/202-523-1694.

Health Careers
Health Careers and Guidebook offers an overview of the health field, along with a brief picture of what is happening in the field today and basic facts about the industry. It discusses new and changing job opportunities and provides information for career planning. Individual career descriptions for more than 100 occupations and a reference list of 150 health organizations that provide career information are also included. The 220-page publication (#029-000-00343-2) is available for $7.50 from the Superintendent of Documents, U.S. Government Printing Office, Washington, DC 20402, 202-783-3238. It can also be obtained from your local Employment and Training Administration office which you can locate by checking the "U.S. Government" listing in your telephone book or contacting: Employment and Training Administration, U.S. Employment Service, U.S. Department of Labor, Washington, DC 20213, 202-376-6289.

Job Listing
Job Bank Openings Seminar is a monthly report providing information about job opportunities listed the preceding month with the public employment service Job Bank System. It includes openings data for all occupational categories. The *Job Bank Frequently Listed Openings* is a monthly publication providing information on "high volume occupations" for which there is a relatively

large number of job listings in the preceding month. Information is also provided on the industries requiring new workers, the numbers of openings listed in these high volume occupations, average pay and employee education and experience requirements. Contact: Division of Occupational Analysis, Office of Technical Support, Education and Training Administration, Department of Labor, 601 D St. N.W., Room 8421, Washington, DC 20213/202-376-6578.

Labor Market Conditions Analysis and Services
There are approximately 595 state, local, or regional Federal Job Training Centers throughout the U.S. and most can provide information about labor market conditions in their geographical area. The Centers are designed to assist the economically disadvantaged, dislocated workers, unemployed, underemployed and those facing special barriers to employment. As each Center offers different services, it is best to call your local office to find out about the eligibility and training programs offered in your area. The Employment and Training Administration Office oversees the federal employment training program. Its staff can provide you with statistical information about the training programs they have analyzed and can refer you to an office in your area. Contact: Employment and Training Administration (ETA), U.S. Department of Labor (DOL), 601 D Street, NW, Washington, DC 20213, 202-376-6093.

Publications
See also "Publications Worth Writing For" which follows "Education."

Women
The government provides several services especially for women. For more information about what's available, see "Especially For. . . . Women" in the Free Help and Information For You and Your Family section of the Sampler.

Education
Described below are services and publications which will help you in educating yourself or your child, including financing higher education.

College Money Hotline
Many middle- and higher-income college students don't realize they may be eligible for government programs offering free money or low-interest loans for financing their education. Experts are available to show you how to take advantage of a variety of student grant and loan programs offered by the

government. Contact: Grants, Department of Education, P.O. Box 84, Washington, DC 20044/(301) 984-4070.

Continuing Education For Women
Information is available on programs which allow women to study part-time in school or at home in order to get formal education credentials. A free publication, *How To Get Credit for What You Know: Alternative Routes to Educational Credit,* lists organizations which offer information on adult education programs and opportunities. Contact: Women's Bureau, Department of Labor, 200 Constitution Ave. N.W., Room S3005, Washington, DC 20210/202-523-6668.

Educational Grants Information Clearinghouse
Information and expertise is available for those who wish to submit grant proposals on education research. Contact: Clearinghouse for National Institute of Education, Department of Education, 1200 19th St. N.W., Room 619B, Washington, DC 20208/202-254-5600.

Educational Programs That Work
Teachers and developers of programs that are deemed educationally significant are sponsored to go into the field and lend their expertise in repeating their programs. A free directory, called *Educational Programs that Work,* describes these programs. Contact: National Diffusion Network, U.S. Department of Education, Room 613, Brown Building, 400 Maryland Ave., S.W., Washington, DC 20202/202-653-7000.

ERIC Educational Reference and Information Center
ERIC is the largest database in the world devoted entirely to educational literature and materials. Coverage includes bibliographies, professional reports, conference papers, statistical reports, literature surveys, federally funded programs descriptions, innovative programs, and curriculum materials. The full text of ERIC is available on microfiche in over 700 public libraries across the country, and monthly indexes facilitate a manual search of the database. In addition, the database is available on-line through several major commercial vendors. Two publications, *A Pocket Guide to ERIC* and *All About ERIC,* are available free of charge to explain the ERIC system, and a free directory of the facilities handling the database is also available.

The ERIC database collection has also been divided into 16 subject oriented information clearinghouses on specific areas of special interest. The

User-Services staff of these Clearinghouses will assist the public in identifying and accessing information within their particular area of interest. Information can be obtained about: grants, loans and other government benefit programs available; literature sources including bibliographies; and curriculum listings; referrals and experts in various fields; teaching aids including free publications and audiovisuals; current research and development; and other topics of value to educational professionals, students, parents, and the public in general. A listing of these clearinghouses is located in the Information on Anything and Everything section of the Sampler. See the Department of Education section for further information about the clearinghouses. For additional information or to request one of the above free publications contact: Educational Reference and Information Center (ERIC), Information Resources, National Institute of Education, Washington, DC 20208/202-254-7934.

Job Corps Advanced General Education Program

This published program is designed to help prepare adult students with the information, concepts, and general knowledge needed to pass the American Council on Education's "Test of General Educational Development" (GED) for high school equivalency certification. The program kit consists of 126 booklets and is available for $40 from: Superintendent of Documents, Government Printing Office, Washington, DC 20401/202-783-3238. For more detailed information on the program, contact: Division of Technical Assistance, Office of Job Corps and Young Adult Conservation Corps, Office of Youth Programs, Office of National Programs, Employment and Training Administration, Department of Labor, 601 D St N.W., Room 6114, Washington, DC 20213/202-376-7053.

Social Security Checks for Students

This free pamphlet shows how qualified unmarried students can receive monthly benefits when a parent insured under Social Security dies or receives disability checks. Available from your local Social Security Office.

Student Guide—Federal Financial Aid Programs

This informative booklet, published annually, by the Department of Education, contains descriptions of the major types of financial assistance available to students of higher education. Coverage includes Pell Grants, Work Study Programs, National Direct Student Loans, Guaranteed Student Loans, and other Supplemental Educational Grants. General information is given on topics such as eligibility, applications, deadlines, and contacts for student aid. The publication is free from: Federal Student Aid Programs, Department DEA-85, Pueblo, CO 81109, or contact: Federal Student Aid Programs, U.S. Department of Education, Washington, DC 20202/301-984-4070.

Vocational and Technical Education

For information on programs and funding for vocational and technical education in occupations that do not require college degrees, contact: Division of Innovation and Development, Office of Vocational and Adult Education, Department of Education, 7th and D Sts. S.W., Room 5108, Washington, DC 20202/ 202-245-2617.

Women and Minority Education Programs

A publication entitled "Higher Education Opportunities for Minorities and Women—Annotated Selections" lists higher-education programs and explains types of funding available. It can be purchased for $6.00 from: Superintendent of Documents, U.S. Government Printing Office, Washington, DC 20402/202-783-3238.

Career and Education Publications

Consumer Information Center

Described below are examples of career and education publications available from: Consumer Information Center, P.O. Box 100, Pueblo, CO 81002.

Children's Books (109N)—$1.00. A descriptive listing of the best books published in 1983 for preschool through junior high school age children.

College Costs: Basic Student Charges (120N)—$1.75. Compare college and graduate school costs for 1983–84 at 2,000 public and private four-year colleges and at 1,300 public and private two-year schools.

Computer and Mathematics-Related Occupations (121N)—$1.00. Everything you want to know about training, earnings, and job outlook for accountants, statisticians, programmers, analysts, and many other jobs in this booming field.

Current Bureau of Labor Statistics Publications (509N)—Free. Listing of titles on area wage surveys, female-male earnings gap, the Consumer Price Index, and major collective bargaining agreements. Some single copies free from BLS regional offices; order blank for subscriptions.

How to Help Your Children Achieve in School

(111N)—$3.75. Ways to help your children perform to the best of their ability in school. Tips include techniques for learning and remembering and strategies for test taking.

The Job Market for Engineers (407N)—50¢. An analysis of market demand and salary trends for engineers.

Job Options for Women in the 80's (123N)—$3.50. Sensible advice and information for women who want help choosing a career and finding a job.

The Job Outlook in Brief (124N)—$1.50. Prospects to the mid-1990's for almost 200 occupations.

Merchandising Your Job Talents (126N)—$2.75. How to prepare a resume, write a letter of application, and have a successful interview.

Occupational Outlook Quarterly (127N)—$11.00. Practical information for job seekers and employment counselors on career counseling programs, new occupations, salary and job trends, and much more. Use subscription blank on page 14. Annual subscription—4 issues.

Your Guide to International Youth Exchange (512N)—Free. Guidelines for selecting the right exchange program as a student, host family, or community volunteer. Directory of selected programs and services included.

Government Printing Office (GPO)
Described below are examples of career and education publications available from GPO. Many of these materials are also available in libraries, especially at schools and guidance centers. Most are updated on a regular basis, either yearly or quarterly. Contact: Superintendent of Documents, Government Printing Office, Washington, DC 20402/202-783-3238, or the GPO Bookstore in your area.

Counselor's Guide to Occupational Information— This publication is an annotated listing of federal government publications. It includes information about occupations, describing job duties, entry requirements, advancement opportunities, job outlook, earnings, etc. It also includes information on overseas jobs; special programs or jobs for minorities, women, veterans, and young workers; education and financial aid; job search; career education, statistics and bibliographies useful to counselors. Available for $4.50.

Dictionary of Occupational Titles—A comprehensive directory, which lists, defines, and describes all the occupations currently in existence in the U.S. Each occupational entry also includes the educational requirements and work experience generally needed to obtain a job. The publication was prepared by the Department of Labor's Employment and Training Administration. This publication (#029-013-0079-9) is available for $23.00.

Exploring Careers—Describes the qualifications an individual must have to be successful in 250 different occupations. The publication (#029-001-02224-7) is available for $11.00.

Occupational Outlook Quarterly—Published four times yearly, this covers employment trends, training and educational opportunities, new and emerging jobs and salary trends. Examples of recent articles are: Careers in Commodity Futures Trading; Fringe Around the Paycheck: Employee Benefits; The Job Hunter's Guide to the Library; and A Checklist for Going Into Business. This publication is available at most libraries and schools. Single copies can be purchased from GPO for $4.50. Annual subscription rate is $9.00.

Occupational Projections and Training Data, 1984 Edition—Provides information about job openings in 240 occupations. Supply and demand data are provided for each job category, including projected employment for 1990, percentage change from 1978 to 1990, average annual openings for 1978 to 1990 and the number of people being trained each year for these jobs. The publication (#029-001-02804-1) costs $6.00.

Occupations Outlook Handbook—Updated yearly, this describes nearly 300 occupations and 25 industries. For each job, information is provided about the nature of the work, working conditions, training and qualifications required, employment outlook, earnings, related occupations and sources of additional information. For each industry, the handbook describes the nature and location of the industry, occupations in the industry, working conditions, employment outlook, earnings and sources of additional information. This publication (#029-001-02325-1) can be found in most libraries. It can be purchased for $8.50 paperback and $10.00 hardback.

Banking, Credit and Finance

Several educational materials, including comic books, are available to help you understand the principles of banking and finance. Some of these items also explain your rights—such as what a bill collector can or can't do, what the consumer credit laws mean, and how to safeguard your investments.

The ABC's of Borrowing
Although aimed at people in business, this book is of interest to the general public. It explains the basics of credit, the different types of loans available, what banks use a rule of thumb for making loans, and tips for filling out loan applications. This free booklet is available from your local Small Business Administration Office or by writing: U.S. Small Business Administration, 1441 L Street NW, Washington, DC 20416.

The Arithmetic of Interest Rates
This 33 page book shows how to calculate the true cost of money if you are borrowing and the true return on your money if you are investing. Available free from: Federal Reserve Bank of New York, Public Information Department, 33 Liberty Street, New York, NY 10045.

Banking Electronically
Alice in Debitland is a free publication which explains the pros and cons of electronic funds transfer and how to use bank debit cards at automatic teller machines and point of sale terminals. It also explains your rights and responsibilities when dealing with lost or stolen cards. Write: Board of Governors, Federal Reserve System, 20th and Constitution Avenue NW, Washington, DC 20405.

Bill Collectors and Your Rights
A free pamphlet entitled *The Fair Debt Collection Practices Act* shows how this law prohibits bill collectors from using tactics such as publicizing your debt, making annoying or repetitive phone calls, or threatening violence or harm to your person, property or reputation. To order a copy send a self-addressed, stamped envelope to: Federal Reserve Bank of Philadelphia, Department of Consumer Affairs, P.O. Box 66, Philadelphia, Pa 19105.

Comic Books
The following comic books are available free of charge from: Federal Reserve Bank of New York, Publications Sections, 33 Liberty Street, New York, New York 10045.

The Story of Money—describes how coin, paper, and checkbook money have evolved over the ages.

The Story of Banks—shows how banks serve as financial supermarkets in our society as well as acting as go-betweens linking savers with borrowers.

The Story of Checks and Electronic Payments—describes in simple terms how checks are used in our society and how they are processed in our banking system.

The Story of Inflation—shows how inflation is one of the most damaging of all economic ills and the most difficult to end because its roots are so deeply entwined in our economic and political system.

The Story of Consumer Credit—describes the impact that consumer credit has on all of our lives.

Credit Complaints
How to File a Consumer Credit Complaint, is a free pamphlet which shows you how and when the Federal Reserve Board will help you resolve a problem you may have with your banker. A form is included to send in your complaint. Write: Federal Reserve System, Publications Section, 20th and Constitution Avenue NW, Washington, DC 20551.

Credit Protection Laws
Find out how you can profit from the new credit laws by obtaining a free copy of the *Consumer Handbook of Credit Protection Laws* from: Publication Services, Board of Governors of the Federal Reserve System, 20th Street and Constitution Avenue NW, Washington, DC 20551/202-452-3245.

Family Economics
A staff of experts research such topics as the economic aspects of family living, family resources, economic problems of families, the relationship of family budget items to each other, the use of food, clothing and textiles and the efficient management of money and time. Low-cost publications are available. Contact: Family Economics

Research Group, ARS/NER, 6505 Belcrest Road, Federal Building, Room 442A, Hyattsville, MD 20782/301-436-8461.

Investing in Commodities

The following free publications will aid in explaining the basics to anyone who is considering an investment in one of the commodities markets. They are available from: Commodities Futures Trading Commission, Office of Public Affairs, 2033 K Street NW, Washington, DC 20581.

Before Trading Commodities Get the Facts—shows how to deal with a commodities broker and how to investigate a broker's background.

Basic Facts About Commodities Futures Trading—this 24 page booklet provides a primer in commodities investing. It shows you how to read and understand various figures that are published and where to get additional sources of information.

Glossary of Trading Terms—lists and defines over 350 terms used by investors and traders in the commodities market.

United States Treasury Securities

This easy-to-read booklet provides basic information for investing in U.S. Treasury bills, notes and bonds. Available free from: Federal Reserve Bank of Dallas, Public Affairs Department, Station K, Dallas, TX 75222.

Consumer Publications

A wide variety of finance-related publications are available, many free of charge, from the Consumer Information Center. Examples of these materials are listed below. Contact: Consumer Information Center, P.O. Box 100, Pueblo, CO 81002.

Consumer Credit Handbook (591N)—Free. How to apply for credit, what to do if you are denied, and how consumer credit laws can help you.

A Consumer's Guide to Life Insurance (592)—Free. Comprehensive guide to different types of policies, costs, and coverage; includes a glossary of commonly used terms.

Fair Credit Billing (419)—50¢. How to resolve a billing dispute on credit card purchases.

Fair Credit Reporting Act (420N)—50¢. How to check the data in your credit file; what to do if you are denied credit because of incorrect information. Includes a Spanish translation.

Fair Debt Collection (421N)—50¢. Methods of debt collection that are prohibited by law and where to complain.

A Guide to Individual Retirement Accounts (183N)—$2.00. Who is eligible, where to invest, federal tax savings, and shopping tips.

Know Your Pension Plan (511N)—Free. Checklists to help you understand your rights and benefits under your retirement plan.

What Every Investor Should Know (185N)—$4.50. Provides basic information on choosing investments; trading securities; safeguarding your investments; and protections guaranteed by law. Describes the different types of securities—stocks, bonds, mutual funds, Treasury notes, etc. (185N) $4.50.

Buying and Maintaining Your Automobile

Next to buying a home, purchasing a car is probably the most important financial investment you will make. The skyrocketing cost of gasoline has made consumers more aware of the importance of this investment. The free services and publications described below will assist you in purchasing and maintaining a safe and economical automobile.

Auto Emissions

A free pamphlet, *What You Should Know About Your Auto Emissions Warranty,* explains how the law requires manufacturers to replace or repair a defective part on cars less than 5 years old with less than 50,000 miles if the part failure causes your car to exceed Federal emissions standards. Write: Public Inquiries Center (PM211B), U.S. Environmental Protection Agency, Washington, DC 20460.

Auto Safety Hotline

This hotline can help in the following ways:

Staff will register your complaint about an automobile safety problem and investigate the problem with the manufacturer.

Provide you with on-the-spot information about safety recalls that might affect your car.

Refer you to experts who can answer your questions about federal safety standards and regulations.

Contact: Auto Safety Hotline, Department of Transportation, National Highway Traffic Safety Administration, Washington, DC 20590/ toll-free 800-424-9393/202-426-0123 in DC.

Brakes
The following publications are available free of charge from the National Highway Traffic Safety Administration, General Services Division, 400 7th St. S.W., Washington, DC 20590:

Brakes: A comparison of Braking Performance for New Passenger Cars and Motorcycles
Safety Tips on the Purchase and Use of Hydraulic Brake Fluids
Passenger Car Brakes
Brake Fluids

Child Restraint Systems For Your Automobile
This free booklet answers such questions as: Why are child safety seats needed? and What kind of restraint systems are available? Write: National Highway Traffic Safety Administration, Publications Dept, 400 7th Street, SW, Washington, DC 20590.

Consumer Information Publications
The following publications are available from the Consumer Information Center, Pueblo, CO 81002.

The Backyard Mechanic Set (104N)—$7.00. Three booklets on auto maintenance full of car-saving and cost-saving tips. The 39 illustrated chapters—useful for the beginner and the expert—start with changing the oil, move on to tune-ups, rebuilding the carburetor, brake and body repairs, and more. They also include consumer tips to help you avoid rip-offs when having your car repaired or buying a used car.
Cost of Owning and Operating Automobiles and Vans (401N)—50¢. Cost breakdown for purchase, depreciation, maintenance, gas, insurance, and taxes; includes worksheet for figuring your own costs.
Gasoline Engine Tune-Up (105N)—$1.50. A three-part, illustrated guide for tune-ups beginning with basic inspection and cleaning; checking the engine's internal condition, spark plugs, and ignition system; getting the fuel and ignition systems to work together; and detailed instructions for valve adjustment necessary for today's smaller engines.
Simple Self-Service (106N)—$1.00. How to perform the simple but important routine maintenance you might miss at the self-service pump: checking the oil, tire pressure, battery, and more.

Crash Protection
The following free publications are available from the National Highway Traffic Safety Administration, General Services Division, (NAD-42), 400 7th St. S.W., Washington, DC 20590/202-426-9550:

Safety Belts: A Step Closer to Automatic Crash Survival
Safety Belts—How Many of These Fairy Tales Have You Told?
Safety Belt Message

Do You Own A Car?
This free booklet offers advice on dealing with a mechanic when it comes to adjusting your emission control equipment. It describes how an auto repairman can be subject to a $2,500 fine for tampering with the equipment. Write: Public Inquiries Center, (PM211B), U.S. Environmental Protection Agency, Washington, DC 20460.

Drunk Driving
A free pamphlet tells "How You Can Help Fight Drunk Drivers." Contact: National Highway Transportation Safety Administration, Public Affairs, DOT, 400 7th Street, SW, Washington, DC 20590/202-426-9550.

Facts on Auto Emission Standards and Warranties
The Environmental Protection Agency (EPA) establishes and monitors pollution requirements in automobiles and offers the following free publications to aid the public in complying with the laws:

What You Should Know About Your Auto Emissions Warranty
Buying A Car Overseas? Beware
Mechanics . . . A New Law Affects You

Contact: Public Inquiries Center, EPA, Washington, DC 20460/202-755-0707.

Gas Mileage Guide
This handy guide gives the estimated mileage per gallon for nearly every model of car. It also has a chart showing what your annual fuel costs may be for a given fuel economy estimate. Produced by the U.S. Dept. of Energy, this is available free from any new car or light truck dealer.

How to Buy a New or Used Car
The following publications are available free of charge from the Consumer Information Center, Pueblo, CO 81009:

Common Sense in Buying A New Car—covers how to compare prices, dealer services, and warranties; how to inspect and test drive; and how to avoid new car problems.

Common Sense in Buying A Used Car—discusses how to inspect before you buy; and how to understand the odometer law and used-car warranties.

Motor Vehicle Defects and Recall Campaigns
This publication describes why recall campaigns are initiated, the rights and responsibilities of consumers when a vehicle is recalled, and how consumers can report safety related problems to the National Highway Traffic Safety Administration. Free from: National Highway Traffic Safety Administration, Publications Dept., 400 7th St, SW, Washington, DC 20590.

Motorcycle Safety
The booklet, *Motorcycle Safety,* answers questions like: Is motorcycling safe? How does it compare to driving a car? What are the causes of motorcycle accidents and how can they be reduced? Free from U.S. Dept. of Transportation, NHTSA, NTS/31, 400 7th Street SW, Washington, DC 20590.

Odometer Tampering
Federal law prohibits tampering with a vehicle's odometer (the instrument, often called a speedometer, that measures the distance traveled by a vehicle). No one, including the vehicle owner, is permitted to turn back or disconnect the odometer, unless performing repairs. When a broken odometer cannot be adjusted to reflect the true mileage, the odometer must be set at zero and a sticker indicating the true mileage before service and the date of service must be attached to the left door frame. Federal law also requires disclosure of the vehicle mileage upon transfer of ownership. Automobile purchasers who suspect tampering should contact: Chief Counsel's Office, National Highway Traffic Safety Administration, Department of Transportation, Washington, DC 20590/202-426-0670, or, Department of Justice, Washington, DC 20530/202-724-6786, or local or state law enforcement authorities.

Police Radar—Is It Reliable?
A free issue paper entitled *Police Traffic Radar* examines the use of police radar, the effects of interference from CB radios and car ignitions, etc., and makes recommendations about improving the effectiveness of radar trafficking. For a copy write: National Bureau of Standards, Public Information Division, Department of Commerce, Washington, DC 20234/301-921-3161.

Ridesharing Hotline and Information Center
The National Ridesharing Information Center (NRIC) provides free information, experts, speakers, newsletters, conferences, and other events to aid individuals and organizations in organizing carpools, vanpools, and other ridesharing programs. Contact: NRIC, Federal Highway Administration, Room 3301, Washington, DC 20590/202-426-0210 in DC.

Safety Publications
The following publications are available free of charge from the National Highway Traffic Safety Administration, General Services Division, 400 7th Street S.W., Washington, DC 20590/202-426-0874.

Travel and Camper Trailer Safety
Consumer Protection Under the New Anti-Tampering Odometer Law
55: Judge for Yourself
Motorhome and Pickup Camper Safety Standards, Federal Motor Vehicle Safety Standards
How to Deal With Motor Vehicle Emergencies
Safe Driving in Winter

Tips on Saving Gas
The following free publications are available from the TIC Request Services, Technical Information Center, Department of Energy, P.O. Box 62, Oak Ridge, TN 37830/615-576-1305:

Gas Mileage Guide: Annual information on EPA miles per gallon estimates for vehicles and a chart for calculating annual fuel costs for all new model cars.

How to Save Gasoline and Money: Basic money- and gas-saving tips, including choosing your next car, driving more effectively, planning your trips and caring for your car.

Starting a Driver-Owned and Operated Vanpool: Tips on ways to start, operate, and finance a vanpool in your neighborhood.

Gasoline More Miles Per Gallon: Shows methods of selecting gas, maintaining your car, improving performance, and lowering costs. The booklet also contains information on the workings of a car engine. Free from the Consumer Information Center, Pueblo, Colorado 81009.

Tires—Safety and Saving Money

Study Says $50 K-Mart Tire Better Than $90 Michelin! The Department of Transportation has rated over 2,500 tires on aspects of wear and safety. The results of this study, called the *Uniform Tire Quality Grading List,* is made available to the public through credit unions, public libraries, recreation associations, and consumer information offices. *Consumer Tire Guide* and *Tire Load: Inflation Labels for Popular Tire Sizes* are free booklets explaining the grading system. To obtain a copy or further information contact: National Highway Traffic Safety Administration, 400 7th St. S.W., Washington, DC 20590/202-426-0874 or 202-426-2768.

Warranties

Information and expertise are available to help you understand your rights under automobile manufacturers' and repair services' warranties and guarantees. The following publications are available free of charge from the Bureau of Consumer Protection, Office of Consumer Education, Federal Trade Commission, Washington, DC 20580:

Service Contracts (Fact Sheet)
Warranties: There Ought To Be A Law
Magnuson-Moss Warranty Act—Private Consumer Remedies Fact Sheet: Explains how the law provides for attorney's fees to aid consumers in bringing suit for failing to honor warranties.
Warranties: Making Business Sense Out of Warranty Law

Purchasing, Renting and Remodeling Your Home

The biggest purchase most of us make in our lifetime is our home. With inflation having a devastating effect on both the cost of housing and the cost of money to purchase a home, we can use all the help we can get. The following free services, publications and government subsidies may prove to be just the assistance you have been waiting for to help make your dream house come true.

Information and Complaints: Where to Go

Energy and Conservation Information

Free publications, information services, referrals, and a hotline service are available to help you learn how to save energy in the home. Available from: Conservation and Renewable Energy Inquiry and Referral Service, P.O. Box 8907, Silver Spring, MD 20807/800-462-4963 in Pennsylvania and 800-523-2929 elsewhere.

Federal Housing Programs

For information about federal housing programs, contact your local Department of Housing and Urban Development or the Program Information Center, Department of Housing and Urban Development, 451 7th Street SW, Room 1104, Washington, DC 20410/202-755-6420.

Housing Discrimination Hotline

If you think you are being discriminated against because of your race, color, sex, religion, age or national origin you can call 800-424-8590 (in DC call 202-426-3500) for assistance. Staff will help people who are the victim of discriminatory practices such as: being directed to buy in a particular neighborhood or building; being denied a mortgage for a home in a location boycotted by lending institutions; being rejected as the buyer of a home for other than financial reasons. For free publications or to report a possible violation, call the hotline or write: Fair Housing and Equal Opportunity, U.S. Department of Housing and Urban Development, Washington, DC 20410.

Land Sales

The government will investigate complaints from individuals who feel that they have been cheated in their purchase of land. A free booklet, *Before Buying Land . . . Get the Facts* provides information about what to watch out for.

Developers offering 50 or more unimproved lots are required to offer you a property report describing in detail the facts about the land you are thinking of buying. As this report must also be filed with the U.S. Department of Housing and Urban Development, if the developer will not give you a copy of his report you can obtain it from HUD.

For further information, or to file a complaint contact: Office of Lender Activities and Land Sales Registration, Room 6278, 451 7th Street SW, Washington, DC 20410/202-755-0502.

Lead Poisoning

Houses built before 1960 may contain lead-based paint which if picked up and swallowed by children can cause brain damage, mental retardation, behavior problems, blindness or even death. A law now requires that these hazards be identified and eliminated in all buildings rehabilitated or refurbished with Department of Housing and Urban Development funds. Many communities have local ordinances barring the sale and use of lead-based paint for housing. If you suspect your children have been exposed, or your house presents a lead hazard, contact your local Department of Housing and Urban Development Office, or Lead-Based Paint Poisoning Prevention, Office of Public Housing, Department of Housing and Urban Development, 451 7th Street SW, Room 4130, Washington, DC 20410/202-755-6640.

Mobile Homes

If you believe that your mobile home does not meet government safety standards and you are unable to obtain satisfaction from the manufacturer or local authorities contact: Office of Mobile Home Construction and Safety Standards, Department of Housing and Urban Development, 451 7th Street SW, Room 3248, Washington DC 20410/202-755-6584.

Moving and Movers

The Interstate Commerce Commission (ICC) regulates interstate movers of household goods. To evaluate a mover before using its services, the commission requires that, on request, consumers be given copies of carrier performance reports. In addition, movers are required to provide each consumer with an ICC booklet explaining the consumer's rights and obligations on signing papers, estimates, weighing of shipments, payment for the move, and filing claims. Contact: Director, Consumer Assistance Office, Interstate Commerce Commission, Washington, DC 20423/202-275-0860.

Settlement Costs

In order to protect you from unnecessary and exhorbitant settlement or closing costs, the Real Estate Settlement Procedures Act requires that you receive some advance notice of what your settlement costs are going to be, plus an itemized account of the total costs. At the time you apply for a loan, the lender is required to furnish you with "good faith" estimates for each of the settlement charges likely to be incurred, as well as a free copy of *A Guide to Settlement Costs*. For further information, or to register a complaint contact: Real Estate Practices Division, Office of Voluntary Associations and Consumer Protection, Department of Housing and Urban Development, 451 7th Street SW, Room 9266, Washington, DC 20410/202-426-0070.

Money For . . . .

Country Homes

If you live in the country you may be eligible to receive financial assistance from the U.S. Department of Agriculture. Its housing and loan guarantee programs include: Rural Housing Site Loans; Low-to-Moderate Income Housing Loans; and Farm Ownership Loans.

For additional information on these programs contact your local Department of Agriculture Office, or: Farmers Home Administration, Department of Agriculture, 14th and Independence Avenue SW, Room 5503 South, Washington, DC 20250/202-447-4323.

Cooperatives and Condominiums

FHA insured loans for up to $67,500 are available to those who wish to purchase cooperatives or condominiums. For further information on these programs contact: your local field office of Department of Housing and Urban Development or: Program Information Center, Department of Housing and Urban Development, 451 7th Street, SW, Room 1104, Washington, DC 20410/202-755-6420.

A free publication entitled *Let's Consider Cooperatives* as well as information is available from: Program Information Center, Department of Housing and Urban Development, 451 7th Street SW, Room 1104, Washington, DC 20410/202-755-6420.

Homesteading

Under the Urban Homesteading program, the U.S. Department of Housing and Urban Development gives cities and towns single-family homes the government has insured but which the owners let run down and left without paying back the loan. Rather than let these homes stand empty, the government then turns these houses over to local communities, which in turn sell them to lower-income families for just a small amount of money (usually only one dollar). To find out whether your community is participating in the program and whether you qualify, contact your local government officials at the Department of Housing and Urban Development office nearest to you, or: Urban Homesteading Division, Office of Urban Rehabilitation, Community Planning and Development, Department of Housing and Urban Development, 451 7th Street SW, Room 7168, Washington, DC 20410/202-755-6880.

Housing—All Types
The Department of Housing and Urban Development (HUD) administers approximately 60 government programs which provide grants, loans, loan guarantees, and direct payments for various forms of housing. A free 87-page book entitled *Programs of HUD* describes these opportunities. The Department of Housing and Urban Development chapter of *Information USA* also provides information about what's available. To contact HUD write: HUD Service Center, U.S. Department of Housing and Urban Development, Room B-258, Washington, DC 20410.

Mobile Homes
GOVERNMENT INSURED LOANS—If you cannot obtain a conventional loan, the government will insure your loan for up to $27,000 for the purchase of a mobile home. For information contact your local Department of Housing and Urban Development field office or the Office of Title I Insured Loans, Department of Housing and Urban Development, 451 7th Street SW, Room 9160, Washington, DC 20410/202-755-6880.

VETERAN'S LOANS—Veterans can receive loan guarantees for mobile home financing of up to $20,000 or 50%, whichever is less. Contact your local Veterans Administration Office or Veterans Administration, Central Office, Washington, DC 20420/202-389-2356.

Remodeling and Improving Your Home
INSURED LOANS—Insured loans of up to $90,000 are available to homeowners for remodeling and rehabilitation. The following publications are free as long as supplies last: *Fixing Up Your Home—And How To Finance It,* and *HUD's Role in Home Improvement.*

Contact your local Department of Housing and Urban Development field office or Program Information Center, Department of Housing and Urban Development, 451 7th Street SW, Room 1104, Washington, DC 20410/202-755-7353.

HELP FOR HOMEOWNERS IN SMALL TOWNS—Those living in small towns should investigate programs in the Department of Agriculture and the Veterans Administration. The offices are listed under "Housing Information" in this section.

Renters, the Elderly, and the Handicapped
Special subsidies, as well as loans and loan guarantees are available to renters, the elderly and the handicapped. For further information contact: Office of the Elderly and Handicapped, Department of Housing and Urban Development, 451 7th Street SW, Washington, DC 20410/202-755-5318 or 755-7149.

Solar Energy Devices for Homeowners
Many states and U.S. territories now give federally-funded low-interest loans or grants to homeowners who want to install solar energy devices. The Solar Energy and Energy Conservation Bank program is for low and moderate income families owning single and multi-family dwellings. For specific information about currently available equipment, contact: Solar Energy and Energy Conservation Bank, U.S. Department of Housing and Urban Development, 451 7th Street SW, Room 7110, Washington, DC 20410/202-755-7166.

Upgrading Your Neighborhood
There are a large number of federal programs available under which communities can receive government assistance to upgrade the quality of homes in a given neighborhood. For example, in order to improve the appearance of homes in a low-income area of Indianapolis, a community group worked through the city government to receive a Community Development Block Grant in order to subsidize home improvements for both poor and higher-income homeowners. A 400-page free publication, *People Power: What Communities Are Doing to Counter Inflation,* describes available programs and provides countless stories showing how individuals have used these programs to improve housing conditions in their neighborhoods. Available from: Consumer Information Center, Pueblo, CO 81009.

Veterans
Veterans can receive special loans and loan guarantees that have no maximum limit. For further information contact your local Veterans Administration Office, or: Veterans Administration Central Office, Washington, DC 20420/202-389-2356.

Publications Worth Writing For

A wide variety of housing-related publications are available from several federal agencies. Listed below, by topic and agency, are materials you can obtain either free of charge or for a minimal fee.

BUILDING, BUYING AND FINANCING

HUD Program Information Center

The following publications are available free of charge, as long as the supply lasts, from: Program Information Center, Department of Housing and Urban Development, 451 7th Street SW, Room 1104, Washington, DC 20410/202-755-6420.

Homeowner's Glossary of Building Terms
Should You Rent or Buy A Home?
Your Housing Rights—Live Where You Want To Live
Home Buying Members of the Armed Services

Consumer Information Center

The following publications are available, either free of charge or for a minimal fee, from: Consumer Information Center, P.O. Box 100, Pueblo, CO 81002.

Buying Lots from Developers (165N)—$2.50. What you're entitled to know—and should ask—before you sign a contract.
Can I Really Get Free or Cheap Public Land — $2.25. The answer is "no" despite some advertising claims to the contrary; here is the real story on public lands available for purchase or homesteading.
Consumer Handbook on Adjustable Rate Mortgages (610N)—Free. A guide to understanding the basic features, advantages and risks, and terminology associated with adjustable rate mortgages.
House Construction: How to Reduce Costs (169N)—$2.50. Advice on savings in selection of materials, utilities, location, style, and more.
The Mortgage Money Guide (414N)—50¢. Handy guide to different types of mortgages and loan financing options; includes a table of monthly mortgage costs at various rates.
Remodeling a House—Will It Be Worthwhile? (444N)—50¢. What to consider when deciding whether a wood-frame house is worth restoring.
Sales of Federal Surplus Read Estate (585N)— Free. Listing of when, where, and how surplus properties will be sold within the next three months; and where to go for more information on specific pieces of property.
Selecting and Financing a Home (170N)—$3.00.

Brief comparison of renting with buying; how to figure what you can afford and apply for a loan; what to look for in homeowner's insurance.
Turning Home Equity into Income for Older Americans (172N)—$1.25. Three plans to help homeowners convert their capital into income, with examples of how the plans work and what the costs and risks are.
When You Move—Do's and Don'ts (433N)—50¢. Planning; what to expect during the move; and how to handle a loss or damage claim; and tips for the do-it-yourselfer.
Selling Property: Brokers, Title, Closing, and Taxee (432N)—50¢. Advantages and disadvantages of using a real estate broker; some costs of selling; tax implications.
Settlement Costs (171N)—$3.50. What they are; documents to expect; sample forms and worksheets to compare costs; how to avoid unfair practices when purchasing a home.

HUD Service Center

If you are buying, or thinking of buying, a new or used home you will find *The Energy Wise Home Buyer* to be a helpful publication. The free 60-page book is an easy-to-read guide for choosing a home that is energy efficient. Write: HUD Service Center, U.S. Department of Housing and Urban Development, Room B-258, Washington, DC 20410.

Consumer Information Center

The publications listed below are available either free or for a minimal fee, from: Consumer Information Center, P.O. Box 100, Pueblo, CO 81002.

Your Keys to Energy Efficiency (587N)—Free. Tips for saving energy at home and in your car; health related issues; state and local consumer and energy offices; and an energy bibliography.
The Do's and Don'ts of Home Insulation (434N)— 50¢. How to determine the type and amount of insulation needed and tips for installation; importance of moisture retarders; other ways to save including storm windows, weather-stripping, and caulking.
Heat Recovery Ventilation for Housing (174N)— $2.25. How newly developed air-to-air heat exchangers work; how to choose and install a system that fits homeowner needs.
Landscaping to Cut Fuel Costs (435N)—50¢. How to plant trees and shrubs to reduce heating and cooling costs as well as noise and air pollution; discusses foundation planting, windbreak benefits, location and choice of plants.

Money Saving Tips for Home Appliances (445N)—
50¢. How to buy, including information on
energy usage, warranties, service contracts, and
how to complain.

Solar Greenhouses and Sunspaces (176N)—$2.25.
How to design, build, and use greenhouses and
sunspaces to help heat your house; advice on
ventilation, growing plants, and safety. Lists
demonstration projects and other sources of
help.

Weatherize Your Mobile Home (422N)—50¢. How
to heat and cool efficiently; discusses overall
thermal performance standards; reinsulating the
roof cavity, side walls, and floors; best location
for comfort and safety.

Window Insulation (177N)—$2.50. Because glass
is a very poor insulator, windows let in much
heat and cold. This book will help you sort
through the options that are now available to cut
that energy loss.

HOME HEATING AND ENERGY CONSERVATION

EPA Inquiries Center

Below are several freebies available from: Public
Inquiries Center (PM211b), U.S. Environmental
Protection Agency, Washington, DC 20460.

Get the Most From Your Gas Heating Dollar—this
pamphlet answers the most commonly asked
questions about conservation, pollution, and
potential safety hazards of typical gas-heating
equipment.

Get the Most From Your Heating Oil Dollar—this
booklet shows how proper servicing can cut
costs as well as pollution.

*Wood Stove Features and Operation Guides for
Cleaner Air*—this pamphlet gives tips for choosing and installing a stove. It also shows how to
choose the best kind of wood as well as proper
operating procedures.

Energy Technical Information Center

The following publications are available free, as
long as supplies last, from: Department of Energy,
Technical Information Center, P.O. Box 62, Oak
Ridge, TN 37830/615-576-1305.

*Conserve Hot Water—Residential Hot Water Con-
servation Tips*

*Consumers Resource Handbook—General Publi-
cation on Wide-Ranging Conservation Materials
and Actions*

*How to Improve the Efficiency of Your Oil-Fired
Furnace*

How to Keep Warm and Cut Your Fuel Bill
How to Understand Your Utility Bill
*Infrared–An Energy Tool—Infrared Photography
System That Pinpoints Heat Loss*
Insulation
*Model Code for Energy Conservation in New
Building Construction*
Tips For Energy Savers
Winter Survival

Energy Office, Department of Agriculture

The following publications are available free of
charge, as long as supplies last, from: Energy
Office, Department of Agriculture, Washington,
DC 20250.

How to Determine Your Insulation Needs
*Save Heating and Cooling Dollars with Weather-
stripping and Caulking*
*How to Save Money with Storm Doors and
Windows*
What to Look for in Selecting Insulation
How to Install Insulation for Ceilings
How to Install Insulation for Walls
*How to Install Insulation for the Floor and Base-
ment*
*Solving Moisture Problems with Vapor Barriers
and Ventilation*
*Weatherize Your Mobile Home to Keep Costs
Down, Comfort Up*
Tips on Financing Home Weatherization
*Keeping Home Heating and Cooling Equipment in
Top Shape*
Landscaping to Cut Fuel Costs
Home Management Tips to Cut Heating Costs
*Firewood for Your Fireplace, Selection, Purchase,
Use*

HOME MAINTENANCE AND SAFETY

Department of Agriculture

The following publications are available, as long as
supplies last, from: Department of Agriculture,
Office of Governmental and Public Affairs, Publications Division, Washington, DC 20250/202-447-
2791.

Roofing Farm Buildings ($1.50)
Home Heating-Systems, Fuels, and Controls
($1.75)
*Wood Siding, Installing, Finishing, and Maintain-
ing* ($1.50)
*Wood Decay in Houses—How to Prevent and
Control It* ($2.75)
Home Construction—How to Reduce Costs ($2.50)
Renovate an Old House? ($3.00)

Consumer Information Center

The publications listed below are available, either free of charge or for a minimal fee, from: Consumer Information Center, P.O. Box 100, Pueblo, CO 81002.

Aluminum and Vinyl Sidings on Historic Buildings (193N)—$1.00. Also useful for anyone who is thinking about adding siding. Tells about costs, energy, durability, safety, and other factors.

Asbestos in the Home (178N)—$2.75. What asbestos is and the dangers; how you can tell if there is asbestos in your home; and what to do about it.

Chain Saw Safety (415N)—50¢. Important safety tips for selection and use.

Family Work and Storage Areas Outside the Home (446N)—50¢. How to use space more efficiently and build different types of sheds.

Home Electrical Safety Audit (416N)—50¢. How to identify and correct electrical safety problems.

Home Fire Safety (417N)—50¢. How to reduce the risk, including installation of a smoke detector, what to do if a fire breaks out.

How to Crimeproof Your Home (179N)—$2.50. How to use landscaping, lighting, doors, windows, locks, and alarm systems to protect your home or apartment; special safeguards while on vacation.

In the Event of a Flood (588N)—Free. What to do during a flood and how to minimize loss of life and property.

Subterranean Termites (181N)—$2.50. How to recognize them and identify damage to wood; how to prevent and control them.

Wood Siding (182N)—$1.50. Tells why wood siding is still a good choice and gives tips for selecting, installing, maintaining, and refinishing.

Federal Emergency Management Agency

The 2 publications described below are available free of charge from: Federal Emergency Management Agency, P.O. Box 8181, Washington, DC 20024.

Fire Safety in Your Mobile Home—this provides safety tips and procedures for dealing with potential fire hazards in a mobile home.

What You Should Know About Smoke Detectors—this describes why you need a detector, how they work, which types are the most effective and why, and where to install them.

HUD Service Center

A free booklet entitled *Fixing Up Your Home and How To Finance It* provides tips for dealing with contractors and describes the government's Title I Home Improvement Loans which finance up to $51,000 for 15 years. To obtain a copy write: HUD Service Center, U.S. Department of Housing and Urban Development, Room B-258, Washington, DC 20410.

TAX CONSIDERATIONS FOR HOMEOWNERS

Internal Revenue Service

A variety of publications of interest to homeowners are available free of charge from your local Internal Revenue Service Office, or by calling 1-800-555-1212 and asking the operator to give you the toll-free Internal Revenue Service number for your area. Examples of publications include:

Condominiums and Cooperative Apartments, Tax Information on
Energy Tax Credits for Individuals
Homeowners, Tax Information for
Moving Expenses
Rental Property
Sales and Other Disposition of Assets
Selling or Buying Your Home, Tax Information on

Household Tips and Information

Uncle Sam offers several resources helpful to the homemaker, a few of which are described below.

Extension Service

The Department of Agriculture's extension program has a wealth of information available ranging from creating a better home to curing diseases of pets, plants and lawns. You can get information in person, by telephone and by mail. For help in finding your local county agent contact: Executive Officer, USDA/ES, Room 340A, Administration Building, Washington, DC 20250. 202-447-4111.

Family Economics
A staff of experts researches such topics as the economic aspects of family living, family resources, economic problems of families, the relationship of family budget items to each other, the use of food, clothing and textiles, and the efficient management of money and time. Free publications are also available. Contact: Family Economics Research Group, ARS, 6505 Belcrest Rd., Federal Building, Room 442A, Hyattsville, MD 20782/ 301-436-8461.

Help For The Homemaker
The U.S. Department of Agriculture publishes hundreds of books to aid the farmer, suburbanite, homemaker and consumer. The most popular publications include:

Your Money's Worth in Foods ($2.25)
Home Canning of Fruits and Vegetables ($3.25)
Home Freezing of Fruits and Vegetables ($3.50)
Nutritive Value of Foods ($2.25)
Growing Vegetables in the Home Garden ($3.25)

For copies of any of the above publications contact: Superintendent of Documents, Government Printing Office, Washington, DC 20402/ 202/783-3238.

Household Employees and Social Security
This booklet shows how to comply with the law requiring you to deduct Social Security taxes and report wages of your household employee (such as a maid, cook, cleaning lady or gardener) and pay them $50 or more in wages during a 12-month calendar year. Free from your local Social Security Administration office listed in your telephone book.

Publications from the Consumer Information Center
These publications are available from the Consumer Information Center, Pueblo, CO 81002:

Can Your Kitchen Pass the Food Storage Test? (537N)—Free. Checklist of food storage hazards and how to correct them.
Do Yourself a Flavor (538N)—Free. Tips for cooking with herbs and spices; includes chart on herb blends, saltless seasonings, and herbs that go well with different meats.
How to Buy Economically: A Food Buyer's Guide (436N)—50¢. How to cut costs on meat, poultry, eggs, milk, fruits and vegetables; months during which you can get the best buys on a variety of fruits and vegetables.
Irradiation Proposed to Treat Food. (525N)—Free. FDA's proposal to expand the use of radiation treatment for foods such as fresh fruits, vegetables, and spices.
Making Food Dollars Count (409N)—50¢. Two-week plan, including recipes, to help the shopper on a limited budget meet nutritional needs.
Microwave Oven Radiation (539N)—Free. Information on microwave radiation and safe oven operation.
What's New About Care Labels (443N)—50¢. How to read and understand the instructions on care labels for washing, drying, ironing, bleaching, and cleaning newly purchased clothing.

Stains and Spots
Help is available for consumers who want to know how to remove stains from all types of fabric. For a free booklet and information, contact: Superintendent of Documents, Government Printing Office, Washington, DC 20402/202/783-3238.

Pets and Plants

Concerned about how to care for your pets and plants? The government has lots of expertise it will share with you for the asking. Described below are some examples.

Animal and Plant Health Inspection Service
This agency protects and improves animal and plant health by administering federal laws and regulations dealing with animal and plant health and quarantine, humane treatment of animals and the eradication of pests and diseases. APHIS also administers laws concerning the humane handling of livestock and poultry in interstate commerce, and governing the transportation, sale and handling of dogs, cats, and circus and zoo animals

intended for use in laboratory research or for exhibition. Contact: Information Division, Animal and Plant Health Inspection Service, Department of Agriculture, Washington, DC 20250/202-447-3977.

Food and Drug Administration (FDA)

FDA insures that veterinary preparations, drugs and devices are safe and effective and also insures that animal and pet food is safe and properly labeled. Contact: Bureau of Veterinary Medicine, Department of Health and Human Services, 5600 Fishers Lane, Rockville, MD 20857/301-443-5363.

Help for Sick Plants or Animals

Free technical assistance is available to aid in diagnosing and curing diseases of plants or animals. Services range from telephone consultations and free literature to analyzing your pet's stool or your plant's leaves or soil. For help in locating your local County Cooperative Extension Service office contact: Executive Officer, Department of Agriculture, SEA, Room 33A, Administration Building, Washington, DC 20250/202-447-3304.

Gardening Publications

Described below is a sampling of gardening literature available from: Consumer Information Center, P.O. Box 100, Pueblo, CO 81002.

Growing Cauliflower and Broccoli (191N)—$1.00. Covers the different strains of both vegetables plus their growing needs, fertilizing, weed and insect control, harvesting, and packing.

Growing Fruits and Nuts (439N)—50¢. Illustrated guide to selecting, planting, and maintaining fruit trees, nut trees, and berry plants.

Growing Vegetables in Containers (440N)—50¢. For the small-scale gardener, tips on types of containers, soil, planting, and care.

Growing Vegetables in the Home Garden (142N)—$3.25. Everything you need to know about planning, planting, and caring for more than 50 different kinds of vegetables.

Landscaping Around Home—Get Help, Plan Carefully (431N)—50¢. What to consider when planning for a small yard or a few acres; how to draw a landscape design; other information sources.

Plant A Tree (441N)—50¢. Twenty questions to ask yourself when choosing a tree for your yard; plus advice on planting and caring for it.

Pruning Shade Trees and Repairing Their Injuries (144N)—$1.00. The basics of caring for trees: seasons and techniques for pruning, repairing

tree injuries, necessary equipment, and much more.

Selecting and Growing House Plants (145N)—$2.50. Illustrated guide for 61 varieties of foliage, succulent and flowering plants; instructions on potting, watering, fertilizing and propagating.

Weed Control in Lawns and Other Turf (146N)—$2.00. How to discourage weed growth and help the lawn to flourish. Includes sketches of 23 common weeds and identifies the most effective herbicides for treatment.

Year-Round Gardening with a Greenhouse (442N)—50¢. Where to get building plans, how to heat, ventilate, and shade; how to plant and cultivate flowers and tomatoes.

Organic Farming and Gardening

A free bibliography on this subject containing over two hundred citations is available from: National Agricultural Library, 10301 Baltimore Boulevard, Beltsville, MD 20705/301-344-3704.

Pet and Plant Publications

Technical reports and literature of interest to animal dealers, farmers, travel agents, animal and plant professionals, and pet owners are available free of charge from: Animal and Plant Health Inspection Service (APHIS). Described below are freebies of interest to the general public. For information, a copy of these materials or APHIS' free publications catalogue, contact: USDA, APHIS, Information Division, 6505 Belcrest Road, Room 732, Hyattsville, MD 20782/301-436-7776.

Travelers' Tips—written for overseas travelers, this lists what food, plant, and animal products can and cannot be brought into the United States from foreign countries. It is available in English, Spanish, Italian and Japanese.

Don't Move Gypsy Moth—directed toward individuals moving out of a gypsy-moth infested area, this describes regulations governing the movement of outdoor household articles that may harbor gypsy moths and ways to inspect these articles. Color illustrations and a checklist are included.

Importing a Pet Bird—this describes the rules for bringing in a pet bird, identifies government agencies involved, and lists addresses of ports where pet birds may enter. It also discusses fees, the quarantine period and special exceptions.

Plant Protection and Quarantine—this publication discusses overall Plant Protection and Quarantine missions, specific programs, and the people who carry them out.

Veterinary Services: Protecting America's Animal Health—written for farmers and the general public, this provides basic information on the activities and programs of APHIS' Veterinary Services.

Careers for Veterinarians—designed for recruiting college students, this offers descriptions of positions for veterinarians in the Department of Agriculture.

The Animal Welfare Act, How it Protects Your Dog and Cat—this leaflet explains how the law provides for the humane handling, shipping,

care, and treatment of dogs, cats, and other warmblooded animals.

Licensing and Registration Under the Animal Welfare Act—this publication tells those who buy or sell animals, exhibit them to the public, or use them in experiments, whether or not their activities are regulated by the Animal Welfare Act.

Pets—They Need Proper Care to Travel by Air—this freebie tells shippers, airlines, veterinarians, and others involved in preparing and consigning animals for shipment what the Animal Welfare Act requires.

Travel and Recreation in the USA

Whether you enjoy diving, bird-watching, hiking, camping or visiting historical sites, the Federal Government has something for you. It has prepared hundreds of freebies—from maps to safety guides—to help you plan your trips and recreational activities. You can also be a guest of Uncle Sam at parks and wildlife refuges throughout the U.S.—including the U.S. Virgin Islands.

Aids to Navigation
Your U.S. Coast Guard district can give you a free copy of "Local Notice to Mariners" which includes: information on establishments, changes and discontinuances of aids to navigation in the United States, its territories and possessions; and reports on channel conditions, obstructions to navigation, danger areas and new charts. Another free publication, "Aids to Navigation," explains the significance of the colors of beacons and buoys, of the variety of light and fog signal characteristics, and of the system of electronic aids to navigation. Contact: Marine Information Branch, Short Range Aids to Navigation Division, Office of Navigation, Coast Guard, Department of Transportation, 2100 2nd Street NW, Room 1414, Washington, DC 20593/202-426-9566.

Airline Passenger Services
This office is responsible for airline consumer protection matters including consumer assistance and consumer protection regulations. Staff will provide information and resolve complaints with regard to delayed and cancelled flights, overbooking, lost baggage, smoking, flight cancellation, refunds, and charter flights. Contact: Consumer Affairs Division, Office of Governmental Affairs, Department of Transportation, 400 7th Street SW,

Room 10405, Washington, DC 20590/202-755-2220.

Airline Safety
Airline passengers who have inquiries or complaints regarding airplane safety should contact: Community and Consumer Liaison Division, Office of Public Affairs, Federal Aviation Administration, Department of Transportation, 800 Independence Avenue, SW, Washington, DC 20591/202-426-1960.

Airline Tariffs and Routes
Information on airline carriers' passenger and cargo operations can be obtained from: Public Reference Room, Department of Transportation, 400 7th Street SW, Room 4107, Washington, DC 20590/202-426-7634.

Archeological Projects
For information on archeologic projects being conducted in the Western states, contact: Preservation Office, Bureau of Reclamation, Office of Environmental Affairs, MS D-151, Department of the Interior, P.O. Box 25007, Denver Federal Center, Denver, CO 80225/303-234-4348.

Atlas, National

The National Atlas of the U.S., a wonderful vacation planning aid, is a looseleaf collection of full-color maps and charts showing physical features such as landforms, geology, soil, vegetation, climate and environmental hazards such as landslides. Economic, social and cultural data are also presented. Sixty percent of the Atlas is digitized. Contact: National Atlas Program Manager, Geological Survey, National Center, MS 514, Reston, VA 22092/703-860-6283.

Automobile Energy Efficiency

For information on the energy efficiency of new passenger cars and approaches to improving it, contact: Office of Automotive Fuel Economy Standards, Rulemaking, National Highway Traffic Safety Administration, Department of Transportation, 400 7th Street SW, Room 6124, Washington, DC 20590/202-426-0846.

Biking and Hiking Maps

Brochures with maps of trails throughout the National Park Service are available free of charge. When placing your order, specify the geographical area you are interested in. Contact: U.S. Department of the Interior, 18th and C Streets NW, Room 1013, Washington, DC 20240/202-343-4747. (Note: If you call, you will at first hear a recording. Stay on the line if you wish to speak with someone.)

Boating Information

Information and technical assistance is available on boating. The following free publications can also be obtained:

Federal Requirements for Recreational Boats— detailed information on such items as fire extinguishers, personal flotation devices, lighting, safe boating tips, and marine sanitation devices.
Suddenly in Command—basics of how to run a boat, how to use emergency equipment, and what to do in case of trouble.
Marine Communication for the Recreational Boater
Trailer-Boating—A Primer
Visual Distress Signals
Passport to Pleasure Cruising
U.S. Coast Guard Boating Safety Newsletter
Boating Statistics
Cold Water Drowning—A New Lease on Life
First Aid for the Boatman
Hypothermia and Cold Water Survival
This Is the Seal of Safety
Emergency Repairs Afloat

Safety Standards for the Backyard Boat Builders
Navigational Rules—International—Inland

Contact: Boating Information Branch, Office of Boating Safety, Coast Guard, Department of Transportation, G-BA2, 2100 2nd Street SW, Washington, DC 20593/202-472-2373.

Boating Lessons

A variety of free courses, ranging from 1 to 13 classes, on safe boating are offered by the U.S. Coast Guard. For further information contact: Your local U.S. Coast Guard Office or Commandant (G-BAU-1), U.S. Coast Guard, Washington, DC 20592/202-426-1077.

Boating on the Saint Lawrence River

Boating information is given in the publication *Pleasure Craft Guide—the Seaway.* Available free from: Public Information Office, St. Lawrence Seaway Corporation, P.O. Box 520, Massena, NY 13662/315-764-3200.

Camping—Accommodations

Are you planning a camping trip? The book *Visitor Facilities and Services in the National Parks* will give you ideas on where to go and what to expect once you get there. It even tells you about the campground in the Virgin Islands. The cost of the book is $3.00 plus $1.05 postage and handling. Available from: Conference of Concessioners, Mammoth Cave, KY 42559.

Camping in the National Forests and Grasslands

For general information and a list of addresses for camping facilities in the country's 154 national forests and 19 national grasslands, contact: Office of Information, Forest Service, Department of Agriculture, Room 3238, South Building, Washington, DC 20250/202-447-3957.

Camping on the Public Lands

A fold-out map and charts with practical information on 275 campgrounds in the western United States is available for $2.00 from: Consumer Information Service, Pueblo, CO 81009.

Camping Publications:

The following publications are published by the Department of the Interior and are useful for campers:

Camping in the National Park System—$1.50
Guide and Map, National Parks of the U.S.—$.70.
Campground Reservations—free from: Department of the Interior, National Park Service,

18th and C Streets NW, Room 3043, Washington, DC 20240/203-343-7394.

The Complete Guide to America's National Parks—available from: National Park Foundation, P.O. Box 57473, Washington, DC 20037/202-785-4500 for $9.25.

Diving Guides
If you are planning to do some serious diving, two useful manuals are available. Put out by the U.S. Navy, they are recognized worldwide as the most authoritative works on the subject. Volume I on Air Diving is $11.00 and Volume II on Mixed-Gas Diving is $12.00. Contact: Superintendent of Documents, U.S. Government Printing Office, Washington, DC 20402/202-783-3238.

Free Accommodations for Youth Groups
Youth groups can obtain free overnight accommodations—ranging from camp sites to beds in barracks—from the U.S. Air Force. Food service is often available on a cost recovery basis. The Air Force will also provide special programs for youth, including participation in training exercises, airplane rides and tours—also free of charge. For more details see entry "Free Accommodations, Airplane Rides and more for Youth Groups" in the Best of the Freebies section of the Sampler.

Great Outdoors
Recreation and Outdoor Activities (SB-017) catalogs Federal government publications on biking, water sports, national recreation areas, winter activities and more. It can be obtained at no cost from: Superintendent of Documents, U.S. Government Printing Office, Washington, DC 20402.

Happy Trails
There are 452 recreational, scenic and historical trails within the National Park System, the National Forest System and State Park Systems. Trail guides and other information about these trails is available from: Division of Natural Resource System Planning, HCRS, Department of the Interior, 440 G Street NW, Room 203, Washington, DC 20243/202-272-3566.

Historic Landmarks Directory
If you are interested in visiting historic landmarks on your vacation, you may be interested in a complete listing of all certified historic properties subtitled "National Registry of Historic Places." The cost is $22.00 for Volume I and $19.00 for Volume II. Available from: Superintendent of Documents U.S. Government Printing Office, Washington, DC 20402/202-783-3238.

Historical Site Brochures
Illustrated brochures are available describing individual sites of historic and cultural value which have made significant contributions to American history. Contact: Office of Public Affairs, Water and Power Resources Service, Department of the Interior, Room 7642, Washington, DC 20240/202-343-4662.

How's the Weather?
The following publications will help you better identify and cope with potential weather hazards, you may encounter in your travel.

The Amateur Weather Forecaster—the basics for observing, recording and forecasting present, past and future weather.

Spotter's Guide for Identifying and Reporting Severe Local Storms—describes and illustrates important cloud features which commonly precede tornadoes and severe weather events.

Winter Storms and *Rules for Riding Out Winter Storms Wallet Card*—shows how to deal with storms on the road or in your car.

Lightning the Under-rated Killer and *Lightning Safety Wallet Card*—describes causes and effects of lightning and how it is the chief killer in stormy weather.

Tornado Safety—helps to understand the tornado hazard, and provides lifesaving safety precautions.

Floods, Flash Floods and Warnings—describes safety rules and warning signs for the hazard which annually drives about 75,000 people from their homes, and damages more than $250 million worth of property.

For copies contact: Office of Public Affairs, National Oceanic and Atmospheric Administration, U.S. Department of Commerce, Room 6013, Washington, DC 20230.

Indian Arts and Crafts Development
Visit an Indian Arts and Crafts Museum on your vacation! Three museums are operated by the Indian Arts and Crafts Board. They serve Indians and the general public, and their locations are: the Sioux Indian Museum in Rapid City, South Dakota; the Museum of the Plains Indian in Browning, Montana; and the Southern Plains Indian Museum in Anadarko, Oklahoma, Contact: General Manager, Indian Arts and Crafts Board, Department of the Interior, Washington, DC 20240/202-343-2773.

Land Between the Lakes

Land Between the Lakes is 40-mile-long peninsula located between Kentucky and Barkley Lakes in west Kentucky and Tennessee. In its 18th year of operation, Land Between the Lakes is managed by TVA to provide an outstanding outdoor recreation experience as well as a living laboratory for the study of fundamental conservation and resource use principles. A visitors' center features solar-assisted systems which provides most of the facility's heating and hot water needs and 30 percent of the cooling. The center also has a windmill that produces power which is stored in batteries used by electric cars operated at Land Between the Lakes. The Center is used for exhibits on solar energy and other areas of interest, and there is a domed theatre for special presentations. TVA offers recreation programs at Land Between the Lakes for everyone, but tailors many programs to groups with special needs. Contact: Land Between the Lakes, Office of Natural Resources, Tennessee Valley Authority, Golden Pond, Kentucky 42231/502-924-5602.

Maps and Brochures

Most Congressmen have an abundant supply of free pamphlets and tourist information about resorts and national parks in their home state. Contact: Your Congressman for information and maps about your home area and the Congressional representative of other places in the U.S. you want to visit.

Maps and Charts

Recreation maps of TVA lakes, which indicate detailed routes to shoreline recreation areas, are available. Single copies are free on request. Each request should specify the lake(s) of interest. Navigation charts and maps for the major lakes have also been published by TVA. They show water depths, the location of public recreation areas, boat docks, resorts, and roads. Charts for the mainstream lakes of the Tennessee River show navigation channels, buoys, lights, and other navigation aids. Maps for tributary lakes show the numbered signs TVA has installed at strategic locations on shore to aid fishermen and recreation boaters in locating their position. Navigation maps and charts may be purchased from: TVA Maps, Knoxville, TN 37902/615-632-2357 or Chattanooga, TN 37401/615-755-2133, or use the hotline 800-362-9250 in Tennessee; 800-251-9242 outside Tennessee.

National Park Information Center

The Technical Information Center has information on National Park properties including 300,000 maps and design drawings, and 25,000 scientific and technical reports. Contact: Technical Information Center, National Park Service, Department of the Interior, Denver Service Center, 755 Parfet Street, Denver, CO 80225/303-234-2653.

National Recreation Data Base

Recreation Information Management (RIM) contains data about every National Forest recreation site—22,000 in total—in the U.S. The following data can be retrieved for each site: name, location, capacity, size, description of environment and facilities, hours of use, number of visitors, dates when area is least populated, and travel directions for reaching site.

Most of the RIM data is available in the form of reports, booklets, books and periodicals. Special searches will be done if material does not already exist in hard copy. All services and materials are free. Contact: U.S. Department of Agriculture, Forest Service, Recreation Management Staff, P.O. Box 2417, Washington, DC 20013/202-447-4313.

Natural Resource Management System

The National Resource Management System (NRMS) contains information and statistics about 400 recreation areas in the U.S. Information provided about each site includes data on camping, picnicking, boating, fishing, land and water resources, facilities, location and travel distance, ownership, use by month in recreation days, staffing, activities pursued by visitors, fees charged and much more. Information can be retrieved by site name, geographical area and other data cited.

Data is collected annually and available from 1978 to the present. Searches and printouts are available free of charge. The Corps of Engineers also has free attractive brochures with maps and information about each of its sites. Contact: Army Corps of Engineers, HQ USACE (DAEN-CWO-R), 20 Massachusetts Avenue NW, Washington, DC 20314/202-272-0247.

Nautical Charts

Nautical charts, in various scales, cover the coastline of the United States, its territories and possessions, and the Great Lakes. Six free catalogs, which provide descriptions and ordering information are: 1) Atlantic and Gulf coasts; 2) Pacific Coast including Hawaii, Guam and Samoa Islands; 3) Alaska, including Aleutian Islands; 4) Great Lakes and Adjacent Waterways; 5) Bathymetric Maps and Special Purpose Charts, and 6) Catalog of Aeronautical Charts and Related Publications. Contact: National Ocean Service, Distribution Branch, Riverdale, MD 20737/ 301-436-6990.

Outdoor Activities

General information is available on camping, fishing, hiking, and backpacking trips on 475 million acres of public land. Assistance is available on recreational resources, cultural resources, visual resources, and natural history resources. Contact: Division of Recreation, Bureau of Land Management, Department of the Interior, 18th and C Streets NW, Room 3660, Washington, DC 20240/202-343-9353.

Outdoor Recreation

For information on National Park Service facilities for camping, swimming, boating, mountain climbing, hiking, and fishing, contact: Office of Public Affairs, National Park Service, Department of the Interior, Room 3043, Washington, DC 20240/ 202-343-7394.

Outdoor Survival

Survival, Evasion, and Escape was intended for Army personnel. However, this manual contains useful information for outdoorsmen as well. It covers firemaking and cooking, finding food and water, survival in cold weather, and much more. Available for $9.00 from: Superintendent of Documents, U.S. Government Printing Office, Washington, DC 20402/ 202-783-3238.

Park Passport

The Golden Eagle Passport ($10) allows holders and people accompanying them to enter national parks, monuments and recreation areas free. People over 62 years of age can receive a free lifetime passport. Passport may be purchased at most federally operated recreation areas, National Park Service regional offices or at: Information Office, Department of the Interior, 18th and C Streets NW, Room 1013, Washington, DC 20240/202-343-4747. The Golden Eagle Passport is good for one year only.

Park Rangers

Most National Parks offer free educational programs for visitors. Taught by Park Rangers, the programs generally introduce visitors of all ages to the natural, cultural, and historical significance of a park. Classes range from bodysurfing lessons to nature walks, to slide shows of an area's history. For further information check with the Park's Information Office or contact: Activities and Protection Division, National Park Service, Department of the Interior, Room 3324, Washington, DC 20240/202-343-4874.

Physical Fitness and Sports

The President's Council on Physical Fitness and Sports will supply information and expertise to help you establish physical fitness programs. Available free publications include:

> *Aqua Dynamics: Physical Conditioning*
>   *Through Water Exercise*
> *Exercise and Weight Control*
> *An Introduction to Physical Fitness*
> *Physical Education—A Performance Checklist*
> *An Introduction to Physical Fitness*
> *The Physically Underdeveloped Child*
> *Youth Physical Fitness—$4.75*

Contact: President's Council on Physical Fitness and Sports, Department of Health and Human Services, 450 5th Street, Suite 7103, Washington, DC 20001/202-272-3430.

Police Radar

For those traveling by car, a new study has recently been released on the reliability of police radar. For a copy of the report *Police Traffic Radar* contact: National Bureau of Standards, Public Information Division, Department of Commerce, Washington, DC 20234/301-921-3161.

Presidential Libraries and Museums

Each of the seven libraries below exhibit historic documents and provide reference services on presidential papers. The presidential museums are all housed in the same building as the library, except for the Gerald R. Ford Museum. Besides free pamphlets and other publications, historical memorabilia and souvenirs are sold at all of the Museums. The locations of these are:

Herbert Hoover Presidential Library—West Branch, IA 52358/319-643-5301.
Franklin D. Roosevelt Library—259 Albany Post Road, Hyde Park, NY 12538/914-229-8114.
Harry S. Truman Library—Highway 24 at Delaware Street, Independence, MO 64050/816-833-1400.
Dwight D. Eisenhower Library—Southeast 4th Street, Abilene, KS 67410/913-263-4751.
John F. Kennedy Library—Columbia Point, Boston, MA 02125/617-929-4500.
Lyndon B. Johnson Library—2313 Red River Street, Austin, TX 78705/512-482-5137.
Gerald R. Ford Library—1000 Beal Avenue, Ann Arbor, MI 48109/313-668-2218; Museum—303

Pearl Street NW, Grand Rapids, MI 49504/616-456-2675.

For information regarding the Richard M. Nixon Library or the James E. Carter Library contact: National Archives and Records Administration, 8th and Pennsylvania Avenue NW, Washington, DC 20408/202-523-3212.

Recreation Information Clearinghouse
The Heritage Conservation and Recreation Service (HCRS) Information Exchange is designed to assist practitioners, government agencies, nonprofit organizations, and individuals involved in recreation, cultural, and natural preservation. A free newsletter, *Technical Assistance Notifications,* announces the availability of studies, handbooks, audiovisuals, films, surveys, case studies, publications and training manuals. All services are free. Contact: National Park Service, Department of the Interior, 440 G Street NW, Room 307, Washington, DC 20243/202-272-3761.

Resort Guides
Free resort guides are available for various areas of the United States. They contain seasonal breakdown of weather and recreational opportunities. The guides stress elements of interest for each season, along with tables of activities best suited for each season. Contact: Resort Guides, National Oceanographic Data Center, NOAA/NESDIS, Department of Commerce, Washington, DC 20535/202-634-7500.

Sailing Correspondence Course
A $5.50 book, *The Skipper's Course,* includes an examination on water safety. Those who pass the exam are awarded a water safety certificate. The book is available from: Government Book Store#15, Majestic Building, 720 N. Main Street, Pueblo, CO 81003. For more details on the course, contact: Boating Auxiliary Division, Coast Guard, Department of Transportation, G-BAU, 2100 2nd Street SW, Washington, DC 20593/202-426-1077.

Saint Lawrence Seaway
The following publications are free:

The St. Lawrence Seaway—contains general and historical information in French and English; economic and port data, tool schedules for skippers and potential skippers; information in French and English for tourists traveling by automobile.
St. Lawrence Seaway Development Corporation Annual Report
Annual Traffic Report in the St. Lawrence Seaway—provides calendar year statistics on cargo vessels between Montreal and Lake Erie.
Seaway Regulations—operating manual and chart booklet for commercial vessels, rules and regulations and seaway toll schedule.

Contact: Public Information Office, St. Lawrence Seaway Development Corporation, P.O. Box 520, Massena, NY 13662/315-764-3200.

Space Shuttle Trips
While NASA is not yet taking reservations for the space shuttle, it does have an office coordinating opportunities for private citizens to fly on space shuttle missions. As opportunities develop, such as the first teacher in space, they will be announced in newspapers and on television. For a free fact sheet "Space Flight Participant Program" contact: Manager, Space Flight Participant Program, Mail Code ME, NASA Headquarters, Washington, DC 20546/202-453-2556.

Tips on Saving Gas
The following publications are free from the TIC Request Service, Technical Information Center, Department of Energy, P.O. Box 62, Oak Ridge, TN 37830/615-576-1305:

Gas Mileage Guide—annual information on EPA miles per gallon estimates for vehicles and a chart for calculating annual fuel costs for all new model cars.
How to Save Gasoline and Money—basic money and gas-saving tips, including choosing your next car, driving more effectively, planning your trips and caring for your car.
Gasoline More Miles per Gallon—shows methods of selecting gas, maintaining your car, improving performance, and lowering costs.

Tires—Safety and Saving Money
The Department of Transportation has rated over 2,500 tires on aspects of wear and safety. The results of the study, called the *Uniform Tire Quality Grading List,* is made available to the public through credit unions, public libraries, recreation associations, and consumer information offices. Free booklets explaining the grading system are available from the National Highway Traffic Safety Administration, 400 7th Street SW, Washington, DC 20590/202-426-0874 or 202-426-2768.

Toys for the Young Traveler—Free
Free litter bags, coloring sheets, song sheets,

photographs, posters, bike stickers, and wallet cards are available from: Woodsy Owl, Forest Service, USDA, Room 3248, South Building, P.O. Box 2417, Washington, DC 20013/ 202-475-3785.

Free badges, stickers and other children's toys are available by contacting: Smokey Bear Headquarters, U.S. Forest Service, P.O. Box 2417, Washington, DC 20013/202-235-8160.

Traffic Trends
The following publications are free:

Weekly Traffic Trends Press Release—monitors travel trends especially during periods of fuel shortfall;
Monthly Traffic Volume Trends—monitors travel trends over time.

Contact: Traffic Monitoring Branch, Highway Statistics Division, Office of Highway Planning, Federal Highway Administration, Department of Transportation, 400 7th Street SW, Room 3300, Washington, DC 20590/202-426-0160.

Transporting Plants Between States
Each state has separate rules and regulations for transporting plants across state boundaries. For information on a specific state's regulations, contact: Animal and Plant Health Inspection Service, Plant Protection and Quarantine, USDA, Room 1148, South Building, Washington, DC 20250/ 202-447-6190.

Travel Bibliographies
Travel and Tourism and *Recreational and Outdoor Activities* are free subject bibliographies which together list all travel publications sold by the U.S. government. To order contact: Superintendent of Documents, U.S. Government Printing Office, Washington, DC 20402/202-783-3238.

Travel by Bus
Discrimination, preferential treatment or prejudicial actions by interstate buses is illegal and should be reported to the Interstate Commerce Commission. Contact: Director, Office of Consumer Affairs, Interstate Commerce Commission, Washington, DC 20423/202-275-0860.

Travelers' Airline Rights
Fly Rights describes important consumer information about air fares, reservations and tickets, delayed and cancelled flights, overbooking, baggage, smoking and airline safety. This pamphlet (stock #003-006-00106-5) is available for $2.75 from: Superintendent of Documents, U.S. Gov-ernment Printing Office, Washington, DC 20402/202-783-3238.

Travel for the Handicapped
The Information on Handicapped Center has a guide to The National Capital Area called, *Access Washington Guide*. The office can also refer handicapped individuals to the appropriate centers for information on access to federal parks and recreation centers. Contact: Information on Handicapped, 605 G Street NW, Suite 202, Washington, DC 20001/ 202-347-4986.

Vacations Unlimited
This free leaflet catalogs many low-cost ($2.20–$7.00) travel publications available from the Federal government. Write for: *Vacations Unlimited,* Superintendent of Documents, U.S. Government Printing Office, Washington, DC 20402.

VIP Tours for Washington, DC Visitors
If you are planning to visit Washington, your congressman can arrange special VIP tours for you at the White House, the Federal Bureau of Investigation, the Department of State and other agencies. It means that you will not have to wait in lines, which can be very long during the tourist season. He or she can also arrange a pass for you to see Congress in session and see the U.S. Capitol.

Visiting Washington, DC
While in the nation's capital you might consider visiting the following popular sites; the Bureau of Engraving, the 13 Smithsonian Institution sites and zoo, the National Archives, the Library of Congress, the Botanic Garden, the National Aquarium in the Department of Commerce Building, the Museum and Indian Craft Shop in the Department of the Interior Building, the Pentagon and Arlington Cemetary, and the world's largest printing plant, the Government Printing Office, all described elsewhere in this book.

Visit Ghost Towns and Mines
The first ironmaking furnace in the original 13 colonies, replicas of early wooden derricks used for oil drilling in East Texas, Sutter's Mill in Northern California, open-pit iron mines in Minnesota and off-shore oil and gas wells in the Gulf Coast can all be visited by the public. For information on these and other new and old mines, contact: Office of Technical Information, Bureau of Mines, Department of the Interior, Columbia Plaza, Room 1035, Washington, DC 20241/202-634-1001.

Water Recreation Activities

A series of free brochures is available with a comprehensive list of dams and reservoirs showing available recreational facilities and principal recreational uses. There are 291 recreation areas, 4.4 million acres of land, 1.7 million acres of water surface, 12,268 miles of shoreline, 842 campgrounds, 767 picnic sites, 29,191 tent and trailer spaces, 142 swimming beaches, 704 boat ramps, and 13,852 boat slips. Available brochures include:

"Map No. 1"—recreation areas of Idaho, Oregon, and Washington

"Map No. 2"—recreation areas of Montana, Nebraska, South Dakota, North Dakota, and Wyoming

"Map No. 3"—recreation areas of Arizona, California, Utah, and Nevada

"Map No. 4"—recreation areas of Colorado, Kansas, Texas, Oklahoma, and New Mexico

Contact Office of Public Affairs, Bureau of Reclamation, Department of the Interior, Room 7644, Washington, DC 20240/202-343-4662.

Wilderness

The National Wilderness Preservation System consists of 25.5 million acres of roadless undeveloped lands which represent America's natural heritage. The land is open to the public, contains no commercial enterprises, and motorized access is prohibited. Contact: Recreation, Forest Service, USDA, Box 2417, Washington, DC 20013/202-447-3760.

Wildlife Refuges

A descriptive listing of more than 400 federally run wildlife refuges is available. The descriptions include location, types of recreation available, size of refuge and its primary species. Contact: Division of National Wildlife Refuges, Fish and Wildlife Service, Department of the Interior, Room 2024, Washington, DC 20240/202-343-4305.

Wild Rivers

For maps and other information describing the National Wild and Scenic River System contact: Rivers and Trails Division, National Park Service, Department of the Interior, 440 G Street NW, Room 203, Washington, DC 20243/ 202-426-6700.

Traveling Abroad

Thinking of going abroad? Through the Federal Government you can obtain country information, travel tips, cost-estimates, maps, foreign language training, partially subsidized travel, and much more. And once you get to your destination American Embassies and Consulates can be a source of assistance, too.

American Embassies and Consulates

As an American traveling abroad, you can obtain assistance from the American Embassy or Consulate closest to where you are staying. Embassy staff will help you if you suddenly become ill, are arrested, want to register your baby's birth, need an American document notarized, or if you need to make arrangements concerning a death. When possible, it is best to call the embassy to make an appointment to visit. For a complete listing of American Embassies, see the next section of the Sampler entitled "Selling Overseas."

American Schools and Hospitals Abroad

The Agency for International Development assists private U.S.-sponsored nonprofit schools, libraries and hospitals overseas that serve as study and demonstration centers for American ideas and practices in education and medicine. For a list of schools and hospitals contact: Office of American Schools and Hospitals Abroad, Bureau for Food for Peace and Voluntary Asssistance, Agency for International Development, 1400 Wilson Boulevard, Room 260, Rosslyn, VA 20523/703-235-1966.

Arts America

The International Communication Agency assists qualified artists and performers in arranging private tours overseas. Its aim is to present a balanced portrayal of the American scene. Some past activities have included: a major exhibition of American crafts shown in China; a modern dance company in the USSR, Spain, and Portugal; and a jazz ensemble in Nigeria, Senegal and Kenya. Contact: Arts Liaison Advisor, Office of the Associate Director for Programs, International Communication Agency, United States

Intelligence Agency, 301 4th Street SW, Room 568, Washington, DC 20547/202-485-2779.

Citizens Arrested Overseas

The Arrest Unit: monitors arrests and trials of Americans abroad to see that United States citizens are not abused; acts as a liaison with family and friends in the United States; sends money, messages, etc. (with written consent of arrestee); offers lists of lawyers; will forward money from the United States to a detainee; tries to assure that an American's rights under local laws are observed. Under the Emergency Medical and Dietary Assistance Program the federal government provides vitamin supplements to arrestees when necessary; grants emergency transfer for emergency medical care; and gives short-term feeding of two or three meals a day when arrestee is detained without funds to buy his or her own meals. Contact: Arrests Unit, Citizens Emergency Center, Overseas Citizens Service, Bureau of Consular Affairs, Department of State, 2201 C Street NW, Room 4800, Washington, DC 20520/202-632-5225.

Citizens Emergency Center

Emergency telephone assistance is available to United States citizens abroad needing help in the following areas:

ARRESTS—202-632-5225.

DEATHS—202-632-5225; staff will notify interested parties in the United States of the death abroad of United States citizens and assist in the arrangements for disposition of remains.

FINANCIAL ASSISTANCE—202-632-5225; money is provided for repatriation of destitute United States nationals, coordination of medical evacuation of nonofficial United States nationals from abroad; transmission of private funds in emergencies to destitute United States nationals abroad when commercial banking facilities are unavailable (all costs must be reimbursed).

SHIPPING AND SEAMEN—202-632-5225; this office is concerned with the protection of American vessels and seamen.

WELFARE AND WHEREABOUTS—202-632-5225; staff are involved in the search for nonofficial United States nationals who have not been heard from for an undue length of time and/or about whom there is special concern; transmission of emergency messages to United States nationals abroad. Contact: Overseas Citizen Services, Bureau of Consular Affairs, Department of State, 2201 C Street NW, Washington, DC 20520/202-632-3444.

Costs of Living Overseas

"U.S. Department of State Indexes of Living Costs Abroad and Quarter Allowances: A Technical Description" is a free quarterly publication which provides technical descriptions of the methods of compiling the indexes of living costs abroad, and gives post allowances based on these indexes, and quarter allowances and their use in the government overseas allowance program. Contact: Office of Productivity and Technology, Bureau of Labor Statistics, Department of Labor, 200 Constitution Avenue NW, Room S4214, Washington, DC 20212/202-523-9291.

Country Information Studies

For someone who wants to learn more than the typical travel books tell about a specific country, this series of books provide in-depth knowledge of the country being visited. The books describe the origins and traditions of the people and their social and national attitudes, as well as the economic, military, political and social systems, books you would enjoy reading both before and after visiting the country. For a more complete listing of the countries covered and price contact: Superintendent of Documents, U.S. Government Printing Office, Washington, DC 20402/202-783-3238.

Customs

For information on customs declarations and other legal issues of concern to overseas travelers, write for: *Know Before You Go,* U.S. Customs, P.O. Box 7407, Washington, DC 20044.

Foreign Country Background Notes

Background Notes on the Countries of the World is a series of short, factual pamphlets with information about a country's land, people, history, government, political conditions, economy, foreign relations, and U.S. policy. Each pamphlet also includes a factual profile, brief travel notes, a country map, and a reading list. Contact: Public Affairs Bureau, Department of State, Room 4827A, 2201 C Street NW, Washington, DC 20520/202-632-6575 for a free copy of *Background Notes* for the countries you plan to visit. This material is also available from the: Superintendent of Documents, U.S. Government Printing Office, Washington, DC 20402/202-783-3238. Single copies cost $1.50 or $32.00 for a set.

Foreign Language Materials

The Defense Language Institute Foreign Language Center (DLIFLC) has an academic library with holdings of about 100,000 books and periodicals in 50 different foreign languages. These materials are available through national inter-library loan programs. Your local librarian can furnish you with loan information.

Foreign Language Training
The Foreign Service Institute is an in-house educational institution for foreign service officers, members of their families and employees of other government agencies. It provides special training in 50 foreign languages. Its instructional materials (books and tapes) designed to teach modern foreign languages are available to the public. Lists of books, tapes and prices are available. Tapes are obtained through: National Audio Visual Center, General Services Administration, Order Section/AV, Washington, DC 20409/202-763-1891. Books are available from: Superintendent of Documents, U.S. Government Printing Office. Washington, DC 20402/202-783-3238.

Free Booklets for Travelers
The following book is available from: Publications Distribution, Bureau of Public Affairs, Department of State, 2201 C Street NW, Room 5815A, Washington, DC 20520/202-632-9859.

Travel Information: Your Trip Abroad—contains basic information, such as how to apply for a passport, customs tips, lodging information and how American consular officers can help you in an emergency.

The following publications are available from: Customs Office, P.O. Box 7118, Washington, DC 20044:

Customs Information
Bureau of Consular Affairs: Your Trip Abroad
Visa Requirements of Foreign Governments—lists entry requirements of U.S. citizens traveling as tourists, as well as where and how to apply for visas and tourist cards. Available from: Passport Services, Bureau of Consular Affairs, Department of State, 1425 K Street NW, Room G-62, Washington, DC 20524/202-783-8170.

Maps—Worldwide
Multicolor reference maps and wall charts on both communist and non-communist countries are produced by the Central Intelligence Agency. The maps identify a country's major roads, population density, major industries, locations of natural resources, and other specific features. Some maps are on specific topics such as clothing factories in China. They are available in a variety of sizes. GPO sells many of the maps for $3.50 and NTIS

for $7.50. Contact: Superintendent of Documents, U.S. Government Printing Office, Washington, DC 20402/202-783-3238 or National Technical Information Service, 5285 Port Royal Road, Springfield, VA 22161/703-487-4650.

Marriage, Birth and Death Records
The Bureau of Consular Affairs will provide upon request:

Consular Certificates of Witness to Marriage—This is merely a certificate indicating that a U.S. officer was present at a U.S. citizen's marriage abroad.
Reports of Birth—children born of American parents in a foreign country can have a Report of Birth Abroad on file with the Consular Affairs office if the parents have made a report to the American consul in the country of birth.
Reports of Death—since 1979 reports of death of Americans abroad are on file with the Passport Services files if the death is brought to the attention of an American consul.

Contact: Bureau of Consular Affairs, Department of State, 2201 C Street NW, Room 4800, Washington, DC 20520/202-632-3666, or contact the consul in the American Embassy if you are overseas.

Overseas Citizen Services
This office is responsible for activities relating to the protection and assistance of U.S. citizens abroad. It provides help in the event of an arrest, the death of a U.S. citizen, conservation of his/her personal estate abroad, and the repatriation to the U.S. of citizens who are destitute or ill. The Bureau serves as liaison with other government agencies in such matters as payment of benefits to beneficiaries residing abroad, and in determinations of the acquisition or loss of U.S. citizenship by persons outside the U.S. It provides notarial functions and related services to U.S. citizens abroad including coordinating with the U.S. Department of Justice to bring witnesses to U.S. courts. Contact: Overseas Citizen Services, Bureau of Consular Affairs, Department of State, 2201 C Street NW, Room 4800, Washington, DC 20520/202-632-3816.

Overseas Schools
For information about schooling and also teaching positions at U.S. Department of State schools, contact: International School Services (ISS), 126 Alexandria, P.O. Box 5910, Princeton, NJ 08540. For other information, contact: Office of Overseas

Schools, Bureau of Administration, Department of State, SAG, Room 234, Washington, DC 20520/703-235-9600.

Passport Information—Recorded Message
A recorded telephone message provides general information about what you need to apply for a passport. Call 202-783-8200. U.S. citizens and nationals can apply for passports at all passport agencies as well as post offices and federal and state courts authorized to accept passport applications.

Services For Americans Visiting, Living, and Voting Abroad
The Citizens Consular Services offers help for Americans visiting, living and doing business abroad. Examples of assistance are:

NOTARY PUBLIC SERVICES—includes administering oaths in depositions, affidavits, and other documents, and takes acknowledgement of signatures.

VOTING ASSISTANCE—includes help in obtaining absentee ballots and election information.

JUDICIAL ASSISTANCE—offers help in determining particular foreign laws, transmits letters, authenticates foreign documents, obtains documents abroad for legal purposes, retains lists of English-speaking lawyers, helps in the whereabouts and welfare search in child custody cases, in property claims, and in nationality and expatriation cases.

PASSPORT AND REGISTRATION SERVICES ABROAD—issues U.S. passports and travel documents to United States citizens and nationals abroad and registers U.S. citizens abroad.

CLAIMS ASSISTANCE—in the protection of property and other interests owned by U.S. nationals abroad. Answers claims inquiries including those regarding foreign government restitution/compensation. Provides advice on methods of obtaining documents from abroad as property claims evidence. Handles inquiries concerning private trade complaints.

CHILD CUSTODY DISPUTES—provides welfare and whereabouts information concerning children involved in custody disputes.

ESTATES—guidance to consular office and heirs concerning estates in foreign countries of U.S. nationals who die abroad when there is no qualified legal representative present. Consular services include handling inquiries on the transfer of estates from the United States to foreign countries.

FEDERAL BENEFITS FUNCTION—assures the receipt of U.S. federal checks abroad.

Other services include providing tax forms and tax information and protecting a person's material remains should he or she die while traveling alone overseas. Contact: Citizens Consular Services, Bureau of Consular Affairs, Department of State, 2201 C Street NW, Room 4800, Washington, DC 20520/202-632-3666 for a brochure and more detailed information about these services.

If you are an American in need of assistance while traveling in a foreign country, contact a consular officer at the American Embassy or Consulate nearest you at once. They will be most willing to assist you. In the U.S. you might contact the Citizens Emergency Assistance number before departure for any last-minute updates on the country you are visiting. That office can be reached by calling: 202-632-5225.

Smithsonian National Associate Program
Participants in the Smithsonian's National Associate Program (SNAP) can take advantage of foreign travel opportunities. For information contact: Smithsonian National Associate Program, Smithsonian Institution, 900 Jefferson Drive SW, Washington, DC 20560/ 202-357-1350.

Status of the World's Nations
This geographic bulletin, revised in September 1980, and a separate map entitled "Political Map of the World" provide country name, United Nations membership, capital, population, area, dependencies and areas of special sovereignty, and date of independence (since 1943) for nations of the world. Cost is $3.25. Contact: Superintendent of Documents, U.S. Government Printing Office, Washington, DC 20402/202-783-3238.

Tax Help
Although you may be out of the country during filing season, the IRS will still help you figure out your taxes. They make it easier for Americans living and traveling abroad by extending the filing date (but not payment date) to June 15. The following services are available:

EMBASSY TAX ASSISTANCE OFFICES—during the filing season temporary tax assistance offices are set up at centrally located embassies in cities with a heavy concentration of Americans. IRS officials also spend a large part of January through June traveling through their post's neighboring towns and cities to conduct workshops and help U.S. citizens prepare their taxes. Often it is possible to schedule an appointment to meet with the IRS tax assistant by contacting the American Embassy closest to you.

FOREIGN OPERATIONS DISTRICT OFFICE—Washington, DC, assists taxpayers living or traveling abroad. The office will answer any question you may have about your taxes, and they will send you copies of IRS forms or publications you need. Upon request, the office also will send you a complete schedule of where its IRS representatives will be during the filing season. To contact the office write: Foreign Operations District Office, Internal Revenue Service, 1325 K Street NW, Washington, DC 20225.

OBTAINING TAX FORMS—most embassies have copies of the basic tax forms and packets, but if your embassy does not have a tax form or publication you need, the fastest way to obtain a copy is by writing to the IRS Distribution Center. Depending on where you live you would write: (European residents) Forms Distribution Center, Caller Number 848, Atlanta, GA 20270 and (Pacific residents) Forms Distribution Center, P.O. Box 12626, Fresno, CA 93778.

VITA CENTERS—are located on most military bases overseas. The program usually is run from the Judge Advocate General's Office, and it consists of IRS-trained volunteers helping military personnel prepare their taxes. VITA volunteers on military bases are knowledgeable about the special deductions available to members of the military and their families.

Temporary Office Space Overseas
While traveling abroad, you can obtain temporary office space and help at the U.S. Department of Commerce's Export Development offices. Translation services and local market information are also available. A nominal fee is charged. Contact: Office of Event Management, Event Management Division, International Trade Administration, Department of Commerce, Room 2111, Washington, DC 20230/202-377-2741.

Terrorism Abroad
Assistance is available to help design corporate security programs for business operations in foreign countries. "Countering Terrorism" is a free pamphlet providing security suggestions for U.S. business representatives abroad, and it describes precautionary measures as well as suggested behavior in case of kidnapping. Additional information is also available from: Executive Committee and Working Group on Terrorism, D/CT, Department of State, 2201 C Street NW, Room 2238, Washington, DC 20520/202-632-9892. Contact: Foreign

Operations, Office of Security, Bureau of Administration, Department of State, 2201 C Street NW, Room 3422, Washington, DC 20520/202-632-3122.

Trade Missions—Business
The International Trade Administration sponsors small tours of U.S. businessmen offering a single product. The groups make three or four stops overseas in order to evaluate market potential. These trips are prepared by the staff of the U.S. Department of Commerce and take up to two years of planning. Contact: Office of Export Management Support Services, Export and Foreign Commercial Service, International Trade Administration, Department of Commerce, Room 2806, Washington, DC 20230/ 202-377-4908.

Travel Advisories
Advisories on travel to foreign countries are available, including information on civil disturbances, natural disasters, epidemic diseases, strikes, shortages of hotel rooms and anything else that may affect a traveler. Write for publications describing consular services, visa requirements and special features of a particular country. Contact: Overseas Citizens Services, Bureau of Consular Affairs, Department of State, 2201 C Street NW, Room 4800, Washington, DC 20520/202-632-3732, or the Citizens Emergency Assistance at: 202-632-5225.

Travel an Icebreaker to the Arctic
Scientists and researchers can travel on U.S. Coast Guard Icebreaker expeditions into the Arctic. Passage is granted on a space-available basis, and applicants are selected according to the value of the project they are working on. Occasionally representatives of government agencies, academic institutions, and nonprofit organizations can travel free of charge; for the most part, though, travel is on a reimbursement basis. For details contact: Ice Operations Division, U.S. Coast Guard Headquarters, Washington, DC 20593/202-426-1881.

Travelers' Airline Rights
Fly Rights describes important consumer information about air fares, reservations and tickets, delayed and cancelled flights, overbooking, baggage, smoking and airline safety. This pamphlet (stock #003-006-00106-5) is available for $2.75 from: Superintendent of Documents, U.S. Government Printing Office, Washington, DC 20402/202-783-3238.

Travel Bibliographies
Subject Bibliographies are available from the

Government Printing Office on two aspects of travel. They are:

Customs, Immunization, and Passport Publications
Travel and Tourism

These free catalogues list all publications that can be purchased from the Government Printing Office relating to travel. To order contact: Superintendent of Documents, U.S. Government Printing Office, Washington, DC 20402/ 202-783-3238.

Travel Tips for Senior Citizens
A variety of information is available including: health advice, emergency help, general information, customs hints for returning U.S. residents, visa requirements of foreign governments, foreign country information, passports and visas, and clothing to pack. Contact: Bureau of Consular Affairs, Office of Public Affairs, Department of State, 2201 C Street NW, Room 6811, Washington, DC 20520/202-632-1489.

Wall Charts
The Central Intelligence Agency has prepared wall charts showing the government structure of nations throughout the world. Many charts contain pictures of government leaders. Contact: Superintendent of Documents, U.S. Government Printing Office, Washington, DC 20402/202-783-3238 or National Technical Information Service, 5285 Port Royal Road, Springfield, VA 22161/703-487-4650.

World Climate Data
The National Climatic Data Center has world monthly surface climatological data for over 2,500 weather stations. Data for some stations go back to the mid-1700's. The Center supplies information on a cost-recovery basis. A professional staff of 10 meteorologists functioning as request analysts is available to assist potential customers. Contact: National Climatic Data Center, NOAA, Department of Commerce, Federal Building, Asheville, NC 28801/ 704-259-0682.

World Factbook
Each year the Central Intelligence Agency issues a *World Factbook* which provides information about a variety of countries. Examples of country facts include: size, natural resources, population, type of government, government leaders, elections, international organizations to which country belongs, military budget and size, data about number of railroads, airfields, telephones, and more. The book is available for $10.00 from GPO or $23.50 from NTIS. Contact: Superintendent of Documents, U.S. Government Printing Office, Washington, DC 20402/202-783-3238; or National Technical Information Service, 5285 Port Royal Road, Springfield, VA 22161/703-487-4650.

World Import/Export Statistics
For the latest information on any product imported or exported from any foreign country, contact: Foreign Trade Reference Room, Department of Commerce, Room 2233, Washington, DC 20230/202-377-4855.

Your Trip Abroad (189N)
Practical tips on international travel, including information on customs, visas, shots, and insurance are given in this booklet. Available for $1.00 from: Consumer Information Center, Pueblo, CO 81009.

Free Help and Information for Business

The Federal Government is very interested in helping businesses, especially small ones, grow and thrive. It provides all sorts of services—from loans to counseling to overseas marketing assistance—and often this help is free for the asking.

This section is designed to introduce you to what is available from the Federal Government. Although the listings here are fairly comprehensive, they are only "the tip of the iceberg" in terms of what is available. Therefore, this section should be used as a starting point, an enticement, to help you delve into Department and Agency chapters such as Commerce, Small Business Administration, International Trade Administration, General Services Administration, and more. You should also consult the Sampler Section entitled "Finding Free Information on Anything and Everything" as it provides helpful tips for finding and using experts, identifying statistical resources, and obtaining government reports.

As you begin your research you will be astonished at the overwhelming amount of free and low-cost information available, as long as you are resourceful. And, with a little skill, the Federal Government just might become your best marketing information resource!

Starting a Business

Several years ago the Federal Government began programs designed to insure small business survival. Additional programs have since been instituted to aid "socially and economically disadvantaged minorities" entering the business world. The underlying concept behind many of these programs is that big business has grown so huge and powerful in the United States that the Federal Government must step in to help preserve small business. The scope of the federal assistance, including loans, loan guarantees, and other aid programs has already reached over $100 billion annually. Unfortunately, the government does not publicize the availability of these programs very well, so very few people are aware of the assistance, both financial and informational, available to them at little or no charge. "Starting A Business" highlights services of interest to small businesses and beginning entrepreneurs. It is divided into 3 sections: Small Business Administration; U.S. Department of Commerce; and Publications Worth Writing For.

Small Business Administration (SBA)

The best known among federal agencies established to aid small businesses, SBA, offers financial assistance such as direct loans, guaranteed
loans and direct participation loans to small
businesses for virtually any legitimate business
purpose. SBA also offers a variety of business
publications, either free or at a nominal charge,
designed to aid small businesses in nearly every
facet of their development. Staff provide counseling and consulting services, training programs and
seminars on every conceivable topic of interest to
the small business person. Other forms of assistance available include help in developing loan
packages and programs to help small businesses
doing business with the Federal Government. The
SBA works closely with other federal agencies,
state and local governments,and with financial,
educational, professional, and trade institutions
and associations in the private sector. As such, the
SBA is an excellent initial contact for locating
sources of assistance. It has more than 100 field
offices located in major cities across the country. A
list of these offices is printed in the "Resources
Close-to-Home" section of the Sampler. To find
the SBA office in your city, you can also look in
the telephone directory under "U.S. Government,
Small Business Administration" or contact: Office
of Public Affairs, Small Business Administration,
1441 L Street NW, Washington, DC 20416/
202-653-6832. Described below are SBA services
especially helpful for those starting a business.

• Answer Desk Hotline

This toll-free hotline for information and referral
services was established by the Small Business
Administration (SBA) to assist entrepreneurs
throughout the U.S. The Answer Desk has access
to thousands of information sources at all levels of
government that can be helpful to the small
business sector. This is an excellent resource for
locating field offices, SBIC locations, procurement
representatives, bond and loan guarantee officers,
Small Business Innovation Research (SBIR)
grants, and venture capital funding, Minority
Business Development Agency (MBDA) offices,
Small Business Institute (SBI), as well as other
SBA officials in Washington, DC and all of the 50
states. The office also provides contact information for other government agencies which may be
of assistance to businesses. The Answer Desk can
give you updated information about licenses,
lenders, copyrights, franchises, incubators, insur-

ance, interest rates, publications, taxes and numerous other topics of interest to business people. The
Answer Desk is open Monday through Friday, 9
a.m. to 5 p.m. Eastern time. It can also be reached
on Telecommunication Devices for the Deaf
(TDD) for persons with hearing or speech impediments. Contact:1-800-368-5855 (in Washington,
DC 202-653-7561).

• Advocacy Office

The SBA's Office of Advocacy is specifically
mandated to protect, strengthen, and effectively
represent the interests of small business when
dealing with the federal government. If informs
the small business community of issues that affect
it, and assists the entrepreneur with questions and
problems regarding federal laws, regulations, and
assistance programs. It makes available research in
a number of areas, including tax and procurement
issues. This office also serves as a conduit through
which small businesses can make suggestions and
criticisms for policy consideration. Contact: The
Office of Advocacy, U.S. Small Business Administration (SBA), 1441 L Street NW, Washington,
DC 20416/800-368-5855 (SBA Answer Desk)
202-653-7561.

• Computer-Assisted Management Courses

Under an agreement between the Small Business
Administration (SBA) and Control Data Corporation (CDC) the federal government will assume
most of the fees for small businesses taking
computer-assisted management courses offered by
CDC. Training under the program called
"PLATO" (Program Logic For Automatic Teaching Operations) involves 4 series of learning topics:
building your own business; the psychological
approach to selling; accounts receivable collection
techniques; and contract bidding. Students enrolled in the program work with both printed
material and a computer terminal. Contact: your
local U.S. Small Business Administration field
office listed in your telephone book, or U.S. Small
Business Administration, 1441 L Street NW,
Room 317, Washington, DC 20416/202-653-6894.

• Incubators

Business incubators, a fairly recent phenomenon
in the United States, are developing throughout
the country at a rapid rate. These facilities and
services are intended to assist promising businesses
in getting started and expanding. An "incubated"

business is often provided free rent or other physical facilities, free or cooperative utilization of business equipment and machinery, business and technical advice, and even assistance in acquiring venture capital.

SBA'S OFFICE OF PRIVATE SECTOR INITIATIVES (OPSI) serves as a Clearinghouse on incubators. Staff can provide you with information about projects around the country, refer you to experts, and send you free publications, examples of which are described below. This office also sponsors conferences and educational programs on how to develop and manage successful incubator facilities. Publications include:

SMALL BUSINESS INCUBATORS—a resource summary prepared in cooperation with the National Council for Urban Economic Development, this publication includes an overview of what an incubator is and how it functions. It also provides a listing of SBA publications relating to incubators as well as relevant publications produced by other organizations. A contact list of people and organizations that can supply information is also included. The 8-page publication is available free of charge.

STARTING A SMALL BUSINESS—this is a handbook for sponsors and developers. The majority of the text concerns state programs available to businesses in Illinois. The book describes the role and characteristics of an incubator and the steps of development, including where to get help in starting and managing an incubator. The 60-page publication is available free of charge.

To obtain more information, or the publications listed above, contact: Office of Advocacy, Office of Private Sector Initiatives, U.S. Small Business Administration, 1441 L Street NW, Washington, DC 20416/202-653-7880.

• **Score/ACE Program**
The Service Corps of Retired Executives (SCORE) and the Active Corps of Executives (ACE) are two groups of volunteers who offer management counseling and other advice to small business owners. A volunteer's expertise is matched to the specific needs of the business in question, and individual analysis of the problems —as well as solutions—is offered at no charge. Contact: Office of Management Counseling Services, SCORE or ACE Program, Small Business Administration, 1441 L Street NW, Washington, DC 20416/202-653-6768.

• **Small Business Development Centers (SBDC)**
These centers are sponsored by the SBA in cooperation with universities, state, local and Federal Government agencies and the private sector. Each provides assistance in managing small businesses, technical help, research studies and other types of specialized assistance. SBDC's are located primarily at colleges and universities throughout the country. Contact: Office of Small Business Development Centers, Small Business Administration, 1441 L Street NW, Washington, DC 20416/202-653-6768.

• **Small Business Institute (SBI)**
Through the SBI, seniors and graduate students from the country's leading business schools provide on-site management counseling to small business owners and fledgling entrepreneurs, at no charge. Available to all, these services are provided at hundreds of locations throughout the nation. Contact: Small Business Institute, Small Business Administration, 1441 L Street NW, Washington, DC 20416/202-653-6668.

U.S. Department of Commerce

This Department offers many services useful to businesspeople, a few of which are described below. A detailed listing of these services, as well as offices that can be of help, is provided in a free guide entitled: *Business Service Directory*. Sources listed in the directory (each of which is also described in the Department of Commerce chapter of *Information USA*) include: the Office of Business Liaison for information and general direction in business; Bureau of the Census for statistical material on population, demographics, construction and other business, manufacturing, retail trade, foreign trade, and other useful subjects; Economic Development Administration for financial assistance available from the Federal Government; National Bureau of Standards for measurement services for commercial and manufacturing businesses; International Trade Administration for export assistance and statistics; National Technical Information Service for specialized information; Minority Business Development Agency for assistance to minority entrepreneurs; Patent and Trademark Office for innovation and product information; Office of Productivity, Technology and Innovation for research and technology, information and assistance; and the Bureau of Economic Analysis for industry experts and statistical business information. For a copy of the directory, or for more specific information on any Department of Commerce office, contact: Office of Business

Liaison, U.S. Department of Commerce, Washington, DC 20230/202-377-3176.

• **Business Assistance at the Local Level**
The U.S. Department of Commerce maintains 47 district offices throughout the United States to provide a local contact for all Commerce services. Most of these offices also maintain a business reference library containing market research information, business-related materials, foreign trade data, census reports, and "how-to" guides for starting and managing a business. For further information, contact: U.S. and Foreign Commercial Service, ITA, Department of Commerce, Washington, DC 20230/202-377-4767, or check with your telephone book under "U.S. Government, Department of Commerce.

• **Help Finding Your Way Through The Government Maze**
The *Roadmap Program,* an information resource for all potential and small businesses, is an excellent starting point in any search for Federal Government assistance. In addition to directing you through the government maze, staff can provide information, answers, contacts, government reports and direct you to other sources for all types of business information. Contact: Roadmap, Office of Business Liaison, U.S. Department of Commerce, Washington, DC 20230.

• **Productivity Information**
The Productivity Center can provide you with information about how to improve your organization's productivity, competitiveness, and quality. It can also give you information about other nations, including Japanese productivity and management techniques. Staff can provide you with literature, reference/referral services and reading lists—all free of charge. Contact: Commerce Productivity Center, U.S. Department of Commerce, 14th and Constitution Avenue NW, Room 7413, Washington, DC 20230/202-377-0940.

• **Data Bases**
The following computerized data bases are maintained by the Federal Government to help small businesses obtain new opportunities. These data bases are also useful to large corporations seeking the services of small business.

WHO'S WHO RESOURCE FILE (WWRF) contains resource information about more than 24,000 U.S. organizations and individuals involved in minority business development. Collected data includes name of resource, address, telephone number, Standard Industrial Classification (SIC) if applicable, specialty code, and is retrievable by 26 major categories. WWRF is updated monthly by approximately 500 new entries. The Minority Business Development Agency will run searches and provide printouts or mailing labels free of charge. Service is restricted to individuals and organizations advocating minority business development. Contact: Department of Commerce, Minority Business Development Agency, Room 5710, Washington, DC 20230/202-377-5997.

THE BUSINESS DEVELOPMENT REPORT SYSTEM (BDRS) contains information collected quarterly from recipients of federal grants under the Minority Business Development Center Program. As Grantees must report data about clients (over 15,000) assisted, services provided and accomplishments, the data base contains information about minority business activities and services, minority-group breakdowns, business trends, capital and market brokering activities, and new start/acquisition brokering that occurs.

Searches and printouts are available free of charge. Contact: III, U.S. Department of Commerce, Minority Business Development Agency, Room 5708, Washington, DC 20230/202-377-5997.

PROFILE: THE NATIONAL AUTOMATED MINORITY BUSINESS SOURCE LIST SERVICE is a minority business locator system established to help match minority firms with large government contractors needing services or products. The data base contains information about more than 27,000 minority-owned businesses nationwide. Profile can be searched by specific minority ownership (i.e., black, veteran, etc.), type of firm, size, geographic location and product or service supplied. Any company or organization wanting to purchase the services of a minority-owned business can obtain a search free of charge. Companies wanting to be listed in Profile should contact The Minority Business Development Agency (MBDA) to find out if they are eligible. Listing is free of charge. Contact: Information Clearinghouse, Minority Business Development Agency, Room 6708, U.S. Department of Commerce, Washington, DC 20230/202-377-2414 or any of the numerous MBDA Offices throughout the United States. The Agency has seven regional offices, and 33 district offices, and it supports 100 Business Development Centers nationwide. Check your phone book under "U.S. Department of Commerce, Minority Business Development Agency."

Publications Worth Writing For

SBA Hotline to Publications
The Small Business Administration's free publications include management aids, starting out series, and small business bibliographies. These publications are geared to all types of businesses and many are excellent reference guides to for other publications, business organizations, and trade associations. For additional information or a list of publications available on a specific topic, contact: Publications, Small Business Administration, 1441 L Street NW, Room 100, Washington, DC 20416/202-653-7561, or call toll free 800-368-5855.

Advertising, Packaging, and Labeling
For small businesses that prepare their own ads, this provides the basics: standards; suggestions for successful ads, packaging, and labeling; public and private regulatory institutions. Stock Number (129N, $2.25). Available from: Consumer Information Center, Pueblo, CO 81009.

Catalogue of Federal Domestic Assistance Programs
This publication describes all federally funded domestic assistance programs. These include seven financial types (i.e., formula grants, project grants, and direct loans), as well as eight non-financial types, including provision of specialized services. The programs span twenty functional categories and 176 sub-categories, such as: agriculture, community development, consumer protection, education, employment, labor and training, and health. The Catalog contains program descriptions, appendices, and indices, as well as information about application procedures, eligibility of applicants and forms required to apply for assistance. Each program description contains the following information: authorization that funds the program; federal agency that administers the program; objectives and uses of the program; eligibility requirements; applications and awards process; financial information for past, present and future years; and information contacts. The 1000-page publication is published annually in May, with a supplement issued in December. The latter covers new programs, changes to program identification numbers, etc. The Catalogue plus supplement are available for $40.00 from: Superintendent of Documents, U.S. Government Printing Office, Washington, DC 20402/202-783-3238. For information about the Catalogue's contents contact: General Services Administration, Federal Program Information Branch, 1825 Connecticut Avenue NW, Room 804, Washington, DC 20405/202-673-5302.

Checklist for Going Into Business
This handy checklist will help you think through a number of items you must consider before deciding to start your own business, e.g. your character, money, customers, etc. Available free of charge from: U.S. Small Business Administration, 1441 L Street NW, Washington, DC 20416.

Guide to Innovation Resources Planning for the Smaller Business
The guide identifies more than 50 federal and 85 state government offices that assist smaller businesses. The guide has two basic sections. The first examines the many steps in the innovation process and the skills and resources needed. The second section identifies a wide range of resources (federal, state and private) available to assist the smaller business in areas such as financing, information gathering, and management. The capabilities of these resources are summarized and contact phone numbers and addresses given. Each resource has been identified by the stage of the innovation process to which it applies. The 85-page publication is available for $13.50 from: National Technical Information Service, U.S. Department of Commerce, 5285 Port Royal Road, Springfield, VA 22161/703-487-4650. Contact: Small Business Technology Liaison Division, Office of Productivity, Technology and Innovation, U.S. Department of Commerce, Room 4816, Washington, DC 20230/202-377-1093.

Ideas into Dollars (133N)
This publication advises the small business person on patenting, financing, and marketing a new invention or product. It lists sources of assistance including universities, inventors' associations, government offices, etc. It is available for $3.00 from: Consumer Information Center, Pueblo, CO 81009.

Incubator Times
A quarterly newsletter, this will keep you up-to-date about incubator programs, literature, conferences and more. Available free of charge from: Office of Private Initiatives, Small Business Administration, 1441 L Street, N.W. Room 720A, Washington, DC 20416/202-653-7880.

Minority Business Today
Published bimonthly, this newsletter covers assistance and government contracts designed for minority businesses. Contact: Information Center, Minority Business Development Agency, Department of Commerce, Room 6708, Washington, DC 20203/202-377-2217.

Small Business Guide to Federal Research and Development Opportunities

This publication provides scientifically and technically oriented small businesses with information about opportunities for obtaining federal funding for research and development activities. It contains information about: the substantive priorities of federal R & D programs; the criteria that companies must meet in order to do business with the federal government; the procedures used by federal R & D programs to publicize funding opportunities, to solicit ideas from the private sector, and to fund extramural R & D activities; the federal laws, regulations and policies that affect small business participation in federally funded R & D activities; and points of contact for obtaining additional information about each R & D program. The 136-page publication is available for $6.00 from: Superintendent of Documents, U.S. Government Printing Office, Washington, DC 20402/202-783-3238. Refer to stock number 038-000-00522-7. It is also available for $9.50 from: National Technical Information Service, 5285 Port Royal Road, Springfield, VA 22161/703-487-4650. Refer to number PB83-192401. For additional information about the contents of the guide, contact: Office of Small Business R & D, National Science Foundation, 1800 G Street NW, Washington, DC 20550/202-357-7464.

Starting and Managing a Small Service Business

The publication tells how to pick a saleable service by assessing your skills and the market. It includes information on financing and organizing. Available for $4.50 (order #135N) from: Consumer Information Center, Pueblo, CO 81009.

Thinking About Going Into Business

This pamphlet tells you what you will need to know about the many aspects of small business: taxes, pricing, the market, finances, and where to get help. Write: U.S. Small Business Administration, 1441 L Street NW, Washington DC 20416, or contact your local SBA office.

Women's Handbook (518N)

A free booklet, this tells how the Small Business Administration can help a woman establish a business. Available from: Consumer Information Center, Pueblo, CO 81009.

Inventions, Patents, Copyrights and Trademarks

Protecting and licensing your invention, copyrighting your work, and obtaining a patent or trademark are often a necessary part of doing business. Described below are government sources you can consult when you need information about any of these procedures.

Inventions

Protect Your Idea

To protect your idea or invention for up to 2 years, you can officially record evidence of the date you conceived your invention. You can do this by filing a "Disclosure Document," which will be kept in confidence by the Patent and Trademark Office. The cost is $10, and it is a much simpler process than applying for a patent. Contact: Commissioner of Patents and Trademarks, Patent and Trademark Office, Department of Commerce, Washington, DC 20231/703-557-3225.

Licensing

You can identify new products and technology that have been invented by the Federal government and are available for licensing by subscribing to a National Technical Information Service (NTIS) newsletter titled *"Government Inventions for Licensing."* It is available for $205 a year from: NTIS, Department of Commerce, 5285 Port Royal Road, Springfield, VA 22161/703-487-4600.

Energy-Related Invention Assistance

Inventors can get technical assistance from the National Bureau of Standards. A staff of trained specialists evaluate thousands of energy-related inventions and make recommendations to the Department of Energy for grant money. Contact: Office of Energy-Related Inventions, National Bureau of Standards, Department of Commerce, Building 202—Room 209, Gaithersburg, MD 20899/301-921-3694.

Publications

Can You Make Money With Your Idea or Invention?—this free publication tells you how to identify an idea that has some value and what to do to exploit its fullest potential. Write: U.S. Small Business Administration, 1441 L Street NW, Washington, DC 20416, or contact your local SBA office.

Ideas Into Dollars—a 24-page booklet, this can act as a companion piece to the above *Can You Make Money With Your Idea or Invention?*. It describes a variety of government and private organizations and programs that can help ensure a good idea turns into a success. Write: U.S. Small Business Administration, 1441 L Street NW, Washington, DC 20416, or contact your local SBA office.

Patents

Where to Begin
The Patent Office (PTO) administers U.S. patent and trademark laws. The Office examines patent and trademark applications, grants protection for qualified inventions, and registers trademarks. It also collects, assembles, and disseminates the technological information disclosed on patent grants.

The Patent and Trademark Office maintains a collection of more than 4 million U.S. patents issued to date, several million foreign patents, and 1.2 million trademarks, together with supporting documentation. For information contact: Office of Public Affairs, Patent and Trademark Office, U.S. Department of Commerce, 2021 Jefferson Davis Highway, Crystal Plaza Building 3, Arlington, VA 22202/703-557-3428. The Patent and Trademark Office's services include:

SEARCHES—PTO's Office of Technology Assessment and Forecast (OTAF) is part of the U.S. Patent and Trademark Office. Its job is to stimulate the use and enhance the usability of the more than 25 million documents which make up the categorized U.S. patent file. In carrying out its mission OTAF has a master data base which covers all U.S. patents, and searches are available for a fee. OTAF extracts information about the U.S. patent file from its data base, analyzes the information and makes it available in a variety of formats, including publications, custom patent reports, and statistical reports.

ATTORNEYS LIST—for a listing of patent attorneys contact: Office of Enrollment and Discipline, Patent and Trademark Office, Department of Commerce, Washington, DC 20231/703-5570-1728.

COPIES—copies of the specifications and drawings of all patents are available: design patents, trademark copies and plant patents not in color are $1.00 each, plant patents in color are $8.00 each. For copies contact: Patent and Trademark Office, Department of Commerce, P.O. Box 9, Washington, DC 20231/202-377-2540.

TRAINING—Patent Academy provides training for patent examiners in patent practices and procedures. Government agencies can attend sessions for free; there is a charge for those in the private sector or in foreign agencies. Contact: Phase II Patent Academy, Patent and Trademark Office, Department of Commerce, Building 6, Room 1261, Crystal Plaza, Arlington, VA 22202/703-557-2086.

Federal Agencies
The following agencies can provide information and licensing for patents falling under their jurisdiction.

ARMY—the Army grants licenses under government-owned, Army-administered patents. For further information, contact: Patents, Copyrights and Trademarks Division, U.S. Army, Legal Services Agency, 5611 Columbia Pike, Room 332A, Falls Church, VA 22041-5013/202-756-2430.

DEPARTMENT OF AGRICULTURE—Government patents resulting from agricultural research discoveries are available for licensing to U.S. companies and citizens. There is no charge for licensing. For a description of the types of patents available, contact: Acquisition and Assistance, Department of Agriculture, Room 528A, 6505 Belcrest Road, Hyattsville, MD 20782/301-436-8402.

NAVY—the Navy grants licenses and administers patents on a partial, nonexclusive, revocable, royalty or royalty-free, nontransferable basis to any American citizen or business entity capable of introducing the invention into commercial use. Contact: Director, Navy Patent Program, Patent Counsel for the Navy, Office of Naval Research, Department of the Navy, Department of Defense, 800 North Quincy Street, Arlington, VA 22217/202-696-4000.

JUSTICE DEPARTMENT—advice is available about government patent policy. Work is also done on the improper uses of copyrights and patents as they affect marketing competition and policy. Contact: Intellectual Property Section, Antitrust Division, Department of Justice, 521 12th Street NW, Room 704, Washington, DC 20530/202-724-7966.

NATIONAL SCIENCE FOUNDATION—each NSF research grant is subject to a patent and invention clause. This clause governs, in a manner calculated to protect the public interest and the equities of the grantee, the disposition of inventions made or conceived under the grant. Information on patents or inventions, Institutional Patent Agreements, licenses and rights is available. Contact: Office of the General Counsel, National Science Foundation, 1800 G Street NW, Room 501, Washington, DC 20550/202-357-9435.

NATIONAL AERONAUTICAL AND SPACE ADMINISTRATION—detailed information concerning patent policies and procedures as well as available forms for petitioning for waivers of rights to contract inventions, and for making applications for licenses under NASA patents is available. *NASA Patent Abstracts Bibliography,* a semi-annual, contains abstracts of all NASA inventions, and can be purchased from National Technical Information Service, Springfield, VA 22161. Contact: Patent Matters, Office of General Counsel, National Aeronautics Space Administration, 400 Maryland Avenue SW, Room F7037, Washington, DC 20546/202-453-2424.

Foreign Countries Applying for U.S. Patents

Agreements have been made with 31 countries, including Japan, Australia, Russia, most of Western Europe and Brazil, to allow a single patent application to be applied to all 31 countries. Contact: Patent and Trademark Office, Department of Commerce, P.O. Box PCT, Washington, DC 20231/703-557-2003.

Foreign Countries and Patent Filings

For information on patents filed in other countries

contact: Business Practices Division, Office of International Finance and Investments, ITA, Department of Commerce, Room 1128, Washington, DC 20230/202-377-4471.

NASA Inventions for Foreign Licensing

There is a patent coverage on NASA-owned inventions introduced to various foreign countries to further the interests of the United States industry in foreign commerce. Licenses are negotiated individually and may be granted to any applicant, foreign or domestic. *Significant NASA Inventions Available for Licensing in Foreign Countries* includes abstracts of those inventions in which NASA owns the principal or exclusive rights and which have been made available for patent licensing in the countries indicated. The corresponding United States patent number is also listed. For additional information, contact: Patent Matters, Office of General Counsel, Assistant for Patent Matters, National Aeronautics and Space Administration, 400 Maryland Avenue SW, Room F7035, Washington, DC 20546/202-453-2424.

Patent Depository Libraries

The libraries listed below, designated as Patent Depository Libraries, receive current issues of U.S. patents and maintain collections of earlier-issued patents. The scope of these collections varies from library to library, ranging from patents of only certain years in some libraries to all or most of the patents issued since 1790, in other libraries. All of these libraries offer CASSIS (Classification and Search Support Information System), which provides direct, on-line access to Patent and Trademark Office data. For information about the Patent Depository Library Program call toll free on 1-800-368-2532.

State	Name of Library	Telephone Contact
Alabama	Auburn University Libraries	(205) 826-4500 Ext. 21
	Birmingham Public Library	(205) 254-2555
Arizona	Tempe:Science Library, Arizona State University	(602) 965-7140
California	Los Angeles Public Library	(213) 626-7555 Ext. 273
	Sacramento: California State Library	(916) 322-4572
	San Diego Public Library	(619) 236-5813
	Sunnyvale: Patent Information Clearinghouse	(408) 738-5580
Colorado	Denver Public Library	(303) 571-2122
Delaware	Newark: University of Delaware	(302) 738-2238
Georgia	Atlanta: Price Gilbert Memorial Library, Georgia Institute of Technology	(404) 894-4508
Idaho	Moscow: University of Idaho Library	(208) 885-6235
Illinois	Chicago Public Library	(312) 269-2865
	Springfield: Illinois State Library	(217) 782-5430
Indiana	Indianapolis-Marion County Public Library	(317) 269-1706

Louisiana	Baton Rouge: Troy H. Middleton Library, Louisiana State University	(504) 388-2570
Maryland	College Park: Engineering and Physical Sciences Library, University of Maryland	(301) 454-3037
Massachusetts	Boston Public Library	(617) 536-5400 Ext. 265
Michigan	Ann Arbor: Engineering Transportation Library, University of Michigan	(313) 704-7494
	Detroit Public Library	(313) 833-1450
Minnesota	Minneapolis Public Library & Information Center	(612) 372-6570
Missouri	Kansas City: Linda Hall Library	(816) 363-4600
	St. Louis Public Library	(314) 241-2288 Ext. 390 Ext. 391
Nebraska	Lincoln: University of Nebraska-Lincoln, Engineering Library	(402) 472-3411
Nevada	Reno: University of Nevada Library	(702) 784-6579
New Hampshire	Durham: University of New Hampshire Library	(603) 862-1777
New Jersey	Newark Public Library	(201) 733-7815
New Mexico	Albuquerque: University of New Mexico Library	(505) 277-5441
New York	Albany: New York State Library	(518) 474-5125
	Buffalo and Erie County Public Library	(716) 856-7525 Ext. 267
	New York Public Library (The Research Libraries)	(212) 930-0850
North Carolina	Raleigh: D. H. Hill Library, N.C. State University	(919) 737-3280
Ohio	Cincinnati & Hamilton County, Public Library of	(513) 369-6936
	Cleveland Public Library	(216) 623-2870
	Columbus: Ohio State University Libraries	(614) 422-6286
	Toledo/Lucas County Public Library	(419) 255-7055 Ext. 212
Oklahoma	Stillwater: Oklahoma State University Library	(405) 624-6546
Pennsylvania	Cambridge Springs: Alliance College Library	(814) 398-2098
	Philadelphia: Franklin Institute Library	(215) 448-1321
	Pittsburgh: Carnegie Library of Pittsburgh	(412) 622-3138
	University Park: Patee Library, Pennsylvania State University	(814) 865-4861
Rhode Island	Providence Public Library	(401) 521-7722 Ext. 226
South Carolina	Charleston: Medical University of South Carolina	(803) 792-2372
Tennessee	Memphis & Shelby County Public Library and Information Center	(512) 471-1610
Texas	Austin: McKinney Engineering Library, University of Texas	(409) 845-2551
	College Station: Sterling C. Evans Library, Texas A & M University	(214) 749-4176
	Houston: The Fondren Library, Rice University	(713) 527-8101
Washington	Seattle: Engineering Library, University of Washington	(206) 543-0740
Wisconsin	Madison: Kurt F. Wendt Engineering Library, University of Wisconsin	(608) 262-6845
	Milwaukee Public Library	(414) 278-3043

Patent Bibliographic Database

Computer assisted searches of the Patent Bibliographic Database are available from National Technical Information Service. Intended as information tools, these searches do not constitute "legal patent searches." For more information, request a free catalog #PTS-186 or contact: National Technical Information Service, Department of Commerce, 5285 Port Royal Road, Springfield, VA 22161/703-487-4640.

Publications

Guide to the Public Patent Search Facilities and what you need to know of the U.S. Patent and Trademark Office—describes the patent search facilities and what you need to know before you begin a patent search in the Patent and Trademark Office. It explains all of the jargon used by the office as well as the types and locations of the available documents. It also tells how to conduct your own patent search. Contact: Commissioner of Patents and Trademarks, Patent and Trademark Office, Department of Commerce, Washington, DC 20231/703-557-2276. If you wish to start immediately on your own search, the Patent Office will provide you with the necessary documentation and direct you to the nearest patent depository.

Official Gazette (Stock No. 003-004-8001-1)—the weekly listing from the Patent and Trademark Office, this describes all new patents and includes drawings when available. Annual subscription fee is $250.00 Fourth Class and $360.00 First Class. Contact: Superintendent of Documents, U.S. Government Printing Office, Washington, DC 20402/202-783-3238.

The following publications are available from: Superintendent of Documents, U.S. Government Printing Office, Washington, DC 20402/202-783-3238.

Annual Indexes—patents are indexed by patentees and by subject matter. Trademarks are indexed by registrant and by type of goods registered. Price varies from year to year.

Attorneys and Agents Registered to Practice Before the United States Patent and Trademark Office—names, addresses, telephone numbers and registration numbers of attorneys and agents, listed alphabetically by surname and by geographical location (Stock number 003-004-00594-7, $9.00)

General Information Concerning Patents—(Stock number 003-004-00596-3, $3.50)

General Information Concerning Trademarks—(Stock number 003-004-00588-2, $3.25)

Guide for Patent Draftsmen—(Stock number 003-004-00570-0, $2.25)

Manual of Classification—lists numbers and descriptive titles of Patent Office class and subclasses, as well as Design Classes (Stock number 003-004-81001-7, $44.00 domestic, $55.00 foreign)

Manual of Patent Examining Procedure—information on practices and procedures relative to prosecution of patent applications (Stock number 003-004-81002-5, $70.00 domestic, $87.50 foreign)

Patents and Inventions—an information aid to inventors in deciding whether to apply for patents, in obtaining patent protection, and in promoting their inventions (Stock number 003-004-00545-9, $3.25)

Patent Laws—(Stock number 003-004-00561-1, $6.00)

Copyrights

Copyrightable Works

All copyrightable works, whether published or unpublished, are subject to a single system of statute protection which gives the copyright owner the exclusive right to reproduce the copyrighted work in copies or phonorecords and distribute them to the public by sale, rental, lease or lending. Works of authorship include books, periodicals, and other literary works, musical compositions, song lyrics, dramas and dramatico-musical compositions, pantomimes and choreographic works, motion pictures and other audiovisual works, and sound recordings. The Library of Congress provides information on copyright registration procedures and copyright card catalogs which cover 16 million works that have been registered since 1870. For general information contact: Copyright Office, Library of Congress, Room 401, Washington, DC 20540/202-287-6840.

Catalogs of Copyright Entries

The following catalogs list the material registered during the period covered by each issue. The publications are sold as individual subscriptions by the Superintendent of Documents, U.S. Government Printing Office, Washington, DC 20402/202-783-3238.

Part 1:   Nondramatic Literary Works (quarterly) $30.00 per year.

Part 2:   Serials and Periodicals (semi-annually) $6.50 per year.

Part 3:   Performing Arts (quarterly) $27.00 per year.

Part 4:   Motion Pictures and Filmstrips (semi-annually) $7.00 per year.

Part 5:   Visual Arts (excluding maps) (semi-annually) $10.00 per year.

Part 6:   Maps (semi-annually) $4.75 per year.

Part 7:   Sound Recordings (semi-annually) $14.00 per year.

Part 8:   Renewal (semi-annually) $8.00 per year.

For additional information contact: Cataloging Division, Copyright Office, Library of Congress, LM 400, Washington, DC 20540/202-287-8040.

General Information

The Copyright Office will research the copyright you need and send you the information by mail. Requests must be in writing and you must specify exactly what it is you need to know. Contact: Copyright Office, Reference & Bibliographic Section, Library of Congress, Washington, DC 20559/202-387-8700.

Trademarks

General Information

For information on trademarks, the book *General*

Information Concerning Trademarks is available for $3.00 from: Superintendent of Documents, U.S. Government Printing Office, Washington, DC 20402/202-783-3238.

Searches

There is only one office which has all the data necessary for searching a trademark. If you yourself cannot go to this Virginia office, it will recommend someone you can hire to do the searching for you. Contact: Trademark Search Room, Patent and Trademark Office, Department of Commerce, 2011 Crystal Plaza Building #2, Arlington, VA 22202/703-557-3268.

State and Local Assistance

Following the example set by the Federal Government, most states and many local governments have already set up, or announced intentions of setting up, programs geared to assist small businesses, minority enterprises, and women entrepreneurs. Taken as a whole, these state and local programs are probably greater in both number and size than the Federal programs available, and even less well known or advertised. The scope of these programs varies widely, including forms of assistance ranging from loans to free services such as assistance in preparing loan packages or locating suitable sources for funding. The programs are conducted by various agencies of state and local governments under a wide variety of titles. Given space limitations we are unable to print a complete listing of these resources; therefore, in this section we have described services and publications which are good starting points for finding out about state and local initiatives for small business.

Local Assistance

City and County Assistance

Most major U.S. cities and localities have some form of assistance for small and newly developing businesses located or operating within their jurisdiction. As with the state programs, the forms of assistance available vary widely from city to city and the exact titles of the agency or programs sponsored do not conform to any standard guidelines. Good initial contact points would be Chamber of Commerce offices, city planning agencies, local library reference sections, economic opportunity offices, development authorities, city or county public information offices, or consumer affairs or information offices. Most of these sources can be located through city or county government listings in local phone books. The U.S. Conference of Mayors, 1620 I Street NW, Washington, DC 20006/202-293-7330 can also direct you to city programs.

Innovation Centers or Research Incubator Facilities

In an attempt to foster closer university/industry research linkages and to increase university involvement in the innovation process, many states have established innovation centers or research incubator facilities. Generally associated with state universities, these innovation centers usually provide management and business assistance, technical and market evaluation, and in some instances financing. The research incubators provide low-cost physical space, equipment and technical services to assist start up businesses in their early development. Many of these organizations are state operated, others fall under the auspices of local or regional authorities, but the majority are associated with a state educational institute. A good source for locating these organizations and centers is the director of extension activities at state universities. Other sources of information include a State's Department of Commerce and

Development, economic planning offices, small business development centers, industrial development offices, financing offices, and technology authorities.

State Assistance

The following resources will help you locate assistance in your state, or a state in which you might consider setting up a business.

"One-Stop-Shops" for Small Businesses
Most state governments have established small business service/help/action centers often called "one-stop-shops" for small businesses. Many of these offices are involved in creating a research and development environment, and promoting partnerships between business, industry and universities. Staff can provide information, publications, and referrals. Since the Center often tries to entice new businesses to their state, their services are for both in-state and out-of-state residents. These centers are often part of a state's Department of Commerce. To find a particular state's small business help center, contact the appropriate state capitol or a state representative's office. (Note: The names of these centers vary from state to state.)

National Governor's Association (NGA)
Organized to promote interests of the states and territories of the United States, the National Governor's Association (NGA) has several task forces which are an excellent source of information about state assistance programs for small businesses. In addition to providing details of specific programs already established in each state, staff at NGA can also direct you to specific state agencies, associations, universities and other organizations which may be of assistance. This office also has several publications pertaining to cooperative programs, technology centers and other assistance resources which are available free of charge or at a nominal expense. Contact: National Governor's Association, Hall of States, 444 North Capitol Street NW, Washington, DC 20009/ 202-624-5300.

State Agencies Providing Help
Each state or territory of the United States has one or more agencies, within its Department of Commerce, operating for the assistance of small, minority or developing businesses. The exact title of the agencies varies from state to state as do the types of assistance available. Examples of titles include: state small business assistance centers, economic development and planning departments, offices of minority business enterprise, business development centers, and office of business liaison.Types of aid include comprehensive loan programs, loan guarantees, assistance in winning state procurement contracts and subcontracts, preparation of loan packages, employment incentive programs, financial packaging, management and technical assistance, counseling and training programs, product development incentives, industrial development assistance, venture capital and business start-up funds, and general information and referral services. Most local phone books provide a 'State Government' section listing major state agency addresses and phone numbers. Other sources of contact include local library reference sections, Small Business Administration business centers and field offices, governor's offices, federal and state congressional representatives, and other state information systems normally located in a state's capitol and its major cities.

State Technical Assistance Centers
These centers offer direct technical assistance to technology oriented businesses. In addition, many of these centers serve as a link to state programs and services providing financial, management and innovation assistance programs designed to help small companies become more competitive. Forms of assistance include information gathering, market feasibilities, and referrals to expert help. A listing of over 100 currently operating facilities appears in the publication *State Technical Assistance Centers and Federal Technical Information Centers Available to U.S. Businesses* PR-767. This brochure is available at no charge. Request Number PR-767 from: Center for the Utilization of Federal Technology, National Technical Information Service, U.S. Department of Commerce, Springfield, VA 22161/703-557-4600.

Doing Business With the Feds

The Federal Government is the world's largest buyer of materials, equipment and supplies. Opportunities for doing business are plentiful for large or small firms in both major categories of government purchasing: general use items and specialized, mission oriented items. While all agencies need the items in the general use category, the General Services Administration (GSA) is the primary purchaser. Therefore, an excellent initial point of contact is with the GSA Business Service Center serving your location (see list in this section). For the specialized items and services, you must contact the purchasing agents in each appropriate federal unit. A detailed list of nationwide procurement offices is available from the GSA Business Service Centers.

The following agencies and publications may be of assistance in initiating or maintaining your business with the Federal Government.

Where To Go

General Services Administration

GSA is the Federal Governnment's realtor and housekeeper: it builds, rents, maintains, and protects federal workspace; it buys, stores and distributes items government workers need to do their jobs; it contracts for services to maintain, repair, transport and manage these items. Altogether, GSA spends $4 billion annually on goods and services and another $1 billion on construction, leases and repairs. GSA Business Service Centers have counselors to provide individuals and firms with detailed information about all types of government contracting opportunities. They issue bidder's mailing list applications, furnish specifications for bids, maintain current displays of bidding opportunities, receive and safeguard bids, and furnish copies of free publications designed to assist business representatives in doing business with the government. For more information contact: The General Services Administration (GSA) Business Service Center in your region, or General Services Administration, 18th and F Streets NW, Washington, DC 20405/202-523-1250.

National Capital Region
Washington, D.C. and nearby
Maryland and Virginia
7th and D Sts. SW
Washington, DC 20407
(202) 472-1293/1804

Region 1
Maine, Vermont, New Hampshire, Massachusetts, Connecticut, Rhode Island

GSA Business Service Center
John W. McCormack Post Office
and Courthouse
Boston, MA 02109
(617) 223-2868

Region 2
New York, New Jersey, Puerto Rico, Virgin Islands

GSA Business Service Center
26 Federal Plaza
New York, NY 10278
(212) 264-1234

Region 3
Pennsylvania, Delaware, West Virginia, Maryland, Virginia

GSA Business Service Center
9th and Market Sts.
Philadelphia, PA 19107
(215) 597-9613

Region 4
North Carolina, South Carolina, Georgia, Tennessee, Kentucky, Florida, Alabama, Mississippi

GSA Business Service Center
75 Spring St. SW
Atlanta, GA 30303
(404) 221-5103/3032

Region 5
Ohio, Indiana, Illinois, Michigan, Minnesota, Wisconsin

GSA Business Service Center
230 South Dearborn St.
Chicago, IL 60604
(312) 353-5383

Region 6
Missouri, Iowa, Kansas, Nebraska

GSA Business Service Center
1500 East Bannister Rd.
Kansas City, MO 64131
(816) 926-7203

Region 7 Arkansas, Louisiana, Texas, New
Mexico, Oklahoma

GSA Business Service Center
819 Taylor St.
Fort Worth, TX 76102
(817) 334-2321

Region 8 Colorado, North Dakota, South
Dakota, Utah, Montana, Wyoming

GSA Business Service Center
Building 41, Denver Federal Center
Denver, CO 80225
(303) 234-2216

Region 9 Northern California, Hawaii, Nevada
(except Clark County)

GSA Business Service Center
525 Market St.
San Francisco, CA 94105
(415) 974-9000

Los Angeles, Southern California,
Arizona, Nevada (Clark County)

GSA Business Service Center
300 North Los Angeles St.
Los Angeles, CA 90012
(213) 688-3210

Region 10 Alaska, Idaho, Oregon, Washington

GSA Business Service Center
440 Federal Building
915 Second Ave.
Seattle, WA 98174
(206) 442-5556

National Aeronautics and Space Administration
The Technology Utilization Division (TU) of the
National Aeronautics and Space Administration
(NASA) is involved in transferring its developed
technology to industry for the development of
useful commercial products. The division can
provide you with information about technologies
developed under NASA funded projects. A variety of services and publications are available from
this office. (Note: NASA TU information and
services are restricted to U.S. citizens and U.S.
based industry.) Contact: Technology Utilization
Division (NASA TU), Code I, NASA Headquarters, National Aeronautics and Space Administration, 400 Maryland Avenue SW, Washington, DC 20546/202-453-8415.

Preferential Contracting Programs
The Federal Government is required by law to give
preference to certain businesses in awarding contracts. These enterprises include small businesses,
socially and economically disadvantaged small
businesses, firms that operate in areas of above
average unemployment, and workshops for the
blind and severely handicapped. Additionally,
although not required by law, the Federal Government is trying to increase its volume of business
with firms owned by women and Vietnam Veterans. Information on the following programs is
available form the GSA Business Service Centers
or your SBA Field Office:

8-A PROGRAM—Section 8(a) of the Small Business
Act, as amended, authorizes the SBA to contract for goods and services for federal agencies.
SBA then subcontracts the actual performance
of the work to socially and economically disadvantaged small businesses certified as eligible to
receive these contracts. SBA also offers managerial, technical, and financial support to participating firms.

LABOR SURPLUS AREA SET-ASIDES—under this program, competition for contracts is restricted to
firms with production facilities in labor surplus
areas (areas of higher than average unemployment). The firms must agree to perform most of
the contract work in the labor surplus areas.
Contracts are set aside until enough qualified
firms are expected to bid to ensure adequate
competition.

MANDATORY SOURCE PROGRAMS—the Federal Government must purchase certain goods and services from workshops for the blind and severely
handicapped. The committee for purchase from
the blind and other severely handicapped was
created by law to coordinate such government
procurement and publishes a list of the mandatory goods and services.

SMALL BUSINESS SET-ASIDES—this program requires
agencies to limit competition on certain contracts to qualified small businesses so small firms
are not forced to compete with large firms.
However, because the government is required
to buy at competitive prices, contracts are set
aside only when enough qualified firms are
expected to bid to ensure adequate competition.
The SBA establishes size standards which determine a firm's eligibility to bid on set-asides.

SUBCONTRACTS FOR SMALL AND SMALL DISADVANTAGED BUSINESSES—federal agencies are required
to ensure that their prime contractors establish
goals for awarding subcontracts to qualified
small and small disadvantaged businesses. Each

prime contract, or subcontract, with a value of $500,000 or more ($1 million for construction), unless awarded to a small business, must include a plan and percentage goals for subcontracts with such firms.

VIETNAM VETERANS—although there are no statutory requirements for awarding contracts to businesses owned by Vietnam Veterans, federal agencies actively encourage them to seek government contracts and to participate, where eligible, in preferential programs.

WOMEN-OWNED BUSINESSES—executive order 12138 of May 18, 1979, requires federal agencies to take affirmative action in support of businesses owned by women. To carry out this order, agencies are making special efforts to advise women of business opportunities and preferential contracting programs for which they may be eligible.

Small Business Innovation Research Program

The Small Business Innovation Research Program (SBIR) stimulates technological innovation, encourages small science and technology based firms to participate in government funded research, and provides incentives for converting research results into commercial applications. Twelve federal agencies with research and development budgets greater than $100 million are required by law to participate. They are the Departments of Defense, Health and Human Services, Energy, Agriculture, Commerce, Transportation, Interior, and Education, the National Aeronautics and Space Administration, the National Science Foundation, the Nuclear Regulatory Commission, and the Environmental Protection Agency.

Businesses of 500 or fewer employees that are organized for profit are eligible to compete for SBIR funding. They must be in business for profit by the time they receive the award. Non-profit organizations and foreign-based firms are not eligible to receive awards. Contact: Small Business Innovation Research Program, U.S. Small Business Administration, Office of Innovation, Research and Technology, 1441 L Street NW, Room 500-A, Washington, DC 20416/202-653-6458. You may also contact one of the SBIR representatives listed below who can answer questions and send you materials about their agency's SBIR plans and funding:

DEPARTMENT OF AGRICULTURE
Office of Grants and Program Systems
1300 Rosslyn Commonwealth Building, Suite 103
Arlington, VA 22209
703-235-2628

DEPARTMENT OF DEFENSE
Small Business and Economic Utilization
Office of Secretary of Defense
Pentagon, Room 2A340
Washington, DC 20301
202-697-9383

DEPARTMENT OF EDUCATION
The Brown Building
1900 M Street NW, Room 722
Washington, DC 20208
202-254-8247

DEPARTMENT OF ENERGY
SBIR Program
Washington, DC 20545
301-353-5867

DEPARTMENT OF HEALTH AND HUMAN SERVICES
Office of Small and Disadvantaged Business Utilization
200 Independence Avenue, SW, Room 513D
Washington, DC 20201
202-245-7300

DEPARTMENT OF INTERIOR
Bureau of Mines
2401 E Street, NW
Washington, DC 20241
202-634-1305

DEPARTMENT OF TRANSPORTATION
Transportation System Center
Kendall Square
Cambridge, MA 02142
616-494-2222

ENVIRONMENTAL PROTECTION AGENCY
Office of Research Grants and Centers (RD-675)
Office of Research and Development
401 M Street, SW
Washington, DC 20460
202-382-5744

NATIONAL AERONAUTICS AND SPACE ADMINISTRATION
SBIR Office—Code A
600 Independence Avenue, SW
Washington, DC 20546
202-755-2306

NATIONAL SCIENCE FOUNDATION
SBIR Program Managers
1800 G Street, NW
Washington, DC 20550
202-357-7527

NUCLEAR REGULATORY COMMISSION
Administration and Resource Staff
Office of Nuclear Regulatory Research
Washington, DC 20555
301-427-4301

Small and Disadvantaged Business Utilization Offices (OSDBU's)

Each agency of the Federal Government has an office responsible for assuring that the agency complies with federal regulations to purchase a certain percentage of products and services from small and minority owned and operated businesses. If you cannot obtain the information or assistance required from the procurement center of a particular agency, then contact the appropriate Small and Disadvantaged Business Utilization Office listed below. These offices offer small businesses information and guidance on procurement procedures, how to be placed on a bidders list, and identification of both prime contractor and subcontracting opportunities.

DEPARTMENT OF AGRICULTURE
Director, OSDBU
Administration Building, 127W
Washington, DC 20250
(202) 447-7117

DEPARTMENT OF COMMERCE
Director, OSDBU
Room 6411
Washington, DC 20230
(202) 377-1472

DEFENSE DEPARTMENT
Director, OSDBU
Room 2A330, The Pentagon
Washington, DC 20301
(202) 694-1151

U.S. AIR FORCE
Director, OSDBU
Room 4C255, The Pentagon
Washington, DC 20330
(202) 697-4126

ARMY
Director, OSDBU
Room 2A712, The Pentagon
Washington, DC 20310
(202) 697-7753

NAVY
Director, OSDBU
Room 604, Crystal Plaza
Bldg. 6, The Pentagon
Washington, DC 20360
(202) 692-7122

DEFENSE LOGISTICS AGENCY
Director, OSDBU
Cameron Station
Alexandria, VA 22314
(202) 274-6471

HEALTH & HUMAN SERVICES
Director, OSDBU
Room 5130
Washington, DC 20201
(202) 245-7300

HOUSING & URBAN DEVELOPMENT
Director, OSDBU
Room 10226
Washington, DC 20410
(202) 755-1428

INTERIOR DEPARTMENT
Director, OSDBU
Room 2527
Washington, DC 20240
(202) 343-8493

JUSTICE DEPARTMENT
Director, OSDBU
Room 1022 Todd
Washington, DC 20530
(202) 724-6271

LABOR DEPARTMENT
Director, OSDBU
Room S-1004
Washington, DC 20210
(202) 523-9148

STATE DEPARTMENT
Director, OSDBU
M/SDBU, Room 513 SA-6
Washington, DC 20520
(202) 235-9579

AGENCY FOR INTERNATIONAL RELATIONS
Director, Business Relations
Room 648, State Annex 14
Washington, DC 20523
(202) 235-1720

EDUCATION DEPARTMENT
Director, OSDBU
400 Maryland Ave. SW, Rm. 3021
Washington, DC 20202
(202) 245-9582

ENERGY DEPARTMENT
Director, OSDBU
Room 1E061
Washington, DC 20585
(202) 252-8201

ENVIRONMENTAL PROTECTION AGENCY
Director, OSDBU
401 M St. SW A-149-C
Washington, DC 20460
(202) 557-7777

EXPORT-IMPORT BANK
Director, OSDBU
811 Vermont Avenue NW
Room 1031
Washington, DC 20571
(202) 566-8951

FEDERAL HOME LOAN BANK BOARD
Director, OSDBU
1700 G Street NW
4th Floor 3G
Washington, DC 20552
(202) 377-6245

FEDERAL TRADE COMMISSION
Director, OSDBU
6th & Pa. Avenue NW
Suite 700
Washington, DC 20580
(202) 523-5532

GENERAL SERVICES ADMINISTRATION
Director, OSDBU
Room 6013
Washington, DC 20405
(202) 566-1021

TRANSPORTATION DEPARTMENT
Director, OSDBU
Room 10222
Washington, DC 20590
(202) 426-1930

TREASURY DEPARTMENT
Director, OSDBU
Room 1320
15th & Pennsylvania Avenue NW
Washington, DC 20220
(202) 566-9616

PERSONNEL MANAGEMENT OFFICE
Office of Management
Room 1307, 1900 E Street NW
Washington, DC 20415
(202) 632-6161

EXECUTIVE OFFICE OF THE PRESIDENT
Office of Procurement and Contracts
Room 424, OEOB
Washington, DC 20500
(202) 395-3314

TENNESSEE VALLEY AUTHORITY
Director, OSDBU
1000 Commerce Union Bank Bldg.
Chattanooga,TN 37401
(615) 751-2624—FTS 858-2623

U.S. INFORMATION AGENCY
Director, OSDBU
1717 H Street NW, Room 613
Washington, DC 20547
(202) 653-5570

NUCLEAR REGULATORY COMMISSION
Director, OSDBU
Maryland National Bank Building
Washington, DC 20555
(202) 492-4665

INTERSTATE COMMERCE COMMISSION
Small Business Assistance Office
12th & Constitution Avenue NW
Washington, DC 20423
(202) 275-7597

NATIONAL AERONAUTICS & SPACE ADMINISTRATION
Director, OSDBU
NASA Headquarters, Code K
Washington, DC 20546
(202) 453-2088

NATIONAL CREDIT UNION ADMINISTRATION
Director, OSDBU
1776 G Street NW, Room 6021
Washington, DC 20456
(202) 357-1025

NATIONAL SCIENCE FOUNDATION
Director, OSDBU
1800 G Street NW, Room 511A
Washington, DC 20550
(202) 357-7464

POSTAL SERVICE
Director, OSDBU
475 L'Enfant Plaza West SW
Room 2012
Washington, DC 20260
(202) 245-5663

VETERANS ADMINISTRATION
OSDBU
810 Vermont Avenue NW
Washington, DC 20420
(202) 389-2192

Small Business Administration
One of SBA's major functions is to insure that small business concerns receive a fair portion of government purchases, contracts and subcontracts, as well as of the sales of government property. The SBA Procurement center works closely with procurement officials in government agencies and also private contractors to help them award federal work to small businesses. The SBA is responsible for certifying the eligibility and capability to carry

out specific government contracts. The next 2 entries describe SBA offices particularly helpful to business. For more information contact: Small Business Administration, 1441 L Street NW, Washington, DC 20416/202-653-6832.

Procurement Assistance Office

This office offers counseling on obtaining prime contracts and subcontracts with the Federal Government. It has information on government "set asides" and other procurement opportunities, new research and development projects, surplus real and personal property, and natural resources available from the Federal Government. The office also assists small businesses in preparing bids and getting their names on bidders lists, and its staff can refer small businesses to federal contracting officers or assist small concerns with contracting problems. It also maintains a computerized master list, Procurement Automated Source System (PASS), of small companies capable of performing work on federal contracts and subcontracts. PASS is used by many federal agencies and contractors. Upon your request SBA will add your business to PASS free of charge. Contractors can obtain information from PASS data base at no charge. Contact: Procurement Assistance, Small Business Administration, 1441 L Street NW, Room 600, Washington, DC 20416/202-653-6635 or a procurement specialist in an office listed below.

AREAS AND OFFICE LOCATIONS

Maine, New Hampshire, Rhode Island, Massachusetts, Vermont, Connecticut

Procurement Specialist
60 Batterymarch
10th Floor
Boston, MA 02110
617-223-3162

New York, New Jersey, Puerto Rico, Virgin Islands

Procurement Specialist
26 Federal Plaza
New York, NY 10278
212-264-7770

Pennsylvania, Maryland, West Virginia, Virginia, Delaware, District of Columbia

Procurement Specialist
Suite 646-West Lobby
231 S. Asaphs Road
Bala Cynwyd, PA 19004
215-596-0172

North Carolina, South Carolina Georgia, Florida, Mississippi, Alabama, Kentucky, Tennessee

Procurement Specialist
1375 Peachtree St. NE
5th Floor
Atlanta, GA 30367
404-881-7587

Ohio, Illinois, Indiana, Wisconsin, Michigan, Minnesota

Procurement Specialist
219 S. Dearborn Street
Room 858
Chicago, IL 60604
312-886-4727

Texas, Louisiana, Arkansas, Oklahoma, Michigan, Minnesota

Procurement Specialist
8625 King George Dr.
Bldg. C
Dallas, TX 75235-3391
214-767-7639

Kansas, Missouri, Nebraska, Iowa

Procurement Specialist
911 Walnut Street
23rd Floor
Kansas City, MO 64106
816-374-5502

Colorado, Wyoming, Utah, Montana, North Dakota, South Dakota

Procurement Specialist
1405 Curtis Street
22nd Floor
Denver, CO 80202
303-837-5441

Southern California (Zip Codes 90000-93599), Arizona

Procurement Specialist
350 S. Figueroa Street
6th Floor
Los Angeles, CA 90071
213-688-2946

Northern California (Zip Codes
93600-95999), Hawaii, Nevada,
Guam

Procurement Specialist
Box 36044
450 Golden Gate Ave.
San Francisco, CA 94102
415-556-9616

Oregon, Idaho, Washington,
Alaska

Procurement Specialist
4th and Vine Bldg.
2615 4th Ave.
Seattle, WA 98121
206-442-0390

Small Business Administration Field Offices

These offices offer counseling, training, information resources and other assistance to qualified
small businesses seeking business with the Federal
Government. The offices will provide details about
available procurement opportunities, refer small
businesses to specific federal contracting offices,
give information on standards and specifications
required on contracts, assist in obtaining preferential contracting for small and disadvantaged businesses, and help small businesses which have
problems with the activities, regulations or policies
of a Federal Government agency. Staff also will
provide details and information on availability of
grants, loans and guarantees, and other funding
programs available to small businesses. To find
your SBA field office, check the "Small Business
Administration" under the federal government
section of your telephone book.

Helpful Publications

Commerce Business Daily—published weekdays
by the Department of Commerce, this publication lists most proposed civilian agency procurements over $5,000 and most Department of
Defense procurements over $10,000. It identi-
fies contracts with subcontracting opportunities
and those that are set aside under any of the
preferential contracting programs. GSA Business Service Centers, as well as most libraries,
have copies of this publication for review, or a
subscription can be purchased for $160 annually
by First Class Mail, or $81 by Regular Mail.
Contact: Superintendent of Documents, U.S.
Government Printing Office, Washington, DC
20402/202-783-3238. Commerce Business Daily
is also available electronically.

Doing Business with the Federal Government—
This GSA publication explains the procurement
policies and procedures of GSA, the Department of Defense, and 16 other agencies. It also
contains the locations and telephone numbers of
GSA Business Service Centers and GSA Small
Business Information Offices across the country. It is available free of charge from the GSA
Business Service Centers.

*Guide to Specifications, Standards and Commercial
Item Descriptions of the Federal Government*—
this booklet is published as a guide for the
business community, particularly small businesses, who may not be familiar with the types
of government standards and specifications developed and issued by GSA, or their purpose
and methods of use. Copies are available without charge from the GSA Business Service
Centers.

*Procurement Publications from Individual
Agencies*—many federal agencies with procurement authority issue their own publications
explaining the agency's contracting needs, policies and procedures. Examples are:

Selling to the Military (Department of Defense),
stock #008-000-00345-0 for $6.00 available
from: Superintendent of Documents, U.S. Government Printing Office, Washington, DC
20402/202-783-3238.

Selling to the Department of the Treasury, free
from: Department of the Treasury, 15th and
Pennsylvania Avenue NW, Washington, DC
20220/202-566-5252.

Doing Business with the Veterans Administration,
free from: Veterans Administration, Office of
Procurement and Supply, RS 90, 810 Vermont
Avenue NW, Washington, DC 20420/202-389-
3313.

*Small Business Guide to Federal Research and
Development Funding Opportunities*—designed
to help small businesses take advantage of
government research and development, the
guide provides contact information, application
criteria, and program purpose for all government
research and development programs. Advice is
given as to how to approach the agencies, how to
become aware of new opportunities, and more.
The 136-page publication is available for $6.00
from: Superintendent of Documents, U.S. Government Printing Office, Washington, DC
20402/202-783-3238.

Washington, DC, Federal Buying Directory—this
brochure gives the names, addresses and telephone numbers of offices to contact in each

federal agency about sales opportunities and procurements. It is available free of charge from the GSA Business Service Centers.

U.S. Government Purchasing and Sales Directory—this directory, published by the Small Business Administration, lists the nationwide offices of federal agencies with procurement authority. It also contains an explanation of SBA assistance to small businesses in obtaining government prime contracts and subcontracts. Contact: Prime Contracts Division, Small Business Administration, 1441 L Street NW, Washington, DC 20416/202-653-6826.

Data Bases
The following data bases maintained by the Federal Government contain information you may find helpful in your business endeavors.

PROCUREMENT AUTOMATED SOURCE SYSTEM (PASS)— Pass is a centralized inventory and referral system of small businesses interested in being a prime contractor for federal agencies or a subcontractor for companies. More than 77,000 firms nationwide are listed in the fields of research and development, manufacturing, construction and services. PASS uses a keyword system which identifies the capabilities of the company. The system can be searched for firms by geographic location, type of ownership, labor surplus area, zip code, minority type and over 3,000 keywords.

Pass has been operational since October 1978 and it is increased by 200 firms monthly. Anyone seeking to purchase a product or service from a small business can contact SBA to have a search run. Searches and printouts are privided free of charge. Small firms wanting to be listed (no charge) in PASS should contact SBA also. Contact: Your local SBA office or: Procurement Automated Source System, Small Business Administration, 1441 L Street NW, Room 627, Washington, DC 20416/202-653-6586.

FEDERAL PROCUREMENT DATA BASE—The Federal Procurement Data Center (FPDC) stores information about federal procurement actions, from 1979 to present, that totaled $10,000 or more. The system contains 24 data elements, including: purchasing or contracting office: date of award; principal place of performance; dollars obligated; principal product or service; business and labor requirements; type of procurement action; methods of contracting; socioeconomic data; name and address of contractor; and foreign trade data. Examples of federal buying

range from research and development to supplies and equipment.

Searches and printouts are available on a cost-recovery basis. Requests should be made in writing. Contact: Federal Procurement Data Center, 4040 North Fairfax Drive, Suite 900, Arlington, VA 22203/703-235-1634.

MINORITY BUSINESS DEVELOPMENT DATA BASE—The Who's Who Resource File (WWRF) contains resource information about more than 24,000 U.S. organizations and individuals involved in minority business development. Collected data includes name of resource, address, telephone number, Standard Industrial Classification (SIC) if applicable, specialty code and, is retrievable by 26 major categories. WWRF is updated monthly by approximately 500 new entries. The Minority Business Development Agency will run searches and provide printouts or mailing labels free of charge. Service is restricted to individuals and organizations advocating minority business development. Contact: Department of Commerce, Minority Business Development Agency, Room 5710, Washington, DC 20230/202-377-5997.

MINORITY BUSINESS INFORMATION DATA BASE—The Business Development Report System (BDRS) contains information collected quarterly from recipients of federal grants under the Minority Business Development Center Program. As Grantees must report data about clients assisted (over 15,000), services provided and accomplishments, the data base contains information about minority business activities and services, minority-group breakdowns, business trends, capital and market brokering activities, and new start/acquisition brokering that occurs. BDRS currently has 50,000 records and is updated quarterly by approximately 15,000 records. Searches and printouts are available free of charge. Contact: III, U.S. Department of Commerce, Minority Business Development Agency, Room 5708, Washington, DC 20230/202-377-5997.

MINORITY BUSINESS LOCATOR DATA BASE—Profile: The National Automated Minority Business Source List Service is a minority business locator system established to help match minority firms with large government contractors needing services or products. The data base contains information about more than 27,000 minority-owned businesses nationwide. Profile can be searched by specific minority ownership (i.e., black, veteran, etc.), type of firm, size, geographic location and product or service supplied. Any company or organization wanting to purchase the services of a minority-owned business can obtain a search free of charge. Companies wanting to be listed in Profiles should contact The Minority Business Development Agency (MBDA) to find out if they are eligible. Listing is free of charge. Contact: Information Clearinghouse, Minority Business Development Agency, Room 6708, U.S. Department of Commerce, Washington, DC 20230/202-377-2414 or any of the numerous MBDA Offices throughout the United States. The Agency has seven regional offices, and 33 district offices, and it supports 100 Business Development Centers nationwide. Check your phone book under "U.S. Department of Commerce, Minority Business Development Agency."

Federal Money Programs

Direct payments, loans and grants are available to qualified small businesses. The listing below represents the programs we have described in INFORMATION USA under the appropriate sponsoring Department. For example, to locate the first program "Commodity Loans and Purchases" look up that title under the "Direct Payments" section of the chapter "Department of Agriculture." The entry will provide information such as program purpose, eligibility requirements, range of financial assistance, and who you should contact for further details and application.

For a listing of federal money program information sources see "Federal Money Programs: Finding What's Available" in the Finding Free Information on Everything and Anything section of the Sampler.

Department of Agriculture

Direct Payments
Commodity Loans & Purchases
Cotton Direct Pay
Dairy Indemnity Program
Feed Grain Production Stabilization
Wheat Production Stabilization
Wool Act Payments
Forestry Incentive Program
Rice Production Stabilization
Grain Reserve Program
Rural Rental Assistance

Loans
Commodity Loans & Purchases
Storage Facility Loans
Emergency Loans
Farm Labor Loans & Grants
Farm Operating Loans
Farm Ownership Guaranteed Loans
Rural Rental Housing
Soil & Water Loans
Indian Tribes Corporation Loans
Business & Industrial Loans
Economic Emergency Loans
Rural Telephone
Rural Telephone Bank

Grants
Farm Labor Loans & Grants

Department of Commerce

Direct Payments
Fisherman's Contingency
Fishing Vessel and Gear Damage

Loans
Trade Adjustment Assistance
Economic Development
Fishing Vessel

Grants
Economic Development
Research & Evaluation Program
Fish Conservation
Marine Pollution Research Grants
Fisheries Development
Minority Business Development

Department of Health and Human Services

Loans
HOM's Loans and Loan Guarantees
National Health Service

Direct Payments
Rent Supplements

Loans

Mortgage Insurance—Cooperative Projects

Mortgage Insurance—Investor Cooperative Housing

Mortgage Insurance—Land Development

Mortgage Insurance—Mobile Home Parks

Mortgage Insurance—Hospitals

Mortgage Insurance—Construct or Improve Nursing Homes

Rental Housing Mortgage Insurance

Mortgage Insurance—Rental Housing for Moderate Income Families

Mortgage Insurance—Rental Coop Housing—Low- and Moderate-Income

Mortgage Insurance—Rental Housing for Elderly

Mortgage Insurance—Rental Multifamily in Urban Renewal

Property Improvement—New Commercial Buildings

Supplemental Loan Insurance

Mortgage Insurance—Multifamily Experimental Housing

Mortgage Insurance—New Kinds of Construction Technology

Department of the Interior

Loans

Indian—Business Loans

Grants

Historic Preservation Grants

Department of Transportation

Direct Payments

Maritime Direct Payment—Ship Building

Am Transport & Cruise Ship Subsidy

Ship Buying for Business

Maritime Construction Reserve Fund

Loans

Railroad Guaranteed Loans

Railroad Loans—to Build or Improve

Maritime Loan

Grants

Transportation Resource Development

Maritime—R & D for Marine Firms, Shipyards

Department of the Treasury

Direct Payments

CAB Essential Air Services

Overseas Travel

Loans

Physical Disaster Loans

Small Business Loan Guarantees

Small Business Loans

Local Development

Bond Guarantees

Handicapped Assistance Loans

Pollution Control Loans

Small Business Energy Loans

Veterans Business Loans

Foreign Investment Loan Guarantees

Direct Investment Loans

Grants

Women's Business Ownership Training

Small Business Development Centers

Department of Energy

Loans

Coal Loan Guarantees

Minority Business Loans

Grants

Energy Related Inventions

Energy Research Grants

Appropriate Energy Technology

Biomass Energy Technology Research

Industrial Energy Conservation

Radio Station: Emergency Broadcast Assistance

Department of Education

Direct Payments

Handicapped Media Services

Grants

International Business

Minority Institutions Science Improvement

Research Library Resources Strenghtening

National Diffusion Network

Vocational Education Projects

Library Research

Interlibrary Cooperation

Handicapped Information Dissemination

Handicapped Media Services

Sources of Putting Together a Loan Package

Your eventual success in getting a loan approved or in persuading a venture capitalist to invest money in your business will be heavily dependent on your preparation of a loan package or proposal. In addition to compensated financial planners or financial brokers, there are many other sources of assistance in preparing loan presentation requests and business plans. Some of the following sources offer help to small or new businesses at either no cost or a nominal charge. Sources of help for putting together a loan package include:

Catalogue of Federal Domestic Assistance
This is the single best starting point for information on researching grants as well as procedures for requesting grants. It is the most complete source of information on government programs. It is published annually with updates by the Office of Management and Budget. Subscriptions are available for $36.00 from: Superintendent of Documents, U.S. Government Printing Office, Washington, DC 20402/202-783-3238.

Small Business Investment Companies
These corporations are licensed, regulated and sometimes funded by the SBA to provide both venture capital and long term financing to new or small businesses for expansion, modernization and sound financing for their organizations. There are also Minority Enterprise Small Business Investment Companies (MESBICs) to provide capital and assistance to minority owned small businesses. A free booklet *Money for Growth—SBIC Financing for Small Businesses* is available from SBA, and it describes methods of obtaining this financing. Staff will also direct you to volunteer professionals, such as members of SCORE or ACE, who can assist in requesting financing. Contact: Office of Investment, Small Business Administration, 1441 L Street NW, Washington, DC 20416/202-653-6584.

Small Business Administration Field Offices
As mentioned elsewhere in this section, the SBA offers a wide variety of free and nominal charge services and publications to small businesses. Of significance in this area are the numerous pamphlets available from SBA on developing and writing a business plan for use in obtaining financing. Titles include: *Small Marketeer Aid; Business Plan for Retailers; Management Aid for Small Manufacturers; Business Plan for Small Manufacturers; The ABC's of Borrowing;* and *How to Prepare for a Pre-Award Survey.* These are available either free or for a minimal charge from any SBA Field Office. In addition, staff at these offices can either offer free counseling or direct you to a professional volunteer for assistance in preparing your loan request packages. A list of these field offices is included in this section, or contact: Office of Public Affairs, Small Business Administration, 1441 L Street NW, Washington, DC 20416/202-653-6832.

General Service Administration Business Service Centers
Counselors at these centers provide individuals and firms with detailed information about government contracting opportunities, and assist them in doing business with the government. They can aid in the preparation of paperwork and applications necessary for government contracting and awards. A list of these centers is located elsewhere in this section, or contact: Office of Small and Disadvantaged Business Utilization, U.S. General Services Administration, 18th and F Streets NW, Washington, DC 20405/202-566-0776.

Where to Get Market Studies

Each year the U.S. government invests millions of dollars conducting market studies on subjects ranging from citizens' band radios to nuclear waste. But because the government spends very little to announce its reports, few people are aware of them.

Such studies can prove invaluable to any business searching for new markets or investigating opportunities in existing markets. Over the years I have used these little-known reports to satisfy clients' information requests. I once was asked by a client to define the total size of the market for golf carts in the United States along with the approximate sales volume of the major manufacturers. I reviewed all the typical sources and interviewed all of the major manufacturers and turned up very little information. However, we finally found all the information we needed at the U.S. Customs Service of the Department of the Treasury. Customs had investigated a Polish golf cart manufacturer for a possible violation of the Anti-Dumping Act. The investigation involved a number of public hearings that included testimony from major manufacturers. This testimony was printed, and it gave our researchers all that was necessary to piece together a substantial market study on the industry.

Although all of these studies are available to you for free or at every little cost, they are costing you, as a taxpayer, a lot more than you think. We all pay large amounts of taxes to finance the production of these reports, yet few of us get our money's worth. The government does not inform us of their availability and therefore we do not know where to go or what to get.

Described below are eight organizations that regularly publish market studies and topical reports. All but two of these offices can be contacted directly for free listings of reports or topics covered. Armed with such lists, you can request specific reports or documentation related to a topic. For copies of committee hearings available from the U.S. Senate or House of Representatives, you can contact your congressional representative's office and request a listing of committees of both the House and Senate. (See Sampler Section "Help and Information from Your Congressional Representatives") Then contact each committee separately and request lists of their hearings. If the committee will not produce a listing, ask your representative's office for further assistance. Committees should be contacted directly for further information on obtaining documentation and reports.

Copies of Congressional Research Service reports can only be obtained through the office of your member of Congress. Ask your Representative for a copy of the Congressional Research Service's annual index of reports, and with that you can then request copies of specific reports through your congressional-representative's office.

Market studies and other topical reports are available from the following government offices:

International Trade Commission

Part of the function of this agency is to study the volume of imports in comparison to domestic production and consumption. As a result, it produces close to 100 market studies each year on topics such as:

Ice Hockey Sticks
Leather Wearing Apparel
Nonrubber Footwear
Unalloyed Unwrought Zinc
Motorcycles
Clothespins

Reports are free, but a listing of available reports costs 10¢ per page. Contact: Office of the Secretary, International Trade Commission, Washington, DC 20436/202-523-5178.

International Trade Administration (ITC)

Investigates a few dozen industries each year for possible violations of the Anti-Dumping Act. Such industries have included:

Offset Printing Paper
Household Incandescent Lamps
45 RMP Adapters
Carbon Steel Plates

A free listing of industries investigated is available and copies of documents on file can be made for 10¢ per page after the first 50 pages. Contact: Central Records Unit, International Trade Administration, Department of Commerce, 14th St. & Constitution Ave. NW, Room 8099, Washington, DC 20230/202-377-1248.

Congressional Committee Hearings

There is hardly a topic that has not been covered by a Senate or House committee hearing. If a hearing has been held on a topic, it is very likely that the top experts have presented their viewpoints and all major information sources on the topic have been identified. Some 2,000 hearings are held annually on such topics as:

Administration's Comprehensive Program for the Steel Industry
Alcohol Fuels
Technology and the Cost of Health Care
Passive Solar Energy Programs and Plans
Capital Formation Problems Confronting Small Business
Nuclear Waste Management
Amateur Sports
Effects of the Baby Boom
U.S. Coal Production
Problems in the Sale of Travel Insurance at Airport Locations

To find out if a subject you are interested in has been researched by a congressional committee, call the House Bill Status Office: 202-225-8646, or the Capitol Hill Operator 202-224-3121.

You may also find it useful to consult the *Congressional Information Service Index,* which covers all publications (including hearing transcripts) of Congress. It can be found at most libraries, or can be purchased from: Congressional Information Service, 4520 East-West Highway, Bethesda, MD 20814/807/301-654-1550.

Once identified, hearing transcripts are generally available for free from the committee directly, or for a small charge from: Superintendent of Documents, Government Printing Office, Washington, DC 20402/202-783-3238.

Central Intelligence Agency (CIA)

Each year, the CIA declassifies 50 to 100 reports, which are then available to the public. Topics include:

International Energy Statistics
Soviet Chemical Equipment Purchases from the West
Relating Climate Change to Its Effects

A price listing of reports released from 1972 to the present is available free from: Photoduplication Service, Library of Congress, Washington, DC 20540/202-287-5650.

General Accounting Office

This office conducts special audits, surveys and reviews at the request of the U.S. Congress. It produces as many as 600 reports each year on such topics as:

Foreign Ownership of U.S. Farmland-Much Concern, Little Data
Fossil Energy Research, Development and Demonstration: Opportunities for Change
Timber Harvest Levels for National Forests—How Good Are They?
Deep Ocean Mining—Actions Needed to Make it Happen
What Causes Food Prices to Rise? What Can Be Done About It?
U.S. Statistics on International Technology Transfer—Need for Additional Measures
Computer Topography Scanning: Opportunity for Coordinated Federal Planning Before Substantial Acquisitions
Why Are New House Prices So High, How Are They Influenced by Government Regulations, and Can Prices Be Reduced?

Single copies of reports are available free of charge and additional copies can be obtained for $1 each. GAO also has a Bibliographic Data Base containing citations for every GAO document produced since 1976. Searches and printouts are available free of charge. For a free annual index to available reports contact: General Accounting Office, Distribution Section, 441 G St. NW, Room 1000, Washington, DC 20548/202-275-6241.

Congressional Research Service

This division of the Library of Congress services the legislative branch of the government exclusively with a wide variety of research and expertise. It generates more than 1,000 reports each year on such topics as:

A Legal Overview of the Antitrust Aspects of Mergers
The Future of American Agriculture
Future Higher Education Enrollments: An Analysis of Enrollment Projections
Incentives and Disincentives for U.S. Exporters
Taxes in 2000: A Projection of the Major Taxes Paid Directly by the Median Income Family for the Remainder of the 20th Century

Copies of these reports can be obtained through your congressional representative's office. A free annual index can be requested and specific reports can be obtained at no charge. You can contact your representative by writing, in care of his or her name, to: Senate, Washington, DC 20510, or, House of Representatives, Washington, DC 20515. You can also contact your representative through the Capitol Hill switchboard at 202-224-3121.

Federal Trade Commission (FTC)

Along with the Department of Justice, the FTC also investigates possible antitrust violations. Industries under investigation include:

Debt Collection
Auto Insurance
Rustproofing Industry Warranty Practices

For a listing of industries investigated and procedures for obtaining documents at 10¢ per page contact: Public Reference Division, Federal Trade Commission, 6th & Pennsylvania Ave. NW, Room 130, Washington, DC 20580/202-523-3598.

Department of Justice

The antitrust division of this department investigates a number of industries every year. The industries investigated include:

Dairy Products
Corrugated Containers
Armored Car and Related Services
Adult Motion Pictures
Lumber Products

For a listing of industries investigated and procedures for obtaining documents at 10¢ per page contact: Legal Procedure Unit, Department of Justice, 10th & Constitution Ave. NW, Room 7416, Washington, DC 20530/202-633-2481.

Other Information Sources

In addition to the offices described above, there are two government organizations that actively promote their publications. These organizations should be contacted to see how they might be helpful. Contact: Superintendent of Documents, Government Printing Office, Washington, DC 20402/202-783-3238, and, National Technical Information Service, 5285 Port Royal Road, Springfield, VA 22161/703-487-4650.

Also contact those Federal agencies that you think are involved with your subject area.

Getting Information About Competitors

The federal government is regulating and investigating more and more companies, both privately and publicly held. The result of this increased governmental activity has been additional disclosure information, nearly all of which is available to the public. Listed below are the major federal agencies that keep public information on companies. The information held at each federal office varies from agency to agency; however, most of the offices maintain financial or other information that most researchers would consider sensitive. The list is arranged by type of company or industry covered. The "Other Information Sources" category lists those agencies that only occasionally collect information on companies in a variety of industries.

Sources For Specific Industries

Airlines, Air Freight Commuter Carriers, and Air Taxis

Office of Community and Consumer Affairs, Dept. of Transportation Room 10405, 400 7th St. SE, Washington, DC 20590/202-755-2220.

Airports

Air Traffic Service Division, National Flight Data Center, Federal Aviation Administration, 800 Independence Ave. SW, Washington, DC 20591/202-426-3666.

Bank Holding Companies and State Members of the Federal Reserve System

Freedom of Information, Board of Governors of the Federal Reserve System, 20th St. and Constitution Ave. NW, Room B1122, Washington, DC 20551/202-452-3684.

Banks, National
Communications Division, Public Affairs, Comptroller of the Currency, 490 L'Enfant Plaza East SW, Washington, DC 20219/202-447-1800.

Bank Savings and Loan Associations
Federal Home Loan Bank Board, 1700 G St. NW, Washington, DC 20552/202-377-6000.

Barge and Vessel Operators
Financial Analysis, Tariffs, Federal Maritime Commission, 1100 L St. NW, Washington, DC 20573/202-523-5876.

Cable Television System Operators
Cable TV Bureau, Federal Communications Commission, 1919 M St. NW, Room 242, Washington, DC 20554/202-632-7480.

Colleges, Universities, Vocational Schools, and Public Schools
National Center for Educational Statistics, 1200 19th St. NW, Washington, DC 20208-1404/202-254-6503.

Commodity Trading Advisors, Commodity Pool Operators, and Futures Commission Merchants
Commodity Futures Trading Commission, 2033 K St. NW, Washington, DC 20581/202-254-8630.

Consumer Products
Corrective Actions Division, Consumer Product Safety Commission, 5401 Westbard Ave., Bethesda, MD/Mailing Address: 5401 Westbard Ave., Bethesda, MD 20816/301-492-6608.

Electric and Gas Utilities and Gas Pipeline Companies
Federal Energy Regulatory Commission, Department of Energy, 825 North Capitol St. NE, Washington, DC 20426/202-357-8370.

Exporting Companies
American International Traders Register, World Traders Data Reports Section, Department of Commerce, Washington, DC 20230/202-377-4203.

Federal Land Bank Associations and Production Credit Association
Farm Credit Administration, 1501 Farm Credit Drive, McLean, VA 22102-5090/703-883-4000.

Foreign Corporations
World Traders Data Reports, Department of Commerce, Washington, DC 20230/202-377-4203.

Hospitals and Nursing Homes
National Center for Health Statistics, 3700 East-West Highway, Hyattsville, MD 20782/301-436-8500.

Land Developers
Office of Interstate Land Sales Registration, Department of Housing and Urban Development, 451 7th St. SW, Room 6262, Washington, DC 20410/202-755-7077.

Mining Companies
Mine Safety and Health Administration, Department of Labor, 4015 Wilson Blvd., Arlington, VA 22203/703-235-1452.

Nonprofit Institutions
Internal Revenue Service, Freedom of Information Reading Room, 1111 Constitution Ave. NW, Washington, DC 20224/202-566-3770.

Nuclear Plants
Nuclear Regulatory Commission, 1717 H St. NW, Washington, DC 20555/301-492-7715.

Pension Plans
Division of Inquiries and Technical Assistance, Office of Pension and Welfare Benefits Programs, Department of Labor, 200 Constitution Ave. NW, Washington, DC 20210/202-523-8776.

Pharmaceutical, Cosmetic, and Food Firms
Associate Commissioner for Regulatory Affairs, Food and Drug Administration, 5600 Fishers Lane, Rockville, MD 20857/301-443-1594.

Pesticide and Chemical Manufacturers
Environmental Protection Agency, Office of Pesticides and Toxic Substances, 401 M St. SW, Washington, DC 20460/202-382-2902.

Public Companies
Securities and Exchange Commission, 150 5th St. NW, Washington, DC 20549/202-272-7450.

Radio and Television Stations
Broadcast Bureau, Federal Communications Commission, 1919 M St. NW, Washington, DC 20554/202-632-7136.

Railroads, Trucking Companies, Bus Lines, Freight Forwarders, Water Carriers, Oil Pipelines, Transportation Brokers, and Express Agencies
Interstate Commerce Commission, Room 3145, 12th St. and Constitution Ave. NW, Washington, DC 20423/202-275-7524.

Telephone Companies, Overseas Telegraph Companies, Microwave Companies, Public Land, and Mobile Services
Common Carrier Bureau, Federal Communications Commission, 1919 M St. NW, Washington, DC 20554/202-632-6910.

Other Information Sources

Central Records Unit, International Trade Administration, Department of Commerce, 14th St. and Pennsylvania Ave. NW, Washington, DC 20230/202-377-4679.

Patent Office Search Room, Patent Office, Department of Commerce, 2021 Jefferson Davis Hwy., Building 3, Crystal Plaza, Arlington, VA 22202/703-557-2276. Mailing Address: Washington, DC 20231.

Public Reference Division, Federal Trade Commission, 6th St. and Pennsylvania Ave. NW, Room 130, Washington, DC 20580/202-523-3598.

Reference Room, International Trade Commission, 701 E St. NW, Room 154, Washington, DC 20436/202-523-0430.

State governments-check state government offices for more information on companies.

Technology Resources

Information about Technology and Technology Transfer is available from many agencies of the Federal Government. The sources identified below can answer your questions, put you in touch with experts, or send you literature.

Congress

Congressional Caucus for Science and Technology
Established to serve the U.S. Congress, the Caucus' staff provides selected representatives with accurate and timely data about the impact of science and technology on U.S. economic growth. The Caucus also sponsors seminars to increase U.S. scientific literacy and to identify scientists, technologists, educators and others who can advise Congress about scientific and technological issues. The Caucus publishes newsletters, summaries and other materials. Contact: The Congressional Caucus for Science and Technology, House Annex Building #2, H2-226, 2nd and D Streets SW, Washington,, DC 20515/202-226-7788.

House Committee on Science and Technology
This Committee has overall jurisdiction for science and technology legislation under consideration by the U.S. House of Representatives. It is comprised of several subcommittees, each responsible for a different aspect of the field. Members are very knowledgeable about the subject matter they cover, and they can recommend information sources. Subcommittee publications, such as newsletters, bills and hearing records, are available at no cost while the committee's supply lasts. A listing of publications appears in the overall committee's *Legislative Calendar*. Contact: House Committee on Science and Technology, U.S.

House of Representatives, 2321 Rayburn HOB (House Office Building), Washington, DC 20515/202-225-6371, and publications 202-225-6275.

Office of Technology Assessment
This non-partisan analytical agency prepares objective analysis of major policy issues related to scientific and technological change. OTA's staff are available to answer questions and provide information about the subjects they have researched. Upon request, OTA will send you a free catalogue of its publications, as well as descriptions of new projects under way. Summaries of most OTA reports are available, at no cost, directly from the agency. Full text of the reports must be purchased from: Superintendent of Documents, U.S. Government Printing Office, Washington, DC 20402/202-783-3238. Described below are OTA reports relating to R & D funding.

Census of State Government Initiatives for High Technology Industrial Development, $4.50.
Encouraging High Technology Development #1, Background Paper, $4.75.
Technology, Innovation and Regional Economic Development, $4.50.

Contact: Office of Technology Assessment, U.S. Congress, Washington, DC 20510/202-224-9241.

Senate Subcommittee on Science, Technology and Space

This Subcommittee has primary jurisdiction over science and technology legislation under consideration by the Senate. Staff members are very knowledgeable about the subject matter they cover and they can recommend information sources. Subcommittee publications such as bills, printed hearings, and reports are available at no cost while the committee's supply lasts. Contact: Science, Technology and Space Subcommittee, Committee on Commerce, Science and Transportation, U.S. Senate, Washington, DC 20510/ 202-224-5115 (Publications and Documents), or 202-224-8172 (Inquiries).

Department of Commerce

Computers and Software Standards Experts

The National Bureau of Standards (NBS) provides the measurement standards and data necessary to create, make and sell U.S. products and services at home and abroad. This involves the in-house research and development necessary to understand the physical quantities involved and to develop means of characterizing and measuring them. It also involves extensive interactions with users at every level to assure that the system is meeting their needs.

The NBS has several offices which specialize in computers and software. Staff in these offices can be extremely useful in identifying new trends, technology, or other related information sources. Contact: National Bureau of Standards, U.S. Department of Commerce, Route 270, Gaithersburg, MD 20234/301-921-1000.

Data Centers—NSRDS

The National Standards Reference Data System's data centers support the National Bureau of Standards' responsibility to promote numerical data in the physical sciences. Its evaluations are carried out through a national network of 22 NSRDS Centers. The Center's activities are aggregated into three application-oriented program areas: (1) Energy and Environmental Data, (2) Industrial Process Data, and (3) Materials Properties Data. Information about database searches, printouts, publications and data tapes is available from NSRDS' Washington Office. Searches are also available from its 22 Centers. A cost-recovery fee may be charged for services. For a complete listing of the centers see the Department of Commerce chapter, entry titled "Data Centers—NSRDS." Contact: Office of Standard Reference Data, 320 Physics Building, National Bureau of Standards, Washington, DC 20234/ 301-921-2228.

Directory of Responsibilities in Trade Development

Updated approximately every six months, this directory provides the names of industry specialists. It includes the following information: area of responsibility; name of the person; phone number; room number; and cluster or industry sector represented. The 10-page publication is available free of charge by sending a self-addressed, stamped envelope to: Office of Program and Resource Management ITA/TD, International Trade Administration, Room 3015B, U.S. Department of Commerce, Washington, DC 20230/ 202-377-3197.

Industry Specialists

Staff in the following office can refer you to an industry specialist for nearly every industry in the U.S.: Industry Publications, Department of Commerce, International Trade Administration (ITA), Room 442, 14th and Constitution Avenue NW, Washington, DC 20230/202-377-4356.

Institute for Computer Science and Technology (ICST)

This Institute is involved in the overall area of computer science and technology, and in the establishment of standards and guidelines for the field. Staff knowledgeable about internal computer security, computer security communications and cryptology are available to answer questions. Upon request, staff will add you to the mailing list for the ICST newsletter, a free publication which keeps readers up-to-date on the Institute's current activities. It provides information about new publications, conferences, seminars, guides and standards. A free listing of ICST publications is also available. Contact: Institute for Computer Science and Technology, National Bureau of Standards (NBS), Technology Building, Gaithersburg, MD 20899/301-921-3427.

International Trade Administration Reports

ITA has issued several reports profiling U.S. high technology industries and more are in the planning. Studies have been done on biotechnology, computers, robotics, semiconductors, telecommunications, and the overall high tech industry. Information about these reports and their findings can be obtained by contacting: International Trade Administration (ITA), U.S. Department of Commerce, 14th and Constitution Avenue NW, Washington, DC 20230/202-377-3888 (Public Affairs).

Japanese Trade
The Department of Commerce has four offices
that handle the various aspects of trade with
Japan. Staff is knowledgeable about matters concerning high tech industries and trade investment
policy. They will answer questions when possible
and make reference to experts in other government agencies and publications. These offices are:

JAPAN TRADE FACILITATION COMMITTEE
International Trade Administration
Department of Commerce
14th and E Streets NW
Washington, DC 20230/202-377-5722

OFFICE OF JAPAN
International Trade Administration
Department of Commerce
14th and E Streets NW
Washington, DC 20230/202-377-4527

JAPAN WORK GROUP ON HIGH TECHNOLOGY
INDUSTRIES
International Trade Administration
Department of Commerce
14th and E Streets NW
Washington, DC 20230/202-377-5251

COMMERCE PRODUCTIVITY CENTER
Department of Commerce
14th and Constitution Avenue NW
Washington, DC 20230/202-377-0940.

National Technical Information Service
NTIS is the central source for the public sale of
U.S. Government-sponsored research, development and engineering reports as well as computer
software and data files. The NTIS collection
exceeds one million titles with 60,000 new reports
being released yearly. NTIS provides a variety of
information, awareness products and services to
keep the public abreast of the technologies developed by the U.S. government's multi-billion dollar
annual research and engineering effort. The following is a sample of publications available from
NTIS. To order, or obtain further information
contact: National Technical Information Service,
Department of Commerce, 5285 Port Royal Road,
Springfield, VA 22161/703-557-4600.

Federal Technology Transfer—OnLine—This free
   booklet is a reference guide for searching two
   federally produced databases—Government Inventions and NTIS Tech Notes.
Foreign Technology—(NTIS)
(NTIS) offers a weekly newsletter providing summaries to technical reports issued by foreign
governments including Japan, West Germany,

France, Great Britain, and Sweden. Available on
subscription, this newsletter alerts U.S. businesses
to the more than 10,000 new reports NTIS receives
annually. Write for the free descriptive brochure,
PR-733.
Technology Catalogues—Each annual *Federal
   Technology Catalogue* offers a compilation and
   index to more than 1,200 new technologies
   chosen as having potential commercial or practical application. These technologies represent
   some of the best Government research and
   engineering efforts for the year. Ordering information: 1983 Catalogue: Order Number
   PB84-105634 ($23.50), 1984 Catalogue: Order
   Number PB85-106987 ($23.50).
Technology Fact Sheets—A subscription product,
   NTIS Tech Notes, brings readers single-page
   fact sheets (often illustrated) of new processes,
   equipment, inventions for licensing, software,
   and research advances. The input has been
   screened as having potential practical application with much of the material coming from
   R&D activities at Federal laboratories. To
   receive additional information, ask for the free
   descriptive brochure, PR-365.
Technology Newsletters—Available on subscription are the 27 weekly NTIS *Abstract Newsletters*
   providing current and easy-to-read summaries
   of Federal research. These summaries are selected from the more than 70,000 new technical
   reports NTIS receives annually and grouped
   into subject areas of high interest; for example,
   *Manufacturing Technology, Communications,
   and Materials Sciences*. It offers comprehensive
   coverage of the multibillion-dollar Government
   R & D programs. Foreign technology developed
   by other countries also is included. To receive
   additional information, ask for the free descriptive brochure, PR-733.

Roadmap Program
This program helps small and medium-sized businesses get the information they need from the
federal government. Staff are familiar with business and they can respond to questions about
trade, government, procurement, finding sources,
product standards, business licenses, franchising,
etc. They will either answer your questions or put
you in contact with the proper expert. There is no
fee for the service itself, although staff may direct
you to a publication or other source for which
there is a charge. A free brochure describing the
Roadmap Program is available upon request.
Contact: Roadmap Program, Office of Business
Liaison, U.S. Department of Commerce, Room
5898-C, Washington, DC 20230/202-377-3176.

U.S. Industrial Outlook
Published each January, this book provides an overview and prospectus for more than 300 U.S. industries. The book gives the name, telephone number and address of an expert for nearly every industry in the country. These specialists can tell you about the latest developments in the field and refer you to other experts and literature. The 1,000-page book costs $14.00 and is available from: Superintendent of Documents, U.S. Government Printing Office, Washington, DC 20402/202-783-3238. For information about the book's contents, contact: *U.S. Industrial Outlook,* Department of Commerce, International Trade Administration, Industry Publications, Room 442, 14th and Constitution Avenue NW, Washington, DC 20230/202-377-4356.

Department of Defense

Information Analysis Centers (IAC's)
The Department of Defense funds several centers specializing in the analysis of scientific and technical information. Many of the centers maintain on-line data bases and can provide reference services for the specialized area they cover. Staff can also provide evaluative engineering and/or analytical services. Services are generally provided on a cost-recovery basis. Listed below are the names of these centers. Each is described in the DOD Chapter. For a Center's description, look its name up in the proper alphabetical spot in the Department of Defense Chapter.

Aerospace Structures Information and Analysis Center
Coastal Engineering Research Center
Cold Regions Research
Concrete Technology Information Analysis Center
Guidance and Control Information Analysis Center
Hydraulic Engineering Information Analysis Center
Infrared Information and Analysis Center
Manufacturing Technology Information Analysis Center
Metals Matrix Composites Information Analysis Center
Metals and Ceramic Information Center
Nondestructive Testing Information Analysis Center
Nuclear Information Analysis Center
Pavements and Soil Trafficability Information Analysis Center

Plastics Technical Evaluation Center
Reliability Analysis Center
Shock and Vibration Information Center
Soil Mechanics Information Analysis Center
Survivability/Vulnerability Information Analysis Center
Tactical Technology Center
Thermophysical and Electronic Properties Information Analysis Center

Department of Health and Human Services

Biotechnology Resources
This free directory lists and describes biotechnology-related research programs being carried out across the United States. Contact information, services available, and a description of research emphasis or application is provided for each entry. Contact: Research Resources Information Center, 1776 East Jefferson Street, Rockville, MD 20852/301-984-2870.

Medical Technology Experts
The National Institutes of Health consist of 12 separate Institutes, each covering a specific area of medicine. Staff in the following offices can refer you to experts in their Institute who are knowledgeable about specific medical technologies. Most of these offices also have scientific reports and patient-oriented materials they can send you, often free of charge.

NATIONAL INSTITUTE ON AGING
Building 31, Room 5C35
Bethesda, MD 20205/301-496-1752

NATIONAL INSTITUTE OF ALLERGY AND INFECTIOUS DISEASES
Office of Research Reporting and Public Response
Building 31, Room 7A32
Bethesda, MD 20205/301-497-5717

NATIONAL INSTITUTE ON ARTHRITIS, DIABETES, AND DIGESTIVE AND KIDNEY DISEASES
Information Office
Building 31, Room 9A04
9000 Rockville Pike
Bethesda, MD 20205/301-496-3585

NATIONAL INSTITUTE OF CANCER
Cancer Information Service
Building 31, Room 10A18
Bethesda, MD 20205/202-636-5700
Alaska 800-633-6070
Hawaii 800-524-1234
Elsewhere 800-4 CANCER

NATIONAL INSTITUTE OF CHILD HEALTH AND HUMAN
DEVELOPMENT
9000 Rockville Pike
Bethesda, MD 20205/301-496-1848

NATIONAL INSTITUTE OF DENTAL RESEARCH
Public Inquiries and Report Section
Building 31, Room 2C35
Bethesda, MD 20205/301-496-4261

NATIONAL INSTITUTE OF ENVIRONMENTAL HEALTH
SCIENCES
Public Affairs Office
PO Box 12233
Research Triangle Park, NC 27709/919-541-3345

NATIONAL EYE INSTITUTE
Office of Scientific Reporting
Building 31, Room 6A32
Bethesda, MD 20205/301-496-5238

NATIONAL INSTITUTE OF GENERAL MEDICAL SCIENCES
Office of Research Reports
Building 31, Room 4A52
9000 Rockville Pike
Bethesda, MD 20205

NATIONAL HEART, LUNG, AND BLOOD INSTITUTE
Information Office
Building 31, Room 4A21
Bethesda, MD 20205/301-496-4236

NATIONAL INSTITUTE OF MENTAL HEALTH
Public Communications Branch
Division of Communications and Education
Parklawn Building, Room 15-102
5600 Fishers Lane
Rockville, MD 20857/301-443-4536

NATIONAL INSTITUTE OF NEUROLOGICAL AND
COMMUNICATIVE DISORDERS AND STROKE
Office of Scientific and Health Reports
Building 31, Room 8A06
Bethesda, MD 20205/301-496-5924

For further information contact: Division of Public
Information, National Institutes of Health (NIH),
9000 Rockville Pike, Bethesda, MD 20205/
301-496-5787.

Department of Labor

Office of Productivity and Technology Studies
The Office of Productivity and Technology Studies
investigates trends in technology and their impact
on employment and productivity. Staff will send
you an inventory of available statistics, and they
can tell you about both industries affected and
occupations displaced by technological innovations. The Office frequently issues reports and
updates about the impact of technological changes
and the manpower trends of various industries. A
publications list is available upon request. Contact:
Office of Productivity and Technology Studies,
Bureau of Labor Statistics, U.S. Department of
Labor, 441 G Street NW, Washington, DC
20212/202-523-9294.

Department of State

High Technology in Developed Countries
The Division of Developed Country Trade tracks
high technology activities in a developed country.
Staff can provide you with a general overview of a
specific country's activities. Contact: Division of
Developed Country Trade, Office of Trade, U. S.
Department of State, Room 3822, Washington,
DC 20520/202-632-2718.

Department of Transportation

Japanese High Speed Rail System Resource
The U.S. Office of the Japanese government's
transportation system, Japanese National Railway,
can provide you with information about its high
speed rail system. Upon written request, staff will
send you technical information and illustrated
brochures about the Japanese high speed bullet
train called *Shinkansen.* Contact: Japanese National Railroad Assistance Team to the Northeast
Corridor Improvement Project, c/o Federal Railroad Administration, RPF-1, 400 7th Street SW,
Washington, DC 20590/202-472-5597.

Federal Laboratory Consortium
The Federal Laboratory Consortium (FLC) is a
national network of 300 individuals from federal
labs and centers representing 11 federal agencies.
Each FLC member is responsible for taking
inventory and assessing the technology developed
at his/her facility and then passing the research
information on to industry, state and local governments, and to the general public. Through the
FLC, the public has access to virtually every aspect
of unclassified research activity within the federal
government. This office can refer you to an FLC
member in your specialty or geographical area.
The directories listed below will help you locate
FLC members.
Federal Lab Directory, 1985 provides information about 388 federal labs with ten or more
full-time professionals engaged in research and

development. Summary data arranged by federal agency and by state provide a broad overview of the federal lab system. Lab lists by staff size, by state and by agency provide a cross reference. For each lab a contact for obtaining technical information is given by name, address, and phone number. Major mission and major scientific or testing equipment is listed for each laboratory. This directory is available free of charge from: Office of Research and Technology Applications, National Bureau of Standards, Room 402, Administration Building, Washington, DC 20234/301-921-3814.

Directory of Federal Technology Resources describes the hundreds of federal laboratories, agencies, and engineering centers willing to share their expertise, equipment, and sometimes even facilities. It includes descriptions of 70 technical information centers and is indexed by subject, geographical location and resource name. It was prepared by the Center for the Utilization of Federal Technology, a division of the National Technical Information Center (NTIC). Cost is $25, and it can be purchased from NTIS, 5285 Port Royal Road, Springfield, VA 22161/703-487-4650. (Order number is PB84-100015/AAW.)

Listed below are the names and addresses of the consortium's chairman and vice chairman, the executive director, the two Washington, DC representatives, six regional coordinators, and the technical specialty coordinator. To locate the representative nearest you, contact the coordinator for your region:

Federal Laboratory Consortium Chairman
Dr. Eugene Stark, Los Alamos National Laboratory, Los Alamos, NM 87545/505-667-4960.

Federal Laboratory Consortium Vice Chairman
Ms. Margaret McNamara, Naval Underwater Systems Center, Code 10, Building 80T, New London, CT 06320/203-440-4590.

Northeast Region
Dr. William Marcuse, Brookhaven National Laboratory, Building 197, Upton, NY 11973/ 516-282-2103.

Mid-Atlantic Region
Jerome Bortman, Naval Air Development Center, Warminster, PA 18974/215-441-3100.

Southeast Region
Mr. Donald Jared, Oak Ridge National Laboratory Research Application Office, P.O. Box Y, Oak Ridge, TN 37831/615-574-4192.

Midwest Region
Dr. G. R. Williamson, Attention CERL-ZG, Army Construction Engineering Research Laboratory, P.O. Box 40005, Champaign, IL 61820-1305/217-373-7206.

Mid-Continent Region
Mr. Robert Stromberg, Sandia National Laboratory, Technology Transfer Officer, Organization 400, Albuquerque, NM 87185/505-844-5535.

Far West Region
Dr. Loren C. Schmid, Batelle Pacific Northwest, P.O. Box 999, Richland, WA 99352/ 509-375-2559.

Technical Specialty Coordinator
Clifford E. Lanham, Harry Diamond Laboratory, 2800 Powder Mill Road, Adelphi, MD 20783/ 301-394-2296.

Executive Office of the President

Japan/U.S. Industrial Policies and Negotiations
The White House Office, U.S. Special Trade Representative of the Executive Branch is responsible for bilateral affairs between the U.S. and Japan in regard to trade policy development and coordination. Contact: U.S. Special Trade Representative, Director for Japan, White House Office, 600 17th Street NW, Washington, DC 20506.

Office of Science and Technology Policy
This office advises the President of the United States and his administration about science and technology policy and issues. Speeches by the President's science advisor are available free of charge. A listing of publications, many which must be purchased from the U.S. Government Printing Office, is also available at no cost. Contact: Office of Science and Technology Policy, Executive Office of the President, White House, Washington, DC 20506/202-395-3840 or 202-395-4692 (publications).

General Service Administration

Federal Information Center
The Federal Government sponsors a network of information centers throughout the U.S. to help citizens find their way through the federal bureaucracy. By calling, writing, or visiting your local Federal Information Center you will be directed to a government expert who can provide information about high tech industries, government programs, research centers and publications. See "Re-

sources—Close-To-Home" section of the Sampler for a complete listing of the centers. For further information contact: Federal Information Center, General Service Administration (GSA), 7th and D Streets SW, Washington, DC 20405/202-783-3238.

Library of Congress

National Referral Center (NRC)
NRC maintains an on-line data bank of more than 12,000 qualified organizations or individuals willing to provide information to the general public on topics in science, technology, and the social sciences. The Center can refer you to appropriate associations, government agencies, literature and data bases. Staff will perform computer searches and send you a printout free of charge.

The Federal Government supports approximately 130 Information Analysis Centers involved in science and technology. These IAC's provide a variety of services such as publication of critical data compilations, state-of-the-art reviews, bibliographies, current awareness services, and newsletters. Many Centers answer inquiries and provide consulting and literature search services. The National Referral Center can direct you to an appropriate IAC or send you a listing of all the Centers. Contact: National Referral Center (NRC), Library of Congress, Washington, DC 20540/202-287-5670.

Science and Technology Career Materials

Tracer Bullets
A brief guide to information sources covering careers in science and technology, *Career Opportunities in Science and Technology Tracer Bullet* #ISSN 0090-5232 includes a bibliographic listing of books, journals, articles and abstracting and indexing services. The publication is updated as needed and available free of charge. Contact: Reference Section, Science and Technology Division, Library of Congress, 10 First Street SW, Washington, DC 20540/202-287-5639.

Science and Technology Division
This Division offers reference services based on its collection of 3 million scientific and technical books and pamphlets and 2.5 million technical reports. Reference librarians will assist researchers in using the library's book and on-line catalogs as well as its abstracting and indexing services. The Division publishes:

LC Science Tracer Bullets—series of free bibliographic guides to selected scientific and technical topics such as high technology, computer science, and robotics. Contact: Science and Technology division, Library of Congress, 2nd Street and Independence Avenue SE, Washington, DC 20540/202-287-5639—Reference Section and 202-287-5580.

National Aeronautics and Space Administration

Industrial Application Centers
To promote technology transfer, NASA operates a network of dissemination centers whose job is to provide information retrieval services and technical assistance to industrial and government clients. Literature searches are available as well as current awareness services tailored to individual needs. A nominal fee is charged for these services. A free pamphlet, *Search Before Research,* describes the Centers and their services. For further information contact the nearest Industrial Applications Center listed below, or Industrial Applications, National Aeronautics and Space Administration, 400 Maryland Avenue, Room 5113, Washington, DC 20546/202-755-8430.

AEROSPACE RESEARCH APPLICATIONS CENTER, 611 N. Capital Avenue, Indianapolis, IN 46207/317-264-4644.

KERR INDUSTRIAL APPLICATIONS CENTER, Southeastern Oklahoma State University, Station A—Box 2584, Durant, OK 74701/405-924-6822.

NASA INDUSTRIAL APPLICATIONS CENTER, 701 LIS Building, University of Pittsburgh, Pittsburgh, PA 15260/412-624-5211.

NASA INDUSTRIAL APPLICATIONS CENTER, University of Southern California, Research Annex, Room 200, 3716 S. Hope Street, University Park, Los Angeles, CA 90007/213-743-6132.

NEW ENGLAND RESEARCH APPLICATIONS CENTER, Mansfield Professional Park, Storrs, CT 06268/203-486-4533.

NORTH CAROLINA SCIENCE AND TECHNOLOGY RESEARCH CENTER, P.O. Box 12235, Research Triangle Park, NC 27709/919-549-0671.

TECHNOLOGY APPLICATIONS CENTER (TAC), University of New Mexico, 2500 Central Avenue SW, Albuquerque, NM 87131/505-277-3622.

Technology Utilization Office
The Technology Utilization Office is involved in transferring NASA-developed technology to industry for the development of useful commercial

products. A variety of services and publications are available, and staff will answer questions and make referrals. For additional information about the program, see entry for Technology Utilization and Industry Affairs Division under National Aeronautics and Space Administration chapter.

The NASA Tech Brief Journal, a quarterly publication covering 125 new technologies each issue, is available free of charge by contacting: Scientific and Technical Information Facility, Baltimore-Washington International Airport, P.O. Box 8757, BWI Airport, MD 21240/301-621-8241 04 8242—Walter Heiland, Director.

For further information contact: Technology Utilization Office (NASA TU), Code I, NASA Headquarters, National Aeronautics and Space Administration, 400 Maryland Avenue SW, Washington, DC 20546/202-453-8415.

National Science Foundation (NSF)

Services and Publications
An independent federal agency, NSF supports research in science and technology; educational activities in science and engineering; and surveys about the general state of science and technology in the U.S. The Public Affairs staff will refer you to an NSF Program Officer who can tell you about the latest research and development efforts in your field of interest.

Described below are several important NSF publications. They are available by calling the Division of Science Resource Studies at 202-634-4622. All publications are available free of charge from NSF as long as the supply lasts.

> *Grants and Awards for Fiscal Year*
> *Grants for Scientific and Engineering Research*
> *Science Indicators*
> *National Patterns of Science and Technology*
> *Science and Engineering Personnel: A National Overview*

For information about NSF programs, contact: National Science Foundation (NSF), 1800 G Street NW, Washington, DC 20550/202-357-9498—Office of Public Affairs.

Science and Engineering Training and Deployment
The Scientific and Technical Personnel Studies Section office of the National Science Foundation (NSF) conducts studies of scientific and technical personnel in the U.S. The resulting reports are available and provide data about the training and deployment of individuals in science and engineer-

ing fields. Staff in the Studies Section are highly specialized and they will respond to written inquiries. A listing of reports is available by writing the Studies Section or by calling NSF's Editorial and Inquiries Unit. The following publications are available free of charge:

> *Science and Engineering Personnel*
> *Women and Minorities in Science and Engineering*
> *Survey of Recent Science and Engineering Graduates*
> *Survey of Doctoral Scientists and Engineers*
> *Survey of Experienced Scientists and Engineers*
> *U.S. Scientists and Engineers*

Contact: Editorial and Inquiries Unit for Publications, Scientific and Technical Personnel Studies Section, Division of Science Resource Studies, National Science Foundation (NSF), 1800 G Street NW, Washington, DC 20550/202-634-4622.

University of California Data Bases

Directory of Persons Interested in Technology Transfer
The Directory is a listing of more than 2,000 scientists, engineers, technicians, professionals, managers, etc., interested in technology transfer. Everyone included has agreed to respond to a telephone call concerning a technical question related to their area of expertise. Searches and printouts are available free of charge. The university will also generate mailing lists by zip code or area of expertise. Mailing lists are not compiled for advertising purposes. The Directory is also available in hard copy, free of charge.

Federal Laboratory Technological Innovation Cases Data Base (TECLAB)
TECLAB contains cases of technology innovations generated in a federal laboratory that (according to the laboratory) have commercial potential. Searches and printouts are available free of charge. A free monthly newsletter containing information from the data base is also available upon request.

Federal Technological Innovation Transfer Cases Data Base (TECTRA)
TECTRA contains cases of technology innovations that have been transferred from a federal laboratory to a second user and have a high potential for commercialization.

Searches and printouts are available free of charge. A free monthly newsletter containing information from the data base is also available upon request.

University Technological Innovation Cases Data Base
TECUNI contains cases of technology innovations developed by a University School of Engineering and for which the originator believes there is a high likelihood of commercialization.

The data base currently has 200 records. Six new cases are added monthly. Searches and printouts are available free of charge. A free monthly newsletter containing information from the data base is also available upon request. For further information contact: School of Business, University of California, Sacramento, CA 95819/916-454-6640.

Selling Overseas

International trade is becoming increasingly important to the economic well-being of the United States. Five million jobs depend on our exporting goods—1 in 8 manufacturing jobs depends on it, and 1 in 4 farm acres is planted for it. The Federal Government is doing more and more to promote and assist American businesses, especially small businesses, in their efforts to market overseas.

In this section we have identified federal offices offering assistance; unique services, such as temporary office space overseas; country experts; sources which will help you learn about living abroad; a variety of helpful publications; and American embassies you can turn to throughout the world.

Federal Agencies Offering Assistance
Several government offices are particularly good resources for businesses exploring overseas opportunities. In addition to the listing below, also consult the chapter Department of Commerce, especially the section "Exporting—Business Opportunities Abroad."

Agency for International Development (AID)
AID provides information to U.S. suppliers, particularly small, independent enterprises, regarding purchases to be financed with AID funds. U.S. small businesses can obtain special counseling and services related to AID-financed projects. AID sponsors Development Technologies Exhibitions, where technical firms in the U.S. are matched up with those in lesser developed countries for the purpose of forming joint ventures or exploring licensing possibilities. AID provides loans and grants to finance consulting services that support project activities related to areas such as agriculture, rural development, health, and housing. Contact: Office of Business Relations, Agency for International Development, State Annex 14, Room 648, Washington, DC 20523/202-235-1720.

Bureau of the Census
American exporters can obtain detailed statistical profiles of foreign trade and demographic topics, as well as import/export statistics, and marketing research consultation from the Bureau. Contact: Bureau of the Census, Department of Commerce, Washington, DC 20230/202-377-3523.

Export-Import Bank of the United States
This agency facilitates and aids in the financing of exports of U.S. goods and services. Its programs include: short-term, medium-term, and long-term credits; small business support; financial guarantees and insurance. In addition, it sponsors conferences on small business exporting, maintains credit information on thousands of foreign firms, supports feasibility studies of overseas programs, and offers export and small business counseling. It also operates a hotline to assist small businesses in exporting. Call: 800-424-5201 (in DC 202-566-8860). Contact: Export-Import Bank, 811 Vermont Avenue NW, Washington, DC 20571/202-566-8990. (See also the chapter on Export-Import Bank of the United States).

Foreign Agriculture Service
This office is charged with maintaining and expanding export sales of U.S. agricultural commodities and products. Staff can provide information about foreign agricultural production, trade and consumption, marketing research including areas of demand for specific commodities in foreign countries, and analyses of foreign competition in agricultural areas. Other services include

financing opportunities, contributions to export promotion costs and test marketing assistance. This office also handles U.S. representation to foreign governments and participates in formal trade negotiations. Contact: Foreign Agricultural Service, U.S. Department of Agriculture, Washington, DC 20250/202-447-3935. (See also Department of Agriculture section).

International Prices Division
The International Prices Division of the Department of Labor makes available export price indexes for both detailed and aggregate product groups on a quarterly basis, as well as price trend comparisons of U.S. exports with those of Japan and Germany. Contact: International Prices Division, Bureau of Labor Statistics, Department of Labor, 600 E Street NW, Washington, DC 20212/202-272-5025.

International Trade Administration
The International Trade Administration (ITA) assists American exporters in locating and gaining access to foreign markets. It furnishes information about foreign markets available for U.S. products and services, requirements which must be fulfilled, economic conditions in foreign countries, foreign market and investment opportunities, etc. Operations are divided into four major areas covered by the following offices:

OFFICE OF INTERNATIONAL ECONOMIC POLICY—promotes U.S. exports geographically by helping U.S. businesses market products in various locations abroad and by solving the trade and investment problems they encounter. This office is staffed by Country Desk Officers knowledgeable in marketing and business practice for almost every country in the world. (See list of Country Desk Officers in Department of Commerce section). Contact: Office of International Economic Policy, ITA, Department of Commerce, Washington, DC 20230/202-377-3022.

TRADE ADMINISTRATION OFFICE—supervises the enforcement provisions of the Export Administration Act, and administers the Foreign Trade Zone Program. Personnel in its export enforcement and its administration, policy and regulations offices can offer technical advice and legal interpretations of the various export legislation which affect American businesses. Contact: Trade Administration Office, ITA, Department of Commerce, Washington, DC 20230/202-377-1427.

OFFICE OF TRADE DEVELOPMENT—advises businesses on trade and investment issues, and promotes U.S. exports by industry or product classifications. The Office offers assistance and information on export counseling, statistics and trade data, licensing, trading companies, and other services. Contact: Office of Trade Development, ITA, Department of Commerce, Washington, DC 20230/202-377-1461.

OFFICE OF U.S. AND FOREIGN COMMERCIAL SERVICE—provides information on government programs to U.S. businesses, and uncovers trade opportunities for U.S. exporters. Staff also locate representatives and agents for U.S. firms, assist U.S. executives in all phases of their exporting, and help enforce export controls and regulations. They operate through 47 district offices located in major U.S. cities (see list in Department of Commerce section), and in 124 posts in 68 foreign countries. Contact: Office of U.S. and Foreign Commercial Service, ITA, Department of Commerce, Washington, DC 20230/202-377-8220.

National Technical Information Service (NTIS)
In addition to technical reports on foreign research and development, NTIS sells foreign market airgrams and foreign press and radio translations. Contact: NTIS, Department of Commerce, 5285 Port Royal Road, Springfield, VA 22161/703-557-4650.

Overseas Private Investment Corporation
This agency promotes market and investment interest in about 80 developing countries. Its programs include direct loans, loan guarantees and insurance, feasibility studies of investment opportunities, and other financial assistance. It also sponsors market studies, seminars for investment executives, investment missions to developing countries and disseminates information about specific investment opportunities and trends in various countries. In addition, it operates a Small Business Service Information Hotline at: 800-424-OPIC (6742). In DC call: 202-653-2800. Contact: Overseas Private Investment Corporation, U.S. International Development Cooperation Agency. 1129 29th Street NW, Washington, DC 20527/202-653-2800.

Small Business Administration
This agency makes loans and guarantees to small business concerns and small business investment companies, including those who sell overseas. It also offers technical assistance, counseling, training, management assistance, and information resources, including several excellent publications to small and minority businesses in export opera-

tions. Contact: Small Business Administration, 1441 L Street NW, Washington, DC 20416/202-653-6832.

Special Services

A variety of special services are available to help you overseas, some of which are described below. To take advantage of them, it is advisable to contact the program offices well in advance of your trip overseas.

New Product Information Service (NPIS)

NPIS offers a free export promotion service that will: (a) publicize the availability of your new product to foreign markets, and (b) test foreign market interest in your new product. Contact: Export Communication Section, Room 1620, Department of Commerce, Washington, DC 20230/202-377-2440.

Planning Services for U.S. Exporters

In its effort to promote economic development in Third World countries, the Trade and Development Program finances planning services for development projects leading to the export of U.S. goods and services. The purpose of the services is to assist U.S. firms in meeting competition from the U.S. export competitors so that U.S. firms can increase exports and improve the U.S. balance of trade.

A free pamphlet is available that describes the planning services offered by the Trade and Development Program. To obtain a copy contact: Trade and Development Program, State Annex 16, Washington, DC 20523/703-235-3663.

Temporary Office Space Abroad

For a small fee per day, you can lease an office from the U.S. government in ten major foreign cities. The office includes free telephones for local calls, audio-visual equipment, and a list of key business prospects. Secretarial and interpreter services are also available at your company's expense. Contact: International Trade Administration, Office of Export Promotion, Department of Commerce, Washington, DC 20230/202-377-4811 or 4814.

Terrorism Abroad

Assistance is available to help businesses design corporate security programs for protecting employees in foreign countries. "Countering Terrorism" is a free pamphlet providing security suggestions for U.S. business representatives abroad, and describes precautionary measures as well as suggested behavior in case of kidnapping. Additional information is also available from: Executive Committee and Working Group on Terrorism, D/CT, Department of State, 2201 C Street NW, Room 2238, Washington, DC 20520/202-632-9892. Contact: Foreign Operations, Office of Security, Bureau of Administration, Department of State, 2201 C Street NW, Room 3422, Washington, DC 20520/202-632-3122.

Trade Missions for Businessmen

The International Trade Administration sponsors small tours of U.S. businessmen offering a single product. The groups make three or four stops overseas in order to evaluate market potential. These trips are prepared by the staff of the U.S. Department of Commerce and take up to two years of planning. Contact: Office of Export Management Support Services, Export and Foreign Commercial Service, International Trade Administration, Department of Commerce, Room 2806, Washington, DC 20230/ 202-377-4908.

Trade Remedy Assistance Center

The Center provides information on remedies available under the Trade Remedy Law. It also offers technical assistance to eligible small businesses to enable them to bring cases to the International Trade Commission. Contact: ITC Trade Remedy Assistance Center, International Trade Commission, 701 E Street NW, Washington, DC 20436/202-523-0488.

Country Specialists

Specialists are located in several government agencies. Each is responsible for following a particular aspect (or aspects) of specific foreign countries. The specialists offer years of experience in answering information requests and possess knowledge far wider in scope than their assignments require. Because of their comprehensive understanding of the countries they study, these experts are invaluable sources of information for the researcher and the services they provide are free of charge. Country specialists are available in the following areas:

Overseas Markets and Trade Practices

Office of Export Promotion, Department of Commerce, Room 4015B, Washington, DC 20230/202-377-4231.

Political, Economic, and Cultural Affairs of Specific Countries
Department of State, 2201 C Street NW, Washington, DC 20520/202-632-6575.

Energy Resources
Office of International Affairs, Department of Energy, 1000 Independence Avenue SW, Washington, DC 20585/202-252-5918.

Mineral Resources
Bureau of Mines, Department of Interior, Foreign Data Branch, 2401 E Street NW, Washington, DC 20241/202-632-8970.

Foreign Agriculture
Economics and Statistics Service, Department of Agriculture, International Economic Division, 500 12th Street SW, Washington, DC 20250/202-447-8219.

Economic Assistance to Foreign Countries
Agency for International Development, 320 21st Street NW, Washington, DC 20523/ 202-632-8628.

Information Programs
United States Information Agency, 301 4th Street SW, Washington, DC 20547/202-485-2355.

International Expertise
Staff in the following offices will prove helpful information sources regarding the international scope of their respective subject areas.

Economics
International Economics, Bureau of Economic Analysis, Department of Commerce, Washington, DC 20230/202-523-0695.

Productivity and Technology Statistics
Bureau of Labor Statistics, Department of Labor, 441 G Street NW, Washington, DC 20212/202-523-9294.

Environment
National Environmental Referral Center, 3300 Whitehaven Street NW, Washington, DC 20235/202-634-7722.

Investments and Other Monetary Matters
Office of Assistant Secretary for International Affairs, Department of the Treasury, Washington, DC 20220/202-566-5363.

Life in Europe
European Community Information Service, 2100 M Street NW, Suite 707, Washington, DC 20037/202-862-9500.

Population
International Population Division, Center for International Research, Bureau of Census, Department of Commerce, Washington, DC 20233/ 202-763-2870, and Population Reference Bureau, Inc., 2213 M Street NW, Washington, DC 20037/ 202-785-4664.

Country Development
Inter-American Development Bank, 808 17th Street NW, Washington, DC 20577/202-634-8000, and International Monetary Fund, 700 19th Street NW, Washington, DC 20531/202-477-7000, and World Bank, 1818 H Street NW, Washington, DC 20433/202-477-1234.

Helpful Publications

Basic Guide to Exporting—this publication outlines the sequence of steps necessary to determine whether to, and how to, use foreign markets as a source of profits. It describes the various problems which confront small firms engaged in, or seeking to enter, international trade as well as the types of assistance available. It also provides a guide to appraising the sales potential of foreign markets and to understanding the requirements of foreign markets and to understanding the requirements of local business practices and procedures in overseas markets. The booklet is available for $6.50 from: Superintendent of Documents, U.S. Government Printing Office, Washington, DC 20402/202-783-3238.

Expand Overseas Sales with Commerce Department Help—this free booklet describes the types of assistance available for small businesses interested in international trade opportunities. It is available from any of the Small Business Administration field offices or contact: Office of International Trade, Small Business Administration, 1441 L Street NW, Room 602G, Washington, DC 20416/202-653-6544.

Export Information System (EIS) Data Report—this free pamphlet provides data on world markets for over 2000 product categories. It is available from any of the Small Business Administration field offices or contact: Advisory Service for Small Business, Export-Import Bank of the United States, Room 1031, 811 Vermont Avenue NW, Washington, DC 20571/202-566-8660.

Foreign Market Reports—offer information on markets for specific products in foreign countries. Contact: Department of Commerce, International Trade Administration, Office of Export Marketing Assistance, Washington, DC 20230/202-377-2185.

Global Market Surveys—identify the highest export potential markets overseas. Contact: Department of Commerce, Market Research Division, Washington, DC 20230/202-377-5037.

Markets Overseas with U.S. Government Help—this free booklet describes the various agencies of the Federal Government which offer programs of assistance for those businesses involved in, or contemplating, international trade. It is available free from any of the Small Business Administration field offices.

The New Product Information Service (NPIS)—offers a free export promotion service that will: (a) publicize the availability of your new product to foreign markets, and (b) test foreign market interest in your new product. Contact: Export Communication Section, Room 1620, Department of Commerce, Washington, DC 20230/202-377-2440.

The World Traders Data Report—provides a profile on an individual foreign firm for $75.00 per report. Contact: Department of Commerce, Washington, DC 20230/202-377-2988.

Services Provided By American Embassies and the State Department

The following is a list of U.S. embassies with whom American business representatives would most likely have contact. At larger embassies, the Commercial Officers represent U.S. commercial interests within their country of assignment. Specializing in U.S. export promotion, the Commercial Officers assist American business through: arranging appointments with local business and government officials; providing counsel on local trade regulations, laws, and customs; identifying importers, buyers, agents, distributors, and joint venture partners for U.S. firms; and other business assistance.

Business representatives planning a trip overseas should include in their preparations a visit or telephone call to their nearest U.S. Department of Commerce District Office. Some of the services jointly provided by the Departments of State and Commerce to U.S. business firms interested in establishing a market for their products, or expanding sales abroad, include:

THE TRADE OPPORTUNITIES PROGRAM (TOP)—which provides specific export sales leads of U.S. products and services;

WORLD TRADERS DATA REPORT (WTDR)—which pro-

vides detailed financial and commercial information on individual firmd abroad upon request from U.S. companies;

AGENT DISTRIBUTOR SERVICE (ADS)—which helps U.S. firms find agents or distributors to represent their firms and market their products abroad; and

INFORMATION ABOUT FOREIGN MARKETS—for U.S. products and services and U.S.-sponsored exhibitions abroad in which American firms can participate and demonstrate their products to key foreign buyers.

For additional information about Foreign Service activities overseas, or for specialized assistance with unusual problems, write: Office of Business and Export Affairs, Bureau of Economic and Business Affairs, U.S. Department of State, Washington, DC 20520/202-632-0354.

Listed below are all the embassies currently maintained by the U.S. Government.

Afghanistan
Economic/Commercial Section
American Embassy
Wazir Akbar Khan Mina
Kabul, Afghanistan

Algeria
Economic/CommercialSection
American Embassy
B.P. Box 549 (Alger-Gare)
Algiers, Algeria

Antigua and Barbuda
Economic/Commercial Section
American Embassy
FPO Miami 34054
St. Johns, Antigua and Barbuda

Argentina
Economic/Commercial Section
American Embassy
4300 Colombia, 1425
Buenos Aires, Argentina

Australia
Economic/Commercial Section
American Embassy
Moonah Pl., Canberra, A.C.T.,
Canberra, Australia

Austria
Economic/Commercial Section
American Embassy
A-1091, Boltzmanngasse 16
Vienna, Austria

Bahamas
Economic/Commercial Section
American Embassy
P.O. Box N-8197
Nassau, Bahamas

Bahrain
Economic/Commercial Section
American Embassy
P.O. Box 26431
Manama, Bahrain

Bangladesh
Economic/Commercial Section
American Embassy
G.P.O. Box 323, Ramna
Dhaka, Bangladesh

Barbados
Economic/Commercial Section
American Embassy
P.O. Box 302
Bridgetown, Barbados

Belgium
Economic/Commercial Section
American Embassy
27 Boulevard du Regent: B-1000 Brussels
Brussels, Belgium

Belize
Economic/Commercial Section
American Embassy
Gabourel Lane and Hutson St.
Belize City, Belize

Benin
Economic/Commercial Section
American Embassy
Rue Caporal Anani Bernard; B.P. 2012
Cottonou, Benin

Bermuda
Economic/Commercial Section
American Embassy
Vallis Bldg., Front Street
Hamilton, Bermuda

Bolivia
Economic/Commercial Section
American Embassy
P.O. Box 425
La Paz, Bolivia

Botswana
Economic/Commercial Section
American Embassy
P.O. Box 90
Gaborone, Botswana

Brazil
Economic/Commercial Section
American Embassy
Avenida das Nocoes, Lote 3
Brasilia, Brazil

Brunei
Economic/Commercial Section
American Embassy
P.O. Box 2991
Bandar Seri Begawau, Brunei

Bulgaria
Economic/Commercial Section
American Embassy
1 A. Stamboliski Blvd.,
Sofia, Bulgaria

Burkina Faso
Economic/Commercial Section
American Embassy
B.P. 35
Quagadougou, Burkina Faso

Burma
Economic/Commercial Section
American Embassy
581 Merchant Street
Rangoon, Burma

Burundi
Economic/Commercial Section
American Embassy
Chaussee Prince Louis Rwagasore; B.P.1720
Bujumbura, Burundi

Cameroon
Economic/Commercial Section
American Embassy
Rue Nachitigal; B.P.817
Yaounde, Cameroon

Canada
Economic/Commercial Section
American Embassy
100 Wellington St., KIP ST1
Ottawa, Canada

Republic of Cape Verde
Economic/Commercial Section
American Embassy
Rua Hoji Ya Yenna 81; C.P. 201
Praia, Republic of Cape Verde

Central African Republic
Economic/Commercial Section
American Embassy
Avenue President Dacko; B.P. 924
Bangui, Central African Republic

Chad
Economic/Commercial Section
American Embassy
Ave. Felix Eboue, B.P. 413
N'djamena, Chad

Chile
Economic/Commercial Section
American Embassy
Codina Bldg., 1343 Agustinas
Santiago, Chile

China
Economic/Commercial Section
American Embassy
Guang Hua Lu 17
Beijing, China

Colombia
Economic/Commercial Section
American Embassy
Calle 38, No. 8-61
Bogota, Colombia

People's Republic of the Congo
Economic/Commercial Section
American Embassy
Avenue Amilcar Cabral; B.P. 1015, Box C
Brazzaville, People's Republic of the Congo

Costa Rica
Economic/Commercial Section
American Embassy
Avenida 3 and Calle 1
San Jose, Costa Rica

Cuba
Economic/Commercial Section
Swiss Embassy
Calzada entre L & M, Vedado Seccion
Havana, Cuba

Cyprus
Economic/Commercial Section
American Embassy
Therissos St. and Dositheos St.
Nicosia, Cyprus

Czechoslovakia
Economic/Commercial Section
American Embassy
Trziste 15-12548 Praha
Prague, Czechoslovakia

Denmark
Economic/Commercial Section
American Embassy
Dag Hammarskjolds Alle 24; 2100
Copenhagen, Denmark

Republic of Djibouti
Economic/Commercial Section
American Embassy
Villa Plateau du Serpent Blvd.,
Marechal Joffre; B.P. 185
Djibouti, Republic of Djibouti

Dominican Republic
Economic/Commercial Section
American Embassy
Corner of Calle Cesar Nicolas Penson & Calle
Leopoldo Navarro
Santo Domingo, Dominican Republic

Ecuador
Economic/Commercial Section
American Embassy
120 Avenida Patria
Quito, Ecuador

Egypt
Economic/Commercial Section
American Embassy
5 Sharia Latin America
Cairo, Egypt

El Salvador
Economic/Commercial Section
American Embassy
25 Avenida Norte No. 1230
San Salvador, El Salvador

Equatorial Guinea
Economic/Commercial Section
American Embassy
Calle de Los Ministros
Malabo, Equatorial Guinea

Ethiopia
Economic/Commercial Section
American Embassy
P.O. Box 1014
Addis Ababa, Ethiopia

Fiji
Economic/Commercial Section
American Embassy
P.O. Box 218
Suva, Fiji

Finland
Economic/Commercial Section
American Embassy
Itainen Puistotie
Helsinki, Finland

France
Economic/Commercial Section
American Embassy
2 Avenue Gabriel, 75382 Paris Cedex 08
Paris, France

French Caribbian Department
Economic/Commercial Section
American Embassy
14 rue Blenac
Martinique, French Caribbean Department

Gabon
Economic/Commercial Section
American Embassy
Blvd. de la Mer; B.P. 4000
Libreville, Gabon

The Gambia
Economic/Commercial Section
American Embassy
P.O. Box 2596, Serrekunda
Banjul, The Gambia

German Democratic Republic
Economic/Commercial Section
American Embassy
108 Berlin, Neustaedtische Kirchstrasse 4-5;
USBER Box E
Berlin, German Democratic Republic

Federal Republic of Germany
Economic/Commercial Section
American Embassy
Deichmannsaue, 5300 Bonn 2
Bonn, Federal Republic of Germany

Ghana
Economic/Commercial Section
American Embassy
P.O. Box 194
Accra, Ghana

Greece
Economic/Commercial Section
American Embassy
91 Vasillissis Sophias Blvd.
Athens, Greece

Guatemala
Economic/Commercial Section
American Embassy
7-01 Avenida de la Reforma, Zone 10
Guatemala, Guatemala

Guinea
Economic/Commercial Section
American Embassy
2d Blvd., and 9th Ave.; B.P. 603
Conakry, Guinea

Guinea-Bissau
Economic/Commercial Section
American Embassy
Avenida Domingos Ramos
Bissau, Guinea-Bissau

Guyana
Economic/Commercial Section
American Embassy
31 Main Street
Georgetown, Guyana

Haiti
Economic/Commercial Section
American Embassy
Harry Truman Blvd.
Port-au-Prince, Haiti

The Holy See
Economic/Commercial Section
American Embassy
Piazza Giovanni XXIII No. 1, Rome
Vatican City, The Holy See

Honduras
Economic/Commercial Section
American Embassy
Avenida La Paz
Tegucigalpa, Honduras

Hong Kong
Economic/Commercial Section
American Embassy
26 Garden Road; Box 30
Hong Kong, Hong Kong

Hungary
Economic/Commercial Section
American Embassy
V. Szabadsag Ter. 12; Am. Embassy
Budapest, Hungary

Iceland
Economic/Commercial Section
American Embassy
Laufasvegur 21
Reykjavik, Iceland

India
Economic/Commercial Section
American Embassy
Shanti Path, Chanakyapuri 21
New Delhi, India

Indonesia
Economic/Commercial Section
American Embassy
Medan Merdeka Selatan 5
Jakarta, Indonesia

Iraq
Economic/Commercial Section
American Embassy
P.O. Box 2447, Alwiyah
Baghdad, Iraq

Ireland
Economic/Commercial Section
American Embassy
42 Elgin Rd., Ballsbridge
Dublin, Ireland

Israel
Economic/Commercial Section
American Embassy
71 Hayarkon Street
Tel Aviv, Israel

Italy
Economic/Commercial Section
American Embassy
Via Veneto 119/A, 00187-Rome
Rome, Italy

Ivory Coast
Economic/Commercial Section
American Embassy
5 Rue Jesse Owens; 01 B.P. 1712
Abidjan, Ivory Coast

Jamaica
Economic/Commercial Section
American Embassy
Jamaica Mutual Life Center, 2 Oxford
Rd., 3rd Floor
Kingston, Jamaica

Japan
Economic/Commercial Section
American Embassy
10-1. Akasaka 1-chome, Minato-ku
Tokyo, Japan

Jerusalem
Economic/Commercial Section
American Embassy
18 Agron Road
Jerusalem, Jerusalem

Jordan
Economic/Commercial Section
American Embassy
P.O. Box 354
Amman, Jordan

Kenya
Economic/Commercial Section
American Embassy
P.O. Box 30137
Nairobi, Kenya

Korea
Economic/Commercial Section
American Embassy
82 Sejong-Ro; Chongro-ku
Seoul, Korea

Kuwait
Economic/Commercial Section
American Embassy
P.O. Box 77 Safat
Kuwait, Kuwait

Laos
Economic/Commercial Section
American Embassy
Rue Bartholonie; B.P. 114, Box V
Vientiane, Laos

Lebanon
Economic/Commercial Section
American Embassy
P.O. Box 11-301
Beirut, Lebanon

Lesotho
Economic/Commercial Section
American Embassy
P.O. Box MS 333, Maseru 100
Maweru, Lesotho

Liberia
Economic/Commercial Section
American Embassy
P.O. Box 98
Monrovia, Liberia

Libya
Economic/Commercial Section
American Embassy
P.O. Box 289
Tripoli, Libya

Luxembourg
Economic/Commercial Section
American Embassy
22 Blvd. Emmanuel-Servais, 2535 Luxembourg
Luxembourg, Luxembourg

Madagascar
Economic/Commercial Section
American Embassy
14 and 16 Rue Rainitovo, Antsahavola;
B.P. 620
Antananariva, Madagascar

Malawi
Economic/Commercial Section
American Embassy
P.O. Box 30016
Lilongwe, Malawi

Malaysia
Economic/Commercial Section
American Embassy
P.O. Box No. 10035, Kuala Lumpur 01-02
Kuala Lumpur, Malaysia

Mali
Economic/Commercial Section
American Embassy
Rue Testard and Rue Mohamed V; B.P. 34
Bamako, Mali

Malta
Economic/Commercial Section
American Embassy
P.O. Box 535, Valletta
Valletta, Malta

Mauritania
Economic/Commercial Section
American Embassy
B.P. 222
Nouakchott, Mauritania

Mauritius
Economic/Commercial Section
American Embassy
Rogers Bldg. 4th Fl., John Kennedy St.
Port Louis, Mauritius

Mexico
Economic/Commercial Section
American Embassy
Paseo de la Reforma 305, Mexico 5, D.F.
Mexico, D.F., Mexico

Morocco
Economic/Commercial Section
American Embassy
P.O. Box 120
Rabat, Morocco

Mozambique
Economic/Commercial Section
American Embassy
P.O. Box 783
Maputo, Mozambique

Nepal
Economic/Commercial Section
American Embassy
Pani Pokhari
Kathmandu, Nepal

Netherlands
Economic/Commercial Section
American Embassy
Lange Voorhout 102
The Hague, Netherlands

Netherlands Antilles
Economic/Commercial Section
American Embassy
P.O. Box 158, Willemstad, Curacao
Curacao, Netherlands Antilles

New Zealand
Economic/Commercial Section
American Embassy
29 Fitzherbert Terrace, Thorndon
Wellington, New Zealand

Nicaragua
Economic/Commercial Section
American Embassy
Km. 4-1/2 Carretera Sur.;
Managua, Nicaragua

Niger
Economic/Commercial Section
American Embassy
B.P. 11201
Niamey, Niger

Nigeria
Economic/Commercial Section
American Embassy
P.O. Box 554
Lagos, Nigeria

Norway
Economic/Commercial Section
American Embassy
Drammensvelen 18, Oslo 2
Oslo, Norway

Oman
Economic/Commercial Section
American Embassy
P.O. Box 966
Muscat, Oman

Pakistan
Economic/Commercial Section
American Embassy
P.O. Box 1048
Islamabad, Pakistan

Panama
Economic/Commercial Section
American Embassy
Avenida Balboa Y Calle 38, Apartado 6959,
R.P. 5; Box E
Panama, Panama

Papua New Guinea
Economic/Commercial Section
American Embassy
P.O. Box 1492
Port Moresby, Papua New Guinea

Paraguay
Economic/Commercial Section
American Embassy
1776 Mariscal Lopez Ave.
Asuncion, Paraguay

Peru
Economic/Commercial Section
American Embassy
P.O. Box 1995, Lima 100
Lima, Peru

Philippines
Economic/Commercial Section
American Embassy
1201 Roxas Blvd.
Manila, Philippines

Poland
Economic/Commercial Section
American Embassy
Aleje Ujazdowskie 29/31
Warsaw, Poland

Portugal
Economic/Commercial Section
American Embassy
Avenida das Forcas Armadas, 1600 Lisbon
Lisbon, Portugal

Qatar
Economic/Commercial Section
American Embassy
P.O. Box 2399
Doha, Qatar

Romania
Economic/Commercial Section
American Embassy
Strada Tudor Arghezi 7-9
Bucharest, Romania

Rwanda
Economic/Commercial Section
American Embassy
Blvd. de la Revolution, B.P. 28
Kigali, Rwanda

Saudi Arabia
Economic/Commercial Section
American Embassy
P.O. Box 9041
Riyadh, Saudi Arabia

Senegal
Economic/Commercial Section
American Embassy
B.P. 49, Avenue Jean XXIII
Dakar, Senegal

Seychelles
Economic/Commercial Section
American Embassy
Box 148
Victoria, Seychelles

Sierra Leone
Economic/Commercial Section
American Embassy
Corner Walpole and Siaka Stevens St.
Freetown, Sierra Leone

Singapore
Economic/Commercial Section
American Embassy
30 Hill Street
Singapore, Singapore

Somalia
Economic/Commercial Section
American Embassy
Corso Primo Luglio
Mogadishu, Somalia

South Africa
Economic/Commercial Section
American Embassy
Thibault House, 225 Pretorius St.
Pretoria, South Africa

Spain
Economic/Commercial Section
American Embassy
Serrano 75
Madrid, Spain

Sri Lanka
Economic/Commercial Section
American Embassy
P.O. Box 106
Colombo, Sri Lanka

Sudan
Economic/Commercial Section
American Embassy
P.O. Box 699
Khartoum, Sudan

Suriname
Economic/Commercial Section
American Embassy
P.O. Box 1821
Paramaribo, Suriname

Swaziland
Economic/Commercial Section
American Embassy
P.O. Box 199
Mbabane, Swaziland

Sweden
Economic/Commercial Section
American Embassy
Strandvagen 101
Stockholm, Sweden

Switzerland
Economic/Commercial Section
American Embassy
Jubilaeumstrasse 93, 3005 Bern
Bern, Switzerland

Syria
Economic/Commercial Section
American Embassy
P.O. Box 29
Damascus, Syria

Tanzania
Economic/Commercial Section
American Embassy
P.O. Box 9123
Dar Es Salaam, Tanzania

Thailand
Economic/Commercial Section
American Embassy
95 Wireless Road
Bangkok, Thailand

Togo
Economic/Commercial Section
American Embassy
Rue Pelletier Cabentou & Rue Vouban
Lome, Togo

Trinidad and Tobago
Economic/Commercial Section
American Embassy
P.O. Box 752
Port-of-Spain, Trinidad and Tobago

Tunisia
Economic/Commercial Section
American Embassy
144 Ave. de la Liberte
Tunis, Tunisia

Turkey
Economic/Commercial Section
American Embassy
110 Ataturk Blvd.
Ankara, Turkey

Uganda
Economic/Commercial Section
American Embassy
British High Commission Bldg., Obote Ave.
Kampala, Uganda

Union of Soviet Socialist Republics
Economic/Commercial Section
American Embassy
Ulitsa Chaykovskogo 19/21/23
Moscow, Union of Soviet Socialist Republics

United Arab Emirates
Economic/Commercial Section
American Embassy
P.O. Box 4009
Abu Dhabi, United Arab Emirates

United Kingdom
Economic/Commercial Section
American Embassy
24/31 Grosvenor Sq., W 1A 1AE
London, England

United States
US Mission to the United Nations
799 United Nations Plaza
New York, NY 10017

Uruguay
Economic/Commercial Section
American Embassy
Calle Lauro Muller 1776
Montevideo, Uruguay

Venezuela
Economic/Commercial Section
American Embassy
P.O. Box 62291, Caracas 1060-A
Caracas, Venezuela

Yemen Arab Republic
Economic/Commercial Section
American Embassy
P.O. Box 1088
Sanaa, Yemen Arab Republic

Yugoslavia
Economic/Commercial Section
American Embassy
Kneza Milosa 50
Belgrade, Yugoslavia

Zaire
Economic/Commercial Section
American Embassy
310 Avenue des Aviateurs
Kinshasa, Zaire

Zambia
Economic/Commercial Section
American Embassy
P.O. Box 31617
Lusaka, Zambia

Zimbabwe
Economic/Commercial Section
American Embassy
P.O. Box 3340
Harare, Zimbabwe

Tax Help

IRS provides several special services to help small business-owners understand their tax responsibilities. Some of these services are described below.

Hey, We're In Business
This instructional film, prepared by IRS, stresses the free assistance available to small businesses in areas such as good recordkeeping, obligations to employees, and expenses and depreciation. The film, and others, are loaned free of charge. Contact: Taxpayer Information and Education Branch, Taxpayer Service Division, Internal Revenue Service, Department of the Treasury, 1111 Constitution Avenue NW, Washington, DC 20274/202-566-2136.

Small-Business Workshops
Most IRS offices throughout the U.S. conduct one-day workshops for taxpayers who own small businesses or are about to start one. The workshops cover all aspects of business taxes at the federal level, including: annual income tax returns, Social Security taxes (FICA), and unemployment taxes. The workshop also includes information about: how to cut your tax liability; how, and how long to keep records; what a small-businessperson can do if she or he is headed for financial trouble and can't pay a tax bill; and much more. Contact your local IRS office to find out about the time, date and location of these workshops. You can also contact: Taxpayer Information and Education Branch, Taxpayer Service Division, Internal Revenue Service, Department of the Treasury, 1111 Constitution Avenue NW, Washington, DC 20274/202-566-2136.

Taxpayer Publications
In the Department of Treasury chapter of this

book you will find a complete listing of free publications available from the Internal Revenue Service. Described below are a few of these publications which are particularly helpful for small business owners. For more information, contact your local IRS Office or: Public Affairs Division, Internal Revenue Service, Department of the Treasury, 1111 Constitution Ave. NW, Room 2315, Washington, DC 20224/202-566-4024.

Record Keeping for a Small Business (Publication 583)—this 176-page book covers such subjects as setting up a tax records system, determining net income, tax credits, and business assets.

Tax Guide for Small Business (Publication 334)—this explains what a small-businessperson must know to meet tax obligations such as how to file forms and compute the tax.

Finding Free Information on Anything and Everything

With a little skill, you can use the Federal Government as a resource for expertise and literature on nearly any subject imaginable. The government spends billions of tax dollars performing research on issues of importance to our society—be it counting potatoes in Maine or analyzing Soviet strategic arms capabilities. And as long as you are resourceful, persistent, and somewhat knowledgeable about where to dig for what you need—all this expertise is yours for the asking.

This section of the Sampler, coupled with "The Art of Obtaining Information from Bureaucrats" in the Introduction, will help you develop your skills of finding and using information. (Note: In case you have trouble obtaining government reports you should be aware of your rights under the "Freedom of Information Act." For information on this, see Sampler Section entitled "Your Rights and Benefits.")

Finding an Expert and Information Source

Washington is the largest source of free information and expertise in the world and most of it goes to waste. The federal government supports over 500,000 subject experts and spends billions of dollars a year on specialized studies, of which few people take advantage. For any problem that you may face either professionally or personally, there is likely to be a free expert on the federal payroll who has spent years studying the very same subject. These specialists can save you countless hours in research and many dollars in consulting fees.

Examples of Problem-Solving
The questions and answers below will give you examples of which Washington sources you should tap into to find answers to specific questions.

Contact information for these resources is given in "Information Starting Points," which appears later in this section, and in the relevant chapters throughout the book.

What will be the supply and demand for lawyers for the next 10 years? See: National Center for Education Statistics and the Bureau of Labor Statistics.

What are the opportunities and outlook for the franchising business? See: Bureau of Industrial Economics.

Are Maine potatoes a good investment in the commodities market? See: National Agricultural Library and the U.S. Department of Agriculture.

What are the salaries of computer programmers in the Great Lakes region? See: Bureau of Labor Statistics.

What is the latest technology in preventing acid rain? See: Center for Environmental Services, National Referral Center, and the Library of Congress.

Is there any current legislation which will affect the salaries of teachers? See: Bill Status Office.

What is the best design for building a solar heating unit? See: National Agricultural Library and the Department of Agriculture.

What is the best way to finance a home? See: Department of Housing and Urban Development.

What are the latest developments in the treatment of backaches? See: Department of Health and Human Services.

Write or Call: Bureaucrats Have To Be Nice—It's The Law

You must be persistent in your search for information. Whether you write or telephone, remember you may not reach the appropriate expert on your first try. Normally it takes a number of referrals before you find that one government employee who is devoting his or her time to studying the very subject you are interested in.

Once you find the specialist, you most likely won't have trouble getting information. In fact, expect to be deluged with information. You will probably discover that this expert, who has been concentrating on a particular field for years, often does not get an opportunity to share his or her expertise; therefore he or she will welcome the chance to do so.

Also bear in mind that the recently enacted Civil Service Reform Law makes it mandatory for bureaucrats to be polite to anyone outside the government. If they are impolite, you can report them to their supervisor and this can lead to their dismissal.

Information Starting Points

Experts in the following offices will help you—for free—with your information problems. If they don't have the answers you need, they will also refer you to other experts and information sources.

Agricultural Reference Help
National Agriculture Library, Department of Agriculture, 10301 Baltimore Blvd., Beltsville, MD 20705/301-344-3756. Provides published material and research services on botany, zoology, chemistry, veterinary medicine, forestry, plant pathology, livestock, poultry, entomology, and general agriculture.

Agriculture Information, Clearinghouse
Office of Information Department of Agriculture, Room 402A, Washington, DC 20250/202-447-9005. A staff of research specialists is available to provide specific answers or point you to an expert who can help with almost any agriculture-related subject.

Associations
Information Central, American Society of Association Executives, 1575 Eye St, NW, Washington, DC 20005, 202-626-2723. If you cannot find a relevant association after referring to *Gale's Encyclopedia of Associations* this organization will help find the right one.

Best and Worst Industries and Companies
Department of Commerce, Washington, DC 20230, 202-377-1461. Over 100 analysts who monitor all the major industries in the US and the companies within these industries.

Business Advice
ROADMAP PROGRAM, Department of Commerce,

14th and Constitution Ave. NW, Washington, DC 20230, 202-377-3176. Provides reference services on all aspects of commerce and business.

LIBRARY, Department of Commerce, 14th and Constitution Ave. NW, Washington, DC 20230/202-377-5511. Provides free reference services on commerce and business. See Business section of sampler for more leads.

Country Experts

COUNTRY OFFICERS, Department of State, 2201 C St. NW, Washington, DC 20520, 202-632-9552. Hundreds of experts are available to provide current political, economic, and other background information on the country they study.

COUNTRY MARKETING, International Trade Administration, Department of Commerce, Washington, DC 20230, 202-377-2954. Staff of country experts can provide information on marketing and business practices for almost any country.

INTERNATIONAL AGRICULTURE, Economic Research and Statistical Reporting Service, Office of Information, Department of Agriculture, 14th and Independence Ave. SW, Washington, DC 20250, 202-447-8005. Provides information on agricultural and related aspects of any foreign country.

BRANCH OF FOREIGN DATA, Mineral and Materials Supply and Demand, Bureau of Mines, Department of Interior, 2401 E St. NW, Room W614, Washington, DC 20241, 202-632-8970. Foreign country experts monitor all aspects of foreign mineral industries.

Crime Information
National Criminal Justice Reference Service, National Institute of Justice, Box 6000, Rockville, MD 20850, 301-251-5500. Database and reference service that provides bibliographies and expertise for free or sometimes a nominal fee.

Education Resources
Educational Resource Information Center (ERIC), National Institute of Education, 1200 19th St. NW, Brown Bldg., Washington, DC 20208, 202-254-7934. A network of 16 information clearinghouses that can identify literature, experts, audiovisuals, funding, and more.

Energy Technical Expertise
Department of Energy, Technical Information Center, P.O. Box 62, Oak Ridge, TN 37830/ 615-576-1301. Provides research and other information services for all energy-related topics.

Energy Information Clearinghouse
Energy Information Center, Department of Energy, 1F048 Forrestal Building, 1000 Independence Ave. SW, Washington, DC 20585/202-252-8800. Provides general reference services for all aspects of energy.

Environmental Science Information Center
NOAA, 11400 Rockville Pike, Rockville Building, Rockville, MD 20852/301-443-8910. Provides information services for matters relating to the environment.

Federal Information Centers—Government Assistance
General Services Administration, 7th and D Sts. SW, Room 5716, Washington, DC 20405/202-523-1209. Staff will find you an expert in the government to assist you with almost any topic. For contact information about a Center nearest you, see listing in the "Resources Close-To-Home" section of the Sampler.

Housing—Building, Buying or Renovating
Program Information Center, Department of Housing and Urban Development, 451 7th St. SW, Washington, DC 20410/202-755-6420. This Center provides information about all aspects of housing and staff will direct you to a program which meets your needs.

Help on Health
National Health Information Clearinghouse, P.O. Box 1133, Washington, DC 20013/ toll-free 800-336-4797/703-522-2590 in Virginia. Provides information referral and reference services on health-related topics.

Health and Welfare Information
Information, Department of Health and Human Services, 200 Independence Ave. SW, Room 118F, Washington, DC 20201/202-245-5296. Staff will direct you to an office in Health and Human Services that can help you. Referrals to organizations, Agencies and Publications.

Metals and Minerals
Assistant Directorate of Minerals Information, Bureau of Mines, Department of Interior, Room 1035, Columbia Plaza, Washington, DC 20241, 202-634-1187. Dozens of commodity specialists collect, analyze, and disseminate information on the adequacy and availability of the mineral base for the national economy.

National Referral Center
Library of Congress, Washington, DC 20540/
202-287-5670. Staff will locate an expert or organization that specializes in providing free information in your area of interest.

Performing Arts Information
Performing Arts Library, John F. Kennedy
Center, Washington, DC 20566/202-287-6245.
Offers reference services for any subject dealing
with the performing arts.

Technical Research for Free or a Fee
Science and Technology Division, Reference Section, Library of Congress, Washington, DC
20540/202-287-5639. Offers both free and fee-
based reference and bibliographic services.

Solar Heating and Cooling Information
Conservation and Renewable Energy Inquiry and
Referral Service, P.O. Box 1607, Rockville, MD
20850/toll-free 800-523-2929/800-462-4983 in Penn-
sylvania/800-523-4700/in Alaska and Hawaii. Will
provide research, publications and other information services relating to solar energy.

Current Legislation Information
Bill Status Office, Capitol, House Annex #2,
Room 2650, Washington, DC 20515/202-225-1772.
Can tell you if there is legislation pending on a
particular topic.

Statistical Resources

Below are the major statistics collectors in the federal government. If an office does
not have statistics for your subject area, ask staff to direct you elsewhere.

Agriculture and Food Statistics
Director, Estimates Division and Economics and
Statistics Service, Department of Agriculture, 14th
and Independence Ave. SW, Washington, DC
20250/202-447-2122.

Economic and Demographic Statistics
Customer Services, Bureau of the Census, Data
User Service Division, Washington, DC
20233/301-763-4100.

Crime Statistics
Uniform Crime Reporting Section, FBI, Depart-
ment of Justice, 9th and Pennsylvania Ave. NW,
Room 6212, Washington, DC 20525/202-324-5038.

**Economics—National, Regional and International
Statistics**
Bureau of Economic Analysis, Department of
Commerce, Tower Building, Washington, DC
20230/202-523-0777.

Education Statistics
National Center for Education Statistics, Department of Education, 1200 19th St. NW, Washington, DC 20208/202-254-6057.

Health Statistics
National Center for Health Statistics, Department
of Health and Human Services, 3700 East-West
Highway, Room 1-57, Hyattsville, MD 20782/
301-436-8500.

**Employment, Prices, Living Conditions,
Productivity, and Occupational Safety and Health
Statistics**
Bureau of Labor Statistics, Department of Labor,
441 G St. NW, Washington, DC 20212. For
information: 202-523-1913/ publications: 202-523-
1221/recording: 202-523-9685.

Import and Export Statistics
Foreign Trade Reference Room, Department of
Commerce, Room 2233, Washington, DC
20230/202-377-2185.

World Import and Export Statistics
World Trade Statistics, Department of Commerce,
Washington, DC 20230/202-377-2665.

Reference Rooms You Can Use

In addition to the vast amounts of published information available in Washington, there is also an abundance of information in unpublished form. Major sources of this unpublished information are public document rooms which can give you access to unique documents with very limited circulation. For example, you can obtain financial information on elected officials from the Federal Elections Commission and tax returns of nonprofit organizations from the Internal Revenue Service.

The following list covers the main reference rooms open to the public. If you cannot visit in person, check with the document room to learn how you can obtain copies of the documents you need.

Agency for International Development

Development Information Center
Agency for International Development, Department of State Building, Room 1656, Washington, DC 20523/202-632-9345. Included here are documents covering AID projects overseas, such as contractors' reports, feasibility studies, studies on aspects of foreign aid programs, final reports from AID contractors who have completed work overseas, research done by universities for AID, and AID presentations to Congress for budgetary purposes. (Copying: available at no charge.)

Civil Rights Commission

Clearinghouse Library
Civil Rights Commission, 1121 Vermont Ave. NW, Room 709, Washington, DC 20425/202-376-8110. The Clearinghouse Library contains the Commission's findings covering racial discrimination, minority and women's civil rights and legal reference material; and all books and documents published by the Commission relating to its statutes, regulations, and goals. (Copying: available at no charge.)

Commerce Department

Export Information Reference Room
International Trade Administration, Department of Commerce, Room 1326, 14th St. and Constitution Ave. NW, Washington, DC 20230/202-377-2185. This room has several cabinets of reports, filed by country, which provide information on proposed and approved major projects, particularly overseas construction projects. Notices of overseas construction starts are received by early warning cables from Commerce officials posted abroad. Airgrams are kept on file for three months.

The room also maintains files of press releases on loan approvals, monthly reports of projects under consideration for loans from the World Bank, the Inter-American Development Bank and the Asian Development Bank. (Copying: 15¢ per page in the Commerce Department Library. Bring your own supply of change.)

Minority Business Development Agency (MBDA)
Information Clearinghouse, Department of Commerce, Room 5714, 14th St. and Constitution Ave. NW, Washington, DC 20230/202-377-2414. This room contains a collection of MBDA publications and publications from other agencies relating to minority business enterprise. (Copying: not available.)

Patent Office Search Room
Patent Office, Department of Commerce, 2021 Jefferson Davis Highway, Arlington, VA/703-557-2276/Mailing Address: Washington, DC 20231. In the search room are patents dating back to 1790, arranged numerically and in classified order. The patents are also arranged by classes and subclasses of subject matter. (Copying: 15¢ per page.)

Freedom of Information Records Inspection Facility
International Trade Administration, Department of Commerce, Room 3102, 14th St. and Constitution Ave. NW, Washington, DC 20230/202-377-3031. The documents which may be reviewed in this room include: boycott reporting forms for public inspection, charging letters and news releases involving boycott violations, boycott comments on proposed regulations, administrative staff manuals, instructions to the staff that affect the public, comments concerning countervailing and anti-dumping duties, etc. (Copying: 7¢ per page; 25¢ per microfilm copy.)

Public Information Office
Bureau of the Census, Department of Commerce, Federal Office Building #3, Room 2705, Suitland, MD 20233/301-763-4051. The Public Information Office assists researchers working with historical statistics. The office's collection contains mainly census material published by the Census Bureau itself, but there are some statistical materials published by other U.S. government agencies. Coverage includes financial, growth and production information about numerous industries (including transportation, agriculture and construction), plus the number of employees in each industry and other statistical data. If researchers let the office know in advance what materials they need to see, the office tries to have these ready for them to use. The office can supply most current census materials, either free or priced, and tries to obtain copies of old documents researchers wish to inspect. (Copying: limited copying facilities available at Census Bureau Library.)

Trademark Search Room
Patent and Trademark Office, Department of Commerce, Building #2, 2011 Jefferson Davis Highway, Arlington, VA 22202/703-557-3281. This room contains trademark registrations dating back to 1881. The registrations are arranged numerically and alphabetically by the complete name. (Copying: 15¢ per page; tokens must be purchased in the lobby of Building #4, 2031 Jefferson Davis Highway.)

U.S. Foreign Trade Reference Room
Department of Commerce, Room 2333, 14th St. and Constitution Ave. NW, Washington, DC 20230/202-377-2185. The room contains the most current trade statistics available. It offers a large collection of published and unpublished reports concerning U.S. foreign trade—including import and export data by country and commodity, with quantities and dollar value of exports and imports—prepared mostly by the Bureau of the Census. (Copying: 15¢ per page; microfilm and microfiche—10¢ per copy.)

World Trade Reference Room
Department of Commerce, Room 1315, 14th St. and Constitution Ave. NW, Washington, DC 20230/202-377-1468. Official trade statistics for most countries of the world are kept here. There are publications about importing and exporting, and market share reports which list the leading exporting countries for specific commodities and the countries to which they export. (Copying: 15¢ per page.)

Commodity Futures Trading Commission

Office of Public Information
Commodity Futures Trading Commission, 2033 K St. NW, Washington, DC 20581/202-254-8630. This office has control over documents available to the public. These include copies of hearings and appeals, listings of registered agents, futures commission merchants and brokerage firms, registration applications and financial statements with principals and addresses. (Copying: 10¢ per page.)

Consumer Product Safety Commission

Public Reference Room
Consumer Product Safety Commission, 8th Floor, 1111 18th St. NW, Washington, DC 20207/202-634-7700. The room contains all commission decisions, court cases, and dockets; petitions; comments on proposed regulations and rules; background study reports (these have been sanitized to protect manufacturers); transcriptions and minutes of commission meetings; the weekly public calendar; and other documents regarding work the commission does. There are about 18 open shelves of material. (Copying: the first 250 pages are free; 10¢ per page thereafter.)

Education Department

National Center for Education Statistics
Department of Education, 6525 Belcrest Rd., Presidential Building, Room 1001, Hyattsville, MD 20782/301-254-6057/Mailing Address: 400 Maryland Ave. SW, Washington, DC 20202. The center compiles education statistics and analyses; provides financial data on educational institutions; and makes available numerous publications, most of which must be purchased. (Copying: not available.)

Energy Department

Economic Regulatory Administration
Public Document Room, Office of Public Information, Department of Energy, 1000 Independence Avenue, SW, Washington, DC 20585/202-252-2929. This office contains copies of all Economic Regulatory Administration rules and orders and hearing transcripts. (Copying: 10¢ per page.)

Federal Energy Regulatory Commission

Office of Congressional and Public Affairs, Department of Energy, Room 1000, 825 North Capitol St. NE, Washington, DC 20426/202-357-8118. The office contains copies of annual and monthly reports filed by public utilities, natural gas producers, and interstate oil pipeline companies. These reports cover a wide range of topics from financial information to energy consumption. This room also has copies of special reports produced by the staff of the Federal Energy Regulatory Commission and FERC decisions and rules. (Copying: 10¢ per page.)

Environmental Protection Agency

Public Information Reference Unit
Environmental Protection Agency, 401 M St. SW (PM 213), Washington, DC 20460/202-382-5926. This is a reading room for review and inspection of unpublished materials. Many documents are comments in response to EPA-proposed legislation placed in the Federal Register. Other materials are EPA comments on environmental impact statements; Federal regulations and proposed rules; EPA guidelines, etc. A few published materials are here, but no handouts. (Copying: 10¢ per page after first 25 pages, which are free. Copying must be done by 4:15 P.M., and only checks are accepted—no cash.)

Equal Employment Opportunity Commission

Library
Equal Employment Opportunity Commission, 2401 E St. NW, Washington, DC 20506/202-634-6991. In addition to legal and social science reference materials, the library makes available comments on proposed guidelines, transcripts of commission decisions, annual reports, and budgets. (Copying: 15¢ per page.)

Office of the Executive Secretariat
Equal Employment Opportunity Commission, 2401 E St. NW, Room 4096, Washington, DC 20506/202-634-1356. This office maintains the minutes of all open commission meetings and commission votes; materials are available by appointment. (Copying: 15¢ per page.)

Farm Credit Administration

Congressional and Public Affairs Division
Farm Credit Administration, 1501 Farm Credit Drive, McLean, VA 22101/703-883-4056. This office makes available a number of documents, including copies of regulations and clarifications and in-house reports and publications about the cooperative farm credit system. Special reports by the Farm Credit Administration include such topics as credit and economic outlook, interest rates, surveys, loan profiles, and statistics. Administration and personnel handbooks are also available for inspection. (Copying: 10¢ per page.)

Federal Communications Commission

Industry Analysis
Common Carrier Bureau, Federal Communications Commission, 1919 M St. NW, Room 538, Washington, DC 20554/202-634-6991. This room contains copies of annual reports filed by over 1,200 common carriers in the United States. It also has monthly balance sheets of telephone and telegraph companies, as well as quarterly and annual statistical reports compiled by the office itself. (Copying: 10¢ per page if you make the copies yourself. If they must be mailed, contact: Downtown Copy Center, 1919 M St. NW, Room 239, Washington, DC 20554/202-833-9765. This firm charges 9¢ per page, plus $10 per hour for research and retrieval.)

Domestic Radio Branch
Common Carrier Bureau, Federal Communications Commission, 1919 M St. NW, Room 311, Washington, DC 20554/202-634-1706. This room contains documentation on all point-to-point microwave companies. This includes applications for licenses, annual reports, and applications for new construction facilities. (Copying: 10¢ per page.)

Mobile Services Division
Common Carrier Bureau, Federal Communications Commission, 1919 M St. NW, Room 644, Washington, DC 20554/202-632-6400. This room contains station files on licensing and all new construction for common carriers. (Copying: 10¢ per page if you make the copies yourself. If they must be mailed, contact Downtown Copy Center, 1919 M St. NW, Room 239, Washington, DC 20554/202-833-9765. This firm charges 9¢ per page, plus $10 per hour for research and retrieval.)

Public Reference Room
Federal Communications Commission, 1919 M St. NW, Room 239, Washington, DC 20554/202-632-7566. This room contains complete documentation on all hearings and cases handled by the Federal Communications Commission. An index is available for identifying specific cases or areas covered. (Copying: 10¢ per page.)

Reference Room—Broadcast Bureau
Federal Communications Commission, 1919 M St. NW, Room 239, Washington, DC 20554/202-632-6334. This is a special section within the main reference room which handles documentation on all broadcast matters before it reaches the hearing stage. This room also contains copies of applications and annual reports filed by radio and television stations. (Copying: 10¢ per page.)

Reference Room—Cable Television Bureau
Federal Communications Commission, 2025 M St. NW, Room 239, Washington, DC 20554/202-632-7480. This room contains documentation on cable television companies, including annual reports and applications for licenses. History cards recording all action taken are also available for each company. (Copying: 10¢ per page.)

Tariff Review Branch
Common Carrier Bureau, Federal Communications Commission, 1919 M St. NW, Room 514, Washington, DC 20554/202-632-5550. This reference room provides storage for copies of tariffs filed by more than 1,200 common carriers in the United States. (Copying: 10¢ per page.)

Federal Election Commission

Public Records Office
Federal Election Commission, 1325 K St. NW, Washington, DC 20463/202-523-4181. This room contains all campaign finance reports for House, Senate and Presidential candidates since 1972. If you cannot visit Washington, you can call the commission's information office at toll-free 800-424-9530 to obtain guidance on holdings or copies of the information you need. (Copying: 5¢ per page: 10¢ per page for copies from microfilm.)

Federal Deposit Insurance Corporation
Information Office, Federal Deposit Insurance Corporation (FDIC), 550 17th St. NW, Room 6061-B, Washington, DC 20429/202-389-4221. Popular FDIC materials, available gratis at the Information Office, arc: *Your Insured Deposit* and the FDIC annual report. All published FDIC statistical materials may be reviewed in the FDIC Library. Some publications are free; others are not. (Copying: available only at the FDIC Library, Room 4074; 10¢ each page.)

Federal Home Loan Bank Board

Docket Section
Federal Home Loan Bank Board, 700 G St. NW, Washington, DC 20552/202-377-6262. This room contains documentation related to savings and loan institutions and savings banks, including annual financial reports, applications for new facilities and copies of any correspondence between the bank board and the institution. (Copying: 10¢ per page.)

Information Disclosure Section (Economic Research)
Federal Home Loan Bank Board, 1700 G St. NW, Washington, DC 20252/202-377-6138. This section contains deposit figures, balance sheet income and expense data for branches and home offices of federally insured savings institutions. (Copying: 30¢ per page, plus $2.00 for search and handling.)

Federal Maritime Commission

Office of the Secretary
Federal Maritime Commission, 1100 L St. NW, Room 11101, Washington, DC 20573/202-523-5725. The office has self-policing reports, records of how carriers handled requests and complaints, and tariffs and agreements, including comments and justifications. If you don't know which office under the Commission has the information you need, this is the place to start—you will be referred to the appropriate division. (Copying: no charge.)

Docket Room
Federal Maritime Commission, 1100 L St. NW, Washington, DC 20573/202-523-5760. Contains documentation on all commission proceedings covering complaints, rule making, and investigations. (Copying: 5¢ per page; there is an additional $5 per hour service for copying performed by docket room staff.)

Control Records Center
Federal Maritime Commission, 1100 L St. NW, Room 10223, Washington, DC 20573/202-523-5829. This room contains documentation on all

domestic tariffs for water or water and land for common carriers and others engaged in the foreign and domestic offshore commerce of the United States. (Copying: 30¢ per page.)

Federal Reserve System

Freedom of Information
Board of Governors of the Federal Reserve System, 20th St. and Constitution Ave. NW, Room B-1122, Washington, DC 20551/202-452-3684. This room contains copies of all proposals made by the Board of Governors along with copies of all public comments on these proposals. The room also has available registration statements and annual reports of all bank holding companies and banks that are state members of the Federal Reserve System. (Copying: 10¢ per page after the first 20 pages.)

Federal Trade Commission

Public Reference Division
Federal Trade Commission, 6th St. and Pennsylvania Ave. NW, Room 130, Washington, DC 20580/202-523-3598. Records in this collection are FTC-originated complaints: docket sheets outlining proceedings of a case; FTC economic reports; copies of the Flammability Act and other requirements of manufacturers. Other FTC publications available are of a consumer protection nature. Documentation for all FTC investigations is maintained here. (Copying: 90% of all publications are free. For unpublished materials, a copying charge of 12¢ per page begins at the 80th page, retroactive to the first page.)

Health and Human Services Department

Freedom of Information Office
Food and Drug Administration, Freedom of Information Staff, HF-35, Department of Health and Human Services, 5600 Fishers Lane, Room 12A08, Rockville, MD 20857/301-443-6310. This division has information about food and drugs, including contents, usage and records of investigations. It also has copies of requests for information, replies to these requests, and some FDA manuals (others are available from National Technical Information Service, 5285 Port Royal Road, Springfield, VA 22161/703-557-4650). Other materials available include establishment inspection reports, the Inspectors' Operations Manual, com-

missioners' reports, the FDA Directory, and the *Index to Evaluations,* published in the *Federal Register.* (Copying: 10¢ per page after the first 50 pages, plus postage.)

Dockets Management Branch
Food and Drug Administration, Department of Health and Human Services, 5600 Fishers Lane, Room 4-62, Rockville, MD 20857/301-443-1753. This office holds food and drug contents and labeling information, hearing records, dockets, comments on proposed rules and regulations, and FDA administrative files and manuals. (Copying: 10¢ per page after the first 50 pages, plus postage.)

National Center for Health Statistics
Department of Health and Human Services, 3700 East-West Highway, Room 157, Center Building, Hyattsville, MD 20782/301-436-8500. The center compiles health statistics from surveys and studies about health. It operates a clearinghouse on health indexes that publishes the quarterly "Bibliography on Health Indexes," a free publication. (Copying: available at no charge.)

National Clearinghouse for Alcohol Information
Department of Health and Human Services, 1776 Plaza South, 1776 E. Jefferson St., Rockville, MD 20852/301-468-2600/Mailing Address: P. O. Box 2345, Rockville, MD 20852. Contains over 50,000 items, including published and unpublished documents on the topic of alcoholism. (Copying: limited copying due to contract restrictions.)

Office of Family Planning
Bureau of Community Health Services, Department of Health and Human Services, 330 Independence Ave, SW, Washington, DC 20201/202-245-6335. Materials include pamphlets on family planning, staff research on population, the *Five-Year Plan for Family Planning Services and Population Research* (an annual report to Congress), and some unpublished documents. The office's own documents are not for public distribution; most others are free. (Copying: not available.)

Office of Regulation Management
Health Care Financing Administration, Department of Health and Human Services, 200 Independence Ave. SW, Room 309-G, Washington, DC 20201/202-245-7890. Contains a vast amount of regulatory documents covering Medicare, Medicaid, and Professional Standards Review Organizations (PSROs). (Copying: 10¢ per page.)

Housing and Urban Development Department

Public Reference Room
Office of Interstate Land Sales, Department of Housing and Urban Development, 451 7th St. SW, Room 6262, Washington, DC 20410/202-755-6464. This room contains filings for all developers of 50 or more lots, including articles of incorporation and registration; claims of exemptions; orders of exemptions (applicable to fewer than 300 lots); exemption advisory opinions (partial statements of the HUD Office of Legal Counsel), including those regarding condominiums; inquiries; and free brochures aimed at assisting property buyers. (Copying: 10¢ per page; a property report, complete with description of a property, costs $2.50.)

Interior Department

Public Information Office
Bureau of Indian Affairs, Department of Interior, 19th and E Sts. NW, Room 4627, Washington, DC 20240/202-343-7445. This office has a number of pamphlets about various aspects of Indian life including religion, language, and population and labor statistics. (Copying: not available. Single copies are available free of charge.)

Interstate Commerce Commission

Docket File Reading Room
Interstate Commerce Commission, Constitution Ave. and 12th St. NW, Room 1221, Washington, DC 20423/202-275-7285. The collection includes about 150,000 dockets: records of complaints, protests and cases against railroads, trucking companies and other carriers. (Copying: 10¢ per page.)

Tariff Examining Branch
Public Tariff File Room, Interstate Commerce Commission, 12th St. and Constitution Ave. NW, Room 436, Washington, DC 20423/202-275-0712. The collection consists mainly of bound volumes of thousands of tariffs. There are about 350,000 tariffs (approximately one million pages) issued a year. A cancellation program eliminates outdated tariffs. (Copying: 10¢ per page.)

Public Reference Room
Interstate Commerce Commission, Constitution Ave. and 12th St. NW, Room 3378, Washington, DC 20423/202-275-7343. This room contains bound volumes and vertical files of annual (and some quarterly) reports of transportation companies—motor carriers, railway companies, and freight forwarders—regulated by the ICC. The collection also includes reports of rate bureau organizations regulated by the ICC and stockholder reports on some carriers. (Copying: 10¢ per page.)

Labor Department

Public Disclosure Branch
Office of Pension and Employee Benefits, Department of Labor, 200 Constitution Ave. NW, Room N4677, Washington, DC 20216/202-523-8773. This office maintains annual reports and other disclosure documents filed under the Employee Retirement Income Security Act of 1974. Reports mandated by the Welfare Pension Plans Disclosure Act of 1959 are kept at the Federal Records Center, 4205 Suitland Rd., Suitland, MD 20490/301-763-7010.

National Aeronautics and Space Administration

Information Center
National Aeronautics and Space Administration, 600 Independence Ave. SW, Room 126, Washington, DC 20546/202-453-1000. The Center contains copies of handbooks and scientific and technical documents produced by NASA staff for the various NASA projects. There are also copies of special reports covering new inventions from NASA. (Copying: 10¢ per page.)

National Foundation on the Arts and the Humanities

Library
National Foundation on the Arts and the Humanities, 1100 Pennsylvania Ave. NW, Washington, DC 20506/202-682-5400 Arts and 202-786-0438 Humanities. In addition to its collection of published materials, this room also contains copies of over 150 special reports sponsored by the foundation on such topics as art administration, fund raising, and economic impact studies. (Copying: Available at no charge for 20 copies or less.)

National Labor Relations Board

Division of Information

National Labor Relations Board, 1717 Pennsylvania Ave. NW, Room 710, Washington, DC 20570/202-632-4950. The Division contains decisions, orders and other documentation relating to cases involving unfair labor practices at commercial businesses, private hospitals, some law offices and other firms. This room also contains copies of quarterly reports produced by the board. Records are kept for approximately one year, then bound and sold through the Government Printing Office. (Copying: 10¢ per page at Freedom of Information Office, Room 1100.)

National Mediation Board

National Mediation Board

Department of Research, 1425 K St. NW, Suite 910, Washington, DC 20005/202-523-5995. The board maintains collective bargaining records and hearing documentation for airlines and railroads, and five volumes of determinations by the board. A staff person is available to help with specific requests. (Copying: 15¢ per page, unless you are making fewer than 33 copies.)

National Science Foundation

Engineering Directorate

National Science Foundation, 1800 G St. NW, Room 1152, Washington, DC 20550/202-357-4545. The Directorate for Engineering and Applied Science handles published materials from NTIS, GPO, and some private publishers resulting from research performed under NSF grants and contracts. Extra copies of documents are frequently available on request. The directorate supports research in several areas, including earthquake hazard mitigation, chemical threats, alternative biological sources of materials, managing risks to community water, intergovernmental science and research and development incentives, and various public policy issues. The materials are maintained in the reference section of the NSF Library, Room 1132/202-357-9545. (Copying: available at no charge in the NSF Library, Room 1242.)

National Transportation Safety Board

National Transportation Safety Board

Public Inquiry Section, Room 805-F, 800 Independence Ave. SW, Washington, DC 20594/202-382-6735. Aviation accident information makes up the bulk of the section's collection, but it also includes reports concerning railroad, highway, pipeline, and marine safety. Included are investigators' complete reports on accidents, preliminary reports, probable cause, and transcripts of any hearings. (Copying: 20¢ per page.)

Nuclear Regulatory Commission

Public Document Room

Nuclear Regulatory Commission, 1717 H St. NW, Washington, DC/202-634-3273/Mailing Address: Nuclear Regulatory Commission, Washington, DC 20555. This room holds approximately 900,000 documents, including technical licensing information on nuclear materials, reactor operator licenses, publications of the advisory committee on reactor safeguards, and transcripts of rule-making hearings. Free press releases also available. (Copying: 5¢ per page for paper copies; 22¢ per page for paper copies of microfiche; 24¢ per microfiche copy.)

Occupational Safety and Health Administration

Occupational Safety and Health Administration

Dockets Office, 200 Constitution Ave. NW, Room S-6212, Washington, DC 20210/202-523-7894. This room contains all the comments and transcripts from the private sector on OSHA proposals for new laws governing occupational safety. (Copying: 10¢ per page.)

Occupational Safety and Health Review Commission

Occupational Safety and Health Review Commission

Public Information, Room 701, 1825 K St. NW, Washington, DC 20006/202-634-7943. This adjudicatory body has information on its procedures, as well as specific case transcripts, briefs, and decisions concerning any company which has employees and is engaged in interstate commerce. (Copying: commission decisions are usually free. However, there is a 10¢ per page charge for all briefs and transcripts.)

Panama Canal Commission

Panama Canal Commission
425 13th St. NW, Suite 312, Washington, DC 20004/202-724-0104. The annual report of this organization is a large source of information. It includes: statistics on vessels and cargo, financial statement, and Canal Zone specifics (health, sanitation, schooling, etc.). Also available are consultant studies dealing with the capacity of the Canal and economic impacts. (Copying: not available.)

Pension Benefit Guaranty Corporation

Disclosure Room
Pension Benefit Guaranty Corporation, 2020 K St. NW, Washington, DC 20006/202-254-5527. This room contains copies of the following items: Pension Benefit Guaranty Corporation Trusteeship Plans, opinion letters, opinion manuals, pertinent litigation for review, termination case data sheets, case log terminating plans updated quarterly, and a computer listing of termination cases. In addition, on microfilm there are annual reports filed by pension plans. (Copying: 10¢ per page.)

Postal Rate Commission

Postal Rate Commission, Dockets Section, 333 H St. NW, Washington, DC 20268/202-789-6845. This section contains notices, motions, rulings, transcripts of hearings, and mail classifications, all dealing with postal rate levels. (Copying: 15¢ per page on documents filed by outside organizations. All material published by the commission is free.)

Railroad Retirement Board

Railroad Retirement Board, 425 13th St. NW, Room 444, Washington, DC 20004/202-724-0894. The service's annual report covers amounts paid out, numbers on rolls, and the benefits history of the board. Material pertaining to railroad unemployment and retirement benefits (general, not individual information) is also for public use. (Copying: no charge.)

Securities and Exchange Commission

Public Reference Section, Securities and Exchange Commission, Room 1024, 50 5th Street NW, Washington, DC 20509/202-272-7450. The collection of documents includes annual reports (ten thousand), and quarterly reports (one hundred) of registered companies, as well as current company reports (eight thousand) of significant matters. Also available are registration statements relative to sales of shares and ownership reports concerning personal ownership of 10 percent or more of company stock. (Copying: 10¢ per page.)

Small Business Administration

Small Business Administration, Public Communications, 1441 L St. NW, Washington, DC 20416/202-653-6365. This office contains a list of free management assistance publications and a list of booklets for sale about starting businesses. (Copying: not available).

Transportation Department

Bureau of Domestic Aviation—Licensing Division

Air Traffic Licensing Division, Department of Transportation, Room 6412, 400 7th St. SW, Washington, DC 20590/202-755-3809. The bureau collects information about charter tours, including charter and depository agreements, advertisements and contracts, and insurance data for air taxis and air freight.

Also available are files of registrations for air taxis, scheduled commuter airlines, and charter planes. They show the carriers' names, addresses, types of aircraft operated, services performed, and descriptions of insurance carried. Each registration covers a period of two years; however, proposed rule changes will require carriers to file only an initial registration. (Copying: 15¢ per page.)

Aviation Public Reference Room
Aviation Public Reference Room, Room 4125, Department of Transportation, 400 7th Street SW, Washington, DC 20590/202-426-7888. The Public Reference Room contains all board orders and reports. It also has financial, statistical and performance reports filed by the carriers—commercial airlines, supplementals, foreign airlines and commuter airlines. This office also keeps some Freedom of Information materials, board meeting records, financial data on cargo carriers, and traffic schedules. The Reference Room can obtain other reports from specific offices for public inspection. A few of these publications are free from the publications office. (Copying: 15¢ per page. Bring your own supply of change.)

Financial and Air Traffic Data Section
Data Administration Division, DAI-20-Room 4123, Office of Aviation Information Manage-

ment, Research and Special Programs Administration, Department of Transportation, 400 7th Street SW, Washington, DC 20590/ 202-426-8847. Handbooks and statistical reports cover all traffic data and financial statistics concerning U.S. airlines, U.S. airport activity, and international statistics for U.S. carriers. The section maintains monthly traffic reports, quarterly financial reports showing freight loss and damage, and denied boarding reports on all carriers, including foreign ones. (Copying: 15¢ per page.)

Public Inquiry Center—Federal Aviation Administration
Department of Transportation, 800 Independence Ave. SW, Room 907, E., APA 430, Washington, DC 20591/202-426-8058. The center offers publications describing careers in aviation fields. It acts as a referral service to offices that handle statistical and research and development publications. Some of the statistical books list the number of air miles flown, number of aviation personnel and other figures about airports and aircraft. (Copying: 25¢ for the first page; 5¢ for each additional page, plus a $2 search fee.)

Office of Airport Programs—Federal Aviation Administration
Department of Transportation, 800 Independence Ave. SW, Room 600 E., Washington, DC 20591/ 202-426-3050. The office has copies of the following publications: *General Standards* (i.e., for runways, lighting, etc.), safety standards specifications, *Design Guides, Federal Grant and Aid Programs,* and *Advisory Circulars.* The *Advisory Circulars* and most of the other publications are free. (Copying: 25¢ for the first page; 5¢ for each additional page.)

Public Affairs Office—National Transportation Safety Board
Department of Transportation, 800 Independence Ave. SW, Room 810-D, Washington, DC 20594/ 202-382-6600. This is a central depository of reports about accidents—most involving aircraft, but some pertaining to railroad, marine and pipeline accidents. (Copying: 25¢ per page.)

Technical Reference Branch—National Highway Traffic Safety Administration
Department of Transportation, 400 7th St. SW, Room 5108, Washington, DC 20590/202-426-2768. The Technical Reference Branch collection includes more than 80,000 items pertaining to: highway safety literature (journal articles, monographs, technical reports and other NHTSA publi-

cations, results of contract research, and inhouse publications); reports other than r&d, such as standards enforcement test reports (formerly compliance test reports) issued monthly; certificate information requests; defects investigations; Motor Vehicle Safety Defect Recall Campaigns; Multidisciplinary accident investigation case reports; audio-visual materials engineering specifications; dockets (public records of rule-making activities for motor vehicle and highway safety standards); and general reference materials. The branch also makes available *A Guide to Reference Services in the National Highway Traffic Safety Administration.* (Copying: 25¢ for the first page, 5¢ for each additional page. Microfiche copies cost 15¢ per sheet.)

Office of Vehicle Safety Compliance Enforcement
National Highway Traffic Safety Administration, 400 7th St. SW, Room 6111, Washington, DC 20590/202-426-2820. This office maintains files of ongoing investigations. Documents are filed by number assigned to the case in the standards enforcement test report (formerly compliance test report). Materials in reports identify which vehicles or vehicle parts have failed Transportation Department tests. (Copying: 25¢ for the first page; 5¢ for each additional page.)

Treasury Department

Communications Division—Comptroller of the Currency
Department of the Treasury, 490 L'Enfant Plaza East SW, Washington, DC 20219/202-447-1800. The office contains financial reports by national banks showing conditions and income; some 300 trust reports and shareholder information about banks with 500 or more shareholders: Make a Freedom of Information Act request for materials. (Copying: 10¢ per page.)

Freedom of Information Reading Room—Customs Service
Department of the Treasury, 1301 Constitution Ave. NW, Room 2321, Washington, DC 20229/ 202-566-8681. This room contains two microfilm files; one is a key word index to customs rulings, the other microfilm copies of rulings. (Copying: 10¢ per page.)

Legal Regulations and Rulings—Customs Service
Department of the Treasury, 1301 Constitution Ave. NW, Washington, DC 20229/202-566-8237. Here you can find documents on the legal rulings of the Customs Service. (Copying: 10¢ per page.)

Legal Retrieval Department—Customs Service
Department of the Treasury, 1301 Constitution Ave. NW, Washington, DC 20229/202-566-5095. This room contains the regulations and rulings of the U.S. Customs Service. It publishes the *Listing of Decisions and Rulings* in the Customs Bulletins; microfiche of these rulings are also available. (Copying: 10¢ per page.)

Public Information Department—Customs Service
Department of the Treasury, 1301 Constitution Ave. NW, Room 6303, Washington, DC/202-566-8195 or 8196. Mailing Address: P. O. Box 7118, Washington, DC 20044. This is a public information center for the U.S. Customs Service. It contains pamphlets, publications, brochures, manuals and bulletins on all component activities (i.e., duties, tariffs, regulations, fines, rulings, etc.) of the U.S. Customs Service. (Copying: no charge.)

Freedom of Information Reading Room—Internal Revenue Service
Department of the Treasury, 1111 Constitution Ave. NW, Washington, DC 20224/202-566-3770.

Materials available to the public include: the *IRS Manual,* information concerning tax-exempt organizations, plans approved under the Employee Retirement Income Security Act of 1974, the commissioner's annual report, chief counsel's orders, revenue rulings and revenue procedures, and Treasury decisions, including statistics concerning the income of corporations, estates, and individuals. Individuals outside Washington, DC, may obtain IRS information from public information officers at IRS district offices. (Copying: 10¢ per page.)

International Trade Commission
Office of the Secretary, International Trade Commission, 701 E St. NW, Room 160, Washington, DC 20436/202-523-0161. Publications in this collection date back to January 1961 and relate to the commission's investigation of cases in which U.S. industries sought "import relief." Industries investigated include nonrubber footwear, zippers, mushrooms, stainless steel, wrapper tobacco, nuts, bolts, and screws. Case documentation is available. (Copying: 10¢ per page, however most materials are free.)

Libraries of Federal Agencies

Federal government libraries often have unique holdings in their fields, including photographs and hard-to-find archival material. They are therefore excellent sources of information for researchers. However, some are open to the public by appointment; it is wise to call before scheduling your visit.

Many libraries also offer telephone reference services; the telephone number given in this listing is the reference number unless otherwise noted.

Federal libraries rarely lend materials outside the confines of the government. If you find that you need to borrow materials, you should arrange it through interlibrary loan. Contact your company, university, or public library for assistance in this area.

The following is a list of major federal government libraries, with a few private libraries included whose collections are of special interest. You'll note that most of these libraries are located in Washington, DC. If you live elsewhere check with the federal library to see if it has a regional branch in your area. See also: "Federal Depository Libraries" in the Resources Close-To-Home section of the sampler and the chapter "Library of Congress."

ACTION Library/Room 407, 806 Connecticut Ave. NW, Washington, DC 20525/202-634-9776.
Agriculture Department National Agricultural Library/10301 Baltimore Blvd., Beltsville, MD 20705/301-344-3756.

Armed Forces Institute of Pathology Ash Library/Walter Reed Army Medical Center, Washington, DC 20306/202-576-2983.
Armed Forces Radiobiology Research Institute Library/Building 42, National Naval Medical Center, Bethesda, MD 20814/301-295-0428.

Arms Control and Disarmament Agency/Room 5851, 320 1st St. NW, Washington DC, 20451/202-632-8714.

Belvoir Research and Development Center Technical Library/Building 315, Fort Belvoir, VA 22060/703-664-5179.

Army Office of the Chief of Engineers Library/20 Massachusetts Ave. NW, Room 3119, Washington, DC 20314/202-272-0455.

Bar Association of the District of Columbia Library/Room 3518, District Court Building, Washington, DC 20001/202-426-7087.

Civil Rights Commission Library/Room 709, 1121 Vermont Ave. NW, Washington, DC 20425/202-376-8110.

Commerce Department Library/Room 7046, 14th St. and Constitution Ave. NW, Washington, DC 20230/202-377-5511.

Commerce Department Law Library/Room 1894, Main Commerce Bldg., 14th St. and Constitution Ave. NW, Washington, DC 20230/202-377-5517.

Commerce Department Bureau of the Census Library/Room 2451, Federal Building 3, Suitland, MD. Mailing address: Washington, DC 20233/301-763-5042.

Commerce Department National Oceanic and Atmospheric Administration Library and Information Services Division/OA/D82, 6009 Executive Blvd., Rockville, MD 20852/301-443-8287.

Commerce Department National Oceanic and Atmospheric Administration Page Branch Library/Georgetown Information Center, 3300 Whitehaven St. NW, Room 193, Washington, DC 20235/202-634-7346.

Commerce Department National Telecommunications and Information Administration Library/Room 755, 1800 G St. NW, Washington, DC 20504/202-377-1551.

Commerce Department, Patent and Trademark Office Scientific Library/2021 Jefferson Davis Highway, Crystal Plaza Building 34, 2nd Floor, Arlington, VA 22202/703-557-2955.

Commodity Futures Trading Commission Library/2033 K St. NW, Room 540, Washington, DC 20581/202-254-5901.

Consumer Product Safety Commission Library/5401 Westbard Ave., Bethesda, MD. Mailing address: Washington, DC 20207/301-492-6544.

Congressional Budget Office Library/House Office Building Annex #2, 2nd and D Sts. SW, Room 471, Washington, DC 20515/202-226-2635.

Defense Department Audiovisual Agency Still Picture Depository/Building 168, Naval District Washington, Washington, DC 20374/202-433-2168.

Defense Department Communications Agency Technical Library/Building 12, Arlington, VA 22204. Mailing address: Headquarters DCA, Code 309, Washington, DC 20305/202-692-2468.

Defense Department Technical Information Center Technical Library/Cameron Station, Building #5, Alexandria, VA 22314/703-274-6833.

District of Columbia Government Martin Luther King, Jr. Memorial Library/901 G St. NW, Washington, DC 20001/202-727-1126.

Education Department National Institute of Education, Educational Research Library/1200 19th Street NW, Room 230, Washington, DC 20208/202-254-5060.

Education Department Division of Library Programs, Room 707, 400 Maryland Avenue SW, Washington, DC 20202/202-254-5680.

Education Department Office of Libraries and Learning Technologies/State and Public Library Services Branch, Room 707, 400 Maryland Avenue SW, Washington, DC 20202/202-254-9664.

Energy Department Library/Routes 270, and 118. Germantown, MD. Mailing address: Mailstop A 238021 GTN, Washington, DC 20545/301-353-4166.

Energy Department Federal Energy Regulatory Commission Branch Library/825 N. Capital St. NE, Room 8502, Washington, DC 20545/202-357-5480.

Energy Department Technical Library/Forrestal Bldg., Mailstop A232 Forrestal, 1000 Independence Ave. SW, Washington, DC 20585/202-252-9534.

Environmental Protection Agency Headquarters Library/Room 447, 401 M St. SW, Washington, DC 20460/202-382-3556.

Environmental Protection Agency Information Resources and Services Branch/Room 2904, PM 211A, 401 M St. SW, Washington, DC 20460/202-382-5921.

Equal Employment Opportunity Commission Library/2401 E St. NW, Washington, DC 20507/202-634-6990.

Executive Office of the President, Information Center/Room G102, New Executive Office Building, 726 Jackson Pl. NW, Washington, DC 20503/202-395-3654.

Export-Import Bank of the U.S. Library/Room 1373, 811 Vermont Ave. NW, Washington, DC 20571/202-566-8320.

Farm Credit Administration Reference Library, 1501 Farm Credit Drive, McLean, VA 22101-5090/703-883-4296.

Farm Credit Administration Reference Library/ 490 L'Enfant Plaza, SW, Washington, DC 20578/202-755-2170.

Federal Communications Commission Library/ Room 639, 1919 M St. NW, Washington, DC 20554/202-632-7100.

Federal Deposit Insurance Corporation Library/ Room 4074, 550 17th St. NW, Washington, DC 20429/389-4314.

Federal Home Loan Bank Board Library/1700 G St. NW, Washington, DC 20552/202-377-6296.

Federal Judicial Center Information Service/1520 H St. NW, Washington, DC 20005/202-633-6365.

Federal Maritime Commission Library/1100 L St. NW, Washington, DC 20573/202-523-5762.

Federal Reserve System Board of Governors Research Library/Federal Reserve Building, Washington, DC 20551/202-452-3332.

Federal Trade Commission Library/Room 630, 6th St. and Pennsylvania Ave. NW, Washington, DC 20580/202-523-3871.

Gallaudet College/Edward Miner Gallaudet Library, 800 Florida Ave. NE, Washington, DC 20002/202-651-5566.

General Accounting Office Technical Information Sources and Services Branch/Room 6430, 441 G St. NW, Washington, DC 20548/202-275-5180.

General Services Administration Library/ATRFL-Room 1033, GSA Building, 18th and F Sts. NW, Washington, DC 20405/202-535-7788.

General Services Administration National Archives/8th St. and Pennsylvania Ave. NW, Room 201 NNIL, Washington, DC 20408/202-523-3049.

General Services Administration National Archives and Records Service/Office of Presidential Libraries, NL, 8th St. and Pennsylvania Ave. NW, Washington, DC 20408/202-523-3212.

General Services Administration National Archives and Records/Carter Presidential Materials Project/77 Forsythe St., SW, Atlanta, GA 30203/404-221-3942.

General Services Administration National Archives and Records Service/Dwight D. Eisenhower Library, SE 4th St., Abilene, KS 67410/913-263-4751.

General Services Administration National Archives and Records Service/Gerald R. Ford Library, 1000 Beal Avenue, Ann Arbor, MI 48109/313-668-2218.

General Services Administration National Archives and Records Service/Herbert Hoover Presidential Library, Parkside Drive, P. O. Box 488, West Branch, IA 52358/319-643-5301.

General Services Administration National Archives and Records Service/Lyndon Baines Johnson Library, 2313 Red River St., Austin, TX 78705/512-397-5137.

General Services Administration National Archives and Records Service/John F. Kennedy Library, Columbia Point, Boston, MA 02125/617-929-4534.

General Services Administration National Archives and Records Service/Franklin D. Roosevelt Library, Albany Post Rd., Hyde Park, NY 12538/914-229-8114.

General Services Administration National Archives and Records Service/Harry S. Truman Library and Museum, Highway 24 and Delaware St., Independence, MO 64050/816-833-1400.

General Services Administration National Archives and Records/Motion Picture, Video and Sound, 875 S. Pickett St., Alexandria, VA 22306/703-756-6451.

General Services Administration National Audiovisual Center/ATTN: Reference Section/Washington, DC 20409/301-763-1896.

Government Printing Office-Library Programs Services, North Capital and H Street NW, Washington, DC 20401.

Health and Human Services Department Library/ Room 1436, 330 Independence Ave. SW, Washington, DC 20201/202-245-6791.

Health and Human Services Department Center for Disease Control Library/1600 Clifton Rd. NE, Building 1, Room 4105, Atlanta, GA 30333/404-329-3396.

Health and Human Services Department Food and Drug Administration Medical Library/HFN 98, Room 11B07, 5600 Fishers Lane, Rockville, MD 20857/301-443-3180.

Health and Human Services Department National Institute of Mental Health/Parklawn Building, Room 15C05, 5600 Fishers Lane, Rockville, MD 20852/301-443-4506.

Health and Human Services Department National Institutes of Health Library/Room IL 25, Building 10, 9000 Rockville Pike, Bethesda, MD 20205/301-496-2447.

Health and Human Services Department National Institutes of Health Division of Computer Research and Technology Library/Building 12A, Room 3018, 9000 Rockville Pike, Bethesda, MD 20205/301-496-1658.

Health and Human Services Department National Institute of Health National Library of Medicine/8600 Rockville Pike, Bethesda, MD 20209/301-496-6095.

Health and Human Services Department Public

Health Service Parklawn Health Library/Parklawn Building, Room 1312, 5600 Fishers Lane, Rockville, MD 20853/301-443-2673.

Health and Human Services Department Social Security Administration Library/Washington, DC Branch, 1875 Connecticut Ave. NW, Room 320-0, Washington, DC 20009/202-673-5532.

Housing and Urban Development Department Library/Room 8141, 451 7th St. SW, Washington, DC 20410/202-755-6370.

Interior Department Bureau of Mines Library/ Avondale Research Center, 4900 LaSalle Rd., Avondale, MD 20782/301-436-7552.

Interior Department Geological Survey Library/ Reference Desk, 950 National Center, 12201 Sunrise Valley Dr., Reston, VA 22092/703-860-6671.

Interior Department Geological Survey National Cartographic Geographic Information Service/ 507 National Center, 12201 Sunrise Valley Dr., Reston, VA 22092/703-860-6045.

Interior Department Natural Resources Library (Main Library), Main Interior Building, 18th and C Sts. NW, Washington, DC 20240/202-343-5815.

Interior Department Natural Resources Library Law Branch, PIR-L, Room 7100W, Main Interior Building, 18th and C Sts. NW, Washington, DC 20240/202-343-4571.

Interior Department U.S. Fish and Wildlife Service Patuxent Wildlife Research Center Library/ Laurel, MD 20708/301-498-0235.

International Development Cooperation Agency Information Center/Room 105 SA-18, Washington, DC 20523/703-235-1000.

International Trade Commission, Main Library/ Room 301, 701 E St. NW, Washington, DC 20436/202-523-0013.

International Trade Commission Law Library/ Room 213, 701 E St. NW, Washington, DC 20436/202-523-0333.

Interstate Commerce Commission Library/Room 3392, 12th St. and Constitution Ave. NW, Washington, DC 20423/202-275-7327 or 7328.

Justice Department Main Library/Room 5400, 10th St. and Pennsylvania Ave. NW, Washington, DC 20530/202-633-3148.

Justice Department National Institute of Justice Library/Room 900, 633 Indiana Ave. NW, Washington, DC 20531/202-724-5883 or 301-724-5884.

Labor Department Library/Room N-2439, 200 Constitution Ave. NW, Washington, DC 20210/202-523-6988.

Labor Department Law Library/Room N2439, 200 Constitution Ave. NW, Washington, DC 20210/202-523-7991.

Library of Congress/10 First St. SE, Washington, DC 20540/202-287-5000.

National Aeronautics and Space Administration Goddard Space Flight Center Library/Code 252, Greenbelt, MD 20771/301-344-7218.

National Aeronautics and Space Administration Law Library/Code GL-2, Room 7022, 400 Maryland Ave. SW, Washington, DC 20546/202-755-3896.

National Bureau of Standards Library/Room E01, Administration Building, Gaithersburg, MD 20899/301-921-3451.

National Bureau of Standards, Standards Information Service/Admin. A679, Gaithersburg, MD 20899/301-921-2587.

National Capital Planning Commission Central 1325 G St. NW, Washington, DC 20576/202-724-2870.

National Endowment for the Arts Library/1100 Pennsylvania Avenue NW, Washington, DC 20506/202-682-5485.

National Endowment for the Humanities Library/ 1100 Pennsylvania Avenue NW, Washington, DC 20506/202-786-0245.

National Labor Relations Board Library/Room 900, 1717 Pennsylvania Ave. NW, Washington, DC 20570/202-254-9055.

National Science Foundation Library/Room K300, 1800 G St. NW, Washington, DC 20550/202-357-7811.

Navy Department Library/Building, 44 Washington Navy Yard, 11th & M Sts. SE, Washington, DC 20374-0571/202-433-4131.

Navy Department Center for Naval Analyses Library/4401 Ford Avenue, Alexandria, VA 22302/703-998-3578.

Navy Department Naval Historical Center Operational Archives Branch/Building 210, Washington Navy Yard, 9th & M Sts. SE, Washington, DC 20374/202-433-3171.

Navy Department Naval Medical Research Institute Information Services Branch/National Naval Medical Center, Bethesda, MD 20814-5055/301-295-2186.

Navy Department Naval Sea Systems Command Technical Library SEA098312/National Center #3, Room 1S15, Arlington, VA. Mailing address: Washington, DC 20362/703-692-3305.

Navy Department Office of Naval Research Library/Room 633, Ballston Tower #1, Code 784DL, 800 North Quincy St., Arlington, VA 22217/703-696-4415.

Nuclear Regulatory Commission/7920 Norfolk Ave., Bethesda, MD. Mailing address: Washington, DC 20555/301-492-7748.

Office of Personnel Management Library/Room

5L45, 1900 E St. NW, Washington, DC 20415/202-632-4432. Reference: 202-632-7640.

Office of Technology Assessment Information Center/Congress, 600 Pennsylvania Ave SE, Room 304, Washington, DC 20510/202-226-2160.

Organization of American States Columbus Memorial Library MMB B13/17th St. and Constitution Ave. NW, Washington, DC 20006/202-789-6040.

Overseas Private Investment Corporation Library/ 7th Floor, 1129 20th St. NW, Washington, DC 20527/202-652-2863.

Pension Benefit Guaranty Corporation Library/ Suite 7200, 2020 K St. NW, Washington, DC 20006/202-254-4889.

Pentagon Library/Room 1A518, The Pentagon, Washington, DC 20310/202-695-5346.

Securities and Exchange Commission Library/450 5th Street NW, Room 1C00, Stop C-2, Washington, DC 20549/202-272-2618.

Small Business Administration Law Library/Room 714, 1441 L St. NW, Washington, DC 20416/202-653-6556.

Small Business Administration Reference Library/ 1441 L St. NW, Washington, DC 20416/202-653-6914.

State Department Library/Room 3239NS, 22nd and C Sts. NW, Washington, DC 20520/202-632-0372 or 0486.

State Department Foreign Service Institute Library/Room C2-SA-3, 1400 Key Boulevard, Arlington, VA 22209/703-235-8717.

Supreme Court Library (Information on Records and Briefs only)/1 First St. NE, Washington, DC 20543/202-479-3184.

Tax Court of the U.S. Library/400 2nd St. NW, Washington, DC 20217/202-376-2707.

Transportation Department Library Services Division/Room 2200, 400 7th St. SW, Washington, DC 20590/202-426-1792.

Transportation Department National Highway Traffic Safety Administration Technical Reference Division/400 7th St. SW, Room 5108, Washington, DC 20590/202-426-2768.

Transportation Department Library/General Collection, Information Services/400 7th Street SW, Washington, DC 20590/202-426-2575.

Transportation Department, Coast Guard Library/400 7th Street SW, Washington, DC 20590/202-755-7611.

Transportation Department, FAA Legal Library/ 800 Independence Avenue SW, Washington, DC 20590/202-426-3604.

Transportation Department, Headquarters—Law Library/400 7th Street SW, Washington, DC 20590/202-426-2563.

Treasury Department Library/Room 5310, 15th St. and Pennsylvania Ave. NW, Washington, DC 20220/202-566-2777.

Treasury Department Customs Service Library/ 1301 Constitution Ave. NW, Room 3340, Washington, DC 20229/202-566-5642.

Treasury Department Internal Revenue Service Library/1111 Constitution Ave. NW, Room 4324, Washington, DC 20540/202-566-6342.

United States Information Agency Library/ Room 135, 301 4th Street SW, Washington DC 20547/202-485-8947.

United States Information Agency, Film Library and Shipping Branch/601 D Street NW, Room L-0308, Washington DC 20547/202-376-7817.

United States Information Agency, Voice of America Library/North Building, Room G 510A, Washington, DC 20547/202-755-4649.

Veterans Administration Central Office Library/ Room 976, Administration Building, 810 Vermont Ave. NW, Washington, DC 20420/202-389-3085.

Publications Sold By the Government

There are three main distributors of government publications: the Government Printing Office, the Consumer Information Center and the National Technical Information Services. Below is a brief description of each of these organizations along with a sampling of their best-selling titles.

It should be noted that these organizations only represent about fifty percent of what is published by the federal government. The remaining publications are available directly from the departments or agencies. You should also be aware that many of the titles that are sold by these organizations are also available at no cost, and with much faster service, directly from the publishing department or agency.

Government Printing Office

Superintendent of Documents, Washington, DC 20402/202-783-3238. Sells through mail orders and government bookstores more than 25,000 different publications that originated in various government agencies. (For more complete information see GPO section in "Legislative Branch" portion of book.)

Best-Sellers

Infant Care (017-091-00228-2) $4.75
Prenatal Care (017-091-00237-1) $4.25
Your Child From 1 to 6 (017-091-00219-3) $5.00
Your Child From 6 to 12 (017-091-00070-1) $5.00
Rescue Breathing (wallet-size card) (017-001-00145-7) $1.75 each, $5.50 for 100
Metric Conversion (wallet-size card) (003-003-01068-5) $1.00 each, $35 for 100
United States Postage Stamps (039-000-00224) $8.50
Federal Benefits for Veterans and Dependents (051-000-00170-2) $2.50
U.S. Government Manual (022-003-01109-9) $12.00

Consumer Information Center

Pueblo, Colorado 81009. The Center was established to encourage federal agencies to develop and release useful consumer information and to increase public awareness of this information. Its publications are available by written request. Listed below are the Center's Best Freebies and Booklets for kids.

Best Freebies

Cancer Prevention: Good News, Better News, Best News (571N)—advice on what you can do to help protect yourself against cancer, including latest nutrition information.
Child Support (501N)—help available from the government to enforce child support obligations, locate missing parents, and establish paternity.
Consumer Credit Handbook (591N)—how to apply for credit, what to do if you are denied, and how consumer credit laws can help you.
Student Guide—Five Federal Financial Aid Programs (513N)—important information about five grant and loan programs for college, vocational, and technical school students.
Back Pain (569N)—common causes and treatments of this all too common ailment.
Your Social Security (515N)—all about Social Security and Medicare benefits, including who gets them and how to apply.
Checklist for Going into Business (516N)—important considerations before starting a small business.
A Consumer's Guide to Life Insurance (592N)—comprehensive guide to different types of policies, costs, and coverage, includes a glossary of commonly used terms.
How to Choose and Use a Lawyer (601N)—questions and answers about fees, advertising, referrals, and other legal resources. What to do when you have a problem with a lawyer.
Some Things You Should Know About Prescription Drugs (560N)—even prescription drugs can be dangerous; here are tips for safe use.,
How to Buy a Telephone (600N)—facts about costs, selection, installation, and repair.
Consumer's Guide to Telephone Services (618N)—describes the best area services available.

Best Sellers

The Arithmetic of Interest Rates (418N, 50 cents)—a handy guide to understanding and calculating simple and compound interest rates.
Age Pages (147N, $2.00)—practical health advice for older people on a variety of topics including sexuality, exercise, foot care, incontinence, and more.
How to Buy a Home Computer (426N, 50 cents)—step-by-step guide to selecting a computer (hardware) and the tapes, cartridges, and floppy disks to program it (software); also includes a handy glossary of computer terms.
How to Buy Economically: A Food Buyer's Guide (436N, 50 cents)—how to cut costs on meat, poultry, eggs, milk, fruits and vegetables; months during which you can get the best buys on a variety of fruits and vegetables.
Starting and Managing a Small Service Business (135N, $4.50)—how to pick a salable service by assessing your skills and market. Includes information on financing and organizing.
Federal Benefits for Veterans and Dependents (138N, $2.50)—a comprehensive description of benefits available as of January 1, 1985, including medical, educational, vocational, loan, and insurance programs administered by VA and other agencies. Lists VA facilities nationwide.
The Backyard Mechanic Set (104N, $7.00)—three booklets on auto maintenance full of car-saving and cost-saving tips. The 39 illustrated chapters—useful for the beginner and the expert—start with changing the oil, move on to tune-ups, rebuilding the carburetor, brake and

body repairs, and more. They also include consumer tips to help you avoid rip-offs when having your car repaired or buying a used car.

Help Yourself to a Midlife Career Change (122N, $2.25)—basic steps involved in a career change: assessing your skills, personality, interests, and values: transferring your abilities to new work situations; also lists the "Ten Hottest Transferrable Skills."

How to Help Your Children Achieve in School (111N, $3.75)—ways to help your children perform to the best of their ability in school. Tips include techniques for learning and remembering and strategies for test taking.

Selecting and Financing a Home (170N, $3.00)—brief comparison of renting with buying; how to figure what you can afford and apply for a loan; what to look for in homeowner's insurance.

Booklets For Kids

Comparing the Planets (116N, $3.50)—full-color wall-chart featuring close-up pictures and important data on our neighbors in the solar system. Folded poster.

Dennis Takes a Poke at Poison (507N, free)—Dennis the Menace learns about poisons in the home and how to tell if something is safe to eat.

The New Teen Titans (403N, 50 cents)—this comic book depicts youngsters and their families dealing with alcohol and drug abuse with the help of the superheroes, the Teen Titans. Written for late elementary school children.

The Nine Lives of El Gato (404N, 50 cents)—a comic book to show kids how to avoid the fire hazards El Gato encounters at home and at play.

Space Shuttle (119N, $3.50)—colorful illustration of the orbiter, with details of the interior design and equipment. Also includes a brief history. Folded poster.

Stars in Your Eyes: A Guide to the Northern Skies (195N, $1.50)—how to locate the best known constellations. Relates the legends of how they were named.

Stay-Well Card (508N, free)—coloring book on the importance of immunization with a checklist for parents on vaccinations young children need.

The Story of Checks and Electronic Payments (405N, 50 cents)—comic book for teenagers on how banks started and how they work today.

Think Toy Safety (406N, 50 cents)—coloring book for preschoolers and first graders on safe toy use.

National Technical Information Service (NTIS)

Department of Commerce, 5285 Port Royal Rd., Springfield, Va 22161/703-487-4600. The central source for the public sale of U.S. and foreign government-sponsored research, development and engineering reports and other analyses prepared by national and local government agencies, their contractors or grantees, or by Special Technology Groups. For more complete information see description listed under U.S. Department of Commerce.

Best-Sellers

The Directory of Computer Software and Related Technical Reports (PB 84-134-071) $40.00

Evaluation of Surface Mining Blasting Procedures (PB80-148653) $16.00

Passive Solar Handbook, Volume 1 (MP24992-0127/1) $26.50

Samplers and Sampling Procedures for Hazardous Waste Streams (PB80-135353) $11.50

The Soviet Economy in 1978–1979 and Prospects for 1980 (PB80-928112) $9.50

Siting Handbook for Small Wind Energy Conversion Systems (PNL-2521) $13.00

An Inexpensive Economical Solar Heating System for Homes (N76-27671) $10.00

Electromagnetic Compatibility Standard for Medical Devices (PB80-180284) $10.00

A Private Pension Forecasting Model (PB80-169667) $20.50

ERIC—Educational Resources Information Centers and Database

The Educational Resources Information Center (ERIC) can help you identify literature, experts, audiovisuals, funding and more on nearly any subject imaginable. The ERIC database contains information collected from all 16 ERIC Clearinghouses, and through a database search you can retrieve literature on subjects ranging from how-to stop smoking to ways to prepare for a new career.

ERIC Database

The world's largest educational database, ERIC gives users access to unpublished studies about innovative programs, bibliographies, professional papers, curriculum materials and reports of advances in educational research and development. Many public libraries and schools have access to the ERIC database, and staff will either search it for you or show you how to access the system yourself. A free directory listing more than 500 facilities throughout the U.S. having access to the database is available from: Educational Resources Information Center, National Institute of Education, 1200 19th Street NW, Brown Building, Washington, DC 20208/202-254-7934.

ERIC Clearinghouses

Listed below are the ERIC Clearinghouses, each of which is described in the chapter entitled Department of Education. Staff at these centers can provide you with information falling within the scope of their center. Each clearinghouse is responsible for searching out and acquiring the significant educational literature within its particular scope, screening and selecting the highest quality and most relevant material, processing selected items for input to the database and providing information analysis and other major products and user services. It is important to note that while these Centers are sponsored by the Department of Education, they are an excellent information resource for the general public, as well as teachers, researchers and parents of students. Examples of how you could use the Clearinghouses include:

If you are trying to locate an information resource for a specific subject, be it airplanes or audio-visuals, contact the Clearinghouse on Information Resources for referrals to literature, experts, reading lists, and unpublished materials.

If you are trying to locate reading materials in a specific foreign language, be it French or Japanese, contact the Language and Linguistics Clearinghouse for assistance.

If you are considering a career change and want information about training for a new vocation, contact the Clearinghouse on Adult Career and Vocational Education for information about schools, learning materials, and career prospects.

If you have a child with a reading problem, contact the Reading and Communications Skills Information Clearinghouse and learn the latest techniques in solving that problem.

If you live in a rural area, contact the Rural Education Information Clearinghouse to identify potential programs and available funding.

If you wish to study to teach science, mathematics or environmental education, contact the Clearinghouse on Science. Mathematics, and Environmental Education and investigate the potential opportunities.

Adult and Career Vocation Information
ERIC Clearinghouse on Adult Career and Vocational Education, Ohio State University, 1960 Kenny Road, Columbus, OH 43210/614-486-3655.

Counseling and Personal Services Information
ERIC Clearinghouse on Counseling and Personal Services, University of Michigan, School of Education Building, Room 2108, Ann Arbor, MI 48109/313-764-9492.

Early Childhood Education Information
ERIC Clearinghouse on Elementary and Early Childhood Education, University of Illinois, 805 W. Pennsylvania Avenue, Urbana, IL 61801/217-333-1386.

Educational Management Clearinghouse
ERIC Clearinghouse on Educational Management, University of Oregon, Library, Room 108, Eugene, Oregon 97403/503-686-5043.

Handicapped and Gifted Children Information
Clearinghouse on the Handicapped and Gifted Children, Council for Exceptional Children, 1920 Association Drive, Reston, VA 22091/703-620-3660.

Higher Education Information
ERIC Clearinghouse on Higher Education, One Dupont Circle, Suite #630, Washington, DC 20036/202-296-2597.

Information Resources
ERIC Clearinghouse on Information Resources, Syracuse University, School of Education, Area of Instructional Technology, 130 Huntington Hall, Syracuse, NY 13210/315-423-3640.

Junior College Information
ERIC Clearinghouse for Junior Colleges, Powell Library, Room 96, 405 Hilgard Avenue, Los Angeles, CA 90024/213-825-3931.

Language and Linguistics Clearinghouse
ERIC Clearinghouse on Language and Linguistics, Center for Applied Linguistics, 3520 Prospect Street NW, Washington, DC 20007/202-298-9292.

Reading and Communication Skills Information
ERIC Clearinghouse on Reading and Communication Skills, National Council of Teachers of English, 1111 Kenyon Road, Urbana, IL 61801/217-328-3870.

Rural Education
Rural Education and Small School ERIC Clearinghouse, New Mexico State University, Box 3AP, Las Cruces, New Mexico 88003/505-646-2623.

Science, Mathematics and Environmental Education
Clearinghouse for Science, Mathematics, and Environmental Education, Ohio State University, 1200 Chambers Road, 3rd Floor, Columbus, OH 43212/614-422-6717.

Social Science Information
ERIC Clearinghouse for Social Studies, University of Colorado, Social Science Education, 855 Broadway, Boulder, CO 80302/303-492-8434.

Teacher Education Clearinghouse
Clearinghouse on Teacher Education, American Association of Colleges for Teacher Education, One Dupont Circle NW, Suite 610, Washington, DC 20036/202-293-2450.

Tests, Measurement and Evaluation Information
ERIC Clearinghouse on Tests, Measurements, and Evaluation, Educational Testing Service, Princeton, NJ 08540/609-921-9000, Ext. 5181.

Urban Education Information
ERIC Clearinghouse on Urban Education, Box 40, Teachers College, Columbia University, 525 W. 120th Street, New York, NY 10027/212-678-3433.

Your Rights and Benefits

Described in this section are benefits you have earned as a taxpayer; government offices staffed to handle your complaints about subjects ranging from false advertising to transportation services; and leads to federal money programs. Also included is an explanation of the Freedom of Information Act, an important tool for obtaining information agencies may be reluctant to release. Your rights under the Privacy Act, a law which helps you gain access to information the government may have collected about you, are also explained here.

Benefits You May Be Eligible For

Almost everyone in the United States is entitled to some type of government benefits. Listed below are the major programs and corresponding offices which can help you investigate your eligibility. Should you need additional assistance in obtaining a government benefit you feel you deserve, contact the local office of your U.S. Senator or Congressional Representative. For a listing of these offices see the "Resources-Close-To-Home" Section of the Sampler.

Where To Go

Government Employee Retirement Benefits
Annuities Services Division, Retired Employees Service Section, Office of Personnel Management, 1900 E St. NW, Room 4H23, Washington, DC 20415/202-632-7457.

Handicapped and Disabled Assistance
The federal government, through state and local agencies, provides funding for a wide variety of benefit programs to assist the disabled and the handicapped. Assistance is available through various departments including Mental Health, Rehabilitative Services, Social Security, Health and Human Services, Education, Housing and Labor. For further information on these assistance programs, contact the related state or local authority as listed in the government section of your local phone book.

Medicaid
Director, Inquiries Staff, Health Care Financing Administration, Department of Health and Human Services, 6325 Security Blvd., Room 1P4, Baltimore, MD 21207/301-594-9032, or contact your local Dept. of Social Services.

Medicare
Bureau of Program Policy, Health Care Financing Administration, Department of Health and Human Services, 6325 Security Blvd., Room 1P4, Baltimore, MD 21234/301-594-9032, or see Social Security Administration in your local telephone book.

Social Security

Office of Public Inquiries, Social Security Administration, Department of Health and Human Services, 6401 Security Blvd., Room 4100 Annex Building, Baltimore, MD 21235/301-594-7700, or see Social Security Administration in your local telephone book.

Student Aid

Federal Student Financial Aid Information Center, P.O. Box 84, Washington, DC 20044/301-984-4070.

Unemployment Benefits

Unemployment insurance and benefits are funded by the federal government through state authorities. For information concerning your rights in general or for specific benefit applications, contact the State Unemployment Agency listed under the state government section of your local phone book.

Veterans' Benefits

Department of Veterans' Benefits, Veterans Administration, 810 Vermont Ave. NW, Washington, DC 20420/202-389-2044. The Veterans Administration maintains toll-free numbers in most states. Call 800-555-1212 for a number near you.

Publications Worth Writing For

Consumer Information Center

Described below are several publications which explain your rights to government benefit programs. To order write: Consumer Information Center, P.O. Box 100, Pueblo, CO 81002.

A Brief Explanation of Medicare. (542N)—A free publication which explains how people over 65 and some severely disabled younger persons can get health benefits.

Federal Benefits for Veterans and Dependents. (138N)—$2.50. A comprehensive description of benefits available as of January 1, 1985, including medical, educational, vocational, loan, and insurance programs administered by VA and other agencies. Also lists VA facilities nationwide.

Guide to Health Insurance for People with Medicare. (546N)—This free booklet explains what Medicare pays and doesn't pay, and what to look for in private insurance.

Pocket Guide to Federal Help for the Disabled Person. (150N)—$1.75. Federally funded programs for the disabled include vocational rehabilitation, health care, housing, and much more. Here's how to take advantage of what's available.

Student Guide—Five Federal Financial Aid Programs. (513N)—Important information about five grant and loan programs for college, vocational, and technical school students is described in this free booklet.

A Summary of Veterans Administration Benefits. (427N)—50¢. Highlights of VA programs and services for veterans and their dependents; addresses of VA locations nationwide.

A Woman's Guide to Social Security. (514N)—A free publication that tells what women should know about benefits upon retirement, disability, widowhood, or divorce.

Your Social Security. (515N)—The free booklet explains all about Social Security and Medicare benefits, including who gets them and how to apply.

Consumer Complaints: Where-to-Go

The government offices described below help consumers with specific problems. If an office does not specifically address your problem, but its subject area is similar, contact the office anyway; these offices can usually direct you to other sources of information and help.

If you cannot find an appropriate office listed below, the following organization can tell you if an office exists that can help you: Office of Consumer Affairs, Department of Health and Human Services, 621 Reporters Building, Washington, DC 20201/202-755-8820.

The following information was selected from the *Consumer's Resource Handbook,* which lists hundreds of offices helpful to consumers. Single copies of this publication are available for free by writing: Consumer Information Center, Dept. 532G, Pueblo, CO 81009.

Advertising

The Federal Trade Commission (FTC) is responsible for preventing the use of unfair, false, or deceptive advertisements for consumer products. This includes television, radio and print ads. Although the FTC does not investigate individual complaints, it can and will act when it receives a large number of specific advertising complaints involving substantial consumer harm. Contact: Office of the Secretary, Federal Trade Commission, Washington, DC 20580/202-523-3598. All complaints must be in writing.

Alcohol

The Bureau of Alcohol, Tobacco and Firearms monitors the content, labeling and advertising of alcoholic beverages. The Bureau works to eliminate illegal traffic and trade in alcoholic beverages and sets and monitors collection of taxes due for the sale of these beverages. The Bureau also issues permits to engage in the production of alcohol for industrial purposes, such as gasohol. Contact: Chief, Trade and Consumer Affairs Division, Bureau of Alcohol, Tobacco and Firearms, Department of the Treasury, Washington, DC 20226/ 202-566-7581.

Animals/Pets

Food and Drug Administration (FDA)

Insures that veterinary preparations, drugs and devices are safe and effective and also insures that animal and pet food is safe and properly labeled. Contact: Bureau of Veterinary Medicine. Department of Health and Human Services, 5600 Fishers Lane, Rockville, MD 20857/301-443-5363.

Animal and Plant Health Inspection Service (APHIS) of the Department of Agriculture

Protects and improves animal and plant health by administering federal laws and regulations dealing with animal and plant health and quarantine, humane treatment of animals and the eradication of pests and diseases. APHIS also administers laws concerning the humane handling of livestock and poultry in interstate commerce, and governing the transportation, sale and handling of dogs, cats, and circus and zoo animals intended for use in laboratory research or for exhibition. Contact: Information Division, Animal and Plant Health Inspection Service, Department of Agriculture, Washington, DC 20250/202-447-3977.

Antitrust

The Federal Trade Commission (FTC) and the Antitrust Division of the Department of Justice work to preserve the healthy competition of business in our free enterprise system. These offices share responsibility for enforcement of the antitrust laws. Antitrust violations include price fixing, monopoly, price discrimination and any other anticompetitive practices. Contact: Assistant Director for Evaluation, Bureau of Competition, Federal Trade Commission, Washington, DC 20580/202-523-3404, or Assistant Attorney General, Antitrust Division, Department of Justice, Washington, DC 20530/202-633-3543.

Appliances

Federal Trade Commission (FTC)

Enforces rules that requires refrigerators, refrigerator-freezers, freezers, dishwashers, water heaters, room air conditioners, central air conditioners, clothes washers and furnaces be sold with labels giving consumers the estimated annual energy costs or energy efficiency ratings for each appliance. The label must give: (1) a description of model; (2) the estimated energy cost for air conditioners and heat pumps, or energy efficiency ratings for other appliances; (3) the range of energy costs or efficiency ratings for comparable models; and (4) other useful information that will enable consumers to estimate costs more precisely. The FTC also enforces the Magnuson-Moss Warranty Act which requires that warranties on appliances costing more than $15 be available to consumers for review before purchase, and that the terms of the full and limited warranties be spelled out in clear, easy-to-read language. Contact: Office of the Secretary, Federal Trade Commission, Washington, DC 20580/202-523-3600.

Consumer Product Safety Commission (CPSC)

Protects consumers against the manufacture and sale of hazardous appliances. CPSC can ban or order a recall of products found to be dangerous to the public. For information and fact sheets, contact: Office of Communications, Consumer Product Safety Commission, Washington, DC 20207/toll-free 800-638-2772.

Center for Devices and Radiological Health

Protects consumers against unnecessary exposure to radiation from electronic products including lasers, television sets, X-rays and sunlamps, and microwaves. Contact: Director. Technical Information Staff (HFZ-43), Bureau of Radiological

Health, Food and Drug Administration, Department of Health and Human Services, 5600 Fishers Lane, Rockville, MD 20857/301-443-3434.

Banking and Credit

Federally Chartered Commercial Banks
These are called national banks and have the word "National" or "N.A." in their titles. These banks are supervised by the Office of the Comptroller of the Currency within the Department of the Treasury, which examines banks periodically to assure the soundness of their operation and management and their compliance with laws, rules and regulations. The Office of the Comptroller of the Currency can assist with problems or questions consumers have with a credit card issued through a national bank. This office is interested in learning of any problems consumers may have with any aspect of a national bank's practices. Contact: Consumer Complaint, Consumer Examination Division Office of the Comptroller, Washington, DC 20219/202-447-1600, Department of the Treasury, Washington, DC 20219/202-447-1600.

State-chartered Banks
These can belong to the Federal Reserve System (FRS), which serves as the nation's central bank. Its main responsibilities are to regulate the flow of money and credit and to perform supervisory services and functions for the public, the U.S. Treasury and commercial banks. State banks that are members of the FRS must comply with both federal and state rules and regulations. Contact: Director, Division of Consumer Affairs, Board of Governors of the Federal Reserve System, Washington, DC 20551/202-452-3946.

Insured State Banks
Those that do not hold membership in the Federal Reserve System are subject to supervision by the Federal Deposit Insurance Corporation (FDIC). The FDIC protects bank customers and helps maintain confidence in the banking system by insuring bank deposits up to $100,000. Contact: Director, Office of Consumer Affairs, Federal Deposit Insurance Corporation, Washington, DC 20429/202-389-4767.

Savings and Loan Associations
Regulated by the Federal Home Loan Bank Board (FHLBB), which protects savers against losses on their deposits through the Federal Savings and Loan Insurance Corporation. Contact: Director, Consumer Division, Office of Community Investment, Federal Home Loan Bank Board, Washington, DC 20552/202-377-6237.

National Credit Union Administration
Supervises and examines federal credit unions throughout the country. It can insure accounts in federal or state-chartered credit unions that request and qualify for such coverage. Contact: Director, Division of Consumer Affairs, Office of Examination and Insurance, National Credit Union Administration, Washington, DC 20546/202-357-1050.

Clothing and Fabrics

Federal Trade Commission (FTC)—Care Labels
Enforces the rule that requires garment manufacturers to attach care labels to their products explaining to the consumer how the garment should be cleaned. Fabric manufacturers must provide care labels with their yard goods so that consumers buying fabric can attach the labels to the finished garments. Under the law, care labels must be provided for all textile wearing apparel except hats, gloves and shoes. Leather, suede, fur, plastic and most vinyl fabrics or garments are excluded from this rule.

Federal Trade Commission—Content Labels
Requires content labels to be attached to wool, textile, and down products to protect producers and consumers against misbranding and false advertising. Under these rules, the label must be printed in legible, unabbreviated English; be attached to an easy-to-locate place; and must state the composition of the product. The name or code number of the firm responsible for the accuracy of the label must be on the label or on one close to it. If the manufacturer chooses to use a code number, it must be registered with the FTC; anyone may write or call the FTC and learn the identity of the holder of a registered identification number. Contact: Federal Trade Commission, 1100 Wilshire Blvd., Los Angeles, CA/213-824-7575.

Consumer Product Safety Commission (CPSC)
Protects consumers against unreasonable risks from consumer products, including clothing and fabrics. The CPSC enforces the Flammable Fabrics Act, which sets flammability standards for carpets, rugs, mattresses, children's sleepwear, and general wearing apparel. The CPSC also ensures that clothes will not be cancer-causing or in any other

way harmful to health. Contact: Director, Office of Communications, Consumer Product Safety Commission, Washington, DC 20207/toll-free 800-638-2772.

Communications

The Federal Communications Commission (FCC) is the agency charged with regulating radio, television, wire, cable and satellite communications. FCC rules require that radio and television stations be responsive to the needs of consumers in the communities they serve; that their broadcasts present both sides of a controversial issue; and that misleading advertments are not aired. The FCC does not regulate program content. The FCC regulates and licenses other two-way radio services for marine and aviation safety, and police and fire, business radio and CB service. Telephone companies operating entirely in one state are under the jurisdiction of the state public utility commissions. For information contact: Chief, Consumer Assistance Office, Federal Communications Commission, Washington, DC 20554/202-632-7000.

Cosmetics

The Food and Drug Administration (FDA) insures that cosmetics are safe and pure. The FDA also requires that cosmetics be truthfully and informatively packaged and labeled, and that cosmetic ingredients be listed on each package. If you have an unusual reaction from a cosmetic that you believe is mislabeled, unsanitary, or harmful, report it to the FDA. Contact: Director of Cosmetics Section, FDA, Bureau of Food, 200 C Street SW, Washington, DC 20204/202-245-1144.

Door-to-Door Sales

The Federal Trade Commission (FTC) requires a "cooling off" period for door-to-door sales. The salesperson must (1) inform consumers of their right to cancel the contract; (2) give consumers two copies of the cancellation form, and (3) give consumers a dated receipt or contract that shows the name and address of the seller. Should a consumer decide to cancel the purchase, he or she must sign and date one copy of the form and mail it to the address given for cancellation any time before midnight of the third business day after the contract date. Contact: Office of the Secretary, Federal Trade Commission, Washington, DC 20580/202-523-3598.

Drugs

Foods and Drug Administration (FDA)

Ensures that drugs on the market are properly labeled, safe and effective for their intended uses. The FDA determines whether a drug can be sold over the counter or should be obtainable only with a doctor's prescription. The FDA also regulates advertising of prescription drugs. Injuries and adverse reactions from drugs should be reported to the prescribing doctor and to the FDA, which will investigate and take corrective action when necessary. Contact: Director, Professional and Consumer Relations, Food and Drug Administration, Department of Health and Human Services, 5600 Fishers Lane, Rockville, MD 20857/301-443-1016.

Drug Enforcement Administration (DEA)
Department of Justice

Enforces laws and regulations which apply to legally produced controlled substances (narcotics, amphetamines and barbiturates) handled by registered importers, manufacturers, distributors, pharmacists and doctors. Contact: Director, Diversion Operations, Drug Enforcement Administration, Department of Justice, Washington, DC 20537/202-633-1216.

Education

Office of Civil Rights, Department of Education

Enforces Title IX of the Education Amendments, which prohibit sex discrimination in federally funded educational activities. Contact: Director, Office of Civil Rights, Department of Education, 330 C St. SW, Washington, DC 20202. Elementary/Secondary Division: 202-732-1641. Postsecondary Division: 202-732-1645.

Family Educational Rights and Privacy Act

Enforced by the Department of Education, this Act requires educational institutions that receive funds from the Dept. of Education to allow students over 18 or parents of minors to see their own educational records. The Act also limits disclosure of these records to others. The Department of Education has the power to deny federal funds to any institution in violation of this Act. Contact: Director, Family Educational Rights and Privacy Act Office, Department of Education, Room 3017, 400 Maryland Ave. SW, Washington, DC 20202/202-472-6032.

Energy

Office of Consumer Affairs, Department of Energy (DOE)

Acts as a liaison between consumers, special groups and organizations, and policymakers within DOE. It encourages consumer participation in DOE processes and represents consumers in DOE policy and decision-making. Contact: Director, Office of Consumer Affairs, Department of Energy, Washington, DC 20585/202-252-5141.

Nuclear Regulatory Commission (NRC)

Ensures that the civilian uses of nuclear materials and facilities are consistent with the public health and safety, environmental quality, national security, and the antitrust laws. Contact: Office of Public Affairs, Nuclear Regulatory Commission, Washington, DC 20555/202-492-7715.

Environment

The Environmental Protection Agency (EPA) is charged by Congress to protect the nation's land, air, and water systems. Under the mandate of national environmental laws, the Agency's programs focus on air, noise, radiation, water quality, drinking water, solid waste, hazardous waste, toxic substances, and pesticides. The Agency's goal is achieve a compatible balance between human activities and the natural systems which support life.

The EPA tests automobiles to make sure they meet federal emission standards and compiles information about the gas mileage consumers can expect from their automobiles. Copies of a booklet on these gas mileage figures can be obtained at no charge.

Many people are concerned about the quality of their drinking water and are drinking bottled instead of tap water. The EPA provides information showing that not all bottled water is free from pollutants. The EPA also conducts studies on the effectiveness of home water purifiers and can provide information on study results. Also available is the publication, *Is Your Drinking Water Safe?*

The EPA provides information about proper pesticide storage and disposal; it certifies the safety of all pesticides used in the United States and has information about proper home pesticide use. The EPA also answers questions about chemicals and their dangers.

Asbestos was used in construction of some schools. When this asbestos or its protective covering deteriorates, dangerous particles are released into the air. The EPA has information about a program to identify these schools and help communities remedy this problem. Asbestos 800-424-9065 or 202-724-6711.

For any of the above information contact: Public Information Center, PM-211A, Environmental Protection Agency, Washington, DC 20460/202-382-7550.

Food

Food and Drug Administration (FDA)

Insures that all foods and food additives (other than meat and poultry or those containing meat and poultry) are safe, pure and wholesome, and honestly and informatively packaged and labeled. If you find unsanitary, contaminated, or mislabeled foods, contact: Office of Consumer Affairs (HFE-88), Food and Drug Administration, 5600 Fishers Lane, Rockville, MD 20857/301-443-3170.

Food Safety and Quality Service, Department of Agriculture

Insures that meat and poultry, and products made from them, are safe, wholesome and truthfully labeled. They also provide voluntary grading services and develop grade standards for meat, poultry, eggs, dairy products and fresh or processed fruits and vegetables. In addition, egg products are inspected for freshness and quality. They investigate individual complaints concerning the freshness and quality of egg products and the grading of dairy products, eggs, poultry or meat. Contact: U.S. Department of Agriculture, Agricultural Marketing Service, Commodities Service—Room 3064, South Building, Washington, DC 20250/202-447-5231.

The National Marine Fisheries Service (NMFS) runs a voluntary inspection and grading program for fish and fish products. In addition, NMFS develops standards for quality, conditions, quantity, grade and packaging for fish and fishery plants and products. The NMFS has a consumer education program on the voluntary fishery inspection service and information on nutritional value, preparation and availability of fishery products. Contact: Inspection, National Marine Fisheries Service, Department of Commerce, Washington, DC 20235/202-634-7458.

Housing

Fair Housing and Equal Opportunity Office, Department of Housing and Urban Development (HUD)

Administers the Civil Rights Act of 1968, which prohibits discrimination in housing, employment and business opportunities. In particular, HUD enforces regulations that no one can be denied housing because of race, color, religion, sex, age or national origin. Discriminatory practices include steering (being directed to buy or rent in a particular neighborhood or building), red-lining (being denied a mortgage for a home in a location boycotted by lending institutions), or discriminating in sales (being rejected as the buyer of a home for other than financial reasons) Contact: Fair Housing and Equal Opportunity, Department of Housing and Urban Development, 451 7th Street SW, Washington, DC 20410/toll-free 800-424-8590/202-426-3500 in DC. For poster on "Fair Housing," write: FAGO—FHEO, Room 5110, Washington, DC 20410.

Real Estate Settlement Procedures Act (RESPA)

Also administered by HUD, this requires that homebuyers get an estimate of settlement costs in advance. For information see "Settlement Costs—Information and Complaints" in this section.

Interstate Land Sales

The Department of Housing and Urban Development also administers and enforces disclosure and registration requirements for developers selling land through any means of interstate commerce, including the mails. Under the law, developers having subdivisions containing 50 lots or more must: (1) file a statement of record with the Office of Interstate Land Sales listing information about the ownership of the land, the state of its title, its physical nature, the availability of roads and utilities, and other matters; (2) furnish each purchaser with a printed property report at least 72 hours before signing an agreement for purchase or lease; and (3) not use fraud or misrepresentation in the sale or promotion of the land. Contact: Director, Office of Interstate Land Sales, Department of Housing and Urban Development, Washington, DC 20410/202-755-0502, or 202-755-6716.

Investments and Business Opportunities

Commodity Futures Trading Commission (CFTC)

Regulates trading in commodity futures and certain other transactions such as options, leverage and deferred deliveries that call for future delivery of a commodity. The agency's mission includes preventing market manipulation and protecting consumers who buy and sell contracts. Consumer services include a reparations procedure through which customers can make claims against brokers and salespeople. Contact: Public Reference, Federal Trade Commission, Washington, DC 20580/202-523-3600.

Securities and Exchange Commission (SEC)

The securities laws administered by the SEC protect investors by preventing fraud in the buying and selling of securities. Corporations under the SEC's jurisdiction must disclose financial information in their prospectuses, proxy statements and periodic reports filed with the commission, so investors can make informed investment decisions and vote their shares. The SEC's Office of Consumer Affairs receives and processes complaints and inquiries from individual investors and the public. Contact: Office of Consumer Securities and Exchange Commission, Securities and Exchange Commission, 500 N. Capitol St. NW, Washington, DC 20549/202-523-3952.

Mail

Inspection Service

Headed by the Chief Postal Inspector, this is the law enforcement and audit arm of the Postal Service that performs security, investigative, law enforcement and audit functions. It is responsible for enforcement of approximately 85 federal statutes relating to the Postal Service. Mail fraud, false mail-order advertising, and unsatisfactory mail-order transactions all come under their jurisdiction. Publications are available. Examples include chain letters, work-at-home schemes, pyramid sales promotions, misused credit cards, coupon redemption, false billing and franchising schemes. Contact: Chief Postal Inspector, Postal Service, Room 3509, Washington, DC 20260/202-245-5445.

Federal Trade Commission (FTC)—Mail Orders

Has a rule requiring mail order purchases be shipped within the time stated in the company's printed or broadcast offer. If no time is stated, shipment must be within 30 days after the company receives the order, unless the buyer is contacted and consents to a delay. Contact: Federal Trade Commission Public Reference, Washington, DC 20580/202-523-3600.

Motor Vehicles

National Highway Traffic Safety Administration (NHTSA)

Works to reduce highway deaths, injuries and property losses by writing and enforcing federal vehicle safety standards for vehicles and vehicle equipment, such as tires. NHTSA investigates reports of safety-related defects and substantial equipment failures and enforces laws requiring recall and remedy. NHTSA is also responsible for investigating violations of a law that prohibits anyone, including the vehicle owner, from turning back or disconnecting the odometer of an automobile, unless performing repairs. Contact: Administrator, National Highway Traffic Safety Administration, Department of Transportation, Washington, DC 20590/toll-free 800-424-9393/202-426-0123 in DC.

Department of Justice

Enforces jurisdiction over the federal law requiring the disclosure of new automobile information. The following information must be included on the windshield or side window of the vehicle; make, model, identification number, assembly point, name and location of dealer to whom the vehicle was delivered, method of transportation, total suggested retail price for accessories, and transportation charges. Contact: Consumer Litigation Division, Civil Division, Department of Justice, Washington, DC 20530/202-724-6786.

Moving and Movers

The Interstate Commerce Commission (ICC) regulates interstate movers of household goods. To evaluate a mover before using its services, the commission requires that, on request, consumers be given copies of carrier performance reports. In addition, movers are required to provide each consumer with an ICC booklet explaining the consumer's rights and obligations on signing papers, estimates, weighing of shipments, payment for the move, and filing claims. Contact: Director, Consumer Assistance Office, Interstate Commerce Commission, Washington, DC 20423/202-275-0860.

Pensions

Pension Benefit Guarantee Corporation (PBGC)

Guarantees basic retirement benefits to participants in private pension plans. PBGC has booklets for consumers explaining the guarantee program and publications on program guidelines for plan administrators. Contact: Pension Benefit Guaranty Corporation, 2020 K St. NW, Washington, DC 20006/202-254-4817.

Employee Retirement Income Security Act (ERISA)

The Department of Labor's Labor-Management Services Administration (LMSA) and the Internal Revenue Service (IRS) administer the Employee Retirement Income Security Act (ERISA). ERISA requires managers of pension and welfare plans to manage and invest plan funds prudently and to make sure there is enough money in the plan to pay benefits. If employers elect to set up a pension plan, their employees must be eligible to participate and be entitled to benefits without having to meet unreasonable age or service requirements. Contact: Division of Public Information, Office of Pension and Welfare Benefit Programs, U.S. Department of Labor, 200 Constitution Ave. NW, Washington, DC 20210/202-523-8764.

Product Safety

The Consumer Product Safety Commission (CPSC) protects consumers against unreasonable risks from consumer products used in and around the home, schools and recreation areas, and assists consumers in evaluating product safety. The CPSC develops uniform safety standards for consumer products, promotes research, and investigates product-related deaths, injuries and illnesses. It has the authority to ban hazardous products, set mandatory safety standards and seek court action to have products declared hazardous. Contact: Director, Office of Communications, Consumer Product Safety Commission, Washington, DC 20207/800-638-2772.

Transportation

Office of Community and Consumer Affairs

This office handles complaints against the airlines. Contact: Department of Transportation, Office of Community and Consumer Affairs, Room 10405, 400 7th St. SW, Washington, DC 20590/202-426-1960.

Federal Aviation Administration (FAA)

Establishes and enforces safety standards for air carriers, air taxi operators and other private and commercial aviation enterprises. FAA safety regulations apply to nearly every facet of air travel, ranging from the aircraft and its crew and mechanics to the nation's airways, airports and air traffic control systems. The FAA enforces airport security measures, including passenger screening, to prevent hijacking and threats to safe and secure travel. Contact: Public Information Center, Federal Aviation Administration, Room 907E APA—430, Department of Transportation, Washington, DC 20591/202-426-8058.

Interstate Commerce Commission (ICC)
Ensures that interstate bus lines give the public fair and reasonable rates and services. Discrimination, preferential treatment or prejudicial actions by interstate buses are illegal and should be reported to the ICC. Contact: Director, Office of Compliance and Consumer Assistance, Interstate Commerce Commission, Washington, DC 20423/202-275-0860.

Coast Guard, Department of Transportation
Enforces federal laws on the high seas and navigable waters of the United States. It develops regulations on commercial vessel safety, recreational boating safety, port safety and security and marine pollution. Contact: Commandant (G-B), Office of Boating, Public and Consumer Affairs, U.S. Coast Guard Headquarters, 2100 2nd Street SW, Washington, DC 20593/202-426-1088.

Federal Maritime Commission (FMC)
An independent agency responsible for the regulation of U.S. ocean commerce. Among other duties, the FMC ensures that steamship companies have the required insurance to cover passengers for personal injury or death, and informally assists and counsels passengers who have complaints about companies or service. The commission also assists consumers with problems involving goods transported by ship and advises consumers on appropriate actions. Contact: Office of Informal Inquiries and Complaints, Federal Maritime Commission—Room 11413. 1100 L Street NW, Washington, DC 20573/202-523-5800.

Freedom of Information Act: Key to Unlocking What You Need

The Freedom of Information Act of 1966 is a key to much of the information held by the federal agencies. Under the law, any identifiable records of the administrative agencies in the executive branch of the federal government must be released upon request, unless they fall into one or more of nine exemption categories.

There is nothing difficult about using the Freedom of Information Act. It requires only that you identify the records you desire and write a letter of request. You do not have to state why you want the material.

Cost of Service
The act allows agencies to charge for the services, but the fees cannot be greater than the actual cost of searching for and copying documents. Search fees are roughly $5 per hour, and the average copying cost is 10 cents per page. Some agencies do not charge at all if the total cost is slight.

There are four possible ways to save money when you make a Freedom of Information Act request:

1. If you are indigent, you can ask that the fees be waived.
2. Request a fee waiver if release of the information would benefit the general public.
3. Ask to examine the documents at the agency, rather than purchase them.
4. When writing your request letter, set a dollar amount ceiling on costs.

Your Rights under Freedom of Information Act
The law provides that you must get some response from the agency within 10 working days. This does not mean you will receive the requested information that quickly. To speed the release process, it is wise to write "Freedom of Information Act Request" on the bottom left-hand corner of the envelope in which you send your letter and at the top of the letter itself. (See sample letters in this section.)

If your request is denied, the agency must notify you, giving you reasons for denial, the names and addresses of those responsible for denial and advice about how to appeal.

It is your right to appeal a denial, and appeals often are successful. A Washington Researchers' study of agency reports for 1977 showed that 16 percent of the appeal letters written resulted in full release of the information and 33 percent resulted in partial release. This means that you have nearly a 50 percent chance of obtaining some information, even after your initial request has been denied.

Most agencies require appeals to be filed within 30 days; the agency is required to respond within 20 days of the appeal. Further, if your appeal is denied, you have access to the courts.

Problems for the Information-Seeker

The Freedom of Information Act is not perfect. Administration of the law is handled differently from agency to agency. In almost all agencies, the determination of what meets exemptions is left largely to the discretion of administrators.

Problems for the information-seeker, as well as the bureaucrat, have arisen from the act.

For some offices, utilization of the act has resulted in overkill, and you may be required to submit a formal request for documents you might otherwise have been able to obtain more easily.

Government personnel sometimes become less helpful if you approach the subject by threatening Freedom of Information Act action—it's best to ask for the material informally first.

Often the biggest problem is that you must know what it is you are after. You have to be able "reasonably" to identify what you need.

A Washington Researchers' survey asked members of the Washington press corps to evaluate the effect of the Freedom of Information Act has had on their ability to collect information. These are the results:

45 percent—said the act helped slightly.
36 percent—said it had no significant effect.
11 percent—said the act helped greatly.
 7 percent—said the act hindered them greatly.

Another problem involves time. It can take two weeks, a month, or more to receive the material you request under the act, depending upon whether you need to appeal.

Request Letters

REMEMBER: Under the Freedom of Information Act, your letter of request becomes a public record. For this reason, many companies that don't want their names associated with requests hire attorneys or specialized firms to write the letters. Your company's attorney can write a request letter on his or her stationery or your local bar association lawyer referral service can help you find a qualified lawyer if you prefer one outside your organization.

To find an attorney in the Washington, DC, area, where the Freedom of Information offices are located, contact: Lawyer Referral Service, Bar Association of Washington, DC, 1819 H St. NW, Suite 300, Washington, DC 20036/202-223-1484.

Private firms that will write request letters include Washington Researchers and FOI Services, Inc. The Addresses for Washington Researchers and FOI Services, Inc., are: Washington Researchers, 918 16th St. NW, Washington DC 20006/202-333-3499, and, FOI Services, Inc., 12315 Wilkins Ave., Rockville, MD 20852/301-881-0410.

If you would like to look at request letters to get an idea of what is available under the act, contact the Freedom of Information office for the agency you are interested in. This is perhaps the best way to identify what a department or agency can provide. The letters, sometimes kept in looseleaf binders in reading rooms, are unique shopping lists for researchers.

Exemptions

The act covers only the federal executive branch (not state or local governments); Presidential papers are not available under the act. The Freedom of Information Act does not apply to information kept by the federal legislative and judicial branches. This means that some vital sections of the government, such as Congress, the Library of Congress and the Government Printing Office, are exempt.

The categories of information exempt from the act are:

1. Classified documents concerning the national defense and foreign policy—government secrets and confidential material. If the document you request is classified, however, the agency is required to review it to determine whether it should remain classified.
2. Internal personnel rules and practices. Covered under this exemption are internal rules and practices that do not affect interests outside the agency.
3. Information exempt under other laws. This includes items such as income tax returns, which other laws prohibit releasing.
4. Confidential business information. This exemption provides that trade secrets and confidential commercial or financial data do not have to be released. Determing what does and

does not fall under this exemption has been very controversial. One popular test has been the "competitive harm test," exempting material that could competitively harm the submitter if made public.

5. The confidential business information exemption also has spawned reverse-Freedom-of-Information-Act lawsuits, in which companies that submit information go to court to block agencies from releasing the data. Legislation clarifying this exemption is expected.
6. International communications, including inter- and intra-agency memos. This does not cover factual information or communications about decisions that already have been made.
7. Personal, private information. Covered are personal and medical files and other information which, if released, would constitute invasion of privacy.
8. Investigatory files. These files are records of investigations which, if released, would interfere with enforcement, deprive someone of a fair trial, constitute an invasion of privacy, expose a confidential source, expose investigative techniques, or endanger life or safety.
9. Information about financial institutions, such as Federal Reserve Board records of investigations of federal banks.
10. Information about wells, including some maps.

The act mandates that if only a portion of what you want falls under an exemption, the rest of what you have requested must be released.

Other Sources
If you need more information about the Freedom of Information Act, you can contact:

FOI Clearinghouse, 2000 P St. NW, P. O. Box 19367, Washington, DC 20036/202-785-3704.

House Subcommittee on Government Information and Individual Rights, B349-C Rayburn House Office Building, Washington, DC 20515/202-225-3741.

Senate Subcommittee on Regulatory Reform and Procedure, 104, Russell Building, Washington, DC 20510/202-224-7703.

Congressional Research Service, Government and General Research Division, Library of Congress, 10 First St. SE, Room 115A, Washington, DC 20540/202-287-5700.

Center for National Security Studies, 122 Maryland Ave. NE, Washington, DC 20002/202-544-5380.

Publications include:

The Freedom of Information Act: What It Is and How To Use It—order through the FOI Clearinghouse (see address above). Single copies are free; 2 to 100 cost 10 cents each; for more than 100 the charge is 5 cents each.

Litigation Under the Amended Federal Freedom of Information Act—a lawyer's handbook to the act; this can be purchased for $20 prepaid from the Center for National Security Studies (see address above).

The Federal Register Index—a monthly index bound into quarterly cumulative volumes that list federal agencies' indexes to what is available through the Freedom of Information Act, how much it costs, and where it can be purchased or examined. Not all government agencies submit lists. The index can be ordered from the Government Printing Office for $8 per year (cite order symbol FRSU). Individual cumulative volumes can be ordered for 75 cents each from: Federal Register, Washington, DC 20408/202-523-5240.

Freedom of Information Act Requests for Business Data and Reverse FOIA Lawsuits—by the House Committee on Government Operations; this can be ordered from the Government Printing Office for $2. Cite stock number 052-071-00571-4.

A Citizen's Guide On How To Use The Freedom of Information Act And The Privacy Act in Requesting Government Documents—by the House Committee on Government Operations; it can be ordered from the Government Printing Office for $3. Cite stock number 052-071-00540-4. Orders can be placed with the Government Printing Office by writing or calling: Superintendent of Documents, Government Printing Office, Washington, DC 20402/202-783-3238.

The following sample Freedom of Information Act letters will show you exactly how to write request letters. The Freedom of Information Act Office list of names, addresses, and telephone numbers will tell you to whom you should address them.

Sample Freedom of Information Act Letter

FOIA Officer
Title
Name of Agency
Address of Agency
City, State   Zip Code

Re: Freedom of Information Act Request

Dear   :
Under the provisions of the Freedom of Information Act, 5 U.S.C. 552, I am requesting access to (identify the records as clearly and specifically as possible).

If there are any fees for searching for or copying the records I have requested, please inform me before you fill the request. (Or . . . please supply the records without informing if the fees do not exceed $____.)

(Optional) I am requesting this information (state the reason for your request only if you think it will assist you in obtaining the information).

(Optional) As you know, the act permits you to reduce or waive fees when the release of information is considered as "primarily benefitting the public." I believe that this request fits that category and therefore ask that you waive any fees.

If all or any part of this request is denied, please cite the specific exemption(s) that you think justifies your refusal to release the information and inform me of the appeal procedures available to me under the law.

I would appreciate your handling this request as quickly as possible and I look forward to hearing from you within 10 days, as the law stipulates.

Sincerely,

Signature
Name
Address
City, State   Zip Code

Sample Letter of Appeal

Name of Agency Official
Title
Name of Agency
Address of Agency
City, State   Zip Code

Re: Freedom of Information Act Appeal

Dear   :
This is to appeal the denial of my request for information pursuant to the Freedom of Information Act, 5 U.S.C. 552.

On   (date)   , I received a letter from   (individual's name)   of your agency denying my request for access to   (description of the information sought)   . I am enclosing a copy of this denial along with a copy of my request. I trust that upon examination of these communications you will concede that the information I am seeking should be disclosed.

As provided for in the act, I will expect to receive a reply within 20 working days.

(Optional) If you decide not to release the requested information, I plan to take this matter to court.

Sincerely,

Signature
Name
Address
City, State   Zip Code

Privacy Act: Getting Federal Records About *You!*

As you may know, the government collects information about individual citizens. If you think the government has compiled a record about you, it is within your rights to see exactly what is in the government's file. This is an important right as it gives you the opportunity to correct inaccuracies.

Legislative Background
The underlying purpose of the Privacy Act is to give citizens more control over information collected about them by the federal government and how that information is used. The act accomplishes this in five basic ways. It requires agencies to report publicly the existence of all systems of records maintained on individuals. It requires that the information contained in these record systems be accurate, complete, relevant, and up-to-date. It provides procedures whereby individuals can inspect and correct inaccuracies in nearly all federal files about themselves. It specifies that information about an individual gathered for one purpose not be used for another without the individual's consent. And, finally, it requires agencies to keep

an accurate accounting of the disclosure of records and, with certain exceptions, to make these disclosures available to the subject of the record. In addition, the bill provides sanctions to enforce these provisions.

How To Request Personal Records Information Available Under the Privacy Act

The Privacy Act applies only to personal records maintained by the executive branch of the federal government concerning individual citizens. It does not apply to records held by state and local governments or private organizations. The federal agencies covered by the act include executive departments and offices, military departments, government corporations, government-controlled corporations, and independent regulatory agencies. Subject to specified exceptions, files that are part of a system of records held by these agencies must be made available to the individual subject of the record upon request.* A system of records, as defined by the Privacy Act, is a group of records from which information is retrieved by reference to a name or other personal identifier such as a social security number.

The federal government is a vast storehouse of information concerning individual citizens. For example:

If you have worked for a federal agency or government contractor or have been a member of any branch of the armed services, the federal government has a file on you.

If you have participated in any federally financed project, some agency probably has a record of it.

If you have been arrested by local, state, or federal authorities and your fingerprints were taken, the FBI maintains a record of the arrest.†

If you have applied for a government subsidy for farming purposes, the Department of Agriculture is likely to have this information.

If you have received veterans' benefits, such as a mortgage or education loans, employment op-

portunities, or medical services, the Veterans Administration has a file on you.

If you have applied for or received a student loan or grant certified by the Government, the Department of Health and Human Services has recorded this information.

If you have applied for or been investigated for a security clearance for any reason, there is a good chance that the Department of Defense has a record of it.

If you have received Medicare or social security benefits, the Department of Health and Human Services has a file on you.

In addition, federal files on individuals include such items as:

Investigatory reports of the Federal Communications Commission concerning whether individuals holding citizens band and/or amateur radio licenses are violating operating rules.

Records of the Internal Revenue Service listing the names of individuals entitled to undeliverable refund checks.

Records compiled by the State Department regarding the conduct of American citizens in foreign countries.

This is just a fraction of the information held on individual citizens. In fact, if you have ever engaged in any activity that you think might be of interest to the federal government, there is a good chance that some federal agency has a file on you.

The only information that may be withheld under this act is that which falls within seven designated categories. These exemptions from disclosure are discussed under the section entitled "Reasons Why Access May Be Denied."

Locating Records

If you think that a particular agency maintains records concerning you, you should write to the head of that agency or to the Privacy Act officer. Agencies are required to inform you, at your request, whether or not they have files on you.

If you want to make a more thorough search to determine what records other federal departments may have, you should consult the compilation of Privacy Act notices published annually by the *Federal Register*. This multi-volume work contains descriptions of all federal record systems: it describes the kinds of data covered by the systems and lists the categories of individuals to whom the information pertains. It also includes the procedures that different agencies follow in helping individuals who request information about their

---

*Unlike the FOIA—which applies to anyone making a request, including foreigners as well as American citizens—the Privacy Act applies only to American citizens and aliens lawfully admitted for permanent residence.

†If an individual is arrested more than once, he or she builds up a criminal history called a rap sheet. Rap sheets chronologically list all fingerprint submissions by local, state, and federal agencies. They also contain the charges lodged against the individual and what disposition is made of the case if the arresting agency supplies this information. You can get a copy of your rap sheet by forwarding to the Identification Division of the FBI in Washington, DC, a set of rolled-inked fingerprint impressions along with $5 in the form of a certified check or money order made out to the Treasury of the United States.

records, and it specifies the agency official to whom you should write to find out whether you are the subject of a file.

The compilation is usually available in large reference, law, and university libraries. It can be purchased from the Superintendent of Documents, Government Printing Office, Washington, DC 20402. The cost per volume runs around $6 to $12. If you know which agencies you are interested in, the Superintendent of Documents can help you identify the particular volume or volumes which contain the information you want. However, this word of caution: at the present time, the compilation is poorly indexed and, as a consequence, difficult to use. Therefore, you should examine the work before ordering it.

While it may be helpful to agency officials for you to specify a particular record system which you think contains information concerning you, it is not necessary to provide this information. If you have a general idea of the record you want, don't hesitate to write the agency which you think maintains it.

Making a Request

You can make a request in writing, by telephone, or in person. One advantage to writing is that it enables you to document the date and contents of the request and the agency's reply. This could be helpful in the event of future disputes. Be sure to keep copies of all correspondence concerning the request.

Your request should be addressed to the head of the agency which maintains the records you want or to the agency official specified in the compilation of Privacy Act notices. (See section on Locating Records.) In any event, be sure to write "Privacy Act Request" on the bottom left-hand corner of the envelope. Along with your name and permanent address, you should always give as much information as possible about the record you are seeking.* The more specific the inquiry, the faster you can expect a response. If you want access to a record concerning your application for a government loan, for example, you should give the date of the application, the place where the application was filed, the specific use to which the loan was put, and any relevant identifying numbers. Of course, if you have used the *Federal Register's* compilation of notices and identified a particular record system which you think contains information on you, you should cite the system.

Most agencies require some proof of identity

---

*If you were using a different name at the time the record was compiled, be sure to provide this information.

before they will release records. Therefore, when making your request, it would be a good idea to provide some identifying data such as a copy of an official document containing your complete name and address. Remember, too, to sign your request since a signature provides a form of identification. You might also want to consider having your signature notarized. If you are seeking access to a record which has something to do with a Government benefit, it could be helpful to give your social security number. Some agencies may request additional information such as a document containing your signature and/or photograph depending upon the nature and sensitivity of the material to be released.

Anyone who "knowingly and willfully" requests or receives access to a record about an individual "under false pretenses" is subject to criminal penalties. This means that a person can be prosecuted for deliberately attempting to obtain someone else's records.

Fees

Under the Privacy Act, agencies are permitted to charge fees to cover the actual cost of copying records. However, they are not allowed to charge for the time spent in locating records or in preparing them for your inspection. Copying fees are about 10 cents a page for standard size copies of 8 × 11 inches and 8 × 14 inches.

As mentioned above, fees for locating files can be charged for requests processed under the Freedom of Information Act. Therefore, if you seek access to records under the Privacy Act which can be withheld under the act but are available under the FOIA, you could be charged searching fees. However the legislative histories of both the FOIA and the Privacy Act clearly indicate that Congress intended that access to records not be obstructed by costs. Consequently, if you feel that an agency's fees are beyond your means, you should ask for a reduction or waiver to the charges when making your request.

Sample Privacy Act Request Letter

Agency Head or Privacy Act Officer
Title
Agency
Address of Agency
City, State   Zip Code

Re: Privacy Act Request

Dear   :
Under the provisions of the Privacy Act of 1974,

5 U.S.C. 522a, I hereby request a copy of (or: access to) (describe as accurately and specifically as possible the records you want, and provide all the relevant information you have concerning them).

If there are any fees for copying the records I am requesting, please inform me before you fill the request. (Or: . . . please supply the records without informing me if the fees do not exceed $____.)

If all or any part of this request is denied, please cite the specific exemption(s) which you think justifies your refusal to release the information. Also, please inform me of your agency's appeal procedure.

In order to expedite consideration of my request, I am enclosing a copy of (some document of identification).

Thank you for your prompt attention to this matter.

> Sincerely,
>
> Signature
> Name
> Address
> City, State   Zip Code

Requirements for Agency Responses

Unlike the Freedom of Information Act, which requires agencies to respond within 10 working days after receipt of a request, the Privacy Act imposes no time limits for agency responses. However, the guidelines for implementing the act's provisions recommended by the executive branch state that a request for records should be acknowledged within ten working days of its receipt. Moreover, the acknowledgment should indicate whether or not access will be granted and, if so, when and where. The records themselves should be produced within 30 working days. And, if this is not possible, the agency should tell you the reason and advise you when it is anticipated that access will be granted.

Most agencies will do their best to comply with these recommendations. Therefore, it is probably advisable to bear with some reasonable delay before taking further action.

Disclosure of Records

Agencies are required to release records to you in a form that is "comprehensible." This means that all computer codes and unintelligible notes must be translated into understandable language.

You can examine your records in person or have copies of them mailed to you, whichever you prefer. If you decide that you want to see the records at the agency and for some reason the agency is unable to provide for this, then you cannot be charged copying fees if the records are later mailed to you.

If you view the records in person, you are entitled to take someone along with you. If you do this, you will probably be asked to sign a statement authorizing the agency to disclose and discuss the record in the other person's presence.

Special rules apply to the release of medical records. In most cases, when you request to see your medical record, you will be permitted to view it directly. However, if it appears that the information contained in it could have an "adverse effect" on you, the agency may give it to someone of your choice, such as your family doctor, who would be willing to review its contents and discuss them with you.

Reasons Why Access May Be Denied

Under the Privacy Act, certain systems of records can be exempted from disclosure. Agencies are required to publish annually in the Federal Register the existence and characteristics of all record systems, including those which have been exempted from access. However, records declared exempt are not necessarily beyond your reach, since agencies do not always use the exemptions they have claimed. Therefore, don't hesitate to request any record you want. The burden is on the agency to justify withholding any information from you.

You should familiarize yourself with these exemptions before making a request so you will know in advance what kind of documents may not be available. It will also help you to understand the reasons agencies give for refusing to release information.

General Exemptions

The general exemptions apply only to the Central Intelligence Agency and criminal law enforcement agencies. The records held by these agencies can be exempt from more provisions of the act than those maintained by other agencies. However, even the systems of these agencies are subject to many of the act's basic provisions: (1) the existence and characteristics of all record systems must be publicly reported; (2) subject to specified exceptions, no personal records can be disclosed to other agencies or persons without prior consent of the individual to whom the record pertains; (3) all the disclosures must be accurately accounted for; (4) records which are disclosed must be accurate, relevant, up-to-date, and complete; and (5) no records describing how an individual exercises his First Amendment rights can be maintained unless such maintenance is authorized by statute or by the individual to whom it pertains or unless it is relevant to and within the scope of an authorized law enforcement activity.

General exemptions are referred to as (j)(1) and (j)(2) in accordance with their designations in the act.

Exemption (j)(1): Files maintained by the CIA— Exemption (j)(1) covers records "maintained by the Central Intelligence Agency." This exemption permits the heads of the Central Intelligence Agency to exclude certain systems of records within the agency from many of the act's requirements. The provisions from which the systems can be exempted are primarily those permitting individual access. Consequently, in most instances, you would probably not be allowed to inspect and correct records about yourself maintained by this agency. Congress permitted the exemption of these records from access because CIA files often contain highly sensitive information regarding national security. Nevertheless, you should always bear in mind that agencies are not required to invoke all the exemptions allowed them. Therefore, if you really want to see a record containing information about you that is maintained by this agency, go ahead and make your request.

Exemption (j)(2): Files maintained by Federal criminal law enforcement agencies—Exemption (j)(2) covers records "maintained by an agency or component thereof which performs as its principal function any activity pertaining to the enforcement of criminal laws, including police efforts to prevent, control, or reduce crime or to apprehend criminals, and the activities of prosecutors, courts, correctional, pardon, or parole authorities, and which consist of (A) information compiled for the purpose of identifying individual criminal offenders and alleged offenders and consisting only of identifying data and notations of arrests, the nature and disposition of criminal charges, information compiled for the purpose of a criminal investigation, including reports of informants and investigators; and is associated with an identifiable individual; or (B) reports identifiable to an individual compiled at any stage of the process of enforcement of the criminal laws from arrest or indictment through release from supervision."

This exemption would permit the heads of criminal law enforcement agencies such as the FBI, the Drug Enforcement Administration, and

the Immigration and Naturalization Service to exclude certain systems of records from many of the act's requirements. As with the CIA, the allowed exemptions are primarily those permitting individual access. However, many agencies do not always use the exemptions available to them. Remember, too, the act explicitly states that records available under the FOIA must also be available under the Privacy Act. And under the FOIA, the CIA and FBI and other Federal agencies are required to release all nonexempt portions of their intelligence and investigatory files. Nevertheless, even though Congress intended that Privacy Act requests be coordinated with FOIA provisions, it is still a good idea to cite both these acts when seeking information of an intelligence or investigatory nature.

Specific Exemptions

There are seven specific exemptions which apply to all agencies. Under specified circumstances, agency heads are permitted to exclude certain record systems from the access and challenge provisions of the act. However, even exempted systems are subject to many of the act's requirements. In addition to the provisions listed under General Exemptions (which apply to all record systems), a record system that falls under any one of seven specific exemptions (listed below) is subject to the following requirements: (1) information that might be used to deny a person a right, benefit, or privilege must, whenever possible, be collected directly from the individual; (2) individuals asked to supply information must be informed of the authority for collecting it, the purposes to which it will be put, and whether or not the imparting of it is voluntary or mandatory; (3) individuals must be notified when records concerning them are disclosed in accordance with a compulsory legal process, such as a court subpoena; (4) agencies must notify persons or agencies of any corrections or disputes over the accuracy of the information; (5) and all records must be accurate, relevant, up-to-date, and complete.*

Record systems which fall within the seven exempt categories are also subject to the civil remedies provisions of the act. Therefore, if an agency denies you access to a record in an exempt record system or refuses to amend a record in accordance with your request, you can contest these actions in court. You can also bring suit

*This provision differs from the one pertaining to all record systems which requires that records which are disclosed be accurate, relevant, up-to-date, and complete. Record systems which are subject to the seven specific exemptions must at all times be accurate, relevant, up-to-date, and complete.

against the agency if you are denied a right, benefit, or privilege as a result of records which have been improperly maintained. These remedies are not available under the general exemptions.

Specific exemptions are referred to as (k)(1), (k)(2), etc., in accordance with their designations in the act.

Exemption (k)(1): Classified documents concerning national defense and foreign policy—Exemption (k)(1) covers records "subject to the provisions of section 552(b)(1) of this title."

This refers to the first exemption of the Freedom of Information Act which exempts from disclosure records "(A) specifically authorized under criteria established by an Executive order to be kept secret in the interest of national defense or foreign policy and (B) that are in fact properly classified pursuant to such Executive order." (For further discussion of the provision, see *Exemption 1: Classified documents concerning national defense and foreign policy* under the FOIA section of this guide.)

Exemption (k)(2): Investigatory material compiled for law enforcement purposes—Exemption (k)(2) pertains to "investigatory material compiled for law enforcement purposes, other than material within the scope of subsection (j)(2) of this section: *Provided, however,* that if any individual is denied any right, privilege, or benefit that he would otherwise be entitled by federal law, or for which he would otherwise be eligible, as a result of the maintenance of such material, such material shall be provided to such individual, except to the extent that the disclosure of such material would reveal the identity of a source who furnished information to the Government under an express promise that the identity of the source would be held in confidence, or, prior to the effective date of this section, under an implied promise that the identity of the source would be held in confidence."

This applies to investigatory materials compiled for law enforcement purpose by agencies whose principal function is other than criminal law enforcement. Included are such items as files maintained by the Internal Revenue Service concerning taxpayers who are delinquent in filing Federal tax returns, records compiled by the Customs Bureau on narcotic suspects, investigatory reports of the Federal Deposit Insurance Corporation regarding banking irregularities, and files maintained by the Securities and Exchange Commission on individuals who are being investigated by the agency.

Such files cannot be withheld from you, however, if they are used to deny you a benefit, right, or privilege to which you are entitled by law unless their disclosure would reveal the identity of a confidential source. You should always bear in mind that Congress intended that information available under either the FOIA or the Privacy Act be disclosed. Moreover, since the FOIA requires agencies to release all nonexempt portions of a file, some of the information exempted under this provision might be obtainable under the FOIA. In any event, as mentioned above, when seeking information of an investigatory nature, it is a good idea to request it under both acts.

Exemption (k)(3): Secret Service Intelligence files—Exemption (k)(3) covers records "maintained in connection with providing protective services to the President of the United States or other individuals pursuant to section 3056 of title 18."

This exemption pertains to files held by the Secret Service that are necessary to insure the safety of the President and other individuals under Secret Service protection.

Exemption (k)(4): Files used solely for statistical purposes—Exemption (k)(4) applies to records "required by statute to be maintained and used solely as statistical records."

This includes such items as Internal Revenue Service files regarding the income of selected individuals used in computing national income averages, and records of births, and deaths maintained by the Department of Health and Human Services for compiling vital statistics.

Exemption (k)(5): Investigatory material used in making decisions concerning Federal employment, military service, Federal contracts, and security clearances—Exemption (k)(5) related to "investigatory material compiled solely for the purpose of determining suitability, eligibility or qualifications for Federal civilian employment, military service, Federal contracts, or access to classified information, but only to the extent that the disclosure of such material would reveal the identity of a source who furnished information to the Government under an express promise that the identity of the source would be held in confidence, or, prior to the effective date of this section, under an implied promise that the identity of the source would be held in confidence."

This exemption applies only to investigatory records which would reveal the identity of a confidential source. Since it is not customary for agencies to grant pledges of confidentiality in collecting information concerning employment, Federal contracts, and security clearances, in most instances these records would be available.

Exemption (k)(6): Testing or examination material used solely for employment purposes—Exemption (k)(6) covers "testing or examination material used solely to determine individual qualifications for appointment or promotion in the Federal service, the disclosure of which would compromise the objectivity or fairness of the testing or examination process."

This provision permits agencies to withhold information concerning the testing process that would give an individual an unfair competitive advantage. It applies solely to information that would reveal test questions and answers or testing procedures.

Exemption (k)(7): Evaluation material used in making decisions regarding promotions in the armed services—Exemption (k)(7) pertains to "evaluation material used to determine potential for promotion in the armed services, but only to the extent that the disclosure of such material would reveal the identity of the source who furnished information to the Government under an express promise that the identity of the source would be held in confidence, or, prior to the effective date of this section, under an implied promise that the identity of the source would be held in confidence."

This exemption is used solely by the armed services. Moreover, due to the nature of the military promotion process where numerous individuals compete for the same job, it is often necessary to grant pledges of confidentiality in collecting information so that those questioned about potential candidates will feel free to be candid in their assessments. Therefore, efficiency reports and other materials used in making decisions about military promotions may be difficult to get. But always remember, when seeking information of an investigatory nature it is a good idea to request it under both the Privacy Act and the FOIA.

Appeal Procedure For Denial of Access

Unlike the FOIA, the Privacy Act provides no standard procedure for appealing refusals to release information. However, many agencies have their own regulations governing this. If your request is denied, the agency should advise you of its appeal procedure and tell you to whom to address your appeal. If this information is not provided, you should send your letter to the head of the agency. Include a copy of the rejection letter along with a copy of your original request and state your reason for wanting access, if you think it will help.

If an agency withholds all or any part of your record, it must tell you which Privacy Act exemption it is claiming as a justification. It should also advise you why it believes the record can be withheld under the Freedom of Information Act since Congress intended that information sought under either the Privacy Act or the FOIA be released unless it could be withheld under both acts. Therefore, in making your appeal, it would be a good idea to cite both the FOIA and the Privacy Act. Moreover, if you are able to do so, it might also help you to explain why you think the exemptions used to refuse you access are unjustified.

Sample Letter of Appeal

Agency Head or Appeal Officer
Title
Agency
Agency Address
City, State   Zip Code

Re: Privacy Act Appeal

Dear   :
  On   (date)   , I received a letter from   (individual's name)   of your agency denying my request for access to   (description of the information sought)   . Enclosed is a copy of this denial along with a copy of my original request. By this letter, I am appealing the denial.
  Since Congress intended that information sought under the Privacy Act of 1974, 5 U.S.C. 552a, be released unless it could be withheld under both this Act and the Freedom of Information Act, FOIA, 5 U.S.C. 552, I hereby request that you also refer to the FOIA in consideration of this appeal.
  (Optional) I am seeking access to these records (state the reasons for your request if you think it will assist you in obtaining the information and give any arguments you have to justify its release).

Thank you for your prompt attention to this matter.

Sincerely,

Signature
Name
Address
City, State   Zip Code

Amending Your Records

The Privacy Act requires agencies to keep all personal records on individuals accurate, complete, up-to-date, and relevant. Therefore, if, after seeing your record, you wish to correct, delete, or add information to it, you should write to the agency official who released the information to you, giving the reasons for the desired changes as well as any documentary evidence you might have to justify the changes. Some agencies may allow you to request these corrections in person or by telephone.

Sample Letter for Request to Amend Records

Agency Head or Privacy Officer
Title
Agency
Agency Address
City, State   Zip Code

Re: Privacy Act Request to Amend Records

Dear   :
By letter dated _____, I requested access to (use same descriptions as in request letter).

In viewing the information forwarded to me, I found that it was (inaccurate) (incomplete) (outdated) (not relevant to the purpose of your agency).

Therefore, pursuant to the Privacy Act of 1974, 5 U.S.C. 522a, I hereby request that you amend my record in the following manner: (describe errors, new information, irrelevance, etc.).

In accordance with the Act, I look forward to an acknowledgment of this request within 10 working days of its receipt.

Thank you for your assistance in this matter.

Sincerely,

Signature
Name
Address
City, State   Zip Code

Appeal Procedure for Agency Refusal to Amend Records

If an agency refuses to amend your records, it must advise you of the reasons for the refusal as well as the appeal procedures available to you within the agency. It must also tell you to whom to address your appeal. Amendment appeals are usually handled by agency heads or by a senior official appointed by the agency head.

Your appeal letter should include a copy of your original request along with a copy of the agency's denial. You should also include any additional information you might have to substantiate your claims regarding the disputed material.

A decision on your appeal must be rendered within 30 working days from the date of its receipt. In unusual circumstances, such as the need to obtain information from retired records or another agency, an additional 30 days may be granted.

If the agency denies your appeal and continues to refuse to make the changes you request, you have the right to file a brief statement giving your reasons for disputing the record. This statement of disagreement then becomes part of the record and must be forwarded to all past and future recipients of your file. However, as previously noted, unless the agency has kept some record of disclosures prior to September 27, 1975, it might not be possible to notify all past recipients. The agency is also permitted to place in your file a short explanation of its refusal to change the record. This, too, becomes a part of your permanent file and is forwarded along with your statement of disagreement. If your appeal is denied or if the agency fails to act upon it within the specified time, you can take your case to court.

Sample Letter for Appealing Agency's Refusal to Amend Records

Agency Head or Designated Official
Title
Agency
Agency Address
City, State   Zip Code

Re: Privacy Act Appeal

Dear   :
By letter dated _____ to   (official to whom you addressed your amendment request), I requested that information held by your agency concerning me be amended. This request was denied, and I am hereby appealing that denial. For your information, I am enclosing a copy of my request letter along with a copy of Mr. (Ms.)

————'s reply. (If you have any additional relevant information, send it, too.)

I trust that upon consideration of my reasons for seeking the desired changes, you will grant my request to amend the disputed material. However, in the event you refuse this request, please advise me of the agency procedures for filing a statement of disagreement.

(Optional) I plan to initiate legal action if my appeal is denied.

Thank you for your prompt attention to this matter.

Sincerely,

Signature
Name
Address
City, State   Zip Code

Taking Your Case to Court

Under the Privacy Act, you can sue an agency for refusing to release your records, for denial of your appeal to amend a record, and for failure to act upon your appeal within the designated time. You can also sue if you are adversely affected by the agency's failure to comply with any provisions of the Act. For example, if you are denied a job promotion due to inaccurate, incomplete, outdated, or irrelevant information in your file, you can contest this action in court.

While the Freedom of Information Act requires individuals to use agency appeal procedures before seeking judicial review, the Privacy Act permits individuals to appeal denials of access directly to the courts (although most agencies have their own appeal procedures and you should use them when available). On the other hand, you are required by the Act to use administrative appeal procedures in contesting agency refusals to amend your records.

Judicial rulings favorable to you could result in the release or amendment of the records in question. In addition, you can obtain money damages if it is proven that you have been adversely affected as a result of the agency's intentional and willful disregard of the Act's provisions. You might also be awarded court costs and attorney fees.

The Act provides criminal penalties for the knowing and willful disclosure of personal records to those not entitled to receive them, for the knowing and willful failure to publish the existence and characteristics of all record systems, and for the knowing and willful attempt to gain access to an individual's records under false pretenses.

If and when you do decide to go to court, you can file suit in the Federal district court where you reside or do business or where the agency records are situated. Or you can take the case to the U.S. District Court in the District of Columbia. Under the Privacy Act, you are also required to bring suit within two years from the date of the violation you are challenging. However, in cases where the agency has materially or willfully misrepresented information, the statute of limitations runs two years from the date you discover the misrepresentation. As with lawsuits brought under the FOIA, the burden is on the agency to justify its refusal to release or amend records.

The same advice applies here as with suits filed under the FOIA: if you go to court, you should consult a lawyer. If you cannot afford private counsel, contact your local legal aid society.

Other Rights Provided Under the Privacy Act

One of the most important provisions of the Privacy Act is the one that requires agencies to obtain an individual's written permission prior to disclosing to other persons or agencies information concerning him or her, unless such disclosures are specifically authorized under the Act. Information can be disclosed without an individual's consent under the following circumstances: to employees and officers of the agency maintaining the records who have a need for the information in order to perform their duties; if the information is required to be disclosed under the FOIA; for "routine uses," i.e., uses which are compatible with the purpose for which the information was collected;* to the Census Bureau; to the National Archives; to a law enforcement agency upon the written request of the agency head; to individuals acting on behalf of the health or safety of the subject of the record; to Congress; to the General Accounting Office; or pursuant to court order. In all other circumstances, however, the individual who is the subject of the record must give his or her written consent before an agency can divulge information concerning him or her to others.

Under the Act, you are also entitled to know to whom information about you has been sent. Agencies must keep an accurate accounting of all disclosures made to other agencies or persons except those required under the FOIA. Moreover, this information must be maintained for at least five years or until the record disclosed is destroyed, whichever is longer. With the exception of disclosures requested by law enforcement agencies, a list of all recipients of information

*All federal agencies must publish annually in the Federal Register the "routine uses" of the information they maintain.

concerning you must be made available upon request. Therefore, if you are interested in knowing who has received records about you, you should write to the Privacy Act officer or the head of the agency that maintains the records and request that an accounting of disclosures be sent to you.

Finally, the Privacy Act places a moratorium upon any new uses of your social security number by federal, state, and local government agencies after January 1, 1975.* No agency may deny you a right, benefit, or privilege to which you are

*This is the only provision in the Privacy Act that applies to state and local as well as federal agencies.

entitled by law because of your refusal to disclose your number unless the disclosure is specifically authorized by the statute or regulation adopted before January 1, 1975, or by a later act of Congress. Moreover, in requesting your social security number, agencies are required to tell you whether the disclosure is mandatory or voluntary, under what law or regulation the request is authorized, and what uses will be made of the number. You should bear in mind, however, that this provision applies only to government agencies. It does not apply to the private sector; requests made directly to you for your social security number by private organizations are not prohibited by law.

Federal Money Programs: Finding What's Available

Available government money programs are described under each department and agency. They are listed under the following three headings: Direct Payments; Loans and Loan Guarantees; and Grants. A listing of these programs appears under "Federal Money Programs" in the Sampler Section Free Help and Information For Business.

If you are looking for further information on government programs, you may find one or more of the following sources helpful. Further details about how and where to obtain government money are described in my book, *Getting Yours: The Complete Guide to Government Money* (Penguin, 1984).

Catalog of Federal Domestic Assistance
This 1,000-page document is the most complete source of information on government programs. It is published once a year with updates by the Office of Management and Budget. Subscriptions are available for $20.00 from: Superintendent of Documents, Government Printing Office, Washington, DC 20402/202-783-3238.

Federal Assistance Programs Retrieval System (FAPRS)
This is a computerized information system containing much of the same information as in the Catalog of Federal Domestic Assistance. It is designed to quickly identify specific federal assistance programs for which applicants are eligible. It can be accessed through computer terminals in many government regional offices and in university libraries. The price of a search varies with the request. For an access point near you contact:

FAPRS, Rural Development Service, Department of Agriculture, Washington, DC 20250/202-382-8348.

Federal Information Centers
Staff at these Centers can direct you to appropriate money programs. For more information, see description and listing in next section entitled "Resources Close-To-Home."

Your Senators' and Representative's Home and Washington Offices
This is a good place to turn to when all else fails. Remember your elected representatives work for you. Your Senators and House Member can be reached by contacting the local home office (complete listing is included in the "Resources Close-to-Home" section of the Sampler) or: c/o U.S. Capitol, Washington, DC 20515/202-224-3121.

Help and Information from Your Congressional Representatives

Your Senator, Congressman or Congresswoman and their staff can help you gain access to government resources and benefits. In this section you will find advice about how to use your Congressional Representative, as well as what services you can expect from his/her offices. (A listing of Congressional State and District offices appears in the next section of the Sampler entitled "Resources Close-To-Home".)

Capitol Hill—How to Use It Like a Washington Lobbyist

Capitol Hill, or Congress, the legislative branch of the government, is just beginning to be used as a source of information. Very few people have been aware of this treasure trove of unpublished data. Over the years, the Congress has probably held investigations on any topic you can think of, with experts providing their opinions. The documentation for a given committee or subcommittee hearing provides an unmatched reference source for anyone researching current events or other topics.

The information available from Capitol Hill can be used to serve two ends: to monitor legislation, and to investigate a specific topic. Here is a brief outline on how to use this information to achieve both these purposes.

Monitoring Legislation

The best source for determining if there is specific legislation pending in a given area is the Bill Status Office, Capitol, Washington, DC 20515/202-225-1772. By searching a computerized database, this office can provide you with the answers to such questions as:

Have any bills been introduced covering a given topic?

What is the status of a given bill?
Who sponsored the bill?
On what date was it introduced?
What committee and subcommittees have held hearings on a given bill?
What other bills are similar?

You must provide a key word for the subject you want searched. It is most likely that the legislation you are interested in is pending before a given committee or subcommittee. Armed with the name of the committee provided by the Bill Status Office, you can contact those on it directly in care of: Senate, Capitol, Washington, DC 20510/202-224-3121, or, House of Representatives, Capitol, Washington, DC 20515/202-224-3121.

Once you have reached the committee in question and are able to talk with the staff person covering your bill, you are now in a position to obtain the following information:

A copy of the bill
A copy of any hearings held on the bill
A description of where the bill will go once it leaves the committee
An analysis of the likelihood of the bill moving out of the committee
An estimate of the time involved for the bill to move out of the committee

If your bill is scheduled for action on the floor of the House or Senate, you can monitor its activity by the hour by listening to the recorded messages heard on Cloakroom numbers. It's like being on the floor of Congress yourself. The numbers are:

House of Representatives Cloakroom
    Republican/202-225-7430.
    Democrat/202-225-7400.
Senate Cloakroom
    Republican/202-224-8601.
    Democrat/202-224-8541.

Investigating Topics
See "Senate and House of Representatives Committee Hearings."

What Your Representatives Can Do For You

The federal government is the world's largest storehouse of little-known sources of information, expertise and benefits—and Members of Congress are an important key to this treasure chest. A call to the local office of your congressman or senator can often save you from the many pitfalls that keep people from taking advantage of government resources, e.g., they don't know what's available, they don't know where to look, or they get tired of fighting the bureaucracy and give up.

Most Senators have several offices throughout the state to help constituents with individual problems. In addition to asking your Senators for assistance, ask your Representative who also has one or more district offices. Instead of making a long distance call to Washington, D.C., usually you can get help in the city where you reside.

While the Member's staff in Washington, D.C. essentially works on legislation, the home offices are primarily set up to provide assistance such as help with the Social Security Administration or government student loans. These so-called "case workers" try to resolve problems at the state level but sometimes refer difficult cases to the Washington staff. Although the quantity and quality of the service will vary from office to office, it is still worth your effort to contact them. (A list of all home offices of all 535 Members of Congress can be found later in the "Resources-Close-To-Home" section of the Sampler.)

The following services and benefits are offered by most Representatives and Senators. Some of the books and souvenirs mentioned are available on a first-come-first-served basis.

Celebrate a Special Day By Flying Your Flag Over the Capitol
For the price of a flag ($7.00 to $16.00) your congressman can have the Architect of the Capitol fly your personal Stars and Stripes over the Capitol Building on the day you specify. This makes an unusual birthday gift because you receive the flag

and a certificate noting the date the flag was flown and in whose honor.

VIP Tours
If you are planning to visit Washington, your congressman can arrange special VIP tours for you at the White House, the Federal Bureau of

Investigation, the Department of State and other agencies. It means that you will not have to wait in lines, which can be very long during the tourist season.

Government Benefits

Your Representative and Senator can be very effective in insuring that you receive the government benefits to which you are entitled. He or she can help with such matters as:

A late Social Security check;
A Social Security check for the wrong amount;
Identifying disability, unemployment, or veteran benefits.

Getting the Bureaucracy to Move

If you have applied for a government loan, sent in an unsolicited proposal for government business or requested information from a regulatory agency, and you have waited an unreasonable amount of time for a response, your Representative can help. His or her office can call the agency on your behalf and get them to move. Remember, that although you, a taxpayer, ultimately pay the salaries of all bureaucrats, it is your congressman that actually pulls the purse strings.

Reports on Current Events

The Congressional Research Service publishes and records on cassette hundreds of major issue briefs to keep members of Congress informed on important and current topics. These reports, written in laymen's language, provide an historical perspective in order to increase the understanding of issues. They are updated daily to include latest developments. Members of Congress have computer access to these reports and hard copies are available at no cost through their offices. Call your representative and ask for a listing of Congressional Research Service Current Issue Briefs. It will provide you with a shopping list from which you can then order reports that interest you.

Bills and Laws

For school projects or specific areas of interest, your congressman can send you copies of bills, committee hearings, committee reports, and recently enacted public laws.

Maps and Brochures

Most Congressmen have an abundant supply of free pamphlets and tourist information about resorts and national parks in their home state.

Calendars

Each congressional office has a large stock of free hanging wall calendars, containing beautiful photographs of Washington scenes.

The Capitol: A Pictorial History of the Capitol and the Congress

This free 200-page paperback is full of photographs of the mosaic corridors, the House and Senate Chambers, past members of Congress and many of today's key legislators.

Reports on High School and Intercollegiate Debate Topics

A free report, prepared by the Library of Congress, contains a compilation of pertinent excerpts, bibliographical references and other materials related to the subject selected by the National University Exension Service Association as the national high school debate topic, and the subject selected annually by the American Speech Association as the national college debate topic.

How Our Laws Are Made

This free handbook provides a nontechnical outline of the background and the multiple steps of the legislative process from the origin of a bill through to its publication as a federal statute.

Our American Government: What Is It? How Does It Function? 150 Questions and Answers

This free booklet describes the Legislative, Executive and Judicial branches of government and the relationships among them, and includes such information as the salary of a cabinet member, whether political parties offer legislative guidance to their individual Members of Congress, and the difference between opinions and decisions of the Supreme Court.

The Declaration of Independence and the Constitution of the United States

This free pamphlet also includes amendments and proposed amendments to the Constitution not yet ratified by the States.

Resources Close-To-Home

Washington, DC is the Federal Government's headquarters, but it also has offices throughout the United States which can help you. These include Federal Information Centers, government bookstores and libraries, Congressional offices, and regional branches of federal departments and agencies.

Given space limitations, most entries in INFORMATION USA list Washington, DC as the contact place. However, the corresponding office in your geographical area generally can provide the same services, or contact Washington for you. So, to save yourself toll calls, you might first want to contact a resource "Close-To-Home"!

Federal Information Centers

The Federal Government sponsors a network of information centers throughout the U.S. to help citizens find their way through the federal bureaucracy. By calling, writing, or visiting your local Federal Information Center you will be directed to a government expert who can help you sort through the wide range of services and information provided by hundreds of different departments, agencies and programs of the federal government, the numerous laws it administers, and the multitude of publications and periodicals available. Questions most commonly asked are about jobs, retirement benefits, taxes, Social Security, veterans' benefits and immigration. FIC staff specialists in many cities speak other languages in addition to English.

For information contact the Federal Information Center nearest you. As long as you call a Center within your state, you will either be making a local call or one that will result only in a minimal long distance charge. If you prefer to write to a Center and an address is not listed for your state, direct your correspondence to the closest state Center.

Centers

Alabama
(Write to Atlanta, GA)
Birmingham—205/322-8591
Mobile—205/438-1421

Alaska
Anchorage—907/271-3650

Arizona
Phoenix—602/261-3313

Arkansas
(Write to Fort Worth, TX)
Little Rock—501/378-6177

California
Federal Information Center
300 North Los Angeles Street
Los Angeles, CA 90012/213-688-3800

Federal Information Center
650 Capitol Mall, Room 8543
Sacramento, CA 95814/916-440-3344

Government Information Center
880 Front Street
San Diego, CA 92188/619-293-6030

Federal Information Center
450 Golden Gate Avenue—Box 36082
San Francisco, CA 94102/415-556-6600

Santa Ana—714/836-2386

Colorado
Federal Information Center
Federal Center, P. O. Box 25006
Denver, CO 80225/303-236-7181

Colorado Springs—303/471-9491
Pueblo—303/544-9523

Connecticut
(Write to New York, NY)
Hartford—203/527-2617
New Haven—203/624-4720

Florida
Federal Information Center
144 First Avenue South, Room 105
St. Petersburg, FL 33701/813-893-3495

Ft. Lauderdale—305/522-8531
Jacksonville—904/354-4756
Miami—305/350-4155
Orlando—305/422-1800

Tampa—813/229-7911
West Palm Beach—305/833-7566

Georgia
Federal Information Center
75 Spring Street SW
Atlanta, GA 30303/404-221-6891

Hawaii
Federal Information Center
300 Ala Moana Blvd.—Box 50091
Honolulu, HI 96850/808-546-8620

Illinois
Federal Information Center
230 South Dearborn Street, 33rd Floor
Chicago, IL 60604/312-353-4242

Indiana
(Write to Cincinnati, OH)
Gary—219/883-4110
Indianapolis—317/269-7373

Iowa
(Write to Omaha, NE)
From all points in Iowa—
800/532-1556

Kansas
(Write to St. Louis, MO)
From all points in Kansas—
800/432-2934

Kentucky
(Write to Cincinnati, OH)
Louisville—502/582-6261

Louisiana
(Write to Houston, TX)
New Orleans—504/589-6696

Maryland
(Write to Philadelphia, PA)
Baltimore—301/962-4980

Massachusetts
Federal Information Center
McCormack P.O.C.H. Building, Room 812
Boston, MA 02109/617-223-7121

Michigan
Federal Information Center
477 Michigan Avenue, Room M-25
Detroit, MI 48226/313-226-7016

Grand Rapids—616/451-2628

Minnesota
(Write to Chicago, IL)
Minneapolis—612/349-5333

Missouri
Federal Information Center
1520 Market Street, Room 2616
St. Louis, MO 63103/314-425-4106

From elsewhere in Missouri—
800/392-7711

Nebraska
Federal Information Center
215 North 17th Street
Omaha, NE 68102/402-221-3353

From elsewhere in Nebraska—
800/624-8383

New Jersey
(Northern N.J., write to New York, NY)
(Southern N.J., write to Philadelphia, PA)

Newark—201/645-3600
Trenton—609/396-4400

New Mexico
(Write to Fort Worth, TX)
Albuquerque—505/766-3091

New York
Federal Information Center
111 West Huron
Buffalo, NY 14202/716-846-4010

Federal Information Center
26 Federal Plaza, Room 2-110
New York, NY 10278/212-264-4464

Albany—518/463-4421
Rochester—716/546-5075
Syracuse—315/476-8545

North Carolina
(Write to Atlanta, GA)
Charlotte—704/376-3600

Ohio
Federal Information Center
550 Main Street, Room 7411
Cincinnati, OH 45202/513-684-2801

Akron—216/375-5638
Cleveland—216/522-4040
Columbus—614/221-1014
Dayton—513/223-7377
Toledo—419/241-3223

Oklahoma
(Write to Fort Worth, TX)
Oklahoma City—405/231-4868
Tulsa—918/584-4193

Oregon
Federal Information Center
1220 SW Third Avenue, Room 321
Portland, OR 97204/503-221-2222

Pennsylvania
Federal Information Center
9th and Market Streets, Room 4134
Philadelphia, PA 19107/215-597-7042

Pittsburgh—412/644-3456

Rhode Island
(Write to Boston, MA)
Providence—401/331-5565

Tennessee
(Write to Atlanta, GA)
Chattanooga—615/265-8231
Memphis—901/521-3285
Nashville—615/242-5056

Texas
Federal Information Center
819 Taylor Street
Fort Worth, TX 76102/817-334-3624

Federal Information Center
515 Rusk Avenue
Houston, TX 77002/713/229-2552

Austin—512/472-5494
Dallas—214/767-8585
San Antonio—512/224-4471

Utah
(Write to Denver, CO)
Salt Lake City—801/524-5353

Virginia
(Write to Philadelphia, PA)
Norfolk—804/441-3101
Richmond—804/643-4928
Roanoke—703/982-8591

Washington
(Write to Portland, OR)
Seattle—206/442-0570
Tacoma—206/383-5230

Wisconsin
(Write to Chicago, IL)
Milwaukee—414/271-2273

Government Bookstores

The Superintendent of Documents offers for sale nearly 16,000 of the newest and most popular publications from Government experts in space science, global exporting opportunities, medical research, current Federal law, and much more. In addition, Government bestsellers provide sound, practical answers to a wide variety of questions from child care to saving money on fuel bills. There are 24 Government bookstores all around the country where you can browse through the shelves and take your books home with you. Naturally, these stores can't stock all of the nearly 16,000 titles available, but they do carry the ones you're most likely to be looking for. They'll also be happy to special order any Government book currently offered for sale. All of GPO's bookstores accept VISA, MasterCard, and Superintendent of Documents deposit account orders: (Note: To learn more about what what types of materials and services these GPO Bookstores offer, see the chapter on Government Printing Office.)

GPO Bookstores

Alabama
Roebuck Shopping City
9220-B Parkway East
Birmingham, Alabama 35206
(205) 254-1056
9:00 AM–5:00 PM

California
ARCO Plaza, C-Level
505 South Flower Street
Los Angeles, California 90071
(213) 688-5841
8:30 AM–4:30 PM

Room 1023, Federal Building
450 Golden Gate Avenue
San Francisco, California 94102
(415) 556-0643
8:00 AM–4:00 PM

Colorado
Room 117, Federal Building
1961 Stout Street
Denver, Colorado 80294
(303) 844-3964
8:00 AM–4:00 PM

World Savings Building
720 North Main Street
Pueblo, Colorado 81003
(303) 544-3142
9:00 AM–5:00 PM

District of Columbia
U.S. Government Printing Office
710 North Capitol Street
Washington, DC 20402
(202) 275-2091
8:00 AM–4:00 PM

Commerce Department
Room 1604, 1st Floor
14th & E Streets NW
Washington, DC 20230
(202) 377-3527
8:00 AM–4:00 PM

Dept. of Health and Human Services
Room 1528, North Building
330 Independence Avenue SW
Washington, DC 20201
(202) 472-7478
8:00 AM–4:00 PM

Farragut West
Matomic Building
1717 H Street NW
Washington, DC 20036
(202) 653-5075
9:00 AM–5:00 PM

Pentagon
Room 2E172
Main Concourse, South End
Washington, DC 20310
(703) 557-1821
8:00 AM–4:00 PM

Florida
Room 158, Federal Building
400 W. Bay Street
P.O. Box 35089
Jacksonville, Florida 32202
(904) 791-3801
8:00 AM–4:00 PM

Georgia
Room 100, Federal Building
275 Peachtree Street NE
Atlanta, Georgia 30303
(404) 221-6947
8:00 AM–4:00 PM

Illinois
Room 1365, Federal Building
219 S. Dearborn Street
Chicago, Illinois 60604
(312) 353-5133
8:00 AM–4:00 PM

Massachusetts
Room G25, Federal Building
Sudbury Street
Boston, Massachusetts 02203
(617) 223-6071
8:00 AM–4:00 PM

Michigan
Suite 160, Federal Building
477 Michigan Avenue
Detroit, Michigan 48226
(313) 226-7816
8:00 AM–4:00 PM

Missouri
Room 144, Federal Building
601 East 12th Street
Kansas City, Missouri 64106
(816) 374-2160
8:00 AM–4:00 PM

New York
Room 110
26 Federal Plaza
New York, New York 10278
(212) 264-3825
8:00 AM–4:00 PM

Ohio
1st Floor, Federal Building
1240 E. 9th Street
Cleveland, Ohio 44199
(216) 522-4922
9:00 AM–5:00 PM

Room 207, Federal Building
200 N. High Street
Columbus, Ohio 43215
(614) 469-6956
9:00 AM–5:00 PM

Pennsylvania
Room 1214, Federal Building
600 Arch Street
Philadelphia, Pennsylvania 19106
(215) 597-0677
8:00 AM–4:00 PM

Room 118, Federal Building
1000 Liberty Avenue
Pittsburgh, Pennsylvania 15222
(412) 644-2721
9:00 AM–5:00 PM

Texas
Room 1C50, Federal Building
1100 Commerce Street
Dallas, Texas 75242
(214) 767-0076
7:45 AM–4:15 PM

45 College Center
9319 Gulf Freeway
Houston, Texas 77017
(713) 229-3515
10:00 AM–6:00 PM (Open Sat.)

Washington
Room 194, Federal Building
915 Second Avenue
Seattle, Washington 98174
(206) 442-4270
8:00 AM–4:00 PM

Wisconsin
Room 190, Federal Building
517 E. Wisconsin Avenue
Milwaukee, Wisconsin 53202
(414) 291-1304
8:00 AM–4:00 PM

Retail Sales Outlet
8660 Cherry Lane
Laurel, Maryland 20707
(301) 953-7974
8:00 AM–4:00 PM

Federal Depository Libraries

This national library system is composed of nearly 1,400 public, academic, and law libraries which receive copies of most government publications. Its libraries provide free public access to their government collections. Nearly every state is served by a Regional Depository Library which maintains a collection of all government publications distributed by the Government Printing Office (GPO). If the library in your area does not have a document you need it will borrow the publication for you. The Depository Libraries can also give you information about the price and order numbers for most GPO publications.

List of Depository Libraries by State and City

Alabama

Alexander City

Alexander City State Junior college
Thomas D. Russell Library
P.O. Box 699
35010
(205) 234-6346, ext. 283

Auburn

Auburn University
Ralph Brown Draughon Library
Microforms & Documents Dept.
Mell Street
36849
(205) 826-4500, ext. 23

Birmingham

Birmingham Public Library
Government Documents Department
2020 Park Place
35203
(205) 254-2551

Birmingham-Southern College Library
Documents Department
35254
(205) 328-5250, ext. 242

Jefferson State Junior College
James B. Allen Library
2601 Carson Road
35215
(205) 853-1200, ext. 280

Miles College
C. A. Kirkendoll Learning Resource Center
5500 Avenue G
35208
(205) 923-2771, ext. 241

Samford University Library
800 Lakeshore Drive
35229
(205) 870-2847

Enterprise

Enterprise State Junior College
Learning Resources Center
36331
(205) 347-2623, ext. 281

Fayette

Brewer State Junior College
Learning Resources Center Library
35555
(205) 932-3221, ext. 244

Florence

University of North Alabama
Collier Library
Morrison Avenue
35632
(205) 766-4100, ext. 473

Gadsden

Gadsden Public Library
254 College Street
35999
(205) 547-1611, ext. 7

Huntsville

University of Alabama in Huntsville Library
35899
(205) 895-6526

Jacksonville

Jacksonville State University Library
Houston Cole Building
Pelham Road
36265
(205) 435-9820, ext. 254

Mobile

Mobile Public Library
Government Documents Collection
701 Government Street
36602
(205) 438-7078

Spring Hill College
Thomas Byrne Memorial Library,
Documents Dept.
4307 Old Shell Road
36608
(205) 460-2382

University of South Alabama Library
Government Documents Dept.
36688 (Designated 1968)
(205) 460-7024

Montgomery

Alabama State Department of Archives and History
Library
624 Washington Avenue
36130
(205) 832-6510, ext. 38

Alabama Supreme Court and State Law Library
Judicial Building Capitol
455 Dexter Avenue
36130
(205) 832-6410

Auburn University at Montgomery Library
Documents Department
36193
(205) 271-9650
REGIONAL DEPOSITORY

Air University Library Maxwell Air Force Base
36112
(205) 293-2888

Normal

Alabama Argicultural and Mechanical University
J. F. Drake Memorial Learning Resources
Center
P.O. Box 489
35762
(205) 859-7309

Troy

Troy State University Library
Documents Department
36082
(205) 566-3000, ext. 256

Tuskegee Institute

Tuskegee Institute
Hollis Burke Frissell Library
Documents Department
36088
(205) 727-8891

University

University of Alabama Library
Reference Department/Documents
Box S
35486
(205) 348-6046
REGIONAL DEPOSITORY

University of Alabama School of Law Library
Box 6205
35486
(205) 348-5925

Alaska

Anchorage

Alaska Court Libraries
303 K Street
99501
(907) 264-0585

Anchorage Municipal Libraries
Z. J. Loussac Public Library
524 West 6th Avenue
99501
(907) 264-4481

University of Alaska at Anchorage Library
3211 Providence Drive
99504
(907) 876-1874

U.S. Department of Interior Alaska Resources
Library
701 C Street, Box 36
99513
(907) 271-5025

U.S. District Court Library
701 C Street, Box 4
99513
(907) 271-5655

Fairbanks

University of Alaska
Elmer E. Rasmuson Library
Documents Collection
310 Tanana Drive
99701
(907) 474-7624

Juneau

Alaska State Library
Documents Department
Pouch G
333 Willoughby Avenue
99811
(907) 465-2942

University of Alaska-Juneau Library & Medical Services
11120 Glacier Highway
99803
(907) 789-4440

Ketchikan

Ketchikan Community College Library
Seventh and Madison
99901
(907) 225-4722

Arizona

Coolidge

Central Arizona College
Instructional Materials Center
Signal Peak Campus
Woodruff at Overfield Road
85228
(602) 723-4141, ext. 282

Flagstaff

Northern Arizona University Library
Government Documents Dept.
Box 6022
86011
(602) 523-2171, ext. 24

Mesa

Mesa Public Library
Documents
64 East 1st Street
85201
(602) 834-2207

Phoenix

Department of Library Archives, and Public Records
Third Floor State Capitol
1700 West Washington
85007
(602) 255-4121
REGIONAL DEPOSITORY

Grand Canyon College
Fleming Library
3300 W. Camelback Road
85061
(602) 249-3300, ext. 395

Phoenix Public Library
12 East McDowell Road
85004
(602) 262-4795

U.S. Court of Appeals
9th Circuit Library
Room 6434, U.S. Courthouse
230 North First Avenue
85025
(602) 261-3879

Prescott

Yavapai College Library
1100 East Sheldon Street
86301
(602) 445-7300, ext. 273

Tempe

Arizona State University
College of Law Library
85287
(602) 965-6141

Arizona State University Library
Government Documents Service
85287
(602) 965-3387

Tucson

Tucson Public Library
200 South 6th Avenue
85701
(602) 791-4010

University of Arizona Library
Government Documents Dept.
85721
(602) 621-4871
REGIONAL DEPOSITORY

Yuma

Yuma City-County Library
350 Third Avenue
85364
(602) 782-1871

Arkansas

Arkadelphia

Ouachita Baptist University
Riley Library
410 Ouachita Street
71923
(501) 246-4531, ext. 122

Batesville

Arkansas College Library
Documents Department
72501
(501) 793-9813, ext. 205

Clarksville

College of the Ozarks
Dobson Memorial Library
72830
(501) 754-3964

Conway

Hendrix College
Olin C. Bailey Library
Front and Washington Streets
72032
(501) 450-1303

Fayetteville

University of Arkansas University Libraries
Government Documents Department
72701
(501) 575-5516

University of Arkansas
School of Law Library
72701
(501) 575-5604

Little Rock

Arkansas State Library
Documents Service Section
One Capitol Mall
72201
(501) 371-2090
REGIONAL DEPOSITORY

Arkansas Supreme Court Library
Justice Building
72201
(501) 374-2512

Little Rock Public Library
700 Louisiana Street
72201
(501) 370-5952

University of Arkansas at Little Rock Library
Documents Department
33rd and University Ave.
72204
(501) 569-3120, ext. 38/48

University of Arkansas at Little Rock, School of Law Library
400 West Markham Avenue
72201
(501) 371-1071, ext. 241

Magnolia

Southern Arkansas University
Magale Library
Government Documents
71753
(501) 234-5120, ext. 360

Monticello

University of Arkansas at Monticello Library
Drawer 3599
71655
(501) 367-6811, ext. 80

Pine Bluff

University of Arkansas at Pine Bluff
Watson Memorial Library
University Drive
71601
(501) 541-6500, ext. 6808

Russellville

Arkansas Tech University
Tomlinson Library
72801
(501) 968-0304

Searcy

Harding University
Beaumont Memorial Library
Government Documents Department
Station A, Box 928
900 East Center Street
72143
(501) 268-6161, ext. 354

State University

Arkansas State University
Dean B. Ellis Library
Government Documents
P.O. Box 2040
72467
(501) 972-3077

Walnut Ridge

Southern Baptist College
Felix Goodson Library
72476
(501) 886-6741, ext. 130

California

Anaheim

Anaheim Public Library
500 West Broadway
92805
(714) 999-1880

Arcadia

Arcadia Public Library
20 West Durate Road
91006
(213) 446-7112

Arcata

Humboldt State University Library
Documents Department
95521
(707) 826-3419

Bakersfield

California State College
Bakersfield Library
Government Publications Section
9001 Stockdale Highway
93309 (Designated 1974)
(805) 833-3172, ext. 24

Kern County, Beale Memorial Library
1315 Truxtun Avenue
93301
(805) 861-2136

Berkeley

University of California
General Library
Government Documents Department
94720
(415) 642-2568

University of California
Law Library
Bancroft Way and College Ave.
94720
(415) 642-4044

Carson

California State University
Dominguez Hills Educational Resources Center
800 East Victoria Street
90747
(213) 516-3715

Carson Regional Library
Government Publications Unit
151 East Carson Street
90745
(213) 830-0901

Chico

California State University Merriam Library
Government Publications and Map Department
95929
(916) 895-6802

Claremont

Claremont Colleges' Libraries
Honnold Library
Government Publications Department
8th & Dartmouth
91711
(714) 621-8000, ext. 3990

Coalinga

West Hills Community College Library
300 Cherry Lane
93210
(209) 935-0801, ext. 247

Compton

Compton Public Library
240 West Compton Boulevard
90220
(213) 637-0202, ext. 25

Culver City

Culver City Library
4975 Overland Avenue
90230
(213) 559-1676

Davis

University of California
Shields Library
Government Documents Dept.
95616
(916) 752-1624

University of California at Davis
Law Library
95616
(916) 752-3330

Downey

Downey City Library
11121 Brookshire Avenue
Caller No. 7015
90241
(213) 923-3256

Fresno

**California State University Fresno, Henry Madden
Library**
Documents Department
Shaw & Maple Avenues
93740
(209) 294-2335

Fresno County Free Library
2420 Mariposa Street
93721
(209) 488-3195

Fullerton

California State University at Fullerton Library
P.O. Box 4150
92634
(714) 773-3449

Western State University
College of Law Library
1111 North State College Blvd.
92631
(714) 738-1000

Garden Grove

Garden Grove Regional Library
11200 Stanford Avenue
92640
(714) 530-0711

Gardena

Gardena Public Library
1731 West Gardena Boulevard
90247
(213) 323-6363, ext. 0004

Hayward

California State University at Hayward Library
25800 Carlos Bee Blvd.
94542
(415) 881-3765

Huntington Park

Huntington Park Library
San Antonio Region
6518 Miles Avenue
90255
(213) 583-1461

Inglewood

Inglewood Public Library
Serials Division
101 West Manchester Boulevard
90301
(213) 412-5380

Irvine

University of California at Irvine
General Library
Government Publications Dept.
P.O. Box 19557
92713
(714) 856-7235

La Jolla

University of California at San Diego
Central University Library
Documents Department, C-075-P
92093
(619) 452-3338

Lakewood

Angelo Iacoboni Public Library
Government Publications Collection
5020 Clark Avenue
90712
(213) 866-1777

Lancaster
Lancaster Library
1150 West Avenue J
93534
(805) 948-5020

La Verne

University of La Verne
College of Law Library
1950 Third Street
91750
(714) 593-7184

Long Beach

California State University at Long Beach Library
1250 Bellflower Blvd.
90840
(213) 498-4026

Long Beach Public Library
Ocean and Pacific Avenues
90802
(213) 437-2949, ext. 40

Los Angeles

California State University at Los Angeles
John F. Kennedy Memorial Library
5151 State University Drive
90032
(213) 224-2230

Los Angeles County Law Library
301 West First Street
90012
(213) 629-3531

Los Angeles Public Library
Documents Department
630 West 5th St.
90071
(213) 626-7555

Loyola Marymount University
Charles Von der Ahe Library
Loyola Blvd. at West 80th Street
90045
(213) 642-2790

Loyola Law School Law Library
1440 West Ninth Street
90015
(213) 736-1141

Occidental College Library
Documents Division
1600 Campus Road
90041
(213) 259-2810

Southwestern University
School of Law Library
675 South Westmoreland Ave.
90005
(213) 738-6767

University of California, University Research Library
Public Affairs Service
405 Hilgard Avenue
90024
(213) 825-3135

University of California, Los Angeles
Law Library
405 Hilgard Avenue
90024
(213) 825-6414

University of Southern California
Doheny Memorial Library
Government Documents Dept.
University Park MC-0182
90089
(213) 734-5192

University of Southern California
Law Library
University Park
90089
(213) 743-7448

U.S. Court of Appeals
9th Circuit Library
1702 U.S. Court House
312 North Spring Street
90012
(213) 688-3636

Whittier College
School of Law Library
5353 West Third Street
90020
(213) 938-3621, ext. 24

Malibu

Pepperdine University Library
24255 Pacific Coast Highway
90265
(213) 456-4243

Menlo Park

Department of Interior
Geological Survey Library
345 Middlefield Road MS 55
94025
(415) 323-8111, ext. 2364

Montebello

Montebello Library
1550 West Beverly Boulevard
90640
(213) 722-6551

Monterey

U.S. Naval Postgraduate School
Dudley Knox Library
Code 0142
Sloat & 5th Street
93943
(408) 646-2341

Monterey Park

Bruggemeyer Memorial Library
318 South Ramona Avenue
91754
(213) 307-1368

Northridge

California State University at Northridge,
Oviatt Library
Government Documents
18111 Nordhoff Street
91330
(213) 885-2287

Norwalk

Norwalk Public Library
12350 Imperial Highway
90650
(213) 868-0775

Oakland

Mills College Library
5000 McArthur Blvd.
94613
(415) 430-2116

Oakland Public Library
125 Fourteenth Street
94612
(415) 273-3176, ext. 4

Ontario

Ontario City Library
215 East C Street
91764
(714) 988-8481, ext. 12

Palm Springs

Palm Springs Public Library
Technical Services Section
300 South Sunrise Way
92262
(619) 323-8294

Pasadena

California Institute of Technology
Millikan Memorial Library
1201 East California Blvd.
91125
(213) 356-6419

Pasadena Public Library
285 East Walnut Street
91101
(818) 577-4048

Pleasant Hill

Contra Costa County Library
Documents Section
1750 Oak Park Boulevard
94523
(415) 944-3434

Redding

Shasta County Library
1855 Shasta Street
96001
(916) 246-5756

Redlands

University of Redlands
Armacost Library
1200 East Colton Avenue
92373
(714) 793-2121, ext. 472

Redwood City

Redwood City Public Library
881 Jefferson Avenue
94063
(415) 369-3737

Reseda

West Valley Regional Branch Library
19036 Vanowen Street
91335
(213) 345-4393

Richmond

Richmond Public Library
Civic Center Plaza
94804
(415) 231-2122

Riverside

Riverside City and County Public Library
3581 Seventh Street
92501
(714) 787-7201

University of California at Riverside Library
Government Publications Dept.
900 University Avenue
P.O. Box 5900
92517
(714) 787-3714

Sacramento

California State Library
Government Publications Service
914 Capitol Mall
95814
(916) 322-4572
REGIONAL DEPOSITORY

California State University at Sacramento Library
Documents Section
2000 Jed Smith Drive
95819
(916) 454-6440

Sacramento County Law Library
720 Ninth Street
95820
(916) 444-5910

Sacramento Public Library
828 I Street
95814
(916) 449-5203

University of the Pacific
McGeorge School of Law Library
3282 Fifth Avenue
95817
(916) 739-7300

San Bernardino

San Bernardino County Law Library
Court House Annex, Ground Floor
351 North Arrowhead Avenue
92415
(714) 383-1957

San Bernardino County Library
104 West Fourth Street
92415
(714) 383-1155

San Diego

San Diego County Law Library
1105 Front Street
92101
(714) 236-2172

San Diego County Library
5555 Overland Avenue, Bldg. 15
92123
(714) 565-5750

San Diego Public Library
820 E Street
92101
(714) 236-5552

San Diego State University Library
Government Publications Dept.
92182
(714) 265-5832

University of San Diego
Kratter Law Library
Alcala Park
92110
(714) 293-4542

San Francisco

Golden Gate University
School of Law Library
536 Mission Street, Plaza Level
94105
(415) 442-7000, ext. 7571 or 7260

Hastings College of Law Library
200 McAllister Street
94102
(415) 557-8421

Mechanics' Institute Library
Mechanics' Institute Bldg.
57 Post Street
94194
(415) 421-1750

San Francisco Public Library
Government Documents Dept.
Civic Center
94102
(415) 558-3321

San Francisco State University
J. Paul Leonard Library
Government Publications Dept.
1630 Holloway Avenue
94132
(415) 469-1557

Supreme Court of California Library
State Building Annex
Room 4241
455 Golden Gate Avenue
94102
(415) 557-1922

U.S. Court of Appeals
Ninth Circuit Library
Seventh and Mission Streets
P.O. Box 5731
94101
(415) 556-6129

University of San Francisco
Richard A. Gleeson Library
94117
(415) 666-6686

San Jose

San Jose State University Library
Government Publications Department
One Washington Square
95192
(408) 277-3376

San Leandro

San Leandro Community Library Center
300 Estudillo Avenue
94577
(415) 483-1511

San Luis Obispo

California Polytechnic State University
Robert E. Kennedy Library
Documents and Maps Department
93407
(805) 546-1364

San Rafael

Marin County Free Library
Documents Department
Civic Center Administration Building
94903
(415) 499-6058

Santa Ana

Orange County Law Library
515 North Flower Street
92703
(714) 834-3397

Santa Ana Public Library
Documents Section
26 Civic Center Plaza
92701
(714) 834-4845

Santa Barbara

University of California at Santa Barbara Library
Government Publications Department
93106
(805) 961-2863

Santa Clara

University of Santa Clara
Orradre Library
Documents Division
95053
(408) 984-4415

Santa Cruz

**University of California at Santa Cruz, McHenry
Library**
Government Publications
95064
(408) 429-2347

Santa Rosa

Sonoma County Library
Third and East Streets
95404
(707) 545-0831

Stanford

Stanford University Libraries
Jonsson Library of Government Documents
94305
(415) 497-2727

Stanford University
Robert Crown Law Library
94305
(415) 497-2477

Stockton

**Public Library of Stockton and San Joaquin
County**
605 North El Dorado Street
95202
(209) 944-8221

Thousand Oaks

California Lutheran College Library
60 West Olsen Road
91360
(805) 492-2411, ext. 205

Torrance

Torrance Public Library
3301 Torrance Boulevard
90503
(213) 618-5959

Turlock

California State College Stanislaus Library
801 West Monte Vista Avenue
95380
(209) 667-3233

Vallejo

Solano County Library, John F. Kennedy Library
505 Santa Clara Street
94590
(707) 553-5354

Valencia

Valencia Regional Library
23743 Valencia Boulevard
91355
(805) 259-8942

Ventura

Ventura County Library Services Agency
651 East Main Street
93001
(805) 654-2616

Visalia
Tulare County Free Library
Documents Department
200 West Oak Street
93291
(209) 733-8440, ext. 32

Walnut

Mount San Antonio College Library
1100 North Grand Avenue
91789
(714) 594-5611, ext. 286

West Covina

West Covina Regional Library
1601 West Covina Parkway
91790
(213) 962-3451, ext. 16

Whittier

Whittier College
Wardman Library
13406 East Philadelphia Street
90608
(213) 693-0771, ext. 247

Canal Zone

Balboa Heights

Panama Canal Commission
Library Services Branch
APO Miami, Florida
34011
011-507 52-3502

Colorado

Alamosa

Adams State College
Learning Resources Center
81102
(303) 589-7781

Aurora

Aurora Public Library
14949 Alameda Drive
80012
(303) 695-7450

Boulder

University of Colorado at Boulder
Norlin Library
Government Publications
Campus Box 184
80309
(303) 492-8834
REGIONAL DEPOSITORY

Colorado Springs
Colorado College
Tutt Library
80903
(303) 473-2233, ext. 660

University of Colorado at Colorado Springs Library
Austin Bluffs Parkway
P.O. Box 7150
80933
(303) 593-3295

Denver
Auraria Library
Government Documents Department
Lawrence at Eleventh Street
80204
(303) 629-2741

Colorado State Library
Education Department
1362 Lincoln
80203
(303) 866-2172

Colorado Supreme Court Library
B-112 State Judicial Building
2 East Fourteenth Avenue
80203
(303) 861-1111, ext. 172

Denver Public Library
Government Publications Department
1357 Broadway
80203
REGIONAL DEPOSITORY

Department of the Interior
Bureau of Reclamation Library
D950
P.O. Box 25007
Denver Federal Center
Building 67
80225
(303) 234-3019

Regis College
Dayton Memorial Library
West 50th Avenue and Lowell Boulevard
80221
(303) 458-3552

U.S. Court of Appeals
Tenth Circuit Library
U.S. Court House
Room C-411
80294
(303) 837-3591

University of Denver
Penrose Library
Documents Department
University Park Campus
80208
(303) 753-2422

University of Denver College of Law
Westminster Law Library
1900 Olive Street LTLB
80220
(303) 871-6201

Fort Collins

Colorado State University Libraries
Documents Department
80523
(303) 491-5911, ext. 18

Golden

Colorado School of Mines
Arthur Lakes Library
Fourteenth and Illinois
80401
(303) 273-3695

Grand Junction

Mesa County Public Library
530 Grand Avenue
81501
(303) 243-4442

Greeley

University of Northern Colorado
James A. Michener Library
Government Publications Service
80639
(303) 351-2987

Gunnison

Western State College
Leslie J. Savage Library
81230
(303) 943-2860

La Junta

Otero Junior College
Wheeler Library
81050
(303) 384-4446, ext. 297

Lakewood
Jefferson County Public Library
Lakewood Library
10200 West 20th Ave.
80215
(303) 232-7833

Pueblo
Pueblo Library District
100 East Abriendo Avenue
81004
(303) 542-4636

University of Southern Colorado Library
2200 North Bonforte Boulevard
81001
(303) 549-2451

USAF Academy
U.S. Air Force Academy
Academy Library—DFSEL-D
80840
(303) 472-4774

Connecticut

Bridgeport
Bridgeport Public Library
Business & Technology Dept.
925 Broad Street
06604
(203) 576-7406

University of Bridgeport School of Law Library
Wahlstrom Library—7th Floor
126 Park Avenue
00601
(203) 576-4381

Danbury
Western Connecticut State University
Ruth A. Haas Library
181 White Street
06810
(203) 797-4076

Danielson
Quinebaug Valley Community College
Audrey P. Beck Library
Maple Street
06239
(203) 774-1160

Enfield
Enfield Central Library
104 Middle Road
06082
(203) 749-0766

Hartford

Connecticut State Library
231 Capitol Avenue
06106
(203) 566-4971
REGIONAL DEPOSITORY

Hartford Public Library
500 Main Street
06103
(213) 525-9121, ext. 657

Trinity College Library
300 Summit Street
06106
(203) 527-3151, ext. 395

University of Connecticut
School of Law Library
120 Sherman Street
06105
(203) 241-4615

Middletown

Wesleyan University
Olin Library
06457
(203) 347-9411, ext. 2140

Mystic

Mystic Seaport Museum, Incorporated
G. W. Blunt White Library
06355
(203) 572-0711, ext. 261

New Britain

Central Connecticut State University
Elihu Burritt Library
1615 Stanley Street
06050
(203) 827-7514

New Haven

Southern Connecticut State University
Hilton C. Buley Library
501 Crescent Street
06515
(203) 397-4370

Yale Law Library
P.O. Box 401A, Yale Station
127 Wall Street
06520
(203) 436-4669

Yale University

Seeley G. Mudd Library
38 Mansfield Street
P.O. Box 2491 Yale Station
06520
(203) 436-0176

New London

Connecticut College Library
Reference Department
06320
(203) 447-7622

U.S. Coast Guard Academy Library
Mohegan Avenue
06320
(203) 444-8540

Stamford

Ferguson Library
Stamford's Public Library
96 Broad Street
06901
(203) 964-1000, ext. 225

Storrs

University of Connecticut University Library U-56P
19 Fairfield Road
Government Documents Department
06268
(203) 486-2522

Waterbury

Post College
Traurig Library
800 Country Club Road
06708
(203) 755-0121, ext. 215

Silas Bronson Public Library
267 Grand Street
06702
(203) 574-8225

West Haven

University of New Haven
Peterson Library
300 Orange Avenue
06516
(203) 923-7189

Delaware

Dover

Delaware State College
William C. Jason Library
19901
(302) 736-5393, ext. 28

State Law Library in Kent County
Court House
19901
(302) 736-5467

Georgetown

Delaware Technical and Community College Library
P.O. Box 610
19947
(302) 856-9033

Sussex County Law Library
Court House
Box 486
19947
(302) 856-5483

Newark

University of Delaware Library
Government Documents & Maps Reference
Dept.
19717
(302) 451-2238

Wilmington

Delaware Law School Library
P.O. Box 7475
19803
(302) 478-5280, ext. 247

New Castle County Law Library
Public Building
19801
(302) 571-2437

District of Columbia

Washington

Administrative Conference of the United States Library
Suite 500
2120 L Street NW
20037
(202) 254-7065

Advisory Commission on Intergovernmental Relations Library
Suite 2000, Vanguard Building
1111 20th Street NW
20575
(202) 653-5034

American University
Washington College of Law Library
4400 Massachusetts Avenue NW
20016
(202) 686-2625

Antioch School of Law Library
1624 Crescent Place NW
20009
(202) 265-5219

Catholic University of America
Robert J. White Law Library
102 C. Leahy Hall
620 Michigan Avenue NE
20064
(202) 635-5155

Civil Aeronautics Board Library
1825 Connecticut Avenue NW
Room 912
20428
(202) 673-5101

Department of the Army Pentagon Library AN-RAL
Room 1A518 Pentagon
20310
(202) 697-4658

Department of Commerce Library
Commerce Building, Room H8060
Fourteenth and Constitution Avenue NW
20230
(202) 377-2805

Department of Energy, Energy Library
Room G-034 (MA-442)
20545
(301) 353-2855

Department of Health and Human Services Library
Room 1436 North Building
330 Independence Avenue SW
20201
(202) 472-6575

Department of Housing and Urban Development Library
Room 8233
451 Seventh Street SW
20410
(202) 755-6382

Department of the Interior Library
Natural Resources Library
Serials Section (G/E) 18th & C Streets NW
20240
(202) 343-5815

Department of Justice Main Library
Room 5400
Tenth Street and Constitution Avenue NW
20530
(202) 633-3775

Department of Labor Library
200 Constitution Avenue NW
20210
(202) 523-7670

Department of the Navy Library
Building 44
Washington Navy Yard
11th & M Streets SW
20374
(202) 433-4131

Department of State Library
FAIM/LR, Room 3239 N.S.
2201 C Street NW
20520
(202) 632-2053

Department of State Law Library
Office of Legal Advisor
Room 6422
20520
(202) 632-2628

Department of Transportation Main Library
400 Seventh Street SW
20590
(202) 426-2580

Department of Transportation, U.S. Coast Guard Law Library
M–493.11
Room 4407, Trans Point
2100 Second Street SW
20593
(202) 755-7610

Department of the Treasury Library
Room 5310
Main Treasury Building
Fifteenth Street and Pennsylvania Avenue NW
20220
(202) 566-2777

District of Columbia Court of Appeals Library
6th Level
500 Indiana Avenue NW
20001
(202) 638-5623

District of Columbia Public Library
Documents Department
901 G Street NW
20001
(202) 727-1117

Executive Office of the President, Office of Administration, Library & Information Service Division
Room G220 New Executive Office Building
726 Jackson Place NW
20503
(202) 395-3420

Federal Deposit Insurance Corporation Library
550 Seventeenth Street NW
20429
(202) 389-4314

Federal Election Commission Library
4th Floor
1325 K Street NW
20463
(202) 523-4178

Federal Energy Regulatory Commission Library
Room 8502
825 North Capitol Street NE
20426
(202) 357-5479

Federal Labor Relations Authority Law Library
500 C Street SW
Room 234
20424
(202) 382-0765

Federal Mine Safety & Health Review Commission Library
1730 K Street NW
20006
(202) 653-5459

Federal Reserve System
Board of Governors
Research Library
Twentieth Street and Constitution Avenue NW
20551
(202) 452-3334

Federal Reserve System
Law Library
Twentieth Street and Constitution Avenue NW
20551
(202) 452-3283

General Accounting Office Library
Room 6428
441 G Street NW
20548
(202) 275-2555

General Services Administration Library
BROL, Room 1033
Eighteenth and F Streets NW
20405
(202) 535-7788

Georgetown University Library
Government Documents Dept.
37th and O Streets NW
20057
(202) 625-4213

Georgetown University Law Center
Fred O. Dennis Law Library
600 New Jersey Avenue NW
20001
(202) 624-8033

George Washington University
Melvin Gelman Library
Serials Department
2130 H Street NW
20052
(202) 676-6455

George Washington University
National Law Center
Jacob Burns Law Library
Room 505
716 Twentieth Street NW
20052
(202) 676-6648

Library of Congress
Congressional Research Service
Library Service Division
10 First Street SE
20540
(202) 287-5700

Library of Congress
Serial and Government
Publications Division
Madison Building
1st & Independence Ave. SE
Room 133
20540
(202) 287-6116

Merit Systems Protection Board Library
1717 H Street NW
20419
(202) 254-3036

National Defense University Library
Fort Lesley J. McNair
Bldg. 61, Room 304
4th & P Streets SW
20319
(202) 693-8466

U.S. Court of Appeals
Judges' Library, Room 5518
U.S. Court House
Third & Constitution Ave. NW
20001
(202) 545-3401

U.S. Office of Personnel Management Library
Room 5L45
1900 E Street NW
20415
(202) 632-4434

U.S. Postal Service Library
475 L'Enfant Plaza SW
20260
(202) 245-4021

U.S. Senate Library
S-332, The Capitol
20510
(202) 224-7106

U.S. Supreme Court Library
1 First Street NE
20543
(202) 252-3187

University of the District of Columbia Library
Learning Resources Division
800 Mt. Vernon Place NW
20001
(202) 727-2500

Veterans' Administration
Central Office Library
142D1
810 Vermont Avenue NW
20420
(202) 389-5130

Florida

Boca Raton

Florida Atlantic University S. E. Wimberly Library
Documents Division
P.O. Box 3092
33431
(305) 393-3787

Clearwater

Clearwater Public Library
100 North Osceola Avenue
33515
(813) 462-6800

Coral Gables

University of Miami Library
Government Publications
P.O. Box 248214
33124
(305) 284-3155

Daytona Beach

Volusia County Library Center
City Island
32014
(904) 255-3765

De Land

Stetson University
duPont-Ball Library
421 North Boulevard
32720
(904) 734-4121, ext. 216

Fort Lauderdale

Broward County Main Library
Government Documents Dept.
100 South Andrews Ave.
33301
(305) 357-7439

Nova University, Center for Study of Law/Law Library
3100 S.W. 9th Avenue
33315
(305) 522-2300, ext. 115

Fort Pierce

Indian River Community College Library
3209 Virginia Avenue
33450
(305) 464-2000, ext. 347

Gainesville

University of Florida
College of Law Library
Legal Information Center
Southwest Second Ave. at 25th St.
(904) 392-0417

University of Florida Libraries
Documents Department
Library West
32611
(904) 392-0366
REGIONAL DEPOSITORY

Jacksonville

Haydon Burns Public Library
122 North Ocean Street
32202
(904) 633-3926

Jacksonville University

Swisher Library
University Boulevard North
32211
(904) 744-3950, ext. 263

University of North Florida Thomas G. Carpenter Library
4567 St. John's Bluff Rd. S
32216
(904) 646-2617

Lakeland

Lakeland Public Library
100 Lake Morton Drive
33801
(813) 686-2168

Leesburg

Lake-Sumter Community College Library
5900 S. Highway 44
32788
(904) 787-3747, ext. 33

Melbourne

Florida Institute of Technology Library
P.O. Box 1150
150 West University Blvd.
32901
(305) 723-3701, ext. 412

Miami

Florida International University Library
Tamiami Campus
Documents Section
33199

Miami-Dade Public Library
Documents Division
1 Biscayne Boulevard
33132
(305) 579-3555

North Miami

Florida International University
North Miami Campus Library
Documents Section
33181
(305) 940-5722

Opa Locka

Biscayne College Library
16400 Northwest 32nd Avenue
33054
(305) 625-6000, ext. 219

Orlando

University of Central Florida Library
Documents Department
32816
(305) 275-2563

Palatka

Saint Johns River Community College Library
5001 Saint Johns Avenue
32077
(904) 328-1571, ext. 54

Panama City

Bay County Public Library
25 West Government Street
32401
(904) 769-4131

Pensacola

University of West Florida
John C. Pace Library
32514
(904) 474-2410

Port Charlotte

Charlotte County Library System
801 Northwest Aaron Street
33952
(813) 625-6470

Saint Petersburg

Saint Petersburg Public Library
Reference Department
3745 Ninth Avenue North
33713
(813) 893-7724, ext. 33

Stetson University College of Law
Charles A. Dana Library
1401 61st Street South
33707
(813) 345-1335

Sarasota

Selby Public Library
1001 Boulevard of the Arts
33577
(813) 366-7303

Tallahassee

Florida Agricultural and Mechanical University
Coleman Learning Resources Center
P.O. Box 78-A
32307
(904) 599-3714

Florida State University
College of Law Library
32306
(904) 644-1004

Florida State University
Documents Dept./Strozier Library
32306
(904) 644-6061

Florida Supreme Court Library
Supreme Court Building
32301
(904) 488-8919

State Library of Florida
Documents Section
R. A. Gray Building
32301
(904) 487-2651, ext. 49

Tampa

Tampa-Hillsborough County Public Library
Documents Department
900 North Ashley Street
33602
(813) 223-8969

University of South Florida Library
4202 Fowler Avenue
33620
(813) 974-2726

University of Tampa
Merl Kelce Library
401 West Kennedy Boulevard
33606
(813) 253-8861, ext. 464

Winter Park

Rollins College
Mills Memorial Library
32789
(305) 646-2376

Georgia

Albany

Dougherty County Public Library
Carnegie Branch
215 North Jackson Street
31701
(912) 435-2145

Americus

Georgia Southwestern College
James Earl Carter Library
31709
(912) 928-1352

Athens

University of Georgia Libraries
Government Documents Dept.
30602
(404) 542-8949
REGIONAL DEPOSITORY

University of Georgia
School of Law Library
30602
(404) 542-1922

Atlanta

Atlanta Public Library
Government Documents
1 Margaret Mitchell Square
30303
(404) 688-4636, ext. 203

Atlanta University Center
Robert W. Woodruff Library
111 Chestnut Street SW
30314
(404) 223-5378, ext. 110

Emory University
School of Law Library
North Decatur & Clifton Rds.
30322
(404) 329-6797

Emory University
Woodruff Library
Documents Department
30322
(404) 329-6880

Georgia Institute of Technology
Price Gilbert Memorial Library
225 North Avenue NW
30332
(404) 894-4519

Georgia State Library
Capitol Hill Station
301 Judicial Building
30334
(404) 656-3468

Georgia State University
William Russell Pullen Library
100 Decatur Street SE
30303
(404) 658-2185

Georgia State University
College of Law Library
University Plaza
30303
(404) 658-2479

U.S. Court of Appeals
11th Circuit Library
56 Forsyth Street NW
30303
(404) 221-2510

Augusta

Augusta College
Reese Library
2500 Walton Way
30910
(404) 737-1748

Brunswick

Brunswick-Glynn County Regional Library
208 Gloucester Street
31523
(912) 264-7360

Carrollton

West Georgia College
Irvine Sullivan Ingram Library
Reference Department
30118
(404) 834-1370

Columbus

Columbus College
Simon Schwob Memorial Library
31993
(404) 568-2042, ext. 9

Dahlonega

North Georgia College
Stewart Library
30597
(404) 864-3391, ext. 226

Dalton

Dalton Junior College Library Resource Center
P.O. Box 2168
30720
(404) 278-3113, ext. 237

Decatur

DeKalb Community College
South Campus Learning Resources Center
3251 Panthersville Road
30034
(404) 243-3860, ext. 123

Macon

Mercer University
Stetson Memorial Library
1330 Edgemont Avenue
31207
(912) 744-2961

Mercer University
Walter F. George School of Law Library
1021 Georgia Avenue
31207
(912) 744-2665

Marietta

Kennesaw College Memorial Library
3455 Steve Frey Rd.
30061
(404) 429-2898

Milledgeville

Georgia College at Milledgeville
Ina Dillard Russell Library
231 West Hancock Street
31061
(912) 453-5350

Mount Berry

Berry College Memorial Library
30149
(404) 232-5374, ext. 2434

Savannah

Chatham-Effingham Liberty Regional Library
2002 Bull Street
31499
(912) 234-5127

Statesboro

Georgia Southern College Library
Government Documents
30460
(912) 681-5117

Valdosta

Valdosta State College Library
Patterson Street
31698
(912) 333-5868

Guam

Agana

Nieves M. Flores Memorial Library
P.O. Box 652
254 Martyr Street
96910
(671) 472-6417

Mangilao

University of Guam
Robert F. Kennedy Memorial Library
Federal Documents Dept.
U.O.G. Station
96913
(671) 734-2921, ext 389

Hawaii

Hilo

University of Hawaii at Hilo Library
Government Documents Department
1400 Kapiolani Street
96720
(808) 961-9525

Honolulu

Hawaii Medical Library Incorporated
1221 Punchbowl Street
96813
(808) 536-9302

Hawaii State Library
Federal Documents Section
478 South King Street
96813
(808) 548-2386

Municipal Reference & Records Center
City Hall Annex
558 South King Street
96813
(808) 523-4577

Supreme Court Law Library
Judiciary Bldg., Room 116
417 S. King Street
96813
(808) 548-7434

University of Hawaii Hamilton Library
Government Documents Collection
2550 The Mall
96822
(808) 948-8230
REGIONAL DEPOSITORY

University of Hawaii
William S. Richardson School of Law Library
2525 Dole Street
96822
(808) 948-7583

Laie

Brigham Young University
Hawaii Campus
Joseph F. Smith Library
55-220 Kulanui Street
96762
(808) 293-3850

Lihue

Kauai Regional Library
4344 Hardy Street
96766
(808) 245-3617

Pearl City

Leeward Community College Library
96-045 Ala Ike
96782
(808) 455-0378

Wailuku

Maui County Library
P.O. Box B
251 High Street
96793
(808) 244-3945

Idaho

Boise

Boise Public Library and Information Center
715 Capitol Boulevard
83702
(208) 384-4078

Boise State University Library
Government Documents
1910 University Drive
83725
(208) 385-1264

Idaho State Law Library
Supreme Court Building
451 West State Street
83720
(208) 334-3316, ext. 22

Idaho State Library
325 West State Street
83702
(208) 334-2150

Caldwell

College of Idaho
Terteling Library
2112 Cleveland
83605
(208) 459-5505

Moscow

University of Idaho
College of Law Library
83843
(208) 885-6521

University of Idaho Library
Documents Section
83843
(208) 885-6344
REGIONAL DEPOSITORY

Pocatello

Idaho State University Eli Oboler Library
Documents Division
Box 8089
83209
(208) 236-2940

Rexburg

Ricks College
David O. McKay Library
83440
(208) 356-2351

Twin Falls

College of Southern Idaho Library
315 Falls Avenue
P.O. Box 1238
83303
(208) 733-9554, ext. 238

Illinois

Bloomington

Illinois Wesleyan University Sheean Library
201 East University Street
61702
(309) 556-3175

Carbondale

Southern Illinois University at Carbondale
Morris Library
Documents Center
62901
(618) 536-2163

Southern Illinois University
School of Law Library
Technical Services Department
Documents Section
62901
(618) 536-7711, ext. 240

Carlinville
Blackburn College
Lumpkin Library
62626
(217) 854-3231, ext. 238

Carterville
Shawnee Library System
Greenbriar Road
62918
(618) 985-3711

Champaign
University of Illinois
Law Library
Documents Department
504 East Pennsylvania Avenue
61820
(217) 333-2914

Charleston
Eastern Illinois University
Booth Library
61920
(217) 581-6092

Chicago
Chicago Public Library
Government Publications Department
425 North Michigan Avenue
60611
(312) 269-3021

Chicago State University
Paul and Emily Douglas Library
95th Street at King Drive
60628
(312) 995-2284

DePaul University
Law Library
25 East Jackson Boulevard
60604
(312) 321-7710

Field Museum of Natural History Library
Roosevelt Road and Lake Shore Drive
60605
(312) 992-9410, ext. 281

Illinois Institute of Technology
Chicago-Kent College of Law Library
77 South Wacker Drive
60606
(312) 567-5968

Illinois Institute of Technology
Kemper Libary
Documents Department
3300 South Federal Street
60616
(312) 567-6844

John Marshall Law School Library
315 South Plymouth Court
60604
(312) 427-2737, ext. 484

Loyola University of Chicago
E. M. Cudahy Memorial Library
6525 North Sheridan Road
60626
(312) 274-3000, ext. 2646

Loyola University
School of Law Library
1 East Pearson Street
60611
(312) 670-2950

Northeastern Illinois University Library
Documents Department
5500 N. Saint Louis Avenue
60625
(312) 583-4050, ext. 8178

Northwestern University
School of Law Library
357 East Chicago Avenue
60611
(312) 649-7344

University of Chicago
Law Library
1121 East 60th Street
60637
(312) 962-9612

University of Chicago Library
Documents Section
1100 East 57th Street
60637
(312) 962-7874

University of Illinois at Chicago Library
Documents Department
P.O. Box 8198
801 South Morgan
60607
(312) 996-2738

William J. Campbell Library of the U.S. Courts
219 South Dearborn
Room 1448
60604
(312) 435-5660

Decatur

Decatur Public Library
247 East North Street
62523
(217) 428-6617, ext. 35

De Kalb

Northern Illinois University
Founders' Memorial Library
Government Publications
Department
60115
(815) 753-1932

Northern Illinois University
College of Law Library
Swen Parson Hall
60115
(815) 753-0505

Des Plaines

Oakton Community College Library
1600 East Golf Road
60016
(312) 635-1644

Edwardsville

Southern Illinois University
Lovejoy Memorial Library
62026
(618) 692-2606

Elsah

Principia College
Marshall Brooks Library
62028
(618) 374-2131, ext. 331

Evanston

Northwestern University Library
Government Publications Department
60201
(312) 492-5290

Freeport

Freeport Public Library
318 West Stephenson Street
61032
(815) 235-9606

Galesburg

Galesburg Public Library
40 East Simmons Street
61401
(309) 343-6118

Jacksonville

MacMurray College
Henry Pfeiffer Library
62650
(217) 245-6151, ext. 334

Kankakee

Olivet Nazarene College
Benner Library and Learning Resource Center
Box 592
60901
(815) 939-5355

Lake Forest

Lake Forest College
Donnelley Library
College & Sheridan Rds.
60045
(312) 234-3100, ext. 410

Lebanon

McKendree College
Holman Library
62254
(618) 537-4481, ext. 168

Lisle

Illinois Benedictine College
Theodore F. Lownik Library
5700 College Road
60532
(312) 968-7270, ext. 283

Macomb

Western Illinois University
Government Publications & Legal Reference
    Library
61455
(309) 298-2411, ext. 264

Moline

Black Hawk College
Learning Resources Center
6600 34th Avenue
61265
(309) 796-1311, ext. 282

Monmouth

Monmouth College
Hewes Library
700 West Broadway
61462
(309) 457-2031

Mount Carmel

Wabash Valley College
Bauer Media Center
2200 College Drive
62863
(618) 262-8641, ext. 225

Mount Prospect

Mount Prospect Public Library
Documents Department
Government Information Center
10 South Emerson Street
60056
(312) 253-4646

Normal

Illinois State University
Milner Library
Documents Department
School & College Streets
61761
(309) 438-7442

Oak Park

Oak Park Public Library
834 Lake Street
60301
(312) 383-8200

Oglesby

Illinois Valley Community College
Jacobs Memorial Library
Documents Department
R.R. No. 1
61348
(815) 224-2720, ext. 397

Palos Hills

Moraine Valley Community College Library
10900 South 88th Avenue
60465
(312) 974-4300, ext. 312

Park Forest South

Governors' State University Library
Documents Department
60466
(312) 534-5000, ext. 2232

Peoria

Bradley University
Cullom-Davis Library
61625
(309) 676-7611, ext. 530

Peoria Public Library
107 Northeast Monroe Street
61602
(309) 672-8844

River Forest

Rosary College Library
Rebecca Crown Library
7900 West Division Street
60305
(312) 366-2490, ext. 303

Rockford

Rockford Public Library
215 North Wyman Street
61101
(815) 965-6731, ext. 259

Romeoville

Lewis University Library
Route 53
60441
(815) 838-0500, ext. 300

Springfield

Illinois State Library
Government Documents
Centennial Building
62756
(217) 782-5012
REGIONAL DEPOSITORY

Streamwood

Poplar Creek Public Library
1405 South Park Blvd.
60103
(312) 837-6800

Urbana

University of Illinois
Documents Library
Room 200-D Library
1408 W. Gregory Drive
61801
(217) 333-1056

Wheaton

Wheaton College
Buswell Memorial Library
Government Documents
60187
(312) 260-5169

Woodstock

Woodstock Public Library
414 West Judd
60098
(815) 338-0542

Indiana

Anderson

Anderson College
Charles E. Wilson Library
46012
(317) 649-9071, ext. 2051

Anderson Public Library
32 West Tenth Street
46016
(317) 644-0938

Bloomington
Indiana University Library
Documents Department
47405
(812) 335-6924

Indiana University
Law Library
School of Law
47405
(812) 335-9666

Crawfordsville

Wabash College
Lilly Library
P.O. Box 352
47933
(317) 362-1400, ext. 215

Evansville

Evansville and Vanderburgh County Public Library
22 Southeast Fifth Street
44708
(812) 428-8218

Indiana State University at Evansville
Evansville Campus Library
Documents Department
8600
47712 (Designated 1969)
(812) 464-1907

Fort Wayne

Allen County Public Library
900 Webster Street, Box 2270
46802
(219) 424-7241, ext. 247

Indiana University-Purdue University at Fort Wayne
Helmke Library
2101 East Coliseum Boulevard
46805
(219) 482-5887

Franklin

Franklin College Library
Documents Department
46131
(317) 736-8441, ext. 257

Gary

Gary Public Library
220 West Fifth Avenue
46402
(219) 886-2484, ext. 37

Indiana University
Northwest Campus Library
Documents Department
3400 Broadway
46408
(219) 980-6608

Greencastle

De Pauw University
Roy O. West Library
Box 137
46135
(317) 658-4514

Hammond

Hammond Public Library
564 State Street
46320
(219) 931-5100, ext. 250

Hanover

Hanover College, Duggan Library
Box 287
47243
(812) 866-2151, ext. 338

Huntington

Huntington College
Loew Alumni Library
2303 College Avenue
46750
(219) 356-6000, ext. 159

Indianapolis

Butler University
Irwin Library
4600 Sunset Avenue
46208
(317) 283-9236

Indianapolis-Marion County Public Library
Newspaper & Periodical Division
P.O. Box 211
40 East Saint Clair Street
46206
(317) 269-1728

Indiana State Library
Serials Section
140 North Senate Avenue
(317) 232-3686
REGIONAL DEPOSITORY

Indiana Supreme Court
Law Library
State House Room 316
46204
(317) 232-2546

Indiana University
School of Law Library
735 West New York Street
46202
(317) 264-4028, ext. 25

Indiana University-Purdue University Library
815 W. Michigan Street
46202
(317) 264-8278

Kokomo

Indiana University at Kokomo
Learning Resource Center
Government Documents
2300 South Washington Street
46902
(317) 453-2000, ext. 237

Muncie

Ball State University Library
Government Publications Service
2000 University Avenue
47306
(317) 285-6195

Muncie Public Library
301 East Jackson Street
47305
(317) 747-8204

New Albany

Indiana University
Southeastern Campus Library
4201 Grant Line Road
47150
(812) 945-2731, ext. 368

Notre Dame

University of Notre Dame
Memorial Library
Document Center
46556
(219) 239-5268

Renssaelaer

Saint Joseph's College Library
Documents Department
P.O. Box 813
Highway 231 South
47978
(219) 866-7111, ext. 189

Richmond

Earlham College
Lilly Library
47374
(317) 962-6561, ext. 404

Morrison-Reeves Library
80 North Sixth Street
47374
(317) 996-8291, ext. 20

South Bend

Indiana University at South Bend Library
P.O. Box 7111
1700 Mishawaka Avenue
46634
(219) 237-4440

Terre Haute

Indiana State University
Cunningham Memorial Library
47809
(812) 232-6311, ext. 2772

Valparaiso

Valparaiso University Moellering Memorial Library
46383
(219) 464-5482

Valparaiso University
Law Library
Wesemann Hall
46383
(219) 464-5393

West Lafayette

Purdue University Libraries
Documents Department
47907
(317) 494-2837

Iowa

Ames

Iowa State University Library
Government Publications Department
50011
(515) 294-2834

Cedar Falls

University of Northern Iowa Library
Documents Collection
50613
(319) 273-6327

Council Bluffs

Free Public Library
200 Pearl Street
51501
(712) 323-7553

Iowa Western Community College
Herbert Hoover Library
2700 College Road
Box 4-C
51501
(712) 325-3247

Davenport

Davenport Public Library
321 Main Street
52801
(319) 326-7832

Des Moines

Drake University
Cowles Library
Government Publications Department
28th Street and University Avenue
50311
(515) 271-2814

Drake University
Law Library
27th & Carpenter
50311
(515) 271-3759

Public Library of Des Moines
Documents Department
100 Locust Street
50308
(515) 283-4259

State Library of Iowa
Documents Section
Historical Building
East 12th & Grand
50319
(515) 281-3384

Dubuque

Carnegie-Stout Public Library
Eleventh and Bluff Streets
52001
(319) 556-8270, ext. 25

Loras College
Wahlert Memorial Library
1450 Alta Vista
52001
(319) 588-7163

Fayette

Upper Iowa University
Henderson-Wilder Library
52142
(319) 425-3311, ext. 270

Grinnell

Grinnell College
Burling Library
Documents Department
P.O. Box 805
50112
(515) 236-2521

Iowa City

University of Iowa College of Law
Law Library
52242
(319) 353-5968, ext. 28

University of Iowa Libraries
Government Publications Department
52242
(319) 353-3318
REGIONAL DEPOSITORY

Lamoni
Graceland College
Frederick Madison
Smith Library
50140
(515) 784-5301

Mason City
North Iowa Area Community College Library
Government Documents
500 College Drive
50401
(515) 421-4326

Mount Vernon
Cornell College
Russell D. Cole Library
Government Documents
52314
(319) 895-8811

Orange City
Northwestern College
Ramaker Library
Government Documents Department
51041
(712) 737-4821, ext. 143

Sioux City
Sioux City Public Library
705 Sixth Street
51105
(712) 279-6179

Kansas

Atchison
Benedictine College Library
North Campus
Second and Division Streets
66002
(913) 367-5340, ext. 513

Baldwin City
Baker University
Collins Library
Documents Department
66006
(913) 594-6451, ext. 389

Colby
Colby Community College
H.F. Davis Memorial Library
1255 South Range
67701
(913) 462-3984, ext. 267

Emporia
Emporia State University
William Allen White Library
Government Documents Division
1200 Commercial
66801
(316) 343-1200, ext. 205

Hays
Fort Hays State University
Forsyth Library
Documents Department
600 Park Street
67601
(913) 628-4340

Hutchinson
Hutchinson Public Library
901 North Main Street
67501
(316) 663-5441

Fort Scott
Fort Scott Community College
Learning Resources Center Library
2108 South Horton
66701
(316) 223-2700, ext. 38

Lawrence
University of Kansas
Law Library
Green Hall
66045
(913) 864-3025

University of Kansas
Spencer Research Library
Documents Collection
66045
(913) 864-4662
REGIONAL DEPOSITORY

Manhattan

Kansas State University
Farrell Library
Documents Department
66506
(913) 532-6516, ext. 28

Pittsburg

Pittsburg State University
Leonard H. Axe Library
Government Documents
66762
(316) 231-7000, ext. 431

Salina

Kansas Wesleyan University
Memorial Library
Documents Department
100 East Claflin
67401
(913) 827-5541, ext. 298

Shawnee Mission

Johnson County Library
Documents Department
8700 West 63rd Street
Box 2901
66201
(913) 831-1550

Topeka

Kansas State Historical Society Library
120 West 10th Street
66612
(913) 296-4775

Kansas State Library
3rd Floor, Capitol Bldg.
66612
(913) 296-3296

Kansas Supreme Court Law Library
Kansas Judicial Center
301 West 10th Street
66612
(913) 296-3257

Washburn University of Topeka
Law Library
1700 College Avenue
66621
(913) 295-6688, ext. 628

Wichita

Wichita State University Ablah Library
Documents Department
Box 68
67208
(316) 689-3591

Kentucky

Ashland

Boyd County Public Library
1740 Central Avenue
41101
(606) 329-0090

Barbourville

Union College
Abigail E. Weeks
Memorial Library
40906
(606) 546-4151, ext. 242

Bowling Green

Western Kentucky University
Helm-Cravens Library
42101
(502) 745-3951, ext. 52

Crestview Hills

Thomas More College Library
41017
(606) 341-5800, ext. 60

Danville

Centre College
Grace Doherty Library
40422
(606) 236-5211, ext. 237

Frankfort

Kentucky Department of Libraries and Archives
State Library Services Division
Documents Section
300 Coffee Tree Road
P.O. Box 537
40601
(502) 875-7000

Kentucky State Law Library
Capitol Building Room 200
40601
(502) 564-4848

Kentucky State University
Blazer Library
40601
(502) 564-5852, ext. 8

Highland Heights

Northern Kentucky University
W. Frank Steely Library
41076
(606) 572-5683

Hopkinsville

Hopkinsville Community College Library
North Drive
42240
(502) 886-3921, ext. 122

Lexington

University of Kentucky Law Library
40506
(606) 257-8347

University of Kentucky Libraries
Government Publications Department
40506
(606) 257-3139
REGIONAL DEPOSITORY

Louisville

Louisville Free Public Library
Fourth and York Streets
40203
(502) 584-4154, ext. 379

University of Louisville
Ekstrom Library
Belknap Campus
Government Publications Department
40292
(502) 588-6760

University of Louisville
Law Library
Belknap Campus
40292
(502) 588-6392

Morehead

Morehead State University
Camden-Carroll Library
40351
(606) 783-2160

Murray

Murray State University
Waterfield Library
Government Documents Department
Fifteenth and Olive Streets
42071
(502) 762-4799

Owensboro

Kentucky-Wesleyan College Library Learning Center
3000 Frederica Street
42301
(502) 926-3111, ext. 115

Richmond

Eastern Kentucky University
John Grant Crabbe Library
40475
(606) 622-1791

Williamsburg

Cumberland College
Norma Perkins Hagan Memorial Library
821 Walnut Street
40769
(606) 549-2200

Louisiana

Baton Rouge

Louisiana State Library
760 Riverside North
P.O. Box 131
70821
(504) 342-4927

Louisiana State University Middleton Library
Government Documents Department
70803
(504) 388-2570
REGIONAL DEPOSITORY

Louisiana State University
Paul M. Hebert Law Center Library
70803
(504) 388-5770

Southern University Law School Library
Southern Branch Post Office
70813
(504) 771-4900, ext. 4

Southern University Library
Government Documents Department
Southern Branch Post Office
70813
(504) 771-4990, ext. 5

Eunice

Louisiana State University at Eunice
LeDoux Library
P.O. Box 1129
70535
(318) 457-7311, ext. 64

Hammond

Southeastern Louisiana University
Sims Memorial Library
P.O. Drawer 896
University Station
70402
(504) 549-2034

Lafayette

University of Southwestern Louisiana Library
Documents Division
P.O. 40199
East St. Mary Blvd.
70503
(318) 231-6030

Lake Charles

McNeese State University
Lether E. Frazar Memorial Library
70609
(318) 477-2520, ext. 515

Monroe

Northeast Louisiana University
Sandel Library
Government Publications
71209
(318) 342-3085

Natchitoches

Northwestern State University
Watson Memorial Library
71497
(318) 357-4574

New Orleans

Law Library of Louisiana
100 Supreme Court Building
Civic Center
70112
(504) 568-5705

Loyola University Library
Government Documents Department
6363 Saint Charles Avenue
70118
(504) 865-2158

Loyola University
Law Library
6363 St. Charles Avenue
70118
(504) 865-3373

New Orleans Public Library
Business & Science Division
219 Loyola Avenue
70140
(504) 596-2580

Our Lady of Holy Cross College Library
4123 Woodland Drive
70123
(504) 394-7744

Southern University in New Orleans
Leonard S. Washington Memorial Library
6400 Press Drive
70126
(504) 282-4401, ext. 224

Tulane University Law Library
70118
(504) 865-5994

Tulane University
Howard-Tilton Memorial Library
Documents Department
70118
(504) 865-5683

U.S. Court of Appeals
Fifth Circuit Library
Room 106
600 Camp Street
70130
(504) 589-6510

University of New Orleans Earl K. Long Library
Government Documents Division
Lake Front
70122
(504) 286-6547

Pineville

Louisiana College
Richard W. Norton Memorial Library
1140 College Drive
71359
(318) 487-7201

Ruston

Louisiana Technical University
Prescott Memorial Library
Documents Department
71272
(381) 257-4962
REGIONAL DEPOSITORY

Shreveport

Louisiana State University at Shreveport Library
Documents Department
8515 Youree Drive
71115
(318) 797-5382

Shreve Memorial Library
424 Texas Street
71101
(318) 226-5888

Thibodaux

Nicholls State University
Ellender Memorial Library
Federal Documents
70310
(504) 446-8111, ext. 489

Maine

Augusta

Maine Law and Legislative Reference Library
State House Station 43
04333
(207) 289-2648

Maine State Library
Cultural Building
State House Station #64
04333
(207) 289-3561

Bangor

Bangor Public Library
145 Harlow Street
04401
(207) 947-8336

Brunswick

Bowdoin College Library
Document Department
04011
(207) 725-8731, ext. 298

Castine

Maine Maritime Academy
Nutting Memorial Library
04420
(207) 326-4311, ext. 265

Lewiston

Bates College
George and Helen Ladd Library
Documents Department
04240
(207) 786-6271

Orono

University of Maine
Raymond H. Fogler Library
Tri-State Regional Documents Depository
04469
(207) 581-1680
REGIONAL DEPOSITORY

Portland

Portland Public Library
5 Monument Square
04101
(207) 773-4761, ext. 121

University of Maine School of Law
Garbrect Law Library
246 Deering Avenue
04102
(207) 780-4350

Presque Isle

University of Maine at Presque Isle
Library/Learning Resources Center
181 Main Street
04769
(207) 764-0311, ext. 293

Waterville

Colby College
Miller Library
04901
(207) 873-1131, ext. 2463

Maryland

Annapolis

Maryland State Law Library
Courts of Appeal Building
361 Rowe Boulevard
21401
(301) 269-3395

U.S. Naval Academy
Nimitz Library
Acquisitions Branch
Government Documents Unit
21402
(301) 267-2233

Baltimore

Enoch Pratt Free Library
Documents Department
400 Cathedral Street
21201
(301) 396-5426

Johns Hopkins University
Milton S. Eisenhower Library
Government Publications/Maps/Law Department
34th & Charles Street
21218
(301) 338-8360

Morgan State University
Soper Library
Hillen Road and Cold Spring Lane
21239
(301) 444-3451

University of Baltimore
Langsdale Library
1420 Maryland Avenue
21201
(301) 625-3460

University of Baltimore Law Library
1415 Maryland Avenue
21201
(301) 625-3452

University of Maryland School of Law
Marshall Law Library
20 N. Paca Street
21201
(301) 528-7400

U.S. Court of Appeals
4th Circuit Library
Room 801, U.S. Courthouse
101 West Lombard Street
21201
(301) 962-0997

Bel Air

Harford Community College Library
401 Thomas Run Road
21014
(301) 836-4147

Beltsville

Department of Agriculture
National Agricultural Library
Serials Section, Room 002
20705
(301) 344-4248

Bethesda

Department of Health and Human Services
National Library of Medicine
Documents Room A-58
8600 Rockville Pike
20209
(301) 496-5511

Uniformed Services University of Health Sciences, Learning Resource Center
School of Medicine
4301 Jones Bridge Road
20814
(202) 295-3357

Catonsville

University of Maryland, Baltimore County
Albin O. Kuhn Library & Gallery
21228
(301) 455-2232

Chestertown

Washington College
Clifton M. Miller Library
Washington Avenue
21620
(301) 778-2800, ext. 241

College Park

University of Maryland
McKeldin Library
Documents Division
20742
(301) 454-3034
REGIONAL DEPOSITORY

Cumberland

Allegany Community College Library
Willow Brook Road
21502
(301) 724-7700, ext. 294

Frostburg

Frostburg State College Library
Government Documents
21532
(301) 689-4423

Patuxent River

Patuxent River Central Library
U.S. Naval Air Station
NAS/NARC
Building 407
20670
(301) 863-3686

Rockville

Montgomery County Department of Public Libraries
99 Maryland Avenue
20850
(301) 279-1953

Salisbury

Salisbury State College
Blackwell Library
Camden Avenue
21801
(301) 543-6130

Towson

Goucher College
Julia Rogers Library
21204
(301) 337-6361

Towson State University
Cook Library
21204
(301) 321-3267

Westminster

Western Maryland College
Hoover Library
21157
(301) 848-7000, ext. 281

Massachusetts

Amherst

Amherst College Library
Documents Department
01002
(413) 542-2319

University of Massachusetts
University Library
Government Documents Collection
01003
(413) 545-2765

Boston

Boston Athenaeum Library
10½ Beacon Street
02108
(617) 227-0270, ext. 28

Boston Public Library
Documents Receipts
02117
(617) 536-5400, ext. 226
REGIONAL DEPOSITORY

Boston University School of Law
Pappas Law Library
765 Commonwealth Avenue
02215
(617) 353-4790

Northeastern University Dodge Library
360 Huntington Avenue
02115
(617) 437-2356

State Library of Massachusetts
Documents Department
341 State House
02133
(617) 727-6279

Suffolk University
Law Library
41 Temple Street
02114
(617) 723-4700, ext. 609

Supreme Judicial Court
Social Law Library
1200 Court House
02108
(617) 523-0018

U.S. Court of Appeals
First Circuit Library
1208 John W. McCormick
Post Office and Court House
02109
(617) 223-2891

Brookline

Public Library of Brookline
361 Washington Street
02146
(617) 734-0100

Cambridge

Harvard College Library
Document Receipts
02138
(617) 495-2479

Harvard Law School Library
Langdell Hall
02138
(617) 495-4516

Massachusetts Institute of Technology Libraries
Document Section
Room 14E 210
02139
(617) 253-7057

Chicopee

College of Our Lady of the Elms, Alumnae Library
291 Springfield Street
01013
(413) 598-8351, ext. 297

Lowell

University of Lowell
Alumni-Lydon Library
1 University Avenue
01854
(617) 452-5000, ext. 2383

Lynn

Lynn Public Library
5 North Common Street
01902
(617) 595-0567

Medford

Tufts University Library
Documents Department
02155
(617) 628-5000, ext. 2094

Milton

Curry College, Levin Library
1071 Blue Hill Avenue
02186
(617) 333-0500, ext. 170

New Bedford

New Bedford Free Public Library
613 Pleasant Street
02740
(617) 999-6291, ext. 24

Newton

Boston College
Thomas P. O'Neill Jr. Library
Government Documents
02167
(617) 552-3221

Newton Centre

Boston College Law School Library
885 Centre Street
02159
(617) 552-8605

North Dartmouth

Southeastern Massachusetts
University Library
Documents Section
P.O. Box 6
02747
(617) 999-8740

North Easton

Stonehill College
Cushing-Martin Library
02356
(617) 238-1081, ext. 328

Springfield

Springfield City Library
Documents Section
220 State Street
01103
(413) 739-3871, ext. 6

Western New England College
Law Library
1215 Wilbraham Road
01119
(413) 782-3111, ext. 458

Waltham

Brandeis University Library
Documents Collection
415 South Street
02254
(617) 647-2536

Waltham Public Library
735 Main Street
02154
(617) 893-1750

Wellesley

Wellesley College Library
Documents Collection
02181
(617) 235-0320, ext. 2100

Wenham

Gordon College
Winn Library
255 Grapevine Road
01984
(617) 927-2300, ext. 3345

Williamstown

Williams College Library
Documents Section
01267
(413) 597-2514

Worcester

American Antiquarian Society Library
185 Salisbury Street
01609
(617) 755-5221, ext. 21

University of Massachusetts Medical Center
Lamar Soutter Library
55 North Lake Avenue
01605
(617) 856-2369

Worcester Public Library
Salem Square
01608
(617) 799-1655

Michigan

Albion

Albion College
Stockwell Memorial Library
602 East Cass Street
49224
(517) 629-5511, ext. 384

Allendale

Grand Valley State College
Zumberge Library
College Landing
49401
(616) 895-3252

Alma

Alma College Library
Documents Collection
614 West Superior
48801
(517) 463-7227

Ann Arbor

University of Michigan
Harlan Hatcher Graduate Library
Documents Center
48109
(313) 764-0410

University of Michigan
Law Library
Legal Research Bldg.
801 Monroe
48109
(313) 764-6151

Benton Harbor

Benton Harbor Public Library
213 E. Wall St.
49022
(616) 926-6139

Bloomfield Hills

Cranbrook Institute of Science Library
Documents Department
500 Lone Pine Road
P.O. Box 801
48013
(313) 645-3255

Dearborn

Henry Ford Centennial Library
16301 Michigan Avenue
48126
(313) 943-2337

Henry Ford Community College Library
5101 Evergreen Road
48128
(313) 271-0551, ext. 377

Detroit

Detroit College of Law Library
130 East Elizabeth Street
48201
(313) 965-0150, ext. 20

Detroit Public Library
5201 Woodward Avenue
48202
(313) 833-1409
REGIONAL DEPOSITORY

Marygrove College Library
8425 West McNichols Road
48221
(313) 862-8000, ext. 212

Mercy College of Detroit Library
8200 West Outer Drive
48219
(313) 592-6181

University of Detroit Library
4001 West McNichols Road
48221
(313) 927-1071

University of Detroit
School of Law Library
651 East Jefferson Avenue
48226
(313) 961-5444, ext. 239

Wayne State University
G. Flint Purdy Library
Documents Section
5265 Cass Avenue
48202
(313) 577-4042

Wayne State University
Arthur Neef Law Library
Documents Department
468 West Ferry Mall
84202
(313) 577-3925

Dowagiac

Southwestern Michigan College
Matthews Library
Cherry Grove Road
49047
(616) 782-5113, ext. 27

East Lansing

Michigan State University
Documents Library
48824
(517) 353-8707

Farmington Hills

Oakland Community College
Martin L. King Learning Resources Center
Orchard Ridge Campus
48018
(313) 471-7736

Flint

Flint Public Library
1026 East Kearsley Street
48502
(313) 232-7111, ext. 254

University of Michigan-Flint Library
Documents Unit
48502
(313) 762-3418

Grand Rapids

Calvin College & Seminary Library
Government Documents Collection
3207 Burton Street SE
49506
(616) 957-6312

Grand Rapids Public Library
Library Plaza N.E.
49503
(616) 456-4411

Houghton

Michigan Technological University Library
Documents Department
49931
(906) 487-2506

Jackson

Jackson District Library
244 West Michigan Avenue
49201
(517) 788-4316

Kalamazoo

Kalamazoo Public Library
315 South Rose Street
49007
(616) 342-9837, ext. 43

Western Michigan University
Dwight B. Waldo Library
Government Documents
Department
49008
(616) 383-4952, ext. 24

Lansing

Library of Michigan
Government Documents Unit
P.O. Box 30007
735 E. Michigan Avenue
48909
(517) 373-0640
REGIONAL DEPOSITORY

Thomas M. Cooley Law School Library
U.S. Documents Collection
P.O. Box 13038
217 South Capitol Avenue
48901
(517) 371-5140, ext. 222

Livonia

Schoolcraft College Library
18600 Haggerty Road
48152
(313) 591-6400, ext. 412

Madison Heights

Madison Heights Public Library
240 West Thirteen Mile Road
48071
(313) 588-7763

Marquette

Northern Michigan University
Olson Library
Documents & Map Department
49855
(906) 227-2112

Monroe

Monroe County Library System
Documents Division
3700 South Custer Road
48161
(313) 241-5277

Mount Clemens

Macomb County Library
16480 Hall Road
48044
(313) 286-6660, ext. 27

Mount Pleasant

Central Michigan University Library
Government Documents
Department
48859
(517) 774-3414

Muskegon

Hackley Public Library
316 West Webster Avenue
49440
(616) 722-7276

Olivet

Olivet College Library
Documents Section
49076
(616) 749-7608

Petoskey

North Central Michigan College Library
1515 Howard Street
49770
(616) 347-3973, ext. 240

Port Huron

Saint Clair County Library
210 McMorran Boulevard
48060
(313) 987-7323, ext. 8

Rochester

Oakland University
Kresge Library
48063
(313) 377-2476

Royal Oak

Royal Oak Public Library
222 East Eleven Mile Road
48068
(313) 541-1470

Saginaw

Hoyt Public Library
505 Janes Street
48605
(517) 755-0904

Sault Ste. Marie

Lake Superior State College
Kenneth Shouldice Library
49783
(906) 635-2403

Traverse City

Northwestern Michigan College
Mark Osterlin Library
1701 East Front Street
49684
(616) 922-1065

University Center

Delta College Learning Resources Center
Mackinaw and Delta Roads
(517) 686-9560

Warren

Warren Public Library
Arthur J. Miller Branch
4700 East Thirteen Mile Road
48092
(313) 751-5377

Wayne

Wayne Oakland Library Federation
33030 Van Born Road
48184
(313) 326-8910, ext. 26

Ypsilanti

Eastern Michigan University Library
Documents Department
48197
(313) 487-2280

Micronesia

Community College of Micronesia Library
P.O. Box 159, Kolonia
Ponape, E. Caroline Islands
Federated States of Micronesia
96941

Minnesota

Bemidji

Bemidji State University
A. C. Clark Library
Documents Department
56601
(218) 755-2955

Blaine

Anoka County Library
707 Highway 10
55434
(612) 784-1100

Collegeville

Saint John's University
Alcuin Library
56321
(612) 363-2120

Cottage Grove

Washington County Library-Park Grove
7520-80th Street South
55016
(612) 459-2040

Duluth

Duluth Public Library
520 West Superior Street
55802
(218) 723-3805

University of Minnesota
Library and Learning Resources Service
55812
(218) 726-8102

Eagan

Dakota County Eagan Library
1340 Wescott Road
55123
(612) 452-9600

Edina

Southdale-Hennepin Area Library
Government Documents
7001 York Avenue South
55435
(612) 830-4977

Mankato

Mankato State University Library
Box 19
Government Publications
56001
(507) 389-6201

Minneapolis

Minneapolis Public Library
Government Documents Department
300 Nicollet Mall
55401
(612) 372-6535

University of Minnesota
Law School Library
Documents Department
229 Nineteenth Avenue South
55455
(612) 376-2381

University of Minnesota
Wilson Library
Government Publications
309 Nineteenth Avenue South
55455
(612) 373-7813
REGIONAL DEPOSITORY

Moorhead

Moorhead State University
Livingston Lord Library
Documents Department
56560
(218) 236-2922

Morris

University of Minnesota, Morris, Rodney A. Briggs Library
Documents Department
56267
(612) 589-2211, ext. 6474

Northfield

Carleton College Library
Documents Department
55057
(507) 663-4266

Saint Olaf College
Rolvaag Memorial Library
55057
(507) 663-3226

Saint Cloud

Saint Cloud State University, Learning Resources Center
Documents Department
56301
(612) 255-2084, ext. 15

Saint Paul

Hamline University
School of Law Library
1536 Hewitt Avenue
55104
(612) 641-2349

Minnesota Historical Society Library
690 Cedar Street
55101
(612) 296-9987

Minnesota State Law Library
117 University Avenue
55155
(612) 296-2775

Saint Paul Public Library
Government Publications
90 West 4th Street
55102
(612) 292-6178

University of Minnesota
Saint Paul Campus Library
1984 Buford Avenue
55108
(612) 373-0903

William Mitchell College of Law Library
875 Summit Avenue
55105
(612) 227-9171, ext. 135

Saint Peter

Gustavus Adolphus College Library
Government Documents
56082
(507) 931-7569

Willmar

Pioneerland Library
410 West Fifth Street
56201
(612) 235-3162

Winona

Winona State University
Maxwell Library
Johnson & Sanborn Streets
55987
(507) 457-5148

Mississippi

Cleveland

Delta State University
W. B. Roberts Library
38732
(601) 843-2483

Columbus

Mississippi University for Women
John Clayton Fant Memorial Library
39701
(601) 329-4750, ext. 340

Hattiesburg

University of Southern Mississippi
Joseph A. Cook Memorial Library
Southern Station Box 5053
34901
(601) 266-4252

Jackson

Jackson State University
Henry Thomas Sampson Library
Station C
39217
(601) 968-2123

Millsaps College
Millsaps-Wilson Library
39210
(601) 354-5201, ext. 249

Mississippi College
School of Law Library
151 East Griffith Street
39201
(601) 944-1970

Mississippi Library Commission
1221 Ellis Avenue
P.O. Box 10700
39209
(601) 359-1036, ext. 171

Mississippi State Law Library
P.O. Box 1040
450 High Street
39205
(601) 359-3672

Lorman

Alcorn State University Library
P.O. Box 539
39096
(601) 877-6358

Mississippi State

Mississippi State University
Mitchell Memorial Library
Documents Department
Box 5408
39762
(601) 325-3060

University

University of Mississippi
J. D. Williams Library
Documents Department
38677
(601) 232-5857
REGIONAL DEPOSITORY

University of Mississippi
James O. Eastland Law Library
38677
(601) 232-7361, ext. 316

Missouri

Cape Girardeau

Southeast Missouri State University
Kent Library
Government Documents Dept.
63701
(314) 651-2231

Columbia

University of Missouri at Columbia Library
Government Documents
65201
(314) 882-6733

University of Missouri—Columbia
Law Library
Tate Hall
65211
(314) 882-4597

Fayette

Central Methodist College
George M. Smiley Library
65248
(816) 248-8391, ext. 261

Fulton

Westminster College
Reeves Library
65251
(314) 642-3361, ext. 244

Jefferson City

Lincoln University
Inman E. Page Library
P.O. Box 29
65101
(314) 751-2325, ext. 328

Missouri State Library
308 East High Street
65101
(314) 751-4552

Missouri Supreme Court Library
Supreme Court Building
65101
(314) 751-2636

Joplin

Missouri Southern State College Library
Newman and Duquesne Roads
65801
(417) 624-8100, ext. 261

Kansas City

Kansas City Public Library
Documents Division
311 East Twelfth Street
64106
(816) 221-2685, ext. 150

Rockhurst College
Greenlease Library
5225 Troost Avenue
64110
(816) 926-4143

University of Missouri at Kansas City
General Library
Government Documents Department
5100 Rockhill Road
64110
(816) 276-1536

University of Missouri—Kansas City
Leon E. Bloch Law Library
52nd & Oak Streets
64110
(816) 276-1650

Kirksville

Northeast Missouri State University
Pickler Memorial Library
63501
(816) 785-4534

Liberty

William Jewell College
Charles F. Curry Library
64068
(816) 781-3806, ext. 293

Maryville

Northwest Missouri State University
B.D. Owens Library
64468
(816) 562-1192

Rolla

University of Missouri—Rolla
Curtis Laws Wilson Library
Documents Section
65401
(314) 341-4007

Saint Charles

Lindenwood College
Margaret Leggat Butler Library
63301
(314) 946-6912, ext. 329

Saint Joseph

Saint Joseph Public Library
Tenth and Felix Streets
64501
(816) 232-8151

Saint Louis

Maryville College Library
Documents Department
13550 Conway Road
63141
(314) 576-9496

Saint Louis County Library
1640 South Lindbergh Blvd.
63131
(314) 994-3300

Saint Louis Public Library
1301 Oliver Street
63103
(314) 241-2288, ext. 375

Saint Louis University Law Library
3700 Lindell Boulevard
63108
(314) 658-2756

Saint Louis University
Pius XII Memorial Library
3655 West Pine Boulevard
63108
(314) 658-3105

U.S. Court of Appeals
Eighth Circuit Library
Room 503
1114 Market Street
63101
(314) 425-4930

University of Missouri at Saint Louis
Thomas Jefferson Library
8001 Natural Bridge Road
63121
(314) 553-5061

Washington University
John M. Olin Library
Government Publications Unit
Lindel & Skinker Blvds.
Campus Box 1061
63130
(314) 889-5428

Washington University Law Library
Campus Box 1120
Mudd Building
63130
(314) 889-6484

Springfield

Drury College, Walker Library
65802
(417) 865-8731, ext. 337

Southwest Missouri State University Library
901 South National
65804
(417) 836-5104

Warrensburg

Central Missouri State University
Ward Edwards Library
Government Documents
64093
(816) 429-4149

Montana

Billings

Eastern Montana College Library
Documents Department
1500 North 30th Street
59101
(406) 657-1664

Bozeman

Montana State University Renne Library
Documents Department
59717
(406) 994-3430

Butte

Montana College of Mineral Science and Technology Library
Documents Division
Park Street
59701
(406) 496-4286

Havre

Northern Montana College Library
59501
(406) 265-7821, ext. 3306

Helena

Carroll College Library
Capitol Hill
59625
(406) 442-3450, ext. 342

Montana Historical Society Library
225 North Roberts Street
59620
(406) 444-2681

Montana State Library
1515 East 6th Avenue
59620
(406) 444-3004

State Law Library of Montana
Justice Building
215 North Sanders
59620
(406) 444-3660

Missoula

University of Montana Maurene & Mike Mansfield Library
Documents Division
59812
(406) 243-6700
REGIONAL DEPOSITORY

Nebraska

Blair

Dana College
Dana-LIFE Library
68008
(402) 426-4101, ext. 227

Crete

Doane College Perkins Library
68333
(402) 826-2161, ext. 224

Fremont

Midland Lutheran College Luther Library
Documents Department
68025
(402) 721-5480

Kearney

Kearney State College
Calvin T. Ryan Library
68849
(308) 234-8542

Lincoln

Nebraska Library Commission
Federal Documents Dept.
1420 P Street
68508
(402) 471-2045
REGIONAL DEPOSITORY, in cooperation
with University of Nebraska at Lincoln

Nebraska State Library
Third Floor South
State Capitol Building
68509
(402) 471-3189

University of Nebraska—Lincoln
College of Law Library
East Campus
68583
(402) 472-3547

University of Nebraska—Lincoln
D. L. Love Memorial Library
Documents Department
68588
(402) 472-2562

Omaha

Creighton University
Reinert/Alumni Library
2500 California Street
68178
(402) 280-2227

Creighton University Law Library
2500 California Street
68178
(402) 280-2243

Omaha Public Library
W. Dale Clark Library
Business, Science, Technology Department
215 South Fifteenth Street
68102
(402) 444-4817

University of Nebraska at Omaha
  University Library
  Documents Department
  60th & Dodge Street
  68182
  (402) 554-3202

Scottsbluff

Scottsbluff Public Library
  1809 Third Avenue
  69361
  (308) 632-0050

Wayne

Wayne State College
  U.S. Conn Library
  Documents Division
  68787
  (402) 375-2200, ext. 419

Nevada

Carson City

Nevada State Library
  Capitol Complex
  401 North Carson Street
  89710
  (702) 885-5160

Nevada Supreme Court Library
  Supreme Court Building
  Capitol Complex
  89710
  (702) 885-5140

Las Vegas

Clark County Library District
  1726 East Charleston
  89104
  (702) 382-3493

University of Nevada at Las Vegas
  James Dickinson Library
  4505 Maryland Parkway
  89154
  (702) 739-3512

Reno

National Judicial College
  Law Library
  Judicial College Building
  University of Nevada, Reno
  89557
  (702) 784-6039

Nevada Historical Society Library
  1650 North Virginia Street
  89503
  (702) 789-0190

University of Nevada—Reno Library
  Government Publications Dept.
  89557
  (702) 784-6579
  REGIONAL DEPOSITORY

Washoe County Library
  Government Documents Department
  P.O. Box 2151
  301 South Center Street
  89505
  (702) 785-4010

New Hampshire

Concord

Franklin Pierce Law Center Library
  2 White Street
  03301
  (603) 228-1542, ext. 44

New Hampshire State Library
  20 Park Street
  03301
  (603) 271-2239

Durham

University of New Hampshire Library
  03824
  (603) 862-1777

Hanover

Dartmouth College Library
  03755
  (603) 646-3616

Henniker

New England College Danforth Library
  P.O. Box 638
  03242
  (603) 428-2344

Manchester

Manchester City Library
  405 Pine Street
  03104
  (603) 625-6485

New Hampshire Collge
  H. A. B. Shapiro Memorial Library
  2500 North River Road
  03104
  (603) 668-2211, ext. 223

Saint Anselm's College
Geisel Library
Saint Anselm Drive
03102
(603) 669-1030, ext. 240

Nashua
Nashua Public Library
2 Court Street
03060
(603) 883-4141

New Jersey

Bayonne
Bayonne Public Library
697 Avenue C
07002
(201) 858-6980

Bloomfield
Bloomfield Public Library
90 Broad Street
07003
(201) 429-9292, ext. 39

Bridgeton
Cumberland County Library
800 East Commerce Street
08302
(609) 455-0080

Camden
Rutgers University
Camden Library
300 North Fourth Street
08102
(609) 757-6037

Rutgers University
School of Law Library
5th & Penn Streets
08102
(609) 757-6171

Convent Station
College of Saint Elizabeth
Mahoney Library
07961
(201) 539-1600, ext. 367

East Brunswick
East Brunswick Public Library
2 Jean Walling Civic Center
08816
(201) 390-6767

East Orange
East Orange Public Library
Government Documents
21 South Arlington Avenue
07018
(201) 266-5612

Elizabeth
Elizabeth Free Public Library
11 South Broad Street
07202
(201) 354-6060, ext. 851

Glassboro
Glassboro State College
Savitz Learning Resource Center
08028
(609) 863-6317

Hackensack
Johnson Public Library
275 Moore Street
07601
(201) 343-4169, ext. 15

Irvington
Irvington Public Library
Civic Square
07111
(201) 372-6400

Jersey City
Jersey City Public Library
Documents Department
472 Jersey Avenue
07302
(201) 547-4517

Jersey City State College
Forrest A. Irwin Library
Documents Section
2039 Kennedy Boulevard
07305
(201) 547-3518

Lawrenceville
Rider College, Franklin F. Moore Library
2083 Lawrenceville Road
P.O. Box 6400
08648
(609) 896-5115

Madison

Drew University Library
36 Madison Avenue
07940
(201) 377-3000, ext. 588

Mahwah

Ramapo College Library
5050 Ramapo Valley Road
P.O. Box 542
07430
(201) 825-2800, ext. 275

Mount Holly

Burlington County Library
Woodland Road
08060
(609) 267-9660

New Brunswick

New Brunswick Free Public Library
60 Livingstone Avenue
08901
(201) 745-5175

Rutgers University Alexander Library
Government Documents Dept
College Avenue
08903
(201) 932-7014

Newark

Newark Public Library
U.S. Documents Division
5 Washington Street
P.O. Box 630
07101
(201) 733-7812
REGIONAL DEPOSITORY

Rutgers—The State University of New Jersey
John Cotton Dana Library
185 University Avenue
07102
(201) 648-5911

Rutgers University Law School Library
15 Washington Street
07102
(201) 648-5966

Seton Hall University Law Library
1111 Raymond Boulevard
07102
(201) 642-8766

Passaic

Passaic Public Library
195 Gregory Avenue
07055
(201) 779-0474

Pemberton

Burlington County College Library
Pemberton-Browns Mills Road
08068
(609) 894-9311, ext. 482

Phillipsburg

Phillipsburg Free Public Library
200 Frost Avenue
08865
(201) 454-3712

Plainfield

Plainfield Public Library
Eighth Street at Park Avenue
07060
(201) 757-1111, ext. 24

Pomona

Stockton State College Library
08240
(609) 652-1776, ext. 266

Princeton

Princeton University Library
Documents Division
08544
(609) 452-3178

Randolph

County College of Morris Sherman H. Masten Learning Resource Center
Rt. 10 & Center Grove Road
07869
(201) 361-5000, ext. 478

Rutherford

Fairleigh Dickinson University
Messler Library
Documents Department
207 Montross Avenue
07070
(201) 460-5071

Shrewsbury

Monmouth County Library
Eastern Branch
New Jersey Highway 35
07001
(201) 842-5995

South Orange

Seton Hall University
McLaughlin Library
Government Documents Dept.
07079
(201) 761-9438

Teaneck

Fairleigh Dickinson University
Teaneck/Hackensack Campus Weiner Library
1000 River Road
07666
(201) 692-2290

Toms River

Ocean County College
Learning Resources Center
College Drive
08753
(201) 255-4000, ext. 385

Trenton

New Jersey State Library
Government Reference Office
CN 520
185 W. State Street
08625
(609) 292-4282

Trenton Free Public Library
P.O. Box 2448
120 Academy Street
08608
(609) 392-7188

Union

Kean College of New Jersey
Nancy Thompson Library
P.O. Box 411
Morris Avenue
07083
(201) 527-2112

Upper Montclair

Montclair State College
Harry A. Sprague Library
Government Documents Section
07043
(201) 893-7145

Wayne

Wayne Public Library
475 Valley Road
07470
(201) 694-4272, ext. 29

West Long Branch

Monmouth College
Guggenheim Memorial Library
07764
(201) 222-6600, ext. 251

Woodbridge

Woodbridge Public Library
George Frederick Plaza
07095
(201) 634-4450, ext. 24

New Mexico

Albuquerque

University of New Mexico
Medical Center Library
North Campus
87131
(505) 277-6216

University of New Mexico
School of Law Library
1117 Stanford Drive, N.E.
87131
(505) 277-5131

University of New Mexico
General Library
Government Publications & Maps Department
87131
(505) 277-7180
REGIONAL DEPOSITORY

Hobbs

New Mexico Junior College
Pannell Library
Lovington Highway
88240
(505) 392-4510, ext. 308

Las Cruces

New Mexico State University Library
Documents Division
P.O. Box 3475
88003
(505) 646-3737

Las Vegas

New Mexico Highlands University
Donnelly Library
87701
(505) 425-7511, ext. 331

Portales

Eastern New Mexico University
Golden Library
88130
(505) 562-2650

Santa Fe

New Mexico State Library
325 Don Gaspar Avenue
87503
(505) 827-3800
REGIONAL DEPOSITORY

New Mexico Supreme Court Law Library
P.O. Drawer L
87501
(505) 827-2515

Silver City

Western New Mexico University
Miller Library
88061
(505) 538-6350

Socorro

New Mexico Institute of Mining & Technology
Martin Speare Memorial Library
Government Documents Dept.
Campus Station
87801
(505) 835-5615

New York

Albany

Albany Law School Library
80 New Scotland Avenue
12208
(518) 445-2340

New York State Library
Documents Control
6th Floor, Cultural Education Center, Empire
State Plaza
12230
(518) 474-5563
REGIONAL DEPOSITORY

State University of New York at Albany
University Library
Government Publications Dept.
1400 Washington Ave.
12222
(518) 457-3347

Auburn

Seymour Library
176 Genesee Street
13021
(315) 252-2571

Bayside

CUNY Law School at Queens College
CUNY Law Library
200-01 42nd Avenue
11361
(718) 357-7584

Queensborough Community College Library
222-05 56th Avenue
11364
(718) 631-6225

Binghamton

State University of New York at Binghamton
Glenn G. Bartle Library
Acquisitions Department
Documents Section
Vestal Parkway, East
13901
(607) 798-2368

Brockport

State University of New York at Brockport
Drake Memorial Library
14420
(716) 395-2277

Bronx

Fordham University Library
Public Documents Section
10458
(212) 579-2504

Herbert H. Lehman College Library
Documents Division
Bedford Park Boulevard West
10468
(212) 960-8580

New York Public Library
Mott Haven Branch
321 East 140th Street
10454
(212) 340-0888

State University of New York
Maritime College
Stephen B. Luce Library
Fort Schuyler
10465
(212) 409-7200, ext. 233

Bronxville

Sarah Lawrence College Library
Glen Washington Road
10708
(914) 337-0700, ext. 474

Brooklyn

Brooklyn College Library
Documents Division
Bedford Avenue and Avenue H
11210
(718) 780-5332

Brooklyn Law School Library
250 Joralemon Street
11201
(718) 780-7974

Brooklyn Public Library
Documents: Room 108-D
Grand Army Plaza
11238
(718) 780-7731

Polytechnic Institute of New York
Spicer Library
333 Jay Street
11201
(718) 643-2273

Pratt Institute Library
11205
(718) 636-3686

State University of New York
Downstate Medical Center Library
450 Clarkson Avenue
Box 14
11203
(718) 270-2357

Buffalo

Buffalo and Erie County Public Library
Documents Division
Lafayette Square
14203
(716) 856-7525, ext. 237

State University of New York at Buffalo
Charles B. Sears Law Library
Documents Department
O'Brian Hall, Amherst Campus
14260
(716) 636-2084

State University of New York at Buffalo
Lockwood Memorial Library
Government Documents Department
Amherst Campus
14260
(716) 636-2821

Canton

Saint Lawrence University
Owen D. Young Library
13617
(315) 379-5477

Cheektowaga

Cheektowaga Public Library
Reinstein Memorial Branch
2580 Harlem Road
14225
(716) 892-8089

Corning

Corning Community Center
Arthur A. Houghton Jr. Library
14830
(607) 962-9251

Cortland

State University of New York College at Cortland
Memorial Library
Document Section
13045
(607) 753-2525, ext. 6

Delhi

State University Agricultural and Technical College Library
Documents Department
Main Street, Route 10
13753
(607) 746-4107

Douglaston

Cathedral College Library
7200 Douglaston Parkway
11362
(718) 631-4600, ext. 213

East Islip

East Islip Public Library
381 East Main Street
11730
(516) 286-1600, ext. 76

Elmira

Elmira College
Gannett Tripp Learning Center
14901
(607) 734-3911, ext. 287

Farmingdale

State University of New York at Farmingdale
Library
Melville Road
11735
(516) 420-2420

Flushing

Queens College
Paul Klapper Library
Documents Department
65-30 Kissena Blvd.
11367
(718) 520-7483

Garden City

Adelphi University
Swirbul Library
Documents Department
South Avenue
11530
(516) 663-1036

Geneseo

State University of New York at Geneseo
Milne Library
Documents Department
11454
(716) 245-5593

Greenvale

Long Island University
B. Davis Schwartz Memorial Library
C. W. Post Center
11548
(516) 299-2842

Hamilton

Colgate University, Everett Needham Case
Library
Reference Department
13346
(315) 824-1000, ext. 302

Hempstead

Hofstra University Library
Documents Department
11550
(516) 560-5972

Hofstra University
School of Law Library
11550
(516) 560-5905

Ithaca

Cornell University Library
Serials Department
14853
(607) 256-5118

Cornell Law Library
Myron Taylor Hall
14853
(607) 256-7236

New York State College of Agriculture and Human
Ecology
Albert R. Mann Library
Acquisitions Division
Cornell University
14853
(607) 256-3241

Jamaica

Queens Borough Public Library
Documents Department
89-11 Merrick Boulevard
11432
(718) 990-0769

Saint John's University Library
Grand Central and Utopia Parkway
11439
(718) 990-6161, ext. 6725

Saint John's University
School of Law Library
Grand Central and Utopia Parkway
11439
(718) 990-6161, ext. 6649

Kings Point

U.S. Merchant Marine Academy
Schuyler Otis Bland Library
Steamboat Road
11024
(516) 482-8200, ext. 505

Long Island City

Fiorello H. LaGuardia Community College Library
31-10 Thomson Avenue
11101
(212) 626-5519

Mount Vernon

Mount Vernon Public Library
Reference Department
28 South First Avenue
10550
(914) 668-1840

New Paltz

State University College at New Paltz
Sojourner Truth Library
Government Documents Dept.
12561
(914) 257-2252

New York City

Cardozo Law School Library
Brookdale Center
7th Floor, 55 Fifth Avenue
10003
(212) 790-0467

City University of New York
City College Library
West 138th Street & Convent Avenue
10031
(212) 690-4292

College of Insurance Library
123 William Street
10038
(212) 962-4111, ext. 230

Columbia University Libraries
Documents Service Center
420 West 118th Street, Room 327
10027
(212) 280-5002

Columbia University
School of Law Library
435 West 116th Street
10027
(212) 280-3743

Cooper Union for the Advancement of Science and Arts Library
41 Cooper Square
10003
(212) 254-6300, ext. 360

Medical Library Center of New York
Technical Services
5 East 102nd Street
10029
(212) 427-1630

New York Law Institute Library
120 Broadway
10271
(212) 732-8720

New York Law School Library
57 Worth Street
Government Documents
10013
(212) 789-0281

New York Public Library
Astor Branch
476 Fifth Avenue
10018
(212) 930-0586

New York Public Library
Lenox Branch
476 Fifth Avenue
10018
(212) 930-0586

New York University Law Library
40 Washington Square South
10012
(212) 598-3040

New York University, Elmer Holmes Bobst Library
Documents Department, 7th Floor
70 Washington Square South
10012
(212) 598-7515

U.S. Court of Appeals
Second Circuit Library
Room 2501, U.S. Court House
Foley Square
10007
(212) 791-1052

Yeshiva University
Pollack Library
500 West 185th Street
10033
(212) 960-5378

Newburgh

Newburgh Free Library
124 Grand Street
12550
(914) 561-1836, ext. 22

Niagara Falls

Niagara Falls Public Library
1425 Main Street
14305
(716) 278-8113

Oakdale

Dowling College Library
Government Documents
Idle Hour Boulevard
11769
(516) 589-6100, ext. 216

Oneonta

State University College at Oneonta
James M. Milne Library
13820
(607) 431-2725

Oswego

State University College at Oswego
Penfield Library
Documents Center
13126
(315) 341-3122

Plattsburgh

State University College at Plattsburgh
Benjamin F. Feinberg Library
Government Documents Collection
12901
(518) 564-3180

Potsdam

Clarkston College of Technology
Harriet Call Burnap Memorial Library
Educational Resources Center
13676
(315) 268-2292

State University College at Potsdam
Frederick W. Crumb Memorial Library
Pierrepont Avenue
13676
(315) 267-2477

Poughkeepsie

Vassar College Library
12601
(914) 452-7000, ext. 2131

Purchase

State University of New York, College of Purchase Library
10577
(914) 253-5096

Rochester

Rochester Public Library
115 South Avenue
14604
(716) 428-7343

University of Rochester Rush Rhees Library
Documents Section
River Campus Station
14627
(716) 275-4484

Saint Bonaventure

Saint Bonaventure University
Friedsam Memorial Library
14778
(716) 375-2323 or 4

Saratoga Springs

Skidmore College Library
Documents Department
12866
(518) 584-5000, ext. 642

Schenectady

Union College
Schaffer Library
12308
(518) 370-6281

Southampton

Southampton College Library
Rt. 27, Montauk Highway
11968
(516) 283-4000, ext. 151

Staten Island

Wagner College
Horrmann Library
631 Howard Avenue
10301
(718) 390-3401

Stony Brook

State University of New York at Stony Brook
Main Library
Documents Section
11794
(516) 246-5976

Syracuse

Onondaga County Public Library
Government Documents Section
355 Montgomery Street
13202
(315) 473-4491

Syracuse University Library
Documents Division
222 Waverly Ave.
13210
(315) 423-2093

Syracuse University
William C. Ruger Law Library
E. I. White Hall
13210
(315) 423-2527

Troy

Troy Public Library
100 Second Street
12180
(518) 274-7071

Uniondale

Nassau Library System
Documents Collection
900 Jerusalem Avenue
11553
(516) 292-8920, ext. 260

Utica

Utica Public Library
303 Genesee Street
13501
(315) 735-2279, ext. 26

SUNY College of Technology Library
Documents Section
811 Court Street
13502
(315) 792-3426

West Point

U.S. Military Academy Cadet Library
Documents Department
10996
(914) 968-2230

White Plains

Pace University
Law School Library
78 North Broadway
10603
(914) 681-4272

Yonkers

Yonkers Public Library
Getty Square Branch
Information Services
7 Main Street
10701
(914) 337-1500, ext. 60

Yorktown Heights

Mercy College Library
Yorktown Branch Campus
2651 Strang Boulevard
10598
(914) 245-6100, ext. 18

North Carolina

Asheville

University of North Carolina at Asheville
D. Hiden Ramsey Library
One University Heights
28804
(704) 258-6545

Boiling Springs

Gardner-Webb College
Dover Memorial Library
Documents Department
P.O. Box 836
Highway 150
28017
(704) 434-2361, ext. 301

Boone

Appalachian State University Library
Government Documents
28608
(704) 262-2186, ext. 220

Buies Creek

Campbell University
Carrie Rich Memorial Library
27506
(919) 893-4111, ext. 238

Chapel Hill

University of North Carolina at Chapel Hill
Wilson Library
BA/SS Division-Documents
27514
(919) 962-1151
REGIONAL DEPOSITORY

University of North Carolina Law Library
Van Hecke-Wettach Building,
064-A
27514
(919) 962-1321

Charlotte

Public Library of Charlotte and Mecklenburg County
310 North Tryon Street
28202
(704) 374-2540

Queens College
Everett Library
1900 Selwyn Avenue
28274
(704) 332-7121, ext. 278

University of North Carolina at Charlotte
Atkins Library
Documents Department
UNCC Station
28223
(704) 597-2243

Cullowhee

Western Carolina University
Hunter Library
Documents Division
28723
(704) 227-7252

Davidson

Davidson College Library
28036
(919) 892-2000, ext. 331

Durham

Duke University
School of Law Library
Documents Department
27706
(919) 684-2847

Duke University
William R. Perkins Library
Documents Department
27706
(919) 684-2380 or 684-5435

North Carolina Central University
Law Library
P.O. Box 3557
27702
(919) 683-6244

North Carolina Central University
James E. Shepard Memorial Library
27707
(919) 683-6097

Elon College

Elon College
Iris Holt McEwen Library
Box 187
27244
(919) 584-2338

Fayetteville

Fayetteville State University
Charles W. Chesnutt Library
28301
(919) 486-1233

Greensboro

North Carolina Agricultural and Technical State University
F. D. Bluford Library
1600 East Market Street
27411
(919) 379-7617

University of North Carolina at Greensboro
Walter Clinton Jackson Library
Documents Division
27412
(919) 379-5251

Greenville

East Carolina University, J.Y. Joyner Library
Documents Department
27834
(919) 757-6533

Laurinburg

Saint Andrews Presbyterian College
DeTamble Library
28352
(919) 276-3652, ext. 289

Lexington

Davidson County Public Library
220 South Main Street
27292
(704) 246-2520

Mount Olive

Mount Olive College
Moye Library
28365
(919) 658-2502, ext. 25

Murfreesboro

Chowan College
Whitaker Library
Jones Drive
27855
(919) 398-4101, ext. 241

Pembroke

Pembroke State University
Mary H. Livermore Library
Documents Department
28372
(919) 521-4214, ext. 212

Raleigh

Department of Cultural Resources
Division of State Library
Documents Branch
109 East Jones Street
27611
(919) 733-3343

North Carolina State University
D. H. Hill Library
P.O. Box 5007
27650
(919) 737-3280

North Carolina Supreme Court Library
500 Justice Building
2 East Morgan Street
27601
(919) 733-3425

Wake County Public Library
104 Fayetteville Street
27601
(919) 755-6092

Rocky Mount

North Carolina Wesleyan College Library
Documents Department
College Station
27801
(919) 442-7121, ext. 283

Salisbury

Catawba College Library
Documents Department
2300 West Innes Street
28144
(704) 637-4448, ext. 6

Wilmington

University of North Carolina at Wilmington
William M. Randall Library
601 South College Road
28403
(919) 791-4330, ext. 2760

Wilson

Atlantic Christian College
Hackney Library
Lee Street
27893
(919) 237-3161, ext. 330

Winston-Salem

Forsyth County Public Library
660 West Fifth Street
27101
(919) 727-2220

Wake Forest University
Z. Smith Reynolds Library
Box 7777, Reynolds Station
27109
(919) 761-5473

North Dakota

Bismarck

North Dakota State Library
Liberty Memorial Building
Capitol Grounds
58505
(701) 224-4656

North Dakota Supreme Court Law Library
Second Floor, Capitol Building
58505
(701) 224-2229

State Historical Society of North Dakota
State Archives & Historical Research Library
Heritage Center
58505
(701) 224-2668

Veterans' Memorial Public Library
520 Avenue A East
58501
(701) 222-6410

Dickinson

Dickinson State College
Stoxen Library
58601
(701) 227-2135

Fargo

Fargo Public Library
102 Third Street North
58102
(701) 241-1492

North Dakota State University Library
Government Documents Department
58105
(701) 237-7008
REGIONAL DEPOSITORY, in cooperation
with University of North Dakota, Chester
Fritz Library

Grand Forks

University of North Dakota
Chester Fritz Library
58202
(701) 777-4629

Minot

Minot State College
Memorial Library
58701
(701) 857-3200

Valley City

Valley City State College
58072
(701) 845-7276

Ohio

Ada

Ohio Northern University
J. P. Taggart Law Library
45810
(419) 772-2251

Akron

Akron-Summit County Public Library
55 South Main Street
44326
(216) 762-7621, ext. 463

University of Akron
Bierce Library
Government Documents
44325
(216) 375-7494

University of Akron
School of Law Library
C. Blake McDowell Law Center
44325
(216) 375-6350

Alliance

Mount Union College Library
Documents Department
1972 Clark Avenue
44601
(216) 821-5320, ext. 260

Ashland

Ashland College Library
Documents Department
44805
(419) 289-5181

Athens

Ohio University
Alden Library
Government Documents Department
45701
(614) 594-6063

Batavia

University of Cincinnati at Batavia
Clermont General and Technical College Library
725 College Drive
45103
(513) 732-2990, ext. 13

Bluffton

Bluffton College, Musselman Library
280 West College Avenue
45817
(419) 358-8015, ext. 272

Bowling Green

Bowling Green State University
Jerome Library
Government Documents Department
43403
(419) 372-2142

Canton

Malone College
Everett L. Cattell Library
515 25th Street N.W.
44709
(216) 489-0800, ext. 487

Chardon

Geauga County Public Library
110 East Park Street
44024
(216) 285-7601

Cincinnati

Public Library of Cincinnati and Hamilton County
800 Vine Street
45202
(513) 369-6934

University of Cincinnati
Central Library
Documents Department
45221
(513) 475-5009

University of Cincinnati
College of Law
Marx Law Library, ML 142
45221
(513) 475-3016

Cleveland

Case Western Reserve University
Freiberger Library
11161 East Boulevard
44106
(216) 368-6512

Case Western Reserve University
School of Law Library
11075 East Boulevard
44106
(216) 368-2792

Cleveland Public Library
Documents Collection
325 Superior Avenue
44114
(216) 623-2870

Cleveland State University
Cleveland-Marshall College of Law, Joseph W.
Bartunek III Law Library
44115
(216) 687-2250

Cleveland State University Library
1860 East 22nd Street
44115
(216) 687-2490

Municipal Reference Library
City Hall, Room 100
601 Lakeside Avenue
44114
(216) 664-2656

Cleveland Heights

Cleveland Heights—University Heights Public Library
2345 Lee Road
44118
(216) 932-3600, ext. 31

Columbus

Capital University Law School Library
665 South High Street
43215
(614) 445-8634, ext. 58

Capital University Library
Documents Department
2199 East Main Street
43209
(614) 236-6436

Ohio State University Libraries
Documents Division
1858 Neil Avenue Mall
43210
(614) 422-1232

Ohio Supreme Court Law Library
30 E. Broad Street, 4th Floor
43215
(614) 466-2362

Public Library of Columbus and Franklin County
General Reference Division
96 South Grant Avenue
43215
(614) 222-7180

State Library of Ohio
Documents Section
65 South Front Street
43215
(614) 462-7051
REGIONAL DEPOSITORY

Dayton

Dayton and Montgomery County Public Library
215 East Third Street
45402
(513) 224-1651, ext. 278

University of Dayton
Roesch Library
300 College Park Avenue
45469
(513) 229-4221, ext. 10

Wright State University Library
Government Documents Dept.
45435
(513) 873-2533

Delaware

Ohio Wesleyan University
L. A. Beeghly Library
University Avenue
43015
(614) 369-4431, ext. 315

Elyria

Elyria Public Library
320 Washington Avenue
44035
(216) 323-5747

Findlay

Findlay College
Shafer Library
1000 North Main Street
45840
(419) 422-8313, ext. 330

Gambier

Kenyon College Library
Documents Department
43022
(614) 427-2244, ext. 2187

Granville

Denison University Libraries, William H. Doane Library
Documents Department
43023
(614) 587-0810, ext. 512

Hiram

Hiram College
Teachout-Price Memorial Library
P.O. Box 98
44234
(216) 569-5358

Kent

Kent State University Libraries
Documents Department
44242
(216) 672-2388

Marietta

Marietta College
Dawes Memorial Library
45750
(614) 374-4757

Marion

Marion Public Library
Federal Documents Librarian
445 East Church Street
43302
(614) 387-0992

Middletown

Miami University—Middletown
Gardner-Harvey Library
4200 East University Boulevard
45042
(513) 424-4444, ext. 293

New Concord

Muskingum College Library
43762
(614) 826-8152

Oberlin

Oberlin College Library
44074
(216) 775-8285, ext. 216

Oxford

Miami University Libraries
King Library
Documents Department
45056
(513) 529-3841

Portsmouth

Portsmouth Public Library
1220 Gallia Street
45662
(614) 354-5688

Rio Grande

Rio Grande College and Community College
Jeannette Albiez Davis Library
45674
(614) 245-5353, ext. 322

Springfield

Warder Public Library
P.O. Box 1080
137 East High Street
45501
(513) 323-8616

Steubenville

University of Steubenville
Starvaggi Memorial Library
43952
(614) 283-3771, ext. 208

Public Library of Steubenville and Jefferson County
407 South Fourth Street
43952
(614) 282-9782

Tiffin

Heidelberg College
Beeghly Library
44883
(419) 448-2104

Toledo

Toledo-Lucas County Public Library
Social Science Department
325 Michigan Street
43624
(419) 255-7055, ext. 221

University of Toledo
College of Law Library
2801 West Bancroft Street
43606
(419) 537-2875

University of Toledo Library
Documents Department
2801 West Bancroft Street
43606
(419) 537-2171

University Heights

John Carroll University
Grasselli Library
North Park & Miramar Blvds.
44118
(216) 491-4234

Westerville

Otterbein College
Courtright Memorial Library
138 West Main Street
43081
(614) 890-3000, ext. 115

Wooster

College of Wooster
Andrews Library
Government Publications Department
44691
(216) 263-2279

Youngstown

Public Library of Youngstown and Mahoning County
305 Wick Avenue
44503
(216) 744-8636, ext. 51

Youngstown State University
William F. Maag Library
Government Documents Department
410 Wick Avenue
44555
(216) 742-3126

Oklahoma

Ada

East Central Oklahoma State University
Linscheid Library
74820
(405) 332-8000, ext. 371

Alva

Northwestern Oklahoma State University
J. W. Martin Library
73717
(405) 327-1700, ext. 219

Bethany

Bethany Nazarene College
R. T. Williams Learning Resources Center
4115 North College
73008
(405) 789-6400, ext. 276

Durant

Southeastern Oklahoma State University
Henry G. Bennett Memorial Library
74701
(405) 924-0121, ext. 245

Edmond

Central State University Library
Government Documents
73034
(405) 341-2980, ext. 494

Enid

Public Library of Enid and Garfield County
120 West Maine
P.O. Box 8002
73702
(405) 234-6313

Langston

Langston University
G. Lamar Harrison Library
73050
(405) 466-2231

Muskogee

Muskogee Public Library
801 West Okmulgee Avenue
74401
(918) 682-6657, ext. 43

Norman

University of Oklahoma Libraries
Bizzell Memorial Library
Government Documents Collection
Room 440
401 West Brooks
73019
(405) 325-3141

University of Oklahoma
Law Library
300 Timberdell Road
73019
(405) 325-4311, ext. 11

Oklahoma City

Metropolitan Library System
Main Library
131 Dean A. McGee Avenue
73102
(405) 631-1149

Oklahoma City University Library
2501 North Blackwelder
73105
(405) 521-5073

Oklahoma Department of Libraries
Government Documents
200 NE 18th Street
73105
(405) 521-2502
REGIONAL DEPOSITORY

Shawnee

Oklahoma Baptist University Library
74801
(405) 275-2850, ext. 2255

Stillwater

Oklahoma State University Library
Documents Department
74078
(405) 624-6546
REGIONAL DEPOSITORY

Tahlequah

Northeastern Oklahoma State University
John Vaughan Library
Government Documents Department
74464
(918) 456-5511, ext. 304

Tulsa

Tulsa City-County Library System
400 Civic Center
74103
(918) 592-7977

University of Tulsa College of Law Library
3120 East Fourth Place
74104
(918) 592-6000, ext. 2405

University of Tulsa
McFarlin Library
600 South College
74104
(918) 592-6000, ext. 2874

Weatherford

Southwestern Oklahoma State University
Al Harris Library
Documents Department
73096
(405) 772-6611, ext. 5310

Oregon

Ashland

Southern Oregon State College Library
Documents
1250 Siskiyou Boulevard
97520
(503) 482-6445

Corvallis

Oregon State University Library
Documents Division
97331
(503) 764-2761

Eugene

University of Oregon Law Library
11th & Kincaid
97403
(503) 686-3088

University of Oregon Library
Documents Section
97403
(503) 686-3070

Forest Grove

Pacific University
Harvey W. Scott Memorial Library
2043 College Way
97116
(503) 357-6151, ext. 231

Klamath Falls

Oregon Institute of Technology Library
Ortech Branch P.O.
97601
(503) 882-6321, ext. 182

La Grande

Eastern Oregon College
Walter M. Pierce Library
97850
(503) 963-1546

McMinnville

Linfield College
Northup Library
97128
(503) 472-4121, ext. 261

Monmouth

Western Oregon State College Library
345 Monmouth Avenue
97361
(503) 838-1220, ext. 418

Pendleton

Blue Mountain Community College Library
2411 NW Carden
97801
(503) 276-1260, ext. 214

Portland

Lewis and Clark College
Aubrey R. Watzek Library
615 SW. Palatine Hill Road
97219
(503) 293-2765

Library Association of Portland
Order Department
801 SW. Tenth Avenue
97205
(503) 223-7201

Northwestern School of Law
Lewis and Clark College
Paul L. Boley Law Library
10015 SW. Terwilliger Blvd.
97219
(503) 244-1181, ext. 688

Portland State University Library
P.O. Box 1151
97207
(503) 229-3673
REGIONAL DEPOSITORY

Reed College Library
3203 SE. Woodstock
97202
(503) 771-1112, ext. 338

U.S. Department of Energy Bonneville Power Administration Library
P.O. Box 3621
97208
(503) 230-4160

Salem

Oregon State Library
State Library Building
97310
(503) 378-4368

Oregon Supreme Court Law Library
Supreme Court Bldg.
97310
(503) 378-6030

Willamette University
College of Law Library
Ferry and Winter Streets
97301
(503) 370-6387

Willamette University
Main Library
900 State Street
97301
(503) 370-6312

Pennsylvania

Allentown

Muhlenberg College
Haas Library
18104
(215) 433-3191, ext. 764

Altoona

Altoona Area Public Library
1600 Fifth Avenue
16602
(814) 946-0417, ext. 28

Bethel Park

Bethel Park Public Library
5100 W. Library Avenue
15102
(412) 835-2207

Bethlehem

Lehigh University Libraries
Linderman Library No. 30
18015
(215) 861-3053

Blue Bell

Montgomery County Community College
Learning Resources Center
340 DeKalb Pike
19422
(215) 641-6594

Bradford

University of Pittsburgh at Bradford
Bradford Campus Library
Campus Drive
16701
(814) 362-3801, ext. 126

Carlisle

Dickinson College
Boyd Lee Spahr Library
Government Documents
West High Street
17013
(717) 245-1602

Dickinson School of Law
Sheeley-Lee Law Library
150 South College Street
17013
(717) 243-4611, ext. 225

Cheyney

Cheyney University
Leslie Pinckney Hill Library
19319
(215) 399-2208

Collegeville

Ursinus College
Myrin Library
Main Street
19426
(215) 489-4111, ext. 291

Coraopolis

Robert Morris College Library
Narrows Run Road
15108
(412) 262-8255

Doylestown

Bucks County Free Library
Center County Branch
50 North Main Street
18901
(215) 348-9081

East Stroudsburg

East Stroudsburg University
Kemp Library
18301
(717) 424-3150

Erie

Erie County Library System
3 South Perry Square
Box 1631
16501
(814) 452-2333, ext. 33

Greenville

Thiel College
Langenheim Memorial Library
16125
(412) 588-7700, ext. 234

Harrisburg

State Library of Pennsylvania
Government Publications Section
Box 1601
Walnut Street & Commonwealth Avenue
17105
(717) 787-3752
REGIONAL DEPOSITORY

Haverford

Haverford College
Magill Library
19041
(215) 896-1168

Hazleton

Hazleton Area Public Library
Church and Maple Streets
18201
(717) 454-2961

Indiana

Indiana University of Pennsylvania
Rhodes R. Stabley Library
15701
(412) 357-3002

Johnstown

Cambria County Library System
Glosser Memorial Library Building
248 Main Street
15901
(814) 536-5131

Lancaster

Franklin and Marshall College
Shadek-Fackenthal Library
P.O. Box 3003
17604
(717) 291-4217

Lewisburg

Bucknell University
Ellen Clarke Bertrand Library
17837
(717) 524-1462, ext. 29

Mansfield

Mansfield University Library
Government Documents Department
16933
(717) 662-4257

Meadville

Allegheny College
Lawrence Lee Pelletier Library
North Main Street
16335
(814) 724-3769

Millersville

Millersville University
Helen A. Ganser Library
17551
(717) 872-3617

Monessen

Monessen Public Library
326 Donner Avenue
15062
(412) 684-4750

New Castle

New Castle Public Library
207 East North Street
16101
(412) 658-6659, ext. 24

Newtown

Bucks County Community College Library
Swamp Road
18940
(215) 968-8010

Norristown

Montgomery County—Norristown Public Library
Swede and Elm Streets
19401
(215) 277-3355

Philadelphia

Drexel University Library
Government Documents Section
32d and Chestnut Streets
19104
(215) 895-2782

Free Library of Philadelphia
Government Publications Department
1901 Vine Street
19103
(215) 686-5329

Saint Joseph's University
Drexel Library
5600 City Avenue
19131
(215) 879-7558

Temple University
Paley Library
Documents Unit
13th & Berks Mall
19122
(215) 787-8260

Temple University Law Library
1715 North Broad Street
19122
(215) 787-7891

Thomas Jefferson University
Scott Memorial Library
Eleventh and Walnut Streets
19107
(215) 928-8406

U.S. Court of Appeals Third Circuit Library
22409 U.S. Court House
19106
(215) 597-2009

University of Pennsylvania
Biddle Law Library
3400 Chestnut Street
19104
(215) 898-7056

University of Pennsylvania Library
3420 Walnut Street
19104
(215) 898-7563

Pittsburgh

Allegheny County Law Library
921 City-County Building
15219
(412) 355-5353

Carnegie Library of Pittsburgh
Government Documents Department
4400 Forbes Avenue
15213
(412) 622-3175

Carnegie Library of Pittsburgh
Allegheny Regional Branch
Allegheny Square
15212
(412) 321-0389, ext. 27

Duquesne University Law Library
900 Locust Street
15282
(412) 434-6293

La Roche College
John J. Wright Library
9000 Babcock Boulevard
15237
(412) 367-9300, ext. 168

U.S. Department of Interior
Bureau of Mines Library
4800 Forbes Avenue
15213
(412) 621-4500, ext. 345

University of Pittsburgh
Hillman Library

Documents Office
G-8
15260
(412) 624-4449

University of Pittsburgh
Law Library
409 Law Building
3900 Forbes Avenue
15260
(412) 624-6213

Pottsville

Pottsville Free Public Library
Government Publications Section
Third and Market Streets
17901
(717) 622-8880

Reading

Reading Public Library
Fifth and Franklin Streets
19602
(215) 374-4548

Scranton

Scranton Public Library
Albright Memorial Building
North Washington and Vine Streets
18503
(717) 961-2451, ext. 24

Shippensburg

Shippensburg University
Ezra Lehman Memorial Library
Documents Department
17257
(717) 532-1634

Slippery Rock

Slippery Rock University
Bailey Library
Documents Department
16057
(412) 794-7242

Swarthmore

Swarthmore College Library
Documents Collection
19081
(215) 447-7503

University Park

Pennsylvania State University Libraries
Pattee Library C-207
16802
(814) 865-4861, ext. 233

Villanova

Villanova University Law School
Pulling Law Library
19085
(215) 645-7028

Warren

Warren Library Association
Warren Public Library
205 Market Street
16365
(814) 723-4650, ext. 26

Washington

Washington and Jefferson College
U. Grant Miller Library
15301
(412) 222-4400, ext. 271

Waynesburg

Waynesburg College Library
93 Locust Avenue
15370
(412) 627-8191, ext. 278

West Chester

West Chester University
Francis Harvey Green Library
Documents Department
19383
(215) 436-2869

Wilkes-Barre

King's College
D. Leonard Corgan Library
14 West Jackson Street
18711
(717) 826-5900, ext. 648

Williamsport

Lycoming College Library
Documents Department
Academy Street
17701
(717) 326-1951, ext. 301

York

York College of Pennsylvania
Schmidt Library
321 Country Club Road
17405
(717) 846-7788, ext. 356

Youngwood

Westmoreland County Community College
Learning Resources Center
Armbrust Road
15697
(412) 925-4101

Puerto Rico

Mayaguez

University of Puerto Rico
Mayaguez Campus Library
Documents & Maps Collection
College Station
00708
(809) 832-4040, ext. 3459

Ponce

Catholic University of Puerto Rico
Encarnacion Valdes Library
Las Americas Avenue
00731
(809) 844-4150, ext. 220

Catholic University of Puerto Rico
School of Law Library
Las Americas Avenue
00731
(809) 844-4150, ext. 215

Rio Piedras

University of Puerto Rico
General Library
Documents Section
00931
(809) 764-0000, ext. 3514

Rhode Island

Kingston
University of Rhode Island Library
Government Publications Office
02881
(401) 792-4610

Newport

U.S. Naval War College Library
Documents Department
02841
(401) 841-4345

Providence
Brown University
John D. Rockefeller Jr. Library
Documents Department
Prospect Street
02912
(401) 863-2522

Providence College
Phillips Memorial Library
River Avenue at Eaton Street
02918
(401) 865-2242

Providence Public Library
150 Empire Street
02903
(401) 521-7722, ext. 205

Rhode Island College
James P. Adams Library
600 Mount Pleasant Avenue
02908
(401) 456-9604

Rhode Island State Law Library
Providence County Courthouse
250 Benefit Street
02903
(401) 277-3275

Rhode Island State Library
State House
02903
(401) 277-2473

Warwick
Warwick Public Library
600 Sandy Lane
02886
(401) 739-5440

Westerly
Westerly Public Library
Broad Street
02891
(401) 596-2877, ext. 5

Woonsocket
Woonsocket Harris Public Library
Documents Department
303 Clinton Street
02895
(401) 769-9046

South Carolina

Charleston

Baptist College at Charleston
L. Mendel Rivers Library
Box 10087
29411
(803) 797-4312

The Citadel
Daniel Library
Serials & Documents Dept.
29409
(803) 792-5116

College of Charleston
Robert Scott Small Library
Collection Development Dept.
29424
(803) 792-5530

Clemson

Clemson University Cooper Library
Documents Department
29631
(803) 656-3024, ext. 21

Columbia

Benedict College
Payton Learning Resources Center
Harden and Blanding Streets
29204
(803) 256-4220, ext. 2180

South Carolina State Library
Documents Department
1500 Senate Street
P.O. Box 11469
29211
(803) 758-3138

University of South Carolina
Coleman Karesh Law Library
29208
(803) 777-5944

University of South Carolina
Thomas Cooper Library
Documents/Microform Dept.
Green & Sumter Streets
29208
(803) 777-4841

Conway

University of South Carolina
Coastal Carolina College
Kimbel Library

Reference Department
P.O. Box 1954
29526
(803) 347-3161, ext. 240

Due West

Erskine College
McCain Library
29639
(803) 379-8898

Florence

Florence County Library
319 South Irby Street
29501
(803) 662-8424

Francis Marion College
James A. Rogers Library
29501
(803) 669-4121, ext. 310

Greenville

Furman University Library
Government Documents Department
29613
(803) 294-2195

Greenville County Library
300 College Street
29601
(803) 242-5000, ext. 58

Greenwood

Lander College
Larry A. Jackson Library
29646
(803) 229-8365

Orangeburg

South Carolina State College
Miller F. Whittaker Library
P.O. Box 1991
29117
(803) 536-7045

Rock Hill

Winthrop College
Dacus Library
Documents Department
Oakland Avenue
29733
(803) 323-2131, ext. 25

Spartansburg

Spartansburg County Public Library
P.O. Box 2409
333 South Pine Street
29302
(803) 596-3505

South Dakota

Aberdeen

Northern State College
Beulah Williams Library
Documents Department
57401
(605) 622-2645

Brookings

South Dakota State University
H.M. Briggs Library
University Station
57007
(605) 688-5106, ext. 27

Pierre

South Dakota State Library
Federal Documents Department
State Library Building
800 North Illinois
57501 (Designated 1973)
(605) 773-3131

South Dakota Supreme Court Library
500 East Capitol
57501
(605) 773-4898

Rapid City

Rapid City Public Library
Box 3090
610 Quincy Street
57709
(605) 394-4171

South Dakota School of Mines and Technology
Devereaux Library
500 East St. Joe
57701
(605) 394-2418

Sioux Falls

Augustana College
Mikkelsen Library
57197
(605) 336-4921

Sioux Falls Public Library
201 North Main Avenue
57102
(605) 339-7082

Spearfish
Black Hills State College Library Learning Center
Documents Department
1200 University Avenue
57783
(605) 642-6833, ext. 6

Vermillion
University of South Dakota
I.D. Weeks Library
Documents
57069
(605) 677-5371

Yankton
Yankton College
James Lloyd Library
1016 Douglas
57078
(605) 665-4662

Tennessee

Bristol
King College
E. W. King Library
37620
(615) 968-1187, ext. 238

Chattanooga
Chattanooga-Hamilton County
Bicentennial Library
Government Documents Dept.
1001 Broad Street
37402
(615) 757-5415
U.S. Tennessee Valley Authority
Technical Library
100-401 Building
37401
(615) 751-4915

Clarksville
Austin Peay State University
Felix G. Woodward Library
Documents Department
P.O. Box 4595
601 East College Street
37040
(615) 648-7346

Cleveland
Cleveland State Community College Library
P.O. Box 3570
37311
(615) 472-7141, ext. 278

Columbia
Columbia State Community College
John W. Finney Memorial Library
Highway 99 W
38401
(615) 388-0120, ext. 234

Cookeville
Tennessee Technological University
Jere Whitson Memorial Library
38505
(615) 528-3217

Jackson
Lambuth College
Luther L. Gobbel Library
38301
(901) 427-1500, ext. 293

Jefferson City
Carson-Newman College Library
Documents Department
South Russell Avenue
37760
(615) 475-9061, ext. 337

Johnson City
East Tennessee State University
Sherrod Library
Documents Department
P.O. Box 22450A
37614
(615) 929-5334

Knoxville
Public Libraries Knoxville-Knox County, Lawson McGhee Library
500 West Church Street
37902
(615) 523-0781, ext. 122

University of Tennessee at Knoxville
James D. Hoskins Library
Reference/Documents Dept.
1401 West Cumberland Avenue
37996
(615) 974-6870

University of Tennessee Law Library
1505 West Cumberland Avenue
37996
(615) 974-4381

Martin

University of Tennessee at Martin
Paul Meek Library
University Station
38238
(901) 587-7065

Memphis

Memphis-Shelby County Public Library and Information Center
1850 Peabody Avenue
38104
(901) 725-8800

Memphis State University
Cecil C. Humphreys School of Law Library
38152
(901) 454-2426

Memphis State University Libraries
Government Documents
38152
(901) 454-2206

Murfreesboro

Middle Tennessee State University
Todd Library
Documents Department
37132
(615) 898-2819

Nashville

Fisk University Library
Seventeenth Avenue North
37207
(615) 329-8645

Public Library of Nashville and Davidson County
Eighth Avenue North at Union
37203
(615) 244-4700, ext. 46

Tennessee State Law Library
Supreme Court Building
401 Seventh Avenue North
37219
(615) 741-2016

Tennessee State Library and Archives
State Library Division
403 Seventh Avenue North
37219
(615) 741-2764

Tennessee State University
Brown-Daniel Library
Government Documents Center
3500 John A. Merritt Boulevard
37203
(615) 320-3678

Vanderbilt University Law Library
Documents Department
37203
(615) 322-2568

Vanderbilt University Library
Central Documents Unit
419 21st Avenue South
37240
(615) 322-2838

Sewanee

University of the South
Jessie Ball duPont Library
Government Documents
37375
(615) 598-5931, ext. 368

Texas

Abilene

Abilene Christian University
Margaret and Herman Brown Library
Box 8177
University Station
1600 Campus Court
79699
(915) 677-1911, ext. 2341

Hardin-Simmons University
Rupert and Pauline Richardson Library
Documents Department
2200 Hickory
79698
(915) 677-7281, ext. 245

Arlington

Arlington Public Library
101 East Abram Street
76010
(817) 275-2763, ext. 291

University of Texas at Arlington Library
  Documents Department
  P.O. Box 194497
  701 South Cooper Street
  76019
  (817) 273-3394, ext. 4970

Austin

Texas State Law Library
  P.O.Box 12367
  Capitol Station
  Supreme Court Bldg.
  121 West 14th
  78711
  (512) 475-3807

Texas State Library
  P.O. Box 12927
  Public Services Department
  1201 Brazos
  78711
  (512) 475-2996
  REGIONAL DEPOSITORY

University of Texas at Austin
  Perry-Castañeda Library
  Documents Department
  PCL 2.400
  78712
  (512) 471-3813

University of Texas at Austin
  Edie and Lew Wasserman
  Public Affairs Library
  SRH 3.243
  78712
  (512) 471-4486

University of Texas at Austin
  Tarlton Law Library
  727 E. 26th Street
  78705
  (512) 471-7726, ext. 250

Baytown

Lee College Library
  Documents Department
  Box 818
  77520
  (713) 427-5611, ext. 279

Beaumont

Lamar University
  Mary and John Gray Library
  Box 10021
  Lamar University Station
  East Virginia Street
  77710
  (409) 838-8261

Brownwood

Howard Payne University
  Walker Memorial Library
  76801
  (915) 646-2502, ext. 310

Canyon

West Texas State University
  Cornette Library
  Documents Department
  Second Avenue & 26th Street
  79016
  (806) 656-2761, ext. 39

College Station

Texas Agricultural and Mechanical University Library
  Documents Department
  77843
  (409) 845-2551

Commerce

East Texas State University Library
  East Texas Station
  75428
  (214) 886-5726

Corpus Christi

Corpus Christi State University Library
  6300 Ocean Drive
  78412
  (512) 991-6810, ext. 209

Corsicana

Navarro College
  Gaston T. Gooch Library
  P.O. Box 1170
  75110
  (214) 874-6501, ext. 257

Dallas

Bishop College
  Zale Library
  3837 Simpson-Stuart Road
  75241
  (214) 372-8136

Dallas Baptist College—Vance Memorial Library
  7777 West Kiest Boulevard
  75211
  (214) 331-8311, ext. 220

Dallas Public Library
Government Publications Division
1515 Young St.
75201
(214) 749-4167

Southern Methodist University
Fondren Library
75275
(214) 692-2331

University of Texas Health Science Center—Dallas
Library
5323 Harry Hines Boulevard
75235
(214) 688-2629

Denton

North Texas State University Library
Highland Avenue
Box 5188
North Texas Station
76203
(817) 565-2870

Edinburg

Pan American University Library
Government Documents Division
West University Drive
78539
(512) 381-2769

El Paso

El Paso Public Library
Documents Section
501 North Oregon Street
79901
(915) 541-4873

University of Texas at El Paso
Documents & Maps Library
79968
(915) 747-5685

Fort Worth

Fort Worth Public Library
300 Taylor Street
76102
(817) 870-7721

Texas Christian University
Mary Couts Burnett Library
Box 32904
76129
(817) 921-7117

Galveston

Rosenberg Library
2310 Sealy Avenue
77550
(409) 763-8854, ext. 20

Houston

Houston Public Library
Government Documents Section
500 McKinney Avenue
77002
(713) 224-5441, ext. 298

North Harris County College
Learning Resource Center
2700 W.W. Thorne Drive
77073
(713) 443-6640, ext. 270

Rice University
Fondren Library
Documents Division
P.O. Box 1892
6100 South Main St.
77005
(713) 527-8101, ext. 2587

South Texas College of Law Library
1200 Polk Avenue
77002
(713) 659-8040

Texas Southern University
Thurgood Marshall School of Law Library
3100 Cleburne Avenue
77004
(713) 527-7125

University of Houston-Clear Lake
Alfred R. Neumann Library
2700 Bay Area Boulevard
77058
(713) 488-9295

University of Houston Library
Documents Division
4800 Calhoun Blvd.
77004
(713) 749-1163

University of Houston
School of Law Library
Documents Department
4800 Calhoun Blvd.
77478
(713) 749-3191

Huntsville

Sam Houston State University Library
Govt. Docs. Department
77341
(409) 294-1629

Irving

Irving Public Library System
P.O. Box 2288
915 N. O'Connor Road
75061
(214) 253-2607

Kingsville

Texas Arts and Industries University
Jernigan Library
Documents Department
78363
(512) 595-3916

Laredo

Laredo Junior College
Harold R. Yeary Library
Government Documents
West End Washington Street
78040
(512) 722-0521, ext. 270

Longview

Nicholson Memorial Public Library
400 South Green Street
75601
(214) 758-4252

Lubbock

Texas Tech University Library
Documents Department
79409
(806) 742-2268
REGIONAL DEPOSITORY

Texas Tech University
School of Law Library
79409
(806) 742-3962

Marshall

Wiley College
Thomas Winston Cole Sr. Library
711 Rosborough Springs Road
75670
(214) 938-8341, ext. 70

Nacogdoches

Stephen F. Austin State University
Steen Library
Documents Department
Box 13055
75962
(409) 569-4307

Plainview

Wayland Baptist University
Van Howeling Memorial Library
1900 West Seventh
79072
(806) 296-5521, ext. 481

Richardson

University of Texas at Dallas Library
Government Publications Division
P.O. Box 830643
Campbell & Floyd
75083
(214) 690-2918

San Angelo

Angelo State University
Porter Henderson Library
2601 West Avenue North
76909
(915) 942-2300

San Antonio

Saint Mary's University
Academic Library
One Camino Santa Maria
78284
(512) 436-3441

Saint Mary's University
Law Library
One Camino Santa Maria
78284
(512) 436-3435

San Antonio College Library
1001 Howard Street
78284
(512) 733-2598

San Antonio Public Library
Business, Science, and Technology Department
203 South Saint Mary's Street
78205
(512) 299-7802

Trinity University Library
Documents Department
715 Stadium Drive
78209
(512) 736-7429

University of Texas at San Antonio Library
Government Documents Department
78285
(512) 691-4573, ext. 36

San Marcos

Southwest Texas State University Library
Documents Department
J.C. Kellam Bldg.
78666
(512) 245-2686

Seguin

Texas Lutheran College
Blumberg Memorial Library
1000 West Court Street
78155
(512) 379-4161, ext. 230

Sherman

Austin College
Arthur Hopkins Library
75090
(214) 892-9101, ext. 369

Texarkana

Texarkana Community College
Palmer Memorial Library
1024 Tucker Street
75501
(214) 838-4541, ext. 215

Victoria

Victoria College/University of Houston
Victoria Campus Library
2604 N. Ben Jordan
77901
(512) 576-3151, ext. 283

Waco

Baylor University
Law Library
Government Documents
P.O. Box 6342
76706
(817) 755-2168

Baylor University
Moody Memorial Library
Documents Department
University Station
Box 6307
76706
(817) 755-2111, ext. 6735

Wichita Falls

Midwestern State University
Moffett Library
3400 Taft Street
76308
(817) 692-6611, ext. 4204

Utah

Cedar City

Southern Utah State College Library
Documents Department
351 West Center
84720
(801) 586-7946

Ephraim

Snow College
Lucy A. Phillips Library
84627
(801) 283-4021, ext. 362

Logan

Utah State University
Merrill Library and Learning Resources Center,
UMC-30
Documents Department
84322
(801) 750-2682
REGIONAL DEPOSITORY

Ogden

Weber State College
Stewart Library
Documents Dept. 2901
3750 Harrison Boulevard
84408
(801) 626-6546

Provo

Brigham Young University
Harold B. Lee Library
Documents and Maps Section
84602
(801) 378-6179

Brigham Young University
Law Library
Documents Department
84602 (Designated 1972)
(801) 378-3297

Salt Lake City

University of Utah
Eccles Health Sciences Library
Government Documents
Bldg. 89
10 North Medical Drive
84112
(801) 581-5534

University of Utah
Law Library
84112
(801) 581-6438

University of Utah
Marriott Library
84112
(801) 581-8394

Utah State Library
Document Section
Suite 16
2150 South Third West
84115
(801) 533-5875, ext. 36

Utah State Supreme Court
Law Library
332 State Capitol
84114
(801) 533-5280

Vermont

Burlington

University of Vermont
Bailey/Howe Library
05405
(802) 656-2020, ext. 34

Castleton

Castleton State College
Calvin Coolidge Library
05735
(802) 468-5611, Ext. 255

Johnson

Johnson State College
John Dewey Library
05656
(802) 635-2356, ext. 247

Lyndonville
Lyndon State College
Samuel Reed Hall Library
05851
(802) 626-9371, ext. 149

Middlebury
Middlebury College
Egbert Starr Library
05753
(802) 388-3711, ext. 5488

Montpelier
Vermont Department of
Libraries
Law and Documents Division
State Office Building
111 State Street
05661
(802) 828-3268

Northfield
Norwich University Library
Documents Department
05663
(802) 485-5011, ext. 248

South Royalton
Vermont Law School
Library
Documents Department
Chelsea Street
05068
(802) 763-8303, ext. 246

Virgin Islands

Saint Croix
Florence Williams Public Library
49-50 King Street
Christiansted
00820
(809) 773-5715

Saint Thomas
College of the Virgin Islands
Ralph M. Paiewonsky Library
Charlotte Amalie
00801
(809) 774-9200, ext. 1486

Enid M. Baa Library and Archives
P.O. Box 390
20 Dronnigens Gade
Charlotte Amalie
00801
(809) 774-0630, ext. 25

Virginia

Alexandria

Dept. of the Navy
Office of the Judge Advocate General
Law Library (73)
200 Stovall Street
22332
(202) 325-9565

Arlington

George Mason University School of Law Library
3401 North Fairfax Drive
22201
(703) 841-2653

Blacksburg

Virginia Polytechnic Institute and State University
Carol M. Newman Library
Documents Department
24061
(703) 961-6181

Bridgewater

Bridgewater College
Alexander Mack Memorial Library
Documents Department
East College Street
22812
(703) 828-2501, ext. 512

Charlottesville

University of Virginia
Alderman Library
Government Documents
22901
(804) 924-3133
REGIONAL DEPOSITORY

University of Virginia
Arthur J. Morris Law Library
Documents Department
22901
(804) 924-3504

Chesapeake

Chesapeake Public Library
Civic Center
300 Cedar Road
23320
(804) 547-6591

Danville

Danville Community College
Learning Resources Center
1008 South Main Street
24541
(804) 797-3553, ext. 253

Emory

Emory and Henry College
Kelly Library
24327
(703) 944-3121, ext. 3208

Fairfax

George Mason University
Fenwick Library
Acquisitions Department
4400 University Drive
22152
(703) 323-2877

Fredericksburg

Mary Washington College
E. Lee Trinkle Library
22401
(703) 899-4664

Hampden-Sydney

Hampden-Sydney College
Eggleston Library
P.O. Box 7
23943
(804) 223-4381, ext. 190

Hampton

Hampton Institute
Huntington Memorial Library
23668
(804) 727-5379

Harrisonburg

James Madison University
Carrier Library
22807
(703) 433-6929

Hollins College
Fishburn Library
24020
(703) 362-6591

Lexington

Virginia Military Institute
Preston Library
24450
(703) 463-6228

Washington and Lee University
University Library
24450
(703) 463-9111, ext. 432

Washington and Lee University
Wilbur C. Hall Law Library
24450
(703) 463-3157

Martinsville

Patrick Henry Community College Library
P.O. Drawer 5311
24115
(703) 638-8777, ext. 228

Norfolk

Norfolk Public Library
301 East City Hall Avenue
23510
(804) 441-2579

Old Dominion University Library
Documents Department
Hampton Boulevard
23508
(804) 440-4168

U.S. Armed Forces Staff College Library
Documents Department
7800 Hampton Blvd.
23511
(804) 444-5155

Petersburg

Virginia State University
Johnston Memorial Library
Documents Department
23803
(804) 520-5582

Quantico

Federal Bureau of Investigation
Academy Library
22135
(703) 640-6131, ext. 3047

Marine Corps Development and Education Command
James Carson Breckenridge Library
Education Center
MCDEC
22134
(703) 640-2248

Reston

Department of the Interior
Geological Survey Library
National Center
Mail Stop 950
12201 Sunrise Valley Drive
22092
(703) 860-6614

Richmond

U.S. Court of Appeals
Fourth Circuit Library
U.S. Court House
10th & Main Streets
Room 424
23219
(804) 771-2219

University of Richmond
Boatwright Memorial Library
23173
(804) 285-6452

University of Richmond
Law School Library
23173
(804) 285-6239

Virginia Commonwealth University
James Branch Cabell Library
901 Park Avenue
23284
(804) 257-1104

Virginia State Law Library
Supreme Court Building
100 North Ninth Street
23219
(804) 786-2075

Virginia State Library
Documents Section
12th & Capitol Streets
23219
(804) 786-2175

Salem

Roanoke College Library
Documents Department
24153
(703) 389-2351, ext. 295

Williamsburg

College of William and Mary
Marshall-Wythe Law Library
23185
(804) 253-4637

College of William and Mary
Swem Library
Documents Department
23185
(804) 253-4404

Wise

Clinch Valley College
John Cook Wyllie Library
Documents Division
24293
(703) 328-2431, ext. 233

Washington

Bellingham

Western Washington University
Mable Zoe Wilson Library
Documents Division
516 High Street
98225
(206) 676-3075

Cheney

Eastern Washington University
JFK Library
Documents Section
99004
(509) 359-7894

Ellensburg

Central Washington University Library
Documents Department
98926
(509) 963-1541

Everett

Everett Public Library
2702 Hoyt Avenue
98201
(206) 259-8851, ext. 34

Midway

Highline Community College Library
South 240th & Pacific Highway South
98032
(206) 878-3710, ext. 232

Olympia

Evergreen State College
Daniel J. Evans Library
Documents Department
98505
(206) 866-6000, ext. 6251

Washington State Law Library
Temple of Justice
98504
(206) 753-6525

Washington State Library
Documents Section
98504
(206) 753-4027
REGIONAL DEPOSITORY

Port Angeles

North Olympic Library System
Port Angeles Branch
Documents Division
207 South Lincoln
98362
(206) 452-9953

Pullman

Washington State University Library
Documents Section
99164
(509) 335-9621, ext. 33

Seattle

Seattle Public Library
Documents Department
1000 4th Avenue
98104
(206) 625-4875

University of Washington Libraries
FM-25
Government Documents
98195
(206) 543-4664

University of Washington
Marian Gould Gallagher Law Library
1100 NE Campus Parkway
Condon Hall JB-20
98105
(206) 543-1941

U.S. Court of Appeals
9th Circuit Library
907 U.S. Court House
1010 Fifth Avenue
98104
(206) 442-4475

Spokane

Gonzaga University
School of Law Library
East 600 Sharpe
Box 3528
99220
(509) 328-4220, ext. 3757

Spokane Public Library
Documents Department
West 906 Main Avenue
99201
(509) 838-3361, ext. 300

Tacoma

Tacoma Public Library
Documents Division
1102 Tacoma Avenue South
98402
(206) 591-5666

University of Puget Sound
Collins Memorial Library
1500 North Warner
98416
(206) 756-3257

University of Puget Sound
School of Law Library
950 Broadway Plaza
98402
(206) 756-3320

Vancouver

Fort Vancouver Regional Library
1007 East Mill Plain Boulevard
98663
(206) 695-1561

Walla Walla

Whitman College
Penrose Memorial Library
99362
(509) 527-5191

West Virginia

Athens

Concord College Library
Documents Department
24712
(304) 384-3115, ext. 204

Bluefield

Bluefield State College
Hardway Library
Documents Department
24701
(304) 325-7102, ext. 230

Charleston

Kanawha County Public Library
123 Capitol Street
25301
(304) 343-4646, ext. 15

West Virginia Library Commission
Reference Department
Cultural Center
Capitol Complex
25305
(304) 348-2045

West Virginia Supreme Court Law Library
Room E-404, State Capitol
25305
(304) 348-3637

Elkins

Davis and Elkins College Library
Jennings Randolph Hall
Sycamore Street
26241
(304) 636-1900, ext. 244

Fairmont

Fairmont State College Library
Locust Avenue
26554
(304) 367-4121

Glenville

Glenville State College
Robert F. Kidd Library
Government Documents
26351
(304) 462-7361, ext. 314

Huntington

Marshall University
James E. Morrow Library
1665 Third Avenue
25701
(304) 696-2320, ext. 28

Institute

West Virginia State College
Drain-Jordan Library
25112
(304) 766-3116, ext. 20

Morgantown

West Virginia University Library
Government Documents Section
P.O. Box 6069
26506
(304) 293-3640
REGIONAL DEPOSITORY

Salem

Salem College Library
Documents Department
Pennsylvania Avenue
26426
(304) 782-5238

Shepherdstown

Shepherd College
Ruth Scarborough Library
Documents Department
25443
(304) 876-2511, ext. 217

Weirton

Mary H. Weir Public Library
3442 Main Street
26062
(304) 748-7070

Wisconsin

Appleton

Lawrence University
Seeley G. Mudd Library
Documents Department
54912
(414) 735-6754

Beloit

Beloit College
Col. Robert H. Morse Library
Serials Documents Department
731 College Street
53511
(608) 365-3391, ext. 486

Eau Claire

University of Wisconsin-Eau Claire
William D. McIntyre Library
Park and Garfield Streets
54701
(715) 836-3247

Fond du Lac

Fond du Lac Public Library
32 Sheboygan Street
54935
(414) 921-0066

Green Bay

University of Wisconsin-Green Bay
Learning Resources Center
Government Publications Department
54301
(414) 465-2670

La Crosse

La Crosse Public Library
800 Main Street
54601
(608) 784-5979

University of Wisconsin-La Crosse
Murphy Library
1631 Pine Street
54601
(608) 785-8513

Madison

Madison Public Library
201 West Mifflin Street
53703
(608) 266-6383

State Historical Society of Wisconsin Library
Government Publications Section
816 State Street
53706
(608) 262-4347
REGIONAL DEPOSITORY, in cooperation
with University of Wisconsin-Madison

University of Wisconsin-Madison
Memorial Library
Documents Department
728 State Street
53706
(608) 262-9852

University of Wisconsin-Madison
Law Library
53706
(608) 262-2843

Wisconsin State Law Library
310 East State Capitol
53707
(608) 266-1600

Milwaukee

Alverno College Library Media Center
3401 South 39th Street
53215
(414) 647-3779

Medical College of Wisconsin, Inc.
Todd Wehr Library
P.O. Box 26509
8701 Watertown Plank Road
53226
(414) 257-8302

Milwaukee County Law and Reference Library
Court House, Room 307
901 North 9th Street
53233
(414) 278-4322

Milwaukee Public Library
Documents Division
814 West Wisconsin Avenue
53233
(414) 278-3017
REGIONAL DEPOSITORY

Mount Mary College Haggerty Library
2900 North Menomonee River Parkway
53222
(414) 258-4810, ext. 341

University of Wisconsin-Milwaukee Library
Documents Department
2311 East Hartford
53211
(414) 963-6210

Oshkosh

University of Wisconsin-Oshkosh
Forrest R. Polk Library
Government Documents
800 Algoma Boulevard
54901
(414) 424-3347

Platteville

University of Wisconsin-Platteville
Karrmann Library
Government Publications and Maps
725 West Main Street
53818
(608) 342-1758

Racine

Racine Public Library
75 Seventh Street
53403
(414) 636-9241

Ripon

Ripon College Library
Government Documents
Box 248
300 Seward Street
54971
(414) 748-8330

River Falls

University of Wisconsin-River Falls
Chalmer Davee Library
Documents Department
54022
(715) 425-3874

Sheboygan

Mead Public Library
710 Plaza 8
53081
(414) 459-3422

Stevens Point

University of Wisconsin-Stevens Point
Learning Resources Center
Documents Department
54481
(715) 346-3726

Superior

Superior Public Library
1204 Hammond Avenue
54880
(715) 394-0252

University of Wisconsin-Superior
Jim Dan Hill Library
1800 Grand Avenue
54880
(715) 394-8341

Waukesha

Waukesha Public Library
321 Wisconsin Avenue
53186
(414) 542-4297

Wausau

Marathon County Public Library
400 First Street
54401
(715) 847-5523

Whitewater

University of Wisconsin-Whitewater
Harold Anderson Library
Government Documents Department
53190
(414) 472-4671

Wyoming

Casper

Natrona County Public Library
307 East Second Street
82601
(307) 237-4935

Cheyenne

Wyoming State Law Library
Supreme Court Building
82002
(307) 777-7509

Wyoming State Library
Supreme Court and Library Building
82002
(307) 777-6344
REGIONAL DEPOSITORY

Gillette

Campbell County Public Library
2101 4-J Road
82716
(307) 687-0115

Laramie

University of Wyoming, Coe Library
Documents Division
Box 3334
University Station
13th & Ivinson
82071
(307) 766-2174

University of Wyoming Law Library
Box 3035
University Station
82071
(307) 766-2210

Powell

Northwest Community College
John Taggart Hinckley Library
82435
(307) 754-6207

Riverton

Central Wyoming College Library
2660 Peck Avenue
82501
(307) 856-1165

Rock Springs

Western Wyoming College Library
2500 College Drive
82902
(307) 382-2121, ext. 154

Sheridan

Sheridan College, Griffith Memorial Library
P.O. Box 1500
82801
(307) 674-6446, ext. 213

Regional Depository Libraries by State and City

Alabama

Montgomery

Auburn University at Montgomery Library
Documents Department
36193
(205) 279-9110, ext. 253

University

University of Alabama Library
Reference Department/Documents
Box S
35486
(205) 348-6046

Arizona

Phoenix

Department of Library Archives, and Public Records
Third Floor State Capitol
1700 West Washington
85007
(602) 255-4121

Tucson

University of Arizona Library
Government Documents Department
85721
(602) 621-4871

Arkansas

Little Rock

Arkansas State Library
  Documents Service Section
  One Capitol Mall
  72201
  (501) 371-2090

California

Sacramento

California State Library
  Government Publications Service
  914 Capitol Mall
  95814
  (916) 322-4572

Colorado

Boulder

University of Colorado at Boulder
  Norlin Library
  Government Publications
  Campus Box 184
  80309
  (303) 492-8834

Denver

Denver Public Library
  Government Publications Department
  1357 Broadway
  80203
  (303) 571-2131

Connecticut

Hartford

Connecticut State Library
  231 Capitol Avenue
  06106
  (203) 566-4971
NOTE.—Also serves as Regional for State of Rhode Island.

Florida

Gainesville

University of Florida Libraries
  Documents Department
  Library West
  32611
  (904) 392-0366
NOTE.—Also serves as Regional for Commonwealth of Puerto Rico.

Georgia

Athens

University of Georgia
  Government Documents Department
  30602
  (404) 542-8949

Hawaii

Honolulu

University of Hawaii Hamilton Library
  Government Documents Collection
  2550 The Mall
  96822
  (808) 948-8230

Idaho

Moscow

University of Idaho Library
  Documents Section
  83843
  (208) 885-6344

Illinois

Springfield

Illinois State Library
  Government Documents
  Centennial Building
  62756
  (217) 782-5012

Indiana

Indianapolis

Indiana State Library
  Serials Section
  140 North Senate Avenue
  46204
  (317) 232-3686

Iowa

Iowa City

University of Iowa Libraries
  Government Publications Department
  52242
  (319) 353-3318

Kansas

Lawrence

University of Kansas
Spencer Research Library
Documents Collection
66045
(913) 864-4662

Kentucky

Lexington

University of Kentucky Libraries
Government Publications Department
40506
(606) 257-3139

Louisiana

Baton Rouge

Louisiana State University Middleton Library
Government Documents Department
70803
(504) 388-2570
NOTE.—Also serves as Regional for Virgin Islands.

Ruston

Louisiana Technical University
Prescott Memorial Library
Documents Department
71272
(318) 257-4962

Maine

Orono

University of Maine
Raymond H. Fogler Library
Tri-State Regional Documents Depository
04469
(207) 581-1680
NOTE.—Also serves as Regional for States of New Hampshire and Vermont.

Maryland

College Park

University of Maryland
McKeldin Library
Documents Division
20742
(301) 454-3034
NOTE.—Also serves as Regional for District of Columbia.

Massachusetts

Boston

Boston Public Library
Documents Receipts
02117
(617) 536-5400, ext. 226

Michigan

Detroit

Detroit Public Library
5201 Woodward Avenue
48202
(313) 833-1409

Lansing

Library of Michigan
Government Documents
P.O. Box 30007
735 E. Michigan Avenue
48909
(517) 373-0640

Minnesota

Minneapolis

University of Minnesota
Wilson Library
Government Publications
309 Nineteenth Avenue South
55455
(612) 373-7813

Mississippi

University

University of Mississippi
J.D. Williams Library
Documents Department
38677
(601) 232-5857

Montana

Missoula

University of Montana Maurene & Mike Mansfield Library
Documents Division
59812
(406) 243-6700

Nebraska

Lincoln

Nebraska Library Commission
Federal Documents Dept.
1420 P Street
68508
(402) 471-2045
NOTE.—In cooperation with University of Nebraska-Lincoln
D.L. Love Memorial Library.

Nevada

Reno

University of Nevada-Reno Library
Government Publications Dept.
89557
(702) 784-6579

New Jersey

Newark

Newark Public Library
U.S. Documents Division
5 Washington Street
P.O. Box 630
07101
(201) 733-7812

New Mexico

Albuquerque

University of New Mexico
General Library
Government Publications & Maps Department
87131
(505) 277-7180

Santa Fe

New Mexico State Library
325 Don Gaspar Avenue
87501
(505) 827-3800

New York

Albany

New York State Library
Documents Control
6th Floor, Cultural Education Center, Empire
   State Plaza
12230
(518) 474-5563

North Carolina

Chapel Hill

University of North Carolina at Chapel Hill
Wilson Library
BA/SS Division Documents
27514
(919) 962-1151

North Dakota

Fargo

North Dakota State University Library
Government Documents Department
58105
(701) 237-7008
NOTE.—In cooperation with University of North Dakota,
Chester Fritz Library, Grand Forks.

Ohio

Columbus

State Library of Ohio
Documents Section
65 South Front Street
43215
(614) 462-7051

Oklahoma

Oklahoma City

Oklahoma Department of Libraries
Government Documents
200 NE 18th Street
73105
(405) 521-2502

Stillwater

Oklahoma State University Library
Documents Department
74078
(405) 624-6546

Oregon

Portland

Portland State University Library
P.O. Box 1151
97207
(503) 229-3673

Pennsylvania

Harrisburg

State Library of Pennsylvania
  Government Publications Section
  Box 1601
  Walnut Street & Commonwealth Avenue
  17105
  (717) 787-3752

Texas

Austin

Texas State Library
  Public Services Department
  P.O. Box 12927
  1201 Brazos
  78711
  (512) 475-2996

Lubbock

Texas Tech University Library
  Documents Department
  79409
  (806) 742-2268

Utah

Logan

Utah State University
  Merrill Library and Learning Resources Center,
    UMC-30
  Documents Department
  84322
  (801) 750-2682

Virginia

Charlottesville

University of Virginia
  Alderman Library
  Government Documents
  22901
  (804) 924-3133

Washington

Olympia

Washington State Library
  Documents Section
  98504
  (206) 753-4027

West Virginia

Morgantown

West Virginia University Library
  Government Documents Section
  P.O. Box 6069
  26506
  (304) 293-3640

Wisconsin

Madison

State Historical Society of Wisconsin Library
  Government Publications Section
  816 State Street
  537065
  (608) 252-4347
  NOTE.—In cooperation with University of Wisconsin-Madison,
  Memorial Library.

Milwaukee

Milwaukee Public Library
  Documents Division
  814 West Wisconsin Avenue
  53233
  (414) 278-3017

Wyoming

Cheyenne

Wyoming State Library
  Supreme Court and Library Building
  82002
  (307) 777-6344

Congressional State and District Offices:
The Staff Are There to Serve You

The list below provides the addresses and telephone numbers of the state offices of all U.S. Senators and the district offices of all House Members. This information is based on the 99th Congress and, of course, all 435 Representatives and some 30 Senators must run for reelection in November 1986.

If you do not know the names of your elected representatives call your local information operator. Remember, these offices are good starting places for many types of problems and questions. For more information about the services available from your Congressional Representative, consult the "Capitol Hill" section of the Sampler.

United States Senate

Abdnor, James (R-S.D.)
507 Kansas City St., Rapid City, 57701 (605) 343-5000
P.O. Box 873, Sioux Falls, 57101 336-2980, ext. 474
375 Dakota S., Box 1365, Huron, 57350 352-5117
P.O. Box 9, Mitchell, 57301 996-3601
260 Federal Bldg., Pierre, 57501 224-2891
P.O. Box 588, Aberdeen, 57401 225-0250, ext. 692

Andrews, Mark (R-N.D.)
P.O. Box 1915, Bismarck, 58502 (701) 258-4648
Heritage Place, Minot, 58701 852-2510
106 Federal Bldg., Grand Forks 58201 775-9601
Federal Bldg., P.O. Box 3004, Fargo, 58108 232-8030

Armstrong, William L. (R-Colo.)
215 Federal Bldg., 400 Rood Ave., Grand Junction, 81501 (303) 245-9553
Rm. 722, Thatcher Bldg., Fifth & Main St., Pueblo, 81003 545-9751
Ste. 103, 311 Steel St., Denver, 80206 398-0831
Ste. 106, 228 N. Cascade, Colorado Springs, 80903 634-6071

Baucus, Max (D-Mont.)
62 S. Last Chance Gulch #A, Helena, 59601 (406) 449-5480
Ste. 102, Missoula Bank of Montana Bldg., 2111 N. Higgins, Missoula, 59802 329-3123
320 Securities Bldg., 2708½ First Ave. N, Billings, 59101 657-6790
256 Federal Bldg., Butte, 59701 782-8700
107 Fifth St. N., Great Falls, 59401 761-1574
Federal Bldg., P.O. Box 1689, Bozeman, 59715 586-6104

Bentsen, Lloyd (D-Tex.)
4026 Federal Bldg., 515 Rusk Ave., Houston, 77002 (713) 229-2595
912 Federal Bldg., Austin, 78701 (512) 482-5834
7C30 Earle Cabell Federal Bldg., Dallas, 75242 (214) 767-0577

Biden, Joseph R., Jr. (D-Del.)
6021 J. Caleb Boggs Fed. Bldg., 844 King St., Wilmington, 19801 (302) 573-6345
J. Allen Frear Fed. Bldg., 300 S. New St., Dover, 19901 678-9483
Post Office Bldg., The Circle, P.O. Box 109, Georgetown, 19947 856-9275

Bingaman, Jeff (D-N.M.)
231 Washington Ave., Sante Fe, 87501 (505) 988-6647
9017 Dennis Chavez Federal Bldg., 500 Gold Ave., S.E., Albuquerque, 87102 766-3636
175 Federal Bldg., Roswell, 88201 622-7113
2018 U.S. Courthouse, 200 E. Griggs, Las Cruces, 88002 523-8237

Boren, David L. (D-Okla.)
Ste. 350, 621 N. Robinson, Oklahoma City, 73102 (405) 231-4381
Municipal Bldg., 400 N. Main, Seminole, 74868 382-6480
Robert S. Kerr Fed. Office Bldg., 440 S. Houston, Tulsa, 74127 (918) 481-7785

Boschwitz, Rudolph E. (R-Minn.)
Rm. 210, Bremer Bldg., 419 N. Robert St., St. Paul, 55101 (612) 221-0904
Rm. 704, Marquette Bank Bldg., Rochester, 55901 (507) 288-2384

Bradley, Bill (D-N.J.)
P.O. Box 1720, 1609 Vauxhall Rd., Union, 07083 (201) 688-0960
P.O. Box 1031, Blackhorse Pike & Whitman Dr., Turnersville, 08012 (609) 228-2815

Bumpers, Dale (D-Ark.)
2527 Federal Bldg., Little Rock, 72201 (501)
378-6286

Burdick, Quentin N. (D-N.D.)
266 Federal Office Bldg., 657 Second Ave. N.,
Fargo, 58102 (701) 237-4000
306 Federal Bldg., P.O. Box 2057, Bismarck,
58501 255-2553
319 Federal Bldg., 100 First St., S.W., Minot,
58701 852-4503

Byrd, Robert C. (D-W.Va.)
1006 Federal Bldg., 500 Quarrier St.,
Charleston, 25301 (304) 342-5855

Chafee, John H. (R-R.I.)
301 Pastore Federal Bldg., Kennedy Plaza,
Providence, 02903 (401) 528-5295

Chiles, Lawton (D-Fla.)
Federal Bldg., Lakeland, 33801 (813) 688-6681
24 U.S. P.O. & Courthouse Bldg., 110 E. Park
Ave., Tallahassee, 32301 (904) 681-7514
931 Federal Bldg., 51 S.W. First Ave., Miami,
33130 (305) 350-4891

Cochran, Thad (R-Miss.)
321 Main Post Office Bldg., P.O. Box 22581,
Jackson, 39225 (601) 960-4459

Cohen, William S. (R-Maine)
154 State St., Augusta, 04330 (207) 622-8416
P.O. Box 1384, Bangor, 04401 945-0417
Promenade Mall, 11 Lisbon St., Lewiston, 04240
784-6969
151 Forest Ave., P.O. Box 1938, Portland,
04104 780-3575
523 Main St., Presque Isle, 04769 764-3266
2 Adams St., Biddeford, 04005 283-1101

Cranston, Alan (D-Calif.)
45 Polk St., San Francisco, 94102 (415) 566-8440
Ste. 515, 5757 W. Century Blvd., Los Angeles,
90045 (213) 214-2186

D'Amato, Alfonse M. (R-N.Y.)
Ste. 1635, One Penn Plaza, New York City,
10001 (212) 947-7390
420 Leo O'Brien Federal Office Bldg., Albany,
12207 (518) 463-2244
1259 Federal Bldg., 100 S. Clinton St., Syracuse,
13260 (315) 423-5471
415 Federal Bldg., 100 State St., Rochester,
14614 (716) 263-5866
Federal Bldg., 111 W. Huron St., Buffalo, 14202
846-4111

Danforth, John C. (R-Mo.)
228 Old Post Office Bldg., 815 Olive St., St.
Louis, 63101 (314) 425-6381
1233 Jefferson St., Jefferson City, 65101
635-7292
943 U.S. Courthouse, 811 Grand Ave., Kansas
City, 64106 (816) 374-6101
Ste. 705, Plaza Towers, 1736 E. Sunshine,
Springfield, 65804 (417) 881-7068

DeConcini, Dennis (D-Ariz.)
Ste. 200, 700 E. Jefferson, Phoenix, 85034 (602)
261-6756
Ste. 1540, 33 N. Stone St., Tucson, 85701
629-6831
Ste. 315, 20 E. Main St., Mesa, 85201 261-4998

Denton, Jeremiah A. (R-Ala.)
Ste. B121, 3280 Dauphin St., Mobile, 36616
(205) 690-3222
Rm. 1701, Daniel Bldg., 15 S. 20th St.,
Birmingham, 35233 254-0806
Ste. 118, One Court Sq., Montgomery, 36104
832-7600
Rm. 510, Bank of Huntsville Bldg., 101
Governor Dr., S.E., Huntsville, 35801
895-5105

Dixon, Alan J. (D-Ill.)
3996 Kluczynski Fed. Bldg., 230 S. Dearborn
St., Chicago, 60604 (312) 353-5420
108 Post Office & Courthouse, Sixth & Monroe
Sts., Springfield, 62701 (217) 492-4126
Ste. 227, 105 S. Sixth St., Mount Vernon, 62864
(618) 244-6703
10 E. Washington, Belleville, 62220 235-0998

Dodd, Christopher J. (D-Conn.)
Ste. 802, 60 Washington St., Hartford, 06106
(203) 722-3470
One Landmark Sq., Stamford, 06901 323-3137

Dole, Robert (R-Kan.)
444 S.E. Quincy, Topeka, 66603 (913) 295-2745
Franklin Savings Bldg., 4655 State Ave., Kansas
City, 66102 287-4545
Ste. 102, 76 Parsons Plaza, Parsons, 67357 (316)
421-5380
Fourth Financial Center, 100 N. Broadway,
Wichita, 67202 263-4956

Domenici, Pete V. (R-N.M.)
10013 U.S. Federal Bldg. & Courthouse, 500
Gold Ave., Albuquerque, 87102 (505)
766-3481
140 Federal Bldg., Roswell, 88201 623-6170

307 New Postal Bldg., Santa Fe, 87501 988-6511
202E New Federal Bldg., Las Cruces, 88001
523-8150

Durenberger, David (R-Minn.)
Rm. 1020, Plymouth Bldg., 12 S. Sixth St.,
Minneapolis, 55402 (612) 349-5111

Eagleton, Thomas F. (D-Mo.)
224 Old Post Office Bldg., 815 Olive St., St.
Louis, 63101 (314) 425-5067
320 Jackson, Jefferson City, 65101 634-2488
Rm. 911, 811 Grand, Kansas City, 64106 (816)
374-2747

East, John P. (R-N.C.)
P.O. Box 25009, Raleigh, 27611 (919) 755-4401
P.O. Box 8087, Greenville, 27834 757-1188
P.O. Box 2742, Winston-Salem, 27101 761-3213
P.O. Box 2779, Asheville, 28802 (704) 254-3099
P.O. Box 35555, Charlotte, 28235 371-6800

Evans, Daniel J. (R-Wash.)
3206 Henry M. Jackson Federal Bldg., 915
Second Ave., Seattle, 98174 (206) 442-0350

Exon, J. James (D-Neb.)
287 Federal Bldg., 100 Centennial Mall N.,
Lincoln, 68508 (402) 471-5591
8305 New Federal Building, 215 N. 17th St.,
Omaha, 68102 221-4665
275 Federal Bldg., N. Platte, 69101 (308)
534-2006

Ford, Wendell H. (D-Ky.)
172-C New Federal Bldg., 600 Federal Place,
Louisville, 40202 (502) 582-6251
305 Federal Bldg., Frederica St., Owensboro,
42301 685-5158
Ste. 204, 343 Waller Ave., Lexington, 40504
(606) 233-2484
19 U.S. Post Office & Courthouse, Covington,
41011 491-7929

Garn, Jake (R-Utah)
4225 Federal Bldg., Salt Lake City, 84138 (801)
524-5933
1010 Federal Bldg., Ogden, 84401 625-5676
111 Federal Bldg., 88 W. 100 North, Provo,
84601 374-2929
10 N. Main, P.O. Box 99, Cedar City, 84720
586-8435
Ste. 1, The Cong'l Office Energy Bldg., 98 E.
Center St., Moab, 84532 259-7188

Glenn, John H., Jr. (D-Ohio)
Rm. 600, 200 N. High, Columbus, 43215 (614)
469-6697
104 U.S. Courthouse, 201 Superior Ave.,
Cleveland, 44114 (216) 522-7095

Goldwater, Barry (R-Ariz.)
Ste. 135F, Camel Sq., 4350 E. Camelback Rd.,
Phoenix, 85018 (602) 241-2567
Box 7-C, Federal Bldg., 301 W. Congress,
Tucson, 85701 629-6334

Gore, Albert, Jr. (D-Tenn.)
315 Post Office Bldg, Knoxville, 37902 (615)
673-4595
716 Federal Bldg, Nashville, 37203 271-5129
Smith County Courthouse, Carthage, 37030
735-0173
Post Office Bldg., 9 E. Broad, Cookeville, 38501
528-6475
256 Federal Bldg., Chattanooga, 37402 267-2329
403 Federal Bldg., 167 N. Main, Memphis,
38103 (901) 521-4224

Gorton, Slade (R-Wash.)
2988 Henry M. Jackson Federal Bldg., 915
Second Ave., Seattle, 98174 (206) 442-5545
445 First Fed. Plaza, 1220 Main, Vancouver,
98660 696-7838
770 U.S. Courthouse, W. 920 Riverside Ave.,
Spokane, 99201 (509) 456-6816

Gramm, Phil (R-Tex.)
Suite 570, 900 Jackson, Dallas, 75202 (214)
767-3000
Suite 106, E. Jackson St., Harlingen, 78551
(512) 423-6118
8632 Federal Bldg., 515 Rusk, Houston, 77002
(713) 229-2766
113 Federal Bldg., 1205 Texas Ave., Lubbock,
79401 (806) 743-7533

Grassley, Charles E. (R-Iowa)
Ste. 210, Waterloo Bldg., 531 Commercial St.,
Waterloo, 50701 (319) 232-6657
206 Federal Bldg., 101 First St., S.E., Cedar
Rapids, 52401 399-2555
721 Federal Bldg., 210 Walnut St., Des Moines,
50309 (515) 284-4890
228 Post Office & Courthouse Bldg., 320 Sixth
St., Sioux City, 51101 (712) 233-3331

Harkin, Tom (D-Iowa)
210 Walnut, Room 733 Federal Bldg., Des
Moines 50309 (515) 284-4574
131 East 4th St., 314 B Federal Bldg.,
Davenport, 52801 (319) 322-1338

Lindale Mall, 4444 First Ave. NE, Cedar
Rapids, 52402 393-6374
Box H, 307 Federal Bldg., Council Bluff, 51502
(712) 325-5533

Hart, Gary (D-Colo.)
1748 High St., Denver, 80218 (303) 398-0800
212 Federal Bldg., Main St., Pueblo, 81002
544-9370
105 E. Vermijo, Colorado Springs, 80902
635-0001
Ste. 5, 2004–12th St., Grand Junction, 81501
241-8585

Hatch, Orrin G. (R-Utah)
3438 Federal Bldg., 125 S. State, Salt Lake City,
84138 (801) 524-4380
109 Federal Bldg., 88 W. 100 North, Provo,
84601 375-7881
1410 Federal Bldg., 325–25th St., Ogden, 84401
625-5672
10 N. Main, P.O. Box 99, Cedar City, 84720
586-8435

Hatfield, Mark O. (R-Ore.)
475 Cottage St., N.E., Salem, 97301 (503)
363-1629
114 Pioneer Courthouse, 555 S.W. Yamhill,
Portland, 97204 221-3386

Hawkins, Paula (R-Fla.)
P.O. Box 2000, Winter Park, 32789 (305)
628-1738
817 Federal Bldg., 51 S.W. First Ave., Miami,
33130 350-6952
Ste. 108, 306 E. Park Ave., Tallahassee, 32301
(904) 681-7430

Hecht, Chic (R-Nev.)
426 Federal Bldg., 300 Las Vegas Blvd., Las
Vegas, 89101 (702) 388-6605
2014 Federal Bldg., 300 Booth St., Reno, 89509
784-5007
Rm. 201, 308 N. Curry St., Carson City, 89701
885-9111

Heflin, Howell T. (D-Ala.)
Ste. 111, 555 S. Perry St., Montgomery, 36104
(205) 261-4626
Cardiff Hotel Bldg., 151 N. Main St., P.O. Box
228, Tuscumbia, 35674 381-7060
316 Federal Bldg., 1800 Fifth Ave., N.,
Birmingham, 35203 254-1500
401 Federal Courthouse Bldg., Mobile, 36602
690-3167

Heinz, John (R-Pa.)
9456 William J. Green, Jr., Federal Bldg.,
Philadelphia, 19106 (215) 925-8750
2031 Wm. S. Moorhead Federal Bldg.,
Pittsburgh, 15222 (412) 562-0533
Third & Chestnut Sts., P.O. Box 55, Federal Sq.
Station, Harrisburg, 17108 (717) 233-5849
Rm. 814, Scranton Electric Bldg., 507 Linden
St., Scranton, 18503 347-2341
130 Federal Bldg., Perry Square, Erie, 16501
(814) 454-7114

Helms, Jesse (R-N.C.)
P.O. Box 2888, Raleigh, 27602 (919) 755-4630
P.O. Box 2944, Hickory, 28601 (704) 322-5170

Hollings, Ernest F. (D-S.C.)
Rm. 1551, 1835 Assembly St., Columbia, 29201
(803) 765-5731
112 Customhouse, 200 E. Bay St., Charleston,
29401 724-4525
103 Federal Bldg., Spartanburg, 29301 585-3702
242 Federal Bldg., Greenville, 29603 233-5366
233 Federal Bldg., Florence, 29503 662-8135

Humphrey, Gordon J. (R-N.H.)
1 Pillsbury St., Concord, 03301 (603) 228-0453
730 Norris Cotton Federal Bldg., 275 Chestnut
St., Manchester, 03103 666-7691
209 Federal Bldg., 80 Daniel St., Portsmouth,
03801 431-8760
157 Main St., Berlin, 03570 752-2600

Inouye, Daniel K. (D-Hawaii)
7325 Prince Kuhio Federal Bldg., 300 Ala
Moana, Honolulu, 96850 (808) 546-7550
P.O. Box 4188, Hilo, 96720 959-6021
2853-A Mokoi St., Lihue, 96766 335-5003
P.O. Box 5, Kaunakakai, 96748 567-6107
421 Oahu St., Kahului, 96732 871-4976

Johnston, J. Bennett (D-La.)
7A12 J.D. Waggoner, Jr. Fed. Bldg., 500 Fannin
St., Shreveport, 71161 (318) 266-5085
1010 Hale Boggs Federal Bldg., 500 Camp St.,
New Orleans, 70130 (504) 589-2427
Ste. 1510, One American Place, Baton Rouge,
70825 389-0395

Kassebaum, Nancy Landon (R-Kan.)
111 N. Market, Wichita, 67202 (316) 269-2651
402 N. 7th St., Garden City, 67486 276-3423
444 S.E. Quincy, P.O. Box 51, Topeka, 66683
(913) 295-2888
Ste. 152, 4200 Somerset, Prairie Village, 66208
648-3103

Kasten, Robert W., Jr. (R-Wis.)
H.S. Reuss Fed. Bldg., 517 E. Wisconsin Ave.,
Milwaukee, 53202 (414) 291-4160
Ste. 775, 25 W. Main St., Madison, 53703 (608)
264-5366
107 Federal Bldg., 317 First St., Wausau, 54401
(715) 842-3307

Kennedy, Edward M. (D-Mass.)
2400A John F. Kennedy Federal Bldg., Boston,
02203 (617) 223-2826

Kerry, John F. (D-Mass.)
2003F John F. Kennedy Bldg., Boston, 02203
(617) 223-1890

Lautenberg, Frank R. (D-N.J.)
Gateway One, Gateway Center, Newark, 07102
(201) 645-3030
Rm. 225, The Parkade Bldg., 518 Market St.,
Camden, 08102 (609) 757-5353

Laxalt, Paul (R-Nev.)
U.S. Federal Bldg., 300 Booth St., Reno, 89509
(702) 784-5568
U.S. Federal Bldg., 300 Las Vegas Blvd., S., Las
Vegas, 89101 388-6547
U.S. Federal Bldg., 705 N. Plaza St., Carson
City, 89701 883-1930

Leahy, Patrick J. (D-Vt.)
135 Church St., Burlington, 05401 (802)
863-2525
338 Federal Bldg., P.O. Box 933, Montpelier,
05602 229-0569

Levin, Carl M. (D-Mich.)
500 Federal St., P.O. Box 817, Saginaw, 48606
(517) 754-2494
537 Chisolm St., Alpena, 49707 354-5520
Rm. G30, 124 W. Michigan Ave., Lansing,
48933 377-1508
2409 First Ave. N., Escanaba, 49829 (906)
789-0052
Ste. 101, 180 N. Division, Grand Rapids, 49503
(616) 456-2531
1860 McNamara Fed. Bldg., 477 Mich. Ave.,
Detroit, 48226 (313) 226-6020
26417 Hoover, Warren, 48089 226-3770

Long, Russell B. (D-La.)
220 Federal Post Office Bldg., 750 Florida Blvd.,
Baton Rouge, 70801 (504) 389-0401

Lugar, Richard G. (R-Ind.)
Rm. 447, 46 E. Ohio St., Indianapolis, 46204
(317) 269-5555

Rm. 103, 5530 Sohl Ave., Hammond, 46320
(219) 937-5380
104 Federal Bldg., 1300 S. Harrison, Fort
Wayne, 46802 422-1505
103 Federal Center, Jeffersonville, 47132 (812)
288-3377
Federal Bldg., 127 N.W. Seventh St.,
Evansville, 47708 423-6871,
ext. 440

McClure, James A. (R-Idaho)
Rm. 149, Borah Station, 304 N. Eighth St.,
Boise, 83702 (208) 334-1560
P.O. Box 657, Idaho Falls, 83401 523-5541
216 Federal Bldg., 250 S. Fourth Ave.,
Pocatello, 83201 236-6817
305 Federal Bldg., Coeur d'Alene, 83814
664-3086
Lewis and Clark Motor Inn, Second & Main
Sts., Lewiston, 83501 743-3579
Ste. 106, 401 Second St. N., Twin Falls, 83001
734-6780

McConnell, Mitch (R-Ky.)
600 Federal Place, Room 136-C, Louisville,
40202 (502) 582-6304
307 Federal Bldg., Seventh & Scott Sts.,
Covington, 41011 (606) 431-4028
Irving Cobb Bldg., 608 Broadway, Paducah,
42001 (502) 442-4554
1501 South Main St., Suite N, London, 40741
(606) 864-2026
241 Main St., Bowling Green, 42101 (502)
781-1673

Mathias, Charles McC., Jr. (R-Md.)
1616 Geo. M. Fallon Federal Bldg., 31 Hopkins
Plaza, Baltimore, 21201 (301) 962-4850
Allegany County Office Building, 3 Pershing St.,
Cumberland, 21502 722-4535
Ste. 212, Weber Bldg., 9420 Annapolis Rd.,
Lanham, 20706 344-2453

Matsunaga, Spark M. (D-Hawaii)
3104 Prince Kuhio Federal Bldg., P.O. Box
50124, Honolulu, 96850 (808) 546-7555
P.O. Box 1009, Wailuku, 96793 242-4741
P.O. Box 983, Lihue, 96766 245-6986
P.O. Box 453, Hilo, 96721 329-9355

Mattingly, Mack (R-Ga.)
Ste. 195, 380 Interstate N., Atlanta, 30339 (404)
952-8686
Ste. 1458, 75 Spring St., Atlanta, 30303 221-2700
Ste. 707, 2607 Cross Country Office Park,
Columbus, 31906 563-7444

105 Federal Bldg., 125 Bull St., Savannah, 31412 (912) 944-4230

Ste. 350, Albany Towers, 235 Roosevelt Ave., Albany, 31701 883-3060

Melcher, John (D-Mont.)
1016 Federal Bldg., Billings, 59101 (406) 657-6644

23 S. Last Chance Gulch, Helena, 59601 449-5251

104 Fourth St. N., Great Falls, 59401 452-9585

200 E. Broadway, Box 8568, Missoula, 59807 329-3528

55 W. Granite, Butte, 59701 723-8211

Metzenbaum, Howard M. (D-Ohio)
Rm. 442, 121 E. State St., Columbus, 43215 (614) 469-6774

2915 Anthony J. Celebrezze Fed. Bldg., E. Ninth & Lakeside Ave., Cleveland, 44114 (216) 522-7272

Ste. 510, City Center 1 LTD, 100 Federal Plaza E., Youngstown, 44503 746-1132

8405 Federal Bldg., Cincinnati, 45202 (513) 684-3894

234 Summit St., Toledo, 43603 (419) 259-7536

Mitchell, George J. (D-Maine)
Federal Bldg., 33 College Ave., P.O. Box 786, Waterville, 04901 (207) 873-3361

New Federal Bldg., 151 Forest Ave., P.O. Box 8300, Portland, 04101 780-3561

Federal Bldg., 202 Harlow St., P.O. Box 1237, Bangor, 04401 945-0451

11 Lisbon St., Lewiston, 04240 784-0163

5 Washington St., Biddeford, 04005 282-4144

6 Church St., Presque Isle, 04769 764-5601

387 Main St., Rockland, 04841 596-0311

Moynihan, Daniel P. (D-N.Y.)
733 Third Ave., New York City, 10017 (212) 661-5150

214 Main St., Oneonta, 13820 (607) 433-2310

Federal Office Bldg., 111 W. Huron St., Buffalo, 14202 (716) 846-4097

Murkowski, Frank H. (R-Alaska)
Federal Bldg., 701 C St., Box 1, Anchorage, 99513 (907) 271-3735

Federal Bldg., 101–12th Ave., Box 7, Fairbanks, 99701 456-0233

Federal Bldg., Box 1647, Juneau, 99802 586-7400

501 Federal Bldg., Ketchikan, 99901 225-6880

P.O. Box 3030, Kenai, 99611 283-5808

P.O. Box 2399, Kodiak, 99615 486-5407

P.O. Box 1860, Nome, 99762 443-5511

Nickles, Don (R-Okla.)
Rm. 820, 215 Dean McGee Ave., Oklahoma City, 73102 (405) 231-4941

1916 Lake Rd., Ponca City, 74601 767-1270

106 Federal Bldg., Fifth & E Ave., Lawton, 73501 357-9878

3003 Federal Bldg., 333 W. Fourth St., Tulsa, 74103 (918) 581-7651

Nunn, Sam (D-Ga.)
930 Federal Bldg., 275 Peachtree St., N.E., Atlanta, 30303 (404) 221-4811

361 Federal Bldg., 600 E. First St., Rome 30161 291-5896

130 Federal Bldg., Gainesville, 30501 532-9976

101 U.S. Post Office Bldg., Columbus, 31902 327-3270

915 Main St., Perry, 31069 (912) 987-1458

Federal Bldg., 126 Bull St., Savannah, 31402 944-4300

Packwood, Bob (R-Ore.)
Ste. 385, 1220 S.W. Third, Portland, 97204 (503) 221-3370

Pell, Claiborne (D-R.I.)
418 Federal Bldg., Providence, 02903 (401) 528-5456

Pressler, Larry (R-S.D.)
Empire Mall, Sioux Falls, 57101 (605) 336-2980, ext. 433

520 S. Main St., Aberdeen, 57401 225-0250, ext. 471

Rushmore Mall, Unit 105, Rapid City, 57701 341-1185

P.O. Box 340, Pierre, 57501 224-9552

Proxmire, William (D-Wis.)
344 H.S. Reuss Fed. Bldg., 517 E. Wisconsin, Milwaukee, 53202 (414) 272-0388

Pryor, David (D-Ark.)
3030 Federal Bldg., Little Rock, 72201 (501) 378-6336

Quayle, Dan (R-Ind.)
Rm. 447, 46 E. Ohio St., Indianapolis, 46204 (317) 269-5555

5530 Sohl Ave., Hammond, 46320 (219) 937-5380

340 Federal Bldg., 1300 S. Harrison St., Fort Wayne, 46802 422-1505

Rm. 103, Bldg. #66, Jeffersonville Fed. Depot, 1201 E. 10th St., Jeffersonville, 47132 (812) 288-3377

240 Federal Bldg., 127 N.W. Seventh St.,
Evansville, 47708 423-6871,
ext. 440

Riegle, Donald W., Jr. (D-Mich.)
1850 McNamara Fed. Bldg., 477 Michigan Ave.,
Detroit, 48226 (313) 226-3188
Sabuco Bldg., S-910, 352 S. Saginaw, Flint,
48502 234-5621
Rm. 705, Washington Sq. Bldg., 109 W.
Michigan Ave., Lansing, 48933 (517) 377-1713
323 Post Office Bldg., 200 W. Washington St.,
Marquette, 49855 (906) 228-7457
117 W. Cass Ave., Cadillac, 49601 (616)
775-0951
716 Gerald R. Ford Fed. Bldg. & Courthouse,
110 Michigan St., N.W., Grand Rapids, 49503
456-2592

Rockefeller, John D. (D-W.Va.)
812 Quarrier, Suite 200, Charleston, 25301 (304)
347-5372

Roth, William V., Jr. (R-Del.)
3021 Federal Bldg., 844 King St., Wilmington,
19801 (302) 573-6291
2215 Federal Bldg., 300 S. New St., Dover,
19901 674-3308

Rudman, Warren B. (R-N.H.)
125 N. Main St., Concord, 03301 (603)
225-7115/7116
Norris Cotton Federal Bldg., 275 Chestnut St.,
Manchester, 03103 666-7591
Thos. J. McIntyre Federal Bldg., 80 Daniel St.,
Portsmouth, 03801 431-5900
157 Main St., Berlin, 03570 752-2604

Sarbanes, Paul S. (D-Md.)
1518 Geo. M. Fallon Fed. Ofc. Bldg., 31
Hopkins Plaza, Baltimore, 21201 (301)
962-4436
1110 Fidler Lane, Silver Spring, 20910 589-8800
1906 Frederick St., Cumberland, 21502 722-5369
Rte. 3, 87 Bonhill, Salisbury, 21801 546-4998

Sasser, James R. (D-Tenn.)
569 U.S. Courthouse, Nashville, 37203 (615)
251-7353
237 Federal Bldg., Chattanooga, 37401 756-8836
Tri-City Airport, Blountville, 37617 323-6207
307 U.S. Post Office Bldg., Knoxville, 37902
673-4204
403 Federal Office Bldg., 169 N. Main St.,
Memphis, 38103 (901) 521-4187
B-8 Post Office Bldg., Jackson, 38301 424-6600

Simon, Paul (D-Ill.)
230 South Dearborn, Kluczynski Bldg.,
Chicago, 60604 (312) 353-4952
3 West Old Capitol Plaza, Suite 1, Springfield,
67201 (217) 492-4960
250 West Cherry, Room 115 B, Carbondale,
62901 (618) 457-3653

Simpson, Alan K. (R-Wyo.)
3201 Federal Center, Casper, 82601 (307)
261-5172
2007 Federal Office Bldg., Cheyenne, 82001
772-2477
Ste. 1, 1737 E. Sheridan, P.O. Box 430, Cody,
82414 527-7121
209 Grand Ave., P.O. Box 335, Laramie, 82070
745-5303
Ste. 104, 2632 Foothill Blvd., Rock Springs,
82901 382-5079
P.O. Box 3155, Gillette, 82716 682-7091

Specter, Arlen (R-Pa.)
9400 William J. Green, Jr., Federal Bldg.,
Philadelphia, 19106 (215) 597-7200
201 Post Office Bldg., Fifth & Hamilton St.,
Allentown, 18101 776-4374
2017 Wm. S. Moorhead Federal Bldg., Liberty
Ave., Pittsburgh, 15222 (412) 644-3400
118 Federal Bldg., Sixth & State Sts., Erie,
16501 (814) 453-3010
1159 Federal Bldg., 228 Walnut St., Box 1092,
Harrisburg, 17101 (717) 782-3952
312 Courthouse & Post Office Bldg.,
Washington & Linden Sts., Scranton, 18503
346-2006
Rm. 306, S. Main Towers, 116 S. Main,
Wilkes-Barre, 18701 826-6265

Stafford, Robert T. (R-Vt.)
27 S. Main St., Rutland, 05701 (802) 775-5446
Rm. 45, The Champlain Mill, 1 Main St.,
Winooski, 05404 951-6707

Stennis, John C. (D-Miss.)
303 Post Office Bldg., P.O. Box 39, Jackson,
39205 (601) 353-5494
DeKalb, 39328 743-2631

Stevens, Ted (R-Alaska)
Federal Bldg., 701 C St., Box 2, Anchorage,
99513 (907) 271-5915
Federal Bldg., Box 4, 101–12th Ave.,
Fairbanks, 99701 456-0261
403 Federal Bldg., P.O. Box 149, Juneau, 99801
586-7400
501 Federal Bldg., Ketchikan, 99901 225-6880

P.O. Box 3030, Kenai, 99611 283-5808
Rm. 2, Harbor View Bldg., P.O. Box 2399,
Kodiak, 99615 486-5407
P.O. Box 1860, Nome, 99762 443-2842

Symms, Steven D. (R-Idaho)
338 Borah Post Office, P.O. Box 1190, Boise,
83701 (208) 334-1776
305 Federal Bldg., Coeur d'Alene, 83814
664-5490
Ste. 103, Bollinger Plaza, 301 D St., Lewiston,
83501 743-1492
105 Federal Bldg., Moscow, 83843 882-5560
211 Federal Bldg., Idaho Falls, 83401 522-9779
Rm. 108, 401 Second St. N., Twin Falls, 83301
734-2515
207 Federal Bldg., Pocatello, 83201 236-6775

Thurmond, Strom (R-S.C.)
Strom Thurmond Federal Bldg., 1835 Assembly
St., Columbia, 29201 (803) 765-5496
29 Federal Bldg., 211 York St., N.E., Aiken,
29801 649-2591
Rm. 600, 334 Meeting St., Charleston, 29401
724-4282
McMillan Federal Bldg., 401 W. Evans St.,
Florence, 29501 662-8873

Trible, Paul S., Jr. (R-Va.)
Ste. 1-B, 113–115 Third St., Richmond, 23219
(804) 771-2221
2101 Executive Dr., Tower Box 59, Hampton,
23666 838-3309
Rm. 514, 105 S. Union St., Danville, 24541
792-5444
P.O. Box 869, Roanoke, 24005 (703) 962-4676

Wallop, Malcolm (R-Wyo.)
2201 Federal Bldg., Casper, 82601 (307)
261-5098
2009 Federal Center, Cheyenne, 82001 634-0626
2515 Foothill Blvd., Rock Springs, 82901
382-5127
40 S. Main St., Sheridan 82801 672-6456
P.O. Box 1014, Lander, 82520 332-2293

Warner, John W. (R-Va.)
1100 E. Main St., Richmond, 23219 (804)
771-2579
805 Federal Bldg., 200 Granby Mall, Norfolk,
23510 441-3079
235 Federal Bldg., 180 W. Main St., Abingdon,
24210 (703) 628-8158

Weicker, Lowell P., Jr. (R-Conn.)
102 U.S. Courthouse & Federal Bldg., 915

Lafayette Blvd., Bridgeport, 06604 (203)
579-5830
One Corporate Center, 11th Fl., Hartford,
06103 722-2882
Ste. 3A, 100 Grand St., Waterbury, 06702
575-9537

Wilson, Pete (R-Calif.)
Rm. 6-S-9, 880 Front St., San Diego, 92188
(619) 293-5257
4015 Federal Bldg., 1130 O St., Fresno, 93721
(209) 487-5727
Phillip Burton Fed. Bldg. & U.S. Courthouse,
San Francisco, 94102 (415) 556-4307
11221 Federal Bldg., 11000 Wilshire Blvd., Los
Angeles, 90024 (213) 209-7543

Zorinsky, Edward (D-Neb.)
8311 Federal Bldg., 215 N. 17th St., Omaha,
68102 (402) 221-4381
294 Federal Bldg., 100 Centennial Mall N.,
Lincoln, 68508 471-5246
1811 W. Second St., Grand Island, 68801 (308)
381-5552

United States House of Representatives

This list includes House Members who are serving
in the 99th Congress and must stand reelection in
1986. Two vacancies, 8th District in Indiana and
the 8th District of Louisiana, are absent from this
roster. Party affiliation is in brackets (D stands for
Democrat, R stands for Republican), followed by
state and district.

Ackerman, Gary L. (D/L-N.Y., 7th)
118-35 Queens Blvd., Forest Hills, 11375 (212)
263-1525

Addabbo, Joseph P. (D-N.Y., 6th)
96-11–101st Ave., Ozone Park, 11416 (212)
845-3131
18-36 Mott St., Far Rockaway, 11691 327-2727
186-17 Merrick Blvd., Springfield Gardens,
11413 276-3660

Akaka, Daniel K. (D-Hawaii, 2nd)
5104 Prince Kuhio Federal Bldg., Honolulu,
96850 (808) 546-8952

Alexander, Bill (D-Ark., 1st)
211A Gathings Bldg., 615 S. Main, Jonesboro,
72401 (501) 972-4600
202 Federal Bldg., Batesville, 72501 698-1761
3 St. Francis County Courthouse, Forest City,
72335 633-5226

Anderson, Glenn M. (D-Calif., 32nd)
300 Long Beach Blvd., P.O. Box 2349, Long Beach, 90801 (213) 548-2721

Andrews, Michael A. (D-Tex., 25th)
7707 Fannin, Houston, 77054 (713) 791-1877
4008 Vista, Pasadena, 77504 943-8833

Annunzio, Frank (D-Ill, 11th)
Rm. 201, 4747 W. Peterson Ave., Chicago, 60646 (312) 736-0700
3816 Kluczynski Federal Bldg., 230 S. Dearborn St., Chicago, 60604 353-2525

Anthony, Beryl F., Jr. (D-Ark., 4th)
206 Federal Bldg., P.O. Box 2021, El Dorado, 71730 (501) 863-0121
2521 Federal Bldg., Pine Bluff, 71601 536-3376
201 Federal Bldg., P.O. Box T, Hot Springs, 71901 624-1011

Applegate, Douglas (D-Ohio, 18th)
Rm. 610, Ohio Valley Towers, Steubenville, 43952 (614) 283-3716
150 W. Main St., St. Clairsville, 43950 695-4600
109 W. Third St., East Liverpool, 43920 (216) 385-5921
168 W. High Ave., New Philadelphia, 44663 343-9112

Archer, Bill (R-Tex., 7th)
7501 Federal Bldg., 515 Rusk St., Houston, 77002 (713) 229-2763

Armey, Richard K. (R-Tex., 26th)
250 South Stemmons, #210, Lewistown, 75067 (214) 221-4527
1141 West Pioneer Parkway, #101, Arlington, 76013 (817) 461-2556

Aspin, Les (D-Wis., 1st)
603 Main St., Racine, 53401 (414) 632-4446
12 Post Office Bldg., 210 Dodge St., Janesville, 53545 (608) 752-9074

Atkins, Chester G. (D-Mass., 5th)
134 Middle St., Lowell, 01852 (617) 459-0101
229 Essex St., Room 201, Lawrence, 01840 683-5313
650 Worster Rd., Framingham, 01701 879-4566

AuCoin, Les (D-Ore., 1st)
1716 Federal Office Bldg., 1220 S.W. Third Ave., Portland, 97204 (503) 221-2901

Bedham, Robert E. (R-Calif., 40th)
Ste. 240, 180 Newport Center Dr., Newport Beach, 92660 (714) 644-4040

Barnard, Doug, Jr. (D-Ga., 10th)
128 Stephens Federal Office Bldg., P.O. Box 3, Athens, 30601 (404) 546-2194
407 Telfair St., P.O. Box 10123, Augusta, 30903 724-0739
Ste. 206, 5195 Jimmy Carter Blvd., Norcross, 30093 447-0770

Barnes, Michael D. (D-Md., 8th)
Ste. 302, 11141 Georgia Ave., Wheaton, 20902 (301) 946-6801

Bartlett, Steve (R-Tex., 3rd)
Ste. 4190, 6600 LBJ Fwy, Dallas, 75240 (214) 767-4848

Barton, Joe (R-Tex., 6th)
Interfirst Tower #507, 300 W. Davis, Conroe, 77301 (409) 760-2291
PO Box 4802, Bryon, 77805 846-1985
Interfirst Bank #101, 303 West Knox, Ennis, 77109 (214) 875-8488
3509 Hulen #110, Fort Worth, 76107 (817) 737-7737

Bateman, Herbert H. (R-Va., 1st)
739 Thimble Shoals Blvd., Newport News, 23606 (804) 877-5832
P.O. Box 1183, Tappahannock, 22560 443-4740
Box 447, Accomak, 23301 787-7836

Bates, Jim (D-Calif., 44th)
Rm. 5S35, 880 Front St., San Diego, 92188 (619) 234-2766
Ste. A, 430 Davidson St., Chula Vista, 92010 691-1166

Bedell, Berkley (D-Iowa, 6th)
318 Federal Bldg., Sioux City, 51101 (712) 233-3281
309 Post Office Bldg., Mason City, 50401 (515) 424-3613

Bellenson, Anthony C. (D-Calif., 23rd)
Ste. 14223, 11000 Wilshire Blvd., Los Angeles, 90024 (213) 209-7801
Ste. 222, 18401 Burbank Blvd., Tarzana, 91356 (818) 345-1560

Bennett, Charles E. (D-Fla., 3rd)
Old St. Luke's Bldg., 314 Palmetto St., Jacksonville, 32202 (904) 791-2587

Bentley, Helen Delich (R-Md., 2nd)
200 E. Joppa Rd., #400, Towson, 21204 (301) 337-7222

Bereuter, Doug (R-Neb., 1st)
1045 K St., P.O. Box 82887, Lincoln, 68501 (402) 471-5400

Berman, Howard L. (D-Calif., 26th)
Ste. 506, 14600 Roscoe Blvd., Panorama City, 91402 (213) 891-0543

Bevill, Tom (D-Ala., 4th)
107 Federal Bldg., 600 Broad St., Gadsden, 35901 (205) 546-0201
102-104 Federal Bldg., Cullman, 35055 734-6043
1804 Fourth Ave., Jasper, 35501 221-2310

Biaggi, Mario (D-N.Y., 19th)
3255 Westchester Ave., Bronx, 10461 (212) 931-0100
5 Seminary Ave., Yonkers, 10704 (914) 375-0500

Bilirakis, Michael (R-Fla., 9th)
Ste. 1103, 1100 Cleveland St., Clearwater, 33515 (813) 441-3721
Ste. 5, 608 W. Gulf Dr., New Port Richey, 33552 847-1022
(Mon., Wed. & Fri.) Ste. 107-F, 408 W. Renfro St., Plant City, 33566 752-9280

Billey, Thomas J., Jr. (R-Va., 3rd)
510 E. Main St., Richmond, 23219 (804) 771-2809

Blaz, Ben (Delegate, Guam)
Agana Shopping Ctr., #117, Rt. 4, Agana, 96910 Oversea Opr. 462-6700

Boehlert, Sherwood L. (R-N.Y., 25th)
302 Rome City Hall, Rome 13440 (315) 339-0013
200 Federal Bldg., 10 Broad St., Utica, 13503 793-8146
Rm. 203, 125 Main St., Oneonta, 13820 (607) 432-5524
42 S. Broad St., Norwich, 13815 334-5896
17 Main St., Cortland, 13045 753-9324

Boggs, Lindy (D-La., 2nd)
1012 Hale Boggs Federal Bldg., New Orleans, 70130 (504) 589-2274

Boland, Edward P. (D-Mass., 2nd)
Rm. 309, 1550 Main St., Springfield, 01103 (413) 785-0325
881 Main St., Fitchburg, 01420 (617) 342-8722

Boner, William Hill (D-Tenn., 5th)
552 U.S. Courthouse, Nashville, 37203 (615) 251-5295

Bonior, David E. (D-Mich., 12th)
82 Macomb Pl., Mt. Clemens, 48043
101 Federal Bldg., 526 Water St., Port Huron, 48060 987-8889

Bonker, Don (D-Wash., 3rd)
207 Federal Bldg., Olympia, 98501 (206) 753-9528
Post Office Bldg., Longview, 98632 636-5260
700 E. Evergreen Blvd., Vancouver, 98661 696-7942

Borski, Robert A. (D-Pa., 3rd)
303 Smylie Times Bldg., 8001 Roosevelt Blvd., Philadelphia, 19152 (215)334-3355

Bosco, Douglas H. (D-Calif., 1st)
329 Federal Bldg., 777 Sonoma Ave., Santa Rosa, 95404 (707) 525-4235
Ste. 216, The Eureka Inn, Seventh & F Sts., Eureka, 95501 445-2055

Boucher, Frederick C. (Rick) (D-Va., 9th)
180 E. Main St., Abingdon, 24210 (703) 628-1145
321 Shawnee Ave., E, Big Stone Gap, 24219 523-5450
112 N. Washington Ave., P.O. Box 1268, Pulaski, 24301 980-4310

Boulter, Beau (R-Tex., 13th)
Federal Bldg., #208, 1000 Lamar, Wichita Falls, 76301 (817) 767-0541
205 E. Fifth, Amarillo, 79101 (806) 376-2381

Boxer, Barbara (D-Calif., 6th)
Phillip Burton Federal Bldg. & U.S. Courthouse, 450 Golden Gate Ave., Box 36024, San Francisco, 94102 (415) 556-1333
901 Irwin St., San Rafael, 94901 457-7272
Rm. 8, 823 Marin St., Vallejo, 94590 (707) 552-0720

Breaux, John B. (D-La., 7th)
2530 Federal Bldg., 921 Moss St., Lake Charles, 70601 (318) 437-7251
301 Federal Bldg., 705 Jefferson St., Lafayette, 70501 264-6657

Brooks, Jack (D-Tex., 9th)
230 Jack Brooks Federal Bldg., Beaumont, 77701 (409) 839-2508

217 U.S. Post Office Building, 601–25th St., Galveston, 77550 766-3608

Broomfield, William S. (R-Mich., 18th)
430 N. Woodward, Birmingham, 48011 (313) 642-3800
371 N. Main, Milford, 48042 685-2640

Brown, George E., Jr. (D-Calif., 36th)
657 N. La Cadena Dr., Colton, 92324 (714) 825-2472
Ste. 116, 3600 Lime St., Riverside, 92502 686-8863

Brown, Hank (R-Colo., 4th)
2214 W. 118th Ave., Denver, 80234 (303) 466-3443
Ste. 101-A, 1015–37th Ave. Court, Greeley, 80634 352-4112
203 Federal Bldg., Fort Collins, 80521 493-9132
230 Main St., P.O. Box 767, Fort Morgan, 80701 867-8909
243 Post Office Building, La Junta, 81050 384-7370

Broyhill, James T. (R-N.C., 10th)
224 Mulberry St., S.W., Lenoir, 28645 (704) 758-4247
832 E. Garrison Blvd., Gastonia, 28054 864-9922
133 Federal Bldg., P.O. Box 1830, Hickory, 28601 328-8718

Bruce, Terry L. (D-Ill., 19th)
114 West Chestnut, Olney, 62450 (618) 395-8585
106 N. Vermilon, Danville, 61832 (217) 446-7445
102 E. University, Champaign, 61820 398-0020

Bryant, John (D-Tex., 5th)
Ste. 518, 8035 East R. L. Thornton, Dallas, 75228 (214) 767-6554

Burton, Danny L. (R-Ind., 6th)
Ste. 814, 8900 Keystone at the Crossing, Indianapolis, 46240 (317) 848-0201
922 Meridian Plaza, Anderson, 46016 649-6887

Burton, Sala (D-Calif., 5th)
11104 Phillip Burton Fed. Bldg. & U.S. Courthouse, 450 Golden Gate Ave., San Francisco, 94102 (415) 556-4862

Bustamante, Albert G. (D-Tex., 23rd)
727 E. Durango, San Antonio, 78206 (512) 229-6191
1300 Matamoros, Laredo, 78040 724-7774
Federal Courthouse Bldg., #103, 300 E. Broadway, Del Rio, 78841 774-6515

Uvalde County Courthouse, Uvalde, 78801 278-5821

Byron, Beverly B. (D-Md., 6th)
10 E. Church St., Frederick, 21701 (301) 662-8622
Ste. 110, Franklin Center, 100 W. Franklin St., Hagerstown, 21740 797-6043
P.O. Box 3275, Cumberland, 21504 729-0300
6 N. Court St., Westminster, 21157
From Carroll County   848-5366
From Howard County   962-3348

Callahan, Sonny (R-Ala., 1st)
109 St. Joseph St., #8011, Mobile, Ala. 36602 (205) 690-2811

Campbell, Carroll A., Jr. (R-S.C., 4th)
P.O. Box 1330, Spartanburg, 29304 (803) 582-6422
P.O. Box 10183, Federal Station, Greenville, 29603 232-1141
P.O. Box 479, Union, 29379 427-3172

Carney, William (R-N.Y., 1st)
2400 N. Ocean Ave., Farmingville, 11738 (516) 736-1100

Carper, Thomas R. (D-Del., At Lge.)
5021 J. Caleb Boggs Fed. Office Bldg., 844 King St., Wilmington, 19801 (302) 573-6181
J. Allen Frear Federal Bldg., 300 S. New St., Dover, 19901 736-1666

Carr, M. Robert (D-Mich., 6th)
91 N. Saginaw, Pontiac, 48058 (313) 332-2510
116 Bailey St., East Lansing, 48823 (517) 337-6714

Chandler, Rod (R-Wash., 8th)
3350 161st Ave., S.E., Bellevue, 98008 (206) 442-0116
1025 S. 320th, Federal Way, 98003 593-6371

Chappell, Bill, Jr. (D-Fla., 4th)
575 N. Halifax Ave., Daytona Beach, 32018 (904) 253-7632
Ste. 13, 3015 Hartley Rd., Jacksonville, 32217 262-3570

Chapple, Eugene A. (R-Calif., 2nd)
Ste. 30, 500 Cohasset Rd., Chico, 95926 (916) 893-8363

Cheney, Richard B. (R-Wyo., At Lge.)
4003 Federal Bldg., Casper, 82601 (307) 261-5413

2015 Federal Bldg., Cheyenne, 82001 772-2451
560 Uinta Dr., P.O. Box 1357, Green River,
    82935 875-6969

Clay, William L. (Bill) (D-Mo., 1st)
6197 Delmar Blvd., St. Louis, 63112 (314)
    725-5770
12263 Bellefontaine Rd., St. Louis, 63138
    355-6811

Clinger, William F., Jr. (R-Pa., 23rd)
Ste. 219, 315 S. Allen St., State College, 16801
    (814) 238-1776
Rm. 805, Penn Bank Bldg., Warren, 16365
    726-3910

Coats, Daniel R. (R-Ind., 4th)
326 Federal Bldg., Ft. Wayne, 46802 (219)
    424-3041

Cobey, William W., Jr. (R-N.C., 4th)
200 W. Morgan St, Raleigh, 27601 (919)
    755-4611
910 Airport Rd., Chapel Hill, 27514 942-0444
Rm. 101 Federal Bldg., Sunset Ave., Asheboro,
    27203 625-3060

Coble, Howard (R-N.C., 6th)
P.O. Box 299, Greensboro, 27402 (919)
    378-5005
510 Ferndale Rd., High Point, 27260 886-5106
P.O. Box 814, Graham, 27253 229-0159
P.O. Box 1813, Lexington, 27293 (704) 249-7011

Coelho, Tony (D-Calif., 15th)
Federal Bldg., 415 W. 18th St., Merced, 95340
    (209) 383-4455
2001 Federal Bldg., 1130 O St., Fresno, 93721
    487-5004
Federal Bldg., 1125 Eye St., Modesto, 95354
    527-1914

Coleman, E. Thomas (R-Mo., 6th)
2701 Rockcreek Pkwy., No. Kansas City, 64116
    (816) 474-9035
Post Office & Fed. Bldg., Eighth & Edmond
    Sts., St. Joseph, 64501 364-3900

Coleman, Ronald D. (D-Tex., 16th)
146 U.S. Courthouse, 511 E. San Antonio, El
    Paso, 79901 (915) 541-7650
304 U.S. Post Office, 106 W. Fourth St., Pecos,
    79772 445-6218

Collins, Cardiss (D-Ill., 7th)
3880 Kluczynski Fed. Bldg., 230 S. Dearborn
    St., Chicago, 60604 (312) 353-5754

3851 W. Roosevelt Rd., Chicago, 60624
    522-2444
505 Main St., Maywood, 60153 450-1600

Combest, Larry (R-Tex., 19th)
Federal Bldg., 1205 Texas Ave., #613,
    Lubbock, 79401 (806) 763-1611
400 W. Fourth, Suite 201, Odessa, 79761 (915)
    337-1669

Conte, Silvio O. (R-Mass., 1st)
Federal Bldg., 78 Center St. Arterial, Pittsfield,
    01201 (413) 442-0946
187 High St., Holyoke, 01040 532-7010

Conyers, John, Jr. (D-Mich., 1st)
669 Federal Office Bldg., 231 W. Lafayette
    Blvd., Detroit, 48226 (313) 226-7022

Cooper, James H. (D-Tenn., 4th)
116 Depot St., P.O. Box 725, Shelbyville, 37160
    (615) 684-1114
City Hall, 7 S. High St., Winchester, 37398
    967-4150
Ste. 1, 208 E. First North St., P.O. Box 2025,
    Morristown, 37816 587-9000
106 W. Second St., P.O. Box 845, Crossville,
    38555 484-1864

Coughlin, Lawrence (R-Pa., 13th)
Rm. 607, One Montgomery Plaza, Norristown,
    19401 (215) 277-4040

Courter, Jim (R-N.J., 12th)
Post Office Bldg., 1 Morris St., Morristown,
    07960 (201) 538-7267
41 N. Bridge St., Somerville, 08876 722-8200
14 River Rd., Summit, 07901 273-4855

Coyne, William J. (D-Pa., 14th)
2005 Wm. S. Moorhead Fed. Bldg., Pittsburgh,
    15222 (412) 644-2870

Craig, Larry E. (R-Idaho, 1st)
Rm. 134, 304 N. Eighth St., Boise, 83701 (208)
    334-9046
Ste. 103, 301 D St., Lewiston, 83501 743-0792
103 N. Fourth St., Coeur d'Alene, 83814
    667-6130

Crane, Philip M. (R-Ill., 12th)
Ste. 101, 1450 S. New Wilke Rd., Arlington
    Heights, 60005 (312) 394-0790
Rm. 101, 1415 Cedar Lake Rd., Round Lake
    Beach, 60073 546-1050
56 N. Williams St., Crystal Lake, 60014 (815)
    459-3399

Crockett, George W., Jr. (D-Mich., 13th)
Ste. 106, 8401 Woodward Ave., Detroit, 48202
(313) 874-4900

Daniel, Dan (D-Va., 5th)
301 Post Office Bldg., Danville, 24541 (804)
792-1280
Abbitt Federal Bldg., 103 S. Main St.,
Farmville, 23901 392-8331

Dannemeyer, William E. (R-Calif., 39th)
Ste. 100, 1235 N. Harbor Blvd., Fullerton, 92632
(714) 992-0141

Darden, George (Buddy) (D-Ga., 7th)
301 Federal Bldg., Rome, 30161 (404) 291-7777
Ste. 212, 366 Powder Springs St., Marietta,
30064 422-4480
125 Main St., Lafayette, 30728 638-7042

Deschle, Thomas A. (D-S.D., At Lge.)
800 S. Cliff, P.O. Box 1274, Sioux Falls, 57101
(605) 334-9596
603 S. Main, P.O. Box 1536, Aberdeen, 57401
225-8823
816 Sixth St., P.O. Box 8168, Rapid City, 57709
348-7551

Deub, Harold (Hal) (R-Neb., 2nd)
8424 Federal Bldg., 215 N. 17th St., Omaha,
68102 (402) 221-4216

Davis, Robert W. (R-Mich., 11th)
215 W. Washington St., Marquette, 49855 (906)
228-3700
102 Federal Bldg., Alpena, 49707 (517) 356-2028
215 S. Court St., Gaylord, 49735 732-3151
(Fri.) City County Bldg., 325 Court St., Sault
Ste. Marie, 49783 (906) 635-5261,
ext. 36

de la Garza, E. (D-Tex., 15th)
1418 Beech St., La Posada Village, McAllen,
78501 (512) 682-5545

DeLay, Thomas D. (R-Tex., 22nd)
9000 Southwest Freeway, #205, Houston, 77074
(713) 270-4000
500 North Chenango, #312, Angleton, 77515
(409) 849-4446

Dellums, Ronald V. (D-Calif., 8th)
Rm. 105, 201 13th St., Oakland, 94617 (415)
763-0370
9424 E. 14th St., Oakland, 94603 562-4981

Rm. 217, 2490 Channing Way, Berkeley, 94704
548-7767
3557 Mount Diablo Blvd., Lafayette, 94549
283-8125

de Lugo, Ron (D-V. Isl., Deleg.)
Federal Bldg., Box 808, St. Thomas, 00801 (809)
774-4408
Sunny Isle Shopping Center, P.O. Box LL,
Christiansted, St. Croix, 00820 773-5900

Derrick, Butler (D-S.C., 3rd)
315 S. McDuffie St., P.O. Box 4126, Anderson,
29622 (803) 224-7401
5 Federal Bldg., 211 York St., N.E., Aiken,
29801 649-5571
129 Federal Bldg., Greenwood, 29646 223-8251

DeWine, Michael (R-Ohio, 7th)
220 Post Office Bldg., 150 N. Limestone St.,
Springfield, 45501 (513) 325-0474
144 E. Center St., Marion, 43302 (614) 387-5300

Dickinson, William L. (R-Ala., 2nd)
301 Federal Court Bldg., 15 Lee St.,
Montgomery, 36104 (205) 832-7292
Federal Bldg., 100 W. Troy St., Dothan, 36303
794-9680

Dicks, Norman D. (D-Wash., 8th)
Ste. 604, Security Bldg., 915½ Pacific Ave.,
Tacoma, 98402 (206) 593-6536
Rm. 207, Sheridan Plaza, 2817 Wheaton Way,
Bremerton, 96310 479-4011

Dingell, John D. (D-Mich., 18th)
Rm. 204, 4917 Schaefer Rd., Dearborn, 48126
(313) 846-1276
14 W. First St., Monroe, 48161 243-1849

DioGuardi, Joseph J. (R-N.Y., 20th)
1 North Broadway, #901, White Plains, 10601
(914) 997-6440

Dixon, Julian C. (D-Calif., 28th)
Ste. 301, 111 N. LaBrea Ave., Inglewood, 90301
(213) 678-5424

Donnelly, Brian (D-Mass., 11th)
47 Washington St., Quincy, 02169 (617)
472-1800
61 Main St., Brockton, 02401 583-6300
2307 John F. Kennedy Federal Bldg., Boston,
02203 223-0038

Dorgan, Byron L. (D-N.D., At Lge.)
358 Federal Bldg., Third St. & Rosser Ave.,

P.O. Box 2579, Bismarck, 58502 (701)
255-4011, ext. 618
101 Fed. Sq. Bldg., 112-114 Robert St., P.O.
Box 1664, Fargo, 58107 237-5771,
ext. 5135

Dornan, Robert K. (R-Calif., 38th)
12387 Lewis St., Garden Grove, 92640 (714)
971-9292

Dowdy, Wayne (D-Miss., 4th)
P.O. Box 569, Jackson, 39205 (601) 969-3300
Ste. C-1, Commerce Bldg., 521 Main St.,
Natchez, 39120 446-8628

Downey, Thomas J. (D-N.Y., 2nd)
4 Udall Rd., West Islip, 11795 (516) 661-8777
Contact District Office for Mobile Office
schedule.

Dreier, David (R-Calif., 33rd)
112 N. Second Ave., Covina 91723 (213)
339-9078

Duncan, John J. (R-Tenn., 2nd)
318 Post Office Bldg., Knoxville, 37902 (615)
673-4282
McMinn County Courthouse, Athens, 37303
745-4671
Rm. 419, Blount National Bank Bldg.,
Maryville, 37801 984-5464

Durbin, Richard J. (D-Ill., 20th)
1307 S. Seventh St., P.O. Box 790, Springfield,
62705 (217) 492-4062
531 Hampshire, Quincy, 62301 228-1042
363 S. Main St., P.O. Box 1506, Decatur, 62523
428-4745

Dwyer, Bernard J. (D-N.J., 6th)
214 Smith St., Perth Amboy, 08861 (201)
826-4610
U.S. Post Office, 86 Bayard St., New
Brunswick, 08901 545-5655
628 Wood Ave., N., Linden, 07036 486-4000

Dymally, Mervyn M. (D-Calif., 31st)
322 W. Compton Blvd., Compton, 90220 (213)
536-6930
City Hall, 4455 W. 126th St., Hawthorne, 90250
536-6772
Carson Community Ctr., 801 E. Carson St.,
Carson, 90745 536-6934

Dyson, Roy P. (D-Md., 1st)
1 Plaza E., Salisbury, 21801 (301) 742-9070

Ste. 105, Waldorf Five Center, Rte. 3, P.O. Box
742, Waldorf, 20601 645-4844
38 W. Bel Air Ave., Aberdeen, 21001 272-7070
County Annex B, 206 N. Commerce St.,
Centreville, 21617 758-1113

Early, Joseph D. (D-Mass., 3rd)
Rm. 203, 34 Mechanic St, Worcester, 01608
(617) 752-6718

Eckart, Dennis E. (D-Ohio, 11th)
9040 Mentor Ave., Mentor, 44060 (216)
522-2056

Eckert, Fred J. (R-N.Y., 30th)
311 Federal Bldg., 100 State St., Rochester,
14614 (716) 263-3156
216 Main St., Batavia, 14020 344-2407

Edgar, Robert W. (D-Pa., 7th)
55 N. Landsdowne Ave., Landsdowne, 19050
(215) 626-7000

Edwards, Don (D-Calif., 10th)
Ste. 372, 280 S. First St., San Jose, 95113 (408)
292-0143
38750 Paseo Padre Pkwy., Fremont, 94536 (415)
792-5320

Edwards, Mickey (R-Okla., 5th)
812 Old Post Office Bldg., Oklahoma City,
73102 (405) 231-4541
Ste. 105, 114 N. Fourth, Ponca City, 74601
762-8121
Ste. 102, 1200 S.E. Frank Phillips Blvd.,
Bartlesville, 74003 (918) 336-5436

Emerson, Bill (R-Mo., 8th)
339 Broadway, Cape Girardeau, 63701 (314)
335-0101
614 Pine, P.O. Box 639, Rolla, 65401 364-2455

English, Glenn (D-Okla., 6th)
264 Old Post Office Bldg., 215 Dean A. McGee
Ave., Oklahoma City, 73102 (405) 231-5511
1120 Ninth St., P.O. Box 1927, Woodward,
73801 256-5752
Federal Bldg., Box 3612, Enid, 73702 233-9224

Erdreich, Ben (D-Ala., 6th)
105 Federal Courthouse, 1800 Fifth Ave., N.,
Birmingham, 35203 (205) 254-0956

Evans, Cooper (R-Iowa, 3rd)
162 W. Fourth St., Waterloo, 50704 (319)
234-3295

Rm. 505, 102 S. Clinton, Iowa City, 52240
351-0062
13 W. Main St., Marshalltown, 50158 (515)
753-3172

Evans, Lane (D-Ill., 17th)
3727 Blackhawk Rd., Rock Island, 61201 (309)
793-5760
125 E. Main, Galesburg, 61401 342-4411
Rm. 10, City Hall, Monmouth, 61462 734-9304
208½ N. Lafayette, Macomb, 61455 837-5263

Fascell, Dante B. (D-Fla., 19th)
Ste. 220, 7855 S.W. 104th St., Miami, 33156
(305) 350-5301

Fauntroy, Walter E. (D-D.C., Deleg.)
Rm. 311, 2041 Martin Luther King, Jr., Ave.,
S.E., D.C. 20020 (202) 426-2530

Fawell, Harris W. (R-Ill., 13th)
911 North Elm St., Hinsdale, 60521 (312)
655-2052

Fazio, Vic (D-Calif., 4th)
844B, Union Ave., Fairfield, 94533 (707)
426-4333
Ste. 26, 117 W. Main St., Woodland, 95695
(916) 666-5521
Ste. 503, 4811 Chippendale Dr., Sacramento,
95841 484-4174

Feighan, Edward F. (D-Ohio, 19th)
2951 Federal Office Bldg., 1240 E. Ninth St.,
Cleveland, 44199 (216) 522-4382

Fiedler, Bobbi (R-Calif., 21st)
Ste. 204, 21053 Devonshire St., Chatsworth,
91311 (818) 341-2121
Ste. 165, 100 E. Thousand Oaks Blvd.,
Thousand Oaks, 91360 (805) 496-4700

Fields, Jack (R-Tex., 8th)
Ste. 320, InterFirst Bank Bldg., 12605 E.
Freeway, Houston, 77015 (713) 451-6334

Fish, Hamilton, Jr. (R-N.Y., 21st)
82 Washington St., Poughkeepsie, 12501 (914)
452-4220
343 New Windsor Hwy., New Windsor, 12550
565-5015
36 Gleneida Ave., Carmel, 10512 225-5200

Flippo, Ronnie G. (D-Ala., 5th)
P.O. Box 6065, Huntsville, 35806 (205) 772-0244
301 N. Seminary St., Florence, 35630 766-7692

Florio, James J. (D-N.J., 1st)
Ste. 16–17, 1 Colby Ave., Stratford, 08084 (609)
627-8222

Foglietta, Thomas M. (D-Pa., 1st)
10402 William J. Green, Jr., Federal Bldg.,
Philadelphia, 19106 (215) 925-6840

Foley, Thomas S. (D-Wash., 5th)
574 U.S. Courthouse, Spokane, 99201 (509)
466-4580
28 W. Main St., Walla Walla, 99362 529-6111
12929 E. Sprague, Spokane Valley, 99216
926-4434

Ford, Harold E. (D-Tenn., 9th)
369 Federal Bldg., 167 N. Main, Memphis,
38103 (901) 521-4131
Mallory Post Office Bldg., 193 W. Mitchell Rd.,
Memphis, 38109 521-4141

Ford, William D. (D-Mich., 15th)
Federal Bldg., Wayne, 48184 (313) 722-1411
20155 Goddard Rd., Taylor, 48180 287-4900
31 S. Huron, Ypsilanti, 48197 482-6636

Fowler, Wyche, Jr. (D-Ga., 5th)
Ste. 425, William Oliver Bldg., 32 Peachtree St.,
Atlanta, 30303 (404) 688-8207

Frank, Barney (D-Mass., 4th)
437 Cherry St., West Newton, 02165 (617)
332-3920
10 Purchase St., Fall River, 02722 674-3551
8 N. Main St., Attleboro, 02703 226-4723

Franklin, William (Webb) (R-Miss., 2nd)
219 Federal Bldg., Greenwood, 38930 (601)
453-0126
Ste. G, 207 N. Madison, Kosciusko, 39090
289-5041
Ste. 7, 1720 Clay St., Vicksburg, 39180 638-5429

Frenzel, Bill (R-Minn., 3rd)
Rm. 445, 8120 Penn Ave., S., Bloomington,
55431 (612) 881-4600

Frost, Martin (D-Tex., 24th)
Ste. 1319, Republic Bank, Oak Cliff Tower, 400
Zang Blvd., Dallas, 75208 (214) 767-2816
Ste. 720, Republic Bank of Grand Prairie, 801
W. Freeway, Grand Prairie, 75051 262-1503

Fuqua, Don (D-Fla., 2nd)
Ste. 5015, 227 N. Bronough, Tallahassee, 32301
(904) 681-7434

1990-A S. First St., Lake City, 32055 755-5657
109 U.S. Post Office, Marianna, 32446 526-3525

Fuster, Jaime B. (Resident Commissioner, Puerto Rico)
P.O. Box 4751, Old San Juan, 00902 (809) 722-2121

Gallo, Dean A. (R-N.J., 11th)
22 N. Sussex St., Dover, 07801 (201) 328-7413
140 Littleton Rd., Parsippany, 07054 334-8000

Garcia, Robert (D-N.Y., 18th)
890 Grand Concourse, Bronx, 10451 (212) 860-6200
541 E. 138th St., Bronx, 10454 292-4014
1185 Beacon Rd., Bronx, 10456 542-4273

Gaydos, Joseph M. (D-Pa., 20th)
318 Fifth Ave., McKeesport, 15132 (412) 673-7756/644-2896
Rm. 217, Crown Bldg., 979 Fourth Ave., New Kensington, 15068 339-7070

Gejdenson, Samuel (D-Conn., 2nd)
P.O. Box 2000, Norwich, 06360 (203) 886-0139
94 Court St., Middletown, 06457 346-1123

Gekas, George W. (R-Pa., 17th)
Ste. 302, One Riverside Ofc. Ctr., 2101 N. Front St., Harrisburg, 17110 (717) 232-5123
Herman Schneebeli Federal Bldg., P.O. Box 606, Williamsport, 17703 327-8161
25 N. Fourth St., Sunbury, 17801 286-6417

Gephardt, Richard A. (D-Mo., 3rd)
9959 Gravois Rd., St. Louis, 63123 (314) 631-9959

Gibbons, Sam M. (D-Fla., 7th)
510 Federal Bldg., 500 Zack St., Tampa, 33602 (813) 228-2101

Gilman, Benjamin A. (R-N.Y., 22nd)
223 Rte. 59, Monsey, 10952 (914) 357-9000
44 East Ave., P.O. Box 358, Middletown, 10940 343-6666
190 Broadway, Monticello, 12701 796-1621
32 Main St., Hastings-on-Hudson, 10706 478-5550

Gingrich, Newt (R-Ga., 6th)
Federal Bldg., P.O. Box 848, Griffin, 30224 (404) 228-0389
Carroll County Courthouse, Carrollton, 30117 834-6398

County Office Bldg., 22 E. Broad St., Newnan, 30263 253-8355
Suite E, 6351 Jonesboro Rd, Morrow, 30260 968-3219

Glickman, Dan (D-Kan., 4th)
224 U.S. Courthouse, Box 403, Wichita, 67201 (316) 262-8396
302 Wolcott Bldg., 201 N. Main St., Hutchinson, 67501 669-9011

Gonzalez, Henry B. (D-Tex., 20th)
B124 Federal Bldg., 727 E. Durango Blvd., San Antonio, 78206 (512) 229-6199/6195

Goodling, William F. (R-Pa., 19th)
Federal Bldg., 200 S. George St., York, 17403 (717) 843-8887
212 N. Hanover St., Carlisle, 17013 243-5432
209 Post Office Bldg., Gettysburg, 17325 334-3430
2020 Yale Ave., Camp Hill, 17011 763-1988
44 Frederick St., Hanover, 17331 632-7855

Gordon, Bart (D-Tenn., 6th)
P.O. Box 1986, Murfreesboro, 37133 (615) 896-1986
P.O. Box 1140, Cookeville, 38503 528-5475
102 W. Seventh St., Columbia, 38401 388-8808

Gradison, Willis D., Jr. (R-Ohio, 2nd)
8008 Federal Bldg., 550 Main St., Cincinnati, 45202 (513) 684-2456
190 E. Main St., Batavia, 45103 732-1786

Gray, Kenneth J. (D-Ill., 22nd)
234 W. Main, West Frankfort, 62896 (618) 937-6402
P.O. Box 398, Herrin, 62948 997-3341

Gray, William H., III (D-Pa., 2nd)
6753 Germantown Ave., Philadelphia, 19119 (215) 951-5388
2318 W. Columbia Ave., Philadelphia, 19121 232-2770
22 N. 52nd St., Philadelphia, 19139 476-8725

Green, Bill (R-N.Y., 15th)
110 E. 45th St., 5th Fl., New York City, 10017 (212) 826-4466

Gregg, Judd (R-N.H., 2nd)
N.H. Highway Hotel, Fort Eddy Rd., Concord, 03301 (603) 228-0315
1 Spring St., Nashua, 03060 883-0800

Grotberg, John E. (R-Ill., 14th)
2560 Foxfield Dr., St. Charles, 60174 (312)
584-2071
100 W. Lafayette St., Ottawa, 61350 (815)
434-5666

Guarini, Frank J. (D-N.J., 14th)
15 PATH Plaza, Journal Square, Jersey City,
07306 (201) 659-7700
319 Broadway, Bayonne, 07002 823-2900
3715 Palisades Ave., Union City, 07087 867-8208

Gunderson, Steven (R-Wis., 3rd)
438 N. Water St., P.O. Box 407, Black River
Falls, 54615 (715) 284-7431

Hall, Katie (D-Ind., 1st)
215 W. 35th St., Gary 46408 (219) 884-1177
100 E. Michigan Blvd., Michigan City, 46360
872-0676

Hall, Ralph M. (D-Tex., 4th)
104 San Jacinto, Rockwall, 75087 (214) 722-9118
211 Federal Bldg., Tyler, 75702 597-3729
105 Federal Bldg., McKinney, 75069 542-2618
201 Federal Bldg., Sherman, 75090 892-1112
Rm. 201-A, 402 E. Rusk St., Jacksonville, 75766
586-6387

Hall, Sam B., Jr. (D-Tex., 1st)
P.O. Box 1349, Marshall, 75670 (214) 938-8386
P.O. Box 350, Paris, 75460 785-0723
P.O. Box 1410, Texarkana, 75504 793-6728

Hall, Tony P. (D-Ohio, 3rd)
501 Federal Bldg., 200 W. Second St., P.O. Box
279, Dayton, 45402 (513) 225-2843

Hamilton, Lee H. (D-Ind., 9th)
Rm. 107, 1201 E. 10th St., Jeffersonville, 47130
(812) 288-3999

Hammerschmidt, John Paul (R-Ark., 3rd)
424 Federal Bldg., Fayetteville, 72701 (501)
442-5258
248 Main Post Office Bldg., P.O. Box 1624, Ft.
Smith, 72902 782-7787

Hansen, James V. (R-Utah, 1st)
1017 Federal Bldg., 324–25th St., Ogden, 84401
(801) 625-5677
Ste. 105, Creamer-Noble Bldg., 435 Tabernacle,
St. George, 84770 628-1071

Hartnett, Thomas F. (R-S.C., 1st)
640 Federal Bldg., 334 Meeting St., Charleston,
29403 (803) 724-4175

263 Hampton St., Walterboro, 29488 549-5395
P.O. Box 1538, Beaufort, 29902 524-2166

Hatcher, Charles F. (D-Ga., 2nd)
Rm. 201, 225 Pine Ave., Albany, 31701 (912)
439-8067
P.O. Box 1626, Valdosta, 31601 247-9705
Ste. 218, 404 N. Broad St., P.O. Box 2966,
Thomasville, 31799 228-7359

Hawkins, Augustus F. (D-Calif., 29th)
4509 S. Broadway, Los Angeles, 90037 (213)
750-0260
2710 Zoe Ave., Huntington Park, 90255
587-0421

Hayes, Charles A. (D-Ill., 1st)
7801 S. Cottage Grove Ave., Chicago, 60619
(312) 783-6800

Hefner, W.G. (Bill) (D-N.C., 8th)
101 S. Union St, Concord, 28025 (704) 933-1615
Ste. 225, Home Savings & Loan Bldg., 507 W.
Innes St., P.O. Box 4220, Salisbury, 28144
636-0635
Ste. 200, 202 E. Franklin St., P.O. Box 1503,
Rockingham, 28379 (919) 997-2070

Heftel, Cecil (Cec) (D-Hawaii, 1st)
Rm. 4104, 300 Ala Moana Blvd., Honolulu,
96850 (808) 546-8997

Hendon, Bill (R-N.C., 11th)
202 Executive Park, Asheville, 28801 (704)
253-3406
602 A-1 West Main St., Forest City, 28043
245-5551
109 Federal Bldg., 140 4th Ave. West,
Hendersonville, 28739 693-8366

Henry, Paul B. (R-Mich., 5th)
166 Federal Bldg., Grand Rapids, 49503 (616)
451-8383

Hertel, Dennis M. (D-Mich., 14th)
18927 Kelly Rd., Detroit, 48224 (313) 526-5900
28221 Mound Rd., Warren, 48092 574-9420

Hiler, John P. (R-Ind., 3rd)
Rm. 120, River Glen Ofc. Plaza, 501 E. Monroe
St., South Bend, 46601 (219) 236-8282

Hillis, Elwood H. (Bud) (R-Ind., 5th)
P.O. Box 5048, Kokomo, 46902 (317) 457-4411
323 S. Adams, Marion, 46952 662-7227
2 Indiana Ave., Valparaiso, 46383 (219)
462-6499

Holt, Marjorie S. (R-Md., 4th)
Ste. 509, Arundel Ctr. N., 101 Crane Hwy.,
Glen Burnie, 21061 (301) 261-2008
Ste. 303, Five Star Bldg., 6178 Oxon Hill Rd.,
Oxon Hill, 20745 567-9212

Hopkins, Larry J. (R-Ky., 6th)
Rm. 207, Vine Ctr., 333 W. Vine, Lexington,
40507 (606) 233-2848

Horton, Frank (R-N.Y., 29th)
314 Kenneth M. Keating Fed. Bldg., 100 State
St., Rochester, 14614 (716) 263-6270
304 Metcalf Plaza, Auburn, 13021 (315)
255-1125
Riverfront Bldg., Oswego, 13126 342-4688

Howard, James D. (D-N.J., 3rd)
808 Belmar Plaza, Belmar, 07719 (201) 681-3321
1286 Hwy 35, Middletown, 07748 671-8993

Hoyer, Stany H. (D-Md., 5th)
Citizens Bank Bldg., 6th Fl., 4351 Garden City
Dr., Landover, 20785 (301) 436-5510

Hubbard, Carroll, Jr. (D-Ky., 1st)
307 Federal Bldg., P.O. Box 782, Paducah,
42002 (502) 442-9804
145 E. Center, McCoy Bldg., Madisonville,
42431 825-1371
City Hall Municipal Bldg., P.O. Box 1457,
Henderson, 42420 826-5776
Ste. 1, 109 Hammond Plaza, Hopkinsville, 42240
885-2625
Box 323, Mayfield, 42066 247-7128

Huckaby, Jerry (D-La., 5th)
211 N. Third St., Monroe, 71201 (318) 387-2244
Old Courthouse Bldg., P.O. Box 34,
Natchitoches, 71457 352-9000
Contact District Office for Mobile Office
schedule.

Hughes, William J. (D-N.J., 2nd)
2307 New Rd., Northfield, 08225 (609) 645-7957
151 N. Broadway, P.O. Box 248, Pennsville,
08070 678-3333

Hunter, Duncan L. (R-Calif., 45th)
366 S. Pierce St., El Cajun, 92020 (619) 579-3001
Ste. G, 1101 Airport Rd., Imperial, 92251
353-5420
Ste. D, 430 Davidson St., Chula Vista, 92010
422-0893

Hutto, Earl (D-Fla., 1st)
Courthouse Annex, Shalimar, 32579 (904)
651-3111
P.O. Box 17689, Pensacola, 32522 432-6179
P.O. Box 459, Panama City, 32402 763-0709

Hyde, Henry J. (R-Ill., 6th)
Ste. 305, 701 Lee St., Des Plaines, 60016 (312)
296-4933
Grand Oak Ofc. Ctr. II, 970 N. Oaklawn Ave.,
Elmhurst, 60126 832-5950

Ireland, Andrew P. (R-Fla., 10th)
120 W. Central Ave., P.O. Box 9447, Winter
Haven, 33883 (813) 299-4041
1803 Richmond Rd. at Bartow Hwy., P.O. Box
8758, Lakeland, 33806 687-8018
1101 Sixth Ave. W., P.O. Box 1220, Bradenton,
33506 746-0766

Jacobs, Andrew, Jr. (D-Ind., 10th)
441-A Federal Bldg., 46 E. Ohio St.,
Indianapolis, 46204 (317) 269-7331

Jeffords, James M. (R-Vt., At Lge.)
Champlain Mill, 1 Main St., Winooski, 05404
(802) 951-6732
138 Main St., P.O. Box 676, Montpelier, 05602
223-5273
121 West St., Rutland, 05701 773-3875

Jenkins, Ed (D-Ga., 9th)
P.O. Box 70, Jasper, 30143 (404) 692-2022
P.O. Box 1015, Gainesville, 30503 536-2531
307 Selvidge St., Dalton, 30720 226-5320
Ste. 8, 195 Pike St., Lawrenceville, 30245
963-0675

Johnson, Nancy L. (R-Conn., 6th)
40 S. High St., New Britain, 06051 (203)
223-8412
91 High St., Enfield, 06082 722-2940

Jones, Ed (D-Tenn., 8th)
P.O. Box 128, Yorkville, 38389 (901) 643-6123
B7 Post Office Bldg., Box 2808, Jackson, 38301
423-4848
3179 N. Watkins, Box 27190, Memphis, 38127
358-4094

Jones, James R. (D-Okla., 1st)
4536 Federal Bldg., Tulsa, 74103 (918) 581-7111

Jones, Walter B. (D-N.C., 1st)
108 E. Wilson St., P.O. Drawer 90, Farmville,
27828 (919) 753-3082

Kanjorski, Paul E. (D-Pa., 11th)
10 East South St. Bldg., South Main St., Wilkes-Barre, 18702 (717) 825-2200

Kaptur, Marcy (D-Ohio, 9th)
719 Federal Bldg., 234 Summit St., Toledo, 43604 (419) 259-7500

Kasich, John R. (R-Ohio, 12th)
400 Federal Office Bldg., 200 N. High St., Columbus, 43215 (614) 469-7318

Kastenmeier, Robert W. (D-Wis., 2nd)
Ste. 505, 119 Monona Ave., Madison, 53703 (608) 264-5206

Kemp, Jack F. (R-N.Y., 31st)
1101 Federal Bldg., 111 W. Huron St., Buffalo, 14202 (716) 846-4123
484 S. Main St., Geneva, 14456 (315) 789-3360

Kennelly, Barbara B. (D-Conn., 1st)
618 Federal Bldg., 450 Main St., Hartford, 06103 (203) 722-2383

Kentucky, 7th District (No Representative at press time.)
Post Office Bldg., 2nd Fl., Box 127, Ashland, 41105 (606) 325-8530
Federal Building, Pikeville, 41501 432-4191

Kildee, Dale E. (D-Mich., 7th)
400 N. Saginaw St., Flint, 48502 (313) 239-1437

Kindness, Thomas N. (R-Ohio, 8th)
646 High St., Hamilton, 45011 (513) 895-5656
234 E. Main St., Greenville, 45331 548-8817

Kieczka, Gerald D. (D-Wis., 4th)
5032 W. Forest Home Ave., Milwaukee, 53219 (414) 291-1140
817 Clinton St., Waukesha, 53186 549-6360

Kolbe, Jim (R-Ariz., 5th)
4444 East Grant Rd., Tucson, 85712 (602) 323-1467
222 Cottonwood Lane, Suite 113, Casa Grande, 85222 836-6364
77 Calleportal, Suite B160, Sierra Vista, 85635 459-3115

Kolter, Joseph P. (D-Pa., 4th)
1322 Seventh Ave., Beaver Falls, 15010 (412) 846-3600
104 U.S. Post Office Bldg., Butler, 16001 282-8081

160 McKean St., Kittanning, 16201 543-5136
20 S. Mercer St., New Castle, 16101 658-4525
7 N. Sixth St., Indiana 15701 349-3755

Kostmayer, Peter H. (D-Pa., 8th)
44 E. Court St., Doylestown, 18901 (215) 345-8543
Ste. 700, One Oxford Valley, Langhorne, 19047 757-8181
Quaker Village Shopping Center, 351 W. Broad St., Quakertown, 18951 538-2222

Kramer, Kenneth B. (R-Colo., 5th)
1520 N. Union Blvd., Colorado Springs, 80909 (303) 632-8555
Ste. 104, 10394 W. Chopfield, Littleton, 80127 973-0397

LaFalce, John J. (D-N.Y., 32nd)
Federal Bldg., 111 W. Huron St., Buffalo, 14202 (716) 846-4056
201 Main U.S. Post Office, Niagara Falls, 14302 284-9976
New Federal Bldg., 100 State St., Rochester, 14614 263-6424

Lagomarsino, Robert J. (R-Calif., 19th)
Studio 121, El Paseo, 814 State St., Santa Barbara, 93101 (805) 963-1708
Ste. 101, 5740 Ralston, Ventura, 93003 642-2200
202 Post Office Bldg., 120 W. Cypress St., Santa Maria, 93454 922-2131

Lantos, Tom (D-Calif., 11th)
Rm. 800, 520 El Camino Real, San Mateo, 94402 (415) 342-0300
City Hall, 90th & Sullivan Ave., Daly City, 94015 992-4500,
ext. 235

Latta, Delbert L. (R-Ohio, 5th)
100 Federal Bldg., 280 S. Main St., Bowling Green, 43402 (419) 353-8871
157 Columbus Ave., Sandusky, 44870 625-0052

Leach, Jim (R-Iowa, 1st)
322 W. Third St., Davenport, 52801 (319) 326-1841
306 F. & M. Bank Bldg., Third & Jefferson Sts., Burlington, 52601 752-4584
Rm. 204, Parkview Plaza, 107 E. Second St., Ottumwa, 52501 (515) 682-8549

Leeth, Marvin (D-Tex., 11th)
207 Federal Bldg., Waco, 76701 (817) 752-9609

Lehman, Richard H. (D-Calif., 18th)
Ste. 301, 1900 Mariposa Mall, Fresno, 93721
(209) 487-5760
808 N. Center St., Stockton, 95202 946-6353
9 N. Washington St., Sonora, 95370 533-1426

Lehman, William (D-Fla., 17th)
2020 N.E. 163rd St., N. Miami Beach, 33162
(305) 945-7518
6116 N.W. Seventh Ave., Miami, 33127
758-6377

Leland, Mickey (D-Tex., 18th)
Ste. 101, 4101 San Jacinto, Houston, 77004 (713)
527-9692

Lent, Norman F. (R-N.Y., 4th)
Rm. 300, Baldwin Plaza Bldg., 2280 Grand
Ave., Baldwin, 11510 (516) 223-1616
Massapequa Park Village Hall, 151 Front St.,
Massapequa Park, 11762 795-4454

Levin, Sander (D-Mich., 17th)
Ste. 120, 17117 W. Nine Mile Rd., Southfield,
48075 (313) 559-4444

Levine, Meldon E. (D-Calif., 27th)
Ste. 447, 5250 W. Century Blvd., Los Angeles,
90045 (213) 215-2035

Lewis, Jerry (R-Calif., 35th)
101 S. Sixth St., Redlands, 92373 (714) 862-6030

Lewis, Tom F. (R-Fla., 12th)
Ste. 1, 2700 PGA Blvd., Palm Beach Gardens,
33410 (305) 627-6192
Rm. 104, 50 Kindred St., Stuart, 33497 293-7989
Rm. 105, 700 Virginia Ave., Ft. Pierce, 33450
465-3710

Lightfoot, Jim (R-Iowa, 3rd)
501 West Lowell, Shenandoah, 51601 (712)
246-1984
229 Federal Bldg., Council Bluff, 51501
325-5572
201 W. Salem, Indianola, 50125 (515) 961-0591
908 First Ave. South, Warden Plaza, Fort
Dodge, 50501 955-5319

Lipinski, William O. (D-Ill., 5th)
5832 S. Archer Ave., Chicago, 60638 (312)
886-0481
6700 W. 26th St., Berwin, 60402 788-0331

Livingston, Robert L. (Bob) (R-La., 1st)
642 F. Edward Hebert Federal Bldg., New
Orleans, 70130 (504) 589-2753

(Mon. & Tues.) Rm. 102, 8201 W. Judge Perez
Dr., Chalmette, 70043 589-3747
(Tues.) 432 E. Boston St., Covington, 70433
892-7304
(Thurs.) 401 Pontchartrain Blvd., Slidell, 70458
643-7733

Lloyd, Marilyn (D-Tenn, 3rd)
1211 Federal Bldg., Oak Ridge, 37830 (615)
576-1977
253 J. Solomon Federal Office Bldg.,
Chattanooga, 37401 267-9108

Loeffler, Tom (R-Tex., 21st)
Ste. 415, 40 N.E. Loop 410, San Antonio, 78216
(512) 229-5880
1016-B Junction Hwy., Kerrville, 78028
895-1414
Rm. 301, 33 Twohig, San Angelo, 76903 (915)
653-3971
208 Federal Bldg., 200 E. Wall St., Midland,
79701 687-0188

Lott, Trent (R-Miss., 5th)
P.O. Box 1557, Gulfport, 39501 (601) 864-7670
215 Federal Bldg., Hattiesburg, 39401 582-3246
3100 S. Pascagoula St., Pascagoula, 39567
762-6435

Lowery, William D. (R-Calif., 41st)
Rm. 6-S-15, 880 Front St., San Diego, 92188
(619) 231-0957

Lowry, Mike (D-Wash., 7th)
107 Prefontaine Pl. S., Seattle, 98104 (206)
442-7170

Lujan, Manuel, Jr. (R-N.M., 1st)
10001 Federal Building, 500 Gold Ave., S.W.,
Albuquerque, 87103 (505) 766-2538

Luken, Thomas A. (D-Ohio, 1st)
Ste. 712, 711 Gwynne Bldg., 602 Main St.,
Cincinnati, 45202 (513) 684-2723

Lundine, Stan (D-N.Y., 34th)
122 Federal Bldg., P.O. Box 908, Jamestown,
14702 (716) 484-0252
Rm. 505, 101 N. Union St., Olean, 14760
372-1818
180 Clemens Center Pkwy., Elmira, 14901 (607)
734-0302

Lungren, Daniel E. (R-Calif., 42nd)
Ste. 505, 555 E. Ocean Blvd., Long Beach,
90802 (213) 548-2406

MacKay, Kenneth H. (Buddy) (D-Fla., 6th)
314-316 Federal Bldg., 401 S.E. First Ave.,
Gainesville, 32601 (904) 372-0382
111 S. Sixth St., Leesburg, 32748 326-8285
258 Federal Bldg., 207 N.W. Second St., Ocala,
32670 351-8777

McCain, John (R-Ariz., 1st)
Ste. 151, 1255 W. Baseline Rd., Mesa, 85202
(602) 897-0892
Ste. 201, 411 S. Mill Ave., Tempe, 85281
829-0440

McCandless, Alfred A. (R-Calif., 37th)
6529 Riverside Ave., Riverside, 92506 (714)
682-7127
Ste. A-7, 74-075 El Paseo, Palm Desert, 92660
(619) 340-2900

McCollum, Bill (R-Fla., 5th)
Ste. 301, 1801 Lee Rd., Winter Park, 32789
(305) 645-3100

McCurdy, Dave (D-Okla., 4th)
Ste. 105, 330 W. Gray, Norman, 73069 (405)
329-6500
103 Federal Bldg., Lawton, 73501 357-2131
205 Post Office Bldg., 802 Willow St., Duncan,
73533 252-1434

McDade, Joseph M. (R-Pa., 10th)
Rm. 1223, Bank Tower, Scranton, 18503 (717)
346-3834

McEwen, Bob (R-Ohio, 6th)
202 Federal Bldg., Hillsboro, 45133 (513)
393-4223
Post Office Bldg., Portsmouth, 45662 (614)
353-5171

McGrath, Raymond J. (R-N.Y., 5th)
203 Rockaway Ave., Valley Stream, 11580 (516)
872-9550

McHugh, Matthew F. (D-N.Y., 28th)
201 Federal Bldg., Binghamton, 13902 (607)
773-2768
Terrace Hill-Babcock Hall, Ithaca, 14850
273-1388
292 Fair St., Kingston, 12401 331-4462

McKernan, John R., Jr. (R-Maine, 1st)
262 Middle St., P.O. Box 10240, Portland, 04104
(207) 780-3381
154 State St., Augusta, 04330 622-8303
118 Main St., Sanford, 04073 324-2911

148 Federal Bldg., 21 Limerock St., P.O. Box
469, Rockland, 04801 594-7285

McKinney, Stewart B. (R-Conn., 4th)
Federal Bldg., 915 Lafayette Blvd., Bridgeport,
06604 (203) 579-5870
500 Summer St., Stamford, 06901 357-8277

McMillan, J. Alex (R-N.C., 9th)
401 West Trade St., Charlotte, 28202 (704)
376-1976

McSweeney, Mac (R-Tex., 14th)
1908 North Laurant, Victoria, 77901 (512)
576-6001

Mack, Connie III (R-Fla., 13th)
108 George W. Whitehurst Fed. Bldg. & U.S.
Courthouse, Ft. Myers, 33901 (813) 334-4424
Ste. 204, 2015 Siesta Dr., Sarasota, 33579
366-9482

Madigan, Edward R. (R-Ill., 15th)
2401 E. Washington St., Bloomington, 61701
(309) 662-9371
219 S. Kickapoo, Lincoln, 62656 (217) 735-3521
Ste. 200, 70 Meadowview Center, Kankakee,
60901 (815) 937-3277

Manton, Thomas J. (D-N.Y., 9th)
46-12 Queens Blvd., Sunnyside, 11104 (718)
706-1400

Markey, Edward J. (D-Mass., 7th)
2100A John F. Kennedy Federal Bldg., Boston,
02203 (617) 223-2781
464-B Salem St., Medford, 02155 396-4800

Marlenee, Ron (R-Mont., 2nd)
2717 First Ave. N., Billings, 59101 (406)
657-6753
312 Ninth St. S., Great Falls, 59405 453-3264

Martin, David O'B. (R-N.Y., 26th)
E. J. Noble Medical Ctr., Main St., Canton,
13617 (315) 379-9611
246 N. Main St., Herkimer, 13350 866-1051
Purvine Blvd., N. State St. & Shady Ave.,
Lowville, 13367 376-6446
307 Federal Bldg., Watertown, 13601 782-3150
100 W. Main St., Johnstown, 12095 (518)
762-4975
104 Federal Bldg., Plattsburgh, 12901 563-1406

Martin, Lynn M. (R-Ill., 16th)
416 E. State St., Rockford, 61104 (815) 987-4326
420 Avenue A, Sterling, 61081 626-1616

Martinez, Matthew G. (D-Calif., 30th)
1712 W. Beverly Blvd., Montebello, 90640 (213) 722-7731

Matsui, Robert T. (D-Calif., 3rd)
8058 Federal Bldg., 650 Capitol Mall, Sacramento, 95814 (916) 440-3543

Mavroules, Nicholas (D-Mass., 6th)
70 Washington St., Salem, 01970 (617) 745-5800
140 Union St., Lynn, 01902 599-7105
10 Welcome St., Haverhill, 01830 372-3461

Mazzoli, Romano L. (D-Ky., 3rd)
551 Federal Bldg., 600 Federal Place, Louisville, 40202 (502) 582-5129

Meyers, Jan (R-Kan., 3rd)
204 Federal Bldg., Kansas City, 66101 (913) 621-0832

Mica, Daniel A. (D-Fla., 14th)
Ste. 303, 639 E. Ocean Ave., Boynton Beach, 33435 (305) 732-4000

Michel, Robert H. (R-Ill., 18th)
Rm. 107, 100 N.E. Monroe, Peoria, 61602 (309) 671-7027
236 W. State St., Jacksonville, 62650 (217) 245-1431

Mikulski, Barbara A. (D-Md., 3rd)
1414 Federal Bldg., Baltimore, 21201 (301) 962-4510
235 Wilde Lake Village Green, Columbia, 21044 962-6104
Ste. 104, 6609 Reisterstown Rd., Baltimore, 21215 962-6102
(Mon.–Thurs., 10 a.m. until 2 p.m.) 419 S. Highland Ave., Baltimore, 21224 563-4000

Miller, Clarence C. (R-Ohio, 10th)
212 S. Broad St., Lancaster, 43130 (614) 654-5149
27 S. Park, Newark, 43055 349-8279

Miller, George (D-Calif., 7th)
367 Civic Dr., Pleasant Hill, 94523 (415) 687-3260
4 Alvarado Sq., P.O. Box 277, San Pablo, 94806 231-5791

Miller, John R. (R-Wash., 1st)
2888 Federal Bldg., 715 Second Ave., Seattle, 98174 (206) 442-4220

Mineta, Norman Y. (D-Calif., 13th)
Rm. 310, 1245 S. Winchester, San Jose, 95128 (408) 984-6045

Mitchell, Parren J. (D-Md., 7th)
1018 George Fallon Fed. Ofc. Bldg., 31 Hopkins Plaza, Baltimore, 21201 (301) 962-3223
1903 Bloomingdale Rd., Baltimore, 21216 962-4531

Moekley, Joe (D-Mass., 9th)
1900C John F. Kennedy Federal Bldg., Boston, 02203 (617) 223-5715

Molinari, Guy V. (R-N.Y., 14th)
Bldg. 203, Fort Wadsworth, Staten Island, 10305 (718) 981-9800
9306 Fourth Ave., Brooklyn, 11209 680-1000

Mollohan, Alan B. (D-W.Va., 1st)
603 Deveny Bldg., Fairmont, 26554 (304) 363-3356
209 Post Office Bldg., Clarksburg, 26301 623-4422
316 Federal Bldg., Wheeling, 26003 232-5390
1117 Federal Bldg., Parkersburg, 26101 428-0493

Monson, David S. (R-Utah, 2nd)
125 S. State St., Federal Bldg., Salt Lake City, 84138 (801) 524-4394

Montgomery, G.V. (Sonny) (D-Miss., 3rd)
Federal Bldg., P.O. Box 5618, Meridian, 39301 (601) 693-6681
110-D Airport Rd., Pearl, 39208 932-2410
P.O. Box 412, Laurel, 39440 649-1231
P.O. Box 709, Columbus, 39701 327-2766

Moody, Jim (D-Wis., 5th)
Ste. 618, 135 W. Wells St., Milwaukce, 53203 (414) 291-1331

Moore, W. Henson (R-La., 6th)
236 Federal Bldg., 750 Florida, Baton Rouge, 70801 (504) 344-7679

Moorhead, Carlos J. (R-Calif., 22nd)
Rm. 304, 420 N. Brand Blvd., Glendale, 91203 (213) 247-8445
Rm. 618, 301 E. Colorado Blvd., Pasadena, 91101 792-6168

Morrison, Bruce A. (D-Conn., 3rd)
  85 Church St., New Haven, 06510 (203)
  773-2325

Morrison, Sid (R-Wash., 4th)
  212 East E St., Yakima, 98901 (509) 575-5891
  Ste. 105, 3311 W. Clearwater, Keenewick, 99336
  376-9702
  Ste. 210, Morris Bldg., 23 S. Wenatchee,
  Wenatchee, 98801 662-4294

Mrazek, Robert J. (D-N.Y., 3rd)
  143 Main St., Huntington, 11743 (516) 673-6500
  17 Main St., Rosslyn, 11576 625-0434

Murphy, Austin J. (D-Pa., 22nd)
  70 E. Beau St., Washington, 15301 (412)
  228-2777
  365 McClelland Town Rd., Uniontown, 15401
  438-1490
  306 Fallowfield Ave., Charleroi, 15022 489-4217
  Hopewell Township Municipal Bldg.,
  Aliquippa, 15001 375-1199

Murtha, John P. (D-Pa., 12th)
  Box 780, Johnstown, 15907 (814) 535-2642
  15 Post Office Bldg., 201 N. Center St.,
  Somerset, 15501 445-6041
  206 N. Main St., Greensburg, 15601 (412)
  832-3088

Myers, John T. (R-Ind., 7th)
  107 Federal Bldg., Terre Haute, 47808 (812)
  238-1619
  107 Charles A. Halleck Federal Bldg.,
  Lafayette, 47901 (317) 423-1661

Natcher, William H. (D-Ky., 2nd)
  414 E. 10th St., Bowling Green, 42101 (502)
  842-7376
  50 Public Square, Elizabethtown, 42701
  765-4360

Neal, Stephen L. (D-N.C., 5th)
  421 Federal Bldg., Winston-Salem, 27101 (919)
  761-3125

Nelson, Bill (D-Fla., 11th)
  Ste. 202, 65 E. Nasa Blvd., Melbourne, 32901
  (305) 724-1978
  300 Federal Bldg., 80 N. Hughey, Orlando,
  32801 841-1776
  (Wed.) City Hall, 555 S. Washington Ave.,
  Titusville, 32780 268-1776
  (Tues. & Thurs., 10 a.m. until 2 p.m.) Osceola
  Courthouse, Kissimmee, 32747 847-0723

(Tues.) Indian River County Courthouse, Vero
  Beach, 32960 567-8000, ext. 411
(Thurs.) Merritt Island Branch, Brevard County
  Courthouse, Merritt Island, 32952 459-1776

**New Jersey, 13th District (No Representative at
press time.)**
  301 Mill St., Moorestown, 08057 (609) 235-6622

Nichols, Bill (D-Ala., 3rd)
  Federal Bldg., P.O. Box 2042, Anniston, 36202
  (205) 236-5655
  107 Federal Bldg., Opelika, 36801 745-6222
  115 E. Northside, Tuskegee, 36083 727-6490

Nielson, Howard C. (R-Utah, 3rd)
  Ste. 105, 88 W. 100 North, Provo, 84601 (801)
  377-1776
  1777 E. 90th S., West Jordan, 84084 524-5301
  Rm. 1, 92 E. Center St., Moab, 84532 259-7188

Nowak, Henry J. (D/L-N.Y., 33rd)
  212 U.S. Courthouse, Buffalo, 14202 (716)
  853-4131

Oakar, Mary Rose (D-Ohio, 20th)
  523 Federal Court Bldg., Cleveland, 44114 (216)
  522-4927

Oberstar, James L. (D/F/L-Minn., 8th)
  231 Federal Bldg., Duluth, 55802 (218) 727-7474
  City Hall, 316 Lake St., Chisholm, 55719
  254-5761
  City Hall, 501 Laurel, Brainerd, 56401 828-4400

Obey, David (D-Wis., 7th)
  Federal Bldg., 317 First St., Wausau, 54401
  (715) 842-5606

O'Brien, George M. (R-Ill., 4th)
  Rm. 260, 101 N. Joliet St., Joliet, 60431 (815)
  740-2040
  Ste. 415, 100 First Natl. Plaza, Chicago Heights,
  60211 (312) 754-4111
  Rm. 702, The Aurora Natl. Bank Bldg., 105 E.
  Galena Blvd., Aurora, 60505 844-3444

Olin, James R. (Jim) (D-Va., 6th)
  Rm. 706, First Federal Savings & Loan Bldg.,
  406 First St., Roanoke, 24011 (703) 982-4672
  Masonic Bldg., 2nd Fl., 13 W. Beverly St.,
  Staunton, 24401 885-8178
  Rm. 415, Savian Bank Bldg., Harrisonburg,
  22801 433-9433
  First Federal Savings & Loan Bldg., 3rd Fl., 925
  Main St., Lynchburg, 24504 (804) 845-6546

O'Neill, Thomas P., Jr. (D-Mass., 8th)
2200A John F. Kennedy Federal Bldg., Boston, 02203 (617) 223-2784
85 Main St., Watertown, 02172 926-2400
661 Massachusetts Ave., Arlington, 02174 648-2000

Ortiz, Solomon P. (D-Tex., 27th)
Ste. 438, 3505 Boca Chica Blvd., Brownsville, 78521 (512) 541-1242
Ste. 510, 3649 Leopard, Corpus Christi, 78048 883-5868

Owens, Major R. (D/L-N.Y., 12th)
289 Utica Ave., Brooklyn, 11213 (718) 773-3100

Oxley, Michael G. (R-Ohio, 4th)
3121 W. Elm Plaza, Lima, 45805 (419) 999-6455
Rm. 212, 110 W. Main Cross, Findlay, 45840 423-3210
Rm. 314, 24 W. Third St., Mansfield, 44902 522-5757

Packard, Ronald C. (R-Calif., 43rd)
Ste. 105, 2121 Palomar Airport Rd., Carlsbad, 92008 (619) 438-0443
Ste. 160, 28261 Marguerite Pkwy., Mission Viejo, 92692 (714) 495-1243

Panetta, Leon E. (D-Calif., 16th)
380 Alvarado St., Monterey, 93940 (408) 649-3555
100 W. Alisal, Salinas, 93901 424-2229
701 Ocean St., Santa Cruz, 95060 429-1976
(2nd & 4th Fridays) 335 Fifth St., Hollister, 95023 637-0500
728 Morrow Bay Blvd., Morrow Bay, 93442 (805) 722-2035

Parris, Stan (R-Va., 8th)
Ste. 101, 6901 Old Keene Mill Rd., Springfield, 22150 (703) 644-0004
1525 King St., Alexandria, 22314 548-5288

Pashayan, Charles, Jr. (R-Calif., 17th)
Ste. 103, 1702 E. Bullard, Fresno, 93710 (209) 487-5500
831 W. Center St., Visalia, 93291 627-2700
804 N. Irwin, Hanford, 93230 582-2896
201 High St., Delano, 93215 (805) 725-7371

Pease, Donald J. (D-Ohio, 13th)
1936 Cooper Foster Park Rd., Lorain, 44053 (216) 282-5003
(Wed.) Medina County Admin. Bldg., Ground Fl., Medina, 44256 725-6120

Ste. 101, The Center, 42 E. Main St., Ashland, 44805 (419) 325-4184
Huron County Administration Bldg., 180 Milan Ave., Norwalk, 44857 668-0206
Rm. 7, MOIC Bldg., 445 Bowman St., Mansfield, 44902 526-6663

Penny, Timothy J. (Tim) (D/F/L-Minn., 1st)
Park Towers, 22 N. Broadway, Rochester, 55904 (507) 281-6053
410 S. Fifth St., P.O. Box 3148, Mankato, 56001 656-6921

Pepper, Claude (D-Fla., 18th)
904 Federal Bldg., 51 S.W. First Ave., Miami, 33130 (305) 350-5565

Petri, Thomas E. (R-Wis., 6th)
14 Western Ave., Box 1816, Fond du Lac, 54935 (414) 922-1180
Rm. 112, 105 Washington Ave., Oshkosh, 54901 231-6333

Pickle, J.J. (D-Tex., 10th)
763 Federal Office Bldg., Austin, 78701 (512) 482-5921

Porter, John Edward (R-Ill., 10th)
Ste. 410, 104 Wilmot Rd., Deerfield, 60015 (312) 940-0202
601-A County Bldg., 18 N. County St., Waukegan, 60085 662-0101
Ste. 104, 1650 Arlington Hgts. Rd., Arlington Heights, 60004 392-0303

Price, Melvin (D-Ill., 21st)
Federal Bldg., 650 Missouri Ave., East St. Louis, 62201 (618) 274-2200

Pursell, Carl D. (R-Mich., 2nd)
361 W. Eisenhower Pkwy., Ann Arbor, 48104 (313) 761-7727
111 N. West Ave., Jackson, 49201 (517) 787-0552

Quillen, James H. (Jimmy) (R-Tenn., 1st)
157 Federal Post Office Bldg., Kingsport, 37662 (615) 247-8161

Rahall, Nick Joe II (D-W.Va., 4th)
Rm. 307, Bair Bldg., Beckley, 25801 (304) 252-5000
1005 Elizabeth Kee Federal Bldg., Bluefield, 24701 325-6222
815 Fifth Ave., Huntington, 25701 522-6425
R.K. Bldg., Logan, 25601 752-4934

Rangel, Charles B. (D-N.Y., 18th)
Rm. 737, 163 W. 125th St., New York City,
10027 (212) 663-3900
656 W. 181st St., New York City, 10033
927-5333
2112 Second Ave., New York City, 10029
348-9630

Ray, Richard (D-Ga., 3rd)
200 Carl Vinson Pkwy., Warner Robins, 31056
(912) 929-2764
P.O. Box 2057, Columbus, 31902 (404) 324-0292
Rm. 107, 200 Ridley Ave., LaGrange, 30240
882-9214

Regula, Ralph S. (R-Ohio, 16th)
4150 Beldon St., N.W., Canton, 44718 (216)
489-4414
201 E. Liberty St., Wooster, 44691 264-3585

Reid, Harry (D-Nev., 1st)
420 Federal Bldg., 300 Las Vegas Blvd., S., Las
Vegas, 89101 (702) 388-6545

Richardson, William B. (D-N.M., 3rd)
122 Federal Bldg., Cathedral Pl., Santa Fe,
87501 (505) 988-6177
900 Municipal St., Farmington, 87401 327-7898
Rm. B-8, McKinley County Courthouse, 200 W.
Hill St., Gallup, 87301 722-6522
San Miguel County Courthouse, P.O. Box 1850,
Las Vegas, 87701 425-7270

Ridge, Thomas J. (R-Pa., 21st)
108 Federal Office Bldg., Erie, 16501 (814)
456-2038
305 Chestnut St., Meadville, 16335 724-8414
91 E. State St., Sharon, 16146 (412) 981-8440

Rinaldo, Matthew J. (R-N.J., 7th)
1961 Morris Ave., Union, 07083 (201) 687-4235

Ritter, Don (R-Pa., 15th)
212 Post Office Bldg., Allentown, 18101 (215)
439-8861
Ste. 300, 1 Bethlehem Plaza, Bethlehem, 18018
866-0916
Rm. 705, Alpha Bldg., Easton, 18042 258-8383

Roberts, Pat (R-Kan., 1st)
P.O. Box 550, Dodge City, 67801 (316) 227-2244
P.O. Box 1224, Salina, 67401 (913) 825-5409
P.O. Box 128, Norton, 67654 877-2454

Robinson, Tommy (D-Ark., 2nd)
1527 Federal Bldg., Little Rock, 72201 (501)
378-5941

411 North Spruce, Searcy, 72143 268-4287
115 S. Moose, Conway County Courthouse,
Morrilton, 72110 354-0100

Rodino, Peter W., Jr. (D-N.J., 10th)
1435A Peter W. Rodino, Jr., Fed. Bldg., 970
Broad St., Newark, 07102 (201) 645-3213

Roe, Robert A. (D-N.J., 8th)
Rm. 102, Law Bldg., 66 Hamilton St., Paterson,
07505 (201) 523-5152
158 Boonton Rd., Wayne, 07470 696-2077
U.S. Post Office Bldg., 22 N. Sussex St., Dover,
07801 328-7413

Roemer, Charles (Buddy) (D-La., 4th)
203 E. Texas St., Leesville, 71446 (318) 239-9916
Ste. 100, 228 Spring St., Shreveport, 71101
226-5080

Rogers, Harold (Hal) (R-Ky., 5th)
216 Poplar Ave., Somerset, 42501 (606)
679-8346

Rose, Charlie (D-N.C., 7th)
218 Federal Bldg., Fayetteville, 28301 (919)
323-0260
208 Post Office Bldg., Wilmington, 28401
343-4959

Rostenkowski, Dan (D-Ill., 89th)
2148 N. Damen Ave., Chicago, 60647 (312)
431-1111

Roth, Tobias (Toby) (R-Wis., 8th)
207 Federal Bldg., Green Bay, 54301 (414)
433-3811
126 N. Oneida St., Appleton, 54911 739-4167

Roukema, Marge (R-N.J., 5th)
51 Chestnut St., Ridgewood, 07450 (201)
447-3900
425 Rte. 10, Randolph, 07869 361-1467
9 Main St., Flemington, 08822 782-4422

Rowland, John G. (R-Conn., 5th)
135 Grand St., Rm 210, Waterbury, 06701 (203)
573-1418

Rowland, J. Roy (D-Ga., 8th)
203 Federal Bldg., P.O. Box 2047, Franklin Sq.,
Dublin, 31040 (912) 275-0024
207 Federal Bldg., Waycross, 31501 285-8420
P.O. Box 6258, Macon, 31208 743-0151

Roybal, Edward R. (D-Calif., 25th)
7106 New Federal Bldg., 300 N. Los Angeles
St., Los Angeles, 90012 (213) 688-4870

Rudd, Eldon D. (R-Ariz., 4th)
Ste. 440, 6900 E. Camelback Rd., Scottsdale,
85251 (602) 241-2801
Contact District Office for Mobile Office
schedule.

Russo, Marty (D-Ill., 3rd)
10634 S. Cicero, Oaklawn, 60453 (312)
353-8093/636-4171
8542 S. Pulaski, Chicago, 60652 353-0560

Sabo, Martin Olav (D/F/L-Minn., 5th)
462 Federal Courts Bldg., 110 S. Fourth St.,
Minneapolis, 55401 (612) 349-5110

St Germain, Fernand J. (D-R.I., 1st)
204 John E. Fogarty Fed. Bldg., 24 Weybosset
St., Providence, 02903 (401) 528-5050
(Wed.) 206 Post Office Bldg., Newport, 02840
846-7511

Savage, Gus (D-Ill., 2nd)
11434 S. Halsted St., Chicago, 60628 (312)
660-2000
15146 S. Wood St., Harvey, 60426 333-3030

Schaefer, Dan (R-Colo., 6th)
Rm. 110, 730 W. Hampden Ave., Englewood,
80110 (303) 762-8890
Ste. 200E, 601 Chambers Rd., Aurora, 80011
361-0580
Ste. 303, 950 Wadsworth Blvd., Lakewood,
80215 233-5279

Scheuer, James H. (D-N.Y., 8th)
137-08 Northern Blvd., Flushing, 11354 (718)
445-8770

Schneider, Claudine (R-R.I., 2nd)
30 Rolfe Sq., Cranston, 02910 (401) 528-5020

Schroeder, Patricia (D-Colo., 1st)
1767 High St., Denver, 80218 (303) 398-0970

Schuette, Bill (R-Mich., 10th)
304 East Main St., PO Box 31, Midland, 48640
(517) 631-2552
300 West Main St., Owosso, 48867 723-6759
120 W. Harris St., Parkview Plaza North,
Cadillac 49601 (616) 775-2722

Schulze, Richard T. (R-Pa., 5th)
2 E. Lancaster Ave., Paoli, 19301 (215) 648-0555

Schumer, Charles E. (D-N.Y., 10th)
1628 Kings Hwy., Brooklyn, 11229 (718)
965-5400
1663 - 10th Ave., Brooklyn, 11215 965-5055

Selberling, John F. (D-Ohio, 14th)
Federal Bldg., 2 S. Main St., Akron, 44308 (216)
375-5710

Sensenbrenner, F. James, Jr. (R-Wis., 9th)
120 Bishop's Way, Brookfield, 53005 (414)
784-1111

Sharp, Philip R. (D-Ind., 2nd)
814 W. White River Blvd., Muncie, 47303 (317)
747-5566
Main Post Office Bldg., 400 N. A St.,
Richmond, 47374 966-6125
376 S. Madison Ave., Greenwood, 46142
887-3182

Shaw, E. Clay, Jr. (R-Fla., 15th)
Broward Federal Bldg., 299 E. Broward Blvd.,
Ft. Lauderdale, 33301 (305) 522-1800

Shelby, Richard C. (D-Ala., 7th)
Federal Bldg., P.O. Box 2627, Tuscaloosa,
35403 (205) 752-3578
Courthouse, Bessemer, 35020 425-5031
Federal Bldg., Selma, 36701 872-2684

Shumway, Norman D. (R-Calif., 14th)
Ste. 1-A, 1150 W. Robinhood, Stockton, 95207
(209) 957-7773
Ste. B, 11899 Edgewood Rd., Auburn, 95603
(916) 885-3737

Shuster, Bud (R-Pa., 9th)
Ste. G, Penn Alto Hotel, Altoona, 16601 (814)
946-1653
179 E. Queens St., Chambersburg, 17201 (717)
264-8308

Sikorski, Gerry (D/F/L-Minn., 8th)
8535 Central Ave., N.E., Blaine, 55434 (612)
780-5801

Siljander, Mark D. (R-Mich., 4th)
15788 W. Michigan, Three Rivers, 49093 (616)
279-7125
Ste. 3A, 815 Main St., St. Joseph, 49085
982-0722

Sielsky, Norman (D-Va., 4th)
801 Water St., Portsmouth, 23704 (804)
393-2068

Rm. 607, Va. First S. & L., Franklin & Adams Sts., Petersburg, 23808 732-2544
Chamber of Commerce Bldg., 332 S. Main St., Emporia, 23847 634-5575

Skeen, Joe (R-N.M., 2nd)
Ste. A206, 200 Griggs, Las Cruces, 88001 (505) 523-8245
127 Federal Bldg., Roswell, 88201 622-0055

Skelton, Ike (D-Mo., 4th)
Federal Bldg., 319 S. Lamine, Sedalia, 65301 (816) 826-2675
1700 W. 40 Hwy., Blue Springs, 65015 228-4242
314 Jackson St., Jefferson City, 65101 (314) 635-3499

Slattery, James C. (D-Kan., 2nd)
Ste. 280, 444 S.E. Quincy St., Topeka, 66683 (913) 295-2811

Slaughter, D. French, Jr. (R-Va., 7th)
110 South West St., Culpepper, 22701 (703) 825-3495
112 North Cameron St., Winchester 22601 667-0990
100 Port Square Annex, Charlottesville 22902 (804) 295-2106
#301, 904 Princess Anne St., Fredericksburg 22404 (703) 373-0536

Smith, Christopher H. (R-N.J., 4th)
Ste. H, 2333 Whitehorse, Mercerville Rd., Hamilton, 08619 (609) 890-2800
222 High St., Burlington City, 08016 386-5534
Rm. 404, 402 E. State St., Trenton, 08608 989-2140

Smith, Denny (R-Ore., 5th)
Ste. 20, 4035–12th St. S.E., P.O. Box 13089, Salem, 97309 (503) 399-5756

Smith, Lawrence J. (D-Fla., 16th)
4747 Hollywood Blvd., Hollywood, 33021 (305) 987-6484

Smith, Neal (D-Iowa, 4th)
Rm. 544, Insurance Exchange Bldg., Des Moines, 50309 (515) 284-4634
215 U.S. Post Office Bldg., P.O. Box 1748, Ames, 50010 232-5221

Smith, Robert C. (R-N.H., 1st)
340 Commercial St., Manchester, 03101 (603) 644-3387

90 Washington St., Dover, 03820 742-0404
PO Box 658, Wolfeboro, 03894 569-4993

Smith, Robert F. (Bob) (R-Ore., 2nd)
Ste. K, 1150 Crater Lake Ave., Medford, 97504 (503) 776-4646

Smith, Virginia (R-Neb., 3rd)
Ste. 1, The Town House, 1509 First Ave., Scottsbluff, 69361 (308) 632-3333
Post Office Bldg., Main Fl., P.O. Box 2146, Grand Island, 68802 381-5555

Snowe, Olympia J. (R-Maine, 2nd)
146 Main St., Auburn, 04210 (207) 786-2451
209 Federal Bldg., 202 Harlow St., Bangor, 04401 945-0432
197 State St., P.O. Box 722, Presque Isle, 04769 764-5124

Snyder, Gene (R-Ky., 4th)
125 Chenoweth Lane, St. Matthews, 40207 (502) 895-6949
310 Federal Bldg., Covington, 41011 (606) 491-0105

Solarz, Stephen J. (D-N.Y., 13th)
28 Cadman Plaza W., Brooklyn, 11201 (718) 330-7229
117 Brighton Beach Ave., Brooklyn, 11235 965-5105

Solomon, Gerald B. (R-N.Y., 24th)
Gaslight Square, Saratoga Springs, 12866 (518) 587-9800
419 Warren St., Hudson, 12534 828-0181
21 Bay St., Glens Falls, 12801 792-3031
568 Columbia Tnpk., Second Fl., East Greenbush, 12061 477-2703
14 Center St., Rhinebeck, 12572 (914) 876-2200

Spence, Floyd (R-S.C., 2nd)
1916 Assembly St., Columbia, 29201 (803) 765-5871
372 St. Paul St., N.E., P.O. Box 1609, Orangeburg, 29116 536-4641

Spratt, John (D-S.C., 5th)
P.O. Box 272-CSS, Rock Hill, 29731 (803) 327-1114
17 E. Calhoun St., Sumter, 29150 773-3362
P.O. Box 964, Laurens, 29360 984-5323

Staggers, Harley O., Jr. (D-W.Va., 2nd)
155 Armstrong St., P.O. Box 1096, Keyser, 26726 (304) 788-6311

101 N. Court St., Lewisburg, 24901 645-3188
Harley O. Staggers Federal Bldg., P.O. Box
1255, Morgantown, 26507 291-6001
235 S. Queen St., Martinsburg, 25401 267-2144

Stangeland, Arlan (R-Minn., 7th)
M-F Bldg., 403 Center Ave., Moorhead, 56560
(218) 233-8631
Federal Bldg., 720 Mall Germain, St. Cloud,
56301 (612) 251-0740

Stallings, Richard H. (D-Idaho, 2nd)
304 N. Eighth #434, Boise, 83702 (208) 334-1953
250 South Four, #220, Pocatello, 83201
236-6734
834 Falls Ave., #1180, Twin Falls, 83301
734-6329
482 C St., #212, Idaho Falls, 83402 523-6701

Stark, Fortney H. (Pete) (D-Calif., 9th)
Ste. 1029, 22300 Foothill Blvd., Hayward, 94541
(415) 635-1092
Livermore Municipal Airport Bldg., 636
Terminal Cir., Livermore, 94550 449-0269

Stenholm, Charles W. (D-Tex., 17th)
2101 Federal Bldg., P.O. Box 1101, Abilene,
79604 (915) 673-7221
903 E. Hamilton, P.O. Box 1237, Stamford,
79553 773-3623

Stokes, Louis (D-Ohio, 21st).
2947 New Federal Bldg., 1240 E. Ninth St.,
Cleveland, 44199 (216) 522-4900
Ste. 211, 2140 Lee Rd., Cleveland Heights,
44118 522-4907

Strang, Michael L. (R-Colo., 3rd)
Federal Bldg., Rm 126, 400 Rood Ave., Grand
Junction 81501 (303) 242-2400
228 South Union Ave., Pueblo 81003 543-7572
4 Delwood Circle, Durango, 81301 247-3275

Stratton, Samuel S. (D-N.Y., 23rd)
Post Office Bldg., Schenectady, 12305 (518)
374-4547
Post Office Bldg., Amsterdam, 12010 843-3400
827 Leo O'Brien Federal Office Bldg., Albany,
12207 465-0700
206 Post Office Bldg., Troy, 12180 271-0822

Studds, Gerry E. (D-Mass., 10th)
Post Office Bldg., New Bedford, 02740 (617)
999-1251
193 Rockland St., Hanover, 02339 826-3866
146 Main St., Hyannis, 02601 771-0666

Stump, Bob (R-Ariz., 3rd)
5001 Federal Bldg., Phoenix, 85025 (602)
261-6923

Sundquist, Donald K. (R-Tenn., 7th)
117 S. Second St., Clarksville, 37040 (615)
522-4406
Ste. 112, 5909 Shelby Oaks Dr., Memphis, 38134
(901) 382-5811

Sunia, Fofo I.F. (D-Amer. Samoa, Deleg.)
P.O. Drawer X, Pago Pago, 96799 (011684)
663-1372

Swift, Al (D-Wash., 2nd)
308 Federal Bldg., 104 W. Magnolia,
Bellingham, 98225 (206) 733-4500
201 Federal Bldg., 3002 Colby Ave., Everett,
98201 252-3188
1711 K Gunn Rd., Port Angeles, 98362 452-3211

Swindall, Patrick L. (R-Ga., 4th)
304 N. Eighth #434, Boise, 83702 (208) 334-1953
250 South Fourth, #220, Pocatello, 83201
236-6734
834 Falls Ave., #1180, Twin Falls 83301
734-6329
482 C St., #212, Idaho Falls, 83402 523-6701

Synar, Mike (D-Okla., 2nd)
2B22 New Federal Bldg., 125 S. Main St.,
Muskogee, 74401 (918) 687-2533

Tallon, Robin M. (D-S.C., 6th)
P.O. Box 6286, Florence, 29502 (803) 669-9084
Horry County Courthouse, Conway, 29526
248-7401

Tauke, Thomas J. (R-Iowa, 2nd)
698 Central Ave., Dubuque, 52001 (319)
557-7740
Rm. 209, 1756 First Ave., N.E., Cedar Rapids,
52402 366-8709
116 S. Second St., Clinton, 52732 242-6180

Tauzin, W.J. (Billy) (D-La., 3rd)
107 Federal Bldg., Houma, 70360 (504) 876-3033
Ste. 914, 4900 Veterans Memorial Blvd.,
Metairie, 70002 889-2303
210 E. Main St., New Iberia, 70560 (318)
367-8231

Taylor, Gene (R-Mo., 7th)
Ste. 101, 300 Sherman Pkwy., Springfield, 65806
(417) 862-4317
302 Federal Bldg., Joplin, 64801 781-1041

Thomas, Lindsay (D-Ga., 1st)
202 Federal Bldg., Statesboro, 30458 (912)
489-8797
240 Old Post Office Bldg., P.O. Box 10074,
Savannah, 31412 944-4074
304 Federal Bldg., Brunswick, 31520 264-4040
P.O. Box 767, Jessup, 31545 427-9231

Thomas, William M. (R-Calif., 20th)
Rm. 115, 858 W. Jackman St., Lancaster, 93534
(804) 948-2634
Rm. 200, 1830 Truxtun, Bakersfield, 93301
327-3611
Ste. N, 1160 Marsh St., San Luis Obispo, 93401
544-6698

Torres, Esteban Edward (D-Calif., 34th)
Ste. 117, Saddleback Sq., 12440 Firestone Blvd.,
Norwalk, 90650 (213) 929-2711
Ste. 201, Home Fed. S. & L. Bldg., 1400 W.
Covina Pkwy., West Covina, 91790 (818)
814-1557

Torricelli, Robert (D-N.J., 9th)
Ste. 201, 27 Warren St., Hackensack, 07601
(201) 646-1111

Towns, Eldolphus (D/L-N.Y., 11th)
93 Prospect Pl., Brooklyn, 11217 (718) 622-5700

Traficant, James A. Jr. (D-Ohio, 17th)
11 Overhill Ave., Youngstown, 44512 (216)
788-2414
918 Youngstown-Warren, Niles, 44446 652-9149

Traxler, Bob (D-Mich., 8th)
1052 New Federal Bldg., 100 S. Warren St.,
Saginaw, 48607 (517) 753-6444
317 Post Office Bldg., 1000 Washington Ave.,
Bay City, 48706 894-2906

Udall, Morris K. (D-Ariz., 2nd)
300 N. Main Ave., Tucson, 85705 (602) 629-6404
Ste. 103, 1419 N. Third St., Phoenix, 85004
261-3018

Valentine, Tim (D-N.C., 2nd)
121 E. Parrish St., P.O. Box 3654, Durham,
22702 (919) 541-5201
219 S. Franklin St., Rocky Mount, 27801
446-1147

Vander Jagt, Guy (R-Mich., 9th)
Roosevelt Park, 950 W. Norton Ave.,
Muskegon, 49441 (616) 733-3131
31 W. Eighth St., Holland, 49423 396-3849

Ste. D, 124 N. Division St., Traverse City, 49684
946-3832

Vento, Bruce F. (D/F/L-Minn., 4th)
150 Mears Park Place, 405 Sibley St., St. Paul,
55101 (612) 725-7724

Volkmer, Harold L. (D-Mo., 9th)
370 Federal Bldg., Hannibal, 63401 (314)
221-1200
818 W. Terra Lane, P.O. Box 219, O'Fallon,
63366 272-8272
317 Lafayette, P.O. Box 229, Washington, 63090
239-4001
206 Austin, Columbia, 65203 449-5111
122 Bourke St., Macon, 63552 (816) 385-5615

Vucanovich, Barbara (R-Nev., 2nd)
1139 Fed. Bldg. & U.S. Courthouse, 300 Booth
St., Reno, 89509 (702) 784-5003
443 Fifth St., Elko, 89801 738-4064
Ste. 102, 220 Civic Ctr. Dr., P.O. Box A, North
Las Vegas, 89030 399-3555

Walgren, Doug (D-Pa., 18th)
2117 Wm. S. Moorhead Fed. Bldg., Pittsburgh,
15222 (412) 319-4016

Walker, Robert S. (R-Pa., 16th)
50 N. Duke St., 5th Fl., Lancaster, 17603 (717)
393-0666
307 Municipal Bldg., 400 S. Eighth St.,
Lebanon, 17042 274-1641
P.O. Box 69, Cochranville, 19330 (215) 593-2155

Watkins, Wes (D-Okla., 3rd)
232 Post Office Bldg., Ada, 78420 (405)
436-1980
Ste. 4, 720 S. Husband, Stillwater, 74074
743-1400
118 Federal Bldg., McAlester, 74501 (918)
423-5951

Waxman, Henry A. (D-Calif., 24th)
Ste. 400, 8425 W. Third St., Los Angeles, 90048
(213) 651-1040

Weaver, Jim (D-Ore., 4th)
Federal Bldg., 211 E. Seventh Ave., Eugene,
97401 (503) 687-6732

Weber, Vin (R-Minn., 2nd)
919 S. First St., Willmar, 56201 (612) 235-6820
P.O. Box 279, New Ulm, 56073 (507) 354-6400
1212 E. College Dr., P.O. Box 1214, Marshall,
56258 532-9611

Weiss, Ted (D/L-N.Y., 17th)
37 W. 65th St., New York City, 10023 (212)
787-3480
4060 Broadway, New York City, 10032 927-7726
131 Waverly Pl., New York, 10011 620-3310
490 W. 238th St., Riverdale, 10463 884-0441
655 E. 233rd St., Bronx, 10466 652-0400

Wheat, Alan (D-Mo., 5th)
935 U.S. Courthouse Bldg., 811 Grand Ave.,
Kansas City, 65106 (816) 842-4545
Rm. 221, 301 W. Lexington, Independence,
64050 833-4545

Whitehurst, G. William (R-Va., 2nd)
815 Federal Bldg., Norfolk, 23510 (804)
441-3340
Ste. 801, One Columbus Ctr., Virginia Beach,
23462 490-2393

Whitley, Charles O. (D-N.C., 3rd)
306 Federal Bldg., Goldsboro, 27530 (919)
736-1844

Whittaker, Bob (R-Kan., 5th)
Sixth & School Sts., P.O. Box 280, Augusta,
67010 (316) 775-1127
625 Merchant St., P.O. Box 1102, Emporia,
66801 342-6464
908 N. Broadway, P.O. Box 1111, Pittsburg,
66762 232-2320
109 W. Martin, P.O. Box 1003, McPherson,
67460 241-5797

Whitten, Jamie L. (D-Miss., 1st)
Post Office Bldg., Charleston, 38921 (601)
647-2413
Federal Bldg., P.O. Box 667, Oxford, 38655
234-9064
Box 1482, Tupelo, 38801 844-5437

Williams, Pat (D-Mont., 1st)
23 S. Last Chance Gulch, Helena, 59601 (406)
443-7878
302 W. Broadway, Missoula, 59802 549-5550
Finlen Complex, Broadway & Wyoming Sts.,
Butte, 59701 723-4404

Wilson, Charles (D-Tex., 2nd)
Rm. 201, 701 N. First St., Lufkin, 75901 (409)
639-8642

Wirth, Timothy E. (D-Colo., 2nd)
Ste. 112, 3489 W. 72nd St., Westminster, 80030
(303) 234-5200

Wise, Robert E., Jr. (D-W.Va., 3rd)
Ste. 203, 812 Quarrier St., Charleston, 25301
(304) 347-5267

Wolf, Frank R. (R-Va., 10th)
Ste. 115, 1651 Old Meadow Rd., McLean, 22102
(703) 734-1500
Rm. 48, 19 E. Market St., Leesburg, 22075
777-4422

Wolpe, Howard (D-Mich., 3rd)
1816 W. Columbia, Battle Creek, 49014 (616)
962-6511, ext. 6212
142 N. Kalamazoo Mall, Kalamazoo, 49007
385-0039
316 N. Capitol St., Lansing, 48933 (517)
377-1644

Wortley, George C. (R-N.Y., 27th)
1269 Federal Bldg., 100 S. Clinton St., Syracuse,
13260 (315) 423-5657

Wright, Jim (D-Tex., 12th)
9A10 Lanham Federal Office Bldg., Fort Worth,
76102 (817) 334-3212
536B W. Seminary Dr., Fort Worth, 76115
334-4845

Wyden, Ron (D-Ore., 3rd)
1002 N.E. Holladay, P.O. Box 3621, Portland,
97203 (503) 231-2300

Wylie, Chalmers P. (R-Ohio, 15th)
Rm. 500, 200 N. High St., Columbus, 43215
(614) 469-5614

Yates, Sidney R. (D-Ill., 9th)
3920 Kluczynski Fed. Bldg., 230 S. Dearborn
St., Chicago, 60604 (312) 353-4596
2100 Ridge Ave., Evanston, 60204 328-2610

Yatron, Gus (D-Pa., 8th)
Rm. 622, Abraham Lincoln Motor Inn, P.O.
Box 776, Reading, 19603 (215) 375-4573
603 American Bank Bldg., Pottsville, 17901
(717) 622-4212

Young, C. W. Bill (R-Fla., 8th)
627 Federal Bldg., 144 First Ave., S., St.
Petersburg, 33701 (813) 893-3191
Ste. 606, 801 W. Bay Dr., Largo, 33540 581-0980

Young, Don (R-Alaska, At Lge.)
701-C Federal Bldg. & Courthouse, Box 3,
Anchorage, 99513 (907) 271-5978

Federal Bldg., 101–12th Ave., Box 10,
  Fairbanks, 99701 456-0210
401 Federal Bldg., P.O. Box 1247, Juneau,
  99802 586-7400
501 Federal Bldg., Ketchikan, 99901 225-6880
P.O. Box 3033, Kenai, 99611 283-5808
P.O. Box 177, Kodiak, 99615 486-5407
P.O. Box 1860, Nome, 99762 443-5511

Young, Robert A. (D-Mo., 2nd)
  4150 Cypress Rd., St. Ann, 63074 (314) 425-7200
  12325 Manchester Rd., Des Peres, 63131
  425-3210

Zechau, Edwin V. W. (R-Calif., 12th)
  Ste. 125, 505 W. Olive Ave., Sunnyvale, 94086
  (408) 730-8555

Regional Offices

If you are outside Washington, DC, and looking for information from a particular department or agency, start by contacting its regional office in your area. This can save you a lot of time and money in correspondence and telephone calls. A regional office very often will have the information you need or know exactly where to get it in Washington, DC. However, beware: The regional office may tell you that the information you need is *not* available. Don't necessarily stop your search: Next try looking in Washington, DC. It is impossible for people in the field to be aware of everything that is available in Washington. (The people in Washington often don't even know.)

Following are the names, addresses and telephone numbers of all the government's major regional offices.

Department of Agriculture

Agricultural Marketing Service, Fruit and Vegetable Division, Perishable Agriculture Commodities Branch (PACA)
Fort Worth, TX 76102; 819 Taylor Street, Room
  9C03/817-335-1630
Los Angeles, CA 90017; 845 Figueroa Street,
  Room 520/213-628-7766.
New Brunswick, NJ 08901; 330 Livingston Ave-
  nue/201-846-4798.
Washington, DC 20250: 14th and Independence
  Avenue S.W./202-447-4180.
Wood Dale, IL 60191; Suite 103-330 Georgetown
  Square/312-350-0851.

Agricultural Marketing Service, Livestock Division, Livestock and Grain News Branch
Central: 609 Livestock Exchange Building,
  Omaha, NB 68107/402-731-4520.
Eastern: Room 2623 South Building, 14th and
  Independence Ave. SW, Washington D.C.
  20250/202-447-6231.
Western: Room 2623 South Building, 14th and
  Independence Ave. SW, Washington DC
  20250/202-447-6231.

Agricultural Marketing Service, Livestock Division, Seed Branch
Beltsville, MD 20705/Room 213, Building 306
  BARC-E/301-344-2089.

Agricultural Marketing Service, Packers and Stockyards Division
Bedford, VA 24523: Turnpike Rd., Box 101E/703-
  982-4330.
Atlanta, GA 30309: 1720 Peachtree St., N.W.
  Room 338/404-881-4845.
Denver, CO 80216: 208 Livestock Exchange
  Building/303-294-7050.
Fort Worth, TX 76102: 819 Taylor St. Room 8A36
  Federal Building/817-334-3286.
Indianapolis, IN Room 435-Federal Building US
  Court House 46 E. Ohio Street Indianapolis, IN
  46204/317-269-6424.
Kansas City, MO 64102: 828 Livestock Exchange
  Building/816-374-2368.
Lawndale, CA 90261: 15000 Aviation Blvd Room
  2106 P.O. Box 6102/213-536-6687.
Memphis, TN 38103: 167 N. Main St. Room 459
  Federal Building/901-521-3414.
North Brunswick, NJ 08902: 525 Georges Rd./201-
  246-0060.

Omaha, NB 68107: 909 Livestock Exchange Building/402-221-3391.

Portland, OR 97223: 9370 S.W. Greenburg Rd. Suite E/503-221-2687.

South Saint Paul, MN 55075: 208 Post Office Box 8 Building/612-725-7876.

Agricultural Marketing Service, Tobacco Division

Raleigh, NC 27611: 1306 Annapolis, Dr. P.O. Box 27846/919-755-4584.

Lexington, KY 40504: 333 Waller Ave., Suite 401-407/606-233-2613.

Caparra Heights, Puerto Rico 00922/Box 10365/809-725-2874.

Washington, DC 20250: 300 12th St. S.W., Room 502/202-447-2567.

Agricultural Stabilization and Conservation Service, Warehouse Division

Storage Contract Branch, Director, Room 5968, P.O. Box 2415, 14th and Independence Avenue SW. Washington, DC 20250/202-447-4018.

Warehouse Licensing Branch, Director, Room 5968, P.O. Box 2415, 14th and Independence Avenue S.W. Washington, D.C. 20250/202-447-4018.

Agricultural Stabilization and Conservation Service

Northeast: Room 3720-S, P.O. Box 2415, Washington, DC 20013/202-447-4746.

Southeast: Room 3715-S, P.O. Box 2415, Washington, DC 20013/202-447-3593.

Midwest: Room 3709-S, P.O. Box 2415, Washington, DC 20013/202-447-6625.

Northwest: Room 3716S, P.O. Box 2415, Washington, DC 20013/202-447-6941.

Southwest: Room 37195-S, P.O. Box 2415, Washington DC 20013/202-447-7889.

Animal and Plant Health Inspection Service, Plant Protection and Quarantine

Northeast: Moorestown, NJ 08057: Blason 2-II 1st Floor 505 S. Lenola Road/609-235-9120.

South Central: Brownsville, TX 78521: 2100 Boca Chica Blvd. Suite 400/512-542-7231.

Southeast: Gulfport, MS 39505: P.O. Box 3659/601-863-1813.

Western: Sacramento, CA 95866-0790: PO Box 6607 2nd Floor, 83 Scripps Drive 95825/916-440-2098

Animal and Plant Health Inspection Service, Veterinary Services

Central: 221 Lancaster Ave., Fort Worth, TX 76102/817-870-5566.

Northern: GSA Depot Building 12, Scotia, NY 12302/518-370-5026.

Southeastern: 700 Twiggs St., Rm. 821, Tampa, FL 33601/813-228-2952.

Western: 240 W. 26th Ave., Rm. 237, Denver, CO 80211/303-837-3481.

Federal Crop Insurance Corporation, Field Underwriting Offices

Billings, MT 59102: 4th Floor, 2401 Grande Ave./406-657-6447.

Davis, CA 95616: 1340 Covell Blvd., Suite 101/916-753-1006.

Harrisburg, PA 17110: 3555 N. Progress Ave., 717-782-4807.

Jackson, MS 39201: 656 N. State St., Room 401/601-960-4771.

Oklahoma City, OK 73118: Two Grand Park, 5701 N. Charte/405-231-5057.

Raleigh, NC 27602 P.O. Box 589/919-755-4040.

St. Paul, MN 55101: Room 624, Bremer Bldg. 7th & Robert Sts./612-725-5804.

Spokane, WA 99206: N. 112 University Rd., Suite 200/509-456-2147.

Springfield, IL 62701: 524 S. 2nd St., Suite 675/217-492-4186.

Topeka, KS 66603: 444 S.E. Quincy St., Room 135/913-295-2570.

Valdosta, GA 31601: 401 N. Patterson St., Room M 113/912-242-3044.

Operational Federal Crop Insurance Corporation, Field Offices

Billings, MT 59102: 2401 Grand Ave./406-657-6196.

Bismarck, ND 58501: 220 E. Rosser Ave., Room 234/701-255-4011 Ext. 271.

College Station, TX 77840: USDA Building P.O. Box 1159. 3rd Floor/409-260-9391.

Columbia, MO 65201: 700 E. Cherry Rd., Room 201/314-275-5287

Columbia, SC 29201: Room 1065–Federal Bldg. Assembly St./803-765-5766.

Davis, CA 95616: Alamo West Center Bldg. Suite A, 133 D Street/916-753-7880.

Des Moines, IA 50309: 509 Federal Bldg., 210 Walnut St./515-284-4316.

Harrisburg, PA 17110: 3555 N. Progress Ave./717-782-4803.

Huron, SD 57350: Federal Bldg. 200 4th St. S.W./605-352-8651, Ext. 385.

Indianapolis, IN 46224: 5610 Crawfordsville Rd., Atkinson Square West Suite 1501/317-248-4141.

Jackson, MS 39269: 100 W. Capitol St. Suite 1201/601-960-4328.

Lincoln, NB 68508: 100 Centennial Mall, North Federal Bldg. Room 443/402-471-5531.

Manhattan, KS 66502: 2601 Anderson Ave./913-537-4980.

Nashville, TN 37203: U.S. Courthouse, Room 508/615-251-5591.

Raleigh, NC 27611: P.O. Box 27366/919-755-4470.

St. Paul, MN 55101: 316 Robert St., Room 222/612-725-5871.

Spokane, WA 99201: US Court House, W. 920 Riverside Ave., Room 294/509-456-3763.

Springfield, IL 62701: 320 Washington St., Room 607/217-492-4280.

Federal Grain Inspection Service

Atlanta, GA 30309: 1720 Peachtree St., Suite 338/404-881-7910.

Chicago, IL 60607: 433 W. Van Buren St., Room 929/312-353-2744.

Kansas City, MO 64105: Midland Building, 12th Floor, 1221 Baltimore Ave./816-842-9160.

Rockwell, TX 75087: 2313 Ridge Rd., Suite 105/214-226-7061.

Seattle, WA 98134: Federal Center S. Building 1201, Room 1103, 4735 E. Marginal Way S./206-764-3825.

Food and Nutrition Service

Burlington, MA 01803: 33 North Ave 617-272-4272.

Robbinsville, NJ 08691: Mercer Corporate Park, Corporate Boulevard/609-259-5000

Chicago, IL 60602: 50 E. Washington St./312-353-6664.

Atlanta, GA 30367: 1100 Spring St. N.W. Room 200/404-881-4131.

Dallas, TX 75242: 1100 Commerce St. Room S-C-30/214-767-0222.

San Francisco, CA 94108: 550 Kearny St. Room 400/415-556-4950.

Denver, CO 80211: 2420 W. 26th Ave. Room 430-D/303-964-0410.

Food Safety and Inspection Service, Fruit and Vegetable Division, Fresh Products Standardization and Inspection Branch

Washington, DC 20250: 14th St. & Independence Ave. S.W./202-447-5870.

Chicago, IL 60607: 610 S. Canal St. Room 1012/312-353-6225.

San Francisco, CA 94111: 630 Sansome St./415-556-3845.

Falls Church, VA 22041: 5205 Leesburg Pike/703-756-6781.

Food Safety and Quality Service, Fruit and Vegetable Division, Processed Products Standardization and Inspection

Washington, DC 20250: 14th St. & Independence Ave. S.W./202-447-4693.

Wood Dale, IL 60191: 330 Georgetown Square Room 104/312-353-6217.

Winter Haven, FL 33880, 98 3rd St. S.W./813-294-7416.

San Jose, CA 95113: 111 W. St. John St., Suite 416/408-291-7253.

Food Safety and Inspection Service, Meat and Poultry Inspection

Agricultural Marketing Service, Meat Grading and Certification Branch, Main Stations

Des Moines, IA 50316: 607 E. 2nd St./515-284-4042.

Atlanta, GA 30309: 1718 Peachtree St. N.W., Room 216/404-881-3911.

Alameda, CA 94501: Bldg. 2C, 620 Central Ave./415-273-7402.

Philadelphia, PA 19102: 1421 Cherry St. 7th Floor/215-597-4217.

Dallas, TX 75242: 1100 Commerce St. Room 5F41/214-767-9116.

Food Safety and Inspection Service, Meat Quality Division

Agricultural Marketing Service, Meat Grading and Certification Branch, Main Stations

Amarillo, TX 79120: P.O. Box 30217/806-371-7361.

Atlanta, GA 30309: 1718 Peachtree St. Room 206 N.W./404-881-4158.

Bell, CA 90201: Building 7. Section A, 5600 Rickenbacker Road/213-267-6738.

Chicago, IL 60609: 4101 S. Halsted St. Room 217/312-353-5751.

Denver, CO 80216: 206 Livestock Exchange Building/303-294-7676.

Dallas, TX 75242: Earl Cabell Federal Building, 1100 Commerce St. Room 7C59 214-767-6180.

Food Safety and Inspection Service, Meat and Poultry Inspection

North Central: Des Moines, IA 50316: 607 E. 2nd St./515-284-4042.

Northeastern: Philadelphia, PA 19102: 1421 Cherry St., 7th floor/215-597-4217.

Southeastern: Atlanta, GA 30309: 1718 Peachtree St. N.W., Room 216/404-881-3911.

Southwestern: Dallas, TX 75242: 1100 Commerce St., Room 5F41/214-767-9116.

Agricultural Marketing Service, Meat Grading and Certification Branch, Main Station

Amarillo, TX 79120: P.O. Box 30217/806-376-7361.

Atlanta, GA 30309: 1718 Peachtree St. N.W., Room 206/404-881-4158.

Bell, CA 90201: Building 7, Section A, 5600 Rickenbacker Road/213-267-6738.

Chicago, IL 60609: 401 S. Halsted St., Room 217/312-353-5751.

Dallas, TX 75242: Earl Cabell Federal Building, 1100 Commerce St., Room 7C59/214-767-6180.

Denver, CO 80216: 206 Livestock Exchange Building/303-294-7676.

Omaha, NB 68107: 723 Livestock Exchange Building/402-731-2014.

Princeton, NJ 08540: 1101 State Rd., Building E/609-921-3305.

Sioux City, IA 51107: 225 Livestock Exchange Building, PO Box 2437/712-252-3287.

Agricultural Marketing Service, Dairy Division, Dairy Grading Section

San Francisco, CA 94111: 630 Sansome St. Room 754/415-556-5585.

Chicago, IL 60607: 610 S. Canal St. Room 803/312-353-6680.

Minneapolis, MN 55401: 110 S. 4th St. Room 119/612-349-3504.

Syracuse, NY 13260: 100 S. Clinton St. Room 1221/315-423-5325.

Agricultural Marketing Service, Poultry and Dairy Quality Division, Poultry Grading

Gastonia, NC 28054: 635 Cox Road–Suite F/704-867-3871.

Little Rock, AK 72215: #1 Natural Resources Dr./501-378-5955.

Des Moines, IA 50309: 210 Walnut St./515-284-4581.

Modesto, CA 95355: World Plaza Building, 1508 Coffee Rd./209-522-5251.

Forest Service, Forest and Range Research Experiment Stations

Northeastern: Broomall, PA 19008: 370 Reed Rd./215-461-3008.

Southeastern: Asheville, NC 28804: 200 Weaver Blvd., 704-259-0758.

North Central: St. Paul, MN 55108: 1992 Folwell Ave./612-642-5249.

Southern: New Orleans, LA 70113: 701 Loyola Ave./504-589-6787.

Products Lab: Madison, WI 53705: Box 5130 Gifford Pinchot Drive/608-264-5719.

Rocky Mountain: Fort Collins, CO 80526: 240 W. Prospect St./303-221-4390.

Inter Mountain: Ogden, UT 84401: 507 25th St./801-625-5412.

Pacific Northwest: Portland, OR 97208: 319 SW. Pine St. P.O. Box 3890/503-294-5640.

Pacific Southwest: Berkeley, CA 94701: 1960 Addison St./415-486-3292.

Forest Service, National Forest System

Missoula, MT 59807: Federal Building/406-329-3011.

Lakewood, CO 80225: 11177 W. 8th Ave./303-236-9427.

Albuquerque, NM 87102: 517 Gold Ave. S.W./505-842-3300.

Ogden, UT 84401: 324 25th St./801-625-3011.

Milwaukee, WI 53203: 310 W. Wisconsin Ave./414-291-3693.

Atlanta, GA 30367: 1720 Peachtree Rd. N.W./404-881-4177.

Portland, OR 97208: 319 S.W. Pine St./503-221-3625.

San Francisco, CA 94111: 630 Sansome St./415-556-4310.

Juneau, AK 99802: Federal Office Building/907-586-7263.

Forest Service, State and Private Forestry

Missoula, MT 59807: Federal Building/406-329-3011.

Lakewood, CO 80225/11177 W. 8th Ave./303-234-3711.

Albuquerque, NM 87102: 517 Gold Ave. S.W./505-766-2401.

Ogden, UT 84401: 324 25th St./801-625-5603.

Broomall, PA 19008: 370 Reed Rd./215-461-3125.

San Francisco, CA 94111: 630 Sansome St./415-556-4310.

Portland, OR 97208: 319 S.W. Pine St./503-211-3625.

Atlanta, GA 30367: 1720 Peachtree Rd. N.W./404-881-7930.

Anchorage, AK 99508: Suite 104, 2221 East Northern Lights Blvd./907-276-0939.

Office of the General Counsel

Atlanta, GA 30367: 1371 Peachtree St. N.E. Suite 600/404-881-4161.

Chicago, IL 60604: 230 S. Dearborn St. Room 2920/312-353-5640.

Denver, CO 80202: 1444 Wazee Street Suite 230/303-844-4031.

Harrisburg, PA 17108: 228 Walnut St. P.O. Box 1134/717-782-3713.

Little Rock, AR 72201: 700 W. Capitol St./501-378-5246.

Milwaukee, WI 53203: 310 W. Wisconsin Ave./414-291-3774.

Portland, OR 97204: 1734 Federal Building, 1220 S.W. 3rd Ave./503-221-3115.

San Francisco, CA 94105: 211 Main, Suite 1060/415-974-0471.

Kansas City, MO 64141: 9435 Holmes St. P.O. Box 293/816-926-7710.

Temple, TX 76501: 101 S. Main St., Suite 351/817-774-1204.

Office of the Inspector General, Audit Operations

Hyattsville, MD 20782: Federal Center Building, Room 422/301-436-8763.

Atlanta, GA 30309: 1447 Peachtree St. N.E., Room 900/404-881-3675.

Chicago, IL 60606: 1 N. Wacker Dr., Room 800/312-353-1352.

Temple, TX 76501: 101 S. Main St., Room 324/817-774-1430.

Kansas City, MO 64141: 9435 Holmes St., P.O. Box 293/816-926-7657.

San Francisco, CA 94111: 555 Battery St., Room 522/415-556-4244.

Office of the Inspector General, Investigation Operations

New York, NY 10278: 26 Federal Plaza, Room 1707/212-264-4288.

Hyattsville, MD 20782: Federal Building, Room 432A/301-436-8850.

Atlanta, GA 30309: 1447 Peachtree St. N.E., Room 901/404-881-4377.

Chicago, IL 60606: 165 N Canal St., Suite 1400/312-353-1358.

Temple, TX 76501: 101 S. Main St., Room 311/817-774-1351.

Kansas City, MO 64141: 9435 Holmes St., Room 210, P.O. Box 293/816-926-7606.

San Francisco, CA 94111: 555 Battery St., Room 526/415-556-4245.

Rural Electrification Administration

Telephone Areas: 14th and Independence Ave. S.W., South Building, Room 2815, Washington, DC 20250/202-447-2960.

Electric Areas: 14th and Independence Ave. S.W., South Building, Room 3308, Washington, DC 20250/202-382-1420.

Science and Education Administration, Agricultural Research

Washington, DC 20250: Agricultural Research Center, W. 14th and Independence Ave. S.W./202-447-3918.

Peoria, IL 21615: 2000 W. Pioneer Pkwy./309-671-7176.

New Orleans, LA 70153: P.O. Box 53326/504-589-6753.

Oakland, CA 94612: 1333 Broadway, Suite 400/415-273-4191.

Soil Conservation Service, Technical Service Centers

Lincoln, NB 68508: Federal Building, U.S. Court House, Room 393/402-471-5346.

Portland, OR 97209: 511 N.W. Broadway Room 514/503-423-2824.

Chester, PA 19013: 160 East 7th Street/215-499-3905.

Fort Worth, TX 76115: Fort Worth Federal Center, P.O. Box 6567/817-334-3011.

Department of the Air Force

Air Force Regional Civil Engineers

Interagency/Intergovernmental Coordination for Environmental Planning

Eastern (Standard Federal Regions I–IV): 526 Title Building, 30 Pryor Street, Atlanta, GA 30303/404-221-6776.

Central (Standard Federal Regions V–VIII): 1114 Commerce St., Dallas, TX 75242/217-767-2514.

Western (Standard Federal Regions IX and X): 630 Sansome St., Room 1316, San Francisco, CA 94111/415-556-4828.

Department of the Army

Division Offices

Lower Mississippi Valley: P. O. Box 80, Vicksburg, MS 39180/601-634-5750.

Missouri River: P. O. Box 103, Downtown Station, Omaha, NB 68101/402-221-3207.

New England: 424 Trapelo Rd., Waltham, MA 02154/617-894-2400, ext. 200.

North Atlantic: 90 Church St., New York, NY 10007/212-264-7101.

North Central: 536 S. Clark St., Chicago, IL 60605/312-353-6310.

North Pacific: P. O. Box 2870, Portland, OR 97208/503-221-3700.

Ohio River: P. O. Box 1159, Cincinnati, OH 45201/513-684-3002.

Pacific Ocean: Building 230, Fort Shafter, HI 96858/808-438-1500.

South Atlantic: 510 Title Building, 30 Pryor St. S.W., Atlanta, GA 30303/404-221-6711.

South Pacific: 630 Sansome St., Room 1216, San Francisco, CA 94111/415-556-0914.

Southwestern: 1114 Commerce St., Dallas, TX 75242/214-767-2500.

Memphis: 668 Clifford Davis Federal Building, Memphis, TN 38103/901-521-3221.

New Orleans: P. O. Box 60267, New Orleans, LA 70160/504-838-1200.

St. Louis: 210 N. 12th St., St. Louis, MO 63101/314-263-5660.

Vicksburg: P. O. Box 60, Vicksburg, MS 39180/601-634-5010.

Kansas City: 700 Federal Building, Kansas City, MO 64106/816-374-3201.

Omaha: 6014 U.S. Post Office and Courthouse, 215 N. 17th St., Omaha, NB 68102/402-221-3900.

Baltimore: P. O. Box 1715, Baltimore, MD 21203/301-962-4545.

New York: 26 Federal Plaza, New York, NY 10007/212/264-0100.

Norfolk: 803 Front St., Norfolk, VA 23510/804-441-3601.

Philadelphia: U.S. Custom House, 2d & Chestnut Sts., Philadelphia, PA 19106/215-597-4848.

Buffalo: 1776 Niagara St., Buffalo, NY 14207/716-876-5454.

Chicago: 219 S. Dearborn St., Chicago, IL 60604/312-353-6400.

Detroit: P. O. Box 1027, Detroit, MI 48231/313-226-6762.

Rock Island: Clock Tower Building, Rock Island, IL 61201/309-788-6361.

St. Paul: 1135 U.S. Post Office and Custom House, St. Paul, MN 55101/612-725-7501.

Alaska: P. O. Box 7002, Anchorage, AK 99510/907-752-5233 or 279-1132 (FTS).

Portland: P. O. Box 2946, Portland, OR 97208/503-221-6000.

Seattle: P. O. Box C-3755, Seattle, WA 98124/206-764-3690.

Walla Walla: Building 602, City-County Airport, Walla Walla, WA 99362/509-525-5500.

Huntington: P. O. Box 2127, Huntington, W.VA 25721/304-529-5253.

Louisville: P. O. Box 59, Louisville, KY 40201/502-582-5601.

Nashville: P. O. Box 1070, Nashville, TN 37202/615-251-5626.

Pittsburgh: Federal Building, 1000 Liberty Ave., Pittsburgh, PA 15222/412-644-6800.

Charleston: P. O. Box 919, Charleston, SC 29402/803-724-4229.

Jacksonville: P. O. Box 4970, Jacksonville, FL 32232/904-791-2241.

Mobile: P. O. Box 2288, Mobile, AL 36628/205-690-2511.

Savannah: P. O. Box 889, Savannah, GA 31402/912-944-5224.

Wilmington: P. O. Box 1890, Wilmington, NC 28402/919-343-4624, ext. 466.

Los Angeles: P. O. Box 2711, Los Angeles, CA 90053/213-688-5300.

Sacramento: 650 Capitol Mall, Sacramento, CA 95814/916-440-2232.

San Francisco: 211 Main St., San Francisco, CA 94105/415-556-3660.

Albuquerque: P. O. Box 1580, Albuquerque, NM 87103/505-766-2732.

Fort Worth: P. O. Box 17300, Fort Worth, TX 76102/817-334-2300.

Galveston: P.O. Box 1229, Galveston, TX 77553/713-763-1211.

Little Rock: P. O. Box 867, Little Rock, AR 72203/501-378-5531.

Tulsa: P. O. Box 61, Tulsa, OK 74102/918-581-7311.

Department of Commerce

Bureau of the Census

Boston, MA 02116: 441 Stuart St. 10th Floor/617-223-2327.

New York, NY: 10278 Federal Office Bldg. Room 37-130 26 Federal Plaza/212-264-3860.

Philadelphia, PA 19106: William J. Green, Jr Federal Bldg. 600 Arch St./215-597-4920.

Detroit, MI 48226: Federal Bldg & US Court House 231 W. Lafayette Blvd. Room 565/313-226-7742.

Chicago, IL 60604: 55 E. Jackson Blvd. Suite 1304/312-353-6251.

Kansas City, KS 66101: One Gateway Center 4th & State Sts./816-236-3728.

Seattle, WA 98109: Lake Union Bldg. 1700 Westlake Ave. N./206-442-7828.

Charlotte, NC 28202: 230 S. Tryon St. Suite 800/704-371-6142.

Atlanta, GA 30309: 1365 Peachtree St., N.E. Room 625/404-881-2271.

Dallas, TX 75242: 1100 Commerce St. Room 3054/214-767-0621.

Denver, CO 80226: 7655 W. Mississippi Ave. P.O. Box 26750/303-236-2200.

Los Angeles, CA 90049: 11777 San Vincente Blvd. Room 810/213-209-6616.

Economic Development Administration

Philadelphia, PA 19106: 325 Chestnut St. Mall Bldg. 600/215-597-4603.

Chicago, IL 60604: 175 W. Jackson Blvd., Suite A-1630/312-353-7706.

Denver, CO 80204: Room 300-Tremont Center 333 W. Colfax Ave./303-844-4714.

Atlanta, GA 30309: 1365 Peachtree St., N.E. Suite 750/404-881-7401.

Austin, TX 78701: Suite 201 Grant Bldg. 611 E. 6th Street/512-482-5461

Seattle, WA 98109: Suite 500–Lake Union Bldg. 1700 Westlake Ave. N./206-442-0596.

Minority Business Development Agency

Atlanta, GA 30309: 1371 Peachtree St. N.E./404-881-4091.

Chicago, IL 60603: 55 E. Monroe St./312-353-0182.

Dallas, TX 75242: 1100 Commerce St./214-767-8001.

New York, NY 10278: 26 Federal Plaza/212-264-3262.

San Francisco, CA 94102: 450 Golden Gate Ave./415-566-7234.

Washington, DC 20230: 14th and Constitution Ave. NW/202-377-8275.

National Oceanic and Atmospheric Administration, National Marine Fisheries Service

Juneau, AL 99802: P. O. Box 1668/907-586-7221.

Seattle, WA 98115: 7600 Sand Point Way N.E./206-526-6150.

St. Petersburg, FL 33702: 9450 Koger Blvd./813-893-3141.

Gloucester, MA 01930: 14 Elm St./617-281-3600.

Terminal Island, CA 90731: 300 S. Ferry St./213-548-2575.

National Oceanic and Atmospheric Administration, National Weather Service

Garden City, NY 11530: 585 Stewart Avenue/516-228-5400.

Fort Worth, TX 76102: 819 Taylor St./817-334-2668.

Kansas City, MO 64106: 601 E. 12th St./816-374-5463.

Salt Lake City, UT 84147: 125 S. State St./801-524-5122.

Anchorage, AK 99501: 632 6th Ave./907-271-5136.

Honolulu, HI 96850: 300 Ala Moana Blvd./808-546-5680.

Department of Education

Interim Regional Coordinators

Region I: Office of Educational Programs, John W. McCormack Post Office and Court House Room 526 P.O. Square Boston, MA 02109/617-223-7500.

Region II: Office of Student Financial Assistance, 26 Federal Plaza, Room 3954, New York, NY 10278/212-264-7005.

Region III: Office of Student Financial Assistance, 3535 Market St., Room 16350 Philadelphia, PA 19104/215-596-1001.

Region IV: Office of Rehabilitation Services, 101 Marietta Tower Building, Suite 2221 Atlanta, GA 30323/404-221-2502.

Region V: Office of Rehabilitation Services, 300 S. Wacker Dr., 16th Floor, Chicago, IL 60606/312-353-5215.

Region VI: Office of Educational Programs, 1200 Main Tower Building, Room 1460 Dallas, TX 75202/214-767-3626.

Region VII: Office of Educational Programs, Eleven Oak Building, 324 E. 11th St., 9th Floor Kansas City, MO 64106/816-374-2276.

Region VIII: Office of Rehabilitation Services, U.S. Customs House, 1961 Stout St. Room 380 Denver, CO 80294/303-844-3544.

Region IX: Office of Educational Programs, 50 United Nations Plaza, Room 205, San Francisco, CA 94102/415-556-4920.

Region X: Office of Educational Programs, 3rd and Broad Bldg.–2901 3rd Avenue, Suite 108. Seattle, WA 98121/206-399-0460.

Office for Civil Rights

Region I: John W. McCormack Post Office and Court House Room 2222, Boston, MA 02109/617-223-1154.

Region II: 26 Federal Plaza, 33d Floor, New York, NY 10278/212-264-5180.

Region III: Gateway Building, 3535 Market St., 6th Floor P.O. Box 13716, Philadelphia, PA 19104/215-596-6787.

Region IV: 101 Marietta St., 27th Floor, Atlanta, GA 30323/404-242-2954.

Region V: 300 S. Wacker Dr., 8th Floor, Chicago, IL 60606/312-886-3456.

Region VI: 1200 Main Tower Building, Dallas, TX 75202/214-729-3959.

Region VII: 243 E. 11th Street 24th Floor Kansas City, MO 64102/816-758-2223.

Region VIII: Federal Office Building, Room 1185, 1961 Stout St., Denver, CO 80294/303-564-5695.

Region IX: 1275 Market St., 14th Floor, San Francisco, CA 94103/415-556-9894.

Region X: 2901 3rd Avenue M/s 106, Seattle, WA 98101/206-399-1635.

Office of the Inspector General

Region I: Audit Agency, John W. McCormack Post Office and Court House Room 512, Boston, MA 02109/617-223-1408.

Region II: Audit Agency, Federal Building, Room 3739, 26 Federal Plaza, New York, NY 10278/212-264-8453.

Region III: Audit Agency, 3535 Market St., Room 6100, P. O. Box 13716, Philadelphia, PA 19101/215-596-0262.

Region IV: Division of Compliance, P.O. Box 1598, Atlanta, GA 30301/404-221-5862.

Region V: Audit Agency, 300 S. Wacker Dr., Room 1302, Chicago, IL 60606/312-886-6503.

Region VI: Division of Compliance, 1200 Main Tower 14th Floor, Dallas, TX 75202/214-729-3826.

Region VII: Division of Compliance, 324 E. 11th Street 10th Floor, P. O. Box 15248, Kansas City, MO 64106/816-374-7101.

Region IX: Office of Investigations, 50 United Nations Plaza, Room 105, San Francisco, CA 94102/415-556-2711.

Office of Student Financial Assistance

Region I: John W. McCormack Post Office and Court House Building, Room 510, Boston, MA 02109/617-223-7205.

Region II: 26 Federal Plaza, Room 3954 New York, NY 10278/212-264-4045.

Region III: P. O. Box 13716, 3535 Market St., Philadelphia, PA 19104/215-596-1018.

Region IV: 101 Marietta Tower, Suite 423, Atlanta, GA 30323/404-221-5008.

Region V: 300 S. Wacker Dr. 12th Floor, Chicago, IL 60606/312-353-8102.

Region VI: 1200 Main Tower Building, Room 1645, Dallas, TX 75202/214-767-4359.

Region VII: 324 E. 11th St., 9th Floor, Kansas City, MO 64106/816-374-5875.

Region VIII: 1961 Stout St., 3rd Floor, Federal Office Building, Denver, CO 80294/303-844-4128.

Region IX: 50 United Nations Pl., San Francisco, CA 94102/415-556-8159.

Region X: M/S 102 3rd & Broad Avenue, 2901 Third Avenue, Seattle, WA 98121/206-442-0434.

Regional Directors for Educational Programs

Region I: John McCormack Post Office and Court House, Room 526, Boston, MA 02109/617-223-0308.

Region II: 26 Federal Plaza, Room 3954, New York, NY 10278/212-264-4370.

Region III: P.O. Box 13716 16200, Philadelphia, PA 19101/215-596-0804.

Region IV: 101 Marietta Tower Building, Room 1021, Atlanta, GA 30323/404-242-2099.

Region V: 300 S. Wacker Dr., 15th Floor, Chicago, IL 60606/312-353-1743.

Region VI: 1200 Main Tower Building, Room 1645, Dallas, TX 75202/214-729-3811.

Region VII: Eleven Oak Building, 9th Floor, 324 E. 11th St., Kansas City, MO 64106/816-758-2276.

Region VIII: Federal Regional Office Building, Room 380, 1961 Stout St., Denver, CO 80294/303-327-3676.

Region IX: 50 United Nations Pl., Room 205, San Francisco, CA 94102/415-556-5689.

Region X: OSFA-RX M/S102, 2901 Third Avenue, Seattle, WA 98121/206-399-0434.

Rehabilitation Services Administration

Region I: John F. Kennedy Federal Building, Room E-400, Government Center, Boston, MA 02203/617-223-6820.

Region II: 26 Federal Plaza, Room 410, New York, NY 10278/212-264-4016.

Region III: 3535 Market St., Room 3350 Philadelphia, PA 19101/215-596-0317.

Region IV: 101 Marietta St. N.W., Suite 821 Atlanta, GA 30323/404-221-2352.

Region V: 300 S. Wacker Dr., 15th Floor, Chicago, IL 60606/312-353-5372.

Region VI: 1200 Main Tower Building, Room 1400, Dallas, TX 75202/214-767-2961.

Region VII: 324 E. 11th St., 11 Oak Bldg., 10th Floor West, Kansas City, MO 64106/816-374-2381.

Region VIII: Federal Office Building, Room 982, 1961 Stout Street, Denver, CO 802941/303-844-2135

Region IX: Federal Office Building, Room 480, 50 United Nations Plaza, San Francisco, CA 94102/415-556-7333.

Region X: 2901-3rd Avenue Room 120, Seattle, WA 98121/206-442-5331.

Department of Energy

Operations Division Support Offices

150 Causeway St., Boston, MA 02114/617-223-3701.

26 Federal Plaza, Room 3206, New York, NY/212-264-1021.

1421 Cherry St., Philadelphia, PA 19102/215-597-3890.

1655 Peachtree St. N.E., Atlanta, GA 30309/404-257-2837.

9800 S. Cass Ave. Gonne, IL 60439/312-972-2000.

P.O. Box 35228, Dallas, TX 75235/214-767-7741.

324 E. 11th St., Kansas City, MO 64106/816-758-5533

P.O. Box 26247, Belmar Branch, Lakewood, CO 80226/303-776-2000.

333 Broadway, Oakland, CA 94617/415-556-7216.

P.O. Box 550, Richland, WA 99352/6-444-6222.

Federal Energy Regulatory Commission

Atlanta, GA 30308: 730 Peachtree St. N.E., Room 500/404-881-4134.

Chicago, IL 60604: 230 S. Dearborn St./312-353-6173.

Fort Worth, TX 76102: 819 Taylor St./817-334-2631.

New York, NY 10278: 26 Federal Pl Room 2207/212-264-3687.

San Francisco, CA 94105: 333 Market St. 6th Floor/415-974-7150.

Power Adminstrations

Alaska: P.O. Box 50, Juneau, AK 99802/907-586-7405.

Southeastern: Samuel Elbert Building, Elberton, GA 30635/404-283-3261.

Southwestern: P. O. Drawer 1619, Tulsa, OK 74101/918-581-7474.

Bonneville: P. O. Box 3621, Portland, OR 97208/503-230-5101.

Western Area: P. O. Box 3402, Golden, CO 80401/303-231-1511.

Department of Health and Human Services

Health Care Financing Administration

Region I: John F. Kennedy Federal Building, Room 1309, Boston, MA 02203/617-223-6871.

Region II: 26 Federal Plaza, Room 3811, New York, NY 10278/212-264-4488.

Region III: 3535 Market Street P. O. Box 7760, Philadelphia, PA 19101/215-596-1351.

Region IV: 101 Marietta Tower, Suite 701, Atlanta, GA 30323/404-221-2329.

Region V: 175 W. Jackson Blvd., Room A 835, Chicago, IL 60604/312-353-8057.

Region VI: 1200 Main Tower Bldg., Suite 2400, Dallas, TX 75202/214-767-6427.

Region VII: 601 E. 12th St., Room 235, Kansas City, MO 64106/816-374-5233.

Region VIII: Federal Building 1961 Stout St., Room 574, Denver, CO 80294/303-837-2111.

Region IX: 100 Van Ness Ave., 14th Floor, San Francisco, CA 94102/415-556-0254.

Region X: Mail Stop 502, 2901 Third Avenue Seattle, WA 98121/206-442-0425.

Office of Child Support Enforcement

Region I: 150 Causeway St., Room 1300, Boston, MA 02114/617-223-1137.

Region II: 26 Federal Plaza, Room 21-130, New York, NY 10278/212-264-7170.

Region III: 3535 Market St., P. O. Box 8409, Philadelphia, PA 19101/215-596-1396.

Region IV: 101 Marietta Tower, Suite 2102, Atlanta, GA 30323/404-221-2180.

Region V: 300 Wacker Dr., Chicago, IL 60606/312-353-5415.

Region VI: 1100 Commerce St., Room 2-B-17 Dallas, TX 75242/214-767-3749.

Region VII: 601 E. 12th St., Room 1759, Kansas City, MO 64106/816-374-3584.

Region VIII: Federal Office Building, Room 1137, 19th & Stout Sts., Denver, CO 80202/303-844-5661.

Region IX: 50 United Nations Plaza, Room 338, San Francisco, CA 94102/415-556-5176.

Region X: 2901 Third Avenue, 3rd and Broad Building, M/S 415 Seattle, WA 98120/206-442-0943.

Office of Human Development Services

Region I: John F. Kennedy Federal Building, Boston, MA 02203/617-223-3236.

Region II: 26 Federal Plaza, New York, NY 10278/212-264-1487.

Region III: 3535 Market St., P. O. Box 13716, Philadelphia, PA 19101/215-596-6818.

Region IV: 101 Marietta Tower, Suite 903, Atlanta, GA 30323/404-221-2398.

Region V: 300 S. Wacker Dr., Chicago, IL 60606/312-353-8322.

Region VI: 1200 Main Tower, Dallas, TX 75201/214-767-4540.

Region VII: 601 E. 12th St., Kansas City, MO 64106/816-374-3981.

Region VIII: 1961 Stout St., Room 1194, Denver, CO 80294/303-844-2622.

Region IX: 50 United Nations Pl., San Francisco, CA 94102/415-556-4027.

Region X: 2901 Third Avenue M/S 503, Seattle, WA 98121/206-442-2430.

Principal Regional Officials

Region I: John F. Kennedy Federal Building, Boston, MA 02203/617-223-6830.

Region II: 26 Federal Plaza, New York, NY 10278/212-264-4600.

Region III: 3535 Market St., Room 11460, Philadelphia, PA 19104/215-596-6492.

Region IV: 101 Marietta Tower, Atlanta, GA 30323/404-221-2442.

Region V: 300 S. Wacker Dr., Chicago, IL 60606/312-353-5160.

Region VI: 1200 Main Tower, Dallas, TX 75202/214-767-3301.

Region VII: 601 E. 12th St., Kansas City, MO 64106/816-374-2821.

Region VIII: 1961 Stout St., Denver, CO 80294/303-837-3373.

Region IX: 50 United Nations Pl., San Francisco, CA 94102/415-556-6746.

Region X: 2901 Third Avenue, 3rd and Broad Building, Seattle, WA 98121/206-442-0420.

Public Health Service

Region I: John F. Kennedy Federal Building, Room 1400, Boston, MA 02203/617-223-6827.

Region II: 26 Federal Plaza, Room 3337, New York, NY 10278/212-264-2560.

Region III: P. O. Box 13716, Philadelphia, PA 19101/215-596-6637.

Region IV: 101 Marietta Tower, Suite 1007, Atlanta, GA 30323/404-221-2316.

Region V: 300 S. Wacker Dr., 34th Floor, Chicago, IL 60606/312-353-1385.

Region VI: 1200 Main Tower, Room 1700, Dallas, TX 75202/214-767-3879.

Region VII: 601 E. 12th St., Kansas City, MO 64106/816-374-3291.

Region VIII: 1961 Stout St., Denver, CO 80294/303-844-6163.

Region IX: 50 United Nations Pl., San Francisco, CA 94102/415-556-5810.

Region X: 2901 Third Avenue, Seattle, WA 98101/206-442-0430.

Special Security Administration Regional Commissioners

Region I: John F. Kennedy Federal Building, Room 1100, Boston, MA 02203/617-223-6810.

Region II: 26 Federal Plaza, 40th Floor, New York, NY 10278/212-264-3915.

Region III: P. O. Box 8788, 3535 Market Street Room 8330, Philadelphia, PA 19101/215-596-6941.

Region IV: 101 Marietta Tower, Suite 2001 Room 1704, Atlanta, GA 30301/404-221-2475.

Region V: 300 S. Wacker Dr., 27th Floor, Chicago, IL 60606/312-353-4247.

Region VI: 1200 Main Tower, Room 2535, Dallas, TX 75202/214-767-4210.

Region VII: 601 E. 12th St., Room 436, Kansas City, MO 64106/816-374-3701.

Region VIII: 1961 Stout St., Room 876, Denver, CO 80294/303-844-3489.

Region IX: 100 Van Ness Ave., 28th Floor, San Francisco, CA 94102/415-556-4910.

Region X: 2901 Third Avenue, Room 301, Seattle, WA 98121/206-442-0417.

Health Services Administration, Indian Health Service

Anchorage, AK 99510: P.O. Box 7-741/907-279-6153.

Aberdeen, SD 57401: Federal Building, 115 4th Ave., S.E./605-225-0250.

Albuquerque, NM 87101: 500 Gold Ave., S.W./505-766-2151.

Billings, MT 59103: P. O. Box 2143/406-657-6403.

Oklahoma City, OK 73102: 215 Dean A McGee St. N.W. Building/405-231-4796.

Phoenix, AZ 85016: 3738 N. 16th St., Suite A/602-241-2052.

Portland, OR 97204: 1220 S.W. 3d Ave, Room 476/503-221-2020.

Window Rock, AZ 86515: P. O. Box G/602-871-5811.

Bemidji, MN 56601 (USET Program Office) P. O. Box 489/218-751-7701.

Tucson, AZ 85734 (R & D.): PO Box 11340, 203 Federal Building/602-762-6604.

Nashville, TN 37217 (USET Program Office): Oaks Tower Building, 1101 Kermit Drive, Suite 810/615-251-5132.

Sacramento, CA 95821 (USET Program Office): 2999 Fulton Avenue/916-484-4836.

Department of Housing and Urban Development

Regional Offices

Region I: John F. Kennedy Federal Building, Boston, MA 02203/617-223-4066.

Region II: 26 Federal Plaza, New York, NY 10007/212-264-8068.

Region III: Liberty Square, 105 South 7th Street, Philadelphia, PA 19106/215-597-2560.

Region IV: Richard B. Russell Federal Building, 75 Spring St. S.W., Atlanta, GA 30303/404-221-5136.

Region V: 300 S. Wacker Dr., Chicago, IL 60606/312-353-5680.

Region VI: 221 W. Lancaster Ave., P. O. Box 2905, Ft. Worth, TX 76113/817-870-5401.

Region VII: Professional Building, 1103 Grand Ave., Kansas City, MO 64106/816-374-2661.

Region VIII: 1405 Curtis St., Denver, CO 80202/303-837-4513.

Region IX: 450 Golden Gate Ave., San Francisco, CA 94102/415-556-4752.

Region X: Arcade Plaza Building, 1321 2d Ave., Seattle, WA 98101/206-442-5414.

Department of the Interior

Bureau of Indian Affairs

Aberdeen, SD 57401: 115 4th Ave. S.E./605-225-0250.

Albuquerque, NM 87198: 5301 Central Ave. N.E./505-766-3170.

Anadarko, OK 73005: P. O. Box 368/405-247-6673.

Billings, MT 59101: 316 N. 26th St./406-657-6315.

Eastern Area: 1951 Constitution Avenue, Washington, DC 20245/703-235-2591.

Juneau, AK 99802: P. O. Box 3-8000/907-586-7177.

Minneapolis, MN 55402: 15 S. 5th St., 6th Floor/612-349-3390.

Muskogee, OK 74401: Old Federal Bldg./918-687-2296.

Window Rock, AZ 86515: Navajo Area Office/603-871-5151.

Phoenix, AZ 85011: 3030 N. Central P. O. Box 7007/602-261-2305.

Portland, OR 97208: P. O. Box 3785/503-231-6702.

Sacramento, CA 95825: 2800 Cottage Way/916-484-4682.

Washington, DC 20240: 18th & C Sts. N.W./703-235-2571.

Job Corps Civilian Conservation Centers

Collbran, CO 81624:
Route 1, P.O. Box 307
303-487-3576 or 3581.

Moses Lake, WA 98837:
Building 2402–24th Street
FTS-442-1204.

White Swan, WA 98952
Route 1, Box 137
509-874-2244.

Brooklyn, NY 11234:
Building #74, Floyd Bennett Field
FTS-665-4376 or
212-630-0450.

Mammoth Cave, KY 42259:
Mammoth Cave National Park
502-286-4514.

Harpers Ferry, WV 25425:
P.O. Box 237
FTS-925-6341.

Medina, NY 14103:
Route 1
716-798-3300.

Marsing, Idaho 83639:
Route 1
208-896-4127.

Puxico, MO 63960:
Route 2, Box F
314-222-3537.

Cherokee, NC 28719:
Great Smokey National Park,
P.O. Box 306
704-497-5411.

Indiahoma, Oklahoma 73552:
Route 2, Box 30
405-246-3203.

Ogden, Utah 84403:
RFD #4
FTS-586-5959.

Bureau of Land Management

State Offices

Anchorage, AK 99513: 701 C St., P. O. Box 13/907-271-5555.

Phoenix, AZ 85014: 3707 North 7th Street/602-241-5504.

Sacramento, CA 95825: Federal Office Building, 2800 Cottage Way/916-484-4676.

Denver, CO 80205: 2020 Arapahoe Street/303-294-7092.

Boise, ID 83706: 3380 Americana Terrace/208-334-1770.

Billings, MT 59107: Granite Tower Building, 222 N. 32d St./406-657-6561.

Reno, NV 89520: P.O. Box 36800, 300 Booth Street, P.O. Box 12000/702-784-5311.

Santa Fe, NM 87501: U.S. Post Office & Federal Building/505-988-6316.

Portland, OR 97208: 825 N.E. Multnomah St./P.O. Box 2965/503-231-6274.

Salt Lake City, UT 84111: 324 S. State Street CFS Financial Center Bldg. Suite 301/801-524-5311.

Cheyenne, WY 82001: 2515 Warren Ave/307-778-2220.

Outer Continental Shelf Offices
Anchorage, AK 99510: P.O. Box 101159/907-261-4010.

Los Angeles, CA 90017: 1340 W. 6th Street/213-688-2048.

Metarie, LA 70010: Imperial Bldg., 3301 N. Causeway, P.O. Box 7944/504-838-0589.

Vienna, VA 22180: 1951 Kidwell Drive, Suite 601/703-285-2165.

Geological Survey
Reston, VA 22092: 12201 Sunrise Valley Dr./703-860-7411.

Denver, CO 80225: Denver Federal Center, P.O. Box 25046/303-236-5900.

Menlo Park, CA 94025: 345 Middlefield Rd./415-323-8111, ext. 2711.

National Park Service
North Atlantic: 15 State St., Boston, MA 02109/617-223-3769.

Mid-Atlantic: 143 S. 3d St., Philadelphia, PA 19106/215-597-7013.

Southeast: 75 Spring St. S.W., Atlanta, GA 30303/404-221-5185.

Midwest: 1709 Jackson St., Omaha, NE 68102/402-221-3431.

Rocky Mountain: 655 Parfet St., Denver, CO 80225/303-234-2500.

Southwest: P. O. Box 728, Santa Fe, NM 87501/505-988-6388.

Western: 450 Golden Gate Ave., P.O. Box 36063, San Francisco, CA 94102/415-556-4196.

Alaska: 2525 Gambell Street, Anchorage, AK 99503/907-271-4195.

Pacific Northwest: 2001 6th Street, Seattle, WA 98101/206-442-5565.

National Capital: 1100 Ohio Dr. S.W., Washington, DC 20242/202-426-5720.

Office of Environmental Project Review
Boston, MA 02109: 165 State St./617-223-5517.

Atlanta, GA 30303: 75 Spring St. S.W./404-221-4524.

Chicago, IL 60604: 175 W. Jackson Blvd./312-353-6612.

Albuquerque, NM 87103: 5301 Central Ave. N.E./505-766-3565.

San Francisco, CA 94102: 450 Golden Gate Ave./415-556-8200.

Denver, CO 80225: Denver Federal Center/303-236-6900.

Portland, OR 97232: 500 N.E. Multnomah St./503-231-6157.

Anchorage, AL 99510: C St./907-271-5011.

Philadelphia, PA 19106: Customs House, 2nd and Chestnut Streets/215-597-5378.

Office of the Inspector General
Arlington, VA 22217: BT No. 1 800 N. Quincy, Room 401/703-235-1513.

Lakewood, CO 80228: 134 Union Blvd., Suite 510/303-236-9243.

Sacramento, CA 95825: 2800 Cottage Way, Room W2400/916-484-4874.

Office of the Solicitor
Anchorage, AL 99513: 701 C St, Box 34/907-271-4131.

Denver, CO 80225: Denver Federal Center, P.O. Box 25007/303-236-9327.

Atlanta, GA 30303: 75 Spring Street, SW. Suite 1328/404-221-4447.

Newton Corner, MA 02158: 1 Gateway Center, Suite 612/617-965-5100.

Portland, OR 97232: 500 N.E. Multnomah St., Suite 607/503-231-2134.

Sacramento, CA 95825: 2800 Cottage Way/916-484-4343.

Salt Lake City, UT 84138-1180: 125 S. State St./801-524-5677.

Tulsa, OK 74101: P.O. Box 3156/918-581-7502.

Office of Surface Mining Reclamation and Enforcement
603 Morris Street, Charleston, WV 25301/304-342-8125.

530 Gay St., Knoxville, TN 37902/615-637-8060.

46 E. Ohio St., Indianapolis, IN 46204/317-269-2600.

818 Grand Ave., Kansas City, MO 64106/816-374-2193.

1020 15th St., Denver, CO 80202/303-837-5511.

228 West Valley Avenue, Homewood, AL 34209/

600 East Monroe Street, Room 20, Springfield, IL 62701/

340 Legion Drive, Suite 28, Lexington, KY 40504/

219 Central Avenue, NW, Albuquerque, NM 87102/

2242 South Hamilton Road, 2nd Floor, Columbus, OH 43232

333 West 4th Street, Room 3432, Tulsa, OK 74103

101 South 2nd Street, Suite L-4, Harrisburg, PA 17101/

Fish and Wildlife Service
Portland, OR 97232: 500 N.E. Multnomah St./503-231-6118.

Albuquerque, NM 87103: 500 Gold Ave. S.W./505-766-2321.

Twin Cities, MN 55111: Federal Building/612-725-3563.

Atlanta, GA 30303: 17 Executive Park Dr. N.E./404-881-4671.

Newton Corner, MA 02158: 1 Gateway Center, Suite 700/617-965-5100 Ext 200

Denver, CO 80225: Denver Federal Center, P.O. Box 25486/303-776-7920.

Anchorage, AK 99503: 1011 E. Tudor Rd./907-786-3542

Bureau of Reclamation

Northwest Region: Boise, ID 83724: P.O. Box 043/208-334-1908.

Mid Pacific Region: Sacramento, CA 95825: 2800 Cottage Way/916-484-4571.

Lower Colorado Region: Boulder City, NV 89005: P.O. Box 427 St./702-293-7411.

Upper Colorado Region: Salt Lake City, UT 84147: PO Box 11568/801-524-5592.

Southwest Region: Amarillo, TX 79101: 714 S. Tyler St. Suite 201/806-378-5445.

Upper Missouri Region: Billings, MT 59103: PO Box 2553/406-657-6214.

Lower Missouri Region: Denver, CO 80225: PO Box 25247/303-776-0688.

Engineering and Research Center, P. O. Box 25007, Denver Federal Center, Denver, CO 80225/303-776-6985.

Department of Justice

Community Relations Service

Region I: 9 Broad Street, Room 1116, Boston, MA 02110. 617-223-5170.

Region II: 26 Federal Plaza, Room 3402, New York, NY 10278/212-264-0700.

Region III: 2d & Chestnuts Sts., Philadelphia, PA 19106/215-597-2344.

Region IV: 75 Piedmont Ave. N.E., Room 900, Atlanta, GA 30303/404-221-6883.

Region V: 175 W. Jackson Blvd., Room 1113, Chicago, IL 60604/312-353-4391.

Region VI: 1100 Commerce St., Dallas, TX 75242/214-767-0824.

Region VII: 911 Walnut St., Room 2411, Kansas City, MO 64106/816-374-2022.

Region VIII: 1531 Stout St., Room 401, Denver, CO 80202/303-837-2973.

Region IX: 211 Main St., Suite 1040, San Francisco, CA 94103/415-556-2485.

Region X: Federal Office Building, 915 2d Ave., Room 1891, Seattle, WA 48101/206-442-4465.

Antitrust Division

Atlanta, GA 30309: 1776 Peachtree St. N.W./404-222-3100.

Chicago, IL 60604: 230 S. Dearborn St./312-353-7530.

John C. Kluczynski Building, Room 3820, 230 S. Dearborn Street.

Cleveland, OH 44199: 995 Celebrezze Federal Building, 1240 E. 9th St./216-522-4070.

Dallas, TX 75242: Earle Cabell Federal Building, Room 8C6, 1100 Commerce St./214-767-8051.

New York, NY 10278: 26 Federal Plaza, Room 3630/212-264-0390.

Philadelphia, PA 19106: 11400 U.S. Courthouse, Independence Mall West, 601 Market St./215-597-7405.

San Francisco, CA 94102: 450 Golden Gate Ave., P. O. Box 36046/415-556-6300.

Bureau of Prisons

Northeast: US Customs House, 2nd and Chestnut, Philadelphia, PA 19106/215-597-6317.

Southeast: 5213 McDonough Blvd. S.E., Atlanta, GA 30315/404-624-5202.

North Central: Air World Center, 10920 Ambassador Drive. Kansas City, MO 64153/816-891-7007.

South Central: 1607 Main St., Suite 700, Dallas, TX 75201/214-767-0012.

Western: 330 Primrose Rd., 5th Floor, Burlingame, CA 94010/415-347-0721.

Civil Division

California: 450 Golden Gate Ave., P. O. Box 36028, San Francisco, CA 94102/415-556-3146.

New York: 26 Federal Plaza, Suite 36-100, New York, NY 10278/212-264-0480.

Drug Enforcement Administration

Atlanta, GA 30303: 230 Houston St., NE./404-221-4401.

Boston, MA 02203: J F K Federal Building/617-223-2170.

Chicago, IL 60604: 1800 Dirksen Federal Building, 219 S. Dearborn St./312-353-7875.

Dallas, TX 75235: 1880 Regal Row/214-767-7151.

Denver, CO 80201: P. O. Box 1860/303-844-3951.

Detroit, MI 48226: 357 Federal Building, 231 West Lafayette/313-226-7290.

Houston, TX 77027: 4299 San Felipe/713-229-2950.

Los Angeles, CA 90071: 350 South Figueroa Street/213-688-2650.

Miami, FL 33166: 8400 N.W. 53rd Street/305-591-4870.

Newark, NJ 07102: 970 Broad Street, Federal Office Building/201-645-6060.

New Orleans, LA 70112: 1661 Canal Street/504-589-3894.

New York, NY 10019: 555 West 57th Street/212-399-5151.

Philadelphia, PA 19106: 10224 William J. Green Federal Building, 600 Arch Street/215-597-9530.

Phoenix, AZ 85073: 1980 Valley Bank Center, 201 N. Central/602-261-4866.

San Francisco, CA 94102: 450 Golden Gate Avenue/415-556-6771.

San Diego, CA: 402 West 35th Street, National City/619-585-9600.

Seattle, WA 98119: 220 Mercer, Suite 301/206-442-5443.

St. Louis, MO 63105: 120 South Central Avenue/314-425-3241.

Washington, DC 20224: 400 6th Street, S.W./202-724-7834.

Executive Office for United States Trustees

Maine, Massachusetts, New Hampshire and Rhode Island: 87 Kilby St., Boston, MA 02109/617-223-4754.

Southern New York: Federal Building, Room 306, 26 Federal Plaza, New York, NY 10007/212-264-2858.

Delaware & New Jersey: 1180 Raymond Boulevard, Room 2549, Newark, NJ 07102/201-645-2617.

District of Columbia & Eastern Virginia: 421 King St., Room 410, Alexandria, VA 22314/703-557-0746.

Northern Alabama: Frank Nelson Building, Suite 831, 2d Ave. & 20th St., 500 S. 22nd Street, Suite 316, 500 Bldg., Birmingham, AL 35233/205-254-0047.

Northern Texas: U.S. Courthouse, Room 9C60, 1100 Commerce St., Dallas, TX 75242/214-767-8967.

Northern Illinois: 175 W. Jackson St., Room A1335, Chicago, IL 60604/312-886-5785.

Minnesota, North Dakota, South Dakota: U.S. Courthouse, Room 550, 1100 S. 4th St., Minneapolis, MN 55401/612-349-5300.

Central California: 300 N. Los Angeles Room 3101, Federal Bldg., Los Angeles, CA 90012/213-688-6811.

Colorado & Kansas: Columbine Building, Room 202, 1845 Sherman St., Denver, CO 80203/303-844-5188.

Immigration and Naturalization Service

Burlington, VT 05401: Federal Building Elmwood Avenue/802-951-6223.

St. Paul, MN 55111: Federal Building, Fort Snelling/612-725-4451.

Dallas, TX 75270. Skyline Center Building C 311 N. Stemmons Frwy/214-767-6000.

San Pedro, CA 90731: Terminal Island/213-548-2357.

Tax Division

Texas: 5B31 Federal Office Building, 1100 Commerce St., Dallas, TX 75242/214-767-0293.

Parole Commission

Northeast: Customs House, 2nd and Chestnut Streets, 7th Floor, Philadelphia, PA 19106/215-597-6392.

South Central: 555 Griffin Sq., Suite 820, Dallas, TX 75202/214-767-0024.

Western: Crocker Financial Center Building, 330 Primrose Rd., 5th Floor, Burlingame, CA 94010/415-347-4737.

Southeast: 715 McDonough Blvd. S.E., Atlanta, GA 30315/404-221-3515.

North Central: Air World Center, 10920 Ambassador Dr., Suite 220, Kansas City, MO 64153/816-891-1395.

Department of Labor

Employment Standards Administration

Region I: John F. Kennedy Federal Building, Gov't Center Boston, MA 02203/617-223-4305.

Region II: 1515 Broadway, Room 3300, New York, NY 10036/212-944-3351.

Region III: 3535 Market St., Gateway Bldg, Room 15230, Philadelphia, PA 19104/215-596-1185.

Region IV: 1371 Peachtree St., N.E., Room 105, Atlanta, GA 30367/404-881-2818.

Region V: 230 S. Dearborn St., 8th Floor, Chicago, IL 60604/312-353-7280.

Region VI: 555 Griffin Square Building, Young and Griffin Sts., Room 900, Dallas, TX 75202/214-767-6894.

Region VII: 911 Walnut St., Federal Office Building, Room 2000, Kansas City, MO 64106/816-374-5381.

Region VIII: 1961 Stout St., Federal Office Building, Room 1490, Denver, CO 80294/303-837-5903.

Region IX: 450 Golden Gate Ave., Room 10353, San Francisco, CA 94102/415-556-1318.

Region X: 909 1st Ave., Federal Office Building, Seattle, WA 98174/206-442-1536.

Office of Federal Contract Compliance Programs

Region I: McCormack Post Office and Courthouse, Room 507 Boston, MA 02109/617-223-1481.

Region II: 26 Federal Plaza, Room 24-112, New York, NY 10278/212-264-7745.

Region III: 3535 Market St., Philadelphia, PA 19104/215-596-6168.

Region IV: 1371 Peachtree St. N.E., Atlanta, GA 30367/404-881-4211.

Region V: 411 S. Wells St., Chicago, IL 60607/312-353-0806.

Region VI: 1607 Main Street, Room 201, Dallas, TX 75201/214-767-2911.

Region VII: 1103 Grand St., Room 1400, Kansas City, MO 64106/816-374-2669.

Region VIII: 2500 Curtis St., Suite 100, Denver, CO 80205/303-837-6366.

Region IX: 1375 Sutter St., San Francisco, CA 9409/415-556-6017.

Region X: 909 1st Ave., Seattle, WA 98104/206-442-7182.

Wage and Hour Division

Region I: Park Square Bldg., Room 462, 31 St. James Ave., Boston, MA 02116/617-223-6751.

Region II: 26 Federal Plaza, Room 2946, New York, NY 10278/212-264-8185.

Region III: US Customs House, Room 239, 2nd & Chestnut Streets Philadelphia, PA 19106/215-597-4950.

Region IV: 75 Redmont Ave N.E., Atlanta, GA 30303/404-221-4306.

1931 9th Ave., S., Birmingham, AL 35256/205-254-1305

Region V: 230 S. Dearborn St., 4th Floor, Chicago, IL 60604/312-353-8145.

Region VI: 555 Griffin Square Building, Dallas, TX 75202/214-767-6891.

Region VII: 911 Walnut St., Kansas City, MO 64106/816-374-5721.

Region VIII: US Customs House, Room 228 721-19th Street, Denver, CO 80202/303-837-4405.

Region IX: 211 Main Street, Room 341, San Francisco, CA 94105/415-556-6815.

Region X: 99 1st Ave., Seattle, WA 98174/206-442-4482

Employment and Training Administration

Region I: John F. Kennedy Federal Building, Room 1700-C. Boston, MA 02203/617-223-4684.

Region II: 1515 Broadway, Room 3612, New York, NY 10036/212-944-2990.

Region III: 3535 Market St. Room 12220, Philadelphia, PA 19104/215-596-6301.

Region IV: 1371 Peachtree St. N.E., Room 632, Atlanta, GA 30309/404-881-3178.

Region V: 230 S. Dearborn St., 5th Floor, Chicago, IL 60604/312-353-0313.

Region VI: 555 Griffin Square Building, Dallas, Suite 403, TX 75202/214-767-2567.

Region VII: Federal Office Building, 911 Walnut St., Room 1100, Kansas City, MO 64106/816-374-3661.

Region VIII: Federal Building, 1961 Stout St., Room 1680, Denver, CO 80202/303-837-4807.

Region IX: 450 Golden Gate Ave., Room 9477, San Francisco, CA 94102/415-556-8545.

Region X: Federal Office Building, Room 1131, 909 1st Ave., Seattle, WA 98174/206-442-1133.

Occupational Safety and Health Administration

Region I: 16-18 North St., 1 Dock Sq. 4th Floor, Boston, MA 02109/617-223-6710.

Region II: 1515 Broadway, Room 3445, New York, NY 10036/212-944-3432.

Region III: Gateway Building, Suite 2100, 3535 Market St., Philadelphia, PA 19104/215-596-1201.

Region IV: 1375 Peachtree St. N.E., Suite 587, Atlanta, GA 30367/404-881-3573.

Region V: 230 S. Dearborn St. 32nd Floor, Room 3244, Chicago, IL 60605/312-353-2220.

Region VI: 555 Griffin Square Building, Room 602, Dallas, TX 75202/214-767-4731.

Region VII: 911 Walnut St., Room 406, Kansas City, MO 64106/816-374-5861.

Region VIII: Federal Office Building, 1961 Stout St., Room 1554, Denver, CO 80294/303-837-

Region IX: 450 Golden Gate Ave., P.O. Box 36017, San Francisco, CA 94102/415-556-7260.

Region X: 909 1st Ave., Room 6003 Seattle, WA 98174/206-442-5930.

Office of Assistant Secretary for Administration and Management

Region I: John F. Kennedy Federal Building, Boston, MA 02203/617-944-3074.

Region II: 1515 Broadway, New York, NY 10036/212-399-5357.

Region III: 3535 Market St., Philadelphia, PA 19104/215-596-6560.

Region IV: 1371 Peachtree St. N.E., Atlanta, GA 30367/404-881-3898.

Region V: 230 S. Dearborn St., Chicago, IL 60604/312-353-8373.

Region VI: 555 Griffin Square Building, Dallas, TX 75202/214-767-6801.

Region VII: 911 Walnut St., Kansas City, MO 64106/816-374-3891.

Region VIII: 1961 Stout St., Denver, CO 80294/303-844-2218.

Region IX: 450 Golden Gate Ave., San Francisco, CA 94102/415-556-5417.

Region X: 909 1st Ave., Seattle, WA 98174/206-442-0100.

Regional Representatives of the Secretary of Labor

Region I: John F. Kennedy Federal Building, Boston, MA 02203/617-223-4220.

Region II: 1515 Broadway, New York, NY 10036/ 212-944-3442.

Region III: 3535 Market St., Philadelphia, PA 19104/215-596-1116.

Region IV: 1371 Peachtree St., N.E., Atlanta, GA 30367/404-881-4366.

Region V: 230 S. Dearborn St., Chicago, IL 60604/ 312-353-4703.

Region VI: 555 Griffin Square Building, Griffin and Young Streets, Dallas, TX 75202/214-767-6807.

Region VII: 911 Walnut St., Kansas City, MO 64016/816-374-6371.

Region VIII: 1961 Stout St., Denver, CO 80294/ 303-837-5610.

Region IX: 450 Golden Gate Ave., San Francisco, CA 94102/415-556-9326.

Region X: 909 1st Ave., Seattle, WA 98174/206-442-0574.

Women's Bureau

Region I: John F. Kennedy Building, Boston, MA 02203/617-223-4036.

Region II: 1515 Broadway, New York, NY 10036/ 212-944-3445.

Region III: 3535 Market St., Philadelphia, PA 19104/215-596-1183.

Region IV: 1371 Peachtree St. N.E., Atlanta, GA 30367/404-881-4461.

Region V: 230 S. Dearborn St., 4th Floor, Chicago, IL 60604/312-353-8145.

Region VI: 555 Griffin Square Building, 1607 Main Street, Dallas, TX 75201/214-767-6294.

Region VII: 911 Walnut St., Kansas City, MO 64106/816-374-6108.

Region VIII: 1961 Stout St., Denver, CO 80202/ 303-837-4138.

Region IX: 450 Golden Gate Ave., San Francisco, CA 94102/415-556-2377.

Region X: 909 1st Ave., Seattle, WA 98174/206-442-1534.

Bureau of Labor Statistics

Boston, MA 02203: 1603 Federal Office Building/ 617-223-6727.

New York, NY 10036: 1515 Broadway/212-944-3117.

Philadelphia, PA 19104: 3535 Market St./215-596-1151.

Atlanta, GA 30367: 1371 Peachtree St. N.E./404-881-2161.

Chicago, IL 60604: 230 S. Dearborn St./312-353-7226.

Dallas, TX 75202: 555 Griffin Square Building/ 214-767-6953.

Kansas City, MO 64106: 911 Walnut St./816-374-2378.

San Francisco, CA 94102: 450 Golden Gate Ave./ 415-556-3178.

Employment Standards Administration

Office of Workers' Compensation Programs, Division of Federal Employees' Compensation

Boston, MA 02203: John F. Kennedy Federal Building Room 1800 Gov't Center/617-223-6755.

New York, NY 10036: 1515 Broadway Room 3348/ 212-944-4796.

Philadelphia, PA 19104: Gateway Bldg., 3535 Market St., Room 15100/215-596-1431.

Jacksonville, FL 32202: Federal Office Building, 400 W. Bay St./904-791-3426.

New Orleans, LA 70130: Hale Boggs Federal Building, 500 Camp St., Room 840/504-589-3963.

Cleveland, OH 44199: 1240 E. 9th St., Room 867/ 216-522-3800.

Chicago, IL 60604: 230 S. Dearborn St., 8th Floor/ 312-886-5883.

Kansas City, MO 64106: Federal Office Building, 911 Walnut St., Room 1910/816-374-2723.

Denver, CO 80202: Federal Office Building, 1961 Stout St., Room 1425/303-837-5402.

San Francisco, CA 94102: 450 Golden Gate Ave., Room 10301/415-556-6183.

Seattle, WA 98174: 909 1st Ave./206-442-5521.

Honolulu, HI 96813: 300 Ala Moana Blvd./808-546-8336.

Washington, DC 20211: 666 11th St. N.W./202-724-0702.

Atlanta, GA 30309: 1371 Peachtree St. N.W./404-881-7566.

Dallas, TX 75202: 555 Griffin Square Building, Room 100, Young & Griffin Sts./214-767-4707.

Office of Workers' Compensation Programs, Division of Longshore and Harbor Workers' Compensation

Boston, MA 02203: John F. Kennedy Federal Building/617-223-6755.

New York, NY 10036: 1515 Broadway, Room 3362/212-944-3378.

Philadelphia, PA 19104: 3535 Market St./215-596-5568.

Baltimore, MD 21201: Federal Building, Room 1026/301-962-3677.

Norfolk, VA 23510: 200 Granby Mall, Room 212/804-441-3071.

Jacksonville, FL 32201: 311 W. Monroe St./904-791-2881.

New Orleans, LA 70130: Hale Boggs Federal Building, 500 Camp St./504-589-3963.

Houston, TX 77004: 2320 La Branch St., Room 2108/713-750-1700.

Chicago, IL 60604: 230 S. Dearborn St., 7th Floor/312-353-8883.

Kansas City, MO 64106: 911 Walnut St./816-374-2723.

Denver, CO 80202: 1961 Stout St./303-837-5402.

San Francisco, CA 94102: 450 Golden Gate Ave., Room 10301/415-556-6297.

Seattle, WA 98174: 909 1st Ave./206-442-5521.

Honolulu, HI 96813: 300 Ala Moana Blvd., Room 5108/808-546-8336.

Washington, DC 20211: 1111 20th St. N.W., Room 1014/202-254-3472.

Long Beach, CA 90371/300 S. Ferry St./213-548-2687.

Mine Safety and Health Administration

Coal Mine Safety and Health Districts
Wilkes-Barre, PA 18701: 20 N. Pennsylvania Ave./717-826-6321.

Pittsburgh, PA 15213: 4800 Forbes Ave./412-621-4500.

Morgantown, WV 26505: Mountaineer Mall/304-291-4277.

Mount Hope, WV 25880: P.O. Box 112/304-877-6405.

Norton, VA 24273: P.O. Box 560/703-679-0230.

Pikeville, KY 41501: 219 Ratliff's Creek Road, P.O. Box 3249/606-432-0944.

Barbourville, KY 40906: P.O. Box 572/606-546-5123

Vincennes, IN 47591: 501 Busseron St., P.O. Box 418/812-882-7617.

Denver, CO 80225: P.O. Box 25367/303-236-2740.

Madisonville, KY 42431: P.O. Box 473/502-821-4180.

Metal and Nonmetal Mine Safety and Health Districts
Pittsburgh, PA 15213: 4800 Forbes Ave./412-621-4500.

Birmingham, AL 35209: 228 W. Valley Ave./205-254-1510.

Duluth, MN 55802: 228 Federal Building/218-727-6692.

Dallas, TX 75242: 1100 Commerce St./214-767-8401.

Denver, CO 80225: P.O. Box 25367/303-236-2794.

Alameda, CA 94501: 620 Central Ave., Building 7/415-273-7457.

Office of the Solicitor
Boston, MA 02203: John F. Kennedy Federal Building/617-223-6701.

New York, NY 10036: 1515 Broadway/212-944-3322.

Philadelphia, PA 19104: Gateway Building, 3535 Market St./215-596-5158.

Arlington, VA 22203: Boston Tower/703-235-3610.

Atlanta, GA 30309: 1371 Peachtree St. N.E./404-881-4811.

Chicago, IL 60604: 230 S. Dearborn St./312-353-5744.

Kansas City, MO 64106: 911 Walnut St./816-374-6441.

Dallas, TX 75202: 555 Griffin Square Building/214-767-4902.

San Francisco, CA 94102: 450 Golden Gate Ave./415-556-4042.

Department of Transportation

National Highway Traffic Safety Administration
Region I: Kendall Square—Code 903, 55 Broadway, Cambridge, MA 02142/617-494-2680.

Region II: 222 Mamaroneck Ave., White Plains, NY 10605/914-683-9690 Ext. 311.

Region III: 793 Elkridge Landing Rd., Linthicum, MD 21090/301-962-3877.

Region IV: 1720 Peachtree Rd., N.W., Atlanta, GA 30309/404-881-4537.

Region V: 18209 Dixie Hwy., Homewood, IL 60430/312-799-6076.

Region VI: 819 Taylor St., Room 11A26, Fort Worth, TX 76102/817-334-3653.

Region VII: P.O. Box 19515, Kansas City, MO 64141/816-926-7887.

Region VIII: 555 Zang St., 1st Floor, Denver, CO 80228/303-234-3253.

Region IX: 211 Main Street, Suite 1000, San Francisco, CA 94105/415-974-9840.

Region X: 3140 Federal Building, 915 2nd Ave., Seattle, WA 98174/206-442-5934.

Regional Representatives of the Secretary
Regions I, II, and III: 4304 Walnut St., Suite 1000, Philadelphia, PA 19106/215-597-9430.

Region IV: 1720 Peachtree Rd. N.W., Suite 515, Atlanta, GA 30309/404-881-3738.

Region V: 300 S. Wacker Dr., Room 700, Chicago, IL 60606/312-353-4000.

Region VI: 7A29 Federal Building, 819 Taylor St., Fort Worth, TX 76102/817-334-2725.

Regions VII and VIII: 601 E. 12th St., Room 634, Kansas City, MO 64106/816-374-5801.

Regions IX and X: 211 Main Street, Room 1005, San Francisco, CA 94105/415-974-8464.

Urban Mass Transportation Administration

Region I: c/o Transportation Systems Center, Kendall Sq., 55 Broadway, Cambridge, MA 02142/617-494-2055.

Region II: 26 Federal Plaza, Suite 14-130, New York, NY 10278/212-264-8162.

Region III: 434 Walnut St., Suite 1010, Philadelphia, PA 19106/215-597-8098.

Region IV: 1720 Peachtree Rd. N.W., Suite 400, Atlanta, GA 30309/404-881-3948.

Region V: 300 S. Wacker Dr., Suite 1720, Chicago, IL 60606/312-353-2789.

Region VI: 819 Taylor St., Suite 9A32, Fort Worth, TX 76102/817-334-3787.

Region VII: 6301 Rockhill Rd., Suite 100, Kansas City, MO 64131/816-926-5053.

Region VIII: 1050 17th St., Prudential Plaza, Suite 1822, Denver, CO 80265/303-844-3242.

Region IX: 211 Main Street, Room 1160, San Francisco, CA 94105/415-974-7313.

Region X: 915 2d Ave., Suite 3142, Seattle, WA 98174/206-442-4210.

Federal Aviation Administration

New England: 12 New England Executive Park, Burlington, MA 01803/617-273-7244.

Eastern: Federal Building, JFK International Airport, Jamaica, NY 11430/718-917-1005.

Southern: P.O. Box 20636, Atlanta, GA 30320/404-763-7222.

Great Lakes: O'Hare Lake Office Center, 2300 E. Devon Ave., Des Plaines, IL 60018/312-694-7000.

Central: 601 E. 12th St., Federal Building, Kansas City, MO 64106/816-374-5626.

Southwest: P.O. Box 1689, Fort Worth, TX 76101/817-877-2000.

Western: Worldway Postal Center, P.O. Box 92007, Los Angeles, CA 90009/213-536-6427.

Northwest: Northwest Mountain: 17900 Pacific Highway South, C-68966, Seattle, WA 98168/206-431-2001.

Alaskan: P.O. Box 14, Anchorage, AK 99513/907-271-5645.

Federal Highway Administration

Albany, NY 12207: Clinton Ave. & N. Pearl St./518-472-6476.

Baltimore, MD 21201: 31 Hopkins Plaza/301-962-0093.

Atlanta, GA 30367: 1720 Peachtree Rd. N.W./404-881-4078.

Homewood, IL 60430: 18209 Dixie Hwy./312-799-6300.

Fort Worth, TX 76102: 819 Taylor St./817-334-3908.

Kansas City, MO 64131: 6301 Rockhill Rd./816-926-7563.

San Francisco, CA 94105: 211 Main St., Room 1100/415-974-8450.

Lakewood, CO 80228: 555 Zang St./303-236-3322.

Portland, OR 97204: 708 Southwest 3rd Street/503-221-2053.

Arlington, VA 22201: 1000 N. Glebe Rd./703-557-9070.

Federal Railroad Administration

Region I: 55 Broadway, Cambridge, MA 02142/617-494-2302.

Region II: Independence Building, Room 1020, 434 Walnut St., Philadelphia, PA 19106/215-597-0750.

Region III: North Tower, Suite 440A, 1720 Peachtree Rd. N.W., Atlanta, GA 30309/404-881-2751.

Region IV: 165 N. Canal St., Chicago, IL 60606/312-353-6203.

Region V: Federal Office Building, Room 11A23, 819 Taylor St., Fort Worth, TX 76102/817-334-3601.

Region VI: Federal Office Building, Room 1807, 911 Walnut Street, Kansas City, MO 64106/816-374-2497.

Region VII: 211 Main Street, Room 1085, San Francisco, CA 94105/415-974-9845.

Region VIII: 1500 Southwest First Avenue, Room 250, Portland, OR 97201/603-221-3011.

Federal Assistance

Region I: 55 Broadway, 10th Floor, Cambridge, MA 02142/617-494-2302.

Region II: 434 Walnut St., Philadelphia, PA 19106/215-597-3617.

Region III: North Tower, Suite 440A, 1720 Peachtree Rd. N.W., Atlanta, GA 30309/404-881-2757.

Region IV: 165 N. Canal Street, Suite 1400-3A, Chicago, IL 60605/312-353-6203.

Region V: Federal Office Building, Room 7A35, 819 Taylor St., Ft. Worth, TX 76102/817-334-3601.

Region VI: 1807 Federal Bldg., 911 Walnut Street, Kansas City, MO 64106/816-374-2487.

Region VII: 211 Main Street, Room 1085, San Francisco, CA 94105/415-974-9845.

Region VIII: 1500 Southwest First Avenue, Room 250, Portland, OR 97201/503-221-3011.

Maritime Administration

Eastern Region: New York, NY 10278:Federal Bldg., 26 Federal Plaza/212-264-1300.

Central Region: New Orleans, LA 70130: ITM Building, 2 Canal St./504-589-6556.

Western Region: San Francisco, CA 91402: 450 Golden Gate Ave., Box 3607B/415-556-5621.

Kings Point, NY 11024: U.S. Merchant Marine Academy/516-482-8200.

Great Lakes: Cleveland, OH 44114: 1301 Superior Avenue, Room 260/216-522-3623.

Materials Transportation Bureau, Research and Special Programs Administration

Eastern: 400 7th St. S.W., Washington, DC 20590/ 202-755-9435.

Southern: 1776 Peachtree Rd. N.W., Suite 505N, Atlanta, GA 30309/404-881-2632.

Central: 911 Walnut St., Kansas City, MO 64106/ 816-374-2654.

Southwest: 2320 LaBranch, Houston, TX 77004/ 713-750-1746.

Western: 555 Zang St., Lakewood, CO 80228/303-234-2313.

Coast Guard

Atlantic: Governors Island, New York, NY 10004/ 212-668-7196.

Pacific: Government Island, Alameda, CA 94501/ 415-437-3196.

District 1: 150 Causeway St., Boston, MA 02114/ 617-223-3603.

District 2: 1430 Olive St., St. Louis, MO 63103/ 314-425-4601.

District 3: Governors Island, New York, NY 10004/212-668-7196.

District 5: 431 Crawford St., Portsmouth, VA 23705/804-398-6000.

District 7: 1018 Federal Building, 51 S.W. 1st Ave., Miami, FL 33130/305-350-5654.

District 8: 500 Camp St., New Orleans, LA 70130/ 504-589-6298.

District 9: 1240 E. 9th St., Cleveland, OH 44199/ 216-522-3910.

District 11: 400 Oceangate Blvd., Long Beach, CA 90882/213-590-2311.

District 12: 630 Sansome St., San Francisco, CA 94126/415-556-3860.

District 13: 915 2d Ave., Seattle, WA 98174/206-442-5078.

District 14: 300 Ala Moana Blvd., Honolulu, HI 96813/808-546-5531.

District 17: P. O. Box 3-5000, Juneau, AK 99801/ 907-586-2680.

Action

Regional Offices

Region I: John W. McCormack Building, 441 Stuart St., 9th Floor, Boston, MA 20116/617-223-4501.

Region II: 26 Federal Plaza, 16th Floor, Suite 1611, New York, NY 10278/212-264-4747.

Region II: U.S. Customs House, 2nd and Chestnut, Room 108, Philadelphia, PA 19106/215-597-9972.

Region IV: 101 Marietta St. N.W., Suite 1003, 2524, Atlanta, GA 30323/404-221-2859.

Region V: 0 W. Jackson Blvd., 3rd Floor, Chicago, IL 60604/312-353-5107.

Region VI: 00 Commerce Street, Suite 6B11, Dallas, TX 75242/214-767-9494.

Region VIII: 1845 Sherman St., Room 201, Denver, CO 80203/303-844-2671.

Region IX: 211 Main St., Room 530, San Francisco, CA 94105/415-974-0673.

Region X: 1111 3rd Avenue Building, Suite 330, Seattle, WA 98101/206-442-1558.

Office of Recruitment and Communications

PEACE CORPS—Field Service Centers

Boston (serves MA, VT, RI, ME): 150 Causeway St, Room 1304, Boston, MA 02114/617-223-7366.

New York (serves NY, CT, Northern NJ): 26 Federal Plaza, Room 1605, New York, NY 10278/212-264-7123.

Puerto Rico (serves PR, VI): Mercantil Plaza, Room 710, Stop 27½ Ponce DeLeon Avenue, Hato Rey, PR 00918/809-753-3076.

Miami: 330 Biscayne Blvd., Room 420, Miami, FL 33132/305-350-5273.

Philadelphia (serves PA, DE, Southern NJ): Second & Chestnut Streets, Philadelphia, PA 19106/215-597-0744.

Washington, D.C. (serves DC, MD, NC, WV, VA): 633 Indiana Avenue, NW, Room 600, Washington, D.C. 20004/202-376-2550. Toll Free 800-424-8580, Ext 238 or 226.

Atlanta (serves GA, TN, MS, AL, SC, KY): 101 Marietta Street, NW, Room 2207, Atlanta, GA 30323/404-221-2932.

Chicago (serves IL, IN): 10 West Jackson Boulevard, Third Floor, Chicago, IL 60604/312-353-4990.

Minneapolis (serves MN, WI): Old Federal Building, Room 104, 212 Third Avenue, South, Minneapolis, MN 55401/612-349-3625.

Detroit (serves MI, OH): P.V. McNamara Federal Bldg., 477 Michigan Avenue, Room M-74, Detroit, MI 48226/313-226-7928.

Kansas City (serves KS, MO, NE, IA): II Gateway Centre, Suite 318, 4th & State Streets, Kansas City, KS 66101/913-236-3725.

Dallas (serves NM, OK, LA, TX, AR): 400 North Ervay St, Room 230, P.O. Box 638, Dallas, TX 75221/214-767-5435.

San Francisco (serves NV, HI, Northern CA): 211 Main Street, Room 533, San Francisco, CA 94105/415-974-8754.

Los Angeles (serves AZ, Southern CA): 11000 Wilshire Boulevard, Suite 8104, West Los Angeles, CA 90024/213-209-7444.

Denver (serves CO, MT, SD, ND, UT, WY): 1845 Sherman Street, Room 103, Denver, CO 80203/303-866-1057.

Seattle (serves WA, OR, ID, AK): 1111 3rd Avenue, Suite 360, Seattle, WA 98101/206-442-5490.

San Diego (Southern CA) (out station): VA Building, Room 501-502, 2022 Camino del Rio North, San Diego, CA 92108/619-293-7088.

Environmental Protection Agency

Regional Offices

Region I: John F. Kennedy Federal Building, Boston, MA 02203/617-223-7210.

Region II: 26 Federal Plaza, New York, NY 10007/212-264-2525.

Region III: 6th & Walnut Sts., Philadelphia, PA 19106/215-597-9000.

Region IV: 345 Courtland St N.E., Atlanta, GA 30308/404-881-4727.

Region V: 230 S. Dearborn St., Chicago, IL 60604/312-353-2000.

Region VI: First International Building, 1201 Elm St., Dallas, TX 75270/214-767-2600.

Region VII: 324 E. 11th St., Kansas City, MO 64106/816-374-5493.

Region VIII: 1860 Lincoln St., Denver, CO 80203/303-564-5927.

Region IX: 215 Fremont St., San Francisco, CA 94105/415-974-8153.

Region X: 1200 6th Ave., Seattle, WA 98101/206-442-5810.

Office of Personnel Management

Regional Offices

Region I: John W. McCormack Post Office & Courthouse, Boston, MA 02109/617-223-2538.

Region II: 26 Federal Plaza, New York, NY 10278/212-264-0440.

Region III: 600 Arch St., Philadelphia, PA 19106/215-597-4543.

Region IV: 75 Spring St. S.W., Atlanta, GA 30303/404-221-3459.

Region V: Federal Office Building, 29th Floor, 230 S. Dearborn St., Chicago, IL 60604/312-353-2901.

Region VI: 1100 Commerce St., Dallas, TX 75242/214-767-8227.

Region VII: 300 Old Post Office Building, 815 Olive St., St. Louis, MO 63101/314-425-4262.

Region VIII: Denver Federal Center, Denver, CO 80225/303-236-4022.

Region IX: 525 Market St., San Francisco, CA 94105/415-556-0581.

Region X: 915 2d Ave., Seattle, WA 98174, 206-442-7536.

Small Business Administration

Regional Offices

Region I: 60 Batterymarch, 10th Floor, Boston, MA 02110/617-223-3204.

Region II: 26 Federal Plaza, Room 29-118, New York, NY 10278/212-264-7755.

Region III: 1 Bala Cynwyd Plaza, 231 St. Asaph's Road, Suite 640W, Bala Cynwyd, PA 19004/215-596-5889.

Region IV: 1375 Peachtree St. N.E., 5th Floor, Atlanta, GA 30367/404-881-4999.

Region V: 230 S. Dearborn St., Room 510, Chicago, IL 60604/312-353-6614.

Region VI: 8625 King George Drive, Building C, Dallas, TX 75235/214-767-7643.

Region VII: 911 Walnut St., 13th Floor, Kansas City, MO 64106/816-374-5288.

Region VIII: 1405 Curtis St., Denver, CO 80202/303-844-5441.

Region IX: 450 Golden Gate Ave., Box 36044, San Francisco, CA 94102/415-556-2820.

Region X: 4th and Vine Bldg.—Room 440, 2615 Fourth Avenue, Seattle, WA 98121/206-442-7646.

Department of the Treasury

Bureau of Alcohol, Tobacco and Firearms

Office of Criminal Enforcement
Atlanta, GA 30303: 44 Broad St., NW, Suite 302/404-221-6526.
San Francisco, CA 94105: 525 Market St., 25th Floor/415-984-9589.
Birmingham, AL 35203: 2121 8th Ave. N., Room 1025/205-254-1205.
Charlotte, NC 28202: 222 S. Church St., Suite 404/704-371-6125.
Miami, FL 33166: 5205 N.W. 84th Ave., Suite 108/305-350-4368.
Nashville, TN 37215: 4004 Hillsboro Rd., Room 210/615-251-5412.
New Orleans, LA 70130: Hale Boggs Federal Building, 500 Camp Street, Room 330/504-589-2048.
Cleveland, OH 44114: 55 Erie View Plaza, Suite 500/216-522-7210.
Detroit, MI 48226: 231 W. Lafayette St., Room 533/313-226-7300.
Kansas City, MO 64106: 811 Grand Ave., Room 106/816-374-3886.
Louisville, KY 40202: Bank of Louisville Bldg., 510 West Broadway, Suite 807/502-582-5211.
Oak Brook, IL 60521: 2115 Butterfield Rd., Room 300/312-620-7824.
St. Louis, MO 63101:1114 Market St., Room 611/314-425-5560.
St. Paul, MN 55101: 316 N. Robert St., Room 156/612-725-7092.
Boston, MA 02114: P. O. Box 9115, JFK Post Office/617-223-3817.
Falls Church, VA 22046: 701 W. Broad St./703-285-2551.
New York, NY 10008: P. O. Box 3482, Church St. Station/212-264-4658.
Philadelphia, PA 19106: U.S. Customs House, Room 504, 2d & Chestnut Sts./215-597-7266.
Dallas, TX 75242: 1114 Commerce St., Rm. 718/214-767-2250.
Houston, TX 77205: P. O. Box 60927/713-229-3511.
Los Angeles, CA 90012: P. O. Box 1991, Main Office/213-688-4812.
Seattle, WA 98174: 915 2d Ave., Room 806/206-442-4485.

Office of Regulatory Enforcement, Regional Offices
Chicago, IL 60604: 230 S. Dearborn St./213-353-3778.
New York, NY 10048: 6 World Trade Center/212-264-2328.
Atlanta, GA 30340: 3835 N.E. Expressway/404-455-2631.
Dallas, TX 75242: 1114 Commerce St./214-767-2260.
San Francisco, CA 94105: 525 Market St./415-556-2021.

Comptroller of the Currency
Northeast District: 1211 Avenue of the Americas, Suite 4250, New York, NY 10036/212-944-3495.
Southeast District: 229 Peachtree St. N.E., Suite 2700, Atlanta, GA 30303/404-221-4926.
Central District: Sears Tower, Suite 5750–233S. Wacker Drive, Chicago, IL 60606/312-353-0300.
Midwest District: 911 Main St., Kansas City, MO 64105/816-374-6431.
Southwest District 11: 1201 Elm St., Suite 3800, Dallas, TX 75270/214-767-4400.
Western District: 50 Fremont Street, Suite 3900, San Francisco, CA 94105/415-545-5900.

Internal Revenue Service

Regional Commissioners
Cincinnati, OH 45202: 550 Main St./513-684-3613.
Philadelphia, PA 19107: 841 Chestnut Street/215-597-2040.
Chicago, IL 60606: 1 N. Wacker Dr., 10th Floor/312-886-5600.
New York, NY 10007: 90 Church St./212-264-7061.
Atlanta, GA 30043: 275 Peachtree St. N.E./404-221-6048.
Dallas, TX 75251: 7839 Churchill Way, LB-70/214-767-5855.
San Francisco, CA 94105: 525 Market St., Room 2710/415-974-9492.

Customs Service

Regional Commissioners
Boston, MA 02110: 100 Summer St./617-223-7506.
New York, NY 10048: 6 World Trade Center/212-466-4444.
Miami, FL 33131: 99 S.E. 5th St./305-350-5952.
New Orleans, LA 70130: 423 Canal St./504-589-6324.
Houston, TX 77057: 5850 San Felipe St./713-953-6843.
Los Angeles, CA 90012: 300 N. Los Angeles St./213-688-5900.
Chicago, IL 60603: 55 E. Monroe St./312-353-4733.

Savings Bonds Division

New York, NY 10278: 26 Federal Plaza/212-264-1368.

Atlanta, GA 30309: 1100 Spring St. NW, Room 560/404-881-4895.

Birmingham, AL 35203: 2121 Bldg., Room 1018, 2121 8th Avenue N/205-254-1202.

Boston, MA 02109: 16 North Street, 2nd Floor/617-223-2921.

Cleveland, OH 44114: 1301 Superior Avenue, Room 275/216-522-4012.

Dallas, TX 75242: 1100 Commerce Street, Room 140 44/214-767-0435.

Detroit, MI 48226-2577: 477 Michigan Avenue, Room 835/313-266-7375.

Greensboro, NC 27402: U.S. Courthouse–Room 23, 324 W Market St/919-378-5461.

Los Angeles, CA 90073: PO Box 84-600/213-209-6580.

Minneapolis, MN 55401: Marquette Bldg., Room 490, 400 Marquette Ave/612-349-5400.

Pittsburgh, PA 15222: Federal Building, Room 212, 1000 Liberty Avenue/412-644-2990.

Seattle, WA 98004: 121 10 7th N.E. Suite 123, Bellevue, WA.

Washington, DC 20815: 555 Friendship Blvd–Suite 400A/301-492-5797.

Alameda, CA 94501: Alameda Federal Center, 620 Central Avenue, Bldg 2E/415-273-4477.

Chicago, IL 60604: 230 S. Dearborn St., Room 3948/312-353-6754.

St. Louis, MO 63101: 1114 Market St., Room 757/314-425-5715.

Agencies

Commodity Futures Trading Commission

Regional Offices

Eastern: 1 World Trade Center, Suite 4747, New York, NY 10048/212-466-2071.

Central: 233 S. Wacker Dr., Suite 4600, Chicago, IL 60606/312-353-6642.

Southwestern: 4901 Main St., Room 400, Kansas City, MO 64112/816-374-2994.

Western: 10850 Wilshire Boulevard, Suite 370, Los Angeles, CA 90024/213-209-6783.

Consumer Product Safety Commission

Area Offices

Southeastern: Atlanta, GA 30308: 800 Peachtree St., N.E., Suite 210/404-881-2221

Northeastern: New York, NY 10048: 6 World Trade Center, Vesey Street–6th Floor/212-264-1125.

Midwestern: Chicago, IL 60604: 230 S. Dearborn St., Room 2944/312-353-8260.

Southwestern: Dallas, TX 75242: 1100 Commerce St., Room 1C10/214-767-0841.

Western: San Francisco, CA 94111: 555 Battery St., Room 415/415-556-1816.

Equal Employment Opportunity Commission

Atlanta, GA 30335: 75 Piedmont Ave. N.E., 10th Floor/404-221-6091.

Baltimore, MD 21202: 109 Market Place, Suite 4000/301-962-3932.

Birmingham, AL 35203: 2121 8th Ave. N./205-254-1166.

Charlotte, N.C. 28204: 1301 E. Morehead St./704-371-6137.

Chicago, IL 60605: 536 S. Clark St., Room 938/312-353-2713.

Cleveland, OH 44115: 1375 Euclid Avenue–Room 600/216-522-7425.

Dallas, TX 75247: 8303 Elmbrook Drive/214-767-7015.

Denver, CO 80202: 1531 Stout St., 6th Floor/303-844-2771.

Detroit, MI 48226: 660 Woodward Ave./313-226-7636.

Houston, TX 77002: 2320 La Branch St./713-226-2601.

Indianapolis, IN 46204: 46 E. Ohio St., Room 45b/317-269-7212.

Los Angeles, CA 90010: 3255 Wilshire Blvd., 9th Floor/213-688-3400.

Memphis, TN 38104: 1407 Union Ave., Suite 502/901-521-2540.

Miami, FL 33132: 1 NE 1st St., Metro Mall, 6th Floor/305-350-4491.

Milwaukee, WI 53203: 310 W. Wisconsin Avenue–Suite 800/414-291-1111.

New Orleans, LA 70130: 600 South St./504-589-2329.

New York, NY 10007: 90 Church St., Room 1301/212-264-7161.

Philadelphia, PA 19106: 127 N. 4th St., Suite 300/215-597-7784.

Phoenix, AZ 85063: 135 N 2nd St–4th Floor/602-261-3882.

St. Louis, MO 63108: 625 N. Euclid St./314-425-6585.

San Francisco, CA 94102: 10 United Nations Plaza, 4th Floor/415-556-0260.

Seattle, WA 98104:710 2d Ave., 7th Floor/206-442-0968.

Farm Credit Administration

Office of Examination
St. Louis, MO 63131: 1611 Des Peres Road, Suite 375/314-263-7101.
Bloomington, MN 55420: 2850 Metro Dr., Suite 729/612-854-3703.

Federal Deposit Insurance Corporation

Area Offices
Atlanta, GA 30043: 233 Peachtree St. NE./404-221-6631.
Boston, MA 02109: 60 State St./617-223-6420.
Chicago, IL 60606: 233 S. Wacker Dr./312-353-2600.
Columbus, OH 43215: 1 Nationwide Plaza/614-469-7301.
Dallas, TX 75201: 350 N. St. Paul St./214-767-5501.
Kansas City, MO 64108: 2345 Grand Ave./816-374-2851.
Madison, WI 53703: 1 S. Pinckney St./608-264-5226.
Memphis, TN 38103: 1 Commerce Sq./901-521-3872.
Minneapolis, MN 55402: 730 2d Ave. S./612-340-0746.
New York, NY 10154: 345 Park Ave./212-704-1200.
Omaha, NE 68102: 1700 Farnam St./402-221-3311.
Philadelphia, PA 19103: 5 Penn Center Plaza/215-597-2295.
Richmond, VA 23219: 707 E. Main St./804-771-2395.
San Francisco, CA 94104: 44 Montgomery St./415-546-0160.

Federal Home Loan Bank Board

Area Offices
Boston, MA 02110: 1 Federal St./617-223-5300.
New York, NY 10048: 1 World Trade Center, 103rd Floor/212-432-2000.
Pittsburgh, PA 15222: 11 Stanwix St., 4th Floor, Gateway Center/412-288-3400.
Atlanta, GA 30343: 260 Peachtree St. N.W./404-522-2450.
Cincinnati, OH 45202: 2500 DuBois Tower, 511 Walnut St./513-852-7500.

Indianapolis, IN 46202: 1350 Merchant Plaza, South Tower, 115 W. Washington St./317-269-5200.
Chicago, IL 60601: 111 E. Wacker Dr., Room 8400/312-565-5700.
Des Moines, IA 50309: 907 Walnut St., Room 501/515-243-4211.
Little Rock, AR 72201: 1450 Tower Bldg./501-378-5374.
Topeka, KS 66603: No. 3 Townsite Plaza, 120 E. 6th St./913-233-0507.
San Francisco, CA 94120: 600 California St., Room 310/415-393-1000.
Seattle, WA 98101: 600 Stewart St., Suite 610/206-624-3980.
Irving, TX 75062: 500 E. John Carpenter Freeway/214-659-8500.

Federal Labor Relations Authority

Regional Offices
Region I: 441 Stuart St., 9th Floor, Boston, MA 02116/617-223-0920.
Region II: 26 Federal Plaza, Room 2237, New York, NY 10278/212-264-4934.
Region III: 1118 18th St., Room 700, P.O. Box 33758/202-653-8500.
Region IV: 1776 Peachtree St. N.W., Suite 501, North Wing, Atlanta, GA 30309/404-881-2324.
Region V: 175 W. Jackson Blvd., Suite 1359-A, Chicago, IL 60604/312-353-6306.
Region VI: Old Post Office Building, Room 450, Bryan & Ervay Sts., Dallas, TX 75221/214-767-4996.
Region VII: 1531 Stout Street, Suite 301, Denver, CO 80202/303-837-5224.
Region VIII: 350 S. Figueroa St., 10th Floor, Los Angeles, CA 90071/213-688-3805.
Region IX: 530 Bush St.—Room 542, San Francisco, CA 94108/415-556-8106.

Federal Maritime Commission

Regional Offices
Atlantic: 6 World Trade Center, Suite 614, New York, NY 10048/212-264-1430.
Gulf: 1001 N. American Way, Room 102, Miami, FL 33132/305-350-6963.
Gulf: P.O. Box 30550, New Orleans, LA 70190-0550/504-682-6662.
Pacific: U.S. Customs House Building, 300 S. Ferry St., Room 204D, P.O. Box 3184, Terminal Island Station, San Pedro, CA 90731/213-548-2542.

Pacific: 525 Market St., San Francisco, CA 94105/ 415-974-9756.

Great Lakes: 610 S. Canal St., Chicago, IL 60607/ 312-353-0282.

Puerto Rico: P.O. Box 3168, Carlos Chardon St., Hato Rey, PR 00917/809-753-4198.

Federal Mediation and Conciliation Service

Area Offices

New York, NY 10278: 26 Federal Plaza/212-264-1000.

Philadelphia, PA 19106: 600 Arch St., Room 3456/ 215-597-7690.

Atlanta, GA 30309: 1720 W. Peachtree St., N.W. Suite 318/404-881-2473.

Cleveland, OH 44114: 815 Superior Ave. N.E./ 216-522-4800.

Chicago, IL 60604: 175 W. Jackson Blvd./312-353-7350.

St. Louis, MO 63141: 12140 Woodcrest Executive Dr., Suite 325/314-576-3293.

San Francisco, CA 94105: 525 Market Street, 29th Floor/415-974-9850.

Seattle, WA 98121: Westin Building, Suite 310, 2001 Sixth Avenue/206-442-5800.

Federal Reserve System

Area Offices

Boston, MA 02106: 600 Atlantic Ave./617-973-3000.

New York, NY 10045: 33 Liberty St./212-791-5000.

Philadelphia, PA 19106: Ten Independence Mall, P.O. Box 66, Philadelphia, PA 19105/215-574-6000.

Cleveland, OH 44101: 1455 E. 6th St./216-579-2000.

Richmond, VA 23261: 701 E. Byrd St./804-643-1250.

Atlanta, GA 30303: 104 Marietta St. N.W./404-586-8500.

Chicago, IL 60690: 230 S. La Salle St./312-322-5322.

St. Louis, MO 63166: 411 Locust St./314-444-8444.

Minneapolis, MN 55480: 250 Marquette Ave./612-340-2345.

Kansas City, MO 64198: 925 Grand Ave./816-881-2000.

Dallas, TX 75222: 400 S. Akard St./214-651-6111.

San Francisco, CA 94105: 101 Market St., P.O. Box 7702, San Francisco, CA 94120/415-544-2000.

Federal Trade Commission

Area Offices

Atlanta, GA 30367: 1718 Peachtree St. N.W., Suite 1000/404-881-4836.

Boston, MA 02114: 150 Causeway St./617-223-6621.

Chicago, IL 60603: 55 E. Monroe St./312-353-4423.

Cleveland, OH 44114: 118 Saint Clair Ave., Suite 500/216-522-4207.

Dallas, TX 75201: 2001 Bryan St./214-767-0032.

Denver, CO 80202: 1405 Curtis St., Suite 2900/ 303-837-2271.

Los Angeles, CA 90024: 11000 Wilshire Blvd./213-824-7575.

New York, NY 10278: 26 Federal Plaza, Room 2237/212-264-1207.

San Francisco, CA 94102: 450 Golden Gate Ave./ 415-556-1270.

Seattle, WA 98174: 915 2d Ave./206-442-4655.

General Services Administration

Regional Offices

National Capital: 7th & D Sts. S.W., Washington, DC 20407/202-472-1100.

Region I: John W. McCormack Post Office & Courthouse, Boston, MA 02109/617-223-2601.

Region II: 26 Federal Plaza, New York, NY 10278/ 212-264-0718.

Region III: 9th & Market Sts., Philadelphia, PA 19107/215-597-1237.

Region IV: 75 Spring St. S.W., Atlanta, GA 30303/404-221-3200.

Region V: 230 S. Dearborn St., Chicago, IL 60604/ 312-353-5395.

Region VI: 1500 E. Bannister Rd., Kansas City, MO 64131/816-926-7201.

Region VII: 819 Taylor St., Fort Worth, TX 76102/817-334-2321.

Region VIII: Denver Federal Center, Bldg. 41, Denver, CO 80225/303-234-4171.

Region IX: 525 Market St., San Francisco, CA 94105/415-474-9147,

Region X: GSA Center, Auburn, WA 98002/206-931-7000.

Interstate Commerce Commission

Regional Offices
Boston, MA 02114: 150 Causeway St./617-223-2372.
Philadelphia, PA 19104: Gateway Building, 3535 Market Street, 101 N. 7th St./215-596-4040.
Atlanta, GA 30309: 1776 Peachtree St. N.W./404-881-4371.
Chicago, IL 60604: Everett McKinley Dirksen Building, 219 S. Dearborn Street, Room 1304/312-353-6204.
Fort Worth, TX 76102: 411 W. 7th St./817-334-3101.
San Francisco, CA 94105: 211 Main St./415-974-7011.

Merit Systems Protection Board

Field Offices
Atlanta, GA 30309: 1776 Peachtree St. N.E./404-881-3631.
Boston, MA 02114: 150 Causeway St., Room 1122/617-223-2556.
Chicago, IL 60604: Room 1669, 230 S. Dearborn St./312-353-2923.
Dallas, TX 75242: 1100 Commerce St./214-767-0555.
Denver, CO 80401: 730 Simons, Room 301, Golden, CO 80401/303-236-2710.
Falls Church, VA 22041: 5203 Leesburg Pike, Room 1109/703-756-6250.
New York, NY 10278: 26 Federal Plaza/212-264-9372.
Philadelphia, PA 19106: U.S. Custom House, Room 501/215-597-9960.
St. Louis, MO 63103: 1520 Market St., Room 1740/314-425-4295.
San Francisco, CA 94105: 525 Market St., Room 2800/415-974-9703.
Seattle, WA 98174: 915 2nd Ave., Room 1840/206-442-0394.

National Credit Union Administration

Regional Offices
Region I: 441 Stuart St., Boston, MA 02116/617-223-6807.
Region II: 1776 G Street NW, Suite 700, Washington, DC 20006/202-682-1900.
Region II: 1365 Peachtree St. N.E., Suite 540, Atlanta, GA 30367/404-881-3127.
Region IV: 230 South Dearborn, Suite 3346, Chicago, IL 60604/312-886-9697.
Region V: 611 East 6th Street, Suite 407, Austin, TX 78701/512-482-5131.
Region VI: 2 Embarcadero Center, 2890 North Main Street, Suite 101, Walnut Creek, CA 94596/415-486-3490/415-556-6277.

National Labor Relations Board

District Offices
District 1: Boston, MA 02111: 120 Boylston St./617-223-3300.
District 2: New York, NY 10278: 26 Federal Plaza/212-264-0300.
District 3: Buffalo, NY 14202: 111 W. Huron St./716-846-4931.
District 4: Philadelphia, PA 19106: 615 Chestnut St./215-597-7601.
District 5: Baltimore, MD 21202: 109 Market Place/301-962-2822.
District 6: Pittsburgh, PA 15222: 1501 Wm Moorhead Federal Building, 1000 Liberty Avenue/412-644-2977.
District 7: Detroit, MI 48226: 477 Michigan Ave./313-226-3200.
District 8: Cleveland, OH 44199: 1240 E. 9th St./216-522-3715.
District 9: Cincinnati, OH 45202: 550 Main St./513-684-3686.
District 10: Atlanta, GA 30323: 101 Marietta St. N.W./404-221-2896.
District 11: Winston-Salem, NC 27101: 251 N. Main St./919-761-3201.
District 12: Tampa, FL 33602: 700 Twigg St., Suite 511, P.O. Box 3322/813-228-2641.
District 13: Chicago, IL 60604: 219 S. Dearborn St./312-353-7570.
District 14: St. Louis, MO 63101: 210 Tucker Blvd North/314-425-4167.
District 15: New Orleans, LA 70113: 600 S. Maestri Place/504-589-6361.
District 16: Fort Worth, TX 76102: 819 Taylor St./817-334-2938.
District 17: Kansas City, KS 66101: 4th St. & State Ave./913-236-3846.
District 18: Minneapolis, MN 55401: 110 S. 4th St./612-349-5357.
District 19: Seattle, WA 98174: 915 2d Ave./206-442-4532.
District 20: San Francisco, CA 94102: 450 Golden Gate Ave./415-556-3197.
District 21: Los Angeles, CA 94102: 606 S. Olive St./213-688-5200.
District 22: Newark, NJ 07102: 970 Broad St./201-645-2100.

District 23: Houston, TX 77002: 515 Rusk St./713-229-3748.

District 24: Hata Rey, PR 00918: Carlos E. Chardon Ave./809-753-4347.

District 25: Indianapolis, IN 46204: 575 N. Pennsylvania St./317-269-7430.

District 26: Memphis, TN 38174: 1407 Union Ave./901-521-2725.

District 27: Denver, CO 80202: 721–19th St./303-844-3555.

District 28: Phoenix, AZ 85067: 3030 N. Central Ave./602-241-2350.

District 29: Brooklyn, NY 11241: 16 Court St./212-330-7713.

District 30: Milwaukee, WI 53203: 310 W. Wisconsin Avenue/414-291-3861.

District 31: Los Angeles, CA 90024: 11000 Wilshire Blvd./213-309-7352.

District 32: Oakland, CA 94604: 2201 Broadway/415-273-7200.

District 33: Peoria, IL 61602: 411 Hamilton Boulevard/309-671-7080.

National Transportation Safety Board

Administrative Law Judge Circuits
Aurora, CO 80010: 10255 E. 25th Ave., Suite 8/303-844-4685.

Washington, DC 20594: 800 Independence Ave. S.W./202-382-6764.

Los Angeles, CA 90261: Federal Building, 15000 Aviation Blvd., P.O. Box 6117, Lawndale, CA 90261/213-966-6045.

Aviation Field Office
Jamaica, NY 11430: Federal Building, John F. Kennedy International Airport/212-917-1266.

Atlanta, GA 30309: 1720 Peachtree St. N.W./404-881-7385.

Miami Springs, FL 33166: 4471 N.W. 36th St./305-592-6002.

Des Plaines, IL 60018: 2300 E. Devon Ave./312-827-8858.

Kansas City, MO 64106: 601 E. 12th St./816-374-3576.

Los Angeles, CA 90261: Federal Building, 15000 Aviation Blvd., P.O. Box 6117/213-536-6041.

Anchorage, AK 99513: 701 C St., Room C-415, Box 11/9070-271-5001.

Aurora, CO 80010: 10255 E. 25th Ave./303-837-4492.

Fort Worth, TX 76102: 819 Taylor St./817-334-2616.

Seattle, WA 98188: 19415 Pacific Hwy. S./206-764-3782.

Highway Field Offices
New York, NY 11430: Federal Building, John F. Kennedy International Airport, Jamaica, NY 11430/212-917-1266.

Atlanta, GA 30309: 1720 Peachtree St. N.W., Suite 921/404-881-7385.

Kansas City, MO 64106: 601 E. 12th St./816-374-3576.

Los Angeles, CA 90261: Federal Building, 15000 Aviation Blvd., P.O. Box 6117, Lawndale, CA 90261/213-536-6041.

Pipeline Field Offices
Washington, DC 20594: 800 Independence Ave. S.W./202-472-5973.

Fort Worth, TX 76102: 819 Taylor St./817-334-2616.

Railroad Field Offices
Jamaica, NY 11430: Federal Building, John F. Kennedy International Airport/212-995-3716.

Washington,DC 20594: 800 Independence Ave. S.W./202-472-6091.

Atlanta, GA 30309: 1720 Peachtree St. N.W., Suite 921/404-881-7385.

Des Plaines, IL 60018: 2300 E. Devon Ave./312-827-8858.

Kansas City, MO 64106: 601 E. 12th St./816-374-3576.

Los Angeles, CA 90261: Federal Building, 15000 Aviation Blvd., P.O. Box 6117, Lawndale, CA 90261/213-536-6041.

Aurora, CO 80010: 10255 E. 25th Ave./303-837-4492.

Fort Worth, TX 76102: 819 Taylor St./817-334-2616.

Seattle, WA 98188: 19415 Pacific Hwy. S./206-764-3782.

Nuclear Regulatory Commission

Regional Offices
King of Prussia, PA 19406: 631 Park Ave./215-337-5000.

Atlanta, GA 30323: 101 Marietta St., Suite 3100/404-221-4503.

Glen Ellyn, IL 60137: 799 Roosevelt Rd./312-790-5500.

Arlington, TX 76011: 611 Ryan Plaza Dr., Suite 1000/817-860-8128.

Walnut Creek, CA 94596: 1450 Maria Lane, Suite 210/415-943-3700.

Occupational Safety and Health Review Commission

Area Offices
Boston, MA 02109: 16-18 North Street/617-223-6710.

New York, NY 10036: 1 Astor Plaza, 1515 Broadway, Room 3445/212-944-3432.

Atlanta, GA 30367: 1375 Peachtree St. NE, Suite 587/404-881-3573.

Chicago, IL 60604: 230 S. Dearborn Street/312-353-2220.

Dallas, TX 75202: 32nd Floor, 555 Griffin Square Building, 230 S. Dearborn Street/214-767-4731.

Denver, CO 80294: 1961 Stout Street/303-837-3061.

San Francisco, CA 94102: 11349 Federal Building, 450 Golden Gate Avenue, P.O. Box 36017/415-556-7260.

Railroad Retirement Board

Area Offices
Atlanta, GA 30303: 101 Marietta St. N.W., Suite 2304/404-221-2690.

New York, NY 10278: Federal Building, Room 3415, 26 Federal Plaza/212-264-8495.

Cleveland, OH 44199: Anthony J. Celebrezze Federal Building/216-552-4043.

Kansas City, MO 64106: Federal Building, Room 257, 601 E. 12th St./816-374-3278.

San Francisco, CA 94102: Federal Building, Room 7419, 450 Golden Gate Ave., Box 36043/415-556-2584.

Securities and Exchange Commission

Regional Offices
Atlanta, GA 30367: 1375 Peachtree St. N.E./404-881-4768.

Boston, MA 02114: 150 Causeway St./617-223-2721.

Chicago, IL 60604: 219 S. Dearborn St., Room 1204/312-353-7390.

Denver, CO 80202: 410 17th St., Suite 700/303-844-2071.

Fort Worth, TX 76102: 411 W. 7th St., 8th Floor/817-334-3821.

Los Angeles, CA 90036-3648: 5757 Wilshire Blvd., Suite 500 East/213-468-3107.

New York, NY: 10278: Room 1028, 26 Federal Plaza/212-264-1636.

Seattle, WA 98174: 3040 Federal Building, 915 2d Ave./206-442-7990.

Arlington, VA 22203: Ballston Center, Tower 3, 4015 Wilson Blvd./703-235-3701.

Veterans Administration

Department of Medicine and Surgery
Northeastern: 810 Vermont Ave. N.W., Washington, DC 20420/202-389-2734.

Mid-Atlantic: 810 Vermont Ave. N.W., Washington, DC 20420/202-389-3571.

Southeastern: 810 Vermont Ave. N.W., Washington, DC 20420/202-389-2765.

Great Lakes: 810 Vermont Ave. N.W., Washington, DC 20420/202-389-3754.

Mid-Western: 810 Vermont Ave. N.W., Washington, DC 20420/202-389-2173.

Western: 810 Vermont Ave. N.W., Washington, DC 20420/202-389-5062.

District 1: 150 S. Huntington Ave., Bedford, MA 01730/617-232-9500.

District 2: 3495 Bailey Ave., Buffalo, NY 14215/716-834-9200.

District 3: Castle Point, NY 12511/914-831-2000.

District 4: University & Woodland Ave., Philadelphia, PA 19104/215-384-7711.

District 5: University Dr. C, Pittsburgh, PA 15240/412-683-3000.

District 6: 50 Irving St. N.W., Washington, DC 20422/202-483-6666.

District 7: 1201 Broad Rock Rd., Richmond, VA 23249/804-231-9011.

District 8: Durham, NC 27705/704-298-7911.

District 9: 1670 Clairmont Rd., Atlanta, GA 30033/404-321-6111.

District 10: 700 S. 19th St., Birmingham, AL 35233/205-933-8101.

District 11: Lexington, KY 40511/606-233-4511.

District 12: Archer Rd., Gainesville, FL 32602/904-376-1611.

District 13: 10000 Brecksville Road, Brecksville, OH 44141/216-791-3800.

District 14: 2215 Fuller Rd., P. O. Box 2318, Ann Arbor, MI 48106/313-769-7100.

District 15: 1481 W. 10th St., Indianapolis, IN 46202/317-635-7401.

District 16: 2500 Overlook Terrace, Madison, WI 53705/608-256-1910.

District 17: VA Medical Center, Hines, IL 60141/312-343-7200.

District 18: 54th St. & 48th Ave. S., Minneapolis, MN 55417/612-725-6767.

District 19: North Little Rock, AR 72114/501-372-8361.

District 20: Waco, TX 76703/817-778-4811.

District 21: St. Louis, MO 63125/314-487-0400.

District 33: Leavenworth, KS 66048/913-682-2000.

District 23: Omaha, NB 68105/402-346-8800.

District 24: VA Medical Center, Salt Lake City, UT 84148.

District 25: Building 4, Phoenix, AZ 85012/602-445-4860.

District 26: Los Angeles, CA 90073.

District 27: 211 Main St., San Francisco, CA 94105/415-221-4810.

District 28: Seattle, WA 98108/206-762-1010.

Department of Memorial Affairs

Area Offices

Atlanta, GA 30365: 730 Peachtree St., N.E./404-881-2121.

Philadelphia, PA 19106: Independence Bldg. South–Room 1040, 434 Walnut Street/215-922-5421.

Denver, CO 80235: 3698 South Sheraton Blvd./303-980-2750.

Department of Veterans Affairs

Field Directors

Eastern Region: Room 316 (201A), 810 Vermont Ave. N.W., Washington, DC 20420/202-389-5284.

Central Region: Room 324 (201B), 810 Vermont Ave., N.W., Washington, DC 20420/202-389-5341.

Western Region: Room 332 (201C), 810 Vermont Ave. N.W., Washington, DC 20420/202-389-5335.

DEPARTMENTS

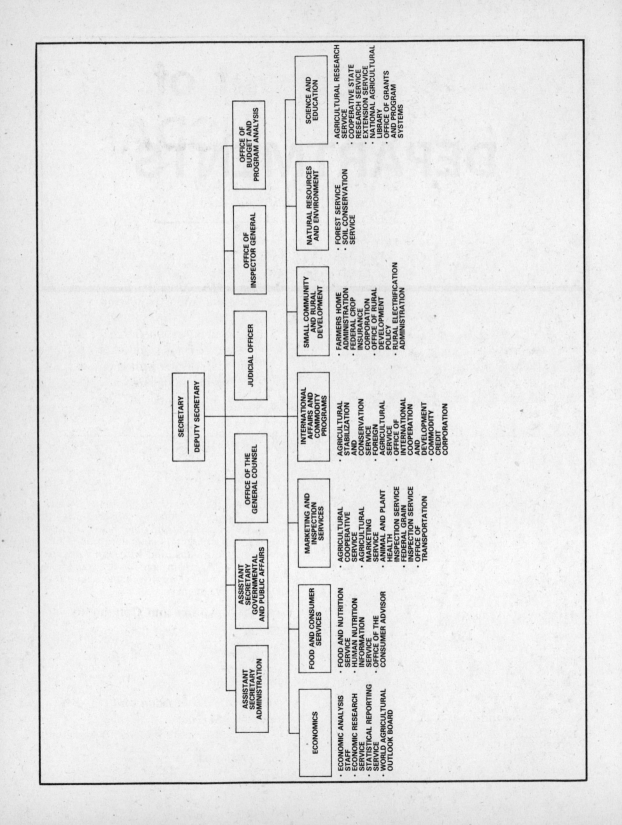

Department of Agriculture (USDA)

**14th St. and Independence Ave. S.W.,
Washington, DC 20250/202-447-2791**

**Established: May 15, 1862
Budget $41,493,143,000
Employees: 89,183**

MISSION: Improve and maintain farm income. Develop and expand markets abroad for agricultural products. Help curb and cure poverty, hunger and malnutrition. Enhance the environment and maintain production capacity by helping landowners protect the soil, water, forests and other natural resources. Aid in carrying out national growth policies with rural development, credit and conservation programs. Provide safeguards and assure standards of quality in the daily food supply by providing inspection and grading services.

Major Divisions and Offices

Natural Resources and Environment

USDA, Room 242-W, Washington, DC 20250/
202-447-7173.
Budget: $2,423,045,000
Employees: 50,612

• *Forest Service*

USDA, Room 3008 South Building, Washington,
DC 20250/202-447-6661.
Budget: $1,904,715,000
Employees: 36,320
Mission: Responsible for national leadership in forestry and provides a continuing flow of natural resource goods and services to help meet the needs of the Nation and to contribute to the needs of the international community.

• *Soil Conservation Service*

USDA, Room 5105 South Building, Washington,
DC 20250/202-447-4525.
Budget: $518,330,000
Employees: 14,292

Mission: Develop and carry out a national soil and water conservation program in cooperation with landowners and operators and other land users and developers, with community planning agencies and regional resource groups, and with other government agencies. Assist in agricultural pollution control, environmental improvement, and rural community development.

International Affairs and Commodity Programs

USDA, Room 212-A, Washington, DC 20250/
202-447-3111.
Budget: $15,538,595,000
Employees: 3,440

• *Agricultural Stabilization and Conservation Service*

USDA, Room 3085 South Building, Washington,
DC 20250/202-447-3467.
Budget: $274,262,000
Employees: 2,414

Mission: Administers commodity and related land use programs designed for voluntary production adjustment, resource protection, and price, market, and farm income stabilization.

• Commodity Credit Corporation

USDA, Room 3085, Washington, DC 20250/202-447-8165.
Budget: $15,185,151,000
Employees: *
Mission: Stabilize and protect farm income and prices. Assist in maintaining balanced and adequate supplies of agricultural commodities and their products. Facilitate the orderly distribution of commodities.

• Foreign Agricultural Service

USDA, Room 5071 South Building, Washington, DC 20250/202-447-3935.
Budget: $75,020,000
Employees: 833
Mission: Maintain and expand export sales. Improve access to foreign markets for U.S. farm products through representations to foreign governments and participation in formal trade negotiations. Operate a global reporting and analysis network covering world agricultural production, trade, competition and policy situations affecting U.S. agriculture.

• Office of International Cooperation and Development

USDA, Room 3049 South Building, Washington, DC 20250/202-447-3157.
Budget: $4,162,000
Employees: 193
Mission: Coordinate, plan and direct the department's efforts in international development and technical cooperation in food and agriculture. Coordinate international organization affairs and scientific exchange programs.

Food and Consumer Services

USDA, Room 207-W, Washington, DC 20250/202-447-7711.
Budget: $17,355,727,000
Employees: 2,317

• Food and Nutrition Service

USDA, 3100 Park Center Drive, Alexandria, Va 22302/202-447-8384.
Budget: $17,347,575,000
Employees: 2,247
Mission: Administer programs to make food assistance available to people who need it.

• Human Nutrition Information Service

USDA, Hyattsville, Md 20782/301-436-7725.
Budget: $8,152,000
Employees: 70

Mission: Performs research in human nutrition to improve professional and public understanding of the nutritional adequacy of diets and food supplies as well as the nutritive value of food; helps develop knowledge needed to improve the nutritional quality of diets, thereby improving the general health of the American public; and collects and disseminates technical, educational and nonprint material and information on food use, food management and human nutritional problems.

• Office of Consumer Advisor

USDA, Room 232W Administrative Building, Washington, DC 20250/202-382-9681.
Budget: **
Employees: ***
Mission: Serves as the focal point for coordinating USDA actions on problems and issues of importance to consumers; consults and advises USDA policymakers on issues and questions of importance to consumers; represents the Department in policy discussions related to consumer-oriented issues before Congress and other public forums; monitors the policies, practices, and procedures of USDA programs in the area of consumer affairs; assists in informing consumers of USDA's functions, policies, and procedures; develops and monitors procedures for handling consumer complaints and followup actions; and analyzes consumer complaints for policy and program evaluation purposes.

Marketing and Inspection Services

USDA, Room 242-E, Washington, DC 20250/202-447-4256.
Budget: $722,958,000
Employees: 9,622

• Agricultural Cooperative Service

USDA, Room 3405 South Building, Washington, DC 20250/202-447-8870.
Budget: $3,860,000
Employees: 77
Mission: Helps farmers to help themselves through the use of cooperative organizations; and conducts studies to support cooperatives that market farm products, purchase production supplies, and perform related business services.

• Agricultural Marketing Service (AMS)

USDA, Room 3071 South Building, Washington, DC 20250/202-447-5115.
Budget: $439,530,000
Employees: 3,885
Mission: Assist producers and handlers of agricultural commodities by administering standardization, grading, voluntary and mandatory inspec-

---

*basically a funding authority.

**This agency does not have individual funding.
***Each of USDA's 40 agencies have assigned consumer responsibilities to member of their staff.

tion, market news, marketing orders, and regulatory and related programs.

• Animal and Plant Health Inspection Service (APHIS)

USDA, Room 312-E, Administrative Building, Washington, DC 20250/202-447-3668.
Budget: $232,607,000
Employees: 4,837
Mission: Conduct regulatory and control programs to protect and improve animal and plant health for the benefit of man and his environment. Administer laws and regulations pertaining to animal and plant health and quarantine, humane treatment of animals, and control eradication of pests and diseases.

• Federal Grain Inspection Service

USDA, Room 1628 South Building, Washington, DC 20250/202-382-0219.
Budget: $5,548,000
Employees: 1,045
Mission: Establish official U.S. standards for grain and other assigned commodities and administration of a nationwide system of official inspection. Regulate the weighing of all grain coming into or going out of any export facility in the United States.

• Food Safety and Inspection Service

USDA, Room 332E Administrative Building, Washington, DC 20250/202-447-7025.
Budget: $328,077,000
Employees: 10,096
Mission: Ensures that meat and poultry products moving in interstate and foreign commerce for human consumption are safe, wholesome, and accurately labeled.

• Office of Transportation

USDA, Room 1405 Auditors Building, Washington, DC 20250/202-447-3963.
Budget: $2,416,000
Employees: 51
Mission: Develops USDA transportation policies for agriculture and rural development, including coordination of USDA programs in education, information, and research to meet policy goals, and representation of agricultural and rural transportation interests before regulatory bodies.

• Packers and Stockyards Administration

USDA, Room 309 South Building, Washington, DC 20250/202-447-7051.
Budget: $8,834,000
Employees: 200
Mission: Maintains effective competition and fair trade practices in livestock, meat, and poultry for the protection of livestock and poultry producers; protects members of the livestock, poultry, and meat industries against unfair or monopolistic practices of competitors; and protects consumers against unfair business practices in marketing of meats and poultry and against restrictions of competition which could unduly raise meat and poultry prices.

Small Community and Rural Development

USDA, Room 5015 South Building, Washington, DC 20250/202-447-4581.
Budget: $3,673,152,000
Employees: 12,106

• Farmers Home Administration

USDA, Room 5014 South Building, Washington, DC 20250/202-447-7967.
Budget: $3,111,435,000
Employees: 10,589
Mission: Provide credit for those in rural America who are unable to get credit from other sources at reasonable rates and terms.

• Rural Electrification Administration

USDA, Room 4051, South Building, Washington, DC 20250/202-382-9540.
Budget: $30,263,000
Employees: 700
Mission: Assists rural electric and telephone utilities to obtain financing.

• Federal Crop Insurance Corporation

USDA, Room 4096 South Building, Washington, DC 20250/202-447-6795.
Budget: $529,424,000
Employees: 775
Mission: Ensures the economic stability of agriculture through a sound system of crop insurance.

• Office of Rural Development Policy

USDA, Room 5042 South Building, Washington, DC 20250/202-382-0044.
Budget: $2,030,000
Employees: 36
Mission: Assists the Under Secretary for Small Community and Rural Development in carrying out the Secretary's responsibilities for rural development leadership, coordination, and strategy preparation and implementation.

Economics

USDA, Room 227-E, Washington, DC 20250/202-447-4164.
Budget: $92,333,000
Employees: 2,061

• Economic Research Service

USDA, 500 12th St. S.W. Room 448, Washington, DC 20250/202-447-8104.
Budget: $38,964,000
Employees: 918
Mission: Provides economic information to aid public policy officials and program managers in developing and administering agricultural and

rural policies and programs; monitors economic activity, makes short-term forecasts of key economic indicators, and develops long-range projections of U.S. and world agricultural production, demand for production resources and demand for agricultural commodities and food products; and measures returns to producers and evaluates how well the agricultural and food sectors meet the needs of domestic and foreign consumers.

• *Statistical Reporting Service*
USDA, Room 4117 South Building, Washington, DC 20250/202-447-2707.
Budget: $51,906,000
Employees: 1,114
Mission: Prepares estimates and reports on production, supply, price, and other items necessary for the orderly operation of the U.S. agricultural economy.

• *World Agricultural Outlook Board*
USDA, Room 5143 S, Washington, DC 20250/202-447-8651.
Budget: $1,463,000
Employees: 29
Mission: Coordinate and review all commodity and aggregate agricultural and food data and analysis used to develop outlook and situation material prepared within the USDA.

• *Economic Analysis Staff*
USDA, Room 227E Administrative Building, Washington, DC 20250/202-447-5955.
Mission: Develops, organizes, coordinates, and synthesizes economic and statistical analyses to be used as a basis for planning and evaluating short and intermediate-range agricultural policy.

Science and Education
USDA, Room 217W Administration Building, Washington, DC 20250/202-447-5923.
Budget: $1,042,961,000
Employees: 9,031

• *Agricultural Research Service*
USDA, Beltsville, Md 20705/301-344-2264.
Budget: $460,626,000
Employees: 8,520
Mission: Administers a basic, applied, and developmental research program in animal and plant protection and production; the use and improvement of soil, water, and air; the processing,

storage, and distribution of farm products; and human nutrition. Applies research to a wide range of goals, commodities, natural resources, fields of science, and geographic, climatic and environmental conditions.

• *Cooperative State Research Service*
USDA, Room 3048, Administrative Building, Washington, DC 20250/202-447-4423.
Budget: $244,949,000
Employees: 131
Mission: Participates in a nationwide system of research program planning and coordination between the States and the Department of Agriculture which encourages and assists in the establishment and maintenance of cooperation within and among the States and between the States and their Federal research partners.

• *Extension Service*
USDA, Room 3428 South Building, Washington, DC 20250/202-447-3029.
Budget: $328,654,000
Employees: 200
Mission: Helps the public learn about and apply to everyday activities, the latest technology developed through research by land-grant universities, the Department of Agriculture, and other sources.

• *National Agriculture Library*
USDA, Beltsville, Md 20705/301-344-3778.
Budget: $8,732,000
Employees: 180
Mission: The largest agricultural library in the United States, covering botany, zoology, chemistry, veterinary medicine, forestry, plant pathology, livestock, poultry, entomology, and general agriculture.

• *Office of Grants and Program Systems*
USDA, Room 324 Administrative Building, Washington, DC 20250/202-475-5720.
Budget: *
Employees: *
Mission: Administers the Department's competitive grants program for small business innovative research and programs in aquaculture, domestic rubber and other critical materials, minority research and teaching and agriculture in the classroom.

---

*Included in figures for Cooperative State Research Service

Data Experts

Agricultural Economists
Staff economists can supply information on a wide variety of agricultural subjects. They are knowledgeable on all aspects of the distribution chain from producer to end user. Each individual below can be reached by mail in care of the Economic Research or Statistical Reporting Service, USDA, or directly by telephone.

Office of Crops, Dairy, Livestock and Poultry
Broilers/Allen Baker/202-447-8636
Catfish/Suzanne Dash/202-447-8636
Cattle/Ron Gustafson/202-447-8636
Coffee/Tea/Fred Gray/202-447-7290
Corn & Feed Grains/Larry Van Meir/202-447-8776
Cold Storage/Bernie Albrecht/202-382-9185
Cotton/Keith Collins/202-447-8776
Dairy Products/Clifford Carman/202-447-8636
Eggs/Alan Baker/202-447-8636
Floriculture/Steve Raleigh/202-447-8661
Hay/George Allen/202-447-8444
Hogs/Leland Southard/202-447-8636
Milk/Clifford Carman/202-447-8636
Oilseeds/Sam Evans/202-447-8444
Peanuts/Verner Grise/202-447-8776
Poultry/Alan Baker/202-447-8636
Potatoes/Michael Stellmacher/202-447-7290
Seeds/George Allen/202-447-8776
Sheep/Leland Southard/202-447-8636
Slaughter/Ron Gustafson/202-447-8636
Soybeans/Sam Evans/202-447-8444
Sugar/Robert Barry/202-447-7290
Turkeys/Alan Baker/202-447-8636
Vegetables/Michael Stellmacher/202-447-7290
Wool/John Lawler/202-447-8776

U.S. Trade and Foreign Agriculture
U.S. Exports and Imports/Thomas Warden/ 202-447-4863

International
World/Cecil Davison/202-447-8054
Trade Policies/Vernon Roningen/202-447-8470
Africa and Mid-East/Cheryl Christensen/ 202-447-3443
Asia/Carmen Nohre/202-447-8860
China/Charles Liu/202-447-8676
Eastern Europe/Anton Malish/202-447-8380
Latin America/Oswald Blaich/202-447-8133
Soviet Union/Anton Malish/202-447-8380
International monetary and financial/Art Morey/ 202-447-8470
North America & Oceania/Don Seaborg/202-447-8376
Western Europe/Reed Friend/202-447-6807
Agricultural Development/Lon Cesal/202-447-8926
Commodities/John Dunmore/202-382-9818
Food Aid/Kevin Lanagan/202-447-8364

Office of Farm Finances
Agricultural Finances/Steve Gabriel/202-447-7340
Farm Credit/Steve Gabriel/202-447-7340
Income/Gary Lucier/202-447-4190
Prices and Parity/LeRoy Rude/202-447-6620
Production Expenditures/Sandra Suddendorf/ 202-447-8342
Wages and Labor/Robert Coltrane/202-447-8621
Cash Receipts/Roger Strickland/202-447-4190
Production Costs/Cole Gustafson/202-447-4190

Office of Farms and Land
Corporate Farming/Donn Reimund/202-447-8168
Farm Numbers/George Patton/202-447-3441
Farm Real Estate/Gene Wunderlich/202-447-9179
Family Farms/Donn Reimund/202-447-8168
Land Ownership/J. Peter DeBraal/202-447-9179
Land Policy/Robert Boxley/202-447-4859
Land Use Planning/William Anderson/202-475-4859
Farm Productivity/Charles Cobb/202-447-3055

Office of Food
Food Assistance Research/Paul Nelson/202-447-6363
Food Consumption/Richard Prescott/202-447-6860
Food Prices/Ralph Parlett/202-447-8801
Food Away From Home/Michael Van Dress/202-447-6363
Food Demand Research/Richard Haidacher/ 202-447-9200
Food Expenditures/Tony Gallo/202-447-8707
Food Manufacturing/Richard Rogers/202-447-6363
Food & Nutrition Policy/Joyce Allen/202-447-8489
Food Retailing/Charles Handy/202-447-6363
Food Safety/Clark Burbee/202-447-8707

Office of Marketing
Marketing Margins and Statistics/Dennis Dunham/ 202-447-8801
Marketing Structure/Charles Handy/202-447-6363
Meat Demand/Richard Stillman/202-447-8636
Price Spreads/Karen Parham/202-447-4997

Other Topics
Agricultural History/Wayne Rasmussen/202-447-8183
Cooperatives/Ralph Richardson (Statistics)/ 202-447-8906
Energy/Tony Prato/202-447-7340
Farm Machinery/Paul Andrilenas/202-447-7340
Fibers/Keith Collins/202-447-8776
Housing/Carol Meeks/202-447-8717
Natural Resource Projections/John Day/202-447-8320
Output and Productivity/Charles Cobb/202-447-3055
Personal Incomes/Tom Carlin/202-447-8366
Pest Control/John Schaub/202-447-8151
Pesticides/Theodore Eichers/202-447-7340
Commodity Programs and Policies/Leroy Rude/ 202-447-6620
Roadside Marketing/Harold Linstrom/202-447-8511
Rural Development/Fred Hines/202-447-9105
State and Local Government Programs/J. Norman Reid/202-447-8874
Transportation/William Gallimore/202-447-8487
Water Policy/Richard Magleby/202-447-2667
Weather/Bill Branner/202-447-7180
Manpower & Employment/Robert Coltrane/ 202-447-8621

Non-Farm Credit/Jim Mikesell/202-447-4215
Population/Calvin Beale/202-447-8200

Office of Situation Reports
Agricultural Exports/Stephen Milmoe/202-447-8054
Agricultural Finance/George Amols/202-447-7340
Farm Real Estate Market Developments/
  Gene Wunderlich/202-447-9179
Inputs/Theodore Eichers/202-447-7340
Cotton and Wool Situation/Keith Collins/202-447-8776
Dairy Situation/Clifford Carman/202-447-8636
Fats and Oils Situation/Sam Evans/202-447-8444
Feed Situation/Larry Van Meir/202-447-8444
Fertilizer Situation/Paul Andrilenas/202-447-7340

Fruit Situation/Ben Huang/202-447-7290
Livestock and Meat Situation/Ron Gustafson/202-447-8636
Poultry and Egg Situation/Leland Southard/202-447-8636
Rice Situation/Barbara Claffey/202-447-8444
Sugar and Sweetener Situation/Robert Barry/202-447-7290
Tobacco Situation/Verner Grise/202-447-8776
Vegetable Situation/Michael Stallmacher/202-447-7290
Wheat Situation (rye included)/Allen Schienbein/202-447-8776
World Agricultural Situation/Cecil Davison/202-447-8054

Major Sources of Information

Agricultural Abstracts
A free newsletter entitled *Economic Research Service Abstracts* describes all ERS publications, their price and how to obtain the publication you select. To be included on the mailing list send your name and address to EMS Information, U.S. Department of Agriculture, Room 4039-S, Washington, DC 20250.

Agricultural Estimates and Forecasts
To assist farmers and associated agriculture businesses and organizations to formulate reliable and objective forecasts, the Statistical Reporting Service publishes, at scheduled times, reports and forecasts. The information provides current data of agricultural business transactions in each state and nationally. For a listing of State Statistical Offices and more information, contact: Administrator, Statistical Reporting Service, U.S. Department of Agriculture, Washington, DC 20250.

Agricultural Research and Technical Expertise
A large staff administers a basic, applied and developmental research program in areas which include pesticides, radiological safety, crop production, plant genetics and breeding, plant introduction and narcotics, plant physiology, crop protection, pest and insect control, plant pathology and nematology, weed science, uses of farm products, processing animal products, soil fertility and plant nutrition, aerospace technology, and livestock and veterinary sciences. For expertise on a specific topic, contact: Agricultural Research Service, USDA, Room 302-A, Administration Building, Washington, DC 20250/202-447-3656.

Agricultural Statistics
Contact specific economists identified under "Statistics Reporting Service" in this section. Room 5829-S, USDA, Washington, DC 20250/202-447-4021.

Agriculture Reference Publications
USDA produces many well respected technical and professional publications for the agricultural and agribusiness community, as well as the general public. Each agency is responsible for publishing its own research reports and informational materials. A free publication list may be obtained by writing each agency directly; by writing for a copy of USDA Fact Book 1984; or by contacting the Government and Publications Office, USDA, Washington, DC 20584/202-447-3298. Documents may be ordered directly from the U.S. Government Printing Office, Washington, D.C. 20402/202-783-3238. Some popular publications are:

Economic Research Service
USDA, Washington, DC 20402/202-447-7255.

Crop Reporting Board Reports, estimates production, stocks, inventories, disposition, utilization and prices of agricultural commodities. (free) Crop Reporting Board, USDA, Rm 5829-S Wash. D.C. 20250/202-447-4021

Outlook and Situation, provides economic analysis of major crops, livestock, dairy and poultry products. Supply, demand, use, trade and prices are discussed. ($8.00 for four quarterly issues)

Foreign Agricultural Trade of the United States, a bimonthly statistical report on farm exports and imports. ($19.00)

Farmline, Written for the general audience.This periodical focuses on farm trends and developments ($16.00)

Human Nutrition Information Service,
USDA, Hyattsville, MD 20782/202-783-3238.

Food Consumption: Households in the U.S. reported by geographical region; these reports provide detailed information on the amount of food purchased and money spent on food purchases per week per household. The survey information is classified by size of family income and whether the family is urban or rural. ($8.50 per report)

Food Commonly Eaten By Individuals: Reports food intake of 200 commonly consumed foods and food groups by men, women, and children of various age groups. Amount per day per meal is reported. ($10.00)

Composition of Foods: This is a series of handbooks, reporting the raw, processed and prepared content of foods. Prices vary per handbook.

Dairy and Eggs Products $7.00
Spices and Herbs $6.50
Baby Foods $8.00
Fats and Herbs $6.50
Poultry Products $9.50
Soups, Sauces, and Gravies $8.00
Sausages and Luncheon Meats $6.00
Breakfast Cereals $7.00
Fruits and Fruit Juices $9.00

Agricultural Marketing Service Reports
USDA, Washington, DC 20250/202-447-5115

AMS Food Purchases, free, issued weekly and quarterly. Reports purchases by the AMS of commodities used in school lunch and other domestic feeding programs.

Facts About: Instant Market News, free. Reports background information on market trading and provides dial-a-market telephone numbers for instant Federal-State market news on various commodities.

Marketing Order Actions, weekly. Describes actions and proposals declared under Federal Marketing orders for fruits, vegetables and specialty crops.

Market News Reports (see separate entry)

Periodicals and Annuals Available from USDA
(Available from Government Printing Office.)

Agricultural Economics Research, $8.00 quarterly. Contains technical articles on methods and findings of agriculture research, including reports on work in progress and articles about new research interests. Each issue contains a book review section.

Agricultural Research, ten issues a year. Reports results of research by Agricultural Research Service scientists.

Extension Review, published quarterly. $12.00. Discusses Extension Service activities at Federal, State and county levels.

Farmer Cooperatives, published monthly. $21.00. Free to cooperative members. Discusses ACS technical assistance and research projects, discusses current issues and reports significant actions of farmer cooperatives across the country.

FGIS UPDATE, free, every other month. Summarizes important activities of the Federal Grain Inspection Service.

Food and Nutrition, $7.00. (single copies @ $2.50) Free to professional agencies and associated members working to further disseminate food and nutrition information. Reports on the Federal Food Assistance Programs.

Food News for Consumers, $7.00. Published by the Food Safety and Inspection Service, USDA.

National Food Review, quarterly, $8.50. Objective, in-depth articles written for economists, nutritionists, educators, consumer advisors, food industry representatives and other professionals in the food economics industry.

Soil and Water Conservation News, $18.00. Free distribution to professionals and organized cooperators of the conservation movement. Presents articles about national programs for conserving and developing land and water resources, promoting rural economic development, developing recreation resources, and improving environmental quality on private land in urban and rural areas.

Weekly Weather and Crop Bulletin, $25.00. Summarizes weather and its effects on crops for the preceding week. Gives weather and farm progress for all states.

Annual Summaries

Agricultural Statistics, a statistical report, revised annually, containing current and historical agricultural data.

Commodity Credit Corporation Charts, free, summarizes financial and program data for preceding fiscal year.

Handbook of Agricultural Charts, key factors in the economic situation and agricultural outlook are examined, using charts and data.

Report of the President of the Commodity Credit Corporation, free distribution to members of Congress. A report authorized by Congress covering operations and financial conditions of the CCC.

Report on Participation in ASCS County Programs and Operations by Racial Groups, free upon request.

U.S. Timber Production, Trade, Consumption and Price Statistics, 1950–1981, free. Statistical information is presented on the production, trade, consumption, and price of timber products in the U.S.

Animal and Plant Health Publications
Technical reports and publications of interest to animal dealers, farmers, travel agents, animal and plant professionals, and pet owners are available free of charge from the Animal and Plant Health Inspection Service. A free publications listing is also available. Materials of interest to the general public include:

Travelers' Tips, October 1983. For the general public, particularly overseas travelers. Lists what food, plant, and animal products can and cannot be brought into the United States from foreign countries. Also available in Spanish, Italian and Japanese.

Don't Move Gypsy Moth, August 1983. For the general public, particularly those moving out of a gypsy-moth infested area. Describes regulations governing the movement of outdoor household articles (OHA) that may harbor gypsy moth and ways to inspect these OHA's. Color illustrations and check list.

Importing a Pet Bird, August 1984. For the general public. Describes rules for bringing in a pet bird, identifies other government agencies involved, and lists addresses of ports where pet birds may enter. Also discusses fees, quarantine period and special exceptions.

Plant Protection and Quarantine, June 1983. For the general public. Describes overall Plant Protection and Quarantine missions, specific programs, and the people who carry them out.

Veterinary Services: Protecting America's Animal Health, September 1982. For farmers and the general public. Provides basic information on the activities and programs of APHIS' Veterinary Services.

Careers for Veterinarians, December 1979. Offers descriptions of positions for veterinarians in USDA. Particularly useful for recruiting college students.

The Animal Welfare Act, How it Protects Your Dog and Cat, November 1979. For the general public. Leaflet on how the law provides for the humane handling, shipping, care, and treatment of dogs, cats and other warm-blooded animals.

Licensing and Registration Under the Animal Welfare Act, January 1980. Tells those who buy or sell animals, exhibit them to the public, or use them in experiments whether or not their activities are regulated by the Animal Welfare Act.

Pets—They Need Proper Care to Travel by Air, August 1983. Tells shippers, airlines, veterinarians, and others involved in preparing and consigning animals for shipment what the Animal Welfare Act requires.

Contact: USDA, APHIS, Information Division, 6505 Belcrest Rd., Rm. 732, Hyattsville, MD 20782/301-436-7776.

Animal Diseases
See "Livestock and Veterinary Sciences."

Animal Products Production
Research is conducted on improving efficiency through plant layout, work methods, equipment design, etc. for livestock markets, commercial feedlots, meatpacking plants, boning plants, poultry plants, egg-packing plants, cheese making and ice cream plants. Contact: Marketing Facilities Branch AMS, Room 130, Building 307, BARC-East, Beltsville, MD 20705/301-344-2800.

Aquaculture
Professional expertise and services are available to those interested in controlled cultivation and harvesting of aquatic animals and plants. Contact: Office of Aquaculture Coordination and Development, S and E, USDA, Room 235W, Wash DC 20250/202-447-7223.

Bees and Beekeeping
Production and price statistics are available. See "Agricultural Statistics" in this section. Technical expertise and advice are available from Bee Breeding and Stock Center, Rte. 3, Box 82B, Ben Hur Rd., Baton Rouge, Louisiana 70820/504-766-6064.

Bibliographies
The National Agricultural Library has free bibliographies available on a wide variety of subjects. Contact the library and request a listing of their Quick Bibliography Series. See "Library."

Brides Information Package
A free package, entitled "Packet for the Bride," is available to new homemakers. The packet consists of an assortment of home and garden bulletins relating to budgeting, consumer tips, cooking, etc. Packets are available from your congressman.

Bull Sperm
For those interested in buying or selling bull semen, information is available from your local county extension agent (see "Extension Service" in this section) or from Animal Science Institute, Agricultural Research Center, 217 B-200 BA E., Beltsville, MD 20705/301-344-3431.

Children and Teenager Loans
Loans are available to children from 10 to 21 years old for projects such as small crop growing, livestock farming, roadside stands, and custom work. See "Best of Government Freebies."

College Courses
The USDA Graduate School offers college courses on nonagricultural subjects and at reasonable prices. The school does not grant degrees; some lectures are available on film, videotape and in manuscript form. Contact: Information Office, USDA Graduate School, Capital Gallery Building, 600 Maryland Ave. S.W., Room 129, Washington, DC 20024/202-447-4419.

Coloring Books
Free coloring books show nutritional value of foods. Contact: Public Information, Food and Nutrition Service, 3101 Park Center Drive, Alexandria, VA 22302/703-756-3284.

Compost and Sludge
For technical assistance on the production and use of compost and sludge, contact: Biological Waste Management and Organic Resources Labs, Building 007, Room 124 BARC-W., Beltsville, MD 20705/301-344-3163.

Computerized Data Bases
The following databases are maintained by the Department of Agriculture.

Agricultural Commodities Data Base
T-DAM is a time series data base of agricultural commodities and macroeconomic data. The system has 77 files with topics ranging from Australian Livestock, Grain and Oilseed to U.S. Dairy Production. International data, food programs, crop information and import/export data are also included. Searches and printouts are available free of charge. Contact: USDA/ERS, Data Resource Center, 500 12th Street, S.W., Room 147, Washington, DC 20250/202-447-4382.

Agricultural Cooperative Extension Service Education Data Base
The Computerized Management Network for Agricultural Cooperative Extension Service Education (CMN) is a software system of more than 60 interactive computer programs in areas such as: utilities; information retrieval; human nutrition and health; home, livestock, farm, and crop management; machinery and equipment; finance and accounting; taxes and estate planning; and much more. It was developed to help farmers, businessmen, consumers and families make decisions. The system is designed to be used by non-computer oriented individuals.

Anyone can get access to CMN through the numerous Cooperative Extension Service offices nationwide. Individuals and organizations can also subscribe to CMN and then use their computer terminal (including microcomputers) to access the systems via local or toll-free telephone lines. A minimum monthly usage fee of $25.00 is charged to everyone. The median cost is approximately $2.00 per analysis. Contact: Computerized Management Network, Plaza 1, Bldg D, Extension Division, Virginia Polytechnic Institute, Blacksburg, VA 24061/703-961-5184 OR your local Cooperative Extension Service listed in the telephone book under "U.S. Government, U.S. Department of Agriculture."

Agricultural Diseases Data Base
The Emergency Program Information Center (EPIC) maintains a computerized data base with bibliographic information for all literature stored on microfilm by the center. The EPIC Data Bank consists of worldwide literature covering diseases of. livestock and poultry exotic to the United States.

Complete services, including bibliographic printouts and copies of cited articles, are primarily for personnel working in federal and cooperating state animal disease-control and eradication programs. Users outside APHIS are generally only provided citations; however, requests are handled on an individual basis. The Center has prepared standard bibliographies on 17 different topics. These are available to the general public. The EPIC Brucellosis file is included in the AGRICOLA system. Contact: Technical Support Staff, Emergency Programs Information Center Data Bank, Veterinary Services, APHIS, USDA, Federal Building, 6505 Belcrest Road, Hyattsville, MD 20782/301-436-8087.

Agriculture and Home Management On-Line Network
AGNET is an on-line information delivery network designed to be used by people with no previous knowledge of computers. The system can assist users in three general areas of application: 1) problem-solving for agricultural and home management questions; 2) retrieving timely information about market conditions, trends, USDA reports, consumer concerns, etc; and 3) facilitating communication via electronic mail and conferencing service. AGNET can be accessed via computer terminals, microcomputers, communicating word processors and some telex machines. AGNET is available to the general public on a subscription basis. Contact: AGNET, University of Nebraska, Lincoln, NE 68583-0713/402-472-1892.

Crop and Livestock Data Base
Crop and livestock production and demand data and forecasts can be obtained through private timesharing services. Contact: Secretary of Crop Reporting Board, Room 5809, USDA, Washington, DC 20250/202-447-2130.

Electric Borrowers Operations Data Base
The Rural Electrification Administration (REA) Data Bases contains financial and statistical information about the operations of approximately 2,160 REA electric borrowers individually and as a group. The following information can be retrieved about each borrower: outstanding loans; REA debit service repayments; balance sheet items; revenue and expense items; operating statements, and sales statistics. REA maintains a variety of files containing information, ranging from loan statistics to accounting data. Searches and printouts are available free of charge. Tapes can be purchased for a cost-recovery fee. Hard copy reports are also available. Contact: Statistics and Data Processing Division, Rural Electrification Administration, U.S. Department of Agriculture, Washington, DC 20250/202-382-8943.

Farm Market News Data Base
The U.S. Department of Agriculture and the Public Broadcasting Service (PBS) have begun a program, Farm Market Infodata Service (FMIS), to provide up-to-the-minute farm market news via PBS's television captioning system. FMIS is carried on PBS Channel 21, and it is exactly the same information that appears on the Agricultural Market News Service teletype circuits. Over 700 reports are broadcast daily about the supply, demand, prices and movement of agricultural products. Commodities include livestock, poul-

try, grain, fruit, vegetables, tobacco, cotton and subdivisions.

Approximately 700 reports are added daily. In areas where FMIS is broadcast, you can gain access by using a television decoder (generally costs less than $300.00) to unscramble the captioned news. Check to see if it's now in your area. Contact: USDA/AMS, Room 0092, 14th and Independence Avenue, S.W., Washington, DC 20250/202-447-7047; your state or regional USDA Office; or your local PBS television station.

Food and Nutrition Data Base
The Food and Nutrition Information Center (FNIC) is a bibliographic data base covering all aspects of current developments in human nutrition, food and related disciplines, including: food service management, consumer economics, food and nutrition programs, nutrition and health education, food composition, food storage, physiology of human nutrition, diet and diet-related diseases, and home economics. The Center will conduct searches, free of charge, for state and local school districts, selected colleges and universities and some non-profit organizations. It can be accessed through DIALOG, SDC, BRS, and, if eligible, the Food and Nutrition Information Center. Contact: Food and Nutrition Information Center, National Agricultural Library Bldg., Room 304, Beltsville, MD 20705/301-344-3719.

Food and Nutrition Data Base-Management and Information
The Management and Information Division: Food and Nutrition Service system contains national, regional and state data on the following programs: food stamps, childcare, school lunch and breakfast programs, WIC (Women, Infants and Children); and nutrition is provided about number and type of meals served; federal costs; race, sex, age, income and employment history of participants; attendance patterns and number of people served; and available nutrition courses, workshops and seminars.

Staff will do searches free of charge and provide a printout (possible charge for lengthy run). The Food and Nutrition Service publishes a Monthly Summary (40–50 pages) about new additions to its data base. Contact: Food & Nutrition Service, USDA, 3101 Park Center Drive, Alexandria, VA 22302/703-756-3100.

General Agriculture Data Base (AGRICOLA)
The USDA's AGRICOLA data base consists of indexes to general agriculture, food and nutrition and agricultural economics information and is available for free from the National Agricultural Library. See "Library" this section.

National Recreation Data Base
Recreation Information Management (RIM) contains data about every National Forest recreation site—in the U.S. The following data can be retrieved for each site: name, location, capacity, size; description of environment and facilities; hours of use; number of visitors; dates when area is least populated; and travel directions for reaching site.

All services and materials are free. Most of the RIM data is available in the form of reports, booklets, books and periodicals. Special searches will be done if material does not already exist in hard copy. Contact: U.S. Department of Agriculture, Forest Service, Recreation Management Staff, P.O. Box 2417, Washington, DC 20013/202-447-4313.

Plant Pest Data Base
The Cooperative National Plant Pest Survey and Detection Program (CNPPDP) maintains a data base of pest data, including information about insects, weeds, plant diseases and nematodes. Thirty-eight states collect data and then transmit it to USDA's National Plant Pest Quarantine Office (PPQ) in Maryland. PPQ stores and processes the data, and produces a weekly summary, by crop and county, for each state. Data elements stored include observation date, state, county, crop, crop growth stage, pest, pest life stage, abundance or incidence, damage or severity, and survey and detection method.

Searches, printouts, and summaries are generally available free from participating states. Decisions on the type and format of information released are made by the particular state. Check with the State's Department of Agriculture (PPQ office) or the state's Land Grant University. Contact: Survey Coordinator, PPQ/APHIS/USDA, Federal Building, Room 654, Hyattsville, MD 20782/301-436-6404.

Soils Series Data Base
Soils Information Retrieval Systems (SIRS) provides interactive data retrieval of soils series data. The data is compiled from the Department of Agriculture's Soil Conservation Service's (SCS) reports on the characteristics and interpretive properties of all soils in the United States. Examples of soil information include use restrictions, potential habitat, description of soil and much more. Information is organized only by soil series. The data base can be accessed directly by remote terminal.

Direct access is available to ETIS subscribers for $100.00 a year, plus $90.00 per hour of connect time. Anyone can become an ETIS subcriber and, thereby, also gain access to three other data bases maintained by ETIS.

ETIS will conduct searches for non-subscribers. A cost-recovery fee based on $110.00 per hour computer time, is charged. The average search generally takes 10 minutes. Contact: U.S. Army Corps of Engineers, ETIS Support Center, 909

West Nevada Street, Urbana, IL 61801/312-333-1369.

Wildland Fire-Bibliographic Data Base

FIREBASE is a collection of bibliographic citations and abstracts of wildland fire-related information. The data base is international in scope and topics include: wildland fire detection, prevention and suppression; fire management analysis, planning and training; and fire statistics, indexes and hazards. The data base contains citations for both the general public and the scientific and technical community. Searches and print-outs are available free of charge. Contact: FIREBASE Operations, USDA Forest Service, Boise Interagency Fire Center, 3905 Vista Avenue, Boise, ID 83705/208-334-9457.

World Agricultural Trade Data Base

The Foreign Agricultural Service (FAS) maintains a data base of U.S. and selected foreign agricultural trade information. The data base contains information from a variety of systems, including United Nations trade tapes and trade data from the U.S. Department of Commerce's agricultural census. Examples of retrievable information include: long-term U.S. export-by-destination; foreign company import and export data; foreign production, supply and distribution of agricultural products; and other export marketing information.

Searches and print-outs are provided on a cost-recovery basis. Staff prefers request by phone so that they can discuss your needs and thereby supply you with appropriate information. Contact; Chief, Trade and Marketing Branch, Foreign Agricultural Service, U.S. Department of Agriculture, 202-382-1295.

Conferences

A free four-day conference is held each fall in Washington, DC covering agricultural supplies, demand for farm products, food prices, land use, and family characteristics. Contact: World Agricultural Outlook Board, USDA, Room 5143 So., Wash DC 20250/202-447-5447.

Conservation

There is a wide range of loan and grant programs which support agricultural conservation. See "Grants" and "Loans and Loan Guarantees" in this section.

Consumer Complaints

If you have a complaint concerning a problem with any meat or poultry product, action can be taken by contacting: FSIS, Meatborne Hazard Control Center, Epidemiology Branch, USDA, BARC-E, Building 322, Beltsville, MD 20705/301-344-2003.

Consumer Publications

Family Fare: A Guide to Good Nutrition. 91 pp.	$5.50
Nutritive Value of Foods. 34 pp.	4.50
Conserving the Nutritive Values in Foods. 11 pp.	2.25
Vegetables in Family Meals: A Guide for Consumers. 31 pp.	3.75
Poultry in Family Meals: A Guide for Consumers. 36 pp.	4.25
Beef and Veal in Family Meals: A Guide for Consumers. 38 pp.	4.25
Lamb in Family Meals: A Guide for Consumers. 22 pp.	3.00
Cereals and Pasta in Family Meals: A Guide for Consumers. 37 pp.	4.25
Pork in Family Meals: A Guide for Consumers. 33 pp.	4.25
Apples in Appealing Ways. 20 pp.	2.75
Keeping Food Safe to Eat: A Guide for Homemakers. 10 pp.	2.25
Your Money's Worth in Foods. 27 pp.	3.50
Breads, Cakes, and Pies in Family Meals: A Guide for Consumers. 38 pp.	4.25
Soybeans in Family Meals. 26 pp.	3.50
FOOD: Sections on Food Guides, Breakfasts, Snacks; 60 recipes. 65 pp.	6.00
Nutrition and Your Health: Dietary Guidelines for Americans. 20 pp.	2.25
Sodium Content of Your Food. 43 pp.	4.25
Calories and Weight: The USDA Pocket Guide. 80 pp.	3.75
Nutrition Labeling—Tools for Its Use. 57 pp.	4.75
Ideas for Better Eating. 30 pp.	4.00
The Hassle-Free Guide to a Better Diet. 2 pp.	2.25

These Human Nutrition Information Service publications are available for sale from the Superintendent of Documents, U.S. Government Printing Office, Washington, DC 20402/202-783-3238.

Cooperative Development

USDA will assist any group interested in starting or developing agcooperatives, and upon request will work with cooperatives in solving any existing organizational, operational, or management problems. They will also assist cooperatives in expanding export markets. Contact: Agricultural Cooperative Service, USDA, Washington, DC 20250/202-447-8353 or your Local Extension Agent.

Cooperative Forest Fire Control

The State and Federal government cooperate to protect non-federal timberland, potential timberland and certain nonforested watershed lands and other rural lands from serious fire damage. For information contact: A regional forester or area director of the USDA Forest Service or Cooperative Fire Protection Staff, Forest Service, USDA, P. O. Box 2417, Washington, DC 20013/202-235-8039.

Cooperative Forest Insect and Disease Management
In order to reduce loss and damage to forests and lands by forest insects and diseases; USDA provides technical and financial assistance in prevention, detection, evaluation and suppression of forest insect and disease outbreaks on State or private lands. Contact: State Foresters or area director of the U.S. Forest Service.

Cooperative Membership Discrimination
If you are an agricultural producer and feel you have been discriminated against because of your membership in a cooperative, the Agricultural Marketing Service will arrange for a hearing and a field investigation by USDA's Office of Inspector General. Contact: Agricultural Marketing Service, USDA, Washington, DC 20250/202-447-5115.

Daily Commodity Prices
With the help of AT&T, USDA offers a wire service of daily market quotations on agricultural products. Contact: AMS, Communications and Operations Branch, USDA, Room 0092, S Building, Washington, DC 20250/202-447-7047.

Department of Agriculture Yearbook
Each year the U.S. Department of Agriculture publishes a yearbook. This lengthy monograph is devoted to a theme associated with farming, agriculture or nature. The past three years topics have been *Using Our Natural Resources—1983, Food From Farm to Table—1982* and *Will There Be Enough Food?—1981.* Available from the Superintendent of Documents, Government Printing Office, Washington, DC 20402/202-783-3238 at a price that varies from year to year, or free from your Congressman (500 copies) or Senator (800 copies) as long as the supply lasts. Contact: Government and Publications Office, U.S. Department of Agriculture, Washington, DC 20250/202-447-3298.

Direct Payments

The programs described below are those that provide financial assistance directly to individuals, private firms and other private institutions to encourage or subsidize a particular activity.

Agricultural Conservation Program
Objectives: Control of erosion and sedimentation, encourage voluntary compliance with Federal and State requirements to solve point and non-point source pollution, achieve priorities in the National Environmental Policy Act, improve water quality, encourage energy conservation measures, and assure a continued supply of necessary food and fiber for a strong and healthy people and economy.
Eligibility: Any person who as owner, landlord, tenant, or sharecropper on a farm or ranch, including associated groups, bears a part of the cost of an approved conservation practice is eligible to apply for cost-share assistance.
Range of Financial Assistance: $3 to $10,000.
Contact: Conservation and Environmental Protection Division, Agricultural Stabilization and Conservation Service, Department of Agriculture, P.O. Box 2415, Washington, DC 20013/202-447-6221.

Accelerated Cooperative Assistance for Forest Programs on Certain Lands Adjacent to the Boundary Waters Canoe Area
Objectives: To provide a system of grants in cooperation with the State of Minnesota, Division of Forestry, for the accelerated management of forest resources on State, county, and private lands adjacent to the Boundary Waters Canoe Area Wilderness.
Eligibility: Director, Minnesota Division of Forestry.
Range of Financial Assistance: Not applicable.
Contact: Deputy Chief, State and Private Forestry, Forest Service, Department of Agriculture, P.O. Box 2417, Washington, DC 20013/202-382-8406.

Commodity Purchases (Price Supports)
Objectives: To improve and stabilize farm income, to assist in bringing about a better balance between supply and demand of the commodities, and to assist farmers in the orderly marketing of their crops.
Eligibility: An owner, landlord, tenant, or sharecropper on a farm that has a history of producing the eligible commodities, and meets program requirements as announced by the Secretary.
Range of Financial Assistance: $50 to $50,000.
Contact: Price Support and Loan Division, Agricultural Stabilization and Conservation Service, Department of Agriculture, P.O. Box 2415, Washington, DC 20013/202-447-8480.

Cotton Production Stabilization
Objectives: To attract the cotton production that is needed to meet domestic and foreign demand for fiber, to protect income for farmers, and to assure adequate supplies at fair and reasonable prices.
Eligibility: An owner, landlord, tenant, or sharecropper on a farm.
Range of Financial Assistance: $3 to $50,000.
Contact: Analysis Division, Agricultural Stabilization and Conservation Service, P.O. Box 2415, Department of Agriculture, Washington, DC 20013/202-447-7951.

Dairy Indemnity
Objectives: To indemnify dairy farmers and manufacturers of dairy products who are directed to remove their milk, milk cows or dairy products from commercial markets because of contamina-

tion by residues of pesticides resulting from no misaction on the part of the dairy farmer or the manufacturer of the dairy product.

Eligibility: Dairy farmers.

Range of Financial Assistance: $1,042 to $6,105.

Contact: Emergency and Indemnity Programs Division, Agricultural Stabilization and Conservation Service, Department of Agriculture, P.O. Box 2415, Washington, DC 20013/202-447-7997.

Emergency Conservation Program

Objectives: To enable farmers to perform emergency conservation measures to control wind erosion on farmlands, or to rehabilitate farmlands damaged by wind erosion, floods, hurricanes or other natural disasters and to carry out emergency water conservation or water enhancing measures during periods of severe drought.

Eligibility: Any person who as owner, landlord, tenant, or sharecropper on a farm or ranch, including associated groups, bears a part of the cost of an approved conservation practice in a disaster area, is eligible to apply for cost-share conservation assistance.

Range of Financial Assistance: $300 to $63,203.

Contact: Conservation and Environmental Protection Division, Agricultural Stabilization and Conservation Service, Department of Agriculture, P.O. Box 2415, Washington, DC 20013/202-447-6221.

Feed Grain Production Stabilization

Objectives: To attract the production needed to meet domestic and foreign demand, to protect income for farmers, and to assure adequate supplies at fair and reasonable prices.

Eligibility: An owner, landlord, tenant, or sharecropper on a farm where the commodity is planted.

Range of Financial Assistance: $3 to $50,000.

Contact: Production Adjustment Division, Agricultural Stabilization and Conservation Service, Department of Agriculture, P.O. Box 2415, Washington, DC 20013/202-447-7633.

Federal-State Marketing Improvement Program

Objectives: To solve marketing problems at the State and local level through pilot marketing service projects conducted by States.

Eligibility: State Department of Agriculture, or other appropriate State agencies.

Range of Financial Assistance: $1,000 to $75,000.

Contact: Staff Officer, Federal-State Marketing Improvement Program, Agricultural Marketing Service, Department of Agriculture, Washington, DC 20250/202-447-2704.

Food Distribution Program Commodities on Indian Reservations

Objectives: To improve the diets of needy persons in households on or near Indian reserva-

tions and to increase the market for domestically produced foods acquired under surplus removal or price support operations.

Eligibility: State agencies designated by the Governor, legislature, or other authority may receive and distribute donated foods.

Range of Financial Assistance: Not applicable.

Contact: Director, Food Distribution Division, Food and Nutrition Service, Department of Agriculture, Alexandria, VA 22302/703-756-3660.

Food Stamps

Objectives: To improve diets of low-income households by supplementing their food purchasing ability. Households receive a free coupon allotment which varies according to household size. The coupons may be used in participating retail stores to buy any food for human consumption and garden seeds and plants to produce food for personal consumption of eligible households.

Eligibility: The state or U.S. territory agency responsible for federally aided public assistance programs submits requests for the program to USDA's Food and Nutrition Service on behalf of local political subdivisions.

Range of Financial Assistance: Average approximately $39.32 per month per person.

Contact: Deputy Administrator, Family Nutrition Programs, Food and Nutrition Service, Department of Agriculture, Alexandria, VA 22302/703-756-3024.

Forestry Incentives Program

Objectives: To bring private non-industrial forest land under intensified management; to increase timber production; to assure adequate supplies of timber; and to enhance other forest resources through a combination of public and private investments on the most productive sites on eligible individual or consolidated ownerships of efficient size and operation.

Eligibility: A private individual, group, association, Indian Tribe or other native group, corporation (except corporations whose stocks are publicly traded) or other legal entity which owns "nonindustrial" private forest lands capable of producing industrial wood crops is eligible to apply for costsharing assistance. Cost-share agreements are limited to eligible ownerships of land of not more than 1000 acres except by special approval. This program is available to eligible landowners in the U.S. or any commonwealth, territory or possession of the U.S.

Range of Financial Assistance: $3 to $10,000.

Contact: Conservation and Environmental Protection Division, Agricultural Stabilization and Conservation Service, Department of Agriculture, P.O. Box 2415, Washington, DC 20013/202-447-6221.

Grain Reserve Program

Objectives: To insulate sufficient quantities of grain from the market to increase price to farmers.

To improve and stabilize farm income and to assist farmers in the orderly marketing of their crops.

Eligibility: All producers or approved cooperatives having a Commodity Credit Corporation loan on wheat, rice, corn, barley, oats, or sorghum from an authorized crop year who provide storage through loan maturity.

Range of Financial Assistance: $25 to $50,000.

Contact: Cotton, Grain and Rice Support Division, Agricultural Stabilization and Conservation Service, Department of Agriculture, P.O. Box 2415, Washington, DC 20013/202-382-8480.

Great Plains Conservation

Objectives: To conserve and develop the Great Plains soil and water resources by providing technical and financial assistance to farmers, ranchers, and others in planning and implementing conservation practices.

Eligibility: Applicant must have control of the land for a period of the contract running from a minimum of three years to a maximum of ten years.

Range of Financial Assistance: Up to $35,000.

Contact: Chief, Soil Conservation Service, Department of Agriculture, P.O. Box 2890, Washington, DC 20013/202-447-7145.

Morrill-Nelson Funds for Food and Agricultural Higher Education

Objectives: Support of instruction in the Food and Agricultural Sciences.

Eligibility: States, in which land-grant colleges are located, are eligible for funds.

Range of Financial Assistance: $50,000 to each State.

Contact: Higher Education Programs, Agricultural Research Service, US Department of Agriculture, 14th & Independence Ave. SW, Washington, DC 20250/202-447-7854.

National Wool Act Payments

Objectives: To encourage increased domestic production of wool at prices fair to both producers and consumers in a way that has the least adverse effect on domestic and foreign trade and to encourage producers to improve the quality and marketing of their wool and mohair.

Eligibility: Any person who owns sheep or lambs for 30 days or more and sells shorn wool or unshorn lambs during the marketing year. Any person who owns angora goats for 30 days or more and sells mohair produced from them.

Range of Financial Assistance: $5 to $240,940.

Contact: Emergency Operations and Livestock Programs Division, Agricultural Stabilization and Conservation Service, Department of Agriculture, P.O. Box 2415, Washington, DC 20013/202-447-7674.

Nutrition Assistance for Puerto Rico

Objectives: To provide a nutritionally adequate diet to needy persons residing in the Commonwealth of Puerto Rico.

Eligibility: The commonwealth of Puerto Rico alone is eligible.

Range of Financial Assistance: The average of financial assistance is $40.07.

Contact: Deputy Administrator, Family Nutrition Programs, Food and Nutrition Service, Department of Agriculture, Alexandria, VA 22303/703-756-3024.

Plant and Animal Disease and Pest Control

Objectives: To protecct US agriculture from economically injurious plant and animal diseases and pests, to insure the humane care and handling of all designated warm-blooded animals, and to insure the safety and potency of veterinary biologics.

Eligibility: State, local and US Territorial government agencies, nonprofit institutions of higher education, and nonprofit associations or organizations requiring Federal support to eradicate, control or assess the status of injurious plant and animal diseases and pests that are a threat to regional or national agriculture and conduct related demonstration projects.

Range of Financial Assistance: Not applicable.

Contact: Budget and Accounting Division, Animal and Plant Health Inspection Service, US Department of Agriculture, Hyattsville, MD 20782/301-436-8635.

Rice Production Stabilization

Objectives: To provide the production needed to meet domestic and foreign demand, to protect income for farmers, and to assure adequate supplies at fair and reasonable prices.

Eligibility: Owner, Landlord, tenant, or sharecropper on a farm where the commodity is planted that meets program requirements as announced by the Secretary.

Range of Financial Assistance: $3 to $50,000.

Contact: Analysis Division, Agricultural Stabilization and Conservation Service, Department of Agriculture, P.O. Box 2415, Washington, DC 20013/202-447-5954.

Rural Abandoned Mine Program

Objectives: To protect people and the environment from the adverse effects of past coal mining practices and to promote the development of soil and water resources of unreclaimed mine lands.

Eligibility: Persons, groups or units of government who own or control the surface or water rights of abandoned coal land or lands and water affected by coal mining practices before August 3, 1977.

Range of Financial Assistance: $1,400 to $303,000.

Contact: Soil Conservation Service, Deputy Chief, State and Local Operations Division, P.O. Box 2890, Washington, DC 20013/202-447-7145.

Rural Clean Water Program

Objectives: To improve water quality in approved project areas in the most cost effective manner, to assist agricultural landowners to reduce agricultural nonpoint source water pollutants; and to develop and test programs, policies, and procedures for controlling agricultural nonpoint source pollution.

Eligibility: RCWP is only applicable to privately owned agricultural lands in approved project areas.

Range of Financial Assistance: Up to $50,000.

Contact: Conservation and Environmental Protection Divsion, Agricultural Stabilization and Conservation Service, Department of Agriculture, P.O. Box 2415, Washington, DC 20013/202-447-6221.

Rural Rental Assistance Payments

Objectives: To reduce the rents paid by low-income families occupying eligible Rural Rental Housing (RRH), Rural Cooperative Housing (RCH), and Farm Labor Housing (FLH) projects financed by the Farmers Home Administration.

Eligibility: The applicant must be the owner or plan to become the owner of an eligible FHA RRH, RH, or LH project operating on a limited profit or nonprofit basis.

Range of Financial Assistance: Not specified.

Contact: Administrator, Farmers Home Administration, Department of Agriculture, Washington, DC 20250/202-382-1604.

Temporary Emergency Food Assistance (Administrative Costs)

Objectives: To make funds available to States for storage and distribution costs incurred by nonprofit eligible recipient agencies in providing nutrition assistance to relieve situations of emergency and distress of needy persons.

Eligibility: Only those State agencies which actually receive the pertinent donated foods are eligible.

Range of Financial Assistance: $24,000 to $3,047,000.

Contact: Food Distribution Division, FNS, USDA, Room 502, Park Office Center 3101 Park Center Drive, Alexandria, VA 22302/703-756-3680.

Water Bank Program

Objectives: To conserve surface waters; preserve and improve migratory waterfowl habitat and wildlife resources; and secure other environmental benefits.

Eligibility: Landowners and operators of specified types of wetlands in designated important migratory waterfowl nesting, breeding and feeding areas.

Range of Financial Assistance: $8 to $65 per acre.

Contact: Conservation and Environmental Protection Division, Agricultural Stabilization and Conservation Service, Department of Agriculture, P.O. Box 2415, Washington, D.C. 20013/202-447-6221.

Wheat Production Stabilization

Objectives: To attract the production that is needed to meet domestic and foreign demand for food, to protect income for farmers, and to assure adequate supplies at fair and reasonable prices.

Eligibility: An owner, landlord, tenant or share-cropper on a farm where the commodity is planted.

Range of Financial Assistance: $3 to $50,000.

Contact: Analysis Division, Agricultural Stabilization and Conservation Service, Department of Agriculture, P.O. Box 2415, Washington, DC 20013/202-447-4146.

Electric Utility Systems

The USDA lends money to approximately 1,106 rural electric companies and maintains a staff which is knowledgeable on both operations and equipment. Contact: Assistant Administrator—Electric, Rural Electrification Administration, USDA, Room 4056, S Building, Washington, DC 20250/202-382-9547.

Emergency Assistance

There are a number of loan, grant, and direct payment programs available to those who need help in an emergency situation. See "Grants," "Direct Payments," and "Loans and Loan Guarantees" in this section.

Emergency Food

The USDA supplies surplus food to relief agencies. Contact: Commodity Credit Corporation, ASCS, USDA, Room 5714, S Building, Washington, DC 20250/202-447-4786.

Excess Food

The Commodity Credit Corporation also buys, stores, and disposes of commodities such as dry milk, wheat, rice and corn, which are acquired through price-support programs. The commodities are sent either overseas as donations or distributed to domestic food programs. Contact: Utilization Branch, Commodity Operations Division, Commodity Credit Corporation, ASCS Room 5764 S Building, USDA, Washington, DC 20250/202-477-5648. Also see "Food for Peace," "Loans," "Grants," and "Direct Payments" in this section.

Export Assistance for Agricultural Products

USDA's Foreign Agricultural Service offers private companies and cooperatives assistance in marketing their products overseas. These include 10–15 overseas food shows per year; a computerized Trade Opportunity Referral Service; and Contacts—a list of new products offered by U.S. companies; label testing; an export credit program; and an export incentive program. Contact: Export Programs Division, FAS, USDA Washington, DC 20250/202-447-6343.

Export Publications

The Foreign Agricultural Service issues various reports and publications for those with an interest in foreign trade:

Foreign Agriculture—a monthly magazine on world agricultural development ($14 per year U.S., $17.50 foreign) Contact: Superintendent of Documents, U.S. Government Printing Office, Washington, DC 20402/202-783-3283.

Export Briefs—a free weekly trade letter listing trade opportunities and foreign trade developments. Contact: Export Trade Services Division, FAS, Room 4945-S, USDA, Washington, DC 20250.

Foreign Agricultural Trade of the United States—a monthly statistical and analytical review of U.S. agricultural trade is free from the Information Division, Economics and Statistics Service, USDA, Washington, DC 20250.

Ocean Liner Cargo Service Directory—a reference of available ocean liner cargo services—free. Contact: Office of Transportation, Room 1405, Auditors Building, USDA, Washington, DC 20250.

The following publications are available free of charge from FAS Information Services, Room 5918-S, USDA, Washington, DC 20250/202-447-3448.

FAS Circulars-specialized commodity reports.
The Weekly Roundup of World Production and Trade— highlights current developments in international agriculture.
World Crop Production Report—monthly report of USDA production estimates for grain, cotton, and oilseeds in major countries and selected regions of the world.
Agricultural Trade Offices: One-Stop Service Overseas—Directory of U.S. agricultural trade offices and what they do to assist exporters of U.S. food and agricultural products.
The U.S. Farmer's Export Arm—Describes the services of the Foreign Agricultural Service.
Partners in Trade Promotion—Directory and description of the FAS market development cooperator program.
Agriculture's Emissaries Overseas—Directory and description of agricultural counselor/attache offices overseas.
Food and Agricultural Export Directory M-201—A

listing of export services and key contacts in the export business.
Commercial Export Financing: An Assist to Farm Product Sales—Describes programs of FAS' General Sales Manager aimed at helping exporters resolve financial problems.
FAS Reports—Press releases announcing potential sales opportunities resulting from the extension of CCC or P.L. 480 credits to foreign countries.

Export Specialist

Following is a list of phone numbers you can call to get help on various types of marketing problems. Call or write to Export Trade Services Division, FAS, USDA, Washington, DC 20250.

Export Trade Services Division

Director	202-447-6343
State-Trade Coordination	202-447-2423
Trade Exhibits and Sales Teams	202-447-3031
Agricultural Trade Offices	202-447-7789
Foreign Visitors	202-447-6725
Trade Opportunity Referral Service (TORS)	202-447-7103
New Products Testing	202-447-2423
Minority and Small Business Coordinator	202-447-3031
Office of Transportation International Transportation Services Room 1405 Auditors Bldg. Washington, DC 20250	202-447-7481
Dairy, Livestock, and Poultry- Marketing Deputy	202-447-3899
Grain and Feed- Marketing Deputy	202-447-4168
Horticultural and Tropical Products- Marketing Deputy	202-447-7931
Oilseeds and Products-Marketing Deputy	202-447-8809
Tobacco, Cotton, and Seeds- Marketing Deputy	202-447-6917

Exporting

A wide variety of assistance is available to exporters of food, livestock and other agricultural products. Information and services available include the following:

Reports on foreign agricultural production, trade and consumption for 200 farm commodities.
Test marketing of new products.
Marketing research.
Contribution to export promotion costs for new products.
Financing for customers.

Contact: Foreign Agricultural Service, USDA, 14th St. and Independence Ave. S.W., Washington, DC 20250/202-447-3448.

Extension Service

The USDA operates an extension program in 3,165 counties located in 50 states and the territories. The program provides education and information to communities on agriculture, family education, food and nutrition, community and rural development, natural resources and 4-H youth clubs. Information ranges from how to operate a better farm, create a better home, or build a better community to diseases of pets, plants and lawns, and is provided in person, by telephone, and by mail. For help in finding your local county agent, contact: Executive Officer, USDA/ES Room 340A Administration Building, Washington, DC 20250/202-447-4111.

Family Economics

A staff of experts researches such topics as the economic aspects of family living, family resources, economic problems of families, the relationship of family budget items to each other, the use of food, clothing and textiles, and the efficient management of money and time. Free publications are also available. Contact: Family Economics Research Group, ARS, 6505 Belcrest Rd., Federal Building, Room 442A, Hyattsville, MD 20782/301-436-8461.

Farmer Cooperatives

There are approximately 6,125 cooperatives in this country that primarily exist to aid in the purchasing of supplies or the marketing of products. Contact: Agricultural Cooperative Service, USDA, 201 14th St. S.W., Room 3300 Washington, DC 20250/202-447-8955.

Films

Motion pictures on a variety of agricultural subjects are available for loan through various State Extension Service film libraries. Contact: National Audio-Visual Center Attn: Info Services Washington, DC 20409/301-763-1896.

Firewood

Where supply exceeds demand, free firewood is available from public lands by contacting your nearest forest ranger.

Food and Nutriton Service Publications

The Food and Nutrition Service publishes materials relating to the Child Nutrition Programs; Food Distribution Program; Women, Infants and Children Program; Food Stamp Program and Nutrition Education. Many of these publications are available free of charge. The "sale only" materials are available from the Government Printing Office. For a free listing of these publications contact your nearest Food and Nutrition Service Regional Office (see Food and Nutrition Service Regional Offices listing in this section).

Food and Nutrition Service Regional Offices

U.S. Department of Agriculture
Food and Nutrition Service
Northeast Region
33 North Avenue
Burlington, Massachusetts 08103

U.S. Department of Agriculture
Food and Nutrition Service
Southeast Region
1100 Spring Street, N.W., Rm 200
Atlanta, Georgia 30367

U.S. Department of Agriculture
Food and Nutrition Service
Southwest Region
1100 Commerce Street, Rm 5-D-22
Dallas, Texas 75242

U.S. Department of Agriculture
Food and Nutrition Service
Western Region
550 Kearny Street
San Francisco, California 94108

U.S. Department of Agriculture
Food and Nutrition Service
Mid-Atlantic Region
Mercer Corporate Park
Corporate Boulevard CN 02150
Trenton, New Jersey 08650

U.S. Department of Agriculture
Food and Nutrition Service
Midwest Region
50 East Washington Street
Chicago, Illinois 60602

U.S. Department of Agriculture
Food and Nutrition Service
Mountain Plains Region
2420 West 26th Avenue, Suite 415-D
Denver, Colorado 80211

Food Assistance

A number of programs are available, which include food stamps; breakfast and lunch in schools; food service for preschool children; meals for needy school-age children; foods for needy expectant mothers, new mothers, and infants and young children at home; donated foods for non-profit summer camps and charitable institutions. See "Free Food for Non-Profit Institutions," "Grants," "Direct Payments," and "Loans and Loan Guarantees" in this section.

Food Consumption Research

Nationwide surveys are conducted every ten years identifying the quantity, type and value of food consumed in U.S. households. The most recent survey was conducted in 1977–78. Contact: Food Consumption Research Group, Consumer Nutrition Center, HNIS, USDA, Federal Building, Room 337, Hyattsville, MD 20782/301-436-8484.

Food Distribution Research Studies

Studies are available on a wide variety of markets covering all aspects of the distribution process—

wholesaling, packaging, transportation, etc. For a list of studies available, contact: Marketing Research and Development Division, USDA, AMS, Room 130, Building 307, BARC-E., Beltsville, MD 20705/301-344-2805.

Food Export and Import
USDA will provide certification to exporters or importers of plants and plant products, animal and animal products or pet birds; to prevent the introduction of agricultural pests and diseases from foreign countries into the United States and to aid exporters meeting foreign importers standards. Contact: for animals, Import—Export Staff Veterinary Services, Animal and Plant Inspection Service, USDA, Hyattsville, MD 20782/301-436-8530; for plants, Permit Unit PRQ, APIS, USDA, Hyattsville, MD 20782/301-436-8247.

Food for Peace
By working with groups like CARE and the World Food Program, this program helps needy people abroad with food and other agricultural commodities. Contact: Food For Peace/II 305 SA8 AID Washington, DC 20523/202-235-9173.

Food Quality and Safety
The Eastern Regional Research Center's six laboratories are involved in applied, basic and developmental research. They are concerned with the effects of post-harvest processing, storage and handling on the quality and safety of consumer products. The laboratories are: 1) Food Safety, 2) Food Science, 3) Plant Science, 4) Animal Biomaterials, 5) Engineering Science, and 6) Physical Chemistry and Instrumentation. The Center sponsors seminars and a workshop series. Primary journals publish their research findings. Contact: Eastern Regional Research Center, Agricultural Research Service, U.S. Department of Agriculture, 600 E. Mermaid Lane, Philadelphia, PA 19118/215-233-6595.

Food Science and Food Service Management Research
The Food and Nutrition Information Center (FNIC) acquires books, journals and audiovisual materials dealing with human nutrition, food service management and food science. Although FNIC resources primarily serve scientists, food service managers, and other professionals, it is open to the general public.

Organizations, agencies and individuals may also request to have journal articles photocopied and sent to them.

Other services include a reference service and 24-hour telephone monitor. The reference staff consists of two or three full-time nutritionists to answer questions and/or make referrals. The reference service also offers computer searches of major data bases. The 24-hour monitor enables

callers to leave messages and have their calls returned. Contact: Food and Nutrition Information Center (FNIC), U.S. Department of Agriculture, National Agricultural Library, 10301 Baltimore Boulevard, Beltsville, MD 20705/301-344-3719.

Food Service Management and Food Science
The Food and Nutrition Information Center acquires books, journals and audiovisual materials dealing with human nutrition, food service management and food science. Although the Center primarily serves professionals including scientists and food service managers, its materials are available to the general public.

Organizations, agencies and individuals may also request that photocopies of journal articles be sent to them. Other services include 1) a 24-hour telephone monitor enabling callers to leave messages and have their calls returned and 2) a Reference Service staff consisting of two or three full-time nutritionists to answer questions and/or make referrals. Computer searches of major data bases are available. Contact: Food and Nutrition Information Center, U.S. Department of Agriculture, National Agricultural Library, 10301 Baltimore Boulevard, Beltsville, MD 20705/301-344-3719.

Food Stamps
See "Direct Payments" in this section.

Food Studies and Food Economics
Studies and expertise on such topics as the convenience food market, food purchases away from home, the fast food industry, the relationship between consumer attitudes about nutrition and actual food expenditures, and the economic effects of food safety regulations are available from Food Economics, National Economic Analysis Division,ERS/USDA, 500 12th St. S.W.,#260, Washington, DC 20250/202-447-8707.

Foreign Agriculture
For supply and demand information of agricultural products in other countries contact: Information Division, Foreign Agricultural Service, USDA, 5074 South Building, Washington, DC 20250/202-447-3448.

Foreign Exchange Students
Students from developing countries can obtain assistance in identifying where to train in agriculture in the United States and in other countries. Contact: Office of International Cooperation, International Training Division, USDA, Room 4118 Auditor's Building, Washington, DC 20250/202-447-4711.

Foreign Investment in the U.S.
Research is conducted identifying the amount of U.S. land owned by foreign interests. Contact:

Land Branch, ERS/USDA, 500 12th St. S.W., #420, Washington, DC 20250/202-447-2628.

Forest Fire Reports
For information on forest fires anywhere in the country, contact: Aviation and Fire Management, Current Forest Fire Situation, 340 COM-W-BG, Washington, DC 20013/703-235-8666.

Forest Products Utilization
Technical assistance is available to wood processors and harvesters of wood products in cooperation with private consultants and state agencies. Contact: Cooperative Forestry, Forest Service, USDA, Room 125-A CW, P.O. Box 2417, Washington, DC 20013/202-235-2212.

Forest Ranger Jobs
For information on becoming a forest ranger, contact: Forest Service, Recruitment, P.O. Box 2417, Washington, DC 20013/703-235-2044.

Forestry Research and Technical Expertise
Basic research is conducted by a large staff of professionals on topics which include forest insects and diseases, forest fire and atmosphere sciences, forest resource economics, timber management, watershed and aquatic habitat, forest recreation, and related human environment, range and wildlife ecology, forest products and engineering research, wood chemistry and fiber products, and structural and forest system engineering. Contact: Deputy for Research, Forest Service, USDA, Room 3007, South Building, Washington, DC 20250/202-447-6665.

Free Food for Non-Profit Institutions
Charitable and rehabilitation institutions are usually eligible to receive surplus commodities stored by USDA. The commodities available are dairy products, oil, grain, and peanuts. Contact: Food Distribution Program, Food and Nutrition Service, 3101 Park Center Dr., Room 502, Alexandria, VA 22302/703-756-3680.

Free Manure
Many of the Extension Service offices offer free manure to gardeners. (See "Extension Service" in this section.) In the Washington, DC area it is available by the barrel or truckload from the College Park Holsteins, University of Maryland Dairy Barns, College Park, MD 20742/301-454-3935.

Freedom of Information Act
Each major division within the USDA has a Freedom of Information Act Office. For a list of these offices, contact: Office of Information, USDA, Room 458A, Washington, DC 20250/202-447-7454. See "Freedom of Information Act" section.

Gardening
See "Plants-Research and Reference" and "Extension Service" in this section.

Gasohol Loans
Anyone interested in producing gasohol can seek financial assistance under the Business and Industry Guaranteed Loan Program. (See "Loans and Loan Guarantees" in this section.) For general policy information, contact: Office of Energy, USDA, Room 144E Admin Bldg., Washington, DC 20250/202-447-2634.

Grading and Inspection
Meat, poultry, and eggs (liquid or frozen) are the only products which are federally inspected on a mandatory basis. All other product grading is voluntary. Grading of meat, poultry, eggs, and dairy products and fresh and processed fruits and vegetables is provided on request for a fee. For further information and descriptions of grading categories, contact the appropriate office below:

Poultry Grading Branch, AMS Poultry Division, USDA, Room 3938, South Building, Washington, DC 20250/202-447-3272.

Dairy Grading Branch Dairy Division, USDA, Room 2750, Wash., DC 20250/202-475-5530.

Meat Grading & Certification Branch, AMS, Room 2638-S, Wash., DC 20250 202-382-1246.

Processed Products Branch, Food and Vegetable Division, AMS/USDA, Room 0709, South Building, Washington, DC 20250/202-447-4693.

Fresh Products Branch, Food and Vegetable Division, AMS/USDA, Room 2052 South Building, Washington, DC 20250/202-447-5870.

Grading Services
USDA provides producers, packers, processors, shippers, wholesalers and consumers with official certification of the quality of food and farm products to aid in establishing a market value for the product. For most commodities a fee is charged to cover the cost of the service; and the service may be conducted during packing or processing or at supply depots. The official grading or inspection certificate is accepted as prima facie evidence in court. Contact: Agricultural Marketing Service or Federal Grain Inspection Service, USDA, Washington, DC 20250/202-447-5115.

Grants
The programs described below are for sums of money which are given by the USDA to initiate and stimulate new or improved activities and to sustain ongoing services.

Additional Lands-Grants to Minnesota

Objectives: To share National Forest Receipts with the state of Minnesota in connection with lands situated in the counties of Cook, Lake, and St. Louis which are withdrawn from entry and appropriation under the public laws of the United States.

Eligibility: State of Minnesota.

Range of Financial Assistance: Grants averaging $711,000.

Contact: Director of Fiscal and Accounting Management, Forest Service, Department of Agriculture, Room 701 RPE, P.O. Box 2417, Washington, DC 20013/703-235-8159.

Agricultural Research—Basic and Applied

Objectives: To make agricultural research discoveries; evaluate alternative ways of attaining goals; and provide scientific and technical information.

Eligibility: Nonprofit institutions of higher education or nonprofit organizations whose primary purpose is conducting scientific research.

Range of Financial Assistance: $15,000 to $113,500.

Contact: Deputy Director for Agricultural Research, Science and Education Administration, USDA, Washington, DC 20250/202-436-8403.

Agricultural Research—Competitive Research Grants

Objectives: To promote research in food, agriculture, and related areas to further the programs of USDA through the award of research grants on a competitive basis.

Eligibility: Individuals, nonprofit organizations, and state governments.

Range of Financial Assistance: $4,000 to $200,000.

Contact: Director, Competitive Grants Office, Science and Education Administration, Department of Agriculture, 1300 Wilson Blvd., Suite 1300, Arlington, VA 22209/703-235-2628.

Agricultural Research—Special Research Grants

Objectives: To carry out research to facilitate or expand promising breakthroughs in areas of the food and agricultural sciences of importance to the nation; to facilitate and expand ongoing state-federal food and agricultural research programs.

Eligibility: Nonprofit organizations and state governments.

Range of Financial Assistance: $5,646 to $296,000.

Contact: Administrator, Cooperative Research, Science and Education, USDA, Washington, DC 20250/202-447-4423.

Agreements with States for Intrastate Meat and Poultry Inspection

Objectives: To supply federal assistance to states desiring to improve the quality of their meat and poultry inspection programs in order to assure the consumer an adequate, safe, supply of wholesale meat and poultry.

Eligibility: An appropriate state or U.S. territory agency administering state or territorial meat or poultry inspection programs under laws comparable to the Federal Meat and Poultry Products Inspection Acts.

Range of Financial Assistance: $39,000 to $3,549,000.

Contact: Executive Officer, Meat and Poultry Inspection Operations, Food Safety and Inspection Service, Department of Agriculture, Washington, DC 20250/202-447-6313.

Alcohol Fuels Research

Objectives: To conduct research on the evaluation, treatment, and conversion of biomass resources for the manufacture of alcohols and industrial hydrocarbons.

Eligibility: Colleges, universities, government corporations.

Range of Financial Assistance: $64,847 to $80,000.

Contact: Administrator, Cooperative State Research Service, Department of Agriculture, Washington, DC 20250/202-447-4423.

Animal Health and Disease Research

Objectives: To support animal health and disease research at eligible schools of veterinary medicine, and state agricultural experiment stations whose purpose is to improve the health and productivity of food animals and horses through effective prevention, control or treatment of disease, reduction of losses from transportation and other hazards, and protect human health through control of animal diseases transmissible to people.

Eligibility: Public non-profit institutions.

Range of Financial Assistance: $341 to $343,157.

Contact: Administrator, Cooperative State Research Service, Department of Agriculture, Washington, DC 20250/202-447-4423.

Child Care Food Program

Objectives: To assist states, through grant-in-aid and other means, to initiate, maintain or expand nonprofit food service programs for children in nonresidential institutions providing child care.

Eligibility: The state and U.S. territory educational agency or other agency within the state and U.S. territory eligible to receive federal funds for disbursement; in states where that agency is not permitted to disburse funds to any institution, the institution may receive funds directly from USDA.

Range of Financial Assistance: Not specified.

Contact: Director, Child Care and Summer Programs Division, Food and Nutrition Service, USDA, Alexandria, VA 22302/703-756-3880.

Commodity Supplemental Food Program

Objectives: To improve the health and nutrition of infants, preschool children, pregnant women, and nursing mothers through the donation of supplemental foods.

Eligibility: Agreements under this program are made between USDA and state distributing agencies or with an Indian tribe, band or group recognized by the Department of the Interior.

Range of Financial Assistance: Not applicable.

Contact: Supplemental Food Program, Food and Nutrition Service, Department of Agriculture, Alexandria, VA 22302/703-756-3746.

Cooperative Extension Service

Objectives: To provide educational programs based upon local needs in the fields of agricultural production and marketing, rural development, home economics, and youth development.

Eligibility: Grants are made to designated land-grant institutions and are administered by the director of the state extension service.

Range of Financial Assistance: $714,086 to $17,781,993.

Contact: Science and Education Administration Extension, Department of Agriculture, Washington, DC 20250/202-447-3377.

Cooperative Forestry Alliance

Objectives: Assistance in the advancement of forest resources management in non-federal forest lands; encouragement of the production of timber; prevention and control of insects and diseases affecting trees and forests; prevention and control of rural fires; efficient utilization of wood and wood residues, including the recycling of wood fiber; improvement and maintenance of fish and wildlife habitat; and planning and conducting of urban forestry programs.

Eligibility: Forestry or equivalent agencies of states and territories.

Range of Financial Assistance: $40,000 to $5,000,000.

Contact: Deputy Chief, State and Private Forestry, Forest Service, USDA, P.O. Box 2417, Washington, DC 20013/202-447-6657.

Cooperative Forestry Research

Objectives: To encourage and assist the states in carrying on a program of forestry research at forestry schools, and to develop a trained pool of forest scientists capable of conducting needed forestry research.

Eligibility: State institutions certified as eligible by a state representative designated by the Governor.

Range of Financial Assistance: $33,105 to $432,073.

Contact: Administrator, Cooperative Research, Science and Education Administration, USDA, Washington, DC 20250/202-447-4423.

1890 Research Facilities

Objectives: To assist in the acquisition and improvement of research facilities and equipment. Available in the states of Alabama, Arkansas, Delaware, Florida, Georgia, Kentucky, Louisiana, Maryland, Mississippi, Missouri, North Carolina, Oklahoma, South Carolina, Tennessee, Texas, and Virginia.

Eligibility: Land-grant colleges and Tuskegee Institute.

Range of Financial Assistance: $232,520 to $564,706.

Contact: Administrator, Cooperative State Research Service, Department of Agriculture, Washington, DC 20250/202-447-4423.

Federal-State Marketing Improvement Program

Objectives: To solve marketing problems at the state and local level through pilot marketing service projects conducted by states.

Eligibility: State departments of agriculture, or other appropriate state agencies.

Range of Financial Assistance: $1,000 to $75,000.

Contact: Director, Federal-State Marketing Improvement Program, Agricultural Marketing Service, USDA, Washington, DC 20250/202-447-2704.

Food Distribution

Objectives: To improve the diets of school children and needy persons in households, on Indian reservations not participating in the Food Stamp Program, and in charitable institutions; the elderly and other individuals in need of food assistance are also included. To increase the market for domestically produced foods acquired under surplus-removal or price-support operations.

Eligibility: Such state and federal agencies that are designated as distributing agencies by the Governor, legislature, or other authority may receive and distribute donated foods.

Range of Financial Assistance: Not applicable. Assistance in the form of grants and goods.

Contact: Food Distribution Division, Food and Nutrition Service, USDA, Alexandria, VA 22302/703-756-3680.

Forestry Research

Objectives: To extend the research activities of the Forest Service by awarding grants primarily to nonprofit institutions of higher education, but also to other institutions and organizations engaged in scientific research.

Eligibility: Grants for basic or applied research may be made to state agricultural experiment stations, state and local governments, and non-profit institutions or organizations.

Range of Financial Assistance: $2,000 to $100,000.

Contact: Deputy, Chief for Research, Forest Service, USDA, P.O. Box 2417, Washington, DC 20013/202-447-7075.

Grants for Agricultural Research—Competitive Research Grants

Objectives: To promote basic research in food, agriculture, and related areas to further the programs of USDA through the award of research grants on a competitive basis.

Eligibility: State Agricultural Experiment Stations, US colleges/universities, other US research institutions and organizations, Federal agencies, private organizations or corporations and individuals.

Range of Financial Assistance: $13,000 to $165,000.

Contact: Director, Competitive Research Grants Office, Department of Agriculture, West Auditors Building, Room 112, 15th and Independence Avenue, SW, Washington, DC 20250/202-475-5022.

Grants for Agricultural Research, Special Research Grants

Objectives: To carry out research to facilitate or expand promising breakthroughs in areas of the food and agricultural sciences of importance to the nation and to facilitate or expand on-going State-Federal food and agricultural research programs.

Eligibility: Land-grant colleges and universities, research foundations established by land-grant colleges and universities,, and State agricultural experiment stations and all colleges and universities having a demonstrable capacity in food and agriculture research as determined by the Secretary of Agriculture.

Range of Financial Assistance: $21,367 to $108,498.

Contact: Administrator, Cooperative State Research Service, Department of Agriculture, Washington, DC 20250/202-447-4423.

Nutrition Education and Training Program (NET Program)

Objectives: To encourage the effective dissemination of scientifically valid information to children participating in or eligible to participate in the school-lunch and related child-nutrition programs.

Eligibility: State and territorial education agencies.

Range of Financial Assistance: $50,000 to $430,000.

Contact: Nutrition and Technical Services Division, Food and Nutrition Service, USDA, Alexandria, VA 22302/703-756-3880.

Payments to Agricultural Experiment Stations Under Hatch Act

Objectives: To support agricultural research at state agricultural experiment stations in order to promote efficient production, marketing, distribution, and utilization of farm products.

Eligibility: Agricultural experiment stations identified and declared eligible by their respective state legislatures.

Range of Financial Assistance: $592,904 to $5,440,316.

Contact: Administrator, Cooperative Research, Science and Education, USDA, Washington, DC 20250/202-447-4423.

Payments to 1890 Land-Grant Colleges and Tuskegee Institute

Objectives: To support continuing agricultural research at eligible colleges including Tuskegee Institute.

Eligibility: Sixteen 1890 Land-Grant Colleges and Tuskegee Institute are eligible in the states of Alabama, Arkansas, Delaware, Florida, Georgia, Kentucky, Louisiana, Maryland, Mississippi, Missouri, North Carolina, Oklahoma, South Carolina, Tennessee, Texas, and Virginia.

Range of Financial Assistance: $451,959 to $2,065,988.

Contact: Administrator, Cooperative State Research Service, USDA, Washington, DC 20250/202-447-4423.

Resource Conservation and Development

Objectives: To assist local people in initiating and carrying out long-range programs of resource conservation and development.

Eligibility: Local governments and nonprofit organizations.

Range of Financial Assistance: $2,400 to $500,000.

Contact: Deputy Chief for Natural Resource Projects, Soil Conservation Service, Department of Agriculture, P.O. Box 2890, Washington, DC 20013/202-447-4554.

Rural Self-Help Housing Technical Assistance

Objectives: To provide financial support for programs of technical and supervisory assistance to aid needy low-income individuals and their families in mutual self-help efforts in rural areas.

Eligibility: State political subdivisions, public nonprofit corporations or private nonprofit corporations. Funds are available in open country and to communities with 10,000 population or less which are rural in character and to places of up to 20,000 population under certain conditions.

Range of Financial Assistance: $49,000 to $747,000.

Contact: Adminstrator, Farmers Home Administration, Department of Agriculture, Washington, DC 20250/202-382-1474.

School Breakfast Program

Objectives: To assist states in providing nutritious breakfasts for school children, through cash grants and food donations.

Eligibility: State and U.S. territory agencies or private schools which are exempt from income tax under the Internal Revenue Code.

Range of Financial Assistance: Average federal cash assistnce is approximately 63¢ per meal.

Contact: Director, School Programs Division, Food and Nutrition Service, USDA, Alexandria, VA 22302/703-756-3590.

School Funds—Grants to Arizona

Objectives: To pay to the state of Arizona a portion of the gross proceeds of all the National Forests in each state.

Eligibility: State of Arizona.

Range of Financial Assistance: Grants averaging $15,600.

Contact: Director of Fiscal and Accounting Management, Forest Service, Department of Agriculture, Room 701 RPE, Box 2417, Washington, DC 20013/703-235-8159.

School Lunch Program

Objectives: To assist states in providing nutritious lunches for school children through cash grants and food donations.

Eligibility: State and agencies and private schools, residential child care centers, and settlement houses which are exempt from income tax under the Internal Revenue Code.

Range of Financial Assistance: Average federal assistance per meal is approximately 11.62 cents in cash and 11.56 cents in food. Special assistance to needy children averages 109.66 cents per meal.

Contact: Director, School Programs Division, Food and Nutrition Service, USDA, Alexandria, VA 22302/703-756-3590.

Schools and Roads—Grants to States

Objectives: To share receipts from the National Forests with the states in which the National Forests are situated.

Eligibility: State governments or U.S. territories.

Range of Financial Assistance: $73 to $69,212,545.

Contact: Director of Fiscal and Accounting Management, Forest Service, Department of Agriculture, P.O. Box 2417, Washington, DC 20013/703-235-8159.

Schools and Roads—Grants to Counties

Objectives: To share receipts from National Grasslands and Land Utilization Projects with the counties in which these are situated.

Eligibility: Counties within the States of the United States.

Range of Financial Assistance: $5 to $4,033,653.

Contact: Director of Fiscal and Accounting Management, Forest Service, Department of Agri-

culture, P.O. Box 2417, Washington, DC 20013/703-235-8159.

Special Milk Program for Children

Objectives: To encourage the consumption of fluid milk by children of high school grade or under through reimbursement to eligible schools and institutions which inaugurate or expand milk-distribution services.

Eligibility: Any state agency or nonprofit private school or child care institution of high school grade or under may participate.

Range of Financial Assistance: Not available.

Contact: Director, School Programs Division, Food and Nutrition Service, USDA, Alexandria, VA 22302/703-756-3590.

Special Supplemental Food Program for Women, Infants and Children (WIC Program)

Objectives: To supply supplemental nutritious foods and nutrition education as an adjunct to good health care to participants identified to be at nutritional risk because of inadequate income and inadequate nutrition.

Eligibility: A local agency is eligible provided (1) it gives health services free or at reduced cost to residents of low-income areas; (2) serves a population of women, infants, and children at nutritional risk; (3) has the personnel, expertise, and equipment to perform measurements, tests and data collection specified for the WIC Program; (4) is able to maintain adequate medical records; and (5) is a public or private nonprofit health or welfare agency.

Range of Financial Assistance: Not specified.

Contact: Supplemental Food Programs Division, Food and Nutrition Service, USDA, Alexandria, VA 22302/703-756-3746.

State Administrative Expenses for Child Nutrition

Objectives: To provide each state educational agency with funds for use for its administrative expenses in supervising and giving technical assistance to the local school districts and institutions in their conduct of child nutrition programs.

Eligibility: State educational agencies responsible for conduct of child nutrition programs, including agencies in the U.S. territories.

Range of Financial Assistance: $120,000 to $3,483,000.

Contact: Director, School Programs Division, Food and Nutrition Service, USDA, Alexandria, VA 22302/703-756-3590.

State Administrative Matching Grants for Food Stamp Program

Objectives: To provide financial aid to state agencies for costs incurred to operate the Food Stamp Program.

Eligibility: Welfare agencies of states and U.S. Territories.

Range of Financial Assistance: $21,000 to $59,343,000.

Contact: Deputy Administrator, Food and Nutrition Service, Family Nutrition Program, USDA, Alexandria, VA 22302/703-756-3046.

Summer Food Service Program for Children

Objectives: To assist states, through grants-in-aid and other means, to initiate, maintain and expand nonprofit food service programs for children in service institutions and camps during the summer months.

Eligibility: The state and U.S. Territory agency applies for and receives federal funds for disbursement, except that in states where that agency is not permitted to disburse funds to any service institution, the institution may receive funds directly from the USDA.

Range of Financial Assistance: Not specified.

Contact: Director, Child Care and Summer Programs Division, Food and Nutrition Service, USDA, Alexandria, VA 22302/703-756-3880.

Very Low-Income Housing Repair

Objectives: To give very low-income rural homeowners an opportunity to make essential minor repairs to their homes to make them safe and remove health hazards to the family or the community.

Eligibility: Applicant must own and occupy a home in a rural area, and be without sufficient income to qualify for a Low- to Moderate-Income Housing Loan to repair or improve his or her dwelling in order to make such dwelling safe and sanitary.

Range of Financial Assistance: $200 to $7,500.

Contact: Administrator, Farmers Home Administration, USDA, Washington, DC 20250/202-382-7967.

Water and Waste Disposal Systems for Rural Communities

Objectives: To provide basic human amenities, alleviate health hazards and promote the orderly growth of the rural areas of the nation by meeting the need for new and improved rural water and waste disposal facilities.

Eligibility: Municipalities, counties and other political subdivisions of a state, such as districts and authorities; associations, cooperatives and corporations operated on a not-for-profit basis; and federally recognized Indian tribes. Facilities should primarily serve rural residents and not include any area in any city or town having a population in excess of 10,000 inhabitants.

Range of Financial Assistance: $3,500 to $6,095,500.

Contact: Community and Business Programs Division, Farmers Home Administration, USDA, Washington, DC 20250/202-382-9583.

Watershed Protection and Flood Prevention

Objectives: To provide technical and financial assistance in planning and carrying out works of improvement to protect, develop, and utilize the land and water resources in small watersheds.

Eligibility: Any state agency, county or groups of counties, municipality, town or township, soil and water conservation district, flood prevention or flood control district, or any other nonprofit agency with authority under state law to carry out, maintain and operate watershed works of improvement may apply for assistance.

Range of Financial Assistance: $300 to $13,000,000.

Contact: Deputy Chief for Natural Resource Projects, Soil Conservation Service, Department of Agriculture, P.O. Box 2890, Washington, DC 20013/202-447-4527.

Great Plains Conservation Work

Land users living in the Great Plains states may seek assistance from the Soil Conservation Service (SCS) which offers technical assistance and cost-sharing funds to farmers, ranchers, and other land users in the Great Plains. Cost-share rates can range up to 80 percent for urgently needed conservation work. Contact: Soil Conservation Service, USDA, Washington, DC 20250-202-382-1868 or your Local Soil Conservation Service Office.

Human Nutrition

A large amount of research is conducted on such topics as human nutrient requirements, food composition, effects of fiber, sugar and fat, child nutrition, diet and aging, and food consumption. For help in identifying specific information and expertise, contact: ARS, Science and Education Administration, USDA, Room 304A Washington, D.C. 20250/202-447-3656.

Human Nutrition Directory

The *Directory of Human Nutrition Activities,* a free 21-page booklet, lists human nutrition services, programs, information sources, research centers and other activities of the U.S. Department of Agriculture. Contact: Agricultural Research Service, U.S. Department of Agriculture, Building 005, BARC—West, Beltsville, MD 20705, 301-344-3216.

Human Nutrition Research

The Agricultural Research Service (ARS) human nutrition research is conducted primarily at five separate Human Nutrition Research Centers and at Regional Utilization Laboratories. Each center has a different research thrust and provides its unique contribution. Contact: U.S. Department of Agriculture, Agricultural Research Service (ARS), National Program Staff, Building 005, BARC—

West, Beltsville, MD 20705. 301-344-3216 or contact a particular center.

Beltsville Human Nutrition Research Center
The Beltsville Human Nutrition Research Center's mission is to define human requirements for the essential nutrients—protein, carbohydrates, lipids, vitamins, and minerals for optimal health and performance, and to identify, through study of their nutrient composition, the foods that meet those nutritional requirements. Emphasis at this center is on the nutritional requirements of adults and on development of food composition analysis methodology. Contact: Beltsville Human Nutrition Research Center, Beltsville Agricultural Research Center, Agricultural Research Service, Department of Agriculture, Beltsville, MD 20705/ 301-344-2157.

Children's Nutrition Research Center
The Children's Nutrition Research Center at Baylor College of Medicine, Houston, TX is the only center to deal exclusively with research on nutrient needs and nutritional status of mothers, infants, and children. Contact: Children's Nutritional Research Center, Agricultural Research Service, Department of Agriculture, 6608 Fannin Street, Suite 601, Houston, TX 77030/713-799-6006.

Human Nutrition Research Center
The mission of the Grand Forks Human Nutrition Research Center, Grand Forks, North Dakota, is to develop recommendations for nutrient intakes in humans and to identify useful nutrient forms, with particular emphasis on mineral requirements. Contact: Human Nutrition Research Center, Agricultural Research Service, Department of Agriculture, 2420 2nd Avenue, N, P. O. Box 7166, University Station, Grand Forks, ND 58202/701-795-8353.

Western Human Nutrition Research Center
The mission of the Western Human Nutrition Research Center, San Francisco, CA is to improve methods for assessing human nutritional status and to study the factors that lead to malnutrition. This center also conducts studies on human nutritional requirements and on factors that influence them, with emphasis on vitamin requirements. Contact: Western Human Nutrition Research Center, Agricultural Research Service, Department of Agriculture, P. O. Box 29997, Presidio of San Francisco, San Francisco, CA 94129/415-556-9699.

Human Nutrition Research Center on Aging
The mission of the center is to examine the relationship of nutrition to aging and the dietary needs of the elderly. For further information contact: Human Nutrition Research Center on Aging, Agricultural Research Service, Department of Agriculture, Tufts University, 711 Washington Street, Boston, MA 02111/617-956-7570.

Human Nutrition Research and Funding
The Cooperative State Research Service (CSRS) is responsible for administering and coordinating funds to 54 state agricultural experiment stations, to 16 landgrant schools and to Tuskegee Institute to carry out research on food and agricultural issues including human nutrition research. These projects often focus heavily on nutrient bioavailability and the composition of foods, determination of nutrient requirements, metabolic functions of nutrients and interactions, dietary and nutritional status of special populations, dietary patterns, and alterations in the nutritional value of food supply resulting from changes in production, processing, or marketing practices. Contact: Cooperative State Research Service (CSRS), U.S. Department of Agriculture, West Auditor's Building, 15th and Independence Avenue, Washington, DC 20251, 202-447-3426.

Human Nutrition Resources
The Food and Nutrition Information Center acquires books, journals and audiovisual materials dealing with human nutrition, food service management and food science. Although the Center primarily serves professionals, including scientists and food service managers, its materials are available to the general public. Organizations, agencies and individuals may also request that photocopies of journal articles be sent to them. Other services include a 24-hour telephone monitor enabling callers to leave messages and have their calls returned, and Reference Service staff consisting of two or three full-time nutritionists to answer questions and/or make referrals. Computer searches of major data bases are available. Contact: Food and Nutrition Information Center, U.S. Department of Agriculture, National Agricultural Library, 10301 Baltimore Boulevard, Beltsville, MD 20705, 301-344-3719.

Hydroponics
Information and expertise on hydroponics, the process of growing crops without soil, is available from: Environmental Research Laboratory, Tucson Int'l Airport, Tucson, AZ 85706/602-621-7962.

Information to Production and Marketing Groups
USDA will provide educational and technical assistance to any agricultural production or marketing association, group or cooperative. They provide the latest USDA land grant university research findings, discuss new technology and share the results of feasibility studies, market analysis reports, and the development of new products and markets. Contact: your Local Cooperative Extension agent or USDA, Science and

Education Department, Washington, D.C. 20250
202-447-5923.

Insects and Pests
Technical assistance is available to aid in identifying and eliminating problems caused by insects and bugs. The USDA encourages that you catch one of your problem insects and send it in for analysis. See "Extension Service" in this section.

Insurance
The USDA runs a Crop Insurance Program whose objective is to improve the economic stability of agriculture through a sound system of crop insurance that provides all-risk insurance for individual farmers to ensure a basic income against droughts, freezes, insects, and other natural causes of disastrous crop losses.
Eligibility: Any owner or operator of farmland who has an insurable interest in a crop in a county where insurance is offered on that crop is eligible unless the land is not classified for insurance purposes.
Contact: Your local ASCS office, or Manager, Federal Crop Insurance Corporation, USDA, Washington, DC 20250/202-447-4603.

Land Grant Colleges
A system of state colleges and universities was established in 1890 from federal government grants of land and funds to each state to encourage practical education in agricultural and urban homemaking, and the mechanical arts. There are 88 land grant colleges. Contact: Extension Div. Info., USDA, Room 3128 S, Washington, DC 20250/202-447-3029.

Landscaping
Assistance is available to help those with problems related to landscaping. Help is available to individuals through the Extension Service (see "Extension Service" in this section). Those who need help with larger projects involving conservation can contact: Landscape Architect, Engineering Division, Soil Conservation Service, USDA, 6129 South Building, Washington, DC 20250/202-447-9155.

Library
The main USDA library provides published material and reference services on botany, zoology, chemistry, veterinary medicine, forestry, plant pathology, livestock poultry, entomology, and general agriculture. Loans of monographs and reference works are available to the public through interlibrary loan. Contact: National Agricultural Library, 10301 Baltimore Blvd., Beltsville, MD 20705/301-344-3755. For additional information, see "Plants—Research and Reference" and "Research and Reference Service" in this section.

Livestock and Veterinary Sciences
A staff of specialists study such topics as domestic animal diseases, beef production, dairy production, foreign animal diseases, poultry production and diseases, production of sheep and fur-bearing animals, swine production, and livestock facilities. Contact: Animal Science Institute, Room 217, Bldg. 200, Beltsville Agricultural Research Center-West, Beltsville, MD 20705/301-344-3431.

Loans and Loan Guarantees
The programs described below are those that offer financial assistance through the lending of federal monies for a specific period of time or programs in which the federal government makes an arrangement to indemnify a lender against part or all of any defaults by the borrower.

Business and Industrial Loans
Objectives: To assist public, private, or cooperative organizations organized for profit or non-profit, Indian tribes or individuals in rural areas to obtain quality loans for the purpose of improving, developing or financing business, industry, and employment and improving the economic and environmental climate in rural communities, including pollution abatement and control, and the conservation, development, and utilization of water for aquaculture purposes.
Eligibility: An applicant may be a cooperative, corporation, partnership, trust or other legal entity organized and operated on a profit or nonprofit basis; an Indian tribe; a municipality, county, or other political subdivision of a state; or an individual in rural areas. Applicants must be located in areas other than cities having a population of more than 50,000 or immediately adjacent to urban areas with a population density of more than 100 persons per square mile.
Range of Financial Assistance: $11,000 to $50,000,000.
Contact: Administrator, Farmers Home Administration, Department of Agriculture, Washington, DC 20250/202-447-7967.

Commodity Loans (Price Supports)
Objectives: To improve and stabilize farm income; to assist in bringing about a better balance between supply and demand of the commodities, and to assist farmers in the orderly marketing of their crops.
Eligibility: Individuals.
Range of Financial Assistance: $50 to $50,000.
Contact: Price Support and Loan Division, USDA-ASCS, P.O. Box 2415, Washington, DC 20013/202-447-8480.

Community Facilities Loans
Objectives: To construct, enlarge, extend, or otherwise improve community facilities providing essential services to rural residents.

Eligibility: State agencies; political and quasi-political subdivisions of states; and associations including corporations, Indian tribes on federal and state reservations and other federally recognized Indian tribes; and existing private corporations operated on a nonprofit basis, have or will have the legal authority necessary for constructing, operating, and maintaining the proposed facility or service and for obtaining, giving security for, and repaying the loan, and are unable to finance the proposed project from its own resources or through commercial credit at reasonable rates and terms. Assistance is authorized for eligible applicants in rural areas.

Range of Financial Assistance: $5,000 to $5,750,000.

Contact: Director, Community Facilities Division, Farmers Home Administration, Department of Agriculture, Washington, DC 20250/202-382-1490.

Economic Emergency Loans

Objectives: To make adequate financial assistance available in the form of loans insured or guaranteed for bona fide farmers, ranchers and aquaculture operators who are primarily and directly engaged in agricultural production.

Eligibility: To be eligible, an applicant must: (1) If an individual, be a citizen of the United States; (2) be a bona fide farmer(owner, operator, or tenant-operator); (3) possess legal capacity to contract for the loans; and (4) be unable to obtain credit elsewhere in order to maintain a viable farm enterprise.

Range of Financial Assistance: Up to $400,000.

Contact: Administrator, Farmers Home Administration, Department of Agriculture, Washington, DC 20250/202-447-4671.

Emergency Loans

Objectives: To assist farmers, ranchers and aquaculture operators with loans to cover losses resulting from a major and/or natural disaster, for annual farm operating expenses, and for other essential needs necessary to return the disaster victims' farming operation(s) to a financially sound basis.

Eligibility: Established farmers, ranchers, or aquaculture operators (either tenant or owner-operator), partnerships, cooperatives and corporations primarily engaged in farming that have suffered severe crop losses or property damage caused by a designated natural disaster, not compensated for fully by insurance or otherwise, and unable to obtain necessary credit from other sources.

Range of Financial Assistance: $500 to $6,400,000.

Contact: Administrator, Farmers Home Administration, Department of Agriculture, Washington, DC 20250/202-382-1632.

Farm Labor Housing Loans

Objectives: To provide decent, safe and sanitary low-rent housing and related facilities for domestic farm laborers.

Eligibility: Loans are available to farmers and associations of farmers. States, political subdivisions of states, broad-based nonprofit organizations, and nonprofit corporations of farm workers may qualify for both loans and grants.

Range of Financial Assistance: $3,000 to $3,000,000.

Contact: Multiple Family Housing Loan Division, Farmers Home Administration, Department of Agriculture, Washington, DC 20250/202-382-1604.

Farm Operating Loans

Objectives: To enable operators of family farms (primarily limited-resource operators, new operators and low-income operators), through the extension of credit and supervisory assistance, to make efficient use of their land, labor, and other resources. Youth loans enable rural youths to establish and operate modest income-producing farm and nonfarm projects. Projects are educational and practical and provide the youth an opportunity to learn basic economic and credit principles.

Eligibility: Individual applicants must have farm experience or training and possess the character, industry and managerial ability to carry out the operation; be unable to obtain sufficient credit elsewhere at reasonable rates and terms; have the ability to repay the loan; and after the loan is closed, be an owner or tenant operating a family farm. Certain corporations, cooperatives and partnerships operating family-sized farms are now eligible for farm operating loans.

Range of Financial Assistance: Up to $200,000.

Contact: Director, Farm Real Estate and Production Division, Farmers Home Administration, USDA, Washington, DC 20250/202-447-4572.

Farm Ownership Loans

Objectives: To assist eligible farmers and ranchers, including cooperatives, partnerships and corporations, through the extension of credit and supervisory assistance, to become owner-operators of family farms, to make efficient use of the land, labor, and other resources, and to carry on sound and successful operations. Farm ownership loans are also available to eligible applicants with limited incomes and resources who are unable to pay the regular interest rate and have special problems such as underdeveloped managerial ability.

Eligibility: An applicant must be unable to obtain adequate credit from other sources at reasonable terms; have the necessary experience, training, and managerial ability to operate a family farm or a nonfarm enterprise; and agree to refinance the balance due on the loan as soon as the borrower is able to obtain adequate credit at reasonable terms from another lender. Individual applicants must not have a combined farm ownership loan, soil and water loan, and recreation loan indebtedness to FmHA of no more than $200,000 for insured loans and $300,000 for guaranteed loans and a total indebtedness against the property securing the loan of more than the market value of the security.

Range of Financial Assistance: Up to $300,000.

Contact: Administrator, Farmers Home Administration, Department of Agriculture, Washington, DC 20250/202-447-7967.

Indian Tribes and Tribal Corporation Loans

Objectives: To enable tribes and tribal corporations to mortgage lands as security for loans from the Farmers Home Administration to buy additional land within the reservation.

Eligibility: Limited to any Indian tribe recognized by the Secretary of the Interior or tribal corporation established pursuant to the Indian Reorganization Act.

Range of Financial Assistance: $750,000 to $3,000,000.

Contact: Office of Indian Affairs, Farmers Home Administration, Department of Agriculture, Washington, DC 20250/202-447-7967.

Income Housing Loans

Objectives: To assist rural families to obtain decent, safe, and sanitary dwellings and related facilities.

Eligibility: Present or prospective owners of dwellings in rural areas. Interest credits may, under certain conditions, be granted to lower-income families that will reduce the effective interest rate paid to as low as one percent, depending on the size of the loan and the size and income of the applicant family.

Range of Financial Assistance: $1,000 to $60,000.

Contact: Single Family Housing, Farmers Home Administration, Department of Agriculture, Washington, DC 20250/202-382-7967.

Resource Conservation and Development Loans

Objectives: To provide loan assistance to local sponsoring agencies in authorized areas where an acceleration of a program of resource conservation, development, and utilization will increase economic opportunities for local people.

Eligibility: State and local governments and nonprofit organizations with authority to plan or carry out activities relating to resource use and development in multijurisdictional areas.

Range of Financial Assistance: $10,000 to $500,000.

Contact: Director, Community Facilities Division, Farmers Home Administration, Department of Agriculture, Washington, DC 20250/202-382-1490.

Rural Electrification Loans and Loan Guarantees

Objectives: To assure that people in eligible rural areas have access to electric services comparable in reliability and quality to the rest of the nation.

Eligibility: Rural electric cooperatives, public utility districts, power companies, municipalities, and other qualified power suppliers, including those located in the U.S. Territories.

Range of Financial Assistance: $250,000 to $1,500,000,000.

Contact: Administrator, Rural Electrification Administration, Department of Agriculture, Washington, DC 20250/202-382-9540.

Rural Housing Site Loans

Objectives: To assist public or private nonprofit organizations interested in providing sites for housing to acquire and develop land in rural areas to be subdivided as building sites and sold on a nonprofit basis to families eligible for low- and moderate-income loans, cooperatives, and nonprofit rural renting housing applicants.

Eligibility: Private or public nonprofit organizations that will provide the developed sites to qualified borrowers on a nonprofit basis in open country and town of 10,000 population or less and areas of up to 20,000 population under certain conditions.

Range of Financial Assistance: $45,200 to $571,000.

Contact: Single Family Housing, Farmers Home Administration, Department of Agriculture, Washington, DC 20250/202-382-1604.

Rural Rental Housing Loans

Objectives: To provide economically designed and constructed rental and cooperative housing and related facilities suited for independent living for rural residents.

Eligibility: Applicants may be individuals, cooperatives, nonprofit organizations, state or local public agencies or nonprofit corporations, trusts, partnership, limited partnerships unable to finance the housing either with their own resources or with credit obtained from private sources.

Range of Financial Assistance: $75,000 to $2,000,000.

Contact: Administrator, Farmers Home Administration, Department of Agriculture, Washington, DC 20250/202-382-1604.

Rural Telephone Bank Loans

Objectives: To provide supplemental financing to extend and improve telephone service in rural areas.

Eligibility: Borrowers, that have received a loan or loan commitment under Section 201 of Rural

Electrification Act or that have been certified by the administrator as qualified to receive such a loan, are eligible to borrow from the Rural Telephone Bank. See "Rural Telephone Loans and Loan Guarantees" in this section.

Range of Financial Assistance: $250,000 to $15,000,000.

Contact: Governor, Rural Telephone Bank, Department of Agriculture, Washington, DC 20250/202-382-9540.

Rural Telephone Loans and Loan Guarantees

Objectives: To assure that people in eligible rural areas have access to telephone service comparable in reliability and quality to the rest of the nation.

Eligibility: Telephone companies or cooperatives, nonprofit associations, limited dividend associations, mutual associations or public bodies.

Range of Financial Assistance: $200,000 to $40,000,000.

Contact: Administrator, Rural Electrification Administration, Department of Agriculture, Washington, DC 20250/202-382-9540.

Soil and Water Loans

Objectives: To facilitate improvement, protection, and proper use of farmland by providing adequate financing and supervisory assistance for soil conservation, water development, conservation and use, forestation, drainage of farmland, establishment and improvement of permanent pasture, and development of pollution abatement and control facilities on farms.

Eligibility: Farming partnerships or cooperatives, domestic corporations, and individual farm owners or tenants.

Range of Financial Assistance: $3,300 to $100,000.

Contact: Administrator, Farmers Home Administration, Department of Agriculture, Washington, DC 20250/202-447-7967.

Storage Facilities and Equipment Loans

Objectives: To complement the commodity loan and grain reserve programs by providing adequate financing for needed on-farm storage facilities, drying equipment, and operating equipment, thereby affording farmers the opportunity for orderly marketing of their crops.

Eligibility: Any person who as owner, landlord, tenant, or sharecropper produces one or more of the applicable commodities.

Range of Financial Assistance: Not specified.

Contact: Cotton, Grain and Rice Price Support Division, Agricultural Stabilization and Conservation Service, Department of Agriculture, P.O. Box 2415, Washington, DC 20013/ 202-447-5094.

Very Low-Income Housing Repair Loans and Grants

Objectives: To give very low-income rural homeowners an opportunity to make essential minor repairs to their homes to make them safe and remove health hazards to the family or the community.

Eligibility: Applicants must own and occupy a home in a rural area; be without sufficient income to qualify for a Section 502 loan; and have sufficient income to repay the loan.

Range of Financial Assistance: $200 to $7,500.

Contact: Administrator, Farmers Home Administration, Department of Agriculture, Washington, DC 20250/202-382-7967.

Watershed Protection and Flood Prevention Loans

Objectives: To provide loan assistance to sponsoring local organizations in authorized watershed areas for share of cost for works of improvement.

Eligibility: Sponsoring local organization, such as municipal corporation, soil and water conservation district, or other nonprofit organization in the approved watershed project, with authority under state law to obtain, give security for and raise revenues to repay the loan and to operate and maintain the facilities to be financed with the loan.

Range of Financial Assistance: $4,000 to $7,500,000.

Contact: Director, Community Facilities Division, Farmers Home Administration, Department of Agriculture, Washington, DC 20250/202-382-1490.

Making the Most of Your Food Dollars

A booklet called *Making Food Dollars Count* is available for fifty cents and contains valuable information for homemakers including nutritious meals for your dollar, recipes, and meal planning. Write: Consumer Information Center, Pueblo, CO 81009 and ask for publication #404M.

Market News Reports

Market news reporters gather and document marketing information on livestock and grain, fruits and vegetables, poultry tobacco and dairy production. The reporting is by personal observation, talking to buyers and sellers and by checking sales records. Information is gathered at the local field offices. A daily, weekly or monthly Market News Report is available, prices vary. Contact: Information Staff, Agricultural Marketing Service, Room 3068- South, United States Department of Agriculture, Washington, D.C. 20250/202-447-6766.

Marketing Orders

Agricultural Marketing Service assists farmers in organizing the distribution of commodities (other than milk) by issuing marketing orders established by an administrative committee. Market stability and fair price standards is the purpose of the market order. Contact: Agricultural Marketing Service, USDA, (commodity) Washington, D.C. 20250.

Meat and Poultry Hotline

If you have a case of meat or poultry food poisoning to report, or a complaint about meat or poultry spoilage that due to improper packaging or processing, you may report in through the Meat and Poultry Hotline, Food Safety and Inspection Service, USDA, Washington, D.C. 20250/800-472-4485.

Meat and Poultry Inspection

USDA's Food Safety and Inspection Service maintains mandatory inspection of all meat and poultry shipped interstate and to foreign countries for human consumption. Inspection starts with approval of service for slaughtering or processing meats or poultry; inspection continues throughout every step of the slaughtering process. Firms interested in attaining the USDA's inspection service may Contact: Meat and Poultry Operations, Food Safety Inspection Service, U.S. Department of Agriculture, Washington, D.C. 20250/202-447-9113.

Market Studies

See "Agricultural Economists," "Computerized Data Bases," "Food Studies and Food Economics," "Library," "Regional Research Facilities," "Research," "Research and Reference Services," "Technology and Innovation."

Mining and Prospecting on Public Land

Under the Mining Law of 1872, qualified prospectors may search for mineral deposits on public domain lands. Contact: Minerals and Geology Mgmt., Forest Service, USDA, P.O. Box 2417, Washington, DC 20013/703-235-8010.

National Arboretum

A variety of woody ornamental and outdoor plants are grown and cared for on the 444 acres comprising the U.S. National Arboretum. Admission is free, and guided tours for 10 or more are available. Many free classes are offered (How to grow a vegetable garden and How to grow Bonsai)along with many special events and functions associated with gardening and growing plants. A free monthly newsletter lists the monthly calendar. Contact: U.S. National Arboretum, 3501 New York Avenue, Educational Department, Washington, DC 20002/202-475-4815.

Natural Disaster Assistance Available From the U.S. Department of Agriculture

This free publication provides an overview of USDA's disaster assistance programs. It describes types of assistance available and where to apply for assistance. USDA's local extension agents in each county can approve disaster applications for: conservation structures (when located on eligible lands); rehabilitation of farm lands destroyed by disaster; crop payment subsidies for disruption caused by disaster to regular crop schedules; sale of animal feed at below market price in emergency situations; animal grazing on reserve or conservation lands in emergency situations; donation of animal feed to Indian reservations when needed; donation of grain to migratory wildfowl domains. The federal government will remove debris from a major disaster from publicly or privately owned lands or waters. Contact: Office of Government and Public Affairs, United States Department of Agriculture, (Program Aid #1328) Washington, D.C. 20250/202-447-3298.

News on Agriculture

For daily news announcements on topics in agriculture, a recorded message can be heard: News Features/202-488-8358.

Nutrition Data Bank

Information from government, university, and industry laboratories on the nutrient content of foods is stored in the national Nutrient Data Bank Tabulations data program. For information in both machine-readable and published forms, contact: Human Nutrition Information Service, U.S. Department of Agriculture, Hyattsville, MD 20782/301-436-8617.

Nutrition Data Tapes and Files

Research of the Consumer Nutrition Division, U.S. Department of Agriculture generates many data sets related to food composition, the food intake of individuals, and the food used by households in the United States. These data sets, in machine-readable form, are available from NTIS. For a free catalog describing these data sets, request free brochure PR-615. Contact: NTIS, U.S. Department of Commerce, Springfield, VA 22161/703-487-4600.

Nutrition Education

The mission of Human Nutrition Information Service (HNIS) is to conduct and interpret research in human nutrition to improve professional and public understanding of the nutritional adequacy of diets and food supplies as well as the nutritive value of food, and to develop knowledge needed to improve the nutritional quality of diets. They also collect and disseminate information, and consult on technical and educational materials on food use, food management and human nutrition problems. Staff have knowledge of published papers, and can answer questions and make referrals. An important public service is the Nutrient Data Research Branch's Nutrient Data Bank. Its publications and magnetic tapes contain data in summary form. It publishes the *Agriculture Handbook No. 8 (The Composition of Foods),* the major Nutrient Data Bank publication. It covers all food groups and gives information on the nutrient composition of foods and is updated continually. It is available from the Government Printing Office, Washington, DC 20402/202-783-3238. Prices range from $6 to $9.50. Contact: Human Nutrition Information Service (HNIS), U.S. Department of Agriculture, 6505 Belcrest Road, Hyattsville, MD 20782/301-436-8457 (Nutrition Monitoring Division),/301-436-8507 (Survey Statistics Division),/301-436-8491 (Nutrient Data Research Branch),/301-436-8474 (Nutrition Education Division),/301-436-8470 (Diet Appraisal Research Board),/301-436-5194 (Guidance and Education Research Branch).

Nutrition Information Center
This information clearinghouse on human nutrition and food service management answers a wide range of inquiries. Contact: Food and Nutrition Information and Education Resources Center, Room 304, National Agricultural Library Building, 10301 Baltimore Blvd., Beltsville, MD 20705/301-344-3719.

Nutrition Publications
A series of publications is available describing the nutritional value of the following food groups: Dairy and Eggs; Spices and Herbs; Baby Foods; Fats and Oils; Poultry; Soups, Sauces and Grains; Sausages and Luncheon Meats; Pork Products; Breakfast Cereals by Brand Name; Nuts and Seeds; Fruits; Vegetables; Legumes; Fish and Shellfish; Beef; Cereal Grain Products; Beverages; Candies and Confections; and Mixed Dishes (TV dinners, pizza, etc.). For detailed information on the content of these publications contact: Nutrient Data Research Branch, CND, HNIS, Federal Building, Room 312, 6505 Belcrest Rd., Hyattsville, MD 20782/301-436-8491. The publications are available for sale at the Government Printing Office, Superintendent of Documents, Washington, DC 20402/202-783-3238.

Nutritional Labeling
The USDA is responsible for labeling requirements for meat and poultry only, and this is done on a voluntary basis. Contact: Meat and Poultry Standards and Labeling Division, FSIS, USDA, Ben Franklin Station, PO Box 7416, Washington, DC 20044/202-447-6043.

Nutrition Monitoring and Food Consumption Surveys
A survey to measure the food intake of individuals, the quality of the diet, and the response of American diets to short term changes in food supplies is being conducted. This "Continuing Survey of Intakes of Individuals", along with additional surveys, will support HNIS research in agricultural planning, the formation of agricultural and food policy, food quality and regulation and nutrition education. Contact: Human Nutrition

Information Service, U.S. Department of Agriculture, Hyattsville, Md. 20782/301-436-8617.

Organic Farming and Gardening
The National Agricultural Library has prepared a free bibliography on this subject containing over 200 citations. See "Library" in this section.

Packers and Stockyards Program
USDA's packers and stockyards specialists work with private producers and trade organizations to investigate complaints and file any complaint that may violate fair and open competition in the marketing of livestock. Contact: Packers and Stockyards Administration, USDA, Washington, DC 20250/202-447-7051.

Patent Licensing Opportunities
Government patents resulting from agricultural research discoveries are available for licensing to U.S. companies and citizens. There is no charge for licensing. For a description of the types of patents available, contact: Acquisition and Assistance, Room 528A, 6505 Belcrest Rd., Hyattsville, MD 20782/301-436-8402.

Patents on Seeds
All unique seeds, with few exceptions, that are sexually reproduced can be patented. The patent provides owners with exclusive rights to sell, reproduce, export and produce the seed; protection extends for 18 years. Contact: Plant Variety Protection Office, Warehouse and Seed Division/AMS, NAL Room 500, Beltsville, MD 20705/301-344-2518.

Perishable Agricultural Commodities
USDA's Agricultural Marketing Service (AMS) prohibits unfair trading practices among buyers and sellers of perishable items. The AMS will provide advice on rights and responsibilities and try to bring quarreling parties together for informal settlements of disputes. Contact: Regulatory Branch Agricultural Marketing Service, USDA Washington, D.C. 20250/202-447-4180.

Pick Your Own Fruits and Vegetables
Many farmers allow consumers to pick products directly from their fields at substantial savings. For a directory of farms which offer these direct marketing programs, contact: the State Department of Agriculture or a state extension service. See "Extension Service" in this section. For statistical information on how many farms direct market what kinds of products, contact: Food Economics, Direct Marketing, 500 12th St. S.W., Room 260, Washington, DC 20250/202-447-6363.

Plant and Entomological Services
A group of specialists study such topics as Biological Control of Pests, Corn and Sorghum Produc-

tion, Crop Mechanization and Pest Control Equipment, Crop Pollination, Bees and Honey, Insect Control, Forage Crop Production, Range Management, Plant Genetics and Breeding, Pest Control, Pest Management, Pesticide Usage and Impacts, Plant Introduction and Narcotics, Plant Pathology and Nematology, Weed Control, Small Grains Production, Sugar Crops Production, Vegetables and Ornamental Crops and Plant Physiology. Contact: Beltsville Agricultural Research Center, Building 003 Room 227, Beltsville, MD 20705/ 301-344-3078.

Plant Variety Protection
Federal legislation protects the ownership rights of breeders of plants that reproduce through seeds; the Agricultural Marketing Service can certify whether a new variety is entitled to protection. The AMS will then issue a certificate. Contact: Plant Variety Protection Office, Livestock, Meat, Grain, and Seed Division, Agricultural Marketing Service, U.S. Department of Agriculture, National Agricultural Library, Beltsville, Maryland 20705/ 202-344-2518.

Plants—Research and Reference
For assistance on topics involving plants, contact: National Arboretum Library, 3501 New York Ave. N.E., Washington, DC 20002/202-475-4815.

Post-Harvest Activity Effects on Consumer Products
The Eastern Regional Research Center's (ERRC) six laboratories are involved in applied, basic and developmental research. They are concerned with the effects of post-harvest processing, storage and handling on the quality and safety of consumer products. The laboratories are: 1) Food Safety, 2) Food Science, 3) Plant Science, 4) Animal Biomaterials, 5) Engineering Science, and 6) Physical Chemistry and Instrumentation. The Center sponsors seminars and a workshop series. Primary journals publish ERRC's research findings. Contact: Eastern Regional Research Center (ERRC), Agricultural Research Service, U.S. Department of Agriculture, 600 E. Mermaid Lane, Philadelphia, PA 19118, 215-233-6595.

Price Supports
This refers to interim financing by government enabling farmers to hold and sell their products at a profit when market prices rise and not at a depressed price when they need money. See "Loans and Loan Guarantees (Commodity Loans)" in this section.

Protection from Animal Pests and Diseases
For control or eradication of livestock/poultry pest or disease a state government and/or industry can receive cooperation from the Federal government to establish quarantines, vaccination procedures and destruction of diseased or exposed animals. Contact: Animal and Plant Health Inspection Service, Veterinary Services, USDA, Washington, DC 20250/ 202-447-3668.

Protection from Plant Pests and Diseases
USDA can assist states and growers control or eradicate pests and diseases that cause plant loss. The Animal and Plant Health Inspection service can cooperate with State agencies to establish quarantines, pesticide spray programs, or release of sterile insects to reduce pest populations. Contact: State Plant Regulatory Officials; or APHIS, USDA Washington, D.C. 20250/202-447-3977.

Quarantine—Plants and Animals
If you bring plants or animals into the country, they may be quarantined because of foreign pests. Contact: Information Division, Room 732, Federal Bldg., APHIS, USDA, Hyattsville, MD 20782/301-436-7776.

Quarterly Report to Congress
This is a free report summarizing research findings of research projects conducted by the Agriculture Department. Reports are about livestock, poultry, crops, insect pest control, soil and water resources, human nutrition and post-harvest technology and commercial uses for commodities. Contact: Current Information Branch, Agricultural Research Service, United States Department of Agriculture, Building 005, Beltsville, MD. 20905/202-344-4296.

Ranches and Fish Farms
Many of the USDA programs are available to ranchers and aquaculture operators. Because program requirements are continually updated, ranchers and aquaculture operators will find it valuable to investigate any farm-related programs.

Regional Research Facilities
The Agricultural Research Division of the Dept. of Science and Education manages 4 regional research facilities, each of which conducts research suitable to its locale. The regional offices are listed below, along with a brief description of subject areas covered:

ARS Northeast Regional Information Office, UDSA, Room 251, Building 003, Beltsville Agricultural Research Center-West, Beltsville, MD 20705/301-344-3530 (animal health, plants, genetics).

ARS North Central Regional Information Office, USDA, 2000 West Pioneer Parkway, Peoria, IL 61615/309-671-7166 (Crops of the north central region; grains).

ARS Southern Regional Information Office, USDA, P.O. Box 53326, New Orleans, LA 70153/504-589-6708 (Southern-region focus on cotton and other southern crops).

ARS Western Regional Information Office, USDA,

1333 Broadway, Suite 400, Oakland, CA 94612/
415-273-6052 (Fruit cropping, irrigation).

Each regional facility matches research needs of
the locale to the center.

Regulatory Activities
Listed below are those organizations within USDA
which are involved with regulating various business activities, with a description of those industries or situations which are regulated by the
office. Regulatory activities generate large
amounts of information on the companies and
subjects they regulate; much of this information is
available to the public. Regulatory activities can
also be used by consumers. A regulatory office
also can tell you your rights when dealing with a
regulated company.

Agriculture Marketing Service
Information Division, USDA, Room 3529 South
Building, Washington, DC 20250/202-447-6766.
Regulates the following segments of the agricultural industry: cotton, dairy products, fruits and
vegetables, livestock, poultry, grains, seeds, tobacco, transportation and warehouses, and
packers and stockyards.

Animal and Plant Health Inspection Service
Information Division, USDA, Room 1143, South
Building, Washington, DC 20250/202-447-3977.
Administers programs which help control and
eradicate diseases and pests that affect animals and
plants. Also administers programs which concentrate on animal and plant health as well as
quarantine.

Federal Grain Inspection Service
Administrator, USDA, Room 1628, South
Building, Washington, DC 20250/202-447-9170.
Establishes federal standards for grain and
performs inspections to ensure compliance. Regu-
lates the weighing of all grain for export.

Food Safety and Inspection Service
Information Division, USDA, Room 327-E,
Washington, DC 20250/202-447-7943.
Inspects all meats, poultry and egg products
shipped interstate and abroad, and insures that
labels on these products are truthful. Develops
official grade standards for meat, poultry, eggs,
dairy products and fresh and processed fruits and
vegetables.

Foreign Agricultural Service
Information Services, USDA, Room 5074, South
Building, Washington, DC 20250/ 202-447-3448.
Regulates the imports of beef, dairy products,
and other commodities by administering quotas
imposed by the President.

Forest Service
Director, Office of Information, USDA, 3244
South Building, Washington, DC 20250/202-
447-3957.
Regulates the activities of commercial foresters
working in national forests.

Other
In addition to the organizations mentioned above,
any office which administers loans, grants, direct
payments, or loan guarantees performs a regulatory function by insuring that the guidelines of the
program are enforced. See "Loans and Loan
Guarantees," "Grants," and "Direct Payments."

Research
The following six agencies conduct and administer
research. Each can be contacted directly for a
more detailed listing of topics covered along with
documentation of findings.

Agricultural Research Service
Science and Education Administration, USDA,
Beltsville, MD 20705/301-344-2264.
Topics: Animal and plant production; use and
improvement of soil water and air; processing,
storage and distribution of farm products; food
safety and consumer service; human nutrition.

Cooperative State Research Service
Science and Education Administration, USDA,
Room 304-A, Washington, DC 20250/202-447-
4423.
Topics: Family and consumer services, natural
resources, grants for research in agriculture,
agriculture marketing, rural development and
forestry.

Soil Conservation Service
USDA, PO Box 2890, Wash., D.C. 20013/-
202-447-4543.

Forest Service
USDA, PO Box 2417, Wash., DC 20013/-
202-447-3760.

Agricultural Marketing Research
Agricultural Marketing Service, USDA, Room
0608, South Building, Washington, DC 20250/
202-447-3075.
Topics: Feasibility studies to determine need for
wholesale distribution facilities; provide technical
and hiring assistance to implement project; research alternative methods of handling, packaging
and distributing food; electronic marketing systems; examine effects and benefits of marketing
news on price reports for agricultural commodities
and retail food prices; provide statistical analysis to
AMS, improve government regulations within
AMS.

Research and Reference Services
Free services are available from the National Agricultural Library. A team of researchers is available to the public to answer questions and provide information on most any topic. Researchers will utilize resources both inside and outside of the library. See "Library" in this section.

Rural Abandoned Mine Program
This program eliminates safety hazards and protects remaining property at abandoned mine sites from becoming safety hazards. USDA aids participants in developing reclamation plans and may provide funding for approved plans up to 100%. The greater benefit to the public provided by the reclamation plan, the more the government will pay. The area to be reclaimed may not exceed 320 acres. Contact: local Soil Conservation Service.

Rural Agricultural Processing Industries
If your community wants to establish and operate an agricultural processing plant, the Science and Education Agency of USDA will help your community to assess the potential for an agricultural processing plant. USDA will also act as a liaison to find needed services, know-how, financial support, and any other assistance need for such a enterprise. Contact: Science and Education Agency, USDA, Washington, D.C. 20250/202-447-5923.

Rural Forestry Assistance
USDA provides assistance to State forestry agencies in a variety of ways. USDA provides technical, financial and related assistance; they will assist in the development of improved tree stands, procure produce and distribute tree seeds and trees, provide technical information and advice to forest landowners and vendors, wood processors and forest operators; determine effects of forestry practices on fish and wildlife and their habitats; effects of harvesting, processing, marketing and utilization of wood and wood products; and conversion of wood to energy. Contact: local Forest Service or Forest Service, U.S. Department of Agriculture, P O. Box 2417, Washington, D.C. 20013/202-447-6661.

Seed Labs
The Federal government can test seeds to determine their quality and that they are free from contamination. They will also prosecute any agent who transfers contaminated or mislabeled seed from state to state. Seeds are examined by/or at a state agent's request at no charge; commercial enterprises are subject to a fee. Contact: Federal Seed Lab, U.S. Department of Agriculture, Beltsville, MD 20705/ 301-344-2089 or Seed Branch, Agricultural Marketing Service, U.S. Department of Agriculture, Washington, DC 20250/202-447-9340.

Sick Pets, House Plants, Gardens, Trees and Lawns
Free technical assistance is available to aid in diagnosing and curing diseases of plants and animals. Services range from telephone consultations and free literature to analyzing your pet's stools or your plant's leaves or soil. See "Extension Service" in this section.

Small and Disadvantaged Businesses
A special office has been established to help small and minority businesses obtain contracts from the USDA. Contact: Office of Small and Disadvantaged Business Utilization, USDA, Room 127W, Administration Building, Washington, DC 20250/ 202-447-7117.

Soil and Farmland Protection Programs
Soil surveys are used not only for conservation purposes but to identify suitable lands for a wide variety of uses, from maintaining crops to urban uses. Information about soil helps prevent major construction mistakes and misuse of land that can be productively put to use. Soil maps identify flood prone areas and sources of water pollutants. One SCS program is the Land Evaluation and Site Assessment program which assists local planning officials in determining use of agricultural land for carbon use. Contact: Soil Conservation Service, USDA, P. O. Box 2890, Washington, D.C. 20250/202-447-4525.

Soil Conservation Technical Expertise
Technical expertise is available in such areas as geology, irrigation, drainage, landscape architecture, construction, sanitary and water quality and hydrology. Contact: Soil Conservation Service.

Soil, Water and Air Sciences
A group of specialists studies such topics as Environmental Quality, Erosion and Sedimentation, Soil Fertility and Plant Nutrition, Organic Wastes, Pesticide Degradation, Water Use Efficiency and Tillage Practices, and Weed Control Technology. Contact: Agricultural Environmental Quality Institute, Room 233, Bldg. 001, BARC, Beltsville, Md. 20705/301-344-3030.

Speakers
Experts will talk to groups for free on a wide variety of agricultural subjects. Contact: Office of Public Liaison, USDA, Washington, DC 20250/ 202-447-2798.

Stains and Spots
Help is available for consumers who wish to know how to remove stains from fabrics. Contact: Textile and Clothing Labs, USDA, 1303 W. Cumberland, Knoxville, TN 37916/615-974-5249.

Technology and Innovation
Studies and expertise on such topics as the application of solar energy to farm production,

new farm machinery technology, and the use of electronic automatic checkout systems in grocery stores are available from Info. Division, SRS/ERS/ USDA, 440-GHI, Washington, DC 20250/202-447-4230.

Telephone and Electricity in Rural Areas
The Rural Electrification Administration assists in providing telephone and electrical services to rural areas. See "Loans and Loan Guarantees" in this section.

Telephone Utility Systems
The USDA lends money to approximately 1,038 rural telephone companies and maintains a staff knowledgeable in both operations and equipment. Contact: Assistant Administrator—Telephone, Rural Electrification Administration, USDA, Room 4048, Washington, DC 20250/202-382-9554.

Tours
Visitors to the Beltsville Agricultural Research Center may arrange for a guided tour or tour the Center in their own car on the self-guided tour. Maps for the self-guided tour are available at the Visitor Unit (Bldg. 186) during the regular working hours of 8 a.m. to 4:30 p.m., Monday through Friday. The Center is closed to the public on Saturdays, Sundays, and holidays. To arrange for your guided tour call 301-344-2483 or write: Tour Coordinator, Agricultural Research Center, Beltsville, Md. 20705.

Toys, Free
Free litter bags, coloring sheets, song sheets, photographs, posters, bike stickers, and wallet cards are available from: Woodsy Owl, Forest Service, USDA, Room 3248, South Building, P.O. Box 2417, Washington, DC 20013/202-475-3785.

Free badges, stickers and other children's toys are available by contacting: Smokey Bear Headquarters, U.S. Forest Service, P.O. Box 2417, Washington, DC 20013/202-235-8160.

Transportation Services
USDA recognizes transportation facilities as being an integral part of the agribusiness system. Farmers, shippers, farm organizations and local or state agencies who feel the need to bring about changes in freight service or rates for food products may seek assistance from the Office of Transportation. This office will hear any complaints and, as necessary, file an appropriate complaint. Contact: Office of Transportation, USDA, Washington, D.C. 20250/202-447-3963.

Transporting Plants Between States
Each state has separate rules and regulations for transporting plants across state boundaries. For information on a specific state's regulations, contact: the USDA office in your state.

Travel and Recreation Information
Travel planning aid and information are available to those wishing to visit one of the country's 154 national forests and 19 national grasslands. A particularly good brochure is "Field Offices of the Forest Service," FS-13. For this and other free brochures, contact: Publications, Forest Service, USDA, Room 3244, South Building, Washington, DC 20250/202-447-3957.

Travelers Tips
USDA will advise travelers about what agricultural and related products may be brought into the United States from foreign countries. Contact: Travelers Tips, USDA, Hyattsville, MD 20782.

Urban Trees and Use of Wood from Trees
USDA will provide financial, technical and related assistance in order to plant and protect trees; maintain and utilize wood from trees in open spaces, green belts, roadside screens, parks, woodlands, curb areas, and residential developments in urban areas. Contact: Local Forest Service, or Forest Service, USDA, P. O. Box 2417, Washington, DC 20013/703-235-2076.

Veterinary Services
A staff of specialists study communicable diseases and pests affecting livestock and poultry. Contact: Veterinary Services, Animal and Plant Health Inspection Service, USDA, Room 320-E, Washington, DC 20250/202-447-5193.

Volume Food Buyers
USDA specialists work with volume food buyers developing specifications for food commodities using specifications, grades and standards that have been developed by USDA for this purpose. USDA graders examine food and certify the food buyers' purchases, prior to delivery. Any processor, wholesaler, retailer, hospital, restaurant, governmental agency, educational institution, airline or other public or private group buying food in large quantities may ask USDA for their inspection services. Contact: Agricultural Marketing Service, USDA, at the appropriate commodity division: Poultry Division, 202-447-3271; dairy products, 202-447-3171; meat and meat products, 202-382-1113; fruits and vegetables, 202-4474693; fresh products, 202-447-4693 for processed products. Washington, DC 20250.

Warehouse Assistance
USDA's Agricultural Stabilization and Conservation Service administers an examination program to assure the quality of warehouses storing agricultural commodities. The Secretary of Agriculture will license public warehouse operators who qualify for a license. Contact: Agricultural Stabilization and Conservation Service, USDA, Room 5962, Washington, DC 20013/202-382-8037 or

Kansas City Commodity Office, P.O. Box 205, Kansas City, MO 64041/816-926-6476.

Water Programs
USDA offers a variety of water reclamation programs to aid landowners and agricultural operators use existing water resources wisely and efficiently and; reclaim or preserve water sources that have been contaminated or allowed to fall into disrepair. Some of the programs are:

Rural Clean Water Program—reduces nonpoint source water pollutants

Watershed Projects—provides flood prevention, watershed protection, agricultural water management, recreation, municipal and industrial water supply management and fish and wildlife development assistance.

Water Bank Program—preserves, restores, and improves inland fresh water sources and adjacent areas in conservation areas.

USDA will provide technical and financial assistance to any approved project that meets its criteria. Contact: Local Agricultural cooperative Service Office, or Soil Conservation Service Ofice, USDA, P.O. Box 2890, Washington, DC 20013/202-447-2847.

Weather Reports
A weekly publication summarizes weather conditions and their effect on crops for the previous week. Single copies are 50¢. Annual subscriptions are $25.00. Contact: Weekly Weather and Crop Bulletin, USDA, Room 5844, South Building, Washington, DC 20250/202-447-7917.

Wholesale Markets
USDA will study, with the cooperation of state and local governments and university research and extension programs, needs for new or additional agricultural marketing facilities. Studies will recommend the development of improved existing market facilities and distribution centers, or recommend new facilities and centers. Contact: Market Research and Development Division, Agricultural Marketing Service, USDA Washington, DC 20250/202-447-3075.

Wilderness
The National Wilderness Preservation System consists of 25.5 million acres of roadless undeveloped lands which represent America's natural heritage. The land is open to the public but contains no commercial enterprises and motorized access is prohibited. Contact: Recreation, Forest Service, USDA, Box 2417, Washington, DC 20013/202-447-3760.

Wildlife and Birds
Bulk grain is available in emergency situations for wildlife and birds at the request of the U.S. Department of Interior. Contact: Administrator, Room 3086, ASCS, USDA, South Building, Washington, DC 20250/202-447-3467.

Wine and Cheese Making at Home
The USDA has accumulated documentation and expertise to assist in making wine and cheese at home. For a literature review on these topics, ask for the wine and cheese Agri-Topics Reports from National Agricultural Library (see "Library" in this section). For expertise in cheese, contact: USDA, Engineering Lab, Eastern Regional Research Center, 600 East Mermaid Lane, Philadelphia, PA 19118/215-233-6516.

Wood Pests
USDA provides technical assistance for insect and disease to wood, be it wood in use, stored wood, wood products and urban trees. All insect and disease suppression projects must meet specific criteria for Federal participation. Contact: the State Foresters or the area director of the U.S. Forest Service.

How Can USDA Help You?
A staff of research specialists is available to get you specific answers or point you to an expert who can help. Ask for a list entitled "How to Get Information from the U.S. Department of Agriculture." If USDA does not have an answer to your question, they will also help in locating another agency who might. Contact: Information Office, Office of Public Affairs, USDA, Room 402-A, Washington, DC 20250/ 202-447-7454.

Department of Commerce

**14th St. between Constitution Ave. and E St. N.W.,
Washington, DC 20230/202-377-2000**

**Established: March 4, 1913
Budget $1,575,882,000
Employees: 25,912**

MISSION: Encourage, serve and promote economic development and technological advancement. Offer assistance and information to help increase exports. Administers programs to prevent unfair foreign trade competition. Provide social and economic statistics and analyses for business and government planners. Provide research and support for the increased use of scientific, engineering and technological development. Grant patent and register trademarks. Aids domestic economic development, seek to improve understanding of the Earth's physical environment and oceanic life. Promote travel to the United States by residents of foreign countries. Assist in the growth of minority business.

Major Divisions and Offices

International Trade Administration (ITA)

Department of Commerce, Room 3850,
Washington, DC 20230/202-377-2867.
Budget: $148,033,000
Employees: 2,411
Mission: Promote world trade; strengthen the international trade and investment position of the U.S.; and coordinate all issues concerning trade administration, international economic policy and programs, and trade development.

National Oceanic and Atmospheric Administration (NOAA)

Department of Commerce, Room 5813,
Washington, DC 20230/202-377-2985.
Budget: $943,936,000
Employees: 12,740
Mission: Explore, map and chart the global ocean and its living resources. Manage, use and conserve those resources and describe, monitor and predict conditions in the atmosphere, ocean, sun and space environment. Issue warnings against impending destructive natural events. Develop beneficial methods of environmental modification and assess its consequences.

United States Travel and Tourism Administration

Department of Commerce, Room 1524,
Washington, DC, 20230/202-377-3811.
Budget: $8,189,000
Employees: 68
Mission: Utilizes the contribution of the tourism and recreation industries to economic prosperity, full employment, and the international trade balance; eliminates unnecessary trade barriers to the U.S. tourism industry operating throughout the world; ensures the compatibility of tourism and

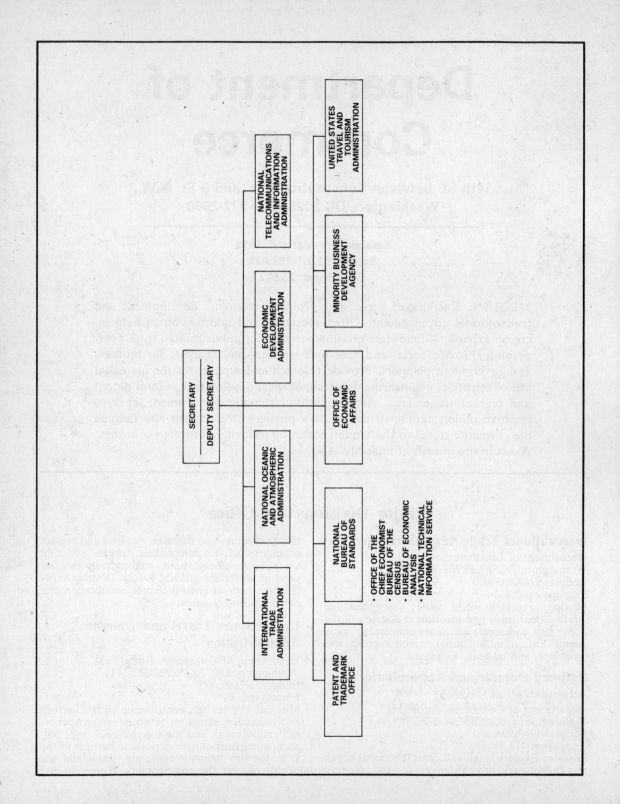

Department of Commerce

recreation with other national interests; and assists in the collection, analysis, and dissemination of tourism data.

Minority Business Development Agency (MBDA)

Department of Commerce, Room 5053, Washington, DC 20230/202-377-1936
Budget: $47,711,000
Employees: 250
Mission: Assists minority business in achieving effective and equitable participation in the American free enterprise system and in overcoming social and economic disadvantages; provides national policies and leadership in forming and strengthening a partnership of business, industry, and government with the Nation's minority businesses; provides management and technical assistance to minority firms on request, primarily through a network of local business development organizations funded by the agency; and promotes and coordinates the efforts of other federal agencies in assisting or providing market opportunities for minority business.

National Bureau of Standards (NBS)

Department of Commerce, Washington, DC 20234/301-921-1000.
Budget: $120,598,000
Employees: 2,849
Mission: Strengthen and advance the nation's science and technology and to facilitate their effective application for public benefit. Conduct research and provide a basis for the nation's physical measurement system, scientific and technological services for industry and government, technical basis for equity in trade, and technical services to promote public safety. Perform technical work at the National Measurement Laboratory, the National Engineering Laboratory, and the Institute for Computer Sciences and Technology.

Patent and Trademark Office

Department of Commerce, Washington, DC 20231/703-557-3158.
Budget: $78,459,000
Employees: 3,140
Mission: Examine patent and trademark applications. Issue patents and register trademarks. Sell printed copies of issued documents. Record and index documents transferring ownership. Maintain a scientific library and search files. Provide search rooms for the public to research their applications.

National Telecommunications and Information Administration

Department of Commerce, 14th and Constitution Ave, NW Room 4898 Washington, DC 20230/ 202-377-1840. Budget: $27,190,000
Employees: 267

Mission: Formulate policies to support the development, growth and regulation of telecommunications information and related industries. Further the efficient development and use of telecommunications and information services. Provide telecommunications facilities grants to public service users.

Office of Economic Affairs

Department of Commerce, Room 4850, Washington, DC 20230/202-377-3523.
Budget: $92,165,000
Employees: 4,444
Mission: Advises the Secretary and other departmental officials on economic affairs; and supervises the Department's statistical economic analysis and economic policy activities.

• *Office of the Chief Economist*

Department of Commerce, Room 4850, Washington, DC 20230/202-337-3727.
Budget: $315,000
Employees: 2

• *Bureau of the Census*

Department of Commerce, Washington, DC 20230/202-763-5190
Budget: $38,450,000
Employees: 3,576
Mission: To provide that a census of population is taken every ten years. To be a general purpose statistical agency which collects, tabulates, and publishes a wide variety of statistical data about the people and the economy of the nation. To have this data utilized by the Congress, by the executive branch, and by the public in the development and evaluation of economic and social programs.

• *Bureau of Economic Analysis (BEA)*

Department of Commerce, Tower Building, Room 704, 14th and K St., N.W., Washington DC, 20230/202-523-0777
Budget: $22,400,000
Employees: 482
Mission: To prepare, develop, and interpret the economic accounts of the United States. To provide a realistic, quantitative view of the production, distribution, and use of the nation's output.

• *National Technical Information Service (NTIS)*

Department of Commerce, 5285 Port Royal Rd., Springfield, Virginia 22161/703-557-4660.
Budget: $31,000,000*
Employees: 384
Mission: Participates in the development of advanced information products and services for the

---

*Funded by sales receipts generated through the sale of products and services and deposited in the Information Product and Services Account, not direct appropriation.

achievement of U.S. productivity and innovational goals; and sells U.S. Government sponsored research, development, and engineering reports, as well as foreign technical reports and other analyses prepared by national and local government agencies, their contractors, or grantees.

Economic Development Administration

Department of Commerce, Room 7800B, Washington, DC 20230/202-377-5081.

Budget: $33,602,000
Employees: 434
Mission: Assist in the long-range economic development of areas with severe unemployment and low family income problems. Aid in developing public facilities and private enterprise to create new, permanent jobs through grants, loans and technical assistance. Provide financial and technical assistance for firms damaged by foreign imports.

Data Experts

Industry Experts

The Bureau of Industrial Economics maintains a staff of some 100 analysts who monitor specific industries. These analysts willingly share their information and industry contacts. They are a terrific resource for researchers beginning their investigation into any industry. If the list below does not present an industry which is of interest to you simply call the Director's office and ask for an expert who specializes in your topic. These experts can also be reached by mail, using the Director's address (Director, Bureau of Industrial Economics, Department of Commerce, Room 4878, Washington, DC 20230/202-377-1405).

Science and Electronics

Medical, Surgical, and Dental Equipment and Supplies, Opthalmic Goods, Horological Instruments/W. Claude Bandy/202-377-2957.
Bearings, Ball and Roller/William Fletcher/202-377-0309.
Telephone Communications Service/William J. Sullivan/202-377-2990.
Broadcast Systems and Service/E. MacDonald Nyhen/202-377-0570.
Electronic Components and Accessories/Jack R. Clifford/202-377-2587.
Computers, Business Equipment, Photographic Equipment/John E. McPhee/202-377-0572.
Science and Electronic Industries Data, Engineering and Scientific Instruments/Thomas F. Flood/202-377-5014.

Consumer Goods and Services Industries

Wholesale Trade, Hotels, Motels, Recreation Malton Evans/202-377-0351.
Insurance, Franchise Regulation in Legislation/Jacob H. Bennison/202-377-0341.
General Merchandise Retail Trade/Marvin J. Margulies/202-377-0345.
Retail Apparel and Accessory Stores/Marvin Margulies/202-377-0345.
Franchising/Andrew Kostecka/202-377-0342.
Advertising, Motion Pictures/Theodore A. Nelson/202-377-0348.

Banking, Consumer Credit, Finance/Wray Candilis/202-377-0339.
Footwear, Hides, Skins/James E. Byron/202-377-4034.
Leather, Tanning and Finishing/James E. Byron/202-377-4034.
Personal Leather Goods, Fur Skins, Luggage, Leather Apparel/James E. Byron/202-377-4034.
Commercial Kitchen Appliances, Primary Batteries, Household Furniture and Appliances, Electric Lamps/John Harris/202-377-1178.
Mopeds, Bicycles, Motorcycles, Sporting Arms and Ammunition, Sporting Goods, Lawn and Garden Equipment, Broomsand Brushes, Wigs, Caskets/Michael Maasen/202-377-2198.
Toys and Games, Jewelry Finding, Costume Jewelry, Silverware, Portable Lamps, Writing Instruments, Stamped Cookware, Flatglass, Novelties, Ceramics, Cutlery, Musical Instruments/Renee Gallop/202-377-1140.
Retail Foods, Wholesale Groceries, Confectionery, Chocolate, Cocoa, Baking/Neil Kenny/202-377-2428.
Dairy Products and Tobacco, Sugar, Grain Mill Products, Fats, Oils/William Janis/202-377-2250.
Meat, Poultry/Donald Hodgen/202-377-3346.
Beverages/Neil Kenny/202-377-2428.

Forest Products, Packaging, and Printing Division

Forest Products/James McElroy/202-377-5158.
Plywood and Veneer/James McElroy/202-377-5158.
Lumber Products/Adair A. Mitchell/202-377-0377.
Poles, Piling, Wood Laminates, Wood Preserving, Logs, Timber Resources/Howard Post/202-377-0378.
Paperboard Grades/Iris Dean/202-377-0380.
Pulp and Raw Materials, Newsprint/Donald W. Burts/202-377-0376.
Converted Paper Products and Paper Packaging/Leonard Smith/202-377-0375.
Plastic Packaging/William Lofquist/202-377-0379.
Commercial Printing/Charles Cook/202-377-0382.
Glass and Metal Containers/William Lofquist/202-377-0379.

Newspapers/William S. Lofquist/202-377-0379.

Book Publishing, Book Printing, Miscellaneous Publishing/William S. Lofquist/202-377-0379.

Periodicals and Greeting Cards, Bookbinding/Rose Marie Bratland/202-377-0381.

Water Resources/Patrick L. McAuley/203-377-4346.

Water Resources, Wastewater Equipment/John Matticks/202-377-4346.

Construction and Building Products, Construction and Building Materials/Abraham Goldblatt/202-377-0132.

Housing Construction/Abraham Goldblatt/202-377-0132.

Building Materials and Products/Charles B. Pitcher/202-377-0132.

Construction Statistics, Construction Review, Building Materials Industries/Nathan Rubinstein/202-377-0132.

Steel Products and Insulation Materials/Ralph Thompson/202-377-0608.

Transportation and Capital Equipment Division

Automotive Equipment/Joseph Kellagher/202-377-0673.

Alumininum and Miscellaneous Metals and Materials/Marie Harris/202-377-0575.

Aluminum and Magnesium/Marie Z. Harris/202-377-0575.

Precious Metals, Mercury, Titanium/James J. Manion/202-377-5157.

Miscellaneous Metals and Minerals, Industrial Diamonds/Neill F. Raab/202-377-2294.

Copper, Lead, Zinc/Robert Reiley/202-377-0575.

Iron and Steel Economic Analysis, Steel Mill Products, Casting and Forgings/Ralph F. Thompson/202-377-0608.

Steel Industry, Raw Materials/William S. Kruppa/202-377-0609.

Textiles/James Bennett/202-377-4058.

Apparel/Laurie McKenna/202-377-4058.

Steel Mill Products/Ralph F. Thompson/202-377-0608.

Automotive Equipment/Robert Coleman/202-377-0609.

Truck and Bus Equipment/Eduardo Japson/202-566-7425.

Aerospace Equipment/Gene Kingsbury/202-377-0677.

Air Conditioning and Refrigeration, Residential Solar Applications/Earl Nettles/202-377-0311.

Ship and Boat Building and Repair/Ralph R. Nordlie/202-377-0305.

Railroad Equipment/Ralph R. Nordlie/202-377-0305.

Power Generating Boilers/David S. Climer/202-377-0681.

Textile and Printing Machinery/T.J. Jackson/202-377-0313.

Agricultural and Construction Machinery and Equipment, Materials Handling Equipment/John A. Lien/202-377-0679.

Mining and Oil Field Machinery, Fluid Power Equipment, Pumps and Compressors/Edward J. McDonald/202-377-0680.

General Components, Ball Bearings, Industrial Fasteners, Power Transmission Equipment/William E. Fletcher/202-377-0309.

Fans and Blowers, Pollution Control Equipment, Plastics and Rubber Machinery/Edward D. Abrahams/202-377-0312.

Electrical Equipment/Richard A. Whitley/202-377-0682.

Metalworking Machinery and Equipment, Including Machine Tools/Thomas Gallogly/202-377-0314.

Abrasives, Tool and Die, Industrial Heating Equipment/Graylin Presbury/202-377-0383.

Cutting Tools, Welding Equipment, Generators, Rolling Mill Equipment/Paul Sacharov/202-377-0611.

Food Processing and Packaging, Machinery and Equipment/Irvin Axelrod/202-377-0310.

Machine Tools, Metal Cutting/Thomas Gallogly/202-377-0314.

Machine Tools, Metal Forming/John A. Mearman/202-377-0315.

Nuclear Power Plants, Turbine Generating Equipment, Power Boilers, and Related Equipment/David S. Climer/202-377-0681.

Basic Industries

Solid Waste/Diana B. Friedman/202-377-0612.

Refractories, and Steel Mill Products and Statistics/Patrick J. Torrilo/202-377-0608.

Chemicals/Harry F. Pfann/202-377-0128.

Fertilizers/Frank P. Maxey/202-377-0128.

Organic Chemicals/Harry Pfann/202-377-0128.

Rubber, Rubber Products/David H. Blank/202-377-0128.

Plastics, Pigments, Paints/David G. Rosse/202-377-0128.

Soaps, Detergents, Toilet Preparations/Leo McIntyre/202-377-0128.

Inorganic Chemicals/Frank Maxey/202-377-0128.

Pharmaceuticals and Miscellaneous Chemicals/-Leo R. McIntyre/202-377-0128.

Economists

A large staff of economists monitors various aspects of the economy. These experts can supply data and expertise for their specific areas of interest. They can be contacted by telephone or by writing to: Bureau of Economic Analysis, Department of Commerce, Washington, DC 20230. Be sure to include the expert's name and subject area on all correspondence.

Division Chiefs

Balance of Payments/Christopher L. Bach/202-523-0620.

Business Outlook/George R. Green/202-523-0701.

Computer Systems and Services/Vincent C. Finelli/202-523-0981.

Current Business Analysis/Carol S. Carson/202-523-0707.

Environmental and Nonmarket Economics/Gary Rutledge/202-523-0687.

Government/Joseph C. Wakefield/202-523-0715.

Interindustry Economics/Paula C. Young/202-523-0683.

International Investment/George R. Kruer/202-523-0657.

National Income and Wealth/Gerald F. Donahoe/202-523-0669.

Regional Economic Analysis/Hugh W. Knox/202-523-0946.

Regional Economic Measurement/Edwin J. Coleman/202-523-0901.

Statistical Indicators/Feliks Tamm/202-523-0535.

National Economics

Antipollution Capital Spending/Gary L. Rutledge/202-523-0687.

Auto Output/J. Daniel McCarron/202-523-0807.

Business Cycle/Feliks Tamm/202-523-0535.

Capital Consumption Allowance/Gerald Silverstein/202-523-0809.

Capital Investment, Plant and Equipment Expenditures/J. Stephen Landefeld/202-523-0874.

National Income and Wealth Division, Investment Branch/John Hinrichs/202-523-0791.

Capital Stock/John C. Musgrave/202-523-0837.

Capacity Utilization, Manufacturing/J. Stephen Landefeld/202-523-0874.

Composite Index of Economic Indicators/Feliks Tamm/202-523-0535.

Construction/Mary E. Joyce/202-523-0802.

Corporate Profits/Kenneth Petrick/202-523-0888.

Depreciation/Gerald Silverstein/202-523-0809.

Disposable Personal Income/Pauline Cypert/202-523-0832.

Econometric Models/Albert A. Hirsch/202-523-0729.

Employee Compensation/Pauline M. Cypert/202-523-0832.

Employee Benefit Plans/Martin Murphy/202-523-0810.

Environmental Studies/Gary L. Rutledge/202-523-0687.

Farm Output/Mary Hook/202-523-0813.

Forecasts and Projections/George R. Green/202-523-0701.

Government

Federal Grants-in-Aid/Deloris T. Tolson/202-523-0896.

Federal Price Measurement/Herman Shelby/202-523-0828.

Federal Purchase of Goods and Services, Currentt Dollars/David T. Dobbs/202-523-0744.

Federal Purchase of Goods and Services, Constant Dollars/Robert T. Mangan/202-523-0522.

Federal Receipts and Expenditures/David T. Dobbs/202-523-0744.

Federal Transfers and Contributions/Kathleen M. Downs/202-523-0885.

State and Local Purchases of Goods and Services/David J. Levin/202-523-0725.

State and Local Receipts and Expenditures/Donald L. Peters/202-523-0725.

Gross National Product, Current Estimates/Leo M. Bernstein/202-523-0824.

Gross National Product by Industry/Milo O. Peterson/202-523-0808.

Gross Private Domestic Investment/John C. Hinrichs/202-523-0791.

Input-Output Analysis/Paula Young/202-523-0683.

Capital Investment and Stocks/John Musgrave/202-523-0837.

Construction/Anne L. Probst/202-523-0703.

Employment and Employee Compensation/Pauline Cypert/202-523-0832.

Finance, Insurance and Real Estate/Carolyn B. Knapp/202-523-0867.

Foreign Trade/Arlene K. Shapiro/202-523-0427.

Government/Claiborne Ball/202-523-0764.

Manufacturing/Jane-Ring F. Crane/202-523-5314.

Mining/Jane-Ring F. Crane/202-523-5314.

Nonprofit Organizations/Nancy W. Simon/202-523-0859.

Retail Trade/Claiborne Ball/202-523-0764.

Services/Anne Probst/202-523-0703.

Input-Output Tables/Mark Planting/202-523-0873.

Transportation/Claiborne M. Ball/202-523-0764.

Utilities/Jane-Ring F. Crane/202-523-5314.

Wholesale Trade/Claiborne Ball/202-523-0764.

Input-Output Computer Tapes/Ray A. Seaton, II/202-523-0686.

Interest Income and Payments/Mary W. Hook/202-523-0813.

Inventories/John Mon/202-523-5421.

Manufacturing Capacity Utilization/J. Stephen Landefeld/202-523-0874.

National Income/Mary Hook/202-523-0813.

Personal Consumption Expenditures/James C. Byrnes/202-523-0819.

Personal Consumption Expenditures Autos/J. Daniel McCarron/202-523-0807.

Personal Consumption Expenditures Other Goods/0/Paul R. Lally/202-523-0829.

Personal Consumption Expenditures Services/-Clinton P. McCully/202-523-0836.

Personal Income/Pauline M. Cypert/202-523-0832.

Plant and Equipment Expenditures/J. Stephen Landefeld/202-523-0874.

Pollution Abatement Capital Spending/Gary L. Rutledge/202-523-0687.

Pollutant Costs and Emissions/Gary L. Rutledge/202-523-0687.

Price Measures—Implicit Price Deflator, Fixed

Weight Price Index, Chain Price Index/Shelby A. Herman/202-523-0828.

Producers' Durable Equipment/Jeffrey W. Crawford/202-523-0782.

Proprietor's Income/Susan Den Herder/202-523-0811.

Rental Income/Mary W. Hook/202-523-0813.

Savings, Personal/Jeannette M. Honsa/202-523-0839.

Seasonal Adjustment Methods/Morton Somer/-202-523-0505.

United Nations and O.E.C.D. System of National Accounts/Jeanette M. Honsa/202-523-0839.

Wealth Accounts/John A. Gorman/202-523-0803.

Regional Economics

BEA Economic Areas/Edward A. Trott, Jr./202-523-0973.

Economic Projections/Kenneth Johnson/202-523-0971.

Economic Situation, Current/Robert B. Bretzfelder/202-523-0948.

Employment Counties, SMSAs, BEA Economic Areas, and States/Linnea Hazen/202-523-0951.

Impact Analysis/Joseph Cartwright/202-523-0594.

Migration Patterns/Bruce Levine/202-523-0938.

Personal Income, Counties, SMSA's BEA Economic Areas, and States/Linnea Hazen/202-523-0951.

Regional Economic Information System/Staff/202-523-0966.

Residence Adjustment/Wallace K. Bailey/202-523-0561.

Shift-Share Analysis/Bruce Levine/202-523-0938.

Work Force Data/Bruce Levine/202-523-0938.

International Economics

Balance of Payments, Current Developments/Christopher L. Bach/202-523-0620.

Capital Expenditures of Majority-Owned Foreign Affiliates of U.S. Companies/Ralph Kozlow/202-523-0661.

Current Account Services/Walter G. Kealy/202-523-0625.

Foreign Direct Investment in the U.S./James L. Bomkamp/202-523-0547.

Government Grants & Capital Transactions/G. Seymour Kerber/202-523-0614.

International Direct Investment/George R. Kruer/202-523-0657.

International Travel/Joan E. Bolyard/202-523-0609.

Merchandise Trade/Howard Murad/202-523-0668.

Multinational Corporations, Analysis of Activities/David Belli/202-523-0645.

Plant and Equipment Expenditures by Foreign Affiliates of U.S. Corporations/Ralph Kozlow/202-523-0661.

Private Capital Transactions/Russell B. Scholl/202-523-0603.

Sources and Applications of Funds of Foreign Affiliates/David Belli/202-523-0645.

U.S. Direct Investment Abroad, Benchmark Survey/John P. Bogumill/202-523-0637.

Quarterly and Annual Data and Analysis/Obie C. Whichard/202-523-0646.

Survey of Current Business

Editor/Carol S. Carson/202-523-0707.

Statistical Series/Kenneth A. Beckman/202-523-0769.

Business and Manufacturing Sales, Inventories, and Orders/Delores Roberts/202-523-0769.

Chemicals and Allied Products/Rita M. Quick/202-523-0783.

Construction and Real Estate/Fred von Batchelder/202-523-0732.

Consumer and Wholesale Prices/Rita Quick/202-523-0783.

Electric Power and Gas/Rita Quick/202-523-0783.

Finance/Fred von Batchelder/202-523-0732.

Food and Kindred Products, Tobacco/Rita M. Quick/202-523-0783.

Foreign Trade of the United States/Rita Quick/202-523-0783.

General Business Indicators/Delores Roberts/202-523-0769.

Industrial Production/Rita Quick/202-523-0783.

Labor Force, Employment, and Earnings/Duhurst Hood/202-523-0788.

Leather and Products/Fred von Batchelder/202-523-0732.

Lumber and Products/Delores Roberts/202-523-0769.

Metals and Manufactures/Duhurst Hood/202-523-0788.

Personal Income/Delores Roberts/202-523-0769.

Petroleum, Coal, and Products/Rita M. Quick/202-523-0783.

Prices Received and Paid by Farmers/Rita Quick/202-523-0783.

Pulp, Paper and Paper Products/Delores Roberts/202-523-0769.

Rubber and Rubber Products/Delores Roberts/202-523-0769.

Stone, Clay, and Glass Products/Rita M. Quick/202-523-0783.

Textile Products/Duhurst Hood/202-523-0788.

Transportation Communication/Duhurst Hood/-202-523-0788.

Transportation Equipment/Rita Quick/202-523-0783.

U.S. Balance of International Payments/Rita Quick/202-523-0783.

Business Conditions Digest

Editor/Feliks Tamm/202-523-0535.

Statistical Series/Betty F. Tunstall/202-523-0589.

Census Data Experts

The individuals listed below are able to tell you exactly what census data are available in their subject areas. They can also be helpful in identifying what information is available on their topics from other sources. They can be contacted directly by telephone or by writing to Bureau of the Census, U.S. Department of Commerce, Washington, DC 20233.

Directorial Staff

Director/Vacant/301-763-5190.
Deputy Director/C. Louis Kincannon/301-763-5192.
Associate Director for Demographic Fields/William P. Butz/301-763-5167.
Associate Director for Economic Fields/Vacant/301-763-5274.
Associate Director for Statistical Standards and Methodology/Barbara A. Bailar/301-763-2562.
Associate Director for Administration/Clifford J. Parker/301-763-2350.
Associate Director for Field Operations/Roland Moore/301-763-7247.
Assistant Director for Demographic Censuses/Peter A. Bounpane/301-763-5613.
Assistant Director for Economic and Agriculture Censuses/Michael G. Farrell/301-763-7356.
Assistant Director for International Programs/Robert A. Bartram/301-763-4014.
Congressional Liaison/Staff/301-763-5360.
Data User Servicers Division/Staff/301-763-4100.
Public Information Office/Staff/301-763-4040.

Demographic Fields

Center for Demographic Studies/James Wetzel, Chief/201-763-7720.
Decennial Census Division/Stanley Matchett, Chief/301-763-7670.
Demographic Surveys Division/Thomas Walsh, Chief/301-763-2776.
Housing Division/Arthur F. Young, Chief/301-763-2863.
International Demographic Statistics Center/Samuel Baum, Chief/301-763-2870.
International Statistical Programs Center/Karl Kindel, Chief/301-763-2832.
Population Division/Roger Herriot, Chief/301-763-7646.
Statistical Methods Division/Charles D. Jones, Chief/301-763-2672.

Population and Housing Subjects

AGE AND SEX
States (age only)/Edwin Byerly/301-763-5072.
United States/Louisa Miller/301-763-5072.
Aliens/Nancy Sweet/301-763-7571.
Annexation Population Counts/Joel Miller/301-763-7955.

Apportionment/Robert Speaker/301-763-7955.
Births and Birth Expectations; Fertility Statistics/Martin O'Connell/301-763-5303.
Census Tract Population/Johanna Barten/301-763-5002.
CITIZENSHIP
Foreign Born Persons, Country of Birth; Foreign Stock Persons/Edward Fernandez/301-763-7571.
Means of Transportation; Place of Work/Philip Fulton/301-763-3850.
Consumer Expenditure Survey/Gail Hoff/301-763-2764.
CRIME SURVEYS
Data Analysis and Publication/Adolfo Paez/301-763-7984.
Victimization, General Information/Robert N. Tinari/301-763-1735.
Current Population Survey/Kenneth Riccini/301-763-2773.
DECENNIAL CENSUS
Content and Tabulations/Earle Knapp/301-763-1840.
General Plans/Rachel F. Brown/301-763-2748.
Minority Statistics Program/Alfred Hawkins/301-763-5987.
Disability/Jack McNeil/301-763-7946.
Education; School Enrollment/Paul Siegel/301-763-1154.
Employment; Unemployment; Labor Force/Thomas Palumbo/202-763-2825.
Farm Population/Diana DeAre/301-763-7955.
Health Surveys/Robert Mangold/301-763-5508.
HOUSEHOLDS AND FAMILIES
Size; Number; Marital Status/Steve Rawls/301-763-7950.
HOUSING
Annual Housing Survey/Edward Montfort/301-763-2881.
Components of Inventory Change Survey/Jane Maynard/301-763-5840.
Contract Block Program/Richard Knapp/301-763-2873.
Housing Information, Decennial Census/Bill Downs/301-763-2873.
Housing Vacancy Data/Paul Harple, Jr/301-763-2880.
Residential Finance/Peter Fronczek/301-763-2866.
INCOME STATISTICS
Current Surveys/Mary Henson/Ed Weiniak/301-763-5060.
Decennial Statistics/George Patterson/G. Lester/301-763-5060.
Household/Robert Cleveland/301-763-5060.
Revenue Sharing/Dan Burkhead/301-763-5060.
Incorporated/Unincorporated Places/Joel Miller/301-763-7955.
Industry and Occupation Statistics (See also Economic Fields)/John Priebe/301-763-5144.
Institutional Population/Arlene Saluter/301-763-7950.

International Populations/Samuel Baum/301-763-2870.

Language, Current; Mother Tongue/Paul Siegel/301-763-1154.

Longitudinal Surveys/Ronald Dopkowski/301-763-2380.

Migration/Kristin Hansen/301-763-3850.

Neighborhood Statistics/Joanne Eitzen/301-763-1818.

Outlying Areas (Puerto Rico, etc.)/Johanna Barten/301-763-5002.

POPULATION:

Decennial Census Count Complaints/Ann Liddle/301-763-1146.

General Information; Census Data; Characteristics; Survey Data/Johanna Barten/301-763-5002.

POPULATION ESTIMATES:

Congressional Districts: SMSAs/Donald Starsinic/301-763-5072.

Counties; Federal-State Cooperative Program for Local Population Estimates/Fred Cavanaugh/301-763-7722.

Estimates Research/Richard Irwin/301-763-7883.

Local Areas; Revenue Sharing/Fred Cavanaugh/301-763-7722.

States/Edward Byerly/301-763-5072.

United States (National)/Louisa Miller/301-763-5072.

POPULATION PROJECTIONS:

Federal-State Cooperative Program for Population Projections/Fred Cavanaugh/301-763-7722.

Household Projections/Robert Grymes/301-763-7950.

National/Gregory Spencer/301-763-5964.

State/Signe Wetrogan/301-763-5964.

Poverty Statistics; Low Income Areas/Arno Windard/301-763-5790.

PRISONER SURVEYS:

National Prisoner Statistics/Robert Tinari/301-763-1735.

Data Analysis and Publication/John Wallerstedt/301-763-7968.

RACE AND ETHNIC STATISTICS:/Nampeo McKenney/301-763-7890.

American Indian Population/Karen Crook/Edna Paisano/301-763-5910.

Asian Americans/Patricia Berman/301-763-2607.

Black Population/Dwight Johnson/301-763-7572.

Ethnic Populations/Edward Fernandez/301-763-7571.

Race/Patricia Berman/301-763-2607.

Spanish Population/Edward Fernandez/301-763-7571.

Religion/Edward Fernandez/301-763-7571.

Revenue Sharing (See also Economic Fields—Governments; Income Statistics)/Douglas Sater/301-763-5178.

Sampling Methods/Charles Jones/301-763-2672.

Social Indicators/Dave O'Neill/301-763-3918.

Social Stratification/Paul Siegel/301-763-1154.

Special Censuses/George Hurn/301-763-7854.

Special Surveys/Ronald Dopkowski/301-763-2380.

SMSAs: Area Definition and Total Population/Johanna Barten/301-763-5002.

SMSAs: New Criteria/Richard Forstall/301-763-5184.

Travel Surveys/John Cannon/301-763-2802.

Urban/Rural Residence/Diana DeAre/301-763-7955.

Veteran Status/Mark Littman/301-763-7962.

Voting and Registration/Jerry Jennings/301-763-5179.

Voting Rights/Paul Siegel/301-763-1154.

Ecnomic Fields

Agriculture Division/John H. Berry, Chief/301-763-5230.

Business Division/Howard Hamilton, Chief/301-763-2360.

Construction Statistics Division/Leonora M. Gross, Chief/301-763-7163.

Economic Census Staff/Michael Farrell, Chief/301-763-7356.

Economic Surveys Division/W. Joel Richardson, Chief/301-763-7735.

Foreign Trade Division/Barry M. Cohen, Chief/301-763-5342.

Governments Division/John R. Coleman, Chief/301-763-7366.

Industry Division/Gaylord E. Worden, Chief/301-763-5850.

Economic Subjects

AGRICULTURE:

Crop Statistics/Donald Jahnke/301-763-1939.

Farm Economics/John Blackledge/301-763-5819.

General Information/Mary Burch/301-763-1113.

Livestock Statistics/Thomas Monroe/301-763-1081.

Special Surveys/Kenneth Norell/301-763-5170.

CONSTRUCTION STATISTICS:

Census/Industries Surveys/Alan Blum/301-763-5435.

Special Trades; Contractors; General Contractor-Builder/Andrew Visnansky/301-763-7546.

Construction Authorized by Building Permits (C40 Series) and Residential Demolitions (C45 Series)/Linda Hoyle/301-763-7244.

Current Programs/William Mittendorf/301-763-7165.

Expenditures on Residential Additions, Alterations, Maintenance and Repairs, and Replacements (C50 Series)/George Roff/301-763-5717.

Housing Starts (C20 Series); Housing Completions (C22 Series); and New Residential Construction in Selected SMSAs (C21 Series)/David Fondelier/301-763-5731.

Price Indexes for New One-Family Homes Sold (C27 Series)/Steve Berman/301-763-7842.

Sales of New One-Family Homes Sold (C27 Series)/Steve Berman/301-763-7842.

Value of New Construction Put in Place (C30 Series)/Allan Meyer/301-763-5717.

County Business Patterns/Stanley Hyman/301-763-5430.

Employment/Unemployment Statistics/Thomas Palumbo/301-763-2825.

Energy Related Statistics/Martin Weingarten/301-763-7184.

Enterprise Statistics/John Dodds/301-763-7086.

Foreign Trade Information/Juanita Noone/301-763-5140.

GOVERNMENTS:

Criminal Justice Statistics/Diana Cull/301-763-7789.

Eastern States Government Sector/Genevieve Speight/301-763-7783.

Employment/Alan Stevens/301-763-5086.

Finance/Henry Wulf/301-763-7664.

Governmental Organization and Special Projects/ Diana Cull/301-763-7789.

Revenue Sharing (See also Demographic Fields)/ James Hogan/301-763-5120.

Taxation/John Behrens/301-763-5308.

Western States Government Sector/Ulvey Harris/ 301-763-5344.

Industry and Commodities Classification/C. Harvey Monk, Jr./301-763-1935.

MANUFACTURES:

Census/Annual Survey of Manufactures/John Govoni/301-763-7666.

Durables/Dale Gordon/301-763-7304.

Nondurables/Michael Zampogna/301-763-2510.

Subject Reports (Concentration, Production Index, Water, etc.)/Bruce Goldhirsch/301-763-1503.

Current Programs/T. Mesenbourg/301-763-7800.

Durables/Malcolm Bernhardt/301-763-2518.

Industry Surveys/Elinor Champion/301-763-5616.

Fuels/Electric Energy Consumed by Manufacturers/Dennis Wagner/301-763-5116.

Nondurables/Carole Ambler/301-763-5911.

Origin of Exports/Brigette Frandenburg/301-763-7860.

Shipments, Inventories, and Orders/Ruth Runyan/ 301-763-2502.

Mineral Industries/John McNamee/301-763-5938.

Minority Business/John Dodds/301-763-7086.

PUERTO RICO:

Census of Retail Trade, Wholesale Trade, and Selected Service Industries/William Wade/301-763-7778.

RETAIL TRADE:

Annual Retail Trade Report; Advance Monthly Retail Sales; Monthly Retail Inventories Survey/ Ronald Piencykoski/301-763-7561.

Census/Mark Wallace/301-763-7038.

Monthly Retail Trade Report: Accounts Receivable; and Monthly Department Store Sales/ Irving True/301-763-7128.

SELECTED SERVICE INDUSTRIES:

Census/Sidney Marcus/301-763-7039.

Current Services Reports/Faran Stoetzel/301-763-3916.

TRANSPORTATION:

Commodity Transportation Survey; Truck Inventory and Use; Domestic Movement of Foreign Trade Data/C. Campbell/J. Schroeder/301-763-1744.

WHOLESALE TRADE:

Census/John Trimble/301-763-5281.

Current Wholesale Sales and Inventories; Green Coffee Survey; Canned Food Survey/Faran Stoetzel/301-763-3916.

Geography and Statistical Research

Geography Division/Robert Marx, Chief/301-763-5636.

Boundaries and Annexations/Brian Scott/301-763-2364.

Census Geography 1970/1980/Staff/301-763-5720.

Computer Graphics and Computer Mapping/Frederick Broome/301-763-7818.

Congressional District Atlas/Kevin Shaw/301-763-5437.

Earth Resources Satellite Technology:

International/Robert Durland/301-763-1996.

United States/James Davis/301-763-2364.

Geographical Base File/Dual Independent Map Encoding (GBF/DIME) System/Staff/301-763-7315.

Geographic Area Measurement and Centers of Population/Roy Borgstede/301-763-7748.

Geographic Statistical Areas/Staff/301-763-2364.

Revenue Sharing Geography/Boo Bukondi/301-763-5720.

User Services

Administrative Services Division/Robert Kirkland, Chief/301-763-5400.

Data User Services Division/Michael G. Garland, Chief/301-763-5820.

Field Division/Lawrence Love, Chief/301-763-5000.

Age Search/Frederick Bohme/301-763-7936.

Bureau of the Census Catalog/John McCall/301-763-1584.

Census Procedures, History of/Frederick Bohme/ 301-763-7936.

Clearinghouse for Census Data Services/John Kavaliunas/301-763-1580.

College Curriculum Support Project/Les Solomon/ 301-763-2370.

Computer Tapes/Customer Service/301-763-4100.

Data User News (Monthly Newsletter)/Neil Tillman/301-763-1584.

DATA USER TRAINING:

Registration/Dorothy Chin/301-763-1510.

Seminars, Workshops, Conferences/Deborah Barrett/301-763-1510.

Exhibits/Joanne Dickinson/301-763-1510.

Guides and Directors/Gary Young/301-763-1584.

Library/Betty Baxtresser/301-763-5040.
Circulation/Jim Thorne/301-763-1175.
Interlibrary Loan/Staff/301-763-1930.
Out of Print Publications and Microfiche/Census Unit/301-763-5511.
Reference Service/Grace Waibel/301-763-5042.
Map Orders/Wendell McManus/812-288-3213.
Microfilm/Customer Service/301-763-4100.
Public Use Samples (Microdata)/Jim Clarke/301-763-5242.
Reapportionment/Redistricting/Marshall Turner/-301-763-1386.
State Data Center Program/Larry Carbaugh/301-763-1580.
Statistical Compendia/Glenn King/301-763-5299.
Publication Orders (Subscriber Services)/Customer Services/301-763-4100.
User Software (CENSPAC, ADMATCH, etc.)/Staff/301-763-4100.

User Assistance in Regional Offices
Atlanta, GA/Forest P. Cawley/404-881-2271.
Boston, MA/Arthur G. Dukakis/617-223-2327.
Charlotte, NC/Joseph F. Harris/704-371-6142.
Chicago, IL/Stanley D. Moore/312-353-6251.
Dallas, TX/John E. Reeder, Jr./214-767-2621.
Denver, CO/William Adams/303-234-3924.
Detroit, MI/Robert G. McWilliam/313-226-7742.
Kansas City, KS/Marvin L. Postma/913-236-3728.
Los Angeles, CA/Dwight P. Dean/213-209-6616.
New York, NY/William Hill/212-264-3860.
Philadelphia, PA/James F. Holmes/215-597-4920.
Seattle, WA/Leo C. Schilling/206-442-7828.

Country Experts
A large staff of experts is available to provide information on marketing and business practices for almost every country in the world. If you are trying to sell goods or services to a specific country, contact the country expert listed below by telephone or by writing to: International Trade Administration, Department of Commerce, Herbert C. Hoover Building, Washington, DC 20230. Be sure to include the expert's name and country name on all correspondence.
Afghanistan/Stan Bilinski/202-377-2954.
Albania/Karen Jurew/202-377-2645.
Algeria/Cynthia McDonald/202-377-5737.
Angola/Simon Bensimon/202-377-0357.
Argentina/Mark Siegelman/202-377-5427.
ASEAN/Kent Stauffer/202-377-3875.
Australia/Stephen Hall/202-377-3646.
Austria/Philip Combs/202-377-2897.
Bahamas/Libby Roper/202-377-2527.
Bahrain/Claude Clement/202-377-5545.
Bangladesh/Naomi Bradshaw/202-377-2954.
Barbados/Desmond Foynes/202-377-2527.
Belgium/Boyce Fitzpatrick/202-377-2920.
Belize (British Honduras)/Desmond Foynes/202-377-2527.
Benin/John Crown/202-377-4564.

Bermuda/Libby Roper/202-377-2527.
Bhutan/Dick Harding/202-377-2954.
Bolivia/Richard Muenzer/202-377-4302.
Botswana/Reginald Biddle/202-377-5148.
Brazil/Wilbur Garges/202-377-5427.
Brunei/Gary Bouck/202-377-3875.
Bulgaria/Karen Jurew/202-377-2645.
Burma/Kyaw Win/202-377-5334.
Burundi/Simon Bensimon/202-377-0357.
Cambodia/JeNelle Matheson/202-377-2462.
Cameroon/Philip Michelini/202-377-0357.
Canada/Thomas Brewer/202-377-3101.
Cape Verde Islands/John Crown/202-377-4564.
Caymans/Libby Roper/202-377-2527.
Central African Republic/Philip Michelini/202-377-0357.
Ceylon (Sri Lanka)/Naomi Bradshaw/202-377-2954.
Chad/Fred Stokelin/202-377-4564.
Chile/Bert Lindow/202-377-4302.
China, People's Republic of (Mainland)/Robert Perito/202-377-3583.
China, Republic of (Taiwan)/Christine Carter/202-377-4957.
Colombia/Richard Muenzer/202-377-4302.
Comoros/Fred Stokelin/202-377-4564.
Congo (Brazzaville)/Philip Michelini/202-377-0357.
Costa Rica/Robert Bateman/202-377-2527.
Cuba/Walter Bastian/202-377-2527.
Cyprus/Ann Corro/202-377-3945.
Czechoslovakia/Karen Jurew/202-377-2645.
Denmark/Maryanne Lyons/202-377-3524.
D'Jibouti/Fred Stokelin/202-377-4564.
Dominican Republic/Robert Bateman/202-377-2527.
Ecuador/Fred Kayser/202-377-4302.
El Salvador/Chai Pegues/202-377-2527.
Equatorial Guinea/Simon Bensimon/202-377-0357.
Egypt/Cheryl McQueen/202-377-4652.
Ethiopia/Fred Stokelin/202-377-4564.
European Economic Community (EEC)/Charles Ludolph/202-377-5276.
Finland/Maryanne Lyons/202-377-3254.
France/Ken Nichols/202-377-4941.
French Guiana/Robert Dormitzer/202-377-2527.
Gabon/Philip Michelini/202-377-0357.
Gambia/John Crown/202-377-4564.
Germany (East)/Delores Harrod/202-377-2645.
Germany (West)/V. Stanoyevitch/202-377-2841.
Ghana/John Crown/202-377-4564.
Greece/Ann Corro/202-377-3945.
Grenada/Desmond Foynes/202-377-2527.
Guatemala/Chai Pegues/202-377-2527.
Guinea/John Crown/202-377-4564.
Guinea-Bissau/John Crown/202-377-4564.
Guyana/Robert Dormitzer/202-377-2527.
Haiti/Libby Roper/202-377-2527.
Honduras/Scott Wylie/202-377-2527.
Hong Kong/Nancy Chen/202-377-2462.

Hungary/John Fogarasi/202-377-2645.
Iceland/Maryanne Lyons/202-377-3254.
India/Dick Harding/202-377-2954.
Indonesia/Don Ryan/202-377-3875.
Iran/Kathleen Keim/202-377-4652.
Iraq/Mark Roth/202-377-5767.
Ireland/Boyce Fitzpatrick/202-377-2920.
Israel/Kathleen Keim/202-377-4652.
Italy/Noel Negretti/202-377-3462.
Ivory Coast/Peter Ryan/202-377-4388.
Jamaica/Scott Wylie/202-377-2527.
Japan/Maureen Smith/202-377-4527.
Jordan/Vicky Eicher/202-377-4652.
Kampuchea/JeNelle Matheson/202-377-2462.
Kenya/Fred Stokelin/202-377-4564.
Korea (South)/Scott Goddin/202-377-4399.
Kuwait/Vicky Eicher/202-377-4652.
Laos/Jeffrey Lee/202-377-4681.
Lebanon/Mark Roth/202-377-5767.
Lesotho/Reginald Biddle/202-377-5148.
Liberia/John Crown/202-377-4564.
Libya/Gwen Brown/202-377-5737.
Luxembourg/Boyce Fitzpatrick/202-377-2920.
Macao/Nancy Chen/202-377-2462.
Madagascar/Simon Bensimon/202-377-0357.
Malaysia/Gary Bouck/202-377-3875.
Malawi/Reginald Biddle/202-337-5148.
Maldives/Naomi Bradshaw/202-377-2954.
Mali/Fred Stokelin/202-377-4564.
Malta/Robert McLaughlin/202-377-5401.
Mauritania/John Crown/202-377-4564.
Mauritius/Simon Bensimon/202-377-0357.
Mexico/Dale Slaght/202-377-2332.
Mongolia/Lillian Monk/202-377-3932.
Morocco/Gwen Brown/202-377-5737.
Mozambique/Reginald Biddle/202-377-5148.
Namibia/Urath Gibson/202-377-5148.
Nepal/Jeff Johnson/202-377-2954.
Netherlands/Robert McLaughlin/202-377-5401.
New Zealand/Stephen Hall/202-377-3646.
Nicaragua/Walter Bastian/202-377-2527.
Niger/Fred Stokelin/202-377-4564.
Nigeria/James Robb/202-377-4388.
Norway/James Devlin/202-377-4414.
Oceania/Stephen Hall/202-377-3646.
Oman/Vicky Eicher/202-377-4652.
Pacific Islands/Stephen Hall/202-377-3646.
Pakistan/Stan Bilinski/202-377-2954.
Panama/Robert Bateman/202-377-2527.
Paraguay/Linda Bawer/202-377-5427.
People's Democratic Republic (Yemen)/Tom
    Sams/202-377-5767.

Peru/Bert Lindow/202-377-4302.
Philippines/George Paine/202-377-3875.
Poland/Delores Harrod/202-377-2645.
Portugal/Randy Miller/202-377-4509.
Puerto Rico/Bruce Sever/202-377-2623.
Qatar/Claude Clement/202-377-6545.
Romania/Edgar Fulton/202-377-2645.
Rwanda/Simon Bensimon/202-377-0357.
Sao Tome and Principe/Simon Bensimon/202-377-
    0357.
Saudi Arabia/Karl Reiner/202-377-5767.
Senegal/John Crown/202-377-4564.
Seychelles/Fred Stokelin/202-377-4564.
Sierra Leone/John Crown/202-377-4564.
Singapore/Gary Bouck/202-377-3875.
Somali/Fred Stokelin/202-377-4564.
South Africa/Urath Gibson/202-377-5148.
Spain/Randy Miller/202-377-4508.
Sri Lanka/Naomi Bradshaw/202-377-2954.
Sudan/Fred Stokelin/202-377-4564.
Surinam/Robert Dormitzer/202-377-2527.
Swaziland/Reginald Biddle/202-377-5148.
Sweden/James Devlin/202-377-4414.
Switzerland/Philip Combs/202-377-2897.
Syria/Vicky Eicher/202-377-4652.
Taiwan/Christine Carter/202-377-4957.
Tanzania/Fred Stokelin/202-377-4564.
Thailand/Don Ryan/202-377-3875.
Togo/John Crown/202-377-4564.
Trinidad and Tobago/Desmond Foynes/202-377-
    2527.
Tunisia/Cynthia McDonald/202-377-5737.
Turkey/Ann Corro/202-377-3945.
Uganda/Fred Stokelin/202-377-4564.
United Arab Emirates (UAE)/Claude Clement/
    202-377-5545.
United Kingdom/Paul Norloff/202-377-3748.
Upper Volta/Fred Stokelin/202-377-4564.
Uruguay/Linda Bawer/202-377-5427.
USSR/Hertha Heiss/202-377-4655.
Venezuela/Carlos Montoulieu/202-377-4302.
Vietnam/JeNelle Matheson/202-377-2462.
Virgin Islands (UK)/Desmond Foynes/202-377-
    2527.
Virgin Islands (U.S.)/Bruce Sever/202-377-2623.
Yemen Arab Republic/Tom Sams/202-377-5767.
Yugoslavia/Geoffrey Jackson/202-377-4508.
Zaire/Simon Bensimon/202-377-0357.
Zambia/Reginald Biddle/202-377-5148.
Zimbabwe/Urath Gibson/202-377-5148.

Major Sources of Information

Abuses and Waste Hotline
A hotline has been established for those who wish
to report to the U.S. Department of Commerce
anything involving mismanagement, fraud, abuse
or waste. Contact: Inspector General's Office,
Department of Commerce, P.O. Box 612, Ben
Franklin Station, Washington, DC 20044/202-377-
2495, 800-424-5197.

Acoustic Research

The Mechanical Production Metrology Division performs research and provides services to both industry and government in the following areas: microphone calibrations; testing and evaluation of acoustical instruments, for example, sound level meters, noise dosimeters, hearing aids. Their special laboratory facilities, called anechoic chambers, are available for cooperative research. Staff have written technical papers which are available to scientists and other professionals in the field. Staff can answer questions and/or make referrals to experts. Contact: Mechanical Production Metrology Division, Room A149, Sound Building, National Bureau of Standards, Gaithersburg, MD 20899, 301-921-3607.

Advisory and Consulting Services

The National Bureau of Standards (NBS) provides advisory and consulting services to assist government and industry in the development of standards. As the national reference for physical measurement, NBS produces measurement standards data necessary to create, make, and sell U.S. products and services at home and abroad. Staff work closely with industry and consumers at every level. Generally, a staffer can lead you to major companies, research centers, experts, and literature. Contact: National Bureau of Standards, Laboratories and Center, Gaithersburg, MD 20899, 301-921-1000. Listed below are NBS' laboratories and centers which can provide scientific and technological services as well as measurement, instrumentation and standards information.

The National Engineering Laboratory provides technology and technical services to the public and private sectors to address national needs and to solve national problems; conducts research in engineering and applied science in support of these efforts; builds and maintains competence in the necessary disciplines required to carry out this research and technical service; develops engineering data and measurement capabilities; provides engineering measurement traceability services; develops test methods and proposes engineering standards and code changes; develops and proposes new engineering practices; and develops and improves mechanisms to transfer results of its research to the ultimate user. Contact: The National Engineering Laboratory, Technology Bldg.—Room B119, National Bureau of Standards, Gaithersburg, MD 20899 301-921-3434. The Laboratory consists of the following centers:

The Center for Applied Mathematics is involved in statistical models, computational methods, math tables, handbooks and manuals. Contact: Center for Appied Mathematics, Administration Bldg.—Room A438, National Bureau of Standards, Gaithersburg, MD 20899, 301-921-2541.

The Center for Building Technology is involved in performance criteria and measurement technology for building owners, occupants, designers, builders, manufacturers and regulatory authorities. Contact: Center for Building Technology, Building Research—Room B250, National Bureau of Standards, Gaithersburg, MD 20899, 301-921-3377.

The Center for Chemical Engineers is involved in measurement data, standards, and services for fluids, solids and gases. Contact: Center for Chemical Engineering, Cryogenics Bldg.—Room 2000, 325 Broadway, Boulder, CO 80303, 303-497-5108.

The Center for Electronics and Electrical Engineering is involved in engineering data, measurement methods, standards and technical services. Contact: Center for Electronics and Electrical Engineering, Metrology Bldg.—Room B358, National Bureau of Standards, Gaithersburg, MD 20899, 301-921-3357.

The Center for Fire Research is involved in engineering data, methods and practices, measurement and test methods for fire safety. Contact: Center for Fire Research, Polymers Bldg.—Room A247, National Bureau of Standards, Gaithersburg, MD 20899, 301-921-3143.

The Center for Manufacturing Engineering tests basic metrology, automation and control support for discrete part manufacturers and others. Contact: Center for Manufacturing Engineering, Metrology Bldg.—Room B322, National Bureau of Standards, Gaithersburg, MD 20899, 301-921-3421.

The Law Enforcement Standards Laboratory is involved in technical data for standards used by law enforcement officials to evaluate commercial products. Contact: Law Enforcement Standards Laboratory, Physics Bldg.—Room B157, National Bureau of Standards, Gaithersburg, MD 20899, 301-921-3161.

The National Measurement Laboratory provides the national system of physical and chemical and materials measurement; coordinates the system with measurement systems of other nations and furnishes essential services leading to accurate and uniform physical and chemical measurement throughout the Nation's scientific community, industry, and commerce; conducts materials research leading to improved methods of measurement, standards, and data on the properties of materials needed by industry, commerce, educational institutions, and Government; provides advisory and research services to other Government agencies; develops, produces, and distributes Standard Reference Materials; and provides calibration services. Contact: The National Measurement Laboratory, Physics Bldg.—Room A363, National Bureau of Standards, Gaithersburg, MD 20899, 301-921-2828.

The Center for Analytical Chemistry is involved in the measurement methods and services for analysis of chemicals of importance in industry, medicine, energy and pollution control. Contact: Center for Analytical Chemistry, Chemistry Bldg.—Room A309, National Bureau of Standards, Gaithersburg, MD 20899, 301-921-2851.

The Center for Basic Standards develops and maintains the scientific competences and laboratory facilities necessary to preserve and continue to refine the base physical quantities upon which the nation's measurement system is constructed. It improves, maintains and transfers the measurement base for time, frequency, electricity, temperature, pressure, and mass and length. Contact: Center for Basic Standards, Physics Bldg.—Room B160, National Bureau of Standards, Gaithersburg, MD 20899, 301-921-2001.

The Center for Chemical Physics is involved in the measurement methods and services for industry in surface science, molecular spectroscopy, chemical kinetics and thermodynamics. Contact: Center for Chemical Physics, Chemistry Bldg.—Room B162, National Bureau of Standards, Gaithersburg, MD 20899, 301-921-2711.

The Center for Materials Science is involved in measurement methods and services to evaluate materials such as gases, ceramics, metals, and polymers; and to deal with failure and substitution questions. Contact: Center for Materials Science, Materials Bldg.—Room B308, National Bureau of Standards, Gaithersburg, MD 20899, 301-921-2891.

The Center for Radiation Research develops methods, calibrations and products essential to the measurement of radiation for health care, nuclear energy, radiation processing and radiation safety. Contact: Center for Radiation Research, Radiation Physics Bldg.—Room C229, National Bureau of Standards, Gaithersburg, MD 20899, 301-921-2551.

The Institute for Computer Sciences and Technology conducts research and provides scientific and technical services to aid Federal agencies in the selection, acquisition, application, and use of computer technology to improve effectiveness and economy in Government operations. Contact: The Institute for Computer Sciences and Technology, Technology Bldg., National Bureau of Standards, Gaithersburg, MD 20899, 301-921-3151. The Institute consists of the following centers:

The Center for Programming Science and Technology is involved in standards and guidelines related to programming languages, software engineering, data management, computer security, and systems selection and evaluation. Contact: Center for Programming Science and Technology, Technology Bldg.—Room A247, National Bureau of Standards, Gaithersburg, MD 20899, 301-921-3436.

The Center for Computer Systems Engineering is involved in standards and guidelines related to computer system components, computer network protocols, local and area networks, and computer-based office systems. Contact: Center for Computer Systems Engineering, Technology Bldg.—Room A231, National Bureau of Standards, Gaithersburg, MD 20899, 301-921-3817.

Aeronomy Research

Information is available on the exotic chemistries in the upper atmosphere, including studies on the destruction of ozone in the stratosphere. Contact: National Oceanic and Atmosphere Administration (NOAA), Environmental Research Lab, Department of Commerce, 325 Broadway, Boulder, CO 80303/303-497-6286.

Air Quality and Atmospheric Research

Studies and expertise are available on subjects including short-term weather phenomena, long-term climate fluctuations, basis atmospheric dynamics, applied weather forecasting technologies and atmospheric pollution. Contact: Public Affairs Office, NOAA, Environmental Research Lab, Department of Commerce, 325 Broadway, Boulder, CO 80303/303-497-6286.

Air Resources Laboratory

For Research and expertise in the use of meteorology to understand and predict human influence on the environment, especially with regard to the atmospheric transport and diffusion of toxic effluents. Contact: ARL, NOAA, Department of Commerce, Environmental Research Laboratories, 6010 Executive Blvd., Rockville MD 20852/301-443-8276.

Appliance Labeling

The National Bureau of Standards (NBS) established methods and standards for measuring appliance efficiency so that labeling is uniform. Contact: Inquiry Service, NBS, Department of Commerce, Administration Building, Room A-537, Washington, DC 20234/301-921-2318.

Arab Boycott

For assistance and information on how to comply with the Arab Boycott laws contact: Antiboycott Compliance Staff, International Trade Administration (ITA), Department of Commerce, Room 2099B, Washington, DC 20230/202-377-2004.

Assistance for Smaller Businesses in New Technologies

The *Guide to Innovation Resources and Planning for the Smaller Business* identifies more than 50 Federal and 85 State government offices that assist smaller businesses bringing new technologies to market. It is written for individuals, companies, and state and local government economic development planners.

The *Guide* has two basic sections. The first examines the many steps in the innovation process and the skills and resources needed. The second section identifies a wide range of resources (Federal, State, and private) available to assist the smaller business in areas such as financing, information gathering, and management.

The 85-page publication is available for $13.50 from the National Technical Information Service, U.S. Department of Commerce, 5285 Port Royal Road, Springfield, VA 22161, phone number (703) 487-4650. Contact: The Small Business Technology Liaison Division, Office of Productivity, Technology and Innovation, U.S. Department of Commerce, Room 4816, Washington, D.C. 20230/202-377-1093.

Automated Sewing Systems and Computer Robotics

Under the Draper Labs Automation Project jointly funded by the government, private industry and the garment union, Draper Laboratories has been studying automated sewing systems and computer robotics. The research and development helps the apparel industry develop new technologies to thereby regain a competitive edge in the marketplace. Although a large portion of the research is classified information, reports are being produced annually for the years 1983 through 1986. Contact: Draper Labs Automation Project, U.S. Department of Commerce, Office of Trade Adjustment Assistance, 14th and Constitution Avenue, NW, Washington, DC 20230. This office can provide information about the project and information about other apparel industry related publications. The Draper report must be purchased from NTIS, 5285 Port Royal Road, Springfield, VA 22161/703-487-4763. The First Year Report (#PB83-155895) is five volumes and costs $50.00.

Bibliographies
Researchers can identify previously published articles and reports on more than 1,000 topics using NTIS *Published Searches*. These bibliographies, prepared from over 20 international data bases, provide full summaries (abstracts) of technical and research reports. To receive additional information, ask for the free descriptive catalog, PR-186. Contact: NTIS, U.S. Department of Commerce, Springfield, VA 22161/703-487-4600.

Biotechnology Industry Minutes and Comparative Analyses
Biotechnology presents the proceedings of meetings between representatives of the biotechnology industry and the federal government. It includes a summary of issues raised at the meetings and transcriptions of industry presentations. Topics covered include the impact of federal research and regulatory policies on the biotechnology industry; export control of biotechnology; technology transfer as the key to the commercialization of biotechnology, and more. A comparison of the development of biotechnology in the United States and other countries is provided. *Biotechnology* is available for $7.00 from the Superintendent of Documents, U.S. Government Printing Office, Washington, DC 20402, 202-783-3238. Refer to stock number 003-009-00430-6. Contact: International Trade Administration, U.S. Department of Commerce, Washington, DC 202-377-3808.

Building Acoustics
The Building Acoustics group of the National Bureau of Standards is involved in research in the following areas: architectural acoustics, performance of acoustical materials, noise generation, and propagation in and around buildings. Staff can answer questions in their areas of expertise and make referrals. Contact: Building Acoustics, Room A105, Sound Building, National Bureau of Standards, Gaithersburg, MD 20899 301-921-3783.

Building Technology
The National Bureau of Standards (NBS) is responsible in an advisory capacity for the usefulness, safety and economy of building through the development of improved technology and is responsible for its applications through improved building practices. It also provides research on construction safety; earthquake, soil collapse and high wind hazards in buildings; durability of construction materials; energy efficiency; and sensory environment. Contact: Center for Building Technology, NBS, Department of Commerce, Bldg. 226, Room B250, Washington, DC 20234/301-921-3106.

Business Assistance at the Local Level
The U.S. Department of Commerce maintains 47 District Offices throughout the United States. These offices provide a local contact for all Department of Commerce services. Most District Offices also maintain a business reference library which contains market research and business related materials, foreign trade data, census reports, and "how to" guides on starting and managing a business, especially exporting information. For a local office consult the white pages of your telephone book under U.S. Government. A list of District Offices is available from U.S. and Foreign Commercial Service, ITA, Department of Commerce, Washington, DC 20230/202-377-4767.

Business Assistance Newsletter
Minority Business Today is a free bi-monthly newsletter for minorities which deals with assistance available for minority business as well as available government contracts. Contact: Information Center, Minority Business Development Agency, Department of Commerce, Room 6708, Washington, DC 20230/202-377-2217.

Business Development
Aid is available in the form of loans; grants and technical assistance to help the economic development of the country. See "Economic Development" under "Grants and Loans and Loan Guarantees," in this section, or contact: Office of Public Affairs, Economic Development Administration, Department of Commerce, Room 7800B, Washington, DC 20230/303-377-5113.

Business Economics—Publications and Data Bases
If you have an interest in macroeconomics you may be interested in one or more of the following publications produced by the Bureau of Economic Analysis.

Business Conditions Digest (SD)
About 300 economic time series are shown in charts covering more than 20 years. Measures the

economic activity on national income and product accounts; prices, wages and productivity; labor force, employment and unemployment; government activities, U.S. international transactions, and multinational transactions. It also describes the leading, lagging and coincident economic indicators. (Monthly, $55.00, Catalog No. C59.9:)

Survey of Current Business (SD)
Provides an interpretation and analysis of the Gross National Product, balance of payments, consumer spending, plant and equipment spending, construction, inventory investment, government spending, foreign trade, price developments, labor markets, and financial flows. Lists some 1,900 statistical series. (Monthly, $50 1st class, $30 2nd class, Catalog No. C 56.109:)

Handbook of Cyclical Indicators (NT's)
Contains all of the economic time series shown in *Business Conditions Digest* as well as historical data, series descriptions, and measures of average variability. ($19.00) PB-273-537

Long-Term Economic Growth 1860–1970 (NTIS)
Amost 1,200 annual time series, from both government and private sources, showing both the aggregator as well as the components based on geographic or industry breakdown. ($26.50) COM73-50869

Business Statistics (SD)
Presents historical data for approximately 1,900 series that appear in the statistical pages of the *Survey of Current Business*. ($9.50, Stock No. 003-010-00089-9)

Detailed Input/Output Structure of the Economy 1972 (NTIS)
The national input-output accounts are a source often overlooked by researchers. This work measures all the repercussions of changes in demand for industrial materials, broken down by standard industrial classification code. If utilities increase their use of coal, the accounts would show that, in addition to the increased output of coal, there will be an increased demand for related products such as explosives and steel products, which in turn will require more basic chemicals, more coal, more petroleum products, more plastics material and rubber, and more iron ore. There will be even further effects: For instance, the increased production of basic chemicals will require more chemical minerals, more steel, more nonferrous metals, and still more coal. With these accounts, one can show the market share for a selected product by end user. Input/output analysis also sheds light on regional implications of changes in the Gross National Product, employment requirements by industry, and cost price relationships. (Vol. I, $9.50, Vol. II, $8.50)

Titles marked SD are available through Superintendent of Documents, U.S. Gov't. Printing Office, Washington, DC 20402/202-783-3238; those marked NTIS are available through NTIS, 5285 Port Royal Road, Springfield, VA 22161/703-487-4650.

Much of the data referenced in the above publications are also available on computerized magnetic tape. Contact: Public Info Office BE-53, BEA, U.S. Dept. of Commerce, Washington, DC 20230.

Business Plans Surveys
The Bureau of Economic Analysis has done pioneer work in its surveys of business plans. The best known are the quarterly and annual surveys of business expenditures for plant and equipment. Contact: Business Outlook Division, Bureau of Economic Analysis, Department of Commerce BE-52, Washington, DC 20230/202-523-0874.

Business Reference Service
The U.S. Department of Commerce Library has a free reference service that will answer quick questions about commerce and business. Services it will perform include consulting standard business reference books for company information and supplying foreign telephone numbers listed in its collection of overseas telephone books. Call or write Library, Department of Commerce, Washington, DC 20230/202-377-2161.

Business Services Directory
Compiled by the Office of Business Liaison, this booklet provides information about Department of Commerce services. Goals of the Departments' diverse agencies is outlined with a brief description of their objectives, types of assistance they can provide, and the phone numbers of each of the various divisions. The publication is available free of charge. Contact: Office of Business Liaison, Department of Commerce, Rm H5898C, Washington DC 20230/202-377-3176.

CAD/CAM Application Research Experts
The Center for Manufacturing Engineering has several specialists in the various areas of CAD/CAM who develop research work in subjects such as application of advances control manufacturing systems, and robot manipulators. For referral to these experts on specific technical topics, please write the Center. A brochure titled "*Publications of Center for Manufacturing Engineering*" lists the papers, books and articles developed by the Center's members. It can help identify experts to contact. A copy of the brochure can be ordered for $10.00 by writing to: National Technical Information Service, Springfield, VA 22161. Contact: Center for Manufacturing Engineering, U.S. Department of Commerce, National Bureau of Standards, Washington, DC 20234 301-921-3421 or Mr.

Brad Smith, Computer Aided Manufacturing, 301-921-3591.

Calibration and Testing Services
The National Bureau of Standards (NBS) works with industry, individuals and government organizations in establishing measurement control and calibration programs. Contact: Office of Measurement Services, NBS, Department of Commerce Physics Building, Room B362, Washington, DC 20234/301-921-2805.

Calibration Program Support Resources
The principal responsibility of the Office of Physical Measurement Services (OPMS) is to provide general administrative support for (NBS) calibration programs and to provide a central point of contact within NBS for resolving calibration issues. This office is the focal point for responding to customer requests for measurement assurance programs (MAPS) and calibration services. OPMS maintains a database on all NBS measurement services and provides information to the public about these services. Their primary publication is *The Calibration Services of NBS. Special Publication 250.* This book lists the services and briefly describes them. The appendix is a price list for calibration services. Special Publication 250 is available free of charge. Contact: Office of Physical Measurement Services, Physics Building, Room B362, National Bureau of Standards, Gaithersburg, MD 20899, 301-921-2805.

Census Data in Convenient Paper Copy Reports
NTIS now offers the opportunity to complete your collection of 1980 Census Data in paper copy conveniently and inexpensively. These reports have been produced for initial use by the Department of Labor's Employment and Training Administration and are now available to the general public. These reports are available in various geographic areas. There are four reports available:

Report 1: Population and Housing Characteristics (PR-726)
Report 2: Employment and Training Indicators (PR-747)
Report 3: Social Indicators for Planning and Evaluation (PR-748)
Report 4: Equal Employment Indicators (PR-739)

To receive a free brochure describing any of these Census reports in detail, request the PR listed after the report title above. Contact: NTIS, U.S. Department of Commerce, Springfield, VA 22161/703-487-4807.

Census Data 1980
Researchers should remember that data from the decennial census will provide what is likely to be the most detailed information available on the demographics of the United States. It is also unique in that data is available for very small geographic areas called census tracts. These tracts represent an area the size of a few city blocks. The major publications generated from a decennial census include: four population reports for each state; two housing reports for each state; a summary of U.S. population; and a summary of U.S. housing. This information is also available in machine-readable (computer and micro) format. Contact: Customer Service, DUSD, Bureau of the Census, Department of Commerce, Washington, DC 20233/301-763-4100.

Census Data, Computerized
Much of the data collected by Census are available in machine-readable (computer and micro) format. For a complete description of available data order *The Directory of Data Files* for $11.00 from Publications Data Users Service Division, Bureau of the Census, Department of Commerce, Washington, DC 20233/301-763-4100. For detailed information on the type of computerized data available contact: Customer Service, Bureau of Census, Data User Services Division, Department of Commerce, Washington, DC 20233/301-763-4100.

Census Data Computer Software
A number of computer programs are available to those using Census computer tapes. The type of programs available include tabulations and cross-tabulations, mapping and address matching. Contact: Customer service, Data Users Service Division, Bureau of the Census, Department of Commerce, Washington, DC 20233/301-763-4100.

Census Data Guides and Indexes
There are a number of guides and indexes to Census publications. Contact: Customer Service, Data User Services Division, Bureau of the Census, Department of Commerce, Washington, DC 20233/301-763-4100.

Census Data on Microformat
Much of Census information is also available on microfiche; some of the data, available on microfiche are not available in printed reports. Contact: Customer Service, Bureau of the Census, Department of Commerce, Washington, DC 20233/301-763-4100.

Census Data Processing
If you would like special manipulation of Census computer data and do not have the proper facilities or expertise, there are a number of private organizations that will help you, for a fee. These organizations are registered with the National Clearinghouse for Census Data Services and provide services ranging from assistance in selecting the right statistical report to sophisticated computer tape processing. For a listing of organiza-

tions contact: Customer Service, Data User Services Division, Bureau of the Census, Department of Commerce, Washington, DC 20233/301-763-4100.

Organizations which are part of a state government system (e.g., state planning agency, state library, or state university) can obtain the same services described above but at a substantially reduced fee (and sometimes for free) from a local State Data Center. Contact the office described above for listing of State Data Centers.

Census Data Seminars
Free seminars are available for librarians and government personnel and at a cost for the general public. The seminars identify the types of statistical data available from Census and other Federal agencies as well as how to use these data. Contact: Bureau of the Census, Department of Commerce, 1649 Federal Building 3, Washington, DC 20233/301-763-1510.

Census Data, Special
The Bureau of the Census will make special tabulations of their data upon request. The purpose of this service is to provide tabulation (not computer program writing) of information which is not already available on tape in the public domain. There is a charge for any special tabulation and the sponsor will be given exclusive rights to the information generated for six months. After that time the tabulations go into the public domain. Contact: Customer Service, Data Users Services Division, Bureau of the Census, Department of Commerce, Washington, DC 20233/301-763-4100.

Census, Economic
Every five years (ending in "2" and "7") a major effort is conducted to identify and classify the economic action within the United States. Subject areas covered include wholesale and retail trade, manufacturers, service industries, mineral industries, construction industries, transportation, enterprise statistics, minority-owned business enterprises and women-owned businesses. For a description of the type of data and reports available contact: Customer Service, Data Users Services Division, Bureau of the Census, Department of Commerce, Washington, DC 20233/301-763-4100.

Census Maps for Data and Art
Computer-generated maps are available for 65 major metropolitan areas. The maps, called "Urban Atlases," display selected census data characteristics such as population density, median family income and median housing value from 1970. Each atlas costs between $2.50 and $5.00 and is printed in brilliant colors. They make fine posters and wall decorations. Contact: Publications Data Users Services Division, Bureau of the Census, Department of Commerce, Washington, DC 20233/301-763-4100.

Census Microdata on Computer Tape
In addition to summary statistics (data already tabulated), microdata are also available from Census. Microdata are untabulated data of individual records. Microdata records do not provide residence identification at the small-area level because of confidentiality guidelines and all confidential information has been deleted. Contact: Tapes, Data Users Service Division, Bureau of the Census, Department of Commerce, Washington, DC 20233/301-763-4100.

Census of Manufacturers' Report
Taken once every 5 years, in the years ending in 7 and 2, this census covers 450 U.S. industries. Major tables in this Report include: a table on employment, payroll, hours worked, value of industry shipments, cost of materials consumed, and new expenditures; a table showing detailed types of products; a table with industry breakdown by geographical areas; and a table detailing the material consumed (i.e., metals, etc.) in the making of the product.

Ordinance and Accessories covers SIC codes 3482, 3483, 3484. The 21-page publication (# 34E) costs approximately $5.00.

Ships and Boat Building and Transportation Equipment provides data on tanks, ships, and other weapons transportation equipment. The 21-page booklet (#37C) costs approximately $5.00.

Aerospace Equipment—Including Parts (# 37B) costs approximately $5.00.

Communication Equipment (#36D) includes data on search, detection and navigation instruments and costs approximately $5.00.

For information about the reports, contact: Census/ASM Durable Goods Branch, Bureau of Census, Washington, DC 20233/301-763-7304. To order a report, Contact: the Superintendent of Documents, U.S. Government Printing Office, Washington, DC 20402/202-783-3238.

Census Publications for Market Research
Listed below are a number of the more popular Census publications subscribed to by market researchers. For further information contact: Publications, Data Users Services Division, Bureau of the Census, Department of Commerce, Washington, D.C. 20233/301-763-4100. (Check for latest edition)

County and City Data Book (SN 003-024-05883-2, $24)
Annual Survey of Manufacturers, $14.50
Current Retail Trade (003-024-80007-1, $39.00)
Monthly Wholesale and Trade (003-001-80013-6, $17)
Current Population Reports

Part 1- includes population characteristics, special studies, and income (C3.186:P20, $90)

Part 2- includes population estimates, projections, and special censuses (C3.186:P25, $22)

Bureau of the Census Catalog (003-024-05768-9, $6.50)

Fact Finders for the Nation-22 separate issues, 25¢–30¢ each

Census Users Guide-3 parts
  A. Text, 003-024-03625-8, $5.50
  B. Glossary, 003-024-05004-8, $6
  C. Index to Summary Tapes, Files 1–4, 003-024-05771-9, $4.25

Guide to '82 Economic Censuses, free

Statistical Abstract of the U.S., 1982–83, $11.00

County Business Patterns, single state-$6, all states-$277.75

Charting and Geodetic Service

This organization collects, maintains, publishes and distributes geodetic and cartographic information pertaining to the National Geodetic Networks. Contact: NOAA, Department of Commerce, Rm 1006, 6001 Rockville Pike, Rockville MD 20852/301-443-8385.

Chemical and Physical Properties of Materials Certification

Updated every two years, the *Standard Reference Materials Catalogue* lists and describes 900 real materials which are certified for their chemical or physical properties. Included under the category of standard reference materials are environmental type and clinical reference materials. For ordering standard reference materials, as well as the free catalog (NBS Special Publication 260), contact: Office of Standard Reference Materials, Chemistry Building, Room B311, National Bureau of Standards, Gaithersburg, MD 20899/301-921-2045.

Climate Monitoring

Information is available estimating trends in climate change and the nature of climates to come. Contact: Public Affairs Office, NOAA, Environmental Research Lab, Department of Commerce, 325 Broadway, Boulder, CO 80303/303-497-6286.

Climatic Information

The National Oceanic and Atmospheric Administration (NOAA) will provide, for a fee, climatological data in either hard-copy or machine-readable formats. Contact: National Climatic Center, Environmental Data Information Service, NOAA, Department of Commerce, Federal Building, Asheville, NC 28801-2696/704-259-0682.

Climatic Summaries

The National Climatic Data Center provides; for the cost of reproduction, climatic summaries for sites in or near a locality. Climatic summaries for major U.S. weather stations, including wind data, are available in different forms, some more detailed than others. Detailed summaries include wind variation by hour of day and month of year. Wind tabulations which present the percentage frequency of the directions and wind-speed groups have been constructed for many of the weather stations. In addition, the office has available raw, unedited solar insolation data for 26 cities in the U.S. Contact: National Climatic Data Center, National Environmental Satellite, Data & Information Service, National Oceanic & Atmospheric Administration, Federal Building, Asheville, NC 28801-2696/703-259-0682.

Coastal Zone Management

Information, expertise, and financial assistance are available on such topics as estuaries, marine sanctuaries, and the effects of offshore drilling. See "Coastal" under "Grants and Loans and Loan Guarantees," in this section or contact: Office of Ocean and Coastal Resource Mgmt. NOAA, Department of Commerce, 3300 Whitehaven St., N.W. Washington, DC 20235/202-634-4232.

Complaints from Businesses

Businesses that have problems or complaints for which government may be of some help or that need aid in finding their way around the government bureaucracy can find assistance at the Office of Business Liaison. Contact: Office of Business Liaison, Department of Commerce, Room 5898C, Washington, DC 20230/202-377-3176.

Coal Gasification

For technical expertise of the conversion of coal into liquid and gaseous fuels contact: Inquiry Service, National Bureau of Standards, Department of Commerce, Administration Building, Room A537, Washington, DC 20234/301-921-2318.

Commerce Business Daily

A publication issued every weekday by the US Department of Commerce, listing all federal procurement invitations. The publication is available in major libraries or by subscription from the Government Printing Office. Current price is $160 annually, by first class mail, or $81 by regular mail. Contact: Superintendent of Documents, Government Printing Office, Washington DC 20402/202-783-3238.

Commercial Materials and International Trade Resources

The Office of Chemical and Allied Products monitors and analyzes economic data on approximately 40 commercial materials and products, with special emphasis on international trade and the promotion of exports. Specialists are available to answer inquiries and make referrals on economic information regarding plastics, chemicals, and allied products. Contact: David Rosse (plastic materials, coatings, adhesives, and allied products), David Blank (miscellaneous plastic products), Office of Chemical and Allied Products, U.S. Department of Commerce, Bureau of Industrial Economics, Washington, DC 20230/202-377-0128.

Communications and Information Policy
For national policy information on such topics as communications legislation, deregulation of common carrier networks, satellite usage for emergency medical networks and public television, and climatic effects on radio waves transmitted at extremely high frequencies contact: National Telecommunications, and Information Administration, Department of Commerce, 14th & Constitution Ave., N.W., Room 4898, Washington, DC 20230/202-377-1832.

Computer Architecture Research
The Center for Computer Systems Engineering of the National Bureau of Standards is concerned with the measurement and prediction of various computer architectures, especially multiprocessor architectures. Staff in the research and development (R&D) office can provide you with information about the latest R&D activities in the field. Contact: Center for Computer Systems Engineering, Systems Components Division, National Bureau of Standards, Gaithersburg, MD 20899.

Computer/Communications Networking Expert
The Systems and Network Architecture Division is responsible for the following activities in computer/communications networking: research, standards development, agency assistance, and technology transfer to government and industry. Contact: Systems and Network Architecture Division, National Bureau of Standards, Bldg. 225, Room B218, Gaithersburg, MD 20899/301-921-3537.

Computer Crime
Technical expertise and published information are available to help organizations establish guidelines for preventing computer crime. Contact: Institute for Computer Science and Technology, Room B64, Technology Bldg., National Bureau of Standards, Washington, DC 20234/301-921-3157.

Computer Integrated Manufacturing
The U.S. Department of Commerce has two divisions within the National Bureau of Standards that are involved in building a small automated factory and developing the principles of computer integrated manufacturing. The Automated Production Technology Division has experts in machine tool metrology or precision machining and robot metrology. The Industrial Systems Division concentrates on high level factory control. Members of this division work on machine vision or robot vision, robotics and data bases. Two-day seminars on a full range of topics are held bimonthly. Staff at both divisions can answer technical questions or refer you to other resources. Contact: Automated Production Technology Division, National Bureau of Standards, Washington, DC 20234, 301-921-2577, or Industrial Systems Division, National Bureau of Standards, Washington, DC 20234/301-921-2381.

Computer/Network Protocol Standards and Technology
The Institute of Computer Science and Technology is a technical center for computers and network technology which primarily serves the federal government, and to a limited extent offers assistance to industry and the general public. Available upon request is the publications listing which includes more than 20 selections on the standardization of network protocols. These can be ordered through the Government Printing Office, Washington, DC 20402 or the National Technical Information Service, 5285 Port Royal Road, Springfield, VA 22161. Contact: Institute of Computer Science and Technology, National Bureau of Standards, Gaithersburg, MD 20899/301-921-2731.

Computer Programming Language Standards
Data Management and Programming Language Division (NMPL) of the Institute for Computer Sciences and Technology administers programming language standards within the federal government. The Division represents federal interests within both national and international standards bodies. Staff can tell you what's happening within the federal government and where to go for information about language programming standards. Contact: Data Management and Programming Language Division, Institute for Computer Sciences and Technology, National Bureau of Standards, Bldg. 225, Room A 265, Gaithersburg, MD 20899/301-921-2431.

Computer Software Directory
The *Directory of Computer Software* announces descriptions of some 600 computer programs in the NTIS software collection. The software covers a broad range of applications including computer graphics, environmental pollution, and engineering. The Directory costs $40 and its order number is PB84-134071. Contact: NTIS, U.S. Department of Commerce, Springfield, VA 22161/703-487-4600.

Computerized Data Bases
These data bases are maintained by the Department of Commerce:

Climate Assessment Data Base
The Climate Assessment Data Base is designed for easy public access and provides users with informa-

tion about short-term climate conditions in the United States and throughout the world. Anyone with a compatible terminal (most home computers are) and telephone linkup can obtain a password and dial directly into the system. Users can then select from a menu of 12 data bases summarizing meterological data on a weekly, monthly and seasonal basis. Examples of data include: temperature, precipitation, weather indexes, heating and cooling days, energy conditions, and assessment of climate on crops. The system contains global surface data collected from 8,000 stations worldwide. Currently most data is in tabular form, but plans are under way to include graphical presentations.

For the price of a phone call, anyone with compatible equipment can use the system. For a password, contact: NOAA, National Meteorological Center, W353, WWB, Room 201, Washington, DC 20233/301-763-8071.

Coastal Zone Color Scanner Data Base
This data base is a computerized catalog of data archived from NASA's experimental satellites. Information stored includes: date, orbit, start and stop time, longitude coordinators, number of channels of information, cloud cover estimate, and the archive number of tape and film frame. Data can be retrieved by time period or geographical area.

Searches and printouts (a listing of satellite data available) are provided free of charge. Actual tapes and films must be purchased from NOAA. Contact: Satellite Data Services Division CC6, NOAA, Room 100, World Weather Building, Washington, DC 20233/301-763-8111.

County Business Data Base
The Bureau of the Census now has available extensive country and city data on diskette from selected 1981 County Business Patterns data (CBP). The County Business Patterns data profiles the economic structure of every U.S. county, showing establishments, employment, and payroll for industries down to two-digit standard industrial classification (SIC) levels. Users can purchase the 5 ¼-inch floppy disks in the following formats:

1) U.S. Summary at the 4-digit SIC level,
2) State Summaries, at the 2-digit SIC level, and
3) County level.

The CPB data disks are available for $45 for the first disk in an order, with additional disks in that order costing $7 each. To receive an order form or for more information, contact: DUSD, Customer Services, Bureau of the Census, Washington, DC 20233/301-763-4100.

Energy, Environment, Industrial and Materials Property Data Bases
(See "Energy, Environment, Industrial and Materials Property Data" this section.)

Environmental Referral Data Base
The National Environmental Data Referral System (NEDRES) is a computerized catalog and index of publicly available environmental data held by federal, state and private organizations throughout the U.S. It contains descriptions of files, published sources, data file documentation references and organizations that make environmental data available. References are provided for climatological, geological, geographic, hydrological and limnological data. Retrievable information includes description of data sets and information about their location, storage medium, availability and cost. NEDRES functions as a cooperating network and grants membership status (free of charge) to organizations willing and able to contribute to the system. NEDRES offers a variety of services on a fee basis, including direct access, searches and printouts. Contact: NEDRES Program Office, Assessment and Information Services Center, NOAA/NESDIS, 3300 Whitehaven Street, N.W., Washington, DC 20235/202-634-7722.

Female/Male Differentials in Countries Worldwide
Women in Development is a computerized database of demographic, social and economic data concerning female/male differentials in 120 countries throughout the world. Variables include: breakdowns by age, sex, urban/rural residence; marital status and fertility; birth and death rates; income and labor statistics; literacy and education levels; religion; ethnicity; and household data. Tables are included.

The system was started in 1980 and contains 52,000 records. Searches and printouts are available free of charge. Tapes can be purchased for $140.00 from the U.S. Census Bureau. Contact: Ellen Jamison, International Demographic Data Center, Scuderi Building, Room 302, U.S. Census Bureau, Washington, DC 20233/301-763-4221.

Foreign Traders Data Base
The Foreign Traders Index (FTI) is a list-building file describing foreign firms, their long-term interests and the types of activities they engage in. The data base can be searched according to agents, sellers, distributors, users, companies, geographic location, date and number of employees.

Information must be purchased. You can purchase country or product tapes of up to 1,000 names for $400.00 (12 cents for each additional name) or the entire FTI file for $5,000. Contact: Your U.S. District Office of the International Trade Administration or Office of Trade Information Services, U.S. Department of Commerce, Washington, DC 20230/202-377-2988.

Government-Industry Phases of Systems and Equipment
The Government-Industry Data Exchange Program (GIDEP) is a data interchange system

whereby participating government agencies and industries exchange information regarding the research, design, development, production, and operational phases of systems and equipment. Currently 656 U.S., Canadian, and European organizations participate. Most organizations willing to contribute information to GIDEP are eligible for membership and access to GIDEP's four data bases. The major data interchanges are: engineering, reliability-maintainability, metrology, failure-experience, and manufacturers test data reports.

The system is updated daily and contains more than 200,000 items. Searches, printouts, and various special services are available to participants only. Membership and services are both free. Contact: Program Director, GIDEP Operations Center, Corona, CA 91720/714-736-4677.

Government Research and Development Projects Data Base

The National Technical Information Service (NTIS) data base has abstracts and bibliographic citations of reports and publications resulting from government sponsored research and development. The materials are all publicly available and cover numerous topics ranging from technology to business procedures. National, state and local government reports are cited along with the works of grantees, contractors, and foreign agencies. Searches can be done by title, keywords, corporate source and categories. NTIS will run a free "cursory search" to give you an idea of how many abstracts exist on a particular topic. Actual searches cost a minimum of $125.00. Contact: Information Analysis Branch, 5285 Port Royal Road, Springfield, VA 22161/703-487-4640.

Hydrology Techniques Data Base

The HOMS Reference Manual documents all operational hydrological techniques offered for technology transfer. The data base contains a contact point and description for more than 300 separate technologies submitted by the meteorological and hydrological services of the World Meteorological Association. Included in each description is the technology's purpose, scientific techniques and procedures.

Searches and printouts are available free of charge. Contact: HOMS National Reference Center, Office of Hydrology, National Weather Service, 8060 13th Street, Room 506, Silver Spring, MD 20910/301-427-7658.

International Demographic Data Base

The International Demographic Center is developing its International Data Base (IDB) which will eventually contain demographic, social, and economic data about every country in the world. Presently, IDB focuses on developing nations, but data on other countries is being added daily. For each country logged, IDB contains 93 different subject tables.

Searches and printouts are available. Currently, both are free, but this may change. Tapes can be purchased. Contact: Center for International Research, Scuderi Building, Room 409, U.S. Bureau of Census, Washington, DC 20233/301-763-4286.

Metals and Ceramics Information Data Base

(See "Metals and Ceramics Information and Technical Assistance" this section.)

Minority Business Development Data Base

The Who's Who Resource File (WWRF) contains resource information about more than 18,000 U.S. organizations and individuals involved in minority business development. Collected data includes name of resource, address, telephone number, Standard Industrial Classification (SIC) if applicable, speciality code and, is retrievable by 26 major categories. WWRF currently has in excess of 18,000 records, with approximately 500 records added monthly. The Minority Business Development Agency will run searches and provide printouts or mailing labels free of charge. Service is restricted to individuals and organizations advocating minority business development. Contact: Department of Commerce, Minority Business Development Agency, Room 5710, Washington, DC 20230/202-377-5997.

Minority Business Information Data Base

The *Business Development Report System (BDRS)* contains information collected quarterly from recipients of federal grants under the Minority Business Development Center Program. As Grantees must report data about clients assisted (over 15,000), services provided and accomplishments, the data base contains information about minority business activities and services, minority-group breakdowns, business trends, capital and market brokering activities, and new start/acquisition brokering that occurs.

BDRS currently has 50,000 records and is updated quarterly by approximately 15,000 records. Searches and printouts are available free of charge. Contact: III, U.S. Department of Commerce, Minority Business Development Agency, Room 5708, Washington, DC 20230/202-377-5997.

Minority Business Locator Data Base

Profile: National Automated Minority Business Source List Service is a minority business locator system established to help match minority firms with large government contractors needing services or products. The data base contains information about more than 27,000 minority-owned businesses nationwide. Profile can be searched by specific minority ownership (i.e., black, veteran, etc.), type of firm, size, geographic location and product or service supplied.

Any company or organization wanting to purchase the services of a minority-owned business can obtain a search free of charge.

Companies wanting to be listed in Profiles should contact MBDA to find out if they are eligible. Listing is free of charge. Contact: Information Clearinghouse, Minority Business Development Agency, Room 6708, U.S. Department of Commerce, Washington, DC 20230/202-377-2414 OR any of the numerous MBDA Offices throughout the United States.

NTIS Data Bases
(See "NTIS Data Base Searches" this section.)

Oceanographic Data Base
The National Oceanic Data Center (NODC) contains the world's largest usable collection of oceanographic data. The Center maintains several informational and bibliographic data bases pertaining to all oceans, seas and estuaries.

NODC also maintains multidisciplinary data base files relating to biology, geology, energy, toxic waste and many more subject areas. Stored and retrievable NODC information is collected from NOAA, private industry, private institutions, universities, private researchers, international cooperative expeditions and other government agencies.

The data bases are updated continually and thousands of records are stored. Searches, printouts, reports, publications and referrals to appropriate information sources are available from NODC. A cost-recovery fee may be charged for services. Contact: The National Oceanographic Data Center, National Oceanic Atmospheric Administration, 2001 Wisconsin Avenue, N.W., Washington, DC 20235/301-634-7232.

Patent Data Base
The Patent & Trademark Office makes available its patent and trademark information on data bases. The Patent Data Base (PDB) contains the following files: *Patent Full-Text Data File,* available on Mead Data Central's LEXPAT system, (202) 785-3550; *Patent Bibliographic Data File,* available from the Bibliographic Retrieval Service, (800) 833-4707; *Patent Bibliographic Data File with Exemplary Claim(s),* available from Dialog Information Services, (800) 227-1960 or Pergamon International Information Corporation, (703) 442-0900; *Patent Bibliographic Data File With All Claims,* available through SDC Information Services, (800) 421-7229; and *Patent Master Classification File (MCF),* available from Pergamon International Information Corporation at, (703) 442-0900, Dialog Information Services, Inc., (800) 227-7229, or SDC Information Services, (800) 421-7229. Contact: Patent Data Base, U.S. Department of Commerce, Patent & Trademark Office, Washington, D.C. 20231.

Physical and Chemical Properties of Substances Data Base (See "Data Centers" this section.)

Selling Overseas—AITS Data Base
The *Automated Information Transfer System (AITS)* is a decentralized data base that matches subscribing U.S. firms with foreign companies and governments interested in purchasing U.S. goods and services. Information connecting buyers and sellers is transmitted via telecommunications between U.S. posts in foreign countries and 16 District Offices in the U.S. District Offices maintain data on the size, products and export capabilities of companies in their locality. Overseas posts collect data about foreign company agents and distributors, and foreign interests in importing U.S. goods or services.

As each District Office and foreign post collects its own data, elements vary with each office. Searches and printouts are available on a cost-recovery basis. Contact: your nearest U.S. Commercial Service District Office, International Trade Administration, U.S. Department of Commerce, OR Automated Information Management Division, U.S. Department of Commerce, 14th & Constitution Ave, N.W., Room #1837, Washington, DC 20230/202-377-4532.

Socio-Economic Demographic Data Base
The Socio-Economic Demographic Information System (SEEDIS), a software and data base storage system, contains more than 30 data bases covering social, economic, environmental, health and demographic subjects. The system contains most of the 1970 and 1980 U.S. Census data, and it has the unique feature of being able to aggregate or disaggregate data from one geographical level to another. SEEDIS has data from 90 different types of geographical areas. SEEDIS products include charts, maps and tabular reports on manpower, population, housing and many other categories. Tables, graphics and computer-readable data files are available, for a fee, from NTIS. Customized searches are available from SEEDIS on a cost-recovery basis. Contact: SEEDIS, National Technical Information Service (NTIS), 5285 Port Royal Road, Springfield, VA 22167/703-487-4631.

Solar Orbit Satellite Digital Data Information System
The Spinner Program is a computerized locator system for digital data transmitted by solar orbit satellite and archived by NOAA. Cataloged data can be retrieved by time period, type of satellite, a particular sensor in a satellite, type of coverage and geographical area.

Searches and printouts (listing of digital data available) are provided free of charge. Actual digital data tapes must be purchased from NOAA. Contact: Satellite Data Services Division, NOAA,

Room 100, World Weather Building, Washington, DC 20233/301-763-8111.

Standards and Certification Data Base

The National Center for Standards and Certification Information (NCSCI) maintains several data bases with up-to-date information about domestic and foreign standards and certification programs. Keyworded indexes retrieve information such as industry and government standards for electric toasters; test methods for determining various characteristics of fireclay brick; whether the nomenclature used in quality control has been defined; and what nationally recognized organization has developed specifications for a specific product. The data bases are used to answer public inquiries about the existence, source and availability of standards, and to produce lists, indices and bibliographies of standards.

Searches and printouts are provided free of charge. Contact: National Center for Standards and Certification Information, Room B166, Technology Building, National Bureau of Standards, Washington, DC 20234/301-921-2587.

World Population Data Base

The World Population data base contains population data for the overall world, its regions (i.e. Latin America, Asia, etc.) and 200 individual countries. Population statistics include: total population, estimated projections, growth rate, migratory rate, and crude (number per 1,000) birth and death rates. Data is collected from a survey conducted every two years. The latest statistics were added in March 1983, and the time span covered is 1950 through 1986 (projections).

Searches and print-outs are provided free of charge and tapes can be purchased. Contact: International Demographic Data Center, Scuderi Building, Room 407, U.S. Census Bureau, Washington, DC 20233/301-763-4086.

Computerized Data File Directory

The National Technical Information Service (NTIS) publishes a directory of all known computerized files within the federal government. The cost of the directory is $40.00 and its order number is PB85-155174. Contact: NTIS, 5285 Port Royal Road, Springfield, VA 22161/703-487-4600.

Consulting for Business

The Trade Adjustment Assistance Program offers business consulting services to firms and industries hurt by import competition. There exists Trade Adjustment Assistance Centers serving 13 geographic areas throughout the country. Areas of expertise and assistance to industries include assessment of opportunities and problems, product diversification, marketing research, increasing productivity, and export promotion. Contact: ITA, Office of Trade Adjustment Assistance,

Technical Assistance Division, Room 4004, Washington, D.C. 20230/202-377-4031.

Cross-Sectoral Trade Policy Issues Experts and Resources

The Office of Industry Assessment is responsible for following industry trade policy issues that are cross-sectoral and for coordinating the Department's Competitive Assessment Program. They also prepare competitive assessments about cross-sectoral issues such as research and development and its impact on industry. Staff can provide information or advice on cross-sectoral international trade policy problems affecting high technology industries and they can discuss the issues and concerns these industries have when dealing with international competition. Staff can also refer you to other sources and experts. The office has produced reports on some specific high tech industries as well as some cross-sectoral reports. This Office also oversees the preparation of the U.S. Industrial Outlook and staff can serve as a source for additional information relating to that publication. Contact: Office of Industry Assessment, International Trade Administration, Department of Commerce, Room 1009, Washington, DC 20230/202-377-5145.

Cryogenic Temperature Measurement

The Temperature Division of the National Bureau of Standards is involved in the measurement of cryogenic temperatures. Standard reference devices are developed based upon the superconducting transition of certain materials. These standard reference materials can be purchased from: The Office of Standard Reference Materials, National Bureau of Standards, Gaithersburg, MD 20899, 301-921-2045. Staff can answer your questions and make referrals. Technical reports can be sent to you upon request. Contact: Temperature Division, National Bureau of Standards, Physics Building, Room B128, Gaithersburg, MD 20899/301-921-3315.

Data Centers—NSRDS

The National Standards Reference Data System (NSRDS) contains data bases of evaluated physical and chemical properties of substances. The system supports NBS' responsibility to promote numerical data in the physical sciences. The evaluations are carried out through a national network of 22 NSRDS Centers and special projects conducted by universities, government laboratories and industry. Each center is responsible for a well-defined technical scope and for compiling a comprehensive indexed bibliographic file with analyses of the world literature within its scope. The Centers assess the accuracy of the data reported in the literature, prepare compilations and recommend best values. The resulting bibliographic and numeric physical, chemical and property data bases are then made available through publications, magnetic tapes and on-line systems.

The Center's activities are aggregated into three application-oriented program areas: (1) Energy and Environmental Data, (2) Industrial Process Data, and (3) Materials Properties Data.

Information about searches, printouts, publications and tapes is available from NSRDS' Washington Office. Searches are also available from the 22 Centers listed below. A cost-recovery fee may be charged for services. Contact: Office of Standard Reference Data, A320 Physics Building, National Bureau of Standards, Washington, DC 20234/ 301-921-2228 OR the appropriate NSRDS Center listed below

Alloy Phase Diagram Data Center
  Center for Materials Science
  Materials Building, Room 150
  National Bureau of Standards
  Washington, DC 20234
  301-921-2917
Aqueous Electrolyte Data Center
  Center for Thermodynamics and Molecular Science
  Chemistry Building, Room A164
  National Bureau of Standards
  Washington, DC 20234
  301-921-3632
Atomic Collision Cross Section Information Center
  Joint Institute for Laboratory Astrophysics
  University of Colorado
  Boulder, CO 80309/303-492-7801
Atomic Energy Levels Data Center
  Center for Radiation Research
  Physics Building, Room A167
  National Bureau of Standards
  Washington, DC 20234
  301-921-2011
Atomic Transition Probabilities Data Center
  Center for Radiation Research
  Physics Building, Room A267
  National Bureau of Standards
  Washington, DC 20234
  301-921-2071
Fluid Mixtures Data Center
  Center for Chemical Engineering
  National Bureau of Standards
  Boulder, CO 80303
Fundamentals Constants Data Center
  Center for Absolute Physical Quantities
  Metrology Building, Room B258
  National Bureau of Standards
  Washington, DC 20234
  301-921-2701
Fundamental Particle Data Center
  Lawrence Berkeley Laboratory
  University of California
  Berkeley, CA 92720
  415-486-5885
High Pressure Data Center
  P.O. Box 7246
  University Station

Provo, UT 84602
  801-378-4442
Ion Energetics Data Center
  Center for Thermodynamics and Molecular Science
  Chemistry Building, Room A139
  National Bureau of Standards
  Washington, DC 20234
  301-921-2439
Isotopes Project
  Lawrence Berkeley Laboratory
  University of California
  Berkeley, CA 96720
  415-486-6152
Center for Information and Numerical Data Analysis and Synthesis (CINDAS)
  Purdue University
  CINDAS
  2595 Yeager Road
  West Lafayette, IN 47906
  317-494-6300
  Direct inquiries to: Mr. W. H. Shafer
Chemical Kinetics Information Center
  Center for Thermodynamics and Molecular Science
  Chemistry Building, Room A166
  National Bureau of Standards
  Washington, DC 20234
  301-921-2565
Chemical Thermodynamics Data Center
  Center for Thermodynamics and Molecular Science
  Chemistry Building, Room A152
  National Bureau of Standards
  Washington, DC 20234
  301-921-2773
Crystal Data Center
  Center for Materials Science
  Materials Building, Room A221
  National Bureau of Standards
  Washington, DC 20234
  301-921-2950
Diffusion in Metals Data Center
  Center for Materials Science
  Materials Building, Room A153
  National Bureau of Standards
  Washington, DC 20234
  301-921-3354
JANAF Thermochemical Tables
  Dow Chemical Company
  1707 Building
  Thermal Research Laboratory
  Midland, MI 48640
  517-636-4160
Molecular Spectra Data Center
  Center for Thermodynamics and Molecular Science
  Physics Building, Room B268
  National Bureau of Standards
  Washington, DC 20234
  301-921-2023
Molten Salts Data Center
  Rensselaer Polytechnic Institute
  Department of Chemistry
  Troy, NY 12181
  518-270-6344
National Center for Thermodynamic Data of Minerals
  U.S. Geological Survey

U.S. Department of the Interior
959 National Center
Reston, VA 22092
Phase Diagrams for Ceramists Data Center
Center for Materials Science
Materials Building, Room A227
National Bureau of Standards
Washington, DC 20234
301-921-2844
Photon and Charged-Particle Data Center
Center for Radiation Research
Radiation Physics Building, Room C313
National Bureau of Standards
Washington, DC 20234
301-921-2685
Radiation Chemistry Data Center
University of Notre Dame
Radiation Laboratory
Notre Dame, IN 46556
219-239-6527
FTS 333-8220
Thermodynamics Research Center
Thermodynamics Research Center
Texas A & M University
College Station, TX 77843
713-845-4971
Thermodynamic Research Laboratory
Department of Chemical Engineering
Washington University
St. Louis, MO 63130
314-889-6011

Data Evaluation Newsletter

An informal newsletter covering recent activities
in the Office of Standard Reference Data is
available for free. Contact: Office of Standard
Reference Data, National Bureau of Standards,
Department of Commerce, Physics Building A320,
Washington, DC 20234/301-921-2228.

Direct Payments

The programs described below are those that
provide financial assistance directly to individuals,
private firms and other private institutions to
encourage or subsidize a particular activity.

Fishermen's Contingency Fund

Objectives: To compensate U.S. commercial fishermen for damage to or loss of fishing gear and resulting economic loss due to oil and gas related activities in any area of the Outer Continental Shelf.
Eligibility: Individuals.
Range of Financial Assistance: $500 to $20,000.
Contact: Chief, Financial Services Division,
National Marine Fisheries Service, 3300 Whitehaven Street, N.W., Washington, D.C. 20235/-
202-634-4688.

Fishing Vessel and Gear Damage Compensation Fund

Objectives: To compensate U.S. fishermen for
the loss, damage, or destruction of their vessels by

foreign fishing vessels and their gear by any vessel
or "act of God."
Eligibility: Individuals.
Range of Financial Assistance: $600 to $150,000.
Contact: Chief, Financial Services Division,
National Marine Fisheries Service, Department of
Commerce, 3300 Whitehaven Street, N.W., Wash-
ington, D.C. 20235/202-634-7496.

Disaster Research

Information is available on improving the designs
of buildings to insure structural safety during
disasters such as earthquakes. Contact: Inquiry
Service, National Bureau of Standards, Department of Commerce, Administration Building,
Room A537, Washington, DC 20234/301-921-
2318.

District Offices

See "Business Assistance at the Local Level" in
this section.

Economic Indicators

The Bureau of Economic Analysis regularly releases current economic data which help business
monitor economic activity. The more popular
indexes released include: Plant and Equipment
Expenditures, Personal Income and Outlays,
Gross National Product, Composite Indexes of
Leading, Coincident, and Lagging Indicators. For
a list of release dates and list of publications
contact: Public Information, Bureau of Economic
Analysis, Department of Commerce, Washington,
DC 20230/202-523-0777.

Educational Materials

The following is a listing of free and inexpensive
educational materials. Inquiries for more than one
copy will be considered on an individual basis.
Classroom quantities are limited to not more than
10 copies per item, and no more than five items per
request. Contact: National Ocean Service (NOS),
Physical Science Services Section, NOAA, Department of Commerce, Riverdale, MD 20737.
Attn: NKG 3341

American History

History of Copperplate Engraving (a look at 19th century
engraving techniques)
A Capital Plan (first maps of Washington, DC)
Three Short Happy Mothers (the story of James Abbott
McNeill Whistler, the artist)
Wilkes Expedition, 1838–1842, of the Pacific Northwest
(exploits of Commander Charles Wilkes)
Hassler's Legacy—History of the National Ocean Survey
(article)
An American Philosopher (the life work of Charles
Sanders Peirce)
The Nation's Chartmaker (History of Nautical Charting)

General

Technology for Surveys and Charts (geodetic and photo-grammetric services)
An Introduction to NOAA's National Ocean Survey
America's Islands (provides data on islands, interesting facts, photos and measurements)
Possible Sources of Shipwreck Information (list)
NOAA Motion Picture Films (list)
Principal Rivers and Lakes of the World (includes a listing of rivers and lakes by depth, size, etc.)
The NOAA Story (all about the National Oceanic and Atmospheric Administration)
Data of the Great Lakes System
National Ocean Survey Pacific Marine Center (organizational functions of the Center)
National Ocean Survey Records for Litigation (Services Available)
NOS Publications can make you a better fisherman

Cartography

A Guide to Books on Maps & Mapping
Map Projections for Modern Charting (elementary school-level approach to projections)
Example of a Nautical Chart (for classroom use)
Obsolete Aeronautical Charts (limit one)
Coastline of the United States (lengths in statute miles of each coastal state)
Map of the United States Continental Shelf (page size)
Map Scales (and How They Differ)

Catalogs

Aeronautical Chart Catalog
Nautical Chart Catalogs (four volumes) Atlantic, Pacific, Alaska, and Great Lakes
Bathymetric and Special Purpose Maps
Cartobibliography of Civil War Maps
Cartobibliography II (Age of Exploration)
World, U.S., and Historical Maps (Government Agencies)
Abstracts-1981 (scientific and technical papers presented by NOS authors)
Summary of NOS Technical Publications and Charts (a complete user list of products, past and present)
NOS Products and Information (current products list)
Facsimiles of Cartographic Treasures (list of maps)

Geodetic Data

Geographic Center of Washington, DC
Geographic Center of the United States (conterminous)
Geographic Center of Hawaii
Geodetic Survey Mark Preservation
NGS-National Geodetic Survey (pamphlet)

Oceanography

List of Institutions Offering Degrees In Oceanography
Our Restless Tides (pamphlet)
Tidal Currents (pamphlet)
Principal Ocean Currents of the World (page size map)
The Gulf Stream (pamphlet)

Oceanography in the National Ocean Survey (pamphlet)
NOS Strategic Petroleum Reserve Support (article)

Photogrammetry

Photogrammetry in the National Ocean Survey (pamphlet)
Aerial Photographs (reproductions for sale)
Requests for priced items must be addressed to the National Ocean Service, Distribution Branch, N/CG33, Riverdale, MD 20737, accompanied by your remittance made payable to the Department of Commerce, NOS.

1/Pamphlet of nautical chart symbols and abbreviations/ $2.00
1210TR/A training chart for use in classroom work; ideal in navigational symbolization/$2.25
116-SC TR/A small-craft training chart for use in classroom work; ideal in navigational symbolization/$2.25
MI 101 Pierce's World Quincuncial Map (buff tint, water tint, boundaries, major cities) size 25 × 49½ inches. $2.00
MI 102 Mercator Projection Map (bufftint) size 8 × 10½ inches. $1.00
MI 103 Miller's Modified Mercator Projection (outline map, black and white, major cities) size 29 × 22½ inches $1.50

Effects of Solar Flaring on Communications

Solar flaring is observed by monitoring conditions of the sun through satellite-borne instrumentation, solar telescopes, and ground-based remote sensors. Observation is made of the development of geo-magnetic storms that affect much of the earth's technology that operates in the ionosphere, such as satellite electronics, short-wave radios, and high-frequency waves used in air navigation as well as on-the-ground communications. Contact: National Oceanic and Atmospheric Administration (NOAA), Environmental Research Lab, 325 Broadway, Boulder, CO 80303/303-497-6286.

Electronic Equipment Manufacturers Shipment Data

Published each fall, the *Current Industrial Report-Selected Electronic and Associated Products Including Telephone and Telegraph Apparatus* report contains product shipment data for all known manufacturers of electronic equipment. The survey is done by the Census Bureau and includes most electronic equipment purchased by the armed forces. Census obtained this information by contacting all known manufacturers in SIC (Standard Industrial Code) 3662. The report (MA 36N), must be ordered in writing and costs $2.65. For information about the figures contact: Data User Services Division, Customer Services (Publications), Bureau of Census, Department of Commerce, Washington, DC 20233/301-763-5353.

Energy Conservation

The National Bureau of Standards (NBS) coordinates energy conservation programs for appliances, and solar heating and cooling of residential and commercial buildings. Contact: Center for Building Technology, National Bureau of Standards, Department of Commerce, Building 226 Room B250, Washington, DC 20234/301-921-3377.

Energy, Environment, Industrial and Materials Property Data

The Office of Standard Reference Data (OSRD) of the National Bureau of Standards is responsible for managing and coordinating the National Standard Reference Data System (NSRDS), a decentralized network of Data Centers and short-term projects conducted at universities, government laboratories, industrial laboratories, and NBS technical divisions. The program's aim is to provide numerical data to the scientific and technical community. Its centers' and special projects are aggregated into three application-oriented areas: (1) Energy and Environmental Data, which includes data from fields, such as spectroscopy and related R&D and environmental modeling; (2) Industrial Process Data, which primarily covers thermodynamic and transport properties of substances important to the chemical and related industries; and (3) Materials Properties Data, which includes structural, electrical, optical and mechanical properties of solid materials of broad interest.

NSRDS' principal output is compilations of evaluated numerical data and critical reviews of the status of data in particular technical areas. It also produces annotated bibliographies and procedures for computerized handling of data. NSRDS' data is stored in a computerized system, and made available to the public via publications, magnetic tapes, and on-line retrieval systems. Staff will answer questions and/or make referrals. Publications lists, as well as information about tapes, printouts and database searches are also available. Contact: National Standard Reference Data System (NSRDS), Office of Standard Reference Data (OSRD), A323 Physics Building, National Bureau of Standards (NBS), Gaithersburg, MD 20899, 301-921-2228 (OSRD Reference Center).

The NSRDS Data Centers throughout the U.S. Staff will supply information and conduct computerized database searches for the public. A cost-recovery fee may be charged for searches. See entry titled "Data Centers—NSRDS" this section for a complete listing of the centers.

Energy-Related Invention Assistance

Inventors can find technical help from the National Bureau of Standards. A staff of trained specialists evaluate thousands of energy related inventions and make recommendations to the Department of Energy for grant money. Contact: Office of Energy-Related Invention, National Bureau of Standards, Department of Commerce, Building 225 A46, Washington, DC 20234/301-921-3694.

Environmental Information Center

Bibliographic information services and expertise are available on meteorology, biology, chemistry, oceanography, and geology. Contact: Assessment and Information Services Center, NOAA, Department of Commerce, Page Building 2, Room 290, Washington, DC 20235/202-634-7251.

Environmental Assessment

Environmental assessment services provided by the National Oceanic and Atmospheric Administration include data base studies and monthly assessments with weekly updates of weather impacts and environmental analysis and assessments to support efficient and effective planning, site selection, design, construction and operation of supertanker ports and offshore drilling rigs. Contact: Assessment and Information Services Center, NOAA, Department of Commerce, Room 290, Washington, DC 20235/202-634-7251.

Environmental Library Services

The National Oceanic and Atmospheric Administration (NOAA) Library and holdings are open to the public on a walk-in basis and through interlibrary loan. The data files contain information on published literature, on-going research projects in the atmospheric sciences, marine and coastal studies, and a wide range of other subjects. Contact: Library Services Branch E/AI21, NOA 6009 Executive Blvd., Rockville, MD 20852/301-443-8330.

Environmental Data Information Service

This service operates a network of specialized service centers along with a computerized environmental data and information retrieval service. The services include managing environmental data and information; acquiring, processing, archiving, analyzing, and disseminating atmospheric marine, solar and solid earth data and information for use by commerce, industry, the scientific and engineering community and the general public as well as by the government; providing experiment design and data management support to large-scale environmental experiments; assessing the impact of environmental changes on food production, energy production and consumption, environmental quality and other economic systems; and assisting national decision makers in solving environment related problems. The centers included in the network are the National Climatic Center, National Oceanographic Data Center, National Geophysical Data Center, Assessment and Information Services Center. Contact: Environmental Data and Information Service, NOAA, Department of Commerce, Room 547, Page Building 2, Washington, DC 20235/202-634-7318.

National Environmental Date Referral Service
This service provides convenient, economic and efficient access to widely scattered environmental data by identifying the existence, location, characteristics and availability conditions of environmental data sets. The NEDRES database is a computer searchable catalog and index of this environmental data. Contact: NOAA, Department of Commerce, NEDRES, 3300 Whitehaven Street NW, Washington DC 20235/202-634-7722.

Environmental Research
Environmental research is conducted at the National Oceanic and Atmospheric Administration (NOAA) with the goal of a better understanding of activities in the oceanic and atmospheric environment which impact on humans. Research includes studies of such topics as what causes changes in ocean thermoclime, how storm systems develop, the exchange of heat and chemicals from the ocean to the atmosphere, and the effects of oil spills on seas and shorelines. Contact: National Oceanic and Atmospheric Administration (NOAA), Environmental Research Lab, 325 Broadway, Boulder, CO 80303/303-497-6286.

Environmental Science Information
For information and expertise on the oceans, the atmosphere and related subjects contact: Assessment and Information Services Center, NOAA, Department of Commerce, Room 290, Washington, D.C. 20235/202-634-7251. The Library Services Branch has information concerning atmospheric, earth and oceanic sciences, energy, environment, pollution and natural resource management. Contact: Library Services Branch, NOAA, Department of Commerce, 6009 Executive Blvd., Rockville, MD 20852/301-443-8330.

Expertise Available at NBS
The National Bureau of Standards (NBS) is the nation's central measurement standards laboratory. The staff of trained specialists who conduct this research is also available to provide information and expertise in their areas of interest. The general subject areas covered include the following: Nondestructive Evaluation; Environmental Measurements; Air and Water; Recycled Materials; Recycled Oil; Resource Recovery; Quantum Physics; Electrical Measurements and Standards; Temperature Measurements and Standards; Length and Mass Measurements and Standards; Time and Frequency; Atomic and Plasma Radiation; Nuclear Radiation; Radiation Physics; Radiometric Physics; Chemical Kinetics; Chemical Thermodynamics; Thermodynamics; Molecular Spectroscopy; Inorganic and Organic Chemistry; Gas and Particulate Science; Chemical Stability and Corrosion;

Polymer Science; Metal Science; Ceramics; Glass and Solid State Science; Reactor Radiation; Computer Sciences and Technology; Computer Programming; Operations Research; Scientific Computing; Statistical Engineering; Applied Mathematics; Electronics and Electrical Engineering; Electron Devices; Electrosystems; Electromagnetic Technology; Mechanical Engineering; Mechanical Processes; Fluid Engineering; Thermal Processes; Industrial Engineering; Acoustical Engineering; Building Technology; Structures and Materials; Building Thermal and Service; Environmental Design; Building Economics; Fire Science; Fire Safety Engineering; Consumer Product Technology; Consumer Sciences; Product Performance; Product Safety and Energy Related Inventions. Contact: National Bureau of Standards, Department of Commerce, Washington, DC 20234/301-921-1000.

Export Regulations
The International Trade Administration (ITA) is responsible for administering expert regulations, as cited in the Export Administration Act, as well as protecting domestic industries from unfair trade practices by other nations. ITA's Office of Export Administration regulates the flow of high technology commodities, services, and technical data applicable to civilian and military uses. This office can give you information about regulations and licensing procedures, as well as product and service export eligibility status. ITA offers seminars and consultations to help businesses become aware of the indications of potential illegal exports. A publication of special interest is the *Business America—ITA Export Services,* a special reprint of four magazine articles about the Trade Administration. It offers information about export regulation, antiboycott compliance, support services, and fair trade. It is available free of charge upon request. Contact: Deputy Assistant Secretary for Export Enforcement, International Trade Administration, U.S. Department of Commerce, Washington, DC 20230/202-377-3618.

Exporting—Business Opportunities Abroad
The items listed below are all helpful to those U.S. firms which are currently doing business overseas or would like to do so.

Agent Distributor Service
For $90 U.S. Foreign Service posts will provide the names and addresses of six foreign firms who are interested in acting as agent or distributor for a company's product. Contact: Office of Trade Information Services U.S. and Foreign Commercial Service, ITA, Department of Commerce, Room 1324, Washington, DC 20230/202-377-2665.

Business America Magazine
This biweekly publication published by the Department of Commerce is an aid to those U.S.

businesses who sell, or wish to sell, goods and services for export. For information on the magazine contact: *Business America*, Public Affairs, International Trade Administration, Department of Commerce, Washington, DC 20230/202-377-3808. Subscriptions are available for $55.00 per year from Superintendent of Documents, Government Printing Office, Washington, DC 20402/202-783-3238.

Catalog and Video Exhibitions

Overseas offices will exhibit company catalogs to potential foreign buyers. There is a fee for their service. Contact: Catalog and Video Catalog Exhibition Program, Department of Commerce, Room 2119, Washington, DC 20230/202-377-3973.

Country Desk Officers

A listing of country desk officers is available free of charge. These specialists are experts in export marketing. Contact: International Economic Policy, ITA, Department of Commerce, Room 3864, Washington, DC 20230/202-377-3022. (See also "Country Experts" in this section under Data Experts).

Country Market Studies

Studies are available that provide broad discussions of long-range opportunities for U.S. businessmen in various countries. Contact: Market Research Division, Export Development, ITA, Department of Commerce, Room 2012, Washington, DC 20230/202-377-3363.

Credit Reports on Foreign Companies

For $75 the World Trade Data Reports will provide financial and background information on any foreign company. Contact: Office of Trade Information Services, ITA, Department of Commerce, Room 1835, Washington, DC 20230/202-377-2665.

Domestic International Sales Corp (DISC)

The DISC program allows exporters to defer 94 percent of its export-related income as incentive for exporting. Contact: Office of Trade Finance, ITA, Department of Commerce, Room 1211, Washington, DC 20230/202-377-4471.

"E" Award Program

Awards are presented to American firms and organizations for excellence in exporting or in export promotion. Contact: U.S. and Foreign Commercial Service, ITA, Department of Commerce, Room 3810, Washington, DC 20230/202-377-5205.

East-West Trade Assistance

A special office has been established to assist U.S. export firms to deal with the special problems which arise when doing business with Eastern European (Communist) countries. Contact: East Europe Division, Office of Eastern Europe and Soviet Affairs, ITA, Department of Commerce, Room 3414, Washington, DC 20230/202-377-2645.

Exhibitions

Commercial exhibitions are listed in an Export Promotion Calendar. Contact: Export Awareness Division, U.S. and Foreign Commercial Service, ITA, Department of Commerce, Washington, DC 20230/202-377-4919.

Exhibitions at Government Trade Fairs

Every year six to nine major product exhibitions are built around a product theme and are presented at overseas U.S. government and other kinds of trade shows. The U.S. Department of Commerce will provide exhibit space, design and construct the exhibit, market and promote the exhibit and advise exhibitors. Contact: Office of Event Management and Support Services, ITA, Department of Commerce, Room 2806, Washington, DC 20230/202-377-4231.

Export Counseling Services

Exporters may receive free personal counseling at any of the U.S. Department of Commerce field offices. These offices offer guidance in the way of in-depth counseling in every phase of international trade. They will also schedule appointments with offices of the International Trade Administration and other government agencies. Contact: Export Counseling Center, U.S. and Foreign Commercial Service, ITA, Department of Commerce, Room 1066, Washington, DC 20230/202-377-3181.

Export Financing Guide

A free booklet is available describing basic programs of international and U.S. government agencies that provide financing and insurance for U.S. exports and investments. Ask for *A Guide to Financing Exports* from Office of Trade Finance, Trade Development, ITA, Room 1211, Department of Commerce, 14th and Constitution N.W., Washington, DC 20230/202-377-3277.

Export Financing Hotline

On-the-spot information is available on sources of export financing, where to find export insurance, how to make maximum use of exporting, and overseas investment assistance programs. Contact: Export-Import Bank, 811 Vermont Ave., N.W., Washington, D.C. 20571/800-424-5201.

Export Mailing Lists

Lists are available on foreign companies by country and/or commodity classification. You can receive such lists as all the advertising agencies in Saudi Arabia or all shoe manufacturers in Brazil. There is a charge for the service. Contact: Export Contact Mailing List, Office of Trade Information

Services, ITA, Department of Commerce, Room 1312, Washington, DC 20230/202-377-2988.

Export Reference Publications
Below is a descriptive listing of publications which will be useful in addition to the special publications described elsewhere.

A Business Guide to the New East and North Africa $4.75 Order from the Superintendent of Documents, Government Printing Office, Washington, DC 20402/202-783-3238

Commerce Publications Update. Biweekly ($31 a year) Order from the Superintendent of Documents, Government Printing Office, Washington, DC 20402/202-783-3238.

Foreign Economic Trends and Their Implications for the United States (Approximately 150 reports a year, $66 per year) Order from the Superintendent of Documents, Government Printing Office, Washington, DC 20402/202-783-3238.

International Economic Indicators (Annual subscription $18) Order from the Superintendent of Documents, Government Printing Office, Washington, DC 20402/202-783-3238.

How To Get the Most From Overseas Exhibitions (free) Order from Publication Distribution, ITA, Department of Commerce, Room 1617D, Washington, DC 20230/202-377-5494.

The Export Management Company—Your Export Department (free) Order from Publication Distribution, ITA, Department of Commerce, Room 1617D, Washington, DC 20230/202-377-5494.

Obtain Tax Deferral Through a Domestic International Sales Corporation (DISC) (free) Order from Publication Distribution, ITA, Department of Commerce, Room 1617D, Washington, DC 20230/202-377-5494.

Foreign Business Practices ($5.50 Order from the Superintendent of Documents, Government Printing Office, Washington, DC 20402/202-783-3238.

Exporting Seminars
Export seminars are conducted periodically in cities across the country. Topics covered vary from one day introductory export overviews to multi-session, "how-to" programs. Contact: Office of Domestic Operations, U.S. and Foreign Commercial Service, ITA, Department of Commerce, Room 3810, Washington, DC 20230/202-377-0300.

Foreign Country Desk Officers
See listing of "Country Experts" in this section under Data Experts.

Foreign Credit Ratings
If you need facts about the credit ratings of foreign firms the World Traders Data Reports may help. For $75 they will provide financial and background information about a foreign firm. Contact: Office of Trade Information Services, ITA, Department of Commerce, P.O. Box 14207, Washington, D.C. 20044/202-377-2432 or your nearest Department of Commerce district office.

Foreign Importers Lists
Lists of foreign importers who want to buy from the United States are available. These lists contain names and addresses of distributors, agents, retailers, manufacturers and potential end-users of American products or services in 130 countries. Lists are also available by industry classification. Information is available on hard copy or computer tapes. Contact: Export List Branch, Office of Trade Information Services, ITA, Department of Commerce, Room 1312, Washington, DC 20230/202-377-2988.

Foreign Investment Services
The U.S. Department of Commerce will match U.S. firms with foreign firms for the purpose of domestic joint ventures. Contact: Invest in the U.S.A. Program, Trade Development, ITA, Department of Commerce, Room 3203, Washington, DC 20230/202-377-2087.

Foreign Press and Radio Translations
Translations of radio news transmissions, newspaper editorials, and magazine articles are regrouped into eight areas of interest and sold through the National Technical Information Service (NTIS). The regions covered are China, Eastern Europe, USSR, Asia and the Pacific, Middle East and North Africa, Latin America, Western Europe, and Sub-Sahara Africa. Contact: NTIS, Department of Commerce, 5285 Port Royal Rd., Springfield, VA 22161/703-487-4630.

Foreign Sales Corporation (FSC)
The Foreign Sales Corporation permits U.S. exporters to gain 32% exemption of export profits through use of foreign corporation. Contact: Office of Trade Finance, ITA, Department of Commerce, Room 1128, Washington, D.C. 20230/202-377-4471.

Global Market Surveys
International market studies are available for 15 industries covering 20 countries. These studies cover past and future market size, names of local producers and technological trends. Both the buyers' and sellers' viewpoint are given. Contact: Market Research Division, Office of Trade Information Services, ITA, Department of Commerce, Room 2012, Washington, DC 20230/202-377-5037.

Guide to Foreign Trade Statistics
This book describes all foreign trade reference tabulations and publications, showing formats, tables and charts. Free copies are available from Trade Information Section, Foreign Trade Division Bureau of the Census, Department of Commerce, Room 2179, Suitland, Md. 20233/301-763-5140.

Import/Export Statistics from Census
If you are unable to find published import/export statistics on a given product, it is possible that the

Bureau of the Census can create the information for you from their vast amounts of raw data. There is a charge for this service. Contact: Trade Information Section, Bureau of the Census, Department of Commerce, Room 2179, Suitland, Md. 20233/301-763-5140.

Industry-Organized Trade Missions
The U.S. Department of Commerce will advise and support industrial trade missions organized by groups such as trade associations, chambers of commerce, and state development agencies. Contact: Office of Export Management Support Services, U.S. and Foreign Commercial Service, ITA, Department of Commerce, Room 2806, Washington, DC 20230/202-377-4908.

In-store Promotions
Consumer goods manufacturers can seek help in having their products promoted within foreign stores. Contact: Office of Consumer Goods, ITA, Department of Commerce, Room 4038, Washington, DC 20230/202-377-3459.

International Trade Fairs
Small and medium-sized businesses can obtain the following assistance in exhibiting at foreign trade fairs: facilities and space; shipping assistance; marketing and promotion; identification of key buyers in specific areas. Contact: Office of Event Management and Support Services, U.S. and Foreign Commercial Service, ITA, Department of Commerce, Room 2806, Washington, DC 20230/202-377-4231.

Licensing of Products Overseas
If you are interested in obtaining licensing agreements to distribute U.S. products overseas, the appropriate foreign country desk officers can aid in identifying specific manufacturers who would be interested in such relationships. See listing of "Country Experts" in this section under Data Experts.

Local Export Councils
Each U.S. Department of Commerce field office has an Export Council comprising community businessmen along with a field officer, in order to foster export interest and expertise. They organize seminars and workshops and also work with schools and colleges to expand their curricula to include coursework on international trade. Contact: U.S. and Foreign Commercial Service, ITA, Department of Commerce, Room 3810, Washington, DC 20230/202-377-2696.

Major Foreign Market Potential
The Office of Major Projects informs U.S. firms of specific large-scale overseas projects which have significant potential for U.S. exports. This office also provides government assistance necessary for successful participation by the American firms. Contact: Office of International Major Projects, Capital Goods International Construction, International Trade Administration, Department of Commerce, Room 2007, Washington, DC 20230/202-377-5225.

Monthly Import/Export Statistics
For the latest in trade statistics contact: Foreign Trade Reference Room, Department of Commerce, Room 2233, Washington, DC 20230/202-377-2185.

Market Share Reports
Reports show the performance of U.S. goods in foreign markets for 88 countries and 1,100 commodities. Contact: Office of Trade and Industry Information, Trade Information and Analysis, ITA, Department of Commerce, Room 2217, Washington, DC 20230/202-377-5242.

New Product Information Service
Free promotion is available to small manufacturers for publicizing new U.S. products abroad. The product information selected for this service is published in the bimonthly Commercial News USA, which is sent to 240 U.S. embassies and consulates. Contact: Export Awareness Division, U.S. and Foreign Commercial Service, ITA, Department of Commerce, Room 2106, Washington, DC 20230/202-377-4919.

Overseas Business Travel Briefings
U.S. firms planning overseas business trips in search of a qualified business contact can get help in the way of in-depth briefings on markets and business practices as well as introductions to appropriate firms and individuals. Notification of travel must be made at least two weeks in advance. Contact: Export Counseling, ITA, Department of Commerce, Room 1066, Washington, DC 20230/202-377-3181.

Overseas Business Reports
Reports are published, by country, one or two times per year, showing the economic and commercial profile of each country. Contact: Publication Distribution, ITA, Department of Commerce, Room 1617D, Washington, DC 20230/202-377-5494.

Overseas Market Research
If you need customized market research performed in a foreign country, or a listing in a foreign country, a customized search can help you find overseas market research organizations. A fee is charged for this service. Contact: Office of Trade Information Services, ITA, Department of Commerce, P.O. Box 14207, Washington, D.C. 20044/202-377-2665.

Overseas Marketing Leads

The Trade Opportunities Program matches, through computers, U.S. suppliers with those overseas who are looking to purchase a specific product or service. The minimum cost is $62.50 for 50 sales leads. Contact: Trade Opportunities, P.O. Box 14207, ITA, Department of Commerce, Room 1324, Washington, DC 20044/202-377-2091.

Target Industry Program

Industries which show the greatest potential for exporting are targeted for detailed marketing research and promotional plans. Contact: Targeting Staff, Industry Research and Forecasting Division, ITA, Department of Commerce, Room 3204, Washington, DC 20230/202-377-5657.

Technical Sales Seminars

For high-technology industries, the U.S. Department of Commerce will set up a special seminar to be given by approximately six U.S. company representatives. These seminars are sponsored and planned by local U.S. Department of Commerce district offices. The seminars are followed by sales-oriented private appointments. Contact: your local U.S. Department of Commerce district office for further information.

Temporary Office Space Overseas

The U.S. Department of Commerce will provide office space in export development offices and services to businessmen as they travel abroad. Translation services and local market information are also available. A nominal fee is charged. Contact: Office of Event Management, Event Management Division, ITA, Department of Commerce, Room 2111, Washington, DC 20230/202-377-3741.

Trade Center Exhibitions

The U.S. Department of Commerce together with the U.S. Department of State operate a network of Trade Centers and East/West Trade Development Facilities. These centers act as commercial showrooms in major marketing centers where there is a high potential for sales of U.S. products. Contact: Office of Event Management and Support Services, U.S. and Foreign Commercial Service, ITA, Department of Commerce, Room 2806, Washington, DC 20230/202-377-2525.

Trade Missions

Small tours of U.S. businessmen offering a single product, make three or four stops overseas in order to evaluate market potential. The missions are prepared by the staff of the U.S. Department of Commerce and take up to two years of planning. Contact: Office of Export Management Support Services, U.S. and Foreign Commercial Service, ITA, Department of Commerce, Room 2806, Washington, DC 20230/202-377-4908.

World Import/Export Statistics

For the latest information on any product imported to or exported from any foreign country, contact: Foreign Trade Reference Room, Department of Commerce, Room 2233, Washington, DC 20230/202-377-4855.

Automated Information Transfer System

(AITS) Program is a computerized data base designed to provide information about U.S. suppliers, as well as trade leads, potential customers and market information on foreign countries. The system comprises three data bases containing business opportunities for exporters and importers, how-to-export information, and descriptions of export promotion activities worldwide. Foreign users can contact U.S. embassies for access to the system. Contact: Office of Trade Information Services, ITA, Department of Commerce, Room 1837, Washington, DC 20230/202-377-4992.

Federal Telecommunications Resource

The National Telecommunications and Information Administration (NTIA) is the Federal Communications Commission (FCC) counterpart for the federal government. The Interdependent Radio Advisory Committee (IRAC) functions on behalf of NTIA for all federal agencies and is responsible for telecommunications protocol. The Chairman and his staff are available to answer questions about federal telecommunications. The Committee publishes *The Manual of Regulations and Procedures for Federal Radio Frequency Management,* designed to cover frequency management responsibilities according to delegated authority under Section 305 of the Communications Act of 1934. The Manual explains who has what authority over federal telecommunications, and how to get a frequency assignment within the federal government. The manual is published three times a year, and each issue runs approximately 600 pages. A three year subscription is $118, or is available free of charge to government agencies. The most frequently requested information is the chapter on national and international allocation tables which is available in a pocket-size excerption from IRAC. Contact: Interdependent Radio Advisory Committee (IRAC), National Telecommunications and Information Administration (NTIA), U.S. Department of Commerce, Herbert C. Hoover Bldg., Room 1605, 14th & Constitution Avenue, NW, Washington, DC 20230/202-377-0599.

Ferrous and Non-Ferrous Issues Experts

The specialists at the Office of Basic Industries advise policy makers in the U.S. Department of Commerce on issues related to ferrous and nonferrous metals. They also make recommendations about how American industries can become more competitive, prepare analyses and comments for the upper management of the Department, and participate in interagency groups and committees on steels.

The Office of Basic Industries also serves as a liaison between industry and government. The specialists listed above can answer inquiries and give referrals to other government and industry sources. Contact: Office of Basic Industries, U.S. Department of Commerce, Bureau of Industrial Economics, Washington, DC, 202-377-0608—Ralph Thompson (ferrous Metals), 212-377-0575—Robert C. Reiley (non-ferrous metals).

Films
A number of offices within the Department of Commerce loan films to the public for free. Titles range from "The Double-Edged Sword" which shows how to guard against x-ray burns, to "Trout, U.S.A." which depicts the farming of trout as food and sport fish. For a free film catalog contact: Audio-Visual, Office of Public Affairs, Department of Commerce, Washington, DC 20230/ 202-377-5610.

Fire Prevention Protection and Research
The National Bureau of Standards (NBS) conducts research in fire prevention and information is given to such groups as the Consumer Product Safety Commission, HHS, Underwriters' Laboratory, and the Fire Administration. NBS works at preventing and reducing fire loss, fire detection, chemistry, and toxology. Contact: Center for Fire Research, NBS, Department of Commerce, Building 224, A247, Washington, DC 20234/301-921-3143.

NBS also sets up methods and standards to test fire protection devices including crash helmets. Tips are available on fire safety and fire prevention. Contact: Inquiry Service, NBS, Department of Commerce, Administration Building, Room A537, Washington, DC 20234/301-921-2318.

For information on research covering all aspects of fire, ranging from the physics and chemistry of combustion to the psychological and motivational characteristics of arsonists, contact: The Center for Fire Research, NBS, Building 224, Room A247, Washington, DC 20234/301-921-3143.

Fish and Seafood Information Center
If you want to know such things as what is the difference between white and light tuna, why some frozen fish are graded "A" while others have no grades, or if you would like to set up a consumer workshop on fish and seafood contact: Office of Utilization Research, National Marine Fisheries Service, NOAA, Department of Commerce, Washington, DC 20235/202-634-7458.

Fisheries
The National Marine Fisheries office provides information on the development of commercial fisheries, along with seafood research and inspection. They also provide help for commercial fishermen and make available statistics on fish catches and provide assessment of fishery resources. Contact: Public Affairs, National Marine Fisheries Service, NOAA, Department of Commerce, Washington, DC 20235/301-634-7281.

Fishing, Commercial
Technical expertise, research, information and financial assistance (see "Fishing" under "Loans") in this section are all available to commercial fishermen. A periodical, *Market News Report,* is published three times a week and is available for $45 per year. It covers such topics as pricing, production, landings, imports and exports, and cold storage holdings. Contact: National Marine Fisheries Service, NOAA, Department of Commerce, 3300 Whitehaven Street, Washington, DC 20235/202-634-7366.

Fishery Products Grading and Inspection
Grading and inspection of fishery products are done on a voluntary basis. The types of inspection services available include plant sanitation; processing methods; lot inspection for weight, condition, etc.; and bacteriological, physical and chemical analysis. Contact: Office of Utilization Research, Nat'l. Seafood Inspection Program, National Marine Fisheries Service, NOAA, Department of Commerce, Washington, DC 20235/202-634-7458.

Fishing, Sport
A good deal of information and expertise is available describing the sport fishing potential of various coastal water. Publications describe the types and amounts of fish found in specific areas. Contact: National Marine Fisheries Service, NOAA, Department of Commerce, Washington, DC 20235/202-634-7366.

Floods
For information on safety precautions for flash floods, community action for flash floods, or flood warning systems contact: Public Affairs—Weather, National Weather Service, Department of Commerce, 8060 13th Street, Room 401, Silver Spring, MD 20910/301-427-7622.

Foreign Investment Statistics
Statistics are kept on the amount of foreign direct investment in the U.S. as well as U.S. direct investment abroad. The kinds of information collected include balance-of-payment data, income and capital flows between U.S. parent companies and their foreign affiliates and between foreign companies and their U.S. affiliates, operating and financial statistics, and balance sheets and income statements of U.S. affiliates abroad and of affiliates of foreign companies in the United States. Contact: International Investment Division, Bu-

reau of Economic Analysis, Department of Commerce, BE-50, Washington, DC 20230/202-523-0657.

Foreign Technology
The National Technical Information Service (NTIS) offers a weekly newsletter providing summaries to technical reports issued by foreign governments including Japan, West Germany, France, Great Britain, and Sweden. Available on subscription, this newsletter alerts U.S. businesses to the more than 10,000 new reports NTIS receives annually. Write for the free descriptive brochure, PR-733. Contact: NTIS, U.S. Department of Commerce, Springfield, VA 22161/703-487-4630.

Franchising
Information and expertise are available from the Bureau of Industrial Economics on the franchising industry. Two publications, *Franchise Opportunities Handbook*, and *Franchising in the Economy*, present industry market data and pinpoint specific franchising opportunities. Contact: Office of Service Industries, ITA, Room 4312, U.S. Dept. of Commerce, Washington, DC 20230/202-377-0342.

Free-trade Zones
More than 100 free ports, free-trade zones or similar customs-privileged facilities are available to U.S. manufacturers or their distributors where they can receive large shipments of goods and reship smaller lots to customers overseas without paying a duty. Contact: Foreign Trade Zones Board, Department of Commerce, Room 1872, Washington, DC 20230/202-377-2862.

Freedom of Information Act
Each major office within the U.S. Department of Commerce handles Freedom of Information Act (FOIA) requests. If you are looking for the address of a specific FOIA office or wish to find a central office, contact: U.S. Dept. of Commerce, Herbert Hoover Bldg., Room 6628, Central Reference and Records Inspection Facility, Washington, DC. 20230/202-377-4217. All correspondence should be clearly marked "FOIA Request."

Geophysical and Solar-Terrestrial Information
Information is available on solid earth and marine geophysics, ionospheric solar and other space environment data, and geomagnetic data. Contact: National Geophysical and Solar-Terrestrial Data Center, Department of Commerce, NOAA/NESDIS, 325 Broadway, Boulder, CO 80303/303-497-6215.

Government Contract Announcements and Awards
The *Commerce Business Daily* lists almost all contracts from all government agencies that are open to bid by interested parties. This is an important publication for anyone who is interested

in doing business with the federal government. Subscriptions are available for $160 (1st class) or $81 (2nd class) annually from Government Printing Office, Superintendent of Documents, Washington, DC 20402/202-783-3238. For further information on content, contact: Commercial Service, ITA, Department of Commerce, Washington, DC 20230/202-377-4878.

Government Productivity Information Sources
Two productivity reports are available from the National Technical Information Service. *The White House Conference on Productivity Growth: A Better Life for America* (Pub #PB84-159144) covers the key areas of the White House conference on productivity, held September 21–23, 1983. The conference focused on four main areas: capital investment, human resources, the role of government, and the role of the private sector. The softcover report is available for $5.00. *Restoring Productivity Growth in America: A Challenge for the 1980's* (Pub # 84-217603) is the final report of the National Productivity Advisory Committee dated 12/30/83 which outlines 46 specific recommendations for improving productivity growth. The report is available for $5.00. Contact: National Technical Information Service (NTIS), 5285 Port Royal Road, Springfield, VA 22161, 703-487-4650.

Grants
The programs described below are for sums of money that are given by the federal government to initiate and stimulate new or improved activities, or to sustain ongoing services.

Anadromous and Great Lakes Fisheries Conservation
Objectives: To cooperate with the states and other non-federal interests in the conservation, development, and enhancement of the nation's anadromous fish and the fish in the Great Lakes and Lake Champlain that ascend streams to spawn, and for the control of sea lampreys.

Eligibility: Any interested person or organization may propose a cooperative undertaking. However, all proposals must be coordinated with the state fishery agency having responsibility for the resource to be affected by the proposal.

Range of Financial Assistance: $2,000 to $533,100.

Contact: Fishery Management Office, National Marine Fisheries Service, Page Building 2, 3300 Whitehaven St. N.W., Washington, DC 20235/202-634-7218.

Coastal Energy Impact Program—Environmental Grants
Objectives: To allow States and units of general purpose local governments to participate effectively in policy, planning and managerial decisions relating to management of Outer Continental Shelf oil and gas resources.

Eligibility: Any coastal state may apply for assistance.

Range of Financial Assistance: $75,000 to $317,000.

Contact: Director, Coastal Energy Impact Program Office, Office of Coastal Zone Management, National Oceanic and Atmospheric Administration, Department of Commerce, 3300 Whitehaven St. N.W., Washington, DC 20235/202-254-8000.

Coastal Energy Impact Program—Formula Grants

Objectives: To provide financial assistance to coastal states to plan and construct public facilities and services and for the amelioration of environmental and recreational loss attributable to Outer Continental Shelf (OCS) energy development activities.

Eligibility: Any coastal state that has or has had adjacent OCS oil and gas leasing and development activities.

Range of Financial Assistance: Dependent upon state's allotment. Allotments ranged from $75,000 to $192,000.

Contact: Office of Ocean and Coastal Resource Mgmt., National Oceanic and Atmospheric Administration, Department of Commerce, 3300 Whitehaven St. N.W., Washington, DC 20235/202-634-1672.

Coastal Energy Impact Program—Outer Continental Shelf State Participation Grants

Objectives: To allow states and units of general purpose local governments to participate effectively in policy, planning, and managerial decisions relating to management of Outer Continental Shelf oil and gas resources.

Eligibility: Any Coastal State that has a management program which has been approved under Section 306.

Range of Financial Assistance: $75,000 to $317,000.

Contact: Director, Coastal Energy Impact Program Office, Office of Coastal Zone Management, National Oceanic and Atmospheric Administration, Department of Commerce, 3300 Whitehaven Street, N.W., Washington, D.C. 20235/202-254-8000.

Coastal Energy Impact Program—Planning Grants

Objectives: To assist the states and units of local government to study and plan for the social, economic, and environmental consequences on the coastal zone of new or expanded energy facilities, and to encourage rational and timely planning and management of energy facility siting and energy resource development.

Eligibility: Any Coastal State that has a management program which has been approved under Section 306.

Range of Financial Assistance: $75,000 to $192,000.

Contact: Office of Ocean and Coastal Resource Management, National Oceanic and Atmospheric Administration, Department of Commerce, 3300 Whitehaven Street, N.W., Washington, D.C. 2035/202-634-1672.

Coastal Zone Management Program Administration

Objective: To assist any coastal state in the implementation and administration of a management program for the land and water resources of its coastal zone.

Eligibility: States in, or bordering on, the Atlantic, Pacific, or Arctic Ocean, the Gulf of Mexico, Long Island Sound, or one or more of the Great Lakes. The Governor will designate the state agency or entity that is to be the applicant.

Range of Financial Assistance: $75,000 to $3,000,000.

Contact: Chief, Coastal Programs Division, Office of Ocean and Coastal Resource Management, National Oceanic and Atmospheric Administration, Department of Commerce, 3300 Whitehaven St. N.W., Washington, DC 20235/202-634-1672.

Coastal Zone Management—Estuarine Sanctuaries

Objectives: To assist states in the acquisition, development and operation of estuarine sanctuaries for the purpose of creating natural field laboratories to gather data and make studies of the natural and human processes occurring within the estuaries of the coastal zone.

Eligibility: Any coastal state. The Governor will designate the state agency or entity that is to be the applicant.

Range of Financial Assistance: $50,000 to $1,252,000.

Contact: Director, Sanctuary Programs Office, Office of Ocean and Coastal Resource Management, National Oceanic and Atmospheric Administration, Department of Commerce, 3300 Whitehaven St. N.W., Washington, DC 20235/202-634-4236.

Commercial Fisheries Research and Development

Objectives: To promote state commercial fishery research and development.

Eligibility: The agency of a state government authorized under its laws to regulate commercial fisheries.

Range of Financial Assistance: $2,000 to $340,000.

Contact: Chief, National Marine Fisheries Service, 3300 Whitehaven St. N.W., Washington, DC 20235/202-634-7218.

Economic Development—District Operational Assistance

Objective: To assist Economic Development Districts in providing professional services (other than by grant) to their local governments.

Eligibility: Chief officers of governing bodies of

Economic Development Districts designated by the Secretary of Commerce.

Range of Financial Assistance: $25,000.

Contact: Deputy Assistant Secretary for Operations, Economic Development Administration, Department of Commerce, Washington, DC 20230/202-377-3081.

Economic Development—Public Works Impact Program

Objective: To provide immediate useful work to unemployed and underemployed persons in designated project areas.

Eligibility: State, cities, counties and other political subdivisions, Indian tribes, and private or public nonprofit organizations representing a redevelopment area or economic development center.

Range of Financial Assistance: Up to $600,000.

Contact: Deputy Assistant Secretary for Operations, Economic Development Administration, Department of Commerce, Washington, DC 20230/202-377-3081.

Economic Development—State and Local Economic Development Planning

Objectives: To develop the capability of state and local governments to undertake comprehensive and coordinated economic development planning that leads to the formulation of development goals and specific strategies to achieve them, with particular emphasis on reducing unemployment and increasing incomes.

Eligibility: Eligible applicants are the governors of states and chief executives of cities and counties meeting Economic Development Administration (EDA) eligibility criteria.

Range of Financial Assistance: $20,000 to $88,000.

Contact: Deputy Assistant Secretary for Operations, Economic Development Administration, Department of Commerce, Washington, DC 20230/202-377-3081.

Economic Development—Support for Planning Organizations

Objective: To foster multi-county district and redevelopment area economic development planning and implementation and thereby promote the creation of full-time permanent jobs for the unemployed and the underemployed.

Eligibility: Areas designated as redevelopment areas or determined by the Secretary of Commerce to have substantial need for planning assistance, groups of adjoining counties, labor market areas, and/or Indian reservations that include at least one area designated as a redevelopment area by the Secretary of Commerce, and one or more centers of growth not over 250,000 population.

Range of Financial Assistance: $25,000 to $120,000.

Contact: Operations Directorate, Economic Development Administration, Department of Commerce, Washington, DC 20230/202-377-3081.

Economic Development—Technical Assistance

Objectives: To solve problems of economic growth in EDA-designated geographic areas and other areas of substantial need through administrative and demonstration project grants, feasibility studies, management and operational assistance, and other studies.

Eligibility: While there are no specific applicant eligibility requirements, most technical assistance applicants are private nonprofit groups of state, municipal or county governments located in economically depressed areas of the country. Technical assistance is also given to small private business firms; however, this technical assistance must be repaid to the government.

Range of Financial Assistance: $7,500 to $500,000.

Contact: Initial contact should be at the regional office, except for projects which are national in scope, in which case initial contact should be with headquarters office, Deputy Assistant Secretary for Operations, Economic Development Administration, Department of Commerce, Washington, DC 20230/202-377-3081.

Economic Development—Grants for Public Works and Development Facilities

Objective: To assist in the construction of public facilities needed to initiate and encourage long-term economic growth in designated geographic areas where economic growth is lagging behind the rest of the nation.

Eligibility: States, cities, counties and other political subdivisions, Indian tribes, and private or public nonprofit organizations or associations representing a redevelopment area or a designated economic development center eligible to receive grants and loans.

Range of Financial Assistance: $50,000 to $5,600,000.

Contact: Deputy Assistant Secretary for Operations, Economic Development Administration, Department of Commerce, Washington, DC 20230/202-377-3081.

Financial Assistance for Marine Pollution Research

Objectives: To determine the ecological consequences of dumping industrial, municipal, and dredged waste materials into the ocean.

Eligibility: Individuals, nonprofit organizations, state and local governments.

Range of Financial Assistance: $15,000 to $180,000.

Contact: Office of Oceanography and Marine Services, N/OMS3, NOS/NOAA, Rockville, MD 20852/301-443-8734.

Fisheries Development and Utilization Research and Development Grants and Cooperative Agreements Program

Objectives: To foster the development and strengthening of the fishing industry of the United States and increase the supply of wholesome, nutritious fish and fish products available to consumers.

Eligibility: Individuals, nonprofit organizations, state and local governments.

Range of Financial Assistance: $5,000 to $2,500,000.

Contact: Office of Utilization and Development, National Marine Fisheries Service, National Oceanic and Atmospheric Administration, Department of Commerce, Washington, D.C. 20235/ 202-634-7451.

Intergovernmental Climate-Demonstration Project

Objectives: To conduct climate-related studies, to provide information to users regarding climate and climatic effects, and to provide advice to regional, state, and local government agencies on climate-related issues.

Eligibility: State and local governments, profit and nonprofit organizations, and individuals.

Range of Financial Assistance: $10,000 to $77,000.

Contact: National Climate Program Office, National Oceanic and Atmospheric Administration, Department of Commerce, 6010 Executive Blvd., Rockville, MD 20852/301-443-8981.

Measurement and Engineering Research and Standards

Objectives: To provide scientific research for measurement and engineering research and standards. Grant money may be used to further scientific research in areas of fire research, precision measurement, building research, automated manufacturing, weights and measures, and other areas of specific research.

Eligibility: Universities, nonprofit organizations, and state and local governments.

Range of Financial Assistance: Not specified.

Contact: National Bureau of Standards, Washington, D.C. 20234/301-921-1000.

Minority Business Development—Management and Technical Assistance

Objectives: To provide free management and technical assistance to economically and socially disadvantaged individuals who need assistance in starting and/or operating a business. Primary objectives of the assistance are to increase the gross receipts and decrease the failure rates of the client firms.

Eligibility: There are no restrictions on who may be funded under this program. This includes state and local governments, state colleges and universities, public, private, junior and community colleges. U.S. Trust Territories, Indian tribes, indi-viduals, other nonprofit organizations and institutions, and profit-making firms.

Range of Financial Assistance: $10,000 to $2,145,000.

Contact: Chief, Grants Administration Division, Room 5099, MBDA, Dept. of Commerce, Washington, DC 20230/202-377-2065.

Public Telecommunications Facilities

Objectives: To assist, through matching grants, in the planning and construction of public telecommunications facilities in order to extend delivery of public telecommunications services to as many citizens as possible by the most efficient and economical means, including the use of broadcast and nonbroadcast technologies; increase public telecommunications services and facilities available to, operated by, and owned by minorities and women; and strengthen the capability of existing public television and radio stations to provide public telecommunications services to the public.

Eligibility: Public broadcast stations, noncommercial and public telecommunications entities, nonprofit foundations, corporations, institutions, or associations organized primarily for education or cultural purposes, and a state or local governmental agencies.

Range of Financial Assistance: $3,000 to $700,000.

Contact: Director, Public Telecommunications Facilities Division/NTIA, Room 4625, Department of Commerce, Washington, DC 20230/ 202-377-5802.

Sea Grant Support

Objectives: To support establishment of major university centers for marine research, education, training, and advisory services, and also individual efforts in these same areas. Limited funds are available for organized national projects and for international cooperative assistance relative to ocean and coastal resources.

Eligibility: Universities, colleges, junior colleges, technical schools, institutes, laboratories, any public or private corporation, partnership, or other association or entity; any state, political subdivision of a state or agency or officer thereof; any individual.

Range of Financial Assistance: $56,000 to $3,100,000.

Contact: Director, National Sea Grant College Program, National Oceanic and Atmospheric Administration, Department of Commerce, 6010 Executive Blvd., Rockville, MD 20852/301-443-8926.

Special Economic Development and Adjustment Assistance Program—Long-Term Economic Deterioration

Objective: To assist state and local areas in the development and implementation of strategies designed to arrest and reverse the problems associated with long-term economic deterioration.

Eligibility: Cities, counties, or other political subdivisions, consortiums of political subdivisions, public or private nonprofit organizations representing redevelopment areas designated under the Public Works and Economic Development Act of 1965, Economic Development Districts established under Title IV of the Act, and Indian tribes and states.

Range of Financial Assistance: Not specified.

Contact: Deputy Assistant Secretary for Operations, Economic Development Administration, Department of Commerce, Washington, DC 20230/202-377-3081.

Special Economic Development and Adjustment Assistance Program—Sudden and Severe Economic Dislocation

Objective: To help state and local areas meet special needs arising from actual or threatened unemployment resulting from sudden and severe economic dislocation.

Eligibility: A public or private nonprofit organization that has been determined to be the representative of a redevelopment area designated under Section 401 of the Public Works and Economic Development Act of 1965, as amended, Economic Development Districts established under Title IV of the Act or Indian tribes, a state, city or other political subdivision of a state, or a consortium of such political subdivisions.

Range of Financial Assistance: Not specified.

Contact: Deputy Assistant Secretary for Operations, EDA, Department of Commerce, Washington, DC 20230/202-377-3081.

Housing Survey, Annual

In addition to the decennial census of housing, other annual surveys are conducted. The results of these surveys are published in six reports. A. General Housing Characteristics ($7, # 003-024-05623-2), B. Indicators of Housing and Neighborhood Quality by Financial Characteristic ($16, # 003-024-05837-5), C. Financial Characteristics ($9, #003-024-05008-1), D. Housing Characteristics of Recent Movers ($6, # 003-024-05770-1), E. Urban and Rural Housing Characteristics ($6.50, # 003-024-05838-3), F. Energy-Related Housing Characteristics ($4.75, # 003-024-05835-9). Copies of these publications are available from Superintendent of Documents, Government Printing Office, Washington, D.C. 20402/202-783-3238. Check for latest edition. For information on content, contact: Housing Division, Bureau of the Census, Dept. of Commerce, Washington, D.C. 20233/202-763-2881.

Industrial Experts Listing

The Bureau of Industrial Economics (BIE) of the U.S. Department of Commerce is responsible for the collection and analysis of both domestic and international data in all categories of industry classifications. Organized into some 300 industries covering producer and consumer goods and services, BIE has staff experts to cover each industry. A listing of each industry and its specialists is available upon request. Individuals and organizations have access to the data and analyses, and all information is available upon request at no charge. Contact: Bureau of Industrial Economics (BIE), U.S. Department of Commerce, 14th & Constitution Avenue, NW, Washington, DC 20230.

Industrial Mobilization

Two defense-related systems, concerning priority of contracts and specified materials which are relevant to defense contractors, are in effect and must be followed at all times. A national emergency results in expansion of the two systems. Contact: Office of Industrial Resource Administration, U.S. Department of Commerce, Washington, D.C. 20230/202-377-3634 or 2233.

Industrial Outlook, U.S.

This annual publication is produced by the Bureau of Industrial Economics. The book shows one- and five-year projections for the economic outlook of some 300 major industries in the United States. It is published each January and is available for $14.00 from Government Printing Office, Attn: Superintendent of Documents, Washington, DC 20402/202-783-3238. (SIN 003-008-00190-4, Check for latest edition.)

Industrial Radio and Television Resources

The U.S. Industrial Outlook is an excellent source of industry information for the radio and television industries. Two chapters are devoted to these topics, "Radio and Television Communications Equipment" and "Broadcasting." Along with the industry forecast are definitions, explanations and descriptions of new technological breakthroughs, referrals to other sources of information, and the name of the BIE industry specialist for radio and television. Published annually, it costs $14.00 from the Government Printing Office, Washington, DC 20402. Also available is Arthur Pleasants, an electronics industry specialist, to answer questions on consumer-oriented products and on all military equipment such as sonars, satellites, etc. Contact: Arthur Pleasants, U.S. Department of Commerce, Bureau of Industrial Economics (BIE), Washington, DC 20042, 202-377-2872.

Industry Technicians Can Use Government Facilities

The National Bureau of Standards (NBS) sponsors a Research Associate Program, which enables technical specialists from industry and professional organizations to work at their facilities under supervision of and consultation with NBS professionals. Contact: Officer, Research Associate Program, Industrial Liaison, National Bureau of

Standards, Department of Commerce, Administration Building, Room A402, Washington, DC 20234/301-921-3591.

Inland Waterways
For a listing of available maps and literature describing the nation's inland waterway system contact: National Ocean Service, Distribution Branch, NOAA, Department of Commerce, 6501 Lafayette Ave., Riverdale, MD 20737/301-436-6980

Innovation and Productivity Enhancement Research
The Office of Productivity, Technology and Innovation (OPTI) reviews issues of industrial innovation and productivity enhancement in the private sector. It provides a variety of information services to the private sector and state and local governments. Its Small Business Technology Liaison Division provides information about the innovation process, resources available, and a financial sensitivity model available for purchase. It links smaller firms, state and local governments, and other organizations involved in innovation, and provides federal policy input on smaller firms and technology. This division also produces the *Guide to Innovation Resources and Planning for the Smaller Business.*

OPTI's Industrial Technology Partnership Program provides information and training on the Research and Development Limited Partnership (RDLP), which is a financing mechanism, prepares feasibility packages to identify high technology projects suitable for RDLPs, assists in the establishment of cooperative R & D projects, and provides federal policy input on R & D tax policy.

OPTI's Productivity Center answers productivity inquiries with off-the-shelf publications. Its staff can provide you with bibliographies, reading lists, and articles, and refer you to other sources.

Contact: Office of Productivity, Technology and Innovation, U.S. Department of Commerce, Room 4816, Washington, DC 20230/202-377-1093.

International Competition Resources and Experts
The Commerce Productivity Center (CPC) provides business and other organizations with information about how to improve competitiveness, productivity, and quality. As part of the Office of Productivity, Technology and Innovation, the Center has access to over 35 professionals having expertise in such diverse areas as economic policy, industrial competitiveness, research and development, technology transfer and patent policy. Its collection includes information on both domestic and foreign experience, data industries and technologies. Upon request, staff can provide publications, articles, reference and referral services, bibliographies and reading lists. CPC's services are available free of charge. Contact: Commerce Productivity Center, U.S. Department of Commerce, 14th St. & Constitution Avenue, NW, Room 7413, Washington, DC 20230/202-377-0940.

International Industrial Competitive Assessment Studies
The Office of General Industrial Machinery prepares articles for the *U.S. Industrial Outlook* as well as competitive assessment studies of selected industries. The office is also involved in international trade development, the capital goods activities of the Industrial Sector Advisory Committee (ISAC), and are responsible for responding to the Secretary of Commerce regarding matters affecting the industries covered by the office. Contact: Capital Goods and International Construction, Office of General Industrial Machinery, International Trade Administration, U.S. Department of Commerce, 14th & Constitution Avenue N.W., Washington, DC 20230/202-377-4382.

International Service Industries
The Office of Service Industries deals with trade policy and promotion matters that affect the foreign business sect of U.S. service industries (hotels, insurance, advertising, tourism, banking, telecommunications and computer services, etc.) and attempts to solve problems that affect such industries. Contact: Office of Service Industries, Department of Commerce, Room 2812, Washington, D.C. 20230/202-377-3575.

International Telecommunications Development Research
The National Telecommunications and Information Administration (NTIA) is an executive branch agency responsible for the development and presentation of domestic and international telecommunications policy. It is also responsible for the administration of telecommunication facility programs receiving capital grants from the federal government. NTIA manages the government use of radio telecommunications, and regulates radio spectrum within the country. Its staff of specialists develop research in support of policy, and provide services in the area of radio frequency. Policy advising staff can be contacted for technical information and referrals. Technical publications and reports are issued by the NTIA, as well as a publications listing. Contact: National Telecommunications and Information Administration, U.S. Department of Commerce, Washington, DC 20230/202-377-1551.

International Trade Experts and Resources
The publications staff of the International Trade Administration can refer you to an industry specialist for nearly every industry in the U.S. These experts can tell you about the latest technological developments; provide you with statistics; give you data on imports and exports; tell you how the U.S.

industry compares with industry abroad; and refer you to appropriate experts and literature.

An expert on high tech international problems and high tech competitiveness issues is on the staff.

Trade reference rooms in libraries located in International Trade Administration (ITA) District Offices across the United States have U.S. import/export data by product, country or both. Foreign data is only available at the ITA trade reference room in Washington, DC. These libraries have all kinds of trade statistics, but you must obtain the information by visiting the library yourself. Contact: International Trade Administration, U.S. Department of Commerce, 14th & Constitution Avenue, NW, Washington, DC 20230, Publications, Room 442, 202-377-4356; High Tech Expert 202-377-5145.

International Trade of High Technology Products

The International Trade Administration puts out several reports on high technology topics, including robotics, the telecommunications industry, the semiconductor industry, the computer industry and biotechnology. One major publication is *An Assessment of U.S. Competitiveness in High Technology Industries* (#003-009-00358-0). This study demonstrates the U.S. challenge to maintain its broad technological preeminence. It examines selected high technology sectors with regard to their importance, their trade performance, and the factors influencing their competitiveness with foreign competitors. Extensive statistical tables support the findings of the study.

Published every January, the *U.S. Industrial Outlook,* provides an overview and prospectus for more than 300 U.S. industries. High tech industries covered include: telecommunications, computing and office equipment, electronic components, aerospace, chemicals, photographic equipment, information services, medical and dental instruments, and more. Also included is the name, phone number and address of Department of Commerce experts for just about every industry in the U.S. These specialists can tell you about the latest developments in the field and refer you to other experts and literature. The 1,000-page book costs $14.00. Both publications are available from the Government Printing Office, Washington, DC 20402/ 202-783-3238. Contact: U.S. Department of Commerce, International Trade Administration, Industry Publications, Room 442, 14th & Constitution Avenue, NW, Washington, DC 20230/202-377-4356; Public Affairs, 202-377-3803.

Invention, Evidence of Conception

For $10 inventors can officially record evidence of the date they conceived an invention. A "Disclosure Document" is filed, which will be kept in confidence by the Patent and Trademark Office. Contact: Commissioner of Patents and Trademarks, Patent and Trademark Office, Department of Commerce, Washington, DC 20231/703-557-3225.

Inventions for Licensing

If you wish to identify new products and technology that have been invented by the Federal government and are available for licensing for $205 a year you can subscribe to a National Technical Information Service (NTIS) newsletter titled "Government Inventions for Licensing." Contact: NTIS, Department of Commerce, 5285 Port Royal Rd., Springfield, VA 22161/703-487-4600.

Inventors Conference and Exposition

Sponsored by the Patents and Trademark Office and the Bureau of National Affairs, the conference is held each February (close to Edison's Birthday) in Washington, DC. The events include speakers addressing inventor's problems and demonstrations by inventors and corporations. Contact: Office of Public Affairs, Patent and Trademark Office, Department of Commerce, 2021 Jefferson Davis Highway, Room 1A05, Arlington, VA 22202/703-557-3341.

Invest in USA

A special program has been developed to provide information to foreign businesses on how, where, who can help, licensing, etc. involving investment in the U.S. "Invest in USA" seminars are held abroad to promote investment. Contact: Invest in USA Program, Investment Advisory Staff—Office of Export Marketing Assistance, ITA, Department of Commerce, Room 4036, Washington, DC 20230/202-377-4831.

Laser Information

Information and expertise are available on such topics as stabilized lasers, measurement of laser frequencies and wave lengths, laser power measurements, and applications of lasers to lengths measurement. Contact: National Bureau of Standards, Technical Information and Publications Division, Department of Commerce, Administration Building, Room A537, Washington, DC 20234/301-921-2318.

Laser Standards and Optical Fiber Research

The Optical Electronics Metrology Group conducts work in the areas of measurements and standards for lasers, the characterization of optical fibers, and device research including detectors, modulators, and wave guide samplers. The staff will respond to inquiries, or can tell you about one of the numerous research reports available. The National Bureau of Standards publishes the *NBS Special Publication 250 and Appendix,* a source for very detailed measurement information regarding optical fibers and lasers. Available free of charge from the Office of Physical Measurement Services, National Bureau of Standards, Physics Building,

RB362, Gaithersburg, MD 20899, 301-921-2805. Contact: Optical Electronics Metrology Group, Mailcode 724.02, National Bureau of Standards (NBS), 325 Broadway, Boulder, CO 80303/303-497-5341.

Law Enforcement Equipment
The National Bureau of Standards has a special division which investigates such products as surveillance cameras, vapor generators, radar, breathohol detection and clothing worn by law enforcement officers. Contact: Law Enforcement Standards Laboratory, National Bureau of Standards, Department of Commerce, Washington, DC 20234/301-921-3161.

Legal Metrology Requirements Experts and Resources
The International Organization for Legal Metrology consists of member nations whose basic purpose is to harmonize legal metrology requirements and to foster international trade. Staff members can answer questions and/or make referrals to the committees. The Organization holds a general conference usually once every four months. An important publication is the *OIML Newsletter* which generally contains brief articles on the status of any harmonization effort going on. The newsletter's coverage includes reports on committee activities. The 6-page publication is free. Contact: International Organization for Legal Metrology, Office of Product Standards Policy, Administration Building, National Bureau of Standards, Gaithersburg, MD 20899/301-921-3287.

Libraries
The libraries within the U.S. Department of Commerce offer a valuable source for information in their respective subject areas. The following is a listing of the major libraries:

Library, Department of Commerce, Washington, DC 20230/202-377-2161.

Library and Information Services (NOAA), Department of Commerce, 6009 Executive Blvd., Rockville, MD 20852/301-443-8330.

National Bureau of Standards Library, Department of Commerce, Washington, DC 20234/301-921-3451.

Patent and Trademark Office, Scientific Library, Department of Commerce, Wash., D.C. 20231

Bureau of the Census Library, Department of Commerce, Federal Office Building No. 3, Room 2451, Washington, DC 20233/202-763-5042.

Bureau of Economic Analysis Reference Room, Department of Commerce, BE 16, 1401 K St. N.W., Washington, DC 20230/202-523-0595.

Technical Information Project, National Telecommunications and Information Administration, Department of Commerce, 1346 Connecticut Ave. N.W., Suite 217, Washington, DC 20036/202-466-2954.

Loans and Loan Guarantees
The programs described below are those that offer financial assistance through the lending of federal monies for a specific period of time or programs in which the federal government makes an arrangement to indemnify a lender against part or all of any defaults by the borrower.

Coastal Energy Impact Program—Loans and Guarantees
Objectives: To provide financial assistance for public facilities necessary to support increased populations stemming from new or expanded coastal energy activity.

Eligibility: Any coastal state may apply for funds for use on public facilities including, but not limited to, highways and secondary roads, parking, mass transit, docks, navigation aids, fire and police protection, water supply, waste collection and treatment (including drainage), schools and education, and hospitals and health care.

Range of Financial Assistance: $200,000 to $38,000,000.

Contact: Director, Coastal Energy Impact Program Office, Office of Coastal Zone Management, National Oceanic and Atmospheric Administration, Department of Commerce, 3300 Whitehaven St. N.W., Washington, DC 20235/202-254-8000.

Economic Development—Business Development Assistance
Objectives: To sustain industrial and commercial viability in designated areas by providing financial assistance to businesses that create or retain permanent jobs, and expand or establish plants in redevelopment areas for projects where financial assistance is not available from other sources.

Eligibility: Any individual, private or public corporation, or Indian tribe, provided that the project to be funded is in an area designated as eligible under the Act at the time the application is filed. Neither business development loans nor guarantees of any kind will be extended to applicants who: 1) have, within the previous three years, relocated any or all of their facilities to another city, or state; 2) contemplate relocating part or all of their existing facilities with a resultant loss of employment at such facilities; and 3) produce a product or service for which there is a sustained and prolonged excess of supply over demand.

Range of Financial Assistance: $260,000 to $111,100,000.

Contact: Office of Business Loans, Economic Development Administration, Department of Commerce, Washington, DC 20230/202-377-5067.

Fishermen's Guaranty Fund
Objectives: To provide for reimbursement of losses incurred as a result of the seizure of a U.S. commercial fishing vessel by a foreign country on

the basis of rights or claims in territorial waters or on the high seas that are not recognized by the United States.

Eligibility: Must be a U.S. citizen and the owner or charter of a fishing vessel documented as such by the United States.

Range of Financial Assistance: $1,000 to $290,000.

Contact: Chief, Financial Services Division, National Marine Fisheries Service, Department of Commerce, 3300 Whitehaven St. N.W., Washington, DC 20235/202-634-4688.

Fishing Vessel Obligation Guarantees
Objectives: To provide government guarantees of private loans to upgrade the U.S. fishing fleet.

Eligibility: Must have an obligee approved by the Secretary of Commerce as able to service the obligation properly; and an obligor approved as possessing the ability, experience, financial resources, and other qualifications necessary to the adequate operation and maintenance of the mortgaged property.

Range of Financial Assistance: $15,000 to $9,000,000.

Contact: Chief, Financial Services Division, National Marine Fisheries Service, Department of Commerce, 3300 Whitehaven St. N.W., Washington, DC 20235, 202-634-7496.

Loans to States for Supplemental and Basic Funding of Titles I, II, III, IV and IX Activities
See "Grants" in this section.

Trade Adjustment Assistance
Objective: To provide trade adjustment assistance to firms and industries adversely affected by increased imports. Financial assistance may be used for capital equipment, buildings, land and working capital.

Eligibility: Firms.

Range of Financial Assistance: Up to $3,000,000.

Contact: Office of Trade Adjustment Assistance, International Trade Administration, Department of Commerce, 14th & E Street, N.W., Washington, D.C. 20230/202-377-5005.

Local Business Statistics
Every year the Bureau of the Census publishes *County Business Patterns,* which shows statistics on business operations for every county in the United States. Fifty-one individual reports are done (50 states and Puerto Rico) and data available include type of business, number of people employed, payroll size and type of industry. Copies of the publication are available from Superintendent of Documents, Government Printing Office, Washington, DC 20402/202-783-3238. For detailed information on content, contact: Publications, DUSD, Bureau of the Census,

Department of Commerce, Washington, DC 20233/301-763-4100.

Life-Cycle Costing
The federal government uses a method of Life-Cycle Costing for making energy-related investment decisions in buildings and building systems. The National Bureau of Standards has published a report which describes how to use this system. Request "Life Cycle Cost Manual for the Federal Energy Management Program" (#All printed copy, AOI microfiche) from NTIS, Dept. of Commerce, 5285 Port Royal Rd., Springfield, VA 22161/703-487-4600.

Local Business Assistance Centers for Minorities
The regional offices of the Minority Business Development Agency (MBDA) manage a network of 100 local business assistance centers. At one of these centers a minority owner can get assistance in preparing a business loan package, securing sales, or solving a particular management problem. Contact: Director MBDA, Department of Commerce, Room 5053, Washington, DC 20230/202-377-2654.

Mammals, Marine
Information is available from the National Oceanic and Atmospheric Administration (NOAA) on marine mammals and on rules and regulations for endangered species. They also issue permits to zoos and aquariums that want to house marine mammals. Contact: Office of Protected Species and Habitat Conservation, National Marine Fisheries Service, NOAA, Department of Commerce, Page Building 2, Washington, DC 20235/202-634-7461.

Manufacturing of Medical and Dental Equipment Data
The Industry Division has data on U.S. manufacturers and their output, including the value and sometimes quantity of products shipped from plants in this country. Reports including those on medical and dental equipment, are available from the Superintendent of Documents, U.S. Government Printing Office, Washington, DC 20402, 202-783-3238. All publications are also available from federal depository libraries throughout the country. Contact: Industry Division, Bureau of the Census, U.S. Department of Commerce, Washington, DC 20233/202-763-5850.

Manufacturing Trends Data
Annual Survey of Manufacturers-Value of Product Shipment provides 5-year trend data for all of manufacturing. This publication can be purchased for $2.75 from the Superintendent of Documents, Government Printing Office, Washington, DC 20233/301-783-3238. For information about the publication contact: Census/ASM Durable Goods

Branch, Bureau of Census, Washington, DC 20233/301-763-7863.

Marine Advisory Service
Through the sea-grant college system a national advisory service disseminates new knowledge from sea-grant researchers to the community and transmits community needs back to the researchers. Contact: National Sea-Grant College Program, NOAA, Department of Commerce, Room 625, 6010 Executive Blvd., Rockville, MD 20852/301-443-8923.

Marine Pollutants
NOAA's Ocean Assessment Division explores the impact of marine pollutants on coasts throughout the entire United States, including the New York-New Jersey Coast, Puget Sound, and Alaska's Prince Williams Sound. Contact: NOAA, N/OMS3, Rockwall Building, Room 652, 6010 Executive Blvd., Rockville, Md. 20852/301-443-8933.

Mariners Weather Log
This quarterly magazine, for those who have a marine-related interest, cost $10 per year. It covers weather in the Atlantic and Pacific oceans for the last three months plus related articles. Contact: Mariners Weather Log, National Oceanographic Data Center, NOAA, Department of Commerce, Washington, DC 20235/202-634-7394.

Market Research Consulting Services
The professional staff at the Bureau of the Census are available on a cost basis to help organizations design and conduct surveys. Contact: Statistical Methods Division, Bureau of the Census, Department of Commerce, FB3, Room 3725, Washington, DC 20233/301-763-2672. See other "Census" listings in this section.

Materials Science Research Laboratories
Under the National Materials Research Laboratory Program (NMRL) the National Science Foundation funds 14 interdisciplinary materials research laboratories at universities across the U.S. Staffed by physicists, chemists, metallurgists, ceramists, polymer scientists, engineers, and materials scientists, the laboratories are an excellent resource for information about all aspects of materials science. In addition to answering technical inquiries, the scientist often can supply you with technical papers and refer you to other resources. Contact: Listed below is contact information for each of the laboratories:

Materials Research Laboratory
Brown University, Box M
Providence, RI 02912
401-863-2318

The Center for the Joining of Materials
Carnegie-Mellon University
Schenley Park

Pittsburgh, PA 15213
412-578-2541

Materials Research Laboratory
Case Western Reserve University
Cleveland, OH 44106
216-368-4225
216-368-4120

Materials Research Laboratory
James Franck Institute
University of Chicago
5640 S. Ellis Avenue
Chicago, IL 60637
312-962-7918

Materials Science Center
Clark Hall
Cornell University
Ithaca, NY 14850
607-256-4272 or 2323

Materials Research Laboratory
Division of Applied Sciences
205 A Pierce Hall
Harvard University
Cambridge, MA 02138
617-495-3213

Materials Research Laboratory
University of Illinois
104 South Goodwin
Urbana, IL 61801
217-333-6186

Center for Materials Science & Engineering
Room 13-2090
Massachusetts Institute of Technology
Cambridge, MA 02139
617-253-6801

Materials Research Laboratory
University of Massachusetts
Amherst, MA 02001
413-545-0433

Materials Research Center
The Technological Institute
Northwestern University
Evanston, IL 60201
312-492-3606

Materials Research Laboratory
Ohio State University
174 West 18th Avenue
Columbus, OH 43210
614-422-5109

Laboratory for Research on the Structure of Matter/K1
3231 Walnut Street
University of Pennsylvania
Philadelphia, PA 19104
215-898-8571

Materials Science Council
Physics Building
Purdue University
West Lafayette, IN 47907
317-494-5567

Center for Materials Research
Stanford University
Stanford, CA 94305
415-497-4118 or 0215

Medical Equipment International Trade Data
The Office of Instrumentation and Medical Sciences has information on how the medical equipment industry is doing in this country and in foreign markets. The kind of information they have include the volume of shipments of domestic manufacturers; level of employment; and international trade data, including exports and imports. Contact: Office of Instrumentation and Medical Sciences, Science and Electronics Cluster, International Trade Administration, U.S. Department of Commerce, Washington, DC 20230/202-377-0550.

Medical Products Foreign Trade Data
The Foreign Trade Division of the Bureau of the Census has import and export data for many products. A significant report is the *Highlights of U.S. Export and Import Trade.*

This publication contains information on the dollar value of products in the broad category of professional, scientific, and controlling instruments and apparatus. Updated monthly, the publication is available for $41 per year from the Superintendent of Documents, U.S. Government Printing Office, Washington, DC 20402/202-783-3238. Contact: Foreign Trade Division, Bureau of the Census, U.S. Department of Commerce, Washington, DC 20233/202-763-5140.

Medical Trade and Production
The International Trade Administration oversees trade and production in the U.S., and monitors developments that affect industry, such as legislative issues and trade policies. Staff can refer you to medical imaging specialists or provide you with information from the annual *Industrial Outlook,* which includes a chapter on instrumentation and medical sciences, and the latest technological equipment, and trade and production figures. The *Outlook* is available from the Government Printing Office, Washington, DC 20402, 202-783-3238. Contact: International Trade Administration, U.S. Department of Commerce, Office of Instrumentation and Medical Sciences, 14th & Constitution Ave., NW, Room 4424, 202-377-5466.

Merchant Marine Jobs
Persons 16 years old and over are eligible for jobs with the merchant marine (those under 18 years old need parental consent). Applicants may or may not have experience at sea. Training is available at the U.S. Merchant Marine Academy, at State Maritime Academies and at Labor union-operated schools. For information on seafaring employment and training contact: Office of Maritime Labor and Training, Maritime Administration, Room 7302, Department of Commerce, Washington, DC 20590/202-426-5755.

Metals and Ceramics Information and Technical Assistance
The Metals and Ceramics Information Center is sponsored by the Department of Defense, and its mission is to provide technical assistance and information about materials within the center's scope, with emphasis on applications to the defense community. The main areas of interest with respect to ceramics at the center include borides, carbides, carbon/graphite, nitrides, oxides, sulfides, silicides, intermetallics, selected glasses and glass ceramics, and other materials mutually agreed upon by Battelle and the government. Battelle has an on-line data base that contains technical journals, reports on government sponsored research, patents, trade literature, and technical books. The data base can be accessed by most terminals. For details about this service, contact the general information number listed below. Contact: Metals and Ceramics Information Center, Battelle Memorial Institute, 505 King Avenue, Columbus, OH 43201/614-424-5000 (General Information), 614-424-6376 (Technical Inquiries Service).

Metals Safety Studies
The Metallurgy Division studies metals and alloys in order to foster their safe, efficient, and economical use to meet the U.S.'s long term needs within the larger framework of the materials cycle.

The division serves as a national resource of metallurgical information through its Diffusion Data Center and Alloy Data Center, and provides consultation and assistance to other government agencies and standards organizations in the development of necessary test methods and standards. Division members can answer questions in their areas of expertise or make referrals. The Annual Report is available free of charge as well as papers, reports, proceedings, and other publications. Contact: Metallurgy Division, Center for Materials Science, National Bureau of Standards, Gaithersburg, MD 20899/301-921-2811.

Meteorological Center
The National Meteorological Center is the primary information source for weather forecasting for the United States. They produce weather analysis charts and numerical forecasts, which are sent to both public and private weather offices. Contact: National Meteorological Center, National Weather Service, NOAA, Department of Commerce, 5400 Auth Rd. #101, Camp Springs, MD 20033/301-763-8016.

Metric Programs
One of the primary functions of the Office of Metric Programs is to work to assure that govern-

ment action, policies and regulations do not present barriers to private enterprises that convert to the metric system. The office coordinates representatives from public and private sectors to solve problems and share information. It also provides general and technical information to the public, including metric requirements of foreign markets. It oversees metric planning within the government and assists the states and private sector in metric transition planning. Contact: Office of Metric Planning, Room 4082, Hoover Building, US Department of Commerce, Washington DC 20230/202-377-0944.

Metric System
For assistance on the technical aspects of the metric system contact: Office of Metric Programs, U.S. Dept. of Commerce, Room 4082, Wash., D.C. 20230/202-377-0944.

Microcomputer Electronics Information Exchange
The Microcomputer Electronics Information Exchange bulletin board, operated by the Systems, Selection and Evaluation Group, is a message board that allows users to communicate about where software can be found, whom to contact, what's the latest technology, etc. It is used as a forum for questions and answers, discussions, news, etc., all related to microcomputers and microprocessors. Contact: Microcomputer Electronics Information Exchange, Institute for Computer Sciences and Technology, National Bureau of Standards, Gaithersburg, MD 20899/301-948-5718.

Minority Business Development Centers
The Minority Business Development Agency has contracted with private firms throughout the nation to sponsor Minority Business Development Centers (MBDC) to provide minority firms with advice and technical assistance on a fee basis. The following is a list of those centers currently operating. For additional information contact: Minority Business Development Agency, Department of Commerce, Washington DC 20230/202-377-1936

MINORITY BUSINESS DEVELOPMENT CENTERS (MBDC)

Alaska Rural Assistance Program
1011 East Tudor Road, Ste. 210
Anchorage, AK 99503
907-562-2322

Birmingham MBDC
2017 Morris Avenue, 2nd Floor
Birmingham, AL 35203
205-252-3682

Mobile MBDC
4321 Downtowner Loop North
Suite D
Mobile, AL 36609
205-344-9650

Montgomery MBDC
503 South Court Street, Ste. 210
Montgomery, AL 36104
205-263-0818

Little Rock MBDC
One Riverfront Place, Rm. 415
North Little Rock, AR 72114
501-372-7312

Tucson MBDC
120 West Broadway
300 United Bank Plaza
Tucson, AZ 85701
602-622-5700

Anaheim MBDC
2700 North Main St., Suite 810
Santa Ana, CA 92701
714-667-8200

California Indian MBDC
NEDA San Joaquin Valley
1541 Wilshire Boulevard
Ste. 418
Los Angeles, CA 90017-2269
213-483-1460

Fresno MBDC
2010 North Fine, Ste. 103
Fresno, CA 93727
209-252-7551

Los Angeles North MBDC
3460 Wilshire Boulevard
Ste. 1006
Los Angeles, CA 90010
213-382-5032

Los Angeles South MBDC
2651 South Western Avenue
Suite 300
Los Angeles, CA 90018
213-731-2131

Riverside/San Bernardino MBDC
341 W. Second Street, Ste. 1
San Bernardino, CA 92401
714-884-8764

Sacramento MBDC
455 Capitol Mall, Ste. 500
Sacramento, CA 95814
916-441-2370

Salinas MBDC
137 Central Avenue, Ste. 1
Salinas, CA 93901
408-422-3701

San Diego MBDC
6363 Alvarado Court, Rm. 225
San Diego, CA 92120
619-265-3684

San Francisco Rural Assistance Program
693 Sutter, 3rd Floor
San Francisco, CA 94102
415-776-0120

San Jose MBDC
4701 Patrick Henry Drive
Bldg. 9
Santa Clara, CA 95054
408-980-0371

Stockton MBDC
2291 West March Lane, Ste. 227D
Stockton, CA 95207
209-474-3553

Denver MBDC
70 W. 6th Avenue, Rm. 400
Denver, CO 80204
303-595-4744

Connecticut MBDC
900 Chapel Street, Ste. 506
New Haven, CT 06510
203-785-8168

Washington MBDC
2100 M Street, N.W., Ste. 607
Washington, D.C. 20037
202-293-1982

Jacksonville MBDC
333 North Laura Street
Ste. 465
Jacksonville, FL 32202-3508
904-353-3826

Miami MBDC
201 Alhambra Circle, 9th Floor
Coral Gables, FL 33134
305-442-2000

Orlando MBDC
132 E. Colonial Drive, Ste. 211
Orlando, FL 32801
305-422-6234

Tampa MBDC
315 East Madison Street
Sun Bank Building, Ste. 617
Tampa, FL 33602
813-273-9145

West Palm Beach MBDC
1675 Palm Beach Lake Boulevard
Ste. 1002
West Palm Beach, FL 33401
305-683-4400

Atlanta MBDC
75 Piedmont Avenue, N.E.
Ste. 256
Atlanta, GA 30303
404-586-0973

Georgia Tech Rural MBDC
Engineering Experiment Station
1005 Life of Georgia Building
Atlanta, GA 30332
404-894-3833

Augusta MBDC
1208 Laney Walker Boulevard
Post Office Box 1283

Augusta, GA 30901
404-722-0994

Columbus MBDC
1214 First Avenue, Ste. 430
Post Office Box 1696
Columbus, GA 31902-1696
404-324-4253

Savannah MBDC
31 W. Congress Street, Ste. 201
Savannah, GA 31401
912-236-6708

Honolulu MBDC
1150 S. King Street, Ste. 203
Honolulu, HI 96814
808-531-7502

Chicago North MBDC
600 Prudential Plaza
Chicago, IL 60601
312-856-0200

Gary MBDC
567 Broadway, P.O. Box 9007
Ste. 4
Gary, IN 46402
219-883-5802

Indianapolis MBDC
1 Virginia Avenue, 2nd Floor
Indianapolis, IN 46204
317-639-6131

Louisville MBDC
835 W. Jefferson Street
Ste. 103
Louisville, KY 40202
502-589-7401

Baton Rouge MBDC
6753 Cezanne Avenue, Ste. 1
Baton Rouge, LA 70806
504-387-1799

New Orleans MBDC
650 South Pierce Street
Ste. 204
New Orleans, LA 70119
504-486-8296

Shreveport MBDC
3003 Knight Street, Ste. 212
Shreveport, LA 71105
318-868-0511

Boston MBDC
15 Court Square, Suite 410
Boston, MA 02108
617-523-4438

Baltimore MBDC
2901 Druid Park Drive, Ste. 203
Baltimore, MD 21215
301-462-3700

Detroit MBDC
1505 Woodward Avenue, Ste. 700

Detroit, MI 48226
313-961-0903

Flint MBDC
708 Root Street, Ste. 325 A
Flint, MI 48503
313-239-5847

Minnesota Chippewa Tribe MBDC
Post Office Box 217
Cass Lake, MN 56633
218-335-2252

Minneapolis/St. Paul MBDC
100 North 6th Street, Ste. 440B
Minneapolis, MN 55403
612-333-3600

Kansas City MBDC
1150 Charterbank Center
920 Main Street
Kansas City, MO 64105
816-221-6500

St. Louis MBDC
1 Center Plaza, Ste. 1900
St. Louis, MO 63101
314-425-0500

Jackson MBDC
Post Office Box 3192
Jackson, MS 39207
601-352-5514

Charlotte/Gastonia MBDC
230 South Tryon Street, Rm. 103
Charlotte, NC 28202
704-372-6966

Cherokee MBDC
Qualla Boundary, P.O. Box 1200
Cherokee, NC 28719
704-497-9335

Fayetteville MBDC
Post Office Box 1387
Fayetteville, NC 28302
919-488-2644

Greensboro MBDC
701 East Market Street
Greensboro, NC 27401
919-273-9461

Raleigh/Durham MBDC
Post Office Box 1088
Durham, NC 27702
919-683-1047

Bismarck MBDC
3315 South Airport Road
Bismarck, ND 58501
701-255-3285

New Brunswick, MBDC
5 Elm Row, Ste. 400
New Brunswick, NJ 08901
201-247-8550

Newark MBDC
60 Park Place, Ste. 1604

Newark, NJ 07102
201-623-7710

Albuquerque MBDC
718 Central S.W.
Albuquerque, NM 87197
505-843-7114

Las Vegas MBDC
618 East Carson
Las Vegas, NV 89101
702-384-3293

Bronx MBDC
349 E. 149th Street
Ste. 702
Bronx, NY 10451
212-665-8583

Brooklyn MBDC
105 Court Street
Brooklyn, NY 11201
718-852-9001

Buffalo MBDC
Convention Tower
43 Court Street, Ste. 200
Buffalo, NY 14202
716-855-0144

Long Island MBDC
150 Broad Hollow Road, Rm. 99
Melville, NY 11747
516-549-5454

Manhattan MBDC
551 Fifth Avenue, Ste. 320
New York, NY 10176
212-661-8044

Opportunity Development Assoc.
MBDC
12 Heyward Street
Brooklyn, NY 11211
718-522-5620

Queens MBDC
97-77 Queens Boulevard, Ste. 708
Forest Hills, NY 11374
718-275-8735

Rochester MBDC
Powers Building
16 W. Main Street, Ste. 215
Rochester, NY 14614
716-546-1930

Cincinnati MBDC
1900 Central Trust Center
Cincinnati, OH 45202
513-621-1900

Cleveland MBDC
601 Lakeside Avenue, Rm. 335
Cleveland, OH 44115
216-664-4152

Columbus MBDC
180 E. Broad Street

Columbus, OH 43215
614-221-8500

Dayton MBDC
350 Gem Plaza
Dayton, OH 45402
513-222-2100

Oklahoma City MBDC
1500 NE 4th Street, Ste. 101
Oklahoma City, OK 73117
405-235-0430

Oklahoma Indian MBDC
555 Constitution Avenue
Norman, OK 73069
405-329-3737

Tulsa MBDC
543 E. Apache, Ste. 204
Tulsa, OK 74106
918-428-2511

Portland MBDC
8959 SW Barbur Boulevard
Ste. 102
Portland, OR 97219
503-245-9253

Philadelphia MBDC
1818 Market Street, 31st Floor
Philadelphia, PA 19103
215-561-7300

Pittsburgh MBDC
1604 Allegheny Building
429 Forbes Avenue
Pittsburgh, PA 15219
412-261-2950

Ponce MBDC
M. L. Prats & Associates MBDC
Ponce, PR 00731
809-840-8110

Mayaguez MBDC
Post Office Box 6015
Marina Station
Mayaguez, PR 00709
809-833-7783

San Juan MBDC
GPO Box 3631
San Juan, PR 00936
809-753-8484

Charleston MBDC
701 East Bay Street, Ste. 539
Charleston, SC 29403
803-723-2771

Columbia MBDC
Post Office Box 5915
Columbia, SC 29250
803-765-9912

Greenville MBDC
300 University Ridge
Suite 110A

Greenville, SC 29601
803-271-8753

Memphis MBDC
1188 Minna Place, Ste. 400
Memphis, TN 38104
901-726-9713

Tennessee State MBDC
1025 Andrew Jackson Building
Nashville, TN 37219
615-741-2545

Austin MBDC
2009 B East Riverside Drive
Austin, TX 78741
512-448-4101

Beaumont MBDC
330 Liberty, 1st Floor
Beaumont, TX 77701
409-833-3426

Brownsville MBDC
855 West Price Road, Ste. 30
Brownsville, TX 78520
512-544-7173

Corpus Christi MBDC
Post Office Box 9339
Corpus Christi, TX 78469
512-852-0909

Dallas Rural MBDC
205 Stemmons Tower South
2720 Stemmons Freeway
Dallas, TX 75207
214-638-6605

Dallas/Ft. Worth MBDC
1800 One Dallas Center
Dallas, TX 75201
214-922-9010

El Paso MBDC
3707 Admiral, Ste., Al
El Paso, TX 79925
915-592-2020

Houston MBDC
2870 Citicorp Center
1200 Smith Street
Houston, TX 77002
713-650-3831

Laredo MBDC
Auto Plaza
800 East Mann Road, Ste. 101
Laredo, TX 78041
512-724-8306

McAllen MBDC
Professional Plaza
4307 N. 10th Street, Ste. F
McAllen, TX 78041
512-687-8336

San Antonio MBDC
University of Texas in
San Antonio

San Antonio, TX 78285
512-224-1945

Salt Lake City MBDC
50 West Broadway, Ste. 800
Salt Lake City, UT 84101
801-328-2300

Newport News MBDC
2601 A Chestnut Avenue
Newport News, VA 23607
804-244-9122

Norfolk MBDC
Plaza One Building
One Main Plaza East, Ste. 801
Norfolk, VA 23510
804-627-5254

Seattle MBDC
10519 NE 38th Place
Kirkland, WA 98033
206-828-0444

Milwaukee MBDC
600 West Walnut Street, Rm. 39
Milwaukee, WI 53212
414-265-6200

EXPORT CENTERS (MEDC)

San Francisco MEDC
6363 Alvarado Court, Ste. 226
San Diego, CA 92120
619-286-5623

Washington MEDC
Caribbean Basin Development Corp.
1523 New Hampshire Avenue, N.W.
Washington, DC 20036
202-462-6752

Atlanta MEDC
825 S. Bayshore Drive, Tower 3
Suite 1744-45
Miami, FL 33131
305-358-7979

Chicago MEDC
2400 Penobscot Building
Detroit, MI 48226
313-965-6320

Puerto Rico MEDC
Caribbean Marketing Overseas Corp.
Post Office Box 6338
Loiza Station
1702 Fernandez Juncos Avenue
Santurce, PR 00914
809-728-1240

Minority Business Publications

The following publications are available free from Information Clearinghouse, Minority Business Development Agency, Department of Commerce, Washington, DC 20230/202-377-2414.

Directory of Regional and District Offices and Funded Organizations
Q & A
MBDA—What You Need To Know
MBDA Minority Business Development Centers
Performance Highlights Report
Federal Agency Performance for Minority Business Development
1982 Guide to Federal Minority Enterprise and Related Assistance Programs
Businessman's Information Guide
Urban Business Profiles
Franchise Opportunities Handbook
How to Build an Export Business

Minority Business Purchasing

The National Minority Supplier Development Council, a private entity under contract with the U.S. Department of Commerce, has been established to increase corporate purchases of supplies and services from minority firms. A network of 45 councils exists throughout the U.S., and is supported by over 2,500 corporations. Contact: National Minority Supplier Development Council, 1412 Broadway, 11th floor, New York, New York 10018/212-944-2430.

Minority Business Regional Assistance

The Minority Business Development Agency conducts most of its management, marketing and technical assistance activities through its Regional and District offices.

REGIONAL OFFICES

Atlanta, Ga., 30309
Suite 505, 1371 Peachtree St. NE
404-881-4091

Chicago, Ill., 60603
Suite 1440, 55 E. Monroe St.
312-363-0182

Dallas, Tex., 75242
Suite 7B-19, 1100 Commerce St.
214-767-8001

New York, N.Y., 10278
Suite 37-20, 26 Federal Plaza
212-284-3262

San Francisco, Calif., 94102
Suite 15045, 450 Golden Gate Ave.
415-666-6351

Washington, D.C. 20230
Suite 6711, 14th and Constitution Ave. NW.
208-377-8278

DISTRICT OFFICES

Boston, Mass. 02117
7th Floor, 441 Stuart St.
617-225-3726

Kansas City, Mo., 64106
Room 501, 911 Walnut St.
616-374-3381

Los Angeles, Calif., 90057
Room 908, 2500 Wilshire Blvd.
213-666-7157

Miami, Fla., 33130
Room 216, Federal Bldg.
306-350-5054

Philadelphia, Pa., 19108
Room 9436, W. J. Green Federal Bldg.
215-597-9236

Minority Business Technology Commercialization
Through a series of nongovernment Technical Commercialization Centers, the MBDA identifies new products that might have long-term growth potential in the marketplace. Contact: Clearinghouse for Minority Business, Minority Business Development Agency, Department of Commerce, Washington, DC 20230/202-377-2414.

Minority Enterprise Small Business Investment Companies (MESBICs)
Private capitalized MESBICs, which invest in minority-owned ventures, receive three dollars of investment funds for every one dollar of private money invested. Contact: Office of Resource Development, Minority Business Development Agency, Department of Commerce, Room 5096, Washington, DC 20230/202-377-3237.

Minority-Owned Financial Institutions
The Minority Business Development Agency encourages the organization of minority-owned financial institutions. They assist with management and technical information in the organizing and structuring of banks and savings and loan associations. They train in how to attract capital and depositors, and how to provide grants to banking associations. Contact: Office of Resource Development, Minority Business Development Agency, Department of Commerce, Room 5096, Washington, DC 20230/202-377-3237.

Nautical Charts
Nautical charts, in various scales, cover the coastline of the United States, its territories and possessions, and the Great Lakes. There are six catalogs, which provide descriptions and ordering information: 1) Atlantic and Gulf Coasts; 2) Pacific Coast including Hawaii, Guam and Samoa Islands; 3) Alaska, including Aleutian Islands; 4) Great Lakes and Adjacent Waterways; 5) Bathymetric Maps and Special Purpose Charts, and 6) Catalog of Aeronautical Charts and Related Publications. Nautical Charts make ideal and inexpensive wall decorations. Contact: National Ocean Service Distribution Branch, Riverdale, Md 20737/310-436-6990.

NOAA Corps
Scientists are recruited from colleges or from the armed services and are trained at the National Oceanic and Atmospheric Administration (NOAA), Officer Training Center in Kings Point, New York. The Corps officers work on and manage such projects as Marine Ecology Analyses, Solar Radiation, Geodesy, and Tide Monitoring, or fly research aircraft. Contact: Commission Personnel Division, NOAA Corps, Department of Commerce, 11400 Rockville Pike, Room 105, Rockville, MD 20852/301-443-8616.

NTIS
National Technical Information Service is the central source for the public sale of U.S. government sponsored research, development and engineering reports, as well as computer software and data files. The NTIS collection exceeds one million titles with 60,000 new reports being published yearly. As the government's central technical information clearinghouse, NTIS provides a variety of information awareness products and services to keep the public abreast of the technologies developed by the federal government's multibillion dollar annual research and engineering effort. To obtain the following publications, contact: National Technical Information Service (NTIS), 5285 Port Royal Road, Springfield, VA 22161/703-487-4600.

Industry Awareness List

The Center for the Utilization of Federal Technology (CUFT) will place the name of any small business on its list. This is a free service to help businesses locate and use federal technology. CUFT alerts people on its mailing list to new federal information services, and in some instances, it forwards the company's name to other government agencies which offer additional technology oriented assistance. To be placed on the CUFT mailing list, send your name, address, company needs and interests, as well as company size, to: Center for the Utilization of Federal Technology, Room 8R at the above address.

Current Awareness Services

Weekly Abstracts Newsletters—a weekly bulletin available on a subscription basis in each of 25 different subject areas. The bulletin announces summaries of newly released government R&D reports and provides complete coverage of broad areas of government research. Price ranges from $50 to $120 per year, depending on subject. For further information, order NTIS' free brochure PR 205.

Government Inventions for Licensing—a weekly subscription bulletin which announces more than 1,500 federally owned patents or patent applications that are available for licensing, often on an exclusive basis. Each issue divides inventions into eleven subject disciplines and provides a summary, and when appropriate, a drawing of the invention. Subscription cost is

$205 per year. For further information, order NTIS' free brochure PR 750.

NTIS Tech Notes—a monthly subscription service alerting readers to new federal technology having practical or commercial potential. *Tech Notes* provides information about newly developed technology in 12 different areas. The publication includes 1–2 page fact sheets, often illustrated, of new processes, equipment, software and material. For further information, order NTIS' free brochure PB 365. Yearly subscription rate is $60 per category or $250 for all 12 categories.

Special Bibliographies
NTIS publishes a free 300-page directory entitled *Published Searches: Master Catalog,* which lists subject searches, with complete citations, from the NTIS bibliographic data base. It also has citations from searches of 20 commercial data bases. Approximately 3,000 NTIS searches are listed, each of which can be ordered in full for $35 from NTIS. For further information, order NTIS' free brochure PR 701.

Computer Software
NTIS' Software Center has a collection of more than 450 computer programs covering an array of subjects. This machine-readable information produced by the government can be purchased by the public.

NTIS Data Base Searches
The National Technical Information Service (NTIS) can search its computerized data base of over 1 million reports on completed government research and analysis and provide a report which identifies all available reports for a specific topic. The fee varies and searches are available in both customized and published formats. Contact: Information Analysis Branch, NTIS, Department of Commerce, 5285 Port Royal Rd., Springfield, VA 22161/703-487-4640.

NTIS Index
The National Technical Information Service (NTIS) publishes an annual index to its publications. The index costs $420 for one year and provides a good starting place for determining if publications are available in your subject area. Many libraries throughout the world subscribe to this index. One can also consult NTIS' computerized data base which contains much of the same information. Contact: NTIS, Department of Commerce, 5285 Port Royal Rd., Springfield, VA 22161/703-487-4600. (Order # NTIS ANNI 83, check for latest edition)

Ocean Structures Research
The NOAA Special Projects Staff identifies critical research needs for Ocean Thermal Energy Conversion (OTEC) ocean structures and conducts a research program. The staff is available to answer technical questions related to ocean thermal energy conversion and ocean engineering problems, and to make referrals. Contact: NOAA Special Projects Staff, Ocean Thermal Energy Conversion (OTEC), Ocean Engineering Technology Development, 11400 Rockville Pike, Rockville, MD 20852/301-443-8655.

Ocean Thermal Energy and Seabed Minerals
The Ocean Mineral and Energy Division of NOAA is concerned with ocean thermal energy conversion and deep seabed hard minerals. They have a licensing and regulatory program and also write environmental impact statements. Staff can answer questions and/or make referrals. Contact: Ocean Mineral and Energy Division, National Ocean Service, National Oceanic and Atmospheric Administration (NOAA), 2001 Wisconsin Avenue, NW, Room 105, Washington, DC 20235/202-254-3483.

Oceanographic Information
The National Oceanic and Atmospheric Administration contains the world's largest collection of oceanographic data. They collect information on all oceans, seas and estuarine from hundreds of domestic and foreign sources. Contact: National Oceanographic Data Center, NOAA/NESDIS E/OC 21 2001 Wisconsin Ave, NW, Washington, DC 20235/202-634-7500.

Oceanography and Marine Services Office
This office collects, analyzes, and disseminates a wide range of data and information that describe the physical properties of the oceans, U.S. coastal waters, estuaries, waterways, and the Great Lakes, including tide and current predictions. Contact: National Ocean Service, Department of Commerce, 6001 Executive Blvd., Rockville, MD 20852/301-443-8487.

Office Automation Resources
An information clearinghouse for techniques and resources pertaining to productivity improvement and quality control, the Commerce Productivity Center can provide you with information about office automation. Upon request and at no cost staff will evaluate your office systems and recommend steps for improving automation, productivity, and quality control. Staff can refer you to government agencies, private firms, and literature pertaining to office automation. Bibliographies, publications, articles and reading lists are all available free of charge from the center. Contact: Commerce Productivity Center, U.S. Department of Commerce, The Assistant Secretary for Economic Affairs, 14th & Pennsylvania Avenue, Room 7413, Washington, DC 20230/202-377-0940.

Packaging and Labeling Expertise
The National Bureau of Standards provides technical assistance to state enforcement agencies and other organizations in establishing proper packaging and labeling regulations. Contact: Office of

Weights and Measures, National Bureau of Standards, Department of Commerce, Washington, DC 20234/301-921-2401.

Patent Academy
Training is available for patent examiners in patent practices and procedures. Government agencies can attend sessions for free; there is a charge for those in the private sector or in foreign agencies. Contact: Phase II Patent Academy, Patent and Trademark Office, Department of Commerce, Building 6, Room 1261, Crystal Plaza, Arlington, VA 22202/703-557-2086.

Patent Applications for Other Countries
Agreements have been made with 31 countries, including Japan, Australia, Russia, most of Western Europe and Brazil, to allow a single patent application to be applied to all 31 countries. Contact: Patent and Trademark Office, Department of Commerce, Box PCT, Washington, DC 20231/703-557-2003.

Patent Attorneys, List of
For a listing of patent attorneys contact: Office of Enrollment and Discipline, Patent and Trademark Office, Department of Commerce, Washington, DC 20231/703-557-1728.

Patent and Trademark Copies
Copies of the specifications and drawings of all patents are available for $1.00 each. Design patents, trademark copies and plant patents not in color are also $1.00 each. Plant patents in color cost $8.00 each. Contact: Patent and Trademark Office, Department of Commerce, Box 9, Washington, DC 20231/202-377-2540.

Patent and Trademark Publications
Annual Indexes. Patents are indexed by patentees and by subject matter. Trademarks are indexed by registrant and by type of goods registered. Price varies from year to year.

Attorneys and Agents Registered to Practice Before the United States Patent and Trademark Office. Names, addresses, telephone numbers and registration numbers of attorneys and agents, listed alphabetically by surname and by geographical location (S/N 003-004-00594-7, $9.00)

General Information Concerning Patents. (S/N 003-004-00596-3, $3.50)

General Information Concerning Trademarks (S/N 003-004-00588-2, $3.25)

Guide for Patent Draftsmen (S/N 003-004-00570-0, $2.25)

Manual of Classification. Lists numbers and descriptive titles of Patent Office class and subclasses, as well as Design Classes (S/N 003-004-81001-7, $44.00 domestic, $55.00 foreign)

Manual of Patent Examining Procedure. Information on practices and procedures relative to prosecution of patent applications (S/N 003-004-81002-5, $70.00 Domestic, $87.50 foreign)

Patents and Inventions. An information aid to inventors in deciding whether to apply for patents, in obtaining patent protection, and in promoting their inventions (S/N 003-004-00545-9, $3.25)

Patent Laws (S/N 003-004-00561-1, $6.00)

Patent Official Gazette, is the official weekly journal of the Patent & Trademark Office which contains a selected figure of the drawings and an abstract of each patent granted, indexes of patents, list of patents available for license or sale, and other general information. It is available for $250 per year.

Trademark Official Gazette is a weekly journal relating to trademarks and is available for $205 per year.

Story of the Patent & Trademark Office costs $4.75.

Above publications are available from Superintendent of Documents, Government Printing Office, Washington, D.C. 20402/202-783-3238.

Patent Bibliographies
Computer assisted searches of the Patent Bibliographic Database are available from NTIS. Intended as information tools, these searches do not constitute "legal patent searches." For more information, request free catalog #PR-186 or contact: National Technical Information Service, Department of Commerce, 5285 Port Royal Road, Springfield Va 22161/703-487-4640.

Patent Catalogs to Government-Owned Inventions
These annual catalogs offer businesses and entrepreneurs opportunities to license and market Government owned inventions—frequently on an exclusive basis. To make it easy for readers to scan and identify promising government inventions, each invention is fully described in one of 43 invention summary sections. Detailed subject and inventor indexes also are included. Each catalog contains more than 1,300 inventions. Ordering information: 1983 Catalog: Order number PB84-117589 ($25.00), 1984 Catalog: Order number PB85-106979 ($25.00). Contact: NTIS, U.S. Department of Commerce, Springfield, VA 22161/703-487-4650. (A free descriptive brochure, number PR-735, is available.)

Patent Depository Libraries
The libraries listed below receive current issues of the U.S. patents and maintain collections of earlier issued patents. All of these libraries offer CASSIS (Classification and Search Support Information System), which provides direct, on-line access to Patent and Trademark Office data. For more information on the Patent Repository Library Program call toll free 1-800-368-2532.

State	Name of Library	Telephone Contact
Alabama	Auburn University Libraries	(205) 826-4500 Ext. 21
	Birmingham Public Library	(205) 254-2555
Arizona	Tempe: Science Library, Arizona State University	(602) 965-7140
California	Los Angeles Public Library	(213) 626-7555 Ext. 273
	Sacramento: California State Library	(916) 322-4572
	San Diego Public Library	(619) 236-5813
	Sunnyvale: Patent Information Clearinghouse*	(408) 738-5580
Colorado	Denver Public Library	(303) 571-2122
Delaware	Newark: University of Delaware	(302) 738-2238
Georgia	Atlanta: Price Gilbert Memorial Library, Georgia Institute of Technology	(404) 894-4508
Idaho	Moscow: University of Idaho Library	(208) 885-6235
Illinois	Chicago Public Library	(312) 269-2865
	Springfield: Illinois State Library	(217) 782-5430
Indiana	Indianapolis—Marion County Public Library	(317) 269-1706
Louisiana	Baton Rouge: Troy H. Middleton Library, Louisiana State University	(504) 388-2570
Maryland	College Park: Engineering and Physical Sciences Library, University of Maryland	(301) 454-3037
Massachusetts	Boston Public Library	(616) 536-5400 Ext. 265
Michigan	Ann Arbor: Engineering Transportation Library, University of Michigan	(313) 704-7494
	Detroit Public Library	(313) 833-1450
Minnesota	Minneapolis Public Library & Information Center	(612) 372-6570
Missouri	Kansas City: Linda Hall Library	(816) 363-4600
	St. Louis Public Library	(314) 241-2288 Ext. 390 Ext. 391
Nebraska	Lincoln: University of Nebraska-Lincoln, Engineering Library	(402) 472-3411
Nevada	Reno: University of Nevada Library	(702) 784-6579
New Hampshire	Durham: University of New Hampshire Library	(603) 862-1777
New Jersey	Newark Public Library	(201) 733-7815
New Mexico	Albuquerque: University of New Mexico Library	(505) 277-5441
New York	Albany: New York State Library	(518) 474-5121
	Buffalo and Erie County Public Library	(716) 856-7525 Ext. 267
	New York Public Library (The Research Libraries)	(212) 930-0850
North Carolina	Raleigh: D. H. Hill Library, N.C. State University	(919) 737-3280
Ohio	Cincinnati & Hamilton County, Public Library of	(513) 369-6936
	Cleveland Public Library	(216) 623-2870
	Columbus: Ohio State University Libraries	(614) 422-6826
	Toledo/Lucas County Public Library	(419) 255-7055 Ext. 212
Oklahoma	Stillwater: Oklahoma State University Library	(405) 624-6546
Pennsylvania	Cambridge Springs: Alliance College Library	(814) 398-2098
	Philadelphia: Franklin Institute Library	(215) 448-1321
	Pittsburgh: Carnegie Library of Pittsburgh	(412) 622-3138
	University Park: Patee Library, Pennsylvania State University	(814) 865-4861
Rhode Island	Providence Public Library	(401) 521-7722 Ext. 226
South Carolina	Charleston: Medical University of South Carolina	(803) 792-2372 1 (901)
Tennessee	Memphis & Shelby County Public Library and Information Center	(512) 471-1610
Texas	Austin: McKinney Engineering Library, University of Texas	(409) 845-2551
	College Station: Sterling C. Evans Library, Texas A & M University	(214) 749-4176

*Collection organized by subject matter.

	Houston: The Fondren Library, Rice University	(713) 527-8101
Washington	Seattle: Engineering Library, University of Washington	(206) 543-0740
Wisconsin	Madison: Kurt F. Wendt Engineering Library, University of Wisconsin	(608) 262-6845
	Milwaukee Public Library	(414) 278-3043

Patent Search, Where to Begin
Before beginning a patent search you may want to obtain a copy of *Guide to the Public Patent Search Facilities of the U.S. Patent and Trademark Office.* It explains all of the jargon used by the office as well as the types and locations of the available documents. It also tells how to conduct your own patent search. Contact: Commissioner of Patents and Trademarks, Patent and Trademark Office, Department of Commerce, Washington, DC 20231/703-557-2276. If you wish to start immediately on your own search, the Patent Office will provide you with the necessary documentation and direct you to the nearest patent depository.

Patent Search Room
The Search Room—Patents will search for any patent, and give the vendor's name, the issue date, and the title. You can also go in and search all patents in any field. The scientific Library contains all U.S. & foreign patents and is open to the public. Contact: Search Room—Patents, 2021 Jefferson Davis Highway, Crystal City, VA 20231/703-557-2276, 703-557-3158 (General information about patents), 703-557-2955 (Scientific Library).

Patents and Trademarks Weekly Listing
The *Official Gazette,* (S/N 003-004-80001-1) published every week describes all new patents and includes drawings when available. Subscriptions are $250.00 Fourth Class and $360 First Class. Contact: Superintendent of Documents, Gov't. Printing Office, Washington, D.C. 20402/202/783-3238.

Patents, Foreign
For information on patents filed in other countries contact: Int'l. Business Practices Division, Office of International Finance and Investments, ITA, Department of Commerce, Room 1128 Washington, DC 20230/202-377-4471.

Photographs
Photographs are available depicting trade shows held in foreign countries. Contact: Office of Publications, ITA, Room 4813, Dept. of Commerce, Washington, DC 20230/202-377-5487.

Plastics Standards Information
The Center for Materials Science is involved in the field of plastics including standards, specifications, and characterization techniques for plastics materials. Specialists at the Center cooperate with the industry in developing national and international standards. The staff can answer technical inquiries and make referrals. Annual reports covering work in progress, as well as technical papers published in professional journals are also available. Contact: Center for Materials Science, National Bureau of Standards, National Measurement Laboratory, Washington, DC 20234/301-921-3336.

Polymer Information Resource
The Polymer, Science and Standards Division of the National Bureau of Standards is involved in the following aspects of plastics: phase behavior and characterization behavior for polymer blends; processing and relation of composites: long-term research for mechanical reliability in low bearing, applications; chemical durability; life time prediction; standards for electric composition; performance and dialectic properties; and reliable data in dental and medical materials.

The staff examines on a scientific basis the material properties which are of concern to the people who design, produce, and use polymer objects. If you are seeking in-depth technical advice, contact NBS' Public Information Division for referral to an appropriate expert. To obtain a list of reports, studies and other literature produced by the Bureau's experts on plastics, contact the Technical Information and Publications Division. Contact: Polymer, Science and Standards Division, National Bureau of Standards, Washington, DC 20234/301-921-3112 (Public Information Division), 301-921-2318 (Technical Information and Publications Division), 301-921-3734.

Population Statistics
Statistics on the total U.S. population are available on a monthly basis. More detailed data are available annually. Contact: Population Division, Bureau of the Census, Department of Commerce, Building 3, Room 2030, Washington, DC 20233/301-763-5002.

Posters, Marine
The National Marine Fisheries Service publishes beautiful, scientifically accurate color posters. Available posters include Marine Fishes of the North Atlantic ($5.50, S/N 003-020-00027-4), Marine Fishes of the North Pacific ($5.50, S/N 003-020-00051-7), Fishes of the Great Lakes ($5.50, S/N 003-020-00069-0), Marine Fishes of the California Current ($5.50, S/N 003-020-00055-0), Mollusks and Crustaceans of the Coastal US ($5.50, S/N 003-020-00087-8), and Sea Turtles of the World ($5.50, S/N 003-020-00152-1). Order from Superintendent of Documents, Government Printing Office, Washington, DC 20402/202-783-3238.

Product Export Promotion Information and Assistance

The main purpose of the International Trade Administration (ITA) is to promote the export of U.S. manufactured products. Counseling is offered to exporters requesting information or assistance, and much of the information is given in personal interviews with specific staff in their area of expertise. There are 47 district offices of the Department of Commerce which can respond to questions. The Trade Development Sector is divided into nine divisions, which are:

Science and Electronics

This office covers the fields of computers and business equipment, components and related equipment, telecommunications, instrumentation and medical sciences. Publications include *A Competitive Assessment of the U.S. Fiber Optics Industry,* a similar assessment of the U.S. digital switching industry, and numerous other statistical assessments of U.S. science and electronic capabilities. 202-377-4466.

Capital Goods and International Construction

This division focuses on: general industrial machinery; special industrial machinery; and international major projects. Periodically technical reports are made available in these fields. 202-377-5023

Automotive Affairs and Consumer Goods

The Auto Industry Affairs office deals with motor vehicles, parts and suppliers. It publishes an annual competitive assessment, *Status of the U.S. Auto Industry,* which is free. The Consumer Goods Office deals with both durable and nondurable goods, and can supply statistical information as to the U.S. competitive position in many major markets. 202-377-0823

Trade Adjustment Assistance

This office is in charge of the certification processes for international trade by U.S. industries. This is the division which pursues unfair practice alllegations and provides both technical and financial assistance to companies that export American made products. 202-377-0150

Trade Information and Analysis

This division is subdivided into five major interest areas: 1) trade finances; 2) trade and investment analysis; 3) trade and industry information; 4) program and resource management; and 5) industrial assessment. 202-377-1316

Textiles and Apparel

This office participates in and provides analytical support for international textile negotiations. It monitors textile and apparel imports, provides studies and analyses of domestic and foreign fiber, textiles and apparel industries, develops and coordinates domestic trade and export expansion programs, and performs several other services. 202-377-3737

Aerospace

This office operates strictly on a consultation basis rather than offering printed material, however, one recent publication of note is *A Competitive Assessment of the U.S. Civil Aircraft Industry.* 202-377-8228

Basic Industries

This office has four divisions divided into 1) chemical and allied products, which published a *Competitive Assessment of the U.S. Advanced Ceramics Industry;* 2) energy; 3) metals, minerals and commodities, which published *A Competitive Assessment of the U.S. Petrochemical Industry;* and 4) forest products and domestic construction. 202-377-0614

Services

This office includes the following service industries: 1) transportation, tourism and marketing industries; 2) finance and management industries; and 3) information industries. The latter has published *A Competitive Assessment of the U.S. Software Industry* and *A Competitive Assessment of the U.S. Information Services Industry,* both available upon request. 202-377-5261

Also contact: Office of Trade Development, International Trade Administration (ITA), Department of Commerce, 14th & E Streets, NW, Washington, DC 20330/202-377-3808.

Product Testing

The Office of Product Standards Policy establishes policy on the development and evaluation of domestic and international standards. They also run a national voluntary accreditation program for labs which are conducting product tests. Contact: Office of Products Standards, NBS, Washington, DC 20234 301-921-3751.

Productivity and Innovation

The Office of Productivity, Technology, and Innovation, whose primary mission it is to strengthen the process of technological innovation, does so by (1) identifying and removing policy barriers to business in areas such as antitrust, (2) provision of incentives, i.e. tax provisions for research and development and granting of titles to inventions to all federal contractors, (3) providing critical information to business, and (4) providing catalytic services, i.e. those in connection with R&D limited partnership model for funding R&D. Contact: Office of Productivity, Technology, and Innovation, Washington, D.C. 20230/202-377-1092.

Productivity Growth Policy Aids
The main purpose of the Office of Productivity, Technology and Innovation (OPTI) is to aid development of new federal policies to create an economical climate conducive to productivity growth. OPTI assists in creating innovative research and development mechanisms to foster large scale R&D projects, and aids in accelerating the transfer of federal technology to the private sector. Additionally, OPTI operates outreach and information programs, chiefly through the Commerce Productivity Center (CPC), to provide productivity, information upon request, and conduct productivity improvement seminars and workshops for the private sector. Contact: Office of Productivity, Technology and Innovation (OPTI), U.S. Department of Commerce, 14th & Constitution Avenue, NW, Washington, DC 20230/202-377-1581.

Productivity Improvement Resource
A part of the Office of Productivity, Technology and Innovation (OPTI), the Commerce Productivity Center (CPC) serves as a clearinghouse for information on all aspects of productivity. With a staff of about 35 professionals with diverse areas of expertise, and access to the information resources of the entire Department of Commerce, CPC can easily provide businesses and other organizations with information on how to improve productivity, quality and competitiveness. The CPC can provide publications, articles, reference and referral services, bibliographies and reading lists on a variety of productivity related topics. All services of the CPC are without charge and a publication list is available upon request. Contact: Commerce Productivity Center (CPC), U.S. Department of Commerce, 14th & Constitution Avenue, NW, Washington, DC 20230/202-377-0940.

Proposed Foreign Regulations for Exporters and Manufacturers
The Standards Code and Information Office assists U.S. exporters and manufacturers by keeping them informed of proposed foreign regulations that may affect U.S. trace opportunities. This office has copies of proposed foreign regulations. Its staff can answer questions and make referrals. The GATT Hotline provides a recording with the most recent information on proposed foreign regulations. An important publication is the *GATT Annual Report* which describes the activities for the year performed by the Standards Code and Information program in support of the GATT Standard Code. The publication is available free of charge. Contact: GATT Agreement on Technical Barriers to Trade (Standards Code), Standards Code and Information Office, Administration Building, Room A629, National Bureau of Standards, Gaithersburg, MD 20899/301-921-2092 (Hotline: 301-921-3200).

Radiated Electromagnetic Fields Measurement Techniques
The Electromagnetic Fields Division of the National Bureau of Standards is primarily responsible for developing measurement techniques for radiated electromagnetic fields irrespective of applications, and has all the measurements related to transmission lines. Staff provides calibration services related to these standards, and make available papers and reports. You can obtain copies of the publications by writing to the Division. If you would like to be kept up-to-date about the Division's publications you can subscribe to the free quarterly, *CEEE Technical Progress Bulletin,* available from the Division's parent, the Center for Electronics and Electrical Engineering (CEEE) in Maryland. The *CEEE Technical Progress Bulletin* provides abstracts and reference information for all publications produced by the Center. The bulletin contains both recently published materials and those released for publication. This free bulletin is only mailed to U.S. addresses. Order from: CEEE, National Bureau of Standards, Metrology Building, Room 9-358, Gaithersburg, MD 20899, 301-921-3357. For other information, contact: Electromagnetic Fields Division, National Bureau of Standards, Boulder, CO 80303/303-497-3131, 303-497-3535.

Radiation
The National Bureau of Standards works on radiation measurement standards for basic research in areas such as health care and energy applications. Contact: Inquiry Service, National Bureau of Standards, Department of Commerce, Administration Building, Room A537, Washington, DC 20234/301-921-2318.

Regional Economic Forecasts
A special division of the Bureau of Economic Analysis regularly publishes forecasts of the future economic conditions for a large number of regions within the country. Contact: Regional Economic Analysis Division, BEA, Department of Commerce, Tower, Room 308, 1401 K St., NW, Washington, DC 20230/202-523-0946.

Research and Development Limited Partnerships
In an effort to promote research in certain targeted industries, the office of Productivity, Technology and Innovation of the Department of Commerce has developed literature to aid US businesses in creating RDLP entities. Request *Information and Steps Necessary to Form Research and Development Limited Partnerships* (PB 83-131516) $10 from National Technical Information Service (NTIS), 5285 Port Royal Road, Springfield, VA 22161/703-487-4650.

Research Journal
The National Bureau of Standards (NBS) pub-

lishes a bimonthly journal which contains papers in math engineering, physics, chemistry, computer science along with citations and abstracts to all NBS publications. Subscriptions to the *Journal of Research of the NBS* are available for $18.00 from Superintendent of Documents, Government Printing Office, Washington, DC 20402/202-783-3238.

Resort Guides
Free resort guides are available for various areas of the United States. They contain seasonal breakdown of weather and recreational opportunities. They stress elements of interest for each season, along with table of activities best suited for each season. Contact: Resort Guides, National Oceanographic Data Center, NOAA,/NESDIS Department of Commerce, Washington, DC 20235/202-634-7500.

Roadmap Through Government Maze
For businesses needing information from the Federal government, the Department of Commerce has established a free information service called Roadmap. Their experts will find the information needed to help a business deal with the government, or at least point you in the right direction. Roadmap can tell you how to obtain a government report, commodity information, or details on a government program, or can answer questions on government procurement, exporting, marketing, statistical sources, and regulatory matters. Roadmap cannot, however, intervene with an agency on your behalf. Contact: Roadmap, Office of Business Liaison, Room 5898C, Department of Commerce, Washington, D.C. 20230/202-377-3176.

Robotics Resource
The International Trade Administration (ITA) has published a report on the robotics industry, *High Techn Industries: Profiles and Outlooks—The Robotics Industry*. For this publication and further assistance identifying sources of information in the field of robotics, contact any of the following government agencies: Machinery-Equipment Division, U.S. International Trade Commission, 701 E Street, N.W., Washington, DC 20436, 202-523-0377; National Bureau of Standards/Industrial Systems Division 739, Bldg. 220, Room A123, Washington, DC 20234/301-921-2381; Office of Producer Goods, Room 4042, Bureau of Industrial Economics, U.S. Department of Commerce, Washington, DC 20230/202-377-0314.

Satellite Data
The National Climate Center makes satellite data available for studies related to climatology, coastal zone management, oceanography, and deep-water port planning. Contact: NESDIS, NOAA/EDIS/NCC, Satellite Data Service, World Weather Building, Room 100, Washington, DC 20233/301-763-8111.

Satellite Information
Environmental satellites, which do such things as track the weather and predict hurricane paths, provide useful data for the agriculture, marine, transportation, and fishing industries. Information is also available from remote sensing satellites showing such land resources as the nation's agricultural inventory. Contact: Public Affairs, NOAA, Department of Commerce, Room 6013, Washington DC 20230/202-377-8090.

Science and Technology Fellowship Programs
Members of upper management within the U.S. Department of Commerce can be assigned, for a period of ten months, to any other government agency. Contact: NBS, Washington, D.C. 20234/301-921-2761.

Scientific and Technical Productivity Services
The Technical Information and Publications Division of the National Bureau of Standards (NBS) provides expertise and assistance in scientific and technical services to aid productivity and innovation. This office can provide publications listing on various topics available through NBS and other agencies of the federal government. Contact: Technical Information and Publications Division, National Bureau of Standards, U.S. Department of Commerce, Route 270, Gaithersburg, MD 20234/301-921-2318.

Sea-Grant Colleges
Sea- or water-related industries may find Sea-Grant Colleges to be an excellent resource for information and expertise on new products and processes. Federal grants are made to colleges to further the development of marine resources through research, education, and advisory services such as information transfer. Subject areas include aquaculture, fisheries, coastal engineering, mineral projects, water recycling and seafood processing. For further information or for listing of Sea-Grant colleges, contact: National Sea-Grant College Program, NOAA, Room 625, 6010 Executive Blvd., Rockville, MD 20852/301-443-8923.

Semiconductor Industry Resource
The Semiconductor Program at the National Bureau of Standards works on measurement-related topics for the semiconductor industry, its suppliers, and its customers in other industries and in the government. The Semiconductor Materials and Processes Division develops measurement methods, data, physical standards, and models and theory characterizing semiconductor materials and processes. The Semiconductor Devices and Circuits Division develops and evaluates measurement methods, data, reference artifacts, models and theory for the design, characterization and performance assurance of electron services and

solid state circuits. Staff within these two divisions are available to answer questions. Workshops and seminars are sponsored, and topical papers are available for sale. A complete listing of these papers is available in the free *NBS List of Publications #72: Semiconductor Measurement Technology.* Contact: Semiconductor Technology Program, U.S. Department of Commerce, National Bureau of Standards, Washington, DC 20234/ 301-921-3357.

Semiconductor Research
The Semiconductor Materials and Processes Division will handle materials-related questions. The secretary can refer callers to an expert who will be able to answer questions or make referrals. Staff at the Semiconductor Devices and Circuits Division can answer highly technical questions. The National Bureau of Standards (NBS) publishes *Semiconductor Measurement Technology.* This list of publications contains reports of work performed at the NBS in the field of semiconductor measurement technology. The publications are grouped by subject matter and within groups are arranged in chronological order. Copies are available for free from NBS. Another NBS publication is *Semiconductor Technology for the Non-Technologist* which covers properties of semiconductor materials, the methods of processing them, and the solid-state products made from them are described in terms intended to be understandable by the lay person. It is available free from the Semiconductor Materials and Processes Division of NBS, 301-921-3786. For further information, contact: Semiconductor Devices and Circuits Division, NBS, Building 225, Room B344, Gaithersburg, MD 20899/301-921-3541/ or -3621.

Shipping Research
Research and expertise is available on commercial ship operations and productivity. Subject areas include safety, efficiency, collision avoidance, navigation, communication, ship, port, and harbor design, and maritime simulation techniques. Contact: National Maritime Research Center, Maritime Administration, Department of Transp. U.S. Merchant Marine Academy, Kings Point, New York 11024/516-482-8200., ext. 600.

Software Catalog
The National Technical Information Service (NTIS) publishes the *Federal Software Exchange Catalog,* which contains the most up-to-date listing and description of all the software available through the Exchange, a Government Services Administration (GSA) controlled software clearinghouse, and NTIS. The catalog presents an abstract and a description of each package, as well as a chapter on software tools, and listings of all the software approved by the GSA for purchase by

government agencies. The directory costs $50 per issue, and is accompanied by a supplement available for $25.00. Contact: National Technical Information Service, U.S. Department of Commerce, 5285 Port Royal Road, Springfield, VA 22161/ 703-487-4650.

Solar Energy and Wind Information
The National Climatic Data Center collects statistical information on solar energy and wind, and other meteorological data and information. It can supply data tapes and publications, and frequently prepares custom tapes to meet requestor needs. Just specify the type of data you need, the time period, and the geographic location. The following data base tape is available: Wind Energy Resource Information System. The Pacific Northwest laboratory, Battelle Memorial Institute, Richland, Washington, regional wind resource assessment data and atlas maps are integrated into this data base, with approximately 975 stations. Standard information given with each table includes the table number, station name, station WBAN number, period of record, number of valid observations, and anamometer height and reference location. The time period covered is variable through 1978. Contact: National Climatic Data Center, National Oceanic and Atmospheric Administration (NOAA), User Services Branch, Federal Building, Asheville, NC 28801/704-259-0682.

Solar Standards
The National Bureau of Standards (NBS) sets up test measurement methods and standards on solar heating and cooling devices. Contact: Inquiry Service, National Bureau of Standards, Department of Commerce, Administration Building, Room A537, Washington, DC 20234/301-921-2318.

Solve Your Identity Crisis
For $12.00 the Bureau of the Census will search its records of one or two censuses to prove one's identity, age, citizenship, or past occupation. Transcripts often can be used in place of a missing birth certificate or to provide proof of occupation needed for collecting government assistance such as black lung benefits for miners. Contact: Age Search Bureau of the Census. Department of Commerce, Washington, D.C. 20233/301-763-7936.

Sources of Information on U.S. Firms
This small booklet is aimed at international traders and describes the major sources of information on U.S. companies. Contact: Export Awareness Division, ITA, Department of Commerce, Room 2108, Washington, DC 20230/202-377-5367.

Space Environment Research
Information and expertise is available on the space environment, the upper atmosphere, and the interactions of the sun and earth. Contact: NOAA, Environmental Research Lab, Department of Commerce, 325 Broadway, Boulder, CO 80303/303-497-6286.

Standard Reference Data System, National
The National Bureau of Standards (NBS) develops data bases of evaluated physical and chemical properties of substances. The NBS works with a number of data centers, located in university, industrial and government laboratories, which compile and evaluate numerical data on physical and chemical properties retrieved from world scientific literature. Contact: Office of Standard Reference Data, NBS, Physics Building, Room A320, Washington, DC 20234/301-921-2228.

Standards Information Service
The National Bureau of Standards—Nat'l Center for Standards and Certification Information (NBS-NCSCI), an information center, is the national repository of standards-related information which maintains a reference collection of engineering and related standards, which includes more than 240,000 standards, specifications, test methods, codes, and recommended practices issued by U.S. technical, trade and professional societies, state and federal agencies, and foreign, national and international standardizing bodies. For information on specific standards, contact: NBS-NCSCI, Technology Building, Room B166, Washington, DC 20234/301-921-2587.

Statistical Abstract of the U.S.
This book comes out at the beginning of each year and is the most popular of Bureau of the Census publications. With more than 1,600 tables and charts it provides data on the social, economic and political organizations of the U.S. For ordering information see "Census Publications" in this section. For detailed information contact Statistical Abstract, Data User Services Division, Bureau of the Census, Department of Commerce, Washington, DC 20233/301-763-4100.

Storm Forecast Center
The Center prepares and releases messages of expected severe local storms including tornadoes. These messages, called Tornado and Severe Thunderstorm Watches, include information for public use and for aviation services. The Center also issues hourly advisories of significant aviation meteorological hazards, writes area forecasts for the nation for pilot briefing purposes, and prepares a National Weather Summary every 6 hours which is used primarily by the media. Contact: National Severe Storms Forecast Center, NOAA, Department of Commerce, 601 East 12th St., Room 1728, Kansas City, MO 64106/816-374-3427.

Superconducting Device Research Resource
The Cryoelectronics Section of the National Bureau of Standards is involved in the research and development of superconducting devices which operate in a cryogenic environment. Among these Josephsen devices are ultra sensitive magnetometers, voltage standards, and high speed digital electronic devices. The staff can answer your questions. Technical reports are available upon request. Contact: Cryoelectronics Section, Division 724.03, National Bureau of Standards, Boulder, CO 80003/303-497-3988.

Surveillance Cameras
The National Bureau of Standards (NBS) has information available on how to select surveillance cameras for specific needs. It includes tips on storing processed film, improving photo quality, selection of film, and lens size. Contact: Law Enforcement Standards Laboratory, National Bureau of Standards, Department of Commerce, Washington, DC 20234/301-921-3161.

Technical Assistance for Businesses
The Economic Development Administration offers grants to businesses. See "Grant" and "Loans and Loan Guarantees" in this section. Those eligible include state and local governments, nonprofit institutions, hospitals, universities and profit-making businesses of all sizes. Contact: Office of Planning, Technical Assistance, Research, and Evaluation, Economic Development Administration, Department of Commerce, Room 7864, Washington, DC 20230/202-377-5111.

Technical Reports (NTIS)
The National Technical Information Service (NTIS) is the central source for obtaining copies of reports generated as a result of U.S. and foreign government sponsored research and development. Some 1.3 million reports are available in hard copy, microfiche and computerized format. Special interest newsletters and other monitoring services are available for those who wish to keep current on a specific topic. A six volume annual index is also available. For a catalogue of available products and services, request brochure PR 154 or contact: NTIS, Department of Commerce, 5285 Port Royal Rd., Springfield, VA 22161/703-487-4600.

Technology Assessment with Patents
Both off-the-shelf and customized reports are available showing domestic and international patent activity. Reports can be produced by product category or by company and can cover both short or long periods of time. It provides excellent data for forecasting future technology. Contact: Office of Technology Assessment and Forecast, Patent and Trademark Office, Department of Commerce, CP6 Room 1225, Washington, DC 20231/703-557-4114.

Technology Catalogs
Each annual *Federal Technology Catalog* offers a compilation and index to more than 1,200 new technologies chosen as having potential commercial or practical application. These technologies represent some of the best Government research and engineering efforts for the year. Brief summaries of the technologies are arranged into subject categories allowing easy browsing. These summaries not only describe the technology but more importantly give a source for further information. The Catalogue costs $23.50. Contact: NTIS, U.S. Department of Commerce, Springfield, VA 22161/703-487-4650. (A free descriptive brochure, number PR-732, also is available.)

Technology Fact Sheets
A subscription product, *NTIS Tech Notes,* brings readers single-page fact sheets (often illustrated) of new processes, equipment, inventions for licensing, software, and research advances. The input has been screened as having potential practical application with much of the material coming from R&D activities at Federal laboratories. To receive additional information, ask for the free descriptive brochure, PR-365. Contact: NTIS, U.S. Department of Commerce, Springfield, VA 22161/703-487-4650.

Technology Newsletters
Available on subscription are the 27 weekly NTIS *Abstract Newsletters* providing current and easy-to-read summaries of Federal research. These summaries are selected from the more than 70,000 new technical reports NTIS receives annually and grouped into subject areas of high interest; for example, *Manufacturing Technology, Communications,* and *Materials Sciences.* No other information source offers you such comprehensive coverage of the multibillion-dollar Government R&D programs. Foreign technology developed by other countries also is included. To receive additional information, ask for the free descriptive brochure, PR-733. Contact: NTIS, U.S. Department of Commerce, Springfield, VA 22161/703-487-4630.

Technology Resources Directory
This reference directory is designed to lead large and small technology oriented businesses to scientific and technical resources provided by Federal agencies and their laboratories. Included in the *Directory of Federal Technology Resources* are expertise at Federal laboratories, unique equipment available for sharing, special services providing materials to the R&D and engineering communities, and descriptions of more that 70 Federal technical information centers. A contact name, address, and telephone are provided for each entry. Some 800 detailed resource summaries are arranged within 30 subject headings for easy browsing along with detailed subject,

state, and resource name indexes. The directory is available for $25 and its NTIS order number is PB84-100015. Contact: NTIS, U.S. Department of Commerce, Springfield, VA 22161/703-487-4650. (A free descriptive brochure, number PR-746, also is available.)

Telecommunication Sciences, Institute for
The Institute performs applied scientific and engineering research on the transmission of radio waves and on their effects on the environment, the interaction among these waves, and problems posed by telecommunications systems and standards. Contact: Institute for Telecommunication Sciences, Department of Commerce, Boulder, CO 80303/303-497-3572.

Telecommunications Expertise for Public Service Groups
Institutions such as schools, hospitals, libraries, police and fire departments and government agencies at all levels can receive help in achieving their goals from the Office of Telecommunications Applications. This office will help public service groups identify their needs and show how these needs can be met through telecommunications. Contact: PTFP, National Telecommunications and Information Administration, Department of Commerce, 14th and Constitution Ave. N.W., Room 4625, Washington, DC 20230/202-377-5802.

Telecommunications Research
The Institute for Telecommunications Science (ITS) is the chief reasearch arm on telecommunications matters of the National Telecommunications Information Administration (NTIA) and serves as the federal resource to assist other agencies of the government in the planning, design, maintenance and improvement of their telecommunications activities. It publishes the *Annual Technical Progress Report* which contains an overview and comprehensive summary of its projects. Many technical reports are also available and can be ordered. Staff at ITS can respond to your inquiries. Contact: Technical Publications Office, Institute for Telecommunications Sciences (ITS), National Telecommunications Information Administration (NTIA), U.S. Department of Commerce, 325 Broadway, Boulder, CO 80303/303-497-3572.

Tourism Revenue
The U.S. Travel and Tourism Administration will work with state and local governments as well as private industry within the United States to help promote and assist travel from abroad. Contact: Marketing and Field Operations, Travel and Tourism Administration, U.S. Department of Commerce, Room 1858, Washington, DC 20230/202-377-4003.

Tours
The National Ocean Service has available tours of its Headquarters in Rockville, Maryland. Requests for information should be addressed to the Visitors Liaison Officer, National Ocean Service, Internal Affairs Staff, Rockville, MD 20852/301-443-8031.

Trace Foreign Economic Trends
The Trade Statistics Division of the U.S. Department of Commerce, produces quarterly comparative economic statistics for the United States, France, West Germany, Italy, Netherlands, United Kingdom, Japan and Canada. Subscriptions to "International Economic Indicators and Competitive Trends" are available for $13.00 (domestic mailing) and $16.25 (foreign mailing). Contact: Trade Statistics Division, Herbert Hoover Bldg., Room 2217, Dept. of Commerce, Washington, D.C. 20230/202-377-4211.

Trace Publications
Office of Trade Information Service (OTIS) provides many reports and services on the marketing of products with an international scope, including a Contact Service, that puts you in contact with distributors, manufacturers, retailers, and wholesalers in the country of your choice that can represent your product. OTIS publishes the following:

Expert Statistical Profile (ESP) is an annual two-volume publication that provides a five-year overview of specific products and export histories. The report shows the percentage of total dollar values and allows for a historical perspective of specific products. A data base is available for more specific information on products, providing a five year export history on certain products. Volume I is $30.00 and Volume II is $70.00.

Market Research—provides a five year projected analysis on the needs for specific products in a particular country. The cost is $10–$250 for the reports, depending on the scope of the product and countries profiles.

Annual Worldwide Industry Review—augments the *Market Research Reports,* providing updated statistical information on products and country profiles. It provides a competitive and market assessment by market officers in the country being profiled. Three different reports are available: Western Hemisphere and Africa, Europe, and the Near East and Asia. Each report is $200, or all three for $500.00.

Trade List—a listing by country and by product and by Standard Industry Classification (SIC) number for easy classification of specific products. It provides a list of agents, manufacturers, distributors, retailers, and wholesalers of products on a worldwide scope. The 126-page publication is available for $40.00.

Trade Opportunities Bulletin—a weekly bulletin produced jointly by the Department of Commerce and the Department of State, consisting of trade leads acquired throughout the world on all types of products. The 50-page publication is available for $175.00

Top Notch Service—a supplement to the Bulletin that provides trade leads on specific countries. The cost is $62.50 for the initial block of 50 leads.

Export Mailing List—provides a custom mailing list of manufacturers of specific products for a country. Prices vary according to the services required.

World Traders Data Report—provides financial reports on companies in foreign markets, presenting information on company history, size, production statistics, credit standings, and overall evaluation. Customized reports are available for $75 per report. Contact: Office of Trade Information Service, Department of Commerce, PO Box 14207, Washington, DC 20044/202-377-2665, 202-377-2432.

Trademark
For information on trademarks one can request a free copy of *General Information Concerning Trademarks* ($3.00) from: Superintendent of Documents, U.S. Government Printing Office, Washington DC, 20402/202-783-3238.

Trademark Search
There is only one office which has all the data necessary for searching a trademark. If you yourself cannot go to this Virginia office, they will recommend someone you can hire to do the searching for you. Contact: Trademark Search Room, Patent and Trademark Office, Department of Commerce, 2011 Crystal Plaza Building #2, Arlington, VA 22202/703-557-3268.

Travel Industry Market Research
The U.S. Travel Service publishes a number of studies describing the potential travel market in a number of countries. Contact: Office of Research, Travel and Tourism Administration, Department of Commerce, Washington, DC 20230/202-377-4028.

Traveling to the United States
If you are in the travel business outside of the United States and you are interested in the United States as a travel destination, the U.S. Travel Service offers help. It has six offices abroad in Mexico City, Toronto, London, Paris, Tokyo and Frankfurt that deal with local tour operators, retail agents and journalists to promote U.S. travel. Those who are not near one of these six offices can contact Washington directly. Contact: Marketing and Field Operations, Travel and Tourism Administration, Department of Commerce, Room 1858, Washington, DC 20230/202-377-4003.

U.S. Government Proposal Requests Listing
The *Commerce Business Daily* contains notices of opportunities and awards for federally sponsored research and development. It provides a daily list of U.S. Government RFPs (Requests for Proposals), invitations for bid, contract awards for possible subcontracting leads, sales of surplus property,

and foreign business opportunities. Generally, this list is accompanied by a brief description of the proposed procurement action and information about how to get a copy of the formal solicitation or announcement. Copies of the publication are available for reference purposes at Department of Commerce field offices and in most public libraries. It may be obtained on a subscription basis for $100 per year via second class mail or $175 via first class mail from the Superintendent of Documents (address listed above). Purchase order must be accompanied by payment.

An electronic, on-line edition of the *Commerce Business Daily* is available from any of several Department of Commerce contractors. Interested parties may contact them for full details. The contractors are Dialog Information Systems, Inc., 3460 Hillview Avenue, Palo Alto, CA 94304/ 800-227-1927; DMS/On-Line, 100 Northfield Street, Greenwich, CT 06830/203-661-7800; and United Communications Group, 8701 Georgia Avenue, Silver Spring, MD 20910/800-638-7728 or call collect 301-589-8875. Contact: Superintendent of Documents, U.S. Government Printing Office, Washington, DC 20402/ 202-783-3238.

Weather
See "Meteorological Center" in this section.

Weather Forecast Messages
In most major cities the National Weather Service has recorded messages on everything from the weather at local recreation areas to two-day forecasts in 30 major cities in the United States. In the white pages of the phone book, look under U.S. Government, then Department of Commerce, then National Oceanic & Atmospheric Administration, *then* the National Weather Service. The numbers for the Washington, DC area:

Aviation Forecast/202-347-4950
Marine Forecast/301-899-3210
MD-VA-DEL five-day forecast/301-899-3240
Ten Eastern Cities/301-899-3244
Ten Western Cities/301-899-3249
General Weather Information for Washington, DC area/202-936-1212

Weather Maps
The Nation Oceanic and Atmospheric Administration publishes a weekly series of daily weather maps. Copies of the maps are free, contact: NOAA Public Affairs, 14th & Constitution Ave, N.W. Room 6013, Washington, D.C. 20230/ 202-377-8090.

The National Oceanic and Atmospheric Administration (NOAA) also has two services for transmitting weather graphics. NAMFAX (National and Aviation Meterological Facsimile Network) offers a comprehensive set of charts depicting analyses, prognoses and selected observed data as well as international high-altitude aviation operations. DIFAX (Digital Facsimile Network) offers 3½ times the products as the NAMFAX system. Contact: NOAA, National Weather Service, WOTS34, 8060 13th St. Silver Spring, Md. 20910/301-436-3962.

Weights and Measurements Information
The Office of Weights and Measures (OWM) of the National Bureau of Standards (NBS) coordinates the weights and measures system in the United States, including state and local government programs. They sponsor the annual National Conference on Weights and Measures, which is held in a different city each year, as well as various committee meetings held in cities across the country throughout the year. The Conference is an association of federal, state and local jurisdictions, as well as industries involved in the manufacturing, processing, and packaging of products for sale at the retail level. Also included are manufacturers of and service companies for measurement and weighing devices. A brochure describing the organization, procedures, and membership plan of the Conference is available from the National Conference on Weights and Measures, P.O. Box 3137, Gaithersburg, MD 20760/301-921-3677. Working directly with the states and industry, and through the National Conference, OWM promotes the standardization of commercial practices; model laws and regulations; and specifications for the design and inspection of measuring and weighing devices. Staff can answer questions and make referrals. The office publishes many technical materials, including handbooks and manuals for weights and measures, administration and training. An important publication is: *NBS Handbook 44—Specification Tolerances and Other Technical Requirements for Weighing and Measuring Devices.* Updated annually, this handbook contains the latest technology in the field. It is used by every state and is incorporated into state regulations for use by inspectors of weighing and measuring devices, for example, gas pumps at gas stations, grocery store scales, and highway truck scales. The publication is available for $6.00 from the Superintendent of Documents, U.S. Government Printing Office, Washington, D.C. 20402/ 202-783-3238. Contact: Office of Weights and Measures, Administration Building—Room A617, National Bureau of Standards (NBS), Gaithersburg, MD 20899/301-921-2401.

World Climate Data
The National Climatic Data Center has world monthly surface climatological data for over 2,500 weather stations. Data for some stations go back to the mid-1700s. The Center operates at full cost recovery for providing products and services and requires pre-payment. A professional staff of 10 meteorologists functioning as request analysts are

available to assist potential customers. Contact: National Climatic Data Center, NOAA, Department of Commerce, Federal Building, Asheville, NC 28801/704-259-0682.

How Can Department of Commerce Help You?
A staff of trained specialists is available to help the public with problems and information needs in the fields of business and economic development. This office is a great place to start in order to determine how the U.S. Department of Commerce can help you. They can also direct you to organizations outside of Commerce which may be helpful. Contact: Office of Business Liaison, Department of Commerce, 14th and Constitution Ave. N.W., Room 5898C, Washington, DC 20230/202-377-3176.

Department of Defense

The Pentagon, Washington, DC 20301/202-545-6700

Established: September 18, 1947
Budget: $258,200,000,000
Employees: 1,065,485*

MISSION: Provide the military forces needed to deter war and protect the security of our country. The major elements of these forces are the Army, Navy, Marine Corps and Air Force, consisting of about two million men and women on active duty, and two-and-one-half million members of the reserve components. Under the President, who is also Commander-in-Chief, the Secretary of Defense exercises direction, authority, and control over the Department of Defense.

Major Divisions and Offices

Department of the Army
Department of Defense, The Pentagon, Washington, DC 20310/202-694-0741
Budget: $61,300,000,000
Employees: 400,000
Mission: Organize, train, and equip active duty and reserve forces for the preservation of peace, security and the defense of our nation; focus on land operations; administer programs aimed at protecting the environment, improving waterway navigation, flood and beach control, and water resource development; and support the National Civil Defense Program by providing military assistance to federal, state, and local government agencies, natural disaster relief assistance, and emergency medical air transportation services.

Department of the Air Force
Department of Defense, The Pentagon, Washington, DC 20330/202-695-4803.
Budget: $86,100,000,000
Employees: 249,000

Mission: Provides an Air Force that is capable, in conjunction with other armed forces, of preserving the peace and security of the United States.

Department of the Navy
Department of Defense, The Pentagon, Washington, DC 20350/202-697-5342.
Budget: $81,900,000,000
Employees: 340,000
Mission: Protects the United States by the effective prosecution of war at sea including with its Marine Corps component, the seizure of defense of advanced naval bases; supports as required the forces of all military departments of the United States; and maintains freedom of the seas.

• United States Marine Corps
Commandant of the Marine Corps, Headquarters, United States Marine Corps, Washington, DC 20380/202-694-2500.
Budget: $7,074,500,000
Employees: 21,509
Mission: Provides Fleet Marine Forces of combined arms, together with supporting air components, for the seizure or defense of advanced naval

---

*Employment and budget estimate for Department of Defense does not include armed forces personnel.

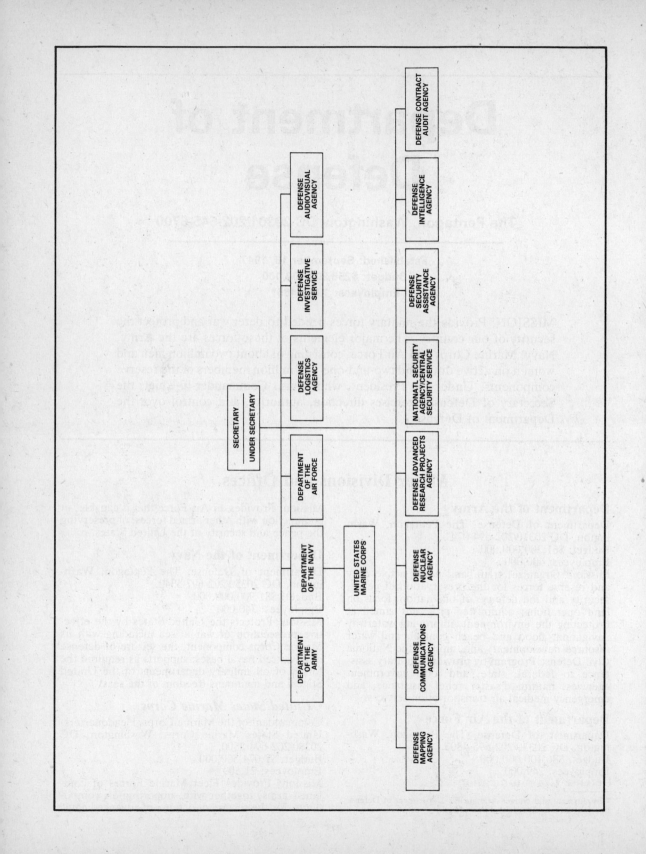

bases and the conduct of land operations essential to the prosecution of a naval campaign; provides detachments and organizations for service on armed vessels of the Navy and provides security detachments for the protection of naval property at naval stations and bases; develops, in coordination with the other services, the tactics, techniques, and equipment for landing forces in amphibious operations; prepares for wartime expansion; and performs such other duties as the President may direct.

Defense Logistics Agency

Department of Defense, Room 3A150, Cameron Station, Alexandria, VA 22314/202-274-6000
Budget: $1,671,141,000
Employees: 48,916
Mission: Provides effective economic support to the military services, other Defense components, federal civil agencies, foreign governments, and others as authorized, for assigned material commodities and items of supply, logistics services directly associated with the supply management function, contract administration services, and other support services as directed by the Secretary of Defense.

Defense Investigative Service

Department of Defense, Buzzard Point, 1900 Half St. S.W., Washington, DC 20324/202-693-1427.
Budget: $22,134,000
Employees: 1,260
Mission: Provides U.S. Department of Defense components, and other U.S. government activities, when authorized, with a single, centrally directed personnel security investigative service.

Defense Nuclear Agency

Department of Defense, Washington, DC 20305/202-325-7047.
Budget: (not available)
Employees: (not available)
Mission: Plans, coordinates, and supervises Defense efforts in nuclear weapons, including tests assessment, construction and management of simulation facilities, and field experiments.

Defense Mapping Agency

Department of Defense, U.S. Naval Observatory Building 56, Washington, DC 20305/202-254-4140.
Budget: $700,000,000
Employees: 8,800
Mission: Provides support to the Secretary of Defense, the military departments, the Joint Chiefs of Staff, and other U.S. Department of Defense components, as appropriate, on matters concerning mapping, charting and geodesy.

Defense Communications Agency

Department of Defense, 8th St. and South Courthouse Rd., Arlington, VA 22204/202-692-0018.

Budget: $258,000,000
Employees: 1,780
Mission: Performs system engineering for the Defense Communication System (DCS) and ensures that the DCS is planned, improved, operated, maintained, and managed effectively, efficiently, and economically to meet the telecommunications requirements of the National Command Authorities, the Department of Defense and, as authorized and directed, other governmental agencies; provides system engineering and technical support to the National Military Command Systems and the Minimum Essential Emergency Communications Network; provides other engineering and technical support to the Worldwide Military Command and Control System; performs system architect functions for current and future Military Satellite Communication systems; provides analytical and automated data processing support to the Joint Chiefs of Staff, the Secretary of Defense and other Defense components; and procures leased communications circuits, services, facilities, and equipment for the U.S. Department of Defense, and other government agencies as directed.

Defense Advanced Research Projects Agency

Department of Defense, 1400 Wilson Blvd., Arlington, VA 22209/202-694-3007.
Budget: $696,085,000
Employees: 132
Mission: Manages high-risk, high-payoff basic research and applied technology programs in projects as may be designated by the Secretary of Defense; and selects and pursues revolutionary technology developments that minimize the possibility of technological surprise and/or offer potential for major increases in national defense capability.

Defense Intelligence Agency

Department of Defense, The Pentagon, Washington, DC 20301/202-695-8844
Budget: Not Available
Employees: Not Available
Mission: Produces and disseminates defense intelligence to satisfy the intelligence requirements of the Secretary of Defense, the Joint Chiefs of Staff, and major components of the Department of Defense.

Defense Audiovisual Agency

Headquarters, Norton Air Force Base, California 92409/714-382-7047 or 202-697-8959 (Washington, DC)
Budget: (not available)
Employees: 300
Mission: Performs centrally managed production, acquisition, and reproduction of motion picture

films, video and audio tapes and discs, still photographs, and multimedia and other audiovisual media products to provide support and services for all Department of Defense components.

Defense Contract Audit Agency

Building 4, Cameron Station, Alexandria, Va. 22314/202-274-7328.
Budget: $157,700,000
Employees: 4,500
Mission: Provides accounting and financial advisory services to all Defense components responsible for procurement and contract administration.

Defense Security Assistance Agency

The Pentagon, Washington, DC 20301/202-695-3291.

Budget: (not available)
Employees: (not available)
Mission: Works closely with the U.S. Military Assistance Advisory Group and Military Groups, worldwide.

National Security Agency/ Central Security Service

Fort George G. Meade, MD 10755/301-688-6311.
Budget: classified
Employees: classified
Mission: Responsible for centralized coordination, direction, and performance of highly specialized technical functions in support of U.S. Government activities to protect U.S. communications, and produce foreign intelligence information.

Major Sources of Information

Aberdeen Proving Ground

This facility provides research and development, production and post-production testing of components and complete items of weapons, systems, ammunition, and combat and support vehicles. Also tests numerous items of individual equipment in use Army-wide. The Proving Ground responds to written inquiries only. Contact: Chief, U.S. Army, TECOM Public Affairs Office (STEAP-10), Aberdeen Proving Ground, MD 21005/301-278-2360.

Abuse and Fraud Reporting Hotline

For reporting alleged abuses and fraud in the Department of Defense, contact: Defense Hotline, The Pentagon, Washington, DC 20301-1900/202-693-5080 or 800-424-9098.

ADA Language Management

The Office of Computer Software and Systems is responsible for the management of the ADA language and the Software Technology for Adaptable Reliable Systems (STARS). ADA is a modern, high-order computer programming language created to be the standard language for software for computer applications at the DOD. It was designed to help reduce the costs of military software systems and to improve athe quality of software engineering. The ADA Information Clearinghouse gathers and disseminates information, and manages the collection and distribution of documentation on all aspects of the ADA language. It maintains a public data base file to announce recent activities and general information on the program. For instructions on obtaining access to the file through MILNET or TELENET, contact: Office of Computer Software and Systems, Office of the Under Secretary of Defense for Research & Advanced Technology, U.S. Depart-

ment of Defense, The Pentagon, Washington, DC 20301/ 202-694-0210 or -0208.

Adjutant General

The Adjutant General is responsible for the development of Army policy and operational management of Army-wide administrative and community life support systems, including the Armed Forces Courier Service, the world-wide Army Publication System, Institute of Heraldry, all Army libraries, and casualty and memorial affairs. For information, contact: Department of the Army, The Adjutant General's Office, The Pentagon, Room 2E532, Washington, DC 20310/202-695-0163.

Advanced Planning Briefings for Industry (APBIs)

These briefings are held periodically by the major subordinate commands of the Army Material Command to inform industry of the U.S. Army's requirements. These briefings are of interest to industrial executives, advance system planners, directors of development, engineering and production, and those concerned with the formulation of corporate long-range objectives. For information, contact: Army Material Command Tri-Service Information Center, Department of the Army, Department of Defense, 5001 Eisenhower Ave., Alexandria, VA 22333-0001/202-274-8948.

Aeronautical and Aeromedical Research

Information is available on the procurement of exploratory, advanced and engineering development in the areas of air breathing; electric and advanced propulsion; fuels and lubricants; power generation: transmission and reception, including (above 15GC) molecular electronics, bionics, lasers, vehicle environment, photo materials and optronics, position and motion sensing devices, navigation, guidance, reconnaissance and avionics, and communications; flight dynamics, including structures; aerodynamics, aerothermodynamics, control displays and crew stations, aerodynamic accelerators and escape, alighting and orbital attachment; airframe and equipment bearing, and flight testing techniques; material sciences, including metals and ceramics, non-metallic materials, and manufacturing technology; subareas of life support, including aerospace medicine and human performance, environmental effects, techniques and equipment for well-being, protection and performance enhancement in subareas of biodynamic forces and energies, altitude thermals, toxic hazards, bionics, and human engineering and training. Basic research in selected areas of applied mathematics, organic and inorganic radiation and molecular chemistry, plasma, atomic, theoretical; nuclear and solid state physics, metallurgy and ceramics, heat transfer, energy conversion and fluid dynamics. For information, contact: Directorate of Research and Development Contracting (ASD/PMR), Aeronautical Systems Division, Air Force Systems Command, Department of the Air Force, Department of Defense, Wright-Patterson Air Force Base, OH 45433/513-255-2358.

Aeronautical Systems
This office develops and acquires aeronautical systems, subsystems, their components and related government-furnished aerospace equipment (GFAE), including, but not limited to, aircraft engines, aircraft wheels and brakes, airborne communications systems, aircraft bombing and navigation systems, aircraft instruments, aeronautical reconnaissance systems, subsystems, special reconnaissance projects and interpretation facilities. Contact: Aeronautical Systems Division, Chief of Staff, Air Force Systems Command, Department of the Air Force, Department of Defense, Wright-Patterson Air Force Base, OH 45433/513-255-2014.

Aerospace Center—Defense Mapping Agency
This center provides mapping, charting and geodetic products and services to the U.S. Armed Forces and other government agencies. Its products and services include aeronautical charts, digital data, flight information, publications, space mission charts and a wide spectrum of technical data about the earth and its aerospace environments vital to navigation on a worldwide basis. DMAAC products are available to the public through: Distribution Division, Office of Aeronautical Charting and Cartography, National Ocean Survey, NOAA, Department of Commerce, Riverdale, MD 20737/301-436-6990. For general information, contact: Public Affairs Office, Defense Mapping Agency, Aerospace Center, Department of Defense, 3200 South 2nd St., St. Louis MO 63118/314-263-4142.

Aerospace Medicine
Research and development is conducted in the life sciences, human factors, aerospace medicine, biosciences, biomedicine, behavioral sciences, space medicine, biotechnology, human engineering, human resources, aviation medicine, space biology and medical equipment. Contact: Aerospace Medical Division, School of Aerospace Medicine (SAM), Air Force Systems Command, Department of the Air Force, Department of Defense, Brooks Air Force Base, TX 78235/512-536-3207.

Aerospace Structures Information and Analysis Center
This center is a central point for the collection and dissemination of aerospace structures information and quick state-of-the-art solutions to structural problems. Its areas of interest include aerospace structural design and analysis; experimental structural data; fracture mechanics; failure analysis; structural history; fatigue; service loads; design criteria; composites. Contact: Aerospace Structures Information and Analysis Center (ASIAC), Air Force Wright Aeronautical Laboratories, Department of the Air Force, FIBRA (ASIAC), Wright-Patterson AFB, OH 45433/513-255-6688.

Air Development Center
This Center acts as the principal Navy research, development, test, and evaluation center for Naval aircraft systems except aircraft-launched weapons systems. Contact: Code 094, Small Business Office, Naval Air Development Center, Department of the Navy, Department of Defense, Warminster, PA 18974/215-441-2456.

Air Force Art Collection
The actions and deeds of Air Force men and women are recorded in paintings which the Air Force puts on continual public display through traveling art shows. The collection includes paintings on World War I aerial combat and U.S. Army Air Force operations in England during World War II. Contact: Art and Museum Branch, Community Relations Division, Office of Public Affairs, Department of the Air Force, Department of Defense, The Pentagon, Room 4A120, Washington, DC 20330/202-697-6629.

Air Force Bands
For information on Air Force Bands, write to: Bands Branch, SAF/PACC The Pentagon, Room 4A120, Washington, DC 20330/202-695-0019.

Air Force Casualties
For information on Air Force personnel missing in action or taken prisoner of war, contact: Casualty Assistance, Personnel HQ AFMPC/MPCC Randolph Air Force Base, TX 78150/512-652-3505.

Air Force Fact Sheets
Fact Sheets published by the U.S. Air Force are

available in limited number for free. A wide range of subjects are covered. A few examples are:

Air Force Broadcasting Service	84-21
Air Force Office of Youth Relations	84-31
B-1B	84-17
C-130 Hercules	84-3
Electronic Security Command	83-16
North Atlantic Treaty Organization	84-26
Thunderbirds	84-7

Contact: Civil Affairs Branch (SAF/PACC), Pentagon, Room 4A120, Washington, DC 20330

Air Force Historical Research Center
This is the principal repository for Air Force historical records. It holds the most extensive collection of documentary source material in the history of U.S. military action in the country. The Historical Reference Branch maintains the Center's document and microfilm collection and provides research services. Contact: Air Force Historical Research Center, HQUSAFHRC/HD), Maxwell Air Force Base, AL 36112/205-293-5958.

Air Force History, Office of
This office manages the Air Force historical program. It publishes scholarly books, monographs and other studies, runs the Air Force Historical Research Center (see listing in this section) and offers the Air Force History Fellowship Program. For a list of the publications and general information, contact: Office of Air Force History, Bolling Air Force Base, Building 5681, Washington, DC 20332/202-767-5089.

Air Force Lithographs
For a listing of Air Force lithographs, mainly of aircraft, contact: Government Printing Office, Washington, DC 20402/202-783-3238.

Air Force Motion Pictures
For information on motion picture film created or acquired by the Air Force and cleared for public distribution, contact: DAVA-N-LD, Norton Air Force Base, CA 92409/714-382-2394. A film catalog, *Air Force Regulations 95-2, Vol. 2*, is available for $10.00 from the Government Printing Office, Superintendent of Documents, Washington, DC 20402-6518/202-783-3238.

Air Force Museum
The Air Force Museum is the largest and oldest military aviation museum in the world. About 140 aircraft are on display including historical, experimental and presidential airplanes. Military uniforms, celebrities in uniform, and space exhibit are also shown. The research library at the museum has still photographs, books, drawings and other historical Air Force material. Contact: United States Air Force Museum, Department of Defense, Wright-Patterson Air Force Base, OH 45433/

513-255-3284. For information on other Air Force museums, contact: Art and Museum Branch, Community Relations Division, Office of Public Affairs, Department of the Air Force, Department of Defense, The Pentagon, Room 4A120, Washington, DC 20330-1000/202-697-6629.

Air Force Publications Program
The Office of Air Force History publishes scholarly books, monographs, and studies designed to meet the needs of the Air Force at all levels. These works stem from a long-term publications effort supporting the development of strategy, plans, and doctrine throughout the Air Force; they also provide Air Force staff members with the historical perspective important in conducting current operations. Air Force students use these materials to further their professional military education, and scholars—military and civilian—find them indispensable in research and teaching. The volumes are also designed to inform the general public about the role of the Air Force in national security. The pamphlet titled Publications lists and describes the works that have been published. To obtain a copy of this free pamphlet write the Civil Affairs Branch (SAF/PACC) Pentagon, Room 4A120, Washington, DC 20330.

Air Force Report
This free annual report describes the Air Force programs. Contact: Office of SAF/PACC, Department of Defense, The Pentagon, Room 4A120, Washington, DC 20330/202-697-2842.

Air Force Reserve
The Reserve trains and serves with active Air Force units. It also controls all active and reserve elements airlifting supplies to victims of hurricanes, tornadoes or other emergencies. Contact: Office of Air Force Reserve, Office of Public Affairs, Department of the Air Force, Department of Defense, The Pentagon, Room 5D323, Washington, DC 20330-5440/202-697-1761.

Air Force Science and Engineering Fair Handbook
This pamphlet describes the role of the Air Force in the Regional and State Science and Engineering Fair Program. This program is sponsored by Science Service, Inc., a non-profit organization based in Washington, DC. It recognizes the scientific accomplishments of America's youth and demonstrates their creativeness and scientific enterprise. Participation in these fairs provides an excellent opportunity for the Air Force to encourage young Americans to seek careers in science and/or engineering and to make these aspiring young scientists and engineers aware of opportunities in Air Force research and development. A copy of the pamphlet may be obtained by writing the Civil Affairs Branch (SAF/PACC) Pentagon, Room 4A120, Washington, DC 20330.

Air Force Speeches
Complete texts of speeches covering current issues and new developments are available for free. The Aerospace Speech Index lists the speeches available. Contact: Civil Affairs Branch (SAF/PACC), Pentagon, Room 4A120, Washington, DC 20330.

Air Force Still Photographs
Some Air Force still photographs are available for duplication. For information, contact: DAVA Still Photo Depository (AF), Anacostia Naval Station, Building 168, NDW, Washington, DC 20374/202-433-2168.

Air Force Stock Footage
Stock footage of Air Force films is available from: DAVA-DAVCOM Division, Building 243, Motion Media Depository, Norton Air Force Base, CA 92409/714-382-2307.

Air Force Technical Publications
Technical publications are available from any one of the following offices:

Air Force Information for Industry Office, Air Force Wright Aeronautical Laboratories (AFWAL/TST), Wright-Patterson AFB, OH 45433/513-258-4259.
Air Force Information for Industry Office, 5001 Eisenhower Ave., Alexandria, VA 22333/202-274-9305
Air Force Information for Industry Office, 1030 East Green Street, Pasadena, CA 91106/213-792-3192

Air Force Logistics Needs
A compilation of those R&D programs that will result in a long-term improvement in operation and support costs. It contains proposed logistics-oriented research and development programs in ten major areas: systems design and development; acquisition; systems management; depot maintenance; field maintenance; supply; transportation; personnel; meteorology; and energy management.

Manufacturing Technology Planning Information
Estimates of long-range plans under consideration by the Manufacturing Technology Division of the Air Force Materials Laboratory. It provides manufacturing processes and techniques in advance of acquisition requirements.

Mission Element Need Statements (MENS)
Identifies a mission deficiency or technological opportunity within a mission area. A MENS is required for each new major system acquisition including system modifications which the U.S. Department of Defense component anticipates will cost in excess of $100 million in research, development, test and evaluation or $500 million in production.

Program Element Descriptive Summaries
Provide information on the Air Force research, development, testing and evaluation (RDT&E) program to congressional committees. They contain supporting data for budget estimates and summarize each program element within the Air Force RDT&E program.

Program Management Directive
The official Air Force management directive used to provide direction to the implementing and participating commands and to satisfy documentation requirements. It is used during the entire acquisition cycle to state requirements and request studies as well as to initiate, approve, change, transition, modify or terminate programs.

R&D Planning Summaries
Prepared by all U.S. Department of Defense component organizations that direct, administer or perform RDT&E work. These documents contain summaries of planned R&D efforts at project and task levels in the following categories: research, exploratory development, advanced development, engineering development, operational system development, management and support. These summaries may be used to identify RDT&E programs in certain scientific or technical areas for a specific budget year.

Research Planning Guide
An annual that consists of research objectives categorized by seven technical areas. Each objective contains a short description of its scope, midterm requirements, the long-term requirements, and points of contact from which any additional technical information may be obtained.

Tactical Air Forces Integrated Information Systems (TAFIIS) Master Plan
Provides in a single-source document the framework for the development of tactical command and control systems. It is intended to bring the operational, developmental, industrial and financial aspects of command and control together in a common document.

Technical Objective Documents
Compilations of technical planning objectives within a specific technical area which describe the technical effort that may satisfy an existing or anticipated Air Force goal. These documents try to stimulate academic, scientific and industrial organizations to participate in Air Force R&D programs by providing them with scientific and technical objectives toward which they can direct their research efforts.

Technology Needs Documents
Identify research and technology barriers to future Air Force systems. They contain specific items of research and technology required for the orderly development of systems, subsystems or capabilities. Each document normally contains a description of the problem and its order of priority.

Vanguard Planning Summary
Summarizes the long-range plans of the Air Force Vanguard System.

Work Unit Information Summaries
Brief descriptions of research and technology efforts currently in progress within the Air Force.

Selling to the United States Air Force
Designed for the small business person, this booklet outlines command contracting responsibilities in sections 1, 2 and 3. Section 3 also provides a list of goods and services typically bought for the day-to-day operation of an air force base. The booklet also provides names and phone numbers of points of contact. It is available free of charge. Request it in writing. Contact: Office of Small and Disadvantaged Business Utilization, Headquarters, U.S. Air Force, Washington, DC 20330/202-697-4126 or Headquarters, Air Force/AF/RDCX, Washington, DC 20330/202-695-6612.

Air Logistics Center
This office conducts, tests and evaluates aircraft weapons systems and their components. Contact: Naval Aviation Logistics Center, Patuxent River, MD 20670/301-863-3637.

Air National Guard
The Air National Guard assists the Air Force in its fighting capabilities with flying and specialized ground support. On a state level, the Guard also protects lives and property while preserving peace and public safety during disasters, civil disorders, and other emergencies. Contact: National Guard Bureau, Public Affairs Office (NGB-PA), Washington, DC 20310/202-695-0421. Contact the Adjutants General in the 50 states, D.C., Puerto Rico, Guam or the Virgin Islands.

Air Propulsion Center
This Center tests and evaluates air-breathing and gas-turbine propulsion systems, components, accessories, fuels, and lubricants. Contact: Naval Air Propulsion Center, Department of the Navy, Department of Defense, P.O. Box 7176, Trenton, NJ 08628-0176/609-896-5600.

Air Research
Research and development is conducted in surveillance, electronic intelligence, communications, computer and data processing techniques, textual data processing, intelligence extraction from aerial reconnaissance, data presentation, high-power electromagnetic generators, receivers, transmission line components, microelectronics applications, reliability and maintainability, survivability, propagation, vulnerability reduction, electronic countermeasures, and electromagnetic weapons. Contact: Small Business Office (BC), Rome Air Development Center, Air Force Systems Command, Griffiss Air Force Base, NY 13411/315-330-4020.

American Forces Information Service
This Service provides information, through print and audiovisual products, to U.S. Department of Defense personnel, including the Armed Forces abroad. It oversees the production of Defense newspapers and periodicals, and information and entertainment radio and television activities on Armed Forces Radio and Television. Contact: American Forces Information Service, 1735 N. Lynn Street, Arlington, VA 22209/202-696-6285.

American Forces Publications
Defense 84 is a monthly publication for $23.00 per year that provides official and professional information on matters related to Defense policies, programs and interests. On sale from the U.S. Government Printing Office, Superintendent of Documents, Washington, DC 20402/202-783-3238. For information on the publication, contact: American Forces Press Service, Armed Forces Information Service, Department of Defense, 1735 N. Lynn St., Arlington, VA 22209/202-696-5295.

Amnesty and Deserter Policies
For information on amnesty programs, contact: Office of the Assistant Secretary of Defense, (MRA and L-MPFM, Legal Policy), The Pentagon, Washington, DC 20301/202-697-3387. For information on deserter programs, contact: Director of Legislation and Legal Policy, 05D(M)(MP and FM) (LLP) Department of Defense, The Pentagon, Room 30823, Washington, DC 20301/202-697-3387.

Annual Report
The U.S. Department of Defense Annual Report describes all Defense programs and provides numerous breakdowns of the Defense budget. Available for $8.00 from U.S. Government Printing Office, Superintendent of Documents, Washington, DC 20402/202-783-3238.

Armament, Munitions and Chemical Command (AMCCOM)
This office is responsible for integrated material readiness management, including follow-on procurement, production, engineering in support of production, industrial management, product assurance, maintenance value and logistics engineering, international logistics, and transportation and traffic management of various Army weapons systems. ARRCOM has responsibility of managing conventional ammunition for the U.S. Department of Defense, and also controls over four arsenals, 26 government owned contractor-operated army ammunition plants (AAP), and three government owned-and-operated AAP activities. Contact: Headquarters, U.S. Army, Armament,

Munitions and Chemical Command, (AMC-COM), Rock Island, IL 61299-6000/309-782-6001.

Armament Research

For information on the procurement of research, development and tests related to the evaluation of guns and other aircraft weapons, new explosives, non-nuclear munitions, bomb warheads, chemical-biological weapons, dispensers, target, and scorers, equipment and the application of equipment or new techniques for counter-insurgency operations testing of Air Force tactics and techniques, test ranges for aircraft and missile systems testing and an electromagnetic test environment for ECM and ECCM, contact: Armament Division, Air Force Systems Command, Department of the Air Force, Department of Defense, Eglin Air Force Base, FLA 32542/904-882-2843.

Armed Forces Health Professions Scholarship Programs (H&E)

A total of 5,000 scholarships are available for award to eligible persons attending accredited educational institutions providing training in approved health professions. The Army, Navy and Air Force each processes applications for their own participants in the program. For general information, contact: Office of the Assistant Secretary of Defense for Health Affairs (Medical Readiness) (Manpower Personnel and Training) Department of Defense, The Pentagon, Room 3E341, Washington, DC 20301/202-694-4705. A student may apply to one, two, or all three military departments. Contact: Commander, Army Medical Department, Personnel Support Agency, Department of the Army, Attn: SGPE-PD M-S, 1900 Half St. S.W., Room 6319, Washington, DC 20314/202-475-1508. Or Commander, Navy Recruiting Command, 4015 Wilson Blvd., Room 1009, Arlington, VA 22203/202-696-4928. Or United States Air Force Recruiting Service, Directorate of Health Professions Recruiting, Randolph Air Force Base, TX 78150/512-652-4334.

Arms Transfer Management Group

The Arms Transfer Management Group advises the Undersecretary of State for Security Assistance, Science and Technology in matters relating to conventional arms transfers. It provides recommendations in the following specific functional areas: provision of systematic and comprehensive policy oversight in the arms transfer field; review of security assistance plans and programs to ensure that they support overall U.S. policies; and preparation of annual program funding levels. Contact: Office of Undersecretary of State for Security Assistance, Science, and Technology, Department of State, Washington, DC 20520/202-632-0004.

Army Aeromedical Research Laboratory

Research efforts have two objectives: enhancement of the individual soldier's combat perfor-mance and efficiency, and the prevention of injury in the operational environment or combat. The laboratory's research and development efforts are channeled toward the safety, efficiency, and effectiveness of the healthy soldier while training or working at his high-risk occupation—training for war and combat. Contact: Army Aeromedical Research Laboratory, Department of the Army, P. O. Box 577, Fort Rucker, AL 36362/205-255-6907.

Army Armament Research and Development Center (ARDC)

This office is responsible for the management of research, development, life-cycle engineering, product assurance, initial acquisition through transition to the U.S. Army Armament Materiel Readiness Command and surety of various nuclear and non-nuclear weapons and ammunition and special tools and test equipment which are a part of or used with assigned materiel. Contact: Army Armament Research and Development Command, Dover, NJ 07801-5001/201-724-4021.

Army Artists

Photos of paintings by Army artists are available through the Defense Audio-visual Agency. For information on what is available, contact: Army Art Activity, Army Center of Military History, Department of the Army, 5001 Eisenhower Ave, Room G2W18, Alexandria, VA 22333/202-274-8290. For information on prices, contact: DAVA, Still Photo Depository Activity, Bldg. 168, Anacostia Naval Station, Washington, DC 20374/202-433-2166.

Army Assets

The Department of the Army has a variety of assets available for participation in activities in the public domain. These assets are used to increase public understanding of the Army's role in national security and assist total Army recruiting and retention. A Public Affairs Office is available at most of the major Army installations throughout the United States to assist in determining the availability and propriety of participation. These assets include, but are not limited to, color guards, drill teams, parachute teams, demonstrations, installation tours, guest speakers, static displays (including weapons, vehicles and aircraft), marching units, bands and other musical units, and exhibits. Contact: Headquarters, Department of the Army, Attn: FAPA-CR, Washington, D.C. 20310/202-697-2707.

Army Aviation Research and Development Command

This office is responsible for research and development of new helicopter systems, support of qualification testing of turbine engines, development and evaluation of prototype hardware for fueling and defueling equipment for use in combat areas and solving of fuel contamination problems. Contact: Army Aviation Research and Development Command (AVRADCOM), Department of the Army, Department of Defense, St. Louis, MO 63120/ 314-263-3901.

Army Community Service Program
This is a community-oriented social service program designed to assist service members and their families. Some of the services include: information and referral, financial planning and assistance, relocation, handicapped dependents' assistance, child-support services and child advocacy programs to prevent child abuse and neglect. Contact: ACS Division Soldier and Family Assistance Directorate, Office of the Adjutant General, Department of the Army, 2461 Eisenhower Ave. Room 1400 Alexandria, VA 22331/202-325-9390.

Army Computer Systems Selection and Acquisition Agency
This office performs automated data processing equipment evaluation, provides Army-wide technical support in the selection, acquisition and installation of the equipment. Contact: Army Computer Systems Selection and Acquisition Agency, Department of the Army, 2461 Eisenhower Ave., Room 954, Alexandria, VA 22331/ 202-325-9490.

Army Corps of Engineers Civil Works Program
The Corps's civil works program provides a broad range of water resources development and management projects. It has constructed major dams, levees, harbors, waterways and locks throughout the United States. Contact: Civil Works, Army Corps of Engineers, Department of the Army, Department of Defense, 20 Massachusetts Ave. N.W., Room 7227, Washington, DC 20314/ 202-272-0099.

Army Corps of Engineers, Audio-Visual Materials and Exhibits
The Corps produces and makes available to the general public informational films on subjects that include navigation, flood control, hydroelectric power, recreation, emergency operations management, environmental enhancement and boating safety. Requests for loan of these films should be sent to: Modern Talking Picture Service, Inc., 5000 Park St. N., St. Petersburg, FLA 33709/ 813-541-7571, or contact: Public Affairs, Army Corps of Engineers, Department of the Army, Department of Defense, 20 Massachusetts Ave. N.W., Room 8122C, HQDA (DAENPAV), Washington, DC 20314/202-272-0017.

Various exhibits and audiovisual presentations produced by the Corps are available for touring. For short, descriptive lists and information, contact the same address as above. 20 Massachusetts Ave. N.W., Room 8122C, HQDA (DAENPAV), Washington, DC 20314/202-272-0017.

Army Corps of Engineers, Military Research and Development
The military research and development conducted by the Corps of Engineers include bulk munitions for engineer obstacles and demolitions; realistic battlefield environmental conditions that affect tactical operations and weapons systems; rapid repair and restoration of bomb-damaged runways; computer-aided architectural and engineering design system; and energy analysis system for estimating fuel consumption in buildings. Contact: Military Programs, Research and Development, Army Corps of Engineers, Department of the Army, Department of Defense, 20 Massachusetts Ave. N.W., Room 6208, Washington, DC 20314/ 202-272-0259.

Army Corps of Engineers, Permits
A Corps permit is required if you plan to locate a structure, excavate or discharge dredged or fill material in waters of the United States, or if you plan to transport dredged material for the purpose of dumping it into ocean waters. Contact District Engineer Offices for current information about nationwide and general permits, or Regulatory Functions Branch, Army Corps of Engineers, Department of the Army, Department of Defense, 20 Massachusetts Ave. N.W., Room 6235, Washington, DC 20314/202-272-0199.

Army Corps of Engineers, Publications
Free pamphlets and brochures on the Corps programs are available. A list of Corps publications on a wide variety of subjects, including archaeology, bicycle trails, camping, canoeing, environment, erosion control, flood control, flood plain management, games for children, history, hunting guides, safety, waste-water treatment and water supply is also available. Contact: Public Affairs, Army Corps of Engineers, Department of the Army, Department of Defense, 20 Massachusetts Ave. N.W., Room 8137, Washington, DC 20314/202-272-0011.

Army Corps of Engineers, Training Programs for Foreign Participants
The Corps conducts training programs in the U.S. in the field of water resource development and related activities such as river basin planning, flood protection, beach erosion control and shore protection, hydroelectric power generation, improvement of waterways for navigation and construction management. The training programs may be long-term, on-the-job training, short-term observation, academic study at a university or research institution and practical training with the Corps's activities or other Federal agencies. For program information, contact: International Affairs Office, Army Corps of Engineers, Department of the Army, Department of Defense, 20 Massachusetts Ave. N.W., Room 8236, Washington, DC 20314/202-272-0006.

Army Films

For Army films available to the public, contact: Commander, U.S. Army AV Center, 1010 MOAV-MO Room 5A470, Pentagon, Washington, DC 20310/202-694-4541

Army Library

This is the U.S. Department of Defense Library funded by the Army. For information on its holdings, contact: The Pentagon Library, Room 1A518, The Pentagon, Washington, DC 20310/202-697-4301.

Army Materials and Mechanics Research Center

This center manages and directs portions of the U.S. Army Development and Readiness Command materials research program conducted within its own laboratories, including basic scientific research and research in metals and ceramics. It also coordinates the total materials research program of the U.S. Army Materiel Command (AMC). Contact: Army Materials and Mechanics Research Center, Department of Defense, Watertown, MA 02172/617-923-5278.

Army Materiel Command

The U.S. Army Materiel Command is responsible for the research, development, procurement, production, supply and maintenance of U. S. Army hardware. Research and development activities are carried out in corporate laboratories and Department of Defense Commands. Contact: Public Affairs, U.S. Army Materiel Command, 5001 Eisenhower Avenue, Alexandria, Virginia 22333-0001/202-274-8010.

Army Materiel Systems Analysis Activity

This office has the overall mission of providing a central technical capability for systems analysis within the Army Materiel Development and Readiness Command (DARCOM) and for continuing improvement in the total command-wide systems analysis activity. This includes the conduct of systems analysis studies, investigations, functions and activities; the evaluation of concepts and proposals on a DARCOM-wide base; and the advancement, improvement and dissemination of techniques and methods of systems analysis. Contact: Army Materiel Systems Analysis Activity, Department of Defense, Aberdeen Proving Ground, MD 21005-5071/301-278-6607.

Army Parachute Team—The Golden Knights

The Golden Knights are the Army's official aerial demonstration team. As part of the Army's recruiting effort, they will participate in those civilian-sponsored events that meet with the Department's approval. Requests should be made at least 1 year prior to the event. Contact U.S. Army Recruiting Support Center, Attn: TAIR, Cameron Station, Building 6, Alexandria, VA 22314/202-274-6666.

Army Posture Statement

The Posture of the Army and the Department of the Army Budget Estimates Fiscal Year 1985 is a joint statement by the Secretary of the Army and the Chief of Staff of the Army. The statement has information on the status and direction of Army forces, the Army budget overview, and Army programs. It is available from: Community Relations Division, Public Affairs, Department of the Army, The Pentagon, Room 2E631, Washington, DC 20310/202-697-5720.

Army Public Affairs

For information on Army programs, personnel and general data, contact: Media Relations Division, Office of the Chief of Public Affairs, Department of the Army, Department of Defense, The Pentagon, Room 2E641, Washington, DC 20310-1507/202-697-7589.

Army Publications

For information on Army publications, contact: Publications, Army Adjutant General Publications Center, Department of the Army, The Pentagon, Room 1B928, Washington, DC 20310/202-695-4739.

Army Recruiting

The U.S. Army Recruiting Command has a variety of recruiting-oriented traveling exhibits, including a mobile theater in expandable vans, equipped for presenting multi-slide, multi-screen shows. Contact: Army Recruiting Support Center, Department of the Army, Department of Defense, Cameron Station, Building 6, Alexandria, VA 22314/202-274-5340.

Army Research and Development Projects

Personnel are available to provide technical consultation, guidance and information on current and long-range research and development projects. Among the planning documents available are:

R&D Long Range Planning—covers Army plans and requirements for the future.

Laboratory Posture Reports—R&D work that has been accomplished during the year by AMC laboratories.

U.S. Army Project Management List—provides command and program manager name, address and telephone number.

Descriptive Summaries of the U.S. Army Development, Test and Evaluation Program—provides a descriptive summary of each program element to be financed for the coming two years.

Science and Technology Objective Guides (STOG)—the principal research, development, testing, and evaluation guidance document for science and technology.

Requirements Documents Listing—a monthly list of approved materiel actuaries.

Catalog of Approved Requirements Documents (CARDS)—lists operational capabilities objectives, currently approved materiel requirements, and materiel requirements deleted for the past 12 months.

Guide for Voluntary Unsolicited Proposals
U.S. Army Research Development and Planning Information

Office Location:
Army Technical Industrial Liaison Office, Army Materiel Command (AMC), (AMCLD-TILO), Hdq., 5001 Eisenhower Ave., Alexandria, VA 22333-0001/202-274-8948.

Army Reserve
The Army Reserve supports the Army contingency plans with units and people. It also conducts projects to improve the environment, work with youth groups and assist the elderly. For additional information on the Reserve's activities and services, contact: Chief, Army Reserve, Department of the Army, DAAR-ZA Washington, DC 20310/202-697-8619.

Army Speaker Programs
Speakers are provided for public audiences interested in presentations on Army matters. The speakers' bureau will arrange for senior Army officials or other appropriate persons to address meetings, conventions, etc. Contact: Speakers Branch, Community Relations Division, Office of the Chief of Public Affairs, Army, The Pentagon, Room 2E631, Washington, DC 20301/202-697-5720.

Arnold Engineering Development Center
This center has test laboratories in which atmospheric conditions, orbital, space flight and ballistic conditions can be simulated. Contact: Arnold Engineering Development Center, Air Force Systems Command, Department of the Air Force, Department of Defense, Arnold Air Force Station, TN 37389/615-455-2611, ext. 7843.

Atmospheric Sciences Laboratory (ASL)
Engaged in the establishment of an atmospheric/environmental technology base for electro-optical military weapons systems, meteorological equipment systems, and intelligence applications; mission focuses upon the enhancement of combat and strategic operations in the following areas: ground combat, air-mobile operations; site defense; ground trafficability; nuclear, biological and chemical operations; and surveillance, target acquisition, night observation and high-energy lasers. ASL is also working to develop automated meteorological data, new atmospheric sensors, improved meteorological techniques, and upper-atmospheric-transmittance modeling. Contact: U.S. Army Atmospheric Sciences Laboratory (ASL), Public Affairs, White Sands Missile Range, White Sands NM 88002/505-678-2811.

Automation and Communications
This office is responsible for all of the Army's Automated Telecommunication System. For information, contact: Assistant Chief of Staff for Information Management, Department of the Army, Washington, DC 20310/202-697-5503.

Aviation Research
Information is available on the research and development of new helicopter systems, support-of-qualification testing of turbine engines, improved Army aircraft support for extreme environments, prototype hardware for fueling and defueling equipment for use in combat areas and solutions to fuel contamination problems. Contact: Army Aviation Research and Development Command (AVRADCOM), Department of Defense, St. Louis, MO 63120/314-263-3901.

Avionics Center
This Center provides research and development on avionics and related equipment. Contact: Naval Avionics Center, Department of the Navy, Department of Defense, Indianapolis, IND 64218/317-359-8471.

Ballistic Missile Defense System Command
This office provides advanced research and development in the fields of radar, interceptors, optics, discrimination data processing, and other technical aspects of ballistic missile defense. Contact: Army Ballistic Missile Defense Systems Command, P.O. Box 1500, Huntsville, AL 35807-3801/205-895-5367.

Ballistic Research Laboratory (BRL)
Basic and applied research in mathematics, physics, chemistry, biophysics, and the engineering sciences related to the solution of problems concerned with ballistics and vulnerability technology. Contact: ARRADCOM Ballistic Research Laboratories, 314 Ryan Building, Aberdeen Proving Ground, MD 21005-5066/301-278-2579.

Beach Erosion Control
The U.S. Army Corps of Engineers designs and constructs projects to control beach and shore erosion to public shores. Contact: U.S. Army Corps of Engineers, DAEN-CWP-F, Washington, D.C. 20314/202-272-0169.

Behavioral and Social Sciences
The U.S. Army Research Institute for Behavioral and Social Sciences conducts research for the military on educational and training methods and organizational effectiveness. It publishes reports and an index. Contact: Army Research Institute for the Behavioral and Social Sciences, Department of the Army, 5001 Eisenhower Ave., Alexandria, VA 22333/202-274-8641.

Budget and Forces Summary
This free publication covers the overall budget for prior and current years, and projections for the

coming year. It contains appropriations for ships, aircraft, etc. Contact: Comptroller of the Navy, NCB32, Crystal City Mall, No. 2, Room 606, Statistical and Report Branch 3224, Washington, D.C. 20350/202-697-7819.

Casualty Services

The Casualty Services Division is responsible for the Army casualty reporting and notification system worldwide. It also runs the survivor and next-of-kin assistance program. For information, contact: Casualty Services Division, Department of the Army, Hoffman Building, Room 920, Alexandria, VA 22331/202-325-7990. A casualty information number (202-325-7990) is available 24 hours a day, seven days a week.

Chemical Propulsion Information Agency (CPIA)

CPIA provides users with products and specialized reference service. The staff can be tasked to provide evaluative engineering and/or analytical service on the following subjects: Solid, liquid, hybrid and electric, rocket and ramjet propulsion systems, fuels, related hardware components, and gun propellants. Data base searches and copies of technical reports are provided on a cost recovery basis. For further information contact: The Johns Hopkins University, Applied Physics Laboratory, Chemical Propulsion Information Agency, Johns Hopkins Road, Laurel, MD 20707/301-992-7307.

Chemical Systems Research and Development Center

Research and development in the fields of chemical, smoke and flame weapons, including defensive aspects; development, production and maintenance engineering related to new and standard chemical, smoke, incendiary, flame and special weapons systems and CBR defense items. Contact: U.S. Army Chemical Systems Research and Development Center, Aberdeen Proving Ground, MD 21010-5423/301-671-4345.

Civil Air Patrol

The Civil Air Patrol is the official civilian auxiliary of the U.S. Air Force. It is a non-profit, benevolent corporation chartered by Congress comprised of volunteers—men and women, boys and girls. For further information contact: HQ Civil Air Patrol, Public Affairs Office, Maxwell Air Force Base, AL 36112.

Civil Engineering

This office is the principal Navy research, development, test and evaluation center for shore and sea-floor facilities and for support of Navy and Marine Corps construction forces. Contact: Naval Civil Engineering Laboratory, Naval Construction Battalion Center, Department of the Navy, Department of Defense, Port Hueneme, CA 93043/805-5336.

Civil Engineering Research

Research and development is conducted on civil engineering aspects systems hardware and techniques, including mobility shelters, environmental engineering, airbase survivability and vulnerability, and numerous other areas. Contact: Public Affairs Office, Air Force Engineering Service Center, Tyndall Air Force Base, FLA 32403/904-283-6476.

Civil Works Programs

The U.S. Army Corps of Engineers conducts many activities under its civil works program. The pamphlet entitled, *Civil Works in Review* describes those activities. Contact: U.S. Army Corps of Engineers, Attn: DAEN-CWM-P, Washington, D.C. 20314/202-272-0162.

Coastal Engineering Research Center

This office conducts research in the materials, utilities, energy, and structures of all buildings except those specifically designed for cold regions and systems-oriented research and development on the life-cycle requirements of military facilities and their management; integrates technological developments into construction; and develops procedures and technology to protect and enhance environmental quality during the course of normal Army missions. Data base searches and copies of technical reports are provided on a cost recovery basis. For further information contact: Army Coastal Engineering Research Center, Office of the Chief of Engineers, Waterways Experiment Station, P.O. Box 631, Vicksburg, Miss. 39180-0631/601-634-2011.

Coastal Systems Center

This office performs research and development, tests and evaluation in support of naval missions and operations that take place primarily in the coastal (Continental Shelf) regions, including mine countermeasures, diving and salvage, coastal and inshore defense swimmer operations and amphibious operations. Contact: Naval Coastal Systems Center, Department of the Navy Department of Defense, Panama City, FL 32407-904-234-4011.

Cold Regions Research

Research is conducted on characteristics and events unique to cold regions, especially winter conditions including the design of facilities, structures and equipment and refining methods for building, traveling, living and working in cold environments. Contact: Army Cold Regions Research and Engineering Laboratory, U.S. Army Corps of Engineers, Department of Defense, 72 Lyme Rd. Hanover, NH 03755-1290/603-646-4100.

Communications and Information Systems

This office is responsible for planning, engineering, installation, operation and maintenance of all assigned Army communications as well as for audiovisual and computer services. Contact: U.S. Army Information Systems Command, Department of the Army, Department of Defense, Fort Huachuca, AZ 85613/602-538-2151.

Communications Research
Information is available on research, development and acquisition of communications tactical data and of command and control systems. Information is also available on research and development on the components and materials of electronic communications, such as integrated circuits, semiconductor devices, display devices, microwave and signal processing, power sources, wire and cable and test maintenance and diagnostic equipment. Contact: Army Communications-Electronics Command (AMSEL-PC-CM) Department of Defense, Fort Monmouth, NJ 07703/201-532-1088.

Computer Security Research and Development
The Department of Defense Computer Security Center is involved with research and development of computer security techniques and procedures. They publish *The Trusted Computer System Evaluation Criteria,* a one-time technical publication dealing with the levels of security in various computer systems, and provides standards of security for both the government and private industry. The 100-page publication is available for free. Contact: Department of Defense Computer Security Center, 9800 Savage Road, Fort Mead, MD 20755-6000/301-859-6883.

Computerized Data Bases
The following data bases are maintained by the Department of Defense.

Aerospace Structures Information Analysis Center (ASIAC)
ASIAC maintains a data base which provides bibliographic information about computer programs, books, journals and conference reports relating to aerospace structures. The Center can search its data base and several commercial systems to provide literature surveys, abstracts, state-of-the-art reviews, technical answers and referrals. ASIAC's most frequently searched topics include: structural analysis, fracture mechanics, fatigue, dynamic response, buckling, vibrations, damping, use of composite materials, stress, strain and loading.

Free searches, print outs and documents are available to U.S. government agencies and contractors upon certification of need to know. In addition to its own data base, ASIAC frequently searches DIALOG, DTIC and CIRC (foreign information). Other services provided by the Center include consulting, loaning of documents and distribution of more than 67 computer software programs designed by DOD. ASIAC will

also help people resolve any problems they may have running the computer software. Contact: AFWAL/FIBRA/ASIAC, Wright Patterson Air Force Base, Dayton, OH 45433/513-255-6688.

Coastal Engineering Bibliographic Data Base
The Coastal Engineering Information Analysis Center has begun automating its data bases containing bibliographic information about books, journals, reports, and eventually computer programs pertaining to coastal engineering. Subject coverage includes wave records, coastal regions, beaches, erosion, ecology, environments, oceanography, tides, estuaries, inlets and hydrodynamics. Searches and printouts are available, generally free of charge. A reproduction fee may be charged for lengthy printouts. The center will loan materials and has thousands of computer software programs available to the public on a cost-recovery basis. CEIAC also provides consulting services to domestic and foreign governments, and information referrals to private companies and individuals. Contact: Coastal Engineering Research Center, U.S. Army Engineers, Waterways Experiment Station, P.O. Box 631, Vicksburg, MS 39180/601-634-2000.

COMPAT/HAZARD-FAILURE Data Base
COMPAT provides rapid access to compatibility data covering the effects of energetic materials (explosives, propellants, pyrotechnics, etc.) on inert materials (polymers, metals, adhesives, coatings, sealants, etc) and vice versa.

COMPAT also contains a supplemental program called HAZARD-FAILURE, which gives information on known deficiencies or problems of polymers, derived from actual experience.

The systems can be accessed easily via remote terminal with a conventional telephone/teletype link. Services are available to the general public on a cost-recovery basis. Use of COMPAT/HAZARD-FAILURE is available either by annual subscription or by single inquiry. A subscription, entitling users to unlimited computer access, costs $400.00. A single inquiry costs $100.00, for which staff will search relevant PLASTEC files plus DTIC, DOE/RECON, NASASTI, DIALOG, and SDC. Subscribers can dial directly in to the PLASTEC data bases or have the Center perform searches. Contact: Armament Research and Development Center, U.S. Army Armament Munitions Chemical command, DRSMCV—SCM—O/D Building 3519N, Dover, NJ 07801/201-724-5859.

Defense Electronic Parts Control Data Base
The Parts Control Automated Support System (PCASS) contains a federally appointed advisory group's (MPCAG's) recommendations about electronic parts to be used in new U.S. defense systems. Historical information about approvals/disapprovals of non-standard/standard electronic

devices such as microcircuits, transistors, diodes, etc. is stored. Data includes input from parts manufacturers, electronic equipment, manufacturers, major defense system contractors and design activities. Searches are done on a cost-recovery basis, and results are printed on microfiche. Hard copy is also available. A Freedom of Information Act is necessary to access data. Contact: DESC/EP, 1507 Wilminston Pike, Dayton, OH 45444/513-296-8207.

Economic Impact Forecast Data Base

Economic Impact Forecast Systems (EIFS) is an information source and analytical tool that allows planners to predict the impacts of proposed changes in an activity on the economy of affected areas. The system, which has statistics for every county in the U.S., can gather this information into any size multicounty region to analyze potential impacts. The data base contains selected Department of Commerce statistics of social and economic characteristics in all U.S. counties and a variety of other types of information, including the Census of Population, Housing, and Manufacturers, the Bureau of Economic Analysis estimates, and County Business Patterson reports. ETIS will conduct searches for non-subscribers. A cost-recovery fee, based on $110.00 per hour computer time, is charged. The average search generally takes 10 minutes. Contact: U.S. Army Corps of Engineers Program, ETIS Support Center, 909 West Nevada Street, Urbana, IL 61801/217-333-1369. Direct access via a remote terminal is available to ETIS subscribers for $100.00 a year plus $90.00 per hour of computer connect time.

Environmental Impact Data Base

The Environmental Impact Computer System (EICS) identifies the consequences of changes in activities occurring in a region and guides the discussion of these consequences in an environmental assessment and impact statement.

Information provided by EICS includes: identification of potential environmental impacts; ramification remarks, which elaborate on each of the impacts of an activity or attribute; and mitigation statements, which provide techniques for minimization, abatement, or avoidance of significant environmental areas such as ecology, health science, air quality, and energy and resource conservation; and 806 basic human activities grouped into seven functional areas such as construction, training and research, development testing and evaluation. Direct access via a remote terminal is available to ETIS subscribers for $100.00 a year, plus $90.00 per hour of computer-connect time. Anyone can become an ETIS subscriber and thereby also obtain direct access to three other data bases maintained by ETIS. ETIS will conduct searches for non-subscribers. A cost-recovery fee, based on $110.00 per hour computer

time, is charged. The average search generally takes ten minutes. Contact: U.S. Army Corps of Engineers Program, ETIS Support Center, 909 West Nevada Street, Urbana, IL 61801/217-333-1369.

Environmental Legislative Data System

The Computer-Aided Environmental Legislative Data System (CELDS) is an information bank of abstracted state and federal environmental laws, regulations and standards. Intended for use by the lay person, legislative information is written in straightforward narrative style. Abstracts are classified in the system by means of 10 environmental sector categories or search fields ranging from air quality to transportation.

Direct access via remote terminal is available to ETIS subscribers for $100.00 a year plus $90.00 per hour of computer connect time. Anyone can become an ETIS subscriber and thereby also obtain direct access to three other data bases maintained by ETIS. A free guest account can be established for individuals and organizations wanting to use the system on a trial basis. ETIS will conduct searches for nonsubscribers. A cost-recovery fee, based on $110.00 per hour computer time, is charged. The average search generally taken ten minutes. Contact: U.S. Army Corps of Engineers Program, ETIS Support Center, 909 West Nevada Street, Urbana, IL 61801/217-333-1369.

Environmental Technical Information Data Base

The Environmental Technical Information System (ETIS) is a computer-based information bank developed by the U.S. Army Corps of Engineers' Construction Engineering Research Laboratory (CERL). ETIS is comprised of three major systems that provide information resources and analysis tools designed as aids in environmental planning and impact statements. The Interactive systems are: the Environmental Impact Computer System (EICS), the Economic Impact Forecast System (EIFS) and the Computer-aided Environmental Legislative Data System (CELDS).

See individual data base listings in this section. Direct access to all ETIS systems is available to the general public for an annual subscription fee of $100.00 a year. Subscribers receive a users manual and can access the system via a terminal in their home or office at their convenience. Subscribers are charged for computer time based on a fee of $90.00 per connect hour. A free guest account can be established for organizations and individuals wanting to use the system on a trial basis. ETIS will conduct searches for non-subscribers. A cost-recovery fee, based on $110.00 per hour computer time, is charged. The average search generally takes 10 minutes. Contact: U.S. Army Corps of Engineers Program, ETIS Support Center, 909 West Nevada Street, Urbana, IL 61801/217-333-1369.

Foreign Geographic Names Data Base

The Branch of Geographic Names (BGN), in collaboration with other federal agencies, has begun to develop a computerized data base to manage and process information about all standardized foreign geographic names approved by BGN. The system is searchable by foreign country and its subdivisions such as listing of a particular country's rivers, populated places, or valleys. Retrievable data include proper name and spelling, longitude/latitude, and type of feature (i.e., city, mountain, administrative area, etc).

The system is not yet fully operational. Eventually, records will exist on all foreign countries. Searches and printouts are expected to be available on a cost-recovery basis. Contact: Chief, Geographic Names Branch, Defense Mapping Agency, Hydro-Graphic Topal-Graphic Center, Washington, DC 20315/ 202-227-3880.

Government and Industry Data Exchange Data Bases

See entry titled "Government and Industry Data Exchange Program" in this section.

Infrared Data Base

The Infrared Information and Analysis Center (IRIA) maintains a data base with bibliographic citations and abstracts for technical literature pertaining to electro-optics technology, with emphasis on military infrared research and development.

The general public can obtain searches and printouts of unclassified information stored in IRIA's data base. U.S. government agencies and contractors with a need to know can obtain searches of the entire data base. A cost-recovery fee is assessed for individuals and organizations that are not subscribers to IRIA's services. Contact: IRIA, Environmental Research Institute of Michigan, Box 8618, Ann Arbor, MI 48107/ 313-994-1200.

Metals and Ceramics Technologies Data Base

Metals and Ceramics Information Center (MCIC), a DOD-sponsored Information Center, maintains a bibliographic data base for worldwide literature pertaining to metals and ceramics technologies. Major emphasis is placed on structural alloys, and retrievable information includes citations, abstracts, and analyses of technical documents from government reports and worldwide open literature. The scope includes selected metals, ceramics, and composite materials of interest to DOD and its contracts and material suppliers. Information cited on all three types of materials covers coatings, environmental effects, physical properties, materials applications, test methods, sources/suppliers, specifications, design characteristics, and various fabrication processes.

MCIC maintains both a computerized and manual data base. MCIS will do searches for the general public. Simple searches are done free of charge, while more complex requests are assessed a cost-recovery fee. DOD agencies and contractors can get direct access to the data base through the Defense Technical Information Center's DTIC on-line system (DROLS). Contact: General Information, Technical Inquiries, Batelle—Columbus Laboratories, 505 King Avenue, Columbus, OH 43201-2693, 614-424-5000/614-424-6376.

Natural Resource Management System

The Natural Resource Management System (NRMS) contains information and statistics about 400 recreational areas in the U.S. Information provided about each site includes data on: camping, picnicking, boating, fishing, land and water resources, facilities, location and travel distance, ownership, use by month in recreation days, staffing, activities pursued by visitors, fees charged and much more. Information can be retrieved by site name, geographical areas and other data cited. Searches and printouts are available free of charge. The Corps of Engineers also has free attractive brochures with maps and information about each of its sites. Contact: Army Corps of Engineers, HQ USACE (DAEN-CWO-R), 20 Massachusetts Avenue, N.W., Washington, DC 20314/202-272-0247.

Pest Management Data Base

The Defense Pest Management Information Analysis Center (DPMIAC), a Department of Defense sponsored center, maintains a bibliographic data base for worldwide literature in the field of pest management and natural resources. Currently 85 percent of the citations cover military and medical entomology, but the natural-resource entries are increasing. U.S. government agencies and certified contractors are eligible for free searches and printouts. Searches are performed for others by the Center, but only on a cost-recovery basis. DTIC users can obtain direct access to the DPMIAC data base. Contact: Chief, Defense Pest Management Information Analysis Center, Forest Glenn Section, WRAMC, Washington, DC 20307/301-427-5365.

Plastics, Adhesives and Organic Matrix Composites Data Base

Plastics Technical Evaluation Center Automated Bibliographic Services (PLASTEC), a DOD-sponsored information and analysis center, maintains a bibliographic data base with abstracts for worldwide technical literature related to plastics, adhesives and organic matrix composites.

In addition to its own bibliographic data base, PLASTEC has on-line access to DTIC, DOE/ RECON, NASA STI, DIALOG and SDC. For a cost-recovery fee, PLASTEC will perform literature searches in all six systems. The fee is based on

vendor charge plus $50.00 per hour to cover staff time for searching and refining output. The PLAS-TEC data base is available on-line to DTIC users. Contact: Plastics Technical Evaluation Center (PLASTEC), U.S. Army Armament Research Development Command, Dover, NJ 07801/201-724-4222.

Reliability Characteristics of Components and Systems Data Base

Reliability Analysis Center (RAC) maintains five data bases with bibliographic and technical information pertaining to the reliability characteristics of components and systems. The data bases are: VLSI, on very large scale circuits; IC, on integrated circuits; Hybrid Circuits; Non-Electronic Devices; and Failures Related to Static Electricity (FRSC).

Searches and printouts are available on a cost-recovery basis. Generally, a bibliographic search runs about $125 to $150.00. Contact: Reliability Analysis Center, RADC/RAC, Griffiss AFB, NY 13441/315-330-4151.

Software Engineering Bibliographic Data Base

The Data and Analysis Center for Software, a DOD-sponsored information center, maintains the Software Engineering Bibliographic Data Base (SEDB) for technical literature pertaining to software engineering.

Searches and printouts are available for a flat fee of $50.00. Searches which return no references are only $20.00. Contact: Data and Analysis Center for Software, Rome Air Development Center, ISISI, Griffiss AFB, NY 13441/315-336-0937.

Software Engineering Data Base

The Data and Analysis Center for Software, a DOD-sponsored information center, maintains a data base with information about many software development and maintenance programs. The data base, Software Engineering Data (SED), contains data relevant to software reliability; software errors, faults and failures; software costs and productivity; and methodologies and tools for software development maintenance.

Searches and printouts are available for a flat fee of $50.00. Searches which return no references are only $20.00. Contact: Data and Analysis Center for Software, Rome Air Development Center, ISISI, Griffiss AFB, NY 13441/315-336-0937.

Software Engineering Research Projects Data Base

Software Engineering Research Projects (SERP) contains description of research projects designed to further the state-of-the-art in software engineering. Projects relating to data collection and analysis, development of quality metrics, analyses of developmental methodologies, the development

or evaluation of programming languages, and model validation are representative of those included in the data base.

Searches and printouts are available for a flat fee of $50.00. Searches which return no references are only $20.00. Contact: Data and Analysis Center for Software, RADC/ISISI, Griffiss AFB, NY 13441/315-336-0937.

Soils Series Data Base

Soils Information Retrieval Systems (SIRS) provides interactive data retrieval of soils series data. The data is compiled from the Department of Agriculture's Soil Conservation Service's (SCS) reports on the characteristics and interpretive properties of all soils in the United States.

Direct access is available to ETIS subscribers for $100.00 a year, plus $90.00 per hour of connect time. Anyone can become an ETIS subscriber and, thereby, also gain access to three other data bases maintained by ETIS. A free guest account can be established for individuals and organizations wanting to use the system on a trial basis. ETIS will conduct searches for non-subscribers. A cost-recovery fee, based on $110.00 per hour computer time, is charged. The average search generally takes 10 minutes. Contact: U.S. Army Corps of Engineers, ETIS Support Center, 909 West Nevada Street, Urbana, IL 61801/312-333-1369.

Tactical Weapons Guidance and Control Data Base

The Tactical Weapons Guidance and Control Information Analysis Center (GACIAC) is a Department of Defense Information Analysis Center which maintains a bibliographic data base of technical information related to the guidance and control of tactical contact weapons. These include missiles, rockets, bombs, submunitions, projectiles and munition-dispensing canisters.

The data base is available on-line to anyone having access to the DTIC on-line data base. The Center serves only Department of Defense agencies and government contractors. Generally, the Center will perform one free search for a contractor needing information. Qualified organizations can subscribe to the Center's services for $300 to $500.00 a year. This entitles them to all the Center's products and four hours of free computer time. Contact: GACIAC, IIT Research Institute, 10 West 35th Street, Chicago, IL 60616/312-567-4345.

Topographic Map Data Base

The Defense Mapping Agency Hydrographic/Topographic Center (DMAHTIC) provides a data base containing maps and data about most of the earth's surface, including: terrain, rivers, coastal and ocean areas, lighthouses, buildings and city plans.

DMAHTIC will perform searches for government contractors, universities, government employees, and selected others. The searches are done on a cost-recovery basis and requests must be in writing. All others must contact NTIS for access to DMAHTIC information. Contact: For government contractors, universities, government employees, and selected others—Data Automation, DMAHTIC, 6500 Brookes Lane, Washington, DC 20315, 202-227-3360; and for all others—National Technical Information Service, 5285 Port Royal Road, Springfield, VA 22161/703-487-4600.

Concrete Technology Information Analysis Center (CTIAC)
CTIAC provides users with products and specialized reference service. The staff can be tasked to provide evaluative engineering and/or analytical service on the following subjects: Concrete, reinforced concrete, reinforcing materials, cements, mixtures, construction materials, aging (materials), loads (force), fracture (mechanics), deformation, degradation, chemical analysis, repair, evaluation, maintenance, rehabilitation. Data base searches and copies of technical reports are provided on a cost recovery basis. For further information contact: U.S. Army Engineer Waterways Experiment Station, Attn: CTIAC, P.O. Box 631, Vicksburg, MS 39180-0631/601-634-3264.

Conscientious Objectors
For general information on conscientious objectors, including reclassification and discharge data, contact: Military Personnel and Force Management, Department of Defense, The Pentagon, Room 3C975, Washington, DC 20301/202-697-9525.

Construction Engineering
Research is conducted on coastal processes, waves, tides, currents, and coastal materials as they affect navigation, recreation, flood and storm protection, beach erosion control, and structures in the coastal zones. The ecological effects of the Corps's coastal zone activities are also studied. Contact: Army Construction Engineering Research Laboratory, Office of the Chief of Engineers, Department of Defense, P.O. Box 4005, Champaign, IL 61820-1305/217-352-6511, ext. 400.

Consumer Programs
For information on Air Force consumer programs, which include disaster relief assistance, air shows, timber and timber product sales, use of public picnic areas, and water recreational facilities, contact: Community Relations Division, Office of Public Affairs, Department of the Air Force, The Pentagon, Room 4A120, Washington, DC 20330/202-697-4008.

Contract Disputes
The Board of Appeals handles appeals of unusual difficulty, dispute or precedential significance re-

garding Defense contracts. Contact: Armed Services Board of Contract Appeals, 200 Stovall St., Hoffman Bldg. 2, Room 9N41, Alexandria, VA 22332/202-325-8000.

Contractors for the Department of Defense
The *100 Companies Receiving the Largest Dollare Volume of Prime Contract Awards* report is published annually by the Office of the Secretary of Defense. It presents summary data about the Department of Defense's top 100 prime contractors for the previous fiscal year. A variety of data is provided about these companies and their subsidiaries, such as dollar amount received, ranking of companies, and a breakdown of dollars awarded subsidiaries. The 21-page publication (# P01) costs $12.00. Contact: Director for Information Operations and Reports, Washington Headquarters Services, The Pentagon, Room 1C535, Washington, DC 20301/202-694-5298.

Correction of Air Force Records
The Air Force can take action to correct Air Force records in order to remove an error or to redress an injustice. For records information, contact: Air Force Board for the Correction of Military Records, Department of the Air Force, Department of Defense, SAF/MICBS, Crystal Square 4, Room 201, Arlington, Va. 20330/202-692-4733.

Correction of Army Records
The Army can take action to correct Army records in order to remove an error or to redress an injustice. For information on the status of the application, contact: Army Board for Correction of Military Records, Department of the Army, The Pentagon, Room 1E517 Washington, DC 20310/202-697-4254.

Correction of Naval Records
The Navy can take action to correct Naval or military records in order to remove an error or to redress an injustice. For information on the status of a case under consideration, contact: Board for correction of Naval Records, Department of the Navy, Washington, DC 20370/202-694-1316.

Data and Analysis Center for Software (DACS)
DACS provides users with products and specialized reference service. The staff can be tasked to provide evaluative engineering and/or analytical service on *Software Engineering and Technology*. DACS maintains a computer database for data collected on software development and maintenance programs. Subsets of the data are available for research purposes and can be obtained on hardcopy and magnetic tape. Data base searches and copies of technical reports are provided on a cost recovery basis. For further information contact: Rome Air Development Center, COED, Griffiss AFB, NY 13441/315-330-3395.

Defense Advanced Research Projects Agency (DARPA)

DARPA supports research and technology development for multi-service applications and potential new defense missions. It pursues high-risk, high-payoff types of programs. Examples of these include research on continuous tracking of a Simulated Quiet Submarine; Aircraft Undersea Sound Experiment; Self-Initiated Antiaircraft Missile; Rapid Solidification Technology; Two-Color Focal Plane Array; Space Defense and Surveillance; and Cruise Missile Technologies. Contact: Defense Advanced Research Projects Agency, Department of Defense, 1400 Wilson Blvd., Arlington, VA 22209/202-695-0192

Defense Audiovisual Material

For information on all U.S. Department of Defense audiovisual material, production, acquisition, operational, testing and evaluation, depository and distribution activities, contact: DAVA-N-D, Norton Air Force Base, CA 92409/714-382-2393.

Defense Communication Publications

For an index to, and information on available publications from the Defense Communications Agency, contact: Publications, Defense Communications Agency, Code 316 Washington, DC 20305/202-692-6965.

Defense Contract Administration Service (DCAS)

This is a post-award service organization responsible for performing contract administration services, including production surveillance, quality assurance, financial services, disbursements and other post-award functions. DCAS regions and management areas are located in the principal sectors of industrial concentration throughout the United States. For a listing of DCAS regional contacts and for further information, contact: Defense Logistics Agency, Deputy Director Acquisition Management, Cameron Station, Alexandria, VA 22314/202-274-7091.

Defense Contract Audits

The Defense Contract Audit Agency performs all necessary contract audit functions for the U.S. Department of Defense. It provides accounting services to all Defense components responsible for procurement and contract administration. These services include evaluating the acceptability of costs claimed or proposed by contractors and reviewing the efficiency and economy of contractor operations. Contact: Defense Contract Audit Agency, Cameron Station, Building 4, Alexandria, VA 22314/202-274-7288.

Defense Fuel

The Defense Fuel Supply Center publishes booklets describing the type, quantity and prices of petroleum fuel products purchased by the U.S. Department of Defense and other Federal agencies. Free brochures are available. Contact: Public Affairs, Defense Fuel Supply Center, DFSC-AP Cameron Station, Alexandria, VA 22314/202-274-6489.

Defense Intelligence Agency Publications

For a list of Defense Intelligence Agency unclassified publications, write to: Freedom of Information Services, Defense Intelligence Agency, Department of Defense, The Pentagon, Attention: RTS4(FOIA) Washington, DC 20301-6111/202-393-3910.

Defense Language Institute Foreign Language Center (DLIFLC)

DLIFLC is one of the largest language training institutions in the world. It provides effective and economical foreign language training for members of the United States Armed Forces and other government agencies. Currently 39 languages and dialects are taught by DLIFLC and the school is capable of arranging training for approximately 57 languages. Almost 600 foreign born instructors are employed to train students of all services in foreign tongues and cultures. The holdings of our academic library—about 100,000 books and periodicals in 50 different foreign languages—are available through the national inter-library loan program. Local librarians can furnish loan information. There is also a nonresident division that provides assistance to government and private agencies worldwide. The nonresident courses are available for sale. Contact: Nonresident Division, Defense Language Institute, Foreign Language Center, Presidio of Monterey, California 93940/408-242-8689.

Defense Logistics Agency, Films

For information on films available for public showing to present and potential contractors, contact: Headquarters, Defense Logistics Agency Department of Defense, Cameron Station, Room 3C547, Alexandria, VA 22314/202-274-6075.

Defense Logistics Agency Introduction

This free publication describes the Agency's operations, supply services, supply centers, defense depots, contract administration services and technical and logistics services. It tells how to do business with the Agency and lists major categories of material under the cognizance of each of the six supply centers. Contact: Public Affairs, (DLA-B) Defense Logistics Agency, Department of Defense, Cameron Station, Alexandria, VA 22304-6100/202-274-6135.

Free publications from the Defense Logistics Agency include:

DLA Index to Forms
DLA Index to Publications

How To Do Business With the Defense Logistics Agency
An Identification of Commodities Purchased by the
  Defense Logistics Agency

Contact: DLA-XPD, Department of Defense, Cameron Station, Building 6, Door 21, Alexandria, VA 22304-6100/202-274-6011.

Defense Management Journal

This quarterly publication is designed for the middle and senior management levels of the U.S. Department of Defense, industry and academia. It covers manpower, logistics, personnel, policy, research and development, and administration. Available for $9.00 per year from Superintendent of Documents, Government Printing Office, Washington, DC 20402/202-783-3238. For information, contact: *Defense Management Journal,* OASD (MI&L), Room 5A201, Defense Logistics Agency, Department of Defense, Cameron Station, Alexandria, VA 22314-6182/202-274-5757.

Defense Mapping School

This school provides training to the military on mapping, geodesy, and charting. Subjects range from basic maps courses to geodetic surveying and terrain analysis. The school offers an apprenticeship program recognized by the U.S. Department of Labor. Contact: Defense Mapping School, Attention: PBO Defense Mapping Agency, Department of Defense, Fort Belvoir, VA 22060-5828/703-664-2383.

Defense Organizational and Functions Guidebook

This publication outlines the functions of the major components of the U.S. Department of Defense. Each functional statement cites the pertinent charter, which provides more detailed information on the authorities and responsibilities of each organization. An organizational chart is also available. Contact: Directorate for Organizational and Management Planning, Department of Defense, The Pentagon, Room 3A326, Washington, DC 20301-1100/202-697-9330.

Defense Research and Development

The U.S. Department of Defense Program for Research, Development and Acquisition is a statement by the Office of Defense Research and Engineering to the Congress in support of a budget request for defense research. It includes information on the major research and development areas, military equipment, international initiatives, strategic and tactical programs, and funding summaries. Contact: Office of the Assistant Secretary of Defense (Public Affairs), Public Correspondence Division, Department of Defense, The Pentagon, Room 2E777, Washington, DC 20301-1400/202-697-5737.

Defense Systems Management College

The College conducts advanced courses of study for military officers and civilian personnel in program management. It also disseminates information on new methods and practices in program management. The College publishes a bimonthly newsletter, *Program Manager,* and *The Defense Systems Management Review,* a quarterly publication. Both publications include articles and reports on policies, trends and events that affect program management and defense systems acquisition. Contact: Defense Systems Management College, Fort Belvoir, VA 22060-5426/703-664-5082.

Defense Technology and Applications

Defense 84, a monthly publication produced by the Department of Defense, covers all aspects of defense technology and applications. Each August issue is devoted to strategic defense initiatives. The publication is distributed free of charge to DOD agencies and contractors. Others can subscribe for $23 per year from the Superintendent of Documents, U.S. Government Printing Office, Washington, DC 20402, 202-783-3238. Contact: American Forces Information Service, 1735 North Lynn Street, Room 210, Arlington, VA 22209/202-696-5294.

Defense Utilization and Disposal Manual

This publication includes the policy and procedures for the disposing of Defense Department surplus property. Contact: Property Disposal Division, Defense Logistics Agency, DLA-SMP Cameron Station, Alexandria, VA 22314/202-274-6763.

Department of Defense Publications

These Department of Defense publications give descriptions of new programs and budget information.

Report of Military Posture by the Chairman of the Joint
  Chiefs of Staff—$4.50
Defense Department Annual Report to Congress—$9.50.

These publications are available from the Superintendent of Documents, Government Printing Office, Washington, DC 20402/202-783-3238.

Dependents Schools

These schools provide education from kindergarten through grade 12, to eligible minor dependents of military and civilian personnel of the U.S. Department of Defense stationed overseas. Contact: Dependents Schools, Department of Defense, 2461 Eisenhower Ave., Alexandria, VA 22331-1100/202-325-0188.

Development and Readiness Command Publications

An Index of Army Development and Readiness Command (DARCOM) Administrative Publications is available from Publication Services AMCAG-AP-DE-S, U.S. Army Materiel Command, Department of the Army, Department of Defense, 5001 Eisenhower Ave., Alexandria, VA 22333/202-274-9663.

Dictionary of American Naval Fighting Ships

This series presents brief histories, arranged alphabetically by name, of all ships commissioned in the U.S. Navy from 1775 to the present. Appendices include discussions and tabulated data on specific ship types, and other related subjects. For prices of individual volumes and to order, contact: Government Printing Office, Superintendent of Documents, Washington, DC 20402/202-783-3238.

Dictionary of Military and Associated Terms

This Dictionary is the U.S. Department of Defense bible for definitions of military terms. It also includes the NATO glossary. Available for $12.00 at the Superintendent of Documents, Government Printing Office, Washington, DC 20402/202-783-3238. For information, contact: Terminology Branch, Personnel Plans and Policy Division, J-1, 1A724C, Washington, DC 20301/202-694-6493

Direct Payments

The program described below provides financial assistance directly to individuals, private firms and other private institutions to encourage or subsidize a particular activity.

Selected Reserve Educational Assistance Program

Objectives: To stimulate enlistment of non-prior service individuals into the selected reserve.

Eligibility: Individuals who have never previously served in the Armed Forces of the United States who enlist in the selected reserve for a term of 6 years.

Range of Financial Assistance: $4,000.

Contact: Deputy Assistant Secretary of Defense, Reserve Affairs, Office of the Assistant Secretary of Defense, (Manpower, Reserve Affairs and Logistics) Pentagon, Washington, D.C. 20301/202-697-4334.

Directives and Instructions

For research and reference service on U.S. Department of Defense directives and instructions, and editorial service on all U.S. Department of Defense publications, contact: The Directives Division, Washington Headquarters Service, Department of Defense, The Pentagon, Room 2A286, Washington, DC 20301/202-697-4111. For free copies of the quarterly index, *DOD Directives & DOD Instructions,* contact: Naval Publications and Forms Center, Department of Defense, 5801 Tabor Ave., Philadelphia, PA 19120/215-697-3321.

Diving Manuals—U.S. Navy

These publications constitute the latest edition of the *Navy Diving Manual,* recognized around the world as one of the most authoritative reference works on the subject. All volumes are looseleaf and punched for three-ring binders.

Volume 1:	Air Diving	$11.00
Volume 2:	Mixed-Gas Diving	$12.00

Both volumes are available from the Superintendent of Documents, Government Printing Office, Washington, DC 20402/202-783-3238.

DOD Budget Reports

Four publications describing the DOD budget for the current fiscal year are available by contacting the National Technical Information Center, Department of Commerce, 5285 Port Royal Road, Springfield, VA 22161/703-487-4600.

Program Acquisition Costs by Weapons System
PB85155307/AS $10.00
Construction Programs (C-1)
PB85155315/AS $15.00
Research, Development, Technical Evaluation Program (R-1)
PB85155323/AS $7.00
Procurement Programs (P-1)
PB85155331/AS $9.00

Drug and Alcohol Abuse in the Military

The Office of Drug Abuse has identification, treatment and educational programs on drug and alcohol abuse. It also provides quarterly reports that include data on the number of people identified, rejected, discharged, tried and courtmartialed by the military. Contact: Office of Professional Affairs and Quality Assurance, Health Affairs, Department of Defense, The Pentagon, Room 3D171, Washington, DC 20301/202-695-6800.

DTIC (Defense Technical Information Center)

DTIC is the clearinghouse for the U.S. Department of Defense's collection of research and development in science and technology and covering subjects that range from aeronautics to zoology. The Center can answer three basic questions related to research, development, testing and evaluation: (1) What research is being planned? (2) What research is currently being performed? and (3) What results were realized by completed research?

There are four data bases at DTIC:

1. R&D Program Planning (RDPP)—planned research at the project and task level. (This data base is in the process of being revised.)
2. R&T Work Unit Information System (WUIS) Data Base—a collection of technically oriented summaries describing research and technology projects currently in progress.
3. Technical Report (TR) Bibliographic Data Base—a collection of bibliographic citations of formally documented scientific and the technical results of Defense-sponsored R&D, testing and evaluation.
4. Independent Research and Development (IR&D) Data Base—describes the technical programs being performed by U.S. Department of Defense contractors as part of their independent research and development programs. This is considered proprietary information and is exempt from disclosure under the Freedom of Information Act.

DTIC services registered users only. For information on registration, see "DTIC—How Does a Potential User Become Eligible?" in this section.

DTIC Data Base Publications and Services
For information on any of the following, contact: Defense Technical Information Center (DTIC) Defense Logistics Agency, Department of Defense, Cameron Station, B St., Building 5, Alexandria, VA 22304-6145/202-274-6871.

Technical Abstract Bulletin (TAB)—classified biweekly listing of all new classified and unclassified but limited scientific and technical reports received by DTIC.

Technical Abstract Bulletin Indexes—issued simultaneously with TAB to assist in identifying accessions of particular interest. Available in paper copy only, there are seven indexes: Corporate Author, Monitoring Agency, Subject, Title, Personal Author, Contract Number, Report Number, and Release Authority.

Automatic Document Distribution Programs—microfiche copies of newly accessioned reports selected according to a user's subject interest, published every two weeks.

Report (Demand) Bibliography—a tailor-made literature search on a particular subject conducted at the request of a user.

Current Awareness Bibliography Program—a customized, automated bibliography service based on the recurring subject needs of DTIC users.

Direct Response Bibliography—a tailor-made response to a specific request.

Bibliography of Bibliographies—publicizes DTIC-scheduled bibliographies, also bibliographies received from military organizations and their educational and industrial contractors.

Technical Vocabulary

DTIC Retrieval and Indexing Terminology—used to index DTIC's scientific and technical literature.

Recurring Management Information System Reports—compiled monthly, quarterly, semiannually or annually from management information systems with formats designed by recipient organizations. They may be requested on a demand basis or with an automated receiving procedure.

Central Registry—a central file of user-authorized access to Defense scientific and technical information.

DTIC—How Does a Potential User Become Eligible?
DTIC provides a Joint Service Regulation called *Certification and Registration for Access to DoD Scientific and Technical Information*. This regulation assists organizations in determining their eligibility for services. It also outlines procedures for registration and includes an explanation of the various forms required to request services and other informational materials concerning programs, products and services offered by the Center. Contact: Defense Technical Information Center, Attn: DTIC-DDR-B, Cameron Station, Alexandria, VA 22304-6145/202-274-6871.

DTIC Referral Data Base
This is a referral data base of information on specialized scientific and technical government-sponsored activities with the capability of serving the defense community. An unclassified directory is available from both DTIC and the National Technical Information Service. It includes information centers, specialized libraries, information exchanges and offices, data base depositories, laboratories, testing directories and similar research facilities. Each entry gives mission, subject areas, services and materials, publications issued, key personnel, access limitations, all updated and verified prior to publication of a new edition. Prices vary according to the size of the document. Refer to Order no. ADA138 400. Contact: DTIC, Defense Logistics Agency, Department of Defense, Cameron Station, B St., Building 5, Alexandria, VA 22304-6145/202-274-6904.

DTIC Tours and Briefings
Visitors are welcomed to DTIC by a tour and briefing held the second Tuesday of every month at 9 A.M. Contact: Defense Technical Information Center (DTIC-V), Office of User Services, Cameron Station, Alexandria, VA 22304-6145/202-272-6728.

DTIC Videotape
A 12-minute videotape called *Your Partner in R&D* depicts DTIC operations, products and services. Copies of the videotape are available on a no-fee loan basis. Contact: Defense Technical Information Center (DTIC-V) Office of User Services, Cameron Station, Alexandria, VA 22304-6145/202-274-6434.

Dugway Proving Ground
This facility conducts field and lab tests to evaluate chemical and radiological weapons and defense systems and materiel, as well as biological defense research. Contact: Public Affairs Dugway Proving Ground, U.S. Army, Department of Defense, Dugway, UT 84022/801-831-2116.

Eastern Space and Missile Center
The Eastern Space and Missile Test Center research and development central procurement program is confined primarily to range test instrumentation. Principal interests are: test range instrumentation; procurement within this broad field may require research, development and product engineering, or any combination of these tasks in radar, telemetry, electro-optics, range instrumentation, ships, aircraft, impact location, data handling, data reduction, communications, range and mission control, range safety, weather timing and firing, and frequency control and analysis. Contact: Public Affairs, Eastern Space and Missile Center, Patrick Air Force Base, FL 32925/305-494-7731.

Economic Adjustment

Economic adjustment programs are devised for alleviating the serious social and economic impact of major U.S. Department of Defense activities, such as base closures, establishment of new installations, conversion of in-house activities to contractual services, or cutbacks or expansion of activities. The Office of Economic Adjustment assists local communities, areas or states affected by U.S. Department of Defense actions. The following free publications are available in limited quantities:

*Communities in Transition—Communities Response to
   Reduced Defense Activity*
Acquiring Former Military Bases
Planning Civilian Reuse of Former Military Bases
*Economic Recovery, Community Response to Defense
   Decisions to Close Bases.*
Defense Procurement and Economic Development

Contact: Office of Economic Adjustment, Department of Defense, The Pentagon, Room 3D968, Washington, DC 20301-4000/202-697-9155.

Electromagnetic Technology Resources

The Public Affairs/Public Correspondence Office of Department of Defense (DOD), is the clearinghouse for public information and correspondence for DOD. The staff can provide general, basic information about electromagnetic technology including annual reports, newsletters, and information sheets. They can also make referrals regarding more specific inquiries. Contact: U.S. Department of Public Affairs/Public Correspondence, R2E777, Washington, DC 20301/202-697-5737.

Electronics Research

For information on research and development associated with communications, communications electronics, intelligence equipment, electronic warfare, aviation electronics, combat surveillance, target acquisition and night vision equipment, identification friend-or-foe systems, automatic data processing, radar (other than weapon use), meteorological and electronic radiological detection materiel, batteries and electric power generation equipment, contact: Army Electronics Research and Development Command (ERADCOM), Department of Defense, 2800 Powder Mill Rd., Adelphi, MD 20783/202-394-1076.

Electronic Systems Command

This office is responsible for the research and development, testing and evaluation for command, control, and communications of undersea and space surveillance; electronic warfare; navigational aids; electronic test equipment; and electronic materials, components and devices. For information contact: Naval Electronic Systems Command, Department of the Navy, Department of Defense, Washington, DC 20363-5100/202-692-6413.

Electronics System Research

Research and development is conducted on command control systems and related equipment; systems for data collection, transmission and display; and the development of weapon command and executive control associated with Air Force aerospace operations. Contact: Electronics Systems Division, Air Force Systems Command, Department of the Air Force, Department of Defense, Hanscom Air Force Base, Bedford, MA 01731/617-861-4973.

Energy Conservation

This office maintains the Defense energy program, environmental and safety policy, and international civil emergency program; provides guidance to the military on the availability of petroleum; represents the U.S. Department of Defense on petroleum matters; conducts U.S. Department of Defense energy consumption studies; and provides information on energy conservation developments. Contact: Defence Energy Programs, Manpower Installations and Logistics, Office of the Assistant Secretary of Defense, The Pentagon, Washington, DC 20301-4000/202-697-2500.

Engineer Museum

The U.S. Army Engineer Museum is open to the public. Its historical collection reflects the contributions of the Corps of Engineers. Contact: Army Engineer Museum, 16th St. and Belvoir Rd., Building 1000, Fort Belvoir, VA 22060/703-664-6104.

Environmental Programs

The environmental mission of the U.S. Army Corps of Engineers is to carry out the mandate of the National Environmental Policy Act with regard to its civil works and military programs, to "... encourage productive and enjoyable harmony between man and his environment; to promote efforts which will prevent or eliminate damage to the environment and biosphere and stimulate the health and welfare of man; and to enrich the understanding of the ecological systems and natural resources important to the nation." Each program the Corps undertakes is preceded by an environmental impact statement which explains in detail the effects that the project will have on man and the environment. Contact: U.S. Army Corps of Engineers, Attn: DAEN-CWZ-P, Washington, D.C. 20314/202-272-0103.

Equipping the Army of the Eighties

This is an annual statement to the Congress that describes the military hardware used by the Army. Available from: Research, Development and Acquisition, Department of the Army, Department of Defense, The Pentagon, 3E412, Washington, DC 20310/202-697-7975.

Explosive Ordnance Disposal

This office is responsible for research and development on the technology base for the consolidated U.S. Department of Defense explosive ordnance disposal (EOD) mission. It defines tool and technology requirements for the development program; it also conducts research and development on EOD tools and equipment for all the Armed Services. Contact: Naval Explosive Ordnance Disposal Technology Center, Department of the Navy, Department of Defense, Indian Head, MD 20640/301-743-4545.

Export Control of U.S. Defense Articles and Services

The Office of Munitions Control (OMC) administers export control of defense articles and services originating in the U.S. It provides licenses and other forms of approval for export. This office can answer questions about whether a product of service is considered to have military implications. Staff will provide companies with advice in the form of written evaluations about licensing approval of their products or services. This office recommends two publications. The *International Traffic in Arms Regulations* (22CFR, parets 121–128) is the operational guide for OMC which contains all the regulations, policies, and procedures for the functioning of OMC. It also explains how to prepare for licenses and agreements. The cost of this guide (order #: 044-000-01603-6) is $4.50 and can be ordered from the Government Printing Office, Superintendent of Documents, Washington, DC 20402, 202-783-3238. The *OMC Newsletter* is published irregularly and contains information about regulations and policy changes. It is available to all manufacturers and exporters registered with OMC as well as organizations involved in munitions exportation. The 8-page publication is available free of charge, and back issues are available. Contact: Office of Munitions Control, PM/MC, SA-6, Room 800, U.S. Department of State, Washington, DC 20520/202-235-9756.

Financing Foreign Military Sales

Foreign military sales financing is provided by the U.S. government in the form of either direct loans or guarantees of Federal Financing Bank loans to assist in the purchase by foreign governments of equipment and services through U.S. government channels or directly from contractors. Contact: Defense Security Assistance Agency, Department of Defense, The Pentagon, Room 4E841, Washington, DC 20301-2800/202-695-3291.

Flight Test Center

The Center supports advanced development programs in four principal areas:

1. Flight testing and evaluation of all new aircraft planned for inventory production and aerospace research vehicles, including fixed wing, VTOL, STOL, lifting body, and other experimental manned flight vehicles.
2. Training experimental and aerospace research pilots.
3. Development, testing and evaluation of new parachutes (Personnel and Cargo), deceleration and retardation devices, and aerial delivery and recovery systems.
4. Development, testing, and evaluation of rocket propulsion systems, including static test of complete engines, and investigation and synthesis of new propellant formulations—liquid, solid, and hybrid.

Contact: Air Force Flight Test Center, Air Force Systems Command, Department of the Air Force, Department of Defense, Edwards Air Force Base, CA 93523/805-277-3510.

Flood Plain Management

The Army Corps of Engineers provides information, guidance, and technical assistance to nonfederal groups in developing regulations for flood plain use. The flood plain management services help communities understand the extent and magnitude of the flood hazards in their areas. Contact: Army Corps of Engineers, Department of the Army, Department of Defense, Attn: DAEN-CWP-F, Washington, DC 20314/202-272-0169.

Foreign Area Studies Series

This is a series of books that deal with a particular foreign country, describing and analyzing its economic, military and political and social systems and institutions, and the ways they are shaped by cultural factors. Origins and traditions of the people and their social and national attitudes are featured. For a list of the books and prices, contact: the Government Printing Office, Superintendent of Documents, Washington, DC 20402/202-783-3238.

Foreign Military Affairs

For information on negotiating for U.S. military installations, properties, and personnel in foreign countries, contact: Foreign Military Rights Affairs, International Security Affairs, Department of Defense, The Pentagon, Room 4D830, Washington, DC 20301/202-695-6386.

Foreign Military Construction Sales

Through the Foreign Military Sales program, the U.S. Army Corps of Engineers provides engineering design and construction services to various foreign governments. All Corps costs under this program are borne by the host country. Contact: U.S. Army Corps of Engineers, Attn: DAEN-ECZ, Washington, D.C. 20314/202-272-0387.

Foreign Military Sales (FMS) Program

This program sells defense articles, and defense services to foreign governments. Contact: Defense Security Assistance Agency, Department of Defense, The Pentagon, Room 4E841, Washington, DC 20301-2800/202-695-3291.

Foreign Military Sales and Military Assistance (FACTS)

This free annual publication includes information and statistics on the Foreign Military Sales (FMS), the Military Assistance (MAP), and the International Military Education and Training programs. Contact: Defense Security Assistance Agency, COMPT/DMD, Department of Defense, The Pentagon, Room 4B659, Washington, DC 20301-2800/202-697-2440.

Freedom of Information

For a list of Freedom of Information contacts within the Department of Defense and the three services, contact: Office of Public Affairs, Freedom of Information and Security Review, Department of Defense, The Pentagon, Room 2C757, Washington, DC 20301/202-697-1180. See also "Freedom of Information Act."

Government and Industry Data Exchange Program

GIDEP (Government Industry Data Exchange Program) is a cooperative activity between government and industry providing participants with a means to exchange information about certain types of technical data, especially the design, development and operational phases of the life cycle of systems and equipment. The program is managed by the U.S. government and participation is open to individuals and organizations able to exchange technical information and willing to abide by GIDEP program guidelines. GIDEP's services, data bases and publications are available free of charge to participants. GIDEP staff will occasionally perform simple data base searches for non-participants, but on a one-time basis. Currently GIDEP members include 444 industry representatives, and 204 U.S. government officials, primarily from NASA and the Departments of Defense, Energy, Transportation, and Labor. Canadian businesses and government officials, mainly from the Department of Defense, also participate. GIDEP services include a bi-monthly newsletter about new developments and an on-line data base. Participants can obtain free direct on-line access to the data base's main computers located in Washington, DC and Corona, CA. Members can also request searches or obtain the entire data base on microfilm and microfiche.

The following are GIDEP data base files:

The Engineering Data Interchange contains engineering evaluation and qualification test reports, non-standard justification data, parts and materials specifications, manufacturing processes, and other related engineering data on parts, components, materials and processes. This data interchange also includes a section of reports on specific engineering methodology and techniques, air and water pollution reports, alternate energy sources, and other subjects.

The Reliability-Maintainability Data Interchange contains failure rate/mode and replacement rate data on parts, components and materials based on field performance information and/or reliability demonstration tests of equipment, subsystems and systems. This data interchange also contains reports on theories, methods, techniques, and procedures related to reliability and maintainability practices.

The Metrology Data Interchange contains metrology related engineering data on test systems, calibration systems, and measurement technology and test equipment calibration procedures, and has been designated as a data repository for the National Bureau of Standards metrology related data. This data interchange also provides a Metrology Information Service (MIS) for its participants.

The Failure Experience Data Interchange contains objective failure information generated when significant problems are identified on parts, components, processed, fluids, materials, or safety and fire hazards. This data interchange includes the ALERT and SAFE-ALERT data, failure analysis and problem information data.

Manufacturer Test Data and Reports includes certified test reports from manufacturers detailing test results and inspections conducted on devices of their manufacturer. Test data pertain to commercial as well as military and high reliability devices. The availability of this test data in GIDEP provides participants the opportunity to apply the data in every phase of system design, development, production and support process.

Contact: GIDEP, Officer in Charge, GIDEP Operations Center, Corona, CA 91720/714-736-4677.

Grants

The programs described below are for sums of money given by the federal government to initiate and stimulate new or improved activities or to sustain on-going services.

Military Construction, Army National Guard

Objectives: To provide a combat-ready reserve force and facilities for training and administering the Army National Guard units.

Eligibility: The state National Guard unit must be federally recognized, and the state must provide real estate for armory projects.

Range of Financial Assistance: $400,000 and up. Maximum based on requirements.

Contact: Chief, Army Installations Division, National Guard Bureau, Pentagon, Washington, DC 20310/202-697-1732.

Military History Grants

Objectives: Assist research in military history.

Eligibility: Educational institutions and scholars.

Range of Financial Assistance: Up to $500.

Contact: Historical Services, Army Military History Institute, Department of Defense, Carlisle Barracks, PA 17013-5008/717-245-3631.

Guidance and Control Information Analysis Center (GACIAC)

GACIAC is responsible for the dissemination and exchange of technical information related to the guidance and control of tactical weapons.

A bimonthly GACIAC Bulletin is available to DOD and DOD contractors that are registered with DTIC. This bulletin covers reports, papers, activities, and conferences of interest to the G & C community. All GACIAC products and services are available at no charge to DOD/Military personnel. DOD contractors may purchase GACIAC reports on an individual basis or obtain all products and services through an annual subscription. GACIAC provides users with products and specialized reference service. The staff can be tasked to provide evaluative engineering and/or analytical service. For further information contact: GACIAC, IIT Research Institute, 10 West 35th Street, Chicago, IL 60616/312-567-4345.

Help to Local Governments

For information on specialized or technical services provided by the U.S. Department of Defense to state and local governments, contact: DOD Washington Headquarters Services, Directorate for Information Operations and Reports, Manpower Management Information Division, 1215 Jefferson Davis Highway, Suite 1204, Arlington, Va. 22202-4302/202-746-0662.

High Energy Laser Program

The Air Force Office of Public Affairs can provide you with information about the Department of Defense's High Energy Laser Program as well as laser weapon technology in general. Staff can answer questions and direct you to the correct government office for further information. *The Department of Defense High Energy Laser Program,* distributed by the office, is a report describing the U.S. military's efforts to develop laser and space laser weapons. It details the technology, program history, and funding of high energy lasers. The 20-page report, which has illustrations, is available free of charge. Contact: Air Force High Energy Laser Program, Air Force Office of Public Affairs, Washington, DC 20330/202-695-5766.

High Tech Smuggling

DOD has prepared several reports about U.S. interest and efforts to prevent the illegal flow of critical high technologies, particularly those which have military implications. Under Congressional mandate, DOD has been submitting an annual report to Congress entitled *The Technology Transfer Control Program,* which summarizes DOD's efforts to control high tech smuggling. The report is available free of charge as long as the supply lasts. Contact: Department of Defense, Public Correspondence Division, OASD (Public Affairs), R2 E777, Washington, DC 20301/202-697-5737.

Historical Budget Data Book

This annual free publication provides a concise array of historical budget data for fiscal year 1974 through the present, broken down by Navy program. Contact: Office of the Comptroller of the Navy, NCB32, Crystal City Mall, No. 2, Room 606, Statistical and Report Branch 3224, Washington, DC 20350-1100/202-697-7819.

Honorary Awards to Private Citizens and Organizations

The U.S. Department of Defense honors private citizens and organizations in recognition of significant achievements that have benefitted one or more Defense components or the U.S. Department of Defense as a whole. Among the awards presented are: U.S. Department of Defense Medal for Distinguished Public Service; Secretary of Defense Award for Outstanding Public Service; and the U.S. Department of Defense Meritorious Award. Contact: Civilian Personnel Policy and Requirements, Manpower Installations and Logistics, Department of Defense, The Pentagon, Room 3D265, Washington, DC 20301-4000/202-695-2330.

Human Engineering

For information on life sciences regarding human factors capabilities and limitations, and human factors engineering applications in relation to Army materiel, contact: Director, Army Human Engineering Laboratories, Army Materiel Command, Department of Defense, Aberdeen Proving Ground, MD 21005-5001/301-278-5820.

Hydraulic Engineering Information Analysis Center (HEIAC)

HEIAC provides users with products and specialized reference service. The staff can be tasked to provide evaluative engineering and/or analytical service on the following subjects: River, harbor, and tidal hydraulics; flow through pipes, conduits, channels, and spillways as related to flood control and navigation; hydraulic design and performance of dams, locks, channels, and other structures; underwater shock effects. Data base searches and copies of technical reports are provided on a cost recovery basis. For further information contact: U.S. Army Engineer Waterways Experiment Station, Attn: HEIAC, P.O. Box 631, Vicksburg, MS 39180-0631/601-634-2608.

Hydroelectric Energy

The Army Corps of Engineers builds and operates hydroelectric power plants in connection with large multipurpose dams. The power is sold through the U.S. Department of Energy. The Corps continues to increase production from its existing dams by adding new units and by using pumped storage. *Hydropower: The Role of the U.S. Army Corps of Engineers* is a free pamphlet that describes hydroelectric projects and lists their locations and functions. Contact: Army Corps of Engineers, Attn: DAEN-CWP, Washington, DC 20314/202-272-0146.

Hydrographic/Topographic Center—Defense Mapping Agency (DMA—HTC)

This center provides mapping, charting and geodetic products and services to the military and navigators in general on the world oceans. It also gathers and processes vast amounts of information about the earth for precise navigation purposes. Contact: DMA Hydrographic/Topographic Center, Department of Defense, PAO, Washington, DC 20315/202-227-2023.

Independent Research and Development— TriService Industry Information Center

Contractors who want to recover the cost of their independent research and development must submit annually a technical plan describing their projects. For information and technical guidelines, contact: U.S. Army Materiel Command, Department of the Army, Department of Defense, 5001 Eisenhower Avenue, Room 10N09, Alexandria, VA 22333-0001/202-274-8671.

Industrial Personnel Security Clearance

The Defense Industrial Security Program provides clearances for industrial facilities and industrial personnel. Inspections are conducted annually to assist contractors to establish and maintain information security systems adequate for the protection of classified information. The Defense Industrial Security Clearance Office determines the eligibility of contractor personnel for access to classified information belonging to the U.S. international treaty organizations and to foreign governments. Contact the regional offices or Defense Investigative Service, Director for Industrial Security, 1900 Half St. S.W., Washington, DC 20324/202-475-0906, or Defense Investigative Service, Defense Industrial Security Clearance Office (S0800), P. O. Box 2499, Columbus, OH 43216/614-236-2133.

Industrial Security Education

The Defense Security Institute presents courses of instruction, both resident and extension, on industrial security. Contact: Defense Investigative Service, Defense Security Institute, c/o Defense General Supply Center, Richmond, VA 23297-5091/804-275-4891.

Information Analysis Centers (IAC's)

The Department of Defense funds several centers specializing in the analysis of scientific and technical information. Many of the centers maintain on-line data bases and can provide reference services for the specialized area they cover. Staff can also provide evaluative engineering and/or analytical services. Services are generally provided on a cost recovery basis. Listed below are the names of these centers, and each is described in this DOD section. For a Center's description, look its name up in the proper alphabetical spot in this section.

Aerospace Structures Information and Analysis Center
Chemical Propulsion Information Agency
Coastal Engineering Research Center
Cold Regions Research
Concrete Technology Information Analysis Center
Guidance and Control Information Analysis Center
Hydraulic Engineering Information Analysis Center
Infrared Information and Analysis Center
Manufacturing Technology Information Analysis Center
Metals Matrix Composites Information Analysis Center
Metals and Ceramic Information Center
Nondestructive Testing Information Analysis Center
Nuclear Information Analysis Center
Pavements and Soil Trafficability Information Analysis Center
Plastics Technical Evaluation Center
Reliability Analysis Center
Shock and Vibration Information Center
Soil Mechanics Information Analysis Center
Survivability/Vulnerability Information Analysis Center
Tactical Technology Center
Thermophysical and Electronic Properties Information Analysis Center

Infrared Information and Analysis Center (IRIA)

IRIA provides users with products and specialized reference service. The staff can be tasked to provide evaluative engineering and/or analytical service on Electro-Optics Technology. IRIA also assists ONR in administering the annual Infrared Information Symposium (IRIS) and the meetings of the seven Specialty Groups of IRIS, and publishes the proceedings and minutes of these conferences and meetings. Data base searches and copies of technical reports are provided on a cost recovery basis. For further information contact: Environmental Research Institute of Michigan, Attn: IRIA, P. O. Box 8618, Ann Arbor, MI 48107/313-994-1200, ext. 214.

Institute of Heraldry

The Institute of Heraldry is responsible for the design, sculpture, development and quality control of heraldic items. It is involved from the concept of design to introduction of items into the federal supply system. It is also concerned with the Department of the Army policy governing flags and other heraldic items (except those worn on uniforms). Heraldic items include decorations, medals, badges, all types of insignia, lapel devices, flags, streamers, and other items of symbolic nature that are worn or displayed. Contact: The Institute of Heraldry, U.S. Army, Department of Defense, Cameron Station, Building 15, Alexandria, VA 22304-5050/202-274-6632.

InterAmerican Geodetic Survey (IAGS)
IAGS was founded to assist Latin American cartographic agencies in performing surveys and producing maps and charts. The training includes classes at the School and on the job covering areas such as geodesy, surveys, photogrammetry, cartography, lithography, photography and computer science. Contact: Inter-American Geodetic Survey Liaison Office, c/o DMA Hydrographic/Topographic Center, Department of Defense, Washington, DC 20315/202-227-2516.

International Affairs
The U.S. Army Corps of Engineers shares its experience and expertise in project planning, engineering, and construction management with friendly nations throughout the world. Programs of the past include managing the completion of the Panama Canal; the design and expansion of highways in Afghanistan; rehabilitation of the port of Inchon in Korea; and helping develop a public works program in the Congo. Current major efforts and services include security assistance and nation building in Saudi Arabia; comprehensive studies for the multipurpose development of the Niger River in West Africa; hydroelectric dam development for the People's Republic of China; and technical assistance to Central and Latin American countries on water resources and port projects. The Corps provides the following management and technical services through both in-house capabilities and by contracting with private industry: project definition and development of conceptual plans; comprehensive project planning, programming and studies; project management covering design, construction, quality control, procurement, operations, and maintenance; training in river basin planning, flood protection, navigation, beach erosion control and shore protection, hydroelectric power generation and construction management. Contact: U.S. Army Corps of Engineers, Attn: DAEN-IA, Washington, D.C. 20314/202-272-0006.

International Exchange of Patents
For information on the International Interchange of Patent Rights and Technical Information, contact: Patents, Copyrights and Trademarks Division, U.S. Army, Legal Services Agency, 5611 Columbia Pike, Room 332A, Falls Church, VA 22041-5013/202-756-2430.

International Military Education and Training Program (IMET)
This program provides military education, training to foreign military personnel as a grant aid. Contact: Defense Security Assistance Agency, Department of Defense, The Pentagon, Room 4B659, Washington, DC 20301/202-697-2297.

Jefferson Proving Ground
This facility processes, assembles, and accepts testing of ammunition and ammunition components, and receives, stores, maintains and issues assigned industrial stocks, including calibrated components. Contact: Jefferson Proving Ground, Department of Defense, Madison, IN 47250/812-273-7211.

Joint Chiefs of Staff
The principal military advisors to the Secretary of Defense, the President and the National Security Council. The Joint Chiefs prepare plans and provisions for the strategic direction of the Armed Forces including the direction of operations conducted by commanders of unified and specified commands. Contact: Public Affairs, Joint Chiefs of Staff, Department of Defense, The Pentagon, Room 2E838, Washington, DC 20301/202-697-4272.

Joint Chiefs of Staff History
For information on Joint Chiefs of Staff history, contact: Historical Division, Joint Chiefs of Staff, Department of Defense, The Pentagon, Room 1A714, Washington, DC 20301/202-697-3088.

Licenses for Army Patents
The Army grants licenses under government-owned, Army-administered patents. For further information, contact: Patents, Copyrights and Trademarks Division, U.S. Army, Legal Services Agency, 5611 Columbia Pike, Room 332A, Falls Church, Va. 22041-5013/202-756-2430.

Licenses for Navy Patents
The Navy grants licenses under government law PL 96517 and administers patents on a partial, nonexclusive, revocable, royalty or royalty-free, nontransferable basis to any American citizen or business entity capable of introducing the invention into commercial use. Contact: Director, Navy Patent Program, Patent Counsel for the Navy, Office of Naval Research, Department of the Navy, Department of Defense, 800 North Quincy St., Arlington, VA 22217/202-696-4000.

Manufacturing Technology Information Analysis Center (MTIAC)
MTIAC is responsible for the collection, analysis and dissemination of manufacturing technology information and data in the following areas: metals, non-metals, inspection and test, electron-

ics and munitions, Computer Aided Design/ Computer Aided Manufacturing (CAD/CAM). MTIAC provides users with products and specialized reference service. The staff can be tasked to provide evaluative engineering and/or analytical service. Data base searches and copies of technical reports are provided on a cost recovery basis. For further information contact: MTIAC Headquarters Office, Case and Company, Inc., Suite 2109, Prudential Plaza, Chicago, IL 60601/312-567-4733.

Map of Military Installations in the United States
This map is available for $3.00 at the Defense Mapping Agency, Office of Distribution Services, Attn: DDCP, Washington, DC 20315/202-227-2534.

Maps and Charts—Defense Mapping Agency
A price list and general information on maps and charts produced by the Defense Mapping Agency is available from: Defense Mapping Agency, Office of Distribution Services, U.S. Department of Defense, Washington, DC 20315/202-227-2816.

Marine Corps Casualty and Missing in Action Information
For casualty and missing-in-action information on Marine Corps personnel, contact: Casualty Section, Code MPH-81, Personnel Service Division, Marine Corps, Headquarters, Arlington Navy Annex, Building #4, Washington, DC 20380/202-694-1787.

Marine Corps Band
For information on the Marine Corps Band and their schedules, contact: Marine Band, Division of Public Affairs (PAB), Headquarters, Marine Corps, Washington, DC 20380/202-694-3502.

Marine Corps Community Relations
For information on Marine Corps community projects and activities, contact: Community Relations Branch, Marine Corps, Department of the Navy, Department of Defense, Room 1133. Washington, DC 20380/202-694-1080.

Marine Corps Information
For general information on Marine Corps programs, contact: Public Affairs Headquarters, Marine Corps, Department of Defense, Washington, DC 20380/202-694-4309.

Marine Corps Museum
The museum exhibits illustrate through the use of uniforms, weapons and other military equipage, graphics, contemporaneous art, and documents a chronological review of the Marine Corps' role in American history. Contact: The Marine Corps Museum, Marine Corps Historical Center, Washington Navy Yard. 9th and M Sts. S.E., Wash-

ington, DC 20374/202-433-3534. A number of additional study collections are located at the Museum's ordinance and technology storage and exhibit facility at Quantico. They include a definitive collection of automatic weapons, uniforms, historic flags and infantry weapons. These collections can be studied by appointment only: Marine Corps Museums Activities, Marine Corps Development and Education Command, Quantico, VA 22134/703-640-2606.

Marine Corps Posture, Plans and Programs Statement
This booklet describes Marine Corps programs, personnel and budget. For a copy, contact: Public Affairs Headquarters, Marine Corps. Department of Defense, Washington, DC 20380/202-694-4309.

Marine Corps Reserve
The Reserve provides units for rapid mobilization and deployment, reinforcing and augmenting active units, and providing air-ground forces of various strengths. In addition to mission-oriented training, specialized training in certain skills is provided through schools and colleges. Contact: Marine Corps Reserve Division, Marine Corps, Headquarters, Department of the Navy, Department of Defense, Navy Annex, Room 1114, Washington, DC 20380/202-694-1161.

Marine Corps Still Photo Archives
The Marine Corps holds about 600,000 still photos dating from December 1941 to the present. The Archives are open to the public. For information, contact: Marine Corps Still Library, Building 168, NDW, Washington, DC 20374/202-433-2168.

Medical Museum
This museum contains specimens representing practically all diseases that affect man, as well as an extensive collection of medical, surgical and diagnostic instruments and related medical items. Contact: Armed Forces Medical Museum of the Armed Forces Institute of Pathology, Department of Defense, Walter Reed Army Medical Center, 6825-16th St. N.W., Building #54, Washington, DC 20306/202-576-2341. For recorded information, call: 202-576-2418.

Medical Research—Army
Research and development in medical sciences, supplies and equipment is conducted at: Army Medical Research and Development Command, Army, Department of Defense, Fort Detrick, Frederick, MD 21701/301-663-2121.

Medical Research—Navy
This office is responsible for research and development, test and evaluation in diving medicine, submarine medicine, aviation medicine, bioeffects of electromagnetic radiation, human performance,

fleet health care, infectious diseases, oral and dental health, and fleet occupational health. Contact: Naval Medical Research and Development Command NMCNCR, Department of the Navy, Department of Defense, Bethesda, MD 20814/202-295-1453.

Medical Research Institute of Chemical Defense
Research, development, test and evaluation is carried out as it relates to medical defense against chemical warfare. Contact: Medical Research Institute of Chemical Defense, Department of the Army, Attn: SGRD-UV-AO, Aberdeen Proving Ground, MD 21010/301-671-3653.

Medical Rsearch Institute for Infectious Diseases
Research is conducted to develop expertise and knowledge of the pathogenesis and characteristics of viruses of military significance and to develop chemical and other agents effective either as preventive vaccines for chemoprophylaxis or drugs effective in the chemotherapy of those virus diseases. Contact: Medical Research Institute for Infectious Diseases, Department of Army, Fort Detrick, Frederick, MD 21701/301-663-2285.

Memorial Affairs
This division operates and maintains Arlington and Soldiers' Home National Cemetery and 28 post cemeteries. It also supervises the worldwide care and disposition of remains and effects of deceased Army personnel. Contact: Memorial Affairs Division, Casualty and Memorial Affairs Directorate, TAGO, 2461 Eisenhower Ave., Alexandria, VA 22331/202-325-7960.

Metal Matrix Composites Information Analysis Center (MMCIAC)
MMCIAC provides users with products and specialized reference service. The staff can be tasked to provide evaluative engineering and/or analytical service on Metal matrix composite materials and technology. The MMCIAC supports the DoD Metal Matrix Composites Steering Committee.

Data base searches and copies of technical reports are provided on a cost recovery basis. For further information contact: Kaman Tempo, 816 State Street, P.O. Drawer QQ, Santa Barbara, CA 93102/805-963-6455.

Metals and Ceramics Information Center (MCIC)
MCIC provides users with products and specialized reference service. The staff can be tasked to provide evaluative engineering and/or analytical service on the following subjects: metals, ceramic, coverages and processes.

Data base searches and copies of technical reports are provided on a cost recovery basis. For further information contact: Battelle-Columbus Laboratories, 505 King Avenue, Columbus, OH 43201/614-424-5000.

Military Assistance Program
See "Foreign Military Sales Program" in this section.

Military Assistance Programs Logistics
This office implements all military assistance programs overseas. It also provides support analysis of the programs. Contact: Directorate of International Logistics and Support Analysis, Office of Assistant Secretary of Defense, Manpower Reserve Affairs and Logistics (PI). The Pentagon, Room 2B329, Washington, DC 20301/202-697-9740.

Military Audiovisual Material
A variety of audiovisual materials is available for sale or on loan through the National Audiovisual Center. The material covers a wide range of subjects that include air defense, air warfare, aviation history, flying exhibitions and competitions, marine strategy and tactics, guided missiles, marine ceremonies, national security, nuclear warfare and military training. *A Reference List of Audiovisual Materials Produced by the U.S. Government* is a free catalog available through the Reference Section, National Audiovisual Center, National Archives and Records Service, General Services Administration, Washington, DC 20409/301-763-1896.

Military Ceremonies
For information on military ceremonies and participation in public events, contact: Community Relations, The Pentagon, Washington, DC 20301/202-697-6005.

Military Construction Programs
This news release lists the current fiscal year construction programs for the Department of Defense. It is available for free by writing: OASD/Public Affairs, Department of Defense, 2E777, Pentagon, Washington, DC 20301-1400.

Military Engineering Programs
The Corps of Engineers provides military engineering support to the Army and other defense agencies. It plans, designs and supervises the construction of housing for soldiers and their families, health, shopping and recreational facilities and facilities for military equipment. The Corps maintains and operates a worldwide network of engineering offices. Contact: Army Corps of Engineers, Attn: DAEN-ECZ, Washington, DC 20314/202-272-0387.

Military Exchange Services
Procurement of resale merchandise for post and base exchanges in the Continental United States (CONUS) is accomplished by five exchange regions. Each exchange region buys for approximately 25 installation exchanges in the region's

general geographical area. To sell to exchanges a firm must, by appointment, offer its product to the buyers at any or all of these five regions, or contact: Army and Air Force Exchange Service, P.O. Box 222305, Dallas, TX 75222/214-780-2011.

Military History Institute
The Institute collects, preserves, and provides to researchers source materials of American military history. It holds more than one million catalogued items relating to military history. Some of the books in the collection date from the 15th century and provide historical background on the American army. Original source material includes diaries, letters, photographs, art work and other records. The Institute provides research and reference assistance. It also publishes bibliographies of its holdings, a biannual anthology titled *Essays in Some Dimensions of Military History,* and collections of short, factual *Vignettes of Military History.* Contact: Army Military History Institute, Department of Defense, Carlisle Barracks, PA 17013/717-245-3611.

Military History on View
A list of Army, Navy, Marine Corps and Air Force museums located throughout the country is available from: Public Affairs, Department of Defense, The Pentagon, Room 2E800, Washington, DC 20301/202-697-5737.

Military History Publications
A free listing of publications is available from: Army Center of Military History, 20 Massachusetts Avenue, N.W., Room 4224, Washington, DC 20314/202-272-0295.

Military Information and Referrals
Staff in the Public Affairs Office of each branch of the military will answer questions from the public and make referrals. You can write or call the following 6 offices: 1) U.S. Department of Defense, Assistant Secretary of Defense for Public Affairs, Public Correspondence Branch, Washington, DC 20301-1100/202-697-5737; 2) U.S. Department of Defense, Defense Logistic Agency, Cameron Station, Alexandria, VA 22314/703-274-6135; 3) U.S. Department of the Army, Office of Chief of Public Affairs, Washington, DC 20310-1501/202-695-5135; 4) U.S. Department of the Navy, Public Affairs, Office of the Secretary, Washington, DC 20350/202-697-7491; 5) U.S. Department of the Air Force, Director of Public Affairs, Office of the Secretary of the Air Force, Washington, DC 20380/202-694-8010; 6) Marine Corps Headquarters, Division of Public Affairs, Washington, DC 20380/202-694-8010.

Military Manpower and Training Report
This report is submitted to Congress annually, and recommends the average student load for each category of training for each component of the armed forces for the next three fiscal years. Contact: Training and Education, Affairs and Logistics, Department of Defense, The Pentagon, Room 3B930. Washington, DC 20301/202-695-6857.

Military Service Records
The National Archives and Records Service (NARS) is the official depository for records of military personnel separated from the U.S. Air Force, Army, Coast Guard, Marine Corps, and Navy. The records are housed in three locations: The National Archives Building, Washington, DC, the Washington National Records Center (WNRC), Suitland, MD; and the National Personnel Records Center, St. Louis, MO. Records relating to military service ended more than 75 years ago are available for public examination, and copies can be provided. Records of military personnel who served within the last 75 years, however, are subject to restrictions imposed by the military under the Public Information Act of 1966. Although such records cannot be made available for public examination or copies provided, information from them may be furnished to searchers on request. A booklet describing the process for obtaining these records is available from the Public Affairs Office, Department of Defense, Pentagon, Washington, DC 20301/202-697-5737.

Military Strength and Defense Contract Publications
For further information on any of the following publications or for a complete publication catalog, contact: Directorate, Information Operations and Reports, Washington Headquarters Service, Department of Defense, The Pentagon, Room 1C535, Washington, DC 20301/202-695-6815.

Catalog of DIOR Reports—contains audited data pertaining to selected procurement, logistics, manpower, economics, financial management, property management, and supply statistical reports (free).
Map Book—Major Military Installations (biannual, $8.50)
Working Capital Funds of the DOD (annual, $9.20)
Military Manpower Statistics (monthly, $6.00)
Worldwide Manpower Distribution by Geographic Areas (quarterly, $5.20)

To obtain copies of the following publications, contact: Public Correspondence, Public Affairs, Office of the Secretary of Defense, The Pentagon, Washington, DC 20301/202-697-5737.

Monthly Report of Military Strength—a press release that provides data on the previous two months and compares the present military strength to that of a year ago (free).
Active Military Duty by Country Worldwide—a quarterly press release that comes out 50 to 60 days after the end of the quarter (free).

100 Companies Receiving the Largest Dollar Volume of Military Prime Contract Awards (annual, $4.40)
Educational and Nonprofit Institutions Receiving Military Prime Contract Awards for Research, Development, Test and Evaluation (annual, $3.90)
Military Prime Contract Awards by State, City and Contractor (annual, $99.90)
Companies Participating in the DoD Subcontracting Programs (quarterly, $5.30)

Military Traffic Management Command MTMC)
This office is responsible for operation of common user CONUS (Continental United States) military ocean terminals and for providing or procuring required terminal services for movement of cargo through other CONUS military or commercial ocean terminal facilities. MTMC is also responsible for the control and maintenance of the Defense Freight Railway Interchange Fleet. Contact: Headquarters, Military Traffic Management Command, 5611 Columbia Pike, Falls Church, VA 22041/202-756-1242.

Missile Research
For information on research and development on rockets, guided missiles, ballistic missiles, targets, air defense weapons systems, fire control coordination equipment, related special purpose and multisystem test equipment, missile launching and ground support equipment, meteorology, calibration equipment, and other associated equipment, contact: U.S. Army Missile Command (MICOM), Department of Defense, Redstone Arsenal, Huntsville, AL 35898/205-876-4759.

Missile Test Facility
This facility is responsible for research and development, testing and evaluation programs on the flight testing of guided missiles, and supports endo- and exo-atmospheric research in the launching of rockets. Contact: Naval Ordnance Missile Test Facility, White Sands Missile Range, NM 88002/505-678-2101.

Missing in Action
For inquiries on military personnel listed as missing in action, see "National Archives."

Mobility Equipment Research
For information on research, development, engineering and first production buys on all varieties and aspects of mobile equipment, contact: US Army Research and Development, Belvoir Center, Department of Defense, Fort Belvoir, VA 22060/703-664-5251.

National Dam Inventory Program
The U.S. Army Corps of Engineers maintains a computer-based detailed inventory of the 68,000 dams over 25 feet high or which impound over 50 acre feet of water. Contact: U.S. Army Corps of Engineers, Attn: DAEN-ECE-S, Washington, D.C. 20314/202-272-0232.

National Defense University
The National Defense University, operated under the Joint Chiefs of Staff, provides the Department of Defense with senior joint professional military education with a focus on national security policy formulation, military strategy development, mobilization, industrial preparedness, and planning for joint and combined operations. The University also provides research in current issues for the national security community. It is composed of the National War College and Industrial College of the Armed Forces, both at Fort McNair in Washington, D.C., the Armed Forces Staff College in Norfolk, Va., plus three institutes with specialized research and education functions. Contact: Public Affairs Officer, National Defense University, Washington, DC 20319-6000/202-475-0811.

National Defense University Press
The University's publication arm makes available through the Government Printing Office a variety of monographs, essays, books and studies on a wide range of national security issues. Popular publications now include:

A T & T: Aftermath of Antitrust, by George H. Bolling $6.00
The Pentagon Reporters, by Robert B. Sims $5.50
Computers on the Battlefield: Can They Survive?, by Richard J. DeBastiani $4.50

To order, contact: Superintendent of Documents, Government Printing Office, Washington, DC 20402/202-783-3238.

National Guard
The National Guard is the primary backup for the U.S. Army, providing it with infantry, armor, artillery, aviation, medical, engineering, communications and electronics support. When not on federal duty, the National Guard is under the control of the state governors to help protect life and property and to preserve peace, order and public safety in their states. Free publications of the National Guard include: *Annual Review,* and *Facts and Fiction About the National Guard.* Contact: Public Affairs, National Guard Bureau, Department of the Army, Department of Defense, The Pentagon, Room 2E258, Washington, DC 20310/202-695-0421.

NATO Programs
A table of key North Atlantic Treaty Organization (NATO) programs including a brief description of the goals, achievements and status of the programs and the countries involved, is included in the U.S. Department of Defense *Program for Research Development and Acquisition Annual Report.* For

more NATO information, contact: NATO Regional Policy, Department of Defense, The Pentagon, Room 1E814, Washington, DC 20301/202-697-7202.

Nautical Charts

The *Catalog of Maps, Charts and Related Products* is a four-part catalog providing a comprehensive reference of all Defense Mapping Agency maps, charts and related products available to U.S. Department of Defense users: Part I, Aerospace Products; Part II, Hydrographic Products; Part III, Topographic Products; Part IV, World—Small- and Medium-Scale Maps. Contact: Defense Mapping Agency, Hydrographic/Topographic Center, Office of Distribution Services, Attn: DDCP, Washington, DC 20315/202-227-2495. Other available charts cover nine regions: 1) United States and Canada; 2) Central and South America and Antarctica; 3) Western Europe, Iceland, Greenland and the Arctic; 4) Scandinavia, Baltic and USSR; 5) Western Africa and the Mediterranean; 6) Indian Ocean; 7) Australia, Indonesia and New Zealand; 8) Oceana; 9) East Asia. (Nautical charts of the U.S., Hawaii, and Alaska are sold through the National Ocean Survey at the Department of Commerce.) Contact: Defense Mapping Agency, Office of Distribution Services, Attn: DDCP, Department of Defense, 6101 MacArthur Blvd., Warren Building, Washington, DC 20315/202-227-3048/3049.

Naval Air Engineering Center

This Center provides research and development, engineering testing and evaluation, system integration, limited production and fleet engineering support in launching recovery and landing aids for aircraft, and in ground support equipment for aircraft and airborne weapons system. It also supports the U.S. Department of Defense standardization and specification programs. Contact: Naval Air Engineering Center, Department of the Navy, Department of Defense, Lakehurst, NJ 08733/201-323-2011.

Naval Air Systems Command

This office is responsible for the design, development, testing and evaluation of naval airframes, aircraft engines, components, and fuels and lubricants; airborne versions of electronic equipment, pyrotechnics and minesweeping equipment; air-launched weapon systems and underwater sound systems; aircraft drone and target systems, catapults, arresting gear, visual landing aids, photographic equipment, meteorological equipment, ground handling equipment for aircraft, parachutes, flight clothing and survival equipment. Contact: Naval Air Systems Command, Department of the Navy, Department of Defense, Washington, DC 20361/202-692-8373.

Naval Facilities Engineering

Research and development is directed toward items of new or improved materials and equipment or engineering techniques pertaining to the technical planning, design, construction, operation, and maintenance of the shore facilities and related material and equipment. Contact: Naval Facilities Engineering Command, Department of the Navy, 200 Stovall St., Alexandria, VA 22332/202-325-8537.

Naval Historical Center

The Naval Historical Center preserves official Navy historical documents and published accounts of naval history. For information and a list of their publications, contact: Naval Historical Center, Department of the Navy, Washington Navy Yard, Washington, DC 20374/202-433-2210.

Naval Observatory

The primary purpose of the Naval Observatory is to provide accurate astronomical data essential for safe navigation at sea, in the air and in space. It is the only observatory in the United States at which fundamental positions of the sun, moon, planets and stars are continually determined. It is also the only observatory to determine time and is the source of all standard time used in the country. The Observatory library contains many rare and periodical sets on astronomy as well as the current literature. It also publishes astronomical and nautical papers. Contact: Naval Observatory, Department of the Navy, 34th and Massachusetts Ave. N.W., Washington, DC 20390/202-653-1499 (library)

Naval Research

This office supports basic research and technology. Contract awards usually result from unsolicited proposals for research on naval vehicles and weapons technology; sensor and control technology; physical sciences; math and information sciences; biological sciences; psychological sciences; arctic and earth sciences; material sciences; ocean science and technology; and analysis of the development and maintenance of future naval power. Contact: Office of Naval Research, Department of the Navy, Code 73 Department of Defense, 800 North Quincy St., Arlington, VA 22217/202-696-5031.

Naval Research Laboratory

The Naval Research Laboratory conducts scientific research and advanced technological development directed toward new and improved materials, equipment, techniques, systems and related operational procedures for the Navy. Major fields of interest are communications, counter-measures, device technology, directed energy devices, energy conversion, environmental effects, hydrodynamics, surveillance systems, undersea technology, navigation, sensor systems, sonar standards, weapons guidance and radiation technology. The *Fact Book* is an annual reference source of factual information about the Naval Research Lab, its personnel and its programs. The *Naval Research Laboratory Review,* an annual, describes programs and includes articles and reports on the research in progress. Contact: Technical Commanding Officer, Naval Research Laboratory, Code 2628, Washington, DC 20375/202-767-2949.

Naval Research Publications

Naval Research Logistic Quarterly—basic original research in mathematical and informational science available for $12.00 per year at the Superintendent of Documents, Government Printing Office, Washington, DC 20402/202-783-3238. For publication information, contact: Operational Research, Mathematical and Physical Sciences Directorate, Office of Naval Research, Department of the Navy, Department of Defense, 800 N. Quincy St., Room 607, Arlington, VA 22217/202-696-4314.

Naval Research Review Quarterly—reviews research in such areas as the physical sciences, mathematics, biology, psychology, metallurgy, oceanography and earth sciences. Available for $10.00 per year at the Superintendent of Documents, Government Printing Office, Washington, DC 20402/202-783-3238. For information, contact: Public Affairs Office, Code 732, Office of Naval Research, Arlington, VA 22217/202-696-5031.

European Scientific Notes (free)—Office of Naval Research Branch Office, Department of the Navy, Department of Defense, Box 39, FPO, New York, NY 09510.

Tokyo Scientific Bulletin (free)—Office Services Branch, Office of Naval Research, Department of the Navy, Department of Defense, 800 N. Quincy St., Room 320, Arlington, VA 22217/202-696-4614.

Naval Reserve

The Reserve prepares for mobilization with equipment and programs that parallel the active Navy. Reservists participate in fleet exercises throughout the year. Contact: Naval Reserve Center, Department of the Navy, Department of Defense, Anacostia S.E., Room 351, Washington, DC 20374/202-433-2623.

Naval Still Picture Depository

Still pictures, taken daily, are available for a small charge. The photos on file range from ships, aircraft, marine crafts, to scenic views and people. Photographic records prior to 1958 are in the National Archives. Prints or reproductions of unclassified official photography may be purchased by the public. The Reference Library is open to the public by appointment only. Contact: Defense Audiovisual Agency, Building 168, Naval District Washington, Washington, DC 20374/202-433-2168.

Naval Stock Footage

Collections of official film photography covering the activities of the U.S. Navy since 1958 (anything prior to that year is kept in the National Archives) are maintained. For information on the collection and ordering, contact: DAVA-N-DDEP, Norton Air Force Base, CA 92409/714-382-2307.

Naval Weapons

This office provides research and development, testing and evaluation on air warfare and missile systems, including technological efforts in missile propulsion, warheads, fuses, avionics, fire control and missile guidance. It is also the lead laboratory on various total weapons system developments. Contact: Naval Weapons Center, Department of the Navy, Department of Defense, China Lake, CA 93555/619-939-9011.

Naval Weapons Support

This office provides research and development as well as support for ships and crafts equipment, shipboard weapons systems, and assigned expendable and nonexpendable ordnance items. Contact: Naval Weapons Support Center, Department of the Navy, Department of Defense, Crane, IN 47522/812-854-2511.

Navy Acquisition Research and Development Information Center (NARDIC)

This office makes Navy research and development planning and requirements information available to current or potential U.S. Department of Defense contractors who are registered for access to U.S. Department of Defense information services. For a list of services and information, contact: Navy Acquisition, Research and Development Information Center (NARDIC), Naval Ocean Systems Center, 5001 Eisenhower Ave., Alexandria, VA 22333/202-274-9315, or 1630 East Green St., Pasadena, CA 91106/213-792-5182. For NARDIC representative, consult a free booklet, *NARDIC,* which describes the services and procedures and lists the contact offices.

Navy Band

There are several performing units of the U.S. Navy Band—Concert Band, Ceremonial Band, Sea Chanters, the Commodores jazz ensemble, Port Authority rock group, Country Current bluegrass unit, Commanders Trio, Classical Clarinet Quartet and Harp-Flute Duo. For information and requests for a Navy Band unit to appear at a civilian program outside Washington, DC, contact: United States Navy Band, Department of the Navy, Department of Defense, Washington, DC 20374/202-433-3676; inside Washington, DC, contact: Chief of Information, Department of the Navy, Department of Defense, The Pentagon, Washington, DC 20350/202-697-9344.

Navy Community Relations

For information on Navy programs for communities, contact: Community Relations, Office of Information, Department of the Navy, Department of Defense, The Pentagon, Room 2O333, Washington, DC 20350/202-695-6915.

Navy Exchange Services

There are two basic methods of doing business with Navy exchanges—directly with each exchange or through the Navy Resale System Office (NAVRESO). All exchange equipment is centrally procured or approved for local procurement by NAVRESO. Contact: Naval Resale Services Support Office, Department of the Navy, Department of Defense, Fort Wadsworth, Staten Island, NY 10305/718-390-3700.

Navy/Industry Cooperative Research and Development Program (NICRAD)

This program provides a mechanism for the interchange of technical information with civilian scientists and engineers and facilitates the transfer of technology. Through the NICRAD program both classified and nonclassified technical information on Navy requirements and Navy research and development is made available to participants. The services of the Navy acquisition Research and Development Information Center (NARDIC) and the Defense Technical Information Center (DTIC) are available to NICRAD participants. For information, contact: Office of Research, Development, Test and Evaluation, Chief of Naval Operations, Department of the Navy, Department of Defense, The Pentagon, Room 5D670, Washington, DC 20350/202-697-4532.

Navy Information

For general information on the Navy and Navy programs, contact: Public Information Division, Office of Information, Department of the Navy, Department of Defense, The Pentagon, Room 2E337, Washington, DC 20350/202-695-0965.

Navy Library

In addition to providing information on their own collection, this library can also provide a complete list of all other Navy libraries. Contact: Library, Department of the Navy, Department of Defense, Washington Navy Yard, 11th and M Sts. S.E., Building 44, Washington, DC 20374/202-433-4131.

Navy Memorial Museum

The exhibits in the museum focus on the fighting ships, aircraft and weapons of each evolving era and on the people who operated them. Contact: Navy Memorial Museum, Washington Naval Yard, Building 76, Washington, DC 20374/202-433-2651.

Navy Prisoner of War and Missing-in-Action Information

For information on Naval personnel either missing in action or prisoners of war, contact: Naval Military Personnel Command, Department of the Navy, Department of Defense, Navy Annex, Arlington, VA 20370/202-694-3197.

Navy Publications

These publications are available for free by contacting: Research and Public Inquiries Branch, Office of Information, Department of the Navy, Washington, DC 20350/202-695-0965.

Annual Testimony on the Posture of the Navy/1986
Bicentennial Issue (1775–1975) of *All Hands* Magazine (Aug 1975)—a special issue containing the history of the development of the Navy.

The following Navy magazines are available for sale by the Superintendent of Documents, Government Printing Office, Washington, DC 20402/202-783-3238.

All Hands—a bimonthly magazine that reports current activities of the Navy. $20.00 a year
Naval Aviation News—bimonthly magazine featuring articles on aviation advances, biographies of noted aviators and naval history. $17.00 a year
Surface Warfare—a bimonthly magazine containing articles of interest to the Surface Warfare community. $15.00 a year

Navy Salvage Assistance

Salvage experts are available to handle spills of oils and hazardous chemicals resulting from vessel casualties. For a list of regional contacts and for general information, contact: Office of Chief of Naval Operations, Department of the Navy, Department of Defense, The Pentagon, Room 4D624, Washington, DC 20350/202-695-0231.

Navy Toll-Free Number

For information on Navy recruitment and Navy recruiting programs, contact: Navy Opportunity Information Center, P. O. Box 5000, Clifton, NJ 07012/1-800-327-NAVY, in Florida call 1-800-432-1884; call collect in Alaska, 272-9133; and in Hawaii call 546-7540.

Night Vision and Electro-Optic Laboratories (NVEOL)

Provides the Army with equipment that will enable it to carry out nocturnal operations with daylight efficiency. The laboratory's attention is directed at image intensification, far infrared, radiation sources, visionics, lower-cost all-whether vision systems and electro-optical low-energy lasers, and associated research and development and first production buys related thereto. Contact: Public Affairs, Night Vision and Electro-Optic Laboratories (NVEOL), Fort Belvoir, VA 22060/703-664-5060.

Nondestructive Testing Information Analysis Center (NTIAC)

NTIAC provides users with products and specialized reference service. The staff can be tasked to provide evaluative engineering and/or analytical service on the following subjects: All Nondestructive Testing (NDT) and/or evaluation techniques and processes, involving material-energy interaction phenomena such as radiographic, holographic, acoustic, magnetic, etc. Data base searches and copies of technical reports are provided on a cost recovery basis. For further information contact: Southwest Research Institute 6220 Culebra Road P.O. Drawer 28510 San Antonio, TX 78284/512-684-5111, Ext. 2362

Nuclear

The Defense Nuclear Agency coordinates nuclear weapons stockpile planning, management and testing in conjunction with the Department of Energy, including nuclear readiness, inspection and safety programs. It develops, coordinates and maintains the National Nuclear Test Readiness Program jointly with the U.S. Department of Energy. It provides nuclear weapon stockpile information to the Joint Chiefs of Staff and nuclear warhead logistic information to authorized Defense organizations. Contact: Director, Defense Nuclear Agency, Washington, DC 20305/202-325-7095 (public affairs).

Nuclear Information and Analysis Center (DASIAC)

DASIAC provides users with products and specialized reference service. The staff can be tasked to provide evaluative engineering and/or analytical service on the following subjects:

Nuclear Weapon Explosion Phenomena
Nuclear Weapons Damage Effects on Military Strategic and Tactical Systems/Components
Military Systems Hardening Design Procedures
Survivability/Vulnerability Analysis
Nuclear Weapon Safety and Physical Security
Military Tactics and Doctrine
Nuclear Weapons Effects Testing

Data base searches and copies of technical reports are provided on a cost recovery basis. For further information contact: Kaman Tempo 816 State Street, P.O. Drawer QQ, Santa Barbara, CA 93102/805-963-6400.

Nuclear Weapons Research

Testing and engineering on nuclear weapons systems equipment with specific focus on nuclear effects simulation; analysis of nuclear effects and the reaction of equipment to these effects; telemetry, instrumentation weapons/aircraft flight characteristics, high-speed camera techniques. This division of the Air Force is also concerned with testing and evaluation of systems, subsystems, and support equipment for nuclear safety, reliability, compatibility, survivability, and vulnerability, and provides Air Force resources to support Atomic Energy Commission/DOD nuclear test operations or training exercises both in the United States and overseas. Kirtland Contracting Center, Air Force Systems Command, Department of the Air Force, Research and Development Contracts Division, Kirtland Air Force Base, NM 87117/505-844-4565.

Ocean Systems

The Naval Oceans Systems Center conducts research and development, testing and evaluation for command control communications, ocean surveillance, surface and air launched undersea weapons systems, and support technologies. Contact: Naval Ocean Systems Center, 271 Catalina Blvd., San Diego, CA 92152/619-225-6011.

Oceanographic Research

The Naval Oceanographic Office conducts research and development in oceanographic, hydrographic, and geodetic equipment, techniques and systems. Contact: Naval Oceanographic Office, Department of the Navy, Department of Defense, NSTL Station, Bay St., Louis, MS 39522/601-688-4312.

Opportunities for Small and Disadvantaged Businesses

This pamphlet describes the Army Corps of Engineers' mission and provides information on Corps procurement, supplies and services. Small and disadvantaged business utilization specialists throughout the United States are also listed. (See listing in this section) For information, contact: DAEN-DB, Army Corps of Engineers, Department of the Army, Department of Defense, 20 Massachusetts Ave. N.W., Room 5112, Washington, DC 20314/202-272-0725.

Ordnance Research

The Naval Ordnance Station conducts research and development, testing and evaluation of ammunition pyrotechnics and solid propellants used in missiles, rockets and guns. Contact: Naval Explosive Ordnance Disposal Technology Center, Department of the Navy, Department of Defense, Indian Head, MD 20640/301-743-4530.

Outdoor Recreation at Army Corps Facilities

The U.S. Army Corps of Engineers administers an extensive system of reservoirs, and camping is provided at many of these installations. For *Lakeside Recreation* brochures that describe corps recreation areas, contact: Army Corps of Engineers, Washington, DC 20314/202-272-0162 Attn: DAEN-CWO-R.

Outleasing Program

The Corps has an active outleasing program, especially in the area of industrial and port facilities. It leases land for agricultural and grazing, wildlife and recreational facilities, and it also leases real property for storage and other purposes. This office keeps records of both land that the Army leases out and the land it leases from others. Contact: Army Corps of Engineers, Washington, DC 20314/202-272-0483. Attn: DAEN-REZ

Pacific Missile Test Center
The Center performs testing and evaluation, development support, follow-on engineering and provides logistics and training support for Naval weapons, weapons systems, and related devices; and provides major range, technical, and base support for fleet users and other U.S. Department of Defense and government agencies. Functions include those related to guided missiles, rockets, free-fall weapons, fire control and radar systems, drones and target drones, computers, electronic warfare devices, countermeasures equipment, range services and instrumentation, test planning, simulations, and data collection. Contact: Pacific Missile Test Center, Code 113, Point Mugu, CA 93042/805-982-7994.

Paternity and Adoption
For general information on paternity claims and adoption proceedings involving members and former members of the Armed Forces, contact: Manpower, Reserve Affairs and Logistics, Department of Defense, The Pentagon, Room 3D823, Washington, DC 20301/202-697-5947.

Pavements and Soil Trafficability Information Analysis Center (PSTIAC)
PSTIAC provides users with products and specialized reference services. The staff can be tasked to provide evaluative engineering and/or analytical service on the following subjects: Pavements, trafficability, vehicle mobility, and terrain, as relevant primarily to military needs. Specific areas of road vehicle mobility, soil trafficability, ground flotation, and terrain evaluation. Data base searches and copies of technical reports are provided on a cost recovery basis. For further information contact: U.S. Army Engineer Waterways Experiment Station, Attn: PSTIAC, P.O. Box 631, Vicksburg, MS 39180/601-634-2734.

Pentagon Building Tours
Tours are available Monday through Friday throughout the day. For information on specific times, contact: Directorate for Community Relations, Public Affairs, Department of Defense, The Pentagon, Room 10c2H, Washington, DC 20301/202-695-1776.

Personnel Administration Research
Applied research is conducted in personnel administration and related behavioral sciences contributing to improved management and utilization of manpower. Contact: Naval Military Personnel Command, Department of the Navy, Washington, DC 20370/202-694-1271 (locator).

Plastics Technical Evaluation Center (PLASTEC)
PLASTEC is responsible for the generation, acquisition, evaluation and exchange of technical information related to plastics, adhesives, and organic matrix composites. Covers technology from applied research through fabrication with emphasis on properties and performance. Subject areas include structural, electrical, electronic and packaging applications. Maintains computerized data file on compatibility of polymers with propellants and explosives (COMPAT), and materials deterioration data. Maintains complete file of standards, specifications, and handbooks in subject areas. Provides following services on a fee basis: Consultation, technical inquiries, state-of-the-art studies, data compilations, handbooks, analysis and evaluations, background studies, bibliographic and literature searches. For further information, contact: Plastics Technical Evaluation Center (PLASTEC), U.S. Army Armament, Materials and Chemicals Command, Dover, NJ 07801/201-724-3189.

Procurement Policies and Programs
For information on the coordination of U.S. Department of Defense procurement policies and programs, contact: Assistant Deputy Under Secretary of Defense for Acquisition, Research and Engineering, Department of Defense, The Pentagon, Room 3E144, Washington, DC 20301/202-697-8177.

Procurement, Small Business
For information and guidance on federal government activities for small businesses, contact: Directorate for Small Business and Economic Utilization, Research and Engineering, Department of Defense, The Pentagon, Room 2A340, Washington, DC 20301/202-697-9383.

Qualitative Requirements Information (QRI) Program
This program is an information exchange between the Army and industry. When the Army has a requirement, a statement is sent to all QRI registrants giving background information, suggested approaches and objectives. Registrants to the QRI Program are listed in the Defense Documentation Center (DTIC) Dissemination Authority List and can request documents in their field of interest. Contact: DARCOM TriService Information Center, Department of the Army, Department of Defense, 5001 Eisenhower Ave., Alexandria, VA 22333/202-274-8948.

Radioactive Material

For information on radiological assistance in the event of an accident involving radioactive material, contact: Assistant to the Secretary of Defense (Atomic Energy), Department of Defense, The Pentagon, Room 3E1074, Washington, DC 20530/202-697-5161.

Radiobiological Research Institute

The Institute publishes an annual report summarizing current work in progress in radiobiological research. Contact: Armed Forces Radiobiology Research Institute, Defense Nuclear Agency, Department of Defense, National Naval Medical Center, Building 42, Bethesda, MD 20814/ 202-295-1210.

Recreational Development and Land Use Management

The U.S. Army Corps of Engineers manages recreation areas and natural resources; archeological, historical and cultural resources; visitors centers; lakeshore management; interagency agreements and master plans for recreation areas. Contact: U.S. Army Corps of Engineers, Attn: DAEN-CWO-R, Washington, D.C. 20314/202-272-0247. The Corps is responsible for leases, licenses and easements at recreational areas and for disposal of land. Contact: U.S. Army Corps of Engineers, Attn: DAEN-REM, Washington, D.C. 20314/202-272-0511.

Recreation Statistics

The U.S. Army Corps of Engineers records the largest outdoor recreation attendances of any single U.S. agency. It manages 453 lakes and waterway projects—approximately 11 million acres of land and water. Data are available which show the number of developed recreation areas under management by the Corps, other federal agencies, states, local public agencies, and private concessionaires. The tables further divide areas into overnight use areas that have camping facilities and day-use areas offering picnic but no camping facilities. Attendance numbers and percentage of activity use is broken down into types of activity; e.g., picnicking, swimming, waterskiing, and fishing. Contact: Army Corps of Engineers, (DAEN-CWO-R), Washington, DC 20314/202-272-0247.

Regulatory Functions

The U.S. Army Corps of Engineers evaluates permit applications with regard to activities within waters of the United States that would impact on navigation, water quality, fish and wildlife and related public interest factors. Contact: U.S. Army Corps of Engineers, Attn: DAEN-CWO-N, Washington, D.C. 20314/202-272-0199.

Reliability Analysis Center (RAC)

RAC provides users with products and specialized reference services. The staff can be tasked to provide evaluation engineering and/or analytical service on the following subjects: Microcircuits, discrete semiconductors, nonelectric devices, and standardized electronic modules. RAC's Reliability Corporate Memory (RCM) contains all reliability and maintainability related information and data on planned and operational systems/equipment. Data base searches and copies of technical reports are provided on a cost recovery basis. For further information contact: Reliability Analysis Center, RADC/RAC, Griffiss AFB, NY 13441/ 315-330-4151.

Research and Development

Research and development programs conducted by the U.S. Army Corps of Engineers include effective solution or improvement of ice problems on waterways; reservoir water quality; coastal ecology; aquatic plant control and environmental impacts of developmental actions; and methods of assessing and designing for effects of earthquakes on dams, locks, floodwalls and other hydraulic structures. Also, two new programs in River Ice Management and Repair, Evaluation, Maintenance and Rehabilitation have been initiated to meet problems of winter navigation and rebuilding of the Corps' water resource infrastructure. In addition, research and development is also performed to support the design, construction, maintenance and operation of Army installations worldwide; combat engineering activities of the Army in the field; and the characterization and analysis of the environment to be encountered on the dirty battlefield such as rain, fog, snow, smoke, dust, terrain and vegetation. Contact: U.S. Army Corps of Engineers, Attn: DAEN-RDZ, Washington, D.C. 20314/202-272-0254.

ROTC

Reserve Officers Training Corps (ROTC) is the single largest source of officers for the Armed Forces. It is used to provide a relatively constant input of officers for active duty. ROTC provides noncareer officers as well as career officers. The program is currently conducted at 531 colleges and universities in the United States. Contact: Training and Education, Manpower, Reserve Affairs and Logistics, Department of Defense, The Pentagon, Room 3B930, Washington, DC 20301/202-695-2618.

Scientific Research

This office accepts unsolicited proposals in the natural sciences, which include aeromechanics and energies, electronic and solid state sciences, life sciences, mathematical and information sciences, physics and geophysics. Contact: Office of Scientific Research Opportunities, Directorate of Contracts (BC) Air Force, Department of the Air Force, Department of Defense, Bolling Air Force Base, Washington, DC 20332/202-767-4943.

Scientific Research Grants

The Army will consider requests for the support of basic research from educational institutions and nonprofit organizations. Proposals should be submitted to the Army activity having primary interest in the research to be undertaken, or to the Army Research Office, Department of Defense, P.O. Box 12211, Research Triangle Park, NC 27709/919-549-0641.

Sea Systems Command

This office is responsible for the research and development, procurement and logistical support and other material functions for all ships and craft, shipboard weapon systems and ordnance, air-launched mines and torpedoes, shipboard components such as propulsion (including nuclear) power-generated, sonar search radar, and auxiliary equipment. It also gives contracts and offers technical guidance and supervision of operations related to salvage of stranded and sunk ships and craft. Contact: Naval Sea Systems Command, Department of the Navy, Department of Defense, Washington, DC 20362/202-692-1574 (Public Affairs and Information).

Selling to the Military

This publication provides businesses with essential information on selling to the military, and buying real and personal surplus property from the federal government. It includes the major buying offices and military exchange services, and details the major research and development programs. It also lists items purchased and includes copies of necessary forms. It is available for $6.00 from the Superintendent of Documents, Government Printing Office, Washington, DC 20402/202-783-3238. For information, contact the small business specialist at the nearest military purchasing activity.

Service Academies

The mission of all three service academies—United States Military Academy, United States Naval Academy and United States Air Force Academy—is to meet a portion of the long-range requirement for career military officers. Their curricula are specifically designed to prepare their students for service as professional officers. The enrollment of each of the academies is established by law. For information, contact any of the service academies, or Training and Education, Manpower, Installation and Logistics, Department of Defense, The Pentagon, Room 3B930, Washington, DC 20301/202-695-2618.

Ship Engineering Center

This office is responsible for the research and development in materials, ship production, safety

and damage control, new ship systems design, hull structures and fluid dynamics, electrical and mechanical and auxiliary systems, ship propulsion (non-nuclear) and control and electronic command surveillance systems. Contact: Ship Design (202-692-2439) or Ship Electronics (202-692-1824) or Ship Production (202-692-9728), Naval Sea Systems Command, Department of the Navy, Washington, DC 20362

Ship Research

Research and development is conducted on naval vehicles, including systems development and analyses, fleet support and investigations into related fields of science and technology including hydromechanics, aeromechanics, structures, computer technology, machinery and materials. Contact: David W. Taylor Naval Ship Research and Development Center, Department of the Navy, Department of Defense, Bethesda, MD 20084/202-227-1417.

Ship Weapons

The Naval Ship Weapons Systems Engineering Station conducts research and development, testing, evaluation and engineering support services for programs for ships' guided weapons systems. Contact: Naval Ship Weapon Systems Engineering Station, Department of the Navy, Department of Defense, Port Hueneme, CA 93043/805-982-5356. (Security and Information.)

Ships Names and Sponsors

For background information on how ships' names and sponsors are chosen, for ship types and basic sources of names, contact: Ships Histories Branch, Naval Historical Center, Washington Navy Yard, Building 57, Washington, DC 20374/202-433-3643.

Shock and Vibration Information Center (SVIC)

SVIC collects, evaluates, and stores information on current and past studies of mechanical shock and vibration technology. This includes shock or vibration effects on structures, equipment, or humans that may be generated by acoustic, mechanical, or other physical phenomena. As a major activity, the Center sponsors, organizes, and conducts the shock and vibration symposia at least once yearly. Data base searches and copies of technical reports are provided on a cost recovery basis. For further information contact: Shock and Vibration Information Center, Naval Research Laboratory, Code 5804, Washington, D.C. 20375/202-767-3306.

Small and Disadvantaged Business Utilization Specialists

This free booklet is designed to assist small, minority and labor surplus area businessmen. It lists main contract offices within the U.S. Department of Defense and the Services, and it lists local contacts by state. Small Business Administration Field Office addresses are also included. Contact: Office of Small and Disadvantaged Business Utilization Policy, Office of the Secretary of Defense, The Pentagon, Room 2A340, Washington, DC 20301/202-697-1481. See also "Opportunities for Small and Disadvantaged Businesses" in this section.

Soil Mechanics Information Analysis Center (SMIAC)
SMIAC provides users with products and specialized reference services. The staff can be tasked to provide evaluative engineering and/or analytical service on the following subjects: Soil mechanics, engineering geology, rock mechanics, soil dynamics, earthquake engineering, earth and rockfill dams, levees, earth retaining structures and building foundations, and laboratory testing of soils and rocks. Data base searches and copies of technical reports are provided on a cost recovery basis. For further information contact: Commander and Director, U.S. Army Engineer Waterways Experiment Station, Attn: SMIAC, P.O. Box 631, Vicksburg, MS 39180-0631/601-634-3475.

Soldiers' and Airmen's Home
The Home was established by an Act of Congress in 1851 for retired or discharged enlisted and warrant officer personnel, both men and women, of the Regular Army and Air Force who have served 20 years or more as warrant officers or enlisted personnel; or have a service-connected disability rendering them unable to earn a livelihood; or have a nonservice-connected disability rendering them unable to earn a livelihood and have served during periods of war. Free information pamphlets are available from: Secretary, Board of Commissioners, U.S. Soldiers' and Airmen's Home, 3700 North Capitol St., Washington, DC 20317/202-722-3336.

Soldiers' Home National Cemetery
For historical and general information on the Soldiers' Home National Cemetery, contact: Memorial Affairs Division, Department of the Army, 2461 Eisenhower Ave., Hoffman Building#1, Room 984, Alexandria, VA 22331/703-325-7960.

Solid State Laser Research Reports
The Naval Research Lab is involved with research of low power and medium power solid state lasers as well as the characterization of infared detectors. Technical reports concerning these areas are available by contacting the branch secretary at the telephone number indicated below. Staff can respond to your questions and refer you to other sources of information. Contact: Naval Research Lab, Code 6550, Washington, DC 20375/202-767-3284.

Soviet Military Power
A previously classified, now unclassified, report on Soviet military strength. This report is available at no cost by writing: OASD/Public Affairs, Department of Defense, 2E777, Pentagon, Washington, DC 20301-1400.

Space and Missile Research
Research and development is conducted in test range instrumentation involving radar, trajectory computers and recorders, tracking and target analysis, wire communications, radio communications, programming timing and firing systems, telemetry receiving, data storage, separation and presentation, optics and telemetry data reduction; develops, maintains, and operates the Test Range and provides support for the U.S. Department of Defense missile and space programs. Contact: ESMC/DC, Patrick Air Force Base, FLA 32925/305-494-5933

For information on research and development and product engineering in radar, telemetry, electro-optics, range instrumentation, ships, aircraft impact location, data handling, data reduction, communications range and mission control, range safety, weather timing and firing and frequency control and analysis, contact: Space and Missile Test, Air Force Systems Command, Department of the Air Force, Department of Defense, Vandenberg Air Force Base, Lompoc, CA 93437/805-866-3016.

Specifications and Standards
The Naval Publications and Forms Center (NPFC) is the U.S. Department of Defense's Single Stock Point (SSP) and Distribution Center for Unclasified Specifications and Standards used throughout the Department for military procurement. It indexes, determines requirements, procures, receives, distributes, warehouses, issues and controls the *Index of Specifications and Standards*. It stocks and distributes the following types of documents:

Military Specifications
Military Standards
Federal Specifications
Federal Standards
Qualified Products Lists
Industry Documents
Military Handbooks
Air Force-Navy Aeronautical Standards
Air Force-Navy Aeronautical Design Standards
Air Force-Navy Aeronautical Specifications
Air Force Specifications
Other Departmental Documents
Air Force-Navy Aeronautical Bulletins
Air Force Specification Bulletins

Contact: Naval Publications and Forms Center (NPEC43), Department of Defense, 5801 Tabor Ave., Philadelphia, PA 19120/215-697-4834.

Star Wars Defense Program
The Office of Assistant Secretary of Defense for Public Affairs can supply you with information about the overall Stars Wars defense program, the Defense Advanced Research Projects Agency's (DARPA) efforts in this area, and the DOD Laser and Space Program. Fact sheets, press releases, congressional testimony, and reports about strategic defense initiative programs and studies are available. Contact: Public Correspondence Branch, Office of Assistant Secretary of Defense for Public Affairs, Department of Defense (DOD), Pentagon, Room 2E777, Washington, DC 20301-1400/202-697-5737 (Public Inquiries), 202-659-0192 (Press Inquiries).

Supercomputers for Nuclear Weapons, Energy Research
Although research in nuclear weapons is the foundation of the work at the Lawrence Livermore National Laboratory (LLNL), their work focuses on five other major programs: magnetic fusion energy, laser isotope separation, laser fusion energy, energy and resources, and biomedical and environmental sciences. Much of the lab's scientific calculations are performed at the Livermore Computer Center (LCC), one of the most powerful computer centers in the world, and also at the National Magnetic Fusion Energy Computer Center (NMFECC) located at Livermore. The Centers will respond to specific questions concerning their computer's capabilities and accessibilities and will forward brochures, pamphlets, reference lists and photographs on the computer center work. Their research findings in various areas are available through the Departments of Energy and Defense. Contact: Lawrence Livermore National Laboratory (LLNL), PO Box 808, Livermore, CA 94550/415-422-1100.

Supply Systems Command
This office is responsible for research and development in supply systems management techniques, including mathematical and statistical analysis, materials handling, clothing, and textiles, transportation and logistics data processing systems. Contact: Naval Supply Systems Command, Department of the Navy, Washington, DC 20376/202-695-4009.

Surface Weapons Center
This office performs research and development, testing and evaluation in the field of exterior, interior and terminal ballistics, surface warfare systems, strategic systems and ordnance systems; also basic and applied research in physics, chemistry, aeroballistics and mathematics in areas that relate to weapons systems development and evaluation of both conventional and nuclear weapons. Contact: Naval Surface Weapons Center, Department of the Navy, Dahlgren, VA 22448/703-633-8531, or 202-394-1488.

Surplus Personal Property Sales
The U.S. Department of Defense sells its surplus and foreign excess property (excluding real property) to individuals, business concerns and other organizations of all sizes and classifications. There are two types of sales—national and local. Two free pamphlets—*How to Buy Surplus Personal Property from the Department of Defense* and *Classes of Surplus Personal Property Sold by the Department of Defense*—as well as a list of regional officers and property locations are available. For further information, contact: Department of Defense Bidders Control Office, Defense Property Disposal Service, Defense Logistics Agency, Department of Defense, Federal Center, Battle Creek, MI 49016/616-962-6511, ext. 6736.

The U.S. Department of Defense donates or lends surplus material to veterans' organizations, soldiers' museums, incorporated museums and incorporated municipalities. Contact the nearest military installation or Property Disposal Division, Defense Logistics Agency, Cameron Station, Room 46541, Alexandria, VA 22314/202-274-6541.

Survivability/Vulnerability Information Analysis Center (SURVIAC)
SURVIAC is the DoD focal point for nonnuclear survivability/vulnerability data, information, methodologies, models and analysis relating to U.S. and foreign aeronautical and surface (excluding ships) targets. SURVIAC maintains and operates the former Combat Data Information Center (CDIC) data bases and Aircraft Survivability Model Repository (ASMR) library of computerized models. SURVIAC provides users with products and specialized reference services. The staff can be tasked to provide evaluative engineering and/or analytical service. Data base searches and copies of technical reports are provided on a cost recovery basis. For further information contact: Survivability/Vulnerability Information Analysis Center, AFWAL/FIES/SURVIAC, Wright-Patterson AFB, OH 45433/513-255-4840.

Survival, Evasion, and Escape
Although intended for Army personnel, this manual contains helpful information for outdoorsmen as well. It covers firemaking and cooking, finding food and water, survival in cold weather, and much more. This publication is available for $9.00 from the Superintendent of Documents, Government Printing Office, Washington, DC 20402/202-783-3238.

Tactical Technology Center (TACTEC)
TACTEC provides users with products and specialized reference services. The staff can be tasked

to provide evaluative engineering and/or analytical service. The IAC holds over 50,000 items covering the technology of tactical warfare from incipient insurgency through tactical nuclear warfare. Data base searches and copies of technical reports are provided on a cost recovery basis. For further information contact: Battelle-Columbus Laboratories, 505 King Avenue, Columbus, OH 43201/ 614-424-7010.

Tank Research
For information on research and development programs on combat, tactical and special purpose vehicles, including automotive subsystems and components, component programs involving engines, transmissions and suspensions, and electrical and miscellaneous vehicular components, contact: Army Tank Automotive Command (TACOM), Dpeartment of Defense, Warren, MI 48090/ 313-574-6307.

Task Force on Equity for Women
The Department of Defense Task Force on Equity for Women has been directed to evaluate the effects of defense policies, programs and practices on opportunities for women and recommend changes where appropriate. The role of women is considered vital to the national security of our country.

The Task Force has been formed to help identify actions, in addition to the many initiatives already underway, to increase opportunities for military and civilian women in DOD, and for civilian spouses of military personnel. Specific duties of the Task Force are to:

Evaluate effects of DOD policies, programs and practices on women, and recommend changes where necessary.

Examine the impact of existing and proposed legislation on equitable opportunities for DOD women.

Ensure that material produced by DOD is free of gender-biased references or effects.

Contact: Assistant Secretary of Defense (Manpower, Installations and Logistics), Department of Defense, Pentagon, Washington, DC 20301-4000/202-695-2431.

Technology Transfer
For information on the technology transfer policy, which includes the transfer of critical technologies to NATO and the tapping of technological resources of U.S. allies, contact: International Programs and Technology Research and Engineering, Department of Defense, The Pentagon, Room 3E1082, Washington, DC 20301/202-697-4172.

Textiles Research and Development
Research and development is conducted in the physical and biological sciences and engineering to meet military requirements in commodity areas of textiles, clothing, body armor, footwear, insecti-

cides and fungicides, subsistence, containers, food service, equipment, tentage, equipage, and air delivery equipment. Contact: Army Natick Research and Development Center (NARADCOM), Department of Defense, Natick, MA 01760/ 617-651-4300.

Thermophysical and Electronic Properties Information Analysis Center (TEPIAC)
TEPIAC provides users with products and specialized reference service. The staff can be tasked to provide evaluative engineering and/or analytical service on the following subjects: Material property data for high energy laser structural and detector vulnerability/hardening assessments. TEPIAC supports the DoD Tri-Service Laser Hardened Materials and Structures Group. Data base searches and copies of technical reports are provided on a cost recovery basis. For further information contact: TEPIAC/CINDAS, Purdue University, 2595 Yeager Road, West Lafayette, IN 47906/317-463-1581.

Tools for Schools
Qualified nonprofit educational institutions and training schools may be loaned idle equipment from the Defense Industrial Reserve. Contact: Directorate of Services, Supply Operations, and Maintenance Depot Operations Division DLA-OWM, Defense Logistics Agency, Cameron Station, Alexandria, VA 22314/202-274-6269.

Topographic Laboratories
Research and development is conducted in the topographic sciences, including mapping, point positioning and military geographic information; scientific and technical advisory services are provided to meet environmental design requirements of military materiel developers and to support the geographic intelligence and environmental resource inventory requirements of military and nonmilitary programs. Contact: Commander, Army Engineer Topographic Laboratories, Fort Belvoir, VA 22060/703-664-3624.

Topographic Maps—Defense Mapping Agency
Topographic maps present the horizontal and vertical positions of the features represented. The shape and elevation of the terrain are normally portrayed by contours and spot elevations. Contact: DMA Office of Distribution Services, Department of the Army, Department of Defense, Washington, DC 20315/202-227-2816.

Training Equipment
The Naval Training Equipment Center is responsible for the procurement of training aids and devices for the Army, Navy, Marines Corps and other government activities, including the following: research and development in simulation technology and techniques; studies in the fields of

training psychology and human engineering; design and engineering development of training devices, weapons system trainers and simulators; and technical data and related ancillary support materials and services. Contact: Naval Training Equipment Center, Department of the Navy, Department of Defense, Orlando, FL 32813/305-646-5464.

Underwater Systems Center
This office plans and conducts programs of warfare and systems analysis, research, development, testing and evaluation and fleet support in underwater warfare systems and components, undersea surveillance systems, navigation, and related science and technology. Contact: Naval Underwater Systems Center, Department of the Navy, Department of Defense, Newport Laboratory, Newport, RI 02840/401-841-2067.

Unfunded Research and Development Studies
Qualified individuals and organizations may conduct studies and projects pertaining to Army research and development as part of its organization-funded, defense-oriented research and development programs. The Army will make its personnel available for consultation. Contact: DARCOM TRI-SERVICE Information Center, Department of the Army, Department of Defense, 5001 Eisenhower Ave., Alexandria, VA 22333/202-274-8948.

Uniform Relocation Assistance Act
This Act provides for payment of certain benefits to landowners, tenants, businesses and farmers who move from real property, or move personal property from real property, as a result of the acquisition of the real property by the government for Federal or federally-assisted programs. The benefits include reimbursement, to the extent allowed by the Act, for moving costs, increased costs of replacement housing, and direct losses of personal property by a farm or business operation. It also establishes fair land acquisition policies. All Federal agencies must comply with this Act. The U.S. Army Corps of Engineers administers this Act on behalf of the Department of the Army. Contact: U.S. Army Corps of Engineers, Attn: DAEN-REH, Washington, D.C. 20314/202-272-0517.

Uniformed Services University of the Health Sciences
This school has been established to educate career-oriented health professionals for the military services and in the case of physicians, for the Public Health Service as well. The university currently incorporates a school of medicine and graduate and continuing education programs. Contact: Uniformed Services University of the Health Sciences, Department of Defense, 4301 Jones Bridge Rd., Room A1045, Bethesda, MD 20814/202-295-3049.

United States Air Force Academy
The Academy offers four years of college education learning to a bachelor of science degree. For further information, contact: Air Force Academy, USAFA, CO 80840/303-472-4040.

United States Army Field Band
The U.S. Army Field Band, the Army's official band, conducts two major tours each year. Components of the band are the Concert Band, Soldiers' Chorus and Jazz Ambassadors. Contact: Office of the Chief of Public Affairs, Department of the Army, Department of Defense, The Pentagon, Room 2E631, Washington, DC 20310/202-697-2707, or United States Army Field Band, Ft. George G. Meade, MD 20755/301-677-2615.

United States Military Academy
The Academy offers four years of college education leading to a bachelor of science degree. Cadets receive a monthly allowance plus tuition, medical care, and room and board. Graduates receive Regular Army commissions and must serve on active duty for at least five years after commissioning. Those interested in securing an appointment should write to their Senators or district Representative in Congress, or contact: Academy Director of Admissions and Registrar, United States Military Academy, West Point, NY 10996/914-938-4011.

United States Naval Academy
The Academy offers a four-year program of academic, military and professional instruction leading to a bachelor of science degree. Completion of the program normally leads to a commission in the United States Navy or the U.S. Merchant Marine. For information, contact: United States Naval Academy, Annapolis, MD 21402/301-267-6100.

Unsolicited Proposals
Industrial organizations, academic institutions, and individuals can participate in research and development programs through unsolicited proposals. These proposals should have no relation to specific solicitation and should contain new ideas. A free guide, *Guide for Voluntary Unsolicited Proposals,* is available from: Army Materiel Development and Readiness Command, Attn: DRCDE-LU, Department of Defense, 5001 Eisenhower Ave., Alexandria, VA 22333/202-274-8333.

Voting Assistance
A *Voting Assistance Guide,* posters and a revised Federal Post Card Application (FPCA) are available to support voting assistance programs enabling United States citizens overseas to register to

vote. The material is available free from U.S. embassies, consulates and U.S. military installations. *Voting Assistance Guide* ($5.50) is also available from the Government Printing Office, Superintendent of Documents, Washington, DC 20402/202-783-3238.

Walter Reed Army Institute of Research
The following topics comprise the major areas of research at the institute: virology, bacteriology, and nicketsiology of tropical diseases; parasite diseases such 'as schistosomiasis, leshmaniaisis, malaria; preventive medicine; monoclonal antibodies for vaccines and rapid identification and detection; serotyping of disease strains; microwave effects on biological systems; drug and vaccine development; human stress studies; effects of transient overpressure on respiratory systems; control of insects important as human disease vectors; laboratory animal care; and pathology research. Contact: Walter Reed Army Institute of Research, Department of the Army, Attn: SGRD-UWZ-I, Washington, DC 20307/ 202-576-3814.

Water Supply and Management
The U.S. Army Corps of Engineers has 169 contractual agreements for water supply storage in 111 reservoirs. For many communities the water that the Corps has reserved from its multipurpose reservoirs is the main water source. Contact: Army Corps of Engineers, Washington, DC 20314/ 202-272-0228. Attn: DAEN-CWP.

Waterways
Research and development is conducted in the fields of hydraulics, soil mechanics, concrete, engineering, geology, rock mechanics, pavements, expedient construction, nuclear and conventional weapons effects, protective structures, vehicle mobility, environmental relationships, aquatic weeds water quality, dredge material research and nuclear and chemical explosives excavation. Contact: Engineer Waterways Experiment Station, Office of the Chief of Engineers, Department of Defense, P.O. Box 631, Vicksburg, MS 39180/601-636-3111.

Weapons Research—Air Force
Research is conducted in the areas of weapons effects, kill mechanisms, radiation hazards, and delivery techniques. Development and evaluation programs for advanced nonconventional weapon and nuclear power systems integration, nuclear weapon components, training devices, suspension and release systems, ground handling equipment, nuclear safety studies and civil engineering research and weapons effects simulation devices and techniques are conducted. Contact: Air Force Weapons Laboratory, Air Force Systems Command, Department of the Air Force, Kirtland Air Force Base, NM 87117/505-844-2664.

White Sands Missile Range
This facility conducts testing and evaluation of Army missiles and rockets and operates the only U.S. land-based national range to support missile and other testing for the Army, Air Force, Navy and National Aeronautics and Space Administration. Contact: Public Affairs Office, White Sands Missile Range, NM 88002/505-678-1134.

Women in Defense
The pamphlet, *Going Strong!,* describes the role of women in defense and the programs within the Department of Defense to promote their position. This pamphlet is available for $1.75 from the Superintendent of Documents, Government Printing Office, Washington, DC 20402/202-783-3238. For further information on women's programs in the Department of Defense. Contact: Office of Assistant Secretary of Defense Manpower, Installations, Logistics, Department of Defense, Washington, DC 20301-4000/202-695-2431.

Worldwide Locator
Each branch of the Armed Services has a worldwide locator number that aids in locating its members. The operator needs the full name and if available the birth date and Social Security number of the military person that is to be located. There is no charge for this service to military personnel or members of the immediate family. All other users of the service must pay a fee of $2.85 and submit their request by mail.

Air Force	512-652-5774	
	Mailing Address:	AF MPC/MPC D003
		9504 IH 35 N
		San Antonio, TX 78233-6636
	Checks payable to Air Force, Randolph Air Force Base	

Army	317-542-3647	
	Mailing Address:	USAEREC
		Attn: Locator Branch
		Ft Harrison, IN 46249-5301
	Checks payable to the U.S. Treasury	

Marine Corps   202-694-1861
                Mailing Address:

                                    CMC MMRB-10
                                    HQs U.S. Marine Corp
                                    Washington, DC 20380
                Checks payable to the U.S. Treasury

Navy   202-694-3155
                Mailing Address:

                                    (for non-family members)
                                    Naval Military Personnel Command N 0216
                                    Washington, DC 20370-5021

                                    (for family members)
                                    Naval Military Personnel Command N 036CC
                                    Washington, DC 20370-5036
                Checks payable to the U.S. Treasury

Yuma Proving Ground
This facility conducts research and development, production and post-production testing of components and complete items of weapons, systems, ammunition and combat and support vehicles, desert environmental tests of some items, air drop and air delivery tests and participation in engineering and expanded service testing of combat and support items. Contact: Commander, Yuma Proving Ground, Yuma AZ 85365/602-328-2163.

How Can the Department of Defense Help You?
If you believe that the U.S. Department of Defense can help you and you cannot find a relevant office listed in this section, contact: Staff Assistant for Public Correspondence, Department of Defense, Office of the Assistant Secretary of Defense, Public Affairs, The Pentagon, Washington, DC 20301/202-697-5737.

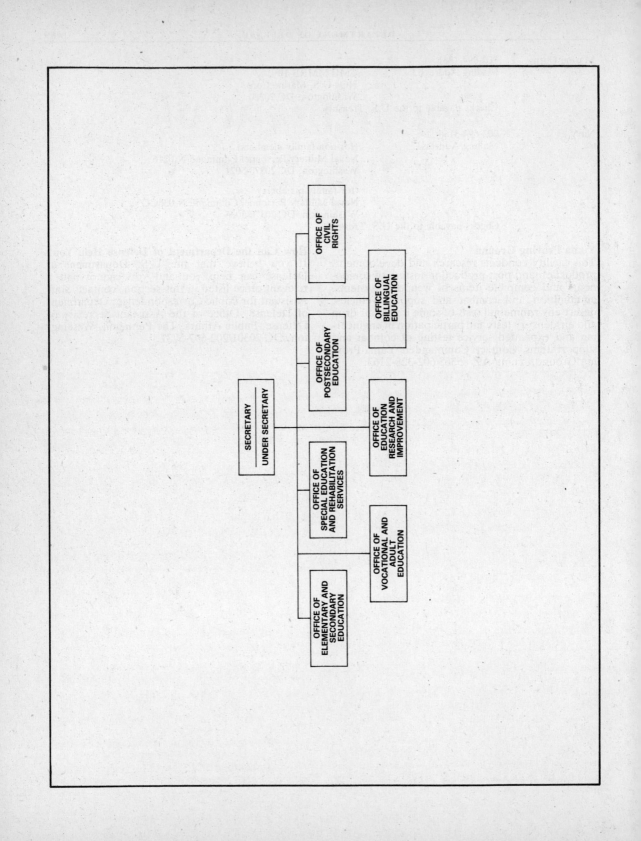

Department of Education

400 Maryland Ave. S.W., FOB 6, Room 4181,
Washington, DC 20202/202-426-6426

Established: May 5, 1980
Budget $13,832,972,000
Employees: 4,990

MISSION: To oversee the federal education effort as outlined by Congress.

Major Divisions and Offices

Office of Civil Rights

Department of Education (ED), 400 Maryland Ave. S.W., Room 5000, Washington, DC 20202/202-245-7680.
Budget: $44,396,000
Employees: 914
Mission: Administers and enforces civil rights laws relating to education and the handicapped; and ensures compliance in programs and activities receiving Federal financial assistance and by employers holding Federal contracts.

Office of Elementary and Secondary Education

Department of Education, 400 Maryland Ave. S.W., Room 2189, Washington, DC 20202/202-245-8720.
Budget: $4,038,149,000
Employees: 257
Mission: Formulates policy for, directs, and coordinates the activities relating to preschool, elementary, and secondary education; and administers programs of grants to State educational agencies and local school districts for Indian and migrant education, programs of financial and technical assistance to school districts to meet special needs incident to the elimination of racial segregation and discrimination, and grants for the education of neglected and delinquent students.

Office of Vocational and Adult Education

Department of Education, ROB#3, 7th and D Sts. S.W., Room 5102, Washington, DC 20202/202-245-8166.
Budget: $823,661,000
Employees: 119
Mission: Administers programs of grants, contracts, and technical assistance for vocational and technical education, education professions development, community schools, and comprehensive employment and training; also responsible for providing a unified approach to rural family education.

Office of Special Education and Rehabilitation Services

Department of Education, 300 C St, S.W. Room 3006, Washington, DC 20202/202-732-1723
Budget: $2,146,979,000
Employees: 429
Mission: Responsible for special education programs and services expressly designed to meet the needs and develop the full potential of handicapped children; and comprehensive rehabilitation service programs specifically designed to reduce human dependency, to increase self-reliance, and to fully utilize the productive capabilities of all handicapped persons.

Office of Postsecondary Education

Department of Education, 400 Maryland Ave. S.W., ROB-3, Room 4082, Washington, DC 20202/202-245-4274
Budget: $6,122,152,000
Employees: 1,194
Mission: Formulates policy and directs and coordinates programs for assistance to postsecondary educational institutions and students pursuing a postsecondary education; and provides assistance for the improvement and expansion of American educational resources for international studies and services, grants to improve instruction in crucial academic subjects, and construction assistance for academic facilities.

Office of Educational Research and Improvement

Department of Education, 1200 19th St., N.W., Room 722 Brown Building, Washington, DC 20208/202-254-8251.
Budget: $138,298,000

Employees: 451
Mission: Administers functions of the Department concerning research, development, demonstration, dissemination, and assessment; also administers a wide variety of discretionary grant programs to maximize individual program impact on school improvement.

Bilingual Education

Department of Education, 400 Maryland Avenue, S.W., Room 421, Reporter Building, Washington, DC 20202/202-245-2600.
Budget: $94,534,000
Employees: 49
Mission: Ensures access to equal educational opportunity and improves the quality of programs for limited English proficiency and minority languages populations by providing support for programs, activities, and management initiatives that meet the special educational needs of those populations; and provides assistance for the development, adoption, and implementation of plans for the desegregation of public schools.

Major Sources of Information

Abroad, Study and Teaching Opportunities
See *"International Education Information Clearinghouse"* in this section.

Adult Career and Vocational Information Clearinghouse
Information services are available on adult, career, and continuing education, and vocational and technical education. Contact: Educational Reference and Information Center (ERIC), Clearinghouse on Adult, Career and Vocational Education, Ohio State University, Center for Vocational Education, 1960 Kenny Rd., Columbus, OH 43210/614-486-3655 or 800-848-4815.

Adult Education
See *"Occupational Education"* in this section.

Adult Education Clearinghouse
This office provides information on adult education programs in The United States. Newsclips about adult education programs are compiled from local newspapers across the U.S. A free information package titled, *Adult Programs That Work,* is available. It contains descriptions of successful adult education programs. Two publications can be ordered free of charge from the clearinghouse. They are:

Bibliography of Clearinghouse Publications
Directory of Clearinghouses of Education in the United States

For further information contact: Adult Education Clearinghouse, Office of Vocational and Adult Education, Division of Adult Education, Department of Education, 400 Maryland Ave, ROB-3, Room 5610, Washington, DC 20202/202-245-9793.

American Education Magazine
Published monthly, except for combined issue in July and August, this magazine keeps educational professionals informed on new funding programs and the results of studies and reports sponsored by the Department of Education. For further information contact: Editor, *American Education Magazine,* 400 Maryland Ave. S.W., Washington, DC 20202/202-245-8907. Subscriptions are available for $20 from the Superintendent of Documents, U.S. Government Printing Office, Washington, DC 202-783-3238.

Architectural and Transportation Barriers
Complaints about federally funded buildings that are inaccessible to handicapped people are handled by the Compliance Board. A free publication called *Access America* tells how and when to file a formal complaint. Contact: Architectural and Transportation Barriers Compliance Board, Switzer Building, 330 C St. S.W., Room 1010, Washington, DC 20202/202-245-1591 (Voice TDD).

Arts and Humanities
For information on programs and funding available for arts and humanities education contact: Arts and Humanities, Special Projects, Department of Education, 400 Maryland Ave, S.W.,

Donohoe Building, Room 3728, Washington, DC 20202/202-472-7960.

Asian and Pacific Americans
A special office provides information to the Asian and Pacific community on grants and other projects that might be of special interest. Contact: Asian and Pacific American Concerns Staff, Department of Education, 400 Maryland Ave. S.W., Reporters Building, Room 501, Washington, DC 20202/202-472-4672

Bilingual Education Information Clearinghouse and Hotline
Along with a free bimonthly newsletter, *Forum,* the Clearinghouse offers data base searches, publications and other information services. Contact: National Clearinghouse for Bilingual Education, Department of Education, 1551 Wilson Blvd., Suite 600, Rosslyn, VA 22209/800-336-4560 (VA: 703-522-0710).

Black Educational Programs
For information on the availability and need for educational programs covering black concerns contact: Black Concerns Unit, Department of Education, 300 7th St. S.W., Reporters Building, Room 507, Washington, DC 20202/202-447-9043.

Braille Books
See "Braille Books" under "Major Sources of Information," "U.S. Department of Health and Human Services."

Captioned Films
A free catalog listing educational and entertainment films for the deaf is available from: Modern Talking Pictures, 500 Park Street N., St. Petersburg, FL 33709/813-541-7571.

Career Education
For information on effective career education techniques at elementary and secondary levels contact: Career Education, Department of Education, 400 Maryland Ave. S.W., Donohoe Building, Room 1725, Washington, DC 20202/202-472-7960.

Class of 1972
The U.S. Department of Education maintains a continual investigation into the education, job training and vocational histories of a nationally representative sample of 22,000 young people who were high school seniors in 1972. The data include: postsecondary education, early vocation and work experiences, social development information, and how all these factors are related to earlier achievement levels, aspirations, attitudes and intervening educational and occupational variables. For information on available publications and other output, contact: National Longitudinal Study of the High School Class of 1972. Longitudinal Studies

Branch, Division of Math-Level Education Statistics, National Center for Education Statistics, Department of Education, Brown Bldg., 1200 19th St., N.W., Washington, DC 20208-1402/202-254-5213.

College and University Directory
A directory entitled *Educational Directory: Colleges and Universities 1981-82* is available offering pertinent data on all colleges and universities in the United States. A 1982-83 *Supplement* is also available. The cost is $9.00 for the directory and $5.50 for the Supplement. Contact: Government Printing Office, Superintendent of Documents, Washington, DC 20202/202-783-3238.

Community Colleges
For information and expertise concerning community college activities, including available programs and funding contact: Office of Higher Education, Bureau of Higher and Continuing Education, Department of Education, 7th and D Sts. S.W., Room 4913, Washington, DC 20202/202-245-9758

Computerized Data Bases
The following data bases are maintained by the Department of Education.

Bilingual Education Data Base
The National Clearinghouse for Bilingual Education (NCBE) has the only data base in the U.S. devoted to bilingual education. The NCBE data base has three sections: a bibliographic file, a directory file and an accessions file. Accessions file is a comprehensive list, with source and availability information, of materials held in selected bilingual education centers throughout the country.

NCBE will perform customized searches of its data base and ERIC for a minimum fee of $10.00, which entitles a requester to up to 100 citations. The Clearinghouse has access to more than 80 other data bases which staff will search for a minimum fee of $10.00 plus 15 cents per citation. NCBE also has 100 prepared "Searches-On-File," which are available for $2.50-$5.00. The NCBE data base is also available on BRS. Contact: National Clearinghouse for Bilingual Education, 1555 Wilson Boulevard, Suite 605, Rosslyn, VA 22209/703-522-0710 or toll-free 800-336-4560.

National Assessment of Educational Progress Data Base
The NAEPIRS data base contains findings from the National Assessment of Educational Programs (NAEP) project. NAEP is an on-going assessment of the achievements of students aged 9, 13 and 17 with periodic coverage of adults. NAEPIRS contains data collected since 1969 on more than ten million students in ten subject areas, including reading, mathematics, science, writing and social

studies. Retrievable data includes: attitudes, background, sex, race, geographical location, economic status, parental education, achievement level and more.

Free copies of NAEP's most recent findings are available to the general public. To obtain a copy, send NIE a blank double-sided, double-density system formatted diskette for the IBM PC computer. Contact: Testing Assessment & Evaluation Division, Teaching and Learning Program, National Institute of Education, 1200 19th St., N.W., Stop 9, Washington, DC 20208.

Continuing Education
The Office of Higher Education supports strengthening of community service programs and the expansion of continuing education programs for adults and other nontraditional students; provides encouragement and assistance to women and minorities to prepare them for careers in academic and other fields in which they have traditionally been underrepresented and to increase the number of persons trained for public service; and helps disadvantaged students train for the legal profession. Contact: Bureau of Higher and Continuing Education, Department of Education, ED, 400 Maryland Ave. S.W., ROB-3, Room 3082, Washington, DC 20202/202-245-9758.

Counseling and Personnel Services Information Clearinghouse
Information services are available on the training, practice and supervision of counselors at all education levels and in all settings; contact: Education Reference and Information Center (ERIC), Clearinghouse on Counseling and Personnel Services, University of Michigan, School of Education Building, Room 2108, Ann Arbor, MI 48109/313-764-9492.

Direct Payments
The programs described below are those that provide financial assistance directly to individuals, private firms, and other private institutions to encourage or subsidize a particular activity.

Bilingual Vocational Instructional Materials, Methods, and Techniques
Objectives: To develop bilingual instructional materials, and encourage research programs and demonstration projects to meet the shortage of such instructional materials available for bilingual vocational training programs.
Eligibility: State agencies, public and private educational institutions, nonprofit organizations, private-for-profit organizations, and individuals (private-for-profit organizations and individuals are only eligible for contracts).
Range of Financial Assistance: Averages $280,000.
Contact: Demonstration Branch, Division of Research and Demonstration, Bureau of Occupa-

tional and Adult Education, Department of Education, 400 Maryland Avenue, S.W., Washington, D.C. 20202/202-447-9227.

Bilingual Vocational Instructor Training
Objectives: To provide training for instructors of bilingual vocational training programs.
Eligibility: State agencies, public and private nonprofit educational institutions, and private-for-profit educational institutions (the last named being eligible only for contracts).
Range of Financial Assistance: $129,234 to $226,377.
Contact: Demonstration Branch, Division of Research and Demonstration, Bureau of Occupational and Adult Education, Department of Education, 400 Maryland Avenue, S.W., Washington, D.C. 20202/202-447-9227.

Bilingual Vocational Training
Objectives: To train individuals of limited English-speaking ability for gainful employment as semiskilled or skilled workers, technicians, or subprofessionals in recognized, new, and emerging occupations.
Eligibility: Local educational agencies, State agencies, post secondary education institutions, private nonprofit vocational training institutions, nonprofit educational or training organizations especially created to serve a group whose language as normally used is other than English, and private-for-profit agencies and organizations (last named being eligible only for contracts).
Range of Financial Assistance: $105,723 to $366,746.
Contact: Office of Bilingual Education, Department of Education, 400 Maryland Avenue, S.W., Washington, D.C. 20202/202-447-9227.

Handicapped Media Services and Captioned Films
Objectives: To maintain a free loan service of captioned films for the deaf and instructional media for the educational, cultural, and vocational enrichment of the handicapped; provide for acquisition and distribution of media materials and equipment; provide contracts and grants for research into the use of media; and train teachers, parents, and others in media utilization.
Eligibility: Public and private agencies, organizations, or groups may submit proposals and applications for projects to the Division of Media Services.
Range of Financial Assistance: $2,400 to $4,650,000.
Contact: Caption Films and Telecommunications Branch, Division of Media Services, Department of Education, Washington, DC 20202/202-732-1172.

Higher Education—Veteran's Cost of Instruction Program
Objectives: To encourage colleges and universi-

ties to serve the special needs of veterans, especially Vietnam era and disadvantaged.

Eligibility: Nationally or regionally accredited insitutions of higher education. Proprietary institutions (i.e. organized for profit) and schools or departments of divinity are not eligible.

Range of Financial Assistance: $879 to $118,000. Contact: Chief, Veterans' Program Branch, Division of Student Services and Veterans' Programs, Department of Education, Washington, DC 20202/202-245-2806.

Higher Education Work-Study

Objectives: To promote the part-time employment of students, particularly those with great financial need, who require assistance to pursue courses of study at institutions of higher education.

Eligibility: Higher education institutions (public, other nonprofit, and proprietary) meeting eligibility requirements (accreditation, postsecondary, etc.).

Range of Financial Assistance: $200 to $9,107,362.

Contact: Campus-Based Branch, Division of Policy and Program Development, Office of Student Financial Assistance, Department of Education, Washington, DC 20202/202-245-9720.

National Defense/Direct Student Loan Cancellations

Objectives: To reimburse institutions for their share of National Defense Student Loan recipients who cancel their loans by becoming teachers or performing active military service in the U.S. Armed Forces.

Eligibility: Nonprofit organizations, state and local governments.

Range of Financial Assistance: $4 to $129,821.

Contact: Campus and State Grant Branch, Division of Program Operations, Bureau of Student Financial Assistance, 400 Maryland Avenue, S.W., Washington, DC 20202/202-245-2320.

National Defense/Direct Student Loans

Objectives: To establish loan funds at eligible higher education institutions to permit needy undergraduate and graduate students to complete their education.

Eligibility: Higher education institutions (public, other nonprofit, and proprietary) meeting eligibility requirements

Range of Financial Assistance: $200 to $12,000.

Contact: Policy Section, Campus-Based Branch, Division of Policy and Program Development, Bureau of Student Financial Assistance, Department of Education, Washington, DC 20202/202-245-9720.

Pell Grant Program

Objectives: To assist in making available the benefits of postsecondary education to qualified students.

Eligibility: Undergraduate students enrolled in eligible institutions of higher education, on at least a half-time basis, who are making satisfactory academic progress. The applicants must be U.S. citizens or eligible noncitizens.

Range of Financial Assistance: $200 to $1,800.

Contact: Division of Policy and Program Development, Basic Grants Branch, Bureau of Student Financial Assistance, Department of Education, 400 Maryland Avenue, S.W., Washington D.C. 20202/800-638-6700; in Maryland call 800-492-6602.

Plus Loans Program

Objectives: To provide additional guaranteed loans for student education expenses, at a rate of 12%, with repayment beginning within 60 days of loan.

Eligibility: Graduate students, independent undergraduates, and parents of dependent undergraduates accepted for enrollment at least half-time in participating schools.

Range of Financial Assistance: From $2,500 per year up to a total of $15,000 above and beyond Guaranteed Student Loan limitations.

Contact: Policy Section, Campus-Based Branch, Division of Policy and Program Development, Office of Student Financial Assistance, U.S. Department of Education, Washington, DC 20202/202-245-9720.

Supplemental Educational Opportunity

Objectives: To enable students of financial need to pursue higher education by providing grant assistance for educational expenses.

Eligibility: Institutions of higher education.

Range of Financial Assistance: $200 to $3,931,226.

Contact: Chief, Policy Section, Campus Based Branch, Division of Policy and Program Development, Office of Student Financial Assistance, Department of Education, Washington, DC 20202/202-245-9720.

Transition Program For Refugee Children

Objectives: To provide Federal Assistance to state and local educational agencies to meet the special educational needs of eligible refugee children enrolled in elementary and secondary schools.

Eligibility: State educational agencies, local educational agencies, institutions of higher education, and nonprofit private organizations.

Range of Financial Assistance: Averages $150 per eligible child.

Contact: Office of Bilingual Education and Minority Languages Affairs, Department of Education, 400 Maryland Avenue, S.W., Room 421, Reporters Building, Washington, D.C. 20020/202-472-3520.

Disadvantaged Children

For information on programs available to expand and improve elementary and secondary school programs for educationally deprived children in low-income areas contact: Division of Student Services, Services for Disadvantaged Students, Department of Education, 400 Maryland Ave. S.W., ROB3, Room 3042, Washington, DC 20202/202-426-8960.

Early Childhood Education Information Clearinghouse

Information services are available on the physical, psychological, social, educational and cultural development of children from birth through the primary grades. Contact: Educational Reference and Information Center (ERIC), Clearinghouse on Elementary and Early Childhood Education, University of Illinois, College of Education, 805 W. Pennsylvania Ave., Urbana, Ilinois 61801/217-333-1386.

Education Research Newletters

The National Institute of Education (NIE) publishes three free newsletters dealing with education research: *NIE Information, Funding Opportunities* and *Information on Unsolicited Proposals.* Contact: Office of Public Affairs, NIE, Department of Education, 1200 19th St. N.W., Room 816, Washington, DC 20208/202-254-5706.

Education Data Bases

For information about computerized data bases related to education, contact: National Center for Educational Statistics, Department of Education, Brown Bldg., 1200 19th St. N.W., Room 418, Washington, DC 20208-1402/202-254-6057.

Educational Development

The National Institute of Education supports research and dissemination activities that will help individuals, regardless of race, sex, age, economic status, ethnic origin, or handicapped condition, realize their full potential through education. Contact: National Institute of Education, Department of Education, 1200 19th St. N.W., Room 639, Washington, DC 20208/202-254-5740.

Educational Management Clearinghouse

Information services are available on the leadership, management and structure of educational organizations; the practice and theory of administration; the training of administrators; and the sites, building, equipping and renovating of educational facilities. Contact: ERIC Clearinghouse on Educational Management, University of Oregon, Library, Room 108, Eugene, Oregon 97403/503-686-5043.

Educational Programs That Work

Teachers and developers of programs that are deemed educationally significant are sponsored to go into the field to lend their expertise in repeating their programs. A directory called *Educational Programs That Work* describes these programs and

is available for free. Contact: National Diffusion Network, Office of Educational Research and Improvement, Department of Education, Brown Bldg., 1200 19th St., N.W., Room 613, Washington, DC 20201/202-653-7000.

Educational Reference and Information Center (ERIC)

ERIC is the largest data base in the world devoted entirely to educational literature and materials. Coverage includes bibliographies, professional reports, conference papers, statistical reports, literature surveys, federally funded programs descriptions, innovative programs, and curriculum materials. The full text of ERIC is available on microfiche in over 700 public libraries across the country, and monthly indexes facilitate a manual search of the data base. In addition, the data base is available on-line through several major commercial vendors. Two publications, *A Pocket Guide to ERIC* and *All About ERIC,* are available free of charge to explain the ERIC system, and a free directory of the facilities handling the data base is also available.

The ERIC data base collection has also been divided into 16 subject oriented information clearinghouses on specific areas of special interest. The User-Services staff members of these Clearinghouses will assist the public in identifying and accessing information within their particular area of interest. Typical requests include: Grants, loans and other government benefit programs available, literature sources including bibliographies, curriculum listings, referrals and experts in various fields, teaching aid including free publications and audiovisuals, current research and development, and other topics of value to educational professionals, students, parents, and the public in general. A listing of these clearinghouses is located in the Information on Anything and Everything section of the Sampler.

For additional information or to request one of the above free publications contact: Educational Reference and Information Center (ERIC), Information Resources, National Institute of Education, Washington, DC 20208/202-254-7934.

Environmental Education

Although there are no funds for new programs in environmental education, information on other resources or existing programs is available from: Office of Division of Educational Support, Elementary and Secondary Education, Department of Education, 400 Maryland Ave. S.W., Mail Stop 6264, Room 1100, Washington, DC 20202/202-245-9231.

Ethnic Heritage Studies

For information and expertise on programs and funding available for helping students become aware of their own heritage contact: Ethnic Heritage Studies, Bureau of School Improvement Program, Department of Education, 400 Maryland Ave. S.W., Donohoe Building, Room 1133, Washington, DC 20202/202-245-8484. For additional information on this topic contact: Ethnic Heritage Studies Clearinghouse, Social Studies Education Consortium, 855 Broadway, Boulder, CO 80302/303-492-8154.

Films, Slides, Video and Other Audiovisual Matter.
For news, information and a listing of audiovisual materials produced by the Education Department, contact: Office of Public Affairs, Department of Education, 400 Maryland Ave., S.W., FOB6, Room 2097, Washington, DC 20202/202-245-8564.

Foreign Language Research
For information about foreign language research grants, including applications and how-to-apply, contact: Center for International Education, Bureau of Higher Education, U.S. Department of Education, Washington, DC 20202/202-485-2555.

Freedom of Information Act
The central office for making a Freedom of Information Act request is: FOI, Department of Education, 400 Maryland Ave. S.W., FOB6. Room 2089, Washington, DC 20202/202-245-8633. See "Freedom of Information Act."

Fulbright Scholarships
See "Grants" in this section.

Gifted and Talented Education
For information on federal government-sponsored programs for gifted and talented children contact: Office of Gifted and Talented Education, Department of Education, 400 6th St. S.W., Room 3835, Washington, DC 20202/202-245-2482.

Grants
The programs described below are for sums of money given by the federal government to initiate and stimulate new or improved activities, or to sustain ongoing services.

Adult Education—State-Administered Program
Objectives: To expand educational opportunities and to encourage the establishment of programs of adult education enabling all adults to acquire basis skills necessary to function in society, to enable those adults who desire to continue their education to at least the level of completion of secondary schools.
Eligibility: Designated state educational agencies.
Range of Financial Assistance: $75,064 to $8,135,355.
Contact: Division of Adult Education, Bureau of Occupational and Adult Education, Department of Education, Washington, DC 20202/202-245-9797.

Aid To Land-Grant Colleges
Objectives: To provide funds to be used for instructor's salaries or instructional equipment in the approved disciplines.
Eligibility: States in which land-grant colleges are located are eligible for funds.
Range of Financial Assistance: Up to $50,000.
Contact: Office of Postsecondary Education, Department of Education, 400 Maryland Avenue S.W., Washington, D.C. 20202/202-245-2806.

Alcohol and Drug Abuse Education Program
Objectives: To develop, through training and technical assistance, local capability to solve problems in the area of alcohol and drug abuse prevention with applicability to other behavior problems such as truancy, vandalism, and disruptive behavior; to alleviate the alcohol and drug abuse crisis amoung youth by promoting awareness and understanding of the nature of the problem and developing and disseminating prevention and early intervention strategies.
Eligibility: Institutions of higher education; state education agencies, local educational agencies, public and private educational and community agencies, institutions, and organizations.
Range of Financial Assistance: $175,000 to $550,000.
Contact: Alcohol and Drug Abuse Program, Office of Elementary and Secondary Education, Department of Education, 400 Maryland Ave. S.W., Donohoe Building, Room 1561, Washington, DC 20202/202-472-7960.

Allen J. Ellender Fellowship Program
Objectives: To provide in the name of Allen J. Ellender an opportunity for participation by students of limited economic means and by their teachers, in the week-long government studies program supported by the Close Up Foundation. To increase understanding of the Federal Government among secondary school students and their teachers and communities.
Eligibility: Close Up Foundation, a nonpartisan, nonprofit, educational foundation; beneficiaries are economically disadvantaged secondary school students and their teachers.
Range of Financial Assistance: Not specified.
Contact: Close Up Foundation, 1235 Jefferson Davis Highway, Arlington, VA 22202/703-892-5400.

Bilingual Education
Objectives: To develop and carry out elementary and secondary school programs, including activities at the preschool level, to meet the educational needs of children of limited English proficiency, and to demonstrate effective ways of providing such children instruction designed to enable them, while using their native language, to achieve competence in English.

Eligibility: State education agencies, local education agencies, and institutions of higher education including junior and community colleges, and private nonprofit organizations that apply jointly or after consultation with one or more local education agencies.

Range of Financial Assistance: $5,000 to $1,800,000.

Contact: Office of Bilingual Education, Department of Education, 400 Maryland Ave. S.W., Washington, DC 20202/202-245-2595.

Bilingual Vocational Instructional Materials, Methods, and Techniques

Objectives: To develop instructional materials and encourage research programs and demonstration projects to meet the shortage of such instructional materials available for bilingual vocational training programs.

Eligibility: State agencies, public and private educational institutions, appropriate nonprofit organizations, and private-for-profit individuals and organizations.

Range of Financial Assistance: Average grant is $200,000.

Contact: Office of Bilingual Education, Department of Education, 400 Maryland Ave. S.W., Reporters Building, Room 421, Washington, DC 20202/202-447-9227.

Bilingual Vocational Instructor Training

Objectives: To provide training for instructions of bilingual vocational training programs.

Eligibility: States, public and private educational institutions, and private for-profit educational institutions.

Range of Financial Assistance: $125,000 to $225,000

Contact: Office of Bilingual Education Branch, Department of Education, 400 Maryland Ave. S.W., Reporters Building, Room 421, Washington, DC 20202/202-447-9227.

Bilingual Vocational Training

Objectives: To train individuals of limited English-speaking ability for gainful employment as semi-skilled or skilled workers or technicians or sub-professionals in recognized, new and emerging occupations.

Eligibility: Local educational agencies, appropriate state agencies, postsecondary education institutions, private nonprofit vocational training institutions, nonprofit organizations, and private-for-profit agencies especially created to serve a group whose language normally used is other than English.

Range of Financial Assistance: $105,723 to $366,746.

Contact: Office of Bilingual Education, Department of Education, 400 Maryland Ave. S.W., Washington, DC 20202/202-447-9227.

Business and International Education

Objectives: To promote innovation and improvement in international education curricula and to serve the needs of the business community.

Eligibility: Accredited institutions of higher education. Applying institutions must enhance international academic programs and provide appropriate service to the business community to expand commercial activities abroad.

Range of Financial Assistance: $3,250 to $110,000.

Contact: International Studies Branch, Division of International Services and Improvement, Department of Education, 400 Maryland Avenue, S.W., Room 3916, ROB-3, Washington, D.C. 20202/202-245-2794.

Centers for Independent Living

Objectives: To provide independent living services to severely handicapped individuals in order for them to function more independently in family and community settings and secure and maintain appropriate employment.

Eligibility: Principal eligible applicant is the State vocational rehabilitation agency; however, if a State agency fails to apply for a grant within six months after they are available, then any local public or private nonprofit agency may apply directly.

Range of Financial Assistance: Averages $150,000.

Contact: Special Assistant for Independent Living Projects, Rehabilitation Services Administration, Office of Human Development Services, Department of Education, 3216 Switzer Building, 400 Maryland Avenue, S.W., Washington, D.C. 20202/202-245-0537.

Civil Rights Technical Assistance and Training

Objectives: To provide direct and indirect technical assistance and training services to school districts to cope with educational problems occasioned by desegregation for race, sex, and national origin.

Eligibility: Any school board, state educational agency, institution of higher education, private nonprofit organization or public agency intended to help solve problems related to the desegregation by race, sex, and national origin of public elementary and secondary schools.

Range of Financial Assistance: $50,000 to $250,000.

Contact: Division of Technical Assistance, Bureau of Elementary and Secondary Education, Department of Education, 400 Maryland Ave. S.W., Washington, DC 20202/202-245-2181.

Client Assistance for Handicapped Individuals

Objectives: To provide assistance in informing and advising clients and client applicants of available benefits under the Rehabilitation Act: and to assist clients and applicants with projects, programs and facilities providing services to them under this Act.

Eligibility: States (through the Governor) are eligible for awards.

Range of Financial Assistance: $30,000 to $562,550.

Contact: Department of Education, Associate Commissioner for Developmental Programs, Rehabilitation Services Administration, Office of Special Education and Rehabilitative Services, Washington, DC 20202/202-732-1353.

College Library Resources

Objectives: To assist and encourage institutions of higher education and other eligible institutions in the acquisition of library materials.

Eligibility: All institutions of higher education, institutions, organizations and all other public or private nonprofit agencies that meet maintenance-of-effort requirements for library purposes. State, local, and private nonprofit library organizations and agencies which on the basis of a formal written agreement with one or more institutions of higher education make available library and information services on a cooperative basis.

Range of Financial Assistance: Average grant is $3,963.

Contact: Library Education and Postsecondary Resources Branch, Office of Library and Learning Resources, Bureau of Elementary and Secondary Education, Department of Education, 400 Maryland Ave. S.W. Washington, DC 20202/202-245-5090.

College Work-Study Program

Objectives: To provide part-time employment to students attending institutions of higher education who need the earnings to help meet their costs of postsecondary education.

Eligibility: Higher education institutions, public, private, nonprofit, postsecondary vocational and proprietary, meeting eligibility requirements.

Range of Financial Assistance: $200 to $7,708,722.

Contact: Division of Policy and Program Development, Student Financial Assistance Programs, Office of Assistant Secretary for Postsecondary Education, Department of Education, 400 Maryland Avenue, S.W. Washington, DC 20202/202-245-9720.

Education of Handicapped Children in State-Operated or Supported Schools

Objectives: To extend and improve comprehensive educational programs for handicapped children enrolled in state-operated or -supported schools.

Eligibility: State agencies and state-supported and state-operated schools for handicapped children. Local educational agencies may also partici-

pate on behalf of children who were formerly enrolled in state agencies.

Range of Financial Assistance; $208,301 to $23,819,704.

Contact: Division of Assistance to States, Bureau of Education for the Handicapped, Department of Education, Washington, DC 20202/202-472-4825.

Education Television and Radio Programming

Objectives: To carry out the development, production, evaluation, dissemination, and utilization of innovative educational television and/or radio programs.

Eligibility: State and local governments, public and private agencies, profit and nonprofit organizations, associations, institutions, and individuals.

Range of Financial Assistance: Not specified.

Contact: Educational Technology Development Branch, Division of Educational Technology, Office of Libraries and Learning Resources, Bureau of Elementary and Secondary Education, Department of Education, 400 Maryland Ave. S.W., Room 3116, Washington, DC 20202/202-245-9228.

Educational Research and Development

Objectives: To improve education in the United States through concentrating the resources of the National Institute of Education on priority research and development needs.

Eligibility: Public and private, profit and nonprofit organizations, institutions, agencies, and individuals, including state educational agencies, local education agencies and international organizations or agencies.

Range of Financial Assistance: $1,500 to $3,900,000.

Contact: National Institute of Education, Department of Education, 1200 19th St. N.W., Washington, DC 20208/202-254-5800.

Educationally Deprived Children in State Administered Institutions Serving Neglected or Delinquent Children

Objectives: To expand and improve educational programs to meet the special needs of institutionalized children for whom the state has an educational responsibility.

Eligibility: Departments of education in states.

Range of Financial Assistance: $2,062 to $2,771,434.

Contact: Director, Bureau of Elementary and Secondary Education, Department of Education, 7th and D Sts. S.W., Washington, DC 20202/202-245-3081.

Educationally Deprived Children—Local Educational Agencies

Objectives: To provide financial assistance to local educational agencies to meet the needs of educationally disadvantaged children in low-income areas whether enrolled in public or private elementary and secondary schools.

Eligibility: Departments of education in states; Bureau of Indian Affairs.

Range of Financial Assistance: $623,586 to $280,628,132.

Contact: Division of Education for the Disadvantaged, Bureau of Elementary and Secondary Education, Department of Education, Washington, DC 20202/202-245-3081.

Educationally Deprived Children—Migrants

Objectives: To expand and improve educational programs to meet the special needs of children of migratory agricultural workers or of migratory fishermen.

Eligibility: Departments of education in states.

Range of Financial Assistance: $36,902 to $55,534,124.

Contact: Migrant Education, Bureau of Elementary and Secondary Education, Department of Education, 400 Maryland Ave. S.W., Washington, DC 20202/202-245-9231.

Educationally Deprived Children—State Administration

Objectives: To improve and expand educational programs for disadvantaged children through financial assistance to state education agencies.

Eligibility: Departments of education in states.

Range of Financial Assistance: $50,000 to $3,299,016.

Contact: Director, Bureau of Elementary and Secondary Education, Department of Education, 7th and D Sts. S.W., Washington, DC 20202/202-245-3081.

Educational Opportunity Centers

Objectives: To provide and coordinate services for residents in areas with a major concentration of low-income people to facilitate their entry into postsecondary educational programs and to provide tutoring, counseling and other supportive services for enrolled postsecondary students from the target community.

Eligibility: Institutions of higher education, combinations of such institutions, public and private nonprofit agencies and organizations (including professional and scholarly organizations) and, in exceptional cases, secondary schools and secondary vocational schools.

Range of Financial Assistance: $124,800 to $467,999.

Contact: Director, Division of Student Services, Bureau of Higher and Continuing Education, Department of Education, 400 Maryland Ave. S.W., Washington, DC 20202/202-426-8960.

Follow Through

Objectives: To sustain and augment in primary grades the gains that children from low-income

families make in Headstart and other quality preschool programs. Follow Through provides special programs of instruction as well as health, nutrition, and other related services which will aid in the continued development of children to their full potential. Active participation of parents is stressed.

Eligibility: For discretionary project grants or contracts, only currently approved public and private institutions of higher education or other currently approved public or private educational or research agencies and organizations. For formula grants or contracts, state educational agencies and/or other appropriate agencies are eligible.

Range of Financial Assistance: $63,000 to $660,000.

Contact: Follow Through Division, Bureau of Elementary and Secondary Education, Department of Education, ROB-3, 7th and D Sts. S.W., Washington, DC 20202/202-245-3081.

Fulbright-Hays Training Grants—Doctoral Dissertation Research Abroad

Objectives: To provide opportunities for advanced graduate students to engage in full-time dissertation research abroad in modern foreign language and area studies. The program is designed to develop research knowledge and capability in world areas not widely included in American curriculums.

Eligibility: Candidate for a Dissertation Research Fellowship must be a citizen or national or permanent resident of the United States.

Range of Financial Assistance: $2,705 to $40,000.

Contact: Division of International Education, Department of Education, Room 3669, ROB-3, 7th and D Streets, S.W., Washington, D.C. 20202/202-245-2761.

Fulbright-Hays Training Grants—Faculty Research Abroad

Objectives: To help universities and colleges strengthen their programs of international studies through selected opportunities for research and study abroad in foreign language and area studies; to enable key faculty members to keep current in their specialties; to facilitate the updating of curricula and to help improve teaching methods and materials.

Eligibility: Candidates for faculty research awards must be U.S. citizens or nationals, educators experienced in a foreign language and area studies, with whom institutions have long-term employment relationships; possess adequate skills in the language of the country or in a language germane to the project or region where project would be undertaken; present detailed description of proposed project significant and feasible for the area and time concerned; and present a statement from the employing institution describing how the project will contribute to institution's plans for developing programs in foreign language or area studies.

Range of Financial Assistance: $6,020 to $18,940.

Contact: Division of International Education, Department of Education, 7th and D Sts. S.W., ROB-3, Washington, DC 20202/202-245-2761.

Fulbright-Hays Training Grants—Foreign Curriculum Consultants

Objectives: To benefit American education at all levels by helping institutions bring specialists from other countries to the United States to assist in planning and developing local curriculums in foreign language and area studies.

Eligibility: State departments of education, local school systems, institutions of higher education accredited by a nationally recognized accrediting agency or association, selected non-profit educational organizations, or a consortium of these institutions.

Range of Financial Assistance: $9,420 to $16,865.

Contact: International Education, Department of Education, ROB-3, Washington, DC 20202/ 202-245-2794.

Fulbright-Hays Training Grants—Group Projects Abroad

Objectives: To help education institutions improve their program in foreign language and area studies.

Eligibility: Universities, four-year colleges, community and junior colleges, state departments of education, nonprofit organizations, or consortiums of these institutions.

Range of Financial Assistance: $13,120 to $281,000.

Contact: Division of International Education, Department of Education, 7th and D Streets, S.W., ROB-3, Washington, DC 20202/202-245-2796.

Fund for the Improvement of Postsecondary Education

Objectives: To provide grants and contracts for innovative programs which increase the effectiveness of postsecondary education.

Eligibility: Postsecondary institutions, agencies and community organizations.

Range of Financial Assistance: $5,000 to $200,000.

Contact: Director, Fund for the Improvement of Postsecondary Education, Department of Education, 7th and D Streets, S.W., ROB-3, Room 3100, Washington, DC 20202/202-245-8091.

Graduate and Professional Opportunities

Objectives: To strengthen and develop programs which would assist in providing graduate profes-

sional education to persons with varied backgrounds and experiences including members of minority groups that are underrepresented in colleges and universities and in academic and professional career fields; to provide fellowships to support full-time graduate and professional training of members of those minority groups and women.

Eligibility: Any accredited institution of higher education with a graduate or professional program leading to an advanced degree, other than a medical degree. For fellowship applicants, any individual accepted by an approved institution as a candidate for an advanced degree.

Range of Financial Assistance: $4,500 to $75,000.

Contact: Bureau of Continuing and Higher Education, Division of Training and Facilities, Graduate Training Branch, Department of Education, 7th and D Sts. S.W., Washington, DC 20202/202-245-2347.

Handicapped Early Childhood Assistance

Objectives: To support experimental demonstration, outreach and state implementation of preschool and early childhood projects for handicapped children.

Eligibility: Public agencies and private non-profit organizations.

Range of Financial Assistance: $50,000 to $150,000.

Contact: Program Development Branch, Handicapped Children's Early Education Assistance, Division of Innovation and Development, Department of Education, 400 Maryland Ave. S.W., Washington, DC 20202/202-245-9405.

Handicapped Innovative Programs—Deaf-Blind

Objectives: To provide technical assistance to state education agencies and to improve services to deaf-blind children and youth.

Eligibility: Public or nonprofit agencies, organizations, or institutions.

Range of Financial Assistance: $1,078,726 to $2,388,854.

Contact: Centers and Services for Deaf-Blind Children, Division of Assistance to States, Department of Education, 400 Maryland Ave. S.W., Washington, DC 20202/202-723-1161.

Handicapped Innovative Programs—Programs for Severely Handicapped Children.

Objectives: To improve and expand innovative educational/training services for severely handicapped children and youth, and improve the general acceptance of such people by the general public, professionals, and possible employers.

Eligibility: Public and nonprofit private agencies, organizations, or institutions including state departments of special education, intermediate or local educational agencies, institutions of higher learning, professional organizations and volunteer associations.

Range of Financial Assistance: $81,662 to $257,156.

Contact: Projects for Severely Handicapped Children and Youth, Special Needs Section, Bureau of Education for the Handicapped, Department of Education, 400 Maryland Ave. S.W., Washington, DC 20202/202-732-1161.

Handicapped Preschool and School Programs

Objectives: To provide grants to states to assist them in providing a free appropriate public education to all handicapped children.

Eligibility: State education agencies.

Range of Financial Assistance: $198,669 to $78,487,252.

Contact: Division of Assistance to States, Department of Education, 400 Maryland Ave. S.W., Washington, DC 20202/202-245-9727.

Handicapped Regional Resource Centers

Objectives: To establish regional resource centers which provide advice and technical services to educators for improving education of handicapped children.

Eligibility: Institutions of higher education, state education agencies, local education agencies, or combinations of such agencies or institutions.

Range of Financial Assistance: $100,000 to $800,000.

Contact: Division of Media Services, Bureau of Education for the Handicapped, Department of Education, 400 Maryland Ave. S.W., Washington, DC 20202/202-732-1052.

Handicapped—Research and Demonstration

Objectives: To improve the education of handicapped children through research and development projects, and demonstrations model programs.

Eligibility: State or local educational agencies, public and private institutions of higher learning, and other public or private educational or research agencies and organizations.

Range of Financial Assistance: $4,000 to $500,000.

Contact: Chief, Research Projects Branch, Division of Innovation and Development, Department of Education, 400 Maryland Ave. S.W., Washington, DC 20202/202-245-9405. See "National Institute of Handicapped Research," and "Rehabilitation" and "Vocational Rehabilitation" listings in this section.

Handicapped—Special Studies

Objectives: To assess progress in implementing the Education of the Handicapped Act, and the effectiveness of State and local efforts to provide a free, appropriate public education to all handicapped children and youth.

Eligibility: State educational agencies are eligible to receive funds through the cooperative agreements program.

Range of Financial Assistance: $50,000 to $200,000.

Contact: Research Projects Branch, Chief, Division of Educational Services, Office of Special Education Programs, 400 Maryland Avenue, SW, Washington, DC 20202/202-472-5040.

Handicapped Teacher Recruitment and Information

Objectives: To disseminate information which can help parents, consumer organizations, professionals and others interested in special education in making decisions that affect the education and general well-being of handicapped children.

Eligibility: Public or nonprofit agencies, organizations, or institutions.

Range of Financial Assistance: $10,000 to $400,000.

Contact: Office of Special Education and Rehabilitative Services, Department of Education, 400 Maryland Ave. S.W., Washington, DC 20202/ 202-732-1167

Health Education Assistance Loans

See "Health Education Assistance Loans," under "Grants"; "Major Sources of Information"; and "U.S. Department of Health and Human Services."

Higher Education—Cooperative Education

Objectives: To provide federal support for cooperative education programs. Cooperative education programs are those which alternate periods of academic study with periods of public or private employment related to the student's academic program or professional goals.

Eligibility: Accredited institutions of higher education, including junior colleges, four-year colleges and universities, and other public or private nonprofit agencies and organizations.

Range of Financial Assistance: $9,700 to $189,200.

Contact: Cooperative Education Branch, Division of Training and Facilities, Bureau of Higher and Continuing Education, Department of Education, Washington, DC 20202/202-245-2146.

Higher Education—Strengthening Developing Institutions

Objectives: To strengthen developing colleges in their acedemic, administrative, and student services programs so that they may participate adequately in the higher education community.

Eligibility: A college or institution of higher learning that qualifies as developing.

Range of Financial Assistance: $37,000 to $2,000,000.

Contact: Division of Institutional Development, Office of Postsecondary Education, Department of Education, Washington, DC 20202/202-245-2384.

Improving School Programs—State Block Grants

Objectives: To assist state and local education agencies to improve elementary and secondary education, through consolidation of 29 elementary and secondary programs into a single authorization. The goal is to reduce paperwork and assign responsibility for the design and implementation of programs to local educational agencies.

Eligibility: All states including the District of Columbia and Puerto Rico; and the Insular Areas, including American Samoa, Guam, Northern Mariana Islands, Trust Territories and Virgin Islands.

Range of Financial Assistance: $2,229,304 to $42,084,402.

Contact: Division of Educational Support, State and Local Educational Programs, Office of Elementary and Secondary Education, Department of Education, 400 Maryland Avenue, S.W., Room 1725, Donohoe Building, Washington, D.C. 20202/202-245-7965.

Indian Education—Adult Indian Education

Objectives: To plan, develop, and implement programs for Indian adults.

Eligibility: State and local educational agencies, and Indian tribes, institutions, and organizations.

Range of Financial Assistance: $24,000 to $261,000.

Contact: Office of Indian Education, Department of Education, 400 Maryland Ave. S.W., Washington, DC 20202/202-245-8020.

Indian Education—Fellowships for Indian Students

Objectives: To provide support which enables American Indian people to study for careers in medicine, law, engineering, natural resources, business administration, education and related fields.

Eligibility: An American Indian who is in attendance, or who has been accepted for admission, as a full-time student at an institution of higher education for study in a graduate or professional program leading to a degree in engineering, medicine, law, business, forestry, or a related field.

Range of Financial Assistance: $2,300 to $13,000.

Contact: Office of Indian Education, Department of Education, 400 Maryland Ave. S.W., Washington, DC 20202/202-245-8020.

Indian Education—Grants to Local Educational Agencies and Tribal Schools

Objectives: To provide financial assistance to tribally controlled schools and local educational agencies to develop and implement elementary and secondary school programs designed to meet the special educational and culturally related academic needs of Indian children.

Eligibility: Local educational agencies which have at least ten Indian children or in which Indians constitute at least 50 percent of the total enrollment.

Range of Financial Assistance: $2,000 to $1,137,000.

Contact: Office of Indian Education, Department of Education, 400 Maryland Ave. S.W., Washington, DC 20202/202-245-8020.

Indian Education Grants to Indian Controlled Schools

Objectives: To provide financial assistance to nonlocal educational agencies to develop and implement elementary and secondary school programs designed to meet the special educational needs of Indian children. Nonlocal educational agencies are schools on or near a reservation which are governed by a nonprofit insititution or organization of an Indian tribe.

Eligibility: Nonlocal educational agencies meeting the eligibility factors; local educational agencies which have been local educational agencies for less than three years and meet the selection criteria may also apply.

Range of Financial Assistance: $50,000 to $295,000.

Contact: Office of Indian Education, Department of Education, 400 Maryland Ave. S.W., Washington, DC 20202/202-245-8020.

Indian Education—Special Programs and Projects.

Objectives: To plan, develop, and implement programs and projects for the improvement of educational opportunities for Indian children.

Eligibility: State and local educational agencies, federally supported elementary and secondary schools for Indian children, tribal and other. Indian community organizations, and institutions of higher education.

Range of Financial Assistance: $31,978 to $500,000.

Contact: Office of Indian Education, Department of Education, 400 Maryland Ave. S.W., Washington, DC 20202/202-245-8020.

International Research and Studies

Objectives: To improve foreign language and area studies training in the United States through support of research and studies, experimentation, and development of specialized instructional materials.

Eligibility: Institutions of higher education; qualified individual researchers; State educational agencies; public school systems; other educational and professional organizations.

Range of Financial Assistance: $6,000 to $100,000.

Contact: Centers and Research Section, Division of International Education, Department of Education, ROB-3, 7th and D Streets, S.W., Washington, D.C. 20202/202-245-2761.

International Studies and Foreign Language, Undergraduate Program

Objectives: To strengthen international and global dimensions in the general education curriculum of institutions of higher education by establishing international and global studies programs at the graduate and undergraduate levels.

Eligiblity: Accredited American colleges and universities, and public and non-profit agencies and organizations.

Range of Financial Assistance: $7,000 to $150,500.

Contact: International Studies Branch, Division of International Education, Department of Education, 7th and D Sts. S.W., ROB-3, Washington, DC 20202/202-245-2356.

Law-Related Education

Objectives: To support programs at the elementary and secondary school levels by developing and implementing model projects designed to institutionalize law-related education.

Eligibility: State educational agencies, local education agencies, public or private nonprofit agencies, organizations, and institutions may apply.

Range of Financial Assistance: $10,000 to $150,000.

Contact: Law-Related Education Program, Office of Elementary and Secondary Education, Division of Educational Support, 400 Maryland Avenue, S.W., Washington, D.C. 20202/202-472-7960.

Law School Clinical Experience Program

Objectives: To establish and expand programs in law schools to provide clinical experience to students in the practice of law, with preference being given to programs providing such experience, to the extent practicable, in the preparation and trial of cases.

Eligibility: Accredited law schools.

Range of Financial Assistance: $14,030 to $23,370.

Contact: Graduate Training Branch, Bureau of Higher and Continuing Education, Department of Education, 7th and D Sts. S.W., Washington, DC 20202/202-245-2347.

Legal Training for the Disadvantaged

Objectives; To provide educationally and economically disadvantaged students, many with marginal or less-than-traditional admissions credentials, an opportunity to attend an ABA-accredited law school, by operating seven six-week institutes.

Eligibility: Applicants must be either U.S. citizens or citizens or permanent residents of the Trust Territory of the Pacific Islands or intend to become permanent residents of the U.S. and reside in this

country for other than temporary purposes. Any person from a low-income or economically disadvantaged background who will have graduated from college by the beginning of the summer of 1983 may apply.

Range of Financial Assistance: Up to $1,000.

Contact: Graduate Training Branch, Office of Postsecondary Education, Division of Institutional and State Incentive Programs, Department of Education, Room 3060, 7th and D Street, S.W., Washington, DC 20202/202-245-2347.

Library Research and Demonstration

Objectives: To award grants and contracts for research and/or demonstration projects in areas of specialized services intended to improve library and information science practices and principles.

Eligibility: All institutions of higher education and all other public or private agencies, institutions, and organizations.

Range of Financial Assistance: Not specified.

Contact: Division of Library Programs, Department of Education, 400 Maryland Ave. S.W., Washington, DC 20202/202-245-5090.

Library Services and Construction Act

Objectives: To assist with public library construction.

Eligibility: State library extension agencies which have authority to administer federal funds, supervise public library service within a state, and together with participating libraries, have financial resources sufficient to match federal funds on a percentage basis according to per capita wealth.

Range of Financial Assistance: Not applicable.

Contact: State and Public Library Services Branch, Division of Library Programs, Center for Education Improvement, Department of Education, 400 Maryland Ave. S.W., Washington, DC 20202/202-254-9664.

Interlibrary Cooperation

Objectives: To provide for the systematic and effective coordination of the resources of school, public, academic, and special libraries and special information centers for improved services of a supplementary nature to the special clientele served by each type of library center.

Eligibility: State library administration agencies which have authority to administer federal funds and supervise library service within a state.

Range of Financial Assistance: Not applicable.

Contact: State and Public Library Services Branch, Office of Libraries and Learning Resources, Bureau of Elementary and Secondary Education, Department of Education, 400 Maryland Ave. S.W., Washington, DC 20202/202-254-9664.

Library Career Training Grants

Objectives: To assist institutions of higher education and library organizations and agencies in training persons in the principles and practices of librarianship and information science.

Eligibility: All institutions of higher education and all other nonprofit library organizations or agencies which have an established program of library education or are planning to begin such a program, or which have sufficient facilities and resources necessary to conduct a training program.

Range of Financial Assistance: $8,000 to $60,000.

Contact: Library Education and Postsecondary Resources Branch, Division of Library Programs, Office of Libraries and Learning Resources, Department of Education, 400 Maryland Ave. S.W., Washington, DC, 20202/202-254-5090.

Migrant Education—College Assistance Migrant Program

Objectives: To assist students who are engaged, or whose families are engaged, in migrant and other seasonal farmwork who are enrolled or are admitted for enrollment on a full-time basis in the first academic year at an institution of higher education.

Eligibility: Institutions of higher education or other public or nonprofit private agencies in cooperation with institutions of higher education.

Range of Financial Assistance: Not specified.

Contact: Migrant Education Programs, Office of Elementary and Secondary Education, Department of Education, 400 Maryland Avenue, S.W., ROB-3, Room 3616, Washington, D.C. 20202/202-245-2722.

Migrant Education—Basic State Formula Grant Program

Objectives: To establish and improve programs to meet the special educational needs of migratory children of migratory agricultural workers or of migratory fishers.

Eligibility: Migratory children of migratory agricultural workers or of migratory fishers.

Range of Financial Assistance: Not applicable.

Contact: Division of Migrant Education, Compensatory Education Program, Office of Elementary and Secondary Education, Department of Education, 400 Maryland Avenue, SW. Washington, DC ROB-3, Room 3616, Washington, DC 20202/202-245-2722.

Migrant Education—High School Equivalency Program

Objectives: To provide assistance to older migratory and seasonal farmworker children to attend college and/or attain a job or high school diploma.

Eligibility: Institutions of higher education or other public or nonprofit private agencies in cooperation with institutions of higher education.

Range of Financial Assistance: Not available.

Contact: Office of Migrant Education, Department of Education, 400 Maryland Avenue, S.W., ROB-3, Room 3616, Washington, D.C. 20202/202-245-2722.

Migrant Education—Interstate and Intrastate Coordination Program

Objectives: To carry out activities, in consultation with the states, to improve the interstate and intrastate coordination among state and local educational agencies serving migratory children and to operate a system for the transfer of migrant student records.

Eligibility: State educational agencies.

Range of Financial Assistance: Not available.

Contact: Office of Migrant Education, Department of Education, 400 Maryland Avenue, S.W., ROB-3, Room 3616, Washington, DC 20202/202-245-2722.

Minority Institutions Science Improvement Program

Objectives: To assist institutions to improve the quality of preparation of their students of minority work or careers in science. To increase the number of minority students graduating with majors in one of the sciences, mathematics, or engineering. To improve access for minorities to careers in science and engineering through community outreach programs at eligible colleges and universities. To improve the capability of minority institutions for self-assessment, management, and evaluation of their science programs and dissemination of their results.

Eligibility: Private and public accredited 2 and 4-year institutions of higher education whose enrollments are predominantly (50 percent or more) American·Indian; Alaskan Native; Black, not of Hispanic origin; Hispanic (including persons of Mexican, Puerto Rican, Cuban, and Central or South American origin); Pacific Islander; or any combination of these or other disadvantaged ethnic minorities who are underrepresented in science and engineering. Proposals may also be submitted by non-profit science-oriented organizations, professional scientific societies, and all non-profit accredited colleges and universities which will render a needed service to a group of MISIP-eligible institutions or provide in-service training for project directors, scientists, or engineers from eligible minority institutions.

Range of Financial Assistance: $15,000 to $500,000.

Contact: Minority Institutions Science Improvement Program, Office of Postsecondary Education, Department of Education, Washington, DC 20202/202-426-9313.

National Diffusion Program

Objectives: To promote and accelerate the systematic, rapid dissemination and adoption of educational practices, products, and programs which were developed in Office of Education, state and discretionary grant programs and whose effectiveness had been certified by the Joint Dissemination Review Panel.

Eligibility: Nonprofit public or private agencies, organizations, group or individuals, local governments.

Range of Financial Assistance: $20,000 to $190,000.

Contact: National Diffusion Network, Department of Education, Room 714F, 1200 19th St. NW Washington, DC 20208/202-653-7003.

National Institute of Handicapped Research

Objectives: To support research and its utilization to improve the lives of people of all ages with physical and mental handicaps, especially the severely disabled.

Eligibility: State, public or private nonprofit agencies and organizations, including institutions of higher education are eligible.

Range of Financial Assistance: $10,000 to $1,500,000.

Contact: National Institute of Handicapped Research, Department of Education, Room 3511, Washington, DC 20202/202-245-0795.

National Resource Centers and Fellowships Program for Language and Area or Language and International Studies.

Objectives: To promote instruction in those modern foreign languages and area and international studies critical to national needs by supporting the establishment and operation of such programs at colleges and universities; to meet the critical needs of American education for experts in foreign languages, area studies, and world affairs by supporting fellowships for advanced study at institutions for higher education.

Eligibility: Centers: Accredited American colleges and universities. Applying institutions must provide evidence of existing resources and institutional commitment to language and area and international studies through a curriculum that provides instruction dealing with a particular world area and its languages, with comparative world area studies, or with the international aspects of professional or other fields of study. Fellowships: Accredited institutions of higher education offering comprehensive graduate language and area and international studies are eligible to apply for award quotas.

Range of Financial Assistance: $35,000 to $80,000.

Contact: International Studies Branch, Division of International Education, Department of Education, ROB-3, 7th and D Streets, S.W., Washington, D.C. 20202/202-245-2794.

Neglected or Delinquent Transition Services.

Objectives: To provide special educational services to facilitate the transition of neglected or delinquent children from state-operated institutions into locally-operated programs.

Eligibility: State and local educational agencies.

Range of Financial Assistance: $46,080 to $3,827,904.

Contact: Compensatory Education Programs, Department of Education, 400 Maryland Avenue, S.W., ROB-3, Room 3616, Washington, D.C. 20202/202-245-3081.

Public Library Services

Objectives: To assist in extending public library services to areas without service or with inadequate service; establishing and expanding state institutional library services; offering library service to the physically handicapped; establishing and expanding library services to the disadvantaged in urban and rural areas, and strengthening the metropolitan public libraries which serve as national or regional resource centers; providing programs and projects to serve areas with high concentrations of persons of limited English-speaking ability; and strengthening major urban resource libraries.

Eligibility: State library administrative agencies which have authority to administer Federal funds, supervise public library service within a State, and together with participating libraries, have financial resources sufficient to match Federal funds on a percentage basis according to per capita wealth.

Range of Financial Assistance: Not available.

Contact: State and Public Library Services Branch, Office of Libraries and Learning Resources, Bureau of Elementary and Secondary Education, Department of Education, 400 Maryland Avenue, S.W., Washington, D.C. 20202/202-254-9664.

Regional Education Programs for Deaf and Other Handicapped Persons

Objectives: To develop and operate specially designed or modified programs of vocational, technical, postsecondary, or adult education for deaf or other handicapped persons.

Eligibility: Institutions of higher education, including junior and community colleges, vocational and technical institutions, and other appropriate nonprofit educational agencies.

Range of Financial Assistance: $25,000 to $50,000.

Contact: Program Development Branch, Regional Education Programs, Division of Innovation and Development, Bureau of Education for the Handicapped, Department of Education, 400 Maryland Ave. S.W., Washington, DC 20202/202-245-4660.

Rehabilitation Services and Facilities—Basic Support

Objectives: To provide vocational rehabilitation services to persons with mental and/or physical handicaps. Priority service is placed on needs of those persons with the most severe disabilities.

Eligibility: State agencies designated as the sole state agency to administer the vocational rehabilitation program.

Financial Assistance: $3,000,000 to $64,318,367.

Contact: Office of Program Operations, Rehabilitation Services Administration, Office of Assistant Secretary for Special Education and Rehabilitation Services, Department of Education, Washington, DC, 20202/202-245-0546.

Rehabilitation Services and Facilities—Service Projects

Objectives: To provide funds to state vocational rehabilitation agencies and public or nonprofit organizations for projects and demonstrations which hold promise of expanding and otherwise improving services for the mentally and physically handicapped over and above those provided by the Basic Support Program administered by states.

Eligibility: Projects with industry-employers and other organizations, and all other public or private nonprofit institutions or organizations. Grants cannot be made directly to individuals.

Range of Financial Assistance: Not available.

Contact: Director, Division of Innovation Programs, Rehabilitation Services Administration, Office of Human Development, Department of Education, Washington, DC 20202/ 202-245-0537.

Rehabilitation Training

Objectives: To support projects to increase the numbers of personnel trained in providing vocational rehabilitation services to handicapped individuals.

Eligibility: State vocational rehabilitation agencies, and other public or nonprofit agencies and organizations, including institutions of higher education.

Range of Financial Assistance: $5,000 to $200,000.

Contact: Division of Manpower Development, Rehabilitation Services Administration, Department of Education, Washington, DC 20201/ 202-245-0079.

Removal of Architectural Barriers to the Handicapped

Objectives: To provide financial assistance to State educational agencies (SEAs), local educational agencies (LEAs), and intermediate educational units to pay all or part of the costs of altering existing buildings and equipment to remove architectural barriers to the handicapped.

Eligibility: State educational agencies in the 50 States, D.C., Puerto Rico, American Samoa, Northern Mariana Islands, Guam, Virgin Islands, Trust Territory of the Pacific Islands, and the Bureau of Indian Affairs. Once States begin participating, local educational agencies and intermediate educational units may apply to the State educational agencies and intermediate educational

units may apply to the State educational agencies for funds.

Range of Financial Assistance: Not available.

Contact: Division of Assistance to States, Special Education Programs, Office of the Assistant Secretary for Special Education and Rehabilitative Services, Dept. of Education, 400 Maryland Ave., SW, Washington, DC 20202/202-732-1024.

School Assistance in Federally Affected Areas— Contruction

Objectives: To provide assistance for the construction of urgently needed minimum school facilities in school districts that have had substantial increases in school membership as a result of new or increased federal activities, or where reconstruction of facilities is necessary because of natural disaster.

Eligibility: Local educational agencies which provide free public elementary or secondary education in federally impacted areas, or which provide technical, vocational, or other special education to children of elementary or secondary school age where school facilities are damaged as a result of a declared natural disaster.

Range of Financial Assistance: $2,000 to $3,000,000.

Contact: Division of School Assistance in Federally Affected Areas, Bureau of Elementary and Secondary Education, Department of Education, 400 Maryland Ave. S.W., Washington, DC 20202/202-245-8427.

School Assistance in Federally Affected Areas— Maintenance and Operation

Objectives: To provide financial assistance to local educational agencies upon which financial burdens are placed due to federal activity, where the tax base of a district is reduced through the federal acquisition of real property, or where there is sudden and substantial increase in school attendance as the result of federal activities. Also to provide major disaster assistance by replacing or repairing damaged or destroyed supplies, equipment or facilities.

Eligibility: Local educational agencies which provide free public elementary or secondary education may apply.

Range of Financial Assistance: $5,000 to $12,000,000.

Contact: Division of Impact Aid, Bureau of Elementary and Secondary Education, Department of Education, 400 Maryland Ave. S.W., Washington, DC 20202/202-245-8427.

Secondary Education and Transitional Services for Handicapped Youth

Objectives: To strengthen and coordinate education, training and related services for handicapped youth.

Eligibility: Institutions of higher education,

State educational agencies, local educational agencies or other appropriate public and private nonprofit institutions.

Range of Financial Assistance: $50,000 to $200,000.

Contact: Research Projects Branch, Division of Educational Services, Office of Special Education Programs, 400 Maryland Avenue, SW, Washington, DC 20202/202-472-5040.

Secretary's Discretionary

Objectives: To assist in research, dissemination, demonstration, improvement of training, and technical assistance activities, which address some national education priority as authorized by Section 583 of the Education Consolidation and Improvement Act (ECIA).

Eligibility: The Secretary of Education is authorized to carry out programs and projects directly or through grants to or contracts with State and local educational agencies, instititutions of higher education, and other public and private agencies, organizations, and institutions.

Range of Financial Assistance: $5,000 to $175,000.

Contact: Secretary's Discretionary Program, Office of the Secretary, Department of Education, Washington, D.C. 20202/202-426-6420.

Secretary's Initiative to Improve the Quality of Chapter 1, ECIA Projects

Objectives: To improve the quality of ECIA, Chapter 1 Compensatory Education programs by assisting State Education Agencies (SEAs) with activities they have designed and to apply the results of evaluation activities. This effort will make use of SEAs and local education agencies (LEAs) evaluating experience and expertise. Emphasis will be placed upon findings related to school and classroom effectiveness.

Eligibility: Interstate Consortia or State Education Agencies are eligible to apply.

Range of Financial Assistance: $25,000 to $75,000.

Contact: Department of Education, Office of Planning, Budget and Evaluation, Office of Elementary and Secondary Education, 400 Maryland Avenue, S.W., Washington, D.C. 20202/202-245-9401.

State Student Incentives

Objectives: To make incentive grants to states to develop and expand assistance to eligible students in attendance at institutions of postsecondary education.

Eligibility: The agency responsible for administering each state's need-based, undergraduate scholarship/grant program.

Range of Financial Assistance: $1,613 to $12,000,000.

Contact: Chief, State Student Incentive Grant Program, Programs Branch, Bureau of Student Financial Assistance, Department of Education, Washington, DC 20202/202-472-4265.

Strengthening Research Library Resources

Objectives: To provide financial assistance to help major research libraries maintain and strengthen their collections; and to assist major research libraries in making their holdings available to individual researchers and scholars outside their primary clientele and to other libraries whose users have need for research materials.

Eligibility: Major research libraries, which may be public or private nonprofit institutions, including the resources of an institution of higher education, independent research libraries, state or public libraries, and individuals.

Range of Financial Assistance: $35,750 to $425,000.

Contact: Division of Library Programs, Office of Libraries and Learning Resources, Bureau of Elementary and Secondary Education, Department of Education, 400 Maryland Ave. S.W., Room 613, Washington, DC 20202/202-254-5090.

Special Services for Disadvantaged Students

Objectives: To assist low-income, educationally or culturally deprived, physically handicapped students and/or students with limited English-speaking ability who are enrolled or accepted for enrollment by institutions which are recipients of grants to initiate, continue, or resume postsecondary education.

Eligibility: Institutions of higher education or combinations of institutions of higher education or agencies created or designated by such combinations.

Range of Financial Assistance: $70,000 to $249,739.

Contact: Division of Student Services, Office of Postsecondary Education, Bureau of Higher and Continuing Education, Department of Education, 400 Maryland Ave. S.W., Washington, DC 20202/202-755-1843.

Talent Search

Objectives: To identify youths of financial or cultural need with exceptional potential for postsecondary educational training and assist them in obtaining admissions to postsecondary schools, with adequate financial aid.

Eligibility: Institutions of higher education, combinations of such institutions, public and private nonprofit agencies and organizations, including professional and scholarly associations, and, in exceptional cases, secondary schools and secondary vocational schools.

Range of Financial Assistance: $50,000 to $150,000.

Contact: Director, Division of Student Services, Office of Postsecondary Education, Department of Education, 400 Maryland Ave. S.W., Washington, DC 20202/202-755-1843.

Teacher Exchange (Fulbright)

Objectives: To increase mutual understanding between the people of the United States and those in other countries by offering qualified American teachers opportunities to teach in elementary and secondary schools and in some instances in teacher training institutions, technical colleges, polytechnics or colleges of art abroad. With the cooperation of American schools, teachers from other countries may teach for an academic year in the United States under the same program. There are also opportunities for American teachers to participate in short-term seminars abroad.

Eligibility: Elementary and secondary school teachers, college instructors, and assistant professors. Applicants must have at least a bachelor's degree and must be U.S. citizens at time of application; have at least three years of successful full-time teaching experience to qualify for teaching position abroad; two years for summer seminars; and must be teaching currently in the subject field.

Range of Financial Assistance: Not applicable.

Contact: Teacher Exchange Section, International Exchange Branch, Division of International Education, Department of Education, 7th and D Sts. S.W., ROB-3, Washington, DC 20202/202-245-9700.

Territorial Teacher Training Assistance Program

Objectives: To provide assistance for the training of teachers in schools in Guam, American Samoa, the Commonwealth of the Northern Mariana Islands, the Trust Territory of the Pacific Islands, and the Virgin Islands.

Eligibility: The State educational agency (SEA) of each territory, or a joint application from an SEA and an institution of higher education with the SEA as the lead agency of the grant.

Range of Financial Assistance: $88,000 to $400,000.

Contact: Territorial Teacher Training Assistance Program, Office of School Improvement, Department of Education, 400 Maryland Avenue, S.W., Washington, D.C. 20202/202-254-6572.

Training for Special Programs—Staff and Leadership Personnel

Objectives: To provide training for staff and leadership personnel associated with projects funded under the Special Programs for Students from Disadvantaged Backgrounds.

Eligibility: Institutions of higher education, public agencies and nonprofit private organizations.

Range of Financial Assistance: $13,149 to $140,001.

Contact: Division of Student Services, Office of Postsecondary Education, Department of Education, 400 Maryland Ave. S.W., Washington, DC 20202/202-755-1843.

Training Interpreters for Deaf Individuals

Objectives: To support projects, increase the numbers and improve the skills of manual and oral interpreters who provide services to deaf individuals.

Eligibility: Public or nonprofit agencies and organizations, including institutions of higher education and State and local governments, are eligible for assistance.

Range of Financial Assistance: $70,000 to $125,000.

Contact: Office of Special Education and Rehabilitative Services, Department of Education, Washington, DC 20202/202-732-1322.

Training Personnel for the Education of the Handicapped

Objectives: To improve the quality and increase the numbers of teachers, supervisors, administrators, researchers, teacher educators, and speech correctionists working with the handicapped, and specialized personnel such as specialists in physical education and recreation, paraprofessionals, and vocational/career education volunteers (including parents and parent coalitions).

Eligibility: Institutions of higher education, both public and private senior colleges and community colleges, and State and local educational agencies. Other nonprofit public and private agencies are eligible for participation.

Range of Financial Assistance: $8,000 to $360,000.

Contact: Director, Division of Personnel Preparation, Department of Education, Bureau of Education for the Handicapped, 400 Maryland Avenue, S.W., Washington, D.C. 20202/202-732-1094.

Upward Bound

Objectives: To generate the skill and motivation necessary for success in education beyond high school among young people from low-income families and with inadequate secondary school preparation.

Eligibility: Institutions of higher education, combinations of such institutions, public and private nonprofit agencies, and, in exceptional cases, secondary schools and secondary vocational schools.

Range of Financial Assistance: $76,055 to $411,033.

Contact: Division of Student Services, Office of Postsecondary Education, Department of Education, 400 Maryland Ave. S.W., Washington, DC 20202/202-755-1843

Vocational Education—Basic Grants to States

Objectives: To assist states in improving planning and in conducting vocational programs for persons of all ages in all communities who desire and need education and training for employment.

Eligibility: State boards for vocational education.

Range of Financial Assistance: $158,247 to $50,017,656.

Contact: Director, Division of State Vocational Program Operations, Office of Vocational and Adult Education, Department of Education, Washington, DC 20202/202-472-3440.

Vocational Education—Consumer and Homemaking

Objectives: To assist states in conducting programs in consumer and homemaking education. Emphasis is placed on programs located in economically depressed areas or areas of high rates of unemployment.

Eligibility: State boards for vocational education.

Range of Financial Assistance: $8,833 to $2,792,030.

Contact: Director, Division of State Vocational Program Operations, Office of Vocational and Adult Education, Department of Education, Washington, DC 20202/202-472-3440.

Vocational Education—Contract Program for Indian Tribes and Indian Organizations

Objective: To make contacts and grants with Indian tribal organizations to plan, conduct, and administer programs or portions of programs authorized by and consistent with the Vocational Education Act.

Eligibility: Indian tribal organizations of Indian tribes.

Range of Financial Assistance: $45,429 to $556,099.

Contact: Indian Vocational Education Program, Special Programs Staff, Office of Vocational and Adult Education. Department of Education, Washington, DC 20202/202-245-2774.

Vocational Education—Program Improvement and Supportive Service

Objective: To assist the states in improving their programs of vocational education and in providing supportive services for such programs.

Eligibility: State boards for vocational education.

Range of Financial Assistance: $27,909 to $8,821,126.

Contact: Division of National Vocational Programs, Office of Vocational and Adult Education, Department of Education, ROB-3, Room 5018, Washington, DC 20202/202-472-3440.

Vocational Education—Program Improvement Projects

Objectives: To provide support for a National Center for Research in Vocational Education, projects for research, curriculum development, and demonstration in vocational education, and six Curriculum Coordination Centers.

Eligibility: Public organizations, institutions, and agencies; nonprofit organizations, institutions, and agencies; individuals.

Range of Financial Assistance: $15,000 to $4,216,927.

Contact: Division of National Vocational Programs, Office of Vocational and Adult Education, Department of Education, Washington, DC 20202/202-245-2278.

Vocational Education—Special Programs for the Disadvantaged

Objectives: To provide special vocational education programs for persons who have academic or economic handicaps and who require special services and assistance in order to enable them to succeed.

Eligibility: State boards for vocational education.

Range of Financial Assistance; $4,009 to $1,267,106.

Contact: Division of National Vocational Programs, Office of Vocational and Adult Education, Department of Education, Washington, DC 20202/202-472-3440.

Vocational Education—State Advisory Councils

Objectives: To advise state boards for vocational education on the development and administration of state plans; evaluate vocational education programs, services, and activities and publish and distribute the results; and prepare and submit through the state boards to the Commissioner and the National Advisory Council an annual evaluation report.

Eligibility: State advisory council.

Range of Financial Assistance: $99,907 to $200,000.

Contact: Division of National Vocational Programs, Office of Vocational and Adult Education, Department of Education, Washington, DC 20202/202-472-3440.

Vocational Education—State Planning and Evaluation

Objectives: To assist the states in fulfilling federally mandated planning and evaluation requirements by providing a special allocation to each which does not have to be matched by state and/or local funds.

Eligibility: State Boards for Vocational Education. Eligible recipients for subgrants are local educational agencies and postsecondary institutions.

Range of Financial Assistance: $1,002 to $316,688.

Contact: Division of State Vocational Program Operations, Office of Vocational and Adult Education, Department of Education, 400 Maryland Avenue, S.W., Washington, D.C. 20202/202-472-3440.

Women's Educational Equity

Objectives: To promote educational equity for girls and women at levels of education, and to provide financial assistance to local educational institutions to meet the requirements of Title IX of the Education Amendments of 1972.

Eligibility: State and local government, private nonprofit organizations and institutions, and individuals.

Range of Financial Assistance: $6,000 to $600,000.

Contact: Women's Program Staff, Division of Educational Support, Department of Education, 400 Maryland Ave. S.W., Washington, DC 20202/ 202-245-7965.

Grants Information Clearinghouse

Information and expertise are available for those who wish to submit grant proposals on education research. Contact: Clearinghouse for National Institute of Education, Department of Education, 1200 19th St N.W., Room 6195, Washington, DC 20208/202-254-5600.

Guide to Department of Education Programs

Published annually, this 37-page guide gives information necessary to begin the process of applying for funding under individual federal education programs. The guide, which generally appears in the April issue of the Department of Education's magazine "American Education" is available for $2.50. Contact: U.S. Superintendent of Documents, Government Printing Office, Washington, DC 20402/202-783-3238.

Handicapped and Gifted Children Information Clearinghouse

Information services are available on gifted children as well as the aurally, visually, mentally, and speech handicapped, the emotionally disturbed and learning disabled. Contact: ERIC Clearinghouse on Handicapped and Gifted Children, Council for Exceptional Children, 1920 Association Dr., Reston, VA 22091/703-620-3660.

Handicapped, Education of the

For information on programs and funding available for the education of the handicapped contact: Special Education Programs. Department of Education, Switzer Building, Room 3086, 300 C Street, SW, Washington, DC 20201/202-732-1007.

Handicap Information Clearinghouse

The Clearinghouse offers the following: 1) information and referral services, 2) monitoring information operations on a national, state and local level, 3) technical assistance to information operations on request, 4) information on federal funding programs and legislation, 5) a Directory of National Information Services on Handicapping Conditions and Related Services, 6) a Directory of

Model Programs for Handicapped Children, and 7) a bimonthly newsletter describing programs for the handicapped. Contact: Clearinghouse on the Handicapped, Office for Handicapped Individuals, Department of Education, 330 C St. N.W., Switzer Building, Room 3132, Washington, DC 20202/202-245-0196.

Head Start

See "Head Start," under "Major Sources of Information," and "U.S. Department of Health and Human Services."

Higher Education Information Clearinghouse

Information services are available on various subjects relating to college and university students, conditions, programs, and problems. Contact: Educational Reference and Information Center (ERIC) Clearinghouse on Higher Education, George Washington University, One Dupont Circle,#630, Washington, DC 20036/202-296-2597.

Higher Education Information System

A computerized data base contains information on all institutions of higher learning. Data include: earned degrees conferred; number, characteristics and salaries of employees; financial statistics; institutional characteristics and enrollment; physical facilities; and residence and migration of students and students enrolled for advanced degrees. Contact: National Center for Education Statistics, Department of Education, 400 Maryland Ave. S.W., Room 418, Washington, DC 20202/301-254-6059.

Hispanic-American Program

The Hispanic Concerns Staff provides a focal point in the Department of Education for directing federal resources toward the education of children and adults of Hispanic-American Communities. This office provides information services and designs methods for informing Hispanic-Americans of ways to gain access to educational and employment opportunities. Contact: Hispanic Concerns Staff, Department of Education, 400 Maryland Ave. S.W., Reporters Building, Room 509, Washington, DC 20202/202-245-8467.

Indian Education

For information on programs and funding for Indian education, contact: Office of Indian Education Programs, Department of Education, 400 Maryland Ave. S.W., Room 2177, Washington, DC 20202/202-245-9159.

International Education and Teacher Exchange Program

The Education Department promotes international education through international teacher exchange and other programs aimed at increasing mutual understanding between the United States and other countries. Contact: Center for International Education, International Education Exchange Branch, Department of Education, 400 Maryland Ave. S.W., Washington, DC 20202/202-485-2555.

International Education Grants Information
For information about grants for foreign language study at U.S. Educational institutions. Contact: Center for International Education, Department of Education, ROB-3, Room 3919, Washington, DC 20202/202-245-7804.

Junior College Information Clearinghouse
Information services are available on the development, administration and evaluation of public and private community junior colleges. Contact: ERIC Clearinghouse for Junior Colleges, UCLA, Math-Science Bldg, Room 8118, Los Angeles, CA 90024/213-825-3931.

Languages and Linguistics Information Clearinghouse
Information services are available on languages and linguistics, including instructional methodology, psychology of language learning, teacher training and qualifications, and taught languages including English for those who speak other languages. Contact: ERIC Clearinghouse on Languages and Linguistics, Center for Applied Linguistics, 3520 Prospect St. N.W., Washington, DC 20007/202-298-9292.

Learning and Development
For information on current developments and programs covering topics such as mathematics learning, how people learn to think and reason, and why women shun mathematics and the sciences, contact: Programs on Learning and Development, National Institute of Education, Department of Education, 1200 19th St. N.W., Room 821K, Washington, DC 20208/202-254-5766.

Libraries
For information about programs and funding opportunities for library resources, education, and improvement, contact: Center for Libraries and Education Improvement, Department of Education, 1200 19th St. N.W., Brown Building, Room 613, Washington, DC 20202/202-245-6572.

Library Resources Information Clearinghouse
Information services are available on the management, operation and use of libraries. Contact: ERIC Clearinghouse on Information Resources, Syracuse University, School of Education, Area of Instructional Technology, Syracuse, New York 13210/315-423-3640.

Loans and Loan Guarantees
The programs, described below offer financial assistance through the lending of federal monies for a specific period of time or to idemnify a lender against part or all of any defaults by the borrower.

Higher Education Act Insured Loans
Objectives: To authorize low-interest deferred loans for educational expenses available from eligible lenders such as banks, credit unions, savings and loan associations, pension funds, insurance companies, and eligible institutions to vocational, undergraduate, and graduate students enrolled at eligible institutions. The loans are insured by a state or private nonprofit agency or the federal government.
Eligibility: Any U.S. citizen, national, or person in the United States for other than a temporary purpose, who is enrolled or accepted for enrollment on at least a half-time basis at a participating postsecondary school may apply. Only U.S. nationals may attend eligible foreign postsecondary schools.
Range of Financial Assistance: $2,500 to $15,000.
Contact: Guaranteed Student Loan Branch, Division of Policy and Program Development, Bureau of Student Financial Assistance, Department of Education, ROB-3, Room 4310, Washington, DC 20202/202-245-9717.

Housing for Educational Institutions
Objectives: To alleviate severe student and faculty housing shortages through construction, acquisition, or rehabilitation to provide student and faculty housing and related dining facilities. To reduce fuel consumption or other operating costs of existing eligible housing and related dining facilities.
Eligibility: Public or private nonprofit colleges and universities offering at least a 2-year program acceptable for full credit toward a bachelor's degree and public or private nonprofit hospitals operating nursing schools or internship and resident programs, public higher educational facility authorities, nonprofit student housing cooperatives and nonprofit corporations established solely to provide student or faculty housing are eligible. Each institution must develop its own plans, subject to local zoning and building codes. Competition for construction contracts is required.
Range of Financial Assistance: $100,000 to $3,500,000.
Contact: Office of Institutional Support, Office of Postsecondary Education, Department of Education, 400 Maryland Avenue, S.W., Washington, D.C. 20202/202-245-3253.

Media Resources
Information and expertise are available on the acquisition of instructional materials and equipment for the use of children and teachers in public and private elementary schools. The following free publications are also available: *Aids to Media Selection for Students,* and *A List of Sources for*

Both Audio-Visual and Printed Material for Teachers and Libraries. Contact: School Media Resource Branch, Center for Libraries and Educational Improvement, Department of Education, Brown Bldg, 400 Maryland Ave. S.W., Room 3125B, Washington, DC 20202/202-245-6752.

Occupational Education
The Office of Occupational and Adult Education maintains a vocational education data base, plans conferences on such topics as adult urban guidance centers, and produces papers and reports. Contact: Office of Vocational and Adult Education, Department of Education, 7th and D Sts. S.W., Room 3682, Washington, DC 20202/202-245-8166.

Reading and Communication Skills Information Clearinghouse
Information services are available on reading, English and communication skills from pre-school through college. Contact: ERIC Clearinghouse on Reading and Communication Skills, National Council of Teachers of English, 1111 Kenyon Rd., Urbana, IL 61801/217-328-3870.

Reading and Language
For information on developments and programs for the development of language and literacy, how cultural factors affect development and information about improving reading and other basic skills contact: Reading and Language Studies, National Institute of Education, Department of Education, 1200 19th St. N.W., Room 722F, Washington, DC 20208/202-254-5766.

Refugees
A number of programs are available for providing educational services to Vietnamese, Cambodian and Laotian children. Contact: Indochinese Refugee Children Assistance, Office of Bilingual Education and Minority Language Affairs, Department of Education, 400 Maryland Ave. S.W., Reporters Building, Room 421, Washington, DC 20202/202-245-2600.

Rural Education Information Clearinghouse
Information services are available on rural education, small schools and outdoor education as well as the education of American Indians, and Mexican Americans. Contact: ERIC Clearinghouse on Rural Education and Small Schools, New Mexico State University, Box 3AP, Las Cruces, NM 88003/505-646-2623.

Scholarships
See "Grants" and "Student Financial Assistance Hotline" in this section.

School Construction
For information and expertise on programs and funding available for school construction contact: School Construction Branch, Impact Aid, Department of Education, 400 Maryland Ave. S.W., Room 2069, Washington, DC 20202/202-245-8198.

Science, Mathematics and Environmental Education Clearinghouse
Information services are available on the development of curriculum and instructional materials for all levels of science, mathematics and environmental education. Contact: ERIC Clearinghouse for Science, Mathematics and Environmental Education, Ohio State University, 1200 Chambers Rd., 3rd Floor, Columbus, OH 43212/614-422-6717.

Social Science Information Clearinghouse
Information services are available on the development of educational programs at all levels of social studies and social science. Contact: ERIC Clearinghouse for Social Studies/Social Science Education, 855 Broadway, Boulder, CO 80302/303-492-8434.

Statistics, National Center for Education (NCES)
Statistics are available on such topics as enrollment, teachers and instructional staff, retention rates, finances, educational achievement, financial aid, adult and vocational education, international education and libraries and public television. Contact: Statistical Information Office, NCES, Brown Bldg. 1200 19th St, NW, Room 418, Department of Education, Washington, DC 20208-1402/202-254-6057.

Statistical Publications on Education
For a free catalog describing available releases, reports, directories and other publications on educational statistics contact: Information Office, National Center for Education Statistics, Department of Education, Brown Bldg. 1200 19th St, NW, Room 600, Washington, DC 20208-1402/202-254-6057.

Student Financial Assistance Hotline
There are a number of federally funded loan and grant programs available to students for financing their education. (See "Grants and Loans and Loan Guarantees" in this section.) A hotline has been established to assist with basic information on available programs. Contact: Student Information, Department of Education, 7th and D Sts. S.W., Washington, DC 20202/301-984-4070 (No collect calls).

Student Guide—Federal Financial Aid Programs
This informative booklet, published annually, by the department of Education, contains descriptive listings of the major types of financial assistance available to students of higher education. Coverage includes Pell Grants, Work Study Programs, National Direct Student Loans, Guaranteed Student Loans, and other Supplemental Educational

Grants. There are also general information topics such as eligibility, applications, deadlines, and contacts for student aid. The publication is free and available upon request from: Federal Student Aid Programs, Department DEA-85, Pueblo, CO 81109, or contact: Federal Student Aid Programs, U.S. Department of Education, Washington, DC 20202/301-984-4070.

Talent Search
The Bureau of Higher Education sponsors a number of programs that are aimed at helping students. They include:

Talent Search—counseling and funds to promising students to help them pursue postsecondary education.
Upward Bound—on-campus program for special training between junior and senior years.
Special Services—tutorial support for those already in college; counseling is also included both on an individual and group basis.
Educational Opportunity Centers—tutorial and counseling support based on community cooperation. (A directory of Centers is also available.)

Contact: Division of Student Services, Office of Postsecondary Education, Department of Education, 7th and D Sts. S.W., Washington, DC 20202/202-426-8960.

Teacher Education Information Clearinghouse
Information services are available on issues concerning school personnel at all levels from selection through preservice and in-service preparation and training to retirement. Contact: ERIC Clearinghouse on Teacher Education, American Association of Colleges for Teacher Education, One Dupont Circle, N.W.,#610, Washington, DC 20036/202-293-2450.

Teacher Exchange
See "Grants" and "International Education" in this section.

Teacher Supply and Demand and College Graduate Employment
Surveys are regularly conducted showing the employment and education status of recent college graduates as well as teacher demand and shortages. Contact: National Center for Educational Statistics, Department of Education, Brown Bldg, Room 600, 1200 19th St, NW, Washington, DC 20208-1402/202-254-6057.

Teaching and Learning
For information and expertise regarding the latest developments on the nature of good teaching or on how children and adults learn, contact: Program on Teaching and Learning, Department of Education, 1200 19th St. N.W., Room 820, Washington, DC 20208/202-254-6000.

Testing, Assessment and Evaluation
For information on developments and programs regarding the measurement of student achievement contact: Program on Testing, Assessment and Evaluation, National Institute of Education, Department of Education, 1200 19th St. N.W., Room 821, Washington, DC 20208/202-254-6271.

Tests, Measurement and Evaluation Information Clearinghouse
Information services are available on topics covering tests and other measurement devices; evaluation procedures and techniques; and application of tests, measurement or evaluation in educational projects or programs. Contact: ERIC Clearinghouse on Tests, Measurement and Evaluation, Educational Testing Service, Princeton, NJ 08540/609-921-9000, ext. 576.

Urban Educational Information Clearinghouse
Information services are available on topics relating to the relationship between urban life and schooling. Contact: ERIC Clearinghouse on Urban Education, Box 40, Teachers College, Columbia University, 525 West 120th St., New York, NY 10027/212-678-3437.

Vocational and Technical Education
For information on programs and funding for vocational and technical education for occupations that do not require college degrees, contact: Division of Innovation and Development, Office of Vocational and Adult Education, Department of Education, 7th and D Sts. S.W., Room 5108, Washington, DC 20202/202-245-2617.

Women's Educational Programs
For information on the availability and need for educational programs covering women's concerns contact: Women's Educational Equity Act Program, Department of Education, 400 Maryland Ave SW, FOB-6, Room 2017, Washington, DC 20202/202-245-2465.

How Can the Education Department Help You?
If you believe that the Department of Education can help you and you are not sure where to start contact: Information Branch, Office of Public Affairs, Department of Education, 400 Maryland Ave. S.W., Room 2097, Washington, DC 20202/202-245-8564.

Department of Energy

1000 Independence Ave. S.W.,
Washington, DC 20585/202-252-5000

Established: August 4, 1977
Budget: $11,660,000,000
Employees: 15,233

Mission: To provide the framework for a comprehensive and balanced national energy plan through the coordination and administration of the energy functions of the federal government; and to be responsible for long term, high risk research, development and demonstration of energy technology, the marketing of federal power, energy conservation, the nuclear weapons program, regulation of energy production and use, a central energy data collection and analysis program.

Major Divisions and Offices

Economic Regulatory Administration

Department of Energy, 1000 Independence Ave, SW, Washington, DC 20585/202-252-4241.
Budget: $23,200,000
Employees: 1,701
Mission: Administer the U.S. Department of Energy's regulatory programs, other than those assigned to the Federal Energy Regulatory Commission.

Energy Information Administration

Department of Energy, 1000 Independence Ave. S.W., Washington, DC 20585/202-252-2363.
Budget: $57,346,000
Employees: 457
Mission: Timely and accurate collection, processing, and publication of data on energy resource reserves, production, demand, consumption, distribution and technology.

Federal Energy Regulatory Commission (FERC) *

Department of Energy, 825 North Capitol St. N.E., Washington, DC 20426/202-357-8300.

Budget: $95,000,000
Employees: 16,000
Mission: Sets rates and charges for the transportation and sale of natural gas, the transmission and sale of electricity and the licensing of hydroelectric power projects, and establishes rates or charges for the transportation of oil by pipeline, as well as the valuation of such pipelines.

Under Secretary of Energy

Department of Energy, Room 7B260, 1000 Independence Ave. S.W., Washington, DC 20585/202-252-2020
Budget: 310,295,000
Employees: 270

1. Conservation

Department of Energy, Room 6A025, 1000 Independence Ave. S.W., Washington, DC 20585/202-252-9232.
Budget: $150,900,000
Employees: 143
Mission: Assists the private sector in developing the technological means to use energy economically by conducting research in areas of energy conservation where new knowledge can expand the technology base.

*Functions independently of the Department of Energy and receives its own funding.

515

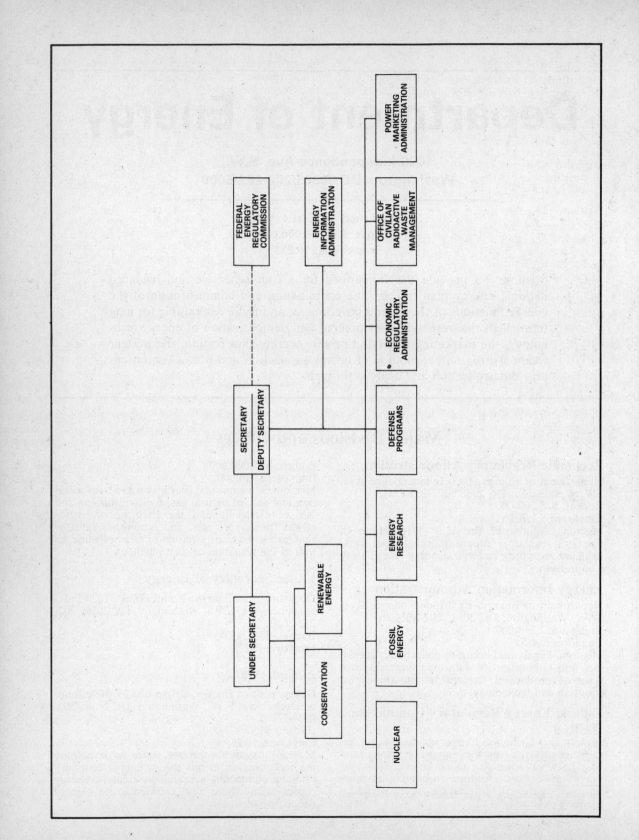

Department of Energy

Renewable Energy

Department of Energy, Room 6C036, 1000 Independence Ave. S.W., Washington, DC 20585/202-252-9275.
Budget: $215,000,000
Employees: 108
Mission: Works toward achieving energy self-sufficiency over the long term by close coordination with industry, to support private sector efforts to develop these resources as competitive energy supply options.

Nuclear Energy

Department of Energy, Room 5A115, 1000 Independence Ave. S.W., Washington, DC 20585/202-252-8728.
Budget: $674,700,000
Employees: 498
Mission: Provides the technological base to revitalize the industry's efforts to continue the development of nuclear power as an economic and environmentally acceptable source of baseload electric power.

Fossil Energy

Department of Energy, Room 4G034, 1000 Independence Ave. S.W., Washington, DC 20585/202-252-4700.
Budget: $260,200,000
Employees: 561
Mission: Establish an adequate scientific and engineering knowledge base to support private sector efforts to develop and deploy these technologies which promote future production of electricity and energy from the direct combustion of coal and coal mixtures.

Office of Energy Research

Department of Energy, Room 7B-058, 1000 Independence Ave. S.W., Washington, DC 20585/202-252-5430.
Budget: $1,684,000,000
Employees: 272
Mission: Advises the Secretary on the physical and energy research and development programs of the Department, the use of multipurpose laboratories, education and training for basic and applied research, and financial assistance and budgetary priorities for these activities.

Defense Programs

Department of Energy, Room 4R014, 1000 Independence Ave. S.W., Washington, DC 20585/202-252-2181.
Budget: $6,560,800
Employees: 2,597
Mission: Supports the national defense through research, development, testing and production of nuclear weapons and materials in support of Department of Defense requirements and nuclear waste generated by these activities, development of improved safeguards, and security systems for nuclear weapons, materials and facilities, and naval nuclear propulsion development.

Office of Civilian Radioactive Waste Management

Department of Energy, Room 5A085, 1000 Independence Ave. S.W., Washington, DC 20585/202-252-6842.
Budget: $11,400,000
Employees: 44
Mission: Encourages and expedites the availability of licensed new atreactor storage technologies; researches alternatives for the permanent disposal of high-level radioactive wastes; and conducts generic research and development studies and efforts to support civilian waste management activities.

Power Marketing Administration

Department of Energy, Room 6B104, 1000 Independence Ave. S.W., Washington, DC 20585/202-252-1040.
Budget: $662,000,000
Employees: 4,912
Mission: Markets electricity generated by Federal hydropower projects.

Data Experts

Energy Data Experts
The Energy Information Administration (EIA) is responsible for collecting, evaluating, analyzing and disseminating energy data. EIA makes available to the public a variety of reports, guides to reports, and data in machine-readable form. Initial inquiries about energy data should be made to the NEIC Subject Specialists listed below under "Information Services." Additional contacts for statistical and analytical information are listed under specific headings below.

INFORMATION SERVICES
Data Collection Forms Design and Clearance/John Gross/202-252-2308
Data Resources Directory (DRD)/Jay Casselberry/202-252-2171
Data Survey Forms/Marion King/202-252-8800
EIA Publications Information/NEIC Staff/202-252-8800
Energy Statistical Inquiries/NEIC Staff/202-252-8800

GPO Sales of EIA Publications/NEIC Staff/202-252-8800

Information on EIA Press Releases/Patricia Jacobus/202-252-1670

Machine-Readable Files and Data/Mark Velander/202-252-1097

Machine-Readable Files and Models/Samuel Cohen/202-252-2396

NEIC Subject Specialists:

Information Research Lead Specialist/Nancy Nicoletti/202-252-8800

Coal and Synthetic Fuel/John Miens/Sarah Doelp/202-252-8800

Electric Power/Mary Kimbrough/Rita Barnett/202-252-8800

Natural Gas/Michael Feld/William Jeffers/202-252-8800

Nuclear Power/Mary Kimbrough/Michael Feld/202-252-8800

Petroleum/Christopher Freitas/Elaine Toye/202-252-8800

Renewable Energy Resources/Paula Altman/Rita Barnett/202-252-8800

News Media Statistical Inquiries/Leola Withrow/202-252-8800

Public Use Energy Statistics Data Base (PU-ESDB)/Jay Casselberry/202-252-2171

Publications Production, Mailing List Services, and Product Dissemination Programs/Maurice R. Berez/202-252-1105

Data Programs

ALTERNATE FUELS:

Solar Collectors and Manufacturing Activity/John Carlin/202-252-9775

Wood and Energy/John Carlin/202-252-9775

COAL:

Anthracite/Consumption, Exports, Inventories/Robert E. Harris/202-252-2982

Bituminous/Consumption, Exports, Inventories, Prices/Robert E. Harris/202-252-2982

Data Development/Robert E. Harris/202-252-2982

Distribution/Mary McNair/202-252-6886

Prices, International/Harold Weisman/202-252-1158

Production, Annual/Clyde Boykins/202-252-5296

Production, Weekly/Robert E. Harris/202-252-2982

Reserves/Richard F. Bonskowski/202-252-5299

Lignite/Consumption/Robert E. Harris/202-252-2982

Lignite/Exports, Inventories, Prices/Robert E. Harris/202-252-2982

Pennsylvania Anthracite/Export/Robert E. Harris/202-252-2982

Supply and Demand, International/Bernadette Michalski/202/252-9412

ELECTRIC POWER:

Data Development/Edward Hill/202-252-6516,

Larry Prete/202-252-6535, Roger Sacquety/202-252-8752, Carol French/202-252-5311, Samuel Brown/202-252-5847

Data Systems/Dean Fennell/202-252-6523

Electricity Prices, International/Harold Weisman/202-252-1158

Generating Unit Reference File (GURF)/Elsie Bess/202-252-6534

Hydropower Generation, International/Patricia Smith/202-252-6925

Net Generation/Melvin Johnson/202-252-6520, Carol French/202-252-5311

Power Plants/Construction Costs, Production Expenses/Elsie Bess/202-252-6534

Privately Owned Electric Utilities/Financial Data/Samuel Brown/202-252-5847

Publicly Owned Electric Utilities/Financial Data/Leon Hood/202-252-5197

Rate Structure/Beverly D. Byrdsong/202-252-6872, Larry Prete/202-252-6535

Sales/Charlene Harris-Russell/202-252-2028

Utilities/Financial Issues/Robert Eynon/202-252-9855, Gerald Price/202-252-9854

Utilities/Fuel Consumption/Melvin Johnson/202-252-6520, Carol French/202-252-5311

Utilities/Fuel Cost, Quality and Receipts/Kenneth McClevey/202-252-5310, Richard Salkov/202-252-6525

Utilities/Installed Capacity Data/Melvin Johnson/202-252-6520, Carol French/202-252-5311

Utilities/Peak Load Capability Power Transmission/Dean Fennell/202-252-6523

Utilities/Retail Prices/Deborah Bolden/202-252-8952

NATURAL GAS:

Consumption (EIA-176)/Charles Readling/202-252-6301, Margaret McDonald/202-252-6303

Deficiencies/Ellis Maupin, Jr./202-252-6178

Demand, Distribution, Domestic Supplies/Gordon Koelling/202-252-6305

Exports/Fay Dillard/202-252-6181

Financial Data (FERC-11)/James Keeling/202-252-6107

Financial Reporting System/Arthur T. Andersen/202-252-1441

High-Btu Gas/Production/Charles Readling/202-252-6301

Imports/Fay Dillard/202-252-6181

Industrial Sales/Fay Dillard/202-252-6181

Interstate Pipeline Companies and Reserves/Jack Arnold/202-252-6135

Interstate Pipeline and Financial Data/Juanita Mack/202-252-6169

Market by State/Gordon Koelling/202-252-6305

Natural Gas Liquids, Ethane/Mary Zitomer/202-252-5130

Natural Gas Liquids and Production/Mary Zitomer/202-252-5130

Price and Class, End-Use, State, Wellhead Value/Gordon Koelling/202-252-6305

Prices, International/Harold Weisman/202-252-1158

Production, Monthly/Charles Readling/202-252-6301

Reserves, Domestic/John Wood/214-767-2200

Supply and Demand, International/Bernadette Michalski/202-252-9412

Underground Storage, Monthly and Annual/Gordon Koelling/202-252-6305

NUCLEAR POWER:

Cost/Mark Gielecki/202-252-4442

Enrichment/Demand/Z.(Dan) Nikodem/202-252-1787

Fuel Cycle/Harold Steinberg/202-252-1332

Generation, Domestic and International/Harold Steinberg/202-252-1332

Power Plants/Operations, Construction/Roger Diedrich/202-252-9407

Reactor Capacity, Domestic and International/ Harold Steinberg/202-252-1332

Spent Fuel Storage and Reprocessing/James Finucane/202-252-2398

Uranium Resources and Reserves, Production/ Taesin Chung/202-252-6331

PETROLEUM AND PETROLEUM PRODUCTS:

Competition/Harold Millie/202-252-6613

Crude Oil and Prices, Historical Spot Contract/ Michael Grillot/202-252-6583

Crude Oil/Production/David Hinton/202-252-9616

Crude Oil/Wellhead Value/Charles Shirkey/202-252-6567

Domestic Crude Oil First Purchase Report (EIA-182)/Charles Shirkey/202-252-6567

Domestic Crude Oil Markets/Charles Shirkey/202-252-6567

Exports/Christine Gray/202-252-8995

Fuel Oils/Deliveries/Mike Griffey/202-252-9601

Geological Field Codes/Robert King/202-252-4787

Imports (EIA-814)/Virginia Anderson/202-252-5788

Inventories/Louise Guey-Lee/202-252-2990

Lease Condensate-Production/David Hinton/202-252-9616

Liquefied Petroleum Gases-Production, Stocks/ Mary Zitomer/202-252-5130

Petroleum Products-Market/Harold Millie/202-252-6613

Petroleum Products (Miscellaneous)/Leonard Fanelli/202-252-8380

Petroleum Products-Prices, Domestic/Charles Riner/202-252-6610, Annie Whatley/202-252-6612

Petroleum Products and Prices, International/ Harold Weisman/202-252-1158

Production/Monthly, International/Patricia Smith/ 202-252-6925

Refineries/Acquisition Cost/Lamar Gowland/202-252-6608

Refineries/Capacity, Production/David Hinton/-202-252-9616

Reserves, Domestic Crude Oil/John Wood/(214)-767-2200

Supply and Disposition, International/Louis DeMouy/202-252-6557

Transportation/Pipeline (EIA-812)/Renee Rowland/202-252-9649

Transportation/Tankers and Barges (EIA-817)/ Renee Rowland/202-252-9649

Forecasting and Analysis

Coal/Export and Import Projections/David Costello/202-252-1199, Ercan Tukenmez/202-252-5253

Coal/Midterm Projections/Robert Schnapp/202-252-1760

Coal/Short-Term Projections/David Costello/202-252-1199

Commercial Energy Use/Midterm Projections/-John Holte/202-252-1471

Distillate Fuel/Short-Term Projections/Scott Sitzer/202-252-5206

Economy Interactions, Inter-Industry/Ronald Earley/202-252-1398

Economy Interactions, International/E. Stanley Paul/202-252-6577

Economy Interactions, National/Gerard Lagace/ 202-252-1452, William Curtis/202-252-1455, Jon A. Rasmussen/202-252-1449

Electric Power/Short-Term Projections/Colleen Cornett/202-252-5243

Electric Power Use/Midterm Projections/Margaret Jess/202-252-9853

Electric Utilities/Midterm Projections/Reginald Sanders/202-252-1466

Electric Utilities/Regulations/Robert Eynon/202-252-9855

Energy Consumption Analysis, International/A. David Sandoval/202-252-6581

Energy Disposition/Short-Term Projections, Domestic/Mark Rodekohr/202-252-5209, Scott Sitzer/202-252-5206

Energy Disposition/Short-Term Projections, International/E. Stanley Paul/202-252-6577, Derriel Cato/202-252-6574

Energy Disposition/Long-Term Projections, International/A.David Sandoval/202-252-6581

Energy Emergency Programs/Calvin Kilgore/202-252-1130

Energy Prices/Short-Term Projections/Scott Sitzer/202-252-5206, Neil Gamson/202-252-2418

Energy Supplies/Short-Term Projections/Edward Flynn/202-252-5748

Energy Taxes/Impacts/Arthur T. Andersen/202-252-1441

Financial Reporting System (FRS)/Arthur T. Andersen/202-252-1441

Fuel Cycle Analysis/Betsy O'Brien/202-252-4320

Gasoline/Short-Term Projections/David Costello/ 202-252-1199

Industrial Energy Use/Long-Term, Year 2000/Paul Werbos/202-252-1197

Industrial Energy Use/Midterm Projections/Paul Werbos/202-252-1197

Liquefied Petroleum Gases/Short-Term Projections/Linda Barber/202-252-4815

Macroeconomic Analysis, Domestic/William Curtis/202-252-1455

Macroeconomic Analysis, International/E. Stanley Paul/202-252-6577

Natural Gas Analysis/Richard O'Neill/202-252-4680

Natural Gas/Midterm Price Projections/Joan Heinkel/202-252-4838

Natural Gas/Midterm Supply Projections/William Trapmann/202-252-6408, Barbara Mariner-Volpe/202-252-4749

Natural Gas Demand/Short-Term Projections/Colleen Cornett/202-252-5243

Nuclear Energy/Policy Issues/Mark Gielecki/202-252-4442

Nuclear Power/Cost, Operations/Mark Gielecki/202-252-4442

Nuclear Power/Projections, Domestic/Roger Diedrich/202-252-9407

Nuclear Power/Projections, International/Mark Gielecki/202-252-4442

Petroleum/Demand Projections, International/A. David Sandoval/202-252-6581

Petroleum/Market Analysis, International/Calvin Kilgore/202-252-1130

Petroleum/Intermediate Future Forecasting Systems (IFFS)/Michael Lehr/202-252-1470

Petroleum/Midterm Supply/William Trapmann/202-252-6408

Petroleum and Price Projections, International/Daniel Butler/202-252-9503

Petroleum/Regulation/Richard Farmer/202-252-9888

Petroleum/Short-Term Projections/Mark Rodekohr/202-252-5209

Public Utilities/Regulation/James Hewlett/202-252-4440

Reactors/Forecasting/Roger Diedrich/202-252-9407

Residential Energy Use/Midterm Projections/John Holte/202-252-1471

Residual Fuel Oil/Short-Term Projections/Neil Gamson/202-252-2418

Short-Term Integrated Forecasting System (STIFS)/Edward Flynn/202-252-5748

Short-Term Projection Series/Assumptions/Mark Rodekohr/202-252-5209, Scott Sitzer/202-252-5206

Supply Shortfalls/Macroeconomic Effects/William Curtis/202-252-1455

Synthetic Fuels (Coal)/Projections/Robert Crockett/202-252-4266

Uranium/Demand/Z. (Dan) Nikodem/202-252-6227

U.S. Contingency Analysis/Calvin Kilgore/202-252-1130

World Crude Oil Prices/A. David Sandoval/202-252-6581

World Oil Price Projections/Calvin Kilgore/202-252-1130

World Oil Price Analysis, International/Erik Kreil/202-252-6573

Conservation and Consumption

Commercial Sector/Energy Consumption/Julia Oliver/202-252-1121

Energy Consumption, State/Nancy Masterson/202-252-5952

Energy Expenditures, State/Coy Lay/202-252-5850

Energy Prices, State/Coy Lay/202-252-5850

Energy Emergency Management Information Program/Calvin Kilgore/202-252-1130

Industrial Sector/Energy Consumption/John L. Preston/202-252-1128

Residential Energy Consumption Analysis Survey/Martha Johnson/202-252-1135

Transportation Sector/Residential Consumption/Leigh Carleton/202-252-1132

Transportation Sector/Non-Residential Consumption/Susan Dillman/202-252-1134

Data Experts

Energy Efficient Building Experts

The following experts are involved in research, development, and demonstration projects in energy conservation for retrofitting and new construction of both residential and commercial buildings. Each expert can be reached at: Energy Efficient Building Program, Berkeley Laboratory, Building 90, Room 3026F, Berkeley, CA 94720.
Building Energy Analysis/Richard Curtis/415-486-5711.
Building Envelopes and Infiltration/Robert Sonderegger/415-486-4029.
Windows and Use of Daylight/Steve Selkowitz/415-486-5064.
Lighting Systems/Sam Berman/415-486-5682.

Building Energy Performance Standards/Mark Levine/415-486-5238.
Building Energy Analysis Compilation/Art Rosenfeld/415-486-4834.

International Energy Experts

A staff of experts is available to provide information on most any aspect of the world supply and demand of energy. They can be called directly or reached by writing. For information on countries not listed below, or for information on other international topics, contact: International Affairs, Department of Energy, 1000 Independence Ave. S.W., Room MSF031, Washington, DC 20585. (Be sure to note name, country and room number when corresponding with experts.)

Energy Statistics at Census

The following are subject matter specialists for energy statistics within the Census Bureau. They can be contacted directly by telephone or by writing in care of Director, Bureau of the Census, Washington, DC 20233.

Agriculture/Frank Shelton/301-763-7280
Business/John McNamee/301-763-5938.
Construction/William Mittendorf/301-763-7165
Economic Surveys/Jerry McDonald/301-763-5182.
Foreign Trade/Gerald Kotwas/301-763-5333
Government/Henry Wolff/301-763-7664.
Manufactures/John McNamee/301-763-5938
Mineral Industries/John McNamee/301-763-5938
Housing/William A. Downs/301-763-2873
Journey to Work/Philip N. Fulton/301-763-3850
Transportation/Carmen Campbell/301-763-1744
Energy Coordinator/Martin Winegarten/301-763-7184

Technology and Commercialization Experts

The following experts can provide information on the latest available technology and commercializa-tion possibilities for their subject areas. They can be reached by writing: Department of Energy, Washington, DC 20585. (Be sure to note name and topic when corresponding with experts.)

Electric/Hybrid Vehicles/Paul Brown/202-252-8027
Cogeneration/Richard Cowles/202-252-9296
Cogeneration (Tech)/John Eustis/202-252-2084
Wind Energy Systems/Lew Devone/202-252-5540
High Efficiency Motors/Albert Hayes/202-252-2378
Active Solar Systems/John Schuler/202-252-8150
Urban Waste/Don Walter/202-252-6104
Low BTU Gasification/Jerald Wheeler/301-353-3511
Geothermal/Hydrothermal/John Mock/202-252-5340
Industrial Atmospheric Fluidized Bed (AFB)/Howard Feibus/301-353-4348
High BTU Gasification/Steve Verikios/301-353-3962
Low Head Hydro/James Bresee/301-353-3962
Coal Gasification/C. Lowell Miller/301-353-3498
Shale Oil/Paul Petzrick/301-353-2700
Enhanced Oil Recovery/Keith Frye/301-353-2703
Unconventional Gas Resources Development/Troyt York/301-353-2713

Major Sources of Information

Agriculture and Food Processing Industry—Conservation

For information on technological developments that conserve energy in agricultural production, irrigation, fertilizer production, food processing, food preservation, food preparation and distribu-tion, farm power systems, and other areas, con-tact: Agriculture and Food Process Branch, Con-servation Research and Development Division, Industrial Programs, Conservation and Renewable Energy, Department of Energy, 1000 Indepen-dence Ave. S.W., MS Rm 59067 Washington, DC 20461/202-252-2075.

Alcohol Fuels

The Office of Alcohol Fuels provides information on the use of liquid fuels from biomass in vehicles; handles the market analysis, market testing, and research and development activities related to the production and use of alcohol fuels from renew-able resources; implements the commercialization programs that are related to accelerating the production and use of alcohol fuels; consolidates information about federal alcohol fuels activities; and works with farmers, businessmen, and repre-sentatives of the financial, scientific, engineering, and educational communities to stimulate activi-ties leading to wider production and use of alcohol fuels. To promote the development of alcohol fuel production, this office also works with the U.S. Departments of Agriculture, Commerce, and Housing and Urban Development on the White House Alcohol Fuels Task Force. Contact: Office of Alcohol Fuels, Department of Energy, 1000 Independence Ave. S.W., Rm 57043, Washington, DC 20585/202-252-9487.

Alcohol Fuels Publications

The following publications are available free from the Solar Energy Research Institute, Document Distribution Service, 1617 Cole Blvd., Golden, CO 80401/303-231-1158:

Alcohol Fuels Reading List
Facts About Gasohol—answers most common questions.
Facts About Ethanol—answers most common questions.

The following publication is available free from the Technical Information Center, Department of Energy, P. O. Box 62, Oak Ridge, TN 27830/615-576-1301:

Fuel from Farms: A Guide to Small-Scale Ethanol Production—information on benefits, market, uses, market assessments, production potential, financial requirements, and equipment selection; also informa-tion on basic ethanol production, feedstock, co-products plant design, analysis of financial require-ments, summary of ethanol legislation, permit require-ments, references, resources, bibliography, glossary and sources of public finance.

Alternative Fuels Utilization

This office aims to reduce transportation depen-dence on imported petroleum fuels by encouraging development of such fuels as coal, biomass, alcohol, and hydrogen, and their applicability to new auto-engine systems. Contact: Alternative Fuels Utilization, Heavy Duty Transport and Fuels Integration Branch, Technology Development and Analysis, Vehicle and Engine R&D. Conservation and Renewable Energy, Department of Energy, 1000 Independence Ave. S.W., Room G064, Washington, D.C. 20585/202-252-8055.

Analysis, Mid-Term and Short-Term

Information is available on mid-term and short-term forecasts of energy production, distribution, consumption and price, including projections of demand growth, resource depletion, and application of new technologies. Contact: Energy Analysis and Forecasting Division, Office of Energy Markets and End Use, Energy Information Administration, Department of Energy, 1000 Independence Avenue S.W., Room 1H050 FB, Washington, D.C. 20585/202-252-6160.

Anthracite Coal

Information is available on the prospects for increased production and use of anthracite coal consistent with environmental needs. The U.S. Department of Energy is involved with underground mining, surface mining, and coal preparation. Contact: Coal Utilization Systems, Utilization, Advanced Conversation and Gasification, Fossil Energy, Department of Energy, 1000 Independence Avenue S.W., Room C-160, Washington D.C. 20585-202-252-4348.

Appliance Labeling

When you shop for a major appliance, look for the yellow and black "Energy Guide" labels which show the yearly energy cost of operating an appliance. The guide enables you to compare competing brands of models of applicances of similar size with similar features. Energy efficiency guides are required by law on major household appliances and on home furnaces. There are three types of Energy Guide labels: Energy Cost Labels, Energy Efficiency labels, and Generic labels. Contact: Consumer Division, Test and Evaluation Branch, Building Equipment Division, Office of Building R&D, Conservation and Renewable Energy, Department of Energy, 1000 Independence Avenue, S.W., Room GF-217, Washington D.C. 20585/202-252-9123.

Architectural and Engineering Systems

Long-term research is conducted on energy phenomena in buildings to advance the understanding of building energy use. Building component parts, as well as whole building energy performance is included in the research. It is intended for use by designers, builders, and owners to improve overall energy use in the building sector. Contact: Building Systems, Building Energy Research and Development, Conservation and Renewable Energy,

Department of Energy, Room GF253, 1000 Independence Ave. SW, Washington, DC 20585/202-252-9837.

Atmospheric Fluidized Bed (AFB)

Information is available on the commercialization of atmospheric fluidized bed combustion technology as well as direct coal combustion applications. The fluidized-bed process burns coal in a bed of limestone with the mixture suspended on an upward-blowing stream of air. Sulphur released from the burning coal is captured by the limestone before it can leave the boiler and pollute the air. Contact: Office of Coal Utilization Systems, Coal Utilization, Advanced Conversion and Gasification, Fossil Energy, Department of Energy, 1000 Independence Avenue, S.W., Room C-160, Washington D.C. 20585/202-353-4348.

Audiovisuals

For information on the availability of U.S. Department of Energy motion pictures and multimedia presentations, contact: Audiovisual Branch, Office of Public Affairs, Department of Energy, 1000 Independence Ave. S.W., MS 1E218, Washington, DC 20585/202-252-4670.

Bartlesville Energy Technology Center

This U.S. Department of Energy-supported center is devoted primarily to research and engineering in petroleum and natural gas, including improvement and demonstration of technologies in exploration, production, refining and utilization. Petroleum production programs are involved with enhanced oil and gas recovery, heavy oil recovery, improved drilling methods, and determinations of residual oil. A data bank on crude oil production and marketed fuel properties is maintained, the Alternative Fuels Utilization Technical Data Bank. Research is also conducted on automotive octane and gasoline blends and automotive fuels from coal liquids. Contact: Bartlesville Energy Technology Center, P.O. Box 1398, Bartlesville, OK 74001/918-336-2400.

Basic Energy Sciences

Research and development is conducted to expand the fundamental knowledge base in science and engineering so that all energy technologies will have a strong scientific foundation for the future. Work is done in metallurgy, ceramics, solid state physics, natural chemistry, chemical science, engineering, mathematics, geoscience, and biological energy. Contact: Basic Energy Sciences, Energy Research, Department of Energy, Germantown, Room J304, Washington, DC 20545/301-353-5565.

Biomass Research

The Conservation and Renewable Energy office manages the research, development, and proof-of-concept activities of biomass, energy technology, energy from municipal waste, and geothermal and small hydropower energy technology. Emphasis is placed on development of renewable technology with potential to increase significantly the supply of fuels, heat, and electricity. Contact: Renewable Technology, Conservation and Renewable Energy, U.S. Department of Energy, Forrestal Bldg., CE-33, Room 5F059, 1000 Independence Avenue, SW, Washington, DC 20559/202-252-5347.

Biomass Systems
This office integrates the U.S. Department of Energy's efforts to promote the commercialization of biomass—organic material such as trees, crops, manure, seaweed and algae that captures and stores energy from the sun. It oversees research and development for converting biomass into energy-intensive products such as methanol (wood alcohol), ethanol (grain alcohol), hydrogen and petrochemical substitutes. Studies are conducted on the production of methane and other fuel sources from the anaerobic digestion of manure and other agricultural wastes. Contact: Biomass Energy Technology, Office of Renewable Technology, Conservation and Renewable Energy, Department of Energy, 1000 Independence Ave. SW., Room SF-059, Washington, D.C. 20585/202-252-6750.

Building Codes and Conservation
New Building codes and standards are evaluated to assess their impact on energy conservation. Contact: Building Services, Building Energy Research and Development, Conservation and Renewable Energy, Department of Energy, 1000 Independence Ave. S.W., Room CE-115, Washington, DC 20585/202-252-9424.

Building Conservation Services
This office promotes the applications of energy-efficient systems in residential and commercial buildings; fosters the utilization in the marketplace of energy systems technologies and efficient operations practices that reduce energy usage in new and existing buildings; and provides incentives or eliminates disincentives to effective energy conservation in buildings. Contact: Federal and Community System, Building Energy Research and Development, Conservation and Renewable Energy, Department of Energy, 1000 Independence Ave. S.W. Room GF217, Washington, DC 20585/202-252-9389.

Building Energy Sciences
This branch focuses on how systems, subsystems, and components of buildings function, both separately and interactively. Their activities are concerned with improving energy efficiency of buildings. Some areas of application are energy efficient window design; ventilation; infiltration; insulation; heating, ventilating, and air-conditioning control systems; diagnostics; heat transfer; infra-red thermography; and energy analysis calculations. Contact: Building Systems, Building Energy Research and Development, Conservation and Renewable Energy, Department of Energy, 1000 Independence Avenue, SW, Room GF253, Washington, DC 20585/202-252-9187.

Building Equipment
This office provides long-range technical support to supply the private sector with the technological basis for developing and testing high efficiency equipment used in the operation of residential and commercial buildings. The equipment supplies heating, cooling, lighting, hot water, and other services needed to operate a building efficiently and give its occupants a comfortable environment. Contact: Building Energy Research and Development, Conservation and Renewable Energy, Department of Energy, 1000 Independence Avenue SW, Room GF217, Washington, DC 20585/202-252-9123.

Citizens' Assistance
Pamphlets, posters and publications on energy production, use and conservation are available free of charge from the Technical Information Center. Examples are:

Citizens' Workshops on Energy and the Environment Handbook
Tips for Energy Savers
Winter Survival: A Consumer's Guide to Winter Preparedness
Careers in Energy Industries
How to Improve the Efficiency of Your Oil-Fired Furnace
How to Understand Your Utility Bill
Insulation
Nuclear Power from Fission Reactors
Ocean Energy
Solar Electricity from Photovoltaic Conversion
Securing America's Energy Future
Solar Energy

Contact: Technical Information Center, Department of Energy, P. O. Box 62, Oak Ridge, TN 37830/615-576-1301.

Civilian Radioactive Waste Management
Responsibility for the establishment of a program of research, development, and demonstration regarding the disposal of high-level radioactive waste and spent nuclear fuel, rests with this office. It is also responsible for the development of repositories for the disposal of high-level radioactive waste and spent nuclear fuel. Contact: Department of Energy, Room 5A085, 1000 Independence Ave. SW, Washington, DC 20585/202-252-6850.

Classified Material
For information on the classification and declassification of restricted data and other energy-related

national security information, contact: Classification Office, Defense Programs, Department of Energy, 1000 Independence Ave. S.W., Room C-377 (germontoron), Washington, DC 20585/202-353-3521.

Coal and Electric Power Analysis
Studies are conducted on various aspects of coal and electric power, including analysis and forecasting of supply and demand balances of coal; exploration of new technologies to derive energy from coal; forecasts of electric power supply and consumption; utility prices and inter-fuel substitution, and detailed examination of existing and proposed legislation affecting coal and electric power production. Contact: Data Analysis and Forecasting, Department of Energy, Room 25-021, Washington, D.C. 20585/202-252-1760.

Coal and Electric Power Statistics
Statistics are collected, compiled, and evaluated on the coal and electric power industries, and reports and publications are issued pertaining to coal reserves, production, and distribution, coke and coal chemicals, electric retail rates, power disturbances, electricity production and rates, and fuel consumption and stocks at generating facilities. More than 200 statistical periodicals are published. Contact: Office of Energy Markets and End Use, Office of Coal, Nuclear, Electric and Alternate Fuels, Department of Energy, 1000 Independence Avenue, S.W., Room 15-077, Washington, DC 20565/202-252-2444.

Coal Conversion Research
Many programs are concerned with the development of coal gasification technology. These include advanced techniques for producing high-BTU gas from eastern caking coals and improvement of two advanced gasifier concepts for high and medium BTU and others. Contact: Division of Surface Coal Gasification, Coal Utilization, Advanced Conversion and Gasification, Fossil Energy, Department of Energy, 1000 Independence Ave. S.W., Room C-178, Washington, DC 20585/202-353-3498.

Coal Division
This office manages data and information systems for all supply and demand aspects of coal. The office also collects and analyzes data and performs analyses and projections relating to coal supply, including production, prices, and distribution; identifies and analyzes coal reserves and examines new technologies which derive energy from coal; and studies existing and proposed legislation and regulations affecting coal supply and demand. Contact: Office of Coal, Nuclear, Electric and Alternate Fuels, Energy Information Administration, Department of Energy, Room 2F021, 1000

Independence Avenue SW, Washington, DC 20285/202-252-6860/202-252-5145.

Coal Liquids
For information on commercial application of liquid coal and coal-derived liquid fuels, contact: Division of Coal Liquids, Coal Liquefaction Technology, Fossil Energy, Department of Energy, Room E151A, Washington, D.C. 20585/301-353-3482.

For information on the latest developments in coal liquefaction, including the technological aspects of coal liquids refining and indirect liquefaction, contact: Department of Energy, Germantown Road, Washington, DC 20545/301-353-3482.

Coal Operators Assistance
The U.S. Department of Energy provides financial and other types of assistance to help small- and medium-sized producers to expand, develop or reopen underground low-sulphur coal mines and to build coal preparation plants. Contact: Coal Utilization Systems, Coal Utilization Advanced Conversation and Gasification, Fossil Energy, Department of Energy, Room B-128 Washington D.C. 20585/301-353-2603.

Coal Supply Data and Information Systems
The Coal, Nuclear, Electric and Alternate Fuels Division manages data and information systems for all supply and demand aspects of coal. It also collects and analyzes data. Staff perform analyses and projections relating to coal supply, including production, prices, and distribution; identify and analyze coal reserves; examine new technologies which derive energy from coal; and study existing and proposed legislation and regulations affecting coal supply and demand. Contact: Coal Division, Office of Coal, Nuclear, Electric and Alternate Fuels, Energy Information Administration, Department of Energy, Forrestal, EI-52-Room 2F021, 1000 Independence Avenue, SW, Washington, DC 20585/202-252-6860.

Coal Utilization Research
Research is conducted into the direct utilization of coal, i.e., use of coal which has not been changed into another form of fuel. The four main areas of interest are: combustion systems, advanced environmental control technology, heat engines and heat recovery, and fuel cells. Contact: Coal US, Utilization, Advanced Conversation and Gasification, Fossil Energy, Department of Energy, Room C-160, Washington, DC 20585/202-353-4348.

Cogeneration
Research is conducted into cogeneration and related waste energy utilization systems. With cogeneration, industrial waste heat is utilized to generate electricity or provide heating. Contact:

Energy Cascading Branch, Waste Energy Reduction, Industrial Programs, Conservation and Renewable Energy, Department of Energy, 100 Independence Ave. S.W. Room 5G-067, Washington, DC 20585/202-252-2084.

Comment on Energy Rules
Twice a year, the U.S. Department of Energy is required to publish an agenda of significant regulations it is currently developing or reviewing on such topics as the environment, conservation and solar, weatherization, equal opportunity, consumer affairs, oil regulation, utility systems, and other areas. These proposed rules are published for public comment. Contact: Office of Public Affairs, Public Reading Room, Department of Energy, 1000 Independence Ave. S.W., Room IE-190, Washington, DC 20585/202-252-6020.

Community Conservation
Studies are conducted on energy conservation at the community level in order to promote sound conservation practices in community planning and design. Contact: Community Research and Development Branch, Federal and Community Programs, Building Energy Research and Development, Conservation and Renewable Energy, Department of Energy, 1000 Independence Ave. S.W., Room GF-277, Washington, DC 20585/202-252-9389.

Competition—Energy
The office provides policy analysis on energy competition. It advocates market-based solutions for energy problems, analyzes the impact of competition for its activities, and identifies studies and proposes alternatives for energy policy. Also provides testimony before Congress. Contact: Congressional, Intergovernmental, and Public Affairs, Department of Energy, Room 8G073, 1000 Independence Avenue SW, Washington, DC 20585/202-252-5523.

Computerized Data Bases:
The following data bases are maintained by the Department of Energy.

Acid Rain Data Base
The Fossil Energy Information Center (FEIC) maintains a data base of information about ongoing federal and state funded research projects in the area of acid rain. Retrievable data includes: principal investigator and affiliation; sponsoring agency; states involved; and a description of the research projects, including its importances, objectives, and estimated duration. Searches are available free of charge from FEIC. Contact: Fossil Energy Information Center, Oak Ridge National Laboratory, P.O. Box X, Building 2001, Oak Ridge, TN 37831/315-574-7782.

Alternative Fuel Data Bank (AFDB)
AFDB, designed for direct public access, can be searched by most home computer users having a telephone linkup. The data bank contains information about the utilization of alternative fuels. It has three types of data: bibliographies of publications, synopses of ongoing research activities and discussions of topics of current interest. AFDB focuses on the use of non-petroleum sources and non-conventional fuels from petroleum sources in transportation. Examples of fuels covered include syncrudes from shale, coal, alcohols, hydrogen, ethers and broadcut. Data retrieval programs are interactive and designed for easy use by the general public.

Searches and direct-access privileges are available free of charge. Contact the Center to find out if your computer and home link-up are compatible (most home computers are) and to obtain a free user's manual and I.D. number. If you don't have the equipment to search AFDB yourself, the Center will query the system for you and send you a printout. Contact: Alternative Fuel Data Bank, Bartlesville Energy Technology Center, P.O. Box 2128, Bartlesville, OK 74005/518-337-4267.

Carbon-Carbon Data Base (CCDB)
CCDB provides up-to-date information on the use and perfomance of carbon-carbon composites in various rocket and space applications. This data base is new and growing rapidly. MCIC will do searches for the general public. Depending upon the complexity of your request, a cost-recovery fee may be charged. Contact: Metals and Ceramics Information Center, Battelle Columbus Laboratories, 505 King Avenue, Columbus, OH 43201-2693/General Information: 614-424-5000, Technical Inquiries: 614-424-6376.

Carbon Dioxide Bibliographic Information System
The Carbon Dioxide Information Center maintains a specialized bibliographic data base on carbon dioxide and climate. Subject areas covered include: carbon cycling, carbon dioxide, and climate. (Note: the Center is in the process of putting on-line an inventory of numeric data for carbon dioxide research.) CDBIS contains more than 6,300 citations. The Center currently conducts searches free of charge, but that policy could change. Eventually, the system may be available on DOE-RECON. Written requests are preferred and letters should be specific. Contact: Carbon Dioxide Information Center (CDIC), Oak Ridge National Laboratory, P.O. Box X, Building 6025, Room 13W, Oak Ridge, TN 38731.

Conservation and Renewable Energy Data Base
The Conservation and Renewable Energy Inquiry and Referral Service (CEIRS) provides information on all aspects of renewable energy technolo-

gies and energy conservation. The data base covers active and passive solar energy, wind, fuel efficiency, wood heating, ocean energy, geothermal energy, alcohol fuels, comparisons of energy sources, and much more. Designed to help staff answer public inquiries, CEIRS contains standardized responses to the most frequently asked questions, bibliographic citations and abstracts, and referrals to appropriate public and private organizations.

While staff uses the CEIRS data base to respond to public inquiries, they do not perform specialized searches. The Center has prepared bibliographies on 50 different topics numerous fact sheets and documents for public use. All services and materials are available free of charge. Contact: Renewable Energy Center, Box 8900, Silver Spring, MD 20907/in Pennsylvania, 800-462-4983; in Alaska and Hawaii, 800-523-4700; elsewhere in the U.S. including the Virgin Islands and Puerto Rico, 800-523-2929.

Crude Oil Analysis Data Bank

Crude Oil Analysis Data Bank (COA), designed for direct public access, can be searched by most home computer users having a telephone linkup. The data bank contains analyses of nearly all crude oils discovered in the United States and representative crude oils from foreign countries. COA is the world's largest collection of data about crude oil physical properties, distillation and refining. Examples of retrievable properties include: gravity, sulphur content, nitrogen content, viscosity, color and pour point. Other retrievable information includes the oil's geochemistry, its source and financial value. The data base can be searched by any parameter in the analyses (i.e., type of oil, location, specific property, etc.). The system is designed for easy use by the general public.

Searches and direct access privileges are available free of charge. Contact the Center to find out if your computer and telephone linkup are compatible (most home computers are) and to obtain a free user's guide. If you don't have the equipment to search COA yourself, the Center will query the system for you and send you a printout. Contact: Crude Oil Analysis Data Bank, Bartlesville Energy Technology Center, U.S. Department of Energy, P.O. Box 1398, Bartlesville, OK 74003/ 918-336-2400, ext. 256.

Energy Conservation Data Base

The Energy and Environment Data Base (EEDB) is a bibliographic data base for worldwide literature pertaining to energy conservation. Examples of topics covered include: transportation, coal, load management, energy conservation and consumption in buildings, emergency planning, and the industrial sector.

Simple searches are done free of charge while more complex searches are assessed a cost-recovery fee. The data base is available on DOE/ RECON. Some of the EEDB information is also in the energy data bases on DIALOG, SDC and BRS. Contact: Center for Energy and Environmental Information, Oak Ridge National Laboratory, Building 4500-N, Room G-9, Oak Ridge, TN 37830/615-574-7470.

Energy Data Base

The Department of Energy's Remote Console Information System (DOE/RECON) comprises the largest and most comprehensive files of worldwide energy information. Its numerous data bases cover such subject areas as energy conservation, storage and conversion, coal, petroleum, natural gas, oil shales, and tar sands; solar, geothermal, and nuclear energy; fusion and reactor technology; other synthetic and natural fuels; wind and tidal power; and energy management and policy. DOE/ RECON also contains data bases with information about completed and in-progress research projects and a data base about sources of federal energy data.

Its largest is the DOE Energy Data Base, containing more than two million bibliographic citations. U.S. government agencies and their contractors, subcontractors, and grantees can obtain direct access to DOE/RECON. To find out if you qualify, contact DOE-TIC in Oak Ridge, TN. DOE is attempting to make its RECON system more accessible to the public by authorizing search centers at various locations in the U.S. WRISC at Lawrence Berkeley Laboratory is the first such center and has been providing search services. Its fees are computer time ($40.00 per connect hour) plus a staff-time charge of $23.00 per hour for DOE contractors and federal agencies, and $27.00 per hour for others. Check with DOE-TIC to find out about other centers or policies that may be in operation. Contact: Office of Science and Technical Information, Department of Energy, P.O. Box 62, Oak Ridge, TN 37831/615-576-1272 OR Western Regional Information Service Center, Building 50, Room 130, Lawrence Berkeley Laboratory, Berkeley, CA 94720/415-486-6307.

Energy Emergency and Fuel Consumption Plans Data Base

The Regional and Urban Studies Data Base contains state plans on meeting energy emergencies and fuel consumption. Examples of retrievable data include conservation plans, statistics and general information.

Simple searches are available free of charge. A cost-recovery fee is charged for complex searches. Contact: Center for Energy and Environmental Information, Oak Ridge National Laboratory, Building 4500-N, Room G-9, Oak Ridge, TN 37830/615-574-7470.

Environmental Mutagen, Carcinogen and Teratogen Data Base

The Environmental Mutagen, Carcinogen and Teratogen Information Department (EMCT) maintains a data base with technically-indexed master files available from the National Library of Medicine's TOXLINE, related EMCT in-house files, and indexed bibliographies. The bibliographic files contain information about world-wide literature evaluating the mutagenic, carcinogenic, and/or teratogenic potential of environmental agents such as food and food additives, drugs, and agricultural and industrial chemicals. All of these files are linked and can be searched on an in-house computer system for environmental agents, organisms tested, assay systems, or any one of many other fields.

Searches of EMCT's data base files are available free of charge. The Center's main data bases EMIC and ETIC are part of the National Library of Medicine's (NLM) TOXLINE data base DOE-RECON. Contact: Environmental Mutagen, Carcinogen and Teratogen Information Department, Oak Ridge National Laboratory, P.O. Box X, Oak Ridge, TN 37830/615-574-0594.

Fusion Data Base

The Controlled Fusion Atomic Data Center Bibliographic Data Base maintains a computerized data base with bibliographic information, including abstracts and evaluations, on more than 120 fusion-related numeric journals. Searches can be done by author, reactants, and reaction process.

Simple searches are done free of charge. The data base is not available on any other system. Contact: P.O. Box X, Controlled Fusion Atomic Data Center, Oak Ridge National Laboratory, Building 6003, Oak Ridge, TN 38371/615-574-4700.

Natural Gas Data Base

The National Gas Division Management Information System (MIS) data base contains information about all U.S. imports/exports of natural gas. Retrievable data includes: a summary of contract terms for all current and pending import/export authorization, who is authorized and information about current cases. Case information includes importer/exporter, contract provisions, price, volume, point of entry, time frame of authorization, and more.

Searches and printouts will soon be available free of charge. Contact: Department of Energy, Natural Gas Division, Economic Regulatory Administration, Forrestal Building, 1000 Independence Avenue, S.W., Washington, DC 20580/202-252-9485.

Nuclear Information Center Data Base

The Nuclear Safety Information Center (NSIC) data base contains the most complete file of U.S. reactor operating events (now called Licensee Event Reports-LER) in existence. It contains about 1,800 descriptions of safety documents. The data base is searchable by keywords.

Searches are available free of charge to government agencies and their contractors/grantees. Others are charged a cost-recovery fee. (Note: utility companies can obtain free searches. Contact is through the Institute for Nuclear Power Operations in Atlanta, GA.) Contact: Nuclear Safety Information Center, Oak Ridge National Laboratory, P.O. Box Y, Oak Ridge, TN 37830/615-574-0398.

Public Comments on Energy Rules for Conservation and Buildings Data Base

The Center for Energy and Environmental Information maintains a data base of public comments about proposed and enacted Department of Energy Rules for residential conservation and buildings. Comments are collected from verbal and written testimony of State Energy Offices, businesses, trade associations, builders, interest groups and any individuals or organizations submitting remarks. Information is retrievable by subject categories such as central heating, solar heating, electric pilots, residential conservation, and commercial and apartment services.

Simple searches are available free of charge. More complex searches may be done on a cost-recovery basis. Contact: Center for Energy and Environmental Information, Oak Ridge National Laboratory, Building 2001, P.O. Box X, Oak Ridge, TN 37830/615-574-7763.

Radiation Shielding Data Base

The Center maintains an information retrieval system which contains abstracts and indexes shielding information selected by its analysts. Topics include radiation from reactors, weapons, and accelerators plus radiation occurring in space.

RSIC's data base is available on DOE-RECON. Staff will search their data base for people not having access to DOE-RECON. Contact: Radiation Shielding, Oak Ridge National Laboratory, P.O. Box X, Oak Ridge, TN 37830/615-574-6176.

Rare-Earth Information Center

The Rare-Earth Information Center (RIC) is a bibliographic data base of worldwide literature concerning the physical and application aspects of rare-earth. RIC's main emphasis is the physical metallurgy and solid state physics of rare-earth metals and their alloys. Citations of journal articles on ceramics, technology, geochemistry, and toxicity of the elements and their compounds are also provided. RIC can be searched by author, title, time period and subject.

Searches and printouts are available for a minimum fee of $25.00 which entitles you to up to 25 citations. Twenty-five dollars is assessed for each additional increment of 25 citations. Fees are waived under special circumstances. Contact: Rare-Earth Information Center, Energy and Minerals Resources Institute, Iowa State University, Ames, IA 50011/515-294-2272.

Solar Energy Data Base

The Solar Energy Research Institute (SERI) maintains the National Solar Technical Audience File (NSTAF), a data base of people who have indicated their interest in solar energy. The data base can be searched by particular solar technologies, i.e. alcohol fuels, biomass energy, photovoltaics, and wind-energy.

SERI uses its data base to notify people about conferences and new publications in the field of solar energy. Upon request, staff will add your name free of charge to their data base. Staff will also search the data base and supply a print-out (on mailing labels) for a charge of 7 cents per name. Staff will also provide referral services to help people find appropriate documents, organizations and their information sources. Contact: Solar Energy Research Institute, Technical Information Branch, 1617 Cole Blvd, Golden, CO 80401/303-231-7355.

Statistical Energy Information Data Base

The Data Resources Directory Publications Subsystem (DRD) is a bibliographic data base for statistical energy information. It contains abstracts of all publications by the Energy Information Administration, selected materials from other federal agencies, and at least one publication from each state. The data base provides individual access to each table and graph stored.

Searches and printouts are available, on a cost-recovery basis, from the Department of Energy. The data base can also be searched on DOE/RECON and BRS. Contact: Department of Energy, 1000 Independence Avenue, S.W., MS 1H023, Washington, DC 20585/202-252-2171.

Toxic Chemicals Data Base

The Carcinogenesis Bioassay Data System contains data about approximately 600 chemical compounds being tested for toxicity. Data is mostly carcinogenic results of tests on rats and mice exposed to environmental chemicals. Retrievable information includes: species of animal, dose of chemical, animal age, results, organs affected and kinds of tumors. Examples of chemicals tested include compounds in pesticides and over-the-counter drugs. CBDS is searchable in batch mode. The system was started in 1973, contains records on 600 compounds and is updated monthly. Searches and printouts are available free of charge. Some of CBDS data is on CHEMTRACK. Contact: National Institute of Environmental Health Sciences, Toxicology Research and Testing Service, MD 18-01, P.O. Box 12233, Research Triangle Park, NC 27709/919-541-3418.

Conservation and Renewable Resources

Analysis is conducted of federal initiatives in energy conservation with respect to the social, economic, environmental and energy impacts of policies. Contact: Conservation and Renewable Resources, Office of Policy and Management, Conservation and Renewable Resources, Department of Energy, 1000 Independence Ave. S.W., Room 6C-036, Washington, DC 20585/202-252-6768.

Conservation and Solar Energy

For information on programs in research, development and demonstration of advanced technologies and financial and technical assistance for conservation-related activities involving solar applications, contact: Conservation and Solar Energy, Department of Energy, 1000 Independence Ave. S.W., CE-6016, Washington, DC 20585/202-252-9220.

Conservation at Home and Energy Audits.

The Building Conservation Service seeks to reduce the energy consumption of single- to four-family residences by requiring the larger electric and gas utility companies to provide information to those customers on energy conservation and renewable resources. Utilities are required to offer energy audits and arrangements for installation and financing of energy-saving measures. Free publications include: *Rating Your Oil Home-Heating System* and *Upgrading Oil Home-Heating Systems*. Contact: Community Residential Conservation Services, Federal and Community Programs, Office of Buildings and Community Systems, Conservation and Renewable Energy, Department of Energy, 1000 Independence Ave. S.W., MS GH068, Washington, DC 20585/202-252-1650.

Conservation Hotline

Information is available on the U.S. Department of Energy's emergency energy conservation efforts, the Standby Federal Conservation Plan and the Emergency Building Temperature Restrictions. The publication *How to Comply With Emergency Building Temperature Restrictions* is available free. Contact: Office of Emergency Conservation Programs, State and Local Programs, Conservation and Solar Energy, Department of Energy, 1000 Independence Ave. S.W., MS GE004, Washington, DC 20585/800-424-9122 (DC: 202-252-4950; Alaska, Hawaii, Virgin Islands and Puerto Rico: 800-424-9088).

Consumer Affairs

This office is responsible for providing policy direction for and oversight of U.S. Department of Energy's consumer and *education activities*. Free publications include: *Energy Insider* (a newspaper); *Winter Survival; A Consumer's Guide; and Winter Preparedness.* Contact: Office of Consumer Affairs, Department of Energy, 1000 Independence Ave. S.W., Washington, DC 20585/202-252-5373.

Consumer Product Technology
The commercialization of energy-efficient design is encouraged in such products as heating furnaces, wood stoves, cooling and ventilation equipment and systems, lighting appliances, building controls, and materials and diagnostic equipment used to determine the efficiency of energy used in buildings. Contact: Technical Information Center, P.O. Box 62, Oak Ridge, TN 37830/615-576-1301.

Consumption Data Bases
The *Residential Energy Consumption System* provides national estimates on vehicle miles traveled, fuel consumption, efficiency of residential vehicle fleets, and energy consumption, storage, and cost by fuel type and housing unit characteristics. The *Commercial and Industrial Energy Consumption System* provides data on age, size, and characteristics of nonresidential buildings by types and amount of energy used or stored in them and by the uses to which the energy is put. Contact: Consumption Data System, National Energy Information Center, Department of Energy, 1000 Independence Ave. S.W., Room 1F-408, Washington, DC 20585/202-634-5641.

Data Base—DOE
Much of the information in the Department of Energy is available on-line on DOE/RECON, a computer retrieval system maintained by the Department of Energy Technical Information Center. The Energy Information Research Inventory (EIRI) data base identifies and describes federal- and state-funded sources of energy information and is used to expedite the updating and revision of DOE information publications. The file is updated biweekly. The *Resource Directory of DOE Information Organizations* was the first publication to be produced from EIRI data. The EIRI file provides the following information:

Federal and State Sources for Energy Information. DOE information centers, libraries, programs, and operations offices; national laboratories; state energy offices and extension services and their programs; territorial and trust energy offices, extension services and their programs; and information sources within DOE contractor organizations are included, along with several other federally funded programs that supply energy-related information of significant value.

Energy-Related Products and Services Within Each State or Federal Source. Existing data bases, on-line retrieval systems, serial publications, newsletters, hot lines, facsimile transmission devices, interlibrary loan services, and restrictions on usage of the source as an information contact are included.

Key Personnel. EIRI identifies an organization's key information personnel, from the director to a specific contact person. FTS and commercial telephone numbers are provided.

Contact: Information Specialist, Energy Information Resource Inventory, The University of Tennessee Energy, Environment and Resources Center, 327 South Stadium Hall, Knoxville, TN 37916.

Data Files
Listed below are several examples of the Energy Data Files (magnetic tapes) available, for a fee, from: National Technical Information Service, U.S. Department of Commerce, 5285 Port Royal Road, Springfield, VA 22161/703-487-4807.

Lifestyles and Household Energy Use: Household Survey 1973/1975 National Surveys (PB-272 448)
National Interim Energy Consumption Survey (Residential), 1978 (PB81-108714)
End Use Energy Consumption-Transportation Sector/ EIA Format (PB81-112161)
End Use Energy Consumption-Transportation Sector/ ORNL Format (PB81-112195)
Residential Energy Consumption Survey: Household Screener Survey, 1979-1980 (PB82-114877)
Residential Energy Consumption Survey: Household Monthly Energy Consumption and Expenditures, 1978–1979 (PB82-114901)
Statistics of Interstate Natural Gas Pipeline Companies (Form 2), 1964–1980 (PB82-186131)
Nonresidential Energy Consumption Survey Building Characteristics, 1979–1980 (PB82-192014)
Large Combustors Energy Consumption Data Base, 1979 (PB83-120477)
Interstate Pipeline Companies Annual Report of Gas Supply (FERC 15), 1981 (PB83-137307)
Oil and Gas Field Code Master List (EIA) (PB83-149500)
Natural Gas Policy Act Notices of Determination (FERC Form 121) Biweekly File (PB83-154971)

Department of Energy Historian
The historical program includes preparing the official history of the U.S. Department of Energy and its predecessors, making archival decisions on the retention of historically important papers and documents and providing policy and analysis information within an historical context. Contact: Chief Historian, Office of the Secretary, Department of Energy, 1000 Independence Ave. S.W., Room MS G033, Washington, DC 20585/202-252-5235.

Driver Efficiency Program
This program offers an intensive instruction training course, regional seminars, workshops and educational materials, including:

To Help You Save Gas—a free publication that describes U.S. Department of Energy's programs and materials in driver awareness and efficiency.

Implementation Manual Handbook—a free publication that serves as a trainer's guide to developing and implementing driver efficiency programs for employees, students and the general public and as a reference book on driver efficiency materials and trainers around the country.

Running on Empty—a 27-minute film covering four basic conservation areas for drivers education: vehicle selection, driving skills, maintenance, and trip planning.

Gas Saver's Kits—for employers.

Contact: National Training Center, (DECAT) P.O. Box 14400 Las Vegas, NV 89114/Driver Efficiency Program/703-295-6535.

Economic Analysis
Econometric models are used to conduct macroeconomic analysis of energy markets with respect to finance, competition, regulation and the effects of government actions on energy supply, demand and price. Contact: Office of Economics and Statistics, Energy Markets and End Use, Energy Information Administration, Department of Energy, 1000 Independence Ave., S.W., Room 1F-077, Washington, DC 20461/202-252-1444.

Economic Regulation
The Economic Regulatory Administration is responsible for the following areas:

Natural Gas—imports/exports and curtailment priorities; and natural gas liquids price and allocation regulations.

Petroleum—crude oil price and allocation regulations; crude oil and refined petroleum imports; licenses for importation of all finished and unfinished petroleum oils and fee-free licenses to refiners, petrochemical companies, and deep-water terminal operators; special investigation and compliance audits of oil companies; and non-Federal Energy Regulatory Commission (FERC) oil pipeline regulation.

Regulatory Programs—regulatory programs allocating petroleum products, crude oil, and liquid natural gas; development, management, and direction of Department of Energy's economic and regulatory programs other than Federal Energy Regulatory Commission; pricing and allocation regulations; the monitoring of supply and price trends; the administration of programs for the conversion of oil- and gas-fired utilities to alternate fuels development; and implementation of standby and emergency regulations and programs.

Contact: Office of Public Information, Economic Regulatory Administration, Department of Energy, 1000 Independence Ave., S.W., Room 5B148, Washington, DC 20461/202-252-2972.

Electric Energy Systems
The Electric Energy Systems Division investigates dispersed generation and storage systems, and resolves transmission corridor siting problems and electric network-related problems. It also tries to control large-scale complex systems. Contact: Electric Energy Systems, Energy Systems Research, Conservation and Renewable Energy, Department of Energy, 1000 Independence Ave., S.W., Room 5E052, Washington, DC 20585/202-252-4564.

Electric Power Supply Information
The Electric Power Division of the Office of Coal, Nuclear, Electric and Alternate Fuels directs programs to collect and analyze data on electric power supply, including capacity, generation, distribution, fuel use, finances, and rates. Staff provide the Federal Energy Regulatory Commission (FERC) with the information that it needs to regulate electric power. FERC develops analytical models and prepares projections of capacity, generation, fuel use, costs, rates, financial requirements and distribution of electric power, including nuclear, hydropower, and new central station technologies. Staff also analyze the effects of policy and regulatory actions on the electric utility rates, costs, capacity, generation, distribution, finance, and consumption of input fuels. Contact: Electric Power Division of the Office of Coal, Nuclear, Electric and Alternate Fuels, Energy Information Administration, Department of Energy, Forrestal, EI-54, Room 2G060, 1000 Independence Ave., S.W., Washington, DC 20585/202-252-9663.

Electric Vehicles
Electric and hybrid vehicles are promoted and research and development is encouraged to improve existing propulsion systems and batteries. Examples include the Near-Term Electric Vehicle designed and developed by General Electric and Chrysler. Contact: Electric and Hybrid Vehicle Systems, Transportation Programs, Conservation and Renewable Energy, Department of Energy, 1000 Independence Ave., S.W., MS 5H063, Washington, DC 20585/202-252-8027.

Energy and the Environment
The Office of Environment supports the energy program offices in identifying environmental health and safety issues; conducts comprehensive health and environmental effects research and development programs; and overviews U.S. Department of Energy's environmental performance to insure compliance with internal and external environmental health and safety requirements. Contact: Environment, Safety and Health, Department of Energy, 1000 Independence Ave., S.W., Room 3G-092, Washington, DC 20585/202-252-2407.

Energy Budget and Annual Report
The Division of Budget and Administration prepares the U.S. Department of Energy's annual budget and *Annual Report,* which contains information on such items as foreign direct investment

in U.S. energy sources and supplies, exports of energy resources by foreign companies, major recipients of funding by name, and future plans. Contact: Budget and Administration, Policy and Evaluation, Department of Energy, 1000 Independence Ave. S.W., 7A-145, Washington, DC 20585/ 202-252-8010.

Energy Conservation Assistance
The National Appropriate Technology Assistance Service (NATAS) is an information and referral service funded by the Department of Energy. Its staff provides three primary services relating to appropriate technology: 1) general information; 2) engineering, scientific and technical assistance to help callers solve problems related to energy conservation and renewable energy uses; and 3) commercial technical assistance to help entrepreneurs develop the business side of energy-related appropriate technology. NATAS works closely with federal, state and local programs to coordinate these activities. Staff can assist with energy conservation planning, design systems, product patent licensing, as well as business planning, organization and development. Staff can provide you with helpful publications, and they will do on-line searching of both commercial and private appropriate technology data bases. Contact: National Appropriate Technology Assistance Service, U.S. Department of Energy, PO Box 2525, Butte, MT 59702-2525/800-428-1718 (Montana residents), 800-428-2525 (elsewhere in the U.S.).

Energy Conservation Audiovisuals
Energy Conservation audiovisual materials are available on such topics as alternative energy sources, gas economy, and solid waste recycling. Contact: Public Affairs, Audiovisual Office, Department of Energy, 1000 Independence Ave., S.W., Washington, DC 20409/202-252-4670.

Energy-Consuming Nations
Policies, strategies and options for bilateral, multilateral and regional energy relations, negotiations and developments with energy-consuming nations are studied at: Energy-Consuming Nations, International Energy, International Affairs, Department of Energy, 1000 Independence Ave., S.W., 7A029 Washington, DC 20585/202-252-6777.

Energy Contingency Planning
This office is responsible for solving practical energy emergency problems, developing new response plans, and analyzing policy issues associated with energy supply emergencies. They are also responsible for developing and conducting tests of emergency response plans and emergency management structure for U.S. involvement in the International Energy Agency emergency sharing system and NATO civil emergency preparedness activities. They also evaluate probable conse-

quences that the planned responses will have for individuals and the international, Federal, State, and local governments. The office operates the 24-hour energy emergency number, available by calling (301) 353-5555. Contact: Deputy Assistant Secretary for Energy Emergencies, Environmental Protection, Safety and Emergency Preparedness, Department of Energy, Room GH060, 1000 Independence Ave., S.W., Washington, DC 20585/ 202-252-4000.

Energy Conversion—Building Equipment
This office conducts research not undertaken in the private sector in high-risk technology areas associated with equipment for residential and commercial buildings. The areas addressed include refrigeration systems, lighting, heat pumps, and heating systems. Contact: Building Equipment, Building Energy Research and Development, Conservation and Renewable Energy, Department of Energy, Room GF217, 1000 Independence Ave., S.W., Washington, DC 20585/ 202-252-9130.

Energy Data Collection
The National Energy Information Center provides statistics and general data services to the offices within the U.S. Department of Energy. It conducts telephone and mail surveys, such as measuring residential heating oil prices of refiners and large companies and on-site surveys of gasoline prices. Contact: National Energy Information Center, Energy Information Administration, Department of Energy, 1000 Independence Ave., S.W., Room 1F048, Washington, D.C. 20585/202-252-8800.

Energy Data Tapes and Files
Energy-related data files produced by the Energy Information Administration (EIA) are available from NTIS in machine-readable form. The data files are based on data collected by surveys of various energy producers and consumers. To receive a listing of the EIA data files available from NTIS, write for the free brochure PR-712. Contact: NTIS, U.S. Department of Commerce, Springfield, VA 22161/703-487-4600.

Energy Economics and Statistics
This office designs, develops, and maintains economic and financial energy statistical and projection information systems. It also performs data collection, quality control, processing, analyses, projection, and report preparation activities associated with economic and financial matters. Assesses the U.S. energy situation periodically and evaluates and interprets current trends and events in matters that concern all aspects of the U.S. and the international energy situation. Contact: Economics and Statistics Division, Office of Energy Markets and End Use, Energy Information Administration, Department of Energy, Room

1F077, 1000 Independence Ave., S.W., Washington, DC 20585/202-252-1441.

Energy Education
The U.S. Department of Energy is concerned with the role of educational processes and institutions in the implementation of the National Energy Plan, and with developing a public understanding of and facility with energy-related subject matters. Free publications include *Guide for the Preparation of Proposals for the Pre-Freshman Engineering Program for Women and Minorities*. Contact: Department of Energy, 1000 Independence Ave., S.W., Washington, DC 20585/202-252-1634.

Energy Efficient Buildings
This program includes research in support of the energy conservation programs of the Department of Energy's Conservation and Renewable Energy. The projects include computer modeling, field measurement, lab testing, and instrumentation development in lighting, indoor air quality, daylighting, and building performance for both residential and commercial buildings. The lab maintains data bases for infiltration and building performance, as well as two computer programs, DOE-2 and CIRA. The Program includes six Areas:

1. Building Energy Simulation—415-486-5711.
2. Energy Performance of Buildings (CIRA-Microcomputer Program for residential auditors and home energy use labels.)—415-486-4029.
3. Ventilation and Indoor Air Quality—415-486-4023.
4. Windows and Use of Daylight—415-486-5064.
5. Lighting Systems—415-486-5682.
6. Building Energy Data—415-486-4362.

Technical and semitechnical reports and descriptive literature on instrumentation and experimental results are prepared and distributed by each program area. The following data bases are maintained and published regularly: new residences, residential retrofit, commercial buildings, appliances, validation of computer programs, and supply curves of potential conserved fuels and electricity. Contact: Lawrence Berkeley Laboratory, Building 90, Room 3028, Berkeley, CA 94720.

Energy Emergencies
This office deals with environmental issues relating to some aspects of nuclear energy, the Strategic Petroleum Reserve, the Naval Petroleum Reserve, and energy emergencies. They also have certain responsibilities for nuclear and operational oversight for specific DOE operations. Contact: Office of Management Services, Environmental Protection, Safety and Emergency Preparedness, Department of Energy, Room 4G064, 1000 Independence Ave., S.W., Washington, DC 20585/202-252-5800.

Energy Emergency Management Information System
This system provides energy information and projections prior to and during energy emergencies. It combines a communication and information handling facility with fast access to information and the analysts who can interpret and analyze the available data. Contact: Energy Emergency Management Information Program, Energy Information Administration, Department of Energy, 1000 Independence Ave., S.W., Washington, DC 20585/202-252-1311.

Energy End-Use
This office designs, develops, and maintains the data information systems on energy consumption in the residential, commercial, industrial, and transportation sectors. The division analyzes and publishes data on energy end-use consumption by sector and by fuel type. Contact: Office of Energy Markets and End Use, Energy Information Administration, Department of Energy, Room 1F093, 1000 Independence Ave., S.W., Washington, DC 20585/202-252-1112.

Energy Forecasting and Analysis
This division designs, develops, and maintains energy statistical and projection information systems concerning energy situations in the short term (up to 18 months) and the intermediate term (primarily within the next 10 years). The division integrates supply and demand data for all energy sources. It also develops analytical models and prepares ad hoc analyses and projections of domestic short-term and intermediate-term energy issues. Contact: Office of Energy Markets and End Use, Energy Information Administration, Department of Energy, Room 1H050, 1000 Independence Ave., S.W., Washington, DC 20585/202-252-5382.

Energy Information Administration Annual Report
This free report includes: *Volume I*—Energy Information Administration activities detailed by office and major publications from each office ($3.75); *Volume II*—Data ($7.00); *Volume III*—Forecasts ($8.00). For more information on content, contact: Energy Information Administration, Department of Energy, 1000 Independence Ave., S.W., Washington, DC 20585/202-252-8800.

Energy Information Center, National
This center serves as the central clearinghouse for providing energy information and assistance in support of federal agencies, state and local governments, the academic community, industrial and commercial organizations, and the general public. The Center is a comprehensive source of information about energy data and information, providing the following services: copies of publications issued by the Energy Information Administration; indices and catalogs of energy information products, sys-

tems, data bases, and models incorporated in the National Energy Information System; compilations of energy data; standard reference materials; an inquiry unit; expertise on energy sources and applications; and online search and retrieval access to both government and commercial data bases. Contact: National Energy Information Center, Energy Information Administration, Department of Energy, 1000 Independence Ave., S.W., MS 1F048, Washington, DC 20585/202-252-8800.

Energy Information Center—National
This office administers publications to support the functions of the Energy Information Administration's energy data and information programs. They work with ten Department of Energy Regional Energy Information Centers and maintain a public reading room which contains examples of their publications and data survey forms. Contact: National Energy Information Center, Publications Services Division, Energy Information Administration, Department of Energy, 1000 Independence Ave., S.W., Room F048, Washington, DC 20585/202-252-1088.

Energy Information, Regional
Access to U.S. Department of Energy information and services are also available through any one of ten regional offices. Contact:

Department of Energy, Region I/150 Causeway St., Boston, MA 02114/617-223-0504.

Department of Energy, Region II/26 Federal Plaza, Room 3200, New York, NY 10007/212-264-1023.

Department of Energy, Region III/1421 Cherry St., 10th Floor, Philadelphia, PA 19102/215-597-3612.

Department of Energy, Region IV/1655 Peachtree St. N.E., Atlanta, GA 30309/404-881-2352.

Department of Energy, Region V, 1655 Peachtree St., NE, 8th Floor, Atlanta, GA 30309/404-257-2837.

Department of Energy, Region VI/P. O. Box 35228, 2626 West Mockingbird Lane, Dallas, TX 75325/214-767-7741.

Department of Energy, Region VII/Regional Representative's Office, 324 East 11th St., Kansas City, MO 64106/816-374-2061.

Department of Energy, Region VIII, P. O. Box 26247-Belmar Branch, 1675 South Yokon Street, Lakewood, CO 80226/303-234-2402/FTS: 234-2420.

Energy Legislation
The Office of Legislative Affairs tracks daily actions by the U.S. Congress on major energy legislation and provides information on the current status of legislation. Contact: Research and Analysis Division, Legislative Affairs, Department of Energy, 8E070, 1000 Independence Ave., S.W., Washington, DC 20585/202-252-8687.

Energy Libraries
The following are the major libraries at the U.S. Department of Energy:

The Energy Library, Department of Energy, 1000 Independence Ave., S.W., Room GA138, Washington, DC 20585/202-252-6919. Administrative and regulatory matters, non-nuclear research and development, and alternative energy sources.

Federal Energy Regulatory Commission Library, Department of Energy, 825 N. Capitol St. N.W., Room 8502, Washington, DC 20426/202-307-5479. Regulatory matters concerning gas and electric utilities and oil and gas pipelines.

Library, Department of Energy, Germantown Branch, GTN, MA-232.2, Room 6034, Washington, DC 20585/301-353-4301. Collects materials on nuclear energy and fossil fuels, energy research, and environmental protection, safety, and emergency preparedness.

Energy Market Analyses
Analyses are conducted of international energy developments and forecasts of relevance to policy formulation mode. Contact: International Marketing and Policy Analysis, Office of International Energy Analysis, International Affairs, Department of Energy, 1000 Independence Ave. S.W., 7G-090, Washington, DC 20585/202-252-6141.

Energy-Producing Nations
Policies, strategies and options for bilateral, multilateral, and regional energy relations, negotiations and developments with energy-producing nations are studied at International Energy Policy Analysis and Integration, International Energy Resources, International Affairs, Department of Energy, 1000 Independence Ave. S.W., 7C-034, Washington, DC 20585/202-252-5915.

Energy Regulation
For information on the implementation of new legislation covering crude oil, petroleum products, natural gas, or coal, contact: Office of Regulations, Economic Regulatory Administration, Department of Energy, 1000 Independence Ave., S.W., Room 5B-168, 7219, Washington, DC 20585/202-252-8900.

Energy Regulation Hotline
The documents hotline provides a recorded listing of all Federal Energy Regulatory Commission orders, notices, opinions, and news releases, issued at 10:00 A.M. and 3:00 P.M. daily. Contact: Public Inquiries Branch, Office of Congressional and Public Affairs, Federal Energy Regulatory Commission, Department of Energy, 1000 Independence Ave., S.W., Room 75-138, Washington, DC 20585/202-357-8555.

Energy Regulatory Liaison
The Energy Liaison Center is the liaison with state and local governments on Economic Regulatory Administration programs. Contact: Energy Liaison Center, Economic Regulatory Administration,

Department of Energy, 2000 M St. N.W., 5B-148, Washington, DC 20461/202-252-2929.

Energy-Related Inventions
Support is provided for energy-related inventions that involve energy conservation or alternative sources of energy. For information on the application process for receiving funds, contact: Energy Related Inventions Program, Office of Inventions and Small-Scale Technology, Conservation and Renewable Energy, Department of Energy, 1000 Independence Ave. S.W., M5C-24, Washington, DC 20585/202-252-9104.

Energy-Related Laboratory Equipment Grants
Used energy-related equipment is donated to nonprofit educational institutions of higher learning for use in energy-oriented programs in the life, physical and environmental sciences and engineering. Contact: University and Industry Programs Division, Office of Field Operations Management, Department of Energy, Room 35-061, 1000 Independence Ave., S.W., Washington, DC 20585/202-252-6833.

Energy Research
The Office of Energy Research provides advice on U.S. Department of Energy physical energy research programs, the Department's overall energy research and development programs, university-based education and training activities, and grants and other forms of financial assistance. Their major programs include high-energy physics, basic energy sciences, university research support, nuclear physics, technical assessment projects and magnetic fusion energy. Contact: Office of Energy Research, Department of Energy, 1000 Independence Ave. S.W., 7B-058, Washington, DC 20585/202-252-5430.

Energy Research Abstracts
This semimonthly publication includes a semiannual and an annual index along with abstracts of all U.S. government-originated literature on energy-related research and development. It contains information on solar, wind, geothermal, fossil, nuclear, energy information, and storage conversion, as well as literature from foreign governments with which the U.S. Department of Energy has cooperative arrangements. Available for $165.00 per year from: Government Printing Office, Superintendent of Documents, Washington, DC 20402/202-783-3238.

Energy Research Development
The Technical Information Center (TIC) manages the technical information program of the Department of Energy (DOE) and collects, evaluates, analyzes, stores, and disseminates energy information resulting from DOE-funded research and development, as well as relevant technical literature produced worldwide for use by the DOE community. TIC is a central processing and distribution point for scientific and technical reports generated by DOE programs, including reports with classified and limited distribution. TIC maintains the DOE Energy Data Base (EDB) with over 1.8 million citations to technical energy literature; maintains the central DOE Research-in-Progress (RIP) data base; publishes abstract journals and bibliographies; provides on-line retrieval through DOE/RECON; offers microfiche publication services for technical reports to DOE and its contractors; works with technical program offices to assist them with special technical information needs; represents DOE in international technical information exchanges; and responds to public requests for energy information on behalf of program offices. Contact: Technical Information Center, U.S. Department of Energy, PO Box 62, Oak Ridge, TN 37830/615-576-6837.

Energy Research Laboratories
For a description of activities at the U.S. Department of Energy's multi-program nonweapons laboratories, contact: Field Operations Management, Energy Research, Department of Energy, 1000 Independence Ave. S.W., 7B-040, Washington, DC 20585/202-252-5447.

Energy Reserves
The U.S. Department of Energy is responsible for managing three naval petroleum reserves and four oil shale reserves. Contact: Office of Naval Petroleum and Oil Shale Reserve, Resource Applications, Department of Energy, 800 Werner Rd., Suite 342, Casper, Wyoming 82610/307/261-5161.

Energy Resources on Federal Land
For information on the leasing of federal public domain lands for the extraction of energy resources of all types, including coal, gas, petroleum, oil shale, geothermal and uranium, contact: Office of Planning and Development, Fossil Energy, Department of Energy, Room B120, 1000 Independence Ave, SW, Washington, DC 20461/202-353-2782.

Energy Review, Monthly
This monthly publication is an inclusive and timely review of statistical trends and developments in energy. Any factor having a bearing on the U.S. energy situation is examined, such as current fuel prices at the various levels of sale; data on petroleum production by OPEC countries; and data on demand for petroleum production in countries of the International Energy Agency. Available at $49.00 per year from: Government Printing Office, Superintendent of Documents, Washington, DC 20402/202-783-3238.

Energy-Saving Architecture and Engineering
The Buildings Division is responsible for information dissemination and outreach programs concerned with energy efficient buildings. It focuses on how systems, subsystems, and components of buildings function both independently and interactively; and develops and promotes research, which includes construction and operation methods and standards for application to new or existing residential and commercial buildings. Areas of application are illumination, ventilation, infiltration, insulation, heating, ventilating, and air-conditioning control systems, diagnostics, heat transfer, and energy analysis calculations. The Division operates demonstration projects to illustrate these principles. Contact: Architecture and Engineering System Branch, Buildings Systems, Buildings and Community Systems, Conservation and Solar Energy, Department of Energy, 1000 Independence Ave. S.W., Washington, DC 20585/202-252-9837.

Energy Software Packages
The Argonne National Laboratory produces a listing of about 1,000 software packages of the National Energy Software Center. Contact the Center for further information about subscription rates and plans. Contact: National Energy Software Center, Argonne National Laboratory, 9700 South Cass Avenue, Argonne, IL 60439/312-972-7250.

Energy Source Analysis
Research is conducted on the applied analyses of petroleum, natural gas, coal electric power, nuclear and other energy sources. Topics considered include resource availability, exploration, extraction and processing, transmission and distribution, costs and pricing, imports and exports, and the integration of short-term supply/demand balances. Contact: Division of Economic Analysis, Policy Planning and Analysis, Energy Information Administration, Department of Energy, 1000 Independence Ave S.W., Room 7H-063, Washington, DC 20585/202-252-5667.

Energy Statistics
The following are some of the major statistical publications published by the Energy Information Administration:

Monthly Energy Review ($36.00)
Short-Term Energy Outlook ($5.00 per copy, vol. 1 and 2)
Quarterly Coal Report ($17.00 per year)
Electric Power Quarterly ($22.00 per year)
Petroleum Marketing Monthly ($65.00)
Weekly Petroleum Status Report ($55.00)
Natural Gas Monthly ($55.00)
Petroleum Supply Monthly ($44.00)

Available from U.S. Government Printing Office, Superintendent of Documents, Washington, DC 20402/202-783-3238. For further information on statistics collected by the Energy Information Administration, contact: National Energy Information Center, Statistical Information, Energy Information Administration, Department of Energy, 1000 Independence Ave, S.W., 1F-048, Washington, DC 20585/202-252-8800.

Energy Storage Systems
Research is conducted on solar and other intermittent energy systems so that they can provide continuous service. Areas of interest include conserving energy by storing industrial and utility waste heat for later use; improving the efficiency of electrochemical processes; and electrochemical, mechanical, thermal and chemical energy storage technologies to be used in solar systems, transportation, building heating and cooling, industry and utilities. Contact: Office of Energy Systems Research, Advanced Conservation Technologies, Conservation and Renewable Energy, Department of Energy, 1000 Independence Ave. S.W., 5E-052, Washington, DC 20585/202-252-1477.

Energy Systems Research and Development
The Solar Electric Technologies office is responsible for the research and development activities of wind energy systems, ocean energy systems, and photovoltaic energy systems, serving as the solar energy program's focal point and interfacing with the electric utility industry. Contact: Solar Electric Technologies, Conservation and Renewable Energy, Department of Energy, Forrestal Bldg, CE-33, Room 5E080, 1000 Independence Ave, SW, Washington, DC 20585/202-252-5540.

Energy Transportation
The Office of Energy Supply Transportation and Coal Exports coordinates U.S. Department of Energy's activities and policies in all matters of energy transportation and coal exports. For example, it provides policy papers on railroad reorganization and coal slurry pipeline legislation, and it completed the U.S. Department of Energy's study on the Northern Tier Pipeline. It helps manage programs for coal exports to Western Europe and coordinates with the U.S. Department of Transportation and Department of Commerce on the National Energy Transportation Study. Contact: Office of Energy Supply Transportation and Coal Exports, Division of Planning and Environment, Department of Energy, 1000 Independence Ave. S.W., 5A-035, Washington, DC 20585/202-252-9689.

Energy Use Analysis
Research is conducted to produce models and forecasts of short-term and mid-term energy demand in the end-use sectors (residential, commercial, transportation, and industrial), including regional and demographic breakdowns and analysis

of market penetration, as well as the impact of conservation and new technologies. Contact: Energy End Use, Office of Energy Markets and End Use, Energy Information Administration, Department of Energy, 1000 Independence Ave. S.W., Washington, DC 20585/202-633-8510.

Energy Use in Buildings
A computer program is available that provides a detailed analysis of building energy consumption. The program can be used by people who have only limited experience with computers, and architects and engineers can apply it to design energy efficient buildings that have low life-cycle costs. Contact: Energy Efficient Building Program, Berkeley Laboratory, Building 90, Berkeley, CA 94720/415-486-4834.

Enhanced Oil Recovery
For information on the commercialization of enhanced oil recovery technologies, contact: Office of Oil, Gas and Shale Technologies, Division for Oil, Gas, Shale and Coal Liquids, Department of Energy, 1000 Independence Ave., S.W., Washington, DC 20585/202-353-2877.

Environmental Energy Liaison
The Office of Environmental Liaison coordinates the participation of Congress, state and local governments and public interest groups in the development of environmental energy programs. Contact: Office of Congressional Affairs, Division of Congressional Inter-governmental and Public Affairs, Department of Energy, 1000 Independence Ave. S.W., Washington, DC 20585/202-252-2869.

Environmental Impacts of Energy Technology
The Office of Public Safety is responsible for identifying and evaluating the equipment, methods and procedures necessary to minimize detrimental impacts from energy systems on the public and environment. It also compiles an annual inventory of U.S. Department of Energy environmental control technology-related projects. Contact: Office of Public Safety, Environment, Department of Energy, Germantown, G-163, Washington, DC 20545/301-353-3016.

Environmental Policy
Information and analysis on environmental energy-related policy is available from: Office of Environmental Analysis and Assessment, Environmental Safety and Health, Department of Energy, 1000 Independence Ave. S.W., 4G-036, Washington, DC 20585/202-252-2061.

Exhibits
The U.S. Department of Energy sells traveling exhibits suitable for malls, shopping centers, conventions, fairs, science centers, museums, libraries, civic clubs, theme parks, and tourist attractions. The exhibits include:

The Energy Laboratories—these exhibits stress energy conservation, driving for dollars, energy tax credits and home insulation.

Energy—looks at the problems with various energy resources—coal, oil, natural gas, nuclear, water— and discusses other alternatives such as oil shale, geothermal energy, nuclear fusion, and energy storage systems.

The Savings Energy Show—how various energy systems can be used to save energy.

The American Energy Pie—looks at where our energy is being used, where it comes from and how we can use less.

Saving Energy in Your Home—demonstrates sources of heat loss in the home, economical uses of insulation, and energy-efficient thermostats.

Extraction of Oil and Gas—informs energy specialists in oil and gas production about the research and development programs for enhanced oil and gas recovery by the U.S. Department of Energy.

Coal Mining—provides information on U.S. Department of Energy's program to develop and test equipment and procedures that safely and economically mine coal by stripping and deep mining.

Contact: Traveling Programs Department, American Museum of Science and Energy, U.S. Department of Energy, P.O. Box 117, Oak Ridge, TN 37830/615-576-3219. Energy-related exhibits are also available from: Exhibits Branch, Office of Public Affairs, Department of Energy, 1000 Independence Ave. S.W., 85073, Washington, DC 20585/202-252-4670.

Extension Service Program
This program is a federal/state partnership to give personalized information and technical assistance to small-scale energy users on energy conservation and the use of renewable and more abundant resources. States receive grants to work personally with families, owners of small companies, and local government officials to help them take practical steps to save energy. Examples of programs include self-help solar workshops; home builders workshops; clearinghouses; hospital energy management; family-business energy audits; hotel/motel energy audits. Available technical assistance includes source books; a computerized information retrieval system; technical materials (posters, pamphlets, media messages, training materials and technical reports); and seminars and workshops. Contact: Extension Service Program, State and Local Programs, Conservation and Renewable Energy, Department of Energy, 1000 Independence Ave. S.W., 6A-087, Washington, DC 20585/202-252-2346.

Federal Energy Management Program
This program oversees and monitors progress of federal agencies in the reduction of energy con-

sumption in federal buildings and federal operations. Contact: Federal and Community Programs, Federal Energy Management Programs Branch, Conservation and Renewable Energy, Department of Energy, 1000 Independence Ave. S.W., MS 1H054, Washington, DC 20585/202-252-9467.

Federal, State and International Energy Statistics
The Office of Interfuels, International and Emerging Energy Statistics provides information on federal and state energy usage, energy indicators and measures of consumption; develops and collects international statistics and coordinates Energy Information Administration data submissions to major international energy agencies; compiles nuclear energy data; designs and conducts special surveys on emerging fuels such as solar energy, wood, geothermal and conservation activities; and compiles financial statistics from natural gas pipeline companies and electric utilities. Contact: International and Contingency Information, Energy Information Administration, Department of Energy, 1000 Independence Ave. S.W., 1H-072, Washington, DC 20585/202-252-1130.

Financial Data on Energy Companies
Financial and operation performance data is collected on companies in energy-related industries. Companies are arranged by energy source, firm size, operational segment and geographic area. Contact: Office of Economics and Statistics, Division of Energy Markets and End Use, Energy Information Administration, Department of Energy, 1000 Independence Ave. S.W., 1F072, Washington, DC 20585/202-252-1447.

Forecasts and Analysis
The Energy Analysis and Forecasting carries out forecasts and analysis functions for the Energy Information Administration. The type of studies available include:

An Analysis of the Natural Gas Policy Act of 1978 and the Powerplant and Industrial Fuel Act of 1978
The Short-Term Costs of Petroleum Imports
The Possible Utility Fuel Use Implications of Alternative Legislative or Regulatory Reactions to the Three Mile Island Nuclear Power Station Accident
The Short-Term Forecasts of Energy Supply and Demand Balances
The Estimated Impacts of Gasoline Deregulation on Household Energy Consumption Expenditures
The Feasibility of Financing Energy Development Through 1990
An Assessment in Terms of World Oil Prices of the Iranian Petroleum Supply Disruption.

Contact: Energy Analysis and Forecasting, Energy Markets and End Use, Energy Information Administration, Department of Energy, 1000 Independence Ave. S.W., 1H-055, Washington, DC 20585/202-252-6160.

Fossil Energy Research
Research is conducted on the capabilities to convert coal to liquid and gaseous fuels; the increase of domestic production of coal, oil and gas; and more efficient and more economically attractive use of fossil energy resources. Contact: Office of Advanced Energy Conversion Systems, Coal Utilization, Advanced Conversion and Gasification, Department of Energy, Room C156, Washington, DC 20545/301-353-5910.

Freedom of Information Act
For information on Freedom of Information and Privacy Act activities within the U.S. Department of Energy, contact: Office of Administrative Services, Department of Energy, 1000 Independence Ave. S.W., Room 1G051, Washington, DC 20585/202-252-6025. See also "Freedom of Information Act."

Fuel Conversion
Information is available on the Powerplants and Industrial Fuel Use Act of 1978, which prohibits utilities and industry from building and operating major new boiler facilities that would burn oil or natural gas unless the Economic Regulatory Administration grants an exemption. Responsibility also includes ordering the conversion of existing power plants and industrial boilers to coal or other alternate fuels. Contact: Division of Coal and Electricity, Office of Fuels Programs, Economic Regulatory Administration, Department of Energy, 1000 Independence Ave. S.W., GA 033, Washington, DC 20461/202-252-1316.

Fusion
For information on the latest technology for safe, economical and environmentally acceptable use of fusion power for the generation of electricity and for the production of synfuels and heat, contact: Office of Fusion Energy, Energy Research, Department of Energy, Germantown, Room J204, Washington, DC 20545/301-353-3347.

Gas Centrifuge and Isotope Separation Research
The Uranium Enrichment Advanced Technology Project is responsible for the research and development of gas centrifuge technology and advanced isotope separation techniques. It publishes the *Uranium Enrichment 1983 Annual Report* which covers statistical information as it pertains to the research and development of uranium. The report also summarizes the ongoing reports published during the year. It is available free of charge. Contact: Uranium Enrichment Advanced Technology Project, U.S. Department of Energy, NE-32, Washington, DC 20545/301-353-5969.

Gas Centrifuge Technology
For information on the latest developments and applications of gas centrifuge technology and on the

construction of the Gas Centrifuge Enrichment Plant at Portsmouth, Ohio, contact: Office of Enrichment Expansion Project, Uranium-Enrichment, Office of Nuclear Energy, Department of Energy, Room A170, NE-36, Washington, DC 20545/301-353-4610.

Gaseous Diffusion Plants

For information on the activities associated with the operation, construction and maintenance of the three existing gaseous diffusion plants operated by the U.S. Department of Energy, contact: Division of Operations and Facility, Office of Uranium Enrichment, Office of Nuclear Energy, Department of Energy, 1000 Independence Ave. S.W., A-184, Washington, DC 20461/202-353-5832.

Gas Mileage Guide

This free booklet provides estimates on fuel economy by vehicle size in order to provide a basis for selecting the most fuel-efficient vehicle to meet basic needs; infomation on relative fuel economy, engines, transmissions, fuel systems, and body types including sizes of passenger compartments, and trunk and storage space; and information on factors affecting fuel economy such as temperature, wind, precipitation, road conditions and driving style. Contact: Advanced Technology and Assessment Branch, Vehicle and Engine R&D, Conservation and Renewable Energy, Department of Energy, 1000 Independence Ave. S.W., CE-131, Washington, DC 20585/202-252-8012.

Gas Resource Development

Information is available on the production and recovery of unconventional gas from all sources, including marginal wells, as well as the commercialization of all gas and unconventional gas resources. Contact: Oil, Gas and Shale Technology, Fossil Energy, Department of Energy, Room D119, 1000 Independence Ave. S.W., Washington, DC 20585/202-353-2817.

Gas Turbines

Work is done in conjunction with the U.S. auto industry toward the development of gas turbine engines that receive 30 percent or better fuel economy by 1985 (as required by the U.S. Congress). Contact: Advanced Gas Turbine Program, Office of Conservation and Renewable Energy, Department of Energy, 1000 Independence Ave. S.W., 5G030, Washington, DC 20585/202-252-8012.

Geothermal and Hydropower Research

The Geothermal and Hydropower Technologies office oversees the implementation of research and development programs to develop the nation's geothermal and small-scale hydropower resources. The office determines the potential of and develops the technology for exploitation of the large geopressured and hot dry rock resources. It makes geothermal resource and reservoir assessments and conducts research and development on advanced geothermal technologies, including conversion systems and improved techniques for environmental control. It also manages the Geothermal Loan Guarantee Program. Contact: Geothermal and Hydropower Technologies, Renewable Technology, Conservation and Renewable Energy, U.S. Department of Energy, FORSTL, CE-324, Room 5F067, 1000 Independence Ave. S.W., M.S. 6B024, Washington, DC 20585/202-252-5340.

Grants

The programs described below are for sums of money which are given by the federal government to initiate and stimulate new or improved activities or to sustain ongoing services.

Appropriate Energy Technology

Objectives: To encourage research and development of energy-related small-scale technologies.

Eligibility: Not applicable.

Range of Financial Assistance: $350 to $50,000.

Contact: Appropriate Energy Technology, Department of Energy, Forrestal Building, Washington, DC 20585/202-252-9104.

Basic Energy Sciences, High Energy/Nuclear Physics, Fusion Energy, and Program Analysis

Objectives: To provide financial support for fundamental research in the basic sciences and advanced technology concepts and assessments in fields related to energy.

Eligibility: Institutions of higher education.

Range of Financial Assistance: $10,000 to $2,000,000.

Contact: Division of Acquisition Management, Office of Energy Research, Department of Energy, Forrestal Building, MS G256, Washington, DC 20585/301-353-5544.

Biomass Energy Technology

Objectives: To conduct a balanced, long-term research effort aimed at providing the generic technology base for both feedstock production and conversion technologies. Grants will be offered to develop and transfer technology to various regions of the U.S.

Eligibility: Profit organizations; private non-profit institutions/organizations.

Range of Financial Assistance: $500,000 to $700,000.

Contact: Biomass Energy Technology Division, Department of Energy, Washington, DC 20585/202-252-6746.

Energy Conservation for Institutional Buildings

Objectives: To provide grants to states and to public and private nonprofit schools, hospitals, units of local government, and public care institutions to identify and implement energy conservation maintenance and operating procedures, and, for schools and hospitals only, to acquire energy conservation measures to reduce consumption.

Eligibility: Individual local governments and institutions are eligible for assistance to conduct technical assistance analyses. Energy conservation grants are available only to schools and hospitals.

Range of Financial Assistance: $2,000 to $1,000,000.

Contact: Institutional Conservation Programs, Office of Conservation and Renewable Energy, CE 5G-070, Department of Energy, Washington, DC 20585/202-252-2198.

Energy Extension Service

Objectives: To encourage individuals and small establishments to reduce energy consumption and convert to alternative energy sources; to assist in building a credible, nonduplicative, state-planned and operated energy outreach program responsive to local needs.

Eligibility: All 50 states and territories.

Range of Financial Assistance: $88,000 to $602,000.

Contact: Chief, State Programs Branch, Department of Energy, Forrestal Building, 1000 Independence Ave. S.W., Washington, DC 20585/202-252-2300.

Energy Policy, Planning and Development

Objectives: To provide financial assistance for gathering outside experts for seminars, conferences and work groups to discuss specific energy policy issues and write recommendations and reports.

Eligibility: Institutions of higher education, nonprofit institutions.

Range of Financial Assistance: $20,000 to $200,000.

Contact: Division of Budget and Administration, Policy, Safety and Environment (PE-3), 7E-090 Forrestal Building, 1000 Independence Avenue SW, Washington, DC 20585/202-252-2431.

Energy-Related Inventions

Objectives: To encourage innovations in developing non-nuclear energy technology by providing assistance to individual inventors and small business research and development companies in the development of promising energy-related inventions.

Eligibility: Small business, individual inventors, and entrepreneurs are especially invited to participate.

Range of Financial Assistance: Up to $70,000.

Contact: Energy-Related Inventions Programs, Department of Energy, MS 6A116, Forrestal Building, 1000 Independence Ave. S.W., Washington, DC 20585/202-252-9104.

Energy Task Force for the Urban Consortium

Objectives: Nation's 37 largest cities and counties; with a sub-group of 21 communities which have a particular interest in energy.

Eligibility: Sponsored organizations.

Range of Financial Assistance: $25,000 to $80,000.

Contact: Chief, Community Research and Development, Federal Community Programs Division, Office of Building Energy Research and Development, Office of Conservation and Renewable Energy, Department of Energy, 1000 Independence Ave. S.W., Room 5G-063, Washington, DC 20585/202-252-9389.

Grants for Offices of Consumer Services

Objectives: To assist in the establishment of state utility consumer offices to represent consumer interests in electric proceedings before utility regulatory commissions.

Eligibility: States, territories, the District of Columbia, Guam, and the Tennessee Valley Authority are eligible to submit a grant application.

Range of Financial Assistance: $40,000 to $244,000.

Contact: Office of Utility Systems, Economic Regulatory Administration, Department of Energy, 2000 M St. N.W., Room 4306, Washington, DC 20461/202-254-8266.

Indian Energy Resources

Objectives: To encourage the development of Indian-owned energy resources.

Eligibility: Federally recognized Indian tribal governments.

Range of Financial Assistance: $1,000 to $200,000.

Contact: Program Manager, Indian Affairs, Intergovernmental Affairs, CP-60, Department of Energy, Washington, DC 20585/202-252-5661.

Industrial Energy Conservation

Objectives: To increase energy use efficiency and to promote the substitution of alternative fuels for conventional fuels in the industrial sector—assist the transfer of energy efficient technologies and practices.

Eligibility: Private nonprofit institutions/organizations, businesses; profit organizations.

Range of Financial Assistance: $10,000 to $250,000.

Contact: Office of Industrial Programs, CE-12, Department of Energy, Washington, DC 20585/202-252-2193.

Minorities Honors Vocational Training

Objectives: To provide scholarship funding to needy minority honor students pursuing vocational training in energy-related technologies.

Eligibility: Minority individuals.

Range of Financial Assistance: $15,000 to $70,000.

Contact: Office of Minority Economic Impact, MI-2, Department of Energy, Forrestal Building, Room 5B-110, Washington, DC 20585/202-252-8383.

Nuclear Waste Disposal Siting

Objectives: To provide for the development of repositories for the disposal of high-level radioactive waste and spent nuclear fuel including the development of interim storage capabilities prior to the availability of a repository for permanent disposal.

Eligibility: States and their political subdivisions, including executive agencies, offices of the State legislature and units of local government in which DOE is conducting nuclear waste disposal siting on site characterization activities; affected Indian tribes; and interstate and intertribe organizations.

Range of Financial Assistance: $40,000 to $400,000.

Contact: Office of Civilian Radioactive Nuclear Waste Management, Department of Energy, Forrestal Building, Washington, DC 20585.

Office of Minority Economic Impact Loans

Objectives: To provide direct loans to minority business enterprises (MBE) to assist them in financing bid or proposal preparation costs they would incur in pursuing Department of Energy work, enabling such MBE's to participate in Department of Energy research, development, demonstration and contract activities.

Eligibility: A firm including a sole proprietorship, corporation, association, or partnership which is at least 50 percent owned or controlled by a member of a minority or group of members of a minority.

Range of Financial Assistance: $1,000 to $25,000.

Contact: Office of Minority Economic Impact, MI-3.2, Department of Energy, Forrestal Building, Room 5B-110, Washington, DC 20585/202-252-8383.

Pre-Freshman Engineering

Objectives: To promote equitable participation of all Americans in energy-related careers—specifically, to increase the educational opportunities available to qualified minority group members and women in the field of engineering.

Eligibility: United States institutions of higher learning offering an engineering degree. Projects of a cooperative nature between engineering degree-granting and non-degree-granting institutions are allowable, but the proposal should be submitted by the degree-granting institution.

Range of Financial Assistance: Up to $20,000.

Contact: Division of University and Industry

Programs, Office of Energy Research, Department of Energy, Forrestal Building, 1000 Independence Ave. S.W., Washington, DC 20585/202-252-1634.

State Energy Conservation

Objectives: To promote the conservation of energy and reduce the rate of growth of energy demand by authorizing the U.S. Department of Energy to establish procedures and guidelines for specific state energy conservation programs and to provide federal financial and technical assistance to states in support of such programs.

Eligibility: All states plus the District of Columbia, the Virgin Islands, Puerto Rico, Trust Territories of the Pacific, American Samoa, Guam, and Northern Mariana Islands are eligible.

Range of Financial Assistance: $104,300 to $1,479,800.

Contact: Office of State Energy Conservation Programs, Conservation and Solar Energy, Department of Energy, Forrestal Building, 1000 Independence Ave. S.W., Washington, DC 20585/202-252-2344.

University Coal Research

Objectives: To improve scientific and technical understanding of the fundamental processes involved in the conversion and utilization of coal.

Eligibility: Institutions of higher education.

Range of Financial Assistance: Up to $175,000 for up to 3½ years.

Contact: Office of Technical Coordination, Office of Fossil Energy, Department of Energy, Washington, DC 20585/301-353-2784.

University-Laboratory Cooperative Program

Objectives: To provide college and university science and engineering faculty and students with energy-related training and experience in areas of energy research at U.S. Department of Energy facilities.

Eligibility: Science, engineering, and technology faculty and students at U.S. institutions of higher education. U.S. citizenship required.

Range of Financial Assistance: Not available.

Contact: Director, University and Industry Division, Office of Energy Research, Department of Energy, Washington, DC 20585/202-252-6833.

University Reactor Sharing and Fuel Assistance

Objectives: To support the fabrication and use of nuclear fuel for university research and training reactors in order to help ensure the continued conduct of nuclear research, development and training activities by educational institutions.

Eligibility: Private and public institutions of higher education.

Range of Financial Assistance: $1,200 to $40,800.

Contact: Division of University and Industry

Programs, Office of Energy Research, Department of Energy, Washington, DC 20585/202-252-6833.

University Research Instrumentation

Objectives: To assist universities and colleges in strengthening their capabilities to conduct long-range research in specific research and development areas of interest to DOE through the acquisition of specialized research instrumentation.

Eligibility: Institutions of highter education which demonstrated their capabilities to conduct research in the designated areas and which, during the past two years, have received a minimum of $150,000 from DOE program offices.

Range of Financial Assistance: About $100,000 and above.

Contact: Division of University and Industry Programs, Office of Energy Research, Department of Energy, Washington, DC 20585/202-252-8949.

Weatherization Assistance for Low-Income Persons

Objectives: To insulate the dwellings of low-income persons, particularly the elderly and handicapped, in order to conserve needed energy and to aid those persons least able to afford higher utility costs.

Eligibility: States, including the District of Columbia, and in certain instances, Native American tribal organizations. In the event a state does not apply, a unit of local government or community action agency within the state becomes eligible to apply.

Range of Financial Assistance: $163,478 to $14,699,396.

Contact: Weatherization Assistance Programs, Conservation and Renewable Energy, Department of Energy, Forrestal Building, Washington, DC 20585/202-252-2204.

Health and Environmental Research

Research is conducted into the health and environmental effects of energy technology development, including medical applications of nuclear technology. Investigations of the physical and chemical interactions of pollutants in the environment and in biological systems are conducted in an attempt to identify and characterize those pollutants to which humans may be exposed. The transportation of pollutants is also studied for possible disruptions to ecosystems. Biological studies are conducted on animals, organ tissues, cells and subcellular material to understand toxic action and to predict the effects on human health. Studies are made on the effects of weather and climate fluctuations on the nation's utilization of its energy resources in order to determine which types of energy use are most sensitive to climate fluctuations. Contact: Office of Health and Environmental Research, Office of Energy Research, Department of Energy, Ger-

mantown, MS E201, Washington, DC 20545/301-353-3153.

Health Effects of Energy Technology

Research is conducted on the health and environmental effects of all phases of the energy technologies under development, including biological energy conversion. Contact: Office of Acquisition Management, Office of Management, Office of Energy Research, Department of Energy, 1000 Independence Ave. S.W., F-227, Washington, DC 20545/301-353-3468.

Hearings and Appeals, Office of

This office deals with U.S. Department of Energy issues that require adjudicatory, trial-type hearings and formal decisions. Individuals or firms adversely affected by a regulatory requirement may apply to this office for an exception from the regulations. Contact: Office of Hearings and Appeals, Department of Energy, 1000 Independence Ave. S.W., Room 6G030, Washington, DC 20585/202-252-5510.

Heavy-Duty Transport and Fuels

This office manages long-term research and development programs for new energy and petroleum saving technology in the heavy-duty transport sector. Also manages projects associated with the use of alternative fuels in advanced and conventional engines. Contact: Technology Development and Analysis, Vehicle and Engine R & D, Conservation and Renewable Energy, Department of Energy, Room 5G030, 1000 Independence Ave. S.W., Washington, DC 20585/202-252-8055.

High BTU Coal Gasification

The Office of Coal Resource Management promotes commercial applications of high BTU gasification. It hopes to have two to three high-BTU gas plants operational by the mid-1980s. Contact: Office of Surface Coal Gasification, Coal Utilization, Advanced Conversion and Gasification, Fossil Energy, Department of Energy, Germantown, Room C-178, Washington, DC 20545/301-353-3498.

High Energy and Nuclear Physics

Information is available on research and development in high-energy physics (the study of the interaction between very-high-energy particle beams with other particles of matter) and nuclear physics. Contact: High Energy and Nuclear Physics Energy Research, Department of Energy, Germantown, Room G306, Washington, DC 20545/301-353-3713.

High Temperature Manufacturing Processes

For information on technological developments in high-temperature manufacturing processes of such materials as steel, aluminum, glass, contact: Office of Industrial Programs, Improved Energy Productivity Division, Conservation and Energy, Department of Energy, 5G067, Washington, DC 20585/202-252-2072.

Hydroelectric Power
The Office of Small Scale Hydroelectric Power is responsible for research, development, demonstration, of small-scale (15 megawatts or less) hydroelectric power systems of existing dams. Contact: Small Scale Hydroelectric Power Branch, Division of Geothermal Hydroelectric Technology, Office of Renewable Technology, Department of Energy, 1000 Independence Ave. S.W., Washington, DC 20585/202-252-4198.

Impact of Energy Technology
The Office of Technology Impact analyzes proposed environmental policies, laws and regulations to determine the effect on energy development and use; assesses the potential impact on the environment of energy technologies being developed by the U.S. Department of Energy and the impact of national energy strategies at both the national and regional level; conducts an analysis of the environmental impacts of synthetic liquid fuels. Contact: Office of Environment Analysis, Environment, Safety and Health, Department of Energy, 1000 Independence Ave. S.W., Room 4G-036, Washington, DC 20585/202-252-2061.

Industrial Conservation Programs
Increased energy efficiency is promoted to U.S. industry. Programs include the identification and ranking of the major energy-consumptive manufacturing industries; workshops, trade shows, and seminars to further industrial energy conservation practices; and publications and films for selected audiences concerning industrial processes. Contact: Office of Industrial Programs, Conservation and Solar Energy, Department of Energy, 1000 Independence Ave. S.W., 5G067, Washington, DC 20585/202-252-2090.

Industrial Energy Consumption
Annual data identifying those manufacturing companies consuming at least one trillion BTUs are collected to measure progress toward the industrial energy efficiency improvement targets as required by the Energy Policy and Conservation Act. The information lists the ten most energy-consumptive industries, which consume over 90 percent of the purchased energy used by U.S. manufacturers. Contact: Integrated Energy Systems and Industrial Reporting Program, Industrial Programs, Conservation and Renewable Energy, Department of Energy, 1000 Independence Ave. S.W., Room 5G063, Washington, DC 20585/202-252-2371.

Industrial Waste Utilization
Research is conducted on technological developments in industrial waste utilization and in the use of alternative materials as either feedstock or as fuels. Funds are provided for marginally economical programs, which are evaluated as to whether they can become economical, and work is done in materials recycling, alternative material usage, and energy and feedstock production. Contact: Waste Products Utilization Branch, Industrial Programs, Conservation and Renewable Energy, Department of Energy, 1000 Independence Ave. S.W., Room 5F035, Washington, DC 20585/202-252-2369.

Institutional Conservation Programs
These programs are designed to increase the level of energy conservation in schools, hospitals, buildings owned and operated by units of local government, and buildings that house public care institutions. Contact: Institutional Conservation Programs, Office of State and Local Assistance Programs, Conservation and Renewable Energy, Department of Energy, 1000 Independence Ave. S.W., Room 5G070, Washington, DC 20585/202-252-2198.

Integrated Passive and Hybrid Solar Systems
The System Research and Development Branch office of the Department of Energy develops integrated passive and hybrid solar heating, cooling, and lighting systems for residential and non-residential buildings. The branch is responsible for the following activities: concept generation, schematic design, development, and system analysis of residential and commercial building systems; energy management; system control, and performance studies of large-scale systems; and development of large-scale hybrid solar systems for a wide range of building applications in different climatic regions. Contact: System Research and Development Branch, Passive and Hybrid Solar Energy, Solar Heat Technologies, Conservation and Renewable Energy, Department of Energy, Forrestal Building, CE-312.1, Room 5H047, 1000 Independence Ave. S.W., Washington, DC 20585/202-252-8121.

International Analysis
Information is available on forecasts of international economic conditions and energy supply demand and prices under various assumptions regarding institutional arrangements and other international factors. Contact: Division of International and Contingency Information, Office of Energy Markets and End Use, Energy Information Administration, Department of Energy, 1000 Independence Ave. S.W., Room 1H0-87, Washington, DC 20585/202-252-1130.

International Energy Technology Cooperation
The Office of Technical Cooperation negotiates, implements, coordinates and evaluates international energy technology cooperation. Contact:

Division of International Research and Development Cooperation, International Affairs, Department of Energy, 1000 Independence Ave. S.W., Room 7A-029, Washington, DC 20585/202-252-6777.

International Statistics

For information on international energy statistics, contact: Economics and Statistics Division, Office of Energy Markets and End Use, Energy Information Administration, Department of Energy, 1000 Independence Ave. S.W., 1H-067, Washington, DC 20585/202-252-6557.

International Visits

An international program controls unclassified visits and assignments of foreign nationals to the U.S. Department of Energy, recruits U.S. nationals for overseas assignments, and coordinates participation in energy-related international meetings. Contact: Division of International Research and Development Cooperation, International Affairs, Department of Energy, 1000 Independence Ave. S.W., Room 7A-029, Washington, DC 20585/202-252-6121.

Large Wind Systems

The Wind Energy Technology coordinates government research and development programs on large wind energy conversion systems. Most research and development for large wind energy systems is done through the NASA. Contact: Wind Energy Technology, Solar Electric Technologies, Conservation and Renewable Energy, Department of Energy, Forrestal Bldg., CE-331.1, Room 5H048, 1000 Independence Ave. S.W., Washington, DC 20585/202-252-1776.

For information on the Darrieus vertical axis wind turbine research and technology program, contact: Large Wind Technology Branch, Forrestal CE-331.1, Room 5H048/202-252-1995.

For information on the small wind energy (100 kilowatts or less) technology program, contact: Small Wind Technology Branch, Forrestal CE-331.2, Room 5H048/202-252-6268.

Loans and Loan Guarantees _____

The program described below is one which offers financial assistance through the lending of federal monies for a specific period of time or in which the federal government makes an arrangement to indemnify a lender against part or all of any defaults by the borrower.

Coal Loan Guarantees

Objectives: To encourage and assist small- and medium-sized coal producers to increase production of underground low-sulfur coal and to enhance competition in the coal industry.

Eligibility: Any individual, partnership, corpo-

ration, association, joint venture, or any other entity can apply for a guaranteed loan. The applicant and its affiliates cannot have produced, in the previous calendar year, more than one million tons of coal, 300,000 barrels of oil, owned an oil refinery, or had gross revenue in excess of $50 million.

Range of Financial Assistance: Up to $30 million.

Contact: Project Manager, Coal Loan Guarantee Programs, Department of Energy, Room C-156, Germantown, MD 20545/301-353-4348.

Local Energy Conservation

Assistance is available to state and local governments to promote laws, ordinances, techniques and practices that promote the conservation of energy on a community-wide basis. Contact: State Program Branch, Conservation and Renewable Energy, Department of Energy, 1000 Independence Ave. S.W., Room 6A-081, Washington, DC 20585/202-252-8288.

Low and Medium BTU Gas

This program promotes research of low- and medium-BTU gasification. The objective is to develop a timely program for the use of these gases resulting from coal gasification as alternatives to natural gas and fuel oil. Contact: Division of Surface Coal Gasification, Coal Utilization, Advanced Conversion and Gasification, Department of Energy, 1000 Independence Ave. S.W., Room C-178, Washington, DC 20585/202-353-3498.

Low Temperature Manufacturing Processes

This office focuses on technological developments in specific industries requiring low-temperature manufacturing processes, such as textile and paper manufacturing, petroleum refining, and chemical and general manufacturing. Contact: Advanced Concentration and Evaporation Branch, Improved Energy Productivity, Industrial Programs, Conservation and Renewable Energy, Department of Energy, 1000 Independence Ave. S.W., 5F034, Washington, DC 20585/202-252-2078.

Metallic Ores—Melting Branch

This office promotes technological developments in advanced extraction and reduction of ores, with its focus on melting, casting, reheating, and other processes. Also concentrates on improved electrode materials, remote high temperature sensing, and other energy intensive processes in steel, aluminum, glass, cement, copper, and lead, to reduce industrial energy consumption. Contact: Improved Energy Productivity, Industrial Programs, Conservation and Renewable Energy, Department of Energy, Room 5F034, 1000 Independence Ave. S.W., Washington, DC 20585/202-252-2080.

Macroeconomics of Energy

Analysis is conducted on the relationships between the energy sectors and the general economy in determining macroeconomic impacts associated with national energy forecasts. Contact: Office of Energy Markets and End Use, Economics and Statistics Division, Macro and Financial Information, Energy Information Administration, Department of Energy, 1000 Independence Ave. S.W., Room 1F-077, Washington, DC 20585/202-252-1447.

Magnetohydrodynamics

For information on the development and commercial applications of magnetohydrodynamics—the process of converting hot gases produced from burning coal directly into electricity, which is potentially more efficient than many other methods—contact: Advanced Energy Conversion Systems, Coal Utilization, Advanced Conversion and Gasification, Fossil Energy, Department of Energy, Room C-161, Washington, DC 20545/301-353-5910.

Minority Business Procurement

Information, advice, and assistance are available to minority business firms that wish to sell to the U.S. Department of Energy. Contact: Minority Business Division, Office of Small and Disadvantaged Business Utilization, Procurement and Assistance Management Directorate, Department of Energy, 1000 Independence Ave. S.W., 1E061, Washington, DC 20585/202-252-8201.

Museum on Energy

The American Museum of Science and Energy is the largest exhibition on energy in the United States. It contains a variety of demonstrations and films, including harnessed atoms and pedal power exhibitions. Contact: Museum Division, Science Applications, Inc., Department of Energy, 300 South Tulene Ave., Oak Ridge, TN 37830/615-576-3211.

National Environmental Policy Act (NEPA)

The Office of Environmental Compliance and Overview provides technical assistance to all U.S. Department of Energy programs on matters pertaining to the NEPA: reviews and approves NEPA documents and reports prepared for the Department's activities; and determines whether Department programs, projects or regulations require Environmental Impact Statements or other environmental impact review. This is the focal point in the Department for reviewing environmental impact statements from other agencies. Contact: Environmental Compliance, Environmental Protection, Safety and Emergency Preparedness, Department of Energy, 1000 Independence Ave. S.W., 4G-064, Washington, DC 20585/202-252-4600.

Natural Gas Policy

Analysis is conducted on such policy issues as the importation of liquified natural gas, the domestic development of natural gas, and alternative regulatory policies to guide natural gas development and marketing. Contact: Office of Natural Gas Policy and Evaluation, Department of Energy, 1000 Independence Ave. S.W., MS 7E088, Washington, DC 20585/202-252-6423. For answers to questions about the provisions of the Natural Gas Policy Act, contact: Natural Gas Division, Office of Fuels Programs, Economic Regulatory Administration, Department of Energy, Washington, DC 20585/202-252-9482.

Natural Gas Regulation

The regulation of the import and export of natural gas controls pipeline imports from Canada and Mexico as well as the import of natural gas in a super-cooled liquid form commonly known as Liquified Natural Gas (LNG). Contact: Natural Gas Division, Office of Fuel Programs, Economic Regulatory Administration, Department of Energy, 1000 Independence Ave. S.W., Washington, DC 20585/202-252-9482.

Naval Petroleum and Oil Shale Reserves

This office is responsible for planning and preparing to meet essential defense, industrial, and military emergency requirements relative to the national safety, welfare, and economy, particularly those resulting from foreign military or economic actions. The organization controls and manages three oil fields in California and Wyoming in order to fulfill this responsibility. Contact: Office of Naval Petroleum and Oil Shale Reserves, Environmental Protection, Safety and Emergency Preparedness, Department of Energy, Room 3E094, 1000 Independence Ave. S.W., Washington, DC 20585/202-252-4685.

Nuclear and Alternate Fuels

This office manages the data information systems on all supply aspects of nuclear power and alternate fuels. The office also prepares analyses and projections on the availability, production, costs, processing, transportation, and distribution of nuclear and alternate energy sources. It prepares projections about energy supply and production from alternate energy forms, including solar, wind, waste, wood, and alcohol. Contact: Office of Coal, Nuclear, Electric and Alternate Fuels, Energy Information Administration, Department of Energy, 1000 Independence Ave. S.W., Washington, DC 20585/202-252-6363.

Nuclear Energy Research

For information on research performed in nuclear energy, including nuclear waste management and administration of nuclear fission power generation and fuel technology, contact: Room A-439, Nuclear Energy, Department of Energy, Washington, DC 20545/301-353-5161.

Nuclear Fuel Efficiency

Research is conducted to improve the efficiency of uranium fuel, reduce occupational exposure to radiation, improve plant productivity and improve reactor safety. Contact: Office of Converter Reactor Deployment, Office of Nuclear Energy, Department of Energy, Germantown, Room E-977, Washington, DC 20545/301-353-3773.

Nuclear Fuel Reprocessing

Information is available on fuel reprocessing technology research and development related to breeder systems. Contact: Division of Office of Spent Fuel, Management and Reprocessing Systems, Nuclear Energy, Department of Energy, Germantown, Room D-415, Washington, DC 20545/301-353-3609.

Nuclear Nonproliferation

For information on U.S. nuclear nonproliferation, cooperation and export policies, contact: Office of International Nuclear Nonproliferation, International Affairs, Department of Energy, 1000 Independence Ave. S.W., Room 7G-049, Washington, DC 20585/202-252-1883.

Nuclear Power and Alternate Fuels Information

The Nuclear and Alternate Fuels Division of the Office of Coal, Nuclear, Electric and Alternate Fuels manages the data information systems on all supply aspects of nuclear power and alternate fuels. The office also prepares analyses and projections about the availability, production, costs, processing, transportation, and distribution of nuclear and alternate energy sources. It prepares projections about energy supply and production from alternate energy forms, including solar, wind, waste, wood, and alcohol. Contact: Nuclear and Alternate Fuels Division, Office of Coal, Nuclear, Electric and Alternate Fuels, Energy Information Administration, Department of Energy, Forrestal, EI-53, Room BG057, 1000 Independence Ave. S.W., Washington, DC 20585/202-252-6363.

Nuclear Reactor Research

The Reactor Research and Technology Division is responsible for U.S. programs and projects for liquid metal fast breeder reactors. It participates in the international nuclear fuel cycle evaluation and working groups, and assists U.S. government agencies and industry in studies and evaluations of breeder reactors. Contact: Breeder Technology Projects, Nuclear Energy, Department of Energy, Germantown, Room H407, Washington, DC 20545/301-353-2915.

Nuclear Safety Information

Nuclear Safety Information Center was established as a focal point for nuclear safety information. It has been especially beneficial to those concerned with the analysis, design, licensing, construction, and operation of nuclear facilities in defining and solving nuclear safety problems. NSIC issues continuing and single-issue topical bibliographies, technical reports, and fact sheets on subjects of particular interest to the safety community. Responses to specific user requests for information are another disseminating function of NSIC. The NSIC Data Base contains summaries of all licensee event reports on unusual operating experience of U.S. reactors. The NSIC acts as the collection and distribution point for all foreign documents received in the NRC Light-Water Reactor Foreign Exchange Program, advises NRC concerning the need for an English translation, microfiches all foreign reports, and distributes them according to an NRC distribution list. The center has access to the DOE/RECON retrieval system. NSIC's services are available free of charge to governmental organizations, and their prime contractors, and on a cost recovery basis to other users. Contact: Nuclear Safety Information Center (NSIC), Oak Ridge National Laboratory, PO Box Y, Oak Ridge, TN 37830/615-574-0391.

Nuclear Space Technology

Nuclear devices are developed for federal agencies for space-oriented scientific experiments in telemetry, navigation, communication and surveillance. Programs continue to analyze data from NASA's Viking, Pioneer 10, Pioneer 11, Voyager 1 and Voyager 2 spacecraft. Contact: Division of Space Reactor Projects and Special Nuclear Projects, Nuclear Energy, Department of Energy, Germantown, A-416, Washington, DC 20545/301-353-3321.

Nuclear Standards Information

The Nuclear Standards Program Information Center (NSPIC) acquires, compiles, develops, stores, retrieves, and disseminates nuclear standards information. The NSPIC maintains a data base on the status of program standards and standards-related activities. Documents maintained and issued by NSPIC include *Nuclear Standards Master Index, Nuclear Standards Program Newsletter, Conversion of NE Standards to National Consensus Standards, First Steps to Standards Development, Guide to the Nuclear Standards Program, What is the Nuclear Standards Program? Monthly Summary of Unusual Occurrence Reports, Semiannual Index of Unusual Occurrence Reports,* and *Requirements for Preparation and Management of DOE Nuclear Energy Program Standards.* The center also publishes a newsletter. NSPIC's services and publications are not available to parties representing a foreign organization or activity or for further distribution by others to foreign interests. Contact: Nuclear Standards Program Information Center (NSPIC),

Nuclear Standards Management Center, Oak Ridge National Laboratory, Mail Stop 10, Building 9204-1, PO Box Y, Oak Ridge, TN 37830/615-574-7886.

Nuclear Task Force
This office translates policy and integrates program strategy to develop and plan the nuclear power plants construction. Contact: Nuclear Task Force, Nuclear Energy, Department of Energy, Room 7B084, 1000 Independence Ave. S.W., Washington, DC 20585/202-252-4710.

Nuclear Test Facility Safety
Safety evaluation of nuclear test facilities are conducted by: Safety, Quality Assurance and Safeguards, Nuclear Energy Programs, Nuclear Energy, Department of Energy, Germantown, Room E 435, Washington, DC 20545/301-353-4567.

Nuclear Waste
Information is available on the planning, development and execution of programs for civilian and defense nuclear waste processing and isolation, as well as for energy waste decontamination. Contact: Office Civilian Radioactive Waste Management, Nuclear Energy, Department of Energy, Germantown, G-451, Washington, DC 20545/301-353-4288.

The Transportation Technology Center is responsible for assuring a national capability to analyze and resolve problems associated with nuclear waste transportation and for assuring the availability of transportation systems for national nuclear waste storage and disposal programs. The Center also maintains information on state legislation upgrading nuclear waste transportation, and hazardous material incident reports. The Center is the national focus point for nuclear waste transportation, integrating U.S. Department of Energy programs with those of other federal agencies and private industries. Contact: Transportation Technology Center, Sandice National Laboratories, P.O. Box 5800, Albuquerque, NM 87185/505-844-4296.

Nuclear Waste Disposal
This office provides direction for the planning, development, and execution of the Department of Energy's programs for civilian nuclear waste processing and isolation, spent fuel storage and transfer, research and corrective actions on contaminated surplus facilities and inactive mill tailings sites, and for research and development of nuclear fuel cycle technology. Contact: Office of Terminal Waste Disposal and Remedial Action, Nuclear Energy, Department of Energy, Room G463, Germantown, Washington, DC 20545/301-353-5006.

Nuclear Weapons
The Office of Military Applications develops and directs programs in research, testing production, and reliability assessment of nuclear weapons. It also directs the U.S. Department of Energy program for the prevention of accidental and unauthorized nuclear detonation; maintains liaison with the U.S. Department of Defense on nuclear weapon matters; and administers international agreements for cooperation involving nuclear weapons. Contact: Program Support Military Application, Defense Programs, Department of Energy, Germantown, Room B310, Washington, DC 20545/301-353-3618.

Nuclear Weapons Data Indexing Program
All U.S. Department of Energy weapons development reports are catalogued, abstracted, and subject-indexed. A monthly abstract bulletin, *Abstracts of Weapons Data Reports,* is also available. A security clearance is required to receive classified information. Contact: Technical Information Center, Department of Energy, P. O. Box 62, Oak Ridge TN 37830/615-576-1302.

Nuclear Weapons Design and Other Science Technical Information
One of the eleven multipurpose laboratories operated by the Department of Energy (DOE), Los Alamos National Laboratory (LANL) forms part of a collective national repository of technical information and basic research. Programs include nuclear weapons design, development and testing; magnetic and inertial fusion; nuclear fission; nuclear safeguards and security; solar, fossil and geothermal energy; environmental studies; and basic sciences. LANL has one of the most powerful computing facilities in the world, and has begun work in two areas of artificial intelligence. Staff at the Laboratory's Computer Center will direct you to the appropriate publications office to obtain documents and technical reports on supercomputer research, that is available through a data base called File 103, DOE Energy, available through DIALOG.

LANL sponsored a conference in 1983 called "Frontiers of Supercomputing" that centered on the government's role in the development of supercomputers and competition with Japan in this area. Copies of conference papers are available upon request directly from LANL. Contact: Los Alamos National Laboratory (LANL), Los Alamos, NM 87545/505-667-7000.

Ocean Energy Systems
Information is available on ocean energy systems. One example is Ocean Thermal Energy Conservation (OTEC), which uses large floating platforms to capture the temperature difference in the ocean, driving turbines to generate electricity. Studies are

also conducted on the feasibility of methods for generating electricity or energy-intensive products through wave energy, ocean currents and salinity gradients. Contact: Ocean Energy Technology Solar Electric Technologies, Conservation and Renewable Energy, Department of Energy, Washington, DC 20585/202-252-5517.

Offshore Technology
Information is available on selected projects concerned with offshore production of oil and gas on the outer continental shelf and with off-shore instrumentation and drilling technology to increase reserves of oil and gas. Contact: Advanced Process Technology, Oil, Gas and Shale and Coal Liquids, Fossil Energy, Department of Energy, Germantown, Room D-128, Washington, DC 20545/301-353-3032.

Oil and Gas Analysis
Detailed analysis is performed on oil and gas, including short-term supply and demand studies, forecasts of domestic supplies and imports of natural gas, crude oil and petroleum products, and the production, distribution, and importation of synthetic oil and gas. Contact: Office of Oil and Gas, Division of Oil and Natural Gas, Office of Analysis and Forecasting, Energy Information Administration, Department of Energy, 1000 Independence Ave. S.W., BE-064, Washington, DC 20585/202-252-4680.

Oil and Gas Information System
A specialized information system has been developed to collect data on proven reserves and production of crude oil, natural gas, and natural gas liquids. Interpretive reports are available on reserve ownership and operation. Contact: Division of Reserves and Natural Gas, Office of Natural Gas, Energy Information Administration, Department of Energy, 1000 Independence Ave. S.W., BE-064, Washington, DC 20585/202-252-6090.

Oil and Gas Statistics
Statistics are collected, interpreted and disseminated on all forms of petroleum and natural gas supply and demand. More than 200 periodicals, special publications, data bases and situation reports are published each year covering such topics as monthly petroleum statistics, petroleum market shares, sales of refined petroleum products, heating oil prices and margins, natural gas production and consumption, and underground storage and refinery capacity. Contact: Office of Data Quality and Support, Division of Reserves and Natural Gas, Office of Oil and Gas, Energy Information Administration, Department of Energy, 1000 Independence Ave. S.W., BE-504, Washington, DC 20585/202-252-6083.

Oil, Gas, and Shale Programs
For information on underground gasification programs, i.e., turning coal into synthetic gas underground, contact: Office of Oil, Gas and Shale Technology, Fossil Energy, Department of Energy, Germantown, D-120, Washington, DC 20545/301-353-2877. This office also develops strategies and plans for enhancing recovery in light oil, heavy oil, and tar sands as well as for upgrading and refining of petroleum drilling, offshore technology, and advanced energy research.

Oil Policy
Analysis is conducted on such topics as crude oil decontrol, refinery policy, strategic petroleum reserves, and alternative demand restraint strategies. Contact: Office of Oil Policy, Oil and Gas Policy, Office of Economic Analysis, Department of Energy, 1000 Independence Ave. S.W., 7H-063, Washington, DC 20585/202-252-5667.

Oil Shale Research
Basic and applied research and development is conducted on oil shale and oil shale reserves. The primary focus of the research is the "in situ" process, which extracts oil by heating shale underground rather than bringing it to the surface. Work is also done on processing shale on the surface. Contact: Office of Oil, Gas and Shale Technology, Fossil Energy, Department of Energy, Germantown, D119, Washington, DC 20545/301-353-2877.

Petroleum and Natural Gas Regulation
The Economic Regulatory Administration is responsible for importing and exporting petroleum and natural gas and for allocating crude oil and petroleum products. The allocation programs include motor gasoline, middle distillant stock buildup and entitlements for crude oil. Contact: Office of Fuel Programs, Division of Natural Gas, Economic Regulatory Administration, Department of Energy, 1000 Independence Ave. S.W., Room 9A-007, Washington, DC 20585/202-252-9482.

Petroleum Marketing
This office designs, develops, and maintains information systems on crude oil and refined petroleum product prices and the petroleum industry market. The Office provides regular statistical reports on heating oil, distillate oil, and other refined product prices and on sales of fuel oil, kerosene, liquefied petroleum gases, and ethane. It also develops analyses, projections, and models that concern petroleum pricing and marketing patterns. Contact: Petroleum Marketing Division, Office of Oil and Gas, Energy Information Administration, Department of Energy, Room 2G051, 1000 Independence Ave. S.W., Washington, DC 20585/202-252-5214.

Petroleum Regulation

For information on such topics as the regulation of the rates charged by oil pipelines for transporting oil in interstate commerce, or the establishment of oil pipeline valuations, contact: Public Inquiries Branch, Office of Congressional, Intergovernmental and Public Affairs, Federal Energy Regulatory Commission, Department of Energy, 825 N. Capitol St. N.E., Room 2214, Washington, DC 20426/ 202-357-8055.

Petroleum Saving Technology

The staff in the Heavy-Duty Transport and Fuels Integration Branch manages long-term research and development programs for new energy and petroleum saving technology in the heavy-duty transport sector. The Branch also manages research and development projects associated with the use of alternative fuels in advanced and conventional engines. Contact: Heavy-Duty Transport and Fuels Integration Branch, Technology Development and Analysis, Vehicle and Engine R&D, Conservation and Renewable Energy, Department of Energy, Forrestal, CE-131, Room 5G030, 1000 Independence Ave. S.W., Washington, DC 20585/202-252-8055.

Petroleum Supply

The agency designs, develops, and maintains statistical and projection information systems for crude oil and refined petroleum products. The office collects, processes, and analyzes the data needed to monitor and report the supplies of crude oil and petroleum products. The office also analyzes and makes projections about the availability, production, imports, processing, transportation, stocks, and distribution of petroleum supplies. Contact: Petroleum Supply Division, Office of Oil and Gas, Energy Information Administration, Department of Energy, Room 2G020, 1000 Independence Ave. S.W., Washington, DC 20285/ 202-252-5844.

Photovoltaic Materials and Devices

The Collector Research and Development Branch of the Department of Energy plans, implements, and evaluates research, development, and testing programs leading toward potentially low-cost, advanced photovoltaic materials and devices. Contact: Collector Research and Development Branch, Photovoltaics Energy Technology, Solar Electric Technologies, Conservation and Renewable Energy, Department of Energy, Forrestal Bldg., CE-333, Room 5E066, 1000 Independence Ave. S.W., Washington, DC 20585/202-252-1725.

Photovoltaic Systems

The Systems Research and Technology Branch of the Department of Energy develops and manages research programs for the design, prototype fabrication, and testing of photovoltaic systems that will be low in cost, reliable, safe, and environmentally acceptable. Contact: Systems Research and Technology Branch, Photovoltaics Energy Technology, Solar Electric Technology, Conservation and Renewable Energy, Department of Energy, Forrestal Bldg., CE-333, Room 5E066, 1000 Independence Ave. S.W., Washington, DC 20585/202-252-1724.

Pipeline and Producers Regulations

This office is responsible for oil pipeline rates, valuations, charges, operating rules, natural gas pipeline curtailments, certifications, mergers, acquisitions, rates, reserve evaluation, preparation and defense of environmental impact statements in administrative proceedings, etc. Contact: Pipeline and Producers Regulations, Federal Energy Regulatory Commission, Department of Energy, 825 N. Capitol St. N.W., Washington, DC 20426/202-357-8500.

Power Marketing

The U.S. Department of Energy sells power to utilities and industries and maintains extensive transmission lines in some areas of the United States. As part of the rate setting procedure, hearings are held where the public and customers of the power marketing administration are invited to comment. The five power marketing administrations are:

Alaska Power Administration/Juneau, AK 99801/907-586-7405

Bonneville Power Administration/Portland, OR 97208/503-230-3361

Southeastern Power Administration/Elberton, GA 30635/404-283-3261

Southwestern Power Administration/Tulsa, OK 74101/918-581-7474

Western Area Power Administration/Golden, CO 80401/303-321-1511.

For additional information contact: Office of Power Marketing Coordination, Conservation and Renewable Energy, Department of Energy, 1000 Independence Ave. S.W., Room 6B-109, Washington, DC 20585/202-252-1040.

Procurement Policy

Information is available on U.S. Department of Energy's procurement and contract policies, procedures, and other business matters. A booklet, *Doing Business with DOE,* is free. Contact: Business Liaison Division, Office of Small and Disadvantaged Business Utilization, Department of Energy, 1000 Independence Ave. S.W., Washington, DC 20585/202-252-8203.

Production and Use of Alcohol Fuels

The Office of Alcohol Fuels handles research and development activities related to the production and use of alcohol fuels from renewable resources. Staff directs long-term high-risk research and development focused on conversion of non-fuel feedstocks (such as cellulose) into fuel-grade alcohol. The office implements the Energy Security Act's loan guarantee program which is designed to encourage the construction of alcohol fuel production facilities by the private sector. Contact: Office of Alcohol Fuels, Conservation and Renewable Energy, Department of Energy, Forrestal, CE-80, Room 5F043, 1000 Independence Ave. S.W., Washington, DC 20585/202-252-1277.

Publications Directory, Energy Information Administration
This user's guide describes periodicals, one-time publications, a list of survey forms, and information available on microfiche file and computer tape. Copies are free from: National Energy Information Center, Department of Energy, 1000 Independence Ave. S.W., Room 1F-048, Washington, DC 20585/202-252-8800.

Publications, Free
For copies of the following publication or for a complete listing of additional publications, contact: Publications Branch, Tech Information Center, Department of Energy, P.O. Box 62, Oak Ridge, TN 37831/615-576-1301.

How To Understand Your Utility Bill

Public Reading/Document Rooms
Copies of U.S. Department of Energy Environmental Assessments and of Draft Environmental Impact Statements, along with comment letters and other material related to the environmental impact stations, may be seen in the Department's public reading room and in public document rooms at the following locations:

Public Reading Room/Department of Energy Headquarters, Room 1E190, Forrestal Building, 1000 Independence Ave. S.W., Washington, DC 20585/202-252-6020.

Albuquerque Operations Office/Kirkland Air Force Base East, Albuquerque, NM 87116.

Chicago Operations Office/9800 South Cass Ave., Argonne, IL 60939

Idaho Operations Office/550 Second St., P.O. Box 14100, Idaho Falls, ID 83901

Nevada Operations Office/2753 South Highland Dr., Las Vegas, NV 39114-400

Oak Ridge Operations Office/Federal Building, P.O. Box E, Oak Ridge, TN 37831

Richland Operations Office/Federal Building, 825 Judwin Ave., Richland, WA 99352

San Francisco Operations Office/1333 Broadway, Oakland, CA 94612

Savannah River Operations Office/Savannah Plant, P.O. Box A, Aiken SC 29891

In individual cases, as appropriate, copies of Environmental Assessments and Draft Environmental Impact States may also be seen at one or more of the following U.S. Department of Energy Technology Centers:

Bartlesville Energy Technology Center/Virginia and Cudahy Sts., Bartlesville, OK

Grand Forks Energy Technology Center/15 North 23rd St., Grand Forks, ND

Laramie Energy Technology Center/Corner of 9th and Lewis Sts., Laramie, WY

Morgantown Energy Technology Center/Collins Ferry Rd., Morgantown, WV

Pittsburgh Energy Technology Center/Cochran Mill Rd., P.O. Box 10940, PA

Radiation and Nuclear Reactors Resource
The Office of Nuclear Energy provides information to the general public about nuclear energy and nuclear energy programs. Staff can provide you with information about available materials, including pamphlets, fact sheets, and booklets relating to all aspects of nuclear energy. They can also answer general questions or refer inquiries to appropriate program offices. The office's basic brochure is *Atoms to Electricity,* a 61-page publication describing the fission process; that is, how electricity is obtained from the atom. It also covers radiation, types of nuclear reactors, etc. Single copies are available free of charge by writing to ENERGY/DOE, PO Box 62, Oak Ridge, TN 37830. Contact: Office of Nuclear Energy, Department of Energy, 1000 Independence Ave. S.W., Washington, DC 20585/202-252-8728.

Radiological Emergency Assistance
Assistance is available at the time of a radiological incident to evaluate the hazardous aspects of the situation, to counsel responsible officials at the incident scene, to bring hazardous conditions under control, and to supplement the radiological emergency capabilities of other government and private organizations involved. Assistance is also available to help federal, state, local, industrial and other organizations to develop their own plans and capabilities for dealing with radiological emergencies. Contact: Radiological Controls Division, Emergency Preparation and Health, Department of Energy, Germantown, Room PE-222, Washington, DC 20545/301-353-4093.

Reactors, High-Temperature Gas-Cooled
For information on advanced high-temperature reactors capable of direct cycle electricity production via a gas turbine and process heat production, contact: High-Temperature Gas Reactor Branch, Nuclear Reactor Programs, Nuclear Energy, Department of Energy, Germantown, Washington, DC 20545/301-353-4331.

Recreation at Hydroelectric Projects
Many of the hydroelectric projects licensed by the U.S. Department of Energy provide various facilities for recreational activities such as swimming,

boating, hiking, camping, picknicking, fishing and hunting. Some also offer historical sites, natural history museums, guided tours of powerhouses and other facilities for enjoyment of the public. Contact: Public Inquiries Branch, Office of Congressional, Intergovernmental and Public Affairs, Federal Energy Regulatory Commission (FERC), Department of Energy, 825 N. Capitol St. N.E., Washington, DC 20426/202-357-8055.

Regional Libraries

U.S. Department of Energy and other energy-related publications are available at the following regional libraries:

Regional Energy Information Center/2626 West Mockingbird Lane, Dallas TX 75235/214-767-7736.
Regional Energy Information Center/1333 Broadway, Oakland, CA 415/273-4428..

Regulatory Activities

Listed below are those organizations within the U.S. Department of Energy that are involved with regulating various activities. With each listing is a description of those industries or situations regulated by the office. Regulatory activities generate large amounts of information on the companies and subjects they regulate; much of this information is available to the public. A regulatory office can also tell you your rights when dealing with a regulated company.

Economic Regulatory Administration/See "Economic Regulation" in this section.
Federal Energy Regulatory Commission/Department of Energy, 825 N. Capitol St. N.W., MS 9200, Washington, DC 20426/202-357-8555. Sets rates and charges for the transportation and sale of natural gas and the transmission and sale of electricity and the licensing of hydroelectric power projects.
Office of Conservation and Renewable Energy/Department of Energy, 1000 Independence Ave. S.W., Washington, DC 20585/202-252-9249. Establishes conservation standards in buildings and consumer products, and monitors energy conservation within industry.

Regulatory Files

Files and records of the Federal Energy Regulatory Commission are available for public inspection or copying in FERC's Division of Public Information in Washington, DC. Photocopies of Commission records may be obtained through a private firm under FERC contract, requiring payment of a fee directly to the firm. Cost information and order forms are available from the Division of Public Information. The following is a summary of information available:

All filings submitted to the Commission comprising formal records, including applications, petitions and other pleadings requesting FERC action; responses, protests, motions, briefs, contracts, rate schedules,

tariffs and related filings; FERC staff correspondence relating to any proceeding.
Transcripts of hearings, hearing exhibits, proposed testimony and exhibits filed with the Commission but not yet offered or received in evidence.
Administrative law judge's actions, orders and correspondence in connection with proceedings.
Commission orders, notices, opinions, decisions, letter-orders and approved Commission minutes.
Agendas and lists of actions taken at Commission meetings, which are open to the public.
Environmental impact statements prepared by FERC staff pursuant to the National Environmental Policy Act of 1969.
Agendas, minutes and draft papers relating to the National Power Survey, Natural Gas Policy Council and other FERC advisory committee meetings, all open to the public.
Accounting files and FERC audits of gas, electric and oil companies.
Legislative matters under consideration by Congress, after release by the Committee or Member of Congress involved.
Filings and recordings in court proceedings to which the Commission is a party and FERC correspondence with the courts.
News releases and announcements issued by FERC.
Subject index of Commission actions.

Contact: Public Reference Branch, Public Information Division, Office of Congressional, Intergovernmental and Public Affairs, Federal Energy Regulatory Commission, Department of Energy, 825 N. Capitol St. N.E., MS 1000, Washington, DC 20426/202-357-8118.

Regulatory Information

For general or specific information on any of the regulatory activities of the Federal Energy Regulatory Commission, contact: Public Inquiries Branch, Office of Congressional, Intergovernmental and Public Affairs, Federal Energy Regulatory Commission, Department of Energy, 825 N. Capitol St. N.W., Room 2214, Washington, DC 20426/202-357-8055.

Regulatory Legislation on Energy

For information on legislation related to energy regulation, contact: Office of Congressional, Intergovernmental and Public Affairs, Federal Energy Regulatory Commission, Department of Energy, 825 N. Capitol St. N.W., Room 9200, Washington, DC 20426/202-357-8370.

Renewable Energy Information Sources

The Energy Library system provides the Department of Energy Headquarters staff with a wide variety of bibliographic and reference services, and is a major repository of energy-related information.
The Forrestal Branch collects materials on administrative and regulatory matters, non-

nuclear research and development, energy conservation, and renewable energy sources.

The Germantown Branch collects materials on nuclear energy and fossil fuels, energy research, and environmental protection, safety, and emergency preparedness. Contact: The Energy Library Department of Energy, Forrestal Branch, Forrestal Bldg, MA-232.2, Room GA138, 1000 Independence Ave. S.W., Washington, DC 20554; Germantown Branch, Energy Library—Germantown, Washington, DC 20545/301-353-4301.

Research and Analysis

This office tracks daily actions by the Congress on major energy legislation, and provides current status of the legislation. The office provides briefing books and issue papers of DOE witnesses and compiles membership lists of congressional committees concerned with DOE programs. Prepares daily reports of congressional actions, which includes hearings, conferences, and committee markups. Contact: Congressional, Intergovernmental, and Public Affairs, Department of Energy, Room 8E070, 1000 Independence Ave. S.W., Washington, DC 20585/202-252-8687.

Research Contracts

A free publication, *The DOE Program Guide for Universities and Other Research Groups,* provides introductory information about U.S. Department of Energy programs, general procedures, energy research needs and potential opportunities. It also describes federal assistance and procurement policies and procedures. Contact: Education Division, Office of Energy Research, Department of Energy, 1000 Independence Ave. S.W., MS 3F032, Washington, DC 20585/202-252-5447.

School Conservation

The National Energy Conservation Act allows for 50 percent federal matching grants for detailed energy audits of schools and certain other public buildings and for the installation of conservation measures recommended in the audit. Contact: Schools and Hospitals Grants Program, Office of Institutional Conservation Programs, Conservation and Renewable Energy, Department of Energy, 1000 Independence Ave. S.W., MS 5G090, Washington, DC 20585/202-252-2343.

Small Business Procurement

A special office fosters U.S. Department of Energy procurement from small business. The staff provides advice and assistance to Energy buying offices and to the private sector. Contact: Small Business Division, Office of Small and Disadvantaged Business Utilization, Procurement and Contracts Management Directorate, Department of Energy, 1000 Independence Ave. S.W., MA-41, Washington, DC 20585/202-252-8203.

Small Wind Systems

The Rocky Flats Area Office manages DOE's small wind energy conversion systems program. It operates Rocky Flats National Test Center for test and evaluation of small wind systems. It also performs and directs research and development directed toward providing information to manufacturers to improve performance of commercially available wind systems. The office answers technical inquiries from system manufacturers and utilities. Contact: Small Wind Energy Conversion Systems Program, Rocky Flats Area Office, Department of Energy, PO Box 928, Golden, CO 80401/303-497-2647.

Software Center, National Energy (NESC)

NESC is the software exchange and information center for the U.S. Department of Energy. It promotes the sharing of computer software among agency offices and contractors to eliminate duplication of effort and costs. NESC facilitates the transfer of computer applications and technology and arranges for acquiring nongovernment software for the U.S. Department of Energy. Contact: National Energy Software Center, Department of Energy, Argonne National Laboratory, 9700 S. Cass Ave., Argonne, IL 60439/312-972-7250.

Solar Education

The National Solar Energy Education Directory is a guide to programs, courses and curricula offered nationwide ($8.00) from: Superintendent of Documents, Government Printing Office, Washington, DC 20404/202-783-3238.

Solar Electric Technology

Responsibility for research and development activities of wind energy systems, ocean energy systems, and photovoltaic energy systems, is the function of this office. Contact: Conservation and Renewable Energy, Department of Energy, Room 5E080, 1000 Independence Ave. S.W., Washington, DC 20585/202-252-5540.

Solar Energy Referral Service

The Solar Energy Research Institute (SERI), a government-owned contractor operated organization, will refer people to appropriate documents, organizations, and other information sources. The institute maintains a data base of people, National Solar Technical Audience File (NSTAF), who have indicated their interest in solar energy. The data base can be searched by particular solar technologies, i.e. alcohol fuels, biomass energy, photovoltaics, and wind energy. Staff uses the data base to notify people about conferences and new publications in the field of solar energy. Upon request, staff will add your name free of charge to their data base. Staff will also search the data base and supply a printout (on mailing labels) for a charge of $.07 per name. Contact: National Solar Technical Audience File (NSTAF), Solar Energy Research Institute, Technical Information Branch, 1617 Cole Boulevard, Golden, CO 80401.

Solar Heat Technology
This branch directs the design and operation of solar thermal pilot plants, experimental systems and field tests. It assesses the feasibility of advanced solar heat systems. Contact: Solar Heat Technology, Solar Heat, Conservation and Renewable Energy, Department of Energy, Room 5H095, 1000 Independence Ave. S.W., Washington, DC 20585/202-252-8084.

Solar High Risk Research and Development
The Materials and Technology Development Branch Office manages high-risk and high pay-off research and development, from concept generation through prototype field tests, for solar passive and hybrid materials and components. Research and development activities are conducted in cost-shared projects with industry, Department of Energy national laboratories, private sector companies, universities, and other federal agencies in order to identify and mitigate system technical barriers and to improve technical performance and cost-effectiveness. Activities include research in the thermal sciences and materials and components concerned with the collection, thermal storage, thermal transport, rejection/dehumidification, and appropriate controls associated with the use of passive and hybrid technologies in buildings. Areas of interest with respect to buildings include apertures/building envelopes, thermal storage in the interior structural elements, and the transfer of energy among these elements. Contact: Materials and Technology Development Branch, Passive and Hybrid Solar Energy, Solar Heat Technologies, Conservation and Renewable Energy, Department of Energy, Forrestal Building, CE-312.2, Room 5H047, 1000 Independence Ave. S.W., Washington, DC 20585/202-252-8110.

Solar Home Awards
For copies of drawings and descriptions of successful passive solar homes, order *The First Passive Solar Home Awards* from: Government Printing Office, Superintendent of Documents, Washington, DC 20402/202-783-3238.

Solar in Federal Buildings Program
This program promotes the use of solar energy in buildings by providing funds to federal agencies for the design and construction of solar applications in new and existing federal buildings. By expanding an important solar market sector, the program will help demonstrate the federal government's confidence and support of the solar industry. Contact: Office of Passive and Hybrid Solar Heating Technology, Office of Solar Applications for Buildings, Conservation and Renewable Energy, Department of Energy, 1000 Independence Ave. S.W., MS 5G033, Washington, DC 20585/202-252-8121.

Solar Information Center
Reference assistance, interlibrary loan, literature searches, and bibliography searches on solar-related subjects are available from: Solar Energy Research Institute, 1617 Cole Blvd., Golden, CO 80401/303-231-1415.

Solar Publications
The following is a listing of some of the more popular publications available from Document Distribution Services, Solar Energy Research Institute, 1617 Cole Blvd., Golden, CO 80401/303-231-1260.

Don't Get Burned with Solar Energy:
A Consumer's Guide to Buying
Solar (free)
Solar Energy Information Locator (free) 1981 ed.
Analysis Methods for Solar Heating and Cooling Applications—aimed at architects to take the guesswork out of solar. $9.00

Available from Superintendent of Documents, Government Printing Office, Washington, DC 20402/202-783-3238:

Reaching Up, Reaching Out: A Guide to Organizing Local Solar Events ($6.00)
Passive Design: It's A Natural ($1.50)

Solar Systems Performance
Assistance is available for research and development technology transfer and commercialization of solar applications in order to reduce solar systems cost and improve performance. Contact: Systems Development Division, Solar Applications for Buildings, Conservation and Renewable Energy, Department of Energy, 1000 Independence Ave. S.W., MS Room 5H065, Washington, DC 20585/202-252-8150.

Solar Technology Information Source
Solar Energy Research Institute (SERI) is a government-owned, contractor-operated research institute funded by the Department of Energy. They will respond to technical questions from researcher, scientists, engineers and educators on the state-of-the-art in the solar technologies. They can also answer questions from those same groups regarding their own activities and research. Services of SERI include an inter-library loan service for researchers and scientists in the field as well as a data base. The institute also issues subcontracts based on competitive bidding to qualified persons and organizations.

SERI has several publications. *In Review,* a monthly technical digest, describes recent discoveries and work in research. It lists publications and conferences sponsored, and is designed for scientists and engineers in the field of solar energy and is free to that group of people. Technical information guides are also available in all areas that SERI covers. A catalog which presents a selected list of documents published by the Institute since its inception, is available for free to scientists in the field. Contact: Solar Energy Research Institute (SERI), 1617 Cole Boulevard, Golden, CO 80401/301-231-1181 (Public Affairs), 303-231-7303 (Technical Inquiry Services).

Solar Thermal Pilot Plants
The Systems Test and Evaluation Branch office of the Department of Energy directs the design, characterization, and operations of solar thermal pilot plants, experimental systems, and field tests. It assesses the technical feasibility of advanced solar thermal systems. Contact: Systems Test and Evaluation Branch, Solar Thermal Technology, Solar Heat Technologies, Conservation and Renewable Energy, Department of Energy, Forrestal Building, CE-314, Room 5H041, 1000 Independence Ave. S.W., Washington, DC 20585/202-326-1234.

Solar Workshops
For information on solar conferences and workshops, contact: Solar Energy Research Institute, 1617 Cole Blvd., Golden, CO 80401/303-231-1465.

Speakers and Conferences
If you are interested in obtaining a speaker for your meeting from the U.S. Department of Energy, or would like a listing of all U.S. Department of Energy meetings, write: Conference Coordination, Speakers Bureau, Office of Public Affairs, Department of Energy, 1000 Independence Ave. S.W., Washington, DC 20585/202-252-5644.

State and Local Government Assistance
For information on energy conservation programs available to state and local governments, contact: Grants Management and Technical Assistance, State and Local Programs, Conservation and Solar Energy, Department of Energy, 1000 Independence Ave. S.W., MS 2H027, Washington, DC 20585/202-252-2302.

Statistical Standards
This office provides services to data collectors in the area of survey and statistical design, develops standards, and coordinates standard definitions that govern collection and documentation of energy information. It assesses the quality and significance of energy information and the processes used in collection, analysis, and projection. Contact: Office of Statistical Standards, Energy Information Administration, Department of Energy, Room 1H023, 1000 Independence Ave. S.W., Washington, DC 20585/202-252-2222.

Stirling Engine
A set of Stirling engines is being developed that will burn a variety of fuels such as synthetic fuels and alcohols. Work is also being performed on an engine that will utilize solar and thermal energy sources. These engines have great potential for high-efficiency, low-cost, low-noise and low-pollution emissions. Copies of the *Annual Report to Congress on the Automotive Technology Development Program* are available. Contact: Office of Vehicle Engine R&D, Advanced Technology and Assessment Division, Transportation Programs, Conservation and Renewable Energy, Department of Energy, 1000 Independence Ave. S.W., Room 5G-046, Washington, DC 20585/202-252-8012.

Strategic Petroleum Reserve
For answers to specific questions on the Strategic Petroleum Reserve program, such as project implementation, site locations, construction and technical problems, contact: New Orleans Project Management Office, Strategic Petroleum Reserve, Department of Energy, 900 Commerce Rd. E., New Orleans, LA 70123/504-734-4265.

Strategic Petroleum Reserve Management
The Department of Energy is responsible for the managing, planning, development and operation of a crude oil and petroleum products storage and distribution system. This includes the acquisition of crude oil or petroleum products for strategic and regional reserves. Contact: Fossil Energy, Strategic Petroleum Reserve, Department of Energy, 1000 Independence Ave. S.W., Room 3G-052, Washington, DC 20585/202-252-4410.

Supercomputers for Nuclear Weapons, Energy Research
Although research in nuclear weapons is the foundation of the work at the Lawrence Livermore National Laboratory (LLNL), their work focuses on five other major programs: magnetic fusion energy, laser isotope separation, laser fusion energy, energy and resources, and biomedical and environmental sciences. Much of the lab's scientific calculations are performed at the Livermore Computer Center (LCC), one of the most powerful computer centers in the world, and also at the National Magnetic Fusion Energy Computer Center (NMFECC) located at Livermore. The Centers will respond to specific questions concerning their computer's capabilities and accessibilities and will forward brochures, pamphlets, reference lists and photographs on the computer center work. Their research findings in various areas are available through the Departments of Energy and Defense. Contact: Lawrence Livermore National Laboratory (LLNL), PO Box 808, Livermore, CA 94550/415-422-1100.

Supercritical Fluids Information and Referral
The Pittsburgh Energy Technology Center works
with projects using supercritical fluids. Staff is
available to answer questions and make referrals
to other sources in the area of supercritical fluids.
Contact: Pittsburgh Energy Technology Center,
Department of Energy, PO Box 10940, Pittsburgh,
PA 15236/412-675-5797.

Tax Incentives for Using Solar
The federal government and many states are
offering tax incentives for adding solar improvements to your home. For free literature, contact: Congressional Affairs, Congressional, Intergovernmental and Public Affairs, Department
of Energy, 1000 Independence Ave., S.W.,
Room 8E-070, Washington, DC 20585/202-252-
2773.

Teacher Training
For information on teacher training and curricu-
lum development in energy education for kinder-
garten through twelfth grade, contact: Education
Division, Office of Energy Research National,
Department of Energy, 1000 Independence Ave.
S.W., Room 3F-077, Washington, DC 20585/
202-252-1634.

Technical Energy Information
The Technical Information Center (TIC) provides
research, publication, and other information services on energy-related topics. These services
include:

Customer Service Branch—provides monthly meeting
lists, announcements of translations received or published by TIC and consultations on request for building
energy data bases; exchanges technical reports with
foreign countries.

Energy Information Outreach Program—provides reports, pamphlets, brochures, posters, special packets,
films, and technology transfer products to industry,
educational institutions, consumers and the general
public.

Energy Abstract Journals—include printed products and
products from energy data base files which contain
U.S. Department of Energy reports, other reports,
monographs, theses, patents, journal articles and
conference literature.

Energy Research Abstracts—a bimonthly that covers a
full range of energy-related literature

Energy Abstracts for Policy Analysis—a monthly that
covers all phases of energy analysis and development
from the nontechnical and quasi-technical literature

Energy Updates—a monthly that announces new items
added to the Energy Data Base files in a particular
subject area, such as Solar Energy Update, Geothermal Energy Update, Fossil Energy Update, Energy
Conservation Update, and Fusion Energy Update.

Bibliographies—provide customized on-line searches
and special subsets of data available upon request.

Contact: Technical Information Center, Department of Energy, P. O. Box 62, Oak Ridge, TN
37830/615-576-1301.

Technology Implementation
This office focuses on transferring new technologies to the appropriate end-use market and
encouraging implementation by the private
sector. It provides technical assistance in implementation of new energy-conserving technologies and solicits proposals and selects cost-sharing contractors for demonstrations of selected
supply and conservation technologies with commercialization in mind. Contact: Industrial Programs, Conservation and Renewable Energy,
Department of Energy, 1000 Independence Ave.
S.W., 5G-067, Washington, DC 20585/202-252-
2072.

Testing and Evaluation
This office develops new or modifies existing test
procedures to accomodate energy saving design
changes in major household appliances, as refrigerators, hot water heaters, air conditioners, and
furnaces—excludes automobiles. The branch also
develops minimum energy efficiency standards for
these appliances. Contact: Building Equipment,
Building Energy Research and Development,
Conservation and Renewable Energy, Department of Energy, Room GF217, Washington, DC
20585/202-252-9127.

Thermal Imaging Technology
Thermal imaging systems offer the potential for
being a significant tool to determine the effectiveness of existing insulation on residential and
commercial buildings and to pinpoint areas where
existing weather stripping, caulking and insulation
is insufficient. Thermal imaging can be processed
through airborne and ground surveys. A report,
*Status of Thermal Imaging Technology As Applied
to Conservation,* describes the state of the art.
Contact: Architectural and Engineering Systems
Branch, Building Systems, Conservation and Renewable Applications, Department of Energy,
1000 Independence Ave. S.W., GF253, Washington, DC 20585/202-252-9837.

Toxicology Data Bases and Other Resources
Staff at the Toxicology Information Response
Center (TIRC) can provide information, extensive
bibliographies, computerized data base searches,
and publications on all aspects of toxicology. Staff
has access to a vast library and more than 100
computerized government and commercial data
bases. A free publication catalog is available from
TIRC. Contact: Toxicology Information Response
Center, Oak Ridge National Laboratory, P.O. Box
X, Building 2024, Oak Ridge, TN 37831/615-576-
1743.

Truck and Bus Fuel Economy

A voluntary program encourages motor carriers, manufacturers, suppliers, trade associations and labor unions to support and publicize voluntary fuel conservation efforts. Contact: Division of Vehicle Engine R&D, Office of Technical Development and Analysis, Conservation and Renewable Energy, Department of Energy, 1000 Independence Ave. S.W., MS 54044, Washington, DC 20585/202-252-8003.

Unconventional Gas Recovery

Research and development is conducted in unconventional gas recovery, including gas from Western Tight sands, Eastern Devonian shales and methane from coal seams. Contact: Unconventional Gas Recovery, Office of Oil, Gas and Shale Recovery, Fossil Energy, Department of Energy, Germantown, Room D119, Washington, DC 20545/301-353-2877.

Unsolicited Proposals, Guide for the Submission of

This free pamphlet describes types of research supported, inventions wanted, and general guidelines and instructions on how to go about submitting unsolicited proposals; description of the various U.S. Department of Energy offices that consider these proposals is also included. Contact: Business Liaison Division, Office of Small and Disadvantaged Business Utilization, Procurement and Contracts Management Directorate, Department of Energy, 1000 Independence Ave. S.W., 1E-061, Washington, DC 20585/202-252-8201.

For information on submitting unsolicited proposals on energy research, contact: Office of Energy Research, Department of Energy, F-227, Washington, DC 20545/301-353-4154.

Uranium Enrichment

The U.S. Department of Energy directs and administers programs to assess U.S. uranium resources and provides uranium enrichment services to domestic and international customers. It also directs the operation of three existing gaseous diffusion plants, a gas centrifuge program and business activities associated with the marketing of enriched uranium. Contact: Uranium Enrichment, Marketing and Business, Department of Energy, 1000 Independence Ave. S.W., Room A-267, Washington, DC 20585/202-353-5836.

Uranium Marketing

For information on the administration, contracting, marketing, planning and financial control activities in support of the uranium resources and enrichment program, contact: Uranium Enrichment, Marketing and Business, Department of Energy, 1000 Independence Ave. S.W., Room A-267, Washington, DC 20585/301-353-5836.

Uranium Mills

This project takes responsibility for clean-up at 25 inactive uranium mill processing sites in ten states and on the Navajo Reservation. After the clean-up is completed, the sites will be licensed by the Nuclear Regulatory Commission. These 25 sites are privately owned, but the uranium milled at the sites was sold to the Nuclear Regulatory Commission. Contact: Uranium Mill Tailings Remedial Action Project Office, Department of Energy, Albuquerque Operations, P. O. Box 5400, Albuquerque, NM 87115/505-844-2185.

Uranium Mining and Milling Information Publications

The Nuclear and Alternate Fuels Division collects data about activity in the uranium mining and milling industry, including data about nuclear power generation. Data and forecasting publications are available from this office. Staff can answer questions and provide copies of reports. Contact: Nuclear and Alternate Fuels Division, Energy Information Administration, Department of Energy, Mailstop 2F021-EI53, 1000 Independence Ave. S.W., Washington, DC 20585/202-252-6363.

Uranium Resource Assessment

This office directs the National Uranium Resource Evaluation (NURE) program in order to make increasingly reliable estimates of the nation's uranium resources, and to determine areas favorable to uranium deposits. It also collects data from the uranium industry on reserves in the western United States; prepares production capability limits based on NURE and reserve data in order to determine the requirements for uranium enrichment facilities; does research and development work on uranium measuring and exploration equipment; accumulates data on uranium tailings sites throughout the West; carries out activities relating to environmental effects of uranium mining and milling operations; and manages uranium leases on lands under U.S. Department of Energy control. Contact: Uranium Resource Assessment, Grand Junction Office, Department of Energy, P. O. Box 2567, Grand Junction, CO 81502/303-242-8621.

Uranium Resources

Information is available on programs to conserve uranium resources by developing a technology that will permit more economical enrichment of uranium for use as fuel in power reactors. The technology includes using laser and plasma techniques. Contact: Advanced Isotope Separation Technology, Nuclear Reactor Programs, Nuclear Energy, Department of Energy, Germantown, Room A-171, Washington, DC 20545/301-353-4781.

Utility Rate Reform

The National Energy Act is based on the principle that electric rates should encourage the conservation of energy and the efficient use of resources. The items under consideration for determining rates should be time-of-day pricing, seasonal rates, cost of service, interruptible rates, and prohibition of decreasing rates for large users. Contact: Public Inquiries Branch, Office of Congressional, Intergovernmental and Public Affairs, Federal Energy Regulatory Commission, Department of Energy, 825 N. Capitol St. N.E., Room 2214, Washington, DC 20426/202-357-8055.

Utility Rates and Systems

The Office of Utility Systems designs utility rates that encourage electric utilities to operate more efficiently with rates that are fair to consumers. The office promotes utility interconnections to improve reliability of bulk power supplies and can require interconnection in an emergency. It also provides technical and financial assistance to state regulatory agencies. Contact: Office of Fuel Programs, Economic Regulatory Administration, Department of Energy, 1000 Independence Ave. S.W., Room 0A007, Washington, DC 20585/202-252-9396.

Utility Regulation Intervention

The Regulatory Intervention Division intervenes in regulatory proceedings before the Federal Energy Regulatory Commission, other federal regulatory bodies and state utility commissions. The interventions are designed to urge the regulatory bodies to take actions consistent with national energy policy objectives such as the elimination of lower rates for large users of electricity. Contact: Office of Fuel Programs, Utility Systems, Economic Regulatory Administration, Department of Energy, 2000 M St. N.W., GA-007, Washington, DC 20585/202-252-9396.

Vehicle and Engine Research and Development

This office conducts research, development, and design for advanced propulsion systems for both auto and heavy-duty transport sectors. It analyzes and assesses new energy concepts and is directly involved in the research and development of high-temperature materials and components. Contact: Vehicle and Engine R & D, Conservation and Renewable Energy, Department of Energy, Room 5G046, 1000 Independence Ave. S.W., Washington, DC 20585/202-252-8053.

Vehicle Performance

This office operates the following programs: prints and distributes gas mileage information for new cars; determines and analyzes the disparities between Environmental Protection Agency's data and this office's end-use auto mileage data; evalu-

ates new concepts in transportation; trains the public and government officials in aspects of fuel efficiency, driving techniques, maintenance, trip planning, and purchasing of new cars; and promotes fuel economy in the car and trucking industry. Contact: Vehicle and Engine R & D, Conservation and Renewable Energy, Department of Energy, 1000 Independence Ave. S.W., Room 5G-030, Washington, DC 20585/202-252-9118.

Waste as an Energy Source

The Energy From Municipal Waste Division conducts research in the area of utilizing municipal waste as an energy source, and is responsible for DOE programs in waste-to-energy research and development. Contact: Energy From Municipal Waste Division, Department of Energy, Forrestal Building, CE-323, Room 5F081, 1000 Independence Ave. S.W., Washington, DC 20585/202-252-6104.

Waste Heat Recovery

For information on technological developments in waste heat recovery, combustion efficiency, advanced industrial cogeneration, waste materials on feedstocks and fuels, and effective reuse of recovered waste heat, contact: Waste Energy Utilization and Cogeneration Branch, Industrial Programs, Conservation and Solar Energy, Department of Energy, 1000 Independence Ave. S.W., Room 5F-035, Washington, DC 20585/202-252-2084.

Waste Utilization

This office is responsible for research and development on technologies for recovery of energy-intensive materials from waste, and converting it into energy and heating and cooling for businesses, residences and manufacturing. Contact: Waste Energy Reduction Division, Conservation and Renewable Energy, Department of Energy, 1000 Independence Ave. S.W., Room 5F-035, Washington, DC 20585/202-252-2098.

Weatherization Assistance

A national program has been developed to weatherize the homes of low-income persons, particularly the elderly and handicapped through the installation of energy-conserving measures in eligible homes and through the provision of training and technical assistance to states, localities, Indian tribes, and program beneficiaries. *Weatherization Bulletin—WX* is a free newsletter describing recent developments. Contact: Weatherization Assistance Programs, State and Local Programs, Conservation and Renewable Energy, Department of Energy, 1000 Independence Ave. S.W., Room 5G-0230K, Washington, DC 20585/202-252-2204.

Wind Energy Conversion

The Wind Energy Conversion program aims to spread the development and commercialization of reliable and cost-effective wind systems yielding significant quantities of energy. They publish a national wind resource atlas as well as the following available from National Technical Information Service.

Wind Energy Systems Program Summary—provides an overview of government-sponsored activities.

Contact: Wind Energy Technology, Conservation and Renewable Energy, Department of Energy, Room 5H-048, Washington, DC 20545/202-252-1776.

Wind Energy Simulation

Analysis Methods of Wind Energy Applications reports on work done in developing wind energy simulation methods. It includes descriptions of 17 computer programs. Contact: National Technical Information Service, Department of Commerce, 5285 Port Royal Road, Springfield, VA 22161/ 703-487-4650.

Wind Instrumentation

Research is conducted on wind instrumentation, wind-measuring machines (anemometers), and other devices for gauging wind characteristics. A free handbook is available describing small wind turbines. Contact: Wind Characteristics Projects, Battelle Memorial Institute, Pacific Northwest Laboratory, P. O. Box 999, Battelle Blvd., Richland, WA 99352/509-375-2121.

How Can the Department of Energy Help You?

To determine how the U.S. Department of Energy can help you, contact: Public Inquiries, Department of Energy, 1000 Independence Ave. S.W., Washington, DC 20585/202-252-5575.

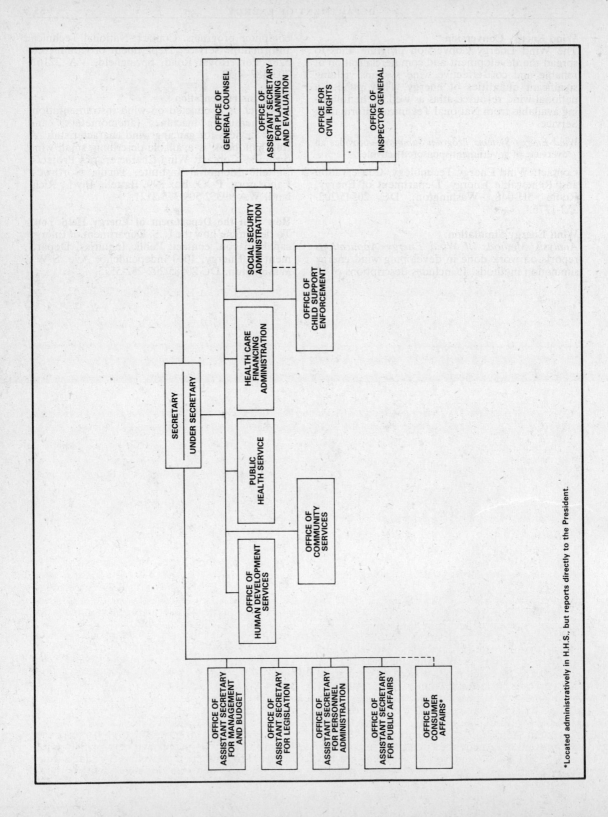

SECRETARY

UNDER SECRETARY

OFFICE OF GENERAL COUNSEL

OFFICE OF ASSISTANT SECRETARY FOR PLANNING AND EVALUATION

OFFICE FOR CIVIL RIGHTS

OFFICE OF INSPECTOR GENERAL

SOCIAL SECURITY ADMINISTRATION

HEALTH CARE FINANCING ADMINISTRATION

OFFICE OF CHILD SUPPORT ENFORCEMENT

PUBLIC HEALTH SERVICE

OFFICE OF HUMAN DEVELOPMENT SERVICES

OFFICE OF COMMUNITY SERVICES

OFFICE OF ASSISTANT SECRETARY FOR MANAGEMENT AND BUDGET

OFFICE OF ASSISTANT SECRETARY FOR LEGISLATION

OFFICE OF ASSISTANT SECRETARY FOR PERSONNEL ADMINISTRATION

OFFICE OF ASSISTANT SECRETARY FOR PUBLIC AFFAIRS

OFFICE OF CONSUMER AFFAIRS*

*Located administratively in H.H.S., but reports directly to the President.

Department of Health and Human Services

200 Independence Ave. S.W., Washington, DC 20201/202-245-6296

Established: May 5, 1980
Budget *(1980 est.):* **$84,845,156,000**
Employees: 135,134

MISSION: Serve as the federal executive branch most concerned with people and most involved with the nation's human concerns. Protect and advance the health of the American people.

Major Divisions and Offices

Office of Human Development Services (OHDS)
Department of Health and Human Services, 200 Independence Ave. S.W., Washington, DC 20201/202-245-7246.
Budget: $5,428,943,000
Employees: 1,210

• Administration for Children, Youth and Families (ACYF)
Department of Health and Human Services, 400 6th St. S.W., Room 5030, Washington, DC. Mailing address—P. O. Box 1182, Washington, DC 20013/202-755-7762.
Budget: $940,220,000
Employees: 380
Mission: Advises the Secretary on matters relating to children, youth, and families; supports and encourages the sound development of children, youth, and families by planning, developing, and implementing a broad range of activities; manages the adoption opportunities program; administers discretionary grant programs providing Head Start services and runaway youth facilities; administers provisions of the Child Abuse Prevention and Treatment Act; supports and encourages services that prevent or remedy the effects of abuse and/or neglect of children and youth; and manages the national clearinghouse on child abuse and neglect

and administers the child abuse and neglect State grant programs.

• Administration for Native Americans
Department of Health and Human Services, 330 Independence Ave. S.W., Room 5300, Washington, DC 20201/202-245-7776.
Budget: $28,000,000
Employees: 13
Mission: Serves as departmental liaison with other Federal agencies on Native American affairs; administers a grant program to promote the social and economic development of Native Americans; ensures that information about departmental services and benefits and eligibility criteria is conveyed to Native Americans; and fosters self-determination in Native Americans and their operation of Native American programs and enterprises.

• Administration on Aging (AOA)
Department of Health and Human Services, 330 Independence Ave. S.W., Room 4760, Washington, DC 20201/202-245-0724.
Budget: $741,726,000
Employees: 164
Mission: Advises the Secretary and other Federal departments and agencies on the characteristics and needs of older people and develops programs designed to promote their welfare; conducts training programs; and provides advice and assistance

to promote the development of State-administered community-based systems of comprehensive social services for older people.

• *Administration of Developmental Disabilities (ADD)*

Department of Health and Human Services, 200 Independence Ave. S.W., Room 348E-5, Washington, DC 20201/202-245-2890.
Budget: $60,500,000
Employees: 25
Mission: Assists States to increase the provision of quality services to persons with developmental disabilities, through the development and implementation of a comprehensive State plan.

Public Health Service (PHS)

Department of Health and Human Services, 200 Independence Ave. S.W., Room 716G, Washington, DC 20201/202-245-6296.
Budget: $7,757,062,000
Employees: 38,810

• *Center for Disease Control (CDC)*

Department of Health and Human Services, 1600 Clifton Rd. N.E., Atlanta, GA 30333/404-329-3311.
Budget: $334,291,000
Employees: 3,782
Mission: Protect the public health of the nation by providing leadership and direction in the prevention and control of diseases and other preventable conditions; administer national programs for the prevention and control of communicable and vectorborne diseases and other preventable conditions; insure safe and healthful working conditions for all working people.

• *Food and Drug Administration (FDA)*

Department of Health and Human Services, 5600 Fishers Lane, HF-1, Rockville, MD 20857/301-443-3380.
Budget: $354,844,000
Employees: 7,140
Mission: Protect the health of the nation against impure and unsafe foods, drugs, and cosmetics; administer regulation of biological products; develop policy with regard to the safety, effectiveness, and labeling of all drugs for human use; develop standards on the composition, quality, nutrition, and safety of foods, food additives, colorings, and cosmetics; reduce human exposure to hazardous ionizing and nonionizing radiation; improve the safety and efficacy of medical devices and veterinary preparations and devices, and conduct research programs to study the biological effects of potentially toxic chemical substances found in man's environment, emphasizing the determination of the health effects resulting from long-term, low-level exposure to chemical toxi-

cants and the basic biological processes for chemical toxicants in animal organisms.

• *Health Resources and Services Administration (HRSA)*

Department of Health and Human Services, 5600 Fishers Lane, Rockville, MD 20857/301-443-2086.
Budget: $2,040,528,000
Employees: 14,641
Mission: Provides leadership and direction to programs and activities designed to improve the health services for all people of the United States; and develops health care and maintenance systems which are adequately financed, comprehensive, interrelated, and responsive to the needs of individuals and families in all levels of society.

• *Agency for Toxic Substances and Disease Registry*

Department of Health and Human Services, 1600 Clifton Road NE, Atlanta, GA 30333/404-452-4111.
Budget: $14,620,000*
Employees: 89
Mission: Provides leadership and direction to programs and activities designed to protect both the public health and worker safety and health from exposure and/or the adverse health effects of hazardous substances in storage sites or released in fires, explosions, or transportation accidents.

• *National Institutes of Health (NIH)*

Department of Health and Human Services, 9000 Rockville Pike, Building 1, Room 124, Bethesda, MD 20205/301-496-4000.
Budget: $4,001,980,000
Employees: 7,953
Mission: Improve the health of the American people by coordinating and supporting biomedical research into the causes, prevention, and cure of diseases; support research training and the development of research resources; and make use of modern methods to communicate biomedical information. The following are major components: National Cancer Institute; National Heart, Lung, and Blood Institute; National Library of Medicine; National Institute of Arthritis, Metabolism, and Digestive Diseases; National Institute of Allergy and Infectious Diseases; National Institute of Child Health and Human Development; National Institute of Dental Research; National Institute of Environmental Health Sciences; National Institute of General Medical Sciences; National Institute of Neurological and Communicative Disorders and Stroke; National Eye Institute; and National Institute on Aging.

---

*Funds provided for this agency included in EPA appropriations for Super Fund Program.

• *Alcohol, Drug Abuse and Mental Health Administration*

Department of Health and Human Services, 5600 Fishers Lane, Room 6C15, Rockville, MD 20857/301-443-2086
Budget: $854,061,000
Employees: 5,205
Mission: Provide leadership in the Federal effort to reduce, and eliminate where possible, health problems caused by the abuse of alcohol and drugs, and improve the mental health of the people of the United States generally.

Health Care Financing Administration

Department of Health and Human Services, Humphrey Building, Room 314G, 200 Independence Ave. S.W., Washington, DC 20201/-202-245-6726.
Budget: $30,236,071,000
Employees: 4,489
Mission: Provide oversight of the Medicare and Medicaid programs and related federal medical care quality control.

Social Security Administration

Department of Health and Human Services, 6401 Security Blvd., Baltimore, MD 21235/301-594-1234

Budget: $41,179,727,000
Employees: 78,090
Mission: Administer national program of contributory, social insurance whereby employees, employers, and the self-employed pay contributions which are pooled in special trust funds; provide research and recommendations oriented to the problems of poverty, insecurity, and health care for the aged, blind, and disabled.

Office of Child Support Enforcement

Department of Health and Human Services, 6110 Executive Blvd., Rockville, MD 20852/301-443-4442.
Budget: $471,000,000
Employees: 361
Mission: Provide leadership in the planning, development, management and coordination of the Department's Child Support Enforcement Programs and activities.

Office of Community Services

Department of Health and Human Services, 1200 Nineteenth Street N.W., Washington, DC 20506/202-653-2010.
Budget: $359,086,000
Employees: 185
Mission: Administers the Community Services block grant and discretionary grant programs.

Data Experts

Disease Information and Developments
For most diseases, the Department of Health and Human Services maintains a staff that keeps current on the latest developments, the best doctors, and the best hospitals available for treating the disease. In many cases literature is available for both the professional and layman. If a disease strikes you or a loved one, it may not be wise to totally trust your local doctor; he or she cannot keep current on everything. Contact the relevant office listed below and ask for the latest facts and developments. This way you will know all the options available to you. If the disease you are interested in is not listed below, contact: Health Information Clearing House, 1555 Wilson Blvd., Suite 600, Rosslyn, VA 22209/800-336-4797. In Virginia, 703-522-2590.

Alcoholism
National Clearinghouse on Alcohol Information, Department of Health and Human Services, P.O. Box 2345, 1776 E Jefferson St, Rockville, MD 20852/ 301-468-2600.
Allergic Diseases
Research Reportive and Public Response, National Institute of Allergy and Infectious Diseases, NIH, Department of Health and Human Services, Building 31, Room 7A32, Bethesda, MD 20205/301-496-5717.

Anemia
Office of Information, National Heart, Lung and Blood Institute, NIH, Department of Health and Human Services, Building 31, Room 4A21, Bethesda, MD 20205/301-496-4236.
Ansomia
National Institute of Arthritis, Metabolism, and Digestive Diseases, NIH, Department of Health and Human Services, Building 31, Room 9A04, Bethesda, MD 20205/301-496-3583.
Arteriosclerosis
See "Anemia."
Arthritis
Arthritis Information Clearinghouse, Box 34427, Bethesda, MD 20817/301-881-9411.
Astigmatism
Office of Program Planning and Scientific Reporting, National Eye Institute, NIH, Department of Health and Human Services, Building 31, Room 6A32, Bethesda, MD 20205/301-496-5248.
Ataxia
Office of Science and Health Reports, National Institute of Neurological and Communicative Disorders and Stroke, NIH, Department of Health and Human Services, Building 31, Room 8A06, Bethesda, MD 20205/301-496-5751.
Birth Defects
Genetic Disease Services Branch, Office of Maternal and

Child Health, Bureau of Community Health Services, Department of Health and Human Services, 5600 Fishers Lane, Room 6–11, Rockville, MD 20857/301-443-1080.

Black Lung Disease
Division of Respiratory Disease, Center for Disease Control, Department of Health and Human Services, 944 Chestnut Ridge Rd., Room 220, Morgantown, WV 26505/304-599-7474.

Bleeding Disorders
See "Anemia."

Blood Diseases
See "Ansomia." See also "Anemia."

Bone Diseases
See "Ansomia."

Brain Trauma
See "Ataxia."

Brain Tumor
See "Ataxia."

Bronchitis, Chronic
See "Anemia."

Cancer
Office of Cancer Communications, National Cancer Institute, NIH, Department of Health and Human Services, Building 31, Room 10A18, Bethesda, MD 20205/301-496-5583. Hotline: toll-free: Alaska/800-638-6070; Hawaii 808-524-1234 (neighboring Islands call collect); Washington, DC area 202-636-5700; elsewhere, 800-638-6694.

Cancer Genetics
See "Birth Defects."

Cardiomyopathus
See "Anemia."

Cataracts
See "Astigmatism."

Cerebral Palsy
See "Ataxia."

Cerebrovascular Disease
See "Anemia."

Chagas Disease
Center for Infectious Diseases, Center for Disease Control, Department of Health and Human Services, Building 4, Room 124, 1600 Clifton Rd. N.E., Atlanta, GA 30333/404-329-3401.

Child Health
Office of Research Reporting and Public Response, National Institute of Child Health and Human Development, NIH, Department of Health and Human Services, Building 31, Room 2a-32, Bethesda, MD 20205/301-496-5133.

Cirrhosis
See "Ansomia."

Clinical Immunology
See "Allergic Diseases."

Clotting Disorders
See "Anemia."

Common Cold
See "Allergic Diseases."

Communicative Disorders
Office of Deafness and Communicative Disorders, Rehabilitation Services Administration, Department of Health and Human Services, 330 C St. S.W., Room 3413, Washington, DC 20201/202-245-0591.
See also "Ataxia."

Cooley's Anemia
See "Birth Defects."

Corneal Disease
See "Astigmatism."

Coronary Artery Disease
See "Anemia."

Cystic Fibrosis
See "Birth Defects."
See also "Ansomia."

Deafness
See "Communicative Disorders." See also "Ataxia."

Dental Disease
Scientific and Health Reports, National Institute of Dental Research, NIH, Department of Health and Human Services, Building 31, Room 2C35, Bethesda, MD 20205/301-496-4261.

Depression
National Clearinghouse for Mental Health Information, National Institute of Mental Health, Department of Health and Human Services, 5600 Fishers Lane, Room 11A33, Rockville, MD 20857/301-443-4517.

Diabetes
National Diabetic Information Clearinghouse, Department of Health and Human Services, E. Jefferson and Executive Blvd., Box NDIC, Bethesda, MD 20205/301-468-2162.

Diabetic Retinopathy
See "Astigmatism."

Digestive Diseases
See "Ansomia."

Down's Syndrome
See "Birth Defects."

Drug Addiction
National Clearinghouse for Drug Abuse Information, Department of Health and Human Services, 5600 Fishers Lane, Room 10A43, Rockville, MD 20857/301-443-6500.

Drug Reactions
See "Allergic Diseases."

Eczema
See "Allergic Diseases."

Emphysema
See "Anemia."

Encephalitis
See "Chagas Disease."

Endocrine Diseases
See "Ansomia."

Epilepsy
See "Ataxia."

Eye Diseases
See "Cataracts."

Food Hypersensitivity
See "Allergic Diseases."

Genetic Diseases
National Clearinghouse for Maternal, Child Health and Human Genetic Diseases, Department of Health and Human Services, 3520 Prospect St, NW, Ground Floor, Suite 1, Washington, DC 20005/202-625-8410.

Glaucoma
See "Astigmatism." See also "Cataracts."

Gonorrhea
See "Sexually Transmissible Diseases."

Hay Fever
See "Allergic Diseases."

Head Injuries
See "Ataxia."
Hearing Disorders
See "Ataxia."
Heart Disease
See "Anemia."
Heart Failure and Shock
See "Anemia."
Heart Infections
See "Anemia."
Hemophilia
See "Birth Defects."
Hepatitis
See "Allergic Diseases."
High Blood Pressure
High Blood Pressure Information Center, National
    Heart, Lung and Blood Institute, NIH, Department
    of Health and Human Services, 1501 Wilson Blvd.,
    2121 Wisconsin Ave., Washington, DC 20007/202-
    944-3163.
Human Development Problems
See "Child Health."
Huntington's Disease
See "Ataxia."
Hyperopia (Farsightedness)
See "Astigmatism."
Hypertension
See "Anemia."
Hypoglycemia
See "Ansomia."
Hypokalemia
See "Anemia."
Influenza
See "Allergic Diseases."
Insect Sting Allergy
See "Allergic Diseases."
Kidney Diseases
See "Ansomia."
Lead Poisoning
Center for Environmental Health, Center for Disease
    Control, Department of Health and Human Services,
    Building C, Room 29-5, 1600 Clifton Rd. N.E.,
    Atlanta, GA 30333/404-452-4111.
Leprosy
U.S. Public Health Hospital, Carville, LA 70721/504-
    642-7771.
Lung Diseases
See "Anemia."
Macular Degeneration
See "Astigmatism."
Malaria
See "Chagas Disease."
Mania
See "Depression."
Mental Illness
See "Depression."
Mental Retardation
See "Child Health."
Metabolic Diseases
See "Ansomia."
Mononucleosis
See "Allergic Diseases."
Multiple Sclerosis
See "Ataxia."

Muscular Dystrophy
See "Ataxia."
Myasthenia Gravis
See "Ataxia."
Myopia (Nearsightedness)
See "Astigmatism."
Nervous System, Infectious Disorders
See "Ataxia."
Neural Trauma
See "Ataxia."
Neuropsychiatric Disorders
See "Depression."
Obesity
See "Ansomia."
Onchoceriasis
See "Chagas Disease."
Oral-Facial Disorders
See "Dental Disease."
Organ Transplantation
See "Allergic Diseases."
Osteoporosis
See "Ansomia."
Parasitic Diseases
See "Allergic Diseases."
Parkinson's Disease
See "Ataxia."
Pituitary Tumors
See "Ataxia."
Poisoning
National Clearinghouse for Poison Control Center,
    Bureau of Drugs, Food and Drug Administration,
    Department of Health and Human Services, 5600
    Fishers Lane, Room 15B-23, Rockville, MD 20857/
    301-443-6260.
Psoriasis
See "Ansomia."
Pulmonary Vascular Disease
See "Anemia."
Red Blood Cell Disorders
See "Anemia."
Reproductive Disorders
See "Child Health."
Respiratory Diseases
See "Black Lung Disease."
Respiratory Distress
See "Ancmia."
Respiratory Failure
See "Anemia."
Retinal Degeneration
See "Cataracts."
Retinal Detachment
See "Astigmatism."
Retinitis Pigmentosa
See "Astigmatism."
Rheumatism
See "Arthritis."
Rheumatoid
See "Ansomia."
Serum Sickness
See "Allergic Diseases."
Sexually Transmissible Diseases
Venereal Disease Section, Center for Disease Control,
    Department of Health and Human Services, Atlanta,
    GA 30333/404-329-2570.

Sickle Cell Anemia
See "Anemia." See also "Birth Defects."
Skin Diseases
See "Ansomia."
Sleep Disturbances
See "Depression."
Speech Disorders
See "Ataxia."
Spinal Cord Injuries
See "Ataxia."
Spinal Cord Tumors
See "Ataxia."
Strabismus
See "Astigmatism."
Stroke
See "Anemia." See also "Ataxia."
Tay-Sachs Disease
See "Birth Defects."

Thyroid Diseases
See "Ansomia."
Tooth Decay
See "Dental Disease."
Trauma
See "Ataxia."
Tropical Diseases
See "Chagas Disease."
Tropical Parasitic Diseases
See "Chagas Disease."
Urologic Diseases
See "Ansomia."
Vasculitis
See "Allergic Diseases."
Venereal Diseases
See "Sexually Transmissible Diseases."
Viral Respiratory Infections
See "Allergic Diseases."

Major Sources of Information

Adolescent Pregnancy
For information on programs and funding available for adolescent health services, pregnancy prevention and care services, contact: Adolescent Pregnancy Programs, Public Health Service, Department of Health and Human Services, 330 Independence Ave. S.W., North Bldg., Room 1351, Washington, DC 20201/202-245-0142.

Adoption
See "Grants—Adoption Opportunities" and "Children's Bureau" in this section.

Aging Information Clearinghouse
The Clearinghouse provides a wide range of services, including collecting statistics on the aging population, custom computerized literature searches, document delivery, and referring users directly to appropriate information sources. Contact: National Clearinghouse on Aging, Administration on Aging, Office of Human Development Services, Department of Health and Human Services, Room 4255, Washington, DC 20201/202-245-0995.

Aging Magazine
This bi-monthly publication at $13 per year is geared to professionals in the field of aging and covers such topics as legislation, projects, book reviews, conferences and international news. Contact: *Aging Magazine,* Administration on Aging, Department of Health and Human Services, Room 4243, Washington, DC 20201/202-245-0641.

Aging—National Institute on
The Institute was established for the conduct and support of biomedical, social, and behavioral research and training related to the aging process and diseases and other special problems of the old. Its mission extends beyond the study of decline, loss and decrement, which do indeed accompany aging, to an examination of the normal processes of development that contribute to the quality of life in the later years. Contact: National Institute on Aging, National Institutes of Health, 9000 Rockville Pike, Bethesda, MD 20205/301-496-1752.

AIDS—-Acquired Immune Deficiency Syndrome
The Center for Disease Control administers the research being conducted on AIDS. The research is dispersed among four agencies within the Department of Health and Human Services. Information on this condition is available free of charge in the form of a question and answer fact sheet and reprints of articles which summarize studies presently being conducted. For further information contact: Office of Public Affairs, Center for Disease Control, 1600 Clifton Road N.E., Building 1, Room 2167, Atlanta, GA 30333.

AIDS Hotline
To obtain information about AIDS (Acquired Immune Deficiency Syndrome) and a free fact sheet call the toll-free number 800-342-2437.

Alcohol Health Magazine
Alcohol Health and Research World is a quarterly magazine intended for professionals involved in treatment of, research into, and prevention of alcohol abuse and alcoholism. It covers developments in the alcohol abuse field, such as new research findings, and prevention, treatment and training programs. Subscriptions are available for $11.00 per year from Superintendent of Documents, Government Printing Office, Washington, DC 20402/202-783-3238.

Alcohol Information Clearinghouse

The Clearinghouse will perform research on alcohol-related topics as well as provide free pamphlets, brochures, books, posters, and films. A newsletter called *NIAA Information and Feature Service* is also available at no charge. Contact: National Clearinghouse for Alcohol Information, National Institute on Alcohol Abuse, Department of Health and Human Services, 1776 East Jefferson Highway, Box 2345, Rockville, MD 20852/301-468-2600.

Alcoholism—Health Insurance Coverage

The National Institute on Alcohol Abuse and Alcoholism (NIAA) works with health agencies and insurance carriers to study the status of alcoholism insurance coverage; to identify barriers to improved coverage; and to develop model benefit provisions. Contact: NIAA, Department of Health and Human Services, 5600 Fishers Lane, Parklawn Building, 16G03, Rockville, MD 20852/301-443-6370.

Alcoholism Treatment on the Job

Nonprofit organizations can receive funds to finance consultants to set up on-the-job programs to help employees deal with alcoholism. Others not eligible for funds can receive a list of consultants, as well as printed material to help set up a program. Contact: Division of Occupational Programs, National Institute on Alcohol Abuse and Alcoholism, Department of Health and Human Services, 5600 Fishers Lane, Room 10055, Parklawn Building, Rockville, MD 20857/301-443-1148.

Allergy and Infectious Diseases—National Institute

The Institute supports world-wide research activities on causes, diagnosis, treatment, and prevention of infections, allergic and other immunologically mediated diseases. Specific aspects of these activities are made the subject of Institute-initiated and directed contract programs. Contact: National Institute of Allergy and Infectious Diseases, Department of Health and Human Services, 9000 Rockville Pike, Bethesda, MD 20205/301-496-5717.

Analytical Toxicology Research Data

Staff at the Center for Disease Control analyze pesticides, arsenic and poisons, trace metals and dioxins. They can provide analytical data about the clinical research performed on certain chemical compounds. Contact: Centers for Disease Control, Clinical Chemistry Division, Toxicology Branch, 1600 Clifton Road, Atlanta, GA 30333/404-452-4176.

Animals and Pets

The Food and Drug Administration (FDA) insures that veterinary preparations, drugs, and devices are safe and effective and that animal and pet food is safe and properly labeled. Contact: Bureau of Veterinary Medicine, Food and Drug Administration, Department of Health and Human Services, 5600 Fishers Lane, Room 7B39, Rockville, MD 20857/301-443-5363.

Arthritis, Diabetes, and Kidney Diseases—National Institute

The Institute supports research into the causes, prevention, diagnosis, and treatment of the various arthritides, and the rheumatic and collagen diseases, and the metabolic diseases such as diabetes; other inborn errors of metabolism, urology and kidney diseases and development of the artificial kidney machine. Contact: National Institute of Arthritis, Diabetes, and Kidney Diseases, National Institutes of Health, 9000 Rockville Pike, Bethesda, MD 20205/301-496-5741.

Arthritis Information Clearinghouse

The Clearinghouse provides information and referral services to both professionals and the general public. It contains a large collection of books and journals, as well as films, slide presentations, videotapes, cassettes, and other audiovisual materials, posters, exhibits and displays. A descriptive listing is available which identifies free bibliographies, catalogues, reference sheets and other guides. Contact: Arthritis Information Clearinghouse, 1700 N. Moore St., Arlington, VA 22209/703-550-8250.

Artificial Intelligence in Medicine

The National Institutes of Health and Stanford University Medical Center share a computer resource facility devoted entirely to designing artificial intelligence application for the biomedical sciences. Contact: National Institutes of Health, Department of Health and Human Services, Stanford University Medical Center, Room TB-105, Stanford, CA 94305/415-497-5569.

Automated Information Systems

Automated information systems include the International Cancer Research Data Bank (ICRDB), the Centralized Cancer Patient Data System (CCPDS), and PDQ. ICRDB facilitates the sharing of cancer information to a worldwide audience through a computerized science information data bank and retrieval system. CCPDS is aimed at developing a uniform data system in the Comprehensive Cancer Centers for capturing data on approximately 50,000 new cancer cases annually. PDQ, a computer data base, makes available information on current methods of cancer therapy. Containing descriptions of approximately 1,000 cancer therapy research programs, PDQ is updated monthly and accessible through the National Library of Medicine's MEDLARS system. Contact: National Cancer Institute, National Institutes of Health, Department of Health and Human Services, Building 82, 9000 Rockville Pike, Bethesda, MD 20205/301-496-5491.

Biologics

The Bureau of Biologics accumulates information and expertise on blood and blood products, coagulation, hepatitis, immunohematology, plasma derivatives, electron microscopy, pathology, cellular physiology, experimental biology, pathobiology, primatology, bacterial products, allergenic products, bacterial toxins, bacterial polysaccharides, biochemistry, mycobacterial and fungal antigens, and mycoplasma. Contact: Bureau of Biologics, Federal Drug Administration, Department of Health and Human Services, 8800 Rockville Pike, Building 29, Room 129, Bethesda, MD 20205/301-496-3556.

Biotechnology Resources

This free directory lists and describes biotechnology-related research programs being carried out across the United States. Contact information for services available, and a description of research emphasis or application is provided for each entry. Contact: Research Resources Information Center, 1776 East Jefferson Street, Rockville, MD 20852/301-984-2870.

Biotechnology Resources Program

This program concentrates on the application of the physical sciences, mathematics, and engineering to biology and medicine. Contact: Biotechnology Resources Program, National Institutes of Health, Division of Research Resources, 1776 East Jefferson Street, Rockville, MD 20852/301-496-5411.

Braille Books

The American Printing House for the Blind is a private nonprofit organization and receives funding from the Department of Health and Human Services. It produces material in Braille, large type, talking books, cassettes, Braille music, and catalogs in Braille. Contact: American Printing House for the Blind, 1839 Frankfort Ave., Louisville, KY 40206/502-895-2405.

Brain Tissue Resource for Neuropsychiatric Research

The program supports the Brain Tissue Bank at the McLean Hospital, Belmont, Massachusetts. This tissue banking resource collects brain tissues obtained at autopsy, stores them cryogenically and in formalin, and distributes these materials to research scientists. Contact: National Institute of Neurological and Communicative Disorders and Stroke, National Institutes of Health, Department of Health and Human Services, Federal Building, Room 714, 7550 Wisconsin Avenue, Bethesda, MD 20205/301-496-1431.

Breast Cancer

For information and expertise on the latest developments concerning breast cancer, contact: Breast Cancer Program Coordinating Branch, National Cancer Institute, NIH, Department of Health and Human Services, Bldg 31, Room 104-18, Bethesda, MD 20205/301-496-5583.

Cancer-Causing Products

To obtain a free listing of 250 trade name products which contain carcinogens (cancer-causing elements), contact: Clearinghouse for Occupational Safety and Health Information, NIOSH, Center for Disease Control, 4676 Columbia Pkwy., Cincinnati, OH 45226/513-684-8326.

Cancer Hotline

This hotline provides information about all aspects of cancer to the general public, cancer patients, and their families. Call: Cancer Information Service, toll-free, Alaska 800-638-6070; Hawaii 808-524-1234 (neighboring Islands call collect); Washington DC area 202-636-5700; Elsewhere in USA 800-4-CANCER.

Cancer Information Clearinghouse

The clearinghouse assists organizations in the treatment and education of cancer patients. It will perform individually tailored searches of its own files as well as other data bases, and will make referrals to specific information sources. *Current Awareness Services* alerts cancer-concerned organizations to new publications, programs, services, data bases and audiovisual material. Contact: Cancer Information Clearinghouse, National Cancer Institute, Building 31, Room 10A18, 9000 Rockville Pike, Bethesda, MD 20205/301-496-4070.

Cancer Information Offices

The National Cancer Institute has established a number of offices throughout the country that provide consultations with cancer experts; help in referring cases to cancer specialists; and information on services and resources available to patients, such as causes of cancer, methods for detecting cancer, medical facilities in local areas, financial aids, and emotional counseling services. For a list of Cancer Information Service Offices or further information, contact: Office of Cancer Communications, National Cancer Institute, NIH, Department of Health and Human Services, Building 31, Room 10A18, Bethesda, MD 20205/301-496-5583.

Cancer Journal

Those who wish to keep abreast of cancer topics, including research, new books, and conferences, can subscribe to *The Journal of the National Cancer Institute*. Subscriptions to this monthly publication are $65 per year, from: Superintendent of Documents, Government Printing Office, Washington, DC 20402/202-783-3238.

Cancer Literature

The following publications are available from National Technical Information Services, 5285 Port Royal Rd., Springfield, VA 22161/703-487-4650:

Cancergrams—More than 60 monthly current awareness publications containing abstracts of recently published articles in major areas of cancer research ($24).

Special Listings—Fifty annual compilations describing ongoing projects in major cancer research areas (prices vary).

Oncology Overviews—Specialized bibliographies containing abstracts of recent articles on cancer research topics of timely interest (prices vary).

Compilation of Clinical Protocol Summaries—800 summaries of clinical protocols currently used for treating cancer ($16.25).

Directory of Cancer Research Information Resources—Describes technical information services and publications in the area of cancer ($10.75).

Cancer Literature Searches

CANCERLINE is a computerized data base containing CANCERLIT (Cancer Literature), CANCERPROS (Cancer Research Projects), CLINPROT (Clinical Cancer Protocols), and PDQ 1 and 2 (Physicians Data Query). (See "Computerized Literature Searches on Health Sciences" in this section for more detailed descriptions.) Searches of this computerized data base are available for a charge from: National Cancer Institute, NIH, Department of Health and Human Services, 9000 Rockville Pike, Bldg 82, Room 103, Bethesda, MD 20205/301-496-7403.

Cancer Pamphlets

Twenty-five free pamphlets are available describing various types of cancer. Pamphlets include information on symptoms, diagnosis, treatment, and rehabilitation. A listing of other free publications which provide information to both cancer patients and professionals is also available. Contact: Office of Cancer Communications, National Cancer Institute, NIH, Department of Health and Human Services, Building 31, Room 10A18, Bethesda, MD 20205/301-496-5583, 1-800-4-CANCER.

Cancer Related Information Service

Funded by the National Cancer Institute, the Cancer Information Service (CIS) has a toll-free telephone inquiry/referral service established to supply cancer-related information to the public, cancer patients and their families, and health professionals. Staff can answer questions about the latest cancer technologies; refer you to experimental programs, experts, local resources, and literature; provide specific information about particular types of cancer and treatment; and give the facts about the patient referral process. Publications, geared toward both the general public and health professionals, are available from CIS. Contact: Cancer Information Service, Office of Cancer Communications, National Cancer Institute, Building 31, Room 10A18, Bethesda, MD 20205/202-636-5700; in Alaska: 800-638-6070, 800-524-1234; elsewhere: 800-4-CANCER.

Cancer Speakers

Specialists will speak for free to both professional and lay groups on such cancer-related topics as environmental causes of cancer, cancer detection and diagnosis, immunology, treatment methods, diet and nutrition, the psychological impact of cancer and public and patient education. Contact: NCP Speakers Bureau, Office of Cancer Communications, National Cancer Institute, Department of Health and Human Services, Building 31, Room 10A18, Bethesda, MD 20014/301-496-4394.

Carcinogenic Toxins Testing

The National Toxicology Program (NTP) studies the effectiveness rate of chemicals and tests for carcinogenic toxins. They publish the following (a mailing list is maintained for all publications):

Annual Report of Carcinogens, an annual publication available each December, provides a detailed rundown on the effectiveness rate and metabolic rate of various chemicals based on controlled dosages. Annual subscription rate is $32.50.

Summary of Annual Report on Carcinogens provides a summary of the research findings of 117 chemicals found to be carcinogenic. The 235-page publication is available free of charge.

Technical Report-Series contains 250 reports, each covering a specific chemical. The reports are issued when final testing of the chemical is completed. The reports run approximately 75–100 pages and are available free of charge.

NTP Annual Plan is a detailed listing of all on-going and projected research studies. Volume I primarily covers NTP research underway, and plans for future projects. Volume II reviews the toxicology research being conducted by other federal agencies. Both volumes are available free of charge.

NTP Technical Bulletins, published every few months, provides updates on current research projects as well as test results. The 25-page publication is available free of charge.

Environmental Health Perspective, a bimonthly publication, deals with the potential health hazards associated with particular elements in the environment. Back issues are available from NIEHS and current issues from the Government Printing Office. The 300-page publication is available for $40 per year, or $8 per issue.

Contact: National Toxicology Program (NTP), National Institute of Environmental Health Sciences, B2-04, P.O. Box 12233, Research Triangle, NC 27709, 919-541-3991 (Information Office).

Chief Nurse
The Office of Chief Nurse serves as an advisor to the Department of Health and Human Services on matters concerning nursing and long-term care. Contact: Office of Chief Nurse, Public Health Service, Department of Health and Human Services, 5600 Fishers Lane, Room 18-67, Rockville, MD 20857/301-443-6497.

Child Abuse and Neglect
Information and expertise are available on improving the prevention, identification and treatment of child abuse and neglect. The services available include data bases describing ongoing research programs, abstracts of public documents and excerpts of state child abuse laws; a listing of available publications, directories and audiovisual materials; and a list of Regional Child Abuse and Neglect Resource Centers. Contact: National Center on Child Abuse and Neglect, Children's Bureau, Administration for Children, Youth and Families, Department of Health and Human Services, P.O. Box 1182, Washington, DC 20013/202-245-2840.

Child Health and Human Development
Information and expertise are available on topics such as birth defects, developmental disabilities, Sudden Infant Death Syndrome, human reproduction, and fertility. Contact: National Institute of Child Health and Human Development, NIH, Department of Health and Human Services, 9000 Rockville Pike, Bethesda, MD 20205/301-496-5133.

Child Support Enforcement
See "Grants" in this section.

Children's Bureau
The Children's Bureau offers information on data sources and programs related to child welfare services, child abuse and neglect, and adoption. Contact: Children's Bureau, Administration for Children, Youth and Families, Office of Human Development Services, Department of Health and Human Services, P.O. Box 1182, Washington, DC 20013/202-755-7418.

Civil Rights Complaints
You can file a formal complaint and have an investigation of a federally funded organization, if you feel your civil rights have been violated (discrimination because of sex, race, or handicap). For further information, contact: Director, Office for Civil Rights, Department of Health and Human Services, 330 Independence Ave. S.W., North Building, Washington, DC 20201/202-245-6403.

Clinical Nutrition Research Units
In a joint effort with the National Cancer Institute and the National Institute on Aging the National Institute of Arthritis, Diabetes, and Digestive and Kidney Diseases has fostered the development and operation of clinical nutrition research units to encourage multidisciplinary approaches to clinical nutrition opportunities and problems. Contact: National Institute of Arthritis, Diabetes, and Digestive and Kidney Diseases, National Institutes of Health, Westwood Building, Room 606, 5333 Westbard Avenue, Bethesda, MD 20205/301-496-7823.

Community Health Services
Community health services are designed to reach those people who are underserved and unserved by the nation's health services systems. For further information on publications, projects or available funding, contact: Bureau of Community Health Services, Health Services Administration, Public Health Service, Department of Health and Human Services, 5600 Fishers Lane, Room 7-05, Rockville, MD 20857/301-443-2320.

Computerized Data Bases
The following data bases are maintained by the Department of Health and Human Services:

Alcohol and Alcoholism Data Base
The National Clearinghouse for Alcohol Information (NCAI)'s data base contains information, collected from worldwide sources, about alcohol and alcoholism. The focus is primarily on the training of personnel and the prevention, treatment and research aspects of the drug and its effects. Searches, printouts, and some documents are available free of charge. Contact: National Clearinghouse for Alcohol Information, P.O. Box 2345, Rockville, MD 20852/301-468-2600.

Arthritis Data Base
AIC is an information storage and retrieval system containing indexes, abstracts, and bibliographies about arthritis and related musculoskeletal diseases. The primary focus of the data base is patient care and patient, public, or professional education. Information about community demonstration programs and federal activities is also stored. Searches and printouts are free and available to health-care professionals only. Contact: Arthritis Information Clearinghouse, P.O. Box 9782, Arlington, VA 22209/703-558-8250.

BIOETHICSLINE Data Base
BIOETHICSLINE contains bibliographic citations and abstracts of literature related to moral or ethical issues in medicine, medical research and health care. Searches and printouts are available free of charge from the Bioethics Library. BIOETHICSLINE is accessible through the Center for

Bioethics Library (free) or the National Library of Medicine (fee charged). Contact: Center for Bioethics Library, Kennedy Institute of Ethics, Georgetown University, Washington, DC 20057/202-625-3383.

Chemical Information Systems

The NIH/EPA Chemicals Information System (CIS) is a collection of scientific and regulatory data bases, as well as data analysis computer programs. It is a large integrative data base system containing numeric, textual, and some bibliographic information in the areas of toxicology, environment, regulations, spectroscopy, chemical and physical properties, and nucleotide sequences. CIS is a subscription service costing $300/year. On-line connect time is $55–85. The subscription and the first $100 connect time charges are waived for degree-granting universities and public libraries. Contact: CIS User Services, Computer Services Corporation, P.O. Box 2227, Falls Church, VA 22042/800-368-3432 (toll-free); 703-237-1333 (VA & DC metro. area).

Child Abuse and Neglect Data Base

The National Clearinghouse on Child Abuse and Neglect provides a data base containing information about child mistreatment, including: abstracts of literature published since 1965, descriptions of programs in the U.S. that serve child-abuse and neglect victims, descriptions of ongoing research in the field, information about available audiovisual items, and neglect laws. Staff will do free searches (within reason) for individuals not having access to the Clearinghouse's Child Abuse and Neglect Data Base on Lockheed/DIALOG. It can be accessed through DIALOG file 64 or the National Clearinghouse on Child Abuse and Neglect. Contact: National Clearinghouse on Child Abuse and Neglect, P.O. Box 1182, Washington, DC 20013/301-251-5157.

Dental Research Projects Data Base

The National Institute of Dental Research maintains a data bank of information about nationwide research activities in all areas of dental health. Limited information is also available on worldwide dental research activities. Searches and printouts are available free of charge and only from NDIR. Contact: Deane Hill, Contracts; Grants, National Institute of Dental Research, Research Data and Management Information Section, 5333 Westbard Avenue, Room 539, Bethesda, MD 20814/301-496-7843.

Diabetes Data Base

The National Diabetes Information Clearinghouse (NDIC)'s on-line data base contains citations and abstracts of diabetic patient education materials including books, audiovisuals, teaching manuals and journal articles. The data base is patient oriented and does not include highly technical, clinical or research materials. NDIC will do searches and provide a bibliographic printout, with abstracts and acquisition source, free of charge). Contact: National Diabetes Information Clearinghouse, 2115 E. Jefferson Street, Rockville, MD 20852/301-468-2162.

Digestive Diseases Data Base

The Clearinghouse maintains a full-text data base of patient-oriented literature about diseases such as heartburn, gallstones, ulcers, colitis and constipation. The state-of-the-art materials, ranging from fact sheets to books, are geared toward both the lay person and health professional. The Clearinghouse will search its data base free of charge. Staff will also provide free copies of material they have in hard copy. Contact: Health Educator, National Digestive Diseases Education & Information Clearinghouse, 1555 Wilson Blvd., Suite 600, Rosslyn, VA 22209/301-496-9707.

Disability and Rehabilitation Data Base

The National Rehabilitation Information Center (NRIC) maintains a bibliographic data base with abstracts of materials on all aspects of disability and rehabilitation. NRIC will search its own data base and several other commercially available data bases. The basic charge is $10 for the first 100 citations, and $6.50 for the next 100. *NRIC also has free fact sheets* and over 100 prepared bibliographies available for $2.00 to $10.00. NRIC's data base is also available on BRS. Contact: National Rehabilitation Information Center, The Catholic University of America, 4407 Eighth Street N.E., Washington, DC 20017/202-635-5822.

Drug Listing Data Base

The Food and Drug Administration maintains a listing of imported and U.S. manufactured drugs. The data base is searchable by drug name, manufacturer, and geographical location. Searches are done on a cost-recovery basis (minimum fee is $50). All searches and information requests must be submitted in writing to the FIO staff. Contact: Freedom of Information Staff, HFW-35, Food and Drug Administration, 5600 Fishers Lane, Rockville, MD 20857.

Emergency Medicine and Crisis Care Data Base

This data base contains bibliographic citations and abstracts of Emergency Medical Services (EMS) literature. Searches and printouts are available free of charge. Contact: Room 13-12, Parklawn Health Library, 5600 Fishers Lane, Rockville, MD 20857/301-443-2673, 436-6147.

Family Planning Data Base

The National Clearinghouse for Family Planning Information maintains a data base of family planning materials and serial publications. The

Clearinghouse will compile bibliographies for family planning health professionals. All services are free of charge. Contact: National Clearinghouse for Family Planning Information, P.O. Box 2225, Rockville, MD 20852/301-251-5153.

Food and Drug Administration Data Base

The Food and Drug Administration (FDA) Electronic Bulletin Board provides subscribers with direct access to up-to-date FDA information. The program is easily accessible by telephone through a word processor, computer or other terminal. Users have access to the following six files: (1) NEWS, which consists of FDA news releases no older than two weeks; (2) ENFORCE, containing weekly recall information; (3) DEVICE, a file listing all medical devices recently approved; (4) IMPORT, containing summary reports of detained imported items; (5) BULLETIN, consisting of the FDA Drug Bulletin, a newsletter geared to physicians and other health professionals; and (6) DRUG, a file of all recently approved drug products.

FDA's Electronic Bulletin Board is established with ITT-Dialcom, and access is available only to Dialcom subscribers. Users are charged a minimum monthly fee of $100.00 and an hourly connect rate ranging from $1–9.00. Contact: FDA Press Office, 301-443-3285; ITT Dialcom, Federal Systems Division, 600 Maryland Avenue S.W., Washington, DC 20024/202-488-0550.

Health Care Data Base

The National Health Planning Information Center (NHPIC) no longer maintains its own data base, but the Center does have access to several data bases dealing with the planning and delivery of health care. The major system searched by NHPIC is the Health Planning and Administration (HPA) Data Base produced by the National Library of Medicine. The HPA data base contains bibliographic citations and abstracts of worldwide literature covering all aspects of health planning.

NHPIC will search a variety of data bases, free of charge, but only for health professionals and selected others. Access to health planning data bases is available, for a fee, through the National Library of Medicine, the National Technical Information Service (NTIS) and DIALOG. Contact: Chief of Clearinghouse Operations Branch, National Health Planning Information Center, 5600 Fishers Lane, Parklawn Building, Room 9A31, Rockville, MD 20857/301-443-1410.

Health Index Data Base

The Clearinghouse on Health Indexes provides a data base containing bibliographic citations and abstracts of literature about health indexes. "Health indexes" refers to the overall health of an individual or group, and concerns measures of health, not disease. Examples of topics covered include: number of cancer deaths, life expectancy,

quality of life, biometry. The data base contains multidisciplinary materials in fields such as sociology, psychology, economics and political science.

Searches and print-outs are available free of charge. Contact: Clearinghouse on Health Indexes, Office of Analysis and Epidemiology, 3700 East-West Highway, Room 27, Hyattsville, MD 20782/301-436-7035.

Human Services Management and Delivery Data Base

Project Share's data base has bibliographic citations and abstracts of literature about improving the delivery and management of human services. Topics include: long-term care, substance abuse, transportation, cost effectiveness, vocational rehabilitation, juvenile delinquency, health insurance, grants, fundings and group homes. Most searches, with print-outs, cost $30.00. Eleven standard searches are available for $10 each. Contact: Reference, Project Share, P.O. Box 2309, Rockville, MD 20852/301-231-9539.

Neurological, Communicative Disorders and Stroke Research Data Base

This section has program data on the National Institute of Neurological and Communicative Disorders and Stroke (NINCDS)' grants/awards, contracts and intramural projects.

Searches and printouts are available on a cost recovery basis. Contact: Management Information and Data Section, Office of Planning and Analysis, Room 904, National Institute of Neurological and Communicative Disorders and Stroke, 7550 Wisconsin Avenue, Bethesda, MD 20205/301-496-9244.

Occupational Safety and Health Bibliographic Data Base

The Document Information Directory System (DIDS) contains a listing of all materials produced by the National Institute for Occupational Safety (NIOSH). The system includes NIOSH: technical-assistance reports, contract and grants reports, health-hazard evaluations, current intelligence bulletins, criteria documents, and speeches by NIOSH personnel.

Printouts are provided free of charge and include: document title, NIOSH publication number, and, if applicable, the document's NTIS or GPO number and price. Upon request, NIOSH will send any document it stocks free of charge. Contact: Information Retrieval and Analyses Section, NIOSH, 4676 Columbia Parkway, Cincinnati, OH 45226/513-684-8317.

Occupational Safety and Health Data Base on Current Research

The National Institute of Occupational Safety and Health maintains a Current Research File which contains information about current research in the area of occupational safety and health. The file includes projects conducted by government agencies, foreign countries and NIOSH. Searches and print-outs are available free of charge. Contact: Information Retrieval and Analysis Section, NIOSH, 4676 Columbia Parkway, Cincinnati, OH 45226/513-684-8317.

Occupational Safety and Toxicology in Health Materials Data Base

NIOSHTIC contains bibliographic citations and abstracts of occupational safety and health materials pertaining mainly to toxicology. Input is gathered from U.S. and foreign literature, the personnel files of several distinguished people in the fields, and foreign trade. Currently searches and printouts are available free of charge. NIOSH is planning to make the data available through Lockheed. Contact: Information Retrieval and Analyses Section, NIOSH, 4676 Columbia Parkway, Cincinnati, OH 45226/513-684-8317.

Poison Control Data Base

The Poison Control Data Base (PCDB) contains information about drugs, household products, industrial compounds and other manufactured or natural substances that pose a threat to the general public. Simple searches are free; more complicated requests may require a cost-recovery fee. Contact: Poison Control Branch, 5600 Fishers Lane, Parklawn Building, Room 15B, Mail Stop HFN720, Rockville, MD 20857/301-443-6260.

Prescription Drugs—Adverse Reaction Data Base

This data base contains all prescription drug adverse reactions reported to the Food & Drug Administration. The data base is searchable by drug name, therapeutic category, and type of reaction. Searches are done on a cost-recovery basis for a minimum fee of $50. All requests must be in writing. Contact: Freedom of Information Staff, HFW-35, Food and Drug Administration, 5600 Fishers Lane, Rockville, MD 20857.

Prescription Drugs—Data Base of Approved Ones

The Food and Drug Administration maintains a data base of approved prescription drugs. The following data is retrievable for each drug: trade and generic name, manufacturer, and date of FDA approval.

Searches are done on a cost-recovery basis for a minimum fee of $50. All searches and information requests must be made in writing. Contact: Freedom of Information Staff, HFW-35, Food and Drug Administration, 5600 Fishers Lane, Rockville, MD 20857.

Product Defect Reporting Data Base

This data base contains data on drug product defects reported to the FDA. It only covers drugs produced in the U.S. Retrievable information includes: drug name, manufacturer and type of defect.

Searches are done on a cost-recovery basis for a minimum fee of $50. Requests must be in writing. Contact: Freedom of Information Staff, HFW-35, Food and Drug Administration, 5600 Fishers Lane, Rockville, MD 20857.

Radiation Experience Data Base

Radiation Experience Data (RED) is a statistical data base containing raw data about patient X-rays, nuclear medicine and ultrasound exams performed in 80 sample hospitals nationwide.

Simple searches and resulting printouts will soon be available free of charge. A cost-recovery fee will be assessed for detailed searches. Contact: Ralph Bunge, FDA (HFZ-250), 5600 Fishers Lane, Rockville, MD 20857/301-443-1002.

Rehabilitation Data Base

The National Rehabilitation Information Center provides a data base, ABLEDATA, which is a national catalog of rehabilitation devices and aids useful to the disabled. The system is accessible only through ABLEDATA and its 10 designated information brokers nationwide. Some brokers will do searches free of charge; others charge a minimal fee if the search cost exceeds $10.00. To find the broker nearest you, contact ABLEDATA's Washington, DC office. Contact: ABLEDATA, National Rehabilitation Information Center, 4407 Eighth Street N.E., Washington, DC 20017/202-635-6090.

Scientific Projects Data Base

The Computer Retrieval of Information on Scientific Projects (CRISP) contains in-depth scientific information about research projects supported by grants and contracts from the Public Health Service, and projects carried out at the National Institutes of Health and the National Institute of Mental Health. Data is also available about campus-based research receiving both public and private funding.

Currently NIH runs searches and printouts free of charge for individuals and non-profit organizations, and on a cost-recovery basis for profit-making institutions. However, this policy may change when CRISP goes on DIALOG in the near future. NIH does plan to continue running searches for groups not having access to DIALOG. Contact: Research Documentation Section, Statistics and Analysis Branch, Division of Research Grants, Westwood Room, Bldg 148, National Institutes of Health, Bethesda, MD 20205/301-496-7543.

Smoking and Health Data Base

The Smoking and Health Clearinghouse maintains a bibliographic data base with abstracts, on all aspects of smoking. Searches and printouts are available free of charge. Contact: Office on Smoking and Health, Technical Information Center, 5600 Fishers Lane, Park Building, Room 116, Rockville, MD 20857/301-443-1690.

Toxic Effects of Chemical Substances Data Base
The Registry of Toxic Effects of Chemical Substances (RTECS) stores data about 56,000 individual chemicals that have been studied for toxicity. NIOSH will run one or two chemicals and provide printouts at no charge. Contact: Information Retrieval and Analyses Section, NIOSH, 4676 Columbia Parkway, Cincinnati, OH 45226/513-684-8317. For more detailed searches (and the fee) contact: National Library of Medicine or EPA Chemical Information System.

Toxicology Self-Search Data Bases
The National Library of Medicine has four data bases that are available on-line to users, who must do their own search.

CHEMLINE is a chemical dictionary that provides registry numbers for over 600,000 chemicals, synonyms of the chemical names and locator information as to where the registry number is used in the other Library of Medicine files. Average cost is $56 per hour.

TOXLINE is a bibliographic data base that covers the literature from 1965 to the present and is a freetext searchable data base, not an indexed file data base. Average cost is $59 per hour.

RTECS, produced by the National Institute of Occupational Safety and Health (NIOSH), is a registry of toxic effects of chemical substances. NIOSH created and maintains the data base. Average cost is $55 per hour.

TOXICOLOGY DATA BANK (TDB) is a comprehensive record of information on manufacturer use, environmental aspects, toxicity aspects (both human and animal), metabolism, antidote and treatment, and poison and pollution potential to soil, water and air. Average cost is $75 per hour.

Cost for the different data bases varies depending upon the extent of the use. The rate is less when the data base is used during non-prime time, but there is an additional charge for printed information. Contact: National Library of Medicine, 9000 Rockville Pike, Bethesda, MD 20814/301-496-1131.

X-Ray Exposure Data Base
The Nationwide Examination of X-Ray Trends (NEXT) contains statistical data and exposure/dose information about diagnostic medical and dental X-rays taken nationwide.

Searches and printouts are available free of charge. Contact: National Center for Devices and Radiology Health, DITP-HFX-230, 5600 Fishers Lane, Rockville, MD 20857/301-443-3446.

Contraception
For information on developments aimed at providing safe and effective methods for regulating fertility in both men and women, contact: Contraceptive Development Branch, Center for Population Research, National Institute of Child Health and Human Development, Department of Health and Human Services, 7910 Woodmont Ave., Room 7A-04, Bethesda, MD 20205/301-496-1661.

Day Care
Information and expertise are available on improving the quality and expanding the availability of day care centers. The following manuals are available for setting up a day care center:

General Information
Day Care Centers Serving Infants
Day Care Centers Serving Pre-Schoolers
Day Care Centers Serving School-Age Children
*Health Services—A Guide to Health Care Personnel and
    Project Directors*
Day Care Centers Serving Children with Special Needs

Contact: Special Projects Branch, Program Support, Head Start, Administration for Children, Youth and Families, Department of Health and Human Services, P.O. Box 1182, Washington, DC 20013/202-755-7724.

Defective Drugs
A list is available from the Food and Drug Administration (FDA), identifying by product or by company name those drug products which have proved defective. Contact: Product Surveillance Branch, Bureau of Foods, Food and Drug Administration, Department of Health and Human Services, 5600 Fishers Lane, Room 9-45, Rockville, MD 20857/301-443-2263.

Dental Care and Research
The National Institute of Dental Research accumulates information and expertise on tooth decay, gum disease, soft tissue diseases and nutrition, tooth implants, control of oral pain, cranio-facial anomalies, cleft lip, cleft palate, and malocclusions. Up to 50 copies each, of the following publications, are available for free:

Good Teeth for You and Your Baby (Spanish)
RX for Sound Teeth
Malocclusion
Tetracycline Stained Teeth
Tooth Decay
Cleft Lip and Palate
Periodontal (Gum) Disease
Research Explores Canker Sores and Fever Blisters
Seal Out Dental Decay

Contact: Scientific and Health Reports, National Institute of Dental Research, NIH, Department of Health and Human Services, Building 31, Room 2C36, Bethesda, MD 20205/301-496-4261.

Developmental Disabilities

For information on mental retardation, autism, epilepsy, cerebral palsy, and other such developmental diseases which are manifested before the age of 22, contact: Administration of Developmental Disabilities, 3730 Health and Human Services Building, Washington, DC 20201/202-245-2890.

Diagnostic and Treatment Techniques

The National Institute for Neurological Communicative Disorders and Stroke (NINCDS) Information Office is available to answer questions about various diseases and the diagnostic and treatment techniques used. The Office publishes informative brochures on the different techniques used to treat diseases, including *Positron Emission Tomography* (PET). This 20-page brochure is available free of charge. Contact: National Institute for Neurological Communicative Disorders and Stroke (NINCDS), National Institutes of Health, Building 31, Room 8A 16, 9000 Rockville Pike, Bethesda MD 20205/301-496-5751.

Diagnostic Imaging Program

The staff of the Diagnostic Imaging Research Grant program is available to provide current information and referrals in the field, and to give further information about the grants available in medical imaging. Contact: National Cancer Institute, Diagnostic Imaging Research Program, Landow Building, Room 8C-19, Bethesda, MD 20205/301-496-9531.

Diabetic Information Clearinghouse

The clearinghouse services the public by supplying references and citations as well as referrals to other information sources. Contact: National Diabetic Information Clearinghouse, 805 15th St. N.W., Room 500, Washington, DC 20005/202-638-7620.

Digestive Diseases Information Clearinghouse

The clearinghouse coordinates the national effort to educate the public, patients, families of patients, physicians, and other health care providers about the prevention and management of digestive diseases. Contact: National Digestive Diseases Education and Information Clearinghouse, National Institute of Arthritis, Diabetes, and Digestive and Kidney Diseases, National Institutes of Health, 1555 Wilson Boulevard, Suite 600, Rosslyn VA 22209/703-496-9707.

Direct Payments

The programs described below are those that provide financial assistance directly to individuals, private firms and other private institutions to encourage or subsidize a particular activity.

Medicare—Hospital Insurance

Objectives: To provide hospital insurance protection for covered services to any person 65 or over and to certain disabled persons.

Eligibility: Persons 65 or over and certain disabled persons are eligible for hospital insurance protection. Nearly everyone who reached 65 before 1968 is eligible for hospital insurance, including people not eligible for cash social security benefits; a person who reached 65 in 1968 or after who is not eligible for such benefits needs some work credit to qualify for hospital insurance benefits. Hospital insurance is also available to persons, age 65 or over, not otherwise eligible through payment of a monthly premium; such coverage is voluntary. Persons under age 65 who have been entitled for at least 24 consecutive months to social security disability benefits or for 29 consecutive months to railroad retirement benefits based on disability, are eligible for hospital insurance benefits. Also, most people who have chronic kidney disease and require kidney dialysis or transport are eligible.

Range of Financial Assistance: Benefits may be paid for most of the reasonable costs of covered inpatient hospital services and post-hospital extended care services incurred in a benefit period. For benefit periods beginning in the calendar year 1979, the beneficiary is responsible for $160 inpatient hospital deductible, a $40 per day coinsurance amount for the 61st through 90th day of inpatient hospital care during the 60 lifetime reserve days, and a $20 per day coinsurance amount after 20 days of care in a skilled nursing facility. Post-hospital home health services are paid in full for 100 visits per benefit period.

Contact: Local Social Security offices or Medicare Bureau, Health Care Financing Administration, Room 700, East High Rise Bldg., 6401 Security Blvd., Baltimore, MD 21235/301-594-9000.

Medicare—Supplementary Medical Insurance

Objectives: To provide medical insurance protection for covered services to persons 65 or over and certain disabled persons who elect this coverage.

Eligibility: All persons 65 and over and those under 65 who are eligible for hospital insurance benefits may voluntarily enroll for supplementary medical insurance. The enrollee pays a monthly premium which is currently $8.70. Some states pay the premium on behalf of qualifying individuals.

Range of Financial Assistance: The beneficiary is responsible for meeting an annual $60 deductible before benefits may begin. Thereafter, Medicare pays 80 percent of the reasonable charges for covered services. Medicare pays 100 percent of reasonable charges for services to hospital inpatients by doctors in the field of radiology or pathology and, after the $60 deductible, 100 percent of the costs for home health services covered under the Supplementary Medical Insurance program.

Contact: Local Social Security offices or Medicare Bureau, Health Care Financing Administration, Room 700, East High Rise Bldg., 6401 Security Blvd., Baltimore, MD 21235/301-594-9000.

Refugee Assistance—State-Administered Programs

Objectives: To help refugees from Cambodia, Vietnam and Laos resettle throughout the country by funding maintenance and medical assistance and social services for needy refugees through state and local public assistance agencies; and to provide grants for special employment training and related projects.

Eligibility: For the public assistance aspects of the program, the state agency responsible for administration of the regular public assistance programs of the state, through agreement with the Social Security Administration, Department of Health and Human Services, is eligible to receive funds for providing cash and medical assistance and social services to needy eligible Indochinese refugees.

Range of Financial Assistance: Not specified.

Contact: Office of Refugee Resettlement, Department of Health and Human Services, Switzer Building, Room 1332, 330 C St. S.W., Washington, DC 20201/202-245-0418.

Social Security—Disability Insurance

Objectives: To replace part of the earnings lost because of a physical or mental impairment severe enough to prevent a person from working.

Eligibility: A disabled worker under age 65 is eligible for social security disability benefits if he or she has worked for a sufficient period of time under social security to be insured. The insured status requirements depend upon the age of the applicant and the date he or she became disabled. Dependents of disabled workers also are eligible for benefits: Unmarried children under age 18; children age 18 through 21 if unmarried and full-time students; unmarried disabled children of any age if disabled before age 22; wife at any age if child in her care is receiving benefits on worker's social security record; wife age 62 or over and husband age 62 or over except those receiving governmental pensions from noncovered employment on their own work record are subject to a pension offset; widows over age 50 who are unable to engage in gainful activity.

Range of Financial Assistance: Up to $1,391.90 monthly.

Contact: Local Social Security offices or Social Security Administration, 6401 Security Blvd., Room 4100, Annex, Baltimore, MD 21235/301-592-3000.

Social Security—Retirement Insurance

Objectives: To replace part of the earnings lost because of retirement.

Eligibility: Retired workers age 62 and over who have worked the required number of years under social security are eligible for monthly benefits. If an eligible worker applies before age 65, the individual will receive permanently reduced benefits. Also certain dependents can receive benefits. They include a wife or husband 62 or over (except those receiving governmental pensions from noncovered earnings on their own record are subject to a pension offset); a wife of any age with a dependent child in her care if the child is entitled to benefits based on the worker's record; unmarried children under 18 (22 if in school); unmarried disabled children if disabled before age 22; and divorced wives or husbands age 62 or over and married to the worker for at least 10 years, except that those receiving governmental pensions from noncovered employment on their own record are subject to a pension offset.

Range of Financial Assistance: Up to $1,000.60 monthly.

Contact: Local Social Security offices or Social Security Administration, 6401 Security Blvd., Room 4100, Annex, Baltimore, MD 21235/301-592-3000.

Social Security—Special Benefits for Persons Aged 72 and Over

Objectives: To assure some regular income to certain persons age 72 and over who had little or no opportunity to earn social security protection during their working years.

Eligibility: Individuals who attained age 72 before 1968 need no work credits under social security to be eligible for special payments. Those who reached age 72 in 1968 or later need some work credits to be eligible. The amount of work credit needed increases gradually each year for people reaching age 72 after 1968, until it is the same as that required for social security retirement benefits. Special payments can also be made to an eligible wife age 72 or over.

Range of Financial Assistance: Up to $138.10 monthly.

Contact: Local Social Security offices or Social Security Administration, 6401 Security Blvd., Room 4100, Annex, Baltimore, MD 21235/301-592-3000.

Social Security—Survivors Insurance

Objectives: To replace part of earnings lost to dependents because of worker's death.

Eligibility: Benefits are payable only if the deceased was insured for survivors' insurance protection. Survivors eligible for monthly cash benefits are the following: widow, widower, surviving divorced wife, or surviving divorced husband age 60 or over who was married to the deceased worker for at least ten years (except those receiving governmental pensions from non-covered employment on their own work record are subject to a pension offset); widow or widower age 50–59 and disabled; young (under age 60) widow, widower, or surviving divorced wife who has in her care a child under age 18 or over age 18 and disabled and entitled to benefits on the deceased worker's social security record; unmarried children under age 18 (22 if in school) or age 18 or over and disabled; and dependent parents age 62 and over.

Range of Financial Assistance: Not specified.

Contact: Local Social Security offices or Social Security Administration, 6401 Security Blvd., Baltimore, MD 21235/301-592-3000.

Special Benefits for Disabled Coal Miners

Objectives: To replace income lost to coal miners because they have become totally disabled due to pneumoconiosis (black lung disease), and replace income lost to widows of miners who were receiving black lung benefits when they died, totally disabled by this disease at the time of death, or who died because of this disease. Where no widow survives the miner, benefits are payable to a miner's children or, if none, to the miner's totally dependent parents or brothers and sisters in that order of priority. Benefits are also payable to children of a deceased widow who was entitled to black lung benefits at the time of her death.

Eligibility: In order to become entitled, the miner must have become "totally disabled" (as defined in the Act) from black lung disease. The applicant may be able to work in areas other than coal mines and still be eligible for benefits. Widows of coal miners whose deaths or total disability at the time of death resulted from black lung disease are also eligible for benefits as are other categories of beneficiaries.

Range of Financial Assistance: Up to $609.80 monthly.

Contact: Local Social Security offices or Social Security Administration, 6401 Security Blvd., Room 4100, Annex, Baltimore, MD 21235/301-592-3000.

Supplemental Security Income

Objectives: To provide supplemental income to persons aged 65 and over and to persons blind or disabled whose income and resources are below specified levels.

Eligibility: The eligibility of an individual who has attained age 65 or over or who is blind or disabled is determined on the basis of quarterly income and resources. In determining income, the first $60 of social security or other income would not be counted. An additional $195 of earned income, plus one-half of any quarterly earnings above $195, would also not be counted. If, after these exclusions, an individual's countable income, effective July 1978, is less than $568.20 per quarter ($852.30 for a couple, both of whom are categorized as above) and resources are less than $1,500 ($2,250 for a couple), the individual is eligible for payments. The value of household goods, personal effects, an automobile, and property needed for self-support are, if found reasonable, excluded in determining value of resources. Life insurance policies with face value of $1,500 or less and the value of a home are excluded in resource valuation.

Range of Financial Assistance: Average $169 per month.

Contact: Local Social Security offices or Social Security Administration, 6401 Security Blvd., Room 4100, Annex, Baltimore, MD 21235/301-592-3000.

Disease Control Training

The Center for Disease Control (CDC) provides training in epidemiologic surveillance, laboratory procedures and public health. Courses are given at the CDC or by CDC personnel in various states and foreign locations. Contact: Center for Professional Development and Training, CDC, Department of Health and Human Services, 1600 Clifton Rd., N.E., Atlanta, GA 30333/404-262-6671.

Doctoral Dissertation Grants

Financial assistance is available to students whose dissertation covers specific topics. See "Grants" in this section.

Drug Abuse Information Clearinghouse

The Clearinghouse will perform free research to answer questions relating to drug abuse. In addition to reference services it also provides drug abuse prevention materials, pamphlets and posters, treatment manuals for medical personnel, and many other publications. Interested persons can be placed on one of the following subject-area mailing lists: epidemiology; laws/policy documents; prevention/education; research papers/reports; and training and treatment. Contact National Clearinghouse on Drug Abuse Information, National Institute on Drug Abuse, Department of Health and Human Services, 5600 Fishers Lane, Room 10A43, Rockville, MD 20857/301-443-6500.

The *National Directory of Drug Abuse Programs* is a compilation of 9,100 federal, state, local and privately funded agencies responsible for the administration or provision of alcoholism or drug abuse services throughout the U.S. Free copies of this directory, as well as more than 300 other free publications that provide information to parents, educators, students, community program workers, trainees, and prevention treatment program personnel are available at the address given above.

Drug Abuse Resource Center

The Center contains more than 10,000 books, magazines and journals, on drug abuse. It also provides a free audiovisual loan service through inter-library loan only on 250 educational films. Contact: National Institute on Drug Abuse Resource Center, Alcohol, Drug Abuse and Mental Health Administration, Department of Health and Human Services, 5600 Fishers Lane, Room 10A54, Rockville, MD 20857/301-443-6614.

Drug Newsletter

This free newsletter is published approximately six times a year and is sent to doctors, hospital administrators, nurses, students and others interested in following drug-related activities at the Food and Drug Administration. Contact: *Drug Bulletin,* Food and Drug Administration, Department of Health and Human Services, HFI-22, 5600 Fishers Lane, Rockville, MD 20857/301-443-1016.

Drug Registration Directory

All registered drugs are given a unique identification number by the Food and Drug Administration, which is used in third-party reimbursement programs. The information, called the *National Drug Code Directory,* is available in hard copy for $90.00 (1 year subscription fee to quarterly) or on magnetic tape, organized by trade name and indexed by company and ingredients. Contact: Government Printing Office, Attn: Superintendent of Documents, Washington, DC 20402/202-783-3238.

Drugs for Cancer Treatment Research

An expert in the field, Mr. Davignon oversees the development, production and distribution of investigational drugs in the division of cancer treatment within the National Cancer Institute (NCI), most products of which are injectable dosage forms. He may be contacted on a limited basis for referrals to other experts in the field of pharmacology. Two NCI publications are *Chemical and Analytical Information,* (842654) a one-time publication that deals with the analytical and chemical information on investigative drugs for laboratory personnel (#842654) and the *Pharmaceutical Data* (#842141) an annual publication that describes data of products for the handling of drugs by pharmacists and nurses. Both are available free of charge. Contact: Pharmaceutical Resources Branch, National Cancer Institute, Landow Building, Room 5C-25, Woodmont Avenue, Bethesda, MD 20205/301-496-8774.

Drugs—Money-Saving Directory

A directory entitled *Approved Prescription Drug List With Therapeutic Equivalent Evaluation* shows how to substitute one drug for another, often at a savings, and sells for $67. Contact: Government Printing Office, Attn: Superintendent of Documents, Washington, DC 20402/201-783-3238.

Drugs—Research and Evaluation

The Bureau of Drugs accumulates information and expertise on new drug evaluation, biometrics, epidemiology, poison control, drug labeling, drug manufacturing, methadone monitoring, pharmaceutical research, drug biology, and drug chemistry. Contact: Advisory Communications Branch, Bureau of Drugs, FDA, Department of Health and Human Services, Room 15B-32, 5600 Fishers Lane, Room 974, Rockville, MD 20857/301-443-1016; or contact Associate Commissioner, Office of Consumer and Public Affairs, Center for Drugs and Biologics, HFE 88, FDA, 5600 Fishers Lane, Rockville, MD 20857.

Education and Training

There are more than 44 programs offering financial assistance to support education and training in health-related careers. Programs range from nursing scholarships to financial distress grants. The listings offer many career opportunities; if a program of interest does not provide assistance directly to individuals, contact the grant-giving office for a listing of local organizations receiving funds. See "Grants" in this section.

Effects of Toxic Substances

The National Institute of Environmental Health Sciences office can supply you with information about the effects of toxic substances on reproduction. The staff can refer you to appropriate experts. The Institute has published *Research Program Booklets,* annual publications that profiles ongoing research at the institute and *Environmental Health Perspective,* a quarterly which profiles specific toxic substances in the environment and their toxic effects on health. Contact: National Institute of Environmental Health Sciences, Public Affairs Office, Research Triangle Park, NC 27709/919-541-3345.

Electromagnetic Energy Resource

The Electromagnetics Branch of Food and Drug Administration is involved in applied research related to sources of electromagnetic energy, product evaluation, the development of measurement techniques and the development of technological control techniques. Technical reports can be ordered. These reports include information about theoretical studies, electromagnetic source evaluations, measurements, measurement techniques, hyperthermia equipment for cancer treatment, and microwave ovens. Staff in this branch can respond to written inquiries. Contact: Electromagnetics Branch, Division of Physical Sciences, Center for Devices and Radiological Health, U.S. Food and Drug Administration, Rockville, MD 20857/301-443-3840, 301-443-3532 (Technical Literature).

Emergency Mental Health

For information and assistance in setting up supplementary counseling services where needed in disaster areas, contact: Disaster Assistance and Emergency Mental Health, National Institute of Mental Health, Department of Health and Human Services, 5600 Fishers Lane, Room 6C-12, Rockville, MD 20857/301-443-1910.

Employee Industrial Hygiene Guides

Information is available describing health and safety rules to be followed by workers involved in such work as foundry operations, metal cleaning, printing, rendering, textile dying, and pesticide applications. Contact: Publications Dissemination, Department of Health and Human Services, 4676 Columbia Pkwy., Cincinnati, OH 45226/513-684-4287.

Energy and Health Facilities

Technical information and expertise are available on energy conservation and costs and how they relate to health facilities. Contact: Division of Energy Policy and Programs, Bureau of Health Facilities, HRA, Department of Health and Human Services, 3700 East-West Hwy., Room 5-50, Hyattsville, MD 20782/301-436-6845.

Environmental Health Sciences

Technical information and expertise are available concerning the effects of chemicals in the environment on human health. Areas of interest include biometry; epidemiology; biochemical, animal and molecular genetics; pharmacokinetics and reproductive, neurological and pulmonary toxicology. Contact: Public Information, National Institute of Environmental Health Sciences, NIH, Department of Health and Human Services, P.O. Box 12233, Research Triangle Park, NC 27709/919-541-3345.

Epidemic Intelligence Service

This special medical intelligence organization tracks and investigates problems of acute diseases that may lead to epidemic situations. In addition to investigating such cases as the Three Mile Island Nuclear Power Plant accident and Legionnaires' Disease, it maintains surveillance programs in infectious diseases, chronic diseases, influenza, parasitic diseases, congenital malformations, and environmental hazards. Contact: Bureau of Epidemiology Program Office, Center for Disease Control, Department of Health and Human Services, Building 1, Room 5009, Atlanta, GA 30330/404-329-3661.

Eye Institute—National

The Institute supports research on the cause, natural history, prevention, diagnosis, and treatment of disorders of the eye and the visual system. Special emphasis is placed on laboratory and clinical research pertaining to glaucoma, retinal diseases, corneal diseases, cataract, and sensory-motor disorders. Support is provided for basic studies, epidemiologic research, instrumentation development, clinical trials, and the development of animal models for vision disorders. Contact: National Eye Institute, National Institutes of Health, 9000 Rockville Pike, Bethesda, MD 20205/301-496-5248.

Family Planning Information Clearinghouse

Information, reference services and other expertise are available on such topics as family planning, birth control, infertility, sex education and related subjects. Other services available include patient and professional education material; books, pamphlets, manuals, films, cassette programs, and models; catalogues of family-planning publications and audiovisual materials; a free newsletter on health education for clinic staff members; and a free newsletter identifying new information services on family planning. Contact: National Clearinghouse for Family Planning Information, Department of Health and Human Services, P.O. Box 2225, Rockville, MD 20852/301-251-5176.

Food and Drug Company and Product Listings

Under the Freedom of Information Act, the Food and Drug Administration makes the following listings available: registered drug establishments; import product list (drugs); product ingredient list (drugs); medical device establishments; radiological health companies. There is a charge for these listings and all requests must be submitted in writing. Contact: Freedom of Information Office, FDA, Department of Health and Human Services, 5600 Fishers Lane, Room 12A16, Rockville, MD 20857/301-443-6310.

Food and Drug Consumer Update

This free quarterly publication lists public hearings, promotes participation in Food and Drug Administration hearings, describes the FDA decision-making process, announces consumer exchange meetings on a national and district level, and lists locations of FDA consumer offices. Contact: Office of Consumer Affairs, Food and Drug Adminstration (HFE-20), Department of Health and Human Services, 5600 Fishers Lane, Rockville, MD 20857/301-443-5006.

Food and Drug Consumer Publications

The Food and Drug Administration publishes more than 200 free publications covering such topics as vitamins, minerals, food labeling, drug regulation, cosmetics, and microwave ovens. You can simply state your food- or drug-related area of interest and relevant publications will be sent to you, or you can request a free catalogue. For current information on the latest topics of interest, subscribe to *The FDA Consumer* at $9 per year. Contact: Office of Public Affairs (HFI-20), Food and Drug Administration, Department of Health and Human Services, 5600 Fishers Lane, Rockville, MD 20857/301-443-3210.

Food and Drug Photographs
The Food and Drug Administration maintains a photo file on food- and drug-related matters which is available for loan. Contact: Office of Public Affairs, Food and Drug Administration, HFW-41, 5600 Fishers Lane, Rockville, MD 20857/301-443-3210.

Food and Drugs—Reporting Problem Products
If you know of any foods, drugs, cosmetics, medical or veterinary products that you think are not properly labeled or packaged or that are harmful or unsanitary, you would perform a public service by reporting it to the Food and Drug Administration. Reports should be made as soon as possible, providing as many details as possible, in writing or by telephone to one of the FDA's 140 regional offices; or to Food and Drug Administration, Department of Health and Human Services, 5600 Fishers Lane (HFO-410), Room 1362, Rockville, MD 20857/301-443-1240. For an emergency call, there is a 24-hour answering service at 202-737-0448.

Food and Drug Small Business Help
The Food and Drug Administration offers special help to the small businesses it regulates. It will explain how the businesses are affected by the regulations and how to complete applications and other forms, describes what manufacturers must do in order to market a new product, and make on-site visits in order to understand special small business problems. Contact: Small Business Coordinator, Food and Drug Administration, Department of Health and Human Services, 5600 Fishers Lane, 1536, Rockville, MD 20857/301-443-1583.

Foods—Research and Evaluation
The Bureau of Foods accumulates information and expertise on food cosmetic microbiology, veterinary pathology, whole animal toxicology, dermal and ocular toxicology, animal resources, genetics toxicology, metabolism, food animal additives, food additives, coloring and cosmetics, contaminants and natural toxicants, packaging technology, food technology, chemical technology, coloring technology, and cosmetics technology. Contact: FDA Press Office, Bureau of Foods, Food and Drug Administration, Department of Health and Human Services, 200 C St. S.W., Room 3807, Washington, DC 20204/202-245-1144.

Frederick Cancer Research Facility
National Cancer Institute supported investigators are studying viruses and chemicals that cause cancer in animals and developing drugs that may be useful in treating cancer. Contact: National Cancer Institute, National Institutes of Health, Frederick, MD 21701/301-695-1108.

Freedom of Information Act
Each major division within the Department of Health and Human Services has a Freedom of Information Act office. For a list of these offices, contact: Office of the Secretary, FOIA, Department of Health and Human Services, 200 Independence Ave. S.W., Room 118F, Washington, DC 20201/202-472-7453. See also "Freedom of Information Act."

General Medical Sciences—National Institute
This institute supports research in the sciences basic to medicine, the behavioral sciences, and in certain clinical disciplines. A major objective is to achieve greater understanding of basic genetic mechanisms and the underlying causes of human inherited diseases. Contact: National Institute of General Medical Sciences, National Institutes of Health, 9000 Rockville Pike, Bethesda, MD 20205/301-496-5230.

Genetic Disease Information Clearinghouse
The clearinghouse provides pamphlets, books, journals, posters, charts, brochures, audio cassettes, film strips, teaching kits, slide and tape lectures, as well as a free directory describing informational and clinical resources. Contact: National Clearinghouse for Human Genetic Diseases, Department of Health and Human Services, Ground Floor, Suite 1, 3520 Prospect St., Washington, DC 20051/202-842-7617.

Gerontology Research Center
Investigations are conducted in a wide range of areas including clinical physiology, behavioral sciences, cellular and molecular biology, molecular aging, neurosciences, and comparative nutrition. Contact: Gerontology Research Center, National Institute on Aging, National Institutes of Health, Department of Health and Human Services, Baltimore City Hospital, Room 1E07, Baltimore, MD 21224/301-496-9419.

Grants
The programs described below are for sums of money which are given by the federal government to initiate and stimulate new or improved activities or to sustain on-going services.

Adolescent Family Life-Demonstration Projects
Objectives: To promote positive family-centered programs promoting self-discipline and other prudent approaches to the problem of adolescent premarital sexual relations, including adolescent pregnancy; with primary emphasis on unmarried

adolescents who are 17 years of age and under and for adolescent parents.

Eligibility: Public organizations and private non-profit organizations.

Range of Financial Assistance: $29,000 to $446,000.

Contact: Office of Adolescent Pregnancy Programs, Office of the Assistant Secretary for Health, DHHS, Room 1351, HHS North Building, 330 Independence Ave. S.W., Washington, DC 20201/202-245-0142.

Adolescent Family Life Research Grants

Objectives: To encourage and support research projects and dissemination activities concerning the societal causes and consequences of adolescent premarital sexual relations, contraceptive use, pregnancy and child rearing.

Eligibility: State and local government agencies; private organizations (nonprofit and profit); institutions of higher education.

Range of Financial Assistance: $25,000 to $145,000.

Contact: Office of Adolescent Pregnancy Programs, Office of the Assistant Secretary for Health, DHHS, Room 1351 HHS-N, 330 Independence Ave. S.W., Washington, DC 20201/202-245-0142.

Adoption Assistance

Objectives: To provide Federal Financial Participation (FFP) to States in the adoption subsidy costs for children with special needs who are adopted.

Eligibility: Only States, the District of Columbia, the Commonwealths of Puerto Rico, and the Northern Marianas, the Virgin Islands and Guam are eligible to receive funds.

Range of Financial Assistance: Not applicable.

Contact: Associate Chief, Children's Bureau, PO Box 1182, Washington, DC 20013/202-755-7418.

Adoption Opportunities

Objectives: To provide financial support for demonstration projects to improve adoption practices; to gather information on adoptions, and to provide training and technical assistance to improve adoption services.

Eligibility: State or local governmental or non-profit institutions of higher learning; state and local government or nonprofit organizations engaged in research on child welfare activities.

Range of Financial Assistance: $50,000 to $500,000.

Contact: Training and Technical Assistance Division, Children's Bureau, Administration for Children, Youth and Families, Department of Health and Human Services, P.O. Box 1182, Washington, DC 20013/202-755-7820.

Advanced Nurse Training Program

Objectives: To prepare registered nurses to teach in the various fields of nurse training and to serve in administrative or supervisory capacities, in nursing specialties, and as nurse clinicians.

Eligibility: Public and nonprofit private collegiate schools of nursing accredited by the appropriate accrediting body.

Range of Financial Assistance: $19,405 to $334,909.

Contact: Division of Nursing, 5600 Fishers Lane, 5C-26, Rockville, MD 20857/301-436-6627.

Aging—Grants for Supportive Services and Senior Centers

Objectives: To provide assistance to state and area agencies for support of programs for older persons through statewide and area planning and provision of social services, including multipurpose senior centers.

Eligibility: All states and territories with approved state plans and state agencies on aging designated by the governors.

Range of Financial Assistance: $121,875 to $22,094,560.

Contact: Office of Program Operations, Administration on Aging, Office of Human Development Services, Department of Health and Human Services, Washington, DC 20201/202-245-0011.

Aging—Nutrition Services

Objectives: To provide older Americans with low-cost nutritious meals, and with appropriate nutrition education services. Meals may be served in a congregate setting or delivered to the home.

Eligibility: All states with approved state plans.

Range of Financial Assistance: $157,500 to $22,602,884.

Contact: Office of Program Operations, Administration on Aging, Office of Human Development Services, Department of Health and Human Services, Washington, DC 20201/202-245-0011.

Aging—Research

Objectives: To support biomedical, social and behavioral research and research training directed toward greater understanding of the aging process and the needs and problems of the elderly.

Eligibility: Universities, colleges, medical, dental and nursing schools, schools of public health, laboratories, hospitals, state and local health departments, other public or nonprofit private institutions, and individuals.

Range of Financial Assistance: $17,720 to $896,204.

Contact: National Institute on Aging, National Institutes of Health, Department of Health and Human Services, Bethesda MD 20205/301-496-4996.

Alcohol and Drug Abuse and Mental Health Services Block Grant

Objectives: To provide financial assistance to States and Territories to support projects for the development of more effective prevention, treatment and rehabilitation programs and activities to deal with alcohol and drug abuse.

Eligibility: State and US Territory Governments; Indian Tribes or Tribal organizations.

Range of Financial Assistance: $9,000 to $44,000,000.

Contact: Office of the Administrator, ADAMHA/PHS, 5600 Fishers Lane, Rockville, MD 20857/301-443-4564.

Alcohol National Research Service Awards for Research Training

Objectives: To provide support to individuals for predoctoral and postdoctoral research training in specified alcohol abuse-related areas.

Eligibility: Support is provided for predoctoral and postdoctoral academic and research training only, in health and health-related areas which are specified by the National Institute of Alcohol Abuse and Alcoholism and include research training in the various aspects of prevention, education and treatment.

Range of Financial Assistance: $6,900 to $108,806.

Contact: Division of Extramural Research, National Institute on Alcohol Abuse and Alcoholism, Department of Health and Human Services, 5600 Fishers Lane, Rockville, MD 20857/301-443-2530.

Alcohol Research Center Grants

Objectives: To provide long-term support for research efforts into the problems of alcohol use and alcoholism by coordinating the activities of investigators from biomedical, behavioral, and social science disciplines.

Eligibility: State and local governments, and any domestic public or nonprofit private institution.

Range of Financial Assistance: $479,000 to $1 million.

Contact: Division of Extramural Research, National Institute on Alcohol Abuse and Alcoholism, Alcohol, Drug Abuse, and Mental Health Administration, Department of Health and Human Services, 5600 Fishers Lane, Rockville, MD 20857/301-443-2530.

Alcohol Research Programs

Objectives: To develop approaches to the causes, diagnosis, treatment, control, and prevention of alcohol abuse and alcoholism through basic, clinical and applied research.

Eligibility: Investigators affiliated with public or nonprofit private agencies, including state, local or regional government agencies, universities, colleges, hospitals, academic or research institutions, and other organizations.

Range of Financial Assistance: $7,200 to $366,000.

Contact: Division of Extramural Research, Director, National Institute on Alcohol Abuse and Alcoholism, Public Health Service, Department of Health and Human Services, 5600 Fishers Lane, Rockville, MD 20857/301-443-2530.

Alcohol Research Scientist Development and Research Scientist Awards

Objectives: To provide support for research relating to the problems of alcohol abuse and alcoholism prevention, treatment, and rehabilitation and to raise the level of competence and increase the number of individuals engaged in such research.

Eligibility: Appropriate research centers, medical schools, community mental health centers, and research institutes with alcoholism programs on behalf of deserving individuals.

Range of Financial Assistance: $33,000 to $50,200.

Contact: Division of Extramural Research, Director, National Institute on Alcohol Abuse and Alcoholism, Public Health Service, Department of Health and Human Services, 5600 Fishers Lane, Rockville, MD 20857/301-443-2530.

Applied Toxicological Research and Testing

Objectives: To develop scientific information about potentially toxic and hazardous chemicals by concentrating on toxicological research, testing and test development and validation efforts.

Eligibility: A university, college, hospital, State or local government, nonprofit research institution, or profit organization.

Range of Financial Assistance: $54,000 to $722,000.

Contact: Associate Director for Extramural Program, National Institute of Environmental Health Sciences, PO Box 12233, Research Triangle Park, NC 27709/919-541-7723.

Area Health Education Centers

Objectives: To improve the distribution, supply, quality, utilization and efficiency of health personnel to increase the regionalization of educational responsibilities of health professions schools.

Eligibility: Accredited public or nonprofit schools of medicine or of osteopathy.

Range of Financial Assistance: $63,867 to $6,380,712.

Contact: Director, Division of Medicine, Bureau of Health Professions, Parklawn Bldg, Department of Health and Human Services, 5600 Fishers Lane, Rockville, MD 20857/301-436-6418.

Arthritis, Musculoskeletal and Skin Diseases Research

Objectives: To support basic laboratory research and clinical investigations and to provide postdoctoral biomedical research training for individuals.

Eligibility: Research grants are available to individuals and public and nonprofit institutions, who propose to establish, expand, or improve research activities. Research contracts are available to public, commercial, and industrial hospitals, and nonprofit and educational institutions.

Range of Financial Assistance: $13,000 to $478,000.

Contact: Associate Director for Extramural Program Activities, National Institute of Arthritis, Metabolism and Digestive Diseases, National Institute of Health, Department of Health and Human Services, Room 607A, Westwood Building, Bethesda, MD 20205/301-496-7277.

Assistance Payments—Maintenance Assistance

Objectives: To set general standards for state administration and to provide the federal financial share to states for aid to families with dependent children, emergency assistance to families with children, assistance to repatriated U.S. nationals.

Eligibility: State and local welfare agencies, which must operate under Health and Human Services-approved state plans and must comply with all Federal regulations governing aid and assistance to needy families with dependent children.

Range of Financial Assistance: $2,025,000 to $1,271,839,000.

Contact: Office of Family Assistance, Social Security Administration, Department of Health and Human Services, 2100 2nd St. S.W., Room B404, Washington, DC 20201/202-245-2736.

Assistance Payments—Research

Objectives: To demonstrate and research new public assistance concepts to reduce dependency and improve living conditions of recipients of public assistance.

Eligibility: Grants may be made to state and local governments and nonprofit organizations.

Range of Financial Assistance: $50,000 to $300,000.

Contact: Director of the Family Assistance Studies and Staff, Office of R&S, Social Security Administration, Department of Health and Human Services, 2221 Switzer Bldg, 330C St. SW, Washington, DC 20201/202-245-8400.

Assistance Payments—State and Local Training

Objectives: To train personnel employed or preparing for employment in state or local agencies administering approved public assistance plans.

Eligibility: States, whose state program is part of its approved state plan and who provide its share of the costs.

Range of Financial Assistance: Up to $7,969,000.

Contact: Director, Office of Procedures, Office of Family Assistance, Social Security Administration, Department of Health and Human Services, 2100 2nd St. S.W., Washington, DC 20201/202-245-2736.

Biological Basis Research

Objectives: Program includes: 1) neurological and communicative science basic research: 2) research on pathological conditions of the nervous system and hearing; 3) research on neurological and communicative disorders: and 4) research training in the basic communicative sciences and basic neurological sciences.

Eligibility: Public or private nonprofit institutions.

Range of Financial Assistance: Not specified.

Contact: Extramural Activities Program, NIH, Department of Health and Human Services, Federal Building, Room 1016, Bethesda, MD 20205/301-496-9248.

Biological Response to Environmental Health Hazards

Objectives: To focus on understanding how chemical and physical agents cause pathological changes in molecules, cells, tissues and organs and become manifested as respiratory disease, neurological, behavioral, and developmental abnormalities, cancer and other disorders.

Eligibility: A university, college, hospital, State or local government, nonprofit research institution, or profit organizations.

Range of Financial Assistance: $8,000 to $965,000.

Contact: Associate Director for Extramural Program, National Institute of Environmental Health Sciences, PO Box 12233, Research Triangle Park, NC 27709/919-541-7723.

Biomedical Research Support and Development

Objectives: To strengthen, balance, and stabilize Public Health Service-supported biomedical and behavioral research.

Eligibility: Health professional schools, other academic institutions, non-federal hospitals, state and municipal health agencies, and other nonprofit, nonacademic research organizations engaged in health-related research.

Range of Financial Assistance: Not specified.

Contact: Biomedical Research Support Program, Division of Research Resources, NIH, Department of Health and Human Services, Room 5B3, Bethesda, MD 20205/301-496-6743.

Biometry and Risk Estimation

Objectives: To conduct a broad scale effort in biometry and risk estimation.

Eligibility: A university, college, hospital, State or local government, nonprofit research institution, or profit organization.

Range of Financial Assistance: $49,000 to $1,923,000.

Contact: Associate Director for Extramural Program, National Institute of Environmental Health Sciences, PO Box 12233, Research Triangle Park, NC 27709/919-541-7723.

Biotechnology Research

Objectives: To assist in developing and sustaining sophisticated research, and biomedical engineering resources.

Eligibility: Public or nonprofit private institutions of higher education, hospitals, and other private, nonprofit institutions with programs of biomedical research, local governments.

Range of Financial Assistance: $10,400 to $1,226,165.

Contact: Biotechnology Resources Branch, Division of Research Resources, NIH, Department of Health and Human Services, Building 31, Room 5B41, Bethesda, MD 20205/301-496-5411.

Blood Diseases and Resources Research

Objectives: To further the development of blood resources and coordinate national and regional activities of blood centers, and to promote research on blood diseases, including sickle cell disease, and develop new scientists for such research.

Eligibility: Any nonprofit organization engaged in biomedical research, individuals, and local governments.

Range of Financial Assistance: $4,712 to $1,962,250.

Contact: Director, Division of Blood Diseases, National Heart, Lung, and Blood Institute, Department of Health and Human Services, Bethesda, MD 20205/301-496-4868.

Cancer Biology Research

Objectives: To provide fundamental information on the cause and nature of cancer in humans in order to develop better methods of prevention, detection, diagnosis, and treatment of neoplastic diseases.

Eligibility: Universities, colleges, hospitals, public agencies or nonprofit research institutions.

Range of Financial Assistance: $9,000 to $1,505,000.

Contact: Chief, Extramural Research Program, Division of Cancer Biology and Diagnosis, National Cancer Institute, Westwood 8A18, Bethesda, MD 20205/301-496-3252.

Cancer Cause and Prevention Research

Objectives: Identification of those factors which cause cancer in humans and the development of mechanisms for preventing cancer.

Eligibility: Universities, colleges, hospitals, public agencies, or nonprofit research institutions, individuals.

Range of Financial Assistance: $4,000 to $3,610,000.

Contact: Division of Cancer Resources and Centers, National Cancer Institute, Department of Health and Human Services, Bethesda, MD 20205/301-496-6618.

Cancer Centers Support

Objectives: To assist in the development and maintenance of multidisciplinary cancer centers for laboratory and clinical research, as well as training and demonstration of the latest diagnostic and treatment techniques.

Eligibility: Universities, colleges, hospitals, public agencies, or nonprofit research institutions.

Range of Financial Assistance: $151,000 to $6,546,000.

Contact: Chief, Cancer Centers Branch, National Cancer Insititute, Department of Health and Human Services, 8300 Colesville Rd, Silver Spring, MD 20910/301-427-8663.

Cancer—Construction

Objectives: To provide new, and expand existing, cancer research facilities and to achieve a geographic distribution of cancer research facilities and centers.

Eligibility: Universities, colleges, hospitals, public agencies or nonprofit research institutions.

Range of Financial Assistance: $146,000 to $640,000.

Contact: Research Facilities Branch, 8300 Colesville Rd, Silver Spring, MD 20910/301-427-8804.

Cancer Control

Objectives: To establish and support demonstration, education and other programs for the detection, diagnosis, prevention, and treatment of cancer and for rehabilitation and counseling related to cancer.

Eligibility: Universities, colleges, hospitals, public agencies, or nonprofit research institutions.

Range of Financial Assistance: $13,000 to $1,503,000.

Contact: Grants Inquiry Office, Division of Research Grants, National Cancer Institute, Department of Health and Human Services, 5333 Westbard Ave, Bethesda, MD 20205/301-496-6616.

Cancer Detection and Diagnosis Research

Objectives: To identify cancer in patients early and precisely enough so that the latest methods of treatment can be applied toward control of the disease.

Eligibility: Universities, colleges, hospitals, public agencies, or nonprofit research institutions, state and local governments.

Range of Financial Assistance: $16,000 to $939,000.

Contact: Extramural Research Program Division of Cancer Research Resources and Centers, National Cancer Institute, Department of Health and Human Services, Room 8A18, Bethesda, MD 20205/301-496-3252.

Cancer Research Manpower

Objectives: To support nonprofit institutions in providing biomedical training opportunities for individuals interested in careers in basic and clinical research in important areas of the National Cancer Program.

Eligibility: Nonprofit organizations, state and local governments.

Range of Financial Assistance: $16,000 to $425,000.

Contact: Chief, Research Manpower Branch, Division of Cancer Resources and Centers, National Cancer Institute, Department of Health and Human Services, Blair 727, Bethesda, MD 20205/301-427-8898.

Cancer Treatment Research

Objectives: To develop the means to cure as many cancer patients as possible and to maintain maximum control of the cancerous process.

Eligibility: Universities, colleges, hospitals, public agencies, or nonprofit research institutions, individuals.

Range of Financial Assitance: $2,000 to $2,819,000.

Contact: Chief, Division of Cancer Treatment, National Cancer Institute, Department of Health and Human Services, Room 8A18, Bethesda, MD 20205/301-496-6404.

Caries Research

Objectives: To develop methods to eliminate dental caries as a major health problem.

Eligibility: Scientists at universities, hospitals, laboratories, and other public or private nonprofit institutions.

Range of Financial Assistance: $10,000 to $300,000.

Contact: Grants and NRSA's, Extramural Programs, National Institute of Dental Research, NIH, Department of Health and Human Services, Bethesda, MD 20205/301-496-7884.

Cataract Research

Objectives: To support research and training to identify the causes of this disorder and develop methods for its prevention and improved treatment.

Eligibility: Universities, colleges, hospitals, laboratories, federal institutions and other public or private nonprofit domestic institutions including state and local units of governments, individuals.

Range of Financial Assistance: $10,000 to $300,000.

Contact: Director for Extramural and Collaborative Programs, National Eye Institute, NIH, Department of Health and Human Services, Bethesda, MD 20205/301-496-4903.

Cellular and Molecular Basis of Disease Research

Objectives: To support research on the structure and function of cells and their component parts, with the expectation that a greater understanding of these aspects will contribute to the ultimate control of human disease.

Eligibility: Public or private nonprofit universities, colleges, hospitals, laboratories, or other institutions, including state and local units of government, and individuals.

Range of Financial Assistance: $16,380 to $871,021.

Contact: Director, Cellular and Molecular Basis of Disease, National Institute of General Medical Sciences, NIH, Department of Health and Human Services, Bethesda, MD 20205/301-496-7021.

Characterization of Environmental Health Hazards

Objectives: To identify and measure the biological, chemical, and physical factors that are hazardous in nature as an essential first step towards establishing the relationship between different levels of exposure to these factors and probable injury.

Eligibility: A university, college, hospital, State or local government, nonprofit research institution, or profit organizations.

Range of Financial Assistance: $14,000 to $838,000.

Contact: Associate Director for Extramural Program, National Institute of Environmental Health Sciences, PO Box 12233, Research Triangle Park, NC 27709/919-541-7723.

Child Abuse and Neglect Prevention and Treatment

Objectives: To assist state, local, and voluntary agencies and organizations in developing programs that will prevent, identify, and treat child abuse and neglect.

Eligibility: State or local governments or other nonprofit institutions of higher learning, and private nonprofit agencies or organizations engaged in related activities.

Range of Financial Assistance: $30,000 to $300,000.

Contact: National Center on Child Abuse and Neglect, Children's Bureau, Department of Health and Human Services, P.O. Box 1182, Washington, DC 20013/202-245-2856.

Child Support Enforcement

Objectives: To enforce the support obligations of absent parents to their children, locate absent parents, establish paternity, and obtain child support.

Eligibility: State child support agencies.

Range of Financial Assistance: $172,603 to $80,017,155.

Contact: Office of Child Support Enforcement, Department of Health and Human Services, 6110 Executive Blvd., Rockville, MD 20852/301-443-4442.

Child Welfare Research and Demonstration

Objectives: To provide financial support for research demonstration projects in the area of child and family development and welfare.

Eligibility: Grants are available to state and local governments, other nonprofit institutions of higher learning, and nonprofit agencies or organizations engaged in research or child welfare activities. Contracts are available to public or private organizations.

Range of Financial Assistance: $50,000 to $500,000.

Contact: Grants Coordinator, Research and Evaluation Division, Administration for Children, Youth and Families, Office of Human Development Services, Department of Health and Human Services, P.O. Box 1182, Washington, DC 20013/202-755-7755.

Child Welfare Service—State Grants

Objectives: To establish, extend, and strengthen services provided by state and local public welfare programs to prevent the neglect, abuse, exploitation or delinquency of children.

Eligibility: State agencies.

Range of Financial Assistance: $112,530 to $4,420,291.

Contact: Children's Bureau, Administration for Children, Youth and Families, office of Human Development Services, Department of Health and Human Services, P.O. Box 1182, Washington, DC 20013/202-755-7418.

Child Welfare Services Training Grants

Objectives: To develop and maintain an adequate supply of qualified and trained personnel for the field of services to children and their families, and to improve educational programs and resources for preparing personnel to work in this field.

Eligibility: Nonprofit organizations and local governments.

Range of Financial Assistance: Averaging $50,000.

Contact: Children's Bureau, Department of Health and Human Services, P.O. Box 1182, Washington, DC 20013/202-755-7418.

Childhood Immunization Grants

Objective: To assist states and communities in establishing and maintaining immunization programs for the control of vaccine-preventable diseases of childhood.

Eligibility: States and local governments, nonprofit organizations.

Range of Financial Assistance: $10,000 to $1,363,000.

Contact: Director, Center for Disease Control, PHS, Department of Health and Human Services, 1600 Clifton Rd., N.E. Atlanta, GA 30333/404-329-3291.

Clinical Research

Objectives: To create and sustain institutional resources in which clinical investigators can observe and study human disease.

Eligibility: Public or nonprofit medical schools, research hospitals, and other medical institutions capable of carrying out well-designed studies working with patients in any preclinical or clinical science.

Range of Financial Assistance: $287,461 to $2,338,014.

Contact: General Clinical Research Centers Program Branch, Division of Research Resources, National Institute of Health, Department of Health and Human Services, Room 5B59, Building 31, Bethesda, MD 20205/301-496-6595.

Coal Miners Respiratory Impairment Treatment Clinics and Services

Objectives: To develop where there are significant numbers of active and inactive miners high quality patient-oriented systems of health care.

Eligibility: State and local government agencies; private nonprofit agencies.

Range of Financial Assistance: $30,000 to $150,000.

Contact: Director, Regional Commissions Health Programs, Health Services Administration, Bureau of Community Health Services, Department of Health and Human Services, 5600 Fishers Lane, Room 7A-55, Rockville, MD 20857/301-443-2270.

Community Health Centers

Objectives: To support the development and operation of community health centers that provide primary, supplemental, and environmental health services to medically underserved populations.

Eligibility: State and local governments, and public or nonprofit private agencies, institutions, or organizations.

Range of Financial Assistance: $25,000 to $4,000,000.

Contact: Associate Bureau Director for Community Health Centers, Bureau of Community Health Service, Department of Health and Human Services, 5600 Fishers Lane, Room 7A-55, Rockville, MD 20857/301-443-2260.

Community Services Block Grant

Objectives: To provide a range of services and activities having a measurable and potential major impact on causes of poverty in the community or those areas of the community where poverty is a particularly acute problem.

Eligibility: States.

Range of Financial Assistance: $123,225 to $29,346,400.

Contact: Director, Office of State and Project Assistance, Office of Community Services, 1200 19th Street, NW, Room 436A, Washington, DC 20506/202-254-7020.

Cooperative Agreements for State-Based Diabetes Control Programs

Objectives: The purpose of the cooperative program is to improve the quality of life and effectiveness of health services for diabetes.

Eligibility: Eligible applicants are the offical state health agencies of the United States, the District of Columbia, the Commonwealth of Puerto Rico, the Virgin Islands, Guam, Trust Territory of the Pacific Islands, the Commonwealth of the Northern Marianna Islands, and American Samoa.

Range of Financial Assistance: $57,000 to $270,000.

Contact: Director, Centers for Disease Control, PHS, DHHS, Atlanta, GA 30333/404-329-3291.

Corneal Diseases Research

Objectives: To reduce the impact of this cause of visual disability through improved methods of treatment, prevention, and diagnosis.

Eligibility: Universities, colleges, hospitals, laboratories, federal institutions and other public or private nonprofit domestic institutions including state and local units of government, individuals.

Range of Financial Assistance: $6,000 to $300,000.

Contact: Director for Extramural and Collaborative Programs, National Eye Institute, NIH, Department of Health and Human Services, Bethesda, MD 20205/301-496-4903.

Craniofacial Anomalies Research

Objectives: To acquire new knowledge for the prevention and treatment of malformations such as cleft lip/palate, acquired malformations from surgery or accident, and malocclusion of teeth and jaws.

Eligibility: Scientists at universities, hospitals, laboratories, and other public or private nonprofit institutions.

Range of Financial Assistance: $5,000 to $300,000.

Contact: Grants and NRSA's, Extramural Programs, National Institute of Dental Research, NIH, Department of Health and Human Services, Bethesda, MD 20205/301-496-7807.

Dental Research Institutes

Objectives: To develop institutes or centers that focus on the problems of oral health.

Eligibility: Nonprofit organizations, state and local governments.

Range of Financial Assistance: $1,000,000 to $1,500,000.

Contact: Extramural Programs, National Institute of Dental Research, Department of Health and Human Services, Bethesda, MD 20205/301-496-7658.

Developmental Disabilities—Basic Support and Advocacy Grants

Objectives: To assist states in the provision of comprehensive services for developmentally disabled persons.

Eligibility: Designated state agencies.

Range of Financial Assistance: $30,000 to $3,581,000.

Contact: Director, Bureau of Developmental Disabilities, Office of Human Development Services, Department of Health and Human Services Building, Washington, DC 20201/202-245-2890.

Developmental Disabilities—Special Projects

Objectives: To provide support for projects to improve the quality of services to the developmentally disabled, and public awareness and informational programs.

Eligibility: States, political subdivisions of states, other public agencies, and nonprofit organizations.

Range of Financial Assistance: $25,000 to $155,238.

Contact: Deputy Assistant Secretary, Office of Human Development, Department of Health and Human Services, Washington, DC 20201/202-245-1961.

Developmental Disabilities—University-Affiliated Facilities

Objectives: To assist with the cost of administration and operation of facilities for providing interdisciplinary training for personnel concerned with developmental disabilities, demonstrations of exemplary services related to the developmentally disabled and of findings related to their provision.

Eligibility: Public or nonprofit facilities associated with a college or university.

Range of Financial Assistance: $150,000 to $348,211.

Contact: Commissioner, Rehabilitation Services Administration, Office of Human Development Services, Department of Health and Human Services, Washington, DC 20201/202-245-1961.

Diabetes, Endocrinology and Metabolism Research

Objectives: To support basic laboratory research and extramural clinical investigations and to provide postdoctoral biomedical research training for individuals interested in careers in health sciences and related fields.

Eligibility: Individuals and public and nonprofit institutions who propose to establish, expand, and improve research activities in health sciences and related fields.

Range of Financial Assistance: $25,000 to $1,448,191.

Contact: Associate Director for Extramural Program Activities, National Institute of Arthritis, Metabolism, and Digestive Diseases, NIH, Department of Health and Human Services, Westwood Building, Room 607A, Bethesda, MD 20205/301-496-7277.

Digestive Diseases and Nutrition Research

Objectives: To support basic laboratory research and extramural clinical investigations and to provide postdoctoral biomedical research training for individuals interested in careers in health sciences and related fields.

Eligibility: Individuals and public and non-profit institutions who propose to establish, expand and improve research activities in health sciences and related fields.

Range of Financial Assistance: $25,000 to $1,069,000.

Contact: Associate Director for Extramural Program Activities, National Institute of Arthritis, Metabolism, and Digestive Diseases, Department of Health and Human Services, Westwood Building, Room 603A, Bethesda, MD 20205/301-496-7277.

Drug Abuse National Research Service Awards for Research Training

Objectives: To provide support to individuals for predoctoral and postdoctoral research training in specified drug related areas, and to enable nonprofit institutions to develop research training opportunities for such individuals.

Eligibility: Support is provided for predoctoral and postdoctoral academic and research training only, in health and health related areas which are specified by the National Institute on Drug Abuse and include both basic and applied studies in all of the life sciences relevant to drug abuse, as well as research on behavioral, societal factors and the epidemiology of drug use and abuse and special training in experimental design and methodology.

Range of Financial Assistance: Not specified.

Contact: Division of Training, Alcohol, Drug Abuse and Mental Health Administration, National Institute on Drug Abuse, Department of Health and Human Services. 5600 Fishers Lane, Rockville, MD 20857/301-443-1887.

Drug Abuse Research Programs

Objectives: To develop new approaches to the control and prevention of narcotic addiction and drug abuse through basic, clinical, and applied research.

Eligibility: State, local or regional government agencies, universities, colleges, hospitals, academic or research institutions and other organizations.

Range of Financial Assistance: $12,000 to $401,000.

Contact: Division of Research, Alcohol, Drug Abuse and Mental Health Administration, National Institute on Drug Abuse, Public Health Service, Department of Health and Human Services, 5600 Fishers Lane, Room 936, Rockville, MD 20857/301-443-1887.

Drug Abuse Research Scientist Development and Research Scientist Awards

Objectives: To provide support for research relating to the problems of narcotic addiction and drug abuse and to raise the level of competence and to increase the number of individuals engaged in such research.

Eligibility: Research Scientist Development and Research Scientist Awards are made on behalf of individuals to research centers, medical schools, community mental health centers and research institutes.

Range of Financial Assistance: $24,000 to $44,000.

Contact: Division of Research, Alcohol, Drug Abuse and Mental Health Administration, National Institute on Drug Abuse, Public Health Service, Department of Health and Human Services, 5600 Fishers Lane, Room 936, Rockville, MD 20857/301-443-1887.

Resource and Manpower Development

Objectives: To provide support for multidisciplinary research and training on environmental health problems in environmental health sciences centers and marine and freshwater biomedical centers.

Eligibility: Nonprofit research institutions, state and local governments.

Range of Financial Assistance: $135,000 to $2,034,000.

Contact: Director for Extramural Programs, National Institute of Environmental Health Sciences, Department of Health and Human Services, P.O. Box 12233, Research Triangle Park, NC 27709/919-541-7723.

Faculty Development in Family Medicine

Objectives: To increase the supply of physician faculty available to teach in family medicine programs and to enhance the pedagogical skills of faculty currently teaching in family medicine.

Eligibility: Public or nonprofit private hospitals, accredited public or nonprofit schools of medicine or of osteopathy, or other public or private nonprofit entities.

Range of Financial Assistance: $45,643 to $371,964.

Contact: Director, Division of Medicine, Department of Health and Human Services, Parklawn Bldg, Room 4C-25, 5600 Fishers Lane, Rockville, MD 20857/301-436-6418.

Family Medicine Departments

Objectives: To assist in establishing, maintaining or improving family medicine academic adminstrative units, to provide clinical instruction in family medicine.

Eligibility: Applicants must be an accredited public or nonprofit private school of medicine or osteopathic medicine.

Range of Financial Assistance: $62,194 to $294,874.

Contact: Director, Division of Medicine, BHPr, HRSA, PHS, DHHS, Parklawn Building, Room 4C25, 5600 Fishers Lane, Rockville, MD 20857/ 301-443-6190.

Family Planning Projects

Objectives: To provide educational, medical and social services to enable individuals to determine freely the number and spacing of their children, to promote the health of mothers and children, and to help reduce maternal and infant mortality.

Eligibility: City, county, and state governments or nonprofit private entities.

Range of Financial Assistance: $20,000 to $1,000,000.

Contact: Assistant Secretary for Population Affairs, HHS, Room 725-H, 200 Independence Ave. S.W., Washington, DC 20201/202-472-9093.

Family Planning Services

Objectives: To provide job-specified training for personnel to improve the delivery of family planning services.

Eligibility: City, county, and state governments or nonprofit private entitites.

Range of Financial Assistance: $15,000 to $600,000.

Contact: Office of Population Affairs, DHHS, Room 725-H, 200 Independence Ave. S.W., Washington, DC 20201/301-472-9093.

Family Planning Services—Delivery Improvement Research Grants

Objectives: To provide techniques for service delivery improvement through demonstration projects, operational research, or technology development and technical assistance.

Eligibility: Public nonprofit entities.

Range of Financial Assistance: $40,000 to $250,000.

Contact: Office of Population Affairs, DHHS, Room 725-H, HH Humphrey Bldg., 200 Independence Ave. S.W., Washington, DC 20205/202-472-9093.

Food and Drug Administration Research

Objectives: To establish, expand, and improve research activities concerned with foods, food additives, shellfish sanitation, poison control, drug and cosmetic hazards, human and veterinary drugs, medical devices and diagnostic products, biologics, and radiation-emitting devices and materials.

Eligibility: Colleges, universities, nonprofit institutions and state and local governments.

Range of Financial Assistance: $50,000 to $500,000.

Contact: Chief, Grants Management Branch, HFA-520, Department of Health and Human Services, 5600 Fishers Lane, Room 12A27, Rockville, MD 20857/301-443-6170.

Foster Care—Title IV-E

Objectives: To provide Federal financial participation (FFP) in assistance on behalf of eligible children needing care away from their families (in foster care) who are in the placement and care of the State agency administering the program and to provide FFP in the cost of proper and efficient adminstrative and training costs.

Eligibility: Only States, the District of Columbia, Guam, The Northern Mariana Islands, Puerto Rico, and the Virgin Islands are eligible.

Range of Financial Assistance: $20,000 to $161,318,000.

Contact: Commission for Children, Youth and Familites, PO Box 1182, Washington, DC 20013/ 202-755-7762.

Genetics Research

Objectives: To support basic research aimed at the prevention, treatment, and control of genetic diseases in humans, including those multifactorial illnesses with a strong hereditary component.

Eligibility: Public or private nonprofit universities, colleges, hospitals, laboratories, or other institutions, including state and local units of government, or individuals.

Range of Financial Assistance: $16,380 to $891,065.

Contact: Program Director (Genetics), National Institute of General Medical Sciences, Department of Health and Human Services, Bethesda, MD 20205/301-496-7087.

Glaucoma Research

Objectives: To support research and training to determine the cause of glaucoma, develop techniques for prevention and detection of the disease, and improve methods of treatment.

Eligibility: Universities, colleges, hospitals, laboratories, federal institutions and other public or private nonprofit domestic institutions, including state and local units of government, individuals.

Range of Financial Assistance: $10,000 to $300,000.

Contact: Director of Extramural and Collaborative Programs, National Eye Institute, Department of Health and Human Services, Bethesda, MD 20205/301-496-4903.

Graduate Programs in Health Administration
Objectives: To support accredited graduate educational programs in health administration, hospital administration, and health planning.
Eligibility: Accredited public or nonprofit private educational entities.
Range of Financial Assistance: Not specified.
Contact: Grants Management Officer, Bureau of Health Professions, HRSA, 5600 Fishers Lane, Rockville, MD 20857/301-443-6915.

Graduate Training in Family Medicine
Objectives: To increase the number of physicians practicing family medicine.
Eligibility: Public and nonprofit private hospitals, accredited public nonprofit private schools of medicine or osteopathy, or nonprofit private health or educational entities.
Range of Financial Assistance: $18,843 to $442,341.
Contact: Director, Division of Medicine, Health Resources and Services Administration, Room 4C25, Parklawn Bldg., 5600 Fishers Lane, Rockville, MD 20857/301-443-6915.

Head Start
Objectives: To provide comprehensive health, educational, nutritional, social and other services primarily to economically disadvantaged preschool children and their families, and to involve parents in activities with their children so that the children will attain social competence.
Eligibility: Local government or private nonprofit agencies.
Range of Financial Assistance: $75,000 to $23 million.
Contact: Administration for Children, Youth and Families/Head Start Bureau, Office of Human Development Services, Department of Health and Human Services, P.O. Box 1182, Washington, DC 20013/202-755-7782.

Health Career Opportunity Program
Objectives: To identify, recruit, and select individuals from disadvantaged backgrounds for education and training in a health profession. To facilitate their entry into such a school and to provide counseling or other services designed to assist them to complete successfully their training.
Eligibility: Public or nonprofit health or educational entities.
Range of Financial Assistance: $13,244 to $528,000.
Contact: Grants Management Office, Bureau of Health Professions, Health Resources Administration, Department of Health and Human Services, 5600 Fishers Lane, Rockville, MD 20857/301-443-6915.

Health Financing Research, Demonstrations and Experiments
Objectives: To discover, test, demonstrate, and promote utilization of health care financing concepts which will provide service to the beneficiary population.
Eligibility: State and local governments, and nonprofit organizations.
Range of Financial Assistance: $25,000 to $1,000,000.
Contact: Office of Policy, Planning, and Research, Health Care Financing Administration, Department of Health and Human Services, 300 Independence Ave. S.W., Washington, DC 20201/202-472-7431.

Health Planning—Health Systems Agencies
Objectives: To provide for effective health resources planning at the area level to meet problems in health care delivery systems, maldistribution of health care facilities and manpower, and increasing cost of health care.
Eligibility: Private nonprofit corporation, single units of local government, or a regional planning body authorized to carry out health planning and resources development activities for its area.
Range of Financial Assistance: Beginning at $100,000.
Contact: Director, Bureau of Health Planning, Parklawn Building, 5600 Fishers Lane, Rockville, MD 20857/301-443-1993.

Health Professions—Capitation Grants
Objectives: To provide financial assistance to schools of medicine, osteopathy, dentistry, public health, veterinary medicine, optometry, pharmacy and podiatry for enrollment goals.
Eligibility: Public or nonprofit private accredited schools, or those that have reasonable assurance of accreditation.
Range of Financial Assistance: $66,650 to $377,872.
Contact: Grants Management Officer, Health Resources and Services Administration, Center Building, 5600 Fishers Lane, Rockville, MD 20857/301-443-1173.

Health Profession—Financial Distress Grants
Objectives: To assist schools of medicine, osteopathy, dentistry, optometry, pharmacy, podiatry, public health and veterinary medicine which are in serious financial distress to meet costs of operation, or which have special financial need to meet accreditation requirements or carry out appropriate operational, managerial and financial reforms.
Eligibility: Public or nonprofit private accredited schools or those that have reasonable assurance of accreditation.
Range of Financial Assistance: $433,000 to $5,506,000.

Contact: Bureau of Health Professions, Health Resources Administration, Room 8C-22, 5600 Fishers Lane, Rockville, MD 20857/301-443-6519.

Health Professions—Preparatory Scholarship Program for Indians

Objectives: To make scholarship grants to Indians for the purpose of completing compensatory preprofessional education in order to qualify for enrollment or re-enrollment in a health professions school.

Eligibility: Individuals.

Range of Financial Assistance: $5,000 to $12,000.

Contact: Office of Grants and Contracts, Indian Health Service, Health Services Administration, Public Health Service, Department of Health and Human Services, 5600 Fishers Lane, Rockville, MD 20857/301-443-5441.

Health Professions—Recruitment Program for Indians

Objectives: To identify Indians with a potential for education or training in the health professions and encourage and assist them to enroll in health or allied health professional schools.

Eligibility: Public or nonprofit health or educational entities or Indian tribes or tribal organizations.

Range of Financial Assistance: $42,170 to $200,000.

Contact: Office of Grants and Contracts, Indian Health Service, Health Services Administration, Public Health Service, Department of Health and Human Services, 5600 Fishers Lane, Room 6A29, Rockville, MD 20857/301-443-5204.

Health Professions—Scholarship Program for Indians

Objectives: To make scholarship grants to Indians and others for the purposes of completing health professional education. Upon completion grantees are required to fulfill an obligated service payback requirement.

Eligibility: Individuals.

Range of Financial Assistance: $7,000 to $14,000.

Contact: Office of Grants and Contracts, Indian Health Service, Health Services Administration, Public Health Service, Department of Health and Human Services, 5600 Fishers Lane, Rockville, MD 20857/301-443-5441.

Health Professions—Special Educational Initiatives

Objectives: To assist allied health professional education programs to prepare allied health personnel for appropriate expanded roles in health promotion and disease prevention and to develop prototypical regional resource centers focused on strengthening multidisciplinary training of health professionals in geriatric health care.

Eligibility: Any health profession, allied health profession, or nurse training institution, or any other public or nonprofit entity.

Range of Financial Assistance: Average award $217,940.

Contact: Health Resources and Services Administration, Public Health Service, Department of Health and Human Services, 5600 Fishers Lane, Rockville, MD 20857/301-443-6887.

Health Professions—Student Loans

Objectives: To increase educational opportunities for students in need of financial assistance to pursue a course of study in specified health professions by providing long-term, low-interest loans.

Eligibility: Accredited public or nonprofit schools of medicine, dentistry, osteopathy, optometry, podiatry, pharmacy, or veterinary medicine.

Range of Financial Assistance: $3,500 to $224,752.

Contact: Division of Student Assistance, Health Resources and Services Administration, Parklawn Bldg., Room 8-44, 5600 Fishers Lane, Rockville, MD 20857/301-443-1173.

Health Programs for Refugees

Objectives: To assist States and localities in providing health assessments to newly arrived refugees and in addressing refugee health problems of public health concern.

Eligibility: Official State health agencies and, in consultation with the State health agency, health agencies of political subdivisions of a State.

Range of Financial Assistance: $1,500 to $5,000,000.

Contact: Director, Centers for Disease Control, PHS, DHHS, Atlanta, GA 30333/404-329-3291.

Health Services Research and Development Grants

Objectives: To support research, development, demonstration and evaluation activities to develop new options for health services delivery policy, to test the assumptions on which current policies and delivery practices are based, and to develop the means for monitoring the performance of the health care system.

Eligibility: States, counties, cities, towns, political subdivisions, universities, hospitals, Native Americans and other public or nonprofit private agencies, institutions, or organizations and individuals.

Range of Financial Assistance: $2,678 to $380,128.

Contact: Public Health Service, Department of Health and Human Services, 5600 Fishers Lane, Rockville, MD 20857/301-443-4033.

Heart and Vascular Diseases Research

Objectives: To foster research, prevention, and education and control activities related to heart and vascular diseases.

Eligibility: Nonprofit organizations engaged in biomedical research, individuals, local governments.

Range of Financial Assistance: $8,300 to $5,023,784.

Contact: Division of Heart and Vascular Diseases, National Heart, Lung and Blood Institute, Department of Health and Human Services, Bethesda, MD 20205/301-496-2553.

Immunology, Allergic and Immunologic Diseases Research

Objectives: To assist public and private nonprofit institutions and individuals in establishing, expanding, and improving biomedical research and research training in allergic and immunologic diseases and related areas.

Eligibility: Universities, colleges, hospitals, laboratories, and other public or private nonprofit domestic institutions including state and local units of government, individuals.

Range of Financial Assistance: $2,000 to $791,148.

Contact: Grants Mangement Branch, National Institute of Allergy and Infectious Diseases, NIH, Department of Health and Human Services, Bethesda, MD 20205/301-496-7075.

Indian Health Services—Health Management Development Program

Objectives: To improve the health of American Indians and Alaskan Natives by providing a full range of curative, preventive and rehabilitative health services, including public health nursing, maternal and child health care, dental and nutrition services, psychiatric care and health education and to increase the Indian communities' capacity to man and manage their own health programs.

Eligibility: Federally recognized tribes and tribal organizations.

Range of Financial Assistance: $100,000 to $2,000,000.

Contact: Director, Indian Health Service, Department of Health and Human Services, 5600 Fishers Lane, Rockville, MD 20857/301-443-5204.

Kidney Diseases, Urology and Hematology Research

Objectives: To support basic laboratory research and extramural clinical investigations and to provide postdoctoral biomedical research training for individuals interested in careers in health sciences and fields related to these programs.

Eligibility: Individuals and public and nonprofit institutions.

Range of Financial Assistance: $25,000 to $650,000.

Contact: Associate Director for Extramural Program Activities, National Institute of Arthritis, Metabolism and Digestive Diseases, NIH, Department of Health and Human Services, Westwood

Building, Room 603A, Bethesda, MD 20205/301-496-7277.

Laboratory Animal Sciences and Primate Research.

Objectives: To provide animal resources with which the biomedical scientist can develop knowledge for prevention and control of disease in man through experimentation with animal models.

Eligibility: Public or nonprofit private institutions of higher education, hospitals, and other private, nonprofit institutions.

Range of Financial Assistance: $2,247,468 to $3,504,063.

Contact: Animal Resources Branch, Division of Research Resources, NIH, Department of Health and Human Services, Building 31, Room 5B59, Bethesda, MD 20205/301-496-5175.

Low-Income Home Energy Assistance

Objectives: To make funds available to States and other jurisdictions to assist eligible households to meet the costs of home energy.

Eligibility: All States, the District of Columbia, Indian Tribal governments which request direct funding, Puerto Rico, the Virgin Islands, Guam, American Samoa, Northern Mariana Islands and the Trust Territories of the Pacific Islands may receive direct grants.

Range of Financial Assistance: The average assistance for heating costs was about $200 nationally.

Contact: Office of Family Assistance, Office of Energy Assistance, Social Security Administration, Department of Health and Human Services, Transpoint Building, 2100 Second Street, S.W., Washington, DC 20201/202-245-2030.

Lung Diseases Research

Objectives: To use available knowledge and technology to solve specific disease problems of the lungs, to promote further studies on the structure and function of the lung, and to improve prevention and treatment of lung disease.

Eligibility: Nonprofit organizations engaged in biomedical research may apply for grant or contract support. Institutions or companies organized for profit may apply for contracts only. An individual may qualify for a research grant if he or she has adequate facilities in which to perform the research.

Range of Financial Assistance: $5,000 to $1,277,359.

Contact: Director, Division of Lung Diseases, National Heart, Lung, and Blood Institute, Department of Health and Human Services, Bethesda, MD 20205/301-496-7208.

Maternal and Child Health Federal Consolidated Programs

Objectives: To carry out special projects of regional and national significance, training, and research; genetic disease testing, counseling, and information development and dissemination programs; and comprehensive hemophilia diagnostic and treatment centers.

Eligibility: Training grants may be made to public ot nonprofit private institutions of higher learning.

Range of Financial Assistance: $50,000 to $1,000,000.

Contact: Division for Maternal and Child Health, Health Resources and Services Administration, Department of Health and Human Services, Room 6-05, Parklawn Building, 56 Fishers Lane, Rockville, MD 20857/301-443-2170.

Maternal and Child Health Services Block Grant

Objectives: To enable States to maintain and strengthen their leadership in planning, promoting, coordinating and evaluating health care for mothers and children and in providing health services for mothers and children who do not have access to adequate health care.

Eligibility: Formula Grants are available to State Health Agencies.

Range of Financial Assistance: $300,000 to $25,000,000.

Contact: Division of Maternal and Child Health, Health Resources and Services Administration, Department of Health and Human Services, Room 6-05, Parklawn Building, 5600 Fishers Lane, Rockville, MD 20857/301-443-2170.

Medical Assistance Program

Objectives: To provide financial assistance to states for payments of Medical Assistance on behalf of cash assistance recipients and, in certain states, on behalf of other individuals, who, except for income and resources, would be eligibile for cash assistance.

Eligibility: State and local welfare agencies operating under an Health and Human Services-approved (Medicaid) state plan and complying with all federal regulations governing aid and medical assistance to the needy.

Range of Financial Assistance: $48 million to $3,754,726,000.

Contact: Local Social Welfare office, or Health Care Financing Administration, Department of Health and Human Services, Meadows East Bldg, 6300 Security Blvd., Baltimore, MD 21207/301-594-9000.

Medical Library Assistance

Objectives: To improve health information services by providing funds to train professional library personnel, strengthen library resources, support biomedical publications, and conduct research in ways of improving information transfer. In addition, funds provide a network of regional medical libraries with the necessary resources and services to provide backup support for local medical libraries.

Eligibility: Public or private nonprofit institutions which maintain or plan to establish a collection or provide services to clientele in the health professions.

Range of Financial Assistance: $4,000 to $200,000.

Contact: Extramural Programs, National Library of Medicine, Department of Health and Human Services, Bethesda, MD 20209/301-496-6131.

Mental Health—Clinical or Service-Related Training Grants

Objectives: To maintain the existing capacity of training institutions to meet mental health manpower needs, while relating the types of personnel trained more closely to service priorities and manpower requirements.

Eligibility: Public or private nonprofit institutions and organizations, and state and local government agencies.

Range of Financial Assistance: $4968 to $346,536.

Contact: Director, Division of Manpower and Training Programs, National Institute of Mental Health, Department of Health and Human Services, 5600 Fishers Lane, Rockville, MD 20857/301-443-4257.

Mental Health—Disaster Assistance and Emergency Mental Health

Objectives: To provide supplemental emergency mental health counseling to individuals affected by major disasters, including the training of volunteers to provide such counseling.

Eligibility: State, local or nonprofit agencies as recommended by the state governor and accepted by the Secretary.

Range of Financial Assistance: $80,000 to $100,000.

Contact: Mental Health Disaster Assistance Section, National Institute of Mental Health, Department of Health and Human Services, 5600 Fishers Lane, Rockville, MD 20857/301-443-1910.

Mental Health—National Research Service Awards for Research Training

Objectives: To provide support to individuals for predoctoral and postdoctoral research training in specified mental health related areas, and to enable nonprofit institutions to develop research training opportunities for individuals interested in careers in a particular specified mental health related field.

Eligibility: Support is provided for predoctoral and postdoctoral academic and research training only, in health and health-related priority areas which are specified by the National Institute of

Mental Health and includes child mental health, depression and suicide; schizophrenia; brain and behavior; psychoactive drugs, crime and delinquency; aging; minorities; program evaluation and mental health services management.

Range of Financial Assistance: grants average $5,040.

Contact: National Institute of Mental Health, Divison of Manpower and Training Programs, Department of Health and Human Services, 5600 Fishers Lane, Rockville, MD 20857/301-443-3533.

Mental Health—Research Grants

Objectives: To develop new knowledge and approaches to the diagnosis, treatment, control and prevention of mental diseases in humans through basic, clinical, and applied research.

Eligibility: Investigators affiliated with public or nonprofit private agencies, including state, local, or regional government agencies, universities, colleges, hospitals, academic or research institutions, and other organizations.

Range of Financial Assistance: $15,000 to $450,000.

Contact: Director, Division of Extramural Research Programs, National Institute of Mental Health, Department of Health and Human Services, 5600 Fishers Lane, Rockville, MD 20857/301-443-3563.

Mental Health—Research Scientists Development and Research Scientist Awards

Objectives: To provide support for research relating to the problems of mental illness and mental health and to raise the level of competence and to increase the number of individuals engaged in such research.

Eligibility: Research centers, medical schools, departments of psychiatry, psychiatric hospitals, community mental health centers, research institutes with mental health programs and behavioral sciences institutes with mental health research programs, on behalf of individuals.

Range of Financial Assistance: $15,000 to $39,852.

Contact: Division of Extramural Research Programs, National Institute of Mental Health, Department of Health and Human Services, 5600 Fishers Lane, Room 10-104, Rockville, MD 20857/301-443-4347.

Microbiology and Infectious Diseases Research

Objectives: To establish, expand, and improve biomedical research and research training in infectious diseases and related areas and to conduct developmental research, produce and test research materials, and provide research services programs in infectious diseases.

Eligibility: Universities, colleges, hospitals, laboratories and other public or private nonprofit domestic institutions, including state and local units of government, individuals.

Range of Financial Assistance: $960 to $517,823.

Contact: Grants Management Branch, National Institute of Allergy and Infectious Diseases, NIH, Department of Health and Human Services, Bethesda, MD 20205/301-496-7075.

Migrant Health Centers Grants

Objectives: To support the development and operation of migrant health centers and projects which provide primary ambulatory and in-patient, supplemental and environmental health services which are accessible to migrant and seasonal farm workers and their families.

Eligibility: Public or nonprofit private entities particularly community-based organizations which are representative of the populations to be served.

Range of Financial Assistance: $30,000 to $1,250,000.

Contact: Associate Bureau Director for Migrant Health, Bureau of Community Health Services, Department of Health and Human Services, 5600 Fishers Lane, Room 7A55, Rockville, MD 20857/301-443-1153.

Minority Access to Research Careers

Objectives: To assist minority institutions to train greater numbers of scientists and teachers in health related fields, increase the number of minority students who can compete successfully for entry into graduate programs in biomedical science fields.

Eligibility: Public or private nonprofit universities, colleges, hospitals, laboratories, or other institutions, including state or local units of government, or individuals.

Range of Financial Assistance: $9,040 to $232,197.

Contact: Program Director (MARC Program), National Institute of General Medical Sciences, NIH, Department of Health and Human Services, Bethesda, MD 20205/301-496-7941.

Minority Biomedical Research Support

Objectives: To increase the numbers of ethnic minority faculty, students, and investigators engaged in biomedical research and to broaden the opportunities for participation in biomedical research of ethnic minority faculty, students and investigators.

Eligibility: Four-year colleges, universities, and health professional schools with over 50 percent minority enrollment, four-year institutions with significant but not necessarily over 50 percent minority enrollment, provided they have a history of encouragement and assistance to minorities; two-year colleges with 50 percent minority enrollment; and Indian tribal schools which have a recognized governing body and which perform substantial governmental functions.

Range of Financial Assistance: $100,000 to $1,000,000 per year for 3 years.

Contact: Minority Biomedical Support Program Branch, Division of Research Resources, NIH, Department of Health and Human Services, Bethesda, MD 20205/301-496-6743.

National Health Promotion

Objectives: To educate the public about environmental, occupational, societal and behavioral factors which affect health in order that individuals may make informed decisions about health related behavior.

Eligibility: Public or private nonprofit organizations.

Range of Financial Assistance: $30,000 to $75,000.

Contact: Program Management Officer, Office of Disease Prevention and Health Promotion, 2132, DHHS, 330 C Street, S.W., Washington, DC 20201/202-472-5370.

National Health Service Corps Scholarship Program

Objectives: To insure an adequate supply of physicians, dentists, and other health professionals for the National Health Service Corps for service in health manpower shortage areas in the United States.

Eligibility: Applicants must be accepted for, or enrolled in, an accredited educational institution, in a full-time course of study leading to a degree in medicine, osteopathy, dentistry, or other participating health professions; be eligible for, or hold, an appointment as a commissioned officer in the Regular or Reserve Corps of the Service or be eligible for selection for civil service employment; and submit application and signed contract to accept payment of a scholarship and to serve for the applicable period of obligated service in a health manpower shortage area.

Range of Financial Assistance: Average of $9,947.

Contact: National Health Service Corps Scholarship Program, Parklawn Building, Room 17A-31, 5600 Fishers Lane, Rockville, MD 20857/301-443-2320 (call collect).

Native American Programs—Research, Demonstration and Evaluation

Objectives: To promote the goal of economic and social self-sufficiency for American Indians, Native Hawaiians, and Alaskan Natives.

Eligibility: Governing bodies of Indian tribes, Alaskan Native villages, and regional corporations and other public or private nonprofit agencies.

Range of Financial Assistance: $10,000 to $185,000.

Contact: Adminstration for Native Americans, Department of Health and Human Services, 330 Independence Ave. S.W., Washington, DC 20201/202-245-7714.

Native American Programs—Training and Technical Assistance

Objectives: To promote the goal of economic and social self sufficiency for American Indians, Native Hawaiians, and Alaskan Natives.

Eligibility: Governing bodies of Indian tribes, Native Alaskan villages, and regional corporations; private organizations and other public or private agencies.

Range of Financial Assistance: $7,400 to $15,000.

Contact: Administration for Native Americans, Department of Health and Human Services, Room 5300, 300 Independence Ave. S.W., Washington, DC 20201/202-245-7714.

Neurological and Communicative Disorders and Stroke

Objectives: Clinical Research in the National Institute of Neurological and Communicative Disorders and Stroke is directed towards the solution of problems directly relevant to patients with neurological disorders or disorders of human communication such as deafness, speech and language.

Eligibility: Any public, private nonprofit, or profit making institution is eligible to apply.

Range of Financial Assistance: $16,000 to $1,576,000.

Contact: Extramural Activities Program, NINCDS,NIH, Federal Building, Room 1016, Bethesda, MD 20205/301-496-9248.

Nurse Practitioner Training Program and Nurse Practitioner Traineeships

Objectives: To educate registered nurses who will be qualified to provide primary health care.

Eligibility: State and local governments, public or nonprofit private schools of nursing, medicine, and public health, public or nonprofit private hospitals, and other public or nonprofit private entities.

Range of Financial Assistance: $3,725 to $88,112

Contact: Division of Nursing, 5600 Fishers Lane, 5C-26, Rockville, MD 20857/301-463-6670.

Nurse Training Improvement—Special Projects

Objectives: To help schools of nursing and other institutions improve the quality and availability of nursing education through projects for specified purposes, such as opportunities for individuals from disadvantaged backgrounds.

Eligibility: Public and nonprofit private schools of nursing and other public or nonprofit private entities.

Range of Financial Assistance: $7,142 to $233,064.

Contact: Division of Nursing, Health Resources and Services Administration, 5600 Fishers Lane, 5C-26, Rockville, MD 20857/301-436-6690.

Nursing Research Project Grants

Objectives: To support basic and applied research activities in nursing education, practice, and administration.

Eligibility: Nonprofit organizations or institutions, government agencies, and occasionally individuals.

Range of Financial Assistance: $11,878 to $394,649.

Contact: Division of Nursing, Health Resources Administration, Department of Health and Human Services, 5600 Fisher Lane, 5C-26, Rockville, MD 20857/301-436-6204.

Nursing Research Sevice Awards

Objectives: To prepare qualified professional nurses to conduct nursing research, collaborate in interdisciplinary research, and function as faculty in schools of nursing at graduate level.

Eligibility: Registered professional nurses with either a baccalaureate and/or a master's degree in nursing.

Range of Financial Assistance: $3,900 to $14,000.

Contact: Chief, Research Training Section, Division of Nursing, BHPR, HRSA Room 5C26 5600 Fisher Lane, Rockville, MD 20857/301-443-6915.

Nursing Student Loans

Objectives: To assist students in need of financial assistance to pursue a course of study in professional nursing education by providing long-term low-interest loans.

Eligibility: Public and nonprofit private schools of nursing that prepare students for practice as registered nurses, and that meet accreditation requirements as defined in the Nurse Training Act of 1975, local governments.

Range of Financial Assistance: $477 to $95,735.

Contact: Division of Student Assistance, Health Resources and Services Administration, Parklawn Building, Room 8-44, 5600 Fishers Lane, Rockville, MD 20857/301-443-1173.

Occupational Safety and Health Research Grants

Objectives: To understand the underlying characteristics of occupational safety and health problems and provide effective solutions in dealing with them.

Eligibility: Individuals, state or local governments, nonprofit organizations, state colleges or universities or public, private, junior or community colleges.

Range of Financial Assistance: $5,000 to $150,000.

Contact: Procurement and Grants Office, Center for Disease Control, Department of Health and Human Services, 1600 Clifton Rd, NE, Atlanta, GA 30333/404-262-6575.

Occupational Safety and Health Training Grants

Objectives: To develop specialized professional personnel with training in occupational medicine, nursing, industrial hygiene and safety.

Eligibility: State, local or private nonprofit institutions or agencies involved in training at technical, professional, or graduate level.

Range of Financial Assistance: $10,000 to $700,000.

Contact: Procurement and Grants Management Branch, Center for Disease Control, Department of Health and Human Services, 1600 Clifton Rd, NE, Atlanta, GA 30333/404-262-6575.

Pain Control and Behavioral Studies

Objectives: To increase knowledge concerning the nature, etiology, pathophysiology, diagnosis and treatment of oral pain problems, and to achieve greater utilization of behavioral sciences knowledge in dental and oral problems.

Eligibility: Scientists at universities, hospitals, laboratories, and other public or private nonprofit institutions.

Range of Financial Assistance: $5,000 to $300,000.

Contact: Grants and NRSA's, Extramural Programs, National Institute of Dental Research, NIH, Department of Health and Human Services, Bethesda, MD 20205/301-496-7491.

Periodontal Diseases Research

Objectives: To develop new knowledge which may lead to the prevention and eradication of periodontal diseases.

Eligibility: Scientists at universities, hospitals, laboratories, and other public or private nonprofit institutions.

Range of Financial Assistance: $10,000 to $600,000.

Contact: Grants and NRSA's, Extramural Programs, National Institute of Dental Research, NIH, Department of Health and Human Services, Bethesda, MD 20205/301-496-7784.

Pharmacological Sciences

Objectives: To improve medical therapy through increased knowledge of the mechanisms of drug action, and of ways to increase efficacy and safety and diminish toxicity.

Eligibility: Public or private nonprofit universities, colleges, hospitals, laboratories, or other institutions, including state and local units of government, or individuals.

Range of Financial Assistance: $16,380 to $1,517,625.

Contact: Program Director (Pharmacological Sciences) National Institute of General Medical Sciences, NIH, Department of Health and Human Services, Bethesda, MD 20205/301-496-7707.

Physiology and Biomedical Engineering

Objectives: To support basic research that applies concepts from mathematics, physics, and engineering to biological systems, uses engineering principles in the development of computers for patient monitoring, and is related to physiology, anesthesiology, trauma and burn studies, and related areas.

Eligibility: Public or private nonprofit universities, colleges, hospitals, laboratories, or other institutions, including states and local units of government, or individuals.

Range of Financial Assistance: $16,380 to $979,633.

Contact: Director (Physiology and Biomedical Engineering), National Institute of General Medical Sciences, NIH, Department of Health and Human Services, Bethesda, MD 20205/301-496-7891.

Population Research

Objectives: To seek solutions to the fundamental problems of the reproductive processes and develop and evaluate safer, more effective, and convenient contraceptives, and to understand how population dynamics affects the health and well-being of individuals and society.

Eligibility: Universities, colleges, medical, dental, and nursing schools, schools of public health, laboratories, hospitals, state and local health departments, other public or private nonprofit institutions, and individuals.

Range of Financial Assistance: $3,225 to $699,817.

Contact: Office of Grants and Contracts, National Institute of Child Health and Human Development, NIH, Department of Health and Human Services, Bethesda, MD 20205/301-496-5001.

Predoctoral Training in Family Medicine

Objectives: To assist schools of medicine and osteopathy in meeting the costs of projects to plan, develop, and operate or participate in professional predoctoral training programs in the field of family medicine.

Eligibility: Accredited public or private nonprofit schools of medicine or of osteopathy, state or local governments.

Range of Financial Assistance: $34,560 to $323,827.

Contact: Director, Division of Medicine, Department of Health and Human Services, Parklawn Bldg, Room 4C-25, 5600 Fishers Lane, Rockville, MD 20857/301-436-6418.

Preventive Health and Health Services Block Grant

Objectives: To provide States with resources for comprehensive preventive health services including: emergency medical services, health incentive activities, hypertension programs, rodent control, fluoridation programs, health education and risk reduction programs, home health services, and services for rape victims.

Eligibility: State governments and, in certain cases, Tribes or Tribal organizations within the States are eligible.

Range of Financial Assistance: $36,349 to $6,267,878.

Contact: Assistant to Director, Centers for Disease Control, Atlanta, GA 30333/404-329-3850.

Preventive Medicine Residence Training Grants

Objectives: To promote the post-graduate education of physicians in preventive medicine to advance the cause of health promotion and disease prevention.

Eligibility: Any accredited public or private school of medicine, osteopathy or public health.

Range of Financial Assistance: $3,310 to $90,056.

Contact: Director, Division of Medicine, Bureau of Health Professions, Health Resources and Services Administration, Parklawn Building, 5600 Fishers Lane, Rockville, MD 20857/301-443-6190.

Primary Care Block Grant

Objectives: To support and strengthen States' capacity to organize and deliver services through Community Health Centers, primary health in medically underserved areas.

Eligibility: Formula grants are available to States, U.S. Territories, and, under certain conditions, federally-recognized Indian Tribal Governments.

Range of Financial Assistance: Not specified.

Contact: Associate Director, Bureau of Health Care Delivery and Assistance, Health Resources and Services Administration, Room 7-05, Parklawn Building, 5600 Fishers Lane, Rockville, MD 20857/301-443-2380.

Professional Nurse Traineeships

Objectives: To prepare registered nurses as administrators, supervisors, teachers, nursing specialists, and nurse practitioners for positions in hospitals and related insititutions, public health agencies, schools of nursing, and other roles requiring advanced training.

Eligibility: Nonprofit institutions providing advanced nurse training, state and local governments.

Range of Financial Assistance: $8,799 to $609,502; students may receive stipends up to $5,040 plus tuition and other expenses.

Contact: Division of Nursing, Bureau of Health Professions, Public Health Service, Department of Health and Human Services, 3700 East-West Highway, Center Building, Room 3-50 Hyattsville, MD 20782/301-436-6681.

Professional Standards Review Organizations

Objectives: To insure that health care services and medical items for which payment may be made in whole or in part conform to appropriate professional standards and are delivered in the most effective, efficient, and economical manner.

Eligibility: Voluntary, nonprofit groups of local physicians organized into Professional Standard Review Organizations meeting the requirements of the Social Security Act as amended, or other public nonprofit private groups that the Secretary of Health and Human Services determines to be of sufficient professional competence and otherwise suitable.

Range of Financial Assistance: $118,222 to $773,071.

Contact: The Office of Professional Standards Review Organization, Standards and Quality Bureau, Health Care Financing Administration, Department of Health and Human Services, 1849 Gwynn Oak Avenue, Dogwood East Bldg, Baltimore, MD 21207/301-594-9207.

Project Grants and Cooperative Agreements for Tuberculosis Control Programs

Objectives: To assist State and local health agencies in carrying out tuberculosis control activities designed to prevent transmission of infection and disease.

Eligibility: Official public health agencies of State and local governments, including the District of Columbia, the Commonwealth of Puerto Rico, the Virgin Islands, Guam, the Trust Territory of the Pacific Islands, the Northern Mariana Islands, and American Samoa. Private individual or profit and private nonprofit agencies are not eligible.

Range of Financial Assistance: $30,000 to $500,000.

Contact: Chief, Grants Management Branch, Procurement and Grants Office, Centers for Disease Control, PHS, DHHS, 1600 Clifton Road, NE, Atlanta, GA 30333/404-262-6575.

Refugee Assistance—Voluntary Agency Programs

Objectives: To assist Soviet and other refugees to become self-supporting and independent members of American society, by providing grants funds to voluntary resettlement agencies currently resettling these refugees in the United States.

Eligibility: National voluntary resettlement agencies currently under contract to the U.S. Department of State to provide reception and initial placement services to the eligible recipient refugees.

Range of Financial Assistance: $100,000 to $2,000,000.

Contact: Office of Refugee Resettlement, Department of Health and Human Services, Switzer Building, 330 C St. N.W., Room 1332 Washington, DC 20201/202-245-0418.

Research for Mothers and Children

Objectives: To improve the health and well-being of mothers, children, and families, through study of the health problems of the period of life from conception through adolescence, centering on the major problems of pregnancy and infancy, developmental biology and nutrition, human learning and behavior, and mental retardation and developmental disabilities.

Eligibility: Universities, colleges, medical, dental and nursing schools, schools of public health, laboratories, hospitals, state and local health departments, other public or private nonprofit institutions, and individuals.

Range of Financial Assistance: $1,405 to $732,633.

Contact: Office of Grants and Contracts, National Institute of Child Health and Human Development, NIH, Department of Health and Human Services, Bethesda, MD 20205/301-496-5001.

Residency Training in General Internal Medicine and/or General Pediatrics

Objectives: To promote the graduate education of physicians who plan to enter the practice of general internal medicine or general pediatrics.

Eligibility: Public or nonprofit private schools of medicine and osteopathy only for approved residency training programs or a new program with provisional approval.

Range of Financial Assistance: $54,000 to $517,004.

Contact: Division of Medicine, Department of Health and Human Services, Parklawn Bldg, Room 4C25, 5600 Fishers Lane, Rockville, MD 20857/301-436-6418.

Residency Training in the General Practice of Dentistry

Objectives: To plan, develop, and operate an approved residency program in the general practice of dentistry.

Eligibility: Public or private nonprofit schools of dentistry or accredited postgraduate dental training institutions, state and local governments.

Range of Financial Assistance: $20,000 to $250,000.

Contact: Dental Health Branch, Division of Associated and Dental Health Professions, DHHS, Parklawn Bldg, 5600 Fishers Lane, Rockville, MD 20857/301-443-6832.

Restorative Materials Research

Objectives: To provide better dental care by fostering the development of improved materials and methods to restore lost oral tissues to normal form and function.

Eligibility: Scientists at universities, hospitals, laboratories, and other public or private nonprofit institutions.

Range of Financial Assistance: $5,000 to $300,000.

Contact: Grants and NRSA's, Extramural Programs, National Institute of Dental Research, NIH, Department of Health and Human Services, Bethesda, MD 20205/301-496-7491.

Retinal and Choroidal Diseases Research

Obejctives: To support research and training to study retinal function and to advance understanding of how the retina is damaged by diseases and to develop methods of prevention, early detection, and treatment.

Eligibility: Universities, colleges, hospitals, laboratories, federal institutions and other public or private nonprofit domestic institutions, including state and local units of government, individuals.

Range of Financial Assistance: $10,000 to $300,000.

Contact: Associate Director for Extramural and Collaborative Programs, National Eye Institute, NIH, Department of Health and Human Services, Bethesda, MD 20205/301-496-4903.

Runaway Youth

Objectives: To develop local facilities to address the immediate needs of runaway youth.

Eligibility: State and local governments, localities or nonprofit private agencies, or coordinated networks of such agencies.

Range of Financial Assistance: $25,000 to $75,000.

Contact: Youth Development Bureau, Administration for Children, Youth and Families, Office of Human Development Services, Department of Health and Human Services, Washington, DC 20201/202-755-0590.

Scholarships for First-Year Students of Exceptional Financial Need

Objectives: To make funds available to authorized health professions schools to award scholarships to full-time, first-year health professions students of exceptional financial need.

Eligibility: Health professions schools fully accredited by a recognized accreditation body or have reasonable first-year health professions students of exceptional financial need.

Range of Financial Assistance: Average $15,625 a year.

Contact: Student and Institutional Assistance Branch, Division of Manpower Training Support, Parklawn Bldg, DHHS, Room 8-44, 5600 Fishers Lane, Rockville, MD 20857/301-443-1173.

Social Services Block Grant

Objectives: To enable each State as far as practicable to furnish a variety of Social services best suited to the needs of the individuals residing in the State in the most efficient and effective method possible by using Federal block grant funds to provide services directed toward one of the five goals specified in the law.

Eligibilty: The 50 States, the District of Columbia, Puerto Rico, Guam, the Virgin Islands and the Northern Mariana Island.

Range of Financial Assistance: $82,759 to $249,402,791.

Contact: Director, Office of Policy Coordination and Review, Office of Human Development Services, 200 Independence Avenue, SW, Washington, DC 20201/202-245-7027.

Strabismus, Amblyopia, and Visual Processing

Objectives: To support laboratory and clinical investigations of the optic nerve and the development and functions of those activities of the brain and the eye muscles which make vision possible, and for the development of rehabilitation techniques and vision substitution devices.

Eligibility: Universities, colleges, hospitals, laboratories, federal institutions and other public or private nonprofit domestic institutions including state and local units of government, and individuals.

Range of Financial Assistance: $10,000 to $300,000.

Contact: Director for Extramural and Collaborative Programs, National Eye Institute, NIH, Department of Health and Human Services, Bethesda, MD 20205/301-496-4903.

Social Services Research and Demonstration

Objectives: To discover, test, demonstrate, and promote new social service concepts which will provide service to the dependent and vulnerable populations such as the poor, the aged, children and youth.

Eligibility: States and nonprofit organizations.

Range of Financial Assistance: $100,000 to $250,000.

Contact: Division of Research, Demonstration, and Evaluation, Administration for Public Services, Department of Health and Human Services, Room 732E, Washington, DC 20201/202-245-6233.

Soft Tissue Stomatology and Nutrition Research

Objectives: To develop new knowledge which may lead to improved treatment and/or prevention of oral soft tissue diseases and conditions.

Eligibility: Scientists at universities, hospitals, laboratories, and other public or private nonprofit institutions.

Range of Financial Assistance: $15,000 to $300,000.

Contact: Extramural Programs, National Institute of Dental Research, NIH, Department of Health and Human Services, Bethesda, MD 20205/301-496-7808.

Special Programs for the Aging—Title VI—Grants to Indian Tribes

Objectives: To promote the delivery of services to older Indians.

Eligibility: Federally recognized Indian tribal organizations which represent at least 75 Indians 60 years of age or older.

Range of Financial Assistance: $65,925 to $102,925.

Contact: Associate Commissioner, Office of State and Tribal Programs, Administration of Aging, Department of Health and Human Services, Washington, DC 20201/202-245-0011.

Special Programs for the Aging—Title IV— Training, Research and Discretionary Projects and Programs

Objectives: To provide adequately trained personnel in the field of aging, improve knowledge of the problems and needs of the elderly, and to demonstrate better ways of improving the quality of life for the elderly.

Eligibility: Grants may be made to any public or nonprofit private agency or organization or institution.

Range of Financial Assistance: $2,183 to $1,890,000.

Contact: Associate Commissioner, Office of Program Development, Administration of Aging, Department of Health and Human Services, Washington, DC 20201/202-245-0441.

State Health Care Providers Survey Certification

Objectives: To provide financial assistance to any state which is able and willing to determine through its state health agency or other appropriate state agency that providers of health care surveys are in compliance with regulatory health and safety standards and conditions of participation in Medicare and Medicaid programs.

Eligibility: The designated state agency performing licensure activities within the state health departments.

Range of Financial Assistance: $7,970 to $3,404,440.

Contact: Office of Standards and Certification, Health Standards and Quality Bureau, Health Care Financing Administration, Department of Health and Human Services, 1849 Gwynn Oak Ave., Dogwood East Building, Baltimore, MD 21207/301-597-2750.

State Health Planning and Development Agencies

Objectives: To provide support to the state health planning agencies conducting physical and mental health planning and development functions.

Range of Financial Assistance: $96,539 to $1,534,916.

Contact: Director, Bureau of Health Planning, Department of Health and Human Services, 5600 Fishers Lane, Rockville, MD 20857/301-443-1993.

State Medicaid Fraud Control Units

Objectives: To control fraud in the states' Medicaid program.

Eligibility: The single state agency which the Secretary certifies as meeting the requirements.

Range of Financial Assistance: Averaging $900,000 per year.

Contact: Division of State Fraud Control, DHHS, Room 5246 North Bldg, 300 Independence Ave SW, Washington, D.C. 20201/202-472-3222.

Traineeships for Students in Health Administration Graduate Programs

Objectives: To support eligible students enrolled in accredited graduate degree programs in health administration, hospital administration, or health policy analysis and planning.

Eligibility: Accredited public or nonprofit private educational entities (excluding Schools of Public Health) offering a graduate program in relevant areas.

Range of Financial Assistance: $4,750 to $83,125

Contact: Grants Management Office, Bureau of Health Professions, HRSA, 5600 Fishers Lane, Rockville, MD 20857/301-443-6915.

Traineeship for Students in Schools of Public Health and Other Graduate Public Health Programs

Objectives: To support traineeships for students in graduate educational programs in schools of public health or other public or nonprofit educational entities (excluding programs eligible for support under program listed above).

Eligibility: Accredited schools of public health and other public or nonprofit educational entities which provide graduate or specialized training in public health.

Range of Financial Assistance: $32,175 to $235,125.

Contact: Grants Management Office, Bureau of Health Professions, HRSA, 5600 Fishers Lane, Rockville, MD 20857/301-443-6915.

Training of Physicians' Assistants

Objectives: To meet the cost of projects to plan, develop, operate or maintain programs for the training of physicians' assistants.

Eligibility: State and local government entities, or nonprofit private health or educational entities.

Range of Financial Assistance: $6,376 to $385,464.

Contact: Division of Medicine, Department of Health and Human Services, Parklawn Bldg, Room 4C-25, 5600 Fishers Lane, Rockville, MD 20857/301-436-6418.

Venereal Disease Control Grants

Objectives: To reduce morbidity and mortality by preventing cases and complications of venereal diseases.

Eligibility: States, and any political subdivisions of a state in consultation with the appropriate state health authority.

Range of Financial Assistance: $30,000 to $2,340,000

Contact: Director, Center for Disease Control, Public Health Service, Department of Health and Human Services, 1600 Clifton Rd. N.E., Atlanta, GA 30333/404-329-3291.

Venereal Disease Research, Demonstration, and Public Information and Education Grants

Objectives: To provide assistance to programs designed for the conducting of research, demonstrations, and public information and education for the prevention and control of venereal disease.

Eligibility: States, and other public or private nonprofit entities.

Range of Financial Assistance: $10,000 to $350,000.

Contact: Grants Management Office, Center for Disease Control, Public Health Service, Department of Health and Human Services, 1600 Clifton Rd. N.E., Atlanta, GA 30333/404-262-6575.

Work Incentive Program

Objectives: To move men, women, and out-of-school youth, age 16 or older, from dependency on grants to economic independence through meaningful, permanent, productive employment by providing appropriate employment training, job placement and other related services, supplemented by child care and other supportive social services when needed to enable a person to participate or secure employment.

Eligibility: States.

Range of Financial Assistance: Not specified.

Contact: Executive Director, National Coordination Committee, Work Incentive Program, Department of Health and Human Services, Washington, DC 20213/202-376-6914.

Head Start

For information and expertise on Head Start programs, contact: Project Head Start, Department of Health and Human Services, P.O. Box 1182, Washington, DC 20013/202-755-7782.

Health Almanac

The National Institutes of Health (NIH) publishes a free almanac covering its activities. Topics covered include historical data on the Institute, biographical sketches of the Institute's research divisions, lists of NIH lectures, Nobel laureates, honors, exhibits, symposia, and major projects. Contact: Editorial Operations Branch, Division of Public Information, NIH, Department of Health and Human Services, Building 31, Room 2B03, Bethesda, MD 20205/301-496-4143.

Health Care Statistics and Publications

Both the Health Care Financing Administration (HCFA) and Social Security Administration collect data and analyze trends related to health and health care. For information on data and publications available, contact: Office of Public Affairs, HCFA, Department of Health and Human Services, 330 C St. S.W., Room 4236, Washington, DC 20201/202-245-8056, and Office of Research and Statistics, Social Security Administration, Department of Health and Human Services, 1875 Connecticut Ave. N.W., Washington, DC 20009/202-673-5602.

Health Care Technology

Information services on the latest technological developments for improving the safety, efficiency, effectiveness and cost effectiveness of health care are available from: National Center for Health Care Technology, Department of Health and Human Services, 5600 Fishers Lane, Room 310, Rockville, MD 20857/301-443-4990.

Health Information Clearinghouse

The Clearinghouse serves as a public referral service for almost any question on health. Contact: National Health Information Clearinghouse, 1555 Wilson Blvd., Suite 600, Rosslyn, VA 22209/703-522-2590.

Health Insurance Guide

A Guide to Health Insurance for People with Medicare is available free from Office of Public Affairs, Health Care Financing Administration, Department of Health and Human Services, 330 C St. S.W., Room 4244, North Bldg, Washington, DC 20201/202-245-8056.

Health Maintenance Organizations (HMOs)

Those considering joining an HMO can obtain free pamphlets and other information to help in making their decision: Private Sector Initiatives, Office of Health Maintenance Organizations, Department of Health and Human Services, 5600 Fishers Lane, Rockville, MD 20857/301-443-2300. For information on programs and funding for Health Maintenance Organizations (HMOs), contact: Office of Health Maintenance Organizations, Public Health Service, Department of Health and Human Services, 5600 Fishers Lane, Room 9-11, Rockville, MD 20857/301-443-4106.

Health Manpower

For information on the education, training and availability of doctors, dentists, nurses, veterinarians, pharmacists, optometrists, nurse practitioners, physician's attendants, dental assistants, dental technicians, allopathic and osteopathic physicians and podiatrists, contact: Office of Information, Bureau of Health Professions, Health Resources and Services Administration, Department of Health and Human Services, Room 8A-03, Rockville, MD /301-443-2060.

Health Planning Information Clearinghouse

Technical assistance and information is provided to state health planning and development agencies, state health coordinating councils, health systems agencies, and centers for health planning to help them develop health planning programs. Contact: National Health Planning Information Center, Office of Health Planning, Health Resources and Services Administration, Department of Health and Human Services, 5600 Fishers Lane, Room 98-33 Rockville, MD 20857/301-443-2183.

Health Publications

A free catalogue of publications produced by the National Institutes of Health is available from: Public Information Division, NIH, Department of Health and Human Services, Room 305, Bethesda, MD 20205/301-496-4143.

Health Related Research and Development

Each of the Institutes of the National Institute of Health (NIH) promote research pertaining to health-related issues. The Office of Extramural Research and Training can refer you to the institute and office most likely to sponsor research in your field of interest. Funding, research reports and technical assistance are often available from NIH. A report which is helpful for determining research and development projects supported by NIH is *The Research Award Index,* an annual catalog of NIH grantees and contractors with descriptions of the research being done. This two-volume set is heavily indexed and cross-indexed by grant or contract number and name of the principal investigator. The publication (stock #017-040-00493-1) is available for $31.00 from the Superintendent of Documents, U.S. Government Printing Office, Washington, DC 20402/202-783-3238. Contact: Office of Extramural Research and Training, National Institutes of Health, U.S. Department of Health and Human Services, Building 1, Room 105, 9000 Rockville Pike, Bethesda, MD 20205/301-496-5126.

Health Research Information System

CRISP (Computer Retrieval of Information on Scientific Projects) provides up-to-date scientific information on research projects supported through various research grants and contracts from the Public Health Service. Contact: Research Documentation Section, Division of Research Grants, NIH, Department of Health and Human Services, 5333 Westbard Ave., Westwood Building, Room 148B, Bethesda, MD 20205/301-496-7543.

Health Service Corps

The National Health Service Corps provides health professionals to those areas designated as having critical shortages of such personnel. Contact: National Health Service Corps, Health Services Administration, 5600 Fishers Lane, Room R640, Rockville, MD 20857/301-443-5630.

Health Services Information

The National Center for Health Services Research is the main source of information and funding for general research on problems related to the quality and delivery of health service. Topics covered include: health promotion and disease prevention; technical assessment; role of market forces in delivery of health services; and health information services, including data systems, medical knowledge and methodology. Contact: National Center for Health Services Research, Park Bldg, Public Health Service, Department of Health and Human Services, 5600 Fishers Lane, Room 1-46, Rockville, MD 20857/301-443-4100.

Health Services Publications

A free directory is available describing those publications obtainable from the Health Services Administration, including those from the Bureau of Community Health Services, Bureau of Medical Services, Bureau of Quality Assurance, and the Indian Health Service. Contact: Office of Public Affairs, Health Resources and Services Administration, Department of Health and Human Services, 5600 Fishers Lane, Room 1443, Rockville, MD 20857/301-443-2086.

Health Statistics

The National Center for Health Statistics (NCHS) is the only federal agency established specifically to collect and disseminate data on health in the United States. The Center designs and maintains national data collection systems, conducts research in statistical and survey methodology, and cooperates with other agencies in the U.S. and in foreign countries in activities to increase the availability and usefulness of health data. Data are available in the form of published reports, computer tapes and specialized tabulations. Described below are those offices within the Center which perform the majority of the data collection activities:

Division of Health Interview Statistics, NCHS, Department of Health and Human Services, 3700 East-West Hwy., Room 2-44, FCB2, Hyattsville, MD 20782/301-436-7085. Conducts a continuing national household interview survey to obtain data on health and demographic factors related to illness, injuries, disability and costs and uses of medical services.

Division of Health Care Statistics, NCHS, Department of Health and Human Services, 3700 East-West Hwy., Room 2-63, FCB2, Hyattsville, MD 20782/301-436-8522. Develops and maintains a national register for primary and allied health personnel, conducts health manpower surveys, establishes inventories of personnel in selected health occupations, and develops statistics on the characteristics of inpatient and outpatient health facilities.

Division of Health Care Statistics, NCHS, Department of Health and Human Services, 3700 East-West Hwy., Room 2-63, Hyattsville, MD 20782/301-436-8522. Compiles data on the utilization of health manpower and facilities providing long-term care, ambulatory care, hospital care, and family planning.

Division of Health Examination Statistics, NCHS, Department of Health and Human Services, 3700 East-West Hwy., Room 2-58, Hyattsville, Md 20782/301-436-7068. Collects data on nutritional status, health-related measurements, prevalence of chronic diseases and related health care needs, and on physical and intellectual growth and development patterns.

Division of Vital Statistics, NCHS, Department of Health and Human Services, 3700 East-West Hwy., Room 1-44, Hyattsville, MD 20782/301-436-8952. Collects data on births, deaths, fetal deaths, marriages, and divorces.

For a central source on health statistics, contact: National Center for Health Statistics, Scientific and Technical Information Branch, 3700 East-West Hwy., Room 1-57, Hyattsville, MD 20782/ 301-436-8500. See also "Health Care Statistics and Publications" in this section.

Healthy Volunteers
The National Institutes of Health operates a number of programs that require healthy persons to provide an index of normal body functions against which to measure the abnormal. These "Normal Volunteers" receive a per diem plus expenses and health services. Many of the volunteers work only during holidays or in their free time. Contact: Normal Volunteer Program, Clinical Center, NIH, Department of Health and Human Services, Building 10, Room 2N230, Bethesda, MD 20205/301-496-4763.

Hearing Aids
A free book entitled *Facts About Hearing and Hearing Aids* is available to consumers and other interested parties from: Office of Consumer Affairs, Food and Drug Administration, Department of Health and Human Services, 5600 Fishers Lane, Rockville, MD 20857/301-443-3170.

Heart and Lung Transplantation Research and Funding
The National Heart, Lung and Blood Institute conducts and funds research pertaining to heart and lung transplantation. Staff in the Public Inquiries and Reports Branch can answer questions and refer you to experts in the field, government programs, and research centers. The office has prepared a 30-page information packet about transplantation, which consists of research reports, papers and articles collected from medical literature as well as publications geared toward the general public. This packet and other transplantation publications are available free of charge. Contact: National Heart, Lung and Blood Institute, Public Inquiries and Reports Branch, National Institutes of Health, Building 31, Room 5A-52, 9000 Rockville Pike, Bethesda, MD 20205/301-496-4236.

Heart, Lung, and Blood Institute—National
The Institute supports basic and clinical research, development and other activities related to the prevention, diagnosis, and treatment of cardiovascular, lung, and blood diseases. Contact: National Heart, Lung, and Blood Institute, National Institutes of Health, 9000 Rockville Pike, Bethesda, MD 20205/301-496-5166.

High Blood Pressure Information Center
The Center acts as a clearinghouse for high blood pressure information. It provides educational materials and technical assistance to those in both the private and public sector who wish to control high blood pressure, and maintains a speaker's roster and manages an exhibit program. A free newsletter, called *Information Memorandum,* is published five times per year, announces new projects and the availability of educational materials. Contact: High Blood Pressure Information Center, National Heart, Lung and Blood Institute, NIH, Department of Health and Human Services, 2121 Wisconsin Ave., Fourth Floor, Washington, DC 20007/202-944-3163.

High Blood Pressure Screening Programs
If you are interested in establishing a high blood pressure screening program in your office or factory, the High Blood Pressure Information Center will send an expert to help with the program. See address directly above.

Human Development Clinical Research
The National Institute of Child Health and Human Development is involved in conducting clinical research on the reproductive development and behavior processes of human development. They support research programs and inform scientists and the public about research advances. Staff can answer questions and make referrals to other information sources. The findings of the research are published in reports, and a free listing of these reports is available from the office. Also published is the *Diagnostic Ultrasound Imaging in Pregnancy,* a free 215-page report on the proceedings of a conference held on ultrasound. Contact: National Institute of Child Health and Human Development (NICHD), Office of Research Reporting, Department of Health and Human Ser-

vices, Bldg. 31, Room 2A-32, 9000 Rockville Pike, Bethesda, MD 20205/301-496-5133.

Human Lenses
The institute supports the Cooperative Cataract Research Group to conduct research studies on human cataracts. For further information contact: Human Lenses, National Eye Institute, National Institutes of Health, Department of Health and Human Services, Building 31, Room 6A49, 9000 Rockville Pike, Bethesda, MD 20205/301-496-5984.

Huntington's Disease Research Roster
The National Institute of Neurological and Communicative Disorders and Stroke supports a research roster for Huntington's disease patients and families based at the Indiana University Medical Center, Indianapolis. The roster is national in scope and its primary purpose is to facilitate research in Huntington's disease. Contact: National Institute of Neurological and Communicative Disorders and Stroke, National Institutes of Health, Federal Building, Room 714, 7550 Wisconsin Avenue, Bethesda, MD 20205/301-496-1431.

Illness and Injury Data Base
See "Occupational Safety and Health Information Clearinghouse" in this section.

Indian Health
Some 51 hospitals, 99 health centers and several hundred field health stations have been established to raise the health status of the American Indian and Alaskan Native. Contact: Indian Health Service, Office of Tribal Affairs, Health Services Administration, Department of Health and Human Services, 5600 Fishers Lane, Room 6A-03, Rockville, MD 20857/301-443-1104.

Industrial Hygiene
The National Institute for Occupational Safety and Health (NIOSH) conducts research on eliminating on-the-job-hazards to the health and safety of workers. Their activities include identifying hazards and determining methods to control them, recommending federal standards to limit hazards, providing training to help alleviate the critical shortage of occupational safety and health manpower, offering a series of courses, supporting education and resource centers at colleges and universities, providing long-term training to upgrade the knowledge and skills of professionals in the field, and making on-the-job investigations in response to requests of reported worker exposures. Contact: NIOSH, Center for Disease Control, Public Health Service, Department of Health and Human Services, 200 Independence Ave. S.W. Room 721B Washington, DC 20201/301-472-7135.

Industry Health Studies
The National Institute for Occupational Safety and Health (NIOSH) conducts in-depth studies on health hazards in specific industries. Approximately 60 studies are being conducted at any one time; topics include causes of death at oil refineries and asbestos-related deaths. Contact: Division of Surveillance, Hazard Evaluation and Field Studies, NIOSH, Center for Disease Control, Public Health Service, Department of Health and Human Services, 4676 Columbia Pky, Cincinnati, OH 45226/513-684-4428.

Instrumentation and Computer Systems Development
The Research Services Branch of the Instramural Research Division of the National Institute of Mental Health is a group of engineers, technicians and computer scientists involved in the design and development of instrumentation and computer systems for neurophysiological, neuropharmacological and neuropsychological research. The staff can answer questions and/or make referrals. Contact: Research Services Branch, Intramural Research Division, National Institute of Mental Health, Building 36, Room 2A03, National Institutes of Health, Bethesda, MD 20205/301-496-4957.

International Health Sciences Studies
The National Institutes of Health provides a forum for study, discussion and dialogue between international scholars and the American biomedical community. They provide access to the international community to their laboratories and libraries. Awards are presented for post-doctoral fellowships to foreign scientists. A free listing of publications on international health science is available upon request. Contact: John E. Fogarty, International Center for Advanced Study in the Health Sciences, NIH, Department of Health and Human Services, Building 38a, Room 609, Bethesda, MD 20205/301-496-1415.

Kidney Disease and Treatment Materials and Seminars
The National Kidney Foundation sponsors research, provides educational materials and seminars for both the health professional and the general public, and compiles statistics relating to kidney disease and treatment. Its affiliates and local groups nationwide provide patient services and educational programs. It has several professional councils, one of which is Clinical Nephrology Dialysis and Transplantation. This Council publishes a quarterly newsletter about developments in the field. In addition to educational pamphlets about kidney dialysis and transplantation, it also publishes *The American Journal of Kidney Diseases,* a monthly publication geared

towards the physician. It covers all aspects of kidney dialysis, transplantation and disease. The journal is available for $70 per year from Grune and Stratton, Inc., 111 5th Avenue, New York, NY 10003, 212-614-3000. *The Kidney,* also published by the Council, is a bimonthly publication written for physicians. It contains medical articles about the kidney. Annual Subscription rate is $20.00. For further information, contact: National Kidney Foundation, 2 Park Avenue, New York, NY 10016/212-889-2210.

Laser Surgery Information
The U.S. Food and Drug Administration publishes *The Surgeon's Newest Scalpel is a Laser* (606-L), a four-page, free booklet that is a catalog of basic information for patients and other laymen. Contact: *The Surgeon's Newest Scalpel is a Laser* (606-L), Consumer Information Center, Pueblo, CO 81009.

Laser Surgery Research
A variety of government institutes, agencies, and private groups are involved in laser surgery research and development. The National Health Information Clearinghouse (NHIC) maintains a data base with information about health-related organizations including federal and state agencies, information centers and private groups. Staff will search their data base to provide you with experts and organizations involved in the particular aspect of laser surgery you are interested in. The federal government alone has several experts at its various health institutes. These officials can tell you about the latest developments in the field and refer you to other information sources. Contact: National Health Information Clearinghouse (NHIC), PO Box 1133, Washington, DC 20013-1133/703-522-2590, 800-336-4797.

Library of Medicine
The National Library of Medicine is the world's largest research library in a single scientific and professional field. The Library collects materials exhaustively in some 40 biomedical areas and, to a lesser degree, in such related subjects as general chemistry, physics, zoology, botany, psychology, and instrumentation. The holdings include three million books, journals, technical reports, documents, theses, pamphlets, microfilms, and pictorial and audiovisual materials. More than 70 languages are represented in the collection. Those who are unable to visit the Library can access the information through:

Interlibrary loans—any library can request a copy of an article or document for you,

MEDLARS (Medical Literature Analysis and Retrieval System)—a computerized data base on medical literature, available in approximately 2,200 medical libraries throughout the country. The public can access this data base; however, there may be a small fee involved. Your local college or university or Veterans Administration Hospital is likely to have access to the system. See "Literature Searches on Health Science" below for a full description.

REGIONAL MEDICAL LIBRARIES Seven Regional Medical Libraries, each responsible for a geographic area, coordinate NLM's online search services in the U.S. These libraries also handle requests for health literature not available locally, passing on to NLM requests they cannot fill. To find out the nearest Online Center, or how your institution can become a Center, write to the Regional Medical Library for your area.

Region 1: Greater Northeastern Regional Medical Library Program (Connecticut, Delaware, Maine, Massachusetts, New Hampshire, New Jersey, New York, Pennsylvania, Rhode Island, Vermont, and Puerto Rico), The New York Academy of Medicine, 2 East 103rd Street, New York, New York 10029.

Region 2: Southeastern/Atlantic Regional Medical Library Services (Alabama, Florida, Georgia, Maryland, Mississippi, North Carolina, South Carolina, Tennessee, Virginia, West Virginia, and District of Columbia), University of Maryland, Health Sciences Library, 111 South Greene Street, Baltimore, Maryland 21201.

Region 3: Regional Medical Library (Iowa, Illinois, Indiana, Kentucky, Michigan, Minnesota, North Dakota, Ohio, South Dakota, and Wisconsin), University of Illinois at Chicago, Library of the Health Sciences, Health Sciences Center, P.O. Box 7509, Chicago, Illinois 60680.

Region 4: Midcontinental Regional Medical Library Program (Colorado, Kansas, Missouri, Nebraska, Utah, and Wyoming), University of Nebraska, Medical Center Library, 42nd and Dewey Avenue, Omaha, Nebraska 68105.

Region 5: South Central Regional Medical Library Program (Arkansas, Louisiana, New Mexico, Oklahoma, and Texas), University of Texas, Health Science Center at Dallas, 5323 Harry Hines Blvd., Dallas, Texas 75235.

Region 6: Pacific Northwest Regional Health Sciences Library Service (Alaska, Idaho, Montana, Oregon, and Washington), Health Sciences Library, University of Washington, Seattle, Washington 98195.

Region 7: Pacific Southwest Regional Medical Library Service (Arizona, California, Hawaii, and Nevada), UCLA Biomedical Library, Center for the Health Sciences, Los Angeles, CA 90024.

Contact: National Library of Medicine, NIH, Department of Health and Human Services, Rockville, MD 20209/301-496-6095.

Literature Searches on Health Sciences

The National Library of Medicine maintains a computerized data base called MEDLARS (Medical Literature Analysis and Retrieval System). The system contains some 4,500,000 references to journal articles and books in health sciences published after 1965. Access to the data base can be made through a number of centers around the country. The charge for a search varies among centers: Some absorb all or more of the costs; others levy a modest fee. The location of local centers can be obtained from the National Library of Medicine. The data bases available on the network include:

MEDLINE—600,000 references to biomedical journal articles published in the current and preceding years.

TOXLINE (Toxicology Information Online)—520,000 references from the last five years on published human and animal toxicity studies, effects of environmental chemicals and pollutants, and adverse drug reactions.

CHEMLINE (Chemical Dictionary Online)—760,000 names for chemical substances, representing 380,000 unique compounds.

RTECS (Registry of Toxic Effects of Chemical Substances)—toxicity data for 31,600 substances.

TDB (Toxicology Data Bank)—chemical, pharmacological, and toxicological information and data on approximately 2,500 substances.

SERLINE (Serials Online)—bibliographic information for about 30,000 serial publications.

AVLINE (Audiovisual Online)—citations to some 6,000 audiovisual teaching packages used in health sciences education at the college level and for the continuing education of practitioners.

HEALTH PLANNING AND ADMINISTRATION—100,000 references to literature on health planning, organization, financing, management, manpower, and related subjects.

HISTLINE (History of Medicine Online)—35,000 references to articles, monographs, symposia, and other publications dealing with the history of medicine and related sciences.

CANCERLIT (Cancer Literature)—140,000 references dealing with various aspects of cancer.

CANCERPRO (Cancer Research Projects)—20,000 descriptions of ongoing cancer research projects from the current and preceding two years.

CLINPROT (Clinical Cancer Protocols)—summaries of clinical investigations of new anticancer agents and treatment techniques.

BIOETHICSLINE —6,500 references to materials on bioethical topics such as euthanasia, human experimentation, and abortion.

Some of the special interest data bases mentioned above are also available through the relevant information clearinghouses described in this section. Contact: Office of Inquiries and Publications Management, National Library of Medicine, Department of Health and Human Services 8600 Rockville Pike, Building 38 Room 25-15, Bethesda, MD 20205/301-496-6308.

Loans and Loan Guarantees _____

The programs described below are those which offer financial assistance through the lending of federal monies for a specific period of time or program in which the federal government makes an arrangement to indemnify a lender against part or all of any defaults by the borrower.

Community Development Credit Union Revolving Loan Fund

Objectives: To support community based credit unions in their efforts to stimulate economic development activities and to provide needed financial and related services to residents of their community.

Eligibility: To community development credit unions and to organizations proposing to form a credit union.

Range of Financial Assistance: $100,000 to $200,000.

Contact: Division of Business Development Loans, Office of Community Services, 1200 19th Street NW, Room 500, Washington, DC 20506/202-653-5675.

Health Education Assistance Loans

Objectives: To authorize loans for educational expenses available from eligible lenders such as banks, credit unions, savings and loan associations, pension funds, insurance companies and eligible educational institutions. Loans are made to graduate students enrolled at eligible health professions institutions. The loans are insured by the federal government.

Eligibility: Generally, any U.S. citizen, national, or person in the United States for other than a temporary purpose, who is enrolled on a full-time basis at an eligible health professions school may apply.

Range of Financial Assistance: Not to exceed $80,000.

Contact: Division of Student Assistance, HRSA, DHHS, Parklawn Bldg, 5600 Fishers Lane, Rockville, MD 20857/301-443-1173.

Health Maintenance Organizations

Objectives: To stimulate the development and increase the number of various models of prepaid, comprehensive health maintenance organizations (HMOs) throughout the United States and the expansion of federally qualified health maintenance organizations.

Eligibility: Public and private nonprofit organizations that plan to develop, operate and expand an HMO, and private organizations including profit-making organizations, that plan to develop or operate and expand an HMO in a medically underserved area.

Range of Financial Assistance: Not specified.

Contact: Office of Health Maintenance Organizations, Public Health Service, Department of

Health and Human Services, 12420 Parklawn Dr., Rockville, MD 20857/301-443-2560.

National Health Service Corps
Objectives: To improve the delivery of health care services to residents in areas critically short of health personnel.
Eligibility: Public or nonprofit private health or health related organization in designated areas.
Range of Financial Assistance: $10,000 to $50,000.
Contact: Director, National Health Service Corps, Health Resources and Services Administration, Parklawn Building, 5600 Fishers Lane, Rockville, MD 20857/301-443-2900.

Rural Development Loan Fund
Objectives: To alleviate rural poverty promoting economic and community development activities through loans to eligible borrowers.
Eligibility: Organizations eligible to receive assistance under this program include; Low income rural families or individuals; business organized for profit; Community Development Corporations; Private nonprofit organizations; Local cooperatives; designated supportive organizations of cooperative eligible for financial assistance; city and county agencies, and State governments; Indian groups; and Community Action Agencies.
Range of Financial Assistance: $80,000 to $2,000,000.
Contact: Director, Division of Business Development Loans, Office of Community Services, Department of Health and Human Services, 1200 19th Street, N.W., Washington, DC 20506/202-653-5675.

Special Loans for National Health Service Corps Members to Enter Private Practice
Objectives: To assist National Health Service Corps scholarship recipients in establishing their own private practice in a health manpower shortage area.
Eligibility: NHSC scholarship recipients who are about to begin or are currently fulfilling the first two years of their scholarship service obligations.
Range of Financial Assistance: Up to $12,500 for one year.
Contact: Director, National Health Resources and Service Corps, Health Services Administration, Parklawn Building, Room 6-40, 5600 Fishers Lane, Rockville, MD 20857/301-443-2900.

Low Dose Radiation Exposure Research
The Ionizing Radiation Branch of the Food and Drug Administration is doing research with low dose radiation exposures delivered over an extended period of time. Studies and experiments are being conducted concerning genetic behavior changes as a result of single doses of radiation. The staff here can answer your questions, and send you technical literature upon request. Contact: Ionizing Radiation Branch, Division of Life Sciences, Center for Devices and Radiological Health, U.S. Food and Drug Administration, Rockville, MD 20857/301-443-7159; Technical Literature, 301-443-3532.

Medicaid
The Medicaid program through grants to states provides medical services to the medically needy. See "Grants—Medical Assistance Program" in this section. For answers to questions on Medicaid, contact your local welfare office or Director, Inquiries Staff, Bureau of Eligibility and Reimbursement, Health Care Financing Administration, Department of Health and Human Services, 6325 Security Blvd., East Lowrise Building, Room 1P4, Baltimore, MD 21207/301-594-9032.

Medicaid Statistics
Medicaid data are available describing such elements as the number of recipients by age, sex and race, the amount of payments by state, and the number of days recipients have been hospitalized. *Medicaid Statistics,* a free monthly publication, keeps subscribers current on latest developments. Contact: Medicaid Program Data Branch, Office of Research, Demonstration and Statistics, Health Care Finance Administration, Department of Health and Human Services, 6325 Security Blvd., Room 2C-14, Oak Meadows Bldg, Baltimore, MD 21207/301-597-1417.

Medical Applications Research
The Office of Medical Applications Research (OMAR) is the focal point, at National Institutes of Health (NIH), for medical technology assessment. The office coordinates the participation of National Institutes of Health and various federal agencies in Concensus Development Conferences at which new drugs, medical procedures, and devices are evaluated for safety and effectiveness. OMAR staff have evaluated more than 44 technologies, and they can provide technical information and reports on the technologies. Staff can also direct you to experts and organizations covering specific medical technologies. Contact: Office of Medical Applications Research (OMAR), National Institutes of Health (NIH), Building 1, Room 216, Bethesda, MD 20205/301-496-1143.

Medical Device Safety Information Source
The Center for Devices and Radiological Health approves new medical devices and radiation-emitting products for use in the U.S. marketplace, and is a good information source for the safety and effectiveness of new medical devices. Publications include two periodical bulletins which are available from the Center and some technical papers can be purchased from the Government Printing Office. The two periodical bulletins are the *Medical*

Devices Bulletin and the *Radiological Health Bulletin*. Both publications cover new developments in the regulation of medical and radiological products. They are designed specifically for health professionals, health agencies, and the industry. Both are available free of charge to these individuals and organizations. Contact: Center for Devices and Radiological Health, Food and Drug Administration (FDA), 5600 Fishers Lane, Rockville, MD 20857/301-443-4690.

Medical Devices

The Bureau of Medical Devices accumulates information and expertise on surgical and rehabilitation devices; gastro/urology and general use devices; anesthesiology and neurology devices; clinical laboratory devices, cardiovascular devices, ophthalmic, ear, nose, throat and dental devices, ob/gyn and radiology devices. Contact: Device Monitoring Branch, Device Experience Network, Bureau of Medical Devices, Food and Drug Administration, Department of Health and Human Services, 8757 Georgia Ave., Room 1222, Silver Spring, Md 20910/301-427-8100.

Medical Devices—Technical Assistance for Small Business

The Food and Drug Administration (FDA) offers free technical assistance to help small manufacturers comply with the new safety and performance requirements for medical devices. Resident experts provide assistance by handling inquiries over the telephone or by mail, presenting workshops and conferences, and by making on-site visits. A free newsletter called *Small Manufacturers Memo* describes new developments in device regulation. Contact: Division of Small Manufacturers Assistance, Center for Devices and Radiological Health, Food and Drug Administration, Department of Health and Human Services, 5600 Fishers Lane, Room 212, Rockville, MD 20851/301-443-6591.

Medical Malpractice

See "Health Standards Information Clearinghouse" in this section.

Medical Sciences

For information on the latest research and training being conducted in the medical sciences, including cellular and molecular basis diseases, genetics, pharmacologic sciences, physiology, and biomedical engineering, contact: Office of Research Reports, National Institute of General Medical Sciences, NIH, Department of Health and Human Services, Bldg 31, Room 48-52, Bethesda, MD 20205/301-496-7301.

Medicare

Medicare is a health insurance program for almost everybody over 65 years old and for certain disabled people under 65. See "Direct Payments" in this section. For answers to questions on Medicare, see "Social Security Administration" in your telephone book. Individual assistance is also available from: Bureau of Program Policy, Health Care Financing Administration, Department of Health and Human Services, 6325 Security Blvd., Room 100, Baltimore, MD 21207/301-594-9324.

Mental Health, National Institute of

Information and expertise are available on a wide variety of topics concerned with mental health and the treatment of mental illnesses. Contact: Public Inquiries, National Institute of Mental Health, Alcohol, Drug Abuse and Mental Health Administration, Department of Health and Human Services, 5600 Fishers Lane, Room 15C-17, Rockville, MD 20857/301-443-4515.

Mental Retardation

The President's Committee on Mental Retardation is a study, evaluation and planning office which coordinates mental retardation programs in agencies and organizations. It answers questions from the public, maintains data bases on trends, population and nature of programs, and publishes reports. Contact: President's Committee on Mental Retardation, Department of Health and Human Services, 330 Independence Ave SW Room 4057, North Building, Washington, DC 20201/202-245-7634.

Mental Retardation Research Centers

The mission of these centers is to conduct research relating to human development, whether biological, medical, social, or behavioral, to assist in finding the causes and means of prevention of mental retardation or in finding means of ameliorating the effects of mental retardation. Contact: Mental Retardation Research Centers, National Institute of Child Health and Human Development, National Institutes of Health, Landow Building, Room 7C16, 7910 Woodmont Avenue, Bethesda, MD 20014/301-496-1383.

Microwave Radiation on Biological Systems Resource

The Electromagnetic Radiation Branch Food and Drug Administration performs and monitors experiments and studies dealing with the effects of radio frequency and microwave radiation on biological systems. This branch also reviews and analyzes similar studies performed in other labs. Staff in this branch can respond to your written inquiries. Technical literature is available upon request. Contact: Electromagnetic Radiation Branch, Division of Life Sciences, Center for Devices and Radiological Health, U.S. Food and Drug Adminstration, Rockville, MD 20857/301-443-7132, 301-443-3532 (Technical Literature).

Minority Group Mental Health

For information and expertise related to the improvement of the quality of life for minority groups—American Indians, Alaskan Natives, Asian Americans, Pacific Islanders, Blacks and Hispanics, the elimination of racism and increasing the quantity and quality of minority mental health professionals, contact: Center for Minority Group Mental Health Programs, National Institute of Mental Health, Alcohol, Drug Abuse, and Mental Health Administration, Public Health Service, Department of Health and Human Services, 5600 Fishers Lane, Room 11-95, Rockville, MD 20857/301-443-3724.

Missing Persons

The Social Security Administration can help you contact a lost loved one, an old friend or other missing person. The procedure is to write a letter to your missing person and send it to the Social Security Administration, along with as much personal information as possible, e.g., date of birth and last place of residence. If it can locate the person in its files, it will forward your letter; it will not give you the current address. For further assistance, call information for the number of your local Social Security Administration office, or send your letter along with pertinent information to Social Security Administration, Public Inquiries, Department of Health and Human Services, 6401 Security Blvd., Baltimore, MD 21235.

Muscularskeletal Diseases

The Muscularskeletal Diseases Program is the single largest funder of orthopedic biomechanics research. Staff can provide you with information about government funding in biomechanics and orthopedics as well as information about on-going research in the field. The staff will also discuss biomedical projects and provide advice and consultation. Much research has been done on head injury as well as kinetics and kinematics of body motion. Contact: Muscularskeletal Diseases Program, NIADDK/National Institutes of Health, Westwood Building, Room 407, Bethesda, MD 20205/301-496-7326.

Narcotic Addition

See "Drug Abuse" in this section.

Neurological and Communicative Disorders and Stroke—National Institute

This Institute conducts, coordinates and supports research concerned with the cause, development, diagnosis, therapy, and prevention of disorders and diseases of the central nervous system and the communicative and sensory systems. Contact: National Institute of Neurological and Communicative Disorders and Stroke, 9000 Rockville Pike, Bethesda, MD 20205/301-496-4697.

New Medical Technologies Reports and Experts

The Office of Health Technology reviews and and analyzes new medical technologies for the Health Care Financing Administration. Staff produce technical reports on specific technologies, gathering their information by talking with experts in government agencies and professional societies, reading periodical literature, and studying clinical evidence. Staff can answer questions or refer you to experts and information sources for topics they have not covered. The office's reports are geared to the medical professional and are available free of charge. Contact: Office of Health Technology, U.S. Department of Health and Human Services, Park Building, Room 310, 5600 Fishers Lane, Rockville, Md 20857/301-443-4990.

New Product Safety Reviews and Recommendations

The Optical Radiation Branch of the Food and Drug Administration reviews and recommends new products on the market on the basis of their safety and efficacy. This Branch conducts research with visible and ultra light using biological systems. Staff in this Branch can answer your questions and make referrals, and will send some technical literature upon request. Contact: Optical Radiation Branch, Division of Life Sciences, Center for Devices and Radiological Health, U.S. Food and Drug Administration, Rockville, MD 20857.

NIH Grant Information

For information on past and current grants and awards made by the National Institutes of Health (NIH), as well as information on policies and procedures for funding, contact: Office of Grants Inquiries, NIH, Department of Health and Human Services, 5333 Westbard Ave., Westwood Building, Room 449, Bethesda, MD 20205/301-496-7441.

Occupational Health Data by Industry and Chemical

The National Institute for Occupational Safety and Health (NIOSH) maintains a data base which analyzes environmental, medical, and demographic data on industrial employees. Special reports can be generated categorized by industry or chemical. Contact: Division of Surveillance Hazard Evaluation, NIOSH, Center for Disease Control, Department of Health and Human Services, 4676 Columbia Pkwy., Cincinnati, OH 45226/513-684-1428.

Occupational Safety and Health College Courses

The National Institute for Occupational Safety and Health (NIOSH) sponsors training courses for professionals independently or through colleges. For a list of available training programs, contact: Division of Training and Manpower Development,

NIOSH, Center for Disease Control, Department of Health and Human Services, 4676 Columbia Pkwy., Cincinnati, OH 45226/513-684-8221.

Occupational Safety and Health Information Clearinghouse

The clearinghouse provides answers to both technical and nontechnical questions. In addition to maintaining a technical library and providing free copies of pamphlets and publications, it also maintains the following data bases:

National Occupational Hazard Survey—identifies those agents to which workers in various industries are commonly exposed; it also includes information on the companies in the industry and the protection equipment required.

NIOSH Technical Information Center—contains information on toxicology, analytical methods, engineering, chemical names, and syndromes.

A catalogue of publications is also available. Contact: Clearinghouse for Occupational Safety and Health Information, NIOSH, Center for Disease Control, 4676 Columbia Pkwy., Cincinnati, OH 45226/513-684-4287.

Periodontal Diseases Centers

The main objective of the centers is to facilitate the application of basic research findings in the areas of microbiology, immunology, and pharmacology in clinical investigations of patients with periodontal disease. These centers pursue studies to establish the causative organisms in periodontal diseases, determine the host response to these causative organisms, improve therapeutic techniques and regiments, and develop preventive measures. Contact: Peridontal Diseases Centers, National Institutes of Health, Westwood Building, Room 504, 5333 Westbard Avenue, Bethesda, MD 20205/301-496-7748.

Pharmacology Studies

National Institute of General Medical Sciences (NIGMS) is a federal agency involved in drug research in synthetic chemical, basic biological and biochemical compounds, and molecular pharmacology. It does comparative studies using laboratory animals and controlled clinical investigations of patients and normal volunteers. NIGMS provides grants for these studies, and supports anesthesiologists, chemists, biologists, and pharmacologists. It has fact sheets available on the programs sponsored, as well as the guidelines for the grants. Two of their publications are *Pharmacological Sciences Program,* an annual report providing highlights on scientific research sponsored by NIGMS (30-page publication is free) and *NIGMS Annual Report,* covering research programs sponsored by the Institute. (The 100-page publication is free). Contact: National Institute of General Medical Sciences (NIGMS), Building 31,

Room 4A52, 9000 Rockville Pike, Bethesda, MD 20205/301-496-7301.

Physical Fitness Award

All schools and youth groups in the United States which have qualified physical education and/or physical fitness personnel can offer the Presidential Physical Fitness Award Program. Youths qualify by passing six test items—a sprint, an endurance run, an agility run, standing long jump, situps, and a test of arm and shoulder strength. Contact: President's Council on Physical Fitness and Sports, Department of Health and Human Services, Suite 7103, 450 5th St, NW, Washington, DC 20001/202-272-3421

Physical Fitness Bibliography

Physical Fitness/Sports Medicine is the most comprehensive bibliographic service available on exercise physiology, sports injuries, physical conditioning, and the medical aspects of exercise. This quarterly publication is available for $10.00 per year from Superintendent of Documents, Government Printing Office, Washington, DC 20402/202-783-3238.

Physical Fitness and Health Promotion

For information and expertise relating to such topics as preventive medicine, health promotion, physical fitness and sports medicine, contact: Office of Disease Prevention and Health Promotion, Public Health Service, Department of Health and Human Services, 330 C St S.W., Room 2132, Washington, DC 20201/202-472-5660.

Physical Fitness and Sports Information

The President's Council on Physical Fitness and Sports will supply information and expertise for those who wish to establish physical fitness programs. Available free publications include *Run for Yourself—An Introduction to Running, Exercise and Weight Control, An Introduction to Physical Fitness, Physical Education—A Performance Checklist, The Physically Undeveloped Child,* and *Youth Physical Fitness.* Contact: President's Council on Physical Fitness and Sports, Department of Health and Human Services, Suite 7103, 450 5th St, NW, Washington, DC 20001/202-272-3421.

Poison Information Clearinghouse

Poisoning case reports are collected by a product's category and trade name, and a directory of local poison control centers is available. Contact: National Clearinghouse for Poison Control Center, Bureau of Drugs, Food and Drug Administration, Department of Health and Human Services, 5600 Fishers Lane, Room 13-45, Rockville, MD 20857/301-443-6260.

Pregnancy

Current information and expertise are available on

such topics as pregnancy, the birth process, intra-uterine development and disorders of infants, including low birth weight, prematurity, Sudden Infant Death Syndrome, and other problems that may originate before birth, at birth, or during early adaption to life outside the womb. Contact: Pregnancy and Perimatology Section, Clinical Nutrition and Early Development Branch, National Institute of Child Health and Human Development, Department of Health and Human Services, Landow Building, Room 7C09, 7910 Woodmont Ave., Bethesda, MD 20205/301-496-5575.

Radiation
Information and expertise are available on radiation and the effects of radiation exposure. Subject areas covered include medical x-rays, medical radiation therapy, lasers, microwave, ionizing radiation, nuclear medicine, radioactive materials, ultra-sound, ultraviolet light, TV radiation, and X-raying baggage. Contact: Bureau of Radiological Health, Center for Devices and Radiological Health, Food and Drug Administration, Department of Health and Human Services, 5600 Fishers Lane, Rockville, MD 20857/301-443-3434.

Rape Information Clearinghouse
Information services are available to assist in identifying projects, funding, publication and other specialized expertise on topics involving the prevention and control of rape. A free directory of rape crisis centers is also available. Contact: National Center for the Prevention and Control of Rape, National Institute of Mental Health, Department of Health and Human Services, 5600 Fishers Lane, Room 6C-12, Rockville, MD 20857/301-443-1910.

Refugee Assistance
A number of grant and direct payment programs are aimed to assist Cuban, Indochinese, and Soviet refugees. See "Grants" and "Direct Payments" in this section.

Regulatory Activities
Listed below are those organizations within the Department of Health and Human Services which are involved with regulating various business activities. Regulatory activities generate large amounts of information on the companies and subjects they regulate, and much of the information is available to the public. A regulatory office also can tell you your rights when dealing with a regulated company.

Food and Drug Administration, Office of Public Affairs, Department of Health and Human Services, 5600 Fishers Lane, Rockville, MD 20857/302-443-4177. Administers programs which protect the public against impure and unsafe foods, drugs and cosmetics, and from the hazards of unsafe medical devices and electronic products which produce radiation exposure.

Office of Civil Rights, Public Affairs Division, Department of Health and Human Services, 300 Independence Ave. S.W., Washington, DC 20201/202-245-6671. Enforces the Civil Rights Act of 1964 which prohibits discrimination with regard to race, color, national origin, sex, age and physical or mental handicap in programs and activities receiving federal financial assistance.

Rehabilitation Magazine
Professionals working with the handicapped can keep current on new programs, innovations and other news in the field by subscribing to *American Rehabilitation*. Subscriptions to the quarterly publication are available for $8.50 from Superintendent of Documents, Government Printing Office, Washington, DC 20402/202-783-3238.

Research Data
The Department of Health and Human Services commissions hundreds of studies every year which contain data and information of value to both the business community and the general public. To identify relevant studies, review the list of grant-giving offices. (See "Grants" in this section.) Then request a listing of recent studies from those offices which cover subjects which may be of interest to you—e.g., on alcoholism if you are a member of the beverage industry. Other sources provide a selected collection of commissioned studies. See "National Institutes of Health Grant Information," "Health Research Information System," "Computerized Data Bases," "Health Related Research and Development" and "Health Statistics," in this section.

Runaway Hotline
The National Runaway Youth Hotline provides advice to both parents and runaways. The service is confidential and operates 24 hours a day. Call toll-free 800-621-4000: 800-972-6004 in Illinois.

Runaway Youths
For information and expertise on Runaway Youth Programs or for a directory of available programs, contact: Division of Runaway Youth Programs, Administration for Children, Youth and Families, Department of Health and Human Services, P. O. Box 1182, Washington, DC 20013/202-755-0593.

Scholarship Hotline for Health Service Corps
Scholarships that pay all tuition and fees at medical, osteopathy or dental schools are available for those willing to serve at least two years in the National Health Corps. Contact: National Health Service Corps, Scholarship Program, Health Resources Administration, Department of Health and Human Services, Room 637, 5600 Fishers Lane, Rockville, MD 20857/301-436-6453

Scholarships—Medical, Dental and Nursing
See "Grants" in this section.

Second Opinion Hotline

The Health Care Financing Administration operates a toll-free hotline referral system for supplying names of physicians who will give second opinions on nonemergency surgery. Contact: Health Care Financing Administration, Health Standards and Quality Bureau, Department of Health and Human Services, 300 C St. S.W., Room 4239, North Bldg, Washington, DC 20201/toll-free 800-638-6833; 800-492-6003 in Maryland.

Sickle Cell Centers Program

The program provides an integrative mechanism for the translation and application of the results of basic and clinical research on sickle cell disease to improved health care at the community level. Contact: National Heart, Lung, and Blood Institute, National Institutes of Health, Federal Building, Room 504D, 7550 Wisconsin Avenue, Bethesda, MD 20205/301-496-6931.

Sickle Cell Directory

A free directory is available describing national, federal and local sickle cell disease programs, along with a listing of comprehensive sickle cell centers, screening and education clinics and national centers for family planning. Contact: Sickle Cell Disease Branch, Division of Blood Disease and Resources, National Heart, Lung and Blood Institute, NIH, Department of Health and Human Services, Federal Building, 7550 Wisconsin Ave., Room 504, Bethesda, MD 20015/301-496-6931.

Small Business Health and Safety Guides

More than 25 handbooks covering the most common violations of Occupational Safety and Health Administration (OSHA) standards in a particular type of business, as well as guidelines for preventing injuries and illnesses are free from: Publications Dissemination, Department of Health and Human Services, 550 Main St, Cincinnati, OH 45226/513-684-3784.

Smoking and Health Information Center

The Office on Smoking and Health handles written and telephone inquiries on scientific and technical aspects of smoking and health. It will perform computerized literature searches on its specialized data base containing over 40,000 records. The following publications are available for free:

Smoking and Health Bulletin
Bibliography on Smoking and Health
Health Consequences of Smoking
Directory of On-Going Research in Smoking and Health
State Legislation on Smoking and Health

Contact: Technical Information Center, Office on Smoking and Health, 5600 Fishers Lane, Room 1-16, Rockville, MD 20857/301-443-1690.

Social Security

Social Security is the basic method of providing a continuing income when family earnings are reduced or stopped because of retirement, disability or death. Monthly benefits include retirement checks, disability checks, survivor checks, and Medicare (see "Direct Payments" in this section). The following pamphlets are available for free:

Your Social Security
Social Security Information for Young Families
Thinking About Retiring
If You Work After You Retire
Applying for a Social Security Number
Check Your Social Security Record
If You Become Disabled
Social Security Benefits for People Disabled Before Age 22
A Brief Explanation of Medicare
How Medicare Helps During a Hospital Stay
Medicare Coverage in a Skilled Nursing Facility
Home Health Care Under Medicare
Social Security Income for the Aged, Blind and Disabled
A Guide to Supplemental Security Income
A Woman's Guide to Social Security
Social Security and Your Household Employee
If You're Self-Employed . . . Reporting Your Income for Social Security
Farmers . . . How to Report Your Income for Social Security
The Advantages of Social Security, A Message for State and Local Government Employee Groups

Information services are also available to handle questions concerning Social Security benefits. Call information in your area for the number of your local Social Security office, or contact: Office of Public Inquiry, Social Security Administration, Department of Health and Human Services, 6401 Security Blvd., Baltimore, MD 21235/301-594-7700.

Social Security Checks

If your Social Security check has been lost, stolen or delayed, contact the nearest office listed in your telephone book under "Social Security Administration," or Social Security Administration, Department of Health and Human Services, 6401 Security Blvd., Baltimore, MD 21235/301-594-7700.

Social Security Health and Welfare Statistics

The Social Security Administration collects and publishes data on a wide variety of health and welfare topics, including health insurance, supplementary security income, social security and the economy, old age survivors and disability health insurance, Black Lung disability, public assistance, Medicare, GNP and social welfare expenditures, and estimates of the labor forces covered under social insurance. Contact: Office of Research and Statistics, Social Security Administration, Department of Health and Human Services, 1875 Connecticut Ave. N.W., Room 1121, Washington, DC 20009/202-673-5602.

Sports
See "Physical Fitness" in this section.

Sports Awards
Anyone over the age of 15 can earn the Presidential Sports Award, which consists of a personalized Presidential Certificate of Achievement, a Presidential Sports Award blazer patch, lapel pin, decal, and membership card. To receive the award you must meet the qualifying standards in one of 43 sports. For an application form, send a stamped self-addressed envelope to: Presidential Sports Award, P.O. Box 5214, FDR Post Office, New York, NY 10022.

Surgeon General
The Surgeon General serves the Department of Health and Human Services as principal advisor to the public on health matters such as smoking and health, diet and nutrition, environmental health hazards, and the importance of immunization and disease prevention. The Surgeon General also oversees the activities of the 6,000-member Public Health Service Commissioned Corps. Contact: Surgeon General, Public Health Service, Department of Health and Human Services, 200 Independence Ave. S.W., Room 716-G, Washington, DC 20201/202-245-6467.

Surplus Property
Health and educational organizations can receive surplus federal property to aid in carrying out their programs. Contact: Division of Realty, Office of Real Property, Office of Facilities Engineering, Office of the Secretary, Department of Health and Human Services, Room 4725, Washington, DC 20201/202-245-1926.

Toxic Effects of Chemicals Registry
The *Registry of Toxic Effects of Chemical Substances* lists chemical information and known biological effects for about 22,000 chemicals currently found in the workplace. Contact: Technical Publication Development Section, Department of Health and Human Services, NIOSH, Division of Standards, Development and Tech. Transfer, Int Acquist. and Data Systems Section, 4676 Columbia Pkwy., Cincinnati, OH 45226/513-684-8317.

Toxicological Effects Research
The National Institute of Environmental Health Sciences (NIEHS) is studying the effect of chemical, physical, and bio-metabolism on health. NIEHS' pharmacology staff conduct research on toxicological effects and metabolic pathways in the body and affected organs. They also explore harmful agents in the environment, neurological and behavioral toxicology, pulmonary functions, genetics, and reproduction and development. NIEHS publishes the *Annual Report to the Science Community,* an annual report providing an overview of the research and developments achieved in the field over the year. The 400-page publication is available free of charge. They also publish *Research Programs of NIEHS,* a biannual publication that outlines the research being conducted by the Institute and new findings. The 80-page publication is available free of charge. Contact: National Institute of Environmental Health Sciences (NIEHS), PO Box 12233, Research Triangle, NC 27709/919-541-3345.

Toxicological Research
The National Center for Toxicological Research accumulates information and expertise, which includes carcinogenic research, mutagenic research, teratogenic research, molecular biology, and microbiology, and immunology. Contact: National Center for Toxicological Research, General Services, Food and Drug Administration, Department of Health and Human Services, Jefferson, AK 72079/501-541-4344.

Toxicology Programs
The Agency for Toxic Substances and Disease Registry, an inter-governmental group, is involved in the coordination and planning with other agencies such as the Food and Drug Administration (FDA), CDC, National Toxicological Program (NTP) and National Institutes of Health (NIH) to ensure the clean up of hazardous waste dump sites and hazardous spills is carried out. The agency oversees a comprehensive environmental program involving testing of chemicals, health studies, testing equipment and clothing for safety, training programs, data base development, and coordinating adequate safety in cleanup sites and cleanup groups. They do not have any publications. Contact: Agency for Toxic Substances and Disease Registry, Super Fund Implementation Group, Atlanta, GA 30333/404-452-4100.

Toxicology Publications
The Center for Environmental Health publishes more than 150 free publications a year on a wide variety of topics. Subjects have included: cancer, laboratory techniques, population studies, lead poisoning, and birth defects. A free publication catalog is available from the Center. Contact: Center for Environmental Health, Centers for Disease Control, Atlanta, GA 30333/404-452-4161.

Training Programs for Careers in Aging
The Department of Health and Human Services funds a number of institutions to provide educational programs for professional careers in aging. (See "Grants" in this section.) For a listing of

institutions which offer training programs for careers in aging, contact: Office of Education and Training, Administration on Aging, Office of Human Development Services, Department of Health and Human Services, North Bldg, 330 Independence Ave SW. Room 4226, Washington, DC 20201/202-472-4226.

Transplantation Publications
The National Institute of Arthritis, Diabetes, Digestive and Kidney Diseases conducts and funds research pertaining to transplantation. Staff can provide information, direct you to government reports, and send you publications. The office's information specialists can refer you to research centers, experts, government programs, and literature in their assigned area. Contact: National Institute of Arthritis, Diabetes, Digestive and Kidney Diseases, Information and Health Research Reports Office, Building 31, Room 9A-04, 9000 Rockville Pike, Bethesda, MD 20205/301-496-3583.

Treatment at Government Expense
The National Institutes of Health (NIH) selects a limited number of patients each month for study and therapy. If your illness is one under investigation at NIH, your doctor can refer you to the program. Travel and housing are supplied to patients. For information on illnesses under investigation or further assistance, contact: Office of the Director, The Clinical Center, Building 10, Room 2C-146, NIH, Department of Health and Human Services, 9000 Rockville Pike, Bethesda, MD 20205/301-496-4891.

Veterinary Medicine
The Food and Drug Administration (FDA), as part of its duties, works to assure the safety and efficiency of drugs, devices and feeds to animals.

Contact: Center for Veterinary Medicine, Food and Drug Administration, Department of Health and Human Services, 5600 Fishers Lane, Room 7-57, Rockville, MD 20857/301-443-3450.

Work Environment Health Examinations
The National Institute on Occupational Safety and Health (NIOSH) will conduct on-site health hazard evaluations at the requesst of employers or employees. It will inspect the work environment and give medical exams when warranted. Contact: Division of Surveillance Hazard Evaluations and Field Studies, NIOSH, Department of Health and Human Services, 4676 Columbia Pkwy., Cincinnati, OH 45226/513-684-4428.

X-Ray and Gamma Ray Research
The Nuclear Medical Department is actively involved in the research and development of scintillation imaging, consisting of gamma rays and X-rays, in an effort to further the use of nuclear medicine. The department oversees hospitals to ensure that the proper specifications and guidelines are followed. Papers with their research findings are submitted to other medical journals. National Institute of Health staff are available to answer questions and make referrals in the field of nuclear medicine. Contact: Nuclear Medicine Department, National Institutes of Health (NIH), Bldg. 10, Room 1C 401, 9000 Rockville Pike, Bethesda, MD 20205/301-496-5675

How Can the Department of Health and Human Services Help You?
If you believe that the Department of Health and Human Services can be of help to you and you cannot find a relevant office listed in this section, contact: Information, Department of Health and Human Services, 200 Independence Ave. S.W., Room 1187, Washington, DC 20201/202-245-6296.

Department of Housing and Urban Development

451 7th St. S.W., Washington, DC 20410/202-755-5111

Established: September 9, 1965
Budget: $10,667,045,000
Employees: 11,910

Mission: Responsible for programs concerned with housing needs, fair housing opportunities, and improving and developing the Nation's communities. To carry out its overall purpose of assisting the sound development of our communities, HUD administers mortgage insurance programs that help families to become home owners; a rental subsidy program for lower income families who otherwise could not afford decent housing; antidiscrimination in housing activities; and programs that aid neighborhood rehabilitation and the preservation of our urban centers from blight and decay. HUD also protects the home buyer in the marketplace and fosters programs that stimulate and guide the housing industry to provide not only housing but a suitable living environment.

Major Divisions and Offices

Policy Development and Research

Department of Housing and Urban Development, 451 7th St. S.W., Room 8100, Washington, DC 20410/202-755-5600.
Budget: $18,000,000
Employees: 155
Mission: Advise the secretary in policy, program evaluation, and research. Evaluate existing programs and policies and analyze potential programs and policies by employing the independent and objective research capabilities of its staff and its consultants.

Fair Housing and Equal Opportunity

Department of Housing and Urban Development, 451 7th St. S.W., Room 5100, Washington, DC 20410/202-755-7252.
Budget: $5,700,000
Employees: 581
Mission: Develops and implements fair housing and equal opportunity policies and programs pursuant to various civil rights laws, Executive orders, and Federal regulations intended to protect affected persons from discrimination based on race, color, sex, national origin, religion, handicap or age.

Government National Mortgage Association

Department of Housing and Urban Development (HUD), 451 7th St. S.W., Room 6100, Washington, DC 20410/202-755-5926.
Budget: $1,880,000
Employees: 53

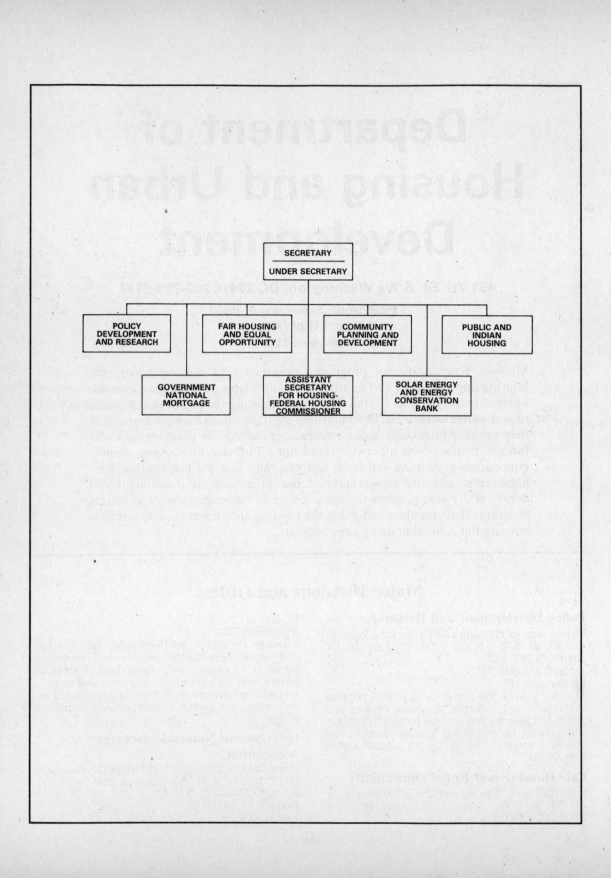

Mission: Provide special assistance in the financing of eligible types of federally underwritten mortgages.

Community Planning and Development

Department of Housing and Urban Development, 451 7th St. S.W., Room 7100, Washington, DC 20410/202-755-6270.
Budget: $3,908,000
Employees: 1,336
Mission: Provide decent housing and a suitable living environment and expanding economic opportunities principally for persons of low and moderate income. Make direct grants to severely distressed cities and urban counties for local economic development projects designed to stimulate new, increased private investment. Assist state and local governments with common or related planning development programs. Insure fair treatment of persons displaced by federally assisted projects. Implement policies and procedures for the protection and enhancement of environmental quality. Provide loans for rehabilitation of property. Provide assistance to the urban homesteading program.

Assistant Secretary For Housing-Federal

Housing Commissioner, Department of Housing and Urban Development, 451 7th St. S.W., Room 9100, Washington, DC 20410/202-755-6600.
Budget: $6,309,594,000
Employees: 5,095
Mission: Direct housing programs and functions of the department including the production, financing, and management of housing, and the conservation and rehabilitation of the housing stock. Provide mortgage insurance. Provide advice and technical assistance to nonprofit sponsors of low- and moderate-income housing. Provide technical and financial assistance in planning, developing and managing housing for low-income families.

Public and Indian Housing

Department of Housing and Urban Development, 451 7th St. S.W., Room 4100, Washington, DC 20410/202-755-6600.
Budget: $5,744,000,000
Employees: 955
Mission: Responsible for administering all public and Indian housing (PIH) programs (including but limited to rental housing, Turnkey III housing, and mutual help housing); and advises the Secretary regarding the production, financing and management of public and Indian housing programs, as well as the preservation, improvement, and upgrading of the management and operation of the existing housing stock.

Solar Energy and Energy Conservation Bank

Department of Housing and Urban Development, 451 7th St. S.W., Room 7110, Washington, DC 20410/202-755-7166.
Budget: $9,000,000
Employees: 6
Mission: Provides loan subsidies and matching grants for low and moderate income individuals to purchase energy conservation and solar energy improvements.

Major Sources of Information

Adjustable Rate Mortgage (ARM)
Department of Housing and Urban Development provides Federal mortgage insurance for Adjustable Rate Mortgages (ARMs). Under this HUD-insured mortgage, the interest rate and monthly payment may change during the life of the loan. The initial interest rate, discount points and the margin are negotiable between the buyer and lender. The one-year Treasury Constant Maturities is the index used for determining the interest rate changes. One percentage point is the maximum amount the interest rate may increase or decrease in any one year. Over the life of the loan, the maximum interest rate change is five percentage points from the initial rate of the mortgage. Lenders are required to disclose to the borrower the nature of the ARM loan at the time of loan application. In addition, borrowers must be informed at least 30 days in advance of any adjustment to the monthly payment. Contact: Assistant Secretary for Housing/Federal Housing Commissioner, Department of Housing and Urban Development, Washington, D.C. 20410/202-755-6604.

Bibliographies, Housing
A number of specialized bibliographies on housing related topics are available from: Library Division, Department of Housing and Urban Development, 451 7th St. S.W., Room 8141, Washington, DC 20410/202-755-6370.

Block Grants
Block grants are provided to local governments to support a variety of programs benefitting lower and middle income people. Projects include: urban renewal; neighborhood development; housing rehabilitation; repairing streets, sidewalks, sewer lines and roads; and parks and recreational centers. See "Grants" or contact: Office of Block Grant Assistance, Office of Community Planning

and Development, Department of Housing and Urban Development, 451 7th St. S.W., Room 7128, Washington, DC 20410/202-755-6587.

Building a House
Homeowner's Glossary of Building Terms is available for free from Program Information, Department of Housing and Urban Development, 451 7th St. S.W., Room 1104, Washington, DC 20410/202-755-6420.

The following books are produced by Housing and Urban Development and are available from Superintendent of Documents, Government Printing Office, Washington, DC 20402/202-783-3238:

All Weather Home Building Manual ($6.50)
Solar Dwellings Design Concepts ($6.50)

See "Consumer Publications on Housing" in this section.

Building Technology
See "Consumer Information" in this section.

Buying a House
The following publications are available for free from: Program Information Center, Department of Housing and Urban Development, 451 7th St. S.W., Room 1104, Washington, DC 20401/202-755-6420.

Buying a Home? Don't Forget the Settlement Costs
Comparison of Condominiums and Cooperatives
Real Estate Settlement Procedures Act—Special Information Booklet
Selling the Solar Home
Fact Sheets—Should You Rent or Buy a Home
Let's Consider Cooperatives
Home Buying Members of the Armed Services
Move in . . . with a Graduated Payment Mortgage

See "Consumer Publications in Housing" in this section.

Citizen Participation in Community Development
For information on reports, studies or surveys on topics of community development contact: Intergovernmental Program, Analysis and Evaluation, Office of Evaluation, Office of Urban Rehabilitation and Community Reinvestment, Department of Housing and Urban Development, 451 7th St. S.W., Room 7144, Washington, DC 20410/202-755-6032.

Consumer Complaints, Land Sales
See "Land Sales" in this section.

Consumer Complaints, Mobile Home
See "Mobile Home Safety and Construction" in this section.

Consumer Complaints—Settlement Costs
If you have a complaint concerning settlement costs on a real estate transaction, assistance is available from Real Estate Practices Division, Office of Voluntary Associations and Consumer Protection, Department of Housing and Urban Development, 451 7th St. S.W., Room 9266, Washington, DC 20410/202-426-0070.

Consumer Information
A wide variety of information is available to consumers on such topics as: home improvement; renting, buying or building a home; building technology; community development; economic development; housing finance; and housing management. Contact: Program Information Center, Department of Housing and Urban Development, 451 7th St. S.W., Room 1104, Washington, DC 20410/202-755-6420.

Consumer Publications on Housing
The following housing publications are available from Consumer Information Center, Pueblo, Colorado 81009:

Avoiding Mortgage Default. 575 M, Free, 5 pp., 1982. Steps to take if you are having trouble making your payments on time.

Buying Lots From Developers 169 H, $2.50 20 pp. 1982. What to ask about a property and contract before you sign; information the developer must give you under law.

Can I Really Get Free or Cheap Public Land? 170M, $2.50, 14 pp. 1981. What public lands are still available for purchase or homesteading; how to go about obtaining them.

Homeowner's Glossary of Building Terms. 603H. Free. 16 pp. 1977. Definitions of everything from acoustical tile to weep holes.

House Construction: How to Reduce Costs. 172M, $2.50 16 pp. 1977. How to save in location, style, interior arrangements, and selection of materials and utilities.

Selecting and Financing A Home. 174M, $3.00 24 pp. 1980. Brief comparison of renting with buying; how to figure what you can afford; how to apply for a loan; what to look for in homeowner's insurance.

Wood-frame House Construction. 148H. $4.25. 223 pp. 1975. Comprehensive, illustrated handbook of detailed instructions and basic principles for building and insulating.

How To Prevent and Remove Mildew. 189M. $2.50, 15 pp. 1980. What it is; how to prevent and remove it from different surfaces; and how to get rid of dampness and musty odors.

Imaginative Ways with Bathrooms. 615H. Free. 6 pp. 1974. Accessories, storage areas, and safety features to consider when planning a new or remodeling an old bathroom.

Painting—Inside and Out. 190M. $2.50 26 pp. 1978. Directions for doing a top-quality paint job, including surface preparation, paint selection, application, use of natural finishes; also lists references.

Buying Lots from Developers. 169M. $2.50. 20 pp. 1982. What you're entitled to know—and should ask—before you sign a contract.(HUD)

Construction Guides for Exposed Wood Decks. 220M. $5.00. 78 pp. 1982. Design, material selection, construction, and finishing of outdoor wood decks; includes step-by-step, illustrated instructions for decks, benches, and stairways. (USDA)

The Mortgage Money Guide. 418M. 50¢. 16 pp. 1982. Handy guide to different types of mortgages and loan financing options; includes a table of monthly mortgage costs at various rates. (FTC)

Sales of Federal Surplus Real Estate. 576M. Free. 18 pp. Revised monthly. Listing of when, where, and how surplus properties will be sold within the next three months; where to go for more information on specific pieces of property. (GSA)

Settlement Costs. 175M. $3.50. 43 pp. 1983. What they are; documents to expect: sample forms and worksheets to compare costs; how to avoid unfair practices when purchasing a home. (HUD)

Turning Home Equity Into Income for Older Americans. 176M. $1.25. 15 pp. 1982. Three plans to help homeowners convert the capital they have built up into income, with examples of how the plans work and what the costs and risks are. (CONG)

Earth Sheltered Housing. 178M. $6.00. 141 pp. 1983. Pros and cons of earth-shelterd construction with extensive information on building codes, zoning, financing, and design ideas. (HUD)

Find and Fix the Leaks. 180M. $2.50. 28 pp. 1982. Energy-efficient ways to plug air leaks and save fuel, as well as tips on maintaining good air quality indoors. (DOE)

Heating with Wood. 181M. $3.00. 20 pp. 1980. Types of fireplaces, stoves, and furnaces; buying, installing, and using wood-stoves; buying and burning wood efficiently and safely. (DOE)

Kerosene Heaters. 577M. Free. 4 pp. 1984. Important safety factors to consider in selection, use, maintenance, refueling, and storage. (CPSC/OCA)

In the Event of a Flood. 600M. Free. 6 pp. 1983. What to do during a flood and how to minimize loss of life and property. (FEMA)

Moisture and Home Energy Conservation. 214M. $4.25. 36 pp. 1983. Illustrated guide to why and where most moisture problems occur and suggested remedies; includes a checklist to help you detect problem areas. (DOE)

Solar Greenhouses and Sunspaces. 223M. $2.25. 35 pp. 1984. How you can design, build, and use greenhouses and sunspaces to help heat your house; advice on ventilation, growing plants, and safety. Lists demonstration projects and other sources of help.(DOE)

Window Insulation. 224M. $2.50. 35 pp. 1984. Because glass is a very poor insulator, windows let in much heat and cold. This book will help you sort through the options that are now available to cut that energy loss (DOE)

Your Keys to Energy Efficiency. 609M. Free. 21 pp. 1984. Tips for saving energy at home and in your car; health related issues; state and local consumer and energy offices; and an energy bibliography. (OCA)

Asbestos in the Home. 183M. $2.75. 12 pp. 1982. What asbestos is and the dangers; how you can tell if there is asbestos in your home; and what to do about it. (CPSC)

Cockroaches. 184M. $2.25. 10 pp. 1980. Getting them out and keeping them out. (USDA)

Home Electrical Safety Audit. 421M. 50¢. 11 pp. 1984. How to identify and correct electrical safety problems in your home. (CPSC)

Home Fire Safety. 405M. 50¢. 9 pp. 1983. Common causes of fire, what to do if fire breaks out, and how to reduce the risk of fire, including installing a smoke detector. (CPSC)

How to Crimeproof Your Home. 188M. $2.50. 18 pp. 1979. How to use landscaping, lighting, doors, windows, locks, and alarm systems to protect your home; tips for apartment dwellers; and special safeguards while you're on vacation. (DOJ)

Subterranean Termites. 194M. $2.50. 40 pp. 1983. How to recognize them and identify damage to wood; how to prevent termites during construction; and how to control termites in existing buildings. (USDA)

Wood Siding. 225M. $1.50. 23 pp. 1983. Tells why wood siding is still a good choice and gives tips for selecting, installing, maintaining, and refinishing. Includes diagrams and photos. (USDA)

Simple Home Repairs . . . Inside. 192M. $3.25. 23 pp. 1979. Guide to repairing and replacing faucets, electric plugs, screens, tiles, etc.

Direct Payments

The programs described below are those which provide financial assistance directly to individuals, private firms and other private institutions to encourage or subsidize a particular activity.

Interest Reduction—Homes for Lower-Income Families

Objectives: To make homeownership more readily available to families displaced by urban renewal or other government actions and to increase homeownership opportunities for low-income and moderate-income families.

Eligibility: All families are eligible.

Range of Financial Assistance: Estimated average $414 per year in interest subsidy payments per unit for the original program and $1,337 per unit per year for the revised program.

Contact: Director, Single Family Development Division, Office of Single Family Housing, Department of Housing and Urban Development, Washington, DC 20410/202-755-6720.

Interest Reduction Payments—Rental and Cooperative Housing for Lower-Income Families

Objectives: To provide good quality rental and cooperative housing for persons of low and moderate income by providing interest reduction payments in order to lower their housing costs.

Eligibility: Eligible mortgagors include nonprofit, cooperative, builder-seller, investor-sponsor, and limited-distribution sponsors. Public bodies do not qualify as mortgagors under this program.

Range of Financial Assistance: The unit mortgage limits are as follows: efficiency, $16,860; one bedroom, $18,648; two bedrooms, $22,356; three bedrooms, $28,152; four or more bedrooms, $31,884.

Contact: Director, Multifamily Development Division, Office of Multifamily Housing Development, Room 6116, Housing, Department of Housing and Urban Development, Washington, DC 20410/202-755-5216.

Lower-Income Housing Assistance Program

Objectives: To aid lower-income families in obtaining decent, safe and sanitary housing in private accommodations and to promote economically mixed existing, and moderately rehabilitated housing.

Eligibility: Any private owner, profit-motivated and nonprofit, cooperative, or an authorized public housing agency, any state, county, municipality or other governmental entity or public body, or agency or instrumentality thereof which is authorized to engage in or assist in the development or operation of housing for low-income families.

Range of Financial Assistance: Amount necessary to lease units and cover related management and maintenance and operating expenses including utilities, not to exceed Housing and Urban Development approved reasonable rents for constructed or existing comparable units, offering equivalent accommodations, utilities and services, for the housing area in which the units will be located.

Contact: Office of Elderly and Assisted Housing, Existing Housing Division, Housing, Department of Housing and Urban Development, Room 6230, Washington, DC 20410/202-755-5597.

Mortgage Insurance—Rental Housing for the Elderly

Objectives: To provide good quality rental housing for the elderly.

Eligibility: Eligible mortgagors include investors, builder developers, public bodies, and nonprofit sponsors.

Range of Financial Assistance: The unit mortgage limits for non-elevator apartments are as follows: efficiency, $18,450; one bedroom, $20,625; two bedrooms, $24,630; three bedrooms, $29,640; four or more bedrooms, $34,846. Limits per family unit are somewhat higher for elevator apartments. In areas where cost levels so require, limits per family unit may be increased up to 75 percent.

Contact: Director, Insurance Division, Office of Insured Multifamily Housing Development, Housing, Department of Housing and Urban Development, Washington, DC 20410/202-755-6223.

Rent Supplements—Rental Housing for Lower-Income Families

Objectives: To make good quality rental housing available to low-income families at a cost they can afford.

Eligibility: Eligible sponsors include nonprofit, cooperative, builder-seller, investor-sponsor, and limited-distribution mortgagors.

Range of Financial Assistance: Assistance covers the difference between the tenant's payment and the basic market rental, but may not exceed 70 percent of the market rental. The tenant's payment is between 25 and 30 percent of the monthly adjusted income or of market rental.

Contact: For Management Information: Director, Office of Multifamily Housing Management, Housing, Department of Housing and Urban Development, Washington, DC 20401/202-755-5216.

Discrimination Hotline

If you feel discriminated against in the rental, purchase or financing of housing HUD will investigate and aid in processing your complaint. Contact: Office of Fair Housing Enforcement and Compliance, Department of Housing and Urban Development, 451 7th St. S.W., Room 5206, Washington, DC 20410/toll-free 800-424-8590, 202-426-3500 in DC.

Elderly Housing

For information and expertise on special problems encountered by the elderly contact: Elderly Housing and Special Programs, Federal Housing Commissioner, Department of Housing and Urban Development, 451 7th St. S.W., Room 10184, Washington, DC 20410/202-755-5318 or Consumer Affairs and the Elderly, Office for Neighborhoods, Voluntary Associations and Consumer Protection, Department of Housing and Urban Development, 451 7th St. S.W., Washington, DC 20410/202-755-5318.

Energy Conservation Research

HUD, in cooperation with the Department of Energy and other agencies, encourages the development and use of new energy conservation designs, methods and standards for all types of existing and new residences including mobile homes. Contact: Building Technology Division, Office of Research, Office of Policy Development and Research, Department of Housing and Urban Development, 451 7th St. S.W., Room 8158, Washington, DC 20410/202-755-6443.

Environmental Quality
Guidance and training in historic preservation and environmental quality are available to local communities from: Environmental Planning Division, Office of Environmental Quality, Community Planning and Development, Department of Housing and Urban Development, 451 7th St. S.W., Room 7152, Washington, DC 20410/202-755-7225.

Experimental Housing
See "Loans and Loan Guarantees (Mortgage Insurance)" in this section.

Fair Housing and Equal Opportunity
For information on expertise on the law which prohibits the discrimination in housing on the basis of race, color, religion, sex or national origin, contact: Office of Fair Housing Enforcement and Compliance, Department of Housing and Urban Development, 451 7th St. S.W., Room 5206, Washington, DC 20410/202-755-5673. See also "Discrimination Hotline" in this section.

Federal Housing Administration (FHA)
The major program of the FHA is the basic home mortgage insurance program which covers 1 to 4 family units. FHA insures private financial institutions against any loss. There is really no FHA. Everything referred to as FHA really means HUD Insured Mortgage. See "Loans and Loan Guarantees" or contact: Office of Single Family Housing, Department of Housing and Urban Development, 451 7th St. S.W., Room 9266, Washington, DC 20410/202-426-7212.

Federal Housing Administration (FHA) Lenders
For information on financial institutions which supply FHA mortgages contact: Single Family Housing, Office of Housing, Department of Housing and Urban Development, 451 7th St. S.W., Room R9282, Washington, DC 20410/202-755-6675.

Financial Institution Regulation and Alternative Housing Finance Mechanisms
Research is conducted to look into capital markets, savings and loan associations, credit unions, mortgage markets, and alternative mortgages to make home buying cheaper. Contact: Division of Housing Finance Analysis, Office of Economic Affairs, Policy Development and Research, Department of Housing and Urban Development, 451 7th St. S.W.. Room 8212, Washington, DC 20410/202-755-5422.

Finance, Housing
The Financial Analysis Division conducts studies and maintains statistics relating to conditions in the mortgage market, municipal securities market, housing finance, taxation, current national housing productions, mortgage market trends, mortgage lending and commitment activity, survey of mortgage interest rates, and capital market forecasts. Contact: Financial Analysis Division, Office of Financial D Management, Office of Housing, Department of Housing and Urban Development, 451 7th St. S.W., Room 9132, Washington, DC 20410/202-755-7270.

Funds to Attract Private Investment
Funds are available to cities to attract private investment in a project in a distressed neighborhood, industrial park or business district. See "Grants" (Urban Development Action Grants) or contact: Urban Development Action Grants, Office of Community Planning and Development, Department of Housing and Urban Development, 451 7th St. S.W., Room 7100, Washington, DC 20410/202-755-6270.

Government National Mortgage Associations (GNMA)
The GNMA program offers government guaranteed securities to investors which are designed to attract non-traditional investors into the residential mortgage market. The minimum size of a security certificate is $25,000. The maturity is typically 30 years. Contact: Office of Corporate Planning, Government National Mortgage Association, Department of Housing and Urban Development, 451 7th St. S.W., Room 6206, Washington, DC 20410/202-755-7141.

Grants
The programs described below are for sums of money which are given by the federal government to initiate and stimulate new or improved activities or to sustain on-going services.

Community Development Block Grants/Entitlement Grants
Objectives: To develop viable urban communities, including decent housing and a suitable living environment, and expand economic opportunities, principally for persons of low and moderate income.

Eligibility: Cities in standard metropolitan statistical areas (SMSAs) with populations in excess of 50,000, and cities with populations of under 50,000 which are central cities in SMSAs.

Range of Financial Assistance: Determined by formula.

Contact: Office of Block Grant Assistance, Community Planning and Development, 451 7th St. S.W., Washington, DC 20410/202-755-9267.

Community Development Block Grants/Small Cities Programs

Objectives: To assist communities in providing decent housing and a suitable living environment for persons of low and moderate income.

Eligibility: All states, counties, and units of general local government, except metropolitan cities and urban counties, may apply for Small Cities Grants.

Range of Financial Assistance: $24,000 to $800,000.

Contact: Office of Block Grant Assistance, Community Planning and Development, Department of Housing and Urban Development, 451 7th St. S.W., Washington, DC 20410/202-755-9267.

General Research and Technology Activity

Objectives: To carry out applied research and demonstration projects of high priority and preselected by the department to serve the needs of housing and community development groups and to improve the operations of the Department's programs.

Eligibility: State and local governments, public and/or private profit and nonprofit organizations which have authority and capacity to carry out projects.

Range of Financial Assistance: $150 to $500,000.

Contact: Assistant Secretary for Policy Development and Research, Department of Housing and Urban Development, 451 7th St. S.W., Washington, DC 20410/1 202-755-6996.

Indian Community Development Block Grant Program

Objectives: To assist Indian Tribes and Alaskan Natives in the development of viable Indian communities principally for persons of low and moderate income.

Eligibility: Approved Indian Tribes.

Range of Financial Assistance: Average grant $235,754.

Contact: Office of Program Policy Development, Department of Housing and Urban Development, 451 7th St. S.W., Washington, DC 20410/202-755-6092.

Low Income Housing—Assistance Program (Public Housing)

Objectives: To provide decent, safe and sanitary housing and related facilities for families of low income through an authorized Public Housing Agency (PHA).

Eligibility: Public Housing Agencies established by a local government in accordance with state law, authorized public agencies, or Indian tribal organizations are eligible.

Range of Financial Assistance: Average obligation per unit is $2,300.

Contact: Director, Office of Elderly and Assisted Housing, Existing Housing Division, Housing, Department of Housing and Urban Development, Room 6230, Washington, DC 20410/202-755-5597.

Low Income Housing—Homeownership for Low-Income Families

Objectives: To provide low-income families with the opportunity of owning their own homes through local public housing agencies.

Eligibility: Public Housing Agencies established by a local government in accordance with state law, authorized public agencies, or Indian tribal organizations are eligible. The proposed program must be approved by the local governing body.

Range of Financial Assistance: Not specified.

Contact: Assistant Secretary for Public Housing and Indian Housing, Housing, Department of Housing and Urban Development, Washington, DC 20410/202-755-8702.

Public Housing—Modernization of Projects

Objectives: To provide annual contributions to modernize existing public housing projects to upgrade living conditions, correct physical deficiencies, and achieve operating efficiency and economy.

Eligibility: Public Housing Agencies (PHAs) operating PHA-owned low income public housing projects under an existing annual contributions contract.

Range of Financial Assistance: Not specified.

Contact: Assistant Secretary for Public and Indian Housing, Department of Housing and Urban Development, Washington, DC 20413/202-755-0950.

Urban Development Action Grants

Objectives: To assist severely distressed cities and severely distressed urban counties in alleviating physical and economic deterioration through economic development and neighborhood revitalization.

Eligibility: Eligible applicants are distressed cities and distressed urban counties.

Range of Financial Assistance: $77,700 to $13,500,000

Contact: Office of Urban Development Action Grants, Community Planning and Development, Department of Housing and Urban Development, 451 7th St. S.W., Room 7132, Washington, DC 20410/202-472-3947.

Handicapped Housing Information Center

For information and expertise on how Housing and Urban Development programs can be used to help disabled individuals contact: Office of Independent Living, Intergovernmental Relations, Office of Housing, Office of Federal Housing Commissioner, Department of Housing and Urban Development, 451 7th St. S.W., Room 10184, Washington, DC 20410/202-755-5857.

Historic Preservation
See "Environmental Quality" in this section.

Home Improvement
The following publications are available free from: Program Information Center, Department of Housing and Urban Development, 451 7th St. S.W., Room 1104, Washington, DC 20410/202-755-6420.

Protecting Your Home Against Theft
Fixing Up Your Home—What You Can Do and How To Finance It
Dealer and Contractor Guide to Property Improvement Loans
Fact Sheet—Home Improvement Loan Insurances

See "Loans (Major Home Improvement)," and "Consumer Publications on Housing" in this section.

Homesteading
The urban Homesteading Program transfers government defaulted properties to a buyer-occupant for $1.00 through a lottery. The homesteader is obliged to rehabilitate the property within 36 months to meet minimum health and safety standards and to live there for at least 5 years. Also available is a listing of publications. Contact: Urban Homesteading Division, Office of Urban Rehabilitation and Community Reinvestment, Community Planning and Development, Department of Housing and Urban Development, 451 7th St. S.W., Room 7168, Washington, DC 20410/202-755-5324.

Housing Assistance Research
Research is conducted on the effectiveness of various housing assistance programs. Contact: Division of Housing Assistance Research, Office of Research, Office of Policy Development and Research, Department of Housing and Urban Development, 451 7th St. S.W., Room 8150, Washington, DC 20410/202-755-6437.

Housing Counseling
Over 600 HUD approved counseling agencies are available throughout the United States to aid with such problems as mortgage defaults, financing and maintaining housing, how to conserve energy, how to budget money, and information on available HUD programs. Contact: Office of the Secretary, HEID and Counseling Services Branch, Single Family Servicing Division, Office of Single Family, Department of Housing and Urban Development, 451 7th St. S.W., Room 9186, Washington, DC 20410/202-755-6664.

Housing Information and Research
The Department of Housing and Urban Development provides the following free information services: 1) Personalized literature searches from HUD User's computerized data base to answer specific questions; 2) *Recent Research Results* a free bimonthly bulletin announcing the latest research reports; 3) bibliographies, brochures, and announcements of important future research; and 4) document distribution service to supply copies of research results. Included in the topical areas covered are: building technology, community development, conserving communities, economic development and public finance, elderly and the handicapped, energy and utilities, environmental research, financial management, housing finance, housing management and housing programs. Contact: Housing and Urban Development User, P.O. Box 280, Germantown, MD 20874/301-251-5154.

Housing Management
Research is conducted on various aspects of housing management, e.g., special user housing, modernization needs, cost of retrofitting for the elderly and handicapped, and cost of retrofitting for energy conservation. Contact: Division of Housing Management and Special User Research, Office of Research, Office for Policy, Development and Research, Department of Housing and Urban Development, 451 7th St. S.W., Room 8156, Washington, DC 20410/202-755-5574.

Housing Market Studies
Local and national studies are conducted on various aspects of the housing market. Contact: Division of Economic Market Analysis, Offices of Economic Affairs, Policy Development and Research, Department of Housing and Urban Development, 451 7th St. S.W., Room 8222, Washington, DC 20410/202-755-5577

HUD Publications
A limited number of these publications are available for free upon request from the U.S. Department of Housing and Urban Development, Information Center, First Floor, 451 7th Street S.W., Washington, DC 20410/202-755-6420.

HUD's Role in Home Improvement
Manufactured Housing: An Opportunity for Affordable Quality Homes
Manufactured Home Financing Through HUD
Dealer and Contractor Guide to Property Improvement Loans
Fair Housing U.S.A.
Fact Sheet: Technical Assistance Program
Fact Sheet: Minority Bank Deposit Program
Fact Sheet: Indian Housing
Changing Environments for People with Disabilities
Fixing Up Your Home—And How To Finance It
Fact Sheet: Neighborhood Strategy Area NSA Program
Fact Sheet: Fact About Relocation of Business Concerns, Farm Operations and Nonprofit Organizations
Group Medical Practice Facilities
Fact Sheet: Lead Poisoning a Constant Danger

Relocation Assistance to Displaced Tenants
Relocation Assistance to Displaced Homeowners
When a Public Agency Acquires Your Property
Nursing Home and Intermediate Care Facility Mortgage
  Insurance
Hospital Mortgage Insurance Program
Let's Consider Cooperatives
Questions About Condominiums
Your Housing Right—Live Where You Want To Live
Home Buying Members of the Armed Services
Buying a Home?" Don't Forget the Settlement Costs!
Move in . . . with a Graduated Payment Mortgage
Fact Sheet: Should You Rent or Buy a Home?
Avoiding Mortgage Default
Before Buying Land . . . Get the Facts
Helping Rehabilitate America
Protecting Your home Against Theft
HUD/FHA Program for Mortgage Insurance for Nursing
  Homes and Related Facilities
HUD/FHA Program for UNSUBSIDIZED Cooperative
  Housing
A Guide to Multifamily Homesteading
Financing Multifamily Rehabilitation
The Impact of Foreign Direct Investment on U.S. Cities
  and Regions
Public Housing Urban Initiatives Program
REDlining: A Bibliography
Neighborhood Conservation and Property Rehabilitation
The Davis-Bacon Act
Community Revitalization Bibliography
FHA Title I Property Improvement Loan Insurance
Small Cities Block Grant Program
Consolidated Annual Report to Congress on Community
  Development Programs
Housing Rehabilitation For Small Cities
Fact Sheet: Small Cities Program
Community Development Block Grant Program
Working Partners—100 Success Stories of Local Commu-
  nity Development
Energy Conserving Features Inherent in Older Homes
The Urban Development Action Grant
Rapid Growth From Energy Projects
Neighborhood Conservation and Property Rehabilitation
Fact Sheet: HUD Assistance to the Elderly
Annual Report—U.S. Department of Housing and Urban
  Development
Block Grant Energy Conservation
The President's National Urban Policy Report
Summary of the Housing and Community Development
  Amendments of 1981
Aids to Understanding the U.S. Department of Housing
  and Urban Development

HUD USER

HUD USER is the research information service sponsored by HUD's Office of Policy Development and Research. This service maintains a data base of about 5,000 documented research reports sponsored by HUD. Two types of data base searches are available. Standard Searches are generalized searches of the data base on 12 recurring topics and Custom Searches are searches of the data base tailored to the specifications of the requestor. Standard Searches are $10.00, and Custom Searches are $50.00. A stock of 270 Current documents are available to the public at a minimal fee. The service can make copies of their other documents on a cost recovery basis. Two publications listing reports available and may be obtained free of charge are *Recent Research Results* and *HUD USER Publication List*. The Service also offers audiovisual materials for purchase or rental to all its users. Audiovisual materials are available offered on topics dealing with Affordable Housing, the Section 8 Program, Community Self-Reliance and Private Delivery of Public Services. Contact: HUD USER, P. O. Box 280, Germantown, MD 20874/301-251-5154.

Indian Housing

For information and expertise concerning the special housing needs for American Indians contact: Office of Indian Housing, Public Housing and Indian Programs, Office of Housing, Department of Housing and Urban Development, 451 7th St. S.W., Room 4232, Washington, DC 20410/202-755-6522.

Joint Venture for Affordable Housing

The Joint Venture for Affordable Housing is a collective effort among public and private sector groups who share a commitment to the creation of more affordable housing, and are linked through a series of coordinated projects and activities. The premise of the Joint Venture is that the key to housing cost reduction at the local level is regulatory relief, which is controlled by elected officials in over 19,000 municipalities and over 3,000 counties. It builds on previous HUD demonstration projects which show that substantial savings are available through reduced site development standards, expedited processing procedures, increased densities, and use of new and improved technologies. Joint Venture projects and activities are currently underway in more than two dozen localities around the country. Contact: Assistant Secretary for Policy Development and Research, Department of Housing and Urban Development, Washington, DC 20410/202-755-6443.

Land Development Assistance

Up-front capital is available to cities for acquiring or rehabilitating property to stimulate industrial, commercial or residential land development. See "Loans (Rehabilitation)" or contact: Financial Management Division, Office of Block Grant Assistance, Office of Community Planning and Development, Department of Housing and Urban Development, 451 7th St. S.W., Room 718, Washington, DC 20410/202-755-1871.

Land Sales

The Department of Housing and Urban Development protects consumers against fradulent practices of land developers. Anyone with 100 lots or more must register with HUD. Consumers have the rights to obtain a copy of the disclosure registration documents from the developer or can view them in the HUD reading room. A free pamphlet, *Before Buying Land . . . Get the Facts,* is available from HUD. Contact: Office of Interstate Land Sales Registration, Department of Housing and Urban Development, 451 7th St. S.W., Room 6278, Washington, DC 204/202-755-0502 Land Sales Documents and Reading Room: Department of Housing and Urban Development, 451 7th St. S.W., Room 6262, Washington, DC 20410/202-755-5945.

Loans and Loan Guarantees

The programs described below are those which offer financial assistance through the lending of federal monies for a specific period of time or programs in which the federal government makes an arrangement to indemnify a lender against part or all of any defaults by the borrower.

Coinsurance for the Purchase or Refinancing of Existing Multifamily Projects

Objectives: To provide mortgage insurance for the purchase or refinancing of existing multifamily housing projects.

Eligibility: The mortgagor may be either private or public.

Range of Financial Assistance: not applicable.

Contact: Director, Office of Insured Multifamily Housing Development, Housing, Department of Housing and Urban Development, Washington, DC 20410/202-755-6223.

Community Development Block Grants—Secretary's Discretionary Fund—Insular Area

Objectives: To provide community development assistance to American Samoa, Guam, The Northern Mariana Islands, the Trust Territory of the Pacific and the Virgin Islands.

Eligibility: American Samoa, Guam, the Northern Mariana Islands, the Trust Territory of the Pacific and the Virgin Islands.

Range of Financial Assistance: not applicable.

Contact: Office of Program Policy Development, Community Planning and Development, Department of Housing and Urban Development, 451 7th St. S.W., Washington, DC 20410/202-755-6090.

Community Development Block Grants—Secretary's Discretionary Fund—Technical Assistance Program

Objectives: To help States, units of general local government, Indian tribes and areawide planning organizations to plan, develop and administer local Community Development Block Grant and Urban Development Action Grant programs.

Eligibility: States, units of general local govern-

ments, Indian tribes and areawide planning organizations may submit unsolicited proposals.

Range of Financial Assistance: not applicable.

Contact: Office of Program Policy Development, Community Planning and Development, Department of Housing and Urban Development, 451 7th St. SW Washington, DC 20410/202-755/6876.

Community Development Block Grants/State's Program

Objectives: The primary objective of this program is the development of viable urban communities by providing decent housing, a suitable living environment, and expanding economic opportunities, principally for persons of low and moderate income.

Eligibility: State governments. States must distribute the funds to units of general local governments in nonentitlement areas.

Range of Financial Assistance: Amount determined by formula.

Contact: State and Small Cities Division, Office of Block Grant Assistance, Community Planning and Development, Department of Housing and Urban Development, 451 7th Street S.W., Washington, DC 20410/202-755-6042.

Community Housing Resource Board Program

Objectives: To fulfill HUD's contractual agreement to provide assistance to local real estate boards in achieving Voluntary Affirmative Marketing Agreement goals by supporting projects that improve Community Housing Resource Boards performance and increase their ability to assist in implementing the VAMA.

Eligibility: The applicant must be a CHRB consisting of HUD appointed representatives of community organizations or agencies formed to fulfill HUD's obligation to provide technical assistance to local real estate boards in the implementation and monitoring of progress under the Voluntary Affirmative Marketing Agreement.

Range of Financial Assistance: $15,000 for CHRBs in communities of 50,000 or less. $25,000 for CHRBs in communities of over 50,000.

Contact: Department of Housing and Urban Development, Office of Fair Housing and Equal Opportunity, Office of Voluntary Compliance, Washington, DC 20410/202-755-5992.

Congregate Housing Services Program

Objectives: To evaluate a new service delivery arrangement designed to 1) prevent premature or unnecessary institutionalization of the elderly-handicapped, non-elderly handicapped, and temporarily disabled, 2) to provide a variety of innovative approaches for the delivery of meals and non-medical supportive services while utilizing existing service programs and 3) to fill gaps in existing service systems and ensure availability of funding for meals, and appropriate services needed to maintain independent living.

Eligibility: Eligible applicants: (1) must be either a conventional public housing project, or housing for the elderly or nonelderly handicapped owned by a nonprofit corporation. (2) must have an accessible central dining facility; (3) must have a need for the program; (4) must be able to demonstrate a record of satisfactory management in housing or services for the elderly or nonelderly handicapped; (5) must have a record of satisfactory performance in areas of equal opportunity.

Range of Financial Assistance: not specified.

Contact: Assisted Elderly and Handicapped Housing Division, Office of Elderly and Assisted Housing, Housing, Department of Housing and Urban Development, Washington, DC 20410/202-755-5597.

Fair Housing Assistance Program—State and Local

Objectives: To provide to those agencies to whom HUD must refer Title VIII complaints both the incentive and resources required to develop an effective workforce to handle complaints.

Eligibility: State and local governments administering State and local fair housing laws.

Range of Financial Assistance: Contribution for Capacity Building and Complaint Processing $20,000-$250,000; Training $1,000-$5,000; Specialized Projects $75,000-$150,000.

Contact: Assistant Secretary for Fair Housing and Equal Opportunity; Department of Housing and Urban Development; 451 7th St. S.W. Washington, DC 20410/202-755-3500.

Graduated Payment Mortgage Program

Objectives: To facilitate early homeownership for households that expect their incomes to rise substantially. Program allows homeowners to make smaller monthly payments initially and to increase their size gradually over time.

Eligibility: All persons are eligible to apply.

Range of Financial Assistance: Up to $60,000

Contact: Director, Single Family Development Division, Office of Single Family Housing, Department of Housing and Urban Development, Room 9270, Washington, DC 20410/202-755-6720.

Housing Counseling Assistance Program

Objectives: To counsel homeowners, homebuyers and tenants under HUD-assisted and insured housing programs in order to assure successful homeownership and thereby prevent and reduce delinquencies, defaults and foreclosures.

Eligibility: An applicant agency must be a public or private nonprofit agency.

Range of Financial Assistance: $5,000 to $50,000 for housing counseling grantees.

Contact: Office of Single Family Housing, Single Family Servicing Division, Secretary-Held and Counseling Services Branch, Department of Housing and Urban Development, Washington, DC 20410/202-755-6664.

Housing Development Grants

Objectives: To support the construction or substantial rehabilitation of rental housing in areas experiencing severe shortages of decent rental housing opportunities for families and individuals without other reasonable and affordable housing alternatives in the private market.

Eligibility: Cities (including closely settled towns and townships with comparable municipal powers), urban counties, and States acting on behalf of, and with the concurrence of, units of general local government may apply.

Range of Financial Assistance: none provided yet.

Contact: Director, Development Grants Division, Office of Elderly and Assisted Housing, Department of Housing and Urban Development, 451 7th St. S.W., Washington, DC 20410/202-755-6142.

Housing for the Elderly or Handicapped

Objectives: To provide for rental or cooperative housing and related facilities (such as central dining) for the elderly or handicapped.

Eligibility: Private nonprofit corporations and consumer cooperatives. Public bodies and their instrumentalities are not eligible.

Range of Financial Assistance: Approximate average award is $2,216,718.

Contact: Assisted Elderly and Handicapped Housing Division, Office of Elderly and Assisted Housing, Housing, Department of Housing and Urban Development, Room 6110, Washington, DC 20410/202-755-5597.

Interest Reduction Payments—Rental and Cooperative Housing for Lower-Income Families

Objectives: To provide good quality rental and cooperative housing for persons of low and moderate income by providing interest reduction payments in order to lower their housing costs.

Eligibility: Eligible mortgagors include nonprofit, cooperative, builder-seller, investor-sponsor, and limited-distribution sponsors. Public bodies do not qualify as mortgagors under this program.

Range of Financial Assistance: Program is now inactive, i.e., no new projects are being approved.

Contact: Director, Office of Multifamily Housing Management, Housing, Department of Housing and Urban Development, Washington, DC 20410/202-755-5216.

Low-Income Housing—Assistance Program (Public Housing)

Objectives: To provide decent, safe and sanitary housing and related facilities for families of low income through an authorized Public Housing Agency.

Eligibility Requirements: Public Housing Agencies established by a local government in accordance with state law, authorized to engage in or assist in the development or operation of housing for low-income families.

Range of Financial Assistance: Amount necessary to lease units and cover related administration, management and maintenance and operating expenses including utilities, offering equivalent accommodations, utilities and services, for the housing area in which the units will be located.

Contact: Director, Office of Elderly and Assisted Housing, Existing Housing Division, Housing, Department of Housing and Urban Development, Washington, DC 20410/202-755-5597.

Mobile Home Loan Insurance—Financing Purchase of Manufactured (Mobile) Homes as Principal Residences of Borrowers

Objectives: To make possible reasonable financing of mobile home purchases.

Eligibility: All persons are eligible to apply.

Range of Financial Assistance: Maximum amount of loan is $40,500.

Contact: Director, Office of Manufactured Housing and Regulatory Functions, Title I Insurance Division, Housing, Department of Housing and Urban Development, Washington, DC 20410/ 202-755-6880.

Mortgage Insurance

Objectives: To help families undertake home ownership.

Eligibility: All families are eligible to apply.

Range of Financial Assistance: Maximum insurable loans for an occupant mortgagor are as follows: One Family, $67,000; two family, $76,000; three-family, $92,000; and four family, $107,000.

Contact: Director, Single Family Development Division, Office of Single Family Housing, Department of Housing and Urban Development, Washington, DC 20410/202-755-6720.

Mortgage Insurance—Combination and Manufactured (Mobile) Home Lot Loans

Objectives: To make possible reasonable financing of mobile home purchase and lot to place it in.

Eligibility: All persons are eligible to apply.

Range of Financial Assistance: Up to $54,000 for a manufactured home and a suitably developed lot; $13,500 for a developed lot only.

Contact: Director, Office of Manufactured Housing and Regulatory Functions, Title I Insurance Division, Department of Housing and Urban Development, Washington, DC 20410/202-755-6880.

Mortgage Insurance—Construction or Substantial Rehabilitation of Condominium Projects

Objectives: To enable sponsors to develop condominium projects in which individual units will be sold to home buyers.

Eligibility: Eligible sponsors include investors, builders, developers, public bodies, and others who meet FHA requirements for mortgagors.

Range of Financial Assistance: Maximum insurable loans are as follows: efficiency, $19,500; one bedroom, $21,600; two bedrooms, $25,800; three bedrooms, $31,800; four or more bedrooms, $36,000. Unit mortgage.

Contact: Director, Insurance Division, Office of Insured Multifamily Housing Development, Housing, Department of Housing and Urban Development, Washington, DC 20410/202-755-6223.

Mortgage Insurance—Cooperative Financing

Objectives: To provide insured financing for the purchase of shares of stock in a cooperative project. Ownership of the shares carries the right to occupy a unit located within the cooperative project.

Eligibility: Owner occupant mortgagors are eligible.

Range of Financial Assistance: The maximum insurable mortgage loan for an occupant mortgagor are as follows: one family, $67,500; two family $76,000; three family $92,000; and four family $107,000, minus the portion of the unpaid balance of the blanket mortgage which is attributable to the dwelling unit.

Contact: Director, Single Family Development Division, Office of Single Family Housing, Department of Housing and Urban Development, Washington, DC 20410/202-755-6720.

Mortgage Insurance—Development of Sales Type Cooperative Projects

Objectives: To make it possible for nonprofit housing cooperatives, ownership housing corporations or trusts to sponsor the development of new housing that will be sold to individual cooperative members.

Eligibility: Eligible mortgagors include nonprofit cooperative ownership housing corporations or trusts, sponsors intending to sell individual units to cooperative members.

Range of Financial Assistance: not specified.

Contact: Director, Insurance Division, Office of Insured Multifamily Housing Development, Housing, Department of Housing and Urban Development, Washington, DC 20410/202-755-6223.

Mortgage Insurance—Experimental Homes

Objectives: To help finance the development of homes that incorporate new or untried construction concepts designed to reduce housing costs, raise living standards, and improve neighborhood design by providing mortgage insurance.

Eligibility: Interested applicants able to prove that the property which is proposed is an acceptable risk for testing advanced housing design or experimental property standards are eligible.

Range of Financial Assistance: Average mortgage is $65,000.

Contact: Assistant Secretary for Policy Development and Research, Department of Housing and Urban Development, 451 7th St. S.W., Washington, DC 20410/202-755-5544.

Mortgage Insurance—Experimental Projects Other Than Housing

Objectives: To provide mortgage insurance to help finance the development of group medical facilities or subdivisions or new communities that incorporate new or untried construction concepts intended to reduce construction costs, raise living standards or improve neighborhood design.

Eligibility: Interested sponsors eligible under HUD/FHA's land development or group practice medical facilities programs are eligible.

Range of Financial Assistance: Not applicable.

Contact: Assistant Secretary for Policy Development and Research, Department of Housing and Urban Development, 451 7th St. S.W., Washington, DC 20410/202-755-5544.

Mortgage Insurance—Experimental Rental Housing

Objectives: To provide mortgage insurance to help finance the development of multifamily housing that incorporates new or untried construction concepts designed to reduce housing costs; raise living standards; and improve neighborhood design.

Eligibility: Interested sponsors, able to prove the property which is proposed is an acceptable risk for testing advanced housing design or experimental property standards, are eligible.

Range of Financial Assistance: Average is $2,314,814 per project.

Contact: Assistant Secretary for Policy Development and Research, Department of Housing and Urban Development, 451 7th St. S.W., Washington, DC 20410/202-755-5544.

Mortgage Insurance for the Purchase or Refinancing of Existing Multifamily Housing Projects

Objectives: To provide mortgage insurance for the purchase or refinancing of existing multifamily housing projects, whether conventionally financed or subject to federally insured mortgages at the time of application for mortgage insurance.

Eligibility: The mortgagors may be either private or public. Property must consist of not less than five living units.

Range of Financial Assistance: The estimated cost of required repairs may not exceed 15 percent of the estimated value after repairs or $6,500 per unit, whichever is greater.

Contact: Director, Office of Insured Multifamily Housing Development, Insurance Division, Housing, Department of Housing and Urban Development, Washington, DC 20410/202-755-6223.

Mortgage Insurance—Group Practice Facilities

Objective: To help develop group practice facilities.

Eligibility: Private nonprofit sponsors 1) undertaking to provide comprehensive health care to members or subscribers on a group practice prepayment or free-for-service basis, or 2) established for the purpose of improving the availability of health care in the community, which will make the group practice facility available to an eligible group.

Range of Financial Assistance: The maximum insurable mortgage would be equal to 90 percent of the estimated replacement cost of the facility, including major movable equipment.

Contact: Director, Insurance Division, Office of Insured Multifamily Housing Development, Housing, Department of Housing and Urban Development, Washington, DC 20110/202-755-6223.

Mortgage Insurance—Growing Equity Mortgages

Objectives: To provide a rapid principal reduction and shorter mortgage term by increasing payments over a 10 year period, thereby expanding housing opportunities to the homebuying public.

Eligibility: All persons are eligible to apply.

Range of Financial Assistance: Not applicable.

Contact: Director, Single Family Development Division, Office of Single Family Housing, Housing, Department of Housing and Urban Development, Washington, DC 20410/202-755-6720.

Mortgage Insurance—Homes for Members of the Armed Services

Objectives: To help members of the armed services on active duty to purchase a home.

Eligibility: Military personnel on active duty for two or more years in any branch of the United States Armed Forces, the Coast Guard or the National Oceanic and Atmospheric Administration may be eligible for mortgage insurance.

Range of Financial Assistance: Maximum $67,500; Average $38,359.

Contact: Director, Single Family Development Division, Office of Single Family Housing, Housing, Department of Housing and Urban Development, Washington, DC 20410/202-755-6720.

Mortgage Insurance—Homes in Outlying Areas

Objectives: To help families purchase homes in outlying areas.

Eligibility: All families are eligible to apply.

Range of Financial Assistance: The maximum insurable loan for an occupant mortgagor on a one-family home is 75 percent of the $67,500 limit in the principal obligation.

Contact: Director, Single Family Development Division, Office of Single Family Housing, Department of Housing and Urban Development, Washington, DC 20410/202-755-6720.

Mortgage Insurance—Homes in Urban Renewal Areas

Objectives: To help families purchase or rehabilitate homes in urban renewal areas.

Eligibility: All families are eligible to apply.

Range of Financial Assistance: Maximum insurable loan for an occupant mortgagor are as follows: one-family, $67,500; two family, $76,000; three-family, $92,000; and four-family, $107,000, plus $9,165 for each family unit over four.

Contact: Director, Single Family Development Division, Office of Single Family Housing, Department of Housing and Urban Development, Washington, DC 20410/202-775-6720.

Mortgage Insurance—Homes—Military Impacted Areas

Objectives: To help families undertake home ownership in military impacted areas.

Eligibility: All families are eligible to apply.

Range of Financial Assistance: Maximum insurable loans for an occupant mortgagor are as follows: one family, $67,500; two family, $76,000; three family, $92,000; and four family, $107,000.

Contact: Director, Single Family Development Division, Office of Single Family Housing, Housing, Department of Housing and Urban Development, Washington, DC 20410/202-755-6720.

Mortgage Insurance—Housing in Older, Declining Areas

Objectives: To help families purchase or rehabilitate housing in older, declining urban areas.

Eligibility: All families are eligible to apply.

Range of Financial Assistance: Range varies. Average is $9,400.

Contact: Director, Single Family Development Division, Office of Single Family Housing, Department of Housing and Urban Development, Washington, DC 20410/202-755-6720.

Mortgage Insurance—Investor Sponsored Cooperative Housing

Objectives: To provide good quality multifamily housing to be sold to nonprofit cooperatives ownership housing corporations or trusts.

Eligibility: Eligible mortgagors include investors, builders, developers, public bodies, and others who meet HUD requirements for mortgagors.

Range of Financial Assistance: The unit mortgage limits for non-elevator buildings are as follows: Efficiency, $19,500; one bedroom, $21,600; two bedroom, $25,800; three bedroom, $31,800; four or more bedroom, $36,000.

Contact: Director, Insurance Division, Office of Insured Multifamily Housing Development, Housing, Department of Housing and Urban Development, Washington, DC 20410/202-755-6223.

Mortgage Insurance—Homes for Disaster Victims

Objective: To help victims of a major disaster undertake homeownership on a sound basis.

Eligibility: Any family which is a victim of a major disaster as designated by the President is eligible to apply.

Range of Financial Assistance: Maximum insurable loan for an occupant mortgagor are as follows: one-family, $67,500; two family, $76,000; three-family, $92,000; and four-family, $107,000, plus $9,165 for each family unit over four.

Contact: Director, Single Family Development Division, Office of Single Family Housing, Department of Housing and Urban Development, Washington, DC 20410/202-755-6720.

Mortgage Insurance—Homes for Low and Moderate Income Families

Objectives: To make home ownership more readily available to families displaced by urban renewal or other government actions as well as other low-income and moderate-income families.

Eligibility: All families are eligible to apply. Displaced families qualify for special terms. Certification of eligibility as a displaced family is made by the appropriate local government agency.

Range of Financial Assistance: Maximum insurable loans for an occupant mortgagor are $31,000 for a single family home, or up to $36,000 for a single family home in high cost areas. For a large family (five or more persons) the limits are $36,000 for a single family home, or up to $42,000 for a single family home in high cost areas.

Contact: Director, Single Family Development Division, Office of Single Family Housing, Department of Housing and Urban Development, Washington, DC 20410/202-755-6720.

Mortgage Insurance—Hospitals

Objectives: To make possible the financing of hospitals.

Eligibility: Eligible applicants are a proprietary facility, or facility of a private nonprofit corporation or association, licensed or regulated by the state, municipality, or other political subdivision.

Range of Financial Assistance: Not specified.

Contact: Insurance Division, Office of Insured Multifamily Housing Development, Housing Development, Housing, Department of Housing and Urban Development, Washington, DC 20410/202-755-6223.

Mortgage Insurance—Land Development

Objectives: To assist the development of subdivisions on a sound economic basis.

Eligibility: Prospective developers, subject to

the approval of HUD, are eligible. Public bodies are not eligible.

Range of Financial Assistance: Not specified.

Contact: Director, Single Family Development Division, Office of Single Family Housing, Department of Housing and Urban Development, Washington, DC 20410/202-755-6720.

Mortgage Insurance—Management Type Cooperative Projects

Objectives: To make it possible for nonprofit cooperatives, ownership housing corporations or trust to acquire housing projects to be operated as management-type cooperatives.

Eligibility: Eligible mortgagors are nonprofit cooperatives, ownership housing corporations or trusts which may either sponsor projects directly, or purchase projects from investor-sponsors.

Range of Financial Assistance: The unit mortgage limits are as follows: Efficiency, $19,500; one bedroom, $21,600; two bedrooms, $25,800; three bedrooms, $31,800; four or more bedrooms, $36,000. Limits per family unit are somewhat higher for elevator apartments. In areas where cost levels so require, limits per family unit may be increased up to 75 percent.

Contact: Director, Insurance Division, Office of Insured Multifamily Housing Development, Housing, Department of Housing and Urban Development, Washington, DC 20410/202-775-6223.

Mortgage Insurance—Manufactured Mobile Home Parks

Objectives: To make possible the financing of construction or rehabilitation of manufactured mobile home parks.

Eligibility: Eligible mortgagors include investors, builders, developers and other who meet HUD requirements for mortgagors.

Range of Financial Assistance: The maximum mortgage limit is $9,000 per space.

Contact: Director, Insurance Division, Office of Insured Multifamily Housing Development, Housing, Department of Housing and Urban Development, Washington, DC 20410/202-755-6223.

Mortgage Insurance—Nursing Homes and Intermediate Care Facilities

Objectives: To make possible financing for construction or rehabilitation of nursing homes and intermediate care facilities, and to provide loan insurance to install fire safety equipment.

Eligibility: Eligible mortgagors include investors, builders, developers, and private nonprofit corporations or associations licensed or regulated by the state for the accommodation of convalescents and person requiring skilled nursing care or intermediate care.

Range of Financial Assistance: Not specified.

Contact: Director, Insurance Division, Office of Insured Multifamily Housing Development, Housing, Department of Housing and Urban Development, Washington, DC 20412/202-755-6223.

Mortgage Insurance—Purchase by Homeowners of Fee-Simple Title From Lessors

Objectives: To help homeowners obtain fee-simple title to the property which they hold under long-term leases and on which their homes are located.

Eligibility: All homeowners whose homes are located on property which is held under long-term ground leases are eligible to apply.

Range of Financial Assistance: Up to $10,000.

Contact: Director, Single Family Development Division, Office of Single Family Housing, Department of Housing and Urban Development, Washington, DC 20410/202-755-6720.

Mortgage Insurance—Purchase of Sales-Type Cooperative Housing Units

Objectives: To provide available, good quality, new housing for purchase by individual members of a housing cooperative.

Eligibility: Eligible mortgagors include members of a nonprofit cooperative, ownership housing corporations or trusts which sponsor such housing.

Range of Financial Assistance: up to $67,500

Contact: Director, Insurance Division, Office of Insured Multifamily Housing Development, Housing, Department of Housing and Urban Development, Washington, DC 20410/202-755-6223.

Mortgage Insurance—Purchase of Units in Condominiums

Objectives: To enable families to purchase units in condominium projects.

Eligibility: All families are eligible to apply.

Range of Financial Assistance: The maximum insurable loan for an occupant mortgagor is $67,500 but may go up to $90,000 in high cost areas.

Contact: Director, Single Family Development Division, Office of Single Family Housing, Housing, Department of Housing and Urban Development, Washington, DC 20410/202-755-6720.

Mortgage Insurance—Rental Housing

Objectives: To provide good quality rental housing.

Eligibility: Eligible mortgagors include investors, builders, developers, and others who meet HUD requirements for mortgagors.

Range of Financial Assistance: The unit mortgage limits for non-elevator apartments are as follow: Efficiency $19,500; one bedroom, $21,600; two bedrooms, $25,800; and three bedrooms, $31,800; four or more bedrooms, $36,000. Limits per family unit are somewhat higher for elevator apartments. In areas where cost levels so require, limits per family unit may be increased up to 75 percent.

Contact: Director, Insurance Division, Office of Insured Multifamily Housing Department, Housing, Department of Housing and Urban Development, Washington, DC 20410/202-755-6223.

Mortgage Insurance—Rental and Cooperative Housing for Low and Moderate Income Families, Market Interest Rate

Objectives: To provide good quality rental or cooperative housing within the price range of low- and moderate-income families.

Eligibility Requirements: Eligible sponsors include public, nonprofit, cooperative, builder-seller, investor-sponsor, and limited distribution mortgagors.

Range of Financial Assistance: The unit mortgage limits for non-elevator apartments are as follows: efficiency, $19,406; one bedroom, $22,195; two bedrooms, $26,985; three bedrooms, $34,541; four or more bedrooms, $38,480. Unit mortgage limits are somewhat higher for elevator apartments. In areas where cost levels so require, limits per family unit may be increased up to 75 percent.

Contact: Director, Insurance Division, Office of Insured Multifamily Housing Department, Housing, Department of Housing and Urban Development, Washington, DC 20410/202-755-6223.

Mortgage Insurance—Rental Housing for Moderate Income Families

Objectives: To provide good quality rental housing within the price range of low- and moderate-income families.

Eligibility: Profit motivated sponsors, limited distribution and nonprofit sponsors, and others who meet HUD requirements for mortgagors.

Range of Financial Assistance: The unit mortgage limits for non-elevator apartments are as follows: Efficiency, $19,406; one bedroom, $22,028; two bedrooms, $26,625; three bedrooms, $33,420; four or more bedrooms, $37,870. Unit mortgage limits are somewhat higher for elevator apartments. In areas where cost levels so require, limits per family unit may be increased up to 75 percent.

Contact: Director, Insurance Division, Office of Insured Multifamily Housing Department, Department of Housing and Urban Development, Washington, DC 20410/202-755-6223.

Mortgage Insurance—Rental Housing for the Elderly

Objectives: To provide good quality rental housing for the elderly.

Eligibility: Eligible mortgagors include investors, builder developers, public bodies, and nonprofit sponsors.

Range of Financial Assistance: The unit mortgage limits for nonelevator apartments are as follows: Efficiency, $18,450; one bedroom, $20,625; two bedroom, $24,630; three bedrooms, $29,640; four or more bedrooms, $34,846. Limits per family unit are somewhat higher for elevator apartments. In areas where cost levels so require, limits per family unit may be increased up to 75 percent.

Contact: Director, Insurance Division, Office of Insured Multifamily Housing Department, Housing, Department of Housing and Urban Development, Washington, DC 20410/202-755-6223.

Mortgage Insurance—Rental Housing in Urban Renewal Areas

Objectives: To provide good quality rental housing in urban renewal areas.

Eligibility: Eligible mortgagors include investors, builders, developers, public bodies, and others who are able to meet HUD requirements for mortgagors.

Range of Financial Assistance: Unit mortgage limits for non-elevator apartments are as follows: Efficiency, $19,500; one bedroom, $21,600; two bedrooms, $25,800; three bedrooms, $31,800; four or more bedrooms, $36,000. Limits per family unit are somewhat higher for elevator apartments. In areas where cost levels so require limits per family unit may be increased up to 50 percent.

Contact: Director, Insurance Division, Office of Insured Multifamily Housing Department, Housing, Department of Housing and Urban Development, Washington, DC 20410/202-755-6223.

Mortgage Insurance—Special Credit Risks

Objective: To make homeownership possible for low-and-moderate-income families who cannot meet normal Housing and Urban Development requirements.

Eligibility: Only families who do not qualify for homeownership under regular HUD credit standards are eligible. The monthly mortgage payment (consisting of principal, interest, MIP, hazard insurance and taxes) may not exceed 25 percent of the borrower's annual income.

Range of Financial Assistance: Up to $18,000 ($21,000 in areas where cost levels so require)

Contact: Director, Single Family Development Division, Office of Single Family Housing, Department of Housing and Urban Development, Washington, DC 20410/202-755-6720.

Mortgage Insurance—Two Year Operating Loss Loans, Section 223 (D)

Objectives: To insure a separate loan covering losses incurred during the first two years following the date of completion of a multifamily project.

Eligibility: Owners of a multifamily project or facility subject to a mortgage insured by HUD or held by HUD are eligible to apply.

Range of Financial Assistance: Average $206,800.

Contact: Director, Office of Insured Multifamily Housing Development, Insurance Division Housing, Housing, Department of Housing and Urban Development, Washington, DC 20410/202-755-5756.

Nonprofit Housing Sponsor Loans—Planning Projects for Low- and Moderate-Income Families

Objective: To assist and stimulate prospective nonprofit sponsors of Section 202 housing to develop sound housing projects for the elderly or handicapped.

Eligibility: Nonprofit organizations as defined by Housing and Urban Development which will qualify as proposed mortgagor corporations.

Range of Financial Assistance: Up to $50,000

Contact: Director, Assisted Elderly and Handicapped Housing Division, Office of Elderly and Assisted Housing, Housing, Department of Housing and Urban Development, Washington, DC 20410/202-755-5597.

Operating Assistance for Troubled Multifamily Housing Projects

Objectives: To provide assistance to restore or maintain, and to assist in the management of low to moderate income projects approved for assistance under the National Housing Act or under the Housing and Urban Development Act of 1965.

Eligibility: Eligible owners include nonprofit, profit-motivated, limited dividend, cooperative owners. Public bodies do not qualify for this program.

Range of Financial Assistance: Based on need of project.

Contact: Director, Management Operations Division, Office of Multifamily Housing Management, Housing, Department of Housing and Urban Development, Washington, DC 20410/202-755-5547.

Property Improvement Loan Insurance for Improving All Existing Structures and Building of New Nonresidential Structures

Objective: To facilitate the financing of improvements to homes and other existing structures and the erection of new nonresidential structures.

Eligibility: Eligible borrowers include the owner of the property to be improved or a lessee having a lease extending at least 6 months beyond maturity of the loan.

Range of Financial Assistance: Up to $17,500 for a one-family dwelling.

Contact: Director, Office of Manufactured Housing and Regulatory Functions, Title I Insurance Division, Department of Housing and Urban Development, Washington, DC 20410/202-755-6880.

Public and Indian Housing

Objectives: To provide and operate cost-effective decent, safe and sanitary dwellings for families of low and very low income through an authorized Public Housing Agency (PHA) or Indian Housing Authority (IHA).

Eligibility: Public Housing Agencies (including Indian Housing Authorities) established in accordance with State Law, authorized public agencies, or Indian tribal organizations are eligible.

Range of Financial Assistance: Average assistance $3,000.

Contact: Assistant Secretary for Public and Indian Housing, Department of Housing and Urban Development, Washington, DC 20410/202-755-0950.

Rehabilitation Loans—Section 312

Objective: To provide funds for rehabilitation of residential, commercial and other nonresidential properties.

Eligibility: Residential or nonresidential property owners, or owners and/or tenants of nonresidential property in neighborhood development, urban renewal, code enforcement areas, Community Development Block Grant areas and Section 810 Urban Homesteading Areas.

Range of Financial Assistance: Loan Limit Maximum of $27,000/Dwelling Unit and $100,000 for Nonresidential Properties.

Contact: Community Planning and Development, Office of Urban Rehabilitation, Department of Housing and Urban Development, 451 7th St. S.W., Washington, DC 20410/202-755-6336.

Rehabilitation Mortgage Insurance

Objectives: To help families repair or improve, purchase and improve, or refinance and improve existing residential structures more than one year old.

Eligibility: All families are eligible to apply.

Range of Financial Assistance: Maximum insurable loans for an occupant mortgagor are as follows: one family, $67,500; two family, $76,000; three family, $92,000; and four family, $107,000.

Contact: Director, Single Family Development Division, Office of Single Family Housing, Housing, Department of Housing and Urban Development, Washington, DC 20410/202-755-6720.

Rental Housing Rehabilitation

Objectives: To increase the stock of standard affordable rental housing available to lower income tenants.

Eligibility: State and local governments except those localities eligible for FmHa Rural Housing Preservation Grant Programs.

Range of Financial Assistance: Maximum of $5,000 per unit for rehabilitation.

Contact: Office of Urban Rehabilitation, Community Planning and Development, Department of Housing and Urban Development, 451 7th St. SW, Washington, DC 20410/202-755-5685.

Single-Family Home Mortgage Coinsurance

Objective: To improve quality and timeliness of service to mortgagers by streamlining HUD mortgage insurance processing.

Eligibility: All persons are eligible to apply.

Range of Financial Assistance: Maximum insurable loans for an occupant mortgagor are as follows: one-family, $67,500; two family, $76,000; three-family, $92,000; and four-family, $107,000.

Contact: Director, Single Family Development Division, Office of Single Family Housing, Department of Housing and Urban Development, Washington, DC 20410/202-755-6720.

Solar Energy and Energy Conservation Bank

Objectives: To reduce the Nation's dependence on foreign sources of oil by offering financial incentives in the form of grants or subsidized loans for the purchase and installation of conservation and solar measures.

Eligibility: The amount of assistance is scaled to applicants' income levels for energy conservation improvements and based on the amount of energy saved for solar measures.

Range of Financial Assistance: Not yet available.

Contact: President, Solar Energy and Energy Conservation Bank, Department of Housing and Urban Development, 451 7th Street, S.W.; Room 7110, Washington, DC 20410/202-755-7166.

Supplemental Loan Insurance Multifamily Rental Housing

Objectives: To finance additions and improvements to any multifamily project, group practice facility, hospital nursing home insured by Housing and Urban Development or held by Housing and Urban Development. Major movable equipment for nursing homes, or group practice facilities or hospital may be covered by a mortgage under this program.

Eligibility: Owners of a multifamily project or facility subject to a mortgage insured by HUD/ or held by Housing and Urban Development are eligible.

Range of Financial Assistance: Not specified.

Contact: Director, Insurance Division, Office of Insured Multi-family Housing Development, Housing, Department of Housing and Urban Development, Washington, DC 20411/202-755-6223.

Urban Homesteading

Objectives: To provide homeownership opportunities to individuals and families utilizing existing housing stock and revitalize neighborhoods through the encouragement of public and private investment.

Eligibility: States or units of general local government are eligible.

Range of Financial Assistance: Determined by formula.

Contact: Director, Urban Homesteading Program, Office of Urban Rehabilitation, Department of Housing and Urban Development, Washington, DC 20410/202-755-5324.

Mobile Homes

See "Loans and Loan Guarantees" in this section.

Mobile Home Safety and Construction

The Department of Housing and Urban Development sets and enforces mobile home construction and safety standards. In addition to providing information on this topic, it will also act on consumer complaints. Contact: State and Consumer Liaison, Manufactured Housing Standards Division, Office of Mobile Home Standards, Department of Housing and Urban Development, 451 7th St. S.W., Room 9152, Washington, DC 20410/202-755-6584.

Modular Housing

For information and expertise on the construction of modular housing, contact: Technical Support Branch, Manufactured Housing and Construction, Standards Division, Office of Manufactured Housing and Regulatory Functions, Department of Housing and Urban Development, 451 7th St. S.W., Room 9156, Washington, DC 20410/202-755-5924.

Mortgage Help

If you are looking for help in obtaining a mortgage the following free publications are available from HUD:

HUD/FHA Program for Home Mortgage Insurance
HUD/FHA Non-Assisted Program for Rental Housing for Moderate Income Families
HUD/FHA Non-Assisted Program for Condominium Housing
Mobile Home Financing thru HUD Graduated Payment Mortgage

Contact: Program Information Center, Department of Housing and Urban Development, 451 7th St. S.W., Room 1104, Washington, DC 20410/202-755-6420.

Neighborhood Reinvestment and Revitalization

See "Grants" ("Community Development Block Grants" and "Urban Development Action Grants").

Partnerships Resource and Referrals

The Community Partnerships Resource Center (NPRC) helps communities and neighborhood groups solve problems through the development of public-private partnerships. NPRC's main goal is to put cities, businesses, neighborhood groups, and leaders in touch with each other to learn about new solutions and set up programs. The staff have researched partnerships throughout the U.S., and they can put you in contact with groups working on a problem similar to yours. The Center maintains an on-line data base of examples of local problem solving groups and partnerships. The NPRC data base is available on LOGIN, a subscriber service, and Partnership Data Net (see next entry), a non-profit membership network with some free services for the public. If time permits, NPRC will also search their data base for interested parties. Contact: Community Partnerships Resource Center, U.S. Department of Housing and Urban Development, Office of Policy Development and Research, 451 Seventh St. S.W., Washington, DC 20410/202-755-4370.

Property for Sale—Multifamily
The Department of Housing and Urban Development-held multifamily properties are sold by sealed-bid auction throughout the country. Contact: Multifamily Sales Division, Office of Multifamily Financing and Preservation, Office of Housing, Department of Housing and Urban Development, 451 7th St. S.W., Room 6151, Washington, DC 20410/202-755-7220.

Property for Sale—Single Family
The Department of Housing and Urban Development held single-family properties are sold by sealed-bid auction throughout the country. Contact: Sales Promotion Branch, Office of Single Family Housing, Office of Housing, Department of Housing and Urban Development, 451 7th St. S.W., Room 9170, Washington, DC 20410/202-755-5832.

Property Standards
The Department of Housing and Urban Development publishes a 5-volume set of *Minimum Property Standards,* which give builders guidance on such items as safety, design, layout, types of windows, etc., to which they must conform if they want to be eligible for VA, and FHA loans. The volumes are: 1) *Single Family Dwelling,* $8.50 2) *Multifamily Dwelling,* $21; 3) *Care Type Housing* (nursing homes) $20; 4) *Manual of Acceptable Practices* (with sketches of designs) $24; and 5) *Solar Heating and Domestic Hot Water Systems,* $12. The 5-volume set is available from Superintendent of Documents, Government Printing Office, Washington, DC 20402/202-783-3238.

Real Estate Practices
See "Settlement Costs" in this section.

Redlining
Redlining is a form of discrimination in which lending institutions boycott investing in certain areas of a city because of race, color, etc. See "Discrimination Hotline" in this section.

Regulatory Activities
Listed below are those organizations within the Department of Housing and Urban Development which are involved with regulating various business activities. With each listing is a description of those industries or situations which are regulated by the office. Regulatory activities generate large amounts of information on the companies and subjects they regulate. Much of the information is available to the public. Regulatory activities can also be used by consumers. A regulatory office can tell you your rights when dealing with a regulated company.

Interstate Land Sales Registration Office. Regulates land developers who sell the land through any means of interstate commerce, including the mails. Contact: Department of Housing and Urban Development, 451 7th St. S.W., Room 6278, Washington, DC 20410/202-755-0502.

Mobile Home Standards. Regulates mobile home construction and safety standards. Contact: Department of Housing and Urban Development, 451 7th St. S.W., Room 9154, Washington, DC 20410/202-755-6920.

Office of Fair Housing and Equal Opportunity. Administers the fair housing program authorized by the Civil Rights Act of 1968. Contact: Department of Housing and Urban Development, 451 7th St. S.W., Room 5208, Washington, DC 20410/202-755-5518.

Real Estate Practices. Regulates real estate settlement procedures used by lenders. Contact: Department of Housing and Urban Development, 451 7th St. S.W., Room 9266, Washington, DC 20410/202-426-0070.

Rental Rates
Fair market rates for various types of dwellings in over 450 market areas are published yearly. Contact: Technical Support Division, Office of Multifamily Housing Development, Office of Housing, Department of Housing and Urban Development, 451 7th St. S.W., Room 6142, Washington, DC 20410/202-426-0035.

Rent Subsidies, Multifamily
Those who are developing or rehabilitating multifamily housing can seek rent subsidies for low-income tenants. See "Direct Payments" in this section or contact: Rehabilitation Division, Office of Multifamily Housing Development, Office of Housing, Department of Housing and Urban Development, 451 7th St. S.W., Room 6132, Washington, DC 20410/202-755-6500.

Research Studies
See "Consumer Information" and "Consumer Publications on Housing" in this section.

Settlement Costs
Lending institutions which deal in FHA or VA loans are required to provide buyers with a special information booklet which describes the settlement and the roles of the realtor, seller and buyer. Copies of the booklet, *Buying a Home? Don't Forget the Settlement Costs,* are also available for free from Housing and Urban Development.

Contact: Program Information Center, Department of Housing and Urban Development, 451 7th St. S.W., Room 1104, Washington, DC 20410/202-755-6420.

Small Cities Assistance
Special financing is available to small cities for improving neighborhood facilities, health facilities, sewer systems, roads, parks, land acquisition, property and rehabilitation. See "Grants" ("Community Development Block Grants/Small Cities Program") or contact: Small Cities Division, Office of Block Grant Assistance, Office for Community Planning and Development, Department of Housing and Urban Development, 451 7th St. S.W., Room 7184, Washington, DC 20410/202-755-6322.

Solar Energy and Energy Conservation Bank
The Solar Energy and Energy Conservation Bank (Solar Bank) operates through States in providing financial assistance to consumers for solar and energy conservation improvements. Eligible consumers apply through a designated State agency which in turn draws funds from the Bank through the Treasury Financial Communication System (TFCS). The amount of financial assistance for solar improvements is based on the amount of energy served by the solar system or a percentage of costs. Contact: Solar Energy and Energy Conservation Bank, Department of Housing and Urban Development, 451 Seventh St. S.W., Suite 7110, Washington, DC 20410/202-755-7166.

Solar Energy Devices for Homeowners
Many states and U.S. territories now give federally-funded low-interest loans or grants to homeowners who want to install solar energy devices. The Solar Energy and Energy Conservation Bank program is for low and moderate income families owning single and multi-family dwellings. For specific information about currently available equipment, contact the Solar Energy and Energy Conservation Bank. Contact: Solar Energy and Energy Conservation Bank, U.S. Department of Housing and Urban Development, 451 7th St. S.W., Room 7110, Washington, DC 20410/202-755-7166.

Solar Information Hotline
The Department of Housing and Urban Development, with the Department of Energy, has established a National Solar Heating and Cooling Information Center to provide free information to both consumers and industry. It serves as a referral point for people needing detailed technical data from a number of sources. Contact: National Solar Heating and Cooling Center, Conservation and Renewable Energy Inquiry and Referral Service, P.O. Box 1900, Silver Spring, MD 70907./toll-free 800-523-2929; 800-462-4983 in Pennsylvania; 800-233-3071 in Alaska or Hawaii.

Statistics, Housing
Each year an *American Housing Survey* is conducted which samples some 80,000 housing units and 60 metropolitan areas and produces information on house inventory, house and neighborhood quality, characteristics of inhabitants, energy retrofitting, condominiums and cooperatives, and condominium conversion. The data from the survey are available in a variety of formats. In addition to the *American Housing Survey,* HUD also:

Analyzes non-financial resources for housing requirements (labor, land, etc.)
Projects housing needs for the next 2 decades
Projects housing inventory to the year 2000
Conducts special research on new usage for increasing housing quality
Assesses housing needs
Conducts research on increasing efficiency
Prepares economic assumptions
Conducts a Product and Marketing Survey in conjunction with the Bureau of Census

Contact: Division of Housing and Demographic Analysis, Office of Economic Affairs, Offices of Policy Development and Research, Department of Housing and Urban Development, 451 7th St. S.W., Room 8224, Washington, DC 20410/202-755-5590. Another source for housing statistics is the Statistical Operations Branch. In addition to general information and expertise the following publication is available for free: *HUD Statistical Yearbook*—annual tallies by state of Housing and Urban Development programs. Contact: Statistical Operations Branch, Data Management Division, Office of Organization and Management Information, Department of Housing and Urban Development, 451 7th St. S.W., Room 3186, Washington, DC 20410/202-755-5194.

Steering
Steering is a type of discrimination in which a person is directed to buy or rent in a particular neighborhood or facility in order to keep him/her from buying in other areas. See "Discrimination Hotline."

Urban Economic Development
See "Grants" ("Community Development Block Grants" and "Urban Development Action Grants").

How Can the Department of Housing and Urban Development Help You?
To determine how the U.S. Department of Housing and Urban Development can help you, first contact: Program Information Center, Department of Housing and Urban Development, 451 7th St. S.W., First Floor, Washington, DC 20410/202-755-6420.

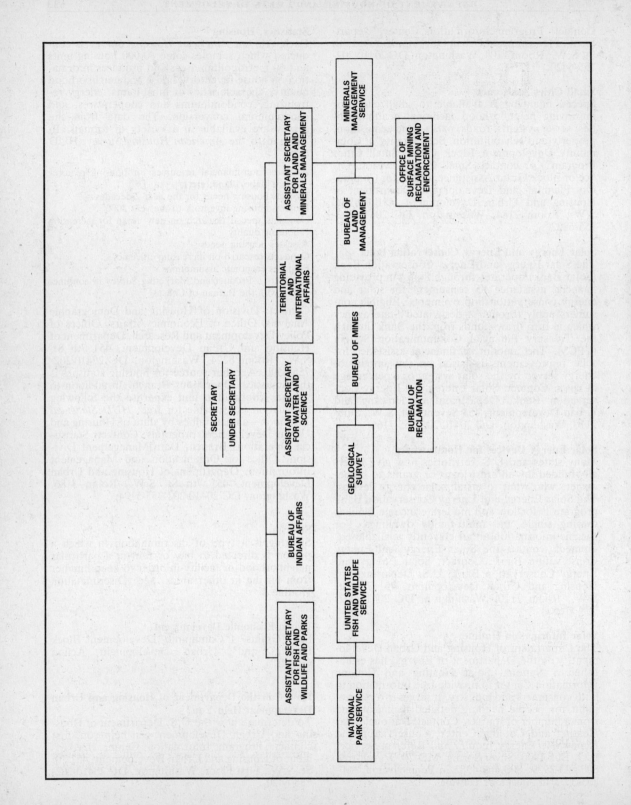

Department of the Interior

**C St. between 18th and 19th Sts. N.W., Washington, DC
20240/202-343-7351**

**ESTABLISHED: March 3, 1849
BUDGET: $5,275,864,000
EMPLOYEES: 63,305**

MISSION: Administration of over 500 million acres of federal land, and trust responsibilities for approximately 50 million acres of land, mostly Indian reservations; the conservation and development of mineral and water resources; the conservation, development, and utilization of fish and wildlife resources; the coordination of federal and state recreation programs; the preservation and administration of the nation's scenic and historic areas; the operation of Job Corps Conservation Centers, and Youth and Young Adult Conservation Corps camps, and coordination of other manpower and youth training programs; the reclamation of arid lands in the West through irrigation; and the management of hydro-electric power systems.

Major Divisions and Offices

Assistant Secretary for Water and Science
Department of the Interior, Room 6654, Washington, DC 20240/202-343-2186.
Budget: $1,332,174,000
Employees: 18,087

• Geological Survey
Department of the Interior, National Center 12201 Sunrise Valley Dr., Reston, VA 22092/703-860-7444.
Budget: $376,684,000
Employees: 7,301
Mission: Identifies the Nation's land, water, energy, and mineral resources; classifies federally owned lands for minerals and energy resources and water power potential; investigates natural hazards such as earthquakes, volcanoes, and landslides; and prepares maps, collects and interprets data on

mineral and water resources, performs fundamental and applied research in the sciences.

• Bureau of Mines
Department of the Interior, 2401 E St. N.W., Washington, DC 20241/202-634-1004.
Budget: $144,568,000
Employees: 2,511
Mission: Help ensure that the nation has adequate mineral supplies for security and other needs; conduct applied and basic research to develop the technology for the extraction, processing, use, and recycling of the nation's mineral resources at a reasonable cost without harm to the environment or the workers involved; and collect, compile, analyze, and publish statistical and economic information on all phases of mineral resource development, including exploration, production,

shipments, demand, stocks, prices, imports and exports.

Bureau of Reclamation

Department of the Interior, Washington, DC 20240/202-343-4662.
Budget: $810,922,000
Employees: 8,275
Mission: Assist States, local governments, and other federal agencies to stabilize and stimulate local and regional economies, enhance and protect the environment, and improve the quality of life through development of water, other renewable resources, and related land resources throughout the 17 contiguous Western States and Hawaii.

Bureau of Indian Affairs

Department of the Interior, Washington, DC 20240/202-343-7445.
Budget: $1,009,812,000
Employees: 13,343
Mission: Encourage and train Indian and Alaskan Native people to manage their own affairs under the trust relationship to the federal government; facilitate with maximum involvement of Indian and Alaskan Native people, full development of their human and natural resource potentials; mobilize all public and private aids to the advancement of Indian and Alaskan Native people for use by them; and utilize the skills and capabilities of Indian and Alaskan Native people in the direction and management of programs for their benefit.

Assistant Secretary for Fish and Wildlife and Parks

Department of the Interior, Washington, DC 20240/202-343-4416.
Budget: $1,350,770,000
Employees: 17,675

• National Park Service

Department of the Interior, Washington, DC 20240/202-343-7394
Budget: $885,576,000
Employees: 11,990
Mission: Administer the properties under its jurisdiction for the enjoyment and education of our citizens; protect the natural environment of the areas; and assist states, local governments, and citizen groups in the development of park areas, the protection of the natural environment and the preservation of historic properties.

• United States Fish and Wildlife Service

Department of the Interior, Washington, DC 20240/202-343-5634.
Budget: $465,194,000
Employees: 5,685
Mission: Responsible for wild birds, endangered species, certain marine mammals, inland sport fisheries, and specific fishery and wildlife resources; insure maximum opportunity for the American people to benefit from fish and wildlife resources as part of their natural environment; assist in the development of an environmental stewardship based on ecological principles, scientific knowledge of wildlife, and a sense of moral responsibility; guide the conservation, development, and management of the nation's fish and wildlife resources; and administer a national program which provides opportunities to the American public to understand, appreciate, and wisely use these resources.

Assistant Secretary for Land and Minerals Management

Department of the Interior, Washington, DC 20243/202-343-2191.
Budget: $1,583,108,000
Employees: 12,311

• Bureau of Land Management

Department of the Interior, Washington, DC 20240/202-343-4151.
Budget: $1,162,421,000
Employees: 9,000
Mission: Total management of 284 million acres of public lands; issue rights-of-way, in certain instances, for crossing federal lands under other agencies' jurisdiction; and survey the federal lands and establish and maintain public land records and records of mining claims.

• Minerals Management Service

Department of the Interior, 12203 Sunrise Valley Drive, Reston, Va. 22091/202-343-3983.
Budget: $198,495,000
Employees: 2,580
Mission: Assesses the nature, extent, recoverability, and value of leasable minerals on the Outer Continental Shelf; ensures the orderly and timely inventory and development, as well as the efficient recovery, of mineral resources; encourages utilization of the best available and safest technology; provides for fair, full, and accurate returns to the Federal Treasury for produced commodities; and safeguards against fraud, waste, and abuse.

• Office of Surface Mining Reclamation and Enforcement

Department of the Interior, Washington, DC 20240/202-343-4953.
Budget: $222,192,000
Employees: 731
Mission: Assist the States in developing a nationwide program that protects society and the environment from the adverse effects of coal mining, while ensuring that coal surface mining can be done without permanent damage to land and water resources; and oversees mining and reclamation in

the States with primary responsibility, to assist the States with primary responsibility, to assist the States in meeting the objectives of the act, and to regulate mining and reclamation activities in those States that choose not to assume primary responsibility.

Territorial and International Affairs

Department of the Interior, Washington, DC 20240/202-343-4822.
Budget: 226,771,000
Employees: 66
Mission: Promotes the economic, social and political development of the U.S. territories of Guam, American Samoa, the Virgin Islands, the Commonwealth of the Northern Mariana Islands, and the Trust Territory of the Pacific Islands, which includes the Marshall Islands, Palau, and Micronesia; and serves as the Department's focal point for analysis, development, and review of the Department's policy and programs pertaining to international activities and the opportunities for support of U.S. foreign policy through the use of the Department's natural resource and environmental expertise.

Data Experts

Foreign Minerals and Metals Experts

Foreign country mineral experts monitor all aspects of foreign mineral industries. Statistics are kept on current and anticipated mineral production. The role of mineral industries in foreign economies is studied along with the legislative and investment climates affecting these industries. These experts can be reached by telephone or by writing in care of: Branch of Foreign Data, Mineral and Materials Supply and Demand, Bureau of Mines, Department of the Interior, 2401 E St. N.W., Room W614, Washington, DC 20241/202-632-8970.

Afghanistan/P. Clarke/202-632-5065
Albania/W. Steblez/202-632-1276
Algeria/P. Clarke/202-632-5065
Angola/G. Morgan/202-632-5065
Argentina/P. Velasco/202-632-9352
Australia/T. Lyday/202-632-1272
Austria/G. Rabchevsky/202-632-5053
Bahamas/D. Hyde/202-632-9352
Bahrein/P. Clarke/202-632-5065
Bangladesh/G. Kinney/202-634-1272
Barbados/D. Hyde/202-632-9352
Belgium/G. Rabchevsky/202-632-5053
Belize/D. Hyde/202-632-9352
Benin/G. Morgan/202-632-5065
Bermuda/D. Hyde/202-632-9352
Bhutan/G. Kinney/202-634-1272
Bolivia/P. Velasco/202-632-9352
Botswana/T. Glover/202-632-5065
Brazil/H. Ensminger/202-632-5062
Brunei/C. Kimbell/202-634-1272
Bulgaria/T. Karpinsky/202-634-1276
Burma/G. Kinney/202-634-1272
Burundi/K. Connor/202-632-5065
Cambodia (Kampucheu)/G. Kinney/202-634-1272
Cameroon/T. Glover/202-632-5065
Canada/H. Newman/202-632-5060
Cape Verde Islands/G. Morgan/202-632-5065
Central African Republic/T. Glover/202-632-5065
Chad/T. Glover/202-632-5065
Chile/E. Chin/202-634-1272
China/E. Chin/202-634-1272
Christmas Island/C. Kimbell 202-634-1713
Columbia/Orlando Martino/202-632-9352
Comoros/K. Conner/202-632-5065
Congo/T. Glover/202-632-5065
Costa Rica/D. Hyde/202-632-9375
Cuba/D. Hyde/202-632-9375
Cyprus/T. Glover/202-632-5065
Czechoslovakia/T. Karpinsky/202-634-1276
Denmark/J. Huvos/202-632-5047
Djibouti (Afars & Issars)/K. Connor/202-632-5065
Dominican Republic/D. Hyde/202-632-9375
Ecuador/P. Velasco/202-632-9352
Egypt/J. Lewis/202-632-5065
El Salvador/O. Martino/202-632-9352
Equatorial Guinea/T. Glover/202-632-5065
Ethiopia/K. Connor/202-632-1272
Fiji/T. Lyday/202-634-1272
Finland/J. Huvos/202-632-5047
France/R. Sondermayer/202-632-5049
French Guiana/H. Ensminger/202-632-5061
Gabon/B. Kornhauser/202-632-5065
Gambia/G. Morgan/202-632-5065
Germany, East/G. Rabchevsky/202-632-5053
Germany, West/G. Rabchevsky/202-632-5053
Ghana/B. Kornhauser/202-632-5065
Greece/W. Steblez/202-634-1276
Greenland/J. Huvos/202-632-5047
Guadaloupe/D. Hyde/202-632-9375
Guatemala/O. Martina/202-632-9352
Guinea/J. Lewis/202-632-5065
Guinea Bissau/G. Morgan/202-632-5065
Guyana/H. Ensminger/202-632-5062
Haiti/D. Hyde/202-632-9352
Honduras/O. Martino/202-632-9352
Hong Kong/E. Chin/202-634-1272
Hungary/W. Steblez/202-634-1276
Iceland/J. Huvos/202-632-5047
India/G. Kinney/202-634-1272
Indonesia/J. Wu/202-634-1272
Iran/J. Lewis/202-632-5065
Iraq/G. Morgan/202-632-5065
Ireland/T. Karpinsky/202-634-1276
Israel/B. Kornhauser/202-632-5065

Italy/R. Sondermayer/202-632-5049
Ivory Coast/G. Morgan/202-632-5065
Jamaica/D. Hyde/202-632-9352
Japan/J. Wu/202-634-1272
Jordan/P. Clarke/202-632-5065
Kenya/T. Glover/202-632-5065
Kampuchea (Cambodia)/G. Kinney/202-634-1272
Kiribati/C. Wyche/202-634-1272
Korea, North/E. Chin/202-634-1272
Korea, South/E. Chin/202-634-1272
Kuwait/P. Clarke/202-632-5065
Kuwait (Neutral Zone)/P. Clarke/202-632-5065
Laos/G. Kinney/202-634-1272
Lebanon/P. Clarke/202-632-5065
Lesotho/K. Connor/202-632-5065
Liberia/B. Kornhauser/202-632-5065
Libya/J. Lewis/202-632-5065
Luxembourg/G. Rabchevsky/202-632-5053
Madagascar (Malagasy Republic)/K. Connor/202-632-5065
Malawi/K. Connor/202-632-5065
Malaysia/J. Wu/202-634-1272
Mali/G. Morgan/202-632-5065
Malta/W. Steblez/202-634-1276
Martinique/D. Hyde/202-632-9352
Mauritania/T. Glover/202-632-5065
Mauritius/K. Connor/202-632-5065
Mexico/O. Martino/202-632-9352
Mongolia/J. Wu/202-634-1272
Morocco/G. Morgan/202-632-5065
Mozambique/K. Connor/202-632-5065
Namibia (South West Africa)/M. Ellis/202-632-5065
Nauru/C. Wyche/202-634-1272
Nepal/G. Kinney/202-634-1272
Netherlands/G. Rabchevsky/202-632-5053
Netherlands Antilles/D. Hyde/202-632-9352
New Caledonia/T. Lyday/202-634-1272
New Zealand/C. Kimbell/202-634-1713
Nicaragua/D. Hyde/202-632-9352
Niger/G. Morgan/202-632-5065
Nigeria/B. Kornhauser/202-632-5065
Norway/J. Huvos/202-632-5047
Oman/P. Clarke/202-632-5065
Pakistan/K. Connor/202-634-5065
Panama/D. Hyde/202-632-9352
Papau New Guinea/T. Lyday/202-634-1272
Paraguay/T. P. Valasco/202-632-5061
Peru/D. Hyde/202-632-9352
Phillipine Islands/J. Wu/202-634-1272
Poland/T. Karpinsky/202-634-1276
Portugal/R. Sondermayer/202-632-5049
Qatar/P. Clarke/202-632-5065
Reunion/K. Connor/202-632-5065
Romania/W. Steblez/202-634-1276
Rwanda/K. Connor/202-632-5065
Sao Tome e Principe/T. Glover/202-632-5065
Saudi Arabia/J. Lewis/202-632-5065
Senegal/G. Morgan/202-632-5065
Seychelles/K. Connor/202-632-5065
Sierra Leone/B. Kornhauser/202-632-5065
Singapore/E. Chin/202-634-1272
Solomon Islands/T. Lyday/202-634-1272
Somalia, Republic of/K. Connor/202-632-5065

South Africa, Republic of/M. Ellis/202-632-5065
Spain/R. Sondermayer/202-632-5049
Sri Lanka/G. Kinney/202-634-1272
Sudan/K. Connor/202-632-5065
Surinam/H. Ensminger/202-632-5062
Swaziland/K. Connor/202-632-5065
Sweden/J. Huvos/202-632-5047
Switzerland/R. Sondermayer/202-632-5049
Syria/P. Clarke/202-632-5065
Taiwan/E. Chin/202-634-1272
Tanzania/K. Connor/202-634-5065
Thailand/G. Kinney/202-634-1272
Togo/G. Morgan/202-632-5065
Trinidad and Tobago/D. Hyde/202-632-9352
Tunisia/K. Connor/202-632-5065
Turkey/P. Clarke/202-632-5065
Uganda/K. Connor/202-632-5065
United Arab Emirates/J. Lewis/202-632-5065
United Kingdom/T. Karpinsky/202-634-1276
Upper Volta/G. Morgan/202-632-5065
Uruguay/P. Velasco/202-632-9352
U.S.S.R./P. Levine/202-632-5060
Vanvatu (New Hebrides)/T. Lyday/202-634-1272
Venezuela/H. Newman/202-632-5060
Vietnam/G. Kinney/202-634-1272
Yemen (Aden)/P. Clarke/202-632-5065
Yemen (Sana)/P. Clarke/202-632-5065
Yugoslavia/R. Sondermayer/202-632-5049
Zaire/G. Morgan/202-632-5065
Zambia/T. Glover/202-632-5065
Zimbabwe Rhodesia/G. Morgan/202-632-5065

Minerals in the World Economy/Charles L. Kimbell/202-634-1713
Soviet Studies/Vasilii V. Strishkov/202-632-5060

Minerals and Metals Experts

Commodity specialists collect, analyze, and disseminate information on the adequacy and availability of the mineral base for the national economy. Fluctuations of supply and demand of particular commodities are studied. These experts can be reached by telephone or writing in care of: Bureau of Mines, Department of the Interior, Washington, DC 20241.

Abrasive Materials/J. F. Smoak/202-634-1206
Aluminum/F. X. McCawley/202-634-1080
Antimony/P. Plunkert/202-634-1083
Arsenic/D. Edelstein/202-634-1053
Asbestos/R. A. Clifton/202-634-1206
Asphalt/Natural/L. Davis/202-634-1184
Barium/S. Ampian/202-634-1081
Bauxite/L. Baumgardner/202-634-1081
Beryllium/J. Carlin/202-634-1083
Bismuth/J. Carlin/202-634-1083
Boron/P. Lyday/202-634-1177
Bromine/P. Lyday/202-634-1177
Cadmium/P. Plunkert/202-634-1083
Calcium/L. Pelham/202-634-1177
Carbon Dioxide/L. Pelham/202-634-1177
Cement/L. Davis/202-634-1184
Cesium/W. Adams/202-634-1082

Chromium/J. Papp/202-634-1028
Clays/S. G. Ampian/202-634-1180
Cobalt/W. S. Kirk/202-634-1028
Columbium/L. Cunningham/202-634-1024
Copper/J. Jolly/202-634-1071
Corundum/J. Smoak/202-634-1206
Diamond (Industrial)/J. Smoak/202-634-1206
Diatomite/A. C. Meisinger/202-634-1184
Explosives/C. Davis/202-634-1190
Feldspar/M. J. Potter/202-634-1180
Ferroalloys/R. Brown/202-634-1015
Fluorspar/L. Pelham/202-634-1177
Gallium/L. Baumgardner/202-634-1081
Garnet/J. Smoak/202-634-1206
Gemstones/J. Pressler/202-634-1206
Germanium/P. Plunkert/202-634-1083
Gold/J. Lucas/202-634-1070
Graphite (Natural)/H. Taylor/202-634-1180
Greensand/J. Searls/202-634-1190
Gypsum/J. W. Pressler/202-634-1206
Hafnium/L. E. Lynd/202-634-1083
Helium/P. Tully/202-376-2604
Indium/J. F. Carlin, Jr./202-634-1063
Iodine/P. Lyday/202-634-1177
Iron Ore/F. L. Klinger/202-634-1023
Iron and Steel/F. Schottman/202-634-1022
Iron and Steel Scrap/F. Cooper/202-634-1022
Kyanite-Mullite/M. J. Potter/202-634-1180
Lead/W. Woodbury/202-634-1083
Lime/J. W. Pressler/202-634-1206
Lithium/J. Ferrell/202-634-1177
Magnesium Compounds/L. Lynd/202-634-1073
Manganese/T. Jones/202-634-7091
Mercury/L. Carrico/202-634-1082
Mica/L. Davis/202-634-1184
Molybdenum/J. Blossom/202-634-1021
Nickel/S. Sibley/202-634-1025
Nitrogen/C. Davis/202-634-1190

Peat/C. Davis/202-634-1190
Perlite (Crude)/A. C. Meisinger/202-634-1190
Phosphate Rock/W. Stowasser/202-634-1190
Platinum Group Metals/J. R. Loebenstein/202-634-1058
Potash/J. Searles/202-634-1190
Pumice/A. Meisinger/202-634-1184
Quartz Crystal/A. Meisinger/202-634-1177
Rare-Earth Metals/J. Hedrick/202-634-1082
Rhenium/J. Blossom/202-634-1021
Rubidium/T. Adams/202-634-1082
Salt/D. Kostick/202-634-1177
Sand and Gravel/V. V. Tepordei/202-634-1185
Selenium/D. L. Edelstein/202-634-1053
Silicon/G. Murphy/202-634-1024
Silver/R. Reese/202-634-1054
Slag (Iron and Steel)/C. T. Collins/202-634-1024
Sodium and NA Compounds/D. S. Kostick/202-634-1177
Staurolite/H. Taylor/202-634-1180
Stone, Crushed/V. Tepordei/202-634-1185
Stone, Dimension/H. Taylor/202-634-1180
Strontium/J. Farrell/202-634-1177
Sulphur/D. Morse/202-634-1190
Talc & Pyrophyllite/R. A. Clifton/202-634-1206
Tantalum/L. Cunningham/202-634-1024
Tellurium/D. L. Edelstein/202-634-1053
Thallium/P. Plunkert/202-634-1083
Thorium/J. B. Hedrick/202-634-1082
Tin/J. F. Carlin/202-634-1083
Titanium/L. E. Lynd/202-634-1073
Tripoli/J. F. Smoak/202-634-1206
Tungsten/P. T. Stafford/202-634-1029
Vanadium/P. Kuck/202-634-1021
Vermiculite/A. Meisinger/202-634-1184
Wollastonite/M. Potter/202-634-1206
Yttrium/J. Hendrick/202-634-1082
Zeolite/R. Clifton/202-634-1206
Zinc/J. Jolly/202-634-1063
Zirconium/W. Adams/202-634-1082

Major Sources of Information

Abandoned Mine Lands Reclamation
The Office of Surface Mining Reclamation and Enforcement is concerned with reclaiming those mines that are either abandoned or not adequately safeguarded against hazards to public health and safety. This office collects fees from every ton of coal mined in order to restore the land and rectify past mistakes. Contact: Abandoned Mine Lands, Office of Surface Mining Reclamation and Enforcement, Department of the Interior, 1951 Constitution Ave. N.W., Room 220, Washington, DC 20245/202-343-4012.

Aerial Photographs of the United States
Aerial photographs are available for most any large or small area of the United States, taken from heights ranging from a few thousand feet to over 60,000 feet. You can probably get a picture of your neighborhood. Contact: User Services, Earth Resources Observation System Data Center, Geological Survey, Department of the Interior, Sioux Falls, SD 57198/605-594-6511.

Animal Damage Control
Information and assistance are available to reduce damage caused by wildlife (birds and mammals) to livestock, crops, forests, wildlife resources; residential, business and industrial properties; and to reduce threats to human health and safety. Examples of damage include: pets killed by coyotes, pigeons living in the eaves of houses, and birds on airport runways. For technical and operational assistance, Contact: Division of Animal Damage Control, Fish and Wildlife Service, Department of the Interior, 1717 H St. N.W., Room 514, Washington, DC 20240/202-632-7463.

Antarctic Maps

The Geological Survey in cooperation with the National Science Foundation prepares and publishes topographic maps of selected areas of Antarctica needed to support the U.S. Antarctic Research Program (USARP) efforts. These maps are prepared from aerial photography by U.S. Navy Air Development Squadron Six (VXE-6) in accordance with USGS specifications. For a catalog of available maps, contact: Branch of Distribution, Geological Survey, Department of the Interior, 1200 South Eads St., Arlington, VA 22202/703-557-2781.

Aquarium, National

The National Aquarium is located in the basement of the Main Commerce Building, 14th St. and Constitution Ave., in Washington, DC, and contains a wide variety of fish from all parts of the country. Admission fee is $1.00 for adults and 50¢ for children. Contact: Fish and Wildlife Service, Department of the Interior, Washington, DC 20240/202-377-2826.

Archeological and Historic Area Studies

See "National Park Service Information" in this section.

Archeological and Historical Publication

The results of National Park Service research on history and archeology are available to the public. Contact: Professional Publications, National Park Service, Department of the Interior, 1100 L St. N.W., Room 2137, Washington, DC 20005/202-343-7071.

Archeological Projects

For information on archeologic projects being conducted in the Western states, contact: Preservation Office, Bureau of Reclamation, Office of Environmental Affairs, MSD-151, Department of the Interior, P.O. Box 25007, Denver Federal Center, Denver, CO 80225/303-234-4348.

Atlas, National

The National Atlas of the U.S. will be a loose-leaf collection of full-color maps and charts showing physical features such as landforms, geology, soil, vegetation, climate and environmental hazards such as landslides. Economic, social and cultural data are also presented. Sixty percent of the Atlas is digitized. Contact: Geographic Research, National Mapping Division, Geological Survey, Department of the Interior, National Center, MS 521; Reston, VA 22092/703-860-6341.

Buffalo and Cattle

Certain nonprofit organizations can obtain free American buffalo or Texas longhorn cattle from government refuges. The government also auctions these animals to the public. Information and expertise are also available on the management of herds of range animals. Contact: Division of Refuge Management, Fish and Wildlife Service, Department of the Interior, Room 2340, Washington, DC 20240/202-343-4311

Bureau of Indian Affairs Area Offices

Aberdeen Area Office
Bureau of Indian Affairs
115 4th Avenue, S.E.
Aberdeen, SD 57401
605-225-0250, ext. 343
(Nebraska, North Dakota and South Dakota)

Albuquerque Area Office
Bureau of Indian Affairs
5301 Central Avenue, N.E.
P.O. Box 8327
Albuquerque, NM 87108
505-766-3170
(Colorado and New Mexico)

Anadarko Area Office
Bureau of Indian Affairs
WCD—Office Complex
P.O. Box 368
Anadarko, OK 73005
405-247-6673
(Kansas and West Oklahoma)

Billings Area Office
Bureau of Indian Affairs
316 North 26th Street
Billings, MT 59101
406-657-6315
(Montana and Wyoming)

Eastern Area Office
Bureau of Indian Affairs
1951 Constitution Ave. N.W.
Washington, DC 20245
703-235-2571
(New York, Maine, Louisiana, Florida, North Carolina and Mississippi)

Juneau Area Office
Bureau of Indian Affairs
Federal Building
P.O. Box 3-8000
Juneau, AL 99802
907-586-7177
(Alaska)

Minneapolis Area Office
Bureau of Indian Affairs
Chamber of Commerce Bldg.
15 South Fifth St.—6th Fl.
Minneapolis, MN 55402
612-349-3383
(Minnesota, Iowa, Mich., & Wisc.)

Muskogee Area Office
Bureau of Indian Affairs
Old Federal Building
Muskogee, OK 74401
918-687-2295
(East Oklahoma)

Navajo Area Office
Bureau of Indian Affairs
P.O. Box M
Window Rock, AZ 86515
602-871-515) (5111)
(Navajo Residents only, Arizona, Utah, and New Mexico)

Phoenix Area Office
Bureau of Indian Affairs
3030 North Central
P.O. Box 7007
Phoenix, AZ 85011
602-241-2305
(Arizona, Nevada, Utah, California and Idaho)

Portland Area Office
Bureau of Indian Affairs
1425 Irving Street, N.E.
P.O. Box 3785
Portland, OR 97208
503-231-6702
(Oregon, Washington, and Idaho)

Sacramento Area Office
Bureau of Indian Affairs
Federal Office Building
2800 Cottage Way
Sacramento, CA 95825
916-484-4682
(California)

Bureau of Land Management Needs You
In order to understand the ecological relationships in an area and to better consider the needs and wishes of the people throughout the Nation, the Bureau of Land Management encourages individuals to visit a local office and offer their ideas. For a complete listing of local offices, contact: Bureau of Land Management, Department of the Interior, Room 5600, Washington, DC 20240/202-343-5717.

Cadastral Survey
The Division of Cadastral Surveys determines boundaries for ownership purposes for the federal government using the "Rectangular System." All original land titles except those in the 13 Colonial States are based on cadastral surveys. Records are in the form of drawings or maps and written descriptions of all land which is now or was once either a part of the public domain or land designated by Congress as within the jurisdiction of the cadastral survey. Contact: Division of Cadastral Survey, Bureau of Land Management, Department of the Interior, 1129 20th St. N.W., Room 309, Washington, DC 20036/202-653-8798.

Camping, Hunting, Fishing, Hiking, Etc.
See "Outdoor Activities," "Outdoor Recreation," and "Trails, National" in this section.

Camping Publications
The following publications are published by the Department of the Interior and are useful for campers:

Camping in the National Park System ($1.50)
Guide and Map, National Parks of the U.S. ($.70)
Campground Reservations. Free from: Department of the Interior, National Park Service, 18th and C Sts. N.W., Room 3043, Washington, DC 20240/202-343-7394.
The Complete Guide to America's National Parks $9.25. Available from National Park Foundation, P.O. Box 57473, Washington, DC 20037/202-785-4500.

Christmas Trees
Free Christmas trees are available from public lands to nonprofit organizations. For the nominal fee of $1.00, an individual can cut his or her own tree. This program is mainly in the 10 western states. Contact: Division of Forestry, Bureau of Land Management, Department of the Interior, Room 901, Premier Bldg, 1725 I St, NW Washington, DC 20240/202-653-8864.

Cloud Seeding
For information and technical expertise on Project Skywater and other cloud seeding programs, contact: Atmospheric Resources Management, Water and Power Resources Service, Department of the Interior, P.O. Box 25007, Denver Federal Center, Denver, CO 80225/303-234-2056.

Computerized Data Base
The following data bases are maintained by the Department of Interior.

Bird Banding Data Base
This data base contains information about game and non-game birds banded and/or recovered since the Banding Program began in 1921. Records exist on all birds banded in North America as well as their recovery from all over the world. The data base is international in scope, as birds have been recovered by participants in countries such as Russia, Brazil and India. Searches and printouts are available. Depending upon the nature of your request, you may or may not be charged a fee. Contact: U.S. Department of Interior, Fish and Wildlife Services, Patuxent Wildlife Research Center, Laurel, MD 20708/301-498-0423.

Birds Breeding Survey Data Base
This data base contains records from the Annual National Bird Survey of the Population of non-game birds. The records are used to analyze population changes from year to year, and to produce range, distribution and abundance maps for non-game bird species.
Searches and printouts are available free of charge. Depending upon the nature of your request, you may or may not be charged a fee. Some information is restricted under the Privacy Act. Contact: U.S. Department of Interior, Fish and Wildlife Service, Patuxent Wildlife Research Center, Laurel, MD 20708/301-498-0280.

Cartographic and Geographic Data Base

The National Cartographic and Geographic Information Center (NCGIC) maintains several computerized data bases with information on aerial photographs, maps, charts, atlases, geographic names and cartographic data. The Center also has on-line access to other data bases of information on aerial/space imagery held at EROS Data Center, geodetic control, and digital cartographic data. From all these data bases, NCGIS generates micrographic indexes and catalogs in various formats. Searches and printouts listing NCGIC's holdings are available free of charge. The actual product (i.e., maps, charts, etc.) must be purchased from NCGIC. Contact: The NCGIC Mapping Center nearest you (there are 34 nationwide—check your phone book under "U.S. Government, Department of the Interior, U.S. Geological Survey") OR National Cartographic and Geographic, Information Center, U.S. Geological Survey, 507 National Center, Reston, VA 22092/703-860-6045.

Earthquake Data Base

Earthquake Data File contains locations of more than 365,000 earthquakes, known or suspected explosions and associated phenomena, coal bumps, rockbursts, quarry blasts, and other disturbances recorded worldwide. Searches, computer listings, mylar, page-size maps, punch cards and magnetic tapes are all available on a cost-recovery basis. Searches generally cost $100.00. Contact: National Geophysical Data Center, NOAA Attn: E/GC1, 325 Broadway, Boulder, CO 80303/303-497-6472.

Earthquake Effect Data Base

Earthquake Effect File contains about 141,000 U.S. earthquake intensity observations (dating back to 1786) gathered from field team reports, canvasses, newspaper clippings, felt and non-felt reports, special catalogs, and other sources. A search can be performed for any geographic area in the United States, including Alaska and Hawaii, for any intensity level. Searches and printouts are provided for a flat fee of $100.00. The complete file can be purchased on magnetic tape for $200.00. Contact: National Geophysical Data Center, National Oceanic And Atmospheric Administration, EDIS/NGSDC D622, 325 Broadway, Boulder, CO 80303/303-497-6472.

Fish and Wildlife Bibliographic Data Base

The Fish and Wildlife reference Service (FWRS) operates a bibliographic data base containing indexed fish and wildlife-related documents from the following sources: the Federal Aid in Fish and Wildlife Restoration Program; the Adronomous Fish Conservation Program; the Endangered Species Grants program; work done at the Cooperative Fishery and Wildlife agencies.

Bibliographic searches and documents can be obtained from FRWS. Individuals working on projects funded by FRWS contributers and full-time employees of state fish and wildlife agencies are eligible for "cooperator" status. Free literature searches are performed for "cooperators" and they are not charged for photocopying and microfiche services unless the cost exceeds $10.00. All others—called "clients"—are charged a flat fee of $30.00 for a new literature search, 10 cents per page for copies of searches on file and 50 cents per fiche for copies of reports. FWRS Data Base may become available on DIALOG in the next year or so. Contact: Fish and Wildlife Reference Service, 1776 East Jefferson St., Room 470-S, Rockville, MD 20852/301-468-1737, 800-582-3421 (except Maryland).

Fishery Statistics Data Base

The Fishery Statistics Data Base (FSDB) contains statistical data pertaining to fishery landings, processed products, employment, value and prices, stocks on hand and foreign trade. Information is stored about commercial and recreational fisheries at the international to regional level. Searches and print-outs are available on a cost-recovery basis. Contact: National Marine Fishery Service, 3300 Whitehaven Street, Washington, DC 20235/202-634-7415.

Geographic Data Base

The Earth Resources Observation System (EROS) Data Center data base is a storage and retrieval system containing images and photographs of the earth's surface features. Geographic searches and print-outs of available materials are available free of charge. Actual photographs and images must be purchased from the Center. Contact: Customer Relations, EROS Data Center, MUNPT Federal Bldg, Sioux Falls, SD 57198/605-594-6511.

Geographic Names Data Base

The National Geographic Names Data Base (NGN) is a collection of geographical names applied to natural and man-made features within the United States. Specialized searches and print-outs are available, on a cost-recovery basis, from Roger Payne's office. Standard alphabetized listings are available for a minimal fee from the National Cartographic and Geological Center. Contact: Manager/Geographic Names Information System, U.S. Geological Survey, 523 National Center, Reston, VA 22092/703-860-6261.

Glacier Photo Data Base

The Glacier Photo Index is an inventory of glacier photographs taken, since the mid-1960s, by the U.S. Geological Survey. The data base contains aerial photographs from the Pacific Northwest of the U.S. (including Alaska) and parts of Canada. Searches and printouts are available on a cost-

recovery basis. Actual photographs must be purchased from the U.S. Geological Survey in Tacoma, WA; 206-593-6502. Contact: World Data Center A: Glaciology, CIRES, Campus Box 449, University of Colorado, Boulder, CO 80309/303-492-5171.

Glaciology Data Base

The Bibliographic Data Base on Glaciology covers all aspects of snow and ice, including: glaciological instruments and methods; physics of ice, glaciers, ice caps and ice sheets; sea, river and lake ice; paleoglaciology; permafrost and frozen-ground studies; seasonal snow cover; avalanches; and snow hydrology.

Searches and printouts are available on a cost-recovery basis. The Center will also provide photocopies of anything in its data base and document delivery. Average search is approximately $25.00. Contact: World Data Center A: Glaciology, CIRES, Campus Box 449, University of Colorado, Boulder, CO 80309/303-492-5171.

Hydrologic Data from U.S. Water Sites

WATSTORE is the U.S. Geological Survey's system for storing the hydrologic data it collects at more than 70,000 water sites nationwide. The system consists of several files. Direct access to the WATSTORE system is available to the general public for a fee. Contact the Water Data Exchange Office for details and a fee schedule. Searches, printouts, etc. can be obtained from the U.S. Government or call the Water Data Exchange office in Washington for a referral to your nearest search service. Contact: Program Manager, National Water Data Exchange, U.S. Geological Survey, 421 National Center, Reston, VA 22092/703-860-6031.

Mineral Deposits and Recovery Operations Data Base

Minerals Availability System (MAS) contains information about worldwide mineral deposits and mineral recovery operations. The system is designed to measure and classify mineral resources according to each deposits' engineering and economic availability. Simple searches, computer print-outs and graphics are available free of charge. Complex searches, etc. are done on a cost-recovery basis with charges based on $600.00 per hour of connect-time. Magnetic tapes of the non-confidential MAS data base are available for $80.00 a reel. Contact: Chief, Division of Mineral Availability, Bureau of Mines, 2401 E. Street, N.W., Washington, DC 20241/202-624-1138.

Minerals Data Base

Automated Minerals Information System (AMIS) is an interactive data base with technical, statistical and bibliographic information about minerals. The system covers domestic and foreign mineral data with emphasis on production, consumption and technological information about approximately 90 commodities. Searches and printouts are available. Simple requests are answered free of charge, while more complicated projects are assessed a cost-recovery fee. Contact: Chief, Division of Minerals Information Systems, Bureau of Mines, 2401 E Street, N.W., Washington, DC 20241/202-634-1117.

Mourning Dove Data Base

The Mourning Dove Data Base contains records, from the results of the Annual Call-Count Survey, which are collected according to various ecological strata. The records are used to produce a meaningful index of the size of the mourning dove breeding population and to set annual mourning dove hunting regulations. Searches and print-outs are available. Depending upon the nature of your request, you may or may not be charged a fee. Some information in the data base is restricted under the Privacy Act. Contact: Chief, Bird Banding Laboratory, U.S. Department of Interior, Fish and Wildlife Service, Patuxent Wildlife Research Center, Laurel, MD 20708/301-498-0205.

Natural Resources Library and Information System

The National Resources Library and Information System (NNRLIS) is a network of 400 libraries and information systems nationwide. Many of its members have access to commercial, government and private data bases—particularly data bases related to natural resources. Search services vary from library to library, but many will search a variety of systems for you. While the National Resources Library in Washington, DC will search only for government employees, staff will refer you to an appropriate library or service in your locality. Contact, for Referral to your local NNRLIS Library, the U.S. Department of Interior, Natural Resources Library, Washington, DC 20240/202-343-5815 OR check your phone book under "U.S. Department of Interior," and then the specific natural resource division you are interested in. The divisions are: National Park Service, Fish and Wildlife, U.S. Geological Survey, Bureau of Land Management, Bureau of Mines, Bureau of Reclamation, Bureau of Indian Affairs and Office of Surface Mining.

Water Data Base

Master Water Base Index (MWDI) is an index file of sites throughout the U.S. from which water data (both surface and ground) is collected. Site information includes: location, organization collecting information, status of collection project and water quality perimeter data. Searches, printouts (including tables) and magnetic tapes are available. Services requiring less than $15.00 computer time are free: otherwise, (with the possible exception of

universities and non-profits) a cost-recovery fee is assessed. Contact: NAWDEX Program Office, U.S. Geological Survey, 421 National Center, Reston, VA 22092/703-860-6031.

Water Data Sources Directory
The Water Data Sources Directory (WDSD) contains information about over 700 organizations that are water data users and collectors. Searches and printouts are available for a cost recovery fee, and a fee is charged for complex requests. The entire data base can be purchased in hard copy for $45.00, and on microfiche for $2.50. Contact: NAWDEX Program Office, U.S. Geological Survey, 421 National Center, Reston, VA 22092/703-860-6031.

Water Resources Bibliographic Data Base
The Water Resources Scientific Information Center (WRSIC) maintains a bibliographic data base covering all scientific and technical information of interest to the water resources community. WRSIC operates five Centers in the United States, and the public can use the terminals at these Centers or have the Centers conduct a search. Some Centers will do a search free of charge, while others will charge a cost-recovery fee. The WRSIC data bases are also available on DOE/RECON and DIALOG (file 17). Contact: Water Resources Scientific Information Center, U.S. Department of the Interior, U.S. Geological Survey, Washington, DC 20240/202-343-8435 OR contact one of the five Water Resource Centers. (see listing of centers in this section.)

Waterfowl Data Base
This May Aerial Survey Data Base contains records from the Annual Aerial Survey of waterfowl in their breeding areas in North America. Searches and printouts are available. Depending upon the nature of your request, you may or may not be charged a fee. Some information in the data base is restricted under the Privacy Act. Contact: Chief, Bird Banding Laboratory, U.S. Department of Interior, Fish and Wildlife Service, Patuxent Wildlife Research Center, Laurel, MD 20708/301-498-0205.

Waterfowl Harvest Surveys Data Base
The Waterfowl data base has two components: (1) Records from the Annual Waterfowl Parts (wing and tail) Collection Survey; and (2) Records from the Annual Male Questionnaire Survey of Waterfowl Hunters. The files are used to determine estimates of waterfowl kill by species, annual production, and a variety of facts about waterfowl kill and hunter activity on a regional and national basis.

The data base was started in 1961 and is updated monthly. Searches and printouts are available. Depending upon the nature of your request, you may or may not be charged a fee. Some information in the data base is restricted under the Privacy Act. Contact: Bird Banding Laboratory, U.S. Department of Interior, Fish and Wildlife Service, Patuxent Wildlife Research Center, Laurel, MD 20708/301-498-0205.

Woodcock Statistical Data Base
The Woodcock Statistical Data Base contains records from two surveys: (1) The Annual Singing-Ground Breeding Population Survey and (2) The Annual Wing-Collection Production Survey. The data base is used to analyze the population dynamics of woodcock species, to provide information for the setting of hunting regulations and for research. Searches and printouts are available. Depending upon the nature of your request, you may or may not be charged a fee. Some information in the data base is restricted under the Privacy Act. Contact: Chief, Bird Banding Laboratory, U.S. Department of Interior, Fish and Wildlife Service, Patuxent Wildlife Research Center, Laurel, MD 20708/301-498-0205.

Conservation Law Enforcement Training
Training assistance is available to state conservation officers in criminal law, and the principles, techniques and procedures of wildlife law enforcement. Contact: Chief, Division of Law Enforcement, Fish and Wildlife Service, Department of the Interior, Box 28006, Washington, DC 20005/202-343-9243.

Cultural Resources
Information is available on all National Park Service historic, cultural, archeological and architectural structures on historic sites and on artifacts considered worthy of preservation. Two computer files are available: 1) List of Classified Structures, and 2) Bibliography Inventory of Park Historical and Architectural Studies. Contact: Cultural Resources, National Park Service, Department of the Interior, Room 3127, Washington, DC 20240/202-343-7625.

Dam Safety
The manual, *Safety Evaluation of Existing Dams,* provides professional personnel with a comprehensive guide to a program of dam safety examination and evaluation. The principles, concepts, and general procedures are readily adaptable by any agency conducting a regulatory or in-house dam safety program for existing dams. This publication is available for $9.50 from the Superintendent of Documents, Government Printing Office, Washington, DC 20402/202-783-3238.

Data Base Directory
The U.S. Geological Survey publishes a comprehensive inventory of its machine-readable scientific and technical, spatial, and bibliographic data

bases. Copies of *Scientific and Technical, Spatial, and Bibliographic Data Bases of the U.S. Geological Survey* can be obtained free of charge from: Branch of Distribution, Geological Survey, Department of the Interior, 1200 South Eads Street, Arlington, VA 22202/703-557-2781. For technical information regarding the data bases, contact: Office of Data Base Administration, Geological Survey, Department of the Interior, Room 806, National Center, Reston, VA 22092/703-860-6086.

Denver Wildlife Research Center
The center conducts research on a wide range of biological sciences topics. Some of the areas of research are animal damage control including damage assessment, laboratory and field studies of behavior and ecology of the damaging species and the development and testing of chemical, physical, or cultural methods for minimizing or eliminating the problem situation; acquisition, care, permanent preservation and systemic study of wildlife species; and developing methods for reducing severe agricultural damage by a variety of rodents, birds, and vampire bats. Contact: Denver Wildlife Research Center, U.S. Fish and Wildlife Service, Department of the Interior, Bldg 16, Federal Center, Denver, CO 80225/303-234-2283.

Desalting Plants Study
A detailed, three-volume study by Burns and Roe for the Office of Water Research and Technology investigated brackish Water Membrane Desalting Plants. Copies are available for $61.50 (NTIS No. PB294-080) from: National Technical Information Service, Department of Commerce, Springfield, VA 22161/703-487-4600 (see, also, "Saline Water Conversion" in this section).

Direct Payments
The programs described below are those which provide financial assistance directly to individuals, private firms and other private institutions to encourage or subsidize a particular activity.

Indian Social Services—Child Welfare Assistance
Objectives: To provide foster home care and appropriate institutional care for dependent, neglected, and handicapped Indian children residing on or near reservations, including those children living in jurisdictions under the BIA in Alaska and Oklahoma, when these services are not available from state or local public agencies.
Eligibility: Dependent, neglected, and handicapped Indian children whose families live on or near Indian reservations or in jurisdictions under the Bureau of Indian Affairs in Alaska and Oklahoma. Applications may be made by a parent or guardian or person having custody of the child.
Range of Financial Assistance: $100 to $1,000; $390. (Assistance per child per month, depending on type of care or treatment required.)

Contact: Division of Social Services, Office of Indian Services, Bureau of Indian Affairs, 18th and C Sts. N.W., Washington, DC 20245/202-343-6434.

Indian Social Services—General Assistance
Objectives: To provide assistance for living needs to needy Indians on or near reservations, including those Indians living in jurisdictions under the Bureau of Indian Affairs in Oklahoma, when such assistance is not available from state or local public agencies.
Eligibility: Needy Indians living on or near Indian reservations or in jurisdictions under the Bureau of Indian Affairs in Oklahoma.
Range of Financial Assistance: Not specified.
Contact: Division of Social Services, Office of Indian Services, Bureau of Indian Affairs, 18th and C Sts. N.W., Washington, DC 20245/202-343-6434.

Regulation of Surface Coal Mining and Surface Effects of Underground Coal Mining
Objectives: To protect society and the environment from the adverse effects of surface coal mining operations consistent with assuring the coal supply essential to the nation's energy requirements.
Eligibility: State governor and tribal chairman designated agencies.
Range of Financial Assistance: Program Development $4,800 to $251,254. Cooperative Agreements $5,230 to $1,135,000. Small Operator Assistance $21,225 to $1,000,000; Administration and Enforcement, $42,370 to $9,000,000; $1,300,000.
Contact: State Grants and Small Operator Assistance, State and Federal Programs, Office of Surface Mining Reclamation and Enforcement, Dept. of the Interior, Washington, DC 20240/202-343-4225.

Dredging and Filling
Wetlands and aquatic culture areas are monitored to avoid unnecessary environmental disruption when there is dumping and discharge. Contact: Permits and License Branch, Ecological Services, Fish and Wildlife Service, Department of the Interior, 1375 K St. N.W., Room 414, Washington, DC 20240/202-343-8814

Duck Stamp
The sale of Duck Stamps is one of the Nation's oldest and most successful wildlife conservation efforts. Duck Stamps (formerly named Migratory Bird Hunting and Conservation Stamp) are required to be purchased each year by anyone age 16 or older who hunts waterfowl. Revenues from the sale of the $7.50 stamps are used to buy wetlands for the National Wildlife Refuge System. Duck Stamps may be purchased at your local Post Office. A free pamphlet, *The Duck Stamp Story,*

presents the background of the Duck Stamp Program. It is available by contacting: Public Affairs, Fish and Wildlife Service, Washington, DC 20240/202-343-5634.

Duck Stamp Contest
The duck stamp contest is held annually from July 1 to October 15. An artist can present a rendition of any living species of North American duck, goose, or swan. The stamps are sold for $7.50 at Post Offices and hunting refuges. The winner receives one sheet of stamps (worth $225) and owns the copyright of the painting, which can be of great value. Contact: Public Affairs, Audio Visual, Fish and Wildlife Service, Department of the Interior, Room 1895A, Washington, DC 20240/202-343-5508.

Earthquake Hazards Reduction Program
This program aims to identify areas of high risk, to acquire the ability to predict the time and intensity of earthquakes and to control them through the gradual release of strain. Contact: Earthquake Hazards Reduction Program, Geological Survey, Department of the Interior, 345 Middlefield Rd., MS 77, Menlo Park, CA 94025/415-323-8111. Two periodicals are published by the program, *Earthquake Information Bulletin* ($14/year) and *Preliminary Determination of Epicenters* ($17/year) are available from: Superintendent of Documents, Government Printing Office, Washington, DC 20402/202-783-3238.

Earthquake Information Center
The National Earthquake Information Service computes and publishes epicenter locations for earthquakes worldwide, and provides general information pertaining to the geographic location, magnitude and intensity of current earthquakes. Contact: National Earthquake Information Centers, Geological Survey, Department of the Interior, Box 25046, Federal Center, MS 967, Denver, CO 80225/303-234-3994.

Earth Resources Observation System (EROS) Data Center
This data center contains a collection of over 6 million images and photographs of the earth's surface features. The data are collected from NASA's Landsat imagery, aerial photography acquired by the Department of the Interior, from NASA research aircraft and the spaceshuttle. The primary functions of the data center are data storage, reproduction and user assistance and training. Contact: User Services, Earth Resources Observation System Data Center, Geological Survey, Department of the Interior, Sioux Falls, SD 57198/605-594-6511, ext. 111.

Earth Resources Observation System (EROS) Regional Center
In addition to the main data center in South Dakota, EROS maintains a number of regional offices which have access to the EROS data files. For a listing of regional *Applications Assistance Facilities,* contact: User Services, Earth Resources Observation System Data Center, Geological Survey, Department of the Interior, Sioux Falls, SD 57198/605-594-6511, ext. 111.

Earth-Science Libraries
The following earth-science libraries contain collections on geology, paleontology, petrology, mineralogy, geochemistry, geophysics, ground and surface water, topography, cartography, mineral resources, physics, chemistry, zoology, earth satellites and remote sensing, geothermal energy, marine geology, land use, lunar geology, and the conservation of resources. Contact:

Library, Geological Survey, 2255 North Gemini Dr., Flagstaff, AZ 86001/602-527-7009
Library, Geological Survey, 345 Middlefield Rd, MS 55, Menlo Park, CA 94025/415-323-8111, ext. 2207.
Library, Geological Survey, Box 25046, Federal Center, Stop 914, Denver, CO 80225/303-236-1060.
Don Lee Kulow Memorial Library, EROS Data Center, Sioux Falls, SD 57198/605-594-6511.
Library, Geological Survey, 950 National Center, Room 4-A-100, 12201 Sunrise Valley Dr., Reston, VA 22092/703-860-6671.

Endangered and Rare Wildlife
For a listing, as well as additional information, on threatened, rare and endangered species, contact: Office of Endangered Species, Fish and Wildlife Service, Department of the Interior, 1000 North Glebe Rd., Arlington, VA 22201/703-235-2771.

Endangered Plants
See "Wildlife Use of Federal Lands" in this section.

Energy Resources, Future
Estimates on the availability of future energy resources, like oil, gas, uranium, and oil shale are available from: Office of Energy and Marine Geology, Geological Survey, Department of the Interior, National Center, Room 3A316, Reston, VA 22092/703-860-6431.

Engineering
Information on environmental engineering and the construction of roads, buildings, recreational complexes, water control and related structures can be obtained from: Division of Engineering, Bureau of Land Management, Department of the Interior, 1129 20th St. N.W., Room 301, Washington, DC 20036/202-653-8811.

Environmental Affairs

The focal point for environmental impact information for the Water and Power Resources Service is: Office of Environmental Affairs, Water and Power Resources Service, Department of the Interior, Room 7622, Washington, DC 20240/202-343-4991.

Environmental Contaminant Evaluation

For information and expertise on pesticide-fish-wildlife ecology, contact: Resource Contaminant Assessment Division, Fish and Wildlife Service, Department of the Interior, Washington, DC 20240/202-343-5452.

Environmental Education

The National Park Service operates a general program for environmental information and education to users of the National Park Service. Visitors to the parks are informed on their surroundings and local elementary and secondary schools are supplied with outdoor classrooms. The programs include National Environmental Study Areas (NESA). Contact: Division of Interpretation and Visitor Services, National Park Service, Department of the Interior, 1100 L St. N.W., Room 4135, Washington, DC 20240/202-523-5270.

Environmental Geology

Basic geological investigations are conducted to help solve engineering, land-use and mining problems which arise from unstable ground conditions and natural hazards. Information is also available on various aspects of engineering and structural geology, physical geography, paleontology, and stratigraphy. Contact: Office of Regional Geology, Geologic Division, Geological Survey, Department of the Interior, National Center, Room 3A100, Reston, VA 22092/703-860-6411.

Environmental Impact Analysis

A special office provides a focal point on environmental matters for the Geological Survey. This office reviews environmental impact statements from other agencies, prepares environmental impact statements for Geological Survey actions, performs research related to environmental consequences (physical, social and economic). Contact: Program of Environmental Affairs, Land Information Analysis, Geological Survey, Department of the Interior, National Center, Room 2D324, MS 423, Reston, VA 22092/703-860-7556.

Environmental Mining

Information is available on strip mining, deep mining, and the reclamation of scarred public lands. Environmental mining research is conducted on better ways to handle overburdened extract minerals and coal; soil handling to prevent slides; the effects of mining on local hydrological systems; and the use of sewage, sludge and effluents in revegetation. Contact: Division of

Conservation and Development, Bureau of Mines, Department of the Interior, 2401 E St. N.W., Room 938, Washington, DC 20241/202-634-1245.

Environmental Research

Studies are conducted on environmental containment evaluation, endangered wildlife research and urban wildlife research at Fish and Wildlife Service, Patuxent Wildlife Research Laboratories, Wildlife Research Laboratories, Wildlife Research Center, Laurel, MD 20708/301-498-0214.

Films

Films are available usually at no cost. Each of the following organizations will provide you with a free catalog:

Office of Public Affairs, Bureau of Land Management, Department of the Interior, 18 & E St, NW Room 5600, Washington, DC 20240/202-343-4151.

Office of Public Affairs, Bureau of Reclamation, Department of the Interior, Room 7644, Washington, DC 20240/202-343-4662.

Harpers Ferry Historical Association, P.O. Box 197, Harpers Ferry, WV 25425/304-535-6371, ext. 6330.

Branch of Visual Services, Geological Survey, Department of the Interior, National Center, Room B-C-10 MS 790, 12201 Sunrise Valley Dr., Reston, VA 22092/703-860-6171.

Films on Mining

Free films are available to acquaint the public with the mineral resources of the United States and to show the need and value of conservation in mineral production and utilization. Most of the films depict mining and metallurgical operations and related manufacturing processes. For a listing of films, contact: Motion Pictures, Bureau of Mines, Department of the Interior, 4800 Forbes Ave., Pittsburgh, PA 15213/412-621-4500, X326.

Fire Management

The Bureau of Land Management is responsible for emergency preparedness and search and recovery coordination for fires on public land. Information is also available on fire prevention, fire suppression, air operations and fire training. Contact: Division of Fire and Aviation Management, Bureau of Land Management, Department of the Interior, 18th and C Sts. N.W., Washington, DC 20240/202-653-8800.

Fish and Wildlife Cooperative Research

For information on the 26 fishery, 18 wildlife and fish and Wildlife research units, contact: Office of Cooperative Research Units, Fish and Wildlife Service, Department of the Interior, Washington, DC 20240/202-653-8766.

Fish and Wildlife Information

For information on hunting and fishing license sales statistics; federal aid to fish and wildlife restoration; fish and wildlife research; duck stamp data; migratory bird hunting regulations; recreation use of National Wildlife Refuges and National Fish Hatcheries; river-basin studies; rare and endangered wildlife; photographs, contact: Public Affairs Office, Fish and Wildlife Service, Department of the Interior, Room 3240, Interior Building, Washington, DC 20240/202-343-5634.

Fish and Wildlife Photographs
An extensive collection of black and white and color slides on fish and wildlife of America is available for education and information purposes. These photographs can be borrowed at no charge. Contact: Public Affairs, Audio Visuals, Fish and Wildlife Service, Department of the Interior, Room 8070, Washington, DC 20240/202-343-5611.

Fish and Wildlife Protection
The Office of Biological Services studies the effects of land and energy development on fish and wildlife, and develops information on how these activities can coexist and compromise with fish and wildlife conservation. Contact: Division of Biological Services, Fish and Wildlife Service, Department of the Interior, Room 555, Washington, DC 20240/202-653-8723.

Fish and Wildlife Publications
For a free listing of fish and wildlife publications, contact: Publications, Fish and Wildlife Service, Department of the Interior, 1717 H St. N.W., Room 148, Washington, DC 20240/202-254-6306.

Fish and Wildlife Reference Service
This reference service maintains a computerized index to reports and files covering fish and wildlife history and management techniques with emphasis on big game, upland game, waterfowl and freshwater sport fish, as well as surveys of species, habitat improvement studies, and recovery plans of endangered species. A free *Fish and Wildlife Reference Service Newsletter* identifies new reports. Literature searches are available for a fee. Contact: Fish and Wildlife Reference Service, Fish and Wildlife Service, Department of the Interior; 1776 East Jefferson St. Rockville, MD 20852/301-468-1737

Fish and Wildlife Service Regional Offices

Region 1 (California, Hawaii, Idaho, Nevada, Oregon, Washington)

U.S. Fish and Wildlife Service
Lloyd 500 Building, Suite 1692
500 N.E. Multnomah Street
Portland, OR 97232
503-231-6118

Region 2 (Arizona, New Mexico, Oklahoma, Texas)

U.S. Fish and Wildlife Service
500 Gold Avenue, S.W. (P.O. Box 1306)
Albuquerque, NM 87103
505-766-2321

Region 3 (Illinois, Iowa, Indiana, Michigan, Minnesota, Missouri, Ohio, Wisconsin)

U.S. Fish and Wildlife Service
Federal Building, Fort Snelling
Twin Cities, MN 55111
612-725-3500

Region 4 (Alabama, Arkansas, Florida, Georgia, Kentucky, Louisiana, Mississippi, North Carolina, South Carolina, Tennessee, Virgin Islands, Puerto Rico)

U.S. Fish and Wildlife Service
Richard B. Russell Federal Building
75 Spring Street, S.W.
Atlanta, GA 30303
404-221-3588

Region 5 (Connecticut, Delaware, Maine, Maryland, Massachusetts, New Hampshire, New Jersey, New York, Pennsylvania, Rhode Island, Vermont, Virginia, West Virginia)

U.S. Fish and Wildlife Service
1 Gateway Center, Suite 700
Newton Corner, MA 02158
617-965-5100

Region 6 (Colorado, Kansas, Montana, Nebraska, North Dakota, South Dakota, Utah, Wyoming)

U.S. Fish and Wildlife Service
134 Union Boulevard
Lakewood, CO 80228
303-234-2209

Region 7 (Alaska)

U.S. Fish and Wildlife Service
1011 E. Tudor Road
Anchorage, AL 99503
907-786-3534

Fish Diseases
For information and expertise on fish virology, bacteriology, parasitology, and immunology as well as tissue culture and related areas including embryology, genetics, histology, and physiology, contact: National Fisheries Center, Technical Information Services, Division of Fishery Research, Fish and Wildlife Service, Department of the Interior, Leetown, Rt. 1, Box 700 Kearneysville, WV 25430/304-725-8461

Fish Production Techniques
The National Fisheries Center's research focuses on the production of healthy fish, including the development of new techniques to produce quality fish. One of its major operations is the Fish Health Research Laboratory located at Leetown with backup from seven other laboratories and field

stations in other parts of the country. Staff in the Technical Assistance Section can provide technical advice. Its library, which participate in inter-library loans, contains 20,000 volumes, reprints of leaflets, articles, etc. Contact: National Fisheries Center—Leetown, Fish and Wildlife Service, Department of the Interior, Box 700—Route 3, Kearneysville, WV 25430/304-725-8461.

Fisheries Academy

The Fisheries Academy provides fishery workers throughout the world with up-to-date training in fisheries management and husbandry. It serves as a distribution point for information on technical training opportunities available from other sources. The Academy develops new computer tools and analytical methodologies. Contact: Fisheries Academy, National Fisheries Center, Fish and Wildlife Service, Department of the Interior, PO Box 700, Kearneysville, WV 25430/304-725-8461.

Fisheries Information Center—National

Literature searches and reference services are provided. The coverage includes culturing of all freshwater organisms, Pond aeration techniques; Pond fertilization; Drug clearance; Water reuse systems; Spawning and rearing techniques; Fish disease identification; treatment and control; Fish nutrition and feed formulation; Genetics; Hybridization; and Strain evaluation. Contact: National Fisheries Information Center, National Fisheries Center, U.S. Fish and Wildlife Service, Department of the Interior, P. O. Box 700, Kearneysville, WV 25430/304-725-8461.

Fishery Ecology

Through a network of one research center, 12 laboratories and 26 field stations, research is conducted on: 1) predicting the impact of land and water development decisions and actions on fish and their habitat; 2) determining the effects of man's impact on ecosystems and the resultant effect on fish populations and their habitat; 3) evaluating and identifying the vast array of chemicals and other environmental pollutants which affect fish and their habitat; 4) sea-lamprey control in the Great Lakes; 5) all phases of ecology of the Great Lakes; 6) improving existing methods for fish husbandry and management of federal reserves; and 7) pursuing the registration of chemicals used in fisheries work. Contact: Division of Fishery Research, Fish and Wildlife Service, Department of the Interior, 1717 H St. N.W., Room 501, Washington, DC 20240/202-653-8772.

Fishery Information

For a central source of technical information on the protection and enhancement of fish and wildlife resources, contact: Deputy Associate Director—Research, Fish and Wildlife Service, Department of the Interior, Washington, DC 20240/202-343-5715.

Fishery Research

The Division of Fishery Research studies population ecology and population dynamics, aqua-culture and fish husbandry, effective contaminants, fish disease and nutrition and fish genetics. Contact: Division of Fishery Research, Fish and Wildlife Service, Department of the Interior, 1717 H St. N.W., Washington, DC 20240/202-653-8772.

Fishery Research Laboratories

Research is conducted on the toxicology and analysis of chemical contaminants in fish and fish food organisms, water management practices regarding fishery resources, crude oil effluents and range management practices regarding salmonids, and sediments' effects on toxicity of herbicides to aquatic organisms. Contact: Columbia National Fishery Research Laboratory, Fish and Wildlife Service, Department of the Interior, Rte. 1, Columbia, MO 65201/314-875-5399, ext. 3201. Research is also conducted on the toxic effects, modes of action, residue dynamics and ecological impacts of chemicals used to manage fishery resources or to culture fishes, and the interrelationships between water chemistry variations, pollutants and contaminants, and biological strains and their effects on the activity of fishery chemicals. Contact: National Fishery Research Laboratory-La Crosse, Fish and Wildlife Service, Department of the Interior, P.O. Box 818, La Crosse, WI 54601/608-783-6451.

Fish Genetics Laboratory

This laboratory genetically characterizes existing strains of rainbow trout and evaluates their suitability for various environment and management uses. It also defines and develops selection and breeding methods for improved maintenance and performance of rainbow trout. Contact: National Fishery Research Center, Division of Fishery Research, Fish and Wildlife, Department of the Interior, PO Box 700, Kearneysville, WV 25430/304-725-8461.

Fish Hatcheries

The National Fish Hatcheries produces and distributes species of fish of the size, number, strain and quantity to meet resource requirements. The anadromous fishery program is primarily concerned with providing juvenile fishes to supplement natural reproduction to improve the quality, abundance and utilization of the fishery resources of coastal areas for recreational and commercial interests. The Great Lake Fishery is committed to producing lake trout and for stocking the Great Lakes. The Inland Fisheries produce and rear inland fish species for stocking federal, state and Indian waters in order to improve, restore and maintain recreational fishing. Contact: National Fish Hatcheries, Division of Program Operations, Fish and Wildlife Service, Department of the Interior, 1717 H St. N.W., Room 637, Washington, DC 20240/202-653-8746.

Forestry
The Bureau of Land Management manages 4.3 million acres of commercial forest lands of which 3.1 million are subject to timber production. It determines which land should be commercially harvested consistent with environmental and other uses (watershed, wildlife, scenic or wilderness). Commercial harvesters bid on the rights at oral auctions and must conform to the regulations. The bureau also maintains past and current information on Bureau of Land Management timber harvest levels, and forest product sales. Contact: Division of Forestry, Bureau of Land Management, Department of the Interior, 1725 I St., Premier Bldg., Room 901, Washington, DC 20006/202-653-8864.

Freedom of Information Act
Each major office within the Department of the Interior handles Freedom of Information Act (FOIA) requests. If you are looking for the address of a specific FOIA office or wish to file with the central office, contact: Freedom of Information Appeals Officer, Department of the Interior, Room 7358, Washington, DC 20240/202-343-6191.

Geographic Names Information Center
The geographic names staff maintains an active national research, coordinating and information center. It provides a single authority in the United States to which all problems and inquiries concerning domestic geographic names may be directed. Staff members furnish assistance to the U.S. Board on Geographic Names, an interdepartmental agency. It manages a names data repository, answers public inquiries, compiles name information and publishes books and lists on domestic names. It also coordinates the name usage between federal and state governments. Any person or organization, public or private, may make inquiries or request the U.S. Board on Geographic Names to render formal decisions on proposed new names, proposed name changes or names that are in conflict. Contact: Geographic Names Section, Geological Survey, Department of the Interior, 523 National Center, Reston, VA 22092/703-860-6262.

Geography Research
Research is conducted on land-use analysis which consists of an inventory of current land uses, monitoring of land-use charges, and explanations of present patterns and changes in land use that occur. Projects include demonstrating the value and use of remote-sensor data received from high-altitude aircraft and satellite platforms, experiments in urban change detection, regional mapping and updating of land-use information, development of a two-level land-use classification system for use with remote-sensor data, and analysis of the effects of land-use patterns and changes on environmental quality. Contact: Office of Geographic and Cartographic Research, National Mapping Division, Geological Survey, Department of the Interior, National Center, Room 2A316, Reston, VA 22092/703-860-6344.

Geological Publications
The Geological Survey publishes a number of books and periodicals. One can receive a free monthly catalog called *New Publications of the Geological Survey*. Subscriptions can be obtained from Geological Survey, Department of the Interior, 329 National Center, Reston, VA 22092/703-860-6781. A host of free publications are available. The following are a few of the more popular titles:

Sources of Information, Products, and Services of the U.S. Geological Survey
John Wesley Powell's Exploration of the Colorado River
The Geology of Caves
Landforms of the United States
The Interior of the Earth
Volcanoes
Permafrost
Collecting Rocks
Suggestions for Prospecting
Why is the Ocean Salty?
Elevations and Distances in the United States
Rain: A Water Resource
Ground Water
Earthquakes
The Naming (and misnaming) of America
The Exclusive Economic Zone: An Exciting New Frontier
The San Andreas Fault
The Great Salt Lake
Measuring the Nation
Tree Rings: Timekeepers of the Past
Water Use in the United States, 1980

For free copies of any of the above publications or for a complete listing of publications, contact: Geological Survey, Branch of Distribution, 1200 South Eads St., Arlington, VA 22202/703-557-2781.

Geological Service Films
Films and videocassettes about geology, topographic mapping, water resources, astrogeology, aerial photography, and other subjects are available. For information and a free film catalogue contact: Visual Information Services, U.S. Geological Survey, 790-National Center, Reston, VA 22092/703-860-6171.

Geological Survey, Regional Information Offices

The Geological Survey's 10 regional offices answer inquiries, recommend publications and refer requests for technical information. They sell limited quantities of maps and books over the counter and distribute circulars, nontechnical publications, catalogs and indexes free of charge. All offices, except those in Reston, VA, Washington, DC, and Menlo Park, CA, maintain small reference libraries. Most are depositories for open-file reports. The Anchorage, Los Angeles, and Spokane offices maintain Landsat reference files and viewers for satellite imagery. The 10 offices are listed below along with a description of their major holdings:

Public Inquiries Office, Geological Survey, 108 Skyline Building, 508 Second Ave., Anchorage, AK 99501/907-277-0577. Maps of and book reports on Alaska.

Public Inquiries Office, Geological Survey, 7638 Federal Building, 300 North Los Angeles St., Los Angeles, CA 90012/213-688-2850. Maps of and book reports on Alaska, Arizona, California, Hawaii, Nevada, Oregon, and Washington.

Public Inquiries Office, Building 3, Mail Stop 533, 345 Middlefield Rd., Menlo Park, CA 94025/415-323-8111, ext. 2817. Maps of and book reports on Alaska, Arizona, California, Hawaii, Idaho, Nevada, Oregon, Utah, and Washington.

Public Inquiries Office, Geological Survey, 504 Customhouse, 555 Battery St., San Francisco, CA 94111/415-556-5627. Maps of and book reports on Alaska, Arizona, California, Hawaii, Idaho, Nevada, Oregon and Washington. (No mail orders)

Public Inquiries Office, Geological Survey, 169 Federal Building, 1961 Stout St., Denver, CO 80294/303-844-4169. Maps of and book reports on Alaska, Arizona, Colorado, Kansas, Montana, Nebraska, New Mexico, North Dakota, South Dakota, Utah, and Wyoming.

Public Inquiries Office, Geological Survey, 1028 General Services Administration Building, 19th and F Sts. N.W., Washington, DC 20244/202-343-8073. Maps of and book reports on all states.

Public Inquiries Office, Geological Survey, 1-C-45 Federal Building, 1100 Commerce St., Dallas, TX 75242/214-767-0198. Maps of and book reports on Arkansas, Louisiana, New Mexico, Oklahoma, and Texas.

Public Inquiries, Geological Survey, 8105 Federal Building, 125 South State St., Salt Lake City, UT 84138/801-524-5652. Maps of and book reports on Arizona, Colorado, Idaho, Montana, Nevada, New Mexico, Utah, and Wyoming.

Pubic Inquiries Office, Geological Survey, 302 National Center, Room 1-C-402, 12201 Sunrise Valley Dr., Reston, VA 22092/703-860-6781. Maps of and book reports on all states.

Public Inquiries Office, Geological Survey, 678 U.S. Courthouse, West 920 Riverside Ave., Spokane, WA 99201/509-456-2524. Maps of and book reports on Alaska, Idaho, Montana, Oregon, and Washington.

Geological Survey

The main purpose of the U.S. Geological Survey is to provide: accurate maps that show the slope of land surface, the location of man-made features, and the present land use; information about the composition and structure of rocks for prospecting, designing engineering and construction works, and identifying natural hazards such as earthquakes and landslides; data on surface and ground water for the development and conservation of water supplies, determination of water quality and reduction of damage from floods; knowledge of earth history and natural processes; appraisals of the nation's energy and mineral resources; classification of federal lands for minerals and waterpower; Contact: Information Office, Geological Survey, Department of the Interior, National Center, Reston, VA 22092/703-860-7444.

Geological Survey Worldwide Directory

The *Worldwide Directory of National Earth-Science Agencies and Related International Organizations* provides addresses of governmental earth-science agencies around the world that have functions similar to those of one or more of the operating divisions of the U.S. Geological Survey; it also lists addresses of major international organizations that are concerned with some phase of the earth sciences. This directory is available free of charge from Distribution Branch, Tex Products Section, U.S. Geological Survey, 604 South Pickett Street, Alexandria, VA 22304.

Geologic Names

For information and expertise on names given to rocks and the arrangement of rocks in layers (stratigraphic nomenclature) contact: Geologic Names Committee, Geological Survey, Department of the Interior, 902 National Center, Room 3A214, Reston, VA 22092/703-860-6511.

Geology Exhibits

Free exhibit panels are available illustrating recent work in conservation, geology, topography and water resources. The exhibits can be obtained for professional meetings, technical conventions and similar gatherings. The panels or three-dimensional exhibits can be obtained with structural supports and lights for free-standing display. Contact one of the following offices:

Branch of Exhibits, Geological Survey, Box 25046, Mail Stop 702, Federal Center, Denver, CO 80225/303-234-3566

Visual Information Service Group, Geological Survey, 301 National Center, 12201 Sunrise Valley Dr., Reston, VA 22092/703-860-6162

Geology, International

The Office of International Geology provides technical assistance and training to developing countries. The Office participates in scientific cooperation and exchange programs with counterpart agencies abroad. Subject areas include mineral resources, marine geology, hydrology, remote sensing, cartography, water resources, geochemistry and geophysics. Contact: Office of International Geology, Geologic Division, Geological Survey, Department of the Interior, National Center, MS 917, Reston, VA 22092/703-860-6418

Geology Questions
A special office handles public inquiries on geology topics such as earthquakes, energy, the geology of specific areas, and geologic maps and mapping. Packets of teaching aids are available for courses at the elementary, secondary and college levels. Contact: Geological Inquiries Group, Geological Survey, Department of the Interior, 907 National Center, 12201 Sunrise Valley Dr., Reston, VA 22092/703-860-6517.

Geology, Unpublished Reports
The Open-File Service of the Geological Survey provides copies of unpublished preliminary reports and other unpublished documents. The monthly newsletter, *New Publications of the Geological Survey*, announces the availability of these reports. Contact: Open-File Service Section, Geological Survey, Department of the Interior, Box 25425, Federal Center, Denver, CO 80225/303-236-7476.

Geothermal Energy
For information and expertise on the use and effects of geothermal energy on fish and wildlife, contact: Ecological Services, Fish and Wildlife Service, Department of the Interior, 1375 K St. N.W., Suite 400, Washington, DC 20240/202-343-2618.

Gold Prospecting
A free book, *How To Mine and Prospect for Gold*, is available from: Publications Department, Bureau of Mines, Department of the Interior, 4900 La Salle Rd., Avondale, MD 20782/703-436-7966.

Grants
The programs described below are for sums of money which are given by the federal government to initiate and stimulate new or improved activities, or to sustain ongoing services.

Abandoned Mine Land Reclamation Program
Objectives: To protect the public and correct the environmental damage caused by coal and noncoal mining practices that occurred before August 3, 1977.
Eligibility: State and Indian Reclamation Program (Project Grants): The program is restricted to states with eligible lands and coal mining operations within their borders that are paying coal reclamation fees into the Abandoned Mine Reclamation Fund. Federal Reclamation Program: Federal reclamation projects are conducted on a national basis through cooperative agreements with states, local governments, or other recipients, and by direct contracting.
Range of Financial Assistance: Not specified.
Contact: Office of Surface Mining, Division of Abandoned Mined Lands, 1951 Constitution Ave. N.W., Washington, DC 20245/202-343-7887.

Anadromous Fish Conservation
Objectives: To conserve, develop, and enhance the anadromous fish resources of the nation and the fish of the Great Lakes and Lake Champlain that ascend streams to spawn.
Eligibility: States and other non-federal interests are eligible. Non-federal interests are eligible if projects are coordinated with the state agency having jurisdiction over the resource. Nineteen inland states are ineligible. Non-federal interests include state, local, nonprofit and individual entities with professional fishery capabilities. Public and private colleges and Indian Tribes are included.
Range of Financial Assistance: $6,000 to $632,800; $74,700.
Contact: Fish and Wildlife Service, Department of the Interior, Washington, DC 20240/202-653-7148.

Assistance to State Water Resources Research Institutes
Objectives: To provide financial support to Water Research and Technology Institutes located at designated state universities in each of the 50 states, Puerto Rico, the District of Columbia, Guam, and the Virgin Islands, to work on one or more aspects of problem-oriented water resources research, disseminate information as to research results, and train scientists.
Eligibility: One State University Water Research and Development Institute in each state, Puerto Rico, the District of Columbia, Guam and the Virgin Islands is designated pursuant to Title I of the Water Research and Development Act of 1978. Other colleges and universities may participate in the program in cooperation with, and administered by, the designated state institute.
Range of Financial Assistance: Up to $115,000.
Contact: Geological Survey, Water Resources Division, MS 424 Department of the Interior, Reston, VA 22092/703-860-7921.

Cooperative Agreements for Research to Public Lands Management
Objectives: To provide for mutually beneficial research and studies that enhance management of resources and other values of the public lands.
Eligibility: Universities, colleges and other tax exempt nonprofit institutions and corporations.

Range of Financial Assistance: Not applicable.

Contact: Chief, Resource Sciences Staff, Bureau of Land Management (201), Department of the Interior, Washington, DC 20240/202-653-9200.

Economic and Political Development of the Territories and the Trust Territory of the Pacific Islands.

Objectives: To promote the economic, social, and political development of the territories, leading toward greater self-government for each of them.

Eligibility: Eligible applicants are Guam, the Virgin Islands, American Samoa, the Trust Territory of the Pacific Islands and the Northern Mariana Islands.

Range of Financial Assistance: Not applicable.

Contact: Assistant Secretary, Office of Territorial and International Affairs, Department of the Interior, Washington, DC 20240/202-343-4822.

Endangered Species Conservation

Objectives: To provide federal financial assistance to any state, through its respective state agency, which has entered into a Cooperative Agreement to assist in the development of programs for the conservation of endangered and threatened species.

Eligibility: Participation limited to state agencies that have entered into a Cooperative Agreement with the Secretary of the Interior. Puerto Rico, Guam, American Samoa, and the Virgin Islands are also eligible to enter into cooperative agreements.

Range of Financial Assistance: $500 to $120,000; $15,000 per project.

Contact: Fish and Wildlife Service, Department of the Interior, Washington, DC 20240/202-235-2760.

Fish Restoration

Objectives: To support projects designed to restore and manage sport fish populations for the preservation and improvement of sport fishing and related uses of these fisheries resources.

Eligibility: Participation limited to state fish and wildlife agencies. State must have passed laws for the conservation of fish which include a prohibition against diversion of license fees paid by fishermen for purposes other than the administration of the State fish and wildlife agency. Also eligible are Puerto Rico, Guam, the Virgin Islands, and American Samoa.

Range of Financial Assistance: $104,600 to $1,569,000.

Contact: Fish and Wildlife Service, Department of the Interior, Washington, DC 20240/703-235-1526.

Grants for Mining and Mineral Resources and Research Institutes

Objectives: Support research and training in mining and mineral resources problems related to the mission of the Department of the Interior; contribute to a comprehensive nationwide program of mining and mineral research having due regard for the protection and conservation of the environment; support specific mineral research and demonstration projects of industrywide application; assist the states in carrying on the work of competent and qualified mining and mineral resources research institutes; and provide scholarships, graduate fellowships and postdoctoral fellowships in mining, mineral resources and allied fields.

Eligibility: The state Governor's designated public college or institute pursuant to Title III of the Surface Mining Control and Reclamation Act of 1977. If a state does not have an eligible public college, then a private college or university may be eligible.

Range of Financial Assistance: $150,000 received by each institute as a formula grant. Project grants average $1,000,000.

Contact: Office of Mineral Institutes, Bureau of Mines, 2401 E Street NW, Washington, DC 20241/202-634-1328.

Historic Preservation Grants-in-Aid

Objectives: Expand and maintain the National Register of Historic Places, the Nation's listing of districts, sites, buildings, structures, and objects significant in American history, architecture, archeology, and culture at the national, state and local levels; provide matching survey and planning grants-in-aid to identify, evaluate, and protect historic properties; provide matching acquisition and development grants-in-aid, to public and private parties for preservation of National Register-listed properties; provide matching grants-in-aid to the National Trust for Historic Preservation to preserve historic resources.

Eligibility: Eligible applicants are the National Trust for Historic Preservation and state and Territories as defined in the National Historic Preservation Act operating programs administered by a State Historic Preservation Officer appointed by the Governor.

Range of Financial Assistance: $33,000 to $620,000.

Contact: Associate Director, National Register Programs, National Park Service, Department of the Interior, Washington, DC 20240/202-343-7625.

Indian Child Welfare Act—Title II Grants

Objectives: To promote the stability and security of Indian tribes and families by the establishment of minimum federal standards for the removal of Indian children from their families and the placement of such children in foster or adoptive homes and providing assistance to Indian tribes in the operation of child and family service programs.

Eligibility: The governing body of any tribe or tribes, or any Indian organization, including multi-service centers, may apply individually or as a consortium for a grant.

Range of Financial Assistance: $25,000 upward.

Contact: Division of Social Services, Office of Indian Services, Bureau of Indian Affairs, Deprtment of the Interior, 1951 Constitution Ave. N.W., Washington, DC 20245/202-343-6434.

Indian Education—Higher Education Grant Program

Objectives: To encourage Indian students to continue their education and training beyond high school.

Eligibility: Must be one-fourth or more degree Indian, Eskimo, or Aleut blood, of a tribe being served by the Bureau, enrolled or accepted for enrollment in an accredited college, have financial need as determined by the institution's financial aid office.

Range of Financial Assistance: $200 to $6,000

Contact: Office of Indian Education Programs, Code 522, 1951 Constitution Ave. NW, Washington, DC 20245/202-343-7387.

Indian Employment Assistance

Objectives: To provide vocational training and employment opportunities for Indians.

Eligibility: The applicant must be a member of a recognized tribe, band, or group of Indians, whose residence is on or near an Indian reservation under the jurisdiction of the Bureau of Indian Affairs; and for vocational training grants, must have one-quarter degree or more of Indian blood.

Range of Financial Assistance: $800 to $5,500 per year.

Contact: Office of Indian Services, Division of Job Placement and Training, Bureau of Indian Affairs, 18th and C Sts. N.W., Room 1350, Washington, DC 20245/202-343, 3668.

Indian Housing Assistance

Objectives: To use the Indian Housing Improvement Program (HIP) and Bureau of Indian Affairs resources to substantially eliminate substandard Indian housing. This effort is combined with the Departments of Health and Human Services and Housing and Urban Development.

Eligibility: Indians in need of financial assistance who meet the eligibility criteria of the HIP regulations (25 CFR, Subchapter X, Part 261). For HUD, Indians who meet the income criteria and other rules and regulations of the legally established local Indian housing authorities.

Range of Financial Assistance: $2,500 to $55,000.

Contact: Division of Housing Assistance, Office of Indian Services, Bureau of Indian Affairs, 18th and C Sts. N.W., Washington, DC 20245/202-343-4876.

Land Acquisition and Development of Comprehensive Management Plan (CMP)—State of New Jersey—Pinelands National Reserve

Objectives: To provide following CMP completion, Federal financial assistance for the acquisition of lands in the Pinelands National Reserve boundaries.

Eligibility: The State of New Jersey.

Range of Financial Assistance: $800,000 to $8,250,000.

Contact: Chief, Division of Recreation Grants, National Park Service, Department of the Interior, Washington, DC 20240/202-343-3700.

National Water Research and Development Program

Objectives: To support needed research and development into any aspects of water-related problems deemed desirable in the national interest.

Eligibility: Educational institutions, private foundations or other institutions, federal, state and local governmental agencies, and private firms and individuals whose training, experience, and qualifications are adequate for conducting water research or development projects.

Range of Financial Assistance: $25,000 to $250,000.

Contact: Bureau of Reclamation, Department of the Interior, Washington, DC 20240/202-343-5975.

Outdoor Recreation—Acquisition, Development, and Planning

Objectives: Provide financial assistance to the states and their political subdivisions for the preparation of comprehensive statewide outdoor recreation plans and acquisition and development of outdoor recreation areas and facilities for the general public to meet current and future needs.

Eligibility: For planning grants, only the state agency formally designated by the Governor or state law as responsible for the preparation and maintenance of the Statewide Comprehensive Outdoor Recreation Plan is eligible to apply. For acquisition and development grants, the designated agency may apply for assistance for itself, or on behalf of other state agencies or political subdivisions such as cities, counties, and park districts. Additionally, Indian tribes which are organized to govern themselves and perform the function of a municipal government qualify for assistance under the program. Individuals and private organizations are not eligible.

Range of Financial Assistance: $150 to $5,450,000

Contact: Chief, Recreation Grants Division, National Park Service, Department of the Interior, Washington, DC 20240/202-343-3700.

Self-Determination Grants—Indian Tribal Governments

Objectives: To improve tribal governing capabilities; to prepare for contracting of Bureau programs; to enable tribes to provide direction to the Bureau, and to have input to other federal programs intended to serve Indian people.

Eligibility: Only governing bodies of federally recognized Indian tribes are eligible to apply for self-determination grants.

Range of Financial Assistance: Not specified.

Contact: Division Chief, Office of Indian Services, Division of Self-Determination Services, 1951 Constitution Ave. N.W., Washington, DC 20240/202-343-4796.

Small Reclamation Projects

Objectives: To provide Federal loans and possible grants to public nonfederal organizations for rehabilitation and betterment or construction of water resource development projects located in the 17 westernmost contiguous States and Hawaii.

Eligibility: Public nonfederal organizations, organized under State law and eligibile to contract with the Federal Government, and who can demonstrate engineering and financial feasibility of project proposal. Private individuals are not eligible.

Range of Financial Assistance: Loans: $700,000 to $26,000,000.

Contact: Commissioner, Bureau of Reclamation, Department of the Interior, Washington, DC 20240/202-343-5501.

Training and Technical Assistance—Indian Tribal Governments

Objectives: To aid Indian Tribes to exercise self-determination in accord with Public Law 93-638.

Eligibility: Governing body of any federally recognized Indian tribe.

Range of Financial Assistance: Not specified.

Contact: Division Chief, Office of Indian Services, Division of Self-Determination Services, 1951 Constitution Ave. N.W., Washington, DC 20240/202-343-2706.

Urban Park and Recreation Recovery Program

Objectives: To provide Federal grants to local governments for the rehabilitation of recreation areas and facilities, and development of improved recreation planning.

Eligibility: Eligible applicants are cities and counties meeting the eligibility requirements and listed in the October 9, 1979, Federal Register.

Range of Financial Assistance: Rehabilitation Grants, $8,438 to $5,250,000; Innovation Grants, $7,000 to $1,100,000; Recovery Action Program Grants, $2,750 to $175,000.

Contact: National Park Service, Recreation Grants Division, Washington, DC 20240/202-343-3700.

Wildlife Habitat Management Technical Assistance

Objectives: To plan, develop, maintain and coordinate programs for the conservation and rehabilitation of wildlife, fish and game on lands administered by the Bureau of Land Management (BLM).

Eligibility: State wildlife and/or State fish and game agencies.

Range of Financial Assistance: Not applicable.

Contact: Division of Wildlife (240), Bureau of Land Management, Department of the Interior, 18th and C Streets, NW., Washington, DC 20240/202-343-4843.

Wildlife Restoration

Objectives: To support projects to 1) restore or manage wildlife populations and the provision of public use of these resources, or 2) provide facilities and services for conducting a hunter safety program.

Eligibility: Participation limited to state fish and wildlife agencies. States must have passed laws for the conservation of wildlife which include a prohibition against diversion of license fees paid by hunters for purposes other than the administration of the state fish and wildlife agency. Also eligible are Puerto Rico, Guam and the Virgin Islands and the Northern Mariana Islands.

Range of Financial Assistance: $121,666 to $4,113,500.

Contact: U.S. Fish and Wildlife Service, Department of the Interior, Washington, DC 20240/202-235-1526.

Grave Robbers

The Bureau of Land Management has an education program to keep the public from plundering and destroying ancient sites. It provides information, brochures, posters, etc. on the importance of drawings, pottery and ruins of the American Indians' ancient civilizations. Contact: Office of Public Affairs, Bureau of Land Management, Department of the Interior, Room 5600, Washington, DC 20240/202-343-5717.

Helium

Information is collected on all aspects of helium including production, sales, distribution, conservation uses, future demand and reserves from 1917 to the present. Contact: Division of Helium, Minerals Research, Bureau of Mines, Department of the Interior, Room 939, Columbia Plaza, 2401 E St. N.W., Washington, DC 20241/202-634-4734.

Historic American Buildings Survey

A national archive of historic architecture is maintained and assistance is provided to public and private organizations to help document structures of historic and architectural merit. Documentation consists of the preparation of architecturally measured drawings, photographs, and written reports which are deposited in the Library of Congress where they are available for public use and reproduction. Contact: Historic American Buildings Survey/Historic American Engineering Records, National Park Service, Department of the Interior, 1100 L. St, NW, Room 6101, Washington, DC 20240/202-343-9625.

Historic Landmarks
The National Historic Landmarks Program studies, identifies, recognizes, and encourages the preservation of nationally significant historic properties which are tangible reminders of the American heritage. If you are interested in having your property designated a national historic landmark, contact the Program for details. If it is accepted, a bronze plaque and certificate are awarded in a presentation ceremony. This provides permanent identification of nationally significant properties. Contact: History Division, National Park Service, Department of the Interior, 100 L. St, NW, Room 4209, Washington, DC 20243/202-343-8168.

Historic Landmarks Directory
A complete listing of all certified historic properties is contained in the *National Register of Historic Places* ($22.00 for Vol. I and $19.00 for Vol II.) Available from: Superintendent of Documents, Government Printing Office, Washington, DC 20402/202-783-3238.

Historic Preservation, Advisory Council on
This independent agency is administered by the Department of the Interior. It advises the President and the Congress on historic preservation policy. It also reviews and comments to the Department of the Interior on the historic preservation program and protects historic places when they are threatened by a federal project. Contact: Advisory Council on Historic Preservation, 1100 Pennsylvania Ave, N.W., Room 309, Washington, DC 20004/202-786-0503.

Hunting Regulations
Each year migratory bird hunting regulations are developed by: Office of Migratory Bird Management, Fish and Wildlife Service, Department of the Interior, 1717 H St. N.W., Room 536, Washington, DC 20006/202-254-3207

Hydroelectric Power
The Department of the Interior operates 50 hydroelectric power plants, including Hoover Dam and Grand Coulee Dam, in the 17 Western States. For information on power matters and related environmental impact statements, contact: Division of Power, Bureau of Reclamation, Department of the Interior, Room 7243, Washington, DC 20240/202-343-4890.

Hydrology, International
An international collection of books, pamphlets and reports is available covering all aspects of hydrology. Topics include the hydrologic cycle, the assessment of water resources, evaluation of the influence of man's activities on water systems, and education and training in hydrology. Contact: Office of International Activities, Water Resources Division, Geological Survey, Department of the Interior, MS 470, Reston, VA 22092/703-860-6547.

Indian Arts and Crafts Development
A special program provides planning assistance to native organizations such as the development of innovative educational, productive, promotion, and economic concepts related to Native culture. Complaints about imitation Native American arts and crafts that are misrepresented as geuine handicrafts are referred to appropriate federal or local authorities for action. The three museums operated by the Board serve Indians and the general public: the Sioux Indian Museum in Rapid City, South Dakota; the Museum of the Plains Indian in Browning, Montana; and the Southern Plains Indian Museum in Anadarko, Oklahoma. Contact: General Manager, Indian Arts and Crafts Board, Department of the Interior, Washington, DC 20240/202-343-2773.

Indian Business Assistance
Indian businesses and tribes can receive technical and financial assistance from the Department of the Interior. Contact: Indian Business Enterprise, Bureau of Indian Affairs, Department of the Interior, 1000 Glebe Rd., Room 129, Arlington, VA 22201/703-343-3651.

Indian Craft Shop
The Interior building contains an Indian craft shop which sells handicrafts of various tribes at commercial prices. Contact: Indian Craft Shop, Department of the Interior, 18th and C Sts. N.W., Room 1023, Washington, DC 20240/202-343-4056.

Indian Development
The Office of Indian Development is responsible for developing and managing programs designed to promote the welfare and development of individual Indians and Indian communities. Programs include: employment and financial assistance, social services, housing, law enforcement, tribal governmental services, and self-determination services. Demographic and cultural data are also available. Contact: Office of Indian Services, Bureau of Indian Affairs, Department of the Interior, Room 4600, Washington, DC 20240/202-343-2111.

Indian Education
For statistical and other information relating to

Indian education, contact: Office of Indian Education Programs, Bureau of Indian Affairs, Department of the Interior, 1951 Constitution Ave. NW, Room 3510 MS 503, Washington, DC 20245/202-343-6364.

Indian Information
Information is available on Indians, their relationship to the federal government, specific reservations, or other items regarding their culture. A list of available publications is also available. Contact: Information Office, Bureau of Indian Affairs, Department of the Interior, Room 4627, Washington, DC 20240/202-343-7445.

Indian Publications
The Bureau of Indian Affairs has a limited supply of free publications on Indians.

BOOKLISTS
Book List for Young Readers
General Reading List on Indian History, Culture, Problems and Relationship to the Federal Government
Languages
Legends and Myths
Music
Religion and Ceremonials
Wars and Local Disturbances
Origin
FACT SHEETS
Acknowledgment
Alaska Natives
American Indian and Alaskan Native Education
Information about American Indians and Alaskan Natives
American Indian Policy Bureau of Indian Affairs 1986 Budget Request
Bureau of Indian Affairs Social Services Program
1980 U.S. Census Count of American Indians
Employment with B.I.A.
Housing Program for Indians
Indian Information
The Indian People
The Law and the Indian
List of Indian Tribal Entities Recognized and Eligible to Receive Services from the U.S. Bureau of Indian Affairs
PAMPHLETS
Education Directory
Indian, Eskimo, Aleut Owned and Operated Arts and Crafts Businesses—Source Directory
Bureau of Indian Affairs—Directory of Area Offices and Field Offices
American Indians: U.S. Indian Policy, Tribes and Reservations, BIA: Past and Present, Economic Development

For further information contact: Public Affairs, Bureau of Indian Affairs, Department of the Interior, Washington, DC 20240/202-343-7445.

International Program
The Office of International Programs acts as a liaison office for the Department of the Interior's international activities. Some of its activities include work with the U.S.-Saudi Arabia Joint Commission on Economic Cooperation on building the first national park in Saudi Arabia; looking for lowgrade iron ore; developing desalinization technology; and developing water resources. Contact: International Programs, Office of Territorial and International Affairs, Department of the Interior, Room 4443, Washington, DC 20240/202-343-3101.

Irrigation
For information or expertise on technical aspects of irrigation facilities, contact: Division of Water and Land, Bureau of Reclamation, Department of the Interior, Room 7416, Washington, DC 20240/202-343-5471.

Job Corps Conservation Centers
Twelve job corps conservation centers throughout the country train disadvantaged youths between the ages of 16 and 22. This residential program provides both formal education and vocational training for 18 months to 2 years. Contact: Job Corps, Office of Youth Programs, Department of the Interior, Room 2415, Washington, DC 20240/202-343-4041.

Land Management
Information is available on wildlife management on 473 million acres of public lands; camping, hunting, fishing, hiking, pack trips on public land, mostly in the West and Alaska; wildlife use of lands; forest and watershed practices aiding wildlife and recreation; adventure-seeking, outdoor pursuits on public land areas; obtaining public lands for state and community parks; photographs; mineral and oil and gas leasing on acquired lands and on the Outer Continental Shelf. Contact: Office of Public Affairs, Bureau of Land Management, Department of the Interior, Room 5600, Washington, DC 20240/202-343-5717.

Land Management Library
The collection at the Bureau of Land Management Library consists of the following areas: engineering, including cadastral engineering surveying; forest resources management; lands and land reserve studies; legislation and public land laws; range management; watershed management; minerals management; mineral, oil, gas and geothermal leasing; history, development, administration, conservation and use of public lands; and management and utilization of the Outer Continental Shelf. Contact: Bureau of Land Management Library, Department of the Interior, Denver Service Center, Building 50, Denver Federal Center, Denver, CO 80225/303-236-6649.

Land Resource Planning

Studies are conducted to translate earth-science information into formats and languages for use by land and resource planners, and the general public. Topics covered include: environmental impact, geological hazards, and land use and land cover. Contact: Publications Section, Text Products, Geological Survey, Department of the Interior, 604 S. Pricketts St., Alexandria, VA 22304/703-756-6141.

Land Resources Management

The Bureau of Reclamation is responsible for recreation, land acquisition, appraisal and relocation, land management and land disposal, archeologic and historic resources, and fish and wildlife enhancement. Contact: Land Resources Management Branch, Division of Operations and Maintenance Policy and Planning, Water and Power Resources Service, Department of the Interior, Room 7424, Washington, DC 20240/202-343-5204.

Loans and Loan Guarantees

The programs described below are those which offer financial assistance through the lending of federal monies for a specfic period of time or programs in which the federal government makes an arrangement to idemnify a lender against part or all of any defaults by the borrower.

Distribution Systems Loans

Objectives: To provide fully reimbursable Federal loans to organized irrigation districts with lands included within congressional authorized Reclamation projects to plan, design, and construct irrigation and municipal and industrial water distribution or drainage systems in lieu of Federal construction.

Eligibility: Irrigation district must be organized under State Law and eligible to contract with the United States; must have water service contract with the Bureau of Reclamation.

Range of Financial Assistance: $3,760,000 to $19,900,000.

Contact: Commissioner, Bureau of Reclamation, Department of the Interior, Washington, DC 20240/202-343-5501.

Indian Education—Assistance to Schools

Objectives: To assure adequate educational opportunities for Indian children attending public schools and tribally operated previously private schools.

Eligibility: Public school districts and previously private schools which have eligible Indian children in attendance and which provide educational services meeting established state standards; and which have established Indian Education Committees to approve operations of programs beneficial to Indians.

Range of Financial Assistance: Not specified.

Contact: Branch of Supplemental Support Services, Office of Indian Education Programs, Bureau of Indian Affairs, 18th and C Sts. N.W., Washington, DC 20240/202-343-6364.

Indian Loans—Claims Assistance

Objectives: To enable Indian tribes or identifiable groups of Indians without available funds to obtain expert assistance in the preparation and processing of claims pending before the U.S. Court of Claims.

Eligibility: An Indian organization must have one or more pending claims of a nature and in a stage of prosecution requiring the services of expert witnesses.

Range of Financial Assistance: $500 to $250,000.

Contact: Director, Office of Indian Services, Bureau of Indian Affairs, Department of the Interior, 18th and C Sts. N.W., Room 4600, Washington, DC 20245/202-343-3657.

Indian Loans—Economic Development

Objectives: To provide assistance to Indians, Alaskan Natives, tribes, and Indian organizations in obtaining financing from private and governmental sources which serve other citizens. When otherwise unavailable, financial assistance through the Bureau is provided eligible applicants for any purpose that will promote the economic development of a Federal Indian Reservation.

Eligibility: Indians, Alaskan Natives, tribes, and Indian organizations. Individual applicants must be a member of a federally recognized tribe and not members of an Indian organization which conducts its own credit program. Organizational applicants must have a form of organization satisfactory to the Commissioner of Indian Affairs.

Range of Financial Assistance: $1,000 to over $1,000,000.

Contact: Director, Office of Indian Services, Bureau of Indian Affairs, 18th and C Sts. N.W., Room 4600, Washington, DC 20245/202-343-3657.

Irrigation Systems Rehabilitation and Betterment

Objectives: To rehabilitate and improve irrigation facilities on projects governed by Reclamation law.

Eligibility: Any water users organization whose irrigation facilites were constructed by the Bureau of Reclamation and to which the United States holds title, and any water users organization on non-federal projects constructed under the Small Reclamation Projects Act of 1956.

Range of Financial Assistance: $9,000 to $64,833,000.

Contact: Commissioner, Bureau of Reclamation, Department of the Interior, Washington, DC 20240/202-343-5471.

Small Reclamation Projects

Objectives: To provide fully reimbursable federal loans and possible grants to public non-federal organizations for rehabilitation and betterment or construction of water resource development projects located in the 17 western-most contiguous states and Hawaii.

Eligibility: Public non-federal organizations, organized under state law and eligible to contract with the federal Government, and who can demonstrate engineering and financial feasibility of project proposal. Private individuals are not eligible.

Range of Financial Assistance: $700,000 to $18,000,000.

Contact: Loan Officer, Water and Power Resources Services, Department of the Interior, Washington, DC 20240/202-343-3125.

Mammals and Nonmigratory Birds

The Division of National Wildlife Refuges protects native wildlife from damage of foreign wildlife, keeps species from becoming endangered, and perpetuates the natural diversity of wildlife species and native habitats on national wildlife refuges. Its area of responsibility includes oxen, elk, sea otters, polar bears, walrus, manatee, non-migratory birds, reptiles, amphibians, mollusks, and crustaceans. Contact: Division of National Wildlife Refuges, Fish and Wildlife Service, Department of the Interior, Room 2343, Washington, DC 20240/202-343-4311.

Mapping Program—National

The U.S. Geological Survey National Mapping Program publishes a variety of multipurpose maps to serve all map users. In addition to published maps, basic map data and open-file map byproducts are available. These include aerial photographs, satellite images, advance and reproducible map materials, geodetic control data, geographic-names data, status maps, microfilm map copies, and map data in digital forms. *An Index to topographic and other Map Coverage* and a companion *Catalog of topographic and other Published Maps* are planned for each State. To obtain these publications contact one of the Mapping Distribution branches.

Eastern Distribution Branch, U.S. Geological Survey, 1200 South Eads St., Arlington, VA 22202/703-557-2781.

Western Distribution Branch, U.S. Geological Survey, Box 52286, Federal Center, Denver, CO 80225/303-776-7477.

Maps and Charts

See "National Cartographic Information Center" in this section.

Market Studies on Recreation Activities

Surveys are conducted periodically to determine such items as what types of recreation are used, what types would be preferred, and what keeps one from recreation. Contact: Recreation and Resource Assistance Division, National Park Service, Department of the Interior, 1100 L St. N.W., Room 2321, Washington, DC 20243/202-343-3780.

Migratory Bird Banding Information

The Office of Migratory Bird Management provides a central repository for all migratory bird banding records in North America. It provides analysis of banding records and production and harvest surveys for use in research and management, and publishes findings of these analyses for public reference. Contact: Office of Migratory Bird Management, Fish and Wildlife Service, Department of the Interior, 1717 H St. N.W., Room 555, Washington, DC 20006/202-254-3207.

Mine Passages

The Bureau's *Mine Map Repository* collection describes old passage-ways in abandoned mines throughout the country. These old mine passages are open to the public. For a free copy, contact: Office of Technology Information, Bureau of Mines, Department of the Interior, Columbia Plaza, Room 1035, Washington, DC 20241/202-634-1004.

Mineral and Water Resources

The Geological Survey is responsible for appraising water, mineral, and mineral fuel resources throughout the United States. For information on the latest available data, contact: Chief Geologist, Geological Survey, Department of the Interior, National Center, 12201 Sunrise Valley Dr., MS 911, Reston, VA 22092/703-860-6531.

Mineral Commodity Summaries

Free up-to-date summaries are available on 91 mineral commodities. These data sheets contain information on the domestic industry structure, government programs, tariffs and statistics, and world resource data. Contact: Office of Technical Information, Bureau of Mines, Department of the Interior, Room 1035, Columbia Plaza, Washington, DC 20241/202-634-1001.

Mineral Extracting and Processing Technology and Research

The Bureau of Mines' activities with respect to minerals include: ensuring the nation has an adequate supply of minerals for the production of metals; conducting applied and basic research to develop the technology for extraction processing, use and recycling of the U.S. mineral resources; gathering data, developing research and preparing reports about the technology of extraction and processing of minerals; improving the conditions related to the health and safety of personnel employed in the mining and processing of minerals.

The Bureau publishes the following:

Mineral Commodity Summaries is an annual publication that covers over 90 non-fuel minerals. The publication is issued every January and it is available free of charge.

Mineral Industries Surveys are short publications on various minerals and metals, presenting the most recent production data. They are available free of charge.

Minerals Yearbook is an annual publication that presents technical and economic trends and statistics, in three hard bound volumes. Volume I covers "Mineral Commodities", and costs $16 per year. Volume II is "Minerals Industry Studies", and costs $14 per year. Volume III is "Minerals International", and costs $20 per year.

Minerals Facts and Products–an "encyclopedia" type of publication issued every five years (next edition in 1986). It covers the technology used in the extraction and processing of minerals. The cost is $23 each.

Several other technical publications such as studies and reports are released periodically. Those seeking specific information about these publications should contact the phone number listed above.

Contact: Bureau of Mines, U.S. Department of the Interior, 2401 E St., N.W., Washington, DC 20244/202-634-1004.

Mineral Industry Location System
This system contains a file of maps and transparent overlays showing mineral deposit locations. Contact: Division of Mineral Availability, Bureau of Mines, Department of the Interior, 2401 E St. N.W., Room 814, Washington, DC 20241/202-634-1138.

Mineral Information Office
The main function of the Bureau of Mines is to 1) collect statistical information on 91 nonfuel mineral commodities (fuel minerals are handled by the Department of Energy); and 2) research health and safety matters in mine and mineral processing, investigate environmental technology and mineral resource technology. For information on free publications and periodicals, contact: Office of Technical Information, Bureau of Mines, Department of the Interior, Columbia Plaza, Room 1035, Washington, DC 20241/202-634-1001.

Mineral Leasing Program—Outer Continental Shelf
This program develops an Outer Continental Shelf oil and gas leasing schedule which tentatively schedules Outer Continental Shelf sales for a five-year period. The schedule is a planning document which outlines the pre-leasing steps to be accomplished that lead to a lease rate decision for designated areas. The five steps are: 1) call for nominations, and comments in the *Federal Register,* 2) tentative tract selection; 3) environmental impact statements available to the public; 4) proposed notice of sale; 5) final notice of sale and opening of submitted bids. Contact: Office of Offshore Leasing Management, Division of Mineral Management Service, Department of the Interior, 18th and C Sts. N.W., Washington, DC 20240/202-343-6906.

Mineral Resource Potential
For information and expertise on national and world mineral resources and resource potential, contact: Office of Mineral Resources, Geologic Division, Geological Survey, Department of the Interior, National Center, MS 913, Reston, VA 22092/703-860-6566.

Minerals and Materials Supply and Demand Analysis
The Minerals Availability System (MAS) consists of a computer-based file and a back-up hard copy file which describes the supply availability as well as the technical and economic feasibility of mining and extractions. It includes a mineral reserve classification system describing ore deposits, processing facilities, available transportation, labor requirements, a variety of economic and statistic data on operative mines producing any of the 30 mineral commodities. Contact: Division of Minerals Availability, Bureau of Mines, Department of the Interior, 2401 E St. N.W., Room 645, Washington, DC 20241/202-634-1026.

Mineral Trends
Free reports containing mineral and metals forecasting and trend information are available from: Division of Publications, Bureau of Mines, Department of the Interior, 4900 La Salle Road, Avondale, MD 20782/301-436-7912.

Mine Reports
Free reports on mining and minerals are available from:

Office of Mineral Information, Bureau of Mines, Department of the Interior, 4900 La Salle Rd, Avondale, MD 20782/301-436-7912.

Branch of Publications, Distribution, Bureau of Mines, Department of the Interior, 4800 Forbes Ave., Pittsburgh, PA 15213/412-621-4500.

Division of Technical Reports, Bureau of Mines, Department of Interior, 2401 E St. N.W., Washington, DC 20241/202-634-4740

Mines Library
The Bureau of Mines Library is open to the public and answers reference questions by telephone and mail. The information it supplies includes all

aspects of mineral production, both domestic and foreign, with economic and statistical emphasis; state and county mineral data; mineral and material supply and demand analysis; mineral-related U.S. Senate and House of Representatives reports; patent gazettes; oil and gas reports and market reports. Contact: Bureau of Mines Library, Division of Publications, Department of the Interior, 2401 E St. N.W., Room 127, Washington, DC 20241/202-634-1116.

Mines, Publications
The Bureau of Mines publishes a large range of periodicals and reports on both a free and fee basis. For a list of available publications, contact: Division of Publications, Bureau of Mines, Department of the Interior, 4900 La Salle Rd., Avondale, MD 20782/301-436-7912.

Mines Technology Transfer
The following disseminate information on the latest mining technology: 1) *Technology News*—a free newsletter; 2) free seminars, conferences, in-mine demonstration projects, and traveling displays and exhibits; 3) technical assistance for mine operators. Contact: Technology Transfer Group, Division of Minerals, Health and Safety Technology, Bureau of Mines, Department of the Interior, 2401 E St. N.W., Washington, DC 20241/202-634-1223.

Mining and Minerals Research
The results of research are available on such topics as: mining, metallurgy and mineral economics, mineral and materials supply/demand analysis, belium activities, mineral processing, hydrometallurgy, pyrometallurgy, metallic and nonmetallic materials, mining health and safety research, dust control, survival and rescue, methane control, explosives and mining environmental research. Contact: Office of Technical Information, Bureau of Mines, Department of the Interior, Room 1035, Columbia Plaza, Washington, DC 20241/202-634-1001.

Mining Claims
All unpatented mining claims, mill or tunnel sites, must be recorded. If the unpatented lode or placer claim, or mill, or tunnel site is located on federal lands, it must be recorded with the Bureau of Land Management state office having jurisdiction over the federal lands where the claim is located. Information is also available on how to file an application for a mineral patent. Contact: Mining Low and Salable Minerals, Bureau of Land Management, Department of the Interior, Room 3538, Washington, DC 20240/202-343-8537.

Museum
The Department of the Interior maintains a collection that reflects the Department's areas of interest and includes National Park Service photos, Indian artifacts, early types of surveying equipment, aerial charts, maps, model of Hoover Dam, photos of wildlife, and handiwork from trust territories. Contact: Departmental Museum, Department of the Interior, 18th and C Sts. N.W., Room 1240, Washington, DC 20240/202-343-5016 (open 8:00 A.M. to 4:00 P.M. weekdays).

National Cartographic Information Center
The Center operates a national information service which organizes maps and charts, aerial and satellite photographs, satellite imagery, map data in digital form and geodetic control data. It also has information about aerial photographic and mapping projects planned by federal agencies. A special teacher's packet emphasizing topographic mapping is available free. Contact: National Cartographic Information Center, Geological Survey, Department of the Interior, 507 National Center, Room 1-C-107, 12201 Sunrise Valley Dr., Reston, VA 22092/703-860-6045.

National Cartographic Information Center (NCIC)—Regional Offices

Eastern Mapping Center
NCIC
U.S. Geological Survey
536 National Center
Reston, VA 22092/702-860-6336

Mid-Continent Mapping Center
NCIC
U.S. Geological Survey
1400 Independence Road
Rolla, MO 65401

Rocky Mountain Mapping Center
NCIC
U.S. Geological Survey
Stop 504
Federal Center
Denver, CO 80225/303-236-5829

Western Mapping Center
NCIC
U.S. Geological Survey
345 Middlefed Road
Menlo Park, CA 94025/415-323-8111, ext. 427

Earth Science Office
NCIC
701-C Street
P. O. Box 53, Room E146
Anchorage, AK 99513/907-271-4159

National Fish and Wildlife Laboratory
This laboratory is responsible for the North American collection of amphibian, reptile, bird and mammal specimens. It performs studies on the ecological relationships and population dynamics of wildlife, especially those forms affected by land use practices. It also works on determining the

ecological effects on marine wildlife and ecosystems of man's activities related to development. Denver Wildlife Research Center, Museum Section, Contact: National Fish and Wildlife Laboratory, Fish and Wildlife Service, Department of the Interior, National Museum of Natural History, 10th St. and Constitution Ave. N.W., Washington, DC 20560/202-357-1930.

National Park Concessions
For information on obtaining a contract to provide goods or services within the National Park System, contact: Concession Management Division, National Park Service, Department of the Interior, 1100 L St. N.W., Room 3209, Washington, DC 20006/202-523-5322.

National Park Information Center
The Technical Information Center contains information on the National Park properties including 300,000 maps and design drawings, and 25,000 scientific and technical reports. Contact: Technical Information Center, National Park Service, Department of the Interior, Denver Service Center, 755 Parfet St., Denver, CO 80225/303-234-2653.

National Park Service Films
The National Park Service has many films on environmental and historical themes. For a list of these films and sales, and information on how to obtain them, contact: National Audiovisual Center, Washington, DC 20409/202-763-1896.

National Park Service Information
The National Park System contains 79 million acres including: 48 national parks; 78 national monuments; 12 national preserves; 4 national lakeshores; 11 national rivers (includes wild and scenic rivers and riverways); 10 national seashores; 63 national historic sites; 24 national memorials; 10 national military parks; 3 national battlefield parks; 10 national battlefields; 1 national battlefield site; 26 national historic parks; 17 national recreation areas; 4 national parkways; 1 national trail; 10 parks (other); 1 national capital park; 1 White House; 1 National Mall. For information on park usage such as camping, swimming, boating, mountain climbing, hiking, fishing, winter activities, wildlife, archeologic and historic area studies, pack trips, or photographs of activities and areas, contact: Office of Public Affairs, National Park Service, Department of the Interior, Room 3043, Washington, DC 20240/202-343-7394.

National Registry of Natural Landmarks
This Registry identifies terrestrial and aquatic communities, landforms, geological features, and habitats of threatened plant and animal species that constitute the Nation's natural history. Official recognition of an area in the National Registry often stimulates its owner to protect the area's nationally significant qualities. Contact: Natural Landmarks, National Park Service, Department of the Interior, 1100 L St. NW Room 6111, Washington, DC 20240/202-343-9525.

Natural Resources Library
Information is available on: conservation and development of natural resources, including scientific, engineering, legal, and social aspects of mining and minerals, land reclamation and management, fish and wildlife management, water resources, parks and outdoor recreation, preservation of scenic and historic sites, Native Americans. Contact: Natural Resources Library, Division of Library and Information Services, Office of Information Resources and Management, Department of the Interior, 18th and C Sts. N.W., Washington, DC 20240/202-343-5815

Natural Water Conditions
This monthly publication provides a summary of the condition of water resources. Subscriptions are free from: Natural Water Conditions, Geological Survey, Department of the Interior, 419 National Center, 12201 Sunrise Valley Dr., Reston, VA 22092/703-860-6884.

Northern Prairie Wildlife Research Center
Areas of interest include factors influencing productivity of upland nesting ducks; breeding biology and migrational ecology of diving ducks; management of wetlands; land management practices for upland nesting waterfowl; relationships of Pacific Flyway wetlands to migratory birds; predator management practices; and nongame birds. Contact: Northern Prairie Wildlife Research Center, U.S. Fish and Wildlife Service, Department of the Interior, P. O. Box 1747, Jamestown, ND 58401/701-252-5363.

Nuclear Waste Disposal
Information and expertise are available on the safe disposal of nuclear waste. Information is also available on the disposal of hazardous, non-nuclear waste. Contact: Office of Hazardous Waste, Water Resources Division, Geological Survey, Department of the Interior, National Center, MS 410, Reston, VA 22092/703-860-6976.

Oil and Gas Lottery
The Department of the Interior runs a lottery to award leases for exploring resources on federally-owned land. For information on the development and implementation of policy procedures, and technology relating to the management of salable, locatable and leasable minerals and other energy resources, contact: Division of Fluid Mineral Leasing, Bureau of Land Management, Department of the Interior, 1717 H St. NW, Room 606, Washington, DC 20240/202-653-2182.

Oil Shale

For information on the impact of fish and wildlife when developing oil shale, contact: Ecological Services, Fish and Wildlife Service, Department of the Interior, 1375 K St. N.W., Suite 403, Washington, DC 20240/202-343-2618.

Older Americans Receive Free Discount Passport

Persons over 62 years of age can receive a free Golden Age Passport which acts as a lifetime entrance permit to those parks, monuments and recreation areas administered by the federal government. The passport also provides for a 50 percent discount on federal use fees charged for facilities and services such as camping, boat launching, parking, etc. Apply in person for passports at most federally operated recreation areas, National Park Service regional offices, or at Information Office, Department of the Interior, 18th and C Sts. N.W., Washington, DC 20240/202-343-4747.

Outdoor Activities

General information is available on camping, fishing, hiking, and pack trips on the 475 million acres of public land. Assistance is available on recreational resources, cultural resources, visual resources, and natural history resources. Contact: Division of Recreation, Bureau of Land Management, Department of the Interior, 18th and C Sts. N.W., Room 3660, Washington, DC 20240/202-343-9353.

Outdoor Recreation

For information on National Park Service facilities for camping, swimming, boating, mountain climbing, hiking, and fishing, contact: Office of Public Affairs, National Park Service, Department of the Interior, Room 3043, Washington, DC 20240/202-343-7394.

Park History

The National Park Service maintains a special library containing archival and artifact collections. The library includes: history of the National Park Service; decorative and useful arts; handicrafts; folk art; historic furnishings; American social history; clothing and dress; military art and science; and the history of agriculture. Contact: Harpers Ferry Center, Division of Reference Services, National Park Service, Department of the Interior, Harpers Ferry, WV 25425/304-925-6588.

Park Index

The *Index to National Park System and Related Areas* describes some 300 national parks, rivers, and trails, and provides information on location and available facilities. Contact: Office of Public Affairs, National Park Service, Department of the Interior, Room 3043, Washington, DC 20240/202-343-7394.

Park Land Acquisitions

The National Park Service buys land for its use with revenues received from off-shore oil leases. Contact: Land Acquisition Division, National Park Service, Department of the Interior, 1100 L St. N.W., Room 3135, Washington, DC 20005/202-523-5252.

Park Passport

The Golden Eagle Passport ($10) allows holders to enter national parks, monuments and recreation areas free. It admits the permit holder and carload of accompanying people. People over 62 years old can receive a free passport. (See "Older Americans Receive Free Discount Passport" in this section.) Passports may be purchased at most federally operated recreation areas, National Park Service regional offices or at Information Office, Department of the Interior, 18th and C Sts. N.W., Room 1013, Washington, DC 20240/202-343-4747.

Park Photographs

Prints and transparencies can be borrowed free of charge on all aspects of the National Parks, including natural history, geologic features, and living history from prehistoric times to the present. Contact: Photo Library, Office of Public Affairs, National Park Service, Department of the Interior, Room 3039, Washington, DC 20240/202-343-7394.

Park Police

The U.S. Park Police are part of the Department of the Interior and most are assigned within the Washington, DC metropolitan area. They have the same police powers as the Washington, DC metropolitan police and act as hosts to park visitors. Contact: National Capital Region, Park Service, Department of the Interior, 1100 Ohio Dr. S.W., Room 177, Washington, DC 20242/202-426-6656.

Park Rangers

The Rangers of the National Park Service plan and carry out conservation efforts to protect plant and animal life from fire, disease and visitor use. They plan and conduct programs of public safety, including law enforcement and rescue work. They set up and direct interpretative programs such as slide shows, guided tours, displays and even dramatic presentations to help visitors become aware of the natural, cultural and historic significance of areas. They coordinate environmental education programs aimed at acquainting visitors, especially school children with how man and nature function. Rangers can be historians, archeologists and naturalists. Contact: Ranger Activities and Protection Division, National Park Service, Department of the Interior, Room 3310, Washington, DC 20240/202-343-3227.

Park Service Publications and Information

Information is available on more than 290 areas

administered by the National Park Service, including national parks, national recreation areas, national seashores, national monuments, historic sites, statistics on park acreage and attendance, types of park usage—camping, swimming, boating, mountain climbing, hiking, fishing, winter activities—wildlife management in parks, archeologic and historic area studies, pack trips, photos of activities, and areas. For assistance or a listing of available publications, contact: Office of Public Affairs, National Park Service, Department of the Interior, Room 3043, Washington, DC 20240/202-343-7394.

Park Statistics
Monthly and yearly data on National Park usage and attendance including visitor hours and number of over-night stays are available from: Statistical Unit, Branch of Scientists, National Park Service, Department of the Interior, Denver Service Center, 755 Parfet St., Denver, CO 80225/303-234-4572.

Patuxent Wildlife Research Center
The Patuxent Wildlife Research Center was established in 1936 to help protect and conserve the Nation's wildlife and natural environment through research on critical environmental problems and issues. It is America's first national wildlife experiment station. Research at the Center and at its field stations throughout the United States focuses on problems of three Fish and Wildlife Service Programs: Environmental Contaminant Evaluation, Endangered Species, and Migratory Birds. The Center occupies 4,700 acres in the Patuxent River valley. Portions of the Center set aside for experimental research now provide one of the few places in the Unites States where investigators have the space to raise and maintain the colonies of wild birds and other animals needed for large-scale controlled studies and the propagation and study of endangered species. A booklet describing the activities at the center is available from the Superintendent of Documents, Government Printing Office, Washington, DC 20402/202-783-3238. For further information regarding the center contact: Research and Development, Fish and Wildlife Service, Department of the Interior, Washington, DC 20240/202-343-5634.

Patuxent Wildlife Research Center Film
There is available a 16 mm motion picture film describing the center. It may be obtained on a free loan basis from a Regional Office of the U.S. Fish and Wildlife Service. Check your phone book under U.S. Government for a listing. This film is also available by contacting: National Audiovisual Center, Washington, DC 20409/202-763-1896.

Pesticide Surveillance
Over 100 sampling stations monitor the effects of pesticides on various species of wildlife. For information, contact: Division of Fishery Research, Fish and Wildlife Service, Department of the Interior, 1717 H St. N.W., Room 511, Washington, DC 20240/202-653-8772 (see "Fishery Research Laboratories" in this section).

Photographs, Aerial
An aerial photograph can be purchased for practically any area of the country. You may even be able to obtain one of your neighborhood. Contact: National Cartographic Information Center, National Mapping Division, Geological Survey, Department of the Interior, 507 National Center, Reston, VA 22092/703-860-6045.

Photographs, Geological
The Geological Survey maintains a collection of some 250,000 photographs of subjects taken during geologic studies of the United States and its territories from 1869 to the present. Prints, copy negatives, duplicate transparencies and enlargements can be purchased from the collection. Contact: Photographic Library, Geological Survey, Department of the Interior, Box 25046, Federal Center, MS 914, Denver, CO 80225/303-236-1010.

Photographs, Land Subjects
Over 10,000 black and white and color slides are available, covering forestry, lands and realty, minerals and range subjects. Contact: Office of Public Affairs, Audio-Visual Support, Bureau of Land Management, Department of the Interior, Room 5600, Washington, DC 20240/202-343-5717.

Presidential Commission Report on Reservation Economies
The complete 200-page report and recommendations made for the President of the United States concerning Indian Reservation Economies is now available for sale at the Government Printing Office (GPO) in Washington, D.C. The report, completed recently by a special commission set up by the President, can be ordered for $7.50 from the Superintendent of Documents, U.S. Government Printing Office at 202-783-3238.

Professional Park Services to Foreign Countries
Foreign governments can receive technical help and assistance in establishing and maintaining national parks from: Office of Cooperative Activities, National Park Service, Department of the Interior, 1100 L St. NW, Room 2138, Washington, DC 20240/202-343-7071.

Public Lands for Sale and Lease
The Department of the Interior is authorized to sell or lease lands in the public domain to state and local governments for recreation and public purposes and to qualified nonprofit organizations for

public and quasi-public purposes, including recreation, education and health. Contact: Division of Lands and Realty, Bureau of Land Management, Department of the Interior, Room 3643, Washington, DC 20240/202-343-8693.

Range Land Management

Information available on grazing on National Resource Lands includes the location of the range, the number of heads of livestock that can run on these public ranges, and the best seasons for grazing. Contact: Division of Range Land Management, Bureau of Land Management, Department of the Interior, Room 909, 1725 I St. NW Premier Bldg., Washington, DC 20006/202-653-9193.

Recreation Planning

The Division of Nationwide Recreation Planning provides technical assistance to federal, state, and local agencies and to the private sector in finding solutions to recreational problems. This division achieves and coordinates statewide Comprehensive Outdoor Recreation Plans. Two major studies are produced by this office:

Nationwide Outdoor Recreation Action Program (annual)—describes what policy the federal government should have on outdoor recreation.

Nationwide Outdoor Recreation Assessment (every 5 years)—presents the state of the nation's recreational needs and facilities report; it includes survey materials with summary and detailed reports.

Contact: Recreation and Resource Assistance, National Park Service, Department of the Interior, 1100 L St. NW, Room 2321, Washington, DC 20243/202-343-3780.

Regulatory Activities

Listed below are those organizations within the Department of the Interior which are involved with regulating various business activities. With each listing is a description of those industries or situations which are regulated by the office. Regulatory activities generate large amounts of information on the companies and subjects they regulate. Much of the information is available to the public. A regulatory office can also tell you your rights when dealing with a regulated company.

Public Affairs Bureau of Reclamation, Department of the Interior, C St. between 18th and 19th Sts. N.W., Washington, DC 20240/202-343-4662. Manages power resource development and management in 17 Western states.

Public Affairs, National Park Service, Department of the Interior, C St. between 18th and 19th Sts. N.W., Washington, DC 20240/202-343-6844. Responsible for

conserving the scenery, natural and historic objects and wildlife in the nation's parks.

Public Affairs, National Park Service, Department of the Interior, 18 and C St. N.W., Washington, DC 20243/202-343-7394. Regulates the development, conservation, and utilization of the nation's natural, cultural, and recreational resources.

Information Office, Geological Survey, Department of the Interior, National Center, 12201 Sunrise Valley Dr., Reston, VA 22092/703-860-6167. Enforces regulations applicable to oil, gas, and other mining leases, permits, licenses, development contracts and gas storage contracts.

Office of Public Affairs, Fish and Wildlife Service, Department of the Interior, C St. between 18th and 19th Sts. N.W., Washington, DC 20240/202-343-5634. Regulates the development of wildlife resources and their habitat.

Office of Public Affairs, Bureau of Land Management, U.S. Department of the Interior, C St. between 18th and 19th Sts. N.W., Washington, DC 20240/202-345-5717. Manages public lands and administers the resources on these lands.

Office of Public Information, Bureau of Indian Affairs, Department of the Interior, C St. between 18th and 19th Sts. N.W., Washington, DC 20240/202-343-7445. Acts as trustee for Indian land and monies held in trust by the United States.

Resources Information Bank

The Computerized Resources Information Bank provides basic information needed to characterize one or more mineral commodities, a mineral deposit, or several related deposits. The data base contains both text and numeric data. Topics covered include name, location, commodity information, geology, production reserves, potential resources, references, status of exploration and development, mining districts, and 1000 largest mines of the world. Contact: Mineral Resources Data Base, Information System Programs, University of Oklahoma, Energy Resources Center, Box 3030, Norman OK 73076/405-360-1600.

Scientific Publications

The Office of Scientific Publications approves all scientific publications, both internal and external to assure scientific quality. Contact: Office of Scientific Publications, Geologic Division, Geological Survey, Department of the Interior, National Center, MS 904, Reston, VA 22092/703-860-6575.

Solar Prints For Your Exhibitions

A large file of "Solar Prints" focusing on a particular architectural or geographic theme can be mounted on request. The prints are sold at $15 per print or are available on loan. Contact: Architectural and Engineering Records, National

Park Service, Department of the Interior, 1100 L St. NW, Room 6101, Washington, DC 20240/202-343-9623.

Space Photographs
Photographs are available from the following space missions:

Landsat—helps users identify and inventory different environmental phenomena such as distribution and general type of vegetation, regional geologic structures, and extent of surface water.

Skylab—data consists of a wide variety of phenomena on the earth's surface, including multispectral photography.

Gemini—photographs taken by a hand-held 70mm camera.

Apollo 9—three types of filtered black and white and one type of false-color infrared photographs, each showing an area approximately 100 miles by 100 miles.

Contact: User Services, Earth Resources Observation System Data Center, Geological Survey, Department of the Interior, Sioux Falls, SD 57198/605-594-6511, ext. 111.

State Mineral Information
The following offices maintain information on state mineral industry activity. The state offices can be contacted directly or a state expert can be reached at: State Mineral Information Program, State Liaison Office, Mineral Data Analysis, Bureau of Mines, Department of the Interior, 2401 E St. N.W., Room West 703, Washington, DC 20240/202-634-1107.

Streams, Measuring the Quality of
The National Stream Quality Accounting Network (NASQAN) compiles regional and nation-wide data on the quality of streams. NASQAN water-quality data measure the quality and quantity of water moving within and from the U.S.; provide a large-scale picture of how stream quality varies from place to place; and detect changes in stream quality. The public can visit the 501 stations throughout the United States by appointment. A list of all stations is available. The types of data collected include: temperature, pH, bacteria indicators, inorganic compounds, biologic nutrients, suspended sediment, trace elements. Contact: Quality of Water Branch, Water Resources Division, Geological Survey, Department of the Interior, National Center, 12201 Sunrise Valley Dr., MS 412, Room 5A420, Reston, VA 22092/703-860-6834.

Strip Mining
The Office of Surface Mine Reclamation provides the following:

Technical Assistance—writes rules, solves problems, and provides legal and technical expertise on reclamation and coal mining.

Environmental Assessment—writes environmental impact statements, rules, guidelines, and handbooks on reclamation, air pollution, water quality, impact on fish and wildlife, climate and geology.

Research—applied and basic research to determine short-term impact of mining.

Technical Training—trains federal inspectors in reclamation assessments.

Contact: Office of Surface Mining Reclamation and Enforcement, Bureau of Mines, Department of the Interior, 1951 Constitution Ave., N.W. Room 228, Washington, DC 20240/202-343-2188.

Surplus Wildlife
Nonprofit organizations can receive surplus wildlife for restocking of wildlife ranges, zoo display, scientific specimens and meat. Contact: Biological Resources Division of Natural Resources, National Park Service, Department of the Interior, 1100 L St. N.W., Room 3317, Washington, DC 20240/202-343-8125.

Technical Preservation Services
The Technical Preservation Services Branch develops and disseminates information on techniques for preserving and maintaining publicly owned historic properties; advises federal agencies on the evaluation, preservation and maintenance of historic properties; evaluates applications for the transfer of surplus federal property for historic monuments; evaluates and certifies rehabilitation of historic structures for tax benefit purposes; plans and specifications; and insures conformance with the standards for historic preservation projects. A free listing of publications is available. Contact: Technical Preservation Services Branch, National Park Service, Department of the Interior, 1100 L St. N.W., Room 6321, Washington, DC 20240/202-343-9573.

Territories of the U.S.
Among the territories administered by the United States are: American Samoa, Northern Mariana Islands, Virgin Islands, and Trust Territory of the Pacific Islands. Contact: Office of Territorial and International Affairs, Department of the Interior, Room 4321, Washington, DC 20240/202-343-6971.

Topographic Maps
Free indexes show available topographic maps published for each state and territory. Indexes for areas east of the Mississippi River and Minnesota, Puerto Rico and the Virgin Islands may be requested from: Branch of Distribution, Geological Survey, 1200 South Eads St., Arlington, VA 22202/703-557-2751. Indexes for areas west of the Mississippi River, including Alaska, Hawaii, Louisiana, Guam, and American Samoa, may be requested from: Branch of Distribution, Geological Survey, P.O. Box 25286, Federal Center, Denver, CO 80225/303-236-7477. Residents of

Alaska may request indexes directly from: Distribution Section, Geological Survey, New Federal Building, P.O. Box 12, 101 12th Ave., Fairbanks, AK 99701/907-456-0244. The indexes contain lists of special maps, addresses of local map reference libraries, local map dealers, and federal map distribution centers. An order blank and detailed instructions for ordering maps are supplied with each index.

Topography Information
Data files are maintained on all phases of topographic mapping and related subjects such as cartography, geodesy, and photogrammetry. These files are kept mainly for reference and include professional journals, technical instructions, research reports, technical papers, photographs and visual aids. Contact: National Mapping Division, Technical Information Office, Geological Survey, Department of the Interior, 521 National Center, Room 2A-316, Reston, VA 22092/703-860-6275.

Visit Ghost Towns and Mines
The first ironmaking furnace in the original 13 colonies, replicas of early wooden derricks used for oil drilling in East Texas, Sutter's Mill in Northern California, open-pit iron mines in Minnesota and off-shore oil and gas wells in the Gulf Coast can all be visited by the public. For information on these and other new and old mines, contact: Office of Technical Information, Bureau of Mines, Department of the Interior, Columbia Plaza, Room 1035, Washington, DC 20241/202-634-1001.

Visitor Information Office
For general information and referrals on the various bureaus within the Department of the Interior, contact: Visitor Information Office, Department of the Interior, Room 1238, Washington, DC 20240/202-434-5278 (open 7:45 A.M. to 4:15 P.M. weekdays).

Volcanos in the U.S.
For information about volcanos in the United States and publications contact: Geologic Inquiries Group, U.S. Geological Survey, 907 National Center, Reston, VA 22092/703-860-6517.

Water and Land Resource Accomplishments
An annual report, *Water and Land Resource Accomplishment Report,* describes new projects of the Water and Power Service including statistical data on physical features of the projects, crop yields resulting from projects, financial status of projects, economic impact on the local community, recreation usage and flood control. For a free copy, contact: Engineering Research Center, Water and Land Technology, Service, Department of the Interior, 2D-450, P.O. Box 25007, Denver, CO 80225/303-236-8098.

Water and Power Photographs
A large collection of black and white prints and color slides, dating back to the early 1900s are free to illustrators, nature lovers, etc. Mobile exhibits, slide shows and other audiovisual presentations, are also available. Contact: Visual Communication Services, Bureau of Reclamation, Department of the Interior, Denver Federal Center, Engineering and Research Center, P.O. Box 25007, Denver, CO 80225/303-236-6973.

Water and Power Resources Library
The library contains information on water resources development, dams, irrigation, environmental control, agriculture, civil engineering, concrete technology, desalinization, drainage, ground water, electrical engineering, fish and wildlife, flood control, hydroelectric power, geothermal, solar and wind energy, materials technology, hydrology, river regulation and control, snow, ice and permafrost, soil mechanics, water quality, weather control and structural engineering. Contact: Bureau of Reclamation Library, Denver Federal Center, Engineering and Research Center, P.O. Box 25007, Denver, CO 80225/303-236-6963.

Water Data Exchange, National (NAWDEX)
NAWDEX is a computerized data system that can identify sources of water data and that indexes the types of water data these sources collect. The primary purpose of the system is to facilitate the exchange of data between the organizations that gather water data and the organizations that need the data. Contact: National Water Data Exchange, Geological Survey, Department of the Interior, 421 National Center, Reston, VA 22092/703-860-6031.

Water Data Storage and Retrieval Systems, National (WATSTORE)
Access of all types of water data is through WATSTORE. These data are organized into five files: 1) Station Header File; 2) Daily Values File; 3) Peak Flow File; 4) Water Quality File; 5) Ground Water Site Inventory File; 6) Unit Values; and 7) Water Use. Contact: Chief Hydrologist, Geological Survey, Department of the Interior, 437 National Center, Reston, VA 22092/703-860-6871.

Water Policy
Research is conducted in water quality and quantity, soil erosion control, improving water yield, snow management for wildlife and livestock and water quality improvement from non-point source. Contact: Soil, Water and Air Branch, Range Land Resources Division, Bureau of Land Management, Department of the Interior, 1725 I St. NW, Premier Bldg, Room 909, Washington, DC 20240/202-653-9210.

Water Recreation Activities

A series of free brochures is available with a comprehensive list of dams and reservoirs showing available recreational facilities and principal recreational uses. There are 291 recreation areas, 4.4 million acres of land, 1.7 million acres of water surface, 12.268 miles of shoreline, 842 campgrounds, 767 picnic sites, 29,191 tent and trailer spaces, 142 swimming beaches, 704 boat ramps, and 13,852 boat slips. Available brochures include:

Map No. 1—recreation areas of Idaho, Oregon, and Washington
Map No. 2—recreation areas of Montana, Nebraska, South Dakota, North Dakota, and Wyoming
Map No. 3—recreation areas of Arizona, California, Nevada, and Utah
Map No. 4—recreation areas of Colorado, Kansas, Oklahoma, New Mexico, and Texas.

Contact: Office of Public Affairs, Bureau of Reclamation, Department of the Interior, Room 7644, Washington, DC 20240/202-343-4662.

Water Research and Development

Information is available on saline water conversion; new and improved technologies and systems to convert unusable water to water suitable for industrial, agricultural and home use; the recovery and beneficial use of byproducts and disposal of residuals; the site selection, design, construction and operation of demonstration desalting plants; providing solar energy from hydropower. A free bimonthly newsletter, *Water Research in Action,* describes current research projects. Contact: Research, Office of Water Research and Technology, Department of the Interior, Room 4210, Washington, DC 20240/202-343-4607.

Water Research and Technology

The Department of the Interior conducts research and development activities to solve current and projected water problems, and a research and development program to convert saline water for beneficial uses; and trains water scientists and engineers through student participation in ongoing research. Contact: Director, Office of Water Research, Bureau of Reclamation, Room 7354, Department of the Interior, Washington, DC 20240/202-343-5975.

Water Resource Centers

The five Water Resource Centers maintain a bibliographic data base covering all scientific and technical information of interest to the water resources community.

Center for Environmental Research,
Cornell University,
468 Hollister Hall,
Ithaca, NY 14850,
607-256-4318.

Water Resources Research Institute of the University of North Carolina,
North Carolina State University,
124 Riddick Building,
Raleigh, NC 27607,
919-737-2683.

Water Resources Research Center,
Virginia Polytechnic Institute and State University,
Blacksburg, VA 24061,
703-961-5624
(Virginia residents only).

Water Resources Research Center,
University of Arizona,
845 North Park Avenue,
Tucson, AZ 85719,
602-626-4925.

Water Resources Center,
University of Wisconsin,
1975 Willows Drive, 2nd Floor,
Madison, WI 53706,
Luedtke: 608-262-0561.

Water Resources

For information and expertise on topics related to water, as a resource, contact: Water Information Group, Geological Survey, Department of the Interior, 420 National Center, Room 5B410, Reston, VA 22092/703-860-6867.

Water Resources in Foreign Countries

For information on activities in foreign countries concerning water resource planning, water treatment and quality alteration, effects and sources of pollution, watershed protection and control of surface water, contact: Division on Foreign Activities, Water and Power Resource Service, Department of the Interior, P.O. Box 25007, Denver Federal Center, Mail Code D 2000, Denver, CO 80225/303-234-3015.

Water, Scientific Publications

Publications are available related to the occurrence, distribution and availability of water resources. Topics include hydrologic data; suspended-sediment data; flood-prone data; drainage areas; watersheds; rainfall fall-off relationships; lake data; surface reservoirs data; temperature and chemical analysis of ground and surface water. For a list of available publications, contact: Scientific Publications and Data Management, Water Resources Division, Geological Survey, Department of the Interior, 440 National Center, MS 440, Reston, VA 22092/703-860-6575.

Water Scientists and Engineers

Water scientists and engineers receive training at 54 water research and technology institutes. For a listing of institutes and information on available research, contact: Research Program Coordinator, Office of Water Research, Bureau of Reclamation, Department of the Interior, Room 7354, Washington, DC 20240/202-343-5975.

Wetlands Inventory

Wetlands and deepwater habitats are vital nursery areas for many forms of wildlife, fish and fowl. They also perform important flood protection and pollution control functions. A computerized data bank describes all the national wetlands in terms of their ecologic and physical characteristics, geographic locations and natural resource values. Contact: National Wetlands Inventory, Fish and Wildlife Service, Department of the Interior, 1730 K St. N.W., Room 818, Washington, DC 20240/ 202-653-8726.

Wetlands Maps

Wetlands maps are produced by the U.S. Fish and Wildlife Service's National Wetlands Inventory. They have produced nearly 10,000 highly detailed maps which cover 30 percent of the lower 48 states, 6 percent of Alaska and all of Hawaii. This includes roughly 75 percent of the coastal zone of the lower 48 states, including the Great Lakes region. Mapping is completed for 7 states, and is under-way in portions of 39 other states. Their goal is to produce maps for an additional 5 percent of the lower 48 states and 2 percent of Alaska each year. Contact: National Wetlands Inventory Office, U.S. Fish and Wildlife Service, Department of the Interior, Washington, DC 20240/202-343-2618

Wetlands of the United States: Current Status and Recent Trends

This report is to inform government agencies, private industry, the scientific community, and the general public about the current status and historical trends of U.S. wetlands. It also identifies regions where wetlands remain in greatest jeopardy and gives recommendations for improving their protection. This book sells for $3.00. Contact: Superintendent of Documents, Government Printing Office, Washington, DC 20402/202-783-3238.

Wetlands Preservation

The U.S. Fish and Wildlife Service is working, through a variety of programs, to conserve our existing wetlands. These programs include Federal permit reviews, waterfowl habitat acquisition, wetlands preservation easements, and environmental education. Contact: Office of Habitat Resource Program, U. S. Fish and Wildlife Service, Department of the Interior, Washington, DC 20240/202-343-4767.

Wild Horses and Burros Up for Adoption

The federal Wild Free Roaming Horses and Burros Act allows people to adopt at no charge excess animals when herds grow too large to be supported by available food supplies. The prospective owners must treat the adopted horses and burros humanely during a one-year trial period before legal title can be obtained. Contact: Wild Horses and Burros, Bureau of Land Management, Department of the Interior, 1725 I St, Premier Bldg, N.W., Room 901, Washington, DC 20240/ 202-653-9215.

Wildlife Ecology Research Information

Through a network of 3 research centers, 3 laboratories, and 54 field stations, research is conducted on: developing techniques for wildlife ecology research; evaluating predator-prey relationships; developing methods for reducing animal damage to crops, livestock, etc.; how to monitor, proprogate, and protect endangered and threatened species; and determining the effects of public use on refuges, parks, and other federal conservation holdings. Contact: Division of Wildlife Research, Fish and Wildlife Service, Department of the Interior, 1717 H St. N.W., Room 515, Washington, DC 20240/202-653-8763.

Wildlife Health Laboratory

This national laboratory develops methods of wildlife and bird disease prevention and control. Its research covers the effects of management practices and environmental changes on the incidence of wildlife diseases. The laboratory compiles statistics on wildlife losses from disease and geographic and species distributions of specific diseases. It provides diagnostic and field assistance to research personnel. Workshops and lectures are also available on the identification, prevention and control of wildlife diseases. Contact: National Wildlife Health Laboratory, Division of Wildlife Research, Fish and Wildlife Service, Department of the Interior, University of Wisconsin, 6006 Schroeder Rd., Madison, WI 53711/608-264-5411.

Wildlife Management

For information on the management of wildlife and other national resources in the National Park System, contact: Division of Natural Resources, National Park Service, Department of the Interior, 1100 L St. N.W., Room 3317, Washington, DC 20240/202-343-8125.

Wildlife of North America Library

Books, pamphlets, reprints, periodicals, and topographic maps are available from: Library, Fish and Wildlife Service, Department of the Interior, Patuxent Wildlife Research Center, Laurel, MD 20811/301-498-0235.

Wildlife Refuges

Information and technical assistance are available to Native Americans, military reservations, other state and federal agencies, and private organizations to improve conditions for the management of wildlife resources. There are over 400 federally run wildlife refuges. Information is available describing their location, the different types of recreation, their size and their primary species. Contact: Division of National Wildlife Refuges, Fish and Wildlife Service, Department of the Interior, Room 2343, Washington, DC 20240/202-343-4312.

Wildlife Use of Federal Lands
The Bureau of Land Management seeks to preserve wildlife habitats on public lands, mainly in 11 Western States and Alaska. It tries to insure that threatened or endangered plants and animals and their critical habitats are not jeopardized by Bureau activities. It also maintains lists of endangered plants and animals, including mammals, birds, reptiles, amphibians, fish, snails, clams, crustaceans, insects, butterflies and plants. Contact: Division of Wildlife, Bureau of Land Management, Department of the Interior, Room 2649, Washington, DC 20240/202-343-6188.

Youth Conservation Corps
Each summer the Department of the Interior employs 15- to 18-year-olds to further develop and maintain the natural resources of the United States. Projects may include clearing streambanks, building trails, planting trees, gathering air and water samples or developing campgrounds. Approximately 1900 young people are involved in this program each summer for an eight week period, on a paid volunteer basis. Listed below are the ten regional National Park Service Offices. Applicants should contact the Office representing their home state, as youth are only eligible for projects in their home area.

Alaska Region (Alaska): Regional Youth Program Coordinator, National Park Service, Alaska Region, 2525 Gambell Street, Anchorage, AK 99503/907-271-4225.

Mid-Atlantic Region (Delaware, Maryland, Pennsylvania, Virginia, West Virginia): Regional Youth Program Coordinator, National Park Service, Mid-Atlantic Region, 143 South 3rd Street, Philadelphia, PA 19106/215-597-7890.

Midwest Region (Illinois, Indiana, Iowa, Kansas, Michigan, Minnesota, Missouri, Nebraska, Ohio, Wisconsin): Regional Youth Program Coordinator, National Park Service, Midwest Region, 1809 Jackson Street, Omaha, NE 68102/402-221-3444.

National Capital Region (District of Columbia, Maryland, Virginia): Regional Youth Program Coordinator, National Park Service, National Capital Region, 1100 Ohio Drive SW, Washington, DC 20242/202-655-6932.

North Atlantic Region (Connecticut, Maine, Massachusetts, New Hampshire, New Jersey, New York, Rhode Island, Vermont): Regional Youth Program Coordinator, National Park Service, North Atlantic Region, 15 State Street, Boston, MA 02109/617-223-3351.

Pacific Northwest Region (Idaho, Oregon, Washington): Regional Youth Program Coordinator, National Park Service, Pacific Northwest Region, Westin Building, 2001 Sixth Avenue, Seattle, WA 98121/206-442-4669.

Rocky Mountain Region (Colorado, Montana, North Dakota, South Dakota, Utah, Wyoming): Regional Youth Program Coordinator, National Park Service, Rocky Mountain Region, 655 Parfet Street, P O Box 25287, Denver, CO 80225/303-234-8744.

Southeast Region (Alabama, Florida, Georgia, Kentucky, Mississippi, North Carolina, South Carolina, Tennessee): Regional Youth Program Coordinator, National Park Service, Southeast Region, 75 Spring Street SW, Atlanta, GA 30303/404-221-4290.

Southwest Region (Arkansas, Louisiana, New Mexico, Oklahoma, Texas): Regional Youth Program Coordinator, National Park Service, Southwest Region, P O Box 728, Santa Fe, NM 87501/505-988-6371.

Western Region (Arizona, California, Hawaii, Nevada): Regional Youth Program Coordinator, National Park Service, Western Region, 450 Golden Gate Avenue, Box 36063, San Francisco, CA 94102/415-556-1866.

Youth Conservation Programs
Employment and on-the-job training are provided to young people in such areas as brick masonry, carpentry, operation of heavy equipment, painting, cement finishing, plastering, caulking and welding. The programs available are: the Youth Conservation Corps (ages 15 to 18). Contact: Youth Conservation Programs, Department of the Interior, Room 2759, Washington, DC 20240/202-343-5951.

How Can the Department of the Interior Help You?
To determine how the Department of the Interior can help you, contact: Office of Public Affairs, Department of the Interior, Room 7211, Washington, DC 20240/202-343-3171.

Department of Justice

**(Attorney General), Constitution Ave. and 10th St. N.W.,
Washington, DC 20530/202-633-2000**

**Established: June 22, 1870
Budget: $2,916,659,000
Employees: 64,833**

MISSION: Serves as counsel for the citizens of the Nation; represents them in enforcing the law in the public interest; through its thousands of lawyers, investigators, and agents it plays a key role in protection against criminals and subversion, in insuring healthy competition of business in our free enterprise system, in safeguarding the consumer, and in enforcing drug, immigration, and naturalization laws; plays a significant role in protecting citizens through its efforts for effective law enforcement, crime prevention, crime detection, and prosecution and rehabilitation of offenders; conducts all suits in the Supreme Court in which the United States is concerned; and represents the Government in legal matters generally.

Major Divisions and Offices

Associate Attorney General

Department of Justice, Constitution Ave. and 10th St. N.W., Washington, DC 20530/202-633-2101.
Budget: $1,322,622,000
Employees: 22,628

• Office of Justice Assistance, Research and Statistics

Department of Justice, 633 Indiana Ave. N.W., Washington, DC 20531/202-724-7782.
Budget: $125,523,000
Employees: 257
Mission: Coordinates and provides staff support for the Juvenile Justice and Delinquency Prevention, the National Institute of Justice and the Bureau of Justice Statistics.

• Bureau of Prisons

Department of Justice, 320 First St. N.W. Washington, DC 20534/202-724-3198.
Budget: $415,139,000
Employees: 10,161
Mission: Protects society through the care and custody of those persons convicted by the courts to serve a period of time incarcerated in a Federal penal institution.

• Marshals Service

Department of Justice, One Tysons Corner Center, McLean, VA 22102/703-285-1131.
Budget: $370,472,000
Employees: 6,814
Mission: Provides support and protection to the Federal courts, including judges, attorneys, and jurors; apprehends most Federal fugitives; operates the witness security program, ensuring the safety of endangered witnesses; transports and cares for thousands of Federal prisoners annually; provides daily service of civil and criminal due process; executes arrest warrants; and prevents civil disturbances and restores order in riot or mob violence situations.

• Parole Commission

Department of Justice, Park Place, 1 N. Park Building, 5550 Friendship Blvd., Bethesda, MD 20015/301-492-5990.
Budget: $6,879,000

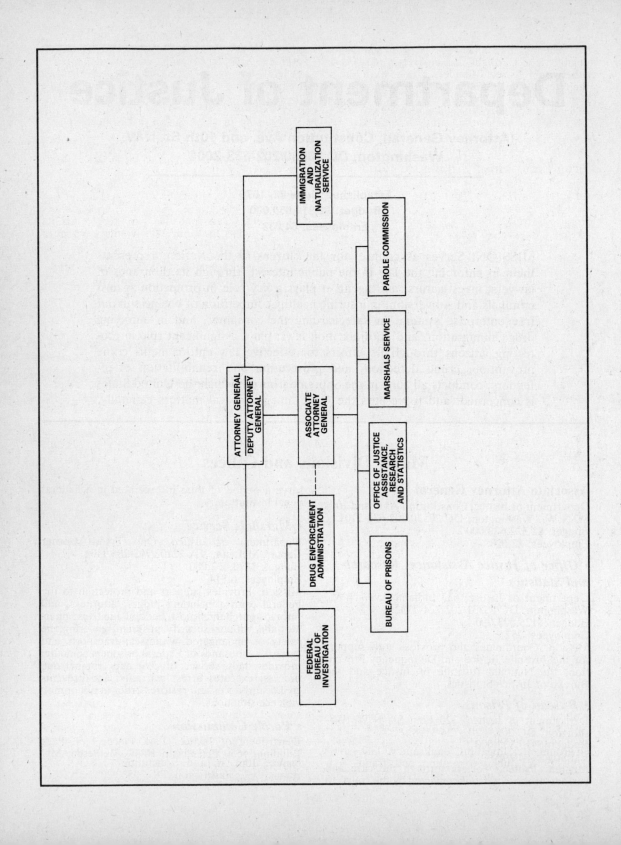

Department of Justice

Attorney General, Constitution Ave. and 10th St. NW.,

- ATTORNEY GENERAL
  DEPUTY ATTORNEY GENERAL

  - IMMIGRATION AND NATURALIZATION SERVICE

  - ASSOCIATE ATTORNEY GENERAL
    - MARSHALS SERVICE
    - PAROLE COMMISSION
    - OFFICE OF JUSTICE ASSISTANCE, RESEARCH AND STATISTICS
    - BUREAU OF PRISONS

  - DRUG ENFORCEMENT ADMINISTRATION
  - FEDERAL BUREAU OF INVESTIGATION

Employees: 157
Mission: Grants, denies, or revokes parole for eligible federal offenders; supervises paroled or otherwise released offenders until expiration of their terms; and determines whether or not persons convicted of certain crimes may serve as officials in the field of organized labor or in labor-oriented management positions and whether or not such persons may provide services to, or be employed by, employment benefit plans.

Drug Enforcement Administration

Department of Justice, 1405 I St. N.W., Washington, DC 20537/202-633-1249.
Budget: $255,496,000
Employees: 4,233
Mission: Investigates major narcotic violators who operate at interstate and international levels; enforces regulations governing the legal manufacture, distribution, and dispensing of controlled substances; manages a national narcotics intelligence system; coordinates with Federal, State, and local law enforcement authorities and cooperates with counterpart agencies abroad; exchanges training, scientific research and information for support of drug traffic prevention and control; concentrates its efforts on high-level narcotics smuggling and distribution organizations in the U.S. and abroad, working closely with such agencies as the Customs Service, the Internal Revenue Service, and the Coast Guard; attempts long-term immobilization of major trafficking organizations through the removal of the leaders and assets upon which these organizations depend; holds concurrent jurisdiction over drug offenses with FBI; enforces

regulation of the legal manufacture and distribution of prescription drugs; and maintains an active training program for narcotics officers in other Federal, State, and local agencies—as well as foreign police.

Federal Bureau of Investigation

Department of Justice, 9th St. and Pennsylvania Ave. N.W., Washington, DC 20535/202-324-3000.
Budget: $853,319,000
Employees: 20,492
Mission: Gathers and reports facts, locates witnesses, and compiles evidence in matters in which the federal government is or may be a party of interest; investigates all violations of federal laws except those assigned to some other federal agency, and is the principal investigation arm of the Department of Justice.

Immigration and Naturalization Service

Department of Justice, 425 St. N.W., Washington, DC 20536/ 202-633-4316.
Budget: $495,694,000
Employees: 10,483
Mission: Administer the immigration and naturalization laws relating to the admission, exclusion, deportation, and naturalization of aliens: inspect aliens to determine their admissibility into the United States; adjudicates requests of aliens for benefits under the law; guards against illegal entry into the United States; investigates, apprehends, and removes aliens in this country in violation of the law; and examines alien applicants wishing to become citizens.

Major Sources of Information

Advanced Criminal Justice Research
Research projects supported by this office investigate the application of advanced analytical techniques to such problems as: estimating the impact of charges in criminal justice policies or procedures; measuring progress or deterioration. Contact: Office of Research and Evaluation Methods, National Institute of Justice, OJARS, Department of Justice, 633 Indiana Ave. N.W., Room 900, Washington, DC 20531/202-724-2945.

Advocacy Institute, Attorney General's
The institute trains Assistant U.S. Attorneys and all U.S. Department of Justice attorneys in trial advocacy. The courses include separate civil and criminal trial advocacy courses, an appellate advocacy course, and seminars on specialized topics, such as white-collar crime, narcotics, conspiracy, environmental litigation, bankruptcy, land condemnations, public corruption and fraud, civil rights, witness security and computer fraud. Con-

tact: Attorney General's Advocacy Institute, Executive Office for U.S. Attorneys, Department of Justice, 10th St. and Constitution Ave. N.W., Room 1342, Washington, DC 20530/202-633-4104.

Antitrust
The mission of this Division is to encourage workable competition throughout the American economy. It brings civil and criminal antitrust cases to promote or maintain competition in particular markets. It participates in proceedings of federal (and sometimes state) regulatory agencies where those proceedings involve important questions of antitrust law or competition policy. It also participates in seminars and speaks before professional organizations, business groups and other organizations as advocates of competition. Contact: Antitrust Division, Department of Justice, 10th St. and Constitution Ave. N.W., Room 3107, Washington, DC 20530/202-633-2401.

Antitrust—Business Reviews
This section coordinates proposed business plans at the written request of interested parties and states its present enforcement intentions. The request and response will be announced at the time a business review letter is issued. These letters and the supporting information supplied by the requesting party are available for public inspection. Case studies of investigations can be seen at this office. Examples of favorable reviews include: a joint venture to build and operate a blood plasma fractionation plant; technical assistance agreement between Chrysler and General Motors whereby Chrysler would receive certain emission control and safety technology; and establishment of prepaid legal services plans. Contact: Business Reviews, Legal Procedure Unit, Antitrust Division, Department of Justice, 10th St. and Constitution Ave. N.W., Room 7416, Washington, DC 20530/202-633-2481.

Antitrust Cases—Information
Researchers can visit the Legal Procedures Unit and thumb through the files for information on companies investigated for antitrust violations. Information includes: pleadings in antitrust cases, formal complaints against companies, and depositions and summaries of legal proceedings. For those who wish more complete information, these documents refer them to the courts in which the cases were tried. Contact: Legal Procedure Unit, Antitrust Division, Department of Justice, 10th St. and Constitution Ave. N.W., Room 7416, Washington, DC 20530/202-633-2481.

Antitrust—Consumer Affairs
This office is responsible for litigation arising, on behalf of government agencies, under the Food, Drug and Cosmetic Act, the Consumer Product Safety Commission Act, and the civil penalty cases arising under the Federal Trade Commission (FTC) Act. It enforces federal criminal provisions prohibiting the turning back of odometers and prohibits certain kinds of actions under the Truth in Lending Act. A free pamphlet, *Antitrust Enforcement and the Consumer,* is available. It explains antitrust laws, describes how antitrust violations hurt the consumer and how the public can actively pursue the violator. Contact: Consumer Litigation, Department of Justice, 666 11th St., N.W., Room 910, Washington, DC 20530/202-724-6786.

Antitrust—Energy Industry
A special division handles antitrust violations within the energy industry. Contact: Energy Section, Antitrust Division, Department of Justice, 414 11th St. N.W., Room 9317, Washington DC 20530/202-724-6410.

Antitrust—Foreign Commerce
This office monitors foreign cartel activity for any effect on U.S. trade and commerce, particularly those activities that may present a significant adverse impact on inflation and prices of vital products for the American consumer. It informs American businessmen on the relationship between export promotion and the antitrust laws. It assists foreign antitrust officials on antitrust laws and enforcement methods, and is involved with the Committee of Experts on Restrictive Business Practices of the Organization for Economic Cooperation and Development (OECD). Contact: Foreign Commerce, Antitrust Division, Department of Justice, 10th St. and Constitution Ave. N.W., Room 7115, Washington, DC 20530/202-633-2464.

Antitrust Guide Concerning Research Joint Ventures
This publication describes ways that corporate cooperation on research can be pursued without violating antitrust laws. The guide is available for $5.50 from the Superintendent of Documents, Government Printing Office, Washington, DC 20402/202-783-3238. For further information on content contact: Antitrust Division, Department of Justice, 10th and Constitution Ave. N.W., Room 3101, Washington, DC 20530/202-633-2401.

Antitrust Issues
The Legislative Unit develops the Antitrust Division's position regarding pending or proposed legislation, including preparation of Congressional testimony by division witnesses and reports to Congress concerning legislative policy issues. Contact: Legislative Unit, Antitrust Division, Department of Justice, 10th St. and Constitution Ave. N.W., Room 3112, Washington, DC 20530/202-633-2497.

Antitrust—Special Industries
For information on antitrust activities concerning businesses involved with telecommunications, securities, and commodity futures, contact: Special Regulated Industries Section, Antitrust Division, Department of Justice, 521 12th St. N.W., Room 504, Washington, DC 20530/202-724-6693.

Antitrust—Transportation
This office has intervened in a variety of regulatory proceedings involving the transportation industry, to act as a procompetitive voice advocating the elimination of unnecessary restraints on entry into markets and the removal of unnecessary restrictions on competitive ratemaking. An example of its involvement is the Airline Deregulation Act. Contact: Transportation Section, Antitrust Division, Department of Justice, 414 11th St. N.W., Room 8120, Washington, DC 20530/202-724-6349.

Applications for Benefits for Immigrants
The Office of Adjudication renders decisions on the various applications and petitions to bestow benefits to aliens. For example, it decides on preference visas for immigrants or for temporary workers and applications for adjustments of status from temporary nonimmigrant statuses to lawful permanent residents of the United States. Contact: Adjudication, Immigration and Naturalization Service, Department of Justice, 425 Eye St. N.W., Room 7116, Washington, DC 20536/202-633-3228.

Bureau of Prisons Publications
The following publications are available: *Annual Report; Statistical Report; Facilities* (describing prison facilities); and *Development of the Federal Prison System.* Contact: Public Information, Bureau of Prisons, Department of Justice, 320 1st St. N.W., Room 554, Washington, DC 20534/202-724-3198.

Citizenship Education
Citizen education films are available at no charge to civic, patriotic, educational and religious groups. There are also about 15 textbooks on citizenship available, consisting of teachers' manuals and student textbooks at various reading levels. These books are distributed free to public schools for applicants for citizenship. Contact: Naturalization, Immigration and Naturalization Service, Department of Justice, 425 Eye St. N.W., Room 7228, Washington, DC 20536/202-633-3320.

Civil Rights—Appeals
This office handles all Division cases in the Supreme Court and court of appeals for legislative matters and for in-house legal counsel such as affirmative action, school desegregation remedies and jury selection. Contact: Appellate Section, Civil Rights Division, Department of Justice, 10th St. and Constitution Ave. N.W., Room 5740, Washington, DC 20530/202-633-2195.

Civil Rights—Criminal
Statutes to preserve personal liberties are enforced to prohibit persons from acting under cover of law or in conspiracy with others to interfere with an individual's federal constitutional rights and to prohibit the holdings of individuals in peonage or involuntary servitude. Contact: Criminal Section, Civil Rights Division, Department of Justice, 10th St. and Constitution Ave. N.W., Room 7627, Washington, DC 20530/202-633-4067.

Civil Rights Enforcement
The Civil Rights Division prosecutes actions under several criminal civil rights statutes; coordinates the civil rights enforcement efforts of the Federal agencies whose programs are covered by Title VI of the 1964 Act; and assists federal agencies in identifying and eliminating sexually discriminatory provisions in their policies and programs. Contact: Civil Rights Division, Department of Justice, 10th St. and Constitution Ave. N.W., Room 5643, Washington, DC 20530/202-633-2151.

Civil Rights—Federal
Statutes are enforced that prohibit employment discrimination by state and local governments, that prohibit discriminatory use of federal funds, and provide equal opportunity among federal contractors. *Questions and Answers on the Uniform Guidelines on Employee Selection Procedures* is a free publication that explains government-wide standards for employers to follow in using selection procedures for employment on a nondiscriminatory basis. Contact: Federal Enforcement Section, Civil Rights Division, Department of Justice, 10th St. and Constitution Ave. N.W., Room 4712, Washington, DC 20530/202-633-3831.

Civil Rights—Special Litigation
This office is responsible for protecting rights secured under the Civil Rights of Institutional Persons Act (42 USC-199. PL 96-247) May 23, 1980, an enforcement tool for the constitutional rights of all institutionalized persons in jail, prisons, mental health and retardation facilities or nursing homes. The Act protects nonstatutory rights to insure adequate treatment and rehabilitation in the setting least restrictive of personal liberty for those persons confined in state or local mental retardation, mental health, juvenile and nursing home facilities. This office enforces part of the Rehabilitation Act of 1973 which prohibits discrimination by recipients of federal funding against qualified handicapped persons in employment and in enjoyment of services and activities. Contact: Special Litigation Section, Civil Rights Division, Department of Justice, 320 1st St. N.W., Room 954, Washington, DC 20530/202-272-6060.

Commercial Litigation
This office pursues the Government's affirmative civil claims arising from fraud, bribery, or other official misconduct and the collection of civil fines or other money judgments awarded to the United States. It also handles improved procedures in collection enforcement activity, contract actions, cases arising under grants, subsidies or insurance undertakings by the government, foreclosures, bankruptcies, negotiations, patent and copyright infringement suits, and customs-related cases. Contact: Commercial Litigation Branch, Civil Division, Department of Justice, 10th and Constitution Ave., N.W., Room 3611, Washington, DC 20530/202-633-3306.

Community Relations Service (CRS)
This service helps communities and groups resolve disputes, disagreements, and difficulties arising from race, color, national origin discrimination. It

employs various techniques of persuasion to defuse tensions and conflicts within communities that arise from racial discrimination. The three fundamental services the CRS provides are technical assistance, conciliation, and mediation. In technical assistance, it identifies and analyzes the roots of community tension and recommends a corrective course of action. In conciliation, the agency informally acts as a third party to disputes to avoid or reduce violence, offer alternatives to involved parties, and influence actions or reactions toward peaceful resolution resulting in a signed document of agreement. In mediation, it acts as a third party intermediary in a more formal sense with sanction from the disputants, assisting them in reaching a settlement of their differences. The Service may enter a community on its own initiative or upon request. Contact: Community Relations Service, Department of Justice, 5500 Friendship Blvd., Suite 330, Chevy Chase, MD 20815/301-492-5929.

Computer Crime and Security Publications
The Bureau of Justice Statistics acts as a clearinghouse for information on computer crime and security and puts out five one-time publications dealing with these topics. The Bureau is an excellent source of legal and technical information. The five volumes are:

Computer Crime: Expert Witness Manual deals with issues relevant to the selection of witnesses to use in computer crime trials;

Computer Crime: Legislative Resource Manual (Pub. #027-000-01135-7) deals with issues relevant to the selection of witnesses to use in computer crime trials;

Computer Crime: Criminal Justice Resource Manual (Pub. #027-000-00870-4) describes different types of computer crime strategies (the 150-page publication is available for $10.00);

Computer Crime: Computer Security Techniques (Pub. #027-000-01169-1) describes different security techniques used to control computer crime (the 150-page publication is $7.50);

Computer Crime: Electronic Fund Transfer Systems and Crime (Pub. #027-000-01170-5) describes electronic fund transfer crimes and discusses available sources of data (the 150-page publication is $7.00).

These reports are available from: Superintendent of Documents, U.S. Government Printing Office, Washington, DC 20402/202-783-3238. Contact: Bureau of Justice Statistics, U.S. Department of Justice, 633 Indiana Ave. N.W., Washington, DC 20531.

Computerized Data Bases
The following data bases are maintained by the Department of Justice

Court Administration and Management Data Base
Information System Indexing System (ISIS) is an in-house data base containing non-book materials about federal court administration and management. Documents by judges, unpublished materials, speeches and remarks are stored. Topics range from workloads to how courts are run. Information can only be accessed by judges and others in the judicial system. Contact: Librarian, Federal Judicial Center, Information Services, 1520 H Street, N.W., Washington, DC 20005/202-633-6011.

Criminal Bibliography Data Base
The National Criminal Justice Referral System (NCJRS) is a bibliographic data base with abstracts on criminal and juvenile justice literature. Subject areas covered include: alternatives to institutionalization; criminology; drug abuse; facility design; police prosecution; reference and statistics, staff resources, and technology. NCJRS will conduct customized searches of its data base for $48. The service also provides topical pre-packaged searches for a fee of $5 for up to 30 citations, and $17.50 for up to 200 citations. The NCJRS data base is also available on Dialog. Contact: Information Specialist, National Criminal Justice Referral Service, National Institute of Justice, Box 6000, Rockville, MD 20850/301-251-5500.

Criminal Justice Data Base
The National Crime Information Center (NCIC) provides information, on-line, to criminal justice agencies concerning wanted persons, missing persons, stolen property and computerized criminal histories. Input and retrieval are performed via federal, state and local computer/terminal interface with a central FBI computer. Retrievable data includes information on criminal careers and permits users to track criminals through the criminal justice system. Searches and printouts are free and restricted to criminal justice agencies. Contact: National Crime Information Center, Technical Services Division, Federal Bureau of Investigation, 10th and Pennsylvania Ave. N.W., Washington, DC 20535/202-324-2606.

Criminal Offense Survey Data Base
The National Crime Survey data base contains all data collected from the National Crime Survey, which is conducted yearly by the Department of Justice. The Survey is based on a representative sample of 135,000 households across the U.S. It focuses on the following offenses (both completed and attempted): the personal crimes of rape, robbery, assault and larceny; and the household crimes of burglary, larceny and motor vehicle theft. Searches and printouts are provided on a cost-recovery basis. Contact: Data Services Section, ICPSR, University of Michigan, Box 1248, Ann Arbor, MI 48106/313-763-5010.

Correctional Assistance
Technical assistance is available to state and local

departments of corrections, institutions, jails, probation and parole agencies, and other correctional units to help upgrade and strengthen the practice of corrections. For technical assistance information specifically related to jails, contact: National Institute of Corrections Jail Center, Bureau of Prisons, Department of Justice, 1790 30th St., Suite 440, Boulder, CO 80301/303-497-6700. For general information on technical assistance, contact: National Institute of Corrections, Bureau of Prisons, Department of Justice, 320 1st St. N.W., Washington, DC 20534/202-724-3106.

Corrections Information Center
The Center provides information in all areas of corrections as well as in specialty areas such as volunteers in corrections, staff development and training and legal matters. Contact: National Institute of Prisons, Department of Justice, 1790 30th St., Suite 130, Boulder, CO 80301/303-444-1101.

Corrections, National Institute of
This office gives technical assistance to state and local correctional programs. Grant funds finance projects in the Institute's priority areas of staff development and training, jails classification systems, offender grievance mechanism, probation and parole programs and clearinghouse activities. Contact: National Institute of Corrections, Bureau of Prisons, Department of Justice, 320 1st St. N.W., Room 200, Washington, DC 20534/202-724-3106.

Crime in the United States
An annual report called, *Uniform Crime Reports,* contains information on the types of crimes committed (murder, rape, robbery, motor vehicle theft, etc), victim/offender relationships, types of weapons, motives, persons arrested, crime trends, and areas in which crimes were committed. Other published reports include: *Bomb Summary,* and *Law Enforcement Officers Killed or Assaulted.* Contact: Uniform Crime Reporting Section, Federal Bureau of Investigation, Department of Justice, 9th St. and Pennsylvania Ave. N.W., Room 7437, Washington, DC 20535/202-324-2820.

Crime Prevention Booklets
Got A Minute? You Can Stop Crime is the first in a series of crime booklets available free of charge from the Distribution Service, National Criminal Justice Reference Service, National Institute of Justice, Department of Justice, P.O. Box 6000, Rockville, MD 20850/301-251-5500.

Criminal Behavior
Research programs conducted on crime and criminal behavior include: 1) *Research Agreements*—longterm grants that allow groups of researchers to focus their collective efforts on fundamental ques-

tions of crime or behavior, e.g., habitual offender, white collar crime, economic studies in criminal justice, unemployment and crime and community reactions to crime, alcohol and drugs, race relations and crime; and 2) *Visiting Fellowships*—which bring researchers to the Institute to work on independent projects of their own choosing. Contact: Office of Research Evaluation and Methodology, National Institute of Justice, Office of Justice Programs, Department of Justice, 633 Indiana Ave. N.W., Room 800, Washington, DC 20531/202-724-7631.

Criminalistics Laboratory Information System (CLIS)
This computerized data base is currently composed of a general Rifling Characteristics File that is used to identify the manufacturer and type of weapon that may have been used to fire a bullet or cartridge. Contact: Laboratory Division, Federal Bureau of Investigation, Department of Justice, 9th St. and Pennsylvania Ave. N.W., Washington, DC 20535/202-324-4410.

Criminal Justice Bibliographies
The National Crime Justice Reference Service maintains the following bibliographies. When requesting a bibliography, ask for the latest available update.

Affirmative Action-Equal Employment Opportunities in the Criminal Justice System (NCJ 61834)
Alternatives to Institutionalization (NCJ 58518)
Arson (NCJ 58366)
Basic Sources in Criminal Justice (NCJ 49417)
Bibliographies in Criminal Justice (NCJ 62014)
Community Crime Prevention (NCJ 43628)
Crime and Disruption in Schools (NCJ 56588)
Crimes Against the Elderly in 26 Cities (NCJ 76709)
Criminal Justice and the Elderly (NCJ 55197)
Criminal Justice Periodicals (NCJ 57168)
Etiology of Criminality: Nonbehavioral Science (NCJ 60117)
Female Offender (NCJ 55637)
Firearm Use in Violent Crime (NCJ 52677)
Halfway Houses (NCJ 46851)
International Policing (NCJ 46190)
Jail-Based Inmate Programs (NCJ 60331)
Jury Reform (NCJ 48232)
Paralegals (NCJ 57986)
Plea Negotiation (NCJ 66559)
Police Consolidation (NCJ 67142)
Police Crisis Intervention (NCJ 48005)
Police Discretion (NCJ 46183)
Police Stress (NCJ 59352)
Prison Industries (NCJ 49701)
Private Security (NCJ 47367)
Publications of the National Institute of Law Enforcement and Criminal Justice (NCJ 49700)
Publications of the National Institute of Law Enforcement and Criminal Justice (NCJ 57987)
Restitution (NCJ 62011)
Speedy Trial (NCJ 48110)

Spouse Abuse (NCJ 54427)
Standards of Care in Adult and Juvenile Correctional Institutions (NCJ 61443)
Strategies for Reintegrating the Ex-Offender (NCJ 61571)
Team Policing (NCJ 35887)
Techniques for Project Evaluation (NCJ 43556)
Terrorism Supplement (NCJ 45005)
Variations on Juvenile Probation (NCJ 62010)
Victimless Crimes (NCJ 43630)
Victim/Witness Assistance (NCJ 49698)
White Collar Crime (NCJ 69331)
Contact: NCJRS Distribution Service, Department of Justice, P.O. Box 6000, Rockville MD 20850/301-251-5500.

Criminal Justice Reference Service

This office act as an international clearinghouse and reference center serving both the criminal justice profession as well as the general public on subjects such as courts, police, corrections, juvenile justice, human resources, fraud and abuse of government programs, evaluations and statistics, service to victims of crime, and civil and criminal dispute resolution. The service provides monthly announcements of significant publications, audiovisual material and events that relate to specific areas of interest. The service maintains a reading room and a reference library which is open to the public. The library contains holdings from NIJ, NIJJ and Delinquency Proceedings Bureau of Justice Statistics, Office for Victims of Crime, and Federal Justice Research Program. A bimonthly journal, *NIJ Reports,* contains news of criminal justice research, abstracts of important publications and announcements of new products and services available from OJARS. Contact: National Criminal Justice Reference Service, National Institute of Justice, Department of Justice, Box 6000, Rockville, MD 20850/301-251-5500.

Criminal Justice Research

Research to explore major problems of crime prevention and criminal justice includes: 1) Police Division research which advances police science and strengthens police effectiveness, e.g., lightweight body armor, police response; 2) Adjudication Division research, which focuses on the prosecution, defense and courts components of the criminal justice system, e.g., improving consistency of sentencing in criminal cases, and better techniques for juror management; 3) Correction Division research projects directed at increasing the knowledge of the custody, treatment, and community supervision of offenders; and 4) Community Crime Prevention Division which focuses on the role of the citizen, the municipality, law enforcement authorities and environmental design factors in preventing crimes of violence, and crimes of special concerns including organized crime, white-collar crime, and rape. The Unsolicited Research Program invites criminal justice

researchers to submit proposals for work on problems of their own choice. Contact: Office of Research Programs, National Institute of Justice, OJARS, Department of Justice, Room 866, Washington, DC 20531/202-724-2965.

Desegregation of Public Facilities

The Attorney General may bring suit for an injunction prohibiting discrimination in operation of public facilities on account of race, color, religion, or national origin when he or she receives, and certifies as meritorious, a written complaint from a person who is unable to bring suit either because of financial reasons or possible intimidation. The Attorney General may intervene in suits of general public importance alleging denial of the equal protection of the laws on account of race, color, religion or national origin and is entitled to the same relief as if he or she had instituted the suit. The Attorney General has the enforcement mission to correct widespread deprivation of civil rights of persons confined in penal and nonpenal institutions. Contact: Chief, Special Litigation Section, Civil Rights Division, Department of Justice, Washington, DC 20530/202-633-3414.

Direct Payments

The program described below provides financial assistance directly to individuals, private firms and other private institutions to encourage or subsidize a particular activity.

Cuban and Haitian Entrant Resettlement Program

*Objectives:*To provide primary and secondary resettlement services to Cuban and Haitian entrants paroled into the community by the Immigration and Naturalization Service.
Eligibility: Public or Private, nonprofit organizations, or institutions may submit proposals, and individuals may apply for individual grants to resettle.
Range of Financial Assistance: $1,200 to $1,600,000.
Contact: Director, Community Relations Service, 5550 Friendship Blvd., Chevy Chase, MD 20815/301-492-5929.

Public Safety Officers' Benefits Program

Objectives: To provide a $50,000 death benefit to the eligible survivors of state and local public safety officers whose death is the direct and proximate result of a personal injury sustained in the line of duty on or after September 29, 1976.
Eligibility: Applicants must be an eligible survivor of a state or local public safety officer whose death is the direct and proximate result of a personal injury sustained in the line of duty on or after September 29, 1976. Public safety officers include law enforcement officers and fire fighters both paid and volunteer. Law enforcement officers

include, but are not limited to, police, corrections, probation, parole and judicial officers.

Range of Financial Assistance: Not applicable.

Contact: Director, Public Safety Officers' Benefits Program, Office of Justice Assistance Research and Statistics, Washington, DC 20531/202-724-7620.

Disaster Squad

The disaster squad identifies, through fingerprints, the victims of disasters. Its services are available upon request of local law enforcement and government agencies or transportation companies following a catastrophe where the identification of victims is a problem. The squad also assists in identifying Americans in disaster abroad only at the specific invitation of the country involved. Contact: FBI Disaster Squad, Identification Division, Federal Bureau of Investigation, Department of Justice, 9th St. and Pennsylvania Ave. N.W., Room 11255, Washington, DC 20537/202-324-5401.

Drug Abuse Warning Network (DAWN)

This network identifies and evaluates the scope and magnitude of drug abuse in the United States. More than 900 hospital emergency rooms and medical examiner facilities supply data to the program. DAWN identifies drugs currently being abused; determines existing patterns and profiles of abuse/abuser in Standard Metropolitan Statistical Areas; monitors systemwide abuse trends; detects new abuse entities and polydrug combinations; provides data for the assessment of health hazards and abuse potential of drug substances; and provides data needed for rational control and scheduling of drugs of abuse. Contact: Information Systems Unit, Office of Diversion Control Drug Enforcement Adm., Department of Justice, 1405 Eye St. N.W., Room 719, Washington, DC 20537/202-633-1316.

Drug Education Materials

Drug education films are available free of charge to civic, educational, private and religious groups. Available publications include:

Drugs of Abuse—a 40-page booklet, written especially for law enforcement officers, educators, health and other professionals, containing full color illustrations of drugs controlled under the Controlled Substances Act 1970 (CSA)-1970, administered by the Drug Enforcement Administration (DEA), it also gives concise, factual, accurate scientific descriptions of the drugs, their effects and the consequences of abuse. It contains a chart summarizing scientific data about controlled licit and illicit drugs and a glossary of slang terms. The Controlled Substances Act-1970 is summarized.

Controlled Substance Chart: Use, Abuse and Effects—a 4-page chart free to the general public in limited quantities (up to 25).

Soozie and Katy—a 26-page activities and coloring book for children ages 5–7, which emphasizes the theme, "Only sick people need drugs."

Contact: Preventive Programs, Office of Public Affairs, Drug Enforcement Administration, Department of Justice, 1405 Eye St. N.W., Room 1204, Washington, DC 20537/202-633-1244.

Drug Enforcement Science and Technology

The Office of Science and Technology provides operational and scientific support and conducts research directly related to enforcement and intelligence efforts. It is responsible for the development of new and improved technical equipment, such as surveillance devices. Provides quick reaction support for ongoing investigations and modifies commercial equipment for special requirements. Manages seven forensic laboratories and a Special Testing and Research Laboratory. Provides forensic support to DEA, FBI, other federal and state and local jurisdictions which do not have laboratory capability. Laboratories analyze drug evidence, provide expert court testimony, and analyze drug evidence for intelligence programs. Contact: Office of Science and Technology, Drug Enforcement Administration, 1405 I St. N.W., Washington, D.C. 20537/202-633-1211.

Drug and Alcohol Prevention Program

This nationwide program, developed in conjunction with the National High School Athletic Coaches Association, is designed to help coaches prevent drug and alcohol abuse among high school athletes and students. Free information packets, publications, a slide show and video tape are all available to coaches. Clinics and workshops for coaches will be held throughout the United States at which the DEA Special Agents, professional athletes, and amateur sports figures will address a variety of topics pertaining to drug and alcohol prevention. Contact: Preventive Programs, Drug Enforcement Administration, Department of Justice, 1405 I St. N.W., Washington, DC 20537/202-633-1437.

Drug Registration

Information is available about registration under the Controlled Substances Act. Every person who manufactures, distributes or dispenses any controlled substance or who proposes to engage in the manufacture, distribution or dispensing of any controlled substance must register annually with the Registration Branch of the DEA (Department of Justice, Box 28083, Central Station, Washington, DC 20005). A schedule of controlled substances is available. The Drug Enforcement Administration has more than 540,000 registrants. It monitors and periodically investigates registrants to ensure that they are accountable for the controlled substances handled. Contact: Registration Section, Office of Compliance and Regulatory Affairs, Drug Enforcement Administration, Department of Justice, 666 11th St. N.W., Room 920, Washington, DC 20001/202-254-8255.

Drug Reporting Systems
Three computerized systems are maintained by this office:

Drug Abuse Warning Network (DAWN)—see listing above.

Automated Reporting and Consolidated Order System (ARCOS)—a comprehensive drug-tracking system that enables the Drug Enforcement Administration to monitor the flow of selected drugs from points of import or manufacture to points of sale, export or distribution.

Project Label—a system that represents a listing of all marketed drug products containing controlled substances.

Contact: Office of Diversion Control, Drug Enforcement Administration, Department of Justice, 1405 Eye St. N.W., Room 419, Washington, DC 20537/202-633-1316.

Drug Situation Indicators
A retail and wholesale heroin price/purity index is available based upon data from the analysis of drug evidence samples submitted to the Drug Enforcement Administration. Reports are available on drug-related emergency room admissions and deaths from metropolitan areas widely distributed throughout the United States. Heroin-related death and injury data are published on a quarterly basis for 21 of these areas. All legal drug handlers are registered with the Drug Enforcement Administration and are required to report thefts or losses of controlled substances. Stolen supplies of controlled drugs comprise a substantial portion of the supply of certain substances in the illicit drug distribution network. Drug Enforcement Administration uses these data to evaluate trends in the overall heroin situation. Contact: Office of Intelligence, Drug Enforcement Administration, Department of Justice, 1405 Eye St. N.W., Room 1013, Washington, DC 20537/202-633-1071.

Drug Statistics
The following statistical information according to subject is available:

Enforcement Activity—domestic drug removals through seizures, through delivery, at posts and borders, immigration and naturalization service illicit drug removals, customs referral drug removals, federal initiated task force arrests and dispositions, domestic arrests and clandestine labs seized, Drug Enforcement Administration foreign cooperative arrests, compliance investigations and regulatory actions;

Drug Abuse Indicators—statistics on heroin, cocaine, stimulants, hallucinogens, depressants;

Contact: Office of Intelligence Services, Drug Enforcement Administration, Department of Justice, 1405 Eye St. N.W., Room 1221, Washington, DC 20537/202-633-1509.

Drug Training
The National Training Institute provides both basic and advanced training in drug law enforcement and related skills to insure that trained personnel are available to perform the necessary functions of Drug Enforcement Administration. It provides training to forensic chemists, intelligence analysts and to the foreign drug law enforcement community. Contact: Office of Training, Drug Enforcement Administration, Department of Justice, FLETC Building 67, Glynco, GA 31524/912-26x2793.

Emergency Programs Center
This office coordinates Department of Justice activities in the three main areas—civil disorder, domestic terrorism, and nuclear incidents (criminal aspects only—extortion, theft, etc.). It also responds to special crises and special security events such as coordinating responsibilities for the Winter Olympics and the Cuban refugees. Contact: Emergency Programs Center, Department of Justice, 10th St. and Constitution Ave. N.W., Room 6101, Washington, DC 20530/202-633-4545.

Equal Opportunity
For information on the Department of Justice's annual affirmative action plan for equal employment opportunity, contact: Equal Opportunity Programs Staff, Justice Management Division, Department of Justice, 10th St. and Constitution Ave. N.W., Room 1230, Washington, DC 20530/202-633-5049.

Fair Housing and Equal Credit Opportunity
Title VIII of the Civil Rights Act of 1968 is designed to insure freedom from discrimination in the sale, rental and financing of housing and other related activities. A private suit alleging discrimination may be filed in the appropriate federal or state court. The Attorney General is authorized to bring civil actions in federal courts when there is reasonable cause to believe that any person or group of persons is engaged in a pattern or practice of discrimination or when there is reasonable cause to believe any group has been denied such rights in a case of general public importance. The Equal Credit Opportunity Act, as amended, is designed to prohibit discrimination in all aspects of credit transactions on a prohibited basis. Persons who believe that they are victims of such discrimination may file complaints with one of the appropriate federal regulatory agencies, or may bring the information to the attention of the Attorney General. The Justice Department is authorized to institute litigation in federal courts when a matter

is referred to the Attorney General by an agency responsible for administrative enforcement of the Act or when there is reasonable cause to believe that one or more creditors are engaged in a pattern or practice in violation of the Act. In addition, an aggrieved person may institute suit in federal court and in such cases, punitive damages in an amount not to exceed $10,000 in addition to actual damages, or in the case of a class action a maximum of the lesser of $500,000 or one percent of the net worth of the creditor, may be granted by the court. Contact: Housing and Civil Enforcement Section, Civil Rights Division, Department of Justice, Room 7525, Washington, DC 20530/ 202-633-4715.

Family Violence Section
This office is responsible for implementation of the recommendations of the Attorney General's Task Force on Family Violence. It develops and funds programs in each area of family violence—child abuse, spouse abuse and elder abuse—and child molestation. The Family Violence Section focuses on the criminal justice aspects of these areas. It takes a leadership position in some of the other systematic areas such as, mental health, social service, education and health. Training of law enforcement personnel in responding to family violence incidents is one of the priorities of the Family Violence Section. Other program areas are:

Prosecution of sexual abuse cases
Media, public awareness campaign
Assistance to child victims
Improvement of court processes for child victims
Improvement of police response to spouse abuse

For further information contact: Family Violence Section, Office of Victims of Crime, Department of Justice, 633 Indiana Ave. N.W., Room 1386, Washington, DC 20531/202-272-6500.

FBI Academy
The programs at the Academy include: new agents' training; in-service program for field agents; training for mid-level and senior police administrators; National Executive Institute for top police executives; Senior Executive Program for top FBI executives; Executive Development Institute for FBI mid-level managers. Custom designed courses are also available. Contact: Federal Bureau of Investigation (FBI) Academy, Quantico, VA 22135/703-640-6131.

FBI Agent Careers
For information on special agent and nonagent positions, contact the nearest FBI field office, or: Federal Bureau of Investigation, Department of Justice, 9th St. and Pennsylvania Ave. N.W., Washington DC 20535.

FBI Guided Tours
Guided tours of the Federal Bureau of Investigation Headquarters, the J. Edgar Hoover FBI Building, are offered Mondays through Fridays, excluding holidays, from 9:00 A.M. to 4:00 P.M. The building is located on E St. between 9th and 10th Sts. N.W., in Washington, DC. No appointments are necessary for groups numbering less than 15. Contact: Office of Public Affairs, Federal Bureau of Investigation, Department of Justice, 9th St. and Pennsylvania Ave. N.W., Room 7116, Washington, DC 20535/202-324-5352.

FBI Laboratory
This laboratory is divided into three major sections:

Document Section—conducts scientific examinations of all documents submitted as physical evidence as well as shoe print, tire tread and other sophisticated examinations. It translates and interprets oral and written foreign language material; performs rhetorical/aural analysis; examines evidence in gambling cases and extortionate credit transactions, administers the FBI Polygraph Examination Program, and conducts cryptanalytic examination of secret/enciphered communications;

Scientific Analysis Section—conducts highly specialized examinations involving chemistry, arson, firearms, tool marks, hairs and fibers, blood, metallurgy, mineralogy, number restoration, glass fracture, instrumental analysis and related matters. It has primary responsibility for physical and biologic science research and forensic science training.

Special Projects Section—provides visual aids such as demonstrative evidence, 2-dimensional graphics and 3-dimensional models used in the prosecution of FBI cases. It designs and fabricates special purpose equipment used for special laboratory applications in investigative techniques and visual aids in the field. It handles photographic research, all necessary scientific and technical photography and direct photographic assistance.

Contact: Laboratory Division, Federal Bureau of Investigation, Department of Justice, 9th St. and Pennsylvania Ave. N.W., Room 3090, Washington, DC 20535/202-324-4410.

FBI Publications
A variety of publications, reports and article reprints are available free of charge from the FBI. Topics cover all aspects of criminal justice, from crime prevention to the history of the FBI. Listed below are examples of current materials. Contact: FBI, Office of Congressional and Public Affairs, Room 6236, 10th Street at Pennsylvania Ave. N.W., Washington, DC 20535.

I Spy at the FBI—is a "Mini Page" publication to help parents and teachers introduce children to the FBI, both its services and building. The 4-page publication contains puzzles, interesting facts, fingerprinting information and more.

Crime Resistance: A Way to Protect Your Family Against Crime—this 16-page booklet provides tips on how you and your family can make yourself safe from crime in your home as well as when you go about your daily routines—commuting to and from work, traveling in the family car, walking to school, and shopping.

You, Yours and Crime Resistance—A self-help booklet with tips for making your home, car and habits safer to avoid being victimized by crime.

The NCIC and You—a booklet describing the National Crime Information Center and the computerized information system the FBI maintains on behalf of law enforcement agencies across the U.S. The NCIC computerized data base contains information about missing children and adults, as well as stolen property such as cars, boats, planes, and guns.

How You Can Help the FBI Combat White Collar Crime—in a question and answer format, this brochure describes what white collar crime is, gives examples, and provides a listing of FBI offices you can contact to report such crime.

99 Facts About the FBI—this 29-page booklet, with sketches, covers all aspects of the FBI including its history, jurisdiction, and operation. Done in a question and answer format, it is geared toward the general public.

The FBI: The First 75 Years—prepared in 1983, this 29 page booklet traces the history of the FBI providing information about topics such as the gangster era, spying, World War II activities, and the training of FBI agents.

Fingerprint Identification—provides a history of how fingerprints came to be.

Federal Prison Industries
UNICOR is the trade name under which the Federal Prison Industries does most of its business. Its mission is to employ and train federal inmates through a diversified program providing products and services exclusively to other federal agencies. Contact: Federal Prison Industries, Department of Justice, 320 1st St. N.W., Room 654, Washington, DC 20534/202-724-3013.

Federal Programs Litigation
This office handles litigation against federal agencies, cabinet officers, and other officials. It handles the enforcement and litigation aimed at remedying statutory or regulatory violations, the defense of employment policies, and personnel actions, and litigation relating to the disposition and availability of government records. Examples of cases include: the injunction to keep *Progressive Magazine* from publishing H-bomb information, the extension of time for the ratification of the Equal Rights Amendment, and declaring California airline regulations unconstitutional in light of federal airline deregulation. Contact: Federal Pro-grams Branch, Civil Division, Department of Justice, 10th St. and Constitution Ave. N.W., Room 3643, Washington, DC 20530/202-633-3354.

Female Offenders
This office monitors programs for female inmates. One major area is the psychiatric unit for women with problems which has been established at the Federal Correctional Institution at Lexington, Kentucky. Contact: Correctional Programs Division, Bureau of Prisons, Department of Justice, 320 1st St. N.W., Room 534, Washington, DC 20534/202-724-3257.

Fingerprint Records to Private Citizens
An individual may obtain a copy of his/her arrest record by submitting a written request directly to the FBI Identification Division, together with a set of rolled, inked fingerprint impressions taken on a fingerprint card which indicates the individual's name and birth date. There is a $11.00 fee. This office also complies with court-ordered expungements and purge requests received from criminal justice agencies. Contact: Identification Division, Federal Bureau of Investigation, Department of Justice, 9th St. and Pennsylvania Ave. N.W., Room 11255, Washington, DC 20535/202-324-5454.

Foreign Agent Information
The public can look through the records of foreign agents for their initial statements upon registration and the six-month follow-ups. These statements provide details on the country, payments, contracts, missions, and everything else that involves the agent's relationship with the foreign country. A list of Public Agents is available for $11.00. Contact: Public Office, Internal Security Section, Criminal Division, Department of Justice, 315 9th St. N.W., Room 100, Washington, DC 20530/202-724-6926.

Foreign Agents Registration
The Internal Security Section administers and enforces the Foreign Agents Registration Act of 1938. For information on registering as a foreign agent, contact: Internal Security Section, Criminal Division, Department of Justice, 315 9th St. N.W., Room 216, Washington, DC 20530/202-724-7109.

Foreign Claims Settlement
This office determines claims of U.S. nationals against foreign governments for losses and injuries sustained by them. Examples include claims by ex-prisoners of the Vietnam War, by United States nationals against the People's Republic of China for losses resulting from nationalization or other taking of property, and claims against the GDR for losses arising out of the nationalization or other taking of property located in the area commonly referred to as East Germany. Contact: Foreign

Claims Settlement Commission of the United States, Department of Justice, 1111 20th St. N.W., Room 400, Washington, DC 20579/202-653-5883.

Foreign Litigation

This office represents the United States before foreign tribunals in civil cases brought by and against the United States. It represents the government in domestic cases involving questions of international and foreign law. Contact: Office of Foreign Litigation, Commercial Litigation Branch, Civil Division, Department of Justice, 550 11th St. N.W., Room 1234, Washington, DC 20530/202-724-7455.

Frauds and White Collar Crimes

This section directs and coordinates the federal effort against white-collar crime. Focuses on frauds involving government programs and procurement, transnational and multi-district trade, the security and commodity exchanges, banking practices, and consumer victimization. Contact: Fraud Section, Criminal Division, Department of Justice, 315 9th St. N.W., Room 832, Washington, DC 20530/202-724-7038.

Freedom of Information Act

This office carries out the Department of Justice's responsibilities under the Freedom of Information Act to encourage agency compliance. It also advises other departments and agencies on all questions of policy, interpretation and application of the Freedom of Information Act. Contact: Office of Information Law and Policy, Department of Justice, 10th St. and Constitution Ave. N.W., Room 6345, Washington, DC 20530/202-724-7400.

Grants

The programs described below are for sums of money which are given by the federal government to initiate and stimulate new or improved activities, or to sustain on-going services.

Corrections—Research and Evaluation and Policy Formulation

Objectives: To conduct, encourage, and coordinate research relating to corrections including the causes, prevention, diagnosis, and treatment of criminal offenders. To conduct evaluation programs which study the effectiveness of new approaches, techniques, systems, programs, and devices to improve the corrections system.

Eligibility: States, general units of local government, public and private agencies, education institutions, organizations and individuals involved in the development, implementation or operation of correction programs and services.

Range of Financial Assistance: $1,500 to $200,000.

Contact: Chief, Community Services Division,

National Institute of Corrections, Department of Justice, 320 1st St. N.W., Room 200, Washington, DC 20534/202-724-3106.

Corrections—Technical Assistance

Objectives: To encourage and assist federal, state, and local government programs and services, and programs and services of other public and private agencies, institutions and organizations in their efforts to develop and implement improved corrections programs. To assist and serve in a consultant capacity to federal, state, and local courts, departments, and agencies in the development, maintenance, and coordination of programs, facilities, and services, training, treatment, and rehabilitation with repect to criminal and juvenile offenders.

Eligibility: States, general units of local government, public and private agencies, education institutions, organizations, and individuals involved in the development, implementation or operation of correction programs and services.

Range of Financial Assistance: $1,500 to $50,000.

Contact: Technical Assistance Coordinator, National Institute of Corrections, 320 1st St. N.W., Room 200, Washington, DC 20534/202-724-3106.

Corrections—Training and Staff Development

Objectives: To devise and conduct, in various geographic locations, seminars, workshops, and training programs for law enforcement officers, judges and judicial personnel, corrections personnel, welfare workers and other personnel, including lay exoffenders and paraprofessionals, connected with the treatment and rehabilitation of criminal and juvenile offenders. To develop technical training teams to aid in the development of seminars, workshops, and training programs within the several states and with the state and local agencies which work with prisoners, parolees, probationers, and other offenders.

Eligibility: States, general units of local government, as well as public and private agencies, education institutions, organizations, and individuals involved in the development, implementation or operation of correction programs and services.

Range of Financial Assistance: $1,500 to $300,000.

Contact: National Institute of Corrections, Department of Justice, 320 1st St. N.W., Room 200, Washington, DC 20534/202-724-3106.

Criminal Justice Research and Development— Graduate Research Fellowships

Objectives: To improve the quality and quantity of knowledge about crime and the criminal justice system, while at the same time, helping to increase the number of persons who are qualified to teach in collegiate criminal justice programs and to conduct research related to criminal justice issues.

Eligibility: Accredited institution of higher education offering a doctoral degree program.

Range of Financial Assistance: $1,600 to $5,000.

Contact: National Institute of Justice, Washington DC 20531/202-724-2965.

Criminal Justice Statistics Development

Objectives: To provide financial and technical assistance to States and local governments regarding the collection, analysis, utilization, and dissemination of justice statistics.

Eligibility: State agencies designated with responsibility for the particular programs.

Range of Financial Assistance: $10,000 to $150,000.

Contact: Bureau of Justice Statistics, Department of Justice, Washington, DC 20531/202-724-7770.

Justice Research and Development Project Grants

Objectives: To encourage and support research and development to further understanding of the causes of crime and to improve the criminal justice system.

Eligibility: State and local governments, private, profit, nonprofit organizations, institutions of higher education and qualified individuals.

Range of Financial Assistance: Not specified.

Contact: National Institute of Justice, Department of Justice, Washington, DC 20531/202-724-2942.

Juvenile Justice and Delinquency Prevention— Allocation to States

Objectives: To increase the capacity of State and local governments for the development of more effective education, training,, research, prevention, diversion, treatment, and rehabilitation programs in the area of juvenile delinquency and programs to improve the juvenile justice system.

Eligibility: States that have established operating State Criminal Justice Councils in accordance with the Justice System Improvement Act of 1979.

Range of Financial Assistance: $56,250 to $225,000.

Contact: Office of Juvenile Justice and Delinquency Prevention, Department of Justice, Washington, DC 20531/202-724-5911.

Juvenile Justice and Delinquency Prevention— Special Emphasis and Technical Assistance Programs

Objectives: Develop and implement programs that support effective approaches, techniques and methods for preventing and controlling juvenile delinquency through development and utilization of community-based alternatives to traditional forms of official justice system processing; suppression of juvenile crime and alcohol and drug involvement; and development of national missing/abducted and serial murder tracking and prevention program. Prosecutorial programs for chronic offenders and gang members have also been announced. Provide technical assistance to federal, state and local governments, courts, public and private agencies, institutions, and individuals, in the planning, establishment, operation or evaluation of juvenile delinquency programs; and assist operating agencies having direct responsibilities for prevention and treatment of juvenile delinquency in the development and promulgation of regulations, guidelines, requirements, criteria, standards, and procedures established through the Office of Juvenile Justice and Delinquency Prevention and the priorities defined for formula grant programs.

Eligibility: Public and private nonprofit agencies, organizations, individuals, state and local units of government, combinations of state or local units.

Range of Financial Assistance: Not specified.

Contact: Office of Juvenile Justice and Delinquency Prevention, Office of Justice Assistance, Department of Justice, Washington, DC 20531/202-724-7753.

National Institute for Juvenile Justice and Delinquency Prevention

Objectives: To encourage, coordinate, and conduct research and evaluation of juvenile justice and delinquency prevention activities; to provide a clearinghouse and information center for collecting, publishing, and distributing information on juvenile delinquency; to conduct a national training program; and to establish standards for the administration of juvenile justice.

Eligibility: Public or private agencies, organizations, or individuals.

Range of Financial Assistance: Not specified.

Contact: National Institute for Juvenile Justice and Delinquency Prevention, Office of Juvenile Justice and Delinquency Prevention, Department of Justice, Washington, DC 20531/202-724-7560.

National Institute of Justice Visiting Fellowships

Objectives: To provide opportunities for experienced criminal justice professionals to pursue promising new ideas for improved understanding of crime, delinquency and criminal justice administration by sponsoring research projects of their own creation and design.

Eligibility: Fellowship grants are awarded to individuals.

Range of Financial Assistance: Not specified.

Contact: National Institute of Justice, Department of Justice, Washington, DC 20531/202-724-2965.

Hazardous Waste

This office deals with hazardous waste disposal problems. It is responsible for litigation, both civil and criminal under the Resource Conservation and

Recovery Act. Contact: Environmental Enforcement Section, Land and Natural Resources Division, Department of Justice, 10th St. and Constitution Ave. N.W., Room 1521, Washington, DC 20530/202-633-5271.

How to Contact the FBI with Important Information
The front page of most telephone directories lists the telephone number of the nearest Federal Bureau of Investigation field offices, all of which are open 24 hours a day, including Saturdays, Sundays, and holidays.

Illegal Sales of Narcotics and Drugs
To report the illegal sale of narcotics or dangerous drugs, contact: Enforcement, Drug Enforcement Administration, Department of Justice, 1405 Eye St. N.W., Room 619, Washington, DC 20537/202-633-1151.

Immigrant Outreach Program
The Outreach Program provides training and guidance to voluntary community groups and agencies which assist aliens in applying for benefits under the Immigration and Naturalization laws. Among the topics included are: basic immigration laws, how to process visas abroad, how to become citizens, how to become permanent residents, and deportation hearings. Contact: Outreach Program, Immigration and Naturalization Service, Department of Justice, 425 Eye St. N.W., Room 6230, Washington, DC 20536/202-633-4123.

Immigration and Naturalization Publications
For a descriptive listing of available publications, contact: Public Information Office, Immigration and Naturalization Service, Department of Justice, 425 Eye St. N.W., Room 5034, Washington, DC 20536/202-633-4330.

Immigration Appeals, Board of
The Board is a quasi-judicial body (independent of the Immigration and Naturalization Service (INS) operating under the supervision and control of the Associate Attorney General that establishes guidelines on immigration procedures and policies. Contact: Board of Immigration Appeals, Department of Justice, 5203 Leesburg Pike, Falls Church, VA 22041/701-756-6168.

Immigration Arrivals
The office of inspections covers the inspections of persons arriving at United States ports of entry to determine admissibility, requests for admission to an immigration status according to immigration law. Contact: Inspections, Immigration and Naturalization Service, Department of Justice, 425 Eye St. N.W., Room 7123, Washington, DC 20536/202-633-3019.

Immigration—Inspections
This office has designed the "one-stop" inspection at airports. Under this new procedure, passengers will be inspected for both immigration and customs purposes at the same time. Contact: Inspections, Immigration and Naturalization Service, Department of Justice, 425 Eye St. N.W., Room 7123, Washington, DC 20536/202-633-3019.

Immigration Statistics
For statistics information on immigration-related topics, contact: Statistical Branch, Information Services, Immigration and Naturalization Service, Department of Justice, 425 Eye St. N.W., Room 5020, Washington, DC 20536/202-633-3665.

Improvements in Administration
The Office of Legal Policy plans, develops and coordinates the implementation of policies and issues that are of special concern to the attorney general's office, as well as administers the Federal Justice Research Program. The kinds of projects the FRP funds are: a large-scale study of the history and characteristics of selected groups of claims to determine why some were taken to court for resolution while others were resolved by alternative mechanisms; the study of the disposition of certain types of criminal cases by U.S. Attorney's offices to improve allocation of prosecutorial responsibility between state and federal authority; a long-range study to develop data required for the formulation and evaluation of sentencing guidelines for the federal courts, and the impact of the Speed Trial Act; and development of proposals for improving the handling of scientific information by courts. Contact: Office for Legal Policy, Department of Justice, 10th St. and Constitution Ave. N.W., Room 4234, Washington, DC 20530/202-633-3824.

Indian Claims
This office defends the United States against legal, equitable and moral claims asserted by Indian tribes under the Indian Claims Commission Act of 1946. Contact: Indian Claims Section, Land and Natural Resources Division, Department of Justice, 550 11th St. N.W., Room 648, Washington, DC 20530/202-724-7376.

Indian Resources
This office is concerned with tribal hunting and fishing rights, both on and off the reservations, assertions of state jurisdiction over activities of Indians, and water rights. Contact: Indian Resources Section, Land and Natural Resources Division, Department of Justice, 550 11th St. N.W., Todd Bldg., Room 624, Washington, DC 20530/202-724-7156.

Interpol
Interpol is a world-wide consortium of 135 coun-

tries. In each member country a point of contact and coordination is established for the Interpol function. It coordinates and facilitates requests between foreign police organizations and law enforcement agencies in the United States for information regarding persons, vehicles, and goods that bear on criminal matters within those respective jurisdictions. Interpol exists as a catalyst to provide efficient police communications between the United States and other member countries, and the General Secretariat Headquarters, which is located outside of Paris, France. Investigations can cover criminal history checks, license plate and drivers' license checks, International Wanted Circulars, weapons trace, locating suspects. Contact: National Central Bureau, Interpol, Department of Justice, 10th St. and Constitution Ave. N.W., Room 6649, Washington, DC 20530/ 202-633-2867.

Justice Assistance News
This newsletter is published 10 times per year and offers information primarily on criminal justice projects of the Law Enforcement Assistance Administration, the National Institute of Law Enforcement and Criminal Justice, and the National Criminal Justice Information and Statistical Service. Available for $15.00 per year, from: Superintendent of Documents, Government Printing Office, Washington, DC 20402/202-783-3238.

Justice Development, Testing and Dissemination
This office links research to action. It publicizes successful local projects and publishes a series entitled "Issues and Practices" that synthesizes research data, experience and expert opinion. "Issues and Practices" includes Police Work Scheduling, Citation Release, and Vehicle Theft Prevention Strategies. Other programs include: *Program Designs,* in managing patrol operations; pre-release centers; neighborhood justice centers; juror usage and management; community response to rape; managing criminal investigations; and *Field Tests,* designed and mounted on experimental projects such as multi-county sentencing guidelines; and *Training Workshops.* Contact: Office of Development, Testing and Dissemination, National Institute of Justice, Office of Justice Assistance Research Statistics, Department of Justice, 633 Indiana Ave. N.W., Room 800, Washington, DC 20531/202-272-6001.

Justice Library
Information and reference services are available on topics related to the Department of Justice. Contact: Justice Library, Department of Justice, 10th St. and Pennsylvania Ave. N.W., Room 5400, Washington, DC 20530/202-633-3775.

Justice Statistics
This office collects and disseminates criminal justice statistics and supports the development of information and communications systems at the state and local level for both statistical and operation purposes. It offers grants to states to develop statistical analysis centers, uniform crime reporting systems, etc. Reports available include:

Myths and Realities About Crime
Parole in the United States, 1967 and 1977
Criminal Victimization in the U.S.: A Comparison of 1976 and 1977 Findings (Advance Report)
Rape Victimization in 26 Cities
Expenditure and Employment Data for the Criminal Justice System: 1979
State Court Statistics: The State of the Art
Sourcebook of Criminal Justice Statistics 1982

Contact: Statistical Division, Bureau of Justice Statistics, Department of Justice, 633 Indiana Ave. N.W., Washington, DC 20531/202-724-7774.

Justice Toll-Free Information Numbers

General Information   800-851-3420

Justice Statistics   800-732-3277

Juvenile Justice   800-638-8736

Written inquiries should also include a daytime phone number. Contact: NCJRS, P. O. Box 6000, Rockville, MD 20850.

Juvenile Justice and Delinquency
This office provides a focal point for programs and policies relating to juvenile delinquency and juvenile justice. It disseminates information on delinquency and juvenile justice programs, gives formula grants to states and Special Emphasis discretionary funds, and provides technical assistance to governmental and nongovernmental agencies. Contact: Office of Juvenile Justice, 633 Indiana Ave. N.W., Room 442, Washington, DC 20531/ 202-724-7751.

Juvenile Justice, National Institute for
This office conducts research on juvenile justice programs, and develops and evaluates programs, including training programs. The institute collects, synthesizes, and disseminates information. Its publications include:

Youth Crime and Delinquency in America—which includes information on the nature and extent of delinquency, justice system operations, and programs.
Foster Parenting—information on selecting and training foster parents; includes an audiovisual list and a bibliography.
Runaway Youth Program Directory—lists selected resources including hotlines, bibliographies, government agencies, general information, and state contracts.

Contact: National Institute for Juvenile Justice and Delinquency Prevention, Office of Juvenile Justice and Delinquency Prevention, Law Enforcement Assistance Administration, Department of Justice, 633 Indiana Ave. N.W., Room 304, Washington, DC 20531/202-724-5893.

Land Acquisition

This office initiates and institutes condemnation proceedings in the District Courts for the acquisition of lands necessary for public use. The issues for decision in a condemnation case are usually either the amount of compensation to be paid by the United States for the property acquired or the authority of the United States to condemn the property and the right to possession. Some client agencies and projects for which this Section acquires land for condemnation are the Army Corps of Engineers, National Park Service, Forest Service, Department of Energy, Federal Aviation Administration, Washington Metro Subway System, General Services Administration, Fish and Wildlife Service, and others. Contact: Land Acquisition Section, Land and Natural Resources Division, Department of Justice, 521 12th St. N.W., Room 315, Washington, DC 20530/202-724-6883.

Land and Natural Resource Case Appeals

This office handles appeals from district court decisions. It prepares briefs on the merits, petitions for certiorari, briefs in opposition, jurisdictional statements, miscellaneous cases involving the Supreme Court. It also prepares amicus curiae briefs in state and federal courts of appeals. Contact: Appellate Section, Land and Natural Resources Division, Department of Justice, 10th St. and Constitution Ave. N.W., Room 2339, Washington, DC 20530/202-633-2748.

Land and Natural Resource Litigation

This office handles cases related to environmental land, natural resources and water law not specifically assigned to other sections. Examples include the protection of Alaska National Interest Land; the development of energy resources and its relation to protection of public values in the environment; and cases involving the National Environmental Policy Act. Contact: General Litigation Section, Land and Natural Resources Division, Department of Justice, 10th St. and Constitution Ave. N.W., Room 2133, Washington, DC 20530/202-633-2704.

Land Appraisal

This office assists in matters relating to establishing the fair market value of real property that is secured by the federal government for public use. Contact: Appraisal Section, Land and Natural Resources Division, Department of Justice, 521 12th St. N.W., Room 336, Washington, DC 20530/202-724-6686.

Law Enforcement—FBI Crime Laboratory Support

FBI Laboratory facilities are made available to duly constituted municipal, county, state, and federal law enforcement agencies in the United States and its territorial possessions. Submitted evidence is examined and the FBI Laboratory also furnishes the experts necessary to testify in connection with the results of these examinations. These examinations are made with the understanding that the evidence is connected with an official investigation of a criminal matter (for federal agencies both criminal and civil matters) and that the laboratory report will be used only for official purposes related to the investigation or a subsequent prosecution. The FBI Laboratory will not accept cases from other crime laboratories which have the capability of conducting the requested examinations. Contact: Director, Federal Bureau of Investigation, Department of Justice, Washington, DC 20535/202-324-3000.

Law Enforcement Assistance—FBI Field Police Training

Courses available from FBI instructors range from basic recruit training to specialized instruction in such areas as fingerprinting, legal topics, police-community relations, hostage negotiation, white collar crime, organized crime, computer fraud, management techniques, etc. FBI training assistance is available in complete programs of instructions or as supplemental courses to already existing local policy training sessions. Contact: Director, Federal Bureau of Investigation, Department of Justice, Washington, DC 20535/202-324-5718.

Law Enforcement Assistance—FBI Fingerprint Identification

This service provides criminal identification by means of fingerprints, determination of the number of previously reported arrests and convictions; fingerprint identification of victims of major disasters; and processing of submitted evidence for latent fingerprint impressions. Information must be used for official purposes only and is not furnished for public dissemination. Contact: Assistant Director, Identification Division, Federal Bureau of Investigation, Department of Justice, Washington, DC 20537/202-324-5401.

Law Enforcement Assistance—Uniform Crime Reports

The FBI collects, analyzes, and publishes certain crime statistics which it receives on a regular and voluntary basis from law enforcement agencies nationwide. These data are published annually in the publication, *Crime in the United States Uniform Crime Reports,* which is supplemented with semi-annual releases. The annual publication provides information on 1) crime trends; 2) offenses known to police; 3) age, sex, and race of persons arrested; 4) police employee information. The information is intended to assist heads of law enforcement agencies in administration and operation of their departments and to be available to judges, penologists, sociologists, legislators, students, and others interested in crime and its social aspects. Contact: Director, Federal Bureau of Investigation, Department of Justice, Washington, DC 20535/202-324-3000.

Law Enforcement Films

The following publication identifies for $25.00 each films on law enforcement subjects:

Criminal Justice Audiovisual Materials Directory—a source directory of materials for education, training, and orientation in the field of criminal justices; covers courts, police techniques and training, prevention, prisons and rehabilitation/corrections and public education.($17.50) 1978 ed.

These films and videotape recordings can be borrowed for education and information purposes. Contact: National Criminal Justice Research Service, 1600 Research Blvd., Rockville, MD 20850/301-251-5500.

Law Enforcement Research Publications

This office is responsible for the publication and distribution of Institute research and evaluation findings and programs. It also oversees the operations of the National Criminal Justice Reference Services. It maintains the NIJ Library, and helps law enforcement agencies to make informed decisions on purchasing equipment. The Law Enforcement Standards Laboratories do research and development on performance standards for equipment. Contact: Reference and Dissemination Division, Office of Development, Testing and Dissemination, National Institute of Justice, Department of Justice, 633 Indiana Ave. N.W., Room 810, Washington, DC 20531/202-272-6001.

Legal Opinions

Since 1977 the legal opinions of the Department of Justice are published by the Office of Legal Counsel and are made available through the Superintendent of Documents, Government Printing Office, Washington, DC 20402/202-783-3238. Contact: Office of Legal Counsel, Department of Justice, 10th St. and Constitution Ave. N.W., Room 5214, Washington, DC 20530/202-633-2041.

Missing and Exploited Children—National Center

The center has been established to initiate a nationwide effort to control the epidemic of missing and exploited children and to provide direct assistance in handling cases of sexual exploitation, child pornography, and child prostitution. The Center is a nonprofit corporation chartered for the purpose of operating a national resource and technical center to deal with child abduction and exploitation issues. A national clearinghouse of information about the problem of missing and

exploited children is offered by the Center. Through the Center, information is collected, compiled, exchanged, and disseminated. Anyone seeking information or wishing to contribute information about the problem should write to the following address: National Center for Missing and Exploited Children, 1835 K Street, N.W., Suite 700, Washington, DC 20006/202-634-9821.

Missing and Exploited Children Publications

The National Center for Missing and Exploited Children has these publications available for free.

Directory of Support Services and Resources for Missing and Exploited Children—a descriptive listing of nonprofit or public support groups throughout the country dedicated to assisting missing and exploited children and their parents.
Parental Kidnapping Handbook—a handbook to assist the parent of a child who has been taken by a noncustodial spouse.
Summary of Selected State Legislation—a guide to the most effective state child-protection laws in the country.
Education and Prevention Guidelines—safety and precaution tips for preventing child abductions and exploitation.

Contact: National Center for Missing and Exploited Children, 1835 K Street N.W., Suite 700, Washington, DC 20006/202-634-9821.

Missing and Exploited Children Toll-Free Hotline

The Center maintains a toll-free number for the use of individuals who believe they have information that could lead to the location and recovery of a missing child. Because these calls literally can be a matter of life or death, the Hotline number should be used by those individuals who have this critical information. If you know the location of a missing child, please call this number: **800-843-5678.**

Missing Persons

The Federal Bureau of Investigation will not look for a missing person but it will post a stop notice in the files of the Identification Division at the request of relatives or law enforcement agencies and will notify the inquirer of any information received regarding the missing person's whereabouts. Contact: Identification Division, FBI, Department of Justice, 9th St. and Pennsylvania Ave. N.W., Room 11255, Washington, DC 20535/202-324-5401.

Narcotics and Dangerous Drugs

This office provides litigation and litigation support for the prosecution and conviction of high-level offenders and members of criminal organizations involved in the manufacture, shipment or distribution of illicit narcotics and other dangerous drugs. It is involved in all facets of drug enforcement policies, including negotiating with foreign governments, prosecuting foreign nationals involved with illicit drug traffic, evaluating narcotic-related legislation, and providing studies for the government on the subject, etc. Contact: Narcotics and Dangerous Drug Section, Criminal Division, Department of Justice, 315 9th St. N.W., Room 901, Washington, DC 20530/202-724-7045.

National Crime Information Center
This Center is a computerized information system established by the FBI as a service to all criminal justice agencies—local, state and federal. Documented information is available on missing persons, serialized stolen property, wanted persons for whom an arrest is outstanding and criminal histories on individuals arrested and fingerprinted for serious or significant offenses. Contact: National Crime Information Center, Technical Services Division, Federal Bureau of Investigation, Department of Justice, 9th St. and Pennsylvania Ave. N.W., Room 7230, Washington, DC 20535/202-324-2606.

National Institute of Justice
The institute supports research on topics that include: violent crime, community crime prevention, career criminals, sentencing, rehabilitation, deterrence, utilization and deployment of police resources, correlates of crime and the determinants of criminal behavior, pretrial process—consistency, fairness and delay reduction—and performance standards and measures. A Visiting Fellowship Program is open to senior-level criminal justice professionals and researchers. Contact: National Institute of Justice, Office of Justice Programs, Department of Justice, 633 Indiana Ave. N.W., Washington, DC 20531/202-724-2942.

National Institute of Justice Library
The Library provides reference services on police, courts, corrections, juvenile justice, community crime prevention, and anything else that relates to the criminal justice field. Contact: National Institute of Justice Library, National Institute of Criminal Justice, Department of Justice, 633 Indiana Ave. N.W., Washington, DC 20531/202-724-5884.

National Partnership to Fight Drug and Alcohol Abuse
The Office of Juvenile Justice and Delinquency Prevention of the Department of Justice has instituted a National Partnership to fight drug and alcohol abuse, particularly among young people. The National Partnership, consisting of members of the media, citizens' groups, businesses, and professionals in the field of drug and alcohol abuse and prevention, will work to coordinate their efforts against substance abuse. Participants in the National Partnership include representatives of all

segments of our society that are particularly concerned about substance abuse. The participants divide into four main groups. The groups are: The Media Group, The Citizen Group, The Business Group, and The Professional Group. The principal objectives of the National Partnership are twofold. First, it will act as a network and information source—a clearinghouse— directing anyone interested in contributing to the attack on the problem to others working in the field and to campaigns that have proven successful on a local, regional, or national basis. The Partnership's second objective is to plan a National Strategy against substance abuse. The National Strategy will be a reference for anyone involved in the reduction of substance abuse. It will be used to coordinate the efforts of all members. Contact: National Partnership, Office of Juvenile Justice and Delinquincy Prevention, Department of Justice, Washington, DC 20530/202-724-5911.

Nazi War Criminals
The Office of Special Investigations detects, identifies, and takes appropriate administrative action leading to denaturalization and/or deportation of Nazi war criminals. It provides historic research, investigations and proceedings before both administrative bodies and United States courts. Contact: Office of Special Investigations, Criminal Division, Department of Justice, Suite 195 1377 K St. NW, Washington, DC 20005/202-633-2502.

New Car Information Disclosure
The Department of Justice enforces jurisdiction over the federal law requiring the disclosure of new automobile information. The following information must be included on the windshield or side window of the vehicle: make, model, identification number, assembly point, name and location of dealer to whom the vehicle was delivered, method of transportation, total suggested retail price for accessories and transportation charges. Contact: Office of Consumer Litigation, Civil Division, Department of Justice, Washington, DC 20530, or U.S. Attorney's Office in each major metropolitan area. Automobile purchasers who suspect tampering with odometers should contact this office or telephone 202-724-6786.

Organized Crime and Racketeering
This office develops and coordinates nationwide enforcement programs to suppress the illicit activities of organized criminal groups, including: narcotics, loan sharking, vice and the illegal infiltration of legitimate businesses, labor unions, and the political process. Attorneys in this section are assigned to Organized Crime Strike Forces operating in major cities. Contact: Organized Crime and Racketeering Section, Criminal Division, Department of Justice, 10th St. and Constitution Ave.

N.W., Room 2515, Washington, DC 20530/202-633-3516.

Pardon Attorney

This office receives and reviews all petitions for Executive Clemency; initiates the necessary investigations and prepares the recommendation of the Attorney General to the President in connection with the consideration of all forms of Executive Clemency, including pardon, commutation, reduction of sentence, remission of fine and reprieve. Contact: Office of the Pardon Attorney, Department of Justice, 5550 Friendship Blvd., Suite 490, Chevy Chase, MD 20815/301-492-5910.

Parole Commission

The Parole Commission is an independent agency in the Department of Justice. Its primary function is to administer a parole system for federal prisoners and develop federal parole policy. The Commission is authorized to: 1) grant or deny parole to any eligible federal prisoner; 2) impose reasonable conditions on the release of any prisoner from custody or discretionary parole or mandatory release by operation of "good-time" laws; 3) revoke parole or mandatory release; and 4) discharge offenders from supervision and terminate the sentence prior to the expiration of the supervision period. Contact: United States Parole Commission, Department of Justice, Park Place, 1 North Park Building, 5550 Friendship Blvd., Chevy Chase, MD 20005/301-492-5990.

Patent and Copyright Policy

Advice is supplied to the Department of Justice and other agencies on government patent policy. Work is also done on the improper uses of copyrights and patents as they effect market competition and marketing power. Contact: Intellectual Property Section, Antitrust Division, Department of Justice, 521 12th St. N.W., Room 704, Washington, DC 20530/202-724-7966.

Pollution Control

This office supervises the defense of civil cases involving the Environmental Protection Agency, Corps of Engineers and other federal agencies. The case load includes civil enforcement actions under the Clean Water Act. The rest is composed of litigation in which regulations, permits, or other determinations by the Environmental Protection Agency and other agencies have been challenged by industry or environmental organization. Contact: Environmental Section, Land and Natural Resources Division, Department of Justice, 12th and Pennsylvania Ave. N.W., Room 4441, Washington, DC 20530/202-633-2219.

Premerger Notification

The Hart-Scott-Rodino Antitrust Improvements Act—Premerger Notification Program requires large enterprises merging or entering into acquisition transactions to notify both the Antitrust Division and the Federal Trade Commission. Contact: Premerger Notification Unit, Operations, Antitrust Division, Department of Justice, 10th St. and Constitution Ave. N.W., Room 3218, Washington, DC 20530/202-633-2558.

Prisons Information

General information is available on prisons including statistics such as percentage of population confined to institutions by offense, and history of federal prisons. Free brochures include: *Federal Prison System Education for Tomorrow* which details the education programs in the Federal Bureau of Prisons. Contact: Public Information, Bureau of Prisons, Department of Justice, 320 1st St. N.W., Room 554, Washington, DC 20534/202-724-3198.

Prisons Library

A free publication, *Correctional Bookshelf,* is a bibliography of some of the books and periodicals in the library and covers such areas as: administration and organization, programs for offenders, community corrections, jails, the prison social system, institutions for female offenders, and law and history. Reference and research services are also available. Contact: Bureau of Prisons Library, Bureau of Prisons, Department of Justice, 117 D St. N.W., Washington, DC 20534/202-724-3029.

Privacy and Information Appeals

This office adjudicates administrative appeals from initial denials from high level offices of data requested under the Freedom of Information and Privacy Acts. It also processes initial requests for records from the attorney general's office, deputy attorney general, and other high level office. Contact: Office of Privacy and Information Appeals, Department of Justice, 550 11th St. N.W., Room 933, Washington, DC 20530/202-724-7400.

Public Safety Officers' Benefits

The Public Safety Officers' Benefits Act pays $50,000 in death benefits to the eligible survivors of a public safety officer who died as the direct result of a personal injury sustained in the line of duty. Contact: Public Safety Officers' Benefits Act, Law Enforcement Assistance Administration, Department of Justice, 633 Indiana Ave. N.W., Room 1042, Washington, DC 20531/202-724-7623.

Race Relations

A special office helps people settle their race-related differences voluntarily rather than in the courts or the streets. Agency professionals enter troubled communities with no investigative power or authority to dispense funds and try to mediate or arrange a voluntary settlement. For instance, they have: mediated a dispute over Chinook salmon fishing; conciliated a Klan/Southern Christian Leadership Conference (SCLC) clash; helped with general community disputes (public housing, revenue sharing); conciliated problems in education; law enforcement and sentencing disparities. Free publications include:

Guidelines for Effective Human Relations Commissions
School Disruptions: Tips for Educators and Police
School Security: Guidelines for Maintaining Safety in School Desegregation
Viewpoints and Guidelines on Court Appointed Citizens Monitoring Commissions in School Desegregation
Desegregation Without Turmoil—the role of multi-racial community coalitions in preparing for smooth transition
Human Relations: A Guide for Leadership Training in the Public Schools
Police Use of Deadly Force—What Police and the Community Can Do About It

Contact: Community Relations Service, Department of Justice, 5550 Friendship Blvd., Suite 330, Chevy Chase, MD 20815/301-492-5929.

Refugees and Parole

This office supervises the refugee and parole programs of Immigration and Naturalization Service including the processing of applicants for conditional entry. It processes humanitarian parole requests which are granted on an individual basis for aliens outside the U.S. Contact: Office of Refugees and Parole, Immigration and Naturalization Service, Department of Justice, 425 Eye St. N.W., Room 7240, Washington, DC 20536/202-633-2361.

Regulatory Activities

Listed below are those organizations within the Department of Justice which are involved with regulating various activities. With each listing is a description of those industries or situations which are regulated by the office. Regulatory activities generate large amounts of information on the companies and subjects they regulate. Much of the information is available to the public. A regulatory office can also tell you your rights when dealing with a regulated company.

Antitrust Division, Department of Justice, 10th St. and Constitution Ave. N.W., Washington, DC 20530/202-633-2421. Enforces laws which punish violations of restraints on the monopolization of trade.
Public Affairs, Civil Rights Division, Department of Justice, 10th St. and Constitution Ave. N.W., Washington, DC 20530/202-633-2017. Enforces laws which prohibit discrimination on the basis of race, national origin, religion, or in some instances, sex, age, or handicap, in the areas of voting, education, employment, housing, credit, the use of public facilities and accommodations, and in federally assisted and conducted programs.

Public Affairs, Drug Enforcement Division, Department of Justice, 1405 Eye St. N.W., Washington, DC 20537/202-633-1249. Enforces laws which regulate narcotics and dangerous drugs.
Public Information Immigration and Naturalization Service, Department of Justice, 425 Eye St. N.W., Washington, DC 20536/202-633-4330. Regulates aliens.

Sex Discrimination

A special task force has been established to assist federal departments and agencies in their reviews and revisions of sexually discriminatory language and practices. The task force also identifies statutory and regulatory bias and studies several systemic problems that disproportionately affect women. Contact: Office of Coordination and Review, Civil Rights Division, Department of Justice, 10th St. and Constitution Ave. N.W., Room 867-A, Washington, DC 20530/202-724-2222.

Solicitor General

The Solicitor General conducts and supervises government litigation in the Supreme Court of the United States. He or she reviews every case litigated by the federal government that a lower court has decided against the United States, to determine whether to appeal and also decides whether the U.S. should file a brief as "amicus curiae" in any appellate court. Contact: Office of the Solicitor General, Department of Justice, 10th St. and Constitution Ave. N.W., Room 5143, Washington, DC 20530/202-633-2201.

Statistical Publications

A large number of statistical reports are available, including:

Criminal Victimization in the United States
The Cost of Negligence
Intimate Victims
Crime and Seasonality
Criminal Victimization of New York State Residents, 1974–77
Criminal Victimization Surveys in 13 American Cities
Public Attitudes About Crime
Public Opinion About Crime
Local Victim Surveys
Compensating Victims of Violent Crime
Crime Against Persons in Urban, Suburban and Rural Areas
Capital Punishment
Profile of Inmates of Local Jails
Characteristics of the Parole Population
Myths and Realities About Crime

For free single copies or for a more complete listing of publications, contact: National Criminal Justice Reference Service, Box 6000, Rockville, MD 20850/301-251-5500.

Statistics—Justice

A variety of statistical services and publications are available. Contact: Statistical Division, Bureau of Justice Statistics, Department of Justice, 633 Indiana Ave. N.W., Room 1158, Washington, DC 20531/202-724-7774.

Take a Bite Out of Crime

This free pamphlet is full of tips and ideas on how to discourage burglars, disappoint muggers and make life tougher for criminals. Contact: National Criminal Justice Reference Service, Department of Justice, P.O. Box 6000, Rockville, MD 20850/301-251-5500.

Tax Criminal Litigation

The Criminal Section controls and supervises all cases involving criminal violations of the Internal Revenue Code. Its responsibilities include the control and supervision of criminal proceedings and collaboration in trial and appellate courts. Contact: Criminal Section, Tax Division, Department of Justice, 10th St. and Constitution Ave. N.W., Room 4611, Washington, DC 20530/202-633-2973.

Tax Litigation

Among the types of litigation in which the Tax Division represents the federal government are:

1. Criminal prosecutions involving attempts to evade taxes, willful failure to file returns or to pay taxes, filing false returns and other deceptive documents, and making false statements to revenue officials.
2. Refund suits brought by taxpayers to recover taxes alleged to have been erroneously or illegally assessed and collected.
3. Suits brought by the United States to collect unpaid assessments, to foreclose federal tax liens or to determine the priority of such liens, to obtain judgments against delinquent taxpayers, to enforce Internal Revenue Service administrative summonses, and to establish tax claims in bankruptcy, receivership, and probate proceedings.
4. Proceedings involving mandamus, injunctions, and other writs arising in connection with Internal Revenue matters.
5. Suits against Internal Revenue Service employees for damages claimed because of alleged injuries caused in the performance of their official duties.
6. Suits against the Secretary of the Treasury, the Commissioner of Internal Revenue, or similar officials to test the validity of regulations or rulings, including declaratory judgment actions pursuant to Section 7428 of the Internal Revenue Code, challenging initial denial or revocation of an organization's tax-exempt status under Code Section 501 (c) 3.
7. Proceedings against the Tax Division and the Internal Revenue Service for disclosure of information under the Freedom of Information Act or for the alleged improper disclosure of information under the Privacy Act.
8. Intergovernmental immunity suits in which the United States resists attempts to apply a state or local tax to some activity or property of the United States.
9. Suits brought by taxpayers pursuant to Code Section 7429 for a judicial determination as to the reasonableness of the use of jeopardy/termination assessment procedures and the appropriateness of the amount so assessed.
10. Suits brought by individuals to foreclose mortgages or to quiet title to property in which the United States is named as a party defendant because of the existence of a federal tax lien on the property.

Contact: Tax Division, Department of Justice, 10th St. and Constitution Ave. N.W., Room 4143, Washington, DC 20530/202-633-2901.

Tax Settlements Review

The Office of Review Section appraises settlement offers in light of litigating potential and policy considerations. It also conducts legal research on pending or proposed legislation on which the Division has been asked to comment. Examples include legislation to revise aspects of the Internal Revenue Code which deal with bankruptcy, insolvency and discharge of indebtedness, privacy legislation, and proposals to allow awards of attorneys' fees against the Government. Contact: Review Tax Division, Department of Justice, 414 11th St. N.W., Room 5121, Washington, DC 20530/202-724-6567.

Ten Most Wanted Fugitives

The selection is based on several items including the fugitive's past criminal record, the threat posed to the community, the seriousness of the crime for which he/she is sought, and whether nationwide publicity is likely to assist in apprehension. Contact: Office of Public Affairs, Federal Bureau of Investigation, 9th St. and Pennsylvania Ave. N.W., Room 7116, Washington, DC 20535/202-324-5353 or Press. Office ex. 3691.

Torts

This office defends the United States, its officers and agents, against suits seeking money damages for negligent and wrongful acts of government employees while acting within the scope of their employment. It also prosecutes affirmative tort claims on behalf of the United States. The docket includes medical malpractice and aircraft accidents, personal injury radiation litigation, and regulatory torts. It has handled claims arising out of the Swine Flu Immunization Program, Teton Dam disaster, and hazards of asbestos manufacture. Contact: Torts Branch, Civil Division, Department of Justice, 9th St. and Constitution Ave. N.W., Room 3137, Washington, DC 20530/202-633-4015.

U.S. Attorneys, Executive Office

This office provides general executive asistance and supervision to 94 officers of the U.S. Attorneys. The U.S. Attorney is the chief law enforcement representative of the Attorney General, enforcing federal criminal law and handling most of the civil litigation in which the United States is involved. The Attorneys are involved with white collar crime, official corruption, controlled substances (narcotics), organized crime, and criminal and civil litigation. Contact: Executive Office for U.S. Attorneys, Department of Justice, 10th St. and Constitution Ave. N.W., Room 1619, Washington, DC 20530/202-633-2121.

U.S. Attorney's Publications

The following publications are published by the Executive Office for U.S. Attorneys:

U.S. Attorney's Manual—consists of nine titles—General Appeals, Office of Justice Management, Civil, Lands and Natural Resources Division, Tax, Antitrust, Civil Rights and Criminal. Available for $714 for the set from Superintendent of Documents, Government Printing Office, Washington, DC 20402/202-738-3238.
Bulletin—This biweekly goes to all U.S. Attorneys and contains notes of recent cases and other Department of Justice information.

Contact: Executive Office for U.S. Attorneys Manual Staff, Department of Justice, Room 1136 1875 Connccticut Ave., Washington, DC 20530/ 202-673-6348.

U.S. Marshals

The U.S. marshals service supports the federal court system and the enforcement of federal law under the direction of the Attorney General. Its activities include daily execution of court ordered arrest warrants, the movement and custody of federal prisoners; the protection of witnesses to organized crime; the seizing and disposing of property under court orders; the security of federal court facilities, judges, jurors, and other trial participants; the prevention of civil disturbances, and the restoration of order in riot or mob violence situations; the collection or disbursal of federal funds; and other special law enforcement functions at the direction of the Attorney General. A free publication, *United States Marshals Service Then . . . And Now,* is available.

Contact: United States Marshals Service, Department of Justice, 1 Tysons Corner Center, Room 202, McLean, VA 22102/703-285-1131.

U.S. Trustees

The U.S. Trustees are charged with administering bankruptcy cases in their respective regions. There is a trustee for each of 10 regions who has the responsibility for appointing private trustees as well as committees of creditors in order to insulate Bankruptcy Judges from the day-to-day adminis- tration of cases. Contact: Executive Office for United States Trustees, Department of Justice, 320 1st St. N.W., Room 812, Washington, DC 20530/202-724-8391.

Victims (of Crime) Initiative Section

This Section implements the recommendations of the President's Task Force on Victims of Crime. Their projects include grants to the National Organization for Victims Assistance, the National Association of Attorneys General, the American Bar Association, the National Sheriff's Association, the Center for Women Policy Studies, and the National Association of State Directors of Law Enforcement Training. In addition, the Section will develop projects in the mental health area under an Interagency Agreement with the National Institute of Mental Health, develop hospital protocols for services to crime victims, establish a model rape evidence kit and a "business information" package on how employers can assist employee-victims, deliver training to criminal justice personnel such as police and prosecutors through grants, for example, to the National College of District Attorneys. The Section also will be developing a training program for staff of victim services providers. Contact: Victims Initiative Section, Office of Victims of Crime, Department of Justice, Room 1386, 633 Indiana Ave. N.W., Room 1386, Washington, DC 20531/202-272-6500.

Victims Resource Center, National

The staff of the National Victims Resource Center is responsible for the information and clearing-house services to the public on victim assistance and compensation programs, state victims legislation, and published victim services materials. Contact: National Victims Resource Center, Office of Victims of Crime, Department of Justice, Room 1386, 633 Indiana Ave. N.W., Washington, DC 20531/202-272-6500.

Voting Laws

This office enforces voting laws designed to insure that all qualified citizens have the opportunity to register and vote without discrimination on account of race, color, membership in a language minority group, or age. It also enforces the Overseas Citizens Voting Rights Act. Contact: Voting Section, Civil Rights Division, Department of Justice, 320 1st St. N.W., Room 700, Washington, DC 20530/202-724-3095.

White Collar Crime Hotline

Each FBI field office maintains a hotline for reporting white collar crimes. The office in Washington, DC is: Federal Bureau of Investigation, 1900 Half St. S.W., Washington, DC 20235/202-252-7801.

Wildlife and Marine Resources

The Wildlife and Marine Resources Section is responsible for civil and criminal litigation arising under statutes which call for federal management of living resources or which regulate private conduct regarding them. Thus, for example, the section handles prosecution of the legal taking, trade or importation of endangered species and other regulated species. The section is also charged with defending cases where clients' ongoing actions affecting wildlife is challenged by environmental groups, industry or development interests. Contact: Wildlife and Marine Resources Section, Land and Natural Resources Division, Department of Justice, 550 11th St. N.W., Room 639, Washington, DC 20530/202-724-7352.

Department of Labor

200 Constitution Ave. N.W., Washington, DC 20210/202-523-6666

Established: March 4, 1913
Budget: $17,387,523,000
Employees: 15,770

Mission: Foster, promote, and develop the welfare of the wage earners of the United States, to improve their working conditions, and to advance their opportunities for profitable employment; protect workers' pension rights; sponsor job training programs; help workers find jobs; strengthen free collective bargaining; and keep track of changes in employment, prices, and other national economic measurements.

Major Divisions and Offices

Employment Standards Administration

Department of Labor, 200 Constitution Ave. N.W., Room S2321, Washington, DC 20210/202-523-6191.
Budget: $513,286,000
Employees: 4,261
Mission: Administer and direct employment standards programs dealing with: minimum wage and overtime standards; registration of farm labor contractors; determining prevailing wage rates to be paid on government contracts and subcontracts; nondiscrimination and affirmative action for minorities, women, veterans, and handicapped workers on government contracts and subcontracts; and workers' compensation programs for federal and certain private employers and employees.

Office of Labor-Management Standards

Department of Labor, 200 Constitution Ave. N.W., Room S2203, Washington, DC 20210/202-523-6045.
Budget: $24,507,000
Employees: 482
Mission: Administers and implements provisions of the Labor-Management Reporting and Disclosure Act of 1959 (Landrum-Griffin Act) as well as certain protections for civil service employees.

Employment and Training Administration

Department of Labor, 200 Constitution Ave. N.W., Room S2307, Washington, DC 20210/202-523-6050.
Budget: $16,626,569,000
Employees: 2341
Mission: Administers a Federal-State employment security system; funds and oversees programs to provide work experience and training for groups having difficulty entering or returning to the work force; formulates and promotes apprenticeship standards and programs; and conducts continuing programs of research, development, and evaluation.

Bureau of Labor Statistics

Department of Labor, 441 G St. N.W., Room 2421 Washington, DC 20212/202-523-1221.
Budget: $123,743,000
Employees: 2002
Mission: Be the Government's principal factfinding agency in the field of labor economics, particularly with respect to the collection and analysis of data on labor requirements, labor force, employment, unemployment, hours of work, wages and employee compensation, price, living conditions, labor-management relations, productivity and

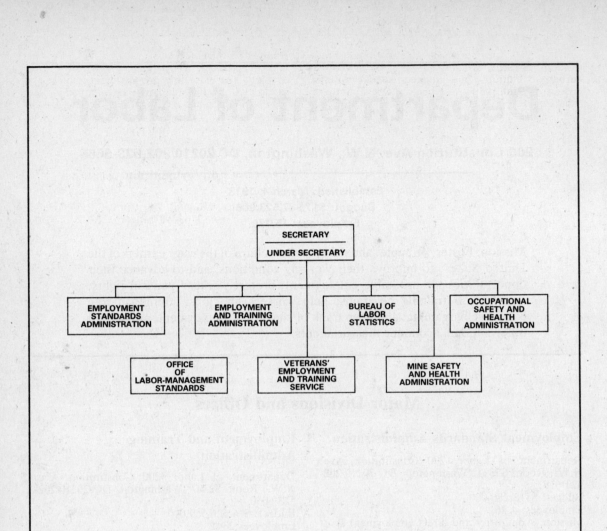

SECRETARY

UNDER SECRETARY

EMPLOYMENT STANDARDS ADMINISTRATION

EMPLOYMENT AND TRAINING ADMINISTRATION

BUREAU OF LABOR STATISTICS

OCCUPATIONAL SAFETY AND HEALTH ADMINISTRATION

OFFICE OF LABOR-MANAGEMENT STANDARDS

VETERANS' EMPLOYMENT AND TRAINING SERVICE

MINE SAFETY AND HEALTH ADMINISTRATION

technological developments, occupational safety and health, structure and growth of the economy, urban conditions and related socio-economic issues, and international aspects of certain of these subjects.

Mine Safety and Health Administration

Department of Labor, 4015 Wilson Blvd., Room 601, Arlington, VA 22203/703-235-1452.
Budget: $152,435,000
Employees: 3,408
Mission: Develop and promulgate mandatory safety and health standards; ensure compliance with such standards; assess civil penalties for violations; investigate accidents; cooperate with and provide assistance to the states in the development of effective state mine safety and health programs; improve and expand training programs in cooperation with the states and the mining industry, and, in coordination with the Department of Health and Human Services, and the Department of the Interior; and contribute to the improvement and expansion of mine safety and health research and development.

Occupational Safety and Health Administration

Department of Labor, 200 Constitution Ave. N.W., Room N3637 Washington, DC 20210/202-523-8151.

Budget: $206,649,000
Employees: 2,354
Mission: Develop and promulgate occupational safety and health standards; develop and issue regulations; conduct investigations and inspections to determine the status of compliance with safety and health standards and regulations; and issue citations and propose penalties for noncompliance with safety and health standards and regulations.

Veterans Employment and Training Service

Department of Labor, 200 Constitution Avenue N.W., Room S1315, Washington, DC 20210/202-523-9116.
Budget: $12,800,000
Employees: 282
Mission: Responsible for seeing that the policies of the Secretary of Labor regarding National Employment and Training Programs for veterans are carried out by the local public employment services and private sector contractors; and also responsible for promulgating policies, procedures, and regulations that provide the maximum employment and training opportunities mandated by legislation to veterans and other eligible persons with priority services given to disabled and Vietnam-era veterans.

Data Experts

Labor Statistical Experts

The following experts are available to answer specific questions concerning their areas of expertise. Call directly or write in care of: Department of Labor, Bureau of Labor Statistics, Washington, DC 20212.

Current Employment Analysis

Assistant Commissioner/Vacant/202-523-1530
Absences from work/John Stensen/202-523-1821
Current employment and unemployment analysis/John Bregger/202-523-1944
Demographic studies/Paul Flaim/202-523-1821 Discouraged workers/Harvey Hamel/202-523-1371
Earnings data from Current Population Survey/Earl Mellor/202-523-1371
Educational attainment and School Enrollment/Anne Young/202-523-1371
Employment and Earnings publications/Gloria Green/202-523-1821
Employment situation—press release/John Bregger/202-523-1944
Family and marital characteristics of labor force/Elizabeth Waldman/202-523-1371
Microdata tapes and analysis/Robert McIntire/202-523-1776
Minorities/Harvey Hamel/202-523-1371

Multiple jobholding/Fran Horvath/202-523-1821
National Commission on Employment and Unemployment Statistics/Harvey Hamel/202-523-1371
Occupational employment and unemployment/Deborah Klein/202-523-1944
Older workers/Philip Rones/202-523-1944
Person-family data/Elizabeth Waldman/202-523-1959
Seasonal adjustment methodology/Robert McIntire/202-523-1776
Students and dropouts/Anne Young/202-523-1959
Veterans/John Stinson/202-523-1959
Women/Elizabeth Waldman/202-523-1371
Work experience/Anne Young/202-523-1371
Work-life estimates/Shirley Smith/202-523-1821
Work schedules (hours of work, shift work, etc.)/John Stensen/202-523-1959

Employment Statistics

Assistant Commissioner/Thomas Piewes/202-523-1695
Earnings—national/Gloria Goings/202-523-1959
Earnings—local area/Raymond Konstant/202-523-1038
Employment and Earnings—periodical/Gloria Goings/202-523-1959
Employment and Wages/Michael Searson/202-523-1339
Employment—local area/Raymond Konstant/202-523-1038
Industry employment statistics/Jerry Storch/202-523-1172

Job vacancy statistics/Brian McDonald/202-523-1949
Labor turnover-press release/Carol Utter/202-523-1146
Local area unemployment statistics/Martin Ziegler/202-523-1919
Occupational classification/Linda Hardy/202-523-1636
Occupational and Administrative Statistics/Brian Mac-Donald/202-523-1949
Thomas Shirk/202-523-1684
Real earnings—press release/Mike Buso/202-523-1821
Seasonal adjustment methodology—industry employment/Carol Utter/202-523-1446
State and area demographic data/Fred Cronkhite/202-523-1720
State and area unemployment—press release/George Stanas/202-523-1227
Unemployment insurance/Sharon Brown/202-523-1809

Economic Growth and Employment Projections

Associate Commissioner/Ronald Kutscher/202-272-5381
Economic growth—projections/Charles Bowman/202-272-5383
Employment requirements/Richard Oliver/202-272-5278
Energy-related questions/Ronald Kutscher/202-272-5381
Industry occupational employment matrix/George Silvestri/202-272-5279
Occupational outlook/Neal Rosenthal/202-272-5382
Occupational outlook handbook/Michael Pilot/202-272-5282
Occupational projections—National/Michael Pilot/202-272-5282

Occupational Safety and Health Statistics

Acting Assistant Commissioner/William Elsenberg/202-272-3467
Annual survey of occupational injuries and illnesses/William Mead/202-272-3467
Characteristics of injuries and illnesses/Lyle Schauer/202-272-3463
Health studies and special projects/Harvey Hilaski/202-272-3467
Industry estimates and incidence rates/John Inzana/202-272-3470
Recordkeeping and reporting in Section 18(b) States/Lee Cooper/202-272-3459
Recordkeeping interpretations/Stephen Newell/202-272-3470
Recordkeeping requirements under the Occupational Safety and Health Act/Lyle Schauer/202-272-3463
Revision of recordkeeping and recording system/Lyle Schauer/202-272-3463
State participation and state reports/Herbert Schaffer/202-272-3463
Supplementary data system/Lyle Schauer/202-272-3463
Workers' compensation data/Lyle Schauer/202-272-3463

Prices and Living Conditions

Associate Commissioner/Kenneth Dalton/202-272-5038
Consumer expenditure surveys, 1960–61 and all public use tapes/Ray Gieseman/202-272-5156
Consumer expenditure survey data, 1972–73/Stephanie Shipp/202-272-5156
Consumer price indexes/Patrick Jackman/202-272-5160

Estimated retail food prices—monthly/Floyd Rabil/202-272-5173
Export and import price indexes—U.S./William Altum/202-272-5020
Family budgets/John Rogers/202-272-5060
PRODUCER PRICE INDEXES
Current analysis/Craig Howell/202-272-5113
Technical information/William Thomas/202-272-5113
Energy and chemicals/Kenneth Lavish/202-272-5210
Nonelectric machinery/Ed Kazanowski/202-272-5115
Electric machinery and transportation equipment/James Sinclair/202-272-5052
Metals/Edward Kazanowski/202-272-5204
Nonmetallic minerals and paper/Kenneth Lavish/202-272-5210
Textiles and leather/Maureen Zoller/202-272-5127
Revision/Thomas Tibbetts/202-272-5110 Methodology/Elliott Rosenberg/202-272-5118
International price indexes/Edward Murphy/202-272-5025
Living conditions studies and consumer expenditure surveys/Eva Jacobs/202-272-5156
Price and index number studies/Joan Greenlees/202-272-5096
Retail prices and indexes of fuels and utilities—monthly report/S. Gibson/202-272-5177
Retail prices—gasoline only/Betty Rice/202-272-5080
Service industry price indexes/Frank Prunella/202-272-5130
Transportation price indexes/John Royse/202-272-5131
Wood/David Wallenstein/202-272-5127

Productivity and Technology

Associate Commissioner/Jerome A. Mark/202-523-9294
Productivity research/William H. Waldouf/202-523-6010
Productivity and costs—press release/Lawrence J. Fulco/202-523-9261
Productivity trends in selected industries and federal government/Charles W. Ardolini/202-523-9244
Foreign countries—productivity, labor costs, industrial disputes, and other economic indicators/Arthur Neef/202-523-9291
Foreign countries—labor force and unemployment/Constance Sorrentino/202-523-9301
Cost-of-living abroad, prices, earnings and compensation in foreign countries/Patricia Capdevielle/202-523-9301
Technological trends in major industries/Richard W. Riche/202-523-9219
Labor and material requirements for different types of construction/Robert L. Ball/202-523-9321

Wages and Industrial Relations

Associate Commissioner/George Stelluto/202-523-1382
Agreements-collective bargaining-public file/Jane Green/202-523-1597
Area wage surveys/John Buckley/202-523-1763
Collective bargaining settlements/Douglas LeRoy/202-523-1921
Compensation expenditures and payroll hours (no longer current)/Patricia Smith/202-523-1313
Current wage developments/George Ruben/202-523-1320

Employee benefit plans—health, insurance, pensions, etc./John Thompson/202-523-9241

Employment cost index/Albert Schwerk/202-523-1220

Federal employees—average salary/William Smith/202-523-1570

Hourly earnings index/Beth Levin/202-523-1165

Industry wage surveys/Sandra King/202-523-1309

Professional, administrative, technical, and clerical pay/ William Smith/202-523-1570

Service contracts surveys/Phil Doyle/202-523-1763

Publications

Bureau of Labor Statistics (BLS) *Handbook of Methods*/ Constance DiCesare/202-523-1554

Current Wage Developments/Rosslyn Springstien/202-523-1139

Olivia Amiss/202-523-1662

Employment and Earnings/Rosalie Epstein/202-523-1554

Handbook of Labor Statistics/Rosslyn Springstien/202-523-1554

Major Programs/Rosslyn Springstien/202-523-1554

Monthly Labor Review/Robert Fisher/202-523-1139

Occupational Outlook Quarterly/Melvin Fountain/202-272-5298

Major Sources of Information

Apprenticeship Programs

Apprenticeship is a combination of on-the-job training and related technical instruction in which workers learn the practical and theoretical aspects of the work required for a skilled occupation, craft, or trade. Programs are conducted by employers, often jointly with labor and management. There are apprenticeship programs available for personnel in the Armed Forces, for veterans, and for female inmates in correction institutions. Contact: Bureau of Apprenticeship and Training, Employment and Training Administration, Department of Labor, 601 D St. N.W., Room 6308, Washington, DC 20213/202-376-2570.

Black Lung Benefits

Monthly payments and medical treatment benefits are available to coal miners totally disabled from pneumoconiosis (black lung) arising from their employment in or around coal mines. Payments are also available to surviving dependents. Contact: Division of Coal Mine Workers' Compensation, Employment Standards Adminstration, Department of Labor, 200 Constitution Ave. N.W., Room C3525, Washington, DC 20210/202-523-6795.

Bureau of Labor Statistics Bulletins Service

These major surveys and research studies include 100 area and industry wage studies each year, and 50 miscellaneous volumes dealing with prices, productivity, economic growth, occupational safety and other subjects including the following:

Bargaining Calendar—a yearly schedule of information on anticipated contract adjustments between labor and management negotiations. Major situations by company and union are identified in which contracts will terminate, deferred wage increases will become due, changes in the Consumer Price Indexes will be reviewed, and contracts will be reopened ($2.00).

Rent or Buy? Evaluating Alternatives in the Shelter Market—describes a method of analyzing the financial costs and benefits of owning a home compared to renting ($3.50).

Directory of National Unions and Employee Associations—a biannual factbook about labor organizations, provides membership figures, names of officers, and other information ($6.00).

Occupational Projections and Training Data—presents both general and detailed information on the relationship between occupational requirements and training needs for over 250 occupations; includes occupational projections to 1985.

Occupational Injuries and Illnesses in the United States by Industry—a detailed annual report with charts and tables showing the job-related injury and illness experience of employees in a wide range of industries ($2.25).

Perspective on U.S. Working Women: A Databook—Sixty-one tables provide a wide array of information on the characteristics of working women in the United States ($5.50).

Available from: Superintendent of Documents, Government Printing Office, Washington, DC 20402/202-783-3238.

Bureau of Labor Statistics—Just Published

This free monthly publication identifies new Bureau of Labor Statistics publications, data tapes and microfiches. Contact: Office of Publications, Bureau of Labor Statistics, Department of Labor, 441 G ST. N.W., Room 2421, Washington, DC 20212/202-523-1239.

Bureau of Labor Statistics News Releases

A free monthly calendar shows dates of future press releases covering such subjects as labor union and employee association membership, urban family budgets and comparative indexes for selected urban areas, white collar salaries, work stoppages, major collective bargaining settlements, employment cost index, productivity and costs, employment situation, state and metropolitan area unemployment, and earnings of workers and their families. Contact: Division of Information Services, Bureau of Labor Statistics, Department of Labor, 441 G St. N.W., Room 2421, Washington, DC 20212/202-523-1239.

Carcinogen Identification

A list is maintained of chemicals that might be cancer-causing agents. The list is made up of 3 categories: 1) those chemicals which, based on epidemiologic and animal studies, are carcinogenic; 2) those chemicals thought to be carcinogenic based on preliminary studies; and 3) those chemicals that appear suspicious that will be studied. Contact: Office of Standards Review, Directorate of Health Standards Programs, Occupational Safety and Health Administration (OSHA), Department of Labor, 200 Constitution Ave. N.W., Room N3718, Washington, DC 20210/202-523-7111.

Child Labor Laws

Certain provisions of the Fair Labor Standards Act apply to minors employed in nonagricultural occupations. Violators of the child labor laws are subject to civil penalties of up to $1,000 for each violation. Contact: Child Labor Branch, Wage and Hour Division, Employment Standards Administration, Department of Labor, 200 Constitution Ave. N.W., Room 3028, Washington, DC 20210/202-523-7640.

Collective Bargaining Agreements

The public has access to copies of some 5,000 agreements in private industry and government, including all those covering 1,000 employees or more, exclusive of railroads and airlines. Contact: Public File of Collective Bargaining Agreements, Union Contracts Section, Industrial Relations Section, Office of Wages and Industrial Relations, Bureau of Labor Statistics, Department of Labor, 441 G St. N.W., Room 1288, Washington, DC 20212/202-523-1597.

Compensation Trends and Current Wage Developments

Data are available showing amount and nature of changes in wages and related benefits. Contact: Division of Occupational Pay and Employee Benefit Levels, Office of Wages and Industrial Relations, Bureau of Labor Statistics, Department of Labor, 441 G. St. N.W., Room 2818, Washington, DC 20212/202-523-1246. For description of the division, call Charles O'Connor, 202-523-1246.

Computerized Data Bases

The following data bases are maintained by the Department of Labor.

Employment and Training Data Base

The Employment and Training Automated Information and Retrieval System (ETAIRS) is a bibliographic data base with citations and abstracts of employment and training (E&T) materials. Most cited literature deals with the training and technical aspect of E&T. Cataloged items include relevant materials from books, journals, government agencies, federal contractors, research and development companies, and all documents housed at the eight E&T clearinghouses across the U.S. Searches, printouts, and many documents are available free of charge. Contact: Department of Labor, Room 6517, 601 D St. N.W., Washington, DC 20213/202-376-3406.

Labor Statistics Data Base

Labor Statistics (LABSTAT) is the Bureau of Labor Statistics (BLS)' overall system for storing, retrieving and manipulating BLS data. The data base contains historic time series data which is generally aggregated at the MACRO level. The system is the repository for data collected from 20 different broad surveys providing data on the labor force, Consumer Price Index, Producer Price Index, Industry Price Index, productivity data for industry and government, international labor comparisons, unemployment data and much more. Information is retrievable by numerous categories.

Each BLS division is responsible for data retrieval in its subject area, so contact the appropriate office for the data you need. Some offices may not be familiar with the term *LABSTAT;* therefore, it's best to simply request the information you need. The office will then try to assist you by consulting its data files, which are actually part of LABSTAT. Depending on the office and your request, you may or may not be charged a fee. Contact: The specific BLS division responsible for the data you are seeking. For referral to the appropriate office, contact: BLS Inquiries and Correspondence, 202-523-1239,; LABSTAT Information Team, 202-523-1975; U.S. Department of Labor, Bureau of Labor Statistics, 44 G St. N.W., Washington, DC 20212.

Labor Statistics—Electronic News Releases

The Bureau of Labor Statistics Electronic News Service (BLS) provides direct dial-in access to subscribers interested in the Bureau's economic indicators. The BLS releases, available on-line as soon as the data is officially released to the public, include: producer price indexes; employment situation; state and metropolitan area employment and unemployment; consumer price index; real earnings; productivity and costs; and the employment cost index.

Cost of the Electronic News Releases, which can be transmitted over telephone lines to computer terminals and other remote-access devices, ranges from $8.00 to $15.00 per release, plus the cost of the telephone call. Contact: Office of Publications, Bureau of Labor Statistics, 441 G St. N.W., Washington, DC 20212/202-523-1913.

Consumer Credit Protection (Federal Wage Garnishment Law)

This law provides restrictions on the amount of an employee's wages or salary which may be garnished, and prohibits employers from discharging employees by reason of garnishment for any one indebtedness. Contact: Administrator, Wage and Hour Division, Employment Standards Administration, 200 Constitution Ave. N.W., Room S3502, Department of Labor, Washington, DC 20210/202-523-8305.

Consumer Expenditure and Family Budget Studies

Income and expenditure studies are available in varying detail for the total U.S. for 1980–81. Selected data are classified by income class, family size and other demographic and economic characteristics of consumer units. Contact: Consumer Expenditure Studies, Living Conditions Studies Division, Bureau of Labor Statistics, Department of Labor, 600 E St. N.W., Room 4216, Washington, DC 20212/202-272-5156.

Consumer Price Index Detailed Report

This monthly publication provides comprehensive data each month on movements in the Consumer Price Indexes by expenditure group, by item and by city. The Consumer Price Index is based on prices of food, clothing, shelter, fuels, transportation fares, charges for doctors, dentists, drugs, and other goods and services that people buy for day-to-day living. Available for $28.00/year from Superintendent of Documents, Government Printing Office, Washington, DC 20402/202-783-3238. For more details on content, contact: Office of Prices and Living Conditions, Bureau of Labor Statistics, Department of Labor, 600 E St. N.W., Washington, DC 20212/202-272-5160.

Consumer Price Index in 24 Hours

This service provides unadjusted and seasonally adjusted data within 24 hours after release via mailgram service. The service is available for $125 per year from: National Technical Information Service, 5285 Port Royal Rd., Springfield, VA 22161/703-487-4630.

Consumer Prices

Monthly indexes are computed for both urban wage earners and urban consumers, including salaried workers, the self-employed, the retired, and the unemployed, and for clerical workers. Both these Computer Price Indexes (CPI) include data for all items and major commodity and service groups and subgroups for the United States and the 5 largest metropolitan areas. Also available are bimonthly indexes for all items. Contact: Consumer Price and Price Indexes Division, Office of Prices and Living Conditions, Bureau of Labor Statistics, Department of Labor, 600 E St. N.W., Room 3216, Washington, DC 20212/202-272-5160.

Continuing Education for Women

Information is available on programs which allow women to study part-time in school or at home in order to get formal educational qualifications. A free publication, *How to Get Credit for What You Know: Alternative Routes to Educational Credit*, list organizations which offer information on adult education programs and opportunities. Contact: Women's Bureau, Department of Labor, 200 Constitution Ave. N.W., Room S3005, Washington, DC 20210/202-523-6668.

Cost of Living Overseas

U.S. Department of State Indexes of Living Costs Abroad and Quarter Allowances: A Technical Description is a free quarterly publication which provides technical descriptions of the methods of compiling the indexes of living costs abroad, post allowances based on these indexes, and quarter allowances and their use in the government overseas allowance program. Contact: Office of Productivity and Technology, Bureau of Labor Statistics, Department of Labor, 200 Constitution Ave. N.W., Room S4325, Washington, DC 20212/202-523-9219.

Current Employment Analysis

Detailed analyses are conducted on data from the Current Population Survey from the Bureau of the Census showing employment, unemployment and the number of persons not in the labor force. Studies include: characteristics of special groups in the labor force, employment status of noninstitutional population 16 years and over; hours of work, annual average employment levels for detailed occupational and industry groups; and employed persons by major occupational and industry groups. Contact: Office of Employment Analysis, Division of Employment and Unemployment, Bureau of Labor Statistics, Department of Labor, 441 G St. N.W., Room 2486, Washington, DC 20212/202-523-1944.

Current Wage Development

This monthly publication reports on collective bargaining settlements, wage and benefit data, and compensation and wage trends. Single copies cost $4 or annual subscription is $23 from: Superintendent of Documents, Government Printing Office, Washington, DC 20402/202-783-3238. For detailed information on content, contact: Office of Wages and Industrial Relations, Bureau of Labor Statistics, Department of Labor, 441 G St. N.W., Room 2132, Washington, DC 20212/202-523-9241.

Dictionary of Occupational Titles (DOT)

This publication contains 12,099 definitions of jobs in the American economy which represent about 20,000 job titles. It offers a system to classify employees and job applicants according to the work they have done and to match them with available jobs. Available for $23 and $4.50 for the 1982 supplement from Superintendent of Documents, Government Printing Office, Washington,

DC 20402/202-783-3238. For more detailed information on content, contact: Division of Occupational Analysis, Employment Service, Employment and Training Administration, Department of Labor, Washington, DC 20213/202-376-6292

Dictionary of Occupational Titles—Computer Tape
Dictionary of Occupational Titles (DOT) data tape contains codes for DOT characteristics; aptitudes; interests; temperaments; general educational development; specific vocational preparation; physical demands and environmental conditions; Standard Occupational Classification (SOC); and Guide for Occupational Exploration (GOE). This tape may be purchased for $140.00 from: National Technical Information Service (NTIS), U.S. Department of Commerce, 5285 Port Royal Road, Springfield, VA 22161/703-487-4650.

Direct Payments
The programs described below are those which provide financial assistance directly to individuals, private firms and other private institutions to encourage or subsidize a particular activity.

Coal Mine Workers' Compensation (Black Lung)
Objectives: To provide benefits to coal miners who have become totally disabled due to coal workers' pneumoconiosis (CWP), and to widows and other surviving dependents of miners who have died of this disease, or who were totally disabled from the disease at the time of death.
Eligibility: The miner must have worked in the nation's coal mines and become "totally disabled" (as defined in the Act) from CWP. The applicant may be able to work in areas other than coal mines and still be eligible for benefits. Widows and other surviving dependents of coal miners totally disabled from or whose death resulted from CWP are also eligible for benefits. Applicants can reside anywhere in the world at the time they apply.
Range of Financial Assistance: Up to $631.10 monthly.
Contact: Division of Coal Mine Workers' Compensation, Office of Workers' Compensation Programs, Employment Standards Administration, Department of Labor, Washington, DC 20210/202-523-6692.

Longshoremen and Harbor Workers' Compensation
Objectives: To provide compensation for disability or death resulting from injury, including occupational disease, to eligible private employees.
Eligibility: Longshoreworkers, harbor workers, and certain other employees engaged in maritime employment on navigable waters of the United States and the adjoining pier and dock areas, employees engaged in activities on the Outer Continental Shelf, employees of nonappropriated fund instrumentalities, employees of private employers engaged in work outside of the United States under contracts with the United States Government, and others as specified, including survivors of the above. Employees of private concerns in the District of Columbia and their survivors are eligible for benefits under extension of the Act. Puerto Rico and the Virgin Islands are not covered by the Longshoremen's and Harbor Workers' Compensation Act.
Range of Financial Assistance: Not specified.
Contact: Office of Workers' Compensation Programs, Division of Longshore and Harbor Workers' Compensation, Department of Labor, Washington, DC 20210/202-523-8721.

Trade Adjustment Assistance—Workers
Objectives: To provide adjustment assistance to workers adversely affected by increase of imports of articles like or directly competitive with articles produced by such workers' firm.
Eligibility: A significant number or proportion of workers in such workers' firm or a subdivision of the firm have become or have been threatened to become totally or partially separated; sales or production, or both, of such firm has decreased absolutely; and increases of imports like or directly competitive with articles produced by the firm have contributed importantly to such total or partial separation, or threat thereof, and to such decline in sales or production. The petition may be filed with the Secretary of Labor by a group of workers or the group's certified or recognized union or other duly authorized representative. Notice of such filing should be promptly published in the *Federal Register*. Within ten days after publication, the petitioner, or any other person found by the Secretary to have a substantial interest, may request a hearing to present evidence and to be heard. Not later than sixty days after receipt of a petition, the Secretary determines whether the petitioning group meets the requirements and may issue a certification of eligibility to apply for adjustment assistance.
Range of Financial Assistance: Weekly allowance payments are the same as amount of weekly state unemployment benefits. *Contact:* Director, Office of Trade Adjustment Assistance, Employment and Training Administration, Department of Labor, 601 D St. N.W., Room 9120, Washington, DC 20213/202-376-6896.

Unemployment Insurance
Objectives: To administer unemployment insurance for eligible workers through federal and state cooperation; to administer payment of worker adjustment assistance.
Eligibility: State unemployment insurance agencies, including Puerto Rico, the Virgin Islands, and the District of Columbia.
Range of Financial Assistance: $1,200,000 to $200,000,000.

Contact: Director, Unemployment Insurance Service, Employment and Training Administration, Department of Labor, Washington, DC 20210/202-376-7228.

Economic Growth Projections
Information is available showing projections of total gross national product and aggregate components of demand specified by 160 industry groups under alternative assumption for basic economic variables (labor force, unemployment, productivity, etc.) and government policies. Projections are also made of the labor force by age, sex, and race under 3 alternative growth scenarios. Contact: Office of Economic Growth and Employment Projections, Bureau of Labor Statistics, Department of Labor, 601 D St. N.W. 4000, Washington, DC 20212/202-272-5381.

Employee Protection
Special protection has been awarded to certain employees who have been adversely affected by legislation. For example, under the Urban Mass Transportation Act fair and equitable arrangements must be established to protect the interests of affected transit employees. These arrangements might include priority employment rights, continuation of pension and other benefits, preservation of collective bargaining rights, paid training programs, etc. Other programs include: Rail Passenger Service Act, Airline Deregulation act, Redwood Park Expansion Act, Hospital Conservation Act, Social Security Disability Program. Contact: Division of Employee Protections, Bureau of Labor-Management Relations Services, and Cooperative Programs, Department of Labor, 200 Constitution Ave. N.W., Room N5639, Washington, DC 20210/202-523-6495.

Employment and Earnings
This monthly publication provides a comprehensive report of current data on unemployment, employment, hours, earnings, and labor turnover. Available for $39.00 per year from: Superintendent of Documents, Government Printing Office, Washington, DC 20402/202-783-3238. For detailed information on content, contact: Employment Structure and Trends, Bureau of Labor Statistics, Department of Labor, 441 G St. N.W., Room 2089, Washington, DC 20212/202-523-1487.

Employment and Unemployment Statistics Analyses
The Employment and Unemployment Analysis Division of the Bureau of Labor Statistics compiles and analyzes U.S. employment and unemployment statistics. This government office investigates trends in employment fluctuation based on such factors as age, sex, race, marital status and education status, as well as regional and industrial variances. Given its sizeable impact on employ-ment, staff currently are researching the effect of high technology infusion in various industries. An inventory of available statistics are available. Contact: Employment and Unemployment Analysis Division, Bureau of Labor Statistics, U.S. Department of Labor, 441 G St. N.W., Washington, DC 20212/202-523-1944.

Employment and Wage Research
Research programs are conducted on such topics as wages and hours, workers' compensation, equal employment opportunities, and older workers and federal contract compliance. Contact: Evaluation and Research Division, Office of Administrative Management, Employment Standards Administration, Department of Labor, 200 Constitution Ave., N.W., Room C3315, Washington, DC 20210/202-523-8493.

Employment Cost Index
Quarterly data measure the change in straight time hourly earnings for the total private non-farm economy excluding households. Data are available for four broad geographic areas, five major industries, and nine occupational groups for metropolitan and nonmetropolitan areas. Contact: Division of Employment Cost Trends, Office of Wages and Industrial Relations, Bureau of Labor Statistics, Department of Labor, 441 G St. N.W., Room 2838, Washington, DC 20212/202-523-1165.

Employment Policy
This quasi-independent organization studies job training programs and advises the President and Congress on employment policy. A free list of its publications is available. Contact: National Commission for Employment Policy, 1522 K St. N.W., Room 300, Washington, DC/202-724-1550.

Employment Projections
Long-term economic projections which include projections of aggregate labor force, potential demand, and industrial output and employment by industry and occupation are available from: Office of Economic Growth, Bureau of Labor Statistics, Department of Labor, 601 D St. N.W., Room 4400, Washington, DC 20212/202-272-5326.

Employment Research and Development
Research and development programs cover various aspects of labor-related subjects including: education, public employment programs, supported employment, training and apprenticeship, upgrading and job restructuring, welfare recipient programs, worker assessment and orientation, supportive services for workers and trainers, worker attitudes, employer practices, labor force, labor demand and economic and social policies. The publication, *Research and Development Projects,* summarizes funded projects. Contact: Office of Research and Development, Office of Policy,

Development and Research, Employment and Training Administration, Department of Labor, 601 D St. N.W., Room 8024, Washington, DC 20213/202-376-6746.

Employment Service
The Employment Service and affiliated state employment service agencies operate nearly 2500 local offices to serve those seeking employment and those providing it. Local offices in most states are now identified as the Job Service. Services include outreach, interviewing, testing, counseling, and referral. Contact: Employment Service, Employment and Training Administration, Department of Labor, 601 D St. N.W., Room 8100, Washington, DC 20213/202-376-6750.

Employment Standards
The Employment Standards Administration has the authority to correct a wide range of unfair employment practices. It enforces wage laws and regulations, setting employment standards providing workers' compensation to those injured on their jobs, and requiring federal contractors and subcontactors to provide equal employment opportunity. Contact: Office of Information and Consumer Affairs, Employment Standards Administration, Department of Labor, 200 Constitution Ave. N.W., Room C4331, Washington, DC 20210/202-523-8743.

Employment Structures and Trends
Detailed data are available on employment, wages, hours, earnings; monthly estimates of states and local area unemployment; occupational employment for most industries; and employment in major nonagricultural industries. Contact: Office of Employment and Unemployment Statistics, Bureau of Labor Statistics, Department of Labor, 441 G St. N.W., Room 2919, Washington, DC 20212/202-523-1694.

Exemplary Rehabilitation Certificates
Exemplary rehabilitation certificates are issued by review board to ex-servicepersons separated from the Armed Forces under conditions other than honorable if it is established that such person has been self-rehabilitated. This Certificate provides tangible evidence of rehabilitation, since discharge, to present to an employer. Certificate does not in any way change the nature of original discharge or alter ex-serviceperson's eligibility for veterans benefits. Contact: Assistant to the Director for Field Operations, Veterans Employment and Training Service, Department of Labor, Room S1316, 200 Constitution Ave. N.W., Washington, DC 202-523-9110

Exploring Careers
This career guidebook is designed for youngsters in their early teens and is designed to help teenagers explore careers. It emphasizes the job as it is experienced by workers, the tasks and the tools. It is an excellent guide for youth service organizations to help with counseling, encouraging teenagers to learn job skills and behaviors, and to familiarize themselves with the work environment. Available for $11.00 from: Superintendent of Documents, Government Printing Office, Washington, DC 20402/202-783-3238. For more detailed information on content, contact: Office of Economic Growth and Employment Projections, Bureau of Labor Statistics, Department of Labor, 601 D St. N.W., Room 4000, Washington, DC 20212/202-272-5282.

Export Price Indexes
Quarterly indexes are available for detailed and aggregate product groups covering machinery and transportation equipment, intermediate manufacturers, chemicals, crude materials, and food. Product categories are based on the Standard International Trade Classification System. Indexes also compare price trends for 34 detailed categories of substitutable products exported by both the U.S. and Germany and 26 detailed categories of substitutable products exported by both the U.S. and Japan. Contact: Division of International Prices, Office of Prices and Living Conditions, Bureau of Labor Statistics, Department of Labor, 600 E St. N.W., Room 3302, Washington, DC 20212/202-272-5020.

Fair Labor Standards Act
This act establishes minimum wages, overtime pay, equal pay, recordkeeping and child labor standards affecting more than 50 million full-time and part-time workers. Contact: Office of Information and Consumer Affairs, Employment Standards Administration, Department of Labor, 200 Constitution Ave. N.W., Room C4331, Washington, DC 20210/202-523-8743.

Farm Worker Protection Law
The Migrant and Seasonal Agricultural Protection Act requires farm labor contractors and other users of migrant labor to observe certain rules in the employment of migrant workers and to register with the Department of Labor before they begin contracting. Contact: Branch of Farm Labor, Wage and Hour Division, Employment Standards Administration, Department of Labor, 200 Constitution Ave. N.W., Room S3028, Washington, DC 20210/202-523-7605.

Federal Contract Compliance Program
This program investigates cases that involve groups of people or indicate patterns of employment discrimination by federal contractors. The program also investigates individual or group complaints under the handicapped workers and veterans laws. Contact: Enforcement Coordination Division, Office of Federal Contract Compliance Pro-

grams, Employment Standards Administration, Department of Labor, 200 Constitution Ave. N.W., Room N5718, Washington, DC 20210/202-523-8767

Federal Employees Workers' Compensation

A free publication, *Federal Injury Compensation,* lists 112 Questions and Answers about the Federal Employees' Compensation Act. For the pamphlet and other information regarding benefits to civilian employees of the United States for disability due to personal injury sustained while in the performance of duty or due to employment-related disease or death, contact: Division of Federal Employees' Compensation, Office of Workers' Compensation Programs, Employment Standards Administration, Department of Labor, 200 Constitution Ave. N.W., Room S3229, Washington, DC 20210/202-523-7552.

Fiduciary Standards

This office monitors exemption from Employee Retirement Income Security Act (ERISA) prohibited transactions provisions. Contact: Office of Fiduciary Standards, Pension and Welfare Benefit Programs, Labor Management Services Administration. Department of Labor, 200 Constitution Ave. N.W., Room C4526, Washington, DC 20216/202-523-7461.

Foreign Economic Research

Research is conducted on such topics as: Review of U.S. Competitiveness in World Trade; Demographic and Occupational Characteristics of Workers in Trade-Sensitive Industries; Trade and Employment Effects of Tariff Reductions Agreed to in the Multilateral Trade Negotiations; An Empirical Analysis of the Structure of U.S. Manufacturing Trade 1964–1976; Shortrun Effects of Trade Liberalization; Productive Strategies and Practices of Foreign Multinationals in the U.S.; and Trends in World Trade with Emphasis on the Trade in the Developing Countries. Contact: Foreign Economics Research Staff, Bureau of International Labor Affairs, Department of Labor, 200 Constitution Ave. N.W., Room S5325, Washington, DC 20210/202-523-7610

Foreign Workers

On the basis of the Immigration and Naturalization Act, employers can request, through local employment offices, foreign workers or foreign individuals who fill a certain void in the labor market. Contact: Alien Labor Certification, Labor Certification Division, Employment Service, Employment and Training Administration, Department of Labor, 601 D St. N.W., Room 8118, Washington, DC 20213/202-376-6846

Freedom of Information Act

For information regarding Freedom of Information Act activities, contact: Assistant Secretary for Administration and Management, Department of Labor, 200 Constitution Ave. N.W., Room S2514, Washington, DC 20210/202-523-9086.

Grants

The programs described below are for sums of money which are given by the federal government to initiate and stimulate new or improved activities, or to sustain on-going services.

Disabled Veterans Outreach Program

Objectives: To provide funds to States to provide job and job training opportunities for disabled and other veterans through contacts with employers; promote and develop on-the-job training and apprenticeship and other on-the-job training positions within VA programs; provide outreach to veterans through all community agencies and organizations; provide assistance to community-based groups and organizations and appropriate grantees under other Federal and federally funded employment and training programs; provide outreach assistance to local employment service offices; develop linkages with other agencies to promote maximum employment opportunites for veterans; promote entry-level and career job opportunities for veterans; and to provide job placement, counseling, testing, job referral to eligible veterans, especially disabled veterans of the Vietnam-era.

Eligibility: State Employment Security Agencies designated under Section 4 of the Wagner Peyser Act.

Range of Financial Assistance: $294,000 to $11.9 million.

Contact: Veterans' Employment and Training Service, Office of the Assistant Secretary for Veterans' Employment and Training, Department of Labor, Room S-1316, 200 Constitution Ave. N.W., Washington, DC 20210/202-523-9110.

Employment and Training Assistance—Dislocated Workers

Objectives: To assist dislocated workers obtain unsubsidized employment through training and related employment services using a decentralized system of State and local programs.

Eligibility: States.

Range of Financial Assistance: Not specified.

Contact: Employment and Training Administration, Department of Labor, 601 D St. N.W., Washington, DC 20213/202-376-6093.

Employment and Training—Indians and Native Americans

Objectives: To reduce the economic disadvantages among Indians and others of Native American descent and to advance the economic and social development of such people in accordance with their goals and life styles.

Eligibility: Indian tribes, bands, or groups, Alaskan Native villages or groups (as defined in the Alaska Native Claims Settlement Act of 1971 [85 Stat. 688]) and Hawaiian Native communities.

Range of Financial Assistance: $50,000 to $7,500,000.

Contact: Office of Indian and Native American Programs, Employment and Training Administration, Department of Labor, 601 D St. N.W., Room 6414, Washington, DC 20213/202-376-6102.

Employment and Training Research and Development Projects

Objectives: To support employment and training studies to develop policy and programs for achieving the fullest utilization of the Nation's human resources; to improve and strengthen the functioning of the nation's employment and training system; to develop new approaches to facilitate employment of the difficult to employ; and to conduct research and development addressing the employment implications of long-term social and economic trends and forces.

Eligibility: State colleges and universities, public, private, junior and community colleges, state and local government organizations including U.S. territories and other organizations and individuals capable of fulfilling the objectives of the programs. There are no formal guidelines or conditions performers must meet other than that they have demonstrated financial responsibility and competence to fulfill the terms of the contract or grant.

Range of Financial Assistance: $1,000 to $1,000,000.

Contact: Director, Office of Research and Evaluation, Employment and Training Administration, Department of Labor, Washington, DC 20213/ 202-376-7335.

Employment and Training Research and Development Projects

Objectives: To provide, foster, and promote training and other employment related services to groups with particular disadvantages in the labor market. To promote and foster new or improved linkages between the network of federal, state, and local employment and training agencies and components of the private sector. To carry out other special federal responsibilities under the act.

Eligibility: State and local governments, federal agencies, private nonprofit and profit-making organizations and education institutions.

Range of Financial Assistance: $200,000 to $7,500,000.

Contact: Administrator, Office of Strategic Planning and Policy Development, Employment and Training Administration, Department of Labor, 601 D St. N.W., Washington, DC 20213/202-376-7341.

Employment Service

Objectives: To place persons in employment by providing a variety of placement-related services to job seekers and to employers seeking qualified individuals to fill job openings.

Eligibility: State employment security agencies, including Virgin Islands, Puerto Rico, and Guam.

Range of Financial Assistance: Determined by Formula.

Contact: Director, Employment Service, Employment and Training Administration, Department of Labor, Washington, DC 20213/202-376-6289.

Job Corps

Objectives: To assist young men and women who need and can benefit from an intensive education and vocation training program operated in a residential group setting in order to become more responsible, employable, and productive citizens.

Eligibility: federal, state, local government agencies including U.S. territories, private profit and nonprofit organizations and Indian tribes and organizations having the capabilities to carry out the objectives of the program.

Range of Financial Assistance: $500,000 to $12,500,000.

Contact: Director, Job Corps, Employment Training Administration (ETA), Department of Labor, 601 D St. N.W., Washington, DC 20213/ 202-376-7139

Job Training Partnership Act

Objectives: To provide job training and related assistance to economically disadvantaged individuals, and others who face significant economic barriers. The ultimate goal of the law is to move trainees into permanent, self-sustaining employment.

Eligibility: States.

Range of Financial Assistance: No established range.

Contact: Employment and Training Administration, Department of Labor, 601 D St. N.W., Washington, DC /202-376-6093.

Labor Force Statistics

Objectives: To provide statistical data for analysis of labor force activities and for Federal funds allocation.

Eligibility: State Employment Security Agencies (SESAs) designated under Section 4 of the Wagner Peyser Act are eligible to apply for cooperative agreement funding to operate CES, LAUS, and OES programs in the State.

Range of Financial Assistance: $49,998 to $2,052,270.

Contact: Bureau of Labor Statistics, Office of Employment and Unemployment Statistics, Department of Labor, Washington DC 20212/202-523-1180.

Local Veterans Employment Representative Program

Objectives: To provide funds to State Employment/Job Service agencies to ensure that there is local supervision of compliance with Federal regulations, performance standards, and grant agreement provisions in carrying out requirements of 38 U.S.C. 2004 in providing veterans with maximum employment and training opportunities.

Eligibility: State Employment Service/Job Service agencies designated under Section 4 of the Wagner Peyser Act.

Range of Financial Assistance: $21,800 to $4.6 million.

Contact: Veterans' Employment and Training Service, Office of the Assistant Secretary for Veterans' Employment and Training, Department of Labor, Room S-1316, 200 Constitution Ave. N.W., Washington, DC 20210/202-523-9110.

Migrant and Seasonal Farm Workers

Objectives: To provide necessary employment, and training and supportive services to help migrant and seasonal farm workers, their families, and youth find economically viable alternatives to seasonal agricultural labor, and improve the live style of seasonal agricultural workers who remain in the agricultural labor market.

Eligibility: 1) Comprehensive Education and Training Act (CETA) prime sponsors whose jurisdictions include significant numbers of individuals meeting the definition of migrant and seasonal farm workers for whom they have committed funds provided under Title II of the Act; or public agencies within the geographic boundaries of CETA prime sponsors who have been designated by such prime sponsors to receive Section 402 funds; 2) private nonprofit organizations authorized by their charters or articles of incorporation to operate Employment and Training programs or such other programs or services as are permitted by Title IV, Section 402 of this Act.

Range of Financial Assistance: $120,000 to $4,444,000.

Contact: Office of Special Targeted Programs, Division of Seasonal Farmworker Programs, Employment and Training Administration, Department of Labor, Room 6122, 601 D St., N.W., Washington DC, 20213/202-376-6225.

Mine Health and Safety Grants

Objectives: To assist states in developing and enforcing effective mine health and safety laws and regulations, to improve state workmen's compensation and occupational disease laws and programs, and to promote federal-state coordination and cooperation in improving health and safety conditions.

Eligibility: Any mining state of the United States through its mine inspection or safety agency.

Range of Financial Assistance: $7,875 to $499,400.

Contact: Assistant Secretary of Labor for Mine Safety and Health, Mine Safety and Health Administration, Department of Labor, Ballston Towers No. 3, Arlington, VA 22203/703-235-8264.

Occupational Safety and Health (OSHA)

Objectives: To assure safe and healthful working conditions.

Eligibility: a) Any employer, employee or representative concerned with OS&H problems; b) state agencies which have federally approved occupational safety and health programs; c) labor unions, trade associations, educational institutions and other nonprofit organizations; d) any employee or employee representative of a business engaged in interstate commerce except those under the jurisdiction of other federal agencies; e) anyone concerned about the OS&H program. f) State agencies or organizations within the State designated by the Governor; and g) workers, employers and their representatives.

Range of Financial Assistance: Not specified.

Contact: Assistant Secretary, Occupational Safety and Health Administration, Department of Labor, Washington, DC 20210/202-523-9361.

Senior Community Service Employment Program

Objectives: To provide, foster, and promote useful part-time work opportunities up to 20 hours per week in community service activities for low income persons ages 55 years old and older, who have poor employment prospects.

Eligibility: The following types of organizations are eligible to receive project grants: 1) States, 2) national public and private nonprofit agencies and organizations other than political parties; and 3) U.S. territories.

Range of Financial Assistance: Not specified.

Contact: Chief, Division of Older Worker Programs, Employment and Training Administration, Department of Labor, 601 D St. N.W., Washington, DC 20213/202-376-7287.

Veterans Employment Program

Objectives: To develop programs to meet the employment and training needs of service-connected disabled veterans, veterans of the Vietnam era, and veterans who were recently separated from military service.

Eligibility: State and local governments, private nonprofit institutions/organizations.

Range of Financial Assistance: Not specified.

Contact: Veterans' Employment and Training Service, Office of the Assistant Secretary for Veterans' Employment and Training, Room S1316, 200 Constitution Ave. N.W., Washington, DC 20210/202-523-9110.

Handbook of Labor Statistics

This publication is a compilation of the major statistics series published by the Bureau of Labor Statistics. Available for $9.50 from: Office of Publications, Bureau of Labor Statistics, Department, 441 G St. N.W., Room 2029, Washington, DC 20212/202-523-1230.

Handicapped Program
This office works on pilot and experimental programs designed to provide employment opportunities for handicapped individuals. Contact: Research and Demonstration Division, Employment and Training Administration, Department of Labor, 601 D St. N.W., Room 8000, Washington, DC 20213/202-376-6289.

Health Careers Guidebook
This publication describes about 100 health-related occupations such as physicians, nurses, medical illustrators, and physical and occupational therapists. Available for $7.50 from: Superintendent of Documents, Government Printing Office, Washington, DC 20402/202-783-3238.

Health Standards
For information on OSHA health standards requirements in general industry, construction or agriculture, contact: Directorate of Health Standards Program, Occupational Safety and Health Administration (OSHA), Department of Labor, 200 Constitution Ave. N.W., Room N3718, Washington, DC 20210/202-523-7075.

Hours and Earnings
Data are available showing gross hours and earnings of production or nonsupervisory workers in private nonagricultural industries. Contact: Office of Employment and Unemployment Statistics, Bureau of Labor Statistics, Department of Labor, 441 G St. N.W., Room 2919, Washington, DC 20212/202-523-1694.

Immigrant Workers Certification
Aliens who seek to immigrate to the United States for employment shall be excluded from admission unless the Secretary of Labor determines and certifies to the Secretary of State and to the Attorney General that there are not sufficient U.S. workers available for the employment and that the employment of such aliens will not adversely affect the wages and working conditions of U.S. workers similarly employed. Contact: Division of Labor Certification, Employment Service, Employment and Training Administration, Department of Labor, Washington, DC 20213/202-376-6295.

Impact of New Office Technology
A sociologist studies the effects of new office technologies on clerical workers, specializing in the secretarial occupation. The particular concern is the impact of word processing technologies on women workers. The staff works as consultants to government and industry. The staff can answer questions in their area of expertise or refer you to colleagues in their office. Contact: Women's Bu-

reau, Room 3307, U.S. Department of Labor, 200 Constitution Ave. N.W., Washington, DC 20210/202-523-6652.

Import Price Indexes
Quarterly indexes are available for detailed and aggregate groups covering food, intermediate manufacturing, machinery, transportation equipment, and crude materials. Product categories are based on Standard International Trade Classification. Contact: International Prices Division, Office of Prices and Living Conditions, Bureau of Labor Statistics, Department of Labor, 600 E St. N.W., Room 3302, Washington, DC 20212/202-272-5025.

Indian Programs
Unemployed, underemployed and disadvantaged Indians and other Native Americans are provided with training, public service employment and a wide range of services to enable them to support themselves and their families. Contact: Office of Special Targeted Programs, Employment and Training Administration, Department of Labor, 601 D St. N.W., Room 6122, Washington, DC 20213/202-376-6225.

Industrial Hygiene Regulation
The Occupational Safety and Health Administration (OSHA) aims to protect U.S. workers in their occupational environment. The major thrust of OSHA's work is setting and enforcing of mandatory standards for employees not only in industry but also construction, maritime and agriculture. In addition to compliance assistance, OSHA also sponsors training and continuing education for hygienists. OSHA maintains a computerized data base containing inspection reports of companies and industries, which staff will search for the public, with the only charge being computer time. Pamphlets covering topics concerning safety hazards and protective equipment and toxicity data are available. Single copies as well as information about general standards are available at no charge directly from OSHA, whereas multiple copies are available at a nominal fee from the Government Printing Office, Washington, DC 20402. Contact: Occupational Safety and Health Administration (OSHA), U.S. Department of Labor, Room N 3637, 200 Constitution Ave. N.W., Washington, DC 20210/202-523-0851—General Information; 202-523-6441—Office of Management Data Systems.

Industrial Hygiene Resources
The National Institute for Occupational Safety and Health (NIOSH) is the research agent which provides the technical information to the Occupational Safety and Health Administration for the promulgation of its regulations on occupational safety and health. Their findings are available to the public as well as to other government agencies,

industry and academia, and are published by NIOSH in continuous technical reports and criteria documents. NIOSH also sponsors training for health professionals and a grant program for educational centers. NIOSH conducted a national occupational environment survey, querying industries and companies as to what types and levels of chemicals workers are exposed to. The published results are available. NIOSHTIC, the technical information center, will make available detailed research on both chemical and physical health and safety hazards and will search their internal document file upon request. NIOSH publishes an annual toxic substances list available at no charge, and supplies information for RTECS, the Register of Toxic Effects of Chemical Substances, available through Medlars. NIOSH also supplies data for a bibliographic data base containing over 106,000 references on occupational environments soon to be available as File 160 through DIALOG. Contact: National Institute for Occupational Safety and Health (NIOSH), 4676 Columbia Parkway, Cincinnati, OH 45226/513-684-8311—Division of Standards Development; 513-684-8328—Technical Information Center.

Industrial Prices and Price Indexes
Monthly prices and indexes are available for 3,000 products by commodity line (end use), and stage of production (degree of fabrication and class of buyer). Contact: Industrial Prices and Price Indexes Division, Office of Prices and Living Conditions, Bureau of Labor Statistics, Department of Labor, 600 E St. N.W., Room 5210, Washington, DC 20212/202-272-5110.

Industry Productivity Measurement
Data are available on output per employee hour, output per employee, output, employment and employee hours. Contact: Industry Productivity and Technology Studies, Office of Productivity and Technology, Bureau of Labor Statistics, Department of Labor, 200 Constitution Ave. N.W., Room S4320, Washington, DC 20210/202-523-9244.

Industry Wages
Data are available showing averages and distribution of straight-time earnings for representative occupations—nationwide, regional and selected areas—by size of establishment and other characteristics depending upon industry. Contact: Division of Occupational Pay and Employee Benefit Levels, Office of Wages and Industrial Relations, Bureau of Labor Statistics, Department of Labor, 441 G St. N.W., Room 2838, Washington, DC 20212/202-523-1309.

Information Processing at Bureau of Labor Statistics
This free publication gives a descriptive account of the evolution and application of machines and computers in the processing of Bureau of Labor Statistics. Contact: Office of Publications, Bureau of Labor Statistics, Department of Labor, 441 G St. N.W., Room 2421, Washington, DC 20212/202-523-1239.

Insured Employment Wages
Data are available showing monthly employment, total quarterly wages, taxable wages and employer contributions by state, industry and size of establishment of workmen covered by state employment insurance laws and program of unemployment compensation for federal employees. Contact: Office of Employment and Unemployment Statistics, Bureau of Labor Statistics, Department of Labor, 441 G St. N.W., Room 2919, Washington, DC 20212/202-523-1694.

International Comparisons of Productivity, Labor Costs, Economic Indicators and Unemployment
Comparative statistics are available on such topics as: output per employee hour, hourly compensation, unit labor costs, real gross product per employed person, rates of change in consumer and producer prices, nominal and real earnings of wage earners, composition and level of earnings and fringe benefits, living costs and quarters allowances, number of stoppages, workers involved, and time lost from industrial disputes, levels of capital investment, and labor force employment and unemployment data. Contact: Division of Foreign Labor Statistics, Office of Productivity and Technology, Bureau of Labor Statistics, Department of Labor, 200 Constitution Ave. N.W., Room S4214, Washington, DC 20210/202-523-9301.

International Labor Programs
For general information on programs from the Bureau of International Labor Affairs, contact: Office of Management, Administration and Planning, Bureau of International Labor Affairs, Department of Labor, 200 Constitution Ave. N.W., Room S5303, Washington, DC 20210/202-523-6274.

Job Corps
This program provides basic education, vocational training, counseling, health care, and similar renewal services to help disadvantaged young men and women 16 through 21 prepare for jobs. Enrollees in Job Corps centers receive room and board, clothing for work, books, supplies, and cash allowances, part of which is paid on leaving the program after satisfactory participation. Training is given in such occupations as: heavy equipment operation, auto repair, carpentry, painting, masonry, nursing and other health care jobs, clerical and office work, and electronic assembly. Basic education includes reading, math, social studies and preparation for the high school equivalency exams. Contact: Office of Job Corps, Em-

ployment and Training Administration, Department of Labor, 601 D St. N.W., Room 6414, Washington, DC 20213/202-376-7139

Job Corps Statistics
Statistics cover new arrivals, terminations, and transfers by Job Corps Centers. Contact: Office of Job Corps and Young Adult Conservation Corps, Office of Youth Programs, Employment and Training Administration, Department of Labor, 601 D St. N.W., Room 6403, Washington, DC 20213/202-376-2572.

Job Discrimination
Veterans and handicapped people who are discriminated against in the job market should file complaints with the nearest state Employment/Job Service office. They can also file a complaint with any of the 10 regional Federal Contract Compliance Program offices, or contact: Veterans/Handicapped Worker Policy, Office of Federal Contract Compliance Programs, Employment Standards Administration, Department of Labor, 200 Constitution Ave. N.W., Room 3422, Washington, DC 20210/202-523-9410.

Job Information Service (JIS)
Job Information Service Centers are located within local employment service centers to enable job-ready applicants to conduct their own job exploration through the *Job Bank Book* and other listings of employment information and opportunities. Contact: Division of Planning and Operations, Office of Program Services, Employment Service, Employment and Training Adminstration, Department of Labor, 601 D St. N.W., Room 8028, Washington, DC 20213/202-376-6185.

Job Requirements Studies
Information is available on job requirements for 160 industries. Contact: Office of Economic Growth, Bureau of Labor Statistics, Department of Labor, 601 D St. N.W., Room 4000, Washington, DC 20212/202-272-5381.

Job Training Partnership Act
This program to provide job training and related assistance to economically disadvantaged individuals, dislocated workers, and others who have difficulty getting employment is administered by state and local governments. This major jobs initiative also includes training services for Native Americans, migrant and seasonal farmworkers, veterans, and older Americans. For further information, contact: Office of Job Training Programs, Employment and Training Administration, Department of Labor 601 D St. N.W., Room 6100, Washington, DC 20213/202-376-6604.

Labor Force Statistics
Data are available on: a) employment and unemployment analysis on the current economic status of workers, based on data from households as well as employment, hours earnings, and labor turnover statistics collected from industrial establishments; b) labor force studies yielding information on such characteristics as educational attainment, work experience and family relationships; c) occupational employment statistics available for a wide variety of occupations, including employment outlook, nature of the work, earnings, working conditions and qualifications; d) national industry/occupational matrices current and projected; e) state and local area labor force employment and unemployment data used to identify areas of high unemployment and for allocations of funds under various federal assistance programs including CETA; and f) long-term projections of labor and employment. Contact: Bureau of Labor Statistics, Office of Employment and Unemployment Statistics, Department of Labor, Washington, DC 20212/202-523-1694.

Labor Foreign Service Attaches
There are about 50 labor attaches in foreign service jobs who report on foreign labor developments and relate U.S. labor activities to foreign audiences. Contact: Bureau of International Labor Affairs, Department of Labor, 200 Constitution Ave. N.W., Room S5016, Washington, DC 20210/202-523-6257.

Labor Historian
For historic information, contact: Historian, Assistant Secretary for Administrative Management, Library, Department of Labor, 200 Constitution Ave. N.W., Room N2439, Washington, DC 20210/202-523-6461.

Labor Library
The Department of Labor Library will provide research services, on-line computer searches, and special bibliographies on labor-related subjects. Contact: Department of Labor Library, 200 Constitution Ave. N.W., Room N2439, Washington, DC 20210/202-523-6988.

Labor-Management Cooperation
Public forums, numerous publications and other resources are sponsored by this Bureau for the purpose of exchanging information on ways to promote worker participation, quality circles and other participative programs. The "Labor Relations Resource Catalog" and "Resource Guide to Labor-Management Cooperation" are available free from: Bureau of Labor-Management Relations and Cooperative Programs, Department of Labor, 200 Constitution Ave. N.W., Room N5677, Washington, DC 20210/202-523-6231.

Labor-Management Disputes
Information is available about labor-management disputes and collective bargaining situations. A

free publication, *Significant Collective-Bargaining Contract Expirations,* lists contract expirations for the coming year. Contact: Industrial Relations Service, Bureau of Labor-Management Relations and Cooperative Program, Department of Labor, 200 Constitution Ave. N.W., Room N5645, Washington, DC 20210/202-523-6475.

Labor-Management Information
For general information on labor-management topics and for a list of available publications, contact: Information Office, Bureau of Labor-Management and Cooperative Programs, Department of Labor, 200 Constitution Ave. N.W., Room N5637, Washington, DC 20216/202-523-7408.

Labor-Management Training Films
The following films are produced by the Department of Labor; *Scenes From the Workplace, Button . . . Button,* and *Out of Conflict . . . Accord.* They are available from: Reference Section, National Audio Visual Center, General Services Administration, Washington, DC 20409/301-763-1896.

Labor Market Information
For information on any local labor market including employment and unemployment information and characteristics of persons in the labor force; intelligence or the characteristics of occupation and jobs; or how and when to find a job, contact: Division of Labor Market Information, Office of Policy and Evaluation and Research, Office of Policy and Planning, Employment and Training Administration, Department of Labor, 601 D St. N.W., Room 9304, Washington, DC 20213/202-376-6263.

Labor Publications
For a listing of publications published by the Department of Labor, contact: Office of Information and Public Affairs, Department of Labor, 200 Constitution Ave. N.W., Room S1030, Washington, DC 20210/202-523-7323.

Labor Review, Monthly
The research journal, *Monthly Labor Review,* includes analytical articles, 40 pages of current labor statistics, reports on industrial relations, court decisions, book reviews and foreign labor developments. Available for $26.00 per year from: Superintendent of Documents, Government Printing Office, Washington, DC 20402/202-783-3238.

Labor Statistics
The Bureau of Labor Statistics for the U.S. Department of Labor is responsible for the compilation, publication and dissemination of a vast assortment of statistical information on U.S. industry. The productivity and technology studies section frequently issues reports and updates on the impact of technological changes and manpower trends of various industries. Publications are available from the Superintendent of Documents. U.S. Government Printing Office, Washington, DC 20402.

Technology and Labor in Four Industries (Bulletin 2104) covers meat products; foundries; metalworking machinery; electrical and electrical and electronic equipment.

Technology and Labor in Five Industries (Bulletin 2033) covers bakery products; concrete; air transportation; telephone communication; insurance.

Technological Change and its Labor Impact in Five Energy Industries (Bulletin 2005) covers coal mining; oil and gas extraction; petroleum refining; petroleum pipeline transportation; electric and gas utilities.

Technological Change and Its Labor Impact in Five Industries (Bulletin 1961) covers apparel; footwear; motor vehicles; railroads; retail trade.

Technological Change and Manpower Trends in Five Industries (Bulletin 1856) covers pulp and paper; hydraulic cement; steel; aircraft and missiles; wholesale trade.

Technical Change and Manpower Trends in Six Industries (Bulletin 1817) covers textile mill products; lumber and wood products; tires and tubes; aluminum; banking; health services.

Contact: Bureau of Labor Statistics, U.S. Department of Labor, 441 G St. N.W., Washington, DC 20212/202-523-9294.

Labor Surplus Areas
The *Area Trends in Employment and Unemployment* is an official list of labor surplus areas as classified by the Department of Labor in which employers are eligible for preference in bidding on certain federal contracts. Contact: Policy, Evaluation and Research, Office of Policy and Planning, Employment and Training Administration, Department of Labor, 601 D St. N.W., Room 9304, Washington, DC 20213/202-376-6263.

Local Area Employment and Unemployment
Statistics are available for labor force employment and unemployment for states, metropolitan areas, counties, cities of 50,000 or more population, and certain local areas. Contact: Local Area Unemployment Statistics Division, Office of Employment and Unemployment Statistics, Bureau of Labor Statistics, Department of Labor, 441 G St. N.W., Room 2083, Washington, DC 20212/202-523-1002.

Longshore and Harbor Workers
The Longshoremen and Harbor Workers' Compensation Act provides compensation benefits to about 1 million workers disabled due to injury or an employment-related occupational disease oc-

curring on the navigable waters of the U.S. or in adjoining shoreside areas. Contact: Division of Longshoremen and Harbor Workers' Compensation, Employment and Standards, Department of Labor, 200 Constitution Ave. N.W., Room 2421, Washington, DC 20210/202-523-1221.

Major Programs of the Bureau of Labor Statistics
This free publication describes the Bureau's principal programs and information sources. Contact: Office of Publications, Bureau of Labor Statistics, Department of Labor, 441 G St. N.W., Room 2421, Washington, DC 20212/202-523-1221.

Matching Personal and Job Characteristics
A chart shows 23 occupational characteristics and requirements which are matched with 281 occupations. The table is designed as an exploratory tool to help compare personal interests, capacities, abilities and educational qualifications with characteristics usually associated with an occupation. Contact: Division of Occupational Outlook, Office of Economic Growth and Employment Projections, Bureau of Labor Statistics, Department of Labor, 601 D St. N.W., Room 4000, Washington, DC 20212/202-272-5382.

Migrant and Seasonal Farmworker Program
This program provides migrant and other seasonal farmworkers and their families with a wide range of services to help them find alternative job opportunities in year-round employment and to improve their living and working conditions. Services include: educational training, job referral, emergency services, residential support, self-help housing, and transportation and relocation assistance. Contact: Migrant and Seasonal Farmworker Programs, Employment and Training Administration, Department of Labor, 601 D St. N.W., Room 6114, Washington DC 20213/202-376-6225.

Mine Health and Safety Academy, National
The primary purpose of the Academy is to design, develop and conduct instructional programs which will assist in government, industry, and labor efforts to reduce accidents and health hazards in the mineral industries. Courses cover subjects such as mandatory health and safety standards, industrial hygiene, mine emergency procedures, safety management, accident prevention techniques, etc. The Academy also provides safety manuals on such subjects as: electrical hazards, accident investigation, job safety analysis, fire safety, coal mine maps, coal mining, laboratory safety, heat stress in mining, gas detectors, and safety tips for underground coal mining. Contact: Continuing Education Department, National Mine Health and Safety Academy, P.O. Box 1166, Beckley, WV 25801/304-255-0451.

Mine Safety Information
Publications, newsletters, training films and educational materials are available on mine safety and health. Contact: Office of Information, Mine Safety and Health Administration, Department of Labor, 4015 Wilson Blvd., Room 601, Arlington, VA 22203/703-235-1452.

Mine Safety Training
Training courses are tailored to the specific conditions of individual mining operations. Course materials include safe mining practices, mine emergency situations, mine rescue techniques, and first aid and equipment operations. Teaching aids include training modules and miner training films. Contact Division of Policy and Program Coordination, Education and Training, Mine Safety and Health Administration, Department of Labor, 4015 Wilson Blvd., Room 576 Arlington, VA 22203/703-235-1400.

Minimum Wage Exemption
This office monitors special certificates which allow employers to pay less than the minimum wage to certain groups of workers, e.g., student learners, full-time students and handicapped workers. Contact: Special Employment Division, Wage and Hour Division, Employment Standards Administration, Department of Labor, 200 Constitution Ave. N.W., Room C4316, Washington, DC 20210/202-523-8727.

Mining Machinery
The office of management research and technology approves new equipment technology, makes assessments and provides technical improvements for safe design of mining machinery, roof control and ventilation systems, mine waste facilities, and instruments used for measuring dust, noise, radiation and other health hazards. Contact: Office of Information, Mine Safety and Health Administration, Department of Labor, 4015 Wilson Blvd., Room 601, Arlington, VA 22203/703-235-1452.

Municipal Government Occupational Surveys
Data are available showing averages and distributions of salary rates for professional, administrative, technical, clerical, data processing, skilled maintenance, custodial, protective service, sanitation and social work occupations. Information is also available on selected work practices and supplementary benefits. Contact: Wage Studies, Division of Occupational Pay and Employee Benefit Levels, Office of Wages and Industrial Relations, Bureau of Labor Statistics, Department of Labor, 441 G St. N.W., Room 2818, Washington, DC 20212/202-523-1268.

National Longitudinal Surveys
These surveys study the relationship of factors influencing the labor force behavior and work experience of four groups: men age 45 to 59 and 14 to 24, and women 30 to 44 and 14 to 24. The

surveys focus on the interaction among economic, sociologic and psychologic variables that permit some members of a given age-education-occupation group to have satisfactory work experience while others do not. Contact: National Longitudinal Surveys, Office of Research and Development, Office of Policy Evaluation and Research, Employment and Training Administration, Department of Labor, 601 D St. N.W., Room 9028, Washington, DC 20213/202-376-7346.

National Occupational Projections
This large matrix shows distribution of employment by occupation and industry for 1500 occupations and occupation groups and 300 industries. It includes projections on job openings by occupation and is used to analyze industry and technologic trends, to evaluate national training policies and for market research. Contact: Office of Economic Growth, Bureau of Labor Statistics, Department of Labor, 601 D St. N.W., Room 4000, Washington, DC 20212/202-272-5383.

National-State-Industry-Occupational Matrix System
The distribution of employment is shown in these matrices which include data on 470 occupations in 260 industries. Matrices for over 1500 occupations in 300 industries provide local information for 27 states. Contact: Office of Economic Growth, Bureau of Labor Statistics, Department of Labor, 600 E St. N.W., Room 4400, Washington, DC 20212/202-272-5279.

Occupational Employment Statistics
For statistics on employment by occupation and industry, contact: Occupational Outlook Division, Office of Employment and Unemployment Statistics, Bureau of Labor Statistics, Department of Labor 441 G St. N.W., Room 2913A, Washington, DC 20212/202-523-1949.

Occupational Injuries and Illnesses
Data are available showing incidence rates by industry, including number of fatal and nonfatal cases without lost workdays, and illness by category of illness. Data are also available showing nature of injury or illness, part of body affected, source of injury or illness, event or exposures which produced the injury or illness, and industry and characteristics of injured or ill workers. Contact: Office of Occupational Safety and Health Statistics, Bureau of Labor Statistics, Department of Labor, 601 D St. N.W., Room 4014, Washington, DC 20210/202-272-3470.

Occupational Injuries and Illnesses Surveys
Data are available on occupational injuries, fatalities, illnesses, and on lost work time. Contact: Surveys Division, Office of Occupational Safety and Health Statistics, Department of Labor, 601 D St. N.W., Room 4014, Washington, DC 20210/202-272-3490.

Occupational Outlook Handbook
This publication shows employment outlook, location of jobs, earnings, nature of the work, training, entry requirements, advancement and working conditions for each occupation, and employment outlook, location, principal occupations, earnings, nature of the industry, training, entry requirements, advancement and working conditions for each industry. It covers several hundred occupations and 35 major industries. Available for $8.50 (paperback) and $10.00 (hard bound). *Occupational Outlook for College Graduates* provides information for more than 100 jobs for which an education beyond high school is necessary or useful. Available for $8.00 from: Superintendent of Documents, Government Printing Office, Washington, DC 20402/202-783-3238. For more detailed information on content, contact: Office of Information and Public Inquiry, Bureau of Labor Statistics, Department of Labor, 441 G St. N.W., Room 4860, Washington, DC 20212/202-523-1221.

Occupational Outlook Handbook Reprints
Individual reprints from the *Occupational Outlook Handbook* are available from the Government Printing Office. The following is a list of reprints available for purchase.

Tomorrow's Jobs: Overview ($1.25)
Business, Managerial, and Legal Occupations ($1.50)
Engineering and Related Occupations ($1.00)
Computer and Mathematics-Related Occupations ($1.00)
Physical and Life Scientists ($1.00)
Education, Social Service, and Related Occupations ($1.50)
Medical and Dental Practitioners and Assistants ($1.25)
Dietetics, Nursing, Pharmacy, and Therapy Occupations ($1.00)
Health Technologists and Technicians ($1.25)
Communications, Design, Performing Arts, and Related Occupations ($1.50)
Sales Occupations ($1.00)
Clerical and Other Administrative Support Occupations ($1.50)
Protective Service Occupations and Inspectors ($1.00)
Service Occupations: Food, Cleaning, Health, and Personal ($1.25)
Mechanics, Equipment Installers, and Repairers ($1.50)
Small Business Occupations ($1.00)
Construction Occupations ($1.50)
Metalworking Occupations ($1.00)
Production Occupations ($1.25)
Transportation and Material Moving Occupations ($1.00)

Contact: Superintendent of Documents, Government Printing Office, Washington, DC 20402/202-783-3238.

Occupational Outlook Quarterly

This publication is designed to help high school students and guidance counselors assess career opportunities. It provides information on several hundred occupations and 35 industries. Available for $11.00. *Job Outlook in Brief* is a companion publication that allows you to compare job prospects. Available for $1.75 from: Superintendent of Documents, Government Printing Office, Washington, DC 20402/202-783-3238.

Occupational Projections and Training Data

This publication shows estimated average annual openings and a summary of available statistics on the number of people completing training in each field for each of several hundred white-collar, blue-collar and service jobs. It also discusses long-term employment prospects for college graduates. Available for $5.50 from: Superintendent of Documents, Government Printing Office, Washington, DC 20402/202-783-3238.

Occupational Safety and Health Subscription Service

This service provides all standards, interpretations, regulations and procedures in easy-to-read loose-leaf form. All changes and additions will be issued for an indefinite period of time. Individual volumes are available at the following rates:

General Industry Standards and Interpretations ($66.00)
Maritime Standards and Interpretations ($41.00)
Construction Standards and Interpretations ($29.00)
Other Regulations and Procedures ($95.00)
Fuel Operations Manual ($28.00)
Industrial Hygiene Field Operation Manual ($27.00)

Available from: Superintendent of Documents, Government Printing Office, Washington, DC 20402/202-783-3238.

Occupational Titles

The *Dictionary of Occupational Titles* lists over 20,000 job definitions that match job requirements to worker skills. It contains occupation classifications for nearly all jobs in the U.S. economy. Available for $21.00 from Superintendent of Documents, Government Printing Office, Washington, DC 20402/202-783-3238. For more detailed information, contact: Division of Occupational Analysis, Office of Technical Support, Employment Service, Employment and Training Administration, Department of Labor, 601 D St. N.W., Room 8430, Washington, DC 20213/202-376-6293.

Occupations, Selected Characteristics

Selected Characteristics of Occupations Defined in the Dictionary of Occupational Titles (DOT) provides additional information about jobs in the DOT such as physical demands, working conditions and specific vocational preparation. Available for $11.50 from Superintendent of Documents, Government Printing Office, Washington, DC 20402/202-783-3238. For more detailed information on content, contact: Division of Occupational Analysis, Employment Service, Employment and Training Administration, Department of Labor, Washington, DC 20213/202-376-6292.

Office Automation and Working Women: Issues for the Decade Ahead

This publication discusses the most important issues women workers face in the electronic office. Single copies can be obtained free of charge. There is a nominal fee for multiple copies. Contact: Women's Bureau, U.S. Department of Labor, 200 Constitution Ave. N.W., Washington, DC 20210/202-523-6611.

Older Workers Program

The Senior Community Service Employment Program (SCSEP) employs economically disadvantaged people 55 years or older in part-time community service jobs. Contact: Office of Special Targeted Programs, Employment and Training Administration, Department of Labor, 601 D St. N.W., Room 6122, Washington, DC 20213/202-376-6225.

OSHA Area Offices—Reporting

An on-the-job accident should be reported within 48 hours to the nearest OSHA office if five or more employees required hospitalization or if one of them dies. A complaint should also be lodged if a worker loses his or her job for reporting a safety or health hazard. *Hazard Alerts* and *Intelligence Reports* are published as needed. For information and for a listing of area offices, contact: Office of Field Coordination and Experimental Programs, Occupational Safety and Health Administration, Department of Labor, 200 Constitution Ave. N.W., Room N3603, Washington, DC 20210/202-523-8116.

OSHA Analytical Laboratory

Samples taken in the field by OSHA staff undergo chemical analysis at Occupational Safety and Health Administration, Salt Lake City Laboratory, 390 Wakara Way, P.O. Box 15200, Salt Lake City, Utah 84115-0200/801-524-5287.

OSHA Cincinnati Laboratory

This laboratory calibrates and tests the technical monitoring equipment used by the OSHA compliance staff. Contact: OSHA Cincinnati Laboratory, U.S. Post Office Building, Room 108, Fifth and Walnut Sts., Cincinnati, OH 45202/513-684-3721.

OSHA Consumer Affairs

The Division of Consumer Affairs is responsible for: 1) managing two advisory committees—National Advisory Committee on Occupational Safety and Health, and National Advisory Committee on Construction Safety and Health; 2) managing all hearings on proposed standards and public factfinding meetings. Contact: Office of Information and Public Affairs, Division of Consumer Affairs, Occupational Safety and Health Administration (OSHA), Department of Labor, 200 Constitution Ave. N.W., Room N3635, Washington, DC 20210/202-523-8024.

OSHA Inspection Data
Data are available on what companies were inspected, when, where, what type of complaint, standards violated (if any), proposed penalties, violations contested, enforcement information, incidents incurred (warrants needed), referrals to health experts, who has been trained, what type of training, etc. Contact: Office of Management Data Systems, Directorate of Administrative Programs, Occupational Safety and Health Administration, Department of Labor, 200 Constitution Ave. N.W., Room N4611, Washington, DC 20210/202-523-7008.

OSHA News and Information
For general information on OSHA programs and developments, contact: Division of News Media Service, Office of Information and Consumer Affairs, Occupational Safety and Health Administration, Department of Labor, 200 Constitution Ave. N.W., Room N4101, Washington, DC 20210/202-523-9667.

OSHA Onsite Consultation
Free consultation on safety and health programs is available to those employers who cannot afford a private consultant. Through these programs, hazardous work conditions can be identified and corrected by the employer. For a free 12-page book listing the offices in each state which offer the service, contact: OSHA Publications Distribution, Office of Administration Services, Occupational Safety and Health Administration, Department of Labor, 200 Constitution Ave. N.W., Room S1212, Washington, DC 20210/202-523-6138.

OSHA Petitions
Employers or employees can petition OSHA for the development of standards as well as for their modification or revocation. Contact: Office of the Assistant Secretary, Occupational Safety and Health Administration, Department of Labor, 200 Constitution Ave. N.W., Room S2315, Washington, DC 20210/202-523-9362.

OSHA Publications and Training Materials
For a complete listing of materials published by OSHA, contact: OSHA Publications Distribution Office, Occupational Safety and Health Administration, Department of Labor, 200 Constitution Ave. N.W., Room N4101, Washington, DC 20210/202-523-9667.

OSHA Regulatory Analysis
Information and analysis are available on issues surrounding major standards such as those for cotton, dust, benzine, and carcinogens. Contact: Office of Regulatory Analysis, Directorate of Policy, Occupational Safety and Health Administration, Department of Labor, 200 Constitution Ave. N.W., Room N3635, Washington, DC 20210/202-523-8018.

OSHA Scientific and Engineering Support
The Directorate of Technical Support provides scientific and engineering support for OSHA's standard-setting and compliance operations. It works on such projects as the health hazards associated with the petro-chemical industry and ionizing and non-ionizing radiation hazards. Contact: Directorate of Technical Support, Occupational Safety and Health Administration, Department of Labor, 200 Constitution Ave. N.W., Room N3651, Washington, DC 20210/202-523-7031.

OSHA Technical Data
Technical data are available on all of OSHA's projects from Technical Data Center, Directorate of Technical Support, Occupational Safety and Health Administration, Department of Labor, 200 Constitution Ave. N.W., Room N2439 Rear, Washington, DC 20210/202-523-9694.

OSHA Technical Laboratory
Technical monitoring equipment used by the OSHA Compliance staff is calibrated and tested at: Occupational Safety and Health Administration, Cincinnati Laboratory, U.S. Post Office Building, Room 108, Fifth and Walnut Sts., Cincinnati, OH 45202/513-684-3721.

OSHA Training Institute
Courses at the Institute are designed to enable OSHA's compliance safety and health officers to learn how to deal with actual workplace situations. Many courses are also open to non-OSHA employees. Contact: OSHA Training Institute, Occupational Safety and Health Administration, Department of Labor, 1555 Times Dr., Des Plaines, IL 60018/312-297-4810.

Pension and Welfare Studies
Research studies include: Multi-Employer Pension Plans, Study of Pension Plan Costs, Reciprocity and Single Employers Plans, Study of National Health Insurance Proposals on Collective Bargaining, Study on the Provisions and Benefits Provided by Health Plans, Study on Encouraging Growth of Health Plans, Pension Plans and Health Plan Coverage, Women and Pensions, Empirical Study of the Effects of Pensions on Savings and Labor, and Supply Decisions of Older Men. Contact: Office of Policy Planning and Research, Pension

and Welfare Benefit Programs, Department of Labor, 200 Constitution Ave. N.W., Room S4220, Washington, DC 20216/202-523-9421.

Pension Plan Publications
The following publications and audiovisual materials are free:

What You Should Know About Your Pension Plan
What You Should Know About the Pension and Welfare Law (Also available in Spanish)
How to File a Claim for Your Benefit
Often Asked Questions About the Employee Retirement Income Security Act
Fiduciary Standards Under the Employee Retirement Income Security Act
Coverage Under the Employee Retirement Income Security Act
ERISA Report to Congress 1982
U.S. Department of Labor Program Highlights (ERISA)
Reporting and Disclosure Guide for Employee Benefit Plans
Know Your Pension Plan
ERISA—General Information About the Employee Retirement Income Security Act of 1974
Identification Numbers Under ERISA
Informacion General De ERISA
Eligibilidad para la Participacion en el Plan de Pensiones
Derechos Inalienables a los Beneficios de Pensiones
Contando anos de Servicios en los Planes de Pensiones
Proteccion Contra la Interrupcion en el Servicio
You and ERISA—a 20-minute presentation designed to help plan participants understand their basic rights under ERISA
This is ERISA—a 20-minute overview of the Act designed for plan administrators and practitioners
The SPD and You—an 11-minute presentation describing the procedures for preparing summary plan descriptions
How to Fill Out the 5500 Annual Report for Small Plans—a 28-minute presentation designed as an aid in helping administrators of small plans complete their annual report as required under ERISA (available only in slide-sound set).

Contact: Division of Public Information, Pension and Welfare Benefit Programs, Department of Labor, 200 Constitution Ave. N.W., Room N5471, Washington, DC 20210/202-523-8921.

Pension Plans—Reports
The Employee Retirement Income Security Act (ERISA) is administered by the Pension Welfare Benefits Division. Every plan covered by ERISA must give each participant a written summary describing in simple language the plan's eligibility requirements, its benefits, and how to file claims for benefits. Each participant must also be given an annual report on the plan's financial activities. A copy of each plan and annual reports must be filed with this Division. Copies are available from: Disclosure Room, Office of Reports and Disclosure, Pension and Welfare Benefit Programs,

Department of Labor, 200 Constitution Ave. N.W., Room 4667, Washington, DC 20216/202-523-8771.

Price and Index Number Studies
In-depth research is conducted on various aspects of price measurements such as adjustment for quality change and cost-of-living indexes. Contact: Prices and Index Number Research Division, Office of Prices and Living Conditions, Bureau of Labor Statistics, Department of Labor, 600 E St. N.W., Room 3306, Washington, DC 20212/202-272-5096.

Prices and Living Conditions
Programs provide information on Consumer Price Indexes, Producer Price Indexes, Export and Import Price Indexes, as well as for retail prices in primary markets, consumer expenditures, income, assets, and liabilities of all U.S. families, and hypothetical budgets at three levels of living in selected areas. Contact: Office of Prices and Living Conditions, Bureau of Labor Statistics, Department of Labor, 600 E St. N.W., Room 3205, Washington, DC 20212/202-272-5038.

Private Pension and Welfare Plans Information
For general information and referrals on topics related to private pension and welfare plans, contact: Office of Communications and Public Services, Pension and Welfare Benefit Programs, Department of Labor, 200 Constitution Ave. N.W., Room N5471, Washington, DC 20216/202-523-8764.

Private Sector Productivity
Quarterly and annual data are available showing percent changes for labor productivity, unit labor cost, real and current dollar compensation per hour and unit labor and nonlabor payments. Contact: Productivity Research Division, Office of Productivity and Technology, Bureau of Labor Statistics, Department of Labor, Washington, DC 20212/202-523-9261.

Producer Prices and Price Indexes
This is a comprehensive monthly report on primary market price movements of both farm and industrial commodities by industry and stage of processing. Available for $34 a year from Superintendent of Documents, Government Printing Office, Washington, DC 20402/202-783-3238. For detailed information on content, contact: Office of Prices and Living Conditions, Bureau of Labor Statistics, Department of Labor, 600 E St. N.W., Room 3001, Washington, DC 20212/202-272-5113.

Productivity and Technology
This office is involved with the following: measuring productivity and labor cost trends in the economy, major sector, individual industries, and

the federal government; providing relevant international comparisons of comparable unemployment rates; investigating the nature and the effect of technology change within industries and across industry lines. Contact: Office of Productivity and Technology, Bureau of Labor Statistics, Department of Labor, 200 Constitution Ave. N.W., Room S4325, Washington, DC 20210/202-523-9294.

Productivity in Federal Government
Annual indexes show output per employee year, unit labor costs, compensation per employee year, and output and employee years for various functional areas within the federal sector. Contact: Industry Productivity Studies Division, Office of Productivity and Technology, Bureau of Labor Statistics, Department of Labor, 200 Constitution Ave. N.W., Room S4320, Washington, DC 20210/202-523-9244.

Productivity Statistics
An inventory of the statistics available from the Office of Productivity and Technology Studies is available upon request. The data centers on three major research programs: 1) the productivity research program provides comprehensive statistics for the U.S. economy, its major component sectors, and individual industries; 2) the technological studies program investigates trends in technology and their impact on employment and productivity; and 3) the international program compiles and analyzes statistics on productivity and related factors in foreign countries for comparison with similar U.S. statistics. Also available as an additional information source is Report 671, *BLS Publications on Productivity and Technology,* free upon request from this office. Contact: Office of Productivity and Technology Studies, Bureau of Labor Statistics, U.S. Department of Labor, 441 G St. N.W., Washington, DC 20212/202-523-9244.

Profiles of Occupational Pay
This publication presents a look at pay relationships within major occupational groups, including profiles of high and low paying metropolitan areas and of high and low paying manufacturing industries. Available for $5.00 from: Office of Publications, Bureau of Labor Statistics, Department of Labor, 441 G St. N.W., Room 2029, Washington, DC 20212/202-523-1239.

Private Sector Initiative Program (PSIP) Clearinghouse
Information services are available on various aspects of the Private Sector Initiative Program (PSIP), including newsletters, bimonthly packets of instructional material, and free publications. Contact: PSIP Clearinghouse, 1015 15th St. N.W., Washington, DC 20005/202-457-0040.

Publications
The following Department of Labor publications may be purchased from the Government Printing Office.

Guide for Occupational Exploration ($12.00)
Job Selection Workbook for Use with Guide for Occupational Exploration (1979) ($4.25)
Selected Characteristics of Occupations Defined in the Dictionary of Occupational Titles ($11.50)
Career Opportunities in the Hotel and Restaurant Industries (1982) ($5.50)
Career Opportunities in Art, Museums, Zoos, and other Interesting Places (1980) ($7.00)
Health Careers Guidebook (1979) ($7.50)
Environmental Protection Careers Guidebook ($7.50)
Criminal Justice Careers Guidebook (1980) ($7.00)
Handbook for Analyzing Jobs (1972) ($9.00)
A Handbook for Job Restructuring (1970) ($0.55)
Standard Industrial Classification Manual ($15.00)
Occupational Outlook Handbook 1984–1985, Paper Edition ($8.50)
Occupational Outlook Handbook 1984–1985, Cloth Edition ($10.00)
Occupational Outlook Quarterly ($11.00 per year's subscription)

Contact: Superintendent of Documents, U. S. Government Printing Office, Washington, DC 20402/202-783-3238.

Quality of Work Life
This office encourages and assists employers and unions in undertaking joint efforts to improve productivity and enhance the quality of life in the workplace. Resource materials, case studies, research reports and monographs as well as other technical assistance are available. Contact: Office of Labor-Management Relations Services, Department of Labor, 200 Constitution Ave. N.W., Room N5677, Washington, DC 20210/202-523-6098.

Regulatory Activities
Listed below are those organizations within the Department of Labor which are involved with regulating various activities. With each listing is a description of those industries or situations which are regulated by the office. Regulatory activities generate large amounts of information on the companies and subjects they regulate. Much of the information is available to the public. A regulatory office can also tell you your rights when dealing with a regulated company.

Division of Public Information, Pension and Welfare Benefit Programs, Department of Labor, 200 Constitution Ave. N.W., Room N5471, Washington, DC 20210/202-523-8921. Monitors and regulates private pension and welfare plans.
Office of Information and Consumer Affairs, Employment Standards Administration, Department of Labor, 200 Constitution Ave. N.W., Washington, DC

20210/202-523-8743. Administers minimum wage and overtime standards, farm labor contractors, wage rates paid on government contracts, nondiscrimination and affirmative action on government contracts, and worker compensation programs. Statistics, Department of Labor, 600 E St. N.W., Room 7216, Washington, DC 20212/202-272-5283.

Office of Information, Office of Labor-Management Standards, Department of Labor, 200 Constitution Ave. N.W., Room N5619, Washington, DC 20210/202-523-7300. Regulates activities of labor unions.

Office of Information, Mine Safety and Health Administration, 4015 Wilson Blvd., Arlington, VA 22203/703-235-1452. Regulates health and safety standards in coal, metal, and other mining.

Office of Information, Occupational Safety and Health Administration, Department of Labor, 3rd St. and Constitution Ave. N.W., Washington, DC 20210/202-523-8148. Regulates safety and health activities at the place of employment for private employers.

Safety Standards

For information on OSHA safety standards requirements in general industry, maritime, construction, or agriculture, contact: Directorate of Safety Standards Program, Occupational Safety and Health Administration, Department of Labor, 200 Constitution Ave. N.W., Room N3605, Washington, DC 20210/202-523-8061.

State and Area Employment Projections

Information is available on current and historic occupational employment estimates, industry and occupation employment projections, and job openings resulting from economic growth and replacement needs for states as a whole and for labor market areas with populations of 50,000 or more. Contact: Office of Economic Growth, Bureau of Labor Statistics, Department of Labor, 600 E St. N.W., Room 7216, Washington, DC 20212/202-272-5283.

Statistical Data Tapes

Bureau of Labor Statistics Machine Readable Data and Statistical Routines provides detailed information on labor force; industry employment, hours, and earnings—national; industry employment, hours, and earnings—state and area; industry employment and wages (covered by unemployment insurance laws); unemployment and labor force—state and area; industry labor turnover—national; consumer price index; producer price index; industry price index; export and import price index; imports; productivity and cost measures; productivity—industry and federal government; international labor and price trend comparisons; and employment cost index. Contact: Data Tapes, Office of Systems and Standards, Bureau of Labor Statistics, Department of Labor, 441 G St. N.W., Room 2045, Washington, DC 20212/202-523-1975.

Statistical Software Programs

The Bureau of Labor Statistics has developed several statistics programs that are for sale to users who have machine processing capabilities. They include: multiple regression programs, seasonal adjustment programs, and table producing language. Contact: Systems Design Division, Office of Systems and Standards, Bureau of Labor Statistics, Department of Labor, 441 G St. N.W., Room 2045, Washington, DC 20212/202-523-1042.

Status of Women, Commissions on the

This office contains information on all commissions organized to improve the status of women. It also acts as liaison for the Department of Labor with the various federal, state, county, or city commissions on women. Contact: Women's Bureau, Department of Labor, 200 Constitution Ave. N.W., Room S3319, Washington, DC 20210/202-523-6631.

Summer Job Tips

Tips on How to Find a Summer Job, along with *A Guide for Young People on How to Get a Job,* are free from: Employment Service, Employment and Training Administration, Department of Labor, 601 D St. N.W., Room 8100, Washington, DC 20213/202-376-6750.

Technological Impact on Employment Resource

The Office of Productivity and Technology Studies investigates trends in technology and their impact on employment and productivity. Staff will send you an inventory of available statistics, and they can tell you about both industries affected and occupations displaced by technological innovations. The Office frequently issues reports and updates about the impact of technological changes and the manpower trends of various industries. A publications list is available upon request. Some of these reports, all available from the Superintendent of Documents, U.S. Government Printing Office, Washington, DC 20402 include:

Technology and Labor in Four Industries: Meat Products /Foundries / Metalworking Machinery / Electrical and Electronic Equipment (Bulletin 2104)

Technology and Labor in Five Industries: Bakery Products / Concrete / Air Transportation / Telephone Communication / Insurance (Bulletin 2033)

Technological Change and Its Labor Impact in Five Energy Industries: Coal Mining / Oil and Gas Extraction / Petroleum Refining / Petroleum Pipeline Transportation / Electric and Utilities (Bulletin 2005)

Technological Change and its Labor Impact in Five Industries: Apparel / Footwear / Motor Vehicles / Railroads / Retail Trade (Bulletin 1961)

Technological Change and Manpower Trends in Five Industries: Pulp and Paper / Hydraulic Cement / Steel / Aircraft and Missiles / Wholesale Trade (Bulletin 1856)

Technical Change and Manpower Trends in Six Industries: Textile Mill Products / Lumber and Wood

Products / Tires and Tubes / Aluminum / Banking / Health Services (Bulletin 1817)

Contact: Office of Productivity and Technology Studies, Bureau of Labor Statistics, Department of Labor, 441 G St. N.W., Washington, DC 20212/ 202-523-9294.

Technological Trends

Studies of employment and occupational implications of technological change are prepared by this Division. One type of summary report appraises some of the major technological changes emerging among selected American industries and discusses the impact of these changes on productivity and labor over the next 5 to 10 years. Another category of study examines the impact of technological innovations such as computers which are being adopted throughout industry. In addition, in-depth studies are prepared periodically for selected major industries where significant changes are taking place on a large scale. Contact: Division of Industry Productivity and Technology Studies, Bureau of Labor Statistics, Department of Labor, 200 Constitution Ave. N.W., Room S4325, Washington, DC 20210/202-523-9219.

Toxic Substances

For information on toxic and hazardous substances such as air contaminants and asbestos, contact: Office of Toxic Substances, Directorate of Health Standards Programs, Occupational Safety and Health Administration, Department of Labor, 200 Constitution Ave. N.W., Room 3718, Washington, DC 20210/202-523-7148.

Trade and Employment Statistics

Information is available on import values and quantities by Trade Schedule United States Annotated (TUSA) number and Standard Industrial Classification (SIC) codes. Information is also available on the ratio of imports to new supply (domestic shipments plus imports), ratio of exports to product shipments, and employment tabulations by SIC industry and industry group. Contact: Office Productivity and Technology, Bureau of Labor Statistics, Department of Labor, 200 Constitution Ave. N.W., Room S4325, Washington, DC 20210/202-523-9294.

Training International Visitors

Each year over 1,000 international visitors participate in customized training programs on such topics as manpower assessment and planning, industrial psychology and industrial economics. Contact: International Visitor Program, Bureau of International Labor Affairs, Department of Labor, 200 Constitution Ave. N.W., Room S5016, Washington, DC 20210/202-523-6301.

Unemployment Compensation, Federal Advisory Council

This advisory body is made up of five employers, five employees, and five members of the general public to study, review and advise the Secretary of unemployment insurance issues. They meet, by law, at least twice a year and issue reports on their meetings. Contact: Federal Advisory Council on Unemployment Compensation, Unemployment Insurance Services, Employment and Training Administration, Department of Labor, 601 D St. N.W., Room 7112, Washington, DC 20213/202-376-6636.

Unemployment Insurance Laws, Comparison of State

This semi-annual review includes information on eligibility, administration, temporary disability insurance, federal training allowances, benefits, taxes, etc. Contact: Unemployment Insurance Service, Employment and Training Administration, Department of Labor, 601 D St. N.W., Room 6326, Washington, DC 20213/202-376-7120.

Unemployment Insurance Programs

This program provides temporary income as partial compensation to employed workers. The programs are administered jointly by the Employment and Training Administration and the individual states. Contact: Unemployment Insurance Programs, Policy and Legislation, Unemployment Insurance Service, Employment and Training Administration, Department of Labor, 601 D St. N.W., Room 7112, Washington, DC 20213/202-376-6636.

Unemployment Insurance Statistics

This monthly report provides data that are collected and reported under the unemployment insurance programs. Data include initial claims, average weekly insured unemployment, weeks compensated, first payments, etc. Additional data may be received from state agencies. Contact: Actuarial Services Division, Office of Research, Legislation and Program Policies, Unemployed Insurance Service, Employment and Training Administration, Department of Labor, 601 D St. N.W., Room 7402, Washington, DC 20213/202-376-6162.

Unions, Information on

Reports filed by unions, employers and labor relations consultants are open to the public. Unions must file copies of their constitutions and by-laws, annual financial reports and certain other information. Union officers and employees must report any payments from employers other than regular wages or other regular payments and employers must report making the payments. Employers must report any expenditures made to interfere with or restrain the right of employees to form a union or bargain collectively. Employers must file reports if they make any agreements with labor relations consultants or other independent contractors to persuade employees not to join a union or exercise their collective bargaining rights or any agreements to obtain certain information about employees' union activities. Labor relations consultants must file reports if they make such agreements with employers. For information on this documentation, contact: Disclosure Room, Office of Labor-Management Standards Enforcement, Department of Labor, 200 Constitution Ave. N.W., Room N5616, Washington, DC 20210/202-523-7393 or 523-8861.

Veterans' Affirmative Action
Veterans are entitled proper consideration for employment by any company that has a federal contract over $10,000. Further information can be obtained from the State Director for Veterans' Employment and Training Service and complaints should be directed to the Employment Standards Administration, Office of Federal Contract Compliance Programs, 200 Constitution Ave. N.W., Room N-3422, Washington, DC 20210/202-523-9447.

Veterans' Employment Programs
The following programs are aimed at veterans:

Disabled Veterans Outreach Program—staff works with the Veterans Administration, veterans' organizations and other groups primarily to find disabled and Vietnam-era veterans in need of job services.
Reemployment Rights—helps qualified veterans obtain their legal rights to return to their former employer with the position and benefits they would have attained had they not been in military service.
Job Training and Partnership Act—veterans who are unemployed and economically disadvantaged are eligible for on-the-job training and public service employment with pay under this law.
Job Placements—local employment Service/Job Service offices offer a variety of assistance to veterans, including counseling, aptitude testing, and referrals to training and jobs.

The Department's field staff and State Directors for Veterans' Employment and Training Service nationwide oversee these programs to make sure state employment agencies and job service offices give priority to veterans. Contact: Assistant Secretary for Veterans' Employment, Veterans' Employment and Training Service, Department of Labor, 200 Constitution Ave. N.W., Room S1315, Washington, DC 20210/202-523-9116.

Veterans' Reemployment Rights
Federal law gives reemployment rights to people who leave their jobs to enter the military services or to train with the National Guard or military reserve units. These rights also apply to people who leave their jobs to enter military service but are rejected. Assistance is available to help veterans exercise these rights. Complaints are investigated and problems are referred to the Department of Justice. Contact: Office of Veterans' Reemployment Rights, Veterans' Employment and Training Service, Department of Labor, 200 Constitution Ave. N.W., Room N5414, Washington, DC 20210/202-523-8611 or 376-6755.

Wages and Industrial Relations Data
This program provides for: a) wage studies made for selected occupations in about 150 areas and about ten industries annually; b) studies of employee benefits such as various types of leave, holidays, insurance and retirement; c) wage trend studies, summarizing wage changes in major industries; and d) industrial relations studies providing collective bargaining settlements, information on work stoppages. Contact: Bureau of Labor Statistics, Office of Wages and Industrial Relations, Department of Labor, Washington, DC 20212/202-523-1382.

Wage Surveys
The following occupational wage surveys are conducted: area surveys for 70 metropolitan areas; industry surveys; national white-collar salary survey. These surveys are meant to measure trends in employee compensation. Contact: Office of Wages and Industrial Relations, Bureau of Labor Statistics, Department of Labor, 441 G St. N.W., Room 2826, Washington, DC 20212/202-523-1382.

Where to Find BLS Statistics on Women
The Bureau of Labor Statistics (BLS) publishes a great variety of statistics on women. It covers the labor force status, employment and unemployment, earnings and hours of work, education, membership in labor organizations and the occupational injuries and illnesses of women. It can also generate special data on the labor force and other socioeconomic variables concerning women. The 1980 edition describes the publications available and how to obtain them. Contact: Bureau of Labor Statistics Regional Offices or Office of Publications, Bureau of Labor Statistics, Department of Labor, 441 G St. N.W., Room 2421, Washington, DC 20212/202-523-1239 or 523-1221.

White-Collar Salary
Data are available showing averages and distribution of salary rates for about 90 professional, administrative, technical and clerical work levels. Contact: Occupational Policy and Employment Benefit Level, Office of Wages and Industrial Relations, Bureau of Labor Statistics, Department of Labor, 441 G St. N.W., Room 2818, Washington, DC 20212/202-523-1246.

Women In Non-Traditional Jobs

This office evaluates how the Job Training Partnership Act and other programs are meeting the job market needs of special target groups such as minority women, older women, rural women, displaced homemakers and young mothers. Contact: Division of Program Evaluation and Review, Women's Bureau, Department of Labor, 200 Constitution Ave. N.W., Room S3315, Washington, DC 20210/202-523-6624.

Women in the U.S. Work Force Information Source

The Women's Bureau of the U.S. Department of Labor follows the impact women have on the U.S. work force as well as the conditions and special problems encountered by working women. The Bureau is currently studying the impact of high technology on labor and its findings will be released in early 1985. The office has studied a variety of issues affecting women, including equal opportunity, women in non-traditional careers, employment goals, and women in management. Staff tracks legislative proposals affecting women such as sex discrimination laws, job training partnerships, and state labor laws. A listing of publications and bibliographies produced by the Bureau, as well as program models, are available upon request. Contact: Women's Bureau, Department of Labor, 200 Constitution Avenue, N.W., Washington, DC 20210/202-523-6611.

Women in the Work Force Statistics

Statistics are compiled on a monthly and annual basis on women in the labor force, e.g., female heads of households, earnings gap, minority women workers, and mature women workers. Contact: Economic Status and Opportunities Branch, Women's Bureau, Department of Labor, 200 Constitution Ave. N.W., Room S3309, Washington, DC 20210/202-523-6652.

Women's Bureau

The Women's Bureau promotes a variety of programs for women to improve their chances for employment, better pay and higher status. Programs include, helping minority women, displaced homemakers, teen-age mothers, American Indian women, women offenders, union women, apprenticeship in nontraditional jobs, and child care facilities. The Bureau also maintains a Resource Center which collects and disseminates information on women's programs throughout the United States. Contact: Information Office, Women's Bureau, Department of Labor, 200 Constitution Ave. N.W., Room S3306, Washington, DC 20210/202-523-6653.

Worker Adjustment Assistance

This program aids workers who have recently been laid off or forced to go on short work weeks because of foreign trade competition. Workers can receive weekly allowances and a variety of help in preparing for and finding new employment. They may also get grants to look for work outside their home areas and money to pay for moving to new jobs. Petitions for group eligibility may be filed by a group of three or more workers through a union or an authorized representative. Contact: Office of Trade Adjustment Assistance, Employment and Training Administration, Department of Labor, 601 D St. N.W., Room 6434, Washington, DC 20213/202-376-2646.

Workers Without Jobs

This publication presents 31 charts covering characteristics of the unemployed by race, education, family, marital status, and occupation. Available for $4.50 from: Superintendent of Documents, Government Printing Office, Washington, DC 20402/202-783-3238.

Work Incentive Program (WIN)

This program provides help in finding jobs to families with dependent children. It provides job information, help in looking for work, and services like child care and medical aid. Contact: Office of Work Incentive Programs, Division of Work Incentive Programs, Employment and Training Administration, Department of Labor, 601 D St. N.W., Room 8028, Washington, DC 20213/202-376-6890.

Work Stoppages

Studies are conducted on the number of work stoppages, workers and days idle, work stoppages by industry and area, issues involved, duration of stoppage and method of settlement. Contact: Division of Developments in Labor-Management Relations, Office of Wage and Industrial Relations, Bureau of Labor Statistics, Department of Labor, 411 G St. N.W., Room 1288, Washington, DC 20212/202-523-1858.

How Can the Department of Labor Help You?

To determine how the Department of Labor can help you, contact: Office of Information, Publications and Reports, Department of Labor, 200 Constitution Ave. N.W., Washington, DC 20210/202-523-9711.

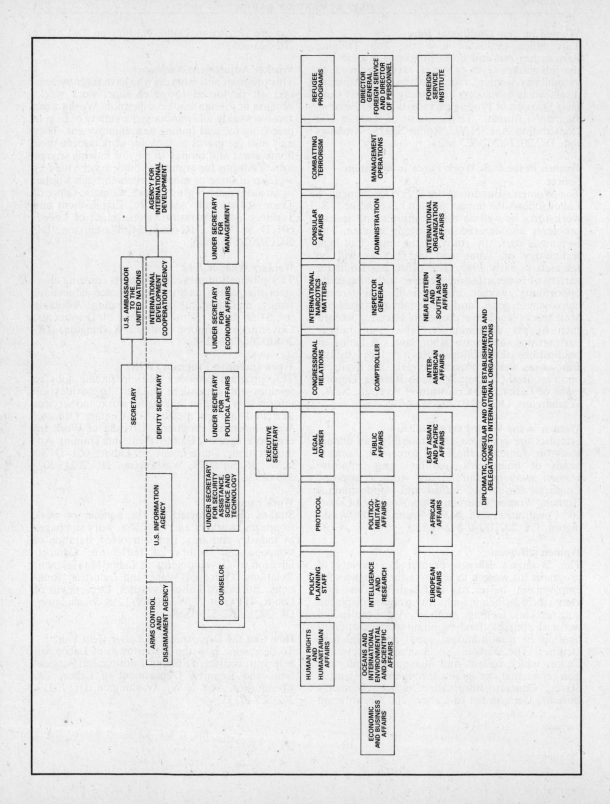

DIPLOMATIC, CONSULAR AND OTHER ESTABLISHMENTS AND
DELEGATIONS TO INTERNATIONAL ORGANIZATIONS

SECRETARY

DEPUTY SECRETARY

U.S. AMBASSADOR
TO THE
UNITED NATIONS

INTERNATIONAL
DEVELOPMENT
COOPERATION AGENCY

AGENCY FOR
INTERNATIONAL
DEVELOPMENT

ARMS CONTROL
AND
DISARMAMENT AGENCY

U.S. INFORMATION
AGENCY

COUNSELOR

UNDER SECRETARY
FOR SECURITY
ASSISTANCE,
SCIENCE AND
TECHNOLOGY

UNDER SECRETARY
FOR
POLITICAL AFFAIRS

UNDER SECRETARY
FOR
ECONOMIC AFFAIRS

UNDER SECRETARY
FOR MANAGEMENT

EXECUTIVE
SECRETARY

POLICY
PLANNING
STAFF

PROTOCOL

LEGAL
ADVISER

CONGRESSIONAL
RELATIONS

INTERNATIONAL
NARCOTICS
MATTERS

CONSULAR
AFFAIRS

COMBATTING
TERRORISM

REFUGEE
PROGRAMS

INTELLIGENCE
AND
RESEARCH

POLITICO-
MILITARY
AFFAIRS

PUBLIC
AFFAIRS

COMPTROLLER

INSPECTOR
GENERAL

ADMINISTRATION

MANAGEMENT
OPERATIONS

DIRECTOR
GENERAL
FOREIGN SERVICE
AND DIRECTOR
OF PERSONNEL

ECONOMIC
AND BUSINESS
AFFAIRS

OCEANS AND
INTERNATIONAL
ENVIRONMENTAL
AND SCIENTIFIC
AFFAIRS

HUMAN RIGHTS
AND
HUMANITARIAN
AFFAIRS

EUROPEAN
AFFAIRS

AFRICAN
AFFAIRS

EAST ASIAN
AND PACIFIC
AFFAIRS

INTER-
AMERICAN
AFFAIRS

NEAR EASTERN
AND
SOUTH ASIAN
AFFAIRS

INTERNATIONAL
ORGANIZATION
AFFAIRS

FOREIGN
SERVICE
INSTITUTE

Department of State

2210 C St. N.W., Washington, DC 20520/202-632-6575

Established: January 10, 1781
Budget: $2,528,106,00
Employees: 23,569

Mission: Advises the President in the formulation and execution of foreign policy; promotes the long-range security and well-being of the United States; determines and analyzes the facts relating to American overseas interest, makes recommendations on policy and future action, and takes the necessary steps to carry out established policy; engages in continuous consultations with the American public, the Congress, other U.S. departments and agencies, and foreign governments; negotiates treaties and agreements with foreign nations; speaks for the United States in the United Nations and in more than 50 major international organizations in which the United States participates; and represents the United States at more than 800 international conferences annually.

Data Experts

Country Desk Officers

The following experts can provide current political, economic, and other background information on the country which they study. These experts can be reached by telephone or by writing in care of: Country Officers, Department of State, 2201 C St. N.W., Washington, DC 20520. Keep in mind that these country desk officers change jobs within the State Department every two years or so.

Afghanistan (Kabul)/Phyllise Oakley/202-632-9552
Albania/William Warren/202-632-4577
Algeria (Algiers)/Thomas Wukitch/202-632-0304
Andorra/Richard Erdman/202-632-2633
Angola (Luanda)/Charles Hall***/202-632-9429
Argentina (Buenos Aires)/Dennise Jett/202-632-9166
Australia (Canberra)/John Glassman/202-632-9690
Austria (Vienna)/Ralph C. Porter III/202-632-2005
Bahamas (Nassau)/Roger Pierce/202-632-6386
Bahrain (Manama)/Janet Sinder/202-632-1794
Baltic States/John Zerolis/202-632-3655
Bangladesh (Dacca)/Jackson McDonald/202-632-0466
Barbados (Bridgetown)/Sondra Marsden/202-632-8451
Belgium (Brussels)/James Huff/202-632-0498
Belize (Belize City)/Gregory Sprow/202-632-0467
Benin (Cotonou)/James Eighmie/202-632-0842
Bermuda (Hamilton)/Carol Staker/202-632-2622

Bhutan/S. Eistman/202-632-0653
Bolivia (La Paz)/Lee Peters/202-632-3076
Botswana (Gaborone)/Peggy Blackford/202-632-0916
Brazil (Brazilia)/Elaine Papzien/202-632-2313
British Honduras/(See Belize)
British Indian Ocean Territory (BIOT)/Robert Snyder/202-632-3040
British Solomon Islands Protectorate/(See Solomon Islands)
Brunei/Thomas Hamilton/202-632-3276
Bulgaria (Sofia)/William Warren/202-632-1457
Burma (Rangoon)/Dee Robinson/202-632-0978
Burundi (Bujumbura)/Alan Tousignent/202-632-3138
Cambodia (Phnom Penh)/Terry Breese/202-632-3132
Cameroon (Yaounde)/Deborah Dell/202-632-0996
Canada (Ottawa)/Sam Fromowitz/202-632-3135
    William Millend/202-632-3189
    Steve Watkins/202-632-1097
    Don Grabenste/202-632-1096
Cape Verde (Praia)/Thomas Burke/202-632-8436
CENTO/Vacant/202-632-3121
Central African Republic (Bangui)/Alan Tousignent/202-632-3138
Central America (ROCAP)/N. Shaw Smith/632-4010
Ceylon (Colombo)/(See Sri Lanka)
Chad (N'Djamena)/Robert Sorenson McMillion/202-632-0725

Chile (Santiago)/David Dbuhy/202-632-2575
China, People's Republic of (Beijing)/Donald Keyser/
202-632-0356
　Howard Lange/202-632-2656
　Hong Kong/James Keith/202-632-1436
Colombia (Bogota)/Gabriel M. Guerra/202-632-3023
Comoros/Robert Snyder/202-632-0668
Congo (Brazzaville)/Ned McMahon/202-632-1637
Congo (Kinshasa)/(See Zaire, Republic of)
Cook Islands/Robert Millspaugh/202-632-3546
Costa Rica (San Jose)/William Togliani/202-632-3385
Council of Europe/Judith Heimann/202-632-0740
CSCE/Michael Klosson/202-632-8050
Cuba (Havana)/Anthony Perkins/202-632-1476
　John Modder/202-632-1658
　John Ritchie/202-632-1503
Cyprus (Nicosia)/Rick Sherman/202-632-1429
Czechoslovakia (Prague)/Paul Hocker/202-632-1457
Dahomey (Cotonou)/(See Benin)
Denmark (Copenhagen)/Alan McKee/202-632-1774
Diego Garcia/Robert Synder/202-632-3040
Djibouti, Republic of (Djibouti)/Randall Lecocq/202-
632-3355
Dominica (Roseau)/Sondra Morsden/202-632-8451
Dominican Republic (Santo Domingo)/David Rogers/
202-632-2130
Economic and Social Commission for Asia and the
Pacific/Kyle Scott/202-632-1654
Economic Commissions for Africa/Kyle Scott/202-632-
1654
Economic Commission for Europe (ECE)/John Garner/
202-632-1656
Economic Commission for Latin America/Kyle Scott/
202-632-1654
Ecuador (Quito)/Steve Ordal/202-632-5864
Egypt, Arab Republic of (Cairo)/Brent Hortley/202-632-
2365
　Donald Booth/202-632-1169
El Salvador (San Salvador)/Robert Boggs/202-632-8148
Equatorial Guinea (Malabo)/Charles Shapiero/202-632-
0996
Estonia/D. Thomas Longo, Jr./202-632-1739
Ethiopia (Addis Ababa)/Randall Lecocq/202-632-3355
European Atomic Energy Commission (Euratom)/Judith
Heimann/202-632-0315
European Coal and Steel Community (ECSC)/Reynold
Reimer/202-632-1708
　Judith Heimann/202-632-0740
European Communities/Reynold Reimer/202-632-1708
European Economic Community (EEC)/Reynold Rei-
mer/202-632-1708
European Free Trade Association (EFTA)/Bryon Blood/
202-632-0457
European Programs
European Space Research Organization (ESRO)/Sher-
wood McGinnis/202-632-0315
Fiji (Suva)/Robert Millspough/202-632-3546
Finland (Helsinki)/Dennis Finnerty III*/202-632-0624
France (Paris)/Dean Curran/202-632-1426
French Antilles/David Rogers/202-632-8451
French Guiana/(See French Antilles)
French Polynesia/Robert Millspaugh/202-632-3546
Gabon (Libreville)/Devron Odell/202-632-0996
Gambia, The (Banjul)/Ken Scott/202-632-2865

Germany, Federal Republic of (Bonn)/Douglas H. Jines/
202-632-2155
　William Salisbury/202-632-0414
　D. Thomas Wolfson/202-632-0415
　Jeffrey Gallop (Berlin affairs)/202-632-2310
German Democratic Republic (Berlin)/Keith McCor-
mack/202-632-2721
Ghana (Accra)/Tom Burke/202-632-8436
Gibraltar/(See Spain)
Gilbert and Ellice Islands/Robert Millspaugh/202-632-
3546
Great Britain/(See United Kingdom)
Greece (Athens)/David Jones/202-632-1563
Greenland/William T. McGlynn/202-632-1774
Grenada/Douglas Rhem/202-632-4195
Guadeloupe/David Rogers/202-632-8541
Guatemala (Guatemala)/James F. Mack/202-632-0467
Guinea (Conakry)/James Eighmie/202-632-0842
Guinea-Bissau (Bissau)/Tom Burke/202-632-8436
Guyana (Georgetown)/Chris Webster/202-632-3449
Haiti (Port-au-Prince)/Susan L. Lysyshyn/202-632-
3447
Honduras (Tegucigalpa)/Mile T. Dirson/202-632-3385
Hong Kong/James Keith/202-632-1322
　David Schear/202-632-2535
Horn of Africa/(See Ethiopia and Somalia)
Hungary (Budapest)/John Zerolis/202-632-1739
Iceland (Reykjavik)/Sam Horsey/202-632-1774
India (New Delhi)/Frances Culpepper/202-632-1289
Indonesia (Jakarta)/Alfred M. Lehn/202-632-3276
Iran (Tehran)/Donald Roberts/202-632-0313
　Peter J. Lydin/202-632-0448
　Mark Johnson*/202-632-0915
Iraq (Baghdad)/Frank Ricciardone/202-632-0695
Ireland (Dublin)/Sam Horsey/202-632-1194
Israel (Tel Aviv)/Keith Loken/202-632-3672
　Barbara Bodine/202-632-3672 Wendy Chamberlain/
202-632-3672 Timothy Hauser/202-632-3672
Italy (Rome)/D. Thomas Long Jr./202-632-2453
　William G. Perett/202-632-8210
　E.J. Beigel*/202-632-3746
Ivory Coast (Abidjan)/James Eighmie/202-632-0842
Jamaica (Kingston)/Chris Webster/202-632-6386
Japan (Tokyo)/Brian Mohler/202-632-3152
　Robert Reis/202-632-3152
　John Scott*/202-632-3152
Jordan (Amman)/Molly Williamson/202-632-0791
Kampuchea/(See Cambodia)
Kenya (Nairobi)/Jay Baker/202-632-0857
Korea, North and South/Spence Richardson**/202-632-
7717 Lee Coldren/202-632-7717 W. David Stroub/202-
632-7717 John Hoog/202-632-7717
Kuwait (Kuwait)/Qwen Loronwry/202-632-1334
Laos (Vientiane)/Terry A. Breese/202-632-3132
Latvia/John Zerolis/202-632-1739
Lebanon (Beirut)/William Stanton/202-632-1018
Lesotho (Maseru)/Susan L. Moots/202-632-8434
Liberia (Monrovia)/Vladimir Sanbaiew/202-632-8354
Libya (Tripoli)/Carol Otis/202-632-9373
Liechtenstein/David Johnson/202-632-2005
Lithuania/John Zerolis/202-632-3655
Luxembourg/James Huff/202-632-0498
　Dennis Finnerty/202-632-0624
Macao/James Keith/202-632-2656

Madagascar, Republic of (Antananarivo)/Robert Snyder/202-632-3040

Malagasy Republic/(See Madagascar, Republic of)

Malawi (Lilongwe)/Sylvia Stenfield/202-632-8851

Malaysia (Kuala Lumpur)/Thomas P. Hamilton/202-632-3276

Maldives/R. Ross Rodgers/202-632-2351

Mali Republic (Bamako)/Stephen Brandage/202-632-3066

Malta (Valletta)/William G. Perett/202-632-1726

Martinique/David F. Rogers/202-632-2130

Mauritania (Nouakchott)/Kenneth Scott/202-632-2865

Mauritius (Port Louis)/Robert Snyder/202-632-3040

Mexico (Mexico, D.F.)/George B. High/202-632-9894
Paul H. Walkerborth/202-632-1865
Nancy W. Masin/202-632-1881

Micronesia/(See Trust Territories of the Pacific Islands)

Monaco/Byron D. Curran/202-632-1726

Mongolia/Steve Young/202-632-1009

Morocco (Rabat)/L. Schermerhorn/202-632-0279

Mozambique (Maputo)/James Libera/202-632-8438

Namibia/Peter Perenyi/202-632-9693

NATO/John Hawes/202-632-1626

Nauru/Tom Allison/202-632-3546

Nepal (Kathmandu)/R. Powell/202-632-0653

Netherlands (The Hague)/James G. Huff/202-632-0498

Netherlands Antilles (Curacao)/Roger Pierce/202-632-7385

New Caledonia and New Hebrides/Robert Millspaugh/202-632-3546

New Zealand (Wellington)/Bruce N. Gray/202-632-9690

Nicaragua (Managua)/Steve G. McFarland/202-632-2205

Niger (Niamey)/Steve Brundage/202-632-3066

Nigeria (Lagos)/F. Marshall McCaller/202-632-3406
Jessie Benjamin/202-632-0647
John Chamberlain/202-632-3468

Northern Rhodesia/(See Zambia)

Norway (Oslo)/Alan McKee/202-632-1774

OECD/James R. Tarrent/202-632-0326

Oman (Muscat)/Qwen Cornway/202-632-1334

Pacific Islands (General)/Robert Millspaugh***/202-632-3546

Pakistan (Islamabad)/James Larocco/202-632-9823

Panama (Panama)/Sherman Hinsen/202-632-4986
Richard Wyrough/202-632-4982

Papua New Guinea (Port Moresby)/Robert Millspaugh/202-632-3546

Paraguay (Asuncion)/Stephanie Kennedy/202-632-1551

Peru (Lima)/Larry Rosser/202-632-3360

Philippines (Manila)/John Muisto/202-632-1669
Alice Straub/202-632-1221

Poland (Warsaw)/David Pozorski/202-632-0575

Portugal (Lisbon)/Murela Micholson/202-632-0719

Portuguese Guinea/(See Guinea-Bissau)

Qatar (Doha)/Qwen Cornway/202-632-1794

Reunion/Brian Curran/202-632-1726

Romania (Bucharest)/Thomas A. Lynch, Jr./202-632-3298

Rwanda (Kigali)/Alan C. Tousignent/202-632-3138

Samoa/(See Western Samoa)

San Marino/William Perett/202-632-2453

Sao Tome and Principe/Deborah Dell/202-632-0996

Saudi Arabia (Jidda)/David L. Litt/202-632-0865
Michael R. Arietti**/202-632-3121

Senegal (Dakar)/Kenneth Scott/202-632-2865

Seychelles (Victoria)/J. T. Baker/202-632-0857

Sierra Leone (Freetown)/Aubrey Verdun/202-632-8354

Singapore (Singapore)/Tom P. Hamilton/202-632-3276

Solomon Islands/Robert Millspaugh/202-632-3546

Somalia (Mogadishu)/Christopher Murray/202-632-0849

South African Republic (Pretoria)/Robert Kott/202-632-3274
Richard Norland/202-632-9693

South Pacific Commission/Robert Millspaugh/202-632-3546

South West Africa/(See Namibia)

Spain (Madrid)/Richard Erdman/202-632-2633

Sri Lanka (Ceylon) (Colombo)/R. Ross Rodgers/202-632-2351

Sudan (Khartoum)/Peter Lindino/202-632-0668

Suriname/Susan Lysyhne/202-632-3449

Switzerland/David T. Johnson/202-632-2005

Syria/Bruce Ehrnman/202-632-4714

Taiwan Coordination/Mark S. Pratt/202-632-7710

Thailand/Nick Mauger/202-632-0978

Tobago/Roger D. Pierce/202-632-7385

Togo/James Eighmie/202-632-0842

Tonga/Robert Millspaugh/202-632-3546

Trinidad/Roger D. Pierce/202-632-7385

Trust Territory of the Pacific Islands/Robert Millspaugh/202-632-3546

Tunisia/Steven Eisenbraun/202-632-3614

Turkey/Arma J. Kovaer/202-632-1562

United Arab Emirates (Abu Dhabi)/Janet Saunderson/202-632-1794

USSR (Moscow)/James F. Schumaker (Bilateral)/202-632-8671
Alex Vershaw (Multilateral)/202-632-0821
Thomas R. Mortens/202-632-3071

United Kingdom (London)/Kay Stocker/202-632-2622

United Republic of Tanzania (Dar es Salaam)/Robert Snyder/202-632-3040

Upper Volta (Ouagadougou)/Stephen Brundage/202-632-3066

Uruguay (Montevideo)/Stephen Kennedy/202-632-1551

Vatican/William G. Perett/202-632-8210

Venezuela (Caracas)/Linda Pfeifle/202-632-3338

Vietnam/Brian Kirkpatrick/202-632-3132

Western European Union (WEU)/John Hamilton/202-632-8051

Western Sahara/Kenneth Scott/202-632-2865

Western Samoa (Apia)/Robert Millspaugh/202-632-3546

Yemen Arab Republic (Sana)/Andrew Steinfeld/202-632-2329

Yemen, People's Democratic Republic of/Andrew Steinfield/202-632-2329

Yugoslavia (Belgrade)/Nicholas Lang/202-632-3655
Ben Fairfax/202-632-3747

Zaire, Republic (Kinshasa)/Ralph Bresler/202-632-2216

Zambia (Lusaka)/Sylvia Stanfield/202-632-8851

Zanzibar/(See United Republic of Tanzania)

Zimbabwe/Simeno Moats/202-632-8252

---

*denotes Economic Officer

**denotes Politico-Military Officer

***denotes Political/Economic Officer

****denotes Economic/Commercial Officer

Major Sources of Information

African Affairs

Regional profiles of Sub Sahara African countries which includes biographical data, relationship with the United States. Information such as background notes on each country; discussion papers—political, economic, historical and ethnographic data; speeches by country experts; press clips; general information on Africa; and current policy speeches, are available on: Angola, Benin, Botswana, British Indian Ocean Territories, Burundi, Cameroon, Cape Verde, Central African Republic, Chad, Comoros, Congo, Republic of Djibouti, Equatorial Guinea, Ethiopia, Gabon, The Gambia, Ghana, Guinea, Guinea-Bissau, Ivory Coast, Kenya, Lesotho, Liberia, Republic of Madagascar, Malawi, Mali Republic, Mauritania, Mauritus, Mozambique, Namibia, Niger, Nigeria, Rwanda, Sao Tome and Principe, Senegal, Seychelles, Sierra Leone, Somalia, South African Republic, Sudan, Swaziland, Togo, Uganda, United Republic of Tanzania, Upper Volta, Western Sahara, Republic of Zaire, Zambia, Zimbabwe. Contact: Bureau of African Affairs, Public Affairs, Department of State, 2201 C St. N.W., Room 3509, Washington, DC 20520/202-632-0362.

Agriculture

This office is the United States link with four Rome-based United Nations agricultural organizations: Food and Agriculture Organization (FAO), World Food Council, World Food Program, and International Fund for Agricultural Development. Contact: Agriculture Office of Economic and Social Affairs, Bureau of International Organization Affairs, Department of State, 2201 C St. N.W., Room 5331, Washington, DC 20520/202-632-0492.

Arms Control—Nuclear Exports

The Office of Non-Proliferation and Export Policy specializes in the arms control and the national security dimension of the nuclear proliferation problem. It pays particular attention to the role of U.S. alliance relationships and security assistance programs within the non-proliferation policy, and formulates the U.S. Department of State policy regarding nonproliferation aspects of other arms control agreements. Contact: Office of Non-Proliferation and Export Policy, Bureau of Oceans, International Environmental and Scientific Affairs, Department of State, 2201 C St. N.W., Room 7828, Washington, DC 20520/202-632-7036.

Arms Transfer

For information on the transfer, selling, giving or licensing of arms or arms technology to foreign countries, contact: Office of Security Assistance and Sales, Bureau of Politico-Military Affairs, Department of State, 2201 C St. N.W., Room 7418, Washington, DC 20520/202-632-3882.

Art in U.S. Embassies

This program borrows art works of all mediums by American artists from museums, corporations and private collections, commercial galleries and artists for a minimum period of two years. Anyone interested in participating in the program by lending art works should contact: Art in Embassies Program, Bureau of Administration, Department of State, 21st and Virginia Ave. N.W., Room B-258, Washington, DC 20520/202-632-1634.

Business Patents and Protection

This office is active in government business dialogues concerning the protection of industrial property, various restrictive business practices, and patent, trademark and copyright protection, as well as various problems relating to licensing agreements. Contact: Office of Business Practices, Bureau of Economics and Business Affairs, Department of State, 2201 C St. N.W., Room 3531A, Washington, DC 20520/202-632-1486.

Certification for Travel Abroad

Foreign governments sometimes require American businesspeople conducting business abroad to receive certification from the American government showing that they represent business entities operating legally within the United States. This certification may be required to register for visa purposes, to obtain work permits, or to license a vehicle. Businesspeople must first obtain from the appropriate official in their states of residence a certificate of incorporation. This office will authenticate that document so that it may be presented to the foreign government. Contact: Authentications, Foreign Affairs Center, Bureau of Administration, Department of State, 2201 C St. N.W., Room 2815 (2813 for mailing), Washington, DC 20520/202-632-0406.

Citizens Arrested Overseas

The Arrest Unit monitors arrests and trials to see that United States citizens are not abused; acts as a liaison with family and friends in the United States; sends money, messages, etc. (with written consent of arrestee); offers lists of lawyers; will forward money from the United States to detainee; tries to assure that your rights under local laws are observed. The Emergency Medical and Dietary Assistance Program includes: providing vitamin supplements when necessary; granting emergency transfer for emergency medical care; and short-term feeding of two or three meals a day when arrestee is detained without funds to buy his or her own meals. Contact: Arrests Unit, Citizens Emergency Center, Overseas Citizens Service, Bureau of Consular Affairs, Department of State, 2201 C St. N.W., Room 4800, Washington, DC 20520/202-632-5225.

Citizens Emergency Center

Emergency telephone assistance is available to United States citizens abroad in the following areas:

Arrests—(See "Citizens Arrested Overseas")—202-632-5225.

Deaths—202-632-5225; notification of interested parties in the United States of the death abroad of United States citizens. Assistance in the arrangements for disposition of remains.

Financial Assistance—202-632-5225; repatriation of destitute United States nationals, coordination of medical evacuation of nonofficial United States nationals from abroad; transmission of private funds in emergencies to destitute United States nationals abroad when commercial banking facilities are unavailable (all costs must be reimbursed).

Shipping and Seamen—202-632-5225; protection of American vessels and seamen.

Welfare and Whereabouts—202-632-5225; search for nonofficial United States nationals who have not been heard from for an undue length of time and/or about whom there is special concern; transmission of emergency messages to United States nationals abroad.

Contact: Overseas Citizen Services, Bureau of Consular Affairs, Department of State, 2201 C St. N.W., Washington, DC 20520/202-632-3444.

Claims Against Foreign Governments

The Government of the United States, at the discretion of the Secretary of State, will act on behalf of U.S. nationals in attempting to settle claims against foreign governments. Assistance is not available: 1) to non-nationals; 2) in cases where there has not been an exhaustion of all local administrative or judicial remedies with a resulting denial of justice; or 3) where the respondent government is not responsible under international law. If the claim is found to be valid by the U.S. Department of State and the Secretary of State chooses to back the claim, the claimant will be informed as to how the claim should be prepared and documented. The U.S. Department of State, using the documentation prepared by the claimant, would then act on behalf of the claimant in pressing for settlement. Settlements (compensation or restitution) result either from direct negotiation through diplomatic channels or from arbitration, which lead to payment by the foreign government. Contact: Assistant Legal Advisor for International Claims, Office of the Legal Advisor, Department of State, 2201 C St. N.W., Washington, DC 20520/202-632-9598.

Commercial Policy

Information is available on such topics as: policy and agreement on developing country trade, General Agreement on Tariffs and Trade (GATT) coordinator, and multilateral trade negotiations. Contact: Developing Countries and Trade Organization Division, International Trade Policy, Bureau of Economic and Business Affairs, Department of State, 2201 C St. N.W., Room 3829, Washington, DC 20520/202-632-0687.

Consumer Affairs

This is the main office at the U.S. Department of State for consumer complaints, advice and information. They bring consumer leaders to Washington to get their opinions on consumer issues such as pricing coffee, etc. It also has consumer advisors as delegates during international negotiations. Contact: Consumer Affairs, Bureau of Economic and Business Affairs, Department of State, 2201 C St. N.W., Room 6822, Washington, DC 20520/202-632-1682.

Consumer Countries—Energy

This office coordinates policies of energy-consuming nations. It also works with the U.S. Department of Energy to coordinate domestic and foreign policy. Contact: Consumer Country Affairs, International Energy Policy, Bureau of Economics and Business Affairs, Department of State, 2201 C St. N.W., Room 3336, Washington, DC 20520/202-632-8097.

Cooperative Science and Technology

This office deals on a bilateral basis with other governments—mainly China, Mexico, USSR, Japan, Brazil, African countries on science and technology, including energy research and development, agriculture, marine science, and space. Contact: Office of Cooperative Science and Technology Programs, Science and Technology Affairs, Bureau of Oceans and International Environmental and Scientific Affairs, Department of State, 2201 C St. N.W., Room 4330, Washington, DC 20520/202-632-2958.

Country Reports on Human Rights

This is an annual report submitted to Congress which lists recipients of United States economic or security assistance, all foreign countries which are United Nations members, and also the amounts of United States bilateral assistance and multilateral development assistance. It provides descriptions of human rights conditions for each country which received such assistance. Bilateral assistance figures are broken down by three basic categories: economic assistance; military assistance; and total economic and military assistance. For additional information contact: Country Reports, Bureau of Human Rights and Humanitarian Affairs, Department of State, 2201

C St. N.W., Room 7802, Washington, DC 20520/202-632-3660.

Decorations and Gifts from Foreign Governments
A list of all decorations and gifts given to federal departments and agencies by foreign governments is published annually in the *Federal Register*. The gifts are described and their value is estimated. If the gifts are not used by the government or are not donated to public institutions, they are sold to the public by the General Services Administration. For information, contact: Office of Protocol, Department of State, 2201 C St. N.W., Room 1238, Washington, DC 20520/202-632-0907.

Digest of U.S. Practices on International Law
This is an annual compendium of U.S. activities, both domestic and international, that have a bearing on international law. Available for $21.00 from the Government Printing Office, Superintendent of Documents, Washington, DC 20402/202-783-3238. For more detailed information on content, contact: Legal Adviser, Department of State, Room 6422, Washington, DC 20520/202-632-2628.

East Asia and Pacific
For information on: Australia, Brunei, Burma, Cambodia, People's Republic of China, Cook Islands, Fiji, French Polynesia, Gilbert and Ellice Islands, Hong Kong, Indonesia, Japan, North Korea, South Korea, Laos, Macao, Malaysia, Mongolia, Nauru, New Caledonia and New Hebrides, New Zealand, Pacific Islands, Papua New Guinea, Phillipines, Singapore, Solomon Islands, Taiwan, Thailand, Tonga, Trust Territory of the Pacific Islands, Vietnam, and Western Samoa, contact: Bureau of East Asian and Pacific Affairs, Public Affairs, Department of State, 2201 C St. N.W., Room 5310, Washington, DC 20520/202-632-2538.

East-West Trade
For policy information on trading with Communist nations, contact: Office of East-West Trade, Bureau of Economic and Business Affairs, Department of State, 2201 C St. N.W., Room 3819, Washington, DC 20520/202-632-0964.

Energy Technology Corporation
This office is concerned mostly with aspects of non-nuclear advanced forms of energy such as extracting low-grade petroleum and coal, solar power and other alternative energy sources, and energy research and development on a multilateral and a bilateral basis. Some examples include: work with coal liquefaction research and development with Japan and Germany, and enhanced oil recovery with Venezuela. The office gives international policy guidance on energy research and development to the U.S. Department of Energy and Interior and to various agencies and it is involved in international energy development programs. Contact: Office of Energy Technology Cooperation, Environment, Health and Natural Resources, Bureau of Oceans and International Environmental and Scientific Affairs, Department of State, 2201 C. St. N.W., Room 7820, Washington, DC 20520/202-632-4413.

Environment and Health
Information is available on environmental and health matters within the international community. Priority attention is given to: toxic chemicals, transboundary air pollution (especially acid-rain problem), and global environmental monitoring systems. Contact: Office of Environment and Health, Bureau of Oceans and International Environmental and Scientific Affairs, Department of State, 2201 C St. N.W., Room 4325, Washington, DC 20520/202-632-9278.

European Affairs
Background notes, speeches and other information are available on all European countries and Canada, and OECD, European Community and Atlantic Political-Economic Affairs, NATO, and Atlantic Political-Military Affairs, Council of Europe, European Atomic Energy (EURATOM), European Coal and Steel Community (ECSC), European Communities, European Economic Community (EEC), European Free Trade Association (EFTA), European Launcher Develop (ELDO), and European Space Research Organization (ESRO). Contact: Bureau of European Affairs, Department of State, 2201 C St. N.W., Room 5229, Washington, DC 20520/202-632-0850.

Executive-Diplomat Seminars
These seminars provide an opportunity for indepth discussions of economic, commercial and other aspects of U.S. foreign policy between business executives and senior U.S. government officials. The seminar consists of a two-day program, with topics that cover: international finance, multilateral trade negotiations, tax reform, code of conduct, energy, commercial services, technology transfer, organization of the U.S. Department of State, International Resources and Food Policy, Human Rights, Ecology and Environmental Affairs. Contact: Executive-Diplomat Seminar, Office of Public Programs, Bureau of Public Affairs, Department of State, 2201 C St. N.W., Room 5831, Washington, DC 20520/202-632-3888.

Export and Import Control
The office coordinates and reviews replies with the Nuclear Regulatory Commission (NRC) for requests they receive to license nuclear export. They are also concerned with transfer of technology, nuclear-related energy and subsequent arrangements. Contact: Office of Export and Import

Control, Nuclear Energy and Energy Technology Affairs, Bureau of Oceans and International Environmental and Scientific Affairs, Department of State, 2201 C St. N.W., Room 7820, Washington, DC 20520/202-632-4101.

Family Planning
The Office of Population Affairs is involved with contraceptive research efforts to improve the technology available for family planning programs throughout the world. Contact: Population Affairs, Bureau of Oceans and International Environmental and Scientific Affairs, Department of State, 2201 C St. N.W., Room 7825, Washington, DC 20520/202-632-3472.

Film—History of U.S. Foreign Relations
A four-part color film series, 30 minutes each, with accompanying discussion guides, may be bought or borrowed without charge.

Part I—begins with the militia diplomacy of the Revolution and ends with the Monroe Doctrine.
Part II—traces expansion of U.S. interests in other nations and its evolution into a world power prior to the events of World War I.
Part III—shows the process by which the United States was finally obliged to accept the role of a major power in the years between World War I and Pearl Harbor.
Part IV—traces the development of U.S. foreign policy from 1945 to 1975.

Contact: Films Officer, Office of Public Communication, Public Affairs, Department of State, 2201 C St. N.W., Room 4827A, Washington, DC 20250/202-632-8203.

Fisheries
This office works principally with the Intergovernmental Oceanographic Commission (IOC), part of UNESCO and the International Council for the Exploration of the Seas (ICES). Their interests include: research in the Caribbean on food from the sea; the North Atlantic fisheries resources; and other oceanographic phenomena. Contact: Office of Fisheries Affairs, Oceans and Fisheries Affairs, Bureau of Oceans and International Environmental and Scientific Affairs, Department of State, 2201 C St. N.W., Room 5806, Washington, DC 20520/202-632-2335.

Food and Natural Resources
The main interest of this office is to maintain long-term productivity of renewable and nonrenewable resources including: forest cover (mostly tropical), arid land management, wildlife conservation, water resources management, protection of crop land and commercialization of new crops. The office coordinates these programs with the other United States agencies and their deals with foreign countries. One program, *Global 2000,* shows conditions and trends of global resources, population and environment. Contact: Office of Food and Natural Resources, Bureau of Oceans and International Environmental and Scientific Affairs, Department of State, Room 7819, Washington, DC 20520/202-632-4325.

Food Policy
This office makes sure that foreign policy concerns are considered where food aid programs are prepared, principally at the U.S. Department of Agriculture and the Agency for International Development. Information is available on the Food for Peace Program. This office also follows activities in other international food programs, such as World Food Program and Food Aid Committee which was recently set up by Food Aid Convention. Contact: Office of Food Policy and Programs, Bureau of Economic and Business Affairs, Department of State, Room 3427, 2201 C St. N.W., Washington, DC 20520/202-632-0563.

Foreign Country Background Notes
Background Notes on the Countries of the World is a series of short, factual pamphlets with information on the country's land, people, history, government, political conditions, economy, foreign relations, and U.S. policy. Each *Notes* also includes a factual profile, brief travel notes, a country map, and a reading list. Contact the Public Affairs Bureau, Department of State, Room 4827A, 2201 C St. N.W., Washington, DC 20520/202-632-6575 for a free copy of *Background Notes* for the countries you plan to visit. This material is also available from the Superintendent of Documents, Government Printing Office, Washington, DC 20402/202-783-3238. Single copies cost $1.50 or $32.00 for a set.

Foreign Language Training
The Foreign Service Institute is an in-house educational institution for foreign service officers, members of their families and employees of other government agencies. It provides special training in public administration, international relations, economics, area studies, consular studies and 50 foreign languages. It puts out instructional materials (books and tapes) designed to teach modern foreign languages. Lists of available books and tapes and their prices are available. Tapes are obtained through: National Audio Visual Center, General Services Administration, Order Section/AV, Washington, DC 20409/301-763-1891. Books are available from: Government Printing Office, Superintendent of Documents, Washington, DC 20402/202-783-3238. Additional available publications include: *Foreign Versions, Variations and Diminutives of English Names; Foreign Equivalents of United States Miltary and Civilian Titles.* This catalog is issued by the Immigration and Naturalization Service. It lists the foreign equivalent names for U.S. military and civilian titles for

45 countries. Available for $3.00 from: Government Printing Office, Superintendent of Documents, Washington, DC 20402/202-783-3238. *Testing Kit—French and Spanish,* contains eight audiocassettes, two-track mono recordings of actual speaking proficiency tests conducted at the Institute. The 140-page manual discusses and describes Foreign Service Institute language testing and techniques. Contact: National Audiovisual Center, National Archives and Records Service, General Services Administration, Order Section AV, Washington, DC 20409/301-763-1896. For more information on the Foreign Service Institute, contact: Foreign Service Institute, Department of State, SA-3, 2201 C St. N.W., Room 604, Washington, DC 20520/703-235-8826.

Foreign Service Officer Careers

Available information includes: description of various careers, eligibility requirements, examination information with sample questions, places where Foreign Service examinations are given, and bibliography about Foreign Service. There are special career opportunities for women and minority group members as mid-level officers and as junior Foreign Service Reserve Officer positions. Contact: Board of Examiners for the Foreign Service, Box 9317, Rosslyn Station, Arlington, VA 22209/703-235-9392.

Free Booklets for Travelers

The following book is available from: Publications Distribution, Bureau of Public Affairs, Department of State, 2201 C St. N.W., Room 5815A, Washington, DC 20520/202-632-9859.

Travel Information: Your Trip Abroad—provides basic information from the U.S. Department of State to help prepare for a trip—how to apply for a passport, customs tips, lodging information and how American consular officers can help you in an emergency.

The following publications are available from: Customs Office, P.O. Box 7118, Washington, DC 20044:

Customs Information
Bureau of Consular Affairs: Your Trip Abroad
Visa Requirements of Foreign Governments—lists the entry requirements for U.S. citizens traveling as tourists, and where and how to apply for visas and tourist cards. Available from: Passport Services, Bureau of Consular Affairs, Department of State, 1425 K St. N.W., Room G-62, Washington, DC 20524/202-783-8170. (See "Foreign Country Information" in this section.)

Freedom of Information

For information concerning requests made under the Freedom of Information Act, contact: Information and Privacy Staff, Foreign Affairs Information Management Center, Department of State, Room 1239, Washington, DC 20520/202-632-8459.

Geographic Data

Precise geographical information is available on boundary locations, territorial sovereignty, and terrain. Available publications include:

International Boundary Studies—land boundaries.
Limits in the Seas—sea boundaries listed by title and number. •
Status of the World's Nations Lists independent countries and gives their official long- and short-form name, capital city, population and area. Also lists dependencies and areas of special sovereignty (e.g., islands that belong to other countries).

Contact: Office of the Geographer, Bureau of Intelligence and Research, Department of State, 2201 C St. N.W., Room 8742, Washington, DC 20523/202-632-2021.

High Technology in Developed Countries

The Division of Developed Country Trade tracks high technology activities in developed country. Staff can provide you with a general overview of a specific country's activities. Contact: Division of Developed Country Trade, Office of Trade, U.S. Department of State, Room 3822, Washington, DC 20520/202-632-2718.

Historian

The Office of the Historian provides historical reference services to government officials, scholars, the press, and the general public. This office prepares, selects, compiles, edits and publishes *Foreign Relations of the United States,* a 260 volume set based on the records of government departments and agencies and includes major telegrams, memoranda, diplomatic notes and other basic papers comprising the official record of U.S. foreign policy. The office also conducts policy-related historical reference for the government. When this material is declassified it goes to the National Archives for Public Research. A list is available of major publications of the U.S. Department of State. Contact: Office of the Historian, Bureau of Public Affairs, Department of State, SA-1, Room 3100, Washington, DC 20520/202-632-8888.

Human Rights

For information on human rights activities within the United Nations and other multilateral organizations such as UNESCO, and International Labor Organization (ILO), contact: Office of Human Rights Affairs, Bureau of International Organization Affairs, Department of State, 2201 C St. N.W., Room 1509, Washington, DC 20520/202-632-0520.

Industrial and Strategic Materials

This office is concerned with all minerals and metals, both U.S.-produced or imported, that are used by U.S. industry and the military (over 90 different materials). It follows developments in the domestic and foreign markets and is involved in the negotiations of agreements. Contact: Industrial and Strategic Materials Division, Office of International Commodities, Bureau of Economic and Business Affairs, Department of State, 2201 C St. N.W., Room 3524A, Washington, DC 20520/202-632-1420.

InterAmerican Affairs
Background information as well as policy matters are available on: Argentina, Bahamas, Barbados, Belize, Bolivia, Brazil, Chile, Colombia, Costa Rica, Cuba, Dominica, Ecuador, El Salvador, French Antilles, Grenada, Guadeloupe, Guatemala, Guyana, Haiti, Honduras, Jamaica, Martinique, Mexico, Netherlands Antilles, Nicaragua, Panama, Paraguay, Peru, Suriname, Trinidad and Tobago, Uruguay and Venezuela. Contact: Bureau of InterAmerican Affairs, Public Affairs, Department of State, 2201 C St. N.W., Room 6913A, Washington, DC 20520/202-632-3048.

International Aviation
This office provides assistance in resolving international operational problems such as overflight and landing clearances. It is the focal point for coordinating U.S. policies on a multilateral basis and for ascertaining whether U.S. aircraft are being discriminated against. Contact: Office of Aviation, Bureau of Economic and Business Affairs, Department of State, 2201 C St. N.W., Room 5830, Washington, DC 20520/202-632-0316.

International Commerce
The Bureau of Economic and Business Affairs deals with international finance and development, trade policy, international resources, including food and energy, transportation and telecommunications. Contact: Bureau of Economic and Business Affairs, Department of State, 2201 C St. N.W., Room 6828, Washington, DC 20520/202-632-0396.

International Communications
This office provides information and reports on bilateral and multilateral agreements and activities of international communications conferences and organizations such as the 1979 Administrative Radio Conference. Contact: Office of International Communications Policy, Bureau of Economic and Business Affairs, Department of State, 2201 C St. N.W., Room 5824, Washington, DC 20520/202-632-3405.

International Conferences
For information on intergovernmental multilateral conferences attended by United States (no bilateral conferences) as accredited delegates, contact: Office of International Conferences, Bureau of International Organization Affairs, Department of State, 2201 C St. N.W., Room 1517, Washington, DC 20520/202-632-1271.

International Conferences
This office can provide information about various multilateral conferences attended by the United States for the next six months. Statistics are also available on such topics as how many people attend conferences and the number of conferences held. Contact: Office of the Budget, Bureau of International Affairs, Department of State, 2201 C St. N.W., Room 1429, Washington, DC 20520/202-632-2738.

International Economic Policy
This office oversees U.S. participation in economic policy making by the whole range of organizations within the United Nations system, mainly the economic and social council of the United Nations. It also maintains a list of "consultative status" organizations at the United Nations. Contact: Office of International Economic Policy, Bureau of International Organization Affairs, Department of State, 2201 C St. N.W., Room 5328, Washington, DC 20520/202-632-1654.

International Environment
This office deals with the foreign policy implications of nuclear and other energy programs, outer space concerns, environmental questions, population problems, technological and scientific relations and various other undertakings such as ocean resources, fisheries and wildlife management. Contact: Bureau of Oceans and International Environmental and Scientific Affairs, Department of State, 2201 C St. N.W., Room 7831, Washington, DC 20520/202-632-1554.

International Finance
The Office of Development Finance is involved in North-South Dialogue in the United Nations concerning rich and poor countries and their prices and commodities; World Bank, African Development Bank, Asian Development Bank, and InterAmerican Bank; following the general foreign aid policy for the U.S. Department of State; and following Export-Import Bank and the issues of negotiations of export credits. Contact: Office of Development Finance, Bureau of Economic and Business Affairs, Department of State, 2201 C St. N.W., Room 2529, Washington, DC 20520/202-632-9426.

International Labor Affairs
For information on foreign policy that has to do with the International Labor Organization, contact: Labor Affairs, Bureau of International Organization Affairs, Department of State, 2201 C St. N.W., Room 5336, Washington, DC 20520/202-632-3049.

International Organizations
This office supervises U.S. participation in the United Nations and in the other international organizations to which the United States belongs. It supports U.S. delegates to over 800 conferences annually. Contact: Bureau of International Organization Affairs, Department of State, 2201 C St. N.W., Room 6334, Washington, DC 20520/202-632-8588.

International Trade Policy
This office works on trade agreements and trade relations with developed countries and is concerned with restrictions that other countries put on U.S. exports. Their major areas are: European Economic Community (EEC), mainly agriculture, Canada and non-EEC European countries (Greece, Scandinavia, etc.), Japan, Australia, New Zealand, and South Africa. It also deals with licensing, aircraft agreements, trade and services (Organization for Economic Cooperation and Development), and customs valuation. Contact: Trade Agreements Division, International Trade Policy, Bureau of Economic and Business Affairs, Department of State, 2201 C St. N.W., Room 3822, Washington, DC 20520/202-632-1718.

Law of the Sea
The U.N. Conference on the Law of the Sea deals with international issues such as navigation, overflight, conservation and management of fisheries resources, the protection of the marine environment, the exploitation of oil and gas in the continental shelf, marine scientific research and a system of compulsory dispute settlement. Contact: Oceans, Law and Policy, Assistant Secretary for Oceans, Environmental and Scientific Affairs, Department of State, 2201 C St. N.W., Room 5805A, Washington, DC 20520/202-632-9098.

Library
The U.S. Department of State Library is open only to those who can enter the State Department Building. It publishes the *International Relations Dictionary*—a dictionary of terms used in foreign affairs. Available for $5.00 from: Government Printing Office, Superintendent of Documents, Washington, DC 20402/202-783-3238. The Library will try to answer mail inquiries. Contact: Library, Department of State, 2201 C St. N.W., Room 3239, Washington, DC 20520/202-632-0372.

Licenses to Export Military Goods
The Office of Munitions Control issues special export licenses to manufacturers and exporters of commercial arms, amunitions, implements of war and related technical data. Contact: Office of Munitions Control, Bureau of Politico-Military Affairs, Department of State, SA-6, Room 800, Washington, DC 20520/703-235-9755.

Man and the Biosphere
The U.S. Man and the Biosphere (MAB) program is aimed at providing a bridge between fundamental science and technological application. Its participants, distinguished scientists, resource administrators, policy makers, academics and others in the environmental community, study management problems arising from the interactions between human activities and natural systems. MAB's structure consists of ten committees with voluntary participants who are experts in their fields. The group produces publications, provides information about resource materials, sponsors consortia, and publishes a free newsletter, *MAB Bulletin*. Published on an as-needed basis, the bulletin provides information about what the MAB is doing, new publications released, resources available, and general information about scholarships, and university, government and industry programs or causes. Contact: The U.S. Man and the Biosphere Program, Secretariat, U.S. Department of State, OES/ENR/MAB, Washington, DC 20520/202-632-2786,-2816, or -7571.

Marine Science
This office deals with oil pollution strategies, assesses biologic damages from spills and blowouts, and works on marine environmental quality. Contact: Office of Marine Science and Technology Affairs, Oceans and Fisheries Affairs, Bureau of Oceans and International Environmental and Scientific Affairs, Department of State, Room 5801, Washington, DC 20520/202-632-0853.

Maritime Affairs
This office informs the U.S. maritime industry ship operators, labor unions and others involved with maritime matters on policy regulations. It deals with such issues as bunkering, detained cargo, and foreign discriminatory practices. Contact: Office of Maritime Affairs, Bureau of Economic and Business Affairs, Department of State, 2201 C St. N.W., Room 5826, Washington, DC 20520/202-632-0704.

Monetary Affairs
This office deals with international monetary issues, primarily with the International Monetary Fund. It also follows the financial conditions of foreign countries and to a lesser degree it follows dollar and gold prices for the U.S. Department of State. Contact: Office of Monetary Affairs, Bureau of Economic and Business Affairs, Department of State, 2201 C St. N.W., Room 4830, Washington, DC 20520/202-632-2580.

Near Eastern and South Asia
For information on: Afghanistan, Algeria, Bahrain, Bangladesh, Bhutan, Arab Republic of Egypt, India, Iran, Iraq, Israel, Jordan, Kuwait, Lebanon, Maldives, Morocco, Nepal, Oman, Pa-

kistan, Qatar, Saudi Arabia, Sri Lanka, Syrian Arab Republic, Tunisia, United Arab Emirates, Yemen Arab Republic, People's Democratic Republic of Yemen, and Central Treaty Organization (CENTO), contact: Bureau of Near Eastern and South Asian Affairs, Department of State, 2201 C St. N.W., Room 4515, Washington, DC 20520/ 202-632-5150.

Nuclear Non-proliferation

For information on U.S. nuclear export laws and agreements, non-proliferation policy, and international organizations concerned with peaceful nuclear development, contact: Office of Nuclear Export Policy, Bureau of Oceans and International Environmental and Scientific Affairs, Department of State, 2201 C St. N.W., Room 7828, Washington, DC 20520/202-632-7036.

Nuclear Technology

The Office of Nuclear Technology and Safeguards makes sure that the nuclear energy exported is used for peaceful purposes. It also works with the International Nuclear Fuel Cycle Evaluation, a technical study of the need for nuclear energy, of the link between nuclear energy programs and weapons proliferation and of means to minimize proliferation risks without jeopardizing the availability of nuclear energy. Contact: Office of Nuclear Technology and Safeguards, Bureau of Oceans and International Environmental and Scientific Affairs, Department of State, 2201 C St. N.W., Room 7828, Washington, DC 20520/202-632-3310.

Oceans and Polar Affairs

For information on U.S. international scientific, environmental, oceanic and marine, arctic and antarctic programs and policies, contact: Office of Oceans and Polar Affairs, Oceans and Fisheries Affairs, Bureau of Oceans and International Environmental and Scientific Affairs, Department of State, 2201 C St. N.W., Room 5801, Washington, DC 20520/202-632-6491.

Organization of American States (OAS)

For documents, reports and other general information on all Organization of American States' activities, contact: Documents and Reference, Permanent Mission of the United States of America to the Organization of American States, Bureau of Inter-American Affairs, Department of State, 2201 C St. N.W., Room 6489, Washington, DC 20520/202-632-8650.

Outer Space Treaties

This office works with: NASA on all the international aspects of the peaceful uses of outer space, with other governments and agencies on the civil space activities of the U.S. government which affect them, and with multilateral organizations such as the European Economic Community (EEC), Organizations for Economic Cooperation and Development (OECD), and the North Atlantic Treaty Organization (NATO). Contact: Office of Advanced Technology, Science and Technology Affairs, Bureau of Oceans and International Environmental and Scientific Affairs, Department of State, 2201 C St. N.W., Room 4333, Washington, DC 20520/202-632-2841.

Overseas Citizen Services

This office is responsible for activities relating to the protection and assistance of U.S. citizens abroad. Among its services are aids to U.S. citizens (including U.S. Merchant Seamen) who are arrested (see "Arrests Units" in this section); assistance, in case of death of a citizen abroad such as the provisional conservation of his/her personal estate abroad, and the repatriation to the United States of citizens who are destitute or ill. The Bureau serves as liaison with other government agencies in matters such as payment of benefits to beneficiaries residing abroad, and in determinations of the acquisition or loss of U.S. citizenship by persons outside the United States. It also provides notarial functions and related services to U.S. citizens abroad including coordinating with the U.S. Department of Justice to bring witnesses to U.S. courts. Contact: Overseas Citizen Services, Bureau of Consular Affairs, Department of State, 2201 C St. N.W., Room 4800, Washington, DC 20520/202-632-3816.

Overseas Schools

Individuals with children who plan to live abroad for an extended period may obtain fact sheets on individual U.S. Department of State supported schools. To apply for jobs at these schools, contact: International School Services (ISS), 126 Alexandria, P.O. Box 5910, Princeton, NJ 08540. For other information, contact: Office of Overseas Schools, Bureau of Administration, Department of State, SA6, Room 234, Washington, DC 20520/ 703-235-9600.

Passport Information

A recorded telephone message provides general information on what is needed when applying for a passport. Call: 202-783-8200. U.S. citizens and nationals can apply for passports at all passport agencies as well as those post offices and federal and state courts authorized to accept passport applications. The office also maintains a variety of records, including:

Consular Certificates of Witness to Marriage—records of those persons at whose marriage abroad a consular officer of the United States was present as a witness. It is merely a certificate indicating that a consular officer was present.

Reports of Birth—children born of American parents in a

foreign country will have a Report of Birth Abroad on file with this office if their parents have made such reports to the American consul in the country of birth.

Reports of Death—Since 1979 reports of death of Americans abroad are on file with the Passport Services files if the death has been brought to the attention of an American consul.

For more specific information on the issuance of passports, contact: Passport Services, Bureau of Consular Affairs, Department of State, 1425 K St. N.W., Room G-62, Washington, DC 20524/202-533-1355.

Passport Offices—Regional
The following is a listing of local passport offices:

John F. Kennedy Building, Government Center, Room E123, Boston, MA 02203/617-223-2946.

Kluczynski Office Building, 230 S. Dearborn St., Room 380, Chicago, IL 60604/312-353-7155.

New Federal Building, 300 Ala Moana Blvd., Room C-106, P.O. Box 50185, Honolulu, HI 96850/808-546-2130

One Allen Center, 500 Dallas St., Houston, TX 77002/713-229-3606.

Federal Building, 11000 Wilshire Blvd., Los Angeles, CA 92061/213-209-7070.

World Trade Center, 350 S. Figueroa St., Room 183, Los Angeles, CA 90071/213-688-3285.

Federal Office Building, 51 Southwest 1st Ave., Room 1616, Miami, FL 33130/305-350-4681.

International Trade Mart, 2 Canal St., Room 400, New Orleans, LA 70130/504-589-6161.

Rockefeller Center, International Building, 630 5th Ave., Room 270, New York, NY 10020/212-541-7710.

Federal Building, 600 Arch St., Room 4426, Philadelphia, PA 19106/215-597-7480.

Federal Building, 450 Golden Gate Ave., Room 1405, San Francisco, CA 94102/415-974-7972.

Federal Building, 915 2nd Ave., Room 906, Seattle, WA 98174/206-442-7945.

One Landmark Square, Broad and Atlantic Sts., Stamford, CT 06901/203-327-9550.

Room G62, 1425 K St. N.W., Washington, DC 20524/202-523-1355.

Political Asylum
For general and specific information on political asylum in the United States, contact: Office of Human Rights, Bureau of Human Rights and Humanitarian Affairs, Department of State, 2201 C St. N.W., Room 7802, Washington, DC 20520/202-632-2551.

Politico-Military Affairs
This office develops and coordinates guidance on issues that affect U.S. security policy, military assistance programs, and arms control and disarmament matters. Contact: Bureau of Politico-Military Affairs, Department of State, 2201 C St. N.W., Room 7317, Washington, DC 20520/202-632-7327.

Producing Countries—Energy
This office urges producing countries (Organization of Petroleum Exporting Countries) to follow "responsible" production and pricing policies. Contact: Producing Country Affairs, International Energy Policy, Bureau of Economic and Business Affairs, Department of State, 2201 C St. N.W., Room 3329, Washington, DC 20520/202-632-3019.

Protection of Ships from Foreign Seizure
Insurance is available to reimburse a financial loss to owners of vessels registered in the United States for fines paid to secure the release of vessels seized for operation in waters that are not recognized as territorial waters by the United States. Owners of private vessels documented or certificated under the laws of the United States whose boats are seized in waters not recognized as the territorial waters of another state by the United States are eligible. No registration or payment of premiums is required prior to the seizure in order to qualify for reimbursement. Contact: Assistant Legal Adviser for International Claims, Office of the Legal Adviser, Department of State, Washington, DC 20520/202-632-7347

Publications
The major publications from the U.S. Department of State include:

Department of State Bulletin (monthly, $35.00 a year)—lists new publications, provides the public, Congress and government agencies with information on developments in U.S. foreign relations as well as on the work of the Department and Foreign Service; its contents include: major addresses and news conferences of the President and Secretary; statements made before Congressional committees; special features and articles on international affairs; selected press releases issued by the White House, the U.S. Department of State, and the U.S. Mission to the United Nations; and treaties and other agreements to which the United States is or may become a party.

Department of State Newsletter (monthly except August, $22.00 a year)—acquaints officers and employees of State, at home and abroad, with developments of interest which may affect operations or personnel. It includes a one-page subject bibliography.

Diplomatic List and List of Foreign Consular Offices in the U.S. (quarterly, $12.00 a year)—a list of foreign diplomatic representatives in Washington, with addresses.

Employees of Diplomatic Missions (quarterly, $9.50 a year)—a quarterly publication listing names and addresses of employees of foreign diplomatic representatives in Washington.

Key Officers of Foreign Service Posts: Guide for Business Representatives ($6.50 a year)—a pocket-size directory, published three times a year, listing key foreign service officers abroad with whom American business representatives would most likely have contact.

The above publications are available from Government Printing Office, Superintendent of Documents, Washington, DC 20402/202-783-3238. For more detailed information on available publications, contact: Publications Distributions, Office of Opinion Analysis and Plans, Bureau of Public Affairs, Department of State, 2201 C St. N.W., Room 5815A, Washington, DC 20520/202-632-9859.

Public Availability of Diplomatic Archives in Foreign Countries

This publication summarizes the policies and practices in most countries of the world concerning access to unpublished diplomatic records. Contact: Office of the Historian, Bureau of Public Affairs, Department of State, SA1, Room 3100, Washington, DC 20520/202-632-8888.

Public Communications

Publications available from this office include:

Current Policy Paper—speeches by the Secretary and other policymakers at the U.S. Department of State (free).

Special Reports—analytical papers on major foreign policy issues including human rights, trade and pollution (free).

Program Notes—information books on individual countries including history, geography, and economy (free).

GIST—quick reference aid to understanding U.S. foreign relations (free).

Background Notes—short factual summaries which describe international organizations and the people, history, government, economy and foreign relations of 160 countries ($32.00 for set).

The Trade Debate—includes information on current U.S. policy, vis-à-vis nontariff barriers, commodities, agricultural trade, adjustment to structural problems, and problems of East-West trade with developing countries (free).

A list of films is also available. Contact: Office of Public Communications, Bureau of Public Affairs, Department of State, 2201 C St. N.W., Room 4827A, Washington, DC 20520/202-632-6575.

Public Programs

Among the programs for the public are:

National Conferences—with opinion leaders from nongovernmental organizations, business and labor, media, education, state and local government and other areas of the private sector.

Seminars—which bring together between 10 and 30 nongovernmental specialists with U.S. Department of State officials for discussions on specific areas of foreign policy.

Briefing and Policy Discussions (on request) for small groups.

Meetings—regional foreign policy conferences across the country.

Speakers Bureau

Contact: Office of Public Programs, Bureau of Public Affairs, Department of State, 2201 C St. N.W., Room 5831, Washington, DC 20520/202-632-6575.

Refugee Affairs

This office coordinates all U.S. Refugee Assistance programs, both foreign and domestic, and oversees all other agency programs involved with refugees. Fact sheets and other publications are available on current refugee problems. Speakers are also available on the subject. Contact: Office of US Coordination for Refugee Affairs, Office of Public Affairs, Department of State, 2201 C St. N.W., Room 7526, Washington, DC 20520/202-632-5203.

Science and Technology

This office deals with overall management, political issues (not substantive scientific and technological issues), for international organizations in science and technology such as: International Energy Administration, International Atomic Energy Administration; World Meteorological Organization; U.N. Environment Program; U.N. Intergovernmental Committee on Science and Technology Development; International Hydrographic Organization; International Organization for Legal Metrology; and International Bureau of Weights and Measures. Contact: Science and Technology, Bureau of International Organization Affairs, Department of State, 2201 C St. N.W., Room 5336, Washington, DC 20520/202-632-2752.

Speakers

The U.S. Department of State officers are available to speak to institutions and groups throughout the country. Contact: Office of Public Programs, Bureau of Public Affairs, Department of State, 2201 C St. N.W., Room 5825, Washington, DC 20520/202-632-6575.

Special Briefings to Groups

A business, group, or other organization can request a special briefing on almost any topic related to foreign affairs. Contact: Office of Public Programs, Bureau of Public Affairs, Department of State, 2201 C St. N.W., Room 5831, Washington, DC 20520/202-632-2406.

Terrorism Abroad

Assistance is available to help design corporate security programs for businesses in foreign countries. Information is available on the security climate within a given country. *Countering Terrorism* is a free pamphlet providing security suggestions for U.S. business representatives abroad, and describes precautionary measures as well as suggested behavior in case of kidnapping. Additional information is also available from: Executive Committee and Working Group on Terrorism, D/

CT, Department of State, 2201 C St. N.W., Room 2238, Washington, DC 20520/202-632-9892. Contact: Foreign Operations, Office of Security, Bureau of Administration, Department of State, 2201 C St. N.W., Room 3422, Washington, DC 20520/202-632-3122.

Textiles

For information on textile agreements with other countries, contact: Textiles Division, Bureau of Economic and Business Affairs, International Trade Policy, Department of State, 2201 C St. N.W., Room 3333, Washington, DC 20520/202-632-0280.

Diplomatic Reception Rooms

These rooms, still used nearly every day for diplomatic receptions, can handle small luncheons or receptions for up to 500 people. The three principal rooms are the John Quincy Adams State Drawing Room, Thomas Jefferson State Reception Room, and the Benjamin Franklin State Dining Room.

Trade Policies

For information on government policies having to do with countervailing codes; government procurement codes; standard problems; escape clause cases; market disruption cases; steel policy; Buy America problems; subsidies codes; and unfair trade practices, contact: Office of International Trade, Bureau of Economic and Business Affairs, Department of State, 2201 C St. N.W., Room 3828, Washington, DC 20520/202-632-1327.

Travel Advisories

Advisories on travel to foreign countries include information on civil disturbances, natural disasters, epidemic diseases, strikes, shortages of hotel rooms and anything else that may affect a traveler. Additonal publications describe consular services, visa requirements and special features of a particular country. Contact: Overseas Citizens Services, Bureau of Consular Affairs, Department of State, 2201 C St. N.W., Room 4800, Washington, DC 20520/202-632-3732.

Travel Tips for Senior Citizens

Information is available including: health advice, emergency help, general information, customs hints for returning U.S. residents, visa requirements of foreign governments, foreign country information, passports and visas, and clothing. Contact: Bureau of Consular Affairs, Office of Public Affairs, Department of State, 2201 C St. N.W., Room 6811, Washington, DC 20520/202-632-1489.

Treaties

The following publications provide data on U.S. treaties:

Treaties in Force ($9.50)—annual publication that lists by name, date, and date of entry into force, all treaties and other international agreements of the United States for that year. It also indicates where a complete text of the cited treaty can be found.

Treaties and Other International Acts ($89.00 a year)—published individually and containing the full text on each treaty.

U.S. Treaties and Other International Agreements—successive volumes (29 thus far) of texts of treaties and international agreements other than treaties to which the United States is a party. The price varies according to the volume.

These publications are available from the Government Printing Office, Superintendent of Documents, Washington, DC 20402/202-783-3238. For more detailed information, contact: Treaty Affairs, Office of the Legal Adviser, Department of State, 2201 C St. N.W., Room 5420, Washington, DC 20520/202-632-1074.

Tropical Products

Tropical products include: sugar, coffee, cocoa, cotton, bananas, and jute and other fibers. For information on international commodity agreements and regulations, and some statistical information (not for customs or domestic information), contact: Tropical Products Division, Office of Food Policy and Programs, Bureau of Economic and Business Affairs, Department of State, 2201 C St. N.W., Room 3527, Washington, DC 20520/202-632-3059.

UN Documents and Reference

The United Nations documents from New York and Geneva are available from: U.N. Documents and Reference, Bureau of International Organization Affairs, Department of State, 2201 C St. N.W., Room 3428, Washington, DC 20520/202-632-7992.

United Nations Educational Scientific and Cultural Organizations (UNESCO)

For UNESCO information within the U.S. Department of State, contact: UNESCO Affairs, Bureau of International Organization Affairs, Department of State, 2201 C St. N.W., Room 4334A, Washington, DC 20520/202-632-3619.

United Nations Mission

The United States office at the United Nations is: United States Mission to the United Nations, 799 United Nations Plaza, New York, NY 10017/212-826-4580.

Visa Information for Aliens Waiting to Enter the United States

This office provides general or specific information on visas for aliens wishing to enter the United States. Inquiries about the status of special cases should be directed to the U.S. consul in the country where the application is made. A list is available of American diplomatic and consular offices that issue visas. Contact: Visa Services, Bureau of Consular Affairs, Department of State, SA, 13th Floor, Washington, DC 20520/202-632-1972.

Visiting and Living Abroad

The Citizens Consular Services offers help for Americans visiting, living and doing business abroad in a number of ways.

Notary Public Services—includes administering oaths in depositions, affidavits, and other documents, and takes acknowledgement of signatures.

Voting Assistance—includes help in obtaining absentee ballots and election information.

Judicial Assistance—offers help in determining particular foreign laws, transmits letters, authenticates foreign documents, obtains documents abroad for legal purposes, retains lists of English-speaking lawyers, helps in the whereabouts and welfare search in child custody cases, in property claims, and in nationality and expatriation cases.

Passport and Registration Services Abroad—issues U.S. passports and travel documents to United States citizens and nationals abroad and registers U.S. citizens abroad.

Claims Assistance—in the protection of property and other interests owned by U.S. nationals abroad. Answers claims inquiries including those regarding foreign government restitution/compensation. Provides advice on methods of obtaining documents from abroad as property claims evidence. Handles inquiries concerning private trade complaints.

Child Custody Disputes—welfare and whereabouts information about children involved in custody disputes.

Estates—guidance to consular office and heirs concerning estates in foreign countries of U.S. nationals who die abroad when there is no qualified legal representative present. Consular services include handling inquiries on the transfer of estates from the United States to foreign countries.

Federal Benefits Function—assures the receipt of U.S. federal checks abroad.

Other services include providing tax forms and tax information and the protection of a person's material remains should he or she die while traveling alone overseas. Contact: Citizens Consular Services, Bureau of Consular Affairs, Department of State, 2201 C St. N.W., Room 4800, Washington, DC 20520/202-632-3666.

Women's Programs

For information on women's programs and women's concerns in international organizations, contact: International Women's Program, Bureau of International Organization Affairs, Department of State, 2201 C St. N.W., Room 4334A, Washington, DC 20520/202-632-2560.

How Can the Department of State Help You?

To determine how the U.S. Department of State can help you, contact: Public Affairs Bureau, Department of State, 2201 C St. N.W., Room 4827A, Washington, DC 20520/202-632-6575.

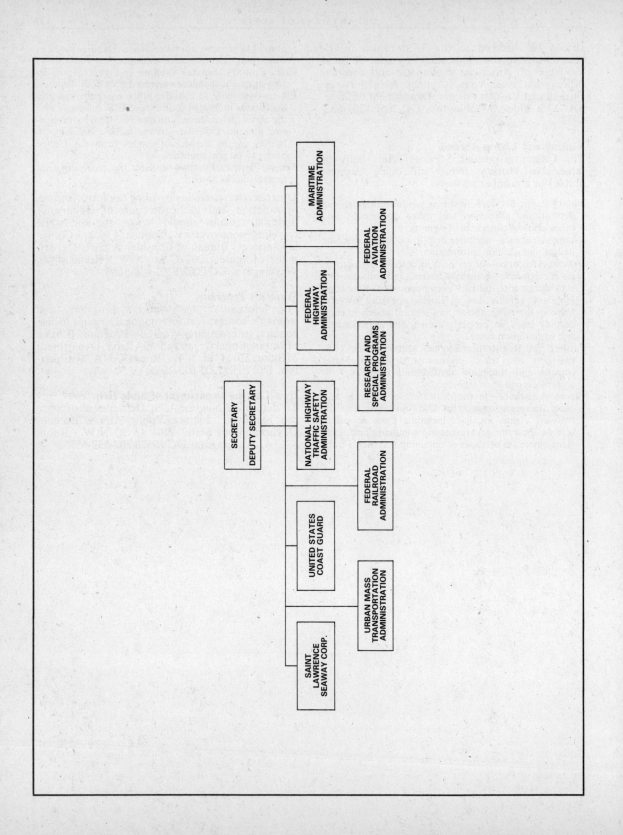

Department of Transportation

400 7th St. S.W., Washington, DC 20590/202-426-4000

Established: October 15, 1966
Budget: $9,548,084,000
Employees: 63,827

Mission: Assures the coordinated, effective administration of the transportation programs of the federal government and develops national transportation policies and programs conducive to the provision of fast, safe, efficient and convenient transportation at the lowest cost consistent therewith.

Major Divisions and Offices

Saint Lawrence Seaway Corporation

Department of Transportation, 400 7th Street S.W., Washington, DC 20540/202-426-3574.
Budget: $11,000,000*
Employees: 190
Mission: Responsible for the development, operation, and maintenance of that part of the Seaway between Montreal and Lake Erie, within the territorial limits of the United States.

Urban Mass Transportation Administration

Department of Transportation, 400 7th St., S.W., Washington, DC 20590/202-426-4043.
Budget: $3,566,166,000
Employees: 525
Mission: Assists in the development of improved mass transportation facilities, equipment, techniques, and methods; encourages the planning and establishment of area-wide urban mass transportation systems; and provides assistance to state and local governments in financing such systems.

Federal Railroad Administration

Department of Transportation, 400 7th St. S.W., Washington, DC 20590/202-426-0881.
Budget: $1,019,679,000

Employees: 1,322
Mission: Consolidates government support of rail transportation activities; provides a unified and unifying national rail transportation policy; administers and enforces rail safety laws and regulations; administers financial assistance programs for certain railroads, conducts research and development in support of improved intercity ground transportation and the future requirements for rail transportation; provides revitalization of the Northeast Corridor rail passenger service; and operates the Alaska Railroad.

National Highway Traffic Safety Administration

Department of Transportation, 400 7th St., S.W., Washington, DC 20590/202-426-1828.
Budget: $52,745,000
Employees: 617
Mission: Carries out programs relating to the safety performance of motor vehicles and related equipment, motor vehicle drivers, and pedestrians, carries out programs and studies aimed at reducing economic losses in motor vehicle crashes and repairs, through general motor vehicle programs; administers the federal odometer law, and a uniform national maximum speed limit; and promulgates average fuel economy standards for passenger and nonpassenger motor vehicles.

*a self supporting agency. Revenues are derived from shipping on the St. Lawrence seaway.

Federal Highway Administration

Department of Transportation, 400 7th St. S.W., Washington, DC 20590/202-426-0677.
Budget: $533,309,000
Employees: 3,500
Mission: Coordinates highways with other modes of transportation to achieve the most effective balance of transportation systems and facilities under cohesive federal transporation policies; and is concerned with the total operation and environment of highway system, with particular emphasis on improvement of highway-oriented aspects of highway safety.

Federal Aviation Administration

Department of Transportation, 800 Independence Ave., Washington, DC 20591/202-426-8058.
Budget: $1,369,535,000
Employees: 49,920
Mission: Regulates air commerce in a manner that promotes its development and safety and fulfills the requirements of national defense; controls the use of navigable airspace of the United States; regulates both civil and military operations in such airspace in the interest of safety and efficiency; and promotes, encourages, and develops civil aeronautics.

United States Coast Guard

Department of Transportation, 2100 2nd St. S.W., Washington, DC 20593/202-426-2158.
Budget: $2,465,126,000
Employees: 5,973
Mission: Maintains a system of rescue vessels, aircraft and communications facilities to carry out its function of saving life and property in and over the high seas and the navigable waters of the United States; is the primary maritime law enforcement agency for the United States; administers and enforces various safety standards for the design, construction, equipment and maintenance of commercial vessels of the United States and off-short structures on the Outer Continental Shelf; regulates pilotage services on the Great Lakes; implements the nation's policies for the protection of the marine environment; administers the Port Safety and Security Program; establishes and maintains United States aids to navigation system;

administers the several statutes regulating the construction, maintenances, and operation of bridges across the navigable waters of the United States; operates the nation's icebreaking vessels, supported by aircraft for ice reconnaisance, to facilitate maritime transportation and aid in prevention of flooding in domestic waters, and supports logistics to U.S. polar installations; administers a licensing and regulatory program governing the construction, ownerships, and operation of deepwater ports on the high seas to transfer oil from tankers to shore; develops and directs a national boating safety program; and maintains a state of readiness to function as a specialized service in the navy in time of war.

Research and Special Programs Administration

Department of Transportation, 400 7th St. S.W., Washington, DC 20590/202-426-4486.
Budget: $20,022,000
Employees: 676
Mission: Serves as a research, analysis, and technical development arm of the U.S. Department of Transportation with emphasis on pipeline safety, transportation of hazardous cargo by all modes of transportation, transportation safety, transportation control, and safety.

Maritime Administration

Department of Transportation, 400 7th St. S.W., NASIF Building, Washington, DC 20590/202-426-5806.
Budget: $525,234,000
Employees: 1,104
Mission: Aids in development, promotion and operation of the United States Merchant Marine and United States Merchant Marine Academy. Organizes and directs emergency merchant ship operations. Administers subsidy programs to ship operators and builders. Constructs or supervises construction of merchant type ships for the federal government. Helps generate increased business for U.S. ships and conducts programs to develop ports, facilities and intermodal transport and domestic shipping. Administers a War Risk Insurance Program. Regulates sales to aliens and transfer to foreign registry of ships.

Major Sources of Information

Accident Prevention—Aviation
This office provides national guidance and policy on accident prevention in general aviation. For information on available publications, tapes, slides, seminars and speakers, contact: Accident Prevention Staff, General Aviation Division, Flight Standards Service, Federal Aviation Administration, Department of Transportation, 800

Independence Ave. S.W., Room 313C, Washington, DC 20591/202-426-8102.

Advanced Marine Vehicle Technology
This office conducts research on the evaluation of new and existing boat designs, including fleet replacement alternatives. Contact: Advanced Marine Vehicle Technology Branch, Technology Di-

vision, Office of Research and Development, Coast Guard, Department of Transportation, 2100 2nd St. S.W., Washington, DC 20593/202-472-5770.

Aeromedical Standards
This office sets policy, regulations and standards for medical certificates required for a pilot's license. Contact: Aeromedical Standards, Office of Aviation Medicine, Federal Aviation Administration, Department of Transportation, 800 Independence Ave. S.W., Room 322, Washington, DC 20591/202-426-3802.

Aids to Navigation
Each U.S. Coast Guard district can provide a free copy of *Local Notices to Mariners* which includes information on establishments, changes and discontinuances of aids to navigation in the United States, its territories and possessions, reports on channel conditions, obstructions to navigation, danger areas and new charts. The publication, *Aids to Navigation*, explains the significance of the colors of beacons and buoys, of the variety of light and fog signal characteristics, and of the system of electronic aids to navigation. Contact: Marine Information Branch, Short Range Aids to Navigation Division, Office of Navigation, Coast Guard, Department of Transportation, 2100 2nd St. N.W., Room 1414, Washington, DC 20593/202-426-9566.

Air Traffic Control System
This system tracks controlled flights automatically and tags each target with a small block of information written electronically on the radar scope used by air traffic controllers. The data block includes aircraft identity, altitude and ground speed and transponder code. Contact: Air Traffic Control System Program Division, Air Traffic Service, Federal Aviation Administration, Department of Transportation, 800 Independence Ave. S.W., Room 400 East, Washington, DC 20591/202-426-3136.

Air Traffic System Errors
A central file is maintained on all system errors chronologically by region. The file consists of reports identifying anything wrong in the air traffic service terminal. Contact: Quality Assurance Division, Air Traffic Services, Federal Aviation Administration, Department of Transportation, 800 Independence Ave. S.W., Room 416, Washington, DC 20591/202-426-3353.

Aircraft Accidents
For information on general aviation accidents and near mid-air collisions, contact: Safety Analysis Division, Office of Aviation Safety, Federal Aviation Administration, Department of Transportation, 800 Independence Ave. S.W., Washington, DC 20591/202-426-8256.

Aircraft Accident Reports
The central file is maintained showing documentation of all accidents and incidents involving aircraft. Contact: Accident/Incident Analysis Branch, Air Traffic Service, Federal Aviation Administration, Department of Transportation, 800 Independence Ave. S.W., Room 417D, Washington, DC 20591/202-426-0928.

Aircraft Maintenance Data
Available aircraft data include maintenance surveillance, mechanical reliability and malfunctions or defects, mechanical interruptions, and inflight mechanical problems. Contact: Maintenance Analysis Center Section, AFO-581, Federal Aviation Administration, Department of Transportation, Aeronautical Center, P.O. Box 25082, Oklahoma City, OK 73125/405-686-4521.

Aircraft Noise
Research is conducted on reducing noise levels of new aircraft, and retrofitting of older aircraft to reduce noise levels. Contact: Noise Abatement Division, Office of Environment and Energy, Federal Aviation Administration, Department of Transportation, 800 Independence Ave. S.W., Room 432, Washington, DC 20591/202-755-9468.

Airline Antitrust Violations
This office investigates mergers and interlocks, unfair methods of competition among airline carriers and also determines antitrust immunity. Contact: Office of Policy and International Affairs, Department of Transportation, 400 7th St. S.W., Room 10223, Washington, DC 20590/202-426-4382.

Airline Data Collection
This office maintains airline data collection, financial and statistical reporting and serves as liaison for public access to air carrier reports. Contact: Research and Special Programs Administration, Department of Transportation, 400 7th St. S.W., Room 4125, Washington, DC 20590/202-426-8969.

Airline Passenger Services
This office is responsible for airline consumer protection matters including consumer assistance and consumer protection regulations. Specific attention is paid to provide information and resolve complaints with regard to delayed and canceled flights, overbooking, lost baggage, smoking, flight cancellation, refunds, charter flights. Contact: Consumer Affairs Division, Office of Governmental Affairs, Department of Transportation, 400 7th St. S.W., Room 10405, Washington, DC 20590/202-755-2220.

Airline Safety
Airline passengers who have inquiries or complaints regarding airplane safety should contact:

Community and Consumer Liaison Division, Office of Public Affairs, Federal Aviation Administration, Department of Transportation, 800 Independence Ave. S.W., Washington, DC 20591/202-426-1960.

Airline Tariffs and Routes
Information about airline carriers' passenger and cargo operations can be obtained from: Public Reference Room, Department of Transportation, 400 7th St. S.W., Room 4107, Washington, DC 20590/202-426-7634.

Airmen and Aircraft Registry
Permanent records are kept on all U.S. civil aircraft and airmen (students, private, commercial and airline transport). Certificates are issued to air carrier personnel involved in international civil aviation. Registration numbers for all civil aircraft are issued and monitored by the Registry. Contact: Airman and Aircraft Registry, Federal Aviation Administration, Department of Transportation, Mike Monroney Aeronautical Center, P.O. Box 25082, Oklahoma City, OK 73125/405-686-4331.

Airport Security
This program insures law enforcement presence in airports, approves the security programs of all airports under FAR 107, certifies walk-through detection devices. Contact: Airport Security Program, Civil Aviation Security Service, Federal Aviation Administration, Department of Transportation, 800 Independence Ave. S.W., Room 319, Washington, DC 20591/202-426-9863.

Airport Standards
Information is available on standards required for constructing and operating airports such as size, length, separation between runways, snow and ice control, and crash and fire rescue equipment. Contact: Design and Operational Criteria Division, Office of Airport Standards, Federal Aviation Administration, Department of Transportation, 800 Independence Ave. S.W., Room 614, Washington, DC 20591/202-426-3446.

Alaska Railroad
This railroad is 478 kilometers of single mainline track from Seward and Whittier to the interior of central Alaska through Anchorage to Fairbanks. It is under mandate from the U.S. Congress to operate within its revenues. Contact: The Alaska Railroad, Federal Railroad Administration, Department of Transportation, 400 7th St. S.W., Room 8218, Washington, DC 20590/202-472-9047.

Automobile Energy Efficiency
For information on the energy efficiency of new passenger cars and approaches to improving it, contact: Office of Automotive Fuel Economy Standards, Rulemaking, National Highway Traffic Safety Administration, Department of Transportation, 400 7th St. S.W., Room 6124, Washington, DC 20590/202-426-0846.

Auto Safety Hotline
The Auto Safety Hotline will tell you if your vehicle has been determined as unsafe and involved in a recall. You can also call the hotline to record a complaint. Computerized literature searches can be made on the files maintained by the Technical Reference Service. However, there is a charge for computer searches. Contact: Office of Defects Investigation, NEF-10, National Highway Traffic Safety Administration, Department of Transportation, 400 7th St. S.W., Room 5326, Washington, DC 20590/800-424-9393 (DC: 202-426-0123).

Aviation Accident Investigations
Pertinent medical data associated with persons involved in aviation accidents are analyzed. Contact: Biomedical and Behavioral Science Division, Office of Aviation Medicine, Federal Aviation Administration, Department of Transportation, 800 Independence Ave. S.W., Room 320, Washington, DC 20591/202-426-3935.

Aviation Consumer Complaints
Complaints on such subjects as safety, noise, pesticide spraying or broken seat belts are handled by: Community and Consumer Liaison Division, Office of Public Affairs, Federal Aviation Administration, Department of Transportation, 800 Independence Ave. S.W., Room 906A, Washington, DC 20591/202-426-1960.

Aviation Equipment Specifications
Information is available on specifications for the manufacturing and installation of such aviation equipment as visual aides associated with landing and taxiing of aircraft, runway lights, approach lights, beacons, etc. Contact: Engineering and Specifications Division, Office of Airport Standards, Federal Aviation Administration, Department of Transportation, 800 Independence Ave. S.W., Room 614, Washington, DC 20591/202-426-3824.

Aviations Forecasts
The following publications are available:

Federal Aviation Administration Aviation Forecast—microfiche provides 12-year projections on all aspects of aviation, including total aircraft, total airborne, statute miles of U.S. air carriers, hours flown in general aviation, and fuel consumed.

Terminal Area Forecasts—microfiche provides 10-year projections on 400 specific airports including in-plane passengers, and operations of air carriers.

Contact: Aviation Forecasts Branch, Office of Aviation Policy, Federal Aviation Administration,

Department of Transportation, 800 Independence Ave. S.W., Room 935F, Washington, DC 20591/ 202-426-3103.

Aviation History

For information on aviation history, contact: Agency Historian, Office of Public Affairs, Federal Aviation Administration, Department of Transportation, 800 Independence Ave. S.W., Room 907A, Washington, DC 20591/202-755-7234.

Aviation Inquiries

For general information concerning subjects covered by the Federal Aviation Administration, contact: Public Inquiry Center, Office of Public Affairs, Federal Aviation Administration, Department of Transportation, 800 Independence Ave. S.W., Room 907E, Washington, DC 20591/202-426-8058.

Aviation Medicine

Aeromedical research is conducted on such topics as: 1) psychology—evaluates spatial disorientation and visual perception in the aviation environment; 2) physiology—performance and health of aircrew and air traffic controllers under diverse environmental conditions; 3) toxicology—toxic hazards such as pesticides used in aerial application, products of combustion and ionizing radiation from air shipment of radioactive cargo in the high altitude environment; and 4) protection and survival—studies of techniques for attenuating or preventing crash injuries, developing concepts and evaluating survival equipment used under adverse environmental conditions, establishing human physical limitations of civil aviation operations and evaluating emergency procedures for downed aircraft. Contact: Biomedical and Behavioral Science Division, Office Of Aviation Administration, Department of Transportation, 800 Independence Ave, S.W., Room 325, Washington, DC 20591/ 202-426-3433

Aviation News

This bimonthly publication is a safety magazine for general aviation pilots. Available for $13.00 per year from: U.S. Government Printing Office, Superintendent of Documents, Washington, DC 20402/202-783-3238. For more detailed information on content, contact: *FAA General Aviation News,* General Aviation and Commercial Division, AFO-807, Flight Standards Service, Federal Aviation Administration, Department of Transportation, 800 Independence Ave. S.W., Washington, DC 20591/202-426-3903.

Aviation Policy

Reports and data are generated from some 18 data bases to aid in aviation policy decisions on such topics as the activities of airlines, seat belt configu-rations, and the number of airports in the United States. Contact: Information Systems Branch, APO-130, Policy Analysis Division, Office of Aviation Policy and Plans, Federal Aviation Administration, Department of Transportation, 800 Independence Ave. S.W., Room 935, Washington, DC 20591/202-426-3374.

Aviation Procedures Periodicals

The following periodicals will keep the reader current on internal directives published by Federal Aviation Administration Headquarters:

Flight Services Handbook—describes the procedures and terms used by personnel providing assistance and communications services ($46.00/subscription).

Data Communications Handbook—describes teletype-writer operating procedures, applicable international teletypewriter procedures and continuous U.S. Service weather schedules ($47.00/subscription).

Contact: Government Printing Office, Superintendent of Documents, Washington, DC 20402/202-783-3238.

Aviation Radio Systems

Work is performed to insure that radio systems have frequencies on which to operate that are compatible with other frequencies. Work is also done in conjunction with international organizations on future plans for radio systems. Contact: Spectrum Engineering Division, Systems Research and Development Service, Federal Aviation Administration, Department of Transportation, 800 Independence Ave. S.W., Room 713, Washington, DC 20591/202-426-3269.

Aviation Small Business Procurement

A small business specialist provides Federal Aviation Administration contracting and procurement support for spare parts, modifications and service contracts for the fleet of aircraft and their air navigation and communication gear operated by the Federal Aviation Administration. Contact: Small Business Specialist Procurement Division, AAC-70A, Federal Aviation Administration, Department of Transportation, Mike Monroney Aeronautical Center, P.O. Box 25082, AVN-120, Oklahoma City, OK 73125/ 405-686-4391.

Aviation Statistics—Accidents

Statistics are maintained on: 1) general aviation accident information; 2) incidents (little damage or minor injury) of both air carrier and general aviation; 3) service difficulty reports; and 4) enforcement data and violations. Contact: Safety Data Branch, Flight Standards, National Field Office, Federal Aviation Administration, Department of Transportation, P.O. Box 25082, AFO 580, Oklahoma City, OK 73125/405-686-4171.

Aviation Statistics—General

Historical and current aviation statistics are available on such topics as: air traffic activities, number of aircraft, flying hours, pilots and passengers. For a listing of available publications, contact: Information Analysis Branch, Management Standards and Statistics Division, Office of Management Systems, Federal Aviation Administration, Department of Transportation, 800 Independence Ave. S.W., Room 607, Washington, DC 20591/202-426-3791.

Bird Strikes

Information is available on where bird strikes occur. Contact: Airport Safety Data Group, Office of Airport Standards, Federal Aviation Administration, Department of Transportation, 800 Independence Ave. S.W., Room 624, Washington, DC 20591/202-426-3854.

Boating Information

Information and technical assistance is available on boating including the following free publications:

Federal Requirements for Recreational Boats—detailed information on such items as fire extinguishers, personal flotation devices, lighting, safe boating tips, and marine sanitation devices.
Suddenly in Command—basics of how to run the boat, how to use emergency equipment, and what to do in case of trouble.
Marine Communication for the Recreational Boater
Trailer-Boating—A Primer
Visual Distress Signals
Passport to Pleasure Cruising
U.S. Coast Guard Boating Safety Newsletters
Boating Statistics
Cold Water Drowning—A New Lease on Life
First Aid for the Boatman
Hypothermia and Cold Water Survival
This is the Seal of Safety
Emergency Repairs Afloat
Safety Standards for Backyard Boat Builders
Navigational Rules—International—Inland

Contact: Boating Information Branch, Office of Boating Safety, Coast Guard, Department of Transportation, G-BA2, 2100 2nd St. S.W., Washington, DC 20593/202-472-2373.

Boating on the Saint Lawrence River

Boating information is available in the publication, *Pleasure Craft Guide—the Seaway*. Available for free from: Public Information Office, St. Lawrence Seaway Corp., P.O. Box 520, Massena, NY 13662/315-764-3200.

Boating Safety and Seamanship Courses—Free

The U.S. Coast Guard Auxiliary offers courses in boating safety and seamanship to the public. They are taught by experienced auxiliary members and the only charge is for materials. Some courses include: Basic Boating, Sailing and Seamanship, Principles of Sailing, Water and Kids, Young Peoples Boating Course, First Aid and the Boatmen, and Introduction to Sailing. Contact: your local auxiliary flotilla, or Auxiliary Division, Office of Boating Safety, Coast Guard, Department of Transportation, 2100 2nd St. S.W., Room 4304, Washington, DC 20593/202-426-1077.

Bus and Paratransit Technology

This office is involved in two major programs:

Paratransit Integration—attempts to find solutions to transportation analysis, management, and operating problems.
Automated Vehicle Monitoring—an electronic system of monitoring the location and status of transit vehicles operating on city streets.

Contact: Office of Bus and Paratransit Systems, Office of Technology Assistance, Urban Mass Transportation Administration, Department of Transportation, 400 7th St. S.W., Room 6432, Washington, DC 20590/202-426-4035.

Civil Aeromedical Institute (CAMI)

This institute conducts research to identify human factor causes of aircraft accidents, prevent future accidents and make accidents that do occur more survivable. It also operates a program for the medical certification of airmen, educates pilots and physicians in matters related to aviation safety, and is responsible for developing and producing brochures, slides, and training films for distribution to aviation groups and organizations. Contact: Civil Aeromedical Institute, Mike Monroney Aeronautical Center, Federal Aviation Administration, Department of Transportation, P.O. Box 25082, Oklahoma City, OK 73125/405-686-4806.

Civil Aviation Security Service

This office maintains information and expertise on domestic and foreign aircraft hijacking, including bomb threats at airports and on carriers, compliance and enforcements of violations of regulations, prevented attempts, explosives and explosive devices found at airports and aircraft, worldwide criminal incidents involving civil aviation, information on number of people screened, number of weapons found, and weapon detection devices. Contact: Civil Aviation Security Services (ACS 400), Federal Aviation Administration, Department of Transportation, 800 Independence Ave. S.W., Room 315, Washington, DC 20591/202-426-8210.

Coast Guard Institute

This Institute trains coast guard personnel in their specialties through a nonresident course program. Most courses are designed to provide training to assist enlisted personnel in preparing for advancement. Contact: Coast Guard Institute, Coast

Guard, Aeronautical Center, MPB 237, P.O. Substation 18, Oklahoma City, OK 73169/405-686-4263.

Coast Guard Publications
For a listing of available publications and photographs, contact: Directives, Publications and Printing Branch, Management Analysis, Chief of Staff, Coast Guard, Department of Transportation, 2100 2nd St. S.W., Room 2604, Washington, DC 20593/202-426-2631.

Coast Guard Research
Information is available on research and development in the following areas: Ice Operations (IO), Ocean Dumping Surveillance; Multi-Mission R&D; Enforcement of Laws and Treaties; Marine Environmental Protection (MEP); Port Safety and Security (PSS); Short Range Aids to Navigation (AN); Radionavigation Aids (RA); Search and Rescue (SAR); Telecommunications R&D (GAC); Commercial Vessel Safety (CVS); Recreational Boating Safety (RBS); Energy Technology (ENG); Command, Control, Surveillance Systems; and Advanced Marine Vehicles. Contact: Planning and Evaluation, Office of Research and Development, Coast Guard, Department of Transportation, 2100 2nd St. S.W., Room 5400J, Washington, DC 20593/202-426-1030.

Coast Guard Reservist Magazine
This free, bimonthly magazine features human interest stories and includes news and information of interest to coast guard reservists. Contact: Office of Readiness and Reserve, Coast Guard, Department of Transportation, 2100 2nd St. S.W., Room 5101, Washington, DC 20593/202-426-2350.

Coast Guard Training
Coast Guard Reserve Training courses are developed and validated for members of the Coast Guard only: 1) correspondence courses; 2) inactive duty training through video and classroom; and 3) active duty schools. Contact: Training Development Branch, Reserve Training Division, Office of the Reserve, Coast Guard, Department of Transportation, 2100 2nd St. S.W., Room 5103, Washington, DC 20593/202-426-1622.

Commuter and Air Taxi
Information is available covering policy, regulations and directives of commuter and air taxi aircraft. A listing is available of air taxi operators and commercial operators of small aircraft. Contact: Commuter and Air Taxi Branch, Air Transportation Division, Office of Flight Operations, Federal Aviation Administration, Department of Transportation, 800 Independence Ave. S.W., Room 304, Washington, DC 20591/202-426-8086.

Computerized Data Base
The Department of Transportation maintains the following data base.

Auto-Safety Data Base
The National Highway Traffic Safety Administration (NHTSA) maintains a data base of safety information about automobiles manufactured in the past 10 years. The system can be searched by car make, model, year, or equipment. Retrievable information includes: crash test results; repairability and damage statistics; safety recall information; insurance and accident costs: consumer complaints filed about a car; used-car information; and tire treadwear and skid resistance.

The data base was started in 1972 and is updated daily. It currently has 150,000 entries. Searches and printouts are available free of charge. Unless your request is complex, you can get the data you need quickly by calling the Hotline. An operator will conduct a search while you are still on the phone and a printout will be mailed within 24 hours. NHTSA encourages individuals to call the Hotline whenever they want to register a safety complaint about their automobile. Often NHTSA will investigate the complaint and if necessary contact the manufacturer on the owner's behalf. Contact: National Highway Traffic Safety Administration, Auto-Safety Hotline, Department of Transportation, 400 7th St. S.W., Washington, DC 20590/800-424-9393; 202-426-0123 (in Washington, DC).

Aviation Standards and Statistics Data Base
The Federal Aviation Administration (FAA) maintains several computerized data files on a variety of aviation-related topics. Examples include data on: aviation safety, air traffic, aviation schools, commercial and government ownership and operation of aircraft, aircraft repair stations, FAA facilities, and procurement.

While the FAA does not conduct searches for anyone outside the agency, if you send them a blank tape they will copy any file you designate. Charge for this service is $38.00. Contact: Federal Aviation Administration, Management Standards and Statistics Division, AMS-400, 800 Independence Ave. S.W., Washington, DC 20591/202-426-3791.

Boating Accident Data Base (BADB)
BADB contains raw data about recreational boating accidents throughout the U.S. More than 30 pieces of information are stored for each accident. Examples include: geographical area, date, size and type of boat, cause of accident, and age of operator. The data base is updated continually. Searches and print-outs are available for a nominal fee. Contact: Statistician, U.S. Coast Guard, G-BP-2, 2100 2nd St. S.W., Washington, DC 20593/202-426-1062.

Transportation Data Base and Referrals

A research and development arm of the Department of Transportation, the Transportation Systems Center is involved in all aspects of transportation, as well as vehicles materials. Technical staff in the Technology Sharing Office can answer inquiries and give referrals. Abstracts of the technical reports produced by the Center can be searched on the data base TRIS, or be obtained from NTIS, 5285 Port Royal Road, Springfield, VA 22161/703-487-4807. Contact: Office of Technology Sharing, Transportation Systems Center, Department of Transportation, Kendall Square, Cambridge, MA 02142/617-494-2486.

Automobiles and Automobile Defects Data Base

The National Highway Traffic Safety Administration (NHTSA) has three data files pertaining to automobiles and their defects. The files are: (1) the Service Bulletin File containing all notices sent out by car manufacturers about correcting automobile problems or defects; (2) the Consumer Complaint file consisting of all letters NHTSA has received from consumers regarding care difficulties; and (3) the Recall File with information about all manufacturers' recalls.

The Service Bulletin File contains 64,000 entries and is updated monthly; the Consumer Complaint File has 128,000 entries and is updated weekly; and the Recall File, which is also updated weekly, contains 4,000 entries. Searches and printouts are available on a cost-recovery basis. Contact: Jerome Holiber, Chief, Technical Reference Division, National Highway Traffic Safety Administration, 400 7th St. S.W., Washington, DC 20590/202-426-2768.

Consumer Liaison

This office assures the coordination of consumer policy within the U.S. Department of Transportation; insures that consumer considerations are incorporated into the Department's policy; and has established systematic procedures for complaint handling. Free publications include:

Transportation Consumer—a bimonthly newsletter on consumer activities and interest in transportation.
Gasoline—More Miles Per Gallon.
Common Sense on Buying a New Car
Rideshare and Save-A-Cost Comparison

Contact: Office of Consumer Liaison, Department of Transportation, 400 7th St. S.W., Room 9402, Washington, DC 20590/202-426-4518.

Cooperative Marine Sciences Program

This program provides optimum utilization of specialized Coast Guard facilities in any area where cooperative efforts may enhance the national marine sciences effort. Space available accommodations for scientists, researchers and students on Coast Guard vessels, aircraft and stations. Joint planning of Coast Guard scientific programs with the programs of others. Accommodation of non-Coast Guard scientific projects on board Coast Guard vessels and aircraft on a "not to interfere with primary mission" basis. Assignment of Coast Guard vessels and aircraft in support of non-Coast Guard scientific projects as a primary mission of that vessel or aircraft. The only restrictions are the availability of suitable ships and aircraft and the pertinence of the project to the national program. Contact: Ice Operations Division, Coast Guard Headquarters, Department of Transportation, Washington, DC 20593/202-426-1881.

Courtesy Marine Examination

To determine if your vessel meets federal and state safety-related equipment requirements as well as further recommended safety standards, contact a member of the U.S. Coast Guard Auxiliary for a free Courtesy Marine Examination or: Boating Information Branch, Office of Boating Safety, Coast Guard, G-BA2, Department of Transportation, 2100 2nd St. S.W., Room 4213, Washington, DC 20593/202-426-1060.

Deepwater Ports

This office has licensing and safety oversight responsibility for deep water port projects. Deep water ports enable off-shore off-loading of all through pipelines into storage. Contact: Office of Economics, Department of Transportation, 400 7th St. S.W., Room 10301, Washington, DC 20590/202-426-4416.

Direct Payments

The programs described below provide financial assistance directly to individuals, private firms and other private institutions to encourage or subsidize a particular activity.

Capital Construction Fund

Objective: To provide for replacement vessels, additional vessels, or reconstructed vessels, built and documented under the laws of the United States for operation in the United States foreign, Great Lakes or noncontiguous domestic trades.

Eligibility: An applicant must be a U.S. citizen, own or lease one or more eligible vessels, have a program for the acquisition, construction or reconstruction of a qualified vessel and demonstrate the financial capabilities to accomplish the program.

Range of Financial Assistance: Applicant receives tax benefits for depositing assets in accordance with the program.

Contact: Associate Administrator for Maritime Aids, Maritime Administration, Department of Transportation, 400 7th St. S.W., Washington, DC 20590/202-382-0364.

Construction-Differential Subsidies

Objective: To promote the development and maintenance of the Merchant Marine by granting financial aid to equalize cost of constructing of a new ship in a U.S. shipyard with the cost of constructing the same ship in a foreign shipyard.

Eligibility: U.S. flagship operators or U.S. shipyards for construction of ships to be used in foreign trade. Prospective purchaser must possess the ability, experience, financial resources, and other qualifications necessary for the acquisition, operation, and maintenance of the proposed new ship.

Range of Financial Assistance: $60,000 to $7,850,000.

Contacts: Associate Administrator for Maritime Aids, Maritime Administration, Department of Transportation, 400 7th St. S.W., Washington, DC 20590/202-382-0364.

Construction Reserve Fund

Objectives: To promote the construction, reconstruction, reconditioning, or acquisition of merchant vessels which are necessary for national defense and to the development of US commerce.

Eligibility. A Construction Reserve Fund (CFR) may be established by any citizen of the United States who owns, in whole or in part, a vessel or vessels operating in the foreign or domestic commerce of the US, or in the fisheries.

Range of Financial Assistance: Not specified.

Contact: Associate Administrator for Maritime Aids, Maritime Administration, Department of Transportation, Washington, DC 20590/202-382-0364.

Operating-Differential Subsidies

Objective: To promote development and maintenance of U.S. Merchant Marine by granting financial aid to equalize cost of operating a competitive foreign flag ship.

Eligibility: Any U.S. citizen who has the ability, experience, financial resources, and other qualifications necessary to enable him to conduct the proposed operation of U.S. flag vessels in an essential service in the foreign commerce of the U.S.

Range of Financial Assistance: $6,612 to $23,079 per day, per ship.

Contact: Associate Administrator for Maritime Aids, Maritime Administration, Department of Transportation, 400 7th St., Washington, DC 20590/202-382-0364.

Ship Sales

Objectives: To sell by competitive bids, merchant ships which become surplus to the needs of the Government.

Eligibility: Those who have a need for ships for non-transportation or dismantling purposes may purchase ships under competitive bids for such purposes.

Range of Financial Assistance: Not applicable.

Contact: Chief, Division of Ship Disposals and Foreign Transfers, Office of Ship Operations, Maritime Administration, Department of Transportation, Washington, DC 20590/202-426-5821.

Driver and Pedestrian Research

Research is conducted to study the interaction between people and machines. The seven basic areas of concentration are: 1) unsafe driving—why, developing countermeasures, public information, detection; 2) occupant restraints—belts, air bags; 3) alcohol—, public information; 4) pedestrian—bicycle research; 5) motorcycles and mopeds—helmet use; 6) driver licenses—developing uniform standards, working with major abuses, special groups; 7) young drivers—risk taking and driver education; 8) drugs and alcohol. Contact: Office of Driver and Pedestrian Research, Research and Development, National Highway Traffic Safety Administration, Department of Transportation, 400 7th St. S.W., Room 6240, (NRD40), Washington, DC 20590/202-426-9591.

Driving Publications and Films

For information on available publications and films for both the consumer and expert, contact: Office of Public Affairs and Consumer Participation, National Highway Traffic Safety Administration, Department of Transportation, 400 7th St. S.W., Room 5232, Washington, DC 20590/202-426-9550.

Driving Records

Each state sends in its suspension and revocation records to a central point in order that other states can make use of the information in granting new licenses. The kind of data included is: name, date of birth, social security number, driver license number, height, weight, eye color, data and reason license was revoked, and date of reinstatement. Not all states participate. Contact: National Driver Register, Traffic Safety Programs, National Highway Traffic Safety Administration, Department of Transportation, 400 7th St. S.W., Room 5119, Washington, DC 20590/202-426-4800.

Environment

This office acts as the environmental contact point for the U.S. Department of Transportation on areas including: the review of environmental impact statements for major projects; resolution of environmental concerns and issues; bicycle-related activities such as studies of their benefits and hazards, and funding for bicycle paths; historic preservation activities; development of regulations for accessibility of mass transportation vehicles for the handicapped and the aged; overseeing highway beautification; art and architecture aesthetic considerations in transportation projects; and air quality. Contact: Office of Environment, Office for Policy and International Affairs, Department of Transportation, 400 7th St. S.W., Room 10228, Washington, DC 20590/202-426-4544.

Environmental Protection Newsletter

Produced by the U.S. Coast Guard, this newsletter is an official medium for information for Coast Guard personnel about developments and matters of general interest in the marine environmental protection field. It is also distributed to federal and state agencies, schools, industries, and individuals interested in marine environment. Contact: Environmental Response Division, Office of Marine Environment and Systems, Coast Guard, Department of Transportation, 2100 2nd St. S.W., Room 1200, Washington, DC 20593/202-426-2010.

Environmental Research

Research is performed on water quality, noise abatement, air quality, vegetation management and corrosion control. Studies are also done on bicycling and pedestrians. Contact: Construction Maintenance and Environmental Design Division, Federal Highway Administration, Department of Transportation, 6300 Georgetown Pike Room T-211, McLean, VA 22101/703-285-2016.

Essential Air Passenger Service

This office guarantees that certain cities will be served by air carriers and it represents community views. Contact: Office of Essential Air Service, Department of Transportation, 400 7th St. S.W., Room 10405, Washington, DC 20590/202-472-5296.

Federal Aviation Administration Academy

The Academy is the principal source of aviation technical knowledge. It conducts training for Federal Aviation Administration personnel through resident or correspondence courses and occasional on-site training. Air traffic training is available for specialists who man the Federal Aviation Administration airport traffic control towers, air route traffic control center, and flight service stations. Electronics training is also available for engineers and technicians who install and maintain navigation traffic control and communications facilities. Initial and recurrent training is also conducted for air carrier and general operations inspectors. Air navigation facilities and flight procedures analysis is provided to flight inspection personnel. Contact: AAC-900, P.O. Box 25082, Oklahoma City, OK 73125/405-686-4317.

Fifty-Five Miles Per Hour Enforcement

A clearinghouse and information center is available on enforcement programs in the United States. They receive and process annual certifications of 55 MPH enforcement that are required by law. It oversees expenditures of Federal Highway Safety Funds allocated annually for 55 MPH enforcement. It also develops research programs which assist state enforcement agencies to improve all police-related traffic enforcement programs. Contact: Police Traffic Services Branch, Enforcement Division, Traffic Safety Programs, National Highway Traffic Safety Administration, Department of Transportation, 400 7th St. S.W., Room 5118, Washington, DC 20590/202-472-5440.

Financial Analysis of Airline Industry

Financial studies and evaluations of the air transport industry are available on such topics as profit margin trends, aircraft cost and performance, domestic jet trends, fuel trends, carrier lenders, passenger yield, used aircraft sales, aircraft seating trends and airline employment. Contact: Industry, Economics and Finance Division, Office of Economics, Office of Assistant Secretary for Policy and International Affairs, Department of Transportation, 400 7th St. N.W., Room 10223, Washington, DC 20590/202-426-4384.

Flight Procedures

Instrument flight procedures are developed and maintained by: Flight Procedures Branch, Federal Aviation Administration, Department of Transportation, P.O. Box 25082, AVN-220, Oklahoma City, OK 73125/405-686-2382.

Freedom of Information Act

Each major division within the Department of Transportation has a Freedom of Information Act office. For a list of these offices, contact: Freedom of Information Office, Office of Public Affairs, Department of Transportation, 400 7th St. S.W., Room 9421, Washington, DC 20590/202-426-4542.

Gasoline Trends

The publication, Monthly Motor Fuels, Reported By States, gives an indication of trends in gasoline sales by month. Contact: Highway Users and Finance Branch, Highway Statistics Division, Office of Highway Planning, Federal Highway Administration, Department of Transportation, 400 7th St. S.W., Room 3300, Washington, DC 20590/202-426-0187.

Grants

The programs described below are for sums of money which are given by the federal government to initiate and stimulate new or improved activities, or sustain on-going services.

Airport Improvement Program

Objectives: To assist sponsors, owners or operators of public-use airports in the development of a nationwide system of public airports adequate to meet the needs of civil aeronautics.

Eligibility: State, country, municipal, and other public agencies including an Indian tribe or pueblo are eligible for airport development grants if the airport on which the development is required is listed in the National Plan of Integrated Airport Systems (NPIAS). Certain units of local governments surrounding airports may be eligible for grants associated with achieving noise compatibility with airports.

Range of Financial Assistance: $25,000 to $9,992,765.

Contact: Grants-in-Aid Division, APP-500, Federal Aviation Administration, Office of Airports Planning and Programming, Department of Transportation, 800 Independence Ave. S.W., Washington, DC 20591/202-426-3831.

Boating Safety Financial Assistance

Objectives: To encourage greater State participation and uniformity in boating safety, particularly to permit the States to assume the greater share of boating safety education, assistance, and enforcement activities, and to assist the States in developing, carrying out and financing their recreational boating safety programs.

Eligibility: States (including Puerto Rico, Virgin Islands, Guam, American Samoa, Northern Marianas, and the District of Columbia) having a Coast Guard approved boating safety program may apply for financial assistance.

Range of Financial Assistance: $35,000 to $703,000.

Contact: Commandant, US Coast Guard, Washington, DC 20593/202-426-1060.

Gas Pipeline Safety

Objectives: To develop and maintain state gas pipeline safety programs.

Eligibility: The Department provides federal matching funds to any state agency with a certificate under Section 5(a) of the Act; an agreement under Section 5(b) of the Act, or to any state acting as a Department of Transportation agent on interstate gas pipelines.

Range of Financial Assistance: $9,565 to $347,560.

Contact: Department of Transportation, Materials Transportation Bureau, 400 7th St. S.W., Washington, DC 20590/202-426-3046.

Grants-in-Aid for Railroad Safety—State Participation

Objectives: To promote safety in all areas of railroad operations, to reduce railroad related accidents, to reduce deaths and injuries to persons, and to reduce damage to property caused by accidents involving any carrier of hazardous materials, by providing for state participation in the enforcement and promotion of safety practices.

Eligibility: A state may participate in carrying out investigative and surveillance activities in connection with regulations promulgated by the Federal Railroad Administrator under this act applicable to track and rolling equipment.

Range of Financial Assistance: Up to $25,000 per State Inspector.

Contact: Associate Administrator for Safety, Federal Railroad Administration, Department of Transportation, 400 7th St. S.W., Washington, DC 20590/202-426-0895.

Highway Beautification—Control of Outdoor Advertising and Control of Junkyards

Objectives: To beautify highways and their vicinities.

Eligibility: State highway agencies.

Range of Financial Assistance: $1,000 to $336,000.

Contact: Office of Right of Way, Federal Highway Administration, 400 7th St. S.W., Washington, DC 20590/202-245-0021.

Highway Educational Grants

Objectives: To assist state and local agencies and the Federal Highway Administration (FHWA) in developing the expertise needed for implementation of their highway programs. The programs are intended to address identified training needs of state and local agencies and FHWA identified national emphasis areas which currently include: highway safety, energy conservation, and civil rights.

Eligibility: Employees of federal, state, and local highway/transportation agencies engaged in or to be engaged in federal-aid highway work.

Range of Financial Assistance: $2,500 to $7,500.

Contact: Director, National Highway Institute, Federal Highway Administration, Department of Transportation, 400 7th St. S.W., Washington, DC 20590/202-426-3100.

Highway Planning and Construction

Objectives: To assist state highway agencies in constructing and rehabilitating the interstate highway system and building or improving primary, secondary and urban systems roads and streets, to provide aid for their repair following disasters, and to foster safe highway design; and to replace or rehabilitate unsafe bridges. Also provides for the improvement of some highways in Guam, the Virgin Islands, American Samoa, and the Northern Mariana Islands.

Eligibility: State highway agencies. Projects related to forest and public lands highway, certain projects in urban areas, or projects of the state highway systems may be proposed by counties or other political subdivisions or agencies through the state highway agencies.

Range of Financial Assistance. $628,560 to $948,486,344.

Contact: Office of Engineering, Federal Highway Administration, Department of Transportation, 400 7th St. S.W., Washington, DC 20590/202-426-4853.

Human Resource Program

Objectives: To provide Financial assistance for national and local programs that address human resource needs as they apply to public transportation activities particularly in furtherance of minority and female needs.

Eligibility: Public bodies, State and local agencies, institutions of higher learning, and nonprofit institutions.

Range of Financial Assistance. None established.

Contact: Director of Civil Rights, Urban Mass Transportation Administration, Department of Transportation, 400 7th ST. S.W., Room 7410, Washington, DC 20590/202-426-4018.

Local Rail Service Assistance

Objectives: To maintain efficient local rail freight services.

Eligibility: States are eligible for assistance.

Range of Financial Assistance: $100,000 to $1,300,000.

Contact: Office of Freight Assistance Programs, Federal Railroad Administration, Department of Transportation, 400 7th St. S.W., Room 5406, Washington, DC 20590/202-426-1677.

Motor Carrier Safety Assistance Program

Objectives: To reduce the number and severity of accidents and hazardous materials incidents involving commercial motor vehicles by substantially increasing the level of enforcement activity and the likelihood that safety defects, driver deficiencies, and unsafe carrier practices will be detected and corrected.

Eligibility: A qualified State or political subdivision thereof, of the United States, the District of Columbia, the Commonwealth of Puerto Rico, the Virgin Islands, American Samoa, Guam, or the Commonwealth of the Northern Marianas.

Range of Financial Assistance: $75,000 to $1,250,000.

Contact: Bureau of Motor Carrier Safety, Federal Highway Administration, Washington, DC 20590/202-426-0701.

Public Transportation for Nonurbanized Areas

Objectives: To improve or continue public transportation service in rural and small urban areas by providing financial assistance for the acquisition, construction, and improvement of facilities.

Eligibility: Eligible recipients may include state agencies, local public bodies and agencies thereof, nonprofit organizations and operators of public transportation services in rural and small urban areas. Urbanized areas, as defined by the Bureau of the Census, are not eligible.

Range of Financial Assistance: Not specified.

Contact: Urban Mass Transportation Administration, Office of Grants Management, State Programs Division, 400 7th St. S.W., Washington, DC 20590/202-426-2360.

Research and Development Assistance

Objectives: To improve the productivity of US shipbuilding, shipping, port, and ancillary industries.

Eligibility: Ship operators, shipbuilders, individuals, universities, State and local governments, US Territories (and possessions), nonprofit organizations and institutions, port authorities, or independent research concerns with marine expertise.

Range of Financial Assistance: Not applicable.

Contact: Assistant for Program Development and Control, Department of Transportation, Washington, DC 20590/202-382-0357.

State and Community Highway Safety

Objectives: To provide a coordinated national highway safety program to reduce traffic accidents, deaths, injuries and property damage.

Eligibility: States, federally recognized Indian tribes, the District of Columbia, and Puerto Rico highway safety programs approved by the Secretary.

Range of Financial Assistance: $499,515 to $8,671,865.

Contact: Chief Program Operations Staff, Traffic Safety Programs, National Highway Traffic Safety Administration, Department of Transportation, Washington, DC 20590/202-426-1634.

Urban Mass Transportation Capital and Operating Assistance Formula Grants

Objectives: To assist in financing the acquisition, construction and improvement of facilities and equipment for use by operation or lease or otherwise in mass transportation service, and the payment of operating expenses to improve or to continue such service by operation, lease, contract or otherwise.

Eligibility: Funds will be made available to urbanized areas (as defined by Bureau of the Census) through designated recipients which must be public entities and legally capable of receiving and dispensing federal funds.

Range of Financial Assistance: Not specified.

Contact: Office of Grants Management, Urban Mass Transportation Administration, Department of Transportation, 400 7th St. S.W., Washington, DC 20590/202-426-2053.

Urban Mass Transportation Capital Improvement Grants

Objectives: To assist in financing the acquisition, construction, reconstruction and improvement of facilities and equipment for use, by operation, lease, or otherwise, in mass transportation service in urban areas and in coordinating service with highway and other transportation in such areas.

Eligibility: Public agencies. Private transporta-

tion companies may participate through contractual arrangements with a public agency grantee.
Range of Financial Assistance: $1,216 to $800,000,000.
Contact: Office of Grants Management, Office of Grants Assistance, Urban Mass Transportation Administration, Department of Transportation, 400 7th St. S.W., Washington, DC 20590/202-472-2440.

Urban Mass Transportation Grants for University Research and Training
Objectives: To sponsor research studies and training in the problems of transportation in urban areas.
Eligibility: Public and private nonprofit institutions of higher learning, offering baccalaureate or higher degrees.
Range of Financial Assistance: Up to $85,000.
Contact: Office of Technical Assistance, Office of Service and Management Demonstration, University Research and Training Division (URT-33), Urban Mass Transportation Administration, Department of Transportation, 400 7th St. S.W., Washington, DC 20590/202-426-0080.

Urban Mass Transportation Managerial Training Grants
Objectives: To provide fellowships for training of managerial, technical and professional personnel employed in the urban mass transportation field.
Eligibility: State and local Public bodies may apply for their employees or those of urban transit companies operating in their areas.
Range of Financial Assistance: $1,091 to $12,000.
Contact: Office of Technical Assistance, Office of Service and Management Demonstrations, Urban Mass Transportation Administration, Department of Transportation, 400 7th St. S.W., Washington, DC 20590/202-426-9274.

Urban Mass Transportation Technical Assistance
Objectives: (1) to conduct technical assistance activities to improve mass transportation facilities, equipment, techniques, methods, management, and planning; (2) to provide technical assistance, including training, to Federal, State, and local governments, transit and planning agencies, private industry, and academia with respect to making such improvements; (3) to ensure the transfer to potential users of the results of the technical assistance; and (4) to administer federally funded programs related to such activities, including training programs.
Eligibility: Public bodies, nonprofit institutions, State and local agencies, universities, and legally constituted public agencies.
Range of Financial Assistance: None established.

Contact: Associate Administrator for Technical Assistance (URT-1), Urban Mass Transportation Administration, Department of Transportation, 400 7th St. S.W., Room 6431, Washington, DC 20590/202-426-4052.

Urban Mass Transportation Technical Studies Grants
Objectives: To assist in planning, engineering, and designing of urban mass transportation projects, and other technical studies in a program for a unified or officially coordinated urban transportation system.
Eligibility: State and other local public bodies and agencies.
Range of Financial Assistance: $10,000 to $6,500,000.
Contact: Director, Office of Planning Assistance (UPM-20), Office of Grants Management, Urban Mass Transportation Administration, Department of Transportation, 400 7th St. S.W., Washington, DC 20590/202-426-2360.

Hazardous Materials
"Special Permits" are required to insure the proper making, packaging, labeling and safe transportation of hazardous materials on U.S. highways. Regulation also requires the safe transportation of migrant workers in interstate commerce. Contact: Regulations Division, Bureau of Motor Carrier Safety, Federal Highway Administration, Department of Transportation, 400 7th St. S.W., Room 3404, Washington, DC 20590/202-426-0033.

High Seas Law Enforcement
The U.S. Coast Guard enforces within the territorial waters, contiguous zones and special interest areas of the high seas, federal laws and international agreements, except those related to pollution, traffic control and port and vessel safety. This includes: minimizing fishing gear loss and damage resulting from conflicts based on the simultaneous use of desirable fishing areas by fishermen, using mobile fishing gear, and other fixed equipment; providing operational assistance enforcement advice and information on offshore activity to other agencies and entities concerned with protecting and preserving ocean resources and national interests; providing fisheries enforcement with random patrols to detect changes in fishing fleet operations, illicit measures of fishing and other illegal activity. Contact: Operational Law Enforcement Division, Office of Operations, Coast Guard, Department of Transportation, 2100 2nd St. S.W., Room 3108, Washington, DC 20593/202-426-1890.

Highway Environment
Information is available on the environment affected by a highway. Areas of concern include archeology, history, architecture, landscape, ecology, geography, and the preservation of historic

sites, wetlands and farm lands. Contact: Environmental Quality Division, Office of Environmental Policy, Federal Highway Administration, Department of Transportation, 400 7th St. S.W., Room 3240, Washington, DC 20590/202-426-0351.

Highway Publications
The following publications are free from: Public Information, Federal Highway Administration, Department of Transportation, 400 7th St. S.W., Room 4208, Washington, DC 20590/202-426-0660.

America on the Move
Consumer's Resource Handbook
Cost of Owning and Operating An Automobile
Driver License Administration Requirements and Fees
Federally Coordinated Programs of Highway Research and Development
Highway Joint Development and Multiple Use
Highway Traffic Noise and Future Land Development
Interstate Transfer Provisions
Junkyards and the Highway and Visual Quality
License Plates—1981
National Highway Institute
National Highway Institute—The First 10 Years—1970–1980
Ridesharing: A Leadership Role
Ridesharing: How It Can Help Your Company
The Sulfur Breakthrough
Surface Transportation Assistance Act of 1978
U.S. Road Symbol Signs
Your Guide to the Freedom of Information Act

Highway Research and Development
For information on administrative documents pertaining to the Federal Highway Administration's research and development program, contact: Administrative Documents, Research and Technology Development, Federal Highway Administration, Department of Transportation, 400 7th St. S.W., Room 214, FHRS, HRD2, Washington, DC 20590/703-285-2107.

Highway Research Implementation
"Implementation Packages" are special publications which document the application of highway research and development results to solving or alleviating problems in highway design, construction and maintenance. The *Implementation Catalog* lists selected publications, visual aids, computer programs, and training materials that are available as part of the Federal Highway Administration implementation program. Contact: Office of Implementation, Federal Highway Administration, Department of Transportation, HDV-20, 400 7th St. S.W., Washington, DC 20590/703-285-2037.

Highway Research Publications
A free listing of publications is available including:

Index to Research and Development Reports
Federally Coordinated Program of Highway Research and Development

Contact: Research and Technology Development, Office of Operations Staff, Federal Highway Administration, Department of Transportation, 400 7th St. S.W., Room 223, FHRS, Washington, DC 20590/202-285-2144.

Highway Statistics
Statistics are available on such topics as: the number of motor vehicles by state; the amount of fuel consumed by state; the number of driver's licenses issued by age, sex, and state; state finances; and vehicle miles traveled. Contact: Highway Statistics Division, Office of Highway Planning, Federal Highway Administration, Department of Transportation, 400 7th St. S.W., Room 3300, HHP 40, Washington, DC 20590/202-426-0180.

Highway Noise
For information and expertise on how to minimize the impact of highway noise, contact: Office of Environmental Policy, Noise and Air Analysis Division, Federal Highway Administration, Department of Transportation, 400 7th St. S.W., Room 3240, Washington, DC 20590/202-426-4836.

Icebreaking
The U.S. Coast Guard is responsible for all icebreaking activities including: a polar icebreaking fleet to support scientific and defense related research in the Arctic and Antarctic regions; the Northslope/DEW Line resupply project which provides logistical support to the Alaskan North Slope oil fields and to isolated northern Alaska defense installations; Operation Deepfreeze which supplies the American Scientific effort in Antarctica, and facilities on the Great Lakes and on the East Coast. Contact: Ice Operations Division, Office of Operations, Coast Guard, Department of Transportation, 2100 2nd St. S.W., Room 3106, Washington, DC 20593/202-426-1881.

Innovations in Public Transportation
This publication describes current research, development and demonstration projects funded by the Urban Mass Transportation Administration. Tables show funding for major program areas. Charts summarize funding and other important information about various individual projects. Contact: Urban Mass Transit Administration, DTS-151, Transportation Systems Center, Research and Special Programs Administration, Department of Transportation, Kendall Square, Cambridge, MA 02142/617-494-2000.

Intercity Passenger Programs
This includes such projects as the Northeast Corridor, Conrail and the Alaska Railroad. Contact: Public Affairs, Federal Railroad Administration, Department of Transportation, 400 7th St. S.W., Room 8125, Washington, DC 20590/202-426-0881.

Intermodal Studies
Research is conducted on analytical and policy studies that involve more than one mode of transportation including the advisability of standardizing weight limits of states. Contact: Economic Studies Division, Office of Assistant Secretary for International Affairs, Office of Economics, Department of Transportation, 400 7th St. S.W., Room 10309, Washington, DC 20590/202-426-4163.

International Aviation
This office is responsible for international aviation including US-Canada Nonscheduled Air Services, negotiations with foreign governments and US Carrier routes with regard to compliance under bilateral agreements. Contact: Office of Policy and International Affairs, Department of Transportation, 400 7th St. S.W., Room 6401, Washington, DC 20590/202-426-2903.

International Cooperation
This office arranges for international cooperation programs that are mutually beneficial or for technical assistance that is reimbursable. Contact: International Cooperation Division, Office of International Policy and Programs, Office of Policy and International Affairs, Department of Transportation, 400 7th St. S.W., Washington, DC 20590/202-426-4398.

International Environment
International environmental coordination and representation to such groups as the United Nations' International Maritime Consultative Organization is handled by: Environmental Coordination Branch, Environmental Response Division, Coast Guard, Department of Transportation, Room 1202, Washington, DC 20593/202-426-9573.

Japanese High Speed Rail System Resource
The U.S. Office of the Japanese government's transportation system, Japanese National Railway, can provide you with information about its high speed rail system. Upon written request, staff will send you technical information and illustrated brochures about the Japanese high speed bullet train called *Shinkansen.* Contact: Japanese National Railroad Assistance Team to the Northeast Corridor Improvement Project, c/o Federal Railroad Administration, RPF-1, 400 7th St. S.W., Washington, DC 20590/202-472-5597.

Junkyard and Outdoor Advertising
This office conducts a program that controls junkyards and outdoor advertising along federally aided primary and interstate highway systems. A publication, *Junkyards, the Highway and Visual Quality,* is also produced by this office. Contact: Real Estate Division, Acquisitions and Special Programs Branch, Office of Right of Way, Federal Highway Administration, Department of Transportation, 400 7th St. S.W., Room 4132, Washington, DC 20590/202-245-0021.

Loans and Loan Guarantees
The programs described below offer financial assistance through the lending of federal monies for a specific period of time or program in which the federal government makes an arrangement to indemnify a lender against part or all of any defaults by the borrower.

Federal Ship Financing Guarantees
Objectives: To promote construction and reconstruction of ships in the foreign and domestic commerce of the United States by providing Government guarantees of obligations so as to make commercial credit more readily available.
Eligibility: Any US citizen with the ability, experience, financial resources, and other qualifications necessary to the adequate operation and maintenance of the vessel.
Range of Financial Assistance: $1,716,000 to $94,833,000.
Contact: Associate Administrator for Maritime Aids, Maritime Administration, Department of Transportation, Washington, DC 20590/202-382-0364.

Railroad Rehabilitation and Improvement—Guarantee of Obligations
Objectives: To provide financial assistance for the acquisition or rehabilitation and improvement of railroad facilities or equipment; and develop new railroad facilities.
Eligibility: Applicant is defined to mean any railroad or other person, including state and local government entities, which submits an application to the Administrator for the guarantee of an obligation under which it is an obligor.
Range of Financial Assistance: $5,000,000 to $75,000,000.
Contact: Office of National Freight Assistance Programs, Department of Transportation, 400 7th St. S.W., Washington, DC 20590/202-426-9657.

Railroad Rehabilitation and Improvement—Redeemable Preference Shares or Notes
Objectives: To provide railroads with financial assistance for the rehabilitation and improvement of equipment and facilities or such other purposes approved by Secretary.
Eligibility: Any common carrier by railroad or express as defined in section 1 (3) of the Interstate Commerce Act (49 U.S.C. 1 (3)) may apply for assistance.
Range of Financial Assistance: $5,000,000 to $100,000,000.
Contact: Office of Freight Assistance Programs, Department of Transportation, 400 7th St. S.W., Washington, DC 20590/202-426-9657.

Marine and Ice Operations
This office collects maritime data for oceanographic, meteorological and hydrographic applications, and emphasizes applied oceanography in support of oceanographic instrumentation on icebreakers and other large cutters. It also collects routine and special weather and oceanographic data for other agencies and furnishes vessels to display and rewire the large environmental data buoys off U.S. coasts. Contact: Ice Operations Division, Operations Division, Office of Operations, Coast Guard, Department of Transportation, 2100 2nd St. S.W., Room 3106, Washington, DC 20593/202-426-1881.

Marine Pollution Data
The Pollution Incident Reporting System (PIRS) lists oil spills and hazardous chemical spills within the United States. This computer-ized data base is designed to provide information on cleanup activities and penalty actions. Information is also available on volume in gallons of oil and other substances spilled, volume in pounds of hazardous and other substances, and incidents by location and month. Contact: Information Analysis Branch, Environmental Response Division, Office of Marine Environment and Systems, Coast Guard, Department of Transportation, 2100 2nd St. S.W., Room 1205, G-WER-4, Washington, DC 20593/202-426-9571.

Marine Safety
The Marine Safety Information System provides computerized information on vessels with safety violations along with records of inspections and port visits. Contact: Safety Information and Analysis Branch, Prevention and Enforcement Division, Office of Marine Environment and Systems, Coast Guard, Department of Transportation, 2100 2nd St. S.W., Room 1106, Washington, DC 20593/202-426-1450.

Marine Technology Research and Development
The U.S. Coast Guard Research and Development Center's research and development activities focus on: ice technology; marine navigation technology; marine fire and safety technology; marine pollution technology; search and rescue technology; and naval engineering and marine systems technology.

They can supply you with technical information and refer you to experts on the above subjects. The Center issues several technical reports and studies that can be obtained from: NTIS, Department of Commerce, 5885 Port Royal Road, Springfield, VA 22161/703-487-4807. Contact: U.S. Coast Guard Research and Development Center, Department of Transportation, Avery Point, Groton, CT 06340/203-445-8501.

Mass Transportation Planning
The Office of Methods and Support aims to research, develop, demonstrate and disseminate computerized and manual techniques to assist federal, state and local agencies in planning, programming, budgeting and implementation of inprovements in their transportation systems. Contact: Office of Methods and Support, Planning Management and Demonstrations, Urban Mass Transportation Administration, Department of Transportation, 400 7th St. S.W., Room 6107, Washington, DC 20590/202-426-9271.

Medical Appeals
For information on appealing medical certification denials, contact: Medical Appeals, Aeromedical Standards Division, Office of Aviation Medicine, Federal Aviation Administration, Department of Transportation, 800 Independence Ave. S.W., Room 322, Washington, DC 20591/202-426-3093

Merchant Marine Safety Data
Computerized files are available on merchant marine safety including: reported vessel casualties, personnel casualties occurring in commercial vessels, and vessels inspected. The information is also available in published format. Contact: Planning Division Automated Systems Branch. Office of Merchant Marine Safety, Coast Guard, Department of Transportation, 2100 2nd St. S.W., Room 1604, Washington, DC 20592/202-426-1483.

Merchant Vessel Documentation
This office administers the laws and regulations on the registration, enrollment and licensing of vessels that are five or more net tons and which are engaged in the coasting trade or fisheries. Vessels engaged in foreign trade must also be registered. Contact: Merchant Vessel Documentation Division, Office of Merchant Marine Safety, Coast Guard, Department of Transportation, 2100 2nd St. S.W., Room 1312, G-MVD/13, Washington, DC 20593/202-426-1494.

Merchant Vessel Inspection
Merchant vessels (including U.S. flag vessels, passenger, freight for hire, dangerous cargo, combustibles and flammables in bulk) are under U.S. Coast Guard regulation from design to construction. Vessels are periodically inspected and records are kept on penalties and violations. Contact: Merchant Vessel Inspection Division, Office of Merchant Marine Safety, Coast Guard, Department of Transportation, 2100 2nd St. S.W., Room 2414, Washington, DC 20593/202-426-2178.

Merchant Vessels of the United States
This publication is issued annually by the U.S. Coast Guard and lists the name, owner, official number, call signs, data and place of construction

and home port of merchant vessels. Available for $47.00 from Superintendent of Documents, Government Printing Office, Washington, DC 20402/202-783-3238.

Merchant Vessel Training
Certain vessels are required to have a specified manning of licensed, qualified crew. The manning of the vessel depends on the route, tonnage, horsepower, and type of trade. The publication, *Rules and Regulations for Licensing and Certification of Merchant Marine Personnel,* includes regulations that are applicable to all persons who want to be licensed, registered or certificated. It also contains rules and regulations concerning shipment and discharge of seamen, allotments of seamen and U.S. shipping commissioners. Contact: Licensing and Evaluation, Merchant Vessel Personnel Division, Office of Merchant Marine Safety, Coast Guard, Department of Transportation, 2100 2nd St. S.W., Room 1316, Washington, DC 20593/202-426-2240.

Merchant Vessel Statistics
Merchant Vessels of the U.S. is an annual publication which lists such information as: names of vessels, home port, names of owners, official number, gross and net tonnage, breadth and length of vessel, and year it was built. Available for $47.00 from Government Printing Office, Superintendent of Documents, Washington, DC 20402/202-783-3238.

Mike Monroney Aeronautical Center
This Center provides much of the Federal Aviation Administration's in-resident flight training. Information is available on airmen and aircraft, human factors research, maintenance and modification of agency aircraft, and flight inspection of airways' electronic and communications equipment. Contact: Public Affairs Office, Mike Monroney Aeronautical Center, Federal Aviation Administration, Department of Transportation, P.O. Box 25082, 6500 S. MacArthur, Oklahoma City, OK 73125/405-686-2562.

Minority Business Opportunities
The Minority Business Resource Center helps to identify business opportunities in all modes of transportation including aviation and railroads. The Center maintains a Marketing Assistance Clearinghouse and provides a free newsletter aimed at assisting business people through the entire procurement process. Contact: Minority Business Resource Center, Office of the Secretary, Department of Transportation, 400 7th St. S.W., Room 9410, Washington, DC 20590/202-472-2438.

Motor Carrier Safety Research
Research projects are sponsored to administer the Motor Carrier Safety Regulations and the Hazardous Materials Regulations governing trucks and buses operating in interstate and foreign commerce which includes for-hire and private carriers of property for-hire carriers of passengers, carriers of agricultural commodities, livestock and horticultural products. The field offices contain staffs of hazardous material specialists and safety investigators which assist in the implementation of the U.S. Department of Transportation's Cargo Security Program. They perform periodic and unannounced roadchecks on the vehicle's condition, loading and documentating. Contact: Operations Division, Bureau of Motor Carrier Safety, Federal Highway Administration, Department of Transportation, 400 7th St. S.W., Room 3408, Washington, DC 20590/202-426-1724.

Motor Vehicle Accident Data
Data are collected on drivers, pedestrians, vehicles, collision types, injuries, environmental factors and exposure. The national data collection systems operated by the National Center for Statistics and Analysis include:

National Accident Sampling System (NASS)—investigates and analyzes data on all types of motor vehicle accidents throughout the country; investigations focus on information such as vehicle crash protection, driver characteristics, roadside hazards, and injury security; data are compiled into national totals based on geographic, population and type of roadway.
Fatal Accident Reporting System (FARS)—provides statistical data on fatal accidents.
National Crash Severity Study (NCSS)—seeks to link vehicle damage with injury severity.
National Electronic Injury Surveillance System (NEISS)—extends the Consumer Product Safety Commission Data System to include traffic accident information.
Contact: National Center for Statistics and Analysis, Research and Development, National Highway Traffic Safety Administration, Department of Transportation, 400 7th St. S.W., Room 6125, Washington, DC 20590/202-426-1470.

Motor Vehicle Diagnostic Inspection Program
This report concludes that car owners can achieve greater safety, lower pollution, improved gas mileage and lower repair and maintenance costs for their cars by using diagnostic inspection. These diagnostic inspections involve running a series of tests on a car and giving the consumer a status report on its conditions, complete enough to serve as a prescription for getting proper repairs. Contact: Traffic Safety Program (NTS-30), National Highway Traffic Safety Adminstration, Department of Transportation, 400 7th St. S.W., Room 5119, Washington, DC 20590/202-426-1760.

Motor Vehicle Safety Standards
The Office of Crashworthiness provides information and sets standards for: air bags, seat belts,

child restraint safety seats, motorcycle helmets, fuel system integrity, odometers, windshield defrosters, rearview mirrors, tire selection and rims, door locks, school bus rollover protection, seating systems, new pneumatic tires, and more. A publication covering this topic, *Federal Motor Vehicle Safety Standards and Regulation,* is available for $120.00 from: Government Printing Office, Superintendent of Documents, Washington, DC 20402/202-783-3238.

National Airport System Plan
Statistical information and interpretation is available on the National Airport System. Contact: Office of Airport Planning and Programming, National Planning Division, Federal Aviation Administration, Department of Transportation, 800 Independence Ave. S.W., Room 616, Washington, DC 20591/202-426-3844.

National Flight Data Center
Information is available on all civilian airports (and those military airports with joint usage), navigation aids, and procedures for the national air space system. A data base is maintained containing such items as the latitude and longitude of airports, airport runways, records of obstruction to air navigation, flight planning information, bearing and distance information, and records of hazards to air navigation. Contact: National Flight Data Center, Air Space-Rules and Aeronautical Information Division, Air Traffic Service, Federal Aviation Administration, Department of Transportation, 800 Independence Ave. S.W., Room 631, Washing-ton, DC 20591/202-426-3288.

National Highway Institute
This Institute develops and administers training programs for Federal Highway Administration, and state and local highway department employees engaged or to be engaged in federal-aided highway work. It administers graduate and undergraduate awards for study in transportation-related fields and compiles information on available training materials, short courses and visual aids. A listing of available films and publications is also available. Contact: National Highway Institute, Training Facility, Federal Highway Administration, Department of Transportation, 400 7th St. S.W., Room 4206, Washington, DC 20590/202-426-4878.

Navigation Aid Research and Testing
A field office of the U.S. Maritime Administration, the National Maritime Research Center conducts research and testing on the following ship control areas navigation aids; certification and training instrumentation; ship maneuvering and instrumentation; general management of ships; satellite communications with ships; preliminary investigation and application of satellite communications in maritime transportation. Its Study

Center plans to have a data base set up and in use shortly. The Center issues technical reports on the topics indicated above. Contact: National Maritime Research Center, U.S. Maritime Administration, Department of Transportation, Kings Point, Long Island, NY 11024/516-482-8200.

No-Fault Insurance
For information and expertise on no-fault automobile insurance, contact: Office of Eco-nomics, Department of Transportation, 400 7th St. S.W., Room 10301, Washington, DC 20590/202-426-4416.

Northeast Corridor Project
This is a major track upgrading program on AMTRAK's main line from Washington, D.C. to Boston. The upgrading is aimed at producing the best high-speed passenger railroad the United States has ever seen. For current progress, contact: Office of Public Affairs, Federal Railroad Administration, Department of Transportation, 400 7th St. S.W., Room 8126, Washington, DC 20590/202-426-0881.

Odometer Law
It is a federal offense to roll back the odometer in a car. An odometer disclosure statement must be signed when you sell a car stating that the mileage on the odometer is accurate. Contact: Office of the Chief Counsel, National Highway Traffic Safety Administration, Department of Transportation, 400 7th St. S.W., Room 5219, Washington, DC 20590/202-426-1835.

Oil and Chemical Spills Hotline
The National Response Center is the clearinghouse for notification of incidents of oil and hazardous substance spills on land or in U.S. waters. It discovers spills through surveillance systems, evaluates the situation, initiates immediate containment action and countermeasures, and provides for cleanup and disposal. Contact: National Response Center, Marine Environment and Response Division, Office of Marine Environment and Systems, Coast Guard, Department of Transportation, 400 7th St. S.W., Room 7402, Washington, DC 20590/202-426-1192 (Hotline: 800-424-8802)

Paratransit
Paratransit includes a broad range of services that lies between conventional fixed route transit and the private automobile (jitneys, taxis, car-pools, etc.). The primary focus is on the use of these alternative travel modes to provide more efficient use of transportation facilities where needed. Testing is also done on specialized services that will provide for the travel needs of transit-dependent people, particularly the elderly, the handicapped and the poor. Contact: Paratransit and

Special User Groups, Office of Service and Methods Demonstration, Urban Mass Transportation Administration, Department of Transportation, 400 7th St. S.W., Room 6100, Washington, DC 20590/202-426-4984.

Passenger Vehicle Research
Research is conducted on vehicles including cars, pick-up trucks and vans. Studies are made on automotive systems, occupant packaging (inside the car), accident avoidance (tires, braking, towing), structures (fuel tanks, crash performance), technology assessment (advanced technology, diesels, emissions, new materials), experimental vehicles projected for 1985 to 1990, downsizing and fuel economy. Contact: Office of Vehicle Research, Research and Development, National Highway Traffic Safety Administration, Department of Transportation, 400 7th St. S.W., Room 6226, Washington, DC 20590/202-426-4862.

Pedestrian Safety
For information on the kind of facilities used to improve pedestrian safety, contact: Environmental Design and Surveys Branch, Highway Design Division, Office of Engineering, Federal Highway Administration, Department of Transportation, 400 7th St. S.W., Room 3124, Washington, DC 20590/202-426-0294.

Pilot Schools
A *List of Certified Pilot Schools* is available for $2.00 from: Government Printing Office, Superintendent of Documents, Washington, DC 20402/202-783-3238.

Pollution Incident Reporting System
The Pollution Incident Reporting System (PIRS) contains information about all spills of hazardous materials, oil and other pollutants that have been reported to the U.S. Coast Guard since 1973. Data is used for management, statistical and public information purposes. Records contain the following type of data: spill dates, location, type, affected resources, cause, source, and quantity; cleanup party, materials, duration, and cost; and penalty action and results. Enviromental impact statements are also stored.

Begun in 1973, PIRS contains 150,000 records and is updated monthly by approximately 1,000 reports. Searches and printouts are available free of charge. All requests must be in writing. Contact: U.S. Coast Guard Headquarters, 2100 2nd St, S.W., Room 1202, Washington, DC 20593/202-426-9571.

Pollution National Strike Force
Marine pollution control experts, specially trained and equipped, provide technical advice and undertake containment and cleanup activities when needed. Contact: National Strike Force, Pollution Response Branch, Environmental Response Division, Office of Marine Environment and Systems, Coast Guard, Department of Transportation, 2100 2nd St. S.W., Room 1205, Washington, DC 20593/202-426-9568.

Pollution Response
The U.S. Coast Guard is the primary federal agency responsible for cleaning up coastal areas. It conducts aerial and surface surveillance patrols for oil discharge pollution, sets policies for the pollution response program, and maintains the Chemical Hazards Response Information System with the following data bases:

Condensed Guide to Chemical Hazards—first aid information.
Hazardous Chemical Data—physical and chemical properties.
Hazard Assessment Handbook—series of formulas that simulate and have access to pollution or spill incidents.
Response Methods Handbook—techniques for cleaning up spills.
Spill Cleanup Equipment Inventory System—inventory of equipment available for pollution response.

Contact: Pollution Response Branch, Marine Environment Response Division, Office of Marine Environment and Systems, Coast Guard, Department of Transportation, 2100 2nd St. S.W., Room 1205, Washington, DC 20593/202-426-9568.

Pollution Surveillance
Surveillance and monitoring activities to pre-vent water pollution are conducted by: Commandant, GWPE, Enforcement Branch, Port and Environmental Safety Division, Coast Guard, Department of Transportation, 2100 2nd St. S.W., Room 1104, Washington, DC 20593/202-755-7917.

Port Facilities
Regulations for pollution prevention and port safety for waterfront facilities are handled by: Port and Environmental Safety Division, Programs Development Branch, Office of Marine Environment and Systems, Coast Guard, Department of Transportation, 2100 2nd St. S.W., Room 1611, Washington, DC 20593/202-755-1354.

Port Safety
Daily checks are made on vessel traffic in the harbor, special transport arrangements, security zone classifications and other special authorizations for port movements. Inspections are also made of commercial vessels for safety of their equipment and cargo stowage, especially when dangerous cargo is listed on the manifest. Contact: Enforcement Branch, Port and Environmental Safety Division, Office of Marine Environment and Systems, Coast Guard, Department of Transportation, 2100 2nd St. S.W., Room 1104, Washington, DC 20593/202-755-7917.

Rail Dynamics Laboratory

This laboratory provides a testing capability to identify improvements for current railroad and transit systems. It is available to governments and to private organizations such as foreign and domestic railroads, car builders, locomotive manufacturing trade associations and universities. Contact: Rail Dynamics Laboratory, Transportation Test Center, Federal Railroad Administration, Department of Transportation, P.O. Box 1130, Pueblo, CO 81001/303-545-5660.

Railroad Accidents

One can obtain access to accident data maintained on a computer data base as well as the following free publications:

Accident-Incident Bulletin (annual)
Railroad Highway Crossing Accident-Incident and Inventory Bulletin
Summary of Accidents Investigated by the Federal Railway Administration (1981)
Railroad Employee Fatalities investigated by the Federal Railway Administration (1981)
Railroad Accident Investigation Reports

Contact: System Support Division, Safety, RRS 22, Federal Railroad Administration, Department of Transportation, 400 7th St. S.W., Room 7401, Washington, DC 20590/202-426-2762.

Railroad Crossings

States receive federal funds to correct railroad grade crossing hazards. Contact: Program Development Division, Office of Highway Safety, Federal Highway Administration, Department of Transportation, 400 7th St. S.W., Room 3413, Washington, DC 20590/202-426-2131.

Railroad Freight and Operations

Studies are made on the use of freight cars, accounting and financial systems of railroads, coal rates, grain transportation and mergers. Available publications include: *Carload Waybill Statistics, Waybill Statistics, Waybill Data Base, Waybill/Freight Commodity Statistics*. Contact: Industry Analysis, Office of Policy, Federal Railroad Administration, Department of Transportation, 400 7th St. S.W., Room 5100, Washington, DC 20590/202-472-7260.

Railroad Information

For information on available programs, publications and other activities, contact: Public Affairs, Federal Railroad Administration, Department of Transportation, 400 7th St. S.W., Room 8125, Washington, DC 20590/202-426-0881.

Railroad Research and Development

Information is available on: developments to improve track and track bed structures; work to reduce the effects of accidents involving tank cars carrying hazardous materials; efforts to gain a better understanding of equipment failures; development of lower cost and more effective grade crossing techniques; and research into human factors in train operation. Contact: Office of Research and Development, Federal Railroad Administration, Department of Transportation, 400 7th St. S.W., Room 5423, Washington, DC 20590/202-426-9601.

Railroad Safety

The Office of Safety Programs inspects tracks, equipment, signals and general railroad operations. It investigates accidents and complaints and makes routine investigations. The office has jurisdiction over such areas as locomotives, signals, safety appliances, power brakes, hours of service, transportation of explosives, and human factors in rail operations. A publication, *Safety Report,* lists federal actions to improve railroad safety and includes statistical compilations of accidents; incident reports, federal safety regulations, orders and standards issued by the Federal Railroad Administration; evaluation of the degree of their observance; summary of outstanding problems; analysis and evaluation of research and related activities; a list of completed or pending judicial actions for the enforcement of any safety rules, regulations, orders or standards issued; and recommendations for additional legislation. Contact: Office of Safety, Federal Railroad Administration, Department of Transportation, 400 7th St. S.W., Room 7330, Washington, DC 20590/202-426-9252.

Rail Transit Safety

The rapid rail and light rail transit safety system consists of the following three elements: 1) Safety Information—Reporting and Analysis System—developing a new rapid rail transit accident/incident reporting system; 2) System Safety—disseminates pertinent information to individuals working in the field of mass transit; 3) Safety Research—research in fire safety, etc. Contact: Office of Safety and Product Qualifications, Technology Development and Deployment, Urban Mass Transportation Administration, Department of Transportation, 400 7th St. S.W., Room 7421, Washington, DC 20590/202-426-2896.

Regulatory Activities

Listed below are those organizations within the U.S. Department of Transportation which are involved with regulating various activities. With each listing is a description of those industries or situations, which are regulated by the office. Regulatory activities generate large amounts of information on the companies and subjects they regulate. Much of the information is available to the public. A regulatory officer can also tell you your rights when dealing with a regulated company.

Public Inquiry Center, Federal Aviation Administration, Department of Transportation, 800 Independence Ave. S.W., Washington, DC 20591/202-426-8058. Regulates civilian and military safety aspects of air commerce.

Public Affairs, Federal Highway Administration, Department of Transportation, 400 7th St. S.W., Washington, DC 20590/202-426-0660. Regulates design, construction, maintenance and use of the nation's highways.

Consumer Affairs, Federal Railroad Administration, Department of Transportation, 400 7th St. S.W., Washington, DC 20590/202-426-0881. Regulates the safety aspects of rail transportation.

Information Services, Materials Transportation Bureau, Research and Special Programs Administration, Department of Transportation, 400 7th St. S.W., Washington, DC 20590/202-755-9260. Regulates hazardous materials transportation and pipeline safety.

Public Affairs, National Highway Traffic Safety Administration, Department of Transportation, 400 7th St. S.W., Washington, DC 20590/202-426-9550. Regulates motor vehicle safety and efficiency.

Public Information, Saint Lawrence Seaway Corporation, Department of Transportation, P.O. Box 520, Massena, NY 13662/315-764-3200. Responsible for operating the U.S. section of the Saint Lawrence Seaway.

Public Affairs, Urban Mass Transportation Administration, Department of Transportation, 400 7th St. S.W., Washington, DC 20590/202-426-4043. Responsible for developing improved mass transportation facilities and equipment.

Public Affairs, Coast Guard, Department of Transportation, 2100 2nd St. S.W., Washington, DC 20593/202-426-2158. Regulates vessels and merchant marine personnel.

Relocation Assistance Near Airports
Assistance is available to airport owners involved with airport develpment projects to provide uniform and equitable treatment of persons displaced from their homes, business or firm by federal or federally assisted programs. Assistance is also available on enviromental impact statements and noise. Contact: Community and Environmental Needs Division, Office of Airport Planning and Programming, Federal Aviation Administration, Department of Transportation, 800 Independence Ave. S.W., Room 617, Washington, DC 20591/202-426-8434.

Rescues at Sea
The Coast Guard resource has the capability to respond effectively to a distress call—about 70,000 calls are made a year. Searches are planned using scientific methods based on experience and statistical foundations. The Guard also maintains a cooperative international and distress response system for open ocean incidents. Contact: Search and Rescue Division, Office of Operation, Coast Guard, Department of Transportation, 2100 2nd St. S.W., Room 3222, Washington, DC 20593/202-426-1948.

Ridesharing Information Center
The Center acts as a clearinghouse for infor-mation on ridesharing. They maintain a list of public ridesharing agencies that help in setting up systems and offer the following free publications:

Bi-Monthly Newsletter—information on new programs such as hitchhiking tax incentives, legislation, matching funds, etc.

Rideshare and Save-a-Cost Comparison a pamphlet for the individual to use in calculating the costs of commuting to work alone, in a carpool or in a vanpool.

Community Ridesharing: A Leadership Role

Contact: Transportation Management and Ride-Sharing Program Branch, Urban Planning and Transportation Division, Federal Highway Administration, Department of Transportation, 400 7th St. S.W., Room 3303, HHP25, Washington, DC 20590/202-426-0210.

Safety Data Management
Hazardous material incident reports are available on gas distribution and transmission and liquid pipeline carriers. Contact: Information Systems Division, Tranportation Programs Bureau, Research and Special Programs Administration, Department of Transportation, 400 7th St. S.W., Washington, DC 20590/202-426-4317.

Sailing Correspondence Course
A $5.50 book, *The Skipper's Course,* includes an examination on water safety. Those who pass the exam are awarded a water safety certificate. The book is available from: Government Book Store 15, Majestic Building, 720 N. Main St., Pueblo, CO 81003. For more details on the course, contact: Boating Auxiliary Division, Coast Guard, Department of Transportation, G-BAU, 2100 2nd St. S.W., Washington, DC 20593/202-426-1077

Saint Lawrence Seaway
The following publications are free:

The St. Lawrence Seaway—general and historic information in French and English; economic and port data, tool schedules for skippers and potential skippers; information in French and English for tourists traveling by automobile.

St. Lawrence Seaway Development Corporation Annual Report

Annual Traffic Report in the St. Lawrence Seaway—calendar year statistics on cargo vessels between Montreal and Lake Erie

Seaway Regulations—operating manual and chart booklet for commercial vessels, rules and regulations and seaway toll schedule.

Contact: Public Information Office, St. Lawrence Seaway Development Corp., P.O. Box 520, Massena, NY 13662/315-764-3200.

Saint Lawrence Seaway Statistics

For statistical and other data on the St. Lawrence Seaway, contact: Office of Trade and Traffic Development, St. Lawrence Seaway Development Corp., Department of Transportation, 400 7th St. S.W., Room 5424, Washington, DC 20590/ 202-426-2884.

Search and Rescue Data

Information is available on all calls for assistance from the U.S. Coast Guard, including: identification of unit that responded, data and time, how they were notified, nature of call, how far off shore was the vessel, position of vessel, method used by distressed unit to call, cause of distress, ownership of vessel, type of vessel, type of propulsion, size, number of lives lost and saved, property lost or damaged, number of people assisted, description of Coast Guard unit, distance from vessel, time spent searching, total amount of time on the sortie, sea height, wind speed, visibility, kind of assistance rendered and mission performance. Contact: Search and Rescue Data Section, Information Systems Staff, Office of Operations, Coast Guard, Department of Transportation, 2100 2nd St. S.W., Room 3222, Washington, DC 20593/202-426-1957.

Shipbuilding

For information on the market for and the cost of shipbuilding, contact: Office of Shipbuilding Costs, Maritime Administration, Department of Transportation, 400 7th St. S.W., Room 6422, Washington, DC 20590, 202-426-5793.

Standard Highway Signs

This publication provides detailed drawings of standard highway signs for the promotion of a national uniform highway sign design. It also includes general design guidelines for developing signs that conform with basic standards. Available for $11.00 from: Government Printing Office, Superintendent of Documents, Washington, DC 20402/202-783-3238.

The Car Book

The publication is a free comprehensive guide to car buying. It includes information on crash test results, fuel economy, maintenance, insur-ance costs, accident fatality rates, safety defects and recalls for foreign and domestic cars. The publication can be obtained by writing: Car Book, Pueblo, CO 81009. For further information on content, contact: Office of Public Affairs and Consumer Participation, National Highway Traffic Safety Administration, Department of Transportation, 400 7th St. S.W., Room 5232, Washington, DC 20590/202-426-9550.

Traffic Accident Information

An extensive computerized list of publications related to accidents and highway safety is maintained by: Accident Analysis Branch, Office of Highway Safety, Federal Highway Administration, Department of Transportation, 400 7th St. S.W., Room 3409, Washington, DC 20590/ 202-755-9035.

Traffic Characteristics

This office collects information on traffic, in-cluding speed volume, effect on traffic flow, width of lane, pavement, highway capacity and the psychological factors on drivers. Contact: Performance Branch, Traffic Engineering Division, Federal Highway Administration, Department of Transportation, 400 7th St. S.W., Room 3101, Washington, DC 20590/202-426-1993.

Traffic Information and Records

Information is available on the following: 1) National Project Reporting System—keeps records of their funded projects; description of the program, amount of money and congressional district; 2) Highway Safety Standards Program—keeps information on what the states are doing, such as periodic car inspections and pedestrian safety. Contact: Information and Records Systems Division, State Program Assistance, Traffic Safety Programs, National Highway Traffic Safety Administration, 400 7th St. S.W., Room 5119, Washington, DC 20590/202-426-4932.

Traffic Safety Publications

The following publications are free:

Pedestrian-Bicycle Safety Study
Marijuana, Other Drugs and Their Relation to Highway Safety

For a copy of these or for a complete list of available publications, contact: General Services Division, Office of Management Services Administration, National Highway Traffic Safety Administration, Department of Transportation, 400 7th St. S.W., Room 6117, Washington, DC 20590/202-426-0874.

Traffic Safety Records

All National Highway Traffic Safety Administration records are available for public examination. This includes research reports, accident investigation case reports, defects investigations, consumer letters, compliance reports listing investigations opened, closed and pending, and compliance test reports accepted, an index to consumer advisories, documentary filmed records of research and testing, consumer films, and a bibliography of Technical Reports of the National Highway Traffic Safety Administration. Subject categories include: tires, fuel tank systems, passive restraint systems, bumpers, pedestrians, fuel economy, youth and driving, emergency medical services, crashworthiness of motor vehicles, vision and visibility in highway driving, brakes, bicycle safety, accident risk forecasting, rollover accidents, and heavy duty vehicles. Contact: Technical Reference Division, Office of Management Services, National Highway Traffic Safety Administration, Department of Transportation, 400 7th St. S.W., Room 5108, Washington, DC 20590/202-426-2768.

Traffic Signs and Markings

Information and expertise is available on the design of traffic control device standards. A free 45-minute slide presentation describes symbol signs and traffic signal meanings. The following publications are available from the Government Printing Office, Superintendent of Documents, Washington, DC 20402/202-783-3238.

Manual on Uniform Traffic Control Devices ($30.00)
Standard Highway Signs Booklet ($11.00)
Road Symbol Signs ($2.25)
Work Zone Traffic Control ($7.00)

Contact: Signs and Markings Branch, Traffic Control System, Office of Traffic Operations, Federal Highway Administration, Department of Transportation, 400 7th St. S.W., Room 3419, Washington, DC 20590/202-426-0411.

Traffic Trends

The following publications are free:

Weekly Traffic Trends Press Release—monitors travel trends especially during periods of fuel shortfall;
Monthly Traffic Volume Trends—monitors travel trends over time.

Contact: Traffic Monitoring Branch, Highway Statistics Division, Office of Highway Planning, Federal Highway Administration, Department of Transportation, 400 7th St. S.W., Room 3300, Washington, DC 20590/202-426-0160.

Transit Pricing

Studies are conducted on ways to increase the number of transit riders so that the transit system is more productive. Contact: Pricing and Marketing Division, Office of Management Research and Transit Services, Planning, Management and Demonstrations, Urban Mass Transportation Administration, Department of Transportation, 400 7th St. S.W., Room 6100, Washington, DC 20590/202-426-4984.

Transit Research Information Center

This office acts as a clearinghouse for Urban Mass Transportation Administration research projects. Topics include: energy and environment; financing; conventional transit services, innovations and improvements; fares, pricing and service innovations; international transportation; paratransit systems; political processes and legal affairs; rural and low-density areas; safety and security; bus and paratransit vehicle technology; rapid rail vehicles; and light rail vehicles. Contact: Transit Research

Information Center, Planning Management and Demonstrations, Urban Mass Transportation Administration, Department of Transportation, 400 7th St. S.W., Room 6419, Washington, DC 20590/202-426-9157.

Transit Service Innovations

This office is responsible for such items as: innovative use of traffic engineering techniques and transit services; policies aimed at improving conventional fixed-route transit systems; more effective utilization of existing transportation and urban resources; and expediting peak period movement of passengers on surface transit vehicles. Contact: Office of Management Research and Transit Services, Urban Mass Transportation Administration, Department of Transportation, 400 7th St. S.W., Room 6100, Washington, DC 20590/202-426-4984.

Transportation and Energy

Technical information is available on energy issues and programs within the U.S. Department of Transportation. A free publication, *Transportation Energy Activities of the U.S. Department of Transportation,* describes available technical assistance, programs, projects, contacts, and conferences. Contact: Office of Technology Sharing, Office of the Secretary of Transportation, Department of Transportation, 400 7th St. S.W., Room 9402 (I.30), Washington, DC 20590/202-426-4208.

Transportation Economic Analysis

This office provides staff analysis of the eco-nomic and institutional aspects of major trans-portation policy issues as they relate to the public transportation sector, rural and urban passengers and freight. They conduct analysis to support policy development in the areas of 1)transportation energy conservation, 2) contingency planning for responses to energy emergencies, and 3) transportation requirements and capabilities for the movement of energy materials by all modes. They develop contingency plans and are responsible for strategic planning for the national transportation system. They also design, carry out, and coordinate studies and assessments of the effect of federal policies and program options upon the performance of intercity, urban and local transportation systems. Contact: Office of Economics, Office of Policy and International Affairs, Department of Transportation, 400 7th St. S.W., Room 10301F, Washington, DC 20590/202-426-1911.

Transportation Engineering Technical Information

The Transportation Laboratory has transportation specialists who develop research in areas such as: transportation engineering; highway materials; testing, research and development; highway safety systems; and pavement design. If you are seeking technical information about a particular topic, you can contact the laboratory's library. Its staff can answer inquiries and make referrals. The library will send you free listings of publications issued by specialists at the laboratory, as well as abstracts of on-going laboratory research. Contact: Transportation Laboratory, Department of Transportation, Office of Engineering Services, P.O. Box 19128/Sacramento, CA 95819, 916-739-2400 (General Information) or 916-739-2452 (Library and Technical Information).

Transportation Library
The Library maintains an extensive collection of literature on all aspects of transportation. In addition to reference services, the library offers a free biweekly compilation of current transportation literature. Contact: Library, Department of Transportation, 400 7th St. S.W., Room 2200, Washington, DC 20590/202-426-1792.

Transportation of Hazardous Materials
Two newsletters are available: 1)*Hazardous Material Regulations,* and 2) *Pipeline Safety Regulations.* Information is also available on packaging, labeling and marketing of hazardous and radioactive materials. Contact: Information Services Division, Office of Operations and Enforcement, Research and Special Programs Administration, Department of Transportation, 400 7th St. S.W., Room 8424, Washington, DC 20590/202-426-2301.

Transportation Safety Institute
This Institute fosters and promotes the development and improvement of transportation safety and security management technology and operating procedures. Some 52 courses are offered to government employees and those in industry and international governments in topics which include aviation safety, highway safety, marine safety, materials analysis, motor carrier safety, pipeline safety, railroad safety, transportation of hazardous materials, and transportation security. Contact: Transportation Safety Institute, Department of Transportation, 6500 S. MacArthur Blvd, MPB-60, Oklahoma City, OK 73125/405-686-2153.

Transportation Systems Center
This center performs research and analysis on all modes of transportation—air, highway, rail, marine, urban and pipeline. Contact: Transportation Systems Center, Research and Special Programs Administration, Department of Transportation, Kendall Sq., Cambridge, MA 02142/617-494-2000.

Transportation System Management
This office provides information on such transportation techniques and methods as exclusive lanes for high occupancy vehicles, parking policies and staggered work hours, and ridesharing. Contact: Transportation System Management Branch, Office of Highway Planning, Federal Highway Administration, Department of Transportation, 400 7th St. S.W., Room 3301, Washington, DC 20590/202-426-0210.

Transportation Test Center
This Center conducts comprehensive testing, evaluation and associated development of ground transportation systems. Such test operations include: determining system feasibility, the validity of designs, the expected operational cost and the environmental impact of new developments. The facilities are available for use by government agencies, private industry and international projects. Contact: Transportation Test Center, Federal Railroad Administration, Department of Transportation, P.O. Box 11130 Pueblo, CO 81001/303-545-5660.

Transportation USA
This quarterly publication covers all aspects of transportation, including information on U.S. Department of Transportation events, news, major actions, legislation, and recent publications. Available for $16.00 per year from: Government Printing Office, Superintendent of Documents, Washington, DC 20402/202-783-3238.

University Transit Research
A list of universities which receive federal money for research is available. Contact: Office of University Research, Research and Special Programs Administration, Department of Transportation, 400 7th St. S.W., Room 10223, Washington, DC 20590/202-426-0190.

Travelers' Airline Rights
Fly Rights describes important consumer information about air fares, reservations and tickets, delayed and canceled flights, overbooking, baggage, smoking and airline safety. This pamphlet (stock # 003-006-00106-5) is available for $2.75 from Superintendent of Documents, Government Printing Office, Washington, DC 20402/202-275-3287.

Urban Mass Transportation Evaluation
For information on evaluation studies of Urban Mass Transportation Administration programs assessing the effectiveness of urban transportation performance, contact: Office of Program Evaluation, Policy, Budget and Program Evaluation, Urban Mass Transportation Administration, Department of Transportation, 400 7th St. S, W., Room 9310, Washington, DC 20590/202-426-4059.

Urban Mass Transportation for the Handicapped
For information on research conducted on the transportation of the handicapped, contact: Special Projects, Office of Service and Methods Demonstration, Planning Management and Demonstrations, Urban Mass Transportation Adminis-

tration, Department of Transportation, 400 7th St. S.W., Room 6100, Washington, DC 20590/202-426-4984.

Urban Mass Transportation Information
The Information Services responds to information requests on the Urban Mass Transportation Administration and other mass transit research; collects statistical information on financial and operational aspects of research programs; maintains an index to and abstracts of all research reports; maintains the Urban Mass Transportation Information Service, which is a data base that includes all transportation research information for national access; and maintains the Transit Research Information Center, which is a repository of all Urban Mass Transportation Administration-sponsored reports. Contact: Information Services, Office of Technical Assistance, Planning Management and Demonstrations, Urban Mass Transportation Administration, Department of Transportation, 400 7th St. S.W., Room 6419, Washington, DC 20590/202-426-9157.

Urban Mass Transportation Planning
For information on the Planning Grant Program and special energy planning research studies, contact: Office of Planning Assistance, Planning Management and Demonstration, Urban Mass Transportation Administration, Department of Transportation, 400 7th St. S.W., Room 9315, Washington, DC 20590/202-426-2360.

U.S. High Speed Rail Feasibility Resource
The Federal Railroad Administration (FRA) has sponsored and jointly funded studies regarding super high speed rail systems. The studies focus on the demand and economic feasibility of such transportation systems in U.S. corridors. Contact: Federal Railroad Administration (FRA), RPF-1, Room 5411, 400 7th St. S.W., Washington, DC 20590/202-426-9660.

Vehicle Defects
Information is available on safety-related complaints, recall data, defects data, investigations, etc. A publication is also available—*Safety Related Recall Campaigns for Motor Vehicle Equipment Including Tires.* Quarterly issues $3.25, annual $3.75, from: Government Printing Office, Superintendent of Documents, Washington, DC 20402/202-783-3238. For further information on content, contact: Office of Defects Investigation, Enforcement, National Highway Traffic Safety Administration, Department of Transportation, 400 7th St. S.W., Room 5326, Washington, DC 20590/202-426-2843.

Vehicle Research and Test Center
This center combines the engineering test facility with safety research. Contact: Vehicle Research and Test Center, Research and Development, National Highway Traffic Safety Administration, Department of Transportation, P.O. Box 37, East Liberty, OH 43319/513-666-4521.

Vehicle Safety Compliance
This office provides the testing, inspection, and investigation necessary to assure compliance with federal motor vehicle safety standards by foreign and domestic vehicle and equipment manufacturers. Contact: Office of Vehicle Safety Compliance, Enforcement, National Highway Traffic Safety Administration, Department of Transportation, 400 7th St. S.W., Room 6113, Washington, DC 20590/202-426-2832.

Vessel Traffic
Through electronic surveillance and shore-based centers, attempts are made to reduce vessel congestion, incidents of collision, rammings and groundings. Contact: Vessel Traffic Services Branch, Waterways Management Division, Office of Marine Environment and Systems, Coast Guard, Department of Transportation, 2100 2nd St. S.W., Room 1606, Washington, DC 20593/202-426-1940.

War-Risk Insurance for Ships
The Maritime Administration offers standby war-risk insurance to ships when such coverage is not available from commercial insurance companies. The program covers material and life loss caused by war involving any of the five major powers or by a hostile nuclear detonation. The plan covers about 600 U.S. flagships and 150 flagships of convenience. Contact: Office of Marine Insurance, Maritime Administration, Department of Transportation, 400 7th St. S.W., NASIF Building, Washington, DC 20590/202-382-0369.

Waterway Safety
This office deals with navigation safety for vessels, navigation equipment, bridge-to-bridge radio telephone requirements, shipping safety fairways, and traffic separation schemes. It publishes *Navigation Rules—International—Inland* available for $6.00. It also writes the regulations and rules for waterway safety. Contact: Waterway Safety Branch, Waterways Management Division, Office of Marine Environment and Systems, Coast Guard, Dept. of Transportation, 2100 2nd St. S.W., Room 1606, Washington, DC 20593/202-426-4958.

How Can the Department of Transportation Help You?
To determine how the U.S. Department of Transportation can help you, contact: Public Information, Office of Public Affairs, Department of Transportation, 400 7th St. S.W., Room 10413, Washington, DC 20590/202-426-4321.

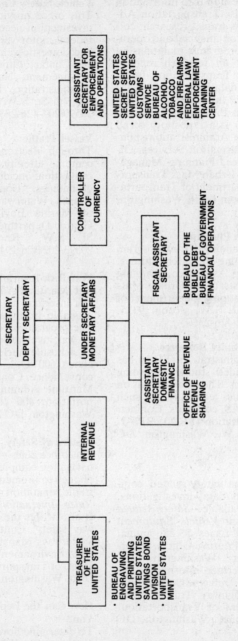

SECRETARY
DEPUTY SECRETARY

TREASURER OF THE UNITED STATES
- BUREAU OF ENGRAVING AND PRINTING
- UNITED STATES SAVINGS BOND DIVISION
- UNITED STATES MINT

INTERNAL REVENUE

UNDER SECRETARY MONETARY AFFAIRS

ASSISTANT SECRETARY DOMESTIC FINANCE
- OFFICE OF REVENUE REVENUE SHARING

FISCAL ASSISTANT SECRETARY
- BUREAU OF THE PUBLIC DEBT
- BUREAU OF GOVERNMENT FINANCIAL OPERATIONS

COMPTROLLER OF THE CURRENCY

ASSISTANT SECRETARY FOR ENFORCEMENT AND OPERATIONS
- UNITED STATES SECRET SERVICE
- UNITED STATES CUSTOMS SERVICE
- BUREAU OF ALCOHOL, TOBACCO AND FIREARMS
- FEDERAL LAW ENFORCEMENT TRAINING CENTER

Department of Treasury

15th St. and Pennsylvania Ave. N.W., Washington, DC 20220/202-566-2041

Established: September 2, 1789
Budget: $119,736,122,000
Employees: 144,165

Mission: Formulates and recommends economic, financial, tax, and fiscal policies; serves as financial agent for the U.S. government; law enforcement; and manufactures coins and currency.

Major Divisions and Offices

Under Secretary for Monetary Affairs

Department of the Treasury, 15th St. and Pennsylvania Ave. N.W., Room 3312, Washington, DC 20220/202-566-5164.
Budget: $4,573,909,000
Employees: 163

Assistant Secretary—Domestic Finance

Department of the Treasury, 15th St. and Pennsylvania Ave. N.W., Room 3321, Washington, DC 20220/202-566-2103.
Budget: $4,573,767,000
Employees: 153
Mission: Advises and assists the Secretary, Deputy Secretary and Under Secretary for Monetary Affairs on matters of federal finance, state and local finance, and financial institutions policy.

• *Office of Revenue Sharing*

Department of the Treasury, 2401 E St. N.W., 14 Floor, Washington, DC 20226/202-634-5157.
Budget: $4,573,567,000
Employees: 135
Mission: Returns specified amounts of federally collected funds to eligible units of general-purpose governments under the general revenue sharing program.

Fiscal Assistant Secretary

Department of the Treasury, 15th St. and Pennsyl-

vania Ave. N.W., Washington, DC 20220/202-566-2112.
Budget: $2,313,989,000
Employees: 5114

Bureau of the Public Debt

Department of the Treasury, 1435 G St. N.W., Room 310, Washington, DC 20226/202-376-0319.
Budget: $199,934,000
Employees: 2,585
Mission: Prepares U.S. Department of the Treasury circulars offering public debt securities; directs the handling of subscriptions and making of allotments; formulates instructions and regulations pertaining to security issues; and conducts or directs the conduct of transactions in outstanding securities.

Bureau of Government Financial Operations

Department of the Treasury, Pennsylvania Ave. and Madison Pl. N.W., Room 618, Washington, DC 20226/202-566-2158.
Budget: $2,114,003,000
Employees: 2,524
Mission: Maintains a system of central accounting and reporting, disclosing the monetary assets and liabilities of the U.S. Treasury and provides for the integration of Treasury cash and funding operations with the financial operations of disbursing

and collecting officers and of federal program agencies; provides disbursing services for most civilian agencies of the government; provides technical support for the system of tax payments by business organizations; supervises the government-wide letter-of-credit system for financing federal grant-in-aid programs; monitors all cash held outside the Treasury; handles claims from the public for the redemption of partially destroyed U.S. currency; and administers functions relating to the qualifications of surety companies.

Assistant Secretary for Enforcement and Operations

Department of Treasury, 15th St. and Pennsylvania Ave. N.W., Room 4308, Washington, DC 20220/202-566-2568.
Budget: $886,888,000
Employees: 22,992

United States Secret Service

Department of the Treasury, 1800 G St. N.W., Room 805, Washington, DC 20223/202-535-5708.
Budget $249,462,000
Employees: 4,001
Mission: Detects and arrests any person committing any offense against the laws of the United States and foreign governments: detects and arrests any person violating any of the provisions of sections 508, 509 and 871, 879 and 1752, of Title 18 of the United States Code; executes warrants issued under the authority of the United States; carries firearms; protects the person of the president of the United States, the members of his immediate family, the president-elect, the vice president or other officer next in the order of succession to the office of president, the Vice President-elect and the members of their immediate families; major Presidential and Vice Presidential candidates and, under certain conditions, their spouses; former presidents and their wives during his lifetime, widows of former presidents until their death or remarriage, and minor children of a former president until they reach age of 16, and visiting heads of a foreign state or foreign government; and performs such other functions and duties as are authorized by law.

United States Customs Service

Department of the Treasury, 1301 Constitution Ave. N.W., Washington, DC 20229/202-566-8195.
Budget: $643,317,000
Employees: 14,420
Mission: properly assesses and collects customs duties, excise taxes, fees, and penalties due on imported merchandise; interdicts and seizes contraband, including narcotics and illegal drugs; processes persons, carriers, cargo, and mail into and out of the United States; administers certain navigation laws; detects and apprehends persons engaged in fraudulent practices designed to circumvent customs and related laws, copyright, patent, and trademark provisions, quotas and marking requirements for imported merchandise.

Bureau of Alcohol, Tobacco and Firearms

Department of the Treasury, 1200 Pennsylvania Ave. N.W., Washington, DC 20226/202-566-7777
Budget: $147,492,000
Employees: 3,016
Mission: Enforces and administers firearms and explosive laws, as well as those covering the production, use, and distribution of alcohol and tobacco products.

Federal Law Enforcement Training Center

Department of the Treasury, Glynco, GA 31524/912-267-2100
Budget: $12,803,000
Employees: 344
Mission: Serves as an interagency training center serving 51 federal law enforcement agencies; conducts common, recruit, advanced, specialized, and refresher law enforcement training for the special agents and police officers from participating agencies, and provides the necessary facilities, equipment and support for the accomplishment of that training; conducts programs to teach common areas of law enforcement skills to police and investigative personnel; conducts advanced and specialized programs in areas of common need, such as courses in white collar crime, advanced law enforcement photography, procurement/contract fraud, marine law enforcement, and several instructor training courses; provides the facilities and support services for participating organizations to conduct advanced and specialized training for their own law enforcement personnel; and offers selective highly specialized training programs to State and local officers as an aid in deterring crime.

Treasurer of the United States

Department of the Treasury, 15th St. and Pennsylvnia Ave. N.W., Room 4328, Washington, DC 20220/202-566-2843.
Budget: $257,843,000
Employees: 114,851

• *Bureau of Engraving and Printing*

Department of the Treasury, 14th and C Sts. S.W., Room 602-11A, Washington, DC 20228/202-447-0917
Budget: $200,000,000
Employees: 2,317
Mission: Designs, engraves and prints all major items of financial character issued by the U.S. Government; and produces paper currency, Treasury bonds, bills, notes, and certificates; postage, revenue and certain customs stamps.

• United States Mint

Department of the Treasury, 501-13th St. N.W., Washington, DC 20220/202-376-0837.
Budget: $57,758,000
Employees: 2,008
Mission: Produces domestic and foreign coins; manufactures and sells proof and uncirculated coin sets and other numismatic items; provides for the custody, processing and movement of bullion.

• Savings Bond Division

Department of the Treasury, 1111 Twentieth St. N.W., Washington, DC 20226/202-634-5350.
Budget: $17,850,000
Employees: 276
Mission: Promotes the sale and retention of U.S. savings bonds; and installs and maintains the payroll savings plan through which nearly 60 percent of total sales are derived.

Internal Revenue Service

Department of the Treasury, 1111 Constitution Ave. N.W., Washington, DC 20224/202-566-5000.
Budget: $6,422,312,000
Employees: 82,879

Mission: Administers and enforces the internal revenue laws and related statutes, except those relating to alcohol, tobacco, firearms, and explosives; encourages and achieves the highest possible degree of voluntary compliance with the tax laws and regulations and to conduct itself so as to warrant the highest degree of public confidence in the integrity and efficiency of the Service; advises the public of its rights and responsibilities, communicates requirements of the law to the public; assists taxpayers in complying with the laws and regulations; and takes those enforcement actions necessary for fair, effective and impartial tax administration.

Office of the Comptroller of the Currency

Department of the Treasury, 490 L'Enfant Plaza E S. W., Washington, DC 20219/202-447-1800.
Budget: $180,000,000
Employees: 2,925
Mission: Responsible for the execution of laws relating to national banks, and promulgates rules and regulations governing the operations of approximately 4,450 national and District of Columbia banks.

Data Experts

Customs Commodity Experts

These important specialists can provide information on tariffs, classifications, and other related topics concerning the commodities they cover. Each can be contacted directly by telephone or by writing in care of the Customs Service, Department of the Treasury, 6 World Trade Center, Room 425, New York, NY 10048/212-466-5821.

Autos, Motorcycles/ E. Lainoff/ 212-466-5667
Valves, Measuring Instruments/K. Riedl/212-466-5493
Heavy Industrial Machinery/A. Horowitz/212-466-5494
Tools, Navigational & Drafting Instruments/R. Losche/ 212-466-5670
Furnaces, Refrigeration/M. Rocks/212-466-5669
Agricultural Implements/W. O'Connell/212-466-5668
Chains, Engines/H. Persky/212-466-5485
T.V., Radios, Tape Players/M. DiCerbo/212-466-5672
Electronic Components/I. Josephs/212-466-5673
Office Machinery, Textile Machinery, Data Processing Equipment/A. Brodbeck/212-466-5490
X-Ray, Transormers, Aircraft, Boats/E. Francke/212-466-5684
Electrical Articles/J. Miller/212-466-5680
Small Appliances, Weighing Machinery/S. DellaVentura/212-466-5678
Cameras, Optical Equipment/C. O'Carroll/212-466-5685
Hand Tools/M. Schulberg/212-466-5487
Metals, Ores, Bearings, Metal Foil/M. Laker/212-466-5491

Steel/P. Ilardi/212-466-5478
Wire, Fasteners/J. Fitzgerald/212-466-5492
Explosives, Cutlery, Medical Instruments/J. Preston/212-466-5488
Metal Household Articles, General Articles of Metal/A. Tytleman/212-466-5480
Plastic & Rubber Articles/D. Masiello/212-466-5794
Musical Instruments/A. Manzella/212-466-5476
Sporting Goods, Bicycles/Y. Tomenga/212-466-5540
Games, Toys/T. McKenna/212-466-5538
Models, Dolls/D. Rainer/212-466-5475
Glass, Stone, Abrasives/A. Arzulowicz/212-466-5794
Ceramics, Chinaware, Earthenware/G. Kalkines/212-466-5794
Fruits & Vegetables/W. Mitchell/212-466-5760
Meat Products, Fish, Dairy Products/T. Brady/ 212-466-5790
Wood Products/R. Conte/212-466-5779
Tobacco Products, Plants, Grain, Coffee, Tea, Spices, Nuts/L. Mushinski/ 212-466-5759
Beer, Distilled Spirits, Juices, Oils, Sugar, Cocoa/W. Springer/212-466-5730
Furniture, Works of Art/L. Mushinski/212-466-5739
Paper, Paper Products/C. Abramowitz-212-466-5733
Chemical Elements, Inorganic & Organic Compounds/J. DiMaria-212-466-5769
Glue, Dyeing & Tanning Products, Pigments, Waxes, Gelatin, Brushes/G. Brownschweig/212-466-5744
Petroleum, Aromatic Substances, Flavoring Extracts, Fertilizers/C. Scavo/212-466-5742
Drugs and Medical Supplies/C. Reilly/212-466-5770

Benzenoid Compounds and Mixtures/W. Winters/212-466-5747

Synthetic Resins & Rubber, Surface-Active Agents, Fatty Substances/R. Valdes/212-466-5768

Luggage, Handbags, Flatgoods, Bags, Cases/K. Gorman/212-466-5893

Artificial Flowers, Christmas Decorations/S. Hantman/212-466-5887

Clasps, Buckles, Zippers, Tires, Tubes/T. Rauch/212-466-5892

Clocks, Watches, Jewelry/L. Piropato/212-466-5895

Miscellaneous Textile Articles (except wearing apparel)/A. Falcone/212-466-5886

Athletic & Casual Footwear/J. Sheridan/212-466-5889

All Other Footwear/W. Raftery/212-466-5890

Tapestries, Wall Hangings, Floor Coverings/G. Shea/212-466-5854

Bedding, Furnishings, Related Articles/R. Eyskens/212-466-5854

Non-Woven Fabrics, Coated or Filled Fabrics, Industrial Fabrics/G. Barth/212-466-5884

Fibers, Yarns, Netting/K. Springer/212-466-5885

Woven Fabrics/A. Masterson/212-466-5896

Animals, Animal Products/J. Faraci/212-466-5881

Apparel Accessories, Intimate Apparel/H. Davis/212-466-5880

Woven Wearing Apparel-Men's and Boys'/V. DeMaio/212-466-5878

Knit Wearing Apparel-Men's and Boys'/M. Ryan/212-466-5871

Knit and Woven Outerwear/S. Berczuk/212-466-5851

Wearing Apparel-Girls' and Infants'/B. Kiefer/212-466-5865

Knit Wearing Apparel-Women's/M. Crowley/212-466-5852

Woven Wearing Apparel-Women's/E. Crowley/212-466-5866

Major Sources of Information

Actuaries, Joint Board for the Enrollment of
This board is responsible for the enrollment of individuals who wish to perform actuarial services under the Act and for the supervision and revocation of the enrollment of such individuals after notice and opportunity for hearings. Contact: Joint Board for the Enrollment of Actuaries, Department of the Treasury, 1325 G St. N.W., Washington, DC 20220/202-535-6787.

Advance Financing
Information and expertise is available to agencies on advance financing of federal grant-in-aid programs under the letter-of-credit procedure whereby recipients draw funds from the U.S. Treasury only as needed for program disbursement. Contact: Bureau of Government Financial Operations, Department of the Treasury, TFCS Program Branch, Room 704-Premier Bldg, Washington, DC 20226/202-634-5770.

Alcohol Fuels Information Director—Gasohol Packet
This free publication provides a brief bibliography as well as lists of alcohol equipment manufacturers, enzyme and yeast suppliers, engineering firms and organizations that can provide the potential alcohol producer with assistance. Contact: Publication Distribution Center, Bureau of Alcohol, Tobacco and Firearms, Department of the Treasury, 3800 S. Four Mile Run Drive, Arlington, VA 22206/703-557-7850.

Alcohol Regulation
For information on the regulation of the production and formulation of distilled spirits, wines, and malt beverages, their distinctive liquor bottles,

case markings and advertising contact: Product Compliance Branch, Office of Compliance Operations, Bureau of Alcohol, Tobacco and Firearms, Department of the Treasury, 1200 Pennsylvania Ave. N.W., Washington, DC 20226/202-566-7595.

Alcohol, Tobacco and Firearms Information
For information concerning any activity in the Bureau of Alcohol, Tobacco and Firearms, contact: Communication Center, Office of Administration, Bureau of Alcohol, Tobacco and Firearms, Department of the Treasury, 1200 Pennsylvania Ave. N.W., Room 1202, Washington, DC 20226/202-566-7777.

Alcohol, Tobacco and Firearms Bulletin
The quarterly publication informs all permit holders and licensees on current alcohol, tobacco, firearms and explosive matter. It contains regulatory, procedural and administrative information as well as items of general interest. Available for $15.00 a year, contact: Government Printing Office, Superintendent of Documents, Washington, DC 20402/202-783-3238.

Alcohol, Tobacco and Firearms Laboratory Services
Information is available on the analysis of tobacco products to distinguish between cigarettes and cigars for taxing purposes; the analysis of alcoholic beverages to distinguish between wines, spirits, medicinal purposes and industrial alcohol for different taxes; and the examination of inks for date verification. Contact: BATF, Laboratory Services, National Laboratory Center, 1401 Research Blvd., Rockville, MD 20850/301-443-1062.

Alcohol, Tobacco and Firearms Regulations
A *Semiannual Agenda* is published that identifies significant and nonsignificant regulations under development and review. Its purpose is to give the public adequate notice of regulatory activities. For information on regulations regarding: Bonded Wineries, Breweries and Federal Alcohol Administration Act contact: FAA Wine and Beer Branch, Office of Compliance Operation, Bureau of Alcohol, Tobacco, and Firearms, Department of the Treasury, 1200 Pennsylvania Ave. NW, Washington, DC 20226/202-566-7626. Distilled Spirits, Plants, Tobacco, Import-Export Regulations and Industrial Alcohol Regulations contact: Distilled Spirit and Tobacco Branch, Office of Compliance Operation, Bureau of Alcohol, Tobacco, and Firearms, Department of the Treasury, 1200 Pennsylvania Ave, NW, Washington, DC 20226/202-566-7351. Firearms and Explosives Regulations contact: Firearms and Explosives Branch, Office of Compliance Operation, Bureau of Alcohol, Tobacco, and Firearms, Department of the Treasury, 1200 Pennsylvania Ave, NW, Washington, DC 20226/202-566-7591.

Alcohol, Tobacco and Firearm Summary Statistics
Data are available on the domestic manufacturing and importation of all types of alcohol, tobacco and firearms. The data are broken down monthly by state and include statistics on establishments qualified to manufacture these items and the number of permits issued. Contact: Information and Management Services Section, Program Planning and Analysis Staff, Office of Administration, Bureau of Alcohol, Tobacco and Firearms, Department of the Treasury, 1200 Pennsylvania Ave. N.W., Room 6202, Washington, DC 20226/202-566-7070.

Alcohol, Tobacco, Firearms Trade Laws
The Bureau of Alcohol, Tobacco, and Firearms provides news releases and information about federal laws and ordinances that affect trade in and licensing of alcohol, tobacco, firearms, and explosives. The Bureau also distributes pamphlets and factsheets about its history, responsibilities, and the production of alcohol fuel and gasohol. Contact: Bureau of Alcohol, Tobacco, and Firearms, Department of the Treasury, 1200 Pennsylvania Ave, NW, Washington, DC 20226/202-566-7268.

Automated Clearing House (ACH) Programs
The Automated Clearing House (ACH) branch mission is to manage, develop, and promote the Direct Deposit/Electronic Funds Transfer Program (DD/EFT). DD/EFT is a payments mechanism by which payments are deposited automatically into recipients' savings or checking accounts. DD/EFT has a role as part of an efficient national payment system, is a major component of effective government cash management, and is to be fully used for appropriate government payments. Contact: Bureau of Government Financial Operations, Department of the Treasury, ACH Programs Branch, Treasury Annex #1, Room 26, Washington, DC 20226/202-535-6337.

Automated Commercial System ACS
This system improves merchandise processing by automatically handling routine entries to it by import specialists. Contact: Duty Assessment Division, Customs Service, Department of the Treasury, 1301 Constitution Ave. N.W., Room 1218, Washington, DC 20209/202-566-2471.

Bank Examiners, District Offices of National
The 6 district offices regulate and examine national banks for their areas. Contact:

Northeastern District, 1211 Ave. of the Americas, Suite 4250, New York, NY 10036/212-944-3495.
Southeastern District, Suite 2700, Peachtree Cain Tower, 229 Peachtree St. N.E., Atlanta, GA 30303/404-221-4926.
Central District, Sears Tower, 233 S. Wacker Dr., Suite 5750, Chicago, IL 60606/312-353-0300. Illinois, Michigan.
Midwestern District, 911 Main St., Suite 2616, Kansas City, MO 64105/816-374-6431. Iowa, Kansas, Missouri, Nebraska.
Southwestern District, 1201 Elm St., Suite 3800, Dallas, TX 75270/214-767-4400.
Western District, 53 Fremont St., Suite 3900, San Francisco, CA 94105/415-545-9400.

The Bureau of Engraving and Printing Tours
The Bureau of Engraving and Printing located at 14th and C St, S.W. has a continuous self-guided tour facility providing the public a view of the operations in the manufacture of U.S. currency. Tour hours are 9:00 a.m. to 2:00 p.m., Monday through Friday except legal holidays. Because of the large number of visitors that come during the peak tourist season from April to September, we are unable to accommodate all visitors during the open hours and must frequently stop the line before 2:00 p.m. Sightseeing buses may discharge passengers at the 14th Street entrance and reload at the 15th Street exit point. The facility is included on the Tourmobile "Washington Mall" Tour. For further information please contact: Public Affairs Office, Bureau of Engraving and Printing, 14th and C Streets, S.W., Washington, DC 22028/202-447-0193

Capital Markets Legislation
This office is concerned with the development and administration of policy and legislation affecting banks and other financial institutions. Its recent reports include *Interagency Task Force Study on Thrift Institutions*. Contact: Capital Markets Policy, Domestic Finance, 15th St. and Pennsylvania

Ave. N.W., Room 3025, Washington, DC 20220/202-566-5337.

Cargo Processing
Research is conducted on the best methods of processing merchandise through Customs. This office also provides a free pamphlet, *Importing A Car,* which explains import requirements for clearing your car or vehicles through U.S. Customs. Contact: Division of Cargo Enforcement and Facilitation, Office of Inspection and Control, Customs Service, Department of the Treasury, 1301 Constitution Ave. N.W., Room 4416, Washington, DC 20229/202-566-5354.

Check Claims
Claims against the United States or U.S. Department of the Treasury for checks that are lost in the mails, or which bear forged endorsements are made at: Check Claims Group, Headquarters Operation, Bureau of Government Financial Operations, Department of the Treasury, 401 14th St. N.W., Room 520, Washington, DC 20227/202-447-1080.

Coin Sets
The following coin sets are sold by the U.S. Mint: 1) Regular Proof Coin Sets—proof claims bear the "S" mint mark and are produced only at the San Francisco area office; proof coins have higher relief than regular issue circulating coins; 2) Regular Uncirculated Coin Sets—these coins represent the best coins which can be made with the same coining techniques used for circulating coinage production; each set contains one of each denomination from the Denver and Philadelphia mints. Only coin sets manufactured and issued during the current year will be available from the U.S. Mint. Contact: Consumer Affairs Staff, Marketing Division, U.S. Mint, Department of the Treasury, 501 13th St. N.W., Room 1021, Washington, DC 20220/202-376-0542.

Combined Annual Wage Reporting
This system has been developed to reduce the reporting burden for employers. Contact local field office for detailed information (see "Local Tax Offices" in this section), or: Returns, Processing and Accounting Division, Internal Revenue Service, Department of the Treasury, 1111 Constitution Ave. N.W., Room 7009, Washington, DC 20224/202-566-6881.

Consumer Bank Examination
This office conducts consumer examiner training schools for outside groups and representatives from trade associations, consumer groups and other federal and state regulatory agencies. They teach examiners what to look for when they examine the bank's activities. They also assist consumer groups in developing their own compli-

ance programs. Contact: Consumer Examinations, Bank Supervision, Comptroller of the Currency, Department of the Treasury, 490 L'Enfant Plaza E.S.W., 5th Floor, Washington, DC 20219/202-447-1600.

Consumer Complaints Against National Bank
Consumer complaints against national banks are handled by district offices and the head office. A free pamphlet, *Do You Have a Complaint Against A National Bank?,* is designed to help consumers notify the Office of Consumer Complaints about any problems they have with national banks. The pamphlet begins with an explanation of how to resolve a complaint and includes a summary of some consumer credit protection and civil rights laws. Contact: Consumer Complaint Information System, Consumer Examinations Division, Comptroller of the Currency, Department of the Treasury, 490 L'Enfant Plaza E.S.W., Washington, DC 20219/202-447-1600.

Consumer Guide
This free guide provides information on a number of Treasury programs: labeling alcoholic beverages, IRS taxpayer assistance, alcohol fuels, drinking and pregnancy, and Customs for travelers. Contact: Treasury Consumer Affairs Guide, Office of Consumer Affairs, Department of the Treasury, 15th St. and Pennsylvania Ave. N.W., Room 1320, Washington, DC 20220/202-566-9623.

Copyrights and Trademarks
This office records copyrights and trademarks for import protection and makes rulings to assure that trademark and copyright items are not too closely copied by imported goods entering the country. A free pamphlet, *Trademark Information for Travelers,* is also available. Contact: Entry Licensing and Restricted Merchandise, Entry Procedures and Penalties Division, Office of Regulation and Rulings, Customs Service, Department of the Treasury, 1301 Constitution Ave. N.W., Room 2417, Washington, DC 20229/202-566-5765.

Corporate Tax Statistics
For information on corporation taxes by industry and size, contact: Corporation Statistics, Internal Revenue Service, Department of the Treasury, 1111 Constitution Ave., N.W., Washington, DC 20224/202-376-0102.

Counterfeit and Forgery Statistics
The free *Annual Statistical Summary* provides counterfeit and forgery statistics and trends. Contact: Public Affairs, Secret Service, Department of the Treasury, 1800 G St. N.W., Room 805, Washington, DC 20223/202-535-5708.

Currency Imports/Exports
There is no limitation in terms of total amount of monetary instruments which may be brought into

or taken out of the United States. However, if you transport or cause to be transported more than $5,000 in the form of a monetary instrument (A monetary instrument would include currency of any nation, endorsed checks, blank travellers checks, stock certificates and bonds in bearer form, etc.) on any occasion into or out of the United States, or if you receive more than that amount you must file a customs report. Contact: Financial Investigation Division, Office of Investigations, U S Custom Service, Department of the Treasury, 1301 Constitution Ave. N.W., Room 5146, Washington, DC 20229/202-566-8005.

Currency Redemption

Mutilated currency may be forwarded to the Office of Currency Standards for examination by trained experts to determine whether it will be exchanged at face value. Final decisions for redemption of such currency rest with the Treasurer of the United States. No relief will be granted on account of lawfully held paper currency of the United States which has been totally destroyed. Mutilated currency should be sent for redemption to the Department of the Treasury, Bureau of Engraving and Printing, OCS, Room 344, BEP A, P.O. Box 37048, Washington, DC 20013. For further information and assistance contact: Public Affairs Office, Bureau of Engraving and Printing, 14th & C St., S.W., Washington, DC 20228/202-447-0193.

Customer and Industry Affairs

This office acts as liaison to bank customer groups, as well as insurance, real estate, securities, small business and other nonbank financial industries. It also provides technical assistance to banks, neighborhood groups, and local governments to develop, implement or expand community or economic development activities. The office encourages bankers and community groups to work together through nonregulatory means. Contact: Customer and Industry Affairs Division, Comptroller of the Currency, 490 L'Enfant Plaza, S.W., Washington, D. C. 20219/202-287-4169.

Customs Audit

The Regulatory Audit Division provides the U.S. Customs Service with an external audit capability to verify transactions and claims of importers, carriers and exporters. Contact: Regulatory Audit Division, Customs Service, Department of the Treasury, 1301 Constitution Ave. N.W., Room 2114, Washington, DC 20229/202-566-2812.

Customs Bonded Warehouse

Customs Bonded Warehouses are buildings or other secured areas (duty-free stores) in which dutiable goods may be stored, manipulated, or may undergo manufacturing operations without payment of duty. Contact: Drawbacks and Bonds Branch, Carrier Drawbacks and Bonds Division,

Office of Regulations and Rulings, Customs Service, Department of the Treasury, 1301 Constitution Ave. N.W., Room 2414, Washington, DC 20229/202-566-5856.

Customs Bulletin

This weekly publication contains current amendments to Customs Regulations and decisions of U.S. Customs Court and the U.S. Court of Customs and Patent Appeals. Available for $89.00 a year, from: Government Printing Office, Superintendent of Documents, Washington, DC 20402/202-783-3238. For more detailed information on the availability of published rulings and decisions in all areas of customs laws, especially tariff classification and value rulings, contact: Legal Retrieval Branch, Office of Regulations and Rulings, Customs Service, Department of the Treasury, 1301 Constitution Ave. N.W., Room 2406, Washington, DC 20229/202-566-5095.

Customs Investigation

U.S. Customs maintains a force of special agents at 66 domestic and 8 foreign offices. They investigate violations of customs and related laws and regulations—fraud, currency reporting violations, cargo theft, neutrality violations, narcotics and bird smuggling. Contact: Office of Investigations, Customs Service, Department of the Treasury, 1301 Constitution Ave. N.W., Room 3124, Washington, DC 20229/202-566-5401.

Customs Laboratory Program

The Technical Services Division manages the Customs Laboratory Program. There are six field laboratories located in New York, Savannah, New Orleans, Los Angeles. San Francisco, and Chicago which analyze a wide range of commodities that are or might be subject to duty such as sugar, oil, textiles, tobacco, alcoholic beverages, and drugs; examine imports of video games and computers for possible copyright infringement; and participate in commercial enforcement operations involving commodities such as steel and textiles. There is also a research laboratory located in Washington, DC. Technical Services maintains the National Commodity Sampling Information System (NCSIS) which provides import data and classification change rates for imported merchandise. Contact: Director, Technical Services Division, U.S. Customs Service, 1301 Constitution Ave., N.W., 7113, Washington, DC 20229/202-566-5853.

Customs Regulations

The Legal Precedent Retrieval System is a comprehensive index to ORR rulings and decisions. Microfiche copies of documents are available for sale. Contact: Legal Retrieval and Dissemination Branch, Office of Regulations and Rulings, Customs Service, Department of the Treasury, 1301

Constitution Ave. N.W., Room 2404, Washington, DC 20229/202-566-5095.

Customs Rulings
An exporter, importer, or any other person who has a direct interest may request an administrative ruling on the application of a Customs law to their specific situation. Contact: Regional Commissoner of Customs, New York Region, 6 World Trade Center, New York, New York 10048/212-466-5821.

Customs Statistics
Statistics are available on merchandise entries, carriers, cargo, passengers, foreign trade, enforcement, seizures of narcotics and dangerous drugs, seizures of violators of the law, and much more from: Program Information and Analysis Branch, Management Analysis and Systems Division, Office of the Controller, Customs Service, Department of the Treasury, 1301 Constitution Ave. N.W., Room 6420, Washington, DC 20229/202-566-5817.

Customs Today
This free quarterly magazine is the official magazine of the U.S. Customs Service. It contains features and information on such items as statistics on merchandise entries, sources of customs operating funds, customs collections by region and district, and by category, and seizures for violations of laws enforced by Customs. Contact: Customs Today, Public Information Division, Customs Service, Department of the Treasury, 1301 Constitution Ave. N.W., Room 6311, Washington, DC 20229/202-566-3962.

Daily Treasury Statement
This publication provides information on the cash and debt operations of the U.S. Treasury, operating cash balance, deposits and withdrawals of operating cash, public debt transactions, federal tax deposit system activities, tax and loan note accounts by depository category, and income tax refunds issued. Available for $125.00 per year from Government Printing Office, Superintendent of Documents, Washington, DC 20402/202-783-3238.

Debt Management
This office deals with federal debts including public debt securities, nonmarketable public issues, federal agency securities, and government-sponsored agency securities. Contact: Federal Finance, Domestic Finance, Department of the Treasury, 15th St. and Pennsylvania Ave. N.W., Room 3315, Washington, DC 20220/202-566-5806.

Detector Dogs
Detector dogs and handlers are assigned to major international sea, air and border ports. These units are flexible and can be detailed to other areas as special needs arise. They screen mail, cargo, baggage, ships, aircraft and vehicles. Customs uses a wide variety of dogs, many of which are recruited from animal shelters. Customs also accepts dogs from individual owners who offer their dogs as a donation or for sale. Dogs may be available to the public when they retire (at age 9), if their handlers do not wish to keep them. Contact: U.S. Customs Service, Canine Training Center, HCR Box 7, Department of the Treasury, Front Royal, VA 22630/703-635-7104.

Developing Nations
This office is involved with the situation in non-OPEC developing countries, including discussions and negotiations between developed and nondeveloped countries, and the operation of multilateral development banks, World Bank, Inter-American Development Bank, Asian Development Bank and the African Development Bank. Contact: Developing Nations, International Affairs, Monetary Affairs, Department of the Treasury, 15th St. and Pennsylvania Ave. N.W., Room 3222, Washington, DC 20220/202-566-8243.

Drawbacks
Drawbacks refer to a partial or entire refund that may be obtained from tax or duty payments on a commodity used in a special way, e.g., imported material used in the manufacture of exported articles. The purpose of drawbacks is to enable a manufacturer to compete in foreign markets. Contact: Drawbacks and Bond Branch, Carrier Drawbacks and Bonds Division, Office of Regulations and Rulings, Customs Service, Department of the Treasury, 1301 Constitution Ave., N.W., Room 2414, Washington, DC 20229/202-566-5856.

Duty Assessment Division
All merchandise imported into the United States is subject to Customs duties. This office determines the dutiable value of each shipment and the applicable rate of duty. Contact: Entry Operations and Trade Control Branch, Office of Commercial Operations, U.S. Customs Service, Department of the Treasury, 1301 Constitution Ave., Room 4117, Washington, D.C. 20229/202-566-5307.

Economic Analysis
Briefings on current economic performance and economic outlook are provided to private groups and organizations. Contact: Office of Financial Analysis, Domestic Economics Policy, Economic Policy, Department of the Treasury, 15th St. and Pennsylvania Ave. N.W., Room 4415, Washington, DC 20220/202-566-5914.

Energy-Related Tax Credits
Tax credits are given to those who purchase energy saving equipment. For detailed information refer

to IRS Publications Investment Credit (#572) or Energy Credits for Individuals (#903) or contact your local Internal Revenue Service Office (see "Local Tax Offices" in this section).

Engraved and Lithographed Printings
Black ink engravings suitable for framing are produced from intaglio plates in a manner similar to currency and postage stamp production. These include: small presidential portraits (6" × 8"); Chief Justice portraits (6" × 8"); large presidential portraits (9" × 12"); vignettes of historic and government buildings (6" × 8"); and government seals (5-⅜" diameter). Special Bureau of Engraving and Printing souvenir cards commemorating participation at numismatic and philatelic exhibits are also available. All of these products are available both at the Bureau of Engraving and Printing's Visitors' Center and through the mail. For information and a complete price list, contact: Public Affairs Office, Bureau of Engraving and Printing, 14th and C St., S.W., Washington, DC 20228/202-447-1391.

ERISA
For information on the tax aspects of the Employee Retirement Income Security Act (ERISA), including determination and notification letter requests and interpretation of appropriate laws and procedures, contact: Employee Plans Division, Employee Plans and Exempt Organizations, Internal Revenue Service, 1111 Constitution Ave. N.W., Room 6526, Washington, DC 20224/202-566-6740.

Estate and Gift Tax
For information on rulings, laws, etc., on estate and gift tax, contact: Estate and Gift Tax Branch, Individual Tax Division, Internal Revenue Service, 1111 Constitution Ave. N.W., Room 5201, Washington, DC 20224/202-566-3549.

Estimates of Income Unreported on Individual Income Tax Returns
This publication presents estimates of total income individuals should have reported to the Internal Revenue Service but did not and the associated tax revenue loss. The estimates include underreporting on individual returns filed and on returns that should have been filed covering legal and selected types of illegal income. Available for $6.50 from: Government Printing Office, Superintendent of Documents, Washington, DC 20402/202-783-3238.

Explosives Data
The *Annual Explosives Incident Report* provides detailed data analysis on explosives incidents, including thefts, discoveries, and explosions. Contact: Explosives Enforcement Branch, Office of Law Enforcement, Bureau of Alcohol, Tobacco and Firearms, Department of the Treasury, 1200 Pennsylvania Ave. N.W., Room 2207, Washington, DC 20226/202-566-7395.

Explosives Hotline
This hotline provides direct contact between citizens and the Bureau of Alcohol, Tobacco, and Firearms field offices for stolen or recovered explosives. Four national response teams can be rushed to the scene of major arson or bombing cases anywhere in the United States within 24 hours. Contact: Explosives Enforcement Branch, Office of Law Enforcement, Bureau of Alcohol, Tobacco and Firearms, Department of the Treasury, 1200 Pennsylvania Ave. N.W., Room 3234, Washington, DC 20226/800-424-9555 (202-566-7143—call collect from Guam, Alaska, Hawaii, Puerto Rico and Virgin Islands).

Explosives Research
Research is conducted in such areas as explosive detection and post detonation identification. Contact: Explosives Technical Branch, Office of Law Enforcement, Bureau of Alcohol, Tobacco and Firearms, Department of the Treasury, 1200 Pennsylvania Ave. N.W., Washington, DC 20226/202-566-4124.

Federal Law Enforcement Training Center
This interagency facility provides basic police and criminal investigator training for officers and agents of 50 participating Federal organizations, as well as advanced training that is common to two or more organizations. In addition, FLETC provides administrative and logistical support to the participating organizations so that they may conduct their own advanced training at Glynco. The basic programs include subject matter in the following areas: law, criminalistic skills, investigative techniques, behavioral science and communications skills, driver training, firearms, and physical training. Their advanced programs address areas such as Marine Law Enforcement, Advanced Law Enforcement Photography, several instructor training programs, and various computer programs including Computer Fraud and Data Processing Investigations. Participating organizations have the opportunity to design and conduct advanced programs to meet their particular training requirements. The Center's resources, support services, and staff expertise are available to assist these organizations in developing and conducting a variety of agency specific training programs. Advanced programs are also available for the personnel from State and local law enforcement agencies through the Center's State and Local Law Enforcement Training Program. Examples of programs include Fraud and Financial Investigations, Cargo Theft, Advanced Arson for Profit, and Undercover Investigative Techniques. Also included are seminars on juvenile justice law enforcement matters and a program on Child Abuse

and Exploitation Investigation Techniques. Participating agencies include the Departments of Agriculture, Health and Human Services, Interior, Justice, State, and Treasury; Congress; the Supreme Court; and various independent agencies. The Center is located on the southeastern coast of Georgia near Brunswick. Contact: Federal Law Enforcement Training Center, Department of the Treasury, Glynco, GA 31524/912-267-2100.

Federal Regulations of Firearms and Ammunition
The four clearly written manuals cover all aspects of firearm and ammunition regulations. They are free from: Publications Distributions Center, Bureau of Alcohol, Tobacco and Firearms, Department of the Treasury, 3800 S. Four Mile Run Drive, Arlington, VA 22206/703-557-7850.

Firearms Enforcement
This office works with state and local agencies in curtailing the flow of firearms to criminal elements. Contact: Firearms Enforcement, Office of Criminal Enforcement, Bureau of Alcohol, Tobacco and Firearms, Department of the Treasury, 1200 Pennsylvania Ave. N.W., Room 3205, Washington, DC 20226/202-566-7457.

Firearm Imports
Information is available on permits required for importing firearms, aummunition and other implements of war. Free publications include: *Federal Laws and Regulations on Firearms and Ammunition* and *Importation of Arms, Ammunition and Implements of War.* Contact: Import Branch, Compliance Operation Division, Office of Regulatory Enforcement, Bureau of Alcohol, Tobacco and Firearms, Department of the Treasury, 1200 Pennsylvania Ave. N.W., Room 7241, Washington, DC 20226/202-566-7151.

Foreign Acquisition of Banks
A series of studies were conducted in 1981 on the effects of foreign acquisition of U.S. banks, the advantages and difficulties of how they operate in the United States and what changes have been made in their banking policies. Contact: Communications Division, Comptroller of the Currency, Department of the Treasury, 490 L'Enfant Plaza E. S.W., Washington, DC 20219/202-447-1768.

Foreign Currency
This office develops guidelines for the funding of cooperative production arrangements for the purchase and sale of technology and equipment between agencies of the U.S. government and foreign nations. Contact: Cash Management Operation Staff, Banking and Cash Management, Bureau of Government Financial Operations, Department of the Treasury, Pennsylvania Ave. and Madison Place, N.W., Room 204, Washington, DC 20226/202-566-8577.

Foreign Exchange
The Department of the Treasury monitors the foreign exchange market. Contact: Foreign Exchange and Gold Operations, Department of the Treasury, 15th St. and Pennsylvania Ave. N.W., Room 5037, Washington, DC 20220/202-566-2773.

Foreign Mail Shipments
For information on merchandise mailed from abroad to the United States, contact: Duty Assessment Division, Customs Service, Commercial Operations, Department of the Treasury, 1301 Constitution Ave. N.W., Room 4114, Washington, DC 20229/202-566-8121.

Foreign Portfolio Investment
This office collects and analyzes data related to international portfolio investment and its effects upon the national security, commerce, employment, inflation, general welfare, and foreign policy of the United States. It also reports on foreigners' portfolio investment in the U.S. Contact: Office of Data Management, Office of the Assistant Secretary for International Affairs, Department of the Treasury, 1500 Pennsylvania Ave. N.W., Room 512, Washington, DC 20220/202-566-5473.

Foreign Statistics
For information on foreign tax credits and citizens living abroad, contact: Foreign Statistics, Internal Revenue Service, Department of the Treasury, 1201 E St. N.W., Washington, DC 20224/202-376-0177.

Foreign Tax Credits
Information is available on guidelines for circumstances under which a payment to a foreign country may be credited against U.S. income tax liabilities. Contact: T.C.R, Internal Revenue Service, Department of the Treasury, 1111 Constitution Ave. N.W., Room 900, Washington, DC 20224/202-566-6275.

Freedom of Information Act
For information on using the Freedom of Information Act throughout the Department of the Treasury, contact: Director, Disclosure Operations Division, IRS, P.O. Box 388, Ben Franklin Station, Washington, DC 20044/202-566-4912.

Gasohol Packet
See "Alcohol Fuels Information Directory" in this section.

Gasohol Permits
Permits are required to operate distilled spirits plants. General information on the production of gasohol is also available. Free publications include: *Alcohol Fuels Information Directory* and *Alcohol Fuel Plants and Distilled Spirits for Fuel Use.* For publications contact: ATF Distribution

Center, 3800 S. Four Mile Run Dr., Arlington, Va 22006/703-557-7850. For general information, contact: Distilled Spirits Branch, Bureau of Alcohol, Tobacco and Firearms, Department of the Treasury, 1200 Pennsylvania Ave. N.W., Room 6235, Washington, DC 20226/202-566-7591.

Gold Medallions and Hotline
A series of 10 gold medallions, ½ ounce and 1 ounce, is being produced to honor 10 specific American artists. The artists and publishing dates are as follows:

Marian Anderson, Grant Wood—1980
Mark Twain, Willa Cather—1981
Louis Armstrong, Frank Lloyd Wright—1982
Robert Frost, Alexander Calder—1983
Helen Hayes, John Steinbeck—1984

Information on which medallions are still available and their prices are available by calling 800-368-5510; 800-368-5500 (Alaska, Hawaii, Puerto Rico, Virgin Islands); 783-3800 (D.C.). For additional information on medallions, contact: Customer Services Branch, Marketing Division, Bureau of the Mint, Department of the Treasury, 501 13th St. N.W., Room 1021, Washington, DC 20220/202-376-0458.

Government Checks
There are seven Regional Financial Centers under the Treasury Department's Bureau of Government Financial Operations which issue payments for over 1,800 federal administrative offices throughout the United States. Contact: Operations Group, Bureau of Government Financial Operations, Department of the Treasury, Treasury Annex, Madison Place & Pennsylvania Avenue, Washington, DC 20226/202-566-9512.

Government Loans Abroad
Information is available on all U.S. government loans from all government agencies to foreign governments and foreign organizations and U.S. government contracts of guarantees or insurance on private loans to foreigners. The following reports are issued quarterly:

Active Foreign Credits of the U.S. Government Contingent Foreign Liabilities of the U.S. Government.
Amounts Due and Unpaid 90 Days or More on Foreign Credits of the U.S. Government.

Contact: Office of Data Management, Office of Assistant Secretary for International Affairs, Department of the Treasury, 15th St. and Pennsylvania Ave. N.W., Room 5127, Washington, DC 20220/202-566-2969.

Government Securities, Lost, Stolen or Destroyed
For claims on account of lost, stolen, destroyed or mutilated securities, contact: Claims Section, Division of Securities Operations, Bureau of the Public Debt, Department of the Treasury, 13th and C Sts. S.W., Room 429-2, Washington, DC 20239/202-447-1339.

Grants
The programs described below are for sums of money which are given by the federal government to initiate and stimulate new or improved activites or to sustain on-going services.

State and Local Government Fiscal Assistance—
General Revenue Sharing
   Objective: To provide financial assistance to general purpose local governments.
   Eligibility: State governments (including the District of Columbia) and general purpose local governments, including the governing bodies of Indian tribes or Alaskan native villages performing substantial governmental functions, and county sheriffs' offices in the State of Louisiana.
   Range of Financial Assistance: Average $200 to $261,462,432.
   Contact: Intergovernmental Relations Division, Office of Revenue Sharing, Department of the Treasury, 2401 E St. N.W., Washington, DC 20226/202-634-5200.

Tax Counseling for the Elderly
   Objectives: To authorize the Internal Revenue Service to enter into agreement with private or public nonprofit agencies or organizations; to establish a network of trained volunteers to provide free income tax information and return preparation assistance to elderly taxpayers.
   Eligibility: Tax Counseling for the Elderly sponsors must be private or public nonprofit organizations with experience in coordinating volunteer programs. Federal, State and local governmental agencies and organizations are not eligible to sponsor a program.
   Range of Financial Assistance: $287–$1,190,119.
   Contact: Tax Counseling for the Elderly, Taxpayer Service Division, D:R:T:I, Internal Revenue Service, 1111 Constitution Avenue, NW, Washington, DC 20224/202-566-4904.

Help for the Deaf
The Internal Revenue Service offers telephone tax assistance to deaf taxpayers with teletypewriter equipment. Call 800-382-4059 (Indiana), 300-428-4732 (elsewhere in U.S. including Alaska, Hawaii, Virgin Islands, and Puerto Rico), or contact: Taxpayer Services Division, Internal Revenue Service, Department of the Treasury, 1111 Constitution Ave. N.W., Room 7324, Washington, DC 20224/202-566-4825.

Import Quotas
Import quotas are enforced on some 940 items. These importations are monitored to determine the quantity of a commodity imported from a

specific country or countries. A free monthly newsletter is available on every commodity subject to import quotas. The U.S. Customs Service administers most, but not all, import quotas. Contact: U.S. Customs Service, Quota Section, Trade Operations, Duty Assessment Division, 1301 Constitution Ave. N.W., Room 4111, Washington, D. C. 20229/202-566-8592.

Importing into the U.S.
This publication provides an explanation of entry procedures, delivery, duty payments, assigned entry numbers and quotas. Available for $3.00 a copy from the Government Printing Office, Superintendent of Documents, Washington, DC 20402/202-783-3238.

Income Tax Statistics
Publications provide a variety of data reported on tax returns. The publications available include:

Individual Income Tax Returns
Small Area Data from Individual Income Tax Returns
Corporation Income Tax Returns
International Income and Taxes, U.S. Corporations and Their Controlled Foreign Corporations
International Income and Taxes, Domestic International Sales Corporations Returns
Sole Proprietorship Returns
Partnership Returns
Fiduciary Income Tax Returns
Estate Tax Returns
Personal Wealth

For information on content and availability of statistical publications, contact: Statistics of Income Branch, Statistics Division, Office of Planning and Research, Internal Revenue Service, Department of the Treasury, 1201 E St. N.W., Room 301, Washington, DC 20224/202-376-0102.

Individual Tax Model
This program provides state tax officials with a tax model to be used in determining their rate structure and possible revenue yields in connection with the "piggybacking" provisions of the Federal-State Tax Collection Act of 1972. Contact: Director, Statistics Division, Internal Revenue Service, Department of the Treasury, 1201 E St. N.W., Room 401, Washington, DC 20224/202-376-0216.

Individual Tax Statistics
For information on individual tax returns (agregate data) by county and Standard Metropolitan Statistical Area, contact: Individual Statistics, Internal Revenue Service, Department of the Treasury, 1201 E St. N.W., Washington, DC 20224/202-376-0155.

Internal Revenue Bulletin
This weekly publication reviews rulings, procedures, announcements, orders, treasury decisions,

tax conventions, legislation, Supreme Court decisions and public laws relating to taxes. For information on content contact: Internal Revenue Service, ATTN: Bulletin and Disclosure Unit, CC:IND:S:3:1, Room 2613, 1111 Constitution Ave. NW, Washington DC 20402/202-783-3238. For information on content, contact: Technical Publications Branch, Tax Forms and Publications, Technical Office, Internal Revenue Service, 1111 Constitution Ave. N.W., Room 2571, Washington, DC 20224/202-566-3129. Available for $82.00 a year from: Government Printing Office, Superintendent of Documents, Washington, DC 20402/202-783-3238.

International Commodities
The International Affairs Office is involved with international commodity developments such as International Rubber Agreement, United Nations Conference on Trade and Development Commodities Issues, including copper, cocoa, coffee, sugar, wheat and grain, Oceans Policy, World Oil Market and International Energy Policy. Contact: Office of Commodity Policy, International Affairs, Department of the Treasury, 15th St. and Pennsylvania Ave. N.W., Room 2221, Washington, DC 20220/202-566-5881.

International Energy Economic Research
This office focuses on the ways in which international flows of energy resources and technologies relate to the U.S. Department of the Treasury's responsibility in the international economic area. Contact: Office of the Director, Regional and Resource Policy, Department of the Treasury, Room 4134, 15th St and Pennsylvania Ave. NW, Washington, DC 20220/202-566-5071.

International Financial Statistics
The U.S. Department of Treasury manages two international financial statistics collection systems: 1) the *Treasury International Capital Reporting System*—collects monthly, quarterly, and semiannual data on U.S. banks' foreign assets and liabilities; U.S. commercial firms' claims and liabilities to unaffiliated foreigners; banks' and brokers' securities transactions with foreign residents; foreign transactions in U.S. securities and U.S. banks' lending activity abroad (these data provide information on all movements of capital between the United States and foreign countries other than direct investment flows and government transfers); 2) *Treasury Foreign Currency Reporting System*—gathers information from banks and nonbanking business firms in the United States and their majority-owned foreign subsidiaries and branches on the assets, liabilities and exchange contracts bought and sold in eight major foreign currencies and U.S. dollars held or owned by their foreign branches and majority-owned subsidiaries.

Contact: Office of Data Management, Office of Assistant Secretary for International Affairs, Department of Treasury, 15 St and Pennsylvania Ave. NW, Room 5127, Washington, DC 20220/202-566-3114.

International Mail Imports

The U.S. Customs Service processes all mail entering the country from overseas. A free pamphlet, *U.S. Customs International Mail Imports,* provides information on mail that originates outside the United States. It deals with duty, damaged goods, and provides a listing of Customs International Mail Branches. Contact: General Programs Branch, Duty Assessment Division, Office of Trade Operations, Customs Service, Department of the Treasury, 1301 Constitution Ave. N.W., Room 4217, Washington, DC 20229/202-566-2957.

International Monetary Affairs

This office is concerned with international bank lending and the Eurocurrency market, including treatment accorded to U.S. banks by foreign governments, gold market developments, international balance of payments, foreign exchange market developments and operations, international monetary arrangements, and the International Monetary Fund. Contact: International Monetary Affairs, International Affairs, Department of the Treasury, 15th St. and Pennsylvania Ave. N.W., Room 3221, Washington, DC 20220/202-566-5232.

IRS Braille

See "Tax Information in Braille for Public Libraries" in this section.

IRS Collections and Returns

Statistics are available on IRS tax collections and tax returns including: IRS collections by sources and by area; number of IRS refunds issued; overassessments of tax as the result of examination; number of returns filed by IRS region; number of returns examined and results; results of collection agencies; civil penalties assessed and abated; number of exempt organizations' returns examined by type of organization. Contact: Returns Processing and Accounting Division, Office of Taxpayer Service and Returns Processing, Internal Revenue Service, Department of the Treasury, 1111 Constitution Ave. N.W., Room 7009, Washington, DC 20225/202-566-6881.

IRS Enrolled Agents

Individuals who are not attorneys or certified public accountants must pass the special enrollment examination in order to represent taxpayers before the Internal Revenue Service. Contact: Office of Director of Practice, Internal Revenue Service, Department of the Treasury, 1111 Constitution Ave. N.W., Washington, DC 20224/202-535-6787.

IRS Films

The following films are offered on a free-loan basis from local Internal Revenue Service Field offices (see "Local Tax Office" in this section), or from: Public Affairs Division, Internal Revenue Service, Department of the Treasury, 1111 Constitution Ave. N.W., Washington, DC 20224/202-566-6860.

The American Way of Taxing—highlights the various services available to taxpayers through local IRS offices and traces the history and current administration of the tax system in the United States.

Hey, We're in Business—stresses the IRS free assistance for small business owners in such areas as good records, obligations to employees, and depreciation, for example (English and Spanish editions).

What Happened to My Paycheck?—explains payroll deductions for taxes and the "pipeline" system at the service centers. While designed for high school students, it need not be restricted to that audience.

A Right Good Thing—is designed for showing to groups of elderly people, those 60 years of age or over, and explains tax counseling available free of charge for these taxpayers. It focuses on those tax problems frequently encountered by older persons, such as what qualifies as taxable income, treatment of Social Security benefits, tax consequences of selling a home, and tax benefits for older taxpayers.

The Subject Was Taxes—narrates the history of taxes throughout the ages from about 5000 BC to Colonial times in various early civilizations.

Money Talks—depicts the history of taxes from Colonial times to post World War II.

A Vital Service—about volunteer income tax assistance.

Why Us, The Lakens?—describes taxpayer examination and appeal rights.

Taking Care of Business—provides information on how to organize a business for tax purposes, recordkeeping, accounting methods, filing of business tax returns, and payment of employment taxes.

A Trip Down the Pipeline—depicts the various steps that occur in the processing cycle, or along the pipeline to illustrate how a tax return is processed at an IRS Service Center.

Porque A Nosotros Los Garcia?—this Spanish film highlights taxpayer examination and appeal rights. The Garcias have been notified by the IRS that their tax return has been selected for examination. Unhappy with the audit finding, the Garcias appeal and the viewer learns how the audit procedure and the appeals system work.

Available in Video Tapes only:

Magnetic Media Reporting—encourages medium size and large business owners to report information returns on magnetic media.

Helping to Recover—focuses on how to claim Disaster, Casualty and Theft Losses.

IRS Help for the Deaf

See "Help for the Deaf" in this section.

IRS Manuals

The following Internal Revenue Service manuals are available from: Freedom of Information Reading Room. Internal Revenue Service, Department of the Treasury, 1111 Constitution Ave. N.W., Room 1569, Washington, DC 20224/202-566-3770.

Organization and Staffing ($38.10)
Policies of the Internal Revenue Service Handbook ($14.10)
Internal Management Document System Handbook ($19.50)
Disclosure of Official Information Handbook ($69.75)
Travel Handbook ($26.25)
General ($20.70)
Income Tax Examinations ($50.70)
Tax Audit Guidelines for Internal Revenue Examiners ($9.60)
Techniques Handbook for Specialized Industries
   Insurance ($15.15)
   Auto Dealers ($2.55)
   Textiles ($4.80)
   Timber ($6.00)
   Brokerage Firms ($11.10)
   Railroads ($8.70)
   Construction ($4.65)
   Oil and Gas ($22.50)
   Financial Institution ($6.95)
   Public Utilities ($8.85)
Tax Audit Guidelines, Partnerships, Estates and Trusts, and Corporations ($24.60)
Techniques Handbook for In-Depth Examinations ($25.35)
Examination Tax Shelters Handbook ($17.85)
Report Writing Guide for Income Tax Examinations ($20.55)
Examination Technique Handbook for Estate Tax Examiners ($27.30)
Handbook for Quality Review ($10.50)
Employment Tax Procedures ($11.40)
Excise Tax Procedure ($13.05)
Handbook for Examination Group Managers ($7.95)
Legal Reference Guide for Revenue Officers ($37.65)
Taxpayer Service Handbook ($35.75)
Exempt Organizations Handbook ($54.00)
Private Foundations Handbook ($40.20)
Employee Plans Master File Handbook ($9.30)
Exempt Organizations Business Master File Handbook ($17.55)
Examination Procedures ($33.15)
Employee Plans Examination Guidelines Handbook ($11.15)
Closing Agreement Handbook ($16.20)
Handbook for Special Agents ($75.90)
Rulings, Determination Letters, Information Letters, and Closing Agreements ($9.45)
Tax Litigation ($105.75)
Penalty and Reasonable Cause ($16.65)

IRS Publications

The following are free from your local Internal Revenue Service Field Office (see Local Tax Office)

Your Federal Income Tax (#17)
Tax Guide for U.S. Citizens Abroad (#54)
Farmer's Tax Guide (#225)
Tax Guide for Small Business (#334)
Federal Highway Use Tax on Trucks, Truck-Tractors and Buses (#349)
Fuel Tax Credits—Nonhighway Business Equipment, Aircraft, Buses, and Taxicabs (#378)
Federal Estate and Gift Taxes (#448)
Travel, Entertainment, and Gift Expenses (#463)
Exemptions (#501)
Medical and Dental Expenses (#502)
Child and Disabled Dependent Care (#503)
Tax Information for Divorced or Separated Individuals (#504)
Tax Withholding and Estimated Tax (#505).
Income Averaging (#506)
Educational Expenses (#508)
Tax Calendar for 1981 (#509)
Excise Taxes for 1981 (#510)
Tax Information for Visitors to the United States (#513)
Foreign Tax Credit for U.S. Citizens and Resident Aliens (#514)
Withholding of Tax on Nonresident Aliens and Foreign Corporations (#515)
Tax Information for U.S. Government Civilian Employees Stationed Abroad (#516)
Social Security for Members of the Clergy and Religious Workers (#517)
Foreign Scholars and Educational and Cultural Exchange Visitors (#518)
U.S. Tax Guide for Aliens (#519)
Tax Information for U.S. Scholars (#520)
Moving Expenses (#521)
Disability Payments (#522)
Tax Information on Selling Your Home (#523)
Credit for the Elderly (#524)
Taxable and Nontaxable Income (#525)
Charitable Contributions (#526)
Rental Property (#527)
Miscellaneous Deductions (#529)
Tax Information for Homeowners (#530)
Reporting Income from Tips (#531)
Self-Employment Tax (#533)
Depreciation (#534)
Business Expenses and Operating Losses (#535)
Net Operating Losses and the At Risk Limits (#536)
Installment and Deferred-Payment Sales (#537)
Accounting Periods and Methods (#538)
Withholding Taxes and Reporting Requirements (#539)
Tax Information on Partnerships (#541)
Tax Information on Corporations (#542)
Sales and Other Dispositions of Assets (#544)
Interest Expense (#545)
Tax Information on Disasters, Casualty Losses, and Thefts (#547)
Deduction for Bad Debts (#548)
Condemnations of Private Property for Public Use (#549)
Investment Income and Expenses (#550)
Basis of Assets (#551)
Recordkeeping Requirements and a List of Tax Publications (#552)

Highlights of 1980 Tax Changes (#553)
Tax Benefits for Older Americans (#554)
Community Property and the Federal Income Tax (#555)
Examination of Returns, Appeal Rights, and Claims for Refund (#556)
Revision de las declaraciones de impuesto, derecho de apelacion y reclamaciones de devolucion (Examination of Returns, Appeal Rights, and Claims for Refund) (#556S)
How to Apply for and Retain Exempt Status for Your Organization (#557)
Tax Information for Sponsors of Contests and Sporting Events (#558)
Tax Information for Survivors, Executors, and Administrators (#559)
Tax Information on Self-Employed Retirement Plans (#560)
Determining the Value of Donated Property (#561)
Mutual Fund Distributions (#564)
Tax Information on U.S. Civil Service Retirement and Disability Retirement (#567)
Tax Guide for U.S. Citizens Employed in U.S. Possessions (#570)
Tax-sheltered Annuity Programs for Employees of Public Schools and Certain Tax-Exempt Organizations (#571)
Investment Credit (#572)
Pension and Annuity Income (#575)
Tax Information for Private Foundations and Foundation Managers (#578)
Como Preparar su declaracion de impuesto federal (#579S)
Federal Use Tax on Civil Aircraft (#582)
Recordkeeping for a Small Business (#583)
Disaster and Casualty Loss Workbook (#584)
Voluntary Tax Methods to Help Finance Political Campaigns (#585)
Preceso de cobro (Deudas del impuesto sobre ingreso) (The Collection Process (Income Tax Accounts) (#586S)
Business Use of Your Home (#587)
Tax Information on Condominiums and Cooperative Apartments (#588)
Tax Information on Subchapter S Corporations (#589)
Tax Information on Individual Retirement Arrangements (#590)
Income Tax Benefits for U.S. Citizens Who Go Overseas (#593)
Tax Guide for Commercial Fishermen (#595)
Earned Income Credit (#596)
Information on the United States-Canada Income Tax Treaty (#597)
Tax on Unrelated Business Income of Exempt Organizations (#598)
Certification for Reduced Tax Rates in Tax Treaty Countries (#686)
Comprehensive Tax Guide for U.S. Civil Service Retirement Benefits (#721)
Guides for Qualification of Pension, Profit-Sharing, and Stock Bonus Plans (#778)
Favorable Determination Letter (#794)
U.S. Tax Treaties (#901)
Energy Credits for Individuals (#903)

Computing the Interrelated Charitable, Marital, and Orphans' Deductions and Net Gifts (#904)
Tax Information on Unemployment Compensation (#905)
Targeted Jobs and WIN Credits (#906)
Tax Information for Handicapped and Disabled Individuals (#907)
Identification Numbers under ERISA (#1004)
Filing Requirements for Employee Benefit Plans (#1048)

IRS Rulings and Technical Advice
Internal Revenue Service rulings and technical advice memoranda are open to public inspection. Contact: Freedom of Information Reading Room, Taxpayer Services and Returns Processing, Internal Revenue Service, Department of the Treasury, 1111 Constitution Ave. N.W., Room 1569, Washington, DC 20224/202-566-3770.

IRS Training Publications
Information is available on all training publications for Internal Revenue Service agent training, including tax auditing, state and gift taxes, fiduciary income tax, international taxes, excise taxes and taxpayer service training. Contact: Training Publications, Taxpayer Service Division, 31 Hopkins Plaza, Baltimore, MD 21203/301-962-2590 or order recording 301-962-0808.

Know Your Money
This publication describes: how to detect counterfeit money; how to guard against forgery losses; what to do when you receive a counterfeit bill or coin; how to print reproductions of paper currency, checks, bonds, revenue stamps and securities of the United States and foreign governments legally; what to do when money burns or wears out. Available from: Government Printing Office, Superintendent of Documents, Washington, DC 20402/202-783-3238.

Library
The main library contains holdings which emphasize both general economics and general law. Contact: Department of the Treasury, Room 5030, Treasury Building, Washington, DC 20220/202-566-2777.

Licensing a Small Still
Permits to build alcohol stills are granted by the Bureau of Alcohol, Tobacco and Firearms. Any person wishing to establish an alcohol fuel plant must obtain an Alcohol Fuels Producers Permit. There are 5 Regional Offices and 2 Field Operations Offices. Contact:

Midwest Region, 230 South Dearborn St., Chicago, IL 60604/312-353-4371. Illinois, Iowa, Kansas, Minnesota, Missouri, Nebraska, North Dakota, South Dakota, and Wisconsin.

North Atlantic Region, 6 World Trade Center, 6th Floor, New York, NY 10048/212-264-2106. Connecticut, Maine, Massachusetts, New Hampshire, New York, Rhode Island, and Vermont.

Southeast Region, 3835 Northeast Expressway, Atlanta, GA 30340/404-232-2670. Alabama, Florida, Georgia, Mississippi, North Carolina, South Carolina, and Tennessee.

Southwest Region, 1114 Commmerce St., Dallas, TX 75242/214-729-2281. Arkansas, Colorado, Louisiana, New Mexico, Oklahoma, Texas, and Wyoming.

Western Region, 525 Market Street, 34th Floor, San Francisco, CA 94105/415-454-9623. Alaska, Arizona, California, Hawaii, Idaho, Montana, Nevada, Oregon, Utah, and Washington.

Philadelphia, Pennsylvania Office, Bureau of Alcohol, Tobacco and Firearms, Fed. Bldg. U.S. Post Office, 6th Floor, 9th and Market Streets, Philadelphia, Pennsylvania 19107/215-597-4107. Delaware, District of Columbia, Maryland, New Jersey.

Cincinnati, Ohio Office, Bureau of Alcohol, Tobacco and Firearms, 550 Main St. Cincinnati, OH 45202/513-684-3334.

Local Tax Offices
For a listing of Internal Revenue Service field offices which provide assistance to taxpayers, in your area, consult your local telephone directory.

Marking of Country of Origin on U.S. Imports
This free pamphlet describes how every article of foreign origin entering the United States must be legally marked with the English name of the country of origin unless an exception from marking is provided for in the law. Contact: Entry Licensing and Restricted Merchandise, Entry Procedures and Penalties Division, Office of Regulations and Rulings, Customs Service, Department of the Treasury, 1301 Constitution Ave. N.W., Room 2417, Washington, DC 20229/202-566-5765.

Medals
The U.S. Mint sells medals authorized by Congress, in recognition of distinguished service, careers or feats of outstanding citizens, e.g., Robert F. Kennedy, John Wagner, Hubert H. Humphrey. There are also official medals of all the United States, miniature presidential medals, secretaries of the Treasury, Director of the Mint, great moments in American military history, great naval heros, national historical events, historic buildings, and chief justices of the Supreme Court. There are four U.S. Mint sales facilities:

Main Treasury Building, 15th St. and Pennsylvania Ave., N.W., Washington, DC 20220/202-566-5221.

United States Mint, Independence Mall, Philadelphia, PA 19106/215-597-7692.

United States Mint, 320 West Colfax Ave., Denver, CO 80204/303-837-3331.

San Francisco Old Mint, 88 Fifth Street, San Francisco, CA 94103/415-974-0788.

For further information contact: Consumer Affairs Office, Marketing Division, Bureau of the Mint, Department of the Treasury, 501 13th St. N.W., Room 1021, Washington, DC 20220/202-376-0458.

Merchandise Restricted From Entering the U.S.
Rulings are made on questionable items that may or may not enter the country, i.e., narcotics and dangerous drugs, pre-Columbian monumental and architectural sculpture or murals, switchblade knives and vehicles not equipped to comply with U.S. safety or clean air emission standards. Contact: Entry, Licensing and Restricted Merchandise, Entry Procedures and Penalties Division, Office of Regulations and Rulings, Customs, Department of the Treasury, 1301 Constitution Ave. N.W., Room 2417, Washington, DC 20229/202-566-5765.

Mint Publications
The following publications are published by the U.S. Mint and are available from: Government Printing Office, Superintendent of Documents, Washington, DC 20402/202-783-3238.

Domestic and Foreign Coins Manufactured by Mints of the United States 1793–1980—presents a complete historical record of the production of domestic coins by United States Mint institutions from 1793–1976. The manufacture of foreign coinage by United States Mints for other governments began in 1876. Coinage statistics reflect the years from 1876–1976 ($4.50).

Annual Report of the Director of the Mint—contains report on operations, functions, and legislation pertaining to the Mint ($1.25).

The World's Monetary Stocks of Gold, Silver, and Coins—giving information on production, specifications and metallic composition of coinage of about 100 foreign countries. Illustrated ($2.00).

Our American Coins (Rev. 1974)—brief introduction to U.S. coins for youngsters aged 6–16. Descriptions of current coin designs ($1.50).

For additional information on U.S. Mint publications, contact: Consumer Affairs Office, Bureau of the Mint, Department of the Treasury, 501 13th St. N.W., Room 1021, Washington, DC 20220/202-376-0871.

Monthly Treasury Statement of Receipts and Outlays of the Government
This publication provides totals of budget results and financing, a summary and detail of budget receipts and outlays, means of financing, analysis of change in excess of liabilities, agency securities issued under special financing authorities, and investment of government accounts in federal securities. Available for $125.00 per year from: Government Printing Office, Superintendent of Documents, Washington, DC 20402/202-783-3238.

Mutilated Currency
Claims are handled from the public for the

redemption of partially destroyed U.S. currency. Old bills may be exchanged for new ones at local banks. Contact: Operations, OCS, Bureau of Printing and Engraving, Department of the Treasury, 13th and C St., S.W., Room 344, P.O. Box 37048, Washington, DC 20013/202-447-0278.

National Firearms Act

This act deals with the manufacture, transfer and exportation of firearms. It covers weapons such as machine guns, short-barreled shotguns and silencers. Special tax stamps can be acquired from your local Internal Revenue Service Center. For transfer or manufacturing stamps and numbers for the purchase of automatic weapons contact: National Firearms Act, National Firearms Branch, Bureau of Alcohol, Tobacco and Firearms, Department of the Treasury, 1200 Pennsylvania Ave. N.W., Room 7240, Washington, DC 20226/202-566-7371.

Ownership of Securities

The Accounts Branch keeps individual ownership accounts of registered government securities and authorizes payment of interest. Contact: Accounts Branch, Securities Operations Division, Bureau of the Public Debt, Department of the Treasury, 13th and C Sts. S.W., Room 634, Washington, DC 20228/202-287-4063.

Passenger Processing

This office deals with anyone entering the United States by air, boat, train, car or foot. They develop new policies and procedures to facilitate the processing of travelers and the detection of law violators. Contact: Office of Passenger Enforcement and Facilitation, Inspection and Control, Customs Service, Department of the Treasury, 1301 Constitution Ave. N.W., Room 4413, Washington, DC 20229/202-566-5607.

Pets and Wildlife, Importing

There are a number of rules and restrictions for importing pets and wildlife. A free publication, *Pets, Wildlife, U.S. Customs*, describes most of the regulations. Contact: Information Division, Customs Service, Department of the Treasury, 1301 Constitution Ave. N.W., Room 6303, Washington, DC 20229/202-566-8195.

Pleasure Boats, Imports

Special rules and regulations are given to boats imported for pleasure. A free pamphlet, *Pleasure Boats*, describes how to import a boat. Contact: U.S. Customs, P.O. Box 7407, Washington, DC 20044/202-566-8195.

Problem Resolution Program—Taxes

This program is designed to cut through the red tape for taxpayers with persistent problems. Each Internal Revenue Service district office has a problem resolution officer who is independent from the operating division. If your problem is not resolved within five working days, you will be informed of its status. Contact a district office (see "Local Tax Office" in this section) or: Problem Resolution Branch, Taxpayer Service Division, Internal Revenue Service, Department of the Treasury, 1111 Constitution Ave. N.W., Room 3331, Washington, DC 20224/202-566-6475.

Publications and Information on Alcohol, Firearms and Tobacco

The Public Information Office provides assistance and free publications. The publications include:

Think First of Your Unborn Child—Rex Morgan, M.D. tells of the dangers of drinking during pregnancy, Fetal Alcohol Syndrome, in comic book format.
Explosives and Laws and Regulations
State Laws and Published Ordinances
Liquor Laws and Regulations for Retail Dealers
Contact: Public Information Office, Bureau of Alcohol, Tobacco and Firearms, Department of the Treasury, 1200 Pennsylvania Ave. N.W., Room 4402, Washington, DC 20226/202-566-7268.

Publications to Travelers and Importers

The following publications are free from Media and Public Services Branch, Public Information Division, Customs Service, Department of the Treasury, 1301 Constitution Ave. N.W., Room 6311, Washington, DC 20229/202-566-8195.

Customs Hints—Know Before You Go—explains customs privileges and lists prohibited and restricted imports. "Know Before You Go."
Customs Hints for Visitors (Nonresidents)—customs exemptions for foreign visitors arriving in the United States (English language only).
Pets, Wildlife, U.S. Customs—summary of customs requirements for importing cats, dogs, birds, and wildlife.
Importing a Car—customs requirements for individuals importing automobiles.
Customs Guide for Private Flyers—outlines principal customs requirements and procedures for private and corporate pilots making business or pleasure flights to and from foreign countries.
Pleasure Boats—information for owners of yachts and pleasure boats on customs procedures for importing a boat, entry and reporting requirements.
Books, Copyrights, and Customs—information about copyright restrictions or prohibitions applying to importation of books.
Currency Reporting—a flyer advising that if you take into or out of the United States more than $5,000, a report must be filed with customs.
Drawback—a nontechnical leaflet to explain drawback; how to obtain a duty refund on certain exports.
Customs Bonded Warehouses—a leaflet that explains the types of bonded warehouses, their use, and how to establish a bonded warehouse.
Customs Tips for Visitors—a leaflet issued in English,

French, Spanish, German, Italian, Hungarian, Polish, Yugoslavian, and Czechoslovakian, Portuguese, Dutch, and Korean languages. Provides foreign visitors basic information on clearing U.S. Customs.

Tourist Trademark Information—list of the most popular tourist items prohibited importation because the trademark owners have recorded their marks with the Treasury Department.

International Mail Imports—information about customs procedures and requirements pertaining to parcels mailed from abroad.

GSP and The Traveler—questions and answers regarding duty-free entry of certain articles brought in by travelers from beneficiary developing countries listed under the Generalized System or Preferences (GSP)—annual update lists popular tourist items and the beneficiary countries.

U.S. Import Requirements—general information on U.S. Customs requirements for imported merchandise.

Customs Rulings on Imports—explains how importers may obtain a binding U.S. Customs duty ruling on items before importation.

Exporting to the United States—a 100-page booklet for foreign exporters planning to ship goods to the United States.

Import Quota—summary of information on import quotas administered by the United States Customs Service.

Notice to Masters of Vessels—precautions masters or owners of vessels should take to avoid penalties and forfeitures.

Notice to Carriers of Bonded Merchandise—precautions carriers and customhouse brokers should take to safeguard merchandise moving in-bond.

T.I.B—Temporary Importation Under Bonds—applies to shipments coming into U.S.

Foreign Trade Zones—explains the advantages and use of foreign trade zones and customs requirements.

Quota Statistics

For statistics on the quota system—what's allowed into the United States, how much, etc.—contact: Data Center Operations, Office of Data Systems, Operations Division, Customs Service, Dept. of the Treasury, 1301 Constitution Ave. N.W., Room 1218, Washington, DC 20229/202-566-8461.

Regulations and Rulings Specialists

If any problem arises regarding the proper interpretation and application of any of the laws administered or enforced by Customs or any of their regulations, legal rulings, decisions, guidelines, etc., a specialist on any specific rule or regulation can be contacted at: Office of Regulations and Rulings, Customs Service, Department of the Treasury, 1301 Constitution Ave. N.W., Room 3117, Washington, DC 20229/202-566-2507.

Regulatory Activities

Listed below are those organizations within the U.S. Department of the Treasury which are involved with regulating various activities. With each listing is a description of those industries or situations which are regulated by the office. Regulatory activities generate large amounts of information on the companies and subjects they regulate. Much of the information is available to the public. A regulatory office can tell you your rights when dealing with a regulated company.

Public Affairs, Bureau of Alcohol, Tobacco and Firearms, Department of the Treasury, 1200 Pennsylvania Ave. N.W., Washington, DC 20226/202-556-7135. Regulates firearms, explosives, alcohol, and tobacco.

Communications Division, Comptroller of the Currency, Department of the Currency, Department of the Treasury, 490 L'Enfant Plaza East S.W., Washington, DC 20219/202-447-1800. Regulates national banks.

Freedom of Information Reading Room, Internal Revenue Service, Department of the Treasury, 1111 Constitution Ave. N.W., Room 1569, Washington, DC 20224/202-566-3770. Determines, assesses and collects taxes.

Information Office, Customs Service, Department of the Treasury, 1301 Constitution Ave. N.W., Washington, DC 20229/202-566-8195. Regulates imports into the United States.

Related Federal Regulators on Alcohol, Tobacco and Firearms

The following agencies administer regulations which are related to the Bureau of Alcohol, Tobacco and Firearms:

Federal Aviation Administration—prohibition against carrying of weapons on aircraft or at National Capital Airports (Washington National and Dulles International Airports).

Department of Transportation—transportation of firearms, ammunition and destructive devices.

Internal Revenue Service—manufacturers' and retailers' tax on firearms.

United States Postal Service—Postal Service Manual, firearms, knives, and sharp instuments.

Bureau of Indian Affairs—Indians carrying concealed weapons; sale of arms and ammunition to Indians.

Department of State—international traffic in arms (importation, exportation, registration, licenses, manufacturing); the Office of Munitions Control, U.S. Department of State, regulates the exportation of arms, ammunition, and implements of war, to the exclusion of any regulation by the U.S. Department of Commerce.

Department of Commerce—export of shotguns with barrels eighteen (18) inches or longer.

Department of Interior—National Park Service—use of firearms in national parks prohibited; possession of firearms in national parks restricted.

Department of the Army—promotion of rifle practice; gun clubs. Contact: Firearms and Explosives Division, Office of Compliance Operations, Bureau of Alcohol, Tobacco and Firearms, Department of the Treasury, 1200 Pennsylvania Ave. N.W., Room 7241, Washington, DC 20226/202-566-7666.

Retirement Bonds

Retirement bonds are no longer available for purchase, but individuals who would like information regarding cashing or reissuing such bonds may contact: Bureau of the Public Debt, Department of the Treasury, 200 Third St., Parkersburg, WV 26101/304-422-8551.

Revenue Sharing

This office administers the Revenue Sharing Program which disburses federal funds with minimum restrictions on use permitting the local decision-making process to determine the programs and activities where the money is most needed. Based upon data furnished by the Bureau of the Census funds are distributed to eligible governments to spend in accordance with law. A free publication, *Revenue Sharing 1981–83,* is also available. Contact: Public Affairs Division, Office of Revenue Sharing, Department of the Treasury, 2401 E St. N.W., Washington, DC 20226/202-634-5248.

Revenue Sharing Demography

Revenue sharing funds are distributed on the basis of a complex allocation formula involving population, per capita income, adjusted taxes and intergovernmental transfers. Contact: Data and Demography Division, Domestic Finance, Department of the Treasury, 2401 E St. N.W., 15th Floor, Washington, DC 20226/202-634-5166.

Revenue Sharing Systems and Operations

This office provides all computer support for the Office of Revenue Sharing. Calculates, issues, controls, and documents payments to recipient governments from the Revenue Sharing Trust Fund. Develops and supports various automated information storage and retrieval systems; issues, records, and controls required recipient reports; and conducts policy-related research on proposals for changes in the Revenue Sharing allocation process. Contact: System and Operations Division, Office of Revenue Sharing, Domestic Finance, Department of the Treasury, 2401 E St. N.W., 15th Floor, Washington, DC 20226/202-634-5170.

Savings Bonds—Lost, Stolen or Destroyed

To apply for relief on account of loss, theft or destruction of U.S. Savings Bonds, contact: Bureau of the Public Debt, Department of the Treasury, P.O. Box 1328, Parkersburg, WV 26106-1328/304-422-8551.

Savings Bonds Statistics

Statistics are available on sales, redemption and retention by state and county from the inception of the program. Some statistical comparisons with other money markets are also published. Contact: Market Analysis Office, Planning and Product Development Branch, Savings Bonds Division, Department of the Treasury, 1111 20th St. N.W., Room 302, Washington, DC 20226/202-634-5360.

Savings Bonds—Volunteer Activities

State and county volunteers are the grassroots "mainstay" of the savings bonds program. For more information contact: Office of Banking and Volunteer Activities, Savings Bonds Division, Department of the Treasury, 1111 20th St. N.W., Room 310, Washington, DC 20226/202-634-5357.

Savings Bonds, Where to Buy or Redeem

Local banks or Federal Reserve Banks can sell or redeem U.S. Savings Bonds. For general information and a list of Federal Reserve banks, contact: Office of Public Affairs, Savings Bonds Division, Department of the Treasury, 1111 20th St., N.W., Washington, DC 20226/202-634-5377.

Savings Notes

These notes are no longer sold, but for those who still hold them and require assistance, contact: Bureau of Public Debt, Department of the Treasury, P.O. Box 1328, Parkersburg, WV 26106/304-422-8551

Secret Service

Under law, uniformed officers of the Secret Service provide protection for: the president of the United States and his immediate family; the vice president of the United States and his immediate family, the White House and grounds; the official residence of the vice president in Washington; buildings in which the presidential offices are located; foreign diplomatic missions located in the metropolitan area of the District of Columbia and in such other areas in the United States, its territories and possessions as the President may direct. Contact: Public Affairs, Secret Service, Department of the Treasury, 1800 G St. N.W., Room 805, Washington, DC 20223/202-535-5708.

Secret Service History

For free copies of illustrated history of the Secret Service, contact: Public Affairs, Secret Service, Department of the Treasury, 1800 G St. N.W., Room 805, Washington, DC 20223/202-535-5708.

Secure Documents

The Bureau of Engraving and Printing is responsible for the design and production of U.S. currency, postage stamps, Treasury obligations, and other U.S. securities. It is also responsible for advising and assisting Federal agencies in the design and production of other government securities which incorporate features to deter counterfeiting and alterations. Agencies requiring assistance in this area should contact: Public Affairs Office, Bureau of Engraving and Printing, 14th and G St., SW, Washington, DC 20228/202-447-0229.

Securities Markets
This office is involved with structure and power activities of commercial banks, thrift institutions, credit unions and securities firms. Contact: Financial Institutions Policy, Domestic Finance, Department of the Treasury, 15th and Pennsylvania Ave. N.W., Washington, DC 20220/202-566-5337.

Selling to the Department of the Treasury
This free booklet provides general information, a listing of procurement offices, a description of the office's functions, and a list of products and services purchased. Contact: Office of Procurement, Office of Administrative Programs, Department of the Treasury, 1331 G St. N.W., Room 900, Washington, DC 20220/202-376-0650.

Special Agents
Special agents of the Secret Service are charged with protection and investigative responsibilities. Their primary duty is protection of the president of the United States. In addition, they also protect: the vice president; immediate families of the president and vice president; president-elect and vice president-elect and their immediate families; a former president and his wife during his lifetime, the widow of a former president until her death or remarriage; minor children of a former president until age 16; major presidential and vice presidential candidates; visiting heads of foreign states or foreign governments. Special agents are also charged with suppressing the counterfeiting of U.S currency and securities. They investigate and arrest thousands of people each year for forging and cashing government checks, bonds and securities. Contact: Public Affairs, Secret Service, Department of the Treasury, 1800 G St. N.W., Room 805, Washington, DC 20223/202-535-5708.

State and Local Finance
This office provides staff support to the Deputy Assistant Secretary (State and Local Finance). In particular, the Office (1) performs studies and policy analyses relating to issues affecting the Revenue Sharing Program, including the reauthorization of the Program; (2) carries out studies as directed by the Department and the Congress concerning such matters as the current fiscal condition and outlook for State-local governments, measures of State-local capacity, Federal tax policies affecting State-local governments, proposals for Federal revenue turnbacks to State-local governments, formulas for allocating federal aid to State-local governments, especially Revenue Sharing, and the cyclical behavior of the State-local sector; (3) monitors New York City's compliance with the terms and conditions of outstanding Treasury guarantees of New York City debt; and (4) monitors trends and conditions in the tax-exempt securities market. Contact: Office of State and Local Finance, Department of the Treasury,

15th Street and Pennsylvania Avenue, N.W., Room 5132, Washington, DC 20220/202-566-5681.

Sureties
For information relating to surety companies, including the examination of applications of companies requesting authority to write bonds and the review of their financial statements to determine underwriting limitations, contact: Audit Staff, Bureau of Government Financial Operations, Department of the Treasury, Pennsylvania Ave. and Madison Pl. N.W., Room 312, Washington, DC 20226/202-634-5010.

Tables of Redemption Values for U.S. Savings Bonds, Series E and Series EE
This semiannual publication is available for $10 a year or $3.75 a single copy for Series E and $1.25 a copy for Series EE, from: Government Printing Office, Superintendent of Documents, Washington, DC 20402/202-783-3238.

Targeted Job Tax Credit
Employees who hire people from any of the eight categories listed below may claim a tax credit: 1) people referred by vocational rehabilitation agencies; 2) economically disadvantaged youth 18–24 years old; 3) economically disadvantaged Vietnam veterans; 4) recipients of supplemental security income; 5) recipients of general assistance payments for 30 days or more; 6) people 16–18 years old participating in a qualified state certified cooperation education program; 7) economically disadvantaged ex-offenders; and 8) economically disadvantaged summer youth employees who are 16 or 17 years of age on the hiring date and who have not worked for the employer previously. The tax credit for this group is 85% of the base wage up to $3000. Contact: Employment and Training Administration, U.S. Employment Service, Department of Labor, 601 D St. N.W., Room 8100, Washington, DC 20213/202-376-6565.

Tax Analysis
This office prepares analyses of proposed tax legislation, assembles statistical and analytical materials for use in the formulation of tax programs, and studies the effects of alternative programs or measures in the light of economic and budgetary requirements. Consideration is given to all aspects of the Federal tax system, including the corporation taxes, the individual income taxes, excise taxes, estate and gift taxes, social security taxes, taxation of foreign income, matters affecting international investment and trade, and Federal-state-local fiscal relations.

The office prepares analytical reports on economic problems in these fields for use by Treasury officials in supplying information requested by the President, the Committee on Ways and Means, the Finance Committee, the Joint Committee on

Internal Revenue Taxation, individual members of Congress, other Government agencies, and the public. Contact: Office of Tax Analysis, International Taxation, Department of the Treasury, Room 5121, 1111 Constitution Ave, N.W., Washington, DC 20224/202-566-8784.

Tax Appeals
The Internal Revenue Service encourages the resolution of tax disputes through an administrative appeals system rather than litigation. Proceedings in the appeals process are informal so that taxpayers can represent themselves. The Appeals Division serves as liaison with field officers on appeal matters and writes the procedures on how to handle cases on appeal. Contact: Procedures and Technical Branch, Appeals Division, Office of Compliance, Internal Revenue Service, U.S. Department of the Treasury, 1111 Constitution Ave. N.W., Room 2313, Washington, DC 20224/202-566-4881.

Tax Exempt Organizations
The Office of Exempt Organizations determines the qualifications of organizations seeking tax exempt recognition, determines their private foundation status and examines returns to ensure compliance with the law. There are over 800,000 tax-exempt organizations. Contact: Exempt Organizations Division, Employee Plans and Exempt Organizations, Internal Revenue Service, Department of the Treasury, 1111 Constitution Ave., N.W., Room 6411, Washington, DC 20224/202-566-6208.

Tax Help for Foreign Governments
The Internal Revenue Service, in cooperation with the Agency for International Development, assists foreign governments in modernizing their tax administration systems. Visitors from about 130 countries have participated in Internal Revenue Service orientation and observation programs. Contact: Foreign Visitor Tax Administration Advisory Services Division, Internal Revenue Service, Department of the Treasury, 1111 Constitution Ave. N.W., Room 1031, Washington, DC 20224/202-566-4042.

Tax Information in Braille
Individual Income Tax Forms 1040, 1040A, 1040EZ, and the Instructions for these forms are available at Regional Libraries for the Blind and Physically Handicapped in conjunction with the Library of Congress. For information, contact: the Regional Libraries or the National Library Service for the Blind and Physically Handicapped, Library of Congress, Washington, D.C.

Taxpayer Assistance and Education
A number of programs provide information to taxpayers and assist them in exercising their tax rights and meeting their tax responsibilities. The programs include:

Volunteer Income Tax Assistance (VITA) provides free tax help to people who cannot afford professional assistance. IRS trained volunteers assist individuals with simple tax returns, particularly lower-income, elderly, non-English speaking, and handicapped taxpayers, at sites conveniently located throughout the community.

Tax Counseling for the Elderly (TCE) supplies free tax assistance to persons age 60 and older. Non-profit organizations administer TCE Programs in cooperation with the IRS. TCE sponsors recruit volunteers who make special efforts to reach taxpayers at sites easily accessible to the elderly, and if necessary, visit the residences of the homebound. Volunteers are reimbursed for out-of-pocket expenses related to their providing assistance.

Community Outreach Tax Assistance offers group self-help tax return preparation sessions and tax information seminars to taxpayers according to their needs and tax situations, such as retirees, small business owners and farmers, etc. The self-help assistance is similar to that provided in walk-in areas of IRS offices, while seminars cover new tax law or technical information to groups sharing a common interest.

Small Business Tax Workshops (SBW) assist new and prospective business owners by providing tax information and instruction they need for complying with the tax laws. Workshops are tailored to the needs of those in attendance, who typically include minority business owners and specialized business groups defined by occupation. Workshop materials include an attendee workbook and a twenty-eight minute videotape.

Understanding Taxes (UT) is an introductory tax course developed with the help of educators from all over the country. It explains how to prepare a simple tax return and covers the history, politics and economics of taxation, and explains the rights and responsibilities of a taxpaying citizen. The course is primarliy designed for 11th and 12th grade students, and is of particular interest to students filing tax returns for the first time. Course materials include student and teacher guides and a new film series developed with the cooperation of the departments of education of all 50 states and the District of Columbia.

Practitioner Institutes provide training to persons who prepare tax returns or counsel taxpayers for a fee. Topics include tax law changes and areas of specific interest to practitioners, such as employee plans and IRAs. Participants are preparers, accountants, CPAs, and tax attorneys. Educational institutions sponsor the institutes, reimbursing the IRS for instructional support provided by IRS employees, under Intergovernmental Personnel Act (IPA) agreements.

Student Tax Clinics serve taxpayers, law and graduate accounting students, and educational institutions by making available free counseling and, at times, representation to taxpayers involved in examinations and appeals proceedings. Students provide the assistance to enhance their professional education with practical experience. Schools and colleges sponsor the clinics to further their educational goals and as a community service.

Contact: Taxpayer Information and Education Branch, Taxpayer Service Division, Internal Revenue Service, Department of the Treasury, 1111 Constitution Ave. N.W., Room 1311, Washington, D.C. 20224/202-566-4904.

Taxpayers Overseas

Taxpayers assistance is available to Americans who live abroad. There are tax assistors in major embassies—London, Paris, Bonn, Rome, Ottawa, Mexico City, Caracas, Sao Paulo, Tokyo, Manila, Sydney, Singapore and Johannesburg. Tax assistors also pass through other cities to provide assistance to American taxpayers. Contact nearby embassy or consulate to learn their schedule. Two free publications are available: *Tax Guide for U.S. Citizens Abroad* and *Foreign Tax Credit for U.S. Citizens and Resident Aliens*. Contact: Taxpayer Service Branch, Foreign Operations District, Office of International Operations, Internal Revenue Service, Department of the Treasury, 1325 K St. N.W., Room 900, Washington, DC 20225/202-566-5941.

Taxpayer Usage Studies

Research is conducted on such topics as: What percentage of taxpayers deduct $1.00 for presidential elections, made payments to an IRS, took the deduction for a married couple when both work, and show child and dependent care expenses. This information is published in the Statistics of Income Bulletin available from the Superintendent of Documents, U.S. Government Printing Office, Washington DC, 20402. Contact: The Statistics of Income Division, Internal Revenue Service, Department of the Treasury, 1201 E St. N.W., Room 401, Washington DC, 20224/202-376-0216.

Tax Projections

The Office of Projections and Special Studies makes workload economic and demographic estimates related to tax administration. Contact: Projections and Special Studies Branch, Office of Planning and Research, Internal Revenue Service, Department of the Treasury, 1201 E St. N.W., Room 405, Washington, DC 20224/202-376-0137.

Tax Returns of Nonprofit Organizations

Tax returns are available on over 700,000 nonprofit organizations who file with the Internal Revenue Service. Contact: Freedom of Information Reading Room, Internal Revenue Service, Department of the Treasury, 1111 Constitution Ave. N.W., Room 1569, Washington, DC 20224/202-566-3770.

Technical Assistance with Firearms

Assistance is available to support criminal investigations. Manufacturers can also get help in classifying and marking of newly designed firearms. Contact: Firearms and Explosives Division, Office of Compliance Operations, Bureau of Alcohol, Tobacco and Firearms, Department of the Treasury, 1200 Pennsylvania Ave. N.W., Room 7241, Washington, DC 20226/202-566-7666.

Tele-Tax

The IRS provides a telephone service called Tele-Tax. This service has Recorded Tax Information tapes on about 150 topics covering such areas as filing requirements, dependents, itemized deductions and tax credits. Recorded Tax Information is available 24 hours a day, 7 days a week to taxpayers using a push-button (tone signalling) phone. It is also available during normal business hours to taxpayers using a rotary (dial) or push-button (pulse dial) phone.

Tele-Tax has been expanded this year to include Automated Refund Information at selected locations. If it has been ten weeks since you mailed your 1984 tax return, we will be able to check the status of your refund. Automated Refund Information will not be available between January 1st and March 15th.

Depending on where you live, calling Tele-Tax may be a long distance call for you. Telephone numbers are listed in the tax form packages and can also be found in the white pages of the telephone directory under U.S. Government, Internal Revenue Service.

Tell the IRS What You Think

If you have a general concern or opinion or view that is broadly related to the federal tax system and you want the federal tax law changed, make your opinion known to: Office of Tax Policy, Tax Correspondence, Department of the Treasury, 15th St. and Pennsylvania Ave. N.W., Washington, DC 20220/202-566-5282.

Toll-Free Tax Assistance

Taxpayers anywhere in the United States can call Internal Revenue Service numbers listed in the tax form packages without paying for a long distance charge. The number can also be found in the white pages of the telephone book under U.S. Government, Internal Revenue Service. If there is no number listed for your specific area please call 1-800-424-1040. Walk in assistance is also available as well as foreign language assistance in Spanish, French, Portuguese, Chinese, and Vietnamese in some offices. For a listing of local offices, contact: Office of the Taxpayer Ombudsman, Internal Revenue Service, Department of the Treasury, 1111 Constitution Ave. N.W., Room 3331, Washington, DC 20224/202-566-6475.

Trade and Investment Policy

This office is involved with multilateral trade negotiations including: East-West trade such as

Romanian Trade Agreements, export credits on multilateral levels, bilateral arrangements and investment incentives and disincentives. Contact: Trade and Investment Policy, International Affairs, Monetary Affairs, Department of the Treasury, 15th St. and Pennsylvania Ave. N.W., Room 3208, Washington, DC 20220/202-566-2748.

Travel Information at U.S. Customs
The U.S. Customs Service provides an informative pamphlet describing its regulations, rules regarding duty-free gifts, prohibitions on bringing food, plant and animal products into the United States. Trademark information and customs declaration forms are also included. The pamphlet is available from: U.S. Customs Service, P.O. Box 7404, Washington, DC 20044/202-566-8195.

Treasury Bills
For a general lesson in government Treasury Bills, call 202-287-4091. For information on recently held and upcoming auctions, call 202-287-4100. Treasury Bills are short-term investments of less than one year in minimum denominations of $10,000. Maturity dates are 13, 26 and 52 weeks. For copies of regulations, application forms or additional information on government securities, contact: Bureau of the Public Debt, Department X, Department of the Treasury, Washington, DC 20239/202-287-4113.

Treasury Bulletin
This quarterly Treasury publication provides statistics on the finances of the U.S. Government and information regarding the operations of the Treasury. It covers in narrative and tabular formats Federal fiscal operations; international financial statistics and information on capital movements and foreign currency positions; cash management/debt collection, including receivables due from the public; and special reports on related topics. For more information on content, contact: Treasury Bulletin Editor, Financial Reports Branch, Financial Reporting Division, Bureau of Government Financial Operations, Department of the Treasury, 441 G St., NW, Rm. 3021, Washington, DC 20226/202-566-4531. Subscriptions are available for $22 annually from: U.S. Government Printing Office, Superintendent of Documents, Washington, DC 20402/202-783-3238.

Treasury Notes and Bonds Hotline
For a general lesson in government notes and bonds, call 202-287-4088. For information on recently held and upcoming auctions, call 202-287-4100. Treasury Notes are medium-term investments of 1 to 10 year maturity dates and Treasury Bonds are long-term investments of 10 to 30 years. For copies of regulations, application forms or additional information on government securities, contact: Bureau of the Public Debt, Department A, Department of the Treasury, Washington, DC 20239/202-287-4113.

Treasury Publications
For a copy of the U.S. Department of the Treasury's Annual Report or for a listing of available publications, contact: Public Affairs, Department of the Treasury, 15th St. and Pennsylvania Ave. N.W., Room 2313, Washington, DC 20220/202-566-2041.

Uncut Currency Sales
Uncut United States currency sheets are available for sale in 32-subject, 16-subject, and 4-subject sizes in the $1 denomination; 16-subject and 4-subject in the $2 denomination. For specific information on Bureau of Engraving and Printing's Visitors' Center and mail order prices, contact: Uncut Currency Sales Program, Bureau of Engraving and Printing, 14th and C St., S.W., Washington, DC 20228/202-447-1391.

Viticulture Areas
Petitions are accepted to establish viticulture areas for wine. Viticulture areas are grape growing regions which have boundaries based on geographic factors such as soil, rainfall and temperature. The name of an approved viticulture area may be cited on labels and in advertising as the wine's place of origin. Augusta, Missouri is the first named viticulture area. There are presently 68 viticultural areas approved. Contact: FAA, Wine and Beer Branch, Office of Compliance Operations, Bureau of Alcohol, Tobacco and Firearms, Department of the Treasury, 1200 Pennsylvania Ave. N.W., Room 6237, Washington, DC 20226/202-566-7626.

Voluntary Disclosure
This office encourages persons and business entities subject to Bureau jurisdiction to voluntarily disclose suspected violators of the Bureau of Alcohol, Tobacco and Firearms (ATF) laws and regulations. Contact: Office of Compliance Division, Bureau of Alcohol, Tobacco and Firearms, Department of the Treasury, 1200 Pennsylvania Ave. N.W., Room 4405, Washington, DC 20226/202-566-7118.

How Can the Department of the Treasury Help You?
To determine how the Department of the Treasury can help you, contact: Assistant Secretary for Public Affairs, Department of the Treasury, 15th St. and Pennsylvania Ave. N.W., Washington, DC 20220/202-566-2041.

AGENCIES, BOARDS, COMMISSIONS, COMMITTEES, AND GOVERNMENT CORPORATIONS

ACTION

806 Connecticut Ave. N.W., Washington, DC 20525/202-634-9282

Established: July 1, 1971
Budget: $729,323,000
Employees: 492

Mission: Administers and coordinates the domestic and international volunteer programs sponsored by the federal government, which are linked by a commitment to a "bottom-up" development program which fosters self-reliance and utilizes available human and economic resources to overcome conditions of poverty; tests new ways of bringing volunteer resources to bear on human, social and economic problems; and identifies and develops the widest possible range of volunteer service opportunities for Americans of all ages and ethnic backgrounds.

Major Sources of Information

Action Resource Center
This library has extensive materials on volunteerism and social activities nationwide. Contact: ACTION Resource Center, 806 Connecticut Ave. N. W., Room M-205, Washington, D.C. 20525/202-634-9772.

Grants
The programs described below are for sums of money which are given by the federal government to initiate and stimulate new or improved activities or to sustain ongoing services.

Foster Grandparent Program (FGP)
Objectives: To provide part-time volunteer service opportunities for low-income persons age 60 and over and to render supportive person-to-person services in health, education, welfare and related settings to children having special or exceptional needs through development of community-oriented, cost-shared projects.
Eligibility: Grants are made only to public or nonprofit private agencies or organizations, including state and local governments.
Range of Financial Assistance: $2,000 to $1,321,444.
Contact: Chief, Foster Grandparent Program, ACTION, 806 Connecticut Ave. N.W., Washington, DC 20525/202-634-9349 or tollfree (800) 424-8580 (x239).

Mini-Grant Program
Objectives: To initiate, strengthen and/or supplement volunteer efforts and to encourage broad-based volunteer citizen participation.
Eligibility: Restricted to state and local government, public or private nonprofit organizations.
Range of Financial Assistance: $500 to $15,000
Contact: National Mini-Grant Program Manager, Office of Volunteer Liaison, Room M-207, ACTION, 806 Connecticut Avenue, N.W., Washington, DC 20525. Telephone 202-634-9772 or toll-free 800-424-8867.

Service-Learning Program
Objectives: To assist secondary and postsecondary educators to begin new, and improve existing local student service-learning programs which provide services to the poverty community.
Eligibility: Any college or high school desiring to create a new service-learning program, or improve an existing program, may apply for services. Any local agency which uses student volunteers, and any state or national organization desiring to assist the development of service-learning programs may also apply.

Range of Financial Assistance: $10,000 to $40,000.

Contact: National Center for Service-Learning, ACTION, 806 Connecticut Ave. N.W., Washington, DC 20525/202-634-9410 or toll-free 800-424-8580 (x289)

Retired Senior Volunteer Program (RSVP)

Objectives: To establish a recognized role in the community and a meaningful life in retirement by developing a wide variety of community volunteer service opportunities for persons 60 years of age or over through development of community oriented, cost-shared projects.

Eligibility: Grants are made only to public and private nonprofit organizations including state and local governments.

Range of Financial Assistance: $10,000 to $450,000.

Contact: Director, Older Americans Volunteer Programs, ACTION, 806 Connecticut Ave. N.W., Washington, DC 20525/202-634-9353 or toll free 800-424-8580 (x239).

Senior Companion Program (SCP)

Objectives: To provide volunteer opportunities for low-income older people which enhance their ability to remain active and provide critically needed community services; to play a critical role in providing long-term care by assisting adults, primarily older persons with mental, emotional and physical impairments, to achieve and maintain their fullest potential to be healthy and to manage their lives independently through development of community-oriented, cost-shared projects.

Eligibility: Grants are made only to public or nonprofit agencies or organizations including state and local governments.

Range of Financial Assistance: $2,000 to $262,000.

Contact: Chief, Senior Companion Program, ACTION, 806 Connecticut Ave. N.W., Washington, DC 20525/202-634-9351 or toll-free 800-424-8580 (x239).

Technical Assistance Program (TAP)

Objectives: Help voluntary and nonprofit organizations respond to training, technical assistance and management needs of volunteers; to facilitate and improve human services that organizations provide through the use of volunteers; and to develop and exchange information related to volunteering.

Eligibility: Restricted to Federal, State and local government, agencies, and nonprofit organizations who are able to develop technical assistance materials.

Range of Financial Assistance: $5,000 to $19,000.

Contact: National Program Manager, Technical Assistance Program, Office of Volunteer Liaison,

ACTION, Room M-207, 806 Connecticut Avenue NW, Washington, DC 20525/202-254-8079 or toll-free 800-424-8867.

Volunteer Demonstration Program: Drug Prevention, Literacy, Runaways and Neighborhood Development

Objectives: To explore areas of human and social concern where citizens, as volunteers, can help toward individual self-reliance and community self-sufficiency; to develop and test program models; to explore new areas of concern; and to develop improved systems to increase the efficiency of existing programs. Priority given to drug-prevention, runaway, literacy and neighborhood development.

Eligibility: State and local government agencies and private nonprofit organizations are eligible.

Range of Financial Assistance: $7,479 to $164,385.

Contact: Policy Development Division, Office of Policy and Planning, ACTION, 806 Connecticut Ave. N.W., Washington, DC 20525/202-9308 or toll-free 800-424-8580 (x281).

State Office of Voluntary Citizen Participation

Objectives: To provide grants to states to establish and/or strengthen offices of volunteer services to improve opportunities for volunteer services at the highest level of State government.

Eligibility: Restricted to Governor's office of each State, the District of Columbia, Puerto Rico, and territories and possessions of the United States.

Range of Financial Assistance: Up to $100,000.

Contact: Office of Voluntary Citizen Participation, ACTION, Suite M-207, 806 Connecticut Ave. N.W., Washington, DC 20525/202-254-8079 or toll free 800-424-8867.

Volunteers in Service to America (VISTA)

Objectives: To supplement efforts of community organizations to eliminate poverty and poverty-related human, social and environmental problems by enabling persons from all walks of life and all age groups to perform meaningful and constructive service as volunteers in situations where the application of human talent and dedication may help the poor to overcome the handicaps of poverty and poverty-related problems and secure opportunities for self-advancement.

Eligibility: Sponsors applying for Volunteers in Service to America (VISTA) volunteers must be nonprofit organizations; they may be public or private and include state and local governments. The project in which they propose to use the volunteers must be designed to assist in the solution of poverty-related problems. Sponsors receiving program grants in excess of $25,000 must be incorporated nonprofit organizations and capable of managing grant funds and maintaining auditable records of disbursements.

Range of Financial Assistance: Not specified.

Contact: Deputy Director of VISTA, Office of Domestic Operations, ACTION, 806 Connecticut Ave. N.W., Washington, DC 20525/202-634-9410 or toll-free 800-424-8580 x289.

National Center for Service-Learning

This program offers free job skills development seminars for educators who run programs that involve students in community service. The Center also offers on-site consultation services to high school and college programs, and groups sponsoring conferences or workshops on various aspects of service-learning. The three-times-a-year newsletter, *Synergist,* is a technical assistance journal for educators who work with programs that integrate coursework and community service. It is available for $5.00 from the Superintendent of Documents, Government Printing Office, Washington, DC 20402/202-783-3238. For general information and dates and location of future seminars, contact: National Center for Service-Learning, ACTION, Room 1106, 806 Connecticut Ave. N.W., Washington, DC 20525/202-254-8370.

Newsletters

The following newsletter is free:

Prime Times—contains articles on action projects plus notices of current consumer events and publications; and *Action Update.* Both available from Office of Communications, ACTION, Room 300, 806 Connecticut Ave. N.W., Washington, DC 202-634-9282.

Older American Volunteer Programs

ACTION runs three senior volunteer programs that are mutually beneficial to the volunteers and their communities. The following is a brief description of each of the three programs:

Retired Senior Volunteer Program (RSVP)—for people over 60 who use their knowledge and talents to provide many needed services their communities could not afford. One of the projects is Fixed Income Consumer Counseling which provides information on such problems as health, energy, food and budget shopping. A variety of practical tips for people on a fixed income are also available through this project.

Foster Grandparents Program—for low-income people over 60 who work with children who have physical, mental, social or emotional health needs. The volunteers serve in institutions for the mentally retarded, correctional facilities, pediatric wards of general hospi-

tals, schools, day care centers, private homes and with handicapped, emotionally disturbed and dependent and neglected children. In return for the service, Foster Grandparents receive a tax-free modest stipend, a transportation allowance, hot meals while in service and an annual physical examination.

Senior Companion Program—offers low-income older Americans the opportunity to assist other elderly people with moderate physical and mental health impairments to maintain or resume independent living. Senior Companions provide peer support, encouragement, outside contact as well as links to appropriate community services. In return for these services, the Senior Companions receive a tax free stipend, transportation allowance, a daily hot meal, medical insurance and an annual physical examination.

For general information on these programs, Contact: Older American Volunteer Programs, ACTION, Room 1006, 806 Connecticut Ave. N.W., Washington, DC 20525/202-634-9349. (Also, see "Grants" in this section.)

Voluntary Citizen Participation

Volunteer opportunities at the state level which are coordinated within the Governor's Office. For further information, contact: Office of Volunteer Liaison, ACTION, Room 207, 806 Connecticut Ave. N.W., Washington, DC 20525/202-634-9772.

Young Volunteers In Action

This office is geared to help students between ages of 14 and 22 years volunteer in their communities for such endeavors as aiding the elderly, refugees and latchkey children. Contact: Office of Domestic Operations, ACTION, Room 600, 806 Connecticut Ave. N.W., Washington, DC 20525/202-634-9410.

Volunteers in Service to America—VISTA

VISTA volunteers serve in rural and urban communities to help people become their own advocates for the resources and services they need. They work together with rural and urban poor to find solutions to community problems. Contact: VISTA, ACTION, Public Information, Room 303 PAR, 806 Connecticut Ave. N.W., Washington, DC 20525/202-634-9424.

How can ACTION Help You?

To determine how ACTION can help you, contact: Office of Communications, ACTION, Room M-300, 806 Connecticut Ave. N.W., Washington, DC 20525/202-634-9282.

Administrative Conference of the United States

2120 L St. N.W., Washington, DC 20037/202-254-7020

Established: 1964
Budget: $1,159,000
Employees: 21

Mission: Develops improvements in the legal procedures by which federal agencies administer regulatory, benefit and other government programs; and provides a forum for agency heads, other federal officials, private lawyers, university professors, and other experts in administrative law and government to conduct continuing studies of selected problems involving these administrative procedures.

Major Sources of Information

Conference Reports
The Conference provides copies of its recent recommendations and reports and a selected bibliography on the Administrative Conference of the United States. It also maintains a library where copies of all official conference documents are available for public inspection. For further information, contact: Administrative Conference of the United States: Suite 500, 2120 L St. N.W., Washington, DC 20037/202-254-7020.

Freedom of Information Act Reports
For Freedom of Information Act requests, con-

tact: Freedom of Information, Administrative Conference of the United States, Suite 500, 2021 L St. N.W., Washington, DC 20037/202-254-7020.

How Can the Administrative Conference of the United States Help You?
To determine how this agency may be of help to you, contact: Public Information, Administrative Conference of the U.S., Suite 500, 2120 L St. N.W., Washington, DC 20037/254-7020.

Agency for International Development

320 21st St. N.W., Washington, DC 20523/202-632-1850

Budget: $4,000,000,000
Employees 5,117

Mission: Carries out economic assistance programs designed to help the people of developing countries develop their human and economic resources, increase productive capacities, and improve the quality of human life as well as to promote economic or potential stability in friendly countries.

Data Experts

Country Desk Officers

The following experts can provide current economic, political and other background information on the country which they study. These experts can be reached by telephone or by writing in care of: Country Officers, Agency for International Development, 320 21st St. N.W., Washington, DC 20523.

Angola/Mike Feldstein/202-632-4326
Argentina/Ken Johnson/202-632-2676
Bahamas/Roger Pierce/202-632-6386
Bangladesh/Vivikka Mollarem/202-632-9604
Barbados/Theoar Batrud/202-632-2116
Belize/Edward Campbell/202-632-3448
Benin/Mabel Meores/202-632-7996
Bolivia/Penelope Farley/202-632-2196
Botswana/Charles Sadler/202-632-4287
Brazil/William Rhodes/202-632-2718
Burkina-Faso/Willy Saulters/202-632-9207
Burma/Tom Kellerman/202-632-8526
Burundi/Beatrice Beyer/202-632-9808
Cameroon/William Faulkner/202-632-9810
Cape Verde/Bill Janaes/202-632-9201

Central African Republic/William Faulkner/202-632-9810
Chad/Yvonne John/202-632-3034
Chile/Ken Johnson/202-632-2676
Colombia/Penelope Farley/202-632-2196
Comoros/Lilly Willens/202-632-4030
Congo (Brazzaville)/Beatrice Beyer/202-632-9808
Cook Islands/William Ackerman/202-632-9842
Costa Rica/Marvin Schwartz/202-632-4794
Cyprus/Marx Sterne/202-632-8152
Djibouti/Richard Erey/202-632-9762
Dominican Republic/John Champagne/202-632-2200
Ecuador/Ken Johnson/202-632-2676
Egypt/Gerald Gower/202-632-3900
El Salvador/Harry Wilkinson/202-632-9158
Equatorial Guinea/William Faulkner/202-632-9810
Ethiopia/Thomas Corner/202-632-2978
Fiji/Bill Ackerman/202-632-9844
Gabon/William Faulkner/202-632-9810
The Gambia/Nick Morani/202-632-8124
Ghana/David Walsh/202-632-3305
Guatemala/Gary Adams/202-632-5221
Guinea/Bernard Lane, Movel Meares/202-632-7996
Guinea-Bissau/Movel Meares/202-632-7996

Guyana/Edward Campbell/202-632-3448
Haiti/Elias Padilla/202-632-2129
Honduras/Neil Billig/202-632-9158
India/Ann McDonald/202-632-2076
Indonesia/Vivikka Mollarem/202-632-9842
Israel/Ann Goech/202-632-3585
Ivory Coast/David Walsh/202-632-3305
Jamaica/John Tucker/202-632-3447
Jordan/Benjamin Hawley/202-632-8237
Kenya/Sidney Chernenkoft, Richard Ency/202-632-9762
Kiribati (Gilbert Islands)/William Ackerman/202-632-9844
Kuwait/Richard Burns/202-632-8237
Lebanon/Ben Hawley/202-632-8327
Lesotho/Robert Thompson/202-632-4737
Liberia/Harold Marwitz/202-632-4287
Madagascar/Richard Ency/202-632-3305
Malawi/Lenard Pompa/202-632-4287
Malaysia/William Nance/202-632-9086
Mali/Louise Werlin/202-632-8125
Malta/Christopher Crowley/202-632-9142
Mauritania/Frank Egi/202-632-3034
Mauritius/Richard Ency/202-632-9762
Morocco/George E. Lewis/202-632-9228
Mozambique/Mike Feldstein/202-632-4326
Namibia/Robert Thompson/202-632-4287
Nepal/Howard Thomas/202-632-8226
Niger/Yvonne John/202-632-3034
Nigeria/David Walsh/202-632-3305
Oman/Ben Hawley/202-632-8237
Pakistan/David Mutcheler/202-632-8226
Panama/Neil Billig/202-632-9158
Papua New Guinea/William Ackerman/202-632-9842
Paraguay/Jerome Hulehan/202-632-2718

Peru/202-632-2718
Phillipines/Bruce O'Dell/202-632-8526
Portugal/Max Stern/202-632-6519
Rwanda/Beatrice Beyer/202-632-1761
Sao Tome and Principe/William Faulkner/202-632-9810
Senegal/Nick Mouriani/202-632-8124
Seychelles/Dale Pfeiffer/202-632-9762
Sierra Leone/David Walsh/202-632-3305
Singapore/William Nance/202-632-9086
Solomon Islands/William Ackerman/202-632-9842
Somalia/Brian Kline/202-632-4030
South Africa/Mike Feltstein/202-632-4326
Sri Lanka/John Gunning/202-632-8226
Sudan/John Gunning/202-632-9714
Suriname/Richard McCoy/202-632-3449
Swaziland/Steve Pulaski/202-632-4326
Syria/Benjamin Hawley/202-632-8327
Thailand/Edward Ploch/202-632-9086
Togo/Mavel Meares/202-632-7996
Tonga/William Ackerman/202-632-9842
Tunisia/Marilyn Arnold/202-632-9228
Turkey/Marx Sterne/202-632-9246
Tuvalu (Ellice Islands)/William Ackerman/202-632-9842
Uganda/Alfred Ford/202-632-4030
Uruguay/Ken Johnson/202-632-2676
Vanatu (New Hebrides)/William Ackerman/202-632-9842
Venezuela/Jerome Hulehan/202-632-2718
Western Samoa/William Ackerman/202-632-9842
Yemen Arab Republic/Christopher Crowley/202-632-8984
Zaire/Beatrice Beyer/202-632-9808
Zambia/Leonard Pompa/202-632-4278
Zimbabwe/Robert Wrin/202-632-4326

Major Sources of Information

Agriculture, Rural Development and Nutrition

To help alleviate starvation, hunger and malnutrition in developing countries, Agency for International Development (AID) personnel overseas include community and area development officers, nutritionists, general agricultural advisors, agricultural economists and agronomy, livestock, research, irrigation, and other specialized advisors. The program includes the following kinds of activities: increasing small farmer income and productivity; creating rural employment; improving nutritional status; enhancing rural infrastructure and environment; and removing institutional and policy impediments. Contact: Office of Nutrition, Bureau for Science and Technology, Agency for International Development, 1601 N. Kent St., Room 320, Rosslyn, VA 20523/703-235-9092.

American Schools and Hospitals Abroad

This program assists private U.S.-sponsored, nonprofit schools, libraries and hospitals overseas that serve as study and demonstration centers for American ideas and practices in education and medicine. A list of schools and hospitals is available. Contact: Office of American Schools and Hospitals Abroad, Bureau for Food for Peace and Voluntary Assistance, Agency for International Development, 1400 Wilson Blvd., Room 260, Rosslyn, VA 20523/703-235-1966.

Catalog of AID Research

Research literature for development can be obtained through AID Research Development, Report Distribution Center, Agency for International Development, P. O. Box 353, Norfolk, VA 23501. For additional information as well as AID quarterly Research and Development Abstracts, contact: Agency for International Development, 7222 47th Street, Suite 100, Chevy Chase, MO 20815/701-951-7191

Computerized Data Base

See entry this section titled "Economic and Social Data Base."

Congressional Presentation

The Agency's requests for authorizations and appropriations are an excellent source for AID programs. For information, contact: Office of Legislative Affairs, Agency for International Development, 320 21st St. N.W., Room 2895, Washington, DC 20523/202-632-8264

Cooperative Development

AID supports cooperative development projects in almost 50 countries through its relationship with U.S. cooperative development organizations and the increased integration of the programs with other technical assistance resources. Contact: Office of Program and Management Support, Bureau for Food for Peace and Voluntary Assistance (SA-8), Agency for International Development, 1400 Wilson Blvd., Room 201, Rosslyn, VA 20523/703-235-1940.

Credit Unions

AID supports the international programs sponsored by the Credit Union National Association (CUNA) and the World Council of Credit Unions. AID's funds are used to improve and expand the technical assistance capability of CUNA's global projects office; expand CUNA's capability to solve problems common to all less developed countries' credit unions; and expedite the development and implementation of a world-wide credit union strategy which combines financial resources from credit unions in both the developed and developing countries. Contact: Food for Peace and Voluntary Assistance, Agency for International Development, Room 1684, Washington, DC 20523/703-235-1823

Development Digest

This is a quarterly journal with articles on AID and non-AID projects, and socioeconomic development and problems in less developed countries. It is sold for $6.75 per year by the Superintendent of Documents, Government Printing Office, Washington, DC 20402/202-783-3238. For additional information, contact: Editor of *Development Digest,* Office of Policy Development and Program Review, Bureau for Program and Policy Coordination, Agency for International Development, 320 21st St. N.W., Washington DC 20523/202-632-8382

Economic and Social Data Base

Economic and Social Data System (ESDS) is a statistical data base consisting of development-related information about 180 countries worldwide. The data is in a time series format, and is collected from government agencies and organizations throughout the world. ESDS can be used to retrieve data about a specific country's economy, financial conditions, demography, poverty indicators, labor force, social characteristics; and the population's education, nutrition, health, and food.

The general public can obtain standardized reports, prepared from ESDS data base searches, for a minimal fee from AID-Document Information and Handling Faculty (DIHF). Contact DIHF to obtain a free listing of available reports. The staff at AID will conduct free specialized searches for AID contractors and federal, state, local and foreign government agencies. Contact: Agency for International Development, State Annex 14, 1735 N Lynn Street, Rosslyn, VA 20523/703-235-9183.

Economic Support Fund

The Economic Support Fund provides economic assistance to countries and organizations, on such terms and conditions as the President may determine to promote economic or political stability. The Fund can finance balance of payments assistance; infrastructure and other capital projects; and development programs of more direct benefit to the poor. Contact: Office of Planning and Budgeting, Bureau for Program and Policy Coordination, Agency for International Development, Virginia and 21st St. N.W., Room 375b NS, Washington, DC 20523/202-632-2088

Education Human Resources Program

This program focuses on increasing the number of children receiving quality primary education; improving the organization and delivery of nonformal education programs; developing communications technology to reach rural communities with appropriate information; encouraging low-cost decentralized programs responsive to community needs; and, assisting Less Developed Countries (LDC) governments to mobilize and use local resources in support of rural development programs. Contact: Office of Education, Bureau for Science and Technology, Agency for International Development, SA-18, Room 609, Washington, DC 20523/703-235-8980

Environment and Natural Resources

The *Country Development Strategy Statement* is prepared by each AID mission and describes the environmental situation in each country as part of the development strategy. It is available from the Program Office, Bureau for Science and Technology, A-10, Room 308, SA-18, Washington, DC 20523/703-235-9070. AID also prepares environmental profiles of selected countries to help missions and host countries assess environmental problems and their ability to manage natural resources. Contact: Environmen, Office of Forestry, Environment and Natural Resources, Bureau for Science and Technology, Agency for International Development, International Development Cooperation Agency, Room 509, Washington, DC 20523/703-235-8956.

Excess Property Program

AID is required to use excess property acquired from other federal agencies in its economic development program wherever practicable in lieu of the procurement of new items. Most of the equipment includes heavy construction equipment, vehicles of all types, heavy machinery, electrical generation equipment, and medical equipment and supplies. This program is not only economical but it also assists eligible recipients (friendly countries, international organizations, and registered private and voluntary organizations) to purchase property with their own resources. For additional information, contact: Government Property Resources Division, Directorate for Program and Management Service, Agency for International Development, Headquarters, New Cumberland Army Depot, New Cumberland, PA 17070/717-782-2288, or Washington Liaison Branch, Room 570, SA-14, 703-235-2173

Famine Prevention

Famine Prevention and Freedom from Hunger program supports activities in agriculture, rural development and nutrition. AID makes extensive use of U.S. land grant, sea grant and other qualified colleges and universities to carry out foreign assistance programs. With assistance from the Board for International Food and Agricultural Development AID officials participate in the formulation of agricultural development policy, the design of projects and the use of U.S. agricultural universities in AID programs. Legislation also provides for "Collaborative Research Support Programs" to enable U.S. institutions and those from less-developed countries to work together on projects to benefit both the less-developed countries and U.S. agriculture. Contact: Title XII, Research University Relations, Food and Nutrition, Agency for International Development, Room 309, ST-RUR, Washington, DC 20523/703-235-8930.

Food for Peace (PL 480)

The Food for Peace program draws upon the abundant production of American farmers to provide food aid for primarily humanitarian and development purposes to poor countries. Food aid may be provided directly to friendly governments or channeled through private voluntary agencies, the World Food Program (United Nations) and the Food and Agriculture Organization. Food for Peace resources can support a variety of programs such as increasing the availability of farm credit, providing price incentives and improving on-farm storage and distribution facilities (Title I). The law also authorizes donations of food for emergency/disaster relief and for programs to help needy people through maternal health, child feeding activities, and food-for-work and other programs designed to alleviate the causes of the need for food assistance. Contact: Food for Peace, Bureau for Food for Peace and Voluntary Assistance, Agency for International Development, Room 402, SA-8, Washington, DC 20523/703-235-9210.

Foreign Currency Programs

Participant training programs enable participants from one country to train in another more developed country. Contact: Office of International Training, Directorate for Human Resources, Bureau of Science and Technology, Agency for International Development, SA-16, Room 209, 1621 North Kent Street, Arlington, VA 20523/703-235-1853.

Foreign Service Retirement and Disability

AID career foreign service employees may become participants in the Foreign Service Retirement and Disability Fund. For additional information, contact: Office of Personnel Management, Agency for International Development, International Development Cooperation Agency, Room 300, Washington, DC 20523/202-632-9608.

Freedom of Information Act Requests

For Freedom of Information Act requests, contact: Information Office, Office of Public Affairs, Agency for International Development, International Development Cooperation Agency, Room 2738, Washington, DC 20523/202-632-9614.

Health

The aim of the health program is to increase access by less developed country populations to preventive and curative health care, family planning and nutrition services; to increase access to use of safe water and adequate sanitation; to reduce debilitating tropical diseases, malnutrition, diarrheal infections, measles and other preventable diseases; and to increase the capacities of less developed countries to manage their health resources. Health, population and nutrition officers around the world help host governments identify and address health problems. Contact: Office of Health, Bureau for Science and Technology, Agency for International Development, Room 709, SA-18, Washington, DC 20523/703-235-8926.

Housing Guarantee Program

The Housing Guarantee Program helps create and organize financing for housing in developing countries for families earning below the median urban income. Under this program, AID guarantees repayment to private U.S. lenders who finance AID approved housing for low-income families. Some of the programs include upgrading squatter settlements through the provision of sewerage, potable water, electricity, and credit for home improvement and low-cost, expandable core housing units. Contact: Office for Housing and Urban Programs, Bureau for Private Enterprise, Agency for International Development, 1875 Connecticut Avenue, Washington, DC 20523/202-632-9637.

Human Rights

The Administrator of AID is responsible for implementing the statutory and policy guidelines for promoting human rights in its bilateral country programs. In consultation with the Assistant Secretary of State for Human Rights and Humanitarian Affairs, the Administrator determines the eligibility of countries to receive foreign assistance and how programs will be formulated to benefit needy people and promote human rights in countries violating internationally recognized human rights. Proposed assistance to such countries is brought before the Interdepartmental Group of Human Rights and Foreign Economic Assistance, chaired by the Deputy Secretary of State. Contact: Office of the Administrator, Agency for International Development, 320 21st St. N.W., Room 5942, Washington, DC 20523/202-632-9620.

International Disaster Assistance

The United States alone maintains a permanent, comprehensive disaster relief capability to assist other countries. The program tries to assure emergency relief within an international context; in-country coordination through AID mission staffs; early assessment by special teams as needed; experienced AID specialists to assist at disaster sites; and regional stockpiles which shorten emergency response time. Contact: Office of U.S. Foreign Disaster Assistance, Agency for International Development, Main State Department Building, Room 1262A, Washington, DC 20903/202-632-8924.

Library

This center has an extensive collection of program and technical information concerning development assistance and AID research programs. A project data base is also available. The library is open to the public but advance notification is advisable. Contact: Library, Bureau for Program and Policy Coordination, Agency for International Development, Room 105, SA-18, State Department Building, Annex 18, Washington, DC 20523/703-235-1000.

Library of Statistical Publications

In addition to automated data banks, Economic and Social Data Services maintains a library of printed data consisting of statistical publications obtained directly from individual country government offices. The library also includes major statistical yearbooks from international organizations and the series of country economic and financial reports published by the World Bank and the International Monetary Fund. Contact: Center for Development Information and Evaluation, Bureau for Program and Policy Coordination,

Agency for International Development, Room 621, SA-14, Washington, DC 20523/703-235-9183.

Macro Economic and Social Data Bank

The Economic and Social Data Services Division provides quantitative indicators of economic and social development in lesser developed countries that are relevant to AID's policy, program and reporting needs. The two types of data bases include macro or country-level data and micro household level data. Contact: Center for Development Information and Evaluation, Bureau for Program and Policy Coordination, Agency for International Development, Room 509, SA-14, Washington, DC 20523/703-235-9170

Multilateral Development Banks

AID advises both the Secretary of the Treasury and the U.S. representatives to the multi-lateral development banks on development programs and policies, and on each development project of the banks. Contact: Donor Coordination, Bureau for Program and Policy Coordination, Agency for International Development, 320 21st St. N.W., Room 3637, Washington, DC 20523/202-632-8249.

Policy and Budget

The Office of Policy and Budget Review has a central role in a wide range of areas of economic relations between the United States and the developing world, including U.S. bilateral development assistance programs, U.S. participation in the multilateral development institutions, and the effects of U.S. international trade and financial policies on the economic development prospects of developing countries. IDCA focuses special attention on a few critically important elements of the process of economic development, including agriculture, energy and human resources. Contact: Bureau for Program and Policy Coordination, Agency for International Development, 320 21st St. N.W., Room 3758, PPC-PB, Washington, DC 20523/202-632-0482.

Population Planning

The population planning program aims to reduce population growth rates that seriously impede economic and social development; and to provide families with effective options in choosing the number and spacing of their children. The program stresses:

Participation of the local community, including women's groups; training of outreach workers, especially in rural areas; effective techniques of communication about family planning to families and communities; and combination of family planning with other programs such as health and nutrition wherever appropriate;

Supplying contraceptives and other family planning commodities;

Country-specific analysis to encourage LDC adoption of informed, comprehensive population policies;

Experimenting with new ways to increase acceptability and cost effectiveness of delivery systems tailored to the needs and existing services of specific country settings;

Technical assistance to LDCs to establish improved management programs and evaluation systems;

Training and equipping LDC physicians, family planning program managers, nurses, midwives, paramedicals and other auxiliary workers with respect to family planning and reproductive health under programs that emphasize local and regional circumstances;

Developing and improving new means of fertility control, and assessing the safety, effectiveness and acceptability of a variety of contraceptive techniques;

Survey, census and vital registration projects and the data analysis needed to evaluate population trends and the impact of family planning programs;

Supporting studies and analyses of the determinants and consequences of fertility, leading to practical program applications.

Total population data are mid-year estimates based on recent census with interpretations of subsequent fertility and mortality trends. Contact: Office of Population, Agency for International Development, Room 511, ST-POP, SA18, Washington, DC 20523/703-235-8117.

Private and Voluntary Organizations
AID provides grants to private and voluntary organizations to help them with their programs of aid to rural and urban poor people. The grants support programs in agriculture, rural development, health, family planning, education and a variety of grassroots collaborative efforts with local groups. The office has information on voluntary agencies such as what they do, and statements of support, revenue, and expenditures. Contact: Office of Private and Voluntary Cooperation, Bureau for Food for Peace and Voluntary Assistance, Agency for International Development, Room 246, SA8, Washington, DC 20523/703-235-1623.

Procurement
For AID procurement information, contact: Office Management Operations, Directorate for Program and Management Services, Agency for International Development, 320 21st St. N.W., Room 113, SA-8 Washington, DC 20523/202-632-2931

Procurement—Small Business
Information on AID procurement for small and disadvantaged businesses is available. Contact: Office of Small and Disadvantaged Business Utilization, Agency for International Development, International Development Cooperation Agency, Room 647, SA14. Washington, DC 20523/703-235-2333

Program Data
Data on all foreign assistance programs that involve AID and all other government agencies, including bilateral and multilateral programs are available. Contact: Development Information, Evaluation Application and Statistical Analysis, Center for Development Information and Evaluation, Bureau for Program and Policy Coordination, Agency for International Development, Room 621, SA-14, Washington, DC 20523/703-235-9183.

Program Evaluation
Evaluation findings are disseminated through two AID publication series:

AID Program Evaluation Discussion Papers Series; and AID Program Evaluation Report Series.

They cover such topics as livestock in Africa, potable water, use of traditional health systems and labor-intensive rural roads. Contact: Center for Development Information and Evaluation, Bureau for Program and Policy Coordination, Agency for International Development, Room 611, SA-14, Washington, DC 20523/703-235-3860

Public Affairs
The Public Affairs Office provides information and the annual Development Policy Statement which outlines IDCA's international economic development priorities and agenda for the coming year. Contact: Public Affairs, 320 21st St. N.W., Room 4898, Washington, DC 20523/202-632-4200.

Public Affairs Publications
The following publications are available:

AID's Challenge—describes the purpose of AID and its programs. Available for free by contacting Office of Public Inquiries (XA/PI), Agency for International Development, Washington, DC 20523/202-632-1850.

AID Highlights —free quarterly newsletter available on a subscription basis. Each issue focuses on a specific AID program. Publication is of interest to the general public and opinion makers. Available by contacting Managing Editor (XA/P), AID Highlights, Agency for International Development, Washington, DC 20523

Facts about AID —two-page summary of AID programs. Available for free by contacting Office of Public Inquiries (XA/PI), Agency for International Development, Washington, DC 20523/202-632-1850.

Frontlines —Monthly newspaper discussing AID's programs and policies. Available only to agency staff and retirees. Copies of the newspaper are retained in the Department of State's library.

Horizons —quarterly subscription of interest to academics and development professionals. Focuses on sources of development funding and the recipients of this funding. Available for free to qualified professionals by contacting Horizons Magazine, Agency for International Development, Washington, DC 20523.

Who to Contact for Press on Development —informs the

user who to contact in the media on development issues. Available for free by contacting Office of Press Relations (XA/PR), Agency for International Development, Washington, DC 20523/202-632-4274.

Contact: Office of Public Affairs, Agency for International Development, 320 21st St. N.W., Room 4894, Washington, DC 20523/202-632-4330.

Sahel Development Program
Sahel occupies an area 2/3 the size of the United States and has a population of 30 million people. It encompasses the eight states of Chad, Mali, Mauritania, Niger, Senegal, Upper Volta, The Gambia, and Cape Verde and is one of the world's poorest regions and faces recurring drought. The program, through a multi-donor approach, promotes self-sustaining development and food self-sufficiency. Contact: Sahel Desk, Bureau for Africa, Agency for International Development, Room 3491, Washington, DC 20523/202-632-0990.

Speakers Program
AID officers will address meetings, brief small groups and serve as resource specialists at conferences. Topics discussed include: Third World economic and social development, agricultural, nutritional and health services, world hunger, diaster relief, and rural and urban development. Contact: Speakers, Office of Public Affairs, Agency for International Development, Room 4898, 320 21st St. N.W., Washington, DC 20523/202-632-4213.

Urban Development
AID projects for urban development include introducing pilot programs to more effectively involve urban areas in development; assisting urban-oriented organizations and government agencies in planning, financing and providing basic social and economic services to the urban poor—

i.e., shelter, water, and income earning opportunities; and extending technical assistance to developing countries' programs providing adequate shelter and related services such as water for the urban poor. Contact: Office of Housing and Urban Programs, Bureau for Private Enterprise, Agency for International Development, 1875 Connecticut Avenue, Room 625, Washington, DC 20523/202-632-9637.

Women in Development
"Women-in-development" projects are designed to benefit women only. They help women gain access to resources and to acquire and use new skills. They also take account of women's needs and participation in larger AID programs. The Office promotes, assists and coordinates women in development activities and projects. Agency-wide seminars, debriefings and workshops are held to exchange program and project information and experiences. Rosters of women-in-development specialists are published. This office also collects, publishes and distributes materials through its Resource Center and provides assistance to individuals and groups working on Agency projects. Some of these materials include mission-produced studies, research reports, project documents, specially commissioned papers and relevant publications. Contact: Office of Women in Development, Bureau for Program and Policy Coordination, Agency for International Development, 320 21st ST. N.W., Room 3243, Washington, DC 20523/202-632-3992.

How Can the Agency for International Development (AID) Help You?
To determine how AID can help you, contact: Public Affairs, Agency for International Development, 320 21st. St. N.W., Washington, DC 20523/202-632-1850.

American Battle Monuments Commission

5127 Pulaski Building, Washington, DC 20314/202-272-0536

Established: March 4, 1923
Budget: $10,696,000
Employees: 387

Mission: Responsible for the design, construction and permanent maintenance of military cemeteries and memorials on foreign soil, as well as for certain memorials on American soil.

Major Sources of Information

American Memorials and Overseas Cemeteries
This free pamphlet outlines the Commission's functions and lists, with brief descriptions and directions, the cemetery memorials and monuments under its care. For further information, contact: American Battle Monuments Commission, 20 Massachusetts Ave. N.W., Room 5127, Washington, DC 20314/202-272-0533.

Freedom of Information Requests
For Freedom of Information Act requests, contact: Freedom of Information, American Battle Monuments Commission, Room 5127, 20 Massachusetts Ave. N.W., Washington, DC 20014/202-272-0533.

How Can the American Battle Monuments Commission Help You?
To determine how this agency can help you, contact: American Battle Monuments Commission, Room 5127, 20 Massachusetts Ave. N.W., Washington, DC 20314/202-272-0533.

Appalachian Regional Commission

1666 Connecticut Ave. N.W., Washington, DC 20235/202-673-7968

Established: 1965
Budget: $2,900,000
Employees: 12

Mission: Concerned with the economic, physical and social development of the 13-state Appalachian region, which includes parts of Alabama, Georgia, Kentucky, Maryland, Mississippi, New York, North Carolina, Ohio, Pennsylvania, South Carolina, Tennessee, Virginia, and all of West Virginia.

Major Sources of Information

Appalachian Regional Commission Library
The Library emphasizes information on the socio-economic aspects of the 13 Appalachian states. Contact: Library, Appalachian Regional Commission, 6th Floor, 1666 Connecticut Ave. N.W., Washington, DC 20235/202-673-7835.

Freedom of Information Requests
For Freedom of Information Act Requests, contact: General Counsel, Appalachian Regional Commission, Room 501, 1666 Connecticut Ave. N.W., Washington, DC 20235/202-673-7871.

Grants

The programs described below are for sums of money which are given by the federal government to initiate and stimulate new or improved activities or to sustain on-going services:

Appalachian Child Development
Objectives: To provide child development services in underserved areas throughout the region which meet the needs of industry and its employees.
Eligibility: Public and private nonprofit organizations are eligible for project grants, if the projects are consistent with the state plan and priorities.

Range of Financial Assistance: $24,763 to $1,433,461.
Contact: Executive Director, Appalachian Regional Commission, 1666 Connecticut Ave. N.W., Washington, DC 20235/202-673-7874.

Appalachian Development Highway System
Objectives: To provide a highway system which, in conjunction with other federally aided highways, will open up areas with development potential within the Appalachian region where commerce and communication have been inhibited by lack of adequate access.
Eligibility: State governments only are eligible for development highways within their Appalachian portions.
Range of Financial Assistance: Not specified.
Contact: Executive Director, Appalachian Regional Commission, 1666 Connecticut Ave. N.W., Washington, DC 20235/202-673-7874.

Appalachian Health Programs
Objectives: To make primary health care accessible, reduce infant mortality, and recruit needed health manpower in designated "health-shortage" areas.
Eligibility: States, and through the states, health systems agencies, local governments and nonprofit

organizations. Construction and operating grants are available only for publicly owned facilities or for facilities owned by public or private nonprofit organizations and not themselves operated for profit.

Range of Financial Assistance: $500 to $516,257.

Contact: Executive Director, Appalachian Regional Commission, 1666 Connecticut Ave. N.W., Washington, DC 20235/202-673-7874.

Appalachian Housing Project Planning Loan, Technical Assistance Grant and Site Development and Off-Site Improvement Grant State Appalachian Housing Programs

Objectives: To stimulate low- and moderate-income housing construction and rehabilitation, and to assist in developing site and off-site improvements for low- and moderate-income housing in the Appalachian Region.

Eligibility: Private nonprofit organizations, limited dividend organizations, cooperative organizations, or public bodies.

Range of Financial Assistance: $300,000 to $1,200,000.

Contact: Executive Director, Appalachian Regional Commission, 1666 Connecticut Ave. N.W., Washington, DC 20235/202-673-7874.

Appalachian Local Access Roads

Objectives: To provide access to industrial, commercial, educational, recreational, residential and related transportation facilities which directly or indirectly relate to the improvement of the areas determined by the states to have significant development potential.

Eligibility: States and, through the states, public bodies and private groups within Appalachia.

Range of Financial Assistance: $9,000 to $1,130,250.

Contact: Executive Director, Appalachian Region Commission, 1666 Connecticut Ave. N.W., Washington, DC 20235/202-673-7874.

Appalachian Local Development District Assistance

Objectives: To provide planning and development resources in multi-county areas; to help develop the technical competence essential to sound development assistance; and to meet the objectives stated under the program entitled Appalachian Regional Development.

Eligibility: Multi-county organizations certified by the State.

Range of Financial Assistance: $7,500 to $121,000

Contact: Executive Director, Appalachian Regional Commission, 1666 Connecticut Ave. N.W., Washington, DC 20235/202-673-7874.

Appalachian Mine Area Restoration

Objectives: To further the economic develop-

ment of the region by rehabilitating areas presently damaged by deleterious mining practices and by controlling or abating mine drainage pollution.

Eligibility: States and, through the states, public bodies or private nonprofit entities organized under state law to be used for public recreation, conservation, community facilities, or public housing owning strip-mined land in need of restoration. The states are eligible to apply for assistance to seal and fill voids in abandoned coal mines, plan and execute projects for the extinguishment and control of underground and outcrop mine fires, seal abandoned oil and gas wells, and control or abate mine drainage pollution.

Range of Financial Assistance: Not specified.

Contact: Executive Director, Appalachian Regional Commission, 1666 Connecticut Ave. N.W., Washington, DC 20235/202-673-7874.

Appalachian Special Transportation Related Planning, Research and Demonstration Program

Objectives: To encourage the preparation of action-oriented plans and programs which reinforce and enhance other transportation, but particularly highway, investments.

Eligibility: State and local governments, and nonprofit agencies.

Range of Financial Assistance: $1,260 to $158,000.

Contact: Executive Director, Appalachian Regional Commission, 1666 Connecticut Ave. N.W., Washington, DC, 20235/202-673-7874.

Appalachian State Research, Technical Assistance, and Demonstration Projects

Objectives: To expand the knowledge of the region to the fullest extent possible by means of state-sponsored research (including investigations, studies, technical assistance and demonstration projects) in order to assist the Commission in accomplishing the objectives of the Act.

Eligibility: Appalachian states alone or in combination with other Appalachian states, local public bodies and state instrumentalities.

Range of Financial Assistance: $2,500 to $80,000

Contact: Executive Director, Appalachian Regional Commission, 1666 Connecticut Ave. N.W., Washington, DC 20235/202-673-7874.

Appalachian Supplements to Federal Grant-in-Aid (Community Development)

Objectives: To meet the basic needs of local areas and assist in providing community development opportunities by funding such development facilities as water and sewer systems, sewage treatment plants, recreation centers, industrial sites and other community development facilities. Grants may supplement other federal grants or, when sufficient federal funds are unavailable, funds may be provided entirely by this program.

Eligibility: States, and through the states, their subdivisions and instrumentalities and private non-profit agencies.

Range of Financial Assistance: $9,000 to $800,000.

Contact: Executive Director, Appalachian Regional Commission, 1666 Connecticut Ave. N.W., Washington, DC 20235/202-673-7874.

Appalachian Vocational and Other Education Facilities and Operations

Objectives: To provide the people of the region with the basic facilities, equipment, and operating funds for training and education necessary to obtain employment at their best capability for available job opportunities, and to meet the objectives stated under the program entitled Appalachian Regional Development.

Eligibility: States, and through the states, public educational institutions and private postsecondary institutions. Most of the proposals are for regional vocational-technical centers serving multicounty areas as well as several school districts. Education demonstration projects must be administered through a public body and be areawide in scope.

Range of Financial Assistance: $7,169 to $600,000.

Contact: Executive Director, Appalachian Regional Commission, 1666 Connecticut Ave. N.W., Washington, DC 20235/202-673-7874.

Publications

Appalachian Regional Commission Annual Report provides financial statistics, activities and programs over the past year. Other publications provide information on economic development activities in the region. Contact: News and Public Affairs, Appalachian Regional Commission, Room 328, 1666 Connecticut Ave. N.W., Washington, DC 20235/202-673-7968.

How Can the Appalachian Regional Commission Help You?

To determine how this agency can help you, contact: News and Public Affairs, Appalachian Regional Commission, Room 328, 1666 Connecticut Ave. N.W., Washington, DC 20235/202-673-7968.

Board for International Broadcasting

Suite 1100, 1201 Connecticut Avenue N.W., Washington, DC
20036/202-254-8040

Established: October 19, 1973
Budget: $120,140,000
Employees: 8

Mission: Oversees the operation of Radio Liberty, which broadcasts to the Union of Soviet Socialist Republics and Radio Free Europe, which broadcasts to Poland, Romania, Czechoslovakia, Hungary and Bulgaria.

Major Sources of Information

Freedom of Information Act
For information on Freedom of Information Act requests, contact: Board for International Broadcasting, 1210 Connecticut Ave. N.W., Suite 1100, Washington, DC 20036/202-254-8040.

Radio Free Europe-Radio Liberty Information and Publications
Information and annual reports detailing the programs provided and the areas covered by Radio Free Europe and Radio Liberty are available.

Contact: Board for International Broadcasting, 1210 Connecticut Ave. N.W., Suite 1100, Washington, DC 20036/202-254-8040.

How Can the Board for International Broadcasting Help You?
To determine how this agency may be of help to you, contact: Board for International Broadcasting, 1210 Connecticut Ave. N.W., Suite 1100, Washington, DC 20036/202-254-8040.

Central Intelligence Agency

Washington, DC 20505/703-351-7676

Established: 1947
Budget: Classified
Employees: Classified

Mission: Collects, evaluates and produces foreign intelligence. Advises the National Security Council on intelligence activities. Produces and disseminates foreign intelligence relating to the national security, including foreign political, economic, scientific, technical, military, geographic and sociological intelligence, to meet the needs of the President, the National Security Council, and other elements of the U.S. government. Collects, produces and disseminates intelligence on foreign aspects of narcotics production and trafficking. Conducts counterintelligence activities outside the United States and coordinates counterintelligence activities conducted outside the United States by other agencies within the intelligence community.

Major Sources of Information

Career and Recruitment Information
Career Information packets are available from the CIA. So that staff can tailor a packet to your needs, your request should include information about your background, experience, and the type of position you would be interested in. The CIA operates a recruitment recorded message number 703-351-2028 with information about job opportunities and application procedures. A staffmember will come on the line at the end of the recording to answer any questions you may have. Contact: Office of Personnel, P.O. Box 1925, Department A, Room 6-03, Washington, DC 20013/703-351-2028.

China—Administrative Atlas
The Administrative Atlas of the People's Republic of China depicts the administrative changes which have occurred in this Republic since 1949. Changes are presented in detailed maps of each province. Pronunciation guides are included in the atlas, and a list of the administrative divisions within the

provinces accompanies each map. Available for $8.00 from: Superintendent of Documents, U.S. Government Printing Office, Washington, DC 20402/202-783-3238.

Country Intelligence Reports and Wall Maps
The CIA produces reports on communist and non-communist countries throughout the world. The reports contain political, statistical, and economical information in subjects such as agriculture, metals, minerals, natural gas, oil, and materials. Information is also provided about the political, economic and military structures of the country. These reports, as well as reference directories, wall charts and other CIA materials, are available from a variety of places, each charging different fees. For a listing of available materials, contact:

Superintendent of Documents, U.S. Government Printing Office (GPO), Washington, DC 20402/202-783-3238. GPO has the most limited selection, but as a rule its publications are the cheapest.

Library of Congress, Photoduplicating Service, Washington, DC 20540/202-287-5650. This office maintains a copy of all publicly available CIA materials and, for a duplicating fee, staff will send you a copy of what you need. *DOCEX,* a 15-page listing of available CIA publications, is available for $8.00 from this office.

National Technical Information Service (NTIS), 5285 Port Royal Road, Springfield, VA 22161/703-487-4780. Upon request NTIS must send you a copy of any government document released to the public. As it produces limited copies of publications, its items are more expensive than GPO's.

Economic and Energy Indicators
Published every two weeks, this provides general indicators for major developed countries. Economic coverage includes: industrial production, GNP, consumer prices, money supply, unemployment rate, agricultural prices. Energy coverage includes: world crude oil production, inland oil consumption of "big 7", crude oil reports, OPEC, and crude oil official price. It contains mostly charts and is available for $70 a year. National Technical Information Service, 5285 Port Royal Road, Springfield, VA 221/61/703-487-4650.

Economic Statistics
The CIA produces the *Handbook of Economic Statistics* which provides statistics for all communist countries as well as selected non-communist countries. Statistics are provided about: general economics, foreign trade and aid, energy, transportation, minerals and metals, chemicals and rubber; manufacturing goods and forestry, and agriculture. Published annually, the Handbook is available for $7.50 from GPO and $15.50 from NTIS. Contact: GPO-Superintendent of Documents, U.S. Government Printing Office, Washington, DC 20402/202-783-3238 or NTIS-National Technical Information Service, 5285 Port Royal Road, Springfield, VA 22181/703-487-4650.

Government Leaders Worldwide
Published monthly, *Briefs of State and Cabinet Members of Foreign Governments* lists the names and positions of top leaders in all governments throughout the world. Annual subscription is $45 and single issues are available for $8. Contact: National Technical Information Service, 5285 Port Royal Road, Springfield, VA 22181/703-487-4630.

Indian Ocean Atlas
This book provides a wide variety of economic, historical, and cultural data in addition to the usual geographic information. It is designed as an introduction and general reference aid for those interested in the natural environment, resources, shipping, and political relationships of the Indian Ocean and its islands. Available for $8.50 from: Superintendent of Documents, U.S. Government Printing Office, Washington, DC 20402/202-783-3238.

Information about the CIA
Free booklets describing the CIA and intelligence gathering are available by writing to: Public Affairs, Central Intelligence Agency, Washington, DC 20505

Intelligence Maps
The CIA produces multicolored general reference maps and wall charts on communist and non-communist countries worldwide. The maps indentify a country's major roads, population density, major industries, locations of natural resources, and other specific features. Some maps are on specific topics such as clothing factories in China. They are available in a variety of sizes. GPO sells many of the maps for $3.50 and NTIS for $7.50. Contact: Superintendent of Documents, U.S. Government Printing Office, Washington, DC 20402/202-783-3238 or National Technical Information Service, 5285 Port Royal Road, Springfield, VA 22161/703-487-4630.

International Energy Statistics
Each month the CIA releases *International Energy Statistical Review* which provides statistical data about a variety of topics pertaining to international energy, particularly aspects of the petroleum and natural gas industry. Areas covered include the free world, OPEC, OAPEC, OECD, selected developed countries, Western Europe, China, Russia and Eastern Europe. It contains many tables, charts and graphs. Yearly subscription is $45 and single issues are available for $6. Contact: National Technical Information Service, 5285 Port Royal Road, Springfield, VA 22161/703-487-4630.

Status of the World's Nations
This geographic bulletin, revised in September 1980, and a separate map entitled "Political Map of the World" provides country name, United Nations membership, capital, population, area, dependencies and areas of special sovereignty, date of independence (since 1943) for nations of the world. Cost is $3.25. Contact: Superintendent of Documents, U.S. Government Printing Office, Washington, DC 20402/202-783-3238.

Subscription Services
Each year the CIA declassifies 50 to 100 reports and more than 100 maps. Anyone can subscribe through either of the services below:

Reference Aid Series—Available from the Library of Congress, this service provides subscribers with copies of all declassified CIA reports, reference directories, wall charts and maps—as soon as they are released by the CIA. The service includes more than 130 titles, both monographs and serials, and subscribers receive all back issues still available. Annual subscription fee is $300. Contact: CIA Subscriptions, Documents Expediting Project, Exchange and Gift Division, Library of Congress, Washington, DC 20540/202-287-9527.

Standing Order Series—This NTIS service provides subscribers with all CIA materials, in selected categories, as they are released to the public. Selected categories are: Communist Countries, Non-Communist Countries, USSR, China, Charts Only, Maps Only. Subscribers must establish an NTIS Deposit Account and they are then billed according to materials received. Contact: NTIS, 5285 Port Royal Road, Springfield, VA 22161/703-487-4630.

USSR Agriculture Atlas
This book examines Soviet agriculture, its role in their economy, the policies that govern it, and how it compares with the U.S. Cost is $4.75. Contact: Superintendent of Documents, U.S. Government Printing Office, Washington, DC 20402/202-783-3238.

Wall Charts
The CIA has prepared wall charts showing the government structure of nations throughout the world. Many charts contain pictures of government leaders. Contact: Superintendent of Documents, U.S. Government Printing Office, Wash-ington, DC 20402/202-783-3238 or National Technical Information Service, 5285 Port Royal Road, Springfield, VA 22161/703-487-4630.

World Factbook
Each year the CIA issues a *World Factbook* which provides information about a variety of countries. Examples of country facts include: size, natural resources, population, type of government, government leaders, elections, international organizations to which country belongs, military budget and size, data about number of railroads, airfields, telephones, and more. The book is available for $10 from GPO or $23.50 from NTIS. Contact: GPO-Superintendent of Documents, U.S. Government Printing Office, Washington, DC 20402/202-783-3238 or NTIS-National Technical Information Service, 5285 Port Royal Road, Springfield, VA 22162/703-487-4630.

How Can the CIA Help You?
To determine how the CIA can help you, contact: Public Affairs, Central Intelligence Agency, Washington, DC 20505/703-351-7676.

Commission of Fine Arts

708 Jackson Pl. N.W., Washington, DC 20006/202-566-1066

Established: May 17, 1910
Budget: $328,000
Employees: 7

Mission: Supplies artistic advice relating to the appearance of Washington, DC; reviews the plans for all public buildings, parks, and other architectural elements in the Capital and for private structures in certain areas of the City.

Major Sources of Information

A Brief History of the Commission of Fine Arts—1910–1980
This publication provides a brief history of the Commission activities, highlighting some of its major accomplishments, including the National Gallery of Art, the Jefferson Memorial, Lafayette Square, the Kennedy Center, and some recent projects. The booklet also includes the legislation related to fine arts and preservation, a list of former and present Commission members, and a list of its publications. Contact: Commission of Fine Arts, 708 Jackson Pl. N.W., Washington, DC 20006/202-566-1066.

How Can the Commission of Fine Arts Help You?
To determine how this agency may be of help to you, contact: Commission of Fine Arts, 708 Jackson Pl. N.W., Washington, DC 20006/202-566-1066.

Commission on Civil Rights

1121 Vermont Ave. N.W., Washington, DC 20425/202-376-8177

Established: 1957
Budget: $11,981,000
Employees: 237

Mission: Advances the cause of equal opportunity; holds public hearings and collects and studies information on discrimination or denials of equal protection of the laws because of race, color, religion, sex, age, handicap, national origin, or in the administration of justice; performs factfinding efforts on voting rights, enforcement of federal civil rights laws, and quality of opportunity in education, employment and housing.

Major Sources of Information

Civil Rights Complaints
For complaints alleging denials of civil rights, contact: Office of Federal Civil Rights Evaluation, Commission on Civil Rights, Room 606, 1121 Vermont Ave. N.W., Washington, DC 20425/202-376-8514

Clearinghouse Services, Civil Rights and Sex Discrimination Complaints
The objective of the Clearinghouse is to communicate civil rights information to the public with emphasis on how federal programs and policy can be used to advance equal opportunities for persons who are subjected to discrimination because of age or handicap, and for minority citizens and women; to receive and refer complaints alleging denial of civil rights because of color, race, religion, sex, age, handicap or national origin; to receive, investigate and refer complaints alleging denial of voting rights. Contact: Commission on Civil Rights, 1121 Vermont Ave. N.W., Washington, DC 20425/202-376-8116 (TTY phone, 202-376-2683 for deaf/hearing impaired persons).

Freedom of Information Requests
For Freedom of Information Act requests, contact: Solicitor Unit, Commission on Civil Rights, Room 710, 1121 Vermont Ave. N.W., Washington, DC 20425/202-376-8339

Library
The Robert S. Rankin Civil Rights Library is open to the public. The staff provides free research assistance to the general public. A monthly list of new acquisitions to the collection may be obtained by request. The collection contains material on voting rights, employment, women and minority issues, aging and handicapped discrimination and civil rights education. Contact: Robert S. Rankin Library, Commission on Civil Rights, Room 709, 1121 Vermont Ave. N.W., Washington, DC 20425/202-376-8110

Publications
The following publications are free from the Commission on Civil Rights, 621 N. Payne St. Alexandria, VA 22314/703-557-1794:

Last Hired, First Fired: Layoffs and Civil Rights—examines the effects of seniority as applied to layoffs of minority and female workers; includes findings and recommendations.
Window Dressing on the Set: Women and Minorities in

Television—assesses the portrayal of women and minorities in television network programming and their employment at television stations; contains findings and recommendations.

The Age Discrimination Study—a study of unreasonable discrimination on the basis of age in the administration of programs or activities receiving federal financial assistance; based on hearings in Denver, Miami, San Francisco and Washington, D.C.

Civil Rights Directory—lists private and public individuals and organizations concerned with civil rights at local, state, federal, and national levels.

Civil Rights Brochure—explains functions of the Commission on Civil Rights.

A Guide to Federal Laws and Regulations Prohibiting Sex Discrimination (revised edition)—summarizes federal laws, policies, and regulations banning sex discrimination and tells how to file complaints.

Mortgage Money: Who Gets It?—a case study of discrimination against minorities and women in the granting of home mortgages in Hartford, CT.

Using the Voting Rights Act—explains how the Voting Rights Act of 1965, as amended in 1975, works. Contains lists of areas covered by the new language provisions, as well as text of the amended act.

Getting Uncle Sam to Enforce Your Civil Rights—a handbook describing where and how to file a discrimination complaint with the Federal Government.

Women—Still in Poverty—describes the operation of the welfare system, job training programs, employment discrimination, and child care availability and their effects on women.

Fair Textbooks: A Resource Guide—lists materials aimed at reducing biases in textbooks, organizations, publishers, and their guidelines, state education departments, state statutes, procedures, and guidelines, and conferences. Materials are identified for grade level, subject matter, and racial, ethnic and gender group, as well as indexed by group.

Civil Rights Digest—a quarterly magazine designed to stimulate ideas and interest on various current issues concerning civil rights.

Catalog of Publications

How Can the Commission on Civil Rights Help You?

To determine how this agency can help you, contact: Commission on Civil Rights, Room 606, 1121 Vermont Ave. N.W., Washington, DC 20425/202-376-8177

Commodity Futures Trading Commission

2033 K St. N.W., Washington, DC 20581/202-254-8630

Established: 1974
Budget: $22,881,000
Employees: 550

Mission: Regulates trading on the 11 U.S. futures exchanges; regulates the activities of commodity exchange members, public brokerage houses (futures Commission merchants), Commission-registered futures advisers and commodity pool operators; ensures that the futures trading process is fair and that it protects both the rights of customers and the financial integrity of the marketplace; approves the rules under which an exchange proposes to operate and monitors exchange enforcement of those rules; reviews the terms of proposed futures contracts, and registers companies and individuals who handle customer funds or give trading advice; and protects the public by enforcing rules that require that customer funds be kept in bank accounts separate from accounts maintained by firms for their own use, and that such customer accounts be marked to present market value at the close of trading each day. Commodity Futures Trading Commission, Room 701, 2033 K St. N.W., Washington, DC 20581/202-254-9703.

Major Sources of Information

Commodity Futures Market Reports
These reports provide traders and members of the public information about the futures markets to assist them in understanding the markets. Contact: Office of Communications and Education Services, Commodity Futures Trading Commission, 2033 K St. N.W., Washington, DC 20581/202-254-8630

Commodity Futures Traders' Registration
Companies and individuals involved in futures trading, including futures commission brokers, commodity trading advisors, and commodity pool operators must register with the Commodity Futures Trading Commission. The office will confirm the registration of a firm or an employee and will advise if the CFTC has any prior or pending legal actions against them. Contact: Audit and Registration Unit, Division of Trading and Markets, Commodity Futures Trading Commission, Room 741, 2033 K St. N.W., Washington, DC 20581/202-254-9703. For a $25 directory of all firms involved in futures trading contact: National Futures Association, 200 West Madison, Suite 1400, Chicago, IL 60606/312-781-1300.

Commodity Futures Trading Commission Library
The Library collection emphasizes law, economics, business and commodities. It is open to the public for limited hours. Contact: Library, Commodity Futures Trading Commission, 5th Floor, 2033 K St. Washington, DC 20581/202-254-5901.

Commodity Research

This office conducts or sponsors long-term research on the functioning of futures markets. It also develops materials and programs explaining the Commodity Futures Trading Commission and its responsibilities. A list of publications is available. Contact: Office of Communications and Education Services, Commodity Futures Trading Commission, 2033 K St. N.W., Washington, DC 20581/202-254-8630

Enforcement

Customer complaints are an important source of information about possible violations and assist the Commodity Futures Trading Commission in its enforcement and regulatory functions. Persons who believe they may have been cheated or defrauded in their trading transactions should advise the Commission so that it may take appropriate action. The Commission also provides a customer reparations forum where monetary awards may be directed to any person who can prove damage received as a result of violation of the Commodity Exchange Act in dealing with persons or companies registered with the Commission. Information on futures trading is also available to the general public upon request. Contact: Division of Enforcement, Reparations Unit, Commodity Futures Trading Commission, 2033 K St. N.W., Washington, DC 20581/202-254-3067

Freedom of Information Requests

For Freedom of Information Act requests, contact: Office of the Secretariat, Commodity Futures Trading Commission, 2033 K St. N.W., Washington, DC 20581/202-254-3382.

Monitoring Commodity Economics

This office reviews proposed futures contracts to determine whether their trade would serve a valid economic purpose. It analyzes the economic ramifications of Commodity Futures Trading Commission policies and regulations. It also monitors trading on all contract markets to detect actual or potential manipulations, congestion and price distortion. Contact: Division of Economics and Analysis, Commodity Futures Trading Commission, 2033 K St. N.W., Washington, DC 20581/202-254-3310

Publications

The following publications are free from the Office of Communication and Education Services, Commodity Futures Trading Commission, 2033 K St. N.W., Washington, DC 20581/202-254-7446:

The CFTC (CFTC 100)
Economic Purposes of Futures Trading (CFTC 102)
Farmers, Futures, and Grain Prices (CFTC 103)
Reading Commodity Futures Price Tables (CFTC 104)
Glossary of Some Trade Terms (CFTC 105)
CFTC Futures Facts Sheets: no. 1—CFTC Reports and Offices; no. 2—CFTC Publications and General Bibliography; no. 3—Commodities Traded and Exchange Addresses; no. 4—Visual Aids (Films and Slides); no. 5—Reporting Levels and Speculative Limits
Grain Pricing

Trading and Markets

This office regulates all exchanges on which commodity futures are traded. It also approves all futures contracts traded or exchanged. Contact: Division of Trading and Markets, Commodity Futures Trading Commission, Room 640, 2033 K St. N.W., Washington, DC 20581/202-254-8955

How Can the Commodity Futures Trading Commission Help You?

To determine how the agency can be of help to you, contact: Office of Communication and Education Services, Commodity Futures Trading Commission, 2033 K St. N.W., Washington, DC 20581/202-254-8630.

Consumer Product Safety Commission

1111 18th St. N.W., Washington, DC 20207/202-634-2772

Established: October 27, 1972
Budget: $34,058,000
Employees: 577

Mission: Protects the public against unreasonable risks of injury from consumer products; assists consumers to evaluate the comparative safety of consumer products; develops uniform safety standards; and promotes research and investigation into the causes and prevention of product-related deaths, illnesses, and injuries.

Major Sources of Information

Consumer Deputy Program
This program trains volunteers to obtain marketplace or household survey information for the Consumer Product Safety Commission. The volunteers look for banned products in retail stores, alert retailers to new regulations, and gain product use information from households. Contact: Office of the Secretary, Consumer Product Safety Commission, Room 332, 5401 Westbard Ave, Washington, DC 20207/301-492-6800

Consumer Education Programs
This office prepares programs to inform consumers of standards issued by the Consumer Product Safety Commission, and to alert them to newly discovered hazards. Contact: Office of the Secretary, Consumer Product Safety Commission, Room 332, 5401 Westbard Ave, Washington, DC 20207/301-492-6800

Consumer Product Hotline
This hotline provides information to the public about product recalls and also handles complaints about hazardous products and product defects. The hotline can also be used to obtain free pamphlets and fact sheets. Contact: 800-638-2772

Consumer Product Publications
The U.S. Consumer Product Safety Commission distributes a large number of publications. Publications that can be obtained free of charge are listed under "Publications" in this section. The Commission also has publications for sale through the Consumer Information Center and the Government Printing Office. The following materials may be purchased from the Consumer Information Center:

Think Toy Safety Coloring Book ($0.50)
The Nine Lives of El Gato the Cat ($0.50)
You Should Know About Home Fire Safety ($0.50)
Asbestos in the Home ($2.75)
Little Leon the Lizard Toy Safety Curriculum ($2.25)
What You Should Know About Smoke Detectors ($2.25)

Contact: Consumer Information Center, Pueblo, Colorado 81009.
The following materials may be purchased from the Government Printing Office:

BICYCLES
  A Bicycle Built for You ($2.50)
  Sprocketman (comic book) ($3.00)
CHILDREN'S PRODUCTS
  Baby Care Kit ($4.50)

For Kids Sake...Think Toy Safety ($5.50)

Safety Sampler: Hazards of Children's Products ($3.00)

The Super Sitter (baby sitter's guide) ($2.75)

Toy and Sports Equipment Safety Guide ($2.25)

Little Leon the Lizard—Toy Safety Curriculum ($2.25)

FIRE AND HOME SAFETY

What You Should Know about Smoke Detectors ($2.25)

What You Should Know about Fire Safety ($35.00 for 100 copies)

Asbestos in the Home ($2.75)

POISON PREVENTION

Guide to Teaching Poison Prevention to Kindergarten & Primary ($4.75)

Perils of Pip Preventing Poisoning ($2.75)

Your Home Could be Full of Poisons ($7.00 for 25 copies)

Annotated Bibliography of Toxic Substances ($4.50)

GENERAL INFORMATION ABOUT PRODUCT SAFETY

Product Safety: It's No Accident (Safety planning guide for teachers of Grades K-6) ($2.75)

Handbook and Standard for Manufacturing Safer Consumer Products ($6.00)

Contact: Superintendent of Documents, Government Printing Office, Washington, DC 20402/202-783-3238.

Consumer Products Human Factors Evaluations

The Human Factors Division of the Consumer Product Safety Commission is comprised of multidisciplinary professionals who conduct human factors evaluations of consumer products. Periodic reports are prepared about how man and machine interface to cause accidents. The division will answer questions and provides free copies of its evaluation reports. Contact: Consumer Product Safety Commission, Human Factors Division, 5401 Westbard Avenue, Bethesda, MD 20207/301-492-6468.

Freedom of Information Office

For making a Freedom of Information Act request, contact: Office of the Secretary, Consumer Product Safety Commission, Room 332, 5401 Westbard Ave. Washington, DC 20207/301-492-6800

Hazard Identification and Analysis

This clearinghouse collects, investigates, analyzes and disseminates injury data and information relating to the causes and prevention of death, injury and illness associated with consumer products. It maintains thousands of detailed investigative reports of injuries that have been reported by a nationwide network of hospital emergency departments. It also maintains supplies of publications such as hazard analyses, special studies, and data summaries. These reports identify hazards, accident patterns and types of products. Contact:

National Injury Information Clearinghouse, Consumer Product Safety Commission, Room 625, 5401 Westbard Ave., Washington, DC 20207/301-492-6424.

Help Write a Standard

Consumers or consumer organizations may offer to develop a proposed mandatory standard. When the Commission is looking for offers to develop a standard for a particular product an announcement is made in the Federal Register. Contact: Office of the Secretary, Consumer Product Safety Commission, Room 332, 5401 Westbard Ave., Washington, DC 20207/301-492-6800.

Library

The CPSC Library collection stresses product safety and liability, consumer affairs, engineering, economics and law. Contact: CPSC Library, Consumer Product Safety Commission, Room 546, 5401 Westbard Ave., Washington, DC 20207/301-492-6544

Petition the CPSC

Any interested person may petition the Commission to begin proceedings to issue, amend or revoke a consumer product safety rule. Contact: Office of the Secretary, Consumer Product Safety Commission, 5401 Westbard Ave., Washington, Dc 20207/301-492-6800.

Priority Projects

Each year the Commissioner designates a list of Priority Projects for the Consumer Product Safety Commission to focus on. For a listing and description of these projects contact: Public Affairs, Consumer Product Safety Commission, 1111 18th Street N.W., Washington, DC 20207/202-492-6580.

Product-Related Injuries Data Base

The National Inquiry Information Clearinghouse (NIIC) has statistics and information about consumer product-related injuries. Data is retrievable by product category only (i.e., hair dryers, knives, lawn mowers, etc.). The system is comprised of the following files: (1) NIECE data which includes information supplied by 73 hospitals nationwide regarding injury type, frequency, severity, treatment, causes and projections; (2) consumer complaints with data on product type, details of incident reported and consumer characteristics such as age and sex; (3) in-depth CPSC investigative reports (full text) of incidents; (4) newspaper clippings; (5) manufacturers' reports submitted to CPSC; and (6) death certificate information.

NIIC's computer files contain nearly three million records and are updated continuously. Searches and printouts are free unless NIIC's cost exceeds $25.00. At that point you will be charged a duplicating fee of 10 cents per page and a search fee of $1.50 per quarter hour. Contact: National Inquiry Information Clearinghouse, Consumer Product Safety Commission, 5401 Westbard Avenue, Room 625, Washington, DC 20207/302-492-6424 (phone calls are preferred).

Publications

Up to 10 copies of the following publications are available free by writing to the U.S. Consumer Product Safety Commission, Washington, DC 20207:

BEDS
Bunk Beds (Fact Sheet No. 71)
BICYCLES
Bicycle Regulations (Technical Fact Sheet No. 5)
Skateboards (Fact Sheet No. 93)
CHILDHOOD SAFETY GENERAL
Baby Rattles (Fact Sheet No. 86)
Buyer's Guide (Nursery furniture and equipment) (also in Spanish)
Children's Sleepwear (Fact Sheet No. 96)
Protect Your Child
The Super Sitter (booklet, baby sitter's guide)
CHILDRENS FURNITURE
Baby Walkers (Fact Sheet No. 66)
Buyers' Guide: It Hurts When They Cry (general information booklet for adults)
Cribs (Fact Sheet No. 43)
High Chairs (Fact Sheet No. 70)
Infant Falls (Fact Sheet No. 20)
Toy Boxes and Toy Chests (Fact Sheet No. 74)
CHRISTMAS SAFETY
Christmas Decorations (Fact Sheet No. 40)
Holiday Safety No. 7T (teacher's guide on decorations, toys and other gifts)
Merry Christmas with Safety (illustrated pamphlet)
CONSUMER PRODUCTS, GENERAL
Consumer Product Safety: What's It All About? (guide for teachers of grades 4-6)
Federal Consumer-Oriented Agencies (Fact Sheet No. 52)
The Home Electrical System (Fact Sheet No. 18)
Safer Products, Safer People
Listing of Education Materials for Use by Schools
What's It All About Teacher's Guide (8-T)
You Make the Difference (Teacher's Resource Guide) Grades 7–9; Grades 10–12
CPSC 1982 Conference on Product Safety
CPSC Hotline Flyer
CPSC Publications List
CPSC Publications for sale by GPO and CIC
Consumer's Resource Handbook
Retailers' Guide
How-To Manual for Product Safety—People Make It Happen (guidebook for organization community programs on product safety)
Misuse of Consumer Products (Fact Sheet No. 68)
ELECTRICAL SAFETY
Antenna Alert
CPSC Guide to Electrical Safety
Clothes Dryers (Fact Sheet No. 73)
Electric Home Workshop Tools (Fact Sheet No. 59)
Home Electrical Systems (Fact Sheet No. 18)

FIRE SAFETY
Hazard Hunt
Kerosene Heaters (Fact Sheet 97)
Wake Up! Smoke Detectors (available also in Spanish)
FIREWORKS
Fireworks (Fact Sheet No. 12)
FLAMMABILITY
Flammable Fabrics (Fact Sheet No. 17)
Flammable Fabrics Curriculum: Student Readings No. 4S
Upholstered Furniture (Fact Sheet No. 53)
What You Should Know About Home Fire Safety (booklet)
HALLOWEEN
Halloween Safety Teacher's Guide No. 9T
HEATERS
Caution! Choosing and Using Your Gas Space Heater (illustrated pamphlet)
Furnaces (Fact Sheet No. 79)
Space Heaters (Fact Sheet No. 34)
Wood and Coal Burning Stoves (Fact Sheet No. 92)
HOUSEHOLD PRODUCTS, GENERAL
Extension Cords and Wall Outlets (Fact Sheet No. 16)
Hair Dryers and Stylers (Fact Sheet No. 35)
Ladders (Fact Sheet No. 56)
Lead in Paint (Fact Sheet No. 14)
Home Safety Checklist for Senior Consumers
Television Fire and Shock Hazards (Fact Sheet No. 11)
HOUSEHOLD STRUCTURES
Home Insulation (Fact Sheet No. 91)
Insulation Installers' Guide
Save Energy Safely
Urea Formaldehyde Foam Insulation—Information Packet
Questions and Answers on Home Insulation (booklet)
KITCHEN PRODUCTS
Electric Blenders, Mixers, Choppers, Grinders (Fact Sheet No. 50)
OUTDOOR POWER EQUIPMENT
Make Your Lawn Easier (and Safer) to Mow (illustrated information sheet)
Shopping for a Power Mower
Tips for Better, Safer Mowing
Power Lawn Mowers (Fact Sheet No. 1)
Power Mower Hazards and Safety Features (poster)
Power Mower Maintenance and Storage Tips (illustrated information sheet)
Safe Mowing is Better Mowing (consumer reference book)
Safety, Sales, and Service—Selling Your Customers on Power Lawn Mower Safety (retail sales training booklet for retailers and technical school students)
PLAYGROUND EQUIPMENT
Handbook for Playground Safety (Volume I—General guidelines; Volume II - Technical guidelines)
Play Happy, Play Safely: Playground Handbook (technical information and other resources for adult leaders and teachers)
Play Happy, Play Safely: Little Big Kids (illustrated read-together book for adults and children ages 3–5)
POISONS
Alternatives for the Older Consumer and the Handicapped (pamphlet, safety closures)
First Aid for Poisoning (card)

Locked Up Poisons
Poison Lookout Checklist and Certificate
What Pharmacists Should Know (pamphlet)
RECREATIONAL AND SPORT EQUIPMENT
Hot Tips for Hot Shots on Skateboarding Safety (illustrated brochure)
Skateboards (Fact Sheet No. 93)
REFUSE BINS
Refuse Bins (Fact Sheet No. 81)
TOYS
Electrically Operated Toys (Fact Sheet No. 61)
For Kids' Sake . . . Think Toy Safety (illustrated pamphlet)
For Kids' Sake . . . Think Toy Safety (coloring book)
Toys (Fact Sheet No. 47)
WORKSHOP PRODUCTS
Electric Home Workshop Tools (Fact Sheet No. 59)
Power Saws (Fact Sheet No. 7)

Public Calendar
Notices of meetings are generally published in the Public Calendar at least seven days before meetings of the Commissioners or Commission staff with persons who are not a part of the agency. The calendar may be obtained free of charge. Contact: Office of the Secretary, Consumer Product Safety Commission, Room 332, 5401 Westbard Ave., Washington, DC 20207/301-492-6800

Regional Offices
The U.S. Consumer Product Safety Commission has five regional offices to serve the consumer.

Northeastern Regional Office: 6 World Trade Center, Vesey Street, 6th Floor, New York, New York 10048/ 212-264-1125
Southeastern Regional Office: 800 Peachtree Street, N.E., Suite 210, Atlanta, Georgia 30308/404-381-2231
Midwestern Regional Office: 230 South Dearborn Street, Room 2944, Chicago, Illinois 60604/312-353-8260
Western Regional Office: 555 Battery Street, Room 415, San Francisco, California 94111/415-556-1816
Southwestern Regional Office: 1100 Commerce Street, Room 1010, Dallas, Texas 75242/214-767-0841

Selected Injury Information Resources
The National Electronic Injury Surveillance System (NEISS) is the main source of injury data for the Consumer Product Safety Commission. It is an injury data collection system which provides national estimates of the number and severity of injuries associated with consumer products treated in hospital emergency departments. It also serves as a means of locating injury victims so that further information can be gathered on the nature and probable cause of the accident. Summaries of these data are available in two regular publications: *Tabulation of DATA from NEISS,* annual reports of the involvement of the product(s) in the injury; and *NEISS Data Highlights.* The other sources of information include:

Death Certificates—information is coded into a computer data base with information on place of death, age and sex of victim, dates of injury and death, narrative extracts of the coroner's or medical examiner's description of the accident preceding death, plus codes for manner of death and accident mechanism, for the nature of the injury and location and for as many as four products.
NEISS Data Highlights—a free yearly summary publication of data tables showing numbers of product-related injuries that were treated in hospital emergency departments during the previous month and during the previous 12 months. The data tables are based on top product categories in CPSC's *Product Hazard Index.*
Consumer Complaint File—contains narrative reports of actual or potential product hazards and of injuries or near injuries from consumer products.
Medical Examiners and Coroners Alert Program (MECAP)—provides CPSC with timely information on product-related deaths and additional facts not recorded on death certificates.

Contact: National Injury Information Clearinghouse, Consumer Product Safety Commission, Room 625, 5401 Westbard Ave., Washington, DC 20207/301-492-6424.

How Can the Consumer Product Safety Commission Help You?
To determine how this agency can help you, contact: Directorate for Communications, Consumer Product Safety Commission, Washington, DC 20207/800-638-2772

Environmental Protection Agency

401 M St. S.W., Washington, DC 20460/202-382-4355

Established: December 2, 1970
Budget: $3,508,892,000
Employees: 9,125

Mission: Protects and enhances our environment today and for future generations to the fullest extent possible under the laws enacted by Congress; controls and abates pollution in the areas of air, water, solid waste, noise, radiation and toxic substances.

Data Experts

The following experts can be contacted directly concerning the topics under their responsibility. When writing to any of these experts, state the full name and topic area in the address and send in care of U.S. Environmental Protection Agency. For the rest of the address, refer to the area code in the telephone number and consult the listing at the end of this section.

Drinking Water

Bottled Water/Frank Bell/202-382-3037
Chlorine/Frank Bell/202-382-3037
Community Water Supply/John Trax/202-382-5526
Fluoridation/Ed O'Hnian/202-382-7571
Home Purifiers/Frank Bell/202-382-3037
Publications/Charlene Stein/202-382-5508
Research/David Kleffman/202-382-7468
   Gordon Robeck/513-684-7201
Subsurface Emplacement/Tom Belk/202-382-5530

Noise

Aircraft Noise/John Schettino/703-557-7550
Budgets/John Degnan/703-557-7600
Control Programs, Federal/John Schettino/703-557-7750
Control Programs, State and Local/John Ropes/703-557-7695
Health Effects/Rudolph Marrazzo/703-557-7305
International Activities/Rudolph Marrazzo/703-557-7305
National Noise Assessments/Joseph Montgomery/703-557-9307

Product Labeling/Kenneth Feith/703-557-2710
Public Information/William Franklin/703-557-9698
Standards and Regulations/Henry Thomas/703-557-7743
Surface Transportation Noise/William Roper/703-557-6666

Radiation

Criteria and Standards/William Mills/703-557-0704
Emergency Procedures/Harry Calley/703-557-7395
Environmental Analysis/Floyd Galpin/703-557-8217
Health Effects/William Ellett/703-557-9380
Monitoring/Raymond Johnson/703-557-7380
Natural Radiation/Allan Richardson/703-557-8927
New Standards/William Mills/703-557-0704
Nonionizing Radiation/David Jones/301-427-7604
Nuclear Power Plants/John Russell/703-557-7604
Over-all Program/Robertson Augustine/703-557-9710
Publications/Lorenz Zelsman/703-557-7715
Relation to Clean Air Act/James Hardin/703-557-8610
Technology Assessment/David Smith/703-557-8950
Uranium Mill Tailings/Allan Richardson/703-557-8927
Wastes, High-Level/Daniel Egan/703-557-8610
Wastes, Other/David Smith/703-557-8950

Research and Development Environmental Engineering and Technology

Acid Precipitation/Mike Maxwell/919-541-3091
Adhesives and Sealants/Ron Turner/513-684-4481
Advanced Energy Conversion (e.g. Combined Cycles,

High Temperature Turbines, Fuel Cells, MHD)/Bill Cain/513-684-4335

Analytical Procedures—Oil and Hazardous Spills/Mike Gruenfeld/201-340-6625

Asbestos, Fibrous Minerals—Metal Finishing/Thomas Powers/202-684-7506

Asbestos in Buildings/William Cain/202-684-7881

Asbestos Manufacturing/Mary Stinson/201-340-6683

Boiler—Utility/Industrial By-Product Marketing/Effects/ Assessment/Mike Osborne/919-541-2476

Fluidized Bed Combustion/Jack Wasser/919-541-2476

NO$_x$ Control (by Combustion Modification)/Bob Hall/ 919-541-2477
 (by Flue Gas Treatment)/David Mobley/919-541-2612

Particulate Control/Norm Plaks/919-541-3084

SO$_2$ Control (Nonregenerable/Regenerable)/Mike Maxwell/919-541-3091

Chemical Engineering
 Industrial Chemicals, Plastics/S. Howell/202-654-7756

Coal Cleaning/Julian Jones/919-541-2489 Gasification/ Bill Rhodes/919-541-2853
 In Situ Gasification/Edward Bates/202-684-7774
 Liquefaction/Bill Rhodes/919-541-2853

Combustion
 Fundamental/Jim Mulholland/919-541-2432
 Modifications/Bob Hall/919-541-2477.

Drinking Water
 Control Technology/Rala Krishman202-382-2583
 Economic Analysis/Robert Clark/513-684-7288
 Field Scale Organics Removal/Ben Lykins/513-684-7460
 Microbiological Treatment/Edwin Geldreich/513-684-7232
 Organics Investigations/Alan Stevens/513-684-7342
 Organics Removal Activities/Oliver Love/513-684-7281
 Particulate Contaminants/Gary Logsdon/513-684-7345
 Treatment Research/Gordon Robeck/513-684-7201

Electronic Product Manufacturing/Charles H. Darvin/ 202-684-7506

Energy Control Technology/Frank Princiotta/202-755-0205

Energy Management (in Conservation)
 Energy Recovery/Power Systems/C. C. Lee /512-684-4334
 Environmental Issues and Policies/Henry Postian/513-684-4318
 Industrial Processes/Bob Mournighan/543-684-4334

Environmental Assessments of Conventional and Advanced Energy Systems/
 Bob Hangebrauck/919-541-4134
 David Stephan/513-684-4402

Ferrous Metallurgy/Bob McCrillis/919-541-2733

Flue Gas Particulate Control/George Rey/202-755-2737
 Norm Plaks/919-541-2084

Flue Gas Sulfur Oxide Control/Everett Plyler/919-541-2918

Food Processing Industries/Ken Dostal/202-684-7502

Fuel Processing, Preparation and Advanced Combustion/Morris Altschuler/202-755-2738
 Robert Hangebrauk/919-541-4134

Fugitive Emissions Control
 (call appropriate industry contact) or Norm Plaks/919-541-3084.

Furnaces—Residential/Commercial/Bob Hall/919-541-2477

Gas Turbines/Internal Combustion Engines/Jack Wasser/919-541-2476

Hazardous Air Pollution Control/Gene Tucker/919-541-2746.

Hazardous Material Spills/Frank Freestone/201-340-6632

Hazardous Waste Management/Clyde Dial/202-684-7528
 Alternative/A. Klee/202-684-7493
 Chemical Detoxification/Charles Rogers/202-684-7757
 Biological Detoxification/P. Sferra/202-684-7618
 Conventional Alternative/Roger Wilmoth/202-684-7506
 Hazardous Waste Incineration and Treatment/Donald Oberacker/202-684-7696
 Hazardous Waste Thermal Destruction/Timothy Oppelt/202-684-7696
 Oceanic Incineration of Hazardous Waste/Donald Oberacker/202-684-7696

Indoor Air Quality/Gene Tucker/919-541-2746

Industrial Air Pollution Control
 Technology/David Graham/202-755-9014
 Bill Plyler/919-541-2818

Industrial Painting Processes/Charles Darvin/202-684-7506

Industrial Pollution Control
 Technology/Tom Pheiffer/202-382-2583
 Alden Christianson/513-684-7406

Inorganic Chemicals/Mary Stinson/201-340-6683

Iron and Steel Foundries/Bob McCrillis/919-541-2733

Lime/Limestone Scrubbing (Power Plants)
 Mike Maxwell/919-541-3443

Limestone Injection (LIMB)/Jim Abbott/919-541-3443

Machinery and Mechanical Products
 General Measurements and Sampling/Jim Dorsey/919-541-2509
 Organic Analysis/Larry Johnson/919-541-7943
 Incineration/Joe McSorley/919-541-2920
 Inorganic Analysis/Frank Briden/919-629-2557
 Particulate Samples/Bruce Harris/919-541-7807
 Instrumentation/Merrill Jackson/919-541-2559

Mining and Other Resource Extraction/Wayne Bloch/ 202-755-0647
 Ronald Hill/513-684-4410

Municipal Waste-to-Energy Systems/Harry Freeman/-202-684-7696

Municipal Wastewater Research/Tom Pheiffer/202-382-2583
 John Convery/513-684-7601

Nitrogen Oxide Control/Robert Statnick/202-755-0205
 Bob Hall/919-541-2477

Oil and Gas Production/Jack Farlow/201-340-6631

Oil Processing
 Petrochemicals/Bruce Tichenor/919-541-2991
 Refineries/Bruce Tichenor/919-541-2991
 Residual Oil/Sam Rakes/919-629-2825

Oil Shale
 Mining and Handling, Retorting, Disposal, Air Pollution Control, In Situ Environmental Impacts, Co-Disposal/Edward R. Bates/202-684-7774

Processing Wastewater Treatment/W. Liherick/202-684-7774
Oil Spills/Jack Farlow/201-340-6631
Organic and Inorganic Chemicals/Clyde R. Dempsey/202-654-7502
Particle Control
Control Devices
  Electrostatic Precipitators/Les Sparks/919-541-2458
  Fabric Filters/Lou Hovis/919-541-3374
  Scrubbers From Specific Sources (call appropriate industry contact)/Dale Harmon/919-541-2429
Paving and Roofing Materials
Pesticides Manufacturing/Bruce Tichenor/919-541-2991
Pctrochemical manufacturing/Bruce Tichenor/919-541-2991
Plastics, Dyes and Pigments/Mark Stutsman/202-684-7502
Petroleum Refineries/Bruce Tichenor/919-541-2991
Remedial Action/Don Sanning/513-684-7871
Pulp and Paper/Ken Dostal/202-684-7502
Solid and Hazardous Waste Disposal/N.B. Shomaker/513-684-7871
Solid and Hazardous Waste Incineration Measurement/Larry Johnson/919-541-7943.
Solid and Hazardous Waste Research/Gary Foley/202-426-4567
  Ron Hill/513-684-7861
Steel Making/Bob McCrillis/919-541-2733
Synthetic Fuel Production
  Coal Gasification
  Surface/Bill Rhodes/919-541-2853
  Coal Liquefaction/Bill Rhodes/919-541-2253
Textile Manufacturing/Dale Denny/919-629-2547
Toxic Chemical Incineration
  At Sea/Merrill Jackson/919-541-2559
  Hazardous Materials Spills Related/John Brugger/201-340-6634
  Specific Sources (call Appropriate Industry Contact)
Toxic Substances Control Technology/Don Tang/202-382-2583
Volatile Organic Carbon Control/Bruce Tichenor/919-541-2991
Wastewater Research
  Urban Systems/Jim Kreissl/513-684-7614
  Storm and Combined Sewers/Richard Field/201-340-6674
  Economic Analysis/Richard Smith/513-684-7624
  Technology Development/D.F. Bishop/513-684-7628
  Treatment Process Development/Carl Brunner/513-684-7809

Research and Development Health

Air Pollutant Health Effects/Lester Grant/919-541-2266
Assessment of Reproductive Effects/Peter Voytek/202-382-7303
Cancer Biostatistics/Todd Thorslund/202-382-7351
Cancer Policy/Elizabeth Anderson/202-382-7317
Cancer Toxicology/Robert McGaughy/202-382-7241
  Dharm Singh/202-382-7344
Water Pollutant Health Effects/Jery Stara/513-684-7531

Research and Development Monitoring and Technical Support

Air Quality/Thomas Stanley/202-426-4153
Animal Physiology (Neurophysiology)/John Santolucito/702-736-2969
Aquatic Biology/Stephen Hern/702-736-2969
Atmospheric Visibility/Wiliam Malm/702-736-2969
Biological Monitoring/Bruce Wiersma/702-736-2969
Budget, Program Planning (Las Vegas)/Walter Petrie/702-736-2969
Carcinogen Field Studies/John Santolucito/702-736-2969
Chesapeake Bay Program—Quality Assurance/Werner Beckert/702-736-2969
Data Systems/Lance Wallace/202-426-2175
DOE Nuclear Testing Monitoring Programs/Richard Stanley/702-736-2969
Drinking Water/Thomas Stanley/202-426-4153
  John Winter/513-684-7325
Emergency Response/William Lacy/202-426-2387
  Phyllis Daly/202-426-2387
  Robert Holmes/202-426-2387
  James Shakelford/202-426-2387
Emergency Response—Air/Thomas Hauser/919-541-2106
  Franz Burman/919-541-2106
  Walter Petrie/701-736-2969
  David McNeils/702-736-2969
Emergency Response—Water/Dwight Ballinger/513-684-7301
  Walter Petrie/702-736-2969
  David McNelis/702-736-2969
Emergency Response—Radiation/Erich Bretthauer/702-736-2969
  Walter Petrie/702-736-2969
Environmental Aerial Photography/Vernard Webb/703-557-3110
Environmental Remote Sensing Systems/John Ecert/702-736-2969
Exposure Monitoring/Lance Wallace/202-426-2175
Geothermal Geology/Hydrology/Donald Gilmore/702-736-2969
Groundwater Impacts from Energy Sources/Leslie McMillion/702-736-2969
Hazardous Wastes/John Koutsandreas/202-426-4478
Hazardous Wastes—Quality Assurance Analytical Methodology/Eugene Whittaker/702-736-2969
Integrated Exposure Assessment Modeling/Joe Behar/702-736-2969
Internal Medicine, Nuclear/Maxwell Kaye/702-736-2969
Laboratory Evaluation Procedures/Earl Whittaker/702-736-2969
Laboratory Practice Guides (Toxics)/Werner Beckert/702-736-2969
Monitoring Systems/David McNelis/702-736-2969
Oil and Hazardous Spill Remote Sensing/Robert Landers/702-736-2969
Pesticides/Charles Plost/202-426-2026
Phytoplankton Biology/William Taylor/702-736-2969
Policy/Charles Brunot/202-426-2027
Public Information (Las Vegas Lab)/Geneva Douglas/702-736-2969
Radiation/James Whitney/202-426-4478

Radiation Exposure Investigations/Maxwell Kaye/702-736-2969

Radiochemical Analytical Methods/Earl Whittaker/702-736-2969

Radiochemical Reference Materials and Methods/Loren Thompson/702-736-2969

Safety Officer (Radiation)/John Coogan/702-736-2969

Satellite and Aircraft Remote Sensing/Gary Shelton/702-736-2969

Technical Publications (Las Vegas Lab)/Geneva Douglas/702-736-2969

Toxic Substances/Robert Medz/202-426-4727

Toxic Substances Control/Maxwell Kaye/702-736-2969

Water Quality/Robert Medz/202-426-4727
John Kopp/513-684-7306

Wetlands System Analysis/Victor Lambou/702-736-2969

Research and Development Processes and Effects

Accounting (RI Lab)/David Hobbs/401-789-1071

Acid Rain/Charles Powers/503-757-4672
Gary Glass/218-783-9526

Administration (FL Lab)/A. Reynolds/904-932-5311

Administration (RI Lab)/Claire Geremia/401-789-1071

Administration (OR Lab)/Charles Frank/503-757-4651

ADP/Bob Payne/401-789-1071
Robert Browning/919-541-2273
Joan Novak/919-541-4545

Agriculture—Forestry Pollution/Robert Swank/404-546-3476

Air
Ecological Effects/Thomas Murphy/503-757-4601
Atmospheric Transport and Fate/Alfred Ellison/919-541-2191

Air Ecology/Larry Raniere/503-757-4622

Air Pollution Meteorology/L.E. Niemeyer/919-541-4541

Air Quality Simulation Modeling/Kenneth Demerjian/919-541-4545
Bruce Turner/919-541-4565
Climatology/George Holzworth/919-541-4551
Charles Hosler/919-541-2230
Fluid Modeling/William Snyder/919-541-2811
Meteorologic Processes/George Holzworth/919-541-4551
Francis Pooler/919-541-2649
Model Application/Bruce Turner/919-541-4565

Analytical Chemistry/Peter Rogerson/401-789-1071
D. Garnas/904-932-5311
Charles Anderson/404-546-3183

Animal Production Wastes/Lynn Shuyler/405-332-8800

Aquaculture/Bill Duffer/405-332-8800

Aquatic Weeds/G. Walsh/904-932-5311

Asbestos Analysis/Charles Anderson/404-546-3183

Atmospheric Chemistry and Physics/A.P. Altshuller/919-541-3795
Basil Dimitriades/919-541-2706
Aerosols—Dynamics & Kinetics/Jack Durham/919-541-2183
William Wilson/919-541-2551
Gases—Dynamics and Kinetics/Joseph Bufalini/919-541-2422
Basil Dimitriades/919-541-2706

Modeling—Transformation/Marcia Dodge/919-541-2374
Kenneth Demerjian/919-541-4545

Biological Monitoring/Don Phelps/401-789-1071

Carcinogen Research/J. Couch/904-932-5311

Characterization and Measurements Methods Development
Air Quality/Lon Swaby/202-426-1810
Toxic Substances/Riz Hague/202-426-4256
Water Quality/Bill Sayers/202-426-0146

Chesapeake Bay Program
Eutrophication/T. Phiffer/301-266-0017
Management Studies/D. DeMoss/301-266-0017
Research/Sam Williams/202-426-2317
Submerged Aquatic Vegetation/T. Nugent/215-597-7943
Toxic Substances/W. Cook/301-266-0017

Chlorination Research/W. Davis/803-559-0371

Clean Lakes Research/Spence Peterson/503-757-4716

Community Studies/M. Tagatz/904-932-5311

Complex Effluents/William Horning/513-684-8601

Computers (FL Lab)/R. Ryder/904-932-5311

Congressional Inquiries (GA Lab)/David Duttweiler/404-546-3134

Consent Decree/J. Lowe/904-932-5311

Consent Decree Chemicals Testing/Richard Siefert/218-727-6692

Cooperative Testing—HERL/Robert Drummond/218-727-6692

Corps of Engineers Coordinator/F. Wilkes/904-932-5311

Cost-Benefit Analysis/James Falco/404-546-3585

Criteria Documents/William Brungs/218-727-6692

Data Processing/David Cline/404-546-3123

Ecological Effects
Air Quality/Hal Bond/202-426-2317
Freshwater/Mel Nolan/202-426-2317
Marine/Sam Williams/202-426-2317
Pesticides/Hal Bond/202-426-2317
Toxic Substances/Ken Hood/202-426-2317

Economics Research/501-757-4716

EEO Coordinator (MN Lab)/Diane Olson/218-727-6692

EEO Coordinator (RI Lab)/Waltt Galloway/401-789-1071

Effluent Permit (Lab)/Stan Berge/401-789-1071

Energy—Fuel Processes/Dave Tingey/503-737-4621

Energy-related Pollutants
Atmospheric Transport and Transformation/Dan Golomb/202-426-0264
Health Effects/Gerald Rausa/202-426-3975
Measurement Systems and Information Development/James Stemmie/202-426-3974
Transport, Fate and Effects/Al Galli/202-426-0288

Energy—Terrestrial/Eric Preston/502-757-4636

Exposure Assessment/H. Pritchard/904-932-5311

Extramural Program (MN Lab)/Kenneth Biesinger/218-727-6692

Extramural Research/Mary Malcolm/401-789-1071

Facilities/Robert Trippel/501-757-4680

Field Studies/Willam Wilson/919-541-2551
Francis Pooler/919-541-2649

Fine Particles/Phillip Cook/218-727-6692

Foreign Research Program/David Duttweiler/405-546-3134

Freedom of Information/Jan Prager/401-789-1071
  Robert Ryans/404-546-3306
Fresh Water
  Ecological Effects/Norbert Jaworski/218-727-6692
  Transport and Fate/Rosemarie Russo/404-546-3134
Freshwater Research/Thomas Maloney/503-757-4605
Great Lakes
  Transport, Fate and Ecological Effects/Norbert Jawor-
    ski/218-727-6692
Great Lakes Research/Bill Sayers/202-426-0146
Groundwater
  Transport and Fate/Clinton Hall/405-332-8800
Groundwater Protection/Jack Kelley/405-332-8800
Groundwater Research/Steve Cordle/202-426-3974
Hazardous Materials/Earl Davey/401-789-1071
Industrial Effluent Survey/Walter Shackelford/404-546-
  3186
Information Services (OR Lab)/Karen Randolph/503-
  757-4609
Instrumentation Development/Robert Stevens/919-541-
  3156
Integrated Pest Management/Darwin Wright/202-426-
  2407
Irrigated Crop Production/J.P. Law/405-332-8800
Joint/Areawide Industrial Wastes/Marvin Wood/405-
  332-8800
Laboratory and Facilities Management/Richard Latimer/
  401-789-1071
Laboratory Safety and Health/William Donaldson/404-
  546-3430
Land Disposal/Jeff Lee/503-757-4758
Land Treatment/Curtis Harlin/405-332-8800
Large Lakes Research/Wayland Swain/313-675-5000
Library (FL Lab) A. Lowry/904-932-5311
Library (OR Lab)/Betty McCauley/503-757-4731
Library (RI Lab)/Rose Ann Gamache/401-789-1071
Management & Administration (RTP)
  Administration/Gloria Koch/919-541-2331
  Management/A.P. Altshuller/919-541-3795
  Alfred Ellison/919-541-2191
  Program Planning/Charles Hosler/919-541-2230
  Technical Information/Charles Hosler/919-541-2230
Marine Biological Systems/Richard Swartz/503-757-4031
Marine Research (General)/Donald Baumgartner/503-
  757-4722
Marine Transport and Transformation/Robert Brice/503-
  757-4709
Marine Water
  Complex Effluent Transport, Fate, and Ecological
    Effects/William Brungs/401-789-1071
  Pesticide and Toxic Substances Transport, Fate and
    Ecological Effects/Henry Enos/904-932-5311
Master Analytical Scheme for Organics in Water/Wayne
  Garrison/404-546-3453
Mathematical Modeling/T. Davies/803-559-0371
  Lee Mulkey/404-546-3581
  Lawrence Burns/404-546-3148
Microcosms/Ken Perez/401-789-1071
Microcosm Studies/Steven Hedtke/513-684-8601
Monticello Field Studies/John Arthur/612-295-5145
Multi-element Analysis/Thomas Hoover/404-546-3524
National Crop Loss Assessment Network (Air)/Ray
  Wilhour/503-757-4634

Nonpoint Source Control Technology/Robert Swank,
  Jr./404-546-3476
Nonpoint Source Pollution/Jack Gakstatter/503-757-4611
Offshore Drilling (Oils, Gases and Muds)/N. Richards/
  904-932-5311
Oil and Hazardous Substances/W. Davis/803-559-0371
Oil Spill Assessment/Bob Payne/401-789-1071
Organic Chemical Identification/John McGuire/404-546-
  3185
OTS Testing and Methods Evaluation/Richard Siefert/
  218-727-6692
PCB, Structure Acticity and ISHOW/Gilman Veith/218-
  727-6692
Pesticides/Jay Gile/503-757-4644
Pesticides Exposure Assessment/Riz Hague/202-426-
  4256
Pesticides Programs/John Eaton/218-727-6692
Petrochemical Production Wastes/Tom Short/405-332-
  8800
Petroleum Refining Wastes/Leon Myers/405-332-8800
Pollutant/Emission Characterization/Jack Wagman/919-
  541-3009
  Ambient Air/William Wilson/919-541-2551
  Mobile Sources / Ronald Bradow / 919-541-3037 Fran-
    cis Black/919-541-3037
  Stationary   Sources/Kenneth   Knapp/919-541-3085
    James Homolya/919-541-3085
Pollutant Transport and Transformation in Soil and
  Water/George Baughman/404-546-3145
Program Operations (RI Lab)/Stan Hegre/401-789-1071
Public Health Initiative/H. Pritchard/904-932-5311
Public Technical Information/Robert Ryans/404-546-
  3306
Quality Assurance/Zell Steever/401-789-1071
Radioisotopes/Eugene Jackin/401-789-1071
Renewable Resources (Water Quality)/Will LaVeille/
  202-426-2407
Research Program Administration (GA Lab)/Connie
  Shoemaker/404-546-3122
Rural Land Use Research/George Bailey/404-546-3307
Safety Officer (RI Lab)/Richard Latimer/401-789-1071
Safety Officer (MN Lab)/Fred Freeman/218-727-6692
Sampling and Analytical Techniques/Andrew O'Keefe/
  919-541-2408
  Carbon Fibers, Asbestos/Jack Wagman/919-541-3009
  Inorganics/Robert Stevens/919-541-3156
  Networks/J.C. Romanovsky/919-541-2887
  Organics/James Mulik/919-541-3064
  Remote Sensing/William Herget/919-541-3034
Screening Committee/N. Cooley/904-932-5311
Statistical Analyst/Robert Andrew/218-727-6692
Subsurface Transport of Pollutants/Bill Dunlap/405-332-
  8800
Technical Assistance/Jan Prager/401-789-1071 William
  Brungs/218-727-6692
Technical Information Coordinator, Public Information
  Office and Health Officer (MN Lab)/Evelyn Hunt/218-
  727-6692
Terrestrial
  Transport Fate and Ecological Effects/Thomas
    Murphy/405-757-4601
Terrestrial Research/Norman Glass/503-757-4671
Toxicology/Jack Gentile/401-789-1071

Toxicology (Fresh-water)/Ron Garton/503-757-4753

Toxic Round-Robin (Effects)/S. Schimmel/904-932-5311

Toxics (Terrestrial)/James Gillett/503-757-4624

Toxic Substances Monitoring Programs/William Donaldson/404-546-3430

Toxic Substances Risk Assessment/James Falco/404-546-3585

Transport and Fate of Pollutants
   Air Quality/Deran Pashayan/202-426-2415
   Toxic Substances/Riz Hague/202-426-4256
   Water Quality/Harry Torno/202-426-0810

Water Quality Criteria/Jack Gentile/404-789-1071
   D. Hansen/904-932-5311

Water Quality Research/Walter Sanders, III/404-546-3171

Watershed Management/Lee Mulkey/404-546-3581

Wetlands/Hal Kibby/503-757-4713

Solid Waste

Administrative/Personnel/Becky Kennedy/202-755-2783

Agency Guidance/Denise Hawkins/202-755-9173

Agricultural Wastes/Kent Anderson/202-755-9125

Air Emissions from Hazardous Waste Facilities/Howard Beard/202-755-9203

Audiovisual/Graphics/Miles Allen/202-755-9157

Budget/Denise Hawkins/202-755-9157

Co-Disposal/David Sussman/202-755-9140

Congressional Correspondence/Henry Norton/202-755-9120

Data/ADP Systems/Essie Horton/202-755-9150

Disposal Facility Safety/Karen Waag/202-755-9128

Disposal Facility Standards S.004/Tim Fiels/202-755-9206

Economic Impacts (Subtitles C & D)/Michael Shannon/202-755-9190

Economics/Frank Smith/202-755-9140

Environmental Impact Statements/202-245-3006

Equivalence of State Programs/Sam Morekas/202-755-9145

Facility Permits S.3005/Arthur Galzer/202-755-9150

Facility Siting/Public Acceptance/Andrea Edelman/202-755-9187

Federal Procurement Guidelines/John Heffelfinger/202-755-9206

Financial Responsibility S. 3004/Ronn Dexter/202-755-9190

Flammability and Corrosion Tests/Chet Ozmar/202-755-9163

Generator Standards S. 3002/Harry Trask/202-755-9150

Groundwater Monitoring/Larry Graves/202-755-9116

Groundwater Policy/Barry Stoll/202-755-9116

Hazardous Waste Basins/Robert Holloway/202-755-9204

Hazardous Waste Characteristics (Chemical)/Donn Viviani/202-755-9187

Hazardous Waste Characterization S. 3001/Alan Corson/202-755-9187

Hazardous Waste Incineration and Recycling Facilities/Howard Beard/202-755-9203

Hazardous Waste Land Disposal/Kenneth Shuster/202-755-9125

Hazardous Waste Listing S. 3001/Matt Strauss/202-755-9187

Hazardous Waste State Program Relations/Ernest Pappajohn/202-755-9145

Industry—Specific Analyses/Jan Auerbach/202-755-9203

International Activities/Elizabeth Cotsworth/202-755-9173

Landfill (METBASE) Gas/Chris Rhyne/202-755-9125

Legal Issues/Anne Allen/202-755-9173

Legislation/Anne Allen/202-755-9173

Liner Technology/Allen Geswein/202-755-9120

Loadfarming S. 3004/Larry Weiner/202-755-9125

Materials Recovery/Source Separation/Charles Miller/202-755-9140

Notification System S. 3010/Harry Trask/202-755-9150

Open Dump Inventory (data)/Martha Madison/202-755-9145

Pesticide Containers Disposal (FIFRA S. 196)/John Knobe/202-755-9145

Polychlorinated Biphenyls—Site Approvals/Arthur Galzer/202-755-9150

Postclosure/Ronn Dexter/202-755-9190

Press Activities/Emily Sano/202-755-8987

Programs Plans/Tony Diecidue/202-755-9173

Publications/Kathy Walters/202-755-9153

Public Education Grants/Gladys Harris/202-755-9157

Public Information/Carol Lawson/202-755-9160

Public Participation/Gerri Wyer/202-755-9157

Resource Conservation and Recovery Act Financial Assistance/Denise Hawkins/202-755-9173

Resource Conservation and Recovery Act Guidance/Truett DeGeare/202-755-9120

Resource Conservation Committee/Frank Smith/202-755-9140

Resource Recovery Planning and Implementation/Steven Levy/202-755-9140

Resource Recovery Technology Evaluations/Dave Sussman/202-755-9140

S. 3001 Criteria/Matt Strauss/202-755-9187

S. 3011 State Grants/Daniel Derkies/202-755-9145

S. 4004 Sanitary Landfill Criteria/Kenneth Shuster/202-755-9125

S. 4008 State Grants/Penny Hansen/202-755-9145

Sludge Regulations/Emery Lazar/202-755-9125

Special Wastes/Jan Auerbach/202-755-9203

State Authorization (Subtitle C)/Sam Morekas/202-755-9145

State—EPA Agreements/Penny Hansen/202-755-9145

State Planning for Resource Recovery/David Gavrich/202-755-9140

State Planning Guidelines (Subtitle D)/Susah Absher/202-755-9150

State Program Assessment (Subtitle D)/Marthan Madison/202-755-9145

Surface Impoundment Technology/Allen Geswein/202-755-9120

Technical Assistance Panels/John Thompson/202-755-9140

Technology Assessment/Jan Auerbach/202-755-9203

Transporter Standards S. 3003/Carolyn Barley/202-755-9145

Urban Policy Grants/Steven Leiry/202-755-9140

User Changes/George Garland/202-755-9190

Waste Analyses and Tests (Biological)/David Friedman/202-755-9163

Waste Exchange/Rolf Hill/202-755-9145
Waste Oil (Epca S. 383)/Howard Beard/202-755-9203
State—EPA Agreements/Penny Hansen/202-755-9145

Toxic Substances and Pesticides

Animal Sciences/William Phillips/703-557-2242
Association of American Pesticides Control Officials Inc./State FIFRA Issues Evaluation Group Liaison/ Philip Gray/703-557-7096
Biological Investigation/Robert Jasper/301-344-2187
Chemical Information/Sidney Siegel/202-395-7285
Congressional Inquiries/Ann Lindsey/703-557-7102
Control Action/Margaret Stasikowski/202-382-3938
Disinfectants/Juanita Wills/703-557-3661
Ecological Monitoring/Frederick Kutz/202-382-3569
Emergency Exemptions/Patricia Critchlow/703-557-7700
Environmental Hazards/Clayton Bushong/703-557-7600
Experimen ' Use Permits/Herbert Harrison/703-557-2200
Federal .gency Certification Programs/John MacDonald/202-382-7846
Health Effects/Richard Hill/202-382-2897
Health Review/Irwin Baumel/202-382-4241
Herbicides and Fungicides/James Akerman/703-557-1650
Industrial Assistance/Edward Klein/202-382-3790
Insecticides and Rodenticides/Herbert Harrison/703-557-2200
Integrated Pest Management/Diana Horne/703-557-0620
Labeling and Standards/Jean Frane/703-557-0592
Laboratory Studies/Warren Bontoyan/301-344-2187
Monitoring/Martin Halper/202-382-3866
Pesticide Applicator Training/William Currie/703-557-5017
Pesticide Classification/Walter Waldrop/703-557-7400
Pesticide Disposal/Raymond Krueger/703-557-7347
Pesticide Incidents/Frank Davido/703-557-0576
Policy Questions (General OPP)/Susan Sherman/703-557-7090
Premanufacturing Review/Blake Biles/202-426-8815
Program Management and Support/Louis True/703-557-2440
Public Education and Communication/W. Grosse/703-557-2613
Rebuttable Presumption Against Registration (RRAR) Procedures/Paul Lapsley/703-557-7420
Registration—General Policy/Douglas Campt/703-557-7760
Residue Chemistry/Charles Trichilo/703-557-7324
Science Advisory Panel/Philip Gray/703-557-7096
Science Policy/Richard Hill/202-382-2897
Special Local Needs Registration (24(c))/Herbert Harrison/703-557-2200
System Support/Elgin Fry/202-382-7777
Toxicology Data Audits/William Burnam/703-557-3710

Water Quality

Areawide Publications/Patti Morris/202-475-8637
Asbestos Coordinator/Robert Carton/202-755-0300
Clean Lakes/Frank Lapensee/202-245-3036
Clean Water Report to Congress/202-382-5389
Coastal Zone Management Act/202-245-3054
Construction Cost Indexes/Weh Huang/202-382-7288

Early Warning/Mark Cohen/202-755-2887
Economics of Clean Water/Courtney Riordan/202-426-0803
Enforcement (Water)/Jim Elder/202-475-8488
Estuaries/Tudor Davies/202-382-7166
Eutrophication/David Flamer/202-426-2317
Facility Plan Requirements/Myron Tiemens/382-7260
Feedlots/Don Anderson/202-426-2707
Fishkills/Ed Biernacki/202-382-7008
Hazardous & Toxic Substances/A. Torsey/202-245-3036
Industrial Permits/Bill Jordan/202-426-7010
Land Treatment/Dick Thomas/202-382-7356
Manpower & Training/John Sampson/382-7384
Marine Protection/Al Wastler/202-245-3051
Mine Acid Operations/Bill Telliard/202-382-7131
Mine Acid Research/Carl Schafer/202-755-9014
Minority Business Enterprise/James Murphy/202-382-5847
Multi-Purpose Projects/Myron Tiemans/202-382-7260
Municipal Construction Grants/Walter Brodtman/202-382-5859
Municipal Wastewater-Needs Survey/Jeff Byron/202-382-7251
Ocean/William Beller/202-245-3054
    Secondary Treatment, BPWTT/Alan Hais/202-382-5853
Pretreatment Systems/Jim Gallup/202-755-0750
Publications/Bernita Starks/ 202-382-7373
Research and Development/Joel Fisher/703-577-7720
Research and Development Publications/Linda Smith/ 202-755-0648
Salt/Frank Condon/202-426-3975
Sewer System Evaluation/Alan Hais/202-382-5853
Sludge/Al Cassel/202-426-8976
Small Community Wastewater Treatment Systems/Keith Dearth/202-382-7263
State Delegation Agreements/James Murphy/202-382-5847
State Priority Lists/Myron Tiemens/202-382-7260
Technical Transfer/Michek Herzner/513-684-7394
Thermal Effluent Guidelines/William Telliard/202-382-7131
Toxic Publications/Joni Repasch/202-755-1188
Toxic Spills/Hans Crump/202-245-3045
Training Grants/John Samson/202-382-7384
Urban Runoff/Dennis Athayde/202-382-7112
Waste Oil/Joe Kaivak/202-755-7000
Waste Oil Nonpoint Sources/Carl Myers/202-382-7100
Water Quality Criteria/Dave Sabock/202-245-3042
Water Quality Management/Carl Myers/202-382-7100
Water Quality Standards/Dave Sabock/202-245-3042
Wetlands/Bill Davis/202-472-3400

Area Code/Address

201   Edison NJ
202   Washington DC
206   Seattle WA
212   New York NY
214   Dallas TX
215   Philadelphia PA
218   Duluth MN
301   Annapolis MD

303	Denver CO
312	Chicago IL
313	Ann Arbor MI
	Gross Ile MI
401	Narragansett RI
404	Athens GA
	Atlanta GA
405	Ada OK
415	San Francisco CA
503	Corvallis OR
513	Cincinnati OH

612	Monticello MN
617	Boston MA
702	Las Vegas NV
703	Arlington VA
803	Charleston SC
816	Kansas City MO
904	Gulf Breeze FL
919	Durham NC
	Research
	Triangle Park NC

Major Sources of Information

Air Quality Planning and Standards
This office provides guidelines and technical assistance for air quality planning, monitors air pollution trends, sets standards for new-source emissions and hazardous pollutants. Contact: Air Quality Planning and Standards, Office of Air, and Radiation, Environmental Protection Agency, Research Triangle Park, NC 27711/919-541-5615

Automatic Bidder Mailing List System
A centralized system for organizing and maintaining a list of bidders and offerors' identifies program element codes and vendor name sources for recurring types of EPA requirements such as basic research, applied research, development, abatement and control, and enforcement. Contact: Procurement and Contracts Management Division, Environmental Protection Agency, 499 S. Capitol St., S.W., Fairchild Bldg., 3rd Floor, Washington DC 20460/202-382-3255

Chemical Control
This office plans, operates and evaluates the Agency's work in controlling toxic substances other than pesticides. Contact: Chemical Control Division, Office of Toxic Substances, Environmental Protection Agency, Room 395, 401 M St., S.W.,Washington, DC 20460/202-382-3938

Clean Lakes
The clean lakes program grants awards related to the restoration of water quality and the prevention of the deterioration of water quality in lake waters. Contact: Clear Lakes Program, Criteria and Standards Division, Office of Water Environmental Protection Agency, Room M 2824, 401 M St. S.W., Washington, DC 20460/202-755-0100

Common Environmental Terms
This excellent little handbook is an alphabetic dictionary of terms. Contact: Public Information Center, Environmental Protection Agency, 820 Quincy St. N.W., Washington, DC 20011/202-829-3535

Computerized Data Bases
The following Data bases are maintained by the Environmental Protection Agency.

Chemical Activities Data Base
The EPA Chemical Activities Status Report (EPACASR) is a listing of chemical related activities, primarily in EPA. Recently, data has been added about activities in the Toxicology Program at the Department of Health and Human Services and at the International Agency for Research on Cancer (IARC). Generally, searches and printouts are available free of charge. A fee may be assessed for complex runs. Contact: Environmental Protection Agency (EPA), Office of Toxics Integration (TS 777), 401 M St, S.W., Washington, DC 20460/202-382-3415.

Chemical Regulations Data Base
The Federal Regulatory Search System is a storage and retrieval system cataloging all federal regulatory efforts (proposed, final, withdrawn) regarding chemicals. The system can be searched by chemical or agency, and information provided includes regulatory citation, not text. Searches and printouts are available free of charge. Contact: Environmental Protection Agency, Chemical Coordination Staff, Office of Toxics Substances, 401 M St, S.W., Washington, DC 20460/202-382-3393.

Chemical Regulations/Guidelines Data Base
The Chemical Regulations/Guidelines System contains summaries and citations of all final federal regulations regarding chemicals. Searches and printouts are available free of charge. Contact: Environmental Protection Agency, Chemicals Coordination Staff, 401 M St, S.W., Room 613, East Tower, Washington, DC 20460/202-382-2249.

Environmental Information Data Bases
INFOTERRA is an information referral service for sources of environmental information. The data base contains government agencies, public and private organizations, universities, individuals, etc. from the U.S. and 115 countries world-

wide. All listees have agreed to answer questions and supply information regarding their particular area(s) of expertise. Sources are provided for 26 categories ranging from air to waste. The data base can be searched by more than 1,000 different subject terms.

Searches and printouts are available free of charge. Contact: U.S. National Focal Point For INFOTERRA, TM 211–A, U.S. Environmental Protection Agency, Washington, DC 20460/202-382-5917.

Industrial Chemical Controls

The Environmental Protection Agency's Industry File consists of information about federal regulations that contain chemical controls and affect industry. Eight-nine industrial categories, as defined by the Standard Industrial Codes manual, are stored. Information can be retrieved by the chemical itself or by industrial categories such as iron or steel. Searches and printouts are available free of charge. Contact: Environmental Protection Agency, Office of Toxics Integration (TS 777), 401 M St, S.W., Washington, DC 20460/202-382-2249.

Toxic Effects of Chemical Substances Data Base

The Registry of Toxic Effects of Chemical Substances (RTECS) stores data about 56,000 individual chemicals that have been studied for toxicity. NIOSH will run one or two chemicals and provide printouts at no charge. For more detailed searches (and the fee) contact: National Library of Medicine or EPA Chemical Information System. Contact: Information Retrieval and Analyses Section, NIOSH, 4676 Columbia Parkway, Cincinnati, OH 45226/513-684-8317.

Drinking Water Information

The Environmental Protection Agency maintains an information program on drinking water. It also develops plans to handle water emergencies. Contact: Technical Support Division, Water and Waste Management, Environmental Protection Agency, 26 West St. Claire St., Cincinnati, OH 45268/513-684-7904

Drinking Water Programs

This office develops standards, rules and guidelines for maintaining the quality of public drinking water supplies. For further information, contact: Office of Drinking Water, Environmental Protection Agency, Room 1011 ET, M.C. WH-550, 401 M St., S.W., Washington, DC 20460/202-382-5508.

Economic Analysis

Analyses of the economic and industrial impacts of pollution control regulations on industries and geographic areas are available. Contact: Economic Analysis Division, Office of Planning and Evaluation, Environmental Protection Agency, Room 425 WT, 401 M St., S.W., Washington, DC 20460/202-382-5484.

Effluent Guidelines

The Environmental Protection Agency defines limiting levels of pollutants in the waste streams of industrial and municipal point sources. Contact: Effluent Guidelines Division, Environmental Protection Agency, Room 913 ET, 401 M St. S.W., Washington, DC 20460/202-382-7120.

Enforcement

This office directs enforcement activities for the Agency's stationary source, pesticides, toxic substances and solid waste programs. For further information, contact: General Enforcement, Office of Enforcement, Environmental Protection Agency, WSMW Room 3109, 401 M St., S.W., Washington, DC 20460/202-475-8304.

Environmental and Engineering Technology

This office develops and assesses methods to control the environmental and economic effects of energy production, mineral extraction and processing, industrial operations, municipal wastewater treatment, solid waste disposal and drinking water treatment. Contact: Environmental Engineering and Technology, Office of Research and Development, Environmental Protection Agency, Room 635, 401 M St. S.W., Washington, DC 20460/202-382-2600.

Environmental Education Programs

The Environmental Protection Agency develops environmental education programs for both graduate and postgraduate courses and training programs. The areas of study include wastewater, drinking water, air, noise, pesticides and toxicology, solid waste, radiation, energy, environmental science, engineering and technology programs. Also available are Federal Education Programs with potential for providing technical or financial assistance to students in environmental studies. Contact: National Workforce Development Staff, Office of Research and Development, Environmental Protection Agency, Room 641 WT, 401 M St., S.W., Washington, DC 20460/202-382-5752

Environmental Events Calendar

This calendar lists conferences, meetings, conventions, workshops, seminars, government actions or other events that deal with the environment. For contributions or information, contact: Environmental Constituency Specialist, Office of Public Affairs, Environmental Protection Agency, Room 806, 401 M St., S.W., Washington, DC 20460/202-352-4361

Environmental Impact Statements

This office oversees the review of environmental impact statements, the preparation of Environmental Protection Agency impact statements and environmental problems of federal and federally supported activities. Contact: Office of Environmental Review, Environmental Protection Agency, Room 2119, 401 M St., S.W., Washington, DC 20460/202-382-5075.

Environmental Impact Statements Information
The Office of Federal Activities of the Environmental Protection Agency can refer you to the appropriate federal agency for environmental impact statements. In order to obtain a referral, you must have specific information about what you are seeking, such as the federal department responsible for the statement and the exact geographical area affected. Contact: Office of Federal Activities, Environmental Protection Agency, 401 M St., S.W., Washington, DC 20460/202-382-5073.

Environmental Processes and Effects Research
This office develops scientific and technological methods and data to predict and manage the entry, movement and fate of pollutants in the environment and the effects of pollutants on ecological systems. Contact: Environmental and Processes Effects, Office of Research and Development, Environmental Protection Agency, Room 3702, 401 M St., S.W., Washington, DC 20460/202-382-5950.

EPA Journal
This journal provides information on national environmental developments involving the Environmental Protection Agency. It also has feature articles on environmental developments, news briefs, reviews of recent major EPA activities in the pollution control program areas. It is published 10 times per year for the subscription price of $12 and is available from: Office of Public Affairs, Environmental Protection Agency, 401 M St., S.W., Washington, DC 20460/202-382-4355.

Finding Your Way Through EPA
This is a free EPA directory listing the offices of the agency and the people in them. A subject index, the agency organizational chart, a map of EPA's 10 regional offices, and brief descriptions of EPA's major programs are also included. Contact: Public Information Center, 820 Quincy St., N.W., Washington, DC 20011/202-829-3535.

Freedom of Information Requests
For Freedom of Information Act requests, contact: Freedom of Information Officer, Environmental Protection Agency, Room 227 WT, 401 M St. S.W., Washington, DC 20460/202-382-4048.

Grants
The programs described below are for sums of money which are given by the federal government to initiate and stimulate new or improved activities or to sustain on-going service:

Air Pollution Control Manpower Training Grants
Objectives: To develop career-oriented personnel qualified to work in pollution abatement and control. Grants are awarded to assist in planning, implementing and improving environmental training programs; increase the number of adequately trained pollution control and abatement personnel; upgrade the level of training among state and local environmental control personnel; and bring new people into the environmental control field.

Eligibility: Training grants are awarded to nonprofit academic institutions in the United States and territories. Traineeships are awarded to individuals by these grantee educational institutions. Trainees may be employees of state or local governmental air pollution control agencies and others who desire a career in governmental air pollution control work.

Range of Financial Assistance: $45,000 to $55,000.

Contact: Control Programs Development Division, Office of Air Quality Planning and Standards, Office of Air, and Radiation, Environmental Protection Agency, Research Triangle Park, NC 27711/919-541-2401.

Air Pollution Control Program Grants
Objectives: To assist state, municipal, intermunicipal and interstate agencies in planning, developing, establishing, improving and maintaining adequate programs for prevention and control of air pollution or implementation of national primary and secondary air quality standards.

Eligibility: Any municipal, intermunicipal, state or interstate agency with legal responsibility for appropriate air pollution planning and control is eligible for grant support provided such organization furnishes funds for the current year in excess of its expenditures for the previous year for its air pollution program. This program is available to each state, territory and possession of the United States, including the District of Columbia.

Range of Financial Assistance: $7,025 to $6,449.000.

Contact: Control Programs Development Division, Office of Air Quality Planning and Standards, Office of Air, and Radiation, Environmental Protection Agency, Research Triangle Park, NC 27711/919-541-5526.

Air Pollution Control Research Grants
Objectives: To support and promote research and development projects relating to the causes, effects, extent, prevention and control of air pollution.

Eligibility: This program is available to each state, territory and possession of the United States, including the District of Columbia, for public, private, state universities and colleges, hospitals, laboratories, state and local health departments, and other public or private nonprofit institutions. Grants may also be awarded to individuals who have demonstrated unusually high scientific ability. Profit-making organizations are not eligible.

Range of Financial Assistance: $20,000 to $542,295.

Contact: Director, Office of Research Grants, RD-675, Environmental Protection Agency, Washington, DC 20460/202-382-5744.

Construction Grants for Wastewater Treatment Works

Objectives: To assist and serve as an incentive in construction of municipal wastewater works which are required to meet state and federal water quality standards.

Eligibility: Any municipality, intermunicipal agency, state or interstate agency having jurisdiction over waste disposal. This program is available to each state, territory and possession of the United States, including the District of Columbia.

Range of Financial Assistance: $675 to $290,800,000.

Contact: Director, Municipal Construction Division, WH-547, Office of Water Programs Operations, Environmental Protection Agency, Washington, DC 20460/202-382-5859.

Construction Management Assistance Grants

Objectives: To assist and serve as an incentive in the process of delegating to the states a maximum amount of authority for conducting day-to-day matters related to the management of the construction grant program. An overriding goal is to eliminate unnecessary duplicative reviews and functions.

Eligibility: State Water Pollution Control Agency, or other agency designated by the governor in any state, territory and possession of the United States, including the District of Columbia.

Range of Financial Assistance: $493,072 to $10,473,744.

Contact: Chief, Program Policy Branch, Municipal Construction Division, WH-547, Office of Water Programs Operations, Environmental Protection Agency, Washington, DC 20460/202-382-7359.

Environmental Protection Consolidated Grants— Program Support

Objectives: To enable states to coordinate and manage environmental approaches to their pollution control activities. Consolidated grants are alternate grant delivery mechanisms. These mechanisms provide for consolidation into one grant instrument those grants awarded separately to states for management of environmental protection activities including but not limited to air pollution control, water pollution control and solid waste management.

Eligibility: Any state-designated entity eligible

to receive and administer funds made available through the applicable statutory authorizations.

Range of Financial Assistance: Not specified.

Contact: Grants Administration Division, PM-216, Environmental Protection Agency, Washington, DC 20460/202-382-5297.

Environmental Protection—Consolidated Research Grants

Objectives: To support research to determine the environmental effects and hence the control requirements associated with energy; to identify, develop and demonstrate necessary pollution control techniques; and to evaluate the economic and social consequences of alternative strategies for pollution control of energy systems. To support research to explore and develop strategies and mechanisms for those in the economic, social, governmental and environmental systems to use in environmental management.

Eligibility: This program is available to each state, territory, and possession of the United States, including the District of Columbia, for public and private state universities and colleges, hospitals, laboratories, state and local government departments, and other public or private nonprofit institutions and individuals who have demonstrated unusually high scientific ability.

Range of Financial Assistance: $4,750 to $175,000.

Contact: Environmental Protection Agency, Grants Administration Division, PM 216, Washington, DC 20450/202-382-5744.

Hazardous Substance Response Trust Fund

Objectives: To undertake remedial planning and remedial implementation actions in response to releases on the National Priorities List contained in the National Oil and Hazardous Substances Contingency Plan, to clean up the hazardous waste sites that are found to pose the most imminent hazards to human health.

Eligibility: State and US Territories.

Range of Financial Assistance: $30,000 to $7,800,000.

Contact: Chief, State and Regional Coordination Branch, Hazardous Site Control Division, Office of Emergency and Remedial Response, Environmental Protection Agency, Washington, DC 20460/202-382-2443.

Marine Combined Sewer Overflow Special Fund

Objectives: To assist and serve as an incentive in construction of municipal wastewater treatment works for abatement of combined sewer overflow pollution which are required to meet State and Federal water quality standards for marine bays and estuaries.

Eligibility: Any municipality, intermunicipal agency, State, or interstate agency, or Federally recognized Indian tribal governments, having jurisdiction over combined sewers discharging into marine bays or estuaries. This program is available to each such State, territory and possession of the US, including the District of Columbia.

Range of Financial Assistance: None

Contact: Deputy Director, Facility Requirements Division, Office of Water Programs Operations, Environmental Protection Agency, Washington, DC 20460/202-382-7260.

Pesticides Control Research Grants

Objectives: To support and promote the coordination of research projects relating to human and ecological effects from pesticides, pesticide degradation products, and alternatives to pesticides.

Eligibility: This program is available to each state, territory and possession of the United States, including the District of Columbia, for public or private state colleges and universities, state and local governments, and individuals.

Range of Financial Assistance: $38,000 to $154,548.

Contact: Director, Office of Research Grants, RD-675, Environmental Protection Agency, Washington, DC 20460/202-382-5744.

Pesticides Enforcement Program Grants

Objectives: 1) to assist states in developing and maintaining comprehensive pesticide enforcement programs; 2) sponsor cooperative surveillance, monitoring and analytical procedures, and 3) encourage regulatory activities within the states.

Eligibility: State agencies having pesticide enforcement responsibilities in each state, territory and possession of the United States, including the District of Columbia, and Indian tribes.

Range of Financial Assistance: $10,000 to $428,000.

Contact: Director, Compliance Monitoring Staff, Office of Pesticides and Toxic Substances Enforcement Division, EN-342, Environmental Protection Agency, Washington, DC 20460/202-382-3807.

Safe Drinking Water Research and Demonstration Grants

Objectives: To conduct research relating to the causes, diagnosis, treatment, control and prevention of physical and mental diseases and other impairments of man resulting directly or indirectly from contaminates in water or to the provision of a dependably safe supply of drinking water. Development and demonstration of any project which will demonstrate a new or improved method, approach or technology for providing a dependably safe supply of drinking water to the public or which will investigate and demonstrate health implications involved in the reclamation, recycling and reuse of waste waters for drinking and/or the preparation of safe and acceptable drinking water.

Eligibility: This program is available to each state, territory and possession of the United States, including the District of Columbia, for public, private state colleges and universities, public agencies, state and local governments, other organizations and individuals. Profit-making organizations are not eligible.

Range of Financial Assistance: $8,200 to $280,000.

Contact: Director, Office of Research Grants, RD-675, Environmental Protection Agency, Washington, DC 20460/202-382-5744

Hazardous Waste Management Financial Assistance to States

Objectives: To assist State governments in the development and implementation of an authorized hazardous waste management program for the purpose of controlling the generation, transportation, treatment, storage and disposal of hazardous wastes.

Eligibility: State agencies within the 50 states, the District of Columbia, the Commonwealth of Puerto Rico, the Virgin Islands, Guam, American Samoa, and the Commonwealth of the Northern Mariana Islands.

Range of Financial Assistance:$208,500 to $4,160,409.

Contact: Grants Administration Division, PM-216, Environmental Protection Agency, Washington, DC 20460/202-382-2210.

Solid Waste Disposal Research Grants

Objectives: To support and promote the coordination of research and development in the area of collection, storage, utilization, salvage or final disposal of solid waste.

Eligibility: This program is available to each state, territory and possession of the United States, including the District of Columbia, for public or private agencies, public, private, state universities and colleges, state and local governments, and individuals. Profit-making organizations are not eligible.

Range of Financial Assistance: $19,389 to $139,146.

Contact: Office of Research Grants, RD-675, Environmental Protection Agency, Washington, DC 20460/202-382-5744.

State Public Water System Supervision Program Grants

Objectives: To foster development of state program plans and programs to assist in implementing the Safe Drinking Water Act.

Eligibility: State agencies designated by the Governor or Chief Executive Officer of one of the states of the United States, the District of Columbia, the Commonwealth of Puerto Rico, the Northern Mariana Islands, the Virgin Islands, Guam, American Samoa, or the Trust Territory of the Pacific Islands.

Range of Financial Assistance: $91,500 to $1,752,800.

Contact: Office of Drinking Water, Office of Water, Environmental Protection Agency, Washington, DC 20460/202-382-5529.

State Underground Water Source Protection Program Grants

Objectives: To foster development and implementation of underground injection control programs under the Safe Drinking Water Act.

Eligibility: States have primary Enforcement Authority as of October 1, 1983.

Range of Financial Assistance: $31,900 to $597,100.

Contact: Chief, Ground Water Protection Branch, Office of Drinking Water, Office of Water, Environmental Protection Agency, Washington, DC 20460/202-426-3934.

Toxic Substances Research Grants

Objectives: To support and promote coordination of research projects relating to the effects, extent, prevention and control of toxic chemical substances or mixtures.

Eligibility: This program is available to each state, territory and possession of the United States, including the District of Columbia, public or private state universities and colleges, hospitals, laboratories, state and local government departments, other public or private nonprofit institutions and individuals who have demonstrated unusually high scientific ability.

Range of Financial Assistance: $30,000 to $196,432.

Contact: Office of Research Grants, RD-675, Environmental Protection Agency, Washington, DC 20460/202-382-5744.

Water Pollution Control—Research, Development and Demonstration Grants

Objectives: To support and promote the coordination and acceleration of research, development, and demonstration projects relating to the causes, effects, extent, prevention, reduction and elimination of water pollution.

Eligibility: This program is available to each state, territory and possession of the United States, including the District of Columbia, for public, private, state, and community universities and colleges, hospitals, laboratories, state water pollution control agencies, interstate agencies, state and local governments, other public or private nonprofit agencies, institutions or organizations; grants may also be awarded to individuals who have demonstrated unusually high scientific ability. Grants under certain section of this law may be awarded to profit-making organizations.

Range of Financial Assistance: $15,000 to $99,213.

Contact: Director, Office of Research Grants, RD-675, Environmental Protection Agency, Washington, DC 20460/202-382-5744.

Water Quality Management Planning

Objective: To encourage and facilitate the development of water quality management plans.

Eligibility: This program is available to State Water Quality Management Agencies.

Range of Financial Assistance: $100,000 to $2,500,000.

Contact: Director, Water Planning Division, Office of Water Program Operations, Office of Water, Environmental Protection Agency, 401 M St., S.W., Washington, DC 20460/202-382-7080.

Water Pollution Control—State and Interstate Program Grants

Objectives: To assist state and interstate agencies in establishing and maintaining adequate measures for prevention and control of water pollution.

Eligibility: State and interstate water pollution control agencies as defined in the Federal Water Pollution Control Act.

Range of Financial Assistance: $8,000 to $2,870,000.

Contact: Director, Water Planning Division, Office of Water Program Operations, Office of Water, Environmental Protection Agency, Washington, DC 20460/202-382-7080

Guideline for Public Reporting of Daily Air Quality-Pollutant Standard Index

This index provides a uniform way to report daily on pollution concentrations, to tell the public about the general health effects associated with these concentrations. It also describes some general precautionary steps that can be taken. Contact: Office of Air Quality Planning and Standards, Environmental Protection Agency, Research Triangle Park, NC 27711/919-541-5615

Health Research

This office conducts research on how pollutants affect human and animal health. Contact: Office of Health Research, Office of Research and Development, Environmental Protection Agency, Room 3100, 401 M St. S.W., Washington, DC 20460/202-426-2382.

Libraries

The Environmental Protection Agency maintains a headquarters library as well as libraries in each of its regional offices that are open to the public. Contact: Headquarters Library, Environmental Protection Agency, Room PM-211A, 2904 Waterside Mall, Washington,DC 20460/202-382-5921.

Mailing List

The Environmental Protection Agency maintains

mailing lists for technical information as well as general information about each of its major programs. Requests to be added to the lists should be made to:

General Information—Mailing List Manager, Office of Public Affairs, Environmental Protection Agency, (A-107), 401 M St., S.W., Washington, DC 20460/202-382-4361

Solid Waste—Mailing List Manager, OSW Publications Distribution, Environmental Protection Agency, 26 West St. Clair, Cincinnati, OH 45268/513-684-7931.

Water Quality—Central Mailing List Service, Municipal Construction Division, Environmental Protection Agency, GSA (8FSS), Building 41, Denver Federal Center, Denver, CO 80225

Distribution Office, Effluent Guidelines Division, Environmental Protection Agency, WH-552, Washington, DC 20460/202-382-7120.

Drinking Water—Mailing List Manager, Office of Drinking Water, Environmental Protection Agency, WH-550, Washington, DC 20460/202-382-5508

Toxic Substance—Industry Assistance Office, Office of Toxic Substances, Environmental Protection Agency, TS-799, Washington, DC 20460/202-554-1404

Pesticides—Mailing List Manager, Operation Division, Office of Pesticides Programs, Environmental Protection Agency, TS-767C, Washington, DC 20460/202-557-7700

Air—Mailing List Manager, Library Services, Environmental Protection Agency, MD-35, Research Triangle Park, NC 27711/929-541-4577.

Radiation—Mailing List Manager, Office of Radiation Programs, Environmental Protection Agency, ANR-458, Washington, DC 20460/202-557-9710

Research and Development—Mailing List Manager, ORD Publications, Environmental Protection Agency, 401 M St., S.W., (A-107), 202-382-4361.

Monitoring Technical Support
This office develops standard references and methods for environmental measurement and oversees EPA's quality assurance programs. Contact: Monitoring Systems and Quality Assurance, Office of Research and Development, Environmental Protection Agency, Room 3100, 401 M St., S.W., Washington, DC 20460/202-382-5767.

Motion Picture Film List
For a free listing of Environmental Protection Agency films available for loan at no cost, contact: Publications, Printing Management Office, Environmental Protection Agency, Room 230, 401 M St. S.W., Washington, DC 20460/202-755-0890. For audiovisual information, contact: Audiovisual, Office of Public Affairs, Environmental Protection Agency, Room W230, 401 M St. S.W., Washington, DC 20460/202-382-2064

Mobile Source Air Pollution
For information on mobile source air pollution, contact: Mobile Source Enforcement Division,

Office of Enforcement, Environmental Protection Agency, Room 3220 WSM, 401 M St. S.W., Washington, D.C. 20460/202-382-4645.

Oil and Special Material Control
This office develops programs and standards to control oil and hazardous material spills. Contact: Hazardous Response Division, Office of Water Program Operations, Environmental Protection Agency, Room 3103, 401 M St. S.W., Washington, DC 20460/202-245-3048.

Pesticide Enforcement
The Pesticide Enforcement Program includes the inspection of pesticide-producing establishments, market surveillance, and the monitoring of experimental use permits. Enforcement may include civil actions, stop sales, criminal prosecutions, and injunctive actions, as well as other methods. Contact: Pesticides and Toxic Substances Enforcement Division, Office of General Enforcement, Environmental Protection Agency, Room 541,ET, 401 M St. S.W., Washington, DC 20460/202-382-3807

Pesticide Programs
This office plans and carries out programs to limit the use of pesticides that are harmful to people or to the environment. Contact: Office of Pesticide Programs, Environmental Protection Agency, Room 539, ET, 401 M St. S.W., Washington, DC 20460/202-557-7090.

Pesticide Registration
Pesticide products are registered to prevent harmful products from entering the market and to require labeling products to assure proper use. Products are registered only if they perform their intended functions without unreasonable adverse effects on humans or the environment. Contact: Registration Division, Office of Pesticide Programs, Environmental Protection Agency, Room TS 767 C, 401 M St. S.W., Washington, DC 20460/202-557-7760.

Pesticide Research and Monitoring
Research and monitoring activities are designed to provide prompt alerts on environmental and human effects and to develop data on the long-term human health effects of exposure to pesticides. Contact: Hazard Evaluation Division, Office of Pesticide Programs, Environmental Protection Agency, Room 1121, TS-769, 401 M St. S.W., Washington, DC 20460/202-557-7351.

Planning and Evaluation
This office monitors and evaluates the progress of Environmental Protection Agency programs. It also reviews new standards and regulations. Contact: Standards and Regulations Division, Office of Planning and Evaluation, Environmental Pro-

ENVIRONMENTAL PROTECTION AGENCY

tection Agency, Room 1017A, WT, 401 M St. S.W., Washington, DC 20460/202-382-4001.

President's Youth Awards
This program has been established to recognize the accomplishments of those young people who, by becoming active in their communities, have become true environmentalists. The program also encourages schools, summer camps and groups to organize local environmental protection programs and other efforts to increase environmental awareness. Contact: President's Environmental Youth Awards Program, Office of Public, Environmental Protection Agency, Room W 305, WT, 401 M St. S.W., Washington, DC 20460/202-382-4367.

Publications . . . A Quarterly Guide
This free guide lists most of EPA's general and technical publications for the past year. Children's publications, posters and bumper stickers are also included. Among the topics covered are air pollution, noise, pesticides, solid waste, toxic substances, water pollution, radiation, and environmental health and safety. Contact: Publications, Environmental Protection Agency, Room 303, 401 M St. S.W., Washington, DC 20460/202-382-2624.

Public Information Center
This Center provides first-line contact for public inquiries including walk-in visits. The Center offers a wide variety of information about the EPA and its programs. It will also refer inquiries to the appropriate technical program or regional office. Contact: The Public Information Center, Environmental Protection Agency, 820 Quincy St., N.W., Washington, DC 20011/202-829-3535

Public Information Reference Unit
The public may inspect documents supporting agency actions at: Public Information Reference Unit, Environmental Protection Agency, Room 2904, 401 M St. S.W., Washington, DC 20460/202-382-5926.

Radiation Exposure Limit Regulations
The Non-ionizing Radiation Branch of the Environmental Protection Agency is involved in the development of federal regulations for establishing maximum, permissible exposure limits for radio frequency radiation including the possible hazards of electromagnetic radiation. Publications, available from the National Technical Information Service, include technical reports on specific areas of investigation. Contact: Non-ionizing Radiation Branch, U.S. Protection Agency, PO Box 18416, Las Vegas, NV 89114/702-798-2440.

Radiation Programs
Criteria and standards for the protection of people and the environment from all sources of radiation, including ambient standards for the total amount of radiation from all facilities in the uranium fuel cycle are developed in this office. Contact: Office of Radiation Programs, Environmental Protection Agency, Room 101, ANR-050, 401 M St. S.W., Washington, DC 20460/202-0704.

Selling to the EPA
A free pamphlet with procurement and research and development program information is available from: Procurement and Contracts Management Division, Environmental Protection Agency, PM-214, 401 M St. S.W., Washington, DC 20460/202-382-5020.

Solid Waste Programs
Federal financial and technical assistance to state and local governments in planning and developing comprehensive solid waste management programs is available. These programs include environmental control on all land disposal of solid wastes, regulation of hazardous waste from point of generation through disposal and resource recovery and activities. (Also, see "Grants.") Contact: Office of Solid Waste, Environmental Protection Agency, Room 2804, 401 M St. S.W., Washington, DC 20460/202-382-4627.

Speakers
For information on available speakers, contact: Speaker's Bureau, Office of Public Affairs, Environmental Protection Agency, Room 209, WT, 401 M St. S.W., Washington, DC 20460/ 202-382-7957.

State Drinking Water Programs
The states work to develop water supply enforcement programs and control the underground injection of contaminants. States also survey the quality and availability of rural drinking water supplies. The Environmental Protection Agency provides grant assistance and technical guidance to facilitate these programs. Contact: States Program Division, Office of Drinking Water, Environmental Protection Agency, Room E1099, 401 M St. S.W., Washington, DC 20460/202-382-5522.

State Solid Waste Programs
State programs include schedules for upgrading or closing all environmentally unacceptable land disposal sites, "open dumps" certified according to EPA criteria, and a nationwide inventory. Contact: State Programs, Office of Solid Waste, Environmental Protection Agency, Room F-256, 401 M St. S.W., Washington, DC 20460/202-382-2210.

Stationary Sources of Pollution Enforcement
Standards for enforcing stationary sources of air pollution, radiation and solid waste such as sewage plants and industrial mills and factories are formulated in this office. For additional information, contact: Stationary Source Enforcement Division, Office of General Enforcement, Environmental

Protection Agency, Room M3202D, 401 M St. S.W., Washington, DC 20460/202-382-2807.

Technical Publications

Many Environmental Protection Agency publications are available free from EPA's technical program offices. Others can be obtained from the Government Printing Office or the National Technical Information Service. For a copy of *Publications: A Quarterly Guide,* which includes both technical and general publications, contact: Publications, Printing Management Office, Environmental Protection Agency, Room 303, 401 M St. S.W., Washington, DC 20460/202-382-2624.

Toll-Free Number

For information on the Environmental Protection Agency's regulation of chlorofluorocarbons (CFCs), contact EPA's regional offices, or Office of Pesticides and Toxic Substances, Environmental Protection Agency, Room 541, ET, 401 M St. S.W., Washington, DC 20460/202-382-3807. (800-424-9065).

Toxic Substances

The Environmental Protection Agency identifies and controls harmful chemicals already in commerce as well as new chemicals prior to their commercial manufacture. EPA requires industry to provide information about the production, distribution, use, exposure and health and environmental effects of chemicals. It also requires industry to test potentially harmful chemicals for health and environmental effects and to control harmful chemicals that pose an unreasonable risk to health or the environment. Contact: Office of Toxic Substances, Environmental Protection Agency, Room 539, ET, 401 M St. S.W., Washington, DC 20460/202-382-3813.

Toxic Substances Tests

The Environmental Protection Agency requires manufacturers and processors to conduct tests on potentially harmful chemicals. The conducted tests evaluate a chemical's characteristics, such as persistence or acute toxicity, and clarify the health and environmental effects of a chemical, including carcinogenic, mutagenic, behavioral and synergistic effects. Contact: Assessment Division, Office of Toxic Substances, Environmental Protection Agency, Room 539,ET, 401 M St. S.W., Washington, DC 20460/202-382-3813.

Unsolicited Proposals

Unsolicited proposals for projects such as fundamental research that might advance the state of the art, present possible development of solutions to problems, or contribute to knowledge of a specific phenomenon is an important method of EPA

business. Contact: Bids and Proposals, Environmental Protection Agency, 3rd Floor, 401 M St. S.W., Washington, DC 20460/202-382-3255.

Water Data

A water program data system with files on water quality, discharge and program data is available. Contact: Monitoring and Data Support Division, Office of Water Program Operations, Environmental Protection Agency, Room WH-553, 401 M St. S.W.,Washington, DC 20460/202-382-7040.

Waste Disposal Methods

The Office of Environmental Protection Agency plans, develops, and manages a comprehensive research program to: 1) develop and demonstrate methods to prevent, manage, or control the discharge of pollutants and the disposal of wastes from municipal, recreational, and other domestic sources; 2) assess the environmental and socioeconomic impact of such methods; 3) develop methods to reduce the production of wastes, including recycling; and 4) provide technical expertise and management assistance in the foregoing areas. Contact: Waste Management Division, Office of Environmental Engineering and Technology, Environmental Protection Agency, RD-681, West Tower, 401 M St, S.W., Washington, DC 20460/202-382-2583.

Water Enforcement

The enforcement program includes discharge permit issuance and compliance activities and enforcement actions to achieve compliance with ocean dumping and oil and hazardous materials discharge regulations. Contact: Enforcement Division, Office of Water Enforcement, Environmental Protection Agency, Room M2108, 401 M St. S.W., Washington, DC 20460/202-475-8488.

Water Program Operations

This office develops national programs, technical policies, regulations and guidelines for water pollution control. For information, contact: Water Program Operations, Office of Water, Environmental Protection Agency, Room 1209, ET, 401 M St. S.W., Washington, DC 20460/202-382-5850.

Water Quality Criteria

The water quality criteria program through which the EPA sets acceptable levels for pollutants in ambient waters which serve to protect aquatic life and the health of organisms, including man, which may contact the water. Contact: Criteria and Standards Division, Office of Water Regulations and Standards, Environmental Protection Agency, 401 M St. S.W., WH 585, Washington, DC 20460/202-382-5400.

Water Quality Program

Water quality program is primarily concerned with controlling the discharge of pollutants into waterways from industrial and municipal point and nonpoint sources. For general information, contact: Office of Water, Environmental Protection Agency, Room 1030, ET, 401 M St. S.W., Washington, DC 20460/202-382-5700.

How Can the Environmental Protection Agency Help You?

For information on how this agency can be of help to you, contact: Office of Public Affairs, General Inquires, Environmental Protection Agency, Room W311, 401 M St. S.W., Washington, DC 20460/202-382-4355.

Equal Employment Opportunity Commission

2401 E St. N.W., Washington, DC 20507/202-634-6922

Established: July 2, 1965
Budget: $147,332,000
Employees: 3,185

Mission: Eliminates discrimination based on race, color, religion, sex, national origin or age in hiring, promotion, firing, wages, testing, training, apprenticeship and all other conditions of employment; promotes voluntary action programs by employers, unions, and community organizations to make equal employment opportunity an actuality; and is responsible for all compliance and enforcement activities relating to equal employment opportunity among federal employees and applicants, including handicap discrimination.

Major Sources of Information

Age Discrimination
The Age Discrimination in Employment Act protects workers aged 40-70 from arbitrary age discrimination in hiring, discharge, pay, promotions, fringe benefits and other aspects of employment. For further information, contact: any Equal Employment Opportunity Commission district or area office, or Public Information Unit, Office of Public Affairs, Equal Employment Opportunity Commission, Room 412, 2401 E St. N.W., Washington, DC 20507/202-634-6922

Equal Work Equal Pay
The Equal Pay Act protects women and men against pay discrimination based on sex. For further information, contact: any Equal Employment Opportunity Commission District or area office, or Public Information Unit, Office of Public Affairs, Equal Employment Opportunity Commis-

sion, Room 412, 2401 E St. N.W., Washington, DC 20507/202-634-6922

Field Services
The Equal Employment Opportunity Commission has 22 district offices and 37 smaller area offices to oversee the case-processing system on a regional basis. For a list of these offices and general information, contact: Office of Field Services, Equal Employment Opportunity Commission, Room 410, 2401 E St. N.W., Washington, DC 20507/202-634-6922

Freedom of Information Requests
For Freedom of Information Act requests contact: Office of General Counsel, Employment Opportunity Commission, Room 230, 2401 E St. N.W., Washington, DC 20507/202-634-6595.

Grants

The programs described below are for a sum of money given by the federal government to initiate and stimulate new or improved activities or to sustain on-going services:

Employment Discrimination Project Contracts— Indian Tribes

Objectives: To insure the protection of employment rights of Indians working on reservations.

Eligibility: Any land based Native American Tribe that has a tribal employment rights office established under an ordinance passed by the tribal council.

Range of Financial Assistance: Not applicable.

Contact: State and Local Section, Special Services Staff, Equal Employment Opportunity Commission, 2401 E Street, NW, Washington, DC 20507/202-634-6806.

Employment Discrimination—State and Local Anti-Discrimination Agency Contracts

Objectives: To assist EEOC in the enforcement of Title VII of the Civil Rights Act of 1964, as amended, by attempting settlement and investigating and resolving charges of employment discrimination based on race, color, religion, sex or national origin, or age.

Eligibility: Official state and local government agencies charged with the administration and enforcement of fair employment practices laws.

Range of Financial Assistance: $35,400 to $1,977,200.

Contact: State and Local Section, Special Services Staff, Equal Employment Opportunity Commission, Room 433, 2401 E Street, NW, Washington, DC 20507/202-634-6806.

Hiring Statistics

Statistics on the hiring of minority groups, including women, for nine job categories such as clerical workers, service workers, blue collar workers, and professional and technical workers, is available by state, Standard Metropolitan Statistical Area (SMSA), industry and nationwide. Statistics are also available on apprentices, union workers, state and local governments, and individuals with elementary and secondary education as well as those with college and university degrees. For further information, contact: Office of Program Research, Equal Employment Opportunity Commission, Washington, DC 20507/202-634-6750.

Meeting Schedule

The Equal Employment Opportunity Commission provides recorded information on the agenda, date, and place of the next meeting of the Commission. Contact: Equal Employment Opportunity Commission, 2401 E St. N.W., Washington, DC 20507/202-634-6748.

Publications and Information

For general information and Equal Employment Opportunity Commission publications, contact: Office of Public Affairs, Equal Employment Opportunity Commission, Room 412, 2401 E St. N.W., Washington, DC 20507/202-634-6922.

Special Projects and Programs

This office develops programs for employers designed to deal with Equal Employment Opportunity Commission laws. Such programs include worker-employer arbitration and development of affirmative action programs. Contact: Office of Special Projects and Programs, Equal Employment Opportunity Commission, Room 316, SKY, 2401 E St. N.W., Washington, DC 20507/703-634-7674

How Can the Equal Employment Opportunity Commission Help You?

For information on how this agency can help you, contact: Resource Management Division, Equal Employment Opportunity Commission, Room 386, 2401 E St. N.W., Washington, DC 20507/202-634-1947.

Export-Import Bank of the United States

811 Vermont Ave. N.W., Washington, DC 20571/202-566-8990

Established: February 2, 1934
Budget: $13,865,000,000
Employees: 350

Mission: Facilitates and aids in financing exports of U.S. goods and services; and lends directly or issues guarantees and insurance so that exporters and private banks can extend appropriate financing without taking undue risks.

Major Sources of Information

Agricultural Exports
The Eximbank provides financial support for the export of agricultural commodities, agribusiness facilities and production equipment. The export support programs applicable to agricultural commodities, capital goods and services include insurance for commodity exports, and both insurance and bank guarantees for capital goods. Small business credits and medium-term credits are also available to provide fixed-rate financing for capital goods exports. Contact: Export-Import Bank of the United States, Room 1275, 811 Vermont Ave. N.W., Washington, DC 20571/202-566-8860 or toll free 1-800-424-5201.

Briefing Programs
Regular briefing programs are held at the Eximbank headquarters to familiarize banks, exporters and others with the Eximbank's financing programs and policies. Two day programs for US commercial bankers and one-day briefings for US exporters are tailored to participants needs. For further information, contact: Office of Public Affairs and Publications, Export-Import Bank of the United States, Room 1275, 811 Vermont Ave. N.W., Washington, DC 20571/202-566-8990.

Claims
This office processes claims filed under the Bank's direct lending, guarantee and insurance programs. It is also responsible for collections and recoveries on claims paid. Contact: Claims Division, Export-Import Bank of the United States, Room 969, 811 Vermont Ave. N.W., Washington, DC 20571/202-566-8822.

Conferences on Small Business Exporting
Eximbank, in coordination with the U.S. Department of Commerce and Small Business Administration, sponsors one day conferences throughout the United States to show smaller firms what opportunities are available in foreign trade and what government services can do to help. For further information, contact: Eximbank's Marketing Division, Room 1278, 811 Vermont Ave. N.W., Washington, DC 20571/202-566-8873.

Congressional Relations
Congressional Relations staff is responsible for Eximbank's liaison with the U.S. Congress on all legislation directly affecting or of interest to the Bank. This office processes requests for information from members of Congress and Congressional committees and monitors the appearance of Bank officers before Congress. Contact: Congressional Relations, Export-Import Bank of the United States, Room 1266, 811 Vermont Ave. N.W., Washington, DC 20571/202-566-8967.

Credit Information
The Credit Information Section maintains over 50,000 credit files on thousands of foreign firms with which Eximbank has had experience. It also administers the exchange of information between Eximbank and other members of the Berne Union, an international association of credit insurers. This information is especially helpful to smaller exporters and to those companies of any size that are relatively new to foreign markets. Contact: Credit Information, Export-Import Bank of the United States, Room 912, 811 Vermont Ave. N.W., Washington, DC 20571/202-566-4690.

Direct Credits and Financial Guarantees
The Direct Credits and Financial Guarantees Division administers the Bank's long-term export financing programs. It is divided into the following geographic areas: Africa and Middle East; Asia; Europe and Canada; and Latin America. For additional information, contact: Office of the Senior Vice President, Direct Credits and Financial Guarantees, Export-Import Bank of the United States, Room 1115, 811 Vermont Ave. N.W., Washington, DC 20571/202-566-8187.

Exporter Credits and Guarantees
This office is responsible for the Bank's program to support U.S. Export sales with repayment terms of five years or less. Programs cover small- and medium-term credits, working capital loans and commercial bank guarantees. Contact: Exporter Credits and Guarantees, Export-Import Bank of the United States, Room 901, 811 Vermont Ave. N.W., Washington, DC 20571/202-566-8819.

Exporter Insurance
This office works in close cooperation with the personnel of the Foreign Credit Insurance Association to provide short- and medium-term credit insurance protection for U.S. exporters. Contact: Exporter Insurance, Export-Import Bank of the United States, Room 919, 811 Vermont Ave. N.W., Washington, DC 20571/202-566-8955.

Feasibility Studies
Eximbank will support U.S. firms undertaking studies of overseas projects. Applications for feasibility studies should be made for the appropriate program. For further information, contact: Eximbank Advisory Service, Export-Import Bank of the United States, Room 1275, 811 Vermont Ave. N.W., Washington, DC 20571/202-566-8860 or toll free 1-800-424-5201.

Freedom of Information Act Requests
For Freedom of Information Act requests, contact: Office of Public Affairs and Publications, Export-Import Bank, Room 1231, 811 Vermont Ave. N.W., Washington, DC 20571/202-566-8990.

Government Affairs
This office is responsible for Eximbank's liaison with other U.S. government agencies and interagency bodies, such as the National Advisory Council on International Monetary and Financial Policies. Contact: Government Affairs, Export-Import Bank of the United States, Room 1228, 811 Vermont Ave. N.W., Washington, DC 20571/202-566-8853.

Library
The Eximbank Library concentrates on economics, finance, export credits, business and statistical information. Contact: Library, Export-Import Bank of the United States, Room 1373, 811 Vermont Ave. N.W., Washington, DC 20571/202-566-8320.

Policy Analysis
The Policy Analysis staff conducts the policy planning and research work of the Bank. It monitors economic developments that may affect the Bank's operations and reviews and evaluates the Bank's programs and policies. Contact: Office of Policy Analysis, Export-Import Bank of the United States, Room 1243, 811 Vermont Ave. N.W., Washington, DC 20571/202-566-8861.

Public Affairs and Publications
Public Affairs and Publications is responsible for the Eximbank's public information and business liaison programs, including press relations, conferences, speaking engagements, export and small business counseling. It is also responsible for Export-Import Bank publications. Contact: Office of Public Affairs and Publications, Export-Import Bank of the United States, Room 1231, 811 Vermont Ave. N.W., Washington, DC 20571/202-566-8990.

Small Business Assistance Hotline
Eximbank has established a hotline service to help small business. This counseling service can answer questions that small business exporters may have concerning assistance in financing goods and/or services for sale to foreign countries. Various programs exist to help small exporters. They include the small business advisory service, briefing programs, financial support programs such as export credit insurance including a new-to-export short-term comprehensive policy, the small business guarantee program, and the small business credit program. Contact: Business Advisory Service, Export-Import Bank of the United States, Room 1275, 811 Vermont Ave. N.W., Washington, DC 20571/202-566-8860.

Technical and Scientific Information

Eximbank's engineers review the technical and scientific aspects of each District Credit and Financial Guarantee proposal before the bank. Contact: Engineering, Export-Import Bank of the United States, Room 1167, 811 Vermont Ave. N.W., Washington, DC 20571/202-566-8802.

How Can the Export-Import Bank of the United States Help You?

To find out how this agency can help you, contact: Business Advisory Service, Export-Import Bank of the United States, Room 1275, 811 Vermont Ave. N.W., Washington, DC 20571/202-566-8860 or toll free 1-800-424-5201.

Farm Credit Administration

1501 Farm Drive, McLean, VA 22102/703-883-4000

Established: December 10,1971
Budget: $18,186,000
Employees: 287

Mission: Responsible for the supervision, examination and coordination of the borrower-owned banks and associations that comprise the cooperative Farm Credit System. These institutions make long-term loans on farm, rural or commercial fishing related real estate through local federal land bank associations; the federal intermediate credit banks which provide short-and intermediate-term loan funds to production credit associations and other institutions financing farmers, ranchers, rural homeowners, owners of farm-related businesses, and commercial fishermen; and the banks for cooperatives which make loans for all kinds of agricultural and aquatic cooperatives.

Major Sources of Information

Farm Credit System Information
The cooperative Farm Credit System provides credit and closely related services to farmers, ranchers, cooperatives, and to selected farm-related businesses. The system also provides credit for rural homes to producers and associations of producers. Detailed information on the Banks and Associations of the Farm System may be found in the following publications available from the Farm Credit Banks and the Farm Credit Administration:

Federal Land Banks and How They Operate
Production Credit Associations—How They Operate
Banks for Cooperatives—How They Operate
Corporate Farm Credit System
Annual Report to Investors
Farm Credit Board Brochure
Yearly Annual Report

For a complete descriptive listing of all publications and films available on the Farm Credit System, contact: Public Affairs Division, Farm Credit Administration, Farm Credit Bldg, 1501 Farm Credit Drive, McLean, VA 22102/703-883-4056.

Freedom of Information Requests
For Freedom of Information Act requests, contact: Freedom of Information, Public Affairs Division, Farm Credit Administration, Farm Credit Bldg, 1501 Farm Credit Drive, McLean VA 22102/703-883-4113.

How Can the Farm Credit Administration Help You?
To determine how this agency can help you, contact: Public Affairs Division, Farm Credit Administration, Farm Credit Bldg, 1501 Farm Credit Drive, McLean, VA 22102/703-883-4056

Federal Communications Commission

1919 M St. N.W., Washington, DC 20554/202-632-7000

Established: 1934
Budget: $82,936,000
Employees: 1896

Mission: Regulates interstate and foreign communications by radio, television, wire and cable; is responsible for the orderly development and operation of broadcast services and the provision of rapid, efficient nationwide and worldwide telephone and telegraph services at reasonable rates; and promotes the safety of life and property through radio and the use of radio and television to strengthen the national defense.

Major Sources of Information

Applications, Bulletins and Forms
For requesting applications, bulletins and forms of the Federal Communications Commission, contact: Federal Communications Commission District Offices, or Services and Supply Branch, Federal Communications Commission, Room B-10, 1919 M St. N.W., Washington, DC 20554/202-632-7272.

Broadcast Stations
The Federal Communications Commission allocates spectrum space for AM and FM radio, and VHF and UHF television broadcast services; assigns frequencies and call letters to stations; designates operating power and sign-on and sign-off times. It also issues construction permits and inspects technical equipment. The FCC also requires licensees to serve the programming tastes, needs and desires of their communities. For further information, contact: Mass Media Bureau, Federal Communications Commission, Room 314,

1919 M St. N.W., Washington, DC 20554/202-632-6460.

Cable Television
For general information and/or complaints on cable television, contact: Complaints and Information Branch, Cable Television Bureau, Federal Communications Commission, Room 6218, 2025 M St. N.W., Washington, DC 20554/202-632-3860.

Citizens and Amateur Radio Rules
For information on citizens and amateur radio rules and how these rules are made, contact: Personal Radio Branch, Private Radio Bureau, Federal Communications Commission, Room 8202, 2025 M St. N.W., Washington, DC 20554/202-632-4964.

Common Carrier Complaints
Consumer Affairs Division will handle informal written or verbal complaints from the public on

interstate and international common carrier matters. It will also provide information services to help you understand common carrier proposals and issues and procedural assistance for participating in common carrier proposals and issues. Contact: Consumer Affairs Division, Common Carrier Bureau, Federal Communications Commission, Room 6324, 2025 M St. N.W., Washington, DC 20554/202-632-7553.

Common Carriers
The Federal Communications Commission supervises charges, practices, classifications and regulations on interstate and foreign communication by radio, wire and cable; considers applications for construction of new facilities and discontinuance or reduction of service; acts on applications for interlocking directorates and mergers, and prescribes and reviews the accounting practices of communication carriers. For information, contact: Consumer Affairs Division, Common Carrier Bureau, Federal Communications Commission, Room 6324, 2025 M St. N.W., Washington, DC 20554/202-632-7553.

Common Carrier Tariffs
Common carrier tariffs for interstate and foreign wire and communications are on file. Contact: Tariff Review Branch, Common Carrier Bureau, Federal Communications Commission, Room 518, 1919 M St. N.W., Washington, DC 20554/202-632-5550.

Computerized Data Base
See entry in this section titled "Low Power Television Data Bases and Experts."

Direct Broadcast Satellite Specialists
The Federal Communications Commission (FCC)'s Video Services Division has several specialists in direct broadcast satellite. Several resource people are available including: engineers who can answer technical inquiries; and attorneys who can answer legal questions as well as some technical inquiries. Contact: Video Service Division, Distribution SVS Branch, Federal Communications Commission (FCC), 1919 M Street, NW, Room 702, Washington, DC 20554/202-632-9356.

Dockets
Information on the status of Federal Communications Commission hearing proceedings is obtainable. History cards for all docketed cases since 1928 are filed, including FCC action setting the case for hearing and all subsequent actions in the case. Information on petitions or requests for rulemaking and on rulemaking proceedings is also available from history cards. Contact: Dockets Branch, The Secretary, Federal Communications Commission, Room 230, 1919 M St. N.W., Washington, DC 20554/202-632-7535.

Equal Time Complaints
To complain about Equal Time in Political Broadcasting, contact: Fairness in Political Programming, Enforcement Division, Media Bureau, Federal Communications, Room 6008, 2025 M St. N.W., Washington, DC 20554/202-632-7586.

Equipment Authorization
Manufacturers of new equipment using spectrum space must obtain an equipment authorization as a legal prerequisite to marketing. Contact: Equipment Authorization, Office of Science and Technology, Authorization and Standards Division, Federal Communications Commission, P.O. Box 429, Columbia, MD 21045/301-725-1585.

Ex-Parte Presentations
For information concerning ex-parte presentations, contact: Office of the Executive Director, Federal Communications Commission, Room 852, 1919 M St. N.W., Washington, DC 20554/202-632-6390.

Federal Telecommunications Services
The Consumer Assistance and Small Business Division of the Federal Communications Commission (FCC) is the place to go if you have questions about FCC telecommunications services, such as the use of radio, broadcast, telephone, cable television, and satellite communications. They will provide you with assistance in locating information concerning FCC rules, policies and procedures. If you need general information about communications issues or background material about the FCC, see entry titled "Information Bulletins" this section for a list of bulletins available from the FCC. Contact: Consumer Assistance and Small Business Division, Federal Communications Commission, 1919 M Street, NW, Room 252, Washington, DC 20054/202-632-7000.

Field Operations
The Field Operations Bureau is engaged largely in engineering work. This includes monitoring the radio spectrum to see that station operation meets technical requirements, inspecting stations of all types, conducting operator examinations and issuing permits or licenses to those found qualified, locating and closing unauthorized transmitters, furnishing radio bearings for aircraft or ships in distress, locating sources of interference and suggesting the remedial measures, doing special engineering work for other government agencies, and obtaining and analyzing technical data for Commission use. For additional information, contact: Field Operations Bureau, Federal Communications Commission, Room 734, 1919 M St. N.W., Washington, DC 20554/202-632-6980.

FM/TV Data Base Lists

The Federal Communications Commission Facilities Division maintains an FM and TV engineering data base containing applications, construction permits and licenses for all U.S. stations, including translators and boosters and traditional broadcast stations. Also included are vacant allocations, proposed rulemakings to amend the Table of Assignments and similar information in Canadian and Mexican stations. The two lists printed from these data bases are sorted by frequency (channel), state and city and vice versa. FM lists are printed each month, with weekly updates, TV lists every two months with biweekly updates. TV lists are in two parts: regular TV stations and translators/boosters. Lists are available in the Public Reference Room, Broadcast Bureau, Federal Communications Commission, Room 239, 1919 M St. N.W., Washington, DC 20554/202-632-7566, or can be obtained at the Downtown Copy Center, 1114 21st St. N.W., Washington, DC 20036/202-452-1422. Note: These lists are unofficial and may contain inadvertent errors.

Freedom of Information Act Requests

For Freedom of Information Act Requests, contact: Internal Review and Security Division, Federal Communications Commission, Room 411, 1919 M St. N.W., Washington, DC 20554/202-632-7143.

Frequency Allocation

Domestic and international frequency allocation is administered through this office. Contact: Spectrum Management Division, Office of Science and Technology, Federal Communications Commission, Room 7218, 2025 M St. N.W., Washington, DC 20554/202-632-7025.

Frequency Assignments

Nongovernment frequency assignment lists give data about radio stations of different classes, including frequency, power and call signal assignments; location of base stations with geographic coordinates, number of mobile units, etc. They include frequency lists for broadcast, aviation, marine, industrial, land transportation, public safety, and common carrier services. Contact: Downtown Copy Center, 1114 21st St. N.W., Washington, DC 20036/202-452-1422, or 452-1419 for the computer printout.

Handicapped Information

The coordinator for handicapped individuals offers a job referral service for the handicapped and provides technical assistance to broadcasters in revising job descriptions of positions of interest to handicapped individuals. Contact: The Consumer Assistance Office, Federal Communications Commission, Room 254, 1919 M St. N.W., Washington, DC 20554/202-632-7000.

Information Bulletins

The Federal Communications Commission publishes a number of information bulletins. The following list of bulletins can be obtained free of charge from the Public Information Division, Office of Public Affairs, Room 254, Federal Communications Commission, 1919 M St. N.W., Washington, DC 20554/202-632-7000:

How to Apply for a Broadcast Station
Broadcast Services
The FCC in Brief
Radio Station and Other Lists
A Short History of Electrical Communication
Safety and Radio Services
Common Carrier Services
Station Identification and Call Signs
Regulation of Wire and Radio Communication
Frequency Allocation
Educational Television
Memo to All Young People Interested in Radio
Letter to a Schoolboy
Field Operations Bureau
Subscription TV
Private Radio Services
Public Radio
Cable Television

Interference Complaints

For complaints of radio and television interference, contact the nearest Federal Communication Commission Field Operations Office of the Investigations Branch, Field Operations Bureau, Federal Communications Commission, Room 744, 1919 M St. N.W., Washington, DC 20554/202-632-6345.

Legal Assistance

The Federal Communications Bar Association has instituted a Legal Aid Program for indigent individuals and groups. For a list of possible sources of legal assistance, contact: Consumer Assistance Office, Federal Communications Commission, Room 254, 1919 M St. N.W., Washington, DC 20554/202-632-7000.

Library

The Library contains books, periodicals and information on research and technical subjects, economics and the mass media. It also keeps a legislative history of the Communications Act and congressional hearings involving the FCC. Contact: FCC Library, Federal Communications Commission, Room 639, 1919 M St. N.W., Washington, DC 20554/202-632-7100.

License Application Status

To obtain information on the status of citizens and amateur radio, aviation and marine licenses, contact: Licensing Processing Section, Federal Communications Commission, Rt. 116 West, Gettysburg, PA 17325/717-337-1511 (citizens band and business, including land transportation) (amateur radio); 717-337-1212 (aviation and marine).

Low Power Television Data Bases and Experts
The Low Power Branch of the U.S. Federal Communications Commission is responsible for following all aspects of Low Power Television (LPTV), including authority to construct licenses, interference policy, and the granting of licenses and renewals. This office will answer questions from the public and make referrals to other sources. The LP Branch has available experts on the legal aspects of LPTV and experts on the engineering aspects of LPTV. The LP Branch maintains several data bases listing information on all applications and licenses for LPTV. The data bases are available on microfiche or tape from International Transcription Service, Inc., 40006 University Drive, Fairfax, VA 22030/703-352-2400. Contact: Low Power Branch, U.S. Federal Communications Commission (FCC), 1919 M Street, NW, Washington, DC 20554/202-632-3894.

Master Lists of Radio Stations
Master lists of radio stations, radio frequencies, construction permits and applicants are available for public reference. Contact: Public Reference Room, License Division, Broadcast Bureau, Federal Communications Commission, Room 239, 1919 M St. N.W., Washington, DC 20554/202-632-7566.

Mobile Communications System Regulation
Staff in the Mobile Division of the Federal Communications Commission (FCC) will answer inquiries about the regulatory aspects of cellular radio and other mobile communications systems, and will make referrals to experts. Contact: Mobile Division, Federal Communications Commission, Room 650, 1919 M St. N.W., Washington,DC 20554/202-632-6450.

Multipoint Distribution Service
The Public Reference Room (No. 331) maintains Multipoint Distribution Service (MDS) station files, an inventory of pending applications, by location and service area, etc. Contact: Federal Communications Commission (FCC), 1919 M St. N.W., Washington, DC 20554/202-634-1798 (Public Reference Room).

Network Studies
Detailed studies are available of network behavior with respect to affiliates, advertisers and program suppliers, analyses of syndicated program distribution and examinations of the factors influencing the profitability of television stations. The historical evolution of the commercial network broadcast system, the structure and business activities of the parent corporations of the major network practices and "network dominance" have also been studied.

Contact: Mass Media Bureau, Federal Communications Commission, Room 314, 1919 M St. N.W., Washington, DC 20554/202-632-6460.

Owning Your Own Phone
This free brochure answers basic questions on the purchase of telephone equipment. Contact: Consumer Assistance Office, Federal Communications Commission, Room 254, 1919 M St. N.W., Washington, DC 20554/202-632-7000.

Private Radio Services
There are eight main categories of private radio services that are regulated by the FCC: Stations on Land in the Maritime Services; Stations on Shipboard in the Maritime Services; Aviation Services; Private Land Mobile Radio Services; Private Operational-Fixed Microwave Service; Personal Radio Services; Amateur Radio Service; and Disaster Communications Service. Contact: Private Radio Bureau, Federal Communications Commission, Room 5002, 2025 M St. N.W., Washington, DC 20554/202-632-6940.

Program and Advertising Complaints
To complain about programs and advertising, contact: Complaints Compliance and Investigation, Federal Communications Commission, Room 6218, 2025 M St. N.W., Washington, DC 20554/202-632-7048.

Public Documents
Copies of public documents such as a Notice of Inquiry or a Notice of Proposed Rulemaking can be obtained by contacting the Consumer Assistance Office, Federal Communications Commission, Room 254, 1919 M St. N.W., Washington, DC 20554/202-632-7000.

Public Reference Rooms
These rooms maintain dockets concerning rulemaking and adjudicatory matters, copies of applications for licenses, and grants and reports required to be filed by licensees and cable system operators. All folders in docketed cases are retained for two years after the proceedings have been closed. Also available for inspection are transcripts of nondocket proceedings such as oral arguments and hearings or various types of committee or group meetings. Public documents are available for inspection by the general public in the following rooms:

Broadcast Public Reference Room, Federal Communications Commission, Room 239, 1919 M St. N.W., Washington, DC 20554/202-632-7566.
Cable TV Public Reference Room, Federal Communications Commission, Room 239, 1919 M St. N.W., Washington, DC 20554/202-469-9312.
Common Carrier Public Reference Room, Federal Communications Commission, Room 628 1919 M St. N.W., Washington, DC 20554/202-254-6810, and Room 528,

2025 M St. N.W., Washington, DC 20554/202-653-7388.

Radio Broadcasting Services
The Federal Communications Commission (FCC) regulates interstate and international communications by radio, and oversees the development and operations of radio broadcasting services nationwide. These services include AM, FM, commercial and noncommercial, educational, and developmental services. Other radio services include: aviation; marine; public safety; industrial; land transportation; amateur, personal disaster and experimental.

Those interested in more details about the FCC may obtain publication lists from the Office of Public Affairs. The FCC also has books, reprints, journals, newsletters, publications lists, bibliographies, regulations and history background. Contact: Federal Communications Commission (FCC), 1919 M Street, NW, Washington, DC 20554/202-632-7000 (Consumer Assistance); 202-632-7100 (Library Branch).

Radio Equipment List
The Federal Communications Commission prepares a list of certain type-approved and type-accepted equipment. The list is sold for $25.00 prepaid or plus postage billed, by Downtown Copy Center, 1114 21st St. N.W., Washington, DC 20036/202-452-1422.

Radio Operator Licenses
The Federal Communications Commission issues seven types of commercial radio operator licenses: Radiotelephone First Class Operator License, Radiotelephone Second Class Operator License, Restricted Radiotelephone Operator Permit, Radiotelegraph First Class Operator License, Radiotelegraph Second Class Operator License, Radiotelegraph Third Class Operator Permit, and Marine Radio Operator Permit. The FCC also issues endorsements on first and second class licenses which extend their authority in certain areas. They are the Radar Endorsement, Six Months Service Endorsement, and Aircraft Radiotelegraph Endorsement. It also provides examination guides for prospective radio operator licensees. Contact: Radio Operator and Public Service Branch, Federal Communications Commission, Room 728, 1919 M St. N.W., Washington, DC 20554/202-632-7240.

Recorded Listings of New Releases and Texts
For recorded announcements of Federal Communications Commission actions, contact: Press and News Media Division, Federal Communications Commission, Room 202, 1919 M St. N.W., Washington, DC 20554/202-632-0002.

Regulation of Radio
The Federal Communications Commission considers applications for construction permits and licenses for all classes of nongovernment stations; assignment of frequencies, power and call signs; authorization of communication circuits; modification and renewal of licenses; inspection of transmitting equipment and regulation of its use; control of interference; review of technical operation; remedial action when necessary and other implementation of the Communications Act. Contact: Private Radio Bureau, Federal Communications Commission, Room 5002, 2025 M St. N.W., Washington, DC 20554/202-632-6930.

Satellite Systems Report
Technical Aspects Related to Direct Broadcasting Satellite Systems (pub. no. PB81-178980), is a collection of technical memoranda relating to Direct Broadcasting Satellite systems. The material gives a general description of a system which includes ground receivers, advances in the technology, some information on satellite planning for the ITU Region 2 and a description of experimental DBS satellite systems. Contact: National Technical Information Service, 5285 Port Royal Road, Springfield, VA 22161/703-487-4850

Subscription Television Licenses and Policies
The Federal Communications Commission (FCC) regulates licenses and policies related to the operation of subscription television stations. The FCC has specialists in the areas of licenses and policies regarding subscription television in its television branch at 202-632-5357. Those looking for information about the FCC may obtain copies of bulletins such as "Subscription Television," "The FCC in Brief," "How to Apply for a Broadcast Station," among others. Single copies are available free of charge. Contact: Federal Communications Commission (FCC), 1919 M Street, NW, Washington, DC 20554/202-632-7000 (Consumer Assistance Division); 202-632-7100 (Library Branch).

Technical Bulletins and Reports
Reports and technical bulletins on standards, types of equipment approved and on topics such as broadcast satellite systems, new television service, noise, audio devices and other technical subjects are available from: Technical Information Specialist, Office of Science and Technology, Federal Communications Commission, Room 7109, 2025 M St. N.W., Washington, DC 20554/202-632-7033.

Telephone and Telegraph Complaints
For notifying the Federal Communications Commission about problems with the telephone and telegraph systems, contact: Consumer Affairs Division, Informal Complaints, Federal Communica-

tions Commission, Room 6318, 2025 M St. N.W., Washington, DC 20554/202-632-7553.

Telephone Directory
The Federal Communications Commission Telephone Directory, which includes a functional listing of offices, is available for $1.71 from the Downtown Copy Center, 1114 21st St. N.W., Washington, DC 20036/202-452-1422. (The directory costs $1.00 if you pick it up in person.)

Transcripts
Transcripts of hearings (including prepared state-ments and oral records but not exhibits) may be ordered at the time of the hearing from the Federal Communications Commission official reporter. Contact: International Transcription Services, Inc., 1307 Prince St., Alexandria, VA 22314

How Can the Federal Communications Commission Help You?
For information on how this agency can help you, contact: Consumer Assistance and Information Division, Federal Communications Commission, Room 254, 1919 M St. N.W., Washington, DC 20554/202-632-7000.

Federal Deposit Insurance Corporation

550 17th St. N.W., Washington, DC 20429/202-389-4221

Established: June 16, 1933
Budget: $741,065,000
Employees: 3,554

Mission: Promotes and preserves public confidence in banks and protects the money supply through provision of insurance coverage for bank deposits.

Major Sources of Information

Bank Liquidation
This office supervises the liquidation of failed insured banks and keeps comprehensive records of each case. Contact: Division of Liquidation, Federal Deposit Insurance Corporation, Room 626 NYAV, 550 17th St. N.W., Washington, DC 20429/202-389-4365.

Community Reinvestment
The Community Reinvestment Act of 1977 requires the Federal Deposit Insurance Corporation to monitor the records of financial institutions in meeting the credit needs of their communities, including low and moderate-income neighborhoods. Contact: Community Reinvestment Specialist, Civil Rights Section, Office of Consumer Programs, Federal Deposit Insurance Corporation, Room F-101, 550 17th St. N.W., Washington, DC 20429/202-389-4473.

Compliance Information
General and consumer information is available on the compliance of insured state nonmember banks with consumer laws and on the enforcement of the Truth-in-Lending Act. For more information, contact any insured bank, Federal Deposit Insurance Corporation regional office, or Office of Consumer and Compliance Programs, Federal Deposit Insurance Corporation, Room F-101, 550 17th St. N.W., Washington, DC 20429/202-389-4512. For a tollfree hotline that handles complaints about consumer rights in banking, call 800-424-5488.

Consumer Information
The Federal Deposit Insurance Corporation has a computerized system to: 1) follow the status and handling of consumer complaints and requests for information; 2) produce one-page summaries of census information for use by examiners and other FDIC personnel evaluating bank compliance with the Community Reinvestment Act; 3) summarize the letters of comment on proposed new Truth-in-Lending guidelines; and 4) tabulate a follow-up survey asking complainants if their problems were satisfactorily resolved. Contact: Office of Consumer and Compliance Programs, Bank Supervision Division, Federal Deposit Insurance Corporation, Room F-101, 550 17th St. N.W., Washington, DC 20429/202-389-4512

Consumer Questions
For questions of interest to bank depositors and customers, contact: Office of Consumer and Compliance Programs, Federal Deposit Insurance Corporation, Room F-101, 550 17th St. N.W., Washington, DC 20429/202-389-4767.

Deposit Data
Deposit data can be generated for all banking offices of a specific bank of a computer printout; all banking offices within a given county, SMSA,

or state on a computer printout; and all banking offices in the country on magnetic tape. Nominal fees are charged for these services. A series of books is available—one for each of the 14 FDIC regions which groups each banking office by state, country and SMSA, with total deposits and the percentage thereof in each of the six categories of deposits. There is a $5.00 charge for each book in the series. Contact: DAX, Information Center Unit, Federal Deposit Insurance Corporation, Room 3070, 550 17th St. N.W., Washington, DC 20429/202-389-4131

Enforcement and Supervision
This office supervises the compliance of an insured bank and can initiate cease-and-desist proceedings if the bank does not correct an unsafe or unsound practice or a violation of a law, rule, regulation or written agreement with the FDIC. Contact: Supervisory Surveillance and Enforcement, Bank Supervision Division, Federal Deposit Insurance Corporation, 550 17th St. N.W., Room 5025, Washington, DC 20429/202-389-4297

Freedom of Information Act
Freedom of Information Act requests are handled by: Office of the Executive Secretariat, Federal Deposit Insurance Corporation, Room 6108, 550 17th St. N.W., Washington, DC 20429/202-389-4446.

International Banking
An insured state nonmember bank must obtain Federal Deposit Insurance Corporation consent before establishing its first branch in a foreign country or before acquiring any ownership interest in a foreign bank or other financial entity. The FDIC and other banking agencies follow uniform procedures for evaluating and commenting on country risk factors in the international loan portfolios of U.S. banks. Contact: International Banking Unit, Bank Supervision Division, Room 5110 NYAV, 550 17th St. N.W., Washington, DC 20429/202-389-4345.

Law, Regulations and Related Acts
Information presented in loose-leaf format in two volumes, including the FDI Act and Rules and Regulations issued as prescribed by the Corporation's Board of Directors, and certain other statutes and regulations that affect the operations of insured banks. The service includes also Report Bulletins issued at two-month intervals that reflect the text of any statutory or regulatory changes that may have occurred and summarizes congressional and federal agency actions affecting insured banks. The charge for this information is $100 for each service per calendar year. Orders and checks (payable to FDIC) should be sent to the Office of Information, Office of Legislative Affairs, Federal Deposit Insurance Corporation, Room 6061, 550

17th St. N.W., Washington, DC 20429/202-389-4221.

Library
The Library collection emphasizes banking, statistics, economics and law. Make an appointment before visiting. Contact: Library, Federal Deposit Insurance Corporation, Room 4074, 550 17th St. N.W., Washington, DC 20429/202-389-4314.

Liquidation
The Legal Division is responsible for regulation of enforcement actions and liquidation litigation. To keep the Division up with their more than 5,000 lawsuits connected with liquidation and other closed-bank matters, outside attorneys are hired. Contact: Legal Division, Federal Deposit Insurance Corporation, Room 4025, 550 17th St. N.W., Washington, DC 20429/202-389-4151.

Lost and Stolen Securities Program
The Federal Deposit Insurance Corporation shares enforcement responsibility with the Securities and Exchange Commission for the computer-assisted reporting and inquiry system for lost, stolen, counterfeit and forged securities. All insured banks and brokers, dealers and other securities firms are required to register with the Securities Information Center, Inc., P.O. Box 421, Wellesley Hills, MA 02181/617-235-8270, where a central data base records reported thefts and losses. Contact: Intelligence Section, Special Activities, Bank Supervision Division, Federal Deposit Insurance Corporation, Room 5100 NYAV, 550 17th St. N.W., Washington, DC 20429/202-389-4412

Pamphlets in English and Spanish
The following pamphlets are free:

Fair Credit Reporting Act—describes the steps you can take to protect yourself if you have been denied credit, insurance, or employment, or if you believe you've had difficulties because of an inaccurate or an unfair consumer report.

Equal Credit Opportunity and Women—describes the provisions of the Equal Credit Opportunity Act that apply to sex and marital status.

Equal Credit Opportunity and Age—describes the provisions of the Equal Credit Opportunity Act that applies to age discrimination.

Truth in Lending—describes the Truth-in-Lending law enforced to let consumers know exactly what their charges are and to require creditors to state such charges in a uniform way.

Consumer Information
Fair Credit Billing
Community Reinvestment Act—(Only in English)

For further information and a publication list, contact: Federal Deposit Insurance Corporation regional offices, or Public Information, Federal Deposit Insurance Corporation, Room 6061-B,

550 17th St. N.W., Washington, DC 20429/202-389-4221 or call 800-424-5488.

Problem Banks

The Federal Deposit Insurance Corporation divides problem banks into three categories based on the degree of insurance risk:

Serious Problem-Potential Payoff—an advanced serious problem with an estimated 50% or more chance of requiring financial assistance by the FDIC.

Serious Problem—a situation that threatens ultimately to involve the FDIC in a financial outlay unless drastic changes occur.

Other Problem—a situation in which a bank has significant weaknesses but where the FDIC is less vulnerable.

For further information, contact: Problem Banks Section, Supervisory Surveillance and Enforcement, Supervision Division, Federal Deposit Insurance Corporation, Room 5025, 550 17th St. N.W., Washington, DC 20429/202-389-4673.

Publications

The following free publications are available from: Public Information Office, Federal Deposit Insurance Corporation, Room 6061-B, 550 17th St. N.W., Washington, DC 20429/202-389-4221:

Summary of Deposits—the aggregate results of a mid-year survey of deposits of commercial and mutual savings banks are published annually. The data are grouped by state, county, SMSA, and FDIC region in the following types of accounts: 1) Demand, IPC (individual, partnership and corporate); 2) Savings, IPC; 3) Other time, IPC; 4) Public funds, demand; 5) Public funds, time and savings; and 6) all other.

Changes Among Operating Banks and Branches—an annual year-end publication that sets forth the changes in number and classification of operating banks and branches.

Trust Assets of Banks and Trust Companies—an annual publication of trust department data collected from all insured commercial banks and presented by type of account, asset distribution, and size of trust department. This publication lists also trust assets by type of account (but not asset distribution) for each of the 300 largest trust departments—ranked according to total trust assets. This is a combined effort of the Federal Deposit Insurance Corporation, the Board of Governors of the Federal Reserve System, and the Office of the Comptroller of the Currency.

Your Insured Deposit—a free pamphlet that provides examples of insurance coverage under the Corporation's rules on certain types of accounts commonly held by depositers in insured banks.

Bank Operating Statistics—Federal Deposit Insurance Corporation presentation of year-end data in a geographical framework based on the *Reports of Condition* and *Reports of Income* submitted by all insured commercial banks.

Annual Report of the Federal Deposit Insurance Corpora-

tion—the FDIC Annual Report contains a narative report of operations, legislation and regulations, and statistics on closed banks and deposit insurance.

Statistics on Banking—this publication encompasses tables formerly found in the FDIC Annual Report. It contains several categories of year-end statistical data, including the number of banks and branches, aggregate statistical information on assets and liabilities of insured banks, and aggregate statistical information on income of insured banks.

Merger Decisions—this publication contains approvals and denials of bank absorptions.

Data Book—contains Summary of Accounts and Deposits in all Commercial and Mutual Savings Banks and Domestic Branches of Foreign Banks plus data about Operating Banks and Branches. Survey results are compiled in a series of 19 books by geographic area. Each book includes a national summary, containing tables on bank structure and tabulations by class and size of bank, and also state, SMSA and county tabulations. The number of accounts and amount of deposits by size of account are shown for total deposits and five deposit categories: Demand, IPC; Savings, IPC; Time, IPC; Public funds, demand; Public funds, time and savings.

Bank Operating Statistics—an annual publication presenting year-end data in a geographical framework based on the Reports of Condition and Reports of Income submitted by all insured commercial banks.

Changes Among Operating Banks and Branches—an annual publication as of year-end which sets forth the changes which occurred during the year in number and classification of operating banks and branches.

The Community Bank Automation Series—includes:
1) A Guide: Small Computer Systems Requirements and Selection; and
2) A Guide: Security Control and Auditing of In-House Mini Computers.
Other publications may be added.

Symbol of Confidence—this booklet gives an account of the highlights of the Corporation's history, functions and operations. It describes how the Corporation protects the accounts of depositors and how it promotes sound banking practices.

Registration and Reporting

The Federal Deposit Insurance Corporation administers and enforces the registration and reporting of the Securities Exchange Act of 1934 for insured nonmember banks. Banks with more than $1 million in assets and 500 or more holders of any class of equity security are required to file an initial registration statement and periodic reports. A public document room files these registration statements and periodic reports. Contact: Securities and Disclosure Activities, Bank Supervision Division, Federal Deposit Insurance Corporation, Room 790, 1709 New York Ave. N.W., Washington, DC 20429/202-389-4651.

Reports of Condition and Reports of Income

The reports must be requested by name of bank—

in writing—addressed to the Division of Management Systems and Financial Statistics. *Reports of Condition* available on quarterly basis; *Reports of Income* available on annual basis through December 1975 and semiannual basis since June 1976. Contact: Information Center Unit, Federal Deposit Insurance Corporation, Room 3070, 550 17th St. N.W., Washington, DC 20429/202-389-4101.

Reports and Surveys

Mutual savings banks must fill out a *Report of Condition* quarterly, and a *Report of Income* semiannually. There are surveys that monitor money market certificates and automatic transfers from savings accounts and a weekly survey of selected nonmember banks for data in estimating the nonmember bank component of the U.S. money supply. Reports for the disclosure of loans are extended to certain bank employees and stockholders by the employing bank and its correspondent banks. The Federal Deposit Insurance Corporation has a toll-free number to assist banks in filling out the required call reports—800-424-5101. Contact: Compliance Examination Section, Bank Supervisory Division, Federal Deposit Insurance Corporation, Room 5134, 550 17th St. N.W., Washington, DC 20429/202-389-4512.

Research

Research activities include monitoring developments in the financial industry and the economy and assessing the implications of existing and proposed regulations and legislation. Studies include: deposit insurance reform, new or modified types of deposit accounts, the condition of commercial and mutual savings banks in the United States, rising inflation and interest rates, state usury ceilings, prospects for the housing industry, Federal Reserve membership, and the impact of payment of interest on transaction accounts (NOW accounts, automatic transfer accounts, telephone transfer services). A listing of research papers by titles and authors, including journals and magazines in which some of the papers have appeared is available. Contact: Research Division, Federal Deposit Insurance Corporation, Room 3088, 550 17th St. N.W., Washington, DC 20429/202-389-4541.

How Can the Federal Deposit Insurance Corporation Help You?

For information on how this agency can help you, contact: Federal Deposit Insurance Corporation, 550 17th St. N.W., Washington, DC 20429/202-389-4221.

Federal Election Commission

1325 K St. N.W., Washington, DC 20463/202-523-4089

Established: 1971
Budget: $9,832,000
Employees: 234

Mission: Seeks to obtain compliance with, and formulate policy with regard to the implementation of the Federal Election Campaign Act of 1971. The Act provides for the financing of presidential elections; disclosure of the financial activities of federal candidates and political committees supporting such candidates; limitations on contributions and expenditures regarding such federal candidates and political committees; and the organization and registration of political committees.

Major Sources of Information

Election Assistance
Information and assistance on procedures for registration and reporting requirements for candidates and committees is available to federal candidates, political committees and the general public. Contact: Public Communications Branch, Information Division, Federal Election Commission, 4th Floor, 1325 K St. N.W., Washington, DC 20463/202-523-4068, or toll-free—800-424-9530.

Federal Campaign Finance Law Complaints
If you believe a candidate or committee has violated a provision of the Federal Campaign Finance Law or Federal Election Commission regulations, you may file a complaint with the Federal Election Commission. For further information, contact: Office of the General Counsel, Federal Election Commission, 7th Floor, 1325 K St. N.W., Washington, DC 20463/202-523-4143.

Federal Election Commission Publications
The National Clearinghouse on Election Administration Information compiles and disseminates election administration information related to federal elections. The reports produced by the Clear-inghouse are available to the public at cost. For a list of publications and their prices, contact: National Clearinghouse for Election Administration Information, Federal Election Commission, 4th Floor, 1325 K St. N.W., Washington, DC 20463/202-523-4183, or toll free—800-424-9530.

Financial Disclosure Data Base on Federal Candidates
The Financial Disclosure data base has both financial and reference information on every candidate for federal office (since 1977) and on contributing Political Action Committees, political parties and selected individuals. The system can be searched by specific candidate or contributor, and retrievable data includes exact dollar amounts and contact information.

Searches and printouts amounting to 20 records or less are available free of charge. Above 22 records, a fee, based on computer time used, is accessed. The fee generally ranges from 80 cents to $3.00 a citation. Contact: Public Records Office, Federal Election Commission, 1325 K Street, N.W., Washington, DC 20463/202-523-4181.

Freedom of Information Act Requests

Freedom of Information Act requests should be made to: Information Division, Federal Election Commission, 4th Floor, 1325 K St. N.W., Washington, DC 20463/202-523-4065.

Free Publications

The Federal Election Commission provides the following free publications:

FEC Annual Report
Federal Election Campaign Laws
FEC Regulations
The FEC Record (monthly newsletter)
Campaign Guide for Congressional Candidates and their Committees
Campaign Guide for Party Committees
Campaign Guide for Nonconnected Political Committees
Campaign Guide for Corporations and Labor Organizations
Bookkeeping and Reporting Manual
FEC and Federal Campaign Finance Law
Public Funding of Elections
Using FEC Campaign Financing Information

Contact: Public Communications Office, Information Division, Federal Election Commission, 4th Floor, 1325 K St. N.W., Washington, DC 20463/202-523-4068.

Journal on Election Administration

This is a free quarterly publication available at the National Clearinghouse, Federal Election Commission, 4th Floor, 1325 K St. N.W., Washington, DC 20463/202-523-4183, or toll-free—800-424-9530.

Library

The Federal Election Commission Library collection includes basic legal research resources, with an emphasis on political campaign financing, corporate and labor political activity and election campaign reform. It is open to the public. Contact: Library, Federal Election Commission, 4th Floor, 1325 K St. N.W., Washington, DC 20463/202-523-4178.

Public Election Records

The Office of Public Records provides for public inspection of all reports and statements relating to campaign finance since 1972. They include campaign finance reports, statistical summaries of campaign finance reports, computer indexes and class indexes to locate documents, advisory opinion requests and advisory opinions, completed compliance cases, audit reports, press releases, Commission memoranda, agenda items and minutes. Contact: The Office of Public Records, Public Disclosure Division, Federal Election Commission, 1st Floor, 1325 K St. N.W., Washington, DC 20463/202-523-4181, or toll-free—800-424-9530.

Voting Equipment Standards

This Clearinghouse is conducting a study on the possible development of voluntary engineering and performance standards for voting systems used in the United States. Contact: Clearinghouse, Federal Election Commission, 4th Floor, 1325 K St. N.W., Washington, DC 20463/202-523-4183, or toll free—800-424-9530.

How Can the Federal Election Commission Help You?

For information on how this agency can help you, contact: Information Division, Federal Election Commission, 4th Floor, 1325 K St. N.W., Washington, DC 20463/202-523-4068.

Federal Emergency Management Agency

500 C Street, S.W., Washington, DC 20472/202-646-2500

Established: April 1, 1979
Budget: $518,382,000
Employees: 2,319

Mission: Provides a single point of accountability for all federal emergency preparedness, mitigation and response activities; enhances the multiple use of emergency preparedness and response resources at the federal, state and local levels of government in preparing for and responding to the full range of emergencies—natural, manmade, and nuclear—and to integrate into a comprehensive framework activities concerned with hazard mitigation, preparedness planning, relief operations and recovery assistance.

Major Sources of Information

Arson Assistance Program
This program provides assistance to state and local agencies to support their arson prevention and control programs. The emphasis is on the development of management systems in the form of arson task forces at the state and local level. Workshops are set up to explain the arson task force concept and to show how task forces are structured and how they function. Contact: Office of Fire Prevention and Arson Control, Federal Emergency Management Agency, National Emergency Training Center, South Seton Ave., Emmitsburg, MD 21727/301-447-6771.

Arson Implementation Kits
These kits provide general models for building various aspects of a local arson program. They provide basic information on applying ideas that have proven successful in fighting arson. The topics covered include: municipal task forces, public education, hotlines, tipsters, juvenile counseling, early warning systems, management of training programs, state task forces, rural arson and federal arson programs. Contact: Office of Fire Prevention and Arson Control, Federal Em-

ergency Management Agency, National Emergency Training Center, South Seton Ave., Emmitsburg, MD 21727/301-447-6771.

Arson Media Guidebook
This guidebook covers "how to" information on preparing media campaigns for arson prevention and control. It includes suggestions on how to write news releases, public service announcements, radio and TV scripts, how to conduct press conferences and how to evaluate media campaigns. Contact: Learning Resource Center, Office of Fire Prevention and Arson Control, Federal Emergency Management Agency, National Emergency Training Center, South Seton Ave., Emmitsburg, MD 21727/301-447-6771.

Arson Resource Center
This Center serves as a national arson reference center providing information to states and localities to help them prevent and control arson. It has information on Arson Task Forces, Arson Investigation and Prosecution Legislation, Preservation of Historic Sights from Arson, Juvenile Firesetters Counseling Programs and Arson Information

Management Systems. These free publications are available:

Arson Resource Directory
Arson Task Force Assistance Program
Arson News Media Guidebook
Interviewing and Counseling Juvenile Firesetters
Fire Insurance: Its Nature and Dynamics
Arson: America's Malignant Crime

Two additional publications, *Overview, Report to the Congress* ($8.00) and *The Federal Role in Arson Prevention and Control* ($20.00) are sold through the National Technical Information Services, Department of Commerce, 5285 Port Royal Rd., Springfield, VA 22161/703-557-4600. For further information, contact: Learning Resource Center, Federal Emergency Management Agency, National Emergency Training Center, South Seton Ave., Emmitsburg, MD 21727/302-447-6771.

Community Eligibility for Flood Insurance
A community qualifies for the National Flood Insurance Program in two ways—Emergency and Regular. To determine whether a community is eligible for the Emergency or Regular Program, contact: National Flood Insurance Program, 9901-A George Palmer Hwy, Lanham, MD 20706/301-731-5300, or the Federal Insurance Administration (FIA) Regional Office or Federal Insurance Administration, Federal Emergency Management Agency, Room 427, 500 C St, S.W., Washington, DC 20472/202-287-0750, or call toll-free, 800-638-6620. (Alaska, Hawaii, Puerto Rico and U.S. Virgin Islands).

Crime Insurance
The Federal Crime Insurance Program enables residents and businesses to purchase affordable insurance against burglary and robbery losses in eligible states. Federal crime insurance applications are available from any licensed property insurance agency or broker in an eligible jurisdiction. For further information, contact: Federal Crime Insurance, Federal Emergency Management Agency, P.O. Box 41033, Bethesda, MD 20815/301-652-2637 (call collect from Maryland); 800-638-8780 (Puerto Rico and Virgin Islands); 800-638-8780 elsewhere.

Disaster Assistance Center
In times of disaster, the Federal Emergency Management Agency establishes one or more Disaster Assistance Centers in the affected area. These centers provide a central location where representatives of federal agencies, state and local governments, and private relief agencies can offer aid to the disaster victims. Contact: Emergency Information and Coordination Center, Federal Emergency Management Agency, 500 C St, S.W., Washington, DC 20472/202-646-2400

Earthquake Insurance
The Federal Insurance Administration is conducting a study of the earthquake insurance market, its capacity, the supports that would be needed if insurance capacity were strained, the reasons for apparent consumer apathy, whether there is a need to promote the purchase of insurance more aggressively in light of that apathy, and the role that insurance might play in promoting increased mitigation efforts by individuals and communities. The thrust of the study is to provide information on which policy making decisions can be based. Federal Emergency Management Agency, Room 427, 500 C St, S.W., Washington, DC 20472/202-646-2781.

Emergency Management
This is a free bimonthly with articles and news on emergency and disaster management. It notes new information sources, publications and conferences. Contact: Office of Public Affairs, Federal Emergency Management Agency, Room 806, 500 C St. S.W., Washington, DC 20472/202-646-4600.

Emergency Management Institute
The Institute offers high-level courses in comprehensive emergency management. It serves as a national academic center for the collection and dissemination of emergency management information. For more information, contact: Emergency Management Institute, Federal Emergency Management Agency, Emmitsburg, MD 21727/301-447-6771.

Federal Insurance
The Federal Insurance Administration is responsible for examining the operations and activities of state regulated Fair Act Access to Insurance Requirement (FAIR) plans. FAIR plans are private property insurance pools. They make essential property insurance available in areas where such insurance is unavailable through the standard market because of environmental conditions surrounding the specific properties. Contact: National Flood Insurance Program, Federal Insurance Administration, Federal Emergency Management Agency, Room 7901 A. George Palmer Highway, Lanham, MD 20706/301-731-5300.

Fire Education
Assistance is available to communities in planning, implementing and evaluating educational programs to reduce incidents, loss, deaths and injuries from fire. Technical assistance is provided in arson prevention and control, comprehensive community master planning and emergency medical service management. Contact: Office of Fire Prevention and Arson Control, U.S. Fire Administration, Federal Emergency Management Agency, Building N, Emmitsburg, MD 21727/301-447-6771.

Flood Insurance
The National Flood Insurance Program makes flood insurance available to property owners at a reasonable cost, in return for which communities are required to carry out flood plain management measures to protect lives and reduce property loss. For more insurance information, contact your local insurance agents, or toll-free, 800-638-6620; or National Flood Insurance Program, 9901-A George Palmer Highway, Lanham, MD 20706.

Freedom of Information Act Requests
Freedom of Information Act requests are handled by the Office of Public Affairs, Federal Emergency Management Agency, Room 806, 500 C St, S.W., Washington, DC 20472/202-646-4600.

Grants
The Programs described below are for sums of money which are given by the federal government to initiate and stimulate new or improved activities or to sustain on-going services:

National Fire Academy Student Stipend Program
Objectives: To provide stipends to students attending Academy courses and programs.
Eligibility: Any student other than a Federal or private industry employee or a foreign student who is a member of a fire department or has significant responsibility for fire prevention and control and has been accepted into a course may apply for stipend reimbursement.
Range of Financial Assistance: Average stipend per student - $285.
Contact: National Emergency Training Center, Office of Admissions and Registration, 16825 S. Seton Avenue, Emmitsburg, MD 21727/301-447-6771.

State and Local Maintenance and Services
Objectives: To maintain emergency preparedness of state and local governments by furnishing matching funds for annual recurring and maintenance costs for state and local direction and control and alerting and warning systems required to conduct a viable emergency management program.
Eligibility: State (includes U.S. territories) or state and political subdivision (city, county, township, etc.) jointly.
Range of Financial Assistance: $1,000 to $236,000.
Contact: Communications and Control Branch, SLPS, Federal Emergency Management Agency, Washington, DC 20472/202-646-3692.

Emergency Management Assistance
Objectives: To develop effective civil defense organizations in the states and their political subdivisions in order to plan for and coordinate emergency activities in the event of attack or natural disaster.
Eligibility: States (including U.S. territories and interstate civil defense authorities) are eligible. Local governments participate under the state's application.
Range of Financial Assistance: $29,900 to $4,608,200.
Contact: Emergency Management Programs Office, State and Local Programs and Support Directorate, Federal Emergency Management Agency, Washington, DC 20472/202-646-3512.

Disaster Assistance
Objectives: To provide assistance to states, local governments, selected private nonprofit facilities, and individuals in alleviating suffering and hardship resulting from emergencies or major disasters declared by the President.
Eligibility: State and local governments in declared emergency or major disaster areas, owners of selected private nonprofit facilities, and individual disaster victims.
Range of Financial Assistance: $21 to $39,202,722.
Contact: Federal Emergency Management Agency, Washington, DC 20472/202-646-3615.

Earthquake and Hurricane Preparedness Planning Grants
Objectives: To prepare plans for all levels of government for preparedness capabilities for severe earthquake or hurricanes in certain high-density, high-risk areas.
Eligibility: State or local governments serving highly populated localities designated as highly vulnerable to earthquakes and/or hurricane disasters are eligible.
Range of Financial Assistance: $10,000 to $450,000.
Contact: Natural Hazards Division, State and Local Programs and Support, Federal Emergency Management Agency, Washington, DC 20472/202-646-3692.

Emergency Broadcast System Guidance and Assistance
Objectives: To enhance and develop an emergency broadcast capability to provide emergency information and direction to the public by national, State and local officials.
Eligibility: Broadcast stations must be a part of the emergency broadcast system and State and Local governments must have an EBS Operational Plan.
Range of Financial Assistance: $25,000 to $75,000.
Contact: Emergency Management Officer, State and Local Programs and Support, Washington, DC 20472/202-646-3512 or 646-2400.

Emergency Management Institute

Objectives: To assist in defraying the expenses of professional training for state and local emergency management defense personnel and training for instructors who conduct courses under contract.

Eligibility: Individuals who need emergency management training and are assigned to an emergency management position in state or local government.

Range of Financial Assistance: not applicable

Contact: Emergency Management Institute, 16825 S. Seton Avenue, Emmitsburg, MD 21727/301-447-6771.

General Research, Development, and Demonstration Activity

Objectives: To carry out basic and applied research and demonstration projects of high priority, usually preselected by the Agency to serve the needs of the Emergency Management Community and to improve and guide the operation of Agency programs.

Eligibility: State and local governments, US Territories, Native Americans, institutions of higher education, hospitals, other nonprofit organizations, individuals and profit making organizations.

Range of Financial Assistance: $500 to $250,000.

Contact: Director, Acquisition Management Division, Federal Emergency Management Agency, 500 C Street, SW, Room 72B, Washington, DC 20472/202-646-3744.

National Emergency Training Center—Field Training Program

Objectives: To provide the trainee with instructional capability for the training of FEMA support staffs (e.g. disaster hires), regional staffs of Federal agencies, and elected State/Local government staffs (e.g., professional development training that is essentially interstate in nature).

Eligibility: Individuals who need emergency management training, as described under the objectives.

Range of Financial Assistance: $203 to $816.

Contact: Emergency Management Institute, 16825 S. Seton Avenue, Emmitsburg, MD 21227/301-447-6771.

Population Protection Planning

Objectives: To assist States and Localities to develop population protection plans to prepare for and respond to the full range of emergencies that a jurisdiction may face. This includes such hazards as earthquakes, floods, hurricanes, tornadoes and large-scale hazardous materials incidents.

Eligibility: States (including US territories) are eligible to participate.

Range of Financial Assistance: $20,000 to $730,000.

Contact: State and Local Programs and Support Directorate, Federal Emergency Management Agency, Washington, DC 20472/202-646-3692.

Radiological Systems Maintenance

Objectives: To assist in developing a capability in every locality for the detection and measurement of hazardous levels of radiation; to maintain all emergency management radiological instruments in a calibrated and operationally ready condition for all types of radiological emergencies.

Eligibility: Each FEMA region has negotiated a cooperative agreement for this service with each of its State emergency management organizations.

Range of Financial Assistance: $42,500 to $405,000.

Contact: Physical Scientist Administrator, Logistics Support Branch, Emergency Management Systems Support, Emergency Management Programs Office, Washington, DC 20472/202-646-4600.

Reimbursement for Firefighting on Federal Property

Objectives: To provide that each fire service which engages in firefighting operations on Federal property may be reimbursed for their direct expenses and direct losses incurred in firefighting.

Eligibility: Fire Departments, Volunteer and paid of the State, District of Columbia, Commonwealth, Territories and Possessions of the United States are eligible to apply.

Range of Financial Assistance: Up to $500,000.

Contact: Office of the Comptroller, Federal Emergency Management Agency, Washington, DC 20472/202-646-3717.

State and Local Emergency Operating Centers

Objectives: To enhance effective, reliable and survivable direction and control capabilities of State and local government.

Eligibility: State (including US territories) or State and political subdivision (city, county, townships, etc.) jointly.

Range of Financial Assistance: Not available.

Contact: Communications and Control Branch, Emergency Management Systems Support Division, State and Local Programs and Support, Federal Emergency Management Agency, Washington, DC 20472/202-646-3692.

State and Local Warning and Communication Systems

Objectives: To maintain the civil defense readiness of State and local governments by furnishing matching funds for the purchase of equipment and supporting materials for State and local direction and control, and alerting and warning systems.

Eligibility: State (includes US Territories) or local government, such as city, county, township.

Range of Financial Assistance: Not applicable.

Contact: Communications Management Officer,

Communications and Control Branch, State and Local Programs and Support, Federal Emergency Management Agency, Washington, DC 20472/202-646-2400.

State Assistance Program

Objectives: To facilitate each State's achievement of a level of expertise in flood hazard management which will enable the State to provide assistance to its constituent communities in discharging local flood hazard management responsibility.

Eligibility: States (includes the District of Columbia, Guam, Puerto Rico, and the Virgin Islands).

Range of Financial Assistance: $34,048 to $162,000.

Contact: Emergency Management Programs Office, Federal Emergency Management Agency, Washington, DC 20472/202-646-3692.

State Disaster Preparedness Grants

Objectives: To assist states in developing state and local plans, programs and capabilities for disaster preparedness and prevention.

Eligibility: All states are eligible (including District of Columbia, Puerto Rico, Virgin Islands, Guam, American Samoa, Trust Territory of the Pacific Islands, the Commonwealth of the Northern Marianas Islands.

Range of Financial Assistance: $6,250 to $25,000.

Contact: Emergency Management Programs Office, State and Local Programs and Support, Federal Emergency Management Agency, Washington, DC 20472/202-646-4600.

State Fire Incident Reporting Assistance

Objectives: To assist states in the establishment and operation of a statewide fire incident and casualty reporting system.

Elgibility: States, the District of Columbia, Commonwealth of Puerto Rico, territories and possessions of the United States and large cities with population of 500,000 or more are eligible to apply.

Range of Financial Assistance: Up to $70,000 per state.

Contact: (Office of Fire Data and Analysis) U.S. Fire Administration, Training and Fire Programs Directorate, Federal Emergency Management Agency, Emmitsburg, MD 21727/301-447-6771.

State Radiological Defense Officers

Objectives: To develop and implement a Radiological Defense (RADEF) Program for the radiological hazards that are a potential threat to the State and Local jurisdictions.

Eligibility: In each of the 50 States, the District of Columbia, and Puerto Rico, the State emergency management (civil defense) organization

must negotiate a Cooperative Agreement for this service with the respective FEMA regional office.

Range of Financial Assistance: $26,200 to $93,250.

Contact: Systems Development Division, Office of Emergency Management Programs, Washington, DC 20472/202-646-4600.

Impact of Earthquakes on Financial Institutions

The Federal Emergency Management Agency's Office of Mitigation is currently studying the impact of earthquakes and their predictions (when science perfects this technology) on financial institutions. This study has three related objectives: to determine the viability of the financial system in the aftermath of a truly catastrophic earthquake in a densely populated area; to understand the effects of a credible earthquake prediction on the behavior of the public and its consequent demand on financial institutions; and to examine the feasibility of effective earthquake mitigation through financial institutions. Contact: Mitigation, Federal Emergency Management Agency, Room 728 500 C St, S.W., Washington, DC 20472/202-646-2871.

In Time of Emergency: A Citizen's Handbook on Emergency Management

This free handbook provides information and guidance on what to do to enhance survival in the event of nationwide nuclear attack or in case of major natural disasters. Contact: Office of Public Affairs, Federal Emergency Management Agency, Room 806, 500 C St. S.W., Washington, DC 20472/202-646-2651.

Juvenile Firesetters Program

This training workshop program is geared to train fire education specialists, fire investigators, counselors, law enforcement and juvenile authorities. The program is scheduled through state fire training offices. Contact: Office of Fire Prevention and Arson Control, National Emergency Training Center, South Seton Ave, Emmitsburg, MD 21727/301-447-6771.

Map Information Facility

Information is provided on Special Flood Hazard Areas and the National Flood Insurance Program Rating Factors to both lenders and insurance agents/brokers. A toll-free phone service is available to answer questions Monday through Friday between the hours of 9:00 a.m. and 8:00 p.m. Eastern Time. Contact: Map Information Facility, Federal Insurance Administration, Federal Emergency Management Agency, P.O. Box 619, Lanham, MD 20706/301-731-5300, or toll-free 800-638-6620 (Continental United States, except Maryland); 800-638-6381 (Puerto Rico, Hawaii, Virgin Islands, Alaska); 800-492-2701 (Maryland) 301-731-5300 (DC metropolitan area).

Maps of Flood-prone Areas

The Law requires the Federal Emergency Management Agency to notify every flood-prone community nationwide that it has one or more flood-prone areas. FEMA publishes a map called a "Flood Hazard Boundary Map" which shows the flood-prone areas within the community, and a free MIF Users' Guide is also available. For map requests and information contact: The National Flood Insurance Program, Federal Insurance Administration, Federal Emergency Management Agency, P.O. Box 619, Lanham, MD 20706/toll-free telephone numbers: 800-638-3100 (Continental United States, except Maryland); 800-638-2151 (Puerto Rico, Hawaii, Virgin Islands, Alaska); 800 492 2701 (Maryland).

Motion Picture Catalog

This catalog contains a current list of public information films. For information on specialized educational, training, research and historical films, contact: Office of Public Affairs, Federal Emergency Management Agency, Room 807, 500 C St. S.W., Washington, DC 20472/202-646-2651 or 646-3480.

National Fire Academy

The Academy trains over 6,000 students a year. Courses include executive development, fire data collection and analysis, fire service technologies, arson investigation and detection, and disaster planning for hazardous materials. Many of the courses will be available to paid and volunteer firefighters through the United States. Contact: National Fire Academy, National Emergency Training Center, Federal Emergency Management Agency, 16825 South Seton Ave., Emmitsburg, MD 21727/301-447-6771.

National Fire Data

The National Fire Data Center collects statistical data and general information on fires, fire research, arson, home and building safety, firefighter safety, health and technology, and fire investigation. Through the state fire incident reporting systems, the fire incident file contains information on over one million fires. For further information, contact: National Fire Data Center, Fire Administration, Federal Emergency Management Agency, National Emergency Training Center, 16825 South Seton Ave., Emmitsbutg MD, 21727/301-447-6105.

National Fire Incident Reporting System

This office collects and analyzes information on the frequency, causes, spread and extinguishment of fires, and on property losses. *The NFIRS Handbook* provides detailed information on how to report into the system. *The National Fire Incident Reporting System News* is published by the Center to promote an exchange of information among state and local users of the National Fire Incident Reporting System. Contact: Data Collection and Analysis, The National Fire Data Center, National Emergency Training Center, Federal Emergency Management Agency, 16825 South Seton Ave., Emmitsburg, MD 21727/301-447-6771.

Radioactive Hazards

The Federal Emergency Management Agency helps local governments deal with peacetime emergencies involving radioactive materials—transportation accidents or (to a limited degree) nuclear power reactor accidents. The FEMA provides radiological detection instruments, maintenance for the instruments and training for personnel to detect radiological hazards, and assess their impact on operations. Contact: Technical Hazards Division, Radiological Emergency Preparedness, Plans and Preparedness, Federal Emergency Management Agency, 500 C St. S.W., Washington, DC 20472/202-287-0200.

Regional Offices

There are 10 Federal Emergency Management Agency Regional Offices to facilitate federal disaster assistance to states and local areas. Contact: Emergency Information and Coordination Center, Federal Emergency Management Agency, 500 C St. S.W., Washington, DC 20472/202-646-2400. Locations, addresses and telephone numbers of the regional offices are as follows:

FEMA Region I, J.W. McCormick P.O. and Court House, Fourth Floor, Boston, MA 20109/617-223-4271.

FEMA Region II, 26 Federal Plaza, New York, NY 10278/212-264-8980.

FEMA Region III, Curtis Building—7th Floor, 6th and Walnut Sts., Philadelphia, PA 19106/215-597-9416.

FEMA Region IV, 1371 Peachtree St. N.E., Suite 700, Atlanta, GA 30309/404-881-3641.

FEMA Region V, 300 S. Walker St., 24th Floor, Chicago, IL 60606/312-353-1500.

FEMA Region VI, Federal Regional Center, 800 N. Loop 2, Denton, TX 76201/817-387-5811.

FEMA Region VII, Old Federal Office Building, 911 Walnut St., Kansas City, MO 64106/816-374-5887

FEMA Region VIII, Denver Federal Center, Building 7, Denver, CO 80225/303-234-2553.

FEMA Region IX, 211 Main St., Room 220, Bldg 105, San Francisco, CA 94129/415-556-8794.

FEMA Region X, Federal Regional Center, Bothell, WA 98011/206-486-0721.

Reporting Claims for Flood Losses (Agents Only)

Policyholders should report claims for flood losses to their agents. Agents should call toll-free 800-638-6620, or contact: National Flood Insurance Program, P.O. Box 619, Lanham, MD 20706/301-731-5300.

Smoke Detectors

It's Alarming is a free brochure on smoke detectors, plus a list of brochures, films, reports and public education campaigns are available from: Federal Emergency Management Agency, Publications, Room 324, 500 C St. S.W., Washington, DC 20472/202-287-0689.

Stockpile Information

The Federal Emergency Management Agency develops national plans necessary for resource management and stabilization of the economy in time of emergency, including policy guidance for stockpiling strategic materials. The office also prepares a stockpile report to the Congress which includes information on strategic and critical materials, and other materials in government inventories; stockpile activities such as procurement, research, legislation, storage and maintenance, and disposal programs; expenditure of stockpile finds by type; and stockpile activities of other agencies. Contact: National Defense Stockpile Policy Division, Plans and Preparedness, Federal Emergency Management Agency, Room 5208 GSA, 1725 Eye St. N.W., Washington, DC 20472/202-566-0280.

Urban Property Insurance and Riot Reinsurance

The Federal Riot Reinsurance Program reinsures the general property insurance business against riots. It is available to insurance companies in states with state-wide plans for fair access to insurance requirements meeting federal criteria in making essential property insurance available. For more information, contact: Urban Property Insurance Operations Division, Federal Insurance Operations, Federal Emergency Management Agency, Room 433 500 C St, S.W., Washington, DC 20472/202-646-2781.

Winter Survival

The Federal Emergency Management Agency has a free leaflet on winter survival: *Winter Storms* discusses the problems and solutions for individuals caught by winter storms on the highway or in their homes. Contact: Office of Public Affairs, Federal Emergency Management Agency, Room 806, 500 C St. S.W., Washington, DC 20472/202-646-3649.

How Can the Federal Emergency Management Agency Help You?

For information on how this agency can be of help to you, contact: Office of Public Affairs, Federal Emergency Management Agency, Room 806, 500 C St. S.W., Washington, DC 20472/202-646-4600.

Federal Home Loan Bank Board

1700 G St. N.W., Washington, DC 20552/202-377-6677

Established: July 22, 1932
Budget: $70,578,000
Employees: 1498

Mission: Encourages thrift and economical home ownership; supervises and regulates savings institutions, which specialize in financing residential real estate and are the country's major private source of funds to pay for building and buying homes; operates the Federal Savings and Loan Insurance Corporation, which protects savings of the more than 84 million Americans with savings accounts in FSLIC-insured savings and loan associations; directs the Federal Home Loan Bank System, which, like the Federal Reserve System for banks, provides reserve credit and the assurance that member savings and loan associations will continue to be a source of economical financing for homes.

Major Sources of Information

Administration
This office handles contractual and leasing issues regarding the Bank Board building, Equal Employment Opportunity (EEO) complaints and adverse action hearings, compliance with Freedom of Information (FOI), the Sunshine Act, and the Ethics in Government Act, as weil as other administrative matters relating to the Bank Board, labor negotiating for the Bank Board, and the tort claims made against the FHLBB. Contact: Administration Division, Office of the General Counsel, Federal Home Loan Bank Board, 3rd Floor, 1700 G St. N.W., Washington, DC 20552/202-377-6462.

Application Evaluation
This office evaluates and processes applications submitted by savings and loan associations. It provides data on application trends, facility applications by district banks, merger applications, etc. Contact: Application Evaluation Division, Office of Industry Development, Federal Home Loan Bank Board, 4th Floor, 1700 G St. N.W., Washington, DC 20552/202-377-6715.

Business Transactions
This office gives advice primarily with regard to legal issues arising in connection with mergers, holding company acquisitions and conversions to federal mutual charter. It also reviews novel legal issues raised by applications for branch offices, remote service facilities, permission to organize, change in control, insurance of accounts, and Federal Home Loan Bank membership. Contact: Business Organizations and Transactions, Office of the General Counsel, Federal Home Loan Bank Board, 3rd Floor, 1700 G St. N.W., Washington, DC 20552/202-377-6450.

Community Investment
This office has been developing broad-based commitments from both public and private interests to further community investment. The activities have been aimed at helping the savings and loan industry recognize the business opportunities that

can stem from community investment. Contact: Office of Community Investment, Federal Home Loan Bank Board, 2nd Floor, 1700 G St. N.W., Washington, DC 20552/202-377-6283.

Compliance
This office conducts investigations of suspected statutory or regulatory violations and unsafe or unsound practices by federally insured savings and loan associations and brings administrative enforcement actions leading to cease-and-desist orders, removal and suspension orders, or the termination of insurance. Contact: Compliance Division, Office of General Counsel, Federal Home Loan Bank Board, 3rd Floor, 1700 G St. N.W., Washington, DC 20552/202-377-6430.

Debt Management
This office is responsible for raising money through the sale of debt instruments. Contact: Debt Management Division, Office of Finance, Federal Home Loan Bank Board, 5th Floor, 1700 G St., N.W., Washington, DC 20552/202-377-6314.

District Banks
The Federal Home Loan Bank system, through its twelve regional banks, provides a reserve credit facility for member savings institutions. These banks provide funds in the form of advances to members for savings withdrawals, seasonal and expansionary needs, and special purposes such as community development. Contact one of the following regional Federal Home Loan Banks or Office of the District Banks, Federal Home Loan Bank Board, 4th Floor, 1700 G St. S.W., Washington, DC 20552/202-377-6650.

Federal Home Loan Bank of Boston P.O. Box 2196, Boston, MA 20106 (Connecticut, Maine, Massachusetts, New Hampshire, Rhode Island and Vermont).

Federal Home Loan Bank of New York, One World Trade Center, Floor 103, New York, NY 10048 (New Jersey, New York, Puerto Rico and Virgin Islands).

Federal Home Loan Bank of Pittsburgh, 11 Stanwix St., 4th Floor, Gateway Center, Pittsburgh, PA 15222 (Delaware, Pennsylvania and West Virginia).

Federal Home Loan Bank of Atlanta, P.O. Box 56527, Atlanta, GA 30343 (Alabama, District of Columbia, Florida, Georgia, Maryland, North Carolina, South Carolina and Virginia).

Federal Home Loan Bank of Cincinnati, P.O. Box 598, Cincinnati, OH 45201 (Kentucky, Ohio and Tennessee).

Federal Home Loan Bank of Indianapolis, 2900 Indiana Tower, One Indiana Square, Indianapolis, IN 46204 (Indiana and Michigan).

Federal Home Loan Bank of Chicago, 111 East Wacker Dr., Chicago, IL 60601 (Illinois and Wisconsin).

Federal Home Loan Bank of Des Moines, 907 Walnut St., Des Moines, IA 50309 (Iowa, Minnesota, Missouri, North Dakota and South Dakota).

Federal Home Loan Bank of Little Rock, 1400 Tower Building, Little Rock, AK 7220 (Arkansas, Louisiana, Mississippi, New Mexico and Texas).

Federal Home Loan Bank of Topeka, P.O. Box 176, Topeka, KS 66601 (Colorado, Kansas, Nebraska and Oklahoma).

Federal Home Loan Bank of San Francisco, P.O. Box 7948, San Francisco, CA 94120 (Arizona, Nevada and California).

Federal Home Loan Bank of Seattle, 600 Stewart St., Seattle, WA 98101 (Alaska, Hawaii and Guam, Idaho, Montana, Oregon, Utah, Washington and Wyoming).

Fact Sheets
The Federal Home Loan Bank Board provides Fact Sheets on such subjects as Renegotiable Rate Mortgages, Deposit Insurance Coverage, Electronic Fund Transfer, Community Reinvestment Act, Early Withdrawal Penalties, Mobile Home Loan, Consumer Protection provisions, types of mortgages, availability of fixed rate mortgages, and other related topics. Contact: Information Officer, Office of Public Affairs, Federal Home Loan Bank Board, 2nd Floor, 1700 G St. N.W., Washington, DC 20552/202-377-6933.

Federal Savings and Loan Insurance Corp.
The purpose of the Federal Savings and Loan Insurance Corp is to provide stability to the savings and loan industry while providing safety to small savers by offering insurance for savings accounts. It is also concerned with helping the industry attract funds for economical home financing. Contact: Office of the Federal Savings and Loan Insurance Corporation, Federal Home Loan Bank Board, 4th Floor, 1700 G St. N.W., Washington, DC 20552/202-377-6612.

Files and Dockets
The Files and Dockets of savings and loan associations are available only through Freedom of Information requests. There are files of over 4,000 active members of the Bank system, including associations insured by FSLIC: files of over 670 service corporations which are owned in part or in whole by various federal savings and loans; plus the files of 191 savings and loan holding companies registered with and regulated by the Bank Board. Contact: Office of the General Counsel, Federal Home Loan Bank Board, 3rd Floor, 1700 G St. N.W., Washington, DC 20552/202-377-6469.

Finance
This office provides analysis and research on forecasting asset growth and in managing liabilities of district banks in an effort to insure that adequate funds are available at a reasonable cost. Contact: Office of Finance, Federal Home Loan Bank Board, 5th Floor, 1700 G St. N.W., Washington, DC 20552/202-377-6308.

Financial Assistance

After a merger or rehabilitation action of an insured savings and loan institution is consummated, the FSLIC administers the financial assistance agreement until its expiration. Contact: Financial Assistance Division, Office of the Federal Savings and Loan Insurance Corporation, Federal Home Loan Bank Board, 4th Floor, 1700 G St. N.W., Washington, DC 20552/202-377-6624.

Freedom of Information Act Requests

For Freedom of Information Act requests, contact: Administrative Division, Office of the General Counsel, Federal Home Loan Bank Board, 3rd Floor, 1700 G St. N.W., Washington, DC 20552/202-377-6462.

Grants

The grant program encourages the use of funds for contracts and special studies for which historical black colleges and universities could be invited to perform. Contact: Administrative Services Division, Federal Home Loan Bank Board, 4th Floor, 1700 G St. N.W., Washington, DC 20552/202-377-6222.

Housing Finance Review

This quarterly journal presents the results of research in housing finance and includes policy issues on that subject. Contact: *Housing Finance Review,* Office of Policy and Economic Research, Federal Home Loan Bank Board, 5th Floor, 1700 G St. N.W., Washington, DC 20552/202-377-6762.

Industry Development

This office provides analyses and recommendations for action on most applications submitted by the savings and loan industry, and develops and implements proposals to improve the agency's regulatory requirements, policies and procedures. Contact: Office of Industry Development, Federal Home Loan Bank Board, 4th Floor, 1700 G St. N.W., Washington, DC 20552/202-377-6707

International Activities

This office deals with thrift institutions and mortgage lending either in or relating to foreign countries. For example, it has a program of liaison and technical assistance with the Agency for International Development's (AID) Office of Housing. Projects in Latin America include the continued development of a secondary mortgage market in Bolivia and the continued monitoring of the Inter-American Savings and Loan Bank. It has also conducted a survey of mortgage finance systems of seven Asian countries. It also monitors housing finance developments in the major industrialized countries of the world. There is also a Visiting Research Scholars Program where academic economists work with staff economists on policy and statistical projects. Contact: International Division, Office of Policy and Economic Research, Federal Home Loan Bank Board, 5th Floor, 1700 G St. N.W., Washington, DC 20552/202-377-6775.

Investment

This office is the portfolio manager for the Consolidated Securities Fund, the Federal Home Loan Mortgage Corporation, and the Federal Savings and Loan Insurance Corporation. It is also the money control operations arm for all FHLBB System portfolios. Contact: Investment Division, Office of Finance, Federal Home Loan Bank Board, 5th Floor, 1700 G St. N.W., Washington, DC 20552/202-377-6330.

Legal Assistance

This office provides legal advice and assistance in connection with the Federal Savings and Loan Insurance Corporation's default prevention and financial assistance activities. For more information, contact: Federal Savings and Loan Insurance Corporation Division, Office of the General Counsel, Federal Home Loan Bank Board, 3rd Floor, 1700 G St. N.W., Washington, DC 20552/202-377-6428.

Libraries

The Federal Home Loan Bank Board Research Library includes material in banking, savings and loan associations, economics, finance and related subjects. The Federal Home Loan Bank Board also has a law library that includes banking and savings and loan laws for all the states. Contact: Research Library, Basement, Federal Home Loan Bank Board, 1700 G St. N.W., Washington, DC 20552/202-377-6296, or Law Library, Federal Home Loan Bank Board, Basement, 1700 G St. N.W., Washington, DC 20552/202-377-6470.

Neighborhood Reinvestment

The Federal Home Loan Bank Board has established the Neighborhood Reinvestment Corporation (NRC) to stimulate local partnerships in an effort to reverse the process of neighborhood deterioration. The main focus is the improvement of housing and public amenities. Contact: Office of Neighborhood Reinvestment, Federal Home Loan Bank Board, 6th Floor, 1700 G St. N.W., Washington, DC 20552/202-377-6366.

Publications

For a list of Federal Home Loan Bank Board publications, contact: Information Office, Office of Public Affairs, Federal Home Loan Bank Board, 2nd Floor, 1700 G St. N.W., Washington, DC 20552/202-377-6933.

Receivership and Liquidation

FSLIC will purchase specified assets if it proves to be more economical as part of the default prevention activity. Contact: Office of the Federal Savings and Loan Insurance Corporation, Federal Home Loan Bank Board, 4th Floor, 1700 G St. N.W., Washington, DC 20552/202-377-6609.

Regulations
This office in cooperation with other Bank Board offices, drafts regulations and policy statements to implement the Bank Board's statutory authority, policies, objectives and directives. Contact: Regulations Division, Office of the General Counsel, Federal Home Loan Bank Board, 3rd Floor, 1700 G St. N.W., Washington, DC 20552/202-377-6440.

Research
This office is responsible for most long-range analytical projects relating to the thrift industry and the savings and mortgage markets. Contact: General Research Division, Office of Policy and Economic Research, Federal Home Loan Bank Board, 5th Floor, 1700 G St. N.W., Washington, DC 20552/202-377-6760.

Research and Analysis
This office is responsible for detailed legal analysis and research of issues of concern to the Bank Board such as questions of constitutional law, tax law issues, issues involving the FHLBB system, and civil rights issues. Contact: Research and Analysis Division, Office of the General Counsel, Federal Home Loan Bank Board, 3rd Floor, 1700 G St. N.W., Washington, DC 20552/202-377-6432.

Securities
This office processes mutual-to-stock and state stock-to-federal stock conversion applications and all debt applications. It also administers and enforces provisions of the Securities Exchange Act relating to securities registration, periodic reporting, proxy solicitation, tender offers and insider trading of stock or registered stock savings and loan institutions. Contact: Securities Division, Office of the General Counsel, Federal Home Loan Bank Board, 3rd Floor, 1700 G St. N.W., Washington, DC 20552/202-377-6459.

Statistics
This office collects and monitors reports for the savings and loan industry and produces special reports on various aspects of savings and loan operations. The statistics include Balance Sheet Data Commitments, Savings Activity, Net Savings Inflow, Mortgage Loan Activity, Mortgage Loans, Closed Mortgage debt held, and maximum rates of return payable on savings of savings and loan associations. Contact: Statistical Division, Office of Policy and Economic Research, Federal Home Loan Bank Board, 5th Floor, 1700 G St. N.W., Washington, DC 20552/202-377-6780.

Supervision
This office monitors compliance with the Community Reinvestment Act by the savings and loan system. It has established a Community Reinvestment Act rating and monitoring system under which every association with an adverse rating at its most recent examination is logged and thereafter closely surveilled. Contact: Supervisor, Office of Examinations and Supervision, Federal Home Loan Bank Board, 3rd Floor, 1700 G St. N.W., Washington, DC 20552/202-377-6545.

Supervisory Agents List for Consumer Complaints
For a list of supervisory agents and their addresses and phone numbers who handle consumer complaints in each of the 12 districts, contact: Department of Consumer and Civil Rights, Office of Examinations and Supervision, Federal Home Loan Bank Board, 3rd Floor, 1700 G St. N.W., Washington, DC 20552/202-377-6947.

There Ought to be a Law . . . There Is
This is a free pamphlet on savings and loan associations with information on consumers' and borrowers' rights. Contact: Consumer Division, Office of Community Investment, Federal Home Loan Bank Board, 2nd Floor, 1700 G St. N.W., Washington, DC 20552/202-377-6209.

How Can the Federal Home Loan Bank Board Help You?
For information on how this agency can help you, contact: Communications Office, Federal Home Loan Bank Board, 1700 G St. N.W., Washington, DC 20552/202-377-6677.

Federal Labor Relations Authority

500 C St. S.W., Washington, DC 20424/202-382-0711

Established: December 28, 1978
Budget: $15,812,000
Employees: 306

Mission: Oversees the federal service labor-management relations program; administers the law that protects the right of employees of the federal government to organize, bargain collectively, and participate through labor organizations of their own choosing in decisions that affect them; and ensures compliance with the statutory rights and obligations of federal employees and the labor organizations which represent them in their dealings with federal agencies.

Major Sources of Information

Administrative Law Judges
Administrative law judges hear unfair labor practice cases prosecuted by the General Counsel. Contact: Office of Administrative Law Judges, Federal Labor Relations Authority, 500 C St. S.W., Washington, DC 20424/202-382-0777.

Annual Report of the Federal Labor Relations Authority and the Federal Service Impasses Panel
The Annual Report describes significant decisions of the Federal Labor Relations Authority under the provisions of Title 7 of the Civil Service Reformate of 1978 and case processing statistics of the General Counsel of the Authority. Contact: Public Information Office of the Executive Director, Federal Labor Relations Authority, 500 C St. S.W., Washington, DC 20424/202-382-0711.

Dockets
Case dockets and decisions can be seen in the Case Management Docket Room, Federal Labor Relations Authority, 500 C St. S.W., Washington, DC 20424/202-382-0876 (call ahead).

Federal Service Impasses Panel
This panel provides assistance in resolving negotiation impasses between agencies and exclusive representatives. A *Subject Matter Index* and a *Table of Cases,* an *Annual Report* and a *Guide to Hearing Procedures of the Federal Services Impasses Panel* are available. For further information, contact: Federal Service Impasses Panel, Federal Labor Relations Authority, 500 C St. S.W., Washington, DC 20424/202-382-0981.

Freedom of Information Act Requests
For Freedom of Information Act Requests, contact: Office of the Solicitor, Federal Labor Relations Authority, 500 C St. S.W., Washington, DC 20424/202-382-0711.

General Counsel
The General Counsel may investigate alleged unfair labor practices, and file and prosecute complaints. For additional information, contact: Office of the General Counsel, Federal Labor Relations Authority, 500 C St. S.W., Washington, DC 20424/202-382-0742.

Library
The Federal Labor Relations Authority Library is a small specialized collection of material dealing with Federal Labor Relations. Contact: Library, Federal Labor Relations Authority, Room 234, 500 C St. S.W., Washington, DC 20424/202-382-0765.

Federal Maritime Commission

1100 L St. N.W., Washington, DC 20573/202-523-5707

Established: August 12, 1961
Budget: $11,770,000
Employees: 290

Mission: Regulates the waterborne foreign and domestic offshore commerce of the United States; assures that U.S. international trade is open to all nations on fair and equitable terms, and protects against unauthorized, concerted activity in the waterborne commerce of the United States; maintains surveillance over steamship conferences and common carriers by water; assures that only the rates on file with the Commission are charged; reviews agreements between persons subject to the Shipping Act, of 1984; guarantees equal treatment to shippers, carriers and other persons subject to the shipping statutes; and ensures that adequate levels of financial responsibility are maintained for indemnification of passengers and clean-up of oil and hazardous substances spills.

Major Sources of Information

Agreements and Trade Activities
All agreements are reviewed in this bureau which is also responsible for the on-going analysis of trade patterns, conference activities, pooling statements and operating reports. The Bureau monitors significant trade activities and forecasts future competitive trade conditions. Contact: Bureau of Agreements, Federal Maritime Commission, 1100 L St. N.W., Washington, DC 20573/202-523-5787.

Common Carrier Tariffs in the Foreign Commerce of the United States
Information on tariff filing requirements for common carrier tariffs in the foreign commerce of the United States is available. Contact: Bureau of Tariffs, Federal Maritime Commission, Room 10319-A, 1100 L St. N.W., Washington, DC 20573/202-523-5796.

Dockets
All official files and records of Commission proceedings, copies of decisions of the administrative law judges, Commission reports, publications and miscellaneous documents as well as informal and special docket proceedings of the Federal Maritime Commission can be seen in the Docket Room. Federal Maritime Commission, Room 11409, 1100 L St. N.W., Washington, DC 20573/202-523-5760.

Economic Analysis
This office coordinates activity between the Commission's economists and transportation industry analysts. It also analyzes trade by geographic areas (U.S./North Atlantic/Europe; U.S./East Asia; U.S./South America; U.S. Mainland/Puerto Rico-Virgin Islands: West Coast/Hawaii; West Coast/

American Samoa). Contact: Office of Policy Planning and International Affairs, Bureau of Agreements, Federal Maritime Commission, Room 9211, 1100 L St. N.W., Washington, DC 20572/202-523-5746.

Energy and Environmental Impact

Information on the Commission's environmental and energy impact programs and other energy considerations are available. Contact: Office of Energy and Environmental Impact, Federal Maritime Commission, Room 1100 L St. N.W., Washington, DC 20543/202-523-5835.

Enforcement

A description of the Commission's achievements in prosecuting claims of illegal rebating and standardizing its monitoring, investigative, settlement and prosecutorial activities is available. Contact: Office of General Counsel, Federal Maritime Commission, Room 12221, 1100 L St. N.W., Washington, DC 20573/202-523-5740.

Formal Complaints

Formal complaints involving alleged violations of shipping laws are received and processed by the Commission. Contact: Office of the Secretary, Federal Maritime Commission, Room 11101, 1100 L St. N.W., Washington, DC 20573/202-523-5725.

Freedom of Information Act

For Freedom of Information Act requests, contact: Office of the Secretary, Federal Maritime Commission, Room 11101, 1100 L St. N.W., Washington, DC 20573/202-523-5725

Freight Forwarding Licenses

Ocean freight forwarding licenses are issued to individuals, partnerships and corporations. Contact: Office of Freight Forwarders, Bureau of Tariffs, Federal Maritime Commission, Room 10131, 1100 L St. N.W., Washington, DC 20573/202-523-5843.

General Information

Information other than described in other paragraphs should be referred to the Office of the Secretary, Room 11101, 1100 L Street, NW, Washington, DC 20573/202-523-5725.

Informal Inquiries and Complaints

This office seeks the resolution of consumer complaints through informal liaison between the shipping public and various aspects of the maritime industry. It also coordinates complaint handling procedures within agency and field offices, and monitors consumer activities in other government agencies. Contact: Office of Informal Inquiries and Complaints, Federal Maritime Commission, Room 11413, 1100 L Street, NW, Washington, DC 20573/202-523-5807.

Intermodal Transportation

Intermodal transportation involves the movement of goods over a route involving two or more modes of transportation. Intermodal tariffs, reflecting rates and charges for intermodal transportation services, are filed with both the Federal Maritime Commission and the Interstate Commerce Commission. Contact: Bureau of Tariffs, Federal Maritime Commission, Room 10223, 1100 L St. N.W., Washington, DC 20573/202-523-5796.

Library

The Library collection contains nautical information, primarily on maritime law. Contact: Library, Federal Maritime Commission, Room 11139, 1100 L St. N.W., Washington, DC 20573/202-523-5762.

Marine Terminals

Marine terminals operated by private parties or state or local governments are currently subject to the Commission's jurisdiction if they provide services in connection with common carriers by water. Agreements entered into between terminal operators and other persons subject to the Shipping Act (e.g., for the lease of property, dock or berthing space, or for services to be performed for carriers) may require the determination of effective date under Section 5 and 6 of the Act of 1984. Contact: Bureau of Agreements, Federal Maritime Commission, Room 10415, 1100 L St. N.W., Washington, DC 20573/202-523-3952.

Ocean Commerce Monitoring

The Commission systematically monitors U.S. ocean commerce in an effort to curtail illegal rebating and other malpractices by carriers, shippers, consignees and other persons subject to the Shipping Act. Contact: Bureau of Investigation, Federal Maritime Commission, Room 11223, 1100 L St. N.W., Washington, DC 20573/202-523-5860.

Passenger Vessel Certification

This office certifies passenger vessels for financial responsibility with respect to liability for death or injury and for nonperformance of transportation. Contact: Passenger Vessel Certification, Bureau of Tariffs, Federal Maritime Commission, Room 10115, 1100 L St. N.W., Washington, DC 20573/202-523-5838.

Pooling Agreements

Pooling agreements provide for equitable apportioning of cargo and/or revenues by a number of carriers in a given trade, enabling the participants to benefit from the increased efficiency and economy accruing from the pooling of vessels, equipment and other resources. Various sailing requirements and other features relative to service efficiency are often included in pooling agreements. Equal access agreements are designed to ensure that national flag carriers maintain access to cargo whose movement is controlled by the government of the reciprocal trading partner through cargo preference laws, import quotas or other restrictions. Contact: Bureau of Agreements, Federal Maritime Commission, Room 10327, 1100 L St. N.W., Washington, DC 20573/202-523-5787.

Publications
A list of Federal Maritime Commission Publications, orders, notices, rulings and decisions is currently available. Contact: Office of the Secretary, Federal Maritime Commission, Room 11101, 1100 L St. N.W., Washington, DC 20573/202-523-5707.

Regulatory Policy and Planning
Policy and planning involves responsiveness to new developments and trends in the U.S. ocean commerce and the liner shipping industry. Transportation industry analysis and management analysts work on long-range policy. They also analyze and review current Commission policies to determine their impact on regulated industries and U.S. ocean commerce. Contact: Office of Policy, Planning and International Affairs, Federal Maritime Commission, Room 11213, 1100 L St. N.W., Washington, DC 20573/202-523-5746.

Space Charter Agreements
Space charter agreements involve the charter (or cross-charter) of space or slots between or among ocean carriers. Space chartering agreements are designed to ensure that a carrier is assured of vessel accommodation beyond that which would be otherwise available. Contact: Bureau of Agreements, Federal Maritime Commission, Room 10472, 1100 L St. N.W., Washington, DC 20573/202-523-5793.

State-Controlled Carriers
All state-controlled carriers operating in the foreign commerce of the United States are identified and classified. Information regarding the registry, ownership and control of the responses received is documented. Changes of ownership, registry and control of carriers, their entry and exit from conferences, and the opening rates within conferences to which controlled carriers belong are also monitored. *Publishing and Filing Tariffs by Common Carriers in the Foreign Commerce of the United States* is the Commission's order on this subject. For additional information, contact: Bureau of Tariffs, Federal Maritime Commission, Room 10223, 1100 L St. N.W., Washington, DC 20573/202-523-5796.

Tariffs
Foreign and domestic tariffs filed with the Commission are analyzed by this Bureau. It also monitors trade conditions and audits tariffs periodically. Contact: Bureau of Tariffs, Federal Maritime Commission, Room 10223, 1100 L St. N.W., Washington, DC 20573/202-523-5796.

Weekly Agenda
The Commission Secretary prepares the Commission agenda for weekly meetings. Contact: Office of the Secretary, Federal Maritime Commission, Room 11101, 1100 L St. N.W., Washington, DC 20573/202-523-5725.

How Can the Federal Maritime Commission Help You?
To determine how the Federal Maritime Commission can help you, contact: Office of the Chairman, Federal Maritime Commission, 1100 L St. N.W., Washington, DC 20573/202-523-5707.

Federal Mediation and Conciliation Service

2100 K St. N.W., Washington, DC 20427/202-653-5290

Established: 1947
Budget: $22,014,000
Employees: 367

Mission: Represents the public interest by promoting the development of sound and stable labor-management relationships; prevents or minimizes work stoppages by assisting labor and management to settle their disputes through mediation; advocates collective bargaining, mediation and voluntary arbitration as the preferred processes for settling issues between employers and representatives of employees; develops the art, science and practice of dispute resolution; and fosters constructive joint relationships of labor and management leaders to increase their mutual understanding and solution of common problems.

Major Sources of Information

Arbitration
Arbitration is a preferred method for resolving disputes arising during the term of a contract. Upon request, the Federal Mediation and Conciliation Service will furnish a panel of professional and impartial arbitrators from which the opposing party may select the one most mutually satisfactory to hear and provide a final decision on their dispute. Contact: Office of Arbitration Services, Federal Mediation and Conciliation Service, Room 700, 2100 K St. N.W., Washington, DC 20427/202-653-5280.

Federal Employee Bargaining
This office provides mediation services and assistance to federal agencies and labor organizations in the resolution of negotiation disputes. It enters state and local collective bargaining situations only where both parties ask for assistance, and only when there is no state or local agency available to provide the service. Contact: Public Sector Coordinator, Federal Mediation and Conciliation Ser-

vice, 2100 K St. N.W., Washington, DC 20427/202-653-5240.

Foreign Visitors
The foreign visitor program involves representatives of labor, management and governments from around the world who want to see how mediation and collective bargaining function in the United States. Contact: Technical Assistance Coordinator, Federal Mediation and Conciliation Service, Room 801, 2100 K St. N.W., Washington, DC 20427/202-653-5290.

Freedom of Information Act Requests
For Freedom of Information Act requests contact: Legal Services Office, Federal Mediation and Conciliation Service, Room 903, 2100 K St. N.W., Washington, DC 20427/202-653-5305.

Grants
The program described below is for sums of money which are given by the Department of

Labor to support the expansion of labor-management relations.

Labor-Management Cooperation

Objectives: To support the establishment or expansion of joint labor-management committees at the plant, area, and industrywide levels in order to improve labor-management relations, job security, economic development, and productivity.

Eligibility: State and local units of government; private nonprofit labor-management committees, private company or public agency.

Range of Financial Assistance: $20,000 to $100,000.

Contact: Division of Labor-Management Grant Programs, Federal Mediation and Conciliation Service, 2100 K Street NW, Washington, DC 20427/202-653-5320.

Legal Services

The Legal Services Office represents the Federal Mediation and Conciliation Service in legal matters. It also participates as needed as part of the mediation team on unusually complex and technical mediation assignments. Contact: Legal Services Office, Federal Mediation and Conciliation Service, Room 903, 2100 K St. N.W., Washington, DC 20427/202-653-5305.

Mediation Training and Development

Collective bargaining workshops are conducted in areas such as group dynamics and communications skills training and instructional skills training. Contact: Federal Mediation and Conciliation Service, 2100 K St. N.W., Washington, DC 20427/ 202-653-5210.

Private Sector Help

The Service helps employers and unions in selecting arbitrators to adjudicate labor-management disputes by maintaining a large roster of qualified arbitrators. When an employer and a union need an arbitrator, they need only notify the FMCS and it will provide, at no charge, a listing of qualified arbitrators in their area who are available to hear the dispute. Mediators are on call 24 hours a day in major cities. Contact your local or regional Federal Mediation and Conciliation Service.

Publications

The following publications are available: *FMCS Annual Report* summarizing major negotiations and important developments; pamphlets on mediation in the private, federal, state and local sectors; a pamphlet on arbitration procedures and policies, and a booklet explaining collective bargaining in the health care industry. For these publications and general information, contact: Office of Information, and Public Affairs, Federal Mediation and Conciliation Service, Room 909, 2100 K St. N.W., Washington, DC 20427/202-653-5290.

Technical Assistance Efforts

Technical assistance to improve relations between labor and management can include such efforts as consultant, training for one or both parties, help in modifying a relationship or forming joint labor-management committee. For further information, contact: Technical Assistance Coordinator, Office of Mediation Services, Federal Mediation and Conciliation Service, Room 400, 2100 K St. N.W., Washington, DC 20427/202-653-5240.

How Can the Federal Mediation and Conciliation Service Help You?

For information on how this agency may be of help to you, contact: Office of Information and Public Affairs, Federal Mediation and Conciliation Service, Room 909, 2100 K St. N.W., Washington, DC 20427/202-653-5290.

Federal Reserve System

20th St. and Constitution Ave. N.W., Washington, DC 20551/202-452-3204

Established: December 23, 1913
Budget: $66,800,000
Employees: 1,554

Mission: Administers and makes policy for the nation's credit and monetary affairs; and helps to maintain the banking industry in a sound condition, capable of responding to the nation's domestic and international financial needs and objectives.

Major Sources of Information

Bank Holding Companies
A company that qualifies as a bank holding company must register with the Federal Reserve System and file reports with the System. A registered bank holding company must obtain the approval of the Board of Governors before acquiring more than 5% of the shares of either additional banks or permissible nonbanking companies. Contact: Bank Holding Companies, Bank Supervision and Regulation Division, Federal Reserve System, Room 3170 MAR, 20th St. and Constitution Ave. N.W., Washington, DC 20551/202-542-2638.

Bank Mergers
All proposed bank mergers between insured state-chartered member banks must receive prior approval from the Federal Reserve Board. Contact: Bank Mergers, Bank Supervision and Regulation Division, Federal Reserve System, Room 3148 MAR, 20th St. and Constitution Ave. N.W., Washington, DC 20551/202-452-3408

Bank Supervision and Regulation
The Federal Reserve Board has supervisory and regulatory responsibility over member banks and bank holding companies. It shares responsibility with the states for the supervision of state-chartered banks that are members of the System and has been designated by Congress to administer Federal laws applicable to branching of state-chartered members and to mergers where the resulting bank is a state member. Under provisions of the Bank Holding Company act the Board establishes guidelines for permitting the common ownership of banks and bank-related business. The Board's supervisory responsibilities extend to the foreign operations of American banks, and under the International Banking Act, to the foreign operations of American banks, and under the International Banking Act, to foreign bank operations in the United States. Contact: Federal Reserve System, 20th St. and Constitution Ave. N.W., Washington, DC 20551/202/452-3614.

Board Meetings
Open and closed Board meetings are announced in the *Federal Register*. A mailing list of meeting announcements is also kept. Bank and bank holding Company schedules are available two business days before a meeting. Minutes of past meetings as well as cassette recordings ($5.00 each) of these meetings are also available upon request. Contact: Freedom of Information, Office of the Secretary, Federal Reserve System, Room

2234, 20th St. and Constitution Ave. N.W., Washington, DC 20551/202-452-3684.

Buying Treasury Securities at Federal Reserve Banks

This free publication offers detailed information on buying treasury bills, notes and bonds. It also includes directions on how to read United States government security quotes, regulations and rules governing book-entry treasury bills and the addresses and phone numbers of Federal Reserve Banks and Treasury. Contact: Federal Reserve Bank of Richmond, P.O. Box 27622, Richmond, VA 23261/804-643-1250.

Complaints about Banks

Complaints about a state-chartered bank in connection with any of the federal credit laws are handled by the Federal Reserve Board. The Board will acknowledge your letter and try to respond in full within 15 days. It will refer complaints about other institutions to the appropriate Federal Bank regulatory agency. Contact: Consumer and Community Affairs Division, Federal Reserve System, 20th St. and Constitution Ave. N.W., Washington, DC 20551/202-452-2631.

Consumer Education Materials

Free publications are available from the Board of Governors and other Federal Reserve Banks. Below is a listing of the Federal Reserve Banks followed by examples of available publications:

Board of Governors of the Federal Reserve System, Publications Services, Room MP-510, Washington, DC 20551/202-452-3244.

Federal Reserve Bank of Boston, Public Information Department, 600 Atlantic Ave, Boston, MA 02106/617-973-3459

Federal Reserve Bank of New York, Public Information Department, 33 Liberty St., New York, NY 10045/212-791-6134.

Federal Reserve Bank of Philadelphia, Public Information Department, Ten Independence Mall, Philadelphia, PA 19106/215-574-6115. Federal Reserve Bank of Cleveland, Research Department, P.O. Box 6387, Cleveland, OH 44101/216-241-2000.

Federal Reserve Bank of Richmond, Bank and Public Relations Department, P.O. Box 27622, Richmond, VA 23261/804-643-1250.

Federal Reserve Bank of Atlanta, Research Department, Publications Unit, 104 Marietta St. N.W., Atlanta, GA 30303/404-586-8788.

Federal Reserve Bank of Chicago, Public Information Department, 230 South LaSalle St., Chicago, IL 60690/312-322-5112.

Federal Reserve Bank of St. Louis, Bank Relations and Public Information Department, P.O. Box 442, St. Louis, MO 63166/314-444-8321.

Federal Reserve Bank of Minneapolis, Public Information Department, 250 Marquette Ave., Minneapolis, MN 55480/612-340-2443.

Federal Reserve Bank of Kansas City, Public Informa-

tion Department, 925 Grand Ave., Kansas City, MO 64198/816-881-2798.

Federal Reserve Bank of Dallas, Public Information Department, 400 South Akard St., Dallas, TX 75222/214-651-6267.

Federal Reserve Bank of San Francisco, Public Information Department, 101 Market St., San Francisco, CA 94105/415-544-2184.

PUBLICATIONS AVAILABLE FROM THE BOARD OF GOVERNORS

Consumer Handbook to Credit Protection Laws—explains how consumer credit laws can help in shopping for credit, applying for it, and keeping a good credit rating.

The Equal Credit Opportunity Act and Age—briefly describes criteria used in determining creditworthiness and provisions of the Act that prevent age from being used against an individual.

The Equal Credit Opportunity Act and Credit Rights in Housing—discusses the Equal Credit Opportunity Act rights of prospective home buyers.

The Equal Credit Opportunity Act and Incidental Creditors—explains the effects of the Equal Credit Opportunity Act on doctors, lawyers, craftsmen and other professionals and small businessmen who grant consumer credit.

Equal Credit Opportunity Act and Women—explains the effects of Equal Credit Opportunity Act on women.

Fair Credit Billing—tells how to deal with billing errors on open-end credit accounts.

How to File a Consumer Complaint—explains how to file a complaint against a bank in connection with federal credit laws.

If You Borrow to Buy Stock—explains margin regulations in nontechnical terms.

If You Use a Credit Card—explains the protection under federal law against lost cards, what to do if goods bought with credit cards are unsatisfactory, and how you can figure out and compare various credit card charges.

What Truth in Leasing Means to You—explains major provisions of Truth in Leasing Act

What Truth in Lending Means to You—explains major provisions of the Truth in Lending Act.

PUBLICATIONS AVAILABLE FROM THE FEDERAL RESERVE BANK OF BOSTON

Checkpoints—gives step-by-step instructions on the proper way to write, deposit and cash checks. Also available in Spanish and Portuguese.

Consumer Education Catalog—Lists consumer education material published by the System and local organizations.

Credit Points—discusses the major credit laws enacted in recent years such as Truth in Lending, and describes consumer's rights and protections.

AVAILABLE FROM THE FEDERAL RESERVE BANK OF NEW YORK

Basic Information on Treasury Bills—describes the procedures to be followed by individual investors purchasing T-Bills.

Basic Information on Treasury Notes and Bonds—describes procedures to be followed by individual investors purchasing T-Notes and Bonds.

Fedpoints 5—Book-Entry Procedure—discusses Treasury program to replace physical securities with computer entries.

Fedpoints 17—Consumer Credit Regulations—explains that although the Federal Reserve is charged with writing most consumer regulations, their administration involves 12 separate federal organizations. Explanations and details of each.

Consumer Credit Terminology Handbook—a collection of consumer credit terms and definitions to assist consumers in everyday credit transactions. English and Spanish.

AVAILABLE FROM THE FEDERAL RESERVE BANK OF PHILADELPHIA

Consumer Affairs Pamphlets—Titles: How the New Equal Credit Opportunity Act Affects You, How to Establish and Use Credit, Fair Debt Collection Practices, The Rule of 78's, Your Credit Rating.

Your Credit Rating—describes importance of a credit history and consumers' rights when using credit. Tells what to do to correct credit record.

AVAILABLE FROM THE FEDERAL RESERVE BANK OF RICHMOND

Mechanics of Buying Original Issues of United States Treasury Securities—basic steps involved in purchasing Treasury bills, notes and bonds together with an explanation of the financial needs of the U.S. Treasury.

AVAILABLE FROM THE FEDERAL RESERVE BANK OF CHICAGO

The A B C's of Figuring Interest—discusses how the various ways of calculating interest affects the dollar amount paid.

Marketable Securities of the U.S. Government—provides facts on U.S. Treasury bills, notes and bonds.

Credit Protection Laws

Find out how you can profit from the new credit laws by obtaining a free copy of *Consumer Handbook to Credit Protection Laws*. Contact Board of Governors of the Federal Reserve System, 20th St. and Constitution Ave. N.W., Washington, DC 20551/202-452-3245.

Electronic Fund Transfers

Only handles complaints against state member banks about Electronic Fund Transfers that have not been resolved by the financial institutions involved. A free booklet, *Alice in Debitland*, deals with consumer protections and the Electronic Fund Transfer Act. Contact: Consumer and Community Affairs Division, Federal Reserve System, 20th St. and Constitution Ave. N.W., Washington, DC 20551/202-452-2631.

Federal Open Market Committee

Open market operations are the principal instrument used by the Federal Reserve to implement national monetary policy. The Federal Open Market Committee is responsible for determining what transactions the Federal Reserve System will conduct in the open market. Through frequent buying and selling of United States Government securities, the Manager of the System Open Market Account provides or absorbs bank reserves in keeping with instructions and directives issued by the Committee. In addition the Committee authorizes and oversees operations in foreign exchange markets. Contact: Office of Staff Director for Monetary and Financial Policy, Federal Reserve System, Room B2001, 20th St. and Constitution Ave. N.W., Washington, DC 20551/202-452-3761.

Financial Statistics

Economic and financial information is available including data on banking, capital markets, government finance, flow of funds and savings, business conditions, wages, prices and productivity. The information is published in a variety of reports and studies. Contact: Research and Statistics Division, Federal Reserve System, Room 3048, 20th St. and Constitution Ave. N.W., Washington, DC 20551/202-452-3301.

Freedom of Information Act Requests

For Freedom of Information Act requests, contact: Office of the Secretary, Federal Reserve System, Room 1122, 20th St. and Constitution Ave. N.W., Washington, DC 20551/202-452-2407.

International Finance

For information on foreign financial markets, international banking, U.S./international transactions, international development, world payments and economic activity, etc., contact: International Finance Division, Federal Reserve System, 20th St. and Constitution Ave. N.W., Washington, DC 20551/202-452-3614.

Monetary Control Act of 1980

The Monetary Control Act of 1980 (P.L. 96-221), enacted on March 31, 1980, is designed to improve the effectiveness of monetary policy by applying new reserve requirements set by the Federal Reserve Board to all depository institutions. Among other key provisions, the Act 1) authorizes the Federal Reserve to collect reports from all depository institutions; 2) extends access to Federal Reserve discount and borrowing privileges and other services to nonmember depository institutions; 3) requires the Federal Reserve Board to set a schedule of fees for Federal Reserve Board services; and 4) provides for the gradual phase-out of deposit interest rate ceilings, coupled with broader powers for thrift institutions. For more detailed information, contact your District Reserve Bank or Public Affairs, Federal Reserve Board, Room 2117-B, 20th St. and Constitution Ave. N.W., Washington, DC 20551/202-452-3204.

Monetary Policy

The office of the Staff Director for Monetary and Financial Policy of the Federal Reserve Board is responsible for the analysis of issues in monetary policy, which includes open market operations, member bank discount borrowing at Federal Reserve Banks and changes in reserve requirements. Contact: Staff Director for Monetary and Financial Policy, Federal Reserve Board, 20th St. and Constitution Ave., N.W., Washington, DC 20551.

Priced Services

The following services are covered by a fee schedule:

Check-clearing and collection
Wire transfer
Automated clearinghouse
Settlement
Securities safekeeping
Federal Reserve float

For information, contact the nearest Federal Reserve Bank, or its Branch, or Public Affairs, Federal Reserve System, Room 2117-B, 20th St. and Constitution Ave. N.W., Washington, DC 20551/202-452-3204.

Public Information Materials of the Federal Reserve System

This is a free guide to Federal Reserve System materials designed for use by educators, bankers and the public. The contents of the items, which include occasional and periodic publications, audiovisual materials and statistical information, are briefly described and applicable charges, if any, are listed. For copies of this booklet, contact your local Federal Reserve Bank, or Publication Services, Federal Reserve System, Room MP-510, 20th St. and Constitution Ave. N.W., Washington, DC 20551/202-452-3244.

Research Library

The research library contains material on banking, finance, economics, and other areas related to the Federal Reserve System. Contact: Library, Federal Reserve Board, Room BC241, 20th St. and Constitution Ave. N.W. (entrance is on C St.), Washington, DC 20551/202-452-3398. The law library concentrates on banking laws. Contact; Law Library, Federal Reserve System, Room B1066, 20th St. and Constitution Ave. N.W., Washington, DC 20551/202-452-3284.

Treasury Securities

The Treasury Department raises much of its funds by selling marketable securities to the general public through the 12 Federal Reserve Banks. These banks receive applications from the public for the purchase of securities, allot the securities among bidders, deliver the securities, collect payment from the buyers, redeem the securities later when they mature, and pay interest coupons. For additional information, contact the nearest Federal Reserve Bank or its branch.

Visitors

Individuals or groups who wish to visit the Federal Reserve Board should contact: Office of the Secretary, Federal Reserve System, Room 2242-A 2234, 20th St. and Constitution Ave. N.W., Washington, DC 20551/202-452-2526.

How Can the Federal Reserve System Help You?

For information on how this agency can be of help to you, contact: Office of Public Affairs, Board of Governors, Federal Reserve System, Room 2117-B, 20th St. and Constitution Ave. N.W., Washington, DC 20551/202-452-3204.

Federal Trade Commission

**Pennsylvania Ave. and 6th St. N.W., Washington, DC 20580/
202-523-3830**

Established: 1914
Budget: $64,871,000
Employees: 1,265

Mission: Responsible for the maintenance of strongly competitive enterprise as the keystone of the American economic system; prevents the free enterprise system from being fettered by monopoly or restraints on trade, or corrupted by unfair or deceptive trade practices.

Major Sources of Information

Administrative Law Judges
Administrative law judges are officials to whom the Commission delegates the initial fact-finding procedures in adjudicative cases. The judges conduct trials and review evidence in the form of documents testimony of witnesses, and issue initial decisions which are overviewed by the Commission. Contact: Administrative Law Judges, Federal Trade Commission, Room 603B, 2120 L St. N.W., Washington, DC 20580/202-254-7730.

Advertising Substantiation
This office monitors national advertisements to make sure their claims are substantiated. Contact: Advertising Practices, Bureau of Consumer Protection, Federal Trade Commission, Room 6124A STAR, 6th. and Pennsylvania Ave. N.W., Washington, DC 20580/202-376-8617.

Advisory Opinions
The Federal Trade Commission established the advisory opinion procedures to enable business people to learn, before implementing a practice, whether the practice might violate the laws the Federal Trade Commission administers. Contact: Secretary of the Commission, Federal Trade Commission, 6th St. and Pennsylvania Ave. N.W., Room 172, Washington, DC 20580/202-523-3383.

Antitrust Compliance
This office is responsible for securing compliance with all final orders the Federal Trade Commission issues to protect and maintain competition. When the orders require companies to divest themselves of certain stock, assets or both, the division oversees the divestitures. It also reviews prospective purchasers of the stock or assets when the Federal Trade Commission approval of the purchases appears necessary to protect free and fair competition. Contact: Compliance, Bureau of Competition, Federal Trade Commission, Suite 301, 1111 18th St. N.W., Washington, DC 20036/202-634-4604.

Children's Advertising
This office monitors advertising directed at children to determine whether or not it is deceptive. Contact: Advertising Practices, Federal Trade Commission, Room 6124A STAR, 6th St. and Pennsylvania Ave. N.W., Washington, DC 20580/202-724-1456.

Cigarette Advertising and Labeling
This office reports regularly to Congress on the effects of cigarette labeling, advertising and promotion. It also operates a tobacco testing laboratory to measure tar, nicotine and carbon monoxide

content. Contact: Advertising Practices, Federal Trade Commission, Room 6124A STAR, 6th St. and Pennsylvania Ave. N.W., Washington, DC 20580/202-724-1458.

Competition and Antitrust
This office enforces antitrust laws. It encourages voluntary compliance with the law, and offers industry guidance. Contact: Bureau of Competition, Federal Trade Commission, Room 372, 6th St. and Pennsylvania Ave. N.W., Washington, DC 20580/202-523-3601.

Compliance with Consumer Protection Orders
This office makes certain that companies which are subject to cease-and-desist orders abide by them. This division is also responsible for the enforcement of various trade regulation rules enforced by the Commission. Included are the funeral rule, mail-order rule, franchise rule, appliance labeling rule, and R value rule. Contact: Enforcement Division, Bureau of Consumer Protection, Federal Trade Commission, Room 425, 600 E. Street N.W., Washington, DC 20580/202-376-3475.

Consumer Bibliography
This free bibliography compiled by the Federal Trade Commission Library includes consumer directors, manuals, law and legislative sources, bibliographies and periodicals as well as Federal Trade Commission publications. Contact: Library, Bureau of Consumer Protection, Federal Trade Commission, Room 630 BCB, 6th St. and Pennsylvania Ave. N.W., Washington, DC 20580/202-523-3871

Consumer Complaints
To offer assistance, make suggestions or report violations, contact: Bureau of Consumer Protection, Federal Trade Commission, 6th St. and Pennsylvania Ave. N.W., Washington, DC 20580/202-523-3598.

Consumer Dispute Resolution
This program is working on ways to increase the consumer's ability to resolve disputes with business. The staff is preparing guidelines for voluntary business complaint-handling systems. For further information and suggestions, contact: Marketing Practices, Bureau of Consumer Protection, Federal Trade Commission, Room 238, 6th St. and Pennsylvania Ave. N.W., Washington, DC 20580/202-523-1670.

Consumer Leasing
This office enforces the Consumer Leasing Act which requires that certain terms be disclosed to consumers. Contact: Credit Practices, Bureau of Consumer Protection, Federal Trade Commission, Room 500 IND, 6th St. and Pennsylvania Ave. N.W., Washington, DC 20580/202-724-1569.

Credit Billing
This office polices unfair and deceptive credit billing practices, according to the Fair Credit Billing Act. Contact: Credit Practices, Bureau of Consumer Protection, Federal Trade Comission, Room 500 IND, 6th St. and Pennsylvania Ave. N.W., Washington, DC 20580/202-724-1188.

Credit Discrimination Complaints
If you feel that you have been discriminated against by a retail store, department store, small loan and finance company, gasoline credit card, travel and expense credit card, state chartered credit union or government lending program, you have recourse. You can complain to, and even sue the creditor. You can also file a complaint with the Federal Trade Commission. For further information, and/or for a copy of the Equal Credit Opportunity Act, contact: Federal Trade Commission, Regional Office, or Equal Credit Opportunity, Federal Trade Commission, Room 500, 633 Indiana Ave. N.W., Washington, DC 20580/202-724-1184.

Creditors' Remedies
This office enforces the Fair Debt Collection Practices Act, which prohibits deception, invasion of privacy, overcharging abuse, harassment, and other unfair practices by debt collectors. Contact: Credit Practices, Bureau of Consumer Protection, Room 500 IND, 6th St. and Pennsylvania Ave. N.W., Washington, DC 20580/202-724-1100.

Design Defects
This office investigates failure to disclose information that would be important to the buyers purchase decision or the owners proper use and care of products. In the past investigations have focused on automobile problems and the more costly consumer products. Contact: Division of Advertising Practices, Federal Trade Commission, 6th St. and Pennsylvania Ave. N.W., Washington, DC 20580/202-376-8720.

Economic Reports
Special economic reports on specific industries or specific industry related topics are available from: Public Reference Branch, Federal Trade Commission, Washington, DC 20580/202-523-3598.

Energy and Product Information
This office attempts to ensure that products designed to save energy are marketed in a fair and nondeceptive manner. It investigates claims for such products as storm windows and doors, solar products, automobile gas-saving devices, electric energy-saving devices, wood-burning products and space heaters. Division of Marketing Practices, Federal Trade Commission, 6th and Pennsylvania Ave. N.W., Washington, DC, 20580/202-523-1642.

Equal Credit Opportunity

This office enforces the Equal Credit Opportunity Act which says that credit may be denied only on the basis of individual credit-worthiness and not on the basis of sex, race, marital status, religion, national origin, age, or whether the applicant receives public assistance. The law also gives the consumer the right to know the specific reasons for denial. Contact: Credit Practices, Bureau of Consumer Protection, Federal Trade Commission, Room 500 IND, 6th St. and Pennsylvania Ave. N.W., Washington, DC 20580/202-724-1094.

Evaluation

This office is responsible for advice on how resources should be allocated to most effectively remedy consumer losses. Contact: Division of Policy and Evaluation, Bureau of Consumer Protection, Federal Trade Commission, Room 461, 6th St. and Pennsylvania Ave. N.W., Washington, DC 20580/202-523-3275.

Fair Credit Reporting

This office enforces the Fair Credit Reporting Act which gives consumers the right to know what information is distributed about them and to challenge and change incorrect information distributed to creditors, insurance companies, and employers. Contact: Credit Practices, Bureau of Consumer Protection, Federal Trade Commission, Room 500 IND, 6th St. and Pennsylvania Ave. N.W., Washington, DC 20580/202-724-1182.

Food and Nutrition Advertising

The staff is working on a trade regulation rule on food advertising to regulate the following types of claims: energy and calorie; fat, fatty acid and cholesterol content, and "natural," "organic," "health food," and related terms. For further information contact: Advertising Practices, Bureau of Consumer Protection, Federal Trade Commission, Room 6124 STAR, 6th St. and Pennsylvania Ave. N.W., Washington, DC 20580/202-376-8617.

Franchising and Business Opportunities

This office enforces the franchise rule which requires sellers of franchises and business opportunities to furnish prospective buyers with presale disclosure of information about the franchisor, the franchise, business, and the terms of the franchise relationship. Contact: Division of Enforcement, Bureau of Consumer Protection, Federal Trade Commission, Room 272, 6th St. and Pennsylvania Ave. N.W., Washington, DC 20580/202-523-3814.

Freedom of Information Act Requests

For Freedom of Information Act requests, contact: Freedom of Information Branch, Planning and Information, Federal Trade Commission,

Room 676, 6th St. and Pennsylvania Ave. N.W., Washington, DC 20580/202-523-3640.

FTC Meetings

A recorded message provides details of FTC meetings. Call: 202-523-3806.

FTC News

A recorded message offers the latest news at the FTC. Call: 202-523-3540.

FTC Will Tell You What It's Doing

To keep on top of what the Federal Trade Commission is doing, ask to be put on its two mailing lists for FTC notes, news releases, and calendar of events. They will keep you advised on reports issued and investigations of companies and industries. The releases are free: Contact: Public Information Office, Federal Trade Commission, Room 496, 6th St. and Pennsylvania Ave. N.W., Washington, DC 20580/202-523-3830.

Funeral Industry

This office enforces the funeral trade regulations rules which require disclosure of price information for funeral goods and services. Contact: Division of Enforcement, Bureau of Consumer Protection, Federal Trade Commission, Washington, DC 20580/202-376-2863.

Housing Problems

This office investigates instances of substantial defects in new houses and builders' failure to remedy those defects. Contact: Marketing Practices, Bureau of Consumer Protection, Federal Trade Commission, Room 238, 6th St. and Pennsylvania Ave. N.W., Washington, DC 20580/202-523-1642

Industry Analysis

This office conducts economic studies of individual industries and trade practices along with broad cross-industry comparisons. Contact: Industry Analysis, Bureau of Economics, Federal Trade Commission, Room 754, 2120 L St. N.W., Washington, DC 20580/202-634-7816.

Land Sale Abuses

This office polices abuses in the sale of subdivisional lots, time sharing and recreational land to customers. For additional information, contact: Marketing Practices, Bureau of Consumer Protection, Federal Trade Commission, Room 238, 6th St. and Pennsylvania Ave. N.W., Washington, DC 20580/202-523-1642.

Library

The Library emphasizes materials on consumer affairs and antitrust matters. Contact: Library, Federal Trade Commission, Room 630, 6th St. and

Pennsylvania Ave. N.W., Washington, DC 20580/202-523-3871.

Mobile Homes
For problems with mobile homes, especially those concerning warranty performance and service or formaldehyde odor, contact: Product Reliability, Bureau of Consumer Protection, Federal Trade Commission, Room 242, 6th St. and Pennsylvania Ave. N.W., Washington, DC 20580/202-523-1642.

New Consumer Problems
To raise a consumer problem not covered by an existing federal Trade Commission program or to suggest consumer issues the Federal Trade Commission should be pursuing in the next few years, contact: Management Planning, Bureau of Consumer Protection, Federal Trade Commission, Room 204, 6th St. and Pennsylvania Ave. N.W., Washington, DC 20580/202-523-3553.

Occupational Deregulation
The Occupational Deregulation program investigates governmental and trade association regulation of professionals that has the effect of impeding the operation of the marketplace, such as restraints on advertising. Subjects of interest include eyeglasses, dentists, denturists, real estate brokers, veterinarians, nurse practitioners and nurse midwives. Contact: Professional Services, Bureau of Consumer Protection, Federal Trade Commission, Room 242, 6th St. and Pennsylvania Ave. N.W., Washington, DC 20580/202-523-3658.

Over-the-Counter Drug (OTC) Advertising
This program investigates complaints and brings law enforcement actions regarding false or deceptive advertising claims for over-the-counter drugs and devices. (Complaints about deceptive labels should be made to the Food and Drug Administration.) For further information, contact: Advertising Practices, Bureau of Consumer Protection, Federal Trade Commission, 6th St. and Pennsylvania Ave. N.W., Room 6124A STAR, Washington, DC 20580/202-376-8617.

Point-of-Sales Practices
This office monitors deceptive and unfair marketing techniques, used by retailers such as advertising specials that are unavailable, bait-and-switch tactics, and calling a regular price a "sale price." Contact: Marketing Practices, Bureau of Consumer Protection, Federal Trade Commission, Room 238, 6th St. and Pennsylvania Ave. N.W., Washington, DC 20580/202-523-1642.

Product Registration Numbers
For registration numbers required by the Wool Products Labeling Act, the Fur Products Labeling Act and the Textile Fiber Products Identification Act, contact: Division of Enforcement, Bureau of Consumer Protection, Federal Trade Commission, 600 E. St. N.W., Washington, DC 20580/202-376-2891.

Publications
For reports, brochures and other public documents, contact: Distribution and Duplication Branch, Federal Trade Commission, Room 720, 6th St. and Pennsylvania Ave. N.W., Washington, DC 20580/202-523-3598. The following is a list of the more popular free publications:

CONSUMER RIGHTS BROCHURES:
Bait and Switch
Care Labeling (washing and drying instructions on clothing)
Credit Shopping Guide (monthly payment table for various rates of interest)
Eyeglasses
Equal Credit Opportunity
Fair Credit Billing (what to do about errors on your bill)
Fair Debt Collection (how not to be harassed if you owe money)
How to Complain and Get Results
Plain Talk About IRAs (Individual Retirement Accounts)
Shopping by Mail
Shopping for Advertised Specials
Three-Day Cooling Off (protection when you buy from a door-to-door seller)
Truth in Leasing
Warranties
Women & Credit Histories (have credit reported in your own name)
Fair Credit Reporting (Federal Deposit Insurance Corporation)
Consumer Credit Handbook (Federal Reserve Board)
FTC INFORMATION:
What's Going on at the FTC? (quarterly description of FTC consumer protection programs with contact person for each)
FTC MANUALS FOR BUSINESSES:
Advertising Consumer Credit and Lease Terms (how to comply with the Truth in Lending Act)
FTC POLICY PLANNING BRIEFING BOOKS (EDITED FOR PUBLIC RELEASE):
State Regulatory Task Force Report (March 1978)
Automobiles (April 1978)
Food and Nutritions (May 1978)
Insurance (June 1978)
Private Health Insurance to Supplement Medicare (July 1978)
Consumer Problems of the Elderly (August 1978)
Housing (November 1978)
Drugs and Medical Devices (December 1978)
Life Insurance Sold to the Poor, Industrial and Other Debt Insurance (January 1979)
Trademarks, Consumer Information, and Barriers to Competition (February 1979)
Tax Policy and Competition (February 1979)
Compliance and Enforcement (March 1979)
Mergers (May 1979)

Customer Information Remedies (June 1979)
Health Services (June 1979)

Public Records
Dockets for Federal Trade Commission proceedings, hearing transcripts, index of orders, opinions and public records of the FTC are available for public view. Contact: Public Section, Office of the Secretary, Federal Trade Commission, Room 136, 6th St. and Pennsylvania Ave. N.W., Washington, DC 20580/202-523-3598.

Regional Offices
The Regional Offices are located in ten cities across the country and act as "mini-FTCs." They recommend cases, provide local outreach services to consumers and businesspersons, and coordinate activities with local, state, and regional authorities. FTC regional offices frequently sponsor conferences for small businesses, local authorities, and consumer groups. The ten regional offices are listed below.

1718 Peachtree Stree, N.W., Atlanta, GA 30367/404-881-4836.

150 Causeway Street, Boston, MA 02114/617-223-6621.

55 East Monroe Street, Chicago, IL 60603/312-353-4423.

118 St. Clair Avenue, Cleveland, OH 44114/216-522-4207.

8303 Elmbrook Drive, Dallas, TX 75247/214-767-7050.

1405 Curtis Street, Denver, CO 80202/303-837-2271.

11000 Wilshire Boulevard, Los Angeles, CA 90024/213-209-7575.

26 Federal Plaza, New York, NY 10278/212-264-1207.

450 Golden Gate Avenue, San Francisco, CA 94102/415-556-1270.

915 Second Avenue, Seattle, WA 98174/206-442-4655.

Standards and Certification
The Standards and Certification Program investigates consumer and competition problems arising out of the development of industry standards and seals of approval. The staff is also monitoring solar standards in warranties. Contact: Division of Service Industry Practice, Bureau of Consumer Protection, Federal Trade Commission, Room 272, 6th St. and Pennsylvania Ave. N.W., Washington, DC 20580/202-523-4695.

Trade Regulation Rules and Industry Guides
These guides are issued periodically as "dos and don'ts" to business and industry. The Federal Trade Commission defines practices that violate the law so that businesspeople may know their legal obligations and consumers may recognize those business practices against which legal recourse is available. The following guides are available:

Advertising Allowances and Other Merchandise Payments and Services, Guides for (May 1969 as amended August 1972)

Bait Advertising, Guides Against (November 1959)
Beauty and Barber Equipment Supplies Industry, Guides for the (July 1968)
Debt Collectioon Deception, Guides Against (June 1965; partial revision, June 1968)
Deceptive Pricing, Guides Against (December 1963)
Dog and Cat Food Industry, Guides for the (February 1969)
Endorsements and Testimonials in Advertising, Guide Concerning Use of (May 1975)
Fallout Shelters, Guides for Advertising (December 1961; amended June 1965)
Feather and Down Products Industry, Guides for the (October 1971)
"Free" in Connection with the Sale of Photographic Film and Film Processing Service, Guides Against Deceptive Use of the Word (May 1968)
"Free," Use of the Word and Similiar Representations, Guides Concerning (November 1971)
Fuel Economy Advertising for New Automobiles (December 1978)
Greeting Card Industry Relating to Discriminatory Practices, Guides for the (October 1968)
Guarantees, Guides Against Deceptive Advertising of (April 1960)
Hosiery Industry, Guides for the
Household Furniture Industry, Guides for the (December 1973)
Jewelry Industry, Guides for the
Ladies' Handbag Industry, Guides for the (June 1969, as amended to August 1969)
Law Book Industry, Guides for the (August 1975)
Luggage and Related Products Industry, Guides for the
Mail Order Insurance Industry, Guides for the (July 1964)
Metallic Watch Band Industry, Guides for the "Mill" in the Textile Industry, Guide for Avoiding Deceptive Use of Word (June 1965)
Mirror Industry, Guides for the
Nursery Industry, Guides for the
Preventing Unlawful Practices, Application of Guides in Radiation-Monitoring Instruments, Guides for Advertising (May 1963)
Rebuilt, Reconditioned and Other Used Automobile Parts Industry, Guides for the
Shell Homes, Guides for Advertising (April 1962)
Shoe Content Labeling and Advertising, Guides for (October 1972; Interpretation, August 1963)
Tire Advertising and Labeling Guides (July 1966; amended to 1968)
Vocation and Home Study Schools, Private, Guides for (1972)
Wall Paneling Industry, Decorative, Guides for (1971)
Watch Industry, Guides for the (May 1968; amended August 1970)
Wigs and Other Hairpieces, Guides for Labeling, Advertising and Sale of (August 1970)

Contact: Distribution and Duplication Branch, Federal Trade Commission, Room 720, 6th St. and Pennsylvania Ave. N.W., Washington, DC 20580/202-523-3598.

Truth-in-Lending
This office enforces the Truth-in-Lending Act which requires creditors to give consumers written disclosures of credit information before they enter into a credit transaction. Most of the enforcement activity is aimed at advertising, credit insurance and disclosure violations. Contact: Credit Practices, Bureau of Consumer Protection, Federal Trade Commission, Room 500 IND, 6th St. and Pennsylvania Ave. N.W., Washington, DC 20580/202-724-1145.

Warranties
The Warranties Section monitors to ensure that the information in warranties on consumer products and houses is clear, complete, understandable and timely; that they are not used deceptively; and that companies meet their obligations. Service contracts are also monitored. The Federal Trade Commission is also studying options on warranty advertising and warranty readability. For further information contact: Division of Marketing Practices, Bureau of Consumer Protection, Federal Trade Commission, Room 242, 6th St. and Pennsylvania Ave. N.W., Washington, DC 20580/202-523-1642.

How Can the Federal Trade Commission Help You?
For information on how this agency can be of help to you, contact: Office of Public Information, Federal Trade Commission, 6th St. and Pennsylvania Ave. N.W., Washington, DC 20580/202-523-3830.

General Services Administration

18th and F Sts. N.W., Washington, DC 20405/202-472-1082

Established: July 1, 1949
Budget: $501,022,000
Employees: 29,313

Mission: Establishes policy and provides the government an economical and efficient system for the management of its property and records, including construction and operation of buildings, procurement and distribution of supplies, utilization and disposal of property, transportation, traffic, and communications management, stockpiling of strategic materials, and the management of the government-wide, automatic data processing resources program.

Major Divisions and Offices

Public Buildings Service
General Services Administration, 18th and F Sts. N.W., Washington, DC 20405/202-566-1100.
Budget: (not specified)
Employees: 13,670
Mission: Responsible for the design, building or leasing, appraisal, operation, protection, and maintenance of most of the federally controlled buildings in the nation, 284 million square feet of space, in about 10,000 federally owned and leased buildings, in addition to the $827 million in construction projects currently underway.

Federal Supply and Services
General Services Administration, Washington, DC 20406/202-557-8667.
Budget: $161,000,000
Employees: 5,186
Mission: Operates a worldwide supply system to contract for and distribute supplies and property to Federal agencies as well as managing Government-wide transportation and travel programs, operating a vehicle fleet program, and administering a Government-wide property management program for the utilization of excess personal property and the donation and/or sale of surplus property.

Federal Property Resources Service
General Services Administration, 18th and F St. N.W., Washington, DC 20405/703-535-7210.
Budget: $467,028,000
Employees: 469
Mission: Responsible for the utilization and disposition of government-owned real property, personal property, acquisition and management of the stockpile of critical and strategic materials, and the sale of excess stockpile material.

Office of Information Resources Management
General Services Administrations, 18th and F Sts. N.W., Washington, DC 20405/202-566-1000.
Budget: $34,542,000
Employees: 2,446
Mission: Responsible for a comprehensive government-wide program for the management, procurement and utilization of automatic data, and telecommunications equipment services.

Major Sources of Information

Art-in-Architecture
The General Services Administration commissions murals, sculptures, paintings, photographs and other forms of artwork for display in Federal buildings. Artists are selected in cooperation with the National Endowment of the Arts. *Art-in-Architecture Bulletin* is a free publication covering this art from 1962 on, which includes information and history on the federal programs for the fine arts. It also includes guidance to artists on the submission of plans for projects, a listing of artists, titles and descriptions of the works, and a pictorial section of color and black-and-white photos. For further information, contact: Art-in-Architecture, Office of the Commissioner, Public Buildings Service, General Services Administration, 6th Floor, Room 6340, 18th and F Sts. N.W. Washington, DC 20405/202-566-0950.

Business Opportunities and Information
The following free booklets are available:

GSA Construction—explains how to bid.
Architect-Engineer Services—outlines bidding procedures on GSA architect-engineer contracts.
Architect-Engineer Selection Procedure—explains selection procedures for contracts.

Contact: the nearest Business Service Center, or Office of Design and Construction, Public Buildings Service, General Services Administration, Room 3341, 18th and F Sts. N.W., Washington, DC 20405/202-566-0574.

Business Service Centers
These centers provide advice and counsel to businesspersons who are interested in contracting with General Services Administration and other federal agencies and departments. Business counselors are available who can contact a suitable business representative in the government. They also provide detailed information about all types of government contracting opportunities. These centers are also responsible for issuing bidders mailing list applications, furnishing invitations for bids and specifications to prospective bidders, maintaining a current display of bidding opportunities, safeguarding bids, providing bid opening facilities, and furnishing free copies of publications designed to assist business representatives in doing business with the federal government. Contact: Business Service Centers, General Services Administration, Room 1050, 7th & D Sts. S.W., Washington, DC 20407/202-472-1804.

Circuit Rider Program
Trained counselors provide information on contract opportunities throughout the federal government as well as step-by-step help with contracting procedures on a rotating schedule of visits to towns with no Business Service Centers. Contact the nearest Business Service Center or Business Service Centers Division, General Services Administration, Room 1050, 7th & D St. S.W., 18th and F Sts. N.W., Washington, DC 20407/472-1804.

Commercial Item Descriptions (CID)
This is a series of simplified technical contract support documents used in the acquisition of commercial off-the-shelf and commercial-type products. CIDs are suitable for either advertised or negotiated procurement. Contact: General Products Commodity Center, Room 809, Crystal Mall, Building 4, Federal Supply & Services, General Services Administration, 1941 Jefferson Davis Highway, Arlington, VA 22202/703-557-8626.

Commodity Managers
A list of commodity managers is available for those who wish to contact a specialist. Contact: Office of Procurement, Federal Supply Service, General Services Administration, Room 809, 1941 Jefferson Davis Highway, Arlington, VA 22202/703-557-7901.

Computerized Data Bases
The General Services Administration maintains these data bases.

Consumer Education Organizations Data Base
The Consumer Education Research Network Directory Data Base (Cern II) is a directory of more than 2,000 organizations involved in consumer education or protection. Listed groups range from government agencies to university programs on the national, state, or local level. Retrieval information includes: address, phone number, contact person, type of organization (25 categories), staff size, funding, subject areas covered, purpose and audiences. Searches and printouts are available free of charge, but only to individuals or organizations involved in consumer education. This category includes classroom teachers, community groups, media, and consumer affairs departments of industry. In the future, access may be extended to all interested parties. Contact: Consumer Information Center, GSA, Room KHC, Washington, DC 20405/202-566-1794.

Consumer Education Research Data Base
The Consumer Education Research Network bibliographic Data Base (CERN I) is a bibliographic data base of consumer-education materials including textbooks, reports, research studies, masters' theses and conference proceedings. Retrievable data consists of bibliographic citations with subject

description and availability information, 1976 to present. Searches and printouts are available free of charge, but only to individuals or organizations involved in consumer education. This category includes classroom teachers, community groups, media, and consumer-affairs departments of industry. In the future, access may be extended to all interested parties. Contact: Consumer Information Center, GSA, Room KHC, Washington, DC 20405/202-566-1794.

Federal Procurement Data Base
The Federal Procurement Data Center (FPDC) stores information about federal procurement actions, from 1979 to present, that totaled $10,000 or more. The system contains 24 data elements, including: purchasing or contracting office; date of award; principal place of performance; dollars obligated; principal product or service; business and labor requirements; type of procurement action; methods of contracting; socioeconomic data; name and address of contractor; and foreign trade data. Examples of federal buying range from research and development to supplies and equipment. Searches and printouts are available on a cost-recovery basis. Requests should be made in writing. Contact: Federal Procurement Data Center, 4040 North Fairfax Drive, Suite 900, Arlington, VA 22203/703-235-1634.

Consumer Information Catalog
This free quarterly catalog (also available in Spanish) lists over 150 free consumer publications and about 100 sales publications popular with the general public. Contact: Office of Consumer Affairs, General Services Administration, Room G-142, 18th and F Sts. N.W., Washington, DC 20405/202-566-1794, or write to: Consumer Information Center, Department B, Pueblo, CO 81009.

Consumer Information Center
The General Services Administration makes consumer information available through the Consumer Information Center. It encourages agencies to provide expert knowledge through informative brochures. It also offers hundreds of publications on subjects ranging from car repairs to home buying. Many are free or available at a small charge. For general information, contact: Office of Consumer Affairs, General Services Administration, Room G-142, 18th and F Sts. N.W., Washington, DC 20405/202-566-1794, or write to: Consumer Information Center, Department B, Pueblo, CO 81009.

Consumer Information Pamphlets
The following consumer information pamphlets are the ones most requested. Those available free of charge are:

Cancer Prevention: Good News, Better News, Best News
Student Guide: Five Financial Aid Programs

Your Social Security
Check List for Going Into Business
Consumer Guide to Life Insurance
How to Choose and Lose a Lawyer

These publications are available for $0.50

The Arithmetic of Interest Rate
Mortgage Money Guide

To obtain the above publications contact: Consumer Information Center, Pueblo, CO 81009.

These publications are for sale by the Government Printing Office:

Starting and Managing a Small Service Business ($4.50)
Federal Benefits for Veterans and Dependents ($2.25)
Help Yourself to a Midlife Career Change ($2.25)

Contact: Superintendent of Documents, Government Printing Office, Washington, DC 20402/202-783-3238.

These Spanish publications are available free of charge:

Cuidado y Servicio del Automovil, 1979, gratis
Baterias de Automovil, 1979, gratis
Como Comprar una Aspiradora, 1978, gratis
Como Comprar una Lavadora, 1979, gratis
Como Comprar una Secadora, 1978, gratis

For the free Spanish publications write to Consumer Information Center, Pueblo, CO 81009. For additional information, contact: Consumer Information Center, General Services Administration, Room G142, 18th and F Sts. N.W., Washington, DC 20405/202-566-1794.

Crime Data
Data on crime incidents occurring in buildings controlled by the General Services Administration are compiled and summarized. The information includes thefts of government and personal property, larceny, rape, murder, bombings, demonstrations and vandalism. Contact: Crime Prevention Section, Office of Federal Protective Service, Public Building Service, General Services Administration, Room, 18th and F Sts. N.W., Washington, DC 20405/202-535-7278.

Customer and Industry
This office attempts to resolve customer and vendor problems beyond the capabilities of the regular complaint system. Contact: Office of Customer Relations, General Services Administration, Room 6115, 18th and F Sts. N.W., Washington, DC 20405/202-523-1200.

Design Contracts
This office contracts with architect-engineers for such projects as office buildings, courthouses and research centers. Design contracts for air-conditioning systems, elevators, repairs and alterations are also negotiated. For additional design information, contact: Management Division, Public Build-

ings Service, General Services Administration, Room 3046, 18th and F Sts. N.W., Washington, DC 20405/202-566-1646.

Doing Business with the Federal Government
A free booklet for large or small companies explaining how the government makes purchases, the role of centralized buying, whom to contact for general information, and the names and needs of agencies with special purchasing requirements. Contracting steps and procedures are outlined. Contact: The nearest Business Service Center, or Business Service Centers Division, General Services Administration, Room 1050, 7 and D Sts. N.W., Washington, DC 20407/202-566-0776. 472-1804.

Energy Conservation in Federal Buildings
A variety of energy conservation programs are being examined and implemented in building designs and construction. Solar energy systems are being installed to supplant fossil fuel systems for heating and cooling. Contact Energy Conservation Division, Office of Buildings Management, Public Buildings Service, General Services Administration, Room 4336, 18th and F Sts. N.W., Washington, DC 20405/202-566-1735.

Excess Real Property
This office directs a continuing survey of all federal real properties to determine if they are not being put to their best use. Property no longer needed by a federal agency is generally reported excess to Federal Property Resources Service for disposal and may be transferred from one federal agency to another. If it is not needed by any federal agency, it may then be made available for acquisition by a local public body (state, county or local government), or a tax-supported or nonprofit medical or educational institution. Any property not disposed of in the above ways may be acquired by local public bodies at fair market value or is otherwise offered for sale, generally by advertising for bids. A free brochure, *Disposal of Surplus Real Property,* explains how private business and nonprofit state and local groups can acquire real property (land and buildings) no longer needed by the federal government. Contact: The Business Service Center nearest you, or Office of Real Property, Federal Property Resources Service, Room 4236, 18th and F Sts., Washington, DC 20405/703-535-7084.

Federal Compiler Testing Center
This Center checks whether federal standard computer languages are being used correctly and compatibly so that programs written for one computer can be used readily by another. Contact: Federal Compiler Testing Center, Office of Soft-

ware Development, Automated Data and Telecommunications Service, General Services Administration, Room 1100 SKY, 18th and F Sts. N.W., Washington, DC 20405/703-756-6153.

Federal Conversion Support Center
This office helps agencies when converting to new equipment by examining their software or program of computer instructions, to smooth the transition to more modern machines. Contact: Federal Conversion Support Center, Office of Software Development, Automated Data and Telecommunications Service, General Services Administration, Room 1100 SKY, 18th and F Sts. N.W., Washington, DC 20405/703-756-6156.

Federal Information Centers
The staff at the Federal Information Centers attempt to be a one-stop source of assistance with federal-government-related questions and problems. Call or visit your local Federal Information Center to get help in sorting out the wide range of services and information provided by hundreds of different departments, agencies and programs of the federal government, the numerous laws it administers, and the multitude of publications and periodicals available. Questions most commonly asked are on jobs, retirement benefits, taxes, Social Security, veteran's benefits and immigration. FIC staff specialists in many cities speak other languages in addition to English. For information contact the Federal Information Center nearest you. See the Sampler section for a complete listing of the centers, or Federal Information Center, Office of Consumer Affairs, General Services Administration, Room G-242, 18th and F Sts. N.W., Washington, DC 20405/202-566-1937.

Federal Motor Vehicle Fleet Report
A free annual statistical world-wide report on Federally owned and leased cars, station wagons, ambulances, buses, trucks and truck tractors, and their uses is available from National Travel and Transportation Regulations Division, Office of Transportation, General Services Administration, Crystal Mall, Building 4, Room 405, Washington, DC 20405/202-557-1253

Federal Procurement Data Center
The Center is trying to become the government's single source of procurement information. Each agency headquarters submits procurement information to the Center showing the same 27 items of information on a uniform basis for every acquisition over $10,000. The Center is responsible for consolidating the information on the individual agencies into a master procurement file, processing the information, and reporting to the Congress, the executive branch and industry. The Center can identify what agencies are buying

(products and services), where they are buying (contractor location or from the General Services Administration), in what volume they are buying, and how they are buying (competition, type of contract, or contract modification). In addition, the system provides information on standard industrial classification (SIC) codes and the parent and subsidiary of each contractor establishment, along with the relationship of each. The data cover all prime contract actions awarded to nonfederal sources for supplies, equipment, construction and services including commercial utilities and communications, commercial rents, and transportation or shipments furnished under government bills of lading and government transportation requests. Acquisitions, including contract changes and modifications of more than $10,000, are reported individually. Acquisitions of $10,000 or less are reported in summary. Contact: Federal Procurement Data Center, General Services Administration, 4040 N. Fairfax Dr. Suite 900, Arlington, VA 22203/703-235-2036.

Federal Acquisitions Regulations

The Federal Acquisitions Regulations contain uniform policies and procedures applicable to procurements by civilian executive agencies of personal property and nonpersonal services, including construction. These regulations are prescribed by the General Services administration and published in one of the daily issues of the Federal Register. They are also published in cumulative form in the Code of Federal Regulations. Contact: Office of Acquisition Policy, General Services Administration, Room 4037, 18th & F Sts. Washington, DC 20405/703-523-4862.

Federal Property Management Regulations (FPMR)

The General Services Administration prescribes policies and procedures and delegates authority for management of government property and records. FPMR issuances are published daily in the Federal Register and are accumulated in the Code of Federal Regulations. Contact: Office of Regulations Management Division, Crystal Mall, Building 4, Federal Supply Service, General Services Administration, Room 1941 Jefferson Davis Highway, Washington, DC 20406/703-557-7990.

Federal Surplus Personal Property Donation Programs

These programs enable certain nonfederal organizations to obtain personal property the federal government no longer needs. Eligible recipients are public agencies, nonprofit educational and public health activities, and educational activities of special interest to the armed services and public airports. Among the types of personal property that may be available are included hand and machine tools, office machines and supplies, furniture, hardware, motor vehicles, boats, airplanes, and construction equipment. Contact: Office of Property, Donation Division, Crystal Mall, Building 4, Room 1019, Federal Property Resource Service, General Services Administration, Crystal Square, Room 802, 1755 Jefferson Davis Highway, Washington, DC 20405/202-557-1234.

Federal Supply Schedules

Schedules are indefinite quantity contracts usually established for a one-year term which permit federal agencies to place orders directly with suppliers. The schedule program provides the agencies with sources for approximately 700,000 products and services such as automotive parts and accessories, tires, batteries, furniture, electric lamps, appliances, photographic and duplicating equipment and supplies, athletic equipment, laboratory equipment and supplies, and audio and video recording equipment and supplies. For information on the supply schedules, contact: Publications Mgmt. Procurement Operations Support Div., Federal Supply and Services, General Services Administration, Room 615, 1941 Jefferson Davis Highway, Washington, DC 20406/703-557-5480.

Federal Supply Service Publications

This office is responsible for the Federal Supply Schedules, the General Services Administration supply catalogues and the *Index of Federal Specifications and Standards.* Contact: Publications Management Division, Office of Item Management, Federal Supply Service, General Services Administration, Room 718, 1941 Jefferson Davis Highway, Washington, DC 20406/703-557-5480.

Finance

The Office of Finance provides publications on public buildings leased and owned by the federal government as well as a detailed listing of real property owned by the United States and used by the Department of Defense for military functions throughout the world. For more information contact: Public Buildings, Office of Finance, General Services Administration, Room 7106, 18th and F Sts. N.W., Washington, DC 20405/202-523-5472.

Fire Safety

Public Buildings Services has programs on fire safety in public buildings. For additional information, contact: Accident and Fire Prevention Division, Public Buildings Service, General Services Administration, Room 4338, 18th and F Sts. N.W., Washington, DC 20405/202-566-1464.

Fraud Hotline

The General Services Administration has a 24-hour hotline for reporting alleged fraud and abuses. Call toll-free 800-424-5210 or 202-566-1780. For additional information, contact: Office of Inspector General, General Services Administration, Room 5340, 18th and F Sts. N.W., Washington, DC 20405/202-566-0450.

Freedom of Information Act Requests
For Freedom of Information Act requests, contact: Information and Privacy, Office of Policy & Management Systems, General Services Administration, Room 3007, 18th and F Sts. N.W., Washington, DC 20405/202-535-7647

General Services Administration Library
The Library has material on government contracts, procurement, specifications, art, and architecture. Consumer publications are also available. Contact: Library, General Services Administration, Room 1033, 18 and F Sts. N.W., Washington, DC 20405/202-535-7788.

Guide to Specifications and Standards of the Federal Government
This is a free booklet that describes the purpose, use, types and how to obtain them before bidding on federal contracts for goods and services. It is available at the nearest Business Service Center, or contact: Publications Management Division, Office of Item Management, Federal Supply Service, General Services Administration, Room 718, 1941 Jefferson Davis Highway, Washington, DC 20406/703-557-7950.

Historic Preservation
Historic structures are restored and preserved for continued federal use and public enjoyment. There is a listing of the names and locations of these buildings. A file on many historic structures, analyses and reports with a background history, guidance for designers, and the purpose of the buildings is also available. For further information, contact: Historic Preservation, Art in Architecture and Historic Preservation Public Buildings Service, General Services Administration, 18th and F Sts. N.W., Room 6340, Washington, DC 20405/566-0950.

How the Government Acquires Land
This is a free brochure that answers questions most frequently asked by owners of real property selected by the General Services Administration for public building construction projects. It explains the agency's policy for determining public needs, selecting sites, arriving at a fair price to pay owners and acquiring the property needed for public use. For further information, contact the General Services Administration regional office in your area on Leasing Division, Office of Space Management, Public Building Service, General Services Administration, Room 2330, 18th and F Sts. N.W., Washington, DC 20405/202-566-0638.

Index of Federal Specifications and Standards
This Index has alphabetical, numerical and federal supply classification (FSC) listings plus useful information and periodic supplements. Sold by the Superintendent of Documents, Government Printing Office, Washington, DC 20402/202-783-3238, or contact: Commodity Management Division, Federal Supply Services, General Services Administration, Room 704, 1941 Jefferson Davis Highway, Washington, DC 20406/703-557-0947

Fleet Management Directory
This is a free booklet providing instructions to federal employees for obtaining vehicles. It lists motor pool locations and rates for types of vehicles at different locations. Contact: Fleet Management Center, General Services Administration, Central GSA Depot, Bldg. A, Loisdale Road, Springfield, VA 22150/703-557-1996.

Jewel Bearing Plant
The William Langer Jewel Bearing Plant, the only plant of its kind in North America, produces jewel bearings for the National Stockpile. It was established to provide a domestic source for jewel bearings and related products in order to eliminate U.S. dependency upon foreign sources of supply. For more information, contact: William Langer Jewel Bearing Plant, Rolla, North Dakota, 701-477-3193, or Office of Stockpile Management, Federal Property Resources Service, General Services Administration, Room 908, Room 5024, 18 & F Sts. N.W., Washington, DC 20405/202-535-7139.

Leasing Space to the Government
The General Services Administration leases general purpose and special purpose space for all federal agencies. Each GSA regional leasing office maintains a current listing, by geographic area, of prospective offerors to which it sends notices or leasing needs when they occur. Property managers or owners interested in offering space to the General Services Administration for lease should write to the regional office indicating the type of space available or an interest in constructing space for lease. Leasing Space to the Government, a free pamphlet, explains how property owners can lease space to the General Services Administration. Contact: Leasing Division, Office of Space Management, Public Buildings Service, General Services Administration, Room 3305, 18th and F Sts. N.W., Washington, DC 20405/202-566-0638.

Life Cycle Costing Program
The Life Cycle Costing Program strives for the lower ownership cost rather than the lowest bid price. The emphasis is on quality. It is being applied in the procurement of gas and electric water heaters, gas and electric ranges, window air conditioners, refrigerators, freezers and high-

speed printer ribbons. A free pamphlet, *Life Cycle Costing,* describes how federal agencies can use this buying technique to save money. For more information, contact: Value Engineering Division, Office of Engineering and Technical Management, Federal Supply Service, General Services Administration, Room 510, 1941 Jefferson Davis Highway, Washington, DC 20406/703-557-7567.

List of Areawide Public Utilities Contracts

A free list, by geographic area, updated approximately three times a year, is available from the Office of Public Utilities, Public Buildings Service, General Services Administration, Room 3007, 425 Eye St. N.W., Washington, DC 20406/202-566-1027

Living Buildings Program

This program encourages the use of federal buildings by individuals and organizations for educational, cultural and recreational activities. It offers free or at-cost space ranging from full-scale auditoriums to seminar-sized classrooms. The buildings have been used for a broad range of activities including art exhibits, solar energy workshops, senior citizen meetings, and Hawaiian dancers. For information, contact GSA Regional Buildings Management Offices or Operations Division, Public Buildings Service, General Services Administration, Room 4326, 18th and F Sts. N.W., Washington, DC 20405/202-566-1563.

Management Information Systems

This office publishes annually the *Automatic Data Processing Equipment Inventory in the United States Government* which includes federally owned or leased digital computers, computer systems, and peripheral equipment, glossary, charts, and summary and inventory tables (1979) $15.00 (M.O. $19.00), and the *Automatic Data Processing Activities Summary in the United States Government,* which identifies the cost, manpower and utilization of federal computers subject to such reporting, glossary, charts and summary and inventory table (1979) $5.00. These publications are available from the Superintendent of Documents, Government Printing Office, Washington, DC 20402/202-783-3238. For additional information contact: Federal Equipment Data Center, Office of Information, Resources Management, General Services Administration, Room 2010, 18th and F Sts. N.W., Washington, DC 20405/202-566-1544.

National Furniture Center

This is the centralized facility for procuring furniture for the federal government. Identification of requirements for a product, formulation of its specifications, contracting procedures, quality assurance, contract administration, and delivery are all supervised from this Center. Contact: National Furniture Center, Federal Supply Service, General Services Administration, Room 1010, 1941 Jefferson Davis Highway, Washington, DC 20406/702-557-8636.

National Tools Center

The central depot for all tools procedure for the federal government is the National Tools Center. It is responsible for nationwide commodity management, including contracting, inventory management, and engineering. Contact: National Tools Center, Federal Supply Service, General Services Administration, Room 605, 1941 Jefferson Davis Highway, Washington, DC 20406/703-557-8575.

Procurement and Contracts

This office monitors the procurement practices of the regional and field offices. For more information, contact: Surveys Branch, Office of Contracts, Public Buildings Service, General Services Administration, Room 1300, 18th and F Sts. N.W., Washington, DC 20405/202-566-1383.

Public Art

This office has information on historic public art, mainly murals and sculptures, up to 1962. It also provides policy advice on the fine arts selection for new projects. Contact: Counselor for Fine Arts, Office of Design and Construction, Public Buildings Service, General Services Administration, Room 3302, 18th and F Sts. N.W., Washington, DC 20405/202-566-1499.

Public Building Contracts

The Office of Contracts reviews all Public Buildings Service contracts for compliance with rules and regulations before a contract is awarded. Contact: Office of Contracts, Public Buildings Service, General Services Administration, Room 1300, 18th and F Sts. N.W., Washington, DC 20405/202-566-0907.

Publications and Information

For a list of the General Services Administration publications and some publications and general information on the GSA, contact: Office of Publications, General Services Administration, Room 6111, 18th anf F Sts. N.W., Washington, DC 20405/202-566-1235.

Quality Approved Manufacturer Program

This program allows manufacturers with approved quality control systems to ship material based on their own test results. Assistance is given to contractors in establishing adequate quality control systems and planning and scheduling products, as well as maintaining a continuing liaison with them to ensure that their quality control systems remain effective. Contact: Office of Quality Assurance and Reliability, Federal Supply Service, General Services Administration, Room 1122,

1941 Jefferson Davis Highway, Washington, DC 20406/703-552-8505.

Renovation and Rehabilitation of Federal Property

This office recycles federal government office machines, furniture, carpet and drapes, vehicles and many other items. Most of the rehabilitation work is done by small businesses, and part of the remaining work goes to workshops for the blind or severely handicapped, and to Federal Prison Industries. A free pamphlet, *Contract Opportunities for Maintenance and Repair of Equipment,* describes how to obtain information on federal contracts for services, maintenance and repairs. For additional information, contact the Business Service Center nearest you, or Property Rehabilitation Division, Office Federal Supply & Services, Federal Property Resources Service, General Services Administration, Room 1121, 1755 Jefferson Davis Highway, Washington, DC 20406/703-557-8667.

Residential Relocation Assistance

Services and payments are available to owners and tenants of residences who are asked by the General Services Administration to move from their homes. *Residential Relocation Assistance,* a free pamphlet, describes these services and payments and how to obtain them. For additional information, contact: the GSA regional office in your area, or Leasing Division, Office of Space Management, Public Buildings Service, General Services Administration, Room 3305, 18th and F Sts. N.W., Washington, DC 20405/202-566-0638.

Security Education

An eight-week basic training course for new recruits and courses in refresher training are provided for federal protective officers and contract guards. For further information, contact: Training and Education Division, Office of Federal Protective Service Management, Public Buildings Service, General Services Administration, Room 2035, 18th and F Sts. N.W., Washington, DC 20405/202-566-0267.

Space Management Research

Space management research studies emphasize efficiency and cost productiveness. A major study on "Systems Furniture" aimed at reducing space consumption has been completed. For additional information, contact: Space Standards and Research Branch, Office of Space Management, Public Buildings Service, General Services Administration, Room 2341, 18th and F Sts. N.W., Washington, DC 20405/202-523-5569.

Speakers

The General Services Administration makes available speakers to trade and educational organizations, small and minority business groups and those groups involved or potentially involved with the General Services Administration. Contact: Office of Public Information, General Services Administration, Room 6205, 18th and F Sts. N.W., Washington, DC 20405/202-566-1231.

Specifications and Standards

Single copies of federal specifications and standards are available at no cost from the Business Service Centers. A complete set can be obtained for $70 from: Specification and Consumer Information Distribution Branch (WFSIS), Washington Navy Yard, Building 197, Washington, DC 20407/703-472-2205.

Stockpile Disposal

This Division sells, when authorized by Congress, precious commodities such as silver, gold bullion, diamond and tungsten ore, as well as agricultural materials and other metals and minerals. To be placed on the bidders' list and for general information, contact: Stockpile Disposal Division, Federal Property Resource Service, General Services Administration, Room 5221, 18th and F Sts. N.W., Washington, DC 20405/703-535-7225.

Stockpile Transactions and Inventories

Data are available describing the strategic and critical material stockpiled by the United States. Contact: Office of Stockpile Transactions, Federal Property Resources Service, General Services Administration, Room 5020, 1755 Jefferson Davis Highway, Washington, DC 20405/703-535-7132.

Surplus Land

The General Services Administration sells real property that is surplus to the Federal Government's needs (e.g. a closed Air Force base). Property can range from unimproved land to housing projects. Contact: Office of Real Property, Federal Property Resources Service, General Services Administration, 18th and F Sts. N.W., Washington, DC 20405/202-535-7074.

Surplus Personal Property Donations

Surplus personal property can be transferred for donation to nonfederal public agencies and other specified recipients such as public agencies, non-profit educational and public health activities, educational activities of special interest to the armed services and public airports. The personal property under this program includes hand and machine tools, office machines and supplies, furniture, hardware, motor vehicles, boats, airplanes, construction equipment and many other times. A free pamphlet, *Federal Surplus Personal Property Donation Programs,* explains eligibility and where and how to apply for additional information. For additional information, contact the regional GSA offices or Donation Division, Office of Personal Property, Federal Supply & Services, General

Services Administration, Room 1019, 1755 Jefferson Davis Highway, Washington, DC 20405/703-557-1234.

Surplus Personal Property Sales

The General Services Administration conducts sales of civil agency personal property which include a wide variety of consumer-type items including automobiles and other motor vehicles, aircraft, hardware, plumbing and heating equipment, paper products, typewriters and other office machines, furniture, medical items, textiles, industrial equipment, and many others. Sales catalogs are mailed to prospective buyers who ask to be put on mailing lists and notices to the public of sales are placed in newspapers, trade journals, public buildings, etc. A free pamphlet, *Buying Government Surplus Personal Property,* outlines basic procedures and rules and describes how to be notified of sale dates and locations. Contact: the nearest Business Service Center or Sales Division, Office of Personal Property, Federal Property Resources Service, General Services Administration, Room 4236, 18th and F Sts. N.W., Washington, DC 20405/703-535-7084.

Utilization of Excess Personal Property

The General Services Administration prescribes policies and methods to promote the maximum utilization of excess property and for transferring excess property among the federal agencies. The GSA regional offices issue Excess Personal Property Catalogs and Bulletins for reported property whenever the property warrants it. A free pamphlet, *The Utilization of Excess Personal Property,* provides information about the program, how the program operates and a guide to action. Contact regional GSA offices or Utilization Division, Office of Personal Property, Federal Property Resources Service, General Services Administration, Room 802, 1755 Jefferson Davis Highway, Washington, DC 20405/703-535-7048.

Value Management

Value management aims at improving the efficiency and effectiveness of an organization while reducing costs. It encourages contractor innovation to provide better and cheaper goods and services. It also allows employees to challenge existing procedures and services in its internal operations. The program offers executive seminars for senior management representatives. The following free publications are also available:

Increase Your Profit—Use the Value Incentive Clause— how suppliers of federal goods and services can save the U.S. Government money and increase their own profits.

Value Management: A Briefing for Executives— introduces executives to the concept of value management, its merits and pitfalls.

Establishing a Value Management Program— outlines methods of implementing the program.

Value Management Guide— a detailed outline of how to implement the program.

For additional information, contact: Office of Acquisitions and Policy, Federal Supply & Services, General Services Administration, Room 4013, 1941 Jefferson Davis Highway, Washington, DC 20406/703-566-0690.

How Can the General Services Administration Help You?

For information on how this agency can help you, contact: Division of Public Affairs, General Services Administration, Washington, DC 20405/202-472-1082.

Inter-American Foundation

1515 Wilson Blvd., Rosslyn, VA 22209/703-841-3800

Established: December 30, 1969
Budget: $12,000,000
Employees: 63

Mission: Supports social and economic development in Latin America and the Caribbean; also makes grants primarily to private, indigenous organizations that carry out self-help projects benefiting poor people.

Major Sources of Information

Fellowships

Each year the Inter-American Foundation awards about 15 fellowships for doctoral dissertation research and postdoctoral study in Latin America and the Caribbean. The purpose is to encourage increased scholarly attention to development issues as they affect poor and disadvantaged groups in the region. Contact: Doctoral and Masters Exchange Programs, Inter-American Foundataion, 1515 Wilson Blvd., Rosslyn, VA 22209/703-841-3800.

Film

Here, Nothing is Impossible is a 28-minute film in Spanish, English and bilingual on three self-management projects in Peru. Contact: Office of Planning and Research, Inter-American Foundation, 1515 Wilson Blvd., Rosslyn, VA 22209/703-841-3835.

Freedom of Information Act Requests

For Freedom of Information Act requests, contact: Freedom of Information Officer, Inter-American Foundation, 1515 Wilson Blvd., Rosslyn, VA 22209/703-841-3869.

Planning and Research

This office monitors and evaluates current Foundation projects; conducts evaluation studies in such areas as rural credit, worker-managed enterprises, nonformal education and cultural expression; coordinates the Foundation's fellowship and publication programs. Contact: Office of Planning and Research, Inter-American Foundation, 1515 Wilson Blvd., Rosslyn, VA 22209/703-841-3835.

Publications

Free publications include:

Bottom-Up Development in Haiti is a monograph with a special focus on the peasant leadership training programs of the Institut Diocesain d'Education des Adultes.

First Steps—The Foundation's first three years.

In Partnership with People: An Alternative Department Strategy.

They Know How—An Experiment in Foreign Assistance.

Journal of the Inter-American Foundation—free quarterly with news features on IAF projects and events in Latin America and the Caribbean.

IAF Annual Report—provides program and financial information on the IAF. It also lists a summary of grants for the past year, and describes the projects.

Contact: Inter-American Foundation, 1515 Wilson Blvd., Rosslyn, VA 22209/703-841-3835.

How Can the Inter-American Foundation Help You?

To determine how this agency can help you, contact: Office of the President, Inter-American Foundation, 1515 Wilson Blvd., Rosslyn, VA 22209/703-841-3811.

Interstate Commerce Commission

**12th St. and Constitution Ave. N.W., Washington, DC 20423/
203-275-7252**

Established: February 4, 1887
Budget: $39,548,000
Employees: 1,378

Mission: Regulates interstate surface transportation, including trains, trucks, buses, water carriers, freight forwarder, transportation brakers and coal slurry pipelines; certifies carriers seeking to provide transportation for the public, rates, adequacy of service, purchases, and mergers; and insures that the carriers it regulates will provide the public with rates and services that are fair and reasonable.

Major Sources of Information

Annual Reports of Carriers
Annual Reports of carriers may be examined in the Public Reference Room, Bureau of Accounts, Interstate Commerce Commission, 12th St. and Constitution Ave. N.W., Room 3378, Washington, DC 20423/202-275-7343.

Applications of Motor Carriers
After an application has been published in the *Federal Register,* an applicant must furnish a copy, for $10, of its application package to any person requesting a copy. A copy of the application can be inspected. Contact the ICC Regional Office of applicant's domicile, or Motor and Rail Docket File, Office of the Secretary, Interstate Commerce Commission, 12th St. and Constitution Ave. N.W., Room 1221, Washington, DC 20423/202-275-7285.

Weekly Digest
This is a free, comprehensive review of significant ICC actions of particular interest to consumers. To be put on the mailing list and for additional information, contact: Office of Public Affairs, Interstate Commerce Commission, 12th St. and Constitution Ave. N.W., Room 1211, Washington, DC 20423/202-275-7252.

Calendar of Upcoming Events
A weekly calendar listing Interstate Commerce Commission conferences, scheduled board meetings, and speeches by commissioners is available. To be placed on the mailing list and for additional information, contact: Office of Public Affairs, Interstate Commerce Commission, 12th St. and Constitution Ave. N.W., Room 1211, Washington, DC 20423/202-275-7252.

Classification
A "class rating" is assigned to hundreds of commonly-shipped products based on their transportation characteristics. Motor carrier rates are based, for the most part, on the National Motor Freight Classification set up by the National Classification Board, a carrier organization. If the Board cannot settle a dispute regarding the correct classification, contact: Rates and Informal Cases, Bureau of Traffic, Interstate Commerce Commission, 12th St. and Constitution Ave. N.W., Room 4317, Washington, DC 20423/202-275-7358.

Commission Reports and Orders

Individual Interstate Commerce Commission Reports and Orders are available on the day of issuance from the Public Records Section, Office of the Secretary, Interstate Commerce Commission, 12th St. and Constitution Ave. N.W., Room 2223, Washington, DC 20423/202-275-7279. In addition, printed reports of the Commission are available. Contact: Certification, Public Records Section, Interstate Commerce Commission, 12th St. and Constitution Ave. N.W., Room 22213, Washington, DC 20423/202-275-7279.

Complaint and Performance Data

Summaries of complaint and performance data relating to the operations of the seventeen nationwide moving companies are available. The data can assist in informing customers of any moving company what to expect in the average move. Contact: Office of Compliance and Consumer Assistance, Interstate Commerce Commission, 12th St. and Constitution Ave. N.W., Room 5321, Washington, DC 20423/202-275-0880

Concurrences and Powers of Attorney

A "concurrence" authorizes one carrier to have another carrier publish its rates or fares. A "power of attorney" authorizes a tariff publishing agent to publish rates for a carrier. For information about filing concurrences and powers of attorney, contact: Section of Tariffs, Bureau of Traffic, Interstate Commerce Commission, 12th St. and Constitution Ave. N.W., Room 4356, Washington, DC 20423/202-275-7739.

Consumer Information and Complaint Centers

The Interstate Commerce Commission operates 6 regional Complaint Centers to help consumers who have a complaint, require assistance or need information about interstate railroads, bus lines, moving companies, and trucking companies. Contact the Center in your area:

Region 1 (Connecticut, Maine, Massachusetts, New Hampshire, New Jersey, New York, Rhode Island, and Vermont): Interstate Commerce Commission, Regional Complaint Center, Room 501, 150 Causeway Street, Boston, MA 02114/617-223-2372.

Region 2 (Delaware, District of Columbia, Maryland, Ohio, Pennsylvania, Virginia, and West Virginia): Interstate Commerce Commission, Regional Complaint Center, Room 16450—Gateway Building, 3535 Market Street, Philadelphia, PA 19104/215-596-4062.

Region 3 (Alabama, Florida, Georgia, Kentucky, Mississippi, North Carolina, South Carolina, and Tennessee): Interstate Commerce Commission, Regional Complaint Center, Room 300, 1776 Peachtree Street, N.W., Atlanta, GA 30309/404-881-2167.

Region 4 (Illinois, Indiana, Michigan, Minnesota, North Dakota, South Dakota, and Wisconsin): Interstate Commerce Commission, Regional Complaint Center, P. O. Box 1304, Chicago, IL 60690/312-886-6434.

Region 5 (Arkansas, Iowa, Kansas, Louisiana, Missouri, Nebraska, Oklahoma, and Texas): Interstate Commerce Commission, Regional Complaint Center, P. O. Box 17150, 411 West 7th Street, Suite 600, Fort Worth, TX 76102/817-334-2794.

Region 6 (Alaska, Arizona, California, Colorado, Hawaii, Idaho, Montana, Nevada, New Mexico, Oregon, Utah, Washington, and Wyoming): Interstate Commerce Commission, Regional Complaint Center, Suite 501, 211 Main Street, San Francisco, CA 94105/415-974-7181.

Entering the Trucking Business

A free booklet designed to inform the consumer of the services and remedies available, as well as the obligations and responsibilities of regulated carriers is available. It addresses some of the basic questions or problems on surface transportation services. It also includes a list of ICC field offices and state commissions regulating motor carriers. Contact: Consumer Assistance Section, Office of Compliance and Programs Bureau, Interstate Commerce Commission, 12th St. and Constitution Ave. N.W., Room 5321, Washington, DC 20423/202-275-0860.

Exempt Commodities

Can They Do That? Hot or Exempt is a free booklet listing commodities that are both "exempt" or "not exempt." For additional information, contact the nearest ICC Field Office, or Operations Branch, Interstate Commerce Commission, 12th St. and Constitution Ave. N.W., Room 5321, Washington, DC 20423/202-275-7148.

Freedom of Information Act Requests

For Freedom of Information Act requests, contact: Office of the Managing Director, Interstate Commerce Commission, 12th St. and Constitution Ave. N.W., Room 3387, Washington, DC 20423/202-275-7076.

Fuel Surcharge Hotline

The fuel recovery surcharge attempts to compensate common carriers for increased fuel costs. The adjusted surcharge rate is determined weekly and issued every Tuesday. For additional information on the surcharge, contact: Cost Development Section, Bureau of Accounts, Interstate Commerce Commission, 12th St. and Constitution Ave. N.W., Room 3315, Washington, DC 20423/202-275-7354.

Insurance

All motor common carriers of property and freight forwarders are required to maintain cargo insurance for the protection of the shipping public. The name of the company insuring these carriers is available. Contact: Insurance Bureau, Bureau of Operations, Interstate Commerce Commission,

12th St. and Constitution Ave. N.W., Room 5315, Washington, DC 20423/202-275-7511.

Legal Assistance
All motor carriers must designate an agent for service of legal process in each state into or through which it may operate. The name of this process agency may be obtained. Contact: Office of the Secretary, Insurance Section, Interstate Commerce Commission, 12th St. and Constitution Ave. N.W., Room B-221, Washington, DC 20423/ 202-275-0783.

Library
The commission library's collection concentrates on law and transportation. Contact: Library, Interstate Commerce Commission, 12th St. and Constitution Ave. N.W., Room 3392, Washington, DC 20423/202-275-7328.

Loss and Damage of Cargo Claims
Assistance is available in the form of information and guidance to help work out agreeable settlements on claims for loss and damage of cargo. Two free consumer pamphlets, *Loss and Damage Claims: Can You Collect?* and *Administrative Ruling 120,* provide helpful information and suggestions. For additional information, contact the nearest ICC office or Bureau of Operations, Interstate Commerce Commission, 12th St. and Constitution Ave. N.W., Room 7221, Washington, DC 20423/202-275-0877.

Motor and Rail Dockets
Records of proceedings can be examined by the public. Contact: Motor and Rail Docket File Room, Office of the Secretary, Interstate Commerce Commission. 12th St. and Constitution Ave. N.W., Room 1221, Washington, DC 20423/ 202-275-7285.

Moving
"Your Rights and Responsibilities When You Move" is a free booklet intended to help avoid the common pitfalls of moving. It includes information on selecting movers, estimating cost, moving by the pound, money-saving tips, methods of packing, bill of lading, inventory, mover's liability, delivery, storage in transit, filing claims and sources of assistance. For the booklet and any additional information, contact: Operations and Consumer Programs Branch, Interstate Commerce Commission, 12th St. and Constitution Ave. N.W., Room 5321, Washington, DC 20423/202-275-0880.

Northeast Railroad Network
Plans and policy are being developed to restructure the Northeast railroad network to provide more efficient and economic service. Contact: Rail Policy Section, Office of Policy and Analysis, Interstate Commerce Commission, 12th St. and

Constitution Ave. N.W., Room 5417, Washington, DC 20423/202-275-7245.

Public Advisories
Public Advisories are a series of free pamphlets designed to address some basic questions and problems related to surface transportation services. The following advisories are available at no cost:

No. 1—*Owner Operator Rights, Responsibilities and Remedies*
No. 2—*Arranging Transportation for Small Shipments: Shipper Rights, Remedies, and Alternatives*
No. 3—*Filing Your Tariff*
No. 4—*Lost or Damaged Household Gods; Prevention and Recovery*
No. 5—*Filing Your Contract and Schedule*
No. 6—*Entering the Trucking Business*
No. 7—*Buying Transportation*

Contact: Office Public Affairs, Consumer Office, Interstate Commerce Commission, 12th St. and Constitution Ave. N.W., Room 1211, Washington, DC 20423/202-275-7252.

Publications
The Interstate Commerce Commission issues many publications of both general and consumer interest. It also publishes technical and statistical publications dealing with transportation regulation. For a publication catalog and general information, contact: Communications and Consumer Affairs Office, Interstate Commerce Commission, 12th St. and Constitution Ave. N.W., Room 1211, Washington, DC 20423/202-275-7252.

Public Tariff File
Copies of all tariffs filed by carriers and regulated by the Interstate Commerce Commission can be inspected. Contact: Tariff Examining Branch, Bureau of Traffic, Interstate Commerce Commission, Room 4360, 12th St. and Constitution Ave. N.W., Washington, DC 20005/202-275-7462.

Rail and Service Abandonments
A railroad must issue a notice of intent to the public before it files an abandonment application. If there is sufficient public opposition to the abandonment, the ICC will hold formal proceedings. For additional information, contact: Rail Services Planning Section, Office of Transportation and Analysis, Interstate Commerce Commission, 12th St. and Constitution Ave. N.W., Room 4210, Washington, DC 20423/202-275-0829, or Rail Section, Office of Proceedings, Interstate Commerce Commission, 12th St. and Constitution Ave. N.W., Room 5417, Washington, DC 20423/ 202-275-7657.

Rates and Charges
Carriers must file their proposed tariffs with the

Interstate Commerce Commission. In case of a dispute on a tariff matter, contact: Rates and Informal Cases, Bureau of Traffic, Interstate Commerce Commission, 12th St. and Constitution Ave. N.W., Room 4310, Washington, DC 20423/ 202-275-7358.

Small Business Assistance
Help for small businesses with problems in surface transportation as well as information and assistance to small businesses planning to enter the transportation field is available from: Small Business Assistance Office, Interstate Commerce Commission, 12th St. and Constitution Ave. N.W., Room 2119, Washington, DC 20423/202-275-7597.

Special Permission Authority
Thirty days' notice must be given to the Interstate Commerce Commission and to the public before a rate or fare can be increased or reduced. Information about applying for Special Permission Authority to file tariffs on less than 30 days' notice is available. Contact: Special Permission Branch, Bureau of Traffic, Interstate Commerce Commission, 12th St. and Constitution Ave. N.W., Room 4355, Washington, DC 20423/202-275-7396.

Statistics Reports
The following statistics reports are prepared by the Office of Secretary, Interstate Commerce Commission, 12th St. and Constitution Ave. N.W., Room B-221, Washington, DC 20423:

Selected Statistics of Class III Motor Carriers of Property A-300-Wage Statistics of Class I Railroads in the United States—Calendar Year—number or employees, service hours, and compensation by occupation: professional, clerical, and general; maintenance of way and structures; maintenance of equipment and stores; etc.

QUARTERLY

Large Class I Motor Carriers of Property Selected Earnings Data—operating revenues, net income revenue tons hauled, operating ratio and rates of return.

Class I Line-Haul Railroads Selected Earnings Data—railway operating revenues, net railway operating income, ordinary income, net income and rate of return.

Large Class I Motor Carriers of Passengers Selected Earnings Data—operating revenues, net income, revenue passengers carried, operating ratio and rate of return.

Large Class I Household Goods Carriers Selected Earnings Data—operating revenues, net income, revenue tons hauled, operating ratio and rate of return.

MONTHLY

M-350-Preliminary Report of Railroad Employment. Class I Line-Haul Railroads—number of employees at middle of month, group totals.

Publications, Office of the Secretary, Interstate Commerce Commission, 12th St. and Constitution Ave. N.W., Room B-221, Washington, DC 20423/ 202-275-7833.

Suspension Procedures
If a carrier fails to comply with Interstate Commerce Commission rules and regulations and if other measures taken by the ICC have failed to make the carrier comply, the Commission may suspend or revoke the carrier's operating permit. For information about suspension procedures and filing protests and replies, contact: Suspension Board, Bureau of Traffic, Interstate Commerce Commission, 12th St. and Constitution Ave. N.W., Room 4336, Washington, DC 20423/202-275-7562.

Tariff Instructional Manual
This is a free step-by-step guide for constructing, publishing and filing a tariff. For a free copy and additional information, contact: Tariffs Section, Bureau of Traffic, Interstate Commerce Commission, 12th St. and Constitution Ave. N.W., Room 4363A, Washington, DC 20423/202-275-7462.

Transport Statistics in the United States
This is an annual compilation of statistics on all modes of transportation in the United States, and on related industries and services. It details data on traffic operations, equipment, finances and employment for carriers subject to the Interstate Commerce Act, and comprises the following five parts: 1) Railroads, their lessors and proprietary companies and electric railways; 2) motor carriers; 3) freight forwarders; 4) private car lines, and 5) carriers by water. Available from the Superintendent of Documents, Government Printing Office, Washington, DC 20402/202-783-3238. For additional information, contact: Publications Branch, Office of the Secretary, Bureau of Accounts, Interstate Commerce Commission, 12th St. and Constitution Ave. N.W., Room B-221, Washington, DC 20423/202-275-7833.

How Can the Interstate Commerce Commission Help You?
For information on how this agency can help you, contact: Office of Public Affairs, Interstate Commerce Commission, 12th St. and Constitution Ave. N.W., Washington, DC 20423/202-275-7252.

Merit Systems Protection Board

1120 Vermont Ave. N.W., Washington, DC 20419/202-653-7124

Established: January 16, 1883
Budget: $24,350,000
Employees: 367

Mission: Protects the integrity of federal merit systems and the rights of federal employees working in the systems; conducts special studies of the merit system, hears and decides charges of wrongdoing and employee appeals of adverse agency actions, and orders corrective and disciplinary actions against an executive agency or employee when appropriate; and investigates, among other things, prohibited personnel practices and allegations of activities prohibited by civil service law, rule and regulation, and prosecutes officials who violate civil service rules and regulations.

Major Sources of Information

Appeals
This office is responsible for the hearing of appeals by employees from adverse actions taken against them. Employees can appeal as a matter of right and are guaranteed a hearing in all cases appealable to the Board. Contact: Office of Appeals, Merit Systems Protection Board, 1120 Vermont Ave. N.W., Washington, DC 20419/202-653-8888.

Freedom of Information Act Requests
For Freedom of Information Act requests, contact: Office of the Secretary, Merit Systems Protection Board, 1120 Vermont Ave. N.W., Room 816, Washington, DC 20419/202-653-7200.

Library
This library, open to the public, has a legal collection emphasizing personnel law. For information, contact: Library, Merit Systems Protection Board, 1120 Vermont Ave. N.W., Washington, DC 20419/202-653-7132.

Merit Systems Review and Studies
Through special studies of the federal civil service and other merit systems in the executive branch, and through its review of the rules, regulations and significant actions of the Office of Personnel Management, the Board studies and reports to the President and the Congress on the federal merit systems, making sure that the principles of fairness embodied in the Civil Service Reform Act are being systematically applied. The office is working on several studies including a *Study of Sexual Harassment* which seeks to determine not only the extent of the problem in the federal workplace but also its impact on productivity. Contact: Office of Merit Systems, Review and Studies, Merit Systems Protection Board, 1120 Vermont Ave. N.W., Washington, DC 20419/202-653-7208.

Publications
The following publications are free:

How to File an Appeal with the U.S. Merit Systems Protection Board
Questions and Answers on the Merit Systems Protection Board

Contact: Public Information, Office of Legislative Counsel, Merit Systems Protection Board, 1120 Vermont Ave. N.W., Washington, DC 20419/202-653-7175.

Special Counsel

The Special Counsel receives and investigates charges of:

1. Prohibited personnel practices, including reprisals against whistleblowers
2. Arbitrary or capricious withholding of information that has been designated as available under the Freedom of Information Act
3. Illegal discrimination occurring in the course of any personnel action when found by a court or under any administrative proceeding

4. Prohibited political activity
5. Activities prohibited by any civil service law, rule or regulation.

The Special Counsel has the authority to initiate disciplinary actions before the Board against employees after any investigation conducted by the Special Counsel, or on the basis of an employee's willful refusal or failure to comply with an order of the Board. Contact: Office of the Special Counsel, Merit Systems Protection Board, Room 1100, Vermont Ave. N.W., Washington, DC 20419/202-653-2253

How Can the Merit Systems Protection Board Help You?

For information on how this agency can help you, contact: Merit Systems Protection Board, 1120 Vermont Ave. N.W., Washington, DC 20419/202-653-7124.

National Aeronautics and Space Administration

400 Maryland Ave. S.W., Washington, DC 20546/202-453-1000

Established: 1958
Budget: $6,830,945,000
Employees: 21,219

MISSION: Carries out the policy of Congress that activities in space should be devoted to peaceful purposes for the benefit of all humankind; conducts research for the solution of problems of flight within and outside the Earth's atmosphere and develops, constructs, tests and operates aeronautic and space vehicles; conducts activities required for the exploration of space with manned and unmanned vehicles, arranges for the most effective utilization of the scientific and engineering resources of the United States in conjunction with other nations engaged in aeronautic and space activites for peaceful purposes; and provides for the widest practicable and appropriate dissemination of information concerning NASA's activities and their results.

Major Sources of Information

Aeronautic Publications
This Facility has information about reports and other publications concerned with aeronautics, space and supporting disciplines. Staff can answer questions about a series of continuing bibliographies covering reports literature in aeronautical engineering, earth resources, management, etc. An important publication of this office is the *Scientific and Technical Aerospace Reports* (STAR), NASA's biweekly announcement journal. Consisting of a collection of reports about various research and development efforts, it provides comprehensive coverage of aeronautics, space and supporting disciplines, including defense applications. Annual subscription price is $90.00.

Order this and other NASA publications from the Superintendent of Documents, U.S. Government Printing Office, Washington, DC 20402, 202-783-3238. Contact: NASA Scientific and Technical Information Facility, P. O. Box 8757, BWI Airport, MD 21240/301-859-5300.

Aeronautics and Space Technology
This office is responsible for the planning, direction, execution, evaluation, documentation, and dissemination of the results of all NASA research and technology programs that are conducted primarily to demonstrate the feasibility of a concept, structure, component, or system and which may have general application to the nation's aeronautic

and space objectives. This office is also responsible for coordinating the agency's total program of supporting research and technology related to carrying out specific flight missions in order to avoid unnecessary duplication, and to insure an integrated and balanced agency research program. This includes technology developments supporting reliable low cost energy systems, as a national priority. Contact: Public Affairs, Aeronautics and Space Technology, National Aeronautics and Space Administration, 600 Independence Ave. S.W., Room B647, Washington, DC 20546/202-453-2754.

Aerospace Careers

NASA has prepared several free booklets describing the preparation and training needed for careers in aerospace as a scientist, technician or engineer. The booklets also include interviews with several people in the field. For copies of the publications or additional information about careers in aerospace, contact: Education Services Branch, Academic Affairs Division, National Aeronautics and Space Administration, Washington, DC 20546/202-453-8388 OR write the Education Programs Officer at the NASA Center serving your state.

NASA Ames Research Center, Moffett Field, CA 94035 (serving Alaska, Arizona, California, Hawaii, Idaho, Montana, Nevada, Oregon, Utah, Washington, and Wyoming)

NASA Goddard Space Flight Center, Greenbelt, MA 20771 (serving Connecticut, Delaware, District of Columbia, Maine, Maryland, Massachusetts, New Hampshire, New Jersey, New York, Pennsylvania, Rhode Island, and Vermont)

NASA Johnson Space Center, Houston, TX 77058 (serving Colorado, Kansas, Nebraska, New Mexico, North Dakota, Oklahoma, South Dakota, and Texas)

NASA Kennedy Space Center, Kennedy Space Center, FL 32809 (serving Florida, Georgia, Puerto Rico, and Virgin Islands)

NASA Langley Research Center, Hampton, VA 23665 (serving Kentucky, North Carolina, South Carolina, Virginia, and West Virginia)

NASA Lewis Research Center, 21000 Brookpark Road, Cleveland, OH 44135 (serving Illinois, Indiana, Michigan, Minnesota, Ohio, and Wisconsin)

NASA Marshall Space Flight Center, Marshall Space Flight Center, AL 35812 (serving Alabama, Arkansas, Iowa, Louisiana, Mississippi, Missouri, and Tennessee)

Annual Procurement Report

This report presents summary data on all procurement actions, including contracts, purchase orders, grants and agreements for the past fiscal year. Information is based on detailed data compiled on all grants, all contracts with educational institutions, and all other procurements of $10,000 and over. Contact: Office of Procurement, National Aeronautics and Space Administration, 600 Inde-

pendence Ave. S.W., Room 125, Washington, DC 20546/202-453-2137.

Astronaut Appearances

Astronauts are available to speak to education, civic, scientific, and similar groups. For information, contact: Astronaut Appearances, Public Services Branch, Public Affairs Division, National Aeronautics and Space Administration, 400 Maryland Ave. S.W., Room F6093, Washington, DC 20546/202-453-8315.

Astronaut Application

Selection and training into the Astronaut Program are handled by the NASA/Lyndon B. Johnson Space Center. A student interested in a career as an astronaut should write for a free fact sheet titled *Guidance Tips for Aerospace Careers,* which will include information on recruitment and training of astronauts. Contact: NASA, Lyndon B. Johnson Space Center, Houston, TX 77058.

Atlas-Centaur Rockets

Lewis Research Center manages the Atlas-Centaur rockets which carry many scientific, planetary and application payloads, including commercial communications satellites, into space. Contact: Lewis Research Center, National Aeronautics and Space Administration, 21000 Brookpark Rd., Cleveland, OH 44135/216-433-4000.

Bid Rooms

Two central "Bid Rooms" are maintained where copies of all open National Aeronautics and Space Administration (NASA) solicitations are available for review by interested firms. Each NASA installation provides "bid room" services for its own procurements. Contact: NASA Resident Procurement Branch, Office of Procurement, National Aeronautics and Space Administration, 4800 Oak Grove Dr., Pasadena, CA 91103/213-354-5359, or: Office of Small and Disadvantaged Business Utilization, National Aeronautics and Space Administration, 600 Independence Ave. S.W., Room 116, Washington, DC 20546/202-453-2088.

Computer Software Management and Information Center (COSMIC)

The center collects all the computer programs NASA has developed (and also some of the best programs developed by other government agencies), verifies that they operate properly, and makes them available at reasonable prices. Program documentation is also available for evaluation prior to purchase. A catalog of over 1,600 available computer programs is published, or individual searches for relevant programs will be performed by COSMIC free of charge. *Computer Program Abstracts,* a quarterly, is available for $6.50 per year from the Superintendent of Documents, Government Printing Office, Washington,

DC 20402/202-783-3238. For further information, contact: COSMIC, 112 Barrow Hall, University of Georgia, Athens, GA 30602/404-542-3265.

Computerized Data Bases
The following data bases are maintained by the National Aeronautics and Space Administration:

Antarctic Meteorite Bibliography (AMB)
AMB provides bibliographic information on Antarctic meteorites, Allan Hill meteorites, and Yamato meteorites. Cited materials cover all aspects of the meteorites including analyses, descriptions, composition, classification, experiments, location, etc. Searches and printouts are available free of charge. Contact: Technical Information Specialist, Lunar and Planetary Institute, Library Information Center, 3303 NASA Road 1, Houston, TX 77058/713-486-2191.

Lunar and Planetary Data Base
Lunar Planetary Bibliography (LPB) consists of bibliographic information on worldwide research in the field of lunar and planetary science, including published literature, government documents, conference papers and books. Input from 1950 to the present covers all research on the moon with particular emphasis on the Apollo Program. Searches and printouts are available free of charge. Contact: Technical Information Specialist, Lunar and Planetary Institute, Library Information Center, 3303 NASA Road 1, Houston TX 77058/713-486-2191.

Marshall Space Flight Center Index
The Marshall Space Flight Center maintains a master index, with bibliographic citations and abstracts, of all documents pertaining to the various technologies that have been developed at its center. The Center will provide searches, printouts, and any documents it has free of charge. Contact: Director, Technology Utilization Office, George C. Marshall Space Flight Center, Huntsville, AL 35812/205-453-2223.

NASA Scientific and Technical Information (NASA STI or NASA-RECON)
NASA maintains a data base, called NASA STI or NASA-RECON, which provides bibliographic information for worldwide literature in aeronautics, space and the vast array of topics NASA is interested in. The broad-based system contains more than 100 different categories ranging from aerodynamics to urban technology. Many of the reports, journals, books and conference papers cited are highly technical. NASA's wide interests in science include the environment and properties of the earth, moon, and planets; the sun and its relationship to the earth and the rest of the solar system, the space environment; the physical nature of the universe; and the search for extraterrestrial life. In technology, NASA's interests include spacecraft and launch vehicles; aircraft; propulsion; auxiliary power; human factors; electronics; and structures and materials. In applications, NASA's interests include astronomical, geophysical, meteorological and communications systems, as well as emphasis on earth resources, air and water pollution, and urban transportation.

NASA offers different levels of service depending upon your needs:

Direct Access to NASA STI. This is available for universities, industries and others receiving NASA approval. Charges include a yearly subscription fee of $120.00 (waived for universities) and $20.00 per hour connect time plus five cents per printed citation. Subscription includes a two-day training session, updated reports and other publications.

NASA Headquarters (STIF). Only organizations registered with STIF are eligible for services. Almost any organization interested in aeronautics and space activities can qualify as a subscriber. STIF provides searches, printouts and other services free of charge to universities. Others must pay for these services, and searches generally cost $80.00.

Searches by NASA STI users. Approximately 120 organizations nationwide—universities, libraries and industries—have direct access to NASA STI. While many only do in-house searches, you may be able to locate a user that will do a search for you, often for a minimal fee.

NASA-sponsored search center. NASA sponsors eight Centers nationwide to search NASA STI for the general public. These Centers also search hundreds of other government (including DOE-RECON) and commercial data bases on topics ranging from art to zoology. Their fees vary greatly, and some offer discounts to students, universities and others. Only the Florida and Kentucky Centers are restricted to serving their respective states, so feel free to check around. Most of the Centers will do analytical work and provide special services such as current awareness bulletins.

For a listing of the centers see "Industrial Application Center" this section. For further information contact: NASA RECON, P. O. Box 8757, BWI Airport, Baltimore, MD 21240/202-621-0140 or 301-859-5300.

Space Science Experiments Data Base
The National Space Service Data Center System for Information Retrieval and Storage (SIRS) is a central repository for reduced data obtained from, or related to, space science experiments worldwide. It contains information from satellite experiments, sounding-rocket probes, and high-altitude aeronautical and balloon investigations. Correlative data, such as magnetograms and ionograms collected from ground-based observatories and stations, is also stored. The information covers a wide range of disciplines: astronomy, earth sci-

ences, meteorology, planetary sciences, aeronomy, particles and fields, solar physics, life sciences and material sciences.

SIRS consists of four main information files. The Automated Internal Management (AIM) file provides characteristics of each spacecraft, experiment and data set that have been identified in a hierarchical arrangement. The Technical Reference File (TRF) contains descriptions of publications and technical documents that are used as reference materials. The Rocket File includes information that names and describes all scientific rocket launchings identified by NSSDC. The Nonsatellite Data file contains data from sources other than satellite experiment flights.

Searches, printouts, documents, etc., are all available to any individual or organization resident in the U.S. and to researchers outside the U.S. Normally, a fee is charged to cover reproduction and processing costs incurred by the Center. However, the Center may waive the fee for modest amounts of data when the information is to be used for scientific studies or for specific college-level educational purposes and when services are requested by an individual affiliated with: non-profit organizations; universities or colleges; state or local governments; and U.S. government agencies, their contractors and their grantees. Contact: Request Coordination Office, National Space Science Data Center, Goddard Space Flight Center, Code 601, Greenbelt, MD 20771/301-344-6695.

"Dear Colleague" Letters
These are periodic notices which disseminate information to members of the scientific and engineering community. These letters outline general research areas in which unsolicited proposals would be of interest and contain appropriate guidance for preparation and submittal of related proposals. To be placed on the mailing list and for additional information, contact: National Aeronautics and Space Administration, 600 Independence Ave. S.W., Room B-209, Washington, DC 20546/202-453-1954.

Deep Space Network (DSN)
This is a worldwide deep space tracking and data acquisition network. Contact: Jet Propulsion Laboratory, National Aeronautics and Space Administration, 4800 Oak Grove Dr., Pasadena, CA 91103/213-354-5011.

Delta Launch Vehicle
Goddard Space Flight Center manages the Delta launch vehicle which has launched numerous unmanned NASA satellites as well as many of the satellites of other federal and communications agencies and foreign governments. Contact: Goddard Space Flight Center, National Aeronautics and Space Administration, Greenbelt MD 20771/301-344-7000.

Education Services
Programs and services provided for the education communities throughout the country include curriculum updating, teacher education courses, institutes, seminars and workshops, educational conferences, youth programs, aerospace education services, educational visits and counseling and career guidance. Contact: Community and Education Services Branch, Public Affairs Division, National Aeronautics and Space Administration, 400 Maryland Ave. S.W., Room F6051, Washington, DC 20546/202-453-8397

Environmental and Earth Science Education
This is an annotated listing providing teachers of environmental education and earth science with an understanding of NASA's programs and technologies which may help in coping with earth resources and environment problems. It includes publications, films and environment-related TV programs. Contact: Education and Community Services, Public Affairs Division, National Aeronautics and Space Administration, 400 Maryland Ave. S.W., Room 605, Washington, DC 20546/202-453-8388.

Experience NASA Yourself
You can experience the space program first hand. Visitor Information Centers at the following NASA facilities around the country showcase the nation's activities in space through exhibits, films and public tours.

Dryden Flight Research Facility, Edwards Air Force Base, California 93523 (805)258-3311 8:00–3:30 Monday–Friday

Goddard Space Flight Center, Greenbelt, Maryland 20771 (301)344-8981 10:00–4:00 Wednesday–Sunday

Johnson Space Center, Houston, Texas 77058, (713)483-4241, 9:00–4:00 daily

Kennedy Space Center, Florida 32899, (305)452-2121, 8:00–7:00 daily

Langley Research Center, Hampton, Virginia 23665, (804)865-2855, 8:30–4:30 Monday–Saturday, noon–4:30 Sunday

Lewis Research Center, Cleveland, Ohio 44135, (216)267-1187, 9:00–4:00 Monday–Friday, 10:00–3:00 Saturday, 1:00–5:00 Sunday,

Marshall Space Flight Center, Huntsville, Alabama 35812, at Alabama Space and Rocket Center, Out of State: 1-800-633-7280, In Alabama: 1-800-572-7234, 8:00–6:00 daily, June–August, 9:00–5:00 daily, September–May

National Space Technology Laboratories, Bay Saint Louis, Mississippi 39529, (601)688-2370, 9:00–4:00 daily

Wallops Flight Facility, Wallops Island, Virginia 23337, (804)824-3411 extension 298 or 579, 10:00–4:00 Thursday–Monday

Films
Films describing research and development pro-

grams in space and aeronautics, and the results of the research can be borrowed at no cost for showings to education, civic, industrial, professional, youth and similar groups. Special and general interest films are listed as well as films for classroom use and series on life science, Skylab science, demonstration, rediscovery, living in space, and the Moon. Films on careers in research are also included. For a list of films, film libraries and information, contact: Public Services Branch, Public Affairs Division, National Aeronautics and Space Administration, 400 Maryland Ave. S.W., Room F6052, Washington, DC 20546/202-453-8383. NASA films and filmstrips can be purchased from the National Audiovisual Center, National Archives and Records Service, General Services Administration, Order Section AP, Washington, DC 20409/202-763-1891.

Field Centers

There are ten principal offices within NASA. Most of these can be toured by the public. For information on center programs, contact the following individual centers, or: Office of Public Affairs Division, 400 Maryland Ave. S.W., Room F6027, Washington, DC 20546/202-755-3936.

Ames Research Center

The Center is responsible for NASA's research in austronontics and the life sciences. It conducts research into the medical problems of manned flight, both within the atmosphere and in space. The Center is developing short take-off and landing (STOL) aircraft for urban-region transportation systems, mounting the first flight to planet Jupiter, and supporting research for NASA's orbiting space station-laboratory facility and for the space shuttle to man and supply the space station. Center scientists are also working toward defining the evolution and characteristics of planetary bodies. They are pursuing an active program of astro-physics studying the sun, pulsars, quasars, and the evolution of the galaxies. Contact: Ames Research Center, National Aeronautics and Space Administration, Moffett Field, CA 94035/415-965-5091.

Ames-Dryden Flight Research Facility

This conducts research on flight and the problems of manned flight within the atmosphere. It includes work on the problems of take-off and landing, low-speed flight, supersonic and hypersonic flight, and re-entry in order to verify predicted characteristics and identify unexpected problems in actual flight. The Center is responsible for the development and operation of instrument systems for the acquisition and dissemination of inflight information collected from various programs. It has also been designated as a secondary recovery site. Contact: Ames-Dryden Flight Research, National Aeronautics and Space Adminis-

tration, P.O. Box 273, Edwards, CA 93523/805-258-8381.

Goddard Space Flight Center

The Goddard Space Flight Center has been assigned the prime responsibility within NASA for the management of applications of satellite projects, unmanned scientific satellite projects, and worldwide NASA tracking and data acquisition operations. It is one of the few installations in the world capable of conducting a full range space-science experimentation program from theory through experimentation, design and construction, satellite fabrication and testing, tracking, and data acquisition and reduction. The Center's scientific staff is concerned primarily with research into magnetic fields, energetic particles, ionospheres and radio physics, planetary atmospheres, meteorology, interplanetary matter, solar physics, communication, and astronomy. An important area of interest to NASA is Goddard's applications satellite program. From this program arose the LANDSAT, formerly Earth Resources Technology Satellite, a modified version of its forerunners, the NIMBUS experimental weather satellite and the TIROS Operational (weather) System (TOS). Contact: Goddard Space Flight Center, National Aeronautics and Space Administration, Greenbelt, MD 20771/301-344-7000.

Jet Propulsion Laboratory

This Laboratory is a government-owned research and development facility, operated for NASA by the California Institute of Technology. The Laboratory carries out research programs and flight projects for NASA, and conceives and executes advanced development and experimental engineering investigation to further the technology required for the Nation's space program. The primary emphasis of the Laboratory's effort is on the carrying out of lunar, planetary and deep-space unmanned scientific missions. Supporting research and advanced development are conducted in electric propulsion, nuclear power, chemical propulsion, aerothermodynamics, fluid physics and electrophysics, applied mathematics, space power generation, optical and radio astronomy, planetary atmospheres fields and particles, long-range communications, guidance and control, and systems simulation and analysis techniques. This Laboratory is also involved in supporting the energy program in the areas of geothermal studies, low-cost silicon solar arrays, solar cells, a high efficiency-low pollution engine(s) and stirling engine for undersea applications. Contact: Jet Propulsion Laboratory, National Aeronautics and Space Administration, 4800 Oak Grove Dr., Pasadena, CA 91109/213-354-5011.

Johnson Space Center

This Center has as its primary mission the development of spacecraft for manned space flight programs and the conduct of manned flight operations. The Center's mission includes an engineering, development, and operational capability to support the Space Shuttle and RFP for Space Station to generate the knowledge required to advance the technology of manned spacecraft development. Engineering and development efforts focus on the conception and implementation of a program of applied research and development in the area of space research, space physics, life systems, and test and evaluation. Space science efforts are devoted to science experiments in flight, lunar research, space environment studies, and further development of the capability to survey the Earth's resources from space. The medical capabilities include experiments in flight, flight crew monitoring, and development of physiologic requirements for spacecraft systems. Contact: Johnson Space Center, National Aeronautics and Space Administration, Houston, TX 77058/ 713-483-5111.

Kennedy Space Center
The Center has launched Apollo and other space vehicles as NASA's major launch organization for manned and unmanned space missions. In addition, it launches a wide variety of lunar, planetary and interplanetary space vehicles as well as scientific, meteorologic, and communications satellites. The Center is responsible for the design of launch and recovery facilities for the Space Shuttle. Supporting this primary mission are a host of technical and administrative activities. These include design engineering; testing, assembly, and check-out of launch vehicles and spacecraft; launch operations; and purchasing and contracting. Contact: Kennedy Space Center, National Aeronautics and Space Administration, Kennedy Space Center, FL 32899/305-867-2468.

Langley Research Center
Langley Research Center conducts scientific investigations on a broad scale in the areas of aeronautics, space technology, electronics and structures, and concentrates on the problems of space travel and reentry, application of new materials, supersonic and hypersonic flight, and other areas to provide the technical background necessary for the accomplishment of NASA aeronautic and space missions. Attention is given to the study of systems and techniques for the recovery of vehicles returning to the Earth's atmosphere from a space mission. Aeronautics research is directed toward improvement in the performance, safety, and utility of airborne flight, supersonic military aircraft, helicopters and low-speed airplanes. The Center designed and built the NASA Tech house to demonstrate new techniques suitable for single family residences including the use of solar energy, water recycling and many other innovative fea-

tures. Also, an office building is being heated and cooled by solar collectors. Contact: Langley Research Center, National Aeronautics and Space Administration, Langley Station, Hampton, VA 23365/804-865-0627.

Lewis Research Center
Activities at NASA's Lewis Research Center are directed at advancing technologies for aircraft propulsion, propulsion and power generation for space flight, space communications systems, new terrestrial energy systems and automotive engines. The Center also manages two major launch vehicles, the Atlas-Centaur and Titan-Centaur. Aeronautics activities at Lewis are aimed principally at development of engines which will operate as quietly, cleanly, and efficiently as possible. Propulsive lift concepts are being explored for aircraft which will take-off and land in short distances and will meet a need for short haul transportation. Specific projects include demonstration of a fuel efficient engine; a quiet, clean experimental engine for short-haul aviation; and an experimental, quiet, clean engine for general aviation. Research on propulsion for spacecraft emphasizes electric rocket engine technology, hydrogen-oxygen systems for the Space Shuttle, and other high energy propellants. Lewis scientists are also conducting studies pertinent to space communications particularly at frequencies above 10 gigahertz and at high levels of transmission power. In support of the Department of Energy's Solar Energy Programs, NASA scientists are working on wind energy systems. Initial testing is on a 100 kw wind turbine, with larger sizes to follow. Solar photovoltaic arrays are also being tested and demonstrated. The object of this work is to reduce costs per kilowatt by technical advances, market development and expanded manufacturing. Engineers also are studying alternative fuels for jet aircraft, and are evaluating advanced energy conversion systems which use coal as fuel. Auto propulsion research is another area of experimentation. In addition, basic and applied research is conducted on materials and metallurgy; cryogenic and liquid-metal heat-transfer fluids; pumps and turbines; combustion processes, propellants, tankage injectors, chambers and nozzles; seals, bearings, gears and lubrication; system control dynamics; plasmas and magnetohydrodynamics to simulate various flight conditions, and includes atmospheric wind tunnels and space environment facilities. Contact: Lewis Research Center, National Aeronautics and Space Administration, 21000 Brookpark Rd., Cleveland, OH 44135/216-433-4000, ext. 415.

Marshall Space Flight Center
The primary mission of the Marshall Space Flight Center is to develop and provide launch vehicle and space transportation systems to meet space program requirements from conception through all

phases of design, fabrication, testing and production. The Center's efforts are devoted to various aspects of the Space Transportation System; the Center has responsibility for the Space Shuttle's main engines, solid Rocket Boosters and External Tank. MSFC is also charged with representing NASA's interests in the Inertial Upper Stage which will be used in conjunction with the Space Shuttle. The Center has the leading role within NASA for the international Spacelab (being developed by the European Space Agency) and is monitoring the first three Spacelab missions. Among other prospective Shuttle "payloads," the Center is charged with developing the Space Telescope. MSFC is also in the early stages of work on pressurized space stations. Other activities include basic research, advanced research in the general fields of astronautics, project improvement and the advancement of launch vehicle technology. For information on this and the latest developments regarding Spacelab missions, contact: Marshall Space Flight Center, National Aeronautics and Space Administration, Huntsville, AL 35812/205-453-0038.

Wallops Flight Facility

Wallops Flight is responsible for planning and conducting applied research and development. Scientific development, instrumentation, facilities and techniques utilized in rocket-borne experiments, aeronautic and airport terminal area research projects and ecologic studies are emphasized. Wallops Flight prepares, assembles, launches, and tracks space vehicles, and acquires and processes resulting scientific data. Its facilities are utilized by scientists and engineers from the laboratories and research centers of NASA, other governmental agencies, colleges and universities, and the worldwide scientific community. Wallops Flight personnel assists these scientific research teams with their projects. As necessary, special types of instrumentation and equipment are developed to support these projects. Wallops Flight exercises project management responsibilities for GEOS-C, the Experimental Inter-American Meteorological Rocket Network (EXAMETNET). Contact: Wallops Flight, National Aeronautics and Space Administration, Wallops Island, VA 23337/804-824-3411.

Foreign Patent Licensing

There is patent coverage on NASA-owned inventions introduced to various foreign countries to further the interests of United States industry in foreign commerce. Licenses are negotiated individually and may be granted to any applicant, foreign or domestic. *Significant NASA Inventions Available for Licensing in Foreign Countries* includes abstracts of those inventions in which NASA owns the principal or exclusive rights and which have been made available for patent licens-

ing in the countries indicated. The corresponding United States patent number is also listed. Copies of the United States patents may be purchased from Assistant for Patent Matters. For additional information, contact: Patent Matters, Office of General Counsel, National Aeronautics and Space Administration, 400 Maryland Ave. S.W., Room F7035, Washington, DC 20546/202-453-2424.

Freedom of Information Act Requests

For Freedom of Information Act requests, contact: Freedom of Information, Public Information Section, Public Affairs Division, National Aeronautics and Space Administration, 400 Maryland Ave. S.W., Room F6133, Washington, DC 20546/202-453-8342.

Get Away Special (GAS)

The main purpose of the Space Shuttle is to carry large, sophisticated instruments into the Earth's orbit. The "get away special" payloads will be accommodated on a space-available basis. Scheduling of GAS payloads will provide for placing payloads on the most appropriate mission based generally on a first-come, first-served sequence. The GAS payloads are to be self-contained, i.e., they will not be allowed to draw upon any Shuttle services beyond on-off controls which will be operated by an astronaut. This program encourages the use of space by all researchers, private individuals and organizations. A free experimenters' handbook, *Get Away Special, Small Self-Contained Payloads,* is available. For a copy of the handbook and other information, contact: Get Away Special Liaison, Goddard Space Flight Center, Greenbelt, MD 20771/301-344-6760.

Historical Photographs

NASA field centers maintain photo files on current projects and those of the recent past. Files covering projects and missions extending back to NASA's creation are also available. Contact NASA's Field Centers or Media Services Broadcast & Audiovisual Branch, Public Affairs Division, National Aeronautics and Space Administration, 400 Maryland Ave. S.W., Room 6035, Washington, DC 20546/202-453-8375

How to Seek and Win NASA Contracts

This is a free booklet which provides some basic guidelines to NASA solicitations and includes information on how to prepare bids, how to submit technical and cost proposals, and ways to seek business as a subcontractor. For a copy of the booklet and for additional information, contact: Office of Small and Disadvantaged Business Utilization, National Aeronautics and Space Administration, 600 Independence Ave. S.W., Room B116, Washington, DC 20546/202-453-2088

Industrial Application Centers

To promote technology transfer, NASA operates a network of dissemination centers whose job is to provide information retrieval services and technical assistance to industrial and government clients. These Centers are backed by off-site representatives and technology coordinators at NASA field centers who seek to match NASA expertise and ongoing research and engineering with client problems and interests. Literature searches are available as well as current awareness services tailored to individual needs. A nominal fee is charged for these services. A free pamphlet, *Search Before Research,* describes the Centers and their services.

Aerospace Research Applications Center, 611 N. Capital Ave. Indianapolis, IN 46204 317-264-4644.

Kerr Industrial Applications Center, Southeastern Oklahoma State University, Station A Box 2584 Durant, OK 74701/405-924-6822

NASA Industrial Applications Center, 701 LIS Building, University of Pittsburgh, Pittsburgh, PA 15260/412-624-5211.

NASA Industrial Applications Center, University of Southern California, Research Annex Room 200, 3716 S. Hope St. University Park, Los Angeles, CA 90007/213-743-6132.

New England Research Applications Center, Mansfield Professional Park, Storrs, CT 06268/203-486-4533

North Carolina Science and Technology Research Center, P.O. Box 12235, Research Triangle Park, NC 27709/919-549-0671.

Technology Applications Center (TAC), University of New Mexico, 2500 Central Ave. S.E., Albuquerque, NM 87131/505-277-3622.

Contact the nearest Industrial Applications Center, or Industrial Applications, National Aeronautics and Space Administration, 400 Morefend Ave. Room 5113, Washington, DC 20546/202-755-453-8430.

Inventions and Innovations

Awards are given for scientific or technical contributions significantly valuable to the conduct of space and aeronautics activities, such as innovations and inventions which have been used with proven value. For information, contact: Inventions and Contributions Board, National Aeronautics and Space Administration, 400 Maryland Ave. S.W., Room F5065, Washington, DC 20546/202-453-2901

Libraries

The library's collection emphasizes aerospace, management, basic science, astronomy, and related fields. For a list of NASA field libraries and additional information, contact: Library, Headquarters Administration Division, National Aeronautics and Space Administration, 600 Independence Ave. S.W., Room FB10B, Washington, DC 20546/202-453-8545

Life Sciences Program

The objectives of the life sciences program in space are to qualify personnel to accomplish more manned space functions for longer time periods, including manning space probes and establishing space colonies; studying the effects of the space environment, primarily weightlessness, on living systems in order to learn more about life processes in general; utilizing space conditions for isolation, purification and synthesis of biologic materials such as antigens, hormones, and antibiotics; and assuring that life sciences technology and hardware developed for space are applied on Earth wherever appropriate. This would include communications and sensing systems to bring medical attention to remote areas, as well as systems technology applicable to public health activities. Contact: Life Sciences Division, Space Science, National Aeronautics and Space Administration, 600 Independence Ave. S.W. Room 600, Washington, DC 20547/202-755-1530

Listing of Special Publications Published by the NASA Technology Transfer Division

This is a listing of documents available for purchase through the National Technical Information Service (NTIS). These include surveys, reports, handbooks, compilations and bibliographies. Contact: Technology Transfer Division, Space and Terrestrial Applications, National Aeronautics and Space Administration, 600 Independence Ave. S.W., Room B147, Washington, DC 20546/202-453-8415

Manned Space Flight Vehicles

This Center is responsible for design, development and testing of the U.S. manned space flight vehicles, for selection and training of space flight crews, for ground control of manned flights and for many of the medical, engineering and scientific experiments carried on aboard the flights. Contact: Johnson Space Center, National Aeronautics and Space Administration, Houston, TX, 713-483-5111.

Michoud Assembly Facility

The primary mission of this facility is the systems engineering, engineering design, manufacture, fabrication, assembly and related work for the Space Shuttle External Tank. Contact: Michoud Assembly Facility, National Aeronautics and Space Administration, P.O. Box 29300, New Orleans, LA 70189/504-255-2603.

NASA Activities

This monthly publication covers space statements, legislative affairs concerning space, and such general NASA activities as agreements, key awards, radio-television programs, new films, new publications, press releases, personnel changes, calendar events (pertaining to space and aeronautics), the current launch schedule, monthly lists of technical briefs, patents resulting from NASA research, and monetary awards for inventions and contributions. It is sold for $23.00 per year by the Superintendent of Documents, Goverment Printing Office, Washington, DC 20402/202-783-3238. For additional information, contact: Public Affairs Division, National Aeronautics and Space Administration, 400 Maryland Ave. S.W., Room 6043, Washington, DC 20546/202-453-8400

NASA Facts
Each pamphlet describes a NASA project or specific technology such as Voyager to Saturn, the Viking mission, living in space, and others. For sale (prices vary) at the Superintendent of Documents, Government Printing Office, Washington, DC 20402/202-783-3238. For additional information, contact: Public Affairs Division, National Aeronautics and Space Administration, 400 Maryland Ave. S.W., Room F6091, Washington, DC 20546/202-453-8364

National Sounding Rocket Program
Engineering support provided for this program includes analytic, feasibility and design studies, payload, vehicle and recovery systems, engineering, test and evaluation, and data analysis and reporting. Contact: Wallops Flight Center, National Aeronautics and Space Administration, Wallops Island, VA 23337/804-824-3411.

National Space Science Data Center
This facility is the central repository of the data collected through space flight experiments. This information provided the basis for studies to increase understanding of basic phenomena. Contact: National Space Science Data Center, Goddard Space Flight Center, National Aeronautics and Space Administration, Greenbelt, MD 20771/ 301-344-7354

National Space Technology Laboratories
This is NASA's prime static test facility for large liquid propellant rocket engine systems. It is also involved in support of the Shuttle Test program; is conducting research in terrestrial applications; and is in charge of managing the base and providing technical and institutional support to federal and state resident agencies on a reimbursable basis. Contact: National Space Technology Laboratories, National Aeronautics and Space Administration, NSTL MS 39529/601-688-3341.

Patents
Detailed information concerning patent policies and procedures as well as available forms for petitioning for waivers of rights to contract inventions, and for making applications for licenses under NASA patents is available. NASA Patent Abstracts Bibliography, a semi-annual, contains abstracts of all NASA inventions, and can be purchased from National Technical Information Service, Springfield, VA 22161. Contact: Patent Matters, Office of General Counsel, National Aeronautics and Space Administration, 400 Maryland Ave. S.W., Room F7037, Washington, DC 20546/202-453-2424

Photographs
NASA black and white, and color photographs are available for purchase from NASA's contract laboratory, Bara Photographs, Inc., P.O. Box 486, Bladensburg, MD 20710. A catalog of photographs is available. Contact: Audiovisual Section, Public Affairs Division, National Aeronautics and Space Administration, 400 Maryland Ave. S.W., Room F6035, Washington, DC 20546/202-453-8375

Pioneer Spacecraft
Ames Research Center manages the Pioneer program. Six Pioneer spacecraft have been launched into solar orbit with two having provided the first closeup views of Jupiter. Contact: Ames Research Center, National Aeronautics and Space Administration, Mountain View, CA 94035/415-965-5091.

Planetary Atmospheres
Study of the solar system including comparative planetology, orbital and physical data, composition, origins, atmospheres, geophysics and geology of planets is conducted by this office. Contact: Planetary Atmospheres Discipline, Space Science, National Aeronautics and Space Administration 600 Independence S.W., Room 168, Washington, DC 20546/202-453-1596

Progress in Aircraft Design Since 1903
This booklet traces the changes in aircraft design and technology from the Wright Flyer to the Supersonic F-15. Photos of 90 aircraft are included. Available for $5.50 from the Superintendent of Documents, Government Printing Office, Washington, DC 20402/202-783-3238.

Publications
A list of NASA publications includes educational and scientific publications, wall display sheets with facts on NASA, and classroom picture sets. Contact: Publication Services, Educational Services Branch, Public Affairs Division, National Aeronautics and Space Administration, 400 Maryland Ave. S.W., Room F6137 Washington, DC 20546/202-453-8330.

Records of Achievement
The catalog, Records of Achievement, lists the special publications produced by NASA since the early 1960's. These publications have enjoyed worldwide recognition. They report on the re-

search and development in communications, energy, materials processing, planetology, and astronomy, as well as in aeronautics and aerospace. This catalog is available free of charge. The order number is N 83-33792. Contact: National Technical Information Service, Department of Commerce, 5285 Port Royal Road, Springfield, VA 22161/703-487-4600.

Remote Sensing. Applications Grants
Through grants to universities, NASA seeks to develop new sources of remote sensing expertise within the states, with the goal of facilitating independent state or local government use of the technology. Contact: University Programs, Earth Science and Applications Division, Science and Applications, National Aeronautics and Space Administration, 600 Independence Ave. S.W., Room B1219, Washington, DC 20546/202-453-1706

Remote Sensing Technology
NASA conducts a Remote Sensing Appications Program to assist states in the use of Landsat technology for operations problems. Information about Landsat capabilities is available. Contact: Regional Remote Sensing Applications Program, Space Science and Applications, National Aeronautics and Space Administration, 600 Independence Ave. S.W., Room B209, Washington, DC 20546/202-453-1754

Report to Educators
This free quarterly is aimed at the community of educators, especially at the elementary and secondary school levels. Contact: Educational Services Branch, Public Affairs Division, National Aeronautics and Space Administration, 400 Maryland Ave. S.W., Room F6052, Washington, DC 20546/202-453-8388

Research and Technology Operations Plan Summary
This yearly summary is designed to facilitate communications and coordination among concerned technical personnel in government, industry and universities. It describes NASA's Research and Development objectives, identifies the installation of primary interest and provides a point of contact for technical information. The summary can be purchased from the National Technical Information Service, Department of Commerce, Springfield, VA 22151/487-4600. Price varies according to year requested. For additional information, contact: Office of Procurement, National Aeronautics and Space Administration, 300 7th St. S.W., Room B101, Washington, DC 20546/202-453-2090

Research Software Engineering Projects
The Goddard Space Flight Center maintains several different ongoing research software engineering projects, some of which are developed in conjunction with the Computer Science Department of the University of Maryland. The personnel can be helpful and refer you to other sources of information. Contact: Goddard Space Flight Center, National Aeronautics and Space Administration, Code 702, Greenbelt, MD 20771/301-344-6846.

Scientific and Technical Aerospace Reports (STAR)
A semi-monthly list of more than 1,000 citations of articles and publications of interest to the aerospace community is available. The annual subscription cost is $100.00. Both are available from the Superintendent of Documents, Government Printing Office, Washington, DC 20402/202-783-3238. For further information, contact: Scientific and Technical Information Branch, Information Systems Division, National Aeronautics and Space Administration, 300 7th St. S.W., Room 823, Washington, DC 20546/202-453-2912

Scientific and Technical Information
This office is responsible for collecting, abstracting, announcing and disseminating the reports resulting from the work performed by NASA and its contractors, subcontractors and grantees. It is also responsible for locating, acquiring, and disseminating to the NASA community scientific and technical information originating outside the NASA complex. For further information on available publications, contact: Scientific and Technical Information Facility, Information Systems Division, National Aeronautics and Space Administration, P.O. Box 8758, Baltimore/Washington International Airport, MD 21240.

Selling to NASA
This is a free brochure which describes NASA, its organization and activities, and provides guidance on doing business with the agency. Contact: Office of Small and Disadvantaged Business Utilization, National Aeronautics and Space Administration, 600 Independence Ave. S.W., Room B116, Washington, DC 20546/202-453-2088

Slidell Computer Complex (SCC)
SCC is primarily responsible for fulfilling the computations requirements of NASA. These include scientific, management, and engineering automated data processing and in static and flight test data reduction evaluation. Contact: Marshall Space Flight Center, National Aeronautics and Space Administration, Marshall Space Flight Center, AL 35812/205-453-0031.

Solar Flare Hotline
A hotline designed to inform the public of solar flares erupting on the sun is provided jointly by NASA and the National Oceanic and Atmospheric Administration. Information on sunspots, solar

flares, geomagnetic storms, and the impact of the sun's behavior on radio transmissions will be provided in daily recorded messages which will include reports on the locations of active regions on the Sun, as well as on experiments being conducted aboard NASA's Solar Maximum Mission Spacecraft during the next 24-hour period. Contact: Solar Maximum Mission's Experiment Operations Facility, Goddard Space Flight Center, National Aeronautics and Space Administration, Greenbelt, MD 20771/301-344-8825

Space Activity Related Cryogenics Resource

The Goddard Space Flight Center is involved with cryogenics related to space activities. Applications include long term storage of cryogens on space stations; long term cooling of infrared instruments with large aperture heat which involve earth observations, atmospheric science, meteorological satellites; gamma ray and x-ray astronomy, and long-term storage of liquid helium which requires thermal shielding and the elimination of aperture heat loads with a mechanical cooler. The staff at Goddard can answer your questions, and technical papers are available upon request. Contact: Goddard Space Flight Center, National Aeronautics and Space Administration, Code 713, Greenbelt, MD 20771/301-344-5405.

Space and Terrestrial Applications

This office is responsible for all research and development activities that demonstrate the application of space related technology, systems and other capabilities which can be effectively applied and used in the civil sector for practical benefits to mankind. The R&D activities are grouped in the following areas: weather and climate, pollution monitoring, Earth resources survey, Earth and ocean physics applications, space processing, communications, data management and applications experiments and studies. Contact: Public Affairs, Space Science and Terrestrial Applications, National Aeronautics and Space Administration, 600 Independence Ave. S.W., Room B168, Washington, DC 20546/202-453-1754

Space, Man & Flight

NASA has prepared many beautifully illustrated publications about space and aerospace activities. Many are geared toward students and the general public. The publications listed below are all available free of charge from: Publications, Public Affairs Division, National Aeronautics and Space Administration, 400 Maryland Ave. S.W., Washington, DC 20546/202-453-8332.

Aboard the Space Shuttle—this describes what it would be like to live in space—how you'd get there, what the trip would be like, what you'd eat, how you'd exercise and sleep and finally how you would return home.
Aerospace Bibliography—provides a listing of fiction and nonfiction books and pamphlets available from both commercial and government sources. Reading level, which ranges from grade 1 through adult, is indicated.
Elementary School Aerospace Activities—a resource guide for teachers, this manual provides activities, research project ideas, bibliographic information and more to help instructors teach students about the story of man and flight, with emphasis on flight into space.
Mars: The Viking Discoveries—includes photographs and information about Mars.
NASA 1958–1983—a beautifully illustrated history of NASA, covering events such as the Apollo mission, Man's landing on the moon, and presenting photographs of the planets as photographed in space.
The Space Shuttle at Work—this booklet describes the space transportation system: how it came to be, why it is designed the way it is, what we expect of it, and how it may grow.
The Voyager Flights to Jupiter and Saturn—describes with pictures and narrative the Voyager Flights to Jupiter and Saturn.
The World of Tomorrow: Aerospace Activities for 8 to 10-year-olds—a guide for leaders of children's groups and teachers of the lower grades, this presents projects kids can work on.
Sun, Earth and Man: the Need to Know and the Quest for Knowledge of Sun-Earth Relations—discusses the relationship of the sun, earth and man covering before Sputnik, the Age of Space, the Eighties, and the future.
Viking: The Exploration of Mars—includes information about Viking's mission and findings. The booklet also displays pictures taken in space.
What's New on the Moon?—answers questions such as: Is there life on the moon? What is the moon made of? How old is the moon? and more.
Spacelab—this publication explains what Spacelab is, introduces you to the crew, describes Spacelab experiments, and takes you through a day aboard the aircraft.
Spacelab Poster—a 3½' × 4' color illustration of Spacelab.
Spacestation: The Next Logical Step—with pictures and narrative, this booklet shows you what the spacestation will look like, how it will work, the ways industry will set up shop in space, and what the spacestation means to nations and individuals.

Space Science

This office is responsible for all NASA activities involving the conduct of scientific investigations in space. These activities include the planning, development and conduct of space missions in physics and astronomy, and lunar and planetary exploration as well as solar terrestrial interactions and life sciences investigations. Contact: Public Affairs, Space Science, National Aeronautics and Space Administration, 400 Maryland Ave. S.W., Room F6051, Washington DC 20546/202-453-1754

Space Shuttle Program (Johnson Space Center)

This Center manages the Space Shuttle Program.

Contact: Johnson Space Center, National Aeronautics and Space Administration, Houston, TX 77058/713-471-3210.

Space Station Program
Plans are underway to develop a permanently manned space station within a decade. Research on this project is dispersed among four NASA Field Centers under the direction of NASA Headquarters. The centers are managing contracts with a number of aerospace companies for definition and preliminary design of the space station. Contact: Office of Space Station, National Aeronautics and Space Administration, 400 Maryland Avenue S.W., Washington, DC 20546/202-453-2958.

Space Tracking and Data Acquisitions
This office is responsible for the development and operation of communications, tracking of launch vehicles and spacecraft, data acquisition, and data processing facilities, systems and services required for support of NASA flight programs. The office is also assigned NASA-wide responsibility for administrative communications management and frequency management. Contact: Public Affairs, Space Aeronautics and Technology, National Aeronautics and Space Administration, 400 Maryland Ave. S.W., Room F6091, Washington, DC 20546/202-453-2754.

Space Transportation Operations
This office operates the space transportation systems for the benefit of all users. It is responsible for the management, direction and coordination of all civil launch capabilities and Spacelab development, procurement and operations. Contact: Public Affairs, Office of Space Flight, National Aeronautics and Space Administration, 400 Maryland Ave. S.W., Room B325 Washington, DC 20546/202-453-8590.

Space Transportation Systems
This office is responsible for NASA activities directly involving manned space flight missions. Its principal mission is to develop a new space transportation system significantly improving man and instrument access to space. The Space Shuttle is the key element of the system that will service a wide variety of users. The Shuttle will provide multipurpose, economic space operations for Earth applications, scientific and technologic payloads. Contact: Public Affairs, Office of Space Flight, National Aeronautics and Space Administration, 600 Independence Ave. S.W., Room B325, Washington, DC 20546/202-453-8590.

Speakers
Speakers are available to address education, civic, scientific and similar groups. For information, contact: Speakers Bureau, Public Affairs Division,

National Aeronautics and Space Administration, 400 Maryland Ave. S.W., Room F6093, Washington, DC 20546/202-453-8315.

Spinoff
Spinoff is an annual report describing the many uses of space-developed technology in everyday products and processes and NASA's program to encourage the transfer of such technology to commercial and industrial markets. Sold, for $4.75 by the Superintendent of Documents, Government Printing Office, Washington, DC 20402/202-783-3238.

State Technology Applications Centers
These centers facilitate technology transfer to state and local governments, as well as to private industry. They provide information retrieval services and technical assistance to industrial and government clients. Contact: Technology Utilization and Industry Division Inter-governmental Branch, National Aeronautics and Space Administration, 600 Independence Ave. S.W., Room 5113, Washington, DC 20546/202-453-8415.

Tech Briefs
This is a free, indexed, quarterly journal containing articles on innovations and improved products or processes developed for NASA which are thought to have commercial potential. Articles are grouped into nine broad technical categories and special sections are included for books and reports, computer programs and new product ideas. Information on NASA's Patent Licensing Program and additional services are also provided. For additional information, contact: Technology Utilization and Industry Division, National Aeronautics and Space Administration, 600 Independence Ave. S.W., Room 5113, Washington, DC 20546/202-453-8415.

Technology Utilization and Industry Affairs
NASA's Technology Utilization program offers a variety of free publications and personnel services to help transfer aerospace technology to nonaerospace applications. NASA TU information is restricted to U.S. citizens and U.S.-based industry. Their publications include:

NASA Tech Briefs—published quarterly and free to engineers in U.S. industry and to other domestic technology transfer agents. It is both a current awareness medium and a problem-solving tool. Potential products, industrial processes, basic and applied research, shop and lab techniques, computer software, new sources of technical data concepts, can be found.

NASA Tech Brief Journal—a free quarterly publication covering 125 new technologies in each issue.
NASA Annual Report—produced to make the public aware of practical investments in aerospace research,

the document contains a section profiling at least 35 companies that have used NASA technologies to improve their products. Issued each June or July.

Special Publications Series—NASA TU publishes technology utilization notes; handbooks and bibliographies on specific technologies; conference proceedings; technology utilization surveys on anything from advanced valve technology to measurement of blood pressure in the human body; and technology utilization reports and compilations which include all types of documents about products, processes, and other topics in the technology utilization field.

For copies of these publications and further information contact: NASA Technology Utilization and Industry Affairs Division, NASA Scientific and Technical Information Facility, PO Box 8757, BWI Airport, MD 21240/301-621-0241.

Wall Display Sheets
Color display sheets of various sizes describe a NASA project or a specific technology. Some examples of Wall Display Sheets include:

Ten Years of Planetary Exploration
WAL-102 Space Lab: 10–15 Years in the Future

These wall displays can be bought (prices vary) from the Superintendent of Documents, Government Printing Office, Washington, DC 20402/202-783-3238. For additional information, contact: Public Affairs Division, National Aeronautics and Space Administration, 400 Maryland Ave. S.W., Room F6037, Washington, DC 20546/202-453-8330.

How Can the National Aeronautics and Space Administration Help You?
For information on how this agency can help you, contact: Headquarters Information Center, National Aeronautics and Space Administration, Lobby, 600 Independence Ave. S.W., Washington, DC 20546/202-453-8400.

National Archives and Records Administration

8th and Pennsylvania Ave. N.W., Washington, DC 20408/202-523-3099

Established: 1934
Budget: $99,109,000
Employees: 1715

Mission: Preserves and makes available for further government use and for private research the nation's records of enduring value; operates the Presidential library system; controls and has custody of the Nixon and Carter Presidential historical materials; administers a regional network of storage facilities for Federal agencies' records, prior to their disposition; and publishes a wide variety of public documents.

Major Sources of Information

Archival Project Grants
Three times a year the Commission reviews proposals and makes grants for the preservation and publication of documentary source materials significant to American history. Major ongoing projects include the papers of Thomas Jefferson, Frederick Douglass, and Jane Addams. The following publications are available free on request: "Publications Program Guidelines and Procedures: Applications and Grants," "Records Program Guidelines and Procedures: Applications and Grants," "Suggestions for Records Program Applicants," and "Fellowships in Historical Editing." Contact: National Historical Publications and Records Commission, National Archives and Records Administration, 8th and Pennsylvania Ave. N.W., Washington, DC 20408/202-523-5384.

Airline Transportation Data Files
The Machine-Readable Branch has records pertaining to the airline industry. Contact: Machine-Readable Branch, National Archives and Records Administration, 8th and Pennsylvania Ave. N.W., Room 20E, Washington, DC 20408/202-523-3267.

Civilian Military Personnel Records
The records of civilian employees in the military service of the Army, Navy and Air Force are part of this archival collection. Contact: National Personnel Records Center, National Archives and Records Administration, 9700 Page Boulevard, St. Louis, Mo 63132/314-263-7247.

Conferences, Workshops and Tours
This office sponsors public lectures, workshops, tours, scholarly conferences ranging from genealogical conferences to ongoing Constitutional Study group meetings. To receive the monthly "Calendar" which lists upcoming events, contact: Office of Public Affairs, National Archives and Records Administration, 8th and Pennsylvania Ave. N.W., Room G-6, Washington, DC 20408/202-523-3099.

Continental Congress and Other Diplomatic Papers
Famous treaties and other diplomatic records dating back to the Continental Congress are part of this archival collection. Contact: Diplomatic Branch, National Archives and Records Administration, 8th and Pennsylvania Ave. N.W., Room 5E, Washington, DC 20408/202-523-3174.

Declassified Government Documents
Security-classified records are reviewed for declassification using guidelines prepared by agencies having jurisdiction over the information. Papers from the Office of Strategic Services pertaining to World War II intelligence are still being processed. Contact: Records Declassification Division, Office of the National Archives, National Archives and Records Administration, 8th and Pennsylvania Ave. N.W., Washington, DC 20408/202-523-3165.

Economics Data
This branch serves as the primary tape distribution point for export/import data as well as other sources of economic data including that generated by the Census Bureau and the Bureau of Economic Analysis. Contact: Machine-Readable Branch, National Archives and Records Administration, 8th and Pennsylvania Ave. N.W., Washington, DC 20408/202-523-3267.

Educational Research
This Special Archives Division maintains a large collection of information generated by the Department of Education and other government agencies involved with educational research. Contact: Machine-Readable Branch, National Archives and Records Administration, 8th and Pennsylvania Ave. N.W., Washington, DC 20408/202-523-3267.

Family/Military Genealogy
This collection has personnel records from the Revolutionary War through 1910 and is the proper branch for doing family research on individuals who served in the military. Contact: Military Service Branch, Military Archives Division, National Archives and Records Administration, 8th and Pennsylvania Ave. N.W., Room 8E, Washington, DC 20408/202-523-3223.

Federal Employees' Attitudes
This collection maintains past surveys of attitudes held by civil servants as well as information pertaining to sexual harassment. Contact: Machine-Readable Branch, National Archives and Records Administration, 8th and Pennsylvania Ave. N.W., Room 20E, Washington, DC 20408/202-523-3267.

Federal Employees' Personnel Records
The pay records as well as other personnel documents of federal employees are held in the National Personnel Records Center. Contact: National Personnel Records Center, National Archives and Records Administration, 111 Winnebago Street, St. Louis, MO 63118/314-425-5722.

Federal Records
Semiactive and noncurrent federal records are in 13 regional records centers, the National Personnel Records Center and the Washington National Records Center. Major holdings include the records of the Department of Defense; Department of the Treasury, primarily IRS; Department of Health and Human Services, mostly the Social Security Administration; and the Veterans Administration. Contact: Office of Federal Records Centers-NC, National Archives and Records Administration, 8th and Pennsylvania Ave. N.W., Washington, DC 20408/202-724-1625.

Federal Rules and Regulations
This office is responsible for publishing the *Federal Register* every federal working day which contains Executive orders and Presidential proclamations, proposed and final agency regulations having general applicability and legal effect, and notices of agency activities of interest to the public. *The Code of Federal Regulations* (CFR) is revised annually and is a codification of all regulations. The *Federal Register* costs $300/year and *CFR* can be purchased for $550/year from Superintendent of Documents, Government Printing Office, Washington, DC 20402/202-783-3238. For more information about the rulemaking process, contact: Office of Federal Register, National Archives and Records Administration, 8th and Pennsylvania Ave. N.W., Room 8401, Washington, DC 20408/202-523-5230.

Fellowships
The Commission selects six individuals each year for its records and publications programs. "Fellowships In Historical Editing" is available free. For application information, contact National Historical Publications and Records Commission, National Archives and Records Administration, 8th and Pennsylvania Ave. N.W., Washington, DC 20408/202-523-5384.

Films
Approximately 91 million feet of documentary and newsreel footage and other government-produced films constitute this collection. Materials can be screened and footage can be purchased. For more information, contact: Motion Picture and Video and Sound Branch, National Archives and Records Administration, 8th and Pennsylvania Ave. N.W., Room G-13, Washington, DC 20408/202-786-0041.

Genealogy Research
A free 17-page booklet, "Genealogy Records In

The National Archives," is a useful guide prior to beginning research on one's family tree. *Genealogical Research In The National Archives,* a valuable and popular paperback can be purchased for $19.00 from National Archives. Your local public, college or genealogical library can obtain certain National Archives Records such as ship passenger records from 1820, military records from the Revolutionary War, and census forms from 1790–1910. One-month rentals at nominal rates are available. For more information and help with your research, contact: Reference Service Branch, National Archives and Records Administration, 8th and Pennsylvania Ave. N.W., Room 205, Washington, DC 20408/202-523-3218.

Grants
The program below describes sums of money which are given by the federal government to initiate or stimulate new or improved activities.

National Historical Publications and Records Grants
Objectives: To carry out the National Historical Documents Program which will help preserve important historical documents.
Eligibility: States, units of local government, educational and other nonprofit institutions (universities, colleges, libraries, historical societies, museums, university presses, archives).
Range of Financial Assistance: $1,000 to $198,000.
Contact: National Historical Publications and Records Commission, National Archives and Records Administration, 8th and Pennsylvania Ave. N.W., Washington, DC 20408/202-523-5384.

Historical Memorabilia and Souvenirs
Numerous books and other materials can be purchased at Presidential libraries or from the National Archives. Facsimiles of treaties and other significant documents such as the Declaration of Independence and the Constitution of the U.S. are also available. Request a free price list as well as a 40-page pamphlet, "Reproductions of Historical Documents in the National Archives." Contact: Publications Sales Branch, National Archives and Records Administration, 8th and Pennsylvania Ave. N.W., Washington, DC 20408/202-523-3181.

Internal Revenue Service Information
This archival collection contains tax models and other relevant material from the U.S. Internal Revenue Service. Contact: Machine-Readable Branch, National Archives and Records Administration, 8th and Pennsylvania Ave. N.W., Room 20E, Washington, DC 20408/202-523-3267.

Machine-Readable Records
This Branch functions as a clearinghouse for information on the existence, location and availability of data created by other federal agencies.

The staff routinely provide researchers with tape copies or printouts of the records in its custody. The fees for such services are relatively low and are set solely to recover the costs involved in preparing and processing files for distribution. A major portion of this collection is from the Vietnam War. The *Catalog of Machine-Readable Records in the National Archives of the United States* contains bibliographic and abstract entries for the files in its holdings and in the Center for Machine-Readable Records. *Computer Data Bulletin,* a supplement to the Catalog, announces the recent and upcoming accessions or additions to the Center. For further information, contact: Machine-Readable Branch, Special Archives Division, National Archives and Records Administration, 8th and Pennsylvania Ave. N.W., Room 20E, Washington, DC 20408/202-523-3267.

Magazines and Newsletters
"Prologue," a quarterly magazine includes articles on topics of American history and culture since 1969. It provides timely information about National Archives conferences, publications and accessions, and the latest on declassified documents. It is for sale for $8 per year from the Publications Sales Branch, National Archives and Records Administration, 8th and Pennsylvania Ave. N.W., Room 505, Washington, DC 20408/202-523-3164. "Annotation" is a free newsletter which reports on archival research projects. Contact the National Historical Publications and Records Commission, National Archives and Records Administration, 8th and Pennsylvania Ave. N.W., Washington, DC 20408/202-523-5384.

Maps and Architectural Drawings
Over 1.6 million maps from early 1792–1981 are part of this archival collection. Census maps from 1880–1960 are also available as well as architectural drawings of forts, government buildings and post offices. For further details and information about purchasing copies, contact: Cartographic and Architectural Branch, Special Archives Division, National Archives and Records Administration, 8th and Pennsylvania Ave. N.W., Room 703, Washington, DC 20408/202-756-6700.

Military Data Files
Approximately 50 machine-readable data files originally created by the Department of Defense are now in the holdings of the Machine Readable Archives Division. Most of the collection deals with the Vietnam War, collected in Vietnam by the military headquarters of General Westmoreland. Other machine-readable files include the "American Soldier," a set of over 200 attitudinal and demographic studies covering more than 500,000 officers and enlisted Army personnel which were conducted by the War Department General Staff during World War II. Contact: Machine-Readable

Archives Branch, Special Archives Division, National Archives and Records Administration, 8th and Pennsylvania Ave. N.W., Room 20E, Washington, DC 20408/202-523-3267.

Modern Archives Institute

A two-week training course is taught jointly by the Library of Congress and the National Archives. The course, which is accredited with many colleges and universities, costs approximately $400 and is held in January and June of each year. Contact: National Archives and Records Administration, 8th and Pennsylvania Ave. N.W., Washington, DC 20408/202-523-3616.

National Archives Publications

Over 200 publications are available and are listed in "Select List of Publications and the National Archives and Records Service." This pamphlet can be obtained free of charge from the Publications Sales Branch, National Archives and Records Administration, 8th and Pennsylvania Ave. N.W., Room 505, Washington, DC 20408/202-523-3164.

National Audiovisual Center

This Center is the central clearinghouse of all federally produced or financed audiovisual materials. Copies of government motion pictures, audio tapes, slide sets and videotapes are for sale, rental or loan to the public. The Archives also contain some great works of American film made by some well-known directors, as well as miles of historical combat footage. Conversions of any of the Center's 16mm titles to videocassette formats are made upon request. Individual "subject listings" on 22 topics are available free including: agriculture, alcohol/drug abuse, business/government management, career education, consumer education, dentistry, emergency medical services, fire and law enforcement, flight/meteorology, foreign language instruction, history, industry safety, library/information science, medicine, nursing, science, social issues, social science, space exploration, special education and vocational education. Also available free from the Center is "A Reference List of Audiovisual Materials Produced by the U.S. Government." Contact: National Audiovisual Center, National Archives and Records Administration, 8700 Edgeworth Drive, Capitol Heights, MD 20743/301-763-1896.

Navy Vessel Muster Rolls

This office has the list of men who served on all naval vessels during World War II. Contact: Military Services Branch, Military Archives Division, National Archives and Records Administration, 8th and Pennsylvania Ave. N.W., Room 8E, Washington, DC 20408/202-523-3223.

New Federal Laws

This office has information about recently enacted laws and publishes the annual *United States Statutes At Large.* Contact: Office of the Federal Register, National Archives and Records Administration, 8th and Pennsylvania Ave. N.W., Room 8401, Washington, DC 20408/202-523-5230.

Patent and Trademark Drawings

Elaborate patent and trademark drawings from the 19th century constitute a part of this particular archival collection. Copies of originals can be purchased for a nominal fee. For further information, contact: Cartographic and Architectural Branch, National Archives and Records Administration, 8th and Pennsylvania Ave. N.W., Washington, DC 20408/202-756-6700.

Photographs

Duplicate negatives and 8 × 10 prints can be purchased for a nominal fee. Included in this archival collection of five million photographs are pictures of the New West taken by the first geologists in the 19th century as well as photos by Ansel Adams and other famous photographers. For details about the availability of particular photographs and prices, contact: Still Pictures Branch, National Archives and Records Administration, 8th and Pennsylvania Ave. N.W., Room 18N, Washington, DC 20408/202-523-3236.

Presidential Documents and Public Papers

The President's public speeches, remarks, letters and memoranda, and a digest of his activities are published each week in the *Weekly Compilation of Presidential Documents,* and annually in the *Public Papers of the Presidents.* For example, *Book One of Public Papers 1983: Ronald Reagan* is available for $31 from the Superintendent of Documents, Government Printing Office, Washington, DC 20402/202-783-3238. For further details, contact: Office of the Federal Register, National Archives and Records Administration, 8th and Pennsylvania Ave. N.W., Room 8401, Washington, DC 20408/2092-523-5230.

Presidential Libraries

The libraries preserve, describe and provide reference service on presidential papers and collections, prepare documentary and descriptive publications, and exhibit historic documents. Besides items that are sold at the Presidential Library Museums, free booklets are available such as "President Truman and The Atomic Bomb" and "The Kennedys: A Reading List for Young People." For additional information, contact the individual library of your interest:

Herbert Hoover Presidential Library, West Branch, IA 52358/319-643-5301.

Franklin D. Roosevelt Library, 259 Albany Post Road, Hyde Park, NY 12538/914-229-8114.

Harry S. Truman Library, Highway 24 at Delaware St., Independence, MO 64050/816-833-1400.

Dwight D. Eisenhower Library, Southeast 4th St., Abilene, KS 67410/913-263-471.

John F. Kennedy Library, Columbia Point, Boston, MA 02125/67-929-4500.

Lyndon B. Johnson Library, 2313 Red River St., Austin, TX 78705/512-482-5137.

Gerald R. Ford Library, 1000 Beal Ave., Ann Arbor, MI 48109/313-668-2218.

For information regarding the Richard M. Nixon Library, contact: Nixon Presidential Materials Project, National Archives and Records Administration, 8th and Pennsylvania Ave, N.W., Washington, DC 20408/703-756-6498. Reference help regarding the Jimmy E. Carter Library, contact: Carter Presidential Materials Project, 77 Forsyth St. SW, Atlanta, GA 30303/404-221-3942.

Prisoner-of-War Records
This collection contains records of POWs through the Korean War. Contact: Military Service Branch, Military Archives Division, National Archives and Records Administration, 8th and Pennsylvania Ave. N.W., Room 8E, Washington, DC 20408/202-523-3223.

Reference Services
Reference help to scholars, the general public and government agencies is provided in a variety of ways: records or microfilm copies of records can be examined in one of the National Archives research rooms: information from or about records is furnished over the phone or by mail; and, for a fee, copies of textual and nontextual records are furnished by mail or in person to researchers. A free *Researchers' Guide to the National Archives* is a helpful introduction to the vast collection and available resources. The Reference Service Branch is the best place to begin when one starts their research at the National Archives. Free orientation and consultation by staff and trained volunteers are available. Contact: Reference Service Branch, Central Information Division, National Archives and Records Administration, 8th and Pennsylvania Ave. N.W., Room 205, Washington, DC 20408/202-523-3218.

Revolutionary War Records to 1940
This collection contains records dating back to the Revolutionary War. For more details, contact: Navy and Old Army Branch, Military Archives Division, National Archives and Records Administration, 8th and Pennsylvania Ave. N.W., Room 8W, Washington, DC 20408/202-523-3229.

Securities and Public Offerings
Magnetic tapes are available pertaining to public offerings of securities and other records held by the Securities and Exchange Commission. Contact: Machine-Readable Branch, National Archives and Records Administration, 8th and Penn-

sylvania Ave. N.W., Room 20E, Washington, DC 20408/202-523-3267.

Social Studies and Curriculum Kits
Curriculum kits for secondary school students which include facsimiles of documents and classroom workbook exercises are available. An example is "The Constitution: Evolution Of A Government." For more information, contact: Office of Public Programs and Exhibits, National Archives and Records Administration, 8th and Pennsylvania Ave. N.W., Washington, DC 20408/202-523-3097.

State Historical Records
State assessment and reporting grants are supporting the preservation and description of historical source materials. A useful publication, "The State Historical Records Coordinator and the State Historical Records Advisory Board: Suggested Roles and Procedures," is available free. Contact the local State Historical Records Advisory Board or the National Historical Publications and Records Administration, 8th and Pennsylvania Ave. N.W., Washington, DC 20408/202-523-5384.

Vice-Presidential Papers
Records including all documentary materials of the Vice President and staff relating to his duties beginning with George Bush are owned by the U.S. Government. Materials related soley to private political associations or purely personal matters are retained by the Vice President. Contact: Office of Presidential Libraries, National Archives and Records Administration, 8th and Pennsylvania Ave. N.W., Room 104, Washington, DC 20408/202-523-3212.

Video and Sound Recordings
This archival collection contains 122,000 video and sound recordings including recordings from such government agencies as the Works Progress Administration, the Office of War Information and the US Information Agency. Private holdings include the ABC Collection. For further information on obtaining copies, contact: Motion Picture and Video and Sound Branch, National Archives and Records Administration, 8th and Pennsylvania Ave. N.W., Washington, DC 20408/202-786-0041.

Vietnam War
These files fall into five general subject areas: government and population and South Vietnam; ground operations; air operations including lists of combat and noncombat air missions in North and South Vietnam; naval operations; and the allied incursion into Cambodia. Contact: Machine-Readable Archives Branch, National Archives and Records Administration, 8th and Pennsylvania

Ave. N.W., Room 20E, Washington, DC 20408/202-523-3267.

Watergate Tapes and Transcripts

Approximately 12½ hours of recorded conversations from the Oval Office between President Richard Nixon and Attorney General John Mitchell as well as others are part of this collection. Transcripts of the Watergate tapes can be purchased and large groups that want to listen to the tapes should make arrangements in advance prior to going directly to 845 South Pickett St., Alexandria, VA 22304. For further information, contact: Nixon Presidential Materials Project, Office of Presidential Libraries, National Archives and Records Administration, 8th and Pennsylvania Ave. N.W., Washington, DC 20408/703-756-6498.

World War II Papers

This collection has records from 1940–1954 including documents of the War Production Board, International Tribunal, War Department and other headquarters records such as those of the Joint Chiefs of Staff. Contact: Modern Military Headquarters, Military Archives Division, National Archives and Records Administration, 8th and Pennsylvania Ave. N.W., Room 13W, Washington, DC 20408/202-523-3340.

How Can The National Archives Help You?

For further information regarding research or resources, contact: Office of Public Affairs, National Archives and Records Administration, 8th and Pennsylvania Ave. N.W., Washington, DC 20408/202-523-3099.

National Capital Planning Commission

1325 G St. N.W., Washington, DC 20576/202-724-0174

Established: 1952
Budget: $2,404,000
Employees: 48

Mission: Responsible for the overall coordination of planning and development activities in the National Capital region and is the central planning agency for the federal government in this region. Its area of jurisdiction includes the District of Columbia and all land areas within the boundaries of Montgomery and Prince George counties in Maryland; and Fairfax, Loudoun, Prince William, and Arlington counties in Virginia.

Major Sources of Information

Commission Activities

Commission responsibilities include review of all proposed zoning regulations, map changes, and amendments to the District of Columbia zoning ordinance in order to insure compatibility of zoning regulations with the federal interest as expressed in the Comprehensive Plan. The Commission also adopts urban renewal area boundaries; prepares, adopts, and modifies urban renewal plans; approves the Permanent System of Highways Plan; makes recommendations on proposed street and alley closings; approves transfers of jurisdiction over properties between federal and district; approves the sale of surplus property and park land, and acquires land for parks and parkways in the National Capital region. Contact: Technical Services and Special Studies Division, National Capital Planning Commission, 1325 G St. N.W., Room 1034, Washington, DC 20576/202-724-0196.

Comprehensive Plan for the National Capital

The Comprehensive Plan is a statement of policies dealing with the growth and development of the National Capital; and consists of both federal and district elements. It provides a framework for policy decisions regarding physical development

proposed by federal, state, local and regional agencies. It describes how the Washington area should appear in future years. The plan includes:

BACKGROUND STUDIES
  Federal Employment
  Federal Building Spaces
  Federal Land
ENVIRONMENT
  Proposed Element
  Implementation Proposals
  Planning Report
FOREIGN MISSIONS AND INTERNATIONAL AGENCIES
  Adopted element and related modification to the elements
  Planning Report and Description of Environmental Impact
REVIEW OF PLANNING POLICIES AND PROPOSALS AFFECTING FEDERAL LAND USE AND EMPLOYMENT IN THE NATIONAL CAPITAL REGION
URBAN DESIGN—TOPOGRAPHIC BOWL—ARLINGTON
  Proposed Element
  Implementation Proposals
  Planning Report
  Environmental Assessment

Contact: Planning and Programming Division, National Capital Planning Commission, 1325 G St.

N.W., Room 1023, Washington, DC 20576/202-724-0171.

Construction Approval
Federal public buildings in the District of Columbia and District of Columbia buildings in the central area of the District must be approved prior to construction. Contact: Review and Implementation Division, National Capital Planning Commission, 1325 G St. N.W., Room 1014, Washington, DC 20576/202-724-0188.

National Capital Planning Commission Quarterly Review of Commission Proceedings
This quarterly review provides a summary of Commission actions and information related to change, growth and development in the Washington, DC area. An index covering each series of four issues is included at the end of every calendar year. Contact: Office of Public Affairs, National Capital Planning Commission, 1325 G St. N.W., Room 1075, Washington, DC 20576/202-724-0174.

Planning Washington 1924–1976: An Era of Planning for the National Capital and Environs
This free publication provides an administrative and legislative history of the National Capital Planning Commission and its predecessor agencies. It also includes a biographic register with biographic sketches of Commission members and Executive Directors. To get a free copy or addi-tional information, contact: Office of Public Affairs, National Capital Planning Commission, 1325 G St. N.W., Room 1075, Washington, DC 20576/202-724-0174.

Publications
A list of publications is available from the National Capital Planning Commission. It includes the comprehensive plans and plans for specific areas, studies subjects such as urban and landscape design and other related subjects. Contact: Office of Public Affairs, National Capital Planning Commission, 1325 G St. N.W., Room 1075, Washington, DC 20576/202-724-0174.

Reviews
Plans and programs proposed by federal, state, regional and local agencies or jurisdictions in the National Capital Region are reviewed in this office. Each federal or district project is also reviewed. Contact: Review and Implementation Division, National Capital Planning Commission, 1325 G St. N.W., Room 1014, Washington, DC 20576/202-724-0188.

How Can the National Capital Planning Commission Help You?
For information on how this agency can help you, contact: National Capital Planning Commission, 1325 G St. N.W., Washington, DC 20576/202-724-0174.

National Credit Union Administration

1776 G St. N.W., Washington, DC 20456/202-357-1000

Established: March 10, 1970
Budget: $55,342,000
Employees: 685

Mission: Responsible for chartering, insuring, supervising, and examining federal credit unions (FCUs), and for administering the National Credit Union Share Insurance Fund, and manages the Central Liquidity Facility, a mixed-ownership government corporation whose purpose is to supply emergency loans to member credit unions. (A credit union [CU] is a financial cooperative which aids its members by improving their economic situation through encouraging thrift among its members and providing them with a source of credit for provident purposes at reasonable rates of interest. Federal CUs serve associations, and occupational and residential groups, thus benefiting a broad range of citizens throughout the country.)

Major Sources of Information

Central Liquidity Facility
This office provides credit unions with a source of funds to meet their liquidity needs. The facility also encourages saving and supports consumer borrowing and mortgage lending. Membership is voluntary and is available to both federal and state-chartered credit unions. For further information, contact: Central Liquidity Facility, National Credit Union Administration, 1776 G St. N.W., Room 7361, Washington, DC 20456/202-357-1132.

Chartering
Federal credit unions are chartered by the National Credit Union Administration after their applications are reviewed and approved. For information on charter requirements, new charters, the numbers and percent of operating Federal Credit Union Charters and other related information, contact: Insurance Division, National Credit Union Administration, 1766 G St. N.W., 7th Floor, Washington, DC 20456/202-357-1010

Credit Union Information
Information on how to start a federal credit union is available. A list of regional National Credit Union Administration offices and a list of publications are also available. Contact: Public Information, National Credit Union Administration, 1776 G St. N.W., Room 6100, Washington, DC 20456/202-357-1050.

Credit Union Supervision
Federal credit unions are supervised in the areas of general ledger accounts, liquidity, investment policy, cash management, data processing and internal control. For additional information, contact: Office of Supervision and Examination Insurance, National Credit Union Administration, 1776 G St. N.W., Room 6670, Washington, DC 20456/202-357-1065.

Examiner Training Programs
The National Credit Union Administration pro-

vides technical training consisting of on-the-job and formalized classroom programs for all examiner staff. The training is available to federal and state examiners. Contact: Training and Program Coordination, Office of Examination and Insurance, National Credit Union Administration, 1776 G St. N.W., Room 6676, Washington, DC 20456/202-357-1055.

Freedom of Information Act Requests
For Freedom of Information Act requests, contact: Freedom of Information, National Credit Union Administration, 1776 G St. N.W., Room 6411, Washington, DC 20456/202-357-1244.

Insured Funds
The share insurance program helps maintain sound conditions in the credit union industry and protects those insured in the event of failure of an insured credit union due to insolvency or bankruptcy. *Your Insured Funds,* a free brochure, describes the National Credit Union Administration share insurance operation. For additional information, contact: Office of Examination and Insurance, National Credit Union Administration, 1776 G St. N.W., 7th floor, Washington, DC 20456/202-357-1010.

Liquidations
Information on Federal Credit Union Charter cancellations includes type of membership and

reason for cancellation, such as poor financial condition, mergers, revocation, etc. Contact: Office of Insurance, National Credit Union Administration, 1776 G St. N.W., 7th floor, Washington, DC 20456/202-357-1010.

Listing of Federal Credit Unions
A master list of the names and addresses of all federal credit unions is available for public scrutiny. Copies of the list may also be obtained. Contact: Freedom of Information Office, National Credit Union Administration, 1776 G St. N.W., Room 6411, Washington, DC 20456/202-357-1242.

Publications
A list of National Credit Union Administration publications, including general, technical and research publications, is available. Contact: Public Information, National Credit Union Administration, 1776 G St. N.W., Room 6100, Washington, DC 20456/202-357-1050.

How Can the National Credit Union Administration Help You?
For information on how this agency can help you, contact: National Credit Union Administration, Public Information, 1776 G St. N.W., Room 6100, Washington, DC 20456/202-357-1050.

National Foundation on the Arts and the Humanities

Institute of Museum Service
1100 Pennsylvania Ave. N.W., Room 510, Washington, DC 20506/202-786-0536.

Established: 1976
Budget: $10,800,000
Employees: 9
Mission: Assists museums in maintaining, increasing and improving their services to the public.

National Endowment for the Arts
1100 Pennsylvania Ave. N.W., Washington, DC 20506/202-682-5400.
Established: 1965
Budget: $144,108,000
Employees: 277
Mission: Fosters professional excellence of the arts in America, nurtures and sustains them, and helps create a climate in which they may flourish so they may be experienced and enjoyed by the widest possible public.

National Endowment for the Humanities
1100 Pennsylvania Ave. N.W., Washington, DC 20506/202-786-0438.
Established: 1965
Budget: $135,447,000
Employees: 253
Mission: Makes grants to individuals, groups, or institutions—schools, colleges, universities, museums, public television stations, libraries, public agencies, and nonprofit private groups—to increase understanding and appreciation of the humanities.

Major Sources of Information

Annual Program Announcement
This free booklet details the humanities programs. It provides information on how to apply for grants and includes a calendar of deadlines and a list of deadlines by program. State Humanities Councils are also listed. Contact: Public Affairs Office, National Endowment for the Humanities, 1100 Pennsylvania Ave, NW Room 617, Washington, DC 20506/202-682-5439.

Artists-in-Education
This program awards education grants in various ways. The national, state-based program places professional artists in elementary and secondary schools: professional and technical assistance is available to specific components of the program; and aid to universities with graduate level programs in arts administration awards fellowships to students. Contact: Artists-in-Education, Public Partnership, National Endowment for the Arts, 1100 Pennsylvania Ave, NW, Room 602, Washington, DC 20506/202-682-5426.

Arts and Artifacts Indemnity
Objectives: To provide for indemnification against loss or damage for eligible art works, artifacts and objects 1) when borrowed from abroad on exhibition in the U.S., and 2) from the U.S. for exhibition abroad when there is an exchange exhibition from a foreign country.
Eligibility: Federal, state and local government entities, nonprofit agencies, institutions and individuals may apply.
Range of Financial Assistance: Up to $50,000,000.
Contact: Director, Museum Program, National Endowment for the Arts, 1100 Pennsylvania Ave, NW, Washington, DC 20506/202-682-5442.

Challenge Grants—Arts
The Challenge Grant Program encourages cultural organizations to achieve financial stability. Grants are awarded only once to institutions who match each government dollar with at least three more dollars raised from other sources. Contact: Chal-

lenge Grants, Private Partnership, National Endowment for the Arts, 1100 Pennsylvania Ave, NW, Room 627, Washington, DC 20506/202-682-5436.

Challenges Grants—Humanities
This program helps institutions increase and broaden their bases of individual and corporate support by offering one federal dollar to match at least three non-federal dollars raised by the institution, either from new sources or from increases beyond the regular contributions of traditional sources. Contact: Challenge Grants Program, National Endowment for the Humanities, National Foundation on the Arts and the Humanities, Room 429, 1100 Pennsylvania Ave, NW, Washington, DC 20506/202-786-0361.

Arts Review, The
The Arts Review is a bimonthly publication, featuring articles on Arts Endowment projects. It includes information on current and upcoming programs, reports of meetings, recent grant recipients, legislative votes, book reviews, and news on the arts from other federal agencies. It also lists grant application deadlines. Available for $10 per year from the Superintendent of Documents, Government Printing Office, Washington, DC 20402/202-783-3238. For additional information, contact: Publications Division, National Foundation on the Arts and Humanities, 1100 Pennsylvania Ave, NW, Room 614, Washington, DC 20506/202-682-5570.

Dance Program
The Endowment is committed to assist American dance. It offers direct support to dance companies and choreographers; it gives grants to strengthen companies' managerial staffs; it promotes and supports dance presentations throughout the country; and it seeks to expose the public to dance. Contact: Dance Program, National Endowment for the Arts, 1100 Pennsylvania Ave, NW, Rm. 621 Washington, DC 20506/202-682-5435.

Design Arts Program
The Design Arts Program aims to support architects, landscape architects, urban designers and city planners, industrial designers, graphic designers, interior designers, and fashion designers in their individual or collective pursuits. Grants are awarded to assist groups in the planning and design of exemplary cultural facilities and to encourage the commitment of local public and private money to carry out projects; to assist the development and dissemination of design ideas and information about design for the public and design professionals; to enable established professionals and those just entering or returning to a design career to take time from their practice for personal career development; to support professional designers who do research on new design concepts or develop ways of educating the public about design; to encourage communities to introduce exemplary design as an integral part of their planning processes; to provide federal and state agencies with professional guidance for upgrading publications; and to assist professional organizations, nonprofit groups and coalitions which advance the cause of design excellence. Superintendent of Documents, Government Printing Office, Washington, DC 20402/202-783-3238. For further information, contact: Design Arts Program, National Endowment for the Arts, 1100 Pennsylvania Ave, NW, Room 625, Washington, DC 20506/202-682-5437.

Elementary and Secondary Education
This program offers support for projects designed to strengthen the teaching of the humanities in elementary and secondary schools. Eligible projects include the development of curricula and curricular material, extended teacher institutes and demonstration projects that will have regional or national impact on the teaching of the humanities. Contact: Elementary and Secondary Education Grants Program Division of Education Program National Endowment for the Humanities, 1100 Pennsylvania Ave, NW, Room 302, Washington, DC 20506/202-786-0377.

Evaluation Reports
Studies and reports provide guidance and technical assistance to the arts programs and to other funders and managers of arts activities. They also demonstrate and document the impact and effectiveness of support for arts programs. Some of the studies include: a study to determine the impact of the Endowments Support to Orchestras; a study to determine the effectiveness of fellowship support to composers and librettists; and an evaluation of the Challenge Grant Program's reporting and grant monitoring system. Contact: Research Division, Policy and Planning, National Endowment for the Arts, 1100 Pennsylvania Ave, NW, Rm. 706, Washington, DC 20506/202-682-5432.

Expansion Arts Program
The Expansion Arts Program supports the development of professionally-directed arts organizations which are deeply rooted in and reflective of the culture of minority, low income, blue collar, rural and tribal communities. Grants are given to help state art agencies and regional arts groups; to help sponsor organizations bring together regional; tour events; to community arts projects for instruction and training; to support public presentations that include community workshops; for special summer projects; for city arts/community arts organizations that serve as models for other groups; to neighborhood arts services; and community arts consortia. Contact: Expansion Arts Program, National Endowment for the Arts, 1100

Pennsylvania Ave., NW, Rm. 761, Washington, DC 20506/202-682-5443.

Federal-State Partnership Program

A variety of grants awarded include Basic State Operating Grants to provide funding for state plans for support of the arts; Basic Regional Operating Grants to support arts programming planned and implemented by state arts agencies on a multi-state basis; Priority Grants on a state and regional level; and Governmental Support Services for projects that assist state and community arts agencies. Contact: State Programs National Endowment for the Arts, 1100 Pennsylvania Ave, NW, Room 602, Washington, DC 20506/202-682-5429.

Fellowships—Arts

The program is designed to acquaint participants with the policies and operations of the Endowment and to help give them an overview of arts activities around the country. Fellows are given the opportunity to learn about the Endowment programs by observing policy development, grant-making procedures, and administration. In addition to working as members of the Endowment's staff, fellows attend a series of seminars and meetings with members of the National Council on the Arts, Endowment panelists, artists, journalists, federal officials, and leading arts administrators. Contact: Fellowship Program, Policy and Planning, National Endowment for the Arts, National Foundation for the Arts and the Humanities, Washington, DC 20506/202-682-5786.

Fellowships—Humanities

Applications for support of individual study and research should be submitted to the Fellowships Division, with these exceptions which should be submitted to the Research Division:

1. The production of reference works and scholarly tools, such as bibliographies, certain editing projects and translations, dictionaries, atlases, and encyclopedias.
2. Any aspect of archeological scholarship.
3. Projects with large research costs other than salary support and travel, such as computer costs, salaries of assistants and consultants' travel costs, and equipment costs.
4. Studies on an aspect of state, local, or regional culture or history where the applicant is not affiliated with an academic institution. College and university applicants with projects of this type should apply to a Fellowships Division program.

Contact: Fellowships Programs Division, National Endowment for the Humanities, Rm. 316, 1100 Pennsylvania Ave., NW, Washington, DC 20506/202-786-0458.

Fellowships at Centers for Advanced Study

This program provides funds to centers for advanced study, research libraries and other equivalent institutions independent of universities to enable them to offer fellowships for study and research in the humanities. Contact: Centers for Advanced Study, Fellowships and Seminars Division, National Endowment for the Humanities, Room 316, 1100 Pennsylvania Ave, NW, Washington, DC 20506/202-786-0466.

Fellowships for College Teachers

These fellowships are intended for teachers in undergraduate colleges and universities and in two-year colleges, especially teachers with heavy teaching loads and limited means of research. Contact: Fellowships for the Professions, Fellowships and Seminar Division, National Endowment for the Humanities, 1100 Pennsylvania Ave, NW, Room 316, Washington, DC 20506/202-786-0466.

Fellowships for Independent Study and Research

Fellowships are awarded to scholars and others who have made significant contributions to humanistic thought and knowledge, or to those whose careers show promise of such contributions. Contact: Fellowship for Independent Study and Research, Division of Fellowships and Seminars, National Endowment for the Humanities, Rm. 316, 1100 Pennsylvania Ave, NW, Washington, DC 20506/202-786-0466.

Folk Arts Program

The Folk Arts Program supports community or family-based arts that have endured through several generations and that carry with them a sense of community aesthetic. The program funds nonprofit, tax-exempt groups such as community and cultural organizations, tribes, media centers, educational institutions, professional societies and state and local government agencies, as well as persons of demonstrated talent who wish to learn traditional music or crafts from a master folk artist. Contact: Folk Arts Program, National Endowment for the Arts, Rm. 724, 1100 Pennsylvania Ave, NW, Washington, DC 20506/202-682-5449.

Freedom of Information Act Requests—Arts

For Freedom of Information Act requests, contact: Office of the General Counsel, National Endowment for the Arts, Rm 522, 1100 Pennsylvania Ave, NW, Washington, DC 20506/202-682-5418.

Freedom of Information Act Requests— Humanities

For freedom of Information Act requests, contact: Office of General Counsel, National Endowment for the Humanities, Rm. 530, 1100 Pennsylvania Ave, NW, Washington, DC 20506/202-786-0322.

Frequent Errors in Applications

Endowment staff members have identified the following seven errors they have encountered frequently while processing applications for grants and fellowships in National Endowment for the Humanities programs:

1. The budget does not relate closely to the activities described in the narrative.
2. The application does not provide all the information requested, including complete identification of the personnel for the project and their qualifications for the assignment.
3. The application is marred by inflated rhetoric and ignorance of similar projects elsewhere.
4. Arguments in support of the application are subjective and unconvincing; application assumes that its reader is familiar with or is predisposed to support the application.
5. The plan of work is missing or is too vague; the application shows disorganization of proposed activities and illogical sequencing of specific tasks.
6. The application is distorted by errors in grammar, fact, spelling, and mathematics; the application is sloppy; a clutter of styles, unreadable copies, and missing papers and cited attachments.
7. The application does not give adequate attention to dissemination/distribution of the products of the project.

Contact: Grants Information, Office of Planning and Policy Assessment, National Endowment for the Humanities, 1100 Pennsylvania Ave. NW, Rm. 205, Washington, DC 20506/202-724-0344/682-5403.

General Research

This program provides support for a wide range of scholarships in the humanities in three major areas: Basic Research, including archeological projects; Research Resources; and Reference Works. Contact: Division of Research Programs National Endowment for the Humanities, 1100 Pennsylvania Ave, NW, Room 316 Washington, DC 20506/202-786-0200.

Gifts and Matching Funds

The National Endowment for the Humanities is authorized to accept gifts which are given to NEH in support of particular projects and to match these gifts with federal funds up to the level of one federal dollar for each gift dollar. For further information, contact: Donations Branch, Grants Office, National Endowment for the Humanities, National Foundation on the Arts and the Humanities, 1100 Pennsylvania Ave, NW, Room 310, Washington, DC 20506/202-786-0310.

Grants

The programs described below are for sums of money which are given by the federal government in order to initiate and stimulate new or improved activities or to sustain various on-going services.

Promotion of the Arts—Advancement Grants

Objectives: To assist arts organizations in strengthening their long-term institutional capacity, and enhancing their artistic quality and diversity.

Eligibility: Grants may be made only to nonprofit organizations if donations to such organizations qualify as a charitable deduction under Section 170 (c) of the Internal Revenue Code of 1954. This definition includes State and local governments and State arts agencies. Individuals are not eligible.

Range of Financial Assistance: $40,000 to $85,000.

Contact: Advancement Grant Program, National Endowment for the Arts, 1100 Pennsylvania Ave., N.W., Washington, DC 20506/202-682-5436.

Promotion of the Arts—Artists-in-Education

Objectives: To provide grants for special innovative projects in arts education.

Eligibility: Grants may be made only to nonprofit organizations if donations to such organizations qualify as a charitable deduction under Section 170 (c) of the Internal Revenue Code of 1954. This definition also includes states, local governments.

Range of Financial Assistance: $2,000 to $211,000.

Contact: Director, Artists-in-Education Program, National Endowment for the Arts, 1100 Pennsylvania Avenue, N.W., Washington, DC 20506/202-682-5426.

Promotion of the Arts—Challenge Grants

Objectives: To provide a special opportunity for arts institutions to stregthen long-term institutional capacity and to enhance artistic qualify and diversity by: broadening the base of contributed support; increasing contribution levels; providing a larger, more secure capital base through endowments, cash reserves, or improved physical plant; eliminating debts or deficit financing; and implementing major long-term artistic initiatives which will further the attainment of the institution's long-term artistic goals and/or advance the state of the art form it represents.

Eligibility: Grants may be made only to nonprofit organizations if donations to such organizations qualify as a charitable deduction under Section 170 (c) of the Internal Revenue Code of 1954.

Range of Financial Assistance: $100,000 to $1,500,000.

Contact: Challenge Grant Programs, National Endowment for the Arts, 1100 Pennsylvania Ave. N.W., Washington, DC 20506/202-682-5436.

Promotion of the Arts—Dance

Objectives: The Dance Program provides support for professional choreographers and dance companies, organizations that present or serve dance, and organizations and individuals involved in dance/film projects.

Eligibility: Grants may be made to 1) nonprofit organizations, including state and local governments and state arts agencies, if donations to such organizations qualify as charitable deductions under Section 170 (c) of the Internal Revenue Code of 1954, and 2) individuals who possess exceptional talent.

Range of Financial Assistance: $3,000 to $15,000.

Contact: Director, Dance Program, National Endowment for the Arts, 1100 Pennsylvania Ave. N.W., Washington, DC 20506/202-682-5435.

Promotion of the Arts—Design Arts

Objectives: To provide grants for projects, including research, education, and professional and public awareness in architecture, landscape architecture, and urban, interior, fashion, industrial, and environmental design. The program attempts to encourage creativity and to make the public aware of the benefits of good design. The program awards grants to community and neighborhood organizations, service organizations, art institutions, colleges and universities, local and state governments, professional designers, design students and other qualified individuals working on design projects.

Eligibility: Grants may be made to: 1) nonprofit organizations, including state and local governments and state arts agencies, if donations to such organizations qualify as charitable deductions under Section 170 (c) of the Internal Revenue Code; and 2) individuals who possess exceptional talent.

Range of Financial Assistance: Up to $15,000.

Contact: Director, Design Arts Program, National Endowment for the Arts, 1100 Pennsylvania Ave. N.W., Washington, DC 20506/202-682-5437.

Promotion of the Arts—Expansion Arts

Objectives: To provide grants to professionally directed, community-based arts organizations involved with urban, suburban, and rural communities. Particular attention is given to these organizations which serve citizens—including ethnic minorities—whose cultural needs are not met by the major arts universities.

Eligibility: Grants may be made only to nonprofit organizations if donations to such organizations qualify as a charitable deduction under Section 170 (c) of the Internal Revenue Code. This definition includes states, local governments, and state arts agencies.

Range of Financial Assistance: $5,000 to $30,000.

Contact: Director, Expansion Arts Program, National Endowment for the Arts, 1100 Pennsyl-

vania Ave. N.W., Washington, DC 20506/202-682-5443.

Promotion of the Arts—Folk Arts

Objectives: To provide grants to assist, foster, and make available publicly throughout the country the diverse traditional American folk arts.

Eligibility: Grants may be made only to nonprofit organizations if donations to such organizations qualify as a charitable deduction under Section 170 (c) of the Internal Revenue Code of 1954. This definition also includes states, local governments, and state arts agencies. Individuals are eligible.

Range of Financial Assistance: $1,000 to $50,000.

Contact: Director, Folk Arts Program, National Endowment for the Arts, 1100 Pennsylvania Ave. N.W., Washington, DC 20506/202-682-5449.

Promotion of the Arts—Literature

Objectives: To provide fellowships for creative writers, and to support organizations devoted to development of the literary arts in America.

Eligibility: Grants may be made to: 1) nonprofit organizations, including state and local governments and state arts agencies, if donations to such organizations qualify as charitable deductions under Section 170 (c) of the Internal Revenue Code of 1954; and 2) individuals who possess exceptional talent.

Range of Financial Assistance: $1,000 to $50,000.

Contact: Director, Literature Program, National Endowment for the Arts, 1100 Pennsylvania Ave. N.W., Washington, DC 20506/202-682-5451.

Promotion of the Arts—Media Arts: Film/Radio/Television

Objectives: To provide grants in support of projects designed to assist individuals and groups to produce films, radio and video of high aesthetic quality, to exhibit and disseminate media arts. The Endowment also assists the American Film Institute which carries out a number of assistance programs for film.

Eligibility: Grants may be made to 1) nonprofit organizations, including state and local governments and state arts agencies, if donations to such organizations qualify as charitable deductions under Section 170 (c) of the Internal Revenue Code of 1954; and 2) individuals who possess exceptional talent.

Range of Financial Assistance: $1,000 to $500,000.

Contact: Director, Media Arts Program, National Endowment for the Arts, 1100 Pennsylvania Ave. N.W., Washington, DC 20506/202-682-5452.

Promotion of the Arts—Museums

Objectives: To provide grants in support of the essential activities of American museums.

Eligibility: Grants may be made to: 1) nonprofit organizations, including state and local governments and state arts agencies, if donations to such organizations qualify as charitable deductions under Section 170 (c) of the Internal Revenue Code of 1954, and 2) individuals (ordinarily U.S. citizens only) who possess exceptional talent.

Range of Financial Assistance: Individuals up to $10,000; organizations up to $150,000.

Contact: Director, Museum Program, National Endowment for the Arts, 1100 Pennsylvania Ave. N.W., Washington, DC 20506/202-682-5442.

Promotion of the Arts—Music

Objectives: To support excellence in music performance and creativity and to develop informed audiences for music throughout the country.

Eligibility: Grants may be made to: 1) nonprofit organizations, including state and local governments and state arts agencies, if donations to such organizations qualify as charitable deductions under Section 170 (c) of the Internal Revenue Code of 1954; and 2) individuals who possess exceptional talent.

Range of Financial Assistance: $500 to $240,000.

Contact: Director, Music Program, National Endowment for the Arts, 1100 Pennsylvania Ave. N.W., Washington, DC 20506/202-682-5445.

Promotion of the Arts—Fellowship Program for Arts Management

Objectives: To provide a limited number of 13-week fellowships in arts administration and related fields for professionals and students. The internship is located at Endowment headquarters in Washington, D.C. The program is designed to acquaint the participants with the policies, procedures, and operations of the Endowment and to give them an overview of arts activities in this country.

Eligibility: Grants made only to individuals.

Range of Financial Assistance: $3,300 stipend plus round trip travel.

Contact: Fellowship Program for Arts Management, Office of Policy, Planning and Research, National Endowment for the Arts, 1100 Pennsylvania Avenue, NW, Washington, DC 20506/202-682-5786.

Promotion of the Arts—Opera and Musical Theater

Objectives: To support excellence in the performance and creation of professional opera and musical theater throughout the nation, including state and local government.

Eligibility: Grants may be made only to professional nonprofit organizations if donations to such organizations qualify as a charitable deduction under Section 170 (c) of the Internal Revenue Code of 1954.

Range of Financial Assistance: $3,000 to $250,000.

Contact: Director, Opera/Musical Theater Program, National Endowment for the Arts, 1100 Pennsylvania Ave. N.W., Washington, DC 20506/202-682-5447.

Promotion of the Arts—Inter-Arts

Objectives: To provide grants for projects which involve two or more art forms or program areas.

Eligibility: Grants may be made only to nonprofit organizations if donations to such organizations qualify as a charitable deduction under Section 170 (c) of the Internal Revenue Code of 1954. This definition also includes states, local governments, and state arts agencies. There are no grants to individuals.

Range of Financial Assistance: $5,000 to $50,000.

Contact: Director Inter-Arts Program, National Endowment for the Arts, 1100 Pennsylvania Ave. N.W., Washington, DC 20506/202-682-5444.

Promotion of the Arts—State Program

Objectives: To assist state and regional public arts agencies in the development of programs for the encouragement of the arts and artists.

Eligibility: Agencies officially designated as the State Arts Agency by the governor in each of the 50 states and six special U.S. jurisdictions, and other specific public arts agencies are eligible.

Range of Financial Assistance: $5,000 to $541,300.

Contact: Directors, State Program, National Endowment for the Arts, 1100 Pennsylvania Ave. N.W., Washington, DC 20506/202-682-5429.

Promotion of the Arts—Test Program of Support for Local Arts Agencies

Objectives: To provide grants which will promote a sustained, higher level of commitment to the arts, contribute to the vitality and excellence of the arts nationwide, and encourage partnership amoung the organizations seeking the development of enhanced support for the arts.

Eligibility: Grants may be made to State arts agencies and local arts agencies, if donations to such organizations qualify as charitable deductions under Section 170 (c) of the Internal Revenue Code. Individuals are not eligible.

Range of Financial Assistance: No less than $150,000 will be awarded for a three-year period.

Contact: Test Program of Support for Local Arts Agencies, National Endowment for the Arts, 1100 Pennsylvania Ave. N.W., Washington, DC 20506/ 202-682-5431.

Promotion of the Arts—Theater

Objectives: To provide grants to aid professional theater companies and theater artists.

Eligibility: Grants may be made only to nonprofit organizations if donations to such organizations qualify as a charitable deduction under Section 170 (c) of the Internal Revenue Code of 1954. This definition includes states, local governments, and state art agencies, and individuals.

Range of Financial Assistance: $2,000 to $275,000.

Contact: Director, Theater Program, National Endowment for the Arts, 1100 Pennsylvania Ave. N.W., Washington, DC 20506/202-682-5425.

Promotion of the Arts—Visual Arts

Objectives: To provide grants to assist painters, sculptors, craftsmen, photographers, and print-makers and to support institutions devoted to the development of the visual arts in America.

Eligibility: Grants may be made to 1) nonprofit organizations, including state and local governments and state arts agencies, if donations to such organizations qualify as charitable deductions under Section 170 (c) of the Internal Revenue Code of 1954; and 2) individuals who possess exceptional talent.

Range of Financial Assistance: $1,000 to $50,000.

Contact: Director, Visual Arts Program, National Endowment for the Arts, 1100 Pennsylvania Ave. N.W., Washington, DC 20506/202-682-5448.

Promotion of the Humanities—Basic Research/ Intercultural Research Program

Objectives: To increase understanding of the history, traditions, culture, and problems of foreign countries as a base for the study of contemporary international affairs and to foster this nation's standing in international scholarship by providing support to American Scholars to pursue research abroad in all fields of the humanities.

Eligibility: State and local governments; sponsored organizations; public and private nonprofit institutions/organizations; other public institutions/organizations; Federally recognized Indian tribal governments; Native American Organizations; US Territories; non-government-general; minority organizations; other specialized groups; and quasi-public nonprofit institutions.

Range of Financial Assistance: $50,000 to $500,000.

Contact: National Endowment for the Humanities, Basic Research/Intercultural Research, 1100 Pennsylvania Ave. N.W., Room 319, Washington, DC 20506/202-786-0200.

Promotion of the Humanities—Basic Research/ Project Research

Objectives: To advance basic research that is interpretative in all fields of the humanities. Collaborative, interdisciplinary scholarship involving the efforts of several individuals at the professional, assistant, and clerical levels is encouraged as well as the use of innovative methodologies.

Foreign and domestic archaeology projects are supported in the Program.

Eligibility: U.S. citizens and residents, U.S. nonprofit organizations, and academic institutions including state colleges and universities, public, private, junior and community colleges.

Range of Financial Assistance: $5,000 to $300,000.

Contact: Assistant Director, Basic Research Program, Basic Research/Project Research, Division of Research Programs, Room 319, National Endowment for the Humanities, 1100 Pennsylvania Ave. N.W., Washington, DC 20506/202-786-0207.

Promotion of the Humanities—Basic Research/ Travel to Collections

Objectives: To advance basic research in the humanities by enabling American scholars to travel to use the research collections of libraries, archives, museums or other research repositories to consult research materials which are of fundamental importance for the progress of their scholarly work. The program is intended to help scholars meet the costs associated with a research trip within North America or Western Europe.

Eligibility: US citizens and residents.

Range of Financial Assistance: All awards are $500.

Contact: Division of Research Programs, Basic Research/Travel to Collections, 1100 Pennsylvania Ave. N.W., Room 319G, National Endowment for the Humanities, Washington, DC 20506/202-786-0207.

Promotion of the Humanities—Central Disciplines in Undergraduate Education

Objectives: To assist colleges and universities establish or sustain the disciplines of the humanities in a central role in undergraduate education.

Eligibility: State and local governments; sponsored organizations; public and private nonprofit institutions/organizations; other public institutions/organizations; Federally recognized Indian tribal governments; Native American Organizations; US Territories; non-government-general; minority organizations; other specialized groups; and quasi-public nonprofit institutions.

Range of Financial Assistance: Not specified

Contact: Central Disciplines in Undergraduate Education, National Endowment for the Humanities, 1100 Pennsylvania Ave. N.W., Room 302, Washington, DC 20506/202-786-0380.

Promotion of the Humanities—Challenge Grant Program

Objectives: To provide financial assistance to institutions that store, research or disseminate learnings in the humanities; to broaden the base of financial support by "challenging" institutions to raise three private dollars for every federal grant dollar; to help secure financial stability in order to maintain existing services and resources.

Eligibility: Local, county, and state governments are eligible to apply on behalf of nonprofit institutions, associations or organizations within their jurisdictions; individuals are not eligible to apply.

Range of Financial Assistance: $2,000 to $1,500,000.

Contact: Challenge Grants Program, Room 429, National Endowment for the Humanities, 1100 Pennsylvania Ave. N.W., Washington, DC 20506/ 202-786-0361.

Promotion of the Humanities—Special Projects: Humanities Projects in Libraries

Objectives: To encourage public interest in libraries' humanities resources and stimulate their use through thematic programs, exhibits, media, publications, and other library activities.

Eligibility: Any library or library-related agency serving the adult public may apply. This includes community libraries, county and regional libraries, library systems, independent nonprofit libraries, state libraries, special libraries, library associations, multi-state library organizations, and library schools.

Range of Financial Assistance: $5,000 to $200,000.

Contact: Division of General Programs, Humanities Projects in Libraries, Special Projects: Humanities Programs for Adults, National Endowment for the Humanities, 1100 Pennsylvania Ave. N.W., Room 426, Washington, DC 20506/ 202-786-0271.

Promotion of the Humanities—Elementary and Secondary Schools

Objectives: To improve classroom teaching in history, foreign languages, English and other disciplines in the humanities by supporting elementary and secondary school projects that can be completed within a specified period of time.

Eligibility: State and local governments; sponsored organizations; public and private nonprofit institutions/organizations; other public institutions/organizations: Federally recognized Indian tribal governments; Native American organizations; US Territories; and other specialized groups.

Range of Financial Assistance: Not Specified.

Contact: Humanities Instruction in Elementary and Secondary Schools, National Endowment for the Humanities, Room 302, Washington, DC 20506/202-783-0373.

Promotion of the Humanities—Exemplary Projects and Humanities Programs for Nontraditional Learners

Objectives: To support activities that improve the teaching of the humanities through faculty development, preparation of teaching materials, and sharing of institutional resources. To assist institutions that wish to improve the quality of education for their nontraditional learners by increasing the rigor of instruction or decreasing the unit cost of instruction.

Eligibility: State and local governments; sponsored organizations; public and private nonprofit institutions/organizations; other public institutions/organizations; Federally recognized Indian Tribal governments.

Range of Financial Assistance: Not specified.

Contact: Exemplary Projects and Nontraditional Programs, National Endowment for the Humanities, 1100 Pennsylvania Ave. N.W., Room 302, Washington, DC 20506/202-786-0384.

Promotion of the Humanities—Fellowships at Centers for Advanced Study

Objectives: To provide fellowships for study and research in the humanities to independent centers for advanced study, in order to increase the opportunities for the uninterrupted and extended interchange of ideas which these centers make possible on an independent basis, not primarily in a college or university setting.

Eligibility: State and local governments; sponsored organizations; public and private nonprofit institutions/organizations; other public institutions/organizations; Federally recognized Indian tribal governments; Native American organizations; US Territories; and other specialized groups.

Range of Financial Assistance: $37,500 to $182,680.

Contact: Division of Fellowships and Seminars, Summer Stipends, National Endowment for the Humanities, 1100 Pennsylvania Ave. N.W., Room 316, Washington, DC 20506/202-786-0466.

Promotion of the Humanities—Fellowships for College Teachers

Objectives: To provide opportunities for college teachers to pursue full-time independent study and research that will enhance their abilities as teachers and interpreters of the humanities.

Eligibility: Since these fellowships are awarded to individuals, state, and local governments, and U.S. territories are ineligible. Applicants must have completed their professional training before applying.

Range of Financial Assistance: Up to $25,000.

Contact: Fellowships for College Teachers, Division of Fellowships and Seminars, Room 316, 1100 Pennslyvania Ave. N.W., National Endowment for the Humanities, Washington, DC 20506/ 202-786-0466.

Promotion of the Humanities—Fellowships for Independent Study and Research

Objectives: To provide time for uninterrupted

study and research to scholars, teachers, and other interpreters of humanities who can make significant contributions to thought and knowledge in the humanities. The fellowships free applicants from the day-to-day responsibilities of teaching and other work for extended periods of uninterrupted, full-time study and research so that fellows may enlarge their contributions and continue to develop their abilities as scholars and interpreters of the humanities.

Eligibility: Applications may come from members of college and university faculties and from others who work in the humanities, from persons with broad interests as well as scholars working in specialties.

Range of Financial Assistance: Up to $25,000.

Contact: Fellowships for Independent Study and Research, Division of Fellowships and Seminars, National Endowment for the Humanities, Room 316, 1100 Pennsylvania Ave. N.W., Washington, DC 20506/202-786-0466.

Promotion of the Humanities—Humanities Projects in Media

Objectives: To encourage and support radio and television production that: 1) advances public understanding and use of the humanities, including such fields as history, jurisprudence, literature, anthropology, philosophy, archaeology; 2) is of the highest professional caliber in terms of scholarship in the humanities and in terms of technical production; and 3) is suitable for national or regional television broadcast and distribution, or for national, regional or local radio broadcast.

Eligibility: State and local governments and nonprofit agencies, institutions, organizations or groups are eligible; each proposal must involve direct collaboration between experienced humanities scholars and producers, screenwriters, directors, and actors of top professional stature.

Range of Financial Assistance: $4,000 to $750,000.

Contact: Division of General Programs, Humanities Projects in Media, National Endowment for the Humanities, Room 420, Washington, DC 20506/202-786-0278.

Promotion of the Humanities—Humanities Projects in Museums and Historical Organizations

Objectives: To assist museums and historical organizations in implementing effective and imaginative programs which convey and interpret to the general public knowledge of the cultural legacies of the United States and other nations.

Eligibility: State and local governments and nonprofit museums, historical organizations, historic sites and other institutions capable of implementing public programs in the humanities.

Range of Financial Assistance: $15,000 to $500,000.

Contact: Humanities Projects in Museums and Historical Organizations, Division of General Programs, Room 420, National Endowment for the Humanities, Washington, DC 20506/202-786-0284.

Promotion of the Humanities—Planning and Assessment Studies Program

Objectives: To aid projects that address national humanistic concerns and that analyze the resources and needs in specific areas of the humanities, develop new sources of information that foster a more critical assessment of the humanities, and design, test, and implement tools for evaluation and policy analysis.

Eligibility: Entities of State and local government, U.S. citizens and residents, U.S. nonprofit orgaizations, and public and private academic institutions at all educational levels are eligible. Foreign institutions are not eligible and foreign nationals are also ineligible unless affiliated with a U.S. institution or organization, or a resident within the U.S. for three consecutive years prior to the time of application.

Range of Financial Assistance: $3,000 to $150,000.

Contact: Planning and Assessment Studies, Office of Program and Policy Studies, National Endowment for the Humanities, Room 402, Washington, DC 20506/202-786-0420.

Promotion of the Humanities—Basic Research/ Research Conferences

Objectives: To support conferences, symposia, and workshops, which enable scholars to discuss and advance the current state of research on a particular topic or to consider means of improving conditions for research.

Eligibility: U.S. citizens and residents, U.S. nonprofit organizations, local governments, and academic institutions are eligible.

Range of Financial Assistance: $5,200 to $10,000.

Contact: Division of Research Programs, Project Research, Room 319, National Endowment for the Humanities, 1100 Pennsylvania Ave. N.W., Washington, DC 20506/202-786-0207.

Promotion of the Humanities—Research Resources/ Access Grants

Objectives: To fund, wholly or partially, projects which will improve and facilitate scholarly access to significant documentary resources in order to contribute to greater knowledge and understanding of the humanities.

Eligibility: State and local governments; sponsored organizations; public and private nonprofit institutions/organizations; other public institutions/organizations and Federally recognized Indian tribal governments; Native American organizations; US Territories; minority organizations; and other specialized groups; quasi-public nonprofit institutions.

Range of Financial Assistance: $1,500 to $150,000.

Contact: Research Resources Programs, Division of Research Programs, 1100 Pennsylvania Ave. N.W., Room 319, National Endowment for the Humanities, Washington, DC 20506/202-786-0204.

Promotion of the Humanities—Research Resources/Publications

Objectives: To insure through grants to publishing entities the dissemination of works of scholarly distinction that without support could not be published.

Eligibility: Nonprofit and commercial presses are eligible.

Range of Financial Assistance: $2,000 to $10,000.

Contact: Division of Research Programs, Research Resources/Publications, Room 319, 1100 Pennsylvania Ave. N.W., National Endowment for the Humanities, Washington, DC 20506/202-786-0204.

Promotion of the Humanities—Reference Works/Editions

Objectives: To fund, wholly or partially, projects which create editions of materials important for scholarly research in the humanities and as cultural documents.

Eligibility: U.S. citizens and residents, U.S. nonprofit organizations, and academic institutions including state colleges and universities, public, private, junior and community colleges are eligible.

Range of Financial Assistance: $2,500 to $150,000.

Contact: Division of Research Programs, Reference Works/Editions, Room 319, 1100 Pennsylvania Ave, NW, Washington, DC 20506/202-786-0210.

Promotion of the Humanities—Reference Works/Tools

Objectives: To fund, wholly or partially, projects which create reference works and resources important for scholarly research as cultural documents.

Eligibility: U.S. citizens and residents, U.S. nonprofit organizations, and academic institutions including state colleges and universities, public, private, junior and community colleges are eligible.

Range of Financial Assistance: $2,500 to $150,000.

Contact: Division of Research Programs, Reference Works/Tools, Room 319, 1100 Pennsylvania Ave. N.W., National Endowment for the Humanities, Washington, DC 20506/202-786-0210.

Promotion of the Humanities—Reference Works/Translations

Objectives: To support the translation into English of texts and documents that will make an important contribution to research in the humanities and to greater public awareness of the traditions and achievements of other cultures.

Eligibility: U.S. citizens and residents, U.S. nonprofit organizations, and academic institutions including state colleges and universities, public, private, junior and community colleges are eligible.

Range of Financial Assistance: $2,500 to $100,000.

Contact: Division of Research Programs, Reference Works/Translations, Room 319, 1100 Pennsylvania Ave. N.W., National Endowment for the Humanities, National Foundation on the Arts and the Humanities, Washington, DC 20506/202-786-0210

Promotion of the Humanities—Research Resources/Preservation Grants

Objectives: To fund, wholly or partially, projects which will improve and facilitate scholarly access to significant resources in order to contribute to greater knowledge and understanding of the humanities.

Eligibility: U.S. citizens and residents, U.S. nonprofit organizations, and academic institutions are eligible. Foreign institutions or organizations are not eligible and foreign nationals are also ineligible unless affiliated with a U.S. institution or organization or a resident within the U.S. for three consecutive years prior to the time of application.

Range of Financial Assistance: $7,500 to $150,000.

Contact: Research Resources Programs, Division of Research Programs, Room 319, National Endowment for the Humanities, 1100 Pennsylvania Ave. N.W., Washington, DC 20506/202-786-0204.

Promotion of the Humanities—Basic Research/Humanities, Science and Technology

Objectives: To support humanities research designated to deepen our understanding of science and technology and its role in our culture.

Eligibility: Entities of state and local government, U.S. citizens and residents, U.S. nonprofit organizations, and academic institutions are eligible. Foreign institutions are not eligible and foreign nationals are also ineligible unless affiliated with a U.S. institution or organization, or a resident within the U.S. for three consecutive years prior to the time of application.

Range of Financial Assistance: $15,000 to $100,000.

Contact: Humanities, Science and Technology, Division of Research Programs, National Endowment for the Humanities, 1100 Pennsylvania Ave. N.W., Room 319, Washington, DC 20506/202-786-0207.

Promotion of the Humanities—Special Projects: Humanities Programs for Adults

Objectives: To support humanities projects addressed to adult, out-of-school audiences and to encourage exceptional projects which are not eligible in other divisions of the Endowment.

Eligibility: State and local governments; sponsored organizations; public and private nonprofit institutions/organizations; other public institutions/organizations and Federally recognized Indian tribal governments; Native American organizations; US Territories; minority organizations; and other specialized groups; quasi-public nonprofit institutions.

Range of Financial Assistance: $5,000 to $200,000.

Contact: Special Projects: Humanities Programs for Adults, Division of General Programs, National Endowment for the Humanities, 1100 Pennsylvania Ave. N.W., Room 426, Washington, DC 20506/202-786-0271.

Promotion of the Humanities—Special Projects: Humanities Projects in Libraries

Objectives: To encourage public interest in academic and public libraries' humanities resources and stimulate their use through thematic programs, exhibits, media, publications, and other library activities.

Eligibility: State and local governments; sponsored organizations; public and private nonprofit institutions/organizations; other public institutions/organizations and Federally recognized Indian tribal governments; Native American organizations; US Territories, minority organizations, and other specialized groups; quasi-public nonprofit institutions.

Range of Financial Assistance: $5,000 to $200,000.

Contact: Division of General Programs, Humanities Projects in Libraries, Special Projects; Humanities Programs for Adults, National Endowment for the Humanities, 1100 Pennsylvania Ave. N.W., Room 426, Washington, DC 20506/ 202-786-0271.

Promotion of the Humanities—Summer Seminars for Secondary School Teachers

Objectives: To provide opportunities for teachers in secondary schools to work during the summer under the direction of a distinguished teacher and active scholar at colleges and universities throughout the country, studying seminal works in the humanities in a systematic and thorough way.

Eligibility: State and local governments; sponsored organizations; public and private nonprofit institutions/organizations; other public institutions/organizations; Federally recognized Indian tribal governments; Native American Organizations; US Territories; non-government-general;

minority organizations; other specialized groups; and quasi-public nonprofit institutions.

Range of Financial Assistance: $34,000 to $61,000.

Contact: Summer Seminars for Secondary School Teachers. Division of Fellowships and Seminars, National Endowment for the Humanities, 1100 Pennsylvania Ave. N.W., Room 326, Washington, DC 20506/202-786-0463.

Promotion of the Humanities—State Programs

Objectives: To promote local humanities programming through renewable program grants to humanities councils within each of the states for the purpose of regranting funds to local organizations, institutions and groups. Under the provisions of Public Law 94-462, only one entity in each state may receive assistance as the state humanities group to administer this program.

Eligibility: Nonprofit citizen councils in the several states which conform to the requirements of Public Law 94-462. If the states matches the federal grant, the governor may appoint up to half the council, otherwise the governor may appoint two members of the council.

Range of Financial Assistance: $300,000 to $639,000.

Contact: Division of State Programs, National Endowment for the Humanities, Room 411, 1100 Pennsylvania Ave. N.W., Washington, DC 20506/ 202-786-0254.

Promotion of the Humanities—Summer Seminars for College Teachers

Objectives: To provide opportunities for teachers at undergraduate private and state colleges and junior and community colleges to work during the summer in their areas of interest under the direction of distinguished scholars at institutions with first-rate libraries.

Eligibility: State and local governments; sponsored organizations; public and private nonprofit institutions/organizations; Federally recognized Indian tribal governments; and Native American organizations.

Range of Financial Assistance: $45,000 to $70,000.

Contact: Summer Seminars for College Teachers, Division of Fellowships and Seminars, National Endowment for the Humanities, Room 316, 1100 Pennsylvania Ave. N.W., Washington, DC 20506/202-786-0463.

Promotion of the Humanities—Summer Stipends

Objectives: To provide time for uninterrupted study and research to scholars, teachers, writers, and other interpreters of the humanities, who have produced or demonstrated promise of producing significant contributions to humanistic knowledge.

Eligibility: College, junior college, and university teachers, and other humanists who have completed their professional training and are not degree candidates.

Range of Financial Assistance: All awards are for $3,000.

Contact: Summer Stipends, Division of Fellowships and Seminars, National Endowment for the Humanities, Room 316, 1100 Pennsylvania Ave, NW., Washington, DC 20506/202-786-0466.

Promotion of the Humanities—Special Projects: Humanities Programs for Youth/Younger Scholars

Objectives: To support humanities projects initiated and conducted by young persons under 21 years of age.

Eligibility: Entities of state and local governments, and individuals who are U.S. citizens, native residents of U.S. territorial possessions, or foreign nationals who have been residents in the U.S. for at least three years immediately preceding the date of the application; and nonprofit U.S. organizations and academic institutions are eligible.

Range of Financial Assistance: $1,800 to $2,200.

Contact: Division of General Programs, Special Projects: Humanities Programs for Youth/Younger Scholars, 1100 Pennsylvania Ave. N.W., Room 426, National Endowment for the Humanities, Washington, DC 20506/202-786-0273.

Promotion of the Humanities—Special Projects: Humanities Programs for Youth/Youth Projects

Objectives: To support humanities projects which provide educational opportunities beyond those of in-school programs for large groups of young people under the direction of experienced professionals in the humanities and professionals in youth work. These may be sponsored by education, cultural, scholarly, civic, media or youth organizations.

Eligibility: Entities of state and local governments, and nonprofit U.S. organizations and academic institutions are eligible.

Range of Financial Assistance: $5,000 to $120,000.

Contact: Division of General Programs, Special Projects: Humanities Programs for Youth/Youth Projects, National Endowment for the Humanities, 1100 Pennsylvania Ave. N.W., Room 426, Washington, DC 20506/202-786-0273.

Higher Education/Regional–National

This program promotes the development, testing and dissemination of imaginative approaches to the teaching of the humanities at many institutions. Contact: Higher Education/Regional-National Grants Program, Educational Program Division, National Endowment for the Humanities, National Foundation on the Arts and the Humanities, 1100 Pennsylvania Ave. N.W., Room 302, Washington, DC 20506/202-786-0384.

Humanities

This is a bimonthly publication that describes current developments at the Humanities Endowment. Each issue includes a calendar of grant deadlines, complete listing of all NEH grants by category, articles by major writers on significant issues in the humanities, features on note-worthy Endowment projects and bibliographic essays on selected books resulting from NEH grants in various humanities disciplines. It is available for $14.00 per year from the Superintendent of Documents, Government Printing Office, Washington, DC 20402/202-783-3238. For additional information, contact: *Humanities* Editor, Public Affairs Office, National Endowment for the Humanities, National Foundation on the Arts and the Humanities, 1100 Pennsylvania Ave. N.W., Room 409, N.W., Washington, DC 20506/202-786-0438.

Inter-Arts Program

The Inter-Arts Program assists arts projects and organizations which involve two or more art disciplines and have national or regional impact. This includes presenting organizations, artists colonies, service organizations and projects and interdisciplinary arts projects. Contact: Inter-Arts Program, National Endowment for the Arts, National Foundation for the Arts and the Humanities, Room 710, 1100 Pennsylvania Ave. N.W., Washington, DC 20506/202-682-5444.

International Fellows

International Fellows grants acquaint arts administrators or potential arts administrators with the policies, procedures and operations of the Endowment, and give them an overview of arts activities in the United States. Contact: International Program, Policy and Planning, National Endowment for the Arts, 1100 Pennsylvania Ave. N.W., Room 615, Washington, DC 20506/202-682-5562.

Libraries Humanities Program

This program aims to explore ways to interest the public in the humanities resources of libraries and to stimulate their use through thematic programs, exhibits, media, publications, and other library activities. Contact: Humanities Projects in Libraries Program, Division of General Programs, Special Projects, National Endowment for the Humanities, Washington, DC 20506/202-786-0438.

Library—Arts

The library reflects the interests of the NEA and has material on public policy and the arts, arts management and endowment matters. Contact: Library, National Endowment for the Arts, 1100 Pennsylvania Ave. N.W., Washington, DC 20506/202-682-5485.

Library—Humanities

The Humanities Library has material on humanities subjects. It is open to the public but an appointment is necessary. Contact: Library, National Endowment for the Humanities, 1100 Pennsylvania Ave., N.W., Room 217, Washington, DC 20506/202-786-0245

Literature Program
The literature program includes fellowships for creative writers; grants for residences for writers in an attempt to put writers in personal contact with their audiences; support for independent literary publishers (books and magazines); and distribution and promotion of contemporary literature. Contact: Literature Program, National Endowment for the Arts, 1100 Pennsylvania Ave. N.W., Room 723, Washington, DC 20506/202-682-5451.

Media Arts: Films/Radio/Television
The Media Arts program has four main priorities: Media Arts Centers, Production Grants, Programming in the Arts and Exhibition Assistance. Programming in the Arts concentrates on bringing the performing arts to broadcast (radio and television) and major media centers. Media Arts Centers undertake a variety of projects to make the arts of film, video and radio more widely appreciated and practiced. Funds are also available to assist organizations in exhibiting high quality film and video art not shown commercially; to enable organizations to invite renowned film and videomakers, radio producers and critics for workshops and lectures; to distribute selected short films to commercial theaters; to support single film, video and radio productions by tax-exempt organizations; and to help independent film and video makers complete their projects. Contact: Media Arts: Film/Radio/Television, National Endowment for the Arts, 1100 Pennsylvania Ave. N.W., Room 720, Washington, DC 20506/202-682-5452.

Media Humanities Projects Program
The Media Humanities Projects Program provides support for innovative television, radio and cable projects. It is solely concerned with project ideas which make substantial use of research and information in the humanities and which focus on subjects and issues that are central to the humanities. Contact: Media Humanities Projects Program, Division of General Programs, National Endowment for the Humanities, 1100 Pennsylvania Ave. N.W., Washington, DC 20506/202-786-0278.

Museum Program
Museum grants are awarded to assist museums in providing general education opportunties that complement the goals of the institution; to promote cooperative endeavors between museums, groups of museums, museums and state or regional arts agencies or similar organizations; to encourage museums to purchase works in all media by living American artists; to enable museums to organize special exhibitions and to borrow exhibitions organized by other museums; to install collections formerly in storage or recently acquired or to more effectively display artifacts already on view; to document permanent collections or to publish catalogues or handbooks on collections; to enable museums to engage outside consultants for such projects as fund-raising, research and public relations activities; to enable museum staff members to take leaves of absence for independent study, research, travel or other activities that contribute to their professional development; to assist museums and universities in training museum professionals and technicians through college-level programs, internships and apprenticeships; to assist museums in their implementation of conservation treatment for permanent collections, in the development of workshops, training centers, and internship programs to train conservation professionals and in the formation or expansion of regional conservation centers; to identify problems and recommend solutions concerning security; to assist with renovation projects where surveys have been completed; and to support services to the field such as research, publications, workshops, and seminars provided by museums or other organizations such as state or regional arts agencies and national or regional museum associations. Contact: Museum Programs, National Endowment for the Arts, 1100 Pennsylvania Ave. N.W., Room 624, Washington, DC 20506/202-682-5442.

Museums and Historical Organizations
This program funds activities that convey ideas and stimulate learning through the use of artifacts, documents, objects of arts, specimens or living collections. Museums, historical organizations, historic sites and other similar cultural institutions can develop programs which interpret humanities themes for the broad general public. Contact: Museums and Historical Organizations, Humanities Projects Program, Programs Division, National Endowment for the Humanities, 1100 Pennsylvania Ave. N.W., Room 426, Washington, DC 20506/202-786-0284.

Music Programs
The music program seeks to encourage excellence in all musical forms by granting funds to assist a limited number of solo artists; to provide support to professional ensembles to improve the quality of chamber music performances and to make the art form widely available; to professional orchestras to support innovative projects; to support the activities of a limited number of fully professional choral organizations; to support scholarship aid, development activities and master teacher residences for eligible music schools; to assist organizations that provide career development and performance op-

portunities for young artists; to provide support to professional ensembles and presenting organizations; to encourage the performance of new music and to increase performance opportunities for the work of American composers; to provide for the creation or completion of musical works; and to enable professional jazz composers and performers to advance their careers, to present jazz performances, educational programs and short-term residences, and to assist individuals and organizations with other projects. Contact: Music Program, National Endowment for the Arts, 1100 Pennsylvania Ave. N.W., Room 702 Washington, DC 20506/202-682-5445.

Opera-Musical Theater Program
This program enables the Endowment to respond to the needs of and opportunities within all forms of lyrical theater. Grants are awarded to help opera companies improve their artistic quality, reach new audiences and broaden their repertories to include more works by American artists; to assist outstanding projects that can be used as models for future developments in opera; to assist organizations that provide services to the opera field; and to assist unique projects of limited duration. Contact: Opera/Musical Theater, National Endowment for the Arts, 1100 Pennsylvania Ave. N.W., Room 703, Washington, DC 20506/202-682-5447.

Planning and Assessment Studies
Support is provided for studies and experiments designed to: collect and analyze data, including information about financial material and human resources which help assess the status of and trends in important sectors of the humanities or which explore significant emerging issues concerning the humanities; and develop models, techniques and tools helpful in conducting policy research and analysis, and in evaluating the effectiveness of institutional programs in the humanities. Contact: Office of Planning and Budget, National Endowment for the Humanities, 1100 Pennsylvania Ave. N.W., Rm 402 Washington, DC 20506/202-786-0420.

Research Materials
This program grants funds for research tools and reference works, editions, translations, and publications to provide support for the preparation of reference works considered important for advanced research in the humanities. Contact: Reference Works Program, Division of Research Programs, National Endowment for the Humanities, 1100 Pennsylvania Ave. N.W., Room 319, Washington, DC 20506/202-786-0201.

Research Resources
This program helps make sources needed for scholarly research in the humanities more accessi-

ble for use. It funds projects to place previously unavailable material in public repositories; to facilitate access by preparing catalogs, inventories, registers, guides, bibliographies, and other finding aids: and to improve the ways in which librarians, archivists and others care for and make available research material. Contact: Research Resources, Division of Research Programs, National Endowment for the Humanities, 1100 Pennsylvania Ave. N.W., Rm 319, Washington, DC 20506/202-786-0201.

Humanities, Science, and Technology
This program (jointly administered with the National Science Foundation) supports scholarly work in the disciplines which underlay the science-values field: the history, philosophy, and sociology of science and the emerging fields of the history and philosophy of technology. Contact: Basic Research Program, Humanities, Science & Technology, National Endowment for the Humanities, 1100 Pennsylvania Ave. N.W., Room 319, Washington, DC 20506/202-786-0207.

Special Constituencies
The program for special constituencies aims to make the arts more accessible to handicapped people, older adults, veterans, the gifted and talented, and people in hospitals, nursing homes, mental institutions and prisons. Information and technical assistance to artists, arts organizations, and consumers concerning accessible arts programs and other federal programs which support cultural activities is available. Contact: Special Constituencies, Policy and Planning, National Endowment for the Arts, 1100 Pennsylvania Ave. N.W., Room 614, Washington, DC 20506/202-682-5496.

Special Projects
Projects funded in the Special Projects category include activities for libraries, young adults, youth projects, and young scholars. Contact: Special Projects, Special Programs Division, National Endowment for the Humanities, 1100 Pennsylvania Ave. N.W., Room 426, Washington, DC 20506/202-786-0271.

State Programs
The State Programs provide support for state humanities councils which in turn support humanities projects at the state and local levels. These programs concentrate their efforts to make humanistic projects accessible to the adult, out-of-school public. Contact: Division of National Endowment for the Humanities, 1100 Pennsylvania Ave. N.W., Room 411, Washington, DC 20506/202-786-0254.

Summer Seminars
This program provides a sum of money for two

months of study and research. Recipients participate in seminars directed by distinguished scholars at institutions with libraries suitable for advanced study. Contact: Summer Seminars, Fellowship and Seminars Division, National Endowment for the Humanities, National Foundation on the Arts and the Humanities 1100 Pennsylvania Ave. N.W., DC 20506/202-786-0463.

Summer Stipends

Summer stipends provide a sum of money for two months of summer study and research. Their purpose is to free college and university teachers from the necessities of summer employment and to provide support for travel and other research expenses necessary for concentrated study. Contact: Summer Stipends, Fellowships and Seminars Division, National Endowment for the Humanities, 1100 Pennsylvania Ave. N.W., Room 316, Washington, DC 20506/202-786-0466.

Theater Projects

Theater grants are awarded to state arts agencies for special projects involving professional theater resources in their areas: to bring high quality professional theater to areas where it has not been available; to assist in the development of a theater company by aiding in artistic development, improving the effectiveness of administration or supporting community service activities; to assist professional theater companies with short seasons; to assist theater for youth; to assist small professional theater companies; to help talented individuals make the transition between professional training and full professional work experience; and to assist organizations that provide services to the theater field. Contact: Theater Program, National Endowment for the Arts, 1100 Pennsylvania Ave. N.W., Room 608, Washington, DC 20506/202-682-5425.

Visual Arts Program

The Visual Arts Program provides money to artists, craftsmen and photographers. Grants are awarded for art in public places such as parks, plazas, riverfronts, airports, subways, and public buildings; for artists' exploration of the potential offered by public sites; for performing arts groups that wish to engage visual artists for the design of sets, costumes or posters for theater, opera or dance productions; to provide for artists, critics, photographers and craftsmen in residence; to help groups organize or borrow photography exhibitions of contemporary or historic significance and publish exhibition catalogues; to help groups organize or borrow crafts exhibitions of contemporary or historic significance; to make possible the publication of important works of photography; to

help organizations commission photographers to document the geography or way of life in a particular city or region; to support workshops and alternative spaces; to enable artists, photographers, craftsmen, and art critics to set aside time, purchase materials, and advance their careers; to encourage craftsmen to find ways of working together and of testing new ideas and media; to assist organizations, artists' groups and individuals concerned with providing services to artists. Contact: Visual Arts Program, National Endowment for the Arts, 1100 Pennsylvania Ave. N.W., Room 729, Washington, DC 20506/202-682-5448.

What Are the Humanities?

The Act of Congress that authorized the Endowment defines the humanities as the study of the following: language; linguistics; literature; history; jurisprudence; philosophy; archaeology; comparative religion; ethics; the history, criticism and theory of the arts; those aspects of the social sciences which have humanistic content and employ humanistic methods; and the study and application of the humanities to the human environment. For additional information, contact: Public Affairs Office, National Endowment for the Humanities, National Foundation on the Arts and the Humanities, Room 409, 1100 Pennsylvania Ave. N.W., Washington, DC 20506/202-786-0438

Youthgrants in the Humanities

This program supports humanities projects developed and conducted by young people: educational projects, humanistic research, media presentations; and community programs. Contact: Youthgrants Programs, Special Projects Office, National Endowment for the Humanities, 1100 Pensylvania Ave. N.W., Room 420, Washington, DC 20506/202-786-0271.

Youth Projects

The purpose of Youth Projects is to stimulate the active participation of young people in humanities projects under the direction of experienced professionals. Contact: Youth Programs, Special Projects Division, National Endowment for the Humanities, 1100 Pennsylvania Ave. N.W., Washington, DC 20506/202-786-0271.

How Can the National Foundation on the Arts and the Humanities Help You?

For information on how this agency can help you, contact: Information Office, National Endowment for the Arts, 1100 Pennsylvania Ave. N.W., Washington, DC 20506/202-682-5400, or Public Information Officer, National Endowment for the Humanities, 1100 Pennsylvania Ave. N.W., Room 409, Washington, DC 20506/202-786-0438.

National Labor Relations Board

1717 Pennsylvania Ave. N.W., Washington, DC 20570/202-632-4950

Established: 1935
Budget: $126,398,000
Employees: 3213

Mission: Administers the Nation's laws relating to labor relations, and safeguards employees' rights to organize, to determine through elections whether workers want unions as their bargaining representatives, and to prevent and remedy unfair labor practices.

Major Sources of Information

Annual Report
This report details the Board's activities for the previous fiscal year with descriptions of the cases handled. Statistical tables of case information are also included. The Annual Report is sold (price varies) by the Superintendent of Documents, Government Printing Office, Washington, DC 20402/202-783-3238. For additional information, contact: Division of Advice, National Labor Relations Board, 1717 Pennsylvania Ave. N.W., Room 820, Washington, DC 20570/202-254-9128.

Bargaining Units
A bargaining unit is a group of two or more employees who share a community of interest and may reasonably be grouped together for purposes of collective bargaining. The National Labor Relations Board (NLRB) determines units of employees appropriate for collective bargaining purposes. For further information, contact the regional office in the area where the unit of employees is located, or Division of Information, National Labor Relations Board, 1717 Pennsylvania Ave. N.W., Room 710, Washington, DC 20570/202-632-4950.

Case Processing System
This system tracks all the cases from the time they are filed to their final disposition. Monthly reports are available providing detailed data on these cases. To be placed on the mailing list, contact: Division of Information, National Labor Relations Board, 1717 Pennsylvania Ave. N.W., Room 710, Washington, DC 20570. The information is also summarized in the Annual Report. It includes a listing of elections conducted by company and industry, who conducted the election, number of votes, number of eligible voters, results, and other related election information. For additional information, contact: Statistical Services, National Labor Relations Board, 1375 K St. N.W., Room 730, Washington, DC 20005/202-633-6737.

Election Results
The National Labor Relations Board conducts secret-ballot elections so employees may decide whether or not a union should represent them for bargaining purposes. The following is a brief description of the six types of petitions that can be filed requesting an election:

Certification of Representative (RC)
This petition, which is normally filed by a union, seeks an election to determine whether employees wish to be represented by a union or not. It must be supported by the signature of 30 percent or more of the employees in the bargaining unit being sought.

Decertification (RD)

This petition, which can be filed by an individual, seeks an election to determine whether the authority of a union to act as a bargaining representative of employees should continue. It must be supported by the signature of 30 percent or more of the employees in the bargaining unit represented by the union.

Withdrawal of Union-Shop Authority (UD)

This petition, which can be filed by an individual, seeks an election to determine whether the union's contractual authority to require the payment of union dues and initiation fees as a condition of employment should be continued. It must be supported by the signatures of 30 percent or more of the employees in the bargaining unit covered by the union-shop agreement.

Employer Petition (RM)

This petition is filed by an employer for an election where one or more unions claim to represent the employer's employees or when the employer has reasonable grounds for believing that the union, which is the current bargaining representative, no longer represents a majority of employees.

Unit Clarification (UC)

This petition seeks to clarify the scope of an existing bargaining unit by, for example, determining whether a new classification is properly a part of that unit. The petition may be filed by either the employer or the union.

Amendment of Certificaton (AC)

This petition seeks the amendment of an outstanding certification of a union to reflect changed circumstances such as changes in the name or affiliation of the union. This petition may be filed by a union or an employer. Contact the Regional Office in the area where the unit of employees is located. For appeals of the regional director's decisions, contact: Office of Representative Appeals, National Labor Relations Board, 1717 Pennsylvania Ave. N.W., Room 760, Washington, DC 20570/202-254-9118.

Executive Secretary's Management Information System

This system tracks those cases before the Board and includes information on the types of allegations, type of industry, geographic location, formal actions taken and other related information. Summaries of this data are available in the Annual Report. Contact: Office of the Executive Secretary, National Labor Relations Board, 1717 Pennsylvania Ave. N.W., Room 701, Washington, DC 20570/202-254-9430.

Formal Complaints

Formal complaints are issued and prosecuted before the Board by the General Counsel. Contact: Office of the General Counsel, National Labor Relations Board, 1717 Pennsylvania Ave. N.W., Room 1001, Washington, DC 20570/202-254-9150.

Freedom of Information Act Requests

For Freedom of Information Act requests, contact: Office of the Executive Secretary, National Labor Relations Board, 1717 Pennsylvania Ave. N.W., Room 701, Washington, DC 20570/202-254-9430.

Legal Research System

This system provides indexes of Board decisions, court decisions and related legal information. *Classified Indexes of the National Labor Relations Board Decisions and Related Court Decisions* is available bi-monthly (price varies) from the Superintendent of Documents, Government Printing Office, Washington, DC 20402/202-783-3238. For additional information, contact: Legal Research and Policy Planning, Division of Advice, National Labor Relations Board, 1717 Pennsylvania Ave. N.W., Room 1107, Washington, DC 20570/202-254-9350.

Library

The library is open to the public. The collection emphasizes labor law and labor relations. Contact: Library, National Labor Relations Board, 1717 Pennsylvania Ave. N.W., Room 900, Washington, DC 20570/202-254-9055.

Meetings

National Labor Relations Board meetings are generally open to the public. Notices of these meetings are available upon request. Contact: Division of Information, National Labor Relations Board, 1717 Pennsylvania Ave. N.W., Room 710, Washington, DC 20570/202-632-4950.

Publications

A free list of National Labor Relations Board publications is available. Contact: Division of Information, National Labor Relations Board, 1717 Pennsylvania Ave. N.W., Room 710, Washington, DC 20570/202-632-4950.

Public Information Room

Decisions, appeals and advice papers are available for public inspection. For further information, contact: Records Management, National Labor Relations Board, 1717 Pennsylvania Ave. N.W., Room 200, Washington, DC 20570/202-254-9488.

Regional Offices

Regional offices are the starting points for all cases coming to the National Labor Relations Board. In addition to processing unfair labor practice cases in the initial stages, regional offices investigate representation petitions, determine units of employees appropriate for collective-bargaining purposes, and conduct elections and pass on objections to the conduct of elections. Regional offices are listed in the telephone directory under the United States Government, National Labor Relations Board, or contact: Division of Operational Management, National Labor Relations Board, 1717 Pennsylvania Ave. N.W., Room 1030, Washington, DC 20570/202-254-9102.

Speakers
Washington and regional personnel participate as speakers or panel members before bar associations, labor organizations, management groups and education, civic and other groups. To request speakers or panelists, contact the nearest regional director, or the Division of Information, National Labor Relations Board, 1717 Pennsylvania Ave. N.W., Room 710, Washington, DC 20570/202-632-4950.

Unfair Labor Practice Charges
Charges that business firms, labor organizations, or both, have committed unfair labor practices are filed with the National Labor Relations Board by employees, unions and employers. Contact the nearest National Labor Relations Board field

office. If the regional directors refuse to issue complaints, contact: Office of Appeals, National Labor Relations Board, 1717 Pennsylvania Ave. N.W., Room 1154. Washington, DC 20570/202-254-9316.

Unfair Labor Practice Hearings
Formal hearings in unfair labor practice cases are conducted by Administrative Law Judges. They make rulings, assign dates for hearings and maintain a calendar of cases to be heard. Contact: Division of Administrative Law Judges, National Labor Relations Board, 1375 K St. N.W., Room 1100, Washington, DC 20005/202-633-0500.

Weekly Summary
Weekly summaries of decisions are available. Contact: Division of Information, National Labor Relations Board, 1717 Pennsylvania Ave. N.W., Room 710, Washington, DC 20570/202-632-4950.

How Can the National Labor Relations Board Help You?
For information on how this agency can help you, contact: Division of Information, National Labor Relations Board, 1717 Pennsylvania Ave. N.W., Washington, DC 20570/202-632-4950.

National Mediation Board

1425 K St. N.W., Washington, DC 20572/202-523-5920

Established: June 21, 1934
Budget: $5,448,000
Employees: 60

Mission: Assists in maintaining a free flow of commerce in the railroad and airline industries by resolving disputes that could disrupt travel or imperil the economy; handles railroad and airline employee representation disputes; and supervises finances for the National Railroad Adjustment Board, which handles rail grievances relating to the interpretation and application of existing contracts.

Major Sources of Information

Clerical Forces and Maintenance of Way Men, Dispatchers
This division has jurisdiction over disputes involving station, tower and telegraph employees, train dispatchers, maintenance of way men, clerical employees, freight handlers, express, station and store employees, signalmen, sleeping car conductors, sleeping car porters and maids, and dining car employees. Contact: Third Division, National Railroad Adjustment Board, National Mediation Board, 10 W. Jackson Blvd., Room 200, Chicago, IL 60604/312-886-7303.

Disputes
The disputes between an employee or a group of employees and a carrier or carriers growing out of grievances or out of the interpretation or application of agreements concerning rates of pay, rules, or working conditions shall be handled in the usual manner up to and including the chief operating officer of the carrier designated to handle such disputes; but, failing to reach an adjustment in this manner, the disputes may be referred by petition of the parties or by either party to the appropriate division of the Adjustment Board with full statement of facts and all supporting data bearing upon the disputes. Contact: Executive Secretary, National Railroad Adjustment Board, National Mediation Board, 10 W. Jackson Blvd., Room 200, Chicago, IL 60604/312-886-7300.

Dockets
Copies of collective bargaining agreements between labor and management of various rail and air carriers and copies of the awards and interpretations issued by the several divisions of the National Railroad Adjustment Board are available for public inspection during office hours. Contact: Executive Secretary, National Mediation Board, 1425 K St. N.W., Room 910, Washington, DC 20572/202-523-5920.

Freedom of Information Act Requests
For Freedom of Information Act requests, contact: Freedom of Information Office, National Mediation Board, 1425 K St. N.W., Room 910, Washington, DC 20572/202-523-5996.

Mediation Publications
A booklet outlining the history and operations of the Board and the act, *Administration of the Railway Labor Act by the National Mediation*

Board 1934–70, is available on request. Also available for public distribution are the following documents: *Determination of Craft or Class* (1–11 volumes); *Interpretations Pursuant to Section 5, Second of the Act* (2 volumes); *Annual Reports of the National Mediation Board including the Report of the National Railroad Adjustment Board; The Railway Labor Act at Fifty.* The National Mediation Board maintains two subscription mailing lists:

Subscription List No. 1—the rate of $140.00 per year will cover all publications issued by the Board. These include: *Certifications and Dismissals; Determinations of Craft or Class; Findings Upon Investigation; Annual Reports of the National Mediation Board; Emergency Board Reports; The Representation Manual;* and all other publications on these topics issued by the Agency.

Subscription List No. 2—the rate of $25.00 per year will cover the following publications: *Annual Reports of the National Mediation Board; Emergency Board Reports;* and *Determinations of Craft or Class* (bound volume).

Upon request, the Executive Secretary may waive payment of the subscription rate, in whole or in part, when it is determined that such reduction or waiver is in the public interest. Contact: Executive Secretary, National Mediation Board, 1425 K St. N.W., Room 910, Washington, DC 20572/202-523-5920.

Shop Craft Disputes

This division has jurisdiction over disputes involving machinists, boilermakers, blacksmiths, sheet metal workers, electrical workers, carmen, the helpers, and apprentices of all of the foregoing, coach cleaners, powerhouse employees and railroad shop laborers. For additional information, contact: Second Division, National Railroad Adjustment Board, National Mediation Board, 10 W. Jackson Blvd., Room 200, Chicago, IL 60604/312-886-7303.

Train and Yard Service Employees

This division has jurisdiction over disputes between employees or groups of employees and carriers involving train and yard service employees, that is, engineers, firemen, hostlers, and outside hostler helpers, conductors, trainmen and yard service employees. Contact: First Division, National Railroad Adjustment Board, National Mediation Board, 10 W. Jackson Blvd., Room 200, Chicago, IL 60604/312-886-7303.

Water Transportation and Miscellaneous Matters

This division has jurisdiction over disputes involving employees of carriers directly or indirectly engaged in transportation of passengers or property by water, and all other employees of carriers, over which jurisdiction is not given to the first, second and third divisions. Contact: Fourth Division, National Railroad Adjustment Board, National Mediation Board, 10 W. Jackson Blvd., Room 200, Chicago, IL 60604/312-886-7303.

How Can the National Mediation Board Help You?

For information on how this agency can help you, contact: Executive Secretary, National Mediation Board, 1425 K St. N.W., Washington, DC 20572/202-523-5920.

National Science Foundation

1800 G. St. N.W., Washington, DC 20550/202-357-9498

Established: 1950
Budget: $1,093,600,000
Employees: 1,135

Mission: Promotes the progress of science through the support of research and education in the sciences, emphasizing basic research, the search for improved understanding of the fundamental laws of nature, upon which our future well-being as a nation is dependent; is involved in applied research directed toward the solution of more immediate problems of our society; its educational programs are aimed at insuring increasing understanding of science at all educational levels and an adequate supply of scientists and engineers to meet our country's needs.

Major Sources of Information

Academic Research and Development Data Base
The OPRM Interactive Data Base provides information about the funding of academic research and development; postdoctoral and graduate student support; PhDs awarded; the employment of academic scientists and engineers; indirect faculty costs; salaries and benefits. Funding sources range from governmental agencies to private industry. Searches and printouts are available free of charge. Contact: National Science Foundation, 1800 G St. N.W., Washington, DC 20550/202-357-9540.

Aeronomy
The aeronomy sciences project supports research on upper and middle atmosphere phenomena of ionization, recombination, chemical reaction, photoemission, and transport; the transport of energy, momentum, and mass in the mesosphere-thermosphere-ionosphere system, including the processes involved and the coupling of this global system to the stratosphere below and magnetosphere above; and the plasma physics of phenomena manifested in the upper atmosphere-ionosphere system, including magnetospheric coupling efforts. Contact:

Aeronomy Program, Division of Atmospheric Sciences, Directorate for Astronomical, Atmospheric, Earth and Ocean Sciences, National Science Foundation, 1800 G St. N.W., Room 644, Washington, DC 20550/202-357-7619.

Algebra and Number Theory
The algebra and number theory program supports research on geometry of surfaces describable by algebraic equations and analogous situations in higher dimensions; algebraic sets and their special transformations; structure of groups and other algebraic entities; discrete mathematics and combinatorial theory; and new algebraic techniques to answer questions raised in other areas of mathematics and science. Contact: Algebra and Number Theory Program, Division of Mathematical and Computer Sciences, Directorate for Mathematical and Physical Sciences, National Science Foundation, 1800 G St. N.W., Room 304, Washington, DC 20550/202-357-9764.

Alternative Biological Sources of Materials
The alternative biological sources of materials program supports research to determine which

biological sources constitute promising alternatives; develop biologically based processes needed to convert the sources to useful materials; and determine the socioeconomic, technical, and environmental impacts of various proposed biological alternative systems. Topics selected for investigation include biological conversion of lignocellulose to useful chemicals and materials and production of specialty chemicals from underutilized plants. Contact: Alternative Biological Resources of Materials Program, Molecular Biosciences Division, Biological Behavioral and Social Sciences Directorate, National Science Foundation, Room 325, 1800 G St. N.W., Washington, DC 20550/202-357-9782.

Antarctic Bibliography
This is a series of compilations presenting abstracts and indexes of current Antarctic literature published worldwide since 1951. A flyer describing the bibliography and the monthly printout of *Current Antarctic Literature* is also available. Contact: Polar Information Division of Polar Programs, Directorate for Astronomical, Atmospheric, Earth and Ocean Sciences, National Science Foundation, 1800 G St. N.W., Room 62, Washington, DC 20550/202-357-7817.

Antarctic Research
Antarctic research is supported in the disciplines of astronomy, biology and medicine, upper atmosphere physics, geology, glaciology, meteorology, and oceanography. Specific objectives of the program are to understand the function, evolution, and adaptations of land and sea species and ecosystems; the geology and geologic history of the continent and its surrounding ocean basins; the structure and dynamics of the magnetosphere and the ionosphere, which are uniquely measurable at the high geomagnetic latitudes of Antarctica; Antarctica's role in past and present global climate through study of surface and upper air processes, the structure, dynamics, and chemistry of the ice sheet, and oceanic circulation; and the physical and chemical oceanography of antarctic seas. Contact: Division of Polar Programs, Directorate for Astronomical, Atmospheric, Earth and Ocean Sciences, National Science Foundation, 1800 G St. N.W., Room 620, Washington, DC 20550/202-357-7766.

Anthropology
The anthropology program supports research on archaeology and cultural, social, and physical anthropology spanning all topics, geographic areas, and methodologies; systematic research collections; human origins; the interaction of population, culture, and the environment; and improved methods of radiocarbon and other techniques of dating and analysis. Contact: Anthropology Program, Division of Behavioral and Neural Sciences, Directorate for Biological, Behavioral and Social Sciences, National Science Foundation, 1800 G St. N.W., Room 320, Washington, DC 20550/202-357-7804.

Applied Mathematics
The applied mathematics program supports research on mathematical description of problems in physical sciences and engineering (e.g., solid and fluid mechanics, wave propagation, bifurcation, galactic phenomena); mathematical formulation of problems in biomedical sciences (e.g., population dynamics, ecological structures, epidemiology, genetics); methodologies of control optimization, optimal allocation of resources including mathematical economics; and development of numerical methods and programming techniques for use of digital computers and mathematical models. Contact: Applied Mathematics Program, Division of Mathematical Sciences, Directorate for Mathematical and Physical Sciences, National Science Foundation, 1800 G St. N.W., Room 304, Washington, DC 20550/202-357-9764.

Arctic Research
Research is supported in the disciplines of geology and geophysics, biology, oceanography, meteorology, glaciology, and upper atmospheric physics. Specific objectives of the program are to gain new knowledge on: mechanisms of energy transfer between the magnetosphere, the ionosphere, and the neutral atmosphere; the role of the Arctic Basin in influencing climate; the interactions of arctic and subarctic seas with the global ocean system; sea-ice occurrence and behavior in coastal waters; the history of climatic changes as revealed in the study of deep ice cores from the Greenland ice sheet; properties and characteristics of permafrost; and the structure, function, and regulation of arctic terrestrial and marine eco-systems. Contact: Division of Polar Programs, Directorate for Astronomical, Atmospheric, Earth and Ocean Sciences, National Science Foundation, Room 620, 1800 G St. N.W., Washington, DC 20550/202-357-7766.

Astronomical Instrumentation and Development
The astronomical instrumentation and development program sponsors the development and construction of state-of-the-art detectors and data-handling equipment; procurement of detection and analysis systems for telescopes at institutions that presently lack such systems; development of interactive picture processing systems; development of very long baseline interferometric instrumentation; and application of new technology and innovative techniques to astronomy. Contact: Astronomical, Atmospheric, Earth and Ocean Sciences, National Science Foundation, 1800 G St. N.W., Room 615, Washington, DC 20550/202-357-7621.

Atmospheric Chemistry
The atmospheric chemistry program supports research on the concentration and distribution of gases and aerosols in the atmosphere; chemical reactions among atmospheric species; interactions of atmospheric species with solar radiation; sources and sinks of important trace gases; precipitation chemistry; transport of gases and aerosols between the troposphere and stratosphere; polluted urban air chemistry; and air transport and transportation of energy-related pollutants. Contact: Atmospheric Chemistry Program, Division of Atmospheric Sciences, Directorate for Astronomical, Atmospheric, Earth and Ocean Sciences, National Science Foundation, Room 644, 1800 G St. N.W., Washington, DC 20550/202-357-9657.

Atomic, Molecular, and Plasma Physics
The atomic, molecular and plasma physics program supports research on properties and interactions of particles at the atomic, molecular, and more complex aggregation levels in which the atomic characteristics dominate. Specific interests include: measurement of precisely defined states of atoms and the interaction of these states with other such atoms; formation and properties of highly perturbed electronic configurations in light and heavy atoms; study of the complex states formed during close collisions of heavy atoms; ultraprecise measurements of atomic properties to verify basic theories and find expressions of new physical laws; and general and collision-free plasmas. Contact: Atomic, Molecular and Plasma Physics Program, Division of Physics, Directorate for Mathematical and Physical Sciences, National Science Foundation, 1800 G. St. N.W., Room 341, Washington, DC 20550/202-357-7997.

Automation, Instrumentation, and Sensing Systems
The electrical, computer, and systems engineering programs support applied research in engineering sciences in medicine and biology, including the areas of microminiaturized sensors, pattern analysis, machine intelligence, and cognitive systems engineering. Contact: Automation, Instrumentation and Sensing Systems Program, Division of Electrical, Computer and Systems Engineering, Directorate for Engineering, National Science Foundation, 1800 G St. N.W., Room 1101, Washington, DC 20550/202-357-9618.

Bilateral Cooperative Science Activities
Bilateral Cooperative Science Activities receive support for three types of activities: 1) Cooperative research projects which are jointly designed and jointly conducted by principal investigators from the United States and the foreign country; 2) Research-oriented seminars (or workshops), which are meetings of small groups of scientists from the United States and from the foreign country, to exchange information, review the current status of a specific field of science and plan cooperative research; and 3) Scientific visits for planning cooperative activities or for research. (Visits of six months or longer are eligible for consideration of support of dependent travel.) The United States Cooperative Science Programs include formal bilateral arrangements with Argentina, Australia, Belgium, Brazil, Bulgaria, Federal Republic of Germany, France, Greece, Hungary, India, Italy, Japan, Republic of Korea, Mexico, New Zealand, Pakistan, Romania, Switzerland, USSR, and Venezuela. Contact: Division of International Programs, Directorate for Scientific, Technological and International Affairs, National Science Foundation, 1800 G St. N.W., Room 1214, Washington, DC 20550/202-357-9552.

Biochemistry
The biochemistry program supports research on chemical composition and structure of proteins, carbohydrates, and nucleic acids, and the identification of the molecular parameters that describe their functions; investigations of the mechanism and regulation of the biosynthesis of proteins, carbohydrates, and nucleic and fatty acids; studies on enzyme structure and function; studies on the biogenesis, topography, and assemblage of membranes and the mutual interactions of their constituent macromolecules; and determination of virus structure, assembly, replication, and expression. Contact: Biochemistry Program, Division of Molecular Biosciences, Directorate for Biological, Behavioral and Social Sciences, National Science Foundation, 1800 G St. N.W., Room 329, Washington, DC 20550/202-357-7945.

Biological Instrumentation
The biological instrumentation program supports the purchase of major biological research instruments for use by groups of investigators; and development of biological instruments that are not presently available commercially and that will increase the accuracy and sensitivity of research observations. Contact: Biological Instrumentation, Division of Molecular Biosciences, Directorate for Biological, Behavioral and Social Sciences, National Science Foundation, 1800 G St. N.W., Room 325, Washington, DC 20550/202-357-7652.

Biological Oceanography
The ocean sciences project supports research on the distribution, abundance, physiology, and life history of pelagic, coastal, and deep sea marine organisms, and their interactions with the chemical, physical, and biological environments; the structure of pelagic and detritus-based food chains; phytoplankton productivity; interactions between deep sea biological processes and the overall ocean ecosystem; biological specialization of deep sea organisms; and the ecology of the Great Lakes and factors regulating phytoplankton productivity in

the Great Lakes. Contact: Biological Oceanography Program, Division of Ocean Sciences, Directorate for Astronomical, Atmospheric, Earth and Ocean Sciences, National Science Foundation, 1800 G St. N.W., Room 611, Washington, DC 20550/202-357-9600.

Biological Research Resources
This program provides operational support for biological research resources including living-organism stock centers, biological field research facilities, and systematic research collections to enhance their use by U.S. scientists. Contact: Biological Research Resources Program, Division of Biotic Systems and Resources, Directorate for Biological, Behavioral and Social Sciences, National Science Foundation, 1800 G St. N.W., Washington, DC 20550/202-357-7475.

Biophysics
The biophysics program supports research on the development and interpretation of data that enhance understanding of the chemical and physical changes that occur in macromolecular compounds (biopolymers) during their functional processes; and determination of molecular structure, dynamics, and interactions and alterations that occur during the functional state. Contact: Biophysics Program, Division of Molecular Biosciences, Directorate for Biological, Behavioral and Social Sciences, National Science Foundation, 1800 G St. N.W., Room 329, Washington, DC 20550/202-357-7777.

Cellular Biosciences
The cell biology program supports research on the biology of prokaryotic and eukaryotic cells *in vivo* and in culture; elucidation of the structure and function of the cytoskeleton, membranes, chromosomes, and other organelles of the cell; investigations of the cell cycle, cell behavior, and cell-cell interactions; and mechanisms and regulation of cell motility. Contact: Cell Biology Program, Division of Cellular Biosciences, Directorate for Biological, Behavioral and Social Sciences, National Science Foundation, 1800 G St. N.W., Room 332, Washington, DC 20550/202-357-7474.

Cellular Physiology
The program on cellular physiology supports research on the reception of signals by cells, emphasizing the mechanisms of hormone action, including hormone receptors, hormone-gene interactions, and hormonal effects on metabolism; intracellular messengers and message transduction; basic mechanisms of the immune response; and cellular physiology of muscle. Contact: Cellular Physiology Program, Divison of Cellular Biosciences, Directorate for Biological, Behavioral, and Social Sciences, National Science Foundation,

1800 G St. N.W., Room 332, Washington, DC 20550/202-357-7377.

Ceramics
The ceramics program supports research on the fundamental properties of ceramic materials, including glass, graphite, refractory oxides, nitrides, and carbides, and other inorganic compounds; deformation and fracture mechanisms of ceramic materials in severe environments; corrosion, erosion and wear; and basic optical phenomena in materials considered for fiber optics, lasers, and solar devices. Contact: Ceramics Program, Division of Materials Research, Directorate for Mathematical and Physical Sciences, National Science Foundation, 1800 G St. N.W., Room 411, Washington, DC 20550/202-357-9789.

Cerro Tololo Inter-American Observatory
The National Science Foundation supports the Cerro Tololo Inter-American Observatory (CTIO) to provide qualified scientists with the telescopes and related facilities required ·for research in ground-based optical astronomy in the Southern Hemisphere. CTIO has eight telescopes, including the 4-meter (158-inch) near-twin to the Kitt Peak 4-meter telescope. Contact: Cerro Tololo Inter-American Observatory, Casila (603), La Serena, Chile, South America, or Cerro Tololo Inter-American Observatory, Division of Astronomical Sciences, Directorate for Astronomical, Atmospheric, Earth and Ocean Sciences, National Science Foundation, 1800 G St. N.W., Room 618, Washington, DC 20550/202-357-9740.

Chemical Analysis
The chemical analysis program supports research on new or improved methods of chemical analysis of all forms of matter and surface and interface species; analytic procedures that couple novel chemistry and advanced instrumentation with computer management; and comprehensive approaches to the analysis of complex materials such as catalysts and airborne particulares. Contact: Chemical Analysis Program, Division of Chemistry, Directorate for Mathematical and Physical Sciences, National Science Foundation, 1800 G St. N.W., Room 340, Washington, DC 20550/202-357-7960.

Chemical and Biochemical Systems
The chemical and process engineering program supports research on the basic aspects of chemical and biochemical processes in a variety of technologic areas undergirding a wide range of process industries, with emphasis on biochemical process fundamentals; food process engineering; polymerization and polymer processing; process synthesis, simulation, optimization, and control; and electrochemical processes. Contact: Chemical and Biochemical Processes Program, Division of Chemical

and Process Engineering, Directorate for Engineering and Applied Science, National Science Foundation, 1800 G St. N.W., Room 1126, Washington, DC 20550/202-357-9606.

Chemical Dynamics

The chemical dynamics program supports research on rates of reactions that are critically important in developing general laws and theories in chemistry; influence of chemical environments, energy sources, and catalysis on rates and products of chemical reactions; transient intermediates produced in reacting systems and their roles in producing chemical changes, correlations and generalizations between molecular structure and reactivity; new techniques and instruments; and fundamental rate data for use in disciplines such as biology and atmospheric sciences. Contact: Chemical Dynamics Program, Chemistry Division, Directorate for Mathematical and Physical Sciences, National Science Foundation, 1800 G St. N.W., Room 340, Washington, DC 20550/202-357-7956.

Chemical Instrumentation

The chemical instrumentation program provides assistance to universities and colleges in acquiring major items of instrumentation essential for the improved conduct of fundamental research in chemistry. Contact: Chemical Instrumentation Program, Division of Chemistry, Directorate for Mathematical and Physical Sciences, National Science Foundation, Room 340, 1800 G St. N.W., Washington, DC 20550/202-357-7960.

Chemical Physics

The chemical physics program supports research on the development of a general chemical theory to aid in the design and interpretation of experimental studies; experimental chemical transformation studies of single collisions of atoms and molecules; and acquisition and interpretation of data on the interaction of radiation with atoms and molecules; and energy transfer within and between individual molecules. Contact: Chemical Physics Program, Division of Chemistry, Directorate for Mathematical and Physical Sciences, National Science Foundation, 1800 G St. N.W., Room 340, Washington, DC 20550/202-357-7951.

Classical Mathematical Analysis

The classical analysis program supports research on the properties and behavior of solutions of ordinary and partial differential equations; relationships between analysis and geometry, particularly between solutions of partial differential equations and geometric properties of surfaces and manifolds; functions of one and several complex variables; real analysis; and special functions and approximation theory. Contact: Classical Analysis Program, Division of Mathematical Sciences, Directorate for

Mathematical and Physical Sciences, National Science Foundation, 1800 G St. N.W., Room 339, Washington, DC 20550/202-357-9764.

Climate Dynamics

The atmospheric sciences project supports research on the development of a basis for predicting climate variations and for assessing the impact of these variations on human affairs. The program supports research that will contribute to knowledge of the natural variability of climate and to understanding of the physical processes governing climate. Specific areas of research supported are: modern climate data assembly and analysis; paleoclimatic data assembly and analysis; climate modeling and simulation; and climate impact assessment. Contact: Climate Dynamics Program, Division of Atmospheric Sciences, Directorate for Astronomical, Atmospheric, Earth and Ocean Sciences, National Science Foundation, 1800 G St. N.W., Room 644, Washington, DC 20550/202-357-9892.

Committee Minutes

Summary minutes of open meetings of the National Science Foundation advisory groups may be obtained. Contact: National Science Board, National Science Foundation, 1800 G St. N.W., Room 545, Washington, DC 20550/202-357-9582.

Computer Engineering

The electrical, computer and systems engineering programs support research on the impact of large-scale and very large-scale integration on special purpose hardware and new computer architectures; classes of algorithms and their hardware implementation; types of computer architectures that lend themselves to better algorithms; distributed processing, parallel processing, computer-aided design, fault tolerance, and man-machine interfaces to computers; computer engineering for mechanical systems; and hardware and software computational issues involved in engineering intelligent systems, including knowledge representation and planning systems, transformations between different representations, 3-D object modeling, and very high-level languages. Contact: Computer Engineering Program, Division of Electrical, Computer and Systems Engineering, Directorate for Engineering, National Science Foundation, 1800 G St. N.W., Room 1101, Washington, DC 20550/202-357-9618.

Computer Sciences Special Projects

The special projects program supports research on general and specialized projects in experimental computer science; computer science research equipment; societal issues in computer science including privacy and security; legal aspects of computing, and social and economic impact; new directions in computer science and applications including computer networks, data bases, and database management; computer-based modeling; and other topics of special interest in computer science. Contact: Special Projects, Computer Programs, Division of Computer Research, Rm 339, Division of Mathematical and Computer Sciences, Directorate for Mathematics and Physical Sciences, National Science Foundation, 1800 G. St. N.W., Washington, DC 20550/202-357-7375.

Computer Systems Design

The program on computer systems design supports research on the principles of computer systems design relating to the structure of computer systems or the process of systems design. Topics include, but are not limited to: computer system architecture; distributed computer systems; integrated hardware/software systems; performance measurement and evaluation; fault tolerant systems; logic design; computer graphics; man-machine interaction; and Very Large Scale Integration (VLSI) design methodology. The scope of this program includes experimental implementation where that is an integral part of the research. Contact: Computer Systems Design, Division of Computer Research, Directorate for Mathematical and Physical Sciences, National Science Foundation, 1800 G St. N.W., Room 339, Washington, DC 20550/202-357-7349.

Condensed Matter Theory

The Condensed Matter Theory program supports theoretical research on condensed matter, involving studies of phase transitions and critical point behavior, elementary excitations, lattice dynamics, defects, surfaces, electronic and magnetic states, transport and optical properties, and macroscopic quantum properties such as superconductivity and superfluidity. Contact: Condensed Matter Theory Program, Division of Materials Research, Directorate for Mathematical and Physical Sciences, National Science Foundation, Room 404, 1800 G St. N.W., Washington, DC 20550/202-357-9737.

Deep Sea Drilling

The deep sea drilling project involves the acquisition of geologic samples from the floor of the deep ocean basins by means of rotary drilling and coring in the sediments and the underlying crystalline rocks. Portions of the core samples are made available to qualified scientists for individual research projects. *Initial Reports of the Deep Sea Drilling Project,* lithologic and paleontologic descriptions and resulting interpretations published in a total of 53 volumes, are on sale from the Superintendent of Documents, Government Printing Office, Washington, DC 20402/202-783-3238. For a list of these reports and further information, contact: Ocean Drilling Programs, Directorate for Astronomical, Atmospheric, Earth and Ocean Sciences, National Science Foundation, 1800 G St., Room 1133, Washington, DC 20550/202-357-9849.

Developmental Biology

The developmental biology program supports studies on the mechanisms involved in determining the growth and form of animals, plants and microorganisms. Areas included are reproduction, embryogenesis, pattern formation, developmental genetics, gene expression, recombinant DNA research, plant regeneration from culture protoplasts and cells, and animal regeneration. Emphasis is on experimental analysis of development. Contact: Developmental Biology Program, Division of Cellular Biosciences, Directorate for Biological, Behavioral and Social Sciences, National Science Foundation, 1800 G St. N.W., Room 332, Washington, DC 20550/202-357-7989.

Earthquake Hazards Mitigation Research

The earthquake hazards mitigation program supports research on improved characterization of earthquake and natural hazard loadings necessary for the economical design of structures subject to dynamic loading; new methods of analysis and design of buildings and structures of all types that will take into account nonlinear and inelastic behavior of materials and structures; methods to assess the hazard potential and risk assessments applicable to existing structures and facilities and to improve performance within economically acceptable bounds; observation of damage to facilities following actual earthquakes and incorporation of this information into standard design practice; improved computational capability for dynamic analysis of structures and facilities and improved user access to any computer software developed; model standards and design criteria for design of structures and facilities subjected to earthquake and natural hazard loadings; and behavior of smaller, nonengineered structures and secondary components of buildings to improve analytic procedures and design guidelines. Contact: Civil and Environmental Engineering, Earthquake Hazard Mitigation Section, Division of Architecture, Planning and Dynamic Structure Experimentation, Directorate for Engineering, National Science Foundation, 1800 G St. N.W., Room 1130, Washington, DC 20550/202-357-7710.

Earthquake Policy

The earthquake hazards mitigation program supports research on alternative social adjustments to earthquakes; social, economic, political, legal, and related factors that facilitate or hinder the adoption of both social and technologic solutions to earthquake hazards; effective techniques for disseminating information on earthquake hazard mitigation to the public and to decisionmakers at the local, state, and national levels; and analyses of measures that will reduce possible negative social, economic, and political consequences of earthquake predictions and warnings. Contact: Civil and Environmental Engineering, Earthquake Hazard Mitigation Section, Dynamic Structure Analysis and Societal Response, Directorate for Engineering, National Science Foundation, 1800 G St. N.W., Room 1130 Washington, DC 20550/202-357-9780.

Earthquake Siting

The earthquake hazards mitigation program supports research on the nature of earthquake motion at typical construction sites and for representative structures; the physical basis for characterizing the nature of earthquake motions and the dynamic forces generated by such motions and by other natural hazards; capabilities for predicting the magnitude and frequencies of strong ground motions; and methodology for qualitative and quantitative estimates of local or regional risk associated with earthquakes and combined hazards; a comprehensive and unified program to improve geotechnical engineering practices applicable to solid dynamics, foundation design failure and instability, and other aspects of earthquake ground motion; and procedures for integrating information on natural hazards into land-use planning, urban and coastal zone planning, offshore engineering, and siting procedures. Contact: Earthquake and Hazards Mitigation Program, Division of Fundamental Research in Emerging and Critical Engineering Systems, Directorate for Engineering, National Science Foundation, 1800 G St. N.W., Room 1130 Washington, DC 20550/202-357-9500.

Ecology

The ecology program supports research on community ecology of land and inland waters, with emphasis on interactions such as competition, herbivory, pollination, predation, other antagonisms and symbiosis in natural and agricultural ecosystems, and coevolution within interacting groups; microbial ecology of soils and sediments, especially in relation to decomposition, nutrient cycling, and productivity; mechanisms that influence the distribution and abundance of communities of animals and plants now and in the recent geological past. Contact: Ecology Program, Division of Biotic Systems and Resources, Directorate for Biological, Behavioral and Social Sciences, National Science Foundation, 1800 G St. N.W., Room 1140, Washington, DC 20550/202-357-9734.

Economics

The economics program supports research on microanalysis of economic aggregates, including national income, the price level, and employment; forces determining the time path of the economy in response to various stimuli; determinants and consequences of market structure; interaction of fiscal and monetary variables in open economies, particularly as these pertain to problems of inflation and unemployment; economic study of renewable and nonrenewable resources; nonmarket decisionmaking; economic history and development; international economics; techniques of quantitative analysis; and empirical validation and assessment of different types of economic models. Contact: Economics Program, Division of Social and Economic Sciences, Directorate for Biological, Behavioral and Social Sciences, National Science Foundation, 1800 G St. N.W., Room 312, Washington, DC 20550/202-357-9675.

Ecosystem Studies

The program on ecosystems supports laboratory, field and mathematical modeling studies of the processes and components of natural, managed, and mandominated terrestrial, freshwater, and wetland ecosystems; research on new methods of predicting ecosystem change, and mathematically analyzing functional interdependencies in complex, highly variable systems; and information on ecosystem management and exploitation. Contact: Ecosystem Studies, Division of Biotic Systems and Resources, Directorate for Biological, Behavioral and Social Sciences, National Science Foundation, 1800 G St. N.W., Room 1140, Washington, DC 20550/202-357-9596.

Electrical and Optical Communications

The electrical, computer and systems engineering program supports research on systems methodology and devices for optical communications and large-scale computer communications networks, information and coding theories, digital signal processing, and speech and image transmission and processing. Contact: Electrical and Optical Communications Program, Division of Electrical, Computer and Systems Engineering, Directorate for Engineering and Applied Science, National Science Foundation, 1800 G St. N.W., Room 1151, Washington, DC 20550/202-357-9618.

Elementary Particle Physics

The program on elementary particle physics supports research on unknown states of matter and their properties and interactions; data that can be compared with theoretical models and ideas regarding the nature of the submicroscopic world. Support is primarily provided to university groups to conduct experimental research at the major accelerator centers at national laboratories or at specialized university-based or university-affiliated laboratories. Contact: Elementary Particle Physics Program, Division of Physics, Directorate for Mathematical and Physical Sciences, National Science Foundation, 1800 G St. N.W., Room 341, Washington, DC 20550/202-357-9575.

Engineering Energetics

The chemical and process engineering program supports research on plasma chemistry and arc technology with emphasis on plasma polymerization, isotope separations, laser-induced chemical processes, arc-heater reactors, electric circuit breakers, and arc light sources; chemical and physical behavior of combustion of coal, oil, gas, and other materials; characterization of flames, environmental control, problems associated with substitute fuels, and efficiency of combustion; basic phenomena of energy conversion processes, including magnetohydrodynamics; and nucleonics with emphasis on fundamental investigations and applications of nuclear science, such as reactor dynamics, neutron transport theory and analysis, radiation transport and radiation effects, and fusion-related topics. Contact: Engineering Energetics Program, Division of Chemical and Process Engineering, Directorate for Engineering and Applied Science, National Science Foundation, 1800 G St. N.W., Room 1126, Washington, DC 20550/202-357-9606.

Environment, Energy and Resource Studies

Research in this area centers on issues definition and assistance to policymakers in finding techniques to deal with critical problems and improving methods for assessing effects of alternative governmental actions. Contact: Technology and Resource Policy Section, Division of Policy Research and Analysis, Directorate for Scientific, Technological and International Affairs, National Science Foundation, 1800 G St. N.W., Room 1229, Washington, DC 20550/202-357-7829.

Ethics and Values in Science and Technology

This program supports projects in ethical issues in the education and professional conduct of scientists and engineers; issues of obligation and constraint associated with scientific and technologic organizations and institutions; ethical and social issues associated with new developments in science and technology; effects of changing ethical and social values upon the conduct of science and technology; and ethical issues and value assumptions in decision-making processes involving science and technology. Contact: Ethics and Values in Science and Technology, Division of Research Initiation and Improvement, Directorate for Scientific Technology and International Affairs, National Science Foundation, 1800 G St. N.W., Room 1144, Washington, DC 20550/202-357-7552.

Experimental Meteorology

The atmospheric sciences project supports field research on the physics and dynamics of the troposphere, including basic research related to international and inadvertent weather modification, precipitation development within cloud systems, the interaction between wind fields within cloud systems and the precipitation process, the development of mesoscale weather systems, the role of mesoscale elements in large-scale cyclone and anticyclone formation, and intentional and unintentional alterations of cloud processes and the cloud environment. Contact: Experimental Meteorology, Division of Atmospheric Sciences, Directorate for Astronomical, Atmospheric, Earth, and Ocean Sciences, National Science Foundation, 1800 G St. N.W., Room 644, Washington, DC 20550/202-357-9431.

Extragalactic Astronomy

The program for extragalactic astronomy sponsors theoretical and observational studies of the interstellar medium (including interstellar molecules), the Milky Way galaxy, distant galaxies, and quasars, including infrared studies of extragalactic objects, the use of millimeter wavelengths to map molecular clouds, the chemistry of interstellar space, and observational cosmology. Contact: Extragalactic Astronomy Program; Division of Astronomical Sciences, Directorate for Astronomical, Atmospheric, Earth and Ocean Sciences, National Science Foundation, 1800 G St. N.W., Room 618, Washington, DC 20550/202-357-7639.

Films

The National Science Foundation produces a limited number of films each year to acquaint the general public and the scientific community with scientific research and its applications. The film topics include astronomy, earth sciences, ecology and environment, education and learning, energy, engineering, ocean sciences, physics, polar research, research applications, weather and climate. A free catalog lists the films available and includes the distributors. Contact: Publications, Office of Public Affairs, National Science Foundation, 1800 G St. N.W., Room 533, Washington, DC 20550/202-357-9498.

Fluid Mechanics

The mechanical sciences and engineering program supports research on structure of turbulence, with emphasis on the role of coherent structure; dynamical interaction of vortices; and formation and convection of vortical structures. Contact: Fluid Mechanics Program, Division of Mechanics and Mechanical Engineering, Directorate for Engineering, National Science Foundation, 1800 G St. N.W., Room 1108, Washington, DC 20550/202-357-9542.

Freedom of Information Act Requests

For information on Freedom of Information Act requests, contact: Public Information Branch, National Science Foundation, 1800 G St. N.W., Room 533, Washington, DC 20550/202-357-9498.

Funding Application Information

Grants for Scientific and Engineering Research, a publication of the National Science Foundation (NSF), contains instructions and applications for submitting a proposal for NSF funding. It goes hand-in-hand with the Foundation's guide to its programs, which is a helpful tool for identifying the various subject areas for which NSF funds research projects. These and other NSF publications are available free of charge while its supply lasts. After that, publications must be purchased from the Superintendent of Documents, U.S. Government Printing Office, Washington, DC 20402/202-783-3238. Contact: Office of Legislative and Public Affairs, Public Affairs and Publications Group, National Science Foundation, 1800 G Street, NW, Washington, DC 20550/202-357-9498.

Funding of Science and Technology

This program provides for the collection, analysis and dissemination of information on the characteristics and patterns of funding for research and development and for other scientific and technologic activities. Support is also provided for the development of modeling and simulation techniques to improve the capability to project R&D funding. Contact: R&D Economic Studies Section, Division of Science Resources Studies, Directorate for Scientific, Technological and International Affairs, National Science Foundation, 2000 L St. N.W., Room L602, Washington, DC 20550/202-634-4625.

Genetic Biology

The genetic biology program supports research on the organization, transmission, function and control of hereditary information, including recombinant DNA research; genetic control of assembly of viruses; control of gene expression; packaging and fundamental structure of the genetic material; division of labor between genetic material as it is distributed among cell organelles, nuclei, chloroplasts and mitochondria; and application of molecular mechanisms to plant cell biology and crop research. Contact: Genetic Biology Program, Division of Physiology, Cellular and Molecular Biology, Directorate for Biological, Behavioral and Social Sciences, National Science Foundation, 1800 G St. N.W., Room 329, Washington, DC 20550/202-357-9687.

Geography and Regional Science

The program on geography and regional science supports research on the explanation and impact of population shifts, migration decisions, industrial location, regional stagnation, and residential choice; effects of public policy, environmental preference, and perceived travel costs on land-use decisions; and geographic diffusion of innovations. Contact: Geography and Regional Science Program, Division of Social and Economic Sciences, Directorate for Biological, Behavioral and Social Sciences, National Science Foundation, 1800 G St. N.W., Room 312, Washington, DC 20550/202-357-7326.

Geology

The earth sciences project supports field and laboratory research on such geological processes as volcanic eruptions, movement of glaciers and erosion and sedimentation; interpretation of ancient environments and organic evolution; studies of the Earth's strata; and regional field studies on plate tectonics. Contact: Geology Program, Division of Earth Sciences, Directorate for Astronomical, Atmospheric, Earth and Ocean Sciences, National Science Foundation, 1800 G St. N.W., Room 602, Washington, DC 20550/202-357-7915.

Geotechnical Engineering

The civil and environmental engineering program supports research on constitutive relations for soils, rocks, and ice; slope stability, subsidence, and expansion; site exploration and characterization based on probabilistic analysis; and use of centrifuge for physical modeling techniques. Contact: Geotechnical Engineering Program, Division of Civil and Environmental Engineering, Directorate for Engineering and Applied Science, National Science Foundation, Room 1130, 1800 G St. N.W., Washington, DC 20550/202-357-7352.

Global Atmospheric Research (GARP)

The global atmospheric research program is a long-term international project designed to acquire knowledge of the physical processes in the troposphere and stratosphere that are essential for an understanding of (a) the transient behavior of large-scale atmosphere phenomena which would lead to increasing the accuracy of forecasting; and (b) the factors that determine the statistical properties of the general circulation of the atmosphere, which would lead to better understanding of the physical basis of climate. Within the United States, the National Science Foundation is the primary agency for the support of nonfederal research in the program, particularly at universities. For additional information, contact: Global Atmospheric Research Program, Division of Atmospheric Sciences, Directorate for Astronomical, Atmospheric, Earth and Ocean Sciences, National Science Foundation, 1800 G St N.W., Room 644, Washington, DC 20550/202-357-9887.

Graduate Fellowships

The graduate fellowships program provides up to 3 years of support to students who are beginning their graduate science studies (masters or doctoral) at their chosen institutions. While approximately one out of eight individual applicants (or 400 individuals) will receive fellowships, the highest rating 1,200 non-awardees (the upper two-fifths of the applicants) will be accorded "honorable mention," citing them as being highly deserving of support. This citation assists applicants in acquiring other sources of funds and thereby aids their pursuit of graduate study. Contact: Office of Research and Career Development, Directorate for Science Engineering Information Education, National Science Foundation, 1800 G St. N.W., Room 414, Washington, DC 20550/202-357-7536.

Grant Policy Manual

This manual is a compendium of basic grant policies and procedures. It contains comprehensive statements of National Science Foundation policy and sets forth the actual terms and conditions under which awards are made. It is available for $9.00 from the Superintendent of Documents, Government Printing Office, Washington, DC 20402/202-783-3238. For additional information, contact: Policy Office, Division of Grants and Contracts, National Science Foundation, 1800 G St. N.W., Room 201, Washington, DC 20550/202-357-7880.

Grants

The programs described below are for sums of money which are given by the federal government to initiate and stimulate new or improved activities or to sustain on-going services:

Astronomical, Atmospheric, Earth and Ocean Sciences

Objectives: To strengthen and enhance the national scientific enterprise through the expansion of fundamental knowledge and increased understanding of the Earth's natural environment and of the universe. Activities include encouragement and support of basic research in the astronomic, atmospheric, Earth and ocean sciences; and in the Antarctic and Arctic. Major objectives include new knowledge of astronomy and atmospheric sciences over the entire spectrum of physical phenomena; a better understanding of the physical and chemical make-up of the Earth and its geologic history; increased insight into the world's oceans, their composition, structure, behavior, and tectonics; and new knowledge of natural phenomena and processes in the Antarctic and Arctic regions.

Eligibility: Public and private colleges and universities, nonacademic research institutions, private profit organizations, and unaffiliated scientists under special circumstances. Grants are made on a competitive basis.

Range of Financial Assistance: $1,200 to $2,700,000.

Contact: National Science Foundation, 1800 G St. N.W., Washington, DC 20550/202-357-9715. Astronomy: 202-357-9488; Atmospheric Sciences: 202-357-9874; Earth Sciences: 202-357-7958; Ocean Sciences: 202-357-9639; and Polar Programs: 202-357-7766.

Biological, Behavioral, and Social Sciences

Objectives: To promote the progress of science and thereby insure the continued scientific strength of the Nation; to increase the store of scientific knowledge and enhance understanding of major problems confronting the nation. Most of the research supported is basic in character. The program includes support of research project grants in the following disciplines: physiology, cellular and molecular biology, behavioral and neural sciences, environmental biology, and social and economic science. Support is also provided for research workshops, symposia and conferences, and for the purchase of scientific equipment. In addition, awards are made to improve the quality of doctoral dissertations in behavioral, social and environmental sciences.

Eligibility: Public and private colleges and universities, nonprofit, nonacademic research institutions, private profit organizations and unaffiliated scientists under special circumstances. Grants are made on a competitive basis.

Range of Financial Assistance: $700 to $600,000.

Contact: Assistant Director, Biological, Behavioral and Social Sciences, National Science Foundation, 1800 G St. N.W., Washington, DC 20550/202-357-9854.

Engineering Grants

Objectives: To strengthen the United States engineering and applied science research base and enhance the links between research and applications in meeting national goals. Areas of research include: automation, instrumentation, electrical and optical communications, computer engineering, quantum electronics, waves and beams, applied social and behavioral sciences; applied physical, mathematical, and biological sciences; intergovernmental program; small business innovation program, industrial programs, and appropriate technology, problem-focused research (programs currently include earthquake hazards mitigation, alternative biological sources of materials, science and technology to aid the handicapped, and human nutrition); integrated basic research and problem analysis; electrical, computer and systems engineering; chemical and process engineering; and civil and mechanical engineering.

Eligibility: Public and private colleges and universities, nonprofit institutions, state and local governments, and profit-making institutions including small businesses, and agencies. The greatest percentage of support goes to academic institutions. Grants to individuals are occasionally made.

Range of Financial Assistance: $1,000 to $1,000,000.

Contact: Programs and Resources Officer, Directorate for Engineering, National Science Foundation, Room 1110, 1800 G St. N.W., Washington, DC 20550/202-357-9774.

Intergovernmental Program

Objectives: To facilitate the integration of scientific and technical resources into the policy formulation, management support, and program operation activities in state and local governments.

Eligibility: Units of state (executive or legislative branch) and local government and their regional or national organizations, special governmental districts, colleges and universities, professional schools, professional societies, nonprofit organizations and institutions, and profit-making organizations including small businesses. Awards may be made also under organizational arrangements that combine two or more of the above.

Range of Financial Assistance: $10,000 to $110,000.

Contact: Director, Intergovernmental Program, Division of Intergovernmental Science and Public Technology, National Science Foundation, Washington, DC 20550/202-357-7560.

Mathematical and Physical Sciences

Objectives: To promote the progress of science and thereby insure the continued scientific strength of the Nation; to increase the store of scientific knowledge and enhance understanding of major problems confronting the Nation. Most of the research supported is basic in character. The program includes support of research project grants in the following disciplines: physics, chemistry, mathematical sciences, materials research, and computer research. Support is also provided for research workshops, symposia and conferences, and for the purchase of scientific equipment.

Eligibility: Public and private colleges and universities, nonprofit, nonacademic research institutions, private profit organizations and unaffiliated scientists under special circumstances. Grants are made on a competitive basis.

Range of Financial Assistance: $10,000 to $4,200,000.

Contact: Assistant Director, Mathematical and Physical Sciences, National Science Foundation, 1800 G St. N.W., Washington, DC 20550/202-357-9742.

Minority Research Initiation

Objectives: To help minority scientists at any U.S. college or university develop greater research capability and encourage them to compete for research funds from all appropriate sources.

Eligibility: Applicants must be full-time minority faculty members at any U.S. college or university with academic programs in the sciences and engineering. Applicants must not have received any prior Federal research support as full-time faculty members and must be citizens of the U.S. or native residents of a possession of the U.S., as American Samoa.

Range of Financial Assistance: $12,000 to $150,000.

Contact: Program Director, Minority Research Initiation, Division of Research Initiation and Improvement, National Science Foundation, 1800 G St. N.W., Washington, DC 20550/202-357-7350.

Precollege Science and Mathematics Education

Objectives: To attract talented men and women to science and mathematics teaching careers, develop teachers' capabilities in these critical areas and keep good teachers employed in school systems.

Eligibility: Public and private colleges and universities and other institutions with an education mission.

Range of Financial Assistance: None established.

Contact: Division of Precollege Education in Science and Mathematics, National Science Foundation, 1800 G St. N.W., Washington, DC 20550/202-357-7452.

Research/Improvement in Minority Institutions

Objectives: To help predominantly minority colleges and universities develop greater research capability on their campuses and encourage participating faculty to compete for research funds from all appropriate sources.

Eligibility: Eligible institutions are those higher education institutions whose enrollments are predominantly (more than 50 percent) composed of Black, Native-American, Spanish-speaking, or other ethnic minorities, underrepresented in science. Institutions may qualify by demonstrating their historical commitment to educating minority students.

Range of Financial Assistance: $20,000 to $100,000,

Contact: Director, Research Improvement in Minority Institutions, National Science Foundation, 1800 G St. N.W., Washington, DC 20550/202-357-7350.

Science Education Development and Research and Resources Improvement

Objectives: To improve capabilities of academic institutions for science education and research training.

Eligibility: Public and private colleges and universities on behalf of their staff members, and individuals acting independently. State and local school systems and industrial organizations generally have not been direct recipients of Foundation support.

Range of Financial Assistance: $1,000 to $250,000.

Contact: National Science Foundation, 1800 G St. N.W., Washington, DC 20550/202-282-7900.

Scientific Personnel Management

Objectives: To help create a more effective supply of scientific manpower by providing a few highly skilled graduate students with resources to pursue their training at the institutions of their choice; encouraging training for research and teaching at all levels; encouraging research participation and short courses for science faculty; providing research experience to a number of talented high school and college students showing early promise in science; and stimulating more participation in science by women, and by minorities and the handicapped.

Eligibility: Applicants are eligible to apply for support in accordance with requirements and procedures specifically described in individual program announcements.

Range of Financial Assistance: $7,000 to $55,000.

Contact: Division of Scientific Personnel Improvement, National Science Foundation, 1800 G St. N.W., Washington, DC 20550/202-282-7754.

Scientific, Technological, and International Affairs

Objectives: To address a broad range of scientific and technological issues of concern to policymakers and to encourage contributions from the private sector to the national research effort. Programs are designed to monitor and analyze the Nation's science and technology enterprise and to improve national and international exchange of scientific information. Objectives are pursued through international cooperative scientific activities, information science and technology, policy research and analysis, and science resources studies.

Eligibility: Public and private colleges and universities, nonprofit organizations, profit-making organizations, national scientific societies, individuals, and (for international cooperative scientific activities) government scientific organizations.

Range of Financial Assistance: $1,000 to $2,500,000.

Contact: Assistant Director, Directorate for Scientific, Technological, and International Affairs, National Science Foundation, 1800 G St. N.W., Washington, DC 20550/202-357-7631.

Two-Year and Four-Year College Research Instrumentation

Objectives: To provide research equipment costing not more than $25,000 to United States colleges and universities having substantial undergraduate programs in sciences, mathematics, and/or engineering but granting fewer than 20 Ph.D. degrees annually in those disciplines.

Eligibility: Eligible institutions are those United States colleges and universities having substantial undergraduate programs in sciences, mathematics and/or engineering but granting fewer than 20 Ph.D. degrees annually in the above disciplines.

Range of Financial Assistance: Up to $25,000.

Contact: Director, Office of Planning and Re-

sources Management, National Science Foundation, 1800 G St. N.W., Washington, DC 20550/202-357-7456.

Visiting Professorships for Women

Objectives: To encourage the full use of the scientific and technical resources of the nation, to encourage careers for women in science and engineering, to provide greater visibility for women scientists and engineers. The hallmark of a visiting professorship is the active participation of the visitor in research and teaching at the host institution.

Eligibility: Women who hold doctorates in science or engineering fields supported by NSF who have independent research experience in academic, industrial or public sectors, who are or have recently been affiliated with a U.S. institution, and who do not have a salaried position with the host institution.

Range of Financial Assistance: $50,000 to $70,000.

Contact: Program Director, Visiting Professorships for Women, Division of Research Initiation and Improvement, National Science Foundation, 1800 G St. N.W., Washington, DC 20550/202-357-7734.

Grants for Scientific Research

This is a free publication that includes the guidelines and instructions directed specifically to the interests of investigators applying for support of projects in fundamental or basic research and other closely related activities such as foreign travel, conferences, symposia, and research equipment and facilities. Contact: Forms and Publications, National Science Foundation, 1800 G St. N.W., Room 235, Washington, DC 20550/202-357-7861.

Gravitational Physics

The gravitational physics program supports research on aspects of the explosive creation of the universe, its present dynamic evolution, and its ultimate fate; strong gravitational fields of X-ray sources, neutron stars, and black holes, fine details of weak gravitational fields; gravitational radiation; gravitational interaction with quantum mechanics; and particle theory. Contact: Gravitational Physics Program, Division of Physics, Directorate for Mathematical and Physical Sciences, National Science Foundation, Room 341, 1800 G St. N.W., Washington, DC 20550/202-357-7979.

Guide to NSF Programs

This guide provides summary information about National Science Foundation programs for the fiscal year. It contains general guidance for institutions and individuals interested in participating in these programs. Program Listings describe the principal characteristics and basic purpose of each activity, eligibility requirements, deadline dates (where applicable), and the address from which more detailed information, brochures or application forms may be obtained. Contact: Public Information Branch, National Science Foundation, 1800 G St. N.W., Room 531, Washington, DC 20550/202-357-9498.

Heat Transfer
The mechanical sciences and engineering program supports research on physical properties and predictive models of multiphase heat transfer phenomena; performance characteristics of high-flux devices; application of high-flux concepts to energy and material conservation; characterization of high-temperature transport mechanisms; and transport phenomena in soils and thermal insulation systems. Contact: Heat Transfer Program, Division of Civil and Mechanical Engineering, Directorate for Engineering, 1800 G St. N.W., Room 1132, Washington, DC 20550/202-357-9545.

History and Philosophy of Science
The history and philosophy of science program supports research on the nature and processes of development of science and technology; the interaction between science and technology; the impact of science and technology on society; the interactions of social and intellectual forces that promote or retard the advance of science; and differences in the nature of theory and evidence in different scientific fields. Contact: History and Philosophy of Science, Division of Social and Economic Sciences, Directorate for Biological, Behavioral and Social Sciences, National Science Foundation, 1800 G St. N.W., Room 312, Washington, DC 20550/202-357-7617.

Industry/University Cooperative Programs
The Industrial Science and Technological Innovation Office of the National Science Foundation (NSF) can provide information about NSF-sponsored industry/university cooperative programs, free publications and other information sources. NSF sponsors two major programs: *Industry/University Cooperative Research Projects Program,* a one-on-one program in which NSF funds collaborative research projects between a university scientist and an industry scientist; and *Industry/University Cooperative Research Centers Program,* a program co-funded by NSF and industry sponsors. The funds are considered seed money and are used to initiate large research programs within a university. Funded programs must address industrially relevant research. Contact: National Science Foundation, Industrial Science and Technological Innovation, Industry/University Cooperative Programs, 1800 G St. N.W., Room 1250, Washington, DC 20550/202-357-7527.

Industry/University Cooperative Research
Grants are awarded for the support of cooperative research projects involving universities and industrial firms. The research focuses on fundamental scientific or engineering questions of a basic or applied nature. Contact: Industry/University Cooperative Research Projects, Division of Industrial Science and Technological Innovation, Directorate for Scientific, Technological and International Affairs, National Science Foundation, 1800 G St. N.W., Room 1250, Washington, DC 20550/202-357-7584.

Industry/University Research Relationships
The Office of Planning and Special Projects of the National Science Foundation (NSF) studies organizational patterns of science and technology. Staff will answer inquiries and make referrals. Two major National Science Board (the policy-making board of NSF) reports about industry/university research relationships are available. Free copies of the following reports can be obtained from this office while the supply lasts: *Industry/University Research Relationships: Myths, Realities and Potentials* (Pub. # NBS82-1), a 35-page report providing an overview of the state of the industry/university research relationships; and *Industry/University Research Relationships: Selected Studies* (Pub. # NBS82-2), a publication that includes six background studies. The six background studies are: a large field study of 450 cases of research relationships; a study of the history of the industry/university relationship in chemistry and chemical engineering; a study of the relationship between non-doctoral schools and industry; a study of intellectual property issues; a paper on industry/university/state government consortia in microelectronics research; and an annotated bibliography with an index of the overall report. Contact: Office of Planning and Special Projects, National Science Foundation, Room 1225, Washington, DC 20550/202-357-7791.

Information Science and Technology
The National Science Foundation supports basic and applied research in information science to advance understanding of the properties and structure of information and to contribute to the store of scientific knowledge which can be applied in the design of information systems. Proposals for research into problems in the following categories are considered: standards and measures for information science; structural properties of information and language; behavioral aspects of information transfer; and information technology. Contact: Division of Information Science and Technology, Directorate for Biological, Behavioral and Social Sciences, National Science Foundation, 1800 G St. N.W., Room 336, Washington, DC 20550/202-357-9572.

Initiation Awards for New Investigators in Information Science

This program is aimed at strengthening research potential in the area of information science and is directed toward young scientists. Contact: Information Science Program, Division of Information Science and Technology, Directorate for Scientific, Technological and International Affairs, National Science Foundation, 1800 G St. N.W., Room 336, Washington, DC 20550/202-357-9569.

Innovative Processes and Their Management

Research is supported on the following topics and issues:

1. Issues related to industrial innovation and innovation process decisions in private firms;
2. Studies of how regional, state and local governments identify problems concerned with science and technology, set priorities, use formal or informal evaluative feedback, and deal with problems of accountability in the acquisition and implementation of innovative technology;
3. Analyses of how civilian sector organizations successfully use government-supported research and development, technical information, and hardware.

Contact: Productivity Improvement Research Section, Industrial Science and Technological Innovation, Directorate for Scientific, Technological and International Affairs, National Science Foundation, 1800 G St. N.W., Room 1237, Washington, DC 20550/202-357-9804.

Intelligent Systems

The program on intelligent systems supports research on computer based systems that have some of the characteristics of intelligence. Relevant areas include: pattern recognition, pattern generation, knowledge representation, problem solving, natural language understanding, theorem proving, and areas related to the automatic analysis and handling of complex tasks. Contact: Intelligent Systems Program, Division of Computer Research, Directorate for Mathematical and Physical Sciences, National Science Foundation, 1800 G St. N.W., Room 339, Washington, DC 20550/202-357-7345.

Intergovernmental Programs

The objective of the intergovernmental programs is to facilitate the integration of scientific and technical resources into the activities of state and local governments. The program assists state and local governments, and the regional and national organizations that represent them, as they investigate alternative approaches toward strengthening their capacity to use scientific and technical resources. Contact: Inter-governmental Affairs, Division of Research Initiation and Improvement, Directorate for Scientific, Technological and International Affairs, National Science Foundation, 1800 G St. N.W., Room 1144, Washington, DC 20550/202-357-7560.

Intermediate Energy Physics

The program on intermediate energy physics supports nuclear structure research studies using beams of high energy particles from accelerators; nuclear structure and fundamental physics research using intermediate energy particle accelerators; and nuclear physics research at the interface between particle and nuclear physics. Contact: Intermediate Energy Physics Program, Division of Physics, Directorate of Mathematical and Physical Sciences, National Science Foundation, 1800 G St. N.W., Room 341, Washington, DC 20550/202-357-7993.

International Economic Policy

This program supports research, modeling, and policy analysis on issues of international economic policy which will affect domestic economic progress and the conduct of foreign relations. Contact: International Economic Policy, Division of Policy Research and Analysis, Directorate for Scientific, Technological and International Affairs, National Science Foundation, 1800 G St. N.W., Room 1229, Washington, DC 20550/202-357-9800.

Investments of Venture Capital Firms

The Venture Capital Investment Trends: 1981–82 report is included in *Science Indicators—1986,* a biannual publication. The report aggregates confidential information on investments of venture capital forms. It covers total transactions and divides them into 40 technological categories. The publication is available free of charge. Contact: Science Indicators Unit, National Science Foundation, 1800 G St. N.W. (L-611), Washington, DC 20550/202-634-4682.

Kinetics, Catalysis, and Reaction Engineering

The chemical and process engineering programs support research on kinetics and mechanisms of reactions and processes of engineering significance; relationships of morphologic, electronic, and chemical properties to catalytic performance; basic principles for the design and fabrication of catalyst systems; reaction engineering, including modeling of chemical and physical processes and the dynamic and stability aspects of their interactions; development of new techniques applicable to the preceding areas; and photo-chemical processes. Contact: Kinetics, Catalysis and Reaction Engineering, Division of Chemical and Process Engineering, Directorate for Engineering and Applied Science, National Science Foundation, 1800 G St. N.W., Room 1126, Washington, DC 20550/202-357-9624.

Kitt Peak National Observatory

The National Science Foundation supports the Kitt

Peak National Observatory (KPNO) as the Nation's center for research in ground-based optical and infrared astronomy. Large optical telescopes, observing equipment, and research support services are made available to qualified scientists. Research carried out at KPNO encompasses fields ranging from solar physics to cosmology. The observatory's basic programs support the operation of 14 telescopes. Many of the telescopes, including the Mayall 4-meter telescope, are used for daytime infrared observations in addition to a wide variety of nighttime observations. The KPNO facilities and instrumentation are available on a competitive basis to all qualified U.S. scientists. Contact: Kitt Peak National Observatory, c/o National Optical Astronomical Observatories, 1002 N. Warren Ave., Tucson, AZ 25719, or: Kitt Peak National Observatory, Division of Astronomical Sciences, Directorate for Astronomical, Atmospheric, Earth and Ocean Sciences, National Science Foundation, 1800 G St. N.W., Room 618, Washington, DC 20550/202-357-9740.

Law and Social Sciences
The Law and Social Sciences program supports research on the processes that enhance or diminish the impact of law; causes and consequences of variations and changes in legal institutions; personal, social, and cultural factors affecting the use of law; effects of traditional and alternative means of dispute resolution; decisionmaking in legal forums and contexts; and conditions and processes that create transformations between formal legal rules and law in action. Contact: Law and Social Sciences Program, Division of Social and Economic Sciences, Directorate for Biological, Behavioral, and Social Sciences, National Science Foundation, 1800 G St. N.W., Room 312, Washington, DC 20550/202-357-9567.

Linguistics
The linguistics program supports research on syntactic, semantic, phonologic, and phonetic properties of individual languages and of language in general; acquisition of language by children; psychologic processes in the production and perception of speech; biologic foundations of language; social influences on and effects of language and dialect variation; and formal and mathematical properties of language models. Contact: Linguistic Program, Division of Behavioral and Neural Sciences, Directorate for Biological, Behavioral and Social Sciences, National Science Foundation, 1800 G St. N.W., Room 320, Washington, DC 20550/202-357-7696.

Low Temperature Physics
The low temperature physics program supports experimental research on condensed matter that requires low and/or ultra-low temperatures, including the study of phase transitions and critical point behavior in the isotopes of helium, hydrogen, and other materials, the occurrence and nature of superconductivity among these new phases of binary and ternary alloys and compounds, nonequilibrium superconducting properties of weak link and Josephson Junction devices, superfluid properties of the isotopes of helium, and these and related phenomena as they pertain to systems of reduced dimensionality and crystalline perfection. Contact: Low Temperature Physics Program, Division of Materials Research, Directorate for Mathematical and Physical Sciences, National Science Foundation, 1800 G St. N.W., Room 404, Washington, DC 20550/202-357-9787.

Marine Chemistry
The ocean sciences project supports research on the equilibria of chemical species and compounds in seawater and their availability for reacting with other chemical phases in the marine environment; fluxes between seafloor sediments, their interstitial waters, and the overlying seawater; the fate of material deposited on the sea floor; alterations of material moving through the water column and the effects of such alterations on the sedimentary record and nutrient availability; interactions and interdependencies between the chemistry and biology of the marine environment; air-sea exchange phenomena related to the sea as a source or sink for manmade and naturally mobilized chemicals; the role of air transport on the chemical properties of the ocean surface; kinetic and thermodynamic reactions in the marine environment; and physical and chemical properties of seawater. Contact: Marine Chemistry Program, Division of Ocean Sciences, Directorate for Astronomical, Atmospheric, Earth and Ocean Sciences, National Science Foundation, 1800 G St. N.W., Room 611, Washington, DC 20550/202-357-7910.

Materials Research Laboratories
Major interdisciplinary laboratories are designed to complement individual research funding. Their essential activities include the development and operation of central experimental facilities for the joint use of faculty and students in such areas as research of high magnetic fields; the study of all forms of matter with an extremely intense source of continuous, electromagnetic radiation reaching into the far ultraviolet and x-ray regions of the spectrum; and the collection of data on small-angle neutron scattering. Contact: Materials Research Laboratory Section, Division of Materials Research, Directorate for Mathematical and Physical Sciences, National Science Foundation, 1800 G St. N.W., Room 408, Washington, DC 20550/202-357-9791.

Measurement Methods and Data Resources
The measurement methods and data improvement

program supports survey operations research; methods and models for the quantitative analysis of social data; improvements in the scientific adequacy and accessibility of social statistics data, including those generated by governments as well as the academic research community. Contact: Measurement Methods and Data Improvement Program, Division of Social and Economic Sciences, Directorate for Biological, Behavioral and Social Sciences, National Science Foundation, 1800 G St. N.W., Room 312, Washington, DC 20550/202-357-7913.

Mechanical Systems
The mechanical sciences and engineering program supports research on kinematics, dynamics, mechanisms and gears; lubrication and surface mechanics; vibrations and acoustics; control theory applied to mechanical systems; computer-aided design and manufacturing; robotics; and optimum design, failure analysis, and reliability. Contact: Mechanical Systems Program, Division of Mechanical Engineering and Applied Mechanics, Directorate for Engineering, National Science Foundation, 1800 G St. N.W., Room 1108, Washington, DC 20550/202-357-9542.

Medal of Science Award
The National Medal of Science is awarded by the President to individuals who in the President's judgment deserve special recognition for their outstanding contributions to knowledge in the physical, biological, mathematical or engineering sciences. Not more than twenty individuals may be awarded the Medal in any one calendar year. For information on the selection committees, Medal recipients, ceremonies and related matters, contact: Medal of Science Award, Division of Personnel Management, National Science Foundation, 1800 G St. N.W., Room 212, Washington, DC 20550/202-357-7512.

Memory and Cognitive Processes
The memory and cognitive processes program supports research on complex human cognitive behavior including memory, attention, concept formation, decisionmaking, reading, thinking, and problem-solving and the development of cognitive processes in infants and children. Contact: Memory and Cognitive Processes Program, Division of Behavioral and Neural Sciences, Directorate for Biological, Behavioral and Social Sciences, National Science Foundation, 1800 G St. N.W., Room 320, Washington, DC 20550/202-357-9898.

Metabolic Biology
The metabolic biology program supports research on biochemical processes in animal, plant, and microbial systems by which energy is provided and through which material is assimilated and broken down, including photosynthesis and nitrogen fixa-

tion, ion transport across membranes, oxidative phosphorylation, chemiosmotic systems, the elucidation of metabolic pathways, and the role of natural products in plant function. Contact: Metabolic Biology Program, Division of Molecular Biosciences, Directorate for Biological, Behavioral and Social Sciences, National Science Foundation, 1800 G St. N.W., Room 325, Washington, DC 20550/202-357-7987.

Metallurgy
The metallurgy program supports research on slags and slag metal reactions; kinetics of gas-metal reactions; metal reactions; shape, property change, and control; predictive property and performance analysis under conditions of variable stress, strain-rate, time, temperature, and environmental conditions; surface corrosion, erosion, abrasion, wear, and hydrogen embrittlement; ion implantation of surface and near-surface structure and resulting property changes; preparation, characterization, property behavior and nature of metastability of amorphous metallic materials; theoretic modeling and computer calculations of multicomponent systems, phase transformations, high temperature metal-hydrogen and metal-sulfur systems, and transition metal/noble metal compounds. Contact: Metallurgy Program, Division of Materials Research, Directorate for Mathematical and Physical Sciences, National Science Foundation, Room 411, 1800 G St. N.W., Washington, DC 20550/202-357-9789.

Meteorology
The atmospheric science program supports studies on how severe storms are initiated, organized, and maintained; the relationship of the electrical budget to the characteristics of cloud and precipitation particles; how tornadoes are initiated; the effects of haze layers and clouds on the radiation balance of the Earth and atmosphere; the role of ice in the formulation of natural clouds and precipitation and how ice crystals and nuclei can be measured; and the major physical processes initiating and maintaining cyclonic storms in middle latitudes and how these developments relate to severe local storms. For additional information, contact: Meteorology Program, Division of Atmospheric Sciences, Directorate for Astronomical, Atmospheric, Earth and Ocean Sciences, National Science Foundation, 1800 G St. N.W., Room 644, Washington, DC 20550/202-357-7624.

Minority Graduate Fellowships
Under this program, support is provided to minority graduate students for study or work toward Masters or Doctoral degrees in science fields that receive National Science Foundation support. For additional information on fellowships, contact: Minority Graduate Fellowship Program, Division of Scientific Personnel Improvement, Directorate

for Science and Engineering Education, National Science Foundation, 1800 G St. N.W., Room 414, Washington, DC 20550/202-357-7536.

Minority Research Initiation
The minority research initiation program provides support for individual full-time minority faculty members who are nationals of the United States and who wish to establish quality research efforts on their campuses, thereby increasing their capability to compete successfully for regular support from the Foundation and other sources. Contact: Minority Research Initiation Program, National Science Foundation, 1800 G St. N.W., Room 1144, Washington, DC 20550/202-357-7350.

Modern Mathematical Analysis
The modern analysis program supports research on linear and nonlinear functional analysis; harmonic analysis; linear topological spaces; operator theory; topological dynamics; ergodic theory; mathematical physics; and measurement theory. Contact: Modern Analysis Program, Division of Mathematical Sciences, Directorate for Mathematical and Physical Sciences, National Science Foundation, 1800 G St. N.W., Room 304, Washington, DC 20550/202-357-9764.

Mosaic
This is a bimonthly magazine containing articles of particular interest to the scientific and educational communities serviced by the National Science Foundation. It is sold for $16.00 per year by the Superintendent of Documents, Government Printing Office, Washington, DC 20402/202-783-3238. For information, contact: Communications Resource Branch, National Science Foundation, 1800 G St. N.W., Room 531, Washington, DC 20550/202-357-9776.

National Astronomy and Ionosphere Center
The National Science Foundation supports the National Ionosphere Center (NAIC), a visitor-oriented National Research Center devoted to scientific investigations in atmospheric sciences and radio and radar astronomy. Its principal observing facilities are located 19 kilometers (12 miles) south of the city of Aercibo, Puerto Rico. NAIC provides telescope users with a wide range of research and observing instrumentation, including receivers, transmitters, movable line feeds, and digital data acquisition and processing equipment. The Center has a permanent staff of scientists, engineers, and technicians who are available to assist visiting investigators with their observing programs. The NAIC facilities and instrumentation are available on a competitive basis to qualified scientists from all over the world. For information, contact: National Astronomy and Ionosphere Center, Cornell University, Ithaca, NY 14853, or National Astronomy and Ionosphere

Center, Division of Astronomical Sciences, Directorate for Astronomical, Atmospheric, Earth and Ocean Sciences, National Science Foundation, 1800 G St. N.W., Room 618, Washington, DC 20550/202-357-9484.

National Center for Atmospheric Research
NCAR serves as a focal point for research in the atmospheric sciences and offers fellowships as well as facilities and research support to qualified scientists working in the atmospheric sciences. NCAR's major efforts include research in: developing and testing of numerical models of large-scale atmospheric circulation; interaction between the properties of clouds and the Earth's surface heat; improved forecasting of severe weather events; relationship among chemical, physical and dynamic processes in the stratosphere and beyond; phenomena occurring in the lower atmosphere; phenomena due to solar variability; and cause-effect relationships among phenomena occurring on and below the solar surface, in the solar atmosphere, and in space out to the Earth's atmosphere. In addition to conducting its own research programs, NCAR participates in a number of atmospheric research efforts conducted by government agencies, university scientists, and research groups on a national or international scale. Contact: National Center for Atmospheric Research, P.O. Box 3000, Boulder, CO 80307, or Centers and Facilities Program, Division of Atmospheric Sciences, Directorate for Astronomical, Atmospheric, Earth and Ocean Sciences, National Science Foundation, 1800 G St. N.W., Room 644, Washington, DC 20550/202-357-9889.

National Radio Astronomy Observatory
The National Science Foundation supports the National Radio Astronomy Observatory (NRAO), which makes radio astronomy facilities available to qualified scientists. The NRAO staff assists visiting scientists with the large radio antennas, receivers, and other equipment needed to detect, measure, and identify radio waves from astronomical objects. Contact: National Radio Astronomy Observatory, Edgemont Rd., Charlottesville, VA 22901, or National Radio Astronomy Observatory, Division of Astronomical Sciences, Directorate for Astronomical, Atmospheric, Earth, and Ocean Sciences, National Science Foundation, 1800 G St. N.W., Room 618, Washington, DC 20550/202-357-9857.

National Science Board
The National Science Board is the policymaking arm of the National Science Foundation. The policies of the board on support of science and development of scientific personnel are generally implemented throughout the various programs of the Foundation. The Board issues the following publications, *National Science Board Booklet* and

Criteria for the Selection of Research Projects by the National Science Foundation, which are available at no cost from: Forms and Publications, National Science Foundation, Washington, DC 20550/202-357-7861. *Science at the Bicentennial—A Report from the Research Community* ($2.95), *Basic Research in the Mission Agencies* and *Science Indicators—1978* are sold by the Superintendent of Documents, Government Printing Office, Washington, DC 20402/202-783-3238. For additional information on the National Science Board, contact: National Science Board, National Science Foundation, 1800 G St. N.W., Room 545, Washington, DC 20550/202-357-9502.

National Scientific Balloon Facility

This facility provides the scientific community with ballooning support for high-altitude experiments, and conducts research and development programs aimed at advancing scientific ballooning technology. It also provides ballooning support to a large number of United States and foreign investigators in order to conduct a broad spectrum of experiments in the fields of cosmic rays, X-rays, infrared astronomy, and particles and fields in the magnetosphere. Support is also provided for the measurement of dynamical atmospheric parameters, trace gases involved in ozone formation and destruction, and condensation nuclei important for aerosol production. Contact: Centers and Facilities Program, Division of Atmospheric Sciences, Directorate for Astronomical, Atmospheric, Earth and Ocean Sciences, National Science Foundation, 1800 G St. N.W., Room 644, Washington, DC 20550/202-357-9695.

NATO Postdoctoral Fellowships

The North Atlantic Treaty Organization sponsors a program of NATO Postdoctoral Fellowships. At the request of the Department of State, the Foundation administers this program for NATO. Contact: Postdoctoral Fellowship Program, Division of Scientific Personnel Improvement, Directorate for Science Education, National Science Foundation, 1800 G St. N.W., Room 414, Washington, DC 20550/202-357-7536.

Neurobiology

The neurobiology program supports research on the development, function, and other aspects of nervous systems at the molecular, cellular, physiological, and behavioral levels; neuroanatomy; neurochemistry; neuroendocrinology; neurophysiology; and neuropsychology. Contact: Neurobiology Program, Division of Behavior and Neural Sciences, Directorate for Biological, Behavioral, and Social Sciences, National Science Foundation, 1800 G St. N.W., Room 320, Washington, DC 20550/202-357-7471.

NSF Bulletin

This publication is issued monthly (except July and August), and disseminates information on National Science Foundation programs, policies and activities, staff changes, meetings, new publications, etc. Contact: Office of Legislative and Public Affairs, National Science Foundation, 1800 G St. N.W., Room 527, Washington, DC 20550/202-357-9498.

Nuclear Physics

The program on nuclear physics supports research on the characteristics of the strong force and its quantitative relationship to the properties and dynamics of nuclei; nuclear reactions; universal symmetry and conservation laws and the nature of the weak interaction; and interdisciplinary applications of nuclear physics. Contact: Nuclear Physics Program, Division of Physics, Directorate for Mathematical and Physical Sciences, National Science Foundation, 1800 G St. N.W., Room 341, Washington, DC 20550/202-357-7992.

Ocean Margin Drilling

A major initiative of the ocean margin drilling program will be an extensive investigation of the ocean margins. The passive margins with their thick sediment cover (e.g., the U.S. east coast) represent a major frontier for geologic exploration. Besides its great scientific importance, work on the deeply submerged ocean margins will constitute the first major effort to establish the geologic framework for determining the natural resource potential of these areas. Contact: Ocean Drilling Programs, Directorate for Astronomical, Atmospheric, Earth and Ocean Sciences, National Science Foundation, 1800 G St. N.W., Room 1100 Washington, DC 20550/202-357-9849. Scientists interested in participating aboard the drilling ship should write to: Chief Scientist, Deep Sea Drilling Project, Scripps Institution of Oceanography, University of California at San Diego, La Jolla, CA 92037. Requests for samples of the core material should be directed to: Curator, Deep Sea Drilling Project, Scripps Institution of Oceanography. Suggestions for scientific planning, including sites to be included on the drilling itinerary, should be addressed to: Manager, Deep Sea Drilling Project, Scripps Institution of Oceanography.

Oceanographic Facilities and Support

The National Science Foundation supports construction, modification, conversion, purchase, and operation of oceanographic facilities that lend themselves to shared usage. Facilities supported under this program are those required for research in the open oceans and in coastal areas. Examples of such facilities are ships, boats, submersibles, and shipboard gear and instruments for data collection and analysis. Contact: Oceanographic Facilities and Support Section, Directorate for

Astronomical, Atmospheric, Earth and Ocean Sciences, National Science Foundation, 1800 G St. N.W., Room 613, Washington, DC 20550/202-357-7837.

Particulate and Multiphase Processes

The chemical and process engineering program supports research on colloidal, interfacial, and hydrodynamic behavior of dispersed solids (colloids, slurries, and aerosols), liquids (emulsions and mists), and gases (froths and foams), and physics, chemistry, and engineering principles governing such solid-processing operations as generation, size modification, transport, classification, and separation. Contact: Particulate and Multiphase Processes Program, Division of Chemical and Process Engineering, Directorate for Engineering, National Science Foundation, 1800 G St. N.W., Room 1126, Washington, DC 20550/202-357-9606.

Patents and Inventions

Each Foundation grant in support of research is subject to a patent and invention clause. This clause governs, in a manner calculated to protect the public interest and the equities of the grantee, the disposition of inventions made or conceived under the grant. Information on patents or inventions, Institutional Patent Agreements, licenses and rights is available. Contact: Office of the General Counsel, National Science Foundation 1800 G St. N.W., Room 501, Washington, DC 20550/202-357-9435.

Physical Oceanography

The ocean sciences project supports research on the description, analysis, and modeling of ocean circulation and transport on the global scale and mesoscale; effects of global and mesoscale circulation on energy momentum transport; physical processes of circulation, eddy generation, and turbulent mixing on the continental shelves; mixing processes and circulation in rivers and bays where fresh water and ocean meet; wind-generated tides and surface and internal waves; small-scale (less than a meter) transport processes such as diffusion, conduction and convection, and three-dimensional turbulence; physical properties of seawater; and physical processes of circulation and mixing in lakes. Contact: Physical Oceanography Program, Ocean Sciences Research Section, Division of Ocean Sciences, Directorate for Astronomical, Atmospheric, Earth and Ocean Sciences, National Science Foundation, 1800 G St. N.W., Room 606, Washington, DC 20550/202-357-7906.

Polar Region Books, Maps, and Folios

A listing of books, maps, and folios concerning the Polar regions is available. Contact: Information Section, Division of Polar Programs, Polor Coordination and Information Section, Directorate for

Astronomical, Atmospheric, Earth and Ocean Sciences, 1800 G St. N.W., Room 627, Washington, DC 20550/202-357-7819.

Policy Research

This office funds policy research, and includes among its research performers small business firms which specialize in areas such as: socio-economic effects of science and technology, innovation processes and their management, environment, energy and resources, international economic policy and technology assessment and risk analysis. Contact: Policy Research and Analysis Division, Directorate for Scientific, Technological and International Affairs, National Science Foundation, 1800 G St. N.W., Room 1233, Washington, DC 20550/202-357-9689.

Political Science

The political science program supports research on local, national, and international governmental institutions; the effects of structural factors on political participation and effectiveness; the impact of economic and social change on political processes; factors influencing bureaucratic decision-making and policy formulation; and processes of conflict and political instability. Contact: Political Science Program, Division of Social and Economic Sciences, Directorate for Biological, Behavioral and Social Sciences, National Science Foundation, 1800 G St. N.W., Room 312, Washington, DC 20550/202-357-9406.

Polymers

The polymers program supports research on the fundamental behavior of single macromolecules and aggregates in amorphous or crystalline arrangements; synthesis of new polymers; new methods of polymerization; reactions of polymers; molecular characteristics and their relation to mechanical, optical, and transport properties; macromolecular chain dynamics; polymer surfaces; biocompatibility; environmental, raw material, and energy considerations; and theoretical treatment of macromolecular behavior. Contact: Polymers Program, Division of Materials Research, Directorate for Mathematical and Physical Sciences, National Science Foundation, 1800 G St. N.W., Room 411, Washington, DC 20550/202-357-9789.

Population Biology and Physiological Ecology

The program on population biology and physiological ecology supports research on general principles that describe the physiological adaptations of animals and plants to their microenvironments; evolutionary and ecologic significance of life history characteristics of plants and animals (including behavioral ecology); theoretic models for ecological genetics; adaptive significance of genetic variability; and physiological aspects of genetically determined enzyme variability. Contact:

Population Biology and Physiological Ecology Program, Division of Biotic Systems and Resources, Directorate for Biological, Behavioral and Social Sciences, National Science Foundation, Washington, DC 20550/202-357-9728.

Priority of Science and Technology Investments

Science Indicators, a 1982 document, is the sixth in a series prepared by the National Science Board, the policymaking body of the National Science Foundation (NSF). It is a quantitative assessment of U.S. science and technology, demonstrating the priority for investment and reflecting their importance to the economy and to national security. Statistics covered in the report include amounts spent nationally on R&D, both industrial and federal, patent applications, stock offerings and venture capital investments in high technology companies, amounts spent on basic and applied research in the education sector, science and engineering education statistics, and public reactions to status and expenditures in the science and technology fields. Copies of the report are available from the Superintendent of Documents, U.S. Government Printing Office, Washington, DC 20402/202-783-3238. Each copy, #038-000-0538-3, is $9.50. Contact: National Science Foundation (NSF), 1800 G St. N.W., Washington, DC 20550/ 202-357-9498.

Probability and Statistics

The program on probability supports research on the mathematical modeling for situations involving change or incomplete information. Major subfields include Markov processes, probability on Banach spaces, limit theorems, interacting particle systems, and stochastic processes. The program on statistics supports the theoretical development and application of methods suitable for extracting information about real events from relevant numerical measurements. Major subfields include testing, design, inference, robustness, sampling, sequential analysis, and multivariate analysis. Contact: Statistics and Probability Program, Division of Mathematical Sciences, Directorate for Mathematical and Physical Sciences, National Science Foundation, 1800 G St. N.W., Room 304, Washington, DC 20550/202-357-9764.

Productivity Improvement Innovations

The major goal of the Productivity Improvement Research Section (PIR) program is to provide information and sponsor research that will assist private and public sector management in enhancing U.S. technological growth. Research ranges from highly focused studies which resolve questions about a specific aspect of technological innovation and productivity to more generalized and fundamental studies. A review of the literature in the field of innovations process research is available upon request. A PIR publication, *The Process of Technological Innovation: Reviewing the Literature,* focuses on the organizational context of technological change, including material/ physical aspects and the social/behavioral implications. The 250-page review is available from National Science Foundation for no charge. Contact: Productivity Improvement Research Section (PIR), Division of Industrial Science and Technological Innovation, National Science Foundation, 1800 G St. N.W., Room 1237, Washington, DC 20550/202-357-9805.

Psychobiology

The psychobiology program supports research on environmental, genetic, hormonal, and motivational determinants of behavior; animal learning, conditioning, stimulus control, preferences, and aversions; migration and homing behavior of animals; and animal ingestive, reproductive, social, and communicative behavior. Contact: Psychobiology Program, Division of Behavioral and Neural Sciences, Directorate for Biological, Behavioral and Social Sciences, National Science Foundation, 1800 G St. N.W., Room 320, Washington, DC 20550/202-357-7949.

Publications of the National Science Foundation

This publication is a list of administrative and statistics publications issued by the National Science Foundation. Contact: Forms and Publications, National Science Foundation, 1800 G St. N.W., Room 232, Washington, DC 20550/202-357-7861.

Quantum Electronics, Waves, and Beams

The electrical, computer and systems engineering program supports research on new and improved coherent sources for the infrared, visible, and ultraviolet spectral laser regions; generation of picosecond laser pulses and interaction of short pulses with materials; novel laser spectroscopic methods; nonlinear optics; free-electron laser studies; analysis of propagation through random media; numerical methods for solving scattering problems; nonlinear wave phenomena, antennas, and waveguides; linear and nonlinear effects in surface acoustic wave structures, acoustic resonators, and other bulk devices; sonar-related studies; generation of plasmas; wave effects on plasmas; and properties of charged particle beams. Contact: Quantum Electronics, Waves and Beams Program, Division of Electrical, Computer and Systems Engineering, Directorate for Engineering and Applied Science, National Science Foundation, 1800 G St. N.W., Room 1151, Washington, DC 20550/202-357-9618.

Radio Astronomy Laboratory Resource

The objective of the Electromagnetic Spectrum Management Unit is to ensure the availability of the radio frequency spectrum for scientific research at radio astronomy laboratories. Research involves areas of communications as well as the tracking of animals. Radio frequency is also used directly to analyze information which is emitted from natural bodies. The staff can answer your questions as well as refer you to other information sources. A summary statement about the usage of radio frequencies at astronomy laboratories can be sent to you free of charge. Contact: Electromagnetic Spectrum Management Unit, National Science Foundation, Washington, DC 20550/202-357-9696.

Radio Spectrum Management
This office coordinates radio spectrum usage for research and frequency assignments for other telecommunications/electronics systems with government agencies. Contact: Radio Spectrum Coordinator, Division of Astronomical Sciences, Directorate for Astronomical, Atmospheric, Earth and Ocean Sciences, National Science Foundation, 1800 G St. N.W., Room 618, Washington, DC 20550/202-357-9696.

Reading Room/Library
A collection of agency policy documents, staff instructions and orders, as well as current indexes, is available to the public for inspection. Contact: Reference and Records Section, Division of Administrative Resources, National Science Foundation, 1730 K St. N.W., Room 30, Washington, DC 20550/202-357-7811.

Regional Instrumentation Facilities
The foundation has established regional instrumentation facilities which will improve the quality and scope of research in the various regions of the United States. These facilities will increase the availability of new and powerful instrumentation to researchers in these regions on a shared basis. Trained staff needed to maintain and operate the equipment is available at each facility. The program will improve geographic distribution of basic research capability and enhance research interactions among university, industry, and government scientists and engineers. A list of regional instrumentation facilities is available upon request. Contact: Regional Instrumentation Facilities Program, Directorate of Mathematical and Physical Sciences, National Science Foundation, 1800 G St. N.W., Room 340, Washington, DC 20550/202-357-9826.

Regulatory Biology
The regulatory biology program supports research on the characteristics and evolution of mechanisms, such as endocrine and neuroendocrine systems, that initiate, integrate, and regulate physiologic functions in tissues, organs, and organisms. Contact: Regulatory Biology Program, Division of Cellular Bioscience, Directorate for Biological,

Behavioral and Social Sciences, National Science Foundation, 1800 G St. N.W., Room 332, Washington, DC 20550/202-357-7975.

Reports and Studies
The following analytic reports are available from the Division of Science Resource Studies:

National Patterns of Science and Technology Resources, 1980, 1981, 1984, free
Federal Funds for Research and Development, Fiscal Years 1977, 1978, and 1979, Volume XXVII, 1982, '83, '84, XXXII, free
Fiscal years, 1978, 1979, and 1980, Volume XVIII, free
Science and Engineering Personnel: A National Overview, free
An Analysis of Federal R&D Funding by Function, Fiscal Years 1969–1979 and Fiscal Years 1980–1982, 1983–85, free
Research and Development in State and Local Governments, Fiscal year 1977 (free)
Research and Development in Industry, 1977, 1978 (free), 1982 (free)
Federal Support to Universities, Colleges and Selected Nonprofit Institutions, Fiscal Year 1977, Fiscal Year 1978 ($5.50), FY 1982 free
Academic Science, 1972–77. R&D Funds, Scientists and Engineers, and Graduate Enrollment and Support 72–83 free
Academic Science, R&D Funds, Fiscal Year 1978, Fiscal Year 1979, Scientists & Engineers, January 1979, January 1980, 1982 free, Jan 1983 free
Graduate Enrollment and Support, Fall 1978, Fall 1980, Fall 1982, free
Employment Patterns of Academic Scientists and Engineers, 1973–78 ($1.75)
R&D Activities of Independent Nonprofit Institutions, 1973 ($1.90)
Characteristics of Experienced Scientists and Engineers in the United States, 1976, 1978
U.S. Scientists and Engineers, 1978, 1982
Projections of Supply and Utilization of Science and Engineering Doctorates, 1982 and 1987 ($2.25)
Scientific and Technical Personnel in Private Industry 1977, 1978–1980 ($2.00)
Occupational Mobility of Scientists and Engineers ($1.75)

Contact: Editorial and Inquiries Unit, Division of Science Resources Studies, Directorate for Scientific, Technological and International Affairs, National Science Foundation, 2000 L St. N.W., Room L611, Washington, DC 20550/202-634-4622.

Research and Development Funding and Economic Data Collection
The Division of Science Resources Studies collects data on all sectors of the economy, on research and development (R & D) funding, and science and engineering personnel. A number of publications are available:

Academic Science/Engineering: Scientists and Engineers, January 1983 (NSF 84-309)—this publication gives sample of 2,190 universities and colleges and 19 university associated federally-funded R & D centers. Detailed statistical tables provide information on basic trends in the employment by field at the top 100 institutions. Numerous other tables round out this overview. The publication is available free of charge.

Characteristics of Recent Science/Engineering Graduates: 1982 (NSF 84-318)—the tables in this publication provide insight into what all those R & D funds and employed scientists and engineers have been producing. A total of 24,956 graduates from 1980 and 1981 responded to the survey, providing data on fields and disciplines, degrees obtained, sex, race, employment, type of employer, and primary work activity. The publication is available free of charge.

Guide to NSF Science/Engineering Resources Data (NSF 84-301)—this contains the instruments NSF used to collect the information covered in the publications discussed above. The instructions for completing the surveys are also provided. Together they prove a useful tool for people interested in collecting related information or using the survey results. The publication is available free of charge.

Contact: Editorial and Inquiries Unit, Division of Science Resources Studies, National Science Foundation, 1800 G St. N.W., Washington, DC 20550/202-634-4622.

Research and Development—Funding of the National Science Foundation

The Science Resources Studies (SRS) office can provide information and publications about research and development (R & D) funding and personnel resources. Staff conduct economic surveys and studies designed to provide national R & D funding totals by economic sector. All publications are available free of charge from the National Science Foundation (NSF) as long as the initial printing lasts. When the NSF supply is exhausted, the publications must be purchased from the U.S. Government Printing Office. The following are primary publications of SRS.

Funds for R & D—published each fall, presents data and analysis based on a survey of all federal agencies supporting R & D programs. The data cover such categories as: basic research; applied R & D; the research performing sectors; fields of science; and geographic distribution. The report is available in two sections, Volume I being 200 pages of tables and Volume II 80 pages of text.

R & D in Industry—published each summer, provides data based on an annual survey conducted for NSF by the Bureau of the Census. The report is available in 2 sections, Volume I being 175 pages of tables and Volume II, 50 pages of text.

Academic Science R & D Funds—this annual report is based on data collected each year from academic institutions spending over $50,000 for separately budgeted R & D. Data are displayed for individual institutions. The report runs approximately 100 pages.

National Patterns of Science and Technology—published each spring, assembles and analyzes data collected in the sectoral studies. It provides a concise and comprehensive summary and estimates for national totals. The publication compliments the National Science Board's *Science Indicators* and NSF's *Science Engineering Personnel: A National Overview.*

Science Indicators—this biannual publication of the National Science Board, is on the overall state of the U.S. for all facets of science and technology. *Science Indicators* also provides comparisons of the scientific and technical activities conducted in the U.S. and other major industrialized countries, primarily Japan, Western Europe, and the Soviet Union.

Contact: National Science Foundation, Science Resources Studies, 1800 G St. N.W., Washington, DC 20550/202-634-4634.

Research and Resources Facility for Submicron Structures

This facility, supported through the solid state and micro-structures engineering program and located at Cornell University, provides the equipment and expertise needed to fabricate structures that have features less than a micrometer in length. The facility's resources include a computer-controlled, electron-beam pattern-generating system, as well as thin-film growth, processing, and characterization systems. Contact: Research and Resources Facility for Submicron Structures, Cornell University, Ithaca NY 14853, or Solid State and Micro-structures Engineering Program, Division of Electrical, Computer and Systems Engineering, Directorate for Engineering, National Science Foundation, 1800 G St. N.W., Room 1151, Washington, DC 20550/202-357-9618.

Research Facilitation Awards

This program is an NSF-wide initiative which provides handicapped scientists and engineers with grant supplements for special equipment or assistance required specifically to perform the proposed research. Contact: Research Facilitation Awards, Division of Research Initiation and Improvement, National Science Foundation, 1800 G St. N.W., Washington, DC 20550/202-357-7456

Research Improvement in Minority Institutions

This program provides funding for improving research capabilities of predominantly minority institutions. The program, which responds to Executive Order 12320, supports faculty research and the acquisition of research equipment. It also supports cooperative research projects among academic institutions and between academic institutions and industry. Contact: Research Improvement in Minority Institutions, Division of Research Initiation and Improvement, National Science Foundation, 1800 G Street N.W., Washington, DC 20550/202-357-7350

Research/Instrumentation Support for Predominantly Undergraduate Institutions

This program is an NSF-wide initiative. Predominantly undergraduate institutions are defined as those which awarded no more than 20 science or engineering doctorates in the most recent two years. Support is provided through the regular research programs and through the Research in Undergraduate Institutions (RUI) Program. RUI proposals must be from investigators in predominantly undergraduate institutions, located in departments which do not offer the doctorate. Investigators must propose specific research projects and describe how the projects strengthen the preparation of undergraduate students. Support may be requested for instrumentation as well as research. The research may be conducted at the home institution or at a host institution. Contact: Research/Instrumentation Support for Predominantly Undergraduate Institutions, Division of Research Initiation and Improvement, National Science Foundation, 1800 G Street N.W., Washington, DC 20550/202-357-7734.

Research Opportunities for Women

This program provides opportunities for women scientists and engineers to undertake independent research. Grants are made to women who have not previously been principal investigators or who are reentering the research community. Contact: Research Opportunities for Women, Division of Research Initiation and Improvement, National Science Foundation, 1800 G Street N.W., Washington, DC 20550/202-357-7734.

Sacramento Peak Observatory

The National Science Foundation supports the Sacramento Peak Observatory (SPO), a National Research Center devoted to studies in the fields of solar physics, solar-terrestrial relationships, and related disciplines. SPO makes available to qualified scientists optical solar research support services. All qualified U.S. scientists and, on occasion, foreign visitors, have access to SPO facilities on a competitive basis. Contact: National Solar Observatory, Sunspot, NM 88349, or Division of Astronomical Sciences, Directorate for Astronomical, Atmospheric, Earth and Ocean Sciences, National Science Foundation, 1800 G St. N.W., Room 618, Washington, DC 20550/202-357-9484.

Science and Engineering Personnel: A National Overview

This publication presents a review of current employment and supply patterns for United States scientists and engineers, details of the status of doctoral scientists and engineers, and an examination of the dynamics of the science and engineering labor markets. Appendices provide technical notes and statistics tables on science and engineering personnel. The report is sold for $5.00 by the Superintendent of Documents, Government Printing Office, Washington, DC 20402/202-783-3238. For additional information, contact: Editorial and Inquiries Unit, Division of Science Resource Studies, 2000 L St. N.W., Room L611, Washington, DC 20550/202-634-4622.

Science and Technology to Aid the Handicapped

The objectives of the science and technology to aid the handicapped program are to:

1. Improve sensory systems (speech, visual, hearing, and tactile) and locomotion and manipulatory capabilities through research projects that encourage the use of the best scientific and engineering developments;
2. Involve the handicapped community in the development of the program to help insure that the research meets the social and economic needs, as well as the physical needs, of the handicapped;
3. Focus the research capabilities of universities, industries, small businesses and nonprofit institutions on new low-cost approaches to bringing scientific and technologic developments to the aid of the handicapped.

Contact: Science and Technology to Aid the Physically Handicapped, Electrical Computer and Systems Engineering, Directorate for Engineering and Applied Science, National Science Foundation, 1800 G St. N.W., Room 1151, Washington, DC 20550/202-357-9618.

Science in Developing Countries

The science in developing countries program is directed toward improvement of the scientific infrastructure of developing countries. Research participation grants support (a) the participation of U.S. scientists or engineers in a research project in an eligible developing country, (b) the participation by scientists or engineers from an eligible developing country in an appropriate U.S.-based research project, or (c) a combination of the two. Conference grants support national, regional and international (a) seminars that are research oriented and focused on the problems of developing countries; (b) workshops concerned with the planning and initiation of cooperative research activities; or (c) colloquia at which U.S. and counterpart scientists or engineers who are involved with state-of-the-art research explore the application of science and technology to development programs. Dissertation improvement grants are for the incremental support of developing-country graduate students who are enrolled at U.S. universities and qualified to undertake a dissertation research project. Contact: Division of International Programs, Directorate for Scientific, Technological and International Affairs, National Science Foundation, 1800 G St. N.W., Room 1212, Washington, DC 20550/202-357-9537.

Scientific and Technical Personnel

This program supports studies to provide the

factual information needed to track the training and distribution of scientists and engineers in the United States. Specific areas of interest are the capability of institutions of higher education to produce scientific and technical personnel, and the changing characteristics of scientists and engineers. Contact: Scientific and Technical Personnel Studies Section, Division of Science Resources Studies, Directorate for Scientific, Technological and International Affairs, National Science Foundation, 1800 G St. N.W., Room L611, Washington, DC 20550/202-634-4691.

Scientific Technological and International Affairs
The largest area of opportunity for small businesses in the National Science Foundation is the applied research area of scientific technology. Principal areas of research interest include: physical sciences; mathematical sciences; biological sciences; electrical, computer and systems engineering; civil and mechanical engineering; economics and social sciences; behavioral sciences, and chemical and process engineering. Typical problem areas funded include: materials research; production research; measurement and advanced instrumentation; deep mineral resources; human nutrition; industrial processes; alternative biological sources of materials; marine research; and science and technology to aid the handicapped. Contact: Program Manager for Innovation and Small Business, Directorate for Scientific, Technological and International Affairs, Division of Industry, Science and Technological Innovation, National Science Foundation, 1800 G St. N.W., Room 1250, Washington, DC 20550/202-357-7527.

Science, Technology and the General Public
The Science Indicators Unit prepares the biannual *Science Indicators Report* which includes a chapter about public attitudes towards science and technology. The report is the result of a survey taken of three sectors: the general public; that portion of the public interested and knowledgeable about science and technology (20%); and non-governmental science policy leaders. The staff at this office can answer questions regarding the public's fear of, and attitudes towards, relating to high technology. Contact: Science Indicators Unit, National Science Foundation, 1800 G St. N.W., Washington, DC 20550/202-634-4682.

Selected List of Fellowship Opportunities and Aids to Advanced Education for U.S. Citizens and Foreign Nationals
This free pamphlet describes in detail a variety of organizations, companies, foundations, etc. that provide fellowships and other financial aids to graduate and postgraduate students. Contact: Publications Office, Public Affairs, National Science Foundation, 1800 G St. N.W., Room 533, Washington, DC 20550/202-357-9498.

Sensory Physiology and Perception
The program on sensory physiology and perception supports research on mechanisms and processes at the molecular, cellular, physiologic, and behavioral levels involved in sensory transduction, neural coding, and information processing; neurobiologic and psychophysical correlates of sensory and perceptual phenomena; and development of sensory and perceptual systems. Contact: Sensory Physiology and Perception Program, Division of Behavioral and Neural Sciences, Directorate for Biological, Behavioral and Social Sciences, National Science Foundation, 1800 G St. N.W., Room 320, Washington, DC 20550/202-357-7428.

Small Business Guide to Federal R&D Funding Opportunities
This guide provides small, technically competent firms and businesses working in the area of research and development with information about business opportunities with the federal government. It also describes criteria businesses must meet in order to participate in federally supported R&D programs and efforts, important changes in federal policy and procedures that could affect small business participation in the federal R&D market, and the level of R&D funding likely to be available in various departments and agencies of the government. Contact: Office of Small Business Research and Development, National Science Foundation, 1800 G St. N.W., Room 517, Washington, DC 20550/202-357-7464.

Small Business Innovation Research
Small, creative science-and-technology-oriented firms have the chance to perform innovative high-risk research on scientific and technical problems that could have significant public benefit. Research topics may range from engineering and the physical sciences to the life sciences with emphasis on advanced research concepts. Contact: Industrial Program, Directorate for Scientific, Technological and International Affairs, Division of Industry, Science and Technological Innovation, National Science Foundation, 1800 G St. N.W., Room 1250, Washington, DC 20550/202-357-7527.

Small Business R&D
The National Science Foundation's Office of Small Business Research and Development exists specifically to provide information and guidance to small research firms that wish to know more about National Science Foundation programs and research opportunities. Contact: Office of Small Business R&D, National Science Foundation, 1800 G St. N.W., Room 517, Washington, DC 20550/202-357-7464.

Social and Developmental Psychology
The program on social and developmental psychology supports laboratory and field studies on how

the behavior of others affects individual behavior, and research on changes in personality, social behavior, and emotional responsiveness that occur throughout the life span. Contact: Social and Developmental Psychology, Division of Behavioral and Neural Sciences, Directorate for Biological, Behavioral and Social Sciences, National Science Foundation, 1800 G St. N.W., Room 320, Washington, DC 20550/202-357-9485.

Socioeconomic Effects of Science and Technology

Research in this area addresses the following issues: the impact on economic performance of private and public investment in science and technology; the effects of government policy instruments on the level and outcome of scientific and technologic activities; the role of science and technology in U.S. private sector international transactions; and the effects of technologic change on individual and social institutions. Contact: Science and Innovation Policy Section, Division of Policy Research and Analysis, Directorate for Scientific, Technological and International Affairs, National Science Foundation, 1800 G St. N.W., Room 1229, Washington, DC 20550/202-357-9800.

Sociology

The sociology program supports research on the processes by which organizations adapt to and produce change in their social context; decision-making in organizations and small groups; social factors in population change; social stratification and the development of careers and work roles; the role of communication and influence networks in individual and community decision; effects of social organization on science and knowledge; variation in the social attributes of cities and their effects on competition for resources and population. Contact: Sociology Program, Division of Social and Economic Sciences, National Science Foundation, 1800 G St. N.W., Room 312, Washington, DC 20550/202-357-7802.

Software Engineering

The program on software engineering supports research on the structure and design process of computer software, especially verification, testing, portability, reliability, and human interfacing to numeric and non-numeric software systems. Areas of emphasis include: program validation and testing; software tools; and human factors in software design and use. The program also supports research in computationally oriented numerical analysis, the design and construction of high quality portable software for scientific research, and experimental implementation where that is an integral part of the research. Contact: Software Engineering, Division of Computer Research, Directorate for Mathematical and Physical Sci-

ences, 1800 G St. N.W., Room 339, Washington, DC 20550/202-357-7345.

Software Systems Science

The program on software systems science supports research on the conceptual basis for the specification of future software systems and the necessary experimentation with such systems, including: advanced programming languages and optimizing compilers; functional and relational specification; program transforming systems; systems for the verification and proof of correctness of programs; the study of the concurrency of operations; and the discovery of new algorithms and improved measures of effectiveness of known algorithms. Contact: Software Systems Science Program, Division of Computer Research, Directorate for Mathematical and Physical Sciences, National Science Foundation, 1800 G St. N.W., Room 339, Washington, DC 20550/202-357-7375.

Solar System Astronomy

The solar system astronomy program sponsors research on the detailed structure and activity of the Sun; planetary surfaces, interiors, atmospheres, and satellites; the nature of small bodies— the asteroids, comets, and meteors—and their relevance to the origin and development of the solar system; and the 1980–81 increase to maximum of the quasi-periodic surface activity of the Sun. Contact: Solar System Astronomy Program, Division of Astronomical Sciences, Directorate for Astronomical, Atmospheric, Earth and Ocean Sciences, National Science Foundation, 1800 G St. N.W., Room 615, Washington, DC 20550/202-357-7620.

Solar-Terrestrial

The atmospheric sciences program supports research on the upper atmosphere (including the magnetosphere), the responses to the energy flux from the Sun; mechanism by which the magnetosphere energizes particles from the Sun and the ionosphere and deposits them into the polar upper atmosphere to form the aurora; the nature of electric currents and particles which flow between the atmosphere, ionosphere and magnetosphere; and the effect of variation in the Sun's radiation on weather and climate. Contact: Solar-Terrestrial Program, Division of Atmospheric Sciences, Directorate for Astronomical, Atmospheric, Earth and Ocean Sciences, National Science Foundation, 1800 G St. N.W., Room 644, Washington, DC 20550/202-357-7618.

Solid Mechanics

The mechanical sciences and engineering program supports research on the measurement and prediction of the mechanical strength and behavior of solid materials used in engineering, medicine, agriculture, forestry, and food processing; the effects of environmental and loading stresses on the mechanical strength of solids; fracture mechanics and drainage theory; and creep and fatigue. Contact: Solid Mechanics Program, Division of Mechanical Engineering and Applied Mechanics, Directorate for Engineering, National Science Foundation, 1800 G St. N.W., Room 1108, Washington, DC 20550/202-357-9542.

Solid State and Microstructures Engineering

The electrical, computer and systems engineering program supports research on the modeling of field effect and bipolar junction devices; noise properties of electronic components; thin-film growth and device fabrication; electron-beam and x-ray lithography; photovoltaic devices; and superconductive electronics. Contact: Solid State and Microstructures Engineering Program, Division of Electrical, Computer and Systems Engineering, Directorate for Engineering, National Science Foundation, 1800 G St. N.W., Room 1151, Washington, DC 20550/202-357-9618.

Solid State Chemistry

The solid state chemistry program supports research on electrical and magnetic properties of anisotropic materials, with emphasis on organometallic compounds; molecular studies of chemisorption of species on surfaces, including heterogeneous catalysis and the chemistry of friction, lubrication and wear; properties and phases of liquid crystals; ionic and superionic conductivity in materials; and solid state chemical synthesis. Contact: Solid State Chemistry Program, Division of Materials Research, Directorate for Mathematical and Physical Sciences, National Science Foundation, 1800 G St. N.W., Room 404, Washington, DC 20550/202-357-9737.

Solid State Physics

The solid state physics program supports experimental research on metals, semiconductors and insulators in the crystalline state, the amorphous state, and intermediate states of disorder, involving studies of phase transitions, critical point phenomena, and electronic, magnetic, and lattice structures and their excitations. Important areas include studies of physical phenomena at surfaces and interfaces; photon, electron, and neutron scattering from solids; transport properties; resonance studies; and nonlinear phenomena. Contact: Solid State Physics Program, Division of Material Research, Directorate for Mathematical and Physical Sciences, National Science Foundation, 1800 G St. N.W., Room 404, Washington, DC 20550/202-357-9737.

Source Book of Projects

This book provides information on the awards made in the past fiscal year. It also provides information on awards given in previous years.

Contact: Directorate for Science and Engineering Education, National Science Foundation, 1800 G Street, N.W., Room 420, Washington, DC 20550/202-357-7557

Special Science and Technology Indicators

This program supports studies of the dynamics of the science and technology resources complex. A major component of this undertaking involves the development of special indicators, primarily of an output nature. This work, along with that of the other science resources studies programs that deal primarily with inputs, provides the basis for the National Science Board's biennial *Science Indicators* publications, which are prepared by the Division. Also included are modeling and simulation activities designed to lead to a better understanding of the factors that are responsible for the changes in the distribution of human and financial resources for science and technology. Contact: Science Indicators Unit, Division of Science Resources Studies, Directorate for Scientific, Technological and International Affairs, National Science Foundation, 2000 L St. N.W., Room L611, Washington, DC 20550/202-634-4682.

Specimens and Core Samples

Ice cores, ocean bottom sedimentary cores, terrestrial sedimentary cores, dredged rocks, biologic specimens, meteorites, and ocean bottom photographs are available for study. For information on "specimen and core-sample distribution policy," contact: Polar Coordination, Information Section, Division of Polar Programs, Directorate for Astronomical, Atmospheric, Earth and Ocean Sciences, National Science Foundation, 1800 G St. N.W., Room 627, Washington, DC 20550/202-357-7819.

Stars and Stellar Evolution

The stars and stellar evolution program sponsors research on all aspects of the stellar life cycle, including observation and theoretic studies of the beginning and end points of stellar evolution; physical properties of various classes of stellar objects, including the effects of mass loss, rotation, and magnetic fields on stellar structure; and theoretic and laboratory studies associated with atoms and molecules in space. Contact: Stars and Stellar Evolution Program, Division of Astronomical Sciences, Directorate of Astronomical, Atmospheric, Earth and Ocean Sciences, National Science Foundation, 1800 G St. N.W., Room 615, Washington, DC 20550/202-357-7622.

Stellar Systems and Motions

The stellar systems and motions program supports research on the studies of stars in the immediate vicinity of the Sun through determining their distances and motions with the highest attainable precision; improved coverage of the southern skies; binary and multiple star systems; and application of recently developed optical and radio techniques. Contact: Stellar Systems and Motions Program, Division of Astronomical Sciences, Directorate of Astronomical, Atmospheric, Earth, and Ocean Sciences, National Science Foundation, 1800 G St. N.W., Room 615, Washington, DC 20550/202-357-7620.

Structural Chemistry and Thermodynamics
The structural chemistry and thermodynamics program supports research on equilibrium and time-dependent macroscopic thermodynamics and statistics mechanics; macroscopic properties of matter; intermolecular interactions in condensed phases; properties of colloidal systems and surfaces; high temperature chemistry; new methods for structure determination; and determination and interpretation of the geometric parameters of chemical species by spectroscopic and diffraction methods. Contact: Structural Chemistry and Thermodynamics, Division of Chemistry, Directorate for Mathematical and Physical Sciences, National Science Foundation, Room 340, 1800 G St. N.W., Washington, DC 20550/202-357-9826.

Structural Mechanics
The civil and environmental engineering program supports research on optimality in structural design and system identification; response to random excitation; structural instability and nonlinear effects; concrete technology, with special emphasis on high strength concrete; and active control of structures. Contact: Structural Mechanics Program, Division of Civil and Environmental Engineering, Directorate for Engineering, National Science Foundation, 1800 G.St. N.W., Room 1130, Washington, DC 20550/202-357-9500.

Submarine Geology and Geophysics
The Ocean Sciences project supports research on the structure of continental margins, oceanic rise systems, and deep sea sedimentary basins; evolution of the ocean basins; processes controlling the exchange of heat and chemical elements between seawater and oceanic rocks; tectonic and volcanic activity at mid-ocean ridges; chemical and mineralogic variations in marine sediments; deposition, erosion, and distribution of marine sediments; geologic and oceanographic processes controlling sedimentary systems; past oceanic circulation patterns and climates; evolution of microfossil groups; effects of water chemistry and temperature controls on fossil groups and sediment types; and interaction of land and oceanic geologic processes. Contact: Submarine Geology and Geophysics Program, Division of Ocean Sciences, Directorate for Astronomical, Atmospheric, Earth and Ocean Sciences, National Science Foundation, 1800 G St. N.W., Room 606, Washington, DC 20550/202-357-7906.

Supercomputer Programs Reference
This office can refer you to experts, literature, and programs involved in supercomputers. Contact: Staff Associate for Supercomputing, National Science Foundation, Office of Advanced Scientific Computers, 1800 G St. N.W., Washington, DC 20550/202-357-7558.

Synthetic Inorganic and Organometallic Chemistry
The synthetic inorganic and organometallic chemistry program supports research on new organometallic and inorganic compounds possessing catalytic behavior; the fixation of small molecules for synthetic catalytic behavior; fuels and biomimetic models; inorganic compounds in chemotherapy and plant and animal nutrition; environmental impacts of heavy ions; and the synthesis of inorganic materials possessing useful electrical and thermal properties. Contact: Synthetic Inorganic and Organometallic Chemistry, Division of Chemistry, Directorate for Mathematical and Physical Sciences, National Science Foundation, 1800 G St. N.W., Room 340, Washington, DC 20550/202-357-7499.

Synthetic Organic and Natural Products Chemistry
The synthetic organic and natural products chemistry program supports research on preparation, characterization, and structural manipulation of organic compounds from plant, animal and human sources and nonbiologic synthetic compounds; development of highly efficient reagents and methods for synthesizing compounds for use in energy storage, medicines, and agricultural chemicals; and design and synthesis of novel theories of structure and bonding. Contact: Synthetic Organic and Natural Products Chemistry Program, Directorate for Mathematical and Physical Sciences, National Science Foundation, 1800 G St. N.W., Room 340, Washington, DC 20550/202-357-7499.

Systemic Biology
The systemic biology program supports research on the identities, relationships, and distributions of living species of plants, animals, and microorganisms; fossil studies of extinct species to determine organic changes throughout the Earth's history; improved methods of gathering, processing, and analyzing the above data; functional morphology; chemosystematics; and paleobiology. Contact: Systemic Biology Program, Division of Biotic Systems and Resources, Directorate for Biological, Behavioral and Social Sciences, National Science Foundation, 1800 G St. N.W., Room 1140, Washington, DC 20550/202-357-9588.

Systems Theory and Operations Research
The electrical, computer and systems engineering program supports the study of mathematical methods useful in the analysis of complex engineering systems and systems management or operations

research, and research related to socioeconomic-technologic systems. Contact: Systems Theory and Operations Research Program, Division of Electrical, Computer and Systems Engineering, Directorate for Engineering and Applied Science, National Science Foundation, 1800 G St. N.W., Room 1151, Washington, DC 20550/202-357-9618.

Technology Assessment and Policy Analysis Research
The Division of Policy Research and Analysis (DPRA) of the National Science Foundation (NSF) supports professional research in technology assessment and policy analysis. Staff can refer you to NSF experts in nearly every field who can serve as resources in technology assessment. The office publishes hundreds of reports, special analyses, abstracts and other documents relating to technology assessment. Periodically DPRA publishes a list of recent publications and abstracts available to the public. Contact: Division of Policy Research and Analysis (DPRA), National Science Foundation (NSF), Washington, DC 20550/202-357-9828.

Technology Assessment and Risk Analysis
Studies in technology assessment seek to systematically identify and examine the planned and unplanned consequences of technology that are indirect, unanticipated, and delayed. Studies in risk analysis seek to understand better how information about risk is used in the science and technology policy decisionmaking process and how considerations of public and private costs and benefits are balanced in the S&T policy decision-making process. Contact: Technology and Resource Policy Section, Division of Policy Research and Analysis, Directorate for Scientific, Technological and International Affairs, National Science Foundation, 1800 G St. N.W., Room 1229, Washington, DC 20550/202-357-7829.

Technology Innovation Reports
The Productivity Improvement Research Section of the National Science Foundation (NSF) conducts and funds technological innovation studies of university/industry relations. The office frequently publishes reports about cooperative research. The staff will answer questions and make referrals. Contact: National Science Foundation, Division of Industrial Science and Technological Innovation, Productivity Improvement Research Section, 1800 G St. N.W., Room 1237, Washington, DC 20550/202-357-9805.

Theoretical Computer Science
The program on probability supports research on theories of computation and formal languages; analysis of algorithms; theoretical models for computation; and other theoretical problems concerned with the foundations of computer science.

Contact: Theoretical Computer Science Program, Division of Computer Sciences, Directorate for Mathematical and Physical Sciences, National Science Foundation, 1800 G St. N.W., Room 339, Washington, DC 20550/202-357-7349.

Theoretical Physics
The program on theoretical physics supports research on quantitative hypotheses to interpret results of experimental physics and to suggest new directions for research on the properties of physical systems, from nuclei to stars. Emphasis is on particle, nuclear, and atomic theories. Contact: Theoretical Physics Program, Division of Physics, Directorate for Mathematical and Physical Sciences, National Science Foundation, 1800 G St. N.W., Room 341, Washington, DC 20550/202-357-7979.

Thermodynamics and Mass Transfer
The chemical and process engineering program supports research on fluid property and phase-equilibrium relating measured thermodynamic and transport properties to molecular structure and interactions; fluid behavior at extreme conditions of temperature and pressure; diffusion in gases, liquids, liquid mixtures, polymer solutions, and solid polymers; mass transfer in microporous materials; separations processes—traditional and unconventional methods; processes taking place at interfaces, such as surface diffusion, surface rheology, absorption and surface instabilities; the effect of turbulence on mass transport; and predicting and correlating mass transfer rates. Contact: Thermodynamics and Phenomena Transfer Program, Division of Chemical and Process Engineering, Directorate for Engineering and Applied Science, National Science Foundation, Room 1126, 1800 G St. N.W., Washington, DC 20550/202-357-9606.

Topology, Geometry and Foundations
The program for topology, geometry and foundations supports research on general topology, algebraic topology, manifolds and cell complexes; finite planes, convex sets and related geometric topics; differential geometry and its relations to Lie representation theory, to dynamical systems theory, and to global analysis and analysis on manifolds; and mathematical logic and foundations of set theory, including proof theory, recursion theory, and nonstandard models. Contact: Topology Foundations Program, Division of Mathematical Sciences, Directorate for Mathematical and Physical Sciences, National Science Foundation, 1800 G St. N.W., Room 304, Washington, DC 20550/202-357-9764.

Undergraduate Research Participation
The program provides support to colleges, universities, and certain nonprofit research organizations with equivalent expertise to bring talented and promising undergraduate students into full-time

scientific and engineering research activities with university science faculty or industrial scientists. Contact: Research in Undergraduate Institutions, Division of Research Initiation and Improvement, Directorate for Scientific, Technological and International Affairs, National Science Foundation, 5225 Wisconsin Ave. N.W., Room 1144, Washington, DC 20550/202-357-7456.

Undergraduate Science Education

The comprehensive assistance to undergraduate science education program's primary objectives are twofold: to strengthen and improve the quality and effectiveness of undergraduate science instruction in colleges and universities, and to enhance institutional capability for self-assessment and continuous updating of science programs. Contact: Comprehensive Assistance to Undergraduate Science Education, Division of Science Education Resources Improvement, Directorate for Science Education, National Science Foundation, 5225 Wisconsin Ave. N.W., Room W418, Washington, DC 20550/202-357-7736.

University/Industry Cooperative Research Centers

The Centers are based on a one university-multicompany relationship which deals with particular scientific areas such as polymer processing or computer graphics. Companies may be from one or more industry. The Centers usually call upon the services of many disciplines and functions within the universities and invite participation by the local business and financial communities. Contact: University/Industry Research Centers, Industrial Programs, Division of Research Initiation and Improvement, Directorate for Scientific, Technological and International Affairs, National Science Foundation, 1800 G St. N.W., Room 1250, Washington, DC 20550/202-357-7527.

U.S.-China Program

The U.S.-China program for cooperation in the basic sciences is being developed. Contact: U.S.-China Program, Division of International Programs, Directorate for Scientific, Technological and International Affairs, National Science Foundation, 1800 G St. N.W., Room 1214, Washington, DC 20550/202-357-7393.

U.S.-Israel Binational Science Foundation

The areas supported by the U.S.-Israel Binational Science Foundation are agriculture, health sciences, natural sciences, social and behavioral sciences, science services, and technologies of interest to both countries, such as mass transportation, energy, arid zone, and environmental research. Contact: U.S.-Israel Binational Science Foundation, Division of International Programs, Directorate for Scientific, Technological and International Affairs, National Science Foundation, Room 1214, 1800 G St. N.W., Washington, DC 20550/202-357-7613.

Visiting Professorships for Women

This program provides opportunities for women to serve as visiting professors at academic institutions in the United States, its possessions, and territories. In addition to expanding their research and teaching opportunities, these professors encourage participation of women in science and engineering by their visibility and by advising and counseling other women about careers in science and engineering. Contact: Visiting Professorships for Women, Division of Research Initiation and Improvement, National Science Foundation, 1800 G St. N.W., Washington, DC 20550/202-357-7734.

Water Resources and Environmental Engineering

The civil and environmental engineering program supports research on erosion and transport of sediment; diffusion, dispersion, and biologic interaction of pollutants; flow-through underground aquifers; the mechanics of jets and plumes; wind/wave interaction; environmental acoustics and aerodynamics; hydrology and water resources; and water and wastewater treatment. Contact: Water Resources and Environmental Engineering Program, Division of Civil and Environmental Engineering, National Science Foundation, 1800 G St. N.W., Room 420, Washington, DC 20550/202-357-9542.

How Can the National Science Foundation Help You?

For information on how this agency can help you, contact: Public Affairs, National Science Foundation, 1800 G St. N.W., Washington, DC 20550/202-357-9498.

National Transportation Safety Board

800 Independence Ave. S.W., Washington, DC 20594/202-382-6600

Established: April 1, 1975
Budget: $19,965,000
Employees: 335

Mission: Seeks to insure that all types of transportation in the United States are conducted safely; investigates accidents, conducts studies, and makes recommendations to government agencies, the transportation industry, and others on safety measures and practices; regulates the procedures for reporting accidents; and promotes the safe transport of hazardous materials by government and private industry.

Major Sources of Information

Accident Briefs

Ten accident reports group civil aviation accident findings by kind of flying, type of aircraft or accident, and accident cause. They include computer-printed accident "briefs" which give the basic accident facts, probable cause, and contributing factors, if any, for all the accidents in each category. Statistics tables analyze the accidents by type, injury and cause. All of the ten reports cover general aviation. They are entitled *Briefs of . . .*

Accidents Involving Midair Collisions
Accidents Involving Alcohol as a Cause/Factor
Accidents Involving Corporate/Excecutive Aircraft
Fatal Weather Involved Accidents
Accidents Involving Rotorcraft
Accidents Involving Turbine-Powered Aircraft
Accidents Involving Aerial Application
Commuter Air Carrier and On-Demand Air Taxi Accidents
Accidents Involving Amateur Home Built Aircraft
Accidents Involving Missing, Later Recovered Aircraft

Contact: Accident Data Branch, National Transportation Safety Board, 800 Independence Ave. S.W., Room 837, Washington, DC 20594/202-382-6536.

Accident Data

An automated accident data system compiles statistics information for world-wide use.

Annual Review of Aircraft Accident Data—U.S. Air Carrier Operations

Statistics data and briefs of accidents compiled from reports of U.S. Air Carrier accidents that occurred during a calendar year. The briefs contain the facts, conditions, circumstances, and probable cause for each accident. The record of individual U.S. Air Carriers, U.S. Certificated Route Air Carriers, and U.S. Supplemental Air Carriers is provided by several types of service. Other statistics data include aircraft hours and miles flown, passengers carried, total and fatal accident rates, causal factors, injuries, and other data related to air accidents.

Annual Review of Aircraft Accident Data—U.S. General Aviation

Statistics information compiled from reports of U.S. General Aviation accidents that occurred during a calendar year. The publication is sectionalized to provide accident statistics on all aircraft accidents, small fixed-wing aircraft, rotorcraft and glider aircraft. Typical accident data include type of accident, phase of operation, kind of flying, causal factors, aircraft damage and injuries.

These reviews are available at no cost as long as the supply lasts. Contact: NTIS, Accident Data Branch, Bureau of Technology, National Transportation Safety Board, 800 Independence Ave. S.W., Room 811C, Washington, DC 20594/703-487-4630.

Accident Investigation

The Bureau of Accident Investigation is responsible for all accident investigations conducted by the Board in rail, pipeline, highway, marine and civil aviation transportation. It recommends whether a public hearing or depositions are to be held to determine the facts, conditions, and circumstances of accidents, and prepares a public report on accidents for submission to the Board for adoption, including a recommendation as to the probable cause. It may also participate in the investigation of civil aviation accidents involving U.S. registered, or U.S. manufactured, aircraft which occur in foreign countries. For general information, contact: Bureau of Accident Investigation, National Transportation Safety Board, 800 Independence Ave. S.W., Room 800, Washington, DC 20594/202-382-6800. For information on:

Civil Aircraft Accidents, contact: Aviation Accident Division, Room 820H, 202-382-6830.
Railroad accidents in which there is a fatality, substantial property damage or passenger train involvement, contact: Railroad Accident Division, Room 820G, 202-382-6840.
Pipeline accidents in which there is a fatality or substantial property damage, contact: Pipeline Accident Division, Room 820C, 202-382-0670.
Major marine casualties, contact: Marine Accident Division, Room 840A, 202-382-6860.
Highway accidents (selected in cooperation with the states), contact: Highway Accident Division, Room 820E, 202-382-6850.

Administration Law Judges

The Office of Administrative Law Judges conducts formal proceedings involving petitions for review from applicants denied airman andmedical certificates by the Federal Aviation Administration and also on appeals from FAA orders suspending or revoking certificates issued to pilots, navigators,

mechanics, dispatchers, air traffic controllers, air carriers, and air agencies authorized by the FAA to perform aircraft maintenance and to certify aircraft as airworthy. Administrative Law Judges function as trial judges, issuing subpoenas, administering oaths, holding prehearing conferences, ruling on procedural requests and motions, receiving relevant evidence, and other duties. Nearly all hearings on petitions for review and certain other appeals are held outside the Washington, DC area since the place of hearing must be convenient to all parties. *Initial Decisions of the Administrative Law Judges* are issued as decisions are released. Copies of decisions are available. Contact: Office of Administrative Law Judges, National Transportation Safety Board, 800 Independence Ave. S.W., Washington, DC 20594/202-382-6760.

Aircraft Flight Data and Voice Recorders Investigation

Vehicle parts, aircraft flight data and voice recorders are examined by the National Transportation Safety Board. Contact: Laboratory Services, Bureau of Technology, National Transportation Safety Board, 800 Independence Ave. S.W., Room 826, Washington, DC 20594/202-382-6686.

Certificate or License Appeal

Petitions from applicants denied airman and medical certificates by the Federal Aviation Administration are reviewed. Appeals from FAA orders suspending or revoking certificates issued to pilots, navigators, mechanics, dispatchers, air traffic controllers, air carriers and air agencies authorized by the FAA to perform aircraft maintenance and to certify aircraft as airworthy are also reviewed. Contact: Office of Administrative Law Judges, National Transportation Safety Board, 800 Independence Ave. S.W., Washington, DC 20594/202-382-6760.

Dockets

The Safety Board maintains a Public Docket which contains records of all accident investigations, all safety recommendations, and all safety enforcement proceedings. These records are all available to the public and may be copied, reviewed or duplicated. The accident records include each individual accident investigation conducted by and for the Board. The safety recommendation records include each recommendation issued and all responses from the recipients of such actions. The enforcement cases include all proceedings involving appeals to the Board from actions taken by Department of Transportation against airmen certificates and marine licenses and documents. Contact: Public Inquiries Section, National Transportation Safety Board, 800 Independence Ave. S.W., Room 805F, Washington, DC 20594/202-382-6735 Information on appeal cases of air and marine personnel is also available. Contact:

Docket Section, Office of Administrative Law Judges, National Transportation Safety Board, 800 Independence Ave. S.W., Room 822, Washington, DC 20594/202-382-6772.

Federal Transportation Safety Recommendations Data Base

The Safety Recommendation Information System is an interactive on-line data base containing information about all federal safety recommendations regarding transportation. The system consists of 10 to 20 categories for each of the following modes of transportation: aircraft, marine, pipeline, highway and railroad. Special studies and evaluations of federal transportation measures and practices are also stored. Searches and printouts are available free of charge. Contact: National Transportation Safety Board, 800 Independence Ave. S.W., Washington, DC 20594/202-382-6817.

Freedom of Information Act Requests

For Freedom of Information Act requests, contact: Freedom of Information Office, Office of General Counsel, National Transportation Safety Board, 800 Independence Ave. S.W., Room 818, Washington, DC 20594/202-382-6540.

Human Performance and Survival Factors

The National Transportation Safety Board has two divisions of professionals who deal with human performance and survival factors in relation to transportation equipment. Questions should be directed to the Office of Government and Public Affairs. Individual accident reports which include the human factors aspect may be purchased from the National Technical Information Service, 5285 Port Royal Road, Springfield, VA 20402/202-783-3238. Contact: National Transportation Safety Board, Office of Government and Public Affairs, 800 Independence Ave. S.W., Washington, DC 20594/202-382-6600.

Listing of Aircraft Accidents/Incidents by Make and Model, U.S. Civil Aviation

This publication includes general aviation and airline accidents identified by make and model. Contact: Safety Studies and Analysis Division, National Transportation Safety Board, 800 Independence Ave. S.W., Room 837, Washington, DC 20594/202-382-6570.

Publications

A free list of National Transportation Safety Board publications is available. It lists opinions and orders, initial decisions of the Administrative Law Judges, general subject publications, aviation safety publications and ordering information. Contact: Publications, National Transportation Safety Board, 800 Independence Ave. S.W., Room 805G, Washington, DC 20594/202-382-6735.

Public Data on Aircraft Accidents—Computer Tapes

Computer tapes containing public data on aircraft accidents or data processing programs are available for a fee. For information on how to order tapes, contact: Accident Data Branch, National Transportation Safety Board, 800 Independence Ave. S.W., Room 827, Washington, DC 20594/202-382-6536.

Public Hearings

The Board may hold a public hearing in which the facts determined in its investigation are presented as evidence and persons involved in the accident testify and are questioned. After all the evidence developed at the accident site, and at the hearing, is analyzed, a report setting forth the facts, conditions and circumstances of the accident is adopted by the Board and released to the public. Contact: Public Inquiries, National Transportation Safety Board, 800 Independence Ave. S.W., Room 805F, Washington, DC 20594/202-382-6735.

Regional Offices

There are twelve National Transportation Safety Board regional offices around the country. For a list of their addresses, contact: Public Inquiries, National Transportation Safety Board, 800 Independence Ave. S.W., Room 805F, Washington, DC 20594/202-382-6735.

Safety Recommendations

Safety recommendations are based on information developed from Board investigative findings and special studies, and are aimed at preventing accidents and correcting unsafe conditions in transportation. Recommendations may be issued at any time, sometimes within a few days after an accident, to initiate quick action to prevent additional accidents. Contact: Safety Recommendations, Bureau of Safety Programs, National Transportation Safety Board, 800 Independence Ave. S.W., Room 815, Washington, DC 20594/202-382-6810.

Speakers

Speakers are available to discuss subjects relating to transportation safety or to the Safety Board's organization functions, activities, procedures and regulations. Contact: Public Affiars, National Transportation Safety Board, 800 Independence Ave. S.W., Room 808, Washington, DC 20594/202-382-6600.

Technical Expertise

Specialists investigate accidents within their specific technical areas and participate in public hearings as members of the technical panel. Contact: Bureau of Technology, National Transportation Safety Board, 800 Independence Ave. S.W., Room 824B, Washington, DC 20594/202-382-6610. For specific technical expertise, contact:

Aviation Engineering Division, Room 826B, 202-382-6676
Operational Factors Division, Room 826A, 202-382-6661
Survival Factors Division, Room 830F, 202-382-6626
Service Engineering Division, Room 829B, 202-382-6651
Human Performance Division, Room 824, 202-382-6835
Laboratory Surveys Division, Room 826C, 202-382-6686

How Can the National Transportation Safety Board Help You?
For information on how this agency can help you, contact: Office of Public Affairs, National Transportation Safety Board, 800 Independence Ave. S.W., Washington, DC 20594/202-382-6600.

Nuclear Regulatory Commission

1717 H St. N.W., Washington DC 20555/301-492-7715

Established: January 19, 1975
Budget: $465,974,000
Employees: 3,280

Mission: Licenses and regulates the uses of nuclear energy to protect the environment and public health and safety; licenses persons and companies to build and operate nuclear reactors and to own and use nuclear materials; makes rules and sets standards for these types of licenses; and fully inspects the activities of the persons and companies licensed to insure that they do not violate the safety rules of the Commission.

Major Sources of Information

Abnormal Occurrences—Quarterly Report to Congress
This report identifies an abnormal occurrence as an unscheduled incident or event which the Nuclear Regulatory Commission determines to be significant from the standpoint of public health or safety. This report is available from the Government Printing Office Sales Program, Division of Technical Information and Document Control, Nuclear Regulatory Commission, 1717 H St. N.W., Washington, DC 20555/301-492-9530. For additional information, contact: Management Information, Office of Management and Program Analysis, Nuclear Regulatory Commission, 7735 Old Georgetown Rd. Room 7602 MNBB, Bethesda, MD 20814/301-492-7834.

Advisory Committee on Reactor Safeguards
This statutory body of fifteen scientists and engineers reviews and makes recommendations to the Commission on all applications for construction and operation of nuclear power reactors and related nuclear safety matters. The views of the ACRS are taken into account in a Supplementary Safety Evaluation Report. Contact: Advisory Committee on Reactor Safeguards, Nuclear Regulatory Commission, Room 1010, 1717 H St. N.W., Washington, DC 20555/301-634-3265.

Annual Reports
A variety of annual reports are issued by this office. They include:

Occupational Radiation Exposure at Light Water Cooled Power Reactors—a compilation of occupational radiation exposures at commercial light water cooled nuclear power reactors.
Radioactive Materials Released from Nuclear Power Plants—releases of radioactive materials in airborne and liquid effluents from commercial light water reactors are compiled and reported.
Occupational Radiation Exposure Report
Nuclear Power Plant Operating Experience—includes power generation statistics, plant outages, reportable occurrences, fuel element performance, and occupational radiation exposure for each plant.
Population Dose Commitments Due to Radioactive Releases from Nuclear Power Plants—fifty-year dose commitments for a one-year exposure were calculated from liquid and atmospheric releases for four population groups—infant, child, teenager and adult—residing between 2 and 80 km from each site.

These reports are available through: Publications,

Office of Administration, Nuclear Regulatory Commission, 1717 H St. N.W., MS058 MNBB, Washington, DC 20555/301-492-8523.

Antitrust Review
Prior to or parallel with other reviews, the Nuclear Regulatory Commission conducts a prelicensing antitrust review of each application for a major nuclear facility in order to insure that the proposed facility is in compliance with antitrust laws. Hearings are held when recommended by the U.S. Attorney General, or they may be held on the petition of an interested party. Contact: Antitrust Division, Office of the Executive Legal Director, Nuclear Regulatory Commission, 7735 Old Georgetown Rd., Bethesda, MD 20555/301-492-7488.

Atomic Safety and Licensing Appeal Panel
Three-member appeal boards are selected from this panel to review decisions of the licensing board. Contact: Atomic Safety and Licensing Appeal Panel, Nuclear Regulatory Commission, 1717 H St. N.W., Room 532, Washington, DC 20555/301-492-7662.

Atomic Safety and Licensing Board Panel
This is a three-member board drawn from the safety and licensing panel which conducts public hearings on nuclear power plant applications. Contact: Atomic Safety and Licensing Board Panel, Nuclear Regulatory Commission, 4350 East West Highway, Room 423, Bethesda, MD 20555/301-492-7842.

Citizen's Guide to the Nuclear Regulatory Commission
This catalog lists all publications available from the Nuclear Regulatory Commission. The catalogue is free of charge. Contact: Publication Ordering Office, Nuclear Regulatory Commission, 1717 H. St. N.W., Washington, DC 20555/301-492-9503.

Construction Permit
A utility or any other company must obtain a Nuclear Regulatory Commission construction permit as the first step in operating a nuclear power reactor or other nuclear facility under NRC license. The process for licensing a nuclear power plant or a fuel reprocessing plant requires extensive technical reviews and public proceedings. Contact: Licensing Division, Office of Nuclear Reactor Regulation, Nuclear Regulatory Commission, 7735 Old Georgetown Road, Room 110, Bethesda, MD 20555/301-492-7425.

Construction Surveillance
Nuclear power plants are inspected by NRC representatives during construction and preoperational testing. This largely involves inspection of the quality assurance program of the licensee. Contact: Reactor Construction Branch, Office of

Inspection and Enforcement, Nuclear Regulatory Commission, 7735 Old Georgetown Rd, Room 312A, Bethesda, MD 20555/301-492-9644

Consumer Products Containing Nuclear Material
The Nuclear Regulatory Commission issues three types of licenses—exemptions, general and specific—for consumer products containing source materials (uranium and thorium), special nuclear materials (plutonium, uranium-233), and byproduct materials. A regulatory guide describing the statistics sampling procedures for exempt and generally licensed items containing byproduct material is also available. Contact: Material Licensing Branch, Office of Nuclear Material Safety and Safeguards, Nuclear Regulatory Commission, 1717 H St. N.W., Washington, DC 20555/301-427-4228 for industrial products, 301-427-4232 medical products.

Docket Breakdown
Each nuclear power generating facility is assigned a docket number, and all documents pertaining to that facility are filed by the facility docket number. Each Docket 50 file is further subdivided and filed in categories that pertain either to different aspects of the licensing process or to document types. The types of documents in each category are described in *NRC*, a free publication. For further information, contact: Public Document Room, Nuclear Regulatory Commission, 1717 H St. N.W., Lobby, Washington, DC 20555/301-634-3273.

Environmental Review
A Nuclear Regulatory Commission staff evaluation of the potential environmental impact of the proposed nuclear plant and the suitability of the site is conducted in advance of, or in parallel with, the safety review. This evaluation, required by the National Environmental Policy Act, considers the effects of construction and operation of the plant on the local environment and weighs the benefits to be gained against the possible risk to the environment. The review—which takes into account comments by expert federal and state agencies and the public—results in an NRC Final Environmental Statement, and this statement may require changes to the plant design or operational mode. Contact: Office of Nuclear Reactor Regulation, Nuclear Regulatory Commission, 1717 H St. N.W., AR 5111, Washington, DC 20555/301-492-7331.

Ergonomics of Nuclear Power Plants
The Nuclear Regulatory Commission (NRC) regulates the ergonomics aspect of nuclear power plants. The agency's involvement includes control room design, man-machine interface, training and qualification of operating staffs, and procedures. The Commission also conducts ergonomics related research to develop a technical basis for regula-

tion. The Division of Human Factors Safety and its five branches are involved in ergonomics and staff can refer you to appropriate people. Contact Division of Human Factor Safety, Office of Nuclear Reactor Regulation, Nuclear Regulatory Commission, 1717 H St. N.W., Washington, DC 21555/301-492-4803.

Export-Import Licensing

This office licenses the export of nuclear reactors, and the export and import of uranium and plutonium. Contact: Export/Import and International Safeguards, Office of International Programs, Nuclear Regulatory Commission, 1717 H St. N.W., Room 418, Washington, DC 20555/301-492-8155.

Freedom of Information Act Requests

For Freedom of Information Act requests, contact: Division of Rules and Records, Office of Administration, Nuclear Regulatory Commission, 1717 H St. N.W., Room 4210, Washington, DC 20555/301-492-8133.

Fuel and Materials Safety

This office performs independent measurements of radioactivity in nuclear facility effluents to insure that the licensee's measurements are accurate and that discharges are maintained at levels that are as low as reasonably possible. Contact: Division of Fuel Facilities, Materials, and Safeguards, Office of Inspection and Enforcement, Nuclear Regulatory Commission, 1717 H St. N.W., Room 3105 EWS, Washington, DC 20555/301-492-8225.

Fuel Cycle and Materials Safety

This office licenses and regulates fuel-cycle facilities and the transport and handling of nuclear materials. Contact: Fuel Cycle and Material Safety Division, Office of Nuclear Materials Safety and Safeguards, Nuclear Regulatory Commission, 1717 H St. N.W., Rm 396, Washington, DC 20555/301-427-4485.

Grants

The program described below is for sums of money which are given by the Department of Energy to stimulate research.

Enhance Technology Transfer and Dissemination of Nuclear Energy Process and Safety Information

Objectives: To stimulate research to provide a technological base for the safety assessment of system and subsystem technologies used in nuclear power applications; to increase public understanding relating to nuclear safety; to enlarge the fund of theoretical and practical knowledge and technical information; to enhance the protection of public health and safety.

Eligibility: Educational institutions, public and private entities, State and local governments and professional societies.

Range of Financial Assistance: $5,000 to $15,000 per project.

Contact: Office of Administration, Division of Contracts, Nuclear Regulatory Commission, Washington, DC 20555/301-492-4297.

Handbook of Acronyms and Initialisms

This is a dictionary of acronyms, initialisms, and similar condensed forms used in the nuclear industry. Available for $5.50 from GPO Sales Program, Division of Technical Information and Document Control, Nuclear Regulatory Commission, Room P130A, 7920 Norfolk Ave, Bethesda, MD 20555 Washington, DC 20555/301-492-9530.

High-Level Waste

The Nuclear Regulatory Commission is developing performance criteria for solidified high-level wastes. These criteria are being developed based on a systems analysis model which considers the potential for accidents during interim storage, transportation, handling, emplacement and post-emplacement. Repository site selection criteria are being developed and will encompass a broad spectrum of concerns including earth science, natural resource, demographic and socioeconomic factors. A study to determine the design and operating requirements for high-level waste repositories will provide a basis for the development of standards and staff review methodologies. Contact: Waste Management Division, Office of Nuclear Materials Safety and Safeguards, Nuclear Regulatory Commission, 1717 H St. N.W., MS Rm 923-SS, Washington, DC 20555/301-427-4069.

Inspection and Enforcement

The Nuclear Regulatory Commission conducts periodic inspection of nuclear plants and other licenses. Enforcement powers include issuance of violation notices, imposition of fines and license suspension, modification or revocation. Contact: Office of Inspection and Enforcement, Nuclear Regulatory Commission, 7735 Old Georgetown Rd., Room 322, Bethesda, MD 20555/301-492-7397.

Inspectors

NRC inspectors check the regulatory compliance of other licenses, including hospital nuclear medicine programs, industrial applications, academic and research activities, and nuclear material processing. Contact: Office of Inspection and Enforcement, Nuclear Regulatory Commission, 1717 H St. N.W., Room 322 EWT, Washington, DC 20555/301-492-7397.

Library

The Nuclear Regulatory Commission Library collection stresses energy, nuclear physics and nuclear chemistry and is open to the public. Contact: Library, Nuclear Regulatory Commission, 7920 Norfolk Ave., Room 160, Bethesda, MD 20555/301-492-8501.

Licensee Event Reports
Monthly licensee event reports (LER), which are entered into the computer, are available on the following topics:

LER monthly report sorted by facility
LER monthly report sorted by component
LER monthly regional report sorted by region, facility and event date
LER monthly report on valves and valve operators sorted by facility
LER monthly report on personnel errors and defective procedures sorted by component and system
LER monthly report on mechanical items sorted by component and system
LER monthly report on electrical items sorted by component and system
LER monthly report on instrumentation and control items sorted by component and system
LER monthly report on civil items sorted by component and system
LER monthly report sorted by system and component
LER monthly report on vibration events sorted by component, system and facility
LER monthly report on construction deficiency reports sorted by facility
LER monthly report on events involving personnel errors sorted by facility type, cause subcode and facility
LER monthly report on events involving personnel errors sorted by component, system and facility
LER monthly report on BWR events sorted by cause, facility and event date
LER monthly report on the offsite power system sorted by facility
LER monthly report on water hammer events sorted by facility
LER monthly report on pipe cracks and breaks sorted by facility type, facility and event date

Contact: Management Informaton, Office of Management and Program Analysis, Nuclear Regulatory Commission, 1717 H St. N.W., Room 12702 MNBB, Washington, DC 20555/301-492-7834.

Licensing
The Nuclear Regulatory Commission reviews and issues licenses for the construction and operation of nuclear power plants and other uses of nuclear materials, including medical, industrial, education and research activities. Contact: Licensing Division, Nuclear Regulatory Commission, 7920 Norfolk Rd., Room 528A PHIL, Bethesda, MD 20555/301-492-7672.

Limited Work Authorization (LWA)
In appropriate cases, the Nuclear Regulatory Commission may grant a Limited Work authoriza-

tion to an applicant in advance of the final decision on the construction permit so certain work at the reactor site can begin sooner. Contact: Licensing Division, Office of Nuclear Reactor Regulations, Nuclear Regulatory Commission, 1717 H St. N.W., Room 528A PHIL, Washington, DC 20555/301-492-7672.

Loss-of-Fluid Test (LOFT)
LOFT is designed to provide additional data on the performance of an emergency core cooling system in a pressurized water reactor. Contact: Idaho Site Representative, Idaho National Engineering Laboratory, Nuclear Regulatory Commission, 550 2nd St., Idaho Falls, ID 83401/208-583-1951, or LOFT Research Branch, Reactor Safety Research Division, Nuclear Regulatory Commission, 7915 Eastern Avenue, Room 1204 WILL, Silver Spring, MD 20555/301-427-4260.

Low-Level Waste Program
This program develops a framework of criteria and regulations for long-term management of commercial low-level waste disposal sites to provide the tools for applicants to prepare license applications and to enable the Nuclear Regulatory Commission to make uniform, timely licensing decisions. Contact: Low-Level Waste & Uranium Recovery Projects Branch, Division of Waste Management, Office of Nuclear Material Safety and Safeguards, Nuclear Regulatory Commission, Room 736 WILL, N.W., Washington, DC 20555/301-427-4433.

Material Licensing
This office licenses the users of radioisotopes in industry, research and medicine in those states which have not assumed this authority under agreements with the Nuclear Regulatory Commission. Contact: Material Safety and Licensing Branch, Office of Nuclear Material Safety and Safeguards, Nuclear Regulatory Commission, 1717 H St. N.W., Room 542 WILL, Washington, DC 20555/301-427-4228 for industrial products, 301-427-4232 for medical products.

Monthly Operating Units Status Reports—Licensed Operating Reactors
This publication provides data on the operation of nuclear units. Available for $120.00 per year from GPO Sales Program, Division of Technical Information and Document Control, Nuclear Regulatory Commission, 1717 H St. N.W., Washington, DC 20555/301-492-9530. For additional information, contact: Management Information, Office of Management and Program Analysis, Nuclear Regulatory Commission, 7735 Old Georgetown Rd, Room 7602 MNBB, Bethesda, MD 20555/301-492-7834.

NRC Order and Issuances
Various types of documents are maintained in the

files of nondocketed materials. These specific types of documents are listed in *Descriptions and Content of Non-Docketed PDR File Categories,* available free of charge. Contact: Public Document Room, Lobby, Nuclear Regulatory Commission, 1717 H St. N.W., Washington, DC 20555/ 301-634-3273.

Nuclear Regulatory Research
This office develops recommendations and determinations for research to be conducted in the fields of nuclear reactor safety, safeguards for nuclear materials and facilities, the nuclear fuel cycle, and environmental protection, waste management, and risk assessment. Contact: Office of Nuclear Regulatory Research, Nuclear Regulatory Commission, 7915 Eastern Ave, Room 1140 WILL, Silver Spring, MD 20555/301-427-4341.

Nuclear Safeguards
This office develops programs for protecting nuclear materials from diversion and nuclear facilities from sabotage. It also licenses and regulates the safeguarding of nuclear facilities and materials. Contact: Safeguards Division, Office of Nuclear Material Safety and Safeguards, Nuclear Regulatory Commission, 7915 Eastern Avenue, Silver Spring, MD 20555; Room 872 WILL, Washington, DC 20555/301-427-4033.

Open and Closed Meetings
The general public is welcome to attend and observe all Commission meetings with ten exceptions. The exceptions include meetings involving: classified documents; internal personnel matters; information that is confidential by statute; trade secrets; accusations of a crime or censure; invasion of personal privacy; investigatory records; regulatory reports of financial institutions; premature disclosure of information which will hinder implementation of agenda action; and adjudicatory matters. An announcement of the time, place, subject matter, whether or not it is open to the public and name and telephone number of the contact is placed in the Public Document Room. If a meeting is to be closed the announcement contains an explanation of the reasons for closing the meeting. Notices of meetings are also published in the *Federal Register.* A transcript or electronic recording is made of all meetings. Transcripts of open meetings are placed in the Public Document Room and are available for public inspection or duplication. A free *Guide for Open Meetings* is available. Contact: Office of the Secretary, Nuclear Regulatory Commission, 1717 H St. N.W., Room 1135, Washington, DC 20555/ 301-634-1498.

PDR Accession List
The *PDR Accession List* is the primary reference tool for finding documents in the Public Document Room (PDR). The accession list permits users to search for documents by docket number or non-docket file level: date; author/recipient name and affiliation; report number, etc. The accession list does not contain a subject index. The accession list, issued daily, announces the documents that have been made available that day. There is a two- or three-week delay in the public availability of newly generated documents. The docket materials are listed by docket number, then by licensing category (Docket 50 only), and date. Non-docket materials are listed alphabetically by non-docket file category and then by date. Each month a special list is issued that describes all documents received during that month. The monthly accession list is sorted by docket number and by non-docket file category and then filed in individual binders in the reading room. For more information about the format and content of the accession list, consult *How to Use the PDR Accession List,* 4/11/ 80, copies of which are available free of charge by writing to the PDR, Lobby, 1717 H St. N.W., Washington, DC 20555/301-634-3273.

Power Reactor Events
This is a free bimonthly summary of selected events that have occurred at nuclear power plants. These events are taken mainly from *Licensee Event Reports* and *NRC Inspection Reports* and are, or have been, under review by the NRC. Contact: Office of Research Management, Division of Automated Information Services, 7735 Old Georgetown Road, Bethesda, MD 20555; Nuclear Regulatory Commission, Room 7602 MNBB, Washington, DC 20555/301-492-7834.

Public Document Room
The Public Document Room maintains facilities for receiving, processing, storing and retrieving documents which the Nuclear Regulatory Commission receives or generates in performing its regulatory functions. Some of these documents include Docket Files which relate mainly to the licensing and inspection of nuclear facilities and to the use, transport and disposal of nuclear materials, and non-docket files, including reports, correspondence, contracts, guides, annual reports, press releases, indexes, bibliographies, notices and handbooks. A free *Public Document Room Users Guide* is available. The staff provides reference services, on-line computer searching, document processing, file maintenance, and microfiching and reproduction services. Guided tours of the Public Document Room and orientation or training sessions for individuals or groups are available upon request. Local Public Document Rooms are located in libraries in cities or towns near proposed and actual nuclear power plant sites across the country. They contain the licensing and regulatory files specific to nearby facilities which are either licensed or under review. For location of LPDRs,

consult the *Local Public Document Room Roster* available for examination and copying in the PRD. For additional information, contact: Public Document Room, Nuclear Regulatory Commission, 1717 H St. N.W., Left Lobby, Washington, DC 20555/301-634-3273.

Public Participation

The law requires that a public hearing be held before a decision can be made to grant or deny a permit to build a nuclear power plant. The Atomic Safety and Licensing Board conducting the proceedings may combine the safety and environmental matters or it may consider them in separate public hearings. Notices of these hearings are published in the *Federal Register,* posted in the nearest public document room and published in the local newspapers. Interested parties should petition the licensing board for the right to participate in public hearings. Contact: Atomic Safety and Licensing Board Panel, 4350 East West Hwy, Bethesda, MD 20555; Nuclear Regulatory Commission, Room 423 EWT, Washington, DC 20555/301-492-7842.

Reactor Operating License

Two or three years before completion of the plant is scheduled, the applicant files an application for an operating license. A process similar to that for the construction permit follows. Contact: Document Control Desk, Operating Reactors, Licensing Division, Office of Nuclear Reactor Regulations, Nuclear Regulatory Commission, PHIL, Room 016, 7920 Norfolk Avenue, Bethesda, MD 20555/301-492-7817.

Reactor Operations Inspection

Once licensed, a nuclear facility remains under NRC surveillance and undergoes periodic inspections throughout its operating life. In cases where the NRC finds that substantial additional protection is necessary for the public health and safety, or the common defense and security, the NRC may require "backlifting" of a licensed plant, that is, the addition, elimination, or modification of structures, systems, or components of the plant. Contact: Division of Reactor Enforcement, Nuclear Regulatory Commission, 1717 H St. N.W., Room 360 EWS, Washington, DC 20555/301-492-9696.

Reactor Safety Research

Research in progress for the purpose of establishing site, structural, and environmental information to be used in nuclear facility safety evaluations includes studies in seismology, geology, hydrology, and meteorology. Research in such areas of natural phenomena as earthquakes and tornadoes is also under way. Contact: Division of Accident and Evaluation, Office of Nuclear Regulatory Research, Nuclear Regulatory Commission,

Room 1130-SS, 7913 Eastern Avenue, Bethesda, MD 20555/301-427-4442.

Regulatory and Technical Reports

Listings of regulatory and technical reports are available:

Vol. 3 ('75–'78) $10.00
Vol. 4 ('79) $7.50
Vol. 5 ('80–'81) $6.50
Vol. 6 ('81) $14.00
Vol. 7 ('82) $14.00
Vol. 8 ('83) $14.00

Contact: GPO Sales Program, Division of Technical Information and Document Control, Nuclear Regulatory Commission, 7920 Norfolk Avenue, Bethesda, MD 20555/301-492-9530.

Regulatory Guides

The Nuclear Regulatory Commission Regulatory Guide Series was developed to describe methods acceptable for implementing specific requirements of the Commission's regulations. The Guides are made available at two stages: 1) Task Draft Guides, available free on subscription; and 2) Active Guides, available through a paid subscription.

The following guides are available:

Division 1—*Power Reactor Guides* ($66.00)
Division 2—*Research and Test Reactor Guides* ($15.00)
Division 3—*Fules and Materials Facilities Guides* ($39.00)
Division 4—*Environmental and Siting Guides* ($31.00)
Division 5—*Materials and Plant Protection Guides* ($26.00)
Division 6—*Product Guides* ($15.00)
Division 7—*Transportation Guides* ($19.00)
Division 8—*Occupational Health Guides* ($37.00)
Division 9—*Antitrust and Financial Review Guides* ($15.00)
Division 10—*General Guides* ($21.00)
Division 1 through 10 inclusive ($232.00)

Contact: GPO Sales Program, Division of Technical Information and Document Control, Nuclear Regulatory Commission, 1717 H St. N.W., Washington, DC 20555/301-492-9530.

Safeguards Inspection

This office also investigates accidents and incidents at licensed facilities as well as complaints or allegations from licensee employees or members of the public concerning activities of NRC licensees. Contact: Division of Nuclear Materials and Safeguards, Office of Inspection, Nuclear Regulatory Commission, 7915 Eastern Avenue, Room 332A EWW, Silver Spring, MD 20555/301-427-4043.

Safety Review

The Nuclear Regulatory Commission staff conducts an in-depth safety review of the proposed design of the plant. When design features do not meet NRC standards, changes by the applicant are required. The staff then prepares a Safety Evaluation Report which is made public. Contact: Safety Program Evaluation, Office of Nuclear Reactor Regulations, Nuclear Regulatory Commission, 7920 Norfolk Avenue, PHIL, Room 223, Bethesda, MD 20555/301-492-7827.

Standards
This office coordinates NRC staff participation in standards-related activities of the International Atomic Energy Agency, and serves as a principal point of contact for the Commission with the American National Standards Institute and technical and professional societies on matters concerning nuclear standards. Contact: Office of Research, Nuclear Regulatory Commission, 1717 H St. N.W., Room 1140, 7915 Eastern Avenue, Silver Spring, MD 20555/301-427-4341.

State Programs
This office develops effective working relationships with the states regarding the regulation of nuclear materials. Contact: Office of State Programs, Nuclear Regulatory Commission, MS AR5307, 5th floor, 4550 Montgomery, Bethesda, MD; Washington, DC 20555/301-492-8170.

Subscription Publication
Nuclear Regulatory Commission Issuances (monthly plus quarterly and semiannual indexes), a compilation of adjudications and other issuances of the NRC, including those of the Atomic Safety and Licensing Boards and the Atomic Safety and Licensing Appeal Boards, is available for sale either on subscription ($90/yr) or on a single-issue basis from NTIS, Springfield, VA 22161/703-557-4600.Hardbound semiannual issuances and indexes are available from the Superintendent of Documents, Government Printing Office, Washington, DC 20402/202-783-3238.

Technical Information Hotline
A technical information clearinghouse responds to inquiries about the availability of technical information on the licensing and regulation of nuclear technologies and applications. The clearinghouse also answers questions on how to obtain various kinds of information available to the public through the NRC, and provides information on meeting schedules, the hearing status of nuclear power plant licensing cases, and the locations of NRC local public document rooms. Call toll-free 800-638-8282, or 800-492-8106 in Maryland, or Contact: Office of Public Affairs, Nuclear Regulatory Commission, 1717 H St. N.W., Room 3709 MNBB, Washington, DC 20555/301-492-7715.

Three Mile Island
For information and reports on Three Mile Island, including the final version of the environmental impact statement on the cleanup, contact: Three Mile Island Program Office, Office of Nuclear Reactor Regulation, Nuclear Regulatory Commission, 7920 Norfolk Ave., Bethesda, MD 20555/301-492-7761.

Title List of Documents Made Publicly Available
The *Title List* is a monthly publication which contains bibliographic descriptions of and indexes to the documentation received and generated by the Nuclear Regulatory Commission. It includes both docketed and non-docketed materials. First issued in January 1979, the *Title List* supersedes *Power Reactor Docket Information* (PRDI). It is indexed by a Personal-Author Index, Corporate-Source Index, and Report-Number Index. The *Title List* is not cumulative and has no subject index. There is a one- to two-month time lag in the publication of the *Title List*. Consult the preface of any volume for further information on this publication. The *Title List* is available for $100.00 per year. For information on how to order this publication, contact: GPO Sales Program, Division of Technical Information and Document Control, Nuclear Regulatory Commission, 1717 H St. N.W., Washington, DC 20555/301-492-9530.

How Can the Nuclear Regulatory Commission Help You?
For information on how this agency can help you, contact: Office of Public Affairs, Nuclear Regulatory Commission, 7735 Old Georgetown Rd, Room 3217, Bethesda, MD 20555/301-492-7715.

Occupational Safety and Health Review Commission

1825 K St. N.W., Washington, DC 20006/202-634-7943

Established: 1970
Budget: $6,316,000
Employees: 113

Mission: Rules on cases forwarded to it by the U.S. Department of Labor when disagreements arise over the results of safety and health inspections performed by the Department's Occupational Safety and Health Administration (OSHA). (Employers have the right to dispute any alleged job safety or health violation found during the inspection by OSHA, the penalties proposed by OSHA, and the time given by OSHA to correct any hazardous situation. Employees and representatives of employees may initiate a case by challenging the propriety of the time OSHA has allowed for correction of any violative condition.)

Major Sources of Information

Amendments to Rules
A citizen may propose an amendment or revocation of the Commission's rules. For additional information, contact: Excecutive Secretary, Occupational Safety and Health Review Commission, 1825 K St. N.W., Room 401, Washington, DC 20006/202-634-7950.

Certificate of Service
Copies of all papers filed with the Commission or a judge must be served on all other parties to the case. A statement that service has been made must be attached to any papers submitted for filing with the Commission. The statement must show the date and manner of service (mail or personal delivery) and the names of the persons served. Contact: Executive Secretary, Occupational Safety and Health Review Commission, 1825 K St. N.W., Room 401, Washington, DC 20006/202-634-7950.

Commission Speakers
Members and officials participate as speakers and panel members before bar associations, safety councils, labor organizations, management associations, and educational, civic, and other groups. Contact: Information Office, Occupational Safety and Health Review Commission, 1825 K St. N.W., Room 316, Washington, DC 20006/202-634-7943.

Dockets
The Executive Secretary files all dockets. Any person may inspect and copy these and any other document filed in any proceeding. Contact: Executive Secretary, Occupational Safety and Health Review Commission, 1825 K St. N.W., Room 401, Washington, DC 20006/202-634-7950.

Freedom of Information Act Requests
For Freedom of Information Act requests, contact: Information and Publications, Occupational Safety and Health Review Commission, 1825 K St. N.W., Room 316, Washington, DC 20006/202-634-7943.

Publications
For a listing of publications, contact: Office of Information, Occupational Safety and Health Review Commission, 1825 K St. N.W., Room 316, Washington, DC 20006, 202-634-7943.

Public Information
This adjudicatory body has information on its procedures, as well as specific case transcripts, briefs and decisions concerning any company which has employees and is engaged in interstate commerce. Contact: Public Information, Occupational Safety and Health Review Commission, 1825 K St. N.W., Room 316, Washington, DC 20006/202-634-7943.

Review Commission Judges
All cases which require a hearing are assigned to a Review Commission Administrative Law Judge. Ordinarily the hearing is held in, or close to, the community where the alleged violation occurred. Contact: Chief Administrative Law Judge, Occupational Safety and Health Review Commission, 1825 K St. N.W., Room 419, Washington, DC 20006/202-634-7980.

Simplified Proceedings
Procedures for resolving contests can be simplified so that parties before the Commission may save time and expense while preserving fundamental procedural fairness. For additional information, contact the nearest regional Occupational Safety and Health Review Commission, or the Executive Secretary, Occupational Safety and Health Review Commission, 1825 K St. N.W., Room 401, Washington, DC 20006/202-634-7950.

How Can the Occupational Safety and Health Review Commission Help You?
To determine how the Occupational Safety and Health Review Commission can help you, contact: Director of Information and Publications, Occupational Safety and Health Review Commission, 1825 K St. N.W., Washington, DC 20006/202-634-7943.

Office of Personnel Management

1900 E St. N.W., Washington, DC 20415/202-632-5491

Established: January 1, 1979
Budget: $16,989,193,000
Employees: 5,114

Mission: Administers a merit system for federal employment, which includes recruiting, examining, training, and promoting people on the basis of their knowledge and skills, regardless of their race, religion, sex, political influence, or other nonmerit factors; insures that the federal government provides an array of personnel services to applicants and employees; and supports government program managers in their personnel management responsibilities and provides benefits to employees directly.

Major Sources of Information

Affirmative Employment
Through its affirmative employment efforts, the Office of Personnel Management seeks to eliminate nonmerit considerations such as race, color, religion, sex, national origin, or age from all aspects of federal employment. It also operates selective placement programs for physically and mentally handicapped persons, and programs for other groups including veterans, youths, and women. Contact: Office of Affirmative Employment Programs, Office of Personnel Management, 1900 E St. N.W., Room 7H07 Washington, DC 20415/202-632-4420.

Alcoholic and Drug Treatment Programs
This office oversees all government employee health and alcoholism/drug abuse programs. Contact: Employee Health Services, Workforce Effectiveness and Development Group, Office of Personnel Management, 1900 E St. N.W., Room 7H39; Washington, DC 20415/202-632-5558.

Annuities
Free pamphlets describing annuity benefits under the civil service retirement system are available. Contact: Retirement Information Center, Office of Personnel Management, 1900 E St. N.W., Room 1323B, Washington, DC 20415/202-632-7700.

Civil Service Exams
The pamphlet, *Current Federal Examination Announcements* (AN-2279), is available free from any Federal Job Information Center.

Contracts
For information on contracts, contact the nearest regional office, or Acquisitions Section, Office of Personnel Management, 1900 E St. N.W., Room 1466, Washington, DC 20415/202-254-8492.

Employee and Annuitant Information Center
Help with a claim and general information are available for employees and annuitants. Free pamphlets are available: *Information for Annuitants about the Federal Employee Health Benefits Program,* and *Information for Survivor Annuit-*

ants. Contact: Employee and Annuitant Information Service, Retirement Programs, Office of Personnel Management, 1900 E St. N.W., Room 1323B, Washington, DC 20415/202-632-7700.

Employee Benefits
Federal employee benefits include health benefits, life insurance programs for the employees, annuitants and survivors, and civil service retirement programs. Contact the Personnel Officer for specific information at the agency or federal department where you are or will be employed.

Employee Conduct Regulations
The "Agency Relations Packet" outlines the Ethics in Government, federal regulations, and a digest of opinions since 1979. Available free from: Office of Government Ethics, Office of Personnel Management, PO Box 14108, Washington, DC 20415/202-632-7642.

Ethics in Government
Overall direction of executive branch policies is provided to prevent conflicts of interest on the part of officers and employees of any executive agency. Public financial disclosure is monitored, and rules and regulations pertaining to employee conduct and post-employment conflicts of interest are developed. For information, contact: Office of Government Ethics, Office of Personnel Management, PO Box 14108, Washington, DC 20415/202-632-7642.

Executive Seminar Center
These Centers are residential interagency training facilities to aid government agencies in meeting programmatic and managerial training needs. The programs offered are open to federal, state and local governments. The curriculum includes seminars on: administration of public policy; public program management; national economy and public policy; science, technology and public policy; intergovernmental relations; environmental quality and natural resources; domestic policies and programs; energy policies and programs; and management and executive development. The centers are located as follows:

Executive Seminar Center, c/o U.S. Merchant Marine Academy, Kings Point, NY 11024/516-487-4500, or, 482-8200, ext. 343.

Executive Seminar Center, Broadway and Kentucky Ave., Oak Ridge, TN 37830/615-576-1730.

For additional information, contact: Executive Seminar Center, Office of Training, Office of Personnel Management, 1121 Vermont Ave. N.W., Room 1200, Washington, DC 20044/202-632-6802.

Exemption
For advice on "exemption" from competitive

service, contact: Examination Services Division, Office of Personnel Management, 1900 E St. N.W., Room 6303, Washington, DC 20415/202-632-6000.

Federal Employee Attitudes
A government-wide attitude survey of federal employees was administered to establish a baseline of employee attitudes about their jobs and work environment. Groupings included federal agencies, pay levels, pay systems and supervisory and non-supervisory personnel. *Federal Employee Attitudes: Phase 2—Follow Up,* a report, can be purchased from the Superintendent of Documents, Government Printing Office, Washington, DC 20402/202-783-3238. For additional information, contact: Office of Planning and Evaluation, Office of Personnel Management, 1900 E St. N.W., Room 3305, Washington, DC 20415/202-254-8920.

Federal Executive Institute (FEI)
This is an interagency executive development center which responds to the training and development needs of federal executives. Courses scheduled in various FeI programs are designed to facilitate executive improvement. Four categories of programs are conducted: the Senior Executive Education Program, the Executive Leadership and Management Program, FEI Alumni Follow-up Conferences, and Special Programs. For additional information, contact: Federal Executive Institute, Office of Personnel Management, Rte. 29, North Charlottesville, VA 22903/804-296-0181.

Federal Job Information Center
A network of Federal Job Information Centers, located in major metropolitan areas, provides information on summer employment, necessary application forms, exams, and all other aspects pertaining to federal employment. To obtain the appropriate telephone number, check the white pages under U.S. Government Office, Office of Personnel Management (some directories may still list the U.S. Civil Service Commission). A free directory, *Federal Job Information Centers,* is available. For additional information, contact: Federal Job Information Center, General Information, Office of Personnel Management, 1900 E St. N.W., Room 1416, Washington, DC 20415/202-737-9616.

Federal Occupational Health Facilities
A free directory of Federal Occupational Health Facilities is available. Contact: Employee Health Service, Workforce Effectiveness and Development, Office of Personnel Management, 1100 L St. N.W., Room 7H39, Washington, DC 20006/202-632-5558.

Federal Pay and Benefits Inquiries
This staff can answer questions about federal

holidays, salary schedules, group life insurance, health benefits, occupational health insurance, sick leave, retirement, etc. Contact: Advisory Services Division, Office of Pay and Benefits Division, Office of Personnel Management, 1900 E St. N.W., Room 4332, Washington, DC 20415/ 202-632-5582.

Federal Personnel Manual
This publication covers all aspects of personnel management and includes letters, bulletins and supplements. It is prepared by the various units within the Office of Personnel Management and is available on a subscription basis ($917) from the Superintendent of Documents, Government Printing Office, Washington, DC 20402/202-783-3238. For additional information, contact: Forms and Publications, Office of Personnel Management, 1900 E St. N.W., Room E453, Washington, DC 20415/202-632-4536.

Federal Salary Schedules
Grades and salary rates are available for General Schedule, Executive Schedule and Senior Executive Schedule employees. Contact: Advisory Services Division, Office of Pay and Benefits, Office of Personnel Management, 1900 E St. N.W., Room 4332, Washington, DC 20415/202-632-5582.

FED Facts Pamphlets
The Office of Personnel Management issues pamphlets that cover a variety of subjects related to government employees. Single copies are available free and multiple copies of *FED Facts* must be purchased from the Government Printing Office, Washington, DC 20402/202-783-3238. They include:

Incentive Awards Program
Political Activity of Federal Employees
The Federal Retirement System
Financial Protection for Federal Employees
The Federal Merit Promotion Policy
Serving the Public: The Extra Step
The Federal Wage System
Meeting Your Financial Obligations
Maternity Leave
Employee Appeals from Actions
The Displaced Employee Program
Reductions in Force in Federal Agencies
Reemployment Rights of Federal Employees Who Perform Duty in the Armed Forces
Federal Labor Relations
Pay Under the General Schedule
The Cost of Living Allowance for Federal Employees
The Intergovernmental Mobility Program
How Your GS Job is Classified
Merit System Principles and Prohibited Personnel Practices
Furlough

Contact: Office of Public Affairs, Office of Personnel Management, 1900 E St. N.W., Room 5F12, Washington, DC 20415/202-632-5491.

Freedom of Information Act Requests
For Freedom of Information Act Requests, contact: Administrative Systems Division, Office of Personnel Management, 1900 E St. N.W., Room 6410, Washington, DC 20415/202-632-7714.

General Schedule Classification
A variety of publications on government service classifications is available. For example, *Handbook of Occupational Group and Series of Classes* ($120.00) is sold by the Superintendent of Documents, Government Printing Office, Washington, DC 20402/202-783-3238. Single copies are free, including: *FED Facts on How Your GS Job Is Classified;* and *A Report on Study of Position Classification Accuracy in Executive Branch on Occupation Under the General Schedule.* Contact: Office of Public Affairs, Office of Personnel Management, 1900 E St. N.W., Room 5F12, Washington, DC 20415/202-632-5491.

Government Affairs Institute
The Government Affairs Institute offers the following services:

Interagency seminars, conducted on Capitol Hill to provide on-site experience with Congress.
Single-agency or single-program projects, tailored to meet the specific needs of an agency or clusters of agencies with related missions.

Courses offered by the Government Affairs Institute are designed to meet developmental needs of current and future executives and managers. Seminars for support staff personnel are also offered. Contact: Government Affairs Institute, Executive Personnel and Management Development Division, Office of Personnel Management, 1121 Vermont Ave. N.W., Room 200, Washington, DC 20415/202-632-5662 (send mail to P.O. Box 988, Washington, DC 20044).

Health Benefits
The federal employees health benefits program provides various types of hospital, surgical and medical benefits for federal employees. Various free publications are available on this subject, for example: *Federal Employee Health Benefits Program*—biweekly and monthly health benefits rates; and *Information to Consider in Choosing a Health Plan.* Contact: Insurance Programs, Office of Personnel Management, 1900 E St. N.W., Room 809H, Washington, DC 20415/202-632-4670.

Incentive Awards
The incentive awards program provides cash and honor awards to employees for effecting improvements in government operations or services

through their suggestions, inventions and superior performance. Free publications on Incentive Awards include: *Federal Incentive Awards Program—Annual Report;* and *Suggest: Your Ideas May Be Worth Money!* For additional information, contact: Incentive Awards Branch, Office of Performance Management, Work Force Effectiveness and Development Group, Office of Personnel Management, 1900 E St. N.W., Room 7H39, Washington, DC 20415/202-653-8436.

Index to OPM Information
This annual index with quarterly supplements is available at no cost by written request only. It lists all Office of Personnel Management publications, including information required to be available under the Freedom of Information Act. Contact: Internal Distribution Subunit, Office of Personnel Management, 1900 E St. N.W., Room B431, Washington, DC 20415/202-632-4677.

Insurance Programs
Information on regular and optional life insurance programs can be obtained from a free pamphlet, *Federal Employees Group Life Insurance Program.* Contact: Insurance Programs, Office of Personnel Management, 1717 H St. N.W., Room 809H, Washington, DC 20415/202-632-4670.

Interagency Training Catalog of Courses
This catalog contains a variety of training programs offered by various federal agencies. These courses are available to federal, state and local government employees. The programs include courses on automated data processing, communications and office skills, general management, labor relations, management sciences, personnel management, and records management. Addresses of Training Centers are also listed. Contact: Office of Training and Development, Work Force Effectiveness and Development Group, Office of Personnel Management, 1121 Vermont Ave. N.W., Room 1216, Washington, DC 20415/202-632-4410.

Job Grading System
Job Grading System for Trades and Labor Occupations is available on a subscription basis ($100) from the Superintendent of Documents, Government Printing Office, Washington, DC 20402/202-783-3238. For additional information, contact: Trades and Labor Occupations, Standards Development Center, Staffing Service Group, Office of Personnel Management, 1900 E St. N.W., Room 3441, Washington, DC 20415/202-632-4441.

Labor Agreement Information Retrieval System (LAIRS)
This system provides current and historic information about the federal labor relations program. The information takes the form of computer searches,

microfiche of full text decisions, published analytic reports, current periodicals and a variety of audio-visual training aids. The file contains negotiated agreements, arbitration awards, and significant federal labor relations decisions. A schedule of fees is provided. LAIRS also publishes labor-management reports, surveys, digests and other related publications. For a list of these and for additional information, contact: Labor Agreement Information Retrieval System, Employee, Labor and Agency Relations, Office of Personnel Management, 1900 E St. N.W., Room 7H29, Washington, DC 20415/202-632-5406.

Labor-Management Relations
Information, guidance and assistance are provided to agencies, unions, and the public on federal labor-management relations. Eligible labor organizations are consulted in the development and revision of government-wide personnel policies. Contact: Employee Labor and Agency Relations, Office of Personnel Management, 1900 E St. N.W., Room 7412, Washington, DC 20415/202-632-5580.

Labor Management Surveys
The Labor Agreement Information Retrieval System (LAIRS) generates numerous surveys and analytical studies. including:

A Survey of Unfair Labor Practice Complaints in The Federal Government
Maternity/Sick Leave Provisions in Federal Agreements
Productivity Clauses in Federal Agreements

Single copies of LAIRS publications are available free of charge. Contact: Labor Agreement Information Retrieval System, Employee, Labor and Agency Relations, Office of Personnel Management, 1900 E St. N.W., Room 7H29, Washington, DC 20415/202-632-5406.

Library
The Office of Personnel Management Library contains a comprehensive collection of materials on personnel management and the federal civil service. It also issues *Personnel Literature,* a monthly with an annual index ($23.00) which is available from the Superintendent of Documents, Government Printing Office, Washington, DC 20402/202-783-3238. For additional information, contact: Library, Office of Management, Office of Personnel Management, 1900 E St. N.W., Room 5L45, Washington, DC 20415/202-632-4432.

Management
This is a quarterly magazine which provides an explanation of personnel management policy and readings of general interest to government managers. Each issue contains four or five features on timely subjects along with continuing coverage of current legal decisions, legislation, and state and

local notes. Personnel and general management developments that affect government management are summarized. Sold for $13.00 per year by the Superintendent of Documents, Government Printing Office, Washington, DC 20402/202-783-3238. For additional information, contact: Office of Public Affairs, Office of Personnel Management, 1900 E St. N.W., Room 5F12, Washington, DC 20415/202-632-5491.

Merit Pay

A merit pay system for supervisors and management officials in grades below Senior Executive Schedules has been developed. *FED Facts on Merit System Principles and Prohibited Personnel Practices* is available at the Office of Public Affairs, Office of Personnel Management, 1900 E St. N.W., Washington, DC 20415/202-632-5491.

Personnel Investigations

Personnel investigations are used in support of the selection and appointment processes. They serve several purposes: to determine the suitability of applicants under consideration for appointment; to check on applicants or employees under consideration for appointment to positions having either national security or special professional or administrative qualifications requirements, or both; and to enforce civil service regulations. The OPM also makes loyalty determinations of United States citizens employed or under consideration for employment by international organizations of which the United States is a member. Contact: Personnel Investigations Division, Office of Personnel Management, 1717 H St. N.W., Room 913, Washington, DC 20415/202-632-6181.

Personnel Literature

This is a monthly publication that includes about 200 or so personnel management subjects such as performance evaluation, productivity, executives, employee training and development, and labor management relations. It includes federal, state and local governments, foreign governments and private organizations. It is sold for $23.00 per year by the Superintendent of Documents, Government Printing Office, Washington, DC 20402/202-783-3238. For additional information, contact: Library, Office of Personnel Management, 1900 E St. N.W., Room 5L44, Washington, DC 20415/202-632-4432.

Personnel Management

Personnel management responsibilities include the government-wide classification system; administration of government pay systems; development and operation of information systems to support and improve federal personnel management decisionmaking; and independent evaluation of agency personnel management systems. Contact: Management Division, Office of Personnel Management, 1900 E St. N.W., Room 1469. Washington, DC 20415/202-632-6118.

Personnel Records

Basic Personnel Records and Files System is available by subscription ($65.00) from the Superintendent of Documents, Government Printing Office, Washington, DC 20402/202-783-3238. For additional information, contact: Agency Relations Group, Office of Personnel Management, 1900 E St. N.W., Room 5305, Washington, DC 20415/202-632-6108.

Presidential and Vice-Presidential Financial Reporting

Top personnel in the Executive Branch, including the President, Vice President and anyone with a basic rate of pay equal to or above a General Schedule-16 is expected to provide financial statements. All appointees file with the agency in which they are employed. The financial statements of the President and Vice President are available. Contact: Office of Government Ethics, Office of Personnel Management, PO Box 14108, Washington, DC 20415/202-632-7642.

Presidential Management Intern Program

This program provides a two-year internship in the federal service for recipients of graduate degrees in general management with a public sector focus. For additional information, contact: Presidential Management Intern Program Office of Personnel Management, 1900 E St. N.W., Room 7H34, Washington, DC 20415/202-254-6080.

Public Reference Room

Labor-management reports, surveys, and analyses can be seen in the Public Reference Room. An appointment is suggested. Contact: Labor Agreement Information Retrieval Systems, Employee, Labor and Agency Relations, Office of Personnel Management, 1900 E St. N.W., Room 7H29, Washington, DC 20415/202-632-5406.

Retirees Health and Life Insurance

Information comparing various types of medical benefits and life insurance plans for retired federal employees are available. Contact: Insurance Division, Office of Personnel Management, Room 3H37, 1900 E St. N.W., Washington, DC 20415/202-632-8438.

Retirement Benefits

All claims for benefits under the retirement system must be adjudicated. Benefits are not paid automatically. For information on how to apply for retirement benefits, death benefits and refunds, contact: Retirement Information Center, Office of Personnel Management, 1900 E St. N.W., Room 1323B, Washington, DC 20415/202-632-7700.

Retirement Programs

Information on government retirement programs as well as a variety of free publications on the subject can be obtained. Some of these include: *Federal Retirement Facts; Your Retirement System*—questions and answers on the federal civil service retirement law; *Information for Annuitants; Retirement Benefits When You Leave the Government Early;* and *Federal Fringe Benefits Facts.* Contact: Retirement Information Center, Office of Personnel Management, 1900 E St. N.W., Room 1323B, Washington, DC 20415/202-632-7700.

Senior Executive Service (SES)

SES gives every eligible senior manager the chance to shift top career managers around to meet the senior executive's needs. For additional information, contact: Senior Executive Service Division, Office of Personnel Management, 1900 E St. N.W., Room 6R48, Washington, DC 20415/202-632-4486.

SES Candidate Development Program

This program prepares senior federal managers and other employees at a certain level to enter the Senior Executive Service by providing opportunities to improve upon and/or acquire the management and executive competencies required for the SES. For details about the program, contact: Executive Personnel and Management Development, Office of Personnel Management, 1900 E St. N.W., Room 6R48, Washington, DC 20415/ 202-632-4486.

Speakers about Public Service

Representatives of the Office of Personnel Management will speak to professional societies, business and labor groups, and other organizations interested in or affected by federal personnel policies and changes. Contact: Office of Public Affairs, Office of Personnel Management, 1900 E St. N.W., Washington, DC 20415/202-632-5491.

Special Benefits

For information on special civil servant benefits, contact: Advisory Service, Office of Pay and Benefits Division, Office of Personnel Management, 1900 E St., N.W., Room 4332, Washington, DC 20415/202-632-5582.

Standards

The Standards Development Center develops standards which are tools for evaluating requirements for most government occupations. It provides the minimum qualification standards to which individual agencies can add more qualifica-

tions. Contact: Standards Development Center, Staffing Services Group, Office of Personnel Management, 1900 E St., N.W., Room 3609, Washington, DC 20415/202-632-4516.

Summer Job Announcements

These announcements describe summer employment opportunities with federal agencies. They are available in the Federal Job Information Center, or contact: Federal Job Information Center General Information, Office of Personnel Management, 1900 E St. N.W., Room 1416, Washington, DC 20415/202-737-9616.

Training Audiovisual Materials

A free annotated list of audiovisual materials for the training of government employees is available. Contact: Audiovisual Resources, Office of Personnel Management, P.O. Box 7230, Washington, DC 20044/202-254-6370.

Washington Management Institute

The Institute provides executive and managerial training and development services to support government agencies in their efforts to achieve greater efficiency and effectiveness in managing federal programs. For further information, contact: Washington Management Institute, Executive Personnel and Management Development, Office of Personnel Management, 1121 Vermont Ave. N.W., Room 308, Washington, DC 20415/ 202-632-6047 (send mail to: P.O. Box 988, Washington, DC 20044).

Work Force Analysis and Statistics

Analyses and statistics are available on the Federal Civilian Work Force. For example, the *Federal Civilian Work Force Statistics Monthly Release* contains information on current employment by branch, agency, and area; trends of employment and payroll, and accessions and separations. Narrative analyses and summary tables are given. This can be purchased for $24/year from the Superintendent of Documents, Government Printing Office, Washington, DC 20402/202-783-3238.

Working for the U.S.A.

This pamphlet is available free from any Federal Job Information Center.

How Can the Office of Personnel Management Help You?

To determine how the Office of Personnel Management can help you, contact: Office of Public Affairs, Office of Personnel Management, 1900 E St. N.W., Washington, DC 20415/202-632-5491.

Overseas Private Investment Corporation

1129 20th St. N.W., Washington, DC 20527/202-653-2800

Established: 1970
Budget: $4,300,000,000*
Employees: 124

Mission: Assists United States investors in making profitable investments in about 96 developing countries; encourages investment projects that will help the social and economic development of these countries; helps the U.S. balance of payments through the profits they return to this country, as well as the U.S. jobs and exports they create; offers U.S. investor assistance in finding investment opportunities, insurance to protect their investments, and loans and loan guarantees to help finance their projects.

Major Sources of Information

Agribusiness
The Overseas Private Investment Corporation (OPIC) is working closely with the Department of Agriculture, the Agribusiness Council, United States cooperative organizations, and others to facilitate the transfer of agribusiness development know-how to raise the efficiency of food systems in the emerging nations. OPIC provides pre-investment study funding, project financing, and insurance. Contact: Office of Development, Overseas Private Investment Corporation, IDCA, 1129 20th St. N.W., 7th Floor, Washington, DC 20527/202-653-2855.

Contractors' and Exporters' Guarantees
Insurance coverage is available for bid, performance and advance payment guarantees posted by U.S. construction and service contractors and exporters in favor of host government owners. OPIC insures such guarantees, which normally take the form of on-demand letters of credit, against drawing which are not justified by the contractor's or exporter's non-performance. *OPIC Program for Insurance Contractors' Bid* is a handbook which describes the program. Contact: Insurance Department, Applications Office, Overseas Private Investment Corporation, 1129 20th St. N.W., 7th Floor, Washington, DC 20527/202-653-2952.

Country and Area List
OPIC has agreements with these listed countries to permit the operation of its insurance and finance programs: Afghanistan, Antigua, Argentina, Bangladesh, Barbados, Belize, Benin (Dahomey), Bolivia, Botswana, Brazil, Burkina Faso (Upper Volta), Burundi, Cameroon, Central Africa Republic, Chad, Chile, Colombia, Congo (Brazzaville), Costa Rica, Cyprus, Dominica, Dominican

*Self-sustaining agency—does not receive congressional appropriations.

Republic, Ecuador, Egypt, El Salvador, Ethiopia, Fiji, Gabon, Gambia, Ghana, Greece, Grenada, Guatemala, Guinea, Haiti, Honduras, India, Indonesia, Iran, Israel, Ivory Coast, Jamaica, Jordan, Kenya, Korea, Lesotho, Liberia, Madagascar, Malawi, Malaysia, Mali, Malta, Mauritania, Mauritius, Morocco, Nepal, Nicaragua, Niger, Nigeria, Oman, Pakistan, Panama, Papua New Guinea, Paraguay, Peru, Philippines, Portugal, Romania, Rwanda, St. Christopher (St. Kitts-Nevis), St. Lucia, St. Vincent, Saudi Arabia, Senegal, Sierra Leone, Singapore, Somali Republic, Sri Lanka (Ceylon), Sudan, Surinam, Swaziland, Syria, Taiwan, Tanzania (excl. Zanzibar), Thailand, Togo, Trinidad-Tobago, Tunisia, Turkey, Uganda, Venezuela, Western Samoa, Yemen (Sanaa), Yugoslavia, Zaire, Zambia. For current information regarding OPIC services offered in specific countries, including their potential availability in nations not listed, or possible temporary limitations due to administrative or underwriting considerations, contact: Information Officer, Overseas Private Investment Corporation, IDCA, 1129 20th St. N.W., 7th Floor, Washington, DC 20527/202-653-2800.

Direct Payments

The program described below provides financial assistance directly to individuals, private firms or other private institutions to encourage or subsidize a particular activity:

Pre-Investment Assistance

Objectives: To initiate and support through financial participation, the identification, assessment, surveying and promotion of private investment opportunities.

Eligibility: U.S. firms capable of carrying project forward if survey indicates feasibility.

Range of Financial Assistance: $10,000 to $300,000.

Contact: Information Officer, Overseas Private Investment Corporation, Washington, DC 20527/202-653-2800.

Feasibility Surveys

On a selective basis, OPIC will enter into cost-sharing arrangements with a U.S. firm to investigate and study the feasibility of an opportunity (other than oil or gas extraction) which that firm has identified through its own reconnaissance in the host country and which offers the basis for a sound and practical investment. Small businesses are eligible for feasibility survey assistance in all countries where OPIC operates. Contact: Finance Department, Overseas Private Investment Corporation, IDCA, 1129 20th St. N.W., 7th Floor, Washington, DC 20527/202-653-2870.

Financial Program

OPIC implements its finance program through a variety of loan and loan guaranty techniques to provide medium-to-long-term funding to ventures involving substantial equity and management participation by U.S. business. OPIC participation often is in the form of "project financing," which is based primarily on the economic, technical, marketing and financial soundness inherent in the project itself. OPIC participates in financing through loans from its Direct Investment Fund and loan guaranties issued to private U.S. financial institutions making eligible loans. *Financial Handbook* details the finance services of OPIC. Contact: Finance Department, Overseas Private Investment Corporation, IDCA, 1129 20th St. N.W., 7th Floor, Washington, DC 20527/202-653-2870.

Hotline—Small Business Services

OPIC encourages investment by U.S. small- and medium-sized companies interested in the growing market potential of the developing countries. Contact: Small Business Office, Finance Department, Overseas Private Investment Corporation, IDCA, 1129 20th St. N.W., 7th Floor, Washington, DC 20527/202-653-2800. Toll-free 800-424-OPIC (6742).

Information

For answers to specific questions on OPIC programs, for details on special programs for smaller businesses, and for the dates of future investment seminars and missions, contact: Public Information, Overseas Private Investment Corporation, IDCA, 1129 20th St. N.W., 7th Floor, Washington, DC 20527/202-653-2800.

Insurance Programs

OPIC is best known for its insurance of private U.S. foreign investment against the political risks of inconvertibility of currency, loss of investment due to expropriation by the host government, and loss due to war, revolution, or insurrection. Insurance is available not only for conventional equity and debt investments, but also for investments under various arrangements such as licensing, management and technical assistance agreements, service contracts, and the production-sharing arrangements sometimes used in energy or raw materials extraction projects. *The Investment Insurance Handbook* provides detailed information on the OPIC Insurance Program. For additional information, contact: Insurance Department, Overseas Private Investment Corporation, IDCA, 1129 20th St. N.W., 7th Floor, Washington, DC 20527/202-653-2952.

Loans and Loan Guarantees

The programs described below are those which offer financial assistance through the lending of federal monies for a specific period of time or programs in which the federal government makes an arrangement to indemnify a lender against part or all of any defaults by the borrower:

Direct Investment Loans

Objectives: To make loans for projects in developing countries sponsored by or significantly involving U.S. small business or cooperatives.

Eligibility: Privately owned firms or firms of mixed private and public ownership sponsored by or significantly involving U.S. small business or cooperatives.

Range of Financial Assistance: $107,000 to $2,500,000.

Contact: Information Officer, Overseas Private Investment Corporation, Washington, DC 20527/ 202-653-2800.

Foreign Investment Guaranties

Objectives: To guarantee loans and other investments made by eligible U.S. investors in developing friendly countries and areas.

Eligibility: Guaranteed eligible investor must be a citizen of the United States; corporation, partnership or other association created under the laws of the United States or any state or territory, and substantially beneficially owned by U.S. citizens or a 95% owned foreign subsidiary of such entity.

Range of Financial Assistance: $1,750,000 to $50,000,000

Contact: Information Officer, Overseas Private Investment Corporation, Washington, DC 20527/ 202-653-2800.

Foreign Investment Insurance

Objectives: To insure investments of eligible U.S. investors in developing friendly countries and areas, against the risks of inconvertibility, expropriation, war, revolution and insurrection and certain types of civil strife.

Eligibility: Citizen of the United States; corporation, partnership or other association created under the laws of the United States or any State or territory, and substantially beneficially owned by U.S. citizens; or wholly owned foreign subsidiary of such corporation.

Range of Financial Assistance: $4,000 to $100,000,000.

Contact: Information Officer, Overseas Private Investment Corporation, Washington, DC 20527/ 202-653-2800.

Pre-Investment Assistance

Objectives: To initiate and support through financial participation, the identification, assessment, surveying and promotion of private investment opportunities.

Eligibility: U.S. firms capable of carrying project forward if survey indicated feasibility.

Range of Financial Assistance: $1,000 to $100,000.

Contact: Information Officer, Overseas Private Investment Corporation, Washington, DC 20527/ 202-653-2800.

OPIC Mineral and Energy Projects

OPIC offers highly flexible and innovative coverage for investments in mineral exploration and development (including processing where it is an integral part of a development project), and in oil and gas exploration, development and production, under terms and conditions tailored to the special needs and concerns of investors in these kinds of projects. Contact: Energy and Minerals, Insurance Department, Overseas Private Investment Corporation, IDCA, 1129 20th St. N.W., 7th Floor, Washington, DC 20527/202-653-2952.

Overseas Opportunities

OPIC promotes market and investment interest in lower income countries which have promising potential and reasonably favorable economic environments. It undertakes studies of a host country's needs and the opportunities it offers, including specific projects which can be brought to the attention of qualified potential U.S. investors. OPIC sponsors seminars for business executives and conducts meetings with a broad spectrum of the business and financial community. OPIC invites host country promotional agencies, development banks, and investment centers to provide information for dissemination to potential investors. It also sponsors investment missions to developing countries for U.S. business executives. Meetings are arranged with local business people, development bankers, governmental officials, and others who may be of assistance. Contact: Investment Promotions, Overseas Private Investment Corporation, IDCA, 1129 20th St. N.W., 7th Floor, Washington, DC 20527/202-653-2800.

Policy

It is OPIC policy to be selective in approving applications for overseas business insurance and financial assistance, so that each project will generate mutual advantages to the host country and the United States. In addition to its humanitarian aspects, economic development through private investment usually creates new markets for U.S. exports. Mutual benefit also is derived from private investment activities that find and develop new sources of raw materials. Contact: Investment Mission Director, Overseas Private Investment Corporation, IDCA, 1129 20th St. N.W., 6th Floor, Washington, DC 20527/202-653-2913.

Publications

OPIC publications include:

Annual Report
Insurance Handbook
Finance Handbook
Smaller Business Directory
Small Business Guide
Country List
TOPICS (Newsletter)

Claims History
Guidelines for Broker/Agent Participation

For additional information on OPIC, free copies of these publications are available on request from the Information Officer, Overseas Private Investment Corporation, IDCA, 1129 20th St. N.W., 6th Floor, Washington, DC 20527/202-653-2800.

TOPICS
This is a free newsletter that disseminates information about specific investment opportunities and trends in various countries. Contact: Public Affairs, Overseas Private Investment Corporation, IDCA, 1129 20th St. N.W., 6th Floor, Washington, DC 20527/202-653-2800.

U.S. Investments in Developing Countries
The public affairs office provides information to encourage U.S. private investments in developing nations. It furnishes kits which include Overseas Private Investment Cooperation's (OPICs) annual report, a country listing and other helpful investment information. Contact: Public Affairs, Overseas Private Investment Corporation, 7th Floor, 1129 20th St. N.W., Washington, DC 20527/202-653-2800.

How Can the Overseas Private Investment Corporation Help You?
To determine how the Overseas Private Investment Corporation can help you, contact: Overseas Private Investment Corporation, 1129 20th St. N.W., Washington, DC 20527/202-653-2800.

Panama Canal Commission

425 13th St. N.W., Washington, DC 20004/202-724-0104

Established: October 1, 1979
Budget: $434,399,000
Employees: 7,814

Mission: Maintains and operates the Panama Canal and the facilities and appurtenances related thereto; coordinates the operation of the waterway and other activities with the Republic of Panama; and correlates joint actions in harbors and port areas, certain housing and public areas, and some civil protection functions.

Major Sources of Information

Commission Files
Official files of the Board of Directors are maintained in this office. Contact: Office of the Secretary, Panama Canal Commission, 425 13th St. N.W., Suite 312, Washington, DC 20004/202-724-0104.

Commission Functional Charts
The Commission issues an organization chart that details the functions of each office within the Panama Canal Commission. It is an excellent source of information on the Commission. Contact: Office of the Secretary, Panama Canal Commission, 425 13th St. N.W., Suite 312, Washington, DC 20004/202-724-0104.

Construction Services
This branch provides the services necessary for the management of construction. These include contract formation and award, quality and safety assurance, resolution of construction problems, contract modifications, etc. Services of experts such as architects, engineers and technical representatives are also procured. Contact: Construction Management Branch, Bureau of Engineering and Construction, Panama Canal Commission, APO Miami 34011.

Dredging Operations
This division is responsible for maintenance and construction dredging; slide removal, inspection and maintenance of the Atlantic breakwater; operation and maintenance of navigational aids in the channel; the detection, containment, recovery, and disposal of oil pollution in the Canal operating areas and the removal and control of aquatic weeds through the use of chemical and biologic means. Contact: Dredging Division, Engineering and Construction Branch, Panama Canal Commission, APO Miami 34011.

Economic Analysis
A variety of economic analyses is prepared by this office. They include: forecasts of Canal traffic and tolls revenue; development of budget premises; economic studies and surveys; balance of payments analysis; development of cost and price indices; analytic review of outside economic analyses and reports; and compilations of Canal traffic data. Contact: Office of Executive Planning, Panama Canal Commission, APO Miami 34011.

Electrical Operations
This division operates and maintains power plants, substations, transmission lines, distribution systems and communication systems. It also operates

the Gatun Spillway and Madden Dam. Contact: Electrical Division, Engineering and Construction Bureau, Panama Canal Commission, APO Miami 34011.

Engineering Plans
This division is responsible for designs, estimates, specifications and all pre-contract functions. It also provides engineering studies and architectural designs and maintains record maps of topography, certain streets, utilities, pipelines, and town sites. For additional information, contact: Engineering Division, Engineering and Construction Bureau, Panama Canal Commission, APO Miami 34011.

Freedom of Information Act Requests
For Freedom of Information Act requests, contact: Administrative Services Division, Panama Canal Commission, APO Miami 34011.

Information
Specific information on the organization and functions of the Commission, the operation and maintenance of the Panama Canal, schedules, announcements and minutes of Board meetings, contact: Office of the Secretary, Panama Canal Commission, 425 13th St. N.W., Suite 312, Washington, DC 20004/202-724-0104.

Library and Museum
The library provides public and technical services to Commission employees and their families, U.S. personnel in other agencies and other Isthmian residents. The museum deals with the history of the Canal. Contact: Library-Museum, General Services Administration, APO Miami 34011.

Marine Accident Investigations
The Board of Local Inspectors is responsible for the investigation of the circumstances surrounding marine accidents which occur in the Canal operating area, harbors, canal anchorages, and areas adjacent to them, involving Commission personnel and/or equipment. Contact: Board of Local Inspectors, Marine Bureau, Panama Canal Commission, APO Miami 34011.

Marine Locks
This office is responsible for the operation and maintenance of the Atlantic and Pacific Locks and related facilities, handling of all vessels in the Locks, and operating and maintaining the Miraflores Spillway and Miraflores Bridge. Contact: Locks Division, Marine Bureau, Panama Canal Commission, APO Miami 34011.

Marine Salvage Operations
This division coordinates the handling of burning, wrecked or damaged vessels. Contact: Canal Support Division, Marine Bureau, Panama Canal Commission, APO Miami 34011.

Marine Traffic
Maritime traffic through the Canal and in the terminal ports of Balboa and Cristobal is controlled by the Commission. It also administers rules and regulations of navigation and transiting of the Canal, its terminal harbors and their adjacent waters. Contact: Marine Bureau, Panama Canal Commission, APO Miami 34011.

Meteorologic and Hydrographic Data
This office improves and develops forecasting and operation techniques to improve water utilization. It also collects records and stores meteorologic and hydrographic data. Contact: Engineering Division, Engineering and Construction Bureau, Panama Canal Commission, APO Miami 34011.

Ombudsman
The Ombudsman receives individual complaints, grievances, requests and suggestions, and reviews and seeks resolution of administrative problems, inefficiencies and conflicts caused within the U.S. government agencies in Panama as a result of the Panama Canal Treaty. Contact: Office of Ombudsman, Panama Canal Commission, Administration Building, Balboa Heights, Panama, or: Panama Canal Commission, 425 13th St. N.W., Suite 312, Washington, DC 20004/202-724-0104.

Panama Canal Commission
The following office of the Panama Canal Commission is located in Panama: Panama Canal Commission, Administration Building, Balboa Heights, Panama. The Secretary's Office is the U.S. Liaison for the Commission. Contact: Office of the Secretary, Panama Canal Commission, 425 13th St. N.W., Suite 312, Washington, DC 20004/202-724-0104.

Potable Water
The Water and Laboratories Branch purifies and distributes potable water through two systems serving the Pacific and Atlantic areas. It also operates a general testing and environmental quality laboratory. Contact: Maintenance Division, Engineering and Construction Bureau, Panama Canal Commission, APO Miami 34011.

Procurement
This office is responsible for procuring supplies, materials and equipment required by the Commission. Supplies include machinery, hardware, vehicles and related parts, industrial rubber goods, cranes, towing locomotives, floating equipment, raw materials, electrical steamship and institutional-type goods. Contact: Procurement Division, Panama Canal Commission, 4400 Dauphine St., New Orleans, LA 70146/504-948-5299.

Publications
Official circulars, regulations, tariffs, reports and other publications are issued by this office. Commission records are also managed by this office. Contact: Administrative Services Division, Panama Canal Commission, APO Miami 34011.

Surveys
Topographic and hydrographic surveys are available; precise level benchmarks are maintained; and topographical maps, and hydrographic charts are compiled and produced. Contact: Surveys Branch, Engineering Division, Engineering and Construction Bureau, Panama Canal Commission, APO Miami 34011.

Tolls and Services
This office bills vessels and agencies for tolls and services such as pilotage, towboat and deckhands. Contact: Canal Support Division, Marine Bureau, Panama Canal Commission, APO Miami 34011.

How Can the Panama Canal Commission Help You?
To determine how the Panama Canal Commission can help you, contact: 425 13th St. N.W., Washington, DC 20004/202-724-0104.

Peace Corps

806 Connecticut Avenue N.W., Washington, DC 20526/202-254-5010

Established: 1961
Budget: $128,600,000
Employees: 1,000

Mission: To promote world peace and friendship, to help the peoples of other countries in meeting their needs for trained manpower, to help promote a better understanding of the American people on the part of the peoples served, and to promote a better understanding of other peoples on the part of the American people. In 1977 the Peace Corps Act was amended to emphasize the Peace Corps' commitment toward programming to meet the basic needs of those living in the poorest areas of the countries in which the Peace Corps operates.

Data Experts

Country Desk Officers

The following country desk officers can provide information on peace corps activities, as well as general political, social and economic information about the countries they cover. They can be contacted at: Office of Public Affairs, Peace Corps, 806 Connecticut Ave. N.W., Room M-1214, Washington, DC 20526/202-254-5010.

Africa

Senegal, Dakar/Elena Hughes/202-254-3185
Gambia, Banjul/Theresa Joiner/202-254-8003
Burkina Faso, Ouagadougou/Jerry Brown/202-254-7004
Ghana, Accra/Barbara Gardner/202-254-5644
Zaire, Kinshasa, Refugee Programs/Kay Kennedy/202-254-8694
Botswana, Gaborone/David Browne/202-251-6046
Kenya, Nairobi/Anika McGee/202-254-9696
Cameroon, Yaounde/Paul Rowe/202-254-8397

Latin America

Ecuador, Quito/Maria Lameiro/202-254-6298
Brazil, Paraguay, Dominican Republic/Noreen O'Mera/202-254-8876
Honduras, Tegucigalpa/
Belize, Belize/Katie Wheatley/202-254-6320

North Africa, Near East, Asia and the Pacific (NANEAP)

Papua New Guinea, Port Moresby/Ed Geibel/202-254-3040
Philippines, Manilla/Rebecca Mushingi/202-254-3290
Micronesia, Ponape/Lisbeth Thomsen/202-254-3231
Fiji, Suva/Steve Prieto/202-254-3227
Tunisia, Morocco, Yemen/Chris Pelton/202-254-3196
Nepal, Kathmandu/Susan Belmont/202-254-3118

Major Sources of Information

Agriculture Programs

Peace Corps volunteers assist in fields ranging from agronomy to wildlife management. They are involved in projects to increase food production and can teach techniques of water control. Contact: Agriculture Coordinator, Office of Training and Program Support, Peace Corps, Room 701, 806 Connecticut Ave. N.W., Washington, DC 20526/202-254-8890.

Childhood Communicable Diseases

Numerous projects are directed toward combatting communicable diseases among children in developing nations. Contact: Combatting Childhood Communicable Diseases Coordinator, Office of Training and Program Support, Peace Corps, Room 701, 806 Connecticut Ave. N.W., Washington, DC 20526/202-254-8400.

Energy Conservation
Peace Corps is involved in many energy projects. Contact: Energy Sector Specialist, Office of Training and Program Support, Peace Corps, Room 701, 806 Connecticut Ave. N.W., Washington, DC 20526/202-254-8890.

Fishery Programs
Fishery specialists work as warm water fish culture extension agents. They help farmers stock, manage, feed and harvest pond fish, usually carp or talapia. They work in fish harvesting, marketing and conservation, and teach local fishermen how to improve their fishing techniques. Contact: Fisheries Programmer, Office of Training and Program Support, Peace Corps, Room 701, 806 Connecticut Ave. N.W., Washington, DC 20526/ 202-254-8890.

Forestry Programs
Experts in forests work in many developing nations. Contact: Forestry Programmer, Office of Training and Program Support, Peace Corps, Room 701, 806 Connecticut Ave. N.W., Washington, DC 20526/202-254-8400.

Freedom of Information Act Requests
For Freedom of Information Act requests, contact: Office of the General Counsel, Peace Corps, Room 607, 806 Connecticut Ave. N.W., Washington, DC 20526/202-254-3116.

Health Programs
Peace Corps volunteers with degrees in health-related fields work on a person-to-person basis, teaching concepts of modern hygiene, preventive health education principles and medical care. Contact: Health Programmer, Office of Program and Training Coordination, Peace Corps, Room 701, 806 Connecticut Ave. N.W., Washington, DC 20525/202-254-7386.

Information Collection and Exchange (ICE)
This program gathers and disseminates practical technical knowledge acquired by Peace Corps volunteers. Manuals and handbooks, reprints, and resource packets are available on appropriate technology to assist Third World development. *Appropriate Technologies for Development* presents practical information from initial project planning in the community setting to on-going needs for maintenance training and cooperative organizations for field workers without specialized

technical training. A list of ICE's recent publications is available free. Titles include:

Freshwater Fish Pond Culture and Management
Small Farm Grain Storage
Programming and Training for Small Farm Grain Storage
Resources for Development—Organizations and Publications
The Photonovel—A Tool for Development
Reforestation in Arid Lands
Self-Help Construction of One-Story Buildings
Teaching Conservation in Developing Nations
Community Health Education in Developing Countries
Health and Sanitation Lessons/Africa
A Glossary of Agricultural Terms
Water Purification, Distribution, and Sewage Disposal
Poultry "New Methods Pay with Poultry"
Lesson Plans for Beekeeping
Pesticide Safety
Disaster Procedures
Small Vegetable Gardens
Cooperatives

Contact: Information Collection and Exchange, Office of Training and Program Support, Room 701, 806 Connecticut Ave. N.W., Washington, DC 20525/202-254-7386.

Newsletters
The following newsletter is free:

Peace Corps Times—free bimonthly news of Peace Corps projects, people and events. Includes technical information. Contact: *Peace Corps Times,* Office of Public Affairs, Peace Corps, Room M-1214, 806 Connecticut Ave. N.W., Washington, DC 20526/202-254-5010.

Peace Corps Volunteers
Peace Corps volunteers provide individual Americans to work with people of developing nations while living as part of their communities. Volunteers go abroad for two years, after being trained to work with agencies of host governments or with private institutions. Among the professions in demand are: foresters, fishery specialists, architects, planners, engineers, health professionals, home economists, teachers. For information, contact: Office of Public Affairs, Peace Corps, Room M-1214, 806 Connecticut Ave. N.W., Washington, DC 20526/202-254-5010. The following is a listing of local recruiting offices:

New York Service Center

Peace Corps/Recruiting Office, 26 Federal Plaza, Room 1605, New York, NY 10278/212-264-1780.
Peace Corps/Boston Area Office, Recruiting Office, 150 Causeway St., Room 1307, Boston, MA 02109/617-223-7366.
Peace Corps/Puerto Rico Area Office, Calla Recinto Sur, Room 128, Recruiting Office, P.O. Box 4752, San Juan, PR 00905/809-753-4694.

Atlanta Service Center

Peace Corps/Washington, DC Area Office, 812 Conn. Ave. N.W., Recruiting Office, Washington, DC 20526/202-376-2550.

Peace Corps/Recruiting Office, 101 Marietta St. N.W., Room 2207, Atlanta, GA 30303/404-221-2932.

Peace Corps/Recruiting Office, Customs House, 2nd and Chestnut Sts. Room 102-A, Philadelphia, PA 19106/ 215-597-0744.

Chicago Service Center

Peace Corps/Recruiting Office, 10 West Jackson Blvd., 3rd Floor, Chicago, IL 60604/312-353-3585.

Peace Corps/Recruiting Office, P.V. McNamara Federal Building, Room M-74, 477 Michigan Ave., Detroit, MI 48226/313-226-7928.

Peace Corps/Recruiting Office, Gateway II Building, Room 318, 4th and State Sts., Kansas City, KS 66101/ 913-236-3725.

Peace Corps/Recruiting Office, Old Federal Building, Room 104, 212 3rd Ave. S., Minneapolis, MN 55401/ 612-349-3625.

Dallas Service Center

Peace Corps/Recruiting Office, P.O. Box 638, Room 230, 400 N. Ervay, Dallas, TX 75221/214-767-5435.

Peace Corps/Recruiting Office, 1845 Sherman St., Room 103, Denver, CO 80203/303-844-4171.

San Francisco Service Center

Peace Corps/Recruiting Office, 211 Main St., Room 533, San Francisco, CA 94102/415-974-0677.

Peace Corps/Recruiting Office, 1111 Third Ave., Room 3601, Seattle, WA 98101/206-442-5490.

Peace Corps/Recruiting Office, 11000 Wilshire, Suite 8104, West Los Angeles, CA 90024/213-209-7444.

Partnership Program

This program is a two-way exchange offering Americans and the overseas community the opportunity to experience a different culture. This cross-cultural exchange typically involves sharing or exchanging letters, music, photos, local artifacts and other items reflecting cultures and lifestyles. Contact: Office of Private Sector Development, Peace Corps, 806 Connecticut Ave. N.W., Room M-1210, Washington, DC 20526/202-254-6360.

Private Sector Development

This office provides information to and between the corporate community and the Peace Corps' Office of Returned Volunteer Services and also seeks in-kind gifts and other contributions for special Peace Corps projects. Contact: Office of Private Sector Development, Peace Corps, 806 Connecticut Ave. N.W., Room M-1210, Washington, DC 20526/202-254-6360.

Water and Sanitation Programs

Peace Corps volunteers assist in a variety of water and sanitation projects throughout the world. Contact: Water/Sanitation Section Specialist, Office of Training and Program Support, Peace Corps, 806 Connecticut Ave. N.W., Room 701, Washington, DC 20526/202-254-8400.

Women in Development

This office oversees specific projects in most countries for the purpose of integrating women into forestry and fisheries programs and other Peace Corps endeavors. Women in Development has a Women-to-Women Partnership Program and publishes the "Women in Development Resource Directory." Contact: Women In Development, Office of Training and Program Support, Peace Corps, 806 Connecticut Ave. N.W., Room M-802, Washington, DC 20526/202-254-6390.

How Can Peace Corps Help You?

To determine how Peace Corps can help you, contact: Peace Corps, Office of Public Affairs, 806 Connecticut Ave. N.W., Room M-1214, Washington, DC 20526/202-254-5010.

Pennsylvania Avenue Development Corporation

425 13th St. N.W., Washington, DC 20004/202-566-1218

Established: October 27, 1972
Budget: $11,100,000
Employees: 36

Mission: Has prepared a comprehensive development plan for Pennsylvania Avenue and the adjacent blocks on the north side of the Avenue between the Capitol and the White House; will carry out the plan through a combination of public improvements with stimulation of private investment; and is to ensure development, maintenance, and use of the area compatible with its historic and ceremonial importance.

Major Sources of Information

Building Permits
The District of Columbia government refers building permits for new construction in the Pennsylvania Avenue Development Area to PADC for approval relating to conformity with the plan. Contact: Pennsylvania Avenue Development Corporation, 425 13th St. N.W., Room 1148, Washington, DC 20004/202-566-1218.

Contracts
For information on contracts negotiated by the Corporation and various parties, contact: Contract Specialist, Pennsylvania Avenue Development Corporation, 425 13th St. N.W., Room 1148, Washington, DC 20004/202-566-1218.

Finances
Financial information on land acquisition, public development, construction in progress, real property assets, liabilities, etc. is available. Contact: Financial Manager, Pennsylvania Avenue Development Corporation, 425 13th St. N.W., Room 1148, Washington, DC 20004/202-523-5485.

Freedom of Information Act Requests
For Freedom of Information Act requests, contact: Pennsylvania Avenue Development Corporation, 425 13th St. N.W., Room 1148, Washington, DC 20004/202-523-1340.

Private Development
The Pennsylvania Avenue Development Corporation will buy and assemble some properties in the area and lease them back to private investors/developers for developing according to the Congressionally approved plan. A private investor may also purchase land directly from a landowner and develop it in accordance with the plan. Contact: Finance and Development, Pennsylvania Avenue Development Corporation, 425 13th St. N.W., Room 1248, Washington, DC 20004/202-523-5485.

Publications

The Pennsylvania Avenue Development Corporation publications include a free quarterly newsletter and an annual report, *Historic Preservation* ($2.25), the *Pennsylvania Avenue Plan—1974* ($3.00); supplementary technical documents and economic studies are sold at cost. Contact: Public Information, Pennsylvania Avenue Development Corporation, 425 13th St. N.W., Room 1148, Washington, DC 20004/202-724-9073.

Relocation

The Corporation is working on a program for a supplemental relocation assistance program that includes rental assistance payments beyond those provided by the 1970 Uniform Relocation Act. It also is working with developers in the area in an attempt to relocate as many displaced businesses as possible. For information on these programs, contact: Relocation Office, Pennsylvania Avenue Development Corporation, 425 13th St. N.W., Room 1248, Washington, DC 20004/202-724-9068.

Youth Employment

The Corporation initiated a youth employment program that gives on-the-job training to minority youth in the area of construction management. Contact: Construction, Office of Operations, Pennsylvania Avenue Development Corporation, 425 13th St. N.W., Room 1148, Washington, DC 20004/202-724-9067.

How Can the Pennsylvania Avenue Development Corporation Help You?

To determine how the Pennsylvania Avenue Development Corporation can help you, contact: Public Information Officer, Pennsylvania Avenue Development Corporation, 425 13th St. N.W., Room 1148, Washington, DC 20004/202-724-9087.

Pension Benefit Guaranty Corporation

2020 K St. N.W., Washington, DC 20006/202-254-4817

Established: September 2, 1974
Budget: $145,652,000*
Employees: 492

Mission: Guarantees basic pension benefits in covered private plans if they terminate with insufficient assets.

Major Sources of Information

Actuarial Programs
The Pension Benefit Guaranty Corporation's Annual Report includes an actuarial evaluation of expected operations and a projection of the status of funds for a five-year period. Contact: Actuarial Policy Division, Corporate Administrative Planning Department, Pension Benefit Guaranty Corporation, 2020 K St. N.W., Room 7519, Washington, DC 20006/202-254-7154.

Filing Reportable Events
The notice of a reportable event must be in writing. It may either be mailed or delivered on weekdays between 9:00 A.M. and 4:00 P.M. Contact: Coverage and Inquiries Branch, Insurance Operations Department, Pension Benefit Guaranty Corporation, 2020 K St. N.W., Room 5314, Washington, DC 20006/202-254-4817.

Financial Statements
The Pension Benefit Guaranty Corporation combined financial statements include the assets and liabilities of all defined benefit pension plans for which the Corporation is trustee. It includes those plans which have terminated and are expected to result in PBGC trusteeship. Contact: Financial Operation Department, Pension Benefit Guaranty Corporation, 2020 K St. N.W., Washington, DC 20006/202-254-7106.

*Self-supporting. Funds received from collection of premiums from pension plans.

Freedom of Information Act Requests
For Freedom of Information Act requests, contact: Disclosure Officer, Pension Benefit Guaranty Corporation, 2020 K St. N.W., Room 7100, Washington, DC 20006/202-254-5527.

Grants
The program described below is for sums of money which are given by the Pension Benefit Guaranty Corporation to encourage voluntary private pension plans.

Pension Plan Termination Insurance
Objectives: To encourage the continuation and maintenance of voluntary private pension plans for the benefit of their participants, to provide for the timely and uninterrupted payment of pension benefits to participants in and beneficiaries of covered plans, and to maintain premiums charged by the PBGC at the lowest level consistent with carrying out its obligations.
Eligibility: Private businesses and organizations who maintain defined benefit plans.
Range of Financial Assistance: Monthly benefit range per retiree is $5 to $1,380.
Contact: Pension Benefit Guaranty Corporation, 2020 K St. N.W., Washington, DC 20006/202-254-4817.

Legal Issues
In addition to developing legal issues through litigation, the General Counsel issues a great many

legal opinions which seek to resolve questions of interpretation that arise under PBGC's regulations. Contact: Legal Department, Pension Benefit Guaranty Corporation, 2020 K St. N.W., Room 7200, Washington, DC 20006/202-254-4864.

Multiemployer Program
Multiemployer plans are maintained under collective bargaining agreements, and they cover employees of two or more unrelated employers. Multiemployer plans that become insolvent may receive financial assistance from PBGC to enable them to pay guaranteed benefits. Contact: Corporate Policy and Regulation Department, Pension Benefit Guaranty Corporation, 2020 K St. N.W., Room 5000, Washington, DC 20006/202-254-4700.

Pension Protection Plan
The Pension Benefit Guaranty Corporation administers two pension protection programs: 1) a plan termination insurance program covering about 29 million people in about 110,000 single employer pension plans; and 2) a plan insolvency insurance program covering about 9 million people in 2,500 multiemployer pension plans. Contact: Coverage and Inquiries Branch, Insurance Operations Department, Pension Benefit Guaranty Corporation, 2020 K St. N.W., Room 5314, Washington, DC 20006/202-254-4817.

Premiums
All covered pension plans are required to pay prescribed annual premium rates to the Pension Benefit Guaranty Corporation. For further information, contact: Coverage and Inquiries Branch, Insurance Operations Department, Pension Benefit Guaranty Corporation, 2020 K St. N.W., Room 5314, Washington, DC 20006/202-254-4817.

Public Records
The following items are available for inspection through the Disclosure Officer: Trusteeship Plans, opinion letters, opinion manuals, litigation, termination case data sheets, and case log terminating plans updated quarterly. In addition, on microfilm, annual reports filed by pension plans may be inspected by the public. Contact: Disclosure Officer, Pension Benefit Guaranty Corporation, 2020 K St. N.W., Room 7100, Washington, DC 20006/202-254-5527.

Reportable Events
The plan administrator of a pension plan covered by the Pension Benefit Guaranty Corporation's single employer plan termination insurance program must notify the PBGC within thirty days after he or she knows or should have known of the occurrence of certain events. Notification of reportable events allows the PBGC to take appropriate action to protect the benefits of plan participants and beneficiaries, or to prevent un-

reasonable loss to the plan termination insurance program. Reportable events include: tax disqualification; non-compliance with Title I of ERISA; decrease in benefits; reduction in number of active participants; termination or partial termination of a plan; failure to meet minimum standards; inability to pay benefits when due; distribution to a substantial owner; merger, consolidation or transfer; alternative compliance with reporting and disclosure requirements; bankruptcy, insolvency or similar settlements; liquidation or dissolution; and transactions involving a change of employer. *Reportable Events,* a free booklet, describes what reportable events should be reported, items of information to be submitted in the notice of a reportable event, and events for which a 30-day reporting requirement has been waived. Contact: Coverage and Inquiries Branch, Insurance Operations Department, Pension Benefit Guaranty Corporation, 2020 K St. N.W., Room 5314, Washington, DC 20006/202-254-4817.

Single Employer Program
Whenever a single employer plan insured by the Pension Benefit Guaranty Corporation terminates, the PBGC reviews the plan to ascertain whether it has sufficient plan assets to pay guaranteed benefits. If plan assets are suffficient, the plan administrator winds up the affairs of the plan. If plan assets are not sufficient to pay guaranteed benefits, the PBGC assumes responsibility for the plan by becoming trustee, administering benefit payments and records, managing plan assets, and making up the financial insufficiency from Corporate insurance funds. In all terminations, plan assets must be allocated as specified by ERISA. Contact: Coverage and Inquiries Branch, Insurance Operations Department, Pension Benefit Guaranty Corporation, Room 5314, 2020 K St. N.W., Washington, DC 20006/202-254-4817.

Statistical History of Claims
A table of total pension liabilities guaranteed by the Pension Benefit Guaranty Corporation includes assets of terminated plans, statutory employer liability (the amount expected to be collected from the plan sponsor), and the resulting net claims. Contact: Financial Operations Department, Pension Benefit Guaranty Corporation, 2020 K St. N.W., Room 6000, Washington, DC 20006/202-254-7106.

Terminations
When a Plan Administrator notifies the Pension Benefit Guaranty Corporation of a plan termination, the plan's assets and guaranteed benefit liabilities are valued to determine the sufficiency of assets to pay guaranteed benefits. PBGC may also institute termination proceedings when certain events indicate that such an action may be necessary. Contact: Coverage and Inquiries Branch,

Insurance Operations Department, Pension Benefit Guaranty Corporation, 2020 K St. N.W., Room 5314, Washington, DC 20006/202-254-4817.

Trusteeships

If a terminated plan does not have sufficient assets to pay guaranteed benefits, the Pension Benefit Guaranty Corporation becomes trustee for the plan and administers the payment of such benefits. Contact: Coverage and Inquiries Branch, Insurance Operations Department, Pension Benefit Guaranty Corporation, 2020 K St. N.W., Room 5314, Washington, DC 20006/202-254-4817.

Your Guaranteed Pension

This publication answers questions most commonly asked by workers and retirees about the Pension Benefit Guaranty Corporation and the specific pension benefits it guarantees. Contact: Coverage and Classification, Insurance Operations Department, Pension Benefit Guaranty Corporation, 2020 K St. N.W., Room 5413, Washington, DC 20006/202-254-4817.

How Can the Pension Benefit Guaranty Corporation Help You?

To determine how the Pension Benefit Guaranty Corporation can help you, contact: Coverage and Inquiries Branch, Insurance Operations Department, Pension Benefit Guaranty Corporation, 2020 K St. N.W., Room 5314, Washington, DC 20006/202-254-4817.

Postal Rate Commission

Suite 300, 1333 H St. N.W., Washington, DC 20268/202-254-3880

Established: August 12, 1970
Budget: Not specified
Employees: 75

Mission: Submits recommended decisions to the United States Postal Service on postage rates and fees and mail classifications; issues advisory opinions to the Postal Service on proposed nationwide changes in postal services; initiates studies and submits recommendations for changes in the mail classification schedule; and receives, studies, and issues recommended decisions or public reports to the Postal Service on complaints received from the mailing public regarding postage rates, postal classifications, postal services on a substantially nationwide basis, and the closing or consolidation of small post offices.

Major Sources of Information

Change Requests
The Postal Service can request from the Commission an advisory opinion on changes in the nature of postal services which will generally affect service on a nationwide basis. These formal requests are then published in the *Federal Register*. Contact: Office of the Secretary, Postal Rate Commission, 2000 L St. N.W., Room 500, Washington, DC 20268/202-254-3880.

Complaints
Those parties who believe the Postal Service is charging improper rates or who believe that they are not receiving proper postal service may file and serve a written complaint with the Commission. Contact: Office of the Commission, Postal Rate Commission, 2000 L St. N.W., Room 500, Washington, DC 20268/202-254-3840.

Consumer Information
Consumer information as well as information on public hearings on rate changes is available. Contact: Office of the Commission, Postal Rate

Commission, 2000 L St. N.W., Room 500, Washington, DC 20268/202-254-3840.

Freedom of Information Act Requests
Contact: Administrative Officer and Secretary, Postal Rate Commission, 2000 L St. N.W., Room 500, Washington, DC 20268/202-254-3880.

Hearing Calendar
A docket of all proceedings and a hearing calendar of all proceedings which have been set up for hearing are available for public inspection. The Section also contains notices, motions, rulings, transcripts of hearings, and mail classifications, all dealing with postal rate levels. For further information, contact: Docket Section, Office of the Secretary, Postal Rate Commission, 2000 L St. N.W., Room 500, Washington, DC 20268/202-254-3800.

Information
For general information on postal rates, changes in postal rates and the Postal Rate Service, contact:

Office of the Secretary, Postal Rate Commission, 2000 L St. N.W., Room 500, Washington, DC 20268/202-254-3880.

Open Commission Meetings
The Commission serves as the legal forum for proposed changes in postal rates, fees, and mail classifications, changes in the nature of services, and the closing or consolidating of small post offices. With some exceptions, the Commission meetings are open to public observation (not participation). Access to the documents considered at these meetings is available. Contact: Office of the Secretary, Postal Rate Commission, 2000 L St. N.W., Room 500, Washington, DC 20268/202-254-3880.

Postal Rate Change
A very detailed flow chart provides all the steps followed in a postal rate case. Contact: Officer of the Commission, Postal Rate Commission, 2000 L St. N.W., Room 500, Washington, DC 20268/202-254-3840.

Rate Classification Records
Records of the Postal Rate Commission hearings on rate classification changes can be examined by the public. Contact: Dockets Section, Postal Rate Commission, 2000 L St. N.W., Room 500, Washington, DC 20268/202-254-3800.

Rules of Practice and Procedure
This free booklet describes in detail the Postal Rate Commission's duties and functions. It includes rules of general applicability; rules applicable to requests for changes in rates and fees, establishing or changing mail classification schedules, and changes in the nature of postal services; rules applicable to rate and service complaints, to filing of testimony by intervenors, and to the filing of periodic reports by the Postal Service; and rules applicable to appeal of postal service determinations to close or consolidate post offices. It also includes a statement of Postal Rate Commission revenue and expenses and a glossary of terms. Contact: Office of the Commission, Postal Rate Commission, 2000 L St. N.W., Room 500, Washington, DC 20268/202-254-3840.

Rural Post Offices
At the Crossroads is a research study into the history and development of postal delivery and the Postal Service, and includes a review of pertinent Congressional legislation. The tables in the Appendix include general population characteristics, U.S. population since 1790, number of rural places and their percentage of U.S. population, population mobility, rural population, education, age and income characteristics, and number of post offices. For additional information on this or other research papers, contact: Office of Technical Analysis and Planning, Postal Rate Commission, 2000 L St. N.W., Room 500, Washington, DC 20268/202-254-3890.

How Can the Postal Rate Commission Help You?
To determine how the Postal Rate Commission can help you, contact, Secretary, Postal Rate Commission, 2000 L St. N.W., Washington, DC 20268/202-254-3880.

Railroad Retirement Board

844 Rush St., Chicago, IL 60611/312-751-4500

Established: August 29, 1935
Budget: $5,356,250,000
Employees: 1,535

Mission: Administers retirement-survivor and unemployment-sickness benefit programs provided by federal laws for the nation's railroad workers and their families. Annuities are paid by the Board to rail employees with at least 10 years of service who retire because of age or disability and to their eligible spouses; annuities are also provided to the surviving spouses and children or parents of deceased employees. (These retirement-survivor benefit programs are closely coordinated with social security benefit programs and include Medicare health insurance coverage. Under the Railroad Unemployment Insurance Act, biweekly benefits are payable by the Board to workers with qualifying railroad earnings who become unemployed or sick. About 100 field offices are maintained across the country.)

Major Sources of Information

Actuarial Assumptions
The Board makes estimates of the liabilities created by the Railroad Retirement Act. Various sets of findings each based on a separate and distinct set of actuarial and economic assumptions. Contact: Chief Actuary, Railroad Retirement Board, 844 Rush St., Room 530, Chicago, IL 60611/312-751-4915.

Appeals
Railroad employees have the right to ask for a review on a determination denying benefits. If the review still denies the benefits, the employee has the right to appeal. Contact: Bureau of Hearings and Appeal, Railroad Retirement Board, 844 Rush St., Chicago, IL 60611/312-751-4792.

Certificate of Service Months and Compensation (Form BA-6)
Each year employees in the railroad industry receive a Certificate of Service Months and Compensation from their employers or from the Board. This annual statement provides a current and cumulative record of an employee's railroad service and compensation. To report erroneous information on Form BA-6, or for additional information, contact: Bureau of Compensation and Certification, Railroad Retirement Board, 844 Rush St., Room 201, Chicago, IL 60611/312-751-4968.

Direct Payments
The program described below provides financial assistance directly to individuals, private firms and other private institutions to encourage or subsidize a particular activity:

Social Insurance for Railroad Workers
Objectives: To protect against loss of income for railroad workers and their families resulting from

retirement, death, disability, unemployment, or sickness of the wage earner.

Eligibility: Under the Railroad Retirement Act, for employee, spouse and survivor benefits the employee must have had 10 or more years of railroad service. For survivors to be eligible for benefits, the employee must also have been insured at death. Under the Railroad Unemployment Insurance Act, and employee must have earned at least $1,500 in railroad wages (counting no more than $600 in any month), and, if a new employee, must have worked for a railroad at least five months in a calendar (base) year to be a qualified employee in the applicable benefit year.

Range of Financial Assistance: Up to $1,287 monthly.

Contact: Information Service, Railroad Retirement Board, 844 Rush St., Chicago, IL 60611/312-751-4777.

Field Service

The Board maintains numerous field offices across the country in localities easily accessible to large numbers of railroad workers. Board personnel in these offices can explain benefit rights and responsibilities on an individual basis, assist employees in applying for benefits and answer questions related to the Board's programs. To locate the nearest Board office, persons should check the telephone directory under "United States Government," or they may get the location from their local Post Office or the nearest Federal Information Center. If a Board office is not located near their home, they should call the closest district office to see if they can meet with a traveling Board representative in their area.

Freedom of Information Act Requests

For Freedom of Information Act requests, contact: Secretary of the Board, Railroad Retirement Board, 844 Rush St., Room 814, Chicago, IL 60611/312-751-4920.

Information

Information on the Railroad Retirement Board operations and on the provisions of the laws it administers is available. Publications include: the *Annual Report,* the *Statistical Supplement,* the *Monthly Benefit Statistics,* and several informational pamphlets. For information on the *Annual Report* contact: Superintendent of Documents, Government Printing Office, Washington, DC 20402/202-783-3238. For information on other publications contact: Division of Public Affairs, Railroad Retirement Board, 844 Rush St., Room 543, Chicago, IL 60611/312-751-4777.

Informational Conferences and Labor Contacts

The Board conducts conferences to describe and discuss the benefits available under the Board's retirement-survivor, unemployment-sickness and

Medicare programs. Each conference attendee receives an *Informational Conference Handbook* (a comprehensive source of information on all of the Board's programs), and containing pamphlets and other materials highlighting various features of the Board's programs. Contact: Labor Member, Railroad Retirement Board, 844 Rush St., Room 825, Chicago, IL 60611/312-751-4905.

Legislative Developments

The Board provides technical assistance to Congress, the Administration, and railroad management and labor officials on various legislative proposals designed to improve the financing of the railroad retirement system. Contact: Legislative Counsel, Railroad Retirement Board, 425 13th St. N.W., Room 630, Washington, DC 20004/202-724-0787.

Library

The Railroad Retirement Board Library is located at 844 Rush St., Room 800, Chicago, IL 60611/312-751-4926.

Placement Service

The Board operates a free placement service directed primarily toward finding employment for experienced railroad workers who have lost their jobs. The placement service is available to those claiming unemployment benefits. Contact: the nearest Railroad Retirement Board office, or: Unemployment and Sickness Insurance, Bureau of Railroad Retirement Board, 844 Rush St., Chicago, IL 60611/312-751-4800.

Retirement Benefits

Railroad retirement benefits include regular employee retirement annuities after 10 years of creditable railroad service, supplemental annuities, spouse annuities, cost-of-living increases in employee and spouse retirement benefits as well as a variety of survivor benefits. *Railroad Retirement and Survivor Benefits* (for railroad workers and their families) describes these benefits and provides practical information on how to claim them. Tax information is also included. Contact the nearest Railroad Retirement Board Office, or Bureau of Retirement Claims, Railroad Retirement Board, 844 Rush St., Room 905, Chicago, IL 60611/312-751-4600.

Service and Earnings Records

The Board maintains a record of all railroad service and earnings after 1936. The information is recorded under the employee's Social Security account number used by the employer to report service and compensation to the Board. Covered businesses include railroads engaged in interstate commerce and certain of their subsidiaries, railroad associations, and national railway labor organizations. Contact: Bureau of Compensation and Certification, Railroad Retirement Board, 844 Rush St., Chicago, IL 60611/312-751-4850.

Unemployment and Sickness Benefits

The railroad unemployment insurance provides two kinds of cash benefits: unemployment benefits and sickness benefits. Under the Railroad Unemployment Insurance Act, an employee must have earned at least $1,500 in railroad wages (counting no more than $600 in any month), and, if a new employee, must have worked for a railroad at least five months in a calendar (base) year to be a

qualified employee in the applicable benefit year. Contact: the nearest Railroad Retirement Board Office, or Bureau of Unemployment and Sickness Insurance, Railroad Retirement Board, 844 Rush St., Room 600, Chicago, IL 60611/312-751-4800.

How Can the Railroad Retirement Board Help You?

To determine how the Railroad Retirement Board can help you, contact: the nearest Railroad Retirement Board Office.

Securities and Exchange Commission

450 5th Street N.W., Washington, DC 20549/202-272-2650

Established: July 2, 1934
Budget: $89,330,000
Employees: 2,021

Mission: Provides for the fullest possible disclosure to the investing public and protects the interests of the public and investors against malpractices in the securities and financial markets.

Major Sources of Information

Accounting

The Chief Accountant consults with representatives of the accounting profession regarding the promulgation of new or revised accounting and auditing standards and drafts rules and regulations which prescribe requirements for financial statements. Many of the rules are embodied in a basic accounting regulation entitled *Regulation S-X* adopted by the Commission which, together with a number of opinions issued as *Accounting Series Releases,* governs the form and content of most of the financial statements filed with the Commission. The releases are available upon written request for ten cents a sheet from the Public Reference Room Section, Office of Reports and Information Services, 450 5th Street N.W., Room 1024, Washington, DC 20549/202-272-7450. For additional information, contact: Office of Chief Accountant, Securities and Exchange Commission, 450 5th St. N.W., Room 4197, Washington, DC 20549/202-272-2050.

Administrative Proceedings Requirements

All formal administrative proceedings are conducted in accordance with SEC Rules of Practice. Included are requirements for timely notice of the proceeding and for a sufficient specification of the issues or charges involved to enable each of the parties to prepare adequately his or her case. Contact: Office of Administrative Law Judges, Securities and Exchange Commission, 450 5th St. N.W., Room 7200, Washington, DC 20549/202-272-7636.

Annual (10-K) Reports

The Annual Report is the official annual business and financial report which must be filed with the Securities and Exchange Commission by most publicly held companies. It provides comprehensive current information about the company such as principal products, services, markets and methods of distribution, summary of operations, properties, parents and subsidiaries, legal proceedings, increases and decreases in outstanding securities, changes in securities and changes in security for registered securities, defaults upon senior securities, approximate number of equity security holders, executive officers, indemnification of directors and officers, financial statements and exhibits filed, directors and remuneration of directors and officers, options granted to management to purchase securities, and interest of management and others in certain transactions. Contact: Office of Consumer Affairs and Information Services, Office of Reports and Information Services, Securities and Exchange Commission, 450 5th St. N.W., Room 2111, Washington, DC 20549/202-272-7440.

Broker-Dealer Registration

Brokers and dealers engaged in an interstate over-the-counter securities business are required to register with the Securities and Exchange Commission. They must conform their business practices to the standards prescribed in the law and the SEC regulations for the protection of investors. Form BD is the form for registration, licensing or membership as a broker or dealer (a person or company trading securities). It shows: form of organization; if it is a corporation, the date and state of incorporation, and class of equity security; if it is a sole proprietorship, the person's residence and Social Security number; if it is a successor to a previous broker or dealer, the SEC file number of the predecessor; persons with controlling interests; how the business is financed; the firm's or person's standing with the SEC and other regulatory agencies, including disclosure of having made false statements to the SEC in the past, been convicted in the last 10 years of a related felony, been enjoined in the last 10 years from financial activities, aided anyone in violating related laws or rules, been barred or suspended as a broker-dealer, been the subject of a cease and desist order, been associated with a similar firm that went bankrupt; information about the person or business that maintains the applicant's records and holds funds of the applicant or its customers; details about companies which control or are controlled by the applicant; whether the applicant is an investment adviser; types of business done (such as floor activity, underwriting or mutual fund retailing); descriptions of any nonsecurity business; and information about principals, including positions, securities held, Social Security numbers, education and background. For information, contact: Broker-Dealer Examination Branch, Division of Market Regulation, Securities and Exchange Commission, 450 5th St. N.W., Room 2154, Washington, DC 20549/202-272-7250.

Clearing Agencies
Clearing agencies must register with the Securities and Exchange Commission. For information on registration and regulations, contact: Clearing Agency Regulation Branch, Division of Market Regulation, Securities and Exchange Commission, 450 5th St. N.W., Room 5170, Washington, DC 20549/202-272-7470.

Complaints and Information
Complaints and inquiries from individual investors and the public are handled by the consumer affairs office. This office represents the interests of individual investors to the Commission. It also insures that investors can get assistance in convenient locations. Contact: Office of Consumer Affairs and Information Service, Securities and Exchange Commission, 450 5th St. N.W., Room 2111, Washington, DC 20549/202-272-7440.

Consumer Information
In addition to providing information about the

activities of certain corporations, Consumer Affairs provides assistance communicating with certain corporations and brokers and dealers. The Office also offers advice on possible remedies to problems, such as grievance procedures available through industry organizations, and issues consumer publications. Contact: Office of Consumer Affairs and Information Services, Securities and Exchange Commission, 450 5th St. N.W., Room 2111, Washington, DC 20549/202-272-7440.

Corporate Disclosure Documents
Quarterly (10-Q) and annual (10-K) reports, registration statements, proxy material and other reports filed by corporations, mutual funds or broker-dealers with the SEC are available for inspection and can be copied for a fee. Current annual and other periodic reports (including financial statements) filed by companies whose securities are listed on exchanges also are available for inspection in the Commission's New York, Chicago and Los Angeles regional offices as are the registration statements (and subsequent reports) filed by those companies whose securities are traded over-the-counter. Moreover, if the issuer's principal office is located in the area served by the Atlanta, Boston, Denver, Fort Worth or Seattle regional offices, its filings also may be examined at the appropriate regional office. In addition, prospectuses covering recent public offerings of securities registered under the Securities Act may be examined in all regional offices; copies of broker-dealer and investment adviser registrations, as well as Regulation A notifications and offering circulars, may be examined in the regional office in which they were filed. Contact: Public Reference Room Section, Office of Reports and Information Services, Securities and Exchange Commission, 450 5th St. N.W., Room 1024, Washington, DC 20549/202-272-7450.

Corporate Reorganizations
The Commission serves as adviser to United States district courts in connection with proceedings for the reorganization of debtor corporations in which there is a substantial public interest. It participates as a party to these proceedings, either at the request or with the approval of the courts. It renders independent, expert advice and assistance to the courts, which do not maintain their own staffs of expert consultants, in connection with the preparation of plans of reorganization. It also presents its views and recommendations on such matters as the qualifications and independence, the need for appointment of trustees or examiners and their fee allowances to the various parties, including the trustees and their counsel, sales of properties and other assets, interim distributions to security holders, and other financial or legal matters. The Commission has no independent right of appeal from court rulings. For additional

information, contact: Office of Chief Counsel, Securities and Exchange Commission, 450 5th St. N.W., Room 6077, 20549/202-272-7530.

Decisions and Reports

The Securities and Exchange Commission's decisions (as well as initial decisions which have become final and are of precedential significance) are printed in the SEC's *Decisions and Reports*. The latest volume, Volume 46 (October 1, 1975–October 31, 1978), is sold for $22.00 by the Superintendent of Documents, Government Printing Office, Washington, DC 20402/202-783-3238. For additional information, contact: Office of Opinions and Review, Securities and Exchange Commission, 450 5th St. N.W., Room 2182, Washington, DC 20549/202-272-7400.

Directory of Companies Required to File Annual Reports with the SEC

This annual directory lists companies alphabetically and classifies them by industry groups according to the Standard Industrial Classification Manual of the Budget. It is available for $12.00 from the Superintendent of Documents, Government Printing Office, Washington, DC 20402/202-783-3238.

Disclosure

The Securities and Exchange Commission requires a company to make "full disclosure" of all material facts (that is, accurate information about the business it conducts or proposes to conduct) before it offers its securities to the public. Most publicly-held companies have an obligation to keep their shareholders informed of their business operations, financial conditions and management on a periodic basis. Contact: Division of Corporation Finance, Securities and Exchange Commission, 450 5th St. N.W., Room 3021, Washington, DC 20549/202-272-2573.

Disclosure Policy

If experience shows that a particular requirement fails to achieve its objective, or if a rule appears unduly burdensome in relation to the benefits resulting from the disclosure provided, the Division of Corporation Finance presents the problem to the Commission for consideration of possible modification of the rule or other requirement. Receives suggestions for rule modifications from industry representatives and others affected. In addition, the Commission normally gives advance public notice of proposals for the adoption of new or amended rules or registration forms and affords opportunity for interested members of the public to comment thereon. The same procedure is followed by the other divisions and offices of the Commission. Contact: Disclosure Policy and Proceedings Office, Division of Corporation Finance, Securities and Exchange Commission, 450 5th St.

N.W., Room 3104, Washington, DC 20549/202-272-2589.

Economic Analysis

The Directorate analyzes rule changes and engages in long-term research and policy planning, builds and maintains diverse computer data bases, designs programs that provide access to data, and develops and tests alternative methodologies. For additional information on the activities of this division, contact: Directorate of Economic and Policy Analysis, Securities and Exchange Commission, 450 5th St. N.W., Room 7169, Washington, DC 20549/202-272-2850.

Economic Monitoring

The Directorate assesses the impact of securities market regulations on issuers (in particular, small or high technology issuers), broker-dealers, investors, and the economy in general. One area monitored is the impact of competitively determined Commission rates and changes in regulations which affect the ability of small businesses to raise capital. Contact: Directorate of Economic and Policy Analysis, Securities and Exchange Commission, 450 5th St. N.W., Room 7169, Washington, DC 20549/202-272-2850.

Enforcement

If the Securities and Exchange Commission investigations turn up facts which show possible fraud, or other law violations, it may pursue several courses of action:

Civil injunction. The Commission may apply to an appropriate United States District Court for an order enjoining those acts or practices alleged to violate the law or Commission rules.

Criminal prosecution. If fraud or other willful law violation is indicated, the Commission may refer the facts to the Department of Justice with a recommendation for criminal prosecution of the offending persons.

Administrative remedy. The Commission may, after a hearing, issue orders suspending or expelling members from exchanges or the over-the-counter dealers association; denying, suspending or revoking the registrations of brokers-dealers and investment advisors, or censuring individuals for misconduct or barring them (temporarily or permanently) from employment with a registered firm.

Contact: Division of Enforcement, Securities and Exchange Commission, 450 5th St. N.W., Room 4000, Washington, DC 20549/202-272-2900.

Exemptions from Registration

The registration requirement applies to securities of domestic and foreign private issuers, as well as to securities of foreign governments or their instrumentalities. There are, however, certain exemptions from the registration requirement. Among these are: 1) private offerings to a limited number of persons or institutions who have access to the kind of information registration would disclose and who do not propose to redistribute the securities; 2) offerings restricted to the residents of the state in which the issuing company is organized and doing business; 3) securities of municipal, state, federal and other governmental instrumentalities, of charitable institutions, of banks, and of carriers subject to the Interstate Commerce Act; 4) offerings not in excess of certain specified amounts made in compliance with regulations of the Commission discussed below; and 5) offerings of "small business investment companies" made in accordance with rules and regulations of the Commission. Anti-fraud provisions apply to all sales of securities involving interstate commerce or the mails, whether or not the securities are exempt from registration. Contact: Office of Chief Counsel, Division of Corporation Finance, Securities and Exchange Commission, 450 5th St. N.W., Room 3021, Washington, DC 20549/202-272-2573.

Foreign Companies
Form 6-K is filed by foreign companies selling stock in this country, which do not have to file Form 8-K. It requires that they submit information that they have made public abroad. Only information not previously furnished to the SEC and information that is important to investors is required. If the information is available only in a foreign language, it does not have to be translated into English. The documents show the financial condition of the company and its subsidiaries; changes in business; major acquisitions or disposition of assets; changes in management or control; remuneration to directors and officers and any transactions with directors, officers or principal stockholders. Contact: International Corporate Finance, Division of Corporation Finance, Securities and Exchange Commission, 450 5th St. N.W., Room 3093, Washington, DC 20549/202-272-3246.

Freedom of Information Act Requests
For Freedom of Information Act requests, contact: Freedom of Information, Office of Reports and Information Services, Securities and Exchange Commission, 450 5th St. N.W., Room 2130, Washington, DC 20549/202-272-7420.

Hearings
Hearings are conducted before a Hearing Officer who is normally an Administrative Law Judge appointed by the Commission; he or she serves independent of the interested Division or Office and rules on the admissibility of evidence and on other issues arising during the course of the hearing. The laws provide that any person or firm aggrieved by a decision order of the Commission may seek review by the appropriate United States court of appeals. All initial decisions of Adminis-

trative Law Judges rendered in connection with public proceedings are made public. Ultimately, the Commission's decisions (and initial decisions may be found in the library of Commission's headquarters or regional and branch offices) are printed by the Government Printing Office and published in the Commission's *Decisions and Reports*. Contact: Office of Administrative Law Judges, Securities and Exchange Commission, 450 5th St. N.W., Room 7200, Washington, DC 20549/202-272-7636.

Insider Trading
The protection provided the investing public through disclosure of financial and related information concerning the securities of registered companies is supplemented by provisions of the law designed to curb misuse of corporate information not available to the general public. To that end, each officer and director of such a company and each beneficial owner of more than 10 percent of its registered equity securities, must file an initial report with the Commission (and with the exchange on which the stock may be listed) showing his or her holdings of each of the company's equity securities. Thereafter, he or she must file reports for any month during which there was any change in such holdings. In addition, the law provides that profits obtained from purchases and sales (or sales and purchases) of such equity securities within any six-month period may be recovered by the company or by any security holders on its behalf. This recovery right must be asserted in the appropriate United States district court. Such "insiders" are also prohibited from making short sales of their company's equity securities. Contact: Corporate Accountability, Division of Corporation Finance, Securities and Exchange Commission, 450 5th St. N.W., Washington, DC 20549/202-272-2553.

Intermarket Trading System
A study on the Intermarket Trading System is available. The system, based on automated communications links among traders on the floors of the New York and American and five regional stock exchanges and the National Association of Security Dealers (NASD), permits participants to execute trades at the best price available on any of the participating markets. Contact: Market Structure and Market Trading Studies Branch, Directorate of Economic and Policy Analysis, Securities and Exchange Commission, 450 5th St. N.W., Room 5193, Washington, DC 20549/202-272-2409.

Investigations
The Security and Exchange Commission investigates complaints or other indications of possible law violations in securities transactions. Investigation and enforcement work is also coordinated by the regional offices and the main Division of

Enforcement. Contact: Division of Enforcement, Securities and Exchange Commission, 450 5th St. N.W., Room 4000, Washington, DC 20549/202-272-2900.

Investment Advisor Regulations

The Commission may recommend prosecution of investment advisors by the Department of Justice for fraudulent misconduct or willful violation of the law or rules of the Commission thereunder. The law contains anti-fraud provisions, and it empowers the Commission to adopt rules defining fraudulent, deceptive or manipulative acts and practices and is designed to prevent such activities. It also requires that investment advisors disclose the nature of their interest in transactions executed for their clients; and, in effect, it prevents the assignment of investment advisory contracts without the client's consent. The law also imposes on investment advisors subject to the registration requirement the duty to maintain books and records in accordance with such rules as may be prescribed by the Commission, and it authorizes the Commission to conduct inspections of such books and records. Contact: Office of Chief Counsel, Division of Investment Management, Securities and Exchange Commission, 450 5th St. N.W., Room 5106, Washington, DC 20549/202-272-2030.

Investment Advisors Registration

Persons or firms who engage for compensation in the business of advising others about their securities transactions must register with the Securities and Exchange Commission, and conform their activities to statutory standards designed to protect the interests of investors. Contact: Investment Advisor Registration, Office of Reports and Information Services, Securities and Exchange Commission, 450 5th St. N.W., Room 2154, Washington, DC 20549/202-272-7250.

Investment Companies Registration

Companies engaged primarily in the business of investing, reinvesting and trading in securities and whose own securities are offered to, sold to, and held by the investing public must register with the Securities and Exchange Commission. A list of registered investment companies, showing their classification, assets, size and location, may be purchased from the Commission in photocopy form. The law requires disclosure of their financial condition and investment policies to afford investors full and complete information about their activities; prohibits such companies from changing the nature of their business or their investment policies without the approval of the stockholders; bars persons guilty of security frauds from serving as officers and directors; prevents underwriters, investment bankers or brokers from constituting more than a minority of the directors of such companies; requires management contracts (and material changes therein) to be submitted to security holders for their approval; prohibits transactions between such companies and their directors, officers, or affiliated companies or persons, except on approval by the Commission as being fair and involving no overreaching; forbids the issuance of senior securities by such companies except under specified conditions and upon specified terms; and prohibits pyramiding of such companies and cross-ownership of their securities. Form N-8A is the notice of registration which investment companies must file. It tells: name of registrant, form of organization (corporation, partnership, trust, etc.), state and date of organization. If the business has directors, it tells the name and address of investment advisors, directors, officers, advisory board members and, if it is an open-end company, the underwriters. If the business is unincorporated and has no board of directors, it shows the name and address of the trustee or custodian, sponsor, and the officers and directors of the sponsoring company. If the business is a management company, the form shows whether it is open-end or closed-end, diversified or nondiversified and whether it is an employee securities company. The form must tell whether the registrant is issuing its securities to the public and whether it has any securities issued and outstanding. The last report to security holders is attached. If the registrant is issuing securities, it tells the name and address of its underwriter and if the registrant has securities issued and outstanding it tells the number of beneficiaries owning its securities and the name of any company owning 10 percent or more of the registrant's outstanding securities. The securities of investment companies are also required to be registered; the companies must file periodic reports and are subject to the Commission's proxy and "insider" trading rules. Contact: Office of Chief Counsel, Division of Investment Management, Securities and Exchange Commission, 450 5th St. N.W., Room 5130, Washington, DC 20549/202-272-2105.

Legal Interpretations and Advice

The Securities and Exchange Commission renders administrative interpretations of the law and regulations to members of the public, prospective registrants and others, to help them decide legal questions about the application of the law and the regulations to particular situations and to aid them in complying with the law. This advice, for example, might include an informal expression of opinion about whether the offering of a particular security is subject to the registration requirements of the law and, if so, advice as to compliance with the disclosure requirements of the applicable registration form. Contact: Office of Chief Counsel, Division of Corporation Finance, Securities and Exchange Commission, 450 5th St. N.W., Room 3021, Washington, DC 20549/202-272-2573.

Library
The Securities and Exchange Commission Library is open to the public. Advance notice is advisable. Contact: Library, Securities and Exchange Commission, 450 5th St. N.W., Room 1602, Washington, DC 20549/202-272-2618.

Lost and Stolen Securities Program
The Securities and Exchange Commission has a computer-assisted reporting and inquiry system for lost, stolen, counterfeit, and forged securities. All insured banks and brokers, dealers and other securities firms are required to register with the Securities Information Center, Inc., P.O. Box 421, Wellesley Hills, MA 02181/617-235-8270, where a central data base records reported thefts and losses. Contact: Division of Market Regulation, Securities and Exchange Commission, 450 5th St. N.W., Room 5186, Washington, DC 20549/202-272-7393.

Market Surveillance
The Securities and Exchange Commission regulates securities trading practices in the exchange and the over-the-counter markets. Thus, the Commission has adopted regulations which, among other things, 1) define acts or practices which constitute a "manipulative or deceptive device or contrivance" prohibited by the statute; 2) regulate short selling, stabilizing transactions and similar matters; 3) regulate the hypothecation of customers' securities; and 4) provide safeguards with respect to the financial responsibility of brokers and dealers. Contact: Market Surveillance, Division of Enforcement, Securities and Exchange Commission, 450 5th St. N.W., Room 4006, Washington, DC 20549/202-272-2230.

Margin Trading
The Securities and Exchange Commission enforces the statute which sets limits on the amount of credit allowed for the purpose of purchasing or carrying securities. Contact: Legal Policies and Trading Practices, Division of Market Regulation, Securities and Exchange Commission, 450 5th St. N.W., Room 5024, Washington, DC 20549/202-272-2844.

Meetings
Notices of open and closed Commission meetings and the agendas of open meetings are published the preceding week in the *SEC News Digest.* For additional information on these weekly meetings, contact: Office of the Secretary, Securities and Exchange Commission, 500 N. Capitol St., Room 6184, Washington, DC 20549/202-272-2600. For minutes of the meetings, contact: Office of Public Affairs, Securities and Exchange Commission, 450

5th St. N.W., Room 1012, Washington, DC 20549/202-272-2650.

Monthly *Statistical Review*
This publication provides data on the financial condition of the securities industry, registered securities issues, private placement of corporate securities, quarterly assets of non-insured pension funds and property and liability insurance companies, volume and value of trading of exchange-listed equity securities, quarterly stock transactions of selected nonfinancial institutions, and annual estimated market value of stock outstanding. It is sold for $22.00 per year by the Superintendent of Documents, Government Printing Office, Washington, DC 20402/202-783-3238. For additional information, contact: *Statistical Review,* Directorate of Economic and Policy Analysis, Securities and Exchange Commission, 450 5th St. N.W., Room 7169, Washington, DC 20549/202-272-2850.

National Securities Exchanges Registration
National securities exchanges, those having a substantial securities trading volume, must register with the Commission. The Commission oversees, inspects and evaluates the exchanges. Contact: Office of Self-Regulatory Oversight, Division of Market Regulation, Securities and Exchange Commission, 450 5th St. N.W., Room 5002, Washington, DC 20549/202-272-2866.

Official Summary
This is a monthly summary of security transactions and holdings reported by "insiders" (officers, directors, and others) pursuant to provisions of the federal securities laws. It is sold for $59.00 per year by the Superintendent of Documents, Government Printing Office, Washington, DC 20402/202-783-3238. For additional information, contact: Office of Reports and Information Services, Securities and Exchange Commission, 450 5th St. N.W., Room 2111, Washington, DC 20549/202-272-7440.

Opinions and Reviews
Securities and Exchange Commissions opinions and decisions are prepared by this office. For additional information, contact: Office of Opinions and Reviews, Securities and Exchange Commission, 450 5th St. N.W., Room 2188, Washington, DC 20549/202-272-7400.

Ponzi or Pyramid Schemes
Warnings against investing in a Ponzi or pyramid scheme is offered. These schemes are varied but usually promise very high yield, quick return, a "once in a lifetime" opportunity, and the chance to "get in on the ground floor." Several free publications are available on the subject: *How to Avoid Ponzi and Pyramid Schemes; Applicability of*

Securities Laws to Pyramid Schemes; and *Warning to Investors About Get-Rich-Quick Schemes.* To notify the Securities and Exchange Commission of a fraudulent scheme and for further information, contact: Office of Consumer Affairs and Information Service, Securities and Exchange Commission, 450 5th St. N.W., Room 2111, Washington, DC 20549/202-272-7440.

Proxy Solicitations
In any solicitation of proxies (votes) from holders of registered securities (listed and over-the-counter), whether for the election of directors or for approval of other corporate action, disclosure must be made of all material facts concerning the matters on which such holders are asked to vote. Where a contest for control of the management of a corporation is involved, the rules require disclosure of the names and interests of all "participants" in the proxy contest. The Commission's rules require that proposed proxy material be filed in advance for examination by the Commission for compliance with the disclosure requirements. Contact: Office of Chief Counsel, Division of Corporation Finance, Securities and Exchange Commission, 450 5th St. N.W., Room 3021, Washington, DC 20549/202-272-2573.

Publications
The Securities and Exchange Commission compiles numerous periodic and irregular reports. For a list of these, contact: Office of Consumer Affairs and Information Services, Securities and Exchange Commission, 450 5th St. N.W., Room 1024, Washington, DC 20549/202-272-7450.

Public Utility Registration
Interstate holding companies engaged through their subsidiaries in the electric utility business or in the retail distribution of natural or manufactured gas are subject to regulation. They must register with the Securities and Exchange Commission and file initial and periodic reports containing detailed data about the organization, financial structure and operations of each such holding company and of its subsidiaries. For further information on public utility registration, contact: Public Utilities Branch, Division of Corporate Regulation, Securities and Exchange Commission, 450 5th St. N.W., Room 7010, Washington, DC 20549/202-272-7676.

Quarterly (10-Q) Reports
The quarterly financial report, filed by most publicly held companies, provides a continuing view of their financial position during the year. The information includes the income statement; balance sheet; description of material changes since the previous quarter; legal processing; changes in securities; default upon senior securities; and other materially important events. Contact: Public Reference Section, Office of Reports and Information Services, Securities and Exchange Commission, 450 5th St. N.W., Room 1024, Washington, DC 20549/202-272-7450.

Regional Offices
For information on Securities and Exchange Commission Regional Offices, contact: Regional Office Operations, Office of the Executive Director, Securities and Exchange Commission, 450 5th St. N.W., Room 6029, Washington, DC 20549/202-272-3090.

Revocations
If exchange or association members, registered brokers or dealers, or individuals who may associate with any such firms engage in securities transactions violative of the law, the Securities and Exchange Commission may invoke administrative remedy, i.e., it may, after a hearing, issue orders suspending or expelling members from exchanges or the over-the-counter-dealers association; denying, suspending or revoking the registrations of broker-dealers; or censuring individuals for misconduct or barring them (temporarily or permanently) from employment with a registered firm. Contact: Office of Chief Counsel, Division of Market Regulation, Securities and Exchange Commission, 450 5th St. N.W., Room 5029, Washington, DC 20549/202-272-2848.

Rules and Regulations
The Securities and Exchange Commission's rules and regulations, *Title 17 of the Code of Federal Regulations* ($14.00), and the *Compilation of the Federal Securities Laws* ($13.00), are sold by the Superintendent of Documents, Government Printing Office, Washington, DC 20402/202-783-3238. For additional information, contact: Office of Reports and Information Services, Securities and Exchange Commission, 450 5th St. N.W., Room 2111, Washington, DC 20549/202-272-7440.

SEC Docket
This is a weekly compilation of the full text of SEC releases, including the full texts of *Accounting Series* releases, corporate reorganization and litigation releases. It is sold for $155.00 per year by the Commerce Clearing House, 4025 West Peterson Avenue, Chicago, IL 60646/312-583-8500. For additional information, contact: Office of Reports and Information Services, Securities and Exchange Commission, 450 5th St. N.W., Room 2111, Washington, DC 20549/202-272-7440.

Securities Information Processors
Securities Information Processors must register with the Securities and Exchange Commission. For additional information on regulations and legislation, contact: National Market System Branch, Division of Market Regulation, Securities and

Exchange Commission, 450 5th St. N.W., Room 5199, Washington, DC 20549/202-272-2857.

Securities Registration

Before the public offering of securities, a registration statement must be filed with the Securities and Exchange Commission by the issuer, setting forth the required information. The securities may be sold when the statement has become effective. The registration provides disclosure of financial and other information on the basis of which investors may appraise the merits of the securities. Investors must be furnished with a prospectus (selling circular) containing salient data set forth in the registration statement to enable them to evaluate the securities. The basic registration form, *Form S-1*, requires, among other things, a description of the company's business; its properties; material transactions between the company and its officers and directors; the plan for distributing the securities and the intended use of the proceeds; capitalization; competition; identification of officers and directors and their remuneration; and any pending legal proceedings. It is not prepared as a fill-in-the-blank form like a tax return, but, rather, is similar to a brochure, with the information provided in a narrative format. In addition, there are detailed requirements concerning financial statements, including that such statements be audited by an independent certified public accountant. In addition to the information expressly required by the form, the company must also provide any other information that is necessary to make the statements complete and not misleading. If there are sufficient adverse or risk factors concerning the offering and the issuer—such as lack of business operating history, adverse economic conditions in a particular industry, lack of market for the securities offered, dependence upon key personnel, etc.—they must be set forth prominently in the prospectus, usually in the very beginning. Contact: Division of Corporation Finance, Securities and Exchange Commission, 450 5th St. N.W., Room 619, Washington, DC 20549/202-272-2579.

Small Business Policy

This office spearheads small business rulemaking initiatives; reviews and comments upon the impact of various Securities and Exchange Commission rule proposals on smaller issuers; and serves as a liaison with Congressional committees, government agencies, and other groups concerned with small business. *Q & A: Small Business and the SEC* is a free booklet which discusses capital formation and federal securities laws. Contact: Office of Small Business Policy, Securities and Exchange Commission, 450 5th St. N.W., Room 3195, Washington, DC 20549/202-272-2644.

Small Issues Registration

In April 1979, the Securities and Exchange Commission adopted, as an experiment, a simplified registration form for use by certain domestic or Canadian corporate issues as an alternative to Form S-1. Form S-18 is available for the registration of securities to be sold to the public for cash not exceeding an aggregate offering price of $7.5 million, provided such issuers are not subject to the SEC's continuous reporting requirements under the Exchange Act. Form S-18 provides for reduced disclosure requirements and has other attributes which are intended to result in a more timely and less expensive registration process for the smaller issuer who wishes to gain access to the public capital markets. Although many of the requirements for an S-18 registration statement are the same as those for a full registration, Form S-18 allows:

1. The issuer to provide audited financial statements for two fiscal years prepared in accordance with generally accepted accounting principles;
2. Less extensive narrative disclosure, particularly in the areas of the description of business;
3. The choice of filing with either the SEC's Regional Office nearest the place where the company's principal business operations are conducted, or with the SEC's Division of Corporation Finance, in Washington, DC, where all Form S-1 registration statements are filed and reviewed. The primary advantage of regional filing is that Regional Office personnel may be more familiar with local economic conditions, the business community, the financial environment and, in some cases, the background and history of the company and the industry.

For further information, contact: Office of Small Business Policy, Division of Corporation Finance, Securities and Exchange Commission, 450 5th St. N.W., Room 3195, Washington, DC 20549/202-272-2644.

Tender Offer Solicitations

Commission rules and amendments require disclosure of pertinent information by the person seeking to acquire over 5 percent of the company's securities by direct purchase or by tender offer, as well as by any person soliciting shareholders to accept or reject a tender offer. Thus, as with the proxy rules, public investors who hold stock in the subject corporation may now make informed decisions on takeover bids. Schedule 14-D1 describes tender offers made to companies trading on a stock exchange, or to those worth more than $1 million or with 500 or more shareholders. It is filed by the target company and identifies: the securities; principals; past major dealings between the two companies or their directors; source and amount of funds required; purpose of the transactions; persons, such as brokers, retained to help with the transactions; material financial information; and documents such as the tender offer itself, loan agreements and contracts. Schedule 14-D must be filed by companies that are the subject of the tender offers if they make recommendations for or against the offer. It tells why the recommendation was made; describes the security and issuer; describes the background of the company; identifies persons retained as a result of the tender offer; and gives information about any transactions with the other company during the previous 60 days. Contact: Tender Offers and Acquisitions Office, Division of Corporation Finance, Securities and Exchange Commission, 450 5th St. N.W., Room 3015, Washington, DC 20549/202-272-3097.

Transfer Agents
Transfer Agents must register with the Securities and Exchange Commission. For information on transfer agents registration and regulation, contact: Transfer Agent Regulation, Division of Market Regulation, Securities and Exchange Commission, 450 5th St. N.W., Room 5173, Washington, DC 20549/202-272-2775.

Trust Indentures
Bonds, debentures, notes and similar debt securities offered for public sale which are pursuant to trust indentures must conform to specified statutory standards. Applications for qualification of trust indentures are examined for compliance with the applicable requirements of the law and the Commission's rules. Contact: Office of the Chief Counsel, Securities and Exchange Commission, 450 5th St. N.W., Room 3026, Washington, DC 20549/202-272-2573:

How Can the Securities and Exchange Commission Help You?
To determine how the Securities and Exchange Commission can help you, contact: Office of Public Affairs, Securities and Exchange Commission, 450 5th St. N.W., Washington, DC 20549/202-272-2650.

Selective Service System

1023 31st St. N.W., Washington, DC 20435/202-724-0790

Established: 1940
Budget: $23,264,000
Employees: 260

Mission: To be prepared to supply to the Armed Forces manpower adequate to insure the security of the United States, with concomitant regard for the maintenance of an effective national economy.

Major Sources of Information

Classification
Classification is a statement of a person's availability for military service. The following are some categories: Conscientious objector, college students, ministers, only-son hardship, occupational deferments, medical specialists, alien or dual national, reservists, veterans and women. Contact: Public Affairs, Selective Service System, 1023 31st St. N.W., Washington, DC 20435/202-724-0790.

Programs
For information on current Selective Service programs contact: Programs, Selective Service System, 1023 31st St. N.W., Washington, DC 20435/202-724-0851.

Recorded Message
The recording provides statistics information on the number of draft registrants for specific periods of time. Call: 202-724-0424. For additional information contact: Public Affairs, Selective Service System, 1023 31st St. N.W., Washington, DC 20435/202-724-0790.

Registrant Information and Management System Manual
The purpose of this manual is to disseminate directives which will govern the operational aspects of the Selective Service System at state and local levels. It contains all necessary information for registration, classification, examination, induction, allied subjects and the procedures relating thereto. For additional information contact: Public Affairs Officer, Selective Service System, 1023 31st St. N.W., Washington, DC 20435/202-724-0790.

Semiannual Report of the Director of Selective Service
This report provides an overview of the Selective Service program every six months. To receive a copy of the report, or for additional information on the Selective Service, contact: Public Affairs, Selective Service System, 1023 31st St. N.W., Washington, DC 20435/202-724-0790.

How Can the Selective Service System Help You?
To determine how this office can help you contact: Public Affairs, Selective Service System, 1023 31st St. N.W., Washington, DC 20435/202-724-0790.

Small Business Administration

1441 L St. N.W., Washington, DC 20416/202-653-6565

Established: 1953
Budget: $739,380,000
Employees: 3,910

Mission: Aids, counsels, assists, and protects interests of small business; insures that small business concerns receive a fair proportion of government purchases, contracts, and subcontracts, as well as of the sales of government property; makes loans to small business concerns, state and local development companies, and the victims of floods or other catastrophes, or of certain types of economic injury; licenses, regulates, and makes loans to small business investment companies; improves the management skills of small business owners, potential owners, and managers; conducts studies of the economic environment; and guarantees surety bonds for small contractors.

Major Sources of Information

Active Corps of Executives (ACE)
Active executives from all major industries, professional and trade associations, educational institutions, and many professionals volunteer their specialized kinds of expertise to help small business owners solve their problems. Contact: ACE, Management Assistance, Small Business Administration, 1441 L St. N.W., Room 602H, Washington, DC 20416/202-653-6768.

Advocacy Publications
A variety of publications, including topical reports on current governmental activities which affect small business interests, economic research, government policy, state activities, and general information, is available. Contact: Office of Advocacy, Small Business Administration, 1441 L St. N.W., Room 1012, Washington, DC 20416/202-634-7584.

Alternative Financing
For information concerning alternative ways of financing small business activities, contact: Office of Chief Counsel for Advocacy, Small Business Administration, 1441 L St. N.W., Room 1010, Washington, DC 20416/202-653-6533.

Basic Guide to Exporting
This publication is not just for large corporations but for the small and medium-sized firm as well. It outlines the sequence of steps necessary to determine whether and how to utilize foreign markets as a source of immediate and future profits. It describes the problems facing smaller firms engaged in or seeking to enter international trade and the many types of assistance available to help them cope with problems which may arise. The booklet also provides a step-by-step guide to the appraisal of the sales potential of foreign markets and to an understanding of the requirements of local business practices and procedures in those overseas markets. It is available for $6.50 from the Superintendent of Documents, Government Print-

ing Office, Washington, DC 20402/202-783-3238. For additional information contact: nearest SBA Field Office (see list of SBA Field Offices this section).

Business Eligibility
The Small Business Administration generally defines a small business as one which is independently owned and operated and is not dominant in its field. To be eligible for an SBA loan, a business must meet a size standard set by the agency. For further information contact: nearest Small Business Administration Field Office (see list of Field Offices this section).

Business Loan Programs
Business loan proceeds can be used for working capital, purchase of inventory, equipment and supplies, or for building construction and expansion. The Small Business Administration offers two basic types of business loans: 1) loans made by private lenders, usually banks, and guaranteed by SBA; and 2) loans made directly by the agency. A free booklet, *Business Loans from the SBA,* is available describing the business loans, eligibility, credit requirements, terms of loans, and collateral. It also outlines how to apply for a loan. Contact: nearest Small Business Administration Field Office (see list of Field Offices this section).

Business Management Training Program
Business management courses in planning, organization, and control of a business are co-sponsored by SBA in cooperation with educational institutions, profit making firms, chambers of commerce, and trade associations. Courses generally take place in the evening and last from six to eight weeks. In addition, conferences covering such subjects as working capital, business forecasting, and marketing are held for established businesses on a regular basis. SBA conducts Pre-Business Workshops, dealing with finance, marketing assistance, types of business organization, and business site selection, for prospective business owners. For additional information, contact: Office of Management Assistance, Small Business Administration, 1441 L St. N.W., Room 317, Washington, DC 20416/202-653-6330.

Case Assistance by Advocacy
Help is available to a small business that has problems with the activities, regulations or policies of a federal government agency, including the Small Business Administration. Contact an SBA Regional Office, or Office of Interagency Affairs, Office of Advocacy, Small Business Administration, 1441 L St. N.W., Room 1012, Washington, DC 20416/202-653-6533.

Certificates of Competency
The Small Business Administration is authorized

to study a firm's capabilities and, if it finds that the firm has the responsibility to carry out the specific government contract, certify to this effect. A responsible concern is one that can meet all contract requirements in a timely manner. When it certifies to the competency of a small firm, the Small Business Administration notifies the government contracting officer that the small business is capable of performing the specific government contract in question. Certificates of competency are issued for manufacturers, purchasers of government property, service concerns or regular dealers. Contact: nearest SBA Field Office or for further information, Certificates of Competency, Office of Industrial Assistance, Office of Procurement and Technical Assistance, Small Business Administration, 1441 L St. N.W., Room 636, Washington, DC 20416/202-653-6582.

Computer-Assisted Management Courses
Under an agreement between the Small Business Administration (SBA) and Control Data Corporation (CDC) the federal government will assume most of the fees for small businesses taking computer-assisted management courses offered by CDC. Training under the program called "PLATO" (Program Logic For Automatic Teaching Operations) involves 4 series of learning topics: building your own business; selling the psychological approach; accounts receivable collection techniques; and contract bidding. Students enrolled in the program work with both printed material and a computer terminal. Contact your local U.S. Small Business Administration field office list in your telephone book, or U.S. Small Business Administration, 1441 L St. N.W., Room 317, Washington, DC 20416/202-653-6894.

Disaster Assistance Loans
For information about SBA disaster assistance loans for homeowners, renters, and small businesses, contact: Disaster Assistance Division, Small Business Administration, 1441 L St. N.W., Room 820, Washington, DC 20416/202-563-6879.

Economic Research
Government statistics on small businesses are available. Contact: Office of Economic Research, Office for Advocacy, Small Business Administration, 1100 Vermont Ave. N.W., Room 1100, Washington, DC 20416/202-634-4885.

8-a Contracts
The Small Business Administration, working with procurement officials in other agencies, serves as a prime contractor for federal goods and service purchases, and then subcontracts this federal work to small firms owned by socially and economically disadvantaged persons. SBA also provides management, technical and bonding assistance to firms holding 8-a contracts. Contact: nearest SBA field

office or for further information, 8-a Contracts, Minority Small Business and Capital Ownership Development, Small Business Administration, 1441 L St. N.W., Room 618, Washington, DC 20416/202-653-6549.

Freedom of Information Act Requests
For Freedom of Information Act requests, contact: Freedom of Information, Public Communications, Small Business Administration, 1441 L St. N.W., Washington, DC 20416/202-653-6460.

Grants
The program described below is for sums of money which are given by the federal government to initiate or stimulate new or improved activities or to sustain on-going research:

Management Technical Assistance for Disadvantaged Businessmen
Objectives: To provide management and technical assistance through public or private organizations to existing or potential businessmen who are economically or socially disadvantaged or who are located in areas of high concentration of unemployment; or are participants in activities by sections 7(i) and 8a of the Small Business Act.
Eligibility: Public or private organizations that have the capability of providing the necessary assistance.
Range of Financial Assistance: $15,000 to $306,250.
Contact: Assistant Administrator for Management Assistance, Small Business Administration, 1441 L St. N.W., Room 600, Washington, DC 20416/202-653-6894.

Hotline to Publications
Small Business Administration free publications include management aids, starting out series, and small business bibliographies. The management aids are generally aimed at manufacturing businesses and retail and service firms; starting out series aids new small businesses; and small business bibliographies list key reference sources for a variety of business management topics, including books, pamphlets and trade associations. Call toll-free 800-368-5855 or for additional information contact: Publications, Public Communications, Small Business Administration, 1441 L St. N.W., Room 100, Washington, DC 20416/202-653-7561.

International Trade
The Small Business Administration works closely with the Department of Commerce, Eximbank, Overseas Private Investment Corporation, and other governmental and private agencies to provide small business with assistance and information on export opportunities. The free pamphlet *Markets Overseas with U.S. Government Help* is available upon request. Also available is the pamphlet, *Export Information System (EIS) Data Report,* which provides data on world markets for 2,000 products. This office also guarantees export bank line of credit and co-guarantees up to $1,000,000 in cooperation with the Export-Import Bank. Contact: nearest SBA Field Office (see list of SBA Field Offices this section).

International Trade Counseling and Training
International trade counseling and training is available to managers of small businesses considering entering the overseas marketplace as well as those desiring to expand current export operations. Emphasis is placed on the practical application of successful exporting and importing procedures to small business. Contact: nearest SBA Field office (see a list of SBA Field offices this section).

Library
The library has reference material pertaining to small businesses. Contact: Library, Small Business Administration, 1441 L St. N.W., Room 218, Washington, DC 20416/202-653-6914.

Loans and Loan Guarantees
The programs described below are those which offer financial assistance through the lending of federal monies for a specific period of time or programs in which the federal government makes an arrangement to indemnify a lender against part or all of any defaults by the borrower:

Bond Guarantees for Surety Companies
Objectives: To encourage the commercial surety market to make surety bonds more available to small contractors unable for various reasons to obtain a bond without a guarantee.
Eligibility: Guarantees are limited to those surety companies holding certificates of authority from the Secretary of the Treasury as an acceptable surety for bonds on federal contracts, or those other companies which can meet the requirements of the Small Business Administration.
Range of Financial Assistance: $2,000 to $1,000,000.
Contact: Chief, Surety Bond Guarantee Division, Small Business Administration, 4040 N. Fairfax Dr., Arlington, VA 22203/703-235-2907.

Certified Development Company Loans
Objectives: To assist small business concerns by providing long term financing through the sale of debentures by the Federal Financing Bank.
Eligibility: Certified Development Companies must be incorporated under general State corporation statute, either on a profit or nonprofit basis, for the purpose of promoting economic growth in a particular area.
Range of Financial Assistance: Up to $500,000.

Contact: Office of Economic Development, Small Business Administration, Room 720, 1441 L St. N.W., Washington, DC 20416.

Disaster Assistance to Nonagricultural Businesses (Major Source of Employment)

Objectives: To enable a nonagricultural business that is a major source of employment in a major disaster area and which is no longer in substantial operation as a result of such disaster to resume operations in order to assist in restoring the economic viability of the disaster area.

Eligibility: Must be a major source of employment, a nonagricultural enterprise and be located in a major disaster area.

Range of Financial Assistance: No limit.

Contact: Office of Disaster Loans, Small Business Administration, 1441 L St. N.W., Washington, DC 20416/202-653-6376.

Economic Injury Disaster Loans

Objectives: To assist business concerns suffering economic injury as a result of certain Presidential, SBA, and Department of Agriculture disaster designations.

Eligibility: Must be a small business concern as described in SBA rules and regulations. Must furnish evidence of economic injury claimed. Must also be unable to obtain credit elsewhere.

Range of Financial Assistance: $5,000 to $500,000.

Contact: Office of Disaster Loans, Small Business Administration, 1441 L St. N.W., Washington, DC 20416/202-653-6879.

Handicapped Assistance Loans

Objectives: To provide loans and loan guarantees for nonprofit sheltered workshops and other similar organizations to enable them to produce and provide marketable goods and services; and to assist in the establishment, acquisition, or operation of a small business owned by handicapped individuals.

Eligibility: For nonprofit organizations, must be organized under the laws of the state, or of the United States, as a nonprofit organization operating in the interests of handicapped individuals and must employ handicapped individuals not less than 75 percent of the man-hours required for the direct production of commodities or in the provision of services which it renders. For small business concerns, must be independently owned and operated, not dominant in its field, meet SBA size standards, and be 100 percent owned by handicapped individuals. Handicap must be of such a nature as to limit the individual's engaging in normal competitive business practices without SBA assistance.

Range of Financial Assistance: $500 to $350,000.

Contact: Director, Office of Business Loans, Small Business Administration, 1441 L St. N.W., Washington, DC 20416/202-653-6570.

Loans for Small Businesses

Objectives: To provide loans to small businesses owned by low-income persons or located in areas of high unemployment.

Eligibility: People with income below basic needs or businesses located in areas of high unemployment which have been denied the opportunity to acquire adequate business financing through normal landing channels on reasonable terms. The business must be independently owned and operated, and not dominant in its field and must meet SBA business size standards.

Range of Financial Assistance: $1,000 to $100,000.

Contact: Director, Office of Business Loans, Small Business Administration, 1441 L St. N.W., Washington, DC 20416/202-653-6570.

Management Assistance to Small Businesses

Objectives: To help the prospective as well as the present small business person improve skills to manage and operate a business.

Eligibility: Existing and potential small business persons and, in some cases, members of community groups are eligible. A small business is one independently owned and operated, and not dominant in its field. Veterans are eligible for all programs and under certain circumstances will receive special consideration for procurement and financial programs.

Range of Financial Assistance: Not specified.

Contact: Associate Administrator for Management Assistance, Small Business Administration, 1441 L St. N.W., Washington, DC 20416/202-653-6881.

Minority Business Development—Procurement Assistance

Objectives: To insure participation of businesses, that are owned and controlled by disadvantaged persons, in Federal contracting and establishing small manufacturing service and construction concerns that will become independent and self-sustaining.

Eligibility: A principal factor in eligibility is qualification as a disadvantaged person—persons who for reasons beyond their control, have been deprived of the opportunity to develop and maintain a position in the competitive economy because of social and economic disadvantage.

Range of Financial Assistance: Not specified.

Contact: Office of Business Development, Small Business Administration, 1441 L St. N.W., Washington, DC 20416/202-653-6813.

Office of Women's Business Ownership

Objectives: To enhance job creation potential and improve profitability among small businesses through developing effective management and financial planning skills in women entrepreneurs and improving the business environment for women-owned businesses.

Eligibility: State and local governments, any for-profit firms or nonprofit organizations are eligible. Proposals from academic institutions will not be accepted.

Range of Financial Assistance: $5,000 to $150,000.

Contact: Director, Office of Special Training and Counseling, Office of Women's Business Ownership, Small Business Administration, 1441 L St. N.W., Washington, DC 20416.

Physical Disaster Loans

Objectives: To provide loans to restore, as nearly as possible, the victims of physical-type disasters to predisaster condition.

Eligibility: Must have suffered physical property loss as a result of floods, riots or civil disturbances, or other catastrophes which occurred in an area designated as eligible for assistance by the Administration. Individuals, business concerns, including agricultural enterprises, churches, private schools, colleges and universities, and hospitals are eligible to apply for assistance.

Range of Financial Assistance: Up to $500,000.

Contact: Office of Disaster Loans, Small Business Administration, 1441 L St. N.W., Washington, DC 20416/202-653-6879.

Small Business Development Center

Objectives: To provide management counseling, training, and technical assistance to the small business community through Small Business Development Centers.

Eligibility: Administration may make grants to any State government or any agency, any State-chartered development, credit or finance corporation, and public or private institution of higher education, including a land-grant college or university.

Range of Financial Assistance: $100,000 to $2,300,000.

Contact: Small Business Administration, Small Business Development Center, 1441 L St. N.W., Room 602, Washington, DC 20416.

Small Business Energy Loans

Objectives: To assist small business concerns in financing plant construction, expansion, conversion, or startup; and in the acquisition of equipment facilities, machinery, supplies or materials to enable such concerns to manufacture, design, market, install or service specific energy measures.

Eligibility: Must be a small business concern as described in SBA regulations. Must furnish evidence of being engaged in an eligible energy measure. State and local governments not eligible.

Range of Financial Assistance: Not specified.

Contact: Office of Business Loans, Small Business Administration, 1441 L St. N.W., Washington, DC 20416/202-653-6570.

Small Business Investment Companies

Objectives: To make equity and venture capital available to the small business community with maximum use of private sector participation, and a minimum of government interference in the free market, to provide advisory services and counseling.

Eligibility: Any chartered small business investment company having a combined paid-in capital and paid-in surplus of not less than $1,000,000, having qualified management, and giving evidence of sound operations.

Range of Financial Assistance: $50,000 to $35,000,000.

Contact: Director, Office of Investment, Small Business Administration, 1441 L St. N.W., Washington, DC 20416/202-653-6879.

Small Business Loans

Objectives: To aid small businesses which are unable to obtain financing in the private credit marketplace, including agricultural enterprises.

Eligibility: A small business which is independently owned and operated and is not dominant in its field. Generally for manufacturers, average employment not in excess of 1,500; wholesalers, annual sales not over $14,500,000; retail and service concerns, revenues not over $2,000,000, and agricultural enterprises, gross annual sales not over $3,500,000.

Range of Financial Assistance: $1,000 to $350,000.

Contact: Director, Office of Business Loans, Small Business Administration, 1441 L St. N.W., Washington, DC 20416/202-653-6570.

Small Business Pollution Control Financing Guarantee

Objectives: To help small businesses meet pollution control requirements and remain competitive.

Eligibility: Must be a small business concern as described in SBA regulations. Applicant together with affiliates meets SBA size standards (industry employees limit, or assets, net worth, and annual earnings dollar limits); applicant has minimum five years in business, three of last five years profitable, has evidence from pollution control regulatory authority that pollution control facilities/equipment are acceptable.

Range of Financial Assistance: Up to $5,000,000.

Contact: Chief, Pollution Control Financing Division, Office of Special Guarantees, Small Business Administration, 4040 N. Fairfax Drive, Suite 500, Arlington, VA 22203/703-235-2902.

State and Local Development Company Loans

Objectives: To make federal funds available to state and local development companies to provide long-term financing to small business concerns located in their areas. Both state and local development companies are corporations chartered for the purpose of promoting economic growth within specific areas.

Eligibility: A state development company must be incorporated under a special state law with authority to assist small businesses throughout the state. Loans are available to local development companies which are incorporated under general state corporation statute, either on a profit, or nonprofit basis, for the purpose of promoting economic growth in a particular community within the state.

Range of Financial Assistance: $15,840 to $500,000.

Contact: Office of Business Loans, Small Business Administration, 1441 L St. N.W., Room 720, Washington, DC 20416/202-653-6570.

Veterans Loan Program

Objectives: To provide financial assistance to Vietnam-era and disabled veterans.

Eligibility: Must be a small business concern, must be owned (51% or more) by an eligible veteran and the daily operation of the business must be directed by one or more of the veteran owners. Vietnam-era veterans who served for a period of more than 180 days, between August 5, 1964 and May 7, 1975 and were honorably discharged are eligible.

Range of Financial Assistance: $1,000 to $350,000.

Contact: Director, Office of Business Loans, Small Business Administration, 1441 L St. N.W., Washington, DC 20416/202-653-6570.

Management and Technical Services

The Management and Technical Services program uses professional management and technical consultants. In some cases, due to the nature of their products and production capabilities, some small or minority businesses will require highly sophisticated marketing information and production technology to identify and service overseas markets. Such specialized export assistance may be provided at no cost to an eligible client through this program. Since the availability of these counseling services will vary, more specific information is available from the local SBA Field Office, or from: the Minority Small Business Office, Small Business Administration, 1441 L St. N.W., Room 602, Washington, DC 20416/202-653-6475.

Management Assistance Publications

Management assistance publications are available on a variety of subjects concerning specific management problems and various aspects of business operations. Most of these publications are available from the Small Business Administration free of charge. Others are sold by the Government Printing Office. For a list of these and for additional information, contact: call toll-free 800-368-5855 or for additional information, Publications, Public Communications, Small Business Administration, 1441 L St. N.W, Room 100, Washington, DC 20416/202-653-7561.

Minority Business Development

Regional and district SBA staff members cooperate with local business development organizations and explain to potential minority entrepreneurs how SBA services and programs can help them become successful business owners. Contact your regional and district SBA office, or: Minority Small Business and Capital Ownership Development, Small Business Administration, 1441 L St. N.W., Room 602, Washington, DC 20416/202-653-6407.

Minority Enterprise Small Business Investment Companies (MESBICs)

MESBICs provide venture capital to minority-owned small businesses. Venture capital is provided in the form of equity capital convertible debentures (long-term loans which can be converted into equity capital) or long-term loans. Lists of MESBICs are available at SBA Branch and District Offices. To receive these lists or for additional information on MESBICs, contact: Office of Investment, Small Business Administration, 1441 L St. N.W., 8th Floor, Washington, DC 20416/202-653-6584.

Pollution Control Financing

Assistance is available to highly qualified small businesses to finance pollution control facilities. Contact: Pollution Control, Financing Branch, Office of Special Guarantee, Small Business Administration, 4040 N. Fairfax Dr., Room 500 Webb, Arlington, VA 22203/703-235-2902.

Prime Contracts

Government purchasing offices set aside some contracts or portions of contracts for exclusive bidding by small businesses. SBA Procurement Center representatives stationed at major military and civilian procurement installations recommend additional "set asides," refer small businesses to federal contracting officers, assist small concerns with contracting problems, and recommend relaxation of unduly restrictive specifications. Contact: Nearest SBA Field Office (See list of SBA Field Offices this section). For additional information Prime Contracts Division, Procurement Assistance, Small Business Administrative, 1441 L St. N.W., Room 634, Washington, DC 20416/202-653-6826.

Private Sector Initiatives Office

This office functions as a broker to assist organizations involved in economic development that will aid small businesses. The office works with state and local governments, agencies, universities and large or small firms, both actively and through referrals or public relations efforts. Contact: Office of Private Sector Initiatives, U.S. Small Business Administration, 1441 L St. N.W., Washington, DC 20416/202-653-7880.

Procurement Assistance
Counsel on how to prepare bids and obtain prime contracts and subcontracts, how to get your business name on bidders' lists and related services such as supplying leads on research and development projects and new technology is available. Contact: SBA Regional Offices, or Procurement Assistance, Small Business Administration, 1441 L St. N.W., Room 600, Washington, DC 20416/202-653-6635.

Procurement Automated Source System (PASS)
PASS makes available a master list of small companies capable of performing work on federal contracts and subcontracts. This computerized system lists the names of small companies and their capabilities to assist federal procurement officers and procurement officials at private contractors in awarding contract and subcontract federal work to small businesses. Many other federal agencies use PASS. Small businesses interested in participating in PASS can get appropriate forms at any SBA office. For further information, contact: Procurement Automated Source System, Procurement Assistance, Small Business Administration, 1441 L St. N.W., Room 628, Washington, DC 20416/202-653-6586.

Property Sales Assistance
The Small Business Administration works with government agencies which sell surplus real and personal property and natural resources to insure that small businesses have an opportunity to buy a fair share of them. SBA also insures that small firms operating in energy-related industries obtain an equitable portion of federal energy-related mineral lease contracts. Contact: Office of Natural Resource Sales Assistance, Procurement and Technical Assistance, Small Business Administration, 1441 L St. N.W., Room 622, Washington, DC 20416/202-653-6078.

Service Corps of Retired Executives (SCORE)
Retired business executives volunteer their time and services to help small businesses solve their operating and management problems. Assigned SCORE counselors visit the owners in their places of business to analyze the problems and offer help. Contact: National SCORE Office, Room 410, 1129 20th St. N.W., Washington, DC 20416/202-653-6279.

Small Business Administration Loans (7a)
No special programs exist for any ethnic group. Anyone is eligible for the 7a loan who obtains SBA general Credit Criteria and has been declined by two banks for the loan they are requesting. The Small Business Administration also guarantees loans made by banks up to 90% of the loan amount. Contact: Nearest SBA Field Office (See list of SBA Field Offices this section).

Small Business Data Base
This Data Base contains data about the trends and conditions of individual segments of the small business community or of the sector as a whole. Included are annual statistics on employment and sales for 3.9 million enterprises, and key balance sheet information for over 900,000 firms. Contact: Office of Economic Research, Office of Advocacy, Small Business Administration, 1100 Vermont Ave. N.W., Room 1100 VTB, Washington, DC 20416/202-634-4885.

Small Business Development Centers
Individual counseling and practical training are available for small business owners. Small Business Development Centers draw from resources of local, state and federal government programs, the private sector and university facilities to provide managerial and technical help, research studies and other types of specialized assistance of value to small businesses. Contact: Office of Small Business Development Centers, Management Assistance, Small Business Administration, 1441 L St. N.W., Room 317, Washington, DC 20416/202-653-6768.

Small Business Economic Research
This office promotes an extramural small business economic research program. Some areas of research interest include fiscal and monetary issues; public finance; managerial economics; industrial organizations; market imperfections and competitive disequilibrium; special needs of women and minority business owners; small business data base; and dynamic studies. *Small Business Economic Research Program Announcement* is available. Contact: Office of Economic Research, Office of the Chief Counsel for Advocacy, Small Business Administration, 1100 Vermont Ave. N.W., Room 1100, Washington, DC 20416/202-634-4885.

Small Business Field Offices

REGION I

60 Batterymarch Street, 10th Floor, Boston, MA 02110/617-223-3204

150 Causeway St., 10th Floor, Boston, MA 02114/617-223-3224

1550 Main Street, Springfield, MA 01103/413-785-0268

40 Western Avenue, Room 512, Augusta, ME 04330/207-622-8378

55 Pleasant Street, Room 211, Concord, NH 03301/603-224-4041

One Hartford Square West, Hartford, CT 06106/203-722-3600

87 State Street, Room 204, Montpelier, VT 05602/802-229-0538

380 Westminster Mall, Providence, RI 02903/401-351-7500

REGION II

26 Federal Plaza, Room 29-118, New York, NY 10278/212-264-7772

26 Federal Plaza, Room 3100, New York, NY 10278/212-264-4355

35 Pinelawn Road, Room 102E, Melville, NY 11747/516-454-0750

Carlos Chardon Avenue, Room 691, Hato Rey, PR 00919/809-753-4002

Veterans Drive, Room 283, St. Thomas, VI 00801/809-774-8530

60 Park Place, 4th Floor, Newark, NJ 07102/201-645-2434

100 South Clinton Street, Room 1071, Syracuse, NY 13260/315-423-5383

111 West Huron Street, Room 1311, Buffalo, NY 14202/716-846-4301

333 East Water Street, Elmira, NY 14901/607-733-4686

REGION III

231 St. Asaphs Rd., Suite 400, Philadelphia, PA 19004/215-596-5889

100 Chestnut Street, Suite 309, Harrisburg, PA 17101/717-782-3840

20 North Pennsylvania Avenue, Wilkes-Barre, PA 18701/717-826-6497

844 King Street, Room 5207, Wilmington, DE 19801/302-573-6294

109 North 3rd St., Room 302, Clarksburg, WV 26301/304-623-5631

628 Charleston National Plaza, Charleston, WV 25301/304-347-5220

960 Penn Avenue, 5th Floor, Pittsburgh, PA 15222/412-644-2780

400 North 8th Street, Room 3015, Richmond, VA 23240/804-771-2617

8600 LaSalle Road, Room 630, Towson, MD 21204/301-962-4392

1111 18th Street, N.W., 6th Floor, Washington, DC 20036/202-634-4950

REGION IV

1375 Peachtree St., N.E., 5th Floor, Atlanta, GA 30367/404-881-4999

1720 Peachtree Road, N.W., 6th Floor, Atlanta, GA 30309/404-881-4749

908 South 20th St., Room 202, Birmingham, AL 35205/205-254-1344

230 S. Tryon Street, Room 700, Charlotte, NC 28202/704-371-6563

1835 Assembly, 3rd Floor, Columbia, SC 29202/803-765-5376

100 West Capitol Street, Suite 322, Jackson, MS 39269/601-960-4378

111 Fred Haise Blvd., 2nd Floor, Biloxi, MS 39530/601-435-3676

400 West Bay Street, Room 261, Jacksonville, FL 32202/904-791-3782

600 Federal Place, Room 188, Louisville, KY 40201/502-582-5971

2222 Ponce De Leon Boulevard, 5th Floor, Miami, FL 33134/305-350-5521

404 James Robertson Parkway, Suite 1012, Nashville, TN 37219/615-251-5881

REGION V

219 South Dearborn Street, Room 838, Chicago, IL 60604/312-353-0359

219 South Dearborn Street, Room 437, Chicago, IL 60604/312-353-4528

1240 East 9th Street, Room 317, Cleveland, OH 44199/216-552-4180

85 Marconi Boulevard, Columbus, OH 43215/614-469-6860

550 Main Street, Room 5028, Cincinnati, OH 45202/513-684-2814

477 Michigan Avenue, Room 515, Detroit, MI 48226/313-226-6075

220 West Washington Street, Room 310, Marquette, MI 49885/906-225-1108

575 North Pennsylvania Street, Room 578, Indianapolis, IN 46204/317-269-7272

501 East Monroe Street, Room 160, South Bend, IN 46601/219-232-8361

212 East Washington Ave., Room 213, Madison, WI 53703/608-264-5261

310 West Wisconsin Ave., Room 400, Milwaukee, WI 53203/414-291-3941

100 North 6th Street, Suite 610, Minneapolis, MN 55403/612-349-3550

Four North, Old State Capital Plaza, Springfield, IL 62701/217-492-4416

REGION VI

8625 King George Drive, Bldg. C, Dallas, TX 75235/214-767-7643

1100 Commerce Street, Room 3036, Dallas, TX 75242/214-767-0605

4100 Rio Bravo, Suite 300, El Paso, TX 79902/915-543-7586

221 West Lancaster Ave., Room 1007, Ft. Worth, TX 76102/817-334-5463

5000 Marble Avenue, N.E., Room 320, Albuquerque, NM 87100/505-766-3430

222 East Van Buren Street, Room 500, Harlingen, TX 78550/512-423-8934

400 Mann Street, Suite 403, Corpus Christi, TX 78408/512-888-3331

2525 Murworth, Room 112, Houston, TX 77054/713-660-4401

320 West Capitol Avenue, Room 601, Little Rock, AR 72201/501-378-5871

1611 Tenth Street, Suite 200, Lubbock, TX 79401/806-762-7466

1661 Canal Street, Suite 2000, New Orleans, LA 70112/504-589-6685

200 N.W. 5th Street, Suite 670, Oklahoma City, OK 73102/405-231-4301

727 East Durango Street, Room A-513, San Antonio, TX 78206/512-229-6250

300 East 8th Street, Room 780, Austin, TX 78701/512-482-5288

911 Walnut Street, 3rd Floor, Kansas City, MO 64106/816-374-5288

818 Grande Avenue, Kansas City, MO 64106/816-374-3419

309 North Jefferson, Room 150, Springfield, MO 65803/417-864-7670

373 Collins Road N.E., Cedar Rapids, IA 52402/319-399-2571

210 Walnut St., Room 749, Des Moines, IA 50309/515-284-4422

300 South 19th Street, Omaha, NB 68102/402-221-4691

815 Olive Street, Room 242, St. Louis, MO 63101/314-425-6600

110 East Waterman Street, Wichita, KS 67202/316-269-6571

1405 Curtis Street, 22nd Floor, Denver, CO 80202/303-844-5441

721 19th Street, Room 407, Denver, CO 80202/303-844-2607

100 East B Street, Room 4001, Casper, WY 82602/307-261-5761

657 2nd Avenue, North, Room 218, Fargo, ND 58108/701-237-5771

301 South Park, Room 528, Helena, MT 59626/406-449-5381

125 South State Street, Room 2237, Salt Lake City, UT 84138/314-524-5800

101 South Main Avenue, Suite 101, Sioux Falls, SD 57102/605-336-2980

450 Golden Gate Avenue, Room 15307, San Francisco, CA 94102/415-556-7487

211 Main Street, 4th Floor, San Francisco, CA 94105/415-556-0642

2202 Monterey Street, Room 108, Fresno, CA 93721/209-487-5189

660 J Street, Room 215, Sacramento, CA 95814/916-440-4461

301 East Steward Street, Las Vegas, NV 89125/702-385-6611

300 Ala Moana, Room 2213, Honolulu, HI 96850/671-472-7277

350 S. Figueroa Street, 6th Floor, Los Angeles, CA 90071/213-688-2956

2700 North Main Street, Room 400, Santa Ana, CA 92701/714-836-2494

3030 North Central Avenue, Suite 1201, Phoenix, AZ 85012/602-241-2200

880 Front Street, Room 4-S-29, San Diego, CA 85701/619-293-5540

2615 4th Avenue, Room 440, Seattle, WA 98121/206-442-5676

915 Second Avenue, Room 1792, Seattle, WA 98174/206-442-5534

701 C Street, Room 1068, Anchorage, AK 99501/907-271-4022

101 12th Avenue, Fairbanks, AK 99701/907-452-0211

1005 Main St., 2nd Floor, Boise, ID 83701/208-334-1696

1220 S.W. Third Avenue, Room 676, Portland, OR 97204/503-221-5221

920 Riverside Avenue, Room 651, Spokane, WA 99210/509-456-5310

Small Business Innovation Research (SBIR)

This program stimulates technological innovation, encourages small science and technology-based firms to participate in government-funded research, and provides incentives for converting research results into commercial applications. The program provides funding and technical assistance in both the Research and Product Development stages, and assistance in obtaining private sector financing in the Commercialization stage. Businesses of 500 or fewer employees that are organized for profit are eligible to compete for SBIR funding. Twelve federal agencies are required by law to participate. Contact:

U.S. Small Business Administration
Office of Innovation, Research and Technology
1441 L St. N.W.
Room 500-A
Washington, DC 20416
202-653-6458

Department of Agriculture
Office of Grants and Program Systems
Department of Agriculture
1300 Rosslyn Commonwealth Building
Suite 103
Arlington, VA 22209
703-235-2628

Department of Defense
Small Business and Economic Utilization
Office of Secretary of Defense
Room 2A340 Pentagon
Washington, DC 20301
202-697-9383

Department of Energy
SBIR Program
U.S. Department of Energy
Washington, DC 20545
301-353-5867

Department of Health and Human Services
Office of Small and Disadvantaged Business Utilization
Department of Health and Human Services
200 Independence Ave. S.W.
Room 513D
Washington, DC 20201
202-245-7300

Department of Interior
Bureau of Mines
U.S. Department of the Interior
2401 E St. N.W.
Washington, DC 20241
202-634-1305

Department of Transportation
Transportation System Center
Department of Transportation
Kendall Square
Cambridge, MA 02142
617-494-2222

Environmental Protection Agency
Office of Research Grants and Centers (RD-675)
Office of Research and Development
Evironmental Protection Agency
401 M St. S.W.
Washington, DC 20460
202-382-5744

National Aeronautics and Space Administration
National Aeronautics and Space Administration
SBIR Office-Code R
600 Independence Ave. S.W.
Washington, DC 20546
202-755-2306

National Science Foundation
SBIR Program Managers
National Science Foundation
1800 G St. N.W.
Washington, DC 20550
202-357-7527

Nuclear Regulatory Commission
Administration and Resource Staff
Office of Nuclear Regulatory Research
Nuclear Regulatory Commission
Washington, DC 20555
301-427-4301

Department of Education
The Brown Building
Room 722
1900 M St. N.W.
Washington, DC 20208
202-254-8247

Small Business Institute
Extended personal counseling is offered to small business owners, at no charge. This resource is available through the cooperation of faculty, senior and graduate students and business schools. For additional information, contact: Small Business Institute, Office of Management Counseling Services, Management Assistance, Small Business Administration, 1441 L St. N.W., Room 317, Washington, DC 20416/202-653-6338.

Small Business Investment Companies (SBICs)
The Small Business Administration licenses, regulates and provides financial assistance to small business investment companies and licensees. The sole function of these investment companies is to provide venture capital in the form of equity financing, long-term loan funds, and management services to small business concerns. *SBIC Industry Review,* an annual, provides summaries and analyses of SBIC data, showing the status and progress of the industry. Contact: Office of Invest-

ment, Small Business Administration, 1441 L St. N.W., 8th Floor, Washington, DC 20416/202-653-6584.

Small Business Management Training Films
A list of training films is available on the following topics: advertising/sales promotion; credit and collection; crime prevention; customer relations; financial management; inventory management; foreign trade; marketing; motivation; personnel; planning; recordkeeping; relocation; selling; site selection; time management; and women in business. To borrow films contact: Nearest SBA Field Office (See list of SBA Field Offices this section). To purchase films contact: National Audio Visual Center, ATTN: Order Section, Washington, DC 20409/301-763-1891.

Small Business as Contractors Data Base
The Procurement Automated Source System (PASS) is a centralized inventory and referral system of small businesses interested in being a prime contractor for federal agencies or a subcontractor for companies. More than 72,000 firms nationwide are listed in the fields of research and development, manufacturing, construction and services. PASS uses a keyword system which identifies the capabilities of the company. The system can be searched for firms by geographic location, type of ownership, labor surplus area, zip code, minority type and over 3,000 keywords. Anyone seeking to purchase a product or service from a small business can contact SBA to have a search run. Searches and printouts are provided free of charge. Small firms can be listed in PASS at no charge. Contact: Your local SBA office OR, Procurement Automated Source System, Small Business Administration, 1441 L St. N.W., Room 627, Washington, DC 20416/202-653-6586.

Starting and Managing Series Publications
This series is designed to hellp the small entrepreneur start a business. *Starting and Managing a Small Business of Your Own* deals with the subject in general terms. Each of the other volumes deals with one type of business in detail. The general booklet is available for $3.50 from the Superintendent of Documents, Government Printing Office, Washington, DC 20402/202-783-3238. For additional information, contact: Nearest SBA Field Office (See list of SBA Field Offices this section).

Subcontracting Assistance Program
The Small Business Administration develops subcontracting opportunities for small businesses by maintaining close contact with prime contractors. It is the means by which SBA endeavors to assure that small business concerns are afforded maximum practicable opportunities to participate, as sub-contractors, in the performance of contracts let by any federal agency. Contact: Subcontracting

Assistance, Procurement Assistance, Small Business Administration, 1441 L St. N.W., Room 622, Washington, DC 20416/202-653-6661.

Surety Bonds
The Small Business Administration makes the bonding process accessible to small and emerging contractors who, for whatever reasons, find bonding unavailable to them. SBA accomplishes this by bonds for private sureties. The bonds may be used for construction, supplies or services provided by either a prime or subcontractor for government or nongovernment work. For further information contact: nearest SBA field office (see list of SBA field offices this section). The bonds may be used for construction, supplies or services provided by either a prime or subcontractor for government or nongovernment work. Contact: Surety Bond Guarantee Division, Office of Special Guarantees, Investment, Small Business Administration, 4040 N. Fairfax Dr., Arlington, VA 22203/703-235-2907.

Technical Assistance
Small Business Development Centers (SBDC)'s are the result of a three-way cooperative agreement between the federal government, a state's Governor's office, and educational institutions. Centers exist in approximately 40 states and part of their role is to provide technical assistance to small businesses through counselling, training, and economic development activities. Small business-owners or potential entrepreneurs can use their state's SBDC's service for little or no cost. Call your local SBA office of SBDC listed in the phone book under "U.S. Government, Small Business Administration" or contact: Small Business Administration, 1441 L St. N.W., Suite 317, Washington, DC 20416/202-653-6768.

Timber Sales
The federal government regularly sells timber from the federal forests. The Small Business Administration, with other federal agencies, sets aside timber sales for bidding by small concerns when it appears that, under open sales, small businesses would not obtain a fair share at reasonable prices. For further information, contact: Office of Natural Resources Sales Assistance, Procurement and Technical Assistance, 1441 L St. N.W., Room 632, Washington, DC 20416/202-653-6078.

U.S. Purchasing and Sales Directory
This directory lists the products and services bought by the military departments, with a separate listing for civilian agencies. It includes an explanation of the ways in which SBA can help a business obtain government prime contracts and subcontracts, data on government sales of surplus property, and comprehensive descriptions of the scope of the government market for research and development. Contact: Prime Contracts Division, Office of Procurement and Technical Assistance, Small Business Administration, 1441 L St. N.W., Room 632, Washington, DC 20416/202-653-6826.

Women in Business
All of the Small Business Administration loan, loan guarantee, management assistance, procurement assistance, and advocacy programs are available to women-owned businesses. *Women's Handbook: How SBA Can Help You Go Into Business* is a free booklet with information on the services offered by SBA to women starting new businesses. It also provides general guidelines for women thinking of going into business on their own. There is an assigned Women's Representative in every SBA Regional and District Office. Information and assistance are provided by the Women's Representative in the nearest field office. Contact: Nearest Field Office (See list of SBA Field Offices this section).

How Can the Small Business Administration Help You?
To determine how the Small Business Administration can help you, contact: Office of Public Affairs, Small Business Administration, 1441 L St. N.W., Washington, DC 20416/202-653-6832.

Tennessee Valley Authority

400 West Summit Hill Drive, Knoxville, TN 37902/615-632-8000

Established: May 13, 1933
Budget: $1,165,967,000.
Employees: 22,760

Mission: Conducts a unified program of resource development for the advancement of economic growth in the Tennessee Valley region. Activities include flood control, navigation development, electric power production, fertilizer development, recreational improvement, and forestry and wildlife development. (While its power program is financially self-supporting, other programs are financed primarily by appropriations from Congress.)

Major Sources of Information

Agricultural and Chemical Development
The Office of Agricultural and Chemical Development plans and manages programs for research in and development of new and improved fertilizers and processes for their manufacture, for testing and demonstrating methods of chemical and organic fertilizer use as an aid to soil and water conservation and to the improved use of agricultural and related resources, and for operating and maintaining facilities to serve as a national laboratory for research and development in chemistry and chemical engineering related to fertilizers and munitions essential to national defense. The Office also plans and manages programs for the preservation and enhancement of the Valley's agricultural resources and soil conservation; for demonstration of new and improved agricultural methods, placing emphasis on the Valley's small and limited resource farmers; and for readjustment of agricultural areas affected by TVA operations. Contact: Office of Agricultural and Chemical Development, Tennessee Valley Authority, National Fertilizer Development Center, Muscle Shoals Reservation, Muscle Shoals, AL 35660/205-386-2601.

Air Quality
The TVA is working on a massive air pollution control program. Several methods are being used at different power plants to reduce sulfur dioxide and fly ash emissions to the levels required. In addition to large purchases of medium- and low-sulfur Eastern coal supplies, the program includes flue gas scrubbers to remove sulfur dioxide at some plants, coal-cleaning plants, and new electrostatic precipitators or fabric filter baghouses for increased control of fly ash emissions. *How Clean is Our Air?* is a water quality report which notes that air pollution in four of the region's largest cities—Knoxville, Nashville, Memphis, and Chattanooga—exceeded standards established to protect public health. The report also says that air pollution in 38 nonurban and rural Tennessee Valley counties exceeded standards for particulates, ozone, or sulfur dioxide. Contact: Air Quality Board, Office of Natural Resources and Economic Development, Tennessee Valley Authority, Multipurpose Building, Knoxville, TN 37901/615-632-2101.

Aquatic Weeds

TVA's two major weapons for controlling the spread of such pesky aquatic plants as Eurasian watermilfoil, spiney-leaf naiad, and hydrilla in its reservoirs is the fluctuation of reservoir levels and the selective spraying of herbicides. Reservoir levels may be lowered several feet in the late summer to dry out and kill the roots of these plants embedded in shallow areas of the reservoirs. At other times, lake levels may be held higher than normal to prevent sunshine from penetrating to the bottom and thus prevent germination and growth of new colonies. Selective use of approved herbicides on heavily infested areas is another effective control method. Several experimental control strategies also are being tested on TVA lakes. One of the most promising is the use of the weed-eating white amur fish in a 400-acre embayment that has been screened off from the main body of one of the reservoirs. Some 4,000 sterilized female fish have been released in the weed infested embayment to test their effectiveness as a control measure. The use of desirable native plants to choke out the undesirable plants is another method being tested for its effectiveness. Contact: Fisheries and Aquatic Ecologies, Division of Air and Water Resources, Office of Natural Resources, Tennessee Valley Authority, 400 W. Summit Hill Dr., Knoxville, TN 37921/615-632-6770.

Atmospheric Fluidized Bed Combustion

Atmospheric fluidized bed combustion burns pulverized coal at high temperatures in a bed of limestone particles. Sulfur dioxide released from the burning coal during combustion reacts with the limestone to form calcium sulfate, which is removed from the bottom of the boiler rather than escaping into the atmosphere. The process holds promise for burning high-sulfur coal—abundant in or near the Tennessee Valley—while still meeting air quality standards. Contact: Fluidized Bed Combustion Projects, Energy Demonstrations and Technology Division, Power and Engineering Program, Tennessee Valley Authority, Chestnut Street Tower II, 6th and Chestnut Sts., Room 1020, Chattanooga, TN 37401/615-751-7458.

Board of Directors

The Board of Directors is vested with all the powers of the Corporation. The Board establishes general policies and programs; reviews and appraises progress and results; approves projects and specific items which are of major importance, involve important external relations, or otherwise require Board approval; approves the annual budget; and establishes the basic organization through which programs and policies are executed. Citizens also can and do write the TVA Board of Directors and the General Manager, collectively and individually. Although the Board fully expects the TVA staff to investigate and handle suggestions and complaints courteously and expeditiously, they certainly want to hear if matters have not been satisfactorily resolved. Contact: Board of Directors, Tennessee Valley Authority, 400 W. Summit Hill Ave., Room #12A7, Knoxville, TN 37902/615-632-2531.

Citizen Action Line

A toll-free line has been established for Tennessee Valley residents who wish to get a question answered quickly or make a complaint. Each complaint is independently investigated. Residents can call to obtain information about camping opportunities, the availability of recreation maps, lake levels, and dozens of other subjects. They can call to express their views on TVA programs, all of which are promptly passed on to the TVA Board and the TVA offices directly involved. Contact: Citizen Action Office, Tennessee Valley Authority, 400 W. Summit Hill Ave., Room EPB20, Knoxville, TN 37902/615-632-4100. The lines are open to all seven TVA states—Tennessee, Mississippi, Georgia, Alabama, Kentucky, North Carolina, and Virginia. The toll-free numbers are: 800-362-9250 in Tennessee (outside the Knoxville area); 800-251-9242 (outside Tennessee).

Citizens' Guide to TVA

This is a free brochure which gives an overview of the major TVA offices. It also provides addresses and phone numbers of the district administrators. Contact: Citizen Action Office, Tennessee Valley Authority, 400 W. Summit Hill Ave., Room EPB6, Knoxville, TN 37902/615-632-4402.

Coal Energy Research

TVA's energy programs emphasize three of the most promising technologies for better use of coal. These are fuel cells using gas from coal, fluidized bed combustion, and advanced sulfur dioxide control processes for conventional coal-fired boilers. Contact: Energy Demonstrations and Technology Division, Power and Engineering Program, Tennessee Valley Authority, Chestnut St. Tower II, 6th and Chestnut Sts., Room 1000, Chattanooga, TN 37401/615-751-4573.

Commercial and Industrial Conservation

The conservation program for businesses, industries and other nonresidential power users offers in-depth energy conservation audits to these power users, with loans available for those businesses and industries who carry out measures recommended in the audits. Contact: Conservation and Energy Management Division, Power and Engineering Program, Energy Conservation and Rates Division, Office of Power, Tennessee Valley Authority, 540 Market St., Chattanooga, TN 37401/615-751-6323.

Community and Industrial Development

For information on community and industrial development, and regional planning, contact: Policy Development, Office of Community Development, Tennessee Valley Authority, Walnut St., Knoxville, TN 37902/615-632-4852.

Community Development

Community-oriented programs are planned and conducted to increase citizen participation in the realization of the Valley's sociologic and economic development. Programs provide technical assistance in community planning and in the accomplishment of orderly and balanced development of industry in the Valley. Contact: Land and Economic Division, Office of Natural Resources and Economic Development, TVA, 400 W. Summit Hill Drive, Knoxville, TN 37921/615-632-4635.

Dams and Steam Plants

The Tennessee Valley Authority has constructed a system of dams and reservoirs to promote navigation on the Tennessee River and its tributaries, and to control destructive flood waters in the Tennessee and Mississippi drainage basins. These dams and reservoirs also produce power. A free map showing TVA dams and steam plants and including important facts about each of them is available. Contact: Information, Tennessee Valley Authority, 400 W. Summit Drive, Room E3D92, Knoxville, TN 37902/615-632-8000, or Washington Representative, Tennessee Valley Authority, 412 1st St., Room 300, Washington, DC 20444/202-245-0101. There is also a Toll-Free Action Line for Tennessee Valley residents: 800-362-9250 in Tennessee; 800-251-9242 in other Valley states.

District Administrators

These seven district administrators oversee all field activities within their areas and act as liaison between local residents and the TVA Board:

Alabama District, Tennessee Valley Authority, 529 First Federal Building, Florence, AL 35630/205-767-4620.

Appalachian District, Tennessee Valley Authority, 4105 Fort Henry Dr., 207 Heritage Federal Building, Kingsport, TN 37663/615-239-5981.

Central District, Tennessee Valley Authority, 1719 West End Building, Suite 100, Nashville, TN 37203/615-327-0643.

Kentucky District, Tennessee Valley Authority, 115 Hammond Plaza, Hopkinsville, KY 42240/502-885-3398.

Mississippi District, Tennessee Valley Authority, 1014 North Gloster, P. O. Box 1623, Tupelo, MS 38801/601-842-5825.

Southeastern District, Tennessee Valley Authority, 68 Mouse Creek Rd., Cleveland, TN 37311/615-476-9131.

Western District, Tennessee Valley Authority, 1804 Watkins Towers, Suite 100, Box 1788, Jackson, TN 38301/901-668-6088.

Electric Power Supply and Rates

For information on electric power supply and rates, contact: Division of Energy Use, Power and Engineering Program, TVA, 535 Chestnut Street Towers II, Chattanooga, TN 37401/615-751-5694.

Energy Publications

TVA provides, at no cost, publications on energy for studies and the public. They contain general information on the Tennessee Valley Authority and specific information on such subjects as dams and steam plants, nuclear power, solar energy, energy alternatives, and energy conservation including buying guides for appliances. Contact: Publications, Tennessee Valley Authority, 400 Commerce Ave., Room EPA1C-K, Knoxville, TN 37902/615-632-8040.

Environmental/Energy Education

Much of TVA's environmental education effort is accomplished through university-based environmental education centers. TVA worked with several universities and colleges across the Valley to develop environmental education teaching aids and programs for schools plus workshops for teachers. In addition, TVA offers teacher workshops and interpretive programs for other groups at its Nolichucky Waterfowl Sanctuary and Environmental Study Area near Greeneville, TN. Nolichucky is an old hydroelectric project, retired in 1972. TVA has completed conversion of the old powerhouse into an energy conservation and education center, complete with classroom and an "indoor trail" which winds along the powerhouse's interior, telling the story of energy production and conservation. An outdoor trail system at Nolichucky was also completed in 1979. Contact: Environmental/Energy Education, Land and Economic Resources Division, Office of Natural Resources and Economic Development, Tennessee Valley Authority, Norris, TN 37828/615-632-6450.

Environmental Quality

The Environmental Quality Staff serves as the focal point for TVA's "environmental conscience." The staff works at a policymaking level and its responsibilities include administration of the National Environmental Policy Act within TVA, planning and coordinating the agency's environmental programs, and the development of new environmental initiatives. EQS focuses on policy implications of programs and projects which are likely to set precedents or are especially significant. Contact: Environmental Quality Staff, Office of Natural Resources and Economic Development, Tennessee Valley Authority, 400 W. Summit Hill Drive, Knoxville, TN 37901/615-632-6578.

Fertilizer Research and Development

At its National Fertilizer Development Center, TVA operates the world's leading facility for developing new fertilizer technology. Major objectives of this program have been to reduce energy requirements for fertilizer production and increase the efficiency of fertilizer use. Contact: National Fertilizer Development Center, Office of Agriculture and Chemical Development, Tennessee Valley Authority, Muscle Shoals Reservation, Muscle Shoals, AL 35660/205-386-2593.

Fertilizer Technology
Most U.S. fertilizers are made with the aid of TVA technology. TVA patents its new developments and then issues licenses to interested companies for nonexclusive use of the patented developments. New TVA technology is also spread throughout the Nation and the world by technical visitors to the National Fertilizer Development Center. TVA manufactures small tonnages of experimental fertilizers at Muscle Shoals for distribution and testing throughout the United States. This program insures that new fertilizer developments get a fair chance of being accepted by the fertilizer industry and farmers. Contact: Office of Agriculture and Chemical Development, Tennessee Valley Authority, National Fertilizer Development Center, Muscle Shoals Reservation, Muscle Shoals, AL 35660/205-386-2593.

Films
The following TVA films can be borrowed at no charge:

FILMS OF GENERAL INTEREST
The Valley—reflecting the changing attitudes of the late 1970s and early 1980s, this film gives an overview of TVA while addressing energy issues, environmental concerns, and the need for job opportunities in the Tennessee Valley. In frank discussions, TVA officials and citizens of the region grapple with the complex issues they face together.
The Valley of the Tennessee (1944)—The problems and attitudes of the farm population in the mid-1930s are the centerpiece of this story of TVA.

CONSTRUCTION FILMS
Power from Paradise—in western Kentucky, TVA completed in 1963 a coal-burning steam plant with the two largest turbogenerators in the world. With colorful photography, the construction story is made interesting to laymen as well as specialists.
Superhighways for Power—TVA's construction of one of the Nation's first EHV (extra-high-voltage) transmission lines, a 500,000-volt line from Johnsonville to Memphis in western Tennessee.

FILMS ON SPECIAL SUBJECTS
Shell Mounds in the Tennessee Valley—along the Tennessee River, mounds of shells marked the villages of prehistoric inhabitants. The film describes archaeologic work in a TVA reservoir area prior to impoundment.
Strip Mined Land Can Be Reclaimed—coal is America's most abundant fuel, and strip mining is often the only economically feasible way to extract it. TVA has long advocated legislation that would require mine opera-

tors to reclaim strip mined land, and in this film demonstrates what can—and has—been done to restore such land after mining.

Contact: Film Services, Tennessee Valley Authority, Knoxville, TN 37902/615-632-8040.

Flood Damage Prevention
TVA's local flood damage prevention program is designed to help communities avoid flood damages through a variety of measures, with heavy emphasis on nonstructural remedies such as floodplain zoning, flood proofing, and flood insurance. Contact: Floodplain Management, Division of Air and Water Resources, Office of National Resources and Economic Development, TVA, 400 W. Summit Hill Drive, Knoxville, TN 37901/615-632-4017.

Freedom of Information Act Requests
For Freedom of Information Act requests, contact: Director of Information, Tennessee Valley Authority, 400 W. Summit Hill Drive, Knoxville, TN 37902/615-632-6315.

Home Insulation Program
The program provides energy conservation surveys in the home without charge, with written recommendations on how consumers can make homes more energy-efficient. Interest-free loans are available through TVA distributors to finance weatherization measures with payback spread out over several years as part of the electric bill. Contact: Division of Conservation and Energy Management, Office of Energy Use, Tennessee Valley Authority, 540 Market St., Chattanooga, TN 37401/615-751-2061.

Land Between The Lakes
Land Between The Lakes is a 40-mile-long peninsula located between Kentucky and Barkley Lakes in west Kentucky and Tennessee. In its 20th year of operation, Land Between The Lakes is managed by TVA to provide an outstanding outdoor recreation experience as well as a living laboratory for the study of fundamental conservation and resource use principles. A living history farm exhibit called "Homeplace-1850," recreates life as it existed on a typical farmstead in the area before the Civil War. Exhibitors tend crops and animals, prepare meals and perform hundreds of other farm chores in the same manner as their forebears. TVA offers recreation programs at Land Between The Lakes for everyone, but tailors many programs to groups with special needs. Contact: Land Between The Lakes, Office of Natural Resources and Economic Development, Tennessee Valley Authority, Golden Pond, Kentucky 42231/502-924-5602.

Load Management
TVA and power distributors are trying out a

number of ways to flatten out the peaks in power demand that require the use of more expensive generating facilities. One of these load management demonstrations involves remote "cycling" of hot water heaters and space-conditioning units in homes. TVA is also testing three separate methods of heat storage in the home. This concept puts to work electricity generated at night, when demands are lowest, to produce heat, which is stored for use in the day. Some new and existing homes are being used to test the offpeak storage systems, which include pressurized water, special ceramic brick, and a eutectic salt solution heat storage system. Contact: Load Management, Division of Conservation and Energy Management, Office of Energy Use, Tennessee Valley Authority, Chattanooga, TN 37401/615-751-2061.

Maps and Charts

Recreation maps of TVA lakes which indicate detailed routes to shoreline recreation areas are available. Single copies are free on request. Each request should specify the lake(s) of interest. Navigation charts and maps for the major lakes have also been published by TVA. They show water depths, the location of public recreation areas, boat docks, resorts, and roads. Charts for the mainstream lakes of the Tennessee River show navigation channels, buoys, lights, and other navigation aids. Maps for tributary lakes show the numbered signs TVA has installed at strategic locations on shore to aid fishermen and recreation boaters in locating their position. Navigation maps and charts may be purchased from TVA Maps, Knoxville, TN 37902/615-632-2357, or Chattanooga, TN 37401/615-755-2133, or use the hotline: 800-362-9250 in Tennessee; 800-251-9242 outside Tennessee.

Natural Resources Program

Programs are aimed at providing the people of the region with the multiple benefits of timber, wildlife, fish, and associated recreation and environmental amenities such as clear air and water, healthy vegetation, stable soil, natural beauty, environmental education, and protection of historic and archaeologic resources. There are also programs for water resources conservation, development, and management; waste treatment and disposal; and biologic vector and aquatic plant control. Contact: Office of Natural Resources and Economic Development, TVA, 400 W. Summit Hill Drive, Knoxville, TN 37921/615-632-8109.

Nuclear Power Plants

TVA has two nuclear plants with a total of five reactors in operation. Two additional plants, with a total of four reactors, are under construction. For information, contact: Office of Nuclear Power, Tennessee Valley Authority, Chattanooga, TN 37401/615-751-4560.

Occupational Health and Safety

TVA operates a program of occupational health and safety for employees and others affected by their activities, including the provision of medical services to employees; administration of the hazard control plan and compliance with relevant standards; studies and services related to industrial hygiene; and the radiologic hygiene program at planned and operating nuclear facilities. It conducts independent reviews of TVA's nuclear safety program and insures TVA compliance with agency environmental commitments and standards. Contact: Office of Occupational Health and Safety, Tennessee Valley Authority, Muscle Shoals, AL 35660/205-386-2091.

Power System

The electric system supplies power at wholesale to 160 municipal electric systems and rural electric cooperatives in Tennessee and parts of six neighboring states. Contact: Power and Engineering Information Staff, TVA, Chattanooga, TN 37401/615-751-3376.

Procurement

Procurement services for the Tennessee Valley Authority include procurement, transfer, disposal and shipping of equipment, materials, supplies, fuels and management services. Purchases are principally for construction and operation of electric power plants and transmission systems, construction of dams and locks, and development and experimental production of fertilizers. Items required include electrical generating equipment such as turbogenerators, steam-generating units, nuclear plant equipment, hydraulic turbines and generators, transformers, boilers, piping systems, and switchgear. Coal, coke, and nuclear fuel are bought. Electrical and electronic supplies, equipment and spare parts, and communications equipment are stocked. Supplies procured include structural and milled steel, phosphate rock and chemicals, and items for medical laboratory, and photographic purposes. Contact: Purchasing Division, Tennessee Valley Authority, 633 Chestnut St., Room 1000, Chattanooga, TN 37401/615-751-2623.

Publications List

For lists of TVA publications that are available at no cost, or for a small fee, contact: Publications, Tennessee Valley Authority, 400 W. Summit Hill Drive, Room EPA1, Knoxville, TN 37902/615-632-8040.

Public Board of Directors Meetings

Public Board of Directors meetings are conducted approximately twice a month. Meetings are sometimes held in Knoxville and the others outside of Knoxville to provide local citizens in various towns and cities in the region a convenient opportunity to see how the Agency conducts business. The sessions also provide private citizens the opportunity to talk directly with the Board. For advance notice of these meetings and for further information, contact: Information Office, Tennessee Valley Authority, 400 W. Summit Hill Drive, Knoxville, TN 37901/615-632-6000.

Public Meetings
Public meetings, workshops, and consumer forums are held about specific topics or issues such as large-scale construction projects, electric rates, use of public lands, or proposed modifications in recreation policy for TVA reservoirs. Emphasis is on obtaining citizens' views and opinions and providing information. Contact: Citizen Action Office, Tennessee Valley Authority, 400 W. Summit Hill Drive, Knoxville, TN 37901/615-632-4402.

Rapid Adjustment Farms
Rapid adjustment farms are experimental. University researchers and extension specialists analyze resources on these selected farms and develop management options from which the farmer can choose. TVA supplies fertilizer and some capital to help make the changes, and specialists work with the farmer over a four-year program period. Contact: Agricultural Development Division, Office of Agricultural and Chemical Development, Tennessee Valley Authority, National Fertilizer Development Center, Muscle Shoals Reservation, Muscle Shoals, AL 35660/205-386-2915.

Rates
TVA is required by law to establish electric rates as low as feasible, while providing sufficient revenue to operate the power system in a sound, self-supporting and self-liquidating basis. Contact: Power and Engineering Information Staff, Tennessee Valley Authority, Chattanooga, TN 37401/615-751-3376.

Recreation Areas
A pamphlet listing and describing recreation areas on the Tennessee Valley Authority lakeshores is available. Included are boat docks, resorts, state-parks, U.S. Forest Service camp areas and those county and municipal parks which have docks or camping areas. Contact: Publications, Information Office, TVA, 400 W. Summit Hill Drive, Knoxville, TN 37901/615-632-8090, or use hotline: 800-362-9250 in Tennessee/800-251-9242 elsewhere.

Resident Environmental Education
The Youth Station at Land Between The Lakes operates the residential environmental education program. It is open year-round and accommodates kindergarten through college-level groups. Teacher training accounted for about 15 percent of the programs at the center. Land Between The Lakes staff also worked with Murray (Kentucky) State University Center for Environmental Education in

providing four additional workshops for area teachers and inservice students. LBL's interpretation efforts provide diverse programs to promote better environmental understanding and aesthetic appreciation. Contact: Environmental/Energy Education, Land Between The Lakes, Office of Natural Resources and Economic Development, Tennessee Valley Authority, Golden Pond, Kentucky, 42231/502-924-5602.

Scenic River Study
The Recreation Resources Staff completed an evaluation of the river system of the Valley. The study identifies streams with recreation and aesthetic values, such as the French Broad River in western North Carolina and the eastern Tennessee and the Bear Creek streams in north Alabama. And it addresses one of the major problems to full enjoyment of these resources by Valley residents—a lack of easy access to the rivers. Contact: Recreation Resources Staff, Land and Economic Resources Division, Office of Natural Resources and Economic Development, Tennessee Valley Authority, Norris, TN 37828/615-632-6450.

Small Coal Operator Assistance
The TVA tries to strengthen the position of the small coal operator in the market and to insure more competition and reasonable prices. The assistance program reserves a portion of TVA's coal purchases for small producers. In addition, the program provides mining and reclamation technical assistance activities, some operated by college and university extension programs. For additional information, contact: Small Coal Operator Assistance, Land and Economic Resources Division, Office of Natural Resources and Economic Development, Tennessee Valley Authority, Norris, TN 37828/615-632-6450.

Solar Energy
The TVA is working on the development of solar and renewable energy resources. For examples of and information on its projects, contact: Solar Applications Branch, Division of Conservation and Energy Management, Tennessee Valley Authority, Chattanooga, TN 37401/615-751-6741.

Spent Fuel Options
The TVA is studying alternative facilities needed to store spent fuel from TVA nuclear plants. Contact: Office of Nuclear Power Division, Tennessee Valley Authority, Chestnut St. Tower II, 6th and Chestnut Sts., Room 1750, Chattanooga, TN 37401/615-751-4561.

Technical Library Services
The TVA has library facilities that are open to the public. For information on its holdings and for the location of additional libraries, contact: Library, Tennessee Valley Authority, 400 W. Summit Hill

Drive, Room E2B7, Knoxville, TN 37902/615-632-3466.

Wildlife Management
Information gained from field observation of soil types and geologic formations, dominant plant species, and the nature of the land's water supplies is combined with the management goals for certain types of game animals, such as turkey, deer, squirrels, and others whose habitat preferences are known. The system predicts the effects on wildlife habitat of land management practices, such as timber harvesting. Based on this information, wildlife specialists can map out a program compatible with their management goals. Contact: Land and Economic Resources Division, Office of Natural Resources and Economic Development, Tennessee Valley Authority, Norris, TN 37828/615-632-6450.

Woodland Analysis
WRAP, the Woodland Resource Analysis Program, is a computer-backed land management tool which gives foresters a means of identifying quickly management options based on the desires of the landowner. It helps with decisions concerning how to harvest timber in a manner which would also promote other goals, such as improving wildlife habitat or recreation and scenic values.

Contact: Land and Economic Resources Division, Office of Natural Resources and Economic Development, Tennessee Valley Authority, Norris, TN 37828/615-632-6450.

World Fertilizer Market Data Base
The National Fertilizer Development Center (NFDC) maintains a listing of fertilizer production facilities throughout the world. Plant information includes: name, location (town or city) and capacity of facility. The data can be searched by geographical area or 18 different types of fertilizer materials (i.e., ammonium nitrate, potash, super phosphate, etc.).

The data base is updated annually, and facility information can be provided from 1967 through 1985 (projections). North American listings, including Canada, are available free of charge. A cost-recovery fee is accessed for worldwide listings. Contact: F 226 NFDC, National Fertilizer Development Center, Tennessee Valley Authority, Muscle Shoals, AL 35660/205-386-2821.

How Can the Tennessee Valley Authority Help You?
To determine how the Tennessee Valley Authority can help you, contact: Information Office, Tennessee Valley Authority, Knoxville, TN 37902/615-632-8000.

United States Arms Control and Disarmament Agency

**320 21st St. N.W., Department of State Building, Washington, DC 20451/
202-632-0392**

**Established: September 26, 1961
Budget: $15,443,000
Employees: 154**

Mission: Formulates and implements arms control and disarmament policies which will promote the national security of the United States and its relations with other countries; prepares and participates in discussions and negotiations with the Soviet Union and other countries on such issues as strategic arms limitations, mutual force reductions in Central Europe, preventing the spread of nuclear weapons to countries that do not now possess them, a prohibition on chemical weapons, and monitoring the flow of arms trade throughout the world.

Major Sources of Information

Advanced Technology
Advanced technology includes environmental warfare, chemical and biological weapons, nuclear weapons tests, radiological warfare. This office has technical and policy responsibilities for arms control in advanced technology. Contact: Advanced Technology Division, Bureau of Nuclear and Weapons Control, Arms Control and Disarmament Agency, Department of State Bldg., 320 21st St. N.W., Room 4734, Washington, DC 20451/202-632-3496.

Anti-Satellite Talks
ACDA participates in National Security Council studies on anti-satellite talks policy matters. Contact: Strategic Affairs Division, Bureau of Strategic Programs, Arms Control and Disarmament Agency, Room 4498, 320 21st St. N.W., Washington, DC 20451/202-632-1542.

Arms Control and Europe
The task of arms control in Europe is to reduce the danger of war. For information on the various programs, contact: Theater Affairs Division, Bureau of Strategic Programs, Arms Control and Disarmament Agency, 320 21st St. N.W., Room 4487, Washington, DC 20451/202-632-8253.

Arms Control Impact Statements
Arms control impact statements are issued to analyze the possible impact on arms control and disarmament policy and negotiations for these programs: nuclear weapons related programs; research, development or procurement programs totalling more than $250 million; and other programs involving technology or weapons system. Detailed information about the program includes an analysis of weapon capabilities, stated military requirements and funding. Contact: Defense Pro-

gram Analysis Division, Bureau of Nuclear and Weapons Control, Arms Control and Disarmament Agency, 320 21st St. N.W, Room 5741, Washington, DC 20451/202-632-1296.

Arms Transfer
The arms transfer policy recognizes the defense need of U.S. friends and allies, but calls for restraint to reduce the threat of uncontrolled spread of conventional arms. Contact: Arms Transfer Division, Bureau of Weapons Evaluation and Control, Arms Control and Disarmament Agency, ACDA/NWC/ATD, 320 21st St. N.W., Room 4734, Washington, DC 20451/202-632-3496.

Chemical Weapons Prohibition
ACDA plays a primary role in the negotiations on a chemical weapons prohibition and in discussions of related issues conducted both in the Committee on Disarmament and in the United Nations. Contact: Advanced Science and Technology Division, Bureau of Multilateral Affairs, Arms Control and Disarmament Agency, 320 21st St. N.W., Room 5499, Washington, DC 20451/202-632-2069.

Congressional Liaison
Congressional liaison matters include briefings, hearings and legislative inquiries relating to arms control treaty approval and ACDA legislation. Contact: Congressional Relations, Office of the General Counsel, Arms Control and Disarmament Agency, 320 21st St. N.W., Room 5534, Washington, DC 20451/202-632-8690.

General Advisory Committee
The General Advisory Committee on Arms Control and Disarmament advises the President, the Secretary of State, and the Director of the Arms Control and Disarmament Agency on matters affecting arms control, disarmament and world peace. Contact: General Advisory Committee on Arms Control and Disarmament, 320 21st St. N.W., Room 5927, Washington, DC 20451/202-632-5176.

Hubert H. Humphrey Fellowship
The Hubert H. Humphrey Fellowship Program encourages research in arms control studies and assists in the training of young professionals. The program involves one-year Fellowships in support of doctoral dissertation research in the field of arms control and disarmament. Candidates for law degrees (J.D. or higher) are also eligible for the Fellowships. Contact: Office of Public Affairs, Arms Control and Disarmament Agency, 320 21st St. N.W., Room 5847, Washington, DC 20451/202-632-8714.

Information
For information on all aspects of Arms Control and Disarmament including Strategic Arms Limi-

tations Talks (SALT) I and II and for copies of the following publications:

ACDA Annual Report
World Military Expenditures—how much money is spent on military programs, how much on social programs, what percentage of the GNP is spent on arms, etc.
Arms Control and Disarmament Agreement—update of various arms control agreements, list of signators on past agreements.
Documents on Disarmament—significant papers by U.S. and other officials. Also speeches, press releases, pamphlets, etc.

.Contact: Public Affairs, Arms Control and Disarmament Agency, 320 21st St. N.W., Room 5840, Washington, DC 20451/202-632-9504.

Library
The Library has a collection of documents, reports and other material on arms control and disarmament. It is open to the public but a library card is necessary. To obtain the library card and for general information, contact: Library, Arms Control and Disarmament Agency, 320 21st St. N.W., Room 5051, Washington, DC 20451/202-632-8714.

Multilateral Affairs
This office has policy responsibility for arms control negotiations and discussions that are conducted in multilateral forums such as the Committee on Disarmament and the United Nations General Assembly. Contact: International Relations Division, Bureau of Multilateral Affairs, Arms Control and Disarmament Agency, 320 21st St. N.W., Room 5499, Washington, DC 20451/202-632-7909.

Mutual and Balanced Force Reductions
The agreed objective of the Mutual and Balanced Force Reductions negotiations is to contribute to stability in Central Europe with lower levels of forces without diminishing the security of any party. Contact: Regional Division, Bureau of Strategic Programs, Arms Control and Disarmament Agency, 320 21st St. N.W., Room 5499, Washington, DC 20451/202-632-6957.

Non-Proliferation
The further spread of nuclear weapons constitutes a serious threat to international peace and security. ACDA plays a leading role in the initiation and implementation of U.S. non-proliferation policy. Contact: Bureau of Non-Proliferation, Arms Control and Disarmament Agency, 320 21st St. N.W., Room 4930, Washington, DC 20451/202-632-3466.

Nuclear Exports
This office provides advice, assessments and policy recommendations on the international relations aspects of non-proliferation. It is responsible for

U.S. bilateral initiatives concerning countries of particular non-proliferation interest; for multinational initiatives including those on supplier countries policies; for encouraging additional adherence to the Non-Proliferation Treaty and nuclear-free zone agreements; for non-proliferation aspects of related arms control measures such as testing limitations; for participation in the negotiation of U.S. bilateral nuclear agreements for cooperation; and for work on the development and implementation of U.S. nuclear export policies and procedures. Contact: International Nuclear Affairs, Bureau of Nuclear and Weapons Control, Arms Control and Disarmament Agency, 320 21st St. N.W., Room 4678, Washington, DC 20451/202-632-1160.

Nuclear Safeguards
Efforts are made to improve all phases of nuclear safeguards from seeking better safeguards agreements to providing improved measurement instrumentation for use by International Atomic Energy Agency inspectors. Contact: Nuclear Safeguards and Technology Division, Bureau of Nuclear and Weapons Control, Arms Control and Disarmament Agency, 320 21st St. N.W., Room 4464, Washington, DC 20451/202-632-1140.

Patents and Documents
All operations in the areas of personnel, patents, contracts, procurement, fiscal and administration are handled by Office of the General Counsel, Arms Control and Disarmament Agency, 320 21st St. N.W., Room 5534, Washington, DC 20451/202-632-3582.

Publications
The *Annual Report, Arms Control and Disarmament Agreements, World Military Expenditures and Arms Transfers,* and *Documents on Disarmament* are among the major publications of the U.S. Arms Control And Disarmament Agency. *World Military Expenditures and Arms Transfers* includes arms transfer data as well. The objective is to provide an authoritative source of world-wide statistical data that demonstrates the size and relative costs of military programs. *Documents on Disarmament* is a compilation of U.S. and foreign public statements and documents of significance for arms control, and is issued annually. The Agency also issued the 1980 edition of *Arms Control and Disarmament Agreements: Texts and Histories of Negotiations.* ACDA issued a Special Report on the 1980 Review Conference on the Treaty of the Non-Proliferation of Nuclear Weapons held in Geneva August 11–September 7. The report contained the texts of plenary statements of U.S. delegates and the plenary statements of some 30 delegations on the SALT II Treaty and the Comprehensive Test Ban negotiations. Contact: Office of Public Affairs, Arms Control and Dis-

armament Agency, 320 21st St. N.W., Room 5840, Washington, DC 20451/202-632-9504.

SALT Treaty
The Strategic Arms Limitations Talks (SALT) between the United States and the Soviet Union seek to limit and reduce the strategic nuclear weapons of both countries. Contact: Strategic Affairs Division, Bureau of International Strategic Programs, Arms Control and Disarmament Agency, 320 21st St. N.W., Room 4484, Washington, DC 20451/202-632-1542.

Social Impacts of Arms and Arms Control
The Weapons Evaluation and Control Bureau is devoting increased attention to the arms control implications of various economic and socio-political elements in the Soviet society. Soviet military expenditures and their economic burden are an area of primary interest. Alternative estimating approaches for measuring such expenditures are being studied to assess their respective advantages and disadvantages, uses and misuses. ACDA also participated in a new national effort to reinvigorate Soviet studies, generally by contributing financial support to the National Council for Soviet and East European Research. Contact: Arms Transfer Division, International Nuclear Affairs, Bureau of Nuclear and Weapons Control, Arms Control and Disarmament Agency, 320 21st St. N.W., Room 4734, Washington, DC 20451/202-632-3759.

Speakers
Office of the Agency will address audiences in all parts of the country. Contact: Public Affairs, Arms Control and Disarmament Agency, 320 21st St. N.W., Room 5840, Washington, DC 20451/202-632-9504.

Technology Transfer
Technologies can play a major role in the creation and support of indigenous arms industries in less developed countries, particularly in the latter's capability to manufacture advanced weapons. These dual-use technologies are the subject of arms control deliberations. Contact: Technology Transfer, Bureau of Nuclear and Weapons Control, Arms Control and Disarmament Agency, 320 21st St. N.W., Room 4734, Washington, DC 20451/202-632-3496.

Test Ban Treaty
A treaty imposing a comprehensive ban on nuclear explosions has been on the international arms control agenda since the mid-1950s. ACDA develops and coordinates interagency positions on the test ban. Contact: Advanced Technology Division, Bureau of Multilateral Affairs, Arms Control and Disarmament Agency, 320 21st St. N.W., Room 5499, Washington, DC 20451/202-632-3422.

Theater Nuclear Force

The United States and the Soviet Union are negotiating toward achieving equitable and adequately verifiable limitations on their theater nuclear systems. Contact: Theater Affairs Division, Bureau of Strategic Programs, Arms Control and Disarmament Agency, 320 21st St. N.W., Room 4487, Washington, DC 20451/202-632-8253.

World Military Expenditures and Arms Transfers

The statistical data describe the size, trends and distribution of global military expenditures and the world's arms trade. This annual ACDA publication contains data on the amount of resources devoted to military purposes and to select social purposes by 145 individual states as well as by major alliances. Relative economic expenditure comparisons are shown as well as detailed data on international arms transfers. Also included are brief articles on measuring Soviet military expenditures and on conversion rate comparisons. Contact: Arms Transfer Division, Defense Programs Analysis Division, Bureau of Nuclear and Weapons Control, Arms Control and Disarmament Agency, 320 21st St. N.W., Room 5241, Washington, DC 20451/202-632-0816.

How Can the Arms Control and Disarmament Agency Help You?

To determine how the U.S. Arms Control and Disarmament Agency can help you, contact: Arms Control and Disarmament Agency, 320 21st St. N.W., Washington, DC 20451/202-632-9504.

United States Information Agency (USIA)

400 C Street S.W., Washington, DC 20547/202-485-7860

Established: April 1, 1978
Budget: $597,205,000
Employees: 8,620

Mission: Responsible for the U.S. Government's overseas information and cultural programs, including the Voice of America and the Fulbright scholarship program; responsible for the conduct of international information and educational and cultural affairs, including exchange programs designed to build bridges of mutual understanding between the people of the United States and other peoples of the world; engages in a wide variety of communication activities—from academic and cultural exchanges to press, radio, television, film, seminar, library, and cultural center programs abroad—to accomplish its goals of strengthening foreign understanding of American society and support of United States policies; and reports to the President and the Secretary of State, as well as to advise the National Security Council, on worldwide public opinion as it is relevant to the formulation and conduct of U.S. foreign policy.

Major Sources of Information

Advisory Commission on Public Diplomacy
The Commission provides oversight, assessment and advice for the international information, cultural and education exchange programs for the United States. It also advises the President, Congress, the Secretary of State, and the Director of the U.S. Information Agency on the policies of the U.S.I.A.. Contact: Advisory Commission on Public Diplomacy, 301 4th St. S.W., Room 600, Washington, DC 20547/202-485-2457.

American Participants
The U.S. Information Agency will pay American experts, who can contribute to foreign societies'

understanding of the United States, to travel abroad and participate in seminars, colloquia or symposia. Subjects treated by American participants include economics, international political relations, U.S. social and political processes, arts and humanities, and science and technology. A free booklet, *American Participants,* describing the program is available. Contact: American Participants, Office of Program Coordination and Development, U.S.I.A., 301 4th St. S.W., Room 550, Washington, DC 20547/202-485-2764.

American Studies
This office supports, through ideas, funds and

materials, American Studies Programs abroad. For additional information, contact: Division of the Study of the United States, Office of Academic Programs, Educational and Cultural Affairs, U.S.I.A., 301 4th St. S.W., Room 245, Washington, DC 20547/202-485-2553.

Arts America

The U.S. Information Agency seeks to encourage private-sector involvement and assists qualified artists and performers in arranging private tours overseas. Its aim is to present a balanced portrayal of the American cultural scene. Some of the past activities have included a major exhibition of American crafts shown in China, a modern dance company in the USSR, Spain, and Portugal, and a jazz ensemble in Nigeria, Senegal and Kenya. Contact: Arts Liaison Advisor, Office of the Associate Director for Programs, U.S. Information Agency, U.S.I.A., 301 4th St. S.W., Room 568, Washington, DC 20547/202-485-2779.

Board of Foreign Scholarships

The Board supervises United States government-supported education exchanges. It sets policies and procedures for administration of the program, has final responsibility for approving all grantees and supervises the conduct of the program both in the United States and abroad. The annual report of the Board is available. Contact: Board of Foreign Scholarships Staff, Educational and Cultural Affairs, U.S.I.A., 301 4th St. S.W., Room 247, Washington, DC 20547/202-485-7290.

Book Exhibits

The Agency cooperates with the publishing world to stage six book exhibits annually, which are seen in some 120 cities throughout the world. It also cooperates with American publishers participating in exhibits at international book fairs. Contact: Book Programs Division, Office of Cultural Centers and Resources, U.S. Information Agency, U.S.I.A., 301 4th St. S.W., Room 320, Washington, DC 20547/202-485-2896.

Booklets

The following booklets are available at no cost:

USIA in Brief
The Fulbright Program
American Participants (experts in many professions traveling abroad for USIA)
Arts America (a program to send American arts abroad)
International Visitor Programs
USIA Career Opportunities
Grants to Private Organizations
USIA Program

To receive any of these, write to: Office of Public Liaison, U.S. Information Agency, U.S.I.A., 301 4th St. S.W., Room 602, Washington, DC 20547/202-485-2355.

Book Program

The U.S. Information Agency promotes the publication of books on United States foreign policy, political and social processes, the economy, science and technology, education, and the arts and humanities. Most of the books are sold through commercial channels in developing countries. The agency provides assistance to foreign publishers who bring out editions of American works by absorbing translation and promotion costs or by buying part of the foreign edition for use in its cultural programs. Contact: Book Programs Division, Educational and Cultural Affairs, U.S.I.A., 301 4th St. S.W., Room 320, Washington, DC 20547/202-485-2896.

Career Counseling

For information on a variety of careers available in the Foreign Service, contact: Career Counseling, Office of Personnel Services, U.S.I.A., 301 4th St. S.W., Room 508, Washington, DC 20547/202-485-2713.

Copyright Clearance

The U.S. Information Agency serves as a copyright office for local publishers seeking rights to American books. It will also put them in touch with American publishers. For additional information, contact: Copyright Service Branch, Book Programs Division, Office of Cultural Centers and Resources, Educational and Cultural Affairs, U.S.I.A., 301 4th St. S.W., Room 320, Washington, DC 20547/202-485-2898.

Directory of Resources for Cultural and Educational Exchanges and U.S. Information

This is a free list of contacts in United States government agencies and non-profit organizations. It includes departments and agencies of the federal government, federal boards, commissions, committees and advisory groups, intergovernmental organizations, and private organizations. Acronyms and symbols are also listed. Contact: Office of Public Liaison, U.S.I.A., 301 4th St. S.W., Room 602, Washington, DC 20547/202-485-2355.

Donated Book Programs

American publishers donate books to developing nations and to certain education specialists overseas. Contact: Book Programs Division, Donated Book Service, Office of Cultural Centers and Resources, Educational and Cultural Affairs, U.S.I.A., 301 4th St. S.W., Room 320, Washington, DC 20547/202-485-2902.

Exhibits

Approximately ten international exhibitions a year are held combining the efforts and resources of the federal government and the private sector. The exhibitions focus on a variety of subjects such as the arts, agriculture, communications, and computers. For additional information, contact: Exhibits Service, U.S.I.A., Room 349, 301 4th St. S.W., Washington, DC 20547/202-485-7167.

Films and Television

The U.S. Information Agency acquires and produces videotape programs and films for distribution through posts. Almost 100 videotape programs a year are produced in U.S.I.A. studios; others are acquired from United States broadcast networks. These products are shown by U.S.I.A. posts to audiences overseas and are sometimes also distributed through foreign media and commercial theaters abroad. It also provides foreign TV stations with newsclips of events in the United States. Another important function involves assisting foreign TV teams in producing programs about the United States for telecast abroad. Contact: Television and News Service, U.S.I.A., 601 D St., Washington, DC 20547/202-376-7801.

Foreign Press Centers

Two Foreign Press Centers, one in Washington and one in New York, assist journalists from all parts of the world in covering stories in the United States. For example, the Centers make appointments for foreign journalists, assist them with credentials and make the daily State Department press briefings available through closed circuit radio to correspondents who cannot be at the Department. Similar arrangements are made for White House and other major press conferences. Contact: New York Foreign Press Center, U.S.I.A., 18 E. 50th St., New York, NY 10022/ 212-826-4721, or Washington Foreign Press Center, U.S.I.A., Room 225, Washington, DC 20045/202-724-1640.

Fulbright Program

The Fulbright Program is the United States government's international education exchange program. Scholarships are awarded to American students, teachers and scholars to study, teach, lecture and conduct research abroad and to foreign nationals to engage in similar activities in the United States. Citizens of other countries who would like information about the Fulbright exchange opportunities should contact the Fulbright Commission or the American Embassy Public Affairs Officer in their countries. For information in this country, contact: Academic Exchange Programs Division, Office of Academic Programs, U.S.I.A., 301 4th St. S.W., Room 234, Washington, DC 20547/202-485-7360.

Grants

The programs described below are for sums of money which are given by the federal government to initiate and stimulate new or improved activities or to sustain on-going services:

Educational Exchange—Graduate Students

Objectives: To improve and strengthen international relations with the United States by promoting better mutual understanding among the peoples of the world through education exchanges.

Eligibility: To individuals with the following qualifications: (a) U.S. citizenship at the time of application; (b) with certain exceptions, B.A. degree or its equivalent before the beginning date of the grant; (c) candidates may not hold a doctoral degree at the time of application; (d) applicants must have received the majority of their high school and their undergraduate college education at education institutions in the United States; (e) language proficiency sufficient to communicate with the people of the host country and to carry out the proposed study; language proficiency is especially important for students wishing to undertake projects in the social sciences and the humanities; and (f) good health.

Range of Financial Assistance: $1,000 to $15,000.

Contact: Institute of International Education, 809 United Nations Plaza, New York, NY 10017/ 212-883-8200.

Educational Exchange—University Lecturers (Professors) and Research Scholars

Objectives: To improve and strengthen international relations with the United States by promoting mutual understanding among the peoples of the world through education exchanges.

Eligibility: To individuals with the following qualifications: (a) U.S. citizenship at the time of application; (b) for lecturing—college or university teaching experience at the level for which application is made; (c) for research—a doctoral degree or, in some fields, recognized professional standing as demonstrated by faculty rank, publications, compositions, exhibition record, concerts, etc.

Range of Financial Assistance: $2,000 to $40,000.

Contact: Council for International Exchange of Scholars, 11 Dupont Circle, Suite 300, Washington, DC 20036/202-833-4950.

Hubert H. Humphrey North-South Fellowship Program

This program offers mid-career professionals an opportunity to enhance their capabilities by emphasizing practical experience and developing professional skills. Workshops, seminars, and field trips are provided. Contact: Academic Exchange Programs, Office of Academic Programs, Educational and Cultural Affairs, U.S.I.A., 301 4th St. S.W., Room 234, Washington, DC 20547/202-485-7360.

International Visitors Program

Under the U.S. Information Agency's International Visitors Program, some 2,400 foreign leaders in government, labor, mass media, science, education and other fields come to the United States annually to see American society firsthand and to confer with their counterparts in this country. They are chosen by U.S.I.A. posts abroad on the basis not only of their present influence, but of their potential influence within their own communities. Most visitors come here individually and follow specially tailored itineraries. Others come in small groups to participate in projects on such topics as energy, food systems, environment, communications, the role of women, etc. Contact: Office of International Visitors Programs, Educational and Cultural Affairs, U.S. Information Agency, U.S.I.A., 301 4th St. S.W., Room 266, Washington, DC 20547/202-485-7217.

Junior Officer Trainee Program
Candidates enter this program by taking the Foreign Service Officer Examination given each December at many locations in the United States and overseas. For information on the Junior Officer Trainee Program, contact: Training and Development Division, Office of Personnel Services, U.S.I.A., Room 800, 1425 K St. N.W., Washington, DC 20547/202-523-4390.

Library
The agency library maintains a collection on a wide variety of subjects and includes a Russian language section. Permission to use the library must be obtained through the Office of Congressional and Public Liaison, Room 1016, 202-485-2355. For additional information about the library, contact: Library, U.S.I.A., 301 4th St. S.W., Room 130, Washington, DC 20547/202-485-8947.

Library Programs
There are some 200 U.S. Information Agency libraries in 95 countries. Some collections are general in nature while others are designed exclusively for reference by lawmakers, officials, university students, American studies specialists, etc. Services may include interlibrary loans, preparation of special bibliographies, technical advice and loan of books by mail. For further information, contact: Library Programs, Educational and Cultural Affairs, U.S.I.A., 301 4th St. S.W., Room 324, Washington, DC 20547/202-485-2929.

Overseas Publications Program
With one exception, the U.S. Information Agency publishes the following magazines for overseas distribution only.

Dialogue—a quarterly journal of opinion and analysis on subjects of current intellectual interest in the United States. Published in eight languages during fiscal year 1979, it contains both reprints and original articles.
Topic—a bimonthly magazine published in French and English for distribution in sub-Saharan Africa. It highlights significant aspects of American life and of U.S.-African relations.
al-Majal—published monthly in Arabic for distribution in North Africa and the Near East. It focuses on various aspects of American society and U.S. foreign policy, especially relations with Arab populations.
America Illustrated—an illustrated monthly journal designed to present a balanced and varied picture of American life. It is published in Russian and sent to the Soviet Union in exchange for *Soviet Life,* a magazine from the USSR which is distributed here.
Problems of Communism—a bimonthly scholarly periodical on communist affairs, published in English, available for $16.00 per year from the Superintendent of Documents, Government Printing Office, Washington, DC 20402/202-783-3238.

For additional publications, contact: Publications Division, Press and Publications Service, U.S.I.A., 301 4th St. S.W., Room 408, Washington, DC 20547/202-485-2265.

Press
A radioteletype network known as the Wireless File sends five regional transmissions, five days a week, of policy statements and interpretive material to 159 United States International Communication Agency (USICA) posts overseas. Each regional transmission averages 12,000 to 16,000 words in English. There are also Spanish, French and Arabic language versions. Features, by-line articles, reprints from U.S. publications and photographs are regularly mailed to all posts. This material is used for the background information of U.S. Mission personnel abroad, for distribution to foreign opinion leaders, and for media placement abroad. Contact: Press Division, Press and Publications Service, U.S.I.A., 301 4th St. S.W., Room 450, Washington, DC 20547/202-485-2136.

Private Sector Programs
These programs provide selective assistance and grant support to nonprofit activities of United States organizations outside the federal government that support the enhancement of United States competence in world affairs. For further information, contact: Office of Private Sector Programs, Educational and Cultural Affairs, U.S.I.A., 301 4th St. S.W., Room 216, Washington, DC 20547/202-485-7348.

Research
The research staff is concerned with the attitudes and perceptions of foreign peoples. The researchers try to identify the issues of greatest importance to influential persons in foreign countries, their attitudes and opinions, their views of the United States, and the media and other sources of information they rely on. The research staff reviews foreign social science and literary publications, talks with United States scholars returning from abroad and reviews foreign media output.

Contact: Office of Research, U.S.I.A., 301 4th St. S.W., Room 352, Washington, DC 20547/202-485-2965.

Research Reports
The International Communication Agency's research and media-reaction staffs prepare material for the White House, the Department of State and other departments and agencies of the United States government, and for the Agency's own use in assessing issues. The Agency's research reports are available to interested persons at 46 depository libraries in universities and other institutions throughout the country. For a list of these depositories, write to the Office of Research, U.S.I.A., 301 4th St. S.W., Room 352, Washington, DC 20547/202-485-2965.

Student Support Services
Programs aimed at enhancing the academic experiences of foreign students in the United States are developed and available. For additional information, contact: Student Support Services, Office of Academic Programs, Educational and Cultural Affairs, U.S.I.A., 301 4th St. S.W., Room 246, Washington, DC 20547/202-485-7434.

VOA Broadcasts
Voice of America programs are broadcast in the following 39 languages: Albanian, Arabic, Armenian, Bengali, Bulgarian, Burmese, Chinese, Czech, Dari, English, Estonian, French, Georgian, Greek, Hausa, Hindi, Hungarian, Indonesian, Khmer, Korean, Lao, Latvian, Lithuanian, Persian, Polish, Portuguese, Romanian, Russian, Serbo-Croatian, Slovak, Slovenian, Spanish, Swahili, Thai, Turkish, Ukranian, Urdu, Uzbek, Vietmanese. They include direct broadcasts (about 850 hours a week) and indirect broadcasts. Indirect broadcast programs are those prepared by VOA and/or U.S.I.A. posts abroad and put on by local radio stations. The backbone of VOA's programming is news and news analysis. Some of the other programs include:

VOA Morning—morning program moves westward through breakfast hours in time zones around the world, bringing listeners interviews, popular music and answers to their questions about the United States.
Press Conference USA—features leading figures in the news who face a panel of distinguished American and foreign journalists.
Critics' Choice—presents listeners with discussions of and critiques about the arts in America, including literature, theater, painting, dance, cinema, architecture and music.

English broadcast schedules to the Americas, the Middle East, East Asia and Pacific, South Asia, Africa and Europe are available. For additional information, contact: Programs Office, Voice of America, 330 Independence Ave. S.W., Room 2051, Washington, DC 202-755-4222.

VOA Facilities
The VOA facilities comprise the Master Control in Washington, DC, three facilities in New York City, one each in Chicago, Los Angeles and Miami, 33 domestic and 68 overseas transmitters plus 15 satellite circuits which beam programs to Europe, the Middle East, East Asia and the Pacific Area. A Table of VOA Relay Stations in the United States and overseas showing location, transmitters, power range and area reached, and a Frequency Schedule are available at no cost. For additional information, contact: Office of Engineering and Technical Operations, Voice of America, U.S.I.A., 330 Independence Ave. S.W., Room 3348, Washington, DC 20547/202-485-8048.

VOA Public Tours
Regularly scheduled guided tours are available to show visitors how the VOA communicates with people around the world. Visitors watch broadcasts in session, and see excerpts of motion pictures and TV programs. For additional information, contact: Voice of America, U.S.I.A., 330 Independence Ave. S.W., Room 2137, Washington, DC 20547/202-755-4744.

Voluntary Visitors
"Voluntary Visitors" are those foreigners who come to the United States under private auspices but, at the request of a U.S. Information Agency post abroad, receive assistance in planning their trips in the United States. For further information, contact: Office of International Visitors Programs, Educational and Cultural Affairs, U.S.I.A., 301 4th St. S.W., Room 266, Washington, DC 20547/202-485-2582.

How Can the International Communication Agency Help You?
For information on how this agency can help you, contact: Office of Public Liaison, U.S.I.A., 301 4th St. S.W., Room 602, Washington, DC 20547/202-485-2355.

United States International Development Cooperation Agency*

320 21st St. N.W., Washington, DC 20523/202-632-9170

Established: October 1, 1979
Budget: $8,321,000,000
Employees: Not applicable

Mission: Insures that developing goals are taken fully into account in all executive branch decision making on trade, financing and monetary affairs, technology and other economic policy issues affecting the less developed nations; and provides strong direction for U.S. economic policies toward the developing world and a coherent development strategy through the effective use of U.S. bilateral development assistance programs and U.S. participation in multilateral development organizations.

Development Issues
This annual report on Development Coordination discusses the events of the fiscal year. It highlights the development goals and issues. The report represents the cooperative efforts of the member agencies of the Development Coordination Committee (DDC). To obtain a copy of this report

*This agency is the coordinating agency for Overseas Private Development Corporation, Trade and Development Program, and Agency for International Development.

contact: Public Affairs, International Development Cooperation Agency, 320 21st St. N.W., Washington, DC 20523/202-632-9170.

How Can the International Development Cooperation Agency Help You?
To determine how the International Development Cooperation Agency can help you, contact: Public Affairs, International Development Cooperation Agency, 320 21st St. N.W., Washington, DC 20523/202-632-9170.

United States International Trade Commission

701 E St. N.W., Washington, DC 20436/202-532-0161

Established: September 8, 1916
Budget: $19,774,000
Employees: 438

Mission: Furnishes studies, reports and recommendations involving international trade and tariffs to the President, the Congress, and other government agencies, and conducts a variety of investigations, public hearings, and research projects pertaining to the international policies of the United States.

Data Experts

Industry Specialists and Commodity Assignments
The following specialists monitor the imports of various goods as well as their impact on the domestic market. The goods are listed alphabetically with their corresponding analysts. For additional information, contact: Office of Industries, International Trade Commission, 701 E St. N.W., Room 254, Washington, DC 20436/202-523-0146.

Abaca/Cook/202-523-0348
Abrasive/Garil/202-523-0304
ABS Resins/Taylor/202-523-0379
Acetal Resins/Taylor/202-523-0379
Acetates/Conant/202-523-0495
Acetic Acids/Michels/202-523-0293
Acetone/Michels/202-523-0293
Acetoricinoleic Acid Ester/Johnson/202-523-0127
Acid, Oleic/Noreen/202-523-1255
Acid, Stearic/Noreen/202-523-1255
Acid, Inorganic/Emanuel/202-523-0334
Acid, Organic/Michels/202-523-0293
Acrylates/Conant/202-523-0495
Acrylic Resins/Taylor/202-523-3709
Acrylonitrile/Michels/202-523-0293

Activated Carbon/Noreen/202-523-1255
Acyclic Plasticizers/Johnson/202-523-0127
Adding Machines/Fletcher/202-523-0378
Addressing Machines/Fletcher/202-523-0378
Adhesives/Noreen/202-523-1255
Adipic Acid Esters/Johnson/202-523-0127
Agar Agar/Noreen/202-523-1255
Agglomerating Machinery/Fravel/202-523-0411
Agricultural Machinery/Fravel/202-523-0411
Air Conditioners/DeMarines/202-523-0259
Aircraft/Ladomirak/202-523-0131
Albums (Autograph, Photograph and so on)/Stahmer/ 202-724-0091
Alcohol, Oleyl/Noreen/202-523-1255
Alcohols/Conan/202-523-0495
Alcohols, Polyhydric, Fatty Acids of (Surface-Active Agents)/Land/202-523-0491
Aldehydes/Michels/202-523-0293
Alkaloids/Briggs/202-523-1145
Almonds/Burke/202-724-0088
Alpaca/Clayton/202-523-5701
Alternate Energy/Foreso/202-523-1230
Aluminum/Woods/202-523-0277
Aluminum Compound/Greenblatt/202-523-1212

Boron/Palmer/202-523-0270
Boron Compounds/Greenblatt/202-523-1212
Bottles, Pails and Dishes of Plastic or Rubber/Taylor/
  202-523-3709
Braids, Hat/Worrell/202-523-0452
Braids, Other/Sweet/202-523-0394
Brake Fluid/Foreso/202-523-1230
Bread and Other Baked Goods/Grant/202-724-0099
Breeder Reactor/Greenblatt/202-523-1212
Brick, Ceramic/Ruhlman/202-523-0309
Bromine/Emanuel/202-523-0334
Brooms/Leverett/202-724-1725
Brushes/Leverett/202-724-1725
Buckles/Watkins/202-724-0976
Building Boards/Ruggles/202-724-1766
Building Components (Wood)/Ruggles/202-724-1766
Bulbs (Lamps)/Cutchin/202-523-0231
Bunker "C" Fuel Oil/Foreso/202-523-1230
Buses/McElroy/202-523-0258
Butadiene/Raftery/202-523-0453
Butane/Raftery/202-523-0453
Butter/Warren/202-724-0090
Buttons/Watkins/202-724-0976
Butyl Alcohol/Conant/202-523-0495
Butyl Benzyl Phthalate/Johnson/202-523-0127
Butyl Oleate/Johnson/202-523-0127
Butyl Rubber/Taylor/202-523-3709
Butyl Stearate/Johnson/202-523-0127
Butylene/Raftery/202-523-0453
Cadmium/Palmer/202-523-0270
Caffeine and Its Compounds/Briggs/202-523-1145
Calcium/Palmer/202-523-0270
Calcium Carbonate/Johnson/202-523-0127
Calcium Compounds/Greenblatt/202-523-1212
Calcium Pigments/Johnson/202-523-0127
Calcium Sulfate/Johnson/202-523-0127
Calculators/Nelson/202-523-4585
Calendering Machines/Greene/202-523-0265
Cameras (except Television)/Witherspoon/202-724-0978
Cameos/Wilson/202-724-1731
Camphor/Noreen/202-523-1255
Candles/Cunningham/202-724-0980
Canoes/West/202-523-0299
Canes/Leverett/202-724-1725
Capacitors/Cutchin/202-523-0231
Caprolactan Monomer/Cappuccilli/202-523-0490
Caps/Worrell/202-523-0452
Carbon/Johnson/202-523-0127
Carbon, Activated/Noreen/202-523-1255
Carbon Black/Johnson/202-523-0127
Carbon and Graphite Electrodes/Garil/202-523-0304
Carbon Tetrachloride/Conant/202-523-0495
Carboxylic Acids/Michels/202-523-0293
Carboxymethyl Cellulose Salts (Surface-Active Agents)/
  Land/202-523-0491
Card Cases/Seastrum/202-724-1733
Cardiovascular Drugs/Briggs/202-523-1145
Carpets/Borsari/202-523-5703
Carrots/McCarty/202-724-1753
Casein/Noreen/202-523-1255
Cash Registers/Fletcher/202-523-0328
Castile Soap/Land/202-523-0491
Casting Machines/West/202-523-0299

Cattle/Ludwick/202-724-1763
Caulks/Johnson/202-523-0127
Caulks Compounds/Johnson/202-523-0127
Caustic Potash/Greenblatt/202-523-1212
Caustic Soda/Greenblatt/202-523-1212
Cedar Leaf/Land/202-523-0491
Cement, Hydraulic/Garil/202-523-0304
Cements, Dental/Noreen/202-523-1255
Cements of Rubber, Vinyl etc./Noreen/202-523-1255
Centrifuges/Slingerland/202-523-0263
Ceramic Construction Articles/Lukes/202-523-0279
Ceramic Table, Kitchen Articles/McNay/202-523-0445
Cereal Breakfast Foods/Grant/202-523-724-0099
Cereal Grains/Pierre-Benoist/202-724-0074
Cerium/DeSapio/202-523-0283
Cerium Compounds/Greenblatt/202-523-1212
Cesium Compounds/Greenblatt/202-523-1212
Chain, of Base Metal/Rapkins/202-523-0438
Chairs/Leverett/202-724-1725
Chalk (Pigment Grade)/Johnson/202-523-0127
Chalks/Hanlon/202-724-1745
Channel Black/Johnson/202-523-0127
Check-Writing Machines/Fletcher/202-523-0378
Cheese/Warren/202-724-0090
Chemicals/Jonnard/202-523-0345
Chemical Elements/Emanuel/202-523-0334
Chinaware Articles/McNay/202-523-0445
Chlorine/Emanuel/202-523-0334
Chlorofluorocarbons/Conant/202-523-0495
Chloroform/Conant/202-523-0495
Chocolate/Grant/202-724-0099
Chrome Pigments/Johnson/202-523-0127
Chromium/Boszormenyi/202-523-0328
Chromium Compounds/Greenblatt/202-523-1212
Cigars and Cigarettes/Lipovsky/202-724-0097
  Holders/DePauw/202-724-1730
  Cigar and Cigarette Lighters/Depauw/202-724-1730
Cinchona Bark Alkaloids and Their Salts/Briggs/202-523-
  1145
Cinnamon Oil (Essential Oil)/Land/202-523-0491
Citral/Land/202-523-0491
Citrates/Michels/202-523-0293
Citric Acid/Michels/202-523-0293
Citrus Fruits/Burket/202-724-0088
Civet/Land/202-523-0491
Clays/Lukes/202-523-0279
Cleaners, Under 10 lbs. Each/Noreen/202-523-1255
Cleaning Machinery/Slingerland/202-523-0263
Cleaning Machines (Textile)/Greene/202-523-0265
Clocks/Wilson/202-724-1731
Closures, Stoppers, Seal Lids, Caps of Rubber or Plastic/
  Raftery/202-523-0453
Clove (Essential Oil)/Land/202-523-0491
Coal/Foreso/202-523-1230
Coal Tar, Crude/Foreso/202-523-1230
Coal-Tar Pitch/Foreso/202-523-1230
Coating Machines/Greene/202-523-0265
Cobalt/Pam Woods/202-523-0277
Cobalt Compounds/Greenblatt/202-523-1212
Cocoa/Grant/202-724-0099
Cocks and Valves/DeMarines/202-523-0259
Coffee/Lipovsky/202-724-0097
Coin Purses/Seastrum/202-724-1733

Coke, Calcinated (Non-Fuel)/Garil/202-523-0304
Coke for Fuel/Foreso/202-523-1230
Columbium/DeSapio/202-523-0273
Combs/Leverett/202-724-1725
Concrete and Products/Garil/202-523-0304
Condensate, Lease/Foreso/202-523-1230
Conductors/Cutchin/202-523-0231
Conduit/Cutchin/202-523-0231
Confectionery/Grant/202-724-0099
Construction Paper/Rhodes/202-724-1299
Containers (of Wood)/Jensen/202-724-0096
Containers, of Base Metal/Rapkins/202-523-0438
Converters/West/202-523-0299
Copper/Woods/202-523-0277
Copper Compounds/Greenblatt/202-523-1212
Copra and Coconut Oil/Reeder/202-724-1754
Cordage Machines/Greene/202-523-0265
Cork and Cork Products/Westcot/202-724-0095
Corn, Field/Pierre-Benoist/202-724-0074
Cosmetic Creams/Land/202-523-0491
Cosmetics, Perfumery, Toilet Preparations/Land/202-523-0491
Cotton/Taylor/202-523-0365
Cottonseed & Cottonseed Oil/Reeder/202-724-1754
Cranes/DeMarines/202-523-0259
Crayons/Hanlon/202-724-1745
Creams, Cosmetic/Land/202-523-0491
Crude Cresylic Acid/Foreso/202-523-1230
Crude Petroleum/Foreso/202-523-1230
Crushing Machines/Fravel/202-523-0411
Cryolite/Garil/202-523-0304
Cucumbers/McCarty/202-724-1753
Culm/Foreso/202-523-1230
Cuprous Oxide/Johnson/202-523-0127
Curtains/Borsari/202-523-5703
Cushions/Leverett/202-724-1725
Cut Flowers/Burket/202-724-0088
Cutlery/Reed/202-523-0255
Cutting Machines/Greene/202-523-0265
Dairy Products/Warren/202-724-0090
Data Processing Machines/Fletcher/202-523-0378
Decalcomanias (Decals)/Stahmer/202-724-0091
Dental Cements/Noreen/202-523-1255
Dermatological Agents/Briggs/202-523-1145
Detergents/Land/202-523-0491
Dextrine/Noreen/202-523-1255
Di(2-ethylhexyl) Adipate/Johnson/202-523-0127
Di(2-ethylhexyl) Phthalate/Johnson/202-523-0127
Diamonds/Garil/202-523-0304
Diatomite/Garil/202-523-0304
Diisobutylene/Raftery/202-523-0453
Diisodecyl Phthalate/Johnson/202-523-0127
Dinnerware of Ceramic/McNay/202-523-0445
Dioctyl Phthalate/Johnson/202-523-0127
Distillate Fuel Oil/Foreso/202-523-1230
Doll Carriages, Strollers and Parts/Seastrum/202-724-1733
Dolls/Estes/202-724-0977
Dolomite, Dead Burned/Ruhlman/202-523-0309
Draperies/Borsari/202-523-5703
Drawing Instruments/Hagelin/202-724-1746
Dresses/MacKnight/202-523-5585
Dressing Machines (Textile)/Greene/202-523-0265

Drink-Preparing Machines/Jackson/202-523-4604
Drugs, Natural/Briggs/202-523-1145
Drugs, Synthetic/Briggs/202-523-1145
Dry-Cleaning Machines/Jackson/202-523-4604
Drying Machines/Jackson/202-523-4604
Dyeing Machines/Greene/202-523-0265
Dyes/Wanser/202-523-0492
Dynamite/Johnson/202-523-0127
Earth-Moving Machines/DeMarines/202-523-0259
Earthenware, Articles of/McNay/202-523-0445
Economizers/Tsapogas/202-523-0426
Edible Gelatin/Noreen/202-523-1255
Edible Preparations/Grant/202-724-0099
Eggs/Newman/202-724-0087
Elastic Fabrics/Sweet/202-523-0394
Elastomers/Taylor/202-523-3709
Electromechanical Appliances/Jackson/202-523-4604
Electronic Tubes/Hogge/202-523-0377
Electrothermic Appliances/Jackson/202-523-4604
Elements, Chemical/Emanuel/202-523-0334
Elevators/DeMarines/202-523-0259
Embroidery Machines/Greene/202-523-0265
Enamels/Johnson/202-523-0127
Engineering Resins/Taylor/202-523-3709
Engines/Tsapogas/202-523-0426
Enzymes/Briggs/202-523-1145
Epoxides/Conant/202-523-0495
Epoxidized Ester/Johnson/202-523-0127
Epoxidized Linseed Oils/Johnson/202-523-0127
Epoxidized Soya Oil/Johnson/202-523-0127
Epoxy Resins/Taylor/202-523-3709
Essential Oils/Land/202-523-0491
Esters, Fatty-Acid, of Polyhydric Alcohols/Land/202-523-0491
Ethane/Land/202-523-0491
Ethanolamines/Michels/202-523-0293
Ethers/Conant/202-523-0495
Ethers, Fatty-Acid, of Polyhydric Alcohols/Land/202-523-0491
Ethyl Alcohol (Ethanol) for Nonbeverage Use/Conant/202-523-0495
Ethylene/Foreso/202-523-1230
Ethylene Dibromide/Conant/202-523-0495
Ethylene Glycol/Conant/202-523-0495
Ethylene Oxide/Conant/202-523-0495
Ethlene-Propylene Rubber/Taylor/202-523-3709
Explosives/Johnson/202-523-0127
Eye Glasses/Witherspoon/202-724-0978
Fabric Folding Machines/Greene/202-523-0265
Fabrics:
    Billiard Cloth/Cook/202-523-0348
    Bolting Cloth/Cook/202-523-0348
    Coated/Cook/202-523-0348
    Elastic/Sweet/202-523-0394
    Impression/Chiriaco/202-523-0109
    Knit/Sweet/202-523-0394
    Narrow/Sweet/202-523-0394
    Nonwoven/Cook/202-523-0348
    Oil Cloths/Cook/202-523-0348
    Ornamented/Sweet/202-523-0394
    Pile/Sweet/202-523-0394
    Tapestry, Woven/Cook/202-523-0348
    Tire/Cook/202-523-0348

Tracing Cloth/Cook/202-523-0348
Tufted/Sweet/202-523-0394
Woven:
  Cotton/Williams/202-523-5702
  Glass/Chiriaco/202-523-0109
  Jute/Cook/202-523-0348
  Manmade Fibers/Chiriaco/202-523-0109
  Silk/Chiriaco/202-523-0109
  Wool/McGuyer/202-523-0403
Fans/DeMarines/202-523-0259
Fats, Oils & Greases, Coconut, Palm Tallow, Wool Grease, and Other (Surface-Active Agents)/Land/202-523-0491
Fatty Acids/Noreen/202-523-1255
Fatty-Acid Amides/Land/202-523-0491
Fatty-Acid Amines/Land/202-523-0491
Fatty Alcohols of Animal or Vegetable Origin/Noreen/202-523-1255
Fatty Ethers of Animal or Vegetable Origin/Noreen/202-523-1255
Fatty-Acid Esters of Polyhydric Alcohols/Land/202-523-0491
Fatty-Acid Quarternary Ammonium Salts (Surface-Active Agents)/Land/202-523-0491
Fatty Substances Derived from Animal, Marine Animal, or Vegetable Sources/Noreen/202-523-1255
Feather Products/Cunningham/202-724-0980
Feathers/Newman/202-724-0087
Feeds, Animal/Pierre-Benoist/202-724-0074
Ferments/Briggs/202-523-1145
Ferricyanide Blue/Johnson/202-523-0127
Ferrites/Lukes/202-523-0279
Ferroalloys/Boszormenyi/202-523-0328
Ferrocerium/Cunningham/200-724-0980
Ferrocyanide Blue/Johnson/202-523-0127
Fertilizers/Emanuel/202-523-0334
Fibers:
  Abaca/Cook/202-523-0348
  Alpaca/Clayton/202-523-5701
  Angora/Clayton/202-523-5701
  Camel Hair/Clayton/202-523-5701
  Cashmere/Clayton/202-523-5701
  Cotton/Taylor/202-523-0365
  Flax/Cook/202-523-0348
  Jute/Cook/202-523-0348
  Manmade/Clayton/202-523-5701
  Silk/Chiriaco/202-523-0109
  Sisam and Henequen/Cook/202-523-0348
  Wool/Clayton/202-523-5701
Fibrin/Noreen/202-523-1255
Filberts/Burket/202-724-0088
Film (Photographic)/Durkin/202-724-1729
Film, Plastic/Taylor/202-523-3709
Firewood/Hoffmeier/202-724-1766
Firearms/Estes/202-724-0977
Fireworks/Cunningham/202-724-0980
First Aid Kits/Noreen/202-523-1255
Fish/Lopp/202-724-1759
Fish Nets and Netting/Cook/202-523-0348
Fish Oils/Reeder/202-724-1754
Fishing Tackle/Watkins/202-724-0976
Flags/Cook/202-523-0348
Flares/Cunningham/202-724-0980

Flashlights/Cutchin/202-523-0231
Flat Glass and Products/Fulcher/202-523-0290
Flat Goods/Seastrum/202-724-1733
Flaxseed and Linseed Oil/Reeder/202-724-1754
Flight Simulating Machines/Ladomirak/202-523-0131
Floating Structures/West/202-523-0299
Floor Coverings, Non-Textile/Cunningham/202-724-0980
Floor Coverings, Textile/Borsari/202-523-5703
Flooring (Wood)/Ruggles/202-724-1766
Floral Waters/Land/202-523-0491
Flour (Grain)/Pierre-Benoist/202-724-0074
Flourspar/Ruhlman/202-523-0309
Flowers and Foliage:
  Artificial, Plastics/Raftery/202-523-0453
  Preserved, Plastics/Raftery/202-523-0453
Flowers and Foliage:
  Artificial, Other/Cunningham/202-724-0980
  Preserved, Other/Cunningham/202-724-0980
Fluorocarbons/Conant/202-523-0495
Fluxes/Garil/202-523-0304
Foil, Metal:
  Aluminum/Woods/202-523-0277
  Other/Woods/202-523-0277
Food-Preparing Machines/Jackson/202-523-4604
Footwear/Burns/202-523-0200
Forged-Steel Grinding Balls/Tsapogas/202-523-0426
Fork-Lift Trucks/Fravel/202-523-0411
Formaldehyde/Michels/202-523-0293
Freon (Chlorofluorocarbons)/Conant/202-523-0495
Fructose/Noreen/202-523-1255
Fruit, Edible, Ex Citrus/Macomber/202-724-1765
Fuel, Jet/Foreso/202-523-1230
Fuel Oil, Bunker "C"/Foreso/202-523-1230
Fuel Oil, Navy Special/Foreso/202-523-1230
Fuel Oil (Nos. 1, 2, 3, 4, 5, 6)/Foreso/202-523-1230
Fulminates/Johnson/202-523-0127
Fur & Furlike Apparel/Worrell/202-523-0452
Furfural/Michels/202-523-0293
Furnace Black/Johnson/202-523-0127
Furnaces/DeMarines/202-523-0259
Furniture/Leverett/202-724-1725
Furskins/Ludwick/202-724-1763
Fuses/Cunningham/202-724-0980
Fusion Energy/Greenblatt/202-523-1212
Gallium/Palmer/202-523-0270
Game Animals/Ludwick/202-724-1763
Games/Watkins/202-724-0976
Garters and Suspenders/Rudy/202-523-0142
Gas Generators/Tsapogas/202-523-0426
Gas Oil/Foreso/202-523-1230
Gas-Operated Metalworking Appliances/West/202-523-0299
Gasoline/Foreso/202-523-1230
Gauze, Impregnated with Medicinals/Noreen/202-523-1255
Gelatin, Articles of/DePauw/202-724-1730
Gelatin, Edible/Noreen/202-523-1255
Gelatin, Inedible/Noreen/202-523-1255
Gelatin, Photographic/Noreen/202-523-1255
Gems/Garil/202-523-0304
Gemstones, Imitation/Wilson/202-724-1731
Generators/Hogge/202-523-0377

Glace Fruit and Vegetable Substances/Macomber/202-724-1765

Glass/Fulcher/202-523-0290

Glass Ariticles, n.s.p.f./Fulcher/202-523-0290

Glass Fiber/Fulcher/202-523-0290

Glass Yarn/Clayton/202-523-5701

Glassworking Machines/Fravel/202-523-0411

Glassware/McNay/202-523-0445

Glazing Compounds/Johnson/202-523-0127

Gloves/Worrell/202-523-0452

Glue, Articles of/DePauw/202-724-1730

Glue, of Animal or Vegetable Origin/Noreen/202-523-1255

Glue Size/Noreen/202-523-1255

Glue, Vegetable/Noreen/202-523-1255

Glycerine/Conant/202-523-0495

Glycols/Conant/202-523-0495

Gold/Woods/202-523-0277

Gold Compounds/Greenblatt/202-523-1212

Golf Equipment/Watkins/202-724-0976

Grain Products, Milled/Pierre-Benoist/202-724-0074

Grains/Pierre-Benoist/202-724-0074

Granite/Garil/202-523-0304

Grapefruit Oil (Essential Oil)/Land/202-523-0491

Graphite/Garil/202-523-0304

Grease, Lubricating/Foreso/202-523-1230

Grinding Machines/Tsapogas/202-523-0426

Ground Fish/Lopp/202-724-1759

Gums and Resins/Reeder/202-724-1754

Gun Cotton/Johnson/202-523-0127

Gunpowder/Johnson/202-523-0127

Gut, Articles of/DePauw/202-724-1730

Gut; Catgut, Whip Gut, Oriental Gut, and Wormgut/Ludwick/202-724-1763

Gypsum/Garil/202-523-0304

Gypsum Board/Ruggles/202-724-1766

Hafnium/DeSapio/202-523-0273

Hair/Ludwick/202-724-1763

Hair, Articles of/DePauw/202-724-1730

Hair Curlers, Nonelectric/Leverett/202-724-1725

Hair Ornaments/Leverett/202-724-1725

Halogenated Hydrocarbons/Conant/202-523-0495

Handbags/Seastrum/202-724-1733

Handkerchiefs/MacKnight/202-523-5585

Hand Tools:
    Household/Brandon/202-523-5437
    Other/Brandon/202-523-5437

Hand Tools With Self-Contained Motor/Fravel/202-523-0411

Handwork Yarns:
    Cotton/Taylor/202-523-0365
    Manmade Fibers/Clayton/202-523-5701
    Wool/Clayton/202-523-5701

Hardboard/Ruggles/202-724-1766

Hats/Worrell/202-523-0452

Headwear/Worrell/202-523-0452

Health Services Industry/Jonnard/202-523-0345

Heat-Insulating Articles/Ruhlman/202-523-0309

Heat Process Equipment/Slingerland/202-523-0263

Heliotropin/Land/202-523-0491

Hides/Ludwick/202-724-1763

Hide Cuttings/Noreen/202-523-1255

Hogs/Ludwick/202-724-1763

Home Furnishings/Borsari/202-523-5703

Hoof, Articles of/DePauw/202-524-1730

Hoofs, Crude/Ludwick/202-724-1763

Hooks and Eyes/Watkins/202-724-0976

Hormones/Briggs/202-523-1145

Horn, Articles of/DePauw/202-724-1730

Horn, Crude/Ludwick/202-724-1763

Horses/Ludwick/202-724-1763

Horticultural Machinery/Fravel/202-523-0411

Hose, Industrial/Cook/202-523-0348

Hose, of Plastics or Rubber/Raftery/202-523-0453

Hosiery/Worrell/202-523-0452

Hydrocarbons/Raftery/202-523-0453

Hydrochloric Acid/Emanuel/202-523-0334

Hydrofluoric Acid/Emanuel/202-523-0334

Hypnotics/Briggs/202-523-1145

Ignition Equipment/Graves/202-523-0360

Indium/Palmer/202-523-0270

Industrial Ceramics/Lukes/202-523-0279

Industrial Diamonds/Garil/202-523-0304

Inedible Gelatin/Noreen/202-523-1255

Infants' Accessories or Apparel/MacKnight/202-523-5585

Ingot Molds/West/202-523-0299

Ink Powders/Johnson/202-523-0127

Inks/Johnson/202-523-0127

Inorganic Acids/Emanuel/202-523-0334

Inorganic Compounds and Mixtures/Greenblatt/202-523-1212

Instruments:
    Controlling/Moller/202-724-1732
    Dental/Moller/202-724-1732
    Drawing/Hagelin/202-724-1746
    Mathematical Calculating/Hagelin/202-724-1746
    Measuring/Moller/202-724-1732
    Measuring or Checking/Witherspoon/202-724-0978
    Medical/Moller/202-724-1732
    Meteorological/Moller/202-724-1732
    Musical/Witherspoon/202-724-0978
    Navigational/Moller/202-724-1732
    Surgical/Moller/202-724-1732
    Surveying/Moller/202-724-1732
    Testing/Moller/202-724-1732

Iodine/Emanuel/202-523-0334

Insulators, Ceramic/Lukes/202-523-0279

Iron Blues/Johnson/202-523-0127

Iron Compounds/Greenblatt/202-523-1212

Iron Ore/Boszormenyi/202-523-0328

Isinglass/Noreen/202-523-1255

Isobutane/Raftery/202-523-0453

Isobutylene/Raftery/202-523-0453

Isoprene/Raftery/202-523-0453

Isopropyl Myristate/Johnson/202-523-0127

Ivory, Articles of/DePauw/202-724-1730

Ivory, Tusks/Ludwick/202-724-1763

Jackets:
    Men's and Boys'/Worrell/202-523-0452
    Women's and Girls'/MacKnight/202-523-5585

Jams, Jellies, and Marmalades/Macomber/202-724-1765

Jet Fuel/Foreso/202-523-1230

Jewelry/Wilson/202-724-1731

Juices, Fruit/Macomber/202-724-1765

Juices, Vegetable/Lipovsky/202-724-0097

Kaolin/Lukes/202-523-0279
Kerosene/Foreso/202-523-1230
Ketones/Michels/202-523-0293
Key Cases/Seastrum/202-724-1733
Knitting Machines/Greene/202-523-0265
Labels/Cook/202-523-0348
Lace/Sweet/202-523-0394
Lacemaking Machines/Greene/202-523-0265
Lacings/Cook/202-523-0348
Lactose/Noreen/202-523-1255
Lacquers/Johnson/202-523-0127
Lakes/Wanser/202-523-0492
Lamb/Ludwick/202-724-1763
Lamp Black/Johnson/202-523-0127
Lamps (Bulbs)/Cutchin/202-523-0231
Laundry Machines/Jackson/202-523-4604
Lead/Palmer/202-523-0270
Lead Compounds/Greenblatt/202-523-1212
Lead Pigments/Johnson/202-523-0127
Leads/Hanlon/202-724-1745
Lease Condensate/Foreso/202-523-1230
Leather/Ludwick/202-724-1763
Leather Apparel/Worrell/202-523-0452
Lenses/Witherspoon/202-724-0978
Lemon Oil (Essential Oil)/Land/202-523-0491
Levulose/Noreen/202-523-1255
Light Oil/Foreso/202-523-1230
Lighting Equipment/Cutchin/202-523-0231
Ligninsulfonic Acid and Its Salts/Land/202-523-0491
Lignite/Foreso/202-523-1230
Lime/Garil/202-523-0304
Limestone/Garil/202-523-0304
Lithium/Emanuel/202-523-0334
Lithium Compounds/Greenblatt/202-523-1212
Lithium Stearate/Noreen/202-523-1255
Liquefied Natural Gas (LNG)/Land/202-523-0491
Liquefied Petroleum Gas (LPG)/Land/202-523-0491
Liquefied Refinery Gas (LRG)/Land/202-523-0491
Logs, Rough/Ruggles/202-724-1766
Lube Fittings/Tsapogas/202-523-0426
Lubricating Grease/Foreso/202-523-1230
Lubricating Oil/Foreso/202-523-1230
Luggage/Seastrum/202-724-1733
Lumber/Ruggles/202-724-1766
Macaroni and Other Alimentary Pastes/Grant/202-724-0099
Machines and Machinery:
   Adding/Fletcher/202-523-0378
   Addressing/Fletcher/202-523-0378
   Agglomerating/Tsapogas/202-523-0426
   Agricultural or Horticultural/Fravel/202-523-0411
   Bookbinding/Slingerland/202-523-0263
   Calculators/Nelson/202-523-4585
   Cash Registers/Fletcher/202-523-0378
   Casting Machines/West/202-523-0299
   Checkwriting/Fletcher/202-523-0378
   Cleaning (Heat Process Equipment)/Slingerland/202-523-0263
   Cleaning (Textiles)/Greene/202-523-0265
   Coating/Greene/202-523-0265
   Converters/West/202-523-0299
   Cordage/Greene/202-523-0265
   Crushing/Fravel/202-523-0411

   Cutting/Greene/202-523-0265
   Data Processing/Fletcher/202-523-0378
   Dressing/Greene/202-523-0265
   Drink Preparing/Jackson/202-523-4604
   Dry Cleaning/Jackson/202-523-4604
   Drying/Jackson/202-523-4604
   Dyeing/Greene/202-523-0265
   Earth Moving/DeMarines/202-523-0259
   Embroidery/Greene/202-523-0265
   Fabric Folding/Greene/202-523-0265
   Farm (Except Tractors)/Fravel/202-523-0411
   Flight Simulators/Ladomirak/202-523-0131
   Food Preparing/Jackson/202-523-4604
   Horticultural/Fravel/202-523-0411
   Mining/DeMarines/202-523-0259
   Numbering/Fletcher/202-523-0378
   Office Copying/Fletcher/202-523-0378
   Office Machines Not Enumerated/Fletcher/202-523-0378
   Packaging/Slingerland/202-523-0263
   Paperboard/Slingerland/202-523-0263
   Postage Franking/Fletcher/202-523-0378
   Printing/Slingerland/202-523-0263
   Pulp/Slingerland/202-523-0263
   Reeling/Greene/202-523-0265
   Rolling (Metal)/West/202-523-0299
   Rolling n.e.s./Slingerland/202-523-0263
   Rolling (Textile)/Greene/202-523-0265
Screening/DeMarines/202-523-0259
   Sealing/Slingerland/202-523-0263
   Sewing/Greene/202-523-0265
   Shoe/Fravel/202-523-0411
   Sorting/Tsapogas/202-523-0426
   Spraying/Slingerland/202-523-0263
   Stone Processing/Fravel/202-523-0411
   Stoneworking/West/202-523-0299
   Textile:
     Bleaching/Greene/202-523-0265
     Calendering and Rolling/Greene/202-523-0265
     Cleaning/Greene/202-523-0265
     Coating/Greene/202-523-0265
     Drying/Greene/202-523-0265
     Dyeing/Greene/202-523-0265
     Embroidery/Greene/202-523-0265
     Knitting/Greene/202-523-0265
     Lacemaking/Greene/202-523-0265
     Printing/Greene/202-523-0265
     Spinning/Greene/202-523-0265
     Washing/Greene/202-523-0265
     Weaving/Greene/202-523-0265
   Tobacco/Jackson/202-523-4604
   Tools, Machine/West/202-523-0299
   Vending/Jackson/202-523-4604
   Weighing/Slingerland/202-523-0263
Magnesite:
   Caustic Calcined/Garil/202-523-0304
   Crude/Garil/202-523-0304
   Dead Burned/Ruhlman/202-523-0309
Magnesium/DeSapio/202-523-0273
Magnesium Compounds/Greenblatt/202-523-1212
Magnetic Devices/Graves/202-523-0360
Malts/Grant/202-724-0099

Manganese/Boszormenyi/202-523-0328
Manganese Compounds/Greenblatt/202-523-1212
Manmade Fibers/Clayton/202-523-5701
Mantles/Cunningham/202-724-0980
Marble, Breccia, and Onyx/Garil/202-523-0304
Matches/Cunningham/202-724-0980
Mattresses/Leverett/202-724-1725
MBS Resins/Taylor/202-523-3709
Meat, Edible/Ludwick/202-724-1763
Meat, Inedible/Ludwick/202-724-1763
Medical Apparatus/Moller/202-724-1732
Melamine/Michels/202-523-0293
Melamine Resins/Taylor/202-523-3709
Menthol/Land/202-523-0491
Mercury/DeSapio/202-523-0273
Mercury Compounds/Greenblatt/202-523-1212
Metal Rolling Mills/West/202-523-0299
Metal Working Machines/West/202-523-0299
Meteorological/Moller/202-724-1732
Methacrylates/Conant/202-523-0495
Methane/Land/202-523-0491
Methyl Alcohol (Methanol)/Conant/202-523-0495
Methyl Ethyl Ketone/Michels/202-523-0293
Methyl Oleate/Johnson/202-523-0127
Mica/Garil/202-523-0304
Microscopes/Witherspoon/202-724-0978
Milk/Warren/202-724-0090
Millinery Ornaments/Cunningham/202-724-0980
Mineral Oil/Foreso/202-523-1230
Mineral Salts/Noreen/202-523-1255
Mineral Wool/Garil/202-523-0304
Mining/DeMarines/202-523-0259
Mining Machines/DeMarines/202-523-0259
Miscellaneous Animal Products/Ludwick/202-724-1763
Miscellaneous Benzenoid Intermediates/Cappuccilli/202-523-0490
Miscellaneous Articles of Pulp and Paper/Rhodes/202-724-1299
Miscellaneous Fish Products/Lopp/202-724-1759
Miscellaneous Products/Cunningham/202-724-0980
Miscellaneous Vegetable Products/Pierre-Benoist/202-724-0074
Miscellaneous Wood Products/Westcot/202-724-0095
Mixtures (Artificial) of Fatty Substances/Noreen/202-523-1255
Mixtures of Inorganic Compounds/Greenblatt/202-523-1212
Mixtures of Organic Compounds/Conant/202-523-0495
Moccasins/Burns/202-523-0200
Models/Estes/202-724-0977
Molasses/Grant/202-724-0099
Molders' Boxes, Forms, and Patterns/Tsapogas/202-523-0426
Moldings, Wooden/Ruggles/202-724-1766
Molybdenum/Woods/202-523-0277
Molybdenum Compounds/Greenblatt/202-523-1212
Monofilaments, Manmade/Clayton/202-523-5701
Monosodium Glutamate/Land/202-523-0491
Motion Pictures/Witherspoon/202-724-0978
Motorcycles/McElroy/202-523-0258
Motor Oil/Foreso/202-523-1230
Motor Vehicles:
  Buses/McElroy/202-523-0258

Fork-Lift & Other Self-Propelled Work Trucks/Fravel/202-523-0411
Motorcycles & Armored Vehicles/McElroy/202-523-0258
Passenger Autos/McElroy/202-523-0258
Snowmobiles/McElroy/202-523-0258
Tractors, Ex Truck Tractors/DeMarines/202-523-0259
Trailers & Other Vehicles Not Self-Propelled/Ladomirak/202-523-0131
Trucks (Including Truck Tractors)/McElroy/202-523-0258
Motors:
  Electric/Hogge/202-523-0377
  Nonelectric/Tsapogas/202-523-0426
Mufflers (Apparel)/MacKnight/202-523-5585
Mushrooms/McCarty/202-724-1753
Musk, Grained or in Pods/Land/202-523-0491
Musical Instruments, Accessories/Witherspoon/202-724-0978
Musical Instruments, Parts/Witherspoon/202-724-0978
Nails/Brandon/202-523-5437
Naphtha/Foreso/202-523-1230
Naphthalene (Refined)/Cappuccilli/202-523-0490
Napkins, Cloth/Borsari/202-523-5703
Narrow Fabrics/Sweet/202-523-0394
Natural Gas/Land/202-523-0491
Natural Gas Liquids (NGL)/Land/202-523-0491
Natural Pearls/Garbecki/202-724-1731
Natural Rubber/Taylor/202-523-3709
Navigational Instruments/Moller/202-724-1732
Navy Special Fuel Oil/Foreso/202-523-1230
Neckties/MacKnight/202-523-5585
Nettings:
  Fish/Cook/202-523-0348
  Other/Sweet/202-523-0394
Newsprint/Stahmer/202-724-0091
Nickel/Woods/202-523-0277
Nickel Compounds/Greenblatt/202-523-1212
Nitric Acid/Emanuel/202-523-0334
Nitriles/Michels/202-523-0293
Nitrogenous Fertilizers/Emanuel/202-523-0334
Non-Benzenoid Resins/Taylor/202-523-3709
Non-electric Motors and Engines/Tsapogas/202-523-0426
Nonenumerated Products/Cunningham/202-724-0980
Nonmetallic Minerals/Lukes/202-523-0279
Nuclear Energy/Greenblatt/202-523-1212
Numbering Machines/Fletcher/202-523-0378
Nuts, Edible/Burket/202-724-0088
Oakum/Cook/202-523-0348
Odoriferous or Aromatic Substances/Land/202-523-0491
Office Copying Machines/Fletcher/202-523-0378
Office Machines, Not Enumerated/Fletcher/202-523-0378
Oil, Lubricating/Foreso/202-523-1230
Oilcloth/Cook/202-523-0348
Oils, Essential/Land/202-523-0491
Oilseeds/Reeder/202-724-1754
Oleic Acid/Noreen/202-523-1255
Oleic Acid/Esters/Johnson/202-523-0127
Oleyl Alcohols/Noreen/202-523-1255
Onions/McCarty/202-724-1753
Ophthalmic/Witherspoon/202-724-0978
Optical Elements/Witherspoon/202-724-0978

Optical Goods/Witherspoon/202-724-0978
Orange Oil (Essential Oil)/Land/202-523-0491
Organic Acids/Michels/202-523-0293
Organic Chemicals/Jonnard/202-523-0345
Organo-metallic Compounds/Conant/202-523-0495
Ornamented Fabrics/Sweet/202-523-0394
Ossein/Noreen/202-523-1255
Ovens/DeMarines/202-523-0259
Packaging Machines/Slingerland/202-523-0263
Paint Rollers/Leverett/202-724-1725
Paints/Johnson/202-523-0127
Paint Sets, Artist's/Johnson/202-523-0127
Pajamas:
   Men's and Boys'/Worrell/202-523-0452
   Women's, Girls', and Infants'/MacKnight/202-523-5585
Palm Oil/Reeder/202-724-1754
Palmitic Acid Esters/Johnson/202-523-0127
Panty Hose/Worrell/202-523-0452
Paper Machines/Slingerland/202-523-0263
Paperboard/Rhodes/202-724-1299
Paperboard, Products of/Stahmer/202-724-0091
Paperboard Machines/Slingerland/202-523-0263
Papermakers' Felts/Cook/202-523-0348
Papermaking Materials/Rhodes/202-724-1299
Paper/Rhodes/202-724-1299
Paper, Products of/Stahmer/202-724-0091
Parachutes/Ladomirak/202-523-0131
Particle Board/Ruggles/202-724-1766
Party Favors/Estes/202-724-0977
Passenger Autos, Trucks, & Buses/McElroy/202-523-0258
Peanuts/Burket/202-724-0088
Pearl Essence/Johnson/202-523-0127
Pearls/Wilson/202-724-1731
Peat Moss/Emanuel/202-523-0334
Pectin/Noreen/202-523-1255
Pencils/Hanlon/202-724-1745
Penicillin/Briggs/202-523-1145
Pens/Hanlon/202-724-1745
Perchloroethylene/Conant/202-523-0495
Perfumery, Cosmetics, and Toilet Preps/Land/202-523-0491
Personal Leather Goods/Seastrum/202-724-1733
Pesticides/Cappuccilli/202-523-0490
Pet Animals (Live)/Ludwick/202-724-1763
Petroleum/Foreso/202-523-1230
Phenol/Cappuccilli/202-523-0490
Phenolic Resins/Taylor/202-523-3709
Phonograph Records/Witherspoon/202-724-0978
Phonographic Equipment/Witherspoon/202-724-0978
Phonographs/Nelson/202-523-4585
Phosphatic Fertilizers/Emanuel/202-523-0334
Phosphoric Acid/Emanuel/202-523-0334
Phosphoric Acid Esters/Johnson/202-523-0127
Phosphorus/Emanuel/202-523-0334
Phosphorus Compounds/Greenblatt/202-523-1212
Photocells/Hogge/202-523-0377
Photographic Chemicals/Wanser/202-523-0492
Photographic Film:
   Scrap/Witherspoon/202-724-0978
   Waste/Witherspoon/202-724-0978
Photographic Gelatin/Noreen/202-523-1255

Photographic Supplies/Witherspoon/202-724-0978
Photographs/Stahmer/202-724-0091
Phthalic Acid Esters/Johnson/202-523-0127
Phthalic Anhydride/Cappuccilli/202-523-0490
Pig Iron/Boszormenyi/202-523-0328
Pigments, Inorganic/Johnson/202-523-0127
Pigments, Organic/Wanser/202-523-0492
Pillow Blocks/Tsapogas/202-523-0426
Pillowcases/Borsari/202-523-5703
Pillows/Leverett/202-724-1725
Pinane/Raftery/202-523-0453
Pinball Machines/Watkins/202-724-0976
Pins/Watkins/202-724-0976
Pipe of Plastics or Rubber/Raftery/202-523-0453
Pipes/DePauw/202-724-1730
Pitch From Wood/Noreen/202-523-1255
Plants, Live/Burket/202-724-0088
Plaster Products (Except Wallboard)/Garil/202-523-0304
Plasticizers/Johnson/202-523-0127
Plastics/Taylor/202-523-3709
Plastics Products/Raftery/202-523-0453
Plastic Wood/Johnson/202-523-0127
Platinum Compounds/Greenblatt/202-523-1212
Platinum Group Metals/Woods/202-523-0277
Pleasure Boats/West/202-523-0299
Plutonium/Greenblatt/202-523-1212
Plywood/Ruggles/202-724-1766
Polishes Under 10 lbs. Each/Noreen/202-523-1255
Polycarbonate Resins/Taylor/202-523-3709
Polyhydric Alcohol/Conant/202-523-0495
Polyhydric Alcohols, Fatty Acids of, Derived From Animal or Vegetable Oil/Land/202-523-0491
Polyhydric Alcohols of Polysaccharides and Rare Saccharides/Noreen/202-523-1255
Polyisoprene Rubber/Taylor/202-523-3709
Polyester Resins/Taylor/202-523-3709
Polyethylene/Taylor/202-523-3709
Polyethylene Teraphthalate (PET) Resins/Taylor/202-523-3709
Polysaccharides/Noreen/202-523-1255
Polymers/Taylor/202-523-3709
Polypropylene/Taylor/202-523-3709
Polystyrene Resins/Taylor/202-523-3709
Polyurethane Resins/Taylor/202-523-3709
Polyvinyl Alcohol Resins/Taylor/202-523-3709
Polyvinyl Chloride/Taylor/202-523-3709
Pork/Ludwick/202-724-1763
Postage-Franking Machines/Fletcher/202-523-0378
Potash/Emanuel/202-523-0334
Potassic Fertilizers/Emanuel/202-523-0334
Potassium & Sodium Salts From Coconut, Palm, & Other Oils/Land/202-523-0491
Potassium Chloride/Emanuel/202-523-0334
Potassium Compounds/Greenblatt/202-523-1212
Potatoes/McCarty/202-724-1753
Pottery/McNay/202-523-0445
Poultry/Newman/202-724-0087
Powder, Smokeless/Johnson/202-523-0127
Precious Stones/Garil/202-523-0304
Printing Ink/Johnson/202-523-0127
Printing Machines/Slingerland/202-523-0263
Printing Machines (Textiles)/Greene/202-523-0265
Printed Matter/Stahmer/202-724-0091

Projectors (Photographic)/Witherspoon/202-724-0978
Propane/Land/202-523-0491
Propylene Glycol/Conant/202-523-0495
Propylene/Raftery/202-523-0453
Propylene Oxide/Conant/202-523-0495
Psychotherapeutic Agents/Briggs/202-523-1145
Pulleys/Tsapogas/202-523-0426
Pulp, Articles of/Rhodes/202-724-1299
Pulp Machines/Slingerland/202-523-0263
Pulpwood/Ruggles/202-724-1766
Putty/Johnson/202-523-0127
Puzzles/Watkins/202-724-0976
Pumps, Air and Vacuum/DeMarines/202-523-0259
Pumps, Liquid/DeMarines/202-523-0259
Pyrethrum/Cappuccilli/202-523-0490
Pyridine/Cappuccilli/202-523-0490
Pyrotechnics/Cunningham/202-724-0980
Quartzite/Garil/202-523-0304
Quaternary Ammonium Salts, Fatty Acids/Land/202-523-0491
Quebracho/Wanser/202-523-0492
Quill, Articles of/DePauw/202-724-1730
Quilts/Borsari/202-523-5703
Racing Shells/West/202-523-0299
Radar Apparatus/Fletcher/202-523-0378
Radio Navigational Apparatus/Fletcher/202-523-0378
Radio Receivers/Nelson/202-523-4585
Rags/Cook/202-523-0348
Rail, Locomotives/Ladomirak/202-523-0131
Rails/Rapkins/202-523-0438
Railway Rolling Stock/Ladomirak/202-523-0131
Rainwear/Wallace/202-523-0120
Rare-Earth Compounds/Greenblatt/202-523-1212
Rare-Earth Metals/DeSapio/202-523-0273
Rare Saccharides/Noreen/202-523-1255
Rattan/Westcot/202-724-0095
Reconstituted Crude Petroleum/Foreso/202-523-1230
Recording Media/Witherspoon/202-724-0978
Reeling Machines/Greene/202-523-0265
Refractories/Ruhlman/202-523-0309
Refrigeration Equipment/DeMarines/202-523-0259
Regulators/Graves/202-523-0360
Residual Fuel Oil/Foreso/202-523-1230
Resistors/Cutchin/202-523-0231
Rhenium/Woods/202-523-0277
Rhodium Compounds/Greenblatt/202-523-1212
Ribbons:
    Inked/Cook/202-523-0348
    Typewriter/Sweet/202-523-0349
    Other/Sweet/202-523-0349
Rice/Pierre-Benoist/202-724-0074
Ricinoleic Acid Esters/Johnson/202-523-0127
Riding Crops/Leverett/202-724-1725
Rifles/Estes/202-724-0977
Rods, Plastic/Raftery/202-523-0453
Rolling Machines, Except Metal/Slingerland/202-523-0263
Rolling Mills, Metal/West/202-523-0299
Rope/Cook/202-523-0348
Rosemary Oil (Essential Oil)/Land/202-523-0491
Rouges/Land/202-523-0491
Rubber, Natural/Taylor/202-523-3709
Rubber, Synthetic/Taylor/202-523-3709

Rugs/Borsari/202-523-5703
Saccharin/Land/202-523-0491
Salicin/Noreen/202-523-1255
Salt/Greenblatt/202-523-1212
Salts, Inorganic/Greenblatt/202-523-1212
Salts, Organic/Michels/202-523-0293
SAM Resins/Taylor/202-523-3709
Sand/Garil/202-523-0304
Sandals/Burns/202-523-0200
Saran/Taylor/202-523-3709
Sardines/Lopp/202-724-1759
Satin White/Johnson/202-523-0127
Sausages/Ludwick/202-724-1763
Scales/Slingerland/202-523-0263
Scarves/MacKnight/202-523-5585
Scrap Cordage/Cook/202-523-0348
Screening Machines/Fravel/202-523-0411
Screws/Brandon/202-523-5437
Sealing Machinery/Slingerland/202-523-0263
Seat Belts/Cook/202-523-0348
Sebacic Acid Esters/Johnson/202-523-0127
Sedatives/Briggs/202-523-1145
Seeds, Field and Garden/Roeder/202-724-1170
Seeds, Oil-Bearing/Reeder/202-724-1754
Seeds, Spice/Lipovsky/202-724-0097
Selenium/Woods/202-523-0277
Selenium Compounds/Greenblatt/202-523-1212
Semiconductors/Hogge/202-523-0377
Sewing Machines/Greene/202-523-0265
Sewing Machine Needles/Greene/202-523-0265
Sewing Thread:
    Cotton/Taylor/202-523-0365
    Manmade Fibers/Clayton/202-523-5701
    Silk/Chiriaco/202-523-0109
    Wool/Clayton/202-523-5701
Shale Oil/Foreso/202-523-1230
Shawls/MacKnight/202-523-5585
Sheep/Ludwick/202-724-1763
Sheet, Plastic/Raftery/202-523-0453
Sheets, Bed/Borsari/202-523-5703
Shell, Articles of/DePauw/202-724-1730
Shellac and Other Lacs/Reeder/202-724-1754
Shellfish/Newman/202-724-0087
Shells, Freshwater, Crude/Ludwick/202-724-1763
Shells, Marine, Crude/Ludwick/202-724-1763
Shingles, Asphalt/Rhodes/202-724-1299
Shingles and Shakes (Wood)/Westcot/202-724-0095
Shirts:
    Men's and Boys'/Worrell/202-523-0452
    Women's and Girls'/MacKnight/202-523-5585
Shotguns/Estes/202-724-0977
Shoe Machinery/Fravel/202-523-0411
Shoes/Burns/202-523-0200
Shorts:
    Men's and Boys'/Worrell/202-523-0452
    Women's and Girls'/MacKnight/202-523-5585
Shrimp/Newman/202-724-0087
Siding (Wood)/Ruggles/202-724-1766
Silica/Garil/202-523-0304
Silicon/Boszormenyi/202-523-0328
Silicones/Conant/202-523-0495
Silicone Resins/Taylor/202-523-3709
Silk/Chiriaco/202-523-0109

Silver/Woods/202-523-0277
Silver Compounds/Greenblatt/202-523-1212
Sirups/Grant/202-724-0099
Ski Equipment/Watkins/202-724-0976
Skins (Animal)/Ludwick/202-724-1763
Skirts/MacKnight/202-523-5585
Slack/Foreso/202-523-1230
Slacks, Men's and Boys'/Worrell/202-523-0452
Slacks, Women's and Girls'/MacKnight/202-523-5585
Slate/Garil/202-523-0304
Slide Fasteners/Watkins/202-724-0976
Slippers/Burns/202-523-0200
Smokeless Powder/Johnson/202-523-0127
Smokers' Articles/DePauw/202-724-1730
Snap Fasteners/Watkins/202-724-0976
Soap, Castile/Land/202-523-0491
Soap, Surface-Active Agents, Synthetic Detergents/
Land/202-523-0491
Soap, Toilet/Land/202-523-0491
Soapstone/Garil/202-523-0304
Soda Ash/Greenblatt/202-523-1212
Sodium and Potassium Salts of Fats, Oils, and Greases/
Land/202-523-0491
Sodium Benzoate/Cappuccilli/202-523-0490
Solar Energy/Foreso/202-523-1230
Sodium Compounds/Greenblatt/202-523-1212
Sorbitol/Noreen/202-523-1255
Sorting Machines/Fravel/202-523-0411
Sound Signaling Apparatus/Baker/202-523-0361
Soybeans and Soybean Oil/Reeder/202-724-1754
Spacecraft/Ladomirak/202-523-0131
Spectacles/Witherspoon/202-724-0978
Special Classification Provisions/DePauw/202-724-1730
Speed Changers/Tsapogas/202-523-0426
Spices/Lipovsky/202-724-0097
Spinning Machines/Greene/202-523-0265
Sponge, Articles of/DePauw/202-724-1730
Sponges, Marine/Ludwick/202-724-1763
Sporting Goods/Watkins/202-724-0976
Spraying Machinery/Slingerland/202-523-0263
Stains/Johnson/202-523-0127
Staple, Manmade/Clayton/202-523-5701
Starches/Pierre-Benoist/202-724-0074
Starches, Chemically Treated/Noreen/202-523-1255
Stearic Acid/Noreen/202-523-1255
Stearic Acid Esters/Noreen/202-523-1255
Steatite/Garil/202-523-0304
Steel:
    Angles, Shapes, and Sections/DeSapio/202-523-0273
    Bars/DeSapio/202-523-0273
    Ingots, Blooms, and Billets/Newman/202-523-4446
    Pipe and Tube and Fittings/Rapkins/202-523-0438
    Plate/Kavalaukas/202-523-5413
Rails/Rapkins/202-523-0438
    Sheet/Avery/202-523-0342
    Strip/Avery/202-523-0342
    Waste and Scrap/Boszormenyi/202-523-0328
    Wire/Boszormenyi/202-523-0328
    Wire Rods/Boszormenyi/202-523-0328
Stereo Apparatus/Nelson/202-523-4585
Stone and Products/Garil/202-523-0304
Stone-Processing Machines/Fravel/202-523-0411
Stoneworking Machines/West/202-523-0299

Stoneware Articles/McNay/202-523-0445
Strontium/Palmer/202-523-0270
Strontium Compounds/Johnson/202-523-0127
Strontium Pigments/Johnson/202-523-0127
Structures of Base Metals/Rapkins/202-523-0438
Styrene (Monomer)/Cappuccilli/202-523-0490
Styrene Resins/Taylor/202-523-3709
Sugar/Grant/202-724-0099
Sulfur/Emanuel/202-523-0334
Sulfur Dioxide/Greenblatt/202-523-1212
Sulfuric Acid/Emanuel/202-523-0334
Superphosphates/Emanuel/202-523-0334
Surface-Active Agents/Land/202-523-0491
Surgical Apparatus/Moller/202-724-1732
Sutures, Surgical/Noreen/202-523-1255
Sweaters:
    Men's and Boys'/Worrell/202-523-0452
    Women's and Girls'/MacKnight/202-523-5585
Sweatshirts:
    Men's and Boys'/Worrell/202-523-0452
    Women's and Girls'/MacKnight/202-523-5585
Swimwear:
    Men's and Boys'/Worrell/202-523-0452
    Women's and Girls'/MacKnight/202-523-5585
Switchgear/Hogge/202-523-0377
Synthetic Detergents/Land/202-523-0491
Synthetic Iron Oxides and Hydroxides/Johnson/202-523-
0127
Synthetic Natural Gas (SNG)/Land/202-523-0491
Synthetic Organic Chemicals/Jonnard/202-523-0345
Synthetic Rubber/Taylor/202-523-3709
Tablecloths/Borsari/202-523-5703
Talc/Garil/202-523-0304
Tall Oil/Noreen/202-523-1255
Tanning Products and Agents/Wanser/202-523-0492
Tantalum/DeSapio/202-523-0273
Tape Players and Combinations/Reynolds/202-523-
0230
Tape Recordings/Witherspoon/202-724-0978
Tapestries/Borsari/202-523-5703
Taps/DeMarines/202-523-0259
Tar Sands Oil/Foreso/202-523-1230
Tea/Lipovsky/202-724-0097
Telegraph and Telephone Apparatus/Fletcher/202-523-
0378
Television Equipment/Reynolds/202-523-0230
Telescopes/Witherspoon/202-724-0978
Tellurium Compounds/Greenblatt/202-523-1212
Tennis Equipment/Watkins/202-724-0976
Tents and Tarpaulins/Cook/202-523-0348
Tetraethyl Lead/Conant/202-523-0495
Tetramer of Propylene/Raftery/202-523-0453
Tetramethyl Lead/Conant/202-523-0495
Tetrapropylene/Raftery/202-523-0453
Textile Calendering and Rolling Machines/Greene/202-
523-0265
Textile Finishing Agents/Land/202-523-0491
Textile Machines/Greene/202-523-0265
Textile Washing, Bleaching, Dyeing, Cleaning, Dress-
ing, Coating, and Drying Machines/Greene/202-523-
0265
Thallium Compounds/Greenblatt/202-523-1212
Thorium/DeSapio/202-523-0273

Thorium Compounds/Greenblatt/202-523-1212
Thread:
   Cotton/Taylor/202-523-0365
   Manmade Fibers/Clayton/202-523-5701
Silk/Chiriaco/202-523-0109
Ticket-Issuing Machines/Fletcher/202-523-0378
Tiles, Ceramic/Lukes/202-523-0279
Time Switches/Wilson/202-724-1731
Timing Apparatus/Wilson/202-724-1731
Tin/DeSapio/202-523-0273
Tin Compounds/Greenblatt/202-523-1212
Tires and Tubes of Rubber or Plastic/Raftery/202-523-0453
Titanium/DeSapio/202-523-0273
Titanium Compounds/Johnson/202-523-0127
Titanium Dioxide/Johnson/202-523-0127
Titanium Pigments/Johnson/202-523-0127
Tobacco and Tobacco Products/Lipovsky/202-724-0097
Tobacco Machines/Jackson/202-523-4604
Tobacco Pipes/DePauw/202-724-1730
Toilet Preps, Cosmetics, and Perfumery/Land/202-523-0491
Toilet Soaps/Land/202-523-0491
Toluene/Raftery/202-523-0453
Tomatoes/McCarty/202-724-1753
Toners/Wanser/202-523-0492
Topped Crude Petroleum/Foreso/202-523-1230
Tow, Manmade/Clayton/202-523-5701
Towels/Borsari/202-523-5703
Toys/Estes/202-724-0977
Toys for Pets, Christmas Decorations, Figurines, etc/Raftery/202-523-0453
Tractors (Except Truck Tractors)/DeMarines/202-523-0259
Trailers, Other Vehicles Not Self-Propelled/Ladomirak/202-523-0131
Transceivers/Nelson/202-523-4585
Transformers/Hogge/202-523-0377
Travel Goods/Seastrum/202-724-1733
Trichloroethylene/Conant/202-523-0495
Tricks/Estes/202-724-0977
Tricycles/Seastrum/202-724-1733
Trimellitic Acid Esters/Johnson/202-523-0127
Trinitrotoluene/Johnson/202-523-0127
Trousers, Men's/Worrell/202-523-0452
Trucks/McElroy/202-523-0258
Truck Tractors/McElroy/202-523-0258
T-Shirts:
   Men's and Boys'/Worrell/202-523-0452
   Women's and Girls'/MacKnight/202-523-5585
Tubes for Pneumatic Tires/Raftery/202-523-0453
Tubing of Plastic or Rubber/Raftery/202-523-0453
Tuna/Lopp/202-724-1759
Tungsten/Palmer/202-523-0270
Tungsten Compounds/Greenblatt/202-523-1212
Turpentine/Reeder/202-724-1754
Twine/Cook/202-523-0348
Typewriters/Baker/202-523-0361
Umbrellas/Leverett/202-724-1725
Underwear/Wallace/202-523-0120
Unfinished Oils/Foreso/202-523-1230
Universal Joints/Tsapogas/202-523-0426
Upholstery/Borsari/202-523-5703

Uranium/DeSapio/202-523-0273
Uranium Compounds/Greenblatt/202-523-1212
Uranium Oxide/Greenblatt/202-523-1212
Urea/Emanuel/202-523-0334
Urea Resins/Taylor/202-523-3709
Vaccines/Briggs/202-523-1145
Vacuum Cleaners/Jackson/202-523-4604
Valves & Cocks/DeMarines/202-523-0259
Vanadium/DeSapio/202-523-0273
Vanadium Compounds/Greenblatt/202-523-1212
Vanillin/Land/202-523-0491
Varnishes/Johnson/202-523-0127
Vegetable Fibers (Except Cotton)/Cook/202-523-0348
Vegetable Glue/Noreen/202-523-1255
Vegetables/McCarty/202-724-1753
Veiling/Sweet/202-523-0394
Vending Machines/Jackson/202-523-4604
Vests, Men's/Worrell/202-523-0452
Veterinary Instruments/Moller/202-724-1732
Video Games/Watkins/202-724-0976
Vinyl Chloride Monomer/Conant/202-523-0495
Vinyl Resins or Plastics/Taylor/202-523-3709
Visual Signaling Apparatus/Baker/202-523-0361
Vitamins/Briggs/202-523-1145
Walking Sticks/Leverett/202-724-1725
Wall Coverings of Rubber or Plastics/Raftery/202-523-0453
Wallpaper/Stahmer/202-724-0091
Wallets/Seastrum/202-724-1733
Waste and Scrap (Metals)/Boszormenyi/202-523-0328
Waste or Scrap/Cunningham/202-724-0980
Waste, Textile:
   Cotton/Taylor/202-523-0365
   Manmade Fiber/Clayton/202-523-5701
   Silk/Chiriaco/202-523-0109
   Wool/Clayton/202-523-5701
Watches/Wilson/202-724-1731
Wax, Articles of/DePauw/202-724-1730
Waxes/Noreen/202-523-1255
Weaving Machines/Greene/202-523-0265
Weighing Machines/Slingerland/202-523-0263
Welding Apparatus/Graves/202-523-0360
Whalebone, Articles of/DePauw/202-724-1730
Wheat/Pierre-Benoist/202-724-0074
Wheel Goods:
   Motorized/McElroy/202-523-0258
   Non-motorized/Seastrum/202-724-1733
Whips/Leverett/202-724-1725
Whiskey/Lipovsky/202-724-0097
Wines/Lipovsky/202-724-0097
Wire/Boszormenyi/202-523-0328
Wire Rods/Boszormenyi/202-523-0328
Wiring Sets/Cutchin/202-523-0231
Wood (Densified)/Westcot/202-724-0095
Wood Products, Rough Primary/Ruggles/202-724-1766
Wood Pulp/Rhodes/202-724-1299
Wood Veneers/Ruggles/202-724-1766
Wool/Clayton/202-523-5701
Wool Grease, Sulfonated or Sulfated (Surface-Active Agents)/Land/202-523-0491
X-Ray Apparatus/Moller/202-724-1732
Xylene/Raftery/202-523-0453
Xylenol/Cappuccilli/202-523-0490

Yarns:
  Cotton/Taylor/202-523-0365
  Elastic/Sweet/202-523-0394
  Flax/Cook/202-523-0348
  Glass/Clayton/202-523-5701
  Jute/Cook/202-523-0348
  Manmade/Clayton/202-523-5701
  Metalized/Cook/202-523-0348
  Paper/Cook/202-523-0348
  Silk/Chiriaco/202-523-0109

  Tire/Clayton/202-523-5701
  Wool/Clayton/202-523-5701
Yellowcake/Greenblatt/202-523-1212
Zinc/Palmer/202-523-0277
Zinc Compounds/Greenblatt/202-523-1212
Zippers/Watkins/202-724-0976
Zirconium/DeSapio/202-523-0273
Zirconium Compounds/Greenblatt/202-523-1212
Zoris/Burns/202-523-0200

Major Sources of Information

Automotive Trade Statistics
The compilation and publication of the following two series of data began some years ago in response to congressional and general public interest. Series A relates to all motor vehicles (i.e., passenger automobiles, trucks, buses, and so forth), and is published annually, in the spring; Series B relates to new passenger automobiles only and is published annually, in the fall.

Automotive Trade Statistics, 1964–1984: Factory Sales, Imports, Exports, Apparent Consumption, and Trade Balances with Canada and All Other Countries.

Automotive Trade Statistics, 1964–1984: Factory Sales, Retail Sales, Imports, Exports, Apparent Consumption, Suggested Retail Prices, and U.S. Bilateral Trade Balances with Eight Major Producing Countries.

Contact: Machinery and Transportation Equipment Branch, Machinery and Equipment Division, Office of Industries, International Trade Commission, 701 E St. N.W., Room 364, Washington, DC 20436/202-523-0258.

Board Meetings
Board meetings are open to the public and are listed in the *Federal Register*. Agenda of meetings are available. For more information, contact: Office of the Secretary, International Trade Commission, 701 E St. N.W., Room 160, Washington, DC 20436/202-523-0161.

Bounties or Grants on Imports
The Commission determines, with respect to any duty-free article on which the Secretary of the Treasury has determined that a bounty or grant is being paid, whether an industry in the United States is being or is likely to be injured, or is prevented from being established, by reason of the importation of such article. Contact: Office of Investigations, International Trade Commission, 701 E St. N.W., Room 336, Washington, DC 20436/202-523-0301.

Commission Activities
The Commission investigates and reports on many aspects of foreign trade. They include: the administration and fiscal and industrial effects of the customs laws of this country; the relationship between rates of duty on raw materials and finished or partly finished products; the effects of ad valorem and specific duties and of compound (specific and ad valorem) duties; all questions relative to the arrangement of schedules and classification of articles in the several schedules of the customs law; the operation of customs laws, including their relation to the federal revenues and their effect upon the industries and labor of the country; the tariff relations between the United States and foreign countries, commercial treaties, preferential provisions, and economic alliances; the effect of export bounties and preferential transportation rates; the volume of importations compared with domestic production and consumption; and conditions, causes and effects relating to competition of foreign industries with those of the United States. Contact: Office of Operations, International Trade Commission, 701 E St. N.W., Room 338, Washington, DC 20436/202-523-0301.

East-West Trade Statistics Monitoring System
The Commission maintains a program to monitor trade between the United States and the nonmarket economy countries, and to publish a detailed summary of the data collected under the program not less frequently than once every calendar quarter. Contact: Office of Economics, International Trade Commission, 701 E St. N.W., Room 334, Washington, DC 20436/202-523-1995

Freedom of Information Act Requests
For Freedom of Information Act requests contact: Office of the Secretary, International Trade Commission, 701 E St. N.W., Room 156, Washington, DC 20436/202-523-0471.

Generalized System of Preferences
With respect to articles which may be considered for duty-free treatment when imported from designated developing countries, the Commission advises the President as to the probable economic effect of the removal of duty on the domestic

industry and on consumers. Contact: Executive Liaison, International Trade Commission, 701 E St. N.W., Room 71, Washington, DC 20436/202-523-1607.

Harmonized System

The Commission provides technical assistance to government and private industry in understanding and implementing the Harmonized Commodity Description and Coding System ("Harmonized System"), a new international standard nomenclature for tariff and statistical programs, schedule to become effective January 1, 1987. For further information, contact: Office of Tariff Affairs and Trade Agreements, United States International Trade Commission, 701 E St. N.W., Washington, DC 20436/202-523-0370.

Import Relief for Domestic Industries

The Commission conducts investigations upon petition on behalf of an industry by a firm, a group of workers, or other representatives of an industry to determine whether an article is being imported in such increased quantities as to be a substantial cause of serious injury, or the threat thereof, to the domestic industry producing an article like or directly competitive with the imported article. The investigation must be completed not later than six months after receipt of petition. Contact: Investigations, Office of Operations, International Trade Commission, 701 E St. N.W., Room 338, Washington, DC 20436/202-523-0301.

Imports Sold at Less Than Fair Value (Or Subsidized)

The Commission conducts preliminary investigations to determine whether there is a reasonable indication that an industry in the United States is materially injured or is threatened with material injury, or the establishment of an industry in the United States is materially retarded, by reason of imports. Contact: Investigations, Office of Operations, International Trade Commission, 701 E St. N.W., Room 338, Washington, DC 20436/202-523-0301.

Interference with Agricultural Programs

The Commission conducts investigations at the direction of the President to determine whether any articles are being or are practically certain to be imported into the United States under such conditions and in such quantities as to materially interfere with programs of the Department of Agriculture for agricultural commodities or products thereof, or to reduce substantially the amount of any product processed in the United States from such commodities or products, and makes findings and recommendations to the President. The President may restrict the imports in question by imposition of either import fees or quotas. Contact: Office of Investigations, International Trade Commission, 701 E St. N.W., Room 338, Washington, DC 20436/202-724-0301.

Law Library

The Law Library maintains a comprehensive file on documents on legislation affecting U.S. trade. Contact: Law Library, International Trade Commission, 701 E St. N.W., Room 213, Washington, DC 20436/202-523-0333.

Legislation

A list of reports submitted on proposed legislation is available. Contact: Office of Congressional Liaison, International Trade Commission, 701 E St. N.W., Room 314, Washington, DC 20436/202-523-0287.

Library

As the international economic research arm of the Government, it maintains a 80,000-volume library, which subscribes to about 2,400 periodicals. This facility houses not only publications on international trade and U.S. tariff commercial policy, but also many business and technical journals. Contact: Library Division, Office of Data Systems, International Trade Commission, 701 E St. N.W., Room 301, Washington, DC 20436/202-523-0013

Monthly Production Reports

The monthly production reports (Series C/P) add timeliness to the Commission's statistics. A report, containing production data for 91 selected synthetic organic chemicals, plastics and resins, and other trend-setting indicator materials, is issued for each month at a date approximately six weeks after the month covered by the report. Contact: Statistical Unit, Energy and Chemicals Division, Office of Industries, International Trade Commission, 701 E St. N.W., Room 110, Washington, DC 20436/202-523-0456.

Publications

Publications and Investigations of the United States Tariff Commission and United States International Trade Commission is an index of all publications issued by both agencies since their inception. A booklet "Selected Publications of the United States International Trade Commission is also available. Publications may be ordered 24 hours a day, seven days a week by calling 202-523-5178, or contact: Docket Room, Office of the Secretary, International Trade Commission, 701 E St. N.W., Room 152, Washington, DC 20436/202-523-0471.

Public Documents

Publications in this collection date back to January 1961 and relate to the Commission's investigation of cases in which U.S. industries sought "import relief." Industries investigated include nonrubber footwear, zippers, mushrooms, stainless steel, wrapper tobacco, nuts, bolts and screws. Case documentation is available. Contact: Docket Room, Office of the Secretary, International Trade Commission, 701 E St. N.W., Room 158, Washington, DC 20436/202-523-0471.

Summaries of Trade and Tariff Information

The Commission periodically publishes a series of summaries of trade and tariff information to provide the Congress, the courts, government agencies, foreign governments, industrial institutions, research and trade organizations, and the general public with information on each of the commodities listed in the Tariff Schedules of the United States. These summaries provide comprehensive coverage of product uses, manufacturing processes, and commercial practices, and include analysis of the numerous factors affecting U.S. and world trade in each commodity area. This series is updated every two years. The overall summary program will run several years, ultimately covering all items of the TSUS. Contact: Office of Industry, International Trade Commission, 701 E St. N.W., Room 254, Washington, DC 20436/202-523-0146.

Synthetic Organic Chemicals, U.S. Production and Sales—1983

The annual report on United States production and sales of synthetic organic chemicals published since 1918 includes 15 groups of chemicals; tar and tar crudes; primary products from petroleum and natural gas for chemical conversion; cyclic intermediates; dyes; organic pigments; medicinal chemicals; flavor and perfume materials; plastics and resin materials; rubber processing chemicals; elastomers (synthetic rubber), plasticizers; surface-active agents; pesticides and related products; miscellaneous end-use chemicals and chemical products; and miscellaneous cyclic and acyclic chemicals. Approximately 750 manufacturers report data to the Commission on some 8,000 chemical products; these data form the base for the annual report. Also included in the annual report is a directory of manufacturers for each of the named chemicals and chemical products. Contact: Statistical Unit, Energy and Chemicals Division, Office of Industries, International Trade Commission, 701 E St. N.W., Room 104, Washington, DC 20436/202-523-0334.

Tariff Schedules

The Tariff Schedules of the United States Annotated is published periodically by the Commission. It contains the classifications used for reporting import data by commodity and by supplying countries. The schedules delineate some 11,000 commodity classifications for which import statistics are collected. At appropriate intervals the TSUSA is updated to reflect the effects of legislation, presidential proclamations and executive orders, and other modifications of the *Schedules*. The *Schedules* are sold for $47 by the Superinten-

dent of Documents, Government Printing Office, Washington, DC 20402/202-783-3238. For additional information, contact: Office of Tariff Affairs and Trade Agreements, International Trade Commission, 701 E St. N.W., Room 144, Washington, DC 20436/202-523-0370.

Tariff Summaries

The Commission prepares and publishes, from time to time, a series of summaries of trade and tariff information. These summaries contain descriptions (in terms of the Tariff Schedules of the United States) of the thousands of products imported into the United States, methods of production, and the extent and relative importance of U.S. consumption, production and trade, together with certain basic factors affecting the competitive and economic health of domestic industries. Copies of the summaries are available from the Office of the Secretary, International Trade Commission, 701 E St. N.W., Room 254, Washington, DC 20436/202-523-5178.

Trade Agreement Programs

Trade agreement programs include: tariff, commodity and statistical information for negotiations, principally the General Agreement of Tariff and Trade (GATT); preparation of tariff concessions in the complete nomenclature of the tariff schedules of the United States; and preparation of legislation to approve and implement many of the trade agreements and other related matters. Contact: Trade Agreements, U.S. International Trade Commission, 701 E St. N.W., Room 71, Washington, DC 20436/202-523-0232.

Trade and Tariff Issues

The Commission advises the President as to the probable economic effect on the domestic industry and consumers of modification of duties and other barriers to trade which may be considered for inclusion in any proposed trade agreements with foreign countries. In addition, the Commission regularly assists the executive branch of the Government in special issue-oriented studies connected with the trade agreements program, primarily through the Office of U.S. Trade Representative (USTR). Contact: Executive Liaison and Special Advisor for Trade Agreements, International Trade Commission, 701 E St. N.W., Room 71, Washington, DC 20436/202-523-0232.

Trade Remedy Assistance Center

The Center provides information on remedies available under the Trade Remedy Law. It also offers technical assistance to eligible small businesses to enable them to bring cases to the International Trade Commission. Contact: ITC Trade Remedy Assistance Center, International Trade Commission, 701 E St. N.W., Washington, DC 20436/202-523-0488.

Trade With Communist Countries
The Commission makes investigations to determine whether increased imports of an article produced in a Communist country are causing market disruption in the United States. If the Commission's determination is in the affirmative, the President may take the same action as in a case involving injury to an industry, except that the action would apply only to imports of the article from the Communist country. Contact: Office of Investigation, International Trade Commission, 701 E St. N.W., Room 338, Washington, DC 20436/202-523-0301.

Technical Assistance
The Commission provides technical and factual information and data on international trade matters to industry, the press, businesspersons, unions and consumers. Similarly, it receives opinions and comments on issues and policies relating to international trade. Contact: Public Information, International Trade Commission, 701 E St. N.W., Room 160, Washington, DC 20436/202-523-0161.

Unfair Practices in Import Trade
The Commission, after receipt of a complaint under oath from an interested party or upon its own motion, conducts investigations to determine whether unfair methods of competition or unfair acts are being committed in the importation of articles into the United States or in their domestic sale. The investigations must be completed within one year or 18 months in a more complicated case. Contact: Unfair Imports, Investigations Division, Office of Operations, International Trade Commission, 701 E St. N.W., Room 346, Washington, DC 20436/202-523-3019.

Uniform Statistical Data For Imports, Exports and Production
The Commission, in cooperation with the executive departments of the government, establishes for statistical purposes an enumeration of articles for use in the collection of import and export statistics and seeks to establish comparability of such statistics with statistical programs for domestic production and programs for achieving international harmonization of trade statistics. Contact: Office of Tariff Affairs and Trade Agreements, International Trade Commission, 6th and E Sts. N.W., Room 144, Washington, DC 20436/202-523-0370.

World Petroleum Prices
Possible Effects of Changing World Crude Petroleum Prices is a report available from Energy Petroleum Benzenoid Chemical and Rubber and Plastics Branch, Energy and Chemicals Division, International Trade Commission, Room 116, 701 E St. N.W., Washington, DC 20436/202-523-1230.

How Can the International Trade Commission Help You?
To determine how the U.S. International Trade Commission can help you, contact: Secretary, International Trade Commission, 701 E St. N.W., Washington, DC 20436/202-523-0161.

United States Postal Service

475 L'Enfant Plaza West S.W., Washington, DC 20260/202-245-4000

Established: August 12, 1970
Budget: $26,000,000,000
Employees: 702,123

Mission: Provides mail processing and delivery services to individuals and businesses within the United States; develops efficient mail handling systems and operates its own planning and engineering programs; and is responsible for protecting the mails from loss or theft, and apprehending those who violate postal laws.

Major Sources of Information

Administrative Support Manual
This manual describes matters of internal administration in the Postal Service. It includes functional statements as well as policies and requirements regarding security, communications (printing directives, forms, records, newsletters), government relations, procurement and supply, data processing systems, maintenance, and engineering. A subscription is available for $22.00 from the Superintendent of Documents, Government Printing Office, Washington, DC 20402-0001/202-783-3238. For additional information, contact: Public and Employee Communications Department, Postal Service, 475 L'Enfant Plaza West S.W., Room 10736, Washington, DC 20260-3100/202-245-4034.

Aerogramme
An aerogramme is a lightweight stationery item which folds into a mailing envelope and may contain imprinted postage. It is an economical and convenient form of letter mail for corresponding with people in foreign countries except Canada and Mexico (domestic letter rates apply to Canada and Mexico). Aerogrammes are available at any post office. Contact: International Mail Classification Division, Postal Service, 475 L'Enfant Plaza

West S.W., Washington, DC 20260-6321/202-245-4575.

Bulk Mail
There are two types of bulk mail: third and fourth-class mail. Third class mail includes bulk rate regular and bulk rate special. When mailing in bulk, the Postal Service supplies bundle labels, trays, rubber bands, sacks and sack labels, etc. free of charge. For additional information, contact: Office of Processing, Postal Service, 475 L'Enfant Plaza West S.W., Washington, DC 20260-7110/202-245-4087.

Business Reply Mail
Mailers who want to encourage responses by paying the postage for those responses may use business reply mail which is returned to the sender from any U.S. post office to any valid address in the United States. Using one permit, the mailer may provide for return of all replies to one location or several. Business reply mail must be prepaid according to a specified format. There is a small annual fee for each permit issued. The mailer guarantees to pay the postage for all replies returned to him or her. The postage per piece is the regular first class rate plus a business reply fee. For additional information, contact: Office of

1062

Commercial Marketing, Customer Service Department, Postal Service, 475 L'Enfant Plaza West S.W., Room 5621, Washington, DC 20260-6336/202-245-4456.

Business Reply Mailgram

A Business Reply Mailgram is now available for customers who require a quick turnaround response. The Business Reply Mailgram provides all of the features of a regular Mailgram with the addition of a built-in response device using a Business Reply envelope. Contact: Office of Commercial Marketing, Customer Service Department, Postal Service, 475 L'Enfant Plaza West S.W., Room 5547, Washington, DC 20260-6334/202-245-5624.

Carrier Route Information System

For mailers using the Carrier Route Information System, a monthly update capability is provided for hard copy and computer tape information. Contact: Delivery Services Department, Postal Service, 475 L'Enfant Plaza West S.W., Room 7428, Washington, DC 20260-7233/202-245-5788.

Certificate of Mailing

A certificate of mailing provides evidence of mailing only. The fee paid for certificates of mailing does not insure the article against loss or damage. Certificates of mailing are prepared by the mailer, except those mailers living on rural routes. Individual and firm mailing book certificates must show the name and address of both sender and addressee and the amount of postage paid. Identifying invoice or order numbers may also be placed on the certificate. Contact: a local post office, or: Customer Services Department, Postal Service, 475 L'Enfant Plaza West S.W., Room 5621, Washington, DC 20260-6336/202-245-4456.

Certified Mail

Certified mail service provides a receipt to the sender and a record of delivery at the office of address. No record is kept at the office at which mailed. No insurance coverage is provided. Certification may be used only on first class or priority mail containing matter of no intrinsic value. Contact: a local post office, or: Customer Services Department, Postal Service, 475 L'Enfant Plaza West S.W., Room 5621, Washington, DC 20260-6336/202-245-4456.

Collect-on-Delivery (COD) Mail

COD service is used to collect for unpaid merchandise when it is delivered to the addressee. The amount due you for the merchandise, postage, and COD fee is collected from the addressee and returned by the Postal Service. COD service may be used for merchandise sent by parcel post, first class or third class. The merchandise must have been ordered by the addressee. Fees charged for this service include insurance protection against loss or damage. COD items may also be sent as registered mail. COD service is limited, however, to items valued at a maximum of $500. This service is not available to foreign countries. Contact: Customer Services, Postal Service, 475 L'Enfant Plaza West S.W., Room 5621, Washington, DC 20260-6336/202-245-4456.

Consumers Directory of Postal Services and Products

This is a pamphlet to help the consumer become familiar with services and products of the Postal Service. It includes information on classes of mail, size standards, the fastest mail services, consumer protection, ZIP code, passport applications, lockbox and caller services, postage meters, and other common postal questions. Contact: Consumer Advocate, Postal Service, 475 L'Enfant Plaza West S.W., Room 5910, Washington, DC 20260-6320/202-245-4550.

Contracts

Information pertaining to specific solicitations or contracts is available. Contact: Office of Contracts, Procurement and Supply Departments, Postal Service, 475 L'Enfant Plaza West S.W., Room 1010, Washington, DC 20260-6230/202-245-4814.

Criminal Use of the Mail

The Postal Service investigates violations of postal laws such as theft, mail fraud, prohibited mailings, and organized crime in postal-related matters. Contact: Office of Criminal Investigations, Inspection Service Department, Postal Service, 475 L'Enfant Plaza West S.W., Room 3517, Washington, DC 20260-2160/202-245-5449.

Current Mail Rates, Fees and Services

For information on current mail rates, fees and services, contact: Office of Rates, Postal Service, 475 L'Enfant Plaza West S.W., Room 8620, Washington, DC 20260-5350/202-245-4422.

Customer Service Representative

The U.S. Postal Service has a local sales staff of Customer Service Representatives. CSRs are found in main post offices. Their services include: maintaining contact on how to get the most for your postage dollar; how to set up a mailroom; resolving business mail problems and selling services. For additional information, contact: Your Postmaster or Office of Commercial Marketing, Customer Services Department, Postal Service, 475 L'Enfant Plaza West S.W., Room 5516, Washington, DC 20260-6341/202-245-5731.

Design Licenses

Designs of postage stamps issued after January 1, 1978, are copyrighted and may not be reproduced except under license granted by the U.S. Postal Service. Earlier designs are in the public domain and may be reproduced without permission for philatelic, educational, historical and newsworthy purposes. Contact: Patent Counsel, Law Department, Postal Service, 475 L'Enfant Plaza West S.W., Room 9226, Washington, DC 20260-1123/202-245-4062.

Domestic Mail Manual
The manual is designed to assist customers in obtaining maximum benefits from domestic postal services. It includes applicable regulations and information about rates and postage, classes of mail, special services, wrapping and mailing requirements, and collection and delivery services. The subscription is available for $44.00 from the Superintendent of Documents, Government Printing Office, Washington, DC 20402-0001/202-783-3238. For additional information, contact: Customer Services Department, Postal Service, 475 L'Enfant Plaza West S.W., Room 5734, Washington, DC 20260-6300/202-245-5651.

Domestic Money Orders
Domestic money orders may be purchased at all post offices, branches and stations, and from rural carriers in the United States and its possessions, except for certain offices in Alaska. The maximum amount for a single money order is $700. There is no limitation on the number of money orders that may be purchased at one time, except when the Postal Service may impose temporary restrictions. Contact: Customer Services Department, Postal Service, 475 L'Enfant Plaza West S.W., Room 5651, Washington, DC 20260-6330/202-245-5731.

Engineering Support Center
The research and development program within the Postal Service is directed toward the investigation of new concepts for mail handling by utilizing the latest technologies available in systems and equipment to improve service, reduce costs, improve employee working conditions and to process the mail. For additional information, contact: Engineering Support Center, Postal Service, 11711 Parklawn Dr., Rockville, MD 20852-8101.

Express Mail
Express Mail service provides several fast delivery options for letters and packages:

Next Day Service—reliable, overnight delivery available on-demand;
Same Day Airport Service—fast service between 62 Airport Mail Facilities;
Custom Designed Service—scheduled pickup and delivery service tailored to individual needs;
Express Mail International Service—the fastest mail service to 37 countries.

Rates are economical (including flat rates for domestic 2- and 5-pound shipments); an Express Mail Corporate Account provides for mailing by using an account number; all shipments are insured at no additional charge; service is provided 365 days a year.

Other classes of mail may be transported by Express Mail service to speed their receipt and delivery. These services are Express Mail Reshipment (mail addressed to post office boxes in several cities is pouched and sent to the customer via Express Mail service) and Express Mail Drop Ship (mail is sent from a central point via Express Mail service to many post offices for delivery). Contact a local Express Mail post office or the Expedited Mail Services Division, Customer Services Department, U.S. Postal Service, 475 L'Enfant Plaza West S.W., Room 5541, Washington, DC 20260-6334/202-245-5624.

First Class Mail
First Class Mail is used for letters, post cards, postal cards, greeting cards, personal notes, and for sending checks and money orders. First class letter mail may not be opened for postal inspection. First Class Mail over 12 ounces is called priority mail. All First Class Mail is given the fastest transportation service available. If First Class mailing is not letter size, it should be marked "First Class." Contact: Your local Post Office.

Forwarding Mail
A *Change of Address Kit,* available from any post office, notifies the post office, correspondents and publishers of the user's new address. First Class Mail is forwarded free for 18 months. The post office has information about fees for forwarding other classes of mail, holding mail and temporary changes of address. Contact: Customer Services Department, Postal Service, 475 L'Enfant Plaza West S.W., Room 5651, Washington, DC 20260-6330/202-245-5731.

Fourth Class (Parcel Post) Mail
This service is for packages weighing one pound or more. The post office also has information about special mailing rates for books, bound printed matter and international mailings. Domestic Fourth-Class Mail may contain incidental related First-Class Mail. Contact: Your local post office.

Freedom of Information Act Requests
For Freedom of Information Act requests, contact: Freedom of Information Act Office, Records Control Division, Finance Group, Postal Service, 475 L'Enfant Plaza West S.W., Room 8121, Washington, DC/202-245-4142.

Free Mail for the Handicapped
Matter for the use of the blind or other persons who cannot use or read conventionally printed

material because of a physical impairment, and who are certified by competent authority as unable to read normal reading material, may be mailed free of charge. Certain restrictions apply. Please consult your local postmaster. Contact: Customer Services Department, Postal Service, 475 L'Enfant Plaza West S.W., Room 5920 Washington, DC 20260-6321/202-245-3712.

General Delivery
Mail can be delivered through General Delivery service at a specific post office. Generally, General Delivery service is available for a maximum of 30 days. However, in areas where carrier delivery service is not available, extended General Delivery Service can be provided. Contact: the local post office, or: Customer Services Department, Postal Service, 475 L'Enfant Plaza West S.W., Room 5820, Washington, DC 20260-6321/202-245-3712.

Inspection Service
The Inspection Service, headed by the Chief Postal Inspector, is the law enforcement and audit arm of the Postal Service which performs security, investigative, law enforcement, and audit functions. It is responsible for investigations of approximately 85 federal statutes relating to the Postal Service. Mail fraud, false mail order advertising, and unsatisfactory mail order transactions all come under the Inspection Service's jurisdiction. Some examples include: chain letters, work-at-home schemes; pyramid sales promotions; exaggerated cosmetic, diet, medical, and energy saving products; misused credit cards; coupon redemption; false billing; and franchising schemes. Contact: the local postmaster, or Local Postal Inspector, or Chief Postal Inspector, Inspection Service Department, Postal Service, 475 L'Enfant Plaza West S.W., Room 3509, Washington, DC 20260-2100/202-245-5445.

Insured Mail
Insured mail may be used on third and fourth class mail up to a maximum of $500. Official government mail bearing Postage and Fees Paid endorsement may also be insured. First class mail or priority mail containing third or fourth class matter may be insured provided it bears the endorsement "contains third class (or fourth class) matter" in addition to the first class or priority mail endorsement. Contact: Your post office.

Intelpost Service
The Intelpost Service transmits a black and white copy of any information that can be reduced to a maximum of 8½″ × 14″ to other cities (the network is growing) within seconds via satellite. The system transmits, with the confidentiality of international letter mail, anything that can be copied. Contact: Intelpost Service Center, Research and Technology Group, Postal Service, 475 L'Enfant Plaza West S.W., Room 1631, Washington, DC 20260-8116/202-245-4264.

International Mail
Airmail and surface mail can be sent to virtually all countries. There are four types of international mail: Letters and Cards—includes letters, letter packages, aerogrammes, and post cards; Other Articles—includes printed matter, matter for the blind, and small packets; Parcel Post; and Express Mail. A subscription to *International Mail Manual* is available for $34.00 (domestic) and $42.50 (foreign) from the Superintendent of Documents, Government Printing Office, Washington, DC 20402-0001/202-783-3238. Registry services with limited insurance protection is available for letters and cards and other articles to most countries. Insurance is available for parcel post to most countries. Check with your post office for specific information about the country to which you are mailing. Or contact: International Mail Classification Division, Postal Service, 475 L'Enfant Plaza West S.W., Room 8430, Washington, DC 20260/202-245-4575.

International Mail Manual
This manual sets forth the policies, regulations, and procedures governing international mail services offered to the public by the U.S. Postal Service. It includes the postage rates, fees, and mail preparation information for Postal Union mail, parcel post, and International Express Mail, as they apply to each individual country. The subscription is available for $34.00 for domestic addresses and $42.50 for foreign addresses from the Superintendent of Documents, Government Printing Office, Washington, DC 20402-0001/202-783-3238. For additional information, contact: International Mail Classification Division, Postal Service, 475 L'Enfant Plaza West S.W., Room 8430, Washington, DC 20260-5365/202-245-4575.

International Money Order
International money orders may be purchased at most of our larger post offices and some of the smaller ones. International money orders may only be sent to countries having an agreement with the United States to exchange this courtesy. With the exception of Great Britain and Ireland, the maximum amount for an international money order is $700.00. Those two countries have agreed to a separate amount of exchange. Contact: Your local Post Office.

International Surface Air Lift
International Surface Air Lift service provides fast delivery, at a cost lower than airmail, for publications and printed matter sent overseas at the surface rate. Contact: Office of Commercial Marketing, Postal Service, 475 L'Enfant Plaza West S.W., Room 5651, Washington, DC 20260-6330/202-245-5731.

Labor Relations

The Postal Service is the only federal agency whose employment policies are governed by a process of collective bargaining. Labor contract negotiations, affecting all bargaining unit personnel, as well as personnel matters involving employees not covered by collective bargaining agreements, are administered by the Employee and Labor Relations Group. Contact: Special Labor Relations Program, Labor Relations Department, Postal Service, 475 L'Enfant Plaza West S.W., Room 9707, Washington, DC 20260-4101/202-245-4714.

Library

In addition to a working collection of materials in law, the social sciences and technology, the Library contains a unique collection of postal materials; legislative files from the 71st Congress to date, reports, pamphlets, clippings, maps, photographs, general postal histories, periodicals of the national postal employee organizations, Universal Postal Union studies, and the reports of foreign postal administrations. It is open to the public. Contact: Library, Postal Service, 475 L'Enfant Plaza West S.W., Washington, DC 20260-1641/202-245-4021.

Library Rate

Specific items loaned or exchanged between schools, colleges, universities, public libraries, museums, herbaria, nonprofit religious, educational, scientific, philanthropic, agricultural, labor, veterans, or fraternal organizations or sent to or from these associations may be mailed at the fourth class library rate. Material must be labeled Library Rate. Materials include books, printed music, academic theses, sound recordings and others. Check with your postmaster for a specific list of library rate matter.

List Correction and Sequencing Service

The Postal Service provides (for a fee) a series of list correction services. In general, incorrect or nonexistent street addresses will be eliminated on both name and address lists and occupant/resident lists. In addition, for name and address lists, incorrect numbers will be corrected and new addresses furnished for customers who have moved if the customers have left a permanent forwarding order. A list sequencing service is also provided by which addresses on a mailing list are sorted into carrier sequence. Undeliverable addresses will be removed during the sequencing. If the mailing list contains at least 90% of the correct addresses in a five-digit ZIP Code area, missing addresses will be provided and incorrect addresses will be corrected. Otherwise, only a blank card will be inserted to indicate a missing address. For additional information on the various mailing list services available from the Postal Service, please contact your local post master or Customer Service Representative.

Mail Classification

For information on current mail classification, contact: Your local Post Office.

Mail Classification Centers*

Questions regarding the proper classification of mail matter should be directed to local postal officials. There are 37 Mail Classification Centers which have been established to assist local Post Offices in responding to mail classification questions. The Mail Classification Centers may be contacted if the local Post Office is unable to resolve questions. The centers are listed below.

*9599 is the ZIP+4 add-on for all MCCs.

Eastern Region

MCC	Districts	3-Digit ZIP Code Service Area
Rochester, NY 14603	Empire	130-149
Pittsburgh, PA 15219	Allegheny Mountaineer	150-172, 177-179, 195-196, 246-253, 246-268
Philadelphia, PA 19104	Delaware Valley	080-087, 173-176, 180-191, 193-194, 197-199
Washington, DC 20013	Maryland-DC	200, 202-212, 214-223, 226
Richmond, VA 23232	Virginia	224-225, 227-245

Northeast Region

MCC	Districts	3-Digit ZIP Code Service Area
Boston, MA 02109	Boston Portland (ME) White River Junction	014-059
New York, NY 10001	NY City	090-100, 104
Brooklyn, NY 11201	Caribbean Staten Is. Long Is.	006-009 103 110-119
Hartford, CT 06101	Connecticut Valley	010-013, 060-069
Albany, NY 12207	Westchester	105-109, 120-129

Newark, NJ 07102	No. NJ	070-079, 088-089

Central Region

MCC	Districts	3-Digit ZIP Code Service Area
Chicago, IL 60607	Northern Illinois	463-464, 600-606, 609-611, 613-619, 625-627
Columbus, OH 43216	Buckeye	410, 430-438, 448-458, 470
Cleveland, OH 44101	Northeastern Ohio	439-447
Des Moines, IA 50318	Gateway	500-508, 510-514, 520-528, 612
Detroit, MI 48233	Michigan	480-482, 484-497
Indianapolis, IN 46206	Indiana	460-462, 465-469, 472-475, 478-479
Kansas City, MO 64108	Mid-America	640-641, 644-647, 653, 660-662, 664-679
Louisville, KY 40201	Kentuckiana	400-409, 411-418, 420-427, 476-477
Milwaukee, WI 53203	Greater Wisconsin	498-499, 530-532, 534-535, 537-539, 541-545, 549
Minneapolis, MN 55401	North Central	540, 546-548, 550-551, 553-554, 556-562, 565, 567, 570-577, 580-588

Central Region—Continued

MCC	Districts	3-Digit ZIP Code Service Area
Omaha, NE 68101	Mid-America	515-516, 680-681, 683-693
St. Louis, MO 63155	Gateway	620, 622-624, 628-631, 633-639, 648, 650-652, 654-658

Western Region

MCC	Districts	3-Digit Zip Code Service Area
Denver, CO 80202	Rocky Mountain	590-599, 800-816,
	Western Slopes	820-834, 836-837 840-847, 865, 870-871, 873-875, 877-884, 893, 898
	Alaska	995-999

Honolulu, HI 96820	Pacific	967-969
Los Angeles, CA 90052	Angeles Sequoia	900, 902-908, 910-918, 926-928, 930-935
Phoenix, AZ 85026	Sunland	850, 852-853, 855-857, 859-860, 863-864, 890-891, 920-925
San Francisco, CA 94119	Golden State Sierra	894-895, 897, 936 941, 943-966
Seattle, WA 98101	Northwestern	835, 838, 970-978, 980-994

Southern Region

MCC	Districts	3-Digit ZIP Code Service Area
Atlanta, GA 30304	Atlanta	289, 298-299, 300-306, 308-310, 312-319, 350-352, 354-368
Charlotte, NC 28202	Carolina	270-288, 290-297
New Orleans, LA 70113	Delta	369, 387, 389-397 700-714
Dallas, TX 75260	N. Texas	718, 750-769, 795-799
Memphis, TN 38101	Mid-South	307, 370-374, 376 386, 388, 716-717 719-722, 724-729
Miami, FL 33152	Florida	320, 322-331, 333-339
Oklahoma City, OK 73125	Oklahoma	730-731, 734-741 743-749, 790-794
San Antonio, TX 78205	S. Texas	770-779

Mailer's Guide

This free guide contains abridged information on such topics as bulk mailing permits, mail classification items, customer service programs and other facts basic to everyday mailing needs. Contact: Office of Consumer Affairs, Postal Service, 475 L'Enfant Plaza West S.W., Room 5910, Washington, DC 20260-6320/202-245-4550.

Mail Fraud/Mail Order Problems

Help is available for consumers who suspect they have been victims of a fraud or misrepresentation scheme. Some of the schemes include: land sale frauds, charity rackets, investment swindles, work-at-home schemes and medical quackery. Contact: the nearest postmaster or postal inspector, or: Consumer Advocate, Customer Services Department, Postal Service, 475 L'Enfant Plaza West S.W., Room 5910, Washington, DC 20260-6320/ 202-245-4550.

Mailgram
Mailgram is an electronic communications service offered by Western Union and the Postal Service. Mailgrams are transmitted over Western Union's communications network to printers located in post offices. Delivery is made by regular carrier the next business day throughout the United States, except for parts of Alaska. Customers can send Mailgrams over Telex terminals, by a direct computer connection with Western Union, by producing a computer magnetic tape, and by telephone. Western Union provides a toll-free telephone network throughout the United States. Contact: Office of Commercial Marketing, Customer Service Department, Postal Service, 475 L'Enfant Plaza West S.W., Room 5516 Washington, DC 20260-6341/202-245-5731.

Memo to Mailers
This free monthly publication advises business mailers of all rate and classification changes as well as other postal news. It is available from *Memo to Mailers,* Post Office Box 1, Linwood, NJ 08221. Contact: Office of Consumer Affairs, Postal Service, 475 L'Enfant Plaza West S.W., Room 5910, Washington, DC 20260/202-245-4550.

Merchandise Return Service
Merchandise return service provides a method whereby a merchandise return permit holder may authorize individuals and organizations to send parcels to the permit holder and have the return postage and fees paid by the permit holder. It is available for first class mail, and third and fourth class mail. A permit to use it is required at each post office where parcels will be returned. A fee will be charged each calendar year for each permit issued, in addition to the fee for each merchandise return service transaction. Contact: a local post office.

Metered Mail
Many postal customers prefer to use a postage meter which prints prepaid postage either directly on envelopes or on adhesive strips which are then affixed to pieces. The metered mail imprint, or meter stamp, serves as postage payment, postmark, and cancellation mark. It may be used for all classes of mail and for any amount of postage. Any quantity of mail may be metered, and it does not have to be identical in size and shape. *Application for a Postage Meter License* must be approved before obtaining the necessary license. Contact: Your local Post Office.

Military Parcels
PAL (Parcel Airlift Mail) is flown to the overseas destination. You pay the regular parcel post rate to the U.S. exit port, plus a small fee for the air services. SAM (Space Available Mail) is transported by surface means in the United States and flown on a space available basis from the United States to the overseas destination. Contact the local post office.

Mint Set of Commemoratives
The U.S. Postal Service Mint Set of Commemorative and Special Sets is available (price varies). Contact: Philatelic Sales Division, Postal Service, Washington, DC 20265-9997/202-245-5394.

National ZIP Code and Post Office Directory
The *ZIP Code Directory* is an up-to-date and comprehensive listing of ZIP Code information by state and post office. It includes instructions for quickly finding a ZIP Code number when an address is known. Proper ZIP Code information is essential for speedy and economic delivery of your mail. The ZIP Code Directory also includes official lists of post offices, named stations, named branches, and community post offices in the United States. The volume includes a wealth of handy information about ZIP Codes, postal abbreviations, and basic postal procedures and is an indispensable aid that is worth its price many times over. For sale for $9.00 by the Superintendent of Documents, Government Printing Office, Washington, DC 20402-0001/202-783-3238. For additional information, contact: Delivery Services Department, Postal Service, 475 L'Enfant Plaza West S.W., Room 7427, Washington, DC 20260-7235/ 202-245-5788.

Official Mail
Members of Congress are authorized by law to send mail without prepayment of postage. The envelope or wrapper bears a written signature, printed facsimile signature or other required marking instead of a postage stamp. Mail must relate to the official business, activities, and duties of the Congress of the United States. This frank may also be used by the Vice President, Members-elect of Congress, Delegates or Delegates-elect, the Resident Commissioner or Resident Commissioner-elect from Puerto Rico, the Secretary of the Senate, Sergeant at Arms of the Senate, each of the elected officers of the House of Representatives, the Legislative Counsel of the House of Representatives and the Senate, and the Senate Legal Counsel. Penalty mail is official mail sent by officers of the Executive and Judicial branches of the Government: departments, agencies and establishments of the Government, official mail of legislative counsel for the House of Representatives and the Senate; official mail of the Superintendent of Documents, and official correspon-

dence concerning the *Congressional Directory.* The President usually uses regularly printed postage stamps on mail dispatched from his immediate office. Contact: Your local Post Office.

Operating Statistics
Postal Service operating statistics include information on classes of mail by number of pieces, weight and dollars for first class, priority mail, domestic air, express mail, Mailgrams, second class controlled circulation publications, third and fourth class, international surface and air, franked, penalty and free for the blind services. Special services statistics are also available. Contact: Management Information Systems Department, Postal Service, 475 L'Enfant Plaza West S.W., Room 3012, Washington, DC 20260-1500/202-245-4208.

Packaging Pointers
This pamphlet which describes how to package and address parcels, is available at the local post office, or contact: Your local Post Office.

Passport Applications
Many local post offices accept applications for passports. Contact the nearest post office or: Consumer Advocate, Customer Services Department, Postal Service, 475 L'Enfant Plaza West S.W., Room 5910, Washington, DC 20260-6320/ 202-245-4550.

Permit Imprints
An *Application to Mail Without Affixing Postage Stamps* is available in order to use imprints and to pay postage in cash or through an advance Deposit Trust Account at time of mailing. Contact: a local post office.

Plant Loading
When a very large mailing is prepared for one or a few destination points, the postmaster may send a vehicle to the mailer's place of business to pick it up. The mail is loaded, under post office supervision, and usually taken directly to the destination, bypassing all handling at the post office of mailing. Contact: Your local Post Office.

Pornography
Unsolicited sexually oriented advertisements can be halted by filling out Form 2201 (at the local post office). A mailer who sends sexually oriented advertisements to any person whose name has been added to the Postal Service reference listing for 30 days is subject to legal action by the United States government. *Notice for Prohibitory Order Against Sender of Pandering Advertisement in the Mails* can also be filled out to stop any further advertisements considered "erotically arousing or sexually provocative." Contact: the nearest post office.

Post Office Box-Caller Service
Post Office lockboxes and caller services are available at many post offices for a fee. Post Office Box service provides privacy and allows user to get mail any time the post office lobby is open. Caller (pickup) service is available during the hours post office retail windows are open. This service is for customers who receive a large volume of mail or those who need a box number address when no lockboxes are available. For additional information, contact: Your local Post Office.

Postal Bulletin
This weekly publication contains current orders, instructions and information relating to the Postal Service, including philatelic, airmail, money order, parcel post, etc. The subscription is available for $71.00 per year from the Superintendent of Documents, Government Printing Office, Washington, DC 20402-0001/202-783-3238. For further information, contact: Office of Communications, Postal Service, 475 L'Enfant Plaza West S.W., Room 2810 Washington, DC 20260-1571/202-245-3742.

Postal Career Executive Service
The postal career executive program aims at developing qualified managers and supervisors. The program tries to develop executives through training, educational and work experiences. Contact: Postal Career Executive Service, Employee Relations Department, Postal Service, 475 L'Enfant Plaza West S.W., Room 10531, Washington, DC 20260-4270/202-245-4444.

Postal Life: The Magazine for Postal Employees
This bimonthly periodical contains articles, with illustrations, about new methods, techniques and programs of the U.S. Postal Service. Its purpose is to keep postal employees informed and abreast of developments in the U.S. Postal Service. The subscription is available for $14.00 from the Superintendent of Documents, Government Printing Office, Washington, DC 20402-0001/202-783-3238. For additional information, contact Communications Services, Postal Service, 475 L'Enfant Plaza West S.W., Room 10843, Washington, DC 20260-3100/202-245-4234.

Postal Problem
A *Consumer Service Card,* available from letter carriers and at post offices, should be filled out when there is a problem with the mail service. It provides a quick way for Postal Service customers to register a complaint, make a suggestion, or ask a question, or make certain that a complaint gets attention. Contact: Consumer Advocate, Postal Service, 475 L'Enfant Plaza West S.W., Room 5910, Washington, DC 20260-6320/202-245-4550.

Postal Publications and Handbooks
A Postal Service publications list is available which

includes titles of publications and their supply source. Contact: Publications, Public and Employee Communications Department, Postal Service, 475 L'Enfant Plaza West S.W., Room 10907, Washington, DC 20260/202-245-4235.

Postal Service Employment

The *Employee and Labor Relations Manual* sets forth the personnel policies and regulations governing employment with the Postal Service. Topics covered include organization management, job evaluation, employment and placement, pay administration, employee benefits, employee relations, training, safety and health, and labor relations. The subscription is available for $29.00 per year from the Superintendent of Documents, Government Printing Office, Washington, DC 20402-0001/202-783-3238. For additional information, contact: Employee and Labor Relations Group, Postal Service, 475 L'Enfant Plaza West S.W., Room 9903, Washington, DC 20260-4000/ 202-245-4721.

Precanceled Stamps

Precanceling means the canceling of postage stamps, stamped envelopes or postal cards in advance of mailing. The use of precanceled postage reduces the time and costs of mail handling. Precanceled mail, sorted and tied in packages by the mailer, requires less processing time in the post office and is therefore dispatched more quickly. A permit is required. Contact: a local post office.

Presorting

For each advance in level of presorting by the mailer, more handlings are bypassed at the post office, saving time in processing the mail. Presorted mail can be bundled and labeled, or trayed, or sacked depending on the presort requirements for each class of mail. To assist you, the Postal Service normally provides consultation service, mailroom employee training, and certain supplies (trays, labels, rubber bands, etc.) at no cost. Presorted mailings that meet certain requirements are charged reduced postage. Call your postmaster or Customer Service Representative for more details, or contact: Customer Services Department, Postal Service, 475 L'Enfant Plaza West S.W., Room 5667, Washington, DC 20260-6330/ 202-245-5731.

Priority Mail

Priority mail is First Class Mail weighing more than 12 ounces. It is used when fast transportation and expeditious handling are desired. For complete information, contact: Your local Post Office.

Procurement

The Postal Service purchases both supplies and services. Supplies include mail-processing and mail-handling equipment; material transport and delivery service equipment; customer service equipment; office support requirements such as furniture, machines, equipment and supplies, and custodial, protective, building and vehicle maintenance equipment. Cleaning and vehicle maintenance and repair are typical services bought. Details on Postal Service procurement are contained in *Selling to the Postal Service,* a free publication. *Postal Contracting Manual* establishes uniform policies and procedures relating to the procurement of facilities, equipment, supplies and mail transportation services and is available for $750.00 per year from the Superintendent of Documents, Government Printing Office, Washington, DC 20402-0001/202-783-3238. For publication and additional information, contact: Office of Contracts, Procurement and Supply Department, Postal Service, 475 L'Enfant Plaza West S.W., Room 1010, Washington, DC 20260-6230/202-245-4814.

Registered Mail

Registry buys security. It is the safest way to send valuables through the mail system. The full value of the mailing must be declared when mailed up to $25,000. Only mail prepaid at the first class or priority mail rates may be registered. Contact: a local post office.

Return Receipts

A return receipt is your proof of delivery. It is available on mail insured for more than $20 value, and on certified, registered, COD and Express Mail Service. The return receipt identifies the article number, who signed for it and the date it was delivered. For an additional fee you may obtain a receipt showing the exact address of delivery. You may also request restricted delivery service by which delivery is to the addressee only, or to an individual authorized in writing to receive mail of the addressee. Contact a local post office, or: Customer Services Department, Postal Service, 475 L'Enfant Plaza West S.W., Room 5651, Washington, DC 20260-6330/202-245-5731.

Rural or Highway Contract Route

General distribution of third class mail to each boxholder on a rural or highway contract route, or for each family on a rural route, or for all boxholders at a post office that does not have city or village carrier service, may have the mail addressed omitting the names of individuals and box or route numbers if the mailer uses this form of address: "Postal Customer," or, to be more specific: "Rural (or Highway Contract Route) Boxholder, City (or Town), State." A postmaster, on request, will furnish mailers with the number of families and boxes served on each route. Contact: Rural Delivery Division, Delivery Services Department, Postal Service, 475 L'Enfant Plaza West S.W., Room 7226, Washington, DC 20260-7221/ 202-245-5718.

Second Class Mail
Second class mail is generally used by newspaper and other periodical publishers who meet certain Postal Service requirements. There is also a rate for mailing individual copies of magazines and newspapers. Contact the nearest post office for additional information.

Service Standards
Service standards have been established for each area of the country. Contact the postmaster or Customer Service Representative for the specific standards in any local area, or: Office of Consumer Affairs, Customer Services Department, Postal Service, 475 L'Enfant Plaza West S.W., Room 5910, Washington, DC 20260/202-245-4550.

Size Standards
Information is available on nonstandard size mail and minimum size standards. *The Mailer's Guide* and *A Consumer's Directory of Postal Services and Products* provide details on size standards. Contact: Your local post office.

Small Post Office Closings
For information on small post office closings or consolidations, contact: Delivery Services Department, Postal Service, 475 L'Enfant Plaza West S.W., Room 7347, Washington, DC 20260-7230/202-245-4315.

Souvenir Pages
A souvenir page is prepared for each new stamp issue. Each page bears an official first day cancellation of the actual stamp or stamps. Because souvenir pages are prepared in limited quantities, current issues are available on subscription. A minimum deposit of $20.00 is required to open an account. Contact: Souvenir Page Subscription, Philatelic Automatic Distribution Service, Postal Service, 475 L'Enfant Plaza West S.W., Room 5630, Washington, DC 20260/202-245-5778.

Speakers
Postal Service speakers are available to address the public on postal matters and services. To schedule speakers and to coordinate Postal Service participation in meetings of national organizations and associations, contact: Public and Employee Communications Department, Postal Service, 475 L'Enfant Plaza West S.W., Room 10736, Washington, DC 20260-3100/202-245-4034.

Special Delivery
Special delivery may be purchased on all classes of mail except Express Mail to provide prompt delivery. It provides for delivery during prescribed hours which extend beyond the hours for delivery of ordinary mail. Special delivery mail is also delivered on Sundays and holidays at larger post offices. This service is available to all addresses served by city carriers and to addresses within a one-mile radius of other delivery post offices. Contact: Expedited Mail Services, Customer Services Department, Postal Service, 475 L'Enfant Plaza West S.W., Room 5547, Washington, DC 20260-6334/202-245-4498.

Special Fourth Class Mail
Books of at least 8 printed pages, consisting entirely of reading matter, may be sent at the special fourth class rate. Each of the following categories may be sent at this Special Fourth Class rate: 16mm films or narrower width films which must be positive prints; printed music in bound or sheet form; printed objective test materials; sound recordings; manuscripts; educational reference charts; and medical and pre-recorded information. Contact: Your Local Post Office.

Special Handling
Special handling service is available for third and fourth class mail only, including insured and COD mail. It provides for preferential handling in dispatch and transport, but does not provide special delivery. The special handling fee must be paid on parcels that require special care such as baby poultry, bees, etc. Special handling does not mean special care of fragile items. Anything breakable should be packed with adequate cushioning and marked "Fragile." Contact: Customer Services Department, Postal Service, 475 L'Enfant Plaza West S.W., Room 5631, Washington, DC 20260-6336/202-245-4456.

Stamp Collection and Philatelic Services
The Postal Service has certain philatelic products available for purchase, in most post offices, which are useful for those with an interest in starting a collection. These include: *Postal Service Guide to U.S. Stamps* ($3.50)—a comprehensive guide to stamp collecting and all U.S. stamp issues; starter collecting kits; and an annual mint set of all the commemoratives issued in a given calendar year. For the individual already collecting, the Postal Service offers all current issues of stamps, products and postal stationery through its mail order service at face value plus a small handling charge. The following free publications are available:

Philatelic Catalog—Bimonthly, free publication which lists commemorative stamps, souvenir mint sets, and souvenir cards.
Introduction to Stamp Collecting—how to begin a stamp collection; equipment guide; condition and color guide; and glossary of terms.

Contact: Philatelic Sales Division, Postal Service, Washington, DC 20265-9997.

Stamp Design Selection
Suggestions for commemorative postage stamps meeting specific standards outlined by the Citi-

zens' Stamp Advisory Committee should be presented in writing to the Postmaster General, Washington, DC 20260. For additional information, contact: Public Affairs Division, Postal Service, 475 L'Enfant Plaza West S.W., Room 10846, Washington, DC 20260-3122/202-245-5199.

Stamps and Stamped Paper
Yearly announcements for the stamps and stamped paper to be issued for the upcoming year are available. The date, subject and city of issuance is provided. Contact: Stamp Development Branch, Postal Service, 475 L'Enfant Plaza West S.W., Room 5800, Washington, DC 20260/ 202-245-4956.

Stamps by Mail
Postage stamps may be obtained through the mail by using a specially printed envelope available through your post office. This service is for those mailers who cannot get to a post office easily. A check or money order may be used to pay for the stamps. The stamp envelope, with check inside, is presented to the carrier on his or her regular rounds or dropped in any collection box. It must be addressed to the local postmaster using the local ZIP Code. The order is filled and returned to the customer within three days. There is a small handling fee required in addition to the cost of the order. For additional information, contact: Customer Services Department, Postal Service, 475 L'Enfant Plaza West S.W., Room 5651, Washington, DC 20260-6330/202-245-5731.

Third Class Mail
Third class mail, referred to as Bulk Business Mail, may be used by anyone but is used most often by large mailers. This class includes printed materials and merchandise panels which weigh less than 16 ounces and which are not required to be mailed at the First-Class rates. There are two rate structures for this class, a single-piece rate and a bulk rate, which include a Third Class Carrier Route Presort. Many community organizations and businesses find it economical to use this service. Also, individuals may use third class for mailing light weight parcels. The post office has information on which method of third class mail preparation is best suited to your needs. For further information, contact: Your Local Post Office.

Trayed Mail
Metered and permit imprint letter mail can be placed in trays furnished by the post office. This means handling in the mailer's own mailroom, and better protection from possible damage in transit. Trayed mail bypasses handlings at the post office. For more details on the use of letter mail trays, consult your postmaster or customer service representative, or contact: Customer Services Department, Postal Service, 475 L'Enfant Plaza West

S.W., Room 5616, Washington, DC 20260-6341/ 202-245-3922.

United States Postage Stamps Basic Manual
This is an excellent reference source for all stamp collectors, particularly those requiring extensive and authoritative information on U.S. stamps. This official U.S. Postal Service guidebook includes an illustration of every U.S. postage and special service stamp issued from July 1, 1874 to June 20, 1970. Accompanying each illustration is a description of the design, history, and dimensions of the stamp. Tables containing detailed statistics of postage stamps issued from 1933 to the present are appendixed. Listed below are five transmittal letters that update this basic manual ($3.20):

United States Postage Stamps, Transmittal Letter 2— updates the basic manual with information about new stamps issued from May 1970 to December 1971 ($1.50)

United States Postage Stamps, Transmittal Letter 3— updates the basic manual with information about new stamps from February 1972 to December 1973 ($1.30).

*United States Postage Stamps, Transmittal Letter 4—*adds new material for stamps issued during 1974 ($1.30)

United States Postage Stamps, Transmittal Letter 5— includes new information for stamps issued during 1975 ($1.25).

United States Postage Stamps, Transmittal Letter 6— includes new information for stamps issued during 1976 and 1977 ($2.50).

Sold by the Superintendent of Documents, Government Printing Office, Washington, DC 20402-0001. For additional information on stamps, contact: Stamps Division, Customer Services Department, Postal Service, 485 L'Enfant Plaza West S.W., Room 5667, Washington, DC 20260/202-245-5734.

ZIP Code
The ZIP Code helps process the mail quickly and efficiently. Because of population density, transportation patterns and other reasons, key geographic areas are designated as mail-processing centers for mail movement between post offices within their area. The first three digits of any ZIP Code number represent a particular sectional center area or a large metropolis. The last two digits identify a local delivery area. For additional information, contact: Mail Processing Department, Postal Service, 475 L'Enfant Plaza West S.W., Room 7847, Washington, DC 20260-7100/ 202-245-3720.

ZIP + 4
The U. S. Postal Service has introduced the ZIP + 4 CODE program to improve mail processing, reduce handling costs and to stabilize postage rates

over longer periods of time. The ZIP + 4 Code is made up of the current ZIP Code plus a hyphen and four additional numbers. Use of ZIP + 4 Codes is strictly voluntary and the program is geared to First-Class business mailers. Benefits to mailers include more accurate sortation of their mail, more reliable and consistent delivery, reduction in the number of undeliverable pieces of mail and, for those who qualify, postage rate discounts. For additional information, contact your postmaster, customer service representative, or Customer Services Department, U.S. Postal Service, Rm. 5621, 475 L'Enfant Plaza West S.W., Washington, DC 20260-6336/202-245-4456.

Zone Charts
Parcel post postage is computed by weight and by distance zones. The official Zone chart available at any post office shows the complete zone structure from that office. Contact: In-Plant Processing Office, Mail Processing Department, Postal Service, 475 L'Enfant Plaza West S.W., Room 7837, Washington, DC 20260/202-245-4083.

How Can the Postal Service Help You?
To determine how the U.S. Postal Service can help you, contact: Public and Communications Department, Postal Service, Washington, DC 20260-3121/202-245-4089.

United States Tax Court

400 2nd St N.W., Washington, DC 20217/202-376-2754

Established: 1924
Budget: $15,565,000
Employees: 280

Mission: Tries and adjudicates controversies involving the existence of deficiencies or overpayments in income, estate, gift, and personal holding company surtaxes in cases where deficiencies have been determined by the Commission of the Internal Revenue.

Major Sources of Information

Clerk's Office
The Clerk's Office maintains all records of the U.S. Tax Court. After receiving a Notice of Deficiency from the Internal Revenue Service an individual may obtain assistance and information from this office for beginning and handling a case against the Internal Revenue Service. Contact: Clerk's Office, U.S. Tax Court, 400 2nd St. N.W., Washington, DC 20217.

Judges
The court is comprised of 19 judges who are appointed by the President for terms of 15 years. The Chief Judge, who is responsible for the overall administration of the court, is elected by the judges from their membership to serve a term of two years. Retired judges may also be recalled by the Chief Judge for service in the court. Special Trial Judges are appointed by the Chief Judge, who serve under rules and regulations promulgated by the court. They handle the Small Tax cases. Contact: Public Affairs, U.S. Tax Court, 400 2nd St. N.W., Washington, DC 20217/202-376-2754.

Tax Court Rules
A booklet containing the rules of practice and procedure of the U.S. Tax Court. This publication may be obtained for $4.50 by contacting the Superintendent of Documents, Government Printing Office, Washington, DC 20402/202-783-3238 or Office of Public Affairs, U.S. Tax Court, 400 2nd St. N.W., Washington, DC 20217/202-376-2754.

Trials
The Tax Court conducts trials at approximately 110 cities within the United States and each trial session is conducted by a single judge or Special Trial Judge. The court handles cases with disputes in which less than $10,000 is in dispute for any single year. There are no juries in these trials. Contact: Public Affairs, U.S. Tax Court, 400 2nd St. N.W., Washington, DC 20217/202-376-2754.

How Can the U.S. Tax Court Help You?
To determine how the U.S. Tax Court can help you, contact: Public Affairs, U.S. Tax Court, 400 2nd St. N.W., Washington, DC 20217/202-376-2754.

United States Trade and Development Program

State Annex 16, Washington, DC 20523/703-235-3663

Budget: $21,000,000
Employees: 14

Mission: promotes economic development in Third World countries, particularly the middle income developing countries, by financing planning services for development projects leading to the export of U.S. goods and services. In doing so, TDP seeks to assist U.S. firms in meeting competition from the U.S.'s export competitors so that U.S. firms can increase exports and improve the U.S. balance of trade.

Major Sources of Information

Feasibility Studies
Feasibility Studies are one of the project planning services offered by the Trade and Development Program to assist U.S. businesses competing in the foreign market. TDP finances studies to determine the technical, economic, and financial feasibility of projects and to provide detailed data for making decisions on how to proceed with project implementation. These studies provide a sufficient engineering analysis on which to make a firm cost estimate. Contact: Trade and Development Program, State Annex 16, Washington, DC 20523/703-235-3663.

Planning Services for U.S. Businesses
In its effort to promote economic development in Third World countries the Trade and Development Program finances planning services for development projects leading to the export of U.S. goods and services. The purpose of the services is to assist U.S. firms in meeting competition from the U.S. export competitors so that U.S. firms can

increase exports and improve the U.S. balance of trade.

A free pamphlet is available that describes the planning services offered by Trade and Development Program. To obtain a copy contact: Trade and Development Program, State Annex 16, Washington, DC 20523/703-235-3663.

Regional Experts
Trade and Development Program has a staff of experts available to consult with U.S. firms on proposed investor projects. The four major regions are:

Latin America
Asia
Middle East and Caribbean
Africa

For further information contact: Trade and Development Program, State Annex 16, Washington, DC 20523/703-235-3663.

Technology Orientation Missions

Orientation missions are a service provided by Trade and Development Program to assist U.S. businesses competing in the foreign market. TDP will arrange for visits by foreign country decision-makers to review U.S. technology if a country is considering a major project investment. Such visits are typically one to three weeks in length. Itineraries include meetings with U.S. firms and agencies. These visits are often undertaken in conjunction with one or more of the planning services. Industrial associations or foreign countries may initiate these visits. Contact: Trade and Development Program, State Annex 16, Washington, DC 20523/ 703-235-3663.

Technology Symposia

Technology symposia are one of the project planning services offered by the Trade and Development Program to assist U.S. businesses competing in the foreign market. Technology symposia are held when the host country is considering major project investments in a particular sector and is interested in U.S. technological participation. These workshops typically involve: (a) a technical presentation by U.S. experts on the application of U.S. technology to proposed projects, (b) reports by host country officials on their project investment plans and technology needs, and (c) visits to potential project sites. Symposia are planned to lead to pre-feasibility studies and/or direct contracts between U.S. companies and foreign participants. Contact: Trade and Development Program, State Annex 16, Washington, DC 20523/703-235-3663.

How Can the Trade and Development Program Help You?

To determine how the Trade and Development Program can help you, contact: Trade and Development Program, State Annex 16, Washington, DC 20523/703-235-3663.

Veterans Administration

810 Vermont Ave. N.W., Washington, DC 20420/202-393-4120

Established: July 21, 1930
Budget: $24,185,088,000
Employees: 204,040

Mission: Administers a system of benefits for veterans and dependents. These benefits include compensation payments for disabilities or death related to military service; pension based on financial need for totally disabled veterans or certain survivors for disabilities or death not related to military service; education and rehabilitation; home loan guaranty; burial, including cemeteries, markers, flags, etc.; and a comprehensive medical program involving a widespread system of nursing homes, clinics, and more than 172 medical centers.

Major Sources of Information

Academic Affairs
The Veterans Administration conducts the largest coordinated health professions education and training effort of its kind in the United States. Its purpose is to assure high quality veterans' health care and to develop sufficient numbers of all categories of professional and other health personnel. Contact: Academic Affairs, Department of Medicine and Surgery, Veterans Administration, 810 Vermont Ave. N.W., Room 87513, Washington, DC 20420/202-389-3178.

Affiliated Education Program Service
The Veterans Administration has over 2,000 training relationships between VA health care facilities and schools of medicine, dentistry, nursing, pharmacy, social work, and other allied health professions and occupations at the graduate and undergraduate levels. Contact: Affiliated Education Program, Academic Affairs, Department of Medicine and Surgery, Veterans Administration, 810 Vermont Ave. N.W., Room 870, Washington, DC 20420/202-389-3829.

Alcohol and Drug Treatment
The Veterans Administration's Alcohol Dependence Treatment Programs emphasize relatively short hospitalization during which comprehensive health and vocational assessment are accomplished by patient and hospital staff. The outpatient clinic continues the veteran's rehabilitation during which treatment such as group therapy, family therapy, antabuse treatment, and vocational services are provided. Close collaboration with Alcoholics Anonymous is central to all programs. Contact: Alcohol and Drug Dependence, Mental Health and Behavioral Science and Service, Department of Medicine and Surgery, Veterans' Administration, 810 Vermont Ave. N.W., Attn: 116A3, Washington, DC 20420/202-389-5193.

Appellate Review
Claimants not satisfied with determinations made by Veterans Administration field offices may file a written notice of disagreement with the office taking the action. If, after various other steps are followed, the claimant is still dissatisfied, the case

may be sent to the Board of Veteran Appeals for review and final decisions. *Rules of Practice, Board of Veterans Appeals* and an index to appellate decisions (in microfiche only) may be obtained without charge. Contact: Board of Veterans Appeals, Chief of Appellate Index and Retrieval Staff (AIRS), Veterans Administration, 810 Vermont Ave. N.W., Washington, DC 20420/202-389-3365.

Assistance Service
Assistance provides all incoming veterans on their first visit with information about and assistance in applying for various federal benefits. Contact: Veterans Assistance Service, Department of Veterans Benefits, Veterans Administration, 810 Vermont Ave. N.W., Room 132, Washington, DC 20420/202-389-2567.

Building Management
The major functions of the Veterans Administration building management service include environmental sanitation, a laundry/linen program, and interior design. Interior design receives special attention as an integral part of effective medical center operations because of the potential therapeutic effects. The mission of the VA interior designers is to eliminate drab and disheartening environments, with emphasis this year on the admissions/outpatient and clinical support areas of VA medical centers. Contact: Building Management Service, Department of Medicine and Surgery, Veterans Administration, 4040 North Fairfax Dr., Room 640, Arlington, VA 22032/202-235-3010.

Burial Expenses
Eligible veterans may be entitled to a $150 plot or interment allowance and $300 in basic burial allowance. The payment may be greater if the veteran's death is service-connected. Contact: the nearest Veterans Administration Office.

Burial Flags
An American flag may be obtained to drape the casket of a veteran, after which it may be given to next of kin or close friend or associate of the deceased. Contact the nearest Veterans Administration office, or most local post offices, or: the Department of Memorial Affairs, Veterans Administration, 810 Vermont Ave. N.W., Washington, DC 20420/202-389-5202.

Burial in National Cemeteries
Burial is available to any deceased veteran of wartime or peacetime service at all national cemeteries having available grave space. Members of the Reserve and the Army and Air National Guard who die while performing or as a result of performing active duty for training may also be eligible. Burial is also available to the eligible veteran's wife, husband, widow, widower, minor children and, under certain conditions, to unmarried adult children. The eligibility for burial is more restricted for Arlington National Cemetery. A free list of Veterans Administration National Cemeteries showing those with and without available grave space and information on procedures and eligibility for burial in a National Cemetery may be obtained. Contact: the nearest Veterans Administration office or Cemetery Service, Department of Memorial Affairs, Veterans Administration, 941 N. Capitol St. S.E., Room 9500, Washington, DC 20420-202-389-5202.

Canteen Service
The Veterans Canteen Service (VCS) operates retail stores and provides food and other service activities at each VA medical center for the comfort and well-being of the patients. Canteen retail stores offer patients a wide selection of products for their convenience, entertainment, recreation, hygiene and grooming, and leisure use. Food service facilities provide meals and refreshment snacks for patients' families, employees, volunteers and visitors. Contact: Veterans Canteen Service, Department of Medicine and Surgery, Veterans Administration, 7th Floor, 806 15th St. N.W., Washington, DC 20005/202-376-8132.

Central Purchasing
The Veterans Administration has a central purchasing office. It buys medical supplies, textiles, food, paper products, prosthetics, and orthopedic aids, and laundry equipment. Contact: Marketing Center, Veterans Administration, P.O. Box 76, Hines, IL 60141/312-681-6782.

Chaplain Service
Chaplain service provides spiritual and religious ministry for patients in all VA medical centers and for the staff in the medical centers and in Central office. The VA chaplains function as an integral part of the health care team, representing all major faith groups and denominations. Workshops are conducted during the year on death and dying, aging, how to deal with the alcoholic and his or her family, bio-medical ethics, involvement with the medical staff and their needs, and a new area of concern for the chaplain service, the orthopedic patient. The Chaplain School is developing special programs for the aging veteran and support of the national cemetery system. Contact: Chaplain Service, (Routing 125) Department of Medicine and Surgery, Veterans Administration, 810 Vermont Ave. N.W., Washington, DC 20420/202-389-5137.

Civilian Health and Medical Program
This is a medical benefits program through which the Veterans Administration helps pay for medical services and supplies obtained from civilian sources by eligible dependents and survivors of

veterans. A handbook for beneficiaries and health benefits services for dependents and survivors describes the benefits and how to claim them. For the handbook and further information, contact: Public Information, Department of Medicine and Surgery, Veterans Administration, 810 Vermont Ave. N.W., Room 627F, Washington, DC 20420/ 202-389-2337.

Compensation and Pension Service

The Compensation and Pension Service has responsibility for: claims for disability compensation and pension; for automobile allowances and special adaptive equipment; claims for specially adapted housing; special clothing allowance; emergency officer's retirement pay; eligibility determinations based on military service for other VA benefits and services or those of other government agencies; survivor's claims for death compensation, dependency and indemnity compensation, death pension, burial and plot allowance claims; claims for accrued benefits; forfeiture determinations; claims for adjusted compensation in death cases; and claims for reimbursement for headstone or marker. Contact: Compensation and Pension Service, Department of Veterans Benefits, Veterans Administration, 810 Vermont Ave. N.W., Room 400, Washington, DC 20420/202-389-2264.

Construction

Contracts are available to private firms for design, construction and building technology research. New facilities are built and old ones are improved to provide quality medical care for veterans. Design and construction contracts are also given for the National Cemetery System. Veterans Administration design projects requiring services for both design and construction are advertised in the *Commerce Business Daily*. Architect-engineer firms interested in working on VA medical center construction projects may write to the Chairperson, A/E Evaluation Board (OBE). Construction contractors should address their inquiries to the Chief, Administrative Services Division (0802). Contact both at the Veterans Administration Central Office, 810 Vermont Avenue NW., Washington, DC 20420 or the nearest VA Office.

Continuing Education

The Veterans Administration conducts system-wide continuing education programs to bring the latest in scientific, medical and management knowledge to Department of Medicine and Surgery (DM&S) employees. These programs include workshops, seminars and individual training, and all forms of audiovisual, print and transmission media. The activities include the following: 1) instructional design and educational development for all DM&S education activities; 2) management education and patient health education; and 3) coordination and funding support of the following

activities: Regional Medical Education Centers, the Cooperative Health Manpower Education Programs, the Engineering Training Center, Dental Education Centers, Continuing Education Centers, and continuing education activities at VA health care facilities. Contact: Continuing Education Resource Service, Academic Affairs, Veterans Administration, 810 Vermont Ave. N.W., Room 875D, Washington, DC 20420/203-389-2581.

Could You Use a Multimillion Dollar Customer **and** *Let's Do Business*

There are two free bulletins that list management consultant contract opportunities. Contact: Office of Procurement and Supply (91), Veterans Administration, 810 Vermont Ave. N.W., Washington, DC 20420/202-389-2918.

Dietetics

Veterans Administration dieticians are responsible for direct and special nutritional needs of veteran patients. Contact: Dietetic Service, Department of Medicine and Surgery, Veterans Administration, 810 Vermont Ave. N.W., Room 927, Washington, DC 20420/202-389-3376.

Direct Payments

The programs described below are those which provide financial assistance directly to individuals, private firms and other private institutions to encourage or subsidize a particular activity:

Automobiles and Adaptive Equipment for Certain Disabled Veterans and Members of the Armed Forces

Objectives: To provide financial assistance to certain disabled veterans toward the purchase price of an automobile or other conveyance, not to exceed $3,800, and an additional amount for adaptive equipment deemed necessary to insure the eligible person will be able to operate or make use of the automobile or other conveyance.

Eligibility: Veterans with honorable service having a service-connected disability due to loss or permanent loss of use of one or both feet, one or both hands, or a permanent impairment of vision of both eyes to a prescribed degree. Service personnel on active duty also qualify under the same criteria as veterans.

Range of Financial Assistance: Up to $3,800.

Contact: The local Veterans Administration office in your state or, Veterans Administration, Washington, DC 20420/202-389-2356.

Burial Allowance for Veterans

Objectives: To provide a monetary allowance not to exceed $300 toward the funeral and burial expenses plus $150 for plot or interment expenses if not buried in a National Cemetery. If death is service-connected, $1,100 or the amount authorized to be paid in the case of a federal employee whose death occurs as a result of an injury sustained in the performance of duty, is payable for funeral and burial expenses. In addition to the statutory burial allowance, the cost of transporting the remains from place of death to site of burial is paid by the VA if death occurs in a VA facility. The cost of transporting the remains from place of death to the national cemetery in which space is available nearest the veteran's last place of residence may also be paid if death was due to service-connected disability, or at the time of death the veteran was in receipt of disability compensation, and burial is in a national cemetery and the cost of transportation is not fully reimbursable under other provisions. A headstone, marker or the cost of a nongovernment headstone or marker not in excess of the average actual cost of headstones and markers furnished by the VA may be authorized. Also to provide a flag for the burial of a deceased veteran.

Eligibility: The person who bore the veteran's burial expense or the undertaker, if unpaid, is eligible for reimbursement of the burial expense. The next of kin, friend or associate of the deceased veteran is eligible for the flag.

Range of Financial Assistance: Up to $1,100.

Contact: Veterans Administration, Washington, DC 20420/202-389-2356.

Compensation for Service-Connected Deaths for Veterans' Dependents

Objectives: To compensate surviving widows, widowers, children and dependent parents for the death of any veteran who died before January 1, 1957 because of a service-connected disability.

Eligibility: A surviving unmarried widow, widower, child or children, and dependent parent or parents of the deceased veteran who must have died before January 1, 1957 because of a service-connected disability.

Range of Financial Assistance: Starting at $87 monthly.

Contact: The local Veterans Administration office in your state or Veterans Administration, Washington, DC 20420/202-389-2356.

Dependents' Educational Assistance

Objectives: To provide partial support to those seeking to advance their education who are qualifying spouses, surviving spouses, or children of deceased or disabled veterans, or of service personnel who have been listed for a total of more than 90 days as missing in action, or as prisoners of war.

Eligibility: Spouse, surviving spouses, and children between age 18 and 26 of veterans who died from service-connected disabilities, of living veterans whose service-connected disabilities are considered permanently and totally disabling, of those who died from any cause while such disabilities were in existence, of service persons who have

been listed for a total of more than 90 days as missing in action, or of prisoners of war.

Range of Financial Assistance: Not to exceed $2,500 in any one regular academic year.

Contact: The local Veterans Administration office in your state or Veterans Administration Central Office, Washington, DC 20420/202-389-2356.

Pension for Non-Service-Connected Disability for Veterans

Objectives: To assist wartime veterans in need whose non-service-connected disabilities are permanent and total and prevent them from following a substantially gainful occupation.

Eligibility: Those who have had 90 days or more of honorable active wartime service in the Armed Forces or if less than 90 days wartime service were released or discharged from such service because of a service-connected disability, who are permanently and totally disabled for reasons not necessarily due to service, and wartime veterans 65 years of age or older or who became unemployable after age 65 are considered permanently and totally disabled. Income restrictions are prescribed.

Range of Financial Assistance: Starting at $325 monthly.

Contact: The local Veterans Administration office in your state or Veterans Administration, Washington, DC 20420/202-389-2356.

Pension to Veterans Widows or Widowers and Children

Objectives: To provide a partial means of support for needy widows or widowers, and children of deceased wartime veterans whose deaths were not due to service.

Eligibility: Unmarried widows, widowers, and children of deceased veterans who had at least 90 days of honorable active wartime service or, if less than 90 days during wartime, were discharged for a service-connected disability and who have a limited income. A child must be unmarried and 18 or under (23 if in school) or unmarried 18 or over if disabled before 18 and continues to be disabled.

Range of Financial Assistance: Starting at $218 per month.

Contact: The local Veterans Administration office in your state or Veterans Administration, Washington, DC 20420/202-389-2356.

Post-Vietnam Era Veterans' Educational Assistance Program

Objectives: To provide educational assistance to persons first entering the Armed Forces after December 31, 1976, to assist young persons in obtaining an education they might otherwise not be able to afford, to promote and assist the all volunteer military persons to serve in the Armed Forces.

Eligibility: The participant must have served honorably on active duty for more than 180 days beginning on or after January 1, 1977, or have been discharged after such date because of a service-connected disability. Also eligible are participants who serve for more than 180 days and who continue on active duty and have completed their first period of obligated service (or six years of active duty, whichever comes first).

Range of Financial Assistance: Up to $8,100.

Contact: The local Veterans Administration office in your state or Veterans Administration, Central Office, Washington, DC 20420/202-389-2356.

Rehabilitative Research (Prosthetics)

Objectives: To develop new and improved prosthetic devices, sensory aids, mobility aids, automotive adaptive equipment, and related appliances for the primary benefit of disabled veterans. Through comprehensive educational and informational programs, the results of such research are made available for the benefit of the disabled throughout the world.

Eligibility: Any institution, state or local health agency, research organization, university, or rehabilitation center is eligible for contract.

Range of Financial Assistance: $6,000 to $280,000.

Contact: Director, Rehabilitation Engineering Research and Development Service, Veterans Administration, Central Office, Washington, DC 20420/202-389-5177.

Specially Adapted Housing for Disabled Veterans

Objectives: To assist certain totally disabled veterans in acquiring suitable housing units, with special fixtures and facilities made necessary by the nature of the veterans' disabilities.

Eligibility: Veterans with permanent, total and compensable disabilities based on service after April 20, 1898, due to a) loss of use of both extremities, such as to preclude locomotion without the aid of braces, canes, crutches or a wheelchair, or b) which includes 1) blindness in both eyes, having only light perception, plus 2) loss or loss of use of one lower extremity, together with 1) residuals of organic disease and injury, or 2) the loss or loss of use of one upper extremity which so affects the functions of balance or propulsion as to preclude locomotion without the aid of braces, crutches, canes or a wheelchair.

Range of Financial Assistance: Up to $30,000.

Contact: The local Veterans Administration Office in your state or Veterans Administration, Washington, DC 20420/202-389-2356.

Veterans Community Nursing Home Care

Objectives: To provide service-connected veterans with nursing home care and to aid the non-service-connected veteran in making the transition from a hospital to a community care facility by providing up to six months nursing care at VA expense.

Eligibility: A nursing home which 1) must be inspected by VA personnel for compliance with VA standards established for skilled or intermediate care facilities, or 2) is accredited by the Joint Commission on Accreditation of Hospitals.

Range of Financial Assistance: Not specified.

Contact: Assistant Chief Medical Director for Extended Care, Department of Medicine and Surgery, Veterans Administration, Washington, DC 20420/202-389-3692.

Veterans Compensation for Service-Connected Disability

Objectives: To compensate veterans for the disability due to military service according to the average impairment in earning capacity such disability would cause in civilian occupations.

Eligibility: Persons who have suffered disabilities due to service in the armed forces of the United States.

Range of Financial Assistance: Up to $2,536 per month.

Contact: The local Veterans Administration office in your state or Veterans Administration, Washington, DC 20420/202-389-2356.

Veterans Dependency and Indemnity Compensation for Service-Connected Death

Objectives: To compensate surviving widows, or widowers, children and parents for the death of any veteran who died on or after January 1, 1957 because of a service-connected disability.

Eligibility: A surviving unmarried widow, or widower, a child or children, and parent or parents of the deceased veteran who died on or after January 1, 1957, because of a service-connected disability. Dependency and Indemnity Compensation (DIC) payments may be authorized for surviving spouse and children of certain veterans who were totally service-connected disabled at the time of death and whose deaths were not the result of their service-connected disability.

Range of Financial Assistance: Up to $895 monthly.

Contact: The local Veterans Administration office in your state or Veterans Administration, Washington, DC 20420/202-389-2356.

Educational Assistance (GI Bill)

Objectives: To make service in the Armed Forces more attractive by extending benefits of a higher education to qualified young persons who might not otherwise be able to afford such an education; and to restore lost educational opportunities to those whose education was interrupted by active duty after January 31, 1955 and before January 1, 1977.

Eligibility: The veteran must have served honorably on active duty for more than 180 days, any part of which occurred after January 31, 1955 and before January 1, 1977. A veteran with less than 180 days' service may be eligible if he or she was released because of a service-connected disability. A service person who has served on active duty for more than 180 days any part of which was before January 1, 1977, and who continues on active duty is also eligible. Upon completion of 18 continuous months of active duty, the maximum of 45 months of educational assistance will be granted, if the veteran is released under conditions that satisfy his or her active duty obligation, otherwise assistance will be provided for at the rate of 1½ months for each month of service. An initial period of active duty for training under section 511(d), title 10, U.S. Code, served on or after February 1, 1955 when subsequently followed by one year of active duty, may be included in computing active duty time for determining entitlement. Also eligible for benefits are those persons who enter into service under the Delayed Entry Program between January 1, 1977 and January 1, 1978, and who contracted for this program with the Armed Forces prior to January 1, 1977.

Range of Financial Assistance: Not to exceed $2,500 in any one regular academic year.

Contact: The local Veterans Administration office in your state or Veterans Administration, Washington, DC 20420/202-389-2356.

Rehabilitation for Disabled Veterans

Objectives: To train veterans for the purpose of restoring employability, to the extent consistent with the degree of a service-connected disability.

Eligibility: Veterans of World War II and later service who, as a result of a service-connected compensable disability, are determined to be in need of vocational rehabilitation to overcome their handicap.

Range of Financial Assistance. Full cost of tuition, books, fees and supplies, plus monthly full-time allowances.

Contact: The local Veterans Administration office in your state or Veterans Administration, Central Office, Washington, DC 20420/202-389-2356.

Domiciliary

A Veterans Administration domiciliary is a health care facility providing a program of planned living in a sheltered environment and necessary ambulatory medical treatment to veterans who are unable because of their disabilities to earn a living but who are not in need of nursing service, constant medical supervision or hospitalization. Contact: Patient Treatment Service, Department of Medicine and Surgery, Veterans Administration, 810 Vermont Ave. N.W., Room 863, Washington, DC 20420/202-389-3692.

Driver Training for the Handicapped

The Veterans Administration operates driver training centers staffed with trained therapist/instructors and equipped with specially adapted automobiles and vans. Contact: Rehabilitation Medicine Service, Department of Medicine and Surgery, 810 Vermont Ave. N.W., Room 915F, Washington, DC 20420/202-389-2373.

Employment Assistance

The Veterans Administration works with the Department of Labor (DOL) to provide job and job training service to veterans. The VA cooperates in the Disabled Veterans Outreach Program and the Comprehensive Employment and Training Act program by providing names and addresses and by providing veterans' benefits training. VA also provides lists of names and addresses of on-the-job training employers to be used by State Employment Security Administrations (SESAs) in developing job opportunities. Also, Veterans' Employment Representatives are stationed in some U.S. Veterans' Assistance Centers. Contact: the nearest regional VA office by checking the white pages of your phone directory under the heading, U.S. Government.

Equal Opportunity

The Office of Equal Opportunity has responsibility for coordinating and advising on all agency civil rights and equal opportunity matters. The Office coordinates the Federal Women's and Hispanic Employment Programs; processes discrimination complaints, develops and monitors National Equal Employment Opportunity Affirmative Action Plans; develops policy and standards for EEO program review; plans and conducts EEO training; develops National Affirmative Action Plans for minorities and women, handicapped individuals and disabled veterans; monitors VA compliance and enforcement activities to insure nondiscrimination in federally assisted programs; and coordinates VA activities to increase participation of Historically Black Colleges and Universities (HBCU) in federally assisted programs. Contact: Equal Opportunity Staff, Veterans Administration, 810 Vermont Ave. N.W., Washington, DC 20420/202-389-3887.

Exhibits

A variety of exhibits are available for display at Veterans Administration facilities, veterans' organizations, conventions, educational institutions and professional, medical and scientific meetings. Contact: Audio Visual Service, Veterans Administration, 810 Vermont Ave. N.W., Room C76, Washington, DC 20420/202-389-2715.

Extended Care

The Veterans Administration Extended Care programs encompass a broad spectrum of care for veterans of all ages who need such care and is not solely focused on care for elderly veterans. The range of programs, in addition to extended hospital care (intermediate care) and outpatient care, includes: nursing home care, which has three components—the VA's own nursing home care program, the community (contract) nursing home care program, and the state home nursing care program; the domicilliary programs of both the VA and the states; GEU's (geriatric evaluation units); the HBHC (hospital based home care) program; the ADHC (adult day health care) program; the RCH (residential care program); and one prototype hospice program caring exclusively for the terminally ill. The nursing home care units located in VA medical centers provide skilled nursing care and related medical services, as well as opportunities for social, diversional, recreational, and spiritual activities. Nursing home patients typically require a prolonged period of nursing care and supervision, and rehabilitation services to attain and/or maintain optimal function. Contact: Office of Geriatrics and Extended Care (30), Department of Medicine and Surgery, Veterans Administration, 810 Vermont Ave., N.W., Room 865, Washington, DC 20420/202-389-3781.

Federal Benefits for Veterans and Dependents
This pamphlet includes the addresses and phone numbers of all Veterans Administration installations. It is available for $2.00 from the Superintendent of Documents, Government Printing Office, Washington, DC 20402/202-783-3238. For additional information, contact: Public Affairs, Department of Veterans Affairs, Veterans Administration, 810 Vermont Ave. N.W., Room 311, Washington, DC 20420/202-389-5210.

Fee-Basis Medical and Pharmacy Program
This program allows authorized veterans to receive medical services from individuals or organizations. The Veterans Administration compensates participating members for services performed, and pays the veteran for travel expenses incurred for the visit. Make application at your nearest VA Medical Center or contact your nearest regional VA Office by checking the white pages of your phone directory under the heading, U.S. Government.

Fiduciary and Field Examinations
This office supervises the payment of benefits to fiduciaries on behalf of adult beneficiaries who are incompetent or under some other legal disability. It also supervises the payments of benefits to minor beneficiaries who are not in care of a natural or adoptive parent. Contact: Department of Veterans Benefits, Veterans Assistance Service, Veterans Administration, 810 Vermont Ave. N.W., Room 344A, Washington, DC 20420/202-389-3643.

Film Library
The audiovisual activity maintains the VA's centralized motion picture film library consisting of 780 titles and 3,659 prints for use in medical and scientific research, and in orientation, training, information and rehabilitation programs. In addition to VA use, the films are available to other federal and state agencies, veterans' organizations, educational institutions, and professional and scientific groups. Contact: Central Office, Film Library, Veterans Administration, 810 Vermont Ave. N.W., Room B75, Washington, DC 20420/202-389-2780.

Foreign Training
Veterans, in-service students and dependents may pursue training at approved foreign schools. A free pamphlet with information on the program, listing those foreign schools which offer at least one course approved for training is available. Contact: the nearest regional VA office, or Education Service, Department of Veterans Benefits, Veterans Administration, 810 Vermont Ave. N.W., Room 444C, Washington, DC 20420/202-389-5154.

Freedom of Information Act Requests
For Freedom of Information Act requests, contact: Paperwork Management and Regulation Service (73), Veterans Administration, 810 Vermont Ave. N.W., Washington, DC 20420/202-389-3294.

Graduate and Undergraduate Medical and Dental Education
The Veterans Administration health care facilities participate in specialty and subspecialty programs for physicians and dentists. Contact: Academic Affairs, Department of Medicine and Surgery, Veterans Administration, 810 Vermont Ave. N.W., Room 860, Washington, DC 20420/202-389-5093.

Grants
The programs described below are for sums of money which are given by the federal government to initiate and stimulate new or improved activities or to sustain on-going services:

Grants to States for Construction of State Home Facilities
Objectives: To assist states to construct state home facilities for furnishing domiciliary or nursing home care to veterans, and to expand, remodel or alter existing buildings for furnishing domiciliary, nursing home or hospital care to veterans in state homes.
Eligibility: Any state may apply after assuring that the assisted facility will be operated by the state; and will be used primarily for veterans.
Range of Financial Assistance: $47,000 to $16,456,000.

Contact: Assistant Chief Medical Director for Extended Care, Veterans Administration, Central Office, Washington, DC 20420/202-389-3781.

State Cemetery Grants

Objectives: To assist states in the establishment, expansion and improvement of veterans' cemeteries.

Eligibility: Any state may apply.

Range of Financial Assistance: Not specified.

Contact: Director, State Cemetery Grants, Department of Memorial Affairs, Veterans Administration, 810 Vermont Ave. N.W., Washington, DC 20420/202-389-2313.

Veterans State Domiciliary Care

Objectives: To provide financial assistance to states furnishing domiciliary care to veterans in State Veterans' Homes which meet the standards prescribed by the VA Administrator.

Eligibility: Applicant in any state which operates a designated facility to furnish domiciliary care primarily for veterans.

Range of Financial Assistance: $3,947 to $1,490,580.

Contact: Assistant Chief Medical Director for Geriatrics and Extended Care, Veterans Administration, Washington, DC 20420/202-389-3679.

Veterans State Nursing Home Care

Objectives: To provide financial assistance to states furnishing nursing home care to veterans in state veterans' homes which meet the standards prescribed by the VA administrator.

Eligibility: Applicant is any state which operates a designated facility to furnish nursing home care primarily for veterans.

Range of Financial Assistance: $49,283 to $2,835,260.

Contact: Assistant Chief Medical Director for Extended Care, Veterans Administration, Washington, DC 20420/202-389-3781.

Veterans State Hospital Care

Objectives: To provide financial assistance to states furnishing hospital care to veterans in state veterans' homes which meet the standards prescribed by the VA Administrator.

Eligibility: Applicant is any state which operates a state home for veterans and intends to furnish hospital care primarily for veterans.

Range of Financial Assistance: $41,817 to $1,478,806.

Contact: Assistant Chief Medical Director for Geriatrics and Extended Care, Veterans Administration, Washington, DC 20420/202-389-3679.

Headstone or Grave Marker

A headstone or grave marker is available without charge for any deceased veteran of wartime or peacetime service and can be shipped to the consignee designated. Contact: Monument Service, Department of Memorial Affairs, Veterans Administration, 941 N. Capitol St. S.E., Room 9320, Washington, DC 20420/202-275-1480.

Health Services Research and Development

The mission of Health Services Research and Development (HSR&D) is to help VA clinicians and administrators improve veteran health care and save money. It does this by supporting projects to evaluate alternative medical interventions and administrative policies and by providing clinicians and administrators with information that enables them to make intelligent choices. Contact: Health Services Research and Development (152), Research and Development, Department of Medicine and Surgery, Veterans Administration, 810 Vermont Avenue N.W., Washington, DC 20420/202-389-2666.

Insurance

Veterans Administration life insurance operations are for the benefit of service members, veterans and their beneficiaries. Insurance activities include: complete maintenance of all individual insurance accounts (policies); authorization of policy loans, cash surrenders, and matured endowments; exchange and conversion of policy plans; development of insurance death claims and the authorization of payment to the beneficiary; development of disability insurance claims to support waiver of premium or disability insurance award payments in behalf of the insured; allotments from pay for members of the military departments; payroll deductions for employees of large commercial employers; establishing relationship of individual death or disability to extra hazard of military service for assessment to proper funding accounts; any other transaction which may have a bearing upon the total responsibility for the insurance program. Contact: Department of Veterans Benefits (201 A), Veterans Administration, 810 Vermont Ave. N.W., Room 311, Washington, DC 20420/202-389-5284.

Library

The library contains two collections. The medical collection is in the fields of medicine, surgery, dentistry, pharmacy, physical medicine, rehabilitation, nursing, dietetics, social service and hospital administration. Medical periodicals are regularly received. The general reference collection is such fields as veterans affairs, personnel administration, data processing, public administration, accounting, insurance and statistics. General periodicals are regularly received. The collection includes microfilm and microfiche. It is open to the public. Contact: Library Division (142D), Veterans Administration, 810 Vermont Ave. N.W., Room 97, Washington, DC 20420/202-389-3085.

Loan Guaranty

The aim of loan guarantees is to provide credit assistance on more liberal terms than is generally available to nonveterans. Assistance is provided chiefly through substituting the Government's guaranty on loans made by private lenders in lieu of the downpayments, shorter terms, and other requirements generally required in conventional home mortgage transactions. In addition, a system of direct financial grants is operated to help certain permanently disabled veterans to acquire specially adapted housing. The major activities include appraising properties to establish their values; supervising the construction of new residential properties; passing on the ability of a veteran to repay a loan and the credit risk; servicing and liquidating defaulted loans; and disposing of real estate acquired as the consequence of defaulted loans. There are also substantial operations involved in managing and realizing loan assets. A counseling service is conducted to aid potential minority homebuyers both in obtaining housing credit and in discharging their obligations as homeowners and mortgagors. Contact: Loan Guaranty Service (264), Department of Veterans Benefits, Veterans Administration, 810 Vermont Ave. N.W., Room 367, Washington, DC 20420/202-389-3042.

Loans and Loan Guarantees

The programs described below are those which offer financial assistance through the lending of federal monies for a specific period of time or programs in which the federal government makes an arrangement to indemnify a lender against part or all of any defaults by the borrower.

Veterans Housing—Direct Loans and Advances

Objectives: To provide direct housing credit assistance to veterans, service personnel, and certain unmarried widows and widowers of veterans and spouses of service personnel living in rural areas and small cities and towns (not near large metropolitan areas) where private capital is not generally available for VA guaranteed or insured loans.

Eligibility: a) Veterans who served on active duty on or after September 16, 1940 and were discharged or released under conditions other than dishonorable. Veterans of World War II, the Korean Conflict or the Vietnam era must have served on active duty 90 days or more. All other veterans must have served a minimum of 181 days on active duty; b) any veteran in the above classes with less service but discharged with a service-connected disability; c) unmarried widows and widowers of otherwise eligible veterans who died in service or whose deaths were attributable to service-connected disabilities; d) service personnel who have served at least 181 days in active duty status; e) the spouse of any member of the Armed Forces serving on active duty who is listed as missing in action, or is a prisoner of war, and has been so listed for a total of more than 90 days.

Range of Financial Assistance: Up to $33,000.

Contact: Veterans Administration, Washington, DC 20420/202-389-2356.

Veterans Housing—Direct Loans for Disabled Veterans

Objectives: To provide certain totally disabled veterans with direct housing credit, to supplement grants authorized to assist the veterans in acquiring suitable housing units, with special features or movable facilities made necessary by the nature of their disabilities.

Eligibility: Veterans who served on active duty on or after September 16, 1940 with permanent, total and compensable disabilities due to a) loss or loss of use of both lower extremities, such as to preclude locomotion without braces, canes, crutches, or a wheelchair, or b) which includes 1) blindness in both eyes, having only light perception, plus 2) loss or loss of use of one lower extremity, or c) loss or loss of use of one lower extremity, together with 1) residuals of organic disease or injury, or 2) the loss or loss of use of one upper extremity which so affects the function of balance or propulsion as to preclude locomotion without the aid of braces, crutches, canes or a wheelchair.

Range of Financial Assistance: Up to $33,000.

Contact: Veterans Administration, Washington, DC 20420/202-389-2356.

Veterans Housing—Guaranteed and Insured Loans

Objectives: To assist veterans, certain service personnel and certain unmarried widows or widowers of veterans, in obtaining credit for the purchase, construction or improvement of homes on more liberal terms than are generally available to nonveterans.

Eligibility: a) Veterans who served on active duty on or after September 16, 1940 and were discharged or released under conditions other than dishonorable. Veterans of World War II, the Korean Conflict or the Vietnam era must have served on active duty 90 days or more. All other veterans must have served a minimum of 181 days on active duty; b) any veteran in the above classes with less service but discharged with a service-connected disability; c) unmarried widows and widowers of otherwise eligible veterans who died in service or whose deaths were attributable to service-connected disabilities; d) service personnel who have served at least 181 days in active duty status; e) spouses of members of the Armed Forces serving on active duty, listed as missing in action, or as prisoners of war and who have been so listed 90 days or more.

Range of Financial Assistance: $38,500 to $75,550.

Contact: Veterans Administration, Washington, DC 20420/202-389-2356.

Veterans Housing—Manufactured Home Loan

Objectives: To assist veterans, service persons and certain unmarried widows or widowers of veterans in obtaining credit for the purchase of a mobile home on more liberal terms than are available to nonveterans.

Eligibility: a) Veterans who served on active duty on or after September 16, 1940 and were discharged or released under conditions other than dishonorable. Veterans of World War II, the Korean Conflict and the Vietnam era must have served on active duty 90 days or more. All other veterans must have served a minimum of 181 days on active duty; b) any veteran in the above classes with less service but discharged with a service-connected disability; c) unmarried widows and widowers of otherwise eligible veterans who died in service or whose deaths were attributable to service-connected disabilities; d) service personnel who have served at least 181 days in active duty status; e) the spouse of any member of the Armed Forces serving on active duty who is listed missing in action, or as a prisoner of war, and has been so listed for a total of more than 90 days.

Range of Financial Assistance: $15,000 to $24,430.

Contact: Veterans Administration, Washington, DC 20420.

Medical Center

A Veterans Administration medical center provides eligible beneficiaries with medical and other health care services equivalent to those provided by private sector institutions, augmented in many instances by services to meet the special requirements of veterans. For additional information, contact: Operations, Department of Medicine and Surgery, Veterans Administration, 810 Vermont Ave. N.W., Room 814, Washington, DC 20420/202-389-5383.

Medical, Dental and Hospital Benefits

Medical, dental and hospital benefits for veterans include hospitalization in VA hospitals, nursing home care, domiciliary care, outpatient medical care, home health services, outpatient dental treatment, prosthetic appliances, aids for the blind, and alcohol and drug dependence treatment. Contact: the nearest regional VA office, or: Public Information, Department of Medicine and Surgery, Veterans Administration, 810 Vermont Ave. N.W., Room 815F, Washington, DC 20420/202-389-3552.

Medical Library Network (VALNET)

The VALNET (VA Library Network) is made up of 175 Library Services. In addition to operating patient libraries, VALNET supports the information and continuing education needs of medical care, research, clinical administrative, and patient health education programs. Internal networking through the VALNET regional libraries and through external sharing arrangements with community libraries and library consortia makes possible even speedier delivery of materials and eliminates duplication. Library Services act as the major learning resources depository and distribution hub for VA-produced audiovisual programs. Contact: Library (142D), Academic Affairs, Department of Medicine and Surgery, Veterans Administration, 810 Vermont Ave. N.W., Room 975, Washington, DC 20420/202-389-2781.

Medical Media

Audiovisual aids include color transparencies, charts, and drafts, videotape, and motion picture footage. Scientific exhibits are produced and displayed at national meetings. Contact: Medical Media (142B), Learning Resources Service, Academic Affairs, Department of Medicine and Surgery, Veterans Administration, 810 Vermont Ave. N.W., Room 875B, Washington, DC 20420/202-389-3812.

Medical Research

VA medical research plays a key role in fulfilling the Agency's mission to provide the nation's veterans with quality medical care. Research projects are conducted by members of the clinical staff. Currently, the Medical Research Service's high priority program stresses research projects dealing with schizophrenia, alcoholism, spinal cord injury and tissue regeneration, delayed stress, cancer, health problems of female veterans, and Agent Orange. Other significant studies focus on health problems prevalent among veterans; for example, diabetes, chronic heart disease, chronic pulmonary disease, and the health problems of former prisoners of war. Contact: Medical Research Service, Research and Development, Department of Medicine and Surgery, Veterans Administration, 810 Vermont Ave. N.W., Room 744E, Washington, DC 20420/202-389-5041.

Medical Service Activities

Special efforts by Veterans Administration medical service are made in hypertension, sickle cell anemia, dialysis, rheumatology, immunology, cardiology, pulmonary disease and intensive care. Contact: Professional Service, Department of Medicine and Surgery, Veterans Administration, 810 Vermont Ave. N.W., Room 944C, Washington, DC 20420/202-389-3560.

Medical Statistics

The demographic and medical characteristics of VA patients are derived from the Patient Treatment File and the Annual Patient Census. Information includes age, service-connected and VA pensioners, diagnoses, duration of stay and disposition status. Contact: Medical Administration Service, Department of Medicine and Surgery, Veterans Administration, 810 Vermont Ave. N.W., Room 636, Washington, DC 20420/202-389-2180.

Medicine and Law
Copies of the series of the six educational video tape cassettes, entitled *Current Problems in Medicine and the Law* produced by DM&S have been distributed to each VA health care facility. As a supplement to these tapes, study guides are available for distribution. The study guides and the tapes, augmented by directed discussion, provide a highly effective method of giving health care providers timely information on the impact of law on the practice of medicine. Contact your nearest Veterans Administration Library by checking the white pages of your phone directory under the heading of U.S. Government.

Memorial Affairs
The Department of Memorial Affairs administers the National Cemetery system, which provides cemeterial services to veterans and other eligibles. These services also include providing headstones and markers for graves of eligibles in national and private cemeteries and monetary aid to States for establishment, expansion and improvement of veterans' cemeteries. Contact: Department of Memorial Affairs, Veterans Administration, 810 Vermont Ave. N.W., Room 275K, Washington, DC 20420/202-389-5202.

Memorial Markers and Memorial Plots
A memorial headstone or marker may be furnished on application of a close relative recognized as the next of kin to commemorate any eligible veteran (also includes a person who died in the active military, naval or air service) whose remains have not been recovered or identified, or were buried at sea through no choice of the next of kin. The memorial may be erected in a private cemetery in a plot provided by the applicant or in a memorial section of a national cemetery. Contact: Monument Service, Department of Memorial Affairs, Veterans Administration, 941 N. Capitol St. S.E., Room 9320, Washington, DC 20420/202-275-1480.

Mental Health
Mental health services are provided in the Veterans Administration through the use of professionally trained personnel in a multi-disciplinary approach to treatment in most of the Veterans Administration Hospitals. Mental hygiene clinics serve as the basic units in the delivery of ambulatory mental health care. Contact: Mental Health and Behavioral Sciences Service (116), Department of Medicine and Surgery, Veterans Adminis-

tration, 810 Vermont Ave. N.W., Room 963, Washington, DC 20420/202-389-3416.

Mobile Home Loans
The Veterans Administration may guarantee loans made by private lenders to eligible veterans for the purchase of new or used mobile homes with or without a lot. Contact: nearest regional office, or Loan Guaranty Service, Department of Veterans Affairs, Veterans Administration, 810 Vermont Ave. N.W., Room 367, Washington, DC 20420/202-389-2332.

Pointers for the Veteran Homeowner
This is a guide for veterans whose home mortgage is guaranteed or insured under the G.I. Bill. Contact: The nearest regional VA office by checking the white pages of your phone directory under the heading, U.S. Government.

Presidential Memorial Certificate
The certificate expresses the country's grateful recognition of the person's service in the Armed Forces and bears the signature of the President. For information, contact: the VA regional office, or: Department of Memorial Affairs, Veterans Administration, 810 Vermont Ave. N.W., Room 275A, Washington, DC 20420/202-389-5211.

Readjustment Counseling Service
The Veterans Administration conducts a nationwide system of Vet Centers which provide counseling service to Vietnam era veterans. Vet Centers are small (typically with a four-to-six person staff), community-based storefront centers that offer a broad range of services during day and evening hours. Their professional staff addresses problems and concerns of Vietnam era veterans and their families that are related to the veteran's experience while on active duty or during the military-to-civilian transition. Such services include readjustment counseling to individuals, families, and groups; outreach to contact veterans in need of counseling; crisis intervention; counseling related to employment; information and referral regarding available assistance, VA and non-VA services and resources, hospital treatment, benefits, discharge upgrade, Agent Orange, and social services; and community education about post-traumatic stress disorder and other readjustment problems of Vietnam era veterans. Contact: Adjustment Counseling Services (10B/RC), Department of Medicine and Surgery, Veterans Administration, 810 Vermont Ave. N.W., Room 851, Washington, DC 20420/202-389-3317.

Recreation
The Veterans Administration recreational programs attempt to improve the quality of patients' lives and to facilitate their reentry into the community. A film designed to show how disabled

veterans can successfully participate in a multitude of recreation activities has been developed. Contact: Recreation Service, Department of Medicine and Surgery, Veterans Administration, 810 Vermont Ave. N.W., Room 951, Washington, DC 20420/202-389-5389.

Rehabilitative Engineering
Research and development in devices to assist and support physically disabled veterans includes prosthetics research, spinal cord monitoring, sensory aids program, and workshops on maxillofacial prosthetics among others. Contact: Rehabilitation Research and Development Service, Department of Medicine and Surgery, Veterans Administration, 810 Vermont Ave. N.W., Room 642, Washington, DC 20420/202-389-5177.

Reports and Statistics
Reports and statistics are issued on a recurring and nonrecurring basis. Among the reports are the following:

RECURRING REPORTS
Veteran Population
America's Wars
State and County Veteran Population
Veterans Benefits Under Current Educational Programs
Active Compensation, Pension and Retirement Cases by Period of Service
Selected Compensation & Pension Data, by State of Residence
Disability & Death Pension Data
Disability Compensation Data
Employment Data on T.38 Physicians, Dentists and Nurses
Annual Report of the Administrator of Veterans Affairs
VA Trend Data
Directory of Veterans Administration Facilities
Geographic Distribution of VA Expenditures
Statistical Summary of VA Activities
VA Summary of Medical Programs
VA Loan Guaranty Highlights
DVB Field Station Summary
Approved Recurring Reports Bulletin
Active ADP Application Systems
NON-RECURRING REPORTS
National Survey of Veterans
1979 National Survey of Veterans
The Female Veteran Population
Protocol for the Vietnam Veteran Mortality Study
Validating Duty in Vietnam from Automated Military Personnel Files
Historical Data on the Usage of Educational Benefits: 1945–1983
Vietnam Era Veterans Usage of GI Bill Education Entitlement
Work Experience and Income of Male Veterans and Nonveterans in 1981
Employment and Unemployment Among Vietnam Era Veterans, An Analysis of the 1979 National Survey of Veterans

For a description and/or a complete list of these, contact: Report Preparation Division (772), Office of Information Management and Statistics, Veterans Administration, 810 Vermont Ave. N.W., Room 518, Washington, DC 20420.

Social Work
Social work focuses on the social problems of the chronically ill, the disabled and the long-term care patient. Contact: Veterans Administration, Social Work Service (122), 810 Vermont Ave. N.W., Washington, DC 20420/202-389-2613.

Specially Adapted Housing
Veterans who have a service-connected disability may be eligible to receive a Veterans Administration grant toward the cost of a specially adapted housing unit. A free pamphlet, *Questions and Answers on Specially Adapted Housing for Veterans,* is available. Contact: the nearest regional VA office by checking the white pages of your phone directory under the heading, U.S. Government.

State Cemetery Grants
Veterans Administration makes grants to states for the establishment, expansion and improvement of state veterans' cemeteries. Contact: State Cemetery Grants, Department of Memorial Affairs, Veterans Administration, 810 Vermont Ave. N.W., Room 275, Washington, DC 20420/202-389-2313.

Statistical Reporting
The Automated Management Information System (AMIS) is an agency-wide system designed to meet the VA statistical reporting needs. Contact: Report Preparation Division (772), Office of Information Management and Statistics, Veterans Administration, 810 Vermont Ave. N.W., Washington, DC 20420.

Statistical Tables
Tables include statistics on veteran population (number, state, age, period of service), health care and extended care, hospital care, inpatient and ambulatory care, VA and non-VA facilities, pharmacy activity, construction, guardianship and veterans assistance, compensation and pension, national cemetery system, compensation pension, educational assistance, housing assistance, insurance, personnel, employment of minority groups and women, and appeals. These statistical tables appear in the VA annual report. For further information, contact: Report Preparation Division (772), Office of Information Management and Statistics, Controller, Veterans Administration, 810 Vermont Ave. N.W., Washington, DC 20420.

Toll-Free Benefits Information
VA benefits information is available all across the country from a Veterans Benefit Counselor. Other

sources that provide information about veterans benefits are service organizations and state and local office of Veterans Affairs. See the government listing section of the telephone directory for a listing of the nearest VA office. Toll-Free numbers are listed for calls within your state.

Veterans Affairs Toll-Free Information

Veterans Affairs toll-free numbers provide information and help with problems involving GI loans, educational benefits, insurance, disability compensation, medical and dental care, employment, etc. The Veterans Administration also maintains many local offices and medical facilities. Look in your local phone book under "U.S. Government" for a listing of toll-free numbers in your area.

Veterans Benefits

Veterans benefits and services available to older Americans include medical care, disability compensation, disability pension, insurance, death pension, dependency and indemnity compensation, interment allowance, burial in a national cemetery, a burial flag, and headstone or grave marker. Contact the nearest regional VA office.

Vocational Rehabilitation Program

During the period February 1, 1985, through January 31, 1989, veterans awarded pension may be eligible for up to 24 months or more of vocational training to prepare for and enter employment. Under this program every veteran under age 50 who begins to receive a pension award after February 1, 1985, will participate in a vocational evaluation to be arranged by the VA. Veterans who are age 50 and older and are awarded pension after February 1, 1985, may apply for an evaluation of their ability to profit from vocational training. Vocational training for up to 24 months or more and up to 18 months of

employment services will be provided for program participants. A veteran will continue to receive pension during the period of training and employment services. Pension will be reduced or terminated following adjustment in employment when work income exceeds the annual income limitation applicable to pension. However, the veteran's VA health-care eligibility (including any applicable priority) will be preserved for a 3-year period following the date on which pension is terminated. Contact: Nearest VA Regional Office as listed in the phone directory, or Vocational Rehabilitation and Counseling Service (28), Veterans Administration Central Office, 810 Vermont Ave., N.W., Washington, DC 20420/202-389-3935.

Voluntary Service

The Veterans Administration encourages and trains volunteers to work at VA facilities in a variety of assignments that are both beneficial to veterans and rewarding to volunteers. Contact: Chief, Voluntary Service at the nearest VA Medical Center by checking the white pages of your phone directory under the heading, U.S. Government.

Work-Study Program

Veterans enrolled full time in college degree, vocational or professional programs may "earn money while they learn" under the VA work-study program. Contact: the nearest regional VA office by checking the white pages of your phone directory under the heading, U.S. Government.

How Can the Veterans Administration Help You?

To determine how the Veterans Administration can help you, contact the nearest regional VA office by checking the white pages of your phone directory under the heading, U.S. Government.

EXECUTIVE BRANCH

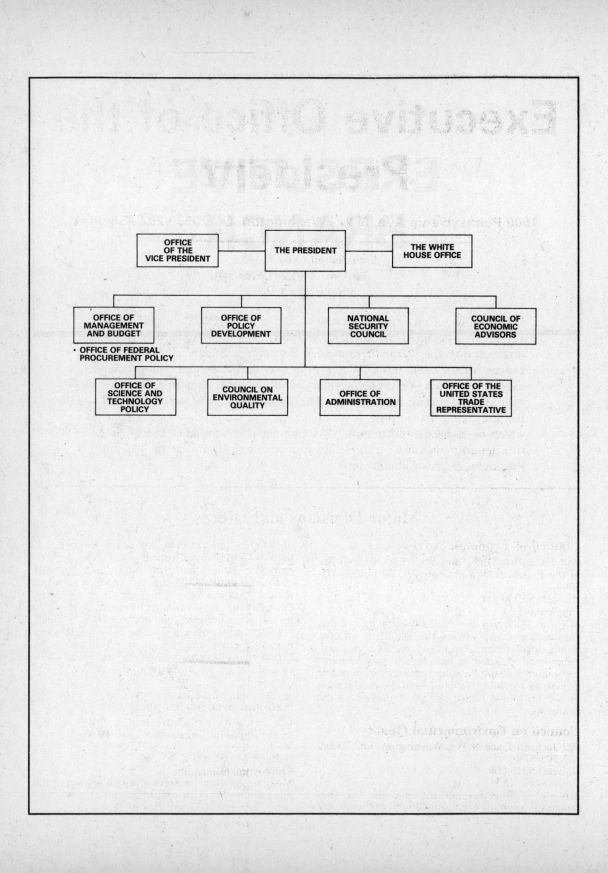

OFFICE OF THE VICE PRESIDENT

THE PRESIDENT

THE WHITE HOUSE OFFICE

OFFICE OF MANAGEMENT AND BUDGET

• OFFICE OF FEDERAL PROCUREMENT POLICY

OFFICE OF POLICY DEVELOPMENT

NATIONAL SECURITY COUNCIL

COUNCIL OF ECONOMIC ADVISORS

OFFICE OF SCIENCE AND TECHNOLOGY POLICY

COUNCIL ON ENVIRONMENTAL QUALITY

OFFICE OF ADMINISTRATION

OFFICE OF THE UNITED STATES TRADE REPRESENTATIVE

Executive Office of the President

1600 Pennsylvania Ave. N.W., Washington, DC 20500/202-456-1414

Established: July 1, 1939
Budget: $101,241,000
Employees:1,503

Mission: The Constitution provides that "the executive power shall be vested in a President of the United States of America. He shall hold his office during the Term of four years—together with the Vice President, chosen for the same term." The President is the administrative head of the executive branch of the Government, which includes numerous agencies as well as 13 executive departments. The Cabinet functions at the pleasure of the President. Its purpose is to advise the President upon any subject on which he requests information. The Cabinet is composed of the 13 executive departments, and certain other executive branch officials to whom the President accords Cabinet rank.

Major Divisions and Offices

Council of Economic Advisors

Old Executive Office Building, Executive Office of the President, Washington, DC 20506/202-395-5084.
Budget: $2,177,000
Employees: 34
Mission: Analyzes the national economy and its various segments; advises the President on economic developments; appraises the economic programs and policies of the federal government; recommends to the President policies for economic growth and stability; and assists in the preparation of the economic reports of the President to the Congress.

Council on Environmental Quality

722 Jackson Place N.W., Washington, DC 20006/202-395-5780
Budget: $926,000
Employees: 15
Mission: Formulates and recommends national policies to promote the improvement of the quality of the environment; develops and recommends to the President national policies which further environmental quality; performs a continuing analysis of changes or trends in the national environment; reviews and appraises programs of the Federal Government to determine their contributions to sound environmental policy; conducts studies, research, and analyses relating to ecological systems and environmental quality; and assists the President in the preparation of the annual environmental quality report to the Congress.

National Security Council

Old Executive Office Building, Executive Office of the President, Washington, DC 20506/202-456-4974.
Budget: $4,064,000
Employees: 60
Mission: Advises the President with respect to the integration of domestic, foreign and military policies relating to national security.

Office of Administration

New Executive Office Building, Executive Office of the President, Washington, DC 20500/202-395-3765
Budget: $13,108,000
Employees: 147
Mission: Provides administrative support services to all units within the Executive Office of the President, except those services which are in direct support of the President.

Office of Management and Budget

Executive Office Building, Executive Office of the President, Washington, DC 20503/202-395-7250
Budget: $37,462,000
Employees: 635
Mission: Assists the President in his program to develop and maintain effective government by reviewing the organizational structure and management procedures of the executive branch to insure that they are capable of producing the intended results; assists in developing interagency cooperation; assists the President in the preparation of the budget and the formulation of the fiscal program of the Government; supervises and controls the administration of the budget; assists the President by clearing and coordinating departmental advice in proposed legislation and by making recommendations as to Presidential action in legislative enactments, in accordance with past practice; assists in the development of regulating reform proposals and in programs for paperwork reduction, especially reporting burdens of the public; assists in the consideration, clearance, and preparation of proposed Executive orders and proclamations; plans and develops information system to provide the President with program performance data; and keeps the President informed of the program of activities by agencies of the government with respect to work proposed, work actually initiated, and work completed, together with the relative timing of work between the several agencies of the Government all to the end that the work programs of the several agencies of the executive branch of the government may be coordinated and that the moneys appropriated by the Congress may be expended in the most economical manner.

Office of Federal Procurement Policy

Office of Management and Budget, New Executive Office Building, Washington, DC 20503/202-395-5802.
Budget: $2,495,000
Employees: 41
Mission: Responsible for improving the economy, efficiency and effectiveness of the procurement process by providing overall direction of procurement policies, regulations, procedures and forms.

Office of Policy Development

Executive Office of the President, 1600 Pennsylvania Ave. N.W., Washington, DC 20500/202-456-1414.
Budget: $2,712,000
Employees: 45
Mission: Formulates, coordinates, and implements economic and domestic policy; and serves as the policy staff for the President's Cabinet Councils.

Office of Science and Technology Policy

Executive Office of the President, New Executive Office Building, Washington, DC 20500/202-395-4697.
Budget: $1,912,000
Employees: 11
Mission: Serves as a source of scientific, engineering and technological analysis and judgement for the President with respect to major policies, plans and programs of the federal government.

Office of the United States Trade Representative

Executive Office of the President, 600 17th St. N.W., Winder Building, Washington, DC 20506/202-395-5123
Budget: $10,509,000
Employees: 115
Mission: Responsible for the direction of all trade negotiations of the United States and for the formulation of trade policy for the United States.

Office of Vice President of the U.S.

New Executive Office Building, Washington, DC 20501/202-456-2326
Budget: $1,506,000
Employees: 23
Mission: Vice President is empowered to succeed to the Presidency, pursuant to Article 11 and the 20th and 25th amendments to the Constitution; serves as President of the Senate; and participates in Cabinet meetings and, by statute, membership in the National Security Council and the Board of Regents of the Smithsonian Institution.

The White House Office

Executive Office of the President, 1600 Pennsylvania Ave., N.W., Washington, DC 20500/202-456-1414.
Budget: $18,973,000
Employees: 351
Mission: Serves the President in the performance of the many detailed activities incident to his immediate office; and facilitates and maintains communication with the Congress, the individual members of the Congress, the heads of the executive departments and agencies, the press and other information media, and the general public.

Major Sources of Information

Additional Key Executive Offices

Office of the Counselor to the President/202-456-2235
Office of the Chief of Staff/202-456-6797
Office of Consumer Affairs/202-634-4310
 1725 I St. N.W. Room 1003 Washington, DC 20201
Office of the Deputy Chief/202-456-6475
Office of the Press Secretary/202-456-2100
Office of Legislative Affairs/202-456-2230
Office of Public Liaison/202-456-2270
Political Affairs Office/202-456-7620
Presidential Personnel Office/202-456-2335
Office of Intergovernmental Affairs/202-456-7007
Office of the Counsel to the President/202-456-2632
Intelligence Oversight Board/202-456-2530
Council on Environmental Quality/202-395-5700
 722 Jackson Place NW Washington, DC 20006
White House Operator 202-456-1414

Correspondence to these offices should be directed in care of: The White House, Executive Office of the President, 1600 Pennsylvania Ave. N.W., Washington, DC 20500.

Catalog of Federal Domestic Assistance

Designed to assist in identifying the types of federal domestic assistance available, describing eligiblity requirements for the particular assistance being sought, and providing guidance on how to apply for specific types of assistance. Also intended to improve coordination and communication between the federal government and state and local governments.

Subscription service includes supplementary material for an intermediate period. It is available for $36.00 from the Superintendent of Documents, Government Printing Office, Washington, DC 20402/202-783-3238. For additional information contact: General Services Administration (GSA) 1825 Connecticut Ave. N.W., Room 804, Washington, DC 20405 202-673-5034.

Consumer Complaint Referral Center

If you need to know which organization can help you with your consumer complaint, contact: Office of Consumer Affairs, 1009 Premiere Building, Washington, DC 20201/202-634-4329.

Consumer Newsletter

The *Consumer News* is published twice monthly to inform American consumers of current and pending legislation and regulation and is available *free* from Office of Consumer Affairs, 1009 Premiere Building, Washington, DC 20201/202-634-4140.

Guide to Publications of the Executive Office of the President

A free quarterly listing the publications issued by the agencies of the Executive Office of the President and available to the public. Contact:

Publications Office, Executive Office of the President, 726 Jackson Pl. N.W., New Executive Office Building, Room 2200, Washington, DC 20503/202-395-7332.

Legislative Information

To find out if and when the President signed a piece of legislation into law, contact: *Executive Clerks Office,* The White House, Washington, DC 20500/202-456-2226.

Middle East Maps

These two maps are available for $3.50 each:

The Middle East—a single-sheet colored reference map, 1:4,500,000 scale, showing status of international boundaries, cities by population category, railroads, roads, airfields, terrain features and bathmyetry. 39 × 36 in.
Middle East Area: Oilfields and Facilities—focusing on an issue of high international interest and concern, this map shows oilfields, pipelines, tanker terminals and refineries against a terrain background. The map is multi-colored and a scale of 1:4,500,000. 39 × 36 in.

Contact: Government Printing Office, Superintendent of Documents, Washington, DC 20402/202-783-3238. For additional information contact: Central Intelligence Agency, Washington, DC 20505/703-351-7676.

News Item from the President

Call 456-7198 in DC area or 800-424-9090 elsewhere to hear the President announce the latest news from the White House.

Office of the Vice President

For information on the office of the Vice President, contact: Press Secretary, Office of the Vice President, 268 Old Executive Office Building, Washington, DC 20501/202-456-6772.

President Reagan's Daily Schedule, see below.

Public Papers of the Presidents

The following nine volumes are part of a series containing documents from specified periods of the Presidency. They include in chronological order the inaugural addresses, statements, executive orders, announcements, nominations, public letters, press conferences, and so on. In addition, weekly digests contain the President's daily public schedule, lists of nominations submitted to the Senate, checklists of White House press releases, and lists of acts approved by the President.

Gerald R. Ford: Book I—January 1 to April 9, 1976 ($23.00)
Gerald R. Ford: Book II—April 9 to July 9, 1976 ($22.00)
Gerald R. Ford: Book III—July 10, 1976 to January 20, 1977 ($22.00)

Jimmy Carter: Book I—June 30 to December 31, 1978
($25.00)
Jimmy Carter: Book II—January 1 to June 30, 1979
($24.00)
Jimmy Carter: Book III—January 1 to June 30, 1980
($21.00)
Ronald Reagan: Book I—June 30 to December 31, 1981
($25.00)
Ronald Reagan: Book II—January 1 to June 30, 1982
($19.00)
Ronald Reagan: Book III—June 30 to December 31, 1982
($25.00)

For additional information and a list of other volumes in the series contact: Superintendent of Documents, Government Printing Office, Washington, DC 20402/202-783-3238.

Publications/Council of Economic Advisors
Reports issued by the Council are available to the public through the Superintendent of Documents, Government Printing Office, Washington, DC 20402/202-783-3238.

Economic Report of the President, Together with the Annual Report of the Council of Economic Advisors Report on Indexing Federal Programs

For additional information contact: Council of Economic Advisors, Old Executive Office Building, Washington, DC 20500/202-395-5107.

Publications/National Security
For any publications available to the public contact: National Security Council, Executive Office of the President, Old Executive Office Building, Washington, DC 20506/202-395-4974.

Publications/OMB
This office issues numerous publications related to the budget and the government's fiscal program. For a history of these contact: Office of Management and Budget, Executive Office of the President, New Executive Office Building, Room 2200, Washington, DC 20503/202-395-7332.

Publications/President
For publications issued by this office contact: Office of Policy Development, Executive Office of the President, 1600 Pennsylvania Ave. N.W., Washington, DC 20500/202-456-2645.

President's Daily Schedule
A recorded message provides the daily schedule of the President. Call: 202-456-2343 or contact: Director of Scheduling, Office of the Deputy Chief of Staff, Executive Office of the President, 1600 Pennsylvania Ave. N.W., Washington, DC 20500/202-456-2343.

First Lady's Daily Schedule
A recorded message provides the daily schedule of the First Lady. Call 202-456-6269. For additional information contact: Scheduling Director, Staff for the First Lady, Office of the Deputy Chief of Staff, Executive Office of the President, 1600 Pennsylvania Ave. N.W., Washington, DC 20500/202-456-7910.

Science and Technology Policy Publications
Scientific engineering and technological analyses are issued regarding major policies, plans and programs of the federal government. Contact: Office of Public Affairs, Office of Science and Technology Policy, Executive Office of the President, Old Executive Office Building, Washington, DC 20506/202-395-3840.

White House Fellows Program
The purpose of the program is to provide gifted and highly motivated young Americans with first hand experience in the process of governing the nation and a sense of personal involvement in the leadership of the society. The Fellows Program seeks to draw exceptional, promising young people from all sectors of our national life—professions, business, government, the arts, and the academic world. The term of the Fellowship is one year. A free brochure is available that explains the program and its purpose. For further information contact: White House Fellows Program, 712 Jackson Place, N.W., Washington, DC 20503/202-395-4522.

White House Publications
For information on White House publications contact: Executive Office of the President, Publications Services, 726 Jackson Pl NW, Suite 2200, Washington DC 20503/202-395-7332.

Women Scientists in Industry and Government, How Much Progress in the 1970's?
This document is for sale at: National Technical Scientific Service (NTIS), Department of Commerce, 5285 Port Royal Rd., Springfield, VA 22161/703-487-4650. For additional information contact: Office of Public Affairs, Office of Science and Technology Policy, New Executive Office Building, Washington, DC 20506/202-395-3840.

World Data Bank II
This cartographic data base, produced by the Central Intelligence Agency, represents natural and manmade features of the world in a digital format. Also available is the (ALC) program that performs a wide variety of cartographic functions and can be used in conjunction with World Data Bank II. Both the World Data Bank II and Cartographic Automatic Mapping Program can be obtained from the *National Technical Information Service,* Department of Commerce, 5285 Port Royal Rd., Springfield, VA 22161/703-487-4650.

How Can the Executive Office of the President Help You?
To determine how this office can help you contact: The White House, 1600 Pennsylvania Ave. N.W., Washington, DC 20500/202-456-1414.

JUDICIAL BRANCH

Judicial Branch

(No Central Office)

Established: September 24, 1789
Budget: $820,567,000
Employees: 11,554

Mission: The judicial power of the United States shall be vested in one supreme court, and in such inferior courts created by the Congress of the United States.

Major Divisions and Offices

Supreme Court of the United States

Supreme Court Building, 1 First St. N.E., Washington, DC 20543/202-479-3000.
Budget: $15,191,000
Employees: 308
Mission: The judicial power extends to all cases, in law and equity, arising under the Constitution, the laws of the United States, and Treaties made, or which shall be made under their authority; to all cases affecting ambassadors; other public ministers and counsels; to all cases of admiralty and maritime jurisdiction; to controversies to which the United States shall be a party; to controversies between two or more states; between a state and citizens of another state; between citizens of different states, between citizens of the same state claiming lands under grants of different states; between a state, or the citizens thereof and foreign states, citizens or subjects; the Supreme Court has appellate jurisdiction, both as the law and fact.

Courts of Appeals and District Courts

c/o Administration Office of the United States Courts, Washington, DC 20544/202-633-6097
Budget: $772,442,000
Employees: 10,442
Mission: District courts are the trial courts with general federal jurisdiction. Each state has at least one district court. Courts of appeals are intermediate appellate courts created to relieve the Supreme Court of considering all appeals in cases originally decided by the federal trial courts.

*Court does not have own appropriations. Its funds are included in General Appropriations for the Judiciary.

United States Claims Court

717 Madison Place N.W., Washington, DC 20005/202-633-7257
Budget*
Employees: 76
Mission: Renders judgment upon any claim against the United States founded upon the Constitution, upon any act of Congress, upon any regulation of an executive Department, upon any expressed or implied contracts with the United States, and for liquidated or unliquidated damages in cases not sounding in tort.

United States Court of International Trade

1 Federal Plaza, New York, NY 10007/212-264-2814
Budget: $5,552,000
Employees: 103
Mission: Jurisdiction over any civil action against the United States arising from Federal laws governing import transactions and exclusive jurisdiction of civil actions to review determinations as to the eligibility of workers, firms, and communities for adjustment assistance under the Trade Act of 1974.

Administrative Office of the United States Courts

811 Vermont Ave. N.W., Washington, DC 20544/202-633-6097
Budget: $24,266,000
Emloyees: 553
Mission: Supervises all administrative matter relat-

ing to the offices of clerks and other clerical and administrative personnel of the courts.

Federal Judicial Center

Dolly Madison House, 1520 H. Street N.W., Washington, DC 20005/202-633-6011.
Budget: (not available)
Employees: (not available)
Mission: To conduct research on the operation of the United States courts, and to stimulate and coordinate such research on the part of other public and private persons and agencies; to stimu-late, create, develop, and conduct programs of continuing education and training for judges and support personnel of the judicial branch; to study and determine ways in which automatic data processing and systems procedures may be applied to the administration of the courts; to provide staff, research, and planning assistance to the judicial Conference and its committees, consistent with the performance of the other functions set forth above; and to develop recommendations for improvement in the administration and management of the courts.

Major Sources of Information

Annual Report of the Director of Administrative Office of the United States Courts

This report provides detailed text and tables on the business of all the federal courts (except the U.S. Court of Military Appeals and the U.S. Tax Courts). It is available for $13.00 from the Superintendent of Documents, Government Printing Office, Washington, DC 20402/202-783-3238. For additional information contact: Administrative Office of the United States Courts, 811 Vermont Ave. N.W., Washington, DC 20544/202-633-6097.

Bankruptcy

The Administrative Office maintains general supervision for the bankruptcy courts. Information on filing fees, preparation and audit of bankruptcy forms, and interpretations of Bankruptcy Act or rules is available. Contact: Bankruptcy Division, Administrative Office of the U.S. Courts, 811 Vermont Ave. N.W., Room 1050, Washington, DC 20544/202-633-6234.

Bench Book

The *Bench Book for United States District Court Judges* is a reference source containing material derived from statutes, and suggestions, recommendations, and reference material useful to judges in the conduct of judicial proceedings. The Bench Book is prepared by the Center under the guidance of experienced district judges and is distributed only to federal judges and magistrates. Contact: Inter-Judicial Affairs and Information Service Division, Federal Judicial Center, 1520 H St. N.W., Washington, DC 20005/202-633-6365.

Constitution of the United States of America: Analysis and Interpretation

This publication provides the text of the Constitution and its amendments preface annotations of those Supreme Court decisions which have a bearing on the way the Constitution is interpreted. It is available for $33.00 from the Superintendent of Documents, Government Printing Office, Washington, DC 20402/202-783-3238. For additional information contact: Supreme Court of the United States, 1 1st St. N.E., Washington, DC 20543/202-252-3000.

Court Reports and Statistics

Reports and statistics are available on bankruptcy, appeal, criminal, civil and trial cases filed, terminated and pending in each district court. An annual wiretap report, speedy trial and court management statistics are also available. For additional information contact: Statistical Analysis and Reports Division, Administrative Office of the United States Courts, 811 Vermont Ave. N.W., Room 671, Washington, DC 20544/202-633-6094.

District Court Publications

Rules of Civil Procedure for the United States District Courts, With Forms—contains the Rules of Civil Procedure for U.S. District Courts as promulgated and amended by the Supreme Court to October 1, 1977, together with the forms adopted by the Court ($4.00).

Rules of Criminal Procedure for the United States District Courts, With Forms—contains the Rules of Criminal Procedure for the U.S. District Courts, together with forms as amended to October 1, 1979 ($2.00).

Federal Rules of Evidence—sets forth Rules of Evidence for use in proceedings in the courts of the U.S. and before U.S. magistrates ($3.50).

Federal Rules of Appellate Procedure—contains the Federal Rules of Appellate Procedure as promulgated and amended by the U.S. Supreme Court to October 1, 1979, together with the forms adopted by the Court ($2.00).

These publications are sold by the Superintendent of Documents, Government Printing Office, Washington, DC 20402/202-783-3238.

Federal Defenders

The Criminal Justice Act provides for the establishment of Federal Public Defender and Federal Community Defender Organizations by the District Courts in districts where at least 200 persons annually require the appointment of counsel.

Defender organizations provide annual reports of their activities to the administrative office. Contact: Administrative Office of the United States Courts, 811 Vermont Ave. N.W., Washington, DC 20544/202-633-6097.

Federal Judicial Center
The Center is the research, development and training arm of the federal judicial system. It also provides continuing education on a wide range of subjects for federal judicial personnel. For additional information contact: Federal Judicial Center, 1520 H St. N.W., Washington, DC 20005/202-633-6011.

Federal Judicial Center Information Service
The collection contains material on all areas of federal judicial administration. The subjects cover court management, civil and criminal procedure, constitutional law and probabilities. For information contact: Federal Judicial Center, 1520 H St. N.W., Washington, DC 20005/202-633-6011.

Federal Magistrates
The Administrative office supervises the administration of the offices of the U.S. magistrates. Statistical and other information on these offices is provided annually to Congress. For additional information contact: Magistrates Division, Administrative Office of the U.S. Courts, 811 Vermont Ave. N.W., Washington, DC 20544/202-633-6097.

Foreign Visitor Service
The Center assembles materials, conducts briefings and makes appropriate arrangements for official visitors from abroad (judges, legislators, legal officers and others). Contact: Inter-Judicial Affairs and Information Services Division, Federal Judicial Center, 1520 H St. N.W., Washington, DC 20005/202-633-6365.

Handbook for Federal Judges' Secretaries
This free handbook contains suggestions for office procedures. It describes the organization and process of the federal courts. Contact: Inter-Judicial Affairs and Information Services Division, Federal Judicial Center, 1520 H St. N.W., Washington, DC 20005/202-633-6365.

Judicial Panel on Multidistrict Litigation
This panel consists of seven federal judges, authorized to temporarily transfer to a single district, for coordinated or consolidated pretrial proceedings, civil actions pending in different districts which involve one or more common questions of fact. Contact: Clerk of the Panel, Judicial Panel on Multidistrict Litigation, 1120 Vermont Ave. N.W., Suite 1002, Washington, DC 20005/202-653-6090.

Library of the Supreme Court of the United States
The library maintains a complete working collection of American, English and Canadian statutes; records and briefs dating back to 1832; a collection of federal tax laws; legislative histories of selected federal acts and other historical and constitutional documents. The library is open to public use. Contact: Supreme Court of the United States Library, 1 1st St. N.E., Washington, DC 20543/202-252-3177.

Probation Officer
The Administrative Office supervises the accounts and practices of federal probation offices. *Federal Probation* is a quarterly journal of correctional philosophy and practice. For additional information contact: Probation Division, Administrative Office of the United States Courts, Washington, DC 20544/202-633-6226.

Publications—Federal Judicial Center
Federal Judicial Center publications report the results of research and analysis done by or for the Center, as well as the products of the Center's seminars and workshops. They include research reports and staff papers, manuals and handbooks, and catalogs and other related material. For a publications catalog and for further information contact: Federal Judicial Center, 1520 H St. N.W., Washington, DC 20005/202-633-6365.

Regional Depositories
There are over 20 regional depositories of Supreme Court records. For further information on their locations contact: Clerk's Office, Supreme Court of the United States, 1 1st St. N.E., Washington, DC 20543/202-252-3029.

Supreme Court Document Copies
Supreme Court documents may be copied either at the Library, Supreme Court of the United States, 1 1st St. N.E., Washington, DC 20543/202-252-3177, or, to obtain copies of Supreme Court documents in the mail, contact: Photoduplication Service, Library of Congress, Washington, DC 20540/202-287-5640.

Supreme Court Information
Information from the Clerk's Office includes the status of pending cases, docket sheet information about briefs filed, and information about admissions to the Supreme Court bar. The office also distributes court opinions. Contact: Clerk's Office, Supreme Court, 1 1st St. N.E., Washington, DC 20543/202-252-3029.

Supreme Court Publications
Individual Slip Opinions—all the Court's opinions as announced from the bench. These are issued irregularly and are available for $140.00 a term of Court.
Preliminary Prints (advance parts)—official United States Reports containing all the opinions with syllabi,

names of counsel, indices, tables of cases, and other editorial additions. These are issued irregularly and are available for $56.00 a term of Court.

For additional information contact: Information, Supreme Court of the United States, Supreme Court Building, 1 1st St. N.E., Washington, DC 20543/202-252-3211.

Temporary Court of Appeals

The court has exclusive jurisdiction of all appeals from the district courts of the United States in cases and controversies arising under the economic stabilization laws, and consists of eight district and circuit judges designated by the Chief Justice. For additional information contact: Clerk, Temporary Emergency Court of Appeals, United States Courthouse, Room 2400, Washington, DC 20001/202-535-3390.

Territorial Courts

Congress has established district courts in the Commonwealth of Puerto Rico, and in the Territories of Guam, the Virgin Islands, the former Canal Zone and the Northern Mariana Islands. For additional information contact: Administrative Office of the United States Courts, 811 Vermont Ave., Washington, DC 20544/202-633-6097.

The Third Branch

The Third Branch is a monthly bulletin for the federal courts. It reports to the federal judicial community and other interested parties on the work of the Judicial Conference and its committees, policies, and projects of the Center and the Administrative Office, innovations undertaken in various courts, and legislative developments. *The Third Branch* also provides a monthly update of

changes in federal judicial personnel. For further information contact: Center Information Services Office, Federal Judicial Center, 1520 H St. N.W., Washington, DC 20005/202-633-6365.

U.S. Court of Military Appeals

The Court, consisting of three civilian judges appointed by the President, is called upon to exercise jurisdiction as to questions of law in all cases:

Affecting a general or flag office or extending to death;
Certified to the Court by the Judge Advocates General of the armed services, and by the General Counsel of the Department of Transportation, acting for the Coast Guard;
Petitioned by accused who have received a sentence of a year or more confinement and/or a punitive discharge.

For additional information contact: Clerk, Court of Military Appeals, 450 E St. N.W., Washington, DC 20442/202-272-1448.

U.S. Tax Court Reports

Each monthly issue is a consolidation of the decisions for a month. The yearly subscription, at $37.00, is available from the Superintendent of Documents, Government Printing Office, Washington, DC 20402/202-783-3238. For additional information contact: United States Tax Court, 400 2nd St. N.W., Washington, DC 20217/202-376-2754.

How Can the Judicial Branch Help You?

To determine how this branch of government can help you contact: Public Information, Supreme Court of the United States, 1 First St. N.E., Washington, DC 20543/202-252-3211.

LEGISLATIVE BRANCH

Congress

(No Central Office)

Established: September 17, 1787
Budget: $758,828,000
Employees: 20,000

Mission: All legislative powers are vested in the Congress of the United States, which consists of the Senate and House of Representatives.

The Senate

The Capitol, Washington, DC 20510/202-224-3121

Budget: $247,019,000
Employees: 7,000

Mission: The Senate is composed of 100 members, 2 from each State, who are elected to serve for a term of six years. One-third of the Senate is elected every two years.

Senate Special Committee on Aging

SDG33 Dirksen Senate Office Building, Washington, DC 20510/202-224-5364.
Jurisdiction: Problems and opportunities of older people, including: health, income, employment, housing and care. The Committee must make annual reports to the Senate describing its studies and giving recommendations. (The Committee has no subcommittees.)

Senate Committee on Agriculture, Nutrition and Forestry

328A Russell Senate Office Building, Washington, DC 20510/202-224-2035.
Jurisdiction: Agriculture, livestock, meat, agricultural products, animal industry and diseases, pests and pesticides, forests and forestry, home economics, soils, farm credits and farm security, rural affairs, human nutrition and school nutrition programs, food stamp programs and foods from fresh water, food and hunger. Subcommittee:

Agricultural Credit and Rural Electrification
Agricultural Production, Marketing and Stabilization of prices
Agricultural Research and General Legislation
Rural Development, Oversight and Investigations
Foreign Agricultural Policy
Nutrition
Soil, Water Conservation, Forestry, and Environment

The subcommittees can be reached at 202-224-2035.

Senate Committee on Appropriations

S-128 Capitol, Washington, DC 20510/202-224-3471.
Jurisdiction: The federal government's revenue, decision of appropriations, new spending and appropriations other than budgetary matters which are handled by the Budget Committee Subcommittees:

Agriculture, Rural Development, and Related Agencies/ 202-224-7240
Defense/202-224-7255
District of Columbia/202-224-2731
Foreign Operations/202-224-7274
HUD—Independent Agencies/202-224-7210
Interior and Related Agencies/202-224-7262
Labor, Health and Human Services, Education and Related Agencies/202-224-7283
Legislative Branch/202-224-7204
Energy and Water Development/202-224-7260
Military Construction/202-224-7271
State, Justice, Commerce, the Judiciary/202-224-7244
Transportation/202-224-0330
Treasury, Postal Service, General Government/202-224-2726.

Senate Committee on the Armed Services

222 Russell Senate Office Building, Washington, DC 20510/202-224-3871.
Jurisdiction: U.S. defense, including the Department of Navy and the Department of the Air Force. Subjects studied include pay, promotion, retirement and other benefits, military research and development, weaponry, the Panama Canal and Selective Service System, national security aspects of nuclear energy, and naval petroleum reserves, except those in Alaska. Subcommittees:

Military Construction/202-224-8631
Manpower and Personnel/202-224-9348
Tactical Warfare/202-224-8636
Strategic and Theater Nuclear Forces/202-224-9349
Preparedness/202-224-8639

Senate Committee on Banking, Housing and Urban Affairs

SD534 Dirksen Senate Office Building, Washington, DC 20510/202-224-7391

Jurisdiction: Banks, banking and financial institutions, financial aid to commerce and industry, deposit insurance, public and private housing, federal monetary policy, currency, notes, control of prices of commodities, rents and services, urban development and mass transit, economic stabilization, exports, nursing home construction, government contract renegotiations. Subcommittees:

Housing and Urban Affairs/202-224-5404
Financial Institutions/202-224-7391
Rural Housing and Development/202-224-5404
Consumer Affairs/202-224-7391
Securities/202-224-7391
International Finance and Monetary Policy/202-224-0891
Economic Policy/202-224-7391

Senate Committee on the Budget

Dirksen Senate Office Building, 6th Floor, Washington, DC 20510/202-224-0642
Jurisdiction: Budget matters, effects of proposed legislation on the budget, tax expenditures and policies and the functions and duties of the Congressional Budget Office. (The Committee has no subcommittees.)

Senate Committee on Commerce, Science and Transportation

Dirksen Senate Office Building, Room 508, Washington, DC 20510/202-224-5115
Jurisdiction: Interstate commerce, transportation, regulation of interstate common carriers, merchant marine and navigation, the Coast Guard, inland waterways, communications, regulation of consumer products, standards and measurement, highway safety, science, engineering and technology, nonmilitary aeronautical and space sciences, marine fisheries, coastal zone management, oceans, weather and atmospheric activities and sports. Subcommittees:

Aviation/202-224-4852
Communications/202-224-8144
Consumer/202-224-4768
Merchant Marine/202-224-4766
Science, Technology and Space/202-224-8172
Surface Transportation/202-224-4852
Business, Trade and Tourism/202-224-8170

Senate Committee on Energy and Natural Resources

Dirksen Senate Office Building, Room 358, Washington, DC 20510/202-224-4971
Jurisdiction: Energy policy, regulation and conservation, solar energy, nonmilitary nuclear energy, naval oil reserves in Alaska, oil and gas, energy aspects of deepwater ports, hydroelectric power, coal, public lands and forests, national parks and wilderness, mining and minerals and territorial possessions of this country. Subcommittees:

Energy, Conservation and Supply/202-224-2366
Energy Research and Development/202-224-4431
Energy and Mineral Resources/202-222-5205
Energy, Conservation and Supply/202-224-2366
Energy Regulation/202-224-5205
Public Lands and Reserved Water/202-224-0613
Water Power/202-224-2366

Senate Committee on Environment and Public Works

410 Dirksen Senate Office Building, Washington, DC 20510/202-224-6176
Jurisdiction: Environmental policy, research and development, ocean dumping, fisheries and wildlife, solid waste, water resources, flood control, water, air and noise pollution, public works, bridges and dams, highways and buildings in Washington, DC.
Subcommittees:

Environmental Pollution
Water Resources
Transportation
Regional and Community Development
Nuclear Regulation
Toxic Substances and Environmental Oversight

The subcommittees can be reached at: 202-224-6167.

Senate Select Committee on Ethics

Second and Constitution Ave. N.E., Hart Senate Office Building, Room 220, Washington, DC 20510/202-224-2981
Jurisdiction: Improper conduct, violations of the law or violations of Senate rules by Senate members, officers and employees. The committee recommends disciplinary action, proposes new regulations and reports violations to federal and state authorities.

Senate Committee on Finance

SD219 Dirksen Senate Office Building, Washington, DC 20510/202-224-4515
Jurisdiction: Social security, certain health programs, the deposit of public money, customs and duties, tariffs, revenue sharing.
Subcommittees:

Health
International Trade
Taxation and Debt Management
Social Security and Income Maintenance Programs
Energy and Agricultural Taxation
Economic Growth, Employment and Revenue Sharing
Estate and Gift Taxation
Oversight of the Internal Revenue Service Code
Pension Plans and Employee Fringe Benefits
Savings, Pensions and Investment Policy

The Subcommittee can be reached at: 202-224-4515.

Senate Committee on Foreign Relations

Dirksen Senate Office Building, Washington, DC 20510/202-224-4651

Jurisdiction: Foreign policy and relations, treaties, U.S. boundaries, U.S. citizens abroad, foreign assistance, the United Nations, declarations of war and interventions abroad, diplomatic service, oceans, international activities of the Red Cross, international aspects of nuclear energy, foreign loans, international commerce, the World Bank, the International Monetary Fund, national security.

Subcommittees:

African Affairs/202-224-5481
Arms Control, Oceans and International Operations and Environment/202-224-4651
East Asian and Pacific Affairs/202-224-5481
European Affairs/202-224-5481
International Economic Policy/202-224-4192
Near East and South Asian Affairs/202-224-5481
Western Hemisphere Affairs/202-224-3866

Senate Committee on Governmental Affairs

340 Dirksen Senate Office Building, Washington, DC 20510/202-224-4751

Jurisdiction: Some federal budget matters, organization of the federal executive branch, intergovernmental relations, government relations, municipal affairs of Washington, DC, federal civil service, postal service, census, the Archives, nuclear export policy and congressional organization.

Subcommittees:

Permanent Subcommittee on Investigations/202-224-3721
Intergovernment Relations/202-224-4718
Governmental Efficiency and the District of Columbia/202-224-4161
Information Management and Regulatory Affairs/202-224-0211
Energy, Nuclear Proliferation, and Government Processes/202-224-9515
Civil Services, Post Office, and General Services/202-224-2254
Oversight of Government Management/202-224-5538

Senate Select Committee on Indian Affairs

SH38 Senate Hart Office Building, Washington, DC 20510/202-224-2251

Senate Select Committee on Intelligence

SH 211 Senate Hart Office Building, Washington, DC 20510/202-224-1700

Jurisdiction: Intelligence activities and programs, oversight over U.S. intelligence activities to ensure they conform with the U.S. Constitution and laws, the Central Intelligence Agency, Federal Bureau of Investigation, Defense Intelligence Agency, National Security Agency and appropriations for intelligence agencies and activities.

Subcommittees:

Analysis and Production
Budget
Legislation and the Rights of Americans
Collection and Foreign Operations
Analysis and Production

The subcommittees can be reached at: 202-224-1700.

Senate Committee on the Judiciary

224 Dirksen Senate Office Building, Washington, DC 20510/202-224-5225

Jurisdiction: Judicial proceedings, constitutional amendments, federal courts and judges, local courts, U.S. statutes, national penitentiaries, monopolies, holidays, bankruptcy, mutiny, espionage and counterfeiting, boundary lines, civil liberties, patents, copyrights and trademarks, immigration and naturalization, appointment of representatives, claims against the United States, interstate compacts and government information.

Subcommittees:

Product and Procurement Administration/202-224-7703
Constitution/202-224-8191
Criminal Law/202-224-5617
Immigration and Refugee Policy/202-224-7878
Juvenile Justice/202-224-8171
Separation of Powers/202-224-6791
Regulatory Reform/202-224-3980
Courts/202-224-1674
Security and Terrorism/202-224-6136
Patents, Copyrights, and Trademarks/202-224-5617

Senate Committee on Labor and Human Resources

4230 Dirksen Senate Office Building, Washington, DC 20510/202-224-5375

Jurisdiction: Education, health, public welfare, labor, including wages and hours, child labor, arbitration, convict labor, foreign laborers, equal employment, handicapped persons, occupational safety and health, private pension plans, aging, student loans, agricultural colleges, Gallaudet College, Howard University and Saint Elizabeth's Hospital and domestic activities of the Red Cross.

Subcommittees:

Labor/202-224-5546
The Handicapped/202-224-6265
Education/202-224-2962
Employment and Productivity/202-224-6306
Children, Families, Drug and Alcoholism/202-224-3491
Aging/202-224-3239

Senate Committee on Rules and Administration

305 Russell Senate Office Building, Washington, DC 20510/202-224-6352

Jurisdiction: Meetings of Congress, attendance and qualifications of members, administration of the congressional offices, federal elections, corrupt practices, the U.S. Capitol, Library of Congress, the Smithsonian Institution, Botanic Gardens and the Government Printing Office. (The Committee has no subcommittees.)

Senate Select Committee on Small Business

428A Russell Senate Office Building, Washington, DC 20510/202-224-5175
Jurisdiction: Research and investigation into the problems of small businesses, and how Congress can help them.
Subcommittees:

Capital Formation and Retention
Export Promotion and Market Development
Government Procurement
Government Regulation and Paperwork
Innovation and Technology
Productivity and Competition
Urban and Rural Economic Development
Small business: Family Farm
Entrepreneurship and Special Problems Facing Small Businesses

The subcommittees can be reached at 202-224-5175.

Senate Committee on Veterans' Affairs

414 Russell Senate Office Building, Washington, DC 20510/202-224-9126
Jurisdiction: Veterans' rehabilitation, hospitals, medical care and treatment, national cemeteries, life insurance for the Armed Forces, petitions of war. (The Committee has no subcommittees.)

Senate Commission on Art and Antiquities

Capitol Building, Room S-411, Washington, DC 20510/202-224-2955.

Joint Committees and Commissions of the Congress

Joint Economic Committee

SD-GO1 Dirksen Senate Office Building, Washington, DC 20510/202-224-5171.
Subcommittees:

Agriculture and Transportation/202-224-5171
Economic Goals and Intergovernmental Policy/202-225-3565
International Trade, Finance and Security Economics/202-226-3230
Investment, Jobs and Prices/202-224-5171
Monetary and Fiscal Policy/202-224-5171
Trade, Productivity, and Economic Growth/202-224-5171

Joint Committee on the Library

SR309 Senate Russell Office Building, Washington, DC 20515/202-224-0291

Commission on Security and Cooperation in Europe

H2-237 House Office Building, Annex #2, 2nd and D Sts. S.W., Washington, DC 20515/202-225-1901.

Joint Committee on Printing

818 Hart Senate Office Building, Washington, DC 20510/202-224-5241.

Joint Committee on Taxation

1015 Longworth House Office Building, Washington, DC 20515/202-225-3621.

Commission for the West Central Front of the U.S. Capitol

Room SB-15 Capitol Building, Washington, DC 20515/202-225-1200

The House of Representatives

The Capitol, Washington, DC 20515/202-224-3121

Budget: $408,357,000
Employees: 12,000

Mission: The House of Representatives comprises 435 representatives, the number representing each state as determined by population but every state is entitled to at least one representative. Members are elected by the people for two-year terms, all terms running for the same period.

House Committee on Agriculture

Room 1301 Longworth House Office Building, Washington, DC 20215/202-225-2171.
Jurisdiction: Agriculture, agricultural chemistry, colleges, economics and research, extension services, production, marketing and price stabilization, the animal industry and animal diseases, crop insurance and soil conservation, dairy industry, plants and seeds, farm credit and security, forestry, nutrition and home economics, livestock and meat inspections, rural electrification and development and commodities exchanges.
Subcommittees:

Conservation and Credit and Rural Development/202-225-1867
Cotton, Rice and Sugar/202-225-1867
Domestic Marketing, Consumer Relations and Nutrition/202-225-8406
Forests, Family Farms and Energy/202-225-8405
Livestock, Dairy and Poultry/202-225-1861
Research and Foreign Agriculture Department Operation/202-225-8408
Tobacco and Peanuts/202-225-8906
Wheat, Soybeans and Feedgrains/202-225-1867

House Select Committee on Aging

712 House Office Building, Annex #1, Washington, DC 20515/202-226-3375
Jurisdiction: The Committee does not prepare legislation. Instead, it holds hearings on problems of the elderly, and submits findings to other committees. In addition, it oversees all federal programs that affect the elderly, such as food stamps, Medicare and Medicaid, and Social Security.
Subcommittees:

Health and Long-Term Care/202-226-3381
Housing and Consumer Interests/202-226-3344
Human Services/202-226-3348
Retirement Income and Employment/202-226-3335

House Committee on Appropriations

H-218, Capitol Building, Washington, DC 20515/202-225-2771
Jurisdiction: Appropriations to support the government, recisions of appropriations, new spending authority and unspent balances.
Subcommittees:

Agriculture and Rural Development Agencies/202-225-2638
Defense/202-225-2847
District of Columbia/202-225-5338
Energy and Water Development/202-225-3421
Foreign Aid Operations/202-225-2041
HUD: Independent Agencies/202-225-3241
Commerce; Judiciary; State; Justice/202-225-3351
Interior/202-225-3081
Labor; Health and Human Services and Education/202-225-3508
Legislative/202-225-5338
Military Construction/202-225-3047
Transportation/202-225-2141
Treasury, Postal Service, General Government/202-225-5834

House Committee on Armed Services

2120 Rayburn House Office Building, Washington, DC 20515/202-225-4151.

Jurisdiction: Defense, the Department of Defense, including the Armed Forces, defense facilities, benefits for members of the Armed Forces, the Selective Service, naval petroleum and oil share reserves.
Subcommittees:

Investigations/202-225-4221
Military Installations and Facilities/202-225-7120
Military Personnel and Compensation/202-225-7560
Procurement and Military Nuclear Systems/202-225-7160
Readiness/202-225-7991
Research and Development/202-225-3168, 202-225-6527
Seapower and Strategic and Critical Materials/202-225-6704

House Committee on Banking, Finance and Urban Affairs

2129 Rayburn House Office Building, Washington, DC 20515/202-225-4247
Jurisdiction: Banks and banking, money and credit, urban development, housing, economic stabilization, defense production, renegotiation, price and rent controls, financial aid to commerce and industry, international financial and monetary organizations.
Subcommittees:

Consumer Affairs and Coinage/202-226-3280
Domestic Monetary Policy/202-226-7315
Economic Stabilization/202-225-7145
Financial Institutions Supervision, Regulation and Insurance/202-225-2924
General Oversight and Renegotiation/202-225-2828
Housing and Community Development/202-225-7054
International Development Institutions and Finance/202-226-7511
International Trade, Investment and Monetary Policy/202-225-1271

House Committee on the Budget

Room 214, House Annex #1, Washington, DC 20515/202-225-7200.
Jurisdiction: The budget and relevant legislation, tax expenditures, policies and programs.
Task Forces:

Budget Process
Capital Resource and Development
Economic Policy and Growth
Education and Employment
Energy and Technology
Entitlements, Uncontrollables, and Indexing
Federalism, and State, Local Relations
International Finance and Trade
Enforcement Credit and Multi-Year Budgeting
Human Resources and Block Grants
National Security and Veterans
Tax Policy
Transportation, Research and Development
Reconciliation

The task forces can be reached at 202-225-7200

House Select Committee on Children, Youth and Families

Room 385, House Annex 2, Washington, DC 20515/202-226-7660.
Jurisdiction: To study public and private sector policies that affect children, youth and families.

Task Force on Crisis Intervention
Task Force on Economic Security
Task Force on Prevention Strategies

House Committee on the District of Columbia

1310 Longworth House Office Building, Washington, DC 20515/202-225-4457.
Jurisdiction: Municipal affairs of Washington, DC, including public health, safety and sanitation, taxes, fiscal policy, transportation, pension funds, National Planning Commission, Home Rule changes, Sewer and Water charges, Workman's Compensation Agency, court system, transfer of Marshal Service, insurance, wills and divorces and transfer of Saint Elizabeth's Hospital.
Subcommittees:

Fiscal and Health Affairs/202-225-4457
Government Operations and Metropolitan Affairs/202-225-1615
Judiciary and Education/202-225-1612

House Committee on Education and Labor

Room 2181, Rayburn House Office Building, Washington, DC 20515/202-225-4527.
Jurisdiction: Education and labor, including: convict labor, child labor, foreign laborers, wages and hours, work incentive programs, the Columbia Institution for the Deaf, Dumb and Blind, Howard University and Freedman's Hospital.
Subcommittees:

Elementary, Secondary and Vocational Education/202-225-4368
Employment Opportunities/202-225-1927
Health and Safety/202-225-6876
Human Resources/202-225-1850
Labor-Management Relations/202-225-5768
Labor Standards/202-226-7594
Postsecondary Education/202-225-8881
Select Education/202-226-7532

House Committee on Energy and Commerce

2125 Rayburn House Office Building, Washington, DC 20515/202-225-2927
Jurisdiction: Interstate and foreign commerce, waterways, oil compacts, petroleum and natural gas, railroads, communications, transmission of power, securities and exchanges, consumer affairs, travel and tourism, public health and health facilities, biomedical research and development.

Subcommittees:

Energy, Conservation and Power/202-226-2424
Fossil and Synthetic Fuels/202-226-2500
Health and the Environment/202-225-4952
Oversight and Investigations/202-225-4441
Telecommunications, Consumer Protection and Finance/
   202-225-9304
Commerce, Transportation, and Tourism/202-226-3160

House Committee on Foreign Affairs

2170 Rayburn House Office Building, Washington, DC 20515/202-225-5021.
Jurisdiction: U.S. foreign relations, embassies, national boundaries, foreign loans, international meetings, interventions and declarations of war, diplomatic service, U.S. business abroad, U.S. citizens abroad, the Red Cross, United Nations, international economic policy, export controls, international commodity agreements and education.
Subcommittees:

Africa/202-226-7807
Asian and Pacific Affairs/202-226-7801
Europe and the Middle East/202-225-3345
Western Hemisphere Affairs/202-225-9404
International Economic Policy and Trade/202-226-7820
International Operations/202-225-3424.
International Organizations/202-226-7825
International Security and Scientific Affairs/202-225-
   8926

House Committee on Government Operations

2157 Rayburn House Office Building, Washington, DC 20515/202-225-5051
Jurisdiction: Budget and accounting measures other than appropriations, the economy and government efficiency, federal procurement, executive branch reorganization, intergovernmental relations, revenue sharing, the National Archives, the Freedom of Information Act and the Privacy Act.
Subcommittees:

Commerce, Consumer and Monetary Affairs/202-225-
   4407
Environment, Energy and Natural Resources/202-225-
   6427
Government Activities and Transportation/202-225-7920
Government Information, Justice and Agriculture/202-
   225-3741
Intergovernmental Relations and Human Resources/202-
   225-2548
Legislation and National Security/202-225-5147
Manpower and Housing/202-225-6751

House Committee on House Administration

H-326 Capitol Building, Washington, DC 20515/202-225-2061.
Jurisdiction: The House contingent fund, House employees, House buildings and facilities, travel and campaign fundraising of House members, the Library of Congress, Botanic Gardens and Smithsonian Institution, the Congressional Record and federal elections.
Subcommittees:

Accounts/202-226-7540
Contracts and Printing/202-226-7310
Office Systems/202-225-1608
Personnel and Police/202-226-2307

House Select Committee on Hunger

Room 507, House Annex 2, Washington, DC 20515/202-226-5470.
Jurisdiction: Studies and reviews problems of hunger and malnutrition; however, committee has no legislative authority.
Subcommittees:

Domestic Task Force
International Task Force

House Permanent Select Committee on Intelligence

H-405 Capitol Building, Washington, DC 20515/202-225-4121.
Jurisdiction: The Committee has oversight and legislative authority over the federal intelligence community including the CIA, the National Security Administration, the Department of Defense's intelligence activities and the counterintelligence activities of the FBI. In addition, it authorizes the annual budget for each intelligence agency.
Subcommittees:

Evaluation and Oversight/202-225-5657
Legislation/202-225-7310
Program and Budget Authorization/202-225-7690

House Committee on Interior and Insular Affairs

1324 Longworth House Office Building, Washington, DC 20515/202-225-2761.
Jurisdiction: Forests and national parks, geologic survey, irrigation and reclamation, Indians, United States insular possessions, military parks and battlefields, national cemeteries within DC, mining and minerals, public lands and prehistoric ruins, domestic nuclear energy industry, petroleum conservation on public and Federal lands, legislation concerning the transportation of natural gas from Alaska.
Subcommittees:

Energy and the Environment/202-225-8331
Insular Affairs/202-225-9297
Mining, Forest Management, and Bonneville Power
   Administration/202-225-1661
Oversight and Investigations/202-226-7610
Public Lands and National Parks/202-225-6044, 202-226-
   7730
Water and Power Resources/202-225-6042

House Committee on the Judiciary

2137 Rayburn House Office Building, Washington, DC 20515/202-225-3951.

Jurisdiction: Judicial proceedings, apportionment, bankruptcy, mutiny, espionage and counterfeiting, civil liberties, constitutional amendments, courts and judges, immigration and naturalization, interstate compacts, claims against the United States, meetings of Congress, penitentiaries, patents, copyrights and trademarks, presidential succession, monopolies, U.S. Statutes, boundaries and subversive activities.

Subcommittees:

Administrative Law and Governmental Relations/202-225-5741
Civil and Constitutional Rights/202-226-1678
Courts, Civil Liberties and the Administration of Justice/202-225-3926
Crime/202-225-1695
Criminal Justice/202-226-2406
Immigrants, Refugees, and International Law/202-225-5727
Monopolies and Commercial Law/202-225-2825

House Committee on Merchant Marine and Fisheries

1334 Longworth House Office Building, Washington, DC 20515/202-225-4047.

Jurisdiction: merchant marine, marine affairs, the Coast Guard, lighthouses, fisheries and wildlife, marine common carriers, navigation laws, the Panama Canal, vessel licensing, and international fishing agreements.

Subcommittees:

Coast Guard and Navigation/202-226-3533
Fisheries and Wildlife Conservation and the Environment/202-226-3522
Merchant Marine/202-226-3500
Oceanography/202-226-3513
Panama Canal and Outer Continental Shelf/202-226-3508

House Select Committee on Narcotics Abuse and Control

H2-234 House Office Building, Annex #2, Washington, DC 20515/202-226-3040.

Jurisdiction: Drug abuse in the United States, including supply, law enforcement, international controls, drug abuse in the military, treatment, rehabilitation and prevention. (The committee has no subcommittees.)

House Committee on the Post Office and Civil Service

309 Cannon House Office Building, Washington, DC 20515/202-225-4054.

Jurisdiction: The census, federal civil service, postal savings bank, the postal service, Hatch Act, holidays, population and demographics.

Subcommittees:

Census and Population/202-226-7523
Civil Service/202-225-4025
Compensation and Employee Benefits/202-226-7546
Human Resources/202-225-2821
Investigation/202-225-6295
Postal Operations and Services/202-225-9124
Postal Personnel and Modernization/202-226-7520

House Committee on Public Works and Transportation

2165 Rayburn House Office Building, Washington, DC 20515/202-225-4472.

Jurisdiction: Flood control, the U.S. Capitol and Senate and House office buildings, construction and maintenance of roads, construction and maintenance of the Botanic Gardens, Library of Congress and the Smithsonian Institution, U.S. government buildings, pollution of navigable water, public works benefiting navigation, water power, transportation other than railroads, roads and road safety, water transportation, and transportation regulatory agencies.

Subcommittees:

Aviation/202-225-9161
Economic Development/202-225-6151
Investigations and Oversight/202-225-3274
Public Buildings and Grounds/202-225-9161
Surface Transportation/202-225-4472
Water Resources/202-225-0060

House Committee on Rules

H-312 Capitol Building, Washington, DC 20515/202-225-9486.

Jurisdiction: Rules and orders of business of the House, recesses and adjournments of Congress.

Subcommittees:

Legislative Processes/202-225-1037
Rules of the House/202-225-9091

House Committee on Science and Technology

2321 Rayburn House Office Building, Washington, DC 20515/202-225-6371.

Jurisdiction: Astronautical matters, the Bureau of Standards and standardization of weights and measures, the metric system, the National Aeronautics and Space Administration, National Aeronautics and Space Council, National Science Foundation, outer space, science scholarships and research and development, energy (nuclear energy, but not including energy for defense purposes), research and development and the National Weather Service.

Subcommittees:

Energy Development and Applications/202-225-4494
Energy Research and Production/202-225-8056
Investigation and Oversight/202-226-3636

Natural Resources, Agriculture Research and Environment/202-226-6980
Science, Research and Technology/202-225-8844
Space Science and Applications/202-225-7858
Transportation, Aviation, and Materials/202-225-9662

House Committee on Small Business

2361 Rayburn House Office Building, Washington, DC 20515/202-225-5821.
Jurisdiction: Assistance, protection and financial aid for small businesses, and federal contracts for small businesses.
Subcommittees:

Antitrust and Restraint of Trade Activities Affecting Small Business/202-225-6026
Energy, Environment and Safety Issues Affecting Small Business/202-225-9368
Export Opportunities and Special Small Business Problems/202-225-3171
SBA and SBIC Authority and Minority Enterprise and General Small Business Problems/202-225-5821
Tax Access to Equity Capital and Business Opportunity/202-225-7797

House Committee on Standards of Official Conduct

HT-2 Capitol Building, Washington, DC 20515/202-225-7103.
Jurisdiction: The Code of Official Conduct, financial disclosure by House members and employees, and activities designed to influence legislation. (The committee has no subcommittees.)

House Committee on Veterans' Affairs

335 Cannon House Office Building, Washington, DC 20515/202-225-3527
Jurisdiction: Veterans' matters, including: Compensation, life insurance, pensions, adjustment to civilian life, hospitals and medical treatment, housing program, and veterans' cemeteries.
Subcommittees:

Compensation, Pension and Insurance
Education Training and Employment
Housing and Memorial Affairs
Hospitals and Health Care
Oversight and Investigations

The subcommittees can be reached at: 202-225-3527.

House Committee on Ways and Means

1102 Longworth House Office Building, Washington, DC 20515/202-225-3625.
Jurisdiction: Customs, reciprocal trade agreements, revenue measures, the U.S. debt, deposit of public money, duties, tax exempt organizations and Social Security.
Subcommittees:

Health/202-225-7785
Oversight/202-225-2743, 202-225-5522
Public Assistance and Unemployment Compensation/202-225-1025 or 202-225-1076
Select Revenue Measures/202-225-9710
Social Security/202-225-9263
Trade/202-225-3943

Major Sources of Information

Bibliographical Directory of the American Congress—1774–1971
This collection of reference material contains biographies and data on every person who served in Congress between 1774 and 1971, a total of more than 10,800 individual biographies. It is out of print, but is in the process of being revised for issuance in 1987 for the Congressional bicentennial for the 100th Congress. Contact Joint Committee on Printing, Congress, the Capitol, Room S-151, Washington, DC 20510/202-224-5241.

Calendar of the House of Representatives and History of Legislation
Contains a list of bills in conference, a list of bills through conference, the Union Calendar, the House Calendar, a history of actions on each bill of the current session, a subject index of active legislation, and more. It is a weekly (when Congress is in session) publication available on subscription for $200.00 per session of Congress from the Superintendent of Documents, Government Printing Office, Washington, DC 20402/202-

783-3238, or it can be picked up free at the House Document Room, Room H-226, 202-225-3456, or contact: Clerk of the House of Representatives, the Capitol, Room H-105, Washington, DC 20515/202-225-7000.

Capitol Hill Switchboard
The switchboard will provide and/or connect you with all the offices in the Capitol, House and Senate. Call: 202-224-3121.

Caucuses—Special Interest Resource Groups
Individual Senators and Representatives have formed numerous special interest groups to exercise a stronger voice about certain regional, ethnic, industry or other concerns related to their state or congressional district. These congressional caucuses have no legislative authority and are totally independent of the 50 House and Senate committees. Some caucuses such as the Congressional Clearinghouse On The Future primarily have a mission of desseminating information. Other coalitions such as the Agricultural Task Force serve as an informal in-house lobby on family farms and

other Federal farm policies. All of the caucuses produce reports, monitor legislation and can serve as useful resources.

Agricultural Task Force-Room 1416 LHOB, Washington, DC 20515/202-225-5725.

Alcohol Fuels, Congressional Caucus–Room 439 CHOB, Washington, DC 20515/202-225-2801.

Arms Control and Foreign Policy Caucus–Room H2-501 HOB Annex 2, Washington, DC 20515/202-226-3440.

Auto, Congressional Caucus–Room 2336 RHOB, Washington, DC 20515/202-225-5037.

Arts, Concerned Senators For The–Room SR-140, Washington, DC 20510/202-224-2315.

Arts, Congressional Caucus–Room H2-338 HOB Annex 2, Washington, DC 20515/202-226-2456.

Baltic States and Ukraine, Ad Hoc Congressional Committee On The–Room 438 CHOB, Washington, DC 20515/202-225-3215.

Black, Congressional Caucus–Room H2-344 HOB Annex 2, Washington, DC 20515/202-226-7790.

Border, Congressional Caucus–Room 1017 LHOB, Washington, DC 20515/202-225-4831.

California Democratic Congressional Delegation–Room 503 HOB Annex 1, Washington, DC 20515/202-226-2313.

Children's, Senate Caucus–Room SH-324, Washington, DC 20510/202-224-2823.

Coal, Senate Caucus–Room SR-277, Washington, DC 20510/202-224-6324.

Copper, Senate Caucus–Room SD-434, Washington, DC 20510/202-224-6621.

Drug Enforcement, Senate Caucus–Room SH-313, Washington, DC 20510/202-224-3041.

Environmental and Energy Study Conference–Room H2-515 HOB Annex 2, Washington, DC 20515/202-226-3300.

Export, Senate Caucus–Room SH-104, Washington, DC 20510/202-224-2441.

Export Task Force–Room H2-337 HOB Annex 2, Washington, DC 20515/202-226-3480.

Family, Senate Caucus On The–Room SH-516, Washington, DC 20510/202-224-5744.

Federal Government Service Task Force–Room H2-301 HOB Annex 2, Washington, DC 20515/202-226-2494.

Future, Congressional Clearinghouse On The–Room H2-555 HOB Annex 2, Washington, DC 20515/202-226-3434.

Hispanic, Congressional Caucus–Room H2-557 HOB Annex 2, Washington, DC 20515/202-226-3430.

Human Rights, Congressional Caucus–Room 1530 LHOB, Washington, DC 20515/202-225-4835.

Long Island Congressional Caucus–Room 2228 RHOB, Washington, DC 20515/202-225-7896.

Military Reform Caucus–Room 325 CHOB, Washington, DC 20515/202-225-5801.

Missing-In-Action, Task Force On–Room 707 HOB Annex 1, Washington, DC 20515/202-226-7801.

New England Congressional Caucus–53 D St., SE, Washington, DC 20003/202-543-3396.

New York State Congressional Delegation–Room 2205 RHOB, Washington, DC 20515/202-225-5076.

North American Trade, Senate Caucus On–Room SH-706, Washington, DC 20510/202-224-2651.

Northeast-Midwest Congressional Coalition–Room H2-530 HOB Annex 2, Washington, DC 20515/202-226-3920.

Northeast-Midwest, Senate Coalition–Room SH-316, Washington, DC 20510/202-224-8803.

Pacific Northwest Trade Task Force–Room 434 CHOB, Washington, DC 20515/202-225-3536.

Pennsylvania Delegation Steering Committee–Room 2366 RHOB, Washington, DC 20515/202-225-1145.

Port, Congressional Caucus–Room H2-531 HOB Annex 2, Washington, DC 20515/202-226-3507.

Pro-Life Caucus–Room 422 CHOB, Washington, DC 20515/202-225-3765.

Rail, Senate Caucus–Room SR-375, Washington, DC 20510/202-224-3244.

Rural, Congressional Caucus–Room H2-595 HOB Annex 2, Washington, DC 20515/202-226-3737.

Science and Technology Caucus–Room H2-226 HOB Annex 2, Washington, DC 20515/202-226-7788.

Solar Coalition–Room 1030 LHOB, Washington, DC 20515/202-225-2726.

South Africa, The Senate/House Ad Hoc Monitoring Group On–Room 303 CHOB, Washington, DC 20515/202-225-3335.

Space, Congressional Caucus–Room 2301 RHOB, Washington, DC 20515/202-225-4906.

Sunbelt, Congressional Council–Room H2-561 HOB Annex 2, Washington, DC 20515/202-226-2374.

Steel, Congressional Caucus–Room H2-556 HOB Annex 2, Washington, DC 20515/202-225-7892.

Steel, Senate Caucus–Room SR-277, Washington, DC 20510/202-224-6324.

Territorial, Congressional Caucus–Room H2-240 HOB Annex 2, Washington, DC 20515/202-226-7780.

Textile, Congressional Caucus–Room H2-368 HOB Annex 2, Washington, DC 20515/202-226-3070.

Tourism, Senate Caucus–Room SR-421, Washington, DC 20510/202-224-6674.

Travel and Tourism, US Congressional Caucus–Room H2-246 HOB Annex 2, Washington, DC 20515/202-225-3935.

Vietnam Veterans in Congress–Room 439 CHOB, Washington, DC 20515/202-225-2801.

Western State Coalition–Room SH-328, Washington, DC 20510/202-224-3542.

Wood Energy, Congressional Caucus–Room 1434 LHOB, Washington, DC 20515/202-225-3561.

Women's Issues, Congressional Caucus For–Room 2471 RHOB, Washington, DC 20515/202-225-6740.

For the latest information about the formation of new congressional caucuses, contact: Capitol Hill Switchboard Operator, 202-224-3121.

Chaplain of the House of Representatives
The Chaplain opens each day's House session with a prayer. Contact: Chaplain of the House of Representatives, The Capitol, Room HB-25, Washington, DC 20515/202-225-2509.

Chaplain of the Senate
Each day's Senate session opens with a prayer. For

information contact: Chaplain of the Senate, Hart Office Building, Room 204, Washington, DC 20510/202-224-2510.

Clerk of the House
The Clerk of the House is the chief administrative, legislative and contracting officer of the House, and presides at the beginning of a Congress until the election of a Speaker. He is a continuing officer whose duties do not terminate with the sine die adjournment of Congress; his duties are largely executive and quasijudicial in nature; he attests bills, resolutions and subpoenas; is custodian of the seal of the House, and prepares the roll of Representatives-elect. Contact: Clerk of the House, House of Representatives, Room H-105, The Capitol, Washington, DC 20515/202-225-7000.

Committee Calendars
Most committees and subcommittees issue their own calendars. These include information on their publications, staff and committee membership, and the legislation that concerns them. They also include a subject index of their legislative activities. To be connected with the individual committee, contact the Capitol Hill Switchboard, 202-224-3121, or see list of Committees under U.S. Senate and U.S. House of Representatives.

Congressional Directory
This congressional directory includes biographies of members of the House and Senate and the Supreme Court. It also lists congressional committees, members of the press admitted to the House and Senate galleries and other pertinent information. It is available for $12.00 from the Superintendent of Documents, Government Printing Office, Washington, DC 20402/202-275-3030, or contact: Joint Committee on Printing, U.S. Congress, The Capitol, Room S-151, Washington, DC 20510/202-224-5241.

Congressional Pages and Interns
Approximately 100 pages work for Members of Congress during the school year. More positions for pages as well as interns are available during the summer months. Contact your Senator and Representative for more information.

Congressional Pictorial Directory
This directory contains photographs of the President, Vice President, members of the Senate and House, Officers of the Senate and House, Officials of the Capitol, and a list of the Senate delegations and an alphabetical list of senators and representatives. Available from the Superintendent of Documents, Government Printing Office, Washington, DC 20402/202-275-3030, or contact: Joint Committee on Printing, U.S. Congress, The Capitol, Room S-151, Washington, DC 20510/202-224-5241.

Congressional Record
This is published daily when Congress is in session in an edited transcript of the House and Senate proceedings and actions. *The Daily Digest* section summarizes the day's activities and includes the next day's schedule of committee hearings. Friday's edition provides the schedule for the following week. Biweekly indexes are published for the Record. The subscription price is $218.00 per year. The Record is sold by the Superintendent of Documents, Government Printing Office, Washington, DC 20402/202-275-3030.

Congressional Staff
Telephone numbers of the members of the Senate staff are available. Contact: Senate Locator, U.S. Capitol, U.S. Senate, The Capitol, Washington, DC 20515/202-224-3207; members of the House Staff telephone numbers are also available. Contact: House Locator Office, Cannon Building, Room 263, Capitol, Washington, DC 20515/202-225-6515.

Congressional Telephone Directory
For a free telephone directory of all the members of both the House of Representatives and the Senate, contact: Clerk of the House, H-105 Capitol Building, Washington, DC 20515/202-225-7000.

Daily Digest
For information on the Senate portion of the *Congressional Record,* call 202-224-2658; for the House portion, call 202-224-5848; for information on the status of bills, call Senate 202-224-2120; House 202-225-4470.

Document Room
The Document Room maintains current files of legislation including public laws (slip laws). Periodic compilations of public laws on a variety of subject areas are available for $150.00 from the Superintendent of Documents, Government Printing Office, Washington, DC 20402/202-275-3030. Contact: House Document Room, House of Representatives, The Capitol Room, H-226, Washington, DC 20515/202-225-3456, or Senate Document Room, Senate, Senate Hart Office Building, Room B 04, Washington, DC 20510/202-224-7860.

Enactment of a Law
This booklet, prepared by the Senate, contains a brief explanation of the procedural steps in the legislative process. It is available for $1.30 from the Superintendent of Documents, Government Printing Office, Washington, DC 20402/202-275-3030.

Government Paper Specification Standards No. 9
Issued by the Joint Committee on Printing, Congress of the United States, for the use of government departments and agencies in the procure-

ment of paper stock for printing. These standards consisting of three parts should also be of value and interest to paper manufacturers, printing establishments and others concerned with paper standards and specifications. Part 1 contains detailed standard specifications; part 2 gives the standards to be used in testing; and part 3 consists of the definitive color standards for all mimeograph, duplicator, writing, manifold, bond ledger and index papers (color standards for other classes of paper will be prepared and issued as such standards are developed). Subscription service includes supplementary material for an indeterminate period and is available for $22.00 from the Superintendent of Documents, Government Printing Office, Washington, DC 20402/202-275-3030, or contact: Joint Committee on Printing, The Capitol, Room S-151, Washington, DC 20510/202-224-5241.

Handbook for Small Business: A Survey of Small Business Programs of the Federal Government

The *Handbook* contains information on programs and services offered to the small businessperson by 25 federal departments and agencies that are directly involved with the support and stimulation of independent enterprise. It includes information on government-sponsored loans and financial guarantees, management and technical assistance programs, government purchasing and sales programs, grants, and entering the world trade markets. It outlines the design of federal programs, describes each program, and indicates how and where further information can be obtained. It is available for $6.50 from the Superintendent of Documents, Government Printing Office, Washington, DC 20402-275-3030, or contact: Senate Select Committee on Small Business, Russell Senate Office Building, Room 424, Washington, DC 20410/202-224-5175.

Hearings on Aquaculture to Zinc

Some 250 House and Senate committees and subcommittees conduct informational and investigative hearings in Washington, D.C. and throughout the country. All of these congressional hearings are published and often available free from the documents clerk of the committee or subcommittee which held the hearings. Many of the hearings are sold by the Superintendent of Documents, Government Printing Office, Washington, DC 20402/202-783-3238.

House and Senate Bills

Free copies of all bills introduced in either house of Congress are available. Legislation approved by committee and also passed by the full House and/or Senate along with committee reports are available free of charge. Requests must include the bill number or report number (no more than six requests at a time). A self-addressed mailing label must be included. For House documents, send written request to: House Documents Room, US Capitol, Washington, DC 20515. For Senate bills and reports, write to Senate Document Room, US Capitol, Washington, DC 20510.

House Library

The Library is the official depository of House documents, reports, bills, etc. Its primary function is to serve House members and their staffs. U.S. House of Representatives and Committees Library, B-18, Cannon House Office Building, Washington, DC 20515/202-225-0462.

House Postmaster

The Postmaster is in charge of postal matters and activities for the Capitol and House offices. Contact: Postmaster of the House of Representatives, The Capitol, Longworth House Office Building, Room B-225, Washington, DC 20515/202-225-3856.

House Telephone Directory

Produced three times a year by the Committee on House Administration, the *House Telephone Directory* provides a listing for representatives, a listing for House committees, an alphabetical staff listing, a listing of staffs by representatives, a listing of staffs by committee, listings for senators and Senate committees, a listing for executive branch leaders, a listing for government agencies, and more. The *House of Representatives Telephone Directory* is available for $9.50 per year from the Superintendent of Documents, Government Printing Office, Washington, DC 20402/202-275-3030, or contact: Committee on House Administration, the Capitol, Room H-326, Washington, DC 20515/202-225-2061.

How Our Laws Are Made

Prepared by the House of Representatives, this booklet provides a plain language explanation of how a legislative idea travels the complex passageways of the federal lawmaking process to become a statute. It is available for $4.50 from the Superintendent of Documents, Government Printing Office, Washington, DC 20402/202-783-3238.

Information on Congressional Publications

The best source of information on congressional publications and for a Subject Bibliography on Congress, contact: Superintendent of Documents, Government Printing Office, Washington, DC 20401/202-275-3030.

Legislative Data Base

LEGIS provides up-to-date information about all bills and resolutions introduced in Congress since 1975. Citations for each piece of legislation contain its date of introduction, sponsor and cosponsors, committee of referral, legislative status, and a summary of the bill's purpose and content. Legislative status includes information about hearings held, markups, amendments added, floor action and vote tallies. LEGIS can be searched by subject, bill number or name, sponsoring member of Congress, committee of referral and public law number.

It is best to call LEGIS to request a search. While you are on the phone, staff will search the data base for you and immediately supply you with needed information over the phone. Printouts cost ten cents a page and, since LEGIS does not have mailing privileges, you must arrange to have the printout picked up or send LEGIS a return envelope with sufficient postage. Contact: Office of Legislative Information, House Office Building, Annex 2, 3rd & D Sts. S.W., Room 696, Washington, DC 20515/202-225-1772.

Legislative Status System

This is a computerized informative book which provides information by topic, member, bill number, etc., on the legislative status of all the bills and resolutions before the House and Senate. Contact: Legislative Status System, LEGIS, House Office Building Annex 2, Room 696, Washington, DC 20515/202-225-1772. By searching a computerized data base, this office provides the answers to such questions as:

Have any bills been introduced covering a given topic?
What is the status of a given bill?
Who sponsored the bill?
What date was it introduced?
What committee and subcommittees have held hearings on a given bill?

List of House Committees

This is a listing of official and unofficial House committees. The members of each committee are included. Contact: Clerk of the House, House of Representatives, The Capitol, Washington, DC 20515/202-225-7000.

Monitoring House Legislation

Both Democrats and Republicans in the House Cloakroom provide a recorded message with daily legislative activity information: 202-225-7400 (Democrat), 202-225-7430 (Republican). A recorded message with the next day's, as well as future, legislative schedule(s) is given; call 202-225-1600 (Democrat), 202-225-2020 (Republican). For additional information or on-going legislative activity, call: 202-225-7330 (Democrat), or 202-225-7350 (Republican).

Monitoring Senate Legislation

Daily legislative action and future scheduling information is available on a tape recording. For the Democratic cloakroom call 202-224-8541. For the Republican cloakroom call 202-224-8601. To monitor the activity of a bill scheduled for activity on the Senate floor contact: 202-224-4691 for the Democratic view and 202-224-5456 for the Republican.

New Laws

The 98th Congress during its two-year session passed only 623 laws. For a complete listing of the new laws passed by the 98th Congress, purchase a copy of the November 14, 1984 issue of the *Congressional Record*. Available for $1.00 from Government Printing Office, Superintendent of Documents, Washington, DC 20402/202-275-3030.

Report of the Clerk of the House

This quarterly report includes the salaries of House members' staffs, committee staffs and House officers and employees. For a copy of this report contact: House Document Room, H226 Capitol Building, Washington, DC 20515/202-225-3456.

Report of The Secretary of the Senate

This biannual report details the salaries of senators' staff, members, committee staff members and officers and employees of the Senate. Contact: Senate Document Room, B-04 Senate Hart Office Building, Washington, DC 20510/202-224-7860.

Sergeant at Arms of the Senate

The Sergeant at Arms of the Senate is elected by and serves as the Executive Officer of that body. He is also the Law Enforcement Office; has statutory power to make arrests; locates absentee senators for a quorum; is a member of Capitol Police Board, serving as chairman each odd year; is a member of the Capitol Guide Board, serving as chairman each odd year; has custody of the Senate gavel; serves subpoenas issued by the Senate or its committees; is responsible for many aspects of ceremonial functions, including the inauguration of the President of the United States; arranges funerals of Senators who die in office and escorts congressional committees to the services; directs and supervises departments and facilities under his jurisdiction; subject to the Presiding Officer, maintains order in the Senate Chamber, prevents admission of any unauthorized person to the senate floor, and prevents quotas of staff members entitled to the floor at one time from being exceeded; escorts the President when he addresses a Joint Session of Congress or attends any function at the Capitol; and escorts members of foreign parliaments into the Senate Chamber when they are to be introduced to the Senate. Contact: Sergeant at Arms, S-321 Senate, The Capitol, Washington, DC 20510/202-224-2341.

Senate Committees

A listing is available of official Senate committees. These include the members of each committee.

Also available is the *Unofficial List of Senators,* which gives the names of all Senators, their states, their party affiliations and the year they are up for reelection. Contact: Office of the Secretary of the Senate, The Capitol, Room S-221, Washington, DC 20510/202-224-2115.

Senate History
The Senate Historical Office collects and disseminates information on Senate history and Senate members, including photographs, unpublished documents and oral history. A free newsletter, *Senate History,* is also available. Contact: Senate Historical Office, Secretary of the Senate, The Capitol, Room SH 201, Washington, DC 20510/202-224-6900.

Senate Library
The Senate Library is the official depository of senate documents. Its primary function is service to Senate members and their staffs. To use the library a researcher must have a letter of introduction from a Senator. Contact: Senate Library, Suite S-332, The Capitol, Washington, DC 20510.

Senate Manual
This biennial manual includes Jefferson's Manual, standing rules, orders, and laws and resolutions affecting the Senate. A list of senators and members of the Executive Branch is also provided. It is published every two years with each new Congress. The manual is sold for $8.50 by the Superintendent of Documents, Government Printing Office, Washington, DC 20402/202-275-3030. For additional information contact: Senate Committee on Rules and Administration, Russell Senate Office Building, 1st St. N.E., Room 305, Washington, DC 20510/202-224-0293.

Senate Procedure: Precedents and Practices
This is a compilation of procedural rules, laws, rulings and practices. It is available for $15.00 from the Superintendent of Documents, Government Printing Office, Washington, DC 20402/202-275-3030, or contact: Parliamentarian of the Senate, The Capitol, Room S-132, Washington, DC 20510/202-224-6128.

Statement on the Senate's History
This is a series of addresses to the Senate on subjects related to its history and traditions. For a list of citations with dates, subjects, and page numbers, contact: Senate Historical Office, Secretary of the Senate, The Capitol, Room SH 201 Washington, DC 20510/202-224-6900.

Televised House Floor Proceedings
Debates and votes in the House Chamber are broadcast gavel-to-gavel. For further information about getting these televised proceedings on your cable system, contact: C-SPAN, 400 North Capitol St. N.W., Suite 1555, Washington, DC 20001/202-737-3220.

Tours
Free guided tours of the interior of the Capitol building are available to the public. Contact: Capitol Guide Service, Sergeant-at-Arms of the Senate, The Rotunda, The Capitol, Washington, DC 20510/202-225-6827.

Treaties and Nominations
For information on and copies of treaties submitted to the Senate for ratification, contact: Senate Document Room, Hart Building, Room B-04, Washington, DC 20510/202-224-7860.

U.S. Policy and Supporting Positions (The Plum Book)
This book lists some 3,000 political appointment jobs and describes type of appointment, tenure, grade and salary. Available for sale at the Superintendent of Documents, Government Printing Office, Washington, DC 20402/202-275-3030, or contact: Senate Government Affairs Committee, Dirksen Office Building, R 340, Washington, DC 20510/202-224-3791.

Visitor Passes
To obtain passes to observe floor debate and votes in the Senate Chamber, contact your Senator's Washington office. Your Representative's office on Capitol Hill can furnish you with passes to the House Chamber.

How Can the Legislative Branch Help You?
To determine how this branch of government can help you contact the local office of your congressman or The Capitol Hill Switchboard, Washington, DC 20510/202-224-3121.

Architect of the Capitol

Capitol Building, Washington, DC 20515/202-225-1200

Budget: $103,452,000
Employees: 2,004

Mission: Is charged with the structural and mechanical care of the U.S. Capitol Building, and making arrangements with the proper authorities for ceremonies and ceremonials held in the building and on the grounds; is responsible for the care, maintenance and improvement of the Capitol grounds, comprising approximately 208.7 acres; has the structural and mechanical care of the Library of Congress Buildings and the U.S. Supreme Court Building; and is responsible for the operation of the U.S. Senate Restaurant.

Major Sources of Information

Fact Sheets
A packet of fact sheets on the various features and artifacts of the Capitol is available free of charge. Includes information on the Statue of Freedom; the tile floor of the Capitol; the history of the old subway transportation system connecting the Capitol and the Russell Office Building; the Rotunda Frieze; the "cornstalk" or "corncob" columns and capitals; the dome; the historic catafalque; Washington's tomb; those who have lain in state in the rotunda; the flags over the east and west central fronts; and the architects and architecture of the Capitol. Contact: Art and Reference Division, Architect of the Capitol, Capitol Building, Room SB15, Washington, DC 20515/202-225-1222.

Raise a Flag Over the Capitol
For the cost of a flag your congressman can have the Architect of the Capitol fly your personal Stars and Stripes over the Capitol Building on the day you specify. This makes an unusual birthday gift because you then receive the flag and a certificate noting the date the flag was flown and for whom. Be sure to state the day to be flown and the recipient. Contact the local office of your congress-

man or c/o Capitol, Washington, DC 20515/202-224-3121.

The Capitol
A pictorial history of the Capitol and of the Congress, *The Capitol* provides a pictorial and narrative history of the Capitol building and the Congresses that have served there. Included are sections devoted to the Architects of the Capitol, the Speaker of the House, House leadership, pages of the U.S. Congress, the Senate, elected officers of the Senate, a profile of the 96th Congress, women in American politics, and related information. $6.50 Contact: your congressman's office for a free copy or Superintendent of Documents, Government Printing Office, Washington, DC 20402/202-275-3030. For additional information contact: Art and Reference Division, Architect of the Capitol, Capitol Building, Room SB15, Washington, DC 20515/202-225-1222.

How Can the Architect of the Capitol Help You?
To determine how this office can help you contact: Architect of the Capitol, Capitol Building, Washington, DC 20515/202-225-1200.

Botanic Gardens

245 1st St. S.W., Washington, DC 20024/202-225-8333

Budget: $1,897,000
Employees: 57

Mission: Collects, cultivates and grows the various vegetable products of this and other countries for exhibition and display to the public and for study material for students, scientists and garden clubs.

Major Sources of Information

Botanic Garden Conservatory
The Botanic Garden Conservatory can be considered an educational facility, for it makes available for study many rare and interesting specimens from all over the world. Every year botanical specimens are received, both foreign and domestic, for identification. The Garden also furnishes, upon request, information relating to the proper care and methods of growing plants. Contact: Botanic Gardens, 1st and Canal St. S.W., Washington, DC 20024/202-225-8333.

Display Information
The Botanic Garden collects and cultivates the various plants of this and other countries for display to the public and for study by students, scientists and garden clubs. Contact: Botanic Gardens, 1st and Canal Sts. S.W., Washington, DC 20024/202-225-7099.

Horticulture Classes
Horticulture classes are offered free of charge and consist of informal lectures followed by a series of demonstrations. For scheduled lectures and other information, contact: Botanic Garden, 1st and Canal Sts. S.W., Washington, DC 20024/202-225-7099.

Plant and Flower Shows
The Botanic Garden sponsors four annual plant and flower shows in display areas totaling 9,000 square feet. The Easter Show, features spring flowering plants. It is held from Palm Sunday through Easter Sunday. The Summer Terrace Display is held on the patio in front of the Conservatory from late May through September. Hundreds of flowering and foliage plants in hanging baskets highlight this event. Mid-November through Thanksgiving Day features a wide variety of chrysanthemums. Poinsettias dominate the show held from mid-December through the Christmas holidays. Each year the Garden hosts plant and flower shows sponsored by area garden clubs and plant societies. Other services sponsored by the U.S. Botanic Garden include group tours which are given during the year by appointment and a series of horticulture classes held from September through May. All services at the Garden are offered free of charge. Contact: Botanic Gardens, 1st and Canal Sts. S.W., Washington, DC 20024/202-225-7099.

Publications
Publications of horticultural interest, schedules of display and horticulture classes and a pamphlet offering a self-guided tour are available. Contact: Botanic Garden, 1st and Canal Sts. S.W., Washington, DC 20024/202-225-7099.

How Can the Botanic Gardens Help You?
To determine how this office can help you contact: Botanic Gardens, 1st and Canal St. SW, Washington, DC 20024/202-225-8333.

General Accounting Office

441 G St. N.W., Washington, DC 20548/202-275-2812

Budget: $254,250,000
Employees: 5,100

Mission: Assists the Congress, its committees, and its members in carrying out their legislative and oversight responsibilities, consistent with its role as an independent, nonpolitical agency in the legislative branch; to carry out legal, accounting, auditing and claims settlement functions with respect to federal government programs and operations as assigned by the Congress; and to make recommendations designed to provide for more efficient and effective government operations.

Major Sources of Information

Annual Report
There are two volumes of the *Annual Report to Congress* published by the General Accounting Office. Volume One highlights the efforts of the General Accounting Office for the present fiscal year. Volume Two contains budget information, a list of recommendations to Congress and a catalog of Audit Reports issued during the fiscal year. Volume One sells for $2.50 and Volume Two sells for $8.00 from the Superintendent of Documents, Government Printing Office, Washington, DC 20402/202-783-3238.

Audit Reference Services Library
The library provides information of GAO interest and has access to data bases, government documents, dissertations, legislative information, research in progress and organizations. *Literature Limelight,* published monthly, lists the latest books acquired. The Law Library is located in Room 7056/202-275-2585. Contact: Technical Library, General Accounting Office, 441 G St. N.W., Room 6536, Washington, DC 20548/202-275-5180.

Auditing
General Accounting Office has the right of access to, and examination of, any books, documents, papers, or records of the departments and agencies.

The Office has statutory authority to investigate all matters relating to the receipt, disbursement, and application of public funds. Additionally, GAO's audit authority covers wholly and partially owned government corporations and certain non-appropriated fund activities.

It makes expenditure analysis of executive agencies to enable the Congress to determine whether public funds are efficiently and economically administered and expended; and to review and evaluate the results of existing government programs and activities. The scope of the audit work extends to the activities of state and local governments, quasi-governmental bodies, and private organizations in their capacity as recipients under, or administrators for federal aid programs financed by loans, advances, grants and contributions. It also covers certain activities of those having negotiated contracts with the government. Contact: Accounting and Financial Management, General Accounting Office, 441 G St. N.W., Washington, DC 20548/202-275-9303.

Bid Protest

Disputes between agencies and bidders for government contracts, including grantee award actions are resolved by the GAO. The free publication, *Bid Protests at GAO—A Descriptive Guide,* contains information on GAO's procedures for deciding legal questions arising from the award of government contracts. Contact: Information Handling and Support Facilities, General Accounting Office, P.O. Box 6015, Gaithersburg, MD 20877-202-275-6241.

Blue Book—Accounting Principles and Standards for Federal Agencies

This free book provides guidance for internal auditing in federal agencies. Contact: Information Handling and Support Facilities, General Accounting Office, P.O. Box 6015, Gaithersburg, MD 20877/202-275-6241.

Checklist for Report Writers and Reviewers (#091-096)

This book standardizes the report format and articulates conceptually how a report should be organized. It breaks a GAO report down to its components—cover, transmittal letter, digest, etc.—and poses questions to use in judging how well each was written. The booklet includes reminders of GAO reporting policies, principles taught in Producing Organized Writing and Effective Reviewing (POWER), recurring reporting problems, and technical reporting requirements. Contact: Superintendent of Documents, GAO, DHIS, P.O. 6015, Gaithersburg, MD 20877/202-275-6241. *From Auditing to Editing* (#095-119) is a guide for teaching report writing. It is sold for $1.45 by the Superintendent of Documents, Government Printing Office, Washington, DC 20402/202-783-3238. Contact: Superintendent of Documents, GAO, DHIS, P.O. 6015, Gaithersburg, MD 20877/202-275-6241

Claims Settlement and Debt Collections

The GAO settles claims by and against the United States. Claims may involve individuals; business entities; or foreign, state and municipal governments as claimant or debtor. Claims are settled by GAO when the departments and agencies have not been given specific authority to handle their own claims and when they involve 1) doubtful questions of law or fact, 2) appeals of agency actions, 3) certain debts which agencies are unable to collect, and 4) waivers of certain erroneous payments for pay, etc. Contact: Claims Group General Government Division, General Accounting Office, 441 G St. N.W., Washington, DC 20548/202-275-3102.

Community and Economic Development

The Community and Economic Development Division coordinates GAO's work in the areas of food, domestic housing and community development, environmental protection, land use planning arrangement and control, transportation systems and policies, and water and water-related programs.

In addition, this division provides GAO audit coverage at the Department of Agriculture, Commerce, Housing and Urban Development, Interior (except energy and materials activities) and Transportation; the Army Corps of Engineers (civil functions); the Environmental Protection Agency; the Small Business Administration; the Interstate Commerce, Federal Martime and Federal Communications Commissions; the National Railroad Passenger Corporation (Amtrak); the Washington Metropolitan Area Transit Authority; the U.S. Railway Association; the Civil Aeronautics Board; the Commodity Futures Trading Commission; the Federal Emergency Management Agency; and a variety of boards, commissions, and quasi-governmental entities. Contact: Resources Community and Economic Development Division, General Accounting Office, 441 G St. N.W., Washington, DC 20548/202-275-3567.

Congressional Sourcebook

The *Sourcebook* is published in three volumes:

Volume I: Requirements for Recurring Reports to the Congress—describes executive agency reports issued regularly. $15.00
Volume II: Federal Program Evaluation—includes evaluation reports on federal agencies' programs. $15.00

Available at the Superintendent of Documents, Government Printing Office, Washington, DC 20402/202-783-3238, or contact: Information, Government Accounting Office, 441 G St. N.W., Washington, DC 20548/202-275-2812.

Congressional Staff Assignments

Each year the Office assigns 50 to 100 staff members directly to committees to help carry out their responsibilities or assist them in using the results of a GAO study. In accordance with the Budget and Accounting Act, GAO provides staff assistance to committees having jurisdiction over revenues, appropriations and expenditures, and often to other committees, as well. However, the agency does not assign staff to individual members. Contact: Congressional Relations, General Accounting Office, 441 G St. N.W., Washington, DC 20548/202-275-5456.

Congressional Testimony

Congressional testimony by GAO officials ranging in topic from "long-term planning for national science policy" to "taking the profit out of crime" is available. Contact: Information Handling and Support Facilities, General Accounting Office,

P.O. Box 6015, Gaithersburg, MD 20877/202-275-6241.

Debarred List
This is a consolidated list of persons or firms currently debarred for violation of various public contract acts incorporating labor standards provisions. It is a free quarterly with interim lists issued semi-monthly. Contact: Information Handling and Support Facilities, General Accounting Office, P.O. Box 6015, Gaithersburg, MD 20877/202-275-6241.

Decisions of the Comptroller General
An annual, bound volume of Comptroller general decisions includes about 10% of the total decisions rendered annually. Digests of decisions not included in this volume are issued quarterly in pamphlet form. Separate pamphlets are issued for Civilian Personnel, General Government Matters, Military Personnel, Procurement, and Transportation; and include decision digests for three-month periods ending in December, March, June and September. They are available on request. The monthly subscription is available for $27.00 per year from the Superintendent of Documents, Government Printing Office, Washington, DC 20402/202-783-3238. Contact: Index-Digest, Information and Legal Reference Services, General Counsel, General Accounting Office, 441 G St. N.W., Room 7510, Washington, DC 20548/202-275-5006.

Discrimination Bars
The General Accounting Office offers a free 72-page book that can help companies avoid discrimination problems. The book, *A Compilation of Federal Laws and Executive Orders for Nondiscrimination and Equal Opportunity Programs,* cites 87 laws and orders relating to equal rights, in employment practices as well as in the provision of services. Each citation names the law or order, describes it briefly, identifies what type of discrimination it prohibits and to whom it applies, and which agencies enforce it.

To order the book (stock number HRD-78-138) write or call: Information Handling and Support Facilities, General Accounting Office, P.O. Box 6015, Gaithersburg, MD 20877/202-275-6241.

Energy and Minerals Division
This division provides GAO audit coverage for the Department of Energy, the Nuclear Regulatory Commission, The Tennessee Valley Authority, energy and minerals programs of the Department of Interior, and energy and materials activities located in numerous other federal entities. Contact: Resources Community and Economic Development Division, General Accounting Office, 441 G St. N.W., Room 4915, Washington, DC 20548/202-275-3567.

Energy Data Verification
GAO conducts verification examinations of energy-related information developed by private business concerns under certain circumstances delineated in the Act. For the purpose of carrying out this authority, the Comptroller General may issue subpoenas, require written answers to interrogations, administer oaths, inspect business premises, and inspect and copy specified books and records. Certain enforcement powers are provided, including for some types of noncompliance the power to assess civil penalties and to collect such penalties through civil action. Contact: Resources Community & Economic Development Division, General Accounting Office, 441 G St. N.W., Washington, DC 20548/202-275-3567.

Federal Personnel and Compensation
This division provides audit coverage for the office of Personnel Management, Merit Systems Protection Board, Federal Labor Relations Authority, and Selective Service System. The division also examines government-wide personnel activities relating to and affecting the federal work force. Contact: General Government Division-Civilian Personnel, General Accounting Office; 441 G St. N.W., Washington, DC 20548/202-275-6209.

Field Operations Division
The Field Operations Division, through its regional offices in 15 cities, provides direct audit support throughout the continental United States, Alaska, Puerto Rico and the Virgin Islands for GAO's other operating divisions. Thus, this division plays a major role in most of the audits and work of GAO. About half of GAO's professional staff is assigned to its regional offices. For addresses of the GAO field offices and for further information contact: Field Operation Division, Assistant Comptroller General, General Accounting Office, 441 G St. N.W., Washington, DC 20548/202-275-5495.

Financial and General Management Studies
The Financial and Financial Management Division is responsible for coordinating GAO's work in the issue areas of automatic data processing, internal audit, accounting and financial reporting, and national productivity.

This division carries out its responsibilities through participation in the Joint Financial Management Improvement Program and its government-wide responsibilities for automatic data processing, accounting systems, internal auditing and fraud prevention, productivity and regulatory accounting and reporting. It provides GAO audit coverage at the Securities and Exchange Commission. It also has primary responsibility for financial statement audits.

In addition, its Claims Group settles and adjudicates claims and demands by or against the United

States and reviews, evaluates, and reports on the claim settlement and debt collection activities of government agencies. Contact: Accounting and Financial Management, General Accounting Office, 441 G St. N.W., Washington, DC 20548/202-275-9303.

Fraud Hotline
A hotline is available to contact GAO about potential problems in government programs involving waste, fraud, abuse and illegal actions. Call: 202-633-6987 (DC area), or 800-424-5454, or contact: Fraud Prevention Group, General Accounting Office, Room 6126, 441 G St. N.W., Washington, DC 20548/202-275-9303.

Fraud Prevention Group
This task force tries to identify root causes and recurring patterns of illegal activities and to see how they can best be prevented and detected. It also probes agency information or accounting systems and programs for weaknesses that invite or allow fraud. Contact: Fraud Prevention Group, Accounting and Financial Management, 441 G St. N.W., Room 6126, Washington, DC 20548/202-275-5824.

GAO—An Administrative History 1966–1981
This book, available for $8, describes the role and operations of the GAO, and the changes it has undergone over the past fifteen years. It details activities of GAO offices and divisions, and describes their functions and their accomplishments. Contact: General Accounting Office, Document Handling & Information Services Facility, PO Box 6015, Gaithersburg, MD 20877/202-275-6241.

The General Government Division is responsible for coordinating GAO's work in the issue areas of intergovernmental policies and fiscal relations, law enforcement and crime prevention, tax administration, data collected from nonfederal sources (statistical and paperwork implications), and federal oversight of financial institutions.

This division provides GAO audit coverage for the Departments of Justice and Treasury, the District of Columbia Government, the United States Postal Service, the judicial and legislative branches of the federal government, and various other agencies and commissions. Contact: General Government Division, General Accounting Office, Room 3866, 441 G St. N.W., Washington, DC 20548/202-275-6059.

General Accounting Office Bibliographic Data Base
The General Accounting Office (GAO) maintains a data base which provides bibliographic information on GAO documents and reports. GAO studies cover a vast array of subjects, as the agency must produce a report on any topic Congress assigns. Reports have ranged from financial audits

of government agencies to policy studies of health-related programs. Searches are generally conducted by subject area and specific time period. Searches and printouts are available free of charge. GAO will also mail you up to five copies of any report listed; this service is also free. Contact: GAO/IHSF, P.O. Box 6015, Gaithersburg, MD 20877/202-275-6241 (to request printouts and searches), 202-275-5042 (for information about contents).

Human Resources
The Human Resources Division coordinates GAO's work in the issue areas of consumer and worker protection, administration of nondiscrimination and equal opportunity programs, education, health, income security, and employment and training.

In addition to its leadership in these issue areas, this division provides GAO audit coverage for the Departments of Labor, Health and Human Services, and Education; the Community Services Administration; the Consumer Product Safety Commission; the Federal Trade Commission; the Pension Benefit Guaranty Corporation; the Legal Services Corporation; ACTION; the Railroad Retirement Board; the Equal Employment Opportunity Commission; the Veterans Administration; all federal health programs; and various small commissions and independent agencies. Contact: Human Resources Division, General Accounting Office, Room 6864, 441 G St. N.W., Washington, DC 20548/202-275-5470.

Index and Files
The Index and Files Section is the correspondence control center for all incoming and outgoing correspondence, reports, decisions, and other documents addressed to or signed by officials in the Office of the Comptroller General and the Office of the General Counsel.

A computerized information system provides immediate access to all case-related information processed since September 1978. Additionally, Index and Files retains manual card files going back to 1921. Thus, a researcher can obtain information by using both the old card system and the new automated system, for any case or group of cases processed by Index and Files since 1921. Contact: Index and Files, Information and Legal Reference Services, General Accounting Office, 441 G St. N.W., Room 7510, Washington, DC 20548/202-275-5436.

International Affairs
The National Security and International Affairs Division serves as lead division for the international affairs issue area.

This division provides GAO audit coverage for the Department of State, the Agency for International Development, the International Development Cooperation Agency, the Central Intelligence Agency, the Export-Import Bank of the United States, the U.S. Information Agency, and the Panama Canal Commission, as well as international activities of numerous other federal entities. International Division personnel staff GAO's overseas offices. Contact: National Security and International Affairs Division, General Accounting Office, Room 4804, 441 G St. N.W., Washington, DC 20548/202-275-5518.

International Auditor Fellowship Program
GAO has made an effort to share its knowledge and experience with other nations, particularly the developing countries. The most visible effort is the Comptroller General's International Auditor Fellowship Program, established in 1979, through which a small number of auditors from developing countries are selected annually to·spend three to six months in an academic and on-the-job experience program. Although GAO cannot pay travel and subsistence for the Fellows, it provides the training itself free of charge and assists many participants in obtaining financial aid from the U.S. Agency for International Development and the United Nations Development Program. Contact: National Security and International Affairs Division, General Accounting Office, Room 4804, 441 G St. N.W., Washington, DC 20548/202-275-5518.

Legal Index-Digest
The Index-Digest Section compiles and maintains the research material related to all legal issuances of the Office of General Counsel. It maintains an in-house research facility by constantly updating the various legal indexes, prepares for printing all legal publications emanating from the Office of General Counsel, and provides research assistance to GAO legal and audit staffs, personnel from other governmental agencies and other interested parties.

This section also produces an annual, bound volume of Comptroller General decisions, and a quarterly pamphlet of decision digests not included in the annual. Contact: Index-Digest Information and Legal Reference Services, General Counsel, General Accounting Office, 441 G St. N.W., Room 7510, Washington, DC 20548/202-275-5006.

Legal Information and Reference Service
The legal information and reference service provides on-going legal support services to the General Counsel, the Comptroller General, the Audit divisions and the public. The service gathers and maintains legal information. Contact: Information and Legal Reference Services, General Counsel, General Accounting Office, 441 G St. N.W., Room 7510, Washington, DC 20548/202-275-4501.

Legislative Branch Audit Site
The Site assists the Congress by doing 15 recurring financial audits of such units as the House Recording Studio and the Senate Restaurant, and offering informal advice and assistance on administrative matters. Contact: Legislative Branch Audit Site, Accounting and Financial Management Division, General Accounting Office, 2nd and D Sts. S.W., Washington, DC 20515/202-226-2480.

Legislative Digest
The Legislative Digest Section provides legislative analyses and research assistance and compiles and maintains legislative history files for each bill and public law since the 1920s. It also maintains subject indexes, enabling a researcher to find legislation or reports dealing with a particular subject, and some subject files containing materials generated by Congress on a particular subject but which are not associated with a specific bill or law. The section also has a file identifying comments made by GAO on bills where the comment deals with a matter of GAO policy, such as its audit authority or new functions the agency might be asked to perform. Contact: Legislative Digest, Information and Legal Reference Service, General Counsel, General Accounting Office, 441 G St. N.W., Room 7510, Washington, DC 20548/202-275-4435.

Periodicals
These periodical subscriptions are available from the Superintendent of Documents, Government Printing Office, Washington, DC 20402/202-783-3238.

GAO Documents. (Monthly.) A comprehensive record of current GAO publications and documents, including audit reports, staff studies, memoranda, opinions, speeches, testimony and Comptroller General decisions. $55.00 per year.

GAO Review (Quarterly.) Contains articles on accounting generally and particularly on accounting and auditing activities of the General Accounting Office, its officials and staff employees. $12.00 per year. *General Accounting Office Policy and Procedures Manual for Guidance of Federal Agencies.* Subscription service of each title listed below includes changes for an indeterminate period. Issued in looseleaf form, with index dividers. Punched for three-ring binder. Title 1, *The United States General Accounting Office,* $14.00; Title 3, *Audit,* Subscription price, $8.00; Title 6. *Pay Leave & Allowances,* $21.00, Title 7. *Policies & Procedures Manual,* $44.00.

Policy and Procedures Manual
The General Accounting Office *Policy and Procedures Manual for Guidance of Federal Agencies* is the official medium through which the Comptroller General promulgates: principles, standards, and related requirements for accounting to be observed by the federal departments and agencies;

uniform procedures for use by the federal agencies; and regulations governing the relationships of the General Accounting Office with other federal agencies and with individuals and private concerns doing business with the government.

All decisions of the Comptroller General of general import are published in monthly pamphlets and in annual volumes. Contact: Office of Policy, General Accounting Office, Room 6800, 441 G St. N.W., Washington, DC 20548/202-275-6172,

Office of Program Planning

This office sees that the audit work of GAO is planned, coordinated and reported in a consistent and effective manner. It works with the audit divisions to implement GAO's policies and planning guidelines across divisional lines. Contact: Office of Program Planning, General Accounting Office, Room 7810, 441 G St. N.W., Washington, DC 20548/202-275-6190.

Procurement and Systems Acquisition

The Procurement and Systems Acquisition Division is responsible for coordinating GAO's work in the issue area of general procurement and the procurement of major systems.

This division monitors the government's entire procurement function and its research and development policies and programs. Most of this division's work is concentrated in the Department of Defense, the National Aeronautics and Space Administration, the defense-related activities of the Department of Energy and the Federal Supply Service of the General Services Administration. Contact: Mission and Systems Acquisition Division, General Accounting Office, 441 G St. N.W., Washington, DC 20548/202-275-3550.

Program Evaluation

The Program Evaluation & Methodology Division performs program evaluation assignments designed to demonstrate new or improved methodologies for program evaluations. The conduct of these evaluations serves to model strategies for similar assignments. The Division also assumes responsibilities for evaluation methods development. In addition, it provides training in evaluation to all GAO personnel.

The Division encourages and maintains contacts with evaluation professionals in other federal agencies, universities, professional societies, and state and local governments, and fosters improved communication within the evaluation community. Contact: Program Evaluation and Methodology Division, General Accounting Office, Room 5868, 441 G St. N.W., Washington, DC 20548/202-275-1854.

Publications

A list of current reports of the Government Accounting Office is available. It includes Comptroller General Reports to Congress and other federal agencies, congressional testimony by GAO officials, speeches by the Comptroller General, and other publications on accounting and auditing procedures, automatic data processing, intergovernmental audit standards and general publications. The subjects covered in the Reports to Congress include:

Accounting and Internal Controls
Financial Integrity Act Reviews
Agriculture and Food
Automatic Data Processing
Civil Service
Defense Procurement
Education
Employment and Training
Environmental Protection
Financial Institution Activities and Regulation
Financial Statements
Foreign Aid
Foreign Military Sales
Fossil Fuels
Government Administrative Management
Government Financial Management
Health and Medicare/Medicaid
Housing
Impoundment Reviews
Income Security and Social Services
Justice and Law Enforcement
Management of Federal Energy Activities
Military Logistics
Military Personnel
Natural Resources
Nuclear Energy
Research and Development
Taxes
Trade
Transportation

These reports are available free of charge. To obtain a current list, contact: Information Officer, General Accounting Office, Room 7015, 441 G St. N.W., Washington, DC 20548/202-275-2812.

Redbook—Guidelines for Financial and Compliance Audits and Federally Assisted Programs

This book indicates which audit standards should be applied, how audits should be planned, and how audit reports and workpapers should be prepared. General procedures for testing compliance with legal and regulatory requirements, studying internal controls, testing account balances, and other audit procedures are also included. Contact: General Accounting Office, Document Handling and Information Services Facility, PO Box 6015, Gaithersburg, MD 20877/202-275-6241.

Regulatory Reports Review

GAO reviews the existing information-gathering practices of independent regulatory agencies. Information report forms designed by these agencies for the collection of information from the public are required to be cleared by GAO before they may be issued. The purposes of the review and clearance functions are to ensure that information is obtained with minimum burden on those businesses required to provide the information, to eliminate duplicate data collection efforts, and to ensure that collected information is tabulated so as to maximize its usefulness. Contact: General Accounting Office, Document Handling and Information Services Facility, PO Box 6015, Gaithersburg, MD 20877/202-275-6241.

Reports
The Comptroller General sends each month to the Congress, its committees, and its members, a list of GAO reports issued or released during the previous month. Copies of GAO reports are provided without charge to Members of Congress and congressional committee staff members; officials of federal, state, local and foreign governments; members of the press; college libraries, faculty members, and students; and nonprofit organizations.

Copies are available from the General Accounting Office, Document Handling and Information Services Facility, PO Box 6015, Gaithersburg, MD 20877/202-275-6241.

Writing Resources
Three levels of courses—introductory, intermediate and advanced—are offered to meet the writing needs of auditors at successive stages in their careers.

The POWER (Producing Organized Writing and Effective Reviewing) course is the heart of the program. POWER is offered to persons in grades GS-12 and up. Its basic principle is that a general-to-specific, or deductive, structure is the easiest for readers. POWER applies the deductive principle at the paragraph level first and then extends it to sections and chapters. The course also includes a unit on report review. Contact: Writing Resources Branch, Publishing Services, General Accounting Office, Room 4428, 441 G St. N.W., Washington, DC 20548/202-275-5864.

Yellow Book—Standards for Audit of Governmental Organizations, Programs, Activities and Functions
This booklet contains a body of audit standards, intended for application to audits of all government organizations, programs, activities, and functions—whether they are performed by auditors employed by federal, state, or local governments; independent public accountants; or others qualified to perform parts of the audit work contemplated under these standards. $4.75.

Supplements include: *Examples of Findings from Governmental Audits.* (Audit Standards Supplement No. 4.) Illustrates audit findings developed during reviews of compliance with applicable laws and regulations, efficiency in using resources, and achievement of program results. $2.00. *Use Auditing to Improve Efficiency and Economy.* (Audit Standards Supplement No. 7) $3.00. These supplements are available from: Superintendent of Documents, Government Printing Office, Washington, DC 20402/202-783-3238. For additional information contact: Accounting and Financial Management, General Accounting Office, 441 G St. N.W., Washington, DC 20548/202-275-9303.

How Can the General Accounting Office Help You?
To determine how this agency can help you, contact: General Accounting Office, 441 G St. N.W., Washington, DC 20548/202-275-2812.

Government Printing Office

North Capitol and H Sts., NW, Washington, DC 20401
GPO main operator: 202-275-2051;
Publications Sales and Information: 202-783-3238

BUDGET: $840,000,000*
EMPLOYEES: 5,638

MISSION: The GPO is often referred to as the largest printing plant under one roof. but it actually has three missions. GPO provides printing and binding services to Congress, the executive agencies, and the judicial branch—including everything from simple letterheads to the massive 9-digit ZIP Code directory. Also, GPO procures private sector composition, printing, and binding services on behalf of the Federal Government. Additionally, GPO's Office of the Superintendent of Documents is the official sales agent for Government publications.

Major Sources of Information

Superintendent of Documents
The Superintendent of Documents offers for sale nearly 16,000 of the newest and most popular publications from Government experts in space science, global exporting opportunities, medical research, current Federal law, and much more. In addition, Government bestsellers provide sound, practical answers to a wide variety of questions from child care to saving money on fuel bills.

The Office of the Superintendent of Documents is also responsible for providing free access to Government documents through the Federal Depository Library Program. There are nearly 1,400 Federal Depository Libraries across the country providing access at no charge to virtually all unclassified Government publications.

Bestsellers
Government publications contain authoritative information on almost every phase of life and offer

*$122,000,000 of this a congressional appropriation

practical answers to almost any question. Some of the most popular publications include the following. Check for current prices by calling Orders and Information 202-783-3238, or write: Superintendent of Documents, Washington, DC 20402.

Infant Care. The latest information on caring for a new baby, including simple guidelines for dealing with common problems most parents face.
Your Child from 1 to 6. Patterns of development, eating, discipline, school readiness, and more.
Your Child from 6 to 12. The role of the parent as family leader, children and money, social involvements, and much more.
Adult Physical Fitness. Outlines two practical, progressive programs of exercise—one for men and one for women. Includes illustrations and a progress chart.
A Meeting With the Universe. A handsome full-color look at the successes and discoveries of America's space program, and the unanswered questions that remain.
Comparing the Planets. A colorful NASA wallchart showing the planets, their differences in size and atmosphere, and the vast distances of the solar system.

Bibliographies

Listings of Government publications on more than 240 subjects ranging from accounting to veteran's affairs can be easily obtained, and they're free. Write for a brochure on the subjects covered: Superintendent of Documents, Research and Analysis Section, Stop: SSOP, Washington, DC 20402/202-783-3238.

Bookdealers

See Discounts.

Bookstores

There are 24 Government bookstores all around the country where you can browse through the shelves and take your books home with you. Naturally, these stores can't stock all of the nearly 16,000 titles available, but they do carry the ones you're most likely to be looking for. They'll also be happy to special order any Government book currently offered for sale. All of GPO's bookstores accept VISA, MasterCard, and Superintendent of Documents deposit account orders. For the Government Bookstore nearest you consult the listing in the Sampler or write: Superintendent of Documents, Bookstore Branch Chief, Stop: SSFB, Washington, DC 20402/202-275-3293.

Catalogs

New Books

It's easy to keep abreast of all new Government publications available for sale from the Superintendent of Documents with this free bimonthly listing. *New Books* is arranged alphabetically by subject category for convenience. Prices and ordering information are included. Write: *New Books,* Superintendent of Documents, Stop: MK, Washington, DC 20402.

U.S. Government Books Catalog

This unique sampling of new and popular publications from the Government "shrinks" the vast quantities of Government information into a convenient resource. For your copy, write: *Catalog,* Superintendent of Documents, Stop: MK, Washington, DC 20402.

Subscriptions

Some of the Government's most valuable information is available in subscription form. More than 600 magazines and periodicals are listed in a free quarterly catalog. For your copy, write: *Government Subscriptions,* Superintendent of Documents, Stop: SSMM, Washington, DC 20402.

Congressional Information

For information on Congressional publications, contact: Superintendent of Documents, Congressional Information Specialist, Stop: SSOI, Washington, DC 20402/202-275-3030.

Customer Information

Although the Office of the Superintendent of Documents cannot offer full research services at this time, answers to general requests for information are provided with bibliographies, catalogs, and current brochures. Call or write: Superintendent of Documents, Research and Analysis Section, Stop: SSOP, Washington, DC 20402/202-783-3238.

If you require extensive research using Government information, contact your nearest Federal Depository Library through your local library. A Federal Depository Librarian can help you obtain access to the information you need at no cost.

Customer Service

The Customer Service staff is available to assist and make appropriate adjustments. For non-subscriptions, write or call: Superintendent of Documents, Publications Service Section, Stop: SSOS, Washington, DC 20402/202-275-3050. For subscriptions, write or call: Subscription Section, Stop: SSOM, Washington, DC 20402/202-275-3054.

Deposit Accounts

To order Government publications quickly and easily, you can establish a Deposit Account with the Superintendent of Documents. A minimum deposit of $50 opens your account so you can charge future purchases. Also, you'll receive a convenient monthly statement. For more information write: Superintendent of Documents, Stop: SSOP, Washington, DC 20402/202-783-3238.

Discounts

Orders of 100 or more copies of a single publication for delivery to one address receive a 25 percent discount off the selling price. Designated bookdealers and educational bookstores are authorized a 25 percent discount on the selling price of any non-subscription offer when delivered to the bookdealer's normal place of business. For more information, write: Superintendent of Documents, Research and Analysis Section, Stop: SSOP, Washington, DC 20402/202-783-3238.

Federal Depository Libraries

This national library system is composed of nearly 1,400 public, academic, and law libraries which receive copies of most Government publications. These libraries provide free public access to their Government collections. Nearly every State is served by a Regional Depository Library which maintains a collection of all Government publications distributed by the GPO. If the library in your area does not have a document you need it will borrow the publication for you. The Depository Libraries can also give you information about the price and order numbers for most GPO publications.

For a complete listing of Depository Libraries across the country, and for the one nearest you consult the Sampler section of this book, your local library, or write: Superintendent of Documents, Library Marketer, Stop: MK, Washington, DC 20402.

International Orders
International mailing regulations require special handling, for which a surcharge of 25 percent of the domestic price will be added on all items shipped to a foreign address. Remittance in U.S. dollars must accompany every order in the form of a check drawn on a bank located in the U.S. or an International Postal Money Order made payable to the Superintendent of Documents. Orders are sent via surface mail unless otherwise requested. All orders must be in English.

Purchases
For information on prices and availability of sale publications, or to charge your orders, call 202-783-3238 between 8 and 4:30 pm (ET), Monday through Friday. Or, write: Superintendent of Documents, Washington, DC 20402. Orders must be prepaid by check, money order, or charged to your VISA, MasterCard or Superintendent of Documents Deposit Account.

Posters, Maps, Charts, Pictures, and Decals
Colorful posters, maps, and more are for sale by the Superintendent of Documents. Facsimiles of the Declaration of Independence, the Constitution, handsome NASA posters, and fascinating wildlife and marine depictions are just some of the possibilities. For a listing of what's available, contact: Superintendent of Documents, Research and Analysis Section, Stop: SSOP, Washington, DC 20402/202-783-3238.

Priority Announcement Lists
You can keep up with what's new from the Government in your area of interest by requesting Priority Announcements. For a complete listing of the nearly 100 subjects covered, contact: Superintendent of Documents, Stop: SSMM, Washington, DC 20402/202-275-3314.

Selling Printing Services to the GPO
Interested in getting a share of the Government's printing business? Last year the Government Printing Office awarded 46,000 printing contracts to commercial printers. Ask for the GPO bidders' information packet which contains everything you'll need to get started. Write or call: U.S. Government Printing Office, Procurement Support Division, Stop: PPS, Washington, DC 20401/202-275-3774.

Standing Order Service
To receive the most current editions of periodically updated Government publications without initiating a purchase order each time, request Standing Order Service. This service includes Federal laws and regulations, statistics, research reports, directories and more. There is no surcharge for this service. For a complete listing of the titles available through Standing Order Service and information on how to open your account, contact: Superintendent of Documents, Stop: SSOP, Washington, DC 20402/202-275-3082.

Tours
For a fascinating look at what is perhaps the largest printing plant in the world, call or write, U.S. Government Printing Office, Office of Legislative and Public Affairs, Stop: LL, Washington, DC 20401/202-275-3541.

Selling Ink and Paper to the GPO
For a pamphlet designed to acquaint commercial contractors with the potential for selling ink to the GPO, write or call: U.S. Government Printing Office, General Procurement Division, Washington, DC 20401/202-275-2470.

For information on selling paper to the GPO, write or call: U.S. Government Printing Office, Paper Procurement Section, Stop: MMG, Washington, DC 20401/202-275-2022.

How Can the Government Printing Office Help You?
To determine how this office can help you contact: Assistant Public Printer, Government Printing Office, North Capitol and H Streets, NW, Washington, DC 20401/202-275-2051.

Library of Congress

10 1st St. S.E., Washington, DC 20540/202-287-5108

Established: April 24, 1800
Budget: $246,917,000
Employees: 4,815

Mission: The Library's first responsibility is service to Congress; one department, the Congressional Research Service, functions exclusively for the legislative branch of the Government; its range of service has come to include the entire governmental establishment in all its branches and the public at large; it has become a national library for the United States.

Major Sources of Information

American Folklife Center
The American Folklife Center coordinates federal, state, local and private programs to support, preserve and present American folklife through such activities as the collection and maintenance of archives, scholarly research, field projects, performances, exhibitions, festivals, workshops, publications and audiovisual presentations. *Folk Life Center News* is a free quarterly newsletter on folklife activites and programs. Contact: American Folklife Center, Library of Congress, 10 1st St. S.E., Washington, DC 20540/202-287-6590.

Archive of Folk Culture
The Archive of Folk Culture maintains and administers an extensive collection of folk music and lore in published and unpublished form. It is a national repository for folk-related recordings, manuscripts and raw materials. The Archive reading room contains over 3,500 books and periodicals; a sizeable collection of magazines, newsletters, unpublished theses, and dissertations; field notes; and many textual and some musical transcriptions and recordings. Contact: Archive of Folk Culture, American Folklife Center, Library of Congress, 10 1st St. S.E., Washington, DC 20540/202-287-5510.

Books for the Blind and Physically Handicapped
Talking books and magazines, and braille books and magazines are distributed through 160 regional and subregional libraries to blind and physically handicapped residents of the United States and its territories. Information is available at public libraries throughout the United States and from the headquarters office. Contact: Library of Congress, National Library Service for the Blind and Physically Handicapped, 1291 Taylor St. N.W., Washington, DC 20542/202-287-5100.

Catalogs of Copyright Entries
The catalogs list the material registered during the period covered by each issue. They are sold as individual subscriptions by the Superintendent of Documents, Government Printing Office, Washington, DC 20402/202-783-3238.

Part 1: Nondramatic Literary Works (quarterly) $30.00 per year.
Part 2: Serials and Periodicals (semi-annually) $6.50 per year.
Part 3: Performing Arts (quarterly) $27.00 per year.
Part 4: Motion Pictures and Filmstrips (semi-annually) $7.00 per year.
Part 5: Visual Arts (excluding maps) (semi-annually) $10.00 per year.
Part 6: Maps (semi-annually) $4.75 per year.
Part 7: Sound Recordings (semi-annually) $14.00 per year.
Part 8: Renewals (semi-annually), $8.00 per year.

For additional information contact: Cataloging Division LM 400, Copyright Office, Library of Congress, Washington, DC 20540/202-287-8040.

Cataloging Data Distribution
Cataloging and bibliographic information in the

form of printed catalog cards, book catalogs, magnetic tapes, bibliographies and other technical publications are distributed to libraries and other institutions. Kits describing the procedure for ordering materials are available from the Library of Congress, Customer Service, Washington, DC 20401/202-287-6100.

Cataloging-in-Publication
Library of Congress card numbers for new publications are assigned by the Cataloging-in-Publication Office. This program is in cooperation with American publishers to print cataloging information in current books. Contact: Cataloging-in-Publication, Library of Congress, Washington, DC 20540/202-287-6372.

Center for the Book
The Center for the Book works closely with other organizations to explore important issues in the book and educational communities, to encourage reading, and to encourage research about books and about reading. Its goal is to serve as a useful catalyst by bringing together authors, publishers, librarians, booksellers, educators, scholars, and readers to discuss common concerns and work toward the solution of common problems. Four committees reflect its primary concerns: television and the printed word, reading development, the international role of the book and publishing. Contact: The Center for the Book, First and Independence St. S.E., Washington, DC 20540/202-287-5221.

Central Intelligence Agency Reports
The Library of Congress distributes CIA reports that the agency has released to the public. The reports detail foreign government structures, trade patterns, economic conditions and industries. Orders must be prepaid or charged to a standing account at the Library of Congress. The Photoduplication Service can also provide a list of CIA reports available; cost is $8.00. For more information and to order reports, contact: Photoduplication Service, Library of Congress, Washington, DC 20540/202-287-5650.

Children's Reference Center
The Center's reference librarians and bibliographies serve as consultants in contemporary, rare, and foreign books to scholars, writers, teachers, librarians, illustrators, and others "serving those who serve children." Lists and scholarly bibliographies are prepared. *Children's Literature: A Guide to Reference Sources* first supplement $13.00, second supplement $12.00 are all sold by the Superintendent of Documents, Government Printing Office, Washington, DC 20402/202-783-3238. For additional information contact: The Children's Center, National Programs, Library of Congress, Washington, DC 20540/202-287-5535.

Color Slides
Color slides featuring the Library's buildings and special items from its collections are also available. Inquiries should be directed to the Library of Congress, Photoduplication Service, 10 1st St. S.E., Washington, DC 20540/202-287-5650.

Compendium of Copyright Office Practices
This compendium is an office manual intended as a general guide for the Copyright Office. It is a condensed digest of office practices in individual cases representing common fact situations. It is available for $35 and includes two semi-annual supplements for an indeterminate period. Available from the Superintendent of Documents, Government Printing Office, Washington, DC 20402/202-783-3238. For additional information contact: Copyright Office, Certifications and Documents, Library of Congress, 1st St. and Independence Ave. S.E., Washington, DC 20540/202-287-6800.

Computer Data Bases
The files listed below may be queried by the public from the computer catalog center or from terminals in the library's reading rooms. Limited searching may be conducted in response to written or telephone inquiries; contact: General Reading Room Division, Library of Congress, Washington, DC 20540/202-287-5522.

BIBL (Bibliographic Information File)
The BIBL file contains references to topical periodical articles, pamphlets, Government Printing Office publications, U.N. documents, and interest/lobby group publications. The Library Services Division of the Congressional Research Service decides which materials to include in the file. Typically, a citation lists the author's name, article title, title of publication, volume, date, date and pagination for periodicals or place of publication, publisher, and the date for monographs, as well as annotations and subject headings and terms (descriptors).

NRCM (National Referral Center Master List)
The NRCM file contains data on organizations qualified and willing to provide information on a large number of scientific and technical topics and issues of interest to social scientists. Information provided usually includes: name of organization, mailing address, location, telephone number, areas of interest, holdings (special collections, data bases), publications, and dissemination services. Researchers should request descriptions of all organizations in the data base related to their field of interest.

LCCC (Library of Congress Computerized Catalog)
The LCCC file contains nearly 3 million records

representing books in the library's MARC (Machine-Readable Cataloging) data base, English-language books printed or catalogued since 1968, French-language books since 1975; additional language titles are being added to the file. A bibliographic reference from this file usually includes the author's name, monograph title, place of publication, publisher, date, descriptive annotations, subject headings, Library of Congress and Dewey Decimal System classification numbers, Library of Congress Card Number, and the International Standard Book Number (ISBN). A free LCCC printout of all publications (since 1968) in your interest area may be obtained from the General Reading Rooms Division, LJ 144, Library of Congress, Washington, DC 20540/202-287-5522.

MUMS (Multiple Use MARC System)
The MUMS file includes the LCCC file as well as maps and serial titles.

CG94, CG95, CG96 (Legislative Information Files for the 94th, 95th and 96th Congresses)
The publication entitled *Digest of General Public Bills and Resolutions,* popularly known as the *Bill Digest,* provides the basic content of these files. In addition to information such as bill content, sponsorship, cosponsorship, and action on a bill, including the most recent action by either chamber of Congress, the files provide the unique number assigned to a bill, the public law number, information concerning the existence of identical bills in both chambers, the revised text of a bill, and other information. Access to these files may be obtained through the Bill Status Office; see "Capitol Hill" section of this volume for additional information.

Congressional Research Service
The Library's primary role is to serve as the research and reference arm of Congress. Through the Congressional Research Service, a separate department, the Library furnishes legislators with the information they need to govern effectively. The Service answers more than 300,000 Congressional inquiries per year, ranging from a simple question on the population of California to an in-depth study on future energy sources. In addition, the Service prepares bill digests, summaries of major legislation, and other tools to help members and their committees stay abreast of the daily flow of legislation.

The work is performed by a staff of over 800—ranging from civil engineers and oceanographers to labor arbitrators and experts on Soviet rocketry. Their most important charge is to provide objective, unbiased information. Services are restricted to Congressional Representatives and their staff. Contact: your Congressional Representative.

Congressional Serial System—Law Library
All Senate and House documents and reports since 1980, indexed numerically with each Congress, can be viewed and studied. Contact: Library of Congress, Washington, DC 20540/202-287-5079.

Copyright
All copyrightable works, whether published or unpublished, are subject to a single system of statute protection which gives the copyright owner the exclusive right to reproduce the copyrighted work in copies or phonorecords and distribute them to the public by sale, rental, lease or lending. Works of authorship include books, periodicals, and other literary works, musical compositions, song lyrics, dramas and dramatico-musical compositions, pantomines and choreographic works, motion pictures and other audiovisual works, and sound recordings. The Library provides information on copyright registration procedures and copyright card catalogs which cover 16 million works that have been registered since 1870. For general information contact: Copyright Office, Library of Congress, LM, Room 401, Washington, DC 20540/202-287-6540.

Copyright Source
The Copyright office will research the copyright you need and send you the information by mail. Requests must be in writing and you must specify exactly what it is you need to know. Contact: Copyright Office, Reference and Bibliographic Section, Library of Congress, Washington, DC 20559/202-387-8700.

CRS Issue Briefs and Reports
Congressional Research Service reports are detailed accounts of issues large and small, foreign and domestic, social and political, etc. An index to these reports is available through your Congressman's office. CRS also publishes and records on cassette tapes hundreds of major issue briefs designed to keep members of Congress informed on timely issues. These briefs, written primarily for the layperson, provide a good deal of background information and are updated daily. Free hard copies may be obtained through your Congressman's office.

Each month, CRS publishes *UPDATE,* a supplement to the *CRS Review. UPDATE* includes a list of new and updated issue briefs of current interest. Briefs that are no longer of intense public or congressional interest are listed in the *Archived Issue Brief List.* Both are available only through your Congressman's office.

Following is a list of issue briefs that were current in late 1985. IB refers to issue brief; MB, mini-brief; and AB, audio brief. All briefs listed below can only be obtained through your Congressional Representative's office.

Issue Brief Menu

AGRICULTURE AND FOOD

Africa Famine Relief Initiatives: A Comparison of Two Proposals [01/10/85] 85-507 F

Agricultural Policies of the EEC: Selected References, 1982–1984 [03/20/84] L0257

Agricultural Policies: Selected References, 1983–1984 [01/18/85] L0389

Agricultural Policy Issues: An Introduction [01/11/84] AB50098

Agricultural Trade: Selected References, 1983–1984 [01/85] 85-568 L

Agriculture and Food: An Alphabetical Microthesaurus of Terms Selected from the Legislative Indexing Vocabulary [12/12/84] 84-820 L

Agriculture: Price Supports and the 1985 Farm Bill IP0295A

Agriculture: The Farm Financial Situation IP0323A

Agriculture: The Payment-in-Kind (PIK) Program; Preliminary Bibliography, 1983–1984 [04/05/84] L0271

Antibiotics in Animal Feeds: Implications for Human Health; Selected References, 1979–1984 [01/08/85] L0397

Aspartame: An Artificial Sweetener [03/23/84] 84-649 SPR

Assistance to Agricultural Producers for Disaster Caused by Plant Pests and Animal Diseases [11/23/84] 84-805 ENR

Barter of Surplus Agricultural Commodities for Strategic and Critical Materials [01/25/85] IB83175

A Brief Look at Federal Milk Marketing Orders [03/09/84] 84-581 ENR

Constitutional Questions: Amending Federal Law to Prohibit Application of State Sales Taxes to Food Purchases by Beneficiaries under the Food Stamp and WIC Programs [01/30/85] 85-551 A

Critical Issues in Agricultural Research, Extension and Teaching Programs [10/31/84] CP 1835

Critical Issues in Agricultural Research, Extension, and Teaching Programs [10/31/84] 84-774 ENR

The Dairy Diversion Program: Should it be Extended [02/19/85] 85-572 ENR

The Dairy Program: Twenty Questions [01/25/85] 85-557 ENR

The Development and Current Status of Federal Farmland Retention Policy [11/21/84] 85-21 ENR

Effect of the Treasury Tax Reform Proposal on Farm Income Taxation [01/30/85] 85-543 E

The Effects of Federal Income Tax Policy on U.S. Agriculture [12/84] CP 1837

Fact Sheet on U.S. Agricultural Exports [01/09/85] 85-505 ENR

Famine in Africa IP0061F

The Famine in Ethiopia: Editorial Commentary on the Relief Efforts [01/25/85] 85-530 L

Farmers Home Administration: Farm Credit Policies and Issues [01/25/85] IB85025

Farm Financial Situation and Credit Problems: Congressional Concerns [02/14/85] IB84126

Farm Income and Debt: Editorial Commentary [02/28/85] 85-563 L

Farm Income and Debt: Selected References, 1982–1985 [02/20/85] L0413'

Federal Farm Programs: A Primer [12/84] 84-232 ENR

Food Banks and the Distribution of Surplus Food [10/05/82] AB50064

Food for Peace, 1954–1984 Major Changes in Legislation [01/20/85] 85-526 ENR

Food Labeling [11/14/84] IB80055

Food Needs in Africa: Selected References, 1982–1984 [02/22/85] L0420

Food Safety and Risk Assessment: Selected References, 1981–1984 [01/02/85] L0396

Food Safety Policy: Scientific and Regulatory Issues [11/13/84] IB83158

Food Safety: Selected References, 1979–1983 [09/23/83] L0137(REV)

The FY85 Farm Bill: Wheat and Feed Grains [02/04/85] IB85033

Glossary of Agricultural Terms [05/84] 84-84 ENR

How the Food Stamp Program Works [11/01/84] 84-190 EPW

Hunger in the United States IP0277H

International Coffee Agreement [12/04/84] 84-224 ENR

International Fund for Agricultural Development (IFAD) [02/13/85] 85-576 ENR

Organic Farming: Legislative Proposals in the 98th Congress [01/24/85] IB83186

Overview of Agriculture Legislation in the 98th Congress [01/28/85] IB83153

Primer on P.L. 480–Program History, Description, and Operations: A Brief Compilation of Explanatory Documents [11/13/84] 84-803 ENR

Proposals for Supplemental Appropriations for African Famine Relief [02/85] 85-558 ENR

The Reagan Administration's Response to Barter [05/23/84] 84-648 ENR

Review of Long-Term Agricultural and Food Policy Legislation; Summary of Hearings Held by the House Committee on Agriculture, February 28 and 29, 1984 [03/30/84] 84-687 ENR

Selected Reports Available from the Food and Agriculture Section [12/84] 84-817 ENR

A Statistical Profile of the Dairy Sector [12/03/84] 84-811 ENR

Sulfites: Food Preservatives [01/09/85] 85-518 SPR

Third World Population Trends [10/24/82] AB50070

U.S. Commodity Surpluses and Food Aid Needs in Selected Regions [01/01/85] 85-574 ENR

USDA's Commodity Inventory [12/03/84] 84-812 ENR

U.S. Grain Sales to the U.S.S.R. [02/06/85] IB75070

U.S. Sugar Price Support Policy Issues: Looking Ahead to the 1985 Farm Bill [07/18/84] 84-689 ENR

Why U.S. Agricultural Exports Have Declined in the 1980s [10/29/84] 84-223 ENR

World Hunger: Selected References [09/05/84] L0337

The 1985 Farm Bill: An Overview [02/22/85] IB85004

The 1985 Farm Bill: Dairy [02/12/85] IB85006

The 1985 Farm Bill: Soil Conservation Issues [02/16/85] IB85016

BUDGET AND GOVERNMENT SPENDING

Balanced Budget Issues IP0011B

The Balanced Budget Proposal: Some Macroeconomic Implications [01/25/85] MB79229

Balanced Budgets: Selected References, 1982–1984 [09/14/84] L0344

Block Grants IP0157B

Block Grants: A Guide to Information Sources [12/03/81] R005

Budget Deficits and Solutions: Editorial Commentary [01/25/85] 85-528 L

Budget Deficits: Causes, Effects and Some Remedial Options [01/06/85] IB84005

Budget Documents Primer [02/02/84] 84-516 L

The Budget for Fiscal Year 1985 IP0285B

Budget for Fiscal Year 1986 IP0322B

Budget Process IP0012B

The Budget Process: 98th Congress [03/29/83] AB50079

Defense Spending IP0028D

Defense Spending: Waste, Fraud, and Abuse IP0279D

The Deficit Reduction Act of 1984 IP0302D

Deficits: A Growing Concern IP0274D

Deficits and Government Spending: Overviews [08/84] VU84011

Do Deficits Influence the Level of Interest Rates [12/28/84] 85-14 E

Economic Policy and Public Finance Issues: Bibliographic Background [12/84] BB04

The Economics of Balancing the Federal Budget [01/14/85] MB84221

The Federal Budget for Fiscal Year 1985 [01/16/85] IB84071

The Federal Budget Process: Selected References [11/84] 84-192 L

Federal Debt and Budget Deficits: Selected References, 1983–1984 [09/11/84] L0345

Federal Debt: Background and Statistics IP0275F

The Federal Debt: Who Bears Its Burdens? [02/05/85] MB84233

Federal Procurement and Contracting-Out Issues [12/20/84] IB82067

Federal Spending Reduction Proposals: Selected References, 1984–1985 [02/19/85] L0414

The Grace Commission IP0281G

Grants and Aid Seminar [04/14/79] AB50025

Lotteries: Proposals for a National Lottery IP0326L

Perspectives on Congressional Budgeting [10/06/83] AB50091

Social Security and the Federal Budget (CRS Review) [02/85] 85-1210 FEB

Summary and Legislative History of Public Law 98-473: Continuing Appropriations for Fiscal Year 1985 (H.J. Res. 648) [12/19/84] 85-12 GOV

Tax Reform Act of 1984 IP0302D

Two United States Deficits: Budgetary and International [01/07/85] AB50119

Waste and Fraud in Government: Preliminary Bibliography, 1981–1984 [08/16/84] L0326

1986 Budget Perspectives: Federal Spending for the Human Resource Programs [02/22/85] 85-52 EPW

BUSINESS, INDUSTRY, AND CONSUMER AFFAIRS

America's Steel Industry: Modernizing to Compete / [04/23/84] 84-786 E

AT&T Divestiture: Restructuring the U.S. Domestic Telephone Industry IP0257A

Comparison of 98th Congress Bills Proposing Enterprise

Zones, Revitalization Areas, or Job Expansion Areas [07/30/84] 84-706 E

Constitutionality of Enforcing Proposed District of Columbia Automobile Lemon Law Against Manufacturers and Sellers Outside the District of Columbia [12/03/84] 84-856 A

Consumer Price Index: Background and Current Data [01/29/85] MB83246

Corporate Mergers: Selected References, 1980–1984 [03/28/84] L0268

Enterprise Zones IP0135E

Foreign Corrupt Practices Act of 1977: Time for Change? [12/27/84] IB81105

The Fortune 500: Names, Addresses, and Offices of the 500 Largest Industrial Corporations in the U.S. Ranked by Sales in 1983 [06/12/84] 84-113 C

Impact of Mergers and Related Phenomena on Shareholders [11/22/84] 84-199 E

Industrial Innovation and High Technology Development: Selected References, 1982–1984 [12/19/84] L0390

Industrial Innovation: The Debate Over Government Policy [02/20/85] IB84004

Industrial Policy IP0254I

Industrial Policy: A Guide to Sources of Information [03/22/84] R012

Industrial Policy in Foreign Countries: Selected References, 1983–1984 [04/22/84] L0273

Industrial Policy in the United States: Selected References, 1983–1984 [04/01/84] L0260

Industry and Labor Issues: Bibliographic Background [12/84] BB11

Legal Analysis of the Product Liability Act (S. 100, 99th Congress) as Introduced [02/12/85] 85-587 A

Leveraged Buyouts: Selected References, 1975–1984 [06/18/84] L0292

Mergers and Acquisitions: A Glossary of Terms [11/23/84] 84-816 E

Products Liability: A Legal Overview [11/09/84] IB77021

Products Liability: Some Legal Issues [11/01/84] 84-189 A

Promoting Economic Recovery [02/18/83] AB50071

Proposed Corporation for Small Business Investment Charter Act: Pro-Con Analysis [10/31/84] 84-791 E

Prospects for the Deregulation of International Airline Markets [11/30/84] 84-213 E

Sex Discrimination in Insurance (ARCHIVED—08/08/84) [06/18/84] IB83184

Small Business: An Overview IP0181S

Small Business: Perceived Economic Problems [12/20/84] IB84141

Some Antitrust Litigation Involving Professional Sports Leagues [01/10/85] 85-531 A

Trade Deficits and Balance of Payments IP0320T

The U.S. Auto Industry: The Situation in the Eighties [01/18/85] IB81054

The U.S. Copper Industry's Declining Competitiveness in the International Economy [02/11/85] IB84129

CIVIL RIGHTS AND LIBERTIES

Abortion IP0001A

Abortion: Judicial and Legislative Control [11/29/84] IB74019

Adoptees' Right to Receive Medical Information on their Birth Parents [12/24/84] 84-848 A

Affirmative Action [05/20/82] AB50054

Awards of Attorneys' Fees Against the United States: The Equal Access to Justice Act, as Amended in 1984 [10/18/84] 84-851 A

Background Information on Equal Access Statute [09/26/84] 84-842 A

Black and Hispanic Appointees in the First Reagan Administration [12/31/84] IB84090

Busing for School Desegregation [02/11/85] IB81010

Busing for School Integration: Selected References, 1980–1984 [10/03/84] L0372

Circumstances under which Grandparents may Petition the Court for Visitation Rights with their Grandchildren [01/24/85] 85-549 A

The Civil Rights Act of 1984 [01/11/85] IB84115

Civil Rights Act of 1984 and Affected Legislation: Preliminary Bibliography, 1972–1984 [08/05/84] L0315

Civil Rights Issues: Bibliographic Background [12/84] BB01

Civil Rights Legislation: Responses to Grove City College v. Bell [02/12/85] IB85048

Civil Rights Legislation: Responses to Grove City College v. Bell IP0324C

The Constitutional Rights of Mental Patients [02/13/85] 85-585 A

Equal Rights Amendment IP0037E

Equal Rights for Women [02/22/85] IB83077

Federal Civil Rights Laws: A Sourcebook [11/84] CP 1822

Legal Right of an Adopted Child to Learn the Identity of His or Her Birth Parents [11/30/84] 84-220 A

Legislative Activity in the 98th Congress Concerning Religious Activities in the Public Schools [10/18/84] 84-843 A

Overview of Recent Judicial Decisions on the Constitutional Right of Mental Patients to Refuse Treatment [01/24/85] 85-548 A

Pay Equity: The Comparable Worth Issue IP0283P

Pension Equity IP0308P

Pornography Depicting Abuse of Women as a Form of Sex Discrimination: A Constitutional Analysis [12/14/84] 84-862 A

Prayer and Religion in U.S. Public Schools: Selected References, 1973–1984 [09/10/84] L0330

Restricting the Sale of "Adult" Video Cassettes to Minors: A Legal Analysis [01/22/85] 85-552 A

Scanlon v. Atascadero State Hospital: Section 504 of the Rehabilitation Act and Eleventh Amendment Sovereign Immunity [12/03/84] 84-849 A

School Desegregation: Selected References, 1978–1984 [01/25/85] L0375

The School Prayer Controversy: Pro-Con Arguments [01/14/85] IB84081

SEC Registration Requirements of Investment Newsletters [10/09/84] 84-844 A

Sex Discrimination and the United States Supreme Court: Developments in the Law [08/84] 84-151 A

A Summary of the Buckley Amendment (Family Educational and Privacy Rights Act) 20 U.S.C. SEC. 1232G (1982) [10/10/84] 84-845 A

The Voting Rights Act of 1965 as Amended [11/16/84] 84-203 GOV

COMMUNICATIONS

AT&T Divestiture: Restructuring the U.S. Domestic Telephone Industry IP0257A

A Brief Overview of Cable Television Law [09/13/84] 84-853 A

Cable Television: Selected References, 1983–1984 [10/19/84] L0377

Cable TV IP0104C

International Data Flow Issues [02/05/85] IB81040

Legality of Receiving Satellite Signals Carrying Cable Programs [12/14/84] 84-846 A

The Legislator as User of Information Technology [12/07/84] 84-170 S

Telephone Industry: Restructuring and Federal Activity [11/14/84] IB81150

ECONOMIC CONDITIONS

Consumer Price Index and the Rate of Inflation IP0025C

Economic Condition of Blacks in America: Decline, Stagnation, or Progress [02/24/84] AB50101

Economic Conditions: Background and Prospects IP0206E

The Economic Expansion: Continued Slowdown or Renewed Growth? [02/04/85] MB84234

The Economic Outlook: A Comparison of Econometric Forecasts [01/10/85] MB83244

Economic Policy and Public Finance Issues: Bibliographic Background [12/84] BB04

Interest Rates IP0107I

Interest Rates: Selected References, 1980–1984 [11/01/84] L0381

Interest Rates: Why Have They Declined Since Mid-1984 and What Does It Imply For Future Economic Activity? [02/20/85] IB85037

The Mexican Economic Crisis [04/25/84] AB50103

The Misery Index [01/28/85] MB84232

Reaganomics and Family Economic Status: Overviews [06/84] VU8406

Selected Economic Indicators [02/15/85] MB81233

Will Our Current Economic Recovery Falter? (CRS Review) [01/85] 85-1119 JAN

Will the Current Economic Upswing Stall? Economic Prospects for 1985 [01/29/85] IB84140

EDUCATION

The Arts and Humanities: Current Federal Funding Issues [02/08/85] IB82026

Bilingual Education: Federal Policy Issues [02/08/85] IB83131

Busing for School Integration: Selected References, 1980–1984 [10/03/84] L0372

Carl D. Perkins Vocational Education Act [02/21/85] IB85036

Chapter 2 Education Block Grants [02/21/85] IB79021

Civil Rights Act of 1984 and Affected Legislation: Preliminary Bibliography, 1972–1984 [08/05/84] L0315

Civil Rights Legislation: Responses to Grove City College v. Bell IP0324C

Computers in Elementary and Secondary Schools: Federal Role [01/15/85] IB84111

Educational Reform: Reports, Responses, and Commentary; Selected References, 1981–1984 [07/02/84] L0295

Education: An Alphabetical Microthesaurus of Terms Selected from the Legislative Indexing Vocabulary [01/31/85] 85-544 L

Education and the 98th Congress: Overview [12/21/84] IB83055

Education and the 99th Congress: Overview [02/21/85] IB85023

Education: Challenges in the 1980s [11/02/84] MB79263

Education for Disadvantaged Children: Federal Aid [02/20/85] IB81142

Education: Funding Issues IP0199E

Education Funding Issues: FY85 and FY86 [02/12/85] IB85040

Education: FY84 and FY85 Funding Issues [11/16/84] IB84050

Education in America: Reports on Its Condition and Recommendations For Change [02/11/85] IB83106

Education of the Handicapped [02/13/85] IB78040

Education: Overviews [04/84] VU8403

Education: Ratings of Colleges and Universities IP0312E

Education Reports and Reform Efforts IP0256E

The Education Reports: Implications for Congressional Action [10/26/83] AB50094

Federal Funds for School Construction, FY 1981 through FY 1985 [12/04/84] 84-834 EPW

Federal School Construction Authorizations: Selected Programs Administered by the Department of Education [12/04/84] 84-833 EPW

Financial Aid to Undergraduate Students IP0042F

Future Status of the Department of Education [02/11/85] IB81021

Guaranteed Student Loans [11/14/84] IB82091

Guide to Selected Federal Assistance Programs for Undergraduate Students [11/15/84] 84-197 EPW

Handicapped Education Act (P.L. 94-142) IP0053H

The Higher Education Act of 1965, as Amended through P.L. 98-558: Summary of Provisions [11/30/84] 84-826 EPW

Higher Education Act: Reauthorization Issues [11/06/84] IB84070

Higher Education: Conditions and Issues in the 1980s [10/18/84] MB83227

Impact Aid For Education: Public Laws 81-874 and 81-815 [02/08/85] IB85018

Impact of Budget Changes in Major Education Programs During the Reagan Administration [12/31/84] 84-838 EPW

Leadership in Educational Administration Development Act of 1984: A Summary of Provisions [12/07/84] 84-831 EPW

Merit Pay for Teachers IP0260M

The Pell Grant Program: 99th Congress [02/01/85] IB85038

Potential Implications of Funding Reductions for Programs Administered by the Department of Education [01/14/85] 85-521 EPW

Prayer and Religion in U.S. Public Schools: Selected References, 1973–1984 [09/10/84] L0330

Private Elementary and Secondary Education: Providing Federal Aid [02/04/85] IB81049

Prohibition of Sex Discrimination in Education: Title IX [11/23/84] IB84091

Resume Writing IP0108R

School Prayer IP0086S

Sex Discrimination in Education: Title IX IP0166S

Standardized Educational Test Scores IP0294S

Student Financial Aid and Draft Registration Compliance [01/09/85] MB83213

Student Financial Aid: FY85 Budget [02/11/85] IB84047

Student Financial Aid Programs: FY86 Budget [02/21/85] IB85056

Student Loan Programs (Federal): Defaults [02/01/85] IB75017

Study Abroad IP0141S

Summary and Analysis of Title VII of the Human Services Reauthorization Act of 1984 (P.L. 98-558), Legislation to Authorize a Carl D. Perkins Scholarship Program and a National Talented Teacher Fellowship [11/05/84] 84-827 EPW

A Summary of "Involvement in Learning: Realizing the Potential of American Higher Education; the Final Report of the Study Group on the Conditions of Excellence in American Higher Education" [12/28/84] 85-506 EPW

Summary of the Adult Education Act, as Amended by the Education Amendments of 1984 (P.L. 98-511) [11/05/84] 84-829 EPW

Title III of the Higher Education Act: FY 1986 Budget Proposal [02/20/85] 85-573 EPW

Town of Burlington v. Department of Education, Commonwealth of Massachusetts: Private School Placement under the Education for All Handicapped Children Act [02/04/85] 85-583 A

Tuition Tax Credits [02/08/85] IB81075

Tuition Tax Credits IP0129T

ELECTIONS

Campaign Finance IP0014C

Campaign Financing/Public Financing [01/07/85] IB73017

Campaign Financing: 98th Congress [06/29/83] AB50085

Delegate Committees in Presidential Elections [02/04/85] 85-550 A

Election Campaigns and the Media: Selected References, 1976–1984 [03/16/84] L0259

Election Night Projections: Selected References, 1981–1984 [06/20/84] L0288

Election Process Issues: Bibliographic Background [12/84] BB05

Electoral College IP0031E

Estimation of Campaign Funds that Might be Generated under Proposed Campaign Finance Reform Legislation [04/17/84] CP 1847

The Fairness Doctrine and the Equal Opportunities Doctrine in Political Broadcasting [01/07/85] IB82087

Federal Election Commission [01/23/85] IB81104

Hatch Act: Selected References, 1976–1984 [06/05/84] L0287

Independent Expenditures in Federal Elections [12/07/84] 84-858 A

Political Action Committees (PACs) IP0196P

Political Action Committees: Selected References, 1980–1984 [09/10/84] L0349

Using as a Model the Recently Negotiated Agreement with Sweden [05/11/84] 84-631 S

Wind Energy [12/26/84] IB80091

ENVIRONMENTAL PROTECTION

The Accident in Bhopal, India: Implications for U.S. Hazardous Chemical Policies [01/22/85] IB85022

Acid Rain IP0134A

Acid Rain: A Dialogue [08/25/80] AB50037

Acid Rain: A Guide to Sources of Information [04/19/84] R013

Acid Rain: Does It Contribute to Forest Decline? [01/24/85] MB84204

Acid Rain: Issues in the 98th Congress [01/18/85] IB83016

Acid Rain: Issues in the 99th Congress [02/05/85] IB85008

Acid Rain: Overviews, Editorials, and Public Opinion Polls [12/84] VU84016

Acid Rain: Selected References, 1983–1984 [06/05/84] L0291(REV)

Air Pollution: Clean Air Act (P.L. 95-95) IP0008A

Clean Air Act: A Guide to Congressional Publications, 1981–1984 [11/21/84] 84-210 L

Clean Air Act: A Guide to Information Sources [08/31/81] R003

Clean Air Act: An Overview [02/11/85] IB83005

Clean Air Act: Can Nonattainment be Cured? [02/11/85] MB84201

Clean Air Act: Preliminary Bibliography, 1982–1984 [09/10/84] L0343

Clean Water Act: Selected References, 1983–1984 [08/10/84] L0313

Clean Water: EPA Municipal Construction Grants Program [01/08/85] IB83013

Clean Water: Section 404 Dredge and Fill Permit Program [02/20/85] IB83011

Comparison of the U.S. Environmental Protection Agency's Groundwater Protection Strategies [02/08/84] CP 1831

Emergency Response and Training for Hazardous Materials Transportation Accidents (CRS Review) [01/85] 85-1121 JAN

Endangered Species IP0192E

Environmental Issues: Bibliographic Background [12/84] BB07

Environmental Protection IP0036E

Environmental Protection Agency Programs: Congressional Activities [01/02/85] IB83018

Environmental Protection Issues of the 99th Congress [01/85] 85-517 ENR

EPA Authority under Existing Law to Regulate Underground Storage Tanks for Petroleum Products [04/09/84] CP 1833

Funding Groundwater Activities [04/17/84] CP 1832

The Global Environment [10/26/82] AB50063

Groundwater Contamination and Protection [01/28/85] IB83091

Groundwater Contamination: Selected References, 1982–1984 [03/22/84] L0265

Hazardous Air Pollutants: A Review of the Statutory Requirements and Their Implementation [02/11/85] MB84212

Hazardous Waste IP0094H

Hazardous Waste Control: RCRA Reauthorization [02/11/85] IB83007

Hazardous Waste Issues: Selected References, 1983–1984 [01/85] 85-540 L

Hazardous Wastes: A Guide to Sources of Information [09/26/83] R009

Indoor Air Quality and Health Impacts of Energy Conservation: Some Congressional Options [01/03/85] IB83074

Low-Level Ionizing Radiation: Preliminary Bibliography, 1978–1982 [05/16/84] L0281

Pesticides Regulation: Current Issues [01/15/85] IB83095

Picking up the Tab: The Cost of Acid Rain Legislation in Indiana [10/15/84] 84-828 ENR

Radioactive Waste Disposal: Selected References, 1981–1984 [11/01/84] L0380

Safe Drinking Water [01/28/85] IB83006

Selected CRS Reports on Environmental Protection [01/85] 85-511 L

The Status of Environmental Economics: The 1984 Update [11/84] CP 1827

Superfund: Hazardous Waste Cleanup [02/21/85] IB83064

Superfund: How Many Sites? How Much Money? [02/06/85] IB85034

Toxic Chemicals: Environmental and Health Issues [05/03/84] AB50104

The Toxic Substances Control Act: Implementation Issues [02/11/85] IB83190

Toxic Waste Incineration at Sea [02/21/85] MB83232

Underground Injection of Wastes [01/28/85] MB83238

Water Pollution: Clean Water Act Revision (P.L. 95-217) IP0154W

Water Quality: Addressing the Nonpoint Pollution Problem [02/20/85] MB83241

Water Quality: Implementing the Clean Water Act [02/20/85] IB83030

FINANCIAL AND FISCAL AFFAIRS

Can the Interest Cost on the Federal Debt be Reduced? Possibilities and Consequences [01/29/85] MB84216

Federal Debt: Background and Statistics IP0275F

The Federal Reserve Discount Window: Selected References [09/20/84] 84-771 E

The Federal Reserve, Interest Rates, and the Economic Expansion [07/27/84] 84-158 E

Federal Reserve System IP0105F

Financial Deregulation IP0291F

Financial Deregulation: Selected References, 1983–1984 [11/30/84] L0382

Financial Institutions' Competition and Regulation: Current Legislative Issues [02/13/85] IB85020

Interest Rates IP0107I

International Debt Problems: Background, Statistics, Proposed Solutions IP0234I

Monetary Policy: Selected References, 1982–1984 [04/20/84] L0272

Rising Interest Rates and the Economic Expansion: Can They Co-Exist [12/05/84] 84-818 E

Secondary Markets for Financial Instruments: Activity in the 98th Congress [12/14/84] 84-212 E

Structural Deficits: Definition and Measurement [02/15/85] MB84217

U.S. Banks and the People's Republic of China [12/31/84] 84-840 E

FOREIGN POLICY AND ASSISTANCE PROGRAMS

Administration Reports on Defense and Foreign Policy Requested by Congress [01/24/85] 85-23 F

Afghanistan after Five Years: Status of the Conflict, the Afghan Resistance and the U.S. Role [01/85] 85-20 F

Africa Famine Relief Initiatives: A Comparison of Two Proposals [01/10/85] 85-507 F

Arms Sales: U.S. Policy IP0214A

Buy American Requirements under Foreign Assistance Legislation and a Summary of Buy American and Buy American-type Laws [01/14/85] 85-533 A

The Caribbean Area: Selected References, 1980–1984 [08/10/84] L0320

Caribbean Basin Initiative IP0190C

The Caribbean Basin Initiative and U.S. Economic Relations with the Caribbean Area: Selected References, 1981–1984 [08/10/84] L0319

Central America and the Caribbean: A Guide to Sources of Information [06/04/82] R008

Central America and U.S. Foreign Assistance: Issues for Congress in 1984 [02/21/85] IB84075

Central America: A Regional Overview IP0271C

Central America: Overviews [06/84] VU8408

Central America: Preliminary Bibliography, 1982–1984 [11/26/84] L0364

Central America: U.S. Economic and Military Assistance IP0288C

China-U.S.-Taiwan Relations IP0021C

China-U.S.-Taiwan Relations: Selected References, 1980–1984 [09/06/84] L0333

China-U.S. Relations: Issues for Congress [01/28/85] IB84135

Congress and Foreign Policy: Selected References [07/05/84] L0298

Cyprus: Turkish Cypriot "Statehood" and Prospects for Settlement [02/13/85] IB84062

Economic Policy Initiative for Africa [03/09/84] CP 1846

El Salvador IP0121E

El Salvador: Overviews, Editorials, and Public Opinion Polls [11/84] VU84015

El Salvador: Policy Issues for Congress [02/08/85] IB83051

El Salvador: Preliminary Bibliography, 1981–1984 [11/05/84] L0334

Ethiopian Food Situation: International Response [02/25/85] IB85061

Famine in Africa IP0061F

The Famine in Ethiopia: Editorial Commentary on the Relief Efforts [01/25/85] 85-530 L

The Fighting in Cambodia: Issues for U.S. Policy [02/01/85] 85-43 F

Food for Peace, 1954–1984 Major Changes in Legislation [01/20/85] 85-526 ENR

Foreign Aid IP0044F

Foreign Aid: Congressional Action in 1984 [02/21/85] IB84078

Foreign Policy: Congress and the President IP0297F

Foreign Policy Issues: Bibliographic Background [12/84] BB08

The Gandhi Assassination: Implications for India and U.S.-Indian Relations (CRS Review) [01/85] 85-1110 JAN

Genocide Convention [01/10/85] IB74129

Genocide Convention IP0170G

Guatemala: Selected References, 1980–1984 [09/05/84] L0335

The Gulf Cooperation Council [11/30/84] 85-516 F

Honduras: Selected References, 1981–1984 [09/05/84] L0336

Honduras: U.S. Military Activities [01/16/85] IB84134

Hong Kong: Issues for U.S. Policy [12/28/84] IB85015

Human Rights and U.S. Foreign Policy IP0187H

India: Political Trends and Issues; Selected References, 1978–1984 [11/13/84] L0383

International Court of Justice—Case concerning Military and Paramilitary Activities in and against Nicaragua (Nicaragua v. United States) [02/11/85] 85-586 A

The Iran-Iraq War: Implications for U.S. Policy [02/05/85] IB84016

Israeli-American Relations [01/29/85] IB82008

The Israeli Economy [02/22/85] IB84138

Japan-U.S. Political and Military Relations: Selected References, 1981–1984 [08/10/84] L0318

Japan-U.S. Relations [01/16/85] IB81026

Lebanon in Crisis IP0136L

Lebanon: Overviews [04/84] VU8404

The Middle East: A Guide to Information Sources [01/84] R011

Middle East Peace Proposals [01/09/85] IB82127

Middle East Peace Proposals IP0176M

The Monroe Doctrine and U.S. Policy Options for the Western Hemisphere [12/12/84] 84-225 F

The Monroe Doctrine and U.S. Policy Options for the Western Hemisphere (CRS Review) [02/85] 85-1202 FEB

Namibia: United Nations Negotiations for Independence/U.S. Interests [02/22/85] IB79073

The National Endowment for Democracy [02/12/85] IB83107

Nicaragua IP0073N

Nicaragua: Conditions and Issues for U.S. Policy [02/20/85] IB82115

Nicaragua: Overviews, Editorials, and Public Opinion Polls [01/85] VU8501

Nuclear Energy: Congressional Consideration of the Proposed Agreement for U.S. Nuclear Cooperation with China [02/11/85] IB84102

Nuclear Non-Proliferation Treaty Conference of 1985 [02/04/85] IB85009

Philippine Internal Conditions: Consequences of the Aquino Assassination [02/20/85] IB84114

Philippine Internal Conditions: Issues for U.S. Policy [07/16/84] IB82102

Philippines: Editorial Commentary [11/13/84] 84-807 L

Philippines in Turmoil: Implications for U.S. Policy [02/20/85] IB84113

Primer on P.L. 480—Program History, Description, and Operations: A Brief Compilation of Explanatory Documents [11/13/84] 84-803 ENR

Radio Marti [02/22/85] IB83105

A Review of the Proposed Agreement for Nuclear Cooperation between the United States and Norway [04/16/84] 84-638 S

Sanctuary Movement: Central American Refugees IP0328S

The Security of U.S. Embassies and Other Overseas Civilian Installations [01/07/85] 85-11 F

South Africa: Editorial Commentary [02/85] 85-562 L

South Africa: Issues for U.S. Policy [02/04/85] IB80032

South Africa: Reform Proposals/U.S. Policy [07/07/83] 83-132 F

South Africa: Selected References, 1977–1985 [01/31/85] L0403

Southern Africa: A Regional Profile IP0303S

Southern Africa: Intraregional and U.S. Relations; Selected References, 1980–1984 [08/07/84] L0314

Soviet Policy and U.S. Response in the Third World [03/12/81] AB50040

Soviet Policy under Chernenko [02/22/85] IB84109

Status of the Contadora Process [02/24/84] 84-547 F

Taiwan and the Killing of Henry Liu: Issue for Congress [02/01/85] 85-42 F

UNESCO-U.S. Withdrawal in Perspective [12/26/84] IB84086

UNESCO: Selected References, 1975–1984 [10/10/84] L0360

The United States and Hong Kong's Future: Important Interests, Limited Options [07/83] 83-149 F

United States Contributions to UNICEF [01/14/85] 85-513 F

United States Policy Toward Vietnam: A Summary Review of its History [01/23/85] 85-16 F

U.S.-Soviet Relations [02/21/85] IB83066

U.S.-Soviet Relations IP0233U

U.S.-Soviet Relations: Overviews [08/84] VU84012

The U.S. Agreement for Nuclear Cooperation with China: An Analysis of Some Likely Major Provisions Using as a Model the Recently Negotiated Agreement with Sweden [05/11/84] 84-631 S

U.S. Assistance to Egypt: Foreign Aid Facts [02/25/85] IB85060

U.S. Assistance to Ethiopia: Foreign Aid Facts [02/21/85] IB85014

U.S. Assistance to Nicaraguan Guerrillas: Issues for the Congress [01/27/85] IB84139

U.S. Assistance to Turkey: Foreign Aid Facts [02/25/85] IB85059

U.S. Foreign Assistance to Central America [03/02/84] 84-34 F

U.S. Foreign Policy Export Controls [11/26/84] IB83097

U.S. Withdrawal from the International Labor Organization: Successful Precedent for UNESCO [11/08/84] 84-202 F

GENERAL INTEREST

Additions to the Major Issues File [02/18/85] IB78300

Archived Issue Brief List [02/05/85] IB77001

Basic Reference Sources for Use by Congressional Offices: An Annotated Selection of Publications and Services [12/84] 84-218 C

Business—Doing Business with the Federal Government IP0305B

Computers for Personal Use IP0238C

Conducting Legislative Research in a Congressional Office [01/07/85] 85-2 GOV

Congressional Liaison Offices of Selected Federal Agencies [12/11/84] 84-226 C

The Congressional Research Service [12/17/84] 85-1 D

The Congressional Scene: Selected Newsletters, Journals, and Other Periodical Publications Covering Congressional Activities [11/84] 84-208 C

CRS Television Program Schedule, Channel 6 House Cable System [02/25/85] IB83145

Form Letters: Tell your Constituents Where to Get Government Publications IP0222F

Fundraising Techniques for Groups: Selected Books and Articles [07/27/83] L0170

Government Publications—How, What, When, Where, and Why IP0264G

Grants and Fund Raising IP0050G

Hotlines and Other Useful Government Telephone Numbers IP0106H

Individual Retirement Accounts (IRAs) IP0177I

Internships IP0063I

Introduction to SCORPIO [01/85] 85-3 AIS

The National Catholic Bishops' Conference and the Poor: Editorials and Commentary [12/84] 85-527 L

Organizations that Rate Members of Congress on their Voting Records [11/84] 84-206 C

Resume Writing IP0108R

Selected Federal Data Bases Available to the Public [10/24/84] 84-183 S

Speechwriting and Delivery IP0139S

State Information: Research Road Map [01/85] R018

Study Abroad IP0141S

Washington, D.C. and the U.S. Capitol Building IP0132W

When Inauguration Day Falls on a Sunday (CRS Review) [01/85] 85-1106 JAN

GOVERNMENT AND POLITICS

Campaign Activities by Congressional Staff [11/01/84] AB500118

Campaign Finance IP0014C

Campaign Funds: Selected References, 1978–1984 [10/19/84] L0357

Changing Profile of America [06/23/83] AB50065

Civil Service Reform Act: Implementation (AR-CHIVED—05/29/84) [05/29/84] IB69094

Civil Service Retirement IP0205C

Closing a Senate Office [01/29/85] 85-30 GOV

Congress IP0022C

Congressional Committee Staff and Funding [01/02/85] IB82006

Congressional Elections—1984 [11/09/84] IB84137

Congressional Foreign Travel: Selected References, 1972–1984 [04/16/84] L0261

Congressional Office Operations IP0151C

Congress: Issues for the 99th Congress IP0319C

Congress (99th, 1st session): Selected Legislative Issues [02/25/85] IB85001

Constitutional Conventions: Political and Legal Questions [02/21/85] IB80062

Contracting Out and OMB Circular A76: Selected References, 1976–1984 [07/02/84] L0285

Critique of Justice Department's FOIA Fee Waiver Policy [01/24/83] CP 1844

HEALTH

Abortion IP0001A

AIDS: Acquired Immune Deficiency Syndrome [02/06/85] IB83162

Alcoholism in the U.S.: Selected References, 1981–1984 [10/19/84] L0369

Alzheimer's Disease [11/23/84] IB83128

Alzheimer's Disease IP0309A

Alzheimer's Disease: Preliminary Bibliography, 1980–1984 [09/10/84] L0348

Antibiotics in Animal Feeds: Implications for Human Health; Selected References, 1979–1984 [01/08/85] L0397

Asbestos in Schools: Program and Policy Issues [02/20/85] IB83160

Asbestos Related Disease: Preliminary Bibliography, 1982–1984 [09/04/84] L0323

Asbestos: Summary of Federal Regulations [02/20/85] MB84215

Aspartame: An Artificial Sweetener [03/23/84] 84-649 SPR

"Baby Doe Rule": Handicapped Infants IP0250B

Biomedical Ethics [06/16/77] AB50004

Cancer and Risk Assessment: Selected References, 1977–1984 [05/11/84] L0279

Cocaine Use in the U.S.: Selected References, 1980–1985 [02/22/85] L0416

Compensation for Victims of Delayed-Manifestation Occupational or Environment-Related Injury or Disease: Selected References [09/25/84] L0361

Data on Disabled Persons (CRS Review) [01/85] 85-1124 JAN

Diabetes Mellitus: Public Health Perspectives, Policy and Programs [12/01/84] 84-235 SPR

Dioxin: Environmental Impacts and Potential Human Health Effects [01/11/85] IB83079

Ethical Issues in Genetic Research: Selected References, 1982–1984 [12/27/84] L0392

Federal Employees Health Benefits Program: Issues and Problems [01/24/85] IB83134

Fetal Research Legislation [11/13/84] 84-804 SPR

The Financing Problem in Medicare's Hospital Insurance Program (CRS Review) [02/85] 85-1219 FEB

Fluoridation Issues: 1972–1985 [01/22/85] 85-524 SPR

Genetic Engineering IP0175G

Handicapped Education Act (P.L. 94-142) IP0053H

Health Care Cost Containment [11/20/84] IB83172

Health Care Costs IP0223H

Health Care Expenditures and Prices [02/05/85] IB77066

Health Effects of Diesel Emissions [01/07/85] IB82010

Health Insurance IP0072H

Health Insurance Issues: Selected References, 1981–1984 [04/04/84] L0263

Health Insurance: Proposals in the 98th Congress [11/02/84] IB84067

Health Insurance: The Pro-Competition Proposals [12/14/84] IB81046

Health Issues: Bibliographic Background [12/84] BB10

Health Maintenance Organizations IP0056H

Health Maintenance Organizations: Selected References, 1980–1984 [09/14/84] L0328

Health Planning: Issues for the Future [11/16/84] IB82023

Health Professions Education Programs, Title VII of the Public Health Service Act [02/08/85] IB85030

Health Services and Resources Programs: FY85 Budget [12/04/84] IB84063

Health Services and Resources Programs: FY86 Budget [02/13/85] IB85046

Hospice Care Under Medicare [01/07/85] IB82042

Hospital Cost Containment [12/14/84] IB82072

Implementation of Medicare's Hospice Benefit [09/19/84] 84-756 EPW

Indian Health Care Improvement Act [12/03/84] IB84107

Infant Formula: National Problems [11/27/84] MB82244

Lead Exposure: Health Effects, Regulatory Actions, and Congressional Options [12/04/84] 84-222 SPR

Medicaid [11/02/84] IB84064

Medicaid: Expansion of Coverage for Pregnant Women and Young Children [11/02/84] IB83179

Medicaid: FY86 Budget [02/20/85] IB85057

Medical Care: Overviews, Editorials, and Public Opinion Polls [10/84] VU84014

Medicare [11/23/84] IB84052

Medicare-Medicaid IP0067M

Medicare-Medicaid: Selected References, 1982–1984 [07/18/84] L0301

Medicare and Physicians: Selected References, 1979–1985 [02/22/85] L0421

Medicare: FY86 Budget [02/14/85] IB85047

Medicare: Physician Payments [12/17/84] IB85007

Medicare: Prospective Payments and DRGs IP 0317 M

Medicare: The Financing Problem in the Hospital Insurance Program [12/27/84] IB85013

Nursing Homes: Selected References, 1981–1984 [10/03/84] L0366

Organ Transplants: Selected References, 1979–1984 [09/19/84] L0356

Prospective Payments for Medicare Inpatient Hospital Services [01/03/85] IB83171

Sulfites: Food Preservatives [01/09/85] 85-518 SPR

Teenage Pregnancy: Selected References, 1979–1985 [02/22/85] L0422

Urea-Formaldehyde Foam Insulation: Health Effects and Regulation [01/07/85] MB82228

HISTORY

Selected Bicentennial Celebrations Commemorating the 200th Anniversaries of the U.S. Constitution and of the U.S. Congress [04/18/84] 84-57 S

HOUSING

Homelessness in the U.S.: Selected References, 1980–1984 [05/14/84] L0280

Homelessness in the U.S.: Selected References, 1981–1985 [02/08/85] L0404

Homeownership—Is Financial Help Available IP 0315 H

Housing and Mortgage Finance Data: News Summary and (26) Statistical Tables [02/19/85] IB84106

Housing Assistance to Low- and Moderate-Income Households [02/25/85] IB79058

Housing Finance: Alternative Mortgages; Selected References, 1981–1984 [09/25/84] L0362

Housing for the Elderly and Handicapped: Section 202 [02/12/85] IB84038

Housing for the Poor [12/14/83] AB50097

Mortgage Subsidy Bonds [01/23/85] IB81136

IMMIGRATION

Enforcement of the Immigration and Nationality Act (INA) by State and Local Officers: An Overview [12/13/84] 84-855 A

Illegal/Undocumented Aliens [01/04/85] IB74137

Illegal Aliens: Selected References, 1980–1984 [07/13/84] L0304

Immigration and Refugee Policy IP0164I

Immigration and Refugee Policy: Selected References, 1982–1984 [07/06/84] L0303

Immigration: Overviews [08/84] VU84010

Refugee Act Reauthorization: Admissions and Resettlement Issues [01/04/85] IB83060

Sanctuary Movement: Central American Refugees IP0328S

The Status of Cuban/Haitian Entrants [12/31/84] IB84084

U.S. Immigration and Refugee Policy: A Guide to Sources of Information [08/84] R016

U.S. Policy Towards Undocumented Salvadorans [01/29/85] MB82223

INCOME MAINTENANCE

Aid to Families with Dependent Children (AFDC): FY86 Budget [02/14/85] IB85045

Aid to Families with Dependent Children: Structural Change [02/17/85] IB74013

Black Lung Benefits: 1985 Legislative Proposals and the FY86 Budget [02/11/85] IB85029

Child Support: Issues and Legislation IP0286C

Civil Service Retirement IP0205C

Civil Service Retirement System: FY85 Budget [01/16/85] IB84048

Civil Service Retirement System: Redesign [01/16/85] IB84049

Constraining Social Security Cost-of-Living Adjustments: Background and Issues; A Report by the Congressional Research Service for the Committee on the Budget, United States Senate [01/85] CP 1839

Designing a Retirement System for Federal Workers Covered by Social Security [12/84] CP 1830

Energy and Fuel Assistance Plans IP0034E

Food Stamps and Distribution Programs IP0043F

Food Stamps: 1985 Legislation and the FY86 Budget [02/11/85] IB85039

How the Food Stamp Program Works [11/01/84] 84-190 EPW

Individual Retirement Accounts (IRAs) IP0177I

Individual Retirement Accounts (IRAs): Selected References, 1983–1985 [01/23/85] L0402

Individual Retirement Accounts: Tax Incentives for Retirement Savings [01/18/85] IB84104

Major Provisions of the Civil Service Retirement System Pertaining to Members of Congress [10/17/84] 84-776 EPW

Military Retirement: Budgetary Implications of the 5th QRMC Proposals [01/31/85] 85-31 F

Pension Equity IP0308P

Pension Plans: Multiemployer Pension Plan Termination Insurance [01/18/85] IB79052

Poverty and Income Statistics IP0327P

Private Pension Plan Standards: A Summary of the Employee Retirement Income Security Act of 1974 (ERISA), as Amended [01/02/85] 84-234 EPW

Progress Against Poverty (1959 to 1983): The Recent Poverty Debate [12/14/84] IB84013

Public Pension Plans: Is Federal Legislation Necessary? [01/18/85] IB82070

Railroad Retirement: Clear Track Ahead? [01/16/85] IB84068

Railroad Unemployment Insurance: Growing Debt to Retirement Program [01/16/85] IB84069

Social Security Amendments of 1983 [01/28/85] IB83070

Social Security and the Federal Budget (CRS Review) [02/85] 85-1210 FEB

Social Security and the Unified Budget [02/15/84] 84-537 EPW

Social Security: Current Law and Benefits IP0153S

Social Security Financing: A Guide to Sources of Information [08/07/81] R002

Social Security Financing: Selected References, 1983–1984 [10/12/84] L0367

The Social Security "Notch" IP0266S

Social Security: Taxing Benefits [02/08/85] IB83164

TEFRA's "Top Heavy" Pension Rules [01/18/85] IB84080

Unemployment Insurance: Financial Problems in the Trust Fund [12/28/84] IB79098

Welfare and Poverty IP0098W

Welfare Reform [02/17/85] IB77069

Women's Pension Equity [01/18/85] IB84077

Women's Pension Equity: A Summary of the Retirement Equity Act of 1984 (REACT) [12/06/84] 84-217 EPW

Workfare [03/30/83] AB50082

Work Incentives in the SSI Program [11/26/84] 84-825 EPW

INFORMATION AND PRIVACY

Computer Crime and Security [02/06/85] IB80047

Computer Crime and Security IP0272C

Copyright: Application Procedures IP0215C

Copyright Law: Legalizing Home Taping of Audio and Video Recordings [02/06/85] IB82075

Freedom of Information Act/Privacy Act: A Guide to Their Use IP0047F

Freedom Of Information Act Amendments [02/08/85] IB82003

Freedom of Information Act: Background and Proposals for Change IP0169F

Freedom of Information Act: Proposals for Change [02/18/82] AB50049

Information Technology for Emergency Operations [11/18/83] AB50117

National Security Controls and Scientific Information [02/08/85] IB82083

Social Security Numbers and Privacy: Selected References, 1973–1983 [07/02/84] L0297

LABOR

Adult Black Workers: The Progress of Some [12/19/84] 84-228 E

Auto Industry Labor-Management Relations: Restore and More in '84? [01/23/85] MB84223

Career Guidance and Federal Job Information IP0016C

Coal Industry Collective Bargaining: The 1984 Round [02/20/85] MB84226

Corporate Bankruptcy and Labor Contracts: Economic

Aspects of the Supreme Court Decisions (NLRB v. Bildisco) [02/20/85] IB84072

Davis-Bacon Act IP0027D

Displaced Homemakers [12/14/84] IB84132

Employment Status of the Nation: Data and Trends [02/15/85] IB82097

Employment Status of the States: Data and Trends [02/19/85] IB82098

Employment Trends to the 1990s: Selected References, 1983–1984 [09/04/84] L0342

Equal Employment Opportunity and the United States Congress [11/08/84] 84-857 A

An International Comparison of Fringe Benefits: Theory, Evidence, and Policy Implications [12/31/84] 84-815 E

Jobs Overseas IP0065J

Job Training and Job Creation Programs IP0246J

Job Training: FY86 Budget Issues [02/15/85] IB85042

Labor Issues in the 99th Congress: Potential Topics of Discussion [01/29/85] 85-525 E

The Labor Market in Recovery [01/23/85] MB84225

Maternity and Parental Leave Benefits: Selected References, 1976–1984 [07/24/84] L0310

Other Nations' Experience with Categorical Employment Subsidies: Are There Options Suggested for the United States [02/04/85] 85-547 E

Pay Equity: The Comparable Worth Issue IP0283P

Plant Closings and Business Relocations [01/22/85] IB83152

Sub-Minimum Wage and Youth Employment IP0304S

Textile and Apparel Workers: A Brief Description [12/03/84] 84-813 E

Unemployment: Problems and Prospects IP0229U

U.S. Wages and Unit Labor Costs in a World Economy [11/09/84] 84-172 E

Women in the Labor Force: Responses to Some Frequent Questions [02/21/85] IB84079

Working Mothers: Selected References, 1978–1984 [11/09/84] L0384

The Youth Sub-Minimum Wage: Proposals of the 98th Congress [10/30/84] 84-185 E

Youth Subminimum Wage: Selected References, 1980–1984 [06/25/84] L0294

LAW, CRIME, AND JUSTICE

Amending the Gun Control Act: 97th Congress [06/03/82] AB50055

Capital Punishment IP0015C

Capital Punishment: Selected References, 1981–1984 [08/10/84] L0317

Child Abuse IP0019C

Compensation for Crime Victims [01/31/85] IB74014

Computer Crime and Security IP0272C

Congressional Response to Prison Conditions [01/04/85] IB81171

Crime and Law Issues: Bibliographic Background [12/84] BB02

Crime and Legislative Efforts: Overviews, Editorials, and Public Opinion Polls [12/84] VU84017

Crime Control: Administration and Congressional Initiatives [02/01/85] IB81172

Crime Control Issues in the 98th Congress [03/29/83] AB50076

Crime: Federal Initiatives in Crime Control IP0310C

Crime: Statistics IP0311C

Drug Abuse and Control of Illicit Trafficking IP0030D

Drunk Driving and Raising the Drinking Age IP0186D

Drunk Driving and the Legal Drinking Age: Selected References, 1982–1984 [08/03/84] L0312

Drunk Driving: Editorial Commentary (September 4, 1984 through December 17, 1984) [12/21/84] 84-830 L

Evolution of the Judicial System in the District of Columbia, 1800–1984 [08/22/84] CP 1845

Federal Efforts to Control Illicit Drug Traffic [02/20/85] IB84011

Federal Initiatives in Crime Control: Selected References, 1981–1984 [10/01/84] L0363

Federal Laws Relating to the Control of Narcotics and Other Dangerous Drugs, Enacted 1961–1984: Brief Summaries [11/13/84] 84-200 GOV

Gun Control [02/19/85] IB74011

Gun Control IP0051G

Gun Control: Selected References, 1981–1985 [02/22/85] L0415

Illicit Drug Trafficking and Law Enforcement Policies: Selected References, 1979–1984 [07/16/84] L0300

Insanity Defense: Selected References, 1981–1984 [09/07/84] L0309

Judicial Reform: A Guide to Information Sources [12/30/83] R010

Lotteries: Proposals for a National Lottery IP0326L

Missing Children IP0178M

National Minimum Drinking Age: Provisions and Analysis [10/29/84] 84-784 E

Overview of State Lottery Operations [01/14/85] 85-520 E

Prisons: Selected References, 1981–1984 [08/24/84] L0329

The Racketeer Influenced and Corrupt Organizations Statute, 18 U.S.C. SEC. 1961–1968 [12/18/84] 84-847 A

Sentencing Reform [12/31/84] IB77108

Smith v. Robinson: The Implications of the Supreme Court's Decision not to Award Attorney's Fees under P.L. 94-142 [11/02/84] 84-860 A

Smith v. Robinson: The Pros, Cons, and Implications of Legislation to Allow Awards of Attorneys' Fees under the Education of the Handicapped Act [01/17/85] 85-519 A

Supreme Court: Church-State Cases, October 1984 Term [12/10/84] MB84229

The Supreme Court This Term [02/01/84] AB50106

Teenage Suicide IP 0318 T

Teenage Suicide: Selected References, 1976–1984 [11/30/84] L0385

The U.S. Supreme Court and the Gender Gap: Legal Developments since Reed v. Reed (CRS Review) [02/85] 85-1212 FEB

MINORITY ISSUES

Benefits for Former Military Spouses IP 0313 B

Comparable Worth and Equal Pay: Editorial Commentary [02/22/85] 85-575 L

Comparable Worth: Selected References, 1983–1985 [02/14/85] L0408

Data on Disabled Persons (CRS Review) [01/85] 85-1124 JAN

Equal Rights Amendment IP0037E

Equal Rights Amendment: Selected References, 1977–1985 [02/07/85] L0407

Indian Education in the United States: 98th Congress [02/11/85] IB83104

Indian Land Claims and Fishing Treaty Rights Issues [02/11/81] AB50043

Japanese American Internment and Reparation: Selected References, 1975–1984 [07/30/84] L0307

Older Women: Selected References, 1976–1984 [09/13/84] L0358

Pay Equity: The Comparable Worth Issue IP0283P

Pension Equity IP0308P

Sex Discrimination in Education: Title IX IP0166S

Sex Discrimination Issues in Pensions and Insurance: Selected References, 1980–1984 [09/06/84] L0327

The U.S. Supreme Court and the Gender Gap: Legal Developments since Reed v. Reed (CRS Review) [02/85] 85-1212 FEB

Women and Minorities: Overviews [05/84] VU8405

Women and Political Office IP0239W

Women's Political Issues: Office Holding and Gender Gap; Selected References, 1973–1983 [12/05/83] L0151(REV)

Working Mothers: Selected References, 1978–1984 [11/09/84] L0384

NATIONAL DEFENSE AND SECURITY

Alternative Defense Posture [09/27/83] AB50096

Arms Sales: U.S. Policy IP0214A

Arms Transfers and Military Assistance: A Guide to Sources of Information [07/84] R015

Arms Transfers: U.S. Policy; Selected References, 1979–1984 [08/10/84] L0321

Battleship Reactivation [01/29/85] IB83053

Benefits for Former Military Spouses IP 0313 B

The C-17 Cargo Plane and the Airlift Shortfall [02/12/85] IB84099

Chemical Warfare IP0146C

Civil Defense [02/13/85] IB84128

Civil Defense and the Effects of Nuclear War IP0174C

The Conference on Disarmament in Europe (CDE) [01/22/85] IB84060

Defense Budget—FY85: Congressional Action to Date [12/28/84] IB84002

Defense Budget—FY86: Congressional Action to Date [02/06/85] IB85021

Defense Contracting: Weapons Warranties; Selected References, 1978–1984 [05/25/84] L0289

Defense Department: Selected References, 1976–1985 [02/15/85] L0410

Defense Petroleum Reserve: Organizational Options for Meeting DOD's Emergency Fuel Supply Requirements [11/09/84] 84-201 F

Defense Spending IP0028D

Defense Spending: A Guide to Information Sources [01/08/82] R006

Defense Spending: an Introduction to Key Questions [02/06/85] IB83169

Defense Spending: Editorial Commentary [01/25/85] 85-529 L

Defense Spending: Preliminary Bibliography, 1983–1985 [02/04/85] L0406

Defense Spending: Waste, Fraud, and Abuse IP0279D

The Draft and Military Manpower Issues IP0029D

Fighter Aircraft Program: F/A-18 [02/08/85] IB78087

The Fiscal Year 1986 Defense Budget Request: Data Summary [02/04/85] 85-38 F

The Future of Nuclear Arms and Arms Control [01/18/85] AB50121

Ground Forces: Apache AH-64 Attack Helicopter (Weapons Facts) [02/21/85] IB84028

Ground Forces: Binary Chemical Munitions (Weapons Facts) [02/21/85] IB84027

Ground Forces: Bradley Infantry/Cavalry Fighting Vehicle (Weapons Facts) [02/21/85] IB84035

Ground Forces: DIVAD (Weapons Facts) [02/21/85] IB84033

Ground Forces: M1 Main Battle Tank (Weapons Facts) [02/21/85] IB84032

Honduras: U.S. Military Activities (CRS Review) [01/85] 85-1113 JAN

International Terrorism [02/12/85] IB81141

M-X Missile IP0070M

Military Balance IP0069M

Military Manpower and Compensation: FY85 Budget Issues [01/24/85] IB84073

Military Procurement Procedures of Foreign Governments: Centralization of the Procurement Function [12/11/84] 84-229 F

Military Readiness IP0307M

Military Readiness: Selected References, 1980–1984 [09/04/84] L0338

Military Uses of Space IP0208M

Military Uses of Space: Selected References, 1979–1984 [10/12/84] L0284

MX, "Midgetman," Minuteman, and Titan Missile Programs [12/11/84] IB77080

National Defense Issues: Bibliographic Background [12/84] BB03

National Defense Stockpile [12/05/84] IB74111

The NATO Allies, Japan and the Persian Gulf (CRS Review) [02/85] 85-1205 FEB

NATO: Selected References, 1979–1985 [01/15/85] L0398

Naval Forces: Arleigh Burke (DDG-51) Guided Missile Destroyer (Weapons Facts) [02/11/85] IB84021

Naval Forces: TOMAHAWK (Weapons Facts) [02/21/85] IB84019

Navy Nuclear Armed TOMAHAWK Cruise Missile [01/29/85] IB84101

The Navy's Proposed Arleigh Burke (DDG-51) Class Guided Missile Destroyer Program: A Comparison with an Equal-Cost Force of Ticonderoga (CG-47) Class Guided Missile Cruisers [11/21/84] 84-205 F

Nuclear Arms Control II: INF IP0227N

Nuclear Arms Control I: START IP0226N

Nuclear Explosions in Space: The Threat of EMP (Electromagnetic Pulse) [12/03/84] MB82221

Nuclear Freeze: Arms Control Proposals [02/14/85] IB82059

Nuclear Weapons and Arms Control: Overviews [08/84] VU8409

Nuclear Weapons Freeze: Issues for National Debate IP0195N

Pros and Cons of Military Intervention [01/08/80] AB50033

The Pros and Cons of the Transfer of the National Defense Stockpile to the Department of Defense [12/20/84] 85-514 ENR

Rapid Deployment Force [02/12/85] IB80027

The Security of U.S. Embassies and Other Overseas Civilian Installations [01/07/85] 85-11 F

Small Single-Warhead Intercontinental Ballistic Missiles: Hardware, Issues, and Policy Choices [05/26/83] 83-106 F

Soviet-U.S. Proposals for Talks on Space Weapons and Nuclear Missiles [12/21/84] IB84121

Soviet Policy on Antisatellite (ASAT) Arms Control [10/23/84] 84-841 S

Space Militarization and Arms Control: Selected References, 1983–1985 [02/85] 85-581 L

Space Policy and Funding: Military Uses of Space [12/18/84] IB82117

Special Operations Forces: Issues for Congress [12/14/84] 84-227 F

Standby Draft Registration [01/24/85] IB82101

START: Ballistic Missile Warhead Portion of the "Build Down" Proposal [01/17/84] 84-8 F

"Star Wars": Antisatellites and Space-Based BMD [02/20/85] IB81123

"Star Wars": The President's Strategic Defense Initiative [06/15/84] AB50105

Strategic Arms Talks: Basic Concepts [07/23/83] AB50088

Strategic Defense Initiative and Arms Control Negotiations: Editorial Commentary [01/25/85] 85-535 L

Strategic Defense Initiative and Star Wars: Current News Coverage [01/85] 85-538 L

The Strategic Defense Initiative and United States Alliance Strategy [02/01/85] 85-48 F

Strategic Forces: Air-launched Cruise Missile (Weapons Facts) [02/01/85] IB84018

Strategic Forces: B-1B Bomber (Weapons Facts) [02/01/85] IB84017

Strategic Forces: MX ICBM (Weapons Facts) [02/06/85] IB84046

Strategic Forces: Small ICBM—"Midgetman" Missile (Weapons Facts) [02/06/85] IB84044

Strategic Forces: Trident II (Weapons Facts) [02/06/85] IB84045

Strategic Mobility: C-17 Cargo Plane (Weapons Facts) [02/12/85] IB84030

Strategic Mobility: C-5B Cargo Plane (Weapons Facts) [02/12/85] IB84029

Tactical Aviation: A-6E Attack Aircraft (Weapons Facts) [02/12/85] IB84022

Tactical Aviation: F/A-18 Fighter/Attack Aircraft (Weapons Facts) [02/12/85] IB84024

Tactical Aviation: F-14 Fighter Aircraft (Weapons Facts) [02/12/85] IB84023

Tactical Aviation: F-15 Fighter Aircraft (Weapons Facts) [02/12/85] IB84025

Tactical Aviation: F-16 Fighter Aircraft (Weapons Facts) [02/12/85] IB84026

Terrorism IP0299T

Terrorism: Selected References, 1982–1984 [02/01/85] L0405

Theater Nuclear Forces: Ground-Launched Cruise Missile (Weapons Facts) [02/21/85] IB84031

Theater Nuclear Forces: Pershing II Missile (Weapons Facts) [02/21/85] IB84034

Trident Program [02/01/85] IB73001

United States Military Installations in Turkey [12/12/84] 84-221 F

U.S./Soviet Military Balance: Statistical Trends, 1970–1983 [08/27/84] 84-163 S

U.S. Chemical Warfare Preparedness Program [02/21/85] IB82125

U.S. Civilian and Defense Research and Development Funding: Some Trends and Comparisons with Selected Industrialized Nations [11/05/84] 84-195 SPR

U.S. Intelligence: Current Issues [02/1/85] IB80097

Verification: Soviet Compliance with Arms Control Agreements [02/14/85] IB84131

The War Powers Resolution: A Retrospective [10/06/83] AB50092

War Powers Resolution: Presidential Compliance [02/15/85] IB81050

Women in the Armed Forces [11/02/79] AB50031

Women in the Armed Forces [02/04/85] IB79045

NATURAL RESOURCES

Analysis of the Conservation Benefits and Costs of Past Youth Conservation Programs and Opportunities for Similar Work in Federal Agencies [01/31/85] 85-561 ENR

Analysis of Timber Contract Relief Legislation [06/26/84] 84-681 ENR

Animal Welfare: Selected References, 1982–1984 [09/11/84] L0352

Aquaculture: Status of Technology and Future Prospects [02/08/85] IB83004

Benefit and Cost Considerations in National Forest Timber Sales [12/17/84] 85-510 ENR

Coal Leasing Policy: Continuing Difficulties [01/24/85] IB83111

Commercial Fisheries Issues: 99th Congress [02/21/85] IB85005

Cost and Revenues of Foreign Fishing in U.S. Waters [05/08/84] 84-676 ENR

Current Status of the U.S. Fishing Industry: Summary Tables of Fisheries Information [01/22/85] 85-522 ENR

Endangered Species Act: Reauthorization [01/17/85] IB85003

Endangered Species Act: Selected References, 1982–1984 [09/11/84] L0351

General Economic Considerations for Policy Decisions Concerning Federal Fish Hatcheries [02/29/84] CP 1828

A Legal Analysis of Congressional Intent as to Issues Relating to Grazing on Lands Managed by the Bureau of Land Management [02/14/85] 85-582 A

The Major Federal Land Management Agencies: Management of Our Nation's Lands and Resources [01/08/85] 85-10 ENR

Marine Mammal Issues: 99th Congress [02/05/85] IB85002

North Pacific Fur Seals: Issues and Options [02/01/85] 85-546 ENR

Ocean Mining [01/29/85] IB74024

Outer Continental Shelf Revenue Sharing [02/08/85] IB85027

Overview of the Outer Continental Shelf Leasing Plan [02/08/85] IB85026

Park and Outdoor Recreation Components in the FY86 Budget [02/20/85] IB85053

Rangeland Condition: Attempts to Chart its Progress [09/25/84] 84-757 ENR

Rangeland Management Issues in the 99th Congress [02/06/85] IB85032

Resource Conservation Issues in the 98th Congress—A Summary [10/29/84] 84-781 ENR

Sport Hunting and Fishing: Major Legislation [01/14/85] IB83020

Tuna: Fishery in Turmoil [02/01/85] IB84092

Wilderness in the 98th Congress (CRS Review) [01/85] 85-1116 JAN

SCIENCE AND TECHNOLOGY

Air Traffic Control: Delays and Near Misses [02/05/85] MB84227

The Availability of Japanese Scientific and Technical Information in the United States [11/84] CP 1829

Biotechnology: Selected References, 1983–1984 [11/01/84] L0373

Computers for Personal Use IP0238C

East-West Technology Transfer: A Congressional Dialog with the Reagan Administration [12/84] CP 1840

East-West Technology Transfer: Selected References, 1979–1984 [09/19/84] L0355

Ethical Issues in Genetic Research: Selected References, 1982–1984 [12/27/84] L0392

Federal Funding for Behavioral and Social Sciences Research [12/13/84] IB82111

Federal Funding for R&D in Major Departments and Agencies, FY85 [11/26/84] IB84051

Fire Safety: Toxicity of Burning Materials [01/11/85] MB83243

Genetic Engineering IP0175G

Government Patent Policy: The Ownership of Inventions Resulting from Federally Funded R&D [02/12/85] IB78057

Human Gene Therapy [02/04/85] IB84119

Industrial Innovation and High Technology Development: Selected References, 1982–1984 [12/19/84] L0390

LANDSAT (Earth Resources Satellite System) [11/13/84] IB82066

The Law of Salvage in Outer Space [01/14/85] 85-532 A

Military Uses of Space: Selected References, 1979–1984 [10/12/84] L0284

Recombinant DNA: Legal Challenges to Deliberate Release Experiments [01/07/85] 85-502 SPR

Research and Development Funding IP0236R

Research and Development Funding: Selected References, 1981–1984 [03/14/84] L0188 (REV)

Risk Assessment in Health and Environmental Regulation [01/29/85] IB84124

Robotics: Selected References, 1982–1984 [09/19/84] L0354

Science Policy and Funding in the Reagan Administration [12/12/84] IB82108

Science Policy in the Reagan Administration: Selected References, 1982–1984 [01/03/85] L0395

Science Policy Issues: Bibliographic Background [12/84] BB12

Soviet Space Activities: A Conversation With Geoffrey Perry [02/24/84] AB50102

Space Exploration and Development: A Guide to Sources of Information [11/84] R017

Space Policy and Funding: NASA and Civilian Space Programs [02/12/85] IB82118

Space Shuttle [02/19/85] IB81175

Space Shuttle IP0128S

Space Station Proposals IP0293S

Space Stations and Space Commercialization [12/10/84] IB83147

Space Stations: Selected References, 1976–1984 [03/30/84] L0267

Strategic and Critical Materials Policy: Research and Development [12/05/84] IB74094

Supercomputers: Foreign Competition and Federal Funding [02/01/85] IB83102

The Tax Credit for Research and Development: An Analysis [01/25/85] 85-6 E

Technology Transfer: Utilization of the Results of Federally Funded Research and Development [02/07/85] IB85031

U.S. Civilian and Defense Research and Development Funding: Some Trends and Comparisons with Selected Industrialized Nations [11/05/84] 84-195 SPR

The Use of Animals in Biomedical Research [02/20/85] IB83161

U.S. Science and Engineering: Education and Manpower [02/01/85] IB82062

SOCIAL SERVICES

Abortion: Selected References, 1983–1985 [02/22/85] L0417

Aged IP0003A

Child Abuse IP0019C

Child Day Care IP0306C

Child Day Care: Selected References, 1980–1984 [09/05/84] L0332

Child Nutrition Issues in the 99th Congress [02/21/85] IB85055

The Child Support Enforcement Amendments of 1984 [10/25/84] 84-796 EPW

Child Support: Issues and Legislation IP0286C

Child Support: Selected References, 1976–1984 [03/02/84] L0256

The Developmental Disabilities Programs: Statutory Authority and Program Operations [11/08/84] 84-196 EPW

Energy and Fuel Assistance Plans IP0034E

The Family: Selected References, 1978–1984 [03/08/84] L0258

Food Stamps and Distribution Programs IP0043F

Handicapped: General Information IP0052H

Handicapped Rehabilitation Act (P.L. 93-112) IP0054H

Homeless in America IP 0314 H

Homelessness in the U.S.: Selected References, 1981–1985 [02/08/85] L0404

Hunger in the United States IP0277H

Legal Services Corporation: Budget and Legislative Issues [02/13/85] IB83096

Medicare-Medicaid IP0067M

Medicare-Medicaid: Selected References, 1982–1984 [07/18/84] L0301

Medicare and Physicians: Selected References, 1979–1985 [02/22/85] L0421

Missing and Runaway Children: Selected References, 1980–1984 [10/03/84] L0370

Missing Children IP0178M

Poverty and Income Statistics IP0327P

Smith v. Robinson: The Implications of the Supreme Court's Decision not to Award Attorney's Fees under P.L. 94-142 [11/02/84] 84-860 A

Smith v. Robinson: The Pros, Cons, and Implications of Legislation to Allow Awards of Attorneys' Fees under the Education of the Handicapped Act [01/17/85] 85-519 A

Social and Community Services Block Grants: FY86 Budget Issues [02/15/85] IB85049

Teenage Pregnancy: Selected References, 1979–1985 [02/22/85] L0422

Teenage Suicide IP 0318 T

Teenage Suicide: Selected References, 1976–1984 [11/30/84] L0385

Welfare and Income Maintenance Issues: Bibliographic Background [12/84] BB15

Welfare and Poverty IP0098W

1986 Budget Perspectives: Federal Spending for the Human Resource Programs [02/22/85] 85-52 EPW

98th Congress Action Affecting the Elderly: Selected Legislation with Program Descriptions [12/31/84] 85-22 EPW

TAXATION

Capital Gains Tax: Selected References, 1983–1985 [02/22/85] L0419

Certain Extraordinary Authority Conferred on the Internal Revenue Service with Regard to Collection of Taxes [01/04/85] 85-534 A

A Comparative Analysis of Five Tax Proposals: Effects of Business Income Tax Provisions [12/27/84] 84-832 E

A Comparative Analysis of the Bradley/Gephardt and Kemp/Kasten Tax Reform Proposals [01/10/85] MB84228

Constitutional Considerations Involved in the Adoption of an Annual Federal Wealth Tax [11/15/84] 84-852 A

Constitutional Questions: Amending Federal Law to Prohibit Application of State Sales Tax to Food Purchases by Beneficiaries under the Food Stamp and WIC Programs [01/30/85] 85-551 A

Consumption Tax: Selected References, 1980–1984 [07/23/84] L0306

The Corporate Income Tax and the U.S. Economy [08/24/84] 84-143 E

Dividend Tax and Tax Integration: Selected References, 1977–1985 [01/25/85] L0401

Effective Tax Burdens on Human Capital Investment under the Income Tax and Proposed Consumption Tax [08/20/84] 84-741 E

Effect of the Treasury Tax Reform Proposal on Farm Income Taxation [01/30/85] 85-543 E

The Effects of Federal Income Tax Policy on U.S. Agriculture [12/84] CP 1837

An Explanation of the Business Energy Investment Tax Credits [01/24/85] 85-25 E

The Extent of Federal Income Tax Liability Generated by a Sale (at a Gain) of Property Held in Trust [10/22/84] 84-850 A

Federal Estate and Gift Taxes: Selected References, 1981–1984 [10/19/84] L0376

Federal Estate, Gift and Generation-Skipping Taxes: A Legislative History and a Description of Current Law [08/20/84] 84-156A

Federal Taxation: A Guide to Information Sources [10/01/81] R004

Federal Tax Provisions Relating to Alcohol Fuels Including Recent Changes under the Tax Reform Act of 1984 [11/06/84] 84-194 E

Flat-Rate Income Tax: Selected References, 1983–1984 [09/18/84] L0350

Foreign-Source Income and Tax Changes [01/07/85] 85-500 E

Imputed Interest on Property Sales [02/01/85] IB84136

National Sales Tax [02/11/85] IB84130

Relationship of the Constitutional Prohibition on Ex Post Facto Laws to Retroactive Tax Legislation [12/31/84] 84-854 A

Renewable Energy Tax Credit Extension Efforts in the 98th Congress [01/01/85] 85-4 SPR

Revenue Generation Through Tax Compliance and Enforcement: Selected References, 1979–1984 [02/03/84] L0243

Revenue Generation Through Tax Initiatives: Selected References, 1979–1984 [02/03/84] L0244

Some Constitutional Questions Regarding the Federal Income Tax Laws [09/26/84] 84-168 A

Summary of the Federal Income Tax Rules Affecting Real Estate [12/18/84] 84-836 A

A Surtax as a Revenue Raiser? [01/08/85] IB84127

Taxation Issues: Bibliographic Background [12/84] BB13

Taxation of Fringe Benefits: Selected References, 1983–1984 [10/19/84] L0378

The Tax Credit for Research and Development: An Analysis [01/25/85] 85-6 E

Taxes: Estate and Gift Tax IP0161T

Taxes in Public Utility Rates: Phantom Taxes or Real Tax Benefits [11/30/84] 84-211 E

Taxes: Overviews, Editorials, and Public Opinion Polls [12/84] VU84018

Tax Indexation: Rate Schedules for 1985 [02/01/85] MB84230

Tax Indexing: Selected References, 1982–1984 [07/30/84] L0311

Taxing Consumption Instead of Income [02/01/85] MB84231

Tax Reform and Federal Subsidy of the State-Local Sector: Is There a Role for State-Local Tax Deductibility [01/28/85] 85-515 E

Tax Reform and Simplification: Selected References, 1983–1984 [12/07/84] L0388

Tax Reform Issues—Flat Rate Tax and Other Proposals IP0267T

Tax Relief for Small Businesses: An Analysis of the Seidman and Seidman Proposal [11/05/84] 84-797 E

Tax Revisions: An Economic Overview [01/18/85] MB84211

Tax Shelters: Selected References, 1983–1985 [02/19/85] L0418

Treatment of State-Local Taxes and Tax-Exempt Bonds under Tax Reform Proposals: Effects on the State-Local Sector [01/18/85] 85-503 E

The Unitary Method of Identifying In-State Income: Basic Concepts and Recent Events [12/18/84] 84-819 E

Unitary Tax: Selected References, 1983–1984 [09/07/84] L0346

The U.S. Tax Structure: Its Level, Composition and Progressivity Compared to Seven Other Nations [12/26/84] 84-233 E

Value-Added Tax Contrasted with a National Sales Tax [02/20/85] IB85054

Value-Added Tax: Estimated Revenue Yields [12/21/84] 84-835 E

Value-Added Tax: Selected References, 1982–1984 [07/25/84] L0308

TRADE AND INTERNATIONAL FINANCE

Automobile Domestic Content Requirements [01/18/85] IB82056

Automobile Import Problems and Solutions: Japanese Export Restraints and U.S. Domestic Content Proposals, Selected References, 1981–1984 [02/13/85] L0411

Automobiles Imported From Japan [02/12/85] IB80030

Deficits, Debt, and World Financial Stability [01/23/85] AB50120

Defining "Country of Origin" as Applied to Textile Import Quotas [09/24/84] 84-751 E

East-West Commercial Issues: The Western Alliance Studies [11/05/84] IB83086

East-West Technology Transfer: Selected References, 1979–1984 [09/19/84] L0355

East-West Trade: Selected References, 1983–1984 [01/02/85] L0394

Exchange Rates: The Dollar in International Markets [01/24/85] IB78033

Exports and Taxes: DISCs and FSCs [02/06/85] IB83122

Fact Sheet on U.S. Agricultural Exports [01/09/85] 85-505 ENR

Finance and Adjustment: The International Debt Crisis, 1982–84 [09/17/84] 84-162 E

Foreign Loans: Selected References, 1983–1984 [06/25/84] L0293

Foreign Loans to Latin America: Selected References, 1983–1984 [07/13/84] L0305

Foreign Trade and Export Promotion: A Guide to Sources of Information [06/84] R014

Foreign Trade Issues: Selected References, 1984 [08/31/84] L0322

The Gray Market for Imported Automobiles [12/27/84] 84-837 E

Import Quotas for Steel: U.S. International Trade Commission Remedy Recommendations vs. "The Fair Trade in Steel Act of 1984" [07/26/84] 84-703 E

International Banking: Selected References, 1983–1984 [06/04/84] L0286

International Coffee Agreement [12/04/84] 84-224 ENR

International Debt Problems: Background, Statistics, Proposed Solutions IP0234I

International Monetary Fund and World Bank IP0245I

International Monetary Fund: Selected References, 1982–1984 [09/11/84] L0340

Japan-U.S. Economic Relations: Selected References, 1983–1984 [09/20/84] L0359

Japan-U.S. Trade IP0201J

Japan-U.S. Trade Relations [02/05/85] IB81011

Market Access in Japan: The U.S. Experience [02/14/85] 85-37 E

Most-Favored-Nation Policy Toward Communist Countries [01/25/85] IB74139

Oil Disruption and the U.S. Economy [07/17/84] AB50107

Overview of Current Provisions of U.S. Trade Law [12/04/84] CP 1838

The Reagan Administration's Response to Barter [05/23/84] 84-648 ENR

Services for Exporters from the U.S. Government [11/84] CP 1823

Sino-Japanese Trade [10/04/84] CP 1841

The Stability of the International Banking System [01/28/85] IB82107

Textiles, Apparel, and Footwear: Import Limitations [02/07/85] IB84110

Trade and Tariff Act of 1984 (P.L. 98-573): A Summary [11/30/84] 84-814 E

Trade Deficits, the Balance of Payments, and the Dollar: Selected References, 1981–1984 [01/02/85] L0393

Trade Issues IP0263T

Trade with the Soviet Union [03/24/83] AB50075

Trading with the Communists [01/20/84] AB50100

United States-Israel Free Trade Area [02/11/85] IB84117

U.S.-Foreign Economic Issues: Bibliographic Background [12/84] BB14

U.S. Issues in International Trade: Overviews, Editorials and Public Opinion Polls [09/20/84] VU84013

U.S. Macroeconomic Policy in an International Context (CRS Review) [01/85] 85-1108 JAN

U.S. Trade and Payments Balances: What Do They Mean [01/23/85] 85-26 E

U.S. Trade Deficit: Data and Analysis [01/28/85] IB83115

U.S. Trade Relations with the Newly Industrializing Countries [10/03/84] 84-173 E

Why U.S. Agricultural Exports Have Declined in the 1980s [10/29/84] 84-223 ENR

TRANSPORTATION

Amtrak: Background and Issues in the 99th Congress [02/19/85] IB85051

Automobile Crash Protection [02/08/85] IB83085

Cargo Preference: Selected References, 1971–1984 [07/02/84] L0302

Commercial Airline Safety [02/05/85] IB84007

CONRAIL—The Proposed Sale IP0325C

Conrail: The Expected Forthcoming Sale [02/25/85] IB84142

Deregulation of Transportation [02/25/85] MB83219

Drunk Driving and the National Driver Register [02/08/85] IB83157

Emergency Response and Training for Hazardous Materials Transportation Accidents (CRS Review) [01/85] 85-1121 JAN

Federal Ownership of National and Dulles Airports: Background, Pro-Con Analysis, and Outlook [01/11/85] 85-504 E

The Gray Market for Imported Automobiles [12/27/84] 84-837 E

Prospects of Non-Compliance with the Automobile Fuel Economy Standards: Some Policy Options and Assessment of their Likelihood [12/21/84] 85-508 ENR

The Staggers Rail Act of 1980: The Outlook for Change During the 99th Congress [01/08/85] IB85017

Summary of the Staggers Rail Act of 1980 [01/07/85] 85-9 E

Trucking Regulation: The Outlook for Change During the 99th Congress [02/20/85] IB76019

Truck Tax Based on Vehicle Weight [11/28/84] MB83247

URBAN AND REGIONAL DEVELOPMENT

Block Grants IP0157B

Block Grants: A Guide to Information Sources [12/03/81] R005

Enterprise Zones IP0135E

Enterprise Zones Legislation in the 98th Congress [12/20/84] IB83188

Enterprise Zones: Selected References, 1981–1984 [12/07/84] L0387

Infrastructure: Current Legislative Proposals [03/29/83] AB50080

Infrastructure: Selected References, 1983–1984 [09/06/84] L0339

Water Project Development: Cost Sharing Issues [02/14/85] IB85044

VETERANS' BENEFITS AND SERVICES

Agent Orange: Veterans' Complaints about Exposure to the Herbicide IP0004A

Agent Orange: Veterans' Complaints and Studies of Health Effects [12/05/84] IB83043

Veterans IP0096V

Veterans' Benefits and Services: FY86 Budget [02/15/85] IB85043

Veterans' Benefits: Selected References, 1983–1984 [12/03/84] L0386

Vietnam Veterans: Selected References, 1979–1984 [10/25/84] L0379

Cultural Programs

Chamber music concerts, poetry festivals, lectures and readings are presented in the 500-seat Coolidge Auditorium and in the adjacent Whittall Pavilion during the fall, winter and spring. Recordings of the concerts and many of the programs are offered to radio stations for broadcast across the country. Lectures are often published in pamphlet form.

Through continually changing exhibitions, the Library shows the public what treasures it holds. Prints and photographs, maps and musical scores, rare books and manuscripts are drawn from the collections and displayed in the Library. In addition, many exhibits are sent on tour to libraries and museums across the nation. A free monthly calendar of events is available by written request. Contact: Information Office, Library of Congress, LM103, Washington, DC 20540/202-287-5108.

Digest of Public General Bills and Resolutions

The Digest provides summaries of each public bill and resolution and its current status in order of their introduction in Congress. It includes subject, author and specific title. Subscriptions service consists of cumulative issues, including a final issue upon adjournment of Congress. Supplements are issued irregularly. Sold for $75.00 per session of Congress by the Superintendent of Documents, Government Printing Office, Washington, DC 20402/202-783-3238. For additional information contact Congressional Research Service, Library of Congress, Madison Building, S.E., Washington, DC 20540/202-287-6996.

Geography and Maps

The Library's cartographic collection, 3,800,000 maps, nearly 48,000 atlases, 500 globes, and some 8,000 reference books is the largest and most comprehensive in the world. It includes atlases for the last five centuries which cover individual continents, countries, states, counties and cities as well as the world. Official topographic, geologic, soil mineral and resource maps and nautical and aeronautical charts are available for most countries of the world. Contact: Geography and Map Division, Library of Congress, LMB 02, Washington, DC 20540/202-287-6277.

Greeting Cards and Other Special Items

Greeting cards, notepaper, bookplates, and posters are for sale at the Library's Information Counter and by mail. For an illustrated brochure, write to the Library of Congress, Central Services Division, Washington, DC 20540/202-287-9691.

Guide to the Library of Congress

Written for both the serious researcher and the casual visitor, this 128-page illustrated guide covers the Library's history, architecture, exhibits, holdings and services. It also provides a map of the Library's tunnel system connecting its buildings and an illustrated location finder of reading rooms and dining facilities. The guide is available for $5.95 at the Library's Information Counter or by mail for $5.95 plus $2 for shipping and handling, from the Library of Congress, Information Office, Box A, Washington, DC, 20540/202-287-5108.

International Division

The Library's international divisions provide reference services on social, economic, and political topics overseas.

African-Middle Eastern Division/202-287-7937
   African Section/202-287-5528
   Hebraic Section/202-287-5422
   Near East Section/202-287-5421
Asian Division/202-287-5420
   Chinese and Korean Section/202-287-5423
   Japanese Section/202-287-5431
   Southern Asia/202-287-5600

European Division/202-287-5414
 Poland and East Europe/202-287-5414
 Czechoslovakia and East Europe/202-287-5414
 Finno-Ugrian/202-287-5414
Hispanic Division/202-287-5400

For additional information contact: Area Studies, Library of Congress, LJ 116, Washington, DC 20540/202-287-5543

Law Library

The Law Library contains the world's largest and most comprehensive collection of foreign international and comparative law. Its legal specialists provide information for all known legal systems present and past including common law, civil law, Roman law, canon law, Chinese law, Jewish and Islamic law, and ancient and medieval law. U.S. legislative documents include the *Congressional Record* (and its predecessors), the serial set, an almost complete set of bills and resolutions, current documents, committee prints, reports, hearings, etc. It also has a complete set of U.S. Supreme Court records and briefs and collections of U.S. Court of Appeals records and briefs. The law library has five major divisions:

American-British Law—United States, Australia, Canada, Great Britain, India, New Zealand, Pakistan, certain other countries of the British Commonwealth and their dependent territories, and Eire: 202-287-5077

European Law—nations of Europe and their possessions, except Spain and Portugal: 202-287-5088

Hispanic Law—Spain and Portugal, Latin America, Puerto Rico, the Philippines, and Spanish- and Portuguese-language states of Africa: 202-287-5070.

Far Eastern Law—nations of East and Southeast Asia, including China, Indonesia, Japan, Korea, Thailand, and former British and French possessions in the area: 202-287-5085.

Near Eastern and African Law—Middle Eastern countries, including the Arab States, Turkey, Iran, and Afghanistan, and all African countries, except Spanish-and Portuguese-language states and possessions, 202-287-5073.

For additional information contact: Law Library, Library of Congress, 10 1st St. S.E., Washington, DC 20540/202-287-5073.

Legislative Histories and Research

For legislative history information contact: Law Library, Library of Congress, LM 235, Washington, DC 20540/202-287-5065.

Librarians of Congress, 1802–1974

The Library of Congress was created in 1800 by an Act of Congress, and in the intervening 178 years there have been only twelve Librarians of Congress. Among them have been politicians, businessmen, newspapermen, a poet (Archibald MacLeish), lawyers, and even one professional librarian! This book discusses the lives and careers of the first eleven Librarians. It is available for $13.00 from the Superintendent of Documents, Government Printing Office, Washington, DC 20402/202-783-3238. For additional information contact: Information Office, Library of Congress, LM 103, Washington, DC 20540/202-287-5108.

Library Services for the Blind and Physically Handicapped

The National Library Services network maintains a collection of books, magazines, journals and music scores in braille, large type and recorded form. The materials are basically recreational in nature and range from best sellers to classics. The network also has information about handicapped conditions and aids. Searches are conducted to help eligible users locate materials and interlibrary loans can be arranged.

The collection contains more than 38,000 titles and is updated frequently. Searches are available from the National Library or its 56 regional and 101 subregional branches. The searches and interlibrary loan services are available free of charge to individuals who have poor eyesight, are blind or physically handicapped. Contact: Your regional or local library or the National Library Services for the Blind and Physically Handicapped, Reference Section, National Library of Congress, Washington, DC 20542/202-287-9287.

Manuscripts

The manuscript collection includes personal papers of eminent and important Americans; manuscripts about the history of Latin America; and records of prominent national organizations. Contact: Manuscript Division, Special Collections, Library of Congress, LM 102, Washington, DC 20540/202-287-5383.

Monthly Checklist of State Publications

This periodical records those documents and publications issued by the various states and received in the Library of Congress. It is available by subscription for $33.00 year. Contact: Superintendent of Documents, Government Printing Office, Washington, DC 20402/202-783-3238.

Motion Picture and Broadcasting

The film and television collections contain over 75,000 titles, with several thousand titles being added each year through copyright deposit, purchase, gift or exchange. Items selected from copyright deposits include feature films and short works of all sorts, fiction and documentary, exemplifying the range of current film and video production. The collections also include some 300,000 stills. Limited viewing facilities are available for specialized research. For additional information and viewing appointments contact: Motion Picture Broadcasting and Recorded Sound Division, Library of Congress, LM 338, Washington, DC 20540/202-287-5840.

Music Division

The collections of music and music literature include over 6,000,000 pieces of music and manuscripts, some 300,000 books and pamphlets and about 350,000 sound recordings reflecting the development of music in Western civilization from earliest times to the present. Every type of printed music is represented. Musicians who wish to play music drawn from the Library's collection may use the piano or the violin available in an adjacent soundproof room. For additional information contact: Music Division, Special Collections, Library of Congress, Room LM 113, Washington, DC 20540/202-287-5504.

National Preservation Program

The Library provides technical information related to the preservation and restoration of library and archival material. New techniques for preservation or restoration are developed and tested in the Restoration Laboratory. Research on longstanding preservation problems is conducted by the Preservation Research and Testing Office. A series of leaflets on various preservation and conservation topics has been prepared by the Preservation Office. Information and publications are available from the Library of Congress, Preservation Office, LMG 21, Washington, DC 20540/202-287-5213.

National Referral Center

The National Referral Center is a free referral service which directs those who have questions concerning any subject to organizations that can provide the answer. Its purpose is to direct those who have questions to resources that have the information and are willing to share it with others. Some of these resources exist within the Library itself. The Center file consists of over 13,000 organizations and includes a description of each, its special fields of interest and the type of information service it provides. Most queries are handled within five days. Contact: National Referral Center, LA 5122, Library of Congress, 10 1st St. S.E., Washington, DC 20540/202-287-5670.

National Referral Center Publications

The National Referral Center occasionally compiles directories of information resources covering a broad area. These are published by the Library of Congress under the general title *A Directory of Information Resources in the United States*. The most recent volume in the series is *Geosciences and Oceanography 1981* (GPO stock number 030-000-00131-1) which costs $8.50. It can be purchased from the Superintendent of Documents, Government Printing Office, Washington, DC 20402. Under the title *Who Knows?*, the Center issues informal lists of resources that have information on specific topics, such as hazardous materials, population or environmental education. The lists are available free of charge from the center as long as the supply lasts. A self addressed mailing label must accompany requests. Available titles include:

SL 80-2   *Pulp and paper.* 27 entries. 13 p. May 80

SL 81-2   *Wood products.* 47 entries. 22 p. Feb. 81

SL 82-1   *Financial assistance & educational opportunity.* 40 p. Rev. Oct. 82

SL 82-2   *Women's health.* 68 entries. 39 p. Rev. Feb. 83

SL 82-3   *Aeronautics & astronautics.* 104 entries. 60 p. Rev. Mar. 83

SL 83-1   *Hazardous materials.* 80 entries. 50 p. Rev. July 83

SL 83-2   *Science education.* 143 entries. 76 p. June 83

SL 83-3   *Vocational education & guidance.* 83 entries. 48 p. Rev. Dec. 83

SL 83-4   *Land use.* 87 entries. 59 p. Sep. 83

SL 83-5   *Solar energy.* 68 entries. 43 p. Aug. 83

SL 83-6   *Inventions & product development.* 38 entries. 20 p. Rev. Dec. 83

SL 84-1   *Motor vehicles.* 76 entries. 45 p. July 84

SL 84-2   *Electricity.* 83 entries. 51 p. July 84

SL 84-3   *Electronics.* 97 entries. 58 p. July 84

SL 84-4   *Foreign policy.* 101 entries. 60 p. July 84

SL 84-5   *International economics.* 115 entries. 76 p. Oct. 84

SL 84-6   *International social affairs.* 98 entries. 59 p. Nov. 84

SL 84   *International scientific affairs*

SL 84   *International education*

SL 84   *The arts*

Contact: Publications Section, National Referral Center, Library of Congress, LA 5122, Washington, DC 20540/202-287-1604.

National Referral Center Register

The National Referral Center invites organizations that have information in specialized fields to participate as information resources. They may register by letter or on a prepared form, available on request from the center. All applications should include the following information which is necessary for referrals: name, address, telephone number, area of interest, type of information available, audience to which information is available, and charge for information (free or fee based). Contact: National Referral Center, LA 5122 Library of Congress, 10 1st St. S.E., 5th Floor, Washington, DC 20540/202-287-5680.

National Union Catalog

The *National Union Catalog* is a register of all the world's books published since 1454 and held in more than 1,100 North American libraries, and other union catalogs which record the location of books in Slavic, Hebraic, Japanese and Chinese languages. It is published in book form so that many libraries have it at hand. Contact: Catalog Management and Publications Division, LA 2004,

Library of Congress Washington, DC 20540/202-287-5965.

Photoduplication Service
Copies of manuscripts, prints, photographs, maps, and book material not subject to copyright and other restrictions are available for a fee. Order forms for photo reproduction and price schedules for this and other copying services are available from the Library of Congress, Photoduplication Service, LA 1007, Washington, DC 20540/202-287-5637.

Printed Catalog Cards
Forms for ordering LC printed catalog cards may be obtained from the Cataloging Distribution Service, Library of Congress, LA 3014W, Washington, DC 20541/202-287-6120.

Prints and Photographs
The collections chronicle American life and society from the invention of photography to the present. Reference librarians will assist researchers doing their own investigations and will furnish names of picture searchers who work for a fee for those who cannot get to the library. Contact: Prints and Photographs Division, Library of Congress, LM 339, Washington, DC 20540/202-287-6394, Architecture Reference 202-287-6399.

Procurement
Persons seeking to do business with the Library of Congress should contact the Library of Congress, Procurement and Supply Division, Landover Center Annex, 1701 Brightseat Rd., Landover, MD 20785/202-287-8717.

Publications in Print
Library of Congress Publications in Print is a free annual list of publications. As new LC publications are issued, they are announced in the Library's weekly *Information Bulletin* and in the Superintendent of Documents' "Checklist of State Publications." The *Annual Report of the Librarian of Congress* contains a list of LC publications issued during the fiscal year covered. Contact: Information Office, Library of Congress, 10 1st St. S.E., Washington, DC 20540/202-287-5108.

Rare Book Division
This division contains about 309,000 volumes and pamphlets. Among the collection are documents of the first fourteen Congresses of the United States; dime novels; incunabula, early American imprints to the year 1801; Adolf Hitler's library; and the Russian Imperial collection. Contact: Rare Book and Special Collections Division, Library of Congress, LJ 256, Washington, DC 20540/202-287-5434.

Reading Rooms
The main reading room is located on the first floor of the main building. It contains material on American history, economics, fiction, language and literature, political science, government documents and sociology. The general reference section is also housed there. Contact: Main Reading Room, Library of Congress, 10 1st St. S.E., Washington, DC 20540/202-287-7478.

The Thomas Jefferson Reading Room contains material on science, technology, medicine, agriculture, fine arts, military science, education, genealogy, American local history, bibliography and library science, world history, philosophy, religion, geography, anthropology and sports. It keeps bound periodicals and also has a general reference section. Contact: Thomas Jefferson Reading Room, Library of Congress, Social Science, Washington, DC 20540/202-287-5538.

Reports on High School and Intercollegiate Debate Topics
A free report, prepared by the Library of Congress, contains a compilation of pertinent excerpts, bibliographical references and other materials related to debate topics. These topics are selected by the National University Extension Service Association as the national high school debate topics, and selected annually by the American Speech Association as the national college debate topics. Contact your local Congressman, or Information Office, LM103 Library of Congress, Washington, DC 20540/202-287-5108.

Research Facilities
Full-time scholars and researchers may apply for study desks in semi-private areas. For additional information contact: Research Facilities Section, General Reading Rooms, Library of Congress, Washington, DC 20540/202-287-5211.

Research Services
Guidance is offered to readers in the identification and use of material in the Library's collections, and reference service in answer to inquiries is offered to those who have exhausted local, state and regional resources. Persons requiring services which cannot be supplied will be furnished with names of private researchers who work on a fee basis. Requests for information should be directed to the Library of Congress, LJ 144 General Reading Rooms Division, Washington, DC 20540/202-287-5543.

Science and Technology
This division offers reference services based on the library's collection of 3 million scientific and technical books and pamphlets and 2.5 million technical reports. Reference librarians assist readers in using the library's book and on-line catalogs and in locating technical reports through abstracting and indexing services housed in the division's reading room. The division's Reference

Section prepares a series of bibliographic guides to selected scientific and technical topics. You can order (at no cost) the *Tracer Bullets* (See *Tracer Bullets* in this section) in your field of interest; they are a handy reference tool. Contact: Science and Technology Division, LA5104, Library of Congress, 110 2nd St. S.E., Room 5008, Washington, DC 20540/202-287-5639.

Science, Technology and Social Science Data Base
The National Referral Center maintains a directory listing of more than 12,000 organizations or individuals qualified and willing to provide information on topics primarily in science, technology and social sciences to the general public. A typical citation contains the name of the resource, mailing address, telephone number, areas of interest, special collections, data bases, publications and special services. Organizations can be located by name or subject.

References are provided for more than 12,000 sources. Searches and printouts are available free of charge. Contact: National Referral Center, Library of Congress, Washington, DC 20540/202-287-5670.

Serial and Government Publications
This collection contains over 70,000 titles of periodicals and government serials, microfilms and newspapers, both domestic and foreign. Contact: Serial and Government Publications Division, LM 133, Library of Congress, Washington, DC 20540/202-287-5647.

Sound Recordings
The sound recording collection reflects the entire spectrum of history of sound from wax cylinders to quadraphonic discs, and includes such diverse media as wire recordings, aluminum discs, zinc discs, acetate-covered glass discs, rubber compound discs and translucent plastic discs. The holdings also reflect a century of American life and culture and include a number of collections of unusual historical interest. Included are the Berliner collection, from the company which invented and introduced disc recording, radio news commentaries from 1944 to 1946, eyewitness descriptions of marine combat and House of Representative debates.

For purchase by researchers, the Division's laboratory is prepared to make taped copies of recordings in good physical condition, when not restricted by copyright, performance rights or provisions of gift or transfer. The requester is responsible for any necessary search—by mail or in person—of Copyright Office records to determine the copyright status of specific recordings.

The Division also offers copies of some of its holdings for sale in disc form. These include a number of LP records of folk music, poetry and other literature. For additional information contact: Motion Picture, Broadcasting and Recording Sound Division, Library of Congress, LM 113, Washington, DC 20540/202-287-5840.

Surplus Books
The Library of Congress makes its surplus duplicate books available to tax-supported and non-profit educational institutions and bodies on a donation basis. These publications are miscellaneous in character and are not listed or arranged in any way. They are shelved for inspection, and any eligible organization can review these surplus publications. Book dealers and other interested individuals may also review the duplicate collection, provided they are willing to offer library materials in exchange for any publication they select. Contact: Exchange and Gift Division, LM 632, Library of Congress, 110 2nd St. S.E., Washington, DC 20540/202-287-5243.

Tours
America's Library, an 18-minute slide/sound introduction to the Library of Congress, is shown hourly every day from 8:45 A.M. to 8:45 P.M. in the Orientation Theatre, Ground Floor, Thomas Jefferson Building. Free tours leave from the Orientation Theatre on the hour from 9 A.M. through 4 P.M. Monday through Friday. Group tours must be arranged in advance with the Tour Office. Contact: Tour Office, LJ G109, Library of Congress, Washington, DC 20540/202-287-5458.

Tracer Bullets
An informal series of free reference guides are issued by the Science and Technology Division under the general title *LC Science Tracer Bullet.* These guides are designed to help a reader begin to locate published material on a subject about which he or she has only general knowledge. New titles in the series are announced in the weekly Library of Congress *Information Bulletin* that is distributed to many libraries. Each *Bullet* is available. Contact Science and Technology Division, Reference Section, Library of Congress, LA 5104, Washington, DC 20540/202-287-5580.

The following titles (Followed by TB number) are available:

Acupuncture (75-1)
Endangered Species (Animals) (72-3)
Fresh-Water Ecology (72-4)
Rose Culture (72-7)
Mars (Planet) (72-8)
Quasars (72-11)
Algae (72-14)
Dolphins (72-15)
Sharks (72-17)
Noise Pollution (72-20)
Venus (73-3)
Artificial Intelligence (73-4)
Optical Illusions (73-5)
Ocean-Atmosphere Interaction (73-6)

Contact: Science and Technology Division, Reference Section, Library of Congress, LA 5104, Washington, DC 20540/202-287-5580.

Telephone Reference Service
Call 202-287-5522 to find out if the Library of Congress has a book you need or one you can borrow through the national inter-library loan system. Staff at this number will also track down answers to simple research questions.

How Can the Library of Congress Help You?
To determine how this office can help you contact: Information Office, Library of Congress, LM 103, Washington, DC 20540/202-287-5108.

Office of Technology Assessment

600 Pennsylvania Ave. S.E., Washington, DC 20510/202-224-8996

BUDGET: $11,284,000
EMPLOYEES: 130

Mission: Helps the Congress anticipate, and plan for, the consequences of uses of technology; provides an independent and objective source of information about the impacts, both beneficial and adverse, of technological applications; and identifies policy alternatives for technology-related issues.

Major Sources of Information

Current Assessment Activities
This booklet provides Members of Congress with brief summaries of OTA's current work projects and their anticipated completion dates. Contact: Publishing Office, Office of Technology Assessment, Congress, 600 Pennsylvania Ave. S.E., Washington, DC 20510/202-224-8996.

Background Papers
OTA Background Papers are documents that contain information believed to be useful to various parties. The information supports formal OTA assessments or is an outcome of internal exploratory planning and evaluation. For information contact: Publishing Office, Office of Technology Assessment, Congress, 600 Pennsylvania Ave. S.E., Washington, DC 20510/202-224-8996.

Congressional Fellowships
OTA awards up to 6 fellowships yearly, providing an opportunity for individuals of demonstrated outstanding ability to gain a better understanding of science and technology issues facing Congress and the ways in which Congress establishes national policy related to these issues. Applications generally must be received by February and stipends range from $25,000 to $41,000 depending upon the individual's background and experience. For further information, write: Congressional Fel-lowships, Personnel Office, Office of Technology Assessment, Congress of the United States, Washington, DC 20510.

Publications
OTA publishes reports, memoranda and background papers which cover such subjects as energy, food and renewable resources, health, international security and commerce, materials, oceans, telecommunications and information systems and transportation. Summaries of these materials are available free of charge from OTA's Publishing Office. Complete text can be purchased from Superintendent of Documents, U.S. Government Printing Office, Washington, DC 20402/202-783-3230. OTA reports include:

Energy, Materials, and International Security Division

ENERGY AND MATERIALS
Application of Solar Technology to Today's Energy Needs
Conservation and Solar Energy Programs of the Department of Energy
Direct Use of Coal
Energy Efficiency of Buildings in Cities
Energy From Biological Processes
Enhanced Oil Recovery Potential in the United States
Environmental Protection in the Federal Coal Leasing Program

Future of Liquefied Natural Gas Imports
Gasohol
Gas Potential From Devonian Shales of the Appalachian Basin
Increased Automobile Fuel Efficiency and Synthetic Fuels
Industrial and Commercial Cogeneration
Industrial Energy Use
Nuclear Power in an Age of Uncertainty
Nuclear Powerplant Standardization
Nuclear Proliferation and Safeguards
Potential U.S. Natural Gas Availability
Residential Energy Conservation
Solar Power Satellite Systems
Technology Assessment of Coal Slurry Pipelines
U.S. Vulnerability to an Oil Import Curtailment
World Petroleum Availability

INDUSTRY, TECHNOLOGY, AND EMPLOYMENT

Access Across Federal Lands: Options for Access in Alaska
Alternative Economic Stockpiling Policies
Conservation of Metals: Case Studies
Continuous Casting in the U.S. Steel Industry
Development and Production Potential of Federal Coal Leases
Engineering Implications of Chronic Materials Scarcity
Habitability of the Love Canal
Information Systems Capabilities Required To Support U.S. Materials Policy Decisions
Management of Minerals in Federal Lands
Materials and Energy From Municipal Waste
Nonnuclear Industrial Wastes
Oil Shale Technologies
Patterns and Trends in Federal Coal Lease Ownership, 1950–80
Technologies and Management Strategies for Hazardous Waste Control
Technologies to Reduce U.S. Materials Impact Vulnerability
Technology and Steel Industry Competitiveness
Wood Use: U.S. Competitiveness and Technology

INTERNATIONAL SECURITY AND COMMERCE

Analysis of Effects of Limited Nuclear Warfare
Directed Energy Missile Defense in Space
Effects of Nuclear War
International Competitiveness in Electronics
International Cooperation and Competition in Civilian Space Activities
MX Missile Basing
Remote Sensing and the Private Sector
Taggants in Explosives
Technology and East-West Trade
Technology and Soviet Energy Availability
Technology Transfer to the Middle East
Unispace '82
U.S. Industrial Competitiveness—A Comparison of Steel, Electronics, and Automobiles

Health and Life Sciences Division

BIOLOGICAL APPLICATIONS

Commercial Biotechnology
Human Gene Therapy

Impacts of Applied Genetics: Micro-Organisms, Plants, and Animals
Impacts of Neuroscience
Role of Genetic Testing in the Prevention of Occupational Disease
Technology and Aging in America
World Population and Fertility Planning Technologies

FOOD AND RENEWABLE RESOURCES

Drugs in Livestock Feed
Emerging Food Marketing Technologies
Environmental Contaminants in Food
Food Information Systems—Summary and Analysis
Impacts of Technology on U.S. Croplands and Rangeland Productivity
Nutrition Research Alternatives
Open Shelf-Life Dating of Food
Organizing and Financing Basic Research To Increase Food Production
Pest Management Strategies in Crop Protection
Technologies To Sustain Tropical Forest Resources
Technology, Renewable Resources, and American Crafts
U.S. Food and Agricultural Research System
Water-Related Technologies for Sustainable Agriculture in U.S. Arid/Semiarid Lands
Workshop Proceedings on Plants: The Potentials for Extracting Protein, Medicines, and Other Useful Chemicals

HEALTH

Abstracts of Case Studies in Health Technology Case Study Series
Blood Policy and Technology
Cancer Testing Technology and Saccharin
Compensation for Vaccine-Related Injuries
Computer Technology in Medical Education and Assessment
Cost-Effectiveness Analysis of Inactivated Influenza Vaccine
Development of Medical Technology: Opportunities for Assessment
Efficacy and Safety of Medical Technologies
Federal Activities Regarding the Use of Pneumoccal Vaccine
Federal Policies and the Medical Devices Industry
    Case Study #27: Nuclear Magnetic Resonance Imaging Technology: A Clinical, Industrial, and Policy Analysis
    Case Study #29: Boston Elbow
    Case Study #30: The Market for Wheelchairs: Innovation and Federal Policy
    Case Study #31: Contact Lenses
    Case Study #32: Hemodialysis Equipment
    Case Study #33: Technologies for Managing Urinary Incontinence
    Procurement and Evaluation of Medical Devices by the Veterans Administration
Forecasts of Physician Supply and Requirements
Impact of Randomized Clinical Trials on Health Policy and Medical Practice
Implications of Cost-Effectiveness Analysis of Medical Technology
    Background Paper #1: Methodological Issues and Literature Review

Background Paper #2: Case Studies of Medical Technologies

Case Study #1: Formal Analysis, Policy Formulation, and End-Stage Renal Disease

Case Study #2: The Feasibility of Economic Evaluation of Diagnostic Procedures: The Case of CT Scanning

Case Study #3: Screening for Colon Cancer: A Technology Assessment

Case Study #4: Cost Effectiveness of Automated Multichannel Chemistry Analyzers

Case Study #5: Periodontal Disease: Assessing the Effectiveness and Costs of the Keyes Technique

Case Study #6: The Cost Effectiveness of Bone Marrow Transplant Therapy and Its Policy Implications

Case Study #7: Allocating Costs and Benefits in Disease Prevention Programs: An Application to Cervical Cancer Screening

Case Study #8: The Cost Effectiveness of Upper Gastrointestinal Endoscopy

Case Study #9: The Artificial Heart: Cost, Risks, and Benefits

Case Study #10: The Costs and Effectiveness of Neonatal Intensive Care

Case Study #11: Benefit and Cost Analysis of Medical Interventions: The Case of Cimetidine and Peptic Ulcer Disease

Case Study #12: Assessing Selected Respiratory Therapy Modalities: Trends and Relative Costs in the Washington, DC Area

Case Study #13: Cardiac Radionuclide Imaging and Cost Effectiveness

Case Study #14: Cost Benefit/Cost Effectiveness of Medical Technologies: A Case Study of Orthopedic Joint Implants

Case Study #15: Elective Hysterectomy: Costs, Risks, and Benefits

Case Study #16: The Costs and Effectiveness of Nurse Practitioners

Case Study #17: Surgery for Breast Cancer

Background Paper #3: The Efficacy and Cost Effectiveness of Psychotherapy

Background Paper #4: The Management of Health Care Technology in Ten Countries

Background Paper #5: Assessment of Four Common X-Ray Procedures

Information Context of Premanufacture Notices

Medical Technology and Costs of the Medicare Program

Case Study #22: The Effectiveness and Costs of Alcoholism Treatment

Case Study #23: The Safety, Efficacy, and Cost Effectiveness of Therapeutic Apheresis

Case Study #24: Variations in Hospital Length of Stay: Their Relationship to Health Outcomes

Diagnosis Related Groups (DRGs) and the Medicare Program: Implications for Medical Technology

Working Paper: Diagnosis Related Groups (DRGs) and the Medicare Program: Using Diagnosis Related Groups in Hospital Payment—The New Jersey Experience

Case Study #28: Intensive Care Units (ICUs): Clinical Outcomes, Costs, and Decisionmaking

Medical Technology Under Proposals To Increase Competition in Health Care

Medlars and Health Information Policy

Policy Implications of the Computed Tomography (CT) Scanner

Policy Implications of Medical Information Systems

Postmarketing Surveillance of Prescription Drugs

Preventing Illness and Injury in the Workplace

Scientific Validity of Polygraph Testing

Selected Topics in Federal Health Statistics

Status of Biomedical Research and Related Technology for Tropical Diseases

Strategies for Medical Technology Assessment

Technologies for Determining Cancer Risks From the Environment

Technology and Handicapped People

Case Study #25: Technology and Learning Disabilities

Case Study #26: Assistive Devices for Severe Speech Impairments

Mandatory Passive Restraint Systems in Automobiles: Issues and Evidence

Selected Telecommunications Devices for Hearing-Impaired Persons

Technology Transfer at the National Institutes of Health

Science, Information, and Natural Resources Division

COMMUNICATION AND INFORMATION TECHNOLOGIES

Computer-Based National Information Systems

Computerized Manufacturing Automation: Employment, Education, and the Workplace

Effects of Information Technology on Financial Services

Electronic Funds Transfer Issues

Electronic Mail and Message Systems for the U.S. Postal Service

Informational Technology and Its Impact on American Education

Information Technology Research & Development

National Computerized Criminal History System

National Crime Information Center and the Computerized Criminal History System

Patent-Term Extension and the Pharmaceutical Industry

Radiofrequency Use and Management: Impacts From the World Administrative Radio Conference of 1979

Review of Postal Automation Strategy

OCEANS AND ENVIRONMENT

Acid Rain and Transported Air Pollutants

Coal Exports and Port Development

Coastal Effects of Offshore Energy Systems

Establishing a 200-Mile Fisheries Zone

Managing Commercial High-Level Radioactive Waste

Maritime Trade and Technology

Ocean Margin Drilling

Oil Transportation by Tankers

Protecting the Nation's Groundwater From Contamination

Renewable Ocean Energy Sources

Technology and Oceanography

Transportation of Liquefied Natural Gas

Use of Models for Water Resources Management, Planning, and Policy
Wetlands: Their Use and Regulation

SCIENCE, TRANSPORTATION, AND INNOVATION
Advanced High-Speed Aircraft
Air Cargo
Airport and Air Traffic Control System
Airport System Development
Air Service to Small Communities
Automated Guideway Transit
Changes in the Future Use and Characteristics of the Automobile Transportation System
Civilian Space Policy and Applications
Civilian Space Stations and the U.S. Future in Space
Evaluation of Railroad Safety
Financing and Program Alternatives for Advanced High-Speed Aircraft
Global Models, World Futures, and Public Policy
Impact of Advanced Group Rapid Transit Technology
Review of the FAA 1982 National Airspace System Plan
Salyut: Soviet Steps Toward Permanent Human Presence in Space
Space Science Research in the United States
Technology for Local Development
Technology, Innovation, and Regional Economic Development
U.S. Passenger Rail Technologies

Specialized Reports
Criteria for Evaluating the Implementation Plan Required by the Earthquake Hazards Reduction Act of 1977

Demographic Trends Influencing Education
Issues and Options in Flood Hazards Management
Technology Assessment in Business and Government
U.S. Disaster Assistance to Developing Countries

Administrative
Annual Reports
Assessment Activities
Information Brochure

For further information and a listing of publications, contact: Publishing Office, Office of Technology Assessment, Congress, 600 Pennsylvania Ave. S.E., Washington, DC 20510/202-224-8996.

Technical Memoranda
OTA Technical Memoranda are issued on specific subjects analyzed in recent OTA reports or in projects presently in process at OTA. They are issued at the request of Members of Congress. Contact: Publishing Office, Office of Technology Assessment, Congress, 600 Pennsylvania Ave. S.E., Washington, DC 20510/202-224-8996.

How Can the Office of Technology Assessment Help You?
To determine how this office can help you, contact: Office of Technology Assessment, 600 Pennsylvania Ave. N.W., Washington, DC 20510/202-224-8996.

Congressional Budget Office

2nd and D Sts. S.W., Washington, DC 20515/202-226-2621

Budget: $15,273,000
Employees: 222

Mission: Provides Congress with basic budget data and with analysis of alternative fiscal, budgetary and programmatic policy issues; and responsibility for economic forecasting and fiscal policy analysis, scorekeeping, cost projections, annual report on the budget and special studies.

Major Sources of Information

Annual Report on the Budget
The Congressional Budget Office is responsible for furnishing the House and Senate Budget Committees by April 1 of each year with a report which includes a discussion of alternative spending and revenue levels and alternative allocations among major programs and functional categories, all in the light of major national needs and the effect on the balanced growth and development of the United States. Contact: Intergovernmental Relations Press and Information, Personnel and Security, Congressional Budget Office, 2nd and D Sts. S.W., Room 405, Washington, DC 20515/202-226-2600.

Budget Analysis
CBO provides periodic forecasts and analyses of economic trends and alternative fiscal policies. Contact: Budget Analysis, Congressional Budget Office, 2nd and D Sts. S.W., Room 429, Washington, DC 20515/202-226-2800.

Cost Projections
The Congressional Budget Office is required to develop five-year cost estimates for carrying out any public bill or resolution reported by congressional committees. At the start of each fiscal year, CBO also provides five-year projections on the costs of continuing current federal and taxation

policies. Contact: Projections, Congressional Budget Office, 2nd and D Sts. S.W., Room 446, Washington, DC 20515/202-226-2880.

Publications
All papers published by CBO are available to the general public as well as to the members of Congress and their staff. A listing of papers by date of publication and by subject area is also available. Some of the areas covered include Agriculture; The Budget and Budget Projections; Budget Procedures; Defense, the Economy and Fiscal Policy; Education; Employment and Training; Energy; Environment and Natural Resources; Federal Work Force and Government Administration; Foreign Affairs; Health; Housing; Income Assistance; International Economic Relations; Law Enforcement and Justice; State and Local Government; Tax Expenditures; Tax Receipts and Distribution; Transportation; and Urban and Regional Development. Contact: Office of Intergovernmental Relations, Congressional Budget Office, House Office Building Annex 2, 2nd and D Sts. S.W., Washington, DC 20515/202-226-2809.

Scorekeeping
CBO "keeps score" for the Congress by monitoring the results of congressional action on individual

authorization, appropriation and revenue bills against the targets or ceilings specified in the concurrent resolutions. Contact: Score-Keeping, Congressional Budget Office, 2nd and D Sts. S.W., Room 439, Washington, DC 20515/202-226-2850.

How Can the Congressional Budget Office Help You?
To determine how this office can help you contact: Congressional Budget Office, Personnel and Security, 2nd and D Sts. S.W., Washington, DC 20515/202-226-2621.

Copyright Royalty Tribunal

Suite 415, 1111 20th St. N.W., Washington, DC 20036/202-653-5175

Budget: $484,000,000
Employees: 10

Mission: Makes determinations concerning the adjustments of copyright royalty rates for records, jukeboxes, and certain cable television transmissions.

Major Sources of Information

Meetings
The Tribunal notifies the public, 30 days in advance, of agency meetings. It publishes a hearing notice in the *Federal Register* and it uses the trade press to publicize proceedings of the Tribunal. Contact: Copyright Royalty Tribunal, 1111 20th St. N.W., Washington, DC 20036/202-653-5175.

Royalty Payments
In addition to records, jukeboxes and certain cable television transmissions, the Tribunal also establishes, and makes determinations concerning terms and rates of royalty payments for the use by public broadcasting stations of published nondramatic compositions and pictorial, graphic and sculptural works. Cost-of-living adjustments are made to these noncommercial broadcasting rates in August of each year. Contact: Copyright Royalty Tribunal, 1111 20th St. N.W., Room 450, Washington, DC 20036/202-653-5175.

Study in Audio Home Taping
The Tribunal published the results of a survey of consumer practices and attitudes concerning the home taping of audio works. Contact: Copyright Royalty Tribunal, 1111 20th St. N.W., Washington, DC 20036/202-653-5175.

Transcripts of Hearings
Transcripts of Tribunal meetings are available to the public. Contact: Copyright Royalty Tribunal, 1111 20th St. N.W., Washington, DC 20036/202-653-5175.

Use of Certain Copyrighted Works in Connection With New Commercial Broadcasting
This report reviews the necessity for a public broadcasting copyright compulsory license for the performance of nondramatic musical works, the recording of nondramatic performances and displays of musical works, and the use of published pictorial, graphic and sculptural works. Contact: Copyright Royalty Tribunal, 1111 20th St. N.W., Washington, DC 20036/202-653-5175.

How Can the Copyright Royalty Tribunal Help You?
To determine how this agency can help you, contact: Copyright Royalty Tribunal, 1111 20th St. N.W., Room 450, Washington, DC 20036/202-653-5175.

QUASI-OFFICIAL AGENCIES

Legal Services Corporation

733 15th St. N.W., Washington, DC 20005/202-272-4030

Established: July 25, 1974
Budget: $241,000,000
Employees: 177

Mission: Provides financial assistance to qualified programs furnishing legal assistance to eligible clients and makes grants to and contracts with individuals, firms, corporations, organizations and state and local governments for the purpose of providing legal assistance to these clients.

Major Sources of Information

Bar Relations
This office works with local and state bar associations and local legal services programs to promote further involvement of private attorneys in the delivery of legal service to the poor. Contact: Office of Bar Relations, Legal Services Corporation, 915 Peachtree St. N.E., 9th Floor, Atlanta, GA 30308/404-881-3049.

Central Records Room
The records room is open to the people and makes available for inspection all final opinions and orders in the adjudication of cases; statements of policy and interpretations; manual and instruction to the staff. There are regional record rooms as well. Contact: General Counsel's Office, Legal Services Corporation, 733 15th St. N.W., Suite 601, Washington, DC 20005/202-272-4010.

Comptroller
The Comptroller's office has developed a set of fundamental criteria for a local program accounting and financial reporting system. Contact: Comptroller, Legal Services Corporation, 733 15th St. N.W., Washington, DC 20005/202-272-4142.

Field Services
The legal services program is decentralized. A *Fact Book,* providing the characteristics of field pro-grams, contains graphs and tables of the main programs which include basic field programs; migrant programs; Native American programs; state support programs; and national support centers. For a listing and information of the legal services corporation's funded field programs contact: Office of Information Management, Legal Services Corporation, 733 15th St. N.W., 6th Floor, Washington, DC 20005/202-272-4276.

Freedom of Information Act
For Freedom of Information Act requests contact: General Counsel's Office, Legal Services Corporation, Room 601, 733 15th St. N.W., Washington, DC 20005/202-272-4010.

LSC News
This is a free bimonthly newsletter with news and features on legal services to the poor. Contact: Office of Public Affairs, Legal Services Corporation, 733 15th St. N.W., Washington, DC 20005/202-272-4030.

Meetings
Board, Committee and Council meetings are announced to the public at least seven days in advance. For minutes of the meeting and any other information contact: General Counsel, Legal Services Corporation, 735 15th St. N.W., Washington, DC 20005/202-272-4010.

National Clearinghouse on Legal Services
The Clearinghouse distributes a wide variety of materials on particular cases, on the practice of law and other issues affecting legal services programs. It also publishes the monthly *Clearinghouse Review*. Contact: National Clearinghouse on Legal Services, Inc., 4075 Dearborn, Suite 400, Chicago, Illinois 60605/312-939-3830.

How Can the Legal Services Corporation Help You?
To determine how this agency can help you contact: Legal Services Corporation, Public Affairs, 1733 15th St. N.W., Washington, DC 20005/202-272-4030.

National Gallery of Art

Constitution at 6th St NW, Washington, DC 20565/202-842-6246

Budget: $33,287,000
Employees: 700

Mission: This museum is devoted to American painting, sculpture and graphic art from the 18th century to today. It is also a major center for research in American art. In addition to its research library, the museum possesses a major archive of photographs and slides and has compiled an inventory of American paintings up to 1914.

Major Sources of Information

Art Courses
The Education Department offers occasional courses in art. The courses are free of charge. Consult the *Calendar of Events* for a listing.

Calendar of Events
A free monthly *Calendar of Events* listing special exhibitions, lectures, concerts and films will be sent upon request. To have your name placed on the mailing list write: Information Office, National Gallery of Art, Washington, DC 20565

Center for Advanced Study in the Visual Arts
The Center is a part of the National Gallery of Art. It was founded in 1979 to facilitate study of the history, theory, and criticism of art, architecture, and urbanism. It has programs for Senior Fellowships, Visiting Senior Fellowships and Pre-doctoral Fellowships. For further information contact: Center for Advanced Study in the Visual Arts, National Gallery of Art, Washington, DC 20565/202-842-6480.

Extension Services
Educational materials, including color slide programs, films and videocassettes based on the works in the Gallery's collection and special exhibitions can be borrowed without charge. A free catalogue is available. Contact: Extension Programs National Gallery of Art, Washington, DC 20565

Films
Free films on art are presented on a varying schedule in the auditorium. For further information, consult the Gallery's *Calendar of Events*.

Gifts and Bequests
Both the buildings and the collections of the National Gallery of Art are the result of private generosity. Offers of gifts or bequests of particular property should be discussed in advance with the Secretary's Office for specific important works of art, or with the Chief Librarian for books of art historical importance. Contact: National Gallery of Art, Washington, DC 20565/202-842-6246.

Lectures
Illustrated Lectures by visiting authorities are scheduled in the Gallery. These lectures are usually related to the National Gallery's collections or to a special exhibition. Admission is free, and no reservations are required. The Andrew W. Mellon Lectures in the Fine Arts is a special series of approximately six lectures that are commissioned yearly by the Gallery and given by a leading scholar. For further information, consult the *Calendar of Events*.

Publications
Books and exhibition catalogues, color reproductions, postcards, slides of works in the National Gallery's collection and posters are for sale through the Gallery's Mail Order Division. A sales catalogue is available for $1, Make checks payable to Publication Service. Contact: Publication Service, National Gallery of Art, Washington, DC 20565/202-842-6466

Slide Lending Service

Slides of the Gallery's collection are available as loans to organizations, schools, and colleges without charge. Contact: Slide Library, National Gallery of Art, Washington, DC 20565/202-737-4215.

Special Exhibition Programs

Under this program, private and public collections are loaned to the National Gallery from sources around the world. All special exhibits are announced in the Gallery's *Calendar of Events*.

Tours

Free tours of the collection and gallery talks are given by the Education Department.

Introductory Tour—lasts about 50 minutes, covers the Gallery's highlights.

Painting of the Week—15 minute gallery talk on a single painting in the collection.

Foreign Language Tours—Regularly scheduled tours are offered in French on Tuesdays at noon and in Spanish on Thursdays at noon. Tours in other foreign languages are offered by appointment through the Education Department. (202-842-6249)

Group Tours—Tours for groups of fifteen or more people may be arranged by booking at least two weeks in advance. (202-842-6246)

For further information contact: Information Office, National Gallery of Art, Washington, DC 20565/202-842-6353.

How Can the National Gallery of Art Help You?

To determine how the National Gallery of Art can help you, contact: Information Office, National Gallery of Art, Washington, DC 20565/202-842-6353.

National Railroad Passenger Corporation (AMTRAK)

400 North Capitol St. N.W., Washington, DC 20001/202-383-3000

Established: 1970
Budget: $684,000,000
Employees: 20,000

Mission: Operates as a for-profit corporation to provide a balanced transportation system by improving and developing intercity rail passenger service.

Major Sources of Information

Financial and Operating Statistics
AMTRAK issues detailed financial and operating statistics which include data on ridership revenue cars, locomotive units, turboliners and metroliner, information on operating grants and AMTRAK's financial position. An Annual Report is also available. For information contact: Corporate Communications, National Railroad Passenger Corporation, 400 North Capitol St. N.W., Washington, DC 20001/202-383-3852.

New Corridor
AMTRAK is studying a new high-speed, high frequency emerging corridor outside the northeast. For information on these potential new corridors contact: Passenger Services, National Railroad Passenger Corporation, 400 North Capitol St. N.W., Washington, DC 20001/202-383-2733.

Passenger Services
For information on AMTRAK passenger service contact: Passenger Service and Communication Group, National Railroad Passenger Corporation, 400 North Capitol St. N.W., Washington, DC 20001/202-383-2733.

How Can AMTRAK Help You?
To determine how this agency can help you contact: Corporate Communications, AMTRAK, 400 North Capitol St. N.W., Washington, DC 20001/202-383-3860.

Smithsonian Institution

1000 Jefferson Dr. S.W., Washington, DC 20560/202-357-2700

Established: 1846
Budget: $303,000,000
Employees: 5,400

Mission: The Smithsonian Institution is an independent trust establishment, performs fundamental research; publishes the results of studies, explorations, and investigations; preserves for study and reference over 100 million items of scientific, cultural and historical interest; maintains exhibits representative of the arts, American history, technology, aeronautics and space explorations and natural history; participates in the international exchange of learned publications; and engages in programs of education and national and international cooperative research and training, supported by its trust endowments and gifts, grants and contracts, and funds appropriated to it by Congress.

Major Sources of Information

Air and Space Museum—National
The Museum is a celebration of flight and a showcase for the evolution of aviation and space technology. The 23 galleries feature history makers from the 1903 Wright Flyer and the Spirit of St. Louis to John Glenn's Friendship 7 and the Apollo 11 command module. Visitors can see the docked Apollo-Soyuz spacecraft, a Viking Lander and a Voyager spacecraft. There are also the backup Skylab Orbital Workshop to enter and a moon rock to touch. In Exploring the Planets, visitors can "fly over" Mars and "descend" to Venus while learning the latest information on the solar system. Special films on flight are projected onto a five-story movie screen in the Museum theater, and visitors can obtain a new insight into the heavens via the presentations in the Albert Einstein Spacearium. Contact: National Air and Space Museum, Smithsonian Institution, 7th Street and Independence Ave. S.W., Washington, DC 20560/202-357-2491.

American and Folklife Studies
The Folklife Program is responsible for research, documentation and presentation of American folklife traditions. It prepares publications based on the papers, films, tapes and other materials amassed during previous Festivals of American Folklife and directs the planning, development and presentation of future folklife programs. Contact: Office of Folklife Programs, Smithsonian Institution, 2600 L'Enfant Plaza, SW, Washington, DC 20560/202-287-3424.

Anacostia Neighborhood Museum
This neighborhood museum serves as a museum exhibition hall and a cultural center. The exhibit, research and educational programs are designed in response to the interest of local residents. Contact: Anacostia Neighborhood Museum, Smithsonian Institution, 2405 Martin Luther King, Jr. Ave. SE, Washington, DC 20020/202-287-3369.

Antarctic Map Folio Series

Knowledge of Antarctica is summarized in this series which includes books, maps and map folios. For a listing of the items in the series and their prices, contact: Oceanographic Sorting Center, Museum of Natural History, Smithsonian Institute, SOSC, Washington, DC 20560/202-287-3302.

Archives

The Smithsonian Archives open to the scholarly community and the general public is the official depository for papers of historic value about the Smithsonian and the fields of science, art, history and the humanities.

The holdings of the Archives are announced by publication of guides which are updated periodically. *Guide to Smithsonian Archives* describes the archival holdings. Contact: Smithsonian Archives, Smithsonian Institution, 900 Jefferson Dr. S.W., Washington, DC 20560/202-357-1420.

Archives Journal

The Archives of American Art publishes a scholarly journal quarterly containing articles and listings of recent acquisitions apprising the research community of newly available resources. Contact: Archives of American Art, Smithsonian Institution, 8th and F Sts. N.W., Washington, DC 20560/202-357-2781.

Archives of American Art

The Archives of American Art contains the nation's largest collection of documentary materials reflecting the history of visual arts in the United States. The Archives gathers, preserves and microfilms the papers of artists, craftsmen, collectors, dealers, critics, museums and art societies. These papers consist of manuscripts, letters, notebooks, sketchbooks, business records, clippings, exhibition catalogs, tape-recorded interviews and photographs of artists and their work. The Archives' chief processing and reference center is in the Smithsonian's Fine Arts and Portrait Gallery Building. The Archives' executive office is in New York; regional branch offices, each with a complete set of microfilm duplicating the Archives' collections are located in Boston, New York, Detroit, San Francisco and Los Angeles. Contact: Archives of American Art, Smithsonian Institution, 8th & F Sts. N.W., Washington, DC 20560/202-357-2781; Boston: 87 Mt. Vernon St. Boston, MA 02108/617-223-0951; Detroit: 5200 Woodward Ave., Detroit, MI 48202/313-226-7544; New York: 41 E. 65th St., New York, NY 10021/212-826-5722; San Francisco: DeYoung Museum, Golden Gate Park, San Francisco, CA 94118/415-556-2530.

Arts in America: A Bibliography

This four-volume set is a systematic presentation of the literature on the visual and performing arts from the colonial period to the present day.

Approximately 25,000 annotated entries, organized into 21 sections, list and describe the resource materials accessible to art historians and curators, students and collectors, librarians and researchers at all levels of interest. Encompassing books, exhibition catalogs, periodical articles, and inventories of pictorial materials, the subject sections cover art of the Native Americans, art of the West, architecture, industrial design and the decorative arts, painting and sculpture, graphic arts and photography, film and theater, dance and music. Special sections of dissertations, serials and periodicals, and visual resources are also included. The four volumes are available for $190.00 from Publications Sales, Smithsonian Institution Press, Smithsonian Institution, 1111 North Capitol St., Washington, DC 20560/202-357-1793. For additional information contact: Smithsonian Archives, Smithsonian Institution, 900 Jefferson Dr. S.W., Washington, DC 20560/202-357-1420.

Astrophysical Observatory

The Harvard-Smithsonian Center for Astrophysics is devoted to research into the basic physical processes which determine the nature and evolution of the Universe. The Observatory conducts this research through a variety of efforts grouped programmatically in seven major divisions:

Atomic and Molecular Processes—laboratory astrophysics, shock tube and ultraviolet vacuum spectroscopy, atomic physics and particle physics.

Radio and Geoastronomy—very long baseline interferometric observations of celestial radio sources and laboratory studies of interstellar molecules; kinematics of the earth, optical and laser satellite tracking, geodesy and geophysics and celestial mechanics.

High-Energy Astrophysics—satellite, balloon and ground observations of high-energy sources emitting x-rays and/or gamma rays.

Optical and Infrared Astronomy—satellite, balloon and ground observation of infrared radiation sources, steller and planetary observations and studies of stellar evolution.

Planetary Sciences—studies of the structure and composition of planetary atmospheres; asteroids, meteorites and cosmic dust; comets; extraterrestrial materials; and studies of solar system evolution.

Solar and Stellar Physics—satellite experiments, observational and theoretical studies of solar and stellar processes, and studies of solar activity.

Theoretical Astrophysics—construction of model stellar atmospheres, investigation of massive and high-density stars, studies of galactic evolution, and the physics of interstellar matters.

Data are obtained from laboratory experiments, ground-based observations and space-borne observations and experiments. The Astrophysical Observatory's data collecting efforts are linked by a global communications center located in Cambridge, MA. The Observatory also maintains extensive laboratory, library and computer facilities to support its research. Research results are published in the *Center Preprint Series, Smithsonian Contributions to Astrophysics,* the *SAO Special Reports* series, and other technical and non-technical bulletins, and distributed to scientific and educational institutions around the world. Contact: Smithsonian Publications, Astrophysical Observatory, 60 Garden St., Cambridge, MA 02138/617-495-7461.

Astronomical Phenomena News
The Central Bureau for Astronomical Telegrams and the Minor Planet Center for the International Astronomical Union issue telegrams and postcard circulars describing news of astronomical phenomena requiring prompt world-wide dissemination to the scientific community, such as asteroid and comet discoveries, novae and supernovae observations, and variable start activity. The Minor Planet Center is the principal source for all positional observations of asteroids as well as for establishing their orbits and ephemendes. Contact: Smithsonian Astrophysical Observatory, Smithsonian Institution, 60 Garden St., Cambridge, MA 02138/617-495-7244

Books
Smithsonian Exposition Books publishes books on Smithsonian art and artifacts and on the results of the Institution's scholarship and expertise for the general reader. Some of its publications include:

Our Green and Living World
Thread of Life
Rhythms of Life
Jungles
A Smithsonian Book of Comic-Book Comics
The National Air and Space Museum
Fire of Life
Treasures of the Smithsonian
The Smithsonian Experience
The Smithsonian Book of Invention
The American Land
The Magnificent Foragers
A Zoo for All Seasons

For a list of additional publications and information, contact: Smithsonian Books, Smithsonian Institution, 475 L'Enfant Plaza, S.W., Washington, DC 20560/202-287-3388. or Toll-Free Order Number 800-247-5072 (in Iowa, 300-532-1426).

Catalogue of American Portraits
This catalog contains documentation including photographs on almost 70,000 portraits of noted Americans located in public and private collections throughout the country. It includes biographical, historical and art-historical data. Contact: Museum Shop, National Portrait Gallery, Smithsonian Institution, 8 and F Sts. N.W., Washington, DC 20560/202-357-1447.

Center for the Study of Man
This center promotes interdisciplinary cultural and anthropological research on man. The Center's National Anthropological Film Center sponsors an effort to record on film the daily life, behavior, adaptations and patterns of various peoples in disappearing cultures. Its Research Institute on Immigration and Ethnic Studies researches various recent immigration patterns to the United States. Contact: Center for the Study of Man, National Museum of Natural History and National Museum of Man, 10th and Constitution Ave. N.W., Washington, DC 20560/202-357-2801.

Comics
The Smithsonian Collection of Newspaper Comics is available for $29.95 (cloth) and $14.95 (paper) from Publications sales, Smithsonian Institution Press, Smithsonian Institution, 1111 North Capitol St., Washington, DC 20560/202-357-1793

Computerized Data Bases
These data bases are maintained by the Smithsonian Institution.

Smithsonian Museum Data Bases
The Smithsonian Institution, the world's largest museum complex, has more than 70 million objects and specimens housed within its museums and the National Zoo. The museum is one of the world's foremost research centers; its huge study collections in the areas of history, technology and science are available to scholars worldwide. Computer data bases exist for every collection and topics range from anthropology to volcanoes. As there are literally hundreds of data bases, it would be impossible to list them all in this directory. If you need information about a specific object or topic, it is best to get in touch with the curator responsible for that particular area. The curator can refer you to the appropriate person who can query the data base for you. Often, the curator can also refer you to experts in your field who are familiar with current research and literature. The majority of data banks are catalogs of Smithsonian collections and, although they vary somewhat in content, most contain the following type of data about objects: donor name; collector's name; date and site of acquistion; object name, type, theme; and sometimes a physical description. Data is retrievable by the aforementioned categories and also by: artist's name, record of artist's works, and sex or race of artist (i.e., all works by women in a certain time period); attributes of museum objects; and utility lists of vendors (i.e., by year, name, etc.).

Searches and printouts are available free of charge. Often, specimens will be lent, free of charge, to researchers. The Smithsonian will also locate, at no charge, objects a donor's relatives would like to view. Contact: The curator responsible for the data in which you are interested. You can obtain the curator's name and phone number from: Public Inquiry Mail Service, Smithsonian Institution Great Hall, Washington, DC 20560/ 202-357-2700.

Taxonomic Organisms Data Base
The Sample Inventory contains taxonomic information about all organisms of algae, plankton, benthic invertebrates and fishes. Specimen data includes: where sample was collected, latitude/ longitude, depth of water in which sample was captured, and date collected. Information can be retrieved by organism, geographical area, or depth of water.

Searches and printouts are available free of charge. Access is available through the Smithsonian Oceanographic Sorting Center. Contact: Smithsonian Institute, SOSC, Washington, DC 20560/202-287-3302.

Conservation-Analytical Laboratory
The Conservation-Analytical Laboratory provides a focus within the Smithsonian Institution for conservation of the millions of artifacts in the collections. It provides chemical analyses to curators for cataloguing purposes, and to conservators for establishing the nature of a particular example of deterioration and for determining whether commercial materials proposed for use in prolonged contact with artifacts are truly safe. It treats many hundreds of artifacts each year and, upon request, supports other conservators in the Institution with advice and specialized materials. It collaborates with archeologists, curators, and university and government laboratories in archeometric studies. Contact: Conservation Analytical Laboratory, Smithsonian Institution, Museum Support Center, Room D, Washington, D.C. 20560/287-3700

Conservation Information
The Conservation Information Program provides data on the preservation of artifacts and specimens which are disseminated to museums, historical societies and other organizations. A series of 80 videotape lectures on the principles of conservation, prepared under the technical direction of the Conservation Analytical Laboratory, is circulating to museums and related organizations. Audiovisual materials on practical aspects of conservation are available. Contact: Conservation Information Program, Office of Museum Programs, Smithsonian Institution, 900 Jefferson Dr. S.W., Washington, DC 20560/202-357-3101.

Contracts and Small Business
Information regarding procurement of supplies; contracts for construction, services, exhibits, research etc.; and property management and utilization services for all Smithsonian Institution organ-

izations may be obtained from Office of Supply Services, Smithsonian Institution, 1000 Jefferson Dr. S.W., Washington, DC 20560/202-287-3238.

Dial-A-Museum
A taped telephone message provides daily announcements on new exhibits and special events. Call 202-357-2020 or contact: Visitor Information Center, Smithsonian Institution, 1000 Jefferson Dr. S.W., Washington, DC 20560/202-357-2700

Dial-A-Phenomenon
A taped telephone message provides weekly announcements on stars, planets and world-wide occurrences of short-lived natural phenomena. 202-357-2000 or contact: Visitor Information Center, Smithsonian Institution, 1000 Jefferson Dr. S.W., Washington, DC 20560/202-357-2700

Discovery Room
Discovery Room allows children to touch and examine objects in the Museum of Natural History. Contact: National Museum of Natural History and National Museum of Man, Smithsonian Institution, 10th and Constitution Ave. N.W., Washington, DC 20560/202-357-2695.

Dwight D. Eisenhower Institute for Historical Research
This institute conducts scholarly studies into the meaning of war, its effect on civilization and on the role of the Armed Forces. Contact: Dwight D. Eisenhower Institute of Historical Research, National Museum of American History, Smithsonian Institution, 12th St. and Constitution Ave. N.W., Washington, DC 20560/202-357-2183.

Elementary and Secondary Education
This office helps make Smithsonian resources for learning available to schools. It coordinates information exchanges between schools and the activities of the Institution's museums, galleries and research centers. Information on the various programs available to schools is published in *Art to Zoo* a newsletter for teachers from 4th through 8th grades and *Learning Opportunities,* a free brochure. Contact: Office of Elementary and Secondary Education, Smithsonian Institution, 900 Jefferson Dr. S.W., Washington, DC 20560/202-357-2425.

Environmental Research Center
The Smithsonian Environmental Research Center pursues basic research programs that quantitatively describe changes in the environment and how these changes influence biological growth and development. Included are problems of photobiology at the cellular, subcellular and molecular levels. It conducts research in the measurement of solar energy and in environmental biology, engages in the study and dating of archeological

specimens by the carbon-14 method, and studies various biological processes that are controlled by light. Predoctoral and postdoctoral research programs in photobiology are encouraged. Contact Smithsonian Environmental Research Center, 12441 Parklawn Dr., Rockville, MD 20852-1773/ 301-443-2306. The program also includes scientific and educational research information transfer and ecological education. The scientific program includes studies of esturarine processes, watershed monitoring and research in terrestrial ecology. The Education programs include workshops on environmental issues for young persons and adults. Educational Services for schools and other groups are available on request. Contact Smithsonian Environmental Research Center, RR 4, P.O. Box 28, Edgewater, MD 21037/301-261-4190.

Exhibits Central
This office provides design editorial, production, installation and other specialized exhibition services for a variety of Smithsonian programs. Some of the services include editing exhibition labels, producing motion pictures on exhibition concepts, and the application of plastics technology to museum exhibitions. Contact: Office of Exhibits Central, Smithsonian Institution, 1111 N. Capitol St., Washington, DC 20560/202-357-3118.

Famous Aircraft of the National Air and Space Museums
Each volume in this series deals with a different historic airplane in the museum's collection. The books are divided into two main sections. Part I covers the background and history of the aircraft. Part II provides details unique to its restoration by skilled craftsmen of the museum.

Excalibur III: The Story of a P-51 Mustang ($4.95)
Aeronca C-2: The Story of the Flying Bathtub ($4.95)
The P-80 Shooting Star—Evolution of a Jet Fighter ($5.95)

These and other publications are available from Publications Sales, Smithsonian Institution Press, Smithsonian Institution, 1111 North Capitol St., Washington, DC 20560/202-357-1793. For additional information on aircraft, contact: National Air and Space Museum, Smithsonian Institution, 7th St. and Independence Ave. N.W., Washington, DC 20560/202-357-2491.

Fellowships and Grants
The Office administers the Smithsonian predoctoral and postdoctoral fellowship programs, which make grants to visiting scholars and students from the United States and abroad. This program is designed to bring developing scholars to the Smithsonian for periods of directed study, to give more senior scholars the benefit of specialized work with staff researchers, and to provide graduates and undergraduates an opportunity for study

visits lasting up to three months. The Office also administers a Special Foreign Currency Program, a nationally competitive grants program for research carried out by U.S. institutions in countries where the United States owns local currencies deemed by the Treasury Department to be in excess of normal U.S. needs. Grants are offered in disciplines in which the Smithsonian has traditional competence and interest: archeology, anthropology and related studies, systematic and environmental biology, astrophysics and earth sciences and museum programs. Contact: Office of Fellowships and Grants, Smithsonian Institution, L'Enfant Plaza, S.W., Suite 3300, AMTRAK Building, Washington, DC 20560/202-287-3271.

Freer Gallery of Art
The Gallery houses one of the world's most renowned collections of oriental art as well as an important group of ancient Egyptian glass, early Christian manuscripts, and the works of James McNeill Whistler together with other late 19th and early 20th century American painters. Over 10,000 objects in the oriental section represent the arts of the Far East, the Near East, Indochina, and India, including paintings, manuscripts, scrolls, screens, pottery, metalwork, glass, jade, lacquer and sculpture. Members of the staff conduct research on objects in the collection and publish results in scholarly journals and books. They arrange special exhibitions and present lectures in their field of specialization. Annually, a series of six lectures on Far and Near Eastern art is given by distinguished scholars.

Technical Laboratory. The laboratory is one of the outstanding centers in the world for research into the materials and methods of ancient craftsmen. Its staff members study the nature and properties of metals, ceramics, lacquers, papers and pigments in an effort to reconstruct the history of ancient technology and to find out how best to preserve and to protect the objects of art in the collection.

The Gallery publishes two scholarly series:

The Freer Gallery of Art Oriental Studies
The Freer Gallery of Art Occasional Papers and Ars Orientalis

Contact: Freer Gallery of Art, Smithsonian Institution, 12th St. and Jefferson Dr. S.W., Washington, DC 20560/202-357-2104.

Grants
The programs described below are for sums of money which are given by the federal government to initiate and stimulate new or improved activities or to sustain on-going services.

Museums—Assistance and Advice:
Objectives: To support the study of museum problems, to encourage training of museum person-

nel, and to assist research in museum techniques, with emphasis on museum conservation.

Eligibility: Science, history and art museums, as well as museum-related organizations and academic institutions are eligible. and individuals employed or sponsored by a museum.

Range of Financial Assistance: $4,000 to $40,000

Contact: Program Coordinator, National Museum Act, Arts and Industries Building, Room 3465, Smithsonian Institution, Washington, DC 20560/202-357-2257.

Smithsonian Institution Programs in Basic Research in Collaboration with Smithsonian Institution Staff:

Objectives: To make available to qualified investigators at various levels of educational accomplishment, the facilities, collections, and professional staff of the Smithsonian Institution.

Eligibility: Appointments are available to advanced students and scholars intending to pursue research and study which relates to Smithsonian Institution research and interests of the professional staff.

Range of Financial Assistance: Up to $18,000.

Contact: Director, Office of Fellowships and Grants, Room 3300, 955 L'Enfant Plaza, Smithsonian Institution, Washington, DC 20560/202-287-3271.

Smithsonian Special Foreign Currency Grants for Museum Programs, Scientific and Cultural Research and Related Educational Activities:

Objectives: To support the research activities of American institutions of higher learning through grants in countries where the U.S. Treasury has determined that the United States holds currencies in excess to its needs as a result of commodity sales under Public Law 480. Limited funds are available for travel to professional meetings.

Eligibility: All American institutions of higher learning are eligible: universities, colleges, museums and research institutions, incorporated in any one of the 50 states or the District of Columbia.

Range of Financial Assistance: $3,000 to $50,000.

Contact: Grants Specialist, Smithsonian Foreign Currency Program, Office of Fellowships and Grants, Smithsonian Institution, Washington, DC 20560/202-287-3321.

Woodrow Wilson International Center for Scholars—Fellowships and Guest Scholar Programs:

Objectives: The theme of the fellowship program is designed to accentuate aspects of Wilson's ideals and concerns for which he is perhaps best known—his search for international peace and his imaginative new approaches in meeting the pressing issues of his day—translated into current terms.

Eligibility: Up to 40 scholars—approximately two thirds from the United States and one third from other countries—will be selected to work at the Center. They will be chosen from academic and nonacademic occupations and professions. Limited to established scholars at the postdoctoral level (or equivalent). There will be no higher degree requirements for nonacademic fellows, but professional standing, writings, honors and advanced degrees will be considered.

Range of Financial Assistance: Not specified.

Contact: Director, Woodrow Wilson International Center for Scholars, Smithsonian Institution Building, Washington, DC 20560/202-357-2841.

Handbook of North American Indians

A major project is the *Handbook of North American Indians,* a comprehensive 20-volume encyclopedia written from anthropological, historical and linguistic perspectives. When completed, it will include the work of more than 1,000 author-contributors. Some volumes will be devoted to tribal cultures and histories by geographic region, such as the Northeast, Southwest and the Plains Indians. Other works will be organized around topics such as languages, technologies and the history of Indian-white relations. The first volume deals with the California tribes. The second volume covers Northeast Indians and the third volume is on the Indians of the Southwest. Contact: National Museum of Natural History and National Museum of Man, Smithsonian Institution, 10th and Constitution Ave. N.W., Washington, DC 20560/202-357-1861

Hirshhorn Museum and Sculpture Garden

The collection consists of modern American and European sculpture, paintings and drawings. It also contains supplementary collections of pre-Columbian sculpture, Benin bronzes, Eskimo carvings and classical antiquities that illustrate some sources of contemporary art. Contact: Hirshhorn Museum and Sculpture Garden, Smithsonian Institution, 8th St. and Independence Ave. S.W., Washington, DC 20560/202-357-3091.

Horticulture

This office is responsible for the development and maintenance of the grounds of the Institution as botanical and horticultural exhibit areas. It coordinates a program of horticultural research, maintains a collection of period garden accessories, documents historic landscape schemes and serves as the Institution's liaison with government organizations for outdoor beautification activities. Contact: Office of Horticulture, Smithsonian Institution, 900 Jefferson Dr. S.W., Washington, DC 20560/202-357-1926.

Insects, National Collection of

The Smithsonian Institution has a large collection

of insects, all of which are mounted and classified. For information on the collection, contact: Systematic Entomological Laboratory, Department of Entomology, Smithsonian Institution, Washington, DC 20560/202-357-2078.

International Center for Scholars
The Center's emphasis is on studies of fundamental political, social, and intellectual issues designed to illuminate man's understanding of critical contemporary and emerging problems and to suggest means of resolving such problems. Special programs focus on such areas as: advanced Russian Studies, Latin American, East Asian, and International Security Studies. The chief concerns of the Center, in its annual choice of fellows through open competition, are with the scholarly capabilities and promise of the prospective fellow. The Center also sponsors a large program of meetings. For additional information contact: Woodrow Wilson International Center for Scholars, Smithsonian Institution, 1000 Jefferson Dr. S.W., Washington, DC 20560/202-357-2763.

International Environmental Science Program
This program is devoted to broad-based ecological studies of tropical and subtropical regions. Contact: Science, Smithsonian Institution, 1000 Jefferson Dr. S.W., Washington, DC 20560/202-357-2903.

International Handbook of Aerospace Awards and Trophies
This *Handbook* is intended to serve as a reference source for aerospace historians, scholars and libraries with collections in science and technology. All aspects of flight, ballooning, manpowered flight, early air racing events and exceptional contributions to the engineering and administration of aerospace achievements are included. One hundred and twenty organizations world-wide are represented. It is available for $15.00. For additional information, contact: National Air and Space Museum, Museum Shop, Smithsonian Institution, 7th St. and Independence Ave. N.W., Washington, DC 20560/202-357-1387.

John F. Kennedy Center for the Performing Arts
Since its opening in 1971, the Center has presented a year-round program of music, dance and drama from the United States and abroad. Facilities include the Concert Hall, the Opera House, the Eisenhower Theater, the Terrace Theater, and a laboratory theater. By special arrangement, the Center also houses the American Film Institute Theater. For additional information contact: John F. Kennedy Center for the Performing Arts, 2700 F St. N.W., Washington, DC 202-872-0466.

Joseph Henry Papers
The Smithsonian is undertaking (with the American Philosophical Society of the National Academy of Sciences) the publication of the papers of Joseph Henry (1797–1878), a major experimental physicist in electricity and magnetism. His papers provide insight into the history of American higher education, the development of federal science policy and American attitudes toward learning and research. Contact: Joseph Henry Papers, Smithsonian Institution, 1000 Jefferson Dr. S.W., Washington, DC 20560/202-357-2787.

Libraries
The Smithsonian Institution libraries system, composed of a central library and 21 bureau and branch libraries, emphasizes multidisciplinary journals, on such topics as ecology, travel exploration and museology, natural history, American ethnology, and cultural, tropical biology, decorative arts and design, astrophysics and the history of science and technology and the history of aeronautics and astronautics. Contact the specialized library or Smithsonian Institution Libraries, Smithsonian Institution, 10th St. and Constitution Ave. N.W., Washington, DC 20560/202-357-2240.

Marine and Estuary Science
The Fort Pierce Bureau sponsors research in marine and estuarine science. Scientists are seeking basic information on life histories, ecology and systematics of vertebrate and invertebrate organisms of the local waters. Contact: Fort Pierce Bureau, Smithsonian Institution, Rt. 1, Box 194-C, Fort Pierce, FL 33450/305-465-6630.

Membership
For information about membership in the Smithsonian Resident Associate Program contact: Resident Associate Program, Smithsonian Institution, 900 Jefferson Dr. S.W., Washington, DC 20560/202-357-3030.

Museum of African Art—National
This museum is dedicated exclusively to the display and study of the creative traditions of Africa. The collection includes 8,000 objects of African sculpture, artifacts, craftworks, traditional costumes, textiles, drums, musical instruments and jewelry, covering almost every art-producing area of Africa but concentrating on West and Central Africa. The library contains some 10,000 titles on African and Afro-American art, culture and history. Contact: Museum of African Art, Smithsonian Institution, 318 A St. N.E., Washington, DC 20002/202-287-3490.

Museum of Natural History
The museum is responsible for the preservation and conservation of the largest collection of natural history specimens and artifacts in the United States. The permanent exhibitions are devoted to ecology; the rise of Western civiliza-

tion; meteorites; moon rocks; mammals; birds, human biology; dinosaurs and other extinct animals and plants; sea life; South American, Asian, African and Pacific cultures; gems and minerals; native Americans; and a live insect zoo. (Nearly 81 million specimens of animals, plants, fossils, rocks, gems and human artifacts.) Scientific research of the museum involves basic work in biology, earth sciences, fossils and anthropology. Contact: National Museum of Natural History, 10th and Constitution Ave. N.W., Washington, DC 20008/202-357-2664.

Museum Programs
This Office provides professional guidance and technical assistance to museums on collections and their management, exhibition techniques, educational activities and operational methods. It conducts training programs for museum professionals, produces and distributes information on museum conservation, and conducts evaluation studies of exhibitions and programs to identify areas and means of improvement. The Office cooperates with American and foreign museums and governmental agencies on museum matters, administers the National Museum Act, and oversees the archival, exhibition, conservation, library, registrial and horticultural activities of the Smithsonian. Contact: Office of Museum Programs, Smithsonian Institution, 900 Jefferson Dr. S.W., Washington, DC 20560/202-357-3101.

Museum Shops
There are museum shops in the major Smithsonian museums. The shops sell books, craft products, reproductions of artifacts and educational games and toys. Mail orders are also available, with spring and fall catalogs. For additional information contact: Business Management Office, Treasurer, Smithsonian Institution, 10th and Constitution Ave. N.W., Washington, DC 20560/202-287-3563. Mail order catalog—202-357-1826.

National Museum of American Art
This museum is devoted to American painting, sculpture and graphic art from the 18th century to today. A portion of its permanent collection of over 23,000 works is exhibited in its extensive galleries, and the remainder is available for study by scholars. It is also a major center for research in American art. In addition to its research library, the museum possesses a major archive of photographs and slides and has compiled an inventory of American paintings up to 1914. A film on the museum has been made. A monthly calendar of events is available. For additional information contact: National Museum of American Art, Smithsonian Institution, 8th and 9th Sts. N.W., Washington, DC 20560/202-357-1959.

National Museum of American History
The museum is a national center for the study and exposition of the history of American civilization through exhibitions research and publications. The museum interprets aspects of American history and culture from folk art to developments in science and technology. Outstanding features include Whitney's cotton gin, Mope's telegraph, the Pioneer locomotive, Thomas Edison's phonograph and a Model T Ford. *Smithsonian Studies in History and Technology* is the museum's publication series. Educational materials include publications, teacher guides, descriptive leaflets and audiovisual packets. Contact: National Museum of American History, Smithsonian Institution, 12th St. and Constitution Ave. N.W., Washington, DC 20560/202-357-3129.

National Museum of Design—Cooper Hewitt Museum
The Museum is the only one in the U.S. devoted exclusively to the study and exhibition of historical and contemporary design. Its collection consists of more than 200,000 items. It maintains a reference library of about 35,000 volumes relating to design, ornament and architecture and a picture library of about 1 million photographs and clippings, as well as a series of archives devoted to color material and industrial design. The Museum is not only a major assemblage of decorative art materials but also a research laboratory serving professionals and students of design. A 14-part series, *The Smithsonian Illustrated Library of Antiques* has been prepared (with the Book-of-the-Month Club) under its direction. Contact: Cooper-Hewitt Museum, Smithsonian Institution, 2 E. 91st St., New York, NY 10128/212-860-6868.

National Portrait Gallery
The National Portrait Gallery was set up "for the exhibition and study of portraiture depicting men and women who have made significant contributions to the history, development, and culture of the people of the United States." Publications include illustrated catalogs for major shows, an illustrated checklist of portraits in the collection, and educational materials designed to be used as teaching guides. Among these are *Fifty American Faces*—a collection of essays of 50 of the Gallery's most significant portraits and the *Collected Papers of Charles Wilson Peale and His Family* in microfiche edition with a letterpress index and guide. *Faces of Freedom* is a 27-minute color film that can be rented. Contact: Publications, National Portrait Gallery, Smithsonian Institution, 8th and G St. N.W., Washington, DC 20560/202-357-2995

National Zoological Park
The Park's collection is outstanding, and comprises about 2,600 living mammals, birds and reptiles of over 600 species. Research objectives

include investigations in animal behavior, ecology, nutrition, reproductive physiology, pathology and clinical medicine. Conservation-oriented studies cover maintenance of wild populations and long-term captive breeding and care of endangered species. Information about activities of the Friends of the National Zoo and their magazine *The Zoogoer,* is available by writing to the Friends of the National Zoological Park, Washington, DC 20008/202-673-4717.

The Department of Animal Health is responsible for the health of the collection. Contact: 202-673-4793.

The Department of Pathology does research to determine causes of death in zoo animals and to understand disease processes. Contact: 202-673-4869.

The Office of Zoological Research studies mammalian behavior, particularly that of primates, birds, rodents, carnivores and ungulates (hoof stock) with special interest in animal communication, olfactory, social bonds and territorial behavior. The office organizes scientific seminars and sponsors training for students and scholars. Contact: 202-673-4825.

The *Front Royal* facility studies propagation and conservation methods for rare and endangered species. Contact: Conservation and Research Center, National Zoological Park, Front Royal, VA 22630/703-635-4166.

Office of Education and Information organizes education programs to promote the understanding of the animal kingdom. It also produces films and publications. Contact: 202-673-4724.

Natural History Education

The Museum has programs for school children and adults. The museum publishes educational materials including booklets, teacher guides and other information. Contact: National Museum of Natural History and National Museum of Man, 10th and Constitution Ave. N.W., Washington, DC 20560/202-357-2664.

Natural History Library

The Museum maintains the largest natural history reference collection in the United States available to qualified scientists. Contact: Library, Museum of Natural History, Smithsonian Institution, 10th and Constitution Ave. N.W., Washington, DC 20560/202-357-1496.

Naturalist Center

This center provides collections which amateur naturalists can touch, examine and study. Amateurs may bring materials or photographs to the Center for identification. Contact: National Museum of Natural History and National Museum of Man, Smithsonian Institution, 10th and Constitution Ave. N.W., Washington, DC 20560/202-357-2804.

Numismatic Collections

The numismatic collections begin with ancient coins from Asia Minor and trace monetary history into the present. Contact: National Numismatics Collection Historian, National Museum of American History, 12th and Constitution Ave. N.W., Washington, DC 20560/202-357-1798.

Office of Publications Exchange

The Service was estabished in 1849 to distribute the publications of the Smithsonian Institution to scientific and learned institutions abroad. Staff accepts addressed packages of publications from libraries, scientific societies and educational institutions in the United States for transmission to similar organizations in foreign countries, and in return receives addressed publications from foreign sources for distribution in the United States. Contact: Office of Publications Exchange, Smithsonian Institution, 1111 North Capitol St. N.E., Washington, DC 20560/202-357-2073.

Philatelic Collection

Philatelic materials include a detailed record of U.S. postage stamps as well as philately from other parts of the world. Contact: National Philatelic Collection, National Museum of American History, 12th and Constitution Ave. N.W., Washington, DC 20560/202-357-1796.

Photographs

Color and black and white photographs and slides (including illustrated slide lectures) are available. Subjects include photographs of the Smithsonian's scientific, technological, historical and art collections as well as pictures dating back more than 130 years taken from its photographic archives. Information, order forms and price lists may be obtained from Photographic Services, Smithsonian Institution, 14th and Constitution Ave, Washington, DC 20560/202-357-1487.

Radio Shows

"Radio Smithsonian," a weekly program presenting a sampling of the research, exhibits, and popular musical concerts of the Smithsonian, is broadcast at varying times over approximately 70 stations in 34 states and Canada. "Smithsonian Galaxy," a series of twice-weekly 2½ minute radio features growing out of the Smithsonian's activities in science, history, and the arts is broadcast by approximately 115 stations in the United States and Canada. Contact: Telecommunication Office, Smithsonian Institution, 600 Maryland Ave. S.W. Washington, DC 20560/202-357-2984.

Reading is Fundamental

Reading is Fundamental develops community projects to motivate young people to read by letting them choose and keep books. It supports these programs with publications, training aids and materials such as a film and public service announcement. For additional information contact: Reading is Fundamental, Smithsonian Institution,

600 Maryland Ave, SW, Suite 500, Washington, DC 20560/202-287-3220.

Reference Center
The Museum Reference Center is a major library source of museological information in the U.S. which includes printed works and other materials. Contact: Museum Reference Center, Office of Museum Programs, Smithsonian Institution, 1000 Jefferson Dr., Washington, DC 20560/202-357-3101.

Registrar
The individual museums are responsible for Institution-wide coordination of their information management efforts and for the development of standards for information storage and retrieval systems. Contact: Office of the Registrar, Smithsonian Institution, 900 Jefferson Dr. S.W., Washington, DC 20560/202-357-2555.

Renwick Gallery
The Gallery is a curatorial department of the National Museum of American Art. It exhibits, with accompanying publications, American design, crafts and decorative arts as well as the arts and crafts of other countries. It maintains an active film and lecture program. Contact: The Renwick Gallery, Smithsonian Institution, 17th & Pennsylvania Ave. N.W., Washington, DC 20560/202-357-2531.

Research Reports
Smithsonian Research Reports containing articles on Smithsonian research in science, art and the humanities are available from the Office of Public Affairs, Smithsonian Institution, 900 Jefferson Dr. S.W., Washington, DC 20560/202-357-2627.

Scholars' Guides to Washington, DC
The Guides are designed to be descriptive and evaluative surveys of research resources. Each work is divided into two parts. Part I examines the holdings of Washington, DC area resource collections: libraries; archives and manuscript depositories; art, film, music and map collections; and data banks. Part II focuses on pertinent activities of Washington-based organizations public and private which are potential sources of information or assistance to researchers. The appendixes include information on press, media, churches and religious organizations, social and recreational clubs, bookstores, etc. The series includes scholars' guides to Washington, DC for:

African Studies ($9.95)
Central and East European Studies ($9.95)
Film and Video Collections ($8.95)
Russian/Soviet Studies ($15.00)
East Asian Studies ($9.95)
Latin American and Caribbean Studies ($9.95)

These guides can be ordered from Publication Sales, Smithsonian Institution Press, Smithsonian Institution, 1111 N. Capitol St., Washington, DC 20560/202-357-1793. For further information contact: Woodrow Wilson International Center for Scholars, Smithsonian Institution, Washington, DC 20560/202-357-2429.

Scientific Event Alert Network
This network provides timely notice of short-lived natural phenomena such as volcanic activity, meteor falls, to scientists and others throughout the world. Contact: Scientific Event Alert Network, Museum of Natural History, 10th and Constitution Ave. N.W., Washington, DC 20560/202-357-1511.

Smithsonian—A Guide for Disabled Visitors
A general information brochure about the Smithsonian detailing special programs and facilities for the disabled. Write to Smithsonian Visitor Information, 1000 Jefferson Drive, Washington, D.C. 20560/202-357-2700.

Smithsonian Collection of Recordings
The Smithsonian Collection of Recordings includes the "Smithsonian Collection of Classic Jazz," "A J.S. Bach Treasury," the "American Musical Theatre Series" and numerous others. For a catalog write Smithsonian Recordings, P.O. Box 10230, Des Moines, IA 50336/800-247-5072.

Smithsonian Institution Press
The Smithsonian Institution Press publishes books and studies related to the sciences, technology, history, air and space, and the arts at a wide range of prices. It also publishes exhibition catalogs, museum guides and various brochures. A free book catalog and a list of studies are available. Contact: Publications Sales, Smithsonian Institution Press, Smithsonian Institution, 1111 North Capitol St., Washington, DC 20002/202-287-3738.

Smithsonian Magazine
This monthly magazine covers the arts, sciences and history. It is available for $18.00 per year. Contact: Smithsonian Associates, Smithsonian Institution, 900 Jefferson Dr., Washington, DC 20560/202-357-2600

Smithsonian Medals
The Smithsonian Institution awards six medals for distinguished achievement in areas of Institutional interest. They include:

1. The Charles Lang Freer Medal for contributions of Oriental civilizations as reflected in their arts.
2. The Henry Medal for outstanding service to the Institution.
3. The Hodgkins Medal for important contributions to knowledge of the physical environment bearing upon the welfare of man.

4. The Langley Gold Medal for meritorious investigations in connection with the science of aerodromics with its application to aviation.
5. The Matthew Fontaine Maury Medal for contributions to the science of oceanography.
6. The Smithson Medal in recognition of exceptional contributions to art, science, history, education and technology.

Contact: Public Office of Affairs, Smithsonian Institution, 1000 Jefferson Dr. S.W., Washington, DC 20560/202-357-2627.

Smithsonian National Associate Program

the Smithsonian National Associate Program (SNAP) is an educational extension of the Institution. Participatory activities available to the National Associates include a Regional Program, a Selected Studies Program, foreign and domestic travel opportunities, and a Contributing Membership Program, including the James Smithson Society. Contact: Smithsonian National Associate Program, Smithsonian Institution, 900 Jefferson Drive, S.W., Washington, DC 20560/202-357-1350

Smithsonian Resident Associate Program

The Resident Associate Program (RAP) was established in 1965 to enable residents of the Washington, D.C., metropolitan area to appreciate Smithsonian resources through in-depth educational experiences, which engage the interest of area families, adults, and young people. These opportunities include: classes in the arts, sciences, humanities, and studio arts; guided tours within the Smithsonian; tours to nearby centers of scientific, artistic, or historial interest; lectures, symposia, and seminars; film series; exhibition previews; poster projects; and an active and varied calendar of performing arts events. Contact: Smithsonian Resident Associate Program, Smithsonian Institute, 900 Jefferson Drive S.W., Washington, DC 20560/202-357-3030.

Symposia and Seminars

The Office of Smithsonian Symposia and Seminars brings together the Smithsonian's own professional staff, visiting investigators and distinguished figures from many areas of intellectual accomplishment in interdisciplinary symposia, colloquia and seminars. It develops the Institution's international symposia series at which leading scholars and specialists from all over the world examine themes of contemporary concern and significance. Some resulting publications include: *Fitness of Man's Environment* ($12.50); and *Kin and Communities* ($22.50). These are available from Publications Distribution, Smithsonian Institution Press, Smithsonian Institution, 1111 North Capitol St., Washington, DC 20560/202-357-1793. For additional information on Symposia and Seminars contact: Office of Smithsonian Symposia and

Seminars, Smithsonian Institution, 1000 Jefferson Dr. S.W., Washington, DC 20560/202-357-2328.

Telecommunications

This office is responsible for all activities in television, radio, films and similar materials created and produced by or for the Smithsonian for external education and information purposes. Contact: Office of Telecommunications, Smithsonian Institution, National Museum of Natural History, Room C222B, Washington, DC 20560/202-357-2984.

Tours

For tour information contact the appropriate office listed below:

Education and Community Outreach Department, Anacostia Neighborhood Museum, 2405 Martin Luther King, Jr. Ave. S.E., Washington, DC 20020/202-287-3369.

Department of Education, National Museum of American Art, Smithsonian Institution, Washington, DC 20560/202-357-3095.

Curator of Education, National Portrait Gallery, 8th and F Sts. N.W., Washington, DC 20560/202-357-2920.

Friends of the National Zoo, National Zoological Park, 3000 Connecticut Ave. N.W., Washington, DC 20008/202-673-4955.

Education Office, National Gallery of Art, Washington, DC 20565/202-842-6249.

Office of Education, National Museum of Natural History, 10th St. and Constitution Ave. N.W., Washington, DC 20560/202-357-2810.

Office of Education and Information, National Museum of American History, 14th St. and Constitution Ave. N.W., Washington, DC 20560/202-357-1481; TDD 357-1563.

Office of Education, Hirshhorn Museum and Sculpture Garden, 8th St. and Independence Ave. S.W., Washington, DC 20560/202-357-3235

Department of Education, Smithsonian Environmental Research Center, RR4, Box 28, Edgewater, MD 21037/202-261-4190, ext. 42.

Membership Department, Cooper-Hewitt Museum, 2 E. 91st St., New York, NY 10028/212-860-6868.

Tour Information, Freer Gallery of Art, 12th St. and Independence Ave. S.W., Washington, DC 20560/202-357-2104.

Tour Office, Education Services Division, National Air and Space Museum, 7th St. and Independence Ave. S.W., Washington, DC 20560/202-357-1400.

Department of Education, National Museum of African Art, 316 A St. N.E., Washington, DC 20002/202-287-3490.

Traveling Exhibition Service

This service (SITES) provides specially designed exhibits to organizations and institutions across the country and abroad at the lowest possible rental fees. More than 120 exhibitions of painting, sculptures, prints, drawings, decorative arts, history, children's art, natural history, photography, science and technology are circulated every year. Lists of available exhibitions and information for future bookings are available. Contact: Smithsonian Institution Traveling Exhibition Service, Smithsonian Institution, 900 Jefferson Dr. S.W., Washington, DC 20560/202-357-3168.

Tropical Research

The Institute, a research organization devoted to the study and support of tropical biology, education and conservation, focuses broadly on the evolution of patterns of behavior and ecological adaptations. Panama offers its unique zoogeographic characteristics—landbridge to terrestrial life forms of two continents and water barrier to marine life of two oceans. A brochure describing the Institute's activities and illustrating some of the facilities and habitats is available. Contact: Smithsonian Tropical Research Institute, Smithsonian Institution, APO Miami 34002 Balboa 52-5669 or 52-2485 or Box 2072, Balboa, Canal Zone.

Visitor Information

The Smithsonian Visitor Information and Associates' Reception Center, located in the original Smithsonian building, provides a general orientation and assistance for members and the public relative to the national collections, museum events and programs. Write to the Visitor Information and Associates' Reception Center, 1000 Jefferson Dr. S.W., Washington, DC 20560/202-357-2700.

Volunteer Services

The Smithsonian Institution welcomes volunteers and offers a variety of service opportunities. Persons may serve as tour guides or information volunteers, or may participate in an independent program in which their educational and professional backgrounds are matched with curatorial or research requests from within the Smithsonian. For information, write to the Visitor Information and Associates' Reception Center, 1000 Jefferson Dr. S.W., Washington, DC 20560/202-357-2700; phone for the hearing-impaired is TTY 381-4448.

"Welcome" Brochure

A general information brochure about the Smithsonian Institution that is distributed to visitors free of charge. It is available in French, German, Spanish and Japanese as well as in English. Write Smithsonian Visitor Information, 1000 Jefferson Drive, Washington, DC 20560/202-357-2700.

Wilson Quarterly

This is a national journal of ideas and information. It is sold on subscription for $17.00 per year from The Wilson Quarterly, P. O. Box 2956, Boulder, CO 80302/303-687-0770. For additional information contact: The Wilson International Center for Scholars, Smithsonian Institution, Washington, DC 20560/202-289-3410.

How Can the Smithsonian Institution Help You?

To determine how this agency can help you contact: Visitor Information, Smithsonian Institution, 1000 Jefferson Dr. S.W., Washington, DC 20560/202-357-2700.

United States Railway Association

955 L'Enfant Plaza N. S.W., Washington, DC 20595/202-488-8777

Established: 1973
Budget: $4,300,000
Employees: 40

Mission: To authorize and direct the maintenance of adequate and efficient rail service in the midwest and northeast regions of the United States.

Major Sources of Information

Documents
The Document Center serves as the official depository of all documents which are involved in the litigation before the Special Court, as well as other courts, in conjunction with the reorganization. It also contains reports and studies dealing with the various issues of rail service. The public is welcome to examine these. Contact: Public Reading Room, Railway Association, 955 L'Enfant Plaza N. S.W., Room 5-500, Washington, DC 20595/202-488-8777.

Publications
USRA prepares reports and studies dealing with rail service. These range from rail planning, light-density lines, productivity, administrative history of the Association, Conrail foreign purchasing policy and practices, trackage rights, employee stock ownership, competitive, Conrail computer service, joint rates and New England freight traffic protection. Contact: Public Affairs, Railway Association, 955 L'Enfant Plaza N. S.W., Washington, DC 20595/202-488-8777 x530.

Meetings
Meetings of the Board of Directors or Committees are open to the public. Notices of the meetings, complete with an agenda, are posted. For additional information contact: Executive Vice President—Law, Railway Association, 955 L'Enfant Plaza N. S.W., Washington, DC 20595/202-488-8777.

How Can the Railway Association Help You?
To determine how this agency can help you contact: Public Affairs Office, Railway Association, 955 L'Enfant Plaza N. S.W., Washington, DC 20595/202-488-8777 x530.

United States Synthetic Fuels Corporation

2121 K Street N.W., Washington, DC 20586/202/822-6600

Established: June 30, 1980
Budget: $5,000,000,000
Employees: 170

Mission: Functions as an investment bank providing financial incentives, but not direct funding, to the private sector for the construction and operation of commercial-scale plants to produce synthetic substitutes for imported fuel.

Major Sources of Information

Annual Report
The U.S. Synthetic Fuels Corporation Annual Report to Congress contains information on past and present projects, recommendations for future actions and budgetary tables. This report is available free of charge. Contact: Public Disclosure Office, U.S. Synthetic Fuels Corporation, 2121 K Street N.W., Washington, DC 20586/202-822-6479.

Public Reading Room
The Corporation maintains a public reading room. It contains the following information: a file on each project receiving financial assistance, original proposals for financial assistance, minutes of every public board meeting, press releases and transcripts made of all public conferences and briefings, and copies of all public speeches, public reports and notices. Contact: Public Reading Room, U.S. Synthetic Fuels Corporation, 2121 K Street N.W., Washington, DC 20586/202-822-6600.

Publications
Two fact sheets, *Questions and Answers About the Synthetic Fuels Corporation* and *Understanding the U.S. Synthetic Fuels Corporation,* are available free of charge. Contact: Office of Public Disclosure, U.S. Synthetic Fuels Corporation, 2121 K Street N.W., Washington, DC 20586/202-822-6479.

How Can the U.S. Synthetic Fuels Corporation Help You?
To determine how the U.S. Synthetic Fuels Corporation can help you, contact: Public Affairs, U.S. Synthetic Fuels Corporation, 2121 K Street, N.W. Washington, DC 20586/202-822-6600.

Other Boards, Committees and Commissions

This listing of federal boards, centers, commissions, councils, panels, study groups and task forces is not described elsewhere in the directory. The organizations were established by congressional or presidential action and their functions are not strictly limited to the internal operations of a parent department or agency.

The organizations listed below are not Federal Advisory Committees, as defined by the Federal Advisory Committee Act. A complete listing of these committees can be found in *Federal Advisory Committees—Annual Report to the President.* Available from Committee Management Secretariat, General Services Administration, Room 7030, 18th & F St. N.W., Washington, DC 20405/202-523-4884.

Administrative Committee of the *Federal Register,* National Archives Building, Washington, DC 20408/202-523-5240.

Advisory Commission on Intergovernmental Relations, Suite 2000, Vanguard Building, 1111 20th St. N.W., Washington, DC 20575/202-653-5536.

Advisory Council on Historic Preservation, Suite 809, 1100 Pennsylvania Ave., N.W., Washington, DC 20004/202-786-0503.

Agricultural and Transportation Barriers Compliance Board, Room 1010, Switzer Building, 330 C St SW, Washington, DC 20202/202-245-1591.

Arthritis Interagency Coordinating Committee, National Institutes of Health, Room 9A35, Building 31, Bethesda, MD 20205/301-496-4353.

Board of Foreign Scholarships, Operations Staff, United States Information Agency, 301 Fourth St. SW, Washington, DC 20547/202-485-7290.

California Debris Commission, 650 Capital Mall, Sacramento, CA 95814/916-440-2327.

Citizens Stamp Advisory Committee, Stamp Division, United States Postal Service, Room 5800, 475 L'Enfant Plaza W. S.W., Washington, DC 20260/202-245-4951.

Commission on Presidential Scholars, Room 2079, Federal Office Bldg 6, 400 Maryland Ave. S.W., Washington, DC 20202/202-245-7792.

Committee on Foreign Investment in the United States, Room 5100, Main Treasury Building, Washington, DC 20220/202-566-2386.

Committee for the Implementation of Textile Agreements, Room 3001, Department of Commerce, 14th St. and Constitution Ave. N.W., Washington, DC 20230/202-377-3737.

Committee for Purchase from the Blind and Other Severely Handicapped, Suite 1107, Jefferson Davis Highway, Arlington, VA 22202/703-557-1145.

Delaware River Basin Commission, Office of the United States. Commissioner: Department of the Interior Guilding, Room 5113, 1100 L St. N.W., Washington, DC 20240/202-343-5761. Office of the Executive Director: P.O. Box 7360, W. Trenton, NJ 08628/609-883-9500.

Development Coordination Committee, Agency for International Development, Room 5942, 320 21st St. N.W., Washington, DC 20523/202-632-9620.

Emergency Mobilization Preparedness Board, Room 417, Donohoe Building, 500 C Street SW., Washington, DC 20472/202-287-0880.

Endangered Species Committee, Room 4423, Department of the Interior Building, Eighteenth and E Streets NW., Washington, DC 20240/202-343-7258.

Export Administration Review Board, Room 1613, Herbert Hoover Bldg., 14th St and Pennsylvania Ave, NW, Washington, DC 20230/202-377-3128.

Federal Financial Institutions, Examination Council, 8th Floor, Comptroller of the Currency Building, 490 L'Enfant Plaza E., Washington, DC 20219/202-447-0939.

Federal Financing Bank, Room 3054, Main Treasury Building, 15th St. and Pennsylvania Ave. N.W., Washington, DC 20220/202-556-2468.

Federal Financing Bank Advisory Council, Room 3124, Main Treasury Building, 15th St. and Pennsylvania Ave. N.W., Washington, DC 20220/202-566-2248.

Federal Interagency Committee on Education, Department of Education, 313H, Hubert H. Humphrey Building, 200 Independence Ave. S.W., Washington, DC 20201/202-245-7904.

Federal Interagency Committee Education, Room 3047, FOB6, 400 Maryland Ave SW, Washington, DC 20202/202-472-6830.

Federal Library Committee, Room 1023, John Adams Bldg, Library of Congress, Washington, DC 20540/202-287-6055.

Federal Mine Safety and Health Review Commission, Sixth Floor, 1730 K St. N.W., Washington, DC 20006/202-653-5633

Franklin Delano Roosevelt Memorial Commission, H2347 House Office Building Annex, No. 2, Washington, DC 20515/202-226-2491.

Harry S Truman Scholarship Foundation, 712 Jackson Pl. N.W., Washington, DC 20006/202-395-4831.

Indian Arts and Crafts Board, Room 4004, Department of the Interior Building, Washington, DC 20240/202-343-2773.

Information Security Oversight Office, Room 6046, General Services Building, 18th and F Sts. N.W., Washington, DC 20405/202-633-6880.

Interagency Committee on Handicapped Employees, Equal Employment Opportunity Commission, Room 422, 2401 E St. N.W., Washington, DC 20507/202-634-6753

Interagency Committee for the Purchase of U.S. Savings Bonds, 1111 Twentieth St NW, Washington, DC 20226/202-634-5347.

Japan-United States Friendship Commission, Room 910, 1875 Connecticut Ave. N.W., Washington, DC 20009/202-673-5295.

Joint Board for the Enrollment of Actuaries, Department of the Treasury, Washington, DC 20220/202-634-5135.

Mailers Technical Advisory Committee, United States Postal Service, Sales Division, Room 5520, 475 L'Enfant Plaza SW, Washington, DC 20260-6341/202-245-5757.

Marine Mammal Commission, Room 307, 1625 Eye St. N.W., Washington, DC 20006/202-653-6237.

Migratory Bird Conservation Commission, Department of the Interior Building, 18th and C Sts, NW, Washington, DC 20240/202-653-7653.

Mississippi River Commission, United States Army Corps of Engineers, P.O. Box 80, Vicksburg, MS 39180/601-634-5000.

National Advisory Council on International Monetary and Financial Policies, Room 5455, Department of the Treasury, Washington, DC 20220/202-566-5227.

National Archives Trust Fund Board, National Archives Building, Room 406, 7th St and Pennsylvania Ave NW, Washington, DC 20408/202-523-3047.

National Commission on Libraries and Information Science, Suite 3122, General Services Administration Regional Office Bldg 3, 7th and D Sts SW, Washington, DC 20024/202-382-0840.

National Coordinating Council on Juvenile Justice and Delinquency Prevention, Office of Juvenile Justice and Delinquency Prevention, Department of Justice, 633 Indiana Ave NW, Washington, DC 20531/202-724-5929.

National Council on the Handicapped, Room 3123, 330 C St SW, Washington, DC 20202/202-732-1276.

National Historical Publications and Records Commission, National Archives Building, Washington, DC 20408/202-724-1083.

National Park Foundation, P.O. Box 57473, Washington, DC 20037/202-785-4500.

Navajo and Hopi Indian Relocation Commission, P.O. Box KK, Flagstaff, AZ 86002/602-779-2721.

Northern Mariana Islands Commission on Federal Laws, Room 4447, Department of the Interior Bldg, Washington, DC 20240/202-343-5617.

Office of the Federal Inspector, Alaska Natural Gas Transportation System, Post Office Building, Room 3412, 1200 Pennsylvania Ave. N.W., Washington, DC 20044/202-275-1100.

Permanent Committee for Oliver Wendell Holmes Devise Fund, Library of Congress, Washington, DC 20540/202-287-5383.

President's Commission on Executive Exchange, 744 Jackson Pl. N.W., Washington, DC 20503/202-395-4616.

President's Committee on Employment of the Handicapped, 1111 20th St. N.W., Washington, DC 20210/202-653-5044.

President's Council on Integrity and Efficiency, Room 3026, Office of Management and Budget, New Executive Office Building, Washington, DC 20503/202-395-4960.

President's Foreign Intelligence Advisory Board, Room 340, Old Executive Office Building, Washington, DC 20500/202-456-2352.

President's Intelligence Oversight Board, Room 331, Old Executive Office Building, Washington, DC 20500/202-456-2530.

Property Review Board, Room 497, Old Executive Office Building, Washington, DC 20500/202-395-3030.

Regulatory Information Service Center, Room 5216, New Executive Office Building, 726 Jackson Place NW., Washington, DC 20503/202-395-4931.

Susquehanna River Basin Commission, Office of the United States Commissioner: Department of the Interior Building, Room 5113, 1100 L St. N.W., Washington, DC 20230/202-343-4091.

Office of the Executive Director: 1721 N. Front St., Harrisburg, PA 17102/717-238-0422.

Task Force on Legal Equity for Women, Room 828, Department of Justice, 320 First Street NW., Washington, DC 20530/202-724-2242.

Textile Trade Policy Group, Room 300, 600 17th St. N.W., Washington, DC 20506/202-395-3026.

Trade Policy Committee, Room 501, 600 17th St. N.W., Washington, DC 20506/202-395-7210.

United States National Commission for UNESCO, Department of State, Room 4334A, Washington, DC 20520/202-632-1534.

Veterans Day National Committee, Room 275C, Veterans Administration, 810 Vermont Ave. N.W., (40B), Washington, DC 20420/202-389-5386.

Index